Marking the Millennium

26th International Conference on Very Large Databases
Cairo, Egypt, 10-14 September 2000

Editors

Amr El Abbadi
Michael L. Brodie
Sharma Chakravarthy
Umeshwar Dayal
Nabil Kamel
Gunter Schlageter
Kyu-Young Whang

This edition includes the correct names of additional reviewers and acknowledges members of the Demonstrations Program Committee (omitted in the previous version).

Ordering Information

Morgan Kaufmann Publishers is the exclusive worldwide distributor for the VLDB proceedings volumes listed below:

	ISBN
2000 Cairo, Egypt	1-55860-715-3
1999 Edinburgh, Scotland	1-55860-615-7
1998 New York, USA	1-55860-566-5
1997 Athens, Greece	1-55860-470-7
1996 Mumbai (Bombay), India	1-55860-382-4
1995 Zurich, Switzerland	1-55860-379-4
1994 Santiago, Chile	1-55860-153-8
1993 Dublin, Ireland	1-55860-152-X
1992 Vancouver, Canada	1-55860-151-1
1991 Barcelona, Spain	1-55860-150-3
1990 Brisbane, Australia	1-55860-149-X
1989 Amsterdam, The Netherlands	1-55860-101-5
1988 Los Angeles, USA	0-934613-75-3
1985 Stockholm, Sweden	0-934613-17-6
1984 Singapore	0-934613-16-8
1983 Florence, Italy	0-934613-15-X
1996 2000 5-year set	1-55860-719-6 ($198)
1991 2000 10-year set	1-55860-720-x ($378)
1988 2000 13-year set	1-55860-718-8 ($486)

Prices are $50 per copy for the 1999 and 2000 volumes, and $40 per copy for all other volumes. Prices for 5-year, 10-year, and 14-year sets reflect a 10% discount.

Shipping is free from Morgan Kaufmann within the U.S. on prepaid orders. International shipping costs are $7 per volume via DHL/regular mail combination, or $20 per volume via international overnight courier. Morgan Kaufmann accepts credit-card payments: the buyer should provide card number, expiration date, and name as it appears on the card for Visa, MasterCard, or American Express credit cards. Morgan Kaufmann also accepts check payments in U.S. dollars only; checks must be drawn on a U.S. bank.

Order from Morgan Kaufmann Publishers

By Mail:	Morgan Kaufmann Publishers
	Attention: Order Fulfillment Department
	6277 Sea Harbor Drive
	Orlando, FL 32887 USA

By Phone:	(800) 745-7323 (from within U.S. and Canada) and (407) 345-3800 (international)
By Fax:	(800) 874-6418 or (407) 345-4060
By Email:	orders@mkp.com
By Web:	http://www.mkp.com

VLDB2000 ISBN 1-55860-715-3
ISSN 0730-9317

Conference Organizers

General Conference Chair	Nabil Kamel, American University at Cairo
Endowment Representative	Maria Orlowska, University Queensland
Program Committee Chair	Michael L. Brodie, GTE

Regional Program Chairs

Americas	Amr El Abbadi, University of California at Santa Barbara
Europe, Africa, and Near East	Gunter Schlageter, University of Hagen
Far East, Asia, and Australia	Kyu-Young Whang, Korea Advanced Institute of Science and Technology
Industrial Track	Umesh Dayal, Hewlett-Packard Labs
Panel and Demonstrations	Ahmed Elmagarmid, Purdue University
	Opher Etzion, IBM Research Laboratory in Haifa
Tutorial	Susan Davidson, University of Pennsylvania
	Divyakant Agrawal, University of California at Santa Barbara
Ten-Year Paper Awards	Mike Carey, Propel

Organizing Committee

Organizing Committee Chair	Samy Gamal Eldin, Military Technical College
Sponsorship Correspondent	Ismail Abdel Ghafar, Military Technical College
Organizing Committee Members	Ismail Abdel Ghafar, Military Technical College
	Ali Moselhi, Regional Information Technology Enterprise
	Ali Ghoneim, Al Ahram
	Ahmed Sameh, American University in Cairo
	Hoda Hosny, American University in Cairo
	Awad Khalil, American University in Cairo
Treasurer	Amany Shehab, American University in Cairo
Publications Chair	Sharma Chakravarthy, University of Texas at Arlington
Publicity Chairs	Magdi Kamel, Naval Postgraduate School
	Erich Neuhold, GMD
Proceedings Editors	Amr El Abbadi, University of California at Santa Barbara
	Michael L. Brodie, GTE
	Sharma Chakravarthy, University of Texas at Arlington
	Umeshwar Dayal, Hewlett-Packard Labs
	Nabil Kamel, American University in Cairo
	Gunter Schlageter, University of Hagen
	Kyu-Young Whang, Korea Advanced Institute of Science and Technology
Local Liaison	Amr Goneid, American University of Cairo
Geographic Area Chairs	Fawaz Al-Anzi, Kuwait University
	Nabeel I. Al-Fayoumi, Yarmouk University
	Paolo Atzeni, Universitá Di Roma Tre
	Catriel Berri, The Hebrew University
	Athman Bougettaya
	Asuman Dogac, Middle East Technical University
	Nabil Kamel, American University of Cairo
	Kamalaker Karapalem, The Hong Kong University of Science and Technology
	Roger King, University of Colorado
	Erich Neuhold, GMD
	Maria Orlowska, University of Queensland
	D.B. Phatak, Indian Institute of Technology at Bombay
	Timos Sellis, National Technical University of Athens

Program Committees

Far East, Asia, and Australia—Regional Chair: Kyu-Young Whang

David John Abel, CSIRO, Australia
Sang K. Cha, Seoul National University, Korea
Chin-Chen Chang, National Chung Cheng University, Taiwan
Arbee L.P. Chen, National Tsing Hua University, Taiwan
Sumit Ganguly, Indian Institute of Technology, India
Eui Kyeong Hong, University of Seoul, Korea
Hyoung-Joo Kim, Seoul National University, Korea
Hideko S. Kunii, Ricoh Company, Ltd., Japan
Chiang Lee, National Cheng-Kung University, Taiwan
Dik Lee, Hong Kong University of Science and Technology, Hong Kong
Frederick H. Lochovsky, Hong Kong University of Science and Technology, Hong Kong
Leszek A. Maciaszek, Macquarie University, Australia
Akifumi Makinouchi, Kyushu University, Japan
Arcot Desai Narasimhalu, Kent Ridge Digital Labs, Singapore
Shojiro Nishio, Osaka University, Japan
Beng Chin Ooi, National University of Singapore, Singapore
Maria Elzbieta Orlowska, The University of Queensland, Australia
Ron Sacks-Davis, RMIT, Australia
Kyuseok Shim, Korea Advanced Institute of Science and Technology, Korea
Kam-Fai Wong, The Chinese University of Hong Kong, Hong Kong
Masatoshi Yoshikawa, Nara Institute of Science and Technology, Japan
Lizhu Zhou, Tsinghua University, China

Europe, Africa, and Middle East—Regional Chair: Gunter Schlageter

Peter Apers, Universiteit Twente, Netherlands
Elisa Bertino, Universitá di Milano, Italy
Wojciech Cellary, The Poznan University of Economics, Poland
Stavros Christodoulakis, Technical University of Crete, Greece
Nihan Kesim Cicekli, Middle East Technical University, Turkey
Christine Collet, LSR/IMAG, France
Peter Dadam, Universität Ulm, Germany
Asuman Dogac, Middle East Technical University, Turkey
Opher Etzion, IBM, Israel
Piero Fraternali, Politecnico di Milano, Italy
Jane Grimson, Trinity College Dublin, Ireland
Arantza Illarramendi Echave, UPV/EHU, Spain
Yannis Ioannidis, University of Athens, Greece
Keith G. Jeffery, Rutherford Appleton Laboratory, United Kingdom
Christian Jensen, Aalborg University, Denmark
Leonid Kalininchenko, Russian Academy of Sciences, Russia
Dimitris Karagiannis, University of Vienna, Austria
Martin Kersten, CWI, The Netherlands
Awad Khalil, The American University in Cairo, Egypt
Gerhard Klett, COMPAREX Informationssysteme, Germany
Klaus Kuespert, University of Jena, Germany
Rivka Ladin, Tandem Labs, Israel
Robert Meersman, Vrije Universiteit Brussel, Belgium
Andreas Meier, University of Fribourg, Switzerland
Mike P. Papazoglou, Tilburg University, The Netherlands
Norman Paton, University of Manchester, United Kingdom
Tore Risch, Linkoping University, Sweden
Martin Rennhackkamp, The Data Base Approach, South Africa
H.-J. Schek, ETH Zentrum Zürich, Switzerland
Marc Scholl, University of Konstanz, Germany
Heinz Schweppe, Free University of Berlin, Germany
Timos Sellis, National Technical University of Athens, Greece
Eric Simon, INRIA, France
Arne Solvberg, IDI-G, Norway
Stefano Spaccapietra, EPFL-DI-LBD, Switzerland
Jukka Teuhola, University of Turku, Finland
Patrick Valduriez, INRIA, France
Jan Van den Bussche, University of Limburg, Belgium
Peter Wood, King's College London, United Kingdom

Americas—Regional Chair: Amr El Abbadi

Walid G. Aref, Purdue University, USA
Daniel Barbara, George Mason University, USA
Claudia Bauzer Medeiros, Instituto Computação, Brazil
Paul Brown, Informix, USA
Surajit Chaudhuri, Microsoft, USA
Sudarshan S. Chawathe, University of Maryland, USA
Panos K. Chrysanthis, University of Pittsburgh, USA
Usama Fayyad, digiMine.com
Dimitrios Georgakopoulos, Microelectronics and
    Computer Technology Center, USA
Shahram Ghandeharizadeh, University of Southern
    California, USA
Luis Gravano, Columbia University, USA
Laura M. Haas, IBM, USA
Jiawei Han, Simon Fraser University, USA
Abdelsalam (Sumi) Helal, University of Florida, USA
Meichun Hsu, Hewlett-Packard Laboratories, USA
H. V. Jagadish, University of Illinois at Urbana-
    Champaign, USA
Theodore Johnson, AT&T Labs, USA
Scott T. Leutenegger, University of Denver, USA
Sharad Mehrotra, University of California at Irvine,
    USA
Richard Muntz, University of California at Los Angeles,
    USA
Marie-Anne Neimat, TimesTen Performance Software,
    USA

Z. Meral Ozsoyoglu, Case Western Reserve University,
    USA
Hamid Pirahesh, IBM, USA
Viswanath Poosala, Bell Labs, USA
Sunil Prabhakar, Purdue University, USA
Michael Rabinovich, AT&T Labs, USA
Prabhu Ram, Mercata, Inc., USA
Raghu Ramakrishnan, University of Wisconsin at
    Madison, USA
Louiqa Raschid, University of Maryland, USA
Rajeev Rastogi, Bell Labs, USA
Frank Olken, Lawrence Berkeley Lab, USA
Kenneth Salem, University of Waterloo, USA
Sunita Sarawagi, IBM, USA
Kenneth C. Sevcik, University of Toronto, Canada
Dennis Shasha, New York University, USA
Jianwen Su, University of California at Santa Barbara,
    USA
Dan Suciu, AT&T Labs, USA
Anthony Tomasic, Digital Integrity, USA
Vassilis Tsotras, University of California at Riverside,
    USA
Victor Vianu, University of California at San Diego,
    USA
Jeffrey S. Vitter, Duke University, USA
Jennifer Widom, Stanford University, USA
Ouri Wolfson, University of Illinois at Chicago, USA
Stan Zdonik, Brown University, USA

Demonstrations Program—Chairs: Opher Etzion and Ahmed Elmagarmid

Asuman Dogac, Middle East Technical University,
    Turkey
Avigdor Gal, Rutgers University, USA
Minos Garofalakis, Lucent Labs, USA
Johannes Gehrke, Cornell University, USA

Bill McIver, Brown University, USA
Aya Soffer, IBM Research Laboratory in Haifa
Vassilios S. Verykios, Drexel University, USA
Aidong Zhang, SUNY at Buffalo, USA

Additional Reviewers

Robert Abarbanel
Serge Abiteboul
Swarup Acharya
Michel Adiba
Divy -Agrawal
Michael Akinde
Mehmet Altinel
Toshiyuki Amagasa
Hirofumi Amano
Stergios Anastasiadis
Thomas Baby
James Bailey
Herman Balsters
Sujata Banerjee
Roger S. Barga
Edgard-Ivan Benitez-Guerrero
Jesús Bermúdez
Kevin Beyer
Alex Biliris
Philip Bohannon
Michael Bohlen
Klemens Böhm
Edward Bortnikov
Peter Bosch
David Botzer
Jihad Boulos
Terje Brasethvik
Yuri Breitbart
Stephane Bressan
Laura Bright
Carlos Brito
D.O. Briukhov
Budiarto
Rolf de By
Don Carney
Malu Castellanos
Barbara Catania
Kaushik Chakrabarti
Chee-Yong Chan
Rahul V. Chari
Qiming Chen
Yaw-Huei Chen
Mitch Cherniack
Rada Chirkova
Junghoo Cho
Parvathi Chundi
Justim Chung
Andrzej Cichocki
Shi Cong
Thierry Coupaye
Arturo Crespo
Yingwei Cui
Bogdan Czejdo
Ricardo Dahab
Theodore Dalamagas
Pascal Déchamboux
Luis Mariano Del Val Cura
Pavan Desikan
Lyman Do
Carlotta Domeniconi
Donko Donjerkovic

Henk Ernst Blok
Kai Essig
L. Feng
Mary Fernandez
Elena Ferrari
Lucas C. Ferreira
J.C. Freytag
Juliana Friere
Xiang Fu
Michael Fuller
Avigdor Gal
Venkatesh Ganti
Dieter Gluche
Bart Goethals
Christoph Gollmick
Alfredo Goñi
Torsten Grabs
Goetz Graefe
Paul Grefen
Torsten Grust
Altay Guvenir
Marios Hadjieleftheriou
Oner N. Hamali
Takahiro Hara
Kaname Harumoto
Kenji Hatano
Jia-Lien Hsu
Andrew Hume
David Hutchionson
Ilyas Ihab
Yoshiharu Ishikawa
Xudong Jiang
Tetsuro Kakeshita
Kunihiko Kaneko
Timour Katchanouov
Timo Kaukoranta
Hiroyuki Kawano
Chih-Horng Ke
Kihong Kim
George Kollios
Flip Korn
Hank Korth
Nick Koudas
Yong Sik Kwon
Alexandros Labrinidis
Joyce Lam
Susan Lauzac
Doheon Lee
Guanling Lee
Kyu-Chul Lee
Wookey Lee
Hong Va Leong
Alon Levy
Eliezer Levy
Chen Li
Chung-Sheng Li
Weifa Liang
Edgar Chia-Han Lin
Lienfa Lin
Xuemin Lin
Shou-Chih Lo

Guy Lohman
Rafael Lozano
Quanwei Lu
Bertram Ludaescher
Jens Lufter
Benny Mandler
Stefan Manegold
Murali Mani
Runying Mao
Arunprasad P. Marathe
Subhasish Mazumdar
Lester McCann
Eduardo Mena
Joris Mihaeli
Renee Miller
Nina Mishra
Gail Mitchell
Sape Mullender
Mario A. Nascimento
Paul Natsev
Surya Nepal
Niels Nes
Jan Nowitzky
Chris Olston
Mike Ortega
Gultekin Ozsoyoglu
Brajendra Panda
Jang Ho Park
Jong Soo Park
Uchang Park
Torben B. Pedersen
Jian Pei
Nitzan Peleg
Arjan Pellenkoft
Frank Pentaris
Helen Pinto
Kringkai Porkaew
Fabio Porto
Cecillia Procopiuc
Octavian Procopiuc
Qing Qian
Timo Raita
Anand Rajaraman
Holger Riedel
Manuel Rodriguez-Martinez
Uwe Röhm
Claudia Lucia Roncancio
Marek Rusinkiewicz
Jarogniew Rykowski
Yasushi Sakurai
Simonas Saltenis
Renato Santos
Ismael Sanz
Hideki Sato
Mehmet Sayal
Heiko Schuldt
Hans Schuster
Greg Seidman
S. Seshadri
Uri Shaft
Bill Shapiro

Yuval Sherman
Jing Shi
Victor Shi
Richard Sidle
A. Prasad Sistla
Steffen Skatulla
N.A. Skvortsov
Giedrius Slivinskas
Aya Soffer
Divesh Srivastava
Emily Su
Kian-Lee Tan
Murat Tasan
Nesime Tatbul
Malcolm Taylor
Dimitri Theodoratos
Yannis Theodoridis
James Thom
Hakki Toroslu
Hallvard Trætteberg
Goce Trajcevski
Shin-Mu Tseng
Arif Tumer
Anthony Tung
Can Türker
Ozgur Ulusoy
Tolga Urhan
Genoveva Vargas-Solar
Vasilis Vassalos
Dirk Vermeir
Arjen P. de Vries
Florian Waas
Botao Wang
Guoren Wang
Ke Wang
Min Wang
Wei Wang
Yuan-Fang Wang
Roger Weber
Jin Wen
Waldemar Wieczerzycki
Jef Wijsen
Man Hon Wong
Xintao Wu
Yi-Hung Wu
Bo Xu
Jianliang Xu
Jun Yang
Ramana Yerneni
Yong-Ik Yoon
Clement Yu
Jeffrey Xu Yu
Gian Piero Zarri
Bin Zhang
Donghui Zhang
Zhili Zhang
Zhong Zhang
Xiaofang Zhou
Hongjun Zhu
Justin Zobel
Qinghua Zou

Additional Demonstrations Reviewers

Phillippe Bonnet	Alin Dobra	Ihab Illyas	Joris Mihaeli
David Botzer	Mohamed Elfeky	Hillel Kolodner	Yucel Saygin
Elena Daseni	Alexandre Evfimievski	Mirette Marzouk	Tali Yatzkar

Sponsors

Main Sponsor[*]

Sponsors[*]

Faisal Islamic Bank

MTC

Misr Exterior Bank

In Cooperation With

Organizers and Supporting Organizations[**]

---

[*]Sponsors have contributed monetarily to the conference and appear in order of their contributions, top to bottom and left to right.
[**]Organizers and supporting organizations have contributed considerably from their resources and staff time to the organization effort of the conference.

VLDB Endowment

Board of Trustees

Preface

In your hands are the results of much effort, beginning with the preparation of papers, panels, demos, and tutorials, going through the review process and the hard work of the program committee and the organizing committee, and ending with the conference itself.

The outstanding results achieved are due largely to the efforts of the dedicated professionals who have spent close to four years preparing for this event, and also to the support of many institutions and individuals. I especially want to thank the VLDB Endowment members for voting in favor of the proposal to bring the conference to Cairo, and for their generosity with offering special support for local and regional participation. Special thanks also go to Peter Lockemann, past VLDB president, for his support for VLDB2000 in Cairo and to John Mylopoulos, the current president, for his continued support of the conference throughout.

We are especially indebted to Maria Orlowska, the VLDB Endowment representative, for all her efforts during the preparation period for the conference.

Special thanks to Dr. Mofied Shehab, Minister of Higher Education and Scientific Research, and Dr. Ahmed Nazif, Minister of Information and Communications, for their support of the conference and for sharing their thoughts and experiences with us during the conference.

Many thanks go to all the members of the Program Committee: Michael L. Brodie, the Program Committee Chair, for his enormous creative effort; Amr El Abbadi, Gunter Schlageter, and Kyu-Young Hwang, the Regional PC Chairs; Umesh Dayal, the Industrial PC Chair; Ahmed ElMagarmid and Opher Etzion, the Panels and Demos Co-chairs; and Susan Davidson and Divvy Agrawal, the Tutorials Co-chairs, for the excellent program they have prepared. Finally, I want to thank Sharma Chakravarthy, the Publications Chair, who was responsible for the final look of the proceedings.

Special thanks to Organizing Committee Chair Dr. Samy Gamal Eldin for his continuous support of the conference, and for a job well done. Thanks to all the members of the Organizing Committee, especially Dr. Ismail Abdel Ghafar, who has shouldered much of the burden; Dr. Ali Moselhi, for managing the VLDB2000 project in the Ministry of Information and Communications; and Dr. Amr Goneid, for his help with local publicity and for supporting our accountant. We are also indebted to Ali Ghoneim and Gamal Gheitas from Al Ahram Newspaper for supporting the conference and helping to promote it and to derive maximum benefit from it locally. Many thanks to Ali Agoza, also from Al Ahram, for his help with the CD-ROM.

Much of the success for raising the participation figures for the conference go to Magdi Kamel and Erich Neuhold, the Publicity Co-chairs, for the energetic and effective international publicity campaign they mounted. Many thanks to all the Geographic Area Chairs for helping to raise awareness about the conference in their local regions.

I would like to thank Rana Ayman for the many hours she spent working on the Web site and for the beautiful logo she designed.

Many others have worked on the conference on a paid basis. I also want to thank them for being part of our team. These include Mrs. Amira Iskander, Star of Egypt Travel; Amany Shehab, our accountant; Hakam Kanafany, Datum; Tamer Kamal and Ramy Farid, the registration form designers; and Khaled Nasrallah and Ayman Al Bayaa, the exhibit organizers.

We are very grateful to all of our sponsors, without whose support this conference would not have been possible.

I would like to offer a few final comments regarding the conference itself. The VLDB conference is a unique conference indeed. Not only because it is the most widely recognized conference in databases, but also because of its long and well-established tradition of quality, innovation, variety, and international orientation.

Holding conferences like this in developing countries is extremely beneficial to the hosting country and its surrounding region. The conference brings important technology to the attention of local scientists and practitioners, and offers them a chance to meet with top scientists and developers in the field. Likewise, it also helps place the technical potential of these countries in the spotlight of the industry at large. It does so at an affordable cost to the local delegates, considering the elimination of travel and lodging costs. In the case of VLDB2000, local fees have been further reduced by a special and generous regional promotional offer, co-sponsored by VLDB2000 and the VLDB Endowment. There are also other side benefits to the hosting country—a small boost in tourism and various conference-related business activities.

Organizing VLDB2000 in Cairo has been a truly large and unforgettable international team effort that required collaboration among multiple institutions. Inevitably, the four years of hard work that was put into the conference preparation and organization entailed personal sacrifices from some of its key volunteer officers. It is to these people who have put in so much effort and time that our deepest gratitude should go.

The location of VLDB2000 was unique, at the foot of the great pyramid of Giza, the only surviving wonder of the ancient world and one of Mankind's most remarkable achievements. Delegates have enjoyed the atmosphere. The VLDB2000 Organizing Committee has also incorporated a number of activities outside of the conference hours to introduce delegates to the local history and culture in their spare time.

On behalf of all conference committees, I hope that you will enjoy the work in these proceedings and find it of much benefit.

Nabil Kamel
General Conference Chair
VLDB2000

Foreword

The 26th International Conference on Very Large Databases addressed some of the most critical challenges and achievements in the research and practice of database applications and management, especially those posed by the current Internet revolution. VLDB2000 continues this conference's 26-year tradition as the premier international forum for database researchers, vendors, practitioners, application developers, and users. VLDB2000 included two keynote presentations, a 10-Year Award paper, 53 papers, 16 demonstrations, 3 panels, 5 industrial sessions, 1 domain session, and a VLDB Endowment-sponsored plenary panel on VLDB directions.

Broadening the Database Field

An objective of VLDB2000 was to contribute to broadening the database field. See *Panel: Future Directions of Database Research—The VLDB Broadening Strategy, Part 2* in this volume for a description of the Broadening Strategy. Initially, the Broadening Strategy was controversial. There was concern that since broadening papers did not have established research methodologies as do core database topics, the quality of broadening papers would be below the quality of papers traditionally accepted by VLDB. The VLDB Endowment unanimously accepted this risk in order to expand the database field, at least in VLDB conferences. To maintain VLDB's traditional strength, a minimum quota was set for papers on core research topics. In addition, a minimum quota was set for papers that contributed to the Broadening Strategy. The Broadening Strategy was unexpectedly successful. More than 77% of submitted papers and more than 88% of accepted papers made modest or strong contributions to broadening in contrast to a range of 2% to 19% of accepted papers in previous years. The quality of these papers was on par with or exceeded papers on core database topics. In fact, the papers with the highest overall scores also had the highest broadening scores. The broadening quotas were exceeded in part by strong core papers that included broadening content. In addition, 56% to 100% of all other contributions also contributed to the Broadening Strategy.

Keynotes

VLDB2000 was honored to have as a keynote speaker Dr. Ebbe Nielsen, one of the world's leading biodiversity scientists and an expert in the developing field of biodiversity informatics. Biodiversity, a theme of VLDB2000 as part of the Broadening Strategy, is an excellent and potentially fruitful domain which poses significant data management challenges and in which database researchers could, in cooperation with biodiversity experts, contribute to both good computer science and to improving the world. The purpose of the keynote and the theme was to encourage database researchers to cooperate with biodiversity experts to address data management research challenges that arise in that domain.

10-Year Paper Award

This prestigious annual award is intended for "the most influential paper in the VLDB Proceedings 10 years ago." VLDB2000. The VLDB Endowment was delighted to honor Dr. Stefano Ceri, Dipartimento Di Elettronica, Politecnico di Milano, and Dr. Jennifer Widom, Computer Science Department, Stanford University, as recipients of the VLDB2000 10-Year Paper Award for their VLDB1990 paper:

> Ceri, S. and J. Widom, *"Deriving Production Rules for Constraint Maintenance."* In Dennis McLeod, Ron Sacks-Davis, Hans-Jorg Schek (Eds.): 16th International Conference on Very Large Databases, August 13–16, 1990, Brisbane, Queensland, Australia.

The honor is well deserved by Stefano and Jennifer given their individual and joint contributions to the area of active databases and to other areas of database research over many years. The award winners invited Roberta J. Cochrane, IBM Almaden Research Center, to co-author the invited paper "Practical Applications of Triggers and Constraints: Success Stories and Lingering Issues," which is included in this volume.

The paper was selected by the 10-Year Paper Award Committee, chaired by Dr. Mike Carey, Propel, and consisting of Prof. Frederick H. Lochovsky, University of Science & Technology–Hong Kong; Prof. Dr. Hans-Jorge Schek, ETH–

Zürich; and Dr. H.V. Jagadish, University of Michigan. After an extensive analysis of 10 years of related research literature, the committee found that the paper has had a significant impact on database research and that it has been formative in initiating research on the application of production rules to various aspects of database systems. The paper was cited more than 60 times on www.vldb.org alone. The award winners also won the Best Paper Award at VLDB1991 in Barcelona, Catalonia, Spain, for their paper "Deriving Production Rules for Incremental View Maintenance." Jennifer also received the Test of Time Award at SIGMOD 2000 for her SIGMOD 1990 paper with Sheldon J. Finkelstein: "Set-Oriented Production Rules in Relational Database Systems."

Papers

The program committee accepted 53 of the 349 papers submitted. The program committee was divided into three regional program committees: the Americas, chaired by Dr. Amr El Abbadi, University of California, Santa Barbara; Europe, Africa, and the Middle East, chaired by Dr. Gunter Schlageter, Fern Universität, Hagen; and the Far East, Asia, and Australia, chaired by Prof. Kyu-Young Whang, Korean Advanced Institute of Science and Technology. The program committee also selected a best paper of VLDB2000 as well as five papers that will be expanded to form a "Best of VLDB2000" issue of the *VLDB Journal*.

Papers were received from more than 22 countries, with more than 750 co-authors submitting papers. The 53 accepted papers had 163 co-authors. We thank the 105 program committee members and the additional 244 reviewers for their diligence and conscientiousness.

Demonstrations

Dr. Opher Etzion, IBM Research Laboratory in Haifa, and Dr. Ahmed Elmagarmid, Purdue University, chaired the demonstrations program committee. Following the trend of recent database conferences, there was an increased emphasis on demonstrations of prototype systems and software. There were twice as many submissions and acceptances as there were for VLDB1999. Of the 33 demonstrations submitted, 16 were accepted. The 16 accepted demonstrations had 69 co-authors; more than 135 co-authors submitted demonstrations. Demonstrations were reviewed by a program committee of 8 and by 12 additional reviewers whom we thank for their work.

Panels

Dr. Opher Etzion, IBM Research Laboratory in Haifa, and Dr. Ahmed Elmagarmid, Purdue University, were the panel chairs. The model management panel discussed the long-overlooked, open problem of translations between schemas or data representations. The 20/20 panel looked at future directions of database research. The third panel discussed how technology can be used to realize social, educational, and governmental policies. This topic could be particularly valuable for Africa, our host continent.

New for VLDB2000 was a plenary on the topic of broadening sponsored by the VLDB Endowment. This was not part of the regular refereed panels. It is a forum for explaining and discussing the Broadening Strategy used in VLDB2000, and possibly future VLDBs, and the ideas being pursued in the VLDB Endowment's Future Directions Committee.

Industrial Sessions

The industrial chair, Dr. Umeshwar Dayal, Hewlett-Packard Laboratories, did a superb job of soliciting and assembling the VLDB2000 industrial program in keeping with the Broadening Strategy. Novel for VLDB2000 was the concept of a domain session. A domain session is a session devoted to a specific application domain that poses significant data management challenges. The first VLDB domain session concentrated on the conference theme of broadening in the rapidly growing field of biodiversity and bio-informatics.

Tutorials

The tutorial chairs, Dr. Susan Davidson, University of Pennsylvania, and Dr. Divyakant Agrawal, University of California, Santa Barbara, accepted 5 of the 16 tutorials submitted. The VLDB2000 tutorials are published in a separate volume.

VLDB2000 Proceedings

The VLDB2000 publications chair, Prof. Sharma Chakravarthy, University of Texas, Arlington, edited and assembled the VLDB2000 Proceedings, which this year is being made available in hard copy, on CD, and on the Web. An innovation this year, spearheaded by Sharma, was to produce a CD version of the proceedings.

With Many Thanks

A program of the quality and magnitude of VLDB2000 requires the contributions and cooperation of many people. First, and foremost, we thank the more than 1,000 contributors who submitted papers or session proposals. Second, we thank those who attended the conference and who, we hope, will continue to benefit from its results. Next, we thank the more than 370 reviewers of papers and proposals. Many thanks to the 105 members of the technical program committee, and to the chairs—Amr, Kyu-Young, Gunter, Ahmed, Opher, Sue, Divy, Umesh, and Sharma. Special thanks to the assistants supporting the regional CP chairs—Chengyu Sun (the Americas), Birgit Feldmann-Pempe assisted by Peter Rosenthal (Europe, Africa, and the Middle East), and Yang-Sae Moon assisted by Seung-Hyun Paek (the Far East, Asia, and Australia). Thanks also to Meichun Hsu for hosting the Americas PC meeting at Hewlett-Packard Laboratories. We thank Microsoft Research and specifically Surajit Chaudhuri and Jonathan Simon for tailoring and operating the Microsoft Conference Management Toolkit, which supported the entire paper submission and review process with no serious problems. Finally, we thank Shirley Blanchard for her cheerful, always reliable development of Web pages for the technical program committee and her editing of lots of other documents, including the Tutorial Notes; and Kathryn Bailey for editing endless documents such as calls for this, that, and the other. With many thanks and gratitude to you all.

Michael L. Brodie
General Program Chair
VLDB2000

CONTENTS

Invited Talks

Regular Papers[1]

Session: Future DBMSs

Session: Data Mining

Session: Publishing, Filtering and Mappings

---

[1] Regular papers are identified, in parenthesis after the title, as one of the following: Research, Vision, Experience, or
Exp/App.

Panels

Industrial Sessions

Rethinking Database System Architecture:
Towards a Self-tuning RISC-style Database System

Surajit Chaudhuri
Microsoft Research
Redmond, WA 98052, USA
surajitc@microsoft.com

Gerhard Weikum
University of the Saarland
D-66123 Saarbruecken, Germany
weikum@cs.uni-sb.de

Abstract

Database technology is one of the cornerstones for the new millennium's IT landscape. However, database systems as a unit of code packaging and deployment are at a crossroad: commercial systems have been adding features for a long time and have now reached complexity that makes them a difficult choice, in terms of their "gain/pain ratio", as a central platform for value-added information services such as ERP or e-commerce. It is critical that database systems be easy to manage, predictable in their performance characteristics, and ultimately self-tuning. For this elusive goal, RISC-style simplification of server functionality and interfaces is absolutely crucial. We suggest a radical architectural departure in which database technology is packaged into much smaller RISC-style data managers with lean, specialized APIs, and with built-in self-assessment and auto-tuning capabilities

1. The Need for a New Departure

Database technology has an extremely successful track record as a backbone of information technology (IT) throughout the last three decades. High-level declarative query languages like SQL and atomic transactions are key assets in the cost-effective development and maintenance of information systems. Furthermore, database technology continues to play a major role in the trends of our modern cyberspace society with applications ranging from web-based applications/services, and digital libraries to information mining on business as well as scientific data. Thus, *database technology* has impressively proven its benefits and *seems* to remain crucially relevant in the new millennium as well.

Proceedings of the 26th International Conference on Very Large Databases, Cairo, Egypt, 2000

Success is a lousy teacher (to paraphrase Bill Gates), and therefore we should not conclude that the *database system*, as the unit of engineering, deploying, and operating packaged database technology, is in good shape. A closer look at some important application areas and major trends in the software industry strongly indicates that database systems have an overly low "gain/pain ratio". First, with the dramatic drop of hardware and software prices, the expenses due to human administration and tuning staff dominate the cost of ownership for a database system. The complexity and cost of these feed-and-care tasks is likely to prohibit database systems from further playing their traditionally prominent role in the future IT infrastructure. Next, database technology is more likely to be adopted in unbundled and dispersed form within higher-level application services.

Both of the above problems stem from packaging all database technology into a single unit of development, maintenance, deployment, and operation. We argue that this architecture is no longer appropriate for the new age of cyberspace applications. The alternative approach that we envision and advocate in this paper is to provide RISC-style, functionally restricted, specialized data managers that have a narrow interface as well as a smaller footprint and are more amenable to automatic tuning.

The rest of the paper is organized as follows. Section 2 puts together some important observations indicating that database systems in their traditional form are in crisis. Section 3 briefly reviews earlier attempts for a new architectural departure along the lines of the current paper, and discusses why they did not catch on. Section 4 outlines the envisioned architecture with emphasis on RISC-style simplification of data-management components and consequences for the viability of auto-tuning. Section 5 outlines a possible research agenda towards our vision.

2. Crisis Indicators

To begin our analysis, let us put together a few important observations on how database systems are perceived by customers, vendors, and the research community.

Observation 1: Featurism drives products beyond manageability. Database systems offer more and more features, leading to extremely broad and thus complex

"

interfaces. Quite often novel features are more a marketing issue rather than a real application need or technological advance; for example, a database system vendor may decide to support a fancy type of join or spatial index in the next product release because the major competitors have already announced this feature. As a result, database systems become overloaded with functionality, increasing the complexity of maintaining the system's code base as well as installing and managing the system. The irony of this trend lies in the fact that each individual customer (e.g., a small enterprise) only makes use of a tiny fraction of the system's features and many high-end features are hardly ever exercised at all.

Observation 2: SQL is painful. A big headache that comes with a database system is the SQL language. It is the union of all conceivable features (many of which are rarely used or should be discouraged to use anyway) and is way too complex for the typical application developer. Its core, say selection-projection-join queries and aggregation, is extremely useful, but we doubt that there is wide and wise use of all the bells and whistles. Understanding semantics of SQL (not even of SQL-92), covering all combinations of nested (and correlated) subqueries, null values, triggers, ADT functions, etc. is a nightmare. Teaching SQL typically focuses on the core, and leaves the featurism as a "learning-on-the-job" life experience. Some trade magazines occasionally pose SQL quizzes where the challenge is to express a complicated information request in a single SQL statement. Those statements run over several pages, and are hardly comprehensible. When programmers adopt this style in real applications and given the inherent difficulty of debugging a very high-level "declarative" statement, it is extremely hard if not impossible to gain high confidence that the query is correct in capturing the users' information needs. In fact, good SQL programming in many cases decomposes complex requests into a sequence of simpler SQL statements.

Observation 3: Performance is unpredictable. Commercial database engines are among the most sophisticated pieces of software that have ever been built in the history of computer technology. Furthermore, as product releases have been driven by the time-to-market pressure for quite a few years, these systems have little leeway for redesigning major components so that adding features and enhancements usually increases the code size and complexity and, ultimately, the general "software entropy" of the system. The scary consequence is that database systems become inherently unpredictable in their exact behavior and, especially, performance. Individual components like query optimizers may already have crossed the critical complexity barrier. There is probably no single person in the world who fully understands all subtleties of the complex interplay of rewrite rules, approximate cost models, and search-space traversal heuristics that underlie the optimization of complex queries. Contrast this dilemma with the emerging need for performance and service quality guarantees in e-commerce, digital libraries, and other Internet applications. The PTAC report has rightly emphasized: "our ability to analyze and predict the performance of the enormously complex software systems that lie at the core of our economy is painfully inadequate" [18].

Observation 4: Tuning is a nightmare and auto-tuning is wishful thinking at this stage. The wide diversity of applications for a given database system makes it impossible to provide universally good performance by solely having a well-engineered product. Rather all commercial database systems offer a variety of "tuning knobs" that allow the customer to adjust certain system parameters to the specific workload characteristics of the application. These knobs include index selection, data placement across parallel disks, and other aspects of physical database design, query optimizer hints, thresholds that govern the partitioning of memory or multiprogramming level in a multi-user environment. Reasonable settings for such critical parameters for a complex application often depend on the expertise and experience of highly skilled tuning gurus and/or time-consuming trial-and-error experimentation; both ways are expensive and tend to dominate the cost of ownership for a database system. "Auto-tuning" capabilities and "zero-admin" systems have been put on the research and development agenda as high priority topics for several years (see, e.g., [2]), but despite some advances on individual issues (e.g., [4,7,8,10,24]) progress on the big picture of self-tuning system *architectures* is slow and a breakthrough is not nearly in sight. Although commercial systems have admittedly improved on ease of use, many tuning knobs are merely disguised by introducing internal thresholds that still have to be carefully considered, e.g., at packaging or installation time to take into account the specific resources and the application environment. In our experience, robust, universally working default settings for complex tuning knobs are wishful thinking. Despite the common myth is that a few rules of thumb could be sufficient for most tuning concerns, with complex, highly diverse workloads whose characteristics evolve over time it is quite a nightmare to find appropriate settings for physical design and the various run-time parameters of a database server to ensure at least decent performance.

Observation 5: We are not alone in the universe. Database systems are not (or no longer) at the center of the IT universe. Mail servers, document servers, web application servers, media servers, workflow management servers, e-commerce servers, auction servers, ERP systems, etc. play an equally important role in modern cyberspace applications. A good fraction of these higher-level services have their own specialized storage engines and, to some extent, simple query engines, and even those that do make use of a database system utilize only a tiny fraction of the functionality up to the extreme point where the database system is essentially used as a luxurious BLOB manager. Thus, while we have been busy building *universal* database management systems, many important applications have simply decided to go on their own. In particular, quite a few vendors of such generic applications view complex SQL and the underlying query optimizer as a burden rather than an opportunity and consequently ignore or circumvent most high-level database system features (e.g., see [17]). Of course, this approach often amounts to "re-inventing" certain query optimization techniques in the layer on top of the database systems, but the vendors of these "value-added" services consider the re-implementation as appropriate given that it can now be streamlined and tailored to a specific application class.

Observation 6: System footprint considered harmful. The market for "classical" database installations may saturate in the near future. On the other hand, significant growth potential for the database system industry lies in embedded applications such as information services in cellular phones, cars, palm-pilots, etc.. These applications need even smaller fractions of the rich feature sets offered by a full-fledged database system. On the other hand, they face much tighter resource constraints in their embedded settings: neither the customer's wallet nor the battery supply of a typical gizmo easily allows purchasing another 256 MB of memory. This implies that the footprint of a system (i.e., code-size and especially memory requirements) is a key issue for lightweight embedded applications. Also, brute-force solutions to performance problems (i.e., adding hardware) are often infeasible. Thus, the current generation of commercial database systems, despite some of them advertising lightweight versions, are not geared for these settings.

Observation 7: System-oriented database research is frustrating. For the academic research (and teaching) community the ever-increasing complexity of commercial database systems makes it very hard to position its individual research efforts in the fast-moving IT world. On one hand, some of the traditional database-engine topics have been almost beaten to death, and the community leaders aim to steer researchers away from studying these seemingly myopic issues (although some of them are still far from a truly satisfactory solution). On the other hand, the success of research is more and more measured in terms of product impact, and for an academic idea to be intriguing to product developers, major prototype implementation and extensive experimentation is often required. With commercial database system being such a highly complex target, this kind of work becomes less and less rewarding and all too often exceeds the available resources in a university environment. Thus, it is no wonder that systems-oriented database research has become so scarce outside the labs of the major vendors. The personal consequence for many academic researchers is that they turn away from database systems and start working on different topics, often in conjunction with startup companies where again the "entrance fee" is much lower than for a new database system). Similar

observations can be made about teaching: teaching interface standards is boring, and teaching database system internals is often unsatisfactory because of the lack of documented knowledge or the indigestibility of the collection of tricks and hacks found in some systems.

All these observations together strongly indicate that database systems are in crisis: they have reached or even crossed a complexity barrier beyond which their lack of manageability and predictability will become so painful that information technology is likely to abandon database systems as a cornerstone of data-intensive applications. The bottom line is that database systems have become unattractive in terms of their *"gain/pain ratio"*: the gain of using a database system versus going on your own is outweighed by the pain of having to cope with overly sophisticated features and a hardly manageable, humongous piece of software.

3. Explanations and Previous Attempts

3.1 Explanations

Database systems (and possibly software technology in general) are susceptible to several "traps": principles that open up both opportunities and complexity (just like Pandora's box in the Greek mythology) and have been overstressed in the evolution of database systems.

Trap 1, the "universality trap": Since a computer is a universal tool, software developers strive for extremely versatile, general-purpose solutions. This attitude of trying to cover as much ground as possible is ambivalent and extremely delicate, however. After all, every good principle can be generalized to the point where it is no longer useful. In the case of database systems, this has led to extremely complex, and hard-to-manage software packages. Contrast this evolution with other fields of engineering: despite the fact that wheels or engines are universal components of cars, the automobile industry has not attempted to develop a universal car that unifies all features of a sports convertible, luxury limousine, 4WD, and economic as well as "ecologically correct" compact into a single product.

Trap 2, the "cost trap": Since software is inexpensive to "manufacture", i.e., copy and distribute to customers, database systems tend to agglomerate too much into a single package of deployment. This approach disregards the cost of maintenance, system operation, and especially the "cost" of gaining confidence in the dependability of the product comprising both correct behavior in all situations and predictable, ideally guaranteed performance. The latter is, of course, more a problem for customers (and also developers of value-added services on top of database systems) than for the vendors.

Trap 3, the "transparency trap": A "transparency trap" arises from very high-level features that hide execution costs. Historically, Algol 68 is a good historic example for this kind of pitfall. This was an extremely powerful language (for the standards of that period), and programmers could easily write code that would end up being a run-time nightmare. A similar phenomenon of hidden execution cost and thus careless programming can be observed with SQL. We teach our students that they can exploit its full expressiveness and rely on the query optimizer producing a miracle, but real life is pretty different. Efficiency should no longer be the main driving force in program designs and coding, but it should not be completely disregarded either. The concepts of a computer language should steer programmers towards reasonably efficient code rather than offering features for which there is little hope that their runtime is acceptable.

Trap 4, the "resource sharing trap": By putting as much functionality as possible into a single software box with certain underlying hardware resources (disks, memory, etc.), we can dynamically share these resources for different purposes. For example, by storing videos in a relational database, video streaming can exploit the space and performance capacity of disks that hold also conventional tables and indexes during daytimes when disks are lightly used for the OLTP or OLAP part of the business. Likewise, by running business-object-style application code, in the form of user-defined functions and abstract data types (ADTs), in the database server, the server's memory and processors are dynamically shared between query and application processing. The flip side of this coin is that such resource sharing introduces interesting but horribly complex tuning problems. Disk configuration planning and disk scheduling for both video streaming and conventional data accesses are much harder than dealing with each of the two data categories separately on two disjoint disk pools. Query optimization in the presence of ADTs is an intriguing research problem, but seems like trying to solve a combined problem before we fully understand each of its constituents.

Some people may argue that we should completely give up building complex software systems, and go back to the roots of programming with every line of code documented by its mathematical properties (e.g., invariants) and not release any software package whose correctness is not rigorously verified. But we should, of course, avoid this unrealistic attitude and the "humble programmer trap", too.

3.2 Previous Attempts

We are surely not the first ones who have made similar observations, have drawn potential conclusions, and have toyed with possible departures from the beaten paths. In the following we briefly discuss some of the most prominent attempts and why we believe they did not achieve their goals.

Attempt 1, database system generators: A common approach in computer science is to address problems by going to a meta level. In the specific case of database system architecture, [3] has proposed to generate customized database systems from a large library of primitive components (see also [13] for a related generator approach). The focus of this interesting but ultimately not so successful work was on storage and index management, but even in this limited context it seems impossible to implement such a generator approach in a practically viable form. Also, once such approaches take into account also cache management, concurrency control, recovery, query optimization, etc., they would inevitably realize the many subtle but critically important interdependencies among the primitive components, which makes the generation of correct and efficient system configurations awfully difficult.

Attempt 2, extensible kernel systems: A related approach that avoids some of the pitfalls of the generator theme has been to put core functionality into a kernel system and provide means for extending the kernel's functions as well as internal mechanisms [5,15,19,23]. This approach has led to the current generation of "data blades", "cartridges", and "extenders" in object-relational products [6]. The extensibility with regard to user-defined functions and ADTs is working reasonably well, but the extensibility with regard to internals, e.g., adding a new type of spatial index, is an engineering nightmare as it comes with all sorts of hardly manageable interdependencies with concurrency control, recovery, query optimization, etc. We would even claim that functional extensibility also creates major problems with respect to managing the overall system in the application environment; especially predicting and tuning the system's performance becomes horribly complex. In fact, it seems that all data-blade-style extensions are written by the database system vendor (or some of their partners) anyway. So extensibility on a per application basis appears to remain wishful thinking, and vendor-provided extensions that are coupled with the "kernel" (actually, a full-fledged database system anyway) are just additional complexity from the customers' viewpoint.

Attempt 3, unbundled technology: More recently several senior researchers have proposed to view database technology, i.e., our know-how about storage management, transaction management, etc., as something that is independent from the packaging of this technology into the traditional form of database systems [1,12,22]. A practical consequence (not necessarily fostered by but fully in line with these positions) is that we see more and more mature, industrial-strength database technology in all sorts of non-database products such as mail servers, document servers, specialized main-memory servers for switching and billing in telecommunication. In contrast to the situation ten years ago, most of these products have state-of-the-art algorithms for recovery, caching, etc. With a broad variety of such services, building applications that span multiple services becomes more difficult. Identifying principles for federating services into value-added information systems is subject of ongoing and future research.

The third approach, unbundling database technology and exploiting it in all sorts of services, is closest to our own position. However, the previous position papers have not said anything about the future role of database systems themselves as a package of installation and operation. We aim to redefine the scope and role of database servers, and outline also a possible path towards a world of composable "RISC"-style data management blocks.

4. Towards RISC-style Components

In computer architecture, the paradigm shift to RISC microprocessors led to a substantial simplification of the hardware-software interface. We advocate a similarly radical simplification of database system interfaces. Our proposal calls for building database systems with components that are built with RISC philosophy in mind. The components need to be carefully designed so that they enable building of richer components on top of the simpler components while maintaining a clear separation among components. Thus, each RISC-style component will have a well defined and relatively narrow functionality (and API). There is a need for "universal glue" as well to enable components to cooperate and build value-added services.

RISC data-management components appear attractive for us for three reasons. First, such components, with their relatively narrow functionality (and API), give us some new hope for predictable behavior and self-tuning capabilities. Second, the narrow functionality, coupled with the ability to build value-added services "on-top" makes such components far more attractive for varied information applications of today compared to a monolithic "universal" database management system. Third, even if we only build a monolithic database management system and no other data management services, building it using RISC data-management components will make it far more predictable and tunable than today's database management systems. All these benefits apply equally to RISC-style componentization within a database system as well as across different kinds of data managers for IT systems in the large.

RISC philosophy for database systems:

We will illustrate our intuition on RISC data components by focusing on querying capabilities of the database system. The simplest class of query engine is *a single-table selection processor*, one that supports single-table selection processing and simple updates with B+-tree indexing built-in. Such a single-table engine can be used in many simple application contexts. Indeed, with transactional support, such a query engine provides an ideal platform that can be used by many applications. In fact, until recently, even SAP R/3 essentially used the underlying DBMS as a storage engine of this kind. Another advantage of such a selection processor is that it can be used with a programmer-friendly API, with little or no knowledge of SQL. Another class of query engine that is quite attractive is the *Select-Project-Join (SPJ) query-processing engine*, suitable for OLTP and simple business applications. Such a RISC-component service can build on top of the simpler single table selection processor, much like how RDS was layered on RSS in System-R. The theory and performance of a SPJ query processor is much more clearly understood than that of a full-blown SQL query engine. In fact, the simplicity of the System-R optimizer has led to a deep understanding of how to process such queries efficiently, with join ordering, local choice of access methods, and interesting orders being the three central concepts. Adding *support for aggregation* to the SPJ engine, through sorting, data-stream partitioning (possibly hierarchical) capabilities, and more powerful local computation within a group (e.g., see [9]) brings it closer to requirements of decision support applications and specifically OLAP. Furthermore, note that the support for aggregation needs to be stronger than what SQL supports today. Yet, layering enables us to view the optimization problem for SPJ+Aggregation query engine as the problem of moving (and replicating) the partitioning and aggregation functions on top of SPJ query sub-trees. The challenge in designing such a RISC-component successfully is to identify optimization techniques that require us to enumerate only a few of all the SPJ query sub-trees. Finally, one could implement a full-fledged *SQL processor* that exploits the SPJ+Aggregation engine. Despite building the same old SQL engine, such an approach offers the hope of decomposing the optimization problem and thus the search complexity. Although in principle such a layered approach can result in inferior plans, it offers the hope of controlling the search space for each layered component much more tightly. Furthermore, the ad-hoc-ness in many of the commercial optimizer search techniques leave us far from being convinced that a global search would necessarily lead to better solutions in most cases. The above discussion illustrates how database technology may be re-packaged into layers of independently usable and manageable components. It should be noted that the vision that such "reduced-functionality" data managers will be available is implicit and anticipated in the OLE-DB API. However, provisions in the API have not led to products with such components yet.

In a similar vein, even the architecture of *storage managers* could be opened up for RISC-style redesign. A number of key mechanisms like disk management, caching, logging and recovery, and also concurrency control are undoubtedly core features in every kind of storage manager. But when we consider also the corresponding strategies that drive the run-time decisions of these mechanisms, we realize that different data or application classes could prefer tailored algorithms, for example, for cache replacement and prefetching, rather than universal algorithms that need more explicit tuning. For example, a media manager that stores video and audio files and needs to provide data-rate guarantees for smooth playback at clients would differ from the storage manager underneath a relational selection processor. Similarly, a semi-structured data storage manager that is geared for variances in record lengths and structures may choose implementation techniques that differ from those of schematic table storage. Finally, we could argue that even an *index manager* should be separated from the primary-data storage. This would make immediate versus deferred index maintenance equal citizens, with the latter being the preferable choice for text or multimedia document management. The price for this extreme kind of specialization and separation would be in additional overhead for calls across components; in the extreme case we may need an explicit two-phase commit between the primary-data and the index storage manager. However, this price seems to be tolerable for the benefit of removing tuning options that a universal storage manager would typically have and a much better chance of automating the remaining fine-tuning issues because of the smaller variance in the per-component workload characteristics.

The "RISC"-style componentization has some important ramifications. First, such componentization limits the interactions among components. For example, the SPJ query engine must use the "selection processor" as an encapsulated engine accessed through the specific APIs. The SPJ engine will have no knowledge of the internals of the selection processor except what can be gleaned via the API published for any consumer of the selection processor. Thus, the SPJ processor will know no more or no less than any other consumer of the "single-table selection" processor. Second, the API provided by any such component must expose at least two classes of interfaces: *functionality* as well as *import/export of meta-information*. For example, in the case of a selection processor, the functionality interface enables specification of a query request (table name and a filter on a column of the table). The import/export interface can expose to external components *limited* information that determines performance of the selection processor. In particular, the selection processor (specifically, the optimizer) should support an interface to return estimated selectivity of (predicates in) a query as well as the estimated run-time and resource consumption of executing the query. Note that obtaining reasonably accurate run-time estimates is important not only for query optimizers to choose an execution plan but also for deciding what priority a query should be given or whether it is worthwhile to submit it all (an issue that frequently arises in OLAP). Conversely, through an import interface, we can empower the application to specify parameters (e.g., response-time or throughput goals) that influence query execution.

RISC philosophy for IT systems in the large:

For building IT systems in the large, we obviously need more building blocks than the various database services discussed above. So we need to apply similar considerations also to web application servers, message queue managers, text document servers, video/audio media servers etc. Each of them should be constructed according to our RISC philosophy, and all of them together would form a library of RISC-style building blocks for composing higher-level, value-added information services. We have to make sure, that the complexity that we aim to reduce by simplifying the components does not reappear at the global application level. Research into principles of service composability should thus be put high on our community's agenda (a serious discussion of these issues is beyond the scope of this paper).

The challenge in adopting a RISC-style architecture is to precisely identify and standardize the functionality and import/export interfaces for each component such that the following objectives are met: (1) these interfaces can be exploited by a multitude of applications, (2) the performance loss due to the encapsulation via the API results is tolerable, and (3) each individual component is self-tuning and exhibits predictable performance. The last point is worth reemphasizing since it attempts to explain as to why RISC-style components are of great importance. It is only when we construct components that can be "locally" understood and explained, that we can hope to achieve predictability of performance and the ability to tune them as a component. As an example, we feel that it is much easier to understand the behavior (and indeed theory) of a single-table selection processor, or that of an SPJ processor that is built using only the narrow interfaces exposed by a selection processor. Of course, use of such narrow interfaces and creation of limited functionality can hamper performance, but as long as the degradation is marginal or even moderate, the need for predictable performance and self-tuning far outweighs such concerns given the cost point of today's commodity hardware. We now describe some of the important ramifications of the architecture we are espousing.

4.1 Notable Departures from Today's Architectures

The new departure that we advocate in this paper follows, in spirit, the earlier approaches of system generators and unbundling (referred to as Attempts 1 and 3 in Section 3.2). However, in contrast to these earlier proposals, we consider the appropriate packaging as a vital aspect of the overall architecture. In comparison to the modules considered by a generator, our RISC-style components are much coarser and ready for self-contained installation, thus avoiding the pitfall of the many subtle inter-dependencies among overly fine-grained modules. Similarly, we go beyond the unbundling theme by striving for components that are self-contained also in terms of predictability and self-tuning, and we aim to reduce the complexity of components and are willing to lose some performance to this end. The following simplifications would be important steps in this direction.

Support only for limited data types: The mantra in our new architecture is predictability and auto-tuning. This strongly argues against support for arbitrary data types. Instead, database systems should focus on the data types that they are best at, namely, tables with attributes of elementary type. Essentially this means going back to the roots of database systems, business data. There is no truly compelling reason for supporting the entire plethora of application-specific and multimedia data types. The initial motivation for adding all these features has been to ease data integration. But integration does not imply universal storage. In fact, what replaces the need for universal storage are data exchange protocols, advanced APIs, and component models that enable specialized storage/query systems to federate with traditional databases, e.g., OLE-DB/COM, EJB, or emerging XML protocols. To reiterate, limiting the responsibilities of the database system to data in table format makes the system much more manageable and give us a significantly better handle on the, still remaining and all but trivial, (automated) tuning problem.

No more SQL: As mentioned in Section 2, there is no demand for much of the complexity of full-fledged SQL, nor for the "Select-From-Where" syntactic sugar that has outlived its original motivation. We advocate a streamlined API through which programs essentially submit *operator trees* to the database server modules. In the example above, a selection processor will accept operator trees that only contain scan and selection; an SPJ processor will be able to process requests for processing trees that contain selection, projection, and join operators. For convenience, these operator trees may be linearized. Moreover, they should avoid the complex forms of nested and correlated subqueries that make current SQL hard to master. However, only changing the syntactic form of SQL is not enough. The language constructs themselves have to be simplified. Given that so many intelligent people have already argued for a simplification for the past two decades without success, we are convinced that the key for simplification lies in substantially limiting the functionality and expressiveness (which most of the previous attempts did not want to compromise).

Disjoint, manageable resources: There should be no dynamic resource sharing among components. This simplifies performance tuning and also provides additional isolation with regard to software failures. For example, when building a news-on-demand service on top of a video server, a text document server, and an SPJ table manager (for simple business issues such as accounting), each of these servers should have its own, dedicated hardware for simpler tuning (although this rules out additional cost/performance gains via dynamic resource sharing). In the extreme this could imply, for example,

that, within a table manager, data pages and index pages should always reside on disjoint disks (which is a commonly used rule of thumb anyway) for the sake of simplicity and at the modest cost of a few additional disks.

Pre-configuration: Each RISC-style data management component could be pre-configured for say five or ten different "power levels" with regard to feature-richness (e.g., "basic", "standard", "advanced", and "full") as well as performance and/or availability levels. Along the latter lines one could support a small spectrum of data server models such as "good for mostly-read workloads", "good for small to medium data volumes". This pre-configuration approach promises a viable compromise between "one size fits all" and complete freedom for configuration and feature selection at the risk of facing a monstrous tuning problem. In many cases the need for customization and tuning could be completely eliminated, at least at installation times. Note that this trend towards pre-packaging can already be observed in the IT industry, definitely as far as marketing and sales are concerned, but to some technical extent also in OS installation. However, database systems are still engineered mostly monolithically for the largest possible feature set. We advocate that the idea of supporting a limited number of different "models" should already be a major consideration in the design and engineering of data management software.

4.2 Prerequisites of Success

Need for "Universal Glue": The problem of composing different data managers into value-added application services is, of course, much more difficult than for standard consumer electronics. As noted earlier, we have to make sure that the complexity that we aim to reduce by simplifying the components does not reappear at the application layer and may become even more monstrous than ever. Simple interfaces with limited functionality and standardized cross-talk protocols are a fundamental prerequisite for composability and manageability of composite systems. Thus, higher-level application servers do need some standardized form of middleware such as OLE-DB or EJB to be able to talk to each underlying data server in a uniform manner. Such "universal glue" is available today. In particular, it is now a standard exercise to coordinate distributed transactions across arbitrary sets of heterogeneous servers by means of standardized 2PC protocols. So one important historical reason for putting all mission-critical data into a centralized, "universal" database for consistency preservation has become obsolete. Even when the classical ACID properties are inadequate for the application at hand, workflow technology is about to become mature and can reliably orchestrate activities on arbitrary servers within long-lived business processes. This is not to say that each and every technical aspect of how to combine arbitrary services into transactional federations is perfectly understood (e.g., see [1] for open issues), but most of the issues are settled and for the remaining ones research solutions are at least within reach.

Apply Occam's Razor: Following Occam's philosophy, we should be extremely careful, even purists, in selecting which features a data manager should support and which internal mechanisms it needs to have to this end, aiming to minimize the complexity of both *interfaces and internals*. Often certain involved features can be implemented on top of a RISC data manager with a moderate loss of performance and a minor increase in programming efforts. So the gain from using a database system would be slightly reduced, but, at the same time, the pain of having to manage a feature-overloaded, complex system could be drastically alleviated. So the win is in improving the gain/pain ratio of database technology. For example, one could argue that null values with all their ramifications should be implemented by the application rather than the underlying data manager: the application understands its specific semantics of missing or undefined values much better, and this would also eliminate a multitude of null-related, often tricky rewrite rules in the data manager's query optimizer.

Likewise, we should avoid an unnecessarily broad repertoire of implementation mechanisms within a single-table, SPJ, or SPJ+Aggregation processor. Often certain mechanisms improve performance by only moderate factors and only in special cases, but significantly add to the complexity of system tuning. For example, hash indexes and hash-based query processing (including the popular hash joins) are probably never better than a factor of two compared to nested-loop variants (including those with index support etc.) or sort-merge-based query processing [14]. Similar arguments could probably be made about pipelined query execution (especially on SMPs with very large memory where the performance impact of pipelining is noise compared to that of data parallelism and may even hamper processor-cache effectively), fancy notions of join indexes etc..

Need for a Self-Tuning Framework: A major incentive for moving towards RISC style data managers is to enable auto-tuning of database components. As explained earlier, tuning must consider the relationship between workload characteristics, knob settings, and the resulting performance in a quantitative manner. Therefore, it is not surprising that the most promising and, to some extent, successful approaches in the past decade have been based on mathematical models and/or feedback control methods (e.g., to dynamically adapt memory partitioning or multiprogramming levels to an evolving, multi-class workload). Unfortunately, these models work only in a limited context, i.e., when focusing on a particular knob (or a small set of inter-related knobs). Attempting to cover the full spectrum of tuning issues with a single, comprehensive model is bound to fail because of the lack of sufficiently accurate mathematical models or the

intractability of advanced models. This is why limiting ourselves to using only RISC data managers is so important: we no longer need to aim for the most comprehensive, elusive performance model, and there is hope that we can get a handle on how to auto-tune an individual data server component. It is much easier to tune a system with a less diverse workload and less dynamic resource sharing among different data and workload classes. Of course, the global tuning problem is now pushed one level above: how do we tune the interplay of several RISC data managers? Fortunately, a hierarchical approach to system tuning appears to be more in reach than trying to solve the entire complex problem in one shot. The main steps of such a hierarchical self-tuning framework are: 1) identifying the need for tuning, 2) identifying the bottleneck, 3) analyzing the bottleneck, 4) estimating the performance impact of possible tuning options, and 5) adjusting the most cost-effective tuning knob.

The hierarchical nature of such a self-tuning procedure is perfectly in line with good practice for manual, or we should better say intellectual, tuning (e.g., [16, 20, 21]). In particular, our approach also adopts a "think globally, fix locally" regime. Further note that mathematical models have been and remain to be key assets also in the practical system tuning community (e.g., [11]). The key to making the mathematics sufficiently simple and thus practical lies in the reduced complexity of the component systems and their interfaces and interplay. We believe that there is a virtue in engineering system components such that their real behavior can be better captured by existing mathematical modeling techniques, even if this may lead to some (tolerable) loss of high-end features and efficiency. The true gain lies in the better predictability and thus tunability and manageability of systems.

5. Towards a Research Agenda

5.1 Evaluation of Success

How should we evaluate the viability and success or failure of the advocated architecture? Actually evaluating an architectural framework would entail designing, building, and operating nontrivial IT systems, which obviously is way beyond the scope of a paper (especially a semi-technical vision paper like this one). So we merely give a rough sketch of how we as a research community may proceed along these lines.

The best measure of success of a RISC-style database system architecture would be to demonstrate the usefulness of the components in a variety of data management scenarios. To start with, we should be able to develop data management components that work well as scalable traditional OLTP systems as well as the basis for OLAP-style data management services. Such systems are likely to use the SPJ query processor and the SPJ+Aggregation query processor, respectively.

Incidentally, recall that the first generation of OLAP services extensively used "multi-statement" SQL, i.e., they fed only simple queries (SPJ with aggregation) to backend servers to ensure that performance characteristics are predictable since database optimizers have been known to behave erratically for complex SQL queries (which should not really be a surprise given that a typical query optimizer is a large bag of tricks).

Another interesting instance of services is metadata management. Such a service is distinguished from traditional OLTP and OLAP in requiring more elaborate conceptual data models, but with relatively simple needs for querying and scalability (for large data volumes). Yet another popular class of services is management of e-mail data. Mail servers require fast insertion of mail messages and "mostly fast" access when queried by attributes. A key characteristic of mail data is that it is sparse, i.e., not all attributes are present and records are of widely variable length. It would be intriguing to consider an SPJ query engine and a separate indexing engine as a mail server's base components. In contrast to traditional relational system designs, however, there should be no limiting necessity of a schema in this setting. Other data services of interest, whose architecture would be worthwhile to re-examine with this paper's philosophy of RISC building blocks in mind, are marketplace data servers (e.g., in E-Bay) or large-scale multimedia information servers for news-on-demand etc.

5.2 Research Opportunities

We wish to encourage researchers to make the system architecture of database technology and the simplification of component interfaces as well as internals (again) a top-priority item on their agenda. Although most of the problems with today's architecture that we have identified refer to industrial products, we believe that the impetus for a new departure must come from academia as product architects and developers are way too busy in their time-to-market issues. To be fair, the database system industry has a lot of stake in maintaining existing products and market shares, and has too little leeway for radical departures. For academic researchers we see ample opportunities of system-oriented exploration that can hopefully drive the community towards a better overall architecture. It is crucial, however, already for component prototyping and systematic experimentation that this research avenue heads for simpler, smaller-scale, RISC-style building blocks.

Along these lines, we propose making major efforts towards the following research (and, to some extent, sociological) challenges:

- Make viable an open, worldwide testbed for RISC-style data-management components to which even small research teams can contribute.

- Work out lean APIs for each of the most important RISC-style components following our discussion of Section 4.1 on different kinds of query processors and storage managers.
- Encourage a worldwide competition for the "best" instantiation of each of these building blocks, for example, with regard to certain standard benchmarks or common test suites for data mining and Web applications. To make this a real challenge and avoid compromising our goal of simplified and auto-tuned components, the rules should limit the code size of each component, limit its footprint, and disallow any kinds of tuning knobs other than what the component does internally based on its own self-assessment.
- To ensure that individual components are not tailored to other components by the same team or even tailored to specific benchmarks, all components that are registered with the worldwide testbed must be able to correctly cooperate, through their official APIs, with all other components from all other teams.
- Identify more precisely the "universal glue" for the above kind of open test bed. Obviously this is already required for setting up the test bed. A bootstrap approach could be that one team provides an initial instantiation of the necessary middleware services and the most important components as a basis for other teams to contribute and plug in individual components or gradually replace some of the "glue" services (e.g., a two-phase commit protocol).

Once the envisioned test bed is operational for database-system components, its scope could and should be broadened to encompass different kinds of data managers for IT solutions in the large (e.g., a media server, a mail server each again built from several RISC-style components). So this worldwide test bed should be extensible beyond the narrow boundaries of what is commonly perceived as the "database community".

6. Concluding Remarks

Universal database systems grew out of our belief that database is the center of the universe and therefore the framework for integration. This is far from true in today's world. Once we are liberated and can accept the fact that the database is one, certainly very important, component in the IT world, programmability and integration of database components with applications become a priority. In such a world, we need to build RISC-style data management components that have predictable performance and can be auto-tuned.

When comparing our field to other areas of engineering that are building extremely complex artifacts such as aircrafts, high-speed trains, or space shuttles, we realize that such an architectural simplification is overdue and critical for the future success of database technology. Few, if any, understand the functions of a modern aircraft (e.g. Boeing 747) completely, but in contrast to the situation with database systems, there is excellent understanding of local components and a good understanding of the interaction across components.

The test for the advocated RISC-style database system architecture will be if it can be used broadly in many more contexts compared to today's database systems. In this paper, we have hinted at some applications that can drive the design of such RISC data management components. These components can be "glued" together using narrow APIs to form powerful data services that have the hope of being effectively manageable.

The bottom line of these challenges is to foster improving the "gain/pain ratio" of database technology with regard to modern cyberspace applications. The key to this goal is to tolerate a moderate degradation of "gain", for example, by tolerating certain overhead for more interface-crossing across components, and reduce the "pain" level by orders of magnitude by ensuring predictable performance and eliminating the need for manual tuning.

References

[1] G. Alonso, C. Hagen, H.-J. Schek, M. Tresch: Distributed Processing Over Stand-alone Systems and Applications, 23rd International Conference on Very Large Data Bases, Athens, Greece, 1997.

[2] P. Bernstein et al. : The Asilomar Report on Database Research, ACM SIGMOD Record Vol.27 No.4, Decemer 1998.

[3] D.S. Batory, T.Y. Leung, T.E. Wise: Implementation Concepts for an Extensible Data Model and Data Language, ACM Transactions on Database Systems Vol.13 No.3, 1988.

[44] K.P. Brown, M. Mehta, M.J. Carey, M. Livny: Towards Automated Performance Tuning for Complex Workloads, 20th International Conference on Very Large Data Bases, Santiago, Chile, 1994.

[5] M.J. Carey, D.J. DeWitt, D. Frank, G. Graefe, M. Muralikrishna, J.E. Richardson, E.J. Shekita: The Architecture of the EXODUS Extensible DBMS, in: K.R. Dittrich, U. Dayal (Eds.), International Workshop on Object-Oriented Database Systems, Pacific Grove, 1986.

[6] M.J. Carey, D.J. DeWitt: Of Objects and Databases: A Decade of Turmoil, 22nd International Conference on Very Large Data Bases, Bombay, India, 1996.

[7] S. Chaudhuri, V. Narasayya : An Efficient, Cost-driven Index Tuning Wizard for Microsoft SQL Server, 23rd International Conference on Very Large Data Bases, Athens, Greece, 1997.

[8] S. Agrawal, S, Chaudhuri, V. Narasayya: Automated Selection of Materialized Views and Indexes, 26th International Conference on Very Large Data Bases, Cairo, Egypt (this proceedings).

[9] D. Chatziantoniou, K.A. Ross: Querying Multiple Features of Groups in Relational Databases, 22nd International Conference on Very Large Data Bases, Bombay, India, 1996.

[10] S. Chaudhuri (Editor): IEEE CS Data Engineering Bulletin, Special Issue on Self-Tuning Databases and Application Tuning, Vol.22 No.2, June 1999.

[11] Computer Measurement Group, Inc., http://www.11.org

[12] A. Geppert, K.R. Dittrich: Bundling: Towards a New Construction Paradigm for Persistent Systems, Networking and Information Systems Journal Vol.1 No.1, 1998.

[13] G. Graefe, D.J. DeWitt: The EXODUS Optimizer Generator, ACM SIGMOD International Conference on Management of Data, San Francisco, 1987.

[14] G. Graefe: The Value of Merge-Join and Hash-Join in SQL Server. 25th International Conference on Very Large Data Bases, Edinburgh, UK, 1999.

[15] L. Haas et al.: Starburst Midflight: As the Dust Clears, IEEE Transactions on Knowledge and Data Engineering Vol.2 No.1, 1990.

[16] D.A. Menasce, V.A.F. Almeida: Capacity Planning for Web Performance – Metrics, Models, and Methods, Prentice Hall, 1998.

[17] R. Munz: Usage Scenarios of DBMS, Keynote, 25th International Conference on Very Large Data Bases, Edinburgh, UK, 1999, http://www.dcs.napier.ac.uk/~vldb99/Industrial SpeakerSlides/SAPVLDB.pdf

[18] US President's Information Technology Advisory Committee Interim Report to the President, August 1998, http://www.ccic.gov/ac/interim

[19] H.-J. Schek, H.-B. Paul, M.H. Scholl, G. Weikum: The DASDBS Project: Objectives, Experiences, and Future Prospects, IEEE Transactions on Knowledge and Data Engineering Vol.2 No.1, 1990.

[20] T. Schneider, SAP R/3 Performance Optimization: The Official SAP Guide, Sybex, 1999.

[21] D.E. Shasha: Database Tuning: A Principled Approach, Prentice Hall, 1992.

[22] A. Silberschatz, S. Zdonik, et al.: Strategic Directions in Database Systems - Breaking Out of the Box, ACM Computing Surveys Vol.28 No.4, December 1996.

[23] M. Stonebraker, L.A. Rowe, M. Hirohama: The Implementation of Postgres, IEEE Transactions on Knowledge and Data Engineering Vol.2 No.1, 1990.

[24] G. Weikum, C. Hasse, A. Moenkeberg, P. Zabback: The COMFORT Automatic Tuning Project, Information Systems Vol.19 No.5, 1994.

PicoDBMS: Scaling down Database Techniques
for the Smartcard

Christophe Bobineau[*], Luc Bouganim[*], Philippe Pucheral[*], Patrick Valduriez[**]

[*]PRiSM Laboratory
78035 – Versailles
France
{Firstname.Lastname}@prism.uvsq.fr

[**]INRIA Rocquencourt
78153 – Le Chesnay
France
Patrick.Valduriez@inria.fr

Abstract

Smartcards are the most secure portable computing device today. They have been used successfully in applications involving money, proprietary and personal data (such as banking, healthcare, insurance, etc.). As smartcards get more powerful (with 32 bit CPU and more than 1 MB of stable memory in the next versions) and become multi-application, the need for database management arises. However, smartcards have severe hardware limitations (very slow write, very little RAM, constrained stable memory, no autonomy, etc.) which make traditional database technology irrelevant. The major problem is scaling down database techniques so they perform well under these limitations. In this paper, we give an in-depth analysis of this problem and propose a PicoDBMS solution based on highly compact data structures and query execution without RAM. We show the effectiveness of our techniques through performance evaluation.

1 Introduction

Smartcards are the most secure portable computing device today. The first smartcard was developed by Bull for the French banking system in the 80s to significantly reduce the losses associated with magnetic stripe credit card fraud. Since then, smartcards have been used successfully around the world in various applications involving money, proprietary data and personal data (such as banking, pay-

Proceedings of the 26th International Conference on Very Large Databases, Cairo, Egypt, 2000

TV or GSM subscriber identification, loyalty, healthcare, insurance, etc.). While today's smartcards handle a single issuer-dependent application, the trend is toward multi-application smartcards. Standards for multi-application support, like the JavaCard [21] and Microsoft's SmartCard for Windows [16], ensure that the card be universally accepted and be able to interact with several service providers. According to DataQuest [8], 990 million smartcards will be shipped in the year 2K and smartcards could become one of the world's highest-volume markets for semiconductors.

As smartcards become more and more versatile, multi-applications and powerful (32 bit processor, more than 1MB of stable storage), the need for database techniques arises. Let us consider a health card storing a complete medical folder including the holder's doctors, blood type, allergies, prescriptions, etc. The volume of data can be important and the queries fairly complex (select, join, aggregate). Sophisticated access rights management using views and aggregate functions are required to preserve the holder's data privacy. Transaction atomicity and durability are also needed to enforce data consistency. More generally, database management helps to separate data management code from application code, thereby simplifying and making application code smaller. Finally, new applications can be envisioned, like computing statistics on a large number of cards, in an asynchronous and distributed way. Supporting database management on the card itself rather than on an external device is the only way to achieve very high security, high availability (anywhere, anytime, on any terminal) and acceptable performance.

However, smartcards have severe hardware limitations which stem from the obvious constraints of small size (to fit on a flexible plastic card and to increase hardware security) and low cost (to be sold in large volumes). Today's microcontrollers contain a CPU, memory including about 96 KB of ROM, 4 KB of RAM and up to 128 KB of stable storage like EEPROM, and security modules [23]. EEPROM is used to store persistent information; it has very fast read time (60-100 ns) comparable to RAM but very slow write time (10 ms/word). Following Moore's law for processor and memory capacities, smartcards will get rapidly more powerful. Existing prototypes, like Gemplus's Pinocchio card [10], bypass the current memory bottleneck by connecting an additional chip of 2MB of Flash memory to the microcontroller. Although a significant improvement over today's cards, this is still very restricted compared to other portable, less secure, devices such as Personal Digital Assistants (PDA). Furthermore, smartcards are not autonomous, *i.e.,* have no independent power supply, thereby precluding asynchronous and disconnected processing.

These limitations (tiny RAM, little stable storage, very costly write and lack of autonomy) make traditional database techniques irrelevant. Typically, traditional DBMS exploit significant amounts of RAM and use caching and asynchronous I/Os to reduce disk access overhead as much as possible. With the extreme constraints of the smartcard, the major problem is scaling down database techniques. While there has been much excellent work on scaling up to deal with very large databases, *e.g.,* using parallelism, scaling down has not received much attention by the database research community. However, scaling down in general is getting very important for commodity computing and is quite difficult [12].

Some DBMS designs have addressed the problem of scaling down. Light versions of popular DBMS like Sybase Adaptive Server Anywhere [22], Oracle 8i Lite [18] or DB2 Everywhere [13] have been primarily designed for portable computers and PDA. They have a small footprint which they obtain by simplifying and componentizing the DBMS code. However, they use relatively much RAM and stable memory and do not address the more severe limitations of smartcards. ISOL's SQLJava Machine DBMS [7] is the first attempt towards a smartcard DBMS and SCQL [15], the standard for smartcard database language, emerges. While both designs are limited to single select, they exemplify the strong interest for dedicated smartcard DBMS.

In this paper, we address the problem of scaling down database techniques and propose the design of what we call a PicoDBMS. This work is done in the context of a new project with Bull Smart Cards and Terminals. The design has been made with smartcard applications in mind but its scope extends as well to any ultra-light computer device based on a secured monolithic chip. This paper makes the following contributions:

- We analyze the requirements for a PicoDBMS based on a typical healthcare application and justify its minimal functionality.
- We give an in-depth analysis of the problem by considering the smartcard hardware trends and derive design principles for a PicoDBMS.

- We propose a new pointer-based storage model that integrates data and indices in a unique compact data structure.
- We propose query execution techniques which handle complex query plans (including joins and aggregates) with no RAM consumption.
- We show the effectiveness of each technique through performance evaluation.

This paper is organized as follows. Section 2 illustrates the use of take-away databases in various classes of smartcard applications and presents in more details the requirements of the health card application. Section 3 analyzes the smartcard hardware constraints and gives the problem definition. Sections 4 - 5 present and assess the PicoDBMS' storage model and query execution model, respectively. Section 6 concludes.

2 Smartcard Applications

In this section, we discuss the major classes of emerging smartcard applications and their database requirements. Then, we illustrate these requirements in further details with the health card application, which we will use as reference example in the rest of the paper.

2.1 Database Management Requirements

Table 1 summarizes the database management requirements of the following typical classes of smartcard applications.

Applications	Volume	Select / Project	Join	Group by / Distinct	Access rights views	Atomicity	Durability	Statistics
Money & identification	*tiny*					✔		
Downloadable DB	*high*	✔	✔	✔				
User environment	*medium*	✔			✔	✔	✔	
Personal folder	*high*	✔	✔	✔	✔	✔	✔	✔

Table 1: *Typical application's profiles*

- *Money and identification:* examples of such applications are credit cards, e-purse, SIM for GSM, phone cards, transportation cards. They are representative of today's applications, with very few data (typically the holder's identifier and some status information). Querying is not a concern and access rights are useless since cards are protected by PIN-codes. Their unique requirement is update atomicity.
- *Downloadable databases:* they are predefined packages of data (*e.g.,* list of restaurants, hotels and tourist sites, catalogs…) that can be downloaded on the card – for example, before traveling – and be accessed from any terminal. Data availability is the major concern here. The volume of data can be important and the queries complex. The data are typically read-only and public.

- *User environment:* the objective is to store in a smartcard an extended profile of the card's holder including, among others, data regarding the computing environment (PC's configuration, passwords, cookies, bookmarks, software licenses…), an address book as well as an agenda. Queries remain simple, as data are not related. However, the data are highly private and must be protected by sophisticated access rights (*e.g.,* the card's holder may want to share a subset of her address book or bookmark list with a subset of persons). Transaction atomicity and durability are also required.
- *Personal folders:* personal folders may be of different nature: scholastic, healthcare, car maintenance history, loyalty. They roughly share the same requirements, which we illustrate next with the healthcare example. Note that queries involving data issued from different folders can make sense. For instance, one may be interested in discovering associations between some disease and the scholastic level of the card holder. This raises the interesting issue of maintaining statistics on a population of cards or mining their content asynchronously.

2.2 The Health Card Application

The health card is very representative of personal folder applications and has strong database requirements. Several countries (France, Germany, USA, Russia, Korea…) are developing healthcare applications on smartcards [5]. The initial idea was to give to each citizen a smartcard containing her identification and insurance data. As smartcard storage capacity increases, the information stored in the card can be extended to the holder's doctors, emergency data (blood type, allergies, vaccination…), surgical operations, prescriptions, insurance data and even links to heavier data (*e.g.,* X-ray examination, scanner images…) stored on hospital servers. Different users may query, modify and create data in the holder's folder: the doctors who consult the patient's past records and prescribe drugs, the surgeons who perform exams and operations, the pharmacists who deliver drugs, the insurance agents who refund the patient, public organizations which maintain statistics or study the impact of drugs correlation in population samples and finally the holder herself.

We can easily observe that: (i) the amount of data is significant (more in terms of cardinality than in terms of volume because most data can be encoded), (ii) queries can be rather complex (*e.g.,* a doctor asks for the last antibiotics prescribed to the patient), (iii) sophisticated access rights management using views and aggregate functions are highly required (*e.g.,* a statistical organization may access aggregate values only but not the raw data), (iv) atomicity must be preserved (*e.g.,* when the pharmacist delivers drugs) and (v) durability is mandatory, without compromising data privacy (logged data stored outside the card must be protected).

One may wonder whether the holder's health data must be stored in a smartcard or in a centralized database. The benefit of distributing the healthcare database on smartcards is threefold. First, health data must be made highly available (anywhere, anytime, on any terminal and without requiring a network connection). Second, storing sensitive data on a centralized server may hurt privacy. Third, maintaining a centralized database is fairly complex due to the variety of data sources. Assuming the health data is stored in the smartcard, the next question is why the aforementioned database capabilities need be hosted in the smartcard rather than the terminals. The answer is again availability (the data must be exploited on any terminal) and privacy. Regarding privacy, since the data must be confined in the chip, so must be the query engine and the view manager. The smartcard being the unique trusted part of the system, access rights and transaction management cannot be delegated to an untrusted terminal.

3 Problem Formulation

In this section, we make clear the smartcard constraints in order to derive design rules for the PicoDBMS and state the problem. Our analysis is based on the characteristics of both existing smartcard products and current prototypes [23, 10], and thus, should be valid for a while. We also discuss how the main constraints of the smartcard will evolve in a near future.

3.1 SmartCard constraints

Current smartcards include in a monolithic chip, a 32 bits RISC processor at about 30 MIPS, memory modules (of about 96 KB of ROM, 4 KB of static RAM and 128 KB of EEPROM), security components and take their electrical energy from the terminal [23]. ROM is used to store the operating system, fixed data and standard routines. RAM is used as working memory for calculating results. EEPROM is used to store persistent information. EEPROM has very fast read time (60-100 ns/word) comparable to RAM, but a dramatically slow write time (10 ms/word).

The main constraints of current smartcards are therefore: (i) the very limited storage capacity; (ii) the very slow write time in EEPROM; (iii) the extremely reduced size of the RAM; (iv) the lack of autonomy and (v) a high security level that must be preserved in all situations. These constraints strongly distinguish smartcards from any other computing devices, including lightweight computers like PDA.

Let us now consider how hardware advances can impact these constraints, in particular memory size. Current smartcards rely on a well established and slightly out-of-date hardware technology (0.35μm) in order to minimize the production cost (less than five dollars) and increase security [20]. Furthermore, up to now, there was not a real need for large memories in smartcard applications like holder's identification. According to major smartcard providers, the market pressure generated by emerging large storage demanding applications will lead to a rapid increase of the smartcard storage capacity. This evolution is however constrained by the smartcard tiny die size fixed to 25 mm² in the ISO standard [14], which pushes for more integration. This limited size is due to security considerations (to minimize the risk of physical attack [2]) and practical constraints (*e.g.*, the chip should not break when the smartcard is flexed). Another solution to relax the storage limit is to extend the smartcard storage capacity with external memory modules. This is being experienced by Gemplus which recently announced Pinocchio [10], a smartcard equipped with 2 MB of Flash memory linked to the microcontroller by a bus. Since hardware security can no longer be provided on this memory, its content must be either non-sensitive or encrypted.

Memory type	EEPROM	FLASH	FeRAM
Read time (/word)	60 to 150 ns	70 to 200 ns	150 to 200 ns
Write time (/word)	10 ms	5 to 10 μs	150 to 200 ns
Erase time (/bank)	None	500 to 800 ms	None
Lifetime [*]	10^5 write cycles per cell	10^5 erase cycles	10^{10} to 10^{12} write cycles

* A memory cell can be overwritten a finite number of times.

Table 2: *Performance of stable memories for the smartcard*

Another important issue is the performance of stable memory. Possible alternatives to the EEPROM are Flash memory and Ferroelectric RAM (FeRAM) [9] (see Table 2 for performance comparisons). Flash is more compact than EEPROM and then represents a good candidate for high capacity smartcards [10]. However, flash banks need be erased before writing, which is extremely slow. This makes Flash memory appropriated for applications with a high read/write ratio (*e.g.*, address books). FeRAM is undoubtedly an interesting option for smartcard as read and write times are both fast. Although its theoretical foundation was set in the early 50s, FeRAM is just emerging as an industrial solution. Therefore, FeRAM is expensive, less secure than EEPROM or Flash, and its integration with traditional technologies (such as CPUs) remains an issue. Thus FeRAM could be considered a serious alternative only in the very long term [9].

Given these considerations, we assume in this paper a smartcard with a reasonable stable storage area (few MB of EEPROM[1]) and a small RAM area (some KB). Indeed, there is no clear interest to have a large RAM area, given that the smartcard is not autonomous, thus precluding asynchronous write operations. Moreover, more RAM means less EEPROM as the chip size is limited.

3.2 Impact on the PicoDBMS architecture

We now analyze the impact of the smartcard constraints on the PicoDBMS architecture, thus justifying why traditional database techniques, and even lightweight DBMS techniques, are irrelevant. The smartcard's properties and their impact are:

- *Highly secure:* smartcard's hardware security makes it the ideal storage support for private data. The PicoDBMS must contribute to the data security by providing access right management and a view mechanism that allows complex view definitions (*i.e.*, supporting data composition and aggregation). The PicoDBMS code must not present security holes due to the use of sophisticated algorithms[2].

- *Highly portable:* the smartcard is undoubtedly the most portable personal computer (the wallet computer). The data located on the smartcard are thus highly available. They are also highly vulnerable since the smartcard can be lost, stolen or accidentally destroyed. The main consequence is that durability cannot be enforced locally.

- *Limited storage resources:* despite the foreseen increase in storage capacity, the smartcard will remain the lightest representative of personal computers for a long time. This means that specific storage models and execution techniques must be devised to minimize the volume of persistent data (*i.e.*, the database) and the memory consumption during execution. In addition, the functionalities of the PicoDBMS must be carefully selected and their implementation must be as light as possible. The lightest the PicoDBMS, the biggest the onboard database.

- *Stable storage is main memory:* smartcard stable memory provides the read speed and direct access granularity of a main memory. Thus, a PicoDBMS can be considered as a *main memory DBMS (MMDBMS)*. However the dramatic cost of writes distinguishes a PicoDBMS from a traditional MMDBMS. This impacts the storage and access methods of the PicoDBMS as well as the way transaction atomicity is achieved.

- *Non autonomous:* compared to other computers, the smartcard has no independent power supply, thereby precluding disconnected and asynchronous processing. Thus, all transactions must be completed while the card is inserted in a terminal (unlike PDA, write operations cannot be cached in RAM and reported on stable storage asynchronously).

3.3 Problem Statement

To summarize, our goal is to design a PicoDBMS including the following components:

- Storage manager: manages the storage of the database and the associated indices.

- Query manager: processes query plans composed of select, project, join and aggregates.

- Transaction manager: enforces the ACID properties and participates in distributed transactions.

- Access right manager: provides access rights on base data and on complex user-defined views.

---

[1] Considering Flash instead of EEPROM will not change our conclusions. It will just exacerbate them.

[2] Most security holes are the results of software bugs [20].

Thus, the PicoDBMS hosted in the chip provides the minimal subset of functionality that is strictly needed to manage in a secure way the data shared by all onboard applications. Other components (*e.g.,* the GUI, a sort operator…) can be hosted in the terminal or be dynamically downloaded when needed, without threatening security. In the rest of this paper, we concentrate on the storage manager and the query manager which are the most impacted by the smarcard constraints. Smartcard-specific transaction manager description can be found in [4], while traditional techniques can be used for access right manager.

When designing the PicoDBMS's components, we must follow several design rules derived from the smartcard's properties:

- *Compactness rule:* minimize the size of data structures and the PicoDBMS code to cope with the limited stable memory area (a few MB).
- *RAM rule:* minimize the RAM usage given its extremely limited size (some KB).
- *Write rule:* minimize write operations given their dramatic cost ($\approx$10 ms/word).
- *Read rule:* take advantage of the fast read operations ($\approx$100 ns/word).
- *Access rule:* take advantage of the low granularity and direct access capability of the stable memory for both read and write operations.
- *Security rule:* never externalize private data from the chip and minimize the algorithms' complexity to avoid security holes.

4 PicoDBMS storage model

In this section, following the design rules for a PicoDBMS, we discuss the storage issues and propose a very compact model based on a combination of flat storage, domain storage and ring storage. We also evaluate the storage cost of our storage model.

4.1 Flat Storage

The simplest way to organize data is *Flat Storage (FS)*, where tuples are stored sequentially and attribute values are embedded in the tuples. Although it does not impose it, the SCQL standard [15] considers FS as the reference storage model for smartcards. The main advantage of FS is access locality. However, in our context, FS has two main drawbacks:

- *Space consuming:* while normalization rules preclude attributes conjunction redundancy to occur, they do not avoid attribute value duplicates (*e.g.,* the attribute *Doctor.Specialty* may contain many duplicates).
- *Inefficient:* in the absence of index structures, all operations are computed sequentially. While this is convenient for old fashion cards (some KB of storage and a mono-relation select operator), this is no longer acceptable for future cards where storage capacity is likely to exceed 1MB and queries can be rather complex.

Adding index structures to FS may solve the second problem while worsening the first one. Thus, FS alone is not appropriate for a PicoDBMS.

4.2 Domain Storage

Based on the critique of FS, it follows that a PicoDBMS storage model should guarantee both data and index compactness. Let us first deal with data compactness. Since locality is no longer an issue in our context, pointer-based storage models inspired by MMDBMS [1, 17, 19] can help reducing the data storage cost. The basic idea is to preclude any duplicate value to occur. This can be achieved by grouping values in domains (sets of unique values). We call this model *Domain Storage (DS)*. As shown in Figure 1, tuples reference their attribute values by means of pointers. Furthermore, a domain can be shared among several attributes. This is particularly efficient for enumerated types, which vary on a small and determined set of values[3].

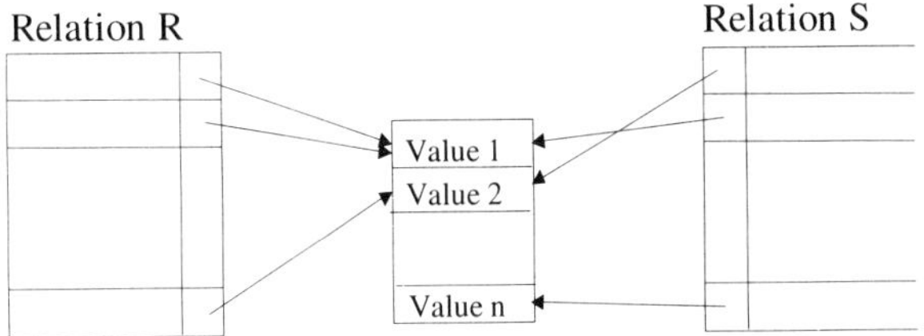

Figure 1 : *Domain Storage*

One may wonder about the cost of tuple creation, update and deletion since they may generate insertion and deletion of values in domains. While these actions are more complex than their FS counterpart, their implementation remains more efficient in the smartcard context, simply because the amount of data to be written is much smaller. To amortize the slight overhead of domain storage, we only store by domain all large attributes (*i.e.,* greater than a pointer size) containing duplicates. Obviously, attributes with no duplicates need not be stored by domain but with FS. Variable-size attributes – generally larger than a pointer – can also be advantageously stored in domains even if they do not contain duplicates. The benefit is not storage savings but memory management simplicity (all tuples of all relations become fixed-size).

4.3 Ring Storage

We now address index compactness along with data compactness. Unlike disk-based DBMS that favor indices which preserve access locality, smartcards should make intensive use of secondary (*i.e.,* pointer-based) indices. The issue here is to make these indices as compact as possible. Let us first consider select indices. A select index is typically made of two parts: a collection of values and a collection of pointers linking each value to all tuples sharing it. Assuming the indexed attribute varies on a domain, the index's collection of values can be saved since

---

[3] Compression techniques can be advantageously used in conjunction with DS to increase compactness [11].

it exactly corresponds to the domain extension. The extra cost incurred by the index is then reduced to the pointers linking index values to tuples.

Let us go one step further and get these pointers almost for free. The idea is to store these *value-to-tuple* pointers in place of the *tuple-to-value* pointers within the tuples (*i.e.,* pointers stored in the tuples to reference their attribute values in the domains). This yields to an index structure which makes a ring from the domain values to the tuples. Hence, we call it *Ring index* (see Figure 2(a)). But the ring index can also be used to access the domain values from the tuples and thus serve as data storage model. Thus we call *Ring Storage (RS)* the storage of a domain-based attribute indexed by a ring. The index storage cost is reduced to its lowest bound, that is, one pointer per domain value, whatever be the cardinality of the indexed relation. This important storage saving is obtained at the price of extra work for projecting a tuple to the corresponding attribute since retrieving the value of a ring stored attribute means traversing in average half of the ring (*i.e.,* up to reach the domain value).

Join indices [24] can be treated in a similar way. A join predicate of the form (*R.a=S.b*) assumes that *R.a* and *S.b* vary on the same domain. Storing both *R.a* and *S.b* by means of rings leads to define a join index. In this way, each domain value is linked by two separate rings to all tuples from *R* and *S* sharing the same join attribute value. However, most joins are performed on key attributes, *R.a* being a primary key and *S.b* being the foreign key referencing *R.a*. In our model, key attributes are not stored by domain but with FS. Nevertheless, since *R.a* is the primary key of *R*, its extension forms precisely a domain, even if not stored outside of *R*. Since attributes *S.b* take their values in *R.a*'s domain, they reference *R.a* values by means of pointers. Thus, the domain-based storage model naturally implements for free a *unidirectional join index* from *S.b* to *R.a* (*i.e.,* each *S* tuple is linked by a pointer to each *R* tuple matching with it). If traversals from *R.a* to *S.b* need be optimized too, a *bi-directional join index* is required. This can be simply achieved by defining a ring index on *S.b*. Figure 2(b) shows the resulting situation where each *R* tuple is linked by a ring to all *S* tuples matching with it and vice-versa. The cost of a bi-directional join index is restricted to a single pointer per *R* tuple, whatever be the cardinality of *S*. Note that this situation resembles the well-known Codasyl model.

4.4 Storage cost evaluation

Our storage model combines FS, DS and RS. Thus, the issue is to determine the best storage for each attribute. If the attributes need not be indexed, the choice is obviously between FS and DS. Otherwise, the choice is between RS and FS with a traditional index. Thus, we compare the storage cost for a single attribute, indexed or not, for each alternative. We introduce the following parameters:

CardRel: *cardinality of the relation holding the attribute*
a: *average length of the attribute (expressed in bytes)*
p: *pointer size (3 bytes will be required to address "large" memory of future cards)*
S: *selectivity factor of the attribute. S=CardDom/CardRel, where CardDom is the cardinality of the attribute domain extension. S measures the redundancy of the attribute (i.e., the same value appears in 1/S tuples).*

$$Cost(FS) = CardRel*a$$
$$Cost(DS) = CardRel*p + S*CardRel*a$$
$$Cost(Indexed\_FS) = Cost(FS) + S*CardRel*a + CardRel*p$$
$$Cost(RS) = Cost(DS) + S*CardRel*p$$

The cost equality between FS and DS gives: $S=(a-p)/a$. The cost equality between Indexed_FS and RS gives: $S=a/p$

Figure 3(a) shows the different values of *S* and *a* for which FS and DS are equivalent. Thus, each curve divides the plan into a gain area for FS (above the curve) and a gain area for DS (under the curve). For values of *a* less than 3 (*i.e., the size of a pointer*), FS is obviously always more compact than DS. For higher values of *a*, DS becomes rapidly more compact than FS except for high values of *S*. For instance, considering *S=0.5*, that is the same value is shared by only two tuples, DS outperforms FS for all *a* larger than 6 bytes. The higher *a* and the lower *S*, the better DS. The benefit of DS is thus particularly important for enumerated type attributes. Figure 3(b) compares Indexed_FS with RS. The superiority of RS is obvious, except for one and two byte long key attributes. Thus, Figures 3(a) and 3(b) are guidelines for the database designer to decide how to store each attribute, by considering its size and selectivity.

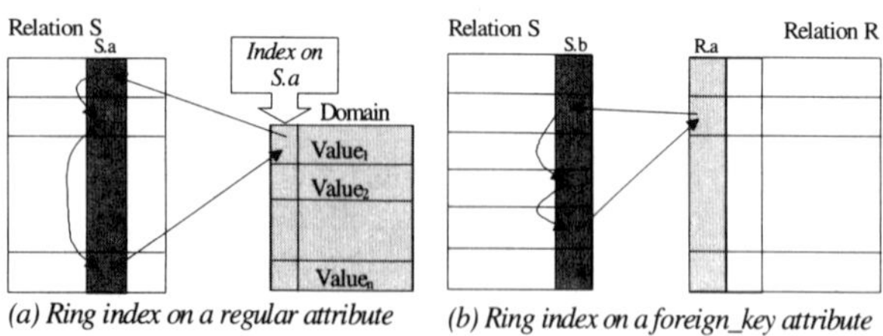

(a) *Ring index on a regular attribute*   (b) *Ring index on a foreign_key attribute*

Figure 2: *Ring Storage*

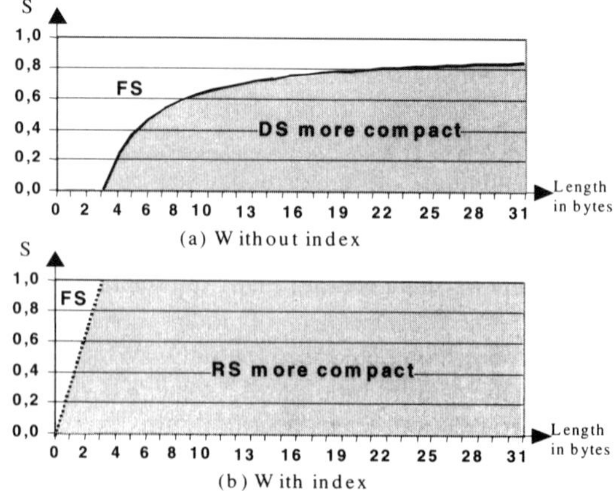

Figure 3: *Storage models tradeoff*

5 Query Processing

Traditional query processing strives to exploit large main memory for storing temporary data structures (*e.g.*, hash tables) and intermediate results. When main memory is not large enough to hold some data, state-of-the-art algorithms resort to materialization on disk to avoid memory overflow. These algorithms cannot be used for a PicoDBMS because:

- Given the write rule and the lifetime of stable memory, writes in stable memory are proscribed, even for temporary materialization;
- Dedicating a specific RAM area does not help since we cannot estimate its size a-priori. Choosing it small increases the risk of memory overflow, thereby leading to writes in stable memory. Choosing it large reduces the stable memory area, already limited in a smartcard (RAM rule). Moreover, even a large RAM area cannot guarantee that query execution will not produce memory overflow [3];
- State-of-the-art algorithms are quite sophisticated, which precludes their implementation in a PicoDBMS whose code must be simple, compact and secure (compactness and security rules).

To solve this problem, we propose query processing techniques that do not use any working RAM area nor incur any writes in stable memory. In the following, we describe these techniques for simple and complex queries, including aggregation and remove duplicates. We show the effectiveness of our solution through a performance analysis.

5.1 Basic Query Execution without RAM

We consider the execution of *SPJ* (*Select-Project-Join*) queries. Query processing is classically done in two steps. The query optimizer first generates an "optimal" *query execution plan* (*QEP*). The QEP is then executed by the query engine which implements an *execution model* and uses a library of relational operators [11]. The optimizer can consider different shapes of QEP: *left-deep*, *right-deep* or *bushy trees* (see Figure 4). In a left-deep tree, operators are executed sequentially and each intermediate result is materialized. On the contrary, right-deep trees execute operators in a pipeline fashion, thus avoiding intermediate result materialization. However, they require materializing in memory all left relations. Bushy trees offer opportunities to deal with the size of intermediate results and memory consumption.

In a PicoDBMS, the query optimizer should not consider any of these execution trees as they incur materialization. The solution is to only use pipelining with *extreme right-deep trees* where all the operators (including select) are pipelined. As left operands are always base relations, they are already materialized in stable memory, thus allowing to execute a plan with no RAM consumption. Pipeline execution can be easily achieved using the well known *Iterator Model* [11]. In this model,

each operator is an *iterator* that supports three procedure calls: *open* to prepare an operator for producing an item, *next* to produce an item, and *close* to perform final clean-up. A *QEP* is activated starting at the root of the operator tree and progressing towards the leaves. The dataflow in the model is demand-driven: a child operator passes a tuple to its parent node in response to a *next* call from the parent.

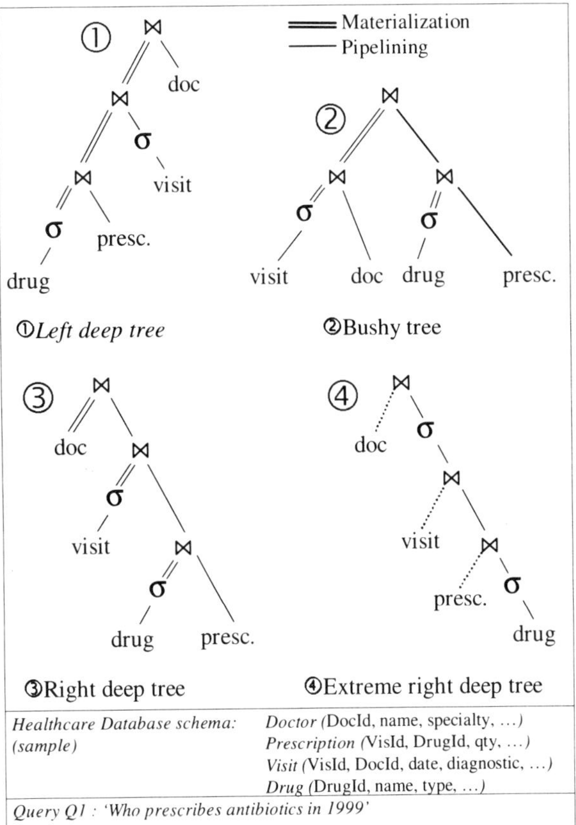

Healthcare Database schema: (sample)

Doctor (DocId, name, specialty, …)
Prescription (VisId, DrugId, qty, …)
Visit (VisId, DocId, date, diagnostic, …)
Drug (DrugId, name, type, …)

Query Q1 : 'Who prescribes antibiotics in 1999'

Figure 4: *Several execution trees for query Q1*

Let us now detail how select, project and join are performed. These operators can be executed either sequentially or with a ring index. Given the access rule, the use of indices seems always to be the right choice. However, extreme right-deep trees allow to speed-up a single select on the first base relation (*e.g.*, *Drug.type* in our example) but using a ring index on the other selected attributes (*e.g.*, *Visit.date*) may slow down execution as the ring need be traversed to retrieve their value. Project operators are pushed up to the tree since no materialization occurs. Note that the final project incurs an additional cost in case of ring attributes. Without indices, joining relations is done by a nested-loop algorithm since no other join technique can be applied without ad-hoc structures (*e.g.*, hash tables) and/or working area (*e.g.*, sorting). The cost of indexed joins depends on the way indices are traversed. Consider the indexed join between *Doctor* (*n* tuples) and *Visit* (*m* tuples) on their key attribute. Assuming a unidirectional index, the join cost is proportional to $n*m$

starting with *Doctor* and to *m* starting with *Visit*. Assuming now a bi-directional index, the join cost becomes proportional to $n+m$ starting with *Doctor* and to $m^2/2n$ starting with *Visit* (retrieving the doctor associated to each visit incurs traversing half of a ring in average). In the latter case, a naïve nested loop join can be more efficient if the ring cardinality is greater than the target relation cardinality (*i.e.*, when $m>n^2$). In that case, the database designer must clearly choose a unidirectional index between the two relations.

5.2 Complex Query Execution without RAM

We now consider the execution of aggregate, sort and duplicate removal operators. At a first look, pipeline execution is not compatible with these operators which are classically performed on materialized intermediate results. Such materialization cannot occur either in the smartcard due to the RAM rule or in the terminal due to the security rule. Note that sorting can be done in the terminal since the output order of the result tuples is not significant, *i.e.*, depends on the DBMS algorithms.

We propose a solution to the above problem by exploiting two properties: (i) aggregate and duplicate removal can be done in pipeline if the incoming tuples are yet grouped by distinct values and (ii) pipeline operators are order-preserving since they consume (and produce) tuples in the arrival order. Thus, enforcing an adequate consumption order at the leaf of the execution tree allows pipelined aggregation and duplicate removal. For instance, the extreme right deep tree of Figure 4 delivers the tuples naturally grouped by *Drug.id*, thus allowing group queries on that attribute.

Let us consider now query Q2 of Figure 5. As pictured, executing Q2 in pipeline requires rearranging the execution tree so that relation *Doctor* is explored first. Since *Doctor* contains distinct doctors, the tuples arriving to the *count* operator are naturally grouped by doctors.

The case of Q3 is harder. As the data must be grouped by *type of drugs* rather than by *Drug.id*, an additional join is required between relation *Drug* and domain *drug.type*. Domain values being unique, this join produces the tuples in the adequate order. If domain *Drug.type* does not exist, an operator must be introduced to sort relation *Drug* in pipeline. This can be done by performing n passes on *Drug* where n is the number of distinct values of *Drug.type*.

The case of Q4 is even trickier. The result must be grouped on two attributes (*Doctor.id* and *Drug.type*), introducing the need to start the tree with both relations! The solution is to insert a Cartesian product operator at the leaf of the tree in order to produce tuples ordered by *Doctor.id* and *Drug.type*. In this particular case, the query response time should be approximately n times greater than the same query without the 'group by' clause, where n is the number of distinct *types of drugs*.

Q5 retrieves the distinct couples of *doctor* and *type of prescribed drugs*. This query can be made similar to Q4 by expressing the distinct clause as an aggregate without function (*i.e.*, the query "*select distinct $a_1,..,a_n$ from ...*" is equivalent to "*select $a_1, .. , a_n$ from ... group by $a_1,.., a_n$*"). The unique difference is that the computation for a given group (*i.e.*, *distinct result tuple*) can stop as soon as one tuple has been produced.

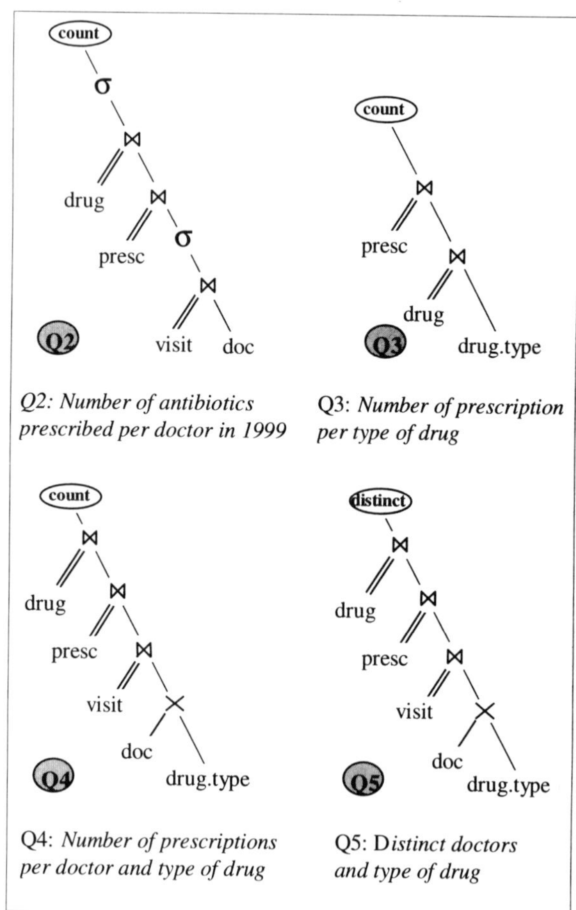

Q2: *Number of antibiotics prescribed per doctor in 1999*

Q3: *Number of prescription per type of drug*

Q4: *Number of prescriptions per doctor and type of drug*

Q5: *Distinct doctors and type of drug*

Figure 5: *Four 'complex' query execution plans*

5.3 Performance Evaluation

Our proposed query engine can handle fairly complex queries, taking advantage of the read and access rules[4] while satisfying the compactness, write, RAM and security rules. We now evaluate whether the PicoDBMS performance matches the smartcard application's requirements, that is any query issued by the application can be performed in reasonable time (*i.e.*, may not exceed the user patience). Since the PicoDBMS code's simplicity is an important consideration to conform to the compactness and security rules, we must also evaluate which acceleration techniques (*i.e.*, ring indices, query optimization) are really mandatory. For instance, an accelerator reducing the response time from 10 ms to 1 ms

---

[4] With traditional DBMS, such techniques will induce so many disk accesses that the system would thrash!

is useless in the smartcard context[5]. Thus, unlike traditional performance evaluation, our major concern is on absolute rather than relative performance.

Evaluating absolute response time is complex in the smartcard environment because all platform parameters (*e.g.*, processor speed, caching strategy, RAM and EEPROM speed) strongly impact the measurements[6]. Measuring the performance of our PicoDBMS on Bull's smartcard technology is attractive but introduces two problems. First, Bull's smartcards compatible with database applications are still prototypes [23]. Second, we are interested in providing the most general conclusions (*i.e.*, as independent as possible of smartcard architectures). Therefore, we prefer to measure our query engine on two old-fashion computers (a PC 486/25Mhz and a Sun SparcStation 1+) which we felt roughly similar to forthcoming smartcard architectures. For each computer, we vary the system parameters (clock frequency, cache) and perform the experimentation tests. The performance ratios between all configurations were roughly constant, the slowest configuration (Intel 486 with no cache) performing 8 times worse than the fastest (RISC with cache). In the following, we present response times for the slowest architecture to check the viability of our solutions in the worst environment.

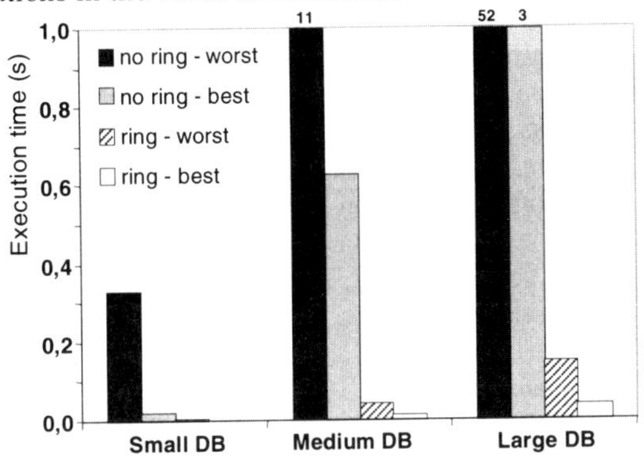

Figure 6: *Performance results for query Q1*

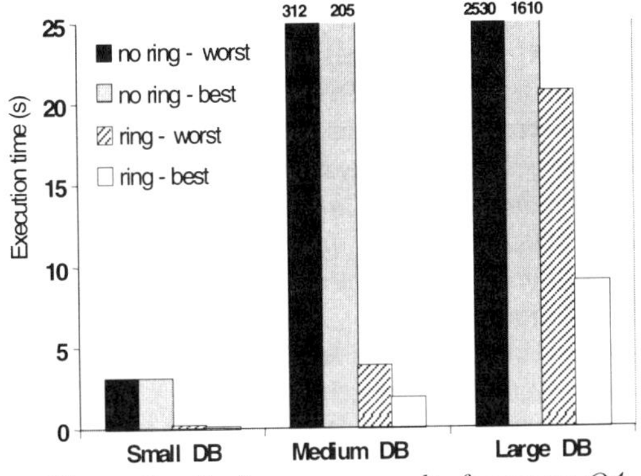

Figure 7: *Performance results for query Q4*

---

[5] With traditional DBMS, such acceleration can improve the transactional throughput.

[6] With traditional DBMS, very slow disk access allows to ignore finer parameters.

We generated three instances of a simplified healthcare database: the *small, medium and large* databases containing respectively (10, 30, 50) doctors, (100, 500, 1000) visits, (300, 2000, 5000) prescriptions and (40, 120, 200) drugs. Although we tested several queries, we describe below only the two most significant. Query Q1, which contains 3 joins and 2 selects on *Visit* and *Drug* (with selectivities of 20% and 5%) is representative of medium-complexity queries. Query Q4, which performs an aggregate on two attributes and requires the introduction of a Cartesian product, is representative of complex queries. For each query, we measure the performance for all possible query execution plans, varying the storage choices (with and without select and join ring indices). Figures 6 and 7 show the results for both best and worst plans on databases built with or without join indices.

Considering SPJ queries, the PicoDBMS performance clearly matches the application's requirements as soon as join rings are used. Indeed, the performance with join rings is at most 146 ms for the largest database and with the worst execution plan. With small databases, all the acceleration techniques can be discarded, while with larger ones, join rings remain necessary to obtain good response time. In that case, the absolute gain (110 ms) between the best and the worst plan does not justify the use of a query optimizer.

The performance of aggregate queries is clearly worst because they introduce a Cartesian product at the leaf of the execution tree. Join rings are useful for medium and large databases. With large databases, the optimizer turns out to be necessary since the worst execution plan with join rings achieves a rather long response time (20,6 s).

The influence of ring indices for selects (not shown) is insignificant. Depending on the selectivity, it can bring slight improvement or overhead on the results. Although it may achieve an important relative speed-up for the select itself, the absolute gain is not significant considering the small influence of select on the global query execution cost (which is not the case in disk-based DBMS). Select ring indices are however useful for queries with aggregates or duplicate removal, that can result in a join between a relation and the domain attribute. In that case, the select index plays the role of a join index, thereby generating a significant gain on large relations and large domains.

Thus, this performance evaluation shows that our approach is feasible and that join indices are mandatory in all cases while query optimization turns out to be useful only with large databases and complex queries.

6   Conclusion

As smartcards become more and more versatile, multi-applications and powerful, the need for database techniques arises. However, smartcards have severe hardware limitations which make traditional database technology irrelevant. The major problem is scaling down database techniques so they perform well under these limitations. In this paper, we addressed this problem and proposed the design of a PicoDBMS, concentrating on the components which require non traditional techniques.

This paper makes several contributions. First, we analyzed the requirements for a PicoDBMS based on a healthcare application which is representative of personal folder applications and has strong database requirements. We showed that the minimal functionality should include select/project/join/aggregate, access right management and views as well as transaction's atomicity and durability.

Second, we gave an in-depth analysis of the problem by considering the smartcard hardware trends. Based on this analysis, we assumed a smartcard with a reasonable stable memory of a few MB and a small RAM of some KB, and we derived design rules for a PicoDBMS architecture.

Third, we proposed a new highly compact storage model that combines Flat Storage (FS), Domain Storage (DS) and Ring Storage (RS). Ring Storage reduces the indexing cost to its lowest bound. Based on storage cost evaluation, we derived guidelines to decide the best way to store an attribute.

Finally, we proposed query processing techniques which handle complex query plans with no RAM consumption. This is achieved by considering extreme right-deep trees which can pipeline all operators of the plan including aggregates. We measured the performance of our execution model with an implementation of our query engine on two old-fashion computers which we configured to be similar to forthcoming smartcard architectures. We showed that the resulting performance matches the smartcard application's requirements.

This work is done in the context of a new project with Bull Smart Cards and Terminals. The next step is to implement our PicoDBMS on Bull's smartcard new technology, called *OverSoft* [6], and to assess its functionality and performance on real world applications. To this end, we are building an experimentation platform, called *Virtual Campus*, to deal with advanced student folders at the University of Versailles. We also plan to address open issues such as protected logging for durability, query execution on encrypted data and statistics maintenance on a population of cards.

References

[1] A. Ammann, M. Hanrahan, and R. Krishnamurthy. Design of a Memory Resident DBMS. *IEEE COMPCON*, 1985.

[2] R. Anderson, M. Kuhn. Tamper Resistance – a Cautionary Note. *USENIX Workshop on Electronic Commerce*, 1996.

[3] L. Bouganim, O. Kapitskaia, P. Valduriez. Memory-Adaptive Scheduling for Large Query Execution. *Int. Conf. on Information and Knowledge Management (CIKM)*, 1998.

[4] C. Bobineau, L. Bouganim, P. Pucheral, P. Valduriez. PicoDBMS: Scaling down Database Techniques for the Smartcard. *PRiSM Technical Report* n°2000/05, 2000.

[5] F. A. van Bommel, J. Sembritzki, H.-G. Buettner. Overview on Healthcard Projects and Standards. *Health Cards Int. Conf.*, 1999.

[6] Bull S.A. Bull unveils iSimplify! the personal portable portal. www.bull.com/bull_news/

[7] L. C. Carrasco. RDBMS's for Java Cards ? What a Senseless Idea ! www.sqlmachine.com, 1999.

[8] DataQuest. *Chip Card Market and Technology Charge Ahead.* MSAM-WW-DP-9808, 1998.

[9] B. Dipert. FRAM: Ready to ditch niche ? *EDN Access Magazine*, Cahners Publishing Company, 1997.

[10] Gemplus. SIM Cards: From Kilobytes to Megabytes. www.gemplus.fr/about/pressroom/, 1999.

[11] G. Graefe. Query Evaluation Techniques for Large Databases. *ACM Computing Surveys*, 25(2), 1993.

[12] G. Graefe. The New Database Imperatives. *Int. Conf. on Data Engineering (ICDE)*, 1998.

[13] IBM Corporation. *DB2 Everywhere – Administration and Application Programming Guide.* IBM Software Documentation, SC26-9675-00, 1999.

[14] International Standardization Organization (ISO). *Integrated Circuit(s) Cards with Contacts – Part 1: Physical Characteristics.* ISO/IEC 7816-1, 1998.

[15] International Standardization Organization (ISO), *Integrated Circuit(s) Cards with Contacts – Part 7: Interindustry Commands for Structured Card Query Language (SCQL).* ISO/IEC 7816-7, 1999.

[16] Microsoft Corporation. Windows for SmartCards Toolkit for Visual Basic 6.0. www.microsoft.com/windowsce/smartcard/, 2000.

[17] M. Missikov, M. Scholl. Relational Queries in a Domain Based DBMS, *ACM SIGMOD Int. Conf. On Management of Data*, 1983.

[18] Oracle Corporation. *Oracle 8i Lite - Oracle Lite SQL Reference.* Oracle Documentation, A73270-01, 1999.

[19] P. Pucheral, J. M. Thévenin, P. Valduriez. Efficient Main Memory Data Management Using the DBGraph Storage Model, *Int. Conf. on Very Large Data Bases (VLDB)*, 1990.

[20] B. Schneier, A. Shostack. Breaking up is hard to do: Modeling Security Threats for Smart Cards. *USENIX Symposium on Smart Cards*, 1999.

[21] Sun Microsystems. *JavaCard 2.1 Application Programming Interface Specification.* JavaSoft documentation, 1999.

[22] Sybase Inc. *Sybase Adaptive Server Anywhere Reference.* CT75KNA, 1999.

[23] J.-P. Tual. MASSC: A Generic Architecture for Multiapplication Smart Cards. *IEEE Micro Journal*, N° 0272-1739/99, 1999.

[24] P. Valduriez. Join Indices, *ACM Trans. on Database Systems*, 12(2), 1987.

The 3W Model and Algebra for Unified Data Mining

Theodore Johnson
AT&T Labs–Research
johnsont@research.att.com

Laks V. S. Lakshmanan
Concordia University and IIT–Bombay
laks@it.iitb.ernet.in

Raymond T. Ng
University of British Columbia
rng@cs.ubc.ca

Abstract

Real data mining/analysis applications call for a framework which adequately supports knowledge discovery as a multi-step process, where the input of one mining operation can be the output of another. Previous studies, primarily focusing on fast computation of *one* specific mining task at a time, ignore this vital issue.

Motivated by this observation, we develop a unified model supporting all major mining and analysis tasks. Our model consists of three distinct worlds, corresponding to intensional and extensional dimensions, and to data sets. The notion of dimension is a centerpiece of the model. Equipped with hierarchies, dimensions integrate the output of seemingly dissimilar mining and analysis operations in a clean manner.

We propose an algebra, called the *dimension algebra*, for manipulating (intensional) dimensions, as well as operators that serve as "bridges" between the worlds. We demonstrate by examples that several real data mining processes can be captured using our model and algebra. We demonstrate the naturality of the algebra by establishing several identities. Finally, we discuss efficient implementation of the proposed framework.

1 Introduction

Data mining studies can be classified broadly into two "generations". Studies in the first generation have fo-

Proceedings of the 26th VLDB Conference, Cairo, Egypt, 2000.

cused primarily on which kinds of patterns to mine, and how fast they can be computed. Examples include associations and variants [3, 4, 20, 14, 8, 22, 29], clustering [24, 31, 2, 5], decision trees [27], and depth contours [18]. Recognizing that mining would be far more effective if not considered in isolation, studies in the second generation have focused on how mining can interact with other "components" in a more general framework of knowledge discovery (KDD). One component is the underlying DBMS. Studies such as [9, 28, 30] explore how association mining can handshake with the DBMS most effectively. Another component is the human analyst. Some studies such as [25, 10, 21], allow the user to express a focus for mining via constraints. Other studies such as [15, 1] provide the user with online feedback, and permit him to make dynamic changes to the parameters of computation.

All previous studies are almost always geared toward one mining task at a time. In real data mining applications, KDD is *rarely a one-shot activity*. Rather, it is a *multi-step process* involving different mining operations, data partitioning, aggregation, and data transformations. Thus, previous work fails to address the fundamental need of *supporting KDD as a multi-step process*. In the following examples, we illustrate several multi-step scenarios, extracted from real mining applications, which call for the ability to manipulate (e.g., analyze, query, transform) the results of mining tasks, making the output of one mining operation the input to another.

Example 1 (Associations and Decision Trees)
Suppose an analyst analyzes the sales data of a chain store to determine which items were co-purchased with a certain promotional item p, generating a collection of frequent sets. As part of his exploration, he decides to roll up this collection of frequent sets from specific items (e.g., specific brands of meat products) to kinds of items (e.g., the general class of meat). He then wishes to determine the "circumstances" (e.g., `location`, `time`, etc.) under which the frequent co-

purchases were made. He does so by constructing a decision tree. The decision tree, when combined with frequent sets, might reveal interesting patterns such as "in northern New Jersey, meat products (not dairy products) are often bought together with p, whereas in southern New Jersey, dairy products (not meat products) are often bought together with p." This example illustrates interesting observations/patterns that can *only* be discovered by freely combining the outcomes of different mining tasks. ∎

Example 2 (Stacking Decision Trees) Suppose T_1 is a decision tree that classifies customers in New Jersey into the categories of `highRisk` and `lowRisk` for credit rating. Let T_2 be a decision tree that predicts under what conditions people in New Jersey live in cities vs. the countryside. The analyst may want to combine the two decision trees so as to be able to predict under what conditions people have a certain credit rating and tend to live in a certain neighborhood.[1] One option is to take a cross product between T_1 and T_2. An alternative is to "stack" T_2 below T_1, i.e. each leaf of T_1 is further classified on the basis of T_2 (see Figure 1). Such a classification may be further analyzed, e.g., used as a basis of a group-by. ∎

Example 3 (Computing Special Regions) Consider a sales data warehouse with measures like `revenue`, `profit`, and dimensions[2] such as `part`, `time`, `location`. The dimensions may have associated hierarchies. For example, a "region" such as `location` = 'quebec/montreal' may be a child of the region `location` = 'quebec'. Suppose the analyst wants to find the minimal regions which satisfy some aggregate property $\mathcal{P}$, e.g., $\mathcal{P} \equiv$ "the total sales exceeds \$100,000", where minimality means children of the region do not satisfy $\mathcal{P}$. The analyst might similarly want to find regions whose sales are significantly different from their siblings. ∎

A key aspect exhibited by the above examples is that the data set/space is split by data mining/analysis operations into (possibly overlapping) subsets or "regions". While the above examples, chosen for the familiarity of most readers, focus on associations, decision trees, and group-bys, similar examples can be drawn based on most known mining tasks like data cubes, data spheres, histograms, and clusters (Table 1 has more details). The main point of the above examples is that *interesting and powerful applications can be supported by allowing different mining, analysis, and aggregation tasks to be combined at will.* This is what a multi-step process for KDD is all about. And this is the kind of *unified* environment in which an analyst would like to operate for real mining applications.

However, such an environment does not exist (yet!). In fact, many of these tasks are supported in isolation by different software packages which may not even share the same data format (ascii, binary, etc.). More fundamentally, there is no *common foundation* for all these tasks to be interfaced with one another, not to mention the difficulty in feeding the output of one operation as input to another. Our contributions, set in this context, answer the following questions:

- **What are the "right" structures for unified mining?:** To ensure the compositionality and closure properties of mining operations, we model and manipulate *regions* and *their descriptions* as first-class objects. We call a set of related regions a *dimension*. Our 3W model consists of three different worlds: the *intensional dimension* world (I-World), the *extensional dimension* world (E-World), and the *data* world (D-World). (See Figure 2.) In the I-World, each region is represented in its intensional form, i.e., as a *description* of its members (Section 2). In the E-World, each region is represented in its extensional form, i.e., by an explicit *enumeration* of its member tuples w.r.t. a given data set (Section 4). The D-World consists of raw data, e.g., in the form of relations, from which regions and dimensions can be created as a result of mining.

- **How to manipulate the structures?:** In each of the three worlds, the structures can be manipulated with an algebra of choice. A significant contribution here is the *dimension algebra* that we develop for the I-World. It forms the key tool for linking various data mining tasks and for applying them in cascade (Section 3). We illustrate the expressive power of the algebra by showing how the key steps in Examples 2 and 3 can be captured using expressions in the dimension algebra.

- **How to move in and out of the worlds?:** Having created the three worlds, we establish the following *"bridges"* between them: the *mine (μ)*, *populate (α)*, *lookup (λ)* operators, and a "macro" called *refresh (γ)* (Section 5). We show how real multi-step data mining and analysis tasks outlined in earlier examples can be fully captured using expressions involving operators of the dimension algebra, and the various operators mentioned above.

- **How good/natural is the model?:** We establish numerous identities involving the dimension algebra and the other operators, thus establishing their naturality. Furthermore, we argue by examples that the model and the operators are expressive enough to support multi-step mining activ-

---

[1] The training data that led to the two trees may be presently unavailable to the analyst, or doing the combined classification from scratch may take too long for his purpose.

[2] As we will show later, the dimensions of warehouses can also be naturally modeled using the notion of dimensions proposed in this paper.

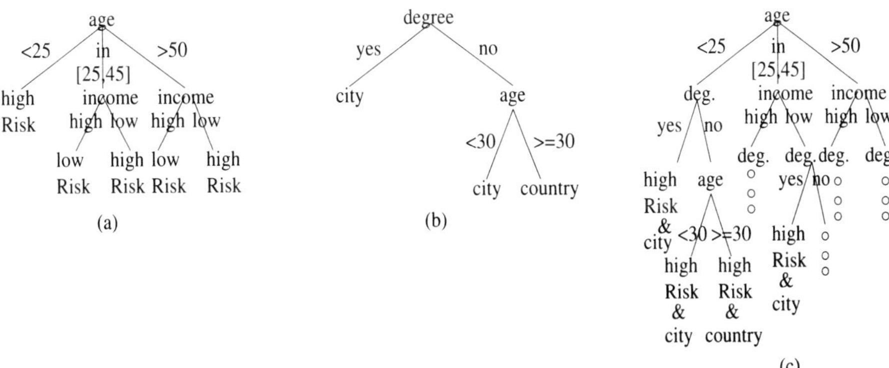

(a)   (b)   (c)

Figure 1: Stacking Decision Trees

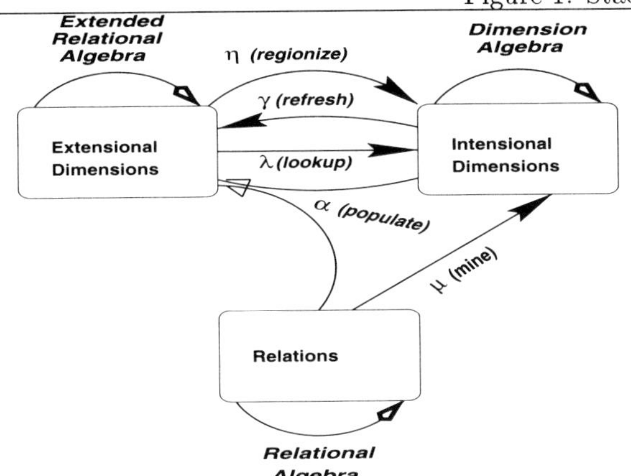

Figure 2: The Different Worlds in the 3W Model, and the Bridges

ities that could not be done before (Sections 3 and 5).

- **How well can the model be implemented?:** Many of these identities enable optimization via query rewriting. In addition, we show that incremental computation is possible for certain operations. In many cases, existing spatial indexing and processing techniques can be applied. (See Section 6.)

2   Regions, Dimensions, and Hierarchical Domains: The I-World

We begin with the question of what the "right" structures should be in a unified mining/analysis model. Our proposed structures center around three key notions – regions, dimensions and hierarchical domains.

2.1   Intuition and Significance

As shown in Examples 1-3, decision trees, data cubes, associations, etc. all serve to split a given data set into a collection of (possibly overlapping) subsets of tuples, i.e., points in the space spanned by the data, which we call "regions". Indeed, most well-known mining and

Task	Shape of Regions	Hierarchies
Dec. Trees	Isothetic	Tree
Freq. Sets	Isothetic	Powerset Lattice
Log-lin. Models	Isothetic	Range Hierarchy
Depth Contours	Convex	Range Hierarchy
Data Spheres	Convex	Range Hierarchy
Data Cubes	Isothetic	Categorical
Histograms	Isothetic	Range Hierarchy
Clusters	can be Non-convex	Adjacent Neighbors

Table 1: Common Data Mining Tasks and the Nature of Their Split Regions

analysis operations effectively do a data space splitting, and create regions to achieve their ends (see Table 1). The regions created vary on their spatial shapes and on whether they overlap. For a majority of the tasks shown, the regions created are axis-parallel and hyper-rectangular. Such regions are called *isothetic*, and admit very efficient manipulation and processing.

The cube operator proposed in [11] at once splits up a data set according to all possible group-bys and computes the required aggregate measure for each group (in our terminology, region). However, for the purpose here, by data cube, we mean the operation of splitting the data set into regions. Computation of the aggregate can always be done by an explicit invocation of an aggregate operation.

Intuitively, a dimension is a set of related regions. With dimensions, an analyst can manipulate sets of regions, often creating new ones. In Example 1, the set of itemsets with support exceeding a given threshold forms a dimension. Furthermore, the set of itemsets containing the promotional item p forms another. The set of frequent sets sought in Example 1 is then the intersection of the two dimensions above.

Example 3 shows that dimensions come with interesting structure that relates their constituent regions in the form of a hierarchy. Examples include categorical hierarchies in data warehouses, set inclusion for frequent sets, and more generally, constraint implication for dimensions produced by most mining tasks.

23

Queries comparing a region to its children, ancestors, siblings, etc. can add significant value to the mining/analysis exercise. To support this, we include hierarchies as an integral part of our 3W model. Table 1 shows the hierarchies associated with dimensions produced by popular mining/analysis tasks.

2.2 Formal Definitions

We next formalize the above notions, first focusing on the I-World (intensional dimensions). Some of these notions assume a different form in the E-World (Section 4).

Definition 1 (Hierarchial Domains) A *hierarchical domain* is any non-empty set H on which the following predicates are defined: (i) equality, interpreted as syntactic identity as usual, and (ii) the predicates $<$ and $\ll$, interpreted as binary relations over H. We require that the graph $(H, <)$ form a DAG, and that $\ll$ be the transitive closure of $<$. ∎

For $x, y \in H$, whenever $x < y$ (resp., $x \ll y$), we say y is a *child* (resp., *descendant*) of x. We abbreviate $x < y \lor x = y$ as $x <= y$ and $x \ll y \lor x = y$ as $x \ll= y$. We say x is an upper bound of y, z whenever $x \ll= y$ and $x \ll= z$. In this paper, we shall assume that hierarchies form either a tree or a lattice. The notion of a least upper bound is well defined on such hierarchies, in the sense that it exists and is unique. In particular, there is a greatest element, denoted *all*. Elements of a hierarchical domain are called hierarchical values. For an attribute A, $dom(A)$ denotes its domain. Attributes whose domains are hierarchical are called hierarchical attributes.

Definition 1 makes precise the notion of a hierarchy in an abstract sense. Here are some concrete and common examples of hierarchies. For the frequent set computation of Example 1, the lattice of all possible subsets of the set of items is a hierarchical domain. Similarly, given a range $[A, B]$ (for a numeric attribute), the set of all subranges of $[A, B]$ forms a hierarchy called the *range hierarchy*, with range containment acting as the $\ll=$ predicate. For decision trees, conjunctions of inequalities form a hierarchy (modulo equivalence) with (reverse) implication acting as $\ll=$. A hierarchical domain is thus an abstraction of such concrete hierarchies found in practice.

In the I-World, a region is represented in the form of descriptions of its members, i.e., region membership criteria. To capture this, we use constraints. The constraints could involve either the attributes of the data sets to be analyzed, or attributes which are computed from those of the given data sets. *In this first paper, we restrict attention to attributes of the base data set.* We sometimes refer to these attributes as coordinates, to emphasize their spatial nature.

Definition 2 (Constraints) Let $\vec{A} = \{A_1, ..., A_n\}$ be the attributes of a given data set (e.g., a relation). Then by LINEAR$(\vec{A})$, we denote the class of linear inequalities with real coefficients over the data set attributes $\vec{A}$. ∎

Regions produced by most mining/analysis operations are convex, which can be modeled as a set of linear inequalities. Non-convex regions can be modeled as a "union" of multiple convex regions.

Definition 3 (Constraint Attributes) A *constraint attribute*, denoted as RDF$_i$, is a special hierarchical attribute, whose domain is a set of constraints drawn from conjunctions over LINEAR$(\vec{A})$, $\vec{A}$ being the data set attributes. Each constraint in $dom(\text{RDF}_i)$ is a conjunction of constraints of the form: $linear(A_1, \ldots, A_n) \geq c$, where c is a constant, and $A_1, \ldots, A_n$ are attributes of the given data set. For a tuple t from the given data set, we say that t *satisfies* $linear(A_1, \ldots, A_n) \geq c$ iff the inequality $linear(t[A_1], \ldots, t[A_n]) \geq c$ evaluates to true. Satisfaction generalizes to a set/conjunction of of constraints as usual.[3] A constraint $\mathcal{C}$ drawn from the domain of a constraint attribute is called a *region description formula* (RDF). ∎

As an example, for the decision tree of Figure 1(a) and Example 2, the first `highRisk` region is described by the constraint `age < 25`, and the second `highRisk` region by the constraint (25 $\leq$ `age` $\leq$ 45) & (`income = low`). Both of these regions are isothetic. As shown in Table 1, there are some commonly used mining tasks that produce regions that are more complex than isothetic, and require their membership criteria to be captured as general linear constraints (e.g. depth contours, clusters, etc.).

Definition 4 (Region Identifiers) Let RDF$_i$ be a constraint attribute. We say that a hierarchical attribute RID$_i$ is the *region identifier* (RID) attribute associated with RDF$_i$, provided the domains of RDF$_i$ and RID$_i$ (together with the hierarchy predicates) are isomorphic, i.e., there is a 1-1 onto function $desc : dom(\text{RID}_i) \rightarrow dom(\text{RDF}_i)$, such that $\forall h, h' \in dom(\text{RID}_i) : h \ll= h'$ iff $desc(h') \Rightarrow desc(h)$. Furthermore, for equivalent constraints $\mathcal{C}, \mathcal{C}'$, $h^{-1}(\mathcal{C}) = h^{-1}(\mathcal{C}')$. ∎

Note that for every constraint attribute RDF, we can always postulate a corresponding RID attribute RID. RID attributes are similar in spirit to the notion of hierarchical attributes introduced by Jagadish et al. [17] in a different context. The intuition is that the RID$_i$ attribute, associated with a given constraint attribute

---

[3] We denote the empty conjucntion as the formula *true*, while *false* is a representative member of the equivalence class of unsatisfiable constraints, e.g., $A < c \land A \geq c$.

RDF_i, allows us to encode the hierarchy relationships such as $<$, $\ll$. For instance, constraints for frequent sets could be of the form $\texttt{beer} = 1 \land \texttt{diaper} = 1$, and they could be encoded using bit vectors as RIDs. The encoding via RIDs serves two purposes. First, in the E-world (Section 4), RIDs will be used as group identifiers to encode the membership of data tuples in specific regions. Second, as will be detailed in Section 6, RIDs enable efficient checking of hierarchy relationships, offering a fast alternative to the expensive implication checking of constraints. Thus, RID attributes help quickly detect hierarchy relatives of specified regions, similar to indices. Below, $\mathcal{V}$ denotes the set of all possible values – both hierarchical and non-hierarchical.

Definition 5 (Regions) A *dimension schema* is a set of attributes $\mathbf{A} = (\text{RID}_1, ..., \text{RID}_m, \text{RDF}_1, ..., \text{RDF}_m, P_1, ..., P_l)$, where RDF_i is a constraint attribute and RID_i is the corresponding RID attribute, $1 \leq i \leq m$. A *region* over $\mathbf{A}$ is a partial function $r : \mathbf{A} \to \mathcal{V}$ such that: (i) whenever $r(A)$ is defined, $A \in \mathbf{A}$, we have $r(A) \in dom(A)$, and (ii) $r(\text{RID}_i)$ is defined iff $r(\text{RDF}_i)$ is. ∎

From now on, we represent the RID and RDF attributes of a dimension schema as the vectors $\vec{\text{RID}}$ and $\vec{\text{RDF}}$. For a region r, we call $r[\vec{\text{RID}}]$ as its RID-value, or simply the RID. A few important remarks are in order.

- The key reason why multiple RDF attributes are allowed is to simplify the process of factoring dimensions.

- There can be other attributes/properties associated with a region. We denote these by the P_i's in the above definition, and refer to them as the *property attributes*. For the decision tree example in Figure 1(a), P_1 may be the `decision-label` attribute indicating whether the region is `highRisk` or `lowRisk`.

- Whenever a region r is undefined over a constraint attribute RDF_i, the intended semantics is that $r(\text{RDF}_i) = true$. This corresponds to $r(\text{RID}_i) = all$.

Definition 6 (Intensional Dimension Instance) An *instance* $\mathcal{D}$ of a dimension schema $\mathbf{A}$ is a set of regions over $\mathbf{A}$. ∎

For the example in Figure 1(a), $\mathcal{D}$ consists of eight regions, corresponding to the eight nodes of the tree, i.e., 5 leaf nodes and 3 non-leaf nodes. Notice that the above definition does not insist that all regions in an instance be defined over the same set of attributes. For instance, for the non-leaf regions, the `decision-label` could be undefined. Thus, a dimension instance can be a heterogeneous collection of regions.

3 The Dimension Algebra

Having defined regions and dimensions, we next address their manipulation in the I-World. Examples 1-3 demonstrate how manipulations of dimensions could add significant value to data mining and analysis. Thereto, we propose the *dimension algebra*. Some operators in the algebra are similar to those in the relational algebra, while others are very different. We start with the latter ones.

3.1 The Selection Operator

The basic idea is to allow selections that invoke various spatial predicates such as overlap, containment, etc. between regions. Any set of predicates that is closed under negation may be chosen for this purpose. The choice will impact the computations expressible in the algebra. For the sake of concreteness, we assume the spatial predicates are overlap ($\|$), containment ($\supset$), disjointness ($\not\|$), and non-containment ($\not\supset$). In addition, for a property attribute P, we let $pred(P)$ be any predicate such as $P \, \theta \, v$, where θ is $=, \leq$, etc. (Allowable predicates on Ps could also include comparison of two property attributes. We suppress the obvious detail here.)

Definition 7 (Selection) Let $\mathcal{D}$ be a dimension instance over the schema $\mathbf{A}$, RDF_a, RDF_b be constraint attributes, $\mathcal{C}$ be a constant constraint drawn from the domain of RDF_a, and $\circ$ be one of the spatial selection predicates mentioned above. Furthermore, let RID_a and RID_b be the corresponding RID attributes in $\mathbf{A}$, $h \in dom(\text{RID}_a)$, and $\triangle$ be any of the hierarchical predicates introduced in Definition 1. Finally, let P be a property attribute in $\mathbf{A}$, and $pred(P)$ be a predicate involving P. We define:

$$\sigma_{\text{RDF}_a \circ \mathcal{C}}(\mathcal{D}) = \{r \mid r \in \mathcal{D} \,\&\, r[\text{RDF}_a] \circ \mathcal{C} \text{ is true }\}.$$
$$\sigma_{\text{RDF}_a \circ \text{RDF}_b}(\mathcal{D}) = \{r \mid r \in \mathcal{D} \,\&\, r[\text{RDF}_a] \circ r[\text{RDF}_b] \text{ is true }\}.$$
$$\sigma_{\text{RID}_a \triangle \text{RID}_b}(\mathcal{D}) = \{r \mid r \in \mathcal{D} \,\&\, r[\text{RID}_a] \triangle r[\text{RID}_b] \text{ is true }\}.$$
$$\sigma_{\text{RID}_a \triangle h}(\mathcal{D}) = \{r \mid r \in \mathcal{D} \,\&\, r[\text{RID}_a] \triangle h \text{ is true }\}.$$
$$\sigma_{pred(P)}(\mathcal{D}) = \{r \mid r \in \mathcal{D} \,\&\, pred(r[P]) \text{ is true }\}. \quad \blacksquare$$

Let $\mathcal{D}$ be the dimension consisting of the eight regions/nodes of the decision tree shown in Figure 1(a), with one RDF attribute RDF_a. The expression $\sigma_{\text{RDF}_a \| (25 \leq age)}(\mathcal{D})$ finds all the regions that overlap with the constant region $25 \leq \texttt{age}$. Similarly, $\sigma_{\texttt{decision-label} = highRisk}(\mathcal{D})$ identifies all `highRisk` regions.

Selection involving boolean combination of conditions should be obvious. A subtle point, however, is that the selection operator as defined above, constrains individual constraint attributes. In practice, we might be interested in constraining the region "bounded" by several constraint attributes. Here, note

$$\sigma_{(\mathrm{RDF}_a \& \mathrm{RDF}_b)\|\mathrm{RDF}_c}(\mathcal{D}) = \sigma_{(\mathrm{RDF}_a\|\mathrm{RDF}_c) \wedge (\mathrm{RDF}_b\|\mathrm{RDF}_c)}(\mathcal{D}).$$
$$\sigma_{(\mathrm{RDF}_a \& \mathrm{RDF}_b)\|\mathcal{C}}(\mathcal{D}) = \sigma_{(\mathrm{RDF}_a\|\mathcal{C}) \wedge (\mathrm{RDF}_b\|\mathcal{C})}(\mathcal{D}).$$
$$\sigma_{(\mathrm{RDF}_a \& \mathrm{RDF}_b)\supset \mathrm{RDF}_c}(\mathcal{D}) = \sigma_{(\mathrm{RDF}_a\supset\mathrm{RDF}_c) \wedge (\mathrm{RDF}_b\supset\mathrm{RDF}_c)}(\mathcal{D}).$$
$$\sigma_{(\mathrm{RDF}_a \& \mathrm{RDF}_b)\supset \mathcal{C}}(\mathcal{D}) = \sigma_{(\mathrm{RDF}_a\supset\mathcal{C}) \wedge (\mathrm{RDF}_b\supset\mathcal{C})}(\mathcal{D}).$$
$$\sigma_{(\mathrm{RDF}_a \& \mathrm{RDF}_b)\nparallel \mathrm{RDF}_c}(\mathcal{D}) = \sigma_{(\mathrm{RDF}_a\nparallel\mathrm{RDF}_c) \vee (\mathrm{RDF}_b\nparallel\mathrm{RDF}_c)}(\mathcal{D}).$$
$$\sigma_{(\mathrm{RDF}_a \& \mathrm{RDF}_b)\nparallel \mathcal{C}}(\mathcal{D}) = \sigma_{(\mathrm{RDF}_a\nparallel\mathrm{RDF}_c) \vee (\mathrm{RDF}_b\nparallel\mathcal{C})}(\mathcal{D}).$$
$$\sigma_{(\mathrm{RDF}_a \& \mathrm{RDF}_b)\not\supset \mathrm{RDF}_c}(\mathcal{D}) = \sigma_{(\mathrm{RDF}_a\not\supset\mathrm{RDF}_c) \vee (\mathrm{RDF}_b\not\supset\mathrm{RDF}_c)}(\mathcal{D}).$$
$$\sigma_{(\mathrm{RDF}_a \& \mathrm{RDF}_b)\not\supset \mathcal{C}}(\mathcal{D}) = \sigma_{(\mathrm{RDF}_a\not\supset\mathcal{C}) \vee (\mathrm{RDF}_b\not\supset\mathcal{C})}(\mathcal{D}).$$

Table 2: A Sample of Identities for the Selection Operator. See Theorem 1 for Precise Assumptions.

that for two constraints $\mathcal{C}_1, \mathcal{C}_2$, the region bounded by $\mathcal{C}_1$ and $\mathcal{C}_2$ is captured by their conjunction $\mathcal{C}_1 \& \mathcal{C}_2$. (We will denote the conjunction of selection conditions Cond_1 and Cond_2 as $\sigma_{\mathrm{Cond}_1 \wedge \mathrm{Cond}_2}$ to avoid confusion.) More precisely, let $\mathrm{RDF}_a, \mathrm{RDF}_b, \mathrm{RDF}_c$ be any constraint attributes of a dimension schema $\mathbf{A}$ with instance $\mathcal{D}$. Then $\sigma_{(\mathrm{RDF}_a \& \mathrm{RDF}_b) \circ \mathcal{C}}(\mathcal{D})$ and $\sigma_{(\mathrm{RDF}_a \& \mathrm{RDF}_b) \circ \mathrm{RDF}_c}(\mathcal{D})$ are defined in the obvious way. The following theorem shows under certain circumstances this complex selection reduces to the simpler one defined above. Similar identities, for boolean combination of selection conditions, are suppressed for brevity.

Theorem 1 Let $\mathcal{D}$ be an instance of the dimension schema $\mathbf{A}$. Let $\mathrm{RDF}_a, \mathrm{RDF}_b, \mathrm{RDF}_c$ be the constraint attributes in $\mathbf{A}$, and $\mathcal{C}$ be a constant constraint drawn from some constraint attribute domain. Then identities (3)-(4) and (7)-(8) listed in Table 2 hold. Furthermore, whenever all constraints are isothetic and $\mathrm{RDF}_a\|\mathrm{RDF}_b$ is true, identities (1)-(2) and (5)-(6) hold. ∎

The identities are non-trivial: for instance, without the isothetic requirement, identities (1)-(2) and (5)-(6) do not always hold. Suppose $\mathrm{RDF}_a, \mathrm{RDF}_b$ are any overlapping axis-parallel rectangles. Unless RDF_c is also isothetic, it could easily overlap the regions $\mathrm{RDF}_a \,\&\, \neg\mathrm{RDF}_b$ and $\mathrm{RDF}_b \,\&\, \neg\mathrm{RDF}_a$, without overlapping $\mathrm{RDF}_a \,\&\, \mathrm{RDF}_b$. On the other hand, we can show that when all three are isothetic, this cannot happen.

3.2 The Projection Operator

Elimination of property attributes is classical and trivial. On the other hand, elimination of constraint attributes must ensure a consistency property in that the corresponding RID attributes should be automatically eliminated.

Definition 8 (Projection) Let $\mathbf{A}$ be a dimension schema, $\mathcal{D}$ an instance of $\mathbf{A}$, and $\mathrm{RDF}_i, ..., \mathrm{RDF}_j, P_k, ..., P_\ell$ a subset of $\mathbf{A}$ consisting of constraint attributes and property attributes. Then $\pi_{\mathrm{RDF}_i,...,\mathrm{RDF}_j,P_k,...,P_\ell}(\mathcal{D}) = \{r[\mathrm{RID}_i, ..., \mathrm{RID}_j, \mathrm{RDF}_i, ..., \mathrm{RDF}_j, P_k, ..., P_\ell] \mid r \in \mathcal{D}\}$.

Intuitively, eliminating a constraint attribute RDF_i amounts to setting this value to *true* in every region.

Similarly, the value of the eliminated RID attribute is essentially *all* in every region.

3.3 The Purge Operator: Generalized Duplicate Elimination

A region is inconsistent provided the conjunction of the RDF formulas defining it (i.e., its description) cannot be satisfied by any data point. For instance, a region r with $r[\mathrm{RDF}_1] = $ "$A \leq 2$" and $r[\mathrm{RDF}_2] = $ "$A \geq 3$" is clearly inconsistent Starting with only consistent regions, our operators can create an inconsistent region. Cartesian product (Section 10) is an example of such an operation, since each of two regions may be consistent by themselves, but not their conjunction (e.g., the third leaf from the left in Figure 1 c). The *purge* operator, defined next, removes inconsistent regions.

Definition 9 (Purge) Let $\mathcal{D}$ be any dimension over the schema $\mathbf{A} = (\mathrm{RID}_1, ..., \mathrm{RID}_m, \mathrm{RDF}_1, ..., \mathrm{RDF}_m, P_1, ..., P_\ell)$. Then the *purge* of $\mathcal{D}$ is defined by $\Upsilon(\mathcal{D}) = \{r \mid r \in \mathcal{D} \ \& \ \bigwedge_{1 \leq i \leq m} r[\mathrm{RDF}_i]$ is satisfiable $\}$. ∎

3.4 Other Operators

The operators introduced so far deal with the spatial aspect of regions and dimensions. Below we discuss the remaining operators, analogous to their relational counterparts, that deal with the set/relation aspect of dimensions.

Definition 10 (Cartesian product) Let $\mathcal{D}_1, \mathcal{D}_2$ be instances of two dimension schemas $\mathbf{A}_1, \mathbf{A}_2$ respectively. For simplicity, assume the attributes in the schemas $\mathbf{A}_1, \mathbf{A}_2$ are distinct. Then $\mathcal{D}_1 \times \mathcal{D}_2 = \{(r_1, r_2) \mid r_i \in \mathcal{D}_i, i = 1, 2\}$, with schema $\mathbf{A}_1 \cup \mathbf{A}_2$. ∎

From a spatial perspective, cartesian product creates new regions which are obtained by taking the pairwise intersection of regions in the two dimension instances. The next operator is union. The main distinction with classical union is the absence of a union-compatibility requirement. This permits a fully heterogeneous union, and hence dimensions that are heterogeneous collections of regions. Recall, whenever a region is not defined on a certain RID attribute, we treat it as the top element *all* of *dom*(RID), whereas when it is not defined on a certain RDF attribute, we treat it as the *true* constraint in *dom*(RDF).

Definition 11 (Union) Let $\mathbf{A}_1, \mathbf{A}_2$ be two dimension schemas and $\mathcal{D}_1, \mathcal{D}_2$ corresponding instances. Then the union of these dimensions has the schema $\mathbf{A}_1 \cup \mathbf{A}_2$. The instance is defined by $\mathcal{D}_1 \cup \mathcal{D}_2 = \{r \mid r \in \mathcal{D}_1 \ \vee \ r \in \mathcal{D}_2\}$. ∎

We say that two regions r_1, r_2 are equivalent provided the conjunctions of the constraint formulas of their RDF attributes are equivalent, i.e., $r_1[\vec{\mathrm{RDF}}] \equiv r_s[\vec{\mathrm{RDF}}]$.

$$\sigma_{Cond}(\pi_{\mathrm{RDF}_i,...,\mathrm{RDF}_j,P_k,...,P_\ell}(\mathcal{D})) =$$
$$\pi_{\mathrm{RDF}_i,...,\mathrm{RDF}_j,P_k,...,P_\ell}(\sigma_{Cond}(\mathcal{D})), \text{ whenever Cond}$$
involves only the attributes $\mathrm{RID}_i, ..., \mathrm{RID}_j, \mathrm{RDF}_i, ..., \mathrm{RDF}_j, P_k, ..., P_\ell$.

$$\sigma_{Cond}(\mathcal{D}_1 \times \mathcal{D}_2) = \sigma_{Cond}(\mathcal{D}_1) \times \mathcal{D}_2, \text{ whenever Cond does}$$
not involve any of the attributes of $\mathcal{D}_2$.

$$\pi_{\mathrm{RDF}_p,...,\mathrm{RDF}_q,\mathrm{RDF}_i,...,\mathrm{RDF}_j,P_a,...,P_b,P_c,...,P_d}(\mathcal{D}_1 \times \mathcal{D}_2) =$$
$$\pi_{\mathrm{RDF}_p,...,\mathrm{RDF}_q,P_a,...,P_b}(\mathcal{D}_1) \times \pi_{\mathrm{RDF}_i,...,\mathrm{RDF}_j,P_c,...,P_d}(\mathcal{D}_2),$$
where $\mathrm{RDF}_p, ..., \mathrm{RDF}_q, P_a, ..., P_b$ are in $\mathbf{A}_1$ but not in $\mathbf{A}_2$ and $\mathrm{RDF}_i, ..., \mathrm{RDF}_j, P_c, ..., P_d$ are in $\mathbf{A}_2$ but not in $\mathbf{A}_1$.

σ and π distribute over $\cup$.

σ distributes over $-$.

$$\pi_{\mathrm{RDF}_p,...,\mathrm{RDF}_q,P_i,...,P_j}(\mathcal{D}_1) - \pi_{\mathrm{RDF}_p,...,\mathrm{RDF}_q,P_i,...,P_j}(\mathcal{D}_2) \subseteq$$
$$\pi_{\mathrm{RDF}_p,...,\mathrm{RDF}_q,P_i,...,P_j}(\mathcal{D}_1 - \mathcal{D}_2).$$

$$\sigma_{Cond_1 \& Cond_2}(\mathcal{D}) = \sigma_{Cond_1}(\mathcal{D}) \cap \sigma_{Cond_2}(\mathcal{D}).$$
$$\sigma_{Cond_1 \& \neg Cond_2}(\mathcal{D}) = \sigma_{Cond_1}(\mathcal{D}) - \sigma_{Cond_2}(\mathcal{D}).$$
$$\sigma_{Cond_1 \vee Cond_2}(\mathcal{D}) = \sigma_{Cond_1}(\mathcal{D}) \cup \sigma_{Cond_2}(\mathcal{D}).$$

Table 3: A Sample of Identities Satisfied by the Operators

Definition 12 (Minus) Let $\mathbf{A}_1, \mathbf{A}_2$ be any dimension schemas and $\mathcal{D}_1, \mathcal{D}_2$ corresponding instances. Then $\mathcal{D}_1 - \mathcal{D}_2 = \{r \mid r \in \mathcal{D}_1 \ \& \ \not\exists s \in \mathcal{D}_2 : s \text{ is equivalent to } r\}$.

Note that just like the union operator, minus does not require union-compatibility between its operands. The result of minus contains exactly those regions in $\mathcal{D}_1$ for which no equivalent region exists in $\mathcal{D}_2$. Thus, the schema of the result is $\mathbf{A}_1$. A natural question is why the minus operator is defined in terms of region equivalence, instead of, e.g., region containment. The next lemma below settles this question, justifying our choice of primitive operators.

Lemma 1 Let $\mathcal{D}_1, \mathcal{D}_2$ be dimension instances of schemas $\mathbf{A}_1, \mathbf{A}_2$, where $\mathbf{A}_i = (\vec{\mathrm{RID}}_i, \vec{\mathrm{RDF}}_i, \vec{P}_i)$. Let $\ominus$ be defined as $\mathcal{D}_1 \ominus \mathcal{D}_2 = \{r \mid r \in \mathcal{D}_1 \ \& \ \not\exists s \in \mathcal{D}_2 : r \text{ is contained in } s\}$. Then $\ominus$ can be simulated using the minus operator. Specifically, $\mathcal{D}_1 \ominus \mathcal{D}_2 = \mathcal{D}_1 - \pi_{\vec{\mathrm{RID}}_1,\vec{\mathrm{RDF}}_1,\vec{P}_1}(\sigma_{\vec{\mathrm{RDF}}_2 \supset \vec{\mathrm{RDF}}_1}(\mathcal{D}_1 \times \mathcal{D}_2))$. But the minus operator cannot be simulated using $\ominus$ and the remaining operators. ∎

Finally, there is the *rename* operator, denoted as $\rho_{B \leftarrow A}(\mathcal{D})$, that renames attribute A of dimension $\mathcal{D}$ to attribute B, for any attributes A, B. Its definition is similar to that in the relational algebra. We sometimes use $\rho_{\mathbf{A}' \leftarrow \mathbf{A}}(\mathcal{D})$ as an abbreviation of the cascade of rename operators which rename each attribute $A \in \mathbf{A}$ to its primed version A'.

3.5 Expressiveness and Naturality of the Operators

Thus far, we have completed the presentation of the operators in the dimension algebra. The theorem below establishes a number of identities analogous to those for the relational algebra. This theorem is significant in two ways. First, it shows that the definitions of the operators are natural. Second, these identities can be used for rewriting algebraic queries into equivalent and more efficient ones.

Theorem 2 The operators of the dimension algebra satisfy the identities listed in Table 3, where $\mathcal{D}, \mathcal{D}_1, \mathcal{D}_2$ are dimension instances of schemas $\mathbf{A}, \mathbf{A}_1, \mathbf{A}_2$. ∎

Example 4 (Revisiting Example 3) In Example 3, the analyst seeks to find a minimal region satisfying some property $\mathcal{P}$, where minimality is defined as a region satisfying $\mathcal{P}$ without any of its children satisfying $\mathcal{P}$. Let $\mathcal{D}$ be a dimension instance consisting of all the regions satisfying property $\mathcal{P}$. ($\mathcal{D}$ itself may be computed as an algebraic expression; but this is not the focus here.) Let $hasChild(\mathcal{D})$ denote those regions in $\mathcal{D}$ such that the region has at least one child also in $\mathcal{D}$. The expression
$$\bigcup_{1 \leq i \leq m} \pi_{\mathbf{A}}(\sigma_{\mathrm{RID}_1=\mathrm{RID}'_1 \wedge \cdots \wedge \mathrm{RID}_{i-1}=\mathrm{RID}'_{i-1} \wedge \mathrm{RID}_i < \mathrm{RID}'_i \wedge \mathrm{RID}_{i+1}=\mathrm{RID}'_{i+1} \wedge ... \wedge \mathrm{RID}_m=\mathrm{RID}'_m}(\mathcal{D} \times \rho_{\mathbf{A}' \leftarrow \mathbf{A}}(\mathcal{D})))$$
precisely computes $hasChild(\mathcal{D})$, where the schema $\mathbf{A}$ contains m RID attributes. This is essentially a "self-join", relying on the hierarchical predicate $<$ defined in Definition 1 to select out those regions with a child in $\mathcal{D}$. The minimal regions in $\mathcal{D}$ that the analyst seeks are found by $\mathcal{D} - hasChild(\mathcal{D})$. It should be obvious that other similar hierarchical relationships can be captured as algebraic expressions, e.g., $hasNoChild(\mathcal{D})$, $hasNoPar(\mathcal{D})$, $hasAnc(\mathcal{D})$. ∎

Example 5 (Revisiting Example 2) In Example 2, we motivate stacking decision tree T_2 below tree T_1, i.e., each leaf of T_1 is further classified based on T_2. We leave it to the reader to verify that the expression $hasNoChild(T_1) \times T_2 \ \cup \ hasChild(T_1) \times hasNoPar(T_2)$ indeed computes the stacking of T_1 on T_2. To take full advantage of the fact that there is no union-compatibility requirement, as shown in Definition 11, we can simplify the above expression to $hasNoChild(T_1) \times T_2 \ \cup \ hasChild(T_1)$. The first part deals with stacking T_2 under each leaf node of T_1, whereas the second part simply includes the non-leaf nodes of T_1 in the final result. ∎

4 The Other Two Worlds

So far, we have introduced regions and dimensions in the I-World, and described how they can be manipulated. In this section, we turn our attention to the E-World and the D-World.

4.1 The E-World and Extensional Dimensions

In the I-world, regions in a dimension are represented by descriptions of their members. However, often times, an *extensional* representation of a dimension is also valuable. By "extensional", we mean that for a given data set E, the dimension is represented by an explicit enumeration of the tuples belonging to each region.

Definition 13 (Extensional Dimension)
An *extensional dimension schema* is a set of attributes
$\mathbf{A} = (\text{RID}_1, ..., \text{RID}_m, A_1, ..., A_n)$, where RIDs are hierarchical attributes and the As are normal attributes.
An *extensional dimension instance* over $\mathbf{A}$ is a set of
tuples over it. ∎

A region $r \in \mathcal{E}$ is identified by its RID-value $r[\vec{\text{RID}}]$,
and its members are precisely those tuples whose RID
equals this value. Note that the As are classical attributes. Thus, an extensional dimension is a generalized partition of a data set (since regions can overlap). For the example illustrated in Figure 1(a), the
intensional dimension $\mathcal{D}$ consists of eight regions, corresponding to the eight nodes. For a given (training or
test) data set E, the analyst may want to "populate"
$\mathcal{D}$ to find out exactly which tuples in E are in each
region (based on which he may take further actions).
While we will formalize the "populate" operation in
Section 5, the result of this operation is an extensional
dimension $\mathcal{E}$. Each tuple in E is assigned an appropriate RID in $\mathcal{E}$, which indicates which region in $\mathcal{D}$ (and
hence in $\mathcal{E}$) it belongs to.

An intensional dimension schema and an extensional dimension schema are *compatible* provided they
have the same set of RID (i.e. hierarchical) attributes.
Let $\mathcal{D}$ be an intensional dimension and $\mathcal{E}$ be an extensional dimension such that their schemas are compati-
ble. We say that a tuple $t_r \in \mathcal{E}$ *corresponds* to a region
$r \in \mathcal{D}$ provided that both of them agree on their RIDs,
i.e., $t_r[\vec{\text{RID}}] = r[\vec{\text{RID}}]$.

For the same reason that we allow intensional dimensions to be manipulated with the dimension algebra, in the E-world, we provide an algebra for the
manipulation of extensional dimensions. Note that ex-
cept for the $\vec{\text{RID}}$ attributes, an extensional dimension is
really like an ordinary relation. Thus, an appropriate
algebra for the E-World is the relational algebra extended with aggregation and with some modifications.
For brevity, we only remark on the adaptations to the
extended (relational) algebra here.

Projection might involve any subset of the RID attributes and/or the classical attributes. Intuitively,
eliminating an RID attribute via projection amounts
to setting the value of that attribute to the top element *all*. Finally, selection might involve any conventional selection predicate over the classical attributes.
In addition, as in Definition 7, we also permit selec-
tion predicates of the form $\text{RID}_i \bigtriangleup \text{RID}_j$ over RID attributes, where $\bigtriangleup$ is one of the hierarchical predicates.
Join can be simulated as usual via Cartesian product
and selection.

4.2 The D-World and Why

Finally, there is the D-World, which can be viewed
as consisting of a relational database (i.e., no RID or
RDF attribtues). Thus, the natural algebra of choice

for this world is the relational algebra (extended with
aggregation). The key difference between extensional
dimensions in the E-world and relations in the D-world
is that the former has a strong region identity, whereas
the latter is completely free of it. One may wonder
why the latter is worth included in the model after all.
From our empirical observation of how a real data mining and analysis process works, an analyst often spends
considerable time operating in the D-World *during the
entire process*. At the beginning, time may be spent on
data integration and data preparation. But even afterwards, considerable time may again be spent in the
D-World for data transformation and renewed preparation. By including the D-World in the 3W model,
we can more faithfully model the interactions among
the worlds, the topic of the next section.

5　Moving In and Out of the Worlds

As discussed above, each of the three worlds has its
unique role to play. And the full power of the 3W
model is only realized when an analyst is allowed to
freely move between the worlds. In this section, we
propose the "bridging" operators to facilitate this.

5.1 The Bridging Operators

The first operation amounts to "populating" the regions in an intensional dimension $\mathcal{D}$ with tuples from a
given data set E, producing an extensional dimension
$\mathcal{E}$. Intuitively, for each region in $\mathcal{D}$, there is a corresponding "extensional" region in $\mathcal{E}$ which contains just
those tuples in E that satisfy the region description.

Definition 14 (Populate) Let $\mathcal{D}$ be an intensional
dimension with dimension schema $(\text{RID}_1, \ldots, \text{RID}_m,$
$\text{RDF}_1, \ldots, \text{RDF}_m, P_1, \ldots, P_l)$ and E be a relation with
schema $(A_1, \ldots, A_n)$, such that the set of (coordi-
nate) attributes included in the constraints in the
domains of each RDF_i is a subset of $\{A_1, \ldots, A_n\}$.
Then $\alpha(\mathcal{D}, E)$ produces an extensional dimension with
schema $(\text{RID}_1, \ldots, \text{RID}_m, A_1, \ldots, A_n, P_1, \ldots, P_l)$, and
instance $\alpha(\mathcal{D}, E) = \{t \mid \exists r \in \mathcal{D} : \exists t_r \in E :$
$t[\vec{\text{RID}}] = r[\vec{\text{RID}}] \ \& \ t[\vec{A}] = t_r[\vec{A}] \ \& \ t[\vec{P}] = r[\vec{P}] \ \&$
t_r satisfies $r[\vec{\text{RDF}}]\}$, where satisfaction is in the sense
formalized in Definition 3. ∎

For instance, populating the decision tree of Figure 1(a) with a test relation would create an extensional dimension, which can be used to evaluate the
accuracy of the decision tree. Similarly, populating a
collection of frequent sets with a transaction database
would give an extensional dimension with each region
containing the set of supporting transactions.

Definition 15 (Mine) The *mine* operation, μ, given
a parameter p, maps a relation E to an intensional
dimension $\mathcal{D}$, i.e., $\mathcal{D} = \mu(E, p)$.

Typical data mining operations create intensional dimensions. We abstract this in the form of the *mine* operation. Examples of μ include decision tree, frequent sets, data cube, depth contour, etc. We may regard p as a number that specifies whether the desired intensional dimension is a decision tree, a depth contour, or any task mentioned in Table 1. For clarity, we use short strings instead of numbers in our examples. For example, $\mu(E, dc)$ corresponds to the data cube computation. Definition 15 above only defines the type of the mine operator at the level of the model. Its exact definition and computation depend entirely on the specific mining task invoked. In practice, invocation of μ would result in the running of a relevant (fast) mining algorithm. When a mining operation is invoked, we sometimes get both an intensional description of regions and an enumeration of the region members. It is convenient to separate these intensional and extensional aspects of a dimension for purposes of algebraic manipulation (as we have done). The extensional dimension $\mathcal{E}$ corresponding to an intensional dimension mined from a relation E can then be captured via the expression $\alpha(\mu(E, p), E)$.

Operation α allows us to relate a data set (D-world) to an intensional dimension (I-world) and, as a result, it lets us move to the E-world. The mine operator lets us move from the D-world to the I-world. (See Figure 2.) Next, we focus on operators bridging the I- and E-worlds. One important such situation is when the analyst has already obtained an extensional dimension $\mathcal{E} = \alpha(\mu(E, p), E)$, but may wish to "recall" or "look up" which intensional dimension gave rise to $\mathcal{E}$. To capture this, we propose a *lookup* operator λ.

Definition 16 (Lookup) Let $\mathcal{E}$ be any extensional dimension over the schema $(\text{RID}_1, \ldots, \text{RID}_m, A_1, \ldots, A_n)$. Then $\lambda(\mathcal{E}) = \{(t[\text{RID}_1], \ldots, t[\text{RID}_m], desc(t[\text{RID}_1]), \ldots, desc(t[\text{RID}_m])) \mid t \in \mathcal{E}\}$, where $desc(\text{RID})$ is the function that represents the 1-1 correspondence between RIDs and constraints (RDFs), as defined in Definition 4. ∎

Whenever the analyst wants to find out the intensional descriptions of regions in $\mathcal{E}$, as opposed to enumerations of their member tuples, λ is used to look up the appropriate hierarchical domain and return the corresponding region description formulas.

Finally, we define the *refresh* macro, below, as a matter of convenience:

Definition 17 (Refresh) Let E be a data set and $\mathcal{D}_1, \ldots, \mathcal{D}_n$ be intensional dimensions based on E. Let $Exp(\mathcal{D}_1, \ldots, \mathcal{D}_n)$ be any expression in the dimension algebra. Then the *refresh* of Exp w.r.t. the data set E is defined as $\alpha(Exp(\mathcal{D}_1, \ldots, \mathcal{D}_n), E)$. ∎

5.2 Completing the Examples

The focus of this section is to show that the machinery in this paper is rich enough to support multi-step mining activities in a clean algebraic framework. We do this by following through with the running examples developed in the earlier sections.

Example 6 (Example 3– The Full Story) Let us return to the task set out in Example 3. To begin, there is the data set E. By applying a data cube operator, the analyst gets $\mathcal{D} = \mu(E, dc)$, from which he also gets the corresponding extensional dimension as $\mathcal{E} = \alpha(\mu(E, dc), E)$. Let $\text{AGG}(\mathcal{E})$ be an expression in extended relational algebra that computes total sales grouped by region ids. (The detail of this standard expression is beside the point here.) Then $\mathcal{E}' = \sigma_{\text{totSales} \geq 100000}(\text{AGG}(\mathcal{E}))$ gives an extensional dimension, containing those regions in $\mathcal{E}$ that grossed a sale over \$100,000. To obtain the intensional descriptions of the regions in $\mathcal{E}'$, the analyst performs a lookup with $\mathcal{D}' = \lambda(\mathcal{E}')$. $\mathcal{D}'$ contains all regions satisfying the predicate on sales. To obtain the minimal regions satisfying this property, all the analyst has to do is plug in $\mathcal{D}'$ in place of the term $\mathcal{D}$ in the dimension algebra expression for $hasNoChild(\mathcal{D})$ given in Example 4. This completes the task. ∎

Example 7 (Example 1 – The Full Story) To perform the task set out in Example 1 with the transaction data set E, the analyst begins with the frequent set mining, with $\mathcal{D} = \mu(E, fs)$. To restrict the computation to those frequent sets containing the promotional item p, the analyst would instead use the expression $\mathcal{D}' = \sigma_{\text{RDF} \supset \{p\}}(\mathcal{D})$, thus finding constrained frequent sets. He can do the rollup on frequent sets (from items to class of items) by computing the parents of the regions in $\mathcal{D}'$ using Cartesian product and selection based on hierarchy predicates. By populating the resulting dimension w.r.t. E, he obtains an extensional dimension, say $\mathcal{E}$, which shows the transaction sets corresponding to $\mathcal{D}'$. By applying a decision tree construction to $\mathcal{E}$, he then obtains another intensional dimension, say $\mathcal{D}''$. This completes the task. ∎

A generic remark about our examples is that in order to facilitate the development of the process within the algebra, we have explained it step by step. In practice, however, an analyst who wishes to conduct such a multi-step mining/analysis process, may wish to evaluate complex expressions in one shot. The system can then exploit the properties of the operators involved, in optimizing the computation effectively. A simple example is the computation of constrained frequent sets via $\sigma_{\text{RDF} \supset \{p\}}(\mathcal{D})$ in Example 7. As pointed out in Section 1, many optimized algorithms have been developed for computing constrained frequent patterns in recent years, which can be leveraged. See Section 6 for more details on optimization.

5.3 Inter-World Interactions

Given the importance of the bridge operators in linking the worlds, a natural question is how do the various

$\alpha((\mathcal{D}_1 \cup \mathcal{D}_2), E) = \alpha(\mathcal{D}_1, E) \cup \alpha(\mathcal{D}_2, E).$

$\alpha(\sigma_{\text{Cond}_1 \wedge \text{Cond}_2}(\mathcal{D}), E) =$
$\quad \alpha(\sigma_{\text{Cond}_1}(\mathcal{D}), E) \cap \alpha(\sigma_{\text{Cond}_2}(\mathcal{D}), E).$

$\alpha(\sigma_{\text{Cond}_1 \wedge \neg\text{Cond}_2}(\mathcal{D}), E) = \alpha(\sigma_{\text{Cond}_1}(\mathcal{D}), E) -$
$\quad \alpha(\sigma_{\text{Cond}_2}(\mathcal{D}), E).$ Similar identities hold for others boolean combinations.

Let $\mathcal{C}$ be a constraint from the domain of RDF_A and $\mathcal{C}'$ from the domain of RDF_B. Then:

(a) $\sigma_{\mathcal{C} \supset \text{RDF}_A}(\mu(E, dc)) = \mu(\sigma_{\mathcal{C}}(E), dc).$
(E.g., all regions contained in $\texttt{location} = \texttt{montreal}$.) A similar identity holds for selection on RID attributes.

(b) $\sigma_{(\text{RDF}_A \& \text{RDF}_B) \supset (\mathcal{C} \& \mathcal{C}')}(\mu(E, dc)) =$
$\mu(\pi_{A,B}(\sigma_{\mathcal{C} \& \mathcal{C}'}(E)), dc).$ (E.g., all regions containing $\texttt{location} = \texttt{montreal}$ & $\texttt{productClass} = \texttt{meat}$.) A similar identity holds for selection on RID attributes.

$\pi_{\text{RDF}_{A_i}, \ldots, \text{RDF}_{A_j}}(\mu(E, dc)) = \mu(\pi_{A_i, \ldots, A_j}(E), dc).$

$\mu(E_1 \cup E_2, dc) = \mu(E_1, dc) \cup \mu(E_2, dc),$ where E_1, E_2 are any union-compatible data sets.

$\mu(E_1 \times E_2, dc) = \mu(E_1, dc) \times \mu(E_2, dc).$

Table 4: A Sample of Inter-World Identities

operators interact. The following theorem answers this question. Identity (1) in Table 4 says the populate operator respects the structure of the I- and E-worlds in that populating the union of two dimensions coincides with taking the union of the two populations. A similar remark holds for product. Similarly, as shown in identities (2) and (3), boolean combinations of selection conditions in the intensional world are faithfully mapped by α to corresponding set-theoretic operations in the extensional world.

Theorem 3 Let $\mathcal{D}_1, \mathcal{D}_2$ be any intensional dimensions and E be a data set. Then identities (1)-(3) in Table 4 hold. ∎

On the one hand, the kinds of identities above attest to the naturality of our definitions. On the other, they are useful for query optimization via query rewriting. Indeed, for some special cases, we can even go beyond the above identities. For instance, consider the data cube operator. Recall that in our framework, the cube operator merely splits up a data set into regions corresponding to all possible group-bys. For cube, we can consider that the attributes mentioned in the constraints (RDFs), as also those used to construct RIDs, are a subset of the attributes of the given relation. To emphasize this, let us use RID_A (resp., RDF_A) to denote the RID (resp., RDF) attribute associated with attribute A of the relation. The following theorem deals with the data cube operator. Similar, but somewhat different, identities hold for the frequent sets operator, but are omitted for lack of space.

Theorem 4 Let E, E_1, E_2 be data sets. Then for data cube computation, identities (4)-(7) in Table 4 hold. ∎

6 Implementation and Optimization Issues

In previous sections, we showed that the framework proposed here can effectively support multi-step min-

1. $\alpha((\mathcal{D}_1 \cup \mathcal{D}_2), E) = \mathcal{E}_1 \cup \mathcal{E}_2.$

2. $\alpha(\sigma_{\text{Cond}}(\mathcal{D}_1), E) = \{t \in \mathcal{E}_1 \mid desc(t[\text{RID}]) \text{ satisfies Cond }\}.$

3. $\alpha(\pi_{\text{RDF}_i, \ldots, \text{RDF}_j, P_k, \ldots, P_\ell}(\mathcal{D}_1), E) = \pi_{\text{RID}_i, \ldots, \text{RID}_j, \vec{A}_1}(\mathcal{E}_1).$

4. $\alpha((\mathcal{D}_1 - \mathcal{D}_2), E) = \mathcal{E}_1 - \mathcal{E}_2.$

5. $\alpha(\Upsilon(\mathcal{D}_1), E) = \{t \mid t \in \mathcal{E}_1, desc(t[\text{RID}]) \text{ is consistent }\}.$

Table 5: Efficient Computation of the Refresh Operation

1. $\lambda(\sigma_{\text{Cond}}(\mathcal{E}_1)) = \{r \in \mathcal{D}_1 \mid \exists t : t \in \sigma_{\text{Cond}}(\mathcal{E}_1), desc(t[\text{RID}]) = r[\text{RDF}], t[\text{RID}] = r[\text{RID}]\}.$

2. $\lambda(\pi_{\vec{X}}(\mathcal{E}_1)) = \pi_{\text{RID}_i, \ldots, \text{RID}_j, \text{RDF}_i, \ldots, \text{RDF}_j}(\mathcal{D}_1),$ where $\vec{X} \cap \mathbf{A}_1 = \{\text{RID}_i, \ldots, \text{RID}_j\}.$

3. $\lambda(\mathcal{E}_1 \cup \mathcal{E}_2) = \mathcal{D}_1 \cup \mathcal{D}_2.$

4. $\lambda(\mathcal{E}_1 - \mathcal{E}_2)) = \mathcal{D}_1 - \mathcal{D}_2.$

5. $\lambda(\mathcal{E}_1 \times \mathcal{E}_2) = \mathcal{D}_1 \times \mathcal{D}_2.$

Table 6: Efficient Computation of the Lookup Operation

ing/analysis activities, that could not be done before within one clean algebraic setting. The question we address in this section is how efficiently we can implement the proposed framework. Some evidence for the possibility for efficient implementation was provided in earlier sections through identities. For space limitations, our discussion here must remain at a somewhat high level. As we argue below, the main reasons behind efficient implementability are: (1) certain key operations admit efficient incremental processing; and (2) many other key operations can benefit from spatial indexing and processing, a strength of the database community.

6.1 Incremental Computation

Two main operations linking different worlds are refresh and lookup, since they help maintain extensional (resp., intensional) dimensions in sync with manipulations being done on the intensional (resp., extensional) dimensions.

Theorem 5 Let $\mathcal{D}_1, \mathcal{D}_2$ be intensional dimensions, E be any data set, and $\mathcal{E}_1, \mathcal{E}_2$ be the corresponding extensional dimensions based on E, i.e., $\mathcal{E}_i = \alpha(\mathcal{D}_i, E)$. Suppose $\vec{A}_1$ is the set of non-RID attributes of $\mathcal{E}_1$. Then the identities listed in Table 5 hold. ∎

The above theorem shows that the refresh macro, as defined in Definition 17, admits efficient incremental processing. Given that the extensional dimension $\mathcal{E}_i$ has been created based on the intensional counterpart $\mathcal{D}_i$, refreshing $\mathcal{E}_i$ w.r.t. an additional dimension algebra operation (and hence a sequence of operations) on $\mathcal{D}_i$, can be done *solely by examining the content of the existing* $\mathcal{E}_i$.

The following result shows that lookup – another key bridging operation – admits incremental processing as well.

Theorem 6 Let $\mathcal{E}_1, \mathcal{E}_2$ be two extensional dimensions and $\mathcal{D}_1, \mathcal{D}_2$ be their intensional counterparts, i.e., $\mathcal{D}_i = \lambda(\mathcal{E}_i)$. Suppose also that the schema of $\mathcal{D}_i$ is $\mathbf{A}_i$. Then the identities listed in Table 6 hold. ∎

6.2 Application of Spatial Techniques

So far, we have considered the optimization of the bridging operations: refresh (which is essentially an incremental version of populate) and lookup. In the previous sections, we established similar identities for other operators including (some special cases of) the mine operator. Next, we turn our attention to efficient implementation of the dimension algebra.

The main problems involving constraints which directly impact the efficiency of dimension algebra at a logical level, are testing constraint implication (and equivalence), consistency checking, and constraint simplification. It is important to note that, as shown in Table 1, numerous existing data mining tasks produce isothetic regions, for which all three problems can be solved efficiently. Specifically, in this case, the constraints are of the form $A_i \theta c$, θ being $\le$ or $\ge$, and the problems can be solved in linear time.

At a physical level, known spatial indexing techniques can be effectively leveraged to help quickly locate points in isothetic regions. Standard multi-dimensional indexing techniques, such as R-trees and its variants [12, 6], are directly applicable to the checking of such spatial predicates as overlap, containment, etc. Note that in traditional spatial processing, indexing structures like R-trees have proved useful for polygons that are not even isothetic (e.g., convex), with the addition of a refinement phase. This suggests that such index structures should prove equally effective in the implementation of key dimension algebra operators, whether the regions are isothetic or not.

Finally, the RID attributes can often be encoded so that the checking hierarchical predicates can be performed efficiently. For example, when the hierarchy in question is a tree or can be factored into a product of tree hierarchies, all hierarchy predicates can be checked in linear time, using the ideas developed in [17]. Examples include categorical hierarchies, e.g., `location`, `product`, as well as decision trees. A hierarchy defined by a tuple of hierarchical attributes, each of which has a tree hierarchy, is a natural example of a hierarchy that can be factored into trees. For range hierarchies (over total orders or partial orders), merely encoding the endpoints of the ranges gives an efficient encoding, from which parents, children, ancestors, etc. can be easily enumerated. For instance, the RID [2, 10] has [1,10] and [2,11] as parents, and [2,9] and [3,10] as children. Finally, for lattices corresponding to powersets (e.g., frequent sets), a number of techniques exist. For instance, we could use a bit vector (made suitably compact to save space) for efficient checking of hierarchy predicates.

7 Related Work

Earlier, we have mentioned numerous data mining studies and how they can be classified into two generations. Below we discuss a few studies that are also very related to the subject matter of this paper – namely, the development of a model and algebra for data mining. In [16], Mannila and Imielinski discussed their vision of manipulating association rules algebraically. The 3W model developed here is a concrete proposal, and is more general, as it models not only association rules, but also many well-known data mining and analysis operations, such as decision trees, data spheres, etc. In [23], Meo et al. proposed adding an association rule operator to SQL. Again, our proposed 3W model is far more general and fundamental.

The dimension algebra developed here is related to constraint query languages in general [19, 7] and geometric query languages in particular [26, 13]. Paredaens et al. [26], and Gyssens et al. [13] consider constraint languages that are in the FO[R] class, i.e., first-order logic augmented with polynomial inequalities over reals, and relation variables with fixed arities. This class of constraints are shown to have nice properties, such as decidability for equivalence checking. Our dimension algebra uses constraints restricted to LINEAR[R], and therefore enjoys at least the properties of FO[R].

The notion of hierarchical domains we use in this paper was first proposed by Jagadish et al. [17]. However, they confine attention to categorical tree hierarchies in data warehouses. By contrast, we use hierarchies (via the notion of dimensions) as a central unifying concept for disparate mining tasks and for warehousing, and permit general lattice-based hierarchies. Finally, the notion of constraint domains was not considered by them, while this notion plays a pivotal role in the I-world. Besides, we propose an algebra for manipulating dimensions (among other things).

8 Summary and Future Work

We have presented the 3W Model and an algebraic framework for unified data mining and analysis. It allows the input of one operation to be the output of another. We have shown via examples and numerous operator identities that the proposed framework is natural and is expressive enough to support multi-step mining processes within one clean algebraic setting, to our knowledge, *for the first time in the literature*. Furthermore, we have also demonstrated and argued that the proposed framework can be efficiently implemented.

This being the first paper on unified mining and analysis within a formal framework, it opens up several important questions for future research. Mining-query optimization needs to be thoroughly investigated – both at the logical level of query rewriting using identities and at the physical level of utilizing spatial database techniques. It is very important to develop a prototype system of the proposed framework for extensive empirical evaluation, which may lead to many interesting algorithmic and optimization problems. A third issue is tight integration of data warehousing and mining, for which we have taken a first step by using dimensions as a unifying concept for warehouses and the result of mining tasks. But much more work remains to be done. Our ongoing work addresses these questions.

References

[1] C. Aggarwal and P. Yu. Online Generation of Association Rules. In *Proc. 1998 ICDE*, pp 402–411.

[2] R. Agrawal, J. Gehrke, D. Gunopolos and P. Raghavan. Automatic Subspace Clustering of High Dimensional Data for Data Mining Applications. In *Proc. 1998 SIGMOD*, pp. 94–105.

[3] R. Agrawal, T. Imielinski, and A. Swami. Mining association rules between sets of items in large databases. In *Proc. 1993 SIGMOD*, pp 207–216.

[4] R. Agrawal and R. Srikant. Fast algorithms for mining association rules. In *Proc. 1994 VLDB*, pp 487–499.

[5] M. Ankerst, M. Breunig, H.P. Kriegel and J. Sander. Optics: Ordering Points to Identify the Clustering Structure. In *Proc. 1999 SIGMOD*, pp. 49–60.

[6] N. Beckmann, H.-P. Kriegel, R. Schneider, and B. Seeger. newblock The R*-Tree: an Efficient and Robust Access Method for Points and Rectangles. In *Proc. 1990 SIGMOD*, pp. 322–331.

[7] M. Benedikt, G. Dong, L. Libkin, and L. Wong. Relational Expressive Power of Constraint Query Languages. Journal of the ACM, 45:1, 1998, pp. 1–34.

[8] S. Brin, R. Motwani, and C. Silverstein. Beyond market basket: Generalizing association rules to correlations. In *Proc. 1997 SIGMOD*, pp 265–276.

[9] S. Chaudhuri. Data mining and database systems: Where is the intersection? *Bulletin of the Technical Committee on Data Engineering*, 21:4–8, March 1998.

[10] M. Garofalakis, R. Rastogi, and K. Shim. SPIRIT: Sequential Pattern Mining with Regular Expression Constraints, In *Proc. 1999 VLDB*, pp 223–234.

[11] J. Gray et al. Data Cube: A relational aggregation operator generalizing group-by, cross-tab, and subtotals. *Proc. 12th ICDE*, 1996, pp. 152–159.

[12] R. Guttmann. A Dynamic Index Structure for Spatial Searching. In *Proc. 1984 SIGMOD*, pp. 47–57.

[13] M. Gyssens, J. Van den Bussche, and D. Van Gucht. Complete Geometric Query Languages. *J. of Comput. & Syst. Sciences* 58:3(483-511) 1999.

[14] J. Han and Y. Fu. Discovery of multiple-level association rules from large databases. In *Proc. 1995 VLDB*, pp 420–431.

[15] C. Hidber. Online Association Rule Mining. In *Proc. 1999 SIGMOD*, pp 145–156.

[16] T. Imielinski and H. Mannila. A database perspective on knowledge discovery. *Communications of ACM*, 39:58–64, 1996.

[17] H. Jagadish, L. Lakshmanan, and D. Srivastava. What can Hierarchies do for Data Warehouses? In *Proc. 1999 VLDB*, pp. 530–541.

[18] T. Johnson, I. Kwok, and R. Ng. Fast Computation of 2-Dimensional Depth Contours. In *Proc. 1998 KDD*, pp. 224–228.

[19] P. Kannellakis, G. Kuper, and P. Revesz. Constraint Query Languages. Journal of Computer and System Sciences, 51:1, 1995, pp. 26–52.

[20] M. Klemettinen, H. Mannila, P. Ronkainen, H. Toivonen, and A.I. Verkamo. Finding interesting rules from large sets of discovered association rules. In *Proc. 1994 CIKM*, pp 401–408.

[21] L. V. S. Lakshmanan, R. Ng, J. Han, and A. Pang. Optimization of constrained frequent set queries with 2-variable constraints. In *Proc. 1999 SIGMOD*, pp. 157–168.

[22] H. Mannila, H Toivonen, and A. I. Verkamo. Discovery of frequent episodes in event sequences. *Data Mining and Knowledge Discovery*, 1, 1997, pp. 259-289.

[23] R. Meo, G. Pasila, and S. Ceri. A New SQL-like Operator for Mining Association Rules. In *Proc. 1996 VLDB*, pp. 122–133.

[24] R. Ng and J. Han. Efficient and Effective Clustering Methods for Spatial Data Mining. In *Proc. 1994 VLDB*, pp. 144-155.

[25] R. Ng, L. V. S. Lakshmanan, J. Han, and A. Pang. Exploratory mining and pruning optimizations of constrained associations rules. In *Proc. 1998 SIGMOD*, pp. 13–24.

[26] J. Paradaens, J. Van dn Bussche, and D. Van Gucht. Towards a Theory of Spatial Database Queries. In *Proc. 1994 PODS*, pp. 279–288.

[27] J. Quinlan. Induction of Decision Trees. Machine Learning, 1, 1986, pp. 81–106.

[28] S. Sarawagi, S. Thomas, and R. Agrawal. Integrating association rule mining with relational database systems: Alternatives and implications. In *Proc. 1998 SIGMOD*, pp 343–354.

[29] C. Silverstein, S. Brin, R. Motwani, and J. Ullman. Scalable techniques for mining causal structures. In *Proc. 1998 VLDB*, pp 594–605.

[30] D. Tsur, J. D. Ullman, S. Abiteboul, C. Clifton, R. Motwani, and S. Nestorov. Query flocks: A generalization of association-rule mining. In *Proc. 1998 SIGMOD*, pp 1–12.

[31] T. Zhang, R. Ramakrishnan and M. Livny. BIRCH: an Efficient Data Clustering Method for Very Large Databases. In *Proc. 1996 SIGMOD*, pp. 103–114.

Design and Implementation of a Genetic-Based Algorithm for Data Mining

Sunil Choenni

National Aerospace Laboratory NLR, P.O. Box 90502, 1006 BM Amsterdam, The Netherlands
and
University of Twente, Dept. of Computer Science, P.O. Box 217, 7500 AE Enschede, The Netherlands
email: choenni@nlr.nl and choenni@cs.utwente.nl

Abstract

Many data mining problems can be considered as search problems. A database is regarded as a search space and a mining algorithm as a search strategy. The search spaces that rise from data mining problems are very large, making an exhaustive search infeasible. Therefore, heuristic search strategies are of vital importance. In this paper, we discuss the design and implementation of a (prototype) data mining tool that is equipped with a genetic algorithm. We have mined two real-life aircraft incident databases with this tool. We report on the obtained mining results as well.

1   Introduction

Research and development in data mining evolves in several directions which are not necessarily divergent. One of these directions is the induction of classification rules from databases [1, 2, 13, 14, 17]. Many data mining problems in this direction can be regarded as search problems. A search problem is characterised by a search space and a search strategy [12]. A search strategy is used to identify specific elements in the search space by walking efficiently through this space.

In the context of data mining, a database is regarded as a set of tuples, and each (projected) subset of tuples is considered as an element in the search space. The problem is to select interesting subsets without inspecting the whole search space, which is the task of a search strategy. For example, in a car insurance environment the identification of profiles of risky drivers, i.e., drivers with (more than average) chances of causing an accident, can be modelled as a search problem. Consider an artificial relation *Driver(gender, age, town, category, price, damage)*, in which the attributes *gender*, *age*, and *town* refer to the driver and the other attributes refer to the car. Attribute *category* records, whether a car is leased or not, and *damage* records, whether a car has been involved in an accident or not. The challenge is to select a conjunction of predicates that represents the group of risky drivers. Assume that young males in leased cars form the group of risky drivers. Then, an expression like: *gender* **is** ('male') $\land$ *age* **in** [19,24] $\land$ *category* **is** ('leased') should be searched for.

In general, the search spaces that should be inspected in order to answer mining questions are very large, making an exhaustive search infeasible. Therefore, heuristic search strategies are of vital importance to data mining. The success of a search strategy is often dependent on the structure of the search space. For example, a hill climber will generally perform better on a search that consists of a few optima, while a genetic algorithm will perform better if the search space consists of many optima. The reason is that a hill climber terminates if it reaches an optimum, while a genetic algorithm does not. In a search space that contains many optima, it will generally be worthwhile to continue searching the space after having found the first optimum. Unfortunately, the search spaces that stem from data mining problems neither have a specific structure nor are the structures known in advance. On the basis of evidence, one should choose for a search algorithm. Therefore, a data mining tool should be equipped with several search algorithms.

This paper is devoted to the design and implementation of a (prototype) data mining tool, called SHARVIND, which is equipped with a genetic algorithm. SHARVIND is primarily developed for data mining problems that give rise to search spaces that consist of expressions. An expression is a conjunction of predicates and each predicate is defined on a database attribute. A genetic algorithm is brought into action to efficiently search for interesting expressions.

In general, a genetic algorithm is characterised by the representation of individuals, a fitness function that evaluates an individual, and the manipulation operators cross-over and mutation [15]. We represent an individual as an expression. This representation fits seamlessly in the field of databases. The fitness function takes care that extracted knowledge from the database is supported by a significant part of the database and that trivial knowledge is discarded before-hand. Furthermore, our fitness function gives rise to the reduction of the number of disk accesses during the mining process. We have implemented the mutation operator such that an expression undergoes a minor modification. The cross-over operator takes two expressions, selects a random point, and exchanges the subexpressions behind this point.

SHARVIND is a re-targetable tool that is currently running in a Microsoft Access environment. Retargetable means that the tool can be integrated with other database management systems, such as ORACLE, without much effort. The tool takes as input a mining question and possibly requirements (e.g., not to use certain attributes in the mining process) posed by a user. Then, a random number of expressions, called initial population, is selected. The initial population is manipulated by applying the cross-over and mutation operators. In order to compute the fitness of individuals, they are translated into corresponding SQL queries which are passed to the MS Access dbms. The fittest individuals are selected to form the next generation and the manipulation process is repeated until no significant improvement of the population can be observed. As output, the tool delivers expressions whose corresponding number of tuples falls in a user-defined interval.

We have mined two real-life databases with SHARVIND. Both databases contain aircraft incident data. The mining question that we have posed to both databases is: "What are the profiles of risky flights?" To one of these databases, we have posed some additional mining questions concerning safety aspects (see Section 7). We have presented the mining results to safety experts at our laboratory and the overall conclusion was that the answers to the mining questions were correct and promising. The mining results helped safety experts to gain insight in the databases and hopefully also knowledge in future.

1.1 Related work

It has been recognised by several researchers that genetic algorithms might be suitable for data mining

tasks [3, 4, 8, 9, 10]. In [3, 10], a genetic approach has been proposed to learn first order logic rules and in [9], a framework is proposed for data mining based on genetic programming. In [4], a genetic algorithm is applied in the context of direct marketing. In [8], a general overview of a pattern search tool is given. Standard statistical measures are used to evaluate patterns.

The efforts in [3, 4, 8, 10] are focussed towards machine learning, and the important data mining issue of integration with databases is superficially discussed or not discussed at all. Although the framework in [9] stresses on the integration of genetic programming and databases, an elaborated approach to implement and to evaluate the framework is not presented. Furthermore, the proposed algorithms in [3, 10] are not implemented as well.

Our work distinguishes from above-mentioned efforts on the following aspects. First, we have implemented our approach and have applied it on two real-life databases. Second, we propose a re-targetable architecture, in which a genetic algorithm is integrated with databases. We note that in [4, 10] individuals are represented as binary strings or as vectors. Third, we have made a first attempt to model a fitness function such that the number of disk accesses may be optimized, which speeds up the mining session.

Other related research has been reported in [13, 14]. In these efforts, the authors use variants of a hill climber to identify the group(s) of tuples satisfying a mining question. Since a genetic-based algorithm is capable of exploring different parts of a search space, it has, by nature, a better chance to escape from a local optimum than a hill climber.

A major advantage of our approach is that we have solved the partitioning of attribute values —which is necessary for many mining algorithms— by choosing a suitable mutation operator (see Section 3). In general, data mining algorithms require a technique that partitions the domain values of an attribute in a limited set of ranges, see amongst others [17], simply because considering all possible ranges of domain values is infeasible. Finding a proper partitioning technique for attribute values is a tough problem [18].

1.2 A guided tour

In Section 2, we discuss the relation between searching and data mining in more detail. In Section 3, we tailor a genetic algorithm for mining purposes. Since our fitness function gives rise to optimization of the number of disk accesses, we discuss, in Section 4, a number of optimization rules. In Section 5, we discuss the overall genetic-based mining algorithm. Section 6 is devoted to the architecture and implementation of SHARVIND. In Section 7, we report on some mining results that we have obtained by mining a number of databases. Section 8 concludes the paper.

tid	gender	age	town	category	price	damage
1	male	20	Rome	leased	70K	yes
2	female	35	Amsterdam	not leased	80K	yes
3	male	24	Amsterdam	leased	75K	yes
4	male	28	Rome	not leased	40K	yes
5	female	28	The Hague	leased	50K	no
...	...	...	...	...	...	...

Table 1: Snapshot of the database *Driver*

2 Data mining and searching

In the following, a database consists of a universal relation [7]. The relation is defined over some independent single valued attributes, such as $att_1, att_2, ..., att_n$, and is a subset of the Cartesian product $\mathbf{dom}(att_1) \times \mathbf{dom}(att_2) \times ... \times \mathbf{dom}(att_n)$, in which $\mathrm{dom}(att_j)$ is the set of values that can be assumed by attribute att_j.

A tuple is an ordered list of attribute values to which a unique identifier, referred as tid, is attached. An expression is defined as a conjunction of predicates, and is used to select a set of tuples from the database, which in turn represents a class in the database. Consider the relation *Driver(gender, age, town, category, price, damage)* and a snapshot of this relation as depicted in Table 1. For example, the expression *gender*='male' selects the tuples corresponding to the males, i.e., the tuples 1, 3 and 4 in Table 1, the expression *age* **in** $[18,24] \wedge$ *category*='leased' selects the set of tuples corresponding to persons between eighteen and twenty four years old driving a leased car, i.e., the tuples 1 and 3, etc. A main advantage of introducing the notion of expression is that we do not have to enumerate explicitly all tuples of a class, and therefore an expression can be regarded as a summary/description of a class. So, a database contains an enormous number of classes, and each class can be represented as an expression or a disjunction of expressions.

Note, the disjunction (*gender*='male' $\wedge$ *age*=20 $\wedge$ *town*='Rome' $\wedge$ *category*='leased' $\wedge$ *price*=70K $\wedge$ *damage*='yes') $\vee$ (*gender*='female' $\wedge$ *age*=35 $\wedge$ *town*='Amsterdam' $\wedge$ *category*='not leased' $\wedge$ *price*=80K $\wedge$ *damage*='yes') is a straightforward way to select the first and the second tuple from Table 1.

Data mining may now be regarded as the search for useful, previously unknown expressions from a space of expressions without inspecting the whole space. The search space is formed by all possible expressions with regard to a database. Note that the number of expressions grows exponentially with the number of attributes and the number of tuples in the database.

Although the usefulness of an expression generally depends on the application, we know before-hand that the following three categories of expressions will not be interesting.

1. Expressions that select zero tuples. An example of such an expression is *age*=20 $\wedge$ *age*=36. Since age is a single valued attribute, no tuples will qualify.

2. Expressions that select a set of arbitrary tuples that do not have any common characteristics. Such a set can easily be obtained by a disjunction of an arbitrary number of expressions.

3. Expressions that consist of a single predicate, called *elementary* expression. Knowledge with regard to these expressions is stored in the data dictionary, which is easily accessible.

Therefore, we discard these categories from the search space by imposing the following restrictions to expressions: 1) an attribute appears at most once in an expression, 2) disjunctions of expressions are not allowed in the search space, and 3) an expression should contain at least one conjunction.

So, the elements of the search space are expressions that satisfy above-mentioned restrictions. The challenge is to come up with search strategies that are able to find the interesting elements by inspecting a relatively small part of the search space.

3 Mining with genetic algorithms

In this section, we discuss the issues that play a role in tailoring a genetic algorithm for data mining. Section 3.1 is devoted to the representation of individuals in a population. Then, in Section 3.2, we discuss a fitness function, which computes the quality of an individual. Finally, in Section 3.3, we discuss the two operators that are used to manipulate an individual.

3.1 Representation

As stated in Section 2, an expression is a conjunction of predicates and a predicate is defined on a database attribute. An individual is defined as an expression to which some restrictions are imposed with regard to the notation of elementary expressions.

The notation of an elementary expression depends on the domain type of the involved attribute. If there exists no ordering relationship between the attribute values of an attribute att, we represent an elementary expression as follows: *expression* := att **is** $(v_1, v_2, ..., v_n)$, in which $v_i \in \mathrm{dom}(att)$, $1 \leq i \leq n$. In this way, we express that an attribute att assumes one of the values in the set $\{v_1, v_2, ..., v_n\}$. If an ordering relationship exists between the domain values of an attribute, an elementary expression is denoted as *expression* := att **in** $[v_i, v_k]$, $i \leq k$, in which $[v_i, v_k]$ represents the values within the range of v_i and v_k.

A population is defined as a set of individuals. An example of a population, based on the relation *Driver*, is given in Figure 1.

3.2 Fitness function

Since a genetic algorithm is aimed to the optimization of a fitness function, this function is one of the keys to

$$
\begin{aligned}
p_1 = &\ \textit{gender } \mathbf{is}\ (\text{'male'}) \wedge \textit{age } \mathbf{in}\ [19,34] \\
p_2 = &\ \textit{age } \mathbf{in}\ [29,44] \wedge \textit{category } \mathbf{is}\ (\text{'leased'}) \\
     &\ \wedge \textit{town } \mathbf{is}\ (\text{'Rome', 'Amsterdam', 'Cairo'}) \\
p_3 = &\ \textit{gender } \mathbf{is}\ (\text{'male'}) \wedge \textit{age } \mathbf{in}\ [29,34] \wedge \\
     &\ \textit{category } \mathbf{is}\ (\text{'leased'}) \\
p_4 = &\ \textit{gender } \mathbf{is}\ (\text{'female'}) \wedge \textit{age } \mathbf{in}\ [29,40] \wedge \\
     &\ \textit{category } \mathbf{is}\ (\text{'leased'}) \wedge \textit{price } \mathbf{in}\ [50K, 100K] \\
p_5 = &\ \textit{gender } \mathbf{is}\ (\text{'male'}) \wedge \textit{price } \mathbf{in}\ [20K,45K]
\end{aligned}
$$

Figure 1: Example of a population

success. Consequently, a fitness function should represent issues that play a role in the optimization of a specific problem. Before enumerating a number of issues that play a role in the context of data mining, we introduce the notions of cover.

Definition 1: Let D be a database and p an individual defined on D. Then, the number of tuples that satisfies the expression corresponding to p is called the cover of p, and is denoted as $\|\sigma_p(D)\|$. The set of tuples satisfying p is denoted as $\sigma_p(D)$.

Note that p can be regarded as a description of a class in D and $\sigma_p(D)$ summarizes the tuples satisfying p. Within a class we can define subclasses. In the following, we regard the classification problem as follows: *Given a target class t, search interesting subclasses, i.e., individuals, within class t.* We note that the target class is the class of tuples in which interesting knowledge should be searched for. Suppose we want to expose the profiles of risky drivers, i.e., the class of persons with (more than average) chances of causing an accident, from the database *Driver*. Then, these profiles should be searched for in a class that records the characteristics of drivers that caused accidents. Such a class may be described as *damage = ('yes')*.

We feel that the following issues play a role in classification problems.

- The cover of the target class. Since results from data mining are used for informed decision making, knowledge extracted from databases should be supported by a significant part of the database. This increases the reliability of the results. So, a fitness function should take into account that small covers are undesired.

- The ratio of the cover of an individual p to the cover of the target class t, i.e., $\frac{\|\sigma_p(D) \cap \sigma_t(D)\|}{\|\sigma_t(D)\|}$. If the ratio is close to 0, this means that only a few tuples of the target class satisfy individual p. This is undesired for the same reason as a small cover for a target class. If the ratio is close to 1, almost all tuples of the target class satisfy p. This is also undesired because this will result in knowledge that is often known. A fitness function should take these properties into account.

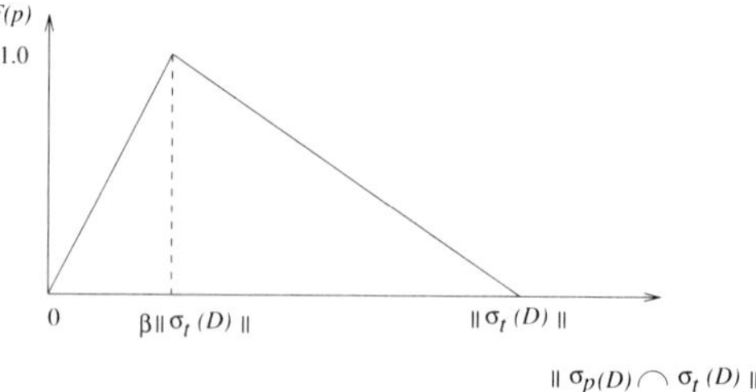

Figure 2: Shape of the fitness function

Taking into account above-mentioned issues, we have defined the following fitness function:

$$
F(p) = \begin{cases}
\dfrac{\|\sigma_p(D) \cap \sigma_t(D)\|}{\beta \|\sigma_t(D)\|} C(t) & \text{if } \|\sigma_p(D) \cap \sigma_t(D)\| \\
& \quad \leq \beta \|\sigma_t(D)\| \\[2ex]
\dfrac{\|\sigma_p(D) \cap \sigma_t(D)\| - \|\sigma_t(D)\|}{\|\sigma_t(D)\| (\beta - 1)} C(t) & \text{otherwise}
\end{cases}
$$

in which $0 < \beta \leq 1$, and

$$
C(t) = \begin{cases}
0 & \text{if } \frac{\|\sigma_t(D)\|}{\|\sigma(D)\|} \leq \alpha \quad \text{with } 0 \leq \alpha \leq 1 \\
1 & \text{otherwise}
\end{cases}
$$

We note that the values for α and β should be defined by the user and will vary for different applications. The value of α defines the fraction of tuples that a target class should contain in order to be a candidate for further exploration. The value β defines the fraction of tuples that an individual should represent within a target class in order to obtain the maximal fitness. In Figure 2, the shape of the fitness function is presented.

The fitness grows linearly with the number of tuples satisfying the description of an individual p as well as satisfying a target class t, i.e., $\|\sigma_p(D) \cap \sigma_t(D)\|$, above a user-defined value α, and decreases linearly with $\|\sigma_p(D) \cap \sigma_t(D)\|$ after reaching the value $\beta \|\sigma_t(D)\|$.

It should be clear that our goal is to search for those individuals that approximate a fitness of $\beta \|\sigma_t(D)\|$. Consider the target class *damage = ('yes')* that consists of 100.000 tuples. Assume that a profile is considered risky if about 30.000 out of 100.000 persons satisfy this profile. This means that $\beta \approx 0.3$. Assuming that 33.000 of the persons that caused an accident are young males, the algorithm should find individuals like *gender* **is** ('male') $\wedge$ *age* **in** [19,28].

3.3 Manipulation operators

In this section, we discuss the effects of the mutation and cross-over operator on an individual.

Mutation. As stated in the introduction of this section, a mutation modifies an individual. In defining the mutation operator, we take into account the domain type of an attribute. If there exists no ordering relationship between the domain values, then we randomly select an attribute value and replace it by another value, which can be a NULL value as well, in an expression that contains this attribute. For example, a mutation on attribute *town* of individual p_2 (see Figure 1) may result into $p'_2 = age$ **in** $[29,44] \wedge town$ **is** ('Rome', 'The Hague', 'Cairo') $\wedge category$ **is** ('leased').

If there exists a relationship between the domain values of an attribute, the mutation operator acts in the case that a single value is associated with this attribute in an expression, i.e., the expression looks as att **is** (v_c), as follows. Let $[v_b, v_e]$ be the domain of attribute att. In order to mutate v_c, we choose randomly a value $\delta_v \in [0, (v_e - v_b)\mu]$, in which $0 \leq \mu \leq 1$. The parameter μ is used to control the maximal increase or decrease of an attribute value. The mutated value v'_c is defined as $v'_c = v_c + \delta_v$ or $v'_c = v_c - \delta_v$ as long as $v'_c \in [v_b, v_e]$. To handle overflow, i.e., if $v'_c \notin [v_b, v_e]$, we assume that the successor of v_e is v_b, and, consequently the predecessor of v_b is v_e. To compute a mutated value v'_c appropriately, we distinguish between whether v_c will be increased or decreased, which is randomly determined. In the case that v_c is increased

$$v'_c = \begin{cases} v_c + \delta_v & \text{if } v_c + \delta_v \in [v_b, v_e] \\ v_b + \delta_v - (v_e - v_c) & \text{otherwise} \end{cases}$$

and in the case v_c is decreased

$$v'_c = \begin{cases} v_c - \delta_v & \text{if } v_c - \delta_v \in [v_b, v_e] \\ v_e - \delta_v + (v_c - v_b) & \text{otherwise} \end{cases}$$

Let us consider the situation in which more than one value is associated with an attribute att in an expression. If a list of non successive (enumerable) values is associated with att, we select one of the values and compute the new value according to one of the above-mentioned formulas. If a range of successive values, i.e., an interval, is associated with att, we select either the lower or upper bound value and mutate it. A potential disadvantage of this strategy for intervals is that an interval may be significantly enlarged, if the mutated value crosses a domain boundary. Suppose that the domain of age is $[18,60]$, and we mutate the upper bound value of the expression age **in** $[55,59]$, i.e., the value 59. Assuming that the value 59 is increased by 6, then 59 is mutated in the value 23. The new expression becomes age **in** $[23,55]$.

We note that the partitioning of attribute values, i.e., the selection of proper intervals in an expression, is simply adjusted by the mutation operator. As noted before, partitioning of attribute values is in general a tough problem [18].

Cross-over. The idea behind a crossover operation is as follows; it takes as input 2 expressions, selects a random point, and exchanges the subexpressions behind this point. To illustrate this idea, we consider a relation $R(att_1, att_2, ..., att_n)$ and two expressions, e^i and e^j, in which *all* attributes are involved. Let e^i be

defined as follows: $(e^i_1 \wedge e^i_2 \wedge e^i_3 \wedge ... \wedge e^i_{k-1} \wedge e^i_k \wedge e^i_{k+1} \wedge ... \wedge e^i_n)$, in which e^i_l represents an elementary expression in which attribute att_l is involved. And, let e^j be defined as $(e^j_1 \wedge e^j_2 \wedge e^j_3 \wedge ... \wedge e^j_{k-1} \wedge e^j_k \wedge e^j_{k+1} \wedge ... \wedge e^j_n)$. Then, a cross-over between e^i and e^j at point k may result into the following two expressions, namely $e^{i'} = (e^i_1 \wedge e^i_2 \wedge e^i_3 \wedge ... \wedge e^i_{k-1} \wedge e^i_k \wedge e^j_{k+1} \wedge ... \wedge e^j_n)$ and $e^{j'} = (e^j_1 \wedge e^j_2 \wedge e^j_3 \wedge ... \wedge e^j_{k-1} \wedge e^j_k \wedge e^i_{k+1} \wedge ... \wedge e^i_n)$.

In general, not all attributes will be involved in an expression. This may have some undesired effects for a cross-over [6]. Solutions to these effects are also discussed in [6].

4 Optimization rules

We discuss two propositions that may be used to prevent the exploration of unprofitable individuals. These propositions are derived from the shape of the fitness function. The complexity of a genetic-based algorithm is determined by the evaluation of the fitness function [16]. Before presenting these propositions, we introduce the notion of a similar of an individual.

Definition 2: Let $length(p)$ be the number of elementary expressions involved in p. An individual p_{sim} is a *similar* of p if each elementary expression of p_{sim} is contained in p or p_{sim} contains each elementary expression of p and $length(p_{sim}) \neq length(p)$.

As stated in the foregoing, we search for individuals with high values for the fitness function F. For the definition of F, we refer to Section 3.2. Note that the computation of $F(p)$ requires the number of tuples that satisfy individual p. So, these tuples should be searched for and retrieved from the database, which is a costly operation [7]. Although several techniques may be used to minimize the number of retrievals from a database [5], still large amounts of tuples have to be retrieved from the database in mining applications.

In the following, two propositions will be presented that may be used to avoid the computation of fitness values of unprofitable individuals. These propositions decide if the fitness value of a similar of an individual p is worse than the fitness of p. If this is the case, this similar can be excluded from the search process.

Proposition 1: Let p_{sim} be a similar of p. If $\|\sigma_p(D) \cap \sigma_t(D)\| \leq \beta \|\sigma_t(D)\|$ and $length(p_{sim}) > length(p)$ then $F(p_{sim}) \leq F(p)$.

Proof. From $length(p_{sim}) > length(p)$ follows that $\sigma_{p_{sim}}(D) \subseteq \sigma_p(D)$. As a consequence, $\|\sigma_{p_{sim}}(D) \cap \sigma_t(D)\| \leq \|\sigma_p(D) \cap \sigma_t(D)\|$. Since $\|\sigma_p(D) \cap \sigma_t(D)\| \leq \beta \|\sigma_t(D)\|$, it follows $F(p_{sim}) \leq F(p)$. $\square$

Proposition 2: Let p_{sim} be a similar of p. If $\|\sigma_p(D) \cap \sigma_t(D)\| \geq \beta \|\sigma_t(D)\|$ and $length(p_{sim}) < length(p)$ then $F(p_{sim}) \leq F(p)$.

Proof. Similar to the proof of Proposition 1. $\square$

Note that the propositions do not require additional retrievals from a database to decide if $F(p_{sim}) \leq F(p)$. The propositions may contribute in optimizing the search process in different ways. Due to space limitation, we discuss an application at population level.

Recall that a cross-over is applied on a mating pair and results into two offsprings. Suppose that a mutation is performed after a cross-over, and the parent and the offspring with the highest fitness values are eligible to be mutated (see Section 5). Consider an offspring p_o resulted from a cross-over, and let p_o be a similar of p, one of its parents. If we can decide that $F(p_o) \leq F(p)$, then it is efficient to mutate p_o. The reason is that computation on an unmutated p_o will be a wasting of effort.

5 Algorithm

Before describing the overall genetic-based mining algorithm, we discuss a mechanism to select an individual for a next generation.

The mechanism to select individuals for a new generation is based on the technique of elitist recombination [19]. According to this technique, the individuals in a population are randomly shuffled. Then, the crossover operation is applied on each mating pair, resulting into two offsprings. The parent and the offspring with the highest fitness value are selected for the next generation. In this way, there is a direct competition between the offsprings and their own parents.

The elitist recombination technique has been chosen for two reasons. First, there is no need to specify a particular cross-over probability, since each individual is involved in exactly one cross-over. Second, there is no need for intermediate populations in order to generate a new population as is the case in a traditional genetic algorithm. These properties simplify the implementation of a genetic algorithm. Let us outline the overall algorithm.

The algorithm starts with the initialization of a population consisting of an even number of individuals, called $P(t)$. The individuals in this population are shuffled. Then, the cross-over operation is applied on two successive individuals. After completion of a crossover, the fitness values of the parents are compared[1]; the parent with the highest value is selected and it may be mutated with a probability c. This parent, p'_{sel}, is added to the next generation, and in case it is mutated its fitness value is computed. Then, for each offspring, p_o, we test if this offspring is a similar of p'_{sel} and if its fitness value is worse or equal than p'_{sel}. If this is the case, p_o is an unpromising individual, and, therefore, we always mutate p_o. Otherwise, we mutate p_o with probability c. Note, to compare the fitness value between p'_{sel} and p_o, the propositions of

---

[1] These values are already computed and stored by the algorithm.

```
program Genetic Algorithm;
initialize(P(t));
FOR p ∈ P(t) DO F(p) OD;
F'(P(t + 1)) := ε + 1; F'(P(t)) := 0;
WHILE F'(P(t + 1)) − F'(P(t)) ≥ ε DO
    F'(P(t)) := F'(P(t + 1)) := 0;
    j := 1;
    shuffle(P(t));
    WHILE j < population_size DO
        cross-over(p_j, p_{j+1}, o_1, o_2);
        IF F(p_j) > F(p_{j+1}) THEN p_sel := p_j
                              ELSE p_sel := p_{j+1}
        FI;
        mutate(p_sel, c, p'_sel);
        IF p'_sel ≠ p_sel THEN F(p'_sel) FI;
        p'_sel → P(t + 1);
        FOR k = 1, 2 DO
            IF (similar(p'_sel, o_k) AND F(o_k) ≤ F(p'_sel))
               THEN mutate(o_k, 1.0, o'_k);
               ELSE  mutate(o_k, c, o'_k);
            FI;
        OD;
        F(o'_1); F(o'_2);
        IF F(o'_1) > F(o'_2) THEN o'_1 → P(t + 1)
                            ELSE o'_2 → P(t + 1);
        FI;
        j := j + 2;
    OD;
    For p ∈ P(t) DO F'(P(t)) := F'(P(t)) + F(p) OD;
    For p ∈ P(t + 1) DO
        F'(P(t + 1)) := F'(P(t + 1)) + F(p)
    OD;
    P(t + 1) := P(t);
OD;
END.
```

Figure 3: Sketch of the genetic-based algorithm

the previous section are used. So, no additional fitness values are computed for this comparison. After possible mutation of the offsprings, their fitness values are computed, and the fittest offspring is added to the new generation. This process is repeated for all individuals in a generation.

Once the new population has been built up, the total fitness of the existing as well as of the new population is computed, and compared. The algorithm terminates if the total fitness of the new population does not significantly improve compared with the total fitness of the existing population, i.e., that the improvement of the total fitness of the new population is less than a threshold value ϵ.

In Figure 3, the algorithm is sketched. We note that the procedure cross-over(p_1, p_2, o_1, o_2) takes two individuals p_1 and p_2 as input, applies a cross-over, and produces two offsprings o_1 and o_2. Procedure mutate(p, c, p') mutates an individual p with probability c into p' and similar(p_1, p_2) is a boolean function that decides whether two individuals are similar or not. The symbol $P(t)$ represents a population at time t, while p_j is the j-th individual in $P(t)$. The total fitness of a population is defined as $F'(P(t)) = \sum_{p \in P(t)} F(p)$.

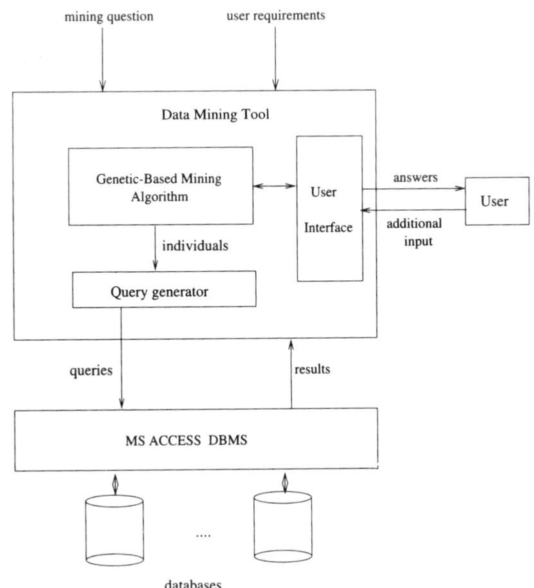

Figure 4: Architecture of SHARVIND

6 SHARVIND: a genetic-based data mining tool

In two successive subsections, we discuss the architecture of and some implementation issues with regard to SHARVIND.

6.1 Architecture

We distinguish three modules in SHARVIND, a user interface, a genetic-based mining algorithm, and a query generator. The overall architecture of SHARVIND is depicted in Figure 4. The input consists of a mining question and additional requirements that may be posed by the user. For example, a user may demand that an attribute in a database should not be involved in the mining process for reasons of privacy (e.g., income of pilots). The user is allowed to request intermediate mining results, and if desired, the user is able to modify the input. We note that this is a useful feature of a mining tool, since, in practice, a user starts a mining session with a rough idea of the information that might be interesting, and during the mining session the user more precisely specifies, based on, amongst others, the mining results obtained so far, which information should be searched for.

Once SHARVIND receives the input, it invokes the genetic-based mining algorithm. To compute the fitness value of an individual, the algorithm needs the number of tuples that satisfies the description of the individual. Therefore, the database should be interrogated. An individual should be translated into queries that are understood by the underlying dbms. This is the task of the query generator.

Since in our case an individual is an expression, the translation of an individual into an equivalent set of SQL queries is straightforward. Note that the individual already forms the WHERE clause of a SQL query. Therefore, the query generator is relatively simple. Suppose that we require the number of tuples in the database *Driver* that satisfies the description of an individual $p = gender$ **is** ('male') $\wedge$ *age* **in** [18,24] then the corresponding SQL query is: SELECT COUNT(*) FROM *Driver* WHERE (*gender* **is** 'male') AND (*age* BETWEEN 18 AND 24).

SHARVIND has as main advantages that it is extensible and re-targetable. For the time-being, SHARVIND is equipped with a genetic-based algorithm but other mining algorithms that are based on e.g., a hill climber, simulated annealing, etc., can be easily plugged in. SHARVIND is re-targetable since the tool can be coupled to other dbmss without much effort. In the case that a dbms does not understand SQL, a new module in the query generator should be built in that translates individuals in the language that is understood by the underlying dbms, while the remainder of the system can be left untouched.

6.2 Implementation

SHARVIND is running in a MS Access 97 environment that uses the Microsoft Jet Engine. The genetic-based algorithm is implemented in Visual Basic and consists of approximately 2000 lines of code. Our choice for this environment is mainly determined by its suitability for rapid application and the fact that the databases we want to mine are stored in MS Access.

As discussed in Section 3, major components in developing a genetic-based algorithm are the representation of individuals, manipulation operators, fitness function, and the translation of an individual into a query that is understood by the MS Access dbms.

Individuals, which are regarded as a conjunction of predicates over attributes, are implemented as binary tables. An ordered attribute, *att* is implemented as two tuples: $<att$, lower bound value$>$ and $<att$, upper bound value$>$. An unordered attribute having n values is implemented as n tuples, having the form $<att$, value$>$ in the table. For each individual, a binary table is built up in this way. So, the individual *gender* **is** ('male') $\wedge$ *age* **in** [18,24] is implemented as follows:

Attribute name	Attribute value
gender	male
age	18
age	24

Once the data structure of an individual was defined, the implementation of the manipulation operators was straightforward. A cross-over is obtained by selecting two tables, splitting each table into two subtables, let's say a head and a tail table. Then, the tail tables are exchanged. A mutation is obtained by deleting and/or inserting one or more tuples. Suppose that in the above-mentioned individual *gender* **is** ('male') should be mutated in *gender* **is** ('female'). This is obtained by removing the tuple *gender* **is** ('male') from the table and inserting the new tuple *gender* **is** ('female').

Due to mutations it may occur that the range interval of an attribute grows to the domain of that attribute. In such a case, the whole database will be covered by that attribute, which is undesired for the search process. To prevent this situation, we have decided that an interval corresponding to an attribute may not grow harder than a user defined threshold value, e.g., (upper bound domain value - lower bound domain value)$\times x$, in which $x \in (0, 1]$.

The implementations of the fitness function as well as the query generator were straightforward. For each generation, we keep track of the average fitness, and the individuals with the highest and lowest fitness.

7 Mining an artificial and two real-life databases

We give an overview of the databases that we have mined with SHARVIND and of the results that have been obtained. Section 7.1 is devoted to an artificial database, in which pre-defined knowledge was hidden. Section 7.2 is devoted to the mining of two real-life incident databases.

7.1 Artificial database

This database consists of the relation *Driver*. For this database 100.000 tuples have been generated of which 50% have a value ('yes') for attribute *damage*, i.e., 50% of the tuples relate to an accident. Furthermore, the following fact was hidden in this database: young men in leased cars have more than average chances of causing an accident. The goal of mining this database was to determine whether the tool is capable of finding the hidden fact. Therefore, we have set the target class as *damage* = ('yes'), and we searched for the profile of risky drivers. The expression for the hidden profile is: *age* **in** [19,24] $\wedge$ *category* **is** ('leased') $\wedge$ *gender* **is** ('male').

We have mined the database with varying initial populations, consisting of 36 individuals. The following classes of initial populations were distinguished. 1) random: this population contained a few individuals that could set the algorithm quickly on a promising route, 2) modified random: individuals that could apparently set the algorithm on a promising route were replaced by other (not promising) individuals, 3) bad converged: this population contained individuals with low fitness values.

We have observed that the algorithm usually finds near optimal solutions, i.e. profiles that look like the hidden one, in less than 1000 fitness evaluations.

The differences between the hidden profile and profiles found by the algorithm (for different initial populations) were mainly caused by variations in the range of attribute *age*.

The type of the initial population plays a role in the number of fitness evaluations required to find a near optimal solution. Running the algorithm on the database with random initial populations, the algorithm was able to find a near optimal expression quite rapidly, i.e., in about 100 fitness evaluations. Starting from modified random initial populations, 300 to 400 fitness evaluations were required for a near optimal solution. Starting from bad converged initial population, 900 to 1000 fitness evaluations were required.

With regard to the settings of the parameters α and β, we note that appropriate values could easily be selected, since the content of the database is precisely known.

7.2 Two real-life databases

The first database, called ECCAIRS is located at the Joint Research Centre in Italy. Currently, this database contains serious incident and accident data that is converted from the Scandinavian accident- and incident reporting system. This database grows with approximately 4% each year. Detailed information can be found on http://eccairs-www.jrc.it, and in [11].

The second database, called the FAA database, contains aircraft incident data that have been recorded from 1978 to 1995. For example, the database contains reports of collisions between aircraft and birds while on approach to or departure from an airport. This database can be obtained from the Internet at http://www.asy.faa.gov/asp/asy_fids.asp.

Both databases are stored in MS Access and contain NULL values and redundant data. Furthermore, integrity rules (e.g., for domain values) are hardly implemented.

In two successive sections, we discuss these databases in more detail. In Section 7.2.3, we report on the mining results.

7.2.1 ECCAIRS

The ECCAIRS database consists of 36 relations and about 300 attributes. Two major relations of the database are the ACS and the $OCCS$ relations. The ACS relation contains information with regard to aircraft, such as manufacturer, motor, speed of the aircraft, etc., and information about the environment in which the aircraft is involved, such as weather conditions. The $OCCS$ relation describes in general terms an occurrence (incident or accident) and contains general information with regard to an occurrence, for example, time and location of an occurrence, etc. The relation $ACCS$ contains 5202 tuples and 186 attributes and $OCCS$ contains 5202 tuples and 27 attributes. Although the number of tuples is not large, mining might be interesting due to the large number of attributes.

However, currently 17 relations do not contain any tuples, while other relations consist of tuples having many NULL values. To gain insight in the number of NULL values in each relation, we define a *filling* factor as follows:

$$filling(R) = \frac{\#values(R)}{max(values(R))} \times 100\%, \text{ in which}$$

$max(values(R)) = \#tuples(R) \times \#attributes(R)$. Note that $\#values(R)$ is the number of values in relation R, $\#tuples(R)$ is the number of tuples in R, etc.

It appears that $filling(ACCS) = 19\%$ which is a bad score especially for mining and $filling(OCCS) = 72\%$. In order to make the database suitable for mining we have removed:

- All attributes with less than 2000 entries filled in.

- All attributes whose values consist of natural language. Although these attributes may expose interesting knowledge, they are removed, since our algorithm is not yet able to handle them.

- Attributes that are fully functional dependent on another attribute. For example, from the latitude/longitude attribute the city name can be derived. So, city name is a redundant attribute

- Attributes with a selectivity factor[2] close to one and attributes with a very low selectivity factor, i.e., close to $\frac{1}{\#tuples(R)}$.

After performing the removals 64 attributes were left and the filling factors for $ACCS$ and $OCCS$ become 81% and 84% respectively. Then, we join these relations into a single relation.

Since the amount of tuples is relatively small, we have mined the whole joined relation.

7.2.2 FAA

At our laboratory, this database is implemented as a single table that is sorted on an attribute, called report number, which served as primary key. In the following, we mean by the FAA database, the database as it is implemented and filled at our laboratory.

The FAA database consists of more than 70 attributes and about 60.000 tuples. As in the case of ECCAIRS, this database contains also NULL values, redundant data, and attributes with very high and low selectivity factors. Therefore, we have cleaned this database in the same way as ECCAIRS, in order to make it suitable for mining. After cleaning 30 attributes were left and 60.000 tuples.

---

[2]The selectivity factor of an attribute att is defined as $\frac{1}{card(att)}$, in which $card(att)$ is the number of distinct values that att assumes.

7.2.3 Mining results

We have mined above-mentioned databases with different values for a number of parameters such as number of individuals of a population, average length of an individual, mutation probability, and the maximal interval to which an attribute is allowed to grow. For the influence of different parameter settings, we refer to [11] and [16]. It appears to be reasonable to set the number of individuals around 50, the average length between 2 and 5 attributes, mutation probability between 0.1 and 0.4, and the maximum interval to which an attribute may grow around 10%.

For the ECCAIRS database, the mining question was: 'What are profiles of risky flights?'. Since the amount of tuples in the ECCAIRS database is relatively small, we have mined the joined relations. So in this case, we have not defined any specific target classes. We have proposed the mining question to SHARVIND with different β values. Recall that β defines the fraction of tuples that an individual should represent within a target class (in this case the whole database) in order to obtain the maximal fitness. The results that we obtain were correct but most of them were trivial. For example, when we set β to 0.2, it appears that male pilots and scattered (1/8 to 4/8) sky conditions are involved in 19% of the incidents. Although most of the results were trivial, it helped to gain insight in the database. For example, we have observed that about 50% of the database consist of incidents where no serious injury occurs and the pilot satisfies the required license. Setting β to 0.3 delivers the following (more complex) association:

$aircraft\_type$ is ('fixed wing') $\land$ $power\text{-}type$ is ('reciprocating') $\land$ $license\_class$ is ('required rating') $\land$ $highest\_degree\_of\_injury$ is ('none') $\rightarrow$ pilot_induced.

This rule says that pilots who hold the required licenses and are flying with fixed wing aircraft and a reciprocating power-type cause about 30% of the accidents. However, these incidents do not cause any injury.

We have mined the FAA database by posing several mining questions to SHARVIND. Our initial mining question was: search for the class of flights with (more than average) chances of causing an incident, i.e., profiles of risky flights. We have searched for this class with different input values. These searches resulted in (valid) profiles that could easily be explained by our flight safety experts. An example of such a profile is that aircraft with 1 or 2 engines are more often involved in incidents. The explanation for this profile is that these types of aircraft perform more flights.

We successively have refined our mining question into a number of questions, such as: 1) given the fact that an incident was due to operational defects not inflicted by the pilot, what is the profile of this type of incident?, 2) given the fact that an incident was due to mistakes of the pilot, what is the profile of this type of incident?, and 3) given the fact that an incident was due to improper maintenance, what is the profile of this type of incident?

The cardinality of the target classes associated with the questions posed to SHARVIND varied from 2500 to 30000 tuples and β varied from 0.10 to 0.20.

The answers to the proposed questions were correct and most of them contained no surprise to our domain expert. In one case the tool came up with an interesting and unexpected result. In this case, we had chosen as target class = 'pilot_induced'. We had chosen to mine this target class in order to find out what type of pilots was causing incidents. The target class contains 26000 tuples. Mining the target class with $\beta = 0.15$ resulted in the following association:

aircraft_damage **is** ('minor') $\wedge$ *primary_flight_type* **is** ('personal') $\wedge$ *type_of_operation* **is** ('general operating rules') $\wedge$ *flight_plan* **is** ('none') $\wedge$ *pilot_rating* **is** ('no rating') $\rightarrow$ pilot_induced.

This association means that pilots without flight certificates and flight plans who are flying in private aircraft are causing more incidents than other groups. This result was on the first glance a bit strange for our safety expert, since pilots without flight certificates are not allowed to fly. After a while it appeared that the association was correct and our safety expert was able to explain the association. The pilots without certificates appeared to be students whose incidents were recorded in the FAA database as well.

8 Conclusions & further research

We have discussed a genetic-based algorithm that may be used for data mining. Contrary to the conventional bit string representation in genetic algorithms, we have chosen a representation that fits better in the field of databases. Furthermore, we have chosen a fitness function that is close to our intuition to rank individuals. The fitness function gives rise to an optimization of the search process.

A genetic-based algorithm for data mining has two major advantages. First, the problem of partitioning attribute values in proper ranges, which is in general a tough problem [18], could be solved by choosing a suitable mutation operator. Second, a genetic-based algorithm is able to escape a local optimum and does not pose any restrictions on the structure of a search space.

We have implemented vital parts of a prototype data mining tool that is based on a genetic algorithm. We have coupled the tool to an MS Access environment in order to mine two aircraft incident databases. Our overall conclusion is threefold. First, both databases could be significantly reduced, especially in the number of attributes, due to NULL values, text attributes, etc. Second, although both databases are significantly reduced after cleaning, we feel that data mining is a promising direction for analysing aircraft incident databases. The mining results helped safety experts to gain insight in these databases. We expect that data mining may expose knowledge from these databases in future, if more and better data will be loaded. We note that data is recently started to be loaded in the EC-CAIRS database. Third, our experience is that a genetic algorithm may rapidly be implemented for data mining, yielding reasonable results. However, to build an operational tool, there is still a significant effort required.

Since many real-life databases contain many unstructured data, i.e., natural language, a topic for further research is to extend our tool with this type of data. Furthermore, to get insight in the results and performance provided by a genetic-based data mining tool, a large scale evaluation is required, which is a topic for further research as well.

Acknowledgments The author is grateful to W. Pelt from the Royal Netherlands Navy, who made this research possible. E. Groenheiden, L. de Penning, and M. Suurd are thanked for their implementation efforts.

References

[1] Agrawal, R., Ghosh, S., Imielinski, T., Iyer, B., Swami, A., An Interval Classiefier for Database Mining Applications, in Proc. of the 18th VLDB Conf., 1992, 560-573.

[2] Agrawal, R., Imielinski, T., Swami, A., Database Mining: A Performance Perspective, IEEE TKDE 5(6), 1993, 914-925.

[3] Augier, S., Venturini, G., Kodratoff, Y., Learning First Order Logic Rules with a Genetic Algorithm, Int. Conf. on KDD, 1995, 21-26.

[4] Bhattacharyya, S., Direct Marketing Performance Modeling Using Genetic Algorithms, INFORMS journal on Computing, 11(3), 248-257, 1999.

[5] Choenni, R., Siebes, A., Query Optimization to Support Data Mining, in Proc. DEXA '97 8th Int. Workshop on Database and Expert Systems Applications, 1997, 658-663.

[6] Choenni, R., On the Suitability of Genetic-Based Algorithms for Data MIning. ER Workshops 1998, LNCS 1552, 55-67.

[7] Elmasri, R., Navathe, S., Fundamentals of Database Systems, The Benjamin/Cummings Publishing Comp., 1989.

[8] Flockhart, I., Radcliffe, N., A Genetic Algorithm-Based Approach to Data Mining, Int. Conf. on KDD, 1996, 299-302.

[9] Freitas, A., A Genetic Programming Framework for two Data Mining Tasks: Classification and Generalized Rule Induction, Conf on Genetic Programming, 1997, 96-101.

[10] Giordana, A., Neri, F., Saitta, L., Botta, M., Integrating Multiple Learning Strategies in First Order Logics, ML 27(3), 1997, 209-240.

[11] Groenheiden, E., A Genetic Data Mining Feasibility Study, internal report, University of Twente, The Netherlands.

[12] Güvner, H., Akman, V., Problem Representation for Refinement, Minds and Machines 2(3), 1992, 267-282.

[13] Han, J., Cai, Y., Cerone, N., Knowledge Discovery in Databases: An Attribute-Oriented Approach, Proc. of the 18th VLDB Conf., 1992, 547-559.

[14] Holsheimer, M., Kersten, M., Architectural Support for Data Mining, AAAI-94 Worksh. on Knowl. Discovery, 217-228.

[15] Michalewicz, Z., Genetic Algorithms + Data Structures = Evolution Programs. Springer-Verlag, New York, USA.

[16] Penning, H. de, Suurd, P., NLR Genetic Search Base, internal report, University of Twente, 1998.

[17] Shafer, J., Agrawal, R., Mehta, M., SPRINT: A Scalable Parallel Clasifier for Data Mining, in Proc. 22nd Int. Conf. on VLDB, 1996, 544-555.

[18] Srikant, R., Agrawal, R., Mining Quantitative Association Rules in Large Relational Tables, in Proc. ACM SIGMOD '96 Int. Conf. on Management of Data, 1996, 1-12.

[19] Thierens, D., Goldberg, D., Elitist Recombination: an integrated selection recombination GA, in 1st IEEE Conf. on Evolutionary Computing, 1994, 508-512.

Mining Frequent Itemsets Using Support Constraints

Ke Wang
National University of Singapore &
Simon Fraser University
wangk@cs.sfu.ca

Yu He
National University of Singapore

hey@comp.nus.edu.sg

Jiawei Han
Simon Fraser University

han@cs.sfu.ca

Abstract

Interesting patterns often occur at varied levels of support. The classic association mining based on a uniform minimum support, such as Apriori, either misses interesting patterns of low support or suffers from the bottleneck of itemset generation. A better solution is to exploit *support constraints*, which specify what minimum support is required for what itemsets, so that only necessary itemsets are generated. In this paper, we present a framework of frequent itemset mining in the presence of support constraints. Our approach is to "push" support constraints into the Apriori itemset generation so that the "best" minimum support is used for each itemset at run time to preserve the essence of Apriori.

1 Introduction

The *association rules mining*, first studied in [AIS93, AS94] for market-basket analysis, is to find all association rules above some user-specified minimum support and minimum confidence. The bottleneck of this problem is finding *frequent itemsets* (and support), i.e., itemsets that have a support above the minimum support. The importance of frequent itemsets goes far beyond market-basket analysis because they serve as an estimation of joint probabilities of events, thereby, useful whenever such estimation is required. For example, several recent studies have leveraged frequent itemsets to build intrusion detection models [LSM98], to con-

struct classifiers [LHM98, MW99], to build Yahoo!-like information hierarchies [WZL99], and to discover emerging patterns [DL99]. We believe that more and more internet/web related data mining will require the ability of finding frequent itemsets.

1.1 Apriori lives on a uniform minimum support

The best known search strategy of frequent itemests, called Apriori [AIS93, AS94], exploits the following property: if an itemset is frequent, so are all its subsets. Thus, Apriori ensures a level-wise generation of itemsets where each candidate k-itemset $\{i_1, \ldots, i_{k-2}, i_{k-1}, i_k\}$ is generated from two frequent $(k-1)$-itemsets $\{i_1, \ldots, i_{k-2}, i_{k-1}\}$ and $\{i_1, \ldots, i_{k-2}, i_k\}$. To make Apriori work, however, it is essential that all itemsets have a uniform minimum support. Consider what happens if the minimum support of $\{coffee, sugar, tea\}$ is 2% and the minimum support of $\{coffee, tea\}$, $\{sugar, tea\}$, $\{coffee, sugar\}$ is 5%: it is possible that $\{coffee, sugar, tea\}$ is frequent with respect to its minimum support, but none of $\{coffee, tea\}$, $\{sugar, tea\}$, $\{coffee, sugar\}$ is frequent with respect to their minimum support!

1.2 The reality is not uniform

In reality, the minimum support is not uniform. First, deviations and exceptions often have much lower support than general trends. For example, rules for accidents are much less supported than rules for non-accidents, but the former are often more interesting than the latter. Second, the support requirement varies with the support of items contained in an itemset. Rules containing *bread* and *milk* usually have higher support than rules containing *food processor* and *pan*. A similar scenario is that dense attributes such as *States* have less support than sparse attributes such as *Gender*. Third, item presence has less support than item absence. Fourth, the support requirement varies at different concept levels of items [HF95, SA95]. Finally, hierarchical classification like

Proceedings of the 26th VLDB Conference, Cairo, Egypt, 2000.

[WZL99] requires feature terms to be discovered at different concept levels, thereby, requiring a non-uniform minimum support.

Given that existing algorithms assume a uniform minimum support, the best one can do is to apply such algorithms at the lowest minimum support ever specified and filter the result using higher minimum supports. This method will generate many candidates that are later discarded. From our experience (see Section 7), the increase of candidates often causes a non-linear increase of execution time and a drastic performance deterioration once page swapping takes place between memory and disk, during the support counting where candidates were read from disk for each transaction. In the world of non-uniform minimum support, we need a technique that finds the itemsets above their minimum supports without forcing the lowest minimum support across all itemsets.

1.3   Our approach

We propose *support constraints* as a way to specify general constraints on minimum support. Informally, a support constraint specifies what itemsets are required to satisfy what minimum support. We consider support constraints of the form $SC_i(B_1, \ldots, B_s) \geq \theta_i$, where $s \geq 0$. Each B_j, called a *bin*, is a set of items that need not be distinguished with respect to the specification of minimum support. θ_i is a minimum support in the range $[0..1]$. The above support constraint specifies that any itemset containing at least one item from each B_j has the minimum support θ_i. The topic of this paper is to "push" such support constraints into the itemset generation to prune candidates as early as possible. We illustrate this approach using an example.

Example 1.1 Consider four support constraints $SC_1(B_1, B_3) \geq 0.2$, $SC_2(B_3) \geq 0.4$, $SC_3(B_2) \geq 0.6$, and $SC_0() \geq 0.8$. Each bin B_i contains a disjoint set of items. We assume that if more than one constraint is applicable to an itemset, the constraint specifying the lowest minimum support is chosen. We will explain the rationale of this choice in Section 3. With this assumption, we have the following specifications. *Case (i)*: $SC_1(B_1, B_3) \geq 0.2$ specifies minimum support 0.2 for any itemset containing (probably more, same below) one item in each of B_1 and B_3. *Case (ii)*: $SC_2(B_3) \geq 0.4$ specifies minimum support 0.4 for any itemset containing one item in B_3, but no item in B_1 (otherwise, Case (i) applies). *Case (iii)*: $SC_3(B_2) \geq 0.6$ specifies minimum support 0.6 for any itemset containing one item in B_2, but no item in B_3 (otherwise, Case (ii) applies). *Case (iv)*: $SC_0() \geq 0.8$ specifies minimum support 0.8 for any other itemset (i.e., the default minimum support). There are two key issues in making use of these specifications:

Constraint pushing. On the one hand, we would like to treat these cases separately so that the highest possible minimum support is applied in each case. On the other hand, we would like to share the work done in different cases so that each itemset is generated at most once. For example, as in Apriori, we like to generate itemset $\{b_0, b_1, b_2\}$ in Case (iii) using $\{b_0, b_1\}$ generated in Case (iv) and $\{b_0, b_2\}$ generated in Case (iii), where b_i denotes an item from B_i. This requires the minimum support 0.6 of $\{b_0, b_1, b_2\}$ to be "pushed" down to $\{b_0, b_1\}$, on the ground that $\{b_0, b_1, b_2\}$ "depends on" $\{b_0, b_1\}$, and further down to $\{b_0\}$ and $\{b_1\}$. The pushed minimum support 0.6 is lower than the minimum support for $\{b_0, b_1\}$, $\{b_0\}$, $\{b_1\}$, i.e., 0.8, but is higher than the lowest minimum support 0.2. In this sense, we have pruned the minimum support 0.2 for certain itemsets and tightened up the search space.

Order sensitivity. The above has implicitly assumed that b_3 does not follow b_2 in the item ordering used by the Apriori itemset generation. If b_3 does follow b_2 in the item ordering, $\{b_0, b_1, b_2, b_3\}$ would depend on $\{b_0, b_1, b_2\}$, and the minimum support 0.2 for $\{b_0, b_1, b_2, b_3\}$ would be pushed down to $\{b_0, b_1, b_2\}$, and transitively, down to $\{b_0, b_1\}$, $\{b_0, b_2\}$, $\{b_0\}$, $\{b_1\}$, $\{b_2\}$. In this case, a lower minimum support is pushed, compared with 0.6, and more itemsets will be generated. The idea of tightening up the search space is to order items in such a way that allows the highest possible minimum support to be pushed. $\square$

Here is the overview of our approach. We define a framework for specifying support constraints in Section 3. We then present a strategy for pushing support constraints into the Apriori itemset generation in Section 4. The constraint pushing exploits the dependency between itemsets, represented by an enumeration tree of sets of bins, and determines the highest minimum support to be pushed to each itemset. This phase makes use of the information of support constraints, but not the database. It turns out that the ordering of nodes in an enumeration tree drastically impacts the pushed minimum support. We present several ordering strategies to maximize the pushed minimum support in Section 5. At the itemset generation phase, candidates are generated as in Apriori and the pushed minimum support is used to determine whether a candidate is frequent. We call this strategy Adaptive Apriori to emphasize that the pushed minimum support is determined *individually* for each itemset and that Adaptive Apriori generalizes Apriori to non-uniform minimum support while preserving the essence of Apriori. An example in Section 6 illustrates our mining algorithm. We evaluate the effectiveness of this approach in Section 7. Finally, we conclude the paper in Section 8.

2   Related work

The support-based Apriori pruning was first studied in [AIS93, AS94], and a similar idea in [MTV94].

Nearly all later frequent itemset minings rely on Apriori as a basic pruning strategy. Another strategy is to push certain constraints into the itemset generation. However, none of these approaches considers non-uniform minimum support. The correlation approach [AY98, BMS97] considers the support requirement relative to the independence assumption, but not general support constraints or constraint pushing. Instead of abandoning the support requirement like in [C*00], our approach is to make it more realistic by allowing different support requirements for different itemsets. [HPY00] generates frequent itemsets without using the Apriori itemset generation, but still critically relies on a uniform support requirement.

To our knowledge, [LHM99] is the only work explicitly dealing with non-uniform minimum support. In [LHM99], a *minimum item support* (or MIS) is associated with each item, and the minimum support of an itemset is defined to be the lowest MIS associated with the items in the itemset. This specification is unnatural for three reasons. (i) The MIS of individual items has to reflect the minimum support of unseen itemsets at the specification time. (ii) In some applications the user may have a minimum support for an itemset, e.g., $\{white, male\}$, as a single concept, but not for individual items in the itemset (e.g., *white* or *male*). The minimum support for $\{white, male\}$ is usually lower than that for *white* or *male*. (iii) Different minimum supports cannot be specified for two itemsets, like $\{white, male\}$ and $\{white, male, grad\}$, if a common item has the lowest MIS, like *white*. We allow the support requirement to be specified directly on itemsets, thereby, overcoming these difficulties.

3 Specifying support constraints

As in [AIS93, AS94], the database is a collection of *transactions*. Each transaction is a set of *items* taken from a fixed universe. A *k-itemset* is a set of k items. The *support* of an itemset I, denoted $sup(I)$, is the fraction of the transactions containing all the items in I.

3.1 The support specification

The task of support specification is to specify the minimum support for each itemset. Clearly, it is not practical to enumerate all itemsets. Our approach is to partition the set of items into *bins*, denoted as B_j, such that items that need not be distinguished in the specification are in the same bin. Therefore, for a bag (i.e., multiset) $\beta = \{B_1, \ldots, B_k\}$ of bins, all k-itemsets $\{i_1, \ldots, i_k\}$, $i_j \in B_j$, have the same minimum support. β is called the *schema* of itemsets $\{i_1, \ldots, i_k\}$. To specify the minimum support for itemsets, we need only to specify the minimum support for schemas. This motivates the notion of support constraints.

Definition 3.1 (Support constraints) A *support constraint (SC)* has the form $SC_i(l_1, \ldots, l_s) \geq \theta_i$ (or simply $SC_i \geq \theta_i$), $s \geq 0$. Each l_j is either a bin or a variable for bins. θ_i, called a *minimum support*, is a function over $l_1, \ldots, l_s$ and returns a real in $[0..1]$. The order of l_j's does not matter and l_j may repeat. A SC is *ground* if it contains no variable, otherwise, *non-ground*. A non-ground SC can be *instantiated* to a ground SC by replacing each variable with a bin. A *support specification* is a non-empty set of SCs. □

There are two considerations in interpreting a SC. First, we can interpret a SC either as specifying *some* items in an itemset, called the *open interpretation*, or as specifying *all* items in an itemset, called the *closed interpretation*. Second, a choice must be made if an itemset "matches" the item specification of more than one SC. Consider itemset $I = \{b_1, b_2, b_3, b_4\}$ of support 0.15, and $SC_1(B_1, B_2) \geq 0.1$ and $SC_2(B_3, B_4) \geq 0.2$, where b_i is an item in B_i. In the open interpretation, I matches the item specification of both SCs. Therefore, whether I is frequent depends on which SC is used as the minimum support for I. Our decision is that the lower minimum support 0.1 prevails. The rationale is simple: the minimum support should not be increased by adding more items.

Definition 3.2 (Frequent itemsets) An itemset I *matches* a ground $SC_i \geq \theta_i$ in the open interpretation if I contains at least one item from each bin in SC_i and these items are distinct. An itemset I *matches* a ground $SC_i \geq \theta_i$ in the closed interpretation if I contains exactly one item from each bin in SC_i and these items are distinct. An itemset I *matches* a non-ground SC if I matches some instantiation of the SC. The *minimum support* of itemset I, denoted $minsup(I)$, is the lowest θ_i of all $SC_i \geq \theta_i$ matched by I. If I matches no SC, $minsup(I)$ is undefined. An itemset I is *frequent* if $minsup(I)$ is defined and $sup(I) \geq minsup(I)$. □

The notion of "match" and *minsup* can be extended to schemas in a natural way. A schema β *matches* a ground $SC_i \geq \theta_i$ in the open interpretation if SC_i is a sub-bag of β [1]. A schema β *matches* a ground $SC_i \geq \theta_i$ in the close interpretation if $SC_i = \beta$. A schema β *matches* a non-ground $SC_i \geq \theta_i$ if β matches some instantiation of the SC.

Let $minsup(\beta)$ denote the minimum support for (the itemsets of) schema β. In the open interpretation, for ground $SC_1(\beta_1) \geq \theta_1$ and $SC_2(\beta_2) \geq \theta_2$, if $\beta_1 \supseteq \beta_2$ and $\theta_1 > \theta_2$, $SC_1(\beta_1) \geq \theta_1$ is never used. In fact, if any itemset I matches $SC_1(\beta_1) \geq \theta_1$, I also matches $SC_2(\beta_2) \geq \theta_2$, and we always use the lower θ_2 as the minimum support for I. In this sense, $SC_1(\beta_1) \geq \theta_1$ is *redundant*. We assume that all redundant SCs are removed. With this assumption, a SC of

---

[1] A bag x is a sub-bag of a bag y if x is a subset of y with duplicates considered.

the form $SC_i() \geq \theta_i$, if specified, must have the highest minimum support, therefore, is used only when no other SC is matched. For this reason, $SC_i() \geq \theta_i$ is called the *default SC*.

Example 3.1 (The running example) Consider the transactions and support specification in Figure 1 in the open interpretation. Each item is represented by an integer from 0 to 8. For any itemset I containing an item from B_1 and an item from B_3, I matches both $SC_1(B_1, B_3) \geq 0.2$ and $SC_2(B_3) \geq 0.4$. But $minsup(I) = 0.2$ because the lowest minimum support of matched SCs is used. Some examples of such I are $\{0, 2\}$, $\{0, 2, 3\}$, and $\{2, 3, 4\}$. $\{0, 2\}$ is frequent, but $\{0, 2, 3\}$ and $\{2, 3, 4\}$ are not. The minimum support of $\{2, 4, 7\}$, $\{2, 4, 8\}$, $\{4, 7, 8\}$, and $\{2, 4, 7, 8\}$ is 0.6 because these itemsets match only $SC_3(B_2) \geq 0.6$. These itemsets are frequent. $\{2, 7\}$ and $\{2, 8\}$ match only $SC_0() \geq 0.8$, and $\{2, 7\}$ is frequent, but $\{2, 8\}$ is not. $\square$

Example 3.2 An example of non-ground SCs in the closed interpretation is $SC_i(V_1, \ldots, V_k) \geq sup(V_1) \times \ldots \times sup(V_k)$, $1 \leq k \leq 4$, where V_i are variables and each bin B_i contains the items of the same support, denoted $sup(B_i)$. Each instantiation $SC_i(B_1, \ldots, B_k) \geq sup(B_1) \times \ldots \times sup(B_k)$ specifies the minimum support relative to the independence assumption about item occurrence. Due to the closed interpretation, any itemset containing more than 4 items has an undefined minimum support. $\square$

In $SC_i \geq \theta_i$, θ_i should be "evaluable" at the *specification time*. For example, $SC(\alpha, \beta) \geq minconf \times sup(\alpha)$ does not satisfy this requirement, where α and β are schemas and each bin contains a single item, because $sup(\alpha)$ is unknown at the specification time. Even at the itemset generation, $sup(\alpha)$ is known only for frequent itemsets α.

The notion of support constraints generalizes several existing classes of constraints. The classic uniform minimum support [AIS93, AS94] can be specified by one default $SC_i() \geq \theta_i$ with θ_i being the usual minimum support. The item constraints [SVA97] can be specified by non-default SCs in which all minimum supports are equal. To model the MIS specification in [LHM99], we can group the items of the same support into a bin and specify the non-ground $SC_i(V_1, \ldots, V_k) \geq min\{sup(V_1), \ldots, sup(V_k)\}$ in the closed interpretation, where V_j are variables for bins. However, it is not hard to see that the MIS specification cannot model the specification in Example 3.2 nor the specification: $SC_1(B_1, B_2, B_3) \geq 0.2$, $SC_2(B_1, B_3) \geq 0.3$, and $SC_2(B_2, B_3) \geq 0.4$.

3.2 Typical scenarios of specification

Until now, we have not said much about how the end user determines bins B_j and minimum support θ_i in a SC. Though this decision largely depends on applications, we consider several typical scenarios and hope that they are indicative to the end user.

Support-based specification. Example 3.2 illustrates three points. (a) A bin B_j contains similarly supported items and θ_i is a function of some representative supports of of bins (such as *max*, *min*, or *avg*). Such bins can be found by computing the support of items in one pass of the transactions and then clustering items based on their support. The number of bins can be optionally specified by the user. (b) θ_i can be either chosen from a menu of built-in functions or supplied by the user. (c) Without a particular schema in mind for specification, a generic specification given by a non-ground SC can be used.

Concept-based specification. In the presence of a item concept hierarchy, it is desirable to specify SCs based on the generality of the concept of items. For example, $SC_1(c_1, c_2) \geq 2 \times \frac{sup(c_1)}{m} \times \frac{sup(c_2)}{n}$ states that any itemset containing at least one child of c_1 and one child of c_2 has the minimum support $2 \times \frac{sup(c_1)}{m} \times \frac{sup(c_2)}{n}$, where c_1 and c_2 are variables representing concepts, and m and n are the number of child concepts of c_1 and c_2.

Attribute-based specification. For a database in the form of a relational table, it makes sense for each bin to correspond to the set of attribute/value pairs from the same attribute. For example, if *States* and *Gender* are attributes in the table, $SC_1(States, Gender) \geq \frac{N}{50} \times \frac{N}{2}$ specifies that any itemset containing a state code and a gender has the minimum support $\frac{N}{50} \times \frac{N}{2}$, where N is the number of tuples in the relational table, $\frac{N}{50}$ and $\frac{N}{2}$ are the average support of state codes and the average support of gender.

Enumeration-based specification. The most flexible specification is explicitly enumerating the items in a bin, on the basis that they are not distinguishable with respect to the specification. For example, $SC_1(B_1, B_2) \geq 0.1$, where $B_1 = \{milk, cheese\}$ and $B_2 = \{boots, sock\}$, says that any itemset containing at least one item in B_1 and one item in B_2 has minimum support 0.1. In this case, the user is interested in only *milk* and *cheese*, rather than all dairy products, and only *boots* and *sock*, rather than all footwear products.

For the rest of the paper, we assume that a support specification is given.

4   Adaptive Apriori

A key idea of our approach is to push SCs following the "dependency chain" in the **Apriori** itemset generation. This dependency is best described by a schema enumeration tree. In a *schema enumeration tree*, each node (except the root) is labeled by a bin B_i. A node v represents the schema given by the labels $B_1 \ldots B_k$ along the path from the root to v. If

database

TID	Items
100	0,2,7
200	0,4,7,8
300	2,4,5,7,8
400	1,2,4,7,8
500	2,4,6,7,8

bins

B_0	1,7,8
B_1	2,6
B_2	4,5
B_3	0,3

a specification

$SC_0() \geq 0.8$
$SC_1(B_1, B_3) \geq 0.2$
$SC_2(B_3) \geq 0.4$
$SC_3(B_2) \geq 0.6$

Figure 1: The running example

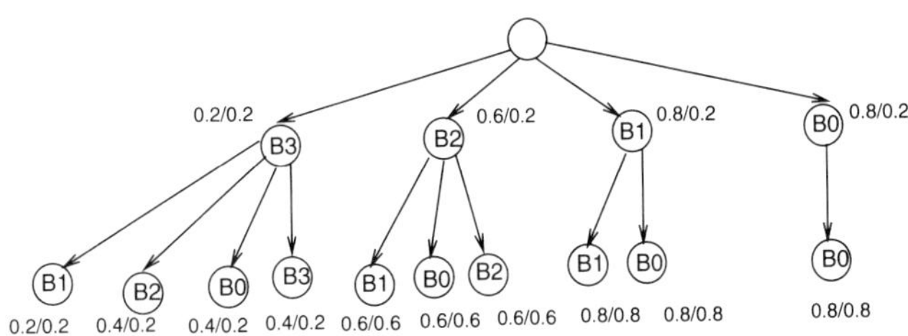

Figure 2: A schema enumeration tree, marked with $Sminsup/Pminsup$

a schema enumeration tree contains two sibling nodes representing schemas $s_1 = B_1 \ldots B_{k-2}B_{k-1}$ and $s_2 = B_1 \ldots B_{k-2}B_k$, where s_1 is on the left of s_2 (if $B_{k-1} \neq B_k$), the schema enumeration tree also contains the node representing schema $s = B_1 \ldots B_{k-2}B_{k-1}B_k$, as a child of the node for s_1. s_1 and s_2 are called *generating schemas* of s. Every schema *depends on* its generating schemas in that the former is constructed by the latter. For example, in Figure 2, $B_2 B_1$ depends on B_2 and B_1, but not on $B_1 B_0$ or B_3.

Several comments follow. (i) Unlike the static lexical ordering in a standard set enumeration tree [R92], the ordering of nodes in a schema enumeration tree is determined dynamically on a per-node basis to achieve a certain optimality of constraint pushing. We will consider the ordering issue in Section 5. (ii) There is an one-to-one correspondence between nodes and schemas represented by nodes, and the terms "schema" and "node" are interchangeable. (iii) There should be no confusion between B_i as a label and B_i as a schema of length 1. As a label, B_i can occur at several nodes (like B_2 in Figure 2), but as a schema, B_i is represented by a unique node. (iv) We can associate *minsup* with nodes, in the way of associating it with schemas. (v) A label B_i is allowed to repeat on a path to cover itemsets containing more than one item from B_i.

4.1 The pushed minimum support

Consider schema $s = B_1 \ldots B_{k-2}B_{k-1}B_k$, and its generating schemas $s_1 = B_1 \ldots B_{k-2}B_{k-1}$ and $s_2 = B_1 \ldots B_{k-2}B_k$. In the case of non-uniform minimum support, $minsup(s)$, $minsup(s_1)$, $minsup(s_2)$ are not always the same, and the Apriori-generation of frequent itemsets of s from those of s_1 and s_2 is lost. Our approach is to replace *minsup* with a new function, denoted by $Pminsup$, such that (i) $Pminsup$ defines a superset of the frequent itemsets defined by *minsup*

and (ii) we can generate this superset in the manner of Apriori. Let us formalize this idea.

For any function f from schemas to $[0..1]$, we say that an itemset I of schema s is $frequent(f)$ if $sup(I) \geq f(s)$. Let $F(f)$ denote the set of $frequent(f)$ itemsets.

Definition 4.1 ($Pminsup$) Let $Pminsup$ be a function from (the schemas of) schema enumeration tree T to $[0..1]$ satisfying:

- *Completeness*: For every schema s in T such that $minsup(s)$ is defined, $Pminsup(s) \leq minsup(s)$;

- *Apriori-like*: For every schema s and its generating schemas s_1 and s_2, whenever $\{i_1, \ldots, i_{k-2}, i_{k-1}, i_k\}$ of s is $frequent(Pminsup)$, so are $\{i_1, \ldots, i_{k-2}, i_{k-1}\}$ of s_1 and $\{i_1, \ldots, i_{k-2}, i_k\}$ of s_2;

- *Maximality*: $Pminsup$ is maximal with respect to the above Completeness and Apriori-like. $\square$

$Pminsup$ is called the *pushed minimum support* with respect to T and *minsup*. $\square$

Completeness ensures that $F(Pminsup)$ is a superset of $F(minsup)$. Apriori-like ensures the Apriori generation of $F(Pminsup)$. Maximality ensures that $F(Pminsup)$ is tightest to satisfy these properties. By replacing *minsup* with $Pminsup$, we are guaranteed to find a tight superset of $F(minsup)$ in the manner of Apriori. This strategy is referred as to Adaptive Apriori. The novelty of Adaptive Apriori is that it breaks the barrier of uniform minimum support by defining the "best" minimum support, i.e., $Pminsup$, for each schema individually while preserving the essence of Apriori.

At this point, two questions need to be answered. First, how do we determine $Pminsup$ with respect

notation	meaning
s	a node or schema
$L(s)$	the label of s
$subtree(s)$	the subtree rooted at s
$\sigma(s)$	the set of SCs in $subtree(s)$
$RS(s)$	the set of right siblings of s plus s itself
$LS(s)$	the set of left siblings of s
$minsup(s)$	the minimum support of s
$Sminsup(s)$	the lowest minimum support in $\sigma(s)$
$Pminsup(s)$	the pushed minimum support of s

Table 1: Notation for a schema enumeration tree

to a *given* schema enumeration tree T? Second, how do we generate a schema enumeration tree for which $Pminsup$ is maximized? We answer the first question in the rest of this section and answer the second question in Section 5.

In the rest of the paper, we shall use the notation in Table 1. For example, for schema $s = B_3 B_2$ in Figure 2, $L(s)$, the label of node s, is the B_2; $subtree(s)$ is the subtree rooted at s (not shown); $\sigma(s)$ contains all SCs except $SC_1(B_1, B_3) \geq 0.2$ because label B_1 does not occur in $subtree(s)$; $Sminsup(s)$ is the lowest minimum support in $\sigma(s)$, i.e., 0.4; $RS(s)$ contains schemas $B_3 B_2, B_3 B_0, B_3 B_3$; and $LS(s)$ contains schema $B_3 B_1$. Notice that while *minsup* only depends on the problem specification, $Pminsup$ and $Sminsup$ also depend on the schema enumeration tree used.

4.2   Determining $Pminsup$

Consider the running example and Figure 2. In $subtree(B_2)$, no schema will match $SC_1(B_1, B_3) \geq 0.2$ and $SC_2(B_3) \geq 0.4$ because label B_3 does not occur in the subtree. In this sense, these SCs or minimum supports are pruned from $subtree(B_2)$. The same goes for $subtree(B_1)$ and $subtree(B_0)$. In general, for generating nodes l and r (which must be siblings) with l on the left and r on the right, the node generated by l and r is a child of l and has label $L(r)$. Therefore, label $L(r)$ occurs in $subtree(l)$, but label $L(l)$ never occurs in $subtree(r)$. This has two implications stated below.

Corollary 4.1 Consider any node v in a schema enumeration tree T.

1. Only the labels of nodes in $RS(v)$ can occur in $subtree(v)$. As such, all SCs containing labels of nodes in $LS(v)$ are pruned from $subtree(v)$.

2. Only the nodes in $subtree(v)$ and in $subtree(u)$ for $u \in LS(v)$ depend on v. Such as, $Pminsup(v) = min\{Sminsup(u) \mid u \in LS(v) \cup \{v\}\}$.

Example 4.1 In Figure 2, each schema s is marked by $Sminsup(s)/Pminsup(s)$. Since label B_3 does not occur in $subtree(B_2)$, all SCs containing B_3 are pruned in $subtree(B_2)$, so $\sigma(B_2) = \{SC_0() \geq 0.8, SC_3(B_2) \geq 0.6\}$ and $Sminsup(B_2) = 0.6$. Similarly, $Sminsup(B_3) = 0.2$. $Pminsup(B_2) = min\{Sminsup(B_3), Sminsup(B_2)\} = 0.2$. Similarly, $Pminsup(s) = 0.6$ for $s = B_2 B_1, s = B_2 B_0, s = B_2 B_2$ because $SC_1 \geq 0.2$ and $SC_2 \geq 0.4$ are pruned in $subtree(s)$, and $Pminsup(s) = 0.8$ for $s = B_1 B_1, s = B_1 B_0, s = B_0 B_0$ because $SC_1 \geq 0.2$, $SC_2 \geq 0.4$, and $SC_3 \geq 0.6$ are pruned from $subtree(s)$. $\square$

4.3   The characteristic of $Pminsup$

To get insights into the benefit of using $Pminsup$, we analyze how $Pminsup$ changes in a schema enumeration tree. Refer to Table 1 for notation. As we move from a left sibling l to a right sibling r, Corollary 4.1(1) implies that $L(l)$ is pruned from $subtree(r)$, thereby, $\sigma(r) \subseteq \sigma(l)$ and $Sminsup(l) \leq Sminsup(r)$. As we move from a parent node p to a child node c, $\sigma(c)$ is the set of SCs in $\sigma(p)$ matched by at least some schema in $subtree(c)$, thereby, $\sigma(c) \subseteq \sigma(p)$ and $Sminsup(p) \leq Sminsup(c)$. The following theorems summarize these characteristics, whose proofs are given in [WHH00].

Theorem 4.1 Consider a schema enumeration tree.

1. Let $s_1, \ldots, s_k$ be the schemas at siblings from left to right. Then (a) $Sminsup(s_i) \leq Sminsup(s_{i+1})$; (b) $Pminsup(s_i) = Pminsup(s_1) = Sminsup(s_1)$.

2. Let $s_1, \ldots, s_k$ be the schemas on a path starting from the root. Then (a) $Sminsup(s_i) \leq Sminsup(s_{i+1})$; (b) $Pminsup(s_i) \leq Sminsup(s_i) \leq Pminsup(s_{i+1})$. $\square$

Theorem 4.1(2b) tells that $Pminsup$ is never decreased by moving from a parent p to a child c. The next theorem characterizes when $Pminsup$ is actually increased.

Theorem 4.2 Consider a parent node p and a child node c. The following are equivalent:

1. p has a left sibling p' such that $Sminsup(p') < Sminsup(p)$;

2. p has a left sibling p' such that $Sminsup(p')$ is pruned in $subtree(p)$;

3. $Pminsup(p) < Pminsup(c)$. $\square$

In Figure 3 (which contains only the nodes for non-empty sets of candidates), since $Sminsup(B_3) < Sminsup(B_i)$, for $i = 2, 1, 0$, every child of schema B_i has a higher $Pminsup$ than B_i does. Similarly, since $Sminsup(B_3 B_1) < Sminsup(B_3 B_2)$, every child of $B_3 B_2$ has a higher $Pminsup$ than $B_3 B_2$ does. The

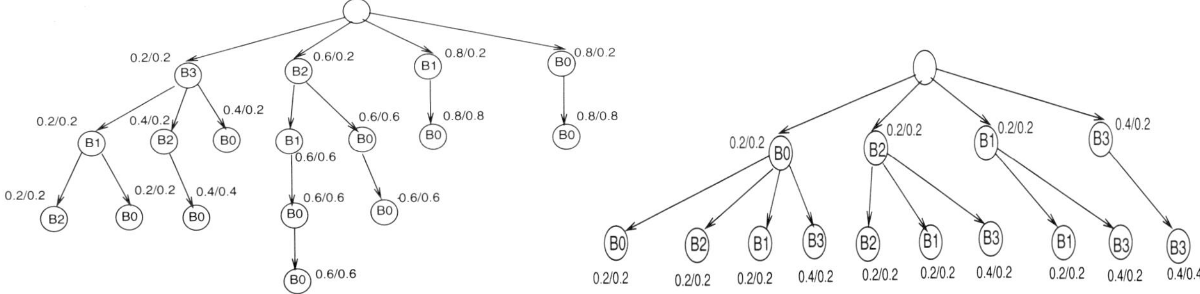

Figure 3: Nodes marked $Sminsup/Pminsup$

Figure 4: Nodes marked $Sminsup/Pminsup$

above theorems give a clear picture of how $Pminsup$ changes in a schema enumeration tree: (a) All sibling nodes have the same $Pminsup$. (b) As we move down from a parent p to a child c, $Pminsup$ never decreases. (c) Whether $Pminsup$ is actually increased, thereby, tightening up the search space, depends on whether p has a left sibling with a lower $Sminsup$. It turns out that the ordering of siblings has a major impact on (c). We now examine how to order siblings to maximize $Pminsup$.

5   The ordering of nodes

Compare Figure 2 with Figure 3. The former is preferred because of higher $Pminsup$ for most schemas. For example, $Pminsup(B_2 B_1)$ and $Pminsup(B_0 B_2)$ are 0.6 in Figure 2, but are 0.2 in Figure 3. This change is caused by placing labels B_1 and B_3 to the right end at level 1 in Figure 4, making $SC_1(B_1, B_3) \geq 0.2$ applicable in $subtree(B_2 B_1)$ and $subtree(B_0 B_2)$. Thus, the order of sibling nodes has a major impact on $Pminsup$. Unfortunately, no "optimal" order exists in general [WHH00]. Therefore, a reasonable thing to do is to order sibling nodes heuristically to maximize $Pminsup$. Let us consider such heuristic orderings.

Assume that $s_1, \ldots, s_k$ are the siblings from left to right. From Corollary 4.1(1), for $i < j$, $L(s_i)$ does not occur in $subtree(s_j)$, and all SCs containing $L(s_i)$ are pruned from $\sigma(s_j)$. Therefore, if we want to prune, as early as possible, the SCs specifying low minimum supports, label $L(s_1)$ for the first sibling s_1 should occur in such SCs. Subsequently, to determine $L(s_2)$ for the second sibling s_2, we remove the SCs containing $L(s_1)$ and repeat the same for the remaining SCs. The strategy is to greedily prune the lowest minimum support from all sibling subtrees on the right. Put another way, this strategy maximizes the chance of $Sminsup(s_i) < Sminsup(s_j)$, for all right siblings s_j of s_i, and thus, the chance of the condition in Theorem 4.2(3). This analysis leads to the first ordering strategy.

Strategy 1 Select the label specifying the lowest minimum support as the next sibling. □

Example 5.1 Consider ordering the child nodes of the root for the example in Figure 1. There is a

tie between B_1 and B_3 as both specify the lowest minimum support in $SC_1(B_1, B_3) \geq 0.2$. Suppose that B_1 is selected as the first child. $SC_1(B_1, B_3) \geq 0.2$ is then pruned from $subtree(B_3)$, $subtree(B_2)$, and $subtree(B_0)$. We select B_3 as the second child because it specifies the lowest minimum support in the remaining SCs. $SC_2(B_3) \geq 0.4$ is then pruned from $subtree(B_2)$ and $subtree(B_0)$. Finally, we select B_2 and B_0 in that order. This gives the order $O_1 = B_1, B_3, B_2, B_0$ at level 1. $Sminsup(B_1) = 0.2$, $Sminsup(B_3) = 0.4$, $Sminsup(B_2) = 0.6$, and $Sminsup(B_0) = 0.8$. If we select B_3 as the first child instead, the order is $O_2 = B_3, B_2, B_1, B_0$. □

The above Strategy 1 is *dynamic* in that there is a separate round of selection for each sibling. In *static* Strategy 1 all siblings are selected in a single round, by ignoring the interaction between siblings. Our second strategy is to greedily prune as many SCs as possible. At each sibling, from left to right, we select the label that occurs in the most number of remaining SCs. In effect, this prunes all the SCs containing this label from the sibling subtrees on the right of the current sibling. By pruning as many SCs as possible, the default SC, which always specifies the highest minimum support, can be used as early as possible.

Strategy 2 Select the label specifying the most number of SCs as the next sibling. □

6   The algorithm

The algorithm expands the schema enumeration tree iteratively, one level per iteration. There are two phases in iteration k. Phase 1 generates new nodes s_i at level k and determines $Pminsup(s_i)$. This phase examines only the support specification and schemas, not the database or itemsets. Phase 2 generates $frequent(Pminsup)$ at nodes s_i, similar to Apriori. We shall focus on Phase 1. Each node p at level $k - 1$ is associated with the set of SCs at p, $\sigma(p)$, and the relation T_p for $frequent(Pminsup)$ itemsets of p. (Refer to Table 1 for notation.) To expand to level k, three steps are performed in Phase 1. Step 1 creates child nodes s_i at level k and Step 2 orders these nodes according to one of the strategies proposed in Section 5.

Step 3 computes $\sigma(s_i)$ and $Pminsup(s_i)$ according to Corollary 4.1. We illustrate Step 3 by an example.

Example 6.1 As in Example 5.1, the nodes at level 1 are in the order $O_2 = B_3, B_2, B_1, B_0$. $\sigma(B_3)$ is initialized to $\sigma(root)$ because B_3 is the left-most child of the root. We delete label B_3 from the SCs in $\sigma(B_3)$ because every schema in $subtree(B_3)$ does contain B_3. Now $\sigma(B_3) = \{SC_0() \geq 0.8, SC_1(B_1) \geq 0.2, SC_2() \geq 0.4, SC_3(B_2) \geq 0.6\}$. $SC_3(B_2) \geq 0.6$ and $SC_0() \geq 0.8$ are redundant in the presence of $SC_2() \geq 0.4$, so deleted from $\sigma(B_3)$. This gives $\sigma(B_3) = \{SC_1(B_1) \geq 0.2, SC_2() \geq 0.4\}$, where $SC_2() \geq 0.4$ becomes the default SC in $subtree(B_3)$. By Corollary 4.1(2), $Pminsup(B_3) = Sminsup(B_3) = 0.2$. Similarly, for sibling B_2, $\sigma(B_2) = \{SC_3() \geq 0.6\}$, $Sminsup(B_2) = 0.6$, $Pminsup(B_2) = 0.2$; for sibling B_1, $\sigma(B_1) = \{SC_0() \geq 0.8\}$, $Sminsup(B_1) = 0.8$, $Pminsup(B_1) = 0.2$; for sibling B_0, $\sigma(B_0) = \{SC_0() \geq 0.8\}$, $Sminsup(B_0) = 0.8$, and $Pminsup(B_0) = 0.2$. $\square$

7 Evaluation

We study the scalability with respect to the lowest minimum support specified. The scalability is measured by the *dead point*, defined as the lowest minimum support at which page swapping between memory and disk starts to takes place. We observed that whenever the available physical memory dropped to only a few Mbytes, the run did not finish within 3 hours and much longer time was needed. So, practically the dead point was taken as the lowest tested minimum support for which a run finishes within 3 hours. All experiments were performed on PII 300-MMX with 128MB memory and NT Server 4.0.

We chose Apriori and Max_Miner for comparison. Apriori provides a baseline for measuring the benefit of our approach. Max_Miner generates only maximal frequent itemsets and is a good candidate to overcome the bottleneck of itemest generation. Since neither Apriori nor Max_Miner handles general support constraints, the lowest minimum support in a support specification was used for them. There are several other high performance algorithms, by being smart in candidate generating and support counting, e.g., [BMUT97, PCY96, SON95]. Like Apriori, thoes techniques can be adopted in our itemset generation phase. So we do not compare with every such algorithm.

We borrowed the census data used in [SBMU98]. The data has 23 attributes, 77 items [2] and 126,229 transactions. Each transaction corresponds to an individual, and each item corresponds to an attribute/value pair. About an half of the items have support less than 10%, and the rest of the items have widely varied support from 10% to more than 90%.

---

[2] originally 63 items, but we explicitly represented the FALSE value of the 14 binary attributes as items, making 77 items in total.

To generate support specifications, we grouped the items from the same attribute into a bin, giving 23 bins $B_1, \ldots, B_{23}$. Let V_i be a bin variable and $S(V_i)$ be the smallest support of the items in the bin represented by V_i. We specified the following SCs in the closed interpretation:

$$SC_i(V_1, \ldots, V_k) \geq \theta_i(V_1, \ldots, V_k) \quad (0 < k \leq K) \quad (1)$$

where K is the maximal itemset size K specified by the user. $\theta_i(V_1, \ldots, V_k) = \gamma^{k-1} \times S(V_1) \times \ldots \times S(V_k)$ if $\gamma^{k-1} \times S(V_1) \times \ldots \times S(V_k)$ is within $[0.0000158, 1]$. If $\gamma^{k-1} \times S(V_1) \times \ldots \times S(V_k)$ is less than the lower bound or larger than the upper bound, the corresponding bound is used. The lower bound 0.0000158 corresponds to the support requirement of at least 2 transactions. Each specification is defined by a pair of γ and K. Since the occurrence of bins is symmetric, Strategy 2 does not impose a bias on the ordering of nodes and we report only "static 1" as the "dynamic 1" did not make a tangible difference. "average" refers to the average of 10 random orders for Adaptive Apriori. A more detailed study of various strategies is reported in [WHH00].

We varied γ and K to simulate different support requirements. In general, as γ decreases and K increases, the lowest minimum support in a specification decreases. The bottom of Figure 7 shows the lowest minimum support for each (γ, K) pair. In Figure 7, on the left are the measures for $\gamma = 5$, and on the right are the measures for $\gamma = 20$. In Figure 7(4a,4b), the y-value for Max_Miner is the number of maximal frequent itemsets. The dead point is represented by the right-most point on a curve. All algorithms were terminated after K iterations for a given K. In general, Apriori and Max_Miner reached the dead point earlier than "static 1" and "average". "static 1" and "average" performed better at $\gamma = 20$ than at $\gamma = 5$. This is because minimum supports are well spread at $\gamma = 20$, as shown in the table in Figure 7.

We plotted $Pminsup$ vs nodes numbered in the breath-first ordering for the dead point of "static 1" at $(\gamma = 20, K = 7)$ and $(\gamma = 5, K = 5)$, shown in Figure 7 and Figure 6, respectively. The two cases have the lowest minimum support, 0.0000158. For the case of $(\gamma = 20, K = 7)$, the minimum supports are well spread and Adaptive Apriori was able to exploit a higher $Pminsup$ for 99% of the nodes expanded! For the case of $(\gamma = 5, K = 5)$, the minimum supports tended to be crowded towards 0.0000158, and only 88% of the nodes expanded have $Pminsup$ higher than 0.0000158. This experiment strongly supports our claim that if itemsets are of varied supports, pushing support constraints is an effective strategy to deal with the bottleneck of itemset generation.

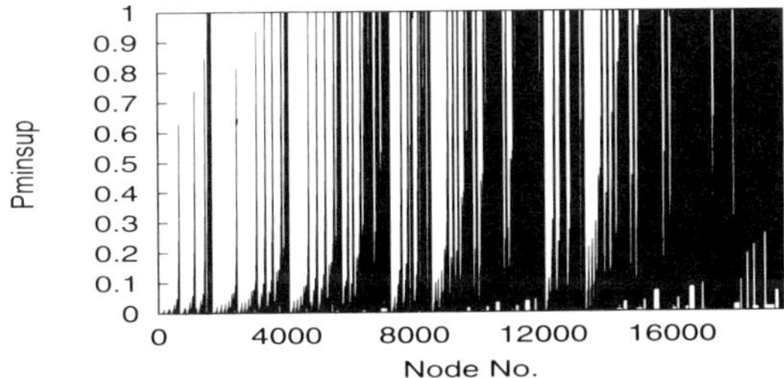

Figure 5: 99.3% nodes above 0.0000158

8 Conclusion

We motivated the need for support constraints and proposed a way of specifying support constraints. We presented a framework for pushing support constraints into the itemset generation. The challenge is that the classic **Apriori** is lost in the presence of non-uniform minimum support. Our approach is to use the best "run time" minimum support for each itemset so as to preserve the **Apriori** itemset generation. We call this strategy **Adaptive Apriori**. Unlike existing constraint pushing strategies, **Adaptive Apriori** does not rely on a uniform support requirement. A key issue for **Adaptive Apriori** is to order items so that the "run time" minimum support is maximized. We proposed several strategies for this. Our experiments showed that pushing support constraints is highly effective in dealing with the bottleneck of itemset generation. A meaningful future work is to study how the non-uniform support framework can be extended to frequent itemset mining without generating candidates like in [HPY00].

References

[AIS93] R. Agrawal, T. Imilienski, and A. Swami. Mining association rules between sets of items in large datasets. SIGMOD 1993, 207-216.

[AS94] R. Agrawal and R. Srikant. Fast algorithm for mining association rules. VLDB 1994, 487-499

[AY98] C. C. Aggarwal and P. S. Yu. A new framework for itemset generation. PODS 1998, 18-24

[BMS97] S. Brin, R. Motwani, and C. Silverstein. Beyond market baskets: generalizing association rules to correlations. SIGMOD 1997, 265-276

[BMUT97] S. Brin, R. Motwani, J.D. Ullman, and S. Tsur. Dynamic itemset counting and implication rules for market basket data. SIGMOD 1997, 255-264

[C*00] E. Cohen, M. Datar, S. Fujiwara, A. Gionis, P. Indyk, R. Motwani, J.D. Ullman, C. Yang. Finding interesting associations without support pruning. ICDE 2000, 489-499

[DL99] G. Dong, J. Li. Efficient mining of emerging patterns: discovering trends and differences. SIGKDD 1999, 43-52

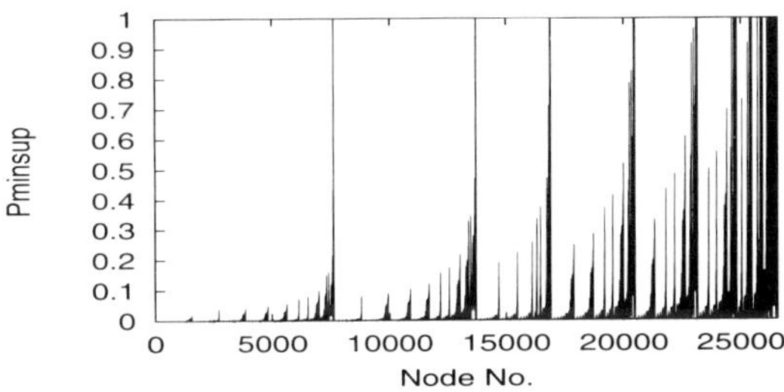

Figure 6: 88.1% nodes above 0.0000158

[HF95] J. Han and Y. Fu. Discovery of multiple-level association rules from large databases. VLDB 1995, 420-431

[HPY00] J. Han, J. Pei, and Y. Yin. Mining Frequent Patterns without Candidate Generation. SIGMOD 2000, 1-12

[LHM98] B. Liu, W. Hsu, Y. Ma. Integrating classification and association rule mining. KDD 1998, 80-86

[LHM99] B. Liu, W. Hsu, Y. Ma. Mining association rules with multiple minimum supports. SIGKDD 1999, 125-134

[LSM98] W. Lee, S.J. Stolfo, K.W. Mok. Mining audit data to build intrusion detection models. KDD 1998, 66-72

[MW99] D. Meretakis, B. Wuthrich. Extending naive Bayes classifiers using long itemsets. SIGKDD 1999, 165-174

[MTV94] H. Mannila, H. Toivonen, A.I. Verkamo. Efficient algorithm for discovering association rules. KDD 1994, 181-192

[PCY96] J.S. Park, M. -S. Chen, P.S. Yu. An efficient hash based algorithm for mining association rules. SIGMOD 1995, 175-186

[R92] R. Rymon. Search through systematic set enumeration. Principles of Knowledge Representation and Reasoning, 1992, 539-550

[SA95] R. Srikant and R. Agrawal. Mining generalized association rules. VLDB 1995, 407-419

[SBMU98] C. Silverstein, S. Brin, R. Motwani, J. Ullman. Scalable techniques for mining causal structures. VLDB 1998, 594-605

[SON95] A. Savasere, E. Omiecinski, S. Navathe. An efficient algorithm for mining association rules in large databases. VLDB 1995, 432-444

[SVA97] R. Srikant, Q. Vu, and R. Agrawal. Mining association rules with item constraints. KDD 1997, 67-73

[WHH00] K. Wang, Y. He, J. Han. Pushing support constraints into frequent itemset mining. School of Computing, National University of Singapore, 2000

[WZL99] K. Wang, S.Q. Zhou, S.C. Liew. Building hierarchical classifiers using class proximity. VLDB 1999, 363-374

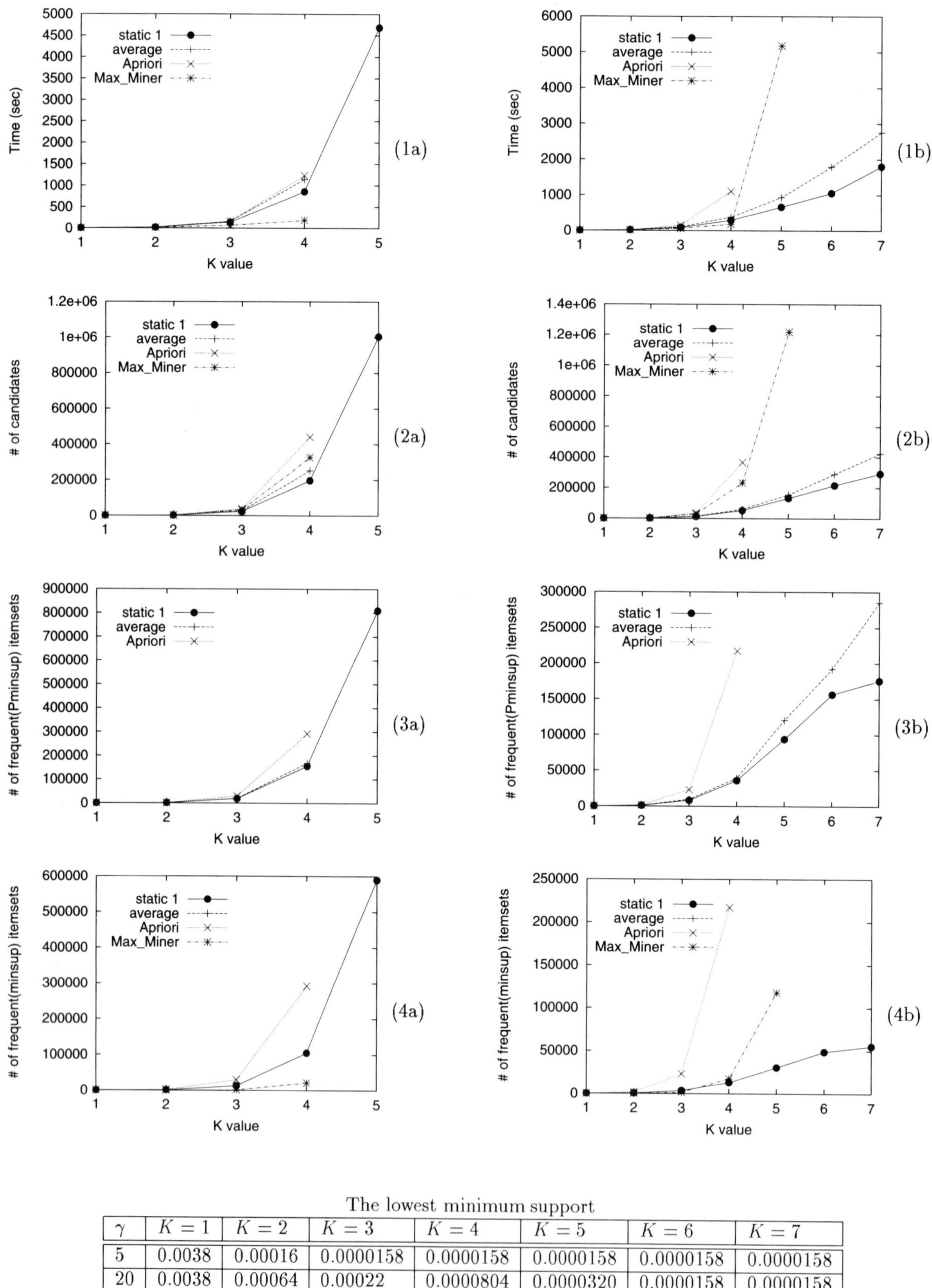

The lowest minimum support

γ	$K=1$	$K=2$	$K=3$	$K=4$	$K=5$	$K=6$	$K=7$
5	0.0038	0.00016	0.0000158	0.0000158	0.0000158	0.0000158	0.0000158
20	0.0038	0.00064	0.00022	0.0000804	0.0000320	0.0000158	0.0000158

Figure 7: The dead points for the census dataset (the left for $\gamma = 5$ and the right for $\gamma = 20$)

Efficient Filtering of XML Documents for Selective Dissemination of Information *

Mehmet Altınel

Department of Computer Science
University of Maryland
altinel@cs.umd.edu

Michael J. Franklin

EECS Computer Science Division
University of California at Berkeley
franklin@cs.berkeley.edu

Abstract

Information Dissemination applications are gaining increasing popularity due to dramatic improvements in communications bandwidth and ubiquity. The sheer volume of data available necessitates the use of selective approaches to dissemination in order to avoid overwhelming users with unnecessary information. Existing mechanisms for selective dissemination typically rely on simple keyword matching or "bag of words" information retrieval techniques. The advent of XML as a standard for information exchange and the development of query languages for XML data enables the development of more sophisticated filtering mechanisms that take structure information into account. We have developed several index organizations and search algorithms for performing efficient filtering of XML documents for large-scale information dissemination systems. In this paper we describe these techniques and examine their performance across a range of document, workload, and scale scenarios.

1 Introduction

The proliferation of the Internet and intranets, the development of wireless and satellite networks, and the availability of asymmetric, high-bandwidth links to home have fueled the development of a wide range of new *dissemination-based* (or *Selective Dissemination of Information (SDI)*) applications. These applications involve timely distribution of data to a large set of customers, and include stock and sports tickers, traffic information systems, electronic

personalized newspapers, and entertainment delivery. The execution model for these applications is based on continuously collecting new data items from underlying data sources, filtering them against user profiles (i.e., user interests) and finally, delivering relevant data to interested users.

In order to effectively target the right information to the right people, SDI systems rely upon user profiles. Current SDI systems typically use simple keyword matching or "bag of words" Information Retrieval (IR) techniques to represent user profiles and match them against new data items. These techniques, however, often suffer from limited ability to express user interests, thereby raising the potential that the users receive irrelevant data while not receiving the information they need. Moreover, work on IR-based models has largely focused on the effectiveness of the profiles rather than the *efficiency* of filtering. In the Internet environment, where huge volumes of input data and large numbers of users are typical, efficiency and scalability are key concerns.

Recently, XML (eXtensible Markup Language) [BPS98, Cov99] has emerged as a standard information exchange mechanism on the Internet. XML allows the encoding of structural information within documents. This information can be exploited to create more focused and accurate profiles of user interests. Of course such benefits come at a cost, namely, an increase in the complexity of matching documents to profiles.

We have developed a document filtering system, named *XFilter*, that provides highly efficient matching of XML documents to large numbers of user profiles. In XFilter, user interests are represented as queries using the XPath language [CD99]. The XFilter engine uses a sophisticated index structure and a modified Finite State Machine (FSM) approach to quickly locate and examine relevant profiles. In this paper we describe these structures along with an event-based filtering algorithm and several enhancements. We then evaluate the efficiency, scalability, and adaptability of the approaches using a detailed experimental framework that allows the manipulation of several key characteristics of document and user profiles. The results indicate that XFilter performs well and is highly scalable. Thus, we believe our techniques represent a promising technology for

*This research has been partially supported by Rome Labs agreement number F30602-97-2-0241 under DARPA order number F078, by the NSF under grant IRI-9501353, and by Intel, Microsoft, NEC, and Draper Laboratories.

**Proceedings of the 26th VLDB Conference,
Cairo, Egypt, 2000.**

the deployment of Internet-scale SDI systems.

The remainder of the paper is organized as follows: In Section 2, we give an overview of an XML-based SDI system and the XPath language, which is used in our user profile model. Related work is discussed in Section 3. In Section 4, we present the profile index structures and an event-based XML filtering algorithm. Enhancements to this algorithm are provided in Section 5. We discuss the experimental results in Section 6. Section 7 concludes the paper.

2 Background

In this section we first present a high-level architecture of an XML-based information dissemination system. We then describe the XPath language, which we use to specify user profiles in XFilter.

2.1 An XML-based SDI Architecture

The process of filtering and delivering documents based on user interests is sometimes referred to as Selective Dissemination of Information (SDI). Figure 1 shows a generic architecture for an XML-based SDI system. There are two main sets of inputs to the system: user profiles and data items (i.e., documents). User profiles describe the information preferences of individual users. In most systems these profiles are created by the users, typically by clicking on items in a Graphical User Interface. In some systems, however, these profiles can be learned automatically by the system through the application of machine learning techniques to user access traces. The user profiles are converted into a format that can be efficiently stored and evaluated by the Filter Engine. These profiles are "standing queries", which are (conceptually) applied to all incoming documents.

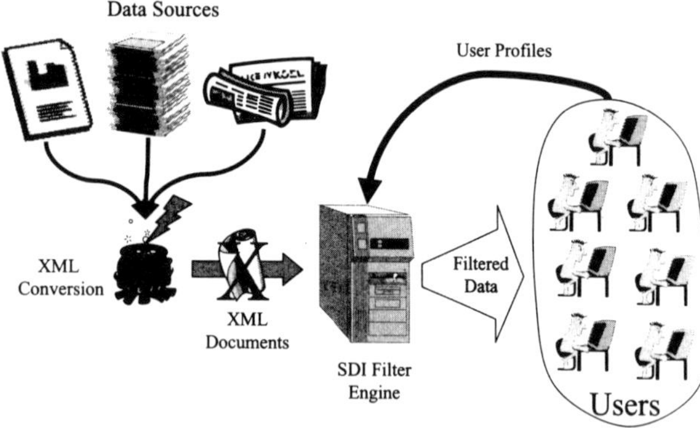

Figure 1: Architecture of an XML Based SDI System

The other key inputs to an SDI system are the documents to be filtered. Our work is focused on XML-encoded documents. XML is a natural fit for SDI because it is rapidly gaining popularity as a mechanism for sharing and delivering information among businesses, organizations, and users on the Internet. It is also achieving importance as a means for publishing commercial content such as news items and financial information.

XML provides a mechanism for tagging document contents in order to better describe their organization. It allows the hierarchical organization of a document as a root element that includes sub-elements; elements can be nested to any depth. In addition to sub-elements, elements can contain data (e.g., text) and attributes. A general set of rules for a document's elements and attributes can be defined in a *Document Type Definition* (DTD). A DTD specifies the elements and attributes names and the nature of their content in the document.

In an SDI system, newly created or modified XML documents are routed to the Filter Engine. When a document arrives at the filter engine, it is matched against the user profiles to determine the set of users to whom it should be sent. As SDI systems are deployed on the Internet, the number of users for such systems can easily grow into the millions. A key challenge in such an environment is to efficiently and quickly search the potentially huge set of user profiles to find those for which the document is relevant. XFilter is aimed at solving exactly this problem. Before presenting the solutions used in XFilter, however, we first describe a model for expressing user profiles as queries of XML documents.

2.2 XPath as a Profile Language

The profile model used in XFilter is based on XPath [CD99], a language for addressing parts of an XML document that was designed for use by both the XSL Transformations (XSLT) [Cla99b] and XPointer [DDM99] languages. XPath provides a flexible way to specify path expressions. It treats an XML document as a tree of nodes; XPath expressions are patterns that can be matched to nodes in the XML tree. The evaluation of an XPath pattern yields an object whose type can be either a node set (i.e., an unordered collection of nodes without duplicates), a boolean, a number, or a string.

Paths can be specified as absolute paths from the root of the document tree or as relative paths from a known location (i.e., the context node). A query path expression consists of a sequence of one or more *location steps*. In the simplest and most common form, a location step specifies a node name (i.e., an element name).[1] The hierarchical relationships between the nodes are specified in the query using parent-child ("/") operators (i.e., at adjacent levels) and ancestor-descendant ("//") operators (i.e., separated by any number of levels). For example the query `/catalog/product//msrp` addresses all `msrp` element descendants of all `product` elements that are direct children of the `catalog` (root) element in the document. XPath also allows the use of a wildcard operator ("*"), which matches any element name, at a location step in a query.

Each location step can also include one or more *filters* to further refine the selected set of nodes. A filter is a predicate that is applied to the element(s) addressed at that location step. All the filters at a location step must evaluate to

---

[1] The full XPath specification [CD99] contains many more options. We do not list them all here due to space considerations.

TRUE in order for the evaluation to continue to the descendant location steps. Filter expressions are enclosed by "[" and "]" symbols. The filter predicates can be applied to the text of the addressed elements or the attributes of the addressed elements and may also include other path expressions. Any relative paths in a filter expression are evaluated in the context of the element nodes addressed in the location step at which they appear. For example, consider the query: `//product[price/msrp<300]/name`. This query selects the `name` elements of the XML document if the `msrp` of the product is less than 300. Here, the path expression `price/msrp` in the filter is evaluated relative to the `product` elements. This example also shows how element contents can be examined in the queries.

In XFilter, XPath is used to select entire documents rather than parts of documents. That is, we treat an XPath expression as a predicate applied to documents. If the XPath expression matches at least one element of a document then we say that the document satisfies the expression.

An alternative to using XPath would be to use one of the query languages that have been proposed for semistructured data such as UnQl [BDHS96], Lorel [AQM+97] or XML-QL [DFF+98]. We chose to use XPath in our work for two reasons: First, we did not need the full functionality of such query languages for our document filtering purposes. In particular, XFilter examines one document at a time, so only path expressions over individual documents are needed. Secondly, the XPath specification is a World Wide Web Consortium (W3C) recommendation, which means W3C considers it appropriate for widespread deployment. In contrast, the standardization process for XML Query Languages is still in progress. Be that as it may, the techniques described in this paper are largely applicable to path expressions in general, and thus, we believe that they can be adapted to suit other languages as the need arises.

3   Related Work

User profile modeling and matching have been extensively investigated by the Information Retrieval community in the context of Information-Filtering (IF) and SDI research (e.g., [AAB+98, FZ98, FD92]). IR-style user profiles are intended for unstructured text-based systems and typically use sets of keywords to represent user interests.[2] In general, IR profile models can be classified as either *Boolean* or *Similarity-based*. The former use an "exact match" semantics over queries consisting of keywords connected with boolean operators. The latter use a "fuzzy match" semantics in which the profiles and documents are assigned a similarity value. A document whose similarity to a profile exceeds a certain threshold is said to match the profile. The Vector Space Model [CFG00, Sal89] and statistical approaches (e.g., [BC92]) are examples of similarity-

based techniques. The Stanford Information Filtering Tool (SIFT) [YM94, YM95] is a text filtering system for Internet News articles that is based on keywords. SIFT originally used Boolean profiles but was later changed to use a Vector Space approach.

Our profile model differs from the IR-based work in SDI in the following ways:

- The application domain of IR-based SDI systems involves only text documents, whereas our system can work for any application domain in which data is tagged using XML.

- Our profile language takes advantage of embedded schema information in the XML documents, providing more precise filtering than is available using only keywords.

- With the notable exception of the SIFT project, work on IR-based models has largely focused on the effectiveness of the profiles rather than the efficiency of filtering [VH98]. For an Internet-scale filtering system, efficiency and scalability are of paramount importance.

Query-based profile models have also been studied by the database community in the context of Continuous Queries (CQ), which are standing queries that allow users to get new results whenever an update of interest occurs in a database. Early work on CQ for relational databases was done by Terry et al. [TGNO92]. More recently, OpenCQ [LPT99] and NiagaraCQ [CDTW00] have been proposed for information delivery on the Internet. The scalability of these systems is fundamentally limited because they apply all standing queries (or at least all non-equivalent ones) to delta increments or to the updated database for each update that arrives at the system. For Internet-scale systems with potentially millions of users, such approaches are simply not feasible. NiagaraCQ provides some measure of scalability by grouping exactly equivalent queries, but does little to improve the efficiency of matching XML documents to profiles beyond that optimization.

The key insight to building high-performance, scalable SDI systems is that in such systems, the roles of queries and data are reversed [YM94]. In a database system large numbers of data items are indexed and stored, and queries are individually applied. In contrast, in SDI systems, large numbers of queries are stored, and the documents are individually matched to the queries. Thus, in an SDI system, it is necessary to *index the queries*. XFilter is unique in that it combines the scalable SDI approach of indexing queries with the ability to reference document structure (i.e., schema information) leading to scalable but precise filtering of documents for Internet-scale systems.

Triggers [SJGP90, WF89, MD89] in traditional database systems are similar to CQ. However, triggers are a more general mechanism which can involve predicates over many data items and can initiate updates to other data items. Thus, trigger solutions are typically not optimized for fast

---

[2]Several recent text retrieval methods aim to take structure information into account for text databases [BN96]. These methods, however, are not as mature as the ones described above and they have not been studied in the context of SDI.

matching of individual items to vast numbers of relatively simple queries. Some recent work has addressed the issue of scalability for simple triggers [HCH+99], however, this work has not addressed the XML-related issues that XFilter handles.

Finally, the C3 project [CAW98] is related to XFilter in that a query subscription service is provided to subscribe to changes in semi-structured information sources. To date this work has focused on developing semantics and basic mechanisms for querying the changes in semi-structured data, rather than on the efficient evaluation of new data items against large numbers of user profiles.

4 XFilter Implementation

In this section, we describe the basic data structures and algorithms used to implement XFilter. We begin by presenting an overview of the XFilter architecture. This architecture, which is depicted in Figure 2, follows the basic SDI architecture presented earlier. The major components include: 1) an event-based parser for incoming XML-encoded documents; 2) an XPath parser for user profiles; 3) the filter engine, which performs the matching of documents and profiles; and 4) the dissemination component, which sends the filtered data to the appropriate users.

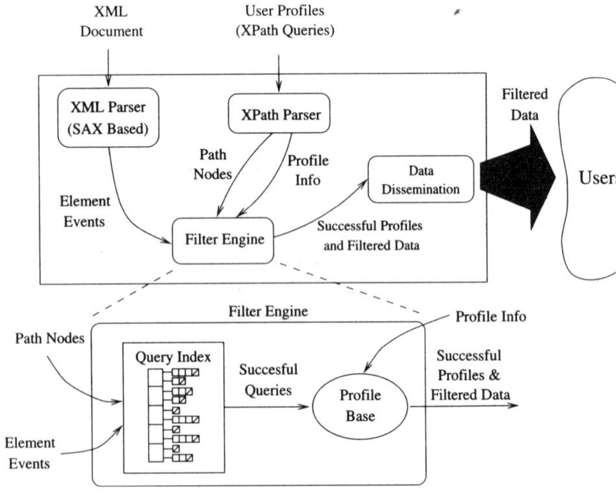

Figure 2: Architecture of XFilter

The heart of the system is the Filter Engine, which uses a sophisticated index structure and a modified Finite State Machine (FSM) approach to quickly locate and check relevant profiles. We first describe the Filter Engine and how it stores the profile information it receives from the XPath parser. The process of checking profiles is driven by an *event-based* XML parser. When an XML document arrives at the system, it is run through the parser, which sends "events" that are responded to by handlers in the filter engine. This process is described in Section 4.2.

Once the matching profiles have been identified for a document, the document must be sent to the appropriate users. The current implementation of XFilter simply uses unicast delivery and sends the entire document to each interested user. Our future work involves the integration of a variety of delivery mechanisms as investigated in our previous work [AAB+98, AAB+99], and the delivery of partial documents. These issues are beyond the scope of this current paper and so are not addressed further here.

4.1 Filter Engine

An XML-based profile model needs efficient algorithms for structure and data filtering to achieve high performance in a large-scale environment such as the Internet. As a result, profile grouping and indexing are crucial for large-scale XML document filtering. For this purpose, similar to traditional SDI systems, the Filter Engine component of XFilter contains an *inverted index* [Sal89], called the *Query Index* (See Figure 2). The Query Index is used to match documents to individual XPath queries. Our implementation also allows for user profiles to be expressed as boolean combinations of XPath queries rather than being restricted to a single XPath query. Such composite profiles are handled by post-processing the matching results at the *Profile Base* to check the boolean conditions. In this paper, due to space limitations, we focus on profiles consisting of a single XPath query.

Filtering XML documents using a structure-oriented path language such as XPath (as opposed to keyword matching) introduces several new problems that must be addressed:

1. Checking the order of the elements in the profiles.

2. Handling wildcards and descendant operators in path expressions.

3. Evaluating filters that are applied to element nodes.

In order to handle these problems efficiently, XFilter converts each XPath query to a *Finite State Machine* (FSM). The events that drive the execution of the Filter Engine are generated by the XML Parser (as described in the following section). In the XFilter execution model, a profile is considered to match a document when the final state of its FSM is reached. The Query Index is built over the states of the XPath queries.

For ease of exposition, we initially describe a solution that addresses the first two problems above (i.e., order checking and wildcard/descendant operators), but only partially addresses the third problem (element node filters). As described in Section 2.2, node filters can themselves contain path expressions, resulting queries with nested path expressions. The handling of element node filters that contain path expressions incurs significant additional complexity. Thus, we first describe a solution that works for filters that do not contain path expressions (e.g., predicates on attribute values or node contents) and postpone the discussion of our solution to handle nested path expressions until Section 4.3.

The main structures used in the Filter Engine are depicted in Figure 3. Each XPath query is decomposed into a

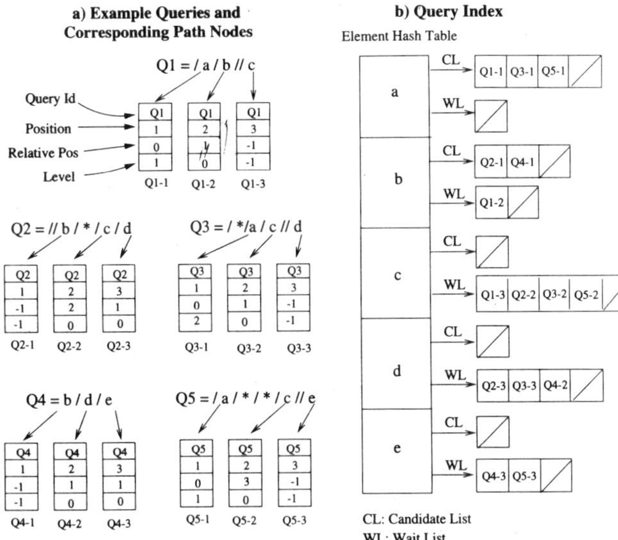

Figure 3: Path Node Decomposition and the content of the Query Index

set of *path nodes* by the XPath parser. These path nodes represent the element nodes in the query and serve as the states of the FSM for the query. Path nodes are not generated for wildcard ("*") nodes. A path node contains the following information:

QueryId: A unique identifier for the path expression to which this path node belongs (generated by the XPath Parser).

Position: A sequence number that determines the location of this path node in the order of the path nodes for the query. The first node of the path is given position 1, and the following nodes are numbered sequentially.

RelativePos: An integer that describes the distance in *document levels* between this path node and the previous (in terms of position) path node. This value is set to 0 for the first node if it does not contain a "Descendant" ('//') operator. A node that is separated from the previous one by a descendant operator is flagged with a special RelativePos value of -1. Otherwise, the RelativePos value of a node is set to 1 plus the number of wildcard nodes between it and its predecessor node.

Level: An integer that represents the level in the XML document at which this path node should be checked. Because XML does not restrict element types from appearing at multiple levels of a document and because XPath allows queries to be specified using "relative" addressing, it is not always possible to assign this value during query parsing. Thus, unlike the previous three items, this information can be updated during the *evaluation* of the query.

The level value is initialized as follows: If the node is the first node of the query and it specifies an absolute distance from the root (i.e., it is either applied to the root node or is a fixed number of wildcard nodes away from the root node), then the level for that node is set to 1 plus its distance from the root. If the RelativePos value of the node is -1, then its level value is also initialized to -1. Otherwise,

the level value is set to 0.

Filters: If a node contains one or more filters, these are stored as expression trees pointed to by the path node.

NextPathNodeSet: Each path node also contains pointer(s) to the next path node(s) of the query to be evaluated. In the restricted case where filters do not include path expressions, there is at most one pointer. Nested path expressions may raise the need for pointers to additional nodes.

Figure 3(a) shows how five example XPath expressions are converted into path nodes by the XPath parser. These nodes are then added to the Query Index. As shown in Figure 3(b), the Query Index is organized as a hash table based on the element names that appear in the XPath expressions. Associated with each unique element name are two lists of path nodes: the *Candidate List* and *Wait List*.

Since each query can only be in a single state of its FSM at a time, each query has a single path node that represents its current state. We refer to this node as the "current node". The current node of each query is placed on the Candidate List of the index entry for its respective element name. All of the path nodes representing future states are stored in the Wait Lists of their respective element names. A state transition in the FSM of a query is represented by promoting a path node from the Wait List to the Candidate List.

The initial distribution of the path nodes to these lists (i.e., which node of each XPath query is initially placed on a Candidate List) is an important contributor to the performance of the XFilter system. We have developed two such placement techniques, which are described in Section 5. Figure 3(b) shows the most straightforward case, where the path nodes for the initial states are placed on the Candidate Lists.

4.2   XML Parsing and Filtering

When a document arrives at the Filter Engine, it is run through an XML Parser which then drives the process of checking for matching profiles in the Index. We use an XML parser that is based on the SAX interface, which is a standard interface for *event-based* XML parsing [Meg98]. We developed the parser using the *expat* toolkit [Cla99a], which is a non-validating XML processor.

The SAX event-based interface reports parsing events (such as encountering the start or end tag of an element) directly to the application through callbacks, and does not usually build an internal tree. To use the SAX interface, the application must implement handlers to deal with the different events, much like handling events in a graphical user interface. For our application, we use the events to drive the profile matching process. Figure 4 shows an example of how a SAX event-based interface breaks the structure of an XML document down into a linear sequence of events.

For XFilter, we implemented callback functions for the parsing events of encountering: 1) a begin element tag; 2) an end element tag; or 3) data internal to an element. All of the handlers are passed the name and document level of the element for (or in) which the parsing event occurred. Ad-

An XML Document	SAX API Events
<?xml version="1.0"> <doc> <para> Hello, world! </para> </doc>	start document start element: doc start element: para characters: Hello, world! end element: para end element: doc end document

Figure 4: SAX API Example

ditional handler-specific information is also passed as described below.

Start Element Handler: When an element tag is encountered by the parser, it calls this handler, passing in the name and level of the element encountered as well as any XML attributes and values that appear in the element tag. The handler looks up the element name in the Query Index and examines all the nodes in the Candidate List for that entry. For each node, it performs two checks: a level check and an attribute filter check.

The purpose of the level check is to make sure that the element appears in the document at a level that matches the level expected by the query. If the path node contains a nonnegative level value, then the two levels must be identical in order for the check to succeed. Otherwise, the level for the node is unrestricted, so the check succeeds regardless of the element level. The attribute filter check applies any simple predicates that reference the attributes of the element.

If both checks succeed and there are no other filters to be checked, then the node passes. If this is the final path node of the query (i.e., its final state) then the document is deemed to match the query. Otherwise, if it is not the final node, then the query is moved into its next state. This is done by *copying* the next node for the query from its Wait List to its corresponding Candidate List (note that a copy of the promoted node remains in the Wait List). If the RelativePos value of the copied node is not -1, its level value is also updated using the current level and its RelativePos values to do future level checks correctly.

End Element Handler: When an end element tag is encountered, the corresponding path node is deleted from the Candidate List in order to restore that list to the state it was in when the corresponding start element tag was encountered. This "backtracking" is necessary to handle the case where multiple elements with the same name appear at the different level in the document.

Element Characters Handler: This handler is called when the data associated with an element is encountered. The data is passed in to the handler as a parameter. It works similarly to the Start Element Handler except that it performs a content filter check rather than an attribute filter check. That is, it evaluates any filters that reference the element content. Like the Start Element Handler, this handler can also cause the query to move to its next state.

4.3 Handling Nested Path Expressions

Recall that the description above was simplified by excluding the processing of element node filters that contain path expressions. Such nested path expressions complicate the filtering process because they introduce non-linearity into the paths. Our implementation of XFilter fully supports such nested path expressions. Due to space limitations, however, we only outline the basic approach to how such expressions are handled.

When the XPath parser encounters an element node filter in a query, it converts it to an expression tree and stores it in the current path node. If the filter contains an XPath query, then that nested query is treated like a separate query from the one it is embedded in. That is, the XPath parser decomposes it into series of path nodes and assigns it a Query ID. A leaf node for the nested query is created in the expression tree of the filter so that its result can be used to evaluate the filter expression. If the filter query starts with an absolute path (i.e. '/' or '//'), that is all that needs to be done. Otherwise, its first path node has to be inserted into the NextPathNodeSet of the current path node to provide relative execution. By doing so, the filter query will be examined relative to current node since its first path node will be copied to Candidate List after the current path node is processed.

If, when evaluating a filter, the result of a nested path expression in that filter is not yet known, we allow the execution for the current path node to continue as if the filter succeeded. At the same time, the filter is marked to be reevaluated when the XML document parsing is finished as the results of all the queries are available at that point. If a query contains nested path expressions that must be evaluated in this manner, it is not considered successful until all of its marked filters are determined to be successful. Likewise, if a query fails after marking a filter, this filter mark is cleared by the system so that the filter need not be reevaluated.

5 Enhanced Filtering Algorithms

In this section we describe several enhancements to the *basic* filtering algorithm described in Section 4. As described in that section, XFilter's basic approach is actually far from "basic" as it incorporates sophisticated indexing and FSM-based evaluation mechanisms. These mechanisms are not strictly necessary to perform SDI filtering, but rather, were developed solely to enhance performance and scalability. Thus, before extending the basic approach it is important to highlight its potential benefits over other, perhaps simpler approaches.

There are two fairly obvious *brute force* strategies that could be employed for performing SDI filtering of XML documents. The first strategy, which is similar to the method used by the database-oriented CQ systems, is to store each profile (query) in an unindexed fashion. When an XML document arrives at the Filter Engine, the document is parsed and indexed. The CQ tool then iterates over all of the profiles, matching them against the document using the document index. This approach is easy to implement and has the benefit of using existing XML search tools, but it is obviously inappropriate for a system with many users, as all profiles must be examined for each new document.

A second brute force strategy applies previous work on keyword-based filtering such as [YM94, YM95] and indexes the profiles using the text, element names, and attribute names that appear in them as keywords. When a new document arrives, this index is used to locate candidate profiles that may possibly be satisfied by the document. These profiles are then checked against the document (i.e., for ordering constraints, etc.) sequentially in a second pass. While this approach is likely to perform better than the first brute force approach, it suffers from the need to perform expensive checks of the document for all candidate profiles.

The main drawback of the brute force methods is that for each input document, they must invoke the profiles individually. XFilter avoids the pitfalls of the brute force approaches by being more careful in the identification of candidate profiles using specialized indexing structures and by more efficiently evaluating those candidate profiles. We now describe two enhancements to the basic XFilter approach: List Balancing and Prefiltering. The performance of XFilter and these enhancements is then examined in Section 6.

5.1 List Balancing

In the basic approach, the Query Index is constructed by simply placing the first path node of each XPath query in the Candidate List for its corresponding element name, and placing the remaining path nodes in the Wait Lists as was shown in Figure 3. For many situations, however, such an approach can be inefficient, as the first elements in the queries are likely to have poorer selectivity due to the fact that they address elements at higher levels in the documents where the sets of possible element names are smaller. In the resulting Query Index, the lengths of the Candidate Lists would become highly skewed, with a small number of very long Candidate Lists that do not provide much selectivity. Such skew hurts performance as the work that is done on the long lists may not adequately reduce the number of queries that must be considered further.

Based on the above observation, we developed the *List Balance* method for choosing a path node to initially place in a Candidate List for each query. This simple method attempts to balance the initial lengths of the Candidate Lists. When adding a new query to the index the element node of that query whose entry in the index has the shortest Candidate List is chosen as the "pivot" node for the query. This pivot node is then placed on its corresponding Candidate List, making it the first node to be checked for that query for any document.

This approach, in effect, modifies the FSM of the query so that its initial state is the pivot node. We accomplish this by representing the portion of the FSM that precedes the pivot node as a "prefix" that is attached to that node. When the pivot node is activated, the prefix of the query is checked

as a precondition in the evaluation of the path node. If this precondition fails, the execution stops for that path node. In order to handle prefix evaluation, List Balance uses a stack which keeps track of the traversed element nodes in the document. We use this stack for fast forward execution of the portion of FSM corresponding to the prefix.

Figure 5 shows example path nodes and a modified Query Index for the List Balance algorithm. Notice that the lengths of the Candidate Lists are the same for each entry of the Query Index. The tradeoff of this approach is the additional work of checking prefixes for the pivot nodes when activated. As we will see in the experiments that follow, this additional cost is far outweighed by the benefits of List Balancing.

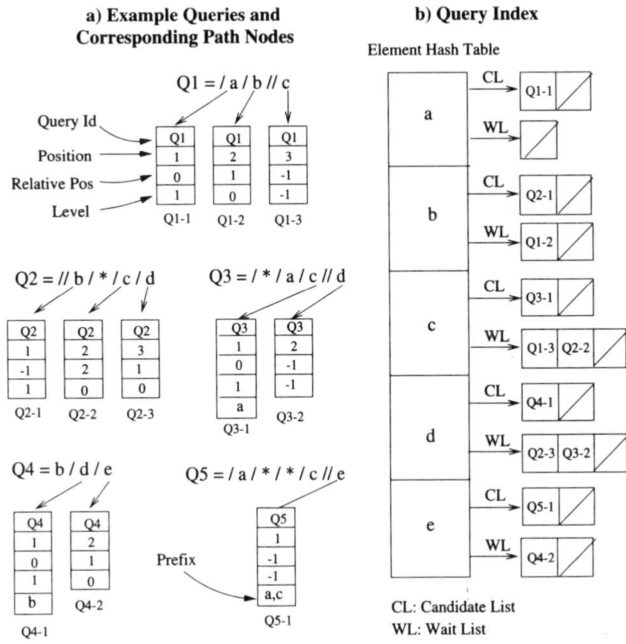

Figure 5: Path Nodes and the content of the Query Index in List Balance

5.2 Prefiltering

Another potential problem with the basic approach is that it proceeds through a path expression one level at a time. Therefore, a considerable amount of unnecessary work may be done for queries that fail due to missing elements late in the evaluation of the path. The idea of Prefiltering is to eliminate from consideration, any query that contains an element name that is not present in the input document. Prefiltering is implemented as an initial pass that is performed before order and filter checking. Thus, in this technique, each incoming document is parsed twice.

Fortunately, previous algorithms developed for the filtering of plain text documents can be used for this purpose. We employed Yan and Garcia-Molina's *Key Based* algorithm [YM94] since it has been shown to be efficient and it fits well with the existing structures used in XFilter. In this method, each query, when initially parsed, is assigned a "key" element name chosen from the element names it contains. In XFilter the key element is chosen using the same algorithm described above for choosing initial nodes in List Balancing.

When a document arrives, an *occurrence table* is constructed, which is a hash table containing an entry of each element name that appears in the document. The entry for an element name in an occurrence table contains a list of all queries whose key is that element name. Once the table has been constructed, the queries referenced by the table are checked to see if all of the element names they contain are in the document. Then, the successful queries are checked further using the normal Basic or List Balance algorithm. That is, the document is parsed a second time during which only queries that have passed the prefiltering step are considered.

The Prefiltering pass introduces an additional cost to the query processing, but can reduce the number of profiles checked by the basic or List Balancing algorithms. The benefits of the Prefiltering method depend on the selectivity of the first step. When the first step discards only small number of profiles, then the advantage of having prefiltering can turn into a disadvantage. We examine the performance of Prefiltering in the next section.

6 Performance Analysis

In this section we evaluate the performance of the basic filtering algorithm and its enhancements. We examine four algorithms: basic, list balance, basic with prefiltering, and list balance with prefiltering.

6.1 Experimental Environment

We implemented XFilter using Gnu C++ version 2.8.1. The experiments were conducted on a Sun Ultra-5 workstation with 128MB memory running Solaris 2.6. All structures are kept in memory in the experiments.

We created our benchmark using the NITF (News Industry Text Format) DTD [Cov99]. The NITF DTD is intended for news copy production, press releases, wire services, newspapers, broadcasters, and Web-based news organizations. It was developed as a joint standard by news organizations and vendors worldwide, and it is supported by most of the world's major news agencies. It is already in use in several commercial applications. For example, the NewsPack product by Wavo corporation [New00] delivers real-time news and information over the Internet in XML format using NITF. The NITF DTD contains 158 elements organized in 7 levels with 588 attributes.

We generated XML documents for our experiments using IBM's XML Generator tool [IBM99], which is a Java program designed to automate creating test cases for XML applications. This tool generates *random* instances of valid XML documents from a single input DTD according to user-provided constraints. In order to create user profiles, we implemented a query generator that takes a DTD as input and creates set of XPath queries based on input parameters similar to IBM's XML Generator. We describe our use of these tools for workload generation in the following section. In the experiments each user profile contains a single XPath query.

We created different workloads by changing the parameters of the document and query generators. For each experiment, we first generated a set of profiles and created the Query Index and other structures from them. Then, we ran the XML generator to produce a random XML document and submitted that document to the system. We measured the "filter time" as the total time to find all matching profiles — the costs of creating the document and profiles and of sending the document to the users are not included in this metric. For each experimental setting we generated and filtered XML documents until the 90% confidence intervals for the measured filter times were within plus or minus 3% of the mean.

6.2 Workload Parameters

Descriptions of the parameters used in the experiments and their value ranges are shown in Table 1. P denotes the number of profiles in the Query Index, which is used to measure the scalability of the system in terms of number of users. The *maximum* depth (i.e., the level number of the lowest level) of the XML document and XPath queries is denoted by D. For a given experiment, D is set to the same value for both documents and queries. However, due to differences in the way the generators work, the actual number of levels in the documents and queries tends to be different. The document generator always starts from the root of the DTD, while the query generator may start at any level depending on which element node it initially chooses. Also, the document generator always includes elements that are identified as "required" in the DTD, so it sometimes generates documents that are deeper than the maximum depth. Thus, for a given value of D the average depths of the documents tend to be larger than the average depths of the queries. Table 2 shows the mean depth values of the documents and queries with various D values. Note that the average depth of a document is 2 for input level 1 due to the presence of required elements at level 2 in the NITF DTD.

Parameter	Range	Description
P	1,000 to 100,000	Number of Profiles
D	1 to 10	Maximum depth of the XML document and queries
W	20% to 80%	Probability of a wildcard ('*') in the element nodes of the queries
F	0 to 3	Level of the element node filter in the queries. 0 means there is no element node filter.
S	1% to 100%	Selectivity of the element node filter
θ	0 and 1	Skewedness of element names in query generation

Table 1: Workload Parameters

Input Max Depth	Avg Doc Depth	Avg Query Depth (Uniform)	Avg Query Depth (Skewed)
1	2	1	1
2	2	2	2
3	2.99	2.65	2.64
4	3.63	3.04	2.96
6	4.36	3.34	3.21
8	4.76	3.4	3.23
10	5.09	3.42	3.24

Table 2: Mean Depth of Workload Document and Queries

Four additional parameters are used to help shape the query workload. W is the probability that a given element node in a query will be a wildcard operator. F and S are used to control the presence and characteristics of filters in the queries. F determines which level of a query (if any) will contain a filter, and S specifies the selectivity of such a filter if it does exist. Finally θ is the parameter of the zipf distribution [Zip49] that is used to determine the skewedness of the choice of element names at each level in query generation. When it is 0, each element name in the query is selected randomly from the set of element names allowed at its level with a uniform distribution, whereas at a setting of 1, the choice is highly skewed. Note that all of the documents are generated with a uniform distribution of element names as provided by the IBM's XML generator.

6.3 Analysis of Experimental Results

We now describe the results of four experiments that investigate the performance of the filtering algorithms for varying 1) number of profiles; 2) depth of queries and documents; 3) probability of wildcards; and 4) filter placement and selectivity.

Experiment 1: Varying P (D=5, W=0, F=0)

In this set of experiments we measure the filter time of the algorithms as the number of profiles in the system is increased. For the results shown we fixed the maximum depth of the input XML documents and queries to 5. Figure 6 shows the results when element names used in queries are chosen with a uniform distribution. As expected, the Basic method has the lowest performance. List Balance provides some improvement, but Prefiltering dramatically improves the performance of both algorithms since most of the profiles are filtered out in the prefiltering step. In this experiment, on average, 2.6% of profiles matched a given document. By itself, the Basic algorithm examined about 12% of the profiles in order to find these. In contrast, when prefiltering was applied, only 3.5% of the profiles were examined in the second phase. In this case (and in virtually all others we have studied) the combination of List Balance and Prefiltering provided the best performance. Here, with 100,000 profiles in the system, that combination was over 5 times faster than the basic approach.[3]

---

[3] Note that we were able to run experiments on our (very modest) hardware configuration with at most 100,000 queries since increasing beyond that point led to swapping, which distorted the results.

The results of running this experiment with the skewed selection of elements are shown in Figure 7. In this case, the execution times are higher for all of the algorithms since more profiles are examined and more match the document due to the element skew. In this case the benefits of Prefiltering are less dramatic than in the uniform case and in fact, List Balance performs substantially better than the combination of Prefiltering and Basic. With element selection skew, the profiles tend to be more similar so the selectivity of prefiltering is lower. In contrast, the List Balance enhancement is highly effective here, as it evens out the distribution of profiles to Candidate Lists. Again in this case, the combination of List Balance and Prefiltering performs the best, although here there is only a slight advantage over List Balance.

Experiment 2: Varying D (P=50,000, W=0, F=0)

The depth of the XML documents and queries in user profiles varies according to application characteristics. In this experiment we evaluated the performance of the algorithms as the maximum depth is varied. Here, we fixed the number of profiles at 50,000 and varied the maximum depth of the XML document and queries from 1 to 10. At each step, the same depth value is used in generating the document and queries.

Figure 8 shows the filter time as D is increased in the case that the element names in queries are selected uniformly. The filter time increases for all the algorithms because the input document contains more elements with each additional level resulting in more checking of path nodes, and because the queries become larger. Again, Basic performs worst while the combination of List Balance and Prefiltering performs best. One interesting aspect of this graph is that beyond a depth of 8, the List Balance and Basic with Prefiltering lines cross. This happens because the increase in levels decreases the effectiveness of prefiltering (more opportunities for element names to appear in queries) while List Balancing benefits slightly by having more choices for the pivot elements.

For the skewed case (Figure 9), there is a sharp increase in the filtering time of Basic because as the number of levels increases, more and more *popular* elements appear in the document, boosting the filtering time. List Balance has a smaller increase compared to Basic, thanks to the presence of less popular elements in the queries which can be used as pivot nodes. After level 4, the presence of element names in the queries does not change much because of skewed distribution, hence the workload characteristics remain similar. As a result, the filtering times of the algorithms increase just slightly. At level 1 and 2 prefiltering discards virtually none of the profiles, so the prefiltering algorithms have worse performance than the others at these points. Starting from level 3, prefiltering becomes more effective due to the presence of less popular elements in queries resulting in better filter time. These experiments indicate that the combination of List Balance and Prefiltering can adapt well to different workload characteristics.

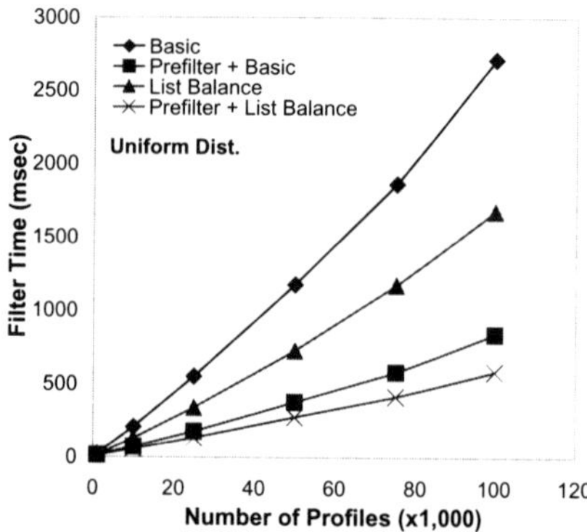

Figure 6: Uniform Dist. Varying P
(D=5, θ=0, W=0, F=0)

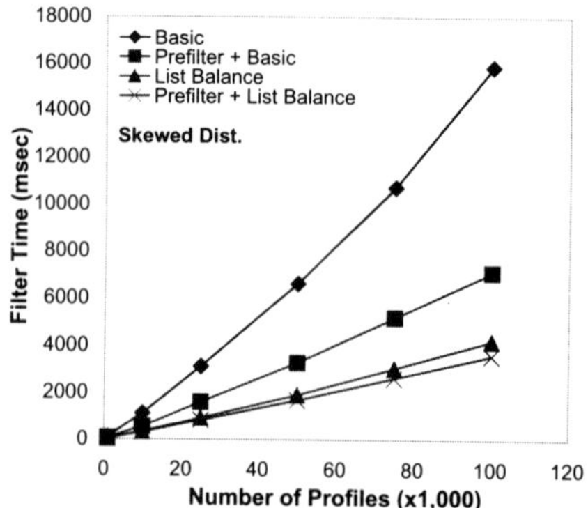

Figure 7: Skewed Dist. Varying P
(D=5, θ=1, W=0, F=0)

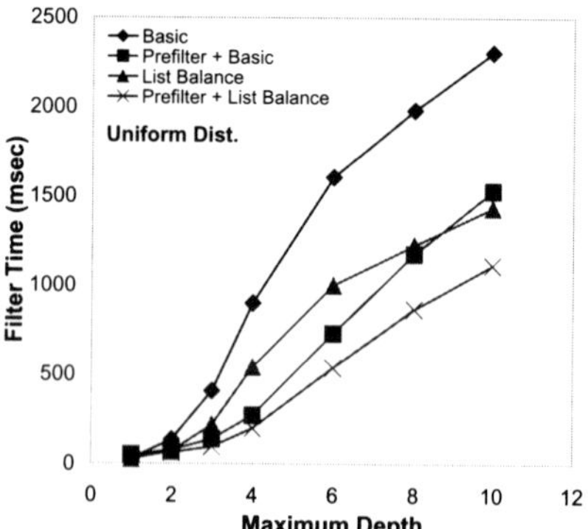

Figure 8: Uniform Dist. Varying D
(P=50,000, θ=0, W=0, F=0)

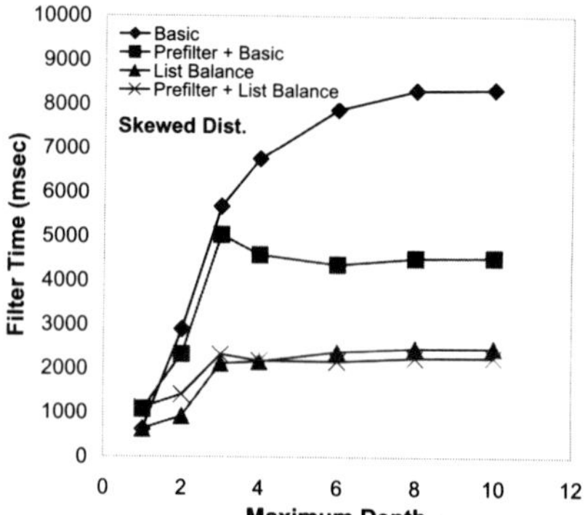

Figure 9: Skewed Dist. Varying D
(P=50,000, θ=1, W=0, F=0)

Experiment 3: Varying W (P=50,000, D=6, F=0)

In this experiment we evaluate the effect of the number of wildcards ('*') that are likely to occur in the queries. We performed this experiment for 50,000 profiles, and set the maximum depth of queries and documents to 6. In each step of the experiment, we varied the probability that an element node may be a wildcard. Figure 10 shows the filtering times of the algorithms as the probability of wildcards is increased. The important result in this experiment is that, with Prefiltering, the algorithms are relatively insensitive to wildcards, while without prefiltering, they are quite sensitive to them. This is because as more wildcards are introduced, the selectivity of prefiltering drops, but the work done in the second step also decreases. List Balance has slightly better performance than List Balance with Prefiltering when the wildcard probability is very high (>60%), but it is unlikely that many profiles will have such a high proportion of wildcards.

Experiment 4: Varying F and S (P=50,000, D=6, W=0)

We performed two experiments to find out the effect of element node filters in the queries. In particular, we examined the effect of the level of the filter and its selectivity on filter time. For this purpose, we modified the NITF DTD and added a fixed attribute named *dummy* to every element.

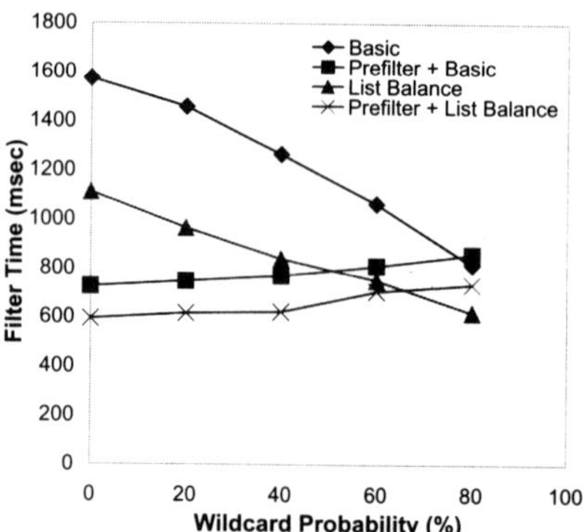

Figure 10: Varying Wildcard Probability
(P=50,000, D=6, θ=0, F=0)

Then, in the queries we created a simple element node filter containing only that fixed attribute. We adjusted the selectivity of the element node filters by changing the appearance probability of *dummy* in the input document using a parameter (called fixedOdds) of the XML document generator.

In the first experiment, we placed a single element node filter in different levels of the query and fixed the query selectivity at 10%. We performed the experiment with 50,000 profiles a maximum depth of 6; No wildcards were used in the queries. The results of this experiment are shown in Figure 11. All the algorithms benefit from the element node filter when it is in the upper levels of the queries as in such cases most of the queries are filtered out in their early level checks. As we move the element node filter to deeper levels, its effect diminishes because the path length of some queries is less than the filter level (so they do not have a filter).

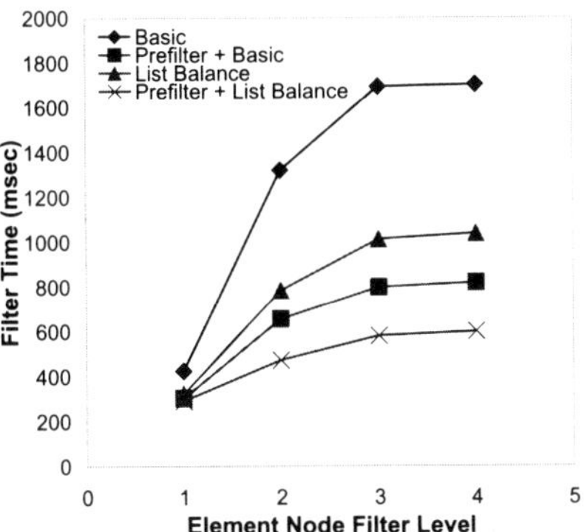

Figure 11: Varying Filter Level
(P=50,000, D=6, θ=0, W=0, S=10)

In the second experiment, we fixed the element node filter at level 2 and varied its selectivity. We assigned selectivity values in logarithmic scale to focus on the behavior of the algorithms when the filter is highly selective. As shown in Figure 12, the selectivity of the element node filter has a relatively small effect on the algorithms and affects all of them to almost the same degree. The slope of the Basic algorithm is a bit sharper than others as it has much worse performance than the others when the effect of the filter diminishes.

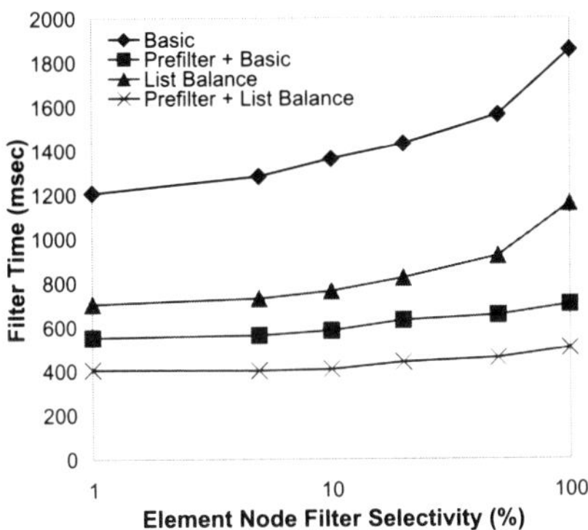

Figure 12: Varying Filter Selectivity
(P=50,000, D=6, θ=0, W=0, F=2)

Summary of Results:
These experiments demonstrate the scalability of the XFilter approach and show that the extensions we proposed for Basic provide substantial improvements to the performance in different document, workload and scale scenarios. In particular, List Balance with Prefiltering has the best filtering performance in virtually all cases. List Balance is also effective by itself when the distribution of elements in queries is highly skewed. Since many SDI applications exhibit such skew, and because List Balance is simpler and requires less space than List Balance with Prefiltering, it may be preferable in many practical cases.

7 Conclusions

In this paper, we have proposed an XML document filtering system, called *XFilter*, for Selective Dissemination of Information (SDI). XFilter allows users to define their interests using the XPath query language. This approach enables the construction of more expressive profiles than current IR-based profile models by exploiting the structural information available in XML documents.

We developed indexing mechanisms and matching algorithms based on a modified Finite State Machine (FSM) approach that can quickly locate and evaluate relevant profiles. By converting XPath queries into a Finite State Machine representation, XFilter is able to (1) handle arbitrary regular expressions in queries, (2) efficiently check element ordering and evaluate filters in queries, and (3) cope with the semi-structured nature of XML documents. We described a detailed set of experiments that examined the performance of the basic XFilter approach and its extensions. The experiments showed that XFilter is effective for different document, workload and scale scenarios, which makes it suitable for use in Internet-scale SDI systems.

XFilter has been implemented in the context of the Dissemination-Based Information Systems (DBIS) project [AAB+99]. This project is developing a toolkit for constructing adaptable, application-specific middleware that incorporates multiple data delivery mechanisms in complex networked environments. We intend to integrate XFilter as the primary filtering mechanism for the toolkit.

Acknowledgments. We would like to thank Fatma Özcan for her useful comments on earlier drafts of the paper.

References

[AAB+98] D. Aksoy, M. Altinel, R. Bose, U. Cetintemel, M. Franklin, J. Wang, S. Zdonik, "Research in Data Broadcast and Dissemination", *Proc. 1st Intl. Conf. on Advanced Multimedia Content Processing*, Osaka, Japan, November, 1998.

[AAB+99] M. Altinel, D. Aksoy., T. Baby, M. Franklin, W. Shapiro, S. Zdonik, "DBIS Toolkit: Adaptable Middleware for Large Scale Data Delivery" (Demo Description), *Proc. ACM SIGMOD Conf.*, Philadelphia, PA, June, 1999.

[AQM+97] S. Abiteboul, D. Quass, J. McHugh, J. Widom, J. Wiener, "The Lorel Query Language for Semistructured Data", *International Journal on Digital Libraries*, 1(1):68–88, April, 1997.

[BC92] N. J. Belkin, B. W. Croft, "Information filtering and information retrieval: Two sides of the same coin?", *CACM*, 35(12):29–38, December 1992.

[BDHS96]   P. Buneman, S. Davidson, G. Hillebrand, D. Suciu, "A Query Language and Optimization Techniques for Unstructured Data", *Proc. ACM SIGMOD Conf.*, Montreal, Canada, June, 1996.

[BN96]   R. Baeza-Yates, G. Navarro, "Integrating Contents and Structure in Text Retrieval", *ACM SIGMOD Record*, 25(1):67-79, 1996.

[BPS98]   T. Bray, J. Paoli, C. M. Sperberg-McQueen, "Extensible Markup Language (XML) 1.0", *http://www.w3.org/TR/REC-xml*, February, 1998.

[CAW98]   S. Chawathe, S. Abiteboul, J. Widom., "Representing and Querying Changes in Semistructured Data", *Proc. 14th ICDE*, Orlando, Florida, February 1998.

[CD99]   J. Clark, S. DeRose, "XML Path Language (XPath) Version 1.0", W3C Recommendation, *http://www.w3.org/TR/xpath*, November, 1999.

[CDTW00]   J. Chen, D. DeWitt, F. Tian, Y. Wang, "NiagaraCQ: A Scalable Continuous Query System for Internet Databases", *Proc. ACM SIGMOD Conf.*, Dallas, TX, May, 2000.

[CFG00]   U. Cetintemel, M. Franklin, C. L. Giles, "Self-Adaptive User Profiles for Large Scale Data Delivery", *Proc. 16th ICDE*, San Diego, February, 2000.

[Cla99a]   J. Clark, "expat - XML Parser Toolkit", *http://www.jclark.com/xml/expat.html*, 1999.

[Cla99b]   J. Clark, "XSL Transformations (XSLT) Version 1.0", *http://www.w3.org/TR/xslt*, November, 1999.

[Cov99]   R. Cover, "The SGML/XML Web Page", *http://www.oasis-open.org/cover/sgml-xml.html*, December, 1999.

[DDM99]   S. DeRose, R. Daniel Jr., E. Maler, "XML Pointer Language (XPointer)", *http://www.w3.org/TR/WD-xptr*, December, 1999.

[DFF+98]   A. Deutsh, M. Fernandez, D. Florescu, A. Levy, D. Suciu, "XML-QL: A Query Language for XML", *http://www.w3.org/TR/NOTE-xml-ql*, August, 1998.

[FZ98]   M. Franklin, S. Zdonik, ""Data in Your Face": Push Technology in Perspective", *Proc. ACM SIGMOD Conf.*, Seattle, WA, June, 1998.

[FD92]   P. W. Foltz, S. T. Dumais, "Personalized information delivery: an analysis of information filtering methods", *CACM*, 35(12):51–60, December 1992.

[HCH+99]   E. N. Hanson, C. Carnes, L. Huang, M. Konyola, L. Noronha, S. Parthasarathy, J. B. Park, A. Vernon, "Scalable Trigger Processing", *Proc. 15th ICDE*, pp. 266-275, Sydney, Australia, 1999.

[IBM99]   A. L. Diaz, D. Lovell, "XML Generator", *http://www.alphaworks.ibm.com/tech/xmlgenerator*, September, 1999.

[LPT99]   L. Liu, C. Pu, W. Tang, "Continual Queries for Internet Scale Event-Driven Information Delivery", *Special Issue on Web Technologies, IEEE TKDE*, January, 1999.

[MD89]   D. McCarthy, U. Dayal, "The Architecture of an Active Database Management System", *Proc. ACM SIGMOD Conf.*, pp. 215-224, May, 1989.

[Meg98]   Megginson Technologies, "SAX 1.0: a free API for event-based XML parsing", *http://www.megginson.com/SAX/index.html*, May, 1998.

[New00]   Newspack, The Wavo Corporation, *http://www.wavo.com*, 2000.

[Sal89]   G. Salton, "Automatic Text Processing", *Addison Wesley*, 1989.

[SJGP90]   M. Stonebraker, A. Jhingran, J. Goh, S. Potamianos, "On Rules, Procedures, Caching and Views in Data Base Systems", *Proc. ACM SIGMOD Conf.*, pp. 281-290, 1990.

[TGNO92]   D. B. Terry, D. Goldberg, D. A. Nichols, B. M. Oki, "Continuous queries over append-only databases", *Proc. ACM SIGMOD Conf.*, pp. 321–330, June 1992.

[VH98]   E. Voorhees, D. Harman, "Overview of the Seventh Text REtrieval Conference (TREC-7)", *NIST*, Gaithersburg, Maryland, November, 1998.

[YM94]   T. W. Yan, H. Garcia-Molina, "Index Structures for Selective Dissemination of Information Under Boolean Model", *ACM TODS*, 19(2):332–364, 1994.

[YM95]   T. W. Yan, H. Garcia-Molina. "Sift - A tool for wide-area information dissemination". *Proc. of the 1995 USENIX Tech. Conf.*, pp. 177-186, 1995.

[WF89]   J. Widom, S. J. Finklestein, "Set-Oriented Production Rules in Relational Database Systems", *Proc. ACM SIGMOD Conf.*, pp. 259-270, 1990.

[Zip49]   G. K. Zipf, *Human Behavior and Principle of Least Effort*, Addison-Wesley, Cambridge, Massachusetts, 1949.

Efficiently Publishing Relational Data as XML Documents

Jayavel Shanmugasundaram*   Eugene Shekita   Rimon Barr[+]

Michael Carey[θ]   Bruce Lindsay   Hamid Pirahesh   Berthold Reinwald

IBM Almaden Research Center
650 Harry Road
San Jose, CA 95139
jai@cs.wisc.edu, shekita@almaden.ibm.com, barr@cs.cornell.edu,
carey@acm.org, bgl@almaden.ibm.com, pirahesh@almaden.ibm.com, reinwald@almaden.ibm.com

Abstract

XML is rapidly emerging as a standard for exchanging business data on the World Wide Web. For the foreseeable future, however, most business data will continue to be stored in relational database systems. Consequently, if XML is to fulfill its potential, some mechanism is needed to publish relational data as XML documents. Towards that goal, one of the major challenges is finding a way to efficiently structure and tag data from one or more tables as a hierarchical XML document. Different alternatives are possible depending on when this processing takes place and how much of it is done inside the relational engine. In this paper, we characterize and study the performance of these alternatives. Among other things, we explore the use of new scalar and aggregate functions in SQL for constructing complex XML documents directly in the relational engine. We also explore different execution plans for generating the content of an XML document. The results of an experimental study show that constructing XML documents inside the relational engine can have a significant performance benefit. Our results also show the superiority of having the relational engine use what we call an "outer union plan" to generate the content of an XML document.

*Also at the University of Wisconsin, Madison, WI 53706.

[+]Work done at the IBM Almaden Research Center while the author was visiting from Cornell University, Ithaca, NY 14850.

[θ]Currently at Propel, 2350 Mission College Blvd., Santa Clara, CA 95054.

Proceedings of the 26th International Conference on Very Large Databases, Cairo, Egypt, 2000

1. Introduction

XML is rapidly emerging as a standard for exchanging business data on the World Wide Web. Its nested, self-describing structure provides a simple yet flexible means for applications to exchange data. In fact, there are already several industry proposals to standardize Document Type Descriptors (DTDs) [1], which are essentially schemas for XML documents. These DTDs are being developed for domains as diverse as electronic commerce [3] and real estate [10]. Despite the excitement surrounding XML, it is important to note that most operational business data, even for new web-based applications, continues to be stored in relational database systems. This is unlikely to change in the foreseeable future because of the reliability, scalability, tools, and performance associated with relational database systems. Consequently, if XML is to fulfil its potential, some mechanism is needed to publish relational data in the form of XML documents.

There are two main requirements for publishing relational data as XML documents. The first is the need for a *language* to specify the conversion from relational data to XML documents. The second is the need for an *implementation* to efficiently carry out the conversion. The language specification describes how to structure and tag data from one or more tables as a hierarchical XML document. One of this paper's contributions is a language specification based on SQL, with minor scalar and aggregate function extensions for XML construction. These extensions can be easily added to existing relational systems without departing from existing SQL semantics. Also, as a result of extending SQL in this manner, standard APIs like ODBC can be used to query and retrieve XML documents. This allows existing tools and applications to easily integrate relational data and XML documents. Other recent proposals, based on a combination of SQL and XML query languages [8], do not share these advantages.

Given a language specification for converting relational tables to XML documents, an implementation to carry out the conversion raises many challenges. Relational tables are flat, while XML documents are tagged, hierarchical and graph-structured. What is the best way to go from the former to the latter? In order to answer this question, we characterize the space of alternatives based on whether tagging and structuring are done early or late in query processing. We then refine this space based on how much processing is done inside the relational engine and explore various alternatives within this space. Our performance comparison of the alternatives using a commercial database system (DB2) shows that an "unsorted outer union" approach – based on late tagging and late structuring – is attractive when the resulting XML document fits in main memory, while a "sorted outer union" approach – based on late tagging and early structuring – performs well otherwise. Our results also show that constructing an XML document inside a relational engine is far more efficient than doing so outside the engine. Thus, constructing an XML document inside the relational engine has a two-fold advantage – not only does it allow existing SQL APIs to be reused for XML documents, but it is also much more efficient.

1.1 Relationship to Related Work

There has been significant recent interest in using relational database systems to store and query XML documents [6][9][13]. The focus of this paper, however, is on efficiently publishing *existing relational data* as XML documents and addressing several of the key difficulties [13] in that conversion.

As mentioned earlier, there are other language proposals for specifying the construction of relational data as XML documents [8]. A distinguishing feature of our approach is that it extends SQL naturally, thus allowing the existing APIs and processing infrastructure of relational database systems to be reused. For example, the relational engine can be used to perform all join/merge operations during the construction of XML documents.

The content of this paper is related to work on set-valued attributes in object-relational databases [15] and nested non-first normal form data models [11]. They each deal with nested structures, much like we deal with nested XML elements. There are, however, some key differences. First, much of that work has been on special-purpose engines to process nested structures. In contrast, our goal is to ride on an underlying relational DBMS. Second, tagging adds an extra dimension to the XML problem that is not present in the O-R set world. Finally, our output is a static XML document rather than a structure accessible through nested cursors. This allows more optimizations to be performed inside the RDBMS.

1.2 Roadmap

The rest of this paper is organized as follows. In Section 2 we provide a brief overview of XML, and in Section 3 we present our SQL-based language approach for publishing relational data as XML. In Section 4 we explore a range of implementation alternatives and in Section 5 we

```
<customer id="C1">
   <name> John Doe </name>
   <accounts>
      <account id="A1"> 1894654 </account>
      <account id="A2"> 3849342 </account>
   </accounts>
   <porders>
      <porder id="PO1" acct="A1">  // first purchase order
         <date>1 Jan 2000</date>
         <items>
            <item id="I1"> Shoes </item>
            <item id="I2"> Bungee Ropes </item>
         </items>
         <payments>
            <payment id="P1"> due January 15 </payment>
            <payment id="P2"> due January 20 </payment>
            <payment id="P3"> due February 15 </payment>
         </payments>
      </porder>
      <porder id="PO2" acct="A2">  // second purchase order
         ...
      </porder>
   </porders>
</customer>
```

Figure 1: An XML Document Describing a Customer

evaluate the performance of the alternatives. We present our conclusions and ideas for future work in Section 6.

2 An XML Primer

Extensible Markup Language (XML) [2] is a hierarchical format for information exchange in the World Wide Web. An XML document consists of nested element structures starting with the root element. Each element has a tag associated with it. In addition to nested elements, an element can have attributes and values or sub-elements. Figure 1 shows an XML document representing a customer in a simple e-commerce application, where each customer has a set of accounts and a set of purchase orders, and each purchase order in turn has a set of items and a set of payments. The customer is represented by the <customer> element, which appears at the root of the document. The customer has an id attribute, which is a special kind of attribute that uniquely identifies an element in an XML document. Each customer has a name, represented by the <name> sub-element nested under customer. A customer element also has nested sub-elements representing the accounts and purchase orders associated with the customer. Each of these has other attributes and sub-elements.

An interesting feature to note in Figure 1 is that the purchase order elements have an attribute called "acct". This is a field that is of type IDREF (such typing information is specified in a Document Type Descriptor [1] – not shown here – associated with an XML document), and it logically points to an element having the same value as its ID. Thus, the first purchase order points to the second account, while the second purchase

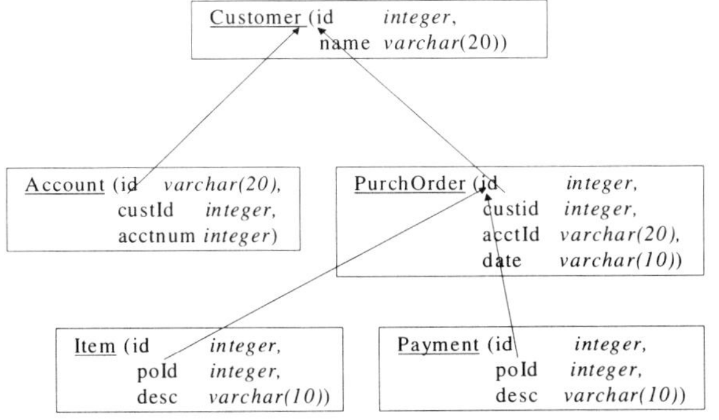

Figure 2: Customer Relational Schema

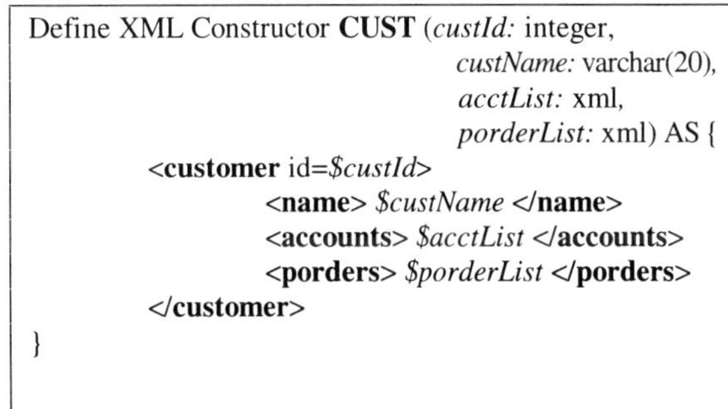

Figure 4: Definition of an XML Constructor

```
01. Select  cust.name, CUST(cust.id, cust.name,
02.                        (Select  XMLAGG(ACCT(acct.id, acct.acctnum))
03.                         From  Account acct
04.                         Where  acct.custId = cust.id),
05.                        (Select  XMLAGG(PORDER(porder.id, porder.acct, porder.date,
06.                                        (Select  XMLAGG(ITEM(item.id, item.desc))
07.                                         From  Item item
08.                                         Where  item.poId = porder.id),
09.                                        (Select  XMLAGG(PAYMENT(pay.id, pay.desc))
10.                                         From  Payment pay
11.                                         Where  pay.poId = porder.id)))
12.                         From  PurchOrder porder
13.                         Where  porder.custId = cust.id))
14. From  Customer cust
```

Figure 3: SQL Query to Construct XML Documents from Relational Data

order points to the first account. Another key feature of the XML model is that elements can be ordered. For example, purchase orders could be ordered by date to make the most recent purchases appear first in the document. More details on XML can be found in [2].

3 A SQL-Based Language Specification

A key requirement for converting relational data to XML documents is a language to specify the conversion. While one approach is to invent a new language specifically for this purpose [8], our approach is to harness and extend the power of SQL to specify the conversion of relational data to XML documents. Nested SQL statements are used to specify nesting, and SQL functions are used to specify XML element construction.

Consider the relational schema shown in Figure 2, which models the customer information of Figure 1 in relational form. As shown, there are customer, account, purchase order, item and payment tables. Each table has an id and other attributes associated with it, and there are foreign key relationships (shown by means of arrows) relating the tables. To convert data in this relational schema to the XML document in Figure 1, we can write a SQL query that follows the nested structure of the document, as shown in Figure 3.

The query in Figure 3 produces both SQL and XML data – each result tuple contains a customer's name together with the XML representation of the customer. The overall query consists of several correlated sub-queries. The easiest way to understand the query is to look at it from the top down. The top-level query retrieves each customer from the customer table. For each customer, a correlated sub-query is used to retrieve the customer's accounts (lines 2-4) and purchase orders (lines 5-13). Assume for the moment that each correlated sub-query returns an XML document fragment. The next step then is to create the customer XML elements. This is done by calling the CUST XML constructor (lines 1-13), which takes a customer name, account information (in XML form), and purchase order information (in XML form) as input and produces a customer XML element as output. The definition of the CUST XML constructor is shown in Figure 4. Conceptually, it should be viewed as a scalar function returning XML. For each input tuple, CUST tags the columns as specified and produces an XML fragment.

The correlated sub-queries can be interpreted similarly, with the ACCT, PORDER, ITEM and PAYMENT constructors defined much like CUST. Each nested query finally has to return one XML fragment. This is done using the aggregate function XMLAGG, which concatenates the XML fragments (e.g., ITEM fragments) produced by XML constructors. To order

XML fragments, the XMLAGG aggregate function needs to work on ordered inputs. Since ordered inputs to aggregate functions are not currently supported in SQL, extensions similar to recent SQL amendments [4] would be necessary to make this possible.

This section has presented one possible language specification for converting relational data to XML documents. The rest of the paper is more general in scope – it examines different *implementations* to carry out the conversion, independent of the specification language.

4 Implementation Alternatives

In order to understand the various alternatives for publishing relational data as XML documents, we characterize the solution space based on the main differences between relational tables and XML documents, namely, XML documents have *tags* and *nested structure,* while relational tables do not. Thus, in converting from relational tables to XML documents, tags and structure have to be added somewhere along the way. One approach is to do tagging as the final step of query processing (*late tagging*), while another approach is to do it earlier in the process (*early tagging*). Similarly, structuring can be done as the final step of query processing (*late structuring*) or it can be done earlier (*early structuring*). These two dimensions of tagging and structuring give rise to a space of alternatives shown pictorially in Figure 5. Each alternative in this space has variants depending on how much work is done inside the relational engine. Note that "inside the engine" means that tagging and structuring are done *completely inside* the relational engine, whereas "outside the engine" means that part, though not necessarily all, of that work is done outside the relational engine. Also note that early tagging with late structuring is not a viable alternative because physically tagging an XML document without having its structure makes no sense. We now explore the space of alternatives in detail by means of concrete examples.

4.1 Early Tagging, Early Structuring

In this class of alternatives, tagging and structuring are both done early in query processing. We first describe an "outside the engine" approach, where a significant amount of processing is done as a stored procedure, and then we describe two approaches where more processing is done inside the relational engine.

4.1.1 The *Stored Procedure* Approach

Perhaps the simplest technique for structuring relational data as an XML document is for an application or stored procedure to explicitly (iteratively) issue a nested set of queries that matches the structure of the desired XML document. Consider the example shown in Figure 1. First a query can be issued to retrieve root level elements (customers). Information about a customer such as their

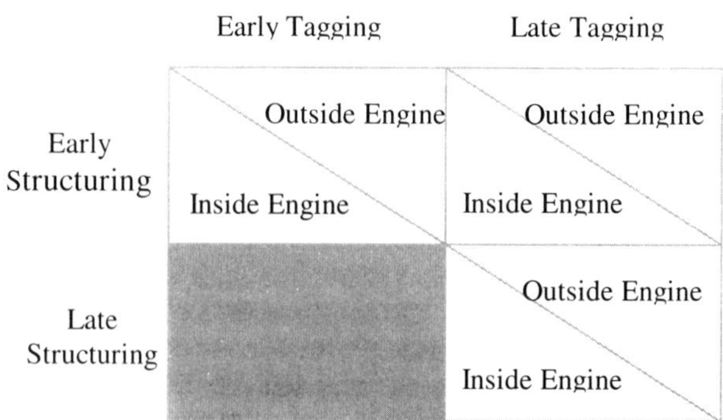

Figure 5: Space of Alternatives for Publishing XML

customer ID and customer name are retrieved, tagged, and output. Then, using the customer's ID, a query is issued to retrieve the customer's account information, which is then tagged and output. Next, while still on the same customer, a query is issued to retrieve the customer's purchase orders. Then, for each purchase order retrieved, a separate query is issued for the purchase order's items and the purchase order's payment information. Once this is done, the processing for one customer is complete. The same procedure is repeated for the next customer until the entire XML document has been constructed. Note that nested structures in the XML document can be ordered using an "order by" clause in the issued SQL queries.

The Stored Procedure approach essentially performs a nested-loop join outside the engine by issuing queries for each nested structure within the desired XML document. It falls under the category of early structuring because the queries that are issued mimic the structure of the result. Also, since tagging is done as soon as each nested structure becomes available, this approach falls under the category of early tagging.

Although the Stored Procedure approach is commonly used today, a major problem with it is that one or more SQL queries are issued *per tuple* for tables that have nested structures in the resulting XML document. The overhead of issuing so many queries can cause serious inefficiencies, as will be confirmed by the performance study in Section 5. Another significant problem with this approach is that it dictates a particular join order and the nested-loop join method, even when other join orders and/or join methods might be superior.

4.1.2 The *Correlated CLOB* Approach

One way to eliminate the overhead of issuing many queries SQL to the relational engine is to move processing inside the relational engine so that one large query with sub-queries, rather than many top-level queries, is executed. The challenge is then to have the relational engine tag and build up the nested structures so that the processing that was previously performed in a stored procedure now occurs inside the engine. This can be accomplished by adding engine support for the XML constructors and XMLAGG function that we described in Section 3. The query to produce the XML result can then

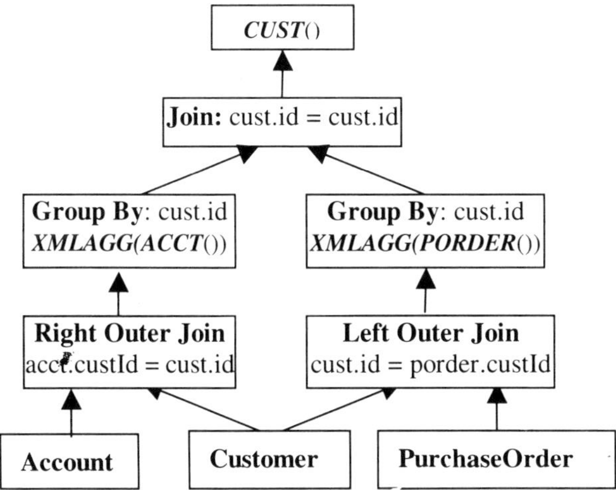

Figure 6: De-Correlated SQL Query with Aggregations

be executed as a nested SQL query. The query's execution would basically follow the language specification shown in Figure 3 by executing correlated sub-queries for nested queries. Since the XML document fragments created by the constructors can be of arbitrary size, the obvious choice is to represent them as large objects, such as Character Large Objects (CLOBs), inside the relational engine.

Because of correlation during execution, the Correlated CLOB approach still performs a nested-loop join. It is likely to out-perform the Stored Procedure approach, however, because a single query is issued to the relational engine. Nonetheless, the fact that intermediate XML structures are represented as CLOBs can lead to performance problems. This is because large objects are typically stored separately from the tuples they belong to. Thus, in parallel environments, fetching these objects (scattered around different nodes) can lead to significant performance degradation. Further, CLOBs may need to be written to a separate storage area on disk during sorts. Finally, each invocation of an XML constructor copies its inputs, which may include CLOBs, to a new CLOB. This repeated creation and copying of CLOBs can be costly.

4.1.3 The *De-Correlated CLOB* Approach

One disadvantage of the Correlated CLOB approach is that, because of its correlated sub-queries, it naturally implies a nested-loop join strategy. This can be avoided by performing query de-correlation [12] inside the relational engine to give the relational optimizer more flexibility. A de-correlated query execution plan for the correlated query of Figure 3 is shown in Figure 6. Though the Item and Payment tables are ignored for clarity, it is easy to see how this approach generalizes to arbitrary depths. First, each path from the root-level table to a leaf-level table is computed by joining the tables along the path (Customer joined with Account, Customer joined with Purchase Order). Outer joins are used because the information about a parent has to be preserved even if it has no children. The set of leaf-level XML elements corresponding to each leaf-level table is then built up (using aggregation) by grouping on the id columns of the parent tables on the path from the root-level table to the leaf-level table (e.g., custId). Higher-level structures are built up by joining on these id fields and using an XML constructor. This is done till the root level is reached.

Despite the fact that this approach is more flexible in allowing the engine to explore join strategies, it shares the same problems as the Correlated CLOB approach with respect to repeated copying, parallelism and materialization of CLOBs. This is because tagging and structuring are done early, thus creating opaque intermediate objects. Is it possible to defer tagging and structuring to arrive at a more efficient alternative? We explore this class of alternatives next.

```
Select cust.*, acct.*, porder.*, pay.*, item.*
From  Customer cust
        left join Account acct on cust.id = acct.custId
        left join PurchOrder porder on cust.id = porder.custId
        left join Item item on porder.id = item.poId
        left join Payment pay on porder.id = pay.poId
```

Figure 7: Query for *Redundant Relation* Content

4.2 Late Tagging, Late Structuring

In the class of alternatives that defer tagging and structuring, both tagging and structuring are done as the final step of constructing an XML document. The construction of an XML document is therefore logically split into two phases: (a) content creation, where relational data is produced, and (b) tagging and structuring, where the relational data is structured and tagged to produce the XML document. We first deal with content creation. We consider only "inside the engine" approaches so that database functionality, such as joins, can be exploited.

4.2.1 Content Creation: *Redundant Relation* Approach

One simple way to produce the needed content is to join all of the source tables. In our example, this would be done by joining the Customer, Accounts, Purchase Order, Item and Payment tables, as shown in Figure 7. Note that the join predicates relate parents to their children.

This approach has the advantage of using regular, set-oriented relational processing, but it also has a serious pitfall – it has both content and processing redundancy. To see this, consider what the result of the query in Figure 7 would look like. Each customer's account information would be repeated PO × IT × PA times, where PO is the number of purchase orders associated with the customer, IT is the number of items per purchase order, and PA is the number of payments per purchase order. The problem here is that multi-valued data dependencies [7] are created when we try to represent a hierarchical structure as a single table. This increases both the size of the result and the amount of processing to produce it, both of which are likely to severely impact performance.

4.2.2 Content Creation: *(Unsorted) Outer Union* Approach

The basic problem with the Redundant Relation approach is that the number of tuples in the relational result grows as the *product* of the number of children per parent. If we could limit the result's size to be the *sum* of the number of children per parent, redundancy could be reduced. To do this, we need to separate the representation of a given child of a parent from the representation of the other children of the same parent. For example, one tuple of the relational result should represent *either* an account *or* a purchase order associated with the customer, not both.

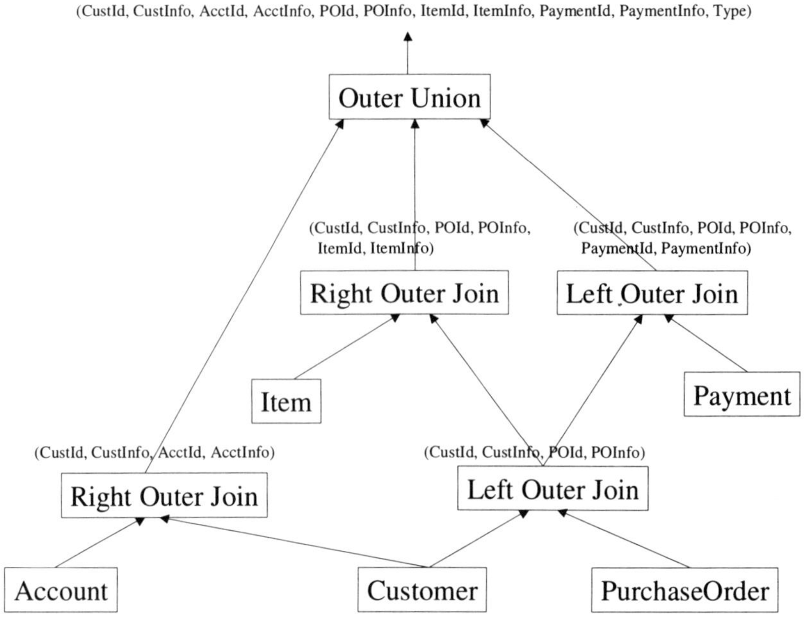

Figure 8 shows a query execution plan that reduces content redundancy for the query of Figure 3. First, as in the De-Correlated CLOB approach of Section 4.1.3, each path from the root-level table to a leaf-level table is computed by means of joins. In our example query, there are three such paths – Customer-Account, Customer-PurchaseOrder-Item and Customer-PurchaseOrder-Payment. Thus, Customers are joined with Accounts (one path), Customers are joined with Purchase Orders which are in turn joined with Items (another path) and Customers are joined with Purchase Orders which are in turn joined with Payments (final path). This computation is shown in Figure 8 (see everything below the outer union). Where possible, common sub-expressions are used so that redundant computation is avoided. Thus, in Figure 8, the join between Customers and Purchase Orders is shared between two path computations.

Each path computation produces one tuple per data item in the leaf level of the XML tree. Each tuple describing a leaf level data item includes the information about all of its ancestors (see the lists of columns above each join box in Figure 8). A separate tuple describing an ancestor needs to be present only if the ancestor has no children. The use of outer joins to relate a parent with its children ensures this semantics.

The final step in the process of creating the relational content is to glue together all the tuples representing leaf level elements in the XML tree (via the outer union in Figure 8) into a single relation. The obvious way to do this is to union the content corresponding to each leaf level element. There are, however, some complications with this strategy since the tuples corresponding to

Figure 8: The Outer Union Plan

different leaf level elements need not have the same number or types of columns. For example, tuples representing accounts need only four columns, while tuples representing items have six columns. In order to handle this heterogeneity, a separate column is allocated in the result of the union for each distinct column in the union's input. For each tuple representing a particular leaf level element and its ancestors, only a subset of these columns will be used and the rest will be set to null (hence the name *outer union* by analogy to outer join).

To keep track of the origin of each tuple, e.g. to distinguish an account tuple from an item tuple, a type column is added to the result of the outer union as well. We call the approach exemplified by Figure 8 the *Path Outer Union* approach because it computes each *path* from the root-level table to a leaf-level table and *outer unions* them.

The Path Outer Union approach eliminates much of the data redundancy (and associated computation redundancy) of the Redundant Relation approach. This is because children of the same parent are represented in separate tuples. However, there is still some data redundancy present. In particular, parent information is replicated with every child of the parent (e.g., customer information is replicated with every account). One way to get around this is to feed the parent information directly into the outer union operator and to carry only parent ids along with the children. This reduces data redundancy, but it increases the number of tuples in the result because each parent is now represented by a separate tuple. We refer to this option as the *Node Outer Union* approach to distinguish it from the earlier Path Outer Union approach.

One concern with the Outer Union approaches is that the number of columns in the result increases with the depth and width of the XML document. Though only a subset of the columns in a given tuple will have data values, with the remaining columns being null, in the absence of null value compression, this may lead to increased processing overhead due to larger tuple widths.

4.2.3 Structuring/Tagging: *Hash-based Tagger*

In the previous two sections, we discussed techniques to produce the relational content necessary for creating an XML document. The final step in the Late Structuring-Late Tagging alternatives is to tag and structure the results. This can be done either inside or outside the relational engine. If it is performed inside the relational engine, it can be implemented as an aggregate function. Such a function would be invoked as the last processing step, after the relational content has been produced, and this (single) aggregate function would logically perform the function of all the XML constructors and XMLAGGs in the user query. This ensures that large objects are not carried around during processing, which was one of the potential disadvantages of the CLOB approaches.

In order to tag and structure the results, either inside or outside the engine, we need to do two things: (a) group all siblings in the desired XML document under the same parent (and eliminate duplicates in the case of the Redundant Relation approach) and (b) extract the information from each tuple and tag it to produce the XML result. An efficient way to group siblings is to use a main-memory hash table to look up the parent of a node, given the parent's type and id information (including the ids of ancestors of the parent). Thus, whenever a tuple containing information about an XML element is seen, it is hashed on the element's type and the ids of its ancestors in order to determine whether its parent is already present in the hash table. If the parent is present, a new XML element is created and added as a child of the parent. If the parent is not present, then a hash is performed on the type and ids of all ancestors *except* that of the parent. This is to determine if the grandparent exists. If the grandparent is present, the parent is created and then the child is created. If the grandparent is also not present, the procedure is repeated until an ancestor is present in the hash table or the root of the document is reached.

After all the input tuples have been hashed, the entire tagged structured can be written out as an XML file. If a specific order is required for the elements of the resulting XML document, then that order can either be maintained as children are added to a parent or it can be enforced by a final sort before writing out the XML document.

The main limitation of using a hash-based tagger is that performance can degrade rapidly when there is insufficient memory to hold the hash table and the intermediate result. However, it may be possible to partition the data into memory-sized chunks, much like in a hash join [14]. Exactly how to do this partitioning (and merging) is left for future work.

4.3 Late Tagging, Early Structuring

The main problem with the Late Tagging-Late Structuring approaches we just considered is that complex memory management needs to be performed in the hash-based tagger when memory is scarce. To eliminate this problem, the relational engine can be used to produce "structured content", which can then be tagged using a *constant space* tagger. We first explore a technique to produce structured content before describing the constant space tagger.

4.3.1 Structured Content Creation: *Sorted Outer Union* Approach

The key to structuring relational content is to order it the same way that it needs to appear in the result XML document. This can be achieved by ensuring that:

1) *All of the information about a node X in the XML tree occurs either before or along with the information about the children of X in the XML tree.* This essentially says that parent information occurs before, or with, child information.

2) *All tuples representing information about a node X and its descendants in an XML tree occur together.* This ensures that information about a particular node and its descendants is not mixed in with information about non-descendant nodes.

3) *The relative order of the tuples matches that of any user-specified order.* This is to handle user defined ordering requests.

We now show that performing a single final relational sort of the unstructured relational content is sufficient to ensure these properties. Our discussion here will be based on the Node (Unsorted) Outer Union approach for constructing unstructured relational content. The solution for the Path Outer Union Approach is actually simpler because it always satisfies condition 1. It is also easy to see how the technique generalizes to the Redundant Relation approach. In the interest of space, we only illustrate how the approach works when there is no user-specified ordering requirement (i.e., considering only conditions 1 and 2)

To ensure conditions 1 and 2, all that is required is to sort the result of the Node Outer Union on its id fields, with the ids of parent nodes occurring higher in the sort order than the ids of children nodes. Thus, in Figure 8, sorting the result on the composite key (CustId, AcctId, POId, ItemId, PaymentId) will ensure that result is in document order. It is also important that tuples having null values in the sort fields occur before tuples having non-null values (i.e., nulls must sort low). Condition 1 is then satisfied because a tuple corresponding to a parent node (say, customer) will have null values for the child id columns (say, account id). Since we ensure that tuples with null values in sort columns occur first, parent tuples (customers) will always occur before child tuples (accounts). Also, because the parent's id (customer id) occurs before a child's id (account id) in the sort order, the children of a parent node are grouped together after the parent, thus satisfying condition 2.

The Sorted Outer Union approach has the advantage of scaling to large data volumes because relational database sorting is disk-friendly. The approach can also ensure user-specified orderings with little additional cost. However, it does do more work than necessary, since a total order is produced when only a partial order is needed. This is because we only require children to occur together with parents and the ordering among siblings is immaterial (without user-specified ordering requirements).

Classification		Approach	Short Name
Early Tag	Outside Engine	Stored Procedure	Stored Proc
Early Structure	Inside Engine	Correlated CLOB	CLOB-Corr
	Inside Engine	De-Correlated CLOB	CLOB-DeCorr
Late Tag	Inside or Outside Engine	Redundant Relation	Redundant R (In/Out)
Late Structure	Inside or Outside Engine	Unsorted Path Outer Union	Unsorted OU (In/Out)
	Inside or Outside Engine	Unsorted Node Outer Union	Unsorted NOU (In/Out)
Late Tag	Inside or Outside Engine	Sorted Path Outer Union	Sorted OU (In/Out)
Early Structure	Inside or Outside Engine	Sorted Node Outer Union	Sorted NOU (In/Out)

Figure 9: Summary of Approaches for Publishing XML

4.3.2 Tagging Sorted Data: *Constant Space Tagger*

Once structured content is created, as described in the previous two sections, the next step is to tag and construct the result XML document. Since tuples arrive in document order, they can be immediately tagged and written out as they are seen. The tagger only requires memory to remember the parent ids of the last tuple seen. These ids are used to detect when all the children of a particular parent node have been seen so that the closing tag associated with the parent can be written out. For example, after all the items and payments of a purchase order have been seen, the closing tag for purchase order (</porder>) has to be written out. To detect this, the tagger stores the id of the current purchase order and compares it with that of the next tuple. It should be clear that the storage required by the constant space tagger is proportional only to the level of nesting and is independent of the size of the XML document.

5. Performance Comparison of Alternatives for Publishing XML

We have now outlined a number of alternatives for creating XML documents from a relational database, which are summarized in Figure 9. Our qualitative assessments indicate that every alternative has some potential disadvantage. In this section, we will conduct a performance evaluation of the alternatives to determine which ones are likely to win in practice (and in what situations). Our focus in this preliminary performance evaluation is to study the effects of nesting flat relational tables as nested XML documents. Towards this end, we will first identify a set of parameters that are simple and yet can model a wide range of relational to XML conversions. In the experiments reported below, we do not consider queries with user-defined sort orders.

5.1 Modeling Relational to XML Transformations

In order to study the effects of nesting relational data as XML documents, we will vary the nesting of the queries specifying the construction of XML documents (see Figure 3 for an example query). In our experiments, the nesting of queries is characterized by two parameters. The first parameter is the *query fan out*. This corresponds to the maximum number of sub-queries directly nested under a parent (sub) query. For example, the query in Figure 3 has a query fan out of two because the (sub) queries in lines 1-15 and lines 5-13 each have two directly nested sub-queries (lines 2-4, 5-13 and lines 6-8, 9-12, respectively) while the other sub-queries (lines 2-4, 6-8, 9-12) have no directly nested sub-queries. The second parameter used to characterize nesting is *query depth*. This corresponds to the maximum nesting level of sub-queries. In our example in Figure 3, the query depth is three because there are three levels of query nesting – the first being the top level query (lines 1-15), the second being queries in lines 2-4 and 5-13 and the third being queries in lines 6-8 and 9-12.

In our experiments, we only consider "balanced" queries, where 1) each non-leaf (sub) query has the same number of directly nested sub-queries and 2) all leaf (sub) queries are at the same depth. This results in a simple set of parameters, each of which can be studied in isolation. Note that the query in Figure 3 is not balanced because it satisfies condition 1 but not condition 2. It is important to note that the query fan out and query depth do not directly specify the fan out or the depth of the result XML document. Even at low values of query fan out and query depth, the result XML document can be wide/deep depending on the XML constructors used (see Figure 4). The query fan out and query depth only specify the structure of the repeating "set" sub-elements, such as the accounts associated with a customer.

Our goal here is to study the effects of nesting relational data as XML documents, and not the complexity of the SQL used to create data for an XML element. Hence, for this performance study, the relational schema we use will reflect the nesting of the SQL query specifying the construction (e.g., like Figure 3 and Figure 2) and each relation in the schema will be a base table (it is, however, important to note that each relation could, in general, be an arbitrarily complex view). Each table has an ID field, which is its primary key. It also has a PJID (parent join id) field that serves as a foreign key for its parent. To match parents with their children, a join is specified between the ID and PJID field of the parent and child tables, respectively. In addition to these two fields, each table has two data fields of different types. The first is an integer field (IntVal) while the second is a 20 character long string field (CharVal).

We now identify two additional parameters that, given a schema, suffice to describe a specific database instance. The first parameter is *number of roots*, which specifies the number of tuples present in the table at the root level. The second parameter is the *number of leaf tuples*, which specifies the total number of tuples present in all the leaf-level tables combined. The number of tuples in each leaf-level table is thus the number of leaf tuples divided by the number of leaf-level tables. These two parameters together determine another important derivative parameter, the *instance fan out*, which specifies the number of children tuples of each type that a parent tuple has (under the assumption that every parent tuple has the same number of child tuples of a given type).

We have chosen to use the number of leaf tuples as the primary parameter and the instance fan out as a derivative parameter because the number of leaf tuples (where the bulk of the data resides) is directly related to the size of the XML document produced. Thus, holding the number of leaf tuples constant allows us to study how the different approaches behave when (essentially) the same amount of data is structured differently.

We now characterize the result XML document created for a given relational database instance. The integer and character column values of each tuple in the relational database instance are tagged as XML elements having a tag name that is 3 characters long. The XML fragments of child tuples are nested under the XML representation of the parent tuples. The result is always a single XML document. This was done to make the experimental results easy to interpret. Note that we do not explicitly consider selections on tables since the same performance effect can be explored by varying the number of roots and the number of leaf tuples.

5.2 Experimental Setup

To conduct our performance comparison, we implemented the various alternatives discussed in Section 4 in the code base of the DB2 Universal Database system. The XML constructors and XMLAGG were implemented as new built-in functions. The Stored Procedure approach was implemented as an "unfenced" stored procedure, i.e., it ran in the same address space as the relational database engine, to maximize performance. The other "outside the engine" approaches were implemented as local embedded-SQL programs, running on the same machine as the database server, to avoid unpredictable network

Parameter	Range of Values	Default
Query Fan Out	2, 3, 4	2
Query Depth	2, 3, 4	2
# Roots	1, 50, 500, 5000, 40000	5000
# Leaf Tuples	160000, 320000, 480000	320000

Figure 10: Parameter Settings for Experiments

delays. (We implemented "outside the engine" approaches as stored procedures as well, but since this did not significantly change their performance, these results are not included here.) A driver program, implemented as a local embedded-SQL program, was used to time the results on a warm DB2 cache. The XML[3] result was always written out as an NT file. All experiments were performed on a Pentium 366 MHz processor with 256 MB of main memory running Windows NT 4.0.

For the experiments, we varied the parameters discussed in Section 5.1 as shown in Figure 10. For each experiment, we varied one of these parameters and used default values for the rest. This enabled us to determine the effect of each parameter on performance. Indexes were created on the ID and PJID fields for all the tables in the relational schema. Detailed optimizer statistics were collected for each table and index before any queries were run. For most experiments, the sort heap and buffer pool sizes were set so that all processing would be done in main memory; the one exception is the experiments in Section 5.7, where the effect of reduced memory is considered. Since the Node and Path Outer Union approaches behave similarly in a wide range of situations, we only show the performance for the Path Outer Union for most of the studies. The relative performance of the Node and Path Outer Union approaches is discussed separately in Section 5.8.

5.3 Testing the Waters: Inside the Engine vs. Outside the Engine Approaches

To get an initial feel for the results, we first explore the effects of varying query fan out while holding the other parameters constant. The resulting time taken to construct the XML document for the "inside the engine" and the "outside the engine" approaches is shown in Figure 11 and Figure 12, respectively. The Redundant Relation approach is not shown in these graphs because it performs very badly with increasing fan out due to large data redundancy. In fact, the time for *just executing* the associated relational query, ignoring the time for tagging and writing the XML result to disk, at a query fan out of 4 was about 155 seconds. The performance of the Redundant Relation approach was also among the worst of all possible approaches throughout our experiments, so will not examine it further in our evaluation results.

The interesting thing to note in Figure 11 and Figure 12 is that while the Stored Procedure approach incurs a significant overhead because it issues many queries to the relational engine; the Correlated CLOB approach, its

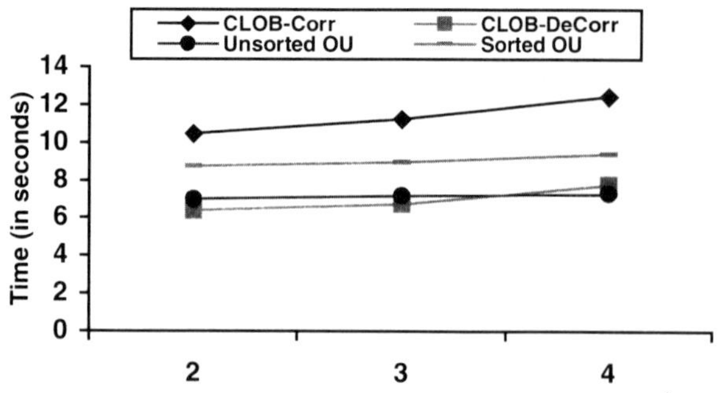

Figure 11: Varying Query Fan Out (Inside the Engine)

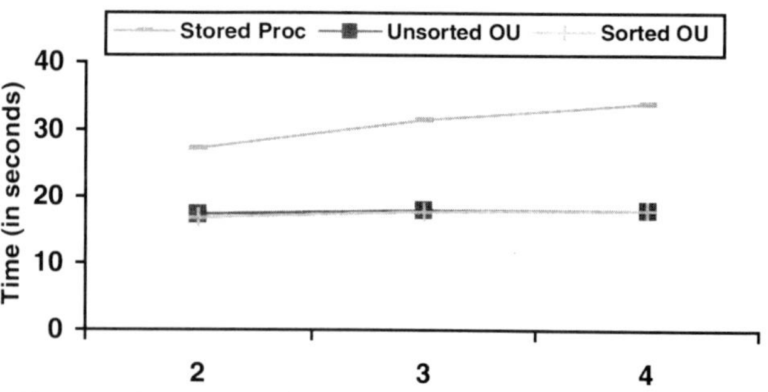

Figure 12: Varying Query Fan Out (Outside the Engine)

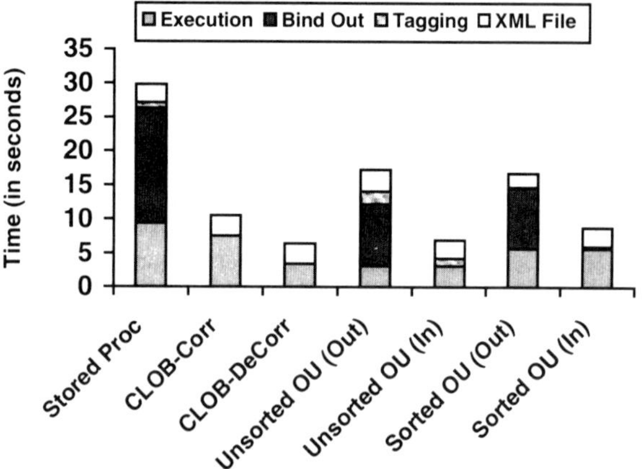

Figure 13: Break Down of XML Construction Time

"inside the engine" counterpart, takes less than one third of the time. This actually points to a more general trend. For the Unsorted and Sorted Outer Union approaches as well, the "inside the engine" versions take less than half the time to execute than the corresponding "outside the engine" versions. In order to explain these results, we broke down the time for creating XML document results.

For the "outside the engine" approaches, there are four components to generating the XML result: 1) the time to produce the relational content, either structured or unstructured, 2) the time to bind out the relational content to host variables outside the engine, 3) the time to tag and possibly structure the relational result, and 4) the time to write the XML result out to a file. For the "inside the engine" approaches, there are the same components except that there is no time spent in binding out the results. We measured each of these components independently for the various approaches. The tagging time for the CLOB approaches was not separated out because it forms an integral part of the computation.

Figure 13 shows this time break down and it is easy to see that the time to bind out (copy) tuples to host variables from the relational engine dominates the cost of the "outside the engine" approaches. These results were found to be true regardless of whether the bind out was done in a local client or in an unfenced stored procedure. Moreover, increasing the size of the communication buffer between the client application and the database server so that larger portions of the result could be copied over to the client address space in one chunk did not significantly reduce the bind-out cost. On the other hand, the "inside the engine" approaches eliminate the host variable bind-out cost for every tuple; their only bind-out is done for the final (single) result document. Consequently, the "inside the engine" approaches give rise to much better performance. This points to our first firm conclusion – *constructing an XML document should be done inside the engine to maximize performance.*

Since "inside the engine" approaches consistently outperform the "outside the engine" approaches, the rest of our experimental results will consider these approaches separately. Note that despite their poor relative performance, "outside the engine" approaches are valuable because they can be used with relational database systems that do not have support for the new XML scalar/aggregate functions mentioned in this paper.

5.4 Effect of Query Fan Out

We now re-examine the effect of varying the query fan out. For the "inside the engine" techniques, increasing the query fan out increases the time for producing the XML result, as shown in Figure 11. This is not surprising since increasing the query fan out increases the number of joins that need to be performed. What is more interesting is the relative performance of the different approaches. The Correlated CLOB approach, which utilizes many correlated sub-queries, performs worse than the other set-oriented plans. This is because the relational optimizer has no choice but to use the nested loop join strategy. Among the Outer Union based plans, the Unsorted Outer Union approach is more efficient than the Sorted Outer Union approach. This implies that the cost of sorting (and using a simple constant space tagger) is more expensive than avoiding the sort and using a more complex hash-based tagger (given sufficient main memory).

A rather surprising result is that the De-Correlated CLOB approach, despite having to repeatedly copy information and carry CLOBs during computation, performs fairly well and in fact, is the best strategy for low query fan outs. This is because the DB2 optimizer picked a plan whereby CLOBs could be retained in main memory without having to be materialized. Also, since

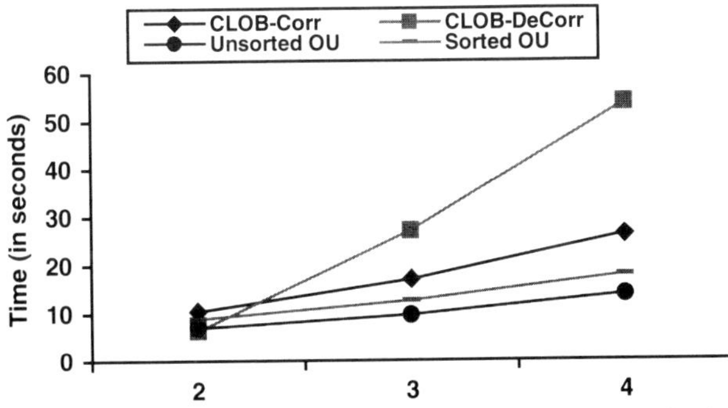

Figure 14: Varying Query Depth (Inside the Engine)

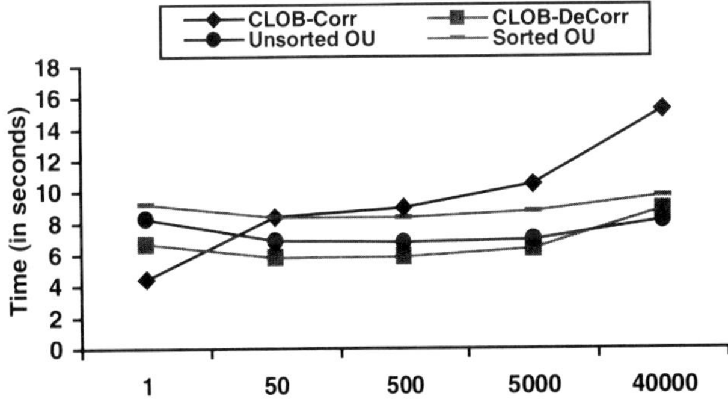

Figure 15: Varying Number of Roots (Inside the Engine)

the query depth is low, the overhead of repeatedly copying CLOBs is not significant.

Figure 12 shows the effects of query fan out on the "outside the engine" approaches. The Stored Procedure approach performs much worse than the Outer Union approaches because of the overhead of issuing many separate queries and using a fixed join strategy. Surprisingly, unlike for the "inside the engine" case, the execution times for the Sorted and Unsorted Outer Union approaches are approximately the same here. This is because the constant space tagger is a streaming operator; i.e., it produces a part of the XML document as soon as it sees a tuple. It can thus overlap tagging with writing the XML document to disk while the hash-based tagger has to process all input tuples before writing anything to disk.

5.5 Effect of Query Depth

We now turn our attention to the next parameter – query depth. Figure 14 shows the effect of varying the query depth parameter for the "inside the engine" approaches. While the execution time for all the approaches increases with query depth, it is interesting to note the dramatic increase for the De-Correlated CLOB approach. This is because, not surprisingly, the relational query optimizer makes mistakes when dealing with very complex queries at higher values of query depth. For instance, the query for a producing an XML document of query depth 4 has 15 aggregations (XMLAGGs) and 12 joins! In these cases, the optimizer makes some wrong decisions such as choosing to sort after an aggregation. This requires CLOBs to be written to a temporary space and materialized again later. This problem is compounded by the fact that the XMLAGG aggregate function is opaque to a traditional relational database optimizer and it thus has no good way to estimate the size of the CLOB result.

The effects of varying query depth for "outside the engine" approaches (not shown) are not very surprising, and essentially have the same form as Figure 12.

5.6 Effect of Number of Roots

The next parameter of interest is the number of roots. When the number of root elements is decreased for the "inside the engine" approaches, the performance of the

Correlated CLOB approach improves dramatically, relative to the other approaches (see Figure 15). This happens because only two correlated sub-queries have to be issued for constructing the XML document with one root element. A similar effect occurs (for similar reasons) with the Stored Procedure approach, the "outside the engine" counterpart of the Correlated CLOB approach (not shown). The relative performance of the outer union approaches remains unchanged.

5.7 Effects of Number of Leaf Tuples, Memory Size

For the next set of experiments, we varied the size of the data set by varying the number of leaf tuples. When there was sufficient memory, the relative performance of the various approaches did not change. However, when the amount of memory available for processing was reduced so that the XML document construction could not be performed entirely in main memory, the Unsorted Outer Union approaches were unable to proceed because our hash-based tagger cannot (currently) handle overflows. In contrast, the Sorted Outer Union approaches, based on the highly scalable relational sort, adapted gracefully.

5.8 Path Outer Unions vs. Node Outer Unions

We now compare the performance of the Node and Path Outer Union approaches. As mentioned earlier, their performance is nearly identical when there is sufficient main memory. In fact, despite its data redundancy, the Path Outer Union approach performs slightly better (by less than a second) because there are fewer tuples to process (and thus to bind out in case of the "outside the engine" approaches). The main difference between the two outer union approaches occurs when memory is scarce. In this case, for bushy trees (having high instance fan out) the Node Outer Union approaches perform better – a difference of up to three seconds – while for non-bushy trees (having low instance fan out), the Path Outer Union approaches perform better. This is because there is greater data redundancy in the Path Outer Union approach for bushy trees, and the overhead of spilling the extra data to disk exceeds the advantage of processing fewer tuples.

5.9 Summary of Experimental Results

To summarize, our performance comparison of the alternatives for publishing XML documents points to the following conclusions:

1) Constructing an XML document inside the relational engine is far more efficient that doing so outside the engine, mainly because of the high cost of binding out tuples to host variables.

2) When processing can be done in main memory, a stable approach that is always among the very best (both inside and outside the engine), is the Unsorted Outer Union approach.

3) When processing cannot be done in main memory, the Sorted Outer Union approach is the approach of choice (both inside and outside the engine). This is because the relational sort operator scales well.

6. Conclusion and Future Work

XML is rapidly emerging as the dominant standard for exchanging data on the World Wide Web, making the ability to publish data as XML increasingly important. In this paper, we have studied ways to publish relational data in the form of structured XML documents. We proposed a SQL language extension (the XML constructor) to specify the construction of XML documents from relational data. By extending SQL in this manner, applications can reuse the existing infrastructure and APIs for SQL to extract XML documents from relational sources.

The bulk of this paper was devoted to exploring efficient mechanisms for publishing relational data as XML documents, independent of the actual language used to specify this mapping. Towards this end, we first characterized the solution space based on the main differences between XML documents and relational tables, namely tags and nested structure. We then explored various alternatives in this space, paying special attention to the amount of processing that can be done inside the relational engine. Our experimental results showed that moving all processing inside the relational engine can provide a significant performance benefit. This is because the high cost of binding out tuples to host variables is eliminated. Our study also showed that the outer union approaches proposed in this paper provide an efficient and robust way to retrieve the relational data needed to construct an XML document.

Possibilities for future work include studying the impact of parallelism, new runtime operators inside the relational engine to enhance the performance of outer union plans, and techniques for efficient memory management to extend the useful range of the Unsorted Outer Union approach. In addition, we believe that the approaches outlined in this paper can be extended to handle the construction of recursive XML documents, such as part hierarchies and bill of material documents. Specifically, this requires modifications to the tagger algorithms so that nested structures of arbitrary depth can be handled and also to the outer union approaches so that information about the unbounded hierachy can be captured using key columns.

7. Acknowledgements

Amrish Lal implemented the initial version of the Correlated CLOB approach. Daniela Florescu provided insightful comments on a draft of this paper.

8. References

[1] J. Bosak, et. al., "W3C XML Specification DTD," http://www.w3.org/XML/1998/06/xmlspec-report.htm.

[2] T. Bray, J. Paoli, C. Sperberg-McQueen, "Extensible Markup Language (XML) 1.0," http://www.w3.org/XML/1998/06/xmlspec-report-19980910.htm.

[3] Commerce XML, http://www.cxml.org.

[4] "Database Language SQL. Amendment 1: On-Line Analytical Processing (SQL/OLAP)", SC32 N00379, November 1999.

[5] A. Deutsch, M. Fernandez, D. Florescu, A. Levy, D. Suciu, "XML-QL: A Query Language for XML," 8th International WWW Conference, Toronto, May 1999.

[6] A. Deutsch, M. Fernandez, D. Suciu, "Storing Semi-Structured Data with STORED," SIGMOD Conference, Philadelphia, May 1999.

[7] R. Fagin, "Multi-valued Dependencies and a New Normal Form for Relational Databases," ACM Transactions on Database Systems, 2(3), 1977.

[8] M. Fernandez, W. Tan, D. Suciu, "SilkRoute: Trading Between Relations and XML," 9th International WWW Conference, May 2000.

[9] D. Florescu, D. Kossman, "Storing and Querying XML Data using a RDBMS," IEEE Data Engineering Bulletin, Vol. 22, No. 3, 1999.

[10] Real Estate Transaction Standard, http://www.rets-wg.org.

[11] M. Scholl, et. al., "VERSO: A Database Machine Based On Nested Relations," Nested Relations and Complex Objects, Germany, April 1987.

[12] P. Seshadri, H. Pirahesh, T. Y. C. Leung, "Complex Query Decorrelation," International Conference on Data Engineering (ICDE), Louisiana, February 1996.

[13] J. Shanmugasundaram, et. al., "Relational Databases for Querying XML Documents: Limitations and Opportunities," Very Large Data Bases (VLDB) Conference, Scotland, September 1999.

[14] L. D. Shapiro, "Join Processing in Database Systems with Large Main Memories," ACM Transactions on Database Systems (TODS), Vol. 11, No. 3, 1986.

[15] M. Stonebraker, D. Moore, P. Brown, "Object-Relational DBMSs: Tracking the Next Great Wave", Morgan Kaufmann Publishers, September 1998.

Schema Mapping as Query Discovery

Renée J. Miller[*]
University of Toronto
miller@cs.toronto.edu

Laura M. Haas   Mauricio A. Hernández
IBM Almaden Research Center
{laura,mauricio}@almaden.ibm.com

Abstract

To enable modern data intensive applications including data warehousing, global information systems and electronic commerce, we must solve the *schema mapping* problem in which a source (legacy) database is mapped into a different, but fixed, target schema. Schema mapping involves the discovery of a query or set of queries that transform the source data into the new structure. We introduce an interactive mapping creation paradigm based on *value correspondences* that show how a value of a target attribute can be created from a set of values of source attributes. We describe the use of the value correspondence framework in *Clio*, a prototype tool for semi-automated schema mapping, and present an algorithm for query derivation from an evolving set of value correspondences.

1 Introduction

Many modern applications such as data warehousing, global information systems and electronic commerce need to take existing data with a particular structure or schema, and re-use it in a different form. These applications start with an understanding of how data will be used and viewed. That is, they start by determining a target schema. They then must create mappings between this target and the schemas of the underlying data sources. Creating those mappings is

today a largely manual (and extremely difficult) process. Transformation of the data is accomplished by complex programs, hand-written or pieced together by specialized tools (*e.g.*, for data warehouses), and these programs must then be carefully tuned to get reasonable performance. While the time required to generate and optimize these programs may be justified for data warehouses, it is unacceptable for e-commerce, where applications must evolve much more quickly, and it is awkward for applications which require direct access to source data (such as global information systems and e-commerce).

We show how the transformation process can be simplified and made more efficient and flexible by using database management systems as transformation engines. Data independent transformations, specified in SQL, can then be automatically optimized and parallelized by the DBMS for better performance. As many DBMS today can process queries over data they do not manage ([IBM97, CHS[+]95, Ora]), the DBMS can effectively handle the inter-source scheduling and data movement needed for transformations as well. Creating mappings becomes a process of query discovery: finding the queries or views that correctly transform the data to the desired schema.

By simplifying the task of mapping creation, we make it possible for DBMS to play a broader role in new applications, not merely as a provider of data, but as a manager of the transformations themselves. Modern DBMS are not only data management tools, they are query management tools. They incorporate a wealth of sophisticated knowledge about queries and query manipulation. While this knowledge has been targeted to the problem of query optimization to produce efficient execution plans, we show how the same infrastructure and similar reasoning can be applied to the problem of query discovery for integrating and transforming data. For both tasks, we are reasoning about the relationships between and equivalences of queries and schemas.

Clio [HMN[+]99] is a research prototype of a schema mapping creation tool. Clio produces view definitions that allow applications to directly access source data using a middleware query engine. Queries posed on

---

[*]Supported by an IBM University Partnership Grant and the Presidential Early Career Award for Scientists and Engineers (PECASE) under NSF Award # 9702974.

**Proceedings of the 26th VLDB Conference,
Cairo, Egypt, 2000.**

these views can be optimized normally by the query engine, so that only the data needed for a particular query is converted. Clio produces the SQL queries for the user, providing users with data samples and other feedback to allow them to understand the mappings produced.

In Section 2, we present a framework for mapping creation based on the notion of *value correspondences*. Value correspondences are an intuitive way of recording the relationships between source and target schemas. Given a set of value correspondences, we show how to compute the query or queries needed to perform the implied transformations (Section 3). Section 4 illustrates the use of our mapping algorithm for a data warehouse. We briefly discuss related work in Section 5 and conclude in Section 6.

2 A Framework for Query Discovery

The focus in schema mapping is on query discovery. By contrast, classical schema integration (including both view integration and database integration) is the activity of integrating a set of schemas into a unified representation [RR99]. Schema integration techniques typically distinguish two key tasks: creation of the integrated schema and creation of queries (mappings) between schemas. In the applications we consider, the target schema does not depend for its definition on the identity and structure of the sources. Hence, the problem of creating the integrated schema is no longer relevant. However, the need to create mappings between the source and the integration remains. Yet the problem of mapping generation between an integrated schema and the source schemas used to derive the integration is inherently different from that of deriving mappings between independently created schemas. In the former problem, the mapping is implicit to the derivation process. Indeed in their comprehensive schema integration survey, Ram and Ramesh devote only a single paragraph to mapping generation [RR99]. This is not an oversight on their part, but rather a true reflection of the methodologies they survey.

As with schema integration, the schema mapping task cannot be fully automated since the syntactic representation of schemas and data do not completely convey the semantics of different databases. For example, it is not possible to know with complete certainty from the schema and data alone whether the `Emp` relation in one schema has the same meaning as the `Employee` relation in another. As a result, for both schema mapping and schema integration, we must rely on an outside source to provide some information about how different schemas (and data) correspond.

However, the different nature and goals of these two tasks necessitate the use of different types of correspondences. For the schema integration, which is predominantly a schema design problem, design level assertions detailing how schema constructs relate are appropriate [RR99]. These assertions state how the **set** of values of a construct in one source schema relate to the **set** of values of a construct in another source schema. For the mapping problem, we claim that a different type of assertion is both more informative and easier to elicit from a user. We call this new type of assertion a *value correspondence*.

2.1 Overview of Value Correspondences

Informally, a value correspondence is a pair, consisting of (1) a function defining how a value (or combination of values) from a source database can be used to form a value in the target, and (2) a filter, indicating which source values should be used. For example, a string concatenation function can be used to indicate that a value of the staff-id attribute of the target schema is formed by concatenating the letter 'E' to an employee number from the source, along with a filter that selects only active employees. Similarly, a value of the appellation attribute may be formed by concatenating together a title and name value from the source. There might be a filter on title, or any other attribute(s), or the filter might be "True". From these examples, it should be clear that schema assertions and value correspondences are related. An attribute assertion that an Attribute A is a subset of Attribute D may imply the use of the identity function and some filter as a value correspondence to map values of A to values of D [RR99]. However, the main focus of schema assertions is on specifying how the values of one attribute (or other schema constructs) **as a set** relate with the set of values of another attribute. It is this set relationship that drives the integration algorithms [RR99].

In contrast, in Clio, the value correspondences drive the integration. This distinction is important for two reasons. First, we argue that it is natural for a DBA to be able to specify value correspondences indicating the form in which a source value should appear in the target. Even DBAs with incomplete knowledge of the schema can specify the correspondences for those values they understand. To be accurate, the set relationships of attribute assertions require a more complete knowledge of the schema and relationships between components of the schema. Inaccurate or imprecise assertions (for example, asserting that two attributes overlap when there is actually a set containment relationship) will lead to incorrect integrations. Second, the knowledge provided by these two different types of statements is very different. This difference gives rise to a new approach to reasoning about and creating schema assertions that has not previously been explored. Specifically, we propose an iterative *integration-by-example* paradigm under which a DBA specifies how example values are mapped and the tool attempts to deduce a likely schema mapping. In the process, the DBA may be prompted for information relevant to choosing between alternative mappings.

This information may sometimes include information about the set relationships (but only if this information is necessary for disambiguating between different mappings).

Note that we are not arguing that the information provided by schema assertions is irrelevant. On the contrary, we are arguing it may not be required to deduce all mappings and that it may be impossible for a DBA to specify *a priori* without having seen even a partial or potential mapping. Furthermore, we do not use schema level assertions to drive the mapping derivation process. Rather, we make use of reasoning about schemas (and queries) and about possible alternative schemas (and queries) to drive this process.

Our thesis is two-fold.

- **Value correspondences are an appropriate abstraction for eliciting information from the user or DBA.** A DBA may easily be able to indicate that distance values are formed by multiplying rate times time. However, (s)he may not readily be able to specify the possibly complex query required to indicate how a specific rate value is paired with a specific time value (perhaps through a complex query involving many relations) without some help or prompting from the mapping tool.

- **Using reasoning about queries and query containment, we can effectively and efficiently help the user derive correct schema mappings.** Specifically, we will employ the same reasoning about queries (and alternative queries) already used in DBMS to do query optimization and semantic query optimization. Traditionally, this knowledge is buried deep within the optimizer and highly tuned to the problem of finding a low cost query plan. To our knowledge, this is the first principled attempt to expose this sophisticated reasoning about queries to a user to help in the schema mapping task.

Value correspondences may be entered by a user or may be suggested using linguistic techniques applied to the data and meta-data such as the names of schema components [BHP94, Joh97]. In Clio, we use a graphical interface that facilitates schema and data browsing to elicit value correspondences from users [HMN+99]. Other data-centric interfaces, including the scalable spreadsheet paradigm proposed by Raman, Chou and Hellerstein [RCH99], would also be appropriate for eliciting the correspondences that drive our algorithms.

2.2 Constructing Schema Mappings

We now turn to the question of constructing a schema mapping from a set of value correspondences. The construction process is one of searching for the most

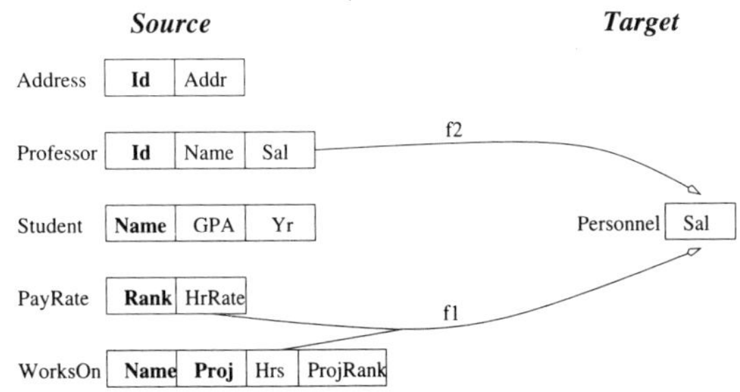

Figure 1: Example schemas to be mapped.

reasonable mapping based on the properties of the correspondences, the properties of the schemas, and the schema or structuring cues that lie buried in the data. We begin with an example that explains intuitively the type of reasoning we will employ.

Example 2.1 *Consider the two schemas of Figure 1. Suppose a user has indicated that the product of the values in the PayRate(HrRate) and WorksOn(Hrs) attributes should also appear in Personnel(Sal). This value correspondence is represented by the function f_1. For this example, we will assume all filters are "True".*

$f_1 : PayRate(HrRate) * WorksOn(Hrs) \rightarrow Personnel(Sal)$

This correspondence indicates how two values from the source can be combined into a target attribute. However, it does not indicate which values should be combined. Intuitively, if HrRate and Hrs belonged to the same relation, then the most likely interpretation of the correspondence is to combine values from the same tuple. However, in general, particularly when HrRate and Hrs belong to different relations, we must define a query that produces pairs of values to be combined.

In this example, to produce a schema mapping we must determine a way of associating a specific tuple of PayRate with a tuple of WorksOn. If ProjRank is a foreign key of PayRate, then the natural way of doing this is through a join on Rank = ProjRank. This produces the following mapping.

```
q₁: SELECT  P.HrRate*W.Hrs
    FROM    PayRate P, WorksOn W
    WHERE   P.Rank = W.ProjRank
```

However, suppose this foreign key is not declared but instead WorksOn.Name is declared as a foreign key of Student and Student.Yr is declared as a foreign key of PayRate. (That is, there is a different HrRate value for Sophomores than for Juniors, etc.) Then the foreign key path $WorksOn \bowtie Student \bowtie PayRate$ would be a better join path to use in the schema mapping.

```
q₁': SELECT  P.HrRate * W.Hrs
     FROM    PayRate P, WorksOn W, Student S
     WHERE   W.Name = S.Name AND S.Yr = P.Rank
```

Note that if, in fact, ProjRank is also declared as a foreign key of PayRate, it is then not clear which join path is better. In some circumstances, the filter of the value correspondence may provide a clue. For example, if our filter were "Student.Yr > 2", the join through Student would make more sense. In the absence of such clues, user input is required. A tool such as Clio can still help, however, by enumerating the options and providing "samples" (that is, instances of the target schema) that are the results of different mappings.

Implicit to the process of deriving the mapping is our intuition that for each HrRate value, there is somewhere in the source database **a** value for the Hrs attribute that can be used to derive **a** value of the Sal attribute in the target. It is certainly possible that a user wished to take the cross product of HrRate and Hrs and form salaries from every pair of these source values. However, this possibility is unlikely, particularly if there is a natural way to pair HrRates with specific Hrs values. So Clio makes use of reasoning about schemas and the semantics conveyed by constraints, such as foreign keys, to deduce likely mappings.

Example 2.2 *Continuing this example, suppose that the user has provided a second value correspondence indicating that values of the Professor(Sal) attribute should appear in Personnel(Sal) in the target.*

$$f_2 : Professor(Sal) \rightarrow Personnel(Sal)$$

Certainly, one interpretation of these correspondences is that we should take the join of salary values produced by f_1 and those produced by f_2 to populate the target. However, this is not the most intuitive mapping since it would mean that many (or perhaps even most) of the source values for salary would not appear in the target. Rather, it is more likely that the user intended the mapping to be a union of these values. The salary for personnel may be derived either from professor salaries or from student pay rates and hours. That is, a better mapping would be the following.

```
q2: SELECT  P.HrRate * W.Hrs
    FROM    PayRate P, WorksOn W, Student S
    WHERE   W.Name = S.Name AND S.Yr = P.Rank
    UNION ALL
    SELECT  Sal
    FROM    Professor
```

While these examples may seem heuristic, there is some principled reasoning going on under the covers. To guide the mapping construction, we are following two key principles. First, if possible, all values in the source appear in the target. This principle guided our decision to use a union rather than a join in the example when two different value correspondences were given for the same attribute. Second, if possible, a value from the source should only contribute once to the target. In other words, associations between values that exist in the source should not be lost. This principle guided our choice to use a join rather than the cross product to compute a salary value using the correspondence f_1.

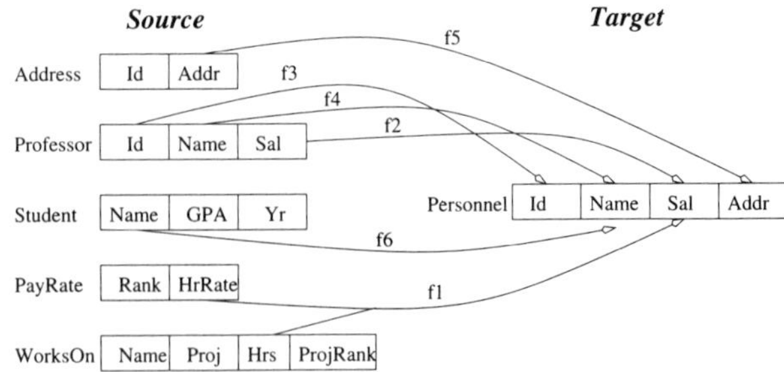

Figure 2: Value Correspondences.

Note that these principles are restatements of common data design principles such as "one fact in one place" [Dat95]. Even in the presence of filters, we try to uphold these principles for those values selected by the filter. Since our goal is schema mapping rather than schema design, we do permit a user to override these principles. For example, in publishing information for a "What-If" scenario, a user might want a cross-product so that (s)he could evaluate all possibilities.

We use these principles to derive an initial mapping, one that preserves, to the extent possible, the information in the source. A user may examine target data derived under this mapping and decide whether to restrict or modify the mapping.

Example 2.3 *To complete our running example, consider the extended schemas of Figure 2 and the following additional value correspondences.*

$$\begin{aligned}
f_3&: Professor(Id) &\rightarrow Personnel(Id)\\
f_4&: Professor(Name) &\rightarrow Personnel(Name)\\
f_5&: Address(Addr) &\rightarrow Personnel(Addr)\\
f_6&: Student(Name) &\rightarrow Personnel(Name)
\end{aligned}$$

Intuitively, these correspondences divide naturally into two groups that coincide with the two different ways in which a Personnel tuple can be created. The first group includes the correspondences from Professor and Address, namely f_2, f_3, f_4, f_5. A Personnel tuple can be created by joining together a Professor tuple and an Address tuple. Such a mapping is suggested by the presence of foreign key constraints between these relations or by the presence of a source query workload that includes a join of these two relations or even by the data itself (if the Id values in the two relations overlap). Depending on the constraint information, we may choose an outer-join, rather than a join to avoid losing information (but we use a join here, to keep our example simple). The second group includes the correspondences from Student, PayRate and WorksOn, namely f_1 and f_6. A Personnel tuple can be created by joining together Student, PayRate and WorksOn. Hence, the most reasonable schema mapping given these specific constraints in the source is the following.

```
s₁: SELECT P.Id, P.Name, P.Sal, A.Addr
    FROM   Professor P, Address A
    WHERE  A.Id = P.Id
    UNION ALL
    SELECT NULL as Id, S.Name, P.HrRate*W.Hrs,
           NULL as Addr
    FROM   Student S, PayRate P, WorksOn W
    WHERE  S.name = W.name AND S.Yr = P.Rank
```

Notice that this is not the only possible mapping. Another option would be to take the outer-union of all the relations in the source and project out attributes from the source that do not participate in any value correspondence. The outer-union is the union where any missing attributes are set to null.

```
s₁′: SELECT NULL as Id, NULL as Name, NULL as Sal, Addr
     FROM   Address A
     UNION ALL
     SELECT P.Id, P.Name, P.Sal, NULL as Addr
     FROM   Professor P
     UNION ALL
     SELECT NULL as Id, Name, NULL as Sal, NULL as Addr
     FROM   Student S ...
```

While possible, it is clear from our understanding of the semantics of the source schema that this would not be a particularly natural mapping. Such a mapping loses associations between data values present in the source. For example, in the source, we can determine the address of a professor (assuming the Id of a professor appears in the Address relation). This would not be true in the target using a mapping based on outer-unions.

In the example, we described the intuition behind the mapping derivation. This intuition, while seeming natural to anyone who has worked with databases, actually has a formal basis that dates back to early theoretical work on database design. Simply put, our goal is to find mappings that do not lose information, or at least lose as little information as possible. In reasoning about mappings, we will consider alternative ways of combining value correspondences to produce mappings. We use formal reasoning about schemas to choose among these alternatives. Due to the vagaries of semantics, we will not always be right. But our goal is not to fully automate this process. Rather, our goal is to present users with a reasonable mapping as a starting point which can be refined. By providing an example mapping, the user can see target values produced by this mapping and identify data values that are missing (or have been included in error). Hence, the mapping refinement process is data- or value-driven. The user does not have to edit SQL to refine the mapping.

We have used a very simple example and enumerated only a few of the possible mappings that would need to be considered. We have not had space to overview the complexities introduced by considering aggregations, groupings or even outer-joins, all of which are important constructs for integrating information. In Example 2.3, if no foreign keys had been specified, we would need to use outer-joins rather than joins to avoid losing information. Because outer-joins are not associative, the differences between alternative outer-join orders can be subtle yet these differences are extremely important in obtaining a semantically correct mapping. There is a considerable literature on these subtleties alone [GL94, RU96, GLR97]. Given this inherent complexity, a systematic search through the large search space of alternative mappings is a job best done by a tool that can eliminate unlikely mappings and identify correct mappings a user might not otherwise have considered.

2.3   Search Space

Having defined the mapping discovery problem as a search through a set of alternative mappings, an important characteristic of the approach is the set of possible mappings considered. We begin by considering mappings that preserve information capacity dominance or equivalence [Hul86]. Such mappings are important in information integration [MIR93]. We are able to take advantage of a solid literature enumerating such mappings [MIR94, RU96, RR94] and providing search procedures for finding such mappings [AH88, MIR94]. From this foundation, we extend the search space in two ways. First, we consider a larger class of mappings, including queries for which the equivalence problem is not decidable. As a result, our algorithm is not complete in that it may not consider all possible mappings. However, this extension is required to consider mappings between schemas with constraints or dependencies. Second, we consider non-equivalence (or dominance) preserving mappings. This extension is a necessity since in practice, the source and target schemas will not represent the same information. To keep our search problem tractable, we attempt to find mappings that minimize the information loss. A formal description of the search space is beyond the scope of this paper. Informally, the mappings we consider can be broadly classified into two groups.

Vertical Compositions Facts or tuples can be combined using the join operator. To avoid having a tuple combine or join with multiple tuples (that is, to avoid having a single tuple contribute multiple times to the result), we favor performing joins where there is a functional (N:1) relationship between the tuples. Dependency theory tells us this can be accomplished using joins across foreign keys. (Indeed this same intuition motivates the relational normal forms.) In addition, to minimize information loss, we use outer-joins unless the constraints in the mapping imply that the outer and inner-joins would be equivalent or unless we can determine that the tuples that could be lost by using a join are included elsewhere in the mapping. Obviously, we will not always be able to determine this since this problem is undecidable for the general constraints we consider. In composing outer-joins, we favor full disjunctions to ensure all information for a single fact is collected in a single tuple [RU96, GLR97]. Note that using an outer-join over a foreign key, we have a mapping that corresponds to the composition transformation of [MIR94]. Such a transformation preserves information (that is, information capacity dominance) in the sense of [Hul86]. We also have an algorithm for determining if such a mapping exists between two schemas and for finding such mappings [MIR94].

Horizontal Compositions Facts or tuples can also be combined using set operators. When we have multiple value correspondences to the same value in the target, we begin by using union to combine the values. To accomplish our information preservation principles, we favor using (multi-set) unions as a starting point, over other set operations such as intersections. If we can determine the sets being unioned are disjoint, a regular (set) union is used. For example, meta-data is often used to create a tag to distinguish a tuple coming from one place in the schema from a tuple coming from a different location. Indeed, the mappings resulting from schematic (or meta-data) heterogeneity between the source and target schemas can often be represented using tagged unions [Mil98].

This framework is an extensible one. Additional classes of mappings and additional heuristics for selecting between mappings can easily be integrated. Furthermore, this framework and the algorithms described below can be used both for traditional applications where the target schema is a (virtual) view specified over one or more (materialized) data sources and for applications where the source schemas are considered to be (materialized) views defined on a (virtual) target schema [LMSS95]. The former is sometimes referred to as the global-as-view approach in the literature and the latter as the local-as-view approach. In the former case, the mapping is a query or set of queries on the source schema that creates an instance of the target. In the latter case, the mapping is a query on the target. A more detailed discussion of this issue and its implications for the mapping can be found in the full version of this paper [MHH00].

3 Query Discovery Algorithm

We now present our mapping construction algorithm. To keep the notation simple, we assume the source and target schemas are represented in the relational model. We discuss generalizations to other models, including semi-structured models such as XML in Section 3.4.

3.1 Notation

Before presenting our algorithm, we outline the notation we will be using.

- Let $S_1, ..., S_n$ represent the n source relations.

- Let $T_1, ..., T_m$ represent the m target relations.

- We use the (possibly subscripted) symbol A to denote source attributes. The domain of an attribute A is denoted $dom(A)$.

- We use the (possibly subscripted) symbol B to denote target attributes.

Each attribute of the source will have associated meta-data. The meta-data includes the attribute name, the relation name, the schema name, the database name, the domain name, statistics such as high and low values of the attribute, and possibly additional annotations provided by a DBA. Hence, the meta-data is extensible. For an attribute A, $\mu(A)$ denotes the meta-data associated with A. Formally, $\mu(A)$ is a tuple $(\mu_1(A), \mu_2(A), ..., \mu_m(A))$ of values. For convenience, we give names to some of these values. The attribute name is denoted $attrname(A)$ and the relation name is denoted $relname(A)$.

We will represent a *value correspondence* as a tuple $v_i = \langle f_i, p_i \rangle$, where f_i is the correspondence function denoting the value substitution and p_i a filter.

When defining a correspondence function f_i, the DBA selects a number of source attributes (and, possibly, meta-data associated with those attributes) and **one** target attribute. Let $Attrs(f_i) = \{A_1, ..., A_q\}$ be the set of all source attributes used in f_i, and $TargetAttr(f_i) = B$ be the (one) target attribute. The correspondence function, f_i, can be expressed as follows.

$$f_i : dom(A_1) \times ... \times dom(A_q) \times \mu(A_1) \times ... \times \mu(A_q) \to dom(B)$$

Example 3.1 *The following correspondence indicates that values of the Distance attribute of the target can be formed by multiplying the Rate value by the Time value and dividing by 1.6 to convert kilometers to miles.*

$$f_1 : Rate * Time/1.6 \to Distance$$

Example 3.2 *The next correspondence indicates that company codes are formed by concatenating the ticker code with the relation name (the name of the stock exchange).*

$$f_2 : concat(relname(Ticker), Ticker) \to CompanyCode$$

Each value correspondence function f_i has an associated filter p_i that determines which subset of values from the source relations will be used by f_i. If we define $Attrs(p_i) = \{A_1, ..., A_r\}$ to be the set of all source attributes used in p_i, we can express p_i as follows.

$$p_i : dom(A_1) \times ... \times dom(A_r) \times \mu(A_1) \times ... \times \mu(A_r) \to boolean$$

By default, p_i is the predicate $True$, indicating the value correspondence is defined for all values in the domain. Note that $Attrs(p_i)$ is not necessarily the same as $Attrs(f_i)$. In the first example above, we could define a $p_1 : Rate \leq 100$ which indicates that the correspondence only holds for small rate values. In the second example, we could have $p_2 : Exchange(Country) = $ "Canada" which would indicate that the correspondence only holds for stocks listed on Canadian exchanges. Here, even though the values involved in the correspondence come from the data and meta-data of a single relation (Ticker), the attributes of the correspondence will also include Exchange(Country). As described below, the algorithm will determine a join path between Exchange and Ticker (for example, $relname(Ticker) \bowtie Exchange(Name)$) to use when applying the filter.

Either the correspondence function or the filter may include aggregate functions. The aggregate is taken as a cue to perform a grouping in the schema mapping. To determine the grouping attributes, we must consider all the value correspondences for a target relation as described in the next section.

3.2 The Core Algorithm

For each target relation T_k we want to construct a query q_k that specifies what values to include in the relation. To do this, we consider the value correspondences $\mathcal{V}_k$ defining attribute values of T_k (*i.e.*, $\mathcal{V}_k = \{v_i = \langle f_i, p_i \rangle \mid TargetAttr(f_i) \in T_k\}$).

The idea behind this algorithm is to divide the set of value correspondences $\mathcal{V}_k$ into subsets of $\mathcal{V}_k$, each of which determines one way of computing the values of T_k. Each of these *candidate sets* can be mapped into a single *candidate SQL query* (that is, a query with a single `select-from-where-group-by` clause). The query q_k is then the horizontal composition (*i.e.*, the application of set operations such as UNION ALL) of these candidate queries.

We present the algorithm for a single target relation T and, thus, $\mathcal{V} = \mathcal{V}_k$ includes all value correspondences. When more that one target relation exists, we repeat the algorithm for each $\mathcal{V}_k$ possibly reusing computations from previous targets.

We divide the algorithm's tasks into four phases (see Figure 3). In the first phase, the value correspondences in $\mathcal{V}$ are partitioned into sets $\{c_1, \ldots, c_p\}$ that contain *at most one* correspondence per attribute of T. We call each such set a *potential candidate set*. In essence, each c_j represents one possible way of mapping the attributes of T. A potential candidate set is *complete* if it includes a value correspondence for every attribute in the target. Potential candidate sets are not necessarily disjoint since the same value mapping can appear in multiple potential candidate sets.

For clarity of exposition, we describe this phase of the algorithm as searching every potential candidate set derived from $\mathcal{V}$ independently (though the computations can be reused across subsets). Although this implies a large search space, potential candidate sets

are generated on demand from the next phase of the algorithm (*i.e.*, pipelined). The order in which potential sets are passed to the next phase is, thus, important. As a heuristic, we give preference to complete potential sets whose value correspondences use the smallest set of source relations. Also, if a particular potential candidate set c_j is selected for use in the schema mapping, we can heuristically prune potential candidates that are proper subsets of c_j since they are unlikely to also appear in the mapping.

Example 3.3 *Consider the following value correspondences (and assume some filter p_i has been defined for each).*
$$f_1 : S_1.A \to T.C \qquad f_2 : S_2.A \to T.D \qquad f_3 : S_2.B \to T.C$$
The collection of complete potential candidate sets is $\mathcal{P} = \{\{v_1, v_2\}, \{v_2, v_3\}\}$. The singleton sets $\{v_1\}$, $\{v_2\}$, $\{v_3\}$ are also potential candidate sets.

It is important to note that we consider potential candidate sets that are not complete. There are two reasons for this. First, as shown in Example 2.3, in the final query mapping, there may not be a value correspondence for every target attribute. Second, we will be using our algorithm incrementally on perhaps incomplete sets of correspondences. We want to permit a user to specify a partial set of correspondences, and have Clio derive a possible mapping. Using the mapping, example tuples in the target can be derived. These tuples can be used by a user to understand how the data is fitting into the target.

The result of the first phase of the algorithm is a collection $\mathcal{P} = \{c_1, \ldots, c_q\}$, where each $c_j \subseteq \mathcal{V}$ represents a different possible way of mapping the attributes in the target relation T.

In the second phase of the algorithm, we prune from the set of potential candidate sets those sets that cannot be mapped into a good query. In particular, if the value correspondences in the potential candidate set map values from several source relations, we need to find a vertical composition (*i.e.*, a way of joining the tuples) of those relations. This composition will satisfy the criteria established in Section 2.3. We search for foreign key paths between these relations.[1] Often there will be at most one such path. If, however, there are multiple paths, we favor the path for which the estimated difference in size of the outer and inner join is the smallest.[2] This heuristic favors (outer-)join paths that produce the fewest dangling tuples. For any ambiguities that remain, we ask the user to choose one of the available join paths. To help in this process, we show the user example target tuples produced by

---

[1] Actually, the search is done only once for all potential candidates and the results of the search reused over different potential candidates.

[2] Note that this measure can be evaluated using common meta-data such as the number of distinct values of an attribute.

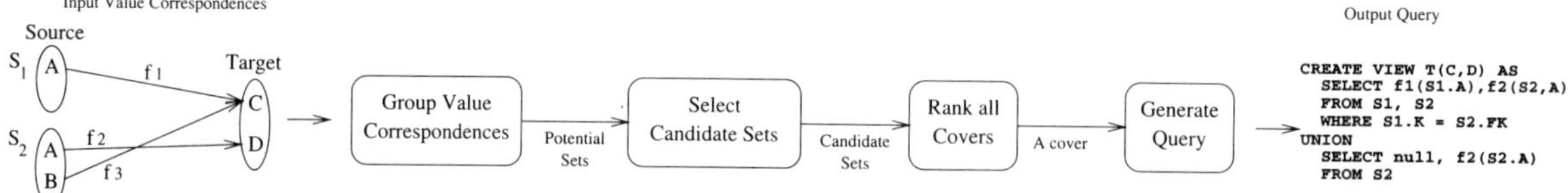

Figure 3: Mapping Algorithm

each of the alternative paths. In the absence of foreign key paths, we could employ data mining techniques to determine if there is an (approximate) foreign key relationship between the relations in question [Bel97, KMRS92] or permit the user to suggest appropriate join paths. If no acceptable join path can be found, the potential candidate set is removed from further consideration. Any potential candidate set that survives this pruning is a *candidate set*.

The result of this second phase is a set $\mathcal{G} \subseteq \mathcal{P}$ of candidate sets. Value correspondences in a candidate set either map attributes from only one source relation, or map attributes from multiple source relations and a join path among those relations is known.

In the third phase of the algorithm, we attempt to find a subset Γ of the candidate sets ($\Gamma \subseteq \mathcal{G}$) that covers all value correspondences in $\mathcal{V}$ (that is, every value correspondence in $\mathcal{V}$ appears at least once in Γ). We permit correspondences to participate in multiple candidates within a cover, but we do not consider a set of candidates Γ if we can remove a candidate set and still have a cover. For instance, in Example 3.3, $\mathcal{G} = \{\{v_1, v_2\}, \{v_2, v_3\}, \{v_1\}, \{v_2\}, \{v_3\}\}$. Possible covers include $\Gamma_1 = \{\{v_1\}, \{v_2, v_3\}\}$ and $\Gamma_2 = \{\{v_1, v_2\}, \{v_2, v_3\}\}$ since all defined value correspondences appear at least once.

If there is more than one cover, Clio ranks them in reverse order of the number of candidate sets in the cover. Since the number of candidates in a cover is the number of candidate SQL queries needed to compute the mapping, we prefer smaller covers which will produce simpler mappings. When two or more covers have the same number of candidate sets, we prefer those that use the largest number of target attributes in all candidate sets and, thus, minimize the number of "null" values in the target. The ranked covers are presented as alternative mappings for the user to evaluate.

The final step is to build the query q from the selected cover. For each candidate set c_j in the selected cover, we create a candidate SQL query such that all correspondence functions f_i mentioned in c_j appear in the **SELECT** clause, all source relations are mentioned in the **FROM** clause, and all predicates p_i appear as a conjunction in the **WHERE** clause. Any join path determined in the second step for this candidate set will be used to determine the appropriate source relations for the **FROM** clause. The join predicates are also added to the **WHERE** clause. For each candidate set that includes aggregate functions (in either the correspondence or

the filter), we select grouping attributes. All attributes (or functions on attributes) in the select clause that are not within the aggregate are selected as the grouping attributes. If the aggregate is in the correspondence function, the aggregate is placed in the select clause. If the aggregate is in the filter, the aggregate is placed in the **HAVING** clause. (We provide an example using aggregation in Section 4.) All candidate SQL queries are then combined into one large query using the multiset **UNION ALL**.

As in query optimization, the search space we consider in this algorithm is exponential. Nevertheless, we are able to provide heuristics that can guide the search towards likely covers and, thus, a correct schema mapping.

3.3 Making the Algorithm Incremental

Often, users will provide value correspondences incrementally and wish to see partial results before adding additional correspondences. We therefore provide an incremental version of the above algorithm. The algorithm takes as input a cover Γ_i and a single change $\Delta \mathcal{V}$ to the set of input value correspondences $\mathcal{V}$. The change $\Delta \mathcal{V}$ can be the addition (denoted $+v$) or the deletion (denoted $-v$) of a single value correspondence v. As output, the user is presented with a ranked set of possible next covers that are produced by the application of $\Delta \mathcal{V}$ to Γ_i. The cover selected by the user becomes the next cover Γ_{i+1}.

The incremental algorithm is divided into three phases (see Figure 4). The first phase does the work of the first and second phases of the batch algorithm presented in the previous section. Given a $+v$, the algorithm tries to insert v into all candidate sets of Γ_i. If the addition of v changes the set of source relations of a candidate set, a new join condition is sought (using the current join condition, if any, as seed for this search). The same heuristics discussed in the previous section to obtain a vertical composition are used here. If no candidate set in the cover can accept v, a new candidate set is created. For a deletion $-v$, the algorithm removes v from all candidate sets where it appears. Candidate sets that become empty, are removed from the cover. The result of this first phase is a set of changes $\Delta \Gamma$ that can be applied to the candidate sets in the current cover Γ_i.

The second phase of the algorithm applies each change in $\Delta \Gamma$ to Γ_i, producing a set of tentative covers Γ_{i+1}. Since the first phase limits the number of

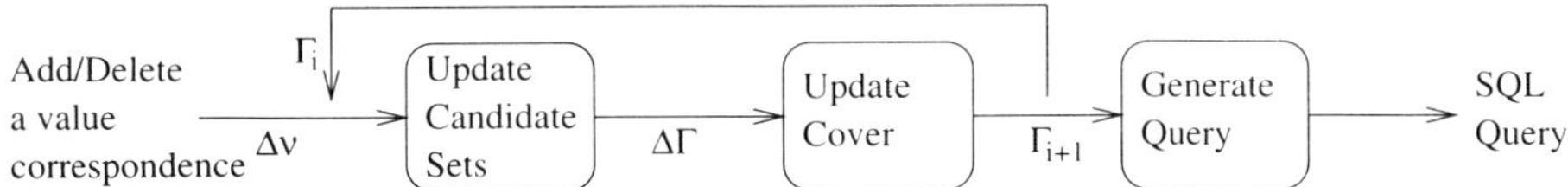

Figure 4: Incremental Mapping Algorithm

changes per candidate set to at most one change, the number of possible new covers is bounded by the number of candidate sets in the cover. This set of new covers are ranked as described in the previous section and presented to the user. The user selects one cover as the next Γ_{i+1}.

The third phase of this algorithm is identical to the fourth phase of the previous algorithm. Given a cover Γ_i, this phase produces an SQL query.

3.4 Nested-Sets in Target Relations

In addition to flat relational schemas, Clio can produce mappings to nested relational targets. Such mappings can be used to populate semi-structured schemas, including XML Schemas [W3C99]. For example, assume one of our target relations is `DeptInfo(number, name, staff:set of row(ename, eaddress))` where `staff` is a set of rows containing the name and address of each staff member. Given source relations `Department(dno, dname)` and `Professors(ssn, name, address, salary, dno)`, we could expect users to map values from `Department` into the outer-level of `DeptInfo` and values from `Professors` into `staff`. This mapping implies a join condition between the source relations `Department` and `Professor`.

Clio considers each target relation as an instance of a collection (or set) of row types. These row types can, in turn, contain collections of other row types. *Candidate sets* represent a possible mapping of the attributes of a particular collection and are maintained for each target collection (including nested collections). This forms a tree of candidate sets. For instance, in the example above, there is one candidate set that defines the mapping for `DeptInfo` and a candidate set under it that defines the maping for `staff`.

Join conditions for nested candidate sets include the extra step of finding (if needed) a way of joining the source relations of a particular candidate set with the source relations of each nested candidate set under it. In the example above, no join condition is needed for the candidate set of `staff`. However, a join condition between the source relations of that candidate set (`Employee`) and the source relation (`Department`) of the candidate set of the parent is needed.

Given a nested cover Γ, we can use a modified version of the procedure described in Section 3.2 to produce an SQL mapping query. The reasoning is similar to that used for flat relations and incorporates explicit knowledge about when nesting preserves the desired information. A nested query is added to the `FROM` clause of the candidate set's query for each of its nested candidate sets. To generate these nested queries, a recursive call is made to this procedure using the nested candidate sets as input. In the example used in this section, the expected output query is the following query.

```
SELECT DI.dno as number, DI.dname as name,
       EmpTable.EmpSet as staff
FROM DeptInfo DI,
     (SELECT SET OF(ROW(E.name, E.address)) AS EmpSet
      FROM    Employee E
      WHERE   E.dno = DI.dnumber) AS EmpTable
```

4   A Data Warehousing Example

We use an example based on a proposed software engineering warehouse for storing and exchanging information extracted from computer programs [BGH99]. Such warehouses have been proposed both to enable new program analysis applications, including data mining applications [MG99], and to promote data exchange between research groups using different tools and software artifacts for experimentation [HMPR97]. Figure 5 depicts a portion of a warehouse schema for this information. This schema has been designed to represent data about a diverse collection of software artifacts that have been extracted using different software analysis tools. The warehouse schema was designed to be as flexible as possible. As a result, it uses a very generic representation of software data as labeled multi-graphs. Conceptually, software artifacts (for example, functions, data types, macros, *etc.*) form the nodes of the graph. Associations or references between artifacts (for example, function calls or data references) form the edges. Two of the main tables for artifacts and references are depicted in the figure. Both tables are specialized with subtables containing specific types of software artifacts and references.

As new software analysis tools are developed, the data from these tools must be mapped into this integrated schema. In Figure 5, we also give a relational representation of facts extracted from the Rigi parser [MOTU93]. This schema may be supported by a wrapper built on top of Rigi [RS97]. Foreign keys are depicted by dashed lines. To map the Rigi data into the warehouse, the correspondences of Figure 6 may be used. In the Schema S, function and data type names are sufficient to disambiguate values within a software system. Within the warehouse, the information must be combined with meta-data describing the software system (for example, the program name and version). In Rigi, the program name and version are given in a header of a text file containing the set of all facts for

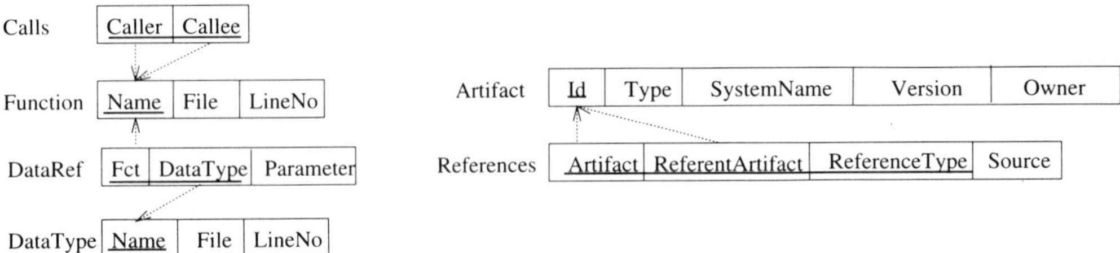

Figure 5: Schema of Rigi Source Database and a Software Engineering Warehouse

the program. The wrapper exposes this information using the meta-data functions dbname and dbversion. The correspondence f_1 is given below and the other correspondences are defined similarly. The function Id is a Skolem Function that produces a unique id for each unique set of values on which it is invoked [HY92]. Note that correspondences f_4 and f_5 map the relation name into the ReferenceType value, effectively transforming schema to data.

$$f_1: Id(dbname(), dbversion(), Calls(Caller))$$
$$\rightarrow References(Artifact)$$

The grouping algorithm of Clio uses the foreign key information in the source to create several candidate subsets. One contains the four correspondences $\{f_1, f_2, f_3, f_4\}$. Note that there are two foreign key join paths between the source relations involved in these correspondences. The first populates the Source attribute of the target with the File attribute of the caller function (Mapping S_1). The second populates the Source attribute of the target with the File attribute of the called function (Mapping S_2).

```
S₁: SELECT Id(dbname(),dbversion(),C.Caller),
           Id(dbname(),dbversion(),C.Callee),
           relname(C), Id(dbname(),dbversion(),F.File)
    FROM   Calls C, Function F
    WHERE C.Caller = F.Name

S₂: SELECT Id(dbname(),dbversion(),C.Caller),
           Id(dbname(),dbversion(),C.Callee),
           relname(C), Id(dbname(),dbversion(),F.File)
    FROM   Calls C, Function F
    WHERE C.Callee = F.Name
```

If we cannot distinguish these paths using the data, both will be presented to the user. The user is given some example values to help evaluate which of the join paths is correct (Figure 7). Based on the data, the user can pick the desired mapping. In this example, the user would choose the first since the source location of a program call is the location of the caller function.

A second candidate subset contains the four correspondences $\{f_5, f_6, f_7, f_3\}$. Note that Clio chooses to use f_3 in both candidates since there is a good foreign key path to use for both candidates. These two correspondences form a cover. Clio combines the Mapping S_1 and the mapping produced for this second candidate subset to produce the following complete schema

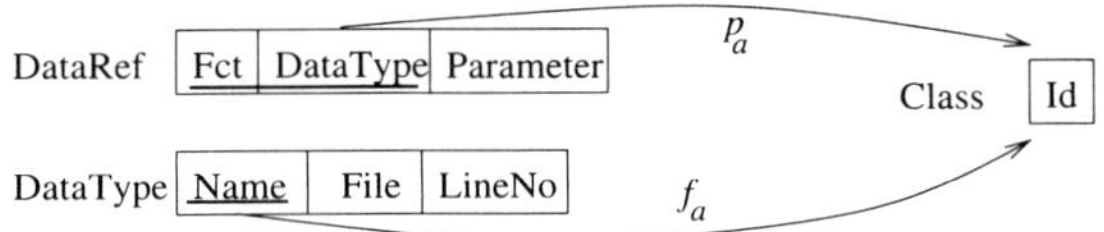

Figure 8: Aggregate filter in a value correspondence. mapping. Since Clio favors grouping correspondences from the same relation, the other covers possible in this example are eliminated.

```
S: SELECT Id(dbname(),dbversion(),C.Caller),
          Id(dbname(),dbversion(),C.Callee),
          relname(C), Id(dbname(),dbversion(),F.File)
   FROM   Calls C, Function F WHERE C.Caller = F.Name
   UNION ALL
   SELECT Id(dbname(),dbversion(),D.Fct),
          Id(dbname(),dbversion(),D.DataType),
          relname(D), Id(dbname(),dbversion(),F.File)
   FROM DataRef D, Function F WHERE D.Fct = F.Name
```

To extend this example, consider the correspondence and filter used to define the Class table (a subtable of the Artifact table). Although the Rigi facts from Figure 7 represent C programs, the warehouse may contain tables like Class for storing information about object-oriented classes. C programs might be "reverse engineered" into C++ programs by grouping together into a class all functions that access a particular data type or set of data types. For brevity, we assume the Class table has a single Id attribute indicating the data type of the class (Figure 8).[3]

$$f_a : Id(dbname(), dbversion(), DataType(Name)) \rightarrow Class(Id)$$
$$p_a : count(DataRef(Fct)) > 5$$

The correspondence f_a maps data types to the Class table. The user also provides a filter p_a restricting the mapping to data types referenced by more than 5 functions. Clio discovers the join paths between DataRef and DataType. Given the aggregate function in the filter, the discovered mapping includes a group by and is depicted below.

```
Sₐ: SELECT Id(dbname(),dbversion(),T.Name)
    FROM   DataType T, DataRef R
    WHERE  T.Name = R.DataType
    GROUP BY Id(dbname(),dbversion(),T.Name)
    HAVING count(R.Fct) > 5
```

[3] While we are over-simplifying the reasoning behind reverse engineering methodologies, we are being faithful to the way these groups can be represented in SQL [MG99].

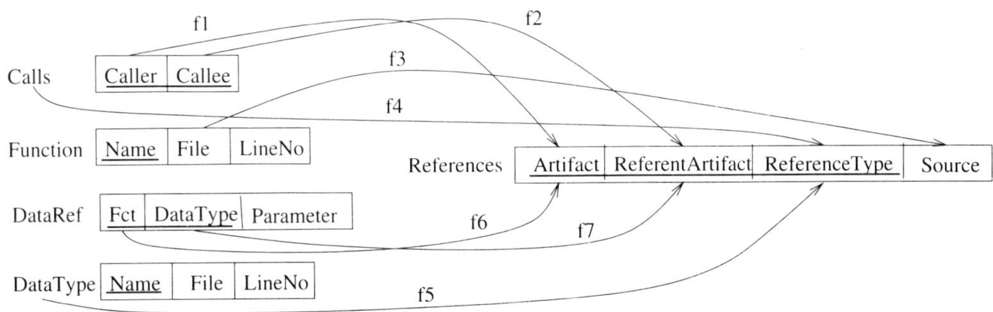

Figure 6: Value correspondences used to map the Rigi Schema to the Warehouse

Source Schema (S)

Function

Name	File	LineNo
sock_wmalloc	sock.c	317
sock_wfree	sock.c	512
alloc_skb	skbuff.c	10
free_skb	skbuff.c	230

Calls

Caller	Callee
sock_wmalloc	alloc_skb
sock_wfree	free_skb

Warehouse Schema (G)

References — **Mapping S1**

Artifact	ReferentArtifact	ReferenceType	Source
sock_wmalloc	alloc_skb	calls	sock.c
sock_wfree	free_skb	calls	sock.c

References — **Mapping S2**

Artifact	ReferentArtifact	ReferenceType	Source
sock_wmalloc	alloc_skb	calls	skbuff.c
sock_wfree	free_skb	calls	skbuff.c

Figure 7: Discovered alternative schema mappings are used to derive example target data. The facts depicted are example facts from Rigi's analysis of the Linux software system. The files sock.c and skbuff.c contain the socket management and socket buffer support, respectively, for the network subsystem of Linux.

Additional real world examples, including an example of using Clio to produce a mapping to an XML schema, are included in the full version of this paper [MHH00].

5 Related Work

We have already described the differences between classical schema integration [RR99], which is primarily a schema design problem, and the schema mapping problem we have addressed here.

Related language-based approaches provide tools for the specification and implementation of data and schema translations. The YAT conversion language [CDSS98] permits the specification of data and schema matching and restructuring operations. The correspondence rules of [ACM97] are another example. These tools also include the schema matching techniques of [MZ98] for simplifying the specifications of matching rules. Our techniques complement and extend these language-based approaches to consider the general problem of query discovery. Finally, the search problem we consider is closely related to the problem of finding the set of all views that can be used to answer a query [LMSS95, DPT99].

6 Conclusions

In this paper, we identified a new problem, *targeted schema mapping*, that is of critical importance to sev-eral increasingly common classes of applications. We distinguished schema mapping from the well-known problem of schema integration, and discussed the similarities and differences between the two. By using queries to represent a mapping, we allow DBMSs to play an expanded role as data transformation engines, as well as data stores. Additionally, we find expanded uses for many techniques from query optimization, as we apply them to the new task of query discovery or mapping creation. Our framework for schema mapping uses *value correspondences* that describe how to populate a single attribute of the target schema. Given a set of value correspondences, we must discover the mapping query needed to transform source data to target data. We presented our algorithm for this often complex task, and introduced Clio, a tool that helps users create a schema mapping. Finally, we showed through extensive examples based on real applications how Clio would process a set of value correspondences to arrive at the mapping query.

Acknowledgements

Discussions with Bartholomew Niswonger helped shape the direction of Clio. Peter Schwarz contributed to the recognition of the importance of value mappings. We thank Periklis Andritsos for providing the Linux data used in our examples, and Ling Ling Yan and anonymous referees for their helpful comments.

References

[ACM97]   S. Abiteboul, S. Cluet, and T.. Milo. Correspondence and Translation for Heterogeneous Data. In *Proc. of the Int'l Conf. on Database Theory (ICDT)*, pages 351–363, 1997.

[AH88]   S. Abiteboul and R. Hull. Restructuring Hierarchical Database Objects. *Theoretical Computer Science*, 62:3–38, 1988.

[Bel97]   Siegfried Bell. Dependency mining in relational databases. In *Proc. of the First Int'l. Joint Conf. on Qualitative and Quantitative Practical Reasoning*, volume 1244 of *LNAI*, pages 16–29, Berlin, June9–12 1997. Springer.

[BGH99]   I. Bowman, M. Godfrey, and R. Holt. Connecting Software Architecture Recovery Frameworks. In *Proc. of the First Int'l Symposium on Constructing Software Engineering Tools (CoSET'99)*, Los Angeles, May 17-18 1999.

[BHP94]   M. W. Bright, A. R. Hurson, and S. Pakzad. Automated Resolution of Semantic Heterogeneity in Multidatabases. *ACM TODS*, 19(2):212–253, June 1994.

[CDSS98]   S. Cluet, C. Delobel, J. Siméon, and K. Smaga. Your Mediators Need Data Conversion. In *ACM SIGMOD Conference*, pages 177–188, 1998.

[CHS$^+$95]   M. J. Carey, L. M. Haas, P. M. Schwarz, M. Arya, W. F. Cody, R. Fagin, M. Flickner, A. W. Luniewski, W. Niblack, D. Petkovic, J. Thomas, J. H. Williams, and E. L. Wimmers. Towards Heterogeneous Multimedia Information Systems: The Garlic Approach. In *Proc. of the Fifth Int'l IEEE Wksp. on Research Issues in Data Eng. (RIDE-95): Distributed Object Mngmt.*, March 1995.

[Dat95]   C. J. Date. *An Introduction to Database Systems*. Addison Wesley, 1995.

[DPT99]   A. Deutsch, L. Popa, and V. Tannen. Physical Data Independence, Constraints, and Optimization with Universal Plans. In *Proc. of the Int'l Conf. on VLDB*, pages 459–470, 1999.

[GL94]   César A. Galindo-Legaria. Outer-joins as Disjunctions. In *ACM SIGMOD Conference*, pages 348–358, 1994.

[GLR97]   César A. Galindo-Legaria and Arnon Rosenthal. Outer-join Simplification and Reordering for Query Optimization. *ACM TODS*, 22(1):43–73, 1997.

[HMN$^+$99]   L. M. Haas, R. J. Miller, B. Niswonger, M. Tork Roth, P. M. Schwarz, and E. L. Wimmers. Transforming Heterogeneous Data with Database Middleware: Beyond Integration. *IEEE Data Engineering Bulletin*, 22(1):31–36, 1999.

[HMPR97]   M. Harrold, R. J. Miller, A. Porter, and G. Rothermel. A Collaborative Investigation of Program-Analysis-Based Testing and Maintenance. In *International Workshop on Experimental Studies of Software Maintenance*, pages 51–56, Bari, Italy, October 1997.

[Hul86]   R. Hull. Relative Information Capacity of Simple Relational Database Schemata. *Society for Industrial and Applied Mathematics (SIAM) Journal of Computing*, 15(3):856–886, August 1986.

[HY92]   R. Hull and M. Yoshikawa. Object Identity and Query Equivalence. In J. D. Ullman, editor, *Theoretical Studies in Computer Science*, pages 253–286. Academic Press, Boston, MA, 1992.

[IBM97]   IBM. DB2 DataJoiner Application Programming and SQL Reference Supplement. Technical report, IBM Corporation, 1997.

[Joh97]   P. Johannesson. Linguistic Support for Analysing and Comparing Conceptual Schemas. *Data and Knowledge Engineering*, 21(2):165–182, 1997.

[KMRS92]   M. Kantola, H. Mannila, K.-J. Rih, and H. Siirtola. Discovering Functional and Inclusion Dependencies in Relational Databases. *International Journal of Intelligent Systems*, 7(7):591–607, September 1992.

[LMSS95]   A. Y. Levy, A. O. Mendelzon, Y. Sagiv, and D. Srivastava. Answering Queries Using Views. In *Proc. of the ACM Symp. on Principles of Database Systems (PODS)*, San Jose, CA, May 1995.

[MG99]   R. J. Miller and A. Gujarathi. Mining for Program Structure. *Int'l Journal on Software Eng. and Knowledge Eng.*, 9(5):499–517, 1999.

[MHH00]   R. J. Miller, L. M. Haas, and M. Hernández. Schema Mapping as Query Discovery. Technical Report CSRG-412, University of Toronto, Department of Computer Science, 2000.

[Mil98]   R. J. Miller. Using Schematically Heterogeneous Structures. *ACM SIGMOD Conference*, 27(2):189–200, June 1998.

[MIR93]   R. J. Miller, Y. E. Ioannidis, and R. Ramakrishnan. The Use of Information Capacity in Schema Integration and Translation. In *Proc. of the Int'l Conf. on VLDB*, pages 120–133, Dublin, Ireland, August 1993.

[MIR94]   R. J. Miller, Y. E. Ioannidis, and R. Ramakrishnan. Schema Equivalence in Heterogeneous Systems: Bridging Theory and Practice. *Information Systems*, 19(1):3–31, 1994.

[MOTU93]   H. A. Müller, M. A. Orgun, S. R. Tilly, and J. S. Uhl. A Reverse Engineering Approach to Subsystem Structure Identification. *Journal of Software Maintenance: Research and Practice*, 5(4):181–204, December 1993.

[MZ98]   T. Milo and S. Zohar. Using Schema Matching to Simplify Heterogeneous Data Translation. In *Proc. of the Int'l Conf. on VLDB*, pages 122–133, NY, NY, 1998.

[Ora]   Oracle. Rdb Distributed Technology Suite. http://oracle.com/rdb/download/rdb7/disttech/sy_dist.pdf.

[RCH99]   V. Raman, A. Chou, and J. M. Hellerstein. Scalable Spreadsheets for Interactive Data Analysis. In *ACM-SIGMOD Workshop on Research Issues in Data Mining and Knowledge Discovery (DMKD)*, Philadelphia, PA, May 1999.

[RR94]   A. Rosenthal and D. Reiner. Tools and Transformations - Rigorous and Otherwise - For Practical Database Design. *ACM TODS*, 19(2), June 1994.

[RR99]   S. Ram and V. Ramesh. Schema Integration: Past, Current and Future. In A. Elmagarmid, M. Rusinkiewicz, and A. Sheth, editors, *Management of Heterogeneous and Autonomous Database Systems*, pages 119–155. Morgan Kaufmann Publishers, 1999.

[RS97]   M. Tork Roth and P. Schwarz. Don't Scrap It, Wrap It! A Wrapper Architecture for Legacy Data Sources. In *Proc. of the Int'l Conf. on VLDB*, pages 266–275, Athens, Greece, August 1997.

[RU96]   A. Rajaraman and J. D. Ullman. Integrating Information by Outerjoins and Full Disjunctions. In *Proc. of the ACM Symp. on Principles of Database Systems (PODS)*, pages 238–248, Montréal, Canada, 1996.

[W3C99]   Xml schema part 1: Structures. http://www.w3.org/TR/xmlschema-1, December 1999.

Local Dimensionality Reduction: A New Approach to Indexing High Dimensional Spaces *

Kaushik Chakrabarti
Department of Computer Science
University of Illinois
Urbana, IL 61801
kaushikc@cs.uiuc.edu

Sharad Mehrotra
Department of Information and Computer Science
University of California
Irvine, CA 92697
sharad@ics.uci.edu

Abstract

Many emerging application domains require database
systems to support efficient access over highly multidimensional datasets. The current state-of-the-art technique to indexing high dimensional data is to first reduce the dimensionality of the data using Principal
Component Analysis and then indexing the reduced-
dimensionality space using a multidimensional index
structure. The above technique, referred to as global
dimensionality reduction (GDR), works well when the
data set is globally correlated, i.e. most of the variation in the data can be captured by a few dimensions.
In practice, datasets are often not globally correlated.
In such cases, reducing the data dimensionality using
GDR causes significant loss of distance information resulting in a large number of false positives and hence a
high query cost. Even when a global correlation does
not exist, there may exist subsets of data that are locally
correlated. In this paper, we propose a technique called
Local Dimensionality Reduction (LDR) that tries to
find local correlations in the data and performs dimensionality reduction on the locally correlated clusters of
data individually. We develop an index structure that
exploits the correlated clusters to efficiently support
point, range and k-nearest neighbor queries over high
dimensional datasets. Our experiments on synthetic as
well as real-life datasets show that our technique (1) reduces the dimensionality of the data with significantly
lower loss in distance information compared to GDR
and (2) significantly outperforms the GDR, original
space indexing and linear scan techniques in terms of
the query cost for both synthetic and real-life datasets.

* This work was supported by NSF CAREER award IIS-9734300, and
in part by the Army Research Laboratory under Cooperative Agreement No.
DAAL01-96-2-0003.

**Proceedings of the 26th VLDB Conference,
Cairo, Egypt, 2000.**

1 Introduction

With an increasing number of new database applications dealing
with highly multidimensional datasets, techniques to support efficient query processing over such data sets has emerged as an
important research area. These applications include multimedia
content-based retrieval, exploratory data analysis/data mining,
scientific databases, medical applications and time-series matching. To provide efficient access over high dimensional feature
spaces (HDFS), many indexing techniques have been proposed
in the literature. One class of techniques comprises of *high dimensional index trees* [3, 15, 16, 5]. Although these index structures work well in low to medium dimensionality spaces (upto
20-30 dimensions), a simple sequential scan usually performs
better at higher dimensionalities [4, 20].

To scale to higher dimensionalities, a commonly used approach is *dimensionality reduction* [9]. This technique has been
proposed for both multimedia retrieval and data mining applications. The idea is to first reduce the dimensionality of the
data and then index the reduced space using a multidimensional
index structure [7]. Most of the information in the dataset is
condensed to a few dimensions (the first few principal components (PCs)) by using principal component analysis (PCA).
The PCs can be arbitrarily oriented with respect to the original
axes [9]. The remaining dimensions (i.e. the later components)
are eliminated and the index is built on the reduced space. To
answer queries, the query is first mapped to the reduced space
and then executed on the index structure. Since the distance in
the reduced-dimensional space lower bounds the distance in the
original space, the query processing algorithm can guarantee no
false dismissals [7]. The answer set returned can have false positives (i.e. false admissions) which are eliminated before it is
returned to the user. We refer to this technique as *global dimensionality reduction* (GDR) i.e. dimensionality reduction over the
entire dataset taken together.

GDR works well when the dataset is *globally correlated* i.e.
most of the variation in the data can be captured by a few orthonormal dimensions (the first few PCs). Such a case is illustrated in Figure 1(a) where a single dimension (the first PC)
captures the variation of data in the 2-d space. In such cases, it
is possible to eliminate most of the dimensions (the later PCs)
with little or no loss of distance information. However, in practice, the dataset may not be globally correlated (see Figure 1(b)).
In such cases, reducing the data dimensionality using GDR will
cause a significant loss of distance information. Loss in distance
information is manifested by a large number of false positives

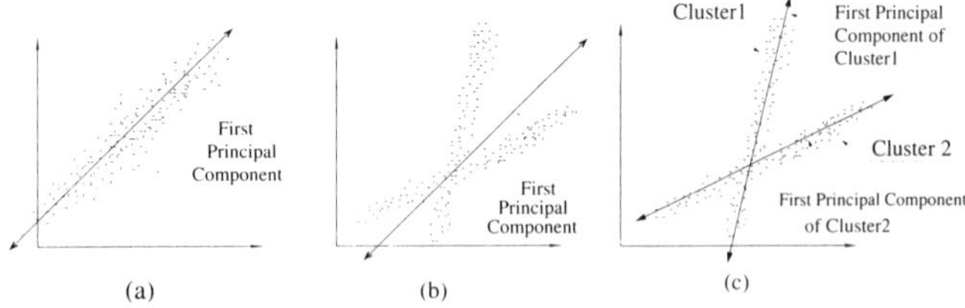

Figure 1: Global and Local Dimensionality Reduction Techniques (a) GDR(from 2-d to 1-d) on globally correlated data (b) GDR (from 2-d to 1-d) on globally non-correlated (but locally correlated) data (c) LDR (from 2-d to 1-d) on the same data as in (b)

and is measured by precision [14] (cf. Section 5). More the loss, larger the number of false positives, lower the precision. False positives increase the cost of the query by (1) causing the query to make unnecessary accesses to nodes of the index structure and (2) adding to the post-processing cost of the query, that of checking the objects returned by the index and eliminating the false positives. The cost increases with the increase in the number of false positives. Note that false positives do not affect the quality the answers as they are not returned to the user.

Even when a global correlation does not exist, there may exist subsets of data that are *locally correlated* (e.g., the data in Figure 1(b) is not globally correlated but is locally correlated as shown in Figure 1(c)). Obviously, the correlation structure (the PCs) differ from one subset to another as otherwise they would be globally correlated. We refer to these subsets as *correlated clusters* or simply *clusters*. [1] In such cases, GDR would not be able to obtain a single reduced space of desired dimensionality for the entire dataset without significant loss of query accuracy. If we perform dimensionality reduction on each cluster *individually* (assuming we can find the clusters) rather than on the entire dataset, we can obtain a set of different reduced spaces of desired dimensionality (as shown in Figure 1(c)) which together cover the entire dataset [2] but achieves it with minimal loss of query precision and hence significantly lower query cost. We refer to this approach as local dimensionality reduction (LDR).

Contributions: In this paper, we propose LDR as an approach to high dimensional indexing. Our contributions can be summarized as follows:

- We develop an algorithm to discover correlated clusters in the dataset. Like any clustering problem, the problem, in general, is NP-Hard. Hence, our algorithm is heuristic-based. Our algorithm performs dimensionality reduction of each cluster individually to obtain the reduced space (referred to as subspace) for each cluster. The data items that do not belong to any cluster are outputted as outliers. The algorithm allows the user to control the amount of information loss incurred by dimensionality reduction and hence the query precision/cost.
- We present a technique to index the subspaces individually. We present query processing algorithms for point, range and k-nearest neighbor (k-NN) queries that execute on the

index structure. Unlike many previous techniques [14, 19], our algorithms guarantee correctness of the result i.e. returns exactly the same answers as if the query executed on the original space. In other words, the answer set returned to the user has no false positives or false negatives.

- We perform extensive experiments on synthetic as well as real-life datasets to evaluate the effectiveness of LDR as an indexing technique and compare it with other techniques, namely, GDR, index structure on the original HDFS (referred to as the original space indexing (OSI) technique) and linear scan. Our experiments show that (1) LDR can reduce dimensionality with significantly lower loss in query precision as compared to GDR technique. For the same reduced dimensionality, LDR outperforms GDR by almost an order of magnitude in terms of precision. and (2) LDR performs significantly better than other techniques, namely GDR, original space indexing and sequential scan, in terms of query cost for both synthetic and real-life datasets.

Roadmap: The rest of the paper is organized as follows. In Section 2, we provide an overview of related work. In Section 3, we present the algorithm to discover the correlated clusters in the data. Section 4 discusses techniques to index the subspaces and support similarity queries on top of the index structure. In Section 5, we present the performance results. Section 6 offers the final concluding remarks.

2 Related Work

Previous work on high dimensional indexing techniques includes development of high dimensional index structures (e.g., X-tree[3], SR-tree [15], TV-tree [16], Hybrid-tree [5]) and global dimensionality reduction techniques [9, 7, 8, 14]. The techniques proposed in this paper build on the above work. Our work is also related to the clustering algorithms that have been developed recently for database mining (e.g., BIRCH, CLARANS, CURE algorithms) [21, 18, 12]. The algorithms most related to this paper are those that discover patterns in low dimensional subspaces [1, 2]. In [1], Agarwal et. al. present an algorithm, called CLIQUE, to discover"dense" regions in all subspaces of the original data space. The algorithm works from lower to higher dimensionality subspaces: it starts by discovering 1-d dense units and iteratively discovers all dense units in each k-d subspace by building from the dense units in (k-1)-d subspaces. In [2], Aggarwal et. al. present an algorithm, called PROCLUS, that clusters the data based on their correlation i.e. partitions the data into disjoint groups of correlated points. The authors use the hill climbing technique, popular in spatial cluster analysis, to determine the projected clusters. Neither CLIQUE, nor PROCLUS can be used as an LDR technique since they cannot discover clusters when the principal components are arbitrarily oriented. They can discover only those clusters that are correlated along one or more of the original dimensions. The above techniques are meant for discovering interesting patterns in the data; since correlation along arbitrarily oriented components is usually not that interesting to the user, they do not attempt to discover such correlation. On the contrary, the goal of LDR is efficient indexing; it must be able to discover such correlation in order to minimize the loss of information and make indexing efficient. Also, since the motivation of their work is pattern discovery and not indexing, they do not address the indexing and query processing issues which we have addressed in this paper. To the best of our knowledge, this is the first paper that pro-

---

[1] Note that correlated clusters (formally defined in Section 3) differ from the usual definition of clusters i.e. a set of spatially close points. To avoid confusion, we refer to the latter as *spatial clusters* in this paper.

[2] The set of reduced spaces may not necessarily cover the entire dataset as there may be outliers. We account for outliers in our algorithm.

Symbols	Definitions
N	Number of objects in the database
M	Maximum number of clusters desired
K	Actual number of clusters found ($K \leq M$)
D	Dimensionality of the original feature space
S_i	The ith cluster
C_i	Centroid of S_i
n_i	Size of S_i (number of objects)
$\mathcal{A}_i$	Set of points in S_i
Φ_i	The principal components of S_i
$\Phi_i^{(j)}$	The jth principal component of S_i
d_i	Subspace dimensionality of S_i
ϵ	Neighborhood range
$MaxReconDist$	Maximum Reconstruction distance
$FracOutliers$	Permissible fraction of outliers
$MinSize$	Minimum Size of a cluster
$MaxDim$	Maximum subspace dimensionality of a cluster
$\mathcal{O}$	Set of outliers

Table 1: Summary of symbols and definitions

poses to exploit the local correlations in data for the purpose of indexing.

3 Identifying Correlated Clusters

In this section, we formally define the notion of correlated clusters and present an algorithm to discover such clusters in the data.

3.1 Definitions

In developing the algorithm to identify the correlated clusters, we will need the following definitions.

Definition 1 (Cluster and Subspace) Given a set $\mathcal{A}$ of N points in a D-dimensional feature space, we define a *cluster S* as a set $\mathcal{A}_S$ ($\mathcal{A}_S \subseteq \mathcal{A}$) of locally correlated points. Each cluster S is defined by $S = \langle \Phi_S, d_S, C_S, \mathcal{A}_S \rangle$ where:

- Φ_S are the principal components of the cluster, $\Phi_S^{(i)}$ denoting the ith principal component.
- d_S is the reduced dimensionality i.e. the number of dimensions retained. Obviously, the retained dimensions correspond to the first d_S principal components $\Phi_S^{(i)}, 1 \leq i \leq d_S$ while the eliminated dimensions correspond to the next $(D - d_S)$ components. Hence we use the terms (principal) components and dimensions interchangeably in the context of the transformed space.
- $C_S = [C_S^{(d_S+1)} \cdots C_S^{(D)}]$ is the centroid, that stores, for each eliminated dimension $\Phi_i, (d_S + 1) \leq i \leq D$, a single constant which is "representative" of the position of every point in the cluster along this unrepresented dimension (as we are not storing their unique positions along these dimensions).
- $\mathcal{A}_S$ is the set of points in the cluster

The reduced dimensionality space defined by $\Phi_S^{(i)}, 1 \leq i \leq d_S$ is called the *subspace* of S. d_S is called the subspace dimensionality of S.

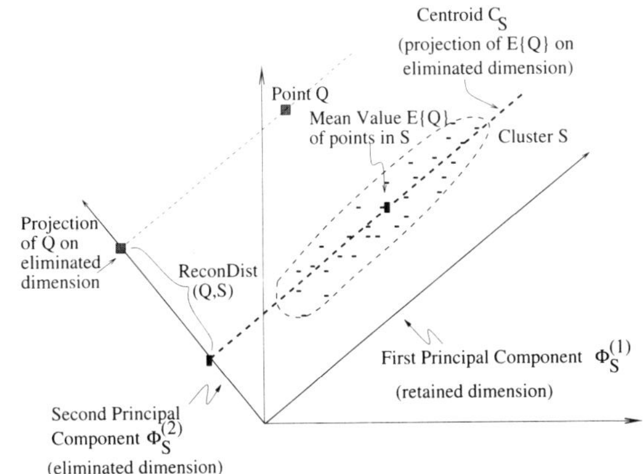

Figure 2: Centroid and Reconstruction Distance.

Definition 2 (Reconstruction Vector) Given a cluster $S = \langle \Phi_S, d_S, C_S, \mathcal{A}_S \rangle$, we define the *reconstruction vector* $\overline{ReconVect}(Q, S)$ of a point Q from S as follows:

$$\overline{ReconVect}(Q, S) = \bar{\Sigma}_{i=(d_S+1)}^{D}(Q \bullet \Phi_S^{(i)} - C_S^{(i)})\Phi_S^{(i)} \quad (1)$$

where $\bar{\Sigma}$ denotes vector addition and $\bullet$ denotes scalar product (i.e. $Q \bullet \Phi_S^{(i)}$ is the projection of Q on $\Phi_S^{(i)}$ as shown in Figure 2). $(Q \bullet \Phi_S^{(i)} - C_S^{(i)})$ is the (scalar) distance of Q from the centroid along each eliminated dimension and $\overline{ReconVector}(Q, S)$ is the vector of these distances.

∎

Definition 3 (Reconstruction Distance) Given a cluster $S = \langle \Phi_S, d_S, C_S, \mathcal{A}_S \rangle$, we now define the *reconstruction distance* (scalar) $ReconDist(Q, S, \mathcal{D})$ of a point Q from S. $\mathcal{D}$ is the distance function used to define the similarity between points in the HDFS. Let $\mathcal{D}$ be an L_p metric i.e. $\mathcal{D}(P, P') = \| P - P' \|_p = [\Sigma_{i=1}^{d}(|P[i] - P'[i]|)^p]^{1/p}$. We define $ReconDist(Q, S, \mathcal{D})$ [3] as follows:

$$
\begin{aligned}
ReconDist(Q, S, \mathcal{D}) &= ReconDist(Q, S, L_p) & (2) \\
&= \| \overline{ReconVect}(Q, S) \|_p & (3) \\
&= [\Sigma_{i=d_S+1}^{D}(|Q \bullet \Phi_S^{(i)} - C_S^{(i)}|)^p]^{1/p} & (4)
\end{aligned}
$$

∎

Note that for any point Q mapped to the d_S-dimensional subspace of S, $\overline{ReconVect}(Q, S)$ (and $ReconDist(Q, S)$) represent the error in the representation i.e. the vector (and scalar) distance between the exact D-dimensional representation of Q and its approximate representation in the d_S-dimensional subspace of S. Higher the error, more the amount of distance information lost.

3.2 Constraints on Correlated Clusters

Our objective in defining clusters is to identify low dimensional subspaces, one for each cluster, that can be indexed separately.

---

[3] Assuming that $\mathcal{D}$ is a fixed L_p metric, we usually omit the $\mathcal{D}$ in $ReconDist(Q, S, \mathcal{D})$ for simplicity of notation.

We desire each subspace to have as low dimensionality as possible without losing too much distance information. In order to achieve the desired goal, each cluster must satisfy the following constraints:

1. **Reconstruction Distance Bound:** In order to restrict the maximum representation error of any point in the low dimensional subspace, we enforce the reconstruction distance of any point $P \in \mathcal{A}_S$ to satisfy the following condition: $ReconDist(P, S) \leq MaxReconDist$ where $MaxReconDist$ is a parameter specified by the user. This condition restricts the amount of information lost within each cluster and hence guarantees a high precision which in turn implies lower query cost.

2. **Dimensionality Bound:** For efficient indexing, we want the subspace dimensionality to be as low as possible while still maintaining high query precision. A cluster must not retain any more dimensions that necessary. In other words, it must retain the minimum number of dimensions required to accommodate the points in the dataset. Note than a cluster S can accommodate a point P only if $ReconDist(P, S) \leq MaxReconDist$. To ensure that the subspace dimensionality d_S is below the critical dimensionality of the multidimensional index structure (i.e. the dimensionality above which a sequential scan is better), we enforce the following condition: $d_S \leq MaxDim$ where $MaxDim$ is specified by the user.

3. **Choice of Centroid:** For each cluster S, we use PCA to determine the subspace i.e. Φ_S is the set of eigenvectors of the covariance matrix of $\mathcal{A}_S$ sorted based on their eigenvalues. [9] shows that for a given choice of reduced dimensionality d_S, the representation error is minimized by choosing the first d_S components among Φ_S and choosing C_S to be the mean value of the points (i.e. the centroid) projected on the eliminated dimensions. To minimize the information loss, we choose $C_S^{(i)} = E\{P \bullet \Phi_S^{(i)}\} = E\{P\} \bullet \Phi_S^{(i)}$ (see Figure 2).

4. **Size Bound:** Finally, we desire each cluster to have a minimum cardinality (number of points) : $n_S \geq MinSize$ where $MinSize$ is user-specified. The clusters that are too small are considered to be outliers.

The goal of the LDR algorithm described below is to discover the set $\mathcal{S} = S_1, S_2, ..., S_K$ of K clusters (where $K \leq M$, M being the maximum number of clusters desired) that exists in the data and that satisfy the above constraints. The remaining points, that do not belong to any of the clusters, are placed in the outlier set $\mathcal{O}$.

3.3 The Clustering Algorithm

Since the LDR algorithm needs to perform *local* correlation analysis (i.e. PCA on subsets of points in the dataset rather than the whole dataset), we need to first identify the right subsets to perform the analysis on. This poses a cyclic problem: how do we identify the right subsets without doing the correlation analysis and how do we do the analysis without knowing the subsets. We break the cycle by using *spatial clusters* as an initial guess of the right subsets. Then we perform PCA on each spatial cluster individually. Finally, we 'recluster' the points based

Clustering Algorithm
Input: Set of Points $\mathcal{A}$, Set of clusters $\mathcal{S}$ (each cluster is either empty or complete)
Output: Some empty clusters are completed, the remaining points form the set of outliers $\mathcal{O}$
FindClusters$(\mathcal{A}, \mathcal{S}, \mathcal{O})$

FC1:	For each empty cluster, select a random point $P \in \mathcal{A}$ such that P is sufficiently far from all completed and valid clusters. If found, make P the centroid C_i and mark S_i valid.
FC2:	For each point $P \in \mathcal{A}$, add P to the closest valid cluster S_i (i.e. $i = argmin(Distance(P, C_i))$) if P lies in the ϵ-neighborhood of C_i i.e. $Distance(P, C_i) \leq \epsilon$.
FC3:	For each valid cluster S_i, compute the principal components Φ_i using PCA. Remove all points from $\mathcal{A}_i$.
FC4:	For each point $P \in \mathcal{A}$, find the valid cluster S_i that, among all the valid clusters requires the minimum subspace dimensionality $LD(P)$ to satisfy $ReconDist(P, S_i) \leq MaxReconDist$ (break ties arbitrarily). If $LD(P) \leq MaxDim$, increment $V_i[j]$ for $j = 0$ to $(LD(P) - 1)$ and n_i.
FC5:	For each valid cluster S_i, compute the subspace dimensionality d_i as: $d_i = \{j \mid F_i[j] \leq FracOutliers$ and $F_i[j - 1] > FracOutliers\}$ where $F_i[j] = \frac{V_i[j]}{n_i}$.
FC6:	For each point $P \in \mathcal{A}$, add P to the first valid cluster S_i such that $ReconDist(P, S_i) \leq MaxReconDist$. If no such S_i exists, add P to $\mathcal{O}$.
FC7:	If a valid cluster S_i violates the size constraint i.e. ($|\mathcal{A}_i| < MinSize$), mark it empty. Remove each point $P \in \mathcal{A}_i$ from S_i and add it to the first succeeding cluster S_j that satisfies $ReconDist(P, S_j) \leq MaxReconDist$ or to $\mathcal{O}$ if there is no such cluster. Mark the other valid clusters complete. For each complete cluster S_i, map each point $P \in \mathcal{A}_i$ to the subspace and store it along with $ReconDist(P, S, \mathcal{D})$.

Table 2: Clustering Algorithm

on the correlation information (i.e. principal components) to obtain the correlated clusters. The clustering algorithm is shown in Table 2. It takes a set of points $\mathcal{A}$ and a set of clusters $\mathcal{S}$ as input. When it is invoked for the first time, $\mathcal{A}$ is the entire dataset and each cluster in $\mathcal{S}$ is marked 'empty'. At the end, each identified cluster is marked 'complete' indicating a completely constructed cluster (no further change); the remaining clusters remain marked 'empty'. The points that do not belong to any of the clusters are placed to the outlier set $\mathcal{O}$. The details of each step is described below:

- **Construct Spatial Clusters**(Steps FC1 and FC2): The algorithm starts by constructing M spatial clusters where M is the maximum number of clusters desired. We use a simple single-pass partitioning-based spatial clustering algorithm to determine the spatial clusters [18]. We first choose a set of $\mathcal{C} \subset \mathcal{A}$ of *well-scattered* points as the centroids such that points that belong to the same spatial cluster are not chosen to serve as centroids to different clusters. Such a set $\mathcal{C}$ is called a *piercing* set [2]. We achieve

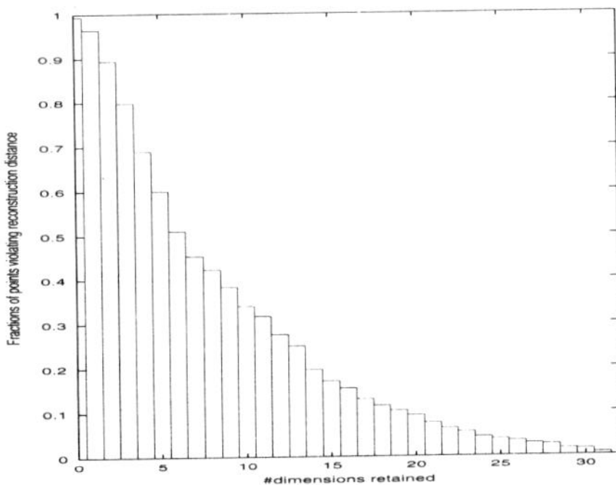

Figure 3: Determining subspace dimensionality (MaxDim=32).

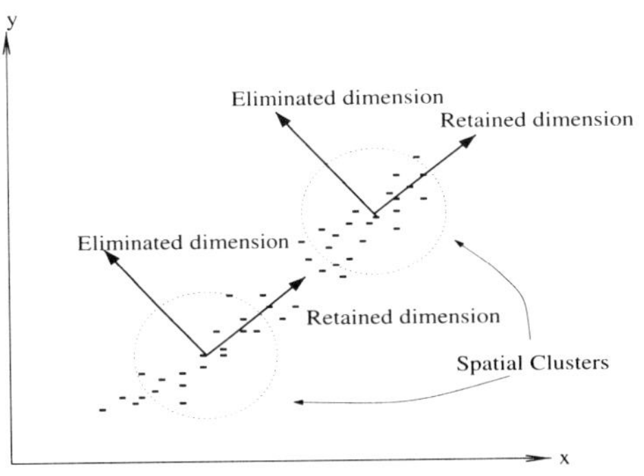

Figure 4: Splitting of correlated clusters due to initial spatial clustering.

this by ensuring that each point $P \in \mathcal{C}$ in the set is sufficiently far from any already chosen point $P' \in \mathcal{C}$ i.e. $Dist(P, P') > threshold$ for a user-defined threshold. [4] This technique, proposed by Gonzalez [10], is guaranteed to return a piercing if no outliers are present. To avoid scanning though the whole database to choose the centroids, we first construct a random sample of the dataset and choose the centroids from the sample [2, 12]. We choose the sample to be large enough (using Chernoff bounds [17]) such that the probability of missing clusters due to sampling is low i.e. there is at least one point from each cluster present in the sample with a high probability [12]. Once the centroids are chosen, we group each point $P \in \mathcal{A}$ with the closest centroid $C_{closest}$ if $Distance(P, C_{closest}) \leq \epsilon$ and update the centroid to reflect the mean position of its group. If $Distance(P, C_{closest}) > \epsilon$, we ignore P. The restriction of the neighborhood range to ϵ makes the correlation analysis *localized*. Smaller the value of ϵ, the more localized the analysis. At the same time, ϵ has to be large enough so that we get a sufficiently large number of points in the cluster which is necessary for the correlation analysis to be robust.

- **Compute PCs**(Step FC3): Once we have the spatial clusters, we perform PCA on each spatial cluster S_i individually to obtain the principal components $\Phi_S^{(i)}$, $i = [1, D]$. We do not eliminate any components yet. We compute the mean value M_i of the points in S_i so that we can compute $ReconDist(P, S_i)$ in Steps FC4 and FC5 for any choice of subspace dimensionality d_i. Finally, we remove the points from the spatial clusters so that they can be reclustered as described in Step FC6.

- **Determine Subspace Dimensionality**(Steps FC4 and FC5): For each cluster S_i, we must retain no more dimensions than necessary to accommodate the points in the dataset (except the outliers). To determine the number of dimensions d_i to be retained for each cluster S_i, we first determine, for each point $P \in \mathcal{A}$, the best cluster, if one exists, for placing P. Let $LD(P, S_i)$ denote the the least dimensionality needed for the cluster S_i to represent P with

---

[4]For subsequent invocations of FindClusters procedure during the iterative algorithm (Step 2 in Table 3), there may exist already completed clusters (does not exist during the initial invocation). Hence P must also be sufficiently far from all complete clusters formed so far i.e. $ReconDist(P, S) > threshold$ for each complete cluster S.

$ReconDist(P, S_i) \leq MaxReconDist$. Formally,

$$LD(P, S_i) = \{d|$$
$$ReconDist(P, S_i) \leq MaxReconDist \text{ if } d_i \geq d$$
$$\text{and } ReconDist(P, S_i) > MaxReconDist \text{ otherwise } \}$$
$$(5)$$

In other words, the first $LD(P, S_i)$ PCs are just enough to satisfy the above constraint. Note that such a $LD(P, S_i)$ always exists for a non-negative $MaxReconDist$. Let $LD(P) = min \{ LD(P, S_i)|S_i \text{ is a valid cluster } \}$. If $LD(P) \leq MaxDim$, there exists a cluster that can accommodate P without violating the dimensionality bound. Let $LD(P, S_i) = LD(P)$ (if there are multiple such clusters S_i, break ties arbitrarily). We say S_i is the "best" cluster for placing P since S_i is the cluster that, among all the valid clusters, needs to retain the minimum number of dimensions to accommodate P. P would satisfy the $ReconDist(P, S_i) \leq MaxReconDist$ bound if the subspace dimensionality d_i of S_i is such that $LD(P, S_i) \leq d_i \leq MaxDim$ and would violate it if $0 \leq d_i < LD(P, S_i)$. For each cluster S_i, we maintain this information as a count array $V_i[j]$, $j = [0, MaxDim]$ where $V_i[j]$ is the number of points that, among the points chosen to be placed in S_i, would violate the $ReconDist(P, S_i) \leq MaxReconDist$ constraint if the subspace dimensionality d_i is j: so in this case (for point P), we must increment $V_i[j]$ for $j = 0$ to $(LD(P, S_i) - 1)$ and the total count n_i of points chosen to be placed in S_i. ($V_i[j]$ and n_i is initialized to 0 before FC4 begins). On the other hand, if $LD(P) > MaxDim$, there exists no cluster in which P can be placed without violating the dimensionality bound; so we do nothing.

At the end of the pass over the dataset, for each cluster S_i, we have computed $V_i[j]$, $j = [0, MaxDim]$ and n_i. We use this to compute $F_i[j]$, $j = [0, MaxDim]$ where $F_i[j]$ is the fraction of points that, among those chosen to be placed in S_i (during FC4), would violate the $ReconDist(P, S_i) \leq MaxReconDist$ constraint if the subspace dimensionality d_i is j i.e. $F_i[j] = \frac{V_i[j]}{n_i}$. An example of F_i from one of the experiments conducted on the real life dataset (cf. Section 5.3) is shown in Figure 3. We choose d_i to be as low as possible without too many points violating the reconstruction distance bound i.e. not more than $FracOutliers$ fraction of points in S_i where $FracOutliers$ is specified by the user. In other words, d_i is the minimum number of dimensions that must be retained so that the fraction of points that violate the $ReconDist(P, S_i) \leq MaxReconDist$ constraint is no more that $FracOutliers$ i.e. $d_i = \{j | F_i[j] \leq FracOutliers$ and $F_i[j-1] > FracOutliers\}$. In Figure 3, d_i is 21 for $FracOutliers = 0.1$, 16 for $FracOutliers = 0.2$ and 14 for $FracOutliers = 0.3$. We now have all the subspaces formed. In the next step, we assign the points to the clusters.

- **Recluster Points**(Step FC6): In the reclustering step, we reassign each point $P \in \mathcal{A}$ to a cluster S that covers P i.e. $ReconDist(P, S) \leq MaxReconDist$. If there exists no such cluster, P is added to the outlier set $\mathcal{O}$. If there exists just one cluster that covers P, P is assigned to that cluster. Now we consider the interesting case of multiple clusters covering P. In this case, there is a possibility that some of these clusters are actually parts of the same correlated cluster but has been split due to the initial spatial clustering. This is illustrated in Figure 4. Since points in a correlated cluster can be spatially distant from each other (e.g., form an elongated cluster in Figure 4) and spatial clustering only clusters spatially close points, it may end up putting correlated points in different spatial clusters, thus breaking up a single correlated cluster into two or more clusters. Although such 'splitting' does not affect the indexing cost of our technique for range queries and k-NN queries, it increases the cost of point search and deletion as multiple clusters may need to searched in contrast to just one when there is no 'splitting'. (cf. Section 4.2.1). Hence, we must detect these 'broken' clusters and merge them back together. We achieve this by maintaining the clusters in some fixed order (e.g., order in which they were created). For each point $P \in \mathcal{P}$, we check each cluster sequentially in that order and assign it to the first cluster that covers P. If two (or more) clusters are part of the same correlated cluster, most points will be covered by all of them but will *always* be assigned to only one them, whichever appears first in the order. This effectively merges the clusters into one since only the first one will remain while the others will end up being almost empty and will be discarded due to the violation of size bound in FC7. Note that the $FracOutliers$ bound in Step FC5 still holds i.e. besides the points for which $LD(P) > MaxDim$, no more that $FracOutliers$ fraction of points can become outliers.

- **Map Points**(Step FC7): In the final step of the algorithm, we eliminate clusters that violate the size constraint. We remove each point from these clusters and add it to the first succeeding valid cluster S_j that satisfies the $ReconDist(P, S_j) \leq MaxReconDist$ bound or to $\mathcal{O}$ otherwise. For the remaining clusters S_i, we map each point $P \in \mathcal{A}_i$ to the subspace by projecting P to $\Phi_i^{(j)}, 1 \leq j \leq d_i$ and refer it as the (d_i-d) image $Image(P, S_i)$ of P:

$$Image(P, S_i)[j] = P \bullet \Phi_i^{(j)} \text{ for } 1 \leq j \leq d_i \qquad (6)$$

We refer to P as the (D-d) original $Original(Image(P, S_i), S_i)$ of its image $Image(P, S_i)$. We store the image of each point along with the reconstruction distance $ReconDist(P, S_i)$.

Since FindClusters chooses the initial centroids from a random sample, there is a risk of missing out some clusters. One way to reduce this risk is to choose a large number of initial centroids but at the cost of slowing down the clustering algorithm. We reduce the risk of missing clusters by trying to discover more clusters, if there exists, among the points returned as outliers by the initial invocation of FindClusters. We iterate the above process as long as new clusters are still being discovered as shown below:

Iterative Clustering
(1)   FindClusters($\mathcal{A}, \mathcal{S}, \mathcal{O}$); /* initial invocation */
(2)   Let $\mathcal{O}'$ be an empty set. Invoke FindClusters($\mathcal{O}, \mathcal{S}, \mathcal{O}'$). Make $\mathcal{O}'$ the new outlier set i.e. $\mathcal{O} \leftarrow \mathcal{O}'$. If new clusters found, go to (2). Else return.

Table 3: Iterative Clustering Algorithm

The above iterative clustering algorithm is somewhat similar to the hill climbing technique, commonly used in spatial clustering algorithms (especially in partitioning-based clustering algorithms like k-means, k-medoids and CLARANS [18]). In this technique, the "bad quality" clusters (the ones that violate the size bound) are discarded (Step FC7) and is replaced, if possible, by better quality clusters. However, unlike the hill climbing approach where all the points are reassigned to the clusters, we do not reassign the points already assigned to the 'complete' clusters. Alternatively, we can follow the hill climbing approach but it is computationally more expensive and requires more scans of the database [18].

Cost Analysis: The above algorithm requires three passes through the dataset (FC2, FC4 and FC6) and a time complexity of $O(ND^2K)$. The detailed analysis can be found in [6].

4 Indexing Correlated Clusters

Having developed the technique to find the correlated clusters, we now shift our attention to how to use them for indexing. Our objective is to develop a data structure that exploits the correlated clusters to efficiently support range and k-NN queries over HDFSs. The developed data structure must also be able to handle insertions and deletions.

4.1 Data Structure

The data structure, referred to as the global index structure (GI) (i.e. index on entire dataset), consists of separate multidimensional indices for each cluster, connected to a single root node. The global index structure is shown in Figure 5. We explain the various components in details below:

- *The Root Node R* of GI contains the following information for each cluster S_i: (1) a pointer to the root node R_i (i.e. the address of disk block containing R_i) of the cluster index I_i (the multidimensional index on S_i), (2) the principal components Φ_i (3) the subspace dimensionality d_i and (4) the centroid C_i. It also contains an access pointer O to the outlier cluster $\mathcal{O}$. If there is an index on $\mathcal{O}$ (discussed later), O points to the root node of that index; otherwise, it points to the start of the set of blocks on which the outlier set resides on disk. R may occupy one or more disk blocks depending on the number of clusters K and original dimensionality D.

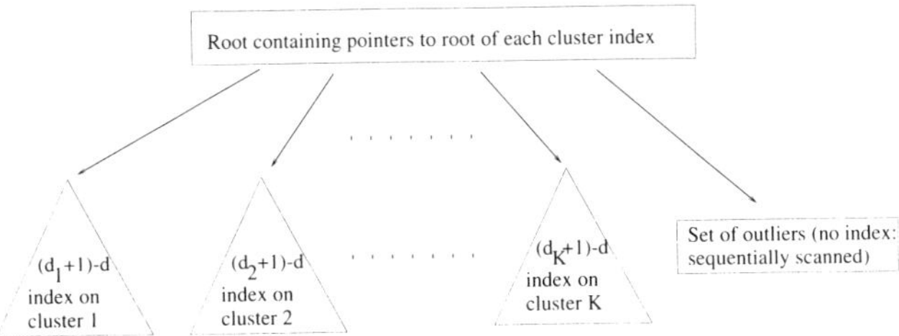

Figure 5: The global index structure

- *The Cluster Indices:* We maintain a multidimensional index I_i for each cluster S_i in which we store the reduced dimensional representation of the points in S_i. However, instead of building the index I_i on the d_i-d subspace of S_i defined by $\Phi_i^{(j)}, 1 \leq j \leq d_i$, we build I_i on the $(d_i + 1)$-d space, the first d_i dimensions of which are defined by $\Phi_i^{(j)}, 1 \leq j \leq d_i$ as above while the $(d_i + 1)$th dimension is defined by the reconstruction distance $ReconDist(P, S_i, \mathcal{D})$. Including reconstruction distance as a dimension helps to improve query precision (as explained later). We redefine the image $NewImage(P, S_i)$ of a point $P \in \mathcal{A}_i$ as a $(d_i + 1)$-d point (rather than a d_i-d point), incorporating the reconstruction distance as the $(d_i + 1)$th dimension:

$$NewImage(P, S_i)[j]$$
$$= Image(P, S_i)[j] = P \bullet \Phi_i^{(j)} \text{ for } 1 \leq j \leq d_i$$
$$= ReconDist(P, S_i, \mathcal{D}) \text{ for } j = d_i + 1 \quad (7)$$

The $(d_i + 1)$-d cluster index I_i is constructed by inserting the $(d_i + 1)$-d images (i.e. $NewImage(P, S_i)$) of each point $P \in \mathcal{A}_i$ into the multidimensional index structure using the insertion algorithm of the index structure. Any disk-based multidimensional index structure (e.g., R-tree [13], X-tree [3], SR-tree [15], Hybrid Tree [5]) can be used for this purpose. We used the hybrid tree in our experiments since it is a space partitioning index structure (i.e. has "dimensionality-independent" fanout), is more scalable to high dimensionalities in terms of query cost and can support arbitrary distance metrics [5].

- *The Outlier Index:* For the outlier set $\mathcal{O}$, we may or may not build an index depending on whether the original dimensionality D is below or above the critical dimensionality. In this paper, we assume that D is above the critical dimensionality of the index structure and hence choose not to index the outlier set (i.e. use sequential scan for it).

Like other database index trees (e.g., B-tree, R-tree), the global index (GI) shown in Figure 5 is disk-based. But it may not be perfectly height balanced i.e. all paths from R to leaf may not be of exactly equal length. The reason is that the sizes and the dimensionalities may differ from one cluster to another causing the cluster indices to have different heights. We found that GI is *almost* height balanced (i.e. the difference in the lengths of *any* two paths from R to leaf is never more than 1 or 2) due to the size bound on the clusters (see [6] for details). Also, its height cannot exceed the height of the original space index by more than 1 (see [6] for details).

To guarantee the correctness of our query algorithms (i.e. to ensure no false dismissals), we need to show that the cluster index distances *lower bounds* the actual distances in the original D-d space [7]. In other words, for any two D-d points P and Q, $\mathcal{D}(NewImage(\text{P},S_i), NewImage(\text{Q},S_i))$ must always lower bound $\mathcal{D}(P, Q)$.

Lemma 1 (Lower Bounding Lemma)
$\mathcal{D}(NewImage(P, S_i), NewImage(Q, S_i))$ *always lower bounds* $\mathcal{D}(P, Q)$. *(Proof in [6]).*

Note that instead of incorporating reconstruction distance as the $(d_i + 1)$th dimension, we could have simply constructed GI with each cluster index I_i defined on the corresponding d_i-d subspace $\Phi_i^{(j)}, 1 \leq j \leq d_i$. Since the lower bounding lemma holds for the d_i-d subspaces (as shown in [7]), the query processing algorithms described below would have been correct. The reason we use $(d_i + 1)$-d subspace is that the distances in the $(d_i + 1)$-d subspace upper bounds the distances in the d_i-d subspace and hence provides a tighter lower bound to distances in the original D-d space:

$$\mathcal{D}(NewImage(P, S_i), NewImage(Q, S_i)) =$$
$$[\mathcal{D}(Image(P, S_i), Image(Q, S_i))^p +$$
$$|(ReconDist(P, S_i, \mathcal{D}) - ReconDist(Q, S_i, \mathcal{D}))|^p]^{1/p}$$
$$\Rightarrow \mathcal{D}(NewImage(P, S_i), NewImage(Q, S_i)) \geq$$
$$\mathcal{D}(Image(P, S_i), Image(Q, S_i)) \quad (8)$$

Furthermore, the difference between the two (i.e. $\mathcal{D}(NewImage(P, S_i)$, $NewImage(Q, S_i))$ and $\mathcal{D}(Image(P, S_i)$, $Image(Q, S_i))$) is usually significant when computing the distance of the query from a point in the cluster: Say, P is a point in S_i and Q is the query point. Due to the reconstruction distance bound, $ReconDist(P, S_i, \mathcal{D})$ is *always* a small number ($\leq MaxReconDist$). On the other hand, $ReconDist(Q, S_i, \mathcal{D})$ can have any arbitrary value and is usually much larger than $ReconDist(P, S_i, \mathcal{D})$), thus making the difference quite significant. This makes the distance computations in the $(d_i + 1)$-d more optimistic than that in the d_i-d index and hence a better estimate of the distances in the original D-d space. For example, for a range query, the range condition ($\mathcal{D}(NewImage(P, S_i), NewImage(Q, S_i)) \leq \rho$) is more optimistic (i.e. satisfies fewer objects) than the range condition ($\mathcal{D}(Image(P, S_i), Image(Q, S_i)) \leq \rho$), leading to fewer false positives. The same is true for k-NN queries. Fewer false positives imply lower query cost. At the same time, adding a new dimension also increases the cost of the query. Our experiments show that decrease in the query cost from fewer false positives offsets the increase of the cost of the adding a dimension, reducing the overall cost of the query significantly (cf. Section 5, Figure 12).

4.2 Query Processing over the Global Index

In this section, we discuss how to execute similarity queries efficiently using the index structure described above (cf. Figure 5). We describe the query processing algorithm for point, range and k-NN queries. For correctness, the query processing algorithm must guarantee that it always returns exactly the same answer as the query on the original space [7]. Often dimensionality reduction techniques do not satisfy the correctness criteria [14, 19].

We show that all our query processing algorithms satisfy the above criteria.

4.2.1 Point Search

To find an object O, we first find the cluster that contains O. It is the first cluster S (in the order mentioned in Step FC6) for which the reconstruction distance bound is satisfied. If such a cluster S exists, we compute $NewImage(O, S)$ and find it in the corresponding index by invoking the point search algorithm of the index structure. The point search returns the object if it exists in the cluster, otherwise it returns null. If no such cluster S exists, O must be, if at all, in $\mathcal{O}$. So we sequentially search through $\mathcal{O}$ and return it if it exists in $\mathcal{O}$.

4.2.2 Range Queries

A range query $\mathcal{Q} = \langle Q, \rho, \mathcal{D} \rangle$ retrieves all objects O in the database that satisfies the range condition $\mathcal{D}(Q, O) \leq \rho$. The algorithm proceeds as follows (see [6] for pseudocode). For each cluster S_i, we map the query anchor Q to its $(d_i + 1)$-d image Q_i (using the principal components Φ_i and subspace dimensionality d_i stored in the root node R of GI) and execute a range query (with the same range ρ) on the corresponding cluster index I_i by invoking the procedure RangeSearchOnClusterIndex on the root node R_i of I_i. RangeSearchOnClusterIndex is the standard R-tree-style recursive range search procedure that starts from the root node and explores the tree in a depth-first fashion. It examines the current node T: if T is a non-leaf node, it recursively searches each child node N of T that satisfies the condition $MINDIST(Q, N, \mathcal{D}) \leq \rho$ (where $MINDIST(Q, N, \mathcal{D})$ denotes the minimum distance of the $(d_i + 1)$-d image of query point to the $(d_i + 1)$-d bounding rectangle of N based on distance function $\mathcal{D}$); if T is a leaf node, it retrieves each data item O stored in T (which is the $NewImage$ of the original D-d object) [5] that satisfies the range condition $\mathcal{D}(Q, O) \leq \rho$ in the $(d_i + 1)$-d space, accesses the full D-dimensional tuple on disk to determine whether it is a false positive and adds it to the result set if it is not a false positive (i.e. it also satisfies the range condition $\mathcal{D}(Q, O) \leq \rho$ in the original D-d space). After all the cluster indices are searched, we add all the qualifying points from among the outliers to the result by performing a sequential scan on $\mathcal{O}$. Since the distance in the index space lower bounds the distance in the original space (cf. Lemma 1), the above algorithm cannot have any false dismissals. The algorithm cannot have any false positives either as they are filtered out before adding to the result set. The above algorithm thus returns exactly the same answer as the query on the original space.

4.2.3 k Nearest Neighbor Queries

A k-NN query $\mathcal{Q} = \langle Q, k, \mathcal{D} \rangle$ retrieves a set $\mathcal{R}$ of k objects such that for any two objects $O \in \mathcal{R}, O' \notin \mathcal{R}, \mathcal{D}(Q, O) \leq \mathcal{D}(Q, O')$. The algorithm for k-NN queries is shown in Table 4. Like the basic k-NN algorithm, the algorithm uses a priority queue $queue$ to navigate the nodes/objects in the database in increasing order of their distances from Q. Note that we use a single queue to navigate the entire global index i.e. we explore the nodes/objects of all the cluster indices in an intermixed fashion and do not require

---

[5] Note that instead of storing the 'NewImage's, we could have stored the original D-d points in the leaf pages of the cluster indices (in both cases, the index is built on the reduced space). Our choice of the former option is explained in [6].

<table>
<tr><td colspan="2">k-NNSearch(Query $\mathcal{Q} = Q, k, \mathcal{D}$))</td></tr>
<tr><td>1</td><td>for (i=1; i $\leq K$; i++)</td></tr>
<tr><td>2</td><td>$Q_{S_i} \leftarrow$ NewImage(Q, S_i);</td></tr>
<tr><td>3</td><td>$queue$.push(S_i, R_i, $MINDIST(Q_i, R_i, \mathcal{D})$);</td></tr>
<tr><td>4</td><td>Add to $temp$ the k closest neighbors of Q among $\mathcal{O}$ (lin. scan)</td></tr>
<tr><td>5</td><td>while (not $queue$.IsEmpty())</td></tr>
<tr><td>6</td><td>top=queue.Top();</td></tr>
<tr><td>7</td><td>for each object O in $temp$ such that $O.dist \leq top.dist$</td></tr>
<tr><td>8</td><td>$temp \leftarrow temp - O$;</td></tr>
<tr><td>9</td><td>$result = result \cup O$;</td></tr>
<tr><td>10</td><td>retrieved++;</td></tr>
<tr><td>11</td><td>if (retrieved = k) return $result$;</td></tr>
<tr><td>12</td><td>queue.Pop();</td></tr>
<tr><td>13</td><td>if $top.T$ is an object</td></tr>
<tr><td>14</td><td>$top.dist = \mathcal{D}(Q, Original(top.T, top.S))$;</td></tr>
<tr><td>15</td><td>$temp = temp \cup top.T$;</td></tr>
<tr><td>16</td><td>else if $top.T$ is a leaf node</td></tr>
<tr><td>17</td><td>for each object O in $top.T$</td></tr>
<tr><td>18</td><td>$queue$.push(top.S, O, $\mathcal{D}(Q_{top.S}, O)$);</td></tr>
<tr><td>19</td><td>else /* $top.T$ is an index node */</td></tr>
<tr><td>20</td><td>for each child N of $top.T$</td></tr>
<tr><td>21</td><td>$queue$.push(top.S, N, $MINDIST(Q_{top.S}, N, \mathcal{D})$);</td></tr>
</table>

Table 4: k-NN Query.

separate queues to navigate the different clusters. Each entry in $queue$ is either a node or an object and stores 3 fields: the id of the node/object T it corresponds to, the cluster S it belongs to and its distance $dist$ from the query anchor Q. The items (i.e. nodes/objects) are prioritized based on $dist$ i.e. the smallest item appears at the top of the queue (min-priority queue). For nodes, the distance is defined by $MINDIST$ while for objects, it is the the point-to-point distance. Initially, for each cluster, we map the query anchor Q to its $(d_i + 1)$-d image Q_i using the information stored in the root node R of GI (Line 2). Then, for each cluster index I_i, we compute the distance $MINDIST(Q_i, R_i, \mathcal{D})$ of Q_i from the root node R_i of I_i and push R_i into $queue$ along with the distance and the id of the cluster S_i to which it belongs (Line 3). We also fill the set $temp$ with the k closest neighbors of Q among the outliers by sequentially scanning through $\mathcal{O}$ (Line 4).

After these initialization steps, we start navigating the index by popping the item from the top of $queue$ at each step (Line 11). If the popped item is an object, we compute the distance of the original D-d object (by accessing the full tuple on disk) from Q and append it to $temp$ (Lines 12-14). If it a node, we compute the distance of each of its children to the appropriate query image $Q_{top.S}$ (where $top.S$ denotes the cluster which top belongs to) and push them into the queue (Lines 15-20). Note that the image for each cluster is computed just once (in Step 2) and is reused here. We move an object O from $temp$ to $result$ only when we are sure that it is among the k nearest neighbors of Q i.e. there exists no object $O' \notin result$ such that $\mathcal{D}(O', Q) < \mathcal{D}(O, Q)$ and $|result| < k$. The second condition is ensured by the exit condition in Line 11. The condition $O.dist \leq top.dist$ in Line 7 ensures that there exists no $unexplored$ object O' such that $\mathcal{D}(O', Q) < \mathcal{D}(O, Q)$. The proof is simple: $O.dist \leq top.dist$ implies $O.dist \leq \mathcal{D}(NewImage(O', S), NewImage(Q, S))$

for any unexplored object O' in a cluster S (by the property of min-priority queue) which in turn implies $\mathcal{D}(O, Q) \leq \mathcal{D}(O', Q)$ (since $D(NewImage(O', S), NewImage(Q, S))$ lower bounds $\mathcal{D}(O', Q)$, see Lemma 1). By inserting the objects in $temp$ (i.e. already explored items) into $result$ in increasing order of their distances in the original D-d space (by keeping $temp$ sorted), we also ensure there exists no *explored* object O' such that $\mathcal{D}(O', Q) < \mathcal{D}(O, Q)$. This shows that the algorithm returns the correct answer i.e. the exact set of objects as the query in the original D-d space. It is also easy to show that the algorithm is I/O optimal.

Lemma 2 (Optimality of k-NN algorithm) *The k-NN algorithm is optimal i.e. it does not explore any object outside the range of kth nearest neighbor. (Proof in [6]).*

4.3 Modifications

We assume that the data is static in order to build the index. However, we must support subsequent insertions/deletions of the objects to/from the index efficiently. We do not describe the insertion and deletion algorithms in this paper due to space limitations but they can be found in [6].

5 Experiments

In this section, we present the results of an extensive empirical study we have conducted to (1) evaluate the effectiveness of LDR as a high dimensional indexing technique and (2) compare it with other techniques, namely, GDR, original space indexing (OSI) and linear scan. We conducted our experiments on both synthetic and real-life datasets. The major findings of our study can be summarized as follows:

- **High Precision:** LDR provides up to an order of magnitude improvement in precision over the GDR technique at the same reduced dimensionality. This indicates that LDR can achieve the same reduction as GDR with significantly lower loss of distance information.
- **Low Query Cost:** LDR consistently outperforms other indexing techniques, namely GDR, original space indexing and sequential scan, in terms of query cost (combined I/O and CPU costs) for both synthetic and real-life datasets.

Thus, our experimental results validate the thesis of this paper that LDR is an effective indexing technique for high dimensional datasets. All experiments reported in this section were conducted on a Sun Ultra Enterprise 450 machine with 1 GB of physical memory and several GB of secondary storage, running Solaris 2.5.

5.1 Experimental Methodology

We conduct the following two sets of experiments to evaluate the LDR technique and compare it with other indexing techniques.

Precision Experiments

Due to dimensionality reduction, both GDR and LDR, cause loss of distance information. More the number of dimensions eliminated, more the amount of information lost. We measure this loss by *precision* defined as $Precision = \frac{|R_{original}|}{|R_{reduced}|}$ where $R_{reduced}$ and $R_{original}$ are the sets of answers returned by the range query on the reduced dimensional space and the original HDFS respectively [14]. We repeat that since our algorithms

guarantee that the user always gets back the correct set $R_{original}$ of answers (as if the query executed in the original HDFS), precision does *not* measure the quality of the answers returned to the user but just the information loss incurred by the DR technique and hence the query cost. For a DR technique, if we fix the reduced dimensionality, the higher the precision, the lower the cost of the query, the more efficient the technique. We compare the GDR and LDR techniques based on precision at fixed reduced dimensionalities.

Cost Experiments

We conducted experiments to measure the query cost (I/O and CPU costs) for each of the following four indexing techniques. We describe how we compute the I/O and CPU costs of the techniques below.

- *Linear Scan:* In this technique, we perform a simple linear scan on the original high dimensional dataset. The I/O cost in terms of sequential disk accesses is $\frac{N*(D*sizeof(float)+sizeof(id))}{PageSize}$. Since $sizeof(id) \ll (D * sizeof(float))$, we will ignore the $sizeof(id)$ henceforth. Assuming sequential I/O is 10 times faster than random I/O, the cost in terms of the random accesses is $\frac{N*sizeof(float)*D}{10*PageSize}$. The CPU cost is the cost of computing the distance of the query from each point in the database.
- *Original Space Indexing (OSI):* In this technique, we build the index on the original HDFS itself using a multidimensional index structure. We use the hybrid tree as the index structure. The I/O cost (in terms of random disk accesses) of the query is the number of nodes of the index structure accessed. The CPU cost is the CPU time (excluding I/O wait) required to navigate the index and return the answers.
- *GDR:* In this technique, we peform PCA on the original dataset, retain the first few principal components (depending on the desired reduced dimensionality) and index the reduced dimensional space using the hybrid tree index structure. In this case, the I/O cost has 2 components: index page accesses (discussed in OSI) and accessing the full tuples in the relation for false positive elimination (post processing cost). The post processing cost can be one I/O per false positives in the worst case. However, as observed in [11], this assumption is overly pessimistic (and is confirmed by our experiments). We, therefore, assume the postprocessing I/O cost to be $\frac{num\_false\_positives}{2}$. The total I/O cost (in number of random disk accesses) is $index\_page\_access\_cost + \frac{num\_false\_positives}{2}$. The CPU cost is the sum of the index CPU cost and the post processing CPU cost i.e. cost of computing the distance of the query from each of the false positives.
- *LDR:* In this technique, we index each cluster using the hybrid tree multidimensional index structure and used a linear scan for the outlier set. For LDR, the I/O cost of a query has 3 components: index page accesses for each cluster index, linear scan on the outlier set and accessing the full tuples in the relation (post processing cost). The total index page access cost is the total number of nodes accessed of all the cluster indices combined. The number of sequential disk accesses for the outlier scan is $\frac{|\mathcal{O}|*D*sizeof(float)}{PageSize}$. The cost of outlier scan in terms of random accesses is $\frac{|\mathcal{O}|*sizeof(float)*D}{10*PageSize}$.

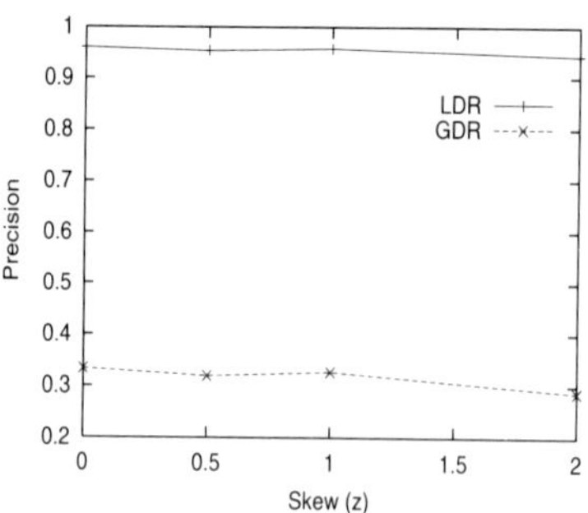

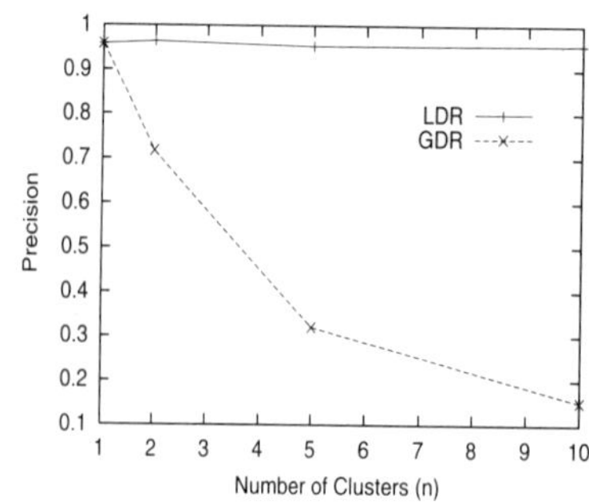

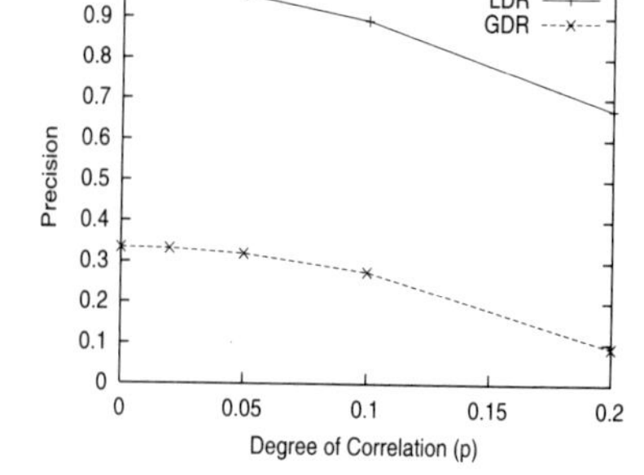

Figure 6: Sensitivity of precision to skew.

Figure 7: Sensitivity of precision to number of clusters.

Figure 8: Sensitivity of precision to degree of correlation.

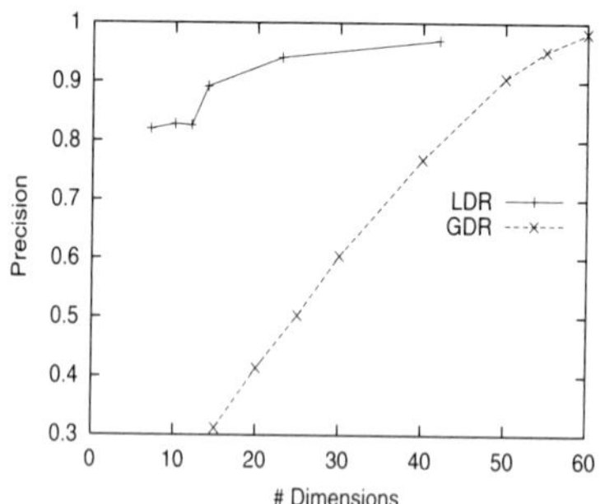

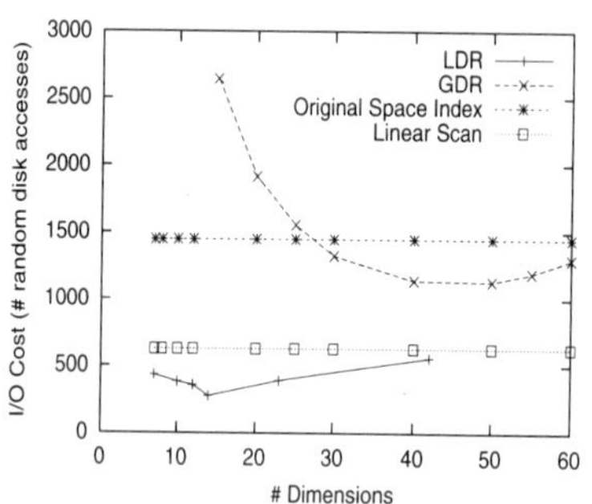

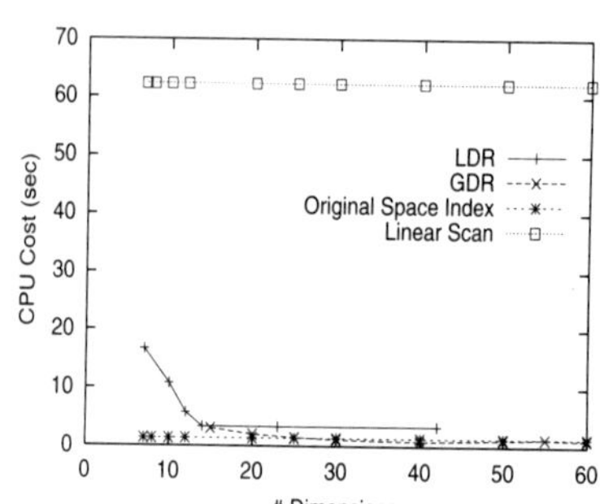

Figure 9: Sensitivity of precision to reduced dimensionality.

Figure 10: Comparison of LDR, GDR, Original Space Indexing and Linear Scan in terms of I/O cost. For linear scan, the cost is computed as: $\frac{num\_sequential\_disk\_accesses}{10}$.

Figure 11: Comparison of LDR, GDR, Original Space Indexing and Linear Scan in terms of CPU cost.

The postprocessing I/O cost is $\frac{num\_false\_positives}{2}$ (as discussed above). The total I/O cost (in number of random disk accesses) is $index\_page\_access\_cost + \frac{|\mathcal{O}|*sizeof(float)*D)}{10*PageSize} + \frac{num\_false\_positives}{2}$. Similarly, the CPU cost is the sum of the index CPU cost, outlier scan CPU cost (i.e. cost of computing the distance of the query from each of the outliers) and the post processing cost (i.e. cost of computing the distance of the query from each of the false positives).

We chose the hybrid tree as the index structure for our experiments since it is a space partitioning index structure ("dimensionality-independent" fanout) and has been shown to scale to high dimensionalities [5]. [6] We use a page size of 4KB for all our experiments.

5.2 Experimental Results - Synthetic Data Sets

Synthetic Data Sets and Queries

In order to generate the synthetic data, we use a method similar to that discussed in [21] but appropriately modified so that we can generate the different clusters in subspaces of different orientations and dimensionalities. The synthetic dataset generator is described in Appendix A. The dataset generated has original dimensionality of 64 and consists of 100,000 points. The input parameters to the data generator and their default values are

shown in Table 5 (Appendix A).

We generated 100 range queries by selecting their query anchors randomly from the dataset and choosing a range value such that the average query selectivity is about 2%. We tested with only range queries since the k-NN algorithm, being optimal, is identical to the range query with the range equal to the distance of the kth nearest neighbor from the query (Lemma 3). We use L_2 distance (Euclidean) as the distance metric. All our measurements are averaged over the 100 queries.

Precision Experiments

In our first set of experiments, we carry out a sensitivity analysis of the GDR and LDR techniques to parameters like skew in the size of the clusters (z_{size}), number of clusters (k) and degree of correlation (p). In each experiment, we vary the parameter of interest while the remaining parameters are fixed at their default values. We fix the reduced dimensionality of the GDR technique to 15. We fix the average subspace dimensionality of the clusters (i.e. $\Sigma_{i=1}^{K} \frac{n_i d_i}{K}$) also to 15 by choosing $FracOutliers$ and $MaxReconDist$ appropriately ($FracOutliers = 0.1$ and $MaxReconDist = 0.5$). Figure 6 compares the precision of the LDR technique with that of GDR for various value of z_{size}. LDR achieves about 3 times higher precision compared to GDR i.e. the latter has more than three times the number of false positives as the former. The precision of neither technique changes significantly with the skew. Figure 7 compares the precision of the two techniques for various values of k. As expected, for one cluster, the two techniques are identical. As k increases, the precision of GDR deteriorates while that of LDR is indepen-

---

[6]The performance gap between our technique and the other techniques was even greater with SR-tree [15] as the index structure due to higher dimensionality curse [5]. We do not report those results here but can be found in the full version of the paper [6].

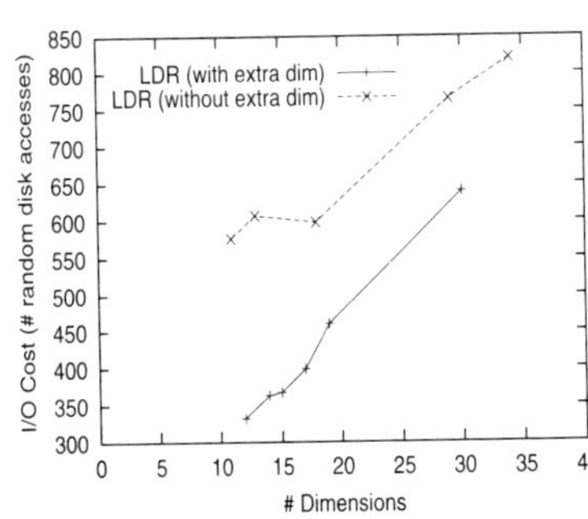

Figure 12: Effect of adding the extra dimension.

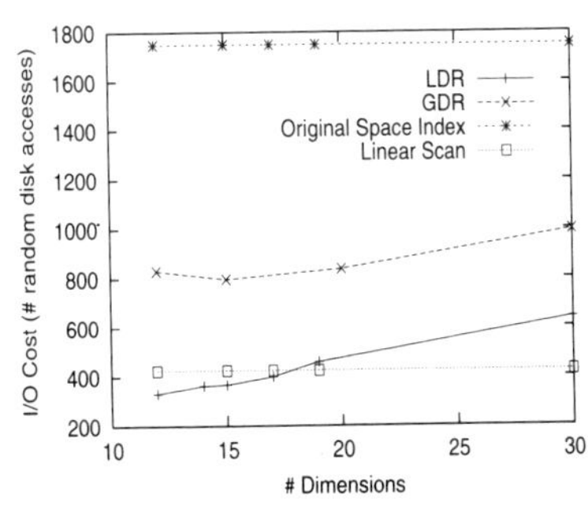

Figure 13: Comparison of LDR, GDR, Original Space Indexing and Linear Scan in terms of I/O cost. For linear scan, the cost is computed as: $\frac{num\_sequential\_disk\_accesses}{10}$.

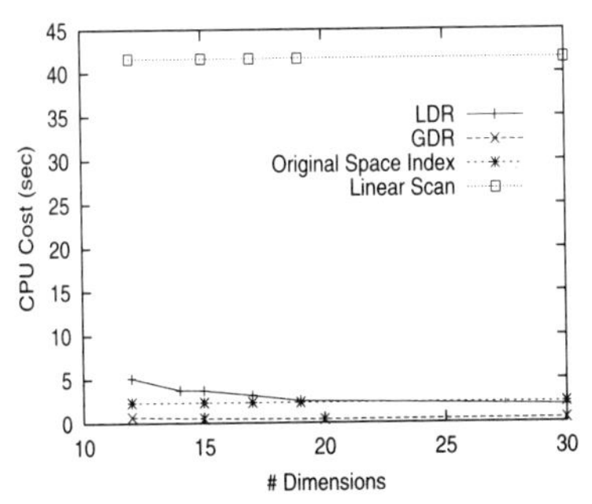

Figure 14: Comparison of LDR, GDR, Original Space Indexing and Linear Scan in terms of CPU cost.

dent of the number of clusters. For $k = 10$, LDR is almost an order of magnitude better compared to GDR in terms of precision. Figure 8 compares the two techniques for various values of p. As the degree of correlation decreases (i.e. the value of p increases), the precision of both techniques drop but LDR outperforms GDR for all values p. Figure 9 shows the variation of the precision with the reduced dimensionality. For the GDR technique, we vary the reduced dimensionality from 15 to 60. For the LDR technique, we vary the $FracOutliers$ from 0.2 to 0.01 (0.2, 0.15, 0.1, 0.05, 0.02, 0.01) causing the average subspace dimensionality to vary from 7 to 42 (7, 10, 12, 14, 23 and 42) ($MaxDim$ was 64). The precision of both techniques increase with the increase in reduced dimensionality. Once again, LDR consistently outperforms GDR at all dimensionalities. The above experiments show that LDR is a more effective dimensionality reduction technique as it can achieve the same reduction as GDR with significantly lower loss of information (i.e. high precision) and hence significantly lower cost as confirmed in the cost experiments described next.

Cost Experiments

We compare the 4 techniques, namely LDR, GDR, OSI and Linear Scan, in terms of query cost for the synthetic dataset. Figure 10 compares the I/O cost of the 4 techniques. Both the LDR and GDR techniques have U-shaped cost curves: when the reduced dimensionality is too low, there is a high degree of information loss leading to a large number of false positives and hence a high post-processing cost; when it is too high, the index page access cost becomes too high due to dimensionality curse. The optimum points lies somewhere in the middle: it is at dimensionality 14 (about 250 random disk accesses) for LDR and at 40 (about 1200 random disk accesses) for GDR. The I/O cost of OSI and Linear Scan is obviously independent of the reduced dimensionality. LDR significantly outperforms all the other 3 techniques in terms of I/O cost. The only technique that comes close to LDR in terms of I/O cost is the linear scan (but LDR is 2.5 times better as the latter performs 6274 sequential accesses ~ 627 random accesses). However, linear scan loses out mainly due to its high CPU cost shown in Figure 11. While LDR, GDR and OSI techniques have similar CPU cost (at their respective optimum points), the CPU cost linear scan is almost two orders of magnitude higher that the rest. LDR has slightly higher CPU cost compared to GDR and OSI since it uses linear scan for the outlier set: however, the savings in the I/O cost over GDR and

OSI (by a factor of 5-6) far offsets the slightly higher CPU cost.

5.3 Experimental Results - Real-Life Data Sets

Description of Dataset

Our real-life data set (COLHIST dataset [5]) comprises of 8×8 color histograms (64-d data) extracted from about 70,000 color images obtained from the Corel Database (http://corel.digitalriver.com/) and is available online at the UCI KDD Archive web site (http://kdd.ics.uci.edu/databases/CorelFeatures). We generated 100 range queries by selecting their query anchors randomly from the dataset and choosing a range value such that the average query selectivity is about 0.5%. All our measurements are averaged over the 100 queries.

Cost Experiments

First, we evaluate the impact of adding $ReconDist$ as an additional dimension of each cluster in the LDR technique. Figure 12 shows that the additional dimension reduces the cost of the query significantly. We performed the above experiment on the synthetic dataset as well and observed a similar result. [7] Figure 13 compares the 4 techniques, namely LDR, GDR, OSI and Linear Scan, in terms of I/O cost. LDR outperforms all other techniques significantly. Again, the only technique that come close to LDR in I/O cost (i.e. number of random disk accesses) is the linear scan. However, again, linear scan turns out to significantly worse compared to LDR in terms of the overall cost due to its high CPU cost as shown in Figure 14.

6 Conclusion

With numerous emerging applications requiring efficient access to high dimensional datasets, there is a need for scalable techniques to indexing high dimensional data. In this paper, we proposed local dimensionality reduction (LDR) as an approach to indexing high dimensional spaces. We developed an algorithm to discover the locally correlated clusters in the dataset and perform dimensionality reduction on each of them individually. We presented an index structure that exploits the correlated clusters to efficiently support similarity queries over high dimensional datasets. We have shown that our query processing algorithms

---

[7]We also analyzed the sensitivity of the LDR technique to the $MaxReconDist$ parameter. The results can be found in [6].

are correct and optimal. We conducted an extensive experimental study with synthetic as well as real-life datasets to evaluate the effectiveness of our technique and compare it to GDR, original space indexing and linear scan techniques. Our results demonstrate that our technique (1) reduces the dimensionality of the data with significantly lower loss in distance information compared to GDR, outperforming GDR by almost an order of magnitude in terms of query precision (for the same reduced dimensionality) and (2) significantly outperforms all the other 3 techniques (namely, GDR, original space indexing and linear scan) in terms of the query cost for both synthetic and real-life datasets.

7 Acknowledgements

We thank David Eppstein and Padhraic Smyth for the useful discussions on the clustering algorithm. We thank Kriengkrai Porkaew for the discussions and his help with the implementation. We thank Corel Corporation for making the large collection of images used in the COL-HIST dataset available to us. Our PCA implementation is built on top of the Meschach Library downloaded from http://www.netlib.org/c/meschach/.

References

[1] R. Agarwal, J. Gehrke, D. Gunopolos, and P. Raghavan. Automatic subspace clustering of high dimensional data for data mining applications. *Proc. of SIGMOD*, 1998.

[2] C. Aggarwal, C. Procopiuc, J. Wolf, P. Yu, and J. Park. Fast algorithms for projected clustering. *Proc. of SIGMOD*, 1999.

[3] S. Berchtold, D. A. Keim, and H. P. Kriegel. The x-tree: An index structure for high-dimensional data. *Proc. of VLDB*, 1996.

[4] K. Beyer, J. Goldstein, R. Ramakrishnan, and U. Shaft. When is "nearest neighbor" meaningful? *Proc. of ICDT*, 1998.

[5] K. Chakrabarti and S. Mehrotra. The hybrid tree: An index structure for high dimensional feature spaces. *Proceedings of the IEEE International Conference on Data Engineering*, March 1999.

[6] K. Chakrabarti and S. Mehrotra. Local dimensionality reduction: A new approach to indexing high dimensional spaces. *Technical Report, TR-MARS-00-04, University of California at Irvine, http://www-db.ics.uci.edu/pages/publications/*, 2000.

[7] C. Faloutsos, W. Equitz, M. Flickner, W. Niblack, D. Petkovic, and R. Barber. Efficient and effective querying by image content. In *Journal of Intelligent Information Systems, Vol. 3, No. 3/4*, pages 231–262, July 1994.

[8] C. Faloutsos and K.-I. D. Lin. Fastmap: A fast algorithm for indexing, data-mining and visualization of traditional and multimedia datasets. In *Proc. ACM SIGMOD*, pages 163–174, May 1995.

[9] K. Fukunaga. *Introduction to Statistical Pattern Recognition*. Academic Press, second edition edition, 1990.

[10] T. Gonzalez. Clustering to minimize the maximum intercluster distance. *Theoretical Computer Science*, 1985.

[11] J. Gray and A. Reuter. *Transaction Processing: Concepts and Techniques*. Morgan Kaufmann, San Mateo, CA, 1993.

[12] S. Guha, R. Rastogi, and K. Shim. Cure: An efficient clustering algorithm for large databases. *Proc. of SIGMOD*, 1998.

[13] A. Guttman. R-trees: A dynamic index structure for spatial searching. In *Proc. ACM SIGMOD Conf., pp. 47–57.*, 1984.

[14] K. V. R. Kanth, D. Agrawal, and A. K. Singh. Dimensionality reduction for similarity searching dynamic databases. *Proc. of SIGMOD*, 1998.

[15] N. Katayama and S. Satoh. The sr-tree: An index structure for high dimensional nearest neighbor queries. *Proc. of SIGMOD*, 1997.

[16] K. Lin, H. V. Jagadish, and C. Faloutsos. The TV-tree - an index stucture for high dimensional data. In *VLDB Journal*, 1994.

[17] R. Motwani and P. Raghavan. *Randomized Algorithms*. Cambridge University Press, 1995.

[18] R. Ng and J. Han. Efficient and effective clustering methods for spatial data mining. *Proc. of VLDB*, 1994.

[19] M. Thomas, C. Carson, and J. Hellerstein. Creating a customized access method for blobworld. *Proc. of ICDE*, 2000.

[20] R. Weber, H. Schek, and S. Blott. A quantitative analysis and performance study for similarity-search methods in high dimensional spaces. *Proc. of VLDB*, 1998.

[21] T. Zhang, R. Ramakrishnan, and M. Livny. Birch: An efficient data clustering method for very large databases. *Proc. of SIGMOD*, 1996.

A Synthetic Data Generation

Param.	Description	Default Value
n	Total number of points	100000
D	Original dimensionality	64
k	Number of clusters	5
d	Avg. subspace dimensionality	10
z_{dim}	Skew in subspace dim. across clusters	0.5
z_{size}	Skew in size across clusters	0.5
c	Number of spatial cluster per cluster	10
r	Extent (from centroid) along subspace dim	0.5
p	Max displacement along non-subspace dim	0.1
o	Fraction outliers	0.05

Table 5: Input parameters to Synthetic Data Generator

The generator generates k clusters with a total of $n.(1 - o)$ points distributed among them using a Zipfian distribution with value z_{size}. The subspace dimensionality of each cluster also follows a Zipfian distribution with value z_{dim}, the average subspace dimensionality being d. Each cluster is generated as follows. For a cluster with size n_i and subspace dimensionality d_i (computed using the Zipfian distributions described above), we randomly choose d_i dimensions among the D dimensions as the subspace dimensions and generate n_i points in that d_i-d plane. Along each of the remaining $(D - d_i)$ non-subspace dimensions, we assign a randomly chosen coordinate to all the n_i points in the cluster. Let f_j be the randomly chosen coordinate along the jth non-subspace dimension. In the subspace, the points are spatially clustered into several regions (c regions on average) with each region having a randomly chosen centroid and an extent of r from the centroid along each of the d_i dimensions. After all the points in the cluster are generated, each point is displaced by a distance of at most p in either direction along each non-subspace dimension i.e. the point is randomly placed somewhere between $(f_j - p)$ and $(f_j + p)$ along the jth non-subspace dimension. The amount of displacement (i.e. value of p) determines the degree of correlation (since r is fixed). Lower the value, more the correlation. To make the subspaces arbitrarily oriented, we generate a random orthonormal rotation matrix (generated using MATLAB) and rotate the cluster by multiplying the data matrix with the rotation matrix. After all the clusters are generated, we randomly generate $N.o$ points (with random values along all D dimensions) as the outliers. The default values of the various parameters is shown in Table 5.

Dynamic Maintenance of Wavelet-Based Histograms

Yossi Matias

Department of Computer Science

Tel Aviv University

Tel Aviv 69978, Israel

matias@math.tau.ac.il

Jeffrey Scott Vitter

Center for Geometric Computing

and Department of Computer Science

Duke University

Durham, NC 27708–0129, USA

jsv@cs.duke.edu

Min Wang

Data Management Department

IBM T. J. Watson Research Center

30 Saw Mill River Road

Hawthorne, NY 10532, USA

min@us.ibm.com

Abstract

In this paper, we introduce an efficient method for the dynamic maintenance of wavelet-based histograms (and other transform-based histograms). Previous work has shown that wavelet-based histograms provide more accurate selectivity estimation than traditional histograms, such as equi-depth histograms. But since wavelet-based histograms are built by a nontrivial mathematical procedure, namely, wavelet transform decomposition, it is hard to maintain the accuracy of the histogram when the underlying data distribution changes over time. In particular, simple techniques, such as split and merge, which works well for equi-depth histograms, and updating a fixed set of wavelet coefficients, are not suitable here.

We propose a novel approach based upon probabilistic counting and sampling to maintain wavelet-based histograms with very little online time and space costs. The accuracy of our method is robust to changing data distributions, and we get a considerable improvement over previous methods for updating transform-based histograms. A very nice feature of our method is that it can be extended naturally to maintain multidimensional wavelet-based histograms, while traditional multidimensional histograms can be less accurate and prohibitively expensive to build and maintain.

1. Introduction

Several important components in a database management system (DBMS) require accurate estimation of the selectivity of a given query. For example, query optimizers use the information to evaluate the costs of different query execution

Proceedings of the 26th VLDB Conference, Cairo, Egypt, 2000.

plans and choose the preferred one. Histograms are a popular way to capture the distribution of the data stored in a database and are used to guide selectivity estimation as well as approximate query processing, load balancing, etc.

In general, there are three issues to be considered when judging a histogram:

1. *Accuracy* of the histogram. Since the accuracy of selectivity estimation depends upon the histograms used, how to build better histograms that approximate the underlying data distributions more accurately is always important. A good histogram should characterize the underlying data distribution with a reasonable accuracy.

2. *Maintenance efficiency* of the histogram. When the underlying data distribution changes, the old histogram needs to be updated to reflect the new distribution; otherwise, significant estimation error could occur because of the outdated histogram. One way to do the update is to recompute and rebuild a new histogram based upon the new data distribution, from scratch, which is costly and still used in most commercial DBMSs. It is very preferable if a histogram can be maintained efficiently on-line. This issue has attracted much attention recently [GMP97, AC99, LKC99, DIR99].

3. *Extension to multidimensional* data. For multidimensional histograms that capture joint distribution of correlated attributes, achieving good accuracy and designing efficient maintenance methods becomes particularly difficult [MD88, PI97, MVW98, AC99, VWI98, VW99].

Equi-depth histograms [PSC84, MRL98] are the most popular histograms and are used in many commercial DBMSs. They are also easy to implement. In some cases they provide good guidance in selectivity estimation and other data processing tasks. Several recent works have dealt with their maintenance and use [GMP97, AC99].

However, equi-depth histograms have major difficulties with complex queries, complex data distributions, and especially multidimensional data. They are built based upon data partitions and maintained by simple mechanisms to keep partition structures. It is very difficult to capture complex multidimensional data distributions with simple partitions. If more advanced partition methods are used, the accuracy becomes better, but the implementation and maintenance become more difficult.

In [MVW98], we introduce a new type of histogram that is based upon the powerful mathematical tool of wavelets and multiresolution analysis. The wavelet-based histogram is fundamentally different from traditional approaches and offers noticeable improvements in accuracy over traditional equi-depth histogram and other leading histogram methods, like the ones in [PIHS96]. A nice feature of the wavelet-based histogram is that it can be naturally extended to the multidimensional case.

While wavelet-based histograms have very little CPU and storage cost at query optimization time, rebuilding a histogram when the underlying data distribution changes is usually very expensive since it involves scanning or sampling the data and performing the wavelet decomposition from scratch. To make the wavelet-based histogram the histogram of choice for future database optimizers, one important step is to design efficient dynamic maintenance methods for both one-dimensional and multidimensional wavelet-based histograms, and we accomplish that goal in this paper.

The rest of the paper is organized as follows: In the next two sections we review related work and formalize our problem. In Section 4, we describe the general ideas of doing dynamic maintenance for wavelet-based histograms and outline our method for one-dimensional case. Our method works for transform methods in general, although for brevity in this paper we confine ourselves to the case of wavelets. We extend our method to the dynamic maintenance of multidimensional wavelet-based histogram in Section 5. We present our experimental results in Section 6 and draw conclusions in Section 7.

2. Previous Work

Histograms are the most widely used form to store succinct statistical information of the data distribution in a database. In addition they can give quality guarantees on the approximations produced. Many different histograms have been proposed in the literature and some of them have been deployed in commercial DBMSs. However, almost all previous histograms have one thing in common, that is, they use buckets to partition the data, although in different ways.

The most popular histogram in today's DBMSs is the equi-depth histogram [PSC84, MRL98]. It partitions the interval between the minimum and maximum attribute value of an attribute into consecutive subintervals so that the total frequency of the attribute values for each subinterval is the same. Poosala et al. [PIHS96, Poo97] give a taxonomy of partition-based histogram methods; new histograms types can be derived by combining effective aspects of different histogram methods. Among the histograms discussed in [PIHS96, Poo97], the MaxDiff(V, A) histogram gives the best overall performance in terms of an accuracy/time trade-off.

When a query involves multiple attributes, its selectivity depends upon the joint distribution of all involved attributes. To simplify things, almost all commercial DBMSs make the *attribute value independence assumption*. This approach, although efficient computationally, is very inaccurate and often leads the query optimizer to generate poor query execution plans. To solve the multidimensional selectivity estimation problem in a better way, Muralikrishna and DeWitt [MD88] propose a spatial index partitioning technique for constructing multidimensional equi-depth histograms. Poosala and Ioannidis [PI97] give two effective alternatives.

All the histograms discussed so far follow the same general guideline, that is, they partition the underlying data in some particular fashion. The effectiveness and accuracy of various partition methods highly depend upon the data distributions and query types. If the data have a simple distribution, the histograms can capture the data distribution effectively. If the data have a very complex distribution, the construction becomes more difficult. In general, using a specific partition method to capture many unpredictable data distributions is a hard job, especially for multidimensional data. It is desirable to study general methods to construct histograms whose usability is more robust.

In [MVW98] we introduce a new type of histograms (wavelet-based histograms) based upon a multidimensional wavelet decomposition. A wavelet decomposition is performed on the underlying data distribution, and the most significant wavelet coefficients are chosen to compose the histogram. In other words, the original data are "compressed" into a set of numbers (wavelet coefficients) via a sophisticated mathematical transformation. Those coefficients constitute the final histogram. This approach offers more accurate selectivity estimation for range-sum queries than do traditional partition-based histogram methods, although there are no analytic quality guarantees. The wavelet decomposition can be extended very naturally to higher-dimensions handle the joint distribution of multiple attributes. Later, a similar approach was discussed using a different mathematical transformation procedure called discrete cosine transform (DCT) [LKC99].

Despite the popularity of histograms, the important issue of their maintenance has attracted attention only recently, and most of the work has been on the maintenance of the traditional partition-based histograms. Gibbons et al. [GMP97] propose sampling-based approaches for incremental maintenance of one-dimensional equi-depth and compressed histograms. In [AC99], a novel approach of building self-tuning histograms is introduced and it can be effectively used for maintaining both one-dimensional and multidimensional equi-depth histograms. Basically, the approach in [AC99] is not about building a new type of histogram, but about adjusting a given partition-based histogram through a learning procedure to be more accurate.

While wavelet-based histograms offer more accuracy than all traditional partition-based histograms, their maintenance is much more difficult because they are built through a non-trivial mathematical transformation procedure. For equi-depth histograms, any change of the data distribution can be easily recorded by updating the summary frequency for the corresponding bucket. The job of the maintenance is to balance the size of the buckets over time through simple operations like splitting and merging [GMP97, AC99]. On the other hand, for wavelet-based histograms, when there is an update in the underlying data distribution, several wavelet coefficients change their values. A significant coefficient could become insignificant over time, and vice versa. Since the histogram should maintain the most significant coefficients in order to ensure accuracy in a robust manner, we must keep track of the most significant coefficient set, and this is a non-trivial job.

The DCT-based histogram method discussed by Lee et al. [LKC99] faces exactly the same problem. The approach in [LKC99] is to maintain a static set of coefficients and update their values in response to the data updates. The same method can be applied to wavelet-based histograms. It is claimed in [LKC99] that any data change will be reflected immediately in the histogram. However, such a claim is true only if the updates follow the same or very similar distribution as the base data. Their method maintains a fixed set of DCT coefficients and only keeps track of the value changes of those coefficients. It never considers the fact that the set of significant coefficients should change over time, and as we shall see in Section 6, this type of dynamic maintenance of a static set of coefficients can introduce very big errors in estimation.

The method of Lee et al. [LKC99] has another fundamental problem. The set of DCT coefficients, which is statically chosen, is not even chosen with respect to the initial set of data, but rather is chosen *a priori* independently of the data by means of static geometrical zonal sampling. The coefficients chosen using the predefined geometrical zonal sampling method may not be significant coefficients, thus resulting in bad histograms.

3. Preliminaries and Problem Formulation

3.1. Wavelet Decomposition

Wavelets are a mathematical tool for the hierarchical decomposition of functions in a space-efficient manner. Wavelets represent a function in terms of a coarse overall shape, plus details that range from coarse to fine. Regardless of whether the function of interest is an image, a curve, or a surface, wavelets offer an elegant technique for representing the various levels of detail of the function in a space-efficient manner.

For readers who are not familiar with wavelets, we borrow a simple example from [VW99] to illustrate the wavelet decomposition procedure. To start the wavelet decomposition procedure, we first need to choose the wavelet basis functions. Haar wavelets are conceptually the simplest wavelet basis functions, and for purposes of exposition in this paper, we focus our discussion on Haar wavelets. They are fastest to compute and easiest to implement. To illustrate how Haar wavelets work, we start with a simple example which will be used throughout the paper. (A detailed treatment of wavelets can be found in any standard reference on the subject, e.g., [JS94, SDS96].) Suppose we have a one-dimensional "signal" of $N = 8$ data items:

$$S = [2, 2, 0, 2, 3, 5, 4, 4].$$

We perform a wavelet transform on it. We first average the signal values, pairwise, to get the new lower-resolution signal with values

$$[2, 1, 4, 4].$$

That is, the first two values in the original signal (2 and 2) average to 2, and the second two values 0 and 2 average to 1, and so on. Clearly, some information is lost in this averaging process. To recover the original signal from the four averaged values, we need to store some *detail coefficients*, which capture the missing information. Haar wavelets store the pairwise differences of the original values (divided by 2) as detail coefficients. In the above example, the four detail coefficients are $(2 - 2)/2 = 0$, $(0 - 2)/2 = -1$, $(3 - 5)/2 = -1$, and $(4 - 4)/2 = 0$. It is easy to see that the original values can be recovered from the averages and differences.

We have succeeded in decomposing the original signal into a lower-resolution version of half the number of entries and a corresponding set of detail coefficients. By repeating this process recursively on the averages, we get the full decomposition:

Resolution	Averages	Detail Coefficients
8	$[2, 2, 0, 2, 3, 5, 4, 4]$	
4	$[2, 1, 4, 4]$	$[0, -1, -1, 0]$
2	$[1\frac{1}{2}, 4]$	$[\frac{1}{2}, 0]$
1	$[2\frac{3}{4}]$	$[-1\frac{1}{4}]$

We define the *wavelet transform* (also called *wavelet decomposition*) of the original eight-value signal to be the single coefficient representing the overall average of the original signal, followed by the detail coefficients in the order of increasing resolution. Thus, for the one-dimensional Haar basis, the wavelet transform of our original signal is given by

$$\widehat{S} = [2\tfrac{3}{4}, -1\tfrac{1}{4}, \tfrac{1}{2}, 0, 0, -1, -1, 0]. \tag{1}$$

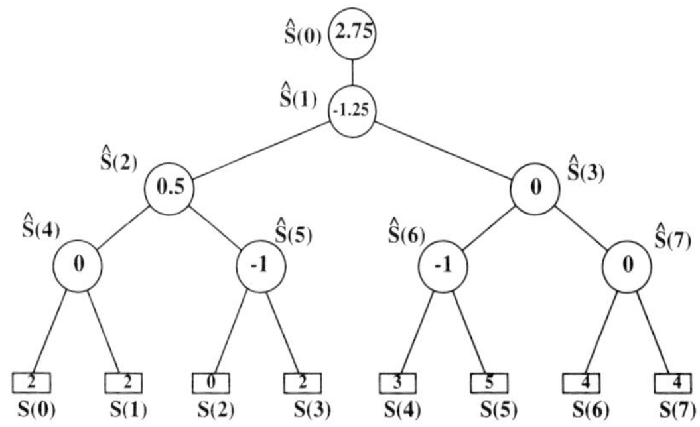

Figure 1: Error tree for $N = 8$

The individual entries are called the *wavelet coefficients*. The wavelet decomposition is very efficient computationally, requiring only $O(N)$ CPU time and $O(N/B)$ I/Os to compute for a signal of N values.

No information has been gained or lost by this process. The original signal has eight values, and so does the transform. Given the transform, we can reconstruct the exact signal by recursively adding and subtracting the detail coefficients from the next-lower resolution.

For compression reasons, the detail coefficients at each level of the recursion are often normalized; the coefficients at the lower resolutions are weighted more heavily than the coefficients at the higher resolutions. One advantage of the normalized wavelet transform is that in many cases a large number of the detail coefficients turn out to be very small in magnitude. Truncating these small coefficients from the representation (i.e., replacing each one by 0) introduces only small errors in the reconstructed signal. We can approximate the original signal effectively by a process of *thresholding*, where we keep only the most significant (normalized) coefficients. Sometimes, especially in high dimensions when the queries specify only a subset of the dimensions, it helps to use a hybrid thresholding policy, which favors coefficients with large absolute value as well as coefficients higher up in the tree. [VW99]. For simplicity in exposition, we assume in this paper that we threshold by choosing the largest coefficients in absolute value. Our dynamic maintenance algorithms can be adapted easily to work with all known hybrid schemes.

The wavelet decomposition procedure can be represented by an *error tree* [MVW98]. The error tree is built based upon the wavelet transform procedure. Figure 1 is the error tree for the example in this section. Each internal node is associated with a wavelet coefficient value, and each leaf is associated with an original signal value. (For purposes of exposition, the wavelet coefficients are unnormalized, but in the implementation the values are normalized and the algorithm is modified appropriately.) Internal nodes and leaves are labeled separately. Their labels are in the domain $\{0, 1, \ldots, N - 1\}$ for a signal of length N. For example, the root is an internal node with label 0 and its node value is 2.75 in Figure 1. For convenience, we shall use "node" and "node value" interchangeably.

The construction of the error tree exactly mirrors the wavelet transform procedure. It is a bottom-up process. First, leaves are assigned original signal values from left to right. Then wavelet coefficients are computed, level by level, and assigned to internal nodes.

The wavelet decomposition generalizes easily to multiple dimensions, which we discuss further in Section 5. The following theorem from [VW99] shows that range-sum queries, which correspond to the sum of the data values within a specified hyperrectangle, can be evaluated extremely quickly:

Theorem 1 ([VW99]) *For a given range-sum query in*

which the rectangle does not span the entire domain in d' of the d dimensions, the approximate query answer can be computed based upon the top m coefficients using a $((d+1)k)$-space data structure in $2d' \times \min\{m, 2\prod_{1 \le i \le d'} \log |D_i|\}$ CPU time, where D_i represents the domain of the ith specified dimension in the query rectangle.

3.2. Problem Formulation

In [MVW98], the wavelet-based histogram is built by first performing wavelet decomposition on the *extended cumulative data distribution* (partial sums) of an attribute, resulting in a sequence of wavelet coefficients. Then the top m coefficients with the largest absolute values are chosen to compose the histogram. (The parameter m depends upon the available storage space for the histogram.) A similar scenario arises in the other transform-based methods, such as those based upon the discrete cosine transform (DCT).

For dynamic maintenance of the wavelet-based histogram, do we have to consider partial-sum based wavelet decomposition, or should we just do the decomposition using the raw data distribution? To answer this question, we need to resolve two issues. First, what would be the accuracy difference between using partial sums and raw data? If the partial-sum-based method gives much higher accuracy for selectivity estimation than the raw-data-based method, we'd better do dynamic maintenance for the partial-sum-based method. The first issue raises the second, that is, intuitively, it would be much harder to do maintenance for the partial-sum-based method because local data changes will propagate globally.

To resolve the first issue, we did an extensive experimental study to compare the accuracy of the two methods using a large collection of Zipf data sets [Zip49]. We don't include the detailed results for lack of space. It turns out that the accuracy of the two methods varies with data distribution, query type, and the choice of different error measurements. We cannot say that one method is always better than another. A similar observation is made in [VW99] for high-dimensional sparse data cube approximation. Both methods give good results, although the partial sum approach tends to work better for low dimensions and for open-sided queries. In this paper, we focus on the dynamic maintenance of histograms based upon raw data distributions, and we do not deal with issues related to processing partial sums.

We formalize the dynamic maintenance problem using the error tree structure for one-dimensional case, as follows. Let T_0 be the initial error tree constructed from the initial data distribution S_{t_0} of an attribute at time t_0. The wavelet-based histogram H_0 is a subset of internal nodes of T_0. Each element of H_0 is of the form $\left(j, \widehat{S}(j)\right)$. Specifically, for a histogram of size m, H_0 contains the top m internal nodes of T_0, ranked by the absolute values of the normalized coefficients. (As mentioned in Section 3.1, our techniques that we will discuss in subsequent sections apply equally well to hybrid coefficient thresholding methods, but for simplicity we will focus our discussion on the simple thresholding policy of choosing the m largest coefficients in absolute value.)

Suppose during a time interval from t_0 to t_1, the data distribution changes from S_{t_0} to S_{t_1}. Based upon S_{t_1} we can construct a new error tree T_1, and consequently we obtain a new histogram H_1. Our *dynamic maintenance problem* is the following: *At any time t_1, how can we efficiently maintain a histogram $\widetilde{H}_1$ that is a good approximation of H_1?*

There are three possible changes in the distribution of an attribute: insertion, deletion, and update. Consider a period from t_0 to t_1. During this time interval, a sequence of insertions, deletions, and updates occur at the leaves, and we can represent them by a list:

$$\Delta = \{\Delta(0), \ldots, \Delta(N-1)\}, \tag{2}$$

where $\Delta(i)$ is the value change at leaf i. The Δ sequence is mainly introduced for simplifying our discussions. We only need to store the non-zero entries in the sequence. (The zero entries correspond to the leaf values that remain unchanged from time t_0 to time t_1.)

4. Dynamic Maintenance of One-Dimensional Wavelet-Based Histograms

In this section, we describe how to dynamically maintain wavelet-based histograms for the one-dimensional case. For convenience in exposition, we give the formulas for the un-normalized wavelet coefficients, but in reality the coefficients are normalized in an online manner.

4.1. Properties of Wavelet-Based Histograms

A value change at a leaf will affect all its ancestors in the error tree. The problem is how those ancestors are affected. It turns out that the error tree has some nice properties and we can use them to figure out the exact changes occurred at internal nodes upon any leaf change.

Inserting a value i is equivalent to increasing $S(i)$ by one. Similarly, deleting a value i is equivalent to decreasing $S(i)$ by one. An update can be considered as one deletion followed by one insertion. (For simplicity, we restrict our attention in this paper to individual value changes of $+1$ and -1, but the method can be extended naturally to general updates.)

Consider an internal node j that is the parent of a leaf node i. At time t_0, leaf i's value is $S_{t_0}(i)$. At time t_1, its value changes to $S_{t_1}(i)$. Letting

$$\Delta(i) = S_{t_1}(i) - S_{t_0}(i), \tag{3}$$

we have

$$\widehat{S}_{t_1}(j) = \begin{cases} \widehat{S}_{t_0}(j) + \dfrac{\Delta(i)}{2} & \text{if leaf } i \text{ is } j\text{'s left child;} \\[2mm] \widehat{S}_{t_0}(j) - \dfrac{\Delta(i)}{2} & \text{if leaf } i \text{ is } j\text{'s right child.} \end{cases} \tag{4}$$

From (4) we can see that from time t_0 to time t_1, the magnitude of $\widehat{S}(j)$ may increase or decrease, depending upon $\widehat{S}_{t_0}(j)$, $\Delta(i)$, and the relative position of j with respect to i (i.e., if i is the left or right child of node j).

In the above example, node j's subtree only contains two leaves, and we are only considering single leaf value change. Now we look at the more general cases. For any leaf i, we use $path(i)$ to denote the set of the internal nodes along the path from i to the root. We use $left(j)$ and $right(j)$ to denote the left and right child of any node j, and we use $leaves(j)$ to denote the set of leaves in the subtree rooted at j. For any internal node j, we define its height as

$$height(j) = \begin{cases} \log N - \lfloor \log j \rfloor & \text{for } 1 \le j < N; \\ \log N & \text{for } j = 0. \end{cases} \tag{5}$$

(By convention, we say that node 0 and 1 have height $\log N$, which is the only difference with the picture in Figure 1.)

Lemma 1 *For any leaf i, we consider the effects of the its value change (3). For each $j \in path(i)$, we have*

$$\widehat{S}_{t_1}(j) = \begin{cases} \widehat{S}_{t_0}(j) + \dfrac{\Delta(i)}{2^{height(j)}} & \text{if } i \in leaves\left(left(j)\right); \\[2mm] \widehat{S}_{t_0}(j) - \dfrac{\Delta(i)}{2^{height(j)}} & \text{if } i \in leaves\left(right(j)\right). \end{cases} \tag{6}$$

From Lemma 1 we obtain the following:

Theorem 2 *From a single leaf value change we can compute the value change of each of its ancestors in constant time using a closed-form formula.*

We can generalize Lemma 2 to the case when there are multiple leaf value changes:

Lemma 2 *For any internal node j, let $\Delta_{\text{int}}(j)$ denote the average of the value changes $\Delta(i)$ among all leaves $i \in leaves(j)$. We have*

$$\widehat{S}_{t_1}(j) = \widehat{S}_{t_0}(j) + \frac{\Delta_{\text{int}}\big(left(j)\big) - \Delta_{\text{int}}\big(right(j)\big)}{2}. \quad (7)$$

Consider the Δ sequence (2). It represents all the leaf value changes from time t_0 to t_1, and it contains N_z non-zero elements. Conceptually, using all the entries in (2) as the leaf values, we may construct a new error tree, and we call it the Δ error tree, denoted by T_Δ. The tree T_Δ has the same structure as the error tree T_0, and it contains at most $\min\{N_z \log N, N\}$ non-zero internal nodes. All the non-zero leaves of T_Δ together with their ancestors compose a partial error tree. We can do a node-wise tree addition between T_0 and T_Δ, that is, we add T_0 and T_Δ, as follows: We construct a new tree with exactly the same structure as T_0. For each node j, its value in the new tree is the sum of the corresponding node values in T_0 and T_Δ. We denote this tree addition by $T_0 + T_\Delta$.

Lemma 3 (Additive property) *If we construct an error tree T_Δ from array Δ (we call T_Δ the Δ error tree), then we can add the values of the corresponding nodes in T_0 and T_Δ to obtain T_1.*

The above lemma summarizes the changes in (2) in a batch. Equivalently, starting from the initial error tree T_0, we can just apply each leaf node change directly and incrementally using (6) to obtain T_1. Alternately, we can also obtain T_1 by updating the internal nodes of T_0 using (7).

4.2. The Difficulties in Dynamic Maintenance

From the discussions in Section 4.1, we can see some difficulties in maintaining wavelet-based histograms. To keep track of the top m coefficients exactly, we must keep all the internal nodes of the error tree, and we must keep their values up to date all the time. Suppose we have kept the top m coefficients at time t_0 in H_0. For any single insertion after time t_0, there are $1 + \log N$ ancestor coefficients in the error tree that will be affected. We can easily use (6) to update those ancestor coefficients that are among H_0. The hard part is how to deal with the coefficients that are *not* in H_0. The only thing we know about those coefficients is that they were not significant enough to be include in H_0 at time t_0. But when the data distribution changes (i.e., after the insertion), they may become significant. Although we can use (6) to compute the *value changes* at those non-H_0 nodes, we still do not know what to do with them because we have no idea about their original values.

A naive way to solve the problem is to recompute the wavelet decomposition from scratch based upon the new data distribution and to choose the top m coefficients whenever the data distribution changes (i.e., when any leaf value changes in the error tree). This approach is not feasible in practice since it invokes too much overhead at query optimization time, even though it maintains the quality of the histogram.

Another approach is to trade accuracy for efficiency. We could build the histogram H_0 at time t_0 and thereafter just keep the values of the coefficients in H_0 up to date using (6). This approach would work fine if the statistics of the underlying data distribution do not change or just have minor

change. This obvious approach is the one used in [LKC99], although the approach in [LKC99] is less sophisticated in its initial choice of coefficients, in that they are chosen independently of the data. The problem is that there is no guarantee that the histogram will still contain the most significant coefficients after the underlying data distribution has changed even modestly. As we shall see in Section 6, histograms maintained using this simple approach often incur very big errors in estimations.

Our goal in this paper is to maintain the histograms efficiently without sacrificing accuracy. We want the histograms to be robust to changing distributions, yet roughly as accurate as a fixed histogram for the case in which the update data follow the same or similar distribution as the base data.

4.3. Our Method

Let the initial error tree at time t_0 be T. We consider the top $m + m'$ internal nodes of T, where $m + m' \ll N$. From those $m + m'$ nodes, we choose the top m to form the histogram H. The other m' nodes are kept as an *auxiliary histogram H'* on disk. We use an *activity log L* to log the insert, delete, and update activities; the log has a maximal size of *Max_Log_Size*.

We shall focus on insertions because deletions are similar and update is one insertion followed by one deletion (or vice versa). We consider a sequence of insertions. When an insertion happens to a leaf node i, according to Lemma 2, the values of all the internal nodes in $path(i)$ change. For any internal node j in $path(i)$, we characterize it into one of three types: (a) $j \in H$, (b) $j \in H'$, and (c) $j \notin H \cup H'$. We will handle different types of nodes differently.

First, we write an entry i into the log L. Then we consider all the internal nodes $j \in path(i)$. If j is a type (a) node, we update its value immediately according to (6). (We have $\Delta(i) = 1$ for an insertion and $\Delta(i) = -1$ for a deletion.) If j is not a type (a) node, we do nothing.

When the number of entries in log L reaches *Max_Log_Size*, we process the entries in the log. For any entry i in L, we update all the corresponding type (b) nodes according to (6). For a type (c) node j, we use a *probabilistic counting* technique [FM85]: We flip a coin with probability $p(j)$ of heads. If the coin flips a head, we set node j's magnitude $\widehat{S}(j)$ to be $v(j)$ (a value to be determined later), and we replace the smallest node (in magnitude) in H' with node j.

When all the entries in the log L have been processed, we adjust H and H'. Whenever the magnitude of the largest node in H' exceeds a threshold value H'_Thresh (to be determined later), we switch it with the smallest node in H.

Once we are done with the current log L, we can start to process new insertions and start over to form a new fresh log L. At any given time, H is the histogram that is used for selectivity estimation.

Our method is motivated by the following tradeoff between update time and space:

- By updating the coefficients in histogram H promptly, we keep the coefficient values in H up to date.
- By keeping and updating the coefficients in H' in a batched fashion, we have reasonable amount of extra information on the possible candidates that are likely to gain entrance later to H.
- By using the probabilistic counting technique for all type (c) nodes, we can detect any "surprising" candidates for H that may later become significant even though they do not appear significant initially.

Let us consider parameters *Max_Log_Size*, H'_Thresh, $p(j)$, and $v(j)$. The parameter *Max_Log_Size* specifies how often we want to check into the situation where we need to do a shake up to include some new nodes into H and exclude some old nodes from H when the data distribution changes. The smaller the Max_Log_Size value is, the more often the shake-up will occur, and the more chance H will get to update. The frequent updating is good for accuracy, but frequent log processing causes slow performance. In our experiments, we choose Max_Log_Size to be 1%–5% of the base data size.

The parameter H'_Thresh specifies how aggressive we are in adjusting H over time. Denote the magnitude of the minimum coefficient in H by $\min(H)$. A reasonable setting would be $H'\_Thresh = \min(H)$. On the other hand, if the magnitudes of two coefficients are very close, it does not really matter which one is in H, because both would be (approximately) equally important. In our experiments, we set $H'\_Thresh = c_1 \times \min(H)$, where c_1 is a constant (typically in the range $[1.0, 3.0]$).

Now let us consider how we should set $p(j)$ and $v(j)$. Intuitively, we want $1/p(j)$ to correspond to the number of insertions needed at leaf i to bring the magnitude of node j from its initial value of zero to $v(j)$, so we need to set $v(j)$ first. The parameter $v(j)$ is similar to the parameter H'_Thresh, and we can set $v(j) = c_2 \times \min(H)$, where c_2 is a constant, typically in the range $[0.2, 0.8]$. The value $v(j)$ is independent of j and we denote $v = c_2 \times \min(H)$. An alternative that also works well is to define $v = c_1 \times \min(H')$. We can easily derive

$$p(j) = \frac{1}{v \times 2^{height(j)}}$$

according to (6). The exact value of node j depends upon its position. When the coin flips a head for node j, the value should be set to v if leaf i is in the left subtree of j and $-v$ otherwise.

The following pseudo code summarizes our algorithm:

Procedure $Dynamic\_Maintenance(H, H', L, m, m',$
$\quad Max\_Log\_Size, c_1, c_2)$
$\quad$ Compute the wavelet decomposition of the base
$\quad\quad$ data distribution;
$\quad$ Compose H by choosing the top m wavelet coefficients;
$\quad$ Compose H' by choosing the $(m+1)$st to $(m+m')$th
$\quad\quad$ coefficients;
$\quad$ **while** (insert value i to the relation)
$\quad\quad$ Write i to log L;
$\quad\quad$ $log\_size + +$;
$\quad\quad$ $path(i) = \{\, j \mid j$ is an internal node on the path from
$\quad\quad\quad$ leaf i to the root$\}$;
$\quad\quad$ **for** each $j \in path(i) \cap H$
$\quad\quad\quad$ Update $\widehat{S}(j)$ using (6);
$\quad\quad$ **if** $(log\_size == Max\_Log\_Size)$
$\quad\quad\quad$ $Process\_Log(L, H', H, log\_size, c_1, c_2)$;
$\quad\quad\quad$ $log\_size = 0$;
Procedure $Process\_Log(L, H', H, log\_size, c_1, c_2)$
$\quad$ **for** $k = 1$ **to** log_size **do**
$\quad\quad$ $i = k$th entry in L;
$\quad\quad$ $v = c_2 \times min\_coeff\_magnitude(H)$;
$\quad\quad$ $path(i) = \{\, j \mid j$ is an internal node on the path from
$\quad\quad\quad$ leaf i to the root$\}$;
$\quad\quad$ **for** each $j \in path(i) \cap H'$
$\quad\quad\quad$ Update $\widehat{S}(j)$ using (6);
$\quad\quad$ **for** each $j \in \big(path(i) - (H \cap H')\big)$
$\quad\quad\quad$ $p = \dfrac{1}{v \times 2^{height(j)}}$;
$\quad\quad\quad$ Flip a coin with probability p of head;
$\quad\quad\quad$ **if** (coin flips a head)
$\quad\quad\quad\quad$ **if** $\big(i \in leaves(left(j))\big)$ $\widehat{S}(j) = v$;
$\quad\quad\quad\quad$ **else** $\widehat{S}(j) = -v$;
$\quad\quad\quad\quad$ Replace the minimum coefficient in H' with
$\quad\quad\quad\quad\quad$ $\big(j, \widehat{S}(j)\big)$;
$\quad$ **while** $\big(max\_coeff\_magnitude(H') >$

$\quad\quad c_1 \times min\_coeff\_magnitude(H)\big)$
$\quad$ Switch the maximum coefficient in H' with
$\quad\quad$ the minimum coefficient in H;

Function $min\_coeff\_magnitude(X)$ returns the magnitude of the smallest coefficient in coefficient set X. Similarly, function $max\_coeff\_magnitude(X)$ returns the magnitude of the largest coefficient in coefficient set X.

A sequence of deletions can be handled in a similar way. For a mixed sequence of deletions and insertions, we may maintain two separate logs, one for insertions and another for deletions. When the total size of these two logs reaches the value of Max_Log_Size, we start to process them, one by one. Or, we just maintain one log for both insertions and deletions. Later, when we need to use the log information to update H and H', we can either split it into two parts, or we just process the single log and handle insertion and deletion differently in our algorithm.

The activity log L is a simplified version of the database transaction log that is used widely in commercial DBMSs. In the above algorithm, we write the inserted entries to the log directly. In our implementation, we use a double buffer in memory to keep the inserted entries instead of writing each entry to the log directly. When the double buffer becomes half full, we write all the entries in the buffer to the log on disk. The number of disk I/O is hence reduced dramatically. (The double-buffer mechanism is indeed used in the implementation of the real database transaction log.) To further facilitate the functions $min\_coeff\_magnitude(X)$ and $max\_coeff\_magnitude(X)$, we maintain H and H' as priority queues throughout the process.

The only storage overhead invoked by our method is the auxiliary histogram H', which is stored on disk. The auxiliary histogram H' is not part of the true histogram used by the optimizer, and it is needed only when we do batch processing of the activity log. Therefore, we can store H' together with the activity log. As we show in Section 6, the overhead can be kept low while achieving very good histogram quality. The time overhead of our method composes two parts: the time for changing the coefficient values for the coefficients in the present histogram and the time for processing the log. The first part is fixed since we can compute each change in constant time using the properties of the error tree structure. Use of random sampling or batch processing of the updates, as discussed in the previous paragraph, would speed up processing even further, at a slight cost in accuracy. The second part, although taking longer time than the first part, is only invoked in batch mode after a significant number of updates and can be tuned by the user.

One way to improve the time performance of our algorithm is to preprocess the log whenever it is full before we invoke the procedure $Process\_Log$. We combine multiple insertions of the same value into a single entries of the form $(value, number\_of\_insertions)$. The preprocessing can speed up $Process\_Log$ significantly when the number of combined entries are much smaller than the original log size, which is likely to happen when Max_Log_Size is set to a big value.

Another speed improvement is to randomly sample the events and process only a random sample. The updates done on the leaves should be adjusted normalized appropriately. Yet another speed improvement is to process the events, whether sampled or not, in batch mode, much like the entries in the log, but at more frequent intervals.

Our method is very stable for various update distributions. The static method in [LKC99] performs reasonably well only when the distribution of the update sequence is *very close* to that of the original base data. Otherwise, the accuracy of the maintained histogram degrades dramatically since the histogram does not contain the set of most significant coefficients anymore.

5. Maintenance of Multidimensional Histograms

The one-dimensional wavelet decomposition and reconstruction procedure in Section 3.1 can be extended naturally to the multidimensional case. One way to do a multidimensional wavelet decomposition is by a series of one-dimensional decompositions. For example, in the two-dimensional case, we first apply the one-dimensional wavelet transform to each row of the data. Next, we treat these transformed rows as if they were themselves the original data, and we apply the one-dimensional transform to each column. We repeat this procedure for each dimension, and the result is the multidimensional wavelet decomposition.

Our method for maintaining one-dimensional wavelet-based histograms can also be extended naturally to multidimensional case. Suppose we want to build a d-dimensional wavelet-based histogram for d attributes. Let $D = \{D_1, D_2, \ldots, D_d\}$ denote the set of attributes. We represent the joint distribution of these attributes by a d-dimensional array S of size $|D_1| \times |D_2| \times \cdots \times |D_d|$, where $|D_i|$ is the size of the domain for D_i. Without loss of generality, we assume that each attribute D_i has domain $\{0, 1, \ldots, |D_i|-1\}$. An array element $S(i_1, i_2, \ldots, i_d)$ is the frequency of the corresponding value combination $(i_1, i_2, \ldots, i_d)$ of the attributes. The wavelet coefficients obtained by performing a d-dimensional wavelet decomposition on S can be represented by a d-dimensional array $\widehat{S}$ of size $|D_1| \times |D_2| \times \cdots \times |D_d|$. The following result from [VW99] gives the I/O complexity of the decomposition as a function of the number N_z of nonzero values in the original multidimensional array. We assume that some data values are coarsely pruned in an online manner so that the number of nonzero coefficients does not increase during the course of the decomposition; the final thresholding is done on the coefficients that make it through the initial filter.

Theorem 3 ([VW99]) *The number of I/Os needed to do a d-dimensional wavelet decomposition of size $N = |D_1| \times |D_2| \times \cdots \times |D_d|$ with internal memory of size M and block size B is*

$$O\left(\frac{N_z}{B} \min\left\{d, \log_{M/B} \frac{N}{B}\right\}\right),$$

where N_z is the number of nonzero coefficients.

To handle dynamic updates, we first extend Lemma 1 to general d-dimensional case.

Lemma 4 *For any array element $S(i_1, i_2, \ldots, i_d)$, we consider the effects of its value change*

$$\Delta(i_1, i_2, \ldots, i_d) = S_{t_1}(i_1, i_2, \ldots, i_d) - S_{t_0}(i_1, i_2, \ldots, i_d). \quad (8)$$

For each $\widehat{S}(j_1, j_2, \ldots, j_d)$ where $j_k \in path(i_k)$ in the error tree of D_k, for $1 \leq k \leq d$, we have

$$\widehat{S}_{t_1}(j_1, j_2, \ldots, j_d) = \widehat{S}_{t_0}(j_1, j_2, \ldots, j_d) + \frac{\Delta(i_1, i_2, \ldots, i_d)}{\prod_{k=1}^{d} sign(i_k, j_k) 2^{height(j_k)}}, \quad (9)$$

where

$$sign(i_k, j_k) = \begin{cases} 1 & \text{if } i_k \in leaves\big(left(j_k)\big) \\ & \text{in the error tree of } D_k; \\ -1 & \text{if } i \in leaves\big(right(j_k)\big) \\ & \text{in the error tree of } D_k. \end{cases} \quad (10)$$

The following algorithm that extends our algorithm in Section 4 to d-dimensional case follows naturally.

Procedure *Multidimensional_Dynamic_Maintenance(H, H', $L, m, m', Max\_Log\_Size, c_1, c_2, d$)*
  Compute the wavelet decomposition of the joint data distribution of the base data;
  Compose H by choosing the top m wavelet coefficients;
  Compose H' by choosing the $(m + 1)$st to $(m + m')$th coefficients;
  $log\_size = 0$;
  while $\big($insert value $(i_1, i_2, \ldots, i_d)$ to the relation$\big)$
    Write $(i_1, i_2, \ldots, i_d)$ to log L;
    $log\_size + +$;
    for $k = 1$ **to** d **do**
      $path(i_k) = \{j_k \mid j_k$ is an internal node on the path from i_k to the root in the error tree of $D_k\}$;
    for each $(j_1, j_2, \ldots, j_d) \in H \cap \prod_{k=1}^{d} path(i_k)$
      Update $S(j_1, j_2, \ldots, j_d)$ using (9);
    if $(log\_size == Max\_Log\_Size)$
      $Multidimensional\_Process\_Log(L, H', H,$
        $log\_size, c_1, c_2, d)$;
      $log\_size = 0$;

Procedure *Multidimensional_Process_Log(L, H', H, log_size, c_1, c_2, d)*
  for $k = 1$ **to** log_size **do**
    $(i_1, i_2, \ldots, i_d) = k$th entry in B;
    $v = c_2 \times min\_coeff\_magnitude(H)$;
    for $k = 1$ **to** d **do**
      $path(i_k) = \{j_k \mid j_k$ is an internal node on the path from i_k to the root in the error tree of $D_k\}$;
    for each $(j_1, j_2 \ldots j_d) \in H' \cap \prod_{k=1}^{d} path(i_k)$
      Update $\widehat{S}(j_1, j_2, \ldots, j_d)$ using (9);
    for each $(j_1, j_2, \ldots, j_d) \in \prod_{k=1}^{d} path(i_k) - (H \cup H')$
      $p = 1/v \prod_{k=1}^{d} 2^{height(j_k)}$;
      Flip a coin with probability p of head;
      if $($coin flips a head$)$
        $\widehat{S}(j_1, j_2, \ldots, j_d) = v \times \prod_{l=1}^{d} sign(i_l, j_l)$;
        Replace the minimum coefficient in H' with $\big(j_1, j_2, \ldots, j_d, \widehat{S}(j_1, j_2, \ldots, j_d)\big)$;
  while $\big(max\_coeff\_magnitude(H') > c_1 \times min\_coeff\_magnitude(H)\big)$
    Switch the maximum coefficient in H' with the minimum coefficient in H;

6. Experimental Results

6.1. Methods of Comparisons

We implement the following three methods for dynamic maintenance of wavelet-based histograms and we compare their performance.

1. *Exact Method.* This *expensive* method corresponds to *recomputing* the histogram from scratch whenever *any* update happens to the data distribution.

2. *Probabilistic Counting Method.* This is the method we introduced in Sections 4 and 5.

3. *Static Method.* At initial time t_0, we compute the exact histogram H_0 for the base data distribution. From then on, the content (the coefficients) of H_0 no longer changes. We only change the values of those coefficients to make them up to date.

At any given time, the histogram maintained using the exact method contains exactly the set of most significant coefficients for the data distribution at that time. Thus, this method usually provides the best accuracy in selectivity estimations. (As mentioned in Section 3.1, our techniques apply equally well to hybrid coefficient thresholding methods, but for simplicity we will focus our discussion on the simple thresholding policy of choosing the largest coefficients in absolute value.)

The static method is similar to that proposed in [LKC99], except that we start with the "right" set of coefficients, chosen in a way corresponding to the distribution of the base data. Its implementation is very simple: After building the initial histogram H_0 based upon the base data distribution at time t_0, in the event of any frequency change for value i, we just need to update the relevant coefficient values for the coefficients that are in $path(i) \cap H_0$ according to (6). For the multidimensional case, when the frequency changes at $(i_1, i_2, \ldots, i_d)$, we use (9) to update the coefficient values for the coefficients that are in $H_0 \cap \big(path(i_1) \times path(i_2) \times \ldots \times path(i_d)\big)$.

6.2.   Error Measures

To define the proper measures for the accuracy of various methods, we first look into the logic in choosing the top m coefficients to form the exact wavelet-based histograms.

With proper normalization (which we always do), the Haar basis is orthonormal. For any orthonormal wavelet basis, choosing the m largest (in absolute value) wavelet coefficients is provably optimal in minimizing the 2-norm of the absolute error *when considering the reconstruction of the original signal values* [SDS96]. Note that the 2-norm of the absolute error for the reconstructed data values corresponds to the 2-norm of the absolute error for all the equal queries. (An equal query is the special case of range-sum queries in which the range corresponds to a single point.) Thus, a useful measurement to evaluate the accuracy of a dynamic maintenance method is the 2-norm average absolute error for all the equal queries using the maintained histogram after a sequence of updates. By using this measure, we can clearly see how "close" a histogram maintained using a certain method is to that maintained using the (expensive) optimal method.

In our experiments, we also use other error measures proposed in [VWI98] and we report the results for one-dimensional case. For the multidimensional case, we only report the results using the 2-norm absolute error for all equal queries. For all the experiments in this section, the errors reported for our probabilistic counting method are the averages of the errors encountered over multiple different runs.

6.3.   Data Distributions

The data we used in our experiments are similar to those of [GMP97]. For one-dimensional data, we model the base data originally in the database and the update data sequence using an extensive set of Zipf distributions. The number of distinct values varies from 128 to 1024. Without loss of generality, we use the integer value domain. The z value for the frequency distribution is chosen from 0.0 to 3.0 to vary the skew. The frequencies are mapped to the values according to three different types of correlations: *positive* (the bigger the value, the higher the frequency), *negative* (the bigger the value, the lower the frequency), and *random*. We refer to a Zipf distribution with parameter z and correlation X as the $Zipf(z, X)$ distribution.

We extend Zipf data distributions to the multidimensional case. To generate a multidimensional data set, we first generate the frequencies for a one-dimensional data set of appropriate size using the Zipf distribution. We then logically map the one-dimensional values to the multidimensional values according to certain dimension order. For example, we

can use the row-major ordering to do the mapping between two-dimensional values and one-dimensional values.

When we model a sequence of insertions, we generate two data sets, one to represent the base data and another to represent the insertion sequence. In our experiments, the size of the insertion sequence varies from the base data size to four times the base data size.

For deletions, we first generate two data sets A and B, as for the insertion case, and we combine A and B to obtain the base data set $A \cup B$. Then we use the second data set B as our deletion sequence. In our experiments, the size of the deletion sequence varies from one quarter of the base data size to three quarters of the base data size.

6.4.   Parameter Settings

Parameters c_1 and c_2 are two very important parameters for our algorithm. They define how aggressive we are in shaking up the coefficients in the maintained histogram. The smaller c_1 and c_2 are, the more aggressive we are in shaking up the histogram. Intuitively, it helps to know the relationship between the distribution of the base data and that of the update sequence in order to choose the proper c_1 and c_2 values. For example, if the two distributions are similar, we should set c_1 and c_2 to bigger values in order to save time.

In our experiments, we find that our algorithm performs very well and is stable for a variety of update distributions as long as we choose c_1 and c_2 from reasonable ranges, and we do not need any *a priori* knowledge on the distribution of the update sequence to guarantee good performance of our algorithm. The appropriate ranges for c_1 and c_2 are 1.0–3.0 and 0.2–0.8, respectively. In our experiments, we use the default values $c_1 = 1.5$ and $c_2 = 0.5$.

The other important parameter is m', the size of the auxiliary histogram. It is obvious that a bigger m' value will give better accuracy but slower performance since we have more extra information in adjusting the histogram. However, our experiments show that it is not necessary to keep a very big auxiliary histogram to achieve good accuracy. For example, in most cases, setting $m' = m/2$ or $m' = 2m$ will not change the accuracy significantly. We use $m' = m/2$ as the default value in our experiments.

The parameter Max_Log_Size is relevant to the size of the base data. In our experiments, we set Max_Log_Size to be between 1% and 5% of the base data size. The default value for Max_Log_Size is 1% of the base data size.

6.5.   Accuracy for Maintaining One-Dimensional Histograms

We experimentally study the accuracy of various methods for a wide range of base data and update data distributions. We use $m = 20$ as the size of our wavelet-based histogram for all the experiments. The size of the value set is 512.

In the first set of experiments, we compare the accuracy of the three methods for the cases when the distribution of the update sequence is the same or very similar to that of the base data. For example, the base data and the update sequence follow the $Zipf(1.0, positive)$ and $Zipf(1.2, positive)$ distributions, respectively. In this case, the set of significant coefficients will either not change or else have some minor changes. As long as we keep the values up to date for the coefficients in the original histogram H_0 (which were built upon the base data), the histogram maintained using the static method is almost the same as the exact histogram. On the other hand, our probabilistic counting method could give less accurate results since it might unnecessarily shake up the coefficients in the histogram because of the probabilistic nature of the method.

Error Norm	Exact	Prob. Counting	Static
$\|e^{\mathrm{abs}}\|_1$	52.13	52.42	52.13
$\|e^{\mathrm{abs}}\|_2$	88.70	88.80	88.70
$\|e^{\mathrm{rel}}\|_1$	0.17	0.17	0.17
$\|e^{\mathrm{comb}}\|_1,$	16.71	16.72	16.71

Table 1: Average errors of various methods for all equal queries for insertions. The $\|e^{\mathrm{comb}}\|_1$ error measures uses the parameter settings $\alpha = 1$, $\beta = 100$.

Error Norm	Exact	Prob. Counting	Static
$\|e^{\mathrm{abs}}\|_1$	1679	1696	1679
$\|e^{\mathrm{abs}}\|_2$	1982	1991	1982
$\|e^{\mathrm{rel}}\|_1$	0.0036	0.0036	0.0036
$\|e^{\mathrm{comb}}\|_1,$	0.36	0.36	0.36

Table 2: Average errors of various methods for all one-sided range queries for insertions. The $\|e^{\mathrm{comb}}\|_1$ error measures uses the parameter settings $\alpha = 1$, $\beta = 100$.

Error Norm	Exact	Prob. Counting	Static
$\|e^{\mathrm{abs}}\|_1$	51.3	55.8	313.9
$\|e^{\mathrm{abs}}\|_2$	81.7	103.1	1899.3
$\|e^{\mathrm{rel}}\|_1$	0.33	0.37	2.20
$\|e^{\mathrm{m\_rel}}\|_1$	0.46	0.59	2.55
$\|e^{\mathrm{comb}}\|_1,$	27.8	29.5	153.0

Table 3: Average errors of various methods for all equal queries for deletions. The $\|e^{\mathrm{comb}}\|_1$ error measures uses the parameter settings $\alpha = 1$, $\beta = 100$.

Error Norm	Exact	Prob. Counting	Static
$\|e^{\mathrm{abs}}\|_1$	4162	6776	22242
$\|e^{\mathrm{abs}}\|_2$	4829	7772	35633
$\|e^{\mathrm{rel}}\|_1$	0.04	0.07	0.21
$\|e^{\mathrm{m\_rel}}\|_1$	0.04	0.07	0.21
$\|e^{\mathrm{comb}}\|_1,$	4.6	7.1	21.4

Table 4: Average errors of various methods for all one-sided range queries for deletions. The $\|e^{\mathrm{comb}}\|_1$ error measures uses the parameter settings $\alpha = 1$, $\beta = 100$.

Our results show that our method gives almost the same accuracy as the exact method even when the distribution of the update sequence is the same as that of the base data. Tables 1–2 show the accuracy of the three methods for one typical case. The base data contain 100K tuples from the $Zipf(1.0, negative)$ distribution; the update data come from the $Zipf(1.2, negative)$ distribution. We measure the errors for different types of range queries—equal queries (which corresponds to the evaluation of a single point in the array) and one-sided queries (in which one of the ends of the range in each dimension is $-\infty$ or $+\infty$)—using the error measures defined in [MVW98] after 400K insertions. (Note that the number of insertions is four times the base data size.)

Now we look into the more interesting cases where the distribution of the update sequence is different from or unrelated to that of the base data. Figure 2 plots the accuracy of different methods for a typical case. In this case, the base data contain 100K tuples and follow the $Zipf(1.0, negative)$ distribution. The insertions follow the $Zipf(1.5, random)$ distribution. We measure the accuracy of the different methods

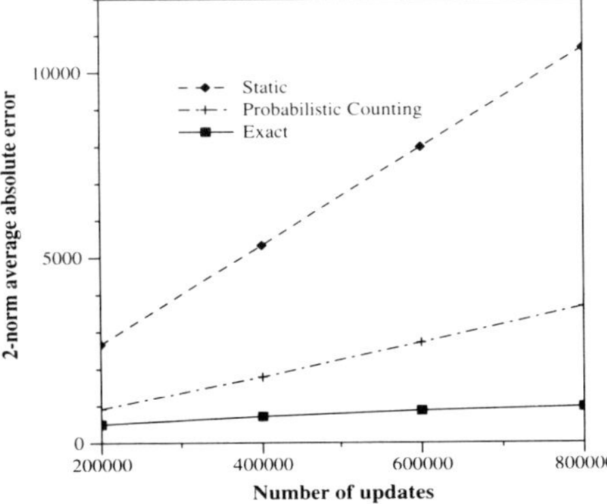

Figure 3: Accuracy of various methods for all equal queries for two-dimensional data

when the insertion sequence contains 100K, 200K, 300K, and 400K entries. The results show that the probabilistic counting method is much better than the static method.

We also compare the methods for deletions. Tables 3–4 show a typical case. In this case, we generate the base data distribution by combining two data sets; one follows $Zipf(1.0, negative)$ and the other follows $Zipf(1.5, positive)$. Each data set contains 100K entries. The deletion sequence follows the same data distribution as the second data set, i.e., $Zipf(1.5, positive)$. Tables 3–4 show the accuracy of the three methods when 100K deletions have been performed.

6.6. Accuracy for Maintenance of Multidimensional Histograms

Figure 3 and Figure 4 depict the accuracy of different methods for typical two-dimensional and three-dimensional data, respectively.

For the two-dimensional case, the value set size is 32×32. The base data follows the distribution $Zipf(1.0, negative)$, and its size is initially 200K. The inserted data follows the $Zipf(1.5, random)$ distribution. We keep $m = 40$ coefficients in the histogram during the process. Figure 3 plot the 2-norm absolute errors of different methods for all equal queries when 200K, 400K, 600K, and 800K entries are inserted.

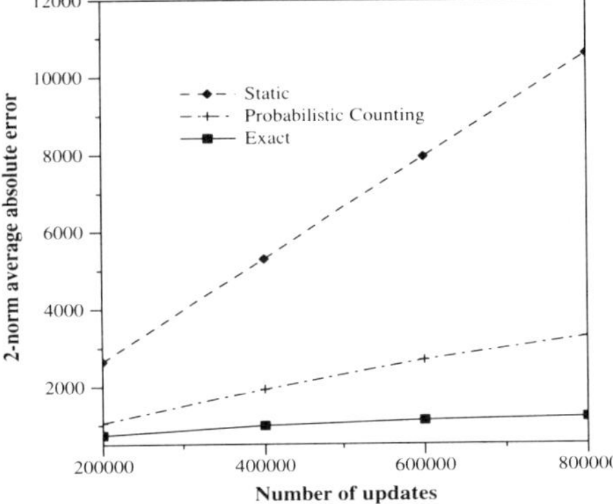

Figure 4: Accuracy of various methods for all equal queries for three-dimensional data

For the three-dimensional case, the value set size is $16 \times 16 \times 16$. The base data follows the $Zipf(1.0, positive)$ distribution, and its size is initially 200K. The distribution of the inserted data follows $Zipf(1.5, random)$. We keep $m = 80$ coefficients in the histogram during the process. Figure 4 plot the 2-norm absolute error of different methods for all equal queries when 200K, 400K, 600K, and 800K entries are inserted.

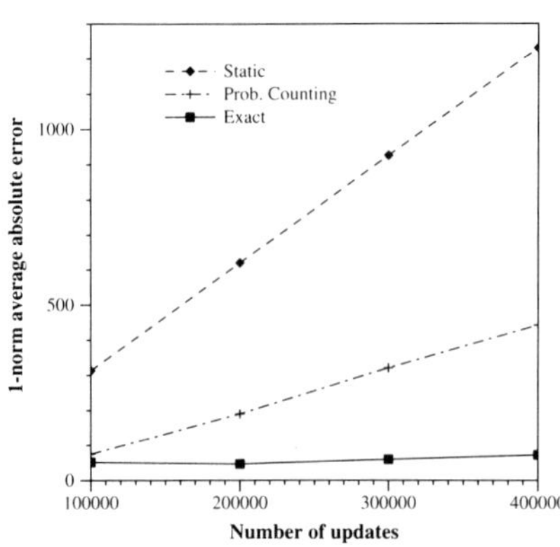

(a) 1-norm average absolute error for all equal queries

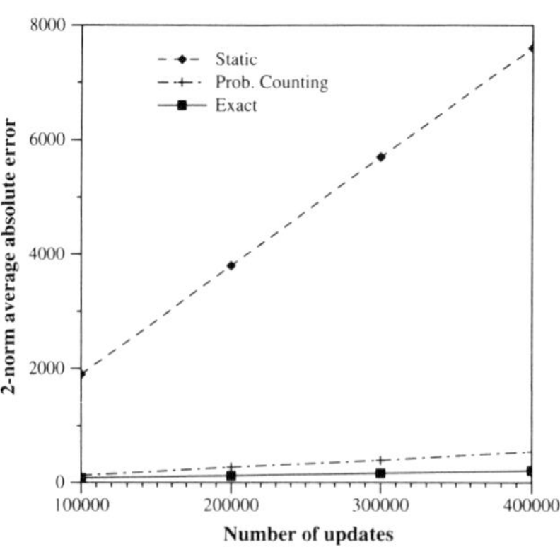

(b) 2-norm average absolute error for all equal queries

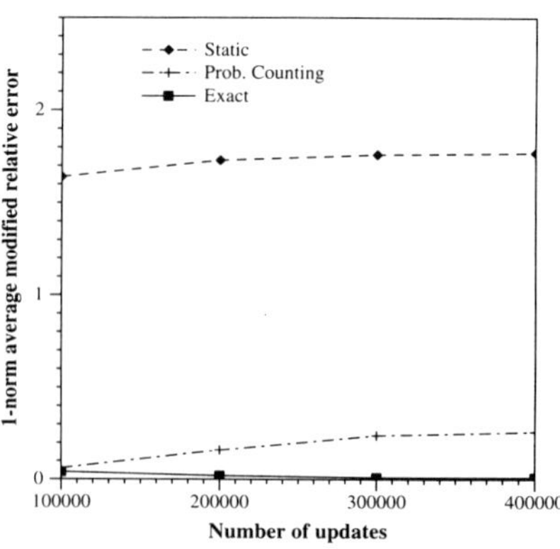

(c) 1-norm average modified relative error for all one-sided range queries

Figure 2: Accuracy of various methods for insertions.

7. Conclusions

In this paper, we present a novel method based upon probabilistic counting to maintain wavelet-based histograms. Experiments show that our method can effectively maintain wavelet-based histograms for a wide variety of update sequences with very little online time and space costs. Our techniques provide much more accurate results than the static maintenance method [LKC99] used in previous work. The accuracy of the histogram maintained using our method is very close to that of the optimal histogram obtained by rebuilding from scratch upon any update.

References

[AC99]   A. Aboulnaga and S. Chaudhuri. Self-tuning histograms: Building histograms without looking at data. In *Proceedings of the 1999 ACM SIGMOD International Conference on Management of Data*, pages 181–192, Phildelphia, June 1999.

[DIR99]   D. Donjerkovic, Y. Ioannidis, and R. Ramakrishnan. Dynamic histograms: Capturing evolving data sets. Technical report, Department of Computer Science, University of Wisconsin-Madison, 1999.

[FM85]   Philippe Flajolet and G. Nigel Martin. Probabilistic counting algorithms for data base applications. *Journal of Computer and System Sciences*, 31(2):182–209, October 1985.

[GMP97]   P. B. Gibbons, Y. Matias, and V. Poosala. Fast incremental maintenance of approximate histograms. In *Proceedings of the 1997 International Conference on Very Large Databases*, Athens, Greece, August 1997.

[JS94]   B. Jawerth and W. Sweldens. An overview of wavelet based multiresolution analyses. *SIAM Rev.*, 36(3):377–412, 1994.

[LKC99]   J. Lee, D. Kim, and C. Chung. Multi-dimensional selectivity estimation using compressed histogram information. In *Proceedings of the 1999 ACM SIGMOD International Conference on Management of Data*, pages 205–214, Phildelphia, June 1999.

[MD88]   M. Muralikrishna and D. J. DeWitt. Equi-depth histograms for estimating selectivity factors for multidimensional queries. In *Proceedings of the 1988 ACM SIGMOD International Conference on Management of Data*, pages 28–36, 1988.

[MRL98]   Gurmeet Singh Manku, Sridhar Rajagopalan, and Bruce G. Lindsay. Approximate medians and other quantiles in one pass and with limited memory. In *Proceedings of the ACM SIGMOD International Conference on Management of Data*, volume 27,2 of *ACM SIGMOD Record*, pages 426–435, New York, June 1–4 1998. ACM Press.

[MVW98]   Y. Matias, J. S. Vitter, and M. Wang. Wavelet-based histograms for selectivity estimation. In *Proceedings of the 1998 ACM SIGMOD International Conference on Management of Data*, pages 448–459, Seattle, WA, June 1998.

[PI97]   V. Poosala and Y. E. Ioannidis. Selectivity estimation without the attribute value independence assumption. In *Proceedings of the 1997 International Conference on Very Large Databases*, Athens, Greece, August 1997.

[PIHS96] V. Poosala, Y. E. Ioannidis, P. J. Haas, and E. Shekita. Improved histograms for selectivity estimation of range predicates. In *Proceedings of the 1996 ACM SIGMOD International Conference on Management of Data*, Montreal, Canada, May 1996.

[Poo97]   V. Poosala. *Histogram-Based Estimation Techniques in Database Systems*. Ph. D. dissertation, University of Wisconsin-Madison, 1997.

[PSC84]   G. Piatetsky-Shapiro and C. Connell. Accurate estimation of the number of tuples satisfying a condition. In *Proceedings of the 1984 ACM SIGMOD International Conference on Management of Data*, pages 256–276, 1984.

[SDS96]   E. J. Stollnitz, T. D. Derose, and D. H. Salesin. *Wavelets for Computer Graphics*. Morgan Kaufmann, 1996.

[VW99]   J. S. Vitter and M. Wang. Approximate computation of multidimensional aggregates of sparse data using wavelets. In *Proceedings of the 1999 ACM SIGMOD International Conference on Management of Data*, pages 193–204, Phildelphia, June 1999.

[VWI98]   J. S. Vitter, M. Wang, and B. Iyer. Data cube approximation and histograms via wavelets. In *Proceedings of Seventh International Conference on Information and Knowledge Management*, pages 96–104, Washington D.C., November 1998.

[Zip49]   G. K. Zipf. *Human Behaviour and the Principle of Least Effort*. Addison-Wesley, Reading, MA, 1949.

Approximate Query Processing Using Wavelets

Kaushik Chakrabarti[*]
University of Illinois
kaushikc@cs.uiuc.edu

Minos Garofalakis
Bell Laboratories
minos@bell-labs.com

Rajeev Rastogi
Bell Laboratories
rastogi@bell-labs.com

Kyuseok Shim
KAIST[†] and AITrc[‡]
shim@cs.kaist.ac.kr

Abstract

Approximate query processing has emerged as a cost-effective approach for dealing with the huge data volumes and stringent response-time requirements of today's decision-support systems. Most work in this area, however, has so far been limited in its applicability and query processing scope. In this paper, we propose the use of multi-dimensional wavelets as an effective tool for general-purpose approximate query processing in modern, high-dimensional applications. Our approach is based on building *wavelet-coefficient synopses* of the data and using these synopses to provide approximate answers to queries. We develop novel query processing algorithms that operate directly on the wavelet-coefficient synopses of relational tables, allowing us to process arbitrarily complex queries *entirely* in the wavelet-coefficient domain. This, of course, guarantees extremely fast response times since our approximate query execution engine can do the bulk of its processing over compact sets of wavelet coefficients, essentially postponing the expansion into relational tuples until the end-result of the query. An extensive experimental study with synthetic as well as real-life data sets establishes the effectiveness of our wavelet-based approach compared to sampling and histograms.

1. Introduction

Approximate query processing has recently emerged as a viable solution for dealing with the huge amounts of data, the high query complexities, and the increasingly stringent response-time requirements that characterize today's Decision-Support Systems (DSS) applications. Typically, DSS users pose very complex queries to the underlying Database Management System (DBMS) that require complex operations over Gigabytes or Terabytes of disk-resident data and, thus, take a very long time to execute to completion and produce exact answers. Due to the *exploratory nature* of many DSS applications, there are a number of scenarios in which an exact answer may not be required, and a user may in fact prefer a fast, approximate answer. For example, during a drill-down query sequence in ad-hoc data mining, initial queries in the sequence frequently have the sole purpose of determining the truly interesting queries and regions of the database [5]. Providing (reasonably accurate) approximate answers to these initial queries gives users the ability to focus their explorations quickly and effectively, without consuming inordinate amounts of valuable system resources.

Prior Work.[1] The strong incentive for approximate answers has spurred a flurry of research activity on approximate query processing techniques in recent years [1, 5, 6, 11, 17, 18]. The majority of the proposed techniques, however, have been somewhat limited in their *query processing scope*, typically focusing on specific forms of aggregate queries. Besides the range of queries, another crucial aspect of an approximate query processing technique is the employed *data reduction mechanism*; that is, the method used to obtain *synopses* of the data on which the approximate query execution engine can then operate. The methods explored in this context include *sampling* and, more recently, *histograms* and *wavelets*.

- *Sampling-based techniques* are based on the use of random samples as synopses for large data sets. Random samples of a data collection typically provide accurate estimates for aggregate quantities (e.g., `counts` or `averages`), as witnessed by the long history of successful applications of random sampling in population surveys [3] and selectivity estimation [8]. Sampling, however, suffers from two inherent limitations that restrict its applicability as an approximate query processing tool. First, a `join` operator applied on two uniform random samples results in a *non-uniform* sample of the join result that typically contains *very few tuples*, even when the join selectivity is fairly high [1]. Thus, `join` operations typically lead to significant degradations in the quality of an approximate aggregate. ("Join synopses" [1] provide a solution, but only for *foreign-key joins that are known beforehand*; that is, they cannot support arbitrary join queries over any schema.) Second, for a *non-aggregate* query, execution over random samples of the data is guaranteed to always produce a small subset of the exact answer which is often empty when `joins` are involved [1, 6].

- *Histogram-based techniques* have been studied extensively in the context of query selectivity estimation [12, 13] and, more recently, as a tool for providing approximate query answers [6, 11]. The very recent work of Ioannidis and Poosala [6] is the first to address the issue of ob-

---

[*] Work done while visiting Bell Laboratories. Author's current address: Univ. of California, Irvine, CA 92697.

[†] Korea Advanced Institute of Science and Technology.

[‡] Advanced Information Technology Research Center at KAIST.

Proceedings of the 26th VLDB Conference,
Cairo, Egypt, 2000.

---

[1] Due to space constraints, we omit a detailed discussion of related work; it can be found in the full version of this paper [2].

taining practical approximations to *non-aggregate* query answers, demonstrating how standard relational operators (like `join` and `select`) can be processed directly over histogram synopses of the data. The experimental results given in [6] prove that certain classes of histograms can provide higher-quality approximate answers compared to random sampling, when considering simple queries over low-dimensional data (one or two dimensions). It is a well-known fact, however, that histogram-based approaches become problematic when dealing with the high-dimensional data sets that are typical of modern DSS applications. The reason is that, as the dimensionality of the data increases, both the *storage overhead* (i.e., number of buckets) and the *construction cost* of histograms that can achieve reasonable error rates increase in an explosive manner [17]. This problem is further exacerbated by `join` operations that can cause the dimensionality of intermediate query results (and the corresponding histograms) to explode.

- *Wavelet-based techniques* provide a mathematical tool for the hierarchical decomposition of functions, with a long history of successful applications in signal and image processing [7, 10, 16]. Recent studies have also demonstrated the applicability of wavelets to selectivity estimation [9] and the approximation of range-sum queries over OLAP data cubes [17, 18]. Briefly, the idea is to apply wavelet decomposition to the input data collection (attribute column(s) or OLAP cube) to obtain a compact data synopsis that comprises a select small collection of *wavelet coefficients*. The results of Vitter et al. [17, 18] have clearly shown that wavelets can be very effective in handling aggregates over high-dimensional OLAP cubes, while avoiding the high construction costs and storage overheads of histograming techniques. Nevertheless, the focus of these earlier studies has always been on a very specific form of queries (i.e., range-sums) over a single OLAP table. Thus, the problem of whether wavelets can provide a solid foundation for general-purpose approximate query processing has hitherto been left unanswered.

Our Contributions. In this paper, we significantly extend the scope of earlier work on approximate query answers, establishing the viability and effectiveness of wavelets as a generic approximate query processing tool for modern, high-dimensional DSS applications. More specifically, we propose a novel approach to general-purpose approximate query processing that consists of two basic steps. First, multi-dimensional Haar wavelets are employed to efficiently obtain effective, compact synopses of general relational tables. Second, using novel query processing algorithms, standard (aggregate and non-aggregate) SQL operators are applied *directly* over the wavelet-coefficient synopses of the data to obtain fast and accurate approximate query answers. The crucial observation here is that, as we demonstrate in this work, our approximate query execution engine can do all of its processing *entirely in the wavelet-coefficient domain*; that is, both the input(s) and the output of our query processing operators are compact collections of wavelet coefficients capturing the underlying relational data. This, of course, implies that we can delay the expansion of our wavelet-coefficient synopses to the very end of an arbitrarily complex query, thus allowing for extremely fast approximate query processing. The contributions of our work are summarized as follows.

- **New, I/O-Efficient Wavelet Decomposition Algorithm for Relational Tables.** The methodology developed in this paper is based on a different form of the multi-dimensional Haar transform than that employed by Vitter et al. [17, 18]. As a consequence, the decomposition algorithms proposed by Vitter and Wang [17] are not applicable. We address this problem by developing a novel, I/O-efficient algorithm for building the wavelet-coefficient synopsis of a relational table. The worst-case I/O complexity of our algorithm matches that of the best algorithms of Vitter and Wang, requiring only a logarithmically small number of passes over the data. Furthermore, there exist scenarios (e.g., when the table is stored in *chunks* [4, 15]) under which our decomposition algorithm can work in a *single pass* over the input.

- **Novel Query Processing Algebra for Wavelet-Coefficient Data Synopses.** We propose a new algebra for approximate query processing that operates *directly over the wavelet-coefficient synopses of relations*, while guaranteeing the correct relational operator semantics. Our algebra operators include the conventional aggregate and non-aggregate SQL operators, like `select`, `join`, `sum`, and `average`. Based on the semantics of Haar wavelet coefficients, we develop novel query processing algorithms for these operators that work *entirely* in the wavelet-coefficient domain. This allows for extremely fast response times, since our approximate query execution engine can do the bulk of its processing over compact wavelet-coefficient synopses, essentially postponing the expansion into relational tuples until the end-result of the query.

- **Extensive Experiments Validating our Approach.** We have conducted an extensive experimental study with synthetic as well as real-life data sets to determine the effectiveness of our wavelet-based approach compared to sampling and histograms. Our results demonstrate that (1) the quality of approximate answers obtained from our wavelet-based query processor is, in general, better than that obtained by either sampling or histograms for a wide range of `select`, `project`, `join`, and aggregate queries, (2) query execution-time speedups of more than two orders of magnitude are made possible by our approximate query processing algorithms; and (3) our wavelet decomposition algorithm is extremely fast and scales linearly with the size of the data.

2. Building Synopses of Relational Data Using Multi-Dimensional Wavelets

2.1 Background: The Wavelet Decomposition

Wavelets are a useful mathematical tool for hierarchically decomposing functions in ways that are both efficient and theoretically sound. Broadly speaking, the wavelet decomposition of a function consists of a coarse overall approximation together with detail coefficients that influence the function at various scales [16]. The wavelet decomposition has excellent energy compaction and de-correlation properties, which can be used to effectively generate compact representations that exploit the structure of data.

The work in this paper is based on the multi-dimensional *Haar wavelet* decomposition. Haar wavelets are conceptually simple, very fast to compute, and have been found to perform well in practice for a variety of applications ranging from image editing and querying [10, 16] to selectivity estimation and OLAP approximations [9, 17]. In this section, we discuss Haar wavelets in both one and multiple dimensions.

One-Dimensional Haar Wavelets. Suppose we are given a one-dimensional data vector A containing the following four values $A = [2, 2, 5, 7]$. The Haar wavelet transform of A can be computed as follows. We first average the values together pairwise to get a new "lower-resolution" representation of the data with the following average values $[2, 6]$. In other words, the average of the first two values (that is, 2 and 2) is 2 and that of the next two values (that is, 5 and 7) is 6. Obviously, some information has been lost in this averaging process. To be able to restore the original four values of the data array, we need to store some *detail coefficients*, that capture the missing information. In Haar wavelets, these detail coefficients are simply the differences of the (second of the) averaged values from the computed pairwise average. Thus, in our simple example, for the first pair of averaged values, the detail coefficient is 0 since 2-2 =0, while for the second we need to store -1 since $6 - 7 = -1$. Note that it is possible to reconstruct the four values of the original data array from the lower-resolution array containing the two averages and the two detail coefficients. Recursively applying the above pairwise averaging and differencing process on the lower-resolution array containing the averages, we get the following full decomposition.

Resolution	Averages	Detail Coefficients
2	[2, 2, 5, 7]	–
1	[2, 6]	[0, -1]
0	[4]	[-2]

We define the *wavelet transform* (also known as the *wavelet decomposition*) of A to be the single coefficient representing the overall average of the data values followed by the detail coefficients in the order of increasing resolution. Thus, the one-dimensional Haar wavelet transform of A is given by $W_A = [4, -2, 0, -1]$. Each entry in W_A is called a *wavelet coefficient*. The main advantage of using W_A instead of the original data vector A is that for vectors containing similar values most of the detail coefficients tend to have very small values. Thus, eliminating such small coefficients from the wavelet transform (i.e., treating them as zeros) introduces only small errors when reconstructing the original data, giving a very effective form of lossy data compression.

Note that, intuitively, wavelet coefficients carry different weights with respect to their importance in rebuilding the original data values. For example, the overall average is obviously more important than any detail coefficient since it affects the reconstruction of all entries in the data array. In order to equalize the importance of all wavelet coefficients, we need to *normalize* the final entries of W_A appropriately. This is achieved by dividing each wavelet coefficient by $\sqrt{2^l}$, where l denotes the *level of resolution* at which the coefficient appears (with $l = 0$ corresponding to the "coarsest" resolution level). Thus, the normalized wavelet transform for our example data array becomes $W_A = [4, -2, 0, -1/\sqrt{2}]$.

Multi-Dimensional Haar Wavelets. There are two common methods in which Haar wavelets can be extended to transform the data values in a *multi-dimensional* array. Each of these transformations is a generalization of the one-dimensional decomposition process described above. To simplify the exposition to the basic ideas of multidimensional wavelets, we assume all dimensions of the input array to be of equal size.

The first method is known as *standard decomposition*. In this method, we first fix an ordering for the data dimensions (say, $1, 2, \ldots, d$) and then proceed to apply the complete one-dimensional wavelet transform for each one-dimensional "row" of array cells along dimension k, for all $k = 1, \ldots, d$. The standard Haar decomposition forms the basis of the recent results of Vitter et al. on OLAP data cube approximations [17, 18].

The work presented in this paper is based on the second method of extending Haar wavelets to multiple dimensions, namely the *nonstandard decomposition*. Abstractly, the nonstandard Haar decomposition alternates between dimensions during successive steps of pairwise averaging and differencing: given an ordering for the data dimensions $(1, 2, \ldots, d)$, we perform *one step of pairwise averaging and differencing* for each one-dimensional row of array cells along dimension k, for each $k = 1, \ldots, d$. (The results of earlier averaging and differencing steps are treated as data values for larger values of k.) This process is then repeated recursively only on the quadrant containing averages across all dimensions. One way of conceptualizing (and implementing [10]) this procedure is to think of a $2 \times 2 \times \cdots \times 2 (= 2^d)$ hyper-box being shifted across the data array, performing pairwise averaging and differencing, distributing the results to the appropriate locations of the wavelet transform array W_A (with the averages for each box going to the "lower-left" quadrant of W_A) and, finally, recursing the computation on the lower-left quadrant of W_A. This procedure is demonstrated pictorially for a $2^m \times 2^m$ data array A in Figure 1(a). More specifically, Figure 1(a) shows the pairwise averaging and differencing step for one positioning of the 2×2 box with its "root"(i.e., lower-left corner) located at the coordinates $[2i_1, 2i_2]$ of A followed by the distribution of the results in the wavelet transform array. This step is repeated for every possible combination of i_j's, $i_j \in \{0, \ldots, 2^{m-1} - 1\}$. Finally, the process is recursed only on the lower-left quadrant of W_A

(containing the averages collected from all boxes). A detailed description of the nonstandard Haar decomposition can be found in any standard reference on the subject (e.g., [7, 16]).

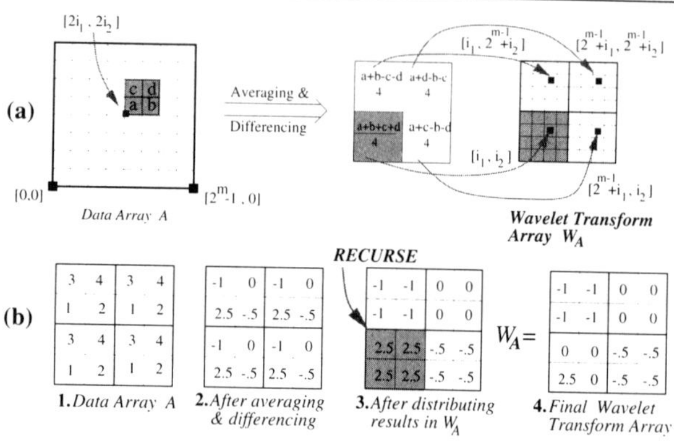

Figure 1. Non-standard decomposition in two dimensions. (a) Computing and distributing pairwise averages and differences. (b) Example decomposition of a 4×4 array.

Example 2.1: Consider the 4×4 array A shown in Figure 1(b.1). Figure 1(b.2) shows the result of the first horizontal and vertical pairwise averaging and differencing on the 2×2 hyper-boxes of the original array. The averages of the values for each positioning of the hyper-box are assigned to the 2×2 lower-left quadrant of the wavelet transform array W_A, while the detail coefficients are distributed in the three remaining 2×2 quadrants of W_A, as shown in Figure 1(b.3). The process is then recursively performed on the lower-left quadrant of W_A, resulting in detail coefficients of 0 and an average value of 2.5 which is stored in the lower-left entry of W_A. The final wavelet transform array W_A is depicted in Figure 1(b.4). ∎

As noted in the wavelet literature, both methods for extending one-dimensional Haar wavelets to higher dimensionalities have been used in a wide variety of application domains and, to the best of our knowledge, none has been shown to be uniformly superior. Our choice of the nonstandard method was mostly motivated by our earlier experience with nonstandard two-dimensional Haar wavelets in the context of effective image retrieval [10]. An advantage of using the nonstandard transform is that, as we explain later in the paper, it allows for an efficient representation of the sign information for wavelet coefficients. This efficient representation stems directly from the construction process for a nonstandard Haar basis [16]. (We often omit the "nonstandard" qualification in what follows.)

Multi-Dimensional Haar Coefficients: Semantics and Representation. Consider a wavelet coefficient W generated during the multi-dimensional Haar decomposition of a d-dimensional data array A. From a mathematical standpoint, this coefficient is essentially a multiplicative factor for an appropriate *Haar basis function* when the data in A is expressed using the d-dimensional Haar basis [16]. The d-dimensional Haar basis function corresponding to W is

defined by (1) a *d-dimensional rectangular support region* in A that essentially captures the region of A's cells that W contributes to during reconstruction; and (2) the *quadrant sign information* that defines the sign ($+$ or $-$) of W's contribution (i.e., $+W$ or $-W$) to any cell contained in a given quadrant of its support rectangle. (Note that the wavelet decomposition process guarantees that this sign can only change across quadrants of the support region.) As an example, Figure 2(a) depicts the support regions and signs of the sixteen nonstandard, two-dimensional Haar basis functions for coefficients in the corresponding locations of a 4×4 wavelet transform array W_A. The blank areas for each coefficient correspond to regions of A whose reconstruction is independent of the coefficient, i.e., the coefficient's contribution is 0. Thus, $W_A[0, 0]$ is the overall average that contributes positively (i.e.,"$+W_A[0, 0]$") to the reconstruction of all values in A, whereas $W_A[3, 3]$ is a detail coefficient that contributes (with the signs shown in Fig. 2(a)) only to values in A's upper right quadrant. Figure 2(a) also depicts the two *levels of resolution* ($l = 0, 1$) for our example two-dimensional Haar coefficients; as in the one-dimensional case, these levels define the appropriate constants for normalizing coefficient values [16].

Example 2.2: In light of Figure 2(a), let us now revisit Example 2.1 and consider how the entries of W_A contribute to the reconstruction of values in A. As we have already observed, coefficient $W_A[0, 0] = 2.5$ is the overall average that contributes $+2.5$ to the reconstruction of all sixteen data values in A. On the other hand, the detail coefficient $W_A[0, 2] = -1$ affects the reconstruction of only the four values in the lower-left quadrant of A, contributing -1 to $A[0, 0]$ and $A[1, 0]$, and $-(-1) = +1$ to $A[0, 1]$ and $A[1, 1]$. Similarly, the detail coefficient $W_A[2, 0] = -.5$ contributes $-.5$ to $A[0, 0]$ and $A[0, 1]$, and $+.5$ to $A[1, 0]$ and $A[1, 1]$. For example, based on Figure 2(a), the data value $A[0, 1]$ can be reconstructed using the formula:

$$A[0, 1] = +W_A[0, 0] + W_A[0, 1] + W_A[1, 0] + W_A[1, 1] - W_A[0, 2] + W_A[2, 0] - W_A[2, 2] = 2.5 - (-1) + (-.5) = 3. ∎$$

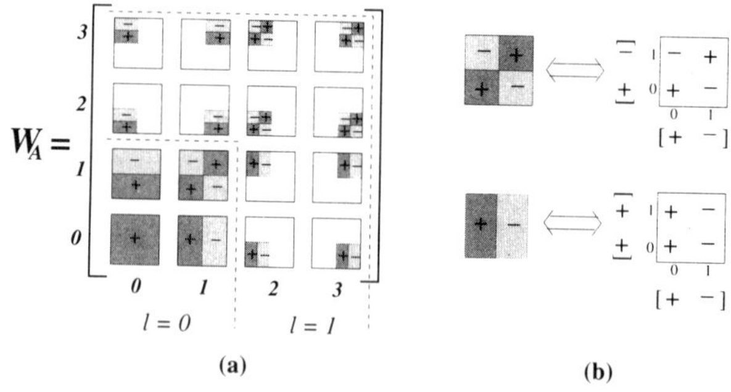

Figure 2. (a) Support regions and signs for the sixteen nonstandard two-dimensional Haar basis functions. (b) Representing quadrant sign information for coefficients using "per-dimension" sign vectors.

To simplify the discussion in this paper, we abstract away the distinction between a coefficient and its corre-

sponding basis function by representing a Haar wavelet coefficient with the triple $W = \langle R, S, v \rangle$, where:

(1) $W.R$ is the *d-dimensional support hyper-rectangle of W* enclosing all the cells in the data array A to which W contributes (i.e., the support of the corresponding basis function). We represent this hyper-rectangle by its low and high boundary values (i.e., starting and ending array cells) along each dimension j, $1 \leq j \leq d$; these are denoted by $W.R.bound[j].lo$ and $W.R.bound[j].hi$, respectively. Thus, the coefficient W contributes to each data cell $A[i_1, \ldots, i_d]$ satisfying the condition $W.R.bound[j].lo \leq i_j \leq W.R.bound[j].hi$ for all dimensions j, $1 \leq j \leq d$. The space required to store the support hyper-rectangle of a coefficient is $2 \log N$ bits, where N denotes the total number of cells of A.

(2) $W.S$ stores the *sign information for all d-dimensional quadrants of W.R.* Storing the quadrant sign information directly would mean a space requirement of $O(2^d)$, i.e., proportional to the number of quadrants of a d-dimensional hyper-rectangle. Instead, we use a more space-efficient representation of the quadrant sign information (using only $2d$ bits) that exploits the regularity of the nonstandard Haar transform. The basic observation here is that a nonstandard d-dimensional Haar basis is formed by scaled and translated products of d one-dimensional Haar basis functions [16]. Thus, our idea is to store a 2-bit *sign vector* for each dimension j, that captures the sign variation of the corresponding one-dimensional basis function. The two elements of the sign vector of coefficient W along dimension j are denoted by $W.S.sign[j].lo$ and $W.S.sign[j].hi$, and contain the sign that corresponds to the lower and upper half of $W.R$'s extent along dimension j, respectively. Given the sign vectors along each dimension and treating a sign of $+$ $(-)$ as being equivalent to $+1$ (resp., -1), the sign for each d-dimensional quadrant can be computed as the product of the d sign-vector entries that map to that quadrant; that is, following exactly the basis construction process. (We will continue to make use of this "+1/-1" interpretation of signs throughout the paper.) Our sign-computation methodology is depicted in Figure 2(b) for two example coefficient hyper-rectangles from Figure 2(a).

(3) $W.v$ is the *(scalar) magnitude of coefficient W*. This is exactly the quantity that W contributes (either positively or negatively, depending on $W.S$) to all data array cells enclosed in $W.R$.

Thus, our view of a d-dimensional Haar wavelet coefficient is that of a d-dimensional hyper-rectangle with a magnitude and a sign that may change across quadrants. Note that, by the properties of the nonstandard Haar decomposition, given *any pair* of coefficients, their hyper-rectangles are either *completely disjoint* or one is *completely contained* in the other; that is, coefficient hyper-rectangles cannot *partially overlap*. It is precisely these containment properties coupled with our sign-vector representation of quadrant signs that enable us to efficiently perform `join` operations directly over wavelet-coefficient synopses.

2.2 Building Wavelet-Coefficient Synopses

Consider a relational table R with d attributes $X_1, X_2, \ldots X_d$. The information in R can be accurately captured as a d-dimensional array A_R, whose j^{th} dimension is indexed by the values of attribute X_j and whose cells contain the count of tuples in R having the corresponding combination of attribute values. (A_R is essentially the *joint frequency distribution* of all the attributes of R.) We have developed a novel, I/O-efficient algorithm for constructing the nonstandard multi-dimensional wavelet decomposition of A_R (denoted W_R). Note that, even though our algorithm computes the decomposition of A_R, it in fact works off the "set-of-tuples" (ROLAP) representation of R. (As noted by Vitter and Wang [17], this is a requirement for computational efficiency since the joint frequency array A_R is typically extremely sparse.) The worst-case I/O complexity of our algorithm matches that of the best algorithms of Vitter and Wang [17], requiring only a logarithmic number of passes over the data. Furthermore, there exist scenarios (e.g., when R is stored in *chunks* [4, 15]) under which our decomposition algorithm can work in a *single pass* over R.

In a nutshell, our algorithm is based on the recursive application of the following key property the nonstandard Haar decomposition: *The decomposition of a d-dimensional array A_R can be computed by <u>independently</u> computing the decomposition for each of the 2^d d-dimensional subarrays corresponding to A_R's quadrants and then performing pairwise averaging and differencing on the computed 2^d averages of A_R's quadrants.* Abstractly, our decomposition algorithm exploits this observation by working in a "depth-first" fashion on d-dimensional chunks of A_R – all the computation required for decomposing a chunk is executed the first time that chunk is loaded into memory.

The size of the wavelet-coefficient synopsis of R is controlled by a *thresholding scheme* that retains only the largest coefficients in absolute normalized value. (This thresholding rule is in fact *provably optimal* with respect to minimizing the overall mean squared error in the data compression [16].) We have also proposed a time- and space-efficient algorithm for *rendering* (i.e., expanding) a synopsis into an approximate "set-of tuples" relation. Due to space constraints, we have chosen to omit the presentation of our wavelet-decomposition and coefficient-rendering algorithms; the details can be found in the full version of this paper [2]. In the remainder of this section, we summarize the notational conventions used throughout the paper.

Notation. Let $\mathcal{D} = \{D_1, D_2, \ldots, D_d\}$ denote the set of dimensions of A_R, where dimension D_j corresponds to the *value domain* of attribute X_j. Without loss of generality, we assume that each dimension D_j is indexed by the set of integers $\{0, 1, \cdots, |D_j| - 1\}$, where $|D_j|$ denotes the size of dimension D_j. Table 1 outlines the notation used in this paper with a brief description of its semantics.

Most of the notation pertaining to wavelet coeffi-

Symbol	Semantics
d	Dimensionality of input relation
R, A_R	Relation and corresponding joint frequency array
X_j, D_j	j^{th} attribute of R and corresponding domain of values ($1 \leq j \leq d$)
$\mathcal{D} = \{D_1, \ldots, D_d\}$	Set of data dimensions of A_R
$W.R.bound[j].\{lo, hi\}$	Support-rectangle boundaries along dimension D_j for W ($1 \leq j \leq d$)
$W.S.sign[j].\{lo, hi\}$	Sign-vector information along dimension D_j for W ($1 \leq j \leq d$)
$W.S.schg[j]$	Sign-change value along dimension D_j for coefficient W ($1 \leq j \leq d$)
$W.v$	Scalar magnitude of coefficient W

Table 1. Notation

cients W has already been described in Section 2.1. The only exception is the *sign-change value vector* $W.S.schg[j]$ that captures the value along dimension j (between $W.R.bound[j].lo$ and $W.R.bound[j].hi$) at which a transition in the value of the sign vector $W.S.sign[j]$ occurs, for each $1 \leq j \leq d$. That is, the sign $W.S.sign[j].lo$ ($W.S.sign[j].hi$) applies to the range $[W.R.bound[j].lo, \ldots, W.S.schg[j] - 1]$ (resp., $[W.S.schg[j], \ldots, W.R.bound[j].hi]$). As a convention, we set $W.S.schg[j]$ equal to $W.R.bound[j].lo$ when there is no "true" sign change along dimension j, i.e., $W.S.sign[j]$ contains $[+, +]$ or $[-, -]$. Note that, for base Haar coefficients with a true sign change along dimension j, $W.S.schg[j]$ is simply the midpoint between $W.R.bound[j].lo$ and $W.R.bound[j].hi$ (Figure 2). This property, however, no longer holds when arbitrary selections and joins are executed over the wavelet coefficients. As a consequence, we need to store sign-change values explicitly in order to support general query processing operations in an efficient manner.

For the remainder of the paper, we use the symbol W_R to denote the set of coefficients *retained (after thresholding)* from the decomposition of R (i.e., the *wavelet-coefficient synopsis of R*).

3 Processing Relational Queries in the Wavelet-Coefficient Domain

In this section, we propose a novel query algebra for wavelet-coefficient synopses. The basic operators of our algebra correspond directly to conventional relational algebra and SQL operators, including the (non-aggregate) `select`, `project`, and `join`, as well as aggregate operators like `count`, `sum`, and `average`. There is, however, one crucial difference: our operators are defined *over the wavelet-coefficient domain*; that is, their input(s) and output are *sets of wavelet coefficients* (rather than relational tables). The motivation for defining a query algebra for wavelet coefficients comes directly from the need for efficient approximate query processing. To see this, consider an n-ary relational query Q over $R_1, \ldots, R_n$ and assume that each relation R_i has been reduced to a (truncated) set

of wavelet coefficients W_{R_i}. A simplistic way of processing Q would be to render each synopsis W_{R_i} into the corresponding approximate relation (denoted `render`(W_{R_i})) and process the relational operators in Q over the resulting sets of tuples. This strategy, however, is clearly inefficient: the approximate relation `render`(W_{R_i}) may contain just as many tuples as the original R_i itself, which implies that query execution costs may also be just as high as those of the original query. Therefore, such a "render-then-process" strategy essentially defeats one of the main motivations behind approximate query processing.

On the other hand, the synopsis W_{R_i} is a highly-compressed representation of `render`(W_{R_i}) that is typically orders of magnitude smaller than R_i. Executing Q in the compressed wavelet-coefficient domain can offer tremendous speedups in query execution cost. We therefore define the operators `op` of our query processing algebra over wavelet-coefficient synopses, while guaranteeing the valid semantics depicted pictorially in the transition diagram of Figure 3. (These semantics can be translated to the equivalence `render`(op($T_1, \ldots, T_k$)) $\equiv$ op(`render`($T_1, \ldots, T_k$)), for each operator op.) Our algebra allows the fast execution of any relational query Q *entirely* over the wavelet-coefficient domain, while guaranteeing that the final (rendered) result is identical to that obtained by executing Q on the approximate input relations.

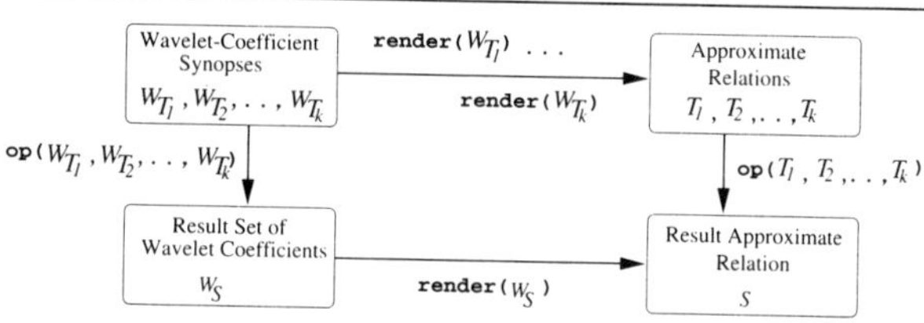

Figure 3. Valid semantics for processing query operators over the wavelet-coefficient domain. ($T_1, \ldots, T_k$ can be base relations or intermediate query results.)

In the following subsections, we describe our algorithms for processing `select`, `project`, and `join` operators in the wavelet-coefficient domain. (Our algorithms for processing aggregate operators can be found in [2].) Each operator takes as input one or more set(s) of multi-dimensional wavelet coefficients and appropriately combines and/or updates the components (i.e., hyper-rectangle, sign information, and magnitude) of these coefficients to produce a "valid" set of output coefficients (Figure 3). Note that, while the wavelet coefficients (generated by our decomposition algorithm) for base relational tables have a very regular structure, the same is not necessarily true for the set of coefficients output by an arbitrary `select` or `join` operator. Nevertheless, we loosely continue to refer to the intermediate results of our algebra operators as "wavelet coefficients" since they are characterized by the exact same components as base-relation coefficients (e.g., hyper-rectangle, sign-vectors) and maintain the exact same semantics with respect to the underlying intermediate relation (i.e., the rendering process remains unchanged).

3.1 Selection Operator (`select`)

Our selection operator has the general form $\texttt{select}_{pred}(W_T)$, where *pred* represents a generic conjunctive predicate on a subset of the d attributes in T; that is, $pred = (l_{i_1} \le X_{i_1} \le h_{i_1}) \wedge \ldots \wedge (l_{i_k} \le X_{i_k} \le h_{i_k})$, where l_{i_j} and h_{i_j} denote the low and high boundaries of the selected range along each selection dimension D_{i_j}, $j = 1, 2, \cdots, k, k \le d$. This is essentially a k-dimensional range selection, where the queried range is specified along k dimensions $\mathcal{D}' = \{D_{i_1}, D_{i_2}, \ldots, D_{i_k}\}$ and left unspecified along the remaining $(d - k)$ dimensions $(\mathcal{D} - \mathcal{D}')$. ($\mathcal{D} = \{D_1, D_2, \ldots, D_d\}$ denotes the set of all dimensions of T.) Thus, for each unspecified dimension D_j, the selection range spans the full index domain along the dimension; that is, $l_j = 0$ and $h_j = |D_j| - 1$, for each $D_j \in (\mathcal{D} - \mathcal{D}')$.

The `select` operator effectively filters out the portions of the wavelet coefficients in the synopsis W_T that do not overlap with the k-dimensional selection range, and thus do not contribute to cells in the selected hyper-rectangle. This process is illustrated pictorially in Figure 4(a). More formally, let $W \in W_T$ denote any wavelet coefficient in the input set of our `select` operator. Our approximate query execution engine processes the selection over W as follows. If W's support hyper-rectangle $W.R$ overlaps the k-dimensional selection hyper-rectangle; that is, if *for every* dimension $D_{i_j} \in \mathcal{D}'$, the following condition is satisfied: $l_{i_j} \le W.R.bound[i_j].lo \le h_{i_j}$ or $W.R.bound[i_j].lo \le l_{i_j} \le W.R.bound[i_j].hi$, then

1. For all dimensions $D_{i_j} \in \mathcal{D}'$ do

   1.1. Set $W.R.bound[i_j].lo := \max\{l_{i_j}, W.R.bound[i_j].lo\}$ and $W.R.bound[i_j].hi := \min\{h_{i_j}, W.R.bound[i_j].hi\}$.

   1.2. If $W.R.bound[i_j].hi < W.S.schg[i_j]$ then set $W.S.schg[i_j] := W.R.bound[i_j].lo$ and $W.S.sign[i_j] := [W.S.sign[i_j].lo, W.S.sign[i_j].lo]$.

   1.3. Else if $W.R.bound[i_j].lo \ge W.S.schg[i_j]$ then set $W.S.schg[i_j] := W.R.bound[i_j].lo$ and $W.S.sign[i_j] := [W.S.sign[i_j].hi, W.S.sign[i_j].hi]$.

2. Add the (updated) W to the set of output coefficients; that is, set $W_S := W_S \cup \{W\}$, where $S = \texttt{select}_{pred}(T)$.

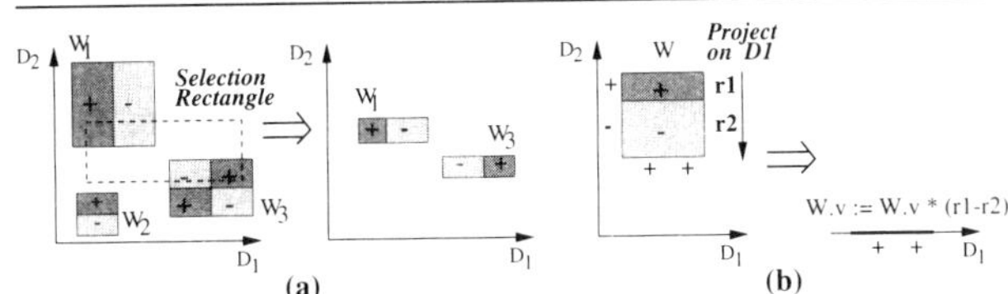

Figure 4. Processing (a) selection and (b) projection operations in the wavelet-coefficient domain.

Our `select` processing algorithm chooses (and appropriately updates) only the coefficients in W_T that overlap with the k-dimensional selection hyper-rectangle. For each such coefficient, our algorithm (a) updates the hyper-rectangle boundaries according to the specified selection range (Step 1.1), and (b) updates the sign information, if such an update is necessary (Steps 1.2-1.3). Briefly, the sign information along the queried dimension D_{i_j} needs to be updated only if the selection range along D_{i_j} is completely contained in either the low (1.2) or the high (1.3) sign-vector range of the coefficient along D_{i_j}. In both cases, the sign-vector of the coefficient is updated to contain only the single sign present in the selection range and the coefficient's sign-change is set to its leftmost boundary value (since there is no change of sign along D_{i_j} after the selection). The sign-vector and sign-change of the result coefficient remain untouched (i.e., identical to those of the input coefficient) if the selection range spans the original sign-change value.

3.2 Projection Operator (`project`)

Our projection operator has the general form $\texttt{project}_{X_{i_1}, \ldots, X_{i_k}}(W_T)$, where the k projection attributes $X_{i_1}, \ldots, X_{i_k}$ form a subset of the d attributes of T. Letting $\mathcal{D}' = \{D_{i_1}, \ldots, D_{i_k}\}$ denote the $k \le d$ projection dimensions, we are interested in *projecting out* the $d - k$ dimensions in $(\mathcal{D} - \mathcal{D}')$. We give a general method for projecting out a single dimension $D_j \in \mathcal{D} - \mathcal{D}'$. This method can then be applied repeatedly to project out all the dimensions in $(\mathcal{D} - \mathcal{D}')$, one dimension at a time.

Consider T's corresponding multi-dimensional array A_T. Projecting a dimension D_j out of A_T is equivalent to summing up the counts for all the array cells in each one-dimensional row of A_T along dimension D_j and then assigning this aggregated count to the single cell corresponding to that row in the remaining dimensions $(\mathcal{D} - \{D_j\})$. Consider any d-dimensional wavelet coefficient W in the `project` operator's input set W_T. Remember that W contributes a value of $W.v$ to every cell in its support hyper-rectangle $W.R$. Furthermore, the sign of this contribution for every one-dimensional row along dimension D_j is determined as either $W.S.sign[j].hi$ (if the cell lies above $W.S.schg[j]$) or $W.S.sign[j].lo$ (otherwise). Thus, we can work directly on the coefficient W to project out dimension D_j by simply adjusting the coefficient's magnitude with an appropriate multiplicative constant $W.v := W.v * p_j$, where p_j is defined as:

$$(W.R.bound[j].hi - W.S.schg[j] + 1) * W.S.sign[j].hi \; + $$
$$(W.S.schg[j] - W.R.bound[j].lo) * W.S.sign[j].lo. \quad (1)$$

A two-dimensional example of projecting out a dimension in the wavelet-coefficient domain is depicted in Figure 4(b). Multiplying $W.v$ with p_j (Equation (1)) effectively projects out dimension D_j from W by summing up W's contribution on each one-dimensional row along dimension D_j. Of course, besides adjusting $W.v$, we also need to discard dimension D_j from the hyper-rectangle and sign information for W, since it is now a $(d-1)$-dimensional coefficient (on dimensions $\mathcal{D} - \{D_j\}$). Note that if the coefficient's sign-change lies in the middle of its support range along dimension D_j (e.g., see Figure 2(a)), then its adjusted magnitude will be 0, which means that it can safely be discarded from the output set of the projection operation.

Repeating the above process for each wavelet coefficient $W \in W_T$ and each dimension $D_j \in \mathcal{D} - \mathcal{D}'$ gives the set of output wavelet coefficients W_S, where $S = \text{project}_{\mathcal{D}'}(T)$. Equivalently, given a coefficient W, we can simply set $W.v := W.v * \prod_{D_j \in \mathcal{D} - \mathcal{D}'} p_j$ (where p_j is as defined in Equation (1)) and discard dimensions $\mathcal{D} - \mathcal{D}'$ from W's representation.

3.3 Join Operator (join)

Our join operator has the general form $\text{join}_{pred}(W_{T_1}, W_{T_2})$, where T_1 and T_2 are (approximate) relations of arity d_1 and d_2, respectively, and *pred* is a conjunctive k-ary equi-join predicate of the form $(X_1^1 = X_1^2) \wedge \ldots \wedge (X_k^1 = X_k^2)$, where X_j^i (D_j^i) ($j = 1, \ldots, d_i$) denotes the jth attribute (resp., dimension) of T_i ($i = 1, 2$). (Without loss of generality, we assume that the join attributes are the first $k \leq \min\{d_1, d_2\}$ attributes of each joining relation.) Note that the result of the join operation W_S is a set of $(d_1 + d_2 - k)$-dimensional wavelet coefficients; that is, the join operation returns coefficients of (possibly) different arity than any of its inputs.

To see how our join processing algorithm works, consider the multi-dimensional arrays A_{T_1} and A_{T_2} corresponding to the join operator's input arguments. Let $(i_1^1, \ldots, i_{d_1}^1)$ and $(i_1^2, \ldots, i_{d_2}^2)$ denote the coordinates of two cells belonging to A_{T_1} and A_{T_2}, respectively. If the indexes of the two cells match on the join dimensions, i.e., $i_1^1 = i_1^2, \ldots, i_k^1 = i_k^2$, then the cell in the join result array A_S with coordinates $(i_1^1, \ldots, i_{d_1}^1, i_{k+1}^2, \ldots, i_{d_2}^2)$ is populated with the *product* of the count values contained in the two joined cells. Since the cell counts for A_{T_i} are derived by appropriately summing the contributions of the wavelet coefficients in W_{T_i} and, of course, a numeric product can always be distributed over summation, we can process the join operator entirely in the wavelet-coefficient domain by considering all pairs of coefficients from W_{T_1} and W_{T_2}. Briefly, for any two coefficients from W_{T_1} and W_{T_2} that overlap in the join dimensions and, therefore, contribute to joining data cells, we define an output coefficient with magnitude equal to the product of the two joining coefficients and a support hyper-rectangle with ranges that are (a) equal to the overlap of the two coefficients for the k (common) join dimensions, and (b) equal to the original coefficient ranges along any of the $d_1 + d_2 - 2k$ remaining dimensions. The sign information for an output coefficient along any of the k join dimensions is derived by appropriately multiplying the sign-vectors of the joining coefficients along that dimension, taking care to ensure that only signs along the overlapping portion are taken into account. (The sign information along non-join dimensions remains unchanged.) An example of this process in two dimensions ($d_1 = d_2 = 2$, $k = 1$) is depicted in Figure 5(a).

More formally, our approximate query execution strat-

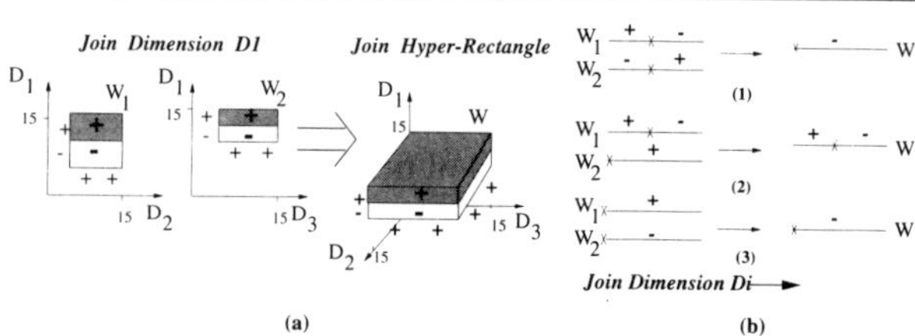

Figure 5. (a) Processing join operations in the wavelet-coefficient domain. (b) Computing sign information for join output coefficients.

egy for joins can be described as follows. (To simplify the notation, we ignore the "1/2" superscripts and denote the join dimensions as $D_1, \ldots, D_k$, and the remaining $d_1 + d_2 - 2k$ dimensions as $D_{k+1}, \ldots, D_{d_1+d_2-k}$.) For each pair of wavelet coefficients $W_1 \in W_{T_1}$ and $W_2 \in W_{T_2}$, if the coefficients' support hyper-rectangles overlap in the k join dimensions; that is, if *for every* dimension D_i, $i = 1 \ldots, k$, the following condition is satisfied:

$$W_1.R.bound.lo[i] \leq W_2.R.bound.lo[i] \leq W_1.R.bound.hi[i] \quad \text{or}$$
$$W_2.R.bound.lo[i] \leq W_1.R.bound.lo[i] \leq W_2.R.bound.hi[i],$$

then the corresponding output coefficient $W \in W_S$ is defined in the following steps.

1. For all join dimensions D_i, $i = 1, \ldots, k$ do

   1.1. Set $W.R.bound[i].lo := \max\{W_1.R.bound[i].lo, W_2.R.bound[i].lo\}$ and $W.R.bound[i].hi := \min\{W_1.R.bound[i].hi, W_2.R.bound[i].hi\}$.

   1.2. For $j = 1, 2$
        /* let s_j be a temporary sign-vector variable */

      1.2.1. If $W.R.bound[i].hi < W_j.S.schg[i]$ then set $s_j := [W_j.S.sign[i].lo, W_j.S.sign[i].lo]$.

      1.2.2. Else if $W.R.bound[i].lo \geq W_j.S.schg[i]$ then set $s_j := [W_j.S.sign[i].hi, W_j.S.sign[i].hi]$.

      1.2.3. Else set $s_j := W_j.S.sign[i]$.

   1.3. Set $W.S.sign[i] := [s_1.lo * s_2.lo, \ s_1.hi * s_2.hi]$.

   1.4. If $W.S.sign[i].lo == W.S.sign[i].hi$ then set $W.S.schg[i] := W.R.bound[i].lo$.

   1.5 Else set $W.S.schg[i] := \max_{j=1,2} \{W_j.S.schg[i] : W_j.S.schg[i] \in [W.R.bound[i].lo, W.R.bound[i].hi]\}$.

2. For each (non-join) dimension D_i, $i = k + 1, \ldots, d_1$ do: Set $W.R.bound[i] := W_1.R.bound[i]$, $W.S.sign[i] := W_1.S.sign[i]$, and $W.S.schg[i] := W_1.S.schg[i]$.

3. For each (non-join) dimension D_i, $i = d_1 + 1, \ldots, d_1 + d_2 - k$ do: Set $W.R.bound[i] := W_2.R.bound[i - d_1 + k]$, $W.S.sign[i] := W_2.S.sign[i - d_1 + k]$, and $W.S.schg[i] := W_2.S.schg[i - d_1 + k]$.

4. Set $W.v := W_1.v * W_2.v$ and $W_S := W_S \cup \{W\}$, where $S = \text{join}_{pred}(T_1, T_2)$.

Note that the bulk of our join processing algorithm concentrates on the correct settings for the output coefficient W along the k join dimensions (Step 1), since the problem becomes trivial for the $d_1 + d_2 - k$ remaining dimensions (Steps 2-3). Given a pair of joining input coefficients and a join dimension D_i, our algorithm starts out by setting the hyper-rectangle range of the output coefficient W along D_i equal to the overlap of the two input coefficients along D_i (Step 1.1). We then proceed to compute W's sign information along join dimension D_i (Steps 1.2-1.3) , which is slightly more involved. (Remember that T_1 and T_2 are (possibly) the results of earlier `select` and/or `join` operators, which means that their rectangle boundaries and signs along D_i can be arbitrary.) The basic idea is to determine, for each of the two input coefficients W_1 and W_2, where the boundaries of the join range lie with respect to the coefficient's sign-change value along dimension D_i. Given an input coefficient W_j ($j = 1, 2$), if the join range along D_i is completely contained in either the low (1.2.1) or the high (1.2.2) sign-vector range of W_j along D_i, then a temporary sign-vector s_j is appropriately set (with the same sign in both entries). Otherwise, i.e., if the join range spans W_j's sign-change (1.2.3), then s_j is simply set to W_j's sign-vector along D_i. Thus, s_j captures the sign of coefficient W_j in the joining range, and multiplying s_1 and s_2 (element-wise) yields the sign-vector for the output coefficient W along dimension D_i (Step 1.3). If the resulting sign vector for W does not contain a true sign change (i.e., the low and high components of $W.S.sign[i]$ are the same), then W's sign-change value along dimension D_i is set equal to the low boundary of $W.R$ along D_i, according to our convention (Step 1.4). Otherwise, the sign-change value for the output coefficient W along D_i is set equal to the maximum of the input coefficients' sign-change values that are contained in the join range (i.e., $W.R$'s boundaries) along D_i (Step 1.5).

In Figure 5(b), we illustrate three common scenarios for the computation of W's sign information along the join dimension D_i. The left-hand side of the figure shows three possibilities for the sign information of the input coefficients W_1 and W_2 along the join range of dimension D_i (with crosses denoting sign changes). The right-hand side depicts the resulting sign information for the output coefficient W along the same range. The important thing to observe with respect to our sign-information computation in Steps 1.3–1.5 is that the join range along any join dimension D_i can contain *at most one* true sign change. By this, we mean that if the sign for input coefficient W_j actually changes in the join range along D_i, then this sign-change value is unique; that is, the two input coefficients cannot have true sign changes at distinct points of the join range. This follows from the *complete containment* property of the base coefficient ranges along dimension D_i (Section 2.1). (Note that our algorithm for `select` retains the value of a true sign change for a base coefficient if it is contained in the selection range, and sets it equal to the value of the left boundary otherwise.) This range containment along D_i ensures that if W_1 and W_2 both contain a true sign change in the join range (i.e., their overlap) along D_i, then that will occur *at exactly the same value* for both (as illustrated in Figure 5(b.1)). Thus, in Step 1.3, W_1's and W_2's sign vectors in the join range can be multiplied to derive W's sign-

vector. If, on the other hand, one of W_1 and W_2 has a true sign change in the join range (as shown in Figure 5(b.2)), then the max operation of Step 1.5 will always set the sign change of W along D_i correctly to the true sign-change value (since the other sign change will either be at the left boundary or outside the join range). Finally, if neither W_1 nor W_2 have a true sign change in the join range, then the high and low components of W's sign vector will be identical and Step 1.4 will set W's sign-change value correctly.

Example 3.1: Consider the wavelet coefficients W_1 and W_2 in Figure 5. Let the boundaries and sign information of W_1 and W_2 along the join dimension D_1 be as follows: $W_1.R.bound[1] = [4, 15]$, $W_2.R.bound[1] = [8, 15]$, $W_1.S.sign[1] = [-, +]$, $W_2.S.sign[1] = [-, +]$, $W_1.S.schg[1] = 8$, and $W_2.S.schg[1] = 12$. In the following, we illustrate the computation of the hyper-rectangle and sign information for join dimension D_1 for the coefficient W that is output by our algorithm when W_1 and W_2 are "joined". Note that for the non-join dimensions D_2 and D_3, this information for W is identical to that of W_1 and W_2 (respectively), so we focus solely on the join dimension D_1.

First, in Step 1.1, $W.R.bound[1]$ is set to $[8, 15]$, i.e., the overlap range between W_1 and W_2 along D_1. In Step 1.2.2, since $W.R.bound[1].lo = 8$ is greater than or equal to $W_1.S.schg[1] = 8$, we set $s_1 = [+, +]$. In Step 1.2.3, since $W_2.S.schg[1] = 12$ lies in between $W.R$'s boundaries, we set $s_2 = [-, +]$. Thus, in Step 1.3, $W.S.sign[1]$ is set to the product of s_1 and s_2 which is $[-, +]$. Finally, in Step 1.5, $W.S.schg[1]$ is set to the maximum of the sign change values for W_1 and W_2 along dimension D_1, or $W.S.schg[1] := \max\{8, 12\} = 12$. ∎

4 Experimental Study

In this section, we present the results of an extensive empirical study that we have conducted using the novel query processing tools developed in this paper. The objective of this study is twofold: (1) to establish the effectiveness of our wavelet-based approach to approximate query processing, and (2) to demonstrate the benefits of our methodology compared to earlier approaches based on sampling and histograms. Our experiments consider a wide range of queries executed on both synthetic and real-life data sets. The major findings of our study can be summarized as follows.

• **Improved Answer Quality.** The quality/accuracy of the approximate answers obtained from our wavelet-based query processor is, in general, better than that obtained by either sampling or histograms for a wide range of data sets and `select`, `project`, `join`, and aggregate queries.

• **Low Synopsis Construction Costs.** Our I/O-efficient wavelet decomposition algorithm is extremely fast and scales linearly with the size of the data (i.e., the number of cells in the MOLAP array). In contrast, histogram construction costs increase explosively with the dimensionality of the data.

- **Fast Query Execution.** Query execution-time speedups of more than two orders of magnitude are made possible by our approximate query processing algorithms. Furthermore, our query execution times are competitive with those obtained by the histogram-based methods of Ioannidis and Poosala [6], and sometimes significantly faster (e.g., for `joins`).

Thus, our experimental results validate the thesis of this paper that wavelets are a viable, effective tool for general-purpose approximate query processing in DSS environments. All experiments reported in this section were performed on a Sun Ultra-2/200 machine with 512 MB of main memory, running Solaris 2.5.

Due to space constraints, the presentation in this paper focuses on the results of our experimental evaluation with real-life data sets, which are indicative of the overall set of experimental results. The details of our experimentation with synthetic data sets can be found in the full version of this paper [2].

4.1 Experimental Testbed and Methodology

Techniques. We consider three approximate query answering techniques in our study.

- *Sampling.* A random sample of the non-zero cells in the multi-dimensional array representation for each base relation is selected , and the counts for the cells are appropriately scaled. Thus, if the total count of all cells in the array is t and the sum of the counts of cells in the sample is s, then the count of every cell in the sample is multiplied by $\frac{t*v}{s}$. These scaled counts give the tuple counts for the corresponding approximate relation.

- *Histograms.* Each base relation is approximated by a multi-dimensional MaxDiff(V,A) histogram. Our choice of this histogram class is motivated by the recent work of Ioannidis and Poosala [6], where it is shown that MaxDiff(V,A) histograms result in higher-quality approximate query answers compared to other histogram classes. We process `selects`, `joins`, and aggregate operators on histograms as described in [6]. For instance, while `selects` are applied directly to the histogram for a relation, a `join` between two relations is done by first partially expanding their histograms to generate the tuple-value distribution of the each relation. An indexed nested-loop `join` is then performed on the resulting tuples.

- *Wavelets.* Wavelet-coefficient synopses are constructed on the base relations (using our decomposition algorithm) and query processing is performed entirely in the wavelet-coefficient domain, as described in Section 3. In our `join` implementation, overlapping pairs of coefficients are determined using a simple nested-loop join. Further, during the rendering step for non-aggregate queries, cells with negative counts are not included in the final answer to the query.

Since we assume d dimensions in the multi-dimensional array for a d-attribute relation, c random samples require $c * (d + 1)$ units of space; d units are needed to store the index of the cell and 1 unit is required to store the cell count. Storing c wavelet coefficients also requires the same amount of space, since we need d units to specify the position of the coefficient in the wavelet transform array and 1 unit to specify the value for the coefficient. (Note that the hyper-rectangle and sign information for a base coefficient can easily be derived from its location in the wavelet transform array.) On the other hand, each histogram bucket requires $3 * d + 1$ units of space; $2 * d$ units to specify the low and high boundaries for the bucket along each of the d dimensions, d units to specify the number of distinct values along each dimension, and 1 unit to specify the average frequency for the bucket [12]. Thus, for a given amount of space corresponding to c samples/wavelet coefficients, we store $b \approx \frac{c}{3}$ histogram buckets to ensure a fair comparison between the methods.

Queries. The workload used to evaluate the various approximation techniques consists of four main query types: (1) SELECT *Queries*: ranges are specified for (a subset of) the attributes in a relation and all tuples that satisfy the conjunctive range predicate are returned as part of the query result, (2) SELECT-SUM *Queries*: the total `sum` of a particular attribute's values is computed for all tuples that satisfy a conjunctive range predicate over (a subset of) the attributes, (3) SELECT-JOIN *Queries*: after performing selections on two input relations, an equi-join on a single join dimension is performed and the resulting tuples are output; and, (4) SELECT-JOIN-SUM *Queries*: the total `sum` of an attribute's values is computed over all the tuples resulting from a SELECT-JOIN.

For each of the above query types, we have conducted experiments with multiple different choices for (a) `select` ranges, and (b) `select`, `join`, and `sum` attributes. The results presented in the next section are indicative of the overall observed behavior of the schemes. Furthermore, the queries presented in this paper are fairly representative of typical queries over our data sets.

Answer-Quality Metrics. In our experiments with aggregate queries (e.g., SELECT-SUM queries), we use the *absolute relative error* in the aggregate value as a measure of the accuracy of the approximate query answer. When deciding on an error metric for non-aggregate results, we considered both the *Match And Compare* (MAC) error of Ioannidis and Poosala [6] and the network-flow-based *Earth Mover's Distance* (EMD) error of Rubner et al. [14]. We eventually chose a variant of the EMD error metric, since it offers a number of advantages over MAC error (e.g., computational efficiency, natural handling of non-integral counts) and, furthermore, we found that MAC error can show unstable behavior under certain circumstances. A more detailed discussion on MAC and EMD errors as well as the actual EMD error calculation formulas used in this paper can be found in the full paper [2].

4.2 Query Execution Times

In order to compare the query processing times for the various approaches, we measured the time (in seconds) for executing a `SELECT-JOIN-SUM` query over synopses of two-dimensional synthetic data sets using each approach. We do not consider the time for random sampling since the join results with samples did not generate any tuples, except for very large sample sizes. The running time of the join query on the original base relations (using an indexed nested-loop join) to produce an exact answer was 3.6 seconds. In practice, we expect that this time will be much higher since in our case, the entire relations fit in main memory. As is evident from Table 2, our wavelet-based technique is more than two orders of magnitude faster compared to running the queries on the entire base relations.

Technique	Number of Coefficients			
	500	1000	2000	5000
Wavelets	0.01	0.02	0.04	0.08
Histograms	9.8	1.48	0.43	1.26

Table 2. `SELECT-JOIN-SUM` Query Execution Times

Also, note that the performance of histograms is much worse than that of wavelets. The explanation lies in the fact that the `join` processing algorithm of Ioannidis and Poosala [6] requires joining histograms to be partially expanded to generate the tuple-value distribution for the corresponding approximate relations. The problem with this approach is that the intermediate relations can become fairly large and may even contain more tuples than the original relations. For example, with 500 coefficients, the expanded histogram contains almost 5 times as many tuples as the base relations. The sizes of the approximate relations decrease as the number of buckets increase, and thus execution times for histograms drop for larger numbers of buckets. In contrast, in our wavelet approach, join processing is carried out exclusively in the compressed domain, that is, joins are performed directly on the wavelet coefficients without ever materializing intermediate relations. The tuples in the final query answer are generated at the very end as part of the rendering step and this is the primary reason for the superior performance of the wavelet approach.

4.3 Experimental Results – Real-life Data Sets

We obtained our real-life data set from the US Census Bureau (`www.census.gov`). We employed the Current Population Survey (CPS) data source and within it the Person Data Files of the March Questionnaire Supplement. We used the 1992 data file for the select and select sum queries, and the 1992 and 1994 data files for the join and join sum queries. For both files, we projected the data on the following four attributes whose domain values were previously coded: *age* (with value domain 0 to 17), *educational attainment* (with value domain 0 to 46), *income* (with value domain 0 to 41) and *hours per week* (with value domain 0 to 13). Along with each tuple in the projection, we stored a count which is the number of times it appears in the file. We rounded the maximum domain values off to the nearest power of 2 resulting in domain sizes of 32, 64, 64 and 16 for the four dimensions, and a total of 2 million cells in the

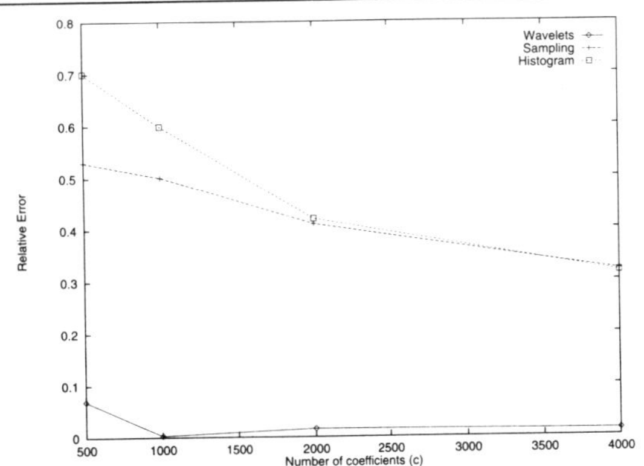

Figure 7. `SELECT-JOIN-SUM` queries on real-life data.

array. The 1992 and the 1994 collections had 16271 and 16024 cells with non-zero counts, respectively, resulting in a density of ≈ 0.001. However, even though the density is very low, we did observe large dense regions within the arrays when we visualized the data – these dense regions spanned the entire domains of the *age* and *income* dimensions.

For all the queries, we used the following select range: $5 \leq age < 10$ and $10 \leq income < 15$ that we found to be representative of several select ranges that we considered (the remaining two dimensions were left unspecified). The selectivity of the query was $1056/16271 = 6\%$. For `sum` queries, the `sum` operation was performed on the *age* dimension. For `join` queries, the `join` was performed on the *age* dimension between the 1992 and 1994 data files.

SELECT Queries. In Figures 6(a) and 6(b), we plot the EMD error and relative error for `SELECT` and `SELECT-SUM` queries, respectively, as the space allocated for the approximations is increased from 3% to 25% of the relation. From the graphs, it follows that wavelets result in the least value for the EMD error, while sampling has the highest EMD error. For `SELECT-SUM` queries, wavelets exhibit more than an order of magnitude improvement in relative error compared to both histograms and sampling (the relative error for wavelets is between 0.5% and 3%). Thus, the results for the select queries indicate that wavelets are effective at accurately capturing both the value as well as the frequency distribution of the underlying real-life data set.

It is interesting to note that the relative error for sampling is better than that of histograms. We conjecture that one of the reasons for this is the higher dimensionality of the real-life data sets, where histograms are less effective.

JOIN Queries. We only plot the results of the `SELECT-JOIN-SUM` queries in Figure 7, since the EMD error graphs for `SELECT-JOIN` queries were similar. Over the entire range of coefficients, wavelets outperform sampling and histograms, in most cases by more than an order of magnitude. With the real-life data set, even after the `join`, the relative aggregate error using wavelets is very low and ranges between 1% to 6%. The relative error of all

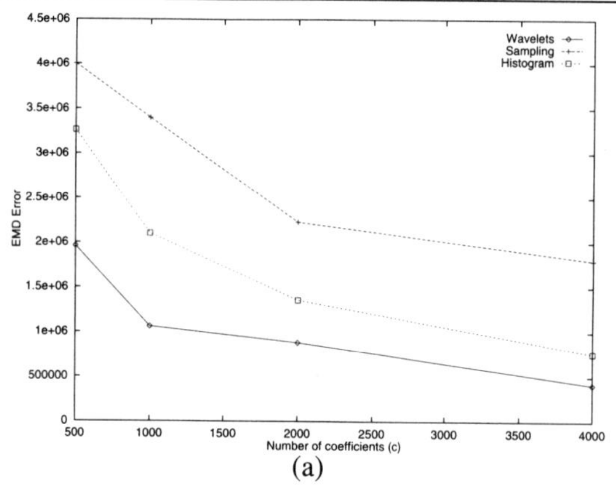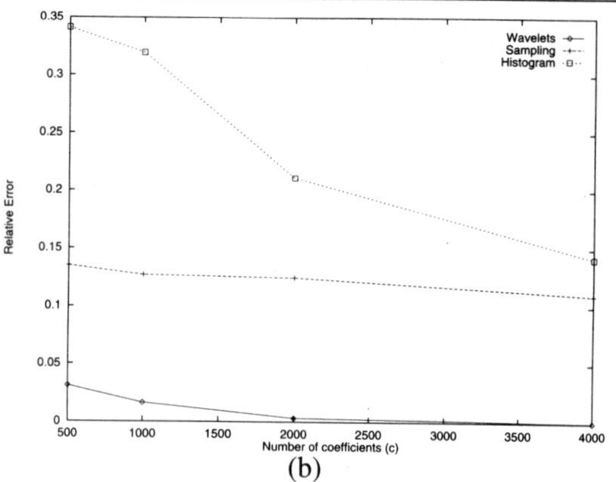

Figure 6. (a) SELECT and (b) SELECT-SUM query errors on real-life data.

the techniques improve as the amount of allocated space is increased. Compared to the synthetic data sets, where the result of a `join` over samples contained zero tuples in most cases, for the real-life data sets, sampling performs quite well. This is because the size of the domain of the *age* attribute on which the join is performed is only 18, which is quite small. Consequently, the result of the `join` query over the samples is no longer empty.

5 Conclusions

In this paper, we have proposed the use of multi-dimensional wavelets as an effective tool for general-purpose approximate query processing in modern, high-dimensional applications. Our approach is based on building wavelet-coefficient synopses of the data and using these synopses to provide approximate answers to queries. We have developed novel query processing algorithms that operate directly on the wavelet-coefficient synopses of relational data, thus allowing for very fast processing of arbitrarily complex queries *entirely* in the wavelet-coefficient domain. We have also proposed a novel I/O-efficient wavelet decomposition algorithm for building the synopses of relational data. Finally, we have conducted an extensive experimental study with synthetic as well as real-life data sets that verifies the effectiveness of our wavelet-based approach compared to both sampling and histograms.

Acknowledgments: We would like to thank Vishy Poosala for providing us with his MaxDiff histogram computation code. This work was partially supported by the Korea Science and Engineering Foundation (KOSEF) through the Advanced Information Technology Research Center (AITrc).

References

[1] S. Acharya, P. B. Gibbons, V. Poosala, and S. Ramaswamy. "Join Synopses for Approximate Query Answering". In *Proc. of the 1999 ACM SIGMOD Intl. Conf. on Management of Data*.

[2] K. Chakrabarti, M. Garofalakis, R. Rastogi, and K. Shim. "Approximate Query Processing Using Wavelets". February 2000. Bell Labs Tech. Memorandum.

[3] W. G. Cochran. *"Sampling Techniques"*. John Wiley & Sons, 1977. (Third Edition).

[4] P. M. Deshpande, K. Ramasamy, A. Shukla, and J. F. Naughton. "Caching Multidimensional Queries Using Chunks". In *Proc. of the 1998 ACM SIGMOD Intl. Conf. on Management of Data*.

[5] J. M. Hellerstein, P. J. Haas, and H. J. Wang. "Online Aggregation". In *Proc. of the 1997 ACM SIGMOD Intl. Conf. on Management of Data*.

[6] Y. E. Ioannidis and V. Poosala. "Histogram-Based Approximation of Set-Valued Query Answers". In *Proc. of the 25th Intl. Conf. on Very Large Data Bases*, 1999.

[7] B. Jawerth and W. Sweldens. "An Overview of Wavelet Based Multiresolution Analyses". *SIAM Review*, 36(3), 1994.

[8] R. J. Lipton, J. F. Naughton, and D. A. Schneider. "Practical Selectivity Estimation through Adaptive Sampling". In *Proc. of the 1990 ACM SIGMOD Intl. Conf. on Management of Data*.

[9] Y. Matias, J. S. Vitter, and M. Wang. "Wavelet-Based Histograms for Selectivity Estimation". In *Proc. of the 1998 ACM SIGMOD Intl. Conf. on Management of Data*.

[10] A. Natsev, R. Rastogi, and K. Shim. "WALRUS: A Similarity Retrieval Algorithm for Image Databases". In *Proc. of the 1999 ACM SIGMOD Intl. Conf. on Management of Data*.

[11] V. Poosala and V. Ganti. "Fast Approximate Answers to Aggregate Queries on a Data Cube". In *Proc. of the 1999 Intl. Conf. on Scientific and Statistical Database Management*.

[12] V. Poosala and Y. E. Ioannidis. "Selectivity Estimation Without the Attribute Value Independence Assumption". In *Proc. of the 23rd Intl. Conf. on Very Large Data Bases*, 1997.

[13] V. Poosala, Y. E. Ioannidis, P. J. Haas, and E. J. Shekita. "Improved Histograms for Selectivity Estimation of Range Predicates". In *Proc. of the 1996 ACM SIGMOD Intl. Conf. on Management of Data*.

[14] Y. Rubner, C. Tomasi, and L. Guibas. "A Metric for Distributions with Applications to Image Databases". In *Proc. of the 1998 IEEE Intl. Conf. on Computer Vision*.

[15] S. Sarawagi and M. Stonebraker. "Efficient Organization of Large Multidimensional Arrays". In *Proc. of the 10th Intl. Conf. on Data Engineering*, 1994.

[16] E. J. Stollnitz, T. D. DeRose, and D. H. Salesin. *"Wavelets for Computer Graphics – Theory and Applications"*. Morgan Kaufmann Publishers, Inc., San Francisco, CA, 1996.

[17] J. S. Vitter and M. Wang. "Approximate Computation of Multidimensional Aggregates of Sparse Data Using Wavelets". In *Proc. of the 1999 ACM SIGMOD Intl. Conf. on Management of Data*.

[18] J. S. Vitter, M. Wang, and B. Iyer. "Data Cube Approximation and Histograms via Wavelets". In *Proc. of the 7th Intl. Conf. on Information and Knowledge Management*, 1998.

Efficient Numerical Error Bounding for Replicated Network Services

Haifeng Yu
Computer Science Department
Duke University
Durham, NC 27708-0129, USA
yhf@cs.duke.edu

Amin Vahdat*
Computer Science Department
Duke University
Durham, NC 27708-0129, USA
vahdat@cs.duke.edu

Abstract

The goal of this work is to support replicated network services that accept updates to numerical records from multiple wide-area locations. Given the high overhead of maintaining strong consistency, many replicated services can tolerate divergence of their shared data, as long as the numerical error is bounded. Target distributed services include replicated stock quotes services, online auctions, distributed sensor systems, wide-area resource accounting and load balancing for replicated servers.

We present two algorithms to efficiently bound absolute error using only local information. Split-Weight AE separately bounds increases and decreases, while Compound-Weight AE bounds them together. The two algorithms can be combined to provide good performance and low space overhead. Our Inductive RE algorithm transforms relative error to absolute error solely based on local knowledge, taking advantage of the fact that the divergence was properly bounded prior to each invocation of the algorithm. We also discuss two optimizations that reduce the space and computational overheads in the algorithms.

* This work is supported in part by the National Science Foundation (EIA-99772879). Vahdat is also supported by an NSF CAREER award (CCR-9984328).

**Proceedings of the 26th VLDB Conference,
Cairo, Egypt, 2000.**

1 Introduction

Many network services store and update numerical records at multiple wide-area sites, which introduces issues of consistency among replicas. Given the high overhead of maintaining strong consistency, many of these services can tolerate divergence from the consistent data, as long as the divergence is bounded. Consider the following replicated services:

Stock Quotes Services Users retrieve stock quotes from replicated stock quotes servers. Each server may also accept updates to the current quotes. Users are concerned with the amount of "error" in the quotes they observe. For example, a user may prefer to see quotes within only ± 1 cent/share (absolute error) or $\pm 1\%$ (relative error) of the accurate quotes.

Online Auctions Each online auction server maintains the highest current bid for a number of items. A user accessing a replica desires guarantees regarding the maximum difference between the highest bid stored locally and the largest global bid.

Distributed Sensor Systems The sensor system takes the average temperature (pollution level, etc.) of an area. Each sensor periodically takes a sample at a fixed point in the area, and updates the average value according to the new sample value taken. User may retrieve the average value at any sensor location. Although users can tolerate approximate value, they may still want an upper bound on the "inaccuracy".

Wide-area Resource Accounting As we move toward global distributed computing, one goal is to account for aggregate consumed resources across multiple providers on a per-user basis[9, 24, 25]. Given the scale of this problem, maintaining accurate resource usage information will incur prohibitive overhead. Allowing bounded error in usage information is a promising approach to solving this problem.

Load Balancing for Replicated Servers For many replicated services, client programs do not directly choose which replica to contact. Instead, a front end forwards requests to the server judged to deliver the highest quality of service for that request. A front end uses its forwarding history to estimate the load of each server. When there are multiple front ends[19, 24], each sees a subset of the request stream, and uses this information to update its estimated load information. Once again, the load information is updated from multiple locations, and it is beneficial to bound the maximum error on load information observed by each front end.

One approach for guaranteeing accurate numerical information is to utilize standard techniques for maintaining strong consistency across wide-area networks. However, the communication costs and latency associated with such techniques often have prohibitively high overhead. We observe that many replicated services, including the ones described above, can tolerate some level of inconsistency in exchange for improved performance and availability, as long as they are provided guarantees regarding the maximum allowable error. In this context, the goal of this work is to develop techniques to efficiently bound numerical inaccuracy by reducing the amount of required wide-area communication.

Despite the importance of bounding numerical error for replicated network services, this topic has not been well studied in the literature. In the context of data caching, [3] proposes the concept of bounded numerical error. However, the authors do not generalize the concept to replicated databases. Efforts exploiting weak consistency [16, 17, 18, 21, 22, 23] concentrate on aspects other than numerical error, such as the number of conflicting transactions. Integrity constraint management algorithms[4, 5, 6, 7, 13, 14] for distributed databases are related to error bounding but are typically inefficient when applied to the special case of bounding numerical error. The demarcation protocol[4] allows easy maintenance of linear inequalities for distributed databases. Error bounding is closely related to enforcing linear inequalities but has three important properties not present in general linear inequalities: i) The copies of a data item are inter-related, ii) servers have approximate information about what writes other servers have seen, iii) during write propagation, writes on all data items are propagated. Because the demarcation protocol addresses a more general problem, it is unable to exploit these properties, resulting in significantly higher communication and space overhead.

In this paper, we present algorithms to efficiently bound numerical error for replicated network services. They are developed in the TACT[26, 27] project, which is a toolkit for building replicated Internet services. Two algorithms *Split-Weight AE* and *Compound-Weight AE* are proposed to bound absolute error. They bound error by limiting the "total weighted writes" accepted by one server but not seen by others. All decisions are based on local information and the algorithms do not incur overhead to acquire global knowledge. Split-Weight AE makes conservative decisions but is amenable to space optimizations, while Compound-Weight AE makes optimal decisions at the cost of higher space overhead. Our *Inductive RE* bounds relative error by transforming it into absolute error and then using Split-Weight AE or Compound-Weight AE to bound the absolute error. By taking advantage of the fact that the divergence was properly bounded prior to each invocation of the algorithm, Inductive RE is able to perform the transformation solely based on local knowledge. We also study the performance of our algorithms through both analysis and simulation.

In summary, this paper makes the following contributions:

- We describe the importance of bounding numerical error to support replicated network services.

- We propose practical algorithms to bound absolute error and relative error using only local information, without incurring the overhead of obtaining global knowledge.

- We explore two optimizations that reduce the space and computational overheads in the algorithms.

The next section describes our replicated database model. We present our error bounding algorithms in Section 3. Section 4 discusses two important optimizations to reduce space and computational overhead for our algorithms. In Section 5, we study the performance of the algorithms. Related work is described in Section 6. In Section 7, we present our conclusions.

2   System Model

The database maintaining the data shared by the network servers is replicated across n servers, $server_1$, $server_2$, ..., $server_n$. The replicated database is composed of multiple *data items*. Each data item has a numerical value for which the service desires to bound *error*. The allowed error for a data item is independent of other data items. We first focus on the case of a single data item and then discuss scalability issues for multiple data items in later sections.

Every server can accept reads (inquires) and writes (updates) from users. Reads return the current value of the data item on the server. A write W increases or decreases the value of a data item by the *weight* ($W.weight$) of the write. $W.weight$ is positive for increases and negative for decreases. While beyond the scope of this paper, our algorithms can be extended to transactions that consist of multiple read/write operations in a straightforward manner.

The server that accepts a write W from a client is the *originating server* of the write, and is denoted by $W.server$. A server updates other servers by propagating writes. The database image itself is never communicated to other servers. Upon accepting a write, a server does not have to update other servers immediately and divergence among replicas is allowed. Writes with the same originating server are always propagated according to the order they are accepted by that server. *Write propagation* can be done in the form of gossip messages[18], anti-entropy sessions[10, 20], broadcast or even unicast. To reduce communication overhead, some write propagation methods allow multiple writes to be merged into one write during propagation. Our algorithms are orthogonal to the write propagation method used by the database, although the freshness of views (defined later in this section) may be affected.

A server may propagate writes to other servers at any time, and such write propagation is called *voluntary write propagation* or *background write propagation*. The error bounding algorithms may require a server to propagate writes, which is called *compulsory write propagation*. Compulsory write propagation is necessary for the correctness of the algorithms, while voluntary write propagation only affects performance.

Each server maintains a write log, which is an ordered list of the writes the server accepts from clients or sees from other servers. Write log recycling can be done using various techniques[10, 18, 20]. We define the functions $twn(i, j)$ and $twp(i, j)$ as:

$$twn(i, j) = \sum \{W.weight \mid W.weight < 0 \ and \ W.server$$
$$= server_j \ and \ W \in write \ log \ of \ server_i\}$$
$$twp(i, j) = \sum \{W.weight \mid W.weight > 0 \ and \ W.server$$
$$= server_j \ and \ W \in write \ log \ of \ server_i\}$$

Intuitively, $twn(i, j)$ is the total negative weight of the writes $server_i$ sees originated from $server_j$, while $twp(i, j)$ is the total positive weight. Distinguishing negative weight and positive weight is necessary because we allow weight on different data items to be totaled in our optimizations. Thus, negative weight on one data item should not offset the positive weight on another data item (see Sections 4.1 and 4.2).

We use V_i to denote the value of the data item on $server_i$, and V_{init} to denote its initial (consistent) value. We use V_{final} to denote the value of the data item if all writes accepted by the system by time t has been applied. Note that as new writes are injected into the system, V_{final} evolves. The following equalities hold for V_i, V_{init} and V_{final}:

$$V_i = V_{init} + \sum_{k=1}^{n}(twn(i, k) + twp(i, k))$$

$$V_{final} = V_{init} + \sum_{k=1}^{n}(twn(k, k) + twp(k, k))$$

For $server_i$, a data item's *absolute error*(AE) is bounded within $[\alpha_i, \beta_i]$ ($\alpha_i \le 0$ and $\beta_i \ge 0$) if and only if at all times, the following inequality holds:

$$\alpha_i \le V_{final} - V_i \le \beta_i \qquad (1)$$

Similarly, we say the *relative error*(RE) is bounded within $[\gamma_i, \delta_i]$ ($\gamma_i \le 0$ and $0 \le \delta_i \le 1$) if and only if:

$$\gamma_i \le 1 - \frac{V_i}{V_{final}} \le \delta_i \qquad (2)$$

For relative error, we assume $V_i > 0$, $1 \le i \le n$.

Each server in the system has approximate knowledge of what writes other servers have seen. We say that each server has its *view* of $twn(i, j)$ and $twp(i, j)$, for $1 \le i \le n, 1 \le j \le n$. The views are either updated during write propagation or updated with explicit view update messages. The actual view update fashion and view freshness depend on the write propagation method. For example, if we use unicast, then during each write propagation, the two parties can inform each other of the writes they see. For anti-entropy sessions, more efficient view update mechanism can be used and details can be found in [10]. The correctness of our algorithms does not depend on the freshness of the views, but performance is affected. We denote $server_k$'s view of $twn(i, j)$ and $twp(i, j)$ as $twn_k(i, j)$ and $twp_k(i, j)$. Intuitively, $twn_k(i, j)$ is the total negative weight of the writes that $server_k$ believes that $server_i$ sees from $server_j$. During a *view advance*, $server_k$ updates $twn_k(i, j)$ and $twp_k(i, j)$. Views are *conservative* in that $server_k$ will never assume that $server_i$ sees a write that $server_i$ actually does not see.

3 Bounding Numerical Error Using Local Information

This section describes two different algorithms for bounding AE and one algorithm for bounding RE. The idea of the AE bounding algorithms is to bound the total weight of writes accepted by one server but not seen by other servers. The first algorithm, *Split-Weight AE*, bounds positive weight and negative weight separately. The second algorithm, *Compound-Weight AE*, keeps track of the possible range of values on other servers and allows negative weight and positive weight to offset. The basic idea of our relative error bounding algorithm, *Inductive RE*, is to transform the relative error into absolute error. The decisions made in the algorithms are all based only on local information, without incurring the overhead of obtaining global knowledge. All three algorithms require cooperation of other servers in the system to enforce local bounds. For each algorithm, we discuss how $server_j$ acts to bound the error for a single data item on $server_i$. Due to space limitations, correctness proofs for the three algorithms are omitted, but can be found in [28].

3.1 Split-Weight AE

In this algorithm, each $server_j$ maintains two local variables x and y for each $server_i, i \neq j$. They are used to record the total negative and positive weight of the writes accepted by $server_j$ but not seen by $server_i$. $server_j$ uses its view to compute x and y. However, since the view is conservative, x and y are also conservative.

Both variables x and y are initially set to zero and are updated in the following fashion:

1. When $server_j$ accepts a new write W, if $W.weight < 0$, $x = x + W.weight$, else $y = y + W.weight$.

2. When $server_j$ advances its view, if $twn_j(i,j)$ and $twp_j(i,j)$ are updated to $twn'_j(i,j)$ and $twp'_j(i,j)$ respectively, then $x = x - (twn'_j(i,j) - twn_j(i,j))$ and $y = y - (twp'_j(i,j) - twp_j(i,j))$. This subtracts weight of the newly propagated writes from x and y.

When $server_j$ receives a write W from a client, it checks the conditions:

$$x + W.weight \geq \alpha_i/(n-1), \; if \; W.weight < 0 \qquad (3)$$
$$y + W.weight \leq \beta_i/(n-1), \; if \; W.weight > 0 \qquad (4)$$

If the conditions do not hold, $server_j$ must advance its view for $server_i$ (potentially propagating writes to $server_i$) before the new write may return.

Split-Weight AE is pessimistic, in the sense that $server_j$ may propagate writes to $server_i$ that are unnecessary for bounding the error. For example, the algorithm does not consider the case where negative weight and positive weight may offset each other. In our simulation study, we will quantify how pessimistic Split-Weight AE is under different workloads. However, this simple design enables several optimizations not applicable to Compound-Weight AE (see Section 3.2). For example, in order to optimize the space overhead, several data items may share the same x and y variables (see section 4.1).

3.2 Compound-Weight AE

In Compound-Weight AE, each $server_j$ maintains three local variables z, min and max for each $server_i, i \neq j$. Intuitively, z is the total weight of the writes accepted by $server_j$ but not seen by $server_i$ in $server_j$'s view. However, since a view can be stale, $server_i$ may actually see more writes than $server_j$ is aware of. So we use min/max to record the minimum/maximum possible total weight of those writes that $server_i$ may see but are not in $server_j$'s view $twn_j(i,j)$ or $twp_j(i,j)$.

All variables z, min and max are initially set to zero and are updated in the following fashion:

1. When $server_j$ accepts a new write W, $z = z + W.weight$. If $z < min$, then $min = z$. If $z >$

(server$_1$: −2)	(server$_1$: 5)	(server$_1$: 1)	(server$_1$: −7)

Before view advance —— The view covers no writes:
z = −3; min = −3; max = 4

(server$_1$: −2)	(server$_1$: 5)	(server$_1$: 1)	(server$_1$: −7)

After view advance —— The view includes the first two writes:
z = −6: min = −6: max = 1

Figure 1: *View Advance in Compound-Weight AE*

max, then $max = z$. Note that since we assume writes from the same originating server are always propagated and applied according to the accept order, min and max are properly maintained in this way.

2. When $server_j$ advances its view for $server_i$, $server_j$ first resets all three variables. Next for each write W in $server_j$'s write log, if $W.server = server_j$ and in $server_j$'s new view, $server_i$ has not seen W, then z, min and max are updated as if W were newly accepted. In this way, z, min and max are re-established for this new view. Rescanning the write log whenever $server_j$ advances its view appears redundant, but is actually necessary for correctness.

Figure 1 illustrates how the three variables on $server_1$ are updated during a view advance. Each write is denoted by the pair ($W.server$: $W.weight$). For simplicity, only writes with $W.server = server_1$ are depicted in the figure. Before the view advance, $server_1$ is not aware of any writes seen by another server, say $server_2$. After the view advance, $server_1$ knows that $server_2$ has seen writes ($server_1$: −2) and ($server_1$: 5). Besides how to update z, min, and max, Figure 1 also explains why rescanning the write log is necessary. Suppose we want to ensure condition $z + W.weight - min \leq 10$ (see inequalities (5) and (6)). Before the view advance, min is −3. If we continue to use this min after the view advance, the algorithm may make incorrect decisions, since min should actually be −6, which makes the condition tighter.

When $server_j$ receives a write W from a client, it checks the following conditions:

$$z + W.weight - max \geq \alpha_i/(n-1) \qquad (5)$$
$$z + W.weight - min \leq \beta_i/(n-1) \qquad (6)$$

If the conditions do not hold, $server_j$ must advance its view for $server_i$ (potentially propagating writes to $server_i$) before the new write may return. According to these two conditions, it is possible that $server_j$ may need to propagate writes to $server_i$ when its view for $server_i$ advances. To avoid this, $server_j$ can be lazy in advancing its view for $server_i$. That is, the need for view advance is not checked until the above two conditions are violated. At that time, $server_j$ can deal with view advance and potentially propagate writes to $server_i$.

As opposed to Split-Weight AE, Compound-Weight AE is optimal given only local information. In other words,

$$\alpha_i/(n-1) \leq$$
$$(twn(j,j) + twp(j,j)) - (twn(i,j) + twp(i,j))$$
$$\leq \beta_i/(n-1)$$

holds if and only if conditions (5) and (6) hold. Please see [28] for the proof.

3.3 Inductive RE

Inductive RE transforms relative error to absolute error using only local information. Recall from definition (2) that relative error is bounded within $[\gamma_i, \delta_i]$ if an only if:

$$\gamma_i \leq 1 - \frac{V_i}{V_{final}} \leq \delta_i$$

This definition requires that V_{final} be a parameter of the transformation. However, knowing V_{final} accurately itself requires strong consistency. Since our goal is to avoid the overhead of strong consistency, the system must be able to bound relative error without knowing V_{final}.

One naive way to overcome this is to transform definition (2) to:

$$\gamma_i/(1-\gamma_i) \times V_i \leq V_{final} - V_i \leq \delta_i/(1-\delta_i) \times V_i$$

By setting:

$$\alpha_i = \gamma_i/(1-\gamma_i) \times V_i$$
$$\beta_i = \delta_i/(1-\delta_i) \times V_i$$

we can apply either of the previous AE algorithms to enforce the inequality. However, since V_i changes over time, $server_i$ must constantly update α_i and β_i and inform other servers in the system of this change. This requires that a consensus algorithm be run among all servers whenever V_i decreases. As a result, the performance could degrade significantly.

Inductive RE is based on the observation that for any j, V_j was properly bounded before the invocation of the algorithm and is an approximation of V_{final}. So $server_j$ may use V_j as an approximate norm to bound γ_i and δ_i. Transforming the definition of RE, we have the following two inequalities:

$$V_{final} - V_i \geq \gamma_i \times V_{final} \tag{7}$$
$$V_{final} - V_i \leq \delta_i \times V_{final} \tag{8}$$

On the other hand, on $server_j$, we know that $\gamma_j \leq 1 - V_j/V_{final}$, so $V_{final} \geq V_j/(1-\gamma_j)$. Figure 2 illustrates the relationship between V_j and V_{final}.

Thus the following two inequalities are sufficient conditions for inequality (7) and (8):

$$V_{final} - V_i \geq \gamma_i \times V_j/(1-\gamma_j)$$
$$V_{final} - V_i \leq \delta_i \times V_j/(1-\gamma_j)$$

Figure 2: *How to Use V_j as an Approximate Norm to Bound RE*

The right-hand side expressions can be evaluated using only local information. So in order to bound relative error for $server_i$, $server_j$ only needs to apply Split-Weight AE or Compound-Weight AE and use:

$$\alpha_i = \gamma_i \times V_j/(1-\gamma_j)$$
$$\beta_i = \delta_i \times V_j/(1-\gamma_j)$$

Note that since the computed α_i and β_i change with V_j, whenever V_j changes, the limits should be recomputed and re-checked. However, no consensus algorithms are necessary because V_j is known locally.

4 Optimizing for Scalability

With the algorithms described in the last section, numerical error can be efficiently bounded for small scale replicated network services. However, since we are interested in extensive replication, in this section we discuss two optimizations that reduce the space and computational overheads in the algorithms.

4.1 Reducing Space Overhead

We have discussed how to bound AE and RE for a single data item. The algorithms incur a per data item space overhead of $O(n)$, where n is the number of servers. If we simply use multiple instances of the algorithms, the size of the data structure maintained by the algorithms can be n times the size of the database itself in the worst case. If a database maintains tens of thousands of data items, this high space overhead can be prohibitive.

To reduce space overhead, we assume that for all data items, $server_i$ has the same α_i and β_i (or γ_i and δ_i), otherwise the space needed simply for storing α_i and β_i will grow linearly with the number of data items. The application may still use several different α_is(β_is) for different data items by using multiple instances of our algorithm. We reduce space overhead by exploiting the fact that during write propagation, writes to all data items on a server are propagated to another server. So we only need to maintain information for those data items accessed between two write propagations. We also take advantage of the locality among the writes accepted by a server. For "hot" data items, we maintain accurate information needed by the algorithms. For data items seldom accessed, we allow them to share the same data structure and maintain conservative information.

We use a hashtable to store the variables needed by our algorithms. Each server maintains one hashtable for every other server in the system. The hashtables are used to maintain the information on "hot" data items. Whenever $server_j$ receives a write on data item D, it uses D as a key to create or update variables in the hashtables. The total space used by a hashtable is bounded. In the case where a hashtable becomes full, a shared entry is created for all other data items without a hashtable entry. On each write propagation, the hashtable and the shared entry corresponding to the receiving server are cleared and the space is freed.

Care must be taken when maintaining the shared entry. For Split-Weight AE, the shared entry simply consists of two variables x and y, which are updated in the same way as normal hashtable entries. For Compound-Weight AE, it is difficult to maintain a shared entry for multiple data items, so we use Split-Weight AE for the shared entry and Compound-Weight AE for hashtable entries. In Inductive RE, the shared entry must also record the smallest V_j of the data items using that entry, so that the computed α_i and β_i values are tight. Using a shared entry may result in conservative behavior, since weight accumulated on multiple items is coalesced to a single item. However, a server can improve performance at the cost of larger hashtables and higher space overhead.

4.2 Reducing Computational Overhead

While less of a concern than memory overhead, in this section we describe techniques for reducing our algorithms' computational overhead. In our algorithms, a server needs to update one hashtable for every other server in the system when accepting a write. These updates are on the critical path for accepting writes. Thus, if there are a large number of servers, the overhead of updating n hashtables on each write can be high. In this section, we discuss how to reduce this computational overhead.

The first possible optimization is to combine the hashtables for multiple servers. We can group together servers with similar bounds, and enforce the tightest bounds for a group of servers. The servers in the group can then share a single hashtable. A server can trade space for performance by using smaller groups. Note that this optimization also reduces space overhead.

Another optimization is to use a cache, so that in most cases, we only need to update the cache rather than n hashtables. We only discuss how to use a cache for bounding error with Split-Weight AE, because the data structures in Compound-Weight AE make it difficult to utilize a cache.

Table 1 describes the information maintained by each cache entry. To create a cache entry for data item D, suppose x_i and y_i are the values in $server_i$'s hashtable entry for D, we scan all hashtables, and set:

$item$	database item
x	total negative weight of newly accepted writes since entry creation
y	total positive weight of newly accepted writes since entry creation
$limitx$	the limit for x
$limity$	the limit for y
$serverx$	the server whose limit we use for this entry's $limitx$
$servery$	the server whose limit we use for this entry's $limity$

Table 1: *Information Maintained by a Cache Entry for Reducing Computational Overhead in Split-Weight AE*

$$limitx = max\{\alpha_i/(n-1) - x_i \mid 1 \leq i \leq n \; i \neq j\}$$
$$limity = min\{\beta_i/(n-1) - y_i \mid 1 \leq i \leq n \; i \neq j\}$$

The variables x and y in the cache entry are set to zero. On each cache hit, we check $x + W.weight \geq limitx$ (if $W.weight < 0$) or $y + W.weight \leq limity$ (if $W.weight > 0$). As long as the condition holds, we only need to update x or y in the cache entry, rather than updating all hashtables. If the condition does not hold, we writeback the cache entry to the hashtables, and potentially perform compulsory write propagation. After that, a new cache entry can be established for the data item with new $limitx$ and $limity$ values. The cache must be flushed whenever $server_i$, $1 \leq i \leq n$ changes α_i or β_i. We consider this an infrequent operation, so the performance penalty will not be excessive.

A further optimization is to use a linked list for each cache entry. The first node in the list has the tightest $limitx$ and $limity$, the second node has the second tightest values and so on. When x or y reaches $limitx$ or $limity$, we remove the first node and update the hashtable corresponding to $serverx$ and $servery$. In this way, we can avoid scanning all hashtables to find the next tightest limits. However, after updating the hashtables for $serverx$ and $servery$, we still need to go through the linked list to see whether $serverx$ or $servery$ now has tighter limits than nodes in the list.

A cache "snapshot" must be made on write propagation. This snapshot is used in the future to create a "diff" when a cache entry is written back. The x and y in the snapshot are subtracted from the cache entry being written back, before the cache entry is added to the hashtable entry.

Applying the cache idea to bounding relative error is subtle. Since the computed α_i and β_i changes with V_j, in order to choose safe $limitx$ and $limity$ for all servers, we must decouple the limits from V_j. Recall the conditions we want to enforce are:

$$x_i \geq \gamma_i/(1-\gamma_j) \times V_j = s_i \times V_j \qquad (9)$$
$$y_i \leq \delta_i/(1-\gamma_j) \times V_j = t_i \times V_j \qquad (10)$$

Notation	Meaning	Case 1	Case 2
n	number of servers	10	20
t_{apply}	CPU time to apply a write to database	3ms	3ms
t_{check}	time to check limits and update n hashtables in error bounding algorithms	2ms	4ms
t_{delay}	round-trip message delay in write propagation	200ms	500ms
t_{setup}	CPU time on one replica for TCP connection setup	10ms	10ms
t_{send}	CPU time to send *one* write	1ms	1ms
t_{recv}	CPU time to receive *one* write	1ms	1ms
$E(L_i)$	expectation of L_i	N/A	N/A
$E(Q_i)$	expectation of Q_i	100ms	100ms

Table 2: *Symbols and Default Values Used in Performance Analysis*

Let the value of x_i, y_i and V_j be x_i^c, y_i^c and V_j^c, respectively, at the time when the cache entry is established. We have $V_j = (V_j^c - x_i^c - y_i^c) + x_i + y_i$, $1 \leq i \leq n$ and $i \neq j$. By using this equation to substitute V_j in (9) and (10), we have:

$$x_i \geq s_i \times ((V_j^c - x_i^c - y_i^c) + x_i + y_i)$$
$$y_i \leq t_i \times ((V_j^c - x_i^c - y_i^c) + x_i + y_i)$$

Next, by solving these two inequalities and choosing a rectangular solution area, we have sufficient conditions for (9) and (10) as:

$$x_i \geq s_i/(1 - s_i) \times (V_j^c - x_i^c - y_i^c)$$
$$y_i \leq t_i/((1 - t_i)(1 - s_i)) \times (V_j^c - x_i^c - y_i^c)$$

Using these two conditions, we can now set:

$$limitx = max\{s_i/(1 - s_i) \times (V_j^c - x_i^c - y_i^c) - x_i^c \mid$$
$$1 \leq i \leq n \text{ and } i \neq j\}$$
$$limity = min\{t_i/((1 - t_i)(1 - s_i)) \times (V_j^c - x_i^c - y_i^c)$$
$$-y_i^c \mid 1 \leq i \leq n \text{ and } i \neq j\}$$

V_j^c only changes when $server_j$ accepts writes from other servers. In that case, the cache should be flushed.

5 Performance Study

In this section, we first build an analytical model to study the performance of the numerical error bounding algorithms. Next through simulation, we gain further understanding on the applicability of the model. We have also implemented a TACT prototype using the algorithms and studied the performance of three applications (Airline Reservation, Bulletin Board and Load Distribution) running across the wide-area network on top of the prototype. Detailed performance results for these applications are available in [27].

5.1 Performance Analysis

We compare our approach to a conventional one-phase protocol in terms of throughput and latency. The one-phase protocol is a variant of a read one, write all quorum system. It achieves strong consistency for most of our target applications by propagating a new write to all other servers before the write may return. For other applications, writes are more complicated than simply increasing or decreasing a numerical value, for example, a write may check the value and decide whether to continue updating or not. In that case, a stronger two-phase update protocol is needed to achieve strong consistency. However, comparing our algorithms against the better performing one-phase protocol understates the potential performance benefits of our algorithms.

Our algorithms and the one-phase protocol treat reads in the same way, so we are mainly interested in the performance for writes and we only consider write workloads. We assume the database consists of a single data item. To simplify discussion, all servers are assumed to have the same error bounds, i.e. α_i and β_i. We also assume that the workload is evenly distributed among the n servers. We do not consider background write propagation or indirect view advance, both of which will improve the performance of our algorithms.

We first describe the terms and notations used in our analysis, as summarized in Table 2. We consider two sets of parameters. Case 1 corresponds to a replicated network service distributed across the United States, while Case 2 models an international replicated network service. An *epoch on $server_i$ for $server_j$* is the period on $server_i$ between two write propagations to $server_j$. We define the *length* of an epoch as the number of writes accepted by a server directly from clients during that epoch.

The performance of the algorithms is dependent on the characteristics of the workload, such as the weight of each write and the inter-arrival time between writes. To make our analysis generally applicable, we abstract the workload characteristics with two high-level random variables L_i and Q_i, where L_i is the length of an epoch on $server_i$ and Q_i is the queuing delay for a write accepted by $server_i$ before the write gets processed by $server_i$. Our goal is to cover the workload spectrum by choosing different distributions for L_i and Q_i. To gain understanding of what $E(L_i)$ and $E(Q_i)$ we can expect in real world cases, we perform simulations for several workloads (see Section 5.2).

We now present the analytical throughput of our algorithms. A detailed analysis is available in [28]. If

129

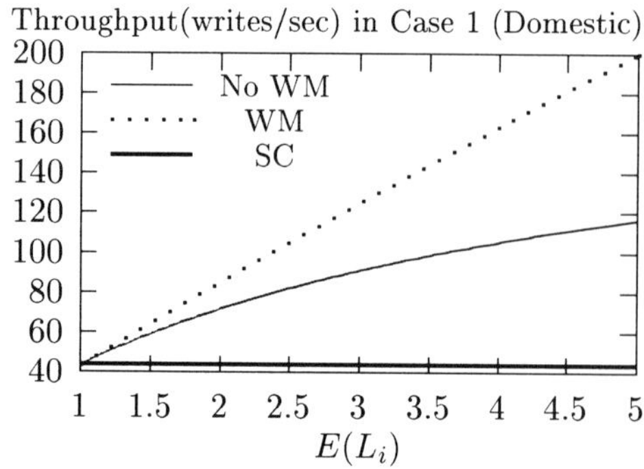

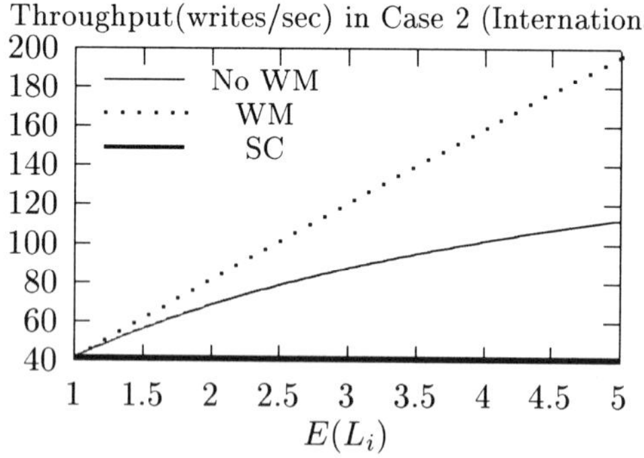

Figure 3: *Throughput of Error Bounding Algorithms vs. Strong Consistency Protocol*

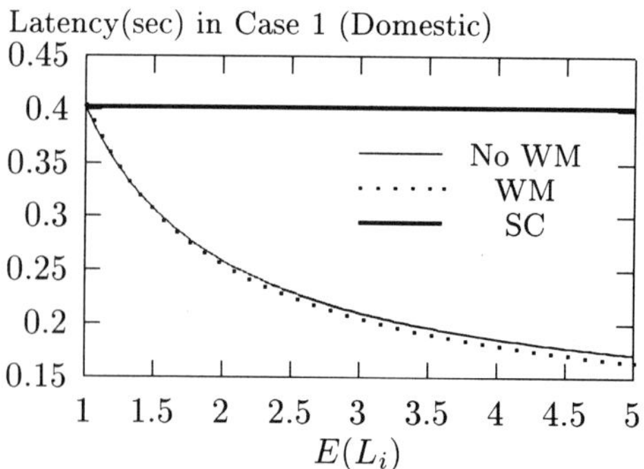

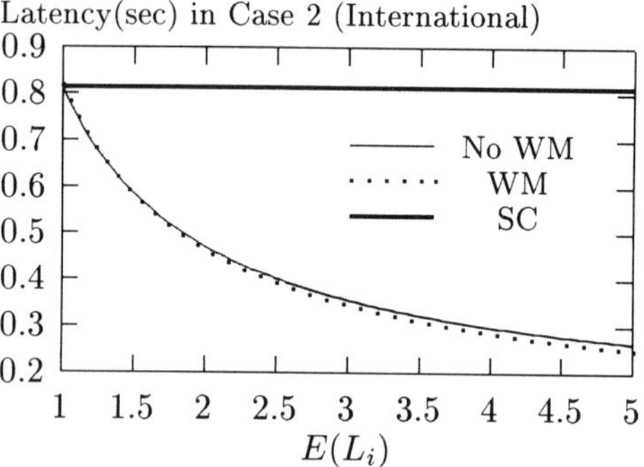

Figure 4: *Latency of Error Bounding Algorithms vs. Strong Consistency Protocol*

writes cannot be merged, we have:

$$Throughput = n/(t_{check} + nt_{apply} + 2(n-1)t_{setup}/E(L_i)$$
$$+ (n-1)t_{send} + (n-1)t_{recv})$$

As mentioned in Section 2, in many cases, it is possible to merge multiple writes into one write in order to save communication overhead. If writes can be merged and in the extreme case where all writes accepted by a server during an epoch can be merged together:

$$Throughput = n \times E(L_i)/(E(L_i)(t_{check} + t_{apply}) +$$
$$2(n-1)t_{setup} + (n-1)(t_{send} + t_{recv} + t_{apply}))$$

The throughput of the conventional one-phase protocol is:

$$Throughput = n/(nt_{apply} + 2(n-1)t_{setup} +$$
$$(n-1)t_{send} + (n-1)t_{recv})$$

Figure 3 shows the throughput of our algorithms versus the one-phase protocol as a function of $E(L_i)$. The key "No WM" stands for error bounding algorithms without write merging, "WM" stands for error bounding algorithms with write merging, and "SC" stands for the strong consistency achieved by the one-phase protocol. We plot the graphs for $E(L_i) \in [1, 5]$. By definition, $E(L_i)$ is greater than 1. Since our algorithms perform better as $E(L_i)$ increases, the graphs are conservative by not considering larger $E(L_i)$, which we expect to be common for many applications. As expected, the error bounding algorithms have considerably higher throughput than a strong

consistency protocol by reducing wide-area communication. As $E(L_i)$ increases, the throughput of the error bounding algorithms also increases, and in the write merging case, the increase is almost linear. The performance improvement, however, does not come without cost. Larger $E(L_i)$ can sometimes only be gained by tolerating larger numerical error (see Section 5.2). Thus, the gains available to a network service depends upon the magnitude of the numerical error it is willing to tolerate.

Having compared the throughput, we now discuss the latency of the system. For numerical error bounding algorithms, the latency with no write merging is:

$$Latency = E(Q_i) + t_{check} + t_{apply} + (n-1)t_{send} +$$
$$((n-1)t_{setup} + t_{delay})/E(L_i)$$

Again, if we consider the possibility of writes merging and in the extreme case where all writes can be merged, the latency will be:

$$Latency = E(Q_i) + t_{check} + t_{apply} + ((n-1)t_{setup} +$$
$$(n-1)t_{send} + t_{delay})/E(L_i)$$

The average latency in the one-phase protocol is:

$$Latency = E(Q_i) + (n-1)t_{setup} + (n-1)t_{send} +$$
$$t_{delay} + t_{apply}$$

Figure 4 shows the latency of the error bounding algorithms versus the one-phase protocol as a function of $E(L_i)$. The keys have the same meaning as in Figure 3. We can see that the error bounding algorithms have

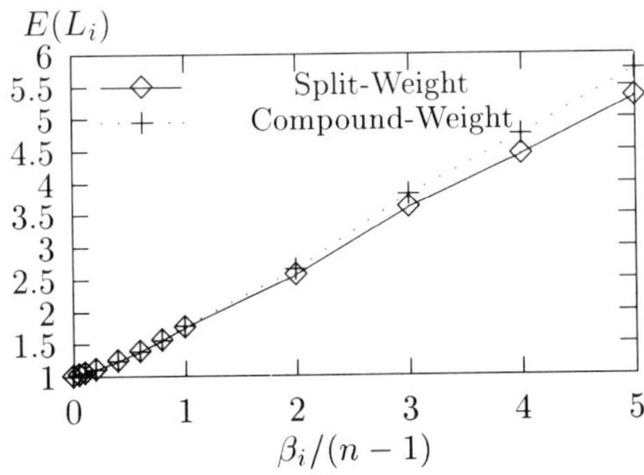

Figure 5: *Split-Weight AE vs. Compound-Weight AE (Weight ~ U(-1, 3))*

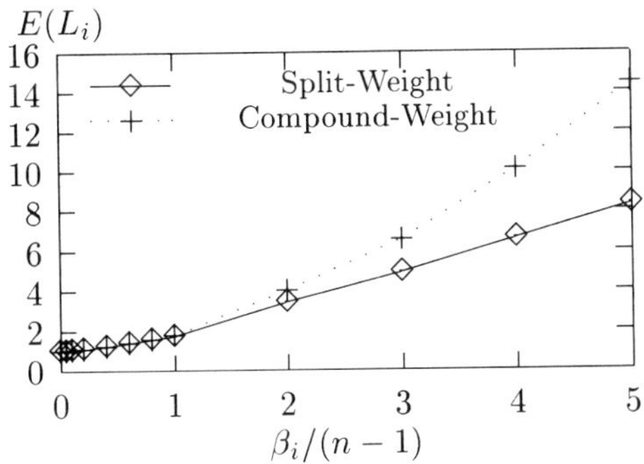

Figure 6: *Split-Weight AE vs. Compound-Weight AE (Weight ~ U(-2, 2))*

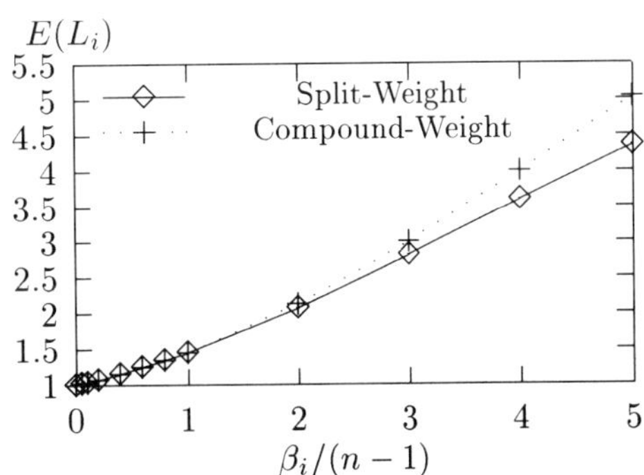

Figure 7: *Split-Weight AE vs. Compound-Weight AE (Weight ~ N(1, 2))*

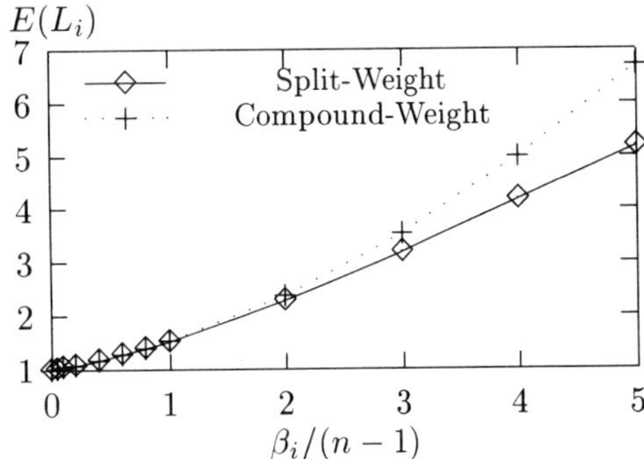

Figure 8: *Split-Weight AE vs. Compound-Weight AE (Weight ~ N(0, 2))*

smaller latency than the strong consistency protocol. Furthermore, the latency in our algorithms decreases rapidly as $E(L_i)$ increases. However, as with throughput, the performance improvement can come at the cost of data accuracy.

5.2 Simulation Results

In this section, we use simulation to determine a range of typical values for $E(L_i)$ based on the distribution of the weight of individual writes. Although numerous factors affect $E(Q_i)$, it is determined by $E(L_i)$ to a large extent. Thus we believe studying $E(L_i)$ can give us insight into $E(Q_i)$ as well. The simulation results on $E(L_i)$ also quantify the performance difference between Split-Weight AE and Compound-Weight AE. As mentioned earlier, the latter is optimal while the former is better suited for space and computational optimizations. The resulting different $E(L_i)$ and $E(Q_i)$ values for the two algorithms directly affect system performance.

$E(L_i)$ is uniquely determined by the distribution of the weight of writes. We consider two different distributions for the weight: uniform distribution and normal distribution. The weight in the first workload is uniformly distributed within $[-1, 3]$, while those in the second are uniformly distributed within $[-2, 2]$. We denote the distributions by $U(-1, 3)$ and $U(-2, 2)$, re-

spectively. For normal distribution, we consider weight conforming to $N(1, 2)$ and $N(0, 2)$. Each workload consists of one million writes and we measure the average epoch length as a function of $\beta_i/(n-1)$. The bound α_i is set to $-\beta_i$ in our experiments. Figures 5, 6, 7 and 8 summarize the simulation results.

The figures show that in most cases, $E(L_i)$ increases roughly linearly with $\beta_i/(n-1)$. For Compound-Weight AE in Figures 6 and 8, $E(L_i)$ increases faster than linearly. As we expect, $E(L_i)$ in Compound-Weight AE is always bigger than that in Split-Weight AE. The conservativeness of Split-Weight AE is quantified here by the difference between the two curves in each figure. The difference is not so obvious when the distribution is biased toward positive weight and becomes clearer when the distribution is symmetric. Note that we do not consider space overhead in the simulations and that the better performance of Split-Weight AE comes at the cost of increased space overhead.

6 Related Work

Alonso et. al.[3] propose four coherency conditions in the context of "quasi-copy" caching. One of the four conditions is "arithmetic condition," which specifies the allowed numerical error. Since in quasi-copy caching only the master database may accept updates, maintaining arithmetic condition is a trivial problem. Relative to this effort, we define numerical error for replicated databases and discuss algorithms for bounding the error when updates are accepted by multiple replicas.

Bounding numerical error in a replicated database is closely related to maintaining integrity constraints in distributed databases. In [7], strong theoretical conclusions are made on how to decompose an arbitrary global constraint into a number of local constraints and communication constraints. The conclusions form the basis of the demarcation protocol[4], which applies a number of optimizations to the special case of linear arithmetic inequalities. Bounding numerical error is intrinsically enforcing an inequality. However, we exploit three special properties in this problem, which makes our algorithms practical and efficient for numerical error bounding. First, in the error bounding problem, the copies of a data item are inter-related. For example, if we want to bound the AE on $server_1$, it is not necessary to limit V_1. However, the demarcation protocol will have to put a limit on every variable present in the inequality. Second, in our algorithms, view advance is automatically incorporated and there is no need to explicitly re-adjust limits. On the other hand, the demarcation protocol does not exploit the fact that servers may have knowledge of what writes other servers have seen and limit re-adjustments are always done explicitly. Also, because the demarcation protocol cannot exploit the fact that copies are brought to consistency through write propagation, it is difficult to design efficient limit re-adjustment policies for it. The third property we utilize is that during a write propagation, all writes are propagated and all limits can be reset. This allows us to optimize the space overhead using hashtables. The demarcation protocol incurs $O(n)$ space overhead for each data item, where n is the total number of servers, limiting scalability. A direct performance comparison between our algorithms and the demarcation protocol would be difficult. Using the general limit re-negotiation policies discussed in [4] would result in poor performance and would be unfair to the demarcation protocol, while designing special policies for bounding numerical error is essentially as hard as designing numerical error bounding algorithms from scratch.

Gupta et.al. [13] describe an algorithm to verify a global constraint using only local information. In the case of a tuple insertion, the algorithm uses other "covering tuples" already in the tuple space to prove that the constraint is not affected by the new tuple. The technique cannot be applied to bounding numerical error, since no "covering tuple" can be obtained when users update a numerical data item.

Maintenance of materialized views[1, 8, 12] is closely related to our work. In fact, if the views are approximations of numerical base data, view maintenance can

be an application of our error bounding algorithms. Various view maintenance algorithms have been proposed, see [12] for a survey on view maintenance. Relative to our work, view maintenance algorithms usually assume that only the base database can accept updates. In this aspect, our algorithms are more general than view maintenance algorithms.

In Section 4.2, we discussed how to efficiently check n conditions given a new write. This is a special case of how to efficiently check local integrity constraints given an update to the database. The general problem has been well studied[5, 6, 14]. However, most of the studies[6, 14] concentrate on how to filter those local constraints that are unaffected by the update. Others[5] only consider a particular class of local constraints and updates. Thus, none of the techniques is applicable to our case. The n conditions we intend to check are all linear conditions, making related techniques[2, 15, 11] developed in computation geometry also applicable. However, in our case, the linear conditions change frequently, making the cost of reconstructing the data structures [2, 11] outweigh the benefits.

7 Conclusion

In this paper, we argue for efficiently bounding numerical error to support replicated network services. Two algorithms, Split-Weight AE and Compound-Weight AE, are proposed to bound absolute error. They can be combined to achieve good performance and low space overhead. Inductive RE bounds relative error by transforming it into absolute error and applying Split-Weight/Compound-Weight AE. Exploiting the fact that V_j is an approximation of V_{final}, we are able to perform the transformation based on local information. We propose two optimizations to improve the scalability of the error bounding algorithms. Through performance analysis and simulation, we show that a replicated network service using our error bounding algorithms has superior performance in terms of latency and throughput compared to a network service using a traditional strong consistency protocol.

8 Acknowledgments

We thank Misha Rabinovich and the anonymous referees for their careful reviews of this paper.

References

[1] Brad Adelberg, Ben Kao, and Hector Garcia-Molina. Database Support for Efficient Maintaining Derived Data. In *International Conference on Extending Database Technology*, 1996.

[2] Pankaj K. Agarwal, Lars Arge, Jeff Erickson Paolo G. Fanciosa, and Jeffrey Scott Vitter. Efficient Searching with Linear Constraints. In *Proceedings of the 17th*

ACM Symposium on Principles of Database Systems, 1998.

[3] Rafael Alonso, Daniel Barbara, and Hector Garcia-Molina. Data Caching Issues in an Information Retrieval System. *ACM Transactions on Database Systems*, September 1990.

[4] Daniel Barbara and Hector Garcia-Molina. The Demarcation Protocol: A Technique for Maintaining Linear Arithmetic Constraints in Distributed Database Systems. In *Proceedings of the International Conference on Extending Database Technology*, 1992.

[5] Philip Bernstein, Barbara Blaustein, and Edmund Clarke. Fast Maintenance of Semantic Integrity Assertions Using Redundant Aggregate Data. In *Proceedings of the 6th Conference on Very Large Data Bases*, 1980.

[6] Peter O. Buneman and Eric K. Clemons. Efficiently Monitoring Relational Databases. *ACM Transactions on Database Systems*, September 1979.

[7] O.S.F. Carvalho and G. Roucairol. On the Distribution of an Assertion. In *Proceedings of the ACM Symposium on Principles of Distributed Computing*, 1982.

[8] Latha S. Colby, Akira Kawaguchi, Daniel F. Lieuwen, and Inderpal Singh Mumick. Supporting Multiple View Maintenance Policies. In *Proceedings of the ACM SIGMOD Conference on Management of Data*, 1997.

[9] Ian Foster and Carl Kesselman. Globus: A Metacomputing Infrastructure Toolkit. In *International Journal of Supercomputer Applications*, volume 11(2), pages 115–128, 1997.

[10] Richard Golding. *Weak-Consistency Group Communication and Membership*. PhD thesis, University of California, Santa Cruz, December 1992.

[11] Jonathan Goldstein, Raghu Ramakrishnan, Uri Shaft, and Jie-Bing Yu. Processing Queries by Linear Constraints. In *Proceedings of the Sixteenth ACM Symposium on Principles of Distributed Computing*, 1997.

[12] Ashish Gupta and Inderpal Singh Mumick. Maintenance of Materialized Views: Problems, Techniques, and Applications. *IEEE Data Engineering Bulletin*, June 1995.

[13] Ashish Gupta and Jennifer Widom. Local Verification of Global Constraints in Distributed Databases. In *Proceedings of the ACM SIGMOD Conference on Management of Data*, 1993.

[14] Robert Kowalshi, Fariba Sadri, and Paul Soper. Integrity Checking in Deductive Databases. In *Proceedings of the 13th Conference on Very Large Data Bases*, 1987.

[15] Norbert Beckmannand Hans-Peter Kriegel, Ralf Schneider, and Bernhard Seeger. The R*-tree: An Efficient and Robust Access Method for Points and Rectangles. In *Proceedings of the ACM SIGMOD Conference on Management of Data*, 1990.

[16] Narayanan Krishnakumar and Arthur Bernstein. Bounded Ignorance in Replicated Systems. In *Proceedings of the 10th ACM Symposium on Principles of Database Systems*, May 1991.

[17] Narayanan Krishnakumar and Arthur Bernstein. Bounded Ignorance: A Technique for Increasing Concurrency in a Replicated System. *ACM Transactions on Database Systems*, 19(4), December 1994.

[18] R. Ladin, B. Liskov, L. Shrira, and S. Ghemawat. Providing High Availability Using Lazy Replication. *ACM Transactions on Computer Systems*, November 1992.

[19] Vivek Pai, Mohit Aron, Gaurav Banga, Michael Svendsen, Peter Druschel, Willy Zwaenepoel, and Erich Nahum. Locality-aware Request Distribution in Cluster-based Network Servers. In *Proceedings of the Eighth International Conference on Architectural Support for Programming Languages and Operating Systems (ASPLOS-VIII)*, 1998.

[20] K. Petersen, M. J. Spreitzer, D. B. Terry, M. M. Theimer, and A. J. Demers. Flexible Update Propagation for Weakly Consistent Replication. In *Proceedings of the 16th ACM Symposium on Operating Systems Principles*, 1997.

[21] Calton Pu and Avraham Leff. Epsilon-Serializability. Technical Report CUCS-054-90, Columbia University, 1991.

[22] Calton Pu and Avraham Leff. Replication Control in Distributed Systems: An Asynchronous Approach. Technical Report CUCS-053-90, Columbia University, January 1991.

[23] D. Terry, K. Petersen, M. Spreitzer, and M. Theimer. The Case for Non-transparent Replication: Examples from Bayou. In *IEEE Data Engineering*, pages 12–20, December 1998.

[24] Amin Vahdat, Thomas Anderson, Michael Dahlin, Eshwar Belani, David Culler, Paul Eastham, and Chad Yoshikawa. WebOS: Operating System Services for Wide-Area Applications. In *Proceedings of the Seventh IEEE Symposium on High Performance Distributed Systems*, Chicago, Illinois, July 1998.

[25] David Wetherall. Active Network Vision and Reality: Lessions from a Capsule-based System. In *Proceedings of the 17th ACM Symposium on Operating Systems Principles*, 1999.

[26] Haifeng Yu and Amin Vahdat. Building Replicated Internet Services using TACT: A Toolkit for Tunable Availability and Consistency Tradeoffs. In *Second International Workshop on Advanced Issues of E-Commerce and Web-based Information Systems*, June 2000.

[27] Haifeng Yu and Amin Vahdat. Design and Evaluation of a Continuous Consistency Model for Replicated Services. Technical Report CS-2000-07, Computer Science Department, Duke University, 2000. See `http://www.cs.duke.edu/~yhf/tr2.pdf`.

[28] Haifeng Yu and Amin Vahdat. Efficient Numerical Error Bounding for Replicated Network Services. Technical Report CS-2000-08, Computer Science Department, Duke University, 2000. See `http://www.cs.duke.edu/~yhf/vldbtr.pdf`.

Don't be lazy, be consistent: Postgres-R,
A new way to implement Database Replication *

Bettina Kemme　　　　　　　Gustavo Alonso

Information and Communication Systems Group, ETH Zürich, Switzerland

{kemme,alonso}@inf.ethz.ch

Abstract

Database designers often point out that eager, update everywhere replication suffers from high deadlock rates, message overhead and poor response times. In this paper, we show that these limitations can be circumvented by using a combination of known and novel techniques. Moreover, we show how the proposed solution can be incorporated into a real database system. The paper discusses the new protocols and their implementation in PostgreSQL. It also provides experimental results proving that many of the dangers and limitations of replication can be avoided by using the appropriate techniques.

1　Introduction

Existing replication protocols can be divided into *eager* and *lazy* schemes [GHOS96]. Eager protocols ensure that changes to copies happen within the transaction boundaries. That is, when a transaction commits, all copies have the same value. Lazy replication protocols propagate changes only after the transaction commits, thereby allowing copies to have different values. While eager replication emphasizes consistency, lazy replication pays more attention to efficiency.

Among database designers, there is the widespread belief that eager replication is not practical. The "dangers" of eager replication have been analyzed by Gray et al. [GHOS96] and, since the publication of those results, the research focus has shifted towards lazy replication [CRR96, PMS99, ABKW98, BKR+99]. The drawback of lazy replication is that, if consistency is necessary, many non trivial problems arise. Namely, in the case of update everywhere (each copy can be updated), maintaining consistency is usually left to the user. If only a primary copy can be updated, consistency is achieved at the price of introducing a bottleneck and a single point of failure. In addition, recent results prove that consistency can only be guaranteed when the system configuration is severely restricted.

We see these as serious limitations. The thesis defended in this paper is that if the goal is to achieve consistency and the computing environment allows it, then eager replication should be used. In spite of what is commonly assumed, eager replication is perfectly feasible in many environments. A good example are the computer clusters which can be found behind many Internet sites. However, in order to circumvent the limitations of traditional solutions, it is necessary to rethink the way transaction and replica management is done. In this paper, we demonstrate how eager replication can be implemented in practice. Some of the techniques we use include executing the transaction first locally on shadow copies and postponing the propagation of updates to the end of the transaction, using group communication primitives for preordering transactions, and acquiring all locks a transaction needs in an atomic step. To prove the feasibility of these ideas, we have implemented them in Postgres-R, an extension of PostgreSQL [Pos98] and tested them extensively. The results prove that eager replication is feasible in clusters of computers and can scale to a relatively large number of nodes.

The paper is organized as follows. Section 2 discusses related work. Section 3 explains the principle techniques of our approach and presents a basic protocol. Section 4 discusses the architecture and implementation of Postgres-R. Section 5 presents performance results. Section 6 discusses configuration management and partial replication. Section 7 concludes the paper.

---

*Part of this work has been funded by ETH Zürich within the DRAGON Research Project (Reg-Nr. 41-2642.5)

**Proceedings of the 26th VLDB Conference,
Cairo, Egypt, 2000.**

2 Related Work

2.1 The dangers of replication ...

Text book eager replication protocols use update everywhere (e.g., *read-one/write-all-available*) and quorums to minimize overhead [BHG87]. With very few exceptions, these protocols have never been used in practice and Gray et al. [GHOS96] have pointed out why. These protocols coordinate each operation individually, using distributed locking and 2-phase commit. As a result, when the number of nodes increases, transaction response times, conflict probability and deadlock rates grow significantly. From these results, Gray et al. concluded that eager replication was not practical and suggested to use lazy approaches instead. Indeed, only few commercial systems implement eager replication. *Oracle Advanced Replication* provides an eager protocol which first executes an update locally and then "after row" triggers are used to synchronously propagate the changes and to lock the corresponding remote copies. Most other solutions mainly focus on availability and represent highly specialized solutions (e.g., Tandem's RDF or Informix's HDR). In general, commercial systems clearly favor lazy approaches [Sta94]. For instance, Sybase provides an extended publish-and-subscribe scheme which tries to minimize the time copies are inconsistent. As another example, IBM Data Replicator uses a pull strategy whereby a client will not see its own updates unless it requests them.

2.2 ... lazy solutions ...

On the research side, lazy replication has been studied using very different approaches like weak consistency models [PL91, KB91, GN95], economic paradigms [SAS$^+$96] or epidemic strategies [AES97]. More recent work has explored lazy strategies that still provide consistency. Thus, Chundi et al. [CRR96] have shown that in lazy primary copy schemes, serializability cannot be guaranteed without restricting the placement of primary and secondary copies in the system. Recent work by Pacitti et al. [PMS99] and Breitbart et al. [BKR$^+$99] has attempted to minimize this limitation. As a major drawback, all these approaches are primary copy. Furthermore, transactions cannot update data items whose primary copies reside on different sites and, in real applications (specially in clusters), the complexities and limitations on replica placement are likely to be a significant liability.

Another way to provide consistency has been to combine eager and lazy approaches. Anderson et al. [ABKW98] have proposed a system that is eager in the sense that the serialization order is determined within the transactional boundaries but updates are propagated only after the commit of the transaction. This approach does not restrict replica placement but is still primary copy and forbids transactions to access data items with primary copies on different sites.

2.3 ... and eager solutions

Parallel to this work, several suggestions [AAES97, PGS97] have been made to implement eager replication using *group communication systems* such as Transis, Totem or Horus [ea96] and initial efforts have been made to optimize the integration of transaction processing and communication management [KPAS99]. In some cases [AAES97, HAA99], the protocols are quite simplistic and suffer from high abort rates. In other cases, the protocols can be quite difficult to implement in a real database [PGS97]. In all cases, the work is simulation based and little effort has been made to tackle the practical aspects of a real implementation. To address these limitations, we have proposed a suite of replication protocols [KA98, KA] where different degrees of isolation are combined with different message delivery guarantees in order to provide a more complete solution that takes into account abort rates, failures and how databases relax consistency. The results presented in this paper are based on this work. In what follows, we discuss how these ideas can be implemented in a database management system and show that the performance reached favorably compares with that of traditional protocols.

3 Replication Model

Our approach is based on a number of techniques and optimizations which we briefly present in this section. For more details see [KA].

3.1 Reducing message and synchronization overhead

Traditional eager replication protocols [BHG87] coordinate copies one operation at a time. In a system with n nodes and where each transaction consists of m operations, a throughput of k transactions per second requires $k \cdot m \cdot n$ messages per second. Such an approach can never scale. One way to avoid this problem is to bundle writes into a single *write set* message [AAES97, ABKW98]. In lazy replication this is somewhat easier since updates are propagated after the transaction commits. One novel aspect of our approach is to apply this technique in eager replication. We use *shadow copies* [BHG87] to perform updates: write operations are executed on private copies in order to check consistency constraints, capture write-read dependencies and fire triggers. These changes to the shadow copies are propagated to the other sites at commit time, thereby greatly reducing the message overhead and the conflict profile of transactions.

3.2 Localizing read operations

Early replication protocols like read-one/write-all [BHG87] already recognized the importance of keeping read operations local. This implies that read operations are executed only at one site and that no information about them is exchanged among the sites. As a result, read operations have no message costs and no overhead at remote sites, and queries can be kept completely local. This is very desirable but it introduces some complexity regarding read/write conflicts since reads are only seen at the local site.

3.3 Pre-ordering transactions

We use a group communication primitive providing *total order* semantics to multicast the write set and to determine the serialization order of the transactions. The total order guarantees that all sites receive the write sets in exactly the same order. Note that a site sends a message also to itself in order to be able to determine the final total order of a transaction. Each transaction manager uses this order to acquire locks. It requests all write locks for a transaction in a single atomic operation, and then proceeds with the execution of the transaction. By granting the locks in the order in which the transactions arrive, it is guaranteed that all sites perform conflicting updates in the same order. Additionally, transactions never get into a deadlock. Note that this does not imply serial execution since non-conflicting transactions are executed in parallel. Only the access to the lock table is serial. With this approach, we also avoid that transaction response time is determined by the slowest machine. The local site can commit a transaction whenever the global serialization order has been determined and does not wait for the other sites to have executed the transaction. Instead it relies on the fact that the other sites will serialize the transaction in the same way.

Group communication primitives provide a variety of execution semantics. These semantics can be used to optimize the protocols as long as the recovery mechanisms are properly adjusted. In this paper we assume *reliable delivery*, which guarantees consistency on all non-faulty sites [KA].

3.4 An eager replication protocol

The replication protocol we use in this paper executes a transaction in four phases:

I. *Local Read Phase:* Perform all read operations locally. Execute write operations on shadow copies. Acquire the appropriate lock before executing the operation.

II. *Send Phase:* If T_i is read-only, then commit. Else bundle all writes into write set WS_i and multicast it to all sites including the sending site (same delivery order at all sites).

III. *Lock Phase:* Upon delivery of WS_i, request all locks for WS_i in an atomic step:
1. For each operation $w_i(X)$ on item X in WS_i:
   a. Perform a conflict test: if a local transaction T_j has a granted lock on X and T_j is still in its read or send phase, abort T_j. If T_j is in its send phase, then multicast the decision message *abort* (decision messages are not ordered).
   b. If there is no lock on X, grant the lock to T_i. Otherwise enqueue the lock request directly after all locks from transactions that are beyond their lock phase.
2. If T_i is a local transaction, multicast the decision message commit (no order requirement).

IV. *Write Phase:* Whenever a write lock is granted apply the corresponding update. A local transaction can commit and release all locks once all updates have been applied to the database. A remote transaction must wait until the decision message arrives and terminates accordingly.

In this protocol, the total order is used to serialize write/write conflicts at all sites. The scheduler has to guarantee that waiting locks are granted in the order in which they appear in the lock queue. Read/write conflicts are also detected during the lock phase (III.1.a). Since read operations are only seen at the local site, we use a straightforward solution and abort local readers when a conflicting writer arrives. This avoids deadlocks and inconsistent executions. The abort is only necessary when the reading transaction is in its read or send phase. In later phases the transaction cannot be involved in a deadlock (see [KA] for details). When a transaction is aborted during the read phase, it is still completely local and no message needs to be sent. When a transaction is aborted during its send phase, the local site must inform the other sites via an abort message. Thus, this protocol requires that the local site sends two messages per transaction, one with the write set and another to confirm that the transaction will commit or abort (this is not a 2PC). The decision messages do not require any ordering semantics. They may be delivered in any order at the different sites and might even arrive before the corresponding write set. Obviously, to abort readers when a writer arrives is problematic. There exist several alternatives [KA], specially using different degrees of isolation like cursor stability or snapshot isolation. For simplicity, we only analyze the presented protocol in this paper.

4 Postgres-R Architecture

Postgres-R has been implemented as an extension to PostgreSQL [Pos98], version 6.4.2, a single node database that supports an extended subset of SQL and uses 2-phase-locking for concurrency control with re-

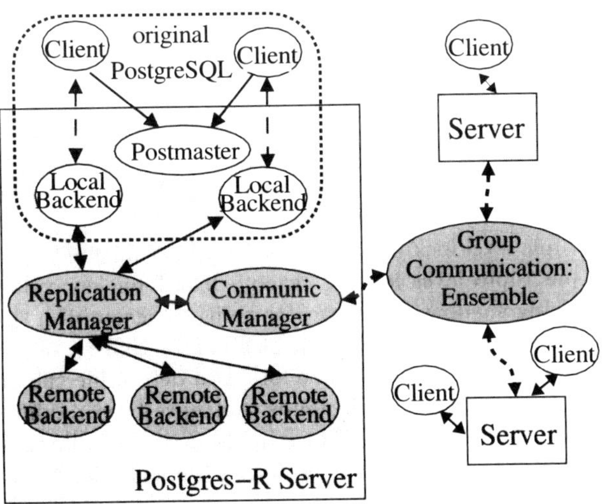

Figure 1: Architecture of Postgres-R

lation level locking. With respect to group communication, we use Ensemble [Hay98], the follow up system to Horus [ea96]. The functionality available in PostgreSQL is still available in Postgres-R but now with replication as an additional feature. All the interfaces provided by PostgreSQL are also available in Postgres-R: embedded SQL, ODBC, etc. The replication features of Postgres-R are usable through SQL, both for data manipulation and data definition. For simplicity, in what follows we assume full replication. In section 6, we discuss how to implement partial replication.

4.1 Basic modules

As shown in Figure 1, a replicated database comprises several nodes (servers), each one of them running an instance of Postgres-R. In the figure, all clear shapes represent original PostgreSQL modules, the shadowed shapes are Postgres-R specific. PostgreSQL is *process-based*. When *clients* want to access the database they send a request to a listener process, called *postmaster*. For each client, the postmaster creates a *backend* process and from then on communication takes place between backend and client. Clients can submit an arbitrary number of transactions (one at a time) until they disconnect. PostgreSQL allows to limit the maximum number of parallel backends. When a given threshold is reached no new clients are admitted.

To implement replication, additional modules are needed to take care of the communication and to deal with remote transactions. In Postgres-R, clients may connect to any server. The transactions of a client are called *local* at the server where the client connects. For each client, the postmaster creates a *local backend* process. To handle *remote* transactions, each Postgres-R server keeps a pool of *remote backend* processes. This

pool is created at system startup (with an adjustable startup pool size). When a message of a remote transaction arrives, it is handed over to one of these remote backends. When all existing remote backends are busy and their number has not reached a given threshold (maximum pool size), a new remote backend is started, otherwise the transaction must wait.

Control of the replication protocol takes place at the *replication manager*. The replication manager is a message handling process. It receives messages from the backends (local and remote) and forwards them to the other sites. It also receives the messages delivered by the communication system and forwards them to the corresponding backends.

4.2 Execution of transactions

For local transactions, as long as they are in their *read phase*, they remain within their corresponding local backend. Once the local backend finishes the execution (over shadow copies), it sends the write set to the replication manager and the transaction enters its *send phase*. The replication manager then broadcasts the write set to all sites. When a write set arrives at a site, its replication manager checks whether the write set corresponds to a local or to a remote transaction. This is done using the host name and a transaction identifier included in the write set message. For write sets of local transactions, the replication manager notifies the corresponding local backend and the transaction enters its *lock phase*. In order to perform the lock phase atomically, the local backend acquires a latch on the lock table and keeps it until all locks are enqueued in the lock table. Additionally, the replication manager stops accepting write sets from the communication system until the backend sends a confirmation that all necessary locks have been requested. This guarantees that the lock phases of concurrent transactions are executed in the same order in which the write sets have been delivered. When the replication manager receives the confirmation from the backend that the locks have been requested, it broadcast a commit message. The transaction then enters its *write phase* and whenever a lock is granted the shadow copies become the valid versions of the items.

Up to the time point at which a local transaction T has acquired the latch on the lock table to start the lock phase, it can be aborted due to a read/write conflict. This happens when another transaction T' tries to set a write lock (during its lock phase) and finds a read lock from T. In this case, T' sets an *abort flag* for T. Local transactions check their abort flags regularly during their read and send phases and abort if they are set. If a transaction is in its send phase, it sends an abort message to the replication manager which broadcasts it to the other sites.

For remote transactions, write and decision messages might arrive in any order. If the write set arrives first, the replication manager passes it to an idle remote backend and proceeds like with local write sets. The remote backend will acquire the locks, confirm this to the replication manager, and apply the updates. However, it will wait to terminate the transaction until the replication manager receives the decision message from the local site and forwards it to the remote backend. Once a remote backend finishes executing a transaction, it sends a *ready*-notification to the replication manager, which will add it to the pool of available remote backends. If the decision message arrives first, the replication manager registers this fact and simply proceeds accordingly when the write set arrives.

To implement these procedures, the PostgreSQL *lock table* had to be modified. Usually, a transaction requests a lock and performs an operation before it requests the next lock. In between the two lock requests, other transactions can also acquire locks. In Postgres-R, it is possible to request all write locks in a single step. As a consequence a transaction can have more than one lock waiting and more than one lock granted without the corresponding operation being executed. Additionally, the *backend coordination* of PostgreSQL needed to be adjusted, but the actual data manipulation and commit actions could be reused.

4.3 Shadow copies

In Postgres-R, updates are executed on a shadow copy during the read phase. This is crucial for several reasons. First, a transaction is able to read what it has previously written by reading the shadow copies. Second, constraints can be checked to assure that the write operation is indeed possible. And finally, triggers can be fired that possibly generate further updates (which are then also performed on shadow copies within the scope of the transaction).

PostgreSQL supports shadow copies quite well since it is a *tuple-based multiversion system*. In PostgreSQL each update invalidates the current physical version of a tuple and creates a new version. To determine the valid version, each tuple has two additional fields which contain the identifiers of the creating and the invalidating transaction. A version is visible to a transaction T_i if T_i itself has created it or the creating transaction T_j has already committed. Furthermore, for the tuple to be visible, the field for the invalidating transaction must be empty or the invalidating transaction is either still running or aborted. Thus, a transaction sees its own updates but not the updates of concurrent transactions. Updates trigger the creation of new entries in all relevant indices. To control the table size, PostgreSQL provides a special garbage collector to physically delete all invisible tuples. Thus, the inte-

gration of the shadow copy approach into PostgreSQL has been rather straightforward. It should be equally feasible in any multiversion database (e.g., Oracle).

4.4 Locking

PostgreSQL uses logical locking at the relation level. For efficiency reasons, however, it is desirable to have tuple level locking. Thus, we have implemented a simple tuple level locking scheme based on key values. Using shadow copies greatly helps to accomplish this. During the read phase, a local site actually executes the transaction and, therefore, can determine the primary key values of all items that have been modified. Including these key values in the write set allows for logical tuple level locking during the lock phase.

Although shadow copies are not visible until commit time, they require a sophisticated handling of locks to avoid **update/update, delete/update** and **insert/insert** conflicts. Assume write operations on shadow copies would not acquire locks and there are two transactions T_1 and T_2:

```
T1:update ATABLE set A1=A1+1 where A-ID=5
T2:update ATABLE set A1=A1+2 where A-ID=5
```

Both might be on the same site or on different sites and they perform the updates concurrently on shadow copies. Now assume, both send their write sets and T_1's write set is delivered before T_2's write set. Since neither T_1 nor T_2 have locks set on the data during the read phase, first T_1's and then T_2's updates will be applied. This results in a non-serializable execution. The problem here is that both operations contain implicit reads. For delete/update conflicts, the problem is incompatible writes. Assume T_1 deleting a tuple and T_2 concurrently updating the tuple and T_1's write set is delivered before T_2's write set. While T_2 could locally update the tuple during the read phase the write phase will fail because T_1 has deleted the tuple. A similar problem arises with two concurrent inserts.

To avoid these problems, we use a similar approach as the multiversion 2-phase-locking scheme proposed in [BHG87]. The approach is also related to *update mode* locks [GR93]. The idea is to obtain a *read-intention-write* (RIW) for all write operations during the read phase. A RIW lock conflicts with other RIW locks and with write locks but not with read locks. As a result, a transaction can perform a write operation on a shadow copy while concurrent transactions can still read the (old) version of the tuple. By using this mechanism, the problems described above are either avoided or are made visible. Conflicts between two local transactions are handled by allowing at most one RIW lock on a data item. Conflicts between local and remote transactions are detected during the lock phase of the remote transactions. In this case RIW locks behave like read locks. If a transaction in its lock phase wants to set a write lock on a data item, it will abort all local transactions in their read or send phases with conflicting read or RIW locks.

The only problem with RIW locks is that they reintroduce deadlocks. Assume transaction T_1 updates data item x and T_2 updates data item y both holding RIW. If now T_1 wants to set a RIW lock on y and T_2 wants to set a RIW lock on x, a deadlock will ensue. However, such a deadlock only occurs among local transactions in their read phases and therefore can be handled locally. Note that, once a transaction is in its send phase, it will not be involved in a deadlock anymore because write locks have precedence over any other type of locks and conflicting transactions will be aborted.

4.5 Index locking

Locks on index structures need further consideration. Most of these locks are usually short locks not following 2-phase-locking and hence, they can be acquired at any time even during the write phase of a transaction. In B-trees, for instance, while searching for an entry to be updated, PostgreSQL searches along a path in the B-tree, locking and unlocking (short read locks) individual pages until the entry is found. When the entry is found, the short read lock is upgraded to a write lock. Two transactions can follow this procedure at the same time and deadlock when they try to upgrade the lock. In PostgreSQL, such deadlocks occur frequently because each update operation creates a new entry in the primary key index. These deadlocks would not be a problem if they involved only local transactions in their read phase. However, since indices are also used during the write phase, remote transactions could also be involved in such deadlocks. To avoid it, Postgres-R immediately acquires write locks on index pages in the case of update operations.

4.6 The write set

Creating, sending and processing the write set plays a crucial role in our protocols and can have a severe impact on performance. In Postgres-R, we have implemented two alternatives to send a write operation. Either the *SQL statement* is sent or the primary key values of the updated tuples along with the new *physical values* of those attributes that have been modified. In the former case, messages are small but remote sites have more work to do since they need to parse the SQL statement and execute the entire operation. In the latter case, remote sites can be very fast installing updates (specific tuples are accessed via the primary key index), but messages can become quite large.

We have evaluated the performance differences between the two alternatives in terms of message size

	1 tuple		50 tuples	
	SQL	**phys.**	**SQL**	**phys.**
Message Size (Byte)	123	105	125	3634
Execution Time (ms)				
Not Replicated	7		125	
Local	7	7	125	140
Remote	7	1	125	40

Table 1: The Write Set

and execution time by running two tests. The results are shown in Table 1. For comparison reasons the table also shows the execution time in a non-replicated system. We have run two tests. In the first test, a write set contains a single operation updating one tuple. The index on the primary key can be used to find the tuple. In the second test, there is one operation updating 50 tuples. This statement performs a table scan. In both cases, two tuple attributes are modified. Regarding message size, in the 1-tuple case, there are no significant differences between sending statements or the physical updates. However, with 50 tuples, the message with physical updates is quite big and might lead to severe latency and buffer problems in the communication system. Regarding execution time, if the SQL statement is sent or if only one tuple is updated the overhead at the local site is not visible and execution takes as long as in the non-replicated case. But even if the local site must include the physical updates of 50 tuples, the overhead is not very high. The most visible difference, however, is how much faster a remote site can apply the physical updates in comparison to executing the SQL statement. Since the overhead at the local site occurs only once while there are many remote sites, we prefer sending the physical updates as long as message size is not the limiting factor.

5 Performance Analysis

5.1 General configuration

PostgreSQL uses a *force* strategy to avoid redo recovery, flushing all dirty buffer pages at the end of each transaction. With this strategy, response times are very poor. This makes it difficult to compare with commercial systems which only flush redo logs to disk. To allow us to use a more "realistic" setting we used the no-flush option offered by PostgreSQL. With this option nothing is forced to disk, not even a log record. This, of course, violates the ACID properties, however the measured response time was better comparable to standard database systems. In future versions of Postgres-R we will correct this limitation.

We have performed 4 experiments. Except for the first experiment, we used a cluster of 15 Unix workstations (SUN Ultra 10, 333 MHz UltraSPARC-IIi CPU, 2MB cache, 256 MB main memory, 9GB IDE disk, switched

Parameters	Ex. 1	Ex. 2	Ex. 3	Ex. 4
Database Size	10 tables of 10000 tuples each			
Tuple Size	appr. 100 Bytes			
# of Servers	1-5	1-15	1-15	1-15
% of Upd. Txn.	100%	100%	100%	varying
# Op. in Upd. Txn.	5	10	1	10
# Op. in Query	-	-	-	1 scan
# of Clients	5	20	20	3 p. serv.
Submission rate in tps in the entire system	10	20-50	40-200	15-225

Table 2: Parameters settings

full-duplex Fast Ethernet). We did not have exclusive access to the cluster. For all our experiments, we use the physical copy approach in which servers only apply the physical updates of remote transactions.

In all our experiments, the database consists of 10 tables each containing 1000 tuples. We did not consider larger databases since this will only reduce the conflict profile. Each table has the same schema: two integers (one being the primary key `t-id`, the other denoted below as `attr1`), one 50-character string (`attr2`), one float (`attr3`) and one date (`attr4`) attribute. For each table there exists one index for the primary key.

Update transactions have operations of the type

```
update t-name set attr1='x', attr2=attr2+4
where t-id=y
```

where x is randomly chosen text and y is a randomly chosen number between 1 and 1000. The relevant tuple is found by searching the index on the primary key.

Transactions are submitted by clients which are evenly distributed among the servers. The interarrival time between two submissions is exponentially distributed. The submission rate (also referred to as workload) is determined by the number of clients and the mean interarrival rate for each client. The system throughput is equal to the submission rate unless the system is saturated. Whenever a transaction is aborted, the client resubmits it immediately.

Table 2 summarizes the parameters of all experiments. As performance indicator, we analyze the response time of local transactions, i.e., the time from which the client starts a transaction until the client receives the commit. For comparison: in a single user, single node system, an update transaction with 10 operations takes around 75 ms, with 1 operation 9 ms.

5.2 Experiment 1: distributed 2 phase locking

In a first experiment we compared standard distributed locking with Postgres-R. To do so we use a commercially available implementation of eager replication based on standard distributed locking. The experiment was conducted with 5 instances of a

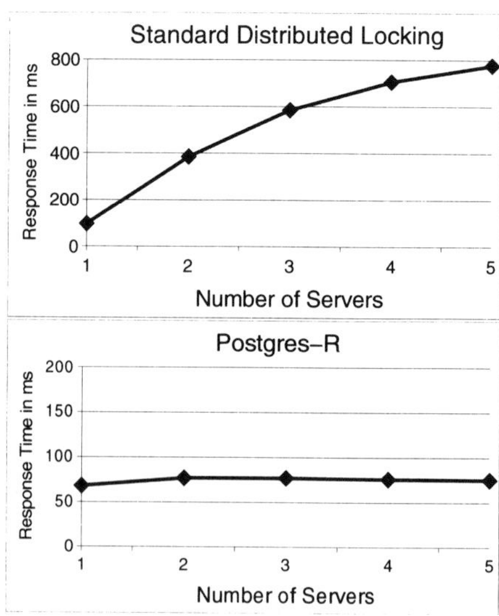

Figure 2: Comparison of distributed locking and Postgres-R

database product installed on PCs (266MHz, 128MB main memory, two local disk [4GB IDE, 4GB SCSI], switched full-duples 100Mbit Fast Ethernet). The workload consists of only update transactions, with 5 operations each. The number of clients was fixed to 5 and the interarrival rate per client to 500 ms for a total submission rate of 10 tps. The number of replicated nodes was varied from 1 (no replication) to 5.

The results are shown in Figure 2. As predicted by Gray et al., we observe a clear degradation in the distributed locking solution as the number of servers increases. In addition to longer response times, we also observe significantly higher abort rates and decreasing throughput beyond 2 nodes.

In comparison, the performance of Postgres-R proved to be stable. Please note, that this comparison can only be relative since different hardware platforms are used and the underlying database systems differ considerably. Still, the test demonstrates that – at least for this relatively small load (10 tps) – the dangers of replication seem to have been circumvented in Postgres-R. To find out whether this is indeed the case, we performed three other experiments varying the workload and communication overhead as well as testing the scalability of Postgres-R.

5.3 Experiment 2: workload

Conventional eager replication protocols do not cope very well with increasing loads. The next step is to analyze the behavior of Postgres-R for high update workloads. To do so, we run tests with different workloads and system sizes from 5 to 15 nodes. For all runs, transactions consist of 10 update operations and

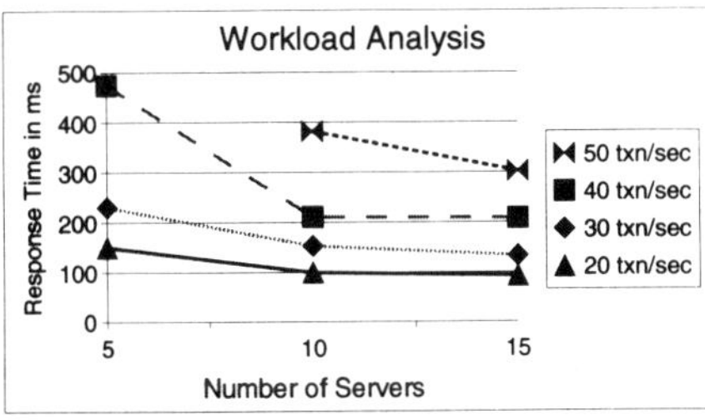

Figure 3: Response time of Postgres-R for different workloads and number of nodes

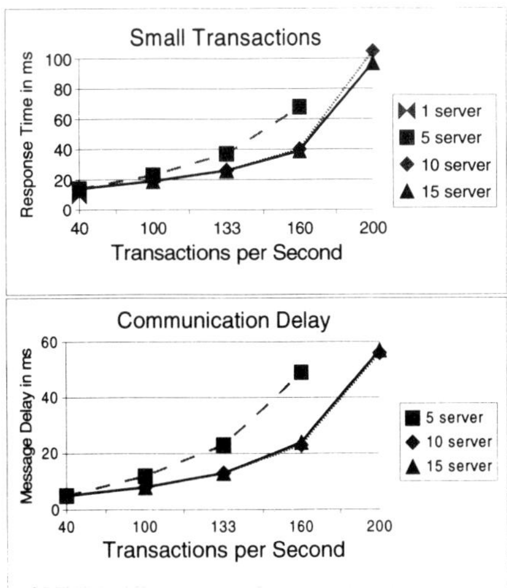

Figure 4: Response time and communication delay for small transactions

there are 20 clients in the system.

As the results in Figure 3 show, for small loads we could run the tests with 5, 10 and 15 nodes. For higher loads, the 5 node configuration was saturated. The results clearly demonstrate that the response times improve as we increase the number of replicated nodes due to the increased processing capacity. This is exactly the behavior that is needed to improve performance by using replication.

To understand why Postgres-R can take advantage of the increased processing capacity, we need to look at how transactions are being processed. Regarding remote transactions, nodes only install the changes without having to execute the SQL statements (see Table 1). As a result, remote transactions use significantly less CPU than local ones which allows to run additional transactions or reduce overall response times. In addition, since updates on remote sites are so fast and applied in a single step, the corresponding locks are held for a very short time. With this, conflict rates are very low (in the tests abort rates never exceeded 5%).

Another important point is that the coordination overhead seems to have very little impact. First, we observed a generally small communication overhead (message delays were between 5 and 10 ms and constructing the write set added only a few milliseconds). Second, the local node does not need to wait until the remote sites have executed the transactions but only waits until the write set is delivered.

We can conclude that the techniques implemented in Postgres-R can be used to increase the processing capacity of a database by using replication. We only tested up to 15 nodes due to the practical limitations of setting up the experiment. With the results obtained we are confident that Postgres-R can cope with both higher loads and more nodes.

5.4   Experiment 3: communication overhead

One of the problems of using group communication systems is the poor performance that many of them exhibit. The claim that Postgres-R can tolerate more than 15 replicated nodes is conditional to proving that the communication system used actually scales up. In this third experiment, we analyze how the communication system handles high message rates. The goal is to test whether high transaction loads can collapse the communication system and whether message delays can severely affect response times.

In the previous experiments, the number of messages never exceeded 100 messages per second. Up to then, the communication system was not the bottleneck. In order to stress test the system, we performed an experiment with very many, very short transactions. These transactions consist of only one operation, thus, the write set is small but the communication overhead has a bigger impact on the overall response time. Again, we use 20 concurrent clients generating a throughput between 40 and 200 transactions per second.

Response times and message delay are shown in Figure 4. Clearly, as the number of messages in the system increases, the communication system becomes slower. Transaction response times vary proportionally to the message delay as the similarity between the slopes in the figures indicate. A resource analysis has shown that the communication process requires the most CPU at high transaction loads. This means, that the message delay is due to increased message processing requirements (for message buffering, determining the total order etc.) and not to a shortage of network bandwidth. Observe, however, that the number of nodes plays no role on the communication congestion. It is only the submission rate that has an effect. Thus, replication can still be used to improve performance. A 1-node system, while slightly faster at 40 tps, cannot cope with 20 clients and a workload of

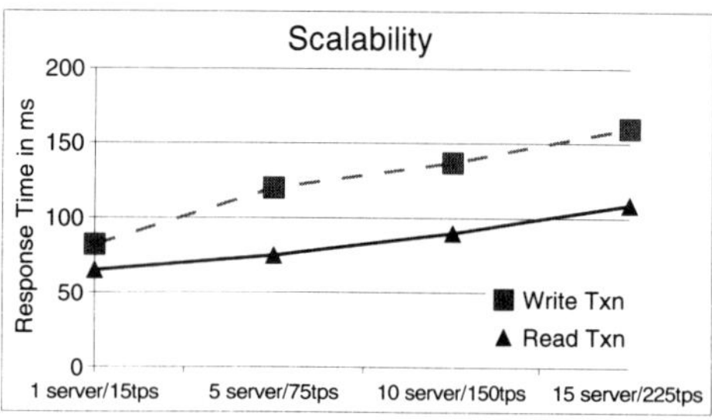

Figure 5: Response time for update transactions and queries

100 tps due to process management and log and data contention while the replicated systems do.

As a summary of this experiment, communication overhead is a factor to take into consideration but it only started to play a limiting role under high update transaction loads (over 150 tps). Then, an efficient communication module is crucial. We believe, however, that when read transactions are considered (which do not require communication), the mechanisms of Postgres-R can provide good performance over an even wider range of loads.

5.5   Experiment 4: scalability

This last experiment tests the scalability of Postgres-R using a more realistic workload of update and read-only transactions (queries). Update transactions have 10 update operations and queries are of the form
`select avg(attr3), sum(attr3) from t-name`
scanning an entire table. There are three clients per site, one submitting an update transaction each 1 second, the two other submitting queries each 150 ms. Thus, the load per node is around 15 tps with a 14 to 1 rate between read and update transactions.

The response times for both read and write transactions are shown in Figure 5. As pointed out above, by considering queries, we are able to achieve higher throughput (up to 225 tps in a 15-node system). The response times increase with the number of nodes but are reasonable if we take into account that the absolute number of update transactions (that must be applied everywhere and create conflicts), increases constantly. In fact, conflicts start to become a problem at higher loads. The way to address this limitation is to use alternative isolation levels. In our specific setting, since the queries only set a single relation level lock they cannot be involved in any deadlock, and hence, we do not abort them. Still, queries and update transactions delay each other. As an alternative, a hybrid protocol could combine serializability for update transactions and provide a snapshot for queries [KA]. In that way, updating transactions never conflict with queries and

are not delayed by them. Such a hybrid protocol practically eliminates conflicts at most loads and will allow to scale Postgres-R even further.

6   Crash Recovery, Administration and Partial Replication

Postgres-R has been designed as a system able to cope with issues like failures and partial replication which are often ignored in research. We have also implemented the administrative tools necessary to set up and maintain the system.

6.1   System configuration

One of the main problems of replication is how to dynamically change the system without having to stop processing. We have designed Postgres-R to work in cluster environments where failures and configuration changes can occur quite frequently. We support this by using the group communication services. As nodes leave (because of failures or shutdowns) or join (new or recovering nodes), the group communication module creates different *views* in the computation. Every time there is a change in the number of nodes, the communication system switches to a new view and informs the replication managers via a view change message.

In the case of failures, when a working sites receives the corresponding view change message, it can identify the active transactions originating at the failed site. In [KA] we show that active transactions from failed nodes can be safely aborted without compromising consistency at the non-faulty nodes.

Upon recovery, or when a new node is added to the system (also triggering a new view), a peer node has to provide a copy of the current database. The transfered data must contain the updates of all write sets that were delivered in the old view (without the joining node). PostgreSQL provides a feature which extracts the database schema and all tuples from a given database to transfer it to another database. We use this feature to install the database in the new node. While the data transfer takes place other nodes in the system can continue processing transactions. The new node will receive these messages (since they execute in the new view) but delay their execution until all data is installed and only then apply the updates. Once all this is done, the new node will allow clients to connect and proceed from then on like a normal node.

6.2   Partial replication

For simplicity in the exposition, we have assumed full replication (all data is replicated at all nodes). Partial replication, however, is an important issue that needs to be addressed. Partial replication means each data item can have one or more copies residing on arbitrary sites. With this, data propagation and enforcing serializability can become quite complex. To tackle this problem Postgres-R implements a *client makes it right* approach where the local node sends all updates of a transaction to all sites, regardless of who has a copy. The nodes receiving this information have to identify which updates need to be done locally and which ones can be ignored. With this strategy, we still can send all updates in a single message and the total order can be used to determine the serialization order following a protocol identical to the one discussed in the paper. The overhead involved is not as high as it may seem. If changes are propagated as physical updates, checking whether a tuple is local or not can be done very quickly. The advantage is that a site does not need to know where the particular copies of a data item reside in order to send the write set. Furthermore, subscribing or unsubscribing to a a data item can be handled with little administrative overhead.

7 Conclusion

Database replication is an increasingly important topic. New computing environments will demand innovative solutions and flexible mechanisms that can support different forms of replication. In particular, eager replication is extremely useful in cluster based systems. Unfortunately, existing commercial products tend to support mainly lazy replication. Similarly, the research focus has shifted towards lazy approaches and this is likely to prevent that future products support eager replication.

In this paper, we prove that eager replication is feasible using the adequate techniques. We have proposed a simple replication protocol, showed how it can be incorporated into a real database management system and analyzed its performance. That is, we have worked out the engineering issues that a protocol needs to address to actually work in practice, issues that have been largely ignored in the literature.

As part of future work, we are developing more sophisticated management tools for Postgres-R and extending the range of replication possibilities by implementing a wide range of eager and lazy protocols.

References

[AAES97] D. Agrawal, G. Alonso, A. El Abbadi, and I. Stanoi. Exploiting atomic broadcast in replicated databases. In *Proc. of Euro-Par*, 1997.

[ABKW98] T. A. Anderson, Y. Breitbart, H. F. Korth, and A. Wool. Replication, consistency, and practicality: Are these mutually exclusive? In *Proc. of the SIGMOD Conf.*, 1998.

[AES97] D. Agrawal, A. El Abbadi, and R. C. Steinke. Epidemic algorithms in replicated databases. In *Proc. of PODS*, 1997.

[BHG87] P. A. Bernstein, V. Hadzilacos, and N. Goodman. *Concurrency Control and Recovery in Database Systems*. Addison Wesley, Massachusetts, 1987.

[BKR+99] Y. Breitbart, R. Komondoor, R. Rastogi, S. Seshadri, and A. Silberschatz. Update propagation protocols for replicated databases. In *Proc. of the SIGMOD Conf.*, 1999.

[CRR96] P. Chundi, D. J. Rosenkrantz, and S. S. Ravi. Deferred updates and data placement in distributed databases. In *Proc. of the Int. Conf. on Data Engineering*, 1996.

[ea96] D. Powel et al. Group communication (special issue). *Communications of the ACM*, 39(4):50–97, 1996.

[GHOS96] J. Gray, P. Helland, P. O'Neil, and D. Shasha. The dangers of replication and a solution. In *Proc. of the SIGMOD Conf.*, 1996.

[GN95] M. Gallersdörder and M. Nicola. Improving performance in replicated databases through relaxed coherency. In *Proc. of the VLDB Conf.*, Zürich, Switzerland, 1995.

[GR93] J. Gray and A. Reuter. *Transaction Processing: Concepts and Techniques*. Morgan Kaufmann, 1993.

[HAA99] J. Holliday, D. Agrawal, and A. El Abbadi. The performance of database replication with group multicast. In *Proc. of the Int. Symp. on Fault-Tolerant Computing (FTCS)*, 1999.

[Hay98] M. Hayden. The ensemble system. Technical report, Departement of Computer Science, Cornell University TR-98-1662, January 1998.

[KA] B. Kemme and G. Alonso. A new approach to developing and implementing eager database replication protocols. *ACM Transactions on Database Systems*. accepted for publication.

[KA98] B. Kemme and G. Alonso. A suite of database replication protocols based on group communication primitives. In *Proc. of the Int. Conf. on Distributed Computing Systems (ICDCS)*, 1998.

[KB91] N. Krishnakumar and A.J. Bernstein. Bounded ignorance in replicated systems. In *Proc. of PODS*, 1991.

[KPAS99] B. Kemme, F. Pedone, G. Alonso, and A. Schiper. Processing transactions over optimistic atomic broadcast protocols. In *Proc. of the Int. Conf. on Distributed Computing Systems (ICDCS)*, 1999.

[PGS97] F. Pedone, R. Guerraoui, and A. Schiper. Transaction reordering in replicated databases. In *Proc. of the Symp. on Reliable Distributed Systems*, 1997.

[PL91] C. Pu and A. Leff. Replica control in distributed systems: An asynchronous approach. In *Proc. of the SIGMOD Conf.*, 1991.

[PMS99] E. Pacitti, P. Minet, and E. Simon. Fast algorithms for maintaining replica consistency in lazy master replicated databases. In *Proc. of the VLDB Conf.*, 1999.

[Pos98] PostgreSQL. *v6.4.2 Released*, January 1998. http://www.postgresql.org.

[SAS+96] J. Sidell, P.M. Aoki, A. Sah, C. Staelin, M. Stonebraker, and A. Yu. Data replication in Mariposa. In *Proc. of the Int. Conf. on Data Engineering*, 1996.

[Sta94] D. Stacey. Replication: DB2, Oracle, or Sybase. *Database Programming & Design*, 7(12), 1994.

Offering a Precision-Performance Tradeoff for Aggregation Queries over Replicated Data[*]

Chris Olston, Jennifer Widom
Stanford University
{olston, widom}@db.stanford.edu

Abstract

Strict consistency of replicated data is infeasible or not required by many distributed applications, so current systems often permit *stale replication*, in which cached copies of data values are allowed to become out of date. Queries over cached data return an answer quickly, but the stale answer may be unboundedly imprecise. Alternatively, queries over remote master data return a precise answer, but with potentially poor performance. To bridge the gap between these two extremes, we propose a new class of replication systems called TRAPP (*Tradeoff in Replication Precision and Performance*). TRAPP systems give each user fine-grained control over the tradeoff between precision and performance: Caches store ranges that are guaranteed to bound the current data values, instead of storing stale exact values. Users supply a quantitative *precision constraint* along with each query. To answer a query, TRAPP systems automatically select a combination of locally cached bounds and exact master data stored remotely to deliver a *bounded answer* consisting of a range that is no wider than the specified precision constraint, that is guaranteed to contain the precise answer, and that is computed as quickly as possible. This paper defines the architecture of TRAPP replication systems and covers some mechanics of caching data ranges. It then focuses on queries with aggregation, presenting optimization algorithms for answering queries with precision constraints, and reporting on performance experiments that demonstrate the fine-grained control of the precision-performance tradeoff offered by TRAPP systems.

1 Introduction

Many environments that replicate information at multiple sites permit *stale replication*, rather than enforcing exact consistency over multiple copies of data. Exact (transactional) consistency is infeasible from a performance perspective in many large systems, for a variety of reasons

---

[*]This work was supported by the National Science Foundation under grant IIS-9811947, by NASA Ames under grant NCC2-5278, and by a National Science Foundation graduate research fellowship.

**Proceedings of the 26th VLDB Conference,
Cairo, Egypt, 2000.**

as outlined in [12], and for many distributed applications exact consistency simply is not a requirement.

The World-Wide Web is a very general example of a stale replication system, where master copies of pages are maintained on Web servers and stale copies are cached by Web browsers. In the Web architecture, reading the stale cached data kept by a browser has significantly better performance than retrieving the master copy from the Web server (accomplished by pressing the browser's "refresh" button), but the cached copy may be arbitrarily out of date. Another example of a stale replication system is a data warehouse, where we can view the data objects at operational databases as master copies, and data at the warehouse (or at multiple "data marts") as stale cached copies. Querying the cached data in a warehouse is typically much faster than querying the master copies at the operational sites.

1.1 Running Example

As a scenario for motivation and examples throughout the paper, we will consider a simple replication system used for monitoring a wide-area network linking thousands of computers. We assume that each node (computer) in the network tracks the average latency, bandwidth, and traffic level for each incoming network link from another node. Administrators at monitoring stations analyze the status of the network by collecting data periodically from the network nodes. For each link $N_i \rightarrow N_j$ in the network, each monitoring station will cache the latest latency, bandwidth, and traffic level figures obtained from node N_j. Administrators want to ask queries such as:

Q1 What is the bottleneck (minimum bandwidth link) along a path $N_1 \rightarrow N_2 \rightarrow \cdots \rightarrow N_k$?

Q2 What is the total latency along a path $N_1 \rightarrow N_2 \rightarrow \cdots \rightarrow N_k$?

Q3 What is the average traffic level in the network?

Q4 What is the minimum traffic level for fast links (*i.e.*, links with high bandwidth and low latency)?

Q5 How many links have high latency?

Q6 What is the average latency for links with high traffic?

While administrators would like to obtain current and precise answers to these kinds of queries, collecting new data values from each relevant node every time a query is posed would take too long and might adversely affect the system. Requiring that all nodes constantly send their updated values to the monitors is also expensive and generally unnecessary. This paper develops a new approach

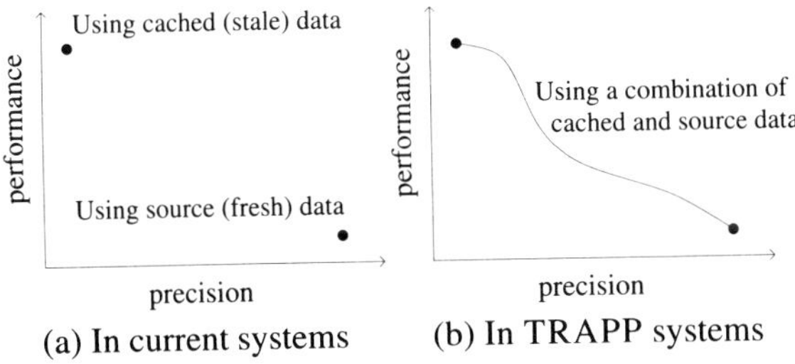

Figure 1: Precision-performance tradeoff.

to replication and query processing that allows the user to control the tradeoff between precise answers and high performance. In our example, the latency, bandwidth, and traffic level figures at each monitor are cached as *ranges*, rather than exact values, and nodes send updates only when an exact value moves outside of a cached range. Queries such as *Q1–Q6* above can be executed over the cached ranges and themselves return a range that is guaranteed to contain the current exact answer. When an administrator poses a query, he can provide a *precision constraint* indicating how wide a range is tolerable in the answer.

For example, suppose the administrator wishes to sample the peak latency periodically in some critical area, in order to decide how much money should be invested in upgrading the network. To make this decision, the administrator does not need to know the precise peak latency at each query, but may wish to obtain an answer to within 5 milliseconds of precision. Our system automatically combines cached ranges with precise values retrieved from the nodes in order to answer queries within the specified precision as quickly as possible.

1.2 Precision-Performance Tradeoff

In general, stale replication systems potentially offer the user two modes of querying. In the first mode, which we call the *precise mode*, queries are sent to the sources to get a precise (up-to-date) answer but with potentially poor performance. Alternatively, in what we call the *imprecise mode*, queries are executed over cached data to get an imprecise (possibly stale) answer very quickly. In imprecise mode, usually no guarantees are given as to exactly how imprecise the answer is, so the user is left to guess the degree of imprecision based on knowledge of data stability and/or how recently caches were updated. Figure 1(a) illustrates the precision-performance tradeoff between these two extreme query modes.

The discrepancy between the extreme points in Figure 1(a) leads to a dilemma: answers obtained in imprecise mode without any precision guarantees may be unacceptable, but the only way to obtain a guarantee is to use precise mode, which can place heavy load on the system and lead to unacceptable delays. Many applications actually require a level of precision somewhere between the extreme points. In our running example (Section 1.1), an administrator posing a query with a *quantitative precision constraint* like "within 5 milliseconds" should be able to find a middle ground between sacrificing preci-

sion and sacrificing performance.

To address this overall problem, we propose a new kind of replication system, which we call TRAPP (*Tradeoff in Replication Precision and Performance*). TRAPP supports a continuous, monotonically decreasing tradeoff between precision and performance, as characterized in Figure 1(b). Each query can be accompanied by a custom precision constraint, and the system answers the query by combining cached and source data so as to optimize performance while guaranteeing to meet the precision constraint. The extreme points of our system correspond to the precise and imprecise query modes defined above.

1.3 Overview of Approach

In addition to introducing the overall TRAPP architecture, in this paper we focus on a specific TRAPP replication system called TRAPP/AG, for queries with aggregation over numeric (real) data. The conventional precise answer to a query with an outermost aggregation operator is a single real value. In TRAPP/AG, we define a *bounded imprecise answer* (hereafter called *bounded answer*) to be a pair of real values L_A and H_A that define a range $[L_A, H_A]$ in which the precise answer is guaranteed to lie. Precision is quantified as the width of the range $(H_A - L_A)$, with 0 corresponding to exact precision and ∞ representing unbounded imprecision. A precision constraint is a user-specified constant $R \geq 0$ denoting the maximum acceptable range width, i.e., $0 \leq H_A - L_A \leq R$.

To be able to give guaranteed bounds $[L_A, H_A]$ as query answers, TRAPP/AG requires cooperation between data sources and caches. Specifically, let us suppose that when a source refreshes a cache's value for a data object O, along with the current exact value for O the source sends a range $[L, H]$ called the *bound* of O. (We actually cover a more general case where the bound is a function of time.) The source guarantees that the actual value for O will stay in this bound, or if the value does exceed the bound then the source will immediately send a new refresh. Thus, the cache stores the bound $[L, H]$ for each data object O instead of an exact value, and the cache can be assured that the current master value of O is within the bound. When the cache answers a query, it can use the bound values it stores to compute an answer, also expressed in terms of a bound.

The small table in Figure 2 shows sample data cached at a network monitoring station (recall Section 1.1), along with the current precise values at the network nodes. The *weights* may be ignored for now. Each row in Figure 2 corresponds to a network link between the *link from* node and the *link to* node. Recall that precise master values for *latency*, *bandwidth*, and *traffic* for incoming links are measured and stored at the *link to* node. In addition, for each link, the monitoring station stores a bounded value for *latency*, *bandwidth*, and *traffic*. The cache can use these bounded values to compute bounded answers to queries.

Suppose a bounded answer to a query with aggrega-

	link		latency		bandwidth		traffic		refresh	weights		
	from	*to*	*cached*	*precise*	*cached*	*precise*	*cached*	*precise*	*cost*	W	W'	W''
1	N_1	N_2	[2, 4]	3	[60, 70]	61	[95, 105]	98	3	2	10	29.5
2	N_2	N_4	[5, 7]	7	[45, 60]	53	[110, 120]	116	6	2	10	2
3	N_3	N_4	[12, 16]	13	[55, 70]	62	[95, 110]	105	6		15	41.5
4	N_2	N_3	[9, 11]	9	[65, 70]	68	[120, 145]	127	8		25	2
5	N_4	N_5	[8, 11]	11	[40, 55]	50	[90, 110]	95	4	3	20	36.5
6	N_5	N_6	[4, 6]	5	[45, 60]	45	[90, 105]	103	2	2	15	31.5

Figure 2: Sample data for network monitoring example.

tion is computed from cached values, but the answer does not satisfy the user's precision constraint, *i.e.*, the answer bound is too wide. In this case, some data must be refreshed from sources to improve precision. We assume that there is a known quantitative *cost* associated with refreshing data objects from their sources, and this cost may vary for each data item (*e.g.*, in our example it might be based on the node distance or network path latency). We show sample refresh costs for our example in Figure 2. Our system uses optimization algorithms that attempt to find the best combination of cached bounds and master values to use in answering a query, in order to minimize the cost of refreshing while still guaranteeing the precision constraint. In this way, TRAPP/AG offers a continuous precision-performance tradeoff: Relaxing the precision constraint of a query enables the system to rely more on cached data, which improves the performance of the query. Conversely, tightening the constraint causes the system to rely more on master data, which degrades performance but yields a more precise answer.

1.4 Contributions

- We define the architecture of TRAPP replication systems, which offer each user fine-grained control over the tradeoff between precision and performance, and propose a method for determining bounds.

- We specify how to compute the five standard relational aggregation functions over bounded data values, considering queries with and without selection predicates, and with joins.

- We present algorithms for finding the minimum-cost set of tuples to refresh in order to answer an aggregation query with a precision constraint, with and without selection predicates. (Joins are discussed but optimal algorithms are not provided.) We analyze the complexity of these algorithms, and in the cases where they are exponential we suggest approximations.

- We have implemented all of our algorithms and we present some initial performance results.

2 Related Work

There is a large body of work dedicated to systems that improve query performance by giving approximate answers. Early work in this area is reported in [22]. Most of these systems use either precomputation (*e.g.*, [26]),

sampling (*e.g.*, [15]), or both (*e.g.*, [11]) to give an answer with statistically estimated bounds, without scanning all of the input data. By contrast, TRAPP systems may scan all of the data (some of which may be bounds rather than exact values), to provide guaranteed rather than statistical results.

The previous work perhaps most similar to the TRAPP idea is *Quasi-copies* [2] and *Moving Objects Databases* [29]. Like TRAPP systems, these two systems are replication schemes in which cached values are permitted to deviate from master values by a bounded amount. However, unlike in TRAPP systems, these systems cannot answer queries by combining cached and master data, and thus there is no way for users to control the precision-performance tradeoff. Instead, the bound for each data object is set independently of any query-based precision constraints. In Quasi-copies, bounds are set statically by a system administrator. In Moving Objects Databases, bounds are set to maximize a single metric that combines precision and performance, eliminating user control of this tradeoff. Furthermore, neither of these systems support aggregation queries.

The *Demarcation Protocol* [3] is a technique for maintaining arithmetic constraints in distributed database systems. TRAPP systems are somewhat related to this work since the bound of a data value forms an arithmetic constraint on that value. However, the Demarcation Protocol is not designed for modifying arithmetic constraints the way TRAPP systems update bounds as needed. Furthermore, the Demarcation Protocol does not deal with queries over bounded data.

Both [19] and [28] consider aggregation queries with selections. The APPROXIMATE approach [19] produces bounded answers when time does not permit the selection predicate to be evaluated on all tuples. However, APPROXIMATE does not deal with queries over bounded data. The work in [28] deals with queries over fuzzy sets. While bounded values can be considered as infinite fuzzy sets, this representation is not practical. Furthermore, the approach in [28] does not consider fuzzy sets as approximations of exact values available for a cost.

In the *multi-resolution relational data model* [27], data objects undergo various degrees of lossy compression to reduce the size of their representation. By reading the compressed versions of data objects instead of the full versions, the system can quickly produce approximate answers to queries. By contrast, in TRAPP systems performance is improved by reducing the number of data objects read from remote sources, rather than by reducing the size of the data representation. In *Divergence Caching* [16], a bound is placed on the number of updates permitted to the master copy of a data object before the cache must be refreshed, but there are no bounds on data values themselves.

Another body of work that deals with imprecision in information systems is *Information Quality (IQ)* research, *e.g.*, [23]. IQ systems quantify the accuracy of data at the granularity of an entire data server. Since no bounds are placed on individual data values, queries have no concrete knowledge about the precision of individual data values from which to form a bounded answer. Therefore, IQ systems cannot give a guaranteed bound on the answer to a particular query.

Finally, data objects whose values are ranges can be considered a special case of constrained values in *Constraint Databases* [20, 6, 7, 21, 4], or as null variables with local conditions in *Incomplete Information Databases* [1]. However, no work in these areas that we know of considers constrained values as bounded approximations of exact values stored elsewhere. Furthermore, aggregation queries over a set with uncertain membership (*e.g.*, due to selection conditions over bounded values) are not considered.

3 TRAPP System Architecture

The overall architecture of a TRAPP system is illustrated in Figure 3. *Data Sources* maintain the exact value V_i of each data object O_i, while *Data Caches* store bounds $[L_i, H_i]$ that are guaranteed to contain the exact values. Source values may appear in multiple caches (with possibly different bounds), and caches may contain bounded values from multiple sources. A user submits a query to the *Query Processor* at a local data cache, along with a precision constraint. To answer the query while guaranteeing the constraint, the query processor may need to send *query-initiated refresh requests* to the *Refresh Monitor* at one or more sources, which responds with new bounds. The Refresh Monitor at each source also keeps track of the bounds for each of its data objects in each relevant cache. (Note that in the network monitoring application we consider in this paper, each source must only keep track of a small number of bounds. In other applications a source may provide a large number of objects to multiple caches, in which case a scalable trigger system would be of great benefit [13].) The Refresh Monitor is responsible for detecting whenever the value of a data object exceeds the bound in some cache, and sending a new bound to the cache (a *value-initiated refresh*).

When the cached bound of a data object is refreshed by its source, some cost is incurred. We consider the general case where each object has its own cost to refresh, although in practice it is likely that the cost of refreshing an object depends only on which source it comes from. (It also may be possible to amortize refresh costs for a set of values, as discussed in Section 8.) These costs are used by our algorithms that choose tuples to refresh in

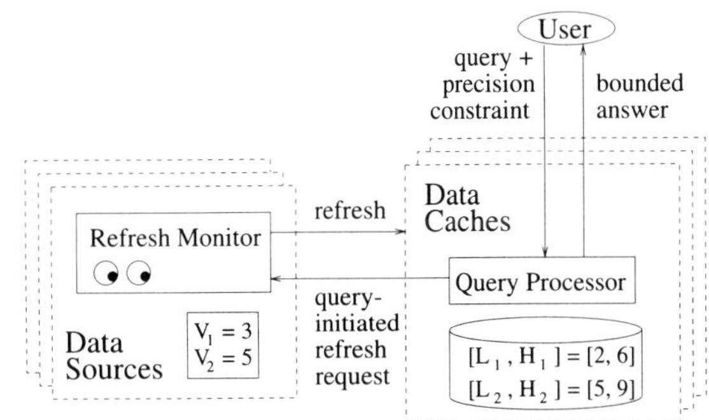

Figure 3: TRAPP system architecture.

order to meet the precision constraint of a query at minimum cost.

The TRAPP architecture as presented in this paper makes some simplifying assumptions. First, although object insertions or deletions do not occur on a regular basis in our example application, insertions and deletions are handled but they must be propagated immediately to all caches. (Section 8.3 discusses how this limitation might be relaxed.) Second, the level of precision offered by our system does not account for elapses of time while sending refresh messages or while processing a single query. We assume that the time to refresh a bound is small enough that the imprecision introduced is insignificant. Furthermore, we assume that value-initiated refreshes do not occur during the time an individual query is being processed. Addressing these issues is a topic for future work as discussed in Section 8.4.

Next, in Section 3.1 we discuss in more detail the mechanics of bounded values and refreshing. Then in Section 3.2 we generalize bound functions to be time-varying functions. In Section 4 we discuss the execution of aggregation queries in the TRAPP/AG system, before presenting our specific optimization algorithms for single-table aggregation queries in Sections 5 and 6. In Section 7 we present some preliminary results for aggregation queries with joins.

3.1 Refreshing Cached Bounds

The master copy of each data object O_i resides at a single source, and for TRAPP/AG we assume it is a single real value, which we denote V_i. Caches store a range of possible values (the *bound*) for each data object, which we denote $[L_i, H_i]$. When a source sends a copy of data object O_i to a cache (a *refresh* event at time $\mathcal{T}_r$), in addition to sending O_i's current precise value, which we denote $V_i(\mathcal{T}_r)$, it sends a bound $[L_i, H_i]$.

As discussed earlier, refreshes occur for one of two reasons. First, if the master value of a data object exceeds its bound stored in some cache (*i.e.*, at current time $\mathcal{T}_c$, $V_i(\mathcal{T}_c) < L_i$ or $V_i(\mathcal{T}_c) > H_i$), then the source is obligated to refresh the cache with the current precise value $V_i(\mathcal{T}_c)$ and a new bound $[L_i, H_i]$—a value-initiated refresh. Second, a query-initiated refresh occurs if a query being executed at a cache requires the current exact value of a data object in order to meet its precision constraint.

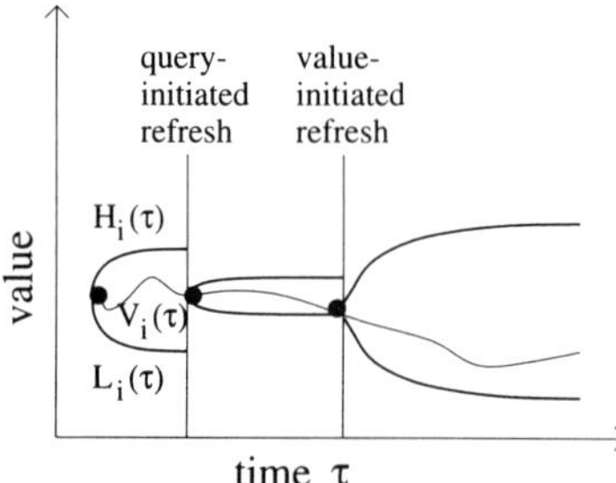

Figure 4: Bound $[L_i(\mathcal{T}), H_i(\mathcal{T})]$ over time, overlaid with precise value $V_i(\mathcal{T})$.

In this case, the source will send $V_i(\mathcal{T}_c)$ along with a new bound to the cache, and the precise value $V_i(\mathcal{T}_c)$ can be used in the query.

3.2 Bounds as Functions of Time

Section 3.1 presented a simple approach where the bound of each data object O_i is a pair of endpoints $[L_i, H_i]$. A more general and accurate approach is to parameterize the bound by time: $[L_i(\mathcal{T}), H_i(\mathcal{T})]$. In other words, the endpoints of the bound are functions of time $\mathcal{T}$. These functions have the property that $L_i(\mathcal{T}_r) = H_i(\mathcal{T}_r) = V_i(\mathcal{T}_r)$, where $\mathcal{T}_r$ is the refresh time. That is, the bound at the time of refresh has zero width and both endpoints equal the current value. As time advances past $\mathcal{T}_r$, the endpoints of the bound diverge from $V_i(\mathcal{T}_r)$ such that the bound contains the precise value at all times $\mathcal{T}_c \geq \mathcal{T}_r$: $L_i(\mathcal{T}_c) \leq V_i(\mathcal{T}_c) \leq H_i(\mathcal{T}_c)$. Eventually, when another refresh occurs, the source sends a new pair of bound functions to the cache that replaces the old pair. Figure 4 illustrates the bound $[L_i(\mathcal{T}), H_i(\mathcal{T})]$ of a data object O_i over time, overlaid with its precise value $V_i(\mathcal{T})$.

All of the subsequent algorithms and results in this paper are independent of how bounds are selected and specified. In fact, in the body of the paper we assume that any time-varying bound functions have been evaluated at the current time $\mathcal{T}_c$, and we write $[L_i, H_i]$ to mean $[L_i(\mathcal{T}_c), H_i(\mathcal{T}_c)]$. Also, we write V_i to mean the exact value at the current time: $V_i(\mathcal{T}_c)$. We have done some preliminary work investigating appropriate bound functions, and have deduced that in the absence of additional information about update behavior, appropriate functions are those that expand according to the square-root of elapsed time. That is: $H_i(\mathcal{T}) - L_i(\mathcal{T}) \propto \sqrt{\mathcal{T} - \mathcal{T}_r}$, where $\mathcal{T}_r$ is the time of the most recent refresh. The proportionality parameter, which determines the width of the bound, is chosen at run-time. The interested reader is referred to [24] for details.

4 Query Execution for Bounded Answers

Executing a TRAPP/AG query with a precision constraint may involve combining precise data stored on remote sources with bounded data stored in a local cache. In this section we describe in general how bounded aggregation queries are executed, and we present a cost model to be used by our algorithms that choose cached data objects to refresh when answering queries. For the remainder of this paper we assume the relational model, although TRAPP/AG can be implemented with any data model that supports aggregation of numerical values.

For now we consider single-table TRAPP/AG queries of the following form. Joins are addressed in Section 7.

```
SELECT  AGGREGATE(T.a) WITHIN R
FROM    T
WHERE   PREDICATE
```

AGGREGATE is one of the standard relational aggregation functions: COUNT, MIN, MAX, SUM, or AVG. PREDICATE is any predicate involving columns of table T and possibly constants. R is a nonnegative real constant specifying the precision constraint, which requires that the bounded answer $[L_A, H_A]$ to the query satisfies $0 \leq H_A - L_A \leq R$. If R is omitted then $R = \infty$ implicitly.

To compute a bounded answer to a query of this form, TRAPP/AG executes several steps:

1. Compute an initial bounded answer based on the current cached bounds and determine if the precision constraint is met. If not:

2. An algorithm CHOOSE_REFRESH examines the cache's copy of table T and chooses a subset of T's tuples T_R to refresh. The source for each tuple in T_R is asked to refresh the cache's copy of that tuple.

3. Once the refreshes are complete, recompute the bounded answer based on the cache's now partially refreshed copy of T.

Our CHOOSE_REFRESH algorithm ensures that the answer after step 3 is guaranteed to satisfy the precision constraint.

Sections 5 and 6 present details based on each specific aggregation function, considering queries with and without selection predicates. For each type of aggregation query we address the following two problems:

- How to compute a bounded answer based on the current cached bounds. This problem corresponds to steps 1 and 3 above.

- How to choose the set of tuples to refresh. This problem corresponds to step 2 above. A CHOOSE_REFRESH algorithm is *optimal* if it finds the cheapest subset T_R of T's tuples to refresh (*i.e.*, the subset with the least total cost) that guarantees the final answer to the query will satisfy the precision constraint for any precise values of the refreshed tuples within the current bounds.

We are assuming that the cost to refresh a set of tuples is the sum of the costs of refreshing each member of the set, in order to keep the optimization problem manageable. This simplification ignores possible amortization due to batching multiple requests to the same source.

Also recall that we assume a separate refresh cost may be assigned to each tuple, although in practice all tuples from the same source may incur the same cost.

Note that the entire set T_R of tuples to refresh is selected before the refreshes actually occur, so the precision constraint must be guaranteed for any possible precise values for the tuples in T_R. A different approach is to refresh tuples one at a time (or one source at a time), computing a bounded answer after each refresh and stopping when the answer is precise enough. See Section 8.2 for further discussion.

5 Aggregation without Selection Predicates

This section specifies how to compute a bounded answer from bounded data values for each type of aggregation function, and describes algorithms for selecting refresh sets for each aggregation function. For now, we assume that any selection predicate in the TRAPP/AG query involves only columns that contain exact values. Thus, in this section we assume that the selection predicate has already been applied and the aggregation is to be computed over the tuples that satisfy the predicate. TRAPP/AG queries with selection predicates involving columns that contain bounded values are covered in Section 6, and joins involving bounded values are discussed in Section 7.

Suppose we want to compute an aggregate over column $T.a$ of a cached table T. The value of $T.a$ for each tuple t_i is stored in the cache as a bound $[L_i, H_i]$. While computing the aggregate, the query processor has the option for each tuple t_i of either reading the cached bound $[L_i, H_i]$ or refreshing t_i to obtain the master value V_i. The cost to refresh t_i is C_i. The final answer to the aggregate is a bound $[L_A, H_A]$.

5.1 Computing MIN with No Selection Predicate

Computing the bounded MIN of $T.a$ is straightforward:

$$[L_A, H_A] = [\min_{t_i \in T}(L_i), \min_{t_i \in T}(H_i)]^1$$

The lowest possible value for the minimum (L_A) occurs if for all $t_i \in T$, $V_i = L_i$, i.e., each value is at the bottom of its bound. Conversely, the highest possible value for the minimum (H_A) occurs if $V_i = H_i$ for all tuples. Returning to our example of Section 1.1, suppose we want to find the minimum bandwidth link along the path $N_1 \rightarrow N_2 \rightarrow N_4 \rightarrow N_5 \rightarrow N_6$, i.e., query $Q1$. Applying the bounded MIN of *bandwidth* to tuples $T = \{1, 2, 5, 6\}$ in Figure 2 yields $[40, 55]$.

Choosing an optimal set of tuples to refresh for a MIN query with a precision constraint is also straightforward, although the algorithm's justification and proof of optimality is nontrivial (see [24]). The CHOOSE_REFRESH$_{\text{NO_SEL/MIN}}$ algorithm chooses T_R to be all tuples $t_i \in T$ such that $L_i <$

$\min_{t_k \in T}(H_k) - R$, where R is the precision constraint, independent of refresh cost. That is, T_R contains all tuples whose lower bound is less than the minimum upper bound minus the precision constraint. If B-tree indexes exist on both the upper and lower bounds[2], the set T_R can be found in time less than $O(|T|)$ by first using the index on upper bounds to find $\min_{t_k \in T}(H_k)$, and then using the index on lower bounds to find tuples that satisfy $L_i < \min_{t_k \in T}(H_k) - R$. Without these two indexes, the running time for CHOOSE_REFRESH$_{\text{NO_SEL/MIN}}$ is $O(|T|)$.

Consider again our example query $Q1$, which finds the minimum bandwidth along path $N_1 \rightarrow N_2 \rightarrow N_4 \rightarrow N_5 \rightarrow N_6$. CHOOSE_REFRESH$_{\text{NO_SEL/MIN}}$ with $R = 10$ would choose to refresh tuple 5, since it is the only tuple among $\{1, 2, 5, 6\}$ whose low value is less than $\min_{t_k \in \{1,2,5,6\}}(H_k) - R = 55 - 10 = 45$. After refreshing, tuple 5's bandwidth value turns out to be 50, so the new bounded answer is $[45, 50]$.

The MAX aggregation function is symmetric to MIN. See [24] for details.

5.2 Computing SUM with No Selection Predicate

To compute the bounded SUM aggregate, we take the sum of the values at each extreme:

$$[L_A, H_A] = [\sum_{t_i \in T} L_i, \sum_{t_i \in T} H_i]$$

The smallest possible sum occurs when all values are as low as possible, and the largest possible sum occurs when all values are as high as possible. In our running example, the bounded SUM of *latency* along the path $N_1 \rightarrow N_2 \rightarrow N_4 \rightarrow N_5 \rightarrow N_6$ (query $Q2$) using the data from Figure 2 is $[19, 28]$.

The problem of selecting an optimal set T_R of tuples to refresh for SUM queries with precision constraints is better attacked as the equivalent problem of selecting the tuples *not* to refresh: $\overline{T_R} = T - T_R$. We first observe that $H_A - L_A = \sum_{t_i \in T} H_i - \sum_{t_i \in T} L_i = \sum_{t_i \in T}(H_i - L_i)$. After refreshing all tuples $t_j \in T_R$, we have $H_j - L_j = 0$, so these values contribute nothing to the bound. Thus, after refresh, $\sum_{t_i \in T}(H_i - L_i) = \sum_{t_i \in \overline{T_R}}(H_i - L_i)$. These equalities combined with the precision constraint $H_A - L_A \leq R$ give us the constraint $\sum_{t_i \in \overline{T_R}}(H_i - L_i) \leq R$. The optimization objective is to satisfy this constraint while minimizing the total cost of the tuples in T_R. Observe that minimizing the total cost of the tuples in T_R is equivalent to maximizing the total cost of the tuples not in T_R. Therefore, the optimization problem can be formulated as choosing $\overline{T_R}$ so as to maximize $\sum_{t_i \in \overline{T_R}} C_i$ under the constraint $\sum_{t_i \in \overline{T_R}}(H_i - L_i) \leq R$.

It turns out that this problem is isomorphic to the well-known *0/1 Knapsack Problem* [8], which can be stated as follows: We are given a set S of items that each have weight W_i and profit P_i, along with a knapsack with capacity M (*i.e.*, it can hold any set of items as long as

---

[1]In this and all subsequent formulas, we define $\min(\emptyset) = +\infty$ and $\max(\emptyset) = -\infty$.

[2]Section 8.3 briefly discusses indexing time-varying range endpoints, a problem on which we are actively working.

their total weight is at most M). The goal of the Knapsack Problem is to choose a subset S_K of the items in S to place in the knapsack that maximizes total profit without exceeding the knapsack's capacity. In other words, choose S_K so as to maximize $\sum_{i \in S_K} P_i$ under the constraint $\sum_{i \in S_K} W_i \leq M$. To state the problem of selecting refresh tuples for bounded SUM queries as the 0/1 Knapsack Problem, we assign $S = T$, $S_K = \overline{T_R}$, $P_i = C_i$, $W_i = (H_i - L_i)$, and $M = R$.

Unfortunately, the 0/1 Knapsack Problem is known to be NP-Complete [10]. Hence all known approaches to solving the problem optimally, such as dynamic programming, have a worst-case exponential running time. Fortunately, an approximation algorithm exists that, in polynomial time, finds a solution having total profit that is within a fraction ϵ of optimal for any $0 < \epsilon < 1$ [17]. The running time of the algorithm is $O(n \cdot \log n) + O((\frac{3}{\epsilon})^2 \cdot n)$. We use this algorithm for CHOOSE_REFRESH$_{\text{NO_SEL/SUM}}$. Adjusting parameter ϵ in the algorithm allows us to trade off the running time of the algorithm against the quality of the solution.

In the special case of uniform costs ($C_i = C_j$ for all tuples t_i and t_j), all knapsack objects have the same profit P_i, and the 0/1 Knapsack Problem has a polynomial algorithm [8]. The optimal answer then can be found by "placing objects in the knapsack" in order of increasing weight W_i until the knapsack cannot hold any more objects. That is, we add tuples to $\overline{T_R}$ starting with the smallest $H_i - L_i$ bounds until the next tuple would cause $\sum_{t_i \in \overline{T_R}}(H_i - L_i) > R$. If an index exists on the bound width $H_i - L_i$ (see Section 8.3), this algorithm can run in sublinear time. Without an index on bound width, the running time of this algorithm is $O(n \cdot \log n)$, where $n = |T|$.

Consider again query *Q2* that asks for the total latency along path $N_1 \rightarrow N_2 \rightarrow N_4 \rightarrow N_5 \rightarrow N_6$. Figure 2 shows the correspondence between our problem and the Knapsack Problem by specifying the knapsack "weight" $W = H - L$ for the *latency* column of each tuple in $\{1, 2, 5, 6\}$. Using the exponential (optimal) knapsack algorithm to find the total latency along path $N_1 \rightarrow N_2 \rightarrow N_4 \rightarrow N_5 \rightarrow N_6$ with $R = 5$, tuples 2 and 5 are "placed in the knapsack" (whose capacity is 5), leaving $T_R = \{1, 6\}$. The bounded SUM of *latency* after refreshing tuples 1 and 6 is [21, 26].

5.2.1 Performance Experiments

CHOOSE_REFRESH$_{\text{NO_SEL/SUM}}$ uses the approximation algorithm from [17] to quickly find a cheap set of tuples T_R to refresh such that the precision constraint is guaranteed to hold. We implemented the algorithm and ran experiments using 90 actual stock prices that varied highly in one day. The high and low values for the day were used as the bounds $[L_i, H_i]$, the closing value was used as the precise value V_i, and the refresh cost C_i for each data object was set to a random number between 1 and 10. Running times were measured on a Sun Ultra-1 Model 140 running SunOS 5.6. In Figure 5 we fix the precision constraint $R = 100$

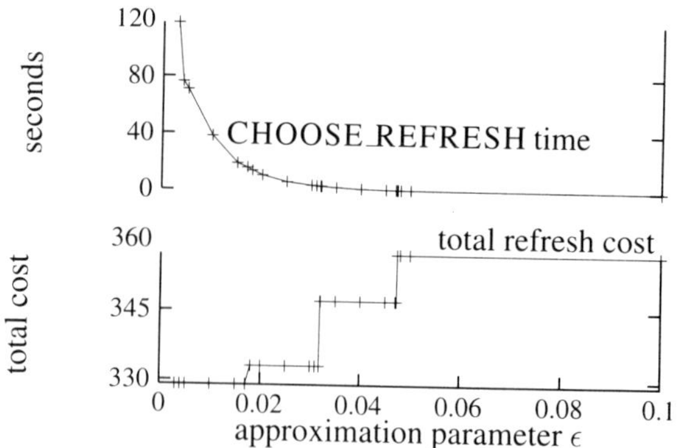

Figure 5: CHOOSE_REFRESH$_{\text{NO_SEL/SUM}}$ time and refresh cost for varying ϵ.

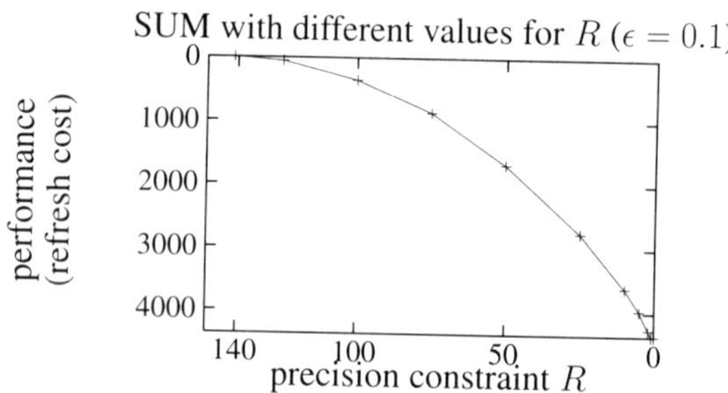

Figure 6: Precision-performance tradeoff for CHOOSE_REFRESH$_{\text{NO_SEL/SUM}}$.

and vary ϵ in the knapsack approximation in order to plot CHOOSE_REFRESH time and total refresh cost of the selected tuples. Smaller values for ϵ increase the CHOOSE_REFRESH time but decrease the refresh cost. However, since the CHOOSE_REFRESH time increases quadratically while the refresh cost only decreases by a small fraction, it is not in general advantageous to set ϵ below 0.1 (which comes very close to optimal) unless refreshing is extremely expensive.

In Figure 6 we fix the approximation parameter $\epsilon = 0.1$ and vary R in order to plot precision (precision constraint R) versus performance (total refresh cost) for our CHOOSE_REFRESH$_{\text{NO_SEL/SUM}}$ algorithm. This graph, a concrete instantiation of Figure 1(b), clearly shows the continuous, monotonically decreasing tradeoff between precision and performance that characterizes TRAPP systems.

5.3 Computing COUNT with No Selection Predicate

When no selection predicate is present, computing COUNT amounts to computing the cardinality of the table. Since we currently require all insertions and deletions to be propagated immediately to the data caches (Section 3), the cardinality of the cached copy of a table is always equal to the cardinality of the master copy, so there is no need for refreshes.

5.4 Computing AVG with No Selection Predicate

When no selection predicate is present, the procedure for computing the AVG aggregate is as follows. First, compute $COUNT$, which as discussed in Section 5.3 is simply the cardinality of the cached T. Then, compute the bounded SUM as described in Section 5.2 with $R = R \cdot COUNT$ to produce $[L_{SUM}, H_{SUM}]$. Finally, let:

$$[L_A, H_A] = [\frac{L_{SUM}}{COUNT}, \frac{H_{SUM}}{COUNT}]$$

Since the bound width $H_A - L_A = \frac{H_{SUM} - L_{SUM}}{COUNT}$, by computing SUM such that $H_{SUM} - L_{SUM} \leq R \cdot COUNT$, we are guaranteeing that $H_A - L_A \leq R$, and the precision constraint is satisfied. The running time is dominated by the running time of the CHOOSE_REFRESH$_{\text{NO_SEL/SUM}}$ algorithm, which is given in Section 5.2.

Consider query *Q3* from Section 1.1 to compute the average traffic level in the entire network, and let precision constraint $R = 10$. We first compute $COUNT = 6$, and then compute SUM with $R = R \cdot COUNT = 10 \cdot 6 = 60$. The column labeled W' in Figure 2 shows the knapsack weight assigned to each tuple based on the cached bounds for *traffic*. Using the optimal Knapsack algorithm, the SUM computation will cause tuples 5 and 6 to be refreshed, resulting in a bounded SUM of $[618, 678]$. Dividing by $COUNT = 6$ gives a bounded AVG of $[103, 113]$.

6 Modifications to Incorporate Selection Predicates

When a selection predicate involving bounded values is present in the query, both computing bounded aggregate results and choosing refresh tuples to meet the precision constraint become more complicated. This section presents modifications to the algorithms in Section 5 to handle single-table aggregation queries with selection predicates. We begin by introducing techniques common to all TRAPP/AG queries with predicates, regardless of which aggregation function is present.

Consider a selection predicate involving at least one column of T that contains bounded values. The system can partition T into three disjoint sets: T^-, $T^?$, and T^+. T^- contains those tuples that cannot possibly satisfy the predicate given current bounded data. T^+ contains tuples that are guaranteed to satisfy the predicate given current bounded data. All other tuples are in $T^?$, meaning that there exist some precise values within the current bounds that will cause the predicate to be satisfied, and other values that will cause the predicate not to be satisfied. The process of classifying tuples into T^-, $T^?$, and T^+ when the selection predicate involves at least one column with bounded values is detailed in [24]. The most interesting aspect is that filters over T that find the tuples in T^+ and $T^?$ can always be expressed as simple predicates over bounded value endpoints, and all of our algorithms for computing bounded answers and choosing tuples to refresh examine only tuples in T^+ and $T^?$. Therefore, the classification can be expressed as SQL queries and optimized by the system, possibly incorporating specialized indexes as discussed in Section 8.3.

For examples in the remainder of this section we refer to Figure 7, which shows the classification for three different predicates over the data from Figure 2, both before and after the exact values are refreshed.

6.1 Computing MIN with a Selection Predicate

When a selection predicate is present, the bounded MIN answer is:

$$[L_A, H_A] = [\min_{t_i \in T^+ \cup T^?} (L_i), \min_{t_i \in T^+} (H_i)]$$

In the "worst case" for L_A, all tuples in $T^?$ satisfy the predicate (*i.e.*, they turn out to be in T^+), so the smallest lower bound of any tuple that might satisfy the predicate forms the lower bound for the answer. In the "worst case" for H_A, tuples in $T^?$ do not satisfy the predicate (*i.e.*, they turn out to be in T^-), so the smallest upper bound of the tuples guaranteed to satisfy the predicate forms the only guaranteed upper bound for the answer. In our running example, consider query *Q4*: find the minimum *traffic* where $(bandwidth > 50) \wedge (latency < 10)$. The result using the data from Figure 2 and classifications from Figure 7 is $[90, 105]$.

CHOOSE_REFRESH$_{\text{MIN}}$ chooses T_R to be exactly the tuples $t_i \in T^+ \cup T^?$ such that $L_i < \min_{t_k \in T^+}(H_k) - R$. This algorithm is essentially the same as CHOOSE_REFRESH$_{\text{NO_SEL/MIN}}$, and is correct and optimal for the same reason (see [24]). The only additional case to consider is that refreshing tuples in $T^?$ may move them into T^-. However, such tuples do not contribute to the actual MIN, and thus do not affect the bound of the answer $[L_A, H_A]$. Hence, the precision constraint is still guaranteed to hold. As with CHOOSE_REFRESH$_{\text{NO_SEL/MIN}}$ the running time for CHOOSE_REFRESH$_{\text{MIN}}$ can be sublinear if B-tree indexes are available on both the upper and lower bounds. Otherwise, the worst-case running time for CHOOSE_REFRESH$_{\text{MIN}}$ is $O(n)$.

For our query *Q4* with precision constraint $R = 10$, CHOOSE_REFRESH$_{\text{MIN}}$ chooses $T_R = \{5, 6\}$, since tuples 5 and 6 may pass the selection predicate and their low values are less than $\min_{t_k \in T^+}(H_k) - R = 105 - 10 = 95$. After refreshing, tuples 5 and 6 turn out not to pass the selection predicate, so the bounded MIN is $[95, 105]$.

The MAX aggregation function is symmetric to MIN. See [24] for details.

6.2 Computing SUM with a Selection Predicate

To compute SUM in the presence of a selection predicate:

$$[L_A, H_A] = [\sum_{\substack{t_i \in T^+}} L_i + \sum_{\substack{t_i \in T^? \\ \wedge L_i < 0}} L_i, \sum_{\substack{t_i \in T^+}} H_i + \sum_{\substack{t_i \in T^? \\ \wedge H_i > 0}} H_i]$$

| | $(bandwidth > 50) \wedge (latency < 10)$ | | $latency > 10$ | | $traffic > 100$ | |
	before refresh	after refresh	before refresh	after refresh	before refresh	after refresh
1	T^+	T^+	T^-	T^-	$T^?$	T^-
2	$T^?$	T^+	T^-	T^-	T^+	T^+
3	T^-	T^-	T^+	T^+	$T^?$	T^+
4	$T^?$	T^+	$T^?$	T^-	T^+	T^+
5	$T^?$	T^-	$T^?$	T^+	$T^?$	T^-
6	$T^?$	T^-	T^-	T^-	$T^?$	T^+

Figure 7: Classification of tuples into T^-, $T^?$, and T^+ for three selection predicates.

The "worst case" for L_A occurs when all and only those tuples in $T^?$ with negative values for L_i satisfy the selection predicate and thus contribute to the result. Similarly, the "worst case" for H_A occurs when only tuples in $T^?$ with positive values for H_i satisfy the predicate.

The CHOOSE_REFRESH$_{SUM}$ algorithm is similar to CHOOSE_REFRESH$_{NO_SEL/SUM}$, which maps the problem to the 0/1 Knapsack Problem (Section 5.2). The following two modifications are required. First, we ignore all tuples $t_i \in T^-$. Second, for tuples $t_i \in T^?$, we set W_i to one of three possible values. If $L_i \geq 0$, let $W_i = H_i - 0 = H_i$. If $H_i \leq 0$, let $W_i = 0 - L_i = -L_i$. Otherwise, let $W_i = (H_i - L_i)$ as before. The idea is that we want to effectively extend the bounds for all tuples in $T^?$ to include 0, since it is possible that these tuples are actually in T^- and thus do not contribute to the SUM (*i.e.*, contribute value 0). In the knapsack formulation, to extend the bounds to 0 we need to adjust the weights as specified above.

6.3 Computing COUNT with a Selection Predicate

The bounded answer to the COUNT aggregation function in the presence of a selection predicate is: $[L_A, H_A] = [|T^+|, |T^+| + |T^?|]$. For example, consider query $Q5$ from Section 1.1 that asks for the number of links that have $latency > 10$. Figure 7 shows the classification of tuples into T^-, $T^?$, and T^+. Since $|T^+| = 1$ and $|T^?| = 2$, the bounded COUNT is $[1, 3]$.

The CHOOSE_REFRESH$_{COUNT}$ algorithm is based on the fact that $H_A - L_A = |T^?|$, and that refreshing a tuple in $T^?$ is guaranteed to remove it from $T^?$. Given these two facts, the optimal CHOOSE_REFRESH$_{COUNT}$ algorithm is to let T_R be the $\lceil |T^?| - R \rceil$ cheapest tuples in $T^?$. Using a B-tree index on cost, this algorithm runs in sublinear time. Otherwise, the worst-case running time for CHOOSE_REFRESH$_{COUNT}$ requires a sort and is $O(n \cdot \log n)$.

Consider again query $Q5$ and suppose $R = 1$. Since $|T^?| = 2$, CHOOSE_REFRESH$_{COUNT}$ selects $T_R = \{5\}$, which is the $\lceil |T^?| - R \rceil = \lceil 2 - 1 \rceil = 1$ cheapest tuple in $T^?$. After updating this tuple (which turns out to be in T^+), the bounded COUNT is $[2, 3]$.

6.4 Computing AVG with a Selection Predicate

6.4.1 Computing the Bounded Answer

Computing the bounded AVG when a predicate is present is somewhat more complicated than computing the other aggregates. With a predicate, COUNT is a bounded value as well as SUM, so it is no longer a simple matter of dividing the endpoints of the SUM bound by the exact COUNT value (as in Section 5.4). To compute the lower bound on AVG, we start by computing the average of the low endpoints of the T^+ bounds, and then average in the low endpoints of the $T^?$ bounds one at a time in increasing order until the point at which the average increases. Computing the upper bound on AVG is the reverse. For example, consider query $Q6$ from Section 1.1 that asks for the average latency for links having $traffic > 100$. To compute the lower bound, we start by averaging the low endpoints of T^+ tuples 2 and 4, and then average in the low endpoints of $T^?$ tuples 1 and then 6 to obtain a lower bound on average latency of 5. We stop at this point since averaging in further $T^?$ tuples would increase the lower bound. This computation is formalized in [24], and has a worst-case running time of $O(n \cdot \log n)$.

A looser bound for AVG can be computed in linear time by first computing SUM as $[L_{SUM}, H_{SUM}]$ and COUNT as $[L_{COUNT}, H_{COUNT}]$ using the algorithms from Sections 6.2 and 6.3, then setting:

$$[L_A, H_A] = [\min(\frac{L_{SUM}}{H_{COUNT}}, \frac{L_{SUM}}{L_{COUNT}}),$$
$$\max(\frac{H_{SUM}}{L_{COUNT}}, \frac{H_{SUM}}{H_{COUNT}})]$$

In our example, $[L_{SUM}, H_{SUM}] = [14, 55]$ and $[L_{COUNT}, H_{COUNT}] = [2, 6]$. Thus, the linear algorithm yields $[2.3, 27.5]$. Notice that this bound is indeed looser than the $[5, 11.3]$ bound achieved by the $O(n \cdot \log n)$ algorithm above.

6.4.2 Choosing Tuples to Refresh

CHOOSE_REFRESH$_{AVG}$ is our most complicated scenario. Details are provided in [24]. Here we give a very brief description.

Our CHOOSE_REFRESH$_{AVG}$ algorithm uses the fact that a loose bound on AVG can be achieved as a function of the bounds for SUM and COUNT, as in the linear algorithm in Section 6.4.1 above. We choose refresh tuples that provide bounds for SUM and COUNT such that the bound for AVG as a function of the bounds for SUM and COUNT meets the precision constraint. This interaction is accomplished by using a modified version of the CHOOSE_REFRESH$_{\text{SUM}}$ algorithm that understands how the choice of refresh tuples for SUM affects the bound for COUNT. This algorithm sets a precision constraint for SUM that takes into account the changing bound for COUNT to guarantee that the overall precision constraint on AVG is met. CHOOSE_REFRESH$_{\text{AVG}}$ preserves the Knapsack Problem structure. Therefore, choosing refresh tuples for AVG can be accomplished by solving the 0/1 Knapsack Problem, and it has the same complexity as CHOOSE_REFRESH$_{\text{NO_SEL/SUM}}$ (see Section 5.2).

In our example query $Q6$ above, if we set $R = 2$ then CHOOSE_REFRESH$_{\text{AVG}}$ chooses a knapsack capacity of $M = 4$ and assigns a weight to each tuple as shown in the column labeled W'' in Figure 2. The knapsack optimally "contains" tuples 2 and 4. After refreshing the other tuples $T_R = \{1, 3, 5, 6\}$, the bounded AVG is $[8, 9]$.

7 Aggregation Queries with Joins

Computing the bounded answer to an aggregation query with a join expression (*i.e.*, with multiple tables in the FROM clause) is no different from doing so with a selection predicate: in most SQL queries, a join is expressed using a selection predicate that compares columns of more than one table. Our method for determining membership of tuples in T^+, $T^?$, and T^- applies to join predicates as well as selection predicates. As before, the classification can be expressed as SQL queries and optimized by the system to use standard join techniques, possibly incorporating specialized indexes as discussed in Section 8.3.

On the other hand, choosing tuples to refresh is significantly more difficult in the presence of joins. First, since there are several "base" tuples contributing to each "aggregation" (joined) tuple, we can choose to refresh any subset of the base tuples. Each subset might shrink the answer bound by a different amount, depending how it affects the T^+, $T^?$, T^- classification combined with its effect on the aggregation column. Second, since each base tuple can potentially contribute to multiple aggregation tuples, refreshing a base tuple for one aggregation tuple can also affect other aggregation tuples. These interactions make the problem quite complex. We have considered various heuristic algorithms that choose tuples to refresh for join queries. Currently, we are investigating the exact complexity of the problem and hope to find an approximation algorithm with a tunable ϵ parameter, as in the approximation algorithm for CHOOSE_REFRESH$_{\text{SUM}}$.

8 Status and Future Work

We have implemented all of the bounded aggregation functions and CHOOSE_REFRESH algorithms presented in this paper, and implementation of the source-cache cooperation discussed in Sections 3.1 and 3.2 is underway. In addition to testing our algorithms in a realistic environment, we plan to study how the choice of bound width (Section 3.2) affects the refresh frequency, and we plan to investigate alternative methods of choosing bound functions.

This paper represents our initial work in TRAPP replication systems, so there are numerous avenues for future work. We divide the future directions into four categories: additional functionality (Section 8.1), choosing tuples to refresh (Section 8.2), improving performance (Section 8.3), and real-time and availability issues (Section 8.4).

8.1 Additional Functionality

- **Expanding the class of aggregation queries we consider.** We want to devise algorithms for other aggregation functions, such as MEDIAN (for which we have preliminary results [9]) and TOP-n. In addition, we would like to extend our results to handle grouping on bounded values, enabling GROUP-BY and COUNT UNIQUE queries. We would also like to handle nested aggregation functions such as MAX(AVG), which requires understanding how the precision of the bounded results of the inner aggregate affects the precision of the outer aggregate.

- **Looking beyond aggregation queries.** We believe that the TRAPP idea can be expanded to encompass other types of relational and non-relational queries having different precision constraints. In our running example (Section 1.1), suppose we wish to find the lowest latency path in the network from node N_i to node N_j. A precision constraint might require that the value corresponding to the answer returned by TRAPP (*i.e.*, the latency of the selected path) is within some distance from the value of the precise best answer.

- **Allowing users to express relative instead of absolute precision constraints.** A relative precision constraint might be expressed as a constant $P \geq 0$ that denotes an absolute precision constraint of $2 \cdot A \cdot P$, where A is the actual answer. The difficulty is that A is not known in advance. Based on the bound on A derived in the first pass from cached data alone, it is possible to find a conservative absolute precision constraint $R \leq 2 \cdot A \cdot P$ to use in our algorithms. However, it might be possible to redesign our algorithms to perform better with relative bounds.

- **Considering probabilistic precision guarantees.** TRAPP systems as defined in this paper improve performance by providing bounded answers, while offering absolute guarantees about precision. As discussed in Section 2, other approaches improve performance by giving probabilistic guarantees about precision. An interesting direction is to combine the two for even better performance: provide bounded answers with probabilistic precision guarantees.

- **Considering applying our TRAPP ideas to *multi-level* replication systems, where each data object resides on one source and there is a hierarchy of data caches.** Refreshes would then occur between a cache and the caches or sources one level below, with a possible cascading effect. A current example of such a scenario is Web caching systems (*e.g.*, *Inktomi Traffic Server* [18]), which reside between Web servers and end-user Web browsers.

- **Extending data visualization techniques to take advantage of TRAPP.** We are currently investigating ways to extend data visualization systems (*e.g.*, [25]) to display images based on bounded data instead of precise data, perhaps by drawing fuzzy regions to indicate uncertainty. A visualization in a TRAPP setting could be modeled as a continuous query in which precision constraints are formulated in the visual domain and upheld by TRAPP.

8.2 Choosing Tuples to Refresh

- **Adapting our CHOOSE_REFRESH algorithms to take refresh batching into account.** If multiple query-initiated refreshes are sent to the same source, the overall cost may be less than the sum of the individual costs. We would like to adapt our CHOOSE_REFRESH algorithms to take into account such cases where refreshing one tuple reduces the cost of refreshing other tuples. In fact, the same adaptation may help us develop CHOOSE_REFRESH algorithms for queries involving join and group-by expressions. In both of these cases, refreshing a tuple for one purpose (one group or joined tuple) may reduce the subsequent cost for another purpose (group or joined tuple).

- **Considering iterative CHOOSE_REFRESH algorithms.** Rather than choosing a set of tuples in advance that guarantees adequate precision regardless of actual exact values, we could refresh tuples iteratively until the precision constraint is met. In addition to developing the alternative suite of algorithms, it will be interesting to investigate in which contexts an iterative method is preferable to the batch method presented in this paper. Also, we could use an iterative method to give bounded aggregation queries an "online" behavior [14], where the user is presented with a bounded answer that gradually refines to become more precise over time. In this scenario, the goal is to shrink the answer bound as fast as possible.

8.3 Improving Performance

- **Delaying the propagation of insertions and deletions to data caches.** We are currently investigating ways in which discrepancies in the number of tuples can be bounded, and the computation of the bounded answer to a query can take into account these bounded discrepancies. Sources will then no longer be forced to send a refresh every time an object is inserted or deleted.

- **Investigating specialized bound functions suitable for update patterns with known properties.** The bound function shape we suggested in this paper (Section 3.2) is based on the assumption that no information about the update pattern is available.

- **Considering ways to amortize refresh costs by *refresh piggybacking* and *pre-refreshing*.** When a (value- or query-initiated) refresh occurs, the source may wish to "piggyback" extra refreshes along with the one requested. These extra refreshes would consist of values that are likely to need refreshing in the near future, *e.g.*, if the precise value is very close to the edge of its bound. The amount of refresh piggybacking to perform would depend on the benefit of doing so versus the added overhead. Additionally, it might be beneficial to perform *pre-refreshing*, by sending unnecessary refreshes when system load is low that may be useful in future processing.

- **Investigating storage, indexing, and query processing issues over bounded values.** We are currently designing and evaluating schemes for indexing bounds that are functions of time with a square-root shape, as discussed in Section 3.2. Also, we plan to weigh the advantages of using functions for bounds versus potential indexing improvements when bounds are constants. We also plan to study ways in which cached data objects stored as pairs of bound functions might be compressed. Without compression, caches must store two values for each data object, and sources must transmit these two values for each tuple being refreshed. Furthermore, the Refresh Monitor at each source must keep track of the bound functions for each remotely cached data object. Compression issues can be addressed without affecting the techniques presented in this paper: our CHOOSE_REFRESH algorithms are independent of which bound functions are used or how they are represented, and we have not yet focused on query processing issues.

8.4 Real-time and Consistency Issues

- **Handling refresh delay.** Since message-passing over a network is not instantaneous, in a value-initiated refresh there is some delay between the time a master value exceeds a cached bound and the time the cache is refreshed. Consequently, a cached bound can be "stale" for a short period of time. One way to avoid this problem is by pre-refreshing a value when it is close to the edge of its bound.

- **Evaluating concurrency control solutions.** If value-initiated refreshes are permitted to occur during the CHOOSE_REFRESH computation or while a query is being evaluated (or in between), the answer could reflect inconsistent data or could fail to satisfy the precision constraint. One solution is to implement multiversion concurrency control [5], which would permit refreshes to occur at any time, while still allowing each in-progress query to read data that was current when the query started.

Acknowledgments

We thank Hector Garcia-Molina, Taher Haveliwala, Rajeev Motwani, and Suresh Venkatasubramanian for useful discussions. We also thank Joe Hellerstein and some anonymous referees for helpful comments on an initial draft. Finally, we thank Sergio Marti for useful discussions about network monitoring.

References

[1] S. Abiteboul, P. Kanellakis, and G. Grahne. On the representation and querying of sets of possible worlds. In *Proceedings of the ACM SIGMOD International Conference on Management of Data*, pages 34–48, San Francisco, California, May 1987.

[2] R. Alonso, D. Barbara, H. Garcia-Molina, and S. Abad. Quasi-copies: Efficient data sharing for information retrieval systems. In *Proceedings of the International Conference on Extending Database Technology*, pages 443–468, Venice, Italy, March 1988.

[3] D. Barbara and H. Garcia-Molina. The Demarcation Protocol: A technique for maintaining linear arithmetic constraints in distributed database systems. In *Proceedings of the International Conference on Extending Database Technology*, pages 373–387, Vienna, Austria, March 1992.

[4] M. Benedikt and L. Libkin. Exact and approximate aggregation in constraint query languages. In *Proceedings of the ACM SIGACT-SIGMOD-SIGART Symposium on Principles of Database Systems*, pages 102–113, Philadelphia, Pennsylvania, May 1999.

[5] P. A. Bernstein, V. Hadzilacos, and N. Goodman. *Concurrency Control and Recovery in Database Systems*. Addison-Wesley, 1987.

[6] A. Brodsky and Y. Kornatzky. The LyriC language: Querying constraint objects. In *Proceedings of the ACM SIGMOD International Conference on Management of Data*, pages 35–46, San Jose, California, May 1995.

[7] A. Brodsky, V. E. Segal, J. Chen, and P. A. Exarkhopoulo. The CCUBE constraint object-oriented database system. In *Proceedings of the ACM SIGMOD International Conference on Management of Data*, pages 577–579, Philadelphia, Pennsylvania, June 1999.

[8] T. H. Cormen, C. E. Leiserson, and R. L. Rivest. *Introduction to Algorithms*. MIT Press, Cambridge, Massachusetts, 1990.

[9] T. Feder, R. Motwani, R. Panigrahy, C. Olston, and J. Widom. Computing the median with uncertainty. In *Proceedings of the 32nd ACM Symposium on Theory of Computing*, Portland, Oregon, May 2000.

[10] M. R. Garey and D. S. Johnson. *Computers and Intractability: A Guide to the Theory of NP-Completeness*. W. H. Freeman and Company, New York, New York, 1979.

[11] P. B. Gibbons and Y. Matias. New sampling-based summary statistics for improving approximate query answers. In *Proceedings of the ACM SIGMOD International Conference on Management of Data*, pages 331–342, Seattle, Washington, June 1998.

[12] J. Gray, P. Helland, P. O'Neil, and D. Shasha. The dangers of replication and a solution. In *Proceedings of the ACM SIGMOD International Conference on Management of Data*, pages 173–182, Montreal, Canada, June 1996.

[13] E. N. Hanson, C. Carnes, L. Huang, M. Konyala, L. Noronha, S. Parthasarathy, J. B. Park, and A. Vernon. Scalable trigger processing. In *Proceedings of the 15th International Conference on Data Engineering*, pages 266–275, Sydney, Austrialia, March 1999.

[14] J. M. Hellerstein, R. Avnur, A. Chou, C. Hidber, C. Olston, V. Raman, T. Roth, and P. Haas. Interactive data analysis with CONTROL. *IEEE Computer*, August 1999.

[15] J. M. Hellerstein and P. J. Haas. Online aggregation. In *Proceedings of the ACM SIGMOD International Conference on Management of Data*, pages 171–182, Tucson, Arizona, May 1997.

[16] Y. Huang, R. Sloan, and O. Wolfson. Divergence caching in client-server architectures. In *Proceedings of the Third International Conference on Parallel and Distributed Information Systems*, pages 131–139, Austin, Texas, September 1994.

[17] O. H. Ibarra and C. E. Kim. Fast approximation algorithms for the knapsack and sum of subset problems. *Journal of the ACM*, 22(4):463–468, October 1975.

[18] Inktomi. Inktomi traffic server, 1999. http://www.inktomi.com/products/network/traffic/product.html.

[19] N. Jukic and S. Vrbsky. Aggregates for approximate query processing. In *Proceedings of ACMSE*, pages 109–116, April 1996.

[20] P. C. Kanellakis, G. M. Kuper, and P. Z. Revesz. Constraint query languages. In *Proceedings of the ACM SIGACT-SIGMOD-SIGART Symposium on Principles of Database Systems*, pages 299–313, Nashville, Tennessee, April 1990.

[21] G. M. Kuper. Aggregation in constraint databases. In *Proceedings of the First Workshop on Principles and Practice of Constraint Programming*, Newport, Rhode Island, April 1993.

[22] J. P. Morgenstein. Computer based management information systems embodying answer accuracy as a user parameter. Ph.D. thesis, U.C. Berkeley Computer Science Division, 1980.

[23] F. Naumann, U. Leser, and J. Freytag. Quality-driven integration of heterogeneous information systems. In *Proceedings of the Twenty-Fifth International Conference on Very Large Data Bases*, Edinburgh, U.K., September 1999.

[24] C. Olston and J. Widom. Offering a precision-performance tradeoff for aggregation queries over replicated data. Technical report, Stanford University Computer Science Department, 2000. http://www-db.stanford.edu/pub/papers/trapp-ag.ps.

[25] C. Olston, A. Woodruff, A. Aiken, M. Chu, V. Ercegovac, M. Lin, M. Spalding, and M. Stonebraker. DataSplash. In *Proceedings of the ACM SIGMOD International Conference on Management of Data*, pages 550–552, Seattle, Washington, June 1998.

[26] V. Poosala and V. Ganti. Fast approximate query answering using precomputed statistics. In *Proceedings of the IEEE International Conference on Data Engineering*, page 252, Sydney, Australia, March 1999.

[27] R. L. Read, D. S. Fussell, and A. Silberschatz. A multi-resolution relational data model. In *Proceedings of the Eighteenth International Conference on Very Large Data Bases*, pages 139–150, Vancouver, Canada, August 1992.

[28] E. A. Rundensteiner and L. Bic. Aggregates in possibilistic databases. In *Proceedings of the Fifteenth International Conference on Very Large Data Bases*, pages 287–295, Amsterdam, The Netherlands, August 1989.

[29] O. Wolfson, B. Xu, S. Chamberlain, and L. Jiang. Moving objects databases: Issues and solutions. In *Proceedings of the Tenth International Conference on Scientific and Statistical Database Management*, pages 111–122, Capri, Italy, July 1998.

Manipulating Interpolated Data
is Easier than You Thought

Stéphane Grumbach   Philippe Rigaux   Luc Segoufin

INRIA   CNAM   INRIA

Abstract

Data defined by interpolation is frequently found in new applications involving geographical entities, moving objects, or spatio-temporal data. These data lead to potentially infinite collections of items, (e.g., the elevation of any point in a map), whose definitions are based on the association of a collection of samples with an interpolation function. The naive manipulation of the data through direct access to both the samples and the interpolation functions leads to cumbersome or inaccurate queries. It is desirable to hide the samples and the interpolation functions from the logical level, while their manipulation is performed automatically.

We propose to model such data using infinite relations (e.g., the map with elevation yields an infinite ternary relation) which can be manipulated through standard relational query languages (e.g., SQL), with no mention of the interpolated definition. The clear separation between logical and physical levels ensures the accuracy and the simplicity of data manipulation. Moreover, we show that the evaluation of queries, which includes the computation of the sampling collections and the interpolation functions of the output, can be done very efficiently. The algorithms operating at the physical level are described.

Proceedings of the 26th VLDB Conference, Cairo, Egypt, 2000.

1 Introduction

The extension of database technology to handle spatial applications raises complex problems related to the modeling of data. One of the difficulties pertains to the logical representation of pointsets allowing user-friendly queries while guaranteeing reasonable complexity for query processing.

In the context of spatial databases, most of the efforts in the last decade has been devoted to 2-dimensional data. The recent emergence of new applications, involving for instance *mobile objects*, *Digital Elevation Models* (DEM), or *spatio-temporal* information, requires the representation of data in a space of higher dimension, and constitutes a new challenge to spatial database modeling.

Mobile objects and DEMs constitute excellent examples of a specific type of spatial data defined by interpolation. Interpolated data are either stored explicitly in the database, or computed from the stored data by applying some interpolation function. The trajectory of objects whose position depends upon time is commonly represented by a sample of points with time and position. The full trajectory can be recovered from these points using linear interpolation. Similarly, DEMs provide, at each point (x, y) of the earth surface, the value of a variable h, typically the height above sea level. It can be represented as a finite set of points P along with their elevation. An interpolation based on some triangulation of P gives the value of h at any location.

Many applications require the manipulation of interpolated data: traffic monitoring, intelligent navigation, mobile communication, as well as earth sciences such as geography, meteorology and geology. Consider an application which tracks the motion of aircrafts in a given area. Typical queries are: "retrieve the aircrafts which are in this region", "show the aircrafts which will be in the same region at the same time", "give the altitude of each aircraft with respect to ground or sea level, as well as its position", etc. These queries address simultaneously several kinds of multidimensional information (space, time, altitude), and existing query languages such as SQL seem at first completely inadequate.

The main contribution of the paper is the design of a data model for interpolated data, based on infinite relations manipulated by standard relational means, which meets the classical requirements of logical database modeling: (i) abstract representation independent from the physical storage, (ii) user-friendly query language, and (iii) reasonable complexity of query evaluation. An important aspect of the model is that the queries (including the examples given above) can be expressed with SQL, and evaluated by an algorithm which relies on a few simple geometric primitives.

One of the main aims of the paper is to demonstrate that it is neither desirable nor necessary to give access to the samples and the interpolation functions to the user for data manipulation purposes. As we show this might indeed lead not only to cumbersome queries, where for instance new samples need to be defined, but more importantly, to inaccurate queries, producing wrong output due to wrong interpolations. There is a need for a clear separation between the logical and the physical levels, to which the samples and the interpolation should be relegated.

To satisfy this requirement, we suggest to extend the relational data model to *abstract* infinite relations, containing all the points in the extension of objects, whether stored explicitly as samples, or computed by interpolation. This framework offers sound modeling of interpolated data. For instance, at this abstract level, the interpolation can be formalized with classical dependencies. The base domain (e.g., space for DEMs, and time for moving objects) is the *key* of an interpolated relation, and there is a functional dependency from the key to the interpolated variables. Moreover, any relational query language can be used to query the database. This defines a very simple interface to the end-user, who does not need to worry about complex data structures or geometric algorithms. A simple data format is introduced to represent the abstract relations at the physical level.

The second fundamental issue is efficient query evaluation. It is well known that the complexity of operations on geometric objects increases dramatically with their dimension [6], and that dimension 2 is the most reasonable for practical purposes. Since interpolated data is described in a d-dimensional space, with an arbitrary d, this raises potentially the problem of expensive manipulation of d-dimensional objects.

Fortunately, interpolated data constitutes a very specific type of object. For instance, a trajectory can be viewed as a 1-dimensional pointset embedded in 4D-space, and a DEM as a 2D pointset in 3D space. More generally, if k is the dimension of the base domain (*space*, *time*, etc.), an interpolated pointset with $d - k$ interpolated attributes can be viewed as a k-dimensional object embedded in a d-dimensional space. The intuition of our technique is that one should be able to evaluate queries with geometric algorithms that operate in dimension k, and not in dimension d.

Our second contribution is to identify a class of queries which can be evaluated over interpolated data with a base of dimension at most 2, using efficient 2D geometric algorithms. This shows that it is possible to manipulate efficiently complex data of higher dimension, without specifying how it should be interpolated, and using standard techniques (geometric algorithms, relational optimization, etc.).

Related work

Interpolated data has been little studied in the database literature. In the area of data modeling, [12] proposes to integrate external interpolation procedures in the SQL language, and to introduce additional clauses to specify new samples. We shall review this approach in Section 2. To the best of our knowledge, no other work aims at integrating in a uniform data model all kinds of interpolated data. However the area of *DEM* is well-established in computational geometry and Geographic Information Systems (GIS) [18]. DEM are used to represent natural phenomena which are continuously variable (temperature, pressure, slope, etc).

Recently the management of mobile objects has received much attention (see for instance the European ChoroChronos Project [5]). The MOST (Moving Objects Spatio-Temporal) model, presented in [16], relies on the concept of *dynamic attributes* which encapsulate motion information (speed + direction) of a mobile object. A prototype, DOMINO [19], has been implemented to test the capabilities of MOST.

An alternative approach is to consider mobile objects as geometric objects embedded in a high-dimensional space, and to specify the appropriate data types and operations [2, 4]. This extends the traditional approach of adding new types to handle geo-referenced objects. In the area of constraint databases [8], some works address the modeling of spatio-temporal data [7, 1]. Relevant research concerns indexing of mobile objects [9, 17, 14] and uncertainty of spatiotemporal information [10, 13].

We investigated the functionalities of some commercial systems regarding the manipulation of interpolated data. Object-relational database systems such as Oracle8 [15] or PostgreSQL [11] provide spatial types (lines, polygons). This clearly relates to the *entity-oriented* modeling of space which focuses on separate entities (parcels, roads, etc), whereas we are rather interested in phenomena that are continuously variable. In geographic applications, this is referred to as *field-oriented* data [20]. To the best of our knowledge, there is currently no support for such data in object-

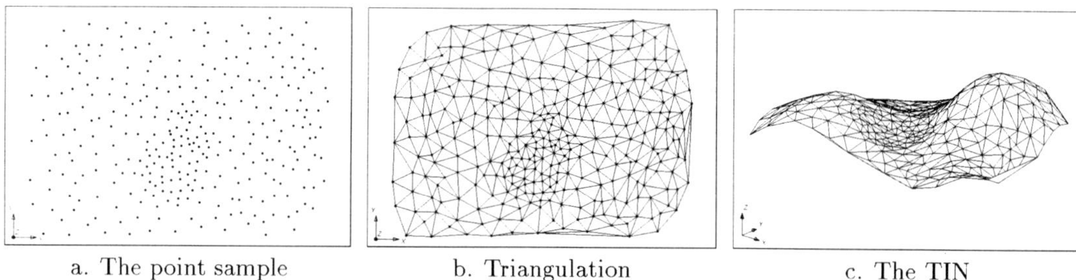

a. The point sample   b. Triangulation   c. The TIN

Figure 1: Triangulated Irregular Network

relational databases.

Regarding commercial GIS, there exists a module (ArcTin) dedicated to the management of DEM in the Arc/Info [3] software. It is possible, through a specific set of commands, to combine elevation data with classical maps. However the user needs to be aware of the physical representation in order to apply the proper operations. The Arc/View product proposes a simpler language, *Avenue*, to create scripts that call spatial operations provided by the core. As in Arc/Info, there is no high level query language.

In contrast, the present paper proposes a quite simple logical model which hides to the end user the internal representation of data and the operations which must be applied to this representation to evaluate a query. In addition, the data model integrates naturally mobile objects with spatial data, and constitutes an innovative approach to the modeling of multi-dimensional applications.

The remainder of the paper is organized as follows. Section 2 presents the general issues related to the modeling of interpolated data. We demonstrate the need for a logical level and describe a generalized relational framework. The algorithms are described in Section 3 together with some practically motivated restrictions of the model. Various extensions of this work are presented in the conclusion.

2 Interpolated data modeling

In this section, we consider different approaches to modeling interpolated data, and their impact on the way queries can be expressed.

2.1 Interpolated data

A *Digital Elevation Model* (DEM) is defined as a continuous function in two (argument) variables, that, for convenience, we shall denote x and y, while h denotes the result of the function. The most common example of a DEM is the elevation (i.e., the height above the sea level), but the model is relevant for any location-dependent attribute (e.g., precipitation, temperature, pollution, etc.).

DEM's are generally based on a finite collection of sample values, from which other values are obtained by interpolation. There are various ways to define the interpolation, which mostly depend on the sampling policy. The most interesting is obtained by *triangulated irregular networks*, TIN's.

A TIN is based on a triangular partition of the space with no assumption on the distribution and position of the vertices of the triangles. The elevation value is recorded at each vertex, and inferred at any point P by linear interpolation of the three vertices of the triangle that contains P (see Figure 1).

Another category of examples originates in spatio-temporal applications with phenomena depending upon time. The trajectory of a moving object shares some fundamental common properties with the previous example. A trajectory can be seen as a triple of functions (f_x, f_y, f_a) from the time t to x, y and a respectively, where a denotes the altitude. A finite representation can be supported by a set of positions $P_i(x, y, a, t)$. The position at any time t can then be approximated by interpolating the two nearest positions.

So the data we consider are represented by:

- A finite collection of sample points, with their associated value;

- An interpolation function.

The manipulation of such data is a priori not easy. Indeed, it imposes to reconstruct the input data needed by interpolation, but also and more importantly to generate the way the output is itself interpolated. Neugebauer proposes in [12] to integrate external interpolation procedures in the SQL language. The syntax of SQL is extended with (i) aggregate functions, and (ii) so-called "table functions", with the nesting of queries in the **from** clause. Interpolated and non-interpolated data are logically modeled differently, and the user has to manage the interpolation.

Consider the example of a cross-section of a TIN with, say, the plane defined by the equation $x = 50$. We assume that a TIN is represented by a relation *Elevation* which contains a collection of triplets (x, y, h), and an interpolation function *my-function*. The syntax of [12] leads to a query of the type:

158

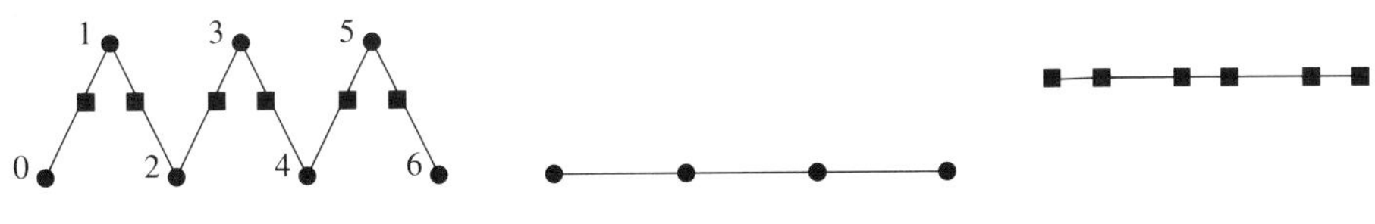

a. The initial sample   b. A sample on even points   c. A sample on middle points

Figure 2: Erroneous samples and interpolation functions

```
select    y, h
from      Elevation by method my–function(h)
              entry (x=50, y= 200)
              step (0, 10)
where     y <= 500
```

The query corresponds to an operation which can be decomposed in two steps. First the user specifies an *output sample*, i.e., a collection of points where the elevation value is required. This is done with the clause **entry** which defines the starting point, the clause **step** which gives the distance for x and y between two consecutively generated points and the clause **where** which gives a bound for y. In summary, these clauses define a set S of 31 points along the segment $[(50, 200), (50, 500)]$.

In the second step a user-defined interpolation function is applied to the input sample in order to get the elevation value at each point of the output sample. This is done with the clause **by method** which specifies the interpolation function *my-function*.

The explicit specification of the interpolation mechanism in the query syntax raises technical problems. The most important one is the dichotomy between the sampling and the interpolation. First it is the responsibility of the user to associate an interpolation function to a sample stored in the database, and second the result consists of a user-defined sample of points, without any associated interpolation function. The distinct manipulation of a sample and its interpolation function might contradict the proper semantics of the data resulting from the integration of the two components.

This may lead to erroneous results and computation. Consider again the cross section of a TIN according to a new user-defined sample of points and the usual linear interpolation function f. The original data is shown in Figure 2.a. In Figure 2.b, the sampling defined by the user returns the even points of the input sample, using the functions f one obtains a flat line which ignores all the mountains. Again Figure 2.c illustrates a bad choice of output sample: by considering only the middle points in each slope, one obtains a result which is not representative either of the actual data.

Although this can be considered as extreme cases, these examples illustrate how a wrong specification of samples and interpolation is likely to result in an important loss of information. Moreover, the output sample must be guaranteed to be finite, and it is preferable not to leave this responsibility to the user. If we forget the **where** clause in the above SQL query, the execution will generate an infinite sample of points.

The specification of the samples and the choice of the interpolation functions should be made during the data acquisition phase. It has an impact on the precision of the data stored in the database. We show that for relational queries, the system can completely handle the samples and the interpolation, and it is preferable to prevent the user from having to take care of the *correctness* of the specifications.

An immediate consequence is that the system should be able to perform the necessary tasks by itself. In particular, it should generate the appropriate output sample supporting the correct representation of the result, and build this result by exploiting properly the interpolation over the input sample(s). This should be managed in a systematic way by maintaining a strong integration of the elements that constitute the semantics of an interpolated dataset: the sample and the interpolation function.

2.2 Abstract modeling

We show how data modeling can be achieved in respect of these principles with the *abstract data model*. It consists simply in the classical relational model with infinite relations instead of finite relations.

Let us give formal definitions. We consider the universe $\mathbb{R}$ of real numbers. A *(database) schema s* is a finite set of relation symbols together with their arity. An *instance I* of s is an interpretation of the relation symbols by relations of the corresponding arity over $\mathbb{R}$. A *query* is a mapping from instances to relations.

In the abstract model, a DEM will be modeled as an infinite ternary relation, with attributes x, y, h, in which for each tuple over x, y, there is a unique value for h. Similarly, a trajectory is modeled as an infinite 4-ary relation, with attributes t, x, y, a, in which for each value of t, there is a unique value for x, y, a. In both cases we have infinite relations satisfying a functional dependency. We will see the importance of these dependencies in Section 3.

Standard relational query languages can be used to query infinite relations, such as relational algebra or SQL. Assume now that the *Elevation* relation is an infinite set of ternary tuples. The cross-section query

159

discussed above can be simply expressed as follows.

```
select    y, h
from      Elevation
where     200 ⩽ y ⩽ 500
and       x= 50
```

Note that neither the collection of samples nor the interpolation function are visible. They are hidden inside the data. This presents numerous advantages.

- **Correctness** The answer to the query is correct since the user cannot use inaccurate samples, or a wrong interpolation function.

- **User-friendliness** It allows the use of standard query languages, with the usual operations (join, intersection, selection, etc.) and a clear meaning. Moreover, no need to worry about samples and interpolation.

- **Safety** The answer to a query can be infinite. The fact that it can be represented by interpolation over a finite collection of samples is considered in the next section.

- **Uniformity** Relations are all dealt with uniformly, whether finite or infinite, interpolated or not.

We next present several examples of queries, expressed in SQL, which combine the various types of relations in the schema. It is not relevant whether a relation is finite or interpolated. The database can be queried in a purely declarative way. We consider a database schema with the following relations.

- A map $Map(x, y, name)$ which gives (attribute $name$) the ground occupancy ('forest', 'pasture', etc.) at location (x, y). The key is (x, y).

- The trajectory of an aircraft, $Traj(t, x, y, a)$, a being the altitude with respect to the sea level at each time t. The key is t.

- A TIN, $TIN(x, y, h)$ for the height above the sea level. The key is (x, y).

1. Give the altitude and location of the aircraft at time $t1$.

   ```
   select  x, y, a from Traj where t = 't1'
   ```

2. Show the trajectory of the aircraft with the altitude above the ground at each point:

   ```
   select    t, t1.x, t1.y, a - h
   from      TIN t1, Traj t2
   where     t1.x = t2.x and t1.y = t2.y
   ```

3. Show the forests between 1000 and 2000m.

   ```
   select    t.x, t.y
   from      TIN t, Map m
   where     t.x = m.x and t.y = m.y
   and       1000 ⩽ h ⩽ 2000
   and       name = 'forest'
   ```

4. Show the parts of the trajectory where the aircraft was above the sea, and higher than 10000m.

   ```
   select    l.x, l.y, l.t
   from      Traj l, Map m
   where     m.x = l.x and m.y = l.y
   and       name = 'sea'
   and       a > 10000
   ```

These queries are very simple to express, in particular because there is no need to think about the internal machinery (interpolation functions or samples). Designing a query just involves viewing the data as infinite relations. This offers a good logical interface to the user's need.

During the evaluation phase, the system must translate automatically a query into operations on the physical storage. Infinite relations need to be encoded in some finite way to be effectively manipulated. The last aspect of the data model is thus a data format which supports the representation of interpolated relations.

2.3 Data format

We distinguish two levels of representation of the data. The *abstract level*, presented above, aims at keeping the essential features of the relational paradigm. The *physical level* supports the finite representation of interpolated relations, and specialized algorithms on this representation.

The finite representation is a compact encoding of all the information pertaining to an interpolated relation, namely the sample and the interpolation function. We first take the example of a TIN. Let $\{T^i \mid i \in [1, n]\}$ be a partition of the plane into finitely many triangles T^i. Inside each triangle T^i, the elevation h can be computed by a linear interpolation from the heights of the three vertices of T^i. In other words, for all points p in T^i we have $h = f_h^i(p)$ where f_h^i is a linear function depending only upon i. Let $t^i(x, y)$ be the Boolean predicate which returns true iff the point (x, y) belongs to T^i. The TIN is symbolically represented by the collection $\{t^i, f_h^i \mid i \in [1, n]\}$ such that:

$$TIN = \{(x, y, h) \mid t^i(x, y) \land h = f_h^i(x, y)\}, \ i \in [1, n]\}$$

The trajectory of a moving object can be represented in a similar way. The position of the object is recorded at finitely many time points. This leads to finitely many time intervals T^i. The speed of the object is assumed to be constant in each interval. The coordinates of its position at time t are defined by $x = u^i t + x^i$, $y = v^i t + y^i$ and $a = w^i t + a^i$, where i is the index of the interval T^i which contains t, and u^i, v^i, w^i the respective speeds on the axis of the object during that interval. The trajectory $Traj(x, y, a, t)$ can thus be symbolically represented by the collection $\{t^i, f_x^i, f_y^i, f_a^i \mid i \in [1, n]\}$ such that:

$$Traj = \{(x, y, a, t) \mid t^i(t) \wedge x = f_x^i(t) \wedge y = f_y^i(t)$$
$$\wedge\, a = f_a^i(t), \; i \in [1, n]\}$$

where $t^i(t)$ is a predicate which is true iff t is in the time interval T^i and where f_x^i, f_y^i and f_a^i are respectively the linear functions $u^i t + x^i$, $v^i t + y^i$ and $w^i t + a^i$.

More generally, let $R(\overline{k_1, \ldots k_p}, h_1, \ldots h_q)$ be an interpolated relation with key $\{k_1, \ldots k_p\}$ and interpolated attributes $\{h_1, \ldots h_q\}$. We use the following terminology: p is the *interpolation dimension*, $p + q$ the *global dimension* and the *key-space* is the p-dimensional space over the variables $\{k_1, \ldots k_p\}$.

Definition 1 *The finite description of R relies on the following components:*

1. *A partition $\{c^i, i \in [1, n]\}$ of $\pi_{k_1, \ldots k_p}(R)$ in cells.*

2. *A set $f_{h_j}^i, i \in [1, n], j \in [1, q]$ of linear functions. Each $f_{h_j}^i$ is defined only on the cell c^i and gives the value of h_j.*

R *is represented as a collection of elements $\langle c^i; f_{h_1}^i, \ldots f_{h_q}^i \rangle$, denoted* blocks.

The relations TIN and $Traj$ described above admit such a representation.

3 Query evaluation

This section is devoted to the evaluation of relational queries on interpolated relations. The main characteristics of the techniques, which allow to compute relational operators on the data format, relies on (complex) geometric computation applied to the convex *cells* of the interpolated relations, followed by (simple) propagation to the other attributes using the interpolation function.

As shown in [18], this principle is verified for many classical operations on interpolated data, such as intersection and difference of TIN's, cross-section of TIN's, window and point queries on TIN's, which require only algorithms for data of the interpolation dimension (generally 2). This suggests that the set of interpolated objects defines a subclass which does not need the full power of geometric computation in the global dimension.

The operations on TIN's mentioned above are easily expressed with a relational query on the abstract relations. If we consider these operations one by one, one can easily find an evaluation strategy which is optimal. We design a general strategy which guarantees that queries are evaluated with geometric operators in low-dimensional spaces.

In fact we need to ensure both reasonable evaluation complexity and query closure. The first requirement implies working on databases consisting of interpolated relations with the interpolation dimension bounded by 2. Indeed, the time complexity of manipulating objects in dimension 2 is low, and the algorithms are rather simple to implement. To this end we require that the keys k_i and k_j of two distinct relations are *orthogonal*, that is either $k_i \subseteq k_j$ or $k_i \cap k_j = \emptyset$. The second requirement of query closure means that queries should deliver interpolated relations. In order to achieve this, we need to restrict the relational queries considered. First we concentrate on conjunctive queries to avoid negation. Second we require that the key of the output relation is a key of some of the input relations. We call *key-restricted* such queries. This is fundamental for the computation which aims at preserving the functional dependencies, and needs to identify the key during the query evaluation process.

In summary, we study the evaluation of conjunctive queries mapping an interpolated database to an interpolated relation, such that the interpolation is always based on one of the well-identified key-spaces of the input schema. Typically these key-spaces will be *space*, *time*, etc. Consequently, the evaluation of queries can be reduced to some operation on the key attributes, followed by an easy propagation to the interpolated attributes via the proper linear interpolation function.

The algorithms relies on a small set of primitives which operate on the *cells* of the *key-space*, and the geometric part of query evaluation is reduced to these primitives. The list of primitives is given below.

1. **Projection**, $proj_v(c)$, projects the cell c on the variable v.

2. **Intersection**, $inter(c_1, c_2)$, computes the cell corresponding to the intersection of c_1 and c_2.

3. **Range**, $range(c, f)$, for any linear function f and convex cell c, computes the interval $[f_{min}, f_{max}]$, image of c by f.

In dimension 2, these primitives enjoy a very low time complexity (and can be found in most systems handling spatial data). For instance, it suffices to scan the n vertices of a convex polygon to compute $proj$ and *range*. The intersection of convex sets in dimension 2 is an easy task, since several simple algorithms compute the intersection of convex polygons in $O(n)$ [6]. Now, the algorithms exploit the interpolated form of the data in order to organize the evaluation as a combination of these primitives.

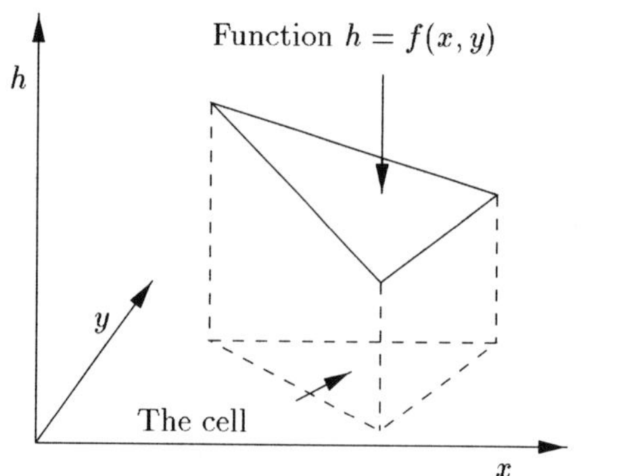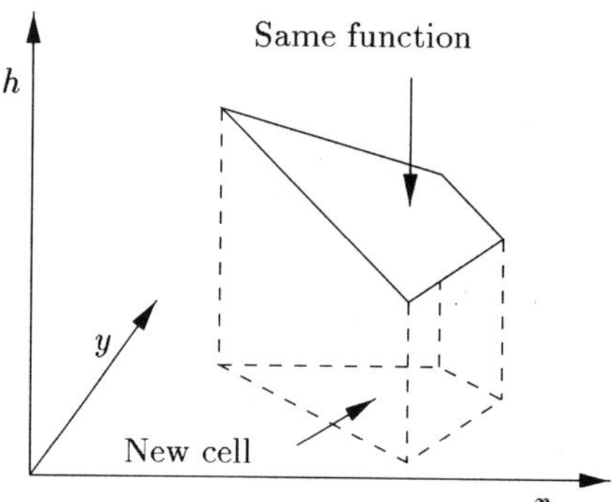

Figure 3: Evaluation of $q = \sigma_{\alpha_x x + \alpha_y y + \alpha_h h = \beta}(TIN)$

We illustrate this intuition with several examples. They are all based on a simple schema with two relations: $TIN(x, y, h)$ which gives the height above the sea, and $Traj(t, x, y, a)$ which describes the trajectory of an aircraft, x, y being the usual variables related to the 2D-space, and a the altitude (w.r.t the sea level). The keys are (x, y) for the relation TIN and t for the relation $Traj$, all the other attributes being interpolated from their respective key.

Selection

The following example illustrates how the selection can be done efficiently by substitution techniques.

Example 1 Consider the query q with the selection $q = \sigma_{\alpha_x x + \alpha_y y + \alpha_h h = \beta}(TIN)$. This computes the part of the TIN which is contained in a sub-space H defined by $\alpha_x x + \alpha_y y + \alpha_h h = \beta$, an operation which a priori involves a 3D object. Let s be one of the blocks of TIN, represented by

$$\langle c^s ; f_h^s \rangle$$

where c^s is the cell (triangle) in the key-space corresponding to the block s and f_h^s the linear function interpolating h on c^s.

Selecting the points of the object represented by s which are *also* in H can be achieved by considering those points in H such that $h = f_h^s(x, y)$. One can thus substitute h by $f_h^s(x, y)$ in the equation of H. This defines a new object H^s as the set of points (x, y) which satisfies $\alpha_x x + \alpha_y y + \alpha_h f_h^s(x, y) = \beta$: a convex object in the 2D key-space.

Finally, the selection is performed by an iteration on the set of blocks which performs at each step the operation $inter(c^s, H^s)$ and returns the block:

$$\langle inter(c^s, H^s) ; f_h^s \rangle$$

The interpolation function remains unchanged, while an intersection is computed upon the key attributes x and y with the $inter$ primitive.

This is depicted in Figure 3. A block s can be seen as consisting of two parts: first a cell $c(x, y)$ in the 2D space defining a "cylinder" in the 3D space, second this cylinder is "cut" by a hyperplane (the function $h = f(x, y)$). Whenever a selection is performed, it suffices to evaluate the operation on the cell. For instance the selection $\sigma_{\alpha_x x + \alpha_y y + \alpha_h h = \beta}(s)$ defines a new object s' as a restriction of the initial convex polygon. This yields a new cylinder, cut by the *same* function f. $\square$

We denote as σ^{subst} this operation. It illustrates a simple substitution technique, based on the interpolation function, which reduces the 3D operation of a selection into a primitive applied to the cells.

Join

We now examine the techniques for more involved queries featuring selection, join and projection. We start with an example of a join which can be processed using substitution techniques similar to the previous example.

Example 2 Consider a query giving the values of t, x and y when the aircraft was over a ground with altitude over 1000. The output key is t.

select	t, Traj.x, Traj.y
from	TIN, Traj
where	h $\geqslant$ 1000
and	TIN.x = Traj.x **and** TIN.y = Traj.y

The algebraic expression is

$$\pi_{t,x,y}(Traj \bowtie \sigma_{h \geqslant 1000}(TIN))$$

First the selection can be evaluated with σ^{subst}, as before. The query involves then a join which delivers pairs of blocks $[r, s]$, from TIN and $Traj$ respectively, of the following form:

$$(r) \qquad \langle c^r(x, y) ; h = f_h^r(x, y) \rangle$$

$$(s) \qquad \langle d^s(t) ; x = g_x^s(t), y = g_y^s(t), a = g_a^s(t) \rangle$$

where c^r and d^s are respectively a triangle in the space (x, y) and a time interval. It is possible to drop out the terms $h = f_h^r(x, y)$ and $a = g_a^s(t)$, which do not play a role in the query anymore. The join operation creates then structures, associating blocks, of the form:

$$[c^r(x, y) \; ; \; d^s(t) \; ; \; x = g_x^s(t) \; , \; y = g_y^s(t)]$$

The join can be evaluated by first performing a general substitution that replaces the variables x and y according to their interpolated definition. One obtains structures of the form:

$$[d^s(t) \; ; \; c^r(g_x^s(t), g_y^s(t)) \; ; \; x = g_x^s(t) \; , \; y = g_y^s(t)]$$

By computing $d' = inter(d^s(t), c^r(g_x^s(t), g_y^s(t)))$, one gets the result of the join as a block in the appropriate format $\langle d'(t); x = g_x^s(t), y = g_y^s(t) \rangle$. Note that the interpolation functions for x and y remain unchanged. $\qquad\square$

So far we have simply exploited the functional dependencies to perform substitutions. We develop a more involved example of application of the substitution mechanism within the next example.

Example 3 Consider the query computing the ground level under the trajectory of the aircraft. One obtains a *profile curvature* which gives the altitude of the ground at each point of the polyline on $[x, y]$. The query is:

select   TIN.x, TIN.y, h
from   TIN , Traj
and   TIN.x= Traj.x **and** TIN.y = Traj.y

The algebraic expression is $\pi_{x,y,h}(TIN \bowtie Traj)$. The query is very similar to the previous one, but the final key is $[x, y]$. We therefore need to rewrite the intermediate structure associating blocks using the dependency functions in order to get the appropriate key. As in the previous example the intermediate structure has the following representation:

$$[c(x, y) \; ; \; h = f_h(x, y) \; ; \; d(t) \; ; \; x = g_x(t) \; , \; y = g_y(t)]$$

All the information pertaining to t is an interval $d \equiv t_{min} \leqslant t \leqslant t_{max}$ and two functions $x = g_x(t)$ and $y = g_y(t)$. These functions[1] can be put in the form $t = g_x^{-1}(x)$ and $t = g_y^{-1}(y)$, and this allows to rewrite the system as follows:

$$[c(x, y) \; ; \; t_{min} \leqslant g_y^{-1}(y) \leqslant t_{max} \; ;$$
$$g_x^{-1}(x) = g_y^{-1}(y) \; ; \; h = f_h(x, y) \; ; \; t = g_y^{-1}(y)]$$

---

[1] Throughout this presentation, we assume that no degenerate case occurs. In particular, a linear function can be inverted, and two distinct functions are assumed to be linearly independent.

The representation $t_{min} \leqslant g_y^{-1}(y) \leqslant t_{max} \; ; \; g_x^{-1}(x) = g_y^{-1}(y)$ describes a segment *seg* in the 2D space. In order to get the correct result of the join in the right data format it suffices to compute $inter(c, seg)$. Finally one removes the last term $(t = g_y^{-1}(y))$ to complete the projection. $\qquad\square$

We can now explain the general computation required for a join operation. It should be noted that *any* join involving two interpolated relations can be reduced to a join involving the key-spaces. Indeed, we can substitute, in each block, any interpolated variable by the proper function on the key. So, during a join $R_1 \bowtie R_2$, the computation is based on intermediate structures of the form:

$$[c^r(x, y) \; ; \; c^s(u, v) \; ; \; f_1, \cdots, f_n]$$

where $c^r(x, y)$ and $c^s(u, v)$ are cells from respectively R_1 and R_2, and the f_i's are linear functions over the variables (x, y, u, v). These functions define a *mapping*, M, which associates the key-space of R_1 to the key-space of R_2 (recall that the key-spaces are orthogonal).

We denote by A the subset of the points of c^r whose image by M intersects c^s, and by B the subset of the points of c^s which are image by M of some point of c^r (see Figure 4.a). Computing A and B (and keeping the functions) is sufficient to evaluate the join. Intuitively, the points in A and B are in relationship via the mapping M, and thus qualify to the join semantics.

Let us assume first that the mapping M contains at least two functions (one for each coordinate). In that case, the first two functions can be rewritten as :

$$m = \begin{cases} u = f(x, y) \\ v = g(x, y) \end{cases}$$

where m defines a one-to-one linear application between the two key-spaces. Now, in the remaining functions, u and v can be replaced by $f(x, y)$ and $g(x, y)$, and this yields a cell $c(x, y)$. The sets A and B can thus be easily obtained as follows:

(1) compute $o = inter(c^r, c)$,

(2) compute $B = inter(m(o), c^s)$,

(3) compute $A = m^{-1}(B)$.

We consider now the case where there is only one function that links two key-spaces of dimension 2: M defines in that case a "loose" connection between the two key-spaces. Imagine, for instance, that the association between the space (x, y) and the space (u, v) is reduced to the function $v = f_v(x, y)$. The computation relies on *range* and *proj*: first one computes $range(c^r, f_v) = I = [v_{min}, v_{max}]$, and $B = inter(I, c^s)$. Then A is obtained as $inter(f^{-1}(proj_v(B)), c^r)$: see Figure 4.b.

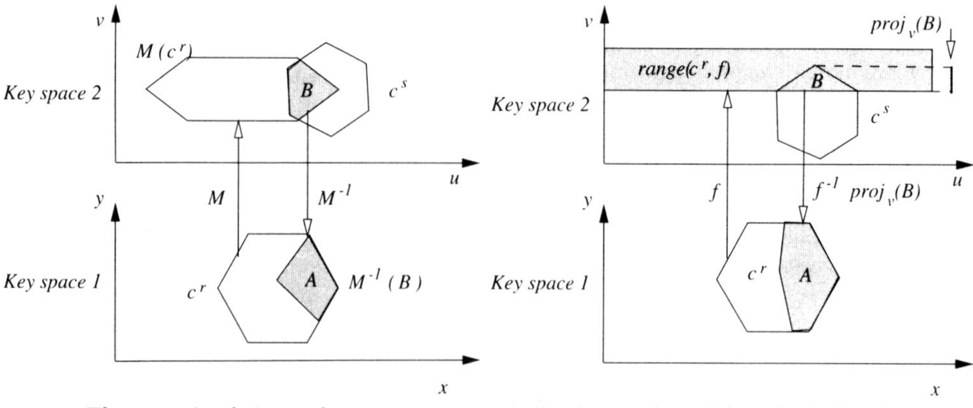

a. The mapping between key-spaces   b. A mapping with a single function.

Figure 4: Evaluation of a join

We denote by JOINCELLS this operator. It takes as input two cells from two distinct key-spaces, a set of functions, and constructs the sets A and B. Essentially, the techniques consist of some simple manipulations from linear algebra to compute the image of a cell by a system of linear functions, and the primitives *inter*, *range* and *proj*. The join algorithm can be described as a simple nested loop which evaluates JOINCELL at each step.

The following example gives a new, general strategy, based on the JOINCELLS algorithm, for evaluating the queries presented in the Examples 2 and 3.

Example 4 We focus on the computation of the join $TIN \bowtie Traj$. The algorithm JOINCELLS operates on a cell $c^r(x,y)$ from TIN, $d^s(t)$ from $Traj$, and the set F of functions $\{g_x, g_y\}$ which link the key-space $time(t)$ to the key-space $space(x,y)$. In order to evaluate the join, we compute JOINCELLS(c^r, F, d^s), which yields $A = inter(d^s(t), c^r(g_x^s(t), g_y^s(t)))$ and $B = inter(c^r(x,y), seg(x,y))$ (seg is the segment defined by $t_{min} \leqslant g_y^{-1}(y) \leqslant t_{max} \ \wedge \ g_x^{-1}(x) = g_y^{-1}(y)$).

By replacing d^s with A, and c^r with B, one obtains the following result:

$$[A \ ; \ x = g_x(t) \ , \ y = g_y(t), a = g_a(t) \ , \ h = f_h(x,y) \ ; \ B]$$

So we computed the correct values on the cells, and kept the interpolation functions unchanged. From this result we can either project on (t,x,y), by removing B, g_a and f_h, or on (x,y,h) by removing A, g_x, g_y and g_a. We get the results of Examples 2 and 3. $\square$

We can directly relate the geometric complexity of queries to the interpolated dimension of the relations involved in the query. The intersection of two trajectories for instance does not even require a computation in the 2D space: operations on time intervals suffice. With opportune restrictions preventing the creation of non-interpolated objects, it is possible to extend the

set of geometric primitives (with 2D union and 2D difference for instance) in order to be able to evaluate more queries.

4 Conclusion

We investigated the modeling of several innovative applications involving for instance mobile objects or digital elevation maps. Our goal has been to develop user-friendly and efficient query languages, based on standard techniques. We demonstrated the need for a logical modeling clearly separated from the physical level. In particular, we proved that the collections of samples together with the interpolation functions should belong to the physical level, and be hidden from the user, therefore resulting in query languages without special primitives.

One of the contributions of the paper is to show that such an approach is possible with simple formalization of these data in the relational framework, together with a data format which provides a compact representation and supports the evaluation of relational queries. A striking aspect of the model is the ability to express SQL queries on geometric data without any geometric skill.

A challenging issue in this context is the complexity of query processing, which strongly depends upon the dimension. Hence, a crucial property of query languages for multidimensional data should be the independence of the complexity of query evaluation from the dimension of the embedding space. Fortunately, interpolated objects can be manipulated at a cost which depends essentially upon the dimension of the key-space, and not of their global dimension. We described a set of algorithms which are used for query evaluation.

The present approach offers a great potential for optimization. First the use of standard relational query languages allows to rely on existing techniques. More

164

importantly, the physical data independence leaves full control to the system over the definition of the sample collections. In some cases it allows the use of indexes in the collection of samples that would not be possible if they were user-defined.

The current setting assumes *keys* of dimension at most 2. This restriction is motivated by complexity reasons. Indeed, objects of dimension 2 can be efficiently manipulated and the implementation of the operators is relatively simple. It is straightforward to generalize the ideas to keys of higher dimension $k > 2$. In this case, the evaluation is performed using operators in dimension k.

Acknowledgments. We are very grateful to Robert M. Wallace who provided the illustrations of Figure 1. We are also indebted to Marlon Dumas, Michel Scholl and Victor Vianu for their useful comments on earlier drafts of this paper.

References

[1] J. Chomicki and P. Revesz. A Geometric Framework for Specifying Spatio-Temporal Objects. In *Proc. Intl. Workshop on Time Representation and Reasoning*, 1999.

[2] M. Erwig, R.H. Güting, M. Schneider, and M. Vazirgiannis. Spatio-Temporal Data Types: An Approach to Modeling and Querying Moving Objects in Databases. *GeoInformatica*, 3(3):269–296, 1999.

[3] ESRI, editor. *Understanding GIS: the Arc/Info method*. ESRI Press, 1996.

[4] L. Forlizzi, R.H. Güting, E. Nardelli, and M. Schneider. A Data Model and Data Structures for Moving Objects Databases. In *Proc. ACM SIGMOD Symp. on the Management of Data*, 2000.

[5] A.U. Frank, S. Grumbach, R. H. Güting, C.S. Jensen, M. Koubarakis, N.A. Lorentzos, Y. Manolopoulos, E. Nardelli, B. Pernici, H.-J. Schek, M. Scholl, T.K. Sellis, B. Theodoulidis, and P. Widmayer. Chorochronos: A Research Network for Spatiotemporal Database Systems. *SIGMOD Record*, 28(3):12–21, 1999. http://www.dbnet.ece.ntua.gr/~choros/.

[6] Jacod E. Goodman and Joseph O'Rourke. *Handbook of Discrete and Computational Geometry*. CRC Press, 1997.

[7] S. Grumbach, P. Rigaux, and L. Segoufin. Spatio-Temporal Data Handling with Constraints. In *Proc. Intl. Symp. on Geographic Information Systems*, 1998.

[8] P. Kanellakis, G Kuper, and P. Revesz. Constraint Query Languages. *Journal of Computer and System Sciences*, 51(1):26–52, 1995. A shorter version appeared in PODS'90.

[9] G. Kollios, D. Gunopolos, and V.J. Tsotras. On Indexing Mobile Objects. In *Proc. ACM Symp. on Principles of Database Systems*, pages 261–272, 1999.

[10] M. Koubarakis. The Complexity of Query Evaluation in Indefinite Temporal Constraint Databases. *Theoretical Computer Science*, 171(1/2), 1997.

[11] Bruce Momjian. *PostgreSQL, Introduction and Concepts*. Addison Wesley, 2000. To appear. See http://postgresql.org.

[12] L. Neugebauer. Optimization and Evaluation of Database Queries Including Embedded Interpolation Procedures. In *Proc. ACM SIGMOD Symp. on the Management of Data*, 1991.

[13] D. Pfoser and C.S. Jensen. Capturing the Uncertainty of Moving-Object Representations. In *Proc. Intl. Conf. on Large Spatial Databases (SSD)*, pages 111–132, 1999.

[14] S. Saltenis, C. S. Jensen, S. T. Leutenegger, and M. A. Lopez. Indexing the Positions of Continuously Moving Objects. In *Proc. ACM SIGMOD Symp. on the Management of Data*, 2000.

[15] J. Sharma. Oracle8i Spatial: Experiences with Extensible Databases. An Oracle Technical White Paper, May 1999.

[16] A. Sistla, O. Wolfson, S. Chamberlain, and S. Dao. Modeling and Querying Moving Objects. In *Proc. IEEE Intl. Conf. on Data Engineering (ICDE)*, pages 422–433, 1997.

[17] Y. Theodoridis, J. R. O. Silva, and M. A. Nascimento. On the Generation of Spatiotemporal Datasets. In *Intl. Conf. on Large Spatial Databases (SSD'99)*, 1999.

[18] M. van Kreveld. Digital Elevation Models and TIN Algorithms. In *Algorithmic foundations of Geographic Information Systems*, number 1340 in LNCS, pages 37–78. Springer Verlag, 1997.

[19] O. Wolfson, A. P. Sistla, B. Xu, J. Zhou, and S. Chamberlain. DOMINO: Databases fOr MovINg Objects tracking. In *Proc. ACM SIGMOD Symp. on the Management of Data*, pages 547–549, 1999. (Demo sessions).

[20] M. Worboys. *GIS: A Computing Perspective*. Taylor and Francis, London, 1995.

Using SQL to Build New Aggregates and Extenders for Object-Relational Systems

Haixun Wang   Carlo Zaniolo

Computer Science Department
University of California at Los Angeles[†]

Abstract

User-defined Aggregates (UDAs) provide a versatile mechanism for extending the power and applicability of Object-Relational Databases (O-R DBs). In this paper, we describe the AXL system that supports an SQL-based language for introducing new UDAs. AXL is easy to learn and use for database programmers because it preserves the constructs, programming paradigm and data types of SQL (whereas there is an 'impedance mismatch' between SQL and the procedural languages of user-defined functions currently used in O-R DBs). AXL will also inherit the benefits of database query languages, such as scalability, data independence and parallelizability. In this paper, we show that, while adding only minimal extensions to SQL, AXL is very powerful and capable of expressing complex algorithms efficiently. We demonstrate this by coding data mining functions and other advanced applications that, previously, had been a major problem for SQL databases.

Due to its flexibility, SQL-compatibility and ease of use, the AXL approach offers a better extensibility mechanism, in several application domains, than the function libraries now offered by commercial O-R DBs under names such as Datablades or DB-Extenders.

† Los Angeles CA 90095, `hxwang|zaniolo@cs.ucla.edu`

**Proceedings of the 26th VLDB Conference,
Cairo, Egypt, 2000.**

1 Introduction

The explosive growth of new database applications has, in several cases, outpaced the albeit dramatic progress made by database technology. In fact, the great success of new application areas often serves as a grim reminder of the limitations from which DBMSs still suffer in terms of power and extensibility. For instance, the newly introduced Object-Relational (O-R) systems offer great improvements in generality, extensibility, and query power; yet O-R systems do not support well data mining applications—a leading growth area for data-intensive applications. Problems also occur in many other application areas, where datablades and similar function libraries need better flexibility and integration with SQL. In this paper, we show that many of these problems can be solved, or ameliorated, by user-defined aggregates (UDAs), which often provide a more flexible and powerful mechanism for extending DBMSs than user-defined functions (UDFs) used today in this role. For instance, an aggregate can take as argument the whole SQL relation rather than fields in individual tuples, as UDFs do. Unfortunately, UDAs are less understood and developed from a technological viewpoint than UDFs, which have greatly benefitted from the ADT advances made in programming languages, while UDAs are primarily a DB-centric concept and have received less attention. In fact, while UDAs were part of Postgres [18] and early SQL3 [11, 10] proposals, and also supported in Informix [12], they have been left out from the recently released SQL-99 specifications.

Therefore, as today, UDAs remain a topic rich with research challenges and opportunities, since they find many important application areas, such as DB-centric data mining. At UCLA, we developed the SQL-AG system that supports UDAs on top of DB2; besides implementing the original SQL3 specifications for U-DAs, SQL-AG extends them to support new forms of aggregation, such as online aggregation, through a mechanism called *early returns* [23]. Aggregates only producing early returns are monotonic with respect to set-containment, and can, therefore, be used in recursive SQL queries with no restriction or modification to the current systems [23]. Monotonic aggregates support efficiently Bill of Materials applications, transitive closures with greedy optimization, and other complex queries that had been a problem for relational query languages since their introduction [23].

In the original SQL3 proposal, new UDAs are actually encoded through three UDFs that, respectively, define the computation to be performed (i) for the first value in the stream, (ii) for each successive value, and (iii) at the end of the stream. Unfortunately, programming UDFs for O-R systems using procedural languages can be exceedingly difficult even for knowledgeable programmers [15]. The difficulty of writing and debugging UDFs is compounded by the fact that, to achieve reasonable performance, these UDFs will normally execute 'unfenced' [2] in the same address space as the database system—thus the use of efficient procedural languages, such as C, could compromise the safety of the system. Clearly, UDAs defined via multiple procedural language UDFs, as suggested in the original SQL3 proposal, will suffer from similar usability problems.

Our approach to solve these problems consists in providing a high-level language for defining new aggregates. Since all users are already familiar with SQL, we will strive to design a language as close as possible to SQL; this will make the new language easier to learn and use, avoid the many problems connected with the introduction of a new language, and eliminate the risk of 'impedance mismatch' in data types and programming styles that is bound to occur if UDAs are written in any other language. In addition, this approach inherits the many advantages of databases and their query languages, including scalability, data independence, and parallelizability.

The main challenge facing this approach was the limited expressive power of SQL, which made us wonder if our objective was achievable at all. Our Simple Aggregate Definition Language (SADL) project [22] represented an important experiment to test the limits and feasibility of our SQL-centric approach. SADL is a 'barebone' language, which only supports basic SELECT statements. Even so, SADL was sufficient to express some aggregates, boosting our confidence that our ultimate goal was achievable. On the other hand, as we explored the issues of performance, scalability, and expressive power required for advanced applications, SADL showed many problems. One is the fact that SADL kept the UDA structure proposed in the original SQL3 specifications, where the definition of a new aggregate is broken down into several functions. This structure leads to poorly structured programs and inefficiency. Another problem with SADL is that it does not support the definition and use of auxiliary tables, nor does it support updates on tables. Therefore, a new language called AXL (for Aggregate Extension Language) was designed to solve all these problems; the AXL system also uses an architecture very different from SADL. For instance, while SADL implementation uses query interpretation, and relies on in-memory tables, AXL relies on compilation and makes full use of secondary memory tables.

This paper is organized as follows. In the next section, we describe our systems SQL-AG and SADL previously developed at UCLA to deal with UDAs and their limitations. Then in Sections 3, 4, 5 and 6 we describe AXL in various application domains. In section 7 we describe its implementation. In section 8 we discuss opportunities for future research.

2   The SQL-AG System and SADL

At UCLA, we have developed the SQL-AG [20] system that supports and extends the UDA specifications originally proposed for SQL3 [11]. For instance, we can define the standard **avg** aggregate as shown in Example 1.

Example 1 *Defining the standard avg aggregate*

```
AGGREGATE myavg(INT)
 RETURNS REAL
 STATE state_type
 INITIALIZE avg_single
 ITERATE avg_multi
 TERMINATE avg_terminate


typedef struct state_s {
   long sum; long cnt;
} state_type;
void avg_single(long *value, state_type *s)
{ s→sum = *value;
   s→cnt = 1;
}
void avg_multi(long *value, state_type *s)
{ s→sum += *value;
   s→cnt++;
}
void avg_terminate(state *s, float *result)
{ *result = s→sum/s→cnt;
}
```

Basically, the user must define the three external procedures, under the labels of INITIALIZE, ITERATE and TERMINATE, which, respectively, specify the computation to be performed for the first value in the stream, for each successive value, and when the end of stream is detected and the final value of the aggregate must be returned. Thus, in our example, the C procedure *avg_single* initializes the current sum to the first value and the current count to 1, *avg_multi* adds the new value to sum and increases count by 1, and *avg_terminate* returns the final average from *state*.

It is important to observe that while traditional SQL2 aggregates are (dependent on repetitions, but) independent of the order in which the computation streams through data, UDAs as defined in the original SQL3 specifications and implemented in SQL-AG can depend on such order. Recent SQL extension for aggregates, supporting partition and windows for OLAP applications [25], also relies on the the order of data. Indeed in many applications, such as cumulative aggregates and moving-windows aggregates used in time-series [14], the fact that the data is sorted by their time stamps is part of the application logic. On the other hand, a direct application of online aggregates on stored data, normally relies on the fact that the data is not skewed [8]. Thus, aggregates that are most useful in advanced applications are often designed to take full advantage on the particular properties of the data.

Two versions of SQL-AG were implemented, the first on Oracle, using PL/SQL, and the second for IBM DB2. Here we describe this second version, which is significantly more powerful and efficient than the other. DB2 supports user-defined functions (UDFs) but not user-defined aggregates. The SQL-AG system supports SQL queries with UDAs by transforming them into DB2 queries that use scratch-pad UDFs to emulate the functionality of the corresponding UDAs [2]. For instance, moving average of stock price in the following query:

```
SELECT company, myavg(price)
FROM stock-closing
GROUP BY company
```

is translated by SQL-AG into the query which can be executed by DB2:

```
SELECT company, myavg_out(company)
FROM stock-closing
WHERE myavg_groupby(company,price)=1
GROUP BY company
```

Each UDA, named say agg, is implemented with two automatically generated DB2 UDFs, namely, agg_groupby and agg_out. The UDF agg_groupby performs the actual computation and it is applied to every record for aggregation. It uses a hash table to keep the aggregate value of each group. The UDF agg_out(group) retrieves from the hash table the last value computed by agg_groupby for group. A detailed description of SQL rewriting can be found in [20].

A key improvement made by the SQL-AG system developed at UCLA [20] with respect to the original proposal of SQL3 is the support for *early returns*. Early returns are basically results returned during the computation of the aggregate, as needed to support online aggregation [8] and other advanced forms of aggregation discussed later in this paper.

Early returns can be supported by allowing the user to add to the aggregate specification a PRODUCE procedure to generate *early returns*, whereas the TERMINATE procedure generates *final returns*. For instance, *avg_multi* in the example below can be used to evaluate the rate of convergence for the computation of average and return values at regular interval.

Example 2 *A UDA with Early Returns*

```
AGGREGATE myavg(INT)
RETURNS REAL
STATE state_type
INITIALIZE avg_single
ITERATE avg_multi
PRODUCE avg_produce
TERMINATE avg_terminate
```

```
int avg_produce(state *s, float *result)
{ if (s→cnt % 100 == 0) {
    *result = s→sum / s→cnt;
    return 1;
  } else
    return 0;
}
```

This version of myavg contains both early returns and final returns. The rules required to map UDAs with both early returns and final returns into equivalent SQL queries with scratchpad UDFs are more complex, as described in [20].

MONOTONIC AGGREGATION. An interesting special case is when the aggregate only contains early returns, i.e., the TERMINATE function avg_terminate is either missing or it has been replaced by NOP. Then, it can be shown that the aggregate is monotonic with respect to set containment and can therefore be used without restrictions in recursive SQL queries to code optimized graph traversal and BoM applications that had been a problem for databases since their introduction [23, 22].

PERFORMANCE. We compared the performance of native DB2 builtins against SQL-AG UDAs on a Ultra SPARC 2 with 128 megabytes memory and reimplemented the SQL built-ins as UDAs. As discussed in [22], when aggregation contains no group-by columns, there is a slight performance penalty resulted from calling UDFs. There are actually situations where the fact that a hash-based aggregation is used instead of a sort-based one yielding better performance than built in aggregates. Thus UDAs can be implemented with nearly the same performance as the standard built-ins.

SADL. UDAs defined using a procedural languages such as C suffer from the same problems as the C-defined user defined functions[15]; these problems include the difficulty of developing and debugging applications, and a loss of optimizability and parallelizability. An obvious solution to these problems consists in providing a high-level language for the definition of aggregates. In [22] we presented a simple aggregate definition language (SADL), which was designed to have SQL-like syntax, data types, and semantics, for ease of learning and use. In SADL, the user codes the INITIALIZE function and the other functions required to introduce a new aggregate using SELECT statements.

While simple aggregates can be expressed easily, more complex ones could not be expressed in SADL, which lacks the ability of introducing temporary tables and calling UDAs recursively. This led to the design of a new language, named AXL, where new tables and aggregates can be defined as part of the definition of an aggregate, and updates on tables are supported along with the recursive invocation of aggregates.

3 AXL

We now introduce AXL by examples; a more complete discussion can be found in [21]. Example 3 defines an online version of **myavg** which returns results for every 100 new values. The first line of this aggregate function declares a local table, **state**, to keep (in memory) the sum and count of the values processed so far. While, for this particular example, **state** contains only one tuple, it is in fact a table that can be queried and updated using SQL statements. These SQL statements are grouped into the three blocks labelled respectively **INITIALIZE** and **ITERATE** and **TERMINATE**. Thus, **INITIALIZE** inserts the value taken from the input stream and sets the count to 1. The **ITERATE** statements update the table by adding the new input value to the sum and 1 to the count. The **TERMINATE** statements return the final result of computation by appending it to **RETURN**; for conformity with SQL, **RETURN** is viewed as a table, and thus an **INSERT INTO** construct is used. We also add intermediate results from the computation to **RETURN** tables as part of the **ITERATE** statements; this eliminates the need for the special **PRODUCE** construct used in SADL.

Example 3 *Return current average for every 100 records*

```
AGGREGATE myavg(Next INT) : REAL
{
    TABLE state(sum INT, cnt INT);
    INITIALIZE : {
        INSERT INTO state VALUES (Next, 1);
    }
    ITERATE : {
        UPDATE state SET sum=sum+Next,
                         cnt=cnt+1;
        INSERT INTO RETURN
            SELECT sum/cnt FROM state
            WHERE cnt % 100 = 0;
    }
    TERMINATE : {
        INSERT INTO RETURN
        SELECT sum/cnt FROM state ;
    }
}
```

We now define a **minpoint** aggregate that returns the point where a minimum occurs rather than the value of the minimum.

Example 4 *Define* minpoint *in AXL*

```
AGGREGATE minpoint(iPoint INT, iValue INT) : INT
{
    TABLE state(point INT, value INT);
    INITIALIZE: {
        INSERT INTO state VALUES(iPoint, iValue);
    }
    ITERATE: {
        UPDATE state
        SET point=iPoint, value=iValue
        WHERE value > iValue;
    }
    TERMINATE: {
        INSERT INTO RETURN
            SELECT point FROM state;
    }
}
```

MONOTONIC COUNT. Another interesting aggregate is the monotonic count **mcount** that returns the running count for each new input value. This aggregate is monotonic with respect set containment. Indeed for a set of cardinality 3 it returns $\{1, 2, 3\}$, and once a new element is added to this set it returns $\{1, 2, 3, 4\}$. Observe that this second set is a superset of the first; the traditional count would instead return singleton sets $\{3\}$ and $\{4\}$, where the second is not a superset of the first. The monotonic aggregate **mcount** can be used freely in recursive SQL queries to express many computations that would be hard or inefficient to express otherwise; several examples are given in [22]. Here we will later use it to assign a sequence number to the tuples of a relation.

Example 5 *Monotonic Count*

```
AGGREGATE mcount(Next INT) : INT
{
    TABLE state(cnt INT);
    INITIALIZE : {
        INSERT INTO state VALUES(1);
        INSERT INTO RETURN VALUES (1);
    }
    ITERATE : {
        UPDATE state SET cnt=cnt+1;
        INSERT INTO RETURN
            SELECT cnt FROM state;
    }
}
```

RECURSIVE AGGREGATES. In AXL, aggregates can call other aggregates. Particularly, an aggregate can call itself recursively. Say we have a relation **children(Parent, Child)**. Example 6 defines a recursive aggregate **alldesc** to find all the descendants of a given person.

Example 6 *Offspring*

```
AGGREGATE alldesc(P CHAR(10)) : CHAR(10)
{
    INITIALIZE:  ITERATE: {
    INSERT INTO RETURN VALUES(P);
    INSERT INTO RETURN
       SELECT alldesc(Child)
       FROM children
       WHERE Parent=P;
    }
}
```

Now, we can use the following query to find all the descendents of Tom.

```
SELECT alldesc(Child) FROM children
WHERE Parent='Tom';
```

AXL also supports a redefinition construct, and SQLCODE construct which are described in the next sections. But, basically, the examples given so far illustrate the complete AXL language. Therefore, AXL manages to be quite powerful using a very small repertoire of new constructs beyond SQL. In the next section, we show how AXL can be used to support OLAPs and other powerful new forms of aggregation; in the section that follows we use AXL to support some data mining functions.

4 Data Mining in AXL

As a first example of the many uses of AXL, consider the data mining methods used for classification. Say for instance, that we want to classify the value of Play as a 'Yes' or a 'No' given a training set such as that shown in Table 1.

Outlook	Temp	Humidity	Wind	Play
Sunny	Hot	High	Weak	No
Sunny	Hot	High	Strong	No
Overcast	Hot	High	Weak	Yes
Rain	Mild	High	Weak	Yes
Rain	Cool	Normal	Weak	Yes
Rain	Cool	Normal	Strong	Yes
Overcast	Cool	Normal	Strong	No
Sunny	Mild	High	Weak	No
Sunny	Cool	Normal	Weak	Yes
Rain	Mild	Normal	Weak	Yes
Sunny	Mild	Normal	Strong	Yes
Overcast	Mild	High	Strong	Yes
Overcast	Hot	Normal	Weak	Yes
Rain	Mild	High	Strong	No

Table 1: The relation **PlayTennis**

We now describe the implementation in AXL of categorical decision tree classifiers. Bayesian classifiers will be discussed in the next section.

DECISION TREE CLASSIFIER. The first step for most decision tree classifiers is to convert the training set into column/value pairs. This conversion, although conceptually simple, is hard to express succinctly in

SQL. Consider the **PlayTennis** relation as shown in Table 1. We want to convert it into a new stream of 4 columns (**RecId, Col, Value, YorN**), meaning that the **Col**-th column of the **RecId**-th tuple in relation **PlayTennis** has value **Value** and its **Play** column has value **YorN**.

In AXL, we can define a new aggregate `dissemble` to solve the problem.

Example 7 *Dissemble a relation into column/value pairs.*

```
AGGREGATE dissemble(v1 INT, v2 INT, v3 INT,
          v4 INT, yorn INT):
          (col INT, val INT, YorN INT)
{
    INITIALIZE: ITERATE: {
        INSERT INTO RETURN
        VALUES(1,v1,yorn), (2,v2,yorn),
          (3,v3,yorn), (4,v4,yorn);
    }
}
```

Following is the query to dissemble the `PlayTennis` table (the `mcount` aggregate is used here to generate a record id for each tuple in the tennis table):

```
SELECT mcount(1),
  dissemble(Outlook, Temp, Humidity, Wind, Play)
FROM PlayTennis;
```

The complete classifier algorithm is shown in Example 8. The INITIALIZE and ITERATE steps share the same block of code. First, we insert the current record into the `treenodes` table. Then we update the class histogram kept in the `summary` table for each column/value pair. If we have not met the column/value pair before, we will insert it on line 17. SQLCODE is a reserved word of AXL, and it keeps the return status of the previous SQL statement. If SQLCODE is 0, then the previous UPDATE statement is unsuccessful and a new record is to be inserted.

The TERMINATE step will first compute the gini index for each column using the histogram we accumulated during the INITIALIZE/ITERATE steps. Then, on line 23, we select the splitting column which has the minimal gini index. A new sub-branch is generated for each value in the column. The UDA used here, `minpointvalue`, is the same aggregate as the `minpoint` defined in Example 4 except that it also returns the minimum value, which will be used as the stop condition for the recursion on line 37. (If gini equals 0, then all the records in the current node has the same class label and no further classification is necessary.) After recording the current split into the `result` table, we call the classifier recursively to further classify the sub nodes. The GROUP-BY clause on line 40 partitions the records in `treenodes` into MAXVALUE subnodes, where MAXVALUE is the largest number of different values in any of the table columns (three for Table 1).

Using the `classify` aggregate, classification on the tennis table can be solved using the following query:

```
SELECT classify(t.RecId, 0, t.Col, t.Val, t.YorN)
FROM (
    SELECT mcount() RecId,
        dissemble(Outlook,Temp,Humidity,Wind,Play)
        AS (Col, Val, YorN)
    FROM PlayTennis) AS t;
```

Example 8 *Using Recursive Aggregates to Implement a Classifier in AXL*

```
[ 1] AGGREGATE classify(RecId INT, iNode INT, iCol INT,
[ 2]                     iValue INT, iYorN INT)
[ 3] {
[ 4]    TABLE treenodes(RecId INT, Node INT,
[ 5]                    Col INT, Value INT, YorN INT);
[ 6]    TABLE mincol(Col INT);
[ 7]    TABLE summary(Col INT, Value INT, Yc INT, Nc INT,
[ 8]                  KEY {Col,Value});
[ 9]    TABLE ginitable(Col INT, Gini INT);
[10]
[11]    INITIALIZE : ITERATE : {
[12]      INSERT INTO treenodes
[13]        VALUES(RecId, iNode, iCol, iValue, iYorN);
[14]      UPDATE summary
[15]        SET Yc=Yc+iYorN, Nc=Nc+1-iYorN
[16]        WHERE Col = iCol AND Value = iValue;
[17]      INSERT INTO summary
[18]        SELECT iCol, iValue, iYorN, 1-iYorN
[19]        WHERE SQLCODE=0;
[20]    }
[21]    TERMINATE : {
[22]      INSERT INTO ginitable
[23]        SELECT Col,
[24]          sum((Yc*Nc)/(Yc+Nc))/sum(Yc+Nc)
[25]        FROM summary GROUP BY Col;
[26]      INSERT INTO mincol
[27]        SELECT minpointvalue(Col, Gini)
[28]        FROM ginitable;
[29]      INSERT INTO result
[30]        SELECT iNode, Col FROM mincol;
[31]      SELECT classify(t.RecId,
[32]          t.Node*MAXVALUE+m.Value+1,
[33]          t.Col, t.Value, t.YorN)
[34]      FROM treenodes AS t,
[35]      ( SELECT tt.RecId RecId, tt.Value Value
[36]        FROM treenodes AS tt, mincol AS m
[37]        WHERE tt.Col=m.Col AND m.MiniGini > 0
[38]      ) AS m
[39]      WHERE t.RecId = m.RecId
[40]      GROUP BY m.Value;
[41]    }
[42] }
```

5 Group-By Modifiers

Powerful aggregate extensions based on modifications and generalizations of group-by constructs have recently been proposed by researchers, OLAP vendors, and standard committees [5, 25]. Here, we show how these aggregate extensions can also be expressed in AXL, as an alternative and more flexible mechanism to achieve their advanced functionality.

Consider the following query to an `employee` relation:

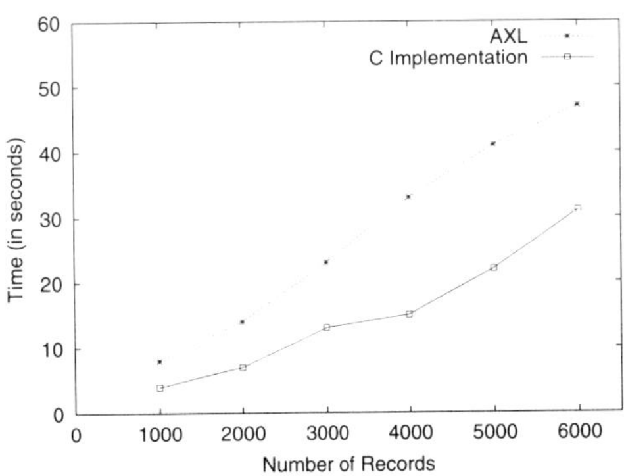

Figure 1: Performance Comparison of AXL and C

For each division, show the average salary of senior managers who make 3 times more than the average employees, and the average salary of senior engineers who make 2 times more than the average employees (in the same output record).

All aggregates in this query are grouped by the same attribute (i.e., division). To express this query in SQL2, we need to use joins and subqueries, and then three passes through the `employee` relation will be needed to produce the answer. To solve these problems, a new construct called SUCH THAT was proposed in [5]. Example 9 shows the use of this construct to express our query. Therefore, this extension uses variables, such as X and Y, that range over groups and are qualified by the SUCH THAT conditions.

Example 9 *SQL extension SUCH THAT proposed in [5]*

```
SELECT division, avg(X.salary), avg(Y.salary)
FROM employee
GROUP BY division : X, Y
SUCH THAT X.title= 'senior manager' AND
          X.salary > 3 * avg(salary) AND
          Y.title= 'senior engineer' AND
          Y.salary > 2 * avg(salary))
```

Queries with SUCH THAT constructs can be implemented in AXL by mapping the queries into UDAs according to simple transformation rules.

Example 10 *Rewriting the SUCH THAT construct using a UDA*

```
AGGREGATE mscan2(title CHAR(20), salary INT,
                 querytitle CHAR(20), INT ratio) : INT
{
    TABLE allstate(sum INT, cnt INT) AS VALUES(0,0);
    TABLE finalstate(fsalary INT);
    INITIALIZE: ITERATE: {
        UPDATE allstate SET sum=sum+salary,
                            cnt=cnt+1;
        INSERT INTO finalstate VALUES(salary)
            WHERE title = querytitle;
    }
    TERMINATE: {
        SELECT avg(fsalary) FROM finalstate
```

```
        WHERE fsalary >
        (SELECT ratio*sum/cnt FROM allstate);
    }
}
```

Then, using aggregate `mscan2` defined above, we rewrite Example 11 into the following query:

```
SELECT  division,
        mscan2(title, salary, 'senior manager', 3),
        mscan2(title, salary, 'senior engineer', 2)
FROM employee
GROUP BY division;
```

We next discuss the implementation of a naive Bayesian classifier, to illustrate both the power and the limitations of OLAP extensions recently introduced in SQL.

BAYESIAN CLASSIFIERS. The Boosted Bayesian Classifier [7] was the winner of the KDD'97 data mining competition. Its derivation algorithm consists of a main phase that produces a *Naive Bayesian* classifiers and of a boosting phase, that normally produces a (modest) performance improvement.

The Naive Bayesian classifier makes probability-based predictions as follows. Let A_1, A_2, ..., A_k be attributes, with discrete values, used to predict a discrete class C. (For the example at hand, we have four prediction attributes, $k = 4$, and $C = $ 'Play'.) For attribute values a_1 through a_k, the optimal prediction is the value c for which $Pr(C = c|A_1 = a_1 \wedge \ldots \wedge A_k = a_k)$ is maximal. By Bayes' rule, and assuming independence of the attributes, this means to classify a new tuple to the value of c that maximize the product of $Pr(C = c)$ with:

$$\prod_{j=1,\ldots,K} Pr(A_j = a_j|C = c)$$

But these probabilities can be estimated from the training set as follows:

$$Pr(A_j = a_j|C = c) = \frac{count(A_j = a_j \wedge C = c)}{count(C = c)}$$

To compute the numerators and denominators in the above formula, we can use the GROUPING SET construct as shown in Example 11. It's AXL UDA equivalent is shown in Example 12.

Example 11 *Using DB2's GROUPING SET*

```
SELECT Outlook, Temp, Humidity, Wind,
       Play, count(*)
FROM PlayTennis
GROUP BY GROUPING SETS ((Outlook, Play),
    (Temp, Play), (Humidity, Play),
    (Wind,Play), (Play));
```

Example 12 *Using a UDA defined in AXL*

```
AGGREGATE assemble(A1 INT, A2 INT, A3 INT,
                   A4 INT, C INT) :
                  (col CHAR(20), class INT)
{
    INITIALIZE: ITERATE: {
       INSERT INTO RETURN VALUES
          (A1, C), (A2, C), (A3, C),
          (A4, C), ('-all-', C);
    }
}
SELECT t.col, t.class, count(*)
FROM (SELECT assemble(Outlook, Temp,
              Humidity, Wind, Play)
      FROM PlayTennis) AS t
GROUP BY t.col, t.class;
```

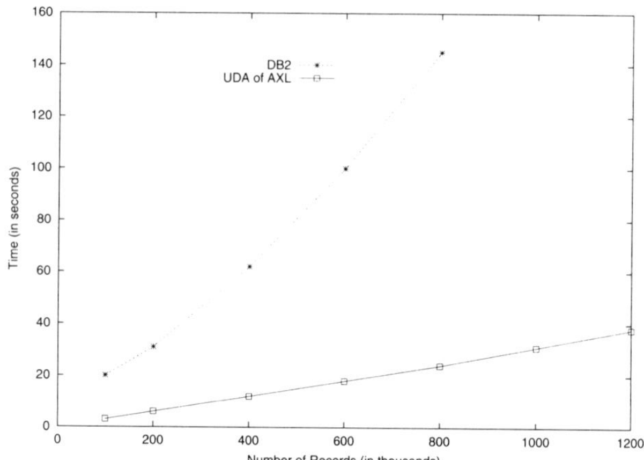

Figure 2: Bayesian Classifiers: grouping sets vs. UDAs

All counts needed in Example 12 are computed in one pass through the data using the hash-based method that is AXL's default approach, while in commercial systems, GROUPING SETS are often implemented as a cascade of sorting operations. As illustrated by Figure 2, AXL's specialized UDA yields a substantial speed-up, and improved scalability (DB2 on our workstation refused to handle more than 800,000 records generated as a synthetic data set).

Therefore, while OLAP extensions recently added to SQL extend its expressive power, their implementation cannot be expected to be optimal for all possible situations. There are many situations, where algorithms other than those used by the database vendor are better for the particular dataset at hand. In the case of categorical classifiers, for instance, the number of possible values is normally such that a hash-based aggregation is applicable and produces the best results.

More powerful OLAP functions are now being added to SQL [25]. But since their implementation can only be optimized for 'typical' situations, there will remain a need for UDAs to serve special situations, and for a high-level language to facilitate their implementation.

6 Datablades and Time Series

Databases are now pulled in different directions by the need to keep the SQL standards while supporting new data types and advanced applications. This has given birth to a proliferation of vendors' packages for new data types and application areas, such as, text, images, video, audio, time-series, spatial data, and others. These packages include IBM's DB2 Extenders, Informix' Data Blades, Oracle's Data Cartridges, and Sybase's Snap-Ins, which are basically libraries of functions that can be called from an SQL query on attribute values and blobs. While this approach is adequate for certain applications, it suffers from several limitations. For instance, the functions take as operands individual tuples rather than tables, and the canned operators provided by a datablade package cannot be extended easily. The first limitation is particularly obvious in data mining applications, which are devoted to finding interesting statistical correlations in the relation. We believe that aggregate-based extenders provide a better basis for data-mining datablades; in fact, AXL provides a powerful facility for writing new data mining functions, or for combining and extending existing ones to match the needs of the application at hand.

An area where the limitations of datablades have long been recognized is that of time-series for which researchers have proposed extensions that are more flexible and better integrated with SQL [17] than commercial time-series datablades. Indeed, a sequence of time-value pairs can naturally be viewed as a relation with ordered tuples, and time-series queries can be formulated via SQL-like query languages [3, 17]. Moreover, it is hard to imagine a more natural model for sequences and ordered relations than the stream model already used by our UDAs. The following examples illustrate the use of temporal UDAs on data that is stored and processed according to their time stamps. Also, we have made much use of UDAs in TEnORs (Temporally Enhanced OR System), to support a valid time extension of SQL [9].

TEMPORAL EXTENDERS. *We have a sequence of events, each of which is active during a certain interval (from, to). Find out at which point of time we have the largest number of active events.*

Example 13 *Active Intervals*

```
AGGREGATE density(from TIME, to TIME)
     : (time TIME, count INT)
{   TABLE state(time TIME, count INT) AS (0,0);
    TABLE active(endpoint TIME);
    INITIALIZE: ITERATE: {
      DELETE FROM active WHERE endpoint < from;
      INSERT INTO active VALUES(to);
```

```
      UPDATE state
        SET time=from, count=count+1
        WHERE count < (SELECT count(*) FROM active);
    }
  TERMINATE: {
    INSERT INTO RETURN
      SELECT time, count FROM state;
  }
}
```

Under the assumption that events are sorted by increasing time, we can use the following query to find the point of time that has the largest number of active events.

Example 14 *Coalescing*

```
SELECT density(from,to) FROM events;
```

When events are not sorted by time, we can create a new aggregate sortdensity that wraps around the aggregate defined in Example 13. In aggregate sortdensity, we specify the ordering of the input stream. Then, in Example 14, we use sortdensity instead of density to find the point of time that has largest number of active events on an unordered stream.

Example 15 *Ordering*

```
AGGREGATE sortdensity(from TIME, to TIME)
     : (time TIME, count INT)
{
    ORDER BY from ASC;
    INSERT INTO RETURN
      SELECT density(from, to);
}
```

This example, illustrates AXL's *redefinition* facility which takes an input stream and transforms it using previously defined aggregates and sorting.

Let us consider now the well-known problem of coalescing after projection in a temporal table. We define the aggregate coalesce, which takes two parameters: from is the start time, to is the end time. Under the assumption that tuples are sorted by increasing start time, then we can perform the task in one scan of the data. In the ITERATE routine, when the new interval overlaps the current interval kept in the state table, we coalesce the two intervals into one interval that ends with the larger of the end time. Otherwise, the current interval is returned while the new interval becomes the current one.

Example 16 *Coalescing*

```
AGGREGATE coalesce(from TIME, to TIME)
     : (start TIME, end TIME)
{   TABLE state(cFrom TIME, cTo TIME);
    INITIALIZE: {
      INSERT INTO state VALUES(from,to);
    }
```

```
ITERATE : {
  UPDATE state SET cTo = to
     WHERE cTo >= from AND cTo < to;
  INSERT INTO RETURN
     SELECT cFrom, cTo FROM state
     WHERE cTo < from;
  UPDATE state
     SET cFrom = from, cTo = to
     WHERE cTo < from;
}
TERMINATE: {
  INSERT INTO RETURN
     SELECT cFrom, cTo FROM state;
}
}
```

7   Implementation of AXL

The AXL compiler translates AXL programs into
C++ code. The classifier algorithm in Example 8,
for instance, is compiled into more than 2100 C++
code. AXL adopts an open interface for its physical
data model, so that the system can link with a variety
of physical database implementations. Currently, we
use the Berkeley DB library[26] as our main storage
manager.

AXL supports both persistent tables and temporary
tables. Temporary tables are declared as local variables in the program and are memory based. Aggregates in AXL are hash-based by default. However, we
also allow the use of predicates like SORT BY column
or SORT BY GROUPBY in a UDA to force sort-based
aggregation.

The runtime model of AXL is based on data pipelining. In particular, all UDAs, including recursive U-
DAs that call themselves, are pipelined, which mean-
s tuples inserted into the RETURN relation during the INITIALIZE/ITERATE steps are returned to
their caller immediately. In order to do this, all local variables (temporary tables) declared inside the
body of a UDA are assembled into a state structure which is passed into the UDA for each INITIAL-
IZE/ITERATE/TERMINATE calls

All the constructs described in this paper, but redefinition facility described in Example 15, are functional
in the current AXL prototype that contains more than
33,000 lines of C++ code. We are now adding more
SQL data types, O-R database extensions and a richer set of supporting indexes and storage structures.
We expect the complete and more robust system will
eventually have 90,000 lines of code.

AXL UDAs can either be used as stand-alone programs or, imported into DB2 using the SQL-AG approach (with limitations due to the fact that we use
UDFs that return a single value for each call).

8   Conclusions

The goal of extending database systems to support
new applications has been the focus of much interest
and activity for database researchers and commercial
vendors. While the previous efforts have concentrated
on UDFs and ADTs, we have shown here that UDAs
can play a major role in supporting new applications—
including datamining applications which have proved
a real challenge for O-R DBs [15]. Since aggregates
can be viewed as query operators on tables, they can
be defined using SQL (while UDFs are basically operators on tuples). The SQL statements defining a UDA
can in turn call other UDAs (often using recursion) to
yield great expressive power and flexibility. The AXL
prototype has turned this simple ideas into an efficient
implementation that builds on the lessons learned from
our two previous UDA prototypes—i.e., the SQL-AG
system [23] and SADL [22].

Using AXL, the database programmer can extend
the functionality of the database system using the
familiar programming style and data types of SQL.
While ease of use is not a small advantage (particularly given the difficulty of extending the database system
through UDFs), many other gains are to be expected.
Indeed, the traditional benefits of SQL, such as data
independence, query optimization and parallelization,
can be inherited by AXL programs. Therefore, in the
same way in which a database query can now be off-
loaded to a remote DB server, it will one day be possible to offload complex AXL programs to remote DB
servers.

The parallelization of AXL programs provides another interesting direction for further work. While
parallelization of aggregates along their group-by partition is easy to achieve, parallelization within the aggregate itself can be difficult achieve for complex aggregate functions [13]. The SQL statements used in AXL
provide more opportunities for compiler analysis and
automatic parallelization than procedural language s-
tatements, and this will provide a direction for future
research.

Another interesting issue to be investigated is the
relationship of AXL with procedural extensions for
SQL, which are now being considered for standards
with the aim of adding the power of procedural languages while retaining some of the benefits of SQL.
These procedural extensions can be added to AXL in
the future to overcome performance or expressiveness
limitations encountered in actual applications. So far
however, AXL proved sufficiently flexible and efficient
for most database applications. In fact, AXL might
also play a role in some data-intensive applications by
replacing languages such as PL/SQL and JDBC used
today.

We are currently working on several fronts. We
are developing a test suite of data mining functions
and database extenders written in AXL to validate

the functionality and performance of our system. At the same time, we are completing and improving the AXL compiler, e.g., by adding more complete support for SQL data types, O-R extensions such as path notation, and a richer set of supporting indexes and storage structures. Issues such as better optimization and parallelization techniques for AXL aggregates provide other important topics for future research.

Acknowledgements

The authors are grateful to Hamid Pirahesh for suggesting a substantial editorial revision, and to the other referees for several improvements.

References

[1] R. Agrawal, R. Srikant. "Fast Algorithm for Mining Association Rules". In *VLDB'94*.

[2] D., Chamberlin, "Using the new DB2, IBM's Object-Relational Database System," Morgan Kaufmann, 1996.

[3] R. Chandra and A. Segev. Managing Temporal Financial Data in an Extensible Database. In *Proc. of the 19th VLDB*, pages 302–313, 1993.

[4] Surajit Chaudhuri, Usama M. Fayyad, Jeff Bernhardt: Scalable Classification over SQL Databases. ICDE 1999: 470-479.

[5] D. Chatziantoniou and K. A. Ross, "Querying Multiple Features of Groups in Relational Databases." Proceedings of the 1996 VLDB Conference, September 1996.

[6] D. Chatziantoniou and K. A. Ross, "Groupwise Processing of Relational Queries." Proceedings of the 1997 VLDB Conference, pages 476-485, August 1997.

[7] Charles Elkan. "Boosting and Naive Bayesian Learning". Technical report no cs97-557, Dept. of Computer Science and Engineering, UCSD, September 1997.

[8] J. M. Hellerstein, P. J. Haas, H. J. Wang. "Online Aggregation". *SIGMOD, 1997*.

[9] Jeijun Kong, Cindy Chen and Carlo Zaniolo: A Temporal Extension of SQL for Object Relational Databases, submitted for publication, 2000.

[10] ISO/IEC JTC1/SC21 N10489, ISO//IEC 9075, "Committee Draft (CD), Database Language SQL", July 1996.

[11] ISO DBL LHR-004 and ANSI X3H2-95-364, "(ISO/ANSI Working Draft) Database language SQL3", Jim Melton (ed), dated 1995.

[12] Informix: Datablade Developers Kid InfoShelf, Informix 1998, http://www.informix.co.za/answers/english/docs/dbdk/infoshelf/index.html

[13] G. S. Manku, S. Rajagopalan, B. G. Lindsay: Approximate Medians and other Quantiles in One Pass and with Limited Memory. SIGMOD Conference 1998: 426-435

[14] I. Motakis, C. Zaniolo, "Temporal Aggregation in Active Database Rules". In *SIGMOD'97*.

[15] S. Sarawagi, S. Thomas, R. Agrawal, "Integrating Association Rule Mining with Relational Database Systems: Alternatives and Implications". In *SIGMOD, 1998*.

[16] J. C. Shafer, R. Agrawal, M. Mehta, "SPRINT: A Scalable Parallel Classifier for Data Mining," In *VLDB 1996*.

[17] P. Seshadri, M. Livny, and R. Ramakrishnan. SEQ: Design and implementation of a sequence database system. submitted for publication, 1996.

[18] M. Stonebraker, L. Rowe, and M. Hirohama, "The Implementation of POSTGRES." *IEEE Transactions on Knowledge and Data Engineering*, **2**(1), March 1990.

[19] H. Wang, C. Zaniolo, "User-Defined Aggregates for Datamining," 1999 ACM SIGMOD Workshop on Research Issues in Data Mining and Knowledge Discovery, Philadelphia, PA, May 30, 1999.

[20] Haixun Wang, The SQL-AG System, http://magna.cs.ucla.edu/~hxwang/sqlag/sqlag.html

[21] Haixun Wang, The AXL System, in "http://vesuvio.cs.ucla.edu/~hxwang/axl"

[22] Haixun Wang, Carlo Zaniolo, "User Defined Aggregates in Object-Relational Systems", in the 16th International Conference on Data Engineering (ICDE'2000), San Diego, USA, 2000.

[23] H. Wang and C. Zaniolo, User Defined Aggregates in Database Languages, 7th Int. Workshop on DB Programming Languages, Kinloch Rannoch, Scotland, Sept. 1999.

[24] C. Zaniolo, S. Ceri, C. Faloutzos, R. Snodgrass, V.S. S ubrahmanian, and R. Zicari, "Advanced Database Systems," Morgan Kaufmann Publishers, 1997.

[25] F. Zemke, K. Kulkarni, A. Witkowski, B. Lyle, "Introduction to OLAP functions" ISO/IEC JTC1/SC32 WG3: YGJ-068 = ANSI NCITS H2-99-154r2.

[26] Sleepycat Software, "The Berkeley Database (Berkeley DB)", http://www.sleepycat.com.

ICICLES: Self-tuning Samples for Approximate Query Answering

Venkatesh Ganti[*]   Mong Li Lee   Raghu Ramakrishnan

{vganti,leeml,raghu}@cs.wisc.edu

Department of Computer Sciences, University of Wisconsin-Madison

Abstract

Approximate query answering systems provide very fast alternatives to OLAP systems when applications are tolerant to small errors in query answers. Current sampling-based approaches to approximately answer aggregate queries over foreign key joins suffer from the following drawback. All tuples in relations are deemed equally important for answering queries even though, in reality, OLAP queries exhibit locality in their data access. Consequently, they may waste precious real estate by sampling tuples that are not required at all or required very rarely.

In this paper, we introduce *icicles*, a new class of samples that tune themselves to a dynamic workload. Intuitively, the probability of a tuple being present in an icicle is proportional to its importance for answering queries in the workload. Therefore, an icicle consists of more tuples from a subset of the relation that is required to answer more queries in the workload. Consequently, the accuracy of approximate answers obtained by using icicles is better than a static uniform random sample. We show, analytically, that for a certain class of queries reflected by the workload, icicles yield more accurate answers. In a detailed experimental study, we examine the validity and performance of icicles.

---

[*]Supported by a Microsoft Graduate Fellowship.

Proceedings of the 26th VLDB Conference,
Cairo, Egypt, 2000.

1 Introduction

Advances in information collection and management have enabled businesses to build large data warehouses containing data about customers and their daily business activity. The realization that careful analysis of this data yields valuable business intelligence led to the emergence of *on-line analytic processing (OLAP)* systems for decision support. The goal of these systems is to provide interactive response times to aggregate queries. However, very large database sizes may not allow true interactivity despite careful design and development of an OLAP system.

Approximate query answering (AQUA) systems are being developed with a goal to reduce response times to true levels of interactivity [VL93, AGPR99b, CMN99, PG99, SFB99, MS00]. That most decision support applications can tolerate approximate answers to queries is exploited by AQUA systems to achieve truly interactive response times.

Several approximate query answering approaches for different data domains have been proposed: sampling-based [AGPR99b, AGPR99a], histogram-based [PG99], clustering-based [SFB99], probabilistic [MS00], and wavelet-based [VW99] approaches. Both histogram-based and wavelet-based approaches assume that attributes of underlying relations are numerical. The sampling-based approach does not require such assumptions. Moreover, only sampling-based approaches have been explored for approximately answering aggregate queries over joins of relations. Therefore, we consider sampling-based techniques in this paper.[1]

Gibbons et al. introduce the concept of a *join synopsis* which, informally, is a uniform random sample over foreign-key joins of relations [AGPR99b]. Depending on the database schema they compute a set of join synopses to approximately answer aggregate queries. However, such a static sampling approach has the following drawback. All tuples within each relation (or a foreign-key join of a set of relations) are assumed to be equally important while collecting a random sample. However, in practice, OLAP

---

[1]This is not to say that the sampling-based approach is qualitatively better than others. In fact, other approaches may be enhanced in the same way we enhance a sampling-based approach.

queries follow a predictable repetitive pattern, and exhibit locality in their data access [DSRN98]. Therefore, treating all tuples uniformly while sampling wastes precious main-memory on tuples that are not required for answering queries.

As an example, consider the data warehouse of the `Widget Tuners` company that maintains all sales information of widgets in United States over the past ten years. A salesperson in the Madison office of `Widget Tuners` may only be interested in analyzing the sale of widgets in Wisconsin over the past one or two years. In such cases, maintaining a uniform random sample over the entire relation wastes real estate because it samples sales information on regions outside of Wisconsin for the last ten years, and the early eight year window of Wisconsin sales. It may waste more than 95% of the available main memory on sampling unnecessary information. But, since we do not a priori know the focus of analysis, a straight-forward approach of jacking up the sampling rate in a given region of the relation cannot be applied.

In this paper, we address the above-mentioned drawback of a static sampling strategy to answer aggregate queries over foreign key joins. The intuition behind our approach is to incrementally maintain a sample, called *icicles*,[2] in which the probability of a tuple being selected is proportional to the frequency with which it is required to answer queries (exactly). That is, the probability is proportional to the number of query predicates in the workload that the tuple satisfies. Therefore, an icicle is expected to consist of more tuples in regions that are accessed more frequently to answer queries. We exploit this property to provide more accurate answers to aggregate queries. Our contributions in this paper are:

1. We introduce a new class of samples, called *icicles*, to capture the data locality exhibited by a set of aggregate queries over foreign key joins.

2. We develop a dynamic algorithm that tunes an *icicle* with respect to the most recent knowledge of the workload (Section 3).

3. We develop estimators for average, count, and sum aggregates to answer queries using icicles (Section 4).

4. We analytically show that icicles are better than static samples for approximately answering a certain class of queries that conform to the workload (Section 6).

5. In an extensive experimental evaluation, we compare the performance of icicles with (static) join synopses (Section 7).

2   Icicles

In this section, we discuss informally the intuition behind icicles, the algorithm for maintaining icicles, and the problem in using traditional estimators with icicles. We start

---

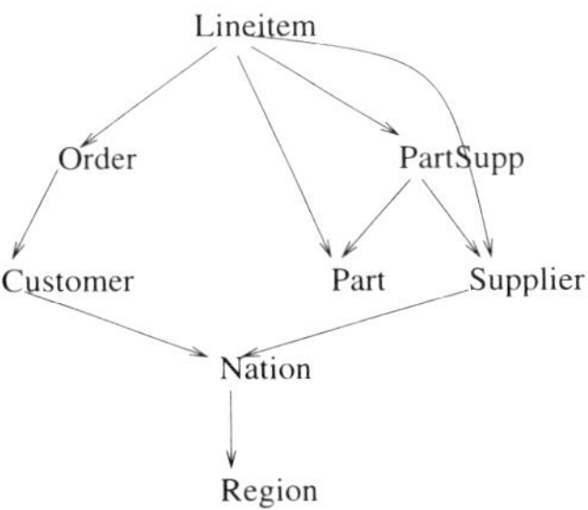

Figure 1: Foreign Key Relationships in TPC-D

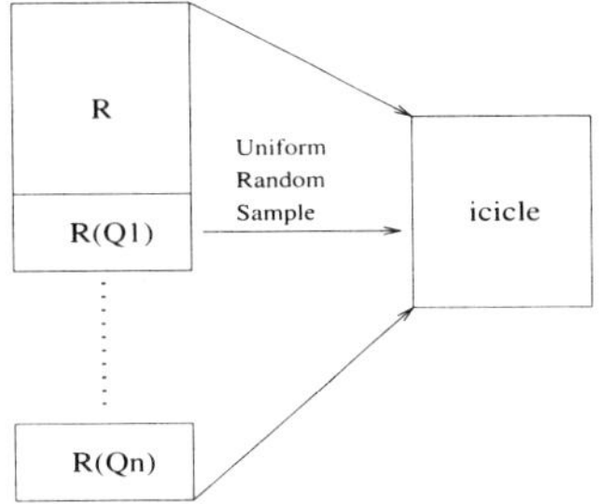

Figure 2: Logical Relation and an icicle

with a brief discussion of earlier work on sampling-based approaches for approximately answering aggregate queries.

Gibbons et al. [AGPR99b] and Chaudhuri et al. [CMN99] showed that a join of random samples of base relations may not be a random sample of the join of base relations. Gibbons et al. exploit the property that relations in many decision support applications are connected by foreign key relationships. For instance, in a star schema, the fact table and dimension tables are connected by foreign key relationships, and queries over such schema typically involve foreign key joins. They introduced the concept of a *join synopsis*, which is the join of a uniform random sample of the fact table with a set of dimension tables. Any aggregate query involving the fact table can now be answered approximately using exactly one of a small number of synopses.

Example 2.1 As a running example, we consider the TPC-D database [Cou95] shown in Figure 1. It consists of the following relations: `Lineitem (LI)`, `Order (O)`, `Customer (C)`, `Part (P)`, `PartSupp (PS)`, `Supplier (S)`, `Nation (N)`, `and Region (R)`. `LI` is the fact table and `O`, `P`, `S` are constrained by foreign key relationships with the `LI` table. The complete schema is shown as a directed graph in Figure 1 wherein a directed edge from relation A to relation B captures the existence of a foreign key constraint from A to B. A query Q derived from query 5 in the TPC-D benchmark is shown below. Note that all joins in the query are foreign key joins. Therefore, this query can be answered approximately using a join synopsis on the join of `LI`, `C`, `O`, `S`, `N`, and `R` relations.

SELECT COUNT(*), AVG(LI_Extendedprice),

---

[2]The number of accesses to tuples in a workload-sensitive sample relative to that over tuples in the relation resembles an *icicle*.

SUM(LI_Extendedprice)
FROM LI, C, O, S, N, R
WHERE C_Custkey=O_Custkey AND O_Orderkey=LI_Orderkey
AND LI_Suppkey=S_Suppkey AND C_Nationkey=N_Nationkey
AND N_Regionkey=R_Regionkey AND R_Name=North America
AND O_Orderdate$\geq$01-01-1998 AND O_Orderdate$\leq$12-31-1998;

In the above TPC-D example query that typifies decision support queries, an analyst is interested in sales in the North American continent for the year 1998. Analysts in North America are unlikely to be very interested in sales in other continents. Therefore, all their queries may be focused on the sales after 1998 in North America. In such cases, a uniform random sample of the entire relation wastes precious main-memory by drawing a significant number of tuples from sets of tuples that are not as "important" for answering queries. The space is better utilized if more sample tuples are gathered from 1998 sales in North America resulting in a significant improvement of the accuracy of approximate answers.

Note that we do not a priori know the subset or sets of subsets on which the analysis is focused. Moreover, the focus may change with time. Therefore, we have to automatically identify the focus of a query workload and sample accordingly. We introduce a new class of workload-sensitive samples, called *icicles*, that capture the data locality exhibited by queries in the workload. *An icicle is a uniform random sample of a multiset of tuples L, which is the union of R and all sets of tuples that were required to answer queries in the workload.* We call L the *extension* of R with respect to the workload.

We maintain an icicle of a relation R (or a foreign key join of relations) as follows. To start with, L is exactly the same as R, and an icicle is a uniform random sample of R. For each query Q on R, we derive a multiset L' by appending to L the set of all tuples in R that satisfy the query predicate (and hence were required to answer Q). The icicle is now updated to be a random sample of the new multiset L'. We use the reservoir sampling algorithm [Vit85] to maintain the invariant that an icicle is a random sample of L. (Note that the algorithm for updating icicles only accesses the new block of data that is logically appended to L.) Therefore, if a particular set of tuples is retrieved for a lot of queries then an icicle is expected to consist of a greater proportion of tuples from this set.

2.1 Icicle-based Estimators

An icicle is a non-uniform sample of the original relation. Hence, traditional estimators for aggregate operators cannot always be applied directly. For instance, consider the TPC-D query Q shown in Example 2.1. Suppose the size of the lineitem relation LI consists of 1000000 tuples and the sample consists of 1000 tuples. Suppose $LI(Q)$ consists of 100000 tuples. A uniform random sample of LI is expected to consist of 100 tuples from $LI(Q)$. Starting with a random sample of relation LI, if the *count query* is executed

five times, the number of tuples from $LI(Q)$ in the icicle is expected to increase by five times to 500. However, the size of the extension of L increases marginally by an amount $5 \cdot |LI(Q)|$ to a value 1500000. It is easy to see that the traditional estimation of scaling up the count from a sample S of LI by a factor of $\frac{|LI|}{|S|}$ is way off the mark!

We need new estimators for providing more accurate answers. In Section 4, we derive icicle-based estimators for the average, count, and sum aggregate operators. The basic idea is to maintain additional information to adjust for the selection bias in an icicle. We maintain a set of *frequencies*, one per tuple in the relation, where the frequency of a tuple is the number of times it was required to answer queries in the workload.

2.2 Quality Guarantees

The accuracy of an approximate answer is expected to increase with the number of tuples in the sample that were actually used to compute it. Since we expect an icicle to contain a greater proportion of tuples from frequently accessed sets of tuples, the quality of answers computed using these sets is better. If the number of queries that use such frequent sets is much greater than the number of queries that do not, the average quality of answers improves as well. Under the assumption that the past workload reflects the future workload, we expect that an icicle provides more accurate answers than a statically collected uniform random sample of the relation. In Section 6, we show analytically that for a broad class of queries computing averages, icicles are expected to provide more accurate answers than simple uniform random samples. However, if an occasional query does not conform to the workload or if the workload changes drastically, then the accuracy of the approximation for that query or for a set of queries is worse than a static sample. But, as shown in Section 7, icicles adapt quickly to a workload. Therefore, such sudden changes in a workload will deteriorate performance only for a short period of time.

2.3 Sampling Over Foreign Key Joins and Base Relations

Due to the results in [AGPR99b, CMN99], we focus on answering aggregate queries involving only foreign key joins (especially, joins between fact tables and dimension tables). Since join synopses are uniform random samples over foreign key joins of a set of base relations, any query in the targeted class can be answered using only one of a small number of join synopses.[3] Therefore, maintaining join synopses is conceptually equivalent to maintaining a set of uniform random samples, each drawn from a single (logical) relation. Therefore, in the algorithmic description, we assume that samples are being drawn from single relations. However, in our experimental study, we evaluate the performance of icicles for answering aggregate queries over foreign-key joins. To avoid any confusion with the precise

---

[3]The total number of such foreign key joins in a star schema is limited ([AGPR99b]).

definition of a join synopsis (see [AGPR99b]), we use the term *static sample* instead of join synopsis.

3 Icicle Maintenance

In this section, we introduce our notation and definitions. We then describe the algorithm for maintaining icicles with respect to a dynamically changing workload.

3.1 Definitions and Notation

We now introduce our terminology beginning with some basic notation. Following the reasons discussed earlier, we assume that icicles are drawn from single relations. In this paper, we study the class of *average, count*, and *sum* aggregate operators.

We use $A(Q)$ to denote a query involving the aggregate A (one of average, count, or sum). A *workload* Q is a set of aggregate queries. If S is a multiset of tuples, we use $\tilde{S}$ to denote the set of distinct tuples in S. Let S_1 and S_2 be two multisets. We use $S_1 \uplus S_2$ to denote the multiset-union of S_1 and S_2. That is, an element is repeated in the result once for every appearance in either S_1 or S_2.

For the remainder of this section, we assume that R is a relation and Q is a workload. We use $A(Q, R)$ to denote the *exact answer* for the aggregate query $A(Q)$ over the relation R.

Given R and a query $A(Q)$, the *query-relevant subset* $R(Q)$ *of* R *for* $A(Q)$ is the set of tuples in R that satisfy the query predicate. $R(Q)$ is also the *minimal set* of tuples in R that are required to exactly answer $A(Q)$. Note that the subset $R(Q)$ of R is independent of the query processing algorithm. An algorithm may scan the entire relation R and determine the (minimal) subset required to answer $A(Q)$, or it may retrieve the minimal subset through an index-scan.

Definition 3.1 The *frequency relation* $F(R, Q) = \{f(t, R, Q) | t \in R\}$ is a set of frequencies one for every tuple $t \in R$ where, $f(t, R, Q) = \sum_{Q \in Q} t \in R(Q)$. That is, the frequency with respect to Q of a tuple $t \in R$ is the number of queries in Q whose query-relevant subsets contain t. The *frequency sum* $\sigma(R, Q)$ is the sum of all frequencies in $F(R, Q)$. That is, $\sigma(R, Q) = \sum_{t \in R} f(t, R, Q)$. $\qquad \odot$

A workload where all tuples in a relation are retrieved equally frequently to answer queries in the workload is called the *uniform workload*. Let $F(R, U)$ represent a uniform workload on R. Then, for any $t \in R$, $f(t, R, U) = c$ for some non-negative integer c. Without loss of generality, we assume that $c = 1$.

Definition 3.2 The *extension* $L(R, Q)$ *of* R *with respect to* Q is defined as follows.

$$L(R, Q) = R \uplus_{Q \in Q} R(Q)$$

An *icicle* $S(R, Q)$ of R with respect to Q is a uniform random sample of $L(R, Q)$. $\qquad \odot$

3.2 Maintenance Algorithm

We now describe our algorithm to maintain an icicle over a single relation. We then generalize it to a set of icicles over a set of relations.

Intuitively, we maintain an icicle such that, at all times, the probability of a tuple's presence in the icicle is proportional to its "importance" in answering queries in a workload. We quantify the importance of a tuple to be its frequency with respect to the workload. Hence, we maintain an icicle such that a tuple is selected with a probability proportional to its frequency. However, we do not want to scan the complete relation whenever we update the icicle. The efficient incremental maintenance of an icicle is possible due to the following two observations. First, a uniform random sample of the extension of a relation R with respect to a workload ensures that each tuple's selection in the icicle is proportional to its frequency. Second, incremental maintenance of a random sample of the extension of R only requires the segment $R(Q)$ of the relation each time a new query $A(Q)$ is answered by the system. We use the *reservoir sampling* algorithm [Vit85] to maintain a random sample of the extension.

As mentioned in Section 2.1, we maintain the frequency relation to derive good estimates for aggregate queries. For clarity in presentation, we treat the maintenance of the frequency relation $F(R, Q)$ independently. However, in Section 5, we describe in detail the maintenance of the frequency relation. For now, we assume that a routine to update frequencies of a set of tuples exists.

Algorithm 3.1 UpdateIcicle($L(R, Q)$, $S(R, Q)$, $A(Q)$)
/* $L(R, Q)$:*extension of* R, $S(R, Q)$:*icicle*, $A(Q)$:*new query* */
begin
    Step 1: *Compute* $R(A(Q))$.
    Step 3: *Set* $L(R, Q) = L(R, Q) \uplus R(A(Q))$.
    Step 2: *Update* $S(R, Q)$ *such that it is a uniform*
                random sample of the updated $L(R, Q)$.
    Step 4: *Increment the frequencies in* $F(R, Q)$ *of*
                each tuple $t \in R(A(Q))$.
end

The pseudocode for the algorithm to update icicles is presented above. At any instant, an icicle $S(R, Q)$ is a uniform random sample of $L(R, Q)$. Conceptually, we stream each tuple being appended to $L(R, Q)$ through a reservoir sampling procedure [Vit85] that maintains a uniform random sample of $L(R, Q)$.[4] When a new query $A(Q)$ is added to the workload Q, we stream tuples in $R(Q)$ through the reservoir sampling procedure to update the icicle $S(R, Q)$ such that it is a uniform random sample of $L(R, Q) \uplus R(Q)$. Even though the pseudocode serializes steps 1 and 2, we pipeline the streaming operator into the

---

[4]The reservoir sampling algorithm maintains a uniform random sample of the relation as follows: it scans the relation one tuple at a time and randomly decides whether to insert it into the sample. If the tuple is added to the sample, another tuple in the sample is kicked out.

reservoir sampling procedure. Thus, we do not need to simultaneously store all of $R(Q)$ in-memory. Also, note that $L(R, \mathcal{Q})$ is not explicitly materialized at all.

3.2.1 Workload Restriction

Note that the icicle-maintenance algorithm accesses all tuples in the set $R(Q)$ that satisfy the query predicate of a query $A(Q)$. Therefore, the amount of work done to update an icicle is almost the same as the work done to answer the query exactly. If the workload includes queries where a user is happy with just an approximate answer, the overhead in maintaining icicles is significant. Therefore, we *restrict* the workload to only consist of queries in the system that require exact answers to queries.[5] This restriction allows us to update icicles for free because tuning an icicle with respect to a new query $A(Q)$ requires the set $R(Q)$ of tuples that satisfy the query predicate. Observe that this set of tuples would have been retrieved anyway for answering the query, and hence we do not perform any additional work for updating the icicle if we piggyback the update with the processing for the query.

Restricting the workload to only consist of exactly answered queries is reasonable because we expect a typical data analysis session to proceed as follows. Analysts derive their initial conclusions on data characteristics based on an approximate or cursory analysis where they can tolerate small errors. To confirm their initial conclusions realized from an interactive exploratory session, they issue one or more queries to be answered exactly. Therefore, the final exactly-answered queries are actual queries of interest and are likely to be representative of the true workload. Because the interactive approximate querying session leads an analyst to the final set of interesting queries, it is indispensable.

Note that duplicates of tuples may be present in an icicle because a tuple may be required several times to answer queries in a workload. It is possible to collapse such duplicates together by maintaining a *count* of the number of times a tuple appears in the icicle. Gibbons et al. showed that this approach is better than maintaining duplicates [GM98]. To avoid muddling the performance study of icicles with improvements due to collapsing duplicates, we stick with the straight-forward implementation of icicles that allows duplicate tuples. However, note that this optimization only improves the performance of icicles.

Example 3.1 We illustrate our icicle-maintenance algorithm through an example. Consider a hypothetical *Widget-Tuners* relation shown in Figure 3. We add a new *frequency* attribute to the schema of the relation to hold frequencies of tuples. A hypothetical icicle created from a hypothetical workload is shown in Figure 4. Suppose the following query is asked by an analyst to compute the average of all sales in the month of April.

```
SELECT average(*) FROM Widget-Tuners
WHERE Date.Month='April';
```

---

[5]Alternative restrictions like choosing only a subset of all queries may also be possible.

We require the two April tuples corresponding to orders 5 and 6 in Figure 3 to answer the above query exactly. The set $\{OrderId = 5, OrderId = 6\}$ consisting of these two tuples is (conceptually) appended to the extension of Widget-tuners. We now update the icicle such that it is a random sample of the updated extension. Suppose the updated icicle is as shown in Figure 5. Note that we increment the frequencies of tuples corresponding to orders 5 and 6, and that these updates are reflected in the updated icicle.

3.2.2 Maintaining Multiple Icicles

Previously, we described an algorithm for maintaining an icicle on a single relation. We now extend it to multiple relations. The extension relies on the partitionability of the workload into a set of workloads, one per relation.

Recall that our target class of queries is the class of aggregate (average, count, and sum) queries over foreign key joins. As discussed earlier, this class is equivalent to a class of single-table queries where tables may be formed from foreign-key joins of a set of relations. Any query may be answered using exactly one icicle on a relation. (It is a fallout of the fact that icicles are "tuned" synopses.) Therefore, the overall workload can be *partitioned* into several independent workloads, one for each relation. Due to the properties that the workload is partitionable and that queries access a single table, we can independently maintain icicles on relations. That is, the maintenance of an icicle on one relation does not depend on how an icicle on a different relation is maintained. Given a certain amount of space to maintain icicles, we distribute the available space among them and maintain each icicle independently. Any space-partitioning strategy to distribute space among icicles may be used here. We refer the reader to the work by Gibbons et al. [AGPR99b] for a detailed discussion of several strategies. We now formalize this procedure.

Let $R_1, \ldots, R_k$ be k relations. Let $\mathcal{Q} = \mathcal{Q}_1 \uplus \cdots \uplus \mathcal{Q}_k$ be a workload where queries in $\mathcal{Q}_i$ only access the relation R_i. Let M be the amount of space allocated for maintaining icicles. We maintain k icicles as follows. Using any space allocation strategy, allocate space M_i to an icicle $S(R_i, \mathcal{Q}_i)$ on relation R_i, $1 \leq i \leq k$. For a query $Q \in \mathcal{Q}_i$, we update the icicle $S(R_i, \mathcal{Q}_i)$ using the *UpdateIcicle* Algorithm.

4 Estimators for Aggregate Queries

In the previous section, we described how we maintain an icicle with respect to a changing workload. We now describe the methodology of answering aggregate queries using the icicle. Due to the presence of duplicates and the selection bias (or non-uniformity) in an icicle, traditional estimators (e.g.,[Olk93, AGPR99b]) do not apply directly. An example was discussed in Section 2.1 to illustrate this problem. We now derive icicle-based estimators for the average, count, and sum aggregate operators. We first discuss the intuition behind our aggregate estimators, and then formalize them in Lemma 4.1. (Due to space constraints, we do not present the proof of the lemma.)

OrderID	Date	Price	Frequency
1	01-Jan-1998	100	3
2	01-Feb-1998	200	1
3	01-Feb-1998	150	1
4	01-Mar-1998	125	1
5	01-Apr-1998	120	$2 \to 3$
6	01-Apr-1998	140	$2 \to 3$

Figure 3: Widget-tuners

OID	Date	Price	Frequency
1	01-Jan-1998	100	3
4	01-Mar-1998	125	1
6	01-Apr-1998	140	2

Figure 4: An icicle of Widget-tuners

OID	Date	Price	Frequency
1	01-Jan-1998	100	3
5	01-Apr-1998	120	3
6	01-Apr-1998	140	3

Figure 5: Updated icicle of Widget-Tuners

When the sum or average is being computed, we use X to denote the aggregated attribute.

Average: We assume that for any query $A(Q)$ the value a tuple $t \in R(Q)$ assumes for the aggregated attribute X is independent of the probability that t is present in the icicle. That is, the distribution of values of X in the set of tuples accessed by the query from the icicle is the same as that in $R(Q)$. Under this assumption, the average of the set of distinct sample tuples that satisfy a given average query is a good estimate of the average. Note that our assumption is similar to the (implicit) assumption made by Gibbons et al. [AGPR99b]. Their assumption was that the value distribution of an attribute is independent of query predicates which, in turn, determine the probability of a tuple's presence in an icicle.

Count: Intuitively, we expect each tuple in an icicle to correspond to a set of tuples in the original relation R. We first compute an estimate of the number of tuples in R that contribute one tuple t in the icicle. We call this value the *expected contribution* of t. We then estimate the count aggregate to be the sum of expected contributions of all tuples in the icicle that satisfy the given query.

Sum: Under the assumption that for any query $A(Q)$, the value a tuple $t \in R(Q)$ assumes for the aggregated attribute X is independent of the probability that t is present in the icicle, the average and the count aggregates are independent of each other. Therefore, the estimate of the sum aggregate is given by the product of the average and count estimates.

Lemma 4.1 Let $A(Q)$ be an aggregate query over the relation R, and $S = S(R, \mathcal{Q})$ be an icicle over R with respect to a workload $\mathcal{Q}$. Let $F(R, \mathcal{Q})$ be the frequency relation. Let the probability of a tuple t being present in S be independent of the probability that t assumes a certain value for an aggregated attribute X. Then $E[A(Q, R)]$

$$= \begin{cases} E[A(Q, \tilde{S})], & \text{if A=avg} \\ \frac{\sigma(R, \mathcal{Q})}{|S|} \sum_{t \in S(Q)} \frac{1}{f(t, R, Q)} & \text{if A=count} \\ E[avg(Q, \tilde{S})] \cdot E[count(Q, S)], & \text{if A=sum} \end{cases}$$

5 Maintaining the Frequency Relation

Recall that we maintain the frequency associated with each tuple for estimating count queries. We now discuss an efficient procedure for maintaining the frequency relation $F(R, \mathcal{Q})$ of a relation R with respect to a workload $\mathcal{Q}$.

To hold the frequency for each tuple, we add a new *frequency* attribute to the relation R. To start with, the frequency of each tuple is set to 1. The frequency of a tuple is incremented whenever it is accessed to answer a query. Therefore, whenever we update an icicle with a new query, we update frequencies of all tuples required to answer the query. Consequently, the frequency column is update-intensive. Even though these updates may be performed off-line when the system is idle, they still constitute a significant overhead. We now describe an efficient procedure for updating frequencies of tuples that exploits the following two properties. First, frequencies need not be maintained up-to-date. That is, it is not absolutely necessary to immediately update the frequency of a tuple whenever it is accessed by a query. Second, data analysis queries exhibit data locality. Therefore, frequencies of a significant portion of often-accessed tuples can be maintained in main memory.

The intuition behind our approach is to delay updating the frequency of a tuple until the magnitude of the change in frequency crosses a certain threshold. The delay helps to batch several related updates (either on the same tuple or on distinct tuples) together thus significantly reducing the overall number of updates. We maintain a main-memory hash table consisting of two attributes: *tuple identifier* and *count*. The *count* for a tuple t in the hash table is the number of times t was required to answer queries since the last time the frequency $f(t, R, \mathcal{Q})$ of t has been updated on disk. The hash table maintains a set of tuples and the counts associated with them.

Whenever a tuple t that is required to answer a query, is read into main memory, we check if t is present in the hash table. If not, we add t to the hash table and set its count to 1. If t is present in the hash table, we increment its count in the hash table. If the count crosses a threshold C (fixed a priori), we update the frequency $f(t, R, \mathcal{Q})$ of t on the disk and delete t from the hash table. We may further optimize this algorithm by updating frequencies of all other tuples in the hash table that belong to the same disk page as t.

5.1 Special Case of the Average Operator

We now discuss a very important optimization for the special case when we are only interested in answering queries that compute averages. We observe that we do ***not*** need to maintain the frequency relation if we restrict ourselves to answering queries with the average operator.

Recall that estimators for the count and the sum aggregate operators require frequencies of tuples in their computation while the computation of the estimate for the average operator does not (Section 4). Also, note that the frequency relation is not required for any purpose other than estimating count and sum aggregate operators. Therefore, if we restrict the class of queries to be answered approximately to the class of aggregate queries computing averages, then we do not need to maintain frequencies of tuples. Thus, restricting the query class significantly reduces the costs for maintaining icicles.

6 Quality Guarantees

In this section, we compare the quality of answers obtained from icicles with answers obtained from static samples. When queries in a workload exhibit data locality, then icicles consist of more tuples from frequently accessed subsets of the relation. The accuracy of an approximate answer improves with the number of tuples used to compute it. Therefore, if a new query reflects the data locality of earlier queries in the workload, then the icicle-based answer to this query is more accurate than that based on a uniform random sample of the relation. We now prove that icicles provide more accurate answers for a certain class of queries computing averages. Intuitively, this class consists of queries "focused" with respect to the workload that created an icicle.

We say that a query $A(Q)$ is *focused* with respect to a workload $\mathcal{Q}$ if any tuple in the set $R(Q)$ is, on an average, accessed more often by queries in $\mathcal{Q}$ than queries in a uniform workload. That is, for a query $A(Q)$ over the relation R, the average frequency with respect to $\mathcal{Q}$ of a tuple in $R(Q)$ is greater than that for a uniform workload. We now formalize this notion below.

Definition 6.1 Let R be a relation and $\mathcal{Q}$ be a workload. Let $F(R, \mathcal{Q})$ be the frequency relation of R with respect to $\mathcal{Q}$. Let $\sigma(R, \mathcal{Q}) = \sum_{t \in R} f(t, R, \mathcal{Q})$. We say that an aggregate query $A(Q)$ is *focused* with respect to $\mathcal{Q}$ if

$$\frac{\sum_{t \in R(Q)} f(R, t, \mathcal{Q})}{\sigma(R, \mathcal{Q})} \geq \frac{|R(Q)|}{|R|}$$

$\odot$

Lemma 6.1 Let R be a relation, $\mathcal{Q}$ be a workload, and $F(R, \mathcal{Q})$ be the frequency relation of R with respect to $\mathcal{Q}$.

Let $\sigma(R, \mathcal{Q}) = \sum_{t \in R} f(t, R, \mathcal{Q})$. Let $S(R, \mathcal{Q})$ be an icicle created by $\mathcal{Q}$ and S be a uniform random sample of R. The expected fraction of $R(Q)$ tuples in S is $\frac{|R(Q)|}{|R|}$, and the expected fraction of $R(Q)$ tuples in $S(R, \mathcal{Q})$ is $\frac{\sum_{t \in R(Q)} f(t, R, \mathcal{Q})}{\sigma(R, \mathcal{Q})}$.

Theorem 6.1 *Let R be a relation, $\mathcal{Q}$ be a workload on R, and $F(R, \mathcal{Q})$ be the frequency relation of R with respect to $\mathcal{Q}$. Let $S(R, \mathcal{Q})$ be an icicle on R. Let S be a uniform random sample on R. If a query $average(Q)$ is focused with respect to $\mathcal{Q}$, then the icicle $S(R, \mathcal{Q})$ yields a more accurate estimate for $average(Q)$ than the uniform random sample S.*

The above theorem follows from Lemma 6.1. We now present a straight-forward extension of Theorem 6.1 to multiple relations. The extension merely relies on the partitionability of the workload and that the amount of space allocated to each icicle and the corresponding uniform static sample on a relation are equal.

Corollary 6.1 *Let $R_1, \ldots, R_k$ be k relations. Let the workload $\mathcal{Q} = \mathcal{Q}_1 \cup \cdots \cup \mathcal{Q}_k$ be such that any query $Q \in \mathcal{Q}_i$ only accesses relation R_i. For $1 \leq i \leq k$, let S_i be a uniform random sample of R_i and $S(R_i, \mathcal{Q}_i)$ be an icicle on R_i with respect to the workload $\mathcal{Q}_i$ such that $|S_i| = |S(R_i, \mathcal{Q}_i)|$. Then a query $average(Q_i)$ focused with respect to the workload $\mathcal{Q}_i$ will be answered more accurately by $S(R_i, \mathcal{Q}_i)$.*

7 Performance Evaluation

In this section, we evaluate the accuracy of answers, obtained from icicles, to aggregate queries for a wide variety of workloads, and their adaptability to the characteristics of a workload.

7.1 Experimental Testbed

We now describe our experimental setup and briefly outline our experimental procedure. We use the TPC-D decision support benchmark to generate a variety of workloads. Using a scale factor of 0.3, we generate 300 megabytes of test data.

Workload Characteristics and Parameters: We fix the number of queries in a workload to be 40. We use the query $Q_{workload}$ shown in Figure 6 to generate workloads. ($Q_{workload}$ is derived from the query Q_5 of the TPC-D benchmark.) The query has two parameters: *region* and *start date*. Region takes values from the set {AFRICA, AMERICA, ASIA, EUROPE, MIDDLE-EAST}. The start date may vary between 01-01-1993 and 06-31-1998. A workload is characterized by the *number of frequently accessed groups* of tuples in a relation, and the *relative size* of each group. The number of frequently accessed groups is varied using the *region* attribute. We vary the sizes of

```
SELECT  COUNT(*), AVG(LI_Extendedprice), SUM(LI_Extendedprice)
FROM  LI, C, O, S, N, R
WHERE  C_Custkey=O_Custkey AND O_Orderkey=LI_Orderkey AND LI_Suppkey=S_Suppkey AND
       C_Nationkey = N_Nationkey AND N_Regionkey = R_Regionkey AND
       R_Name = [region] AND O_Orderdate ≥ Date[startdate] AND O_Orderdate ≤ 12-31-1998
```

Figure 6: $Q_{workload}$: Template for generating workloads

```
SELECT  COUNT(*), AVG(LI_Extendedprice), SUM(LI_Extendedprice)
FROM  LICOS-icicle, N, R
WHERE  C_Nationkey = N_Nationkey AND N_Regionkey = R_Regionkey AND
       R_Name = [region] AND O_Orderdate ≥ Date[startdate] AND O_Orderdate ≤ 12-31-1998
```

Figure 7: Template for obtaining approximate answers

frequently-accessed groups by varying the *start date* parameter (both month and year components) appropriately. Note that the relative size of a group of tuples accessed by a query equals the *selectivity* of the query predicate. We generate queries in the workload by setting (with an element of randomness) the region and start date parameters of $Q_{workload}$.

The join synopsis $LICOS$ we use to answer the query $Q_{workload}$ in Figure 6 is a uniform random sample of the join of lineitem LI, customer C, order O, and supplier S relations. An icicle is a tuned sample of this synopsis. The query, corresponding to $Q_{workload}$, for obtaining an approximate answer from an icicle is shown in Figure 7. (A similar query is used for using a join synopsis.) We fix the sizes of an icicle or a static sample on $LICOS$ join to be 1% of the size of the join of all four relations.

Relative Error: For each query $A(Q)$ on the relation R, we compute the *relative error* for an answer $\hat{A}_S(Q, R)$ obtained using a sample S on R as follows. (We assume that the exact answer $A(Q, R) > 0$.)

$$\text{relative-error}(S, Q) = \frac{|\hat{A}_S(Q, R) - A(Q, R)|}{A(Q, R)}$$

Plots for each Workload: For each workload, we show three plots. The first plot (indexed by the legend *static sample*) corresponds to the errors incurred by a static uniform random sample (join synopsis) of the join of LI, C, O, and S. The second plot (indexed by the legend *icicle*) shows the errors from an icicle as it evolves with the workload. That is, after each query in the workload is answered by the system, we update the icicle; the subsequent query is answered by the updated icicle. The third plot (indexed by the legend *icicle-complete*) shows the errors from a tuned icicle created by executing the entire workload. That is, we first create an icicle "tuned" with respect to queries in a workload. We then answer all queries in the (same) workload (again) using the tuned icicle and compute the error. Intuitively, this plot corresponds to the best possible accuracy from an icicle of a given size. Of course, this is not a feasible evaluation strategy; it is only intended as a way to compare how

our proposed evaluation compares in terms of a sampling strategy that has foreknowledge of the entire workload. We only show the plots for average and count estimators because the behavior of the sum estimator is already captured by these two estimators.

7.2 Quality of Approximate Answers

In this experiment, we study the accuracy of aggregate query answers obtained from icicles on both synthetic and real datasets.

7.2.1 Varying Selectivities

In this experiment, we fix the number of frequently accessed groups at 1, and vary the relative size of a frequently accessed group. Queries in the workload are derived from $Q_{workload}$. We fix the region parameter to be ASIA. We study the behavior on two such workloads. In the first workload, we fix the year component of the start date to 1998 and vary the month component between *January* and *June*. In the second workload, we fix the year component of the start date to 1997 and vary the month component between *January* and *December*. Note that the size of the frequently accessed group in the first workload (year=1998) is much smaller than that for the second workload (year=1997). We first show the 1998 plots (Figures 8 and 9), and then the 1997 plots (Figures 10 and 11).

Figures 8 and 9 demonstrate the *rapid* decrease in relative error of query answers obtained from icicles as more queries focused on a core set of tuples are added to the workload, and the icicle updated with tuples required to answer them. Note that the relative error of query answers obtained from icicles decreases significantly from 25% to 5%. Also, observe that the icicle plot converges to the icicle-complete plot even before 20 queries are answered. The quick convergence of the icicle plot to the icicle-complete plot demonstrates that icicles adapt quickly to the workload characteristics.

The results for the 1997 plots are shown in Figures 10 and 11. The conclusions are similar. Even though the relative error in answers from icicles stabilizes around 5% (as for 1998 plots), the relative improvement in accuracy due to the use of icicles is less than that for 1998 be-

183

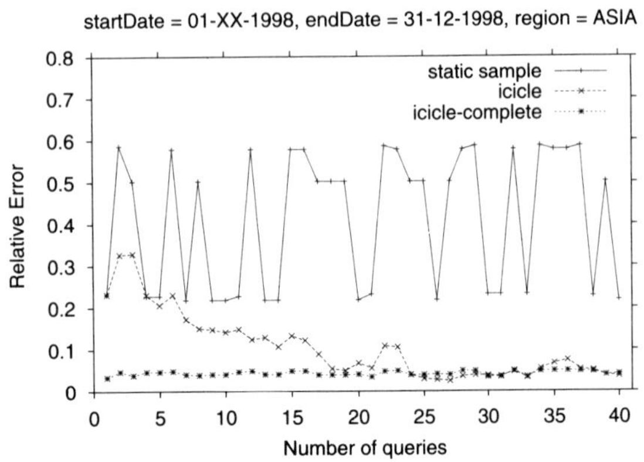

Figure 8: Average Queries

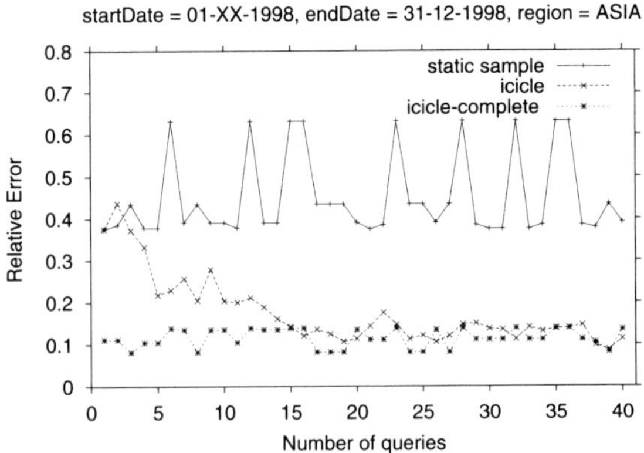

Figure 9: Count Queries

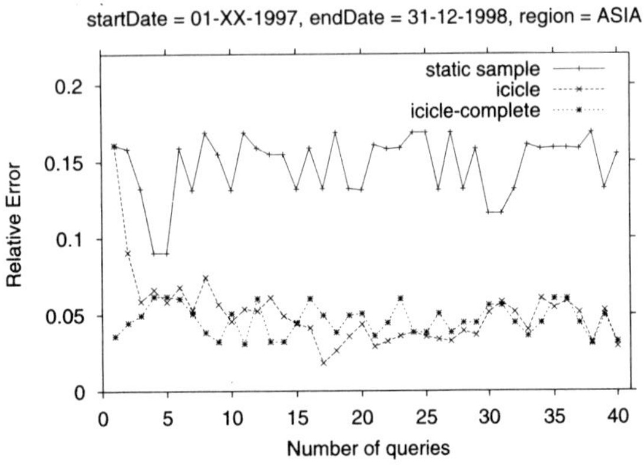

Figure 10: Average Queries

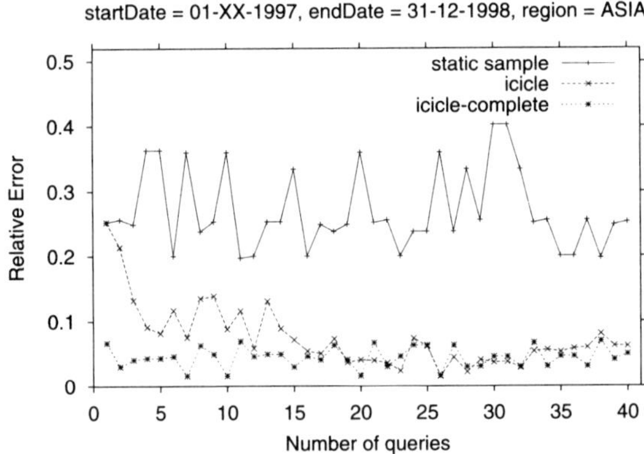

Figure 11: Count Queries

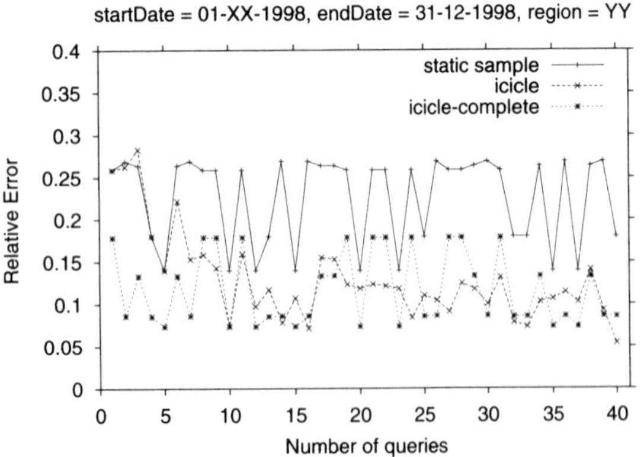

Figure 12: Average Queries

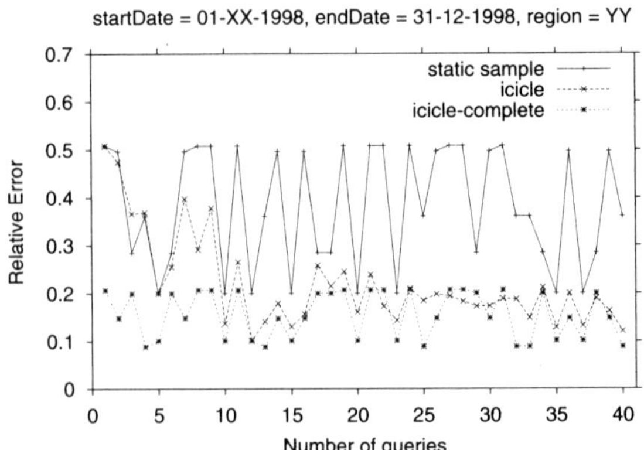

Figure 13: Count Queries

cause both icicles and static samples start at lower error values. Also, the convergence of the icicle plot to the icicle-complete is much faster than that for 1998. These observations are as expected because the absolute number of both 1997 and 1998 tuples in a uniform random sample of the $LICOS$ join is higher than that for 1998 alone.

The plots are not smooth because all queries in the workload are distinct from each other as the values for parameters to $Q_{workload}$ are chosen randomly. Therefore, the exact answers and relative errors of the estimated answers are different and vary significantly from each other. The variation is, in turn, depicted in the plots.[6] The fluctuations in errors are higher when the year component of the start date is fixed at 1998 because the absolute value of the result is much smaller for 1998. And, varying the month component causes relatively larger fluctuations in the exact result as well. These fluctuations are, in turn, exhibited by the relative error plots because the exact answer appears in the denominator of the expression for the relative error.

7.2.2 Varying Number of Groups and Selectivities

In this experiment, we increase the number of frequently accessed groups in a workload. The relative fraction is varied around a fixed constant. We generate such a workload by creating queries from $Q_{workload}$ where the region parameter is uniformly randomly selected from the set {AFRICA, AMERICA, ASIA, EUROPE, MIDDLE-EAST}. As in the previous experiment, we generate two workloads. In the first workload the year component of the start date is fixed at 1998 and the month component varied between $January$ and $June$. In the second workload, the year component is fixed at 1997 and the month component is varied between $January$ and $December$. Each workload has 5 frequently accessed groups, one per region.

The results for the first workload are shown in Figures 12 and 13, and those for the second workload in Figures 14 and 15. The conclusions from these plots are similar to those drawn in the previous section. The relative errors of answers decrease steadily when icicles are used to answer queries. The icicle plot converges quickly to the icicle-complete plot.

7.2.3 A Mixed Workload

In this section, we vary both the number of frequently accessed groups as well as relative sizes of each group. The region is randomly picked from {AFRICA, AMERICA, ASIA, EUROPE, MIDDLE-EAST} while the year component of the start date is randomly picked to be between 1993 and 1998. Note that both the year and region parameters are chosen uniformly at random from their domains. Hence, the workload is not focused on specific sets of tuples. Figures 16 and 17 show the results of this experiment. Therefore, as expected, the improvement due to the use of icicles is not significant. The important point to observe

---

Figure 20: Template Query on Mail Order Data

here though is that *icicles are as good as static samples*, if not better.

7.2.4 Mail Order Dataset

In this section, we present the performance of icicles on a real mail order dataset. Besides other information, the dataset has the following attributes: customer identifier, order date, style, price, quantity, cost, and gender code ('M' for men and 'F' for women). The dataset consists of 45000 tuples. We generate a workload by varying the start date parameter in the template query shown in Figure 20. The start date is varied over an interval of 31 days in May. (Overall, the date attribute varies between 08-01-1995 and 12-31-1996.) The size of the icicles and static samples constructed on this workload are set such that the sample has 3000 tuples.

We present the results from this experiment in Figures 18 and 19. The results and conclusions are similar to those on the TPC-D data. Again, icicles outperform static samples by a significant margin thus validating our approach to maintain more sample tuples from frequently accessed groups.

8 Related Work

The application of statistical techniques to approximate query answering has recently received attention. However, to the best of our knowledge, there is no technique that tunes data summaries (samples or any other class of summaries) with respect to a dynamic workload. We now briefly discuss previous approaches for approximate query answering, which we have not already touched upon.

We have already discussed the approach based on join synopses [AGPR99b]. Chaudhuri et al. explored the issue of introducing sampling as a relational operator [CMN99]. Hellerstein et al. proposed a framework for providing a series of monotonically improving approximate answers to a single query [HHW97].

Barbara et al. [BDF+97] present a survey of various statistical estimation techniques for data reduction, some of which have been applied for approximately answering aggregate queries. For instance, histogram-based approaches [PG99], wavelet-based approaches [VWI98, VW99], mining based approaches [SFB99, MS00] have been explored. We believe that our ideas in this paper are applicable to these summaries as well even though actual (maintenance) techniques will be different. In the APPROXIMATE query processor, Vrbsky and Liu develop notions of approximations to set-valued answers and develop computation techniques [VL92]. Their techniques are not based on statistical summaries of the data.

---

[6]This argument holds for almost all plots that follow.

185

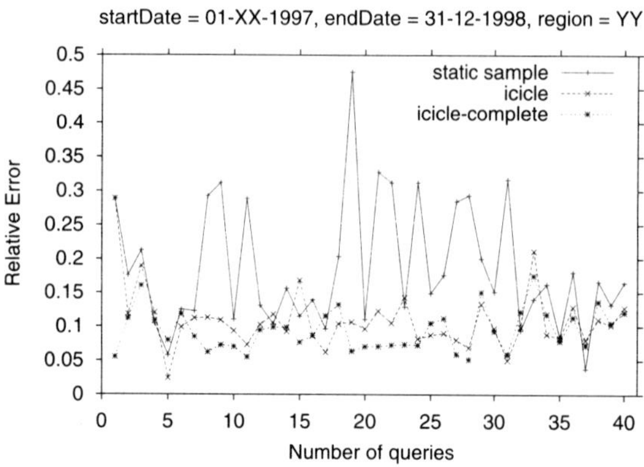

Figure 14: Average Queries

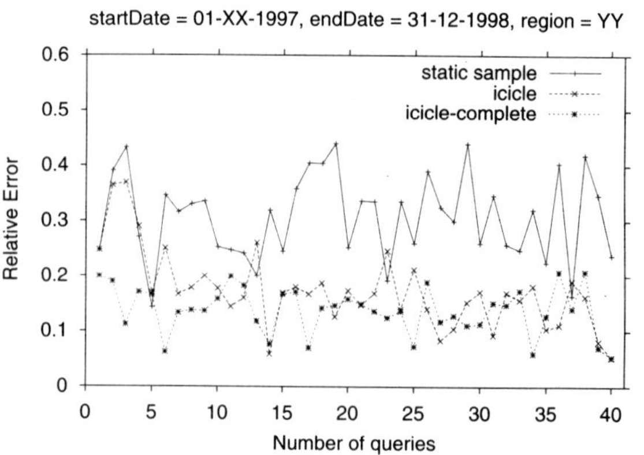

Figure 15: Count Queries

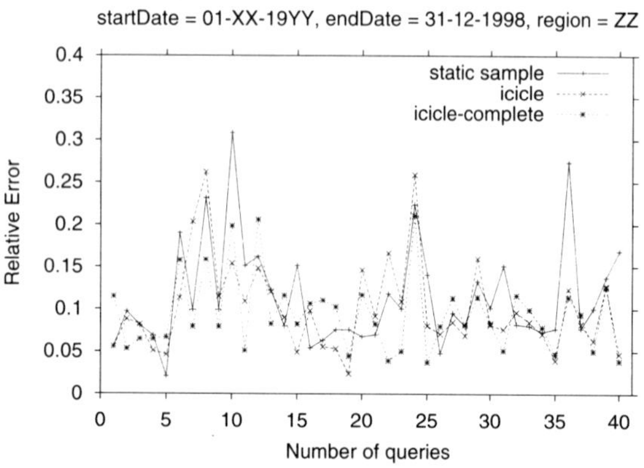

Figure 16: Mixed Workload: Average Queries

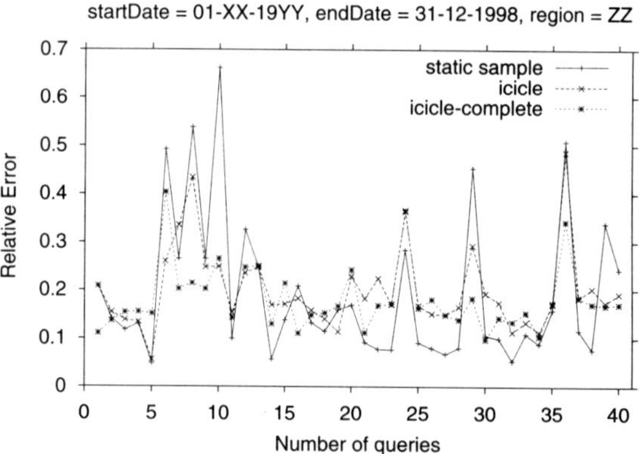

Figure 17: Mixed Workload: Count Queries

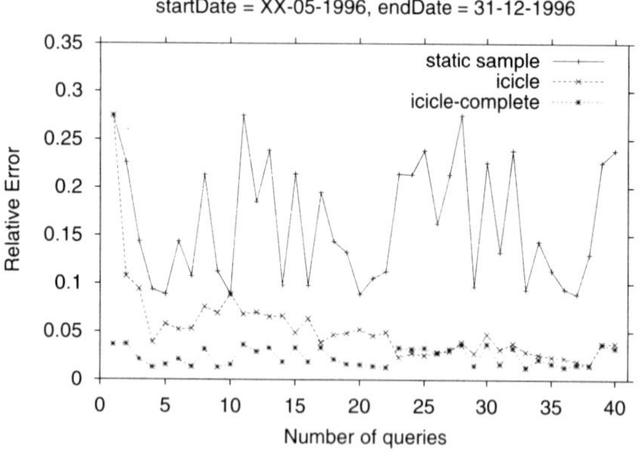

Figure 18: Mail Order Dataset: Average Queries

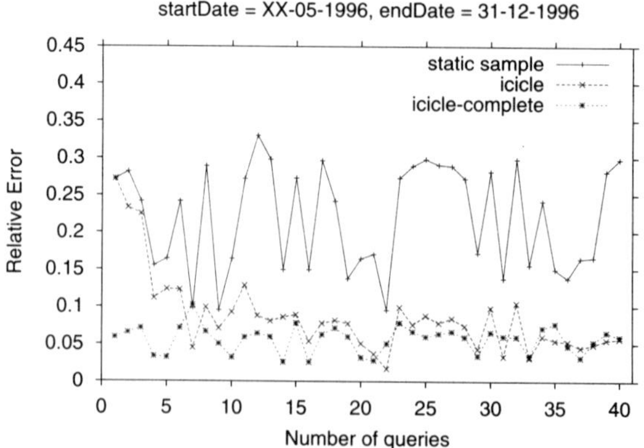

Figure 19: Mail Order Dataset: Count Queries

9 Conclusions and Future Work

We introduced a new class of samples, icicles, that are sensitive to the workload characteristics and described an incremental algorithm to maintain them with respect to a changing workload. We developed new icicle-based estimators for approximately answering aggregate queries. We show analytically and empirically that icicles are better than static samples for a wide variety of workloads. Our empirical studies further show that icicles are especially good when the workload is focused on relatively small subsets of tuples in a relation. In most cases, icicles provide more accurate answers than static samples, and they are at least as good as static samples. Finally, they adapt quickly to the characteristics of a workload.

In future, we intend to extend the maintenance of icicles when the underlying relations are being modified through ad hoc insertions and deletions.

Acknowledgements We thank Donko Donjerkovic for pointing to us that the traditional count estimator is not applicable with icicles. We also thank Kevin Beyer and Prof. Wei-Yin Loh for discussions on statistical estimators.

References

[AGPR99a] S. Acharya, P.B. Gibbons, V. Poosala, and S. Ramaswamy. The aqua approximate query answering system. In *Proceedings of ACM SIGMOD international conference on management of data*, Philadelphia, PA, June 1999. Demonstration paper.

[AGPR99b] S. Acharya, P.B. Gibbons, V. Poosala, and S. Ramaswamy. Join synopses for approximate query answering. In *Proceedings of the ACM SIGMOD International Conference on Managment of Data*, pages 275–286, Philadelphia, PA, June 1999.

[BDF+97] Daniel Barbara, William DuMouchel, Christos Faloutsos, Peter J. Haas, Joseph M. Hellerstein, Yannis E. Ionnidis, H.V. Jagadish, Theodore Johnson, Raymond T. Ng, and Viswanath Poosala. The new jersey data reduction report. *Data Engineering Bulletin*, 20(4), 1997.

[CMN99] Surajit Chaudhuri, Rajeev Motwani, and Vivek Narasayya. On random sampling over joins. In *Proceedings of the ACM SIGMOD International Conference on Managment of Data*, pages 263–274, Philadelphia, PA, June 1999.

[Cou95] Transaction Processing Performance Council, May 1995. http://www.tpc.org.

[DSRN98] Prasad Deshpande, Amit Shukla, Karthik Ramasamy, and Jeffrey Naughton. Caching multidimensional queries using chunks. In *Proceedings of the ACM SIGMOD Conference on Management of Data*, Seattle, WA, June 1998.

[GM98] P.G. Gibbons and Y. Matias. New sampling-based summary statistics for improving approximate query answers. In *Proceedings of the ACM SIGMOD International Conference on Managment of Data*, pages 331–342, Seattle, WA, June 1998.

[HHW97] Joseph M. Hellerstein, Peter J. Haas, and Helen J. Wang. Online aggregation. In Joan M. Peckman, editor, *Proceedings of the 1997 ACM SIGMOD International Conference on Management of Data*, pages 171–182, May 1997.

[MS00] Heikki Mannila and Padhraic Smyth. Approximate query answering with frequent sets and maximum entropy. In *Proceedings of the Sixteenth IEEE International Conference on Data Engineering (ICDE)*, page 309, San Diego, CA, March 2000.

[Olk93] Frank Olken. *Random Sampling from Databases*. PhD thesis, University of California at Berkeley, 1993.

[PG99] Vishy Poosala and Venkatesh Ganti. Fast approximate answers to aggregate queries on a datacube. In *Proceedings of the 11th International Conference on Scientific and Statistical Database Management*, pages 24–33, Cleveland, Ohio, July 1999.

[SFB99] Jayavel Shanmugasundaram, Usama Fayyad, and Paul Bradley. Compressed data cubes for olap aggregate query approximation on continuous dimensions. In *Proceedings of the ACM SIGKDD fifth international conference on knowledge discovery in databases*, pages 223–232, San Diego, CA, August 1999.

[Vit85] Jeffrey Vitter. Random sampling with a reservoir. *ACM Transactions on Mathematical Software*, 11(1):37–57, March 1985.

[VL92] S. Vrbsky and J. Liu. Producing approximate answers to set-valued and single-valued queries with APPROXIMATE. In *Int. Conf. on Information and Knowledge Management, Baltimore*, November 1992.

[VL93] S.V. Vrbsky and J.W.S. Liu. Approximate–a query processor that produces montonically improving answers. *IEEE Transactions on Knowledge and Data Engineering*, 5(6):1056–1068, 1993.

[VW99] Jeffrey Vitter and Min Wang. Approximate computation of multidimensional aggregates of sparse data using wavelets. In *Proceedings of the ACM SIGMOD International Conference on Managment of Data*, Philadelphia, PA, June 1999.

[VWI98] Jeffrey Vitter, Min Wang, and Bala Iyer. Data cube approximation and histogram via wavelets. In *Proceedings of the seventh international conference on information and knowledge management*, pages 96–104, Washington D.C., November 1998.

Caching Strategies for Data-Intensive Web Sites

Khaled Yagoub, Daniela Florescu, Valérie Issarny, Patrick Valduriez

INRIA-Rocquencourt

Domaine de Voluceau, 78153 Le Chesnay Cédex, France

{lastname.firstname}@inria.fr

Abstract.

Data-intensive Web sites serve large volumes of pages whose content is dynamically extracted from a database. Such Web sites have very high software development and maintenance costs and in general offer poor response times due to the heavy interaction with the database system. This paper introduces the Weave management system developed at INRIA, which alleviates the above shortcomings of data-intensive Web sites. Weave relies on the declarative specification of Web sites and offers a number of tools for the easy implementation, deployment and monitoring of the specified site. Weave features a customizable cache system that implements the optimal data materialization strategy according to the Web site's specifics: it can cache database data, XML fragments and HTML files. To explore Weave's performance we have built a Web site based on the TPC/D benchmark database using the WeaveBench test platform. We conducted a number of experiments with various data materialization strategies supported by our system. Results clearly show that in the general case, a mix of different caching policies is required to achieve optimal performance.

1 Introduction

Confronted to the rapid growth of the Internet and the need to quickly deploy effective solutions, many researchers have devoted their energy to improving Web performance by reducing client latency and bandwidth consumption and increasing servers scalability and availability. Proposed solutions include predictive prefetching, caching of Web objects, and the architecting of network and Web servers. Analyses show that existing solutions are beneficial but not yet satisfactory. Proxy caches are currently the most effective mechanism to improve Web performance, and yet

Proceedings of the 26th VLDB Conference, Cairo, Egypt, 2000.

traces clearly show that these caches only manage to attain a maximal hit rate of about 50% [27]. This limitation is mainly due to the dynamic nature of many HTML documents, which prevents them to be cached at the proxy level. Dynamic documents are typically generated using CGI scripts or they include the result of a query to a database. The flourishing of database-centric e-commerce applications is making the current state of affairs even worse, rapidly increasing the percentage of dynamic Web documents.

As more and more Web sites put their data-content under the control of dedicated database management systems (DBMSs) to ensure data's persistence, availability and consistency, improving the access performance to database generated documents becomes a key issue in the improvement of the overall Web performance. This paper addresses the design, implementation and performance of data-intensive Web sites: Web sites that provide access to a large number of pages whose content is extracted from relational databases. Current data-intensive Web sites contain large amounts of ad-hoc code which is application and platform specific, leading to an unbearable system complexity. Complexity translates in very high development and maintenance costs and reduced optimization opportunities. We believe that it is necessary to provide development tools and construction methods based on site's high-level specification. Declarative Web site specifications can dramatically reduce development and maintenance costs while, by making the system's overall structure explicit, they help to automate the detection and deployment of performance improvement solutions. In this paper we describe Weave: a data-intensive Web site management system developed at INRIA[1] that is based on the above principle. Weave supports a high level methodology for the easy design, implementation, profiling and optimization of Web sites built on relational databases.

The performance problem of data-intensive Web sites lies in addressing the latency reduction of pages produced by the site. A system for which every single page would have to be constructed from scratch from the site's underlying DBMS, would surely have very limited performance and would definitely not scale very much. We believe that adequate materialization strategies are mandatory to attain reasonable and scalable performance out of data-intensive Web sites. Improving performance of data-

---

[1] http://caravel.inria.fr/Eprototype_WEAVE.html.

intensive Web sites through data materialization has so far been addressed in two ways: (i) materializing the results of frequently asked SQL queries [13], (ii) selectively materializing pages on the Web server [22]. Although both strategies perform well under certain circumstances, both suffer from lack of generality. The bottlenecks of data-intensive Web sites have large degrees of variation. They typically depend on the hardware and software environment, on the database statistics, and on the Web site's structure and access patterns [13]. We claim that there is no universal evaluation strategy which is optimal for all Web sites and which is independent of their particular parameters. Provisioning data-intensive Web sites requires a management system that is able to implement all the materialization strategies, and which selects the optimal strategy on a case-by-case basis according to the characteristics of the given Web site.

Weave offers a high-level language for Web site specification, and supports an innovative site architecture that is based on a 3-tier customizable cache system. The cache system can cache database data, XML fragments and HTML files, supporting data materialization at various levels. Data materialization is further tailored according to the database characteristics, Web site size, data freshness and response time constraints, and user access patterns. Before going into the particular solution of Weave, Section 2 discusses general issues related to the specification and implementation of data-intensive Web sites. Section 3 describes the particular solution adopted in the Weave system, describing the system's key elements for the easy construction of Web sites running optimal data materialization strategies. Section 4 discusses the experiments we have run so as to assess the benefits of Weave, analyzing the performance of a Weave Web site derived from the TPC/D benchmark database[2]. Section 5 then compares our solution with related work. Finally, Section 6 concludes.

2 Building Declarative Data-Intensive Web Sites

The general architecture of declarative data-intensive Web site management systems can be summarized by the following five fundamental principles:

1. The data content of the Web site is extracted from a (not necessarily dedicated) DBMS. The database can be either a primary database or the result of a data integration process, virtual or materialized.

2. The specification of the Web site is distinguished from its implementation. By specification of a Web site, we mean the description of the site's HTML pages, which must be separated from the code to be executed for solving page requests.

3. The specification of Web site's structure and content is separated from that of the graphical presentation of its pages. The former relates to the set of pages in the Web site, the data content attached to each page and the hyperlinks emanating from each page, while the latter concerns the page's layout.

4. The structure and the data content of the Web site are described in terms of a logical model. Many different models have been considered, most of them being (naturally) based on the notion of graph.

5. The mapping between the raw data and the logical model of the Web site is described via a declarative view definition language.

Concerning the separation between the Web site's content from the graphical presentation, note that this approach is already globally accepted (at least in theory) since the XML standard aims at isolating the data content of a Web site from the graphical presentation, usually described as independent XSLT programs. Hence, in the rest of the paper, we consider XML as the natural candidate language to describe Web site's structure and content and ignore the other possible Web site models. In this context, a Web site specification is done in two steps. First, the specification of the mapping between the raw data (relational in our case) and the Web site's logical model (XML in our case) has to be given. This is equivalent to defining an *XML view* over the relational data[12, 6]. Second, the definition of the Web site graphical presentation is given in terms of a set of XSLT programs.

2.1 Evaluation Strategies for Data-Intensive Web Sites

An important question that we address in this paper is whether it exists an optimal strategy for the evaluation of HTML pages. A multitude of strategies may be applied, ranging from purely dynamic to fully static evaluation.

Under a purely dynamic evaluation strategy, the Web server triggers the generation of an XML fragment corresponding to the requested page upon each request. In order to produce the result, the appropriate parameterized SQL queries have to be executed on the database, according to the site specification, and the result has to be packaged in XML format. The XML fragment is then sent to the HTML generator, which applies the appropriate XSLT program and generates the final HTML file. Under such an evaluation strategy, the total waiting time for a complete Web page can be decomposed as: (1) the *network communication time*, (2) the *HTTP connection time*, (3) the *Web application startup time*, (4) the *DBMS connection time*, (5) the *SQL execution time*, (6) the *XML generation time* and (7) the *HTML generation time*. In the case of dynamic evaluation of HTML pages from large databases, the entire process can be unacceptably slow.

Various solutions have been proposed to reduce the waiting time for a page in this context. Some solutions focus on reducing or eliminating one of the above 7 costs. For example, expensive CGI calls can be replaced by efficient APIs, or servlets. Furthermore, most products avoid systematic database connection through a pool of connections. However, to the best of our knowledge, no previous work studied the ratio between the various components of the response time and analyzed the real bottlenecks of such a system. It is clear that understanding these ratios is a mandatory step prior to considering any work on performance improvement and that the ratios will in general vary depending on the particular Web site. Hence, the local solutions presented above only slightly reduce the performance problem, but do not tackle completely the issues raised in the dynamic evaluation of Web sites.

A more general solution, used by most existing products [22] and prototypes, relies on materializing HTML pages. The materialization can be done either on the fly

---

[2]TPCD Benchmark. http://www.tpc.org.

or off-line, before any user starts browsing. Despite good response times, the static (off-line) evaluation strategy has several major drawbacks. First, it incurs significant space overhead, which can be even greater than duplicating the entire database since the same data item may appear in multiple pages. Furthermore, the same HTML template is replicated for various pages. Second, propagating updates from the database to the Web site is a serious problem once the site has been materialized. Third, the materialization granularity (i.e. a page) is not always appropriate: different fragments in a page can have different update frequencies, and materializing at the page level imposes the recomputation of the entire page, even if some parts of the page did not change. Finally, the static approach cannot always be applied since it cannot accommodate forms (i.e. the page content depends on the values of some parameters which are only known at runtime).

The solution proposed in [13] relies on the observation that, in the case of pure dynamic evaluation, the parameterized queries issued from the Web server and executed on the DBMS server share much of their computation, leading to redundant work. The proposed solution is thus to cache in the DBMS, the results of parameterized SQL computation, under the form of relational tables called cache functions, and reuse the results for subsequent requests. This approach has several advantages. First, if the SQL execution time is the dominant cost and if this cost is high, there are significant performance improvements. Second, since the cached data and the raw data are under the control of the same DBMS, simpler update propagation mechanisms can be deployed. Third, it is possible to control the granularity of the cached data, ranging from entire parameterized SQL queries to simpler sub-queries or combinations of subqueries using outerjoins [13]. However, this solution may alter the Web site's performance under certain conditions. Since the cached data is under the control of the DBMS, every cache action (e.g. search, insert, delete) accesses the DBMS via expensive SQL statements: using a cache with a low hit ratio incurs a large penalty. The SQL execution time is not always the most prominent cost in evaluating a page and may even be negligible. In this case, the overhead of caching tuples in the DBMS may outweigh the performance improvement. Finally, another drawback of this solution is a possible overload the DBMS server.

An alternative to the above solutions is to cache intermediate XML representations of data. Compared to caching HTML files, XML caching has the advantage of storing less data. Moreover, XML representations allow for carefully controlling the granularity of cached data, ranging from complete pages to page fragments. For instance, we can cache the name of a product, which is somehow stable, but not its price which varies a lot over time. However, caching XML data instead of HTML files does not exhibit a clear advantage in terms of space saving when the ratio between the size of the XML representation and that of the corresponding HTML file is close to 1. Under such conditions, caching XML data would not bring any benefit in terms of space saving, and would additionally incur runtime overhead for converting XML data into HTML on the fly. Compared to DBMS caching [13], caching XML has the advantage of eliminating (in the case of a hit) the costs of database connection, SQL execution, and of generating XML data. This technique also allows to reduce the load generated on the DBMS by the Web server. On the other hand, update propagation from the DBMS to the cached data is made more difficult (e.g. [21]).

From the above, we can conclude that there is no universally good solution for improving the performance of a data-intensive Web site. Each of the above materialization techniques (i.e. HTML, XML or DB) will be effective under certain circumstances and disastrous under others. It is thus mandatory for data-intensive Web sites to flexibly support the materialization at all levels: HTML, XML, and DB data. Notice that better response times may be offered to clients by pipelining the operations required to produce an HTML page from a query. Unfortunately, despite some encouraging attempts [20, 26], streaming components are not yet available for XML and HTML generation. In addition, even when such components will be available, this will not solve the overall performance problem of data-intensive Web sites, which requires accommodating the high database and server load. Caching remains here a key solution to address this scalability issue.

2.2 Materialization Strategies

An agreed upon solution for reducing the cost involved in the pure dynamic evaluation of database-generated Web pages seems to be data materialization, reusing intermediate results of various computations to answer subsequent queries. In order to deploy such a solution, the following issues must be addressed.

1. What kind of data should be materialized? As we showed before, data go through various levels of abstraction between the data producer (i.e. relational tables) and the data consumer (i.e. HTML files). Hence, there is a choice of materializing either the result of relational queries (as tables on a DBMS), either XML fragments or directly HTML files.

2. When must materialization be performed? Possible answers to this question are: (i) data items are materialized *proactively*, before users start interacting with the Web site, (ii) data items computed *upon request* are cached, and reused for subsequent requests, (iii) data items are *prefetched* according to their probability of being accessed.

3. Where should the materialized intermediate results be placed for effective performance improvement? Data items can be stored within part or all of the following nodes: *database server*, *Web server*, *proxy*, and *Web client* (in the case of XML fragments and HTML files). Caching a particular data item among eligible nodes then depends both on behavioral information (e.g. access pattern) and on the processing capability of the given node (e.g. Web clients will not support XML generation in general).

4. How are updates from the database propagated to the materialized data? Updates can be propagated in either: (i) a *push* fashion, i.e. an update to the database *immediately* triggers the deletion or the recalculation of the materialized data invalidated by the update, or (ii) a *pull* fashion, i.e. the materialized data items are periodically checked for freshness, and the appropriate action is performed upon inconsistency. There are several comments to make about push *vs.* pull strategies. First, only the push strategy can guarantee up-to-date data delivery. In the case of a pull update propagation strategy, the Web site may eventually deliver outdated data, and this may be unacceptable for certain Web sites, while it can be clearly acceptable for others. On the other hand, a push strategy can only be deployed at the expense of using a costly trigger mechanism. Moreover, the applicability of the push strategy is drastically limited if the data is materialized outside the Web server itself, due to the knowledge that is required (e.g. which data items are materialized and where) [21].

5. Which particular data items must be materialized and which ones must be computed upon request? Intuitively, the data items (i.e. tables, XML fragments or HTML files) satisfying the following three criteria are good candidates for materialization: (i) they are expensive to compute, (ii) they do not require frequent recomputation for update propagation, and (iii) they are requested with high frequency. For the other data items, it is not obvious that the gain obtained from materialization outweighs the overhead.

The right answer to the above questions depends on the database itself, the Web site size, freshness and response time constraints, the Web site usage patterns, and, last but not least, on the particular hardware and software environment. The problem that we are addressing here is how to build a management system that can support all the above evaluation strategies and therefore being useful in most situations.

3 The Weave Web Site Management System

Weave has been designed to support the evaluation strategies described in the previous section. The Web site specification is given in Weave as: (i) a *WeaveL* program that describes the site's structure and content, and (ii) a set of XSLT templates that describe the site's graphical presentation. The WeaveL program describes abstractly the site's pages, the data attached to each type of page, and the links between pages. In the absence of any additional information, the specified Web site is interpreted by Weave as being purely dynamic, and is executed as such. For the cases where complex materialization strategies are desired, Weave offers an extension of WeaveL, called *WeaveRPL*, which allows the specification of complex runtime policies. A runtime policy prescribes which data have to be materialized and under which form, and how the updates are to be propagated from the database to the materialized data, etc. The Weave system includes all the necessary components to deploy and interpret at runtime such complex policies.

In this section we first detail Weave's declarative Web site specification. Subsequently, we describe the Weave site architecture, the associated language for runtime policy customization, and the current implementation of Weave.

3.1 Declarative Web Site Specification using WeaveL

A WeaveL program consists of a set of *site class* specifications. A site class models a collection of homogeneous pages in a Web site (e.g., collections corresponding to pages of customers or suppliers). Each page in the site can then

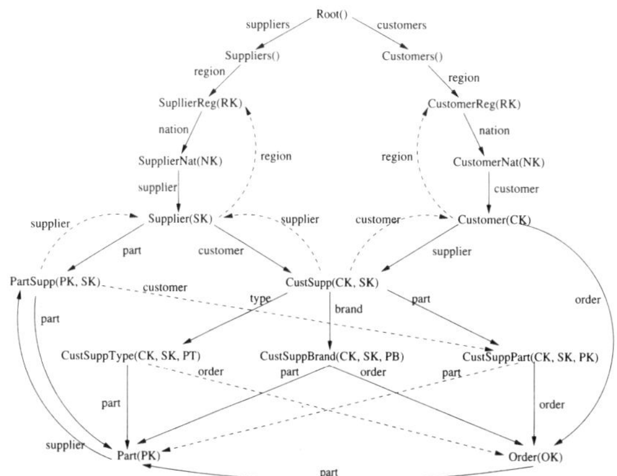

Figure 1: The TPC/D site schema

be seen as an instance of a particular class, and identified and distinguished from the other instances by a set of items from the underlying database (e.g. a page of a particular customer can be identified by the key of the customer in the database). Hence, a page request handled by the Web server must specify the class of the page that is requested and zero or more parameter values, which uniquely identify the content of the requested page.

In WeaveL, the specification of each Web site class includes: (i) the declaration of the parameters identifying an instance of the class, (ii) the SQL query whose result gives all possible instances for the above parameters (describing how to produce all the instances of that class), (iii) the specification of the data contained in an instance of the respective class (i.e. the parameterized query that retrieves this data from the database), (iv) the specification of the hyperlinks emanating from an instance of the respective class (i.e. the database queries that have to be evaluated in order to build the correct links between the pages) and (v) the specification of the forms embedded in the page. Finally, in addition to the WeaveL program which gives the site's XML view definition, a complete Web site specification consists of a set of XSLT programs, all instances of a given class sharing the same XSLT.

Example 3.1 Suppose we want to produce a browsable version of the data contained in the TPC/D benchmark. The database contains information about products, customers and client orders. The desired Web site is organized according to the hyperstructure represented in Figure 1. There is a root page with two links to suppliers (node labeled Suppliers()) and customers (node labeled Customers()). Both suppliers and customers are grouped by geographical region (e.g., CustomerReg(RK)), and within each region by nationality (e.g., CustomerNat(NK)). Suppliers and customers have further links to detailed information about the orders, as depicted in Figure 1. For illustration, we give below the WeaveL specification of the CustomerNat class. A Web page instance of this class depends on a single parameter (i.e. the key in the database of the given nation) and it contains (i) the name of the particular nation and (ii) hyperlinks to all the pages corresponding to customers in that nation. The mapping between the attributes and the hyperlinks contained in an instance of this class and data in the database is described using (parameterized) SQL queries as follows.

```
define class CustomerNat ($NK)
{instances using Q0 }
{
 data  nation_name using Q1 ;
 link customer to Customer($CK) using Q2 ;
}
define query Q0 as select nationkey as $NK from Nation;
define query Q1 as select name as nation_name
                from Nation where nationkey=$NK;
define query Q2 as select custkey as $CK, name as anchor
                from Customer where nationkey=$NK;
```

Given a page request (e.g. a particular binding for the
parameter $NK of the class CustomerNat), it is neces-
sary to first produce the XML fragment corresponding to
the respective Web page. In Weave, the XML Generator
has the task of evaluating the parameterized queries from
the WeaveL specification and producing the corresponding XML data. An important feature of the Weave XML
Generator is that it can be invoked with the request of
generating complete XML pages or only some fragments
of them. In the latter case the resulting fragment keeps
track of the missing pieces, which are computed on the
fly when needed. The XML data produced in Weave adhere to a unique DTD/schema, which is independent of the
database schema and the structure of the Web site. For example, the complete XML fragment describing the content
of the page identified by the class CustomerNat and $NK=6
is the following:

```
<XML_fragment id=" CustomerNat_6 ">
   <class> CustomerNat </class>
   <parameter> 6 </parameter>

   <data_fragment name=" nation_name ">
       <data_value> France </data_value>
   <data_fragment>

   <link_fragment name=" customer ">
       <link_item>
           <XML_fragment id=" Customer_402 ">
               <class> Customer </class>
               <parameter> 402 </parameter>
           </XML_fragment>
           <anchor> Customer#000000402 </anchor>
       </link_item>
           ....
   </link_fragment>
</XML_fragment>
```

3.2 Site Architecture

Declarative Web site specification only worries about what
data will populate the Web site, and how the site is structured, but does not specify how the site is implemented.
This separation of concerns is important because it gives
the freedom of choosing the most adequate evaluation
strategy. In this subsection, we detail the Weave site architecture enabling customized data materialization (or *runtime policy*); the next subsection details the WeaveRPL
language for the specification of customization. The Weave
site architecture is based on the following main components
(see Figure 2):

- The *scheduler* has the task of interpreting the runtime
  policy, and coordinating the behavior of the other
  components. It receives HTTP requests and redirects

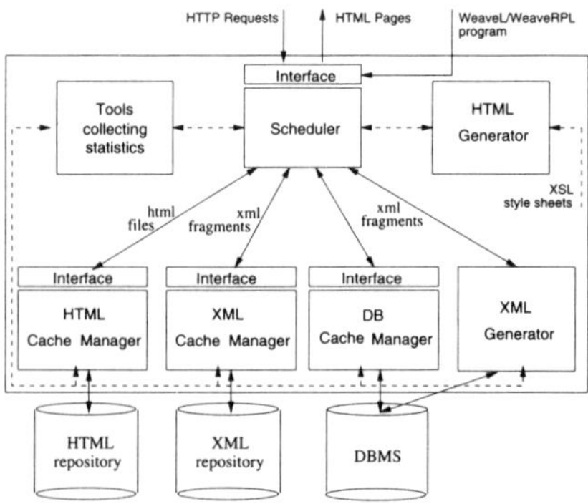

Figure 2: The architecture of the Weave system

them to the *cache manager* components out of which
data relating to a given page may be retrieved.
- The individual *cache managers* enforce the runtime
  policy by handling data requests as forwarded by the
  scheduler. They further undertake appropriate actions regarding environmental constraints (e.g. management of data replacement and of data consistency).
  Environmental constraints are handled through the
  signal of associated events (e.g. time set for a timer
  has elapsed, maximum size set for a data container is
  reached).
- The individual *caches* (or *repositories*), which actually
  store the data and with which the cache managers interact. Notice that there may be various caches related to a given manager, e.g., for scalability purpose.
- The *XML generator* is in charge of issuing queries to
  the DBMS (including the DB cache) and producing
  XML fragments.
- The *HTML generator* generates HTML pages from
  XML fragments and XSLT programs.
- The *statistics manager* is in charge of storing and summarizing the data describing the Web site's runtime
  behavior. These data include: statistics about the
  Web site's traces and access patterns, statistics about
  the response times of the various Weave components
  (e.g. XML generator, XML cache, HTML cache), and
  statistics describing Weave caches usage (e.g. hit ratios, maximum size).

Example 3.2 As an illustration of the interaction patterns among Weave site components, consider a request
for a page whose associated data are asked to be cached
as both XML and HTML. The page is first searched for
within the HTML cache. If present, the page is simply
returned to the scheduler, which returns it as a result of
the HTTP request. If the page is absent from the HTML
cache, the corresponding XML fragment is sought within
the XML cache. If the fragment is present and corresponds
to the entire page, it is returned to the scheduler, which
computes the corresponding HTML page to forward it to
both the HTML cache manager and the initiator of the
HTTP request. Finally, if either the data is absent from
the XML cache or the data retrieved from the XML cache
corresponds to a subset of the page, the missing data is
requested to the XML generator. The XML generator further requests the data to the DB cache manager, the data
being ultimately retrieved from the underlying database.
The retrieved data then serve computing the corresponding
XML fragment, which is processed in order to update the

XML and HTML caches and to service the HTTP request. The above scenario illustrates the interaction among the components of a Weave site when all three data repositories are involved. It is then quite easy to infer alternative interaction patterns when only a subset of the caches is involved.

So far, we have introduced Weave sites with respect to the execution of a given runtime policy. The behavior of Weave sites is dynamically customizable with respect to the enforced runtime policy by taking as input WeaveRPL policy specifications. When the runtime policy is to be modified (or initialized), the new policy is first delivered to the scheduler, which distributes it among the Weave-specific components according to their functionality (see Figure 2).

3.3 Customizing runtime policies

Runtime policies specified using WeaveRPL give the behavior of the three data caches with respect to environmental constraints and data requests, which further implicitly describe the global algorithm that has to be followed in order to solve HTTP requests. This behavioral specification is similar for the three types of caches, and decomposes in three parts:

(1) The specification of the data items that are subject to materialization in each particular data cache. The set of items that are subject to materialization in each cache are logically grouped in a number of *containers*. A container is the unit of storage management and allows grouping together objects (i.e. tuples, XML fragments or HTML files) that have similar access and evolution patterns. Containers enable fine tuning of data materialization and provide a convenient basis for the physical distribution of caches. The definition of a container describes in a declarative fashion the items that are eligible for materialization in that container. In the case of XML or HTML, the items are identified by the name of a site class together with caching conditions upon its instances (e.g. parameter value, instance size, access frequency or computing time). In the case of database tuples, items are identified by the name of a table and a set of key values.

(2) The global constraints over all the data items to be cached in a given container. These constraints relate to the items' size (size), age (age) and access frequency (frequency).

(3) A set of Even-Condition-Action (ECA) rules, which dictates the way the cache manager responds to various events (e.g. request for data, size overflow, data aging, etc). Events that are currently supported relate to initialization (onInit), cache overflow (onFull parameterized with the container size), aging (onTimer parameterized with the timer value). Conditions that may be expressed are as for global constraints. Regarding supported actions, these include: prefetching specified data items within the cache (compute), removing specified items from the cache (remove), applying a given function to the cache content, e.g., for data replacement (apply), and reinitializing the cache content (reinit).

The above specification of containers drives the behavior of the scheduler when servicing HTTP requests. Given an object request, the global scheduler knows from which caches the object can possibly be retrieved, and how it must route the request in order to solve it completely.

Example 3.3 The TPC/D site definition is now complemented with the specification of the associated runtime policy. The specification associated with the HTML cache is given below.

```
Cache HTML:
{   /* Container definition */
    define container contHTML as
      select Part,
        PartSupp(PK) where (PK < 100 and SK < 100),
        CustSupp(PK, SK) where (size < 2KB and
                                frequency > 0.3);
    /* Global constraints */
    frequency > 0.2 and size < 10 KB;
    /* ECA rules */
    onInit compute PartSupp,
                       Part(PK) where PK < 100;
    onTimer(5mn)
           remove Part(PK) where (PK > 100 and
                                  age > 30 mn);
    onFull(200MB) remove all where size > 2KB;
}
```

The HTML cache contains a single container, which stores instances of the site classes that are listed after the select clause. Stored instances must have a size less than 10KB and an access frequency greater than 0.2. Further constraints are set over instances of the PartSup and Cust-Supp classes: instances of the former must have values for PK and SK that are both less than 100, instances of the latter must have a size that is less than 2KB and an access frequency that is greater than 0.3. Upon initialization (handling of the onInit event), the HTML cache is fed with the instances of the Part and PartSupp classes, which meet the aforementioned global constraints over cached instances. The content of the cache is refreshed every 5mn using the onTimer event; stored instances of the Part class whose value for PK is greater than 100 and whose age is greater than 30mn are removed. When the cache is full (space consumption greater than 200MB), all the stored instances whose size is greater then 2KB are removed (see handling of the onFull event). Specification for the XML cache follows.

```
Cache XML:
{   /* Container definition */
    define container contXML as
      select Supplier(SK):fragments{name, customer}
      where SK < 100;
    /* Global constraints */
        frequency > 0.2 and size < 100 KB;
    /* ECA rules */
        onInit compute all;
        onTimer(5mn) reinit;
        onFull(50MB) apply LRU;
}
```

The XML cache also contains a single container, which stores fragments of instances of the Supplier class whose value for SK is less than 100. The stored fragments correspond to parts of the HTML page that give the supplier's name and list of customers. Upon initialization, the cache is fed with all the instances that met the specified conditions until the cache is full. The cache is refreshed every 5mn by removing all the stored instances and recomputing them (reinit action). When the cache is full, a traditional LRU algorithm is applied for the replacement of the instances.

Similarly to the way an XML (resp. HTML) cache holds sets of XML fragments (resp. HTML files) that are logically defined by predicates and physically grouped into containers, a DB cache holds sets of tuples that are logically defined by predicates and physically grouped into tables. The tuples can either belong to some *materialized views*, or be part of *function tables*, which maintain the results of parameterized queries (with their respective inputs) [13]. The DB cache specification contains the definition of the views and/or the cache functions as illustrated below, each of them corresponding in our terminology to a single container. Both the materialized views and the cache functions are tables holding tuples. The difference resides in when the content of the tables is computed: statically (onInit) for the views and upon request (onRequest) for the cache functions. Moreover, views are complete (i.e. they contain *all* the tuples satisfying the given predicate), while cache functions can contain only a subset of the tuples satisfying the given predicate. Hence, both materialized views and cache functions can be specified using the same formalism (i.e. same container definitions and same ECA rules) as for the case of XML and HTML caches. More details about the DB cache can be found in [13].

```
Cache DB:
  { /* Container definition */
    define container CACHE_FUNCTION as
      select o.o_custkey, l.l_supkey, p.p_partkey, p.p_name,
             p.p_type, o.o_orderdate, o.o_orderkey, p.p_brand
      from LINEITEM l, ORDER o, PART p
      where o.o_orderkey = l.l_orderkey and
            p.p_partkey = l.l_partkey
    input o_custkey, l_supkey;
    /* ECA rules */
    onRequest(CustomerSupplier($CK,$SK))
      compute all
          where o_custkey=$CK and l_supkey=$SK;
    onTimer(30mn) remove all;
  }
  { /* Container definition */
    define container VIEW as
      select o.o_custkey, l.l_supkey, l.l_partkey, o.o_orderdate,
             o.o_orderkey, l.l_linenumber
      from ORDER o, LINEITEM l
      where o.o_orderkey = l.l_orderkey
    input custkey, supkey;
    /* ECA rules */
    onInit compute all;
    onTimer(24h) reInit;
  }
```

To conclude this section we note that our final goal is to offer a system, which would analyze the declarative specification and produce automatically the "optimal" runtime policy. At this point, our system still requires a Web site administrator to generate by hand the desired runtime policies. However, in order to help the administrator choosing the best materialization strategy, Weave offers a powerful testing and tracing component. For example, this component analyses and summarizes the Web site execution statistics, and highlights the potential performance problems, hence simplifying considerably the Web site administrator's task.

3.4 Prototype implementation

The Weave site architecture is highly modular, allowing the use of off-the-shelf components for most of the architecture elements but the Weave-specific ones, which are the scheduler and the cache managers. All the Weave site components, presented in Figure 2, are wrapped in Java (JDBC is used for interfacing with the DBMS), using simple but powerful interfaces. Implementing Weave then consists of providing implementations corresponding to the component interfaces, together with the WeaveRPL compiler. In the current Weave implementation, except for the Weave-specific components, we have either reused existing components when available (i.e. IBM LotusXSL for the HTML generator, and IBM XML4J as part of the XML generator, which we enriched for supporting the generation of XML fragments relating to part of a page), or implemented in a quite trivial way some of the others (i.e., we use the underlying file system for the HTML and XML caches).

Particular attention has been devoted to the design and implementation of the three cache managers. Weave contains a single cache manager interface and a single cache manager implementation, which proved to simplify a lot Weave implementation. The three data repositories holding the materialized data share the same interface; changing the real data repository requires only to change the implementation of this interface. This feature allows us, for example, to experiment with several XML repositories (persistent DOM, Excelon and files).

Notice that the specification of XML views over relational databases and their efficient implementation, is a distinct area of active research [26, 12, 6]. Although applicable to the Web domain, the proposed solutions are not specifically designed for it. In particular, they do not allow manipulating entire XML elements and/or fragments. However, Weave is designed such that the XML Generator can easily be replaced in the future when powerful and efficient such components become available. Finally, notice that the current implementation of Weave supports only a subset of all the materialization strategies that were discussed in Section 2. The main limitation concerns data update propagation, currently offered only through a pull model.

3.5 Weave on the Web

Up to this point, we have been concentrating on the use of Weave for building sites at the Web server level. In addition, we have presented an example of Weave site incarnations with exactly one instance of each type of cache (e.g. DB, XML and HTML), all three caches being used and further located on a single site. Unsurprisingly, Weave has been designed to enable the deployment of sites with different configurations, in term of cache components and their location over the various Web nodes (i.e. Web server, proxy, client). We do support the distribution and replication of the Weave site's components over these nodes, and the implementation of sites comprising only a subset of the three caches. Among the benefits of Weave in this context,

Weave site components are valuable for coping with thin Web clients (e.g. wireless PDAs), which are foreseen as future prominent Web actors. Dedicated proxy caches may exploit the XML fragments for the convenient customization of Web pages. Due to the lack of space, we do not discuss any further the usage of Weave in the overall Web environment.

4 Experimentation

To measure the performance of various data materialization strategies, we built a test platform called WeaveBench and performed various experiments. In the following, we present the test platform and its configuration, the experiments and the performance results.

4.1 The WeaveBench test platform

We built our own test platform WeaveBench. WeaveBench generates a load for testing Weave on a Web server by running one or more Web client processes on one or more client computers. Each client process sends requests as fast as it can receive data back from the server. Thus, it generates a load much heavier than that of a single interactive user. A single process manages the testing done by the client processes. It starts the benchmark runs, each one by a different client process, and combines the performance results into a single summary report.

WeaveBench considers a Web site derived from the TPC/D database factor 1 with a database size of 1.2 GB and 15 million pages. The Web site contains in average 5 SPJ queries per page, and no aggregate queries have been used. Each client submits page requests based on a trace file that describes the pages of the TPC/D database. Thus, we must generate a trace file that captures a realistic workload of page accesses. In the experiments, each client sends requests to the Web server according to a trace file. All the trace files for a given run are generated based on the same probability distribution, as follows. First, a workset of N (N=10.000 in the current implementation) distinct pages have been chosen from the entire Web site. In so doing, the pages closer to the root of the Web site are considered with a (slightly) higher probability. Second, C (C being the number of clients) sequences of length M (M=1000 in the current experiments) of pages are chosen from the workset, according to a Zipf distribution.

The database is stored in Oracle v8 on a dedicated Ultra Sparc I machine (143MHz and 384MB of RAM), running SunOS Release 5.5. The cache global manager, the three caches and the Web server, Apache v3.3.3, are all on the same machine, a 300MHz Pentium with 520MB of RAM, running Linux Release 6.1. We use the Apache JServ servlet engine to run the cache global manager, which we implemented as a servlet. Two other machines are used to hold WeaveBench clients. Each machine, a 200MHz Pentium with 96MB of RAM, ran about 1-50 clients in increments of 10. All the machines in the test platform are interconnected by a 10Mbps network that can be isolated from other networks.

4.2 Experiments

We have run the following experiments: dynamic evaluation, static[3] evaluation, DB caching only, XML caching only, HTML caching only, and mixed caching. Notice that the dynamic evaluation is the worst case scenario where client requests always yield access to the database, generation of the XML fragment and generation of the HTML page. On the other hand, the static evaluation is the "ideal" scenario where all the HTML files have been statically generated and put in the HTML cache. This scenario is unrealistic because of the high costs for generating (after each change) and storing the files. For DB caching, XML caching, and HTML caching, the goal is to measure the respective benefit of caching data within the database, the XML cache, and the HTML cache. Finally, mixed caching is the realistic scenario where all three caches are used, each one for a different type of page according to the particular parameters. The goal is to assess the benefit of caching at various levels (database, XML fragment, HTML files).

The results are presented as a two-dimensional table where each row corresponds to a page class (Customer, Supplier, etc.) and gives the percentage of the various execution times (wsconnect, queryexec, etc.) out of the *total Web server response time* for the instances of that class. The table is sorted by decreasing order of response time. We highlighted in bold faces the components that cause performance problems, i.e. the components with execution times that are for more than 30% of the overall processing. All results are shown for 1 client generating 500 page requests and in the absence of data updates. Experiments with up to 50 clients showed large degradations of the HTML generation time. This is mainly due to the fact that existing XSLT processors consume large amounts of memory and do not scale properly. These results suggest that Web site architectures based on XML and XSLT can be used in real applications only when better XSLT processors will be available. However, there is no doubt that this will be the case in the future since efficient XSLT processing is receiving significant attention.

4.3 Performance results

Dynamic pages. Table 1 shows the results when there is no caching. The average response times are between 15 s[4] and 300 ms. For page classes Customer, Supplier, CustSup, CustSuppPart and CustSuppBrand, the query execution time dominates because the queries involve joins with large tables. For page classes CustomerNat and SupplierNat, the XML and HTML generation times dominate because the queries are simple but produce a large amount of data. For the other page classes, the response time drops to 500 ms and below, and is divided between the Web server connection and the HTML generation. These page classes need not be optimized and, thus, they are not shown in the experiments results.

Precomputed pages. Table 2 shows the results when the HTML files have been statically generated. Thus, the only relevant execution times are those for connecting to

---

[3]In this experiment, all the Web pages have been precomputed. However, they are still served through the Weave application, and not by the Web server directly from the file system.

[4]The large response time can be explained by the hardware configuration used for the experiments.

page class	wsconnect(%)	queryexec(%)	xmlgen(%)	htmlgen(%)	resptime(ms)	size(KB)
Customernat	1.52	0.81	**44.36**	**53.32**	15202.34	660
CustSupp	1.84	**97.38**	0.04	0.74	12530.95	2
CustSuppBrand	1.85	**96.73**	0.05	1.37	12459.98	2
CustSuppType	1.91	**96.57**	0.05	1.47	12063.53	2
Supplier	2.30	**82.96**	6.36	8.38	10044.03	100
CustSuppPart	2.52	**96.51**	0.06	0.92	9160.41	2
PartSupp	8.23	**88.40**	0.28	3.09	2802.67	1
Suppliernat	22.30	3.63	25.78	**48.29**	1034.73	60
Customer	30.26	**43.80**	6.73	19.21	762.52	15

Table 1: The results of the dynamic evaluation

page class	wsconnect(%)	transftime(%)	resptime(ms)
Customernat	0.35	**99.65**	3027.30
Supplier	3.30	**96.70**	323.60
Suppliernat	4.87	**95.13**	219.04
Customer	**31.12**	68.88	34.30
CustSuppBrand	**70.22**	29.78	15.20
CustSuppType	**70.65**	29.35	15.11
CustSuppPart	**73.37**	26.63	14.55
CustSupp	**77.46**	22.54	13.78
PartSupp	**78.21**	21.79	13.65

Table 2: The results of the static evaluation

the Web server and transferring the HTML files to the client (transftime). Response times are optimal and are between 3 s and 13 ms for the most expensive pages. For page classes of larger HTML size (**CustomerNat**, Supplier, **SupplierNat** and Customer), the time to transfer the HTML files dominates. For the others (2 KB and below), the Web server connection time dominates and the response time gets quite small.

DB caching. Table 3.a shows the results with DB caching only. We have used three cache containers: one for pages of class Customer only, one for pages of class Supplier and PartSupp and one for pages of class CustSupp, CustSuppPart, CustSuppType and CustSuppBrand. The selection of these containers is close to optimal and was found after several trials. No cache was used for the other page classes because the number of pages or the locality of reference are low. Thus, the results are not shown for those because they are the same as in Table 1. For pages of class CustSupp, CustSuppPart, CustSuppType and CustSuppBrand, the improvement in response time is quite significant (factor 11 or more) The response time for pages of class Supplier has been improved by 2.4. However, that for pages of class PartSupp has been worsened by a factor 1.5 because the hit ratio does not compensate for the cost of inserting tuples in the container.

XML caching. Table 3.b shows the results with XML caching only. In our configuration, the XML cache takes memory away from the Web server. XML caching essentially improves on query execution time and XML generation time. For page classes with a good hit ratio (**CustSuppType**, CustSupp, CustSuppBrand, CustSuppPart, Supplier and PartSupp), the response time can be improved by a factor between 3 and 7. For the other page classes, there is either small improvement or slight degradation due to competing memory access by the Web server. Note that our implementation of an XML cache could be improved by using a persistent XML store. Compared to DB caching, the improvement is not as good mainly because of the relatively high memory consumption.

HTML caching. Table 3.c shows the results with HTML caching only. HTML caching essentially improves on HTML generation time, in addition to the improve-

ments of XML caching. The performance improvement is slightly higher than that of XML caching because the HTML cache consumes less memory (all files are stored on disk). But the improvement is still not as good as that of DB caching.

Mixed caching. Table 3.d shows the results with a mixed strategy where we combine DB caching, XML caching and HTML caching. For each cache, the decision of what to cache and how was taken according to the observations made in separate experiments with either DB, XML or HTML caching only. We use the DB cache for pages of class CustSupp, CustSuppPart, CustSuppType and **CustSuppBrand**. However, we use the XML cache for Supplier and Customer pages. We cache only the fragments corresponding to the customers of a given Supplier and suppliers of a given *Customer*. We assume that these fragments are not frequently updated and worth being cached. The other fragments (i.e. parts of a Supplier and orders of a Customer) are supposed to be frequently updated and so should be built on demand. Finally, the other page classes, except pages of class PartSupp which are computed on the fly without any caching, are statically generated and put in the HTML cache. As a result, the performances are much better than with each cache alone. The highest improvements in response time are with the DB cache (factor 11 or more). The improvement of precomputed pages (e.g., CustomerNat, SupplierNat, etc.) and of XML caching for pages of classes Supplier and Customer is also significant. The results for the uncached pages remain the same as in Table 1. To summarize the results, Figure 3 gives the response times of the different caching strategies for our TPC-D Web site and clearly shows that caching at different levels is a good strategy.

5 Related Work

There is a number of efforts towards easing the construction of data-intensive Web sites through declarative specification [3, 11, 2, 9, 14, 7], and towards optimizing the response times offered by such sites [13, 22]. However, to the best of our knowledge, there is little work addressing both issues in conjunction, which we consider as mandatory

196

page class	wsconnect(%)	queryexec(%)	xmlgen(%)	htmlgen(%)	resptime(ms)
a. Results of DB caching					
PartSupp	5.42	**93.50**	0.18	0.89	4244.72
Supplier	5.64	**58.12**	16.30	19.93	4080.14
CustSupp	26.78	**69.08**	0.53	3.62	859.64
CustSuppPart	28.70	**65.86**	0.67	4.78	802.09
CustSuppBrand	30.22	**62.20**	0.71	6.88	761.79
CustSuppType	**34.74**	**56.94**	0.78	7.54	662.60
Customer	**38.26**	**35.57**	8.63	17.54	601.61
b. Results of XML caching					
Customernat	3.45	0.36	22.18	**74.00**	7337.22
CustSuppType	8.02	**89.27**	0.07	2.64	3157.17
CustSupp	8.37	**90.57**	0.07	0.01	3025.36
CustSuppBrand	8.79	**89.58**	0.07	1.55	2880.49
CustSuppPart	10.01	**88.39**	0.10	1.50	2528.84
Supplier	13.7	21.65	18.09	**46.53**	1843.35
Suppliernat	28.44	1.47	16.67	**53.42**	890.21
Customer	**60.27**	9.46	5.82	24.45	420.05
PartSupp	**68.50**	20.83	0.91	9.76	369.61
c. Results of HTML caching					
Customernat	3.33	0.38	23.40	**72.89**	7517.07
CustSuppType	8.16	**91.02**	0.07	0.75	3071.73
CustSupp	8.62	**90.80**	0.06	0.51	2905.92
CustSuppBrand	9.20	**89.92**	0.07	0.80	2723.02
CustSuppPart	10.96	**88.10**	0.10	0.84	2286.69
Supplier	13.46	24.24	18.51	**43.79**	1862.03
Suppliernat	29.01	1.53	16.70	**52.76**	863.83
PartSupp	**46.33**	**49.66**	0.61	3.39	540.91
Customer	**62.51**	10.66	6.10	20.73	400.92
d. Results of mixed caching					
Customernat	8.07	0.00	0.00	**91.93**	3010.50
PartSupp	8.84	**89.55**	0.29	1.32	2747.78
Supplier	11.63	25.95	18.19	**44.24**	2090.05
CustSupp	29.69	**66.01**	0.57	3.73	818.44
CustSuppPart	30.77	**63.83**	0.62	4.78	789.89
CustSuppBrand	32.02	**60.83**	0.69	6.46	758.88
CustSuppType	**39.82**	**50.23**	0.87	9.08	610.32
Customer	**52.83**	6.71	7.57	**32.89**	460.02
Suppliernat	**97.51**	0.00	0.00	2.49	249.10

Table 3: Results of the dynamic materialization strategies

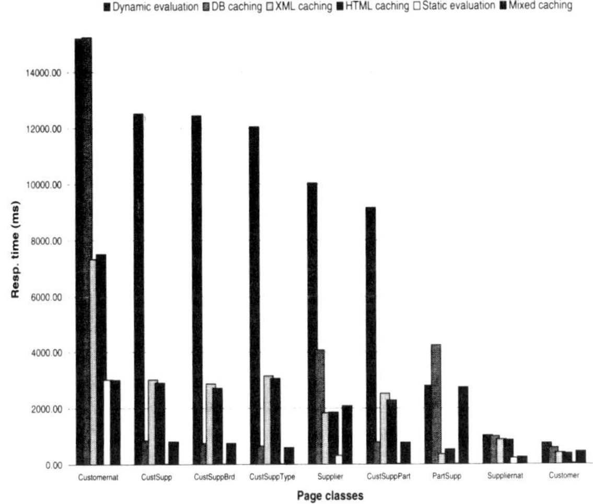

Figure 3: Comparison of different caching strategies for the effective deployment of data-intensive Web sites. In this context, the work proposed in [13] exploits declarative Web site specifications for data caching and lookahead computation within the database system according to the users' access patterns and the update frequency of the data items. This improves the performance of handling database queries, allows for efficient update propagation, and enables caching of data that are shared among various pages. However, this solution addresses only DB caching, which has been shown to be valuable only in certain circumstances.

Related work originates from research results in the Web area, which have been investigating ways to overcome the performance penalty caused by uncacheable dynamic objects. Solutions have been proposed at the level of proxy and server caches. Weave shares common ideas with some of the solutions proposed for proxy caches. In a way similar to combining XML fragments with XSLT programs, the proposal of [10] argues for dividing dynamic objects into a static part (or template) and a dynamic part. Retrieval of the former may then benefit from caching while retrieval of the latter leads to Web server access. In this way, the performance cost of accessing a dynamic object is reduced to the minimum. A more general solution is the introduction of cache applets [5] which customize the caching policy for each document. Cache applets enable Web servers to attach computation with Web objects, which may be conveniently exploited by proxy caches (e.g. the proxy cache may request the server only for the document part that is actually dynamic). Close to this work is the proposal of [4], which introduces the CacheL language for customizing cache management policies according to the specifics of accessed documents and/or services. Regarding proxy cache management, Weave offers features close to the above solutions. Weave additionally deals with the improvement of the Web server latency, which is not addressed by the above work. This aspect is mandatory since, in the case of query processing, the load offered to the Web server remains unchanged and hence still requires adequate management at the server level for effective performance improvement.

Caching of dynamic objects at the level of Web servers has been investigated in [21], which introduces an algorithm for efficient update propagation to caches. It is a first step towards improving Web performance when handling database queries. However, it is aimed at a specific service, i.e., the 1998 Olympic Game Web site. In particular, the targeted service allowed for storing in memory all the dynamic pages without overflow, yielding a cache hit rate close to 100% without applying a replacement algorithm. This assumption cannot be made for all the Web servers interfacing with databases, especially data-intensive Web sites. Furthermore, this solution is a very specific component of the entire Web site, which may easily be integrated within Weave sites given their architectural modularity. On the other hand, our solution is general, providing methods and tools for the easy design, implementation, deployment, and maintenance of efficient data-intensive Web sites.

Close to the Weave system are products that aim at easing the development of Web-based applications. In particular, we find Microsoft Active Server Pages [19], and Sun JavaServer Pages [18] that are component-based architectures offering a number of base components to build Web servers delivering dynamic pages. However, it is up to the developer to tailor the site's implementation by providing the needed additional components. The IBM Websphere [15] and ColdFusion [16] are Web application servers that ease the development of Web sites through the provision of powerful base components for HTML caching, database access, and scheduling. However, customization of the Web site's runtime policy is less flexible than in Weave and is disseminated in the implementation of the various components composing the site. This alters the ease of specification and maintenance of the caching policies; it also diminishes the chances that such caching policies will be generated automatically in the future.

Dynamai [17] is a configurable cache allowing caching dynamic documents. Dynamai sits in front of a site's Web application and intercepts HTTP requests. If a request comes in for content not yet in the cache or that Dynamai cannot cache, Dynamai passes the request to the Web server, caching the response in the first case and ignoring it in the second case. Dynamai allows the site administrator to identify cache-able dynamic content, declare the events that may result in changes to the content, and, notify the cache when these events occur. Weave is close to Dynamai from the standpoint of offering support for the effective caching of dynamic objects. However, Weave is a superset of this product in that it is not only a caching tool, but also provides a framework for the specification of data-intensive Web sites. We believe that a global knowledge of the data supply chain (i.e. from the data producer all the way to the data consumer) is needed in order to derive the appropriate caching policy. By ignoring the source of the data and the way the Web site is generated only limited solutions can be found.

Finally, three other systems explore issues that nicely complement our work. In [7] the authors propose a high level Web site specification model, more powerful then the one we currently support. However, they did not address the performance problem and the supported Web evaluation strategies are the simple ones: static and dynamic. In [22] the authors address the optimization problem. For each particular page, the disadvantages obtained from materialization are compared with the performance improvements, thus deriving an "optimal" materialization strategy. However, due to the large number of (parametrized) Web pages the proposed optimization method cannot be easily adapted to our context. The space of possible materialization policies examined in [22] is also significantly more restricted then the one we would like to explore. Finally, in [1] the authors propose an interesting high level specification methodology for e-commerce applications based on a rule-based language. These systems complement our own; we believe that a complete solution for *fast* and *high quality* Web application deployment can only be obtained by an harmonious combination of these technologies.

6 Conclusions and Future Work

In a data-intensive Web site, returning a Web page may require costly interaction with the database system (connection and querying) to dynamically extract its content. The database interaction cost adds up to the non-negligible base cost of Web page delivery, thereby increasing much the response time. Although useful, techniques for proxy and Web server caches do not help reducing the Web latency in this case since they work at the level of HTML pages. In this paper, we have addressed the performance problem of accessing dynamic Web pages in data-intensive Web sites. This work has been done in the context of the Weave Web site management system developed at INRIA.

Our approach relies on the declarative specification of the Web site through a logical model, and the customization of the site's data materialization strategy based on high-level specification. The logical model of the Web site is based on the XML graph data model. A site schema then represents an XML view definition over a relational database. Thus, we can manage the data of the Web site at three levels: database, XML fragments, HTML files. In this context, we have proposed a customizable cache system architecture and its implementation. Our solution enables data caching at the various levels of data elaboration within the Web site: database data, XML fragments or HTML files. In addition, Weave comes along with the WeaveRPL language for specifying both the Web site's content and customized data materialization within the site. Given a site graph, cache management may be specified at a fine grain by attaching caching actions to each site class. Furthermore, the Web site being specified abstractly, the site's developer is relieved from dealing with low-level implementation details, which further eases the site's maintenance and evolution. Our solution has been illustrated using a Web site derived from the TPC/D benchmark database. Based on the result of our experiments, we have assessed the performance of various caching strategies: dynamic pages (worst case), precomputed pages (best case), DB caching, XML caching, HTML caching, and mixed caching (combining DB, XML and HTML caching). The results clearly show that a mixed strategy is generally optimal.

This paper has presented the building blocks of Weave, which we have further implemented so as to assess our approach. Work still needs to be done for further assessment and improvement of Weave. As a short term objective, we are currently working on the enhancement of the current Weave prototype with respect to optimizing the performance of the components composing a Weave site. As longer term research objectives, we plan to investigate four directions. First, we would like to eliminate a strong limitation of our current system: the fact that our declarative specifications can only model Web sites that *read* data from the database, but not Web sites that *update* a database. It is particularly important (especially for e-commerce Web sites) to be able to model in a declarative fashion data transfers in both directions, from the database to the the Web site and vice versa. Supporting the TPC-W benchmark is our next goal and this functionality will be required. The second interesting direction is to consolidate the replication and distribution of the Weave components on the proxies and/or on the clients. Finally, it is important to be able to generate the run-time policies automatically, based on the information extracted from the execution statistics, from the database statistics and from the Web site constraints in terms of data freshness and response time.

Our ultimate, and ambitious, goal is to obtain a self adaptive Web site management system which dynamically changes its own run-time policies in response to the behavior of a running system.

Acknowledgements: The authors would like to acknowledge Cezar Cristian Andrei for his participation to the implementation and evaluation of the Weave prototype.

References

[1] S. Abiteboul, B. Amann, S. Cluet, A. Eyal, L. Mignet, and T. Milo. Active views for electronic commerce. In *Proc. of the Int. Conf. on Very Large Data Bases (VLDB)*, 1999.

[2] G. Arocena and A. Mendelzon. WebOQL: Restructuring documents, database and Webs. In *Proc. of Int. Conf. on Data Engineering (ICDE)*, 1998.

[3] P. Atzeni, G. Mecca, and P. Merialdo. To weave the Web. In *Proc. of the Int. Conf. on Very Large Data Bases (VLDB)*, 1997.

[4] J. F. Barnes and R. Pandey. Providing dynamic and customizable caching policies. In *Proc. of the USENIX Second Symp. on Internet Technologies and Systems*, 1999.

[5] P. Cao, J. Zhang, and K. Beach. Active cache: Caching dynamic contents on the web. In *Proc. of IFIP Int. Conf. on Distributed Systems Platforms and Open Distributed Processing (Middleware)*, 1998.

[6] M. Carey, D. Florescu, Z. Ives, Y. Lu, J. Shanmugasundaram, E. Shekita, and S. Subramanian. XPERANTO: Publishing object-relational data as XML. In *Proc. of the Int. Workshop on Web and Databases (WebDB)*, 2000.

[7] S. Ceri, Piero, Fraternali, and A. Bongio. Web modeling language (WebML): a modeling language for designing Web sites. In *Proc. of the Int. World Wide Web Conf.*, 2000.

[8] B. Chidlovskii and U. M. Borghoff. Semantic caching of Web queries. *VLDB Journal*, 9(1):2–17, 2000.

[9] S. Cluet, C. Delobel, J. Simeon, and K. Smaga. Your mediators need data conversion. In *Proc. of ACM SIGMOD Int. Conf. on Management of Data (SIGMOD)*, 1998.

[10] F. Douglis, A. Haro, and M. Rabinovich. HPP: HTML macro-preprocessing to support dynamic document caching. In *Proc. of USITS'97 – USENIX Symp. on Internetworking Technologies and Systems*, 1997.

[11] M. Fernandez, D. Florescu, J. Kang, A. Levy, and D. Suciu. Catching the boat with Strudel: Experiences with a Website management system. In *Proc. of ACM SIGMOD Int. Conf. on Management of Data (SIGMOD)*, 1998.

[12] M. Fernandez, W.-C. Tan, and D. Suciu. Silkroute : Trading between relations and XML. In *Proc. of the Int. World Wide Web Conf.*, 2000.

[13] D. Florescu, A. Levy, D. Suciu, and K. Yagoub. Optimization of run time management of data intensive Web sites. In *Proc. of the Int. Conf. on Very Large Data Bases (VLDB)*, 1999.

[14] P. Fraternali. Tools and approches for developing data-intensive Web applications: a survey. *ACM Computing Surveys*, 1999.

[15] http://www-4.ibm.com/software/webservers/appserv/.

[16] http://www1.allaire.com/Products/coldfusion/.

[17] http://www.dynamai.com/home.html.

[18] http://www.java.sun.com/products/jsp/index.html.

[19] http://www.microsoft.com/.

[20] Z. G. Ives, A. Y. Levy, and D. S. Weld. Efficient evaluation of regular path expressions over streaming XML data. Technical Report UW-CSE-2000-05-02, University of Washington, 2000.

[21] A. Iyengar, J. Challenger, and P. Dantzig. A scalable system for consistently caching dynamic Web data. In *Proc. of IEEE INFOCOM*, 1999.

[22] A. Labrinidis and N. Roussopoulos. WebView materialization. In *Proc. of ACM SIGMOD Int. Conf. on Management of Data (SIGMOD)*, 2000.

[23] Q. Luo, J. F. Naughton, R. Krishnamurthy, P. Cao, and Y. Li. Active query caching for database Web servers. In *Proc. of the Int. Workshop on Web and Databases (WebDB)*, 2000.

[24] T. Nguyen and V.Srinivasan. Accessing relational databases from the World Wide Web. In *Proc. of ACM SIGMOD Int. Conf. on Management of Data (SIGMOD)*, 1996.

[25] L. Quan, L. Chen, and E. A. Rudensteiner. Argos: Efficient refresh in an XQL-Based Web caching system. In *Proc. of the Int. Workshop on Web and Databases (WebDB)*, 2000.

[26] J. Shanmugasundaram, E. Shekita, R. Barr, M. Carey, B. Lindsay, H. Pirahesh, and B. Reinwald. Efficient generating XML documents from relational data. In *Proc. of the Int. Conf. on Very Large Data Bases (VLDB)*, 2000.

[27] A. Wolman, G. M. Voelker, N. Sharma, N. Cardwell, A. Karlin, and H. M. Levy. On the scale and performance of cooperative Web proxy cahing. In *Proc. of SOSP'99 – 17th ACM Symp. on Operating Systems Principles*, December 1999.

[28] K. Yagoub, D. Florescu, V. Issarny, and C. Andrei. Building and customizing data-intensive Web sites using Weave. In *Proc. of the Int. Conf. on Very Large Data Bases (VLDB)*, 2000. (software demonstration).

The Evolution of the Web and Implications for an Incremental Crawler

Junghoo Cho   Hector Garcia-Molina

Department of Computer Science
Stanford, CA 94305
{cho, hector}@cs.stanford.edu

Abstract

In this paper we study how to build an effective incremental crawler. The crawler selectively and incrementally updates its index and/or local collection of web pages, instead of periodically refreshing the collection in batch mode. The incremental crawler can improve the "freshness" of the collection significantly and bring in new pages in a more timely manner. We first present results from an experiment conducted on more than half million web pages over 4 months, to estimate how web pages evolve over time. Based on these experimental results, we compare various design choices for an incremental crawler and discuss their trade-offs. We propose an architecture for the incremental crawler, which combines the best design choices.

1 Introduction

A crawler is a program that automatically collects Web pages to create a local index and/or a local collection of web pages. Roughly, a crawler starts off with an initial set of URLs, called *seed URLs*. It first retrieves the pages identified by the seed URLs, extracts any URLs in the pages, and adds the new URLs to a queue of URLs to be scanned. Then the crawler gets URLs from the queue (in some order), and repeats the process.

In general, the crawler can update its index and/or local collection in two different ways. Traditionally, the crawler visits the web until the collection has a desirable number of pages, and stops visiting pages. Then when it is necessary to refresh the collection, the crawler builds a brand new collection using the same process described above, and then replaces the old collection with this brand new one. We refer to this type of crawler as

**Proceedings of the 26th VLDB Conference,
Cairo, Egypt, 2000.**

a *periodic crawler*. Alternatively, the crawler may keep visiting pages after the collection reaches its target size, to *incrementally* update/refresh the local collection. By this incremental update, the crawler refreshes existing pages and replaces "less-important" pages with new and "more-important" pages. When the crawler operates in this mode, we call it an *incremental crawler*.

In principle, the incremental crawler can be more effective than the periodic one. For instance, if the crawler can estimate how often pages change, the incremental crawler may revisit only the pages that have changed (with high probability), instead of refreshing the entire collection altogether. This optimization may result in substantial savings in network bandwidth and significant improvement in the "freshness" of the collection. Also, the incremental crawler may index/collect a new page in a more timely manner than the periodic crawler does. That is, the periodic crawler can index a new page only after the next crawling cycle starts, but the incremental crawler may immediately index the new page, right after it is found. Given the importance of web search engines (and thus web crawlers), even minor improvement in these areas may enhance the users' experience quite significantly.

Clearly, the effectiveness of crawling techniques heavily depends on how web pages change over time. If most web pages change at similar frequencies, the periodic and the incremental crawlers may be equally effective, because both crawlers in fact revisit all pages at the *same* frequencies. Also, if the web is quite static and only a small number of pages appear/disappear every month, the issue of how fast new pages are brought in may be of negligible importance to most users.

In this paper we will study how we can construct an effective incremental crawler. To that end, we first study how the web evolves over time, through an experiment conducted on more than half million web pages for more than 4 months. Based on these results, we then compare various design choices for a crawler, discussing how these choices affect the crawler's effectiveness. Through this discussion, we will also compare relative advantages/disadvantages of a periodic and an incremental crawler. Finally, we propose an architecture for an incremental crawler, which combines the best design choices.

In summary, our contribution is as follows:

- We study how web pages evolve over time, by an

experiment conducted on 720,000 web pages for multiple months (Sections 2 and 3). We use our operational WebBase crawler for this experiment. (An earlier version of this crawler was used for the Google search engine [10].)

- We identify various design choices for an incremental crawler, and using our experimental data, we *quantify* the impact of various choices (Section 4). Our results let us make more informed decisions on the structure of a crawler.

- Based on our observations, we propose an architecture for an incremental crawler, which maintains only "important" pages and adjusts revisit frequency for pages depending on how often they change (Section 5).

2 Experimental setup

Our initial experiment tries to answer the following questions about the evolving web:

- How often does a web page change?
- What is the lifespan of a page?
- How long does it take for 50% of the web to change?
- Can we describe changes of web pages by a mathematical model?

Note that an incremental crawler itself also has to answer some of these questions. For instance, the crawler has to estimate how often a page changes, in order to decide how often to revisit the page. The techniques used for our experiment will shed a light on how an incremental crawler should operate and which statistics-gathering mechanisms it should adopt.

To answer our questions, we crawled around 720,000 pages from 270 sites every day, from February 17th through June 24th, 1999. This was done with the Stanford WebBase crawler, a system designed to create and maintain large web repositories (currently 300GB of HTML is stored). In this section we briefly discuss how the particular sites and pages were selected.

2.1 Monitoring technique

For our experiment, we adopted an *active crawling* approach with a *page window*. With active crawling, a crawler visits pages of interest periodically to see if they have changed. This is in contrast to a passive scheme, where say a proxy server tracks the fraction of new pages it sees, driven by the demand of its local users. A passive scheme is less obtrusive, since no additional load is placed on web servers beyond what would naturally be placed. However, we use active crawling because it lets us collect much better statistics, i.e., we can determine what pages to check and how frequently.

The pages to actively crawl are determined as follows. We start with a list of root pages for sites of interest. We periodically revisit these pages, and visit some predetermined number of pages that are reachable, breadth first, from that root. This gives us a *window of*

pages at each site, whose contents may vary from visit to visit. Pages may leave the window if they are deleted or moved deeper within the site. Pages may also enter the window, as they are created or moved closer to the root. Thus, this scheme is superior to one that simply tracks a fixed set of pages, since such a scheme would not capture new pages.

We considered a variation of the page window scheme, where pages that disappeared from the window would still be tracked, if they still exist elsewhere in the site. This scheme could yield slightly better statistics on the lifetime of pages. However, we did not adopt this variation because it forces us to crawl a growing number of pages at each site. As we discuss in more detail below, we very much wanted to bound the load placed on web servers throughout our experiment.

2.2 Site selection

To select the actual sites for our experiment, we used the snapshot of 42 million web pages in our WebBase repository. Based on this snapshot, we identified top 400 "popular" sites as the candidate sites To measure the popularity of sites, we essentially counted how many pages in our repository have a link to each site, and we used the count as the popularity measure of a site.[1] Then, we contacted the webmasters of all candidate sites to get their permission for our experiment. After this step, 270 sites remained, including sites such as Yahoo (http://yahoo.com), Microsoft (http://microsoft.com), and Stanford (http://www.stanford.edu). Obviously, focusing on the "popular" sites biases our results to a certain degree, but we believe this bias is toward what most people are interested in.

In our site list, 132 sites belong to com and 78 sites to edu. The sites ending with ".net" (11 sites) and ".org" (19 sites) are classified as netorg and the sites ending with ".gov" (28 sites) and ".mil" (2 sites) as gov.

2.3 Number of pages at each site

After selecting the web sites to monitor, we still need to decide the window of pages to crawl from each site. In our experiment, we crawled 3,000 pages at each site. That is, starting from the root pages of the selected sites we followed links in a breadth-first search, up to 3,000 pages per site. This "3,000 page window" was decided for practical reasons. In order to minimize the load on a site, we ran the crawler only at night (9PM through 6AM PST), waiting at least 10 seconds between requests to a single site. Within these constraints, we could crawl at most 3,000 pages from a site every day.

3 Results

From the experiment described in the previous section, we collected statistics on how often pages change (by change we mean *any* change to the textual content of a

---

[1] More precisely, we used PageRank as the popularity measure, which is similar to the link count. To learn more about PageRank, please refer to [10, 4, 7].

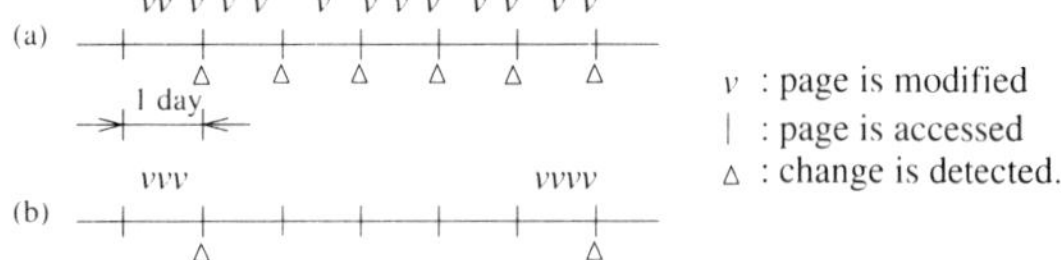

Figure 1: The cases when the estimated change interval is lower than the real value

page) and how long they stay on the web, and we report the result in this section.

3.1 How often does a page change?

Based on the data that we collected, we can analyze how long it takes for a web page to change. For example, if a page existed within our window for 50 days, and if the page changed 5 times in that period, we can estimate the *average change interval* of the page to be 50 days/5 = 10 days. Note that the granularity of the estimated change interval is one day, because we can detect at most one change per day, even if the page changes more often (Figure 1(a)). Also, if a page changes several times a day and then remains unchanged, say, for a week (Figure 1(b)), the estimated interval might be much longer than the true value. In this case, however, we can interpret our estimation as the interval between the *batches of changes*, which might be more meaningful than the average interval of change.

In Figure 2 we summarize the result of this analysis. In the figure, the horizontal axis represents the average change interval of pages, and the vertical axis shows the fraction of pages changed at the given average interval. Figure 2(a) shows the statistics collected over all domains, and Figure 2(b) shows the statistics broken down to each domain. For instance, from the second bar of Figure 2(a) we can see that 15% of the pages have a change interval longer than a day and shorter than a week.

From the first bar of Figure 2(a), we can observe that a surprisingly large number of pages change at very high frequencies: More than 20% of pages had changed whenever we visited them! As we can see from Figure 2(b), these frequently updated pages are mainly from the com domain. More than 40% of pages in the com domain changed every day, while less than 10% of the pages in other domains changed at that frequency (Figure 2(b) first bars). In particular, the pages in edu and gov domain are very static. More than 50% of pages in those domains did not change at all for 4 months (Figure 2(b) fifth bars). Clearly, pages at commercial sites, maintained by professionals, are updated frequently to provide timely information and attract more users.

Note that it is not easy to estimate the *average* change interval over all web page, because we conducted the experiment for a limited period. While we know how often a page changes if its change interval is longer than one day and shorter than 4 months, we do not know exactly how often a page changes, when its change interval is out of this range (the pages corresponding to the first

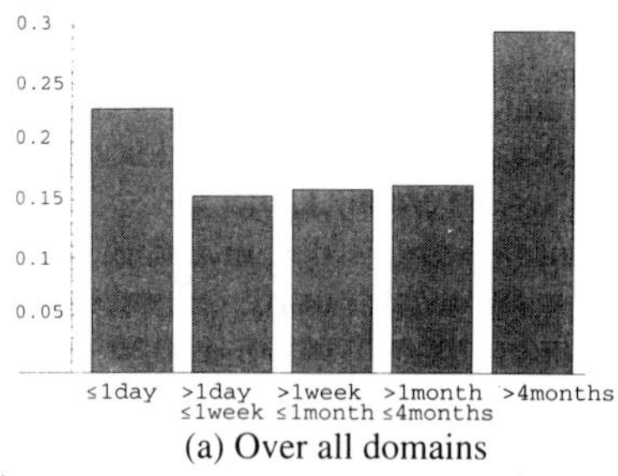

(a) Over all domains

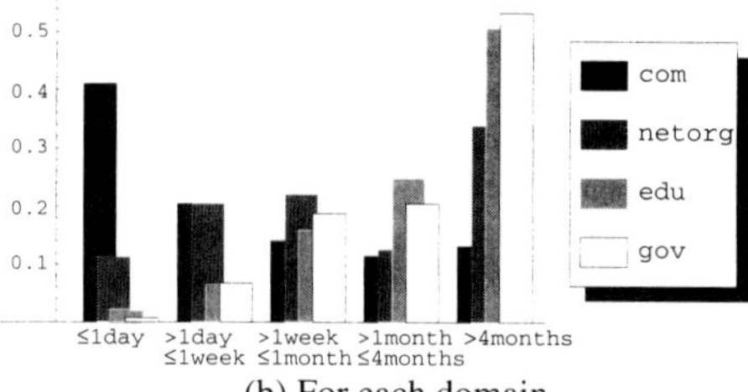

(b) For each domain

Figure 2: Fraction of pages with given average interval of change

or the fifth bar of Figure 2(a)). As a *crude approximation*, if we assume that the pages in the first bar change every day and the pages in the fifth bar change every year the overall average change interval of a web page is about 4 months.

In summary, web pages change rapidly overall, and the actual rates vary dramatically from site to site. Thus, a good crawler that is able to effectively track all these changes will be able to provide much better data than one that is not sensitive to changing data.

3.2 What is the lifespan of a page?

In this subsection we study how long we can access a particular page, once it appears on the web. To address this question, we investigated how long we could detect each page during our experiment. That is, for every page that we crawled, we checked how many days the page was accessible within our window (regardless of whether the page content had changed), and used that number as the *visible lifespan* of the page. Note that the *visible* lifespan of a page is not the same as its *actual* lifespan, because we measure how long the page was visible *within* our window. However, we believe the visible lifespan is a close approximation to the lifespan of a page *conceived by users* of the web. That is, when a user looks for an information from a particular site, she often starts from its root page and follows links. Since the user cannot infinitely follow links, she concludes the page of interest does not exist or has disappeared, if the page is not reachable within a few links from the root page. Therefore, many users often look at only a *window* of pages from a site, not the entire site.

Because our experiment was conducted in a limited time period, measuring the visible lifespan of a page is not as straightforward as we just described. Figure 3 illustrates the problem in detail. For the pages that appeared *and* disappeared during our experiment (Fig-

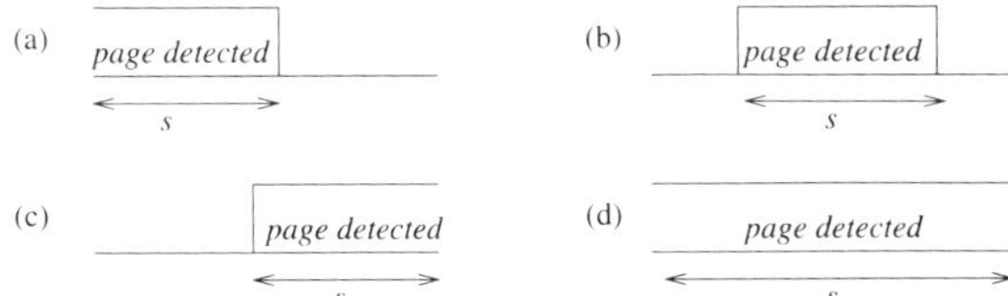

Figure 3: Issues in estimating the lifespan of a page

ure 3(b)), we can measure how long the page stayed in our window precisely. However, for the pages that existed from the beginning (Figure 3(a) and (d)) or at the end of our experiment (Figure 3(c) and (d)), we do not know exactly how long the page was in our window, because we do not know when the page appeared/disappeared. To take this error into account, we estimated the visible lifespan in two different ways. First, we used the length in Figure 3 as the lifespan of a page (Method 1), and second, we assumed that the lifespan is 2 for pages corresponding to (a), (c) and (d) (Method 2). Clearly, the lifespan of (a), (c) and (d) pages can be anywhere between and infinity, but we believe 2 is a reasonable guess, which gives an *approximate* range for the lifespan of pages.

Figure 4(a) shows the result estimated by the two methods. In the figure, the horizontal axis shows the visible lifespan and the vertical axis shows the fraction of pages with given lifespan. For instance, from the second bar of Figure 4(a), we can see that Method 1 estimates that around 19% of the pages have a lifespan of longer than one week and shorter than 1 month, and Method 2 estimates that the fraction of the corresponding pages is around 16%. Note that Methods 1 and 2 give us similar numbers for the pages with a short lifespan (the first and the second bar), but their estimates are very different for longer lifespan pages (the third and fourth bar). This result is because the pages with a longer lifespan have higher probability of spanning over the beginning or the end of our experiment and their estimates can be different by a factor of 2 for Method 1 and 2. In Figure 4(b), we show the lifespan of pages for different domains. To avoid cluttering the graph, we only show the histogram obtained by Method 1.

Interestingly, we can see that a significant number of pages are accessible for a relatively long period. More than 70% of the pages over all domains remained in our window for more than one month (Figure 4(a), the third and the fourth bars), and more than 50% of the pages in the edu and gov domain stayed for more than 4 months (Figure 4(b), fourth bar). As expected, the pages in the com domain were the shortest lived, and the pages in the edu and gov domain lived the longest.

3.3 How long does it take for 50% of the web to change?

In the previous subsections, we mainly focused on how an *individual* web page evolves over time. For instance, we studied how often a page changes, and how long it stays within our window. Now we slightly change our perspective and study how the *web as a whole* evolves

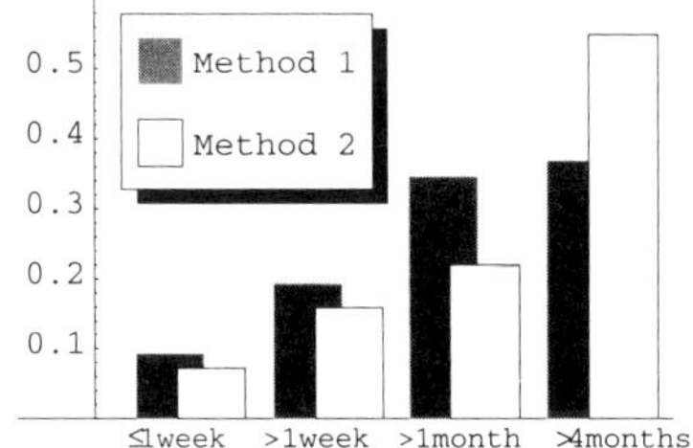

(a) Over all domains

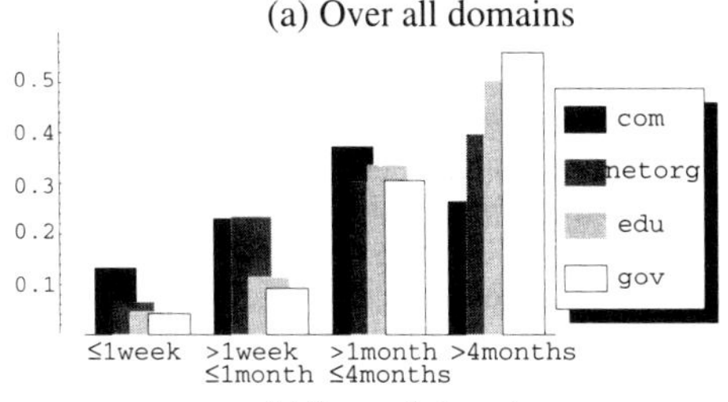

(b) For each domain

Figure 4: Percentage of pages with given visible lifespan

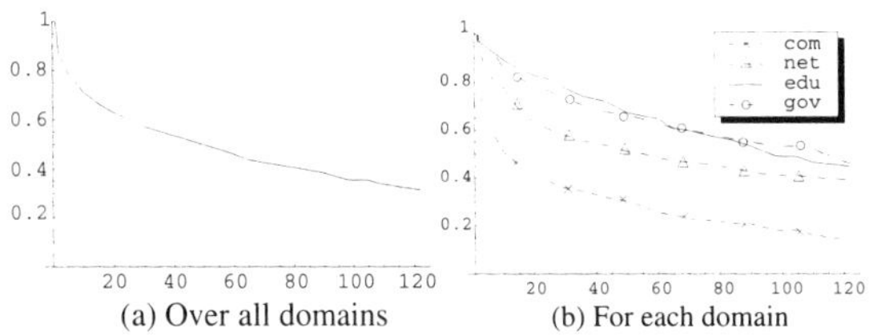

(a) Over all domains   (b) For each domain

Figure 5: Fraction of pages that did not change or disappear until given date.

over time. That is, we investigate how long it takes for % of the pages within our window to change.

To get this information, we traced how many pages in our window remained unchanged after a certain period, and the result is shown in Figure 5. In the figure, the horizontal axis shows the number of days from the beginning of the experiment and the vertical axis shows the fraction of pages that were unchanged by the given day.

From Figure 5(a), we can see that it takes about 50 days for 50% of the web to change or to be replaced by new pages. From Figure 5(b), we can confirm that different domains evolve at highly different rates. For instance, it took only 11 days for 50% of the com domain to change, while the same amount of change took almost 4 months for the gov domain (Figure 5(b)). Similarly to the previous results, the com domain is the most dynamic, followed by the netorg domain. The edu and the gov domains are the most static. Again, our results highlight the need for a crawler that can track these massive but skewed changes effectively.

3.4 Can we describe changes of a page by a mathematical model?

Now we study whether we can describe changes of web pages by a mathematical model. In particular, we study

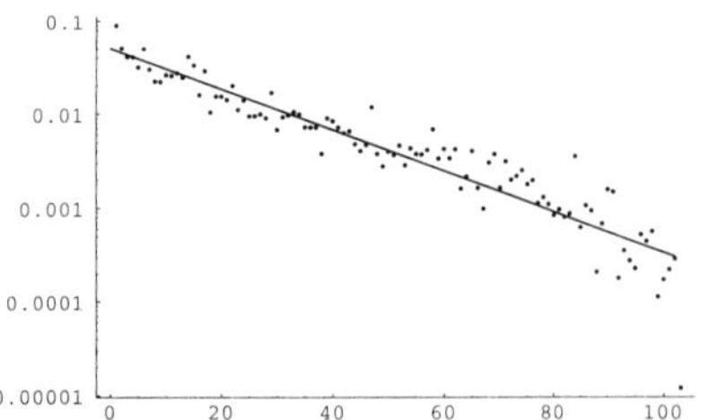

Figure 6: Change intervals of pages (with 20 day average change interval)

whether changes of web pages follow a *Poisson process*. Building a change model of the web is very important, in order to compare how effective different crawling policies are. For instance, if we want to compare how "fresh" crawlers maintain their local collections, we need to compare how many pages in the collection are maintained up-to-date, and this number is hard to get without a proper change model for the web.

A Poisson process is often used to model a sequence of *random* events that happen *independently* with *fixed rate* over time. For instance, occurrences of fatal auto accidents, arrivals of customers at a service center, telephone calls originating in a region, etc., are usually modeled by a Poisson process. We believe a Poisson process is a good model for changes of web pages, because many web pages have the properties that we just mentioned. For instance, pages in the CNN web site change at the *average* rate of once a day, but the change of a particular page is quite random, because update of the page depends on how the news related to that page develops over time.

Under a Poisson process, we can compute the time between two events. To compute this interval, let us assume that the first event happened at time 0, and let be the time when the next event occurs. Then the probability density function of is exponential [12].

Lemma 1 *If is the time to the occurrence of the next event in a* Poisson process *with rate , the probability density function for is* $f(t) = e^{-t}$ *for $t > 0$.* □

We can use Lemma 1 to verify whether web changes follow a Poisson process. That is, if changes to a page follow a Poisson process of rate , its change intervals should follow the distribution e^{-t}. To compare this prediction to our experimental data, we assume that each page i on the web has an *average* rate of change i, where i may differ from page to page. Then we select only the pages whose *average change intervals* are, say, 10 days and plot the distribution of their change intervals. If the pages indeed follow a Poisson process, this graph should be distributed exponentially. In Figure 6, we show one of the graphs plotted this way. We obtained the graph for the pages with 20 day change interval. The horizontal axis represents the interval between successive changes, and the vertical axis shows the fraction of changes with that interval. The vertical axis in the graph is logarithmic to emphasize that the distribution is exponential. The line in the graph is the prediction by a Poisson process. While there exist small variations, we can clearly see that a Poisson process predicts the observed data very well. We also plotted the same graph for the pages with other change intervals and got similar results when we had sufficient data.

Although our results indicate that a Poisson process describes the web page changes very well, they are limited due to the constraint of our experiment. We crawled web pages on a daily basis, so our result does not verify the Poisson model for the pages that change very often. Also, the pages that change very slowly were not verified either, because we conducted our experiment for four months and did not detect any changes to those pages. However, we believe that most crawlers may not have high interest in learning exactly how often those pages change. For example, the crawling interval of most crawlers is much longer than a day, so they do not particularly care whether a page changes exactly once every day or more than once every day.

Also, a set of web pages may be updated at a regular interval, and their changes may not necessarily follow a Poisson process. However, a crawler cannot easily identify these pages when it maintains hundreds of millions of web pages, so the entire set of pages that the crawler manages may be considered to change by a random process on average. Thus, we believe it is safe to use the Poisson model to compare crawler strategies in the next section.

4 Crawler design issues

The results of previous section showed us how web pages change over time. Based on these results, we now discuss various design choices for a crawler and their possible trade-offs. One of our central goals is to maintain the local collection up-to-date. To capture how "fresh" a collection is, we will use the metric *freshness* in [3]. Informally, freshness represents the fraction of "up-to-date" pages in the local collection. For instance, when all pages in the collection are up-to-date (i.e., the same as the *current state* of their real-world counterparts), the freshness of the collection is 1, while the freshness of the collection is 0.5 when a half of the collection is up-to-date. (In [3] we also discuss a second metric, the "age" of crawled pages. This metric can also be used to compare crawling strategies, but the conclusions are not significantly different from the ones we reach here using the simpler metric of freshness.)

4.1 Is the collection updated in batch-mode?

A crawler needs to revisit web pages in order to maintain the local collection up-to-date. Depending on how the crawler updates its collection, the crawler can be classified as one of the following:

Batch-mode crawler: A *batch-mode crawler* runs *periodically* (say, once a month), updating *all* pages in the collection in each crawl. We illustrate how such a

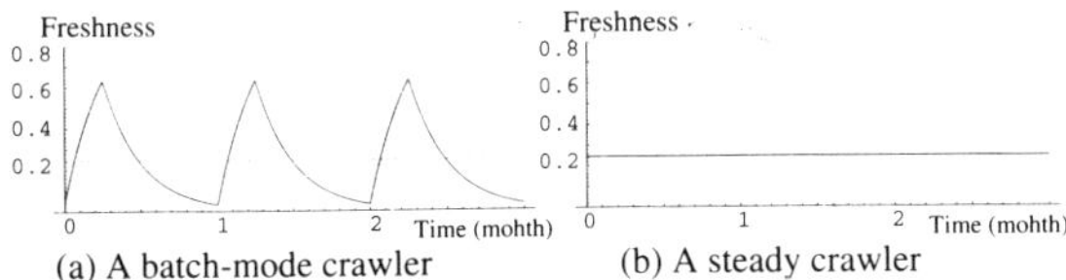

Figure 7: Freshness evolution of a batch-mode/steady crawler

crawler operates in Figure 7(a). In the figure, the horizontal axis represents time and the grey region shows when the crawler operates. The vertical axis in the graph represents the freshness of the collection, and the curve in the graph shows how freshness changes over time. The dotted line shows freshness *averaged over time*. The curves in this section are obtained analytically using a Poisson model. (We do not show the derivation here due to space constraints.) We use a high page change rate to obtain curves that more clearly show the trends. Later on we compute freshness values based on the actual rate of change we measured on the web.

To plot the graph, we also assumed that the crawled pages are immediately made available to users, as opposed to making them all available at the end of the crawl. We believe most of the current crawlers are operating in batch mode.

From the figure, we can see that the collection starts growing stale when the crawler is idle (freshness decreases in white regions), and the collection gets fresher when the crawler revisits pages (freshness increases in grey regions). Note that the freshness is not equal to 1 even at the end of each crawl (the right ends of grey regions), because some pages have already changed during the crawl. Also note that the freshness of the collection decreases exponentially in the white region. This trend is consistent with the experimental result of Figure 5.

Steady crawler: A *steady crawler* runs continuously without any pause (Figure 7(b)). In the figure, the entire area is grey, because the crawler runs continuously. Contrary to the batch-mode crawler, the freshness of the steady crawler is stable over time because the collection is continuously and incrementally updated.

While freshness evolves differently for the batch-mode and the steady crawler, one can *prove* (based on the Poisson model) that their freshness *averaged over time* is the *same*, if they visit pages at the same *average* speed. That is, when the steady and the batch-mode crawler revisit all pages every month (even though the batch-mode crawler finishes a crawl in a week), the freshness averaged over time is the same for both.

Even though both crawlers yield in the same average freshness, the steady crawler has an advantage over the batch-mode one, because it can collect pages at a lower *peak* speed. To get the same average speed, the batch-mode crawler must visit pages at a higher speed when it operates. This property increases the peak load on the crawler's local machine and on the network. From our crawling experience, we learned that the peak crawling

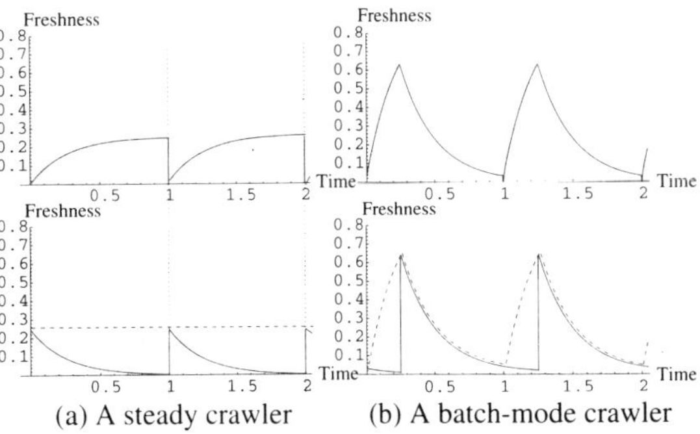

Figure 8: Freshness of the crawler's and the current collection

speed is a *very* sensitive issue for many entities on the web. For instance, when the WebBase crawler ran at a very high speed, it once crashed the central router for the Stanford network. After that incident, Stanford network managers have closely monitored our crawling activity to ensure it runs at a reasonable speed. Also, the webmasters of many web sites carefully trace how often a crawler accesses their sites. If they feel a crawler runs too fast, they sometimes block the crawler completely from accessing their sites.

4.2   Is the collection updated in-place?

When a crawler replaces an old version of a page with a new one, it may update the page *in-place*, or it may perform *shadowing* [9]. With shadowing, a new set of pages is collected from the web, and stored in a *separate space* from the current collection. After all new pages are collected and processed, the current collection is instantaneously replaced by this new collection. To distinguish, we refer to the collection in the shadowing space as the *crawler's collection*, and the collection that is currently available to users as the *current collection*.

Shadowing a collection may improve the availability of the current collection, because the current collection is completely shielded from the crawling process. Also, if the crawler's collection has to be pre-processed before it is made available to users (e.g., an indexer may need to build an inverted-index), the current collection can still handle users' requests during this period. Furthermore, it is probably easier to implement shadowing than in-place updates, again because the update/indexing and the access processes are separate.

However, shadowing a collection may decrease freshness. To illustrate this issue, we use Figure 8. In the figure, the graphs on the top show the freshness of the crawler's collection, while the graphs at the bottom show the freshness of the current collection. To simplify our discussion, we assume that the current collection is instantaneously replaced by the crawler's collection right after all pages are collected.

When the crawler is steady, the freshness of the crawler's collection will evolve as in Figure 8(a), top. Because a new set of pages are collected from scratch

	Steady	Batch-mode
In-place	0.88	0.88
Shadowing	0.77	0.86

Table 1: Freshness of the collection for various choices

say every month, the freshness of the crawler's collection increases from zero every month. Then at the end of each month (dotted lines in Figure 8(a)), the current collection is replaced by the crawler's collection, making their freshness the same. From that point on, the freshness of the current collection decreases, until the current collection is replaced by a new set of pages. To compare how freshness is affected by shadowing, we show the freshness of the current collection *without shadowing* as a dashed line in Figure 8(a), bottom. The dashed line is always higher than the solid curve, because when the collection is not shadowed, new pages are immediately made available. Freshness of the current collection is always higher *without* shadowing.

In Figure 8(b), we show the freshness of a *batch-mode* crawler when the collection is shadowed. The solid line in Figure 8(b) top shows the freshness of the crawler's collection, and the solid line at the bottom shows the freshness of the current collection. For comparison, we also show the freshness of the current collection *without shadowing* as a dashed line at the bottom. (The dashed line is slightly shifted to the right, to distinguish it from the solid line.) The grey regions in the figure represent the time when the crawler operates.

At the beginning of each month, the crawler starts to collect a new set of pages from scratch, and the crawl finishes in a week (the right ends of grey regions). At that point, the current collection is replaced by the crawler's collection, making their freshness the same. Then the freshness of the current collection decreases exponentially until the current collection is replaced by a new set of pages.

Note that the dashed line and the solid line in Figure 8(b) bottom, are the same most of the time. For the batch-mode crawler, freshness is mostly the same, regardless of whether the collection is shadowed or not. Only when the crawler is running (grey regions), the freshness of the *in-place update* crawler is higher than that of *shadowing* crawler, because new pages are immediately available to users with the in-place update crawler.

In Table 1 we contrast the four possible choices we have discussed (shadowing versus in-place, and steady versus batch), using the change rates measured in our experiment. To construct the table, we assumed that all pages change with an *average* 4 month interval, based on the result of Section 3.1. (Even if the average change interval of pages is not exactly 4 months, the result is not much different.) Also, we assumed that the steady crawler revisits pages steadily over a month, and that the batch-mode crawler recrawls pages only in the first week of every month. The entries in Table 1 give the expected freshness of the current collection. From the

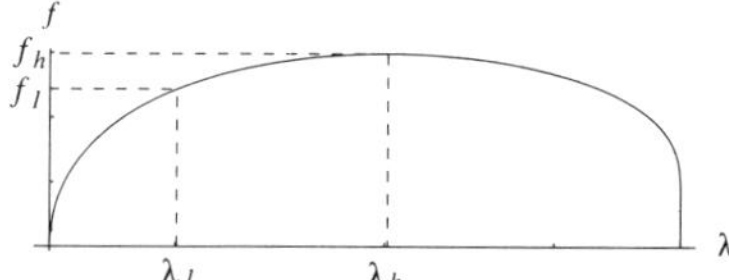

Figure 9: Change frequency of a page vs. optimal revisit frequency of the page

table, we can see that the freshness of the steady crawler significantly decreases with shadowing, while the freshness of the batch-mode crawler is not much affected by shadowing. Thus, if one is building such a crawler, shadowing is a good option since it is simpler to implement, and in-place updates are not a significant win in this case. In contrast, the gains are significant for a steady crawler, so in-place updates may be a good option.

Note that, however, this conclusion is very sensitive to how often web pages change and how often a crawler runs. For instance, consider a scenario where web pages change every month (as opposed to every 4 months), and a batch crawler operates for the first two weeks of every month. Under these parameters, the freshness of a batch crawler with in-place updates is 0.63, while the freshness is 0.50 with a shadowing crawler. Therefore, if a crawler focuses on a dynamic portion of the web (e.g., com domain), the crawler may need to adopt the in-place update policy, even when it runs in batch mode.

4.3 Are pages refreshed at the same frequency?

As the crawler updates pages in the collection, it may visit the pages either at the same frequency or at different frequencies.

Fixed frequency: The crawler revisits web pages at the same frequency, regardless of how often they change. We believe this fixed-frequency policy is often adopted by a batch-mode crawler, since a batch-mode crawler commonly revisits all pages in the collection in every batch.

Variable frequency: The result of Section 3.1 showed that web pages change at widely different frequencies. Given this result, the crawler may optimize the *revisit frequency* for a page, based on how often the page changes. Note that the variable-frequency policy is well suited for the *steady* crawler with *in-place updates*. Since the steady crawler visits pages continuously, it can adjust the revisit frequency with arbitrary granularity and thus increase the freshness of the collection.

If a variable frequency is used, the crawler needs a strategy for deciding at what rate to visit each page. Intuitively, one may suspect that the crawler should revisit a page more often, when it changes more often. However, reference [3] shows that this intuition may not be right, depending on the freshness metric used. For instance, Figure 9 shows how often a crawler should visit a page, to optimize the freshness metric [3]. The horizontal axis represents the change frequency of a page, and the vertical axis shows the optimal revisit frequency

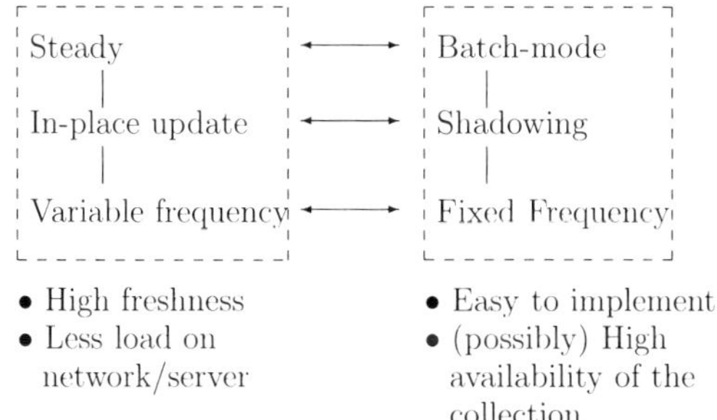

Figure 10: Two possible crawlers and their advantages

for that page. For example, if a page in the collection changes at the frequency λ_1, the crawler should visit the page at the frequency f_1. (We do not show specific numbers in the graph, because the scale of the graph depends on how often pages change and how often the crawler revisits the pages. However, the *shape* of the graph is always the same regardless of the scenario. For details, see [3].) Note that when a page changes at a low frequency (λ), the crawler should visit the page more often as it changes more often (f increases as λ increases). However, when the page changes at a high frequency ($\lambda >$), the crawler should visit the page less often as it changes more often (f decreases as λ increases).

We can understand this unexpected result through the following simple example. Suppose that a crawler maintains two pages, e_1 and e_2, in its collection. Also suppose that page e_1 changes every day and page e_2 changes every second. Due to bandwidth limitations, the crawler can crawl only one page per day, and it has to decide which page to crawl. Probabilistically, if the crawler revisits page e_1, e_1 will remain up-to-date for a half of the day. Therefore, the freshness of the collection will be 0.5 for a half of the day. (One out of two pages remain up-to-date for a half of the day.) Instead, if the crawler revisits page e_2, e_2 will remain up-to-date for a half second, so the freshness will be 0.5 only for a half second. Clearly, it is better to visit e_1 (which changes less often than e_2), than to visit e_2! From this example, we can see that the optimal revisit frequency is not always proportional to the change frequency of a page. The optimal revisit frequency depends on how often pages change and how often the crawler revisits pages, and it should be carefully determined. In reference [3], we study this problem in more detail. The reference shows that one can increase the freshness of the collection by 10%–23% by optimizing the revisit frequencies.

We summarize the discussion of this section in Figure 10. As we have argued, there exist two "reasonable" combinations of options, which have different advantages. The crawler on the left gives us high freshness and results in low peak loads. The crawler on the right may be easier to implement and interferes less with a highly utilized current collection. The left-hand side corresponds to the *incremental crawler* we discussed in

the introduction, and the right-hand side corresponds to the *periodic crawler*. In the next section, we discuss how we can implement an effective incremental crawler, with the properties listed on the left-hand side of the diagram.

5   Architecture for an incremental crawler

In this section, we study how to implement an effective incremental crawler. To that end, we first explain how the incremental crawler conceptually operates and identify two key decisions that an incremental crawler constantly makes. Based on these observations, we propose an architecture for the incremental crawler.

5.1   Operational model of an incremental crawler

In Figure 11 we show pseudo-code that describes how an incremental crawler operates. This code shows the *conceptual* operation of the crawler, not an efficient or complete implementation. (In Section 5.2, we show how an actual incremental crawler operates.) In the algorithm, AllUrls records the set of *all* URLs discovered, and CollUrls records the set of URLs in the collection.

Note that when a crawler continuously crawls the web, the crawler has two important goals in mind. The first goal is to maintain its local collection "fresh" and the second goal is to improve the "quality" of the local collection by replacing "less important" pages with "more important" pages. To achieve these goals, the crawler needs to make a careful decision on what page to crawl next. In the algorithm, the crawler makes decisions in Step [2] and [7] and two decisions are tightly intertwined. That is, when the crawler decides to crawl a new page (Step [2]), it *has to* discard a page from the collection to make room for the new page. Therefore, when the crawler decides to crawl a new page, the crawler should decide what page to discard (Step [7]).

Algorithm 1   *Operation of an incremental crawler*
Input   AllUrls: a set of all URLs known
                    CollUrls: a set of URLs in the local collection
                    (We assume CollUrls is full from the beginning.)
Procedure
```
[1] while (true)
[2]     url ← selectToCrawl(AllUrls)
[3]     page ← crawl(url)
[4]     if (url ∈ CollUrls) then
[5]         update(url, page)
[6]     else
[7]         tmpurl ← selectToDiscard(CollUrls)
[8]         discard(tmpurl)
[9]         save(url, page)
[10]        CollUrls ← (CollUrls − {tmpurl}) ∪ {url}
[11]    newurls ← extractUrls(page)
[12]    AllUrls ← AllUrls ∪ newurls
```

Figure 11: Conceptual operational model of an incremental crawler

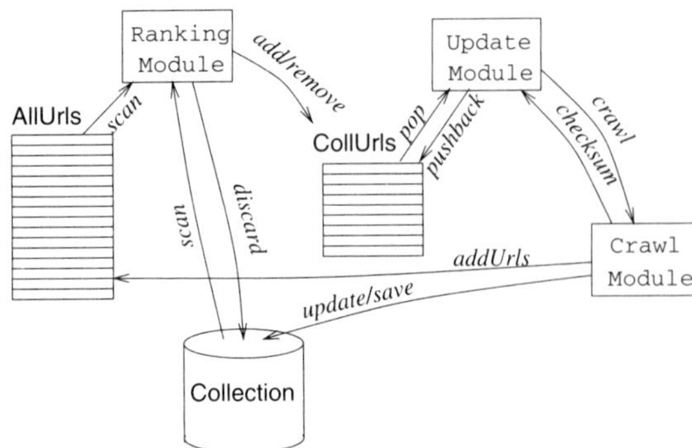

Figure 12: Architecture of the incremental crawler

We refer to this selection/discard decision as the *refinement decision*.

Note that this refinement decision should be based on the "importance" of pages. To measure importance, the crawler can use a number of metrics, including PageRank [4, 10] and Hub and Authority [8]. Clearly, the importance of the discarded page should be lower than the importance of the new page. In fact, the discarded page should have the *lowest* importance in the collection, to maintain the collection of the highest quality.

Together with the refinement decision, the crawler decides on what page to *update* in Step [2]. That is, instead of visiting a new page, the crawler may decide to visit an existing page to refresh its image. To maintain the collection "fresh," the crawler has to select the page that will increase the freshness most significantly, and we refer to this decision as *update decision*.

5.2 Architecture for an incremental crawler

To achieve the two goals for incremental crawlers, and to effectively implement the corresponding decision process, we propose the architecture for an incremental crawler shown in Figure 12. The architecture consists of three major modules (RankingModule, UpdateModule and CrawlModule) and three data structures (AllUrls, CollUrls and Collection). The lines and arrows show data flow between modules, and the labels on the lines show the corresponding commands. Two data structures, AllUrls and CollUrls, maintain information similar to that shown in Figure 11. AllUrls records *all* URLs that the crawler has discovered, and CollUrls records the URLs that are/will be in the Collection. CollUrls is implemented as a priority-queue, where URLs to be crawled early are placed in the front.

The URLs in CollUrls are chosen by the RankingModule. The RankingModule constantly scans through AllUrls and the Collection to make the *refinement decision*. For instance, if the crawler uses PageRank as its importance metric, the RankingModule constantly reevaluates the PageRanks of all URLs, based on the link structure captured in the Collection.[2]

---

[2]Note that even if a page p does not exist in the Collection, the RankingModule can estimate PageRank of p, based on how many pages in the Collection have a link to p.

When a page *not* in CollUrls turns out to be more important than a page within CollUrls, the RankingModule schedules for replacement of the less-important page in CollUrls with that more-important page. The URL for this new page is placed on the top of CollUrls, so that the UpdateModule can crawl the page immediately. Also, the RankingModule discards the less-important page from the Collection to make space for the new page.

While the RankingModule refines the Collection, the UpdateModule maintains the Collection "fresh" (*update decision*). It constantly extracts the top entry from CollUrls, requests the CrawlModule to crawl the page, and puts the crawled URL back into CollUrls. The position of the crawled URL within CollUrls is determined by the page's *estimated* change frequency and its importance. (The closer a URL is to the head of the queue, the more frequently it will be revisited.)

To estimate how often a particular page changes, the UpdateModule records the checksum of the page from the last crawl and compares that checksum with the one from the current crawl. From this comparison, the UpdateModule can tell whether the page has changed or not. In [2], we explain how the UpdateModule can estimate the change frequency of a page based on this change history. In short, we propose two "estimators," E and E , for the change frequency of a page.

Estimator E is based on the Poisson process model verified in Section 3.4, while estimator E is based on a Bayesian inference method. Essentially, E is the same as the method described in Section 3.1. To implement E , the UpdateModule has to record how many times the crawler detected changes to a page for, say, last 6 months. Then E uses this number to get a confidence interval for the change frequency of that page.

The goal of estimator E is slightly different from that of E . Instead of measuring a confidence interval, E tries to categorize pages into different frequency classes, say, pages that change every week (class C) and pages that change every month (class C). To implement E , the UpdateModule stores the probability that page i belongs to each frequency class ($\{ i \in C \}$ and $\{ i \in C \}$) and updates these probabilities based on detected changes. For instance, if the UpdateModule learns that page 1 did not change for one month, the UpdateModule increases $\{ 1 \in C \}$ and decreases $\{ 1 \in C \}$. For details, see [2].

Note that it is also possible to keep update statistics on larger units than a page, such as a web site or a directory. If web pages on a site change at similar frequencies, the crawler may trace how many times the pages on that site changed for last 6 months, and get a confidence interval based on the site-level statistics. In this case, the crawler may get a tighter confidence interval, because the frequency is estimated on *larger* number of pages (i.e., larger sample). However, if pages on a site change at highly different frequencies, this average change frequency may not be sufficient to determine how often to revisit pages in that site, leading to a less-than optimal revisit frequency.

Also note that the `UpdateModule` may need to consult the "importance" of a page in deciding on revisit frequency. If a certain page is "highly important" and the page needs to be always up-to-date, the `UpdateModule` may revisit the page much more often than other pages with similar change frequency. To implement this policy, the `UpdateModule` also needs to record the "importance" of each page.

Returning to our architecture, the `CrawlModule` crawls a page and saves/updates the page in the **Collection**, based on the request from the `UpdateModule`. Also, the `CrawlModule` extracts all links/URLs in the crawled page and forwards the URLs to **AllUrls**. The forwarded URLs are included in **AllUrls**, if they are new. While we show only one instance of the `CrawlModule` in the figure, note that multiple `CrawlModule`'s may run in parallel, depending on how fast we need to crawl pages.

Separating the update decision (`UpdateModule`) from the refinement decision (`RankingModule`) is crucial for performance reasons. For example, to visit 100 million pages every month,[3] the crawler has to visit pages at about 40 pages/second. However, it may take a while to select/deselect pages for **Collection**, because computing the importance of pages is often expensive. For instance, when the crawler computes PageRank, it needs to scan through the **Collection** multiple times, even if the link structure has changed little. (To learn more on the complexity of PageRank computation and how we can efficiently compute PageRank, see [7].) Clearly, the crawler cannot recompute the importance of pages for every page crawled, when it needs to run at 40 pages/second. By separating the refinement decision from the update decision, the `UpdateModule` can focus on updating pages at high speed, while the `RankingModule` carefully refines the **Collection**.

6 Related Work

Several papers investigate how to build an effective crawler. Reference [4] studies what pages a crawler should visit, when it cannot store a complete web image. Reference [1] looks at how to collect web pages related to a *specific* topic, in order to build a specialized web collection. The techniques discussed in these references can be used for the `RankingModule` in our architecture, to improve quality of the collection. In [2], we study how to estimate the change frequency of a web page by revisiting the page periodically. References [3] and [5] study how often a crawler should visit a page when it knows how often the page changes. The algorithms described in these references can be used for the `UpdateModule`, to improve freshness of the collec-

tion. We believe these references are complementary to our work, because we present an incremental-crawler architecture, which can use any of the algorithms in these papers.

References [13] and [6] experimentally study how often web pages change. Reference [11] studies the relationship between the "desirability" of a page and its lifespan. However, none of these studies are as extensive as ours in terms of the scale and the length of the experiment. Also, their focus is different from ours. Reference [13] investigates page changes to improve *web caching policies*, and reference [11] studies how page changes are related to *access patterns*.

7 Conclusion

In this paper we have studied how to build an effective incremental crawler. To understand how the web evolves over time, we first described a comprehensive experiment, conducted on 720,000 web pages from 270 web sites over 4 months. Based on the results, we discussed various design choices for a crawler and the possible trade-offs. We then proposed an architecture for an incremental crawler, which combines the best strategies identified.

References

[1] S. Chakrabarti, M. van den Berg, and B. Dom. Focused crawling: A new approach to topic-specific web resource discovery. In *Proceedings of the 8th World-Wide Web Conference*, 1999.

[2] J. Cho and H. Garcia-Molina. Estimating frequency of change. Technical report, Stanford University, 2000. `http://dbpubs.stanford.edu/pub/2000-4`.

[3] J. Cho and H. Garcia-Molina. Synchronizing a database to improve freshness. In *Proceedings of the 2000 ACM SIGMOD*, 2000.

[4] J. Cho, H. Garcia-Molina, and L. Page. Efficient crawling through URL ordering. In *Proceedings of the 7th World-Wide Web Conference*, 1998.

[5] E. Coffman, Jr., Z. Liu, and R. R. Weber. Optimal robot scheduling for web search engines. Technical report, INRIA, 1997.

[6] F. Douglis, A. Feldmann, and B. Krishnamurthy. Rate of change and other metrics: a live study of the world wide web. In *USENIX Symposium on Internetworking Technologies and Systems*, 1999.

[7] T. Haveliwala. Efficient computation of pagerank. Technical report, Stanford University, 1999. `http://dbpubs.stanford.edu/pub/1999-31`.

[8] J. M. Kleinberg. Authoritive sources in a hyperlinked environment. In *Proceedings of 9th ACM-SIAM Symposium on Discrete Algorithms*, 1998.

[9] M. K. McKusick, W. N. Joy, S. J. Leffler, and R. S. Fabry. A fast file system for UNIX. *ACM Transactions on Computer Systems*, 2(3):181–197, 1984.

[10] L. Page and S. Brin. The anatomy of a large-scale hypertextual web search engine. In *Proceedings of the 7th World-Wide Web Conference*, 1998.

[11] J. Pitkow and P. Pirolli. Life, death, and lawfulness on the electronic frontier. In *Proceedings of International Conference on Computer and Human Interaction*, 1997.

[12] H. M. Taylor and S. Karlin. *An Introduction To Stochastic Modeling*. Academic Press, 3rd edition, 1998.

[13] C. E. Wills and M. Mikhailov. Towards a better understanding of web resources and server responses for improved caching. In *Proceedings of the 8th World-Wide Web Conference*, 1999.

---

[3] Many search engines report numbers similar to this.

CheeTah: a Lightweight Transaction Server for Plug-and-Play Internet Data Management[*]

Guy Pardon   **Gustavo Alonso**

Information and Communication Systems Group

Institute of Information Systems, Swiss Federal Institute of Technology (ETH)

ETH Zentrum, CH-8092 Zürich, Switzerland

{pardon,alonso}@inf.ethz.ch

Abstract

The ability to maintain transactional interaction in a distributed system has proven to be a key feature in information systems. Unfortunately, as technology moves towards more distribution and decentralization, it becomes increasingly difficult to use existing transactional tools. In fact, current solutions are entirely unsuitable for what we call composite systems. Composite systems can be characterized as a collection of distributed, autonomous components, linked in an arbitrary configuration. In this paper, we describe Chee-Tah, a Java based set of tools for building composite components capable of interacting transactionally in arbitrary, dynamically changing configurations. We describe the technology provided, how designers would use it to build composite transactional systems, and examine in detail the performance of the resulting solution. Among the results we have achieved, the performance and the simplicity of use are of particular interest.

1 Introduction

Transactions greatly facilitate the task of dealing with failures, recovery, and concurrency control. They also allow to encapsulate operations and associate concrete semantics to them. Tools that provide transactional primitives for the design and development of information systems have a long history behind them, start-ing with the first TP-monitors [BN97] of almost three decades ago. Today, transactional technology is well understood and widely used.

In spite of this success, there is a growing number of applications for which existing tools are not suitable. The main problem is that current products use a centralized component for scheduling transactions [BK99]. To centralize operations in this way might be exceedingly difficult if the components reside in different organizations or if the components interact over the Internet. It may also be quite difficult in large web-farms or in clusters expanding several LANs. Unfortunately, none of the existing alternatives quite solves the problem. For instance, the TIP protocol [LEK99] provides a limited form of atomicity but no concurrency control. Similarly, persistent queues [IBM99] provide atomic asynchronous interaction but concurrency control cannot be easily enforced. In practice, we do not know of any tool or product that supports transactional interaction without a centralized monitor and without enforcing a static configuration of the components. We see this as a significant limitation in the current state-of-the-art.

At ETH Zürich, we have made this limitation one of our main research themes and have studied its theoretical aspects in great detail [ABFS97, AFPS99a, AFPS99b]. In this paper, we show how a system designer can use the set of tools we provide to build completely autonomous components that, without any centralized coordination, can interact transactionally. The components act as application servers that invoke each other's services to implement increasingly complex application logic. The components can be combined in any configuration and can be dynamically added or removed without compromising correctness. They can be used as wrappers for legacy applications or as infrastructure for transactional agents working across the Internet. They can also be used as EJB containers in the Java Business Components paradigm [EJB]. Our approach has the significant advantage of

*Part of this work has been funded by ETH Zürich within the DRAGON project(Reg-Nr 41-2642.5).

**Proceedings of the 26th VLDB Conference,
Cairo, Egypt, 2000.**

not requiring a very large infrastructure. All a designer has to do is to instantiate and extend a number of classes. In addition, our performance results show that the technology we have developed is not only viable but also quite adequate to the task at hand.

The paper provides an example of composite systems (Section 2), describes CheeTah (section 3), and provides an extensive performance analysis (Section 4), before discussing future work (Section 5). Readers interested in additional information about CheeTah (including a longer version of this work in the form of a technical report) can consult our web pages: *www.inf.ethz.ch/personal/pardon/CheeTah.html*.

2 Motivation: state of the art and related work

2.1 Composite systems

We are interested in distributed and dynamic environments where a collection of different, autonomous information systems interact transactionally. We call such systems composite systems. Figure 1 is an example of such a composite system. The figure illustrates the hierarchy of invocation calls between different services across a variety of components (e.g., *purchase access system, product catalogue server*, etc.). Each component is implemented as an independent entity residing in a different location. These components invoke the services provided by other components (Figure 1.a) forming an arbitrary nested client-server hierarchy in which increasing levels of abstraction and functionality can be introduced (Figure 1.b).

In our model, each component consists of an application logic layer (a *server*) that provides access to a resource manager (usually a database). The aim is to design and implement a mechanism that allows to combine such components in any possible configuration so that transactions can be executed across the resulting system guaranteeing (transactionally) correct results even if the configuration is dynamically altered. Moreover, these application layers must remain independent of each other, that is, there should not be a centralized component controlling their behavior.

2.2 Transactions in composite systems: theoretical aspects

Composite systems pose quite challenging problems from the theoretical point of view. At a first sight (Figure 1.b), one could think that a composite system is simply another version of nested [Mos81] or multilevel transactions [Wei91]. However, there are some fundamental differences that introduce non-trivial problems when deciding on correct executions. One important new aspect is that each scheduler is now entirely independent for concurrency control and recovery purposes. Another key difference is that the structure is not regular: schedules cannot be represented as balanced trees. These problems were first addressed in [ABFS97] where an extension to nested [Mos81, BBG89] and multilevel transaction theory [BSW88, Wei91] was proposed. In [AFPS99b] three basic configurations of composite systems were studied in detail. The basic configurations considered were the *stack*, the *fork*, and the *join*. These cases can be readily identified in Figure 1.b: S_6 forms a fork with S_8, S_{10} and S_7. Similarly, S_1, S_5 and S_{11} form a stack while S_{10}, S_7 and S_{12} form a join. Finally, in [AFPS99a] a general solution to the problem of composite systems was suggested by formulating a correctness criterion for arbitrary, dynamic configurations of composite systems.

2.3 Transactions in composite systems: practical aspects

Most existing systems use a flat transaction model where resources allocated to the transaction (locks, sockets, connections, and context information) are kept until the transaction commits. This is a concern for system designers due to the overhead it introduces [Moh98]. In composite systems, the limitations of the flat model become even more acute. Note that, in theory, one could use open nested transactions [GR93] to avoid these limitations. Open nested transactions allow to release resources of each subtransaction before the global transaction commits. The only requirement is to have a compensation action for the subtransaction in case it needs to be aborted. Although open nested transactions have been discussed in the literature and their theoretical advantages are well known, there are very few examples of successful implementations. Even in those systems where *closed* nested transactions are supported (e.g., Encina [Cor95] or in the CORBA specification where they are an optional feature), there are significant practical problems that have not yet been adequately addressed. As an example, most database products do not support nested transactions. As a result, many of the advantages of nested transactions are lost by having to map them to a flat model. In practice, there are two ways to do this mapping. One is to map each subtransaction to a different local transaction. The other is to map all subtransactions of the same root to a single local transaction. If each subtransaction is converted into a separate local transaction, a transaction will deadlock itself if there are conflicts among the subtransactions. This behaviour can be observed in, e.g., Encina. If all subtransactions are mapped onto a single local transaction, concurrent subcalls are not safe because subtransactions are not isolated from each other. Moreover, this mapping has to be specified as part of the

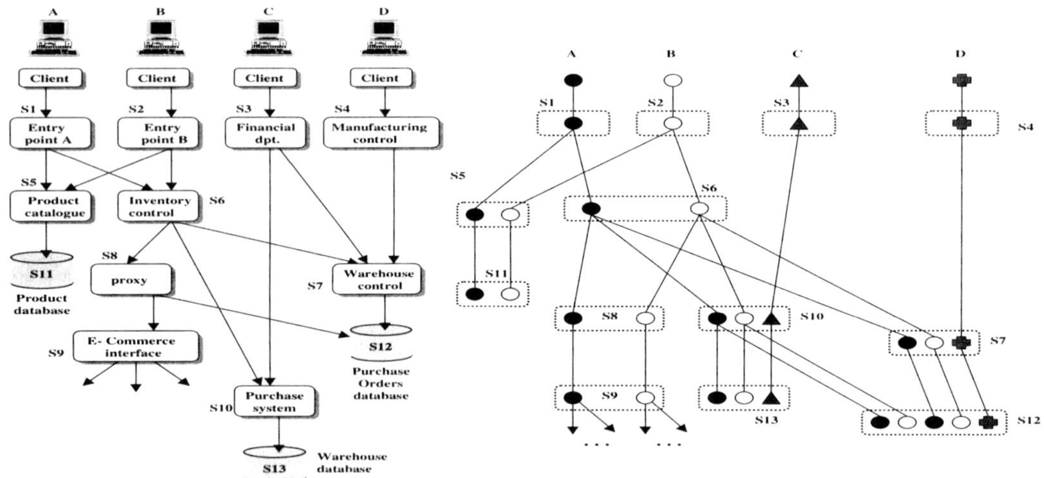

Figure 1: Invocation hierarchy (a, left-hand side) and transactional structure (b, right-hand side) in a composite system

server configuration, meaning that it can not be dynamically changed by a client. For instance, if some client wishes its subtransactions to be executed in parallel, it has no way of asking a server to treat its calls as *different* transactions in the local database. These limitations have often been used to argue that closed nested models are not feasible in practice, let alone open nested models. CheeTah provides an alternative solution to this and many other problems associated with the implementation of nested models. In fact, CheeTah proves that open nested models are feasible and can be used in practice. In CheeTah, we use an open nested model where subtransactions are *always* different local transactions, but we take care of preventing deadlocks while still releasing resources early enough to significantly improve performance.

3 The CheeTah approach to transactional interaction

3.1 System architecture

The main idea behind CheeTah is to provide a lightweight architecture where each component is in itself its own advanced mini-transaction processing monitor. To accomplish this, CheeTah has been implemented as a set of Java classes. The resulting architecture is as follows. In a composite system (Figure 1.b), each server (from S_1 to S_{13}) is an independent component performing its own scheduling and transaction management. These servers are built using Java and inheriting from the classes Cheetah provides. The interface to each server defines the services it implements.

An invocation of one of these services (through RMI) results in the creation of a local transaction (child of the invoking transaction and parent of any transaction that might be triggered by invoking the services of other servers). Each transaction is a thread that can invoke SQL statements in a local database (directly connected to that server) as well as services offered by other servers. All the information required to build a global composite transaction is implicitly added by the system to each call. However, it is important to emphasize that each transaction is independently handled at each server. That is, the servers neither communicate among themselves nor rely on a centralized component to make scheduling or recovery decisions. In this way, components can be dynamically added and removed from the system without compromising correctness. All a new server needs to know is the interface and address of the servers it will invoke. Regardless of the configuration, CheeTah guarantees that transactions executed over these servers will be correct (serializable) and recoverable at a global and local level.

3.2 Scheduling and concurrency control

For notational purposes, t will denote a local transaction in a server. Each incoming RMI invocation triggers a local transaction: $start(t)$ will be the start of the transaction, $commit(t)$ the local commit, $abort(t)$ the local abort, and $globalCommit(T)/globalAbort(T)$ the notification to the server where t runs that T, the root transaction (*root* is the term we generally use for the top-level transaction) of t, has committed/aborted.

In each server, concurrency control and scheduling are based on *call level locking*. That is, checking for conflicts is done at the service level and not merely at the level of the operations used to implement those services. Internally, each server uses traditional 2PL to guarantee correctness using standard mechanisms [GR93] but these resources (including connections and internal locks) are always released upon commitment of a local transaction. Call level locks are also acquired following a 2PL discipline but they are kept until the global transaction terminates or until the server unilaterally aborts the corresponding local transaction.

A call level lock is always acquired when a service is invoked. With each server, a conflict matrix needs to be supplied by the programmer. This matrix considers the effects of the forward operation and also of the compensation of an operation. An important characteristic is that, unlike in classical multilevel models, the conflict matrix for our system needs to take *only local* effects into account: whatever is done by remote calls is handled at the remote server. This greatly simplifies the task of identifying conflicts. Informally, we say that two call level locks, l_1 and l_2, obtained on behalf of two local transactions (service invocations) t_1 and t_2, *conflict* if t_1 conflicts with t_2 or t_2 conflicts with u_1, u_1 being the compensation of t_1. For simplicity, we currently use a symmetric conflict table but this can be easily changed if necessary. There is also the possibility of defining conflicts on item level granularity (i.e., conflicts are only possible if both t_1, t_2 are on the same data item) or on service granularity (invocations of t_1, t_2 always conflict regardless what item is accessed).

Although this locking strategy provides correctness, the arbitrary configurations possible in a composite system require a more sophisticated treatment of call level locks. The key problem is that without any additional information, a server cannot distinguish between invocations that have nothing to do with each other and invocations that actually belong to the same root transaction (*siblings*). In the former case the order of execution is not relevant. In the latter case it is relevant. Not to be able to distinguish between these cases can quickly lead to inconsistencies and incorrect executions. Closed nested transactions avoid these situations by simply blocking all conflicting calls. In a composite system, if a server were to block invocations from siblings, a transaction could easily deadlock itself (which *does* happen in existing implementations of closed nested transactions). Preventing such deadlocks would require to have knowledge of the configuration, which contradicts the spirit of composite systems. To avoid such problems, an additional rule is observed at each server: if t_1 and t_2 conflict but both are children of the same root transaction, they can

both be executed provided that they are not executed in parallel. This implies that $start(t_2)$ must happen after $commit(t_1)$. With this rule, the scheduler can now block conflicting invocations from other transactions and allow conflicting invocations from the same transaction to proceed.

3.3 Implementation of locking

Each incoming request to a server is mapped to a thread (since they are RMI invocations, this happens automatically). Setting the corresponding call level lock is done by the thread by creating an entry in the local lock table. If there is no conflicting lock, the thread proceeds to execute the code implementing the service. Otherwise, the thread returns with an exception (implying rollback of the local transaction). By immediately returning an exception, we force the client to be programmed in such a way so as to take into account that an invocation may not succeed the first time. On the other hand, resources are more readily available and allow ongoing transactions to terminate sooner.

To facilitate the identification of siblings, the system automatically includes the root id with each RMI call. For faster checking, the root id of a transaction is included in the lock table with the corresponding call level lock. Incoming requests are checked against the corresponding call level lock to see if they conflict and whether they are from the same root transaction.

Lock table management in CheeTah is done following Gray and Reuter [GR93], although the conflict information is more detailed (because of the call level mechanism and user-defined semantics).

3.4 Atomicity: Recovery and undo

At each server and for each service there is an undo operation provided by the designer of the service. Undo operations are local: only the local database updates are compensated. In case of abort of siblings, executing all conflicting undo transactions for the same root in the reverse order of their respective executions guarantees that all changes are undone. Any remote calls will be handled by the undo transactions on the remote servers involved. If no undo operation is provided, the invocation of the service will be treated as a closed nested transaction: resources are not released until the termination of the global transaction.

To be informed about the fate of a transaction, we use the root id (automatically propagated with the RMI call). If the local transaction is still being executed and needs to be aborted, it is undone using traditional mechanisms. If the local transaction needs to be aborted after having been committed, the undo operation is used. The call level lock guarantees that the undo operation can be applied. If the root transaction commits, then an optimized form of 2 Phase Commit is used to commit all subtransactions throughout the system (releasing the call level locks). Note that for early committed subtransactions, this termination protocol simply involves releasing call-level locks, write a log entry and cascade the decision to any remaining servers.

3.5 Implementation of Atomicity

A global transaction is committed using a cascaded variant of 2PC: each server assumes the role of coordinator for all servers it invokes. To speed up the process, different servers are contacted in parallel: each communication round in the two-phase commit protocol is implemented by one separate thread per server involved. The two-phase commit protocol uses the root identifier as the label to indicate to each server which subtransactions are to be committed. Just like all other communication in CheeTah, 2PC happens through RMI. This solves problems with firewalls, because RMI calls can automatically be tunneled through http. A negative acknowledgement (a NO vote) is implemented as a RemoteException being thrown.

In addition, and also for reasons of efficiency, it is not always feasible to wait until the root decides to abort or commit. For instance, servers could be disconnected from the rest of the system or network partitions may occur. In those cases, and given that the system is built upon independent components, each server has the right to undo local transactions on its own – as long as it has not heard from any global outcome. After the undo, all local locks and the call level lock can be released. The "right" to undo a local transaction has to be constrained, otherwise a server could undo its local transaction during the time the global commit message travels through the system. Thus, when a server receives a prepare message and agrees to it, it loses the right to perform a server-side undo.

This approach is complicated by the fact that RMI does not provide *exactly once* semantics. More precisely, the failure of a remote call does not necessarily mean that it has not been executed. It could have been executed, leaving behind a locally committed transaction (t_1) and the corresponding call levels locks set. The invoker, however, sees the call fail and may think the transaction has actually aborted. In that case, the server will eventually time out and undo the transaction locally, releasing the call level locks. This might result in incorrect executions if – on that server – later (successful) calls exist for the same root transaction. Let t_2 denote one such sibling subtransaction executed right after t_1. Locally undoing t_1 with u_1 will only be correct if the sequence $t_1\ t_2\ u_1$ is equivalent to the

sequence $t_1\ u_1\ t_2$ or $t_2\ t_1\ u_1$. To avoid these and similar problems, we have taken an expeditive approach. When a server propagates a *globalCommit* operation, it adds to the message the number of invocations it has made to a given server on behalf of the root transaction to be committed. The server that receives the *globalCommit* checks this figure against its own. If they match, then the commit protocol proceeds. Otherwise, the transaction will be aborted. Since in the latter case there are discrepancies about what has been done at each node, aborting seems to be the safest option.

To keep track of all the information needed to perform these operations, CheeTah relies on logging. Each server keeps a log-table and an undo-table inside its local database. As soon as a transaction commits locally, the log-table reflects the fact that the transaction made local changes (needed after recovery). The undo-table contains the needed parameters for executing a compensation if necessary. All this data is written in the same transaction as the user's logic, thereby reducing the number of database transactions to a minimum (one, in this case). A file based log is used to keep track of the two-phase commit status of a transaction after it has been locally committed. On recovery, the system can determine the right action by inspecting the log-table in the database and combining this with the external log file information. For instance, upon restart, a transaction may appear in the database log table but not in the external log file. This is a transaction that locally committed but without a global outcome. The transaction will be compensated as part of the restart procedure, thereby ensuring consistency.

3.6 Dealing with undo operations

Undo operations play an important role in CheeTah. Thus, a key question is whether we can always undo an operation. In this regard, it is important to emphasize that we rely on the service designer to provide the undo operation. Since in CheeTah the programmer only needs to worry about the data integrity of the local server, writing undo operations is relatively straightforward. Nevertheless, if no undo is provided, the system will simply retain resources until the root commits as it is done in existing products. The advantage of CheeTah is that knowledgeable users can exploit open nested transactions to significantly increase the degree of parallelism.

From the concurrency control point of view, executing an undo poses no problem because there is a lock on the corresponding service. If an undo operation needs to be executed, it will always be serialized immediately after the operation it is supposed to undo. However, writing undo operations can be made quite complex by the underlying database system. The typical problems involve dealing with constraints and triggers. In general, as long as there are no non controllable side effects (triggers or constraints that the system – or its programmer – does not know about), CheeTah can handle these cases just like any existing system handles them. That is, by blocking concurrent updates to the same items; so-called *strict* 2PL behaviour.

From our experience working with CheeTah, the knowledge necessary to write undo operations can be compared to what a typical database designer has to know about isolation levels to ensure data consistency in the local database.

3.7 Optimizations of Logging and Locking

Any information that the undo operation may need must be persistently stored (logged). With CheeTah, doing this is quite easy. The programmer only needs to push any information needed for the undo into a *stack object*. This information can be the value of certain variables, the tables used for the undo, transaction id's, and so forth. When the transaction commits, this stack object is written into the log table. In case an abort occurs, the system restores the transaction's undo stack. The undo operation can then read this object and proceed.

When creating the log entry, we use a very important optimization. If this information were saved as an insert into a logging table, and eventually discarded by a corresponding delete, performance would be very poor. Rather, CheeTah uses a pool of undo entries in a fixed-size table (a parameter that can be changed if needed). This table is indexed on a numeric *index* entry. The server component keeps in RAM a list of available entries in the logging table, and allocates them to a transaction when needed. Storing undo data is done by *updating* the log table, rather than *inserting* into it. Without this technique, we would never have been able to reach the current performance.

3.8 A CheeTah Server

With these ideas, the structure of a CheeTah server can be summarized as shown in Figure 2. The structure depends on the particular application, the one shown here being the same one we have used for our experiments.

The server simulates a purchase point where a number of different items can be bought. The interface to the service is a method, *Buy*, that takes as argument the id of the item to be bought, *itemid*. The method is implemented as a Java program that makes calls to a local database and invokes the services of other servers (through RMI calls). This is the code that needs to be implemented by the designer. The lock table provided indicates that two invocations to the *Buy* service con-

flict if they have the same *itemid* (i.e., they are buying the same thing). Each server uses a local database (currently Oracle8) for storing its own data (log and undo tables) and also to act as the local application database. Access to the database takes place through a JDBC interface using connection pooling.

The server also uses the local file system to store additional information (namely, the global log used to track the progress of 2PC). Each server has conceptually (internally they are deeply intertwined) three transaction managers (*incoming TM, internal TM and outgoing TM*). The incoming TM takes care of the incoming RMI calls and uses the call level lock table to determine what to do (whether to proceed or to return an exception). It also produces the entries stored in the file system log (related to 2PC) and the undo table. Context information, root id for the transaction, overall status and any additional information related to the *composite* transaction is stored in main memory and managed by the incoming TM. Messages about termination of global transactions are rerouted to the incoming TM where they are processed as explained above. The internal TM takes care of internal consistency (access to shared variables and internal data, as well as access to the local database). It produces the entries in the database log table and it is in charge of rolling back active transactions if they are aborted. Once a transaction commits locally, the internal TM discards all the information related to this transaction. The outgoing TM is quite limited in that it only adds the root transaction data to each remote call.

4 Performance Analysis

4.1 Application Scenario and Parameters

The tests performed are based on the component shown in Figure 2. For simplicity, the server implements one single service invoked with different items as argument. The service is implemented as a Java program that performs a number of internal operations, including a short local transaction (updating the record with key *itemid*) and one service invocation *for each server on the next level*. Both the local transaction and the Java program itself have been kept as short as possible to make sure the measurements reflect the overhead caused by CheeTah and not that of the database or the JVM.

The experiments conducted were based on a total of 10 different system configurations, ranging from the simple wrapper mode (*1x1*) to complex invocation hierarchies (*3x3* or *4x2*) including well-known structures like federations (*2x5*) (see Figure 3 for an example). The goal of the experiments was to analyze the performance of CheeTah and to better understand the impact of system depth and system width on the overall

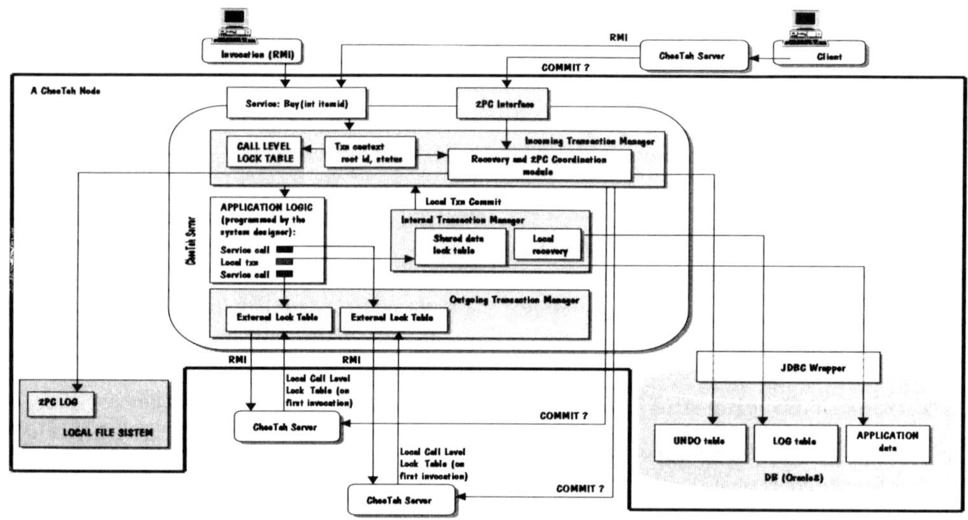

Figure 2: Component Overview

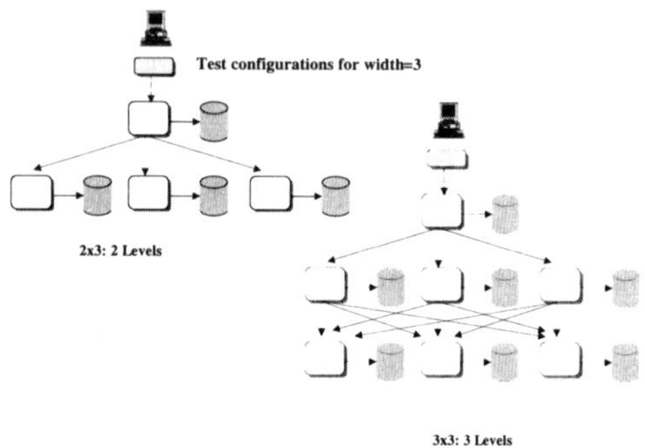

Figure 3: Examples of some configurations used for the tests

performance. For each root transaction, the depth of the system indicates the height of the transaction (how many levels until the leaves are reached). The width of the system indicates how many direct subtransactions each (sub)transaction has. Thus, for instance, in the *3x3* configuration each subtransaction has three children (the root has three children and each one of these subtransactions has another three children). To indicate how many subtransactions are executed on behalf of a given root transaction, we use C, the *cardinality*. Thus, the *3x3* configuration has a cardinality of 13 (the root, plus three children, plus three children for each child of the root). Since invocation of child subtransactions is done serially, the width of the system significantly affects the time it takes to execute a transaction.

In all but two experiments transactions conflict whenever they access the same item. Only for the configuration *4x2* we tested conflict reduction through semantics on the higher level. We considered three cases: no semantics used, half of the servers can use semantics to make conflicts disappear, and all of the servers can make conflicts disappear.

Table 1 summarizes the common settings that apply to our tests. For each one of the tested configurations, we measured throughput, response time and abort rate at the root level and also overall throughput (transactions per minute at all servers). The measurements are based on executions of 10.000 root transactions. For throughput, we measured the time the server needed per 100 transactions, yielding about 100 measurements per experiment in case of our 10.000 roots. The average throughput was obtained by averaging these 100 throughput results for each experiment. The standard deviation represents the confidence (stability) that can be attached to the results. For response times, the average of each of the 10.000 roots' individual response times is given, as well as the standard deviation which reflects the confidence interval.

It is important to emphasize that the tests were all performed on a *worst case scenario* basis. Transactions are made as complex as the system configuration, no semantic information is used to reduce conflict rates (except in two experiments where this technique was tested), and subtransactions are invoked serially. In addition, the load in the system is kept artificially high (as soon as one transaction finishes another one is submitted). The idea behind this approach is that if CheeTah can be made to work on such adverse circum-

Node CPU	Sun Ultra 5, 269MHz UltraSparc IIi CPU
Node RAM	192 MB
Node OS	Solaris 2.6
Node interconnection	100Mbps Ethernet
Java platform	Sun JDK 1.2
Java VM heapsize	16 MB
RDBMS	Oracle 8.0.3
DB Buffersize	64 MB
Database size (per node)	10K tuples
Access path (per node)	unique index on primary key (itemid)
Access mode	80-20 (80% of transactions is on 20% of records)
JDBC Connection pool size (per component)	7
Number of concurrent top-level clients (roots)	25
Root inter-arrival time (per client)	0 (worst possible load)
Total number of *root* transactions per test run	10,000

Table 1: General system parameters

stances, it will certainly work in more realistic, not so demanding environments. In practice, not all transactions will use all servers in the composite system, subtransactions can be executed in parallel, and using semantic information helps to reduce abort rates. Any of these optimizations will improve the results obtained.

4.2 Measurements and Results

Table 2 contains the results of the experiments for the configurations considered (the standard deviation for the overall throughput has been omitted for reasons of space; it is similar to that of the throughput at the root).

strates that the increase in response time is directly related to the complexity of the transaction. Therefore, CheeTah does not add additional overhead as the system becomes more complex. This is surprising since one would expect that longer transactions would block more resources and, therefore, will add more overhead. In practice, CheeTah behaved very well. Observing each individual server, it turned out that the open nested policy allowed servers to free resources quite quickly. The policy of aborting transactions as soon as they run into a conflict also helped in that these transactions could be quickly restarted and, with high probability, succeeded the second time. By aborting them early, the overall delay introduced was minimal, even in those cases with high abort rates (*3x3* and *4x2*).

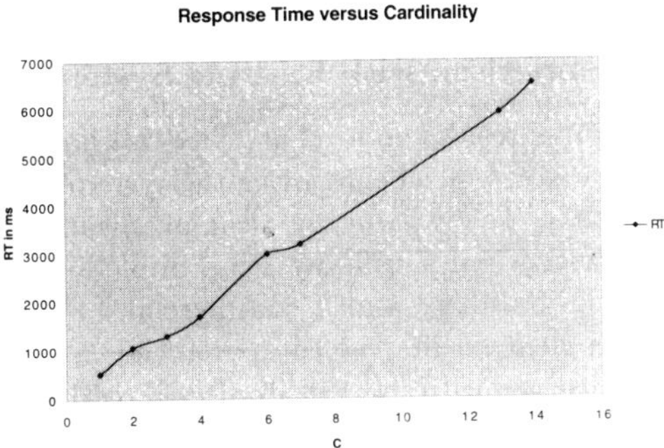

Figure 4: Response Time vs Cardinality

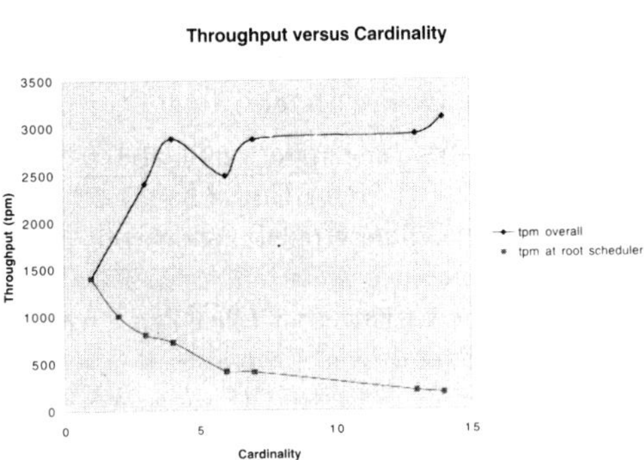

Figure 5: Throughput vs Cardinality

As expected, the throughput at the root decreases and the response time increases with system complexity (i.e., cardinality). This is easier to see in Figures 4 and 5, which show the throughput and response time as a function of the cardinality. In terms of response time, the behavior is obvious. A bigger cardinality implies more complex transactions that naturally take longer to complete. However, the linear relation observed in Figure 4 (almost matching $RT = C \cdot RT_{1x1}$) demon-

The throughput results are also interesting. As the lower curve in Figure 5 shows, the throughput at the root quickly decreases with cardinality. This is an artifact of the experimental setting (we maintained a fixed number of root transactions in the system at all times; the more complex the transaction, implies the longer it takes to complete and, therefore, the less transactions entering the system). In practice, we observed

217

Configuration (Levels x Width)	C	tpm (root) Avg	tpm Stdev	tpm (overall) Avg	Resp.Time Avg (ms)	Resp.Time Stdev (ms)	Abort Rate (%) Avg
1x1	1	1400	150	1400	520	500	0
2x1	2	1000	100	1991	1060	530	1
3x1	3	870	160	2647	1300	380	1.7
4x1	4	720	170	2872	1700	510	5.7
2x2	3	800	60	2402	1650	700	1.6
3x2	7	400	80	2872	3200	1100	7.1
4x2	14	175	25	3096	6500	1100	31
2x3	4	720	70	2882	1800	600	2.1
3x3	13	200	20	2924	5900	1000	22
2x5	6	410	20	2485	3000	800	5.7

Table 2: Results for different configurations

that, even for the highest cardinalities, the servers had enough spare capacity to run additional transactions. This is clear from the results for overall throughput. As the upper curve in Figure 5 shows, the overall throughput increases as we go from cardinality 1 to 3 and then remains stable (the bump in the curve is a result of the different configurations; the low point being cardinality 6, in the *2x5* case). Again, this proves that system complexity does not affect performance. In reality, as the system becomes more complex, there is more processing capacity. If transactions follow different paths from the root to the leaves, then the system will be able to process many more transactions. In fact, in our experiments, we only saturated the server in the *1x1* case.

These results show that CheeTah is very close to having optimal performance. For the range of configurations tested, the response time directly depends on transactional complexity and the throughput remains stable. Both parameters are unaffected by the complexity of the composite system.

For high cardinality, the number of aborted transactions is very high (31 % for the *4x2* and 22 % for the *3x3* configuration). These results, however, are due to the worst case scenario we used for tests and not to any characteristic intrinsic to CheeTah. Any system with this kind of load would have similar abort rates. In more realistic applications, these numbers will go down significantly. To test this hypothesis, we ran a set of experiments using semantic information to reduce conflict rates. The experiments are performed for the *4x2* configuration assuming all transactions accessing the same item conflict (as in Table 2), eliminating half of these conflicts and then eliminating these conflicts entirely. The results are shown in Table 3.

These results show that, once transactions follow different paths, subtransactions are executed in parallel, and the inter-arrival rate is more evenly distributed, the percentage of aborts will drop significantly. Interestingly, throughput and response times do not seem to improve by exploiting semantics. This is due to

the fact that transactions that abort are aborted very quickly (because of conflicts at the higher levels in the system) and then restarted, thereby incurring in a minimal penalty in terms of response time. Similarly, and as pointed out above, since the system is far from its saturation point, abort rates have no influence on the throughput.

The results of the tests were hindered by a feature of the JDBC implementation we were using: not explicitly closing a statement after it has been executed (notably in case of exceptions) causes the server to run out of memory. The only solution (on the level of connection pooling) is to catch this error and re-open the connection. The resulting overhead is quite large. For instance, we have peak results of 2400 transactions per minute (in the 1x1 case), although the average is only 1400 tpm. The difference is largely due to this phenomenon.

4.3 Comparison with Existing Systems

The previous results show that CheeTah has close to an ideal performance behavior as the system complexity increases. To evaluate the basic overhead of CheeTah, we compared similar systems implemented in a commercial database and a commercial TP-Monitor. To obtain clear results, we compared the *1x1* case.

The comparison with the TP-Monitor provides us with a yardstick to test CheeTah against tools used in 3 tier architectures. In the *1x1* configuration, CheeTah achieved more than three times the throughput reachable with the TP-Monitor. The reason is that CheeTah performs all the transaction management inside the server and, unlike in the TP-Monitor, no context changes are necessary to access the different modules of the TP-monitor. We corroborated these results by also comparing performance in the *2x2* case. For root transactions, CheeTah again outperformed the TP-Monitor, a fact that became very clear when the overall throughput in the system is considered. Again, this is due to the fact that the TP-Monitor, like existing commercial products, uses a centralized component for

Configuration (Levels x Width)	C	tpm Avg	tpm (overall) Avg	tpm Stdev	Resp.Time Avg (ms)	Resp.Time Stdev (ms)	Abort Rate (%) Avg
4x2 (all conflict)	14	175	3096	25	6500	1100	31
4x2 (half conflict)	14	210	3300	30	6000	1200	17
4x2 (no conflicts)	14	200	3100	20	6700	1200	1.25

Table 3: Results with high-level semantics advantage

transaction management. Thus, distribution does not bring much in terms of overall performance since the centralized component is the bottleneck and it cannot be distributed. This is where CheeTah excels: each component has its own transaction manager and, therefore, the more components, the more distributed is the load on the transaction manager functionality. These results clearly speak in favor of the language framework approach followed in CheeTah.

The comparison with a commercial database gives us a way to test the performance of CheeTah against 2 tier architectures. For the test, the equivalent to a CheeTah server was implemented in a normal RMI server application that directly uses the database. The database was accessed via a pure JDBC interface and connection pooling (of the same size as in CheeTah) was used. This eliminated the typical CheeTah overhead for propagating transaction context and doing extra logging. The peak rates obtained proved that the performance of CheeTah is comparable to that of commercial databases.

5 Conclusions

We have presented CheeTah, a light weight transaction monitor implemented as a Java framework. CheeTah introduces many novel aspects, the main contributions being the composite systems structure, the use of open nested transactions, and the framework approach. We see composite systems as a key configuration in distributed environments, one that will certainly be promoted by developments like Java, component based design, and standards like Enterprise Java Beans. In such systems, the efficient implementation of transactional interaction requires open nested transactions. To our knowledge, CheeTah is the first working implementation of open nested transactions made publicly available. Finally, the framework approach to building transactional components is an entirely new paradigm. The transactional properties traditionally provided by large systems like TP-Monitors are provided by CheeTah by simply writing services that inherit from certain classes. The development effort is thus significantly reduced. Our results prove that the ideas implemented in CheeTah are feasible in practice and have excellent performance.

References

[ABFS97] G. Alonso, S. Blott, A. Fessler, and H.-J. Schek. Correctness and Parallelism of Composite Systems. In *Proceedings of the 16th ACM Symposium on Principles of Database Systems, Tucson, Arizona, USA. May 12-15.*, May 1997.

[AFPS99a] G. Alonso, A. Fessler, G. Pardon, and H.-J. Schek. Correctness in general configurations of transactional components. In *Proceedings of the ACM Symposium on Principles of Database Systems (PODS'99)*, Philadelphia, PA, May 31 - June 2 1999.

[AFPS99b] G. Alonso, A. Fessler, G. Pardon, and H.-J. Schek. Transactions in stack, fork and join composite systems. In *Int. Conference on Database Theory*, 1999.

[BBG89] C. Beeri, P.A. Bernstein, and N. Goodman. A Model for Concurrency in Nested Transaction Systems. *Journal of the ACM*, 36(2), 1989.

[BK99] K. Boucher and F. Katz. *Essential guide to object monitors*. John Wiley & Sons, 1999.

[BN97] P.A. Bernstein and E. Newcomer. *Principles of Transaction Processing for the Systems Professional*. Morgan Kaufmann, 1997.

[BSW88] C. Beeri, H.-J. Schek, and G. Weikum. Multilevel transaction management, theoretical art or practical need? In *International Conference on Extending Database Technology (EDBT'88), Lecture Notes in Computer Science, Springer-Verlag, LNCS 303, 1988*, 1988.

[Cor95] Transarc Corporation. *Writing Encina Applications*. Transarc Corporation, 1995. ENC-D5012-00.

[EJB] Enterprise javabeans technology. http://java.sun.com/products/ejb/index.html.

[GR93] J. Gray and A. Reuter. *Transaction Processing: Concepts and Techniques*. Morgan Kaufman, 1993.

[IBM99] IBM. *MQSeries*. IBM, March 1999. http://www.software.ibm.com//mqseries/.

[LEK99] J. Lyon, K. Evans, and J. Klein. Transaction Internet Protocol (TIP). Technical report, Tandem and Microsoft, February 1999.

[Moh98] C. Mohan. Transaction processing and distributed computing in the internet age. http://www-rodin.inria.fr/ mohan/abstracts.html, July 1998.

[Mos81] J.E.B. Moss. *Nested Transactions: An Approach to Reliable Distributed Computing*. PhD thesis, M.I.T. Laboratory for Computer Science, Cambridge, Massachusetts, MIT Press, 1981.

[Wei91] G. Weikum. Principles and realization strategies of multilevel transaction management. *ACM Transactions on Database Systems*, 16(1), March 1991.

Hypothetical Queries in an OLAP Environment[*]

Andrey Balmin
Univ. of California, San Diego
abalmin@cs.ucsd.edu

Thanos Papadimitriou
Univ. of California, Los Angeles
apapadim@anderson.ucla.edu

Yannis Papakonstantinou
Univ. of California, San Diego
yannis@cs.ucsd.edu

Abstract

Analysts and decision-makers use what-if analysis to assess the effects of hypothetical scenarios. What-if analysis is currently supported by spreadsheets and ad-hoc OLAP tools. Unfortunately, the former lack seamless integration with the data and the latter lack flexibility and performance appropriate for OLAP applications. To tackle these problems we developed the SESAME system, which models an hypothetical scenario as a list of hypothetical modifications on the warehouse views and fact data. We provide formal scenario syntax and semantics, which extend view update semantics for accomodating the special requirements of OLAP. We focus on query algebra operators suitable for performing spreadsheet-style computations. Then we present SESAME's optimizer and its cornerstone substitution and rewriting mechanisms. Substitution enables lazy evaluation of the hypothetical updates. The substitution module delivers orders-of-magnitude optimizations in cooperation with the rewriter that uses knowledge of arithmetic, relational, financial and other operators. Finally we discuss the challenges that the size of the scenario specifications and the arbitrary nature of the operators pose to the rewriter. We present a rewriter that employs the *"minterms"* and *"packed forests"* techniques to quickly produce plans.

This work was supported by the NSF-IRI 9712239 grant, UCSD startup funds, the Onassis Foundation, and equipment donations from Intel Corp.

**Proceedings of the 26th VLDB Conference,
Cairo, Egypt, 2000.**

We experimentally evaluate the rewriter and the overall system.

1 Introduction

Recently the database community has developed data warehousing and OLAP systems where a business analyst can obtain online answers to complex decision support queries on very large databases. A particularly common and very important decision support process is what-if analysis, which has applications in marketing, production planning, and other areas. Typically, the analyst formulates a possible business scenario deriving a hypothetical "world" that he consequently explores by querying and navigation. What-if analysis is used to forecast future performance under a set of assumptions related to past data. It also enables the evaluation of past performance and the estimation of the opportunity cost taken by not following alternative policies in the past [PC95].

For example, an analyst of a brokerage company may want to investigate *what* the effect on the return and volatility of a customer's portfolios *if* during the last three years that the brokerage had recommended purchasing Intel stock instead of Motorola. According to his scenario, he (hypothetically) eliminates many Motorola buy orders that the customer issued, introduces Intel share orders of equivalent dollar value, then recomputes the newly derived data. Subsequently, he investigates the results of this hypothesis on specific customer categories. More hypothetical modifications and queries will follow as the analyst follows a particular trail of thought.

Spreadsheets or existing OLAP tools are currently used to support such what-if analysis. Surprisingly, despite its importance, what-if analysis is not efficiently supported by either one. Spreadsheets offer a large number of powerful array manipulation functions and an interactive environment that is suitable for specifying changes and reviewing their effects online. However, they lack storage capacity, the functionality of DB query languages, and a seamless integration with the data warehouse; once the data has been exported to the spreadsheet it becomes disconnected from updates that happen in the data warehouse.

OLAP systems offering what-if analysis [CCS] lack the analytical capabilities of spreadsheets and their performance is orders of magnitude worse than what can be achieved by intelligent scenario evaluations, such as thosee ones delivered by our SESAME prototype. To further understand the limitations of current OLAP tools let us walk through a typical implementation of the what-if analysis example above. First, an experienced user or the data warehouse's administrator designs a "scenario" datacube and develops a script (eg, see [CCS] for a scripting language) that populates the scenario datacube with the data corresponding to the hypothetical world developed by the scenario. Consequently, the cross-tabs (sums) and other views are recomputed. Apparently, the creation of the scenario datacube cannot be an online activity.

After the scenario is materialized the analyst will issue queries, drill-down and roll-up [GMUW99] into parts of the hypothetical world. At this point it becomes evident that materializing the full hypothetical world (and hence delaying query submission by as much as a day) may have been an unnecessary overhead. Consider the following two cases where the conventional methodology underperforms. We comment on how SESAME handles such cases.

First, queries and drill-downs on detailed data will typically retrieve only a small part of the hypothetical world. (After all, there is only so much real estate in a monitor.) For example, a query that investigates the consequences of the scenario on the portfolios of the first 50 investors does not have to materialize anything more than the hypothetical portfolios of the specific investors. Indeed, SESAME won't even materialize the hypothetical portfolios; it will simply retrieve the actual portfolios, it will remove the Motorola orders and will dynamically introduce in the result Intel orders of equal dollar value.

Second, queries that retrieve various aggregate measures, such as the SUM, can leverage the corresponding aggregate measures of the "actual" datacube. For example, SESAMEwill compute the hypothetical current value $V'[x]$ of the portfolio of customer x as follows.

$$V'[x] = \begin{array}{l} V[x] - \Sigma_d(O[x,m,d](T[m] - P[m,d])) \\ + \Sigma_d(\frac{P[m,d]}{P[i,d]}O[x,m,d](T[i] - P[i,d]) \end{array}$$

where i stands for Intel, m for Motorola, $V'[x]$ is the hypothetical value of the portfolio of customer x and $V[x]$ is the actual value. The array entry $O[x,y,d]$ stands for the actual number of y shares bought (or sold if the number is negative) by customer x on day d, and $P[y,d]$ stands for the (closing) price of shares of y on day d. $T[y]$ stands for the current value of y. According to the above, the hypothetical value of a portfolio is computed by adding to the portfolio's actual value the profit by each hypothetical investment in Intel and subtracting the profit of each investment in Motorola.

One may actually update the orders table and then propagate the updates, possibly using one of the efficient update propagation techniques suggested by the database community [BLT86, GMS93, RKR97, LYGM99, MQM97]. However, SESAME's no-actual-update policy has the advantage that no backtracking of updates is needed after scenario evaluation is complete nor is it necessary to lock the hypothetically updated parts.

Technical Challenges and Contributions

First, we formally define scenarios as ordered sets of hypothetical modifications on the fact tables or the derived views of the warehouse. As usual, modifications on views may be satisfied by multiple possible fact table modifications. We extend prior work [AHV96] on the semantics of select-project-join (SPJ) view updates by introducing the notion of "minimally modified database", which is necessary for having reasonable semantics in warehouses involving non-SPJ operators, such as aggregation and arithmetic.

Second, we developed an extensible system where arbitrary algebraic array operators can be used. Using the extensible algebra machinery we introduce operators that combine spreadsheet and database functionality. In this paper we present the join arithmetic family of operators. More operators (moving windows and operators for metadata handling) can be found in the extended version [BPP]. Expressions involving the novel operators are optimized by providing to the rewriting optimizer appropriate rewriting rules.

Our most important contribution is SESAME's scenario evaluation, which is based on *substitution* and *rewriting*. Given a scenario s, a query q on the hypothetical database, and information on the warehouse's views, the substitution module delivers a query q' that is evaluated on the actual warehouse and is equivalent to the result of evaluating q on the hypothetical database created by s. Then the rewriter optimizes the query q'. In the spirit of conventional optimizers it pushes selections down and it eliminates parts of q' that do not affect the result (such parts typically correspond to "irrelevant" hypothetical modifications.) It also rewrites the query q' in order to leverage on the warehouse's pre-computed views.

We identify and provide solutions to two major rewriting challenges. First, the query expression q' is typically very large, as a result of the potentially large number of hypothetical modifications. The good news is that q' has a particular structure that is exploited by SESAME's *minterm optimization*. Second, rewriting queries using views, while non-conventional operators are involved in the algebra, is a novel challenge that has not been considered by extensible rewriters [HFLP89] (they have not considered views) or by the "rewriting using views" literature, which has focused on conjunctive queries [LMSS95] or conjunctive with SQL's aggregation operators [SDJL96, CNS99]. We present the *packed forests* extension to System-R-style optimizers that allows the development of rewriters that trade the rewriter's running time with the generality of rewriting axioms, queries, and materialized views for which they can deliver the optimal result.

Finally, we incorporate SESAME as an add-on component to an SQL Server that stores the warehouse and provides the query processing engine for evaluating the optimized scenario/query.

1.1 Related Work

To the best of our knowledge what-if scenarios in an OLAP environment have not been addressed by the database research community. Our work brings together a multitude of concepts and techniques such as substitution, extensible rewriting optimizers, view updates and incomplete data, and logical access path schemas (see below).

[GH97] presents an equational theory for relational queries involving hypothetical modifications and discusses its use in an optimizer that may choose between lazy and eager evaluation. The substitution step of our rewriter extends the lazy evaluation idea of [GH97] by considering an environment including views as well. However, the optimization and rewriting problem is much more challenging in SESAME's case.

The specification of the repercussion of a hypothetical modification on the constituents of a view is influenced by works on the semantics of view updates ([AHV96] provides an overview.) The critical difference from the prior work is the introduction of the "minimally modified datagraph" concept and the corresponding redefinition of "sure" answers. The difference is justified by the intuitive requirement that base relation tuples that do not "contribute" to modified view tuples should remain sure and non-modified. Not surprisingly, our definition of sure and the conventional definition of [AHV96] coincide when we focus on SPJ queries, which have been the focus of prior work, but diverge when we consider aggregate, arithmetic and moving window functions.

The datagraph schema, which helps us rewrite queries using views, inherits from the LAP schemas [SRN90] the idea of guiding the rewriting optimizer by a graph indicating how the views are connected to each other. However, LAP schemas have dealt with SPJ queries only and this makes the rewriter described in [SRN90] much simpler than SESAME's.

The next section introduces the framework, syntax and semantics used. Section 3 describes the architecture and algorithms involved in SESAME.

2 Framework

We first present the *datagraph model*, which is our abstraction of warehouses and datacubes and extends the datacube lattice model of [HRU96] and the logical access path schemas of [SRN90] by allowing derived views to be produced using an extensive set of

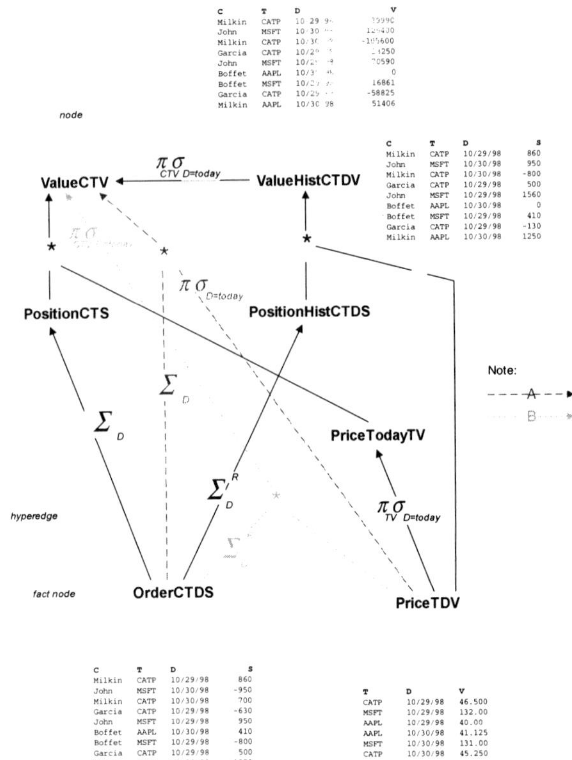

Figure 1: Brokerage House's Datagraph operators.[1] Section 2.1 describes novel operators and Section 2.2 describes the formal syntax and semantics of hypothetical modifications and scenarios.

The datagraph schema is a directed acyclic hypergraph that consists of

1. A set of nodes $\mathcal{V} = \{v_1, \ldots, v_n\}$. Each v_i is a relation schema that has a unique name, zero or more *dimension* attributes and one *measure attribute*. Each dimension attribute a has a domain $D(a)$, which may be ordered (e.g., time) or unordered. Measure attributes are of numeric types only – float or integer. We may use the term *relation* instead of node whenever there is no confusion.

2. A set of directed labeled hyperedges of the form $[v_1, \ldots, v_m] \xrightarrow{e} v_d$, where $[v_1, \ldots, v_m]$ is the tuple of parent nodes and v_d is the *derived* node. The label e is a SESAME algebra expression involving the nodes $v_1, \ldots, v_m$.

We will call *fact* nodes the ones with no incoming hyperedges. They correspond to the fact table(s) of OLAP systems. Internal nodes correspond to the views in a warehouse system and the edge labels correspond to the view definitions. Notice however that, in the same spirit with the lattice model [HRU96] and logical access paths [SRN90], multiple hyperedges may

---

[1] As opposed to the de facto SUM operator of [HRU96] or the SPJ operators of [SRN90].

be leading to the same node/view, hence encoding multiple ways in which the node/view can be derived. The hyperedges assist substitution and rewriting (see Section 3).

Each node v is populated with a bag of tuples $\mathcal{S}(v)$, called the *state* of v. Similarly to relational algebra, each SESAME algebra expression $e(v_1, \ldots, v_m)$, whether it is a hyperedge label or a query, is a mapping $\mathcal{E}$ that given the input nodes' states $\mathcal{S}(v_1), \ldots, \mathcal{S}(v_m)$ it produces an output bag $\mathcal{E}(\mathcal{S}(v_1), \ldots, \mathcal{S}(v_m))$.

The states of the nodes must be such that they satisfy the hyperedge label expressions. Formally, a valid datagraph state (or simply datagraph from now on) is an assignment of a state $\mathcal{S}(v)$ to each node v of the datagraph schema such that for every hyperedge $\{v_1, \ldots, v_m\} \xrightarrow{e} v_d$ it is $\mathcal{S}(v_d) = \mathcal{E}(\mathcal{S}(v_1), \ldots, \mathcal{S}(v_m))$. From now on we will omit mentioning $\mathcal{S}$ explicitly, whenever the context makes clear that we refer to states as opposed to schemas.

The datagraph schema must be *consistent*, in the sense that alternative ways to compute a view have to yield the same result.

Definition 1 *The set of transitive hyperedges $\mathcal{T}$ of a datagraph schema is computed as follows:*

1. *for every node v, $\mathcal{T}$ contains $v \xRightarrow{v} v$,*

2. *if the datagraph schema contains the edge $\{v_1, \ldots, v_m\} \xrightarrow{e} v$ and $\mathcal{T}$ contains the edges $\mathcal{V}_i \xRightarrow{e_i} v_i$, $i = 1, \ldots, m$ then $\mathcal{T}$ also contains the edge $\cup_{i=1,\ldots,m} \mathcal{V}_i \xRightarrow{e'} v$, where e' is the expression created by substituting each v_i in e with e_i.*

Given a transitive hyperedge $\{v_1, \ldots, v_n\} \xRightarrow{e} v_d$ we will say that v_i is an *ancestor* of v_d (for every i) and, vice versa, v_d is a *descendant* of v_i.

EXAMPLE 2.1 Figure 1 illustrates a brokerage house's datagraph that will serve as the running example. A tuple (c, t, d, s) in the *fact node OrderCTDS(Customer, Ticker, Date, Shares)* indicates that customer c, bought s shares of the stock with ticker symbol t on date d. If s has a negative value it indicates selling of shares. For brevity we are writing only the relation name corresponding to the node and, by convention, the capital letters at the relation names' suffix will stand for the initials of the attribute names. The *fact node PriceTDV(Ticker, Date, Value)* has tuples (t, d, v) that stand for the closing price v of stock t on date d.

The current positions node *PositionCTS* is derived from *OrderCTDS* by the hyperedge $\{OrdersCTDS\} \xRightarrow{\Sigma_{Date}} PositionsCTS$. The operator Σ_{Date} (which adapts the summation operator of [GMUW99] to one-measure tables) outputs all dimension attributes of the input except *Date*. For each output tuple (c, t, s) the measure s is the sum

$s_1 + \ldots + s_n$, where the s_i's are the measures of the set of tuples $\{(c, t, d_1, s_1), \ldots, (c, t, d_n, s_n)\}$ that consists of all input tuples where $Customer = c$ and $Ticker = t$. In general, Σ may have multiple parameters, e.g., $\Sigma_{Date, Ticker}$. See [BPP] for a complete definition of Σ as well as all the operators in the current implementation of SESAME.

For brevity we are going to represent attributes by their first letter only and we may not include the full operand names in the edge expression whenever it is obvious from the context.

The hyperedge $OrderCTDS \xRightarrow{\Sigma_D^R} PositionHistCTDS$ declares that the position history is the running sum of orders according to date (D). In particular, *PositionHistCTDS* contains the tuple (c, t, d_n, s) if $\{(c, t, d_1, s_1), \ldots, (c, t, d_n, s_n)\}$ is the set of all *OrderCTDS* tuples such that $d_1 \leq d_2 \leq \ldots \leq d_n$ and $s = s_1 + \ldots + s_n$. Of course, it is necessary that the attribute parameter(s) of Σ^R are of an ordered type.

The hyperedge $\{PositionHistCTDS, PriceTDV\} \xrightarrow{*} ValueHistCTDV$ indicates that *ValueHistCTDV*, the history of the dollar value each customer held in each stock each day, may be derived by multiplying the stock prices with the position history.

Finally as an example of datagraph consistency, observe that *ValueCTV*, which is the current dollar value each customer holds in each stock, may be derived in two ways, corresponding to the hyperedges A and B of Figure 1, from *OrderCTDS* and *PriceTDV*. The first one is the expression $\sum_D(OrderCTDS) * (\pi_{TV}\sigma_{D=today}PriceTDV)$ which first computes the current positions of the customer and then multiplies them with the current stock market prices (depicted by arrow type A of figure 1). The second one is the expression $\pi_{CTV}\sigma_{D=today}((\sum_D^R OrderCTDS) * PriceTDV)$ which first computes the dollar value history for each customer, stock and date (see above) and then selects today's data (depicted by arrow type A of figure 1). The datagraph is consistent because the two expressions always deliver the same result. $\square$

2.1 Novel Operators in SESAME

SESAME is based on an algebra where arbitrary operators can be included as long as their input and output is one-measure bags of tuples (see Section 2.) Besides select, project, semijoin, union, difference and the aggregate operators *sum, min, max, avg* and *count* , we have also included the novel *join arithmetic* family of operators, presented below. Our operators appropriately merge the relational framework of SESAME with array algebras and spreadsheet-style operations. They lead to expressions that are much more concise than relational algebra expressions that are extended with generalized projections [GMUW99] that accomplish arithmetic operations. The conciseness greatly facilitates the development of rewriting rules and speeds up the rewriter, which has to deal with smaller expressions.

Join Arithmetic Operators

The join arithmetic operators $+, *^o, -, /^o$ and $+^s, *, -^s, /$ take two operands, let us call them the $left(D_1, \ldots, D_k, \ldots, D_n, M_l)$ and the $right(D_1, \ldots, D_k, M_r)$. The dimension attributes of $right$ must be a subset of $left$). The result relation has schema $Result(D_1, \ldots, D_k, \ldots, D_n, Measure)$. The semantics depend on whether the operator belongs to the semijoin sub-family $+^s, *, -^s, /$ or the outerjoin sub-family $+, *^o, -, /^o$.

Semijoin Family
For every pair of tuples $left(d_1, \ldots, d_k, \ldots, d_n, m_l)$ and $right(d_1, \ldots, d_k, m_r)$ the result has a tuple $Result(d_1, \ldots, d_k, \ldots, d_n, m_l \odot m_r)$ where $\odot$ is one of the four operators $+, *, -, /$.[2] Note that the without-superscript $*$ and $/$ are "semijoin" operators. For an example of (semijoin) multiplication, consider the contents of $PositionHistCTDS$ and $PriceTDV$ that appear in the Figure 1 and the corresponding content of $ValueHistCTDS = PositionHistCTDS * PriceTDV$.

Outerjoin Family The outerjoin family is defined only when the two operands have identical lists of dimension attributes. For every pair of tuples $left(d_1, \ldots, d_k, \ldots, d_n, m_l)$ and $right(d_1, \ldots, d_k, \ldots, d_n, m_r)$ the result contains the tuple $Result(d_1, \ldots, d_k, \ldots, d_n, m_l \odot m_r)$. For every tuple $left(d_1, \ldots, d_k, \ldots, d_n, m_l)$ with no matching tuple the tuple appears as is in the result and so do tuples of $right$ with no matching left tuples. The no-superscript $+$ is an outerjoin operator.

Notice that, though the result relation name is by default "$Result$" and the result measure is "$Measure$" we may rename them to whatever we like by using the renaming operator ρ. If the operator is used in the datagraph schema then we will omit the ρ, using the convention that the relation name and measure name that have already been given to the view will override "$result$" and "$Measure$".

Based on the above and the special relation $\mathbf{a} = \{(a)\}$, which has no dimensions and its single tuple has measure a, we define the following four "macro" operators that add/subtract/multiply/divide a constant a to the single operand's measure.

$$ADD_a R = R +^s \mathbf{a} \qquad SUB_a R = R -^s \mathbf{a}$$
$$MULT_a R = R * \mathbf{a} \qquad DIV_a R = R / \mathbf{a}$$

Our "implicit join" approach simplifies the expression of array computations and simplifies the axioms and rewriting rules which involve arithmetic (see Appendix).

---

[2] Division by 0 raises an exception.

2.2 Scenarios

A scenario is a set of ordered hypothetical modifications on a datagraph D. The first modification results in a hypothetical datagraph D^1. The second modification uses the state of datagraph D^1 and produces a new hypothetical datagraph D^2, and so on. Eventually a query is evaluated on the last hypothetical datagraph. The following example illustrates the syntax and semantics of scenarios.

$$OrderCTDS^1 \leftarrow$$
$$\hat{\sigma}_{D>'Jan15,97' \wedge T=Intel, MULT_{1.2} OrderCTDS}$$
$$OrderCTDS^2 \leftarrow OrdersCTDS^1$$
$$-\sigma_{D>'Jan15,97' \wedge T=Motorola} OrderCTDS^1$$
$$OrderCTDS^3 \leftarrow OrderCTDS^2$$
$$\cup \pi_{T \mapsto Intel, C, D}$$
$$(\sigma_{T=Motorola \wedge D>'Jan15,97'} ValueHistCTDV)$$

The three modifications above roughly correspond to an update, a delete, and an insert. The first one states that a hypothetical datagraph D^1 is created and its $OrderCTDS^1$ node must be the result of "updating" the fragment $\sigma_{D>'Jan15,97' \wedge T=Intel} OrderCTDS^1$ with $MULT_{1.2}(\sigma_{D>'Jan15,97' \wedge T=Intel} OrderCTDS^1)$.

Notice the select-modify operator $\hat{\sigma}$ that is used for accomplishing the first modification. The function of $\hat{\sigma}$ is to (i) select the tuples satisfying the subscript condition and apply to them the subscript operator and (ii) union the result with the remaining tuples of the input node. Hence, $\hat{\sigma}_{c,f} R = f(\sigma_c R) \cup \sigma_{\neg c} R$

The hypothetical modification will be reverberated to all the nodes of the graph D^1. For example, the $PositionsCTS^1$ will reflect a 20% larger position in Intel. Intuitively D^1 is produced by having $OrderCTDS^1$ be defined directly by the modification and all the nodes that are descendants of $OrderCTDS^1$ are recomputed according to the datagraph hyperedges.

Consequently, the datagraphs D^2 and D^3 are defined. Notice that the definition of D^3 uses both D^2 and D (in particular, the node $ValueHistCTDV$ of D is used.) This facilitates expressing modifications that happen "in parallel". Then queries can be issued against any node of D^1, D^2 or D^3.

We now formalize the semantics of a scenario s on a datagraph G. For uniformity we'll be referring to the actual datagraph G as G^0. The notation $e(\mathcal{V}^{0,1,\ldots,i})$ denotes an expression e whose arguments are nodes of $G^0, G^1, \ldots, G^i$.

$$s : \begin{bmatrix} v_1^1 \leftarrow e_1(\mathcal{V}_1^0), \\ v_2^2 \leftarrow e_2(\mathcal{V}_2^{0,1}), \\ \vdots \\ v_m^m \leftarrow e_m(\mathcal{V}_m^{0,1,\ldots,m-1}) \end{bmatrix}$$

Definition 2 assumes that the first $i-1$ datagraphs are known and uses the i-th modification of s to derive the i-th hypothetical datagraph. Definition 3 specifies the induction that defines G^i from G^0. Note in the following definition that the hypothetical datagraph is not an arbitrary datagraph that satisfies the modification and the edge expressions; in addition, it will have to be in agreement with all minimally changed datagraphs. The intuition behind this definition is illustrated in Example 2.2.

Definition 2
Consider the datagraphs $G^0, G^1, \ldots, G^{i-1}$ and a modification $v_i^i \leftarrow e(\mathcal{V}_i^{0,\ldots,i-1})$. The hypothetical datagraph G^i meets the following properties:

1. *For every node v^0 of G^0 there is a node v^i of G^i with identical schema, modulo having a superscript ^{i} on the relation name. For every edge $\mathcal{V}^0 \xrightarrow{e} v^0$ of G^0 there is a corresponding edge $\mathcal{V}^i \xrightarrow{e} v^i$ of G^i.*

2. $\mathcal{S}(v_i^i) = e(\mathcal{S}(\mathcal{V}_i^{0,\ldots,i-1}))$

3. *Each node v^i of G^i contains the intersection $\cap_{j=1,\ldots,k} v_j^i$ of the corresponding nodes $v_1^i, \ldots, v_k^i$ of all minimally modified datagraphs $M_1^i, \ldots, M_k^i$. A datagraph M^i is called minimal if there is no L^i that meets conditions 1 and 2 and for every node v_l^i of L^i, which corresponds to nodes v^i of M^i and v^{i-1} of G^{i-1}, it is $v_l^i - v^{i-1} \subset v^i - v^{i-1}$ and $v^{i-1} - v_l^i \subset v^{i-1} - v^i$. (I.e., you cannot "cancel" any tuples' insertion or deletion in a minimally changed datagraph and still have a valid modified datagraph that meets conditions 1 and 2.)*

Definition 3 *A hypothetical datagraph G^k given the scenario s is a datagraph such that there is a sequence of datagraphs $G^1, \ldots, G^k$ such that G^i is a hypothetical datagraph of $G^0, \ldots, G^{i-1}$ given the modification $v_i^i \leftarrow e_i(\mathcal{V}_{i-1})$, for each $i = 1, \ldots, k$.*
We denote by $\mathcal{G}(G, s)$ the set of all hypothetical datagraphs given a scenario s and a datagraph G.

Note the following two points which are illustrated in Example 2.2. First, there is no guarantee on the number of hypothetical datagraphs. Second, not all modified datagraphs are hypothetical according to our definition.

EXAMPLE 2.2 Consider the hypothetical modification
$$PositionCTS^1 \leftarrow \hat{\sigma}_{T="Intel".MULT_{1.2}} PositionCTS^0$$
that hypothetically increases by 20% the customer holdings on Intel. There are more than one hypothetical datagraphs because there are multiple ways to derive an $OrderCTDS^1$ state such that the sum of the $OrderCTDS^1$ Intel tuples will be increased by 20%.

There are modified datagraphs that satisfy the modification but affect "irrelevant data". For example, there are datagraphs that lead to the same

$PositionCTS^1$ but they update non-Intel tuples as well. We believe that such datagraphs should not be considered valid hypothetical datagraphs. We exclude them from the set of hypothetical datagraphs by placing the third condition in Definition 2.

Finally note that we do not restrict valid hypothetical datagraphs to the minimally modified ones (see Definition 2.) For example, a valid hypothetical datagraph for the running example is one that increases every Intel order by 20%. However, such a datagraph is not minimal. The only minimal datagraphs are those that assign the full increase of the Intel position to a single order. We believe that being restricted to minimal datagraphs would unnecessarily disqualify meaningful hypothetical datagraphs. $\square$

If a modification is applied on a node with no incoming edge, say the $OrderCTDS$ of Figure 1, and the edge expression operators are total then there is exactly one hypothetical model.

The result of a query or, more general, the result of an expression (say, the expression that is used on the right side of an assignment) is comprised of a sure and a non-sure part as defined below.

Definition 4 (Sure Expressions) *Given a datagraph schema G and a scenario s, consisting of m modifications, the expression $e(\mathcal{V}^m)$ is sure if for every state of G the result of evaluating $e(\mathcal{V}^m)$ on every hypothetical datagraph in the set $\mathcal{G}(G, s)$ is identical.*[3]

It is interesting to note the difference of our definition of "sure" with the one used in [AHV96] for the definition of updating a select-project-join view. The latter one does not use "minimality of changes" and this makes it inappropriate in an OLAP environment with arithmetic and aggregate operators. For example, according to the definition of [AHV96] the updating of a fragment of a sum aggregate node makes the whole source node unsure.

3 Sesame's Algorithms, Implementation and Performance Results

The SESAME system is the middle layer in the 3-tier OLAP architecture of Figure 2. The warehouse is actually stored in a relational database currently Microsoft's SQL Server. On the client side there is a user interface that creates the scenarios and hypothetical queries that are sent to SESAME. A simple GUI is available at www.db.ucsd.edu/projects/sesame/demo.htm and demonstrates the rewriter and the execution engine of SESAME. SESAME processes the hypothetical query (along with the corresponding scenario) in three steps:

---

[3]Note that according to the above definition — and according to SESAME, which follows the above definition — the "sureness" of an expression depends only on the datagraph schema and not on the specific datagraph state. This decision is justified by obvious implementation considerations.

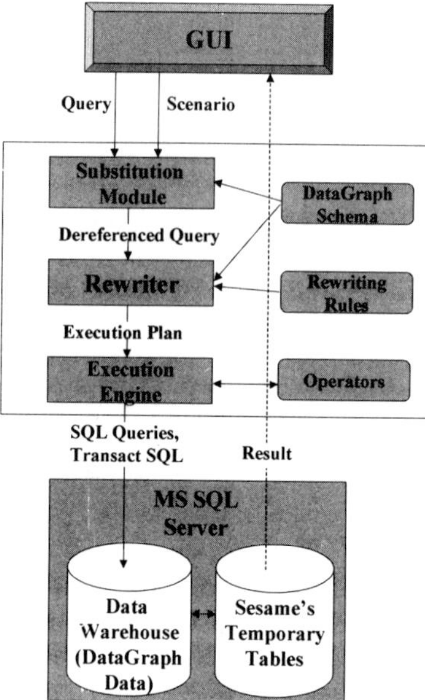

Figure 2: SESAME's Architecture

First, the *substitution* module (see Figure 2) combines the scenario and the original query into a new query, called *dereferenced*, that refers directly to the original datagraph.

Then the *rewriter* turns the dereferenced query into an optimized one, which may even use materialized views. Rewriting is driven by the datagraph and a set of rules related to the involved operators (the complete list can be found in [BPP].)

EXAMPLE 3.1 Consider the single-modification scenario on the *datagraph* shown on Figure 1, where position on the stock "MSFT" is increased by 10%.

$$PositionCTS^1 \leftarrow \hat{\sigma}_{T=MSFT,Mult_{1.1}} PositionCTS^0$$

Then consider the query that retrieves the hypothetical value of the account of client John

$$\sigma_{C=John} ValueCTV^1$$

The substitution module will combine the scenario and the query into the following dereferenced query. The specific steps are explained in Section 3.1 and Example 3.3.

$$\sigma_{C=John}((\hat{\sigma}_{T=MSFT,Mult_{1.1}} PositionCTS^0) \\ * PriceTodayTV^0)$$

Next, the rewriter makes the following transformations:

$$\sigma_{C=John}((\hat{\sigma}_{T=MSFT,Mult_{1.1}} PositionCTS^0) \\ * PriceTodayTV^0)$$
$$= \sigma_{C=John}(\hat{\sigma}_{T=MSFT,Mult_{1.1}} ValueCTV^0)$$
$$= \hat{\sigma}_{T=MSFT,Mult_{1.1}} \sigma_{C=John} ValueCTV^0$$
$$= Mult_{1.1}\sigma_{(T=MSFT) AND (C=John)} ValueCTV^0$$
$$\cup \sigma_{(T \neq MSFT) AND (C=John)} ValueCTV^0$$

At this point the query processor has achieved two goals: (I) It has expressed the query in terms of actual, stored relations. (II) It has optimized the expression by pushing selections down the query tree and by using the appropriate materialized views. In particular it has used the $ValueCTV^0$ – as opposed to the $PositionCTS^0$. $\square$

Finally, SESAME's execution engine treats the expression produced by the rewriter as an execution plan.[4] The engine traverses the plan tree bottom-up. When it locates a subtree t that corresponds to a single SQL statement c it sends c to the SQL server. Consequently the server creates and stores the result table r of c and the engine replaces the subtree t with the table r. However, many SESAME operators cannot be reduced to SQL (e.g., moving windows and financials). For each operator of this kind SESAME has a stored procedure written in Microsoft's Transact-SQL, which has the full power of a programming language. Each procedure implements the functionality of a specific SESAME operator. Note that all processing is done at the SQL Server and no data is moved between SESAME's execution engine and the SQL Server. Only the final result passes through the engine, before it is sent to the client.[5]

EXAMPLE 3.2 The engine will translate the plan produced by the rewriter in the Example 3.1 into the SQL query

```
SELECT C, T, (V * 1.1) AS V
FROM ValueCTV
WHERE T = "MSFT" AND C = "John"
UNION
SELECT * FROM ValueCTV
WHERE T != "MSFT" And C = "John"
```

For the sake of the example, let us assume that SQL does not have a multiplication operator. Then the engine will execute the plan by issuing the following three commands to the SQL Server:

1. `SELECT * INTO #Tmp1 FROM ValueCTV`
   `WHERE T = "MSFT" AND C = "John"` (creates $\#Tmp1 = \sigma_{(T=MSFT) AND (C=John)} ValueCTV$)

2. Run a Transact-SQL procedure that creates a $\#Tmp2$ where V is multiplied by 1.1.

3. `SELECT * FROM ValueCTV`
   `WHERE T != "MSFT" AND C = "John"`
   `UNION`
   `SELECT * FROM #Tmp2`

$\square$

In many real-world situations, substitution and rewriting are not as simple or as fast as the few steps of

---

[4]We have not yet separated the notions of logical and physical plan [GMUW99] mainly because the physical work is passed to the SQL server.

[5]Note also that in order to improve the performance the intermediate tables are stored in a special temporary database which is kept in the main memory.

the Example 3.1 suggest. In the general case they both reduce to combinatorial problems. We have sped up substitution by focusing our algorithms on the class of *structurally sure scenario queries*. For this class substitution is polynomial in the size of the query and the datagraph. Then we present a series of rewriters that address the performance challenges that are special to what-if scenarios.

Section 3.1 describes the substitution step. Section 3.2 gives an overview of a straightforward rewriting algorithm and its performance problems in nontrivial scenarios. Section 3.3 introduces the minterms replacement for efficiently rewriting scenarios with multiple select-modifications. Section 3.4 describes the packed forest rewriter. Section 3.5 provides experiment results.

3.1 Substitution

The substitution module receives (i) a datagraph D^0, (ii) a scenario s illustrated in (SQ5) that produces an hypothetical datagraph D^n and (iii) a query $q = e_q(\mathcal{V}_q^n)$ on D^n. The module derives a query q' that (1) uses exclusively the nodes of the original datagraph D^0, and (2) when evaluated on D^0 it returns the same answer that q returns when it is evaluated on the datagraph D^n. We will call q' the *dereferenced query*.

$$
\begin{aligned}
v_m^1 &\leftarrow e_1(\mathcal{V}_1^0) \\
v_m^2 &\leftarrow e_2(\mathcal{V}_2^{0,2}) \\
&\vdots \\
v_m^n &\leftarrow e_n(\mathcal{V}_n^{0,\dots,n-1})
\end{aligned}
\qquad (SQ5)
$$

$$
e_q(\mathcal{V}_q^n) \% query
$$

The implemented substitution module works for the class of *structurally sure* scenario-queries, which are guaranteed to be sure (as defined in Section 2.) Structural sureness leads to a very efficient substitution algorithm, because it depends on the graph structure of the datagraph schema and scenario modifications, but not on the datagraph's edge expressions and the related axioms.

Given a datagraph D^0 and the scenario-query (SQ5) the following nodes of $D^0, \dots, D^n$ are structurally sure. For each structurally sure node v we also provide a set of expressions $\mathcal{C}(v)$ that compute v using D^0 nodes exclusively.

Initial Nodes Every node v^0 is structurally sure. For each v^0 it is

$$
\mathcal{C}(v^0) = \{v^0\}
$$

Directly Modified Nodes If the nodes $\mathcal{V}_i^{0,\dots,i-1}$ used in the ith modification are structurally sure then the directly modified node v_m^i is also structurally sure. The set of expressions that compute v_m^i is constructed by applying the modification

expression e_i on each expression e' that computes the corresponding node v_m^{i-1} of D^{i-1}, i.e.,

$$
\mathcal{C}(v_m^i) = \{e_i(e')|e' \in \mathcal{C}(v_m^{i-1})\}
$$

Unmodified Nodes If the node v^i is *not* a descendant of an ancestor of the node v_m^i that was modified in the ith step of the scenario then v^i is also structurally sure. One can easily see that such nodes v^i are left unmodified by the ith modification. Hence

$$
\mathcal{C}(v^i) = \mathcal{C}(v^{i-1})
$$

Indirectly Modified Nodes If there is an hyperedge $\mathcal{A}^i \overset{e}{\Rightarrow} v^i$ and all of the nodes $a_j^i \in \mathcal{A}^i$ are structurally sure then v^i is also structurally sure. In general, there are many ways in which we can compute v^i. For example, given the hyperedge labeled by e and given expressions $e_{a_j^i}$ that compute each of the $a_j^i \in \mathcal{A}^i$ one expression that computes v^i is derived by substituting each instance of a_j^i in e with the corresponding $e_{a_j^i}$. However there may be many hyperedges leading to v^i and each source node a_j^i of the hyperedge may be computed by multiple expressions (i.e., $\mathcal{C}(a_j^i)$ will typically have more than one expressions.) Hence $\mathcal{C}(v^i)$ is the following set.

$$
\mathcal{C}(v^i) = \{ \quad e/(a_1^i \mapsto e_{a_1^i}, \dots, a_m^i \mapsto e_{a_m^i}) \\
|\exists \{a_1^i, \dots, a_m^i\} \overset{e}{\Rightarrow} v^i, \\
e_{a_1^i} \in \mathcal{C}(a_1^i), \dots, e_{a_m^i} \in \mathcal{C}(a_m^i)\}
$$

where the notation $e/(a_1^i \mapsto e_{a_1^i}, \dots, a_m^i \mapsto e_{a_m^i})$ stands for the substitution of each $a_j^i, j = 1, \dots, m$, in e with $e_{a_j^i}$.

Finally, a scenario-query is structurally sure if every node in the node set $\mathcal{V}_q^n$, which is used by the query, is structurally sure. It is easy to see that the query can be computed by any expression of the set

$$
\mathcal{C}_q = \{ \quad e_q/(v_1^n \mapsto e_{v_1^n}, \dots, v_l^n \mapsto e_{v_l^n}) \\
|e_{v_1^n} \in \mathcal{C}(v_1^n), \dots, e_{v_l^n} \in \mathcal{C}(v_l^n)\}
$$

The implemented algorithm computes the $\mathcal{C}$ sets top-down — unlike the above definitions that hint a bottom-up algorithm. The top-down derivation computes fewer $\mathcal{C}$ sets than the bottom-up one, because the bottom-up one computes $\mathcal{C}$ sets even for the nodes that are "irrelevant" to the query.

EXAMPLE 3.3 Consider (again) the modification and the query of Example 3.1. The substitution algorithm first locates a transitive hyperedge that leads to $ValueCTV^1$ and contains only directly modified and unmodified nodes. Such a transitive edge is the $\{PositionCTS^1, PriceTodayTV^1\} \overset{*}{\Rightarrow}$

$ValueCTV^1$ since $PositionCTS^1$ is directly modified and $PriceTodayTV^1$ is unmodified. Now we can replace the query with:

$$\sigma_{C=John}(PositionCTS^1 * PriceTodayTV^1)$$

Then $PositionCTS^1$ is replaced by the right hand side of the hypothetical assignment. $PriceTodayTV^1$ is replaced by $PriceTodayTV$ because it is "unmodified". Hence, we end up with the dereferenced query

$$\sigma_{C=John}((\hat{\sigma}_{T=MSFT},MULT_{110\%}\,PositionCTS)*\,PriceTodayTV)$$

$\square$

3.2 SESAME's Rewriters

This section describes the challenges that arise during the rewriting of dereferenced queries and the solutions developed for SESAME's rewriter.

The variety of operators, datagraphs and scenario queries that have to be considered during query rewriting, prompted us to first develop the *ultra-conservative* rewriter that exhaustively searches the space of plans. We configured this rewriter with a set of 9 operators, formally defined in [BPP] and the 15 rewriting rules listed in [BPP].[6]

Although for a small set of inputs the ultra-conservative algorithm might perform reasonably well, in the general case its running time is very poor. An exponential blowup was observed, resulting in poor performance for queries with more than four select-modifications.

The poor performance of the ultra-conservative algorithm is due to challenges that relate to the structure and size of dereferenced queries. We describe next the challenges along with the solutions that SESAME's rewriter gives.

3.3 Exponentiality in the number of Select-Modifications and the Minterms Solution

The first challenge is the exponential size of the dereferenced query after replacing each select modification $\hat{\sigma}_{c_i,f_i}R$ with $f_i\sigma_{c_i}R \cup \sigma_{\neg c_i}R$. For example, the expression $\hat{\sigma}_{c_1,f_1}\hat{\sigma}_{c_2,f_2}\hat{\sigma}_{c_3,f_3}R$ is rewritten as:

$$f_1\sigma_{c_1}(f_2\sigma_{c_2}(f_1\sigma_{c_3}R \cup \sigma_{\neg c_3}R) \cup \sigma_{\neg c_2}(f_1\sigma_{c_3}R \cup \sigma_{\neg c_3}R))$$
$$\cup\sigma_{\neg c_1}(f_2\sigma_{c_2}(f_1\sigma_{c_3}R \cup \sigma_{\neg c_3}R) \cup \sigma_{\neg c_2}(f_1\sigma_{c_3}R \cup \sigma_{\neg c_3}R))$$

One may wonder whether considering common subexpressions could lead to a faster rewriter that would optimize each common subexpression just once. The shortcoming of this approach is that the modifying functions (f_1, f_2 and f_3 above) will make each of the two copies of the common subexpression interact differently with the rest of the expression and hence it

---

[6] This set of rules does not create an infinitely large space of plans.

will become impossible to optimize the common subexpression just once.

SESAME's rewriter, provides an efficient solution to this problem by identifying the *minterms* of R. A *minterm* is a set of tuples on which exactly the same modifying functions are applied. Identifying minterms in a query that involves select-modifications allows the rewriter to remove the exponentiality in the number of select-modifications; instead, the result is exponential only in the number of dimensions referenced in the selections of the query. The *minterms* technique can be applied in the case of scenarios where:

1. The conditions of the select-modifications do not involve measure attributes.

2. The modifying functions in the select-modifications are commutable with selection and union operators.

Though the above requirements seem strict, they are quite common. Indeed, modifying functions consisting of arithmetic operators, which we believe are predominant in what-if practice, meet the above conditions.

Now consider the following scenario/query, which is amenable to the minterms technique because the modifying functions commute with selection and union and the conditions are of the form $A \in range_j$ or $A = c_j$ where A is a dimension. For simplicity let us consider equality conditions as a special case of range conditions.

$$\begin{aligned} \text{scenario} \quad & V^1 \leftarrow \hat{\sigma}_{A\in[l_1,u_1],e_1}V \\ & V^2 \leftarrow \hat{\sigma}_{A\in[l_2,u_2),e_2}V^1 \\ & \quad\vdots \\ & V^n \leftarrow \hat{\sigma}_{A\in[l_n,u_n),e_n}V^{n-1} \\ \text{query} \quad & e_q(V^n) \end{aligned}$$

The dereferenced query for the above is

$$e_q(\hat{\sigma}_{A\in[l_n,u_n),c_n}\cdots\hat{\sigma}_{A\in[l_2,u_2),e_2}\hat{\sigma}_{A\in[l_1,u_1),e_1}V) \quad (Q6)$$

Using the minterm technique this scenario query can be rewritten into the minterm form

$$e_q(\quad (\cup_{j=2,2n}\sigma_{A\in[c_{j-1},c_j)}e_n^j e_{n-1}^j \cdots e_1^j V)\cup \quad (Q7)$$
$$\sigma_{A\notin[c_1,c_{2n})}V)$$

where the points $c_1,\ldots,c_{2n}$ are simply an ordered list of the l_i and u_i points (i.e., $c_1 \leq c_2 \leq \ldots \leq c_{2n}$). e_i^j is e_i if the range $[l_i,u_i)$ covers the range $[c_{j-1},c_j)$ and it is the identity function otherwise (i.e., it can be omitted as well.)

EXAMPLE 3.4 The expression

$$\hat{\sigma}_{D\in[1/1/98,1/15/98),Mult_{1.1}}\hat{\sigma}_{Din[1/10/98,1/25/98),Mult_{1.2}}$$
$$\hat{\sigma}_{D\in[1/20/98,1/30/98),Mult_{1.3}}OrderCTDS$$

reduces to the following after the select modifications are removed using the minterms technique

$$\sigma_{D\in[1/1/98,1/10/98)}Mult_{1.1}OrderCTDS$$
$$\cup\sigma_{D\in[1/10/98,1/15/98)}Mult_{1.2}Mult_{1.1}OrderCTDS$$
$$\cup\sigma_{D\in[1/15/98,1/20/98)}Mult_{1.2}OrderCTDS$$
$$\cup\sigma_{D\in[1/20/98,1/25/98)}Mult_{1.3}Mult_{1.2}OrderCTDS$$
$$\cup\sigma_{D\in[1/25/98,1/30/98)}Mult_{1.3}OrderCTDS$$
$$\cup\sigma_{T\notin[1/1/98,1/30/98)}OrderCTDS$$

$\square$

Note that the above minterm form is linear in the number of select-modifications – as opposed to exponential. We can generalize the above transformation to one where the conditions involve d dimensions. In this case the number of minterms (i.e., the number of operands in the above union) will be less than $((2n+1)/d)^d$. A polynomial time algorithm that performs the above transformation is in [BPP].

3.4 Multi-Operand Operators Challenge and the Packed Forests' Solution

The second challenge arises when the rewriter optimizes unions and other multi-operand operators. In this case, the rewriter produces an exponential number of equivalent expressions.

EXAMPLE 3.5 Assume that the operators a and b are commutative. Then, given the expression $a(b(R))\cup(a(b(S))$ the rewriter will also derive $a(b(R))\cup(b(a(S))$, $b(a(R))\cup(a(b(S)))$, and $b(a(R))\cup(b(a(S)))$. $\square$

System-R style optimizers resolve this problem by optimizing each branch of the union separately, i.e. by employing local optimization (called dynamic programming in the context of System-R.) However, the local optimization algorithms may miss the opportunity to use a materialized view. The following example illustrates the problem.

EXAMPLE 3.6 Consider the dereferenced query $Avg_C(Mult_{1.1}OrderCTDS)*Count_C(OrderCTDS)$ against a datagraph containing the views

$$V_1 = \sum_C OrderCTDS$$
$$V_2 = Avg_C(OrderCTDS)$$

If the optimizer processed each operand of the multiplication operator separately, it would arrive to $Mult_{1.1}V_2 * Count_C(OrderCTDS)$ and would not be able to reach the optimal $Mult_{1.1}V_1$. $\square$

Packed Forests

The above example demonstrates that local optimization may miss the optimal rewriting. Our rewriter tackles the problem by employing the *packed forests* data structure, which efficiently stores all equivalent

```
function buildForest(query q, rules R, datagraph D)
returns forest F

for every hyperedge {v_1,...,v_n} --e--> v_d
    insert e(v_1,...,v_n) -> v_d in R
Queue <- [q]
insert the node q in F
while Queue is not empty
    remove from Queue its first element q'
    for every rule r in R
        if r.match(q')=true
                        and returns the set of bindings B
        for every binding b from the set B
            generate new tree t = r.rewrite(b)
            traverse t's non-forested part bottom-up,
            applying buildForest() to every node.
            if t is not already in F insert t in Queue
            insert the node t in F
```

Figure 3: Packed Forests Optimizer

plans for each subexpression – as opposed to System-R optimizers, which note only the optimal plan and discard the rest.

Technically, a packed forest is a data structure that can encode in a compact way a class of equivalent expressions. A *forest* of an expression E is a set of all expressions equivalent to E. A *packed forest* of E is a forest in which every subtree of each expression is also a forest.

Packed forests have been used to save space in parsing of natural languages [RN95]. To illustrate how packed forests are used to improve efficiency of the query rewriting let us reconsider the union expression of Example 3.5. The packed forest of this expression is $\{a(b(R)),(b(a(R))\}\cup\{a(b(S)),b(a(S))\}$.

Notice that if the union had n operands and the packed forest of each one had two equivalent expressions the packed forest encoding would require space linear in n while it represents 2^n equivalent expressions.

The packed forest rewriting algorithm shown in Figure 3 creates the packed forest of a given query. Let us illustrate this algorithm with the rewriting of the query: $\sum_C(\hat{\sigma}_{[Year=1998,Mult_{1.2}]}(CST))$

In the first step (see Figure 4) , the initial tree is traversed bottom up starting at $\sigma_{Year=1998}$ and a forest is built out of each non-leaf node. In Figure 4 dotted circles indicate the roots of the subtrees for which the *buildForest()* is called, and solid boxes indicate completed forests. Since no rules match any of the nodes, until the rewriter reaches the root node $\sum_C$, every forest contains exactly one tree (step 2 in the figure). At this point the rule $\sum_A(R_1\cup R_2)\Rightarrow(\sum_A R_1)\cup(\sum_A R_2)$ fires and adds the second tree to the forest that is being built (step 3). Note, that the new tree already has forests built for $*_{1.2}$ and $\sigma_{Year\neq1998}$, because these sub-

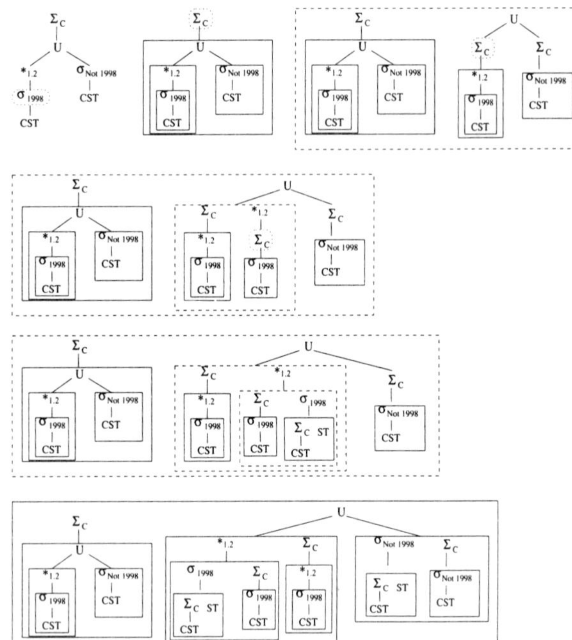

Figure 4: Example of Packed Forest Optimization trees where copied from the original expression without modifications.

Next, the *buildForest()* function is called for every non-forested child of $\cup$ i.e., both its children. It starts with the left $\sum_C$. This instance of buildForest() uses the $\sum_A Mult_k \Rightarrow Mult_k \sum_A$ rewriting and produces the expression $T_1 = Mult_{1.2} \sum_C(\sigma_{Year=1998}(CST))$. Then it recursively calls *buildForest()* on T_1 (step 4). The rest of the forests is produced, in the similar fashion.

By default, SESAME's rewriting rules use only the local optimum plan of each subexpression, thus being almost as fast as local optimization algorithms. However, specially written rules spend extra time to scan (not only the local optimum but also) the equivalent subexpressions and hence find the optimal rewriting. In our current system implementation only the rule $Avg_C R * Count_C R \Rightarrow \sum_C R$ is implemented in this fashion. The *match()* function of this rule looks at the roots of all trees in the operand forests, selecting *Sum*'s in the first operand and *Count*'s in the second. Then pairs of *Sum* and *Count* with the same operands and parameters should be identified, and bindings be produced for each of those pairs.

Packed forests greatly reduce the amount of space required by the rewriter and allow us to trade the rewriter running time with the complexity of rewritings it can do.

3.5   Experiment results

This section presents two sets of experiments. First, we evaluate the running time of an optimizer that employs the techniques described in Sections 3.2, 3.3, and

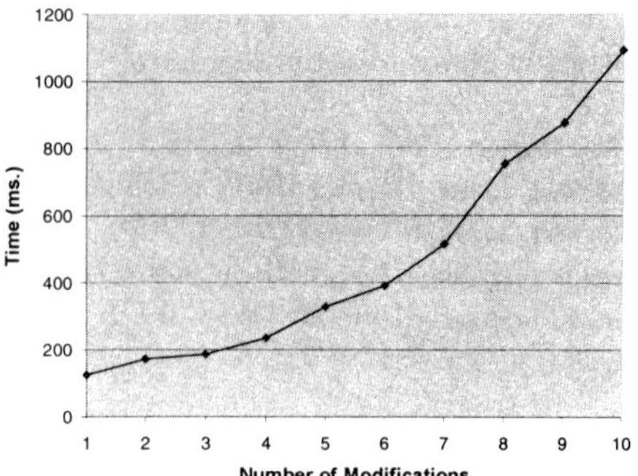

Figure 5: Query on PositionCTS.

3.4 on the performance of the rewriter. Second, we evaluate SESAME's overall performance in comparison with recomputation and incremental update policies in a conventional data warehouse.

The data presented in this section were obtained on the same Pentium II 333 MHz, Windows NT, JDK1.3 with Hotspot Java Virtual Machine configuration where the data for the ultra conservative rewriter were obtained. In all cases the rewriter was set up with the datagraph schema of Figure 1. The same set of rewriting rules listed in [BPP] was used.

Rewriter Running Time Experiments

In this section we evaluate a rewriter employing minterms and the packed forest technique. We do not show results for rewriters without these two techniques, for their performance is non-competitive. For our experiments we report only the running time of the rewriter and not the number of produced plans, because the number of produced expressions is linear with respect to the running time (see [BPP].

For the experiments of Figures 5 and 6 the scenario consists of $N = 1, \ldots, 10$ modifications of the form

$$OrderCTDS^i = \hat{\sigma}_{A_i, MULT_{c_i}} OrderCTDS^{i-1}$$

where A_i were conditions on the dimensions T and C. The first query was $\sigma_{C_S} PositionCST^N$, where C_S was a condition on the T dimension. The second query was $\sigma_{C_S} ValueCTV^N$. Thus the dereferenced queries are of the form:

$\sigma_{C_S} \sum_{Date} \hat{\sigma}_{A_1, MULT_{c_1}} .. \hat{\sigma}_{A_n, MULT_{c_n}} OrderCTDS$, and
$\sigma_{C_S} (\sum_{Date} \hat{\sigma}_{A_1, MULT_{c_1}} ..$
$.. \hat{\sigma}_{A_n, MULT_{c_n}} OrderCTDS) * PriceTodayTV$

Figures 5 and 6 present how the rewriter's running time increases as a function of the number of modifications.

Overall Performance Experiments

In conclusion we present an experiment in which the same hypothetical query $\sigma_{C_S} PositionCST^N$ (where $N = 1, \ldots, 4$ is the number of modifications in the scenario) that was used for the rewriting experiment, was

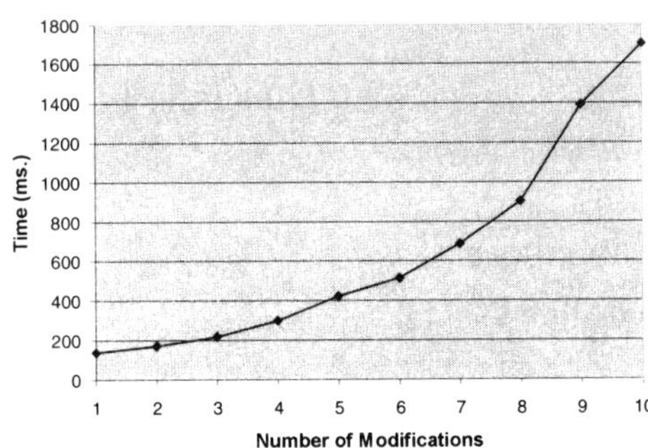

Figure 6: Query on ValueCTV

Modifica-tions	Sesame Exec. time	Incremental Exec. time	Repla cement Exec. Time	Affected tuples
1	0.25 sec	202 sec	630 sec	151 K
2	0.9 sec	225 sec	630 sec	168 K
3	1.1 sec	289 sec	630 sec	249 K
4	1.0 sec	298 sec	630 sec	257 K

Table 1: Overall performance vs. the MS SQL Server

executed by SESAME's execution engine and by Microsoft SQL Server. Since SESAME's rewriter can optimize this query to be answered entirely using the original materialized view *PositionCST*, SESAME's lazy evaluation approach has huge advantage over the eager execution one, as Table 1 clearly demonstrate.

The second column indicates the time that it took SESAME's execution engine to carry out the optimized dereferenced plan.

The third column reflects the time that it took the MS SQL Server to update the fact nodes and relevant views according to the scenario, execute the hypothetical query and roll back the modifications. This result is equal to the time this scenario would take in a warehouse system that supports incremental updates, i.e., the time to create the delta tables for OrderCTDS and PositionCST, run the query and destroy the deltas.

The fourth column reflects the time that it took the MS SQL Server to execute the query without the simulated incremental updates. In this case the hypothetical database was created, all the data was copied from the original fact tables along with the necessary modifications, all the views were recomputed, and the query was executed on the hypothetical database.

The data warehouse used for this experiment contained only one million orders or about 50 MB of data. In a more realistically sized warehouse, SESAME's advantage would be even more striking.

References

[AHV96]   S. Abiteboul, R. Hull, and V. Vianu. *Foundations of Databases*. Addison Wesley, 1996.

[BLT86]   J. Blakeley, P. Larson, and F. Tompa. Efficiently updating materialized views. In *Proc. SIGMOD Conf.*, 1986.

[BPP]   A. Balmin, Y. Papakonstantinou, and T. Papadimitriou. Hypothetical queries in an olap environment. http://www.db.ucsd.edu/ publications/extsesame.pdf.

[CCS]   E.F. Codd, S.B. Codd, and C.T. Salley. Providing OLAP (on-line analytical processing) to user-analysts: An IT mandate. http://www.arborsoft.com/ essbase/wht_ppr/coddTOC.html.

[CNS99]   S. Cohen, W. Nutt, and A. Serebrenik. Rewriting aggregate queries using views. In *Proc. PODS Conf.*, 1999.

[GH97]   T. Griffin and R. Hull. A framework for implementing hypothetical queries. In *Proc. SIGMOD Conf.*, 1997.

[GMS93]   H. Gupta, I. Mumick, and A. Subrahmanian. Maintaining views incrementally. In *Proc. SIGMOD Conf.*, 1993.

[GMUW99]   H. Garcia-Molina, J. Ullman, and J. Widom. *Principles of Database Systems*. Prentice Hall, 1999.

[HFLP89]   L. Haas, J. Freytag, G. Lohman, and H. Pirahesh. Extensible query processing in starburst. In *Proc. SIGMOD Conf.*, 1989.

[HRU96]   V. Harinarayan, A. Rajaraman, and J. D. Ullman. Implementing data cubes efficiently. *ACM SIGMOD Conf. Proc.*, pages 105–216, 1996.

[LMSS95]   A. Levy, A. Mendelzon, Y. Sagiv, and D. Srivastava. Answering queries using views. In *Proc. PODS Conf.*, 1995.

[LYGM99]   W. J. Labio, R. Yerneni, and H. Garcia-Molina. Shrinking the warehouse update window. In *Proc. SIGMOD Conf.*, 1999.

[MQM97]   I. Mumick, D. Quass, and B. Mumick. Mainenance of data cubes and summary tables in a warehouse. In *Proc. SIGMOD Conf.*, 1997.

[PC95]   N. Pendse and R. Creeth. *The OLAP Report*, Business Intelligence, 1995.

[RKR97]   N. Roussopoulos, Y. Kotidis, and M. Roussopoulos. Cubetree: organization of and bulk incremental updates on the data cube. In *Proc. SIGMOD Conf.*, 1997.

[RN95]   S. Russel and P. Norvig. *Artificial Intelligence: a modern approach*. Prentice Hall, 1995.

[SDJL96]   D. Srivastava, S. Dar, H. V. Jagadish, and A. Levy. Answering queries with aggregation using views. In *Proc. VLDB Conf.*, 1996.

[SRN90]   T. Sellis, N. Roussopoulos, and R. Ng. Efficient Compilation of Large Rule Bases Using Logical Access Paths. *Information Systems*, 15(1):73–84, 1990.

Hierarchical Compact Cube for Range-Max Queries

Sin Yeung Lee   Tok Wang Ling   HuaGang Li

School of Computing
National University of Singapore
{jlee,lingtw,lihuagan}@comp.nus.edu.sg

Abstract

A range-max query finds the maximum value over all selected cells of an on-line analytical processing (OLAP) data cube where the selection is specified by ranges of contiguous values for each dimension. One of the approaches to process such queries is to pre-compute a prefix cube (PC), which is a cube of the same dimensionality and size as the original data cube, but with some pre-computed results stored in each cell.

In this paper, we propose a new cube representation called Hierarchical Compact Cube, which is an hierarchical structure that stores not only the maximum value of all the children sub-cubes, but also stores one of the locations of the maximum values among the children sub-cubes. The storage requirement is much less than the prefix cube methods. Furthermore, both of our analysis and experiment results show that the average query time using our method is bounded by a constant independent on the number of data in the data cube, N. For a fixed dimension, the average update cost of our new structure in the worst case is also relatively low. It is only $O(\log N)$.

1 Introduction

Aggregation is a common and computation-intensive operation in on-line analytical processing systems (OLAP) [3, 4, 7], where the data is usually modelled as a multidimensional data cube [5, 6, 10], and queries typically involve aggregations across various cube dimensions. Formally, an n-dimensional data cube is derived from a projection of $n+1$ attributes from some relation R, where one of these attributes is classified as a measure attribute and the remaining n attributes are used as **dimensional attributes**. Each dimension of the data cube corresponds to a dimensional attribute, and the value in each cube cell is an aggregation of the measure attribute value of all records in R having the same dimensional attribute values. For instance, consider the database which stores the sales of each item in each day for each outlets, the data can be stored in a cube having three dimension --- item, date and outlets. The value in each cube will be the actual sales.

Using the data cube model, we can answer many OLAP range queries [11] efficiently. In particular, we propose a new pre-computation technique for a class of OLAP queries called **range-max queries**. A range-max query finds the maximum value over all selected cells of an OLAP data cube where the selection is specified by a range of contiguous values for each dimension [6]. For example, finding the maximum sales of stationary items (each has an item code ranging from 1200 to 1258) between day 130 and day 136 in all the western outlets (branch-no ranging from 45 to 89) is a range-max query. It can be realized using the following SQL statement:

SELECT MAX(amount) FROM sales WHERE
((item>=1200) AND (item <= 1258)) AND
((day>=130) AND (day<=136)) AND
((branch>=45) AND (branch<=89));

The most direct approach is a *naïve* approach. We evaluate a range-max query by accessing each individual cell from the data cube itself and find the maximum value. However, the cost of access is proportional to the size of the sub-cube specified by the range. To illustrate, given a 10-dimension data cube, if we double the size of each dimension in the range, we will increase the total access cost by 1024 times. This is clearly unacceptable.

Proceedings of the 26th Internal Conference on Very Large Databases, Cario, Egypt, 2000.

Note that this naïve method can be applied to other aggregate functions such as SUM.

To improve the range query for the aggregate function SUM, considerable research has been done in the database community [8, 9, 11, 12. 13]. One of the foundation stones for efficient range-sum query algorithm is to pre-compute a set of summary results [9] which will be used to speed up the processing of an OLAP query of arbitrary range. The most commonly found ideas is the Prefix Sum Method. In this method, a prefix cube $\mathcal{PC}$, of the same size as the data cube $\mathcal{DC}$, stores various pre-computed prefix aggregation. In particular, $\mathcal{PC}\langle x_1,\ldots,x_d\rangle$ stores the sum of all the data in $\mathcal{DC}$ ranging from $\langle 0,\ldots,0\rangle$ to $\langle x_1,\ldots,x_d\rangle$. With the use of $\mathcal{PC}$, any range-sum query on d dimension can be answered with a constant (2^d) cell accesses. To illustrate, the sum of all the data in $\mathcal{DC}$ ranging from $\langle 2,4\rangle$ to $\langle 6,9\rangle$ can be computed with only four cell accesses of the $\mathcal{PC}$ by using the formula:

$$\text{sum}(\langle 2,4\rangle, \langle 6,9\rangle) =$$
$$\text{sum}(\langle 0,0\rangle, \langle 6,9\rangle) - \text{sum}(\langle 0,0\rangle, \langle 6,3\rangle) -$$
$$\text{sum}(\langle 0,0\rangle, \langle 1,9\rangle) + \text{sum}(\langle 0,0\rangle, \langle 1,3\rangle)$$

or alternatively,

$$\text{sum}(\langle 2,4\rangle, \langle 6,9\rangle) = \mathcal{PC}\langle 6,9\rangle - \mathcal{PC}\langle 6,3\rangle -$$
$$\mathcal{PC}\langle 1,9\rangle + \mathcal{PC}\langle 1,3\rangle$$

Although the Prefix Sum Method has a very good constant time query cost, it is very expensive to update the prefix sum cube. A single update on the data at $\mathcal{DC}\langle 0,\ldots,0\rangle$ requires to update every cell in the $\mathcal{PC}$. Other methods try to correct this weakness. For example, the Relative Prefix Sum method [12] has a constant query cost and a much reduced $O(n^{d/2})$ update cost. This achieves a better overall effect for frequently updated data cube. The Hierarchical Cubes method [13] further improves [12] to allow a dynamic fine-tuning between the query cost and update cost.

Despite all these works on range-sum query, they cannot be directly applied to the range-max query. In particular, most of the existing range-SUM methods explore the idea that, given two disjointed regions A and B,

$$\text{sum}(B) = \text{sum}(A+B) - \text{sum}(A)$$

where $A + B$ is the union of the two regions. This equality is exactly the corner stone to make prefix sum works. However, for the case of range-max query, even if we know the maximum value of both regions A and $A+B$, we still cannot decide the maximum value of the region B.

Fortunately, there are many other aspects that we can explore to speed up the range-max query that the range-sum query does not process:

1. In a range-sum query, it is possible to prune some processes in the search for the maximum. In particular, given three regions A, B and C. If it is known that $\max(A+B)$ is not more than $\max(C)$, then both $\max(A)$ and $\max(B)$ are smaller than $\max(C)$. Therefore, we do not need to explore regions A nor B to find the exact value of $\max(A)$ nor $\max(B)$. Generalising this idea, if a requested range is covered by regions $A_1,\ldots,A_n$, we can prune off any further investigation on A_i if the maximum value of A_i is not more than the current computed maximum value. This type of pruning allows a great reduction of the IO cost on cube accesses.

2. While the order of the sub-cube visitation for the range-sum query is not very important in terms of IO accesses, it is no longer true in the case of range-max query. Due to the possibility of pruning some searching processes, it is highly beneficial to find a correct order of the evaluation of the sub-range queries so as to increase the probability that a sub-range can be pruned.

3. A maximum data is not just a result of an aggregation function, it is also a data that appears in the data cube. As a result, a maximum data can associate with the location of the data cube cell where the maximum appears. Using the location, some of the range-max query can be done much faster. For example, if we know that the overall maximum is at location $\langle 3,8,4\rangle$, then any range-max query that includes $\langle 3,8,4\rangle$ can be answered in just one cube access --- the access of the cell $\langle 3,8,4\rangle$ itself. In this paper, we shall formulate our algorithm to use this location to further decrease the access cost of range-max query.

2　Hierarchical Compact Cube

Definition 2.2　A data cube $\mathcal{DC}$ of d dimension, is a d-dimensional array. For each dimension, the index can be ranged from 0 till s_i-1 inclusively. We will denote s_i as the size of the ith dimension. In this paper, a cell in the data cube can be expressed in the following form,

$$\mathcal{DC}\langle x_1,\ldots,x_n\rangle \quad \text{where } 0 \leq j_i < s_i$$

Example 2.1　Figure 2.1 shows a data cube of 2 dimension. The size of the first dimension (represented as row in this paper) is 5, and the size of the second dimension (represented as column) is 7.

	0	1	2	3	4	5	6
0	5	24	17	32	9	21	34
1	30	11	2	20	25	8	14
2	16	26	1	13	15	3	28
3	31	4	29	6	33	18	28
4	23	22	12	19	10	27	35

Figure 2.1 A data cube

Definition 2.2 Given a data cube $\mathcal{DC}$ of d dimension, and d integers $m_1,\ldots,m_d$, the **compact cube** of $\mathcal{DC}$, denoted as $\mathcal{CC}$, is another data cube such that

1. it has the same dimension d, and
2. if the size of the ith dimension in $\mathcal{DC}$ is s_i, i.e., it ranges from 0 to s_i-1, then the dimension i in $\mathcal{CC}$ will be ranged from 0 to $\left\lfloor \dfrac{s_i-1}{m_i} \right\rfloor$.
3. Each cell $\mathcal{CC}\langle x_1,\ldots,x_d\rangle$ in $\mathcal{CC}$ stores two items
   - The maximum of all the cells $\mathcal{DC}\langle j_1,\ldots,j_d\rangle$ where $m\,x_i \le j_i < \min(m_i(x_i+1), s_i)$ and
   - the position of one of the cells that holds this maximum value.

In this paper, we shall denote the maximum value stored in $\mathcal{CC}\langle x_1,\ldots,x_d\rangle$ simply as $\mathcal{CC}\langle x_1,\ldots,x_d\rangle$.value, and the maximum location as $\mathcal{CC}\langle x_1,\ldots,x_d\rangle$.location. For simplicity's sake, we assume $m_1 = \ldots = m_d = m$, and we shall call this integer m the **compact factor** of the compact cube. However, our algorithm is equally applicable when m_i are not the same.

Example 2.2 Figure 2.2 shows a compact cube of the data cube shown in Figure 2.1. The compact factor is set to 2. Note that among the data in $\mathcal{DC}\langle i,j\rangle$ where $0 \le i, j \le 1$, the maximum value is 30, and it appears in location $\langle 1,0\rangle$. This information is stored in $\mathcal{CC}\langle 0,0\rangle$ of the compact cube. Note that for $\mathcal{CC}\langle 1,3\rangle$, the maximum value 28, can be derived from $\mathcal{DC}\langle 2,6\rangle$ and $\mathcal{DC}\langle 3,6\rangle$. Our compact cube just randomly picks one of these locations and stores it. Note also that $\mathcal{CC}\langle 2,3\rangle$ only summarises the maximum of only one cell in the data cube: $\mathcal{DC}\langle 4,6\rangle$ and thus $\mathcal{CC}\langle 2,3\rangle$.value is exactly equal to $\mathcal{DC}\langle 4,6\rangle$.

	0	1	2	3
0	30 1 0	32 0 3	25 1 4	34 0 6
1	31 3 0	29 3 2	33 3 4	28 2 6
2	23 4 0	19 4 3	27 4 5	35 4 6

Figure 2.2   A Compact Cube

Definition 2.3 Given a compact cube $\mathcal{CC}$ of dimension d, and d integers $m_1,\ldots,m_d$, its **compact cube**, $\mathcal{CC}_2$, is another compact cube such that

1. it has the same dimension d, and
2. if the dimension i in $\mathcal{CC}$ is ranged from 0 to s_i-1, then the dimension i in $\mathcal{CC}_2$ will be ranged from 0 to $\left\lfloor \dfrac{s_i-1}{m_i} \right\rfloor$.
3. Each cell $\mathcal{CC}\langle x_1,\ldots,x_d\rangle$ in $\mathcal{CC}_2$ stores two items

- The maximum of $\mathcal{CC}\langle j_1,\ldots,j_d\rangle$.value where $m\,x_i \le j_i < \min(m(x_i+1), s_i)$ and
- the location attribute of one of the cells which holds this maximum value.

To simplify the discussion in this paper, we shall again assume that all m_i are the same, and likewise refer it as the **compact factor**.

Example 2.4 With the compact cube $\mathcal{CC}$ as shown in Figure 2.2, we can compact to generate another compact cube $\mathcal{CC}_2$. With compact factor to be 2, $\mathcal{CC}_2\langle 0,0\rangle$ contains the maximum value among $\mathcal{CC}\langle 0,0\rangle$, $\mathcal{CC}\langle 0,1\rangle$, $\mathcal{CC}\langle 1,0\rangle$ and $\mathcal{CC}\langle 1,1\rangle$. From Figure 2.2, we can conclude that the maximum value is 32, and it is at $\mathcal{CC}\langle 0,1\rangle$. Hence, $\mathcal{CC}_2\langle 0,0\rangle$.value will be 32. $\mathcal{CC}_2\langle 0,0\rangle$.location will be equal to the location attribute of $\mathcal{CC}\langle 0,1\rangle$, i.e., $\langle 0,3\rangle$. The completed $\mathcal{CC}_2$ is shown in Figure 2.3.

	0	1
0	32 0 3	34 0 6
1	23 4 0	35 4 6

Figure 2.3
A rank 2 compact cube

Definition 2.4 Given a data cube $\mathcal{DC}$ and an integer m, an **Hierarchical Compact Cube** denoted by $\mathcal{HC}$, is a sequence of compact cubes $\mathcal{CC}_0,\ldots,\mathcal{CC}_h$ such that

1. $\mathcal{CC}_0$ is the data cube $\mathcal{DC}$ itself.
2. $\mathcal{CC}_k$ ($k \ge 1$) is the compact cube of $\mathcal{CC}_{k-1}$ with compact factor m.
3. $\mathcal{CC}_h$ is the only compact cube which contains only one single cell.

We shall call the integer m the **compact factor** of the hierarchical compact cube $\mathcal{HC}$, h the **height** of the $\mathcal{HC}$. We shall refer $\mathcal{CC}_i$ as the rank i compact cube of $\mathcal{HC}$ and $\mathcal{CC}_h$ also as the **topmost** compact cube of $\mathcal{HC}$.

Example 2.4 With the data cube as shown in Figure 2.1, we can construct a hierarchical compact cube $\mathcal{HC}$. The rank 0 compact cube is the data cube itself. The rank 1 compact cube is shown in Figure 2.2, and the rank 2 compact cube is shown in Figure 2.3. Lastly, Figure 2.4 shows the rank 3, the topmost compact cube, which results from compacting the rank 2 compact cube.

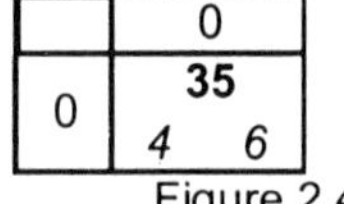

	0
0	35 4 6

Figure 2.4
A rank 3 compact cube

Definition 2.5 A max-range query with respect to a data cube $\mathcal{DC}$ of dimension d can be specified as

$$[<L_1,\ldots,L_d>,<H_1,\ldots,H_d>]$$

such that for each dimension i, $0 \le L_i < H_i \le s_i$ where s_i is the size of the ith dimension of $\mathcal{DC}$. The query returns the maximum value among all the data in $<x_1,\ldots,x_d>$ with $L_i \le x_i < H_i$.

Example 2.5 In Figure 2.5, the shadowed area represents the range $[<1,1>,<4,5>]$.

	0	1	2	3	4	5	6
0	5	24	17	32	9	21	34
1	30	11	2	20	25	8	14
2	16	26	1	13	15	3	28
3	31	4	29	6	33	18	28
4	23	22	12	19	10	27	35

Figure 2.5 The range [<1,1>, <4,5>]

Definition 2.6 Given a cell $CC<x_1,\ldots,x_d>$ of a rth rank compact cube with compacting factor m, a region $R = [<L_1,\ldots,L_d>,<H_1,\ldots,H_d>]$ is said to be contained in the cell if and only if for each i ($1 \le i \le d$),

    1. $m^r x_i \le L_i$ and

    2. $H_i \le \min(m^r(x_i+1), s_i)$.

where s_i is the size of the ith dimension of the compact cube CC_r. The region R is said to be a **full region** with respect to the cell $CC<x_1,\ldots,x_d>$ if all the equality signs in both conditions hold. Otherwise, R is called a **partial region** with respect to the cell $CC<x_1,\ldots,x_d>$.

Example 2.6 Refer to the hierarchical compact cube $\mathcal{HC}$ as described in Example 2.4. The region $[<0,0>,<4,4>]$ is contained in $CC_2[0,0]$ as $2^2*0 \le 0$ and $4 \le 2^2*1$. Indeed, as both the equality signs hold, the region is also a full region. The same region is also contained in $CC_3<0,0>$ as $2^3*0 \le 0$ and $4 \le 2^3*1$. However, the region is only a partial region with respect to $CC_3<0,0>$ as the second equality does not hold. Finally, the region is not contained in $CC_1<0,0>$ as the second condition "$4 \le 2^1*1$" fails.

3 Using the Hierarchical Compact Cube for range query

Before we present the algorithm to handle range-max query, we shall illustrate the idea behind using the following example:

Example 3.1 Refer to the data cube as described in Example 2.1, we want to find the maximum value in the range $R = [<1,1>, <5,5>]$. This range is shown in the shadow area of Figure 3.1.

	0	1	2	3	4	5	6
0	5	24	17	32	9	21	34
1	30	11	2	20	25	8	14
2	16	26	1	13	15	3	28
3	31	4	29	6	33	18	28
4	23	22	12	19	10	27	35

Figure 3.1 A sample query

Instead of accessing the data cube directly to find the maximum, we will first look at the topmost rank of the hierarchical compact cube, the rank 3 compact cube. This compact cube is shown in Figure 3.2. The dotted rectangle represents the region R (ranged [<1,1>, <5,5>]) wrt the Rank 3 compact cube (ranged [<0,0>, <5,7>]).

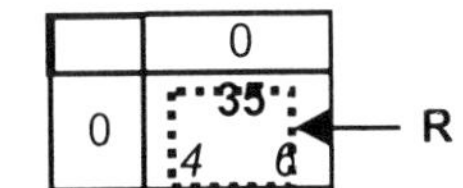

Figure 3.2 Rank 3 compact cube

This compact cube cell reveals that the maximum within the region [<0,0>, <5,7>] is 35 and it is in the location <4,6>. Given any region R that is contained in $CC<0,0>$, there are three possibilities,

    1. R is a full region with respect to $CC<0,0>$,

    2. R is a partial region, but the maximum cell $\mathcal{DC}<4,6>$ is inside R,

    3. R is a partial region, and the maximum cell $\mathcal{DC}<4,6>$ is not inside R.

In either case 1 or case 2, as the maximum element in the cell $\mathcal{DC}<4,6>$ is also inside R, the region R contains the maximum value. We can then return 35 as the answer immediately and do not need to do any further investigation. Only in case 3 do we need to investigate further. In this example, R belongs to case 3.

We now apply the bound and branch [1] and the divide and conquer idea [2] to subdivide the region R into m^d sub-regions. In this example, it is divided into $R1$, $R2$, $R3$ and $R4$ so that each sub-region is contained in exactly one rank 2 compact cube cell. This is shown in Figure 3.3. The original query can now be transformed into four sub-queries to find the maximum values of region $R1$, $R2$, $R3$ and $R4$, and the final result is the largest of these four maximums.

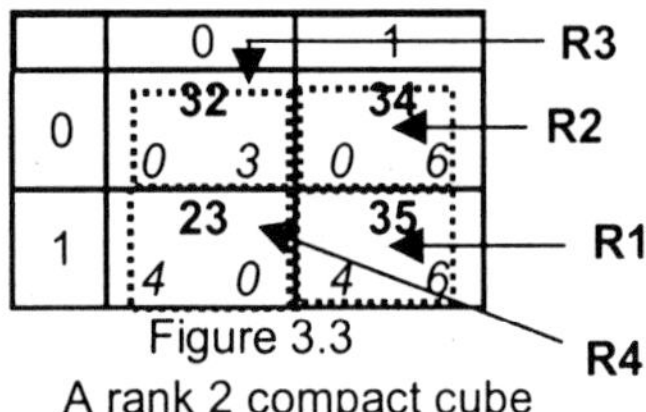

Figure 3.3
A rank 2 compact cube

While the final answer is independent of which four sub-queries is evaluated first, however, if we compute $R1$ and discovers that the maximum is indeed 35, then we can immediately prune the query on $R2$, as its maximum is at best 34. We therefore propose to compute the sub-queries in the following order:

1. All the regions that are full regions first, then
2. All the partial regions with the largest maximum evaluated first and the smallest maximum evaluated last.

The full regions can be computed without any further subdivision. Hence, they should be evaluated first. On the other hand, a partial region may need to investigate furthermore if the maximum location is not inside the partial region. Hence, they are evaluated later. In order to compute the largest maximum first, we need to maintain some sorted order of these partial regions. A complete sorting is quite expensive. For instance, in our example, if 35 is found to be the answer, it is a waste of resources to pre-sort the regions $R2$, $R3$ and $R4$. Consequently, a priority queue implemented using implicit heap is introduced to keep those "to-be-investigated" regions such that the largest cell-maximum can be immediately available in the front of the queue. Note that as we are using heap structure, we do not need all the elements in the queue completely sorted.

In this example, none of the regions $R1$, $R2$, $R3$ or $R4$ is a full region, we therefore proceed to examine the four partial regions. The first region to be investigated is region $R1$. It is contained in the compact cube $CC\langle 1,1 \rangle$ that also holds the largest possible maximum, 35. However, as 35 is at position $\langle 4,6 \rangle$, it is outside the region $R1$. Hence, we cannot immediately conclude the maximum of $R1$. $R1$ is now inserted into the priority queue Q for further analysis. Similarly, regions $R2$, $R3$ and $R4$ are all partial regions and their respective maximums do not fall in their corresponding regions.

Hence, they are all inserted into Q. As Q always ensures that the largest element is in the front of the queue, hence, the elements contained in Q are regions $R1$, $R2$, $R3$ and $R4$, with $R1$ being in the front of the queue.

Now we further investigate the largest element in Q, $R1$. The region can be further sub-divided into only one region $R1a$ in the rank 1 compact cube, as shown in Figure 3.4.

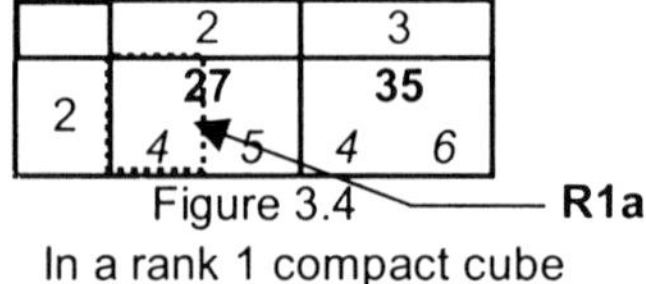

Figure 3.4
In a rank 1 compact cube

Now $R1a$ is still just a partial region, and its maximum, 27, is at position $\langle 4,5 \rangle$, which is outside the region $R1a$. Hence, we again cannot conclude the maximum value of $R1a$ yet and hence $R1$. We need to insert the region $R1a$ into the queue for further processing. Now, the queue Q contains the regions $R2(max=34)$, $R3(max=32)$, $R1a(max=27)$ and $R4(max=23)$ with $R2$ being in the front of the queue.

The next region dequeued from Q is region $R2$. It can be subdivided into $R2a$ and $R2b$, as shown in Figure 3.5.

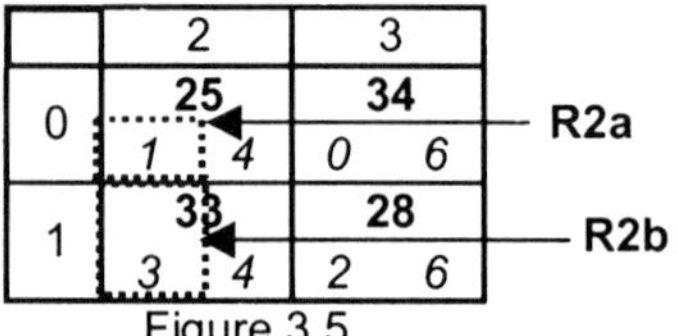

Figure 3.5
In a rank 1 compact cube

None of them is a full region. However, as the maximum value stored in $CC\langle 1,2 \rangle$, 33, is within the region $R2b$, we can conclude that the maximum of region $R2b$ is 33. In other words, the overall maximum of the original query is *at least* 33. Now $R2a$ has a maximum value of 25, which is less than the current maximum, 33. Therefore, we can skip this region. At this moment, the current maximum is 33, and the queue Q contains regions $R3$, $R1a$ and $R4$.

The next region $R3$ has only a maximum of 32, which is smaller than the current maximum, 33. We can skip region $R3$. But since the queue Q always removes the largest element from the queue, the remaining elements in Q are even smaller and can never improve the current maximum, 33. As a result, we can stop our algorithm and conclude that the current maximum is 33.

The following summarizes our algorithm:

Algorithm 3.1 [Maximum Query]

Let $\mathcal{DC}$ be a given data cube and let θ be the smallest domain value of the measure attribute. Let $\mathcal{HC}$ be the hierarchical compact cube of $\mathcal{DC}$ with compacting factor m and height h. We find the result of a range-max query R_0 by the following steps:

1. Let Q be an empty priority queue, which stores tuples of the form $[R, max_{guess}, h_t]$ where R is a range, max_{guess} is an estimated maximum of the range R, and h_t is the smallest height of all the compact cubes in $\mathcal{HC}$ that range R has investigated.

2. To start with, if R_0 covers the entire the data cube, then the topmost compact cube, CC_h, is exactly R_0. We return the maximum value stored in $CC_h<0,...,0>$ as the query result and exit the algorithm.

3. Otherwise, we insert $[R_0, \theta, h]$ inside the priority queue Q. The queue is inserted in a way that a larger max_{guess} will be dequeued first, and the smaller max_{guess} will be dequeued later. We also initialise the current maximum max_{cur} as $\theta - 1$. We now perform the following processes:

4. If Q is empty, then stop the algorithm, and report max_{cur} as the actual maximum.

5. Otherwise, dequeue the largest item $[R, max_{guess}, h_t]$ from the priority queue Q. If the max_{guess} is not more than max_{cur}, stop the algorithm, and report max_{cur} as the actual maximum.

6. Let $\{C_j\}$ be the minimum set of rank $(h_t - 1)^{th}$ compact cubes such that $\bigcup C_j$ covers R. For each j, we denote R_j as the subregion of R that C_j overlaps. In other words, $R_j = R \bigcap C_j \neq \phi$.

7. For each R_j such that R_j is a full region with respect to the compact cube C_j, we query the maximum value stored in the corresponding $(h_t - 1)^{th}$ compact cube C_j, which is exactly the maximum of R_j. If the returned value is more than the current maximum max_{cur}, we update max_{cur} to be the returned value.

8. For the rest of R_j that is only a partial region with respect to the compact cube C_j, we query the $(h_t-1)^{th}$ compact cube to find the maximum of C_j, max_{query}. This value gives the upper bound of the maximum of R_j. We have three cases:

    a. If the returned value max_{query} is not more than the current maximum max_{cur}, then the actual maximum of R_j cannot be more than max_{cur} and we can skip this region. We repeat step 8 for another region $R_{j'}$.

    b. On the other hand, if the returned value is more than the current maximum and if the maximum location is inside R_j, then we confirm that the maximum value of R_j is indeed max_{query}. We update max_{cur} to be max_{query} and continue step 8 with another region $R_{j'}$.

    c. Finally, if the returned value is more than the current maximum, and the maximum location is outside R_j, we need to do further investigation on R_j to confirm its actual maximum. We insert the item $[R_j, max_{query}, h_t-1]$ into Q.

9. After all R_j have been processed, we repeat step 4 of the algorithm until Q is empty.

4 The constant-time average access cost of our method

In this section, we shall first formulate a recurring equation on the average number of compact cube accesses. We then prove that the average number of cube accesses is bounded by a constant that is independent of the size of the compact cube. To start with, we note that during the searching of the maximum value at the rth rank compact cube, the total cost $cost_r$ can be divided into two parts:

1. The query of the maximum values of all the immediate children of the rth rank compact cube, as required in step 7 and step 8 of the Algorithm 3.1. We can assume that there are N such $(r-1)^{th}$ rank children.

2. The possible further query on these N children as described in step 8, part (c) of the Algorithm 3.1.

If k_r is the expected number of children that are required to perform further query, then

$$cost_r = N + k_r \, cost_{r-1}$$

To estimate N, we assume that during the query R on the rth rank compact cube, the rth rank compact cube covers exactly w_i $(r-1)^{th}$ rank compact cubes in the ith dimension where $1 \leq w_i \leq m$. Clearly, the rth rank compact cube covers exactly

$$N = \prod_{i=1}^{d} w_i$$

$(r-1)^{th}$ rank compact cubes. We denote the sub-regions that these compact cubes cover to be $R_1, ..., R_N$. Note that according to Algorithm 3.1, during the processing of any region R of the rth rank cube, we need to access the maximum value stored inside all the sub-cubes R_j in step 7 and 8 of the algorithm. Hence, our algorithm needs to access exactly N compact cubes of rank $(r-1)$.

Given that the compact factor is m, each w_i will be ranged between 1 and m. Thus, the value of N, in the worst case, is at most m^d, which is a constant. Note that in average, the expected value of N is much smaller. If either the starting value or the ending value for the ith dimension of the given range is a random variables, then expected value of each w_i can be shown to be only about $m/2$. Thus, the expected value of N is $1/2^d$ smaller than the worst case. In conclusion, the number of the $(r-1)^{th}$ rank compact cubes needed to be investigated from a rth rank compact is bounded by the constant m^d in the worst case.

To estimate exactly the value of k_r is much more complex. However, we can show that the value of k_r approaches to 0 for lower rank compact cube as the data cube size increases. According to the step 8 of our algorithm, it is required that a sub-region R_p will be inserted into the queue Q for further investigation only if the following conditions are satisfied:

1. The children R_p is a partial region, and
2. the returned maximum on query of R_p is more than the current maximum, and
3. the location of the maximum is not inside R_p.

There can be plenty of compact cubes can do not satisfy the first condition. As illustrated in Figure 4.1, given a region R in the d-dimension r^{th} compact cube, in the worst

case, there are only at most $\prod_{i=1}^{d} w_i - \prod_{i=1}^{d} (w_i - 2)$

partial regions in the $(r-1)^{th}$ compact cube where w_i is the length of the ith dimension that R overlaps with the $(r-1)^{th}$ compact cube. The proportion of partial regions is even smaller when the compact factor m increases, as well as when some dimension ranges falls exactly at the division mark (as shown on the row 5 in figure 4.1) which frequently occurs in lower rank compact cubes.

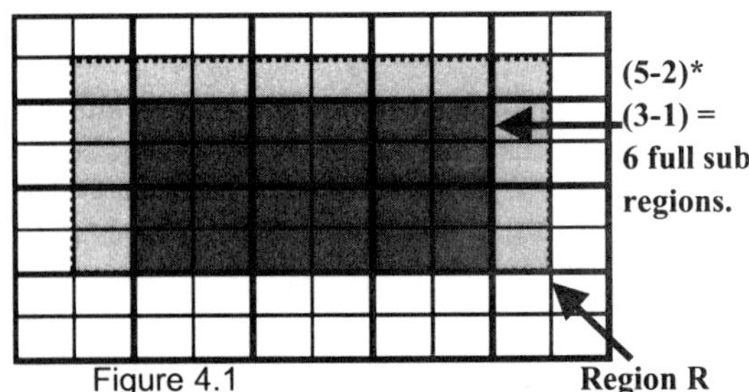

Figure 4.1
Illustration on the numbers of full sub-regions.

To satisfy the second condition, we note that Algorithm 3.1 will first compute the maximum of all the full regions first in step 7. The probability that a partial block R_p has a maximum more than the current maximum is the probability that among all the "explored" regions and the partial block, the largest value is at that partial block. Now, when we start our algorithm by first investigating the topmost rank h compact cube, there are at least

$$\prod_{i=1}^{d} (w_i - 2)$$

sub-regions covered by some rank $(h-1)^{th}$ compact cube being investigated. Each such rank $(h-1)^{th}$

compact cube contains about $m^{(h-1)d}$ data. As a result, we can assume that at least $\left(\prod_{i=1}^{d} (w_i - 2) \right) m^{(h-1)d}$ data has been explored during the visit of these full regions covered by these rank $(h-1)^{th}$ compact cubes. Subsequently, for the remaining partial regions, some full regions of lower rank cubes will also be explored. This further increases the "explored" area and thus decreases the chance that the maximum is found in R_p. However, for simplicity sake, we shall ignore these surpluses in this analysis. In other words, we only assume that at least

$$\left(\prod_{i=1}^{d} (w_i - 2) \right) m^{(h-1)d}$$

data has been explored before accessing the partial block R_p. The size of the partial block of rth rank compact cube is about m^{rd}. Consequently, the probability that the first R_p contains a larger maximum than the current maximum is not more than

$$\frac{m^{rd}}{\left(\prod_{i=1}^{d} (w_i - 2) \right) m^{(h-1)d}}$$

Finally, even if the second condition is satisfied --- R_p has a cell maximum that is greater than the current maximum, as long as this maximum is in the region R_p, it does not fulfil the third condition. In this case, we need not do any further investigation. To estimate this probability, we first illustrate the computation using $d=3$ case. For a partial region in a compact cube of size m, it can fall into three different cases:

1. The region is on the surface. There are $\binom{3}{1} 2^1 (m-2)^2$ such regions. The probability that a chosen point is in the region is ½.
2. The region is on the edge of the cube. There are $\binom{3}{2} 2^2 (m-2)^1$ such regions. The probability that a chosen point is in the region is ¼.
3. Finally, the region can be on the corner of the cube. There are $\binom{3}{3} 2^3 (m-2)^0$ such regions. The probability that a chosen point is in the region is 1/8.

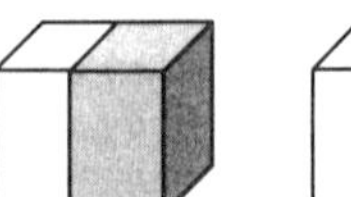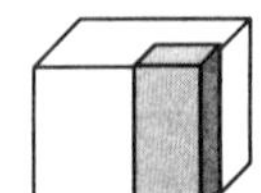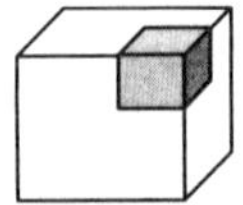

We can generalise the sum for any dimension d, the probability that a particular point is in a partial region is

$$\frac{\sum_{k=1}^{d} \binom{d}{k}(m-2)^{d-k}}{\sum_{k=1}^{d} \binom{d}{k} 2^{k}(m-2)^{d-k}} \approx \left(1 - \frac{1}{m}\right)^{d}$$

Hence, we can deduce that the expected value of k_r is not more than

$$\left(\prod_{i=1}^{d} w_i - \prod_{i=1}^{d}(w_i - 2)\right)\left(\frac{m^{rd}}{\left(\prod_{i=1}^{d}(w_i - 2)\right)m^{(h-1)d}}\right)\left(1 - \frac{1}{m}\right)^{d}$$

Since the value of m, w_i, and d are all independent on the size of the original data cube, we can simply rewrite the above expression as,

$$cm^{(r+1-h)d}$$

where the expected value of the constant c only depends on the value of d and m. With the bound of k_r, we have

$$cost_r < m^d + cm^{(r+1-h)d} cost_{r-1}$$

Expanding the sum, and putting $r = h$, we have,

$$cost_h < m^d \left(1 + cm^d + c^2 m^d + c^3 + \frac{c^4}{m^{2d}} + \frac{c^5}{m^{5d}} + \cdots\right)$$

Note that the sum at the right hand infinite sum converges to a fix number. In other words, for any arbitrary large data cube, the total number of cell accesses, $cost_h$ is bounded by a constant, which is independent on the size of the data cube.

4.1 Experiment Result

The following figures show some of our experiment results.

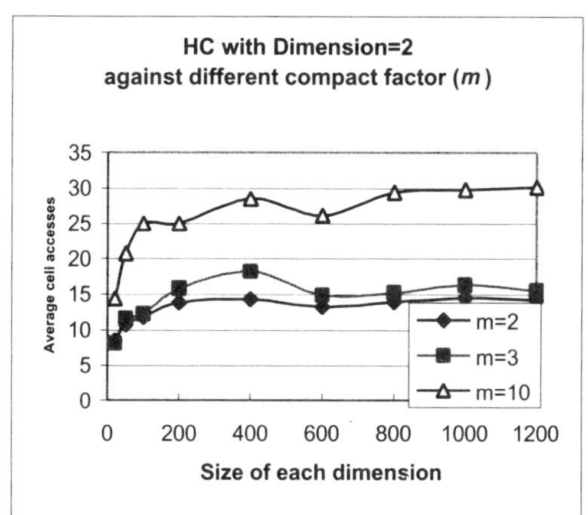

Figure 4.1   Impact of cube size for different compact factor for 2-D Cube

We generated a set of hierarchical compact cubes by varying the data size, compact factor and dimension independently. For simplicity, we consider data cubes with equal sized dimension. We then generate about 100,000 queries of random size and measure the average cell accesses required. The experiment is run in Linux Red hat 6.0 and several observations can be concluded:

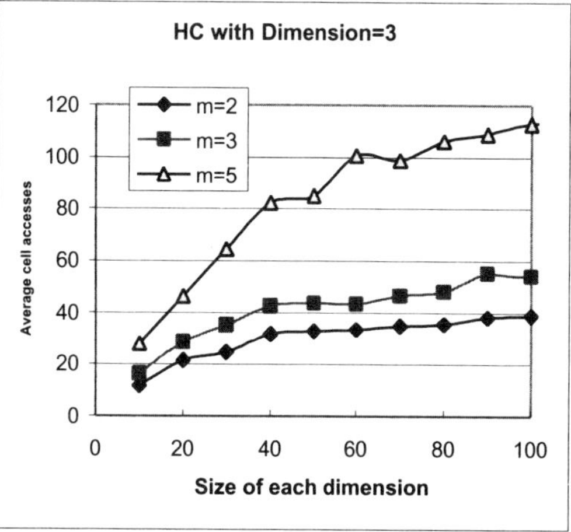

Figure 4.2   Impact of cube size for different compact factor for 3-D Cube

1. From Figure 4,1 and Figure 4.2, there are strong evidences that the average number of cell accesses does converge to a constant when the size of the data cube increases. For large set of data, the performance is not dependent on the number of data in the data cube. This coincides with our analysis. Furthermore, the convergent rate is faster for smaller compact factor and lower dimension.

2. The performance also improves when the compact factor decreases. The best compact factor, as shown in both Figure 4.1 and 4.2, is 2.

As shown in Figure 4.3, the average number of cell accesses grows exponentially as the dimension increases. This also coincides with the factor m^d shown in the analysis result.

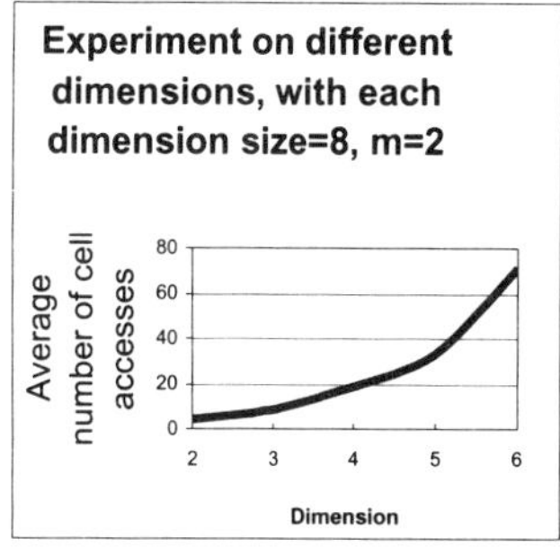

Figure 4.3
Impact of dimension on the overall performance

5 Updates and storage costs of the hierarchical compact cube

When we update a data in the data cube, we may need to update also the hierarchical compact cube. As mentioned in [6,13], our hierarchical compact cube is imperfect if it incurs a huge update cost. Likewise, our method should not incur too much extra storage costs. In this section, we shall show that the maintenance cost of the hierarchical compact cube containing N data is only $O(\log_m N)$. Furthermore, the extra storage cost is a factor smaller as compared to range-sum query methods. [9,13]

There are two types of update to the data cube. We can either increase a value or to decrease a value of a data cube cell. These two updates require a different average update cost analysis on the hierarchical compact cube.

5.1 Maintenance cost for increment

In the case of increment of a cell c in a rth rank compact cube, if the increased value does not exceed the overall maximum of the $(r+1)^{th}$ rank compact cube that c belongs to, then no further update is required. The total update cost is to access the cell c itself, and to query the overall maximum by accessing one cell of the $(r+1)^{th}$ rank compact cube. On the other hand, if the increment affects the overall maximum (for instance, the update is to increase the actual largest value), then the cell of the $(r+1)^{th}$ rank compact cube which contains the overall maximum needed to be updated also. This propagates the update to the $(r+1)^{th}$ rank compact cube, and we now need to query the $(r+2)^{th}$ rank compact cube recursively. The propagation will stop when the update does not affect the maximum stored in its parents or in the worst case, r is the height of the hierarchical compact cube. In other words, in the worst case, the update cost is h. Given that m is the compact factor of the hierarchical compact cube, and d is its dimension, the total number of data in the data cube N, is about m^{hd}. Hence, the update cost h is about

$$\frac{1}{d}\log_m N$$

In other words, for a fixed dimension, the worst case increment cost is only $O(\log_m N)$. The average update case, however, is only a constant. An update of cell c is propagated only when the updated value overtakes the overall maximum. Given that the cell being increased is the kth largest cell, we can assume that with only probability $1/k$, the value of this k^{th} largest cell is increased to overtake the maximum. By summing k from 1 to m^d, and assuming that each cell is updated with the same probability $1/m^d$, the probability that a cell is increased to overtake the overall maximum, and thus propagation to its parent is required, is about

$$\frac{d \ln m + \gamma}{m^d}$$

where γ is the Euler's constant ($=0.5771..$).

As this probability is independent of the rank, hence, an update of a cell in the data cube (a rank 0 cell) can be propagated to a rank 1 parents cell has the same probability that this update will be further propagated to rank 2. It is a geometric progress, and the expected number of cells that requires update is

$$1 \times 1 + 2 \times \frac{d \ln m + \gamma}{m^d} + \cdots + h\left(\frac{d \ln m + \gamma}{m^d}\right)^{h-1} <$$

$$\frac{m^{2d}}{\left(m^d - d \ln m - \gamma\right)^2} = 1 + O(\frac{d \ln m}{m^{2d}})$$

In other words, the average increment cost is bounded by a constant, regardless of the size of the data cube. Furthermore, for data cube with high dimension, the average number of cells that needed to be updated triggered by an increment operation is very closed to 1.

5.2 Maintenance cost for decrement

In the case of decrement of a data cube cell, there are two different cases. If the decrement cell does not appear as a maximum value in some of the compact cubes, then no update on the hierarchical compact cube is required. The total update cost is to access the cell c itself, and to verify that it indeed does not appear as maximum in any compact cube query by an one cell access of its parent rank 1 compact cube. On the other hand, if the decrement cell appears to be a maximum of its parent compact cube, then the cell c itself may not necessarily remain to be the overall maximum. We need to access all the siblings cells of c in the rank 0 compact cube to elect the new overall maximum. This requires an additional m^d queries. As the value of the overall maximum is changed, the update always needs to propagate to the higher level compact cube. The propagation is done recursively until the updated cell is not the maximum cell held by its parents, or in the worst case, when we reach the topmost compact cube. This gives us the average cost to be h cell accesses and the worst cost to be $h \ m^d$ cell accesses. Both the average and worst case decrement costs are $O(\log_m N)$.

5.3 Extra Storage cost

Finally, although our method needs to store a set of compact cubes of different levels, the overall storage cost is still acceptable. For an hierarchical compact cube such that d dimensions are compacted with compacting factor m, the overall number of extra compact cube cells is only

$$\frac{1}{m^d - 1}$$

of the number of data in the data cube. As compared to the prefix sum method where the prefix sum cube is as big as the underlying data cube, our method has a far small extra storage cost then many existing methods [9,12,13,14].

6 Conclusion

Due to an increasing demand for OLAP and data cube applications, efficient calculation of range queries such as the range-max queries has become more important in recent years. Several pre-computations and indexing techniques have been developed to answer the range-sum queries efficiently, but these methods may not be able to apply to the case of range-max. In this paper, we propose the hierarchical compact cube method for processing the range-max queries. We have explored and incorporated the following ideas into our method:

1. We employ an *hierarchical structure* that, applying bound-and-branch as well as divide-and-conquer techniques in multidimensional data, allows an efficient incremental refinement to query the maximum value of any arbitrary range-max query.

2. Different from the range-sum query, we observe that order of the sub-ranges investigation has a huge impact on the overall performance of the query. We propose to use a *priority queue* implemented using heap to store unprocessed regions. This partial ordering process is proven to greatly improve the performance of our algorithm.

3. We introduce the *maximum-location attribute* to further improve the performance of a range-max query. This location allows many early pruning of unnecessary searches.

Both the analysis and experiment results show that our method provides in average a constant time evaluation of range-max queries, and yet incurs only a low $O(log_m N)$ update cost. Finally, the extra storage requirement for the hierarchical compact cube is also much smaller as compared to the prefix cube used in many efficient range-sum queries algorithms.

References

[1] L. Mitten. "Branch and bound methods: General formulation and properties" in Operations Research, 18:24-34, 1970.

[2] Jon Louis Bentley. "Multidimensional divide and conquer". in Comm. ACM, 23(4):214-229,1980

[3] E.F. Codd, "Providing OLAP (on-line analytical processing) to user-analysts: an IT mandate". Technical report, E.F. Codd and Associates, 1993.

[4] Ashish Gupta, Venky Harinarayan, Dallan Quass, "Aggregate-query processing in data warehousing environments". In Proceedings of the 18th Inernational Conference on Very Large Databases, pages 358-369, Zurich, Switzerland, September 1995.

[5] Venky Harinarayan, Anand Rajaraman. Jeffrey D. Ullman. "Implementing Data Cubes Effieciently". In Proceedings of ACM SIGMOD 1996 International Conference on Management of Data, Montreal, Canda, June 1996 pages205-216.

[6] Jim Gray, Adam Bosworth, Andrew Layman, Hamid Pirahesh. "Data cube: A relational aggregation operator generating group-by, cross-tabs and sub-totals". In Proceedings of the 12th International Conference on Data Engineering, pages 152-159, 1996

[7] The OLAP Concil. "MD-API the OLAP Application Program Interface Version 0.5 Specification", September 1996.

[8] Sameet Agarwal, Rakesh Agrawal, Prasad M. Deshpande and Ashish Gupta, "On the Computation of Multidimensional Aggregates", In Proceedings of the 22nd VLDB Conference, Bombay, India, September 1996, pages 506-521.

[9] Inderpal Singh Mumick, Dallan Quass, Barinderpal Singh Mumick, "Maintenance of Data Cubes and Summary Tables in a Warehouse", In Proceedings of ACM SIGMOD 1996 International Conference on Management of Data, June 1997, pages 100-111.

[10] Rakesh Agrawal, Ashish Gupta. Sunita Sarawagi. "Modeling multidimensional databases". In Proc. of the 13th International Conference on Data Engineering, Birmingham, U.K., April 1997.

[11] Ching-Tien Ho, Rakesh Agrawal, Nimrod Megiddo, Ramakrishnan Srikant. "Range Queries in OLAP Data Cubes". In Proceedings of the ACM SIGMOD Conference on the Management of Data, pages 73-88,1997.

[12] Steven Geffner, Divyakant Agrawal, Amr El Abbadi, Terence R. Smith. "Relative Prefix Sum: An Efficient Approach for Querying Dynamic OLAP Data Cubes". In Proceedings of the 15th International Conference on Data Engineering, pages 328-335, 1999

[13] Chee Yong Chan, Yannis E. Ioannidis. "Hierarchical Cubes for Range-Sum Queries". Proceedings of the 25th VLDB Conference, Edinburgh, Scotland, 1999 pages 675-686.

[14] Hua-gang Li, Tok Wang Ling, Sin Yeung Lee, "Range-Max/Min Query in OLAP Data Cube". Appear in Proceedings of the 11th DEXA Conference, Greenwich, 2000.

Temporal Queries in OLAP

Alberto O. Mendelzon

mendel@db.toronto.edu

University of Toronto

Alejandro A. Vaisman

av2n@dc.uba.ar

Universidad de Buenos Aires

Abstract

Commercial OLAP systems usually consider OLAP dimensions as static entities. In practice, dimension updates are often necessary in order to adapt the multidimensional database to changing requirements. We have already defined a taxonomy for these dimension updates in previous works, and a minimal set of operators to perform them. In this paper, we show the need to keep track of the history of the data warehouse. In order to address this problem, we propose a new (temporal) multidimensional model, along with a query language supporting it. We formally define the model, introduce the language by means of examples, and define its syntax and semantics. Finally, we discuss implementation issues, and how a translation into SQL:99, TSQL2 or other SQL-based languages can proceed.

1 Introduction

OLAP (On Line Analytical Processing) has received a lot of attention from the database community in the last few years. As a consequence, several models for OLAP applications have been proposed [Kim96, CT98, Leh98]. In these models, data is organized into *dimensions* and *fact tables* [Kim96]. Dimensions are usually organized as hierarchies, providing a way of defining different levels of data aggregation, a central issue in data analysis. It is a frequent assumption in these works that data in fact tables reflect the dynamic aspect of the data warehouse, while dimension data represent static information. This assumption is often vi-

Proceedings of the 26th VLDB Conference, Cairo, Egypt, 2000.

olated in practice [HMV99a, HMV99b]. For example, a dimension like *Store* (in a retail warehouse application) may change as new stores open and close, or a store is reassigned from one region to another; in addition, the structure of the Store hierarchy itself may change as a level of grouping, such as *Region*, is eliminated, or a new one introduced. Since the schema of the fact table or tables is composed of attributes from the dimensions, such changes may trigger schema evolution in the fact tables. We argue that in an envolving scenario like this, OLAP systems need temporal features to keep track of the different states of a data warehouse throughout its lifespan.

There are many real life situations in which these requirements arise. Consider for example an NBA (professional basketball) warehouse where the fact table *Points* has just two dimensions, *Player* and *Time*, and a measure, *Points Scored*. The *Player* dimension hierarchy is structured by grouping players into teams called *Franchises*. Suppose a user wants to know the total number of points scored by the players of the Portland Blazers. This query could be interpreted in two different ways: the user could be asking for the sum of total points ever scored by all players who are currently on the Blazers, or for the sum of the points scored by these same players since they joined the Blazers. For instance, the points scored by Damon Stoudamire (who is currently on the Blazers) while playing for the Toronto Raptors in the 1998-99 season should only be added under the first interpretation. A query language of a standard commercial OLAP system will not be able to distinguish one interpretation from the other. The reason is that state-of-the-art OLAP systems just record the last value of dimensional attributes and give no access to their historic values. In the language we will introduce in this paper, a query for the first interpretation will be expressed as:

```
Q(x,SUM(p))   <--   Points(x,p,t),
                         Now
                    x -----> franchise:'Blazers'.
```

This means: for each player **x**, add up all the points scored by **x** where **x** currently "rolls up" to the Blazer franchise. The query for the second interpretation will read:

```
Q(x,SUM(p))  ⟵   Points(x,p,t),
               x  --t-->  franchise:'Blazers'.
```

Descriptive attributes make queries like *"total number of points scored by Stoudamire while playing for the Toronto Raptors"* easy to express.

```
Q(SUM(p))  ⟵   Points(x,p,t),
               x  --t-->  franchise:'Raptors',
               x.name=--t--'Stoudamire'.
```

The queries above operate at a high level of abstraction, without requiring low-level knowledge about the database design that underlies the dimensional model.

1.1 Motivating example

We will use the same retail data warehouse throughout the paper, adding dimensions or fact tables when it becomes necessary. For the remainder of this section we will consider dimensions as snapshot relations representing data as of the current time. This is a standard practice in commercial OLAP. Let us start with the following dimensions: *Time, Product, Customer, Salesperson*. Moreover, as dimensions are organized in hierarchies, let us also assume the hierarchy $\{itemId \rightarrow itemType, itemId \rightarrow brand\}$; and the following rollup functions from $itemId$ to $itemType$: $\{(i_1, t_1), (i_2, t_1), (i_3, t_2), (i_4, t_2)\}$ (we will not be using *brand* at this time). The following fact table represents sales facts.

timeId	spId	customerId	itemId	salesAmount
d_1	s_1	c_1	i_1	100
d_2	s_2	c_2	i_1	100
d_3	s_1	c_3	i_3	100
d_4	s_2	c_4	i_4	100

A query asking for the *total sales per salesperson and product type* would return the following table:

spId	itemType	salesAmount
s_1	t_1	100
s_2	t_1	100
s_1	t_2	100
s_2	t_2	100

Suppose now that at an instant immediately after $d4$, product i_1 is reassigned type t_2. A non-temporal star or snowflake schema will store $< i_1, t_2 >$, replacing the tuple $< i_1, t_1 >$, i.e., there will be no memory of the former description of an item. If the user poses the same query, as all the sales occurred before the revision, she would expect to get the same result. However, she gets the following:

spId	itemType	salesAmount
s_1	t_2	200
s_2	t_2	200

What happened is that the contribution of items of type t_1 is ignored, because now all items are of type t_2.

Notice that in order to issue the query above, the user needs to know the schema of the data warehouse, that is, what are the attributes in the fact and dimension tables. This schema may change over time. For instance, *itemId* may not always have been an attribute of the fact and/or dimension tables, if in the early days of this data warehouse data with granularity *itemId* was not available at the sources. In this case, the query above, which is ignorant of this schema change, will only consider total sales made since the time at which *itemId* was added to the fact table, although information is available to obtain the total sales over the whole lifespan of the data warehouse. All these situations must be handled ad-hoc by current OLAP systems, which have no built-in temporal capabilities.

1.2 Related Work

The problem of handling "slowly changing dimensions" was mentioned by Kimball [Kim96], who suggested some partial solutions (which neither take schema evolution into account, nor consider complex dimension updates). Based on this proposal, a *temporal star schema* was introduced [BSSJ98]. This work compares two different temporal implementations against the usual non-temporal star schema, and constitutes a first step toward recognizing the problem. More recently, a multidimensional model for handling complex data has been introduced [PJ99], where the temporal aspect is considered as a modeling issue, and is addressed in conjunction with another data modeling problems. None of these works propose a data warehouse evolution framework or a temporal query language for OLAP. Recent works on maintenance of temporal views [YW98, YW00] present a view definition language operating over non-temporal data sources, along with techniques for maintaining temporal views. Although dealing with temporal databases, these works are orthogonal to ours, as they focus on the data sources and on how a set of temporal views are obtained and maintained, while we focus on querying a temporal multidimensional database.

1.3 Our approach

In light of the above, we introduce a *temporal multidimensional data model* and a temporal query language supporting it, which we called *TOLAP* (*Temporal OLAP*.) TOLAP combines some of the temporal features of query languages like TSQL2 or SQL/TP [Sno95, Tom97] with some of the high-order features of languages like HiLog or Schema-Log [CKW89, LSS97], in the OLAP setting. We introduce *TOLAP* by means of examples, formally define its syntax and semantics, and discuss its expressive power. We show that *TOLAP* allows queries like (a) *"List the amount of sales by product type, using the categorization each item had at the time it was sold"*; (b) *"Were products categorized by brands two years ago?"*; or (c) *"How were customers classified three years ago?"*. Notice that the last two queries are performed over the evolving dimension's metadata. We also introduce an extension to *TOLAP*, allowing queries which *TOLAP* cannot express, like: *"list the total sales per item and region, using only the currently existing regions"*. Finally, we discuss different possible implementations, involving the translation of a *TOLAP* program to SQL.

1.4 Discussion

One might argue, at first sight, that a generic temporal query language like TSQL2 [Sno95] could be used instead of defining a special-purpose one like *TOLAP*. There are two reasons why we prefer to introduce a new language. First, a language designed specifically for the multidimensional model makes typical OLAP queries much more concise and elegant. In a generic language, queries would have to be laboriously encoded using detailed knowledge of the low-level relational structures used to encode the dimensional data. Second, the best-known temporal languages, such as TSQL2, support only a minimal level of schema versioning ([Sno95] p.29).

Another alternative would have been to add temporal features to other languages with schema management features, such as HiLog [CKW89] or Schema-Log [LSS97]. Again, using a language specifically designed for OLAP yields much simpler syntax and semantics, and just the high-order features that are needed to support schema evolution.

The remainder of the paper is organized as follows: in Section 2 we introduce the data model. In Section 3 we define the query language. We discuss its implementation alternatives in Section 4, and conclude in Section 5.

2 Temporal Multidimensional Model

In previous works [HMV99a, HMV99b], we introduced a multidimensional model supporting dimension updates. In that model, dimensions were non-temporal structures, like the ones of Section 1.1. In the *Temporal Multidimensional Model* we introduce here, dimension elements are timestamped at the schema or instance level (or both) in order to keep track of the updates that occur during the dimension's lifespan.

In the rest of the paper we will be dealing with what in temporal databases is called *valid* time [Sno95], that is, the timestamp represents the time when the fact recorded became valid, rather than the time when it was recorded (*transaction time*). The concepts presented here could be easily extended to handle transaction time too. We will consider time as discrete; that is, a point in the time-line, called a *time point*, will correspond to an integer.

2.1 Temporal Dimensions

The following sets are defined : a set of level names $\mathbf{L}$, where each level $l \in \mathbf{L}$ is associated with a set of values $dom(l)$; a set of attribute names $\mathbf{A}$, such that each attribute $a \in \mathbf{A}$ is associated with a set of values $dom(a)$; a set of temporal dimension names $\mathbf{TD}$; and a set of fact table names $\mathbf{F}$. We assume instant t_0 to be the dimension's creation instant.

Definition 1 (Temporal Dimension Schema) *A temporal dimension schema is a tuple (dname,$L,\lambda,\preceq,A,$ $\gg,\mu$) where: (a) dname $\in \mathbf{TD}$ is the name of the temporal dimension; (b) μ is a level in the* Time *dimension. Intuitively, μ defines the granularity of the dimension* dname; *(c) $L \subseteq \mathbf{L}$ is a finite set of levels, which contains a distinguished level name* All, *s.t. $dom(\text{All}) = \{all\}$, where $\{all\}$ is considered valid during the complete lifespan of the dimension; (d) λ is a function with signature $dom(\mu) \to \mathbf{L}$, defining the instants when each level was part of the dimension; (e) $\preceq$ is a function with signature $dom(\mu) \to 2^{\mathbf{L} \times \mathbf{L}}$, such that for each $t \in dom(\mu)$, $\preceq_t$ is a relation s.t. $\preceq_t^*$, the transitive and reflexive closure of $\preceq_t$ is a partial order, with a unique bottom level, $l_{inf} \in \lambda(t)$, and a unique top level,* All, *where, for every level $l \in \lambda(t)$, $l_{inf} \preceq_t^* l$ and $l \preceq_t^*$* All *hold; (f) A is a finite set of attributes; (g)$\gg$ is a function with signature $dom(\mu) \times \mathbf{A} \to \mathbf{L}$, s.t. for every level $l \in \lambda(t)$, a $\gg_t l$ means that if the function is applied to an attribute* a, *it returns the level l, where attribute* a *belongs or belonged to level l at time t.*

Notice that l_{inf} is unique at any time instant t, although it may not be unique across time.

Note In the rest of the paper we will use the retail data warehouse introduced in Section 1.1, with temporal dimensions instead of dimension snapshots.

Example 1 *Let us add a dimension* Store *to our data warehouse, s.t.* dname $= Store$, $\mu = month$, $L = \{storeId, city, region, All\}, \lambda(t) = L, \forall t \geq t_0$, and $\preceq_t = \{StoreId \preceq_t city, city \preceq_t region, \quad region \preceq_t All\}, \forall t \geq t_0$. Also, let us suppose a new level

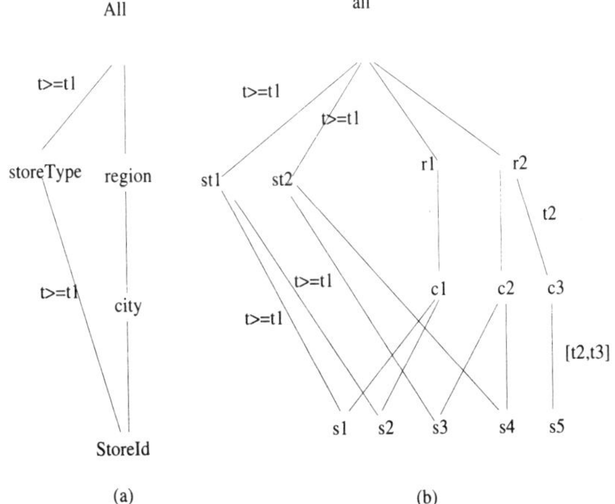

Figure 1: (a) Schema (b) Instance.

storeType is inserted above storeId, at time t_1. Thus, the following holds: $\{storeId \preceq_t StoreType_t,\ storeType \preceq_t All\}, \forall t \geq t_1$. See figure 1(a) [1].

Definition 2 (Temporal Dimension Instance) A temporal dimension instance is a tuple $(D, TRUP, TDESC)$, where D is a temporal dimension schema, and:

- TRUP (temporal rollup) is a set of functions, satisfying the following conditions: (a) for every instant $t \in dom(\mu)$, and for each pair of levels $l_1, l_2 \in \lambda(t)$ such that $l_1 \preceq_t l_2$, there exists in TRUP a rollup function $\rho[t]_{l_1}^{l_2} : dom(l_1) \rightarrow dom(l_2)$; thus, a function is defined for every snapshot taken at any instant $t \in dom(\mu)$; (b) for every instant t in the dimension's lifespan, and for every pair of paths in the graph with nodes in $\lambda(t)$ and edges in $\preceq_t$, $\tau_1 = < l_1, l_2, \ldots, l_k, l_n >$, and $\tau_2 = < l_1, l'_2, \ldots, l'_k, l_n >$, we have $\rho[t]_{l_1}^{l_2} \circ \ldots \circ \rho[t]_{l_k}^{l_n} = \rho[t]_{l_1}^{l'_2} \circ \ldots \circ \rho[t]_{l'_k}^{l_n}$; (c) at every instant t of the dimension lifespan, and for each triple of levels $l_1, l_2, l_3 \in \lambda(t)$ such that $l_1 \preceq_t l_2$ and $l_2 \preceq_t l_3, ran(\rho[t]_{l_1}^{l_2}) \subseteq dom(\rho[t]_{l_2}^{l_3})$.

- TDESC (temporal description) is a set of partial functions $\gg$ with signature $dom(l) \rightarrow dom(a)$, for each level $l \in \lambda(t)$ and attribute a s.t. $a \gg_t l$.

We call condition (b) in the definition of temporal rollup, snapshot consistency, meaning that each element in each level must reach some element in every level above it in the hierarchy, and if there are different paths from one level to another, composing the rollup functions along the different paths must produce the same function.

Example 2 Figure 1(b) shows a temporal dimension instance for dimension Store. The rollup functions with no label are valid for the whole lifespan of Store, while $\rho_{storeId}^{city}[t](s_5) = c_3, \forall t, t_2 \leq t \leq t_3$. Rollup functions with label $t \geq t_1$ suggest that level storeType was created at time t_1.

Clearly, the definitions we gave above are not applicable to the Time dimension. Thus, we will treat it in the usual way.

Definition 3 (Temporal Fact Table) A temporal fact table schema is a tuple $s = (fname, f, m, \mu)$, where m is a level name, called the measure of the fact table, μ is a level in the Time dimension, and f is a function with signature $dom(\mu) \rightarrow 2^{\mathbf{L}}$.

Given a temporal fact table schema $(fname, f, m, \mu)$, a set of levels L in the range of f, and a level μ in the Time dimension, a mapping from each level $l_i \in (L \cup \{\mu\})$ to $dom(l_i)$ is called a point.

Given a temporal fact table schema $s = (fname, f, m, \mu)$, a temporal fact table instance over it is a partial function which maps points of s to elements in $dom(m)$.

Definition 4 (Base Fact Table) Given a set $\mathbf{D}$ of temporal dimensions, a base fact table is a fact table with schema $(fname, f_D, m, \mu)$, such that for each $t \in dom(\mu)$, every level in $f_D(t)$ is a bottom level of its dimension. Thus, a base fact table is a fact table such that its attributes are the bottom levels of each one of the dimensions in $\mathbf{D}$.

Definition 5 (Multidimensional Database)

A temporal multidimensional database schema, denoted $\mathbf{B_s}$, is a pair $(\mathbf{D_s}, \mathbf{F_s})$, where $\mathbf{D_s}$ is a set of temporal dimension schemas, and $\mathbf{F_s}$ is a set of temporal fact table schemas. A temporal multidimensional database instance $I(\mathbf{B})$, is a tuple $(\mathbf{F_I}, \mathbf{D_I})$, where $\mathbf{D_I}$ and $\mathbf{F_I}$ are dimension and fact table instances, respectively, defined as above.

2.2 Temporal OLAP queries

Usually, in an OLAP environment, queries require the computation of aggregates over base fact tables. Moreover, in order to obtain good performance, some systems pre-compute aggregates over different groups of attributes. In the presence of dimensions with hierarchies of levels, queries computing aggregates over various dimension levels are often required. As we claimed that dimensions change over time, this must be taken into account, in order to give the user the desired answer to a query she poses to the system. We will denote by temporal OLAP query, a query over a set of temporal dimensions and fact tables. The example below will show the difference between a temporal OLAP query and a non-temporal one.

Example 3 *Consider a set of dimensions* $\mathbf{D} =$ $\{Product, Store\}$ *from our retail data warehouse, and a base fact table with schema* $(Sales, f, sales, day)$. *Assume no schema update occurred (this will be studied in Section 3.2). Thus,* f *maps each instant to* $\{itemId, storeId\}$. *The instance of dimension* Store *is the one of figure 1, and for the instance of dimension* Product *we have* $\rho_{itemId}^{itemType}[t] = \{i_2 \to t_1, i_3 \to t_2\}, \forall t, t \geq d_0$; $\rho_{itemId}^{itemType}[t] = \{i_1 \to t_1\}, \forall t, d_0 \leq t \leq d_4$ *, and* $\rho_{itemId}^{itemType}[t] = \{i_1 \to t_2\}, \forall t, t \geq d_5$ *(a reclassification occurred at day* d_5). *Assume that in* Time *we have:* $\rho_{day}^{week} = \{d_1 \to w_1, d_2 \to w_1, d_3 \to w_2, d_4 \to w_2, d_5 \to w_2\}$ *(and the rollups from week to All). Finally, we have the following instance for the* Sales *fact table (*Day *is displayed for the sake of clarity, but could have been omitted, like in TSQL2):*

itemId	storeId	day	sales
i_1	s_1	d_1	600
i_2	s_2	d_1	100
i_2	s_1	d_2	100
i_3	s_2	d_2	100
i_3	s_3	d_3	100
i_3	s_4	d_4	100
i_1	s_1	d_5	100

Let us now suppose we are given the query: " list the weekly total sum of sales, by city and item type". As in the example of Section 1, two interpretations could be given to this query. The first one, possibly the most usual one, would expect to get the sum of sales considering the type an item had when it was sold. In this case, for instance, item i_1 *would contribute to the aggregation in the following way: the first three tuples, with a total of 800, will add to the group* $\{t_1, c_1, w_1\}$, *while the last one will contribute to* $\{t_2, c_1, w_2\}$. *The result will be given by the following table:*

itemType	city	week	sales
t_1	c_1	w_1	800
t_2	c_1	w_1	100
t_2	c_2	w_2	200
t_2	c_1	w_2	100

The second interpretation, which is the **only** *one supported by non-temporal systems, would ask for the sum of the sales, considering that each sold item has the* current *type, regardless of the time the sale occurred. The result a user would get under this interpretation is given by the table below, which was computed in the following way: the rollup function for every occurrence of item* i_1 *is set to:* $\rho_{itemId}^{itemType}(i_1) = t_2$. *Thus, all the* i_1 *tuples will contribute to type* t_2. *For instance, the first tuple will now contribute to the group* $\{t_2, c_1, w_1\}$. *In the next Section we present a language*

that lets the user distinguish the two interpretations.

itemType	city	week	sales
t_1	c_1	w_1	200
t_2	c_1	w_1	700
t_2	c_2	w_2	200
t_2	c_1	w_2	100

3 $TOLAP$: A Temporal Multidimensional Query Language

In this section we propose our multidimensional query language $TOLAP$ (standing for Temporal OLAP). We introduce it first by means of examples, and then define its syntax and semantics.

3.1 TOLAP By Example

Let us consider again the set of dimensions $\mathbf{D} = \{Product, Store\}$ from our running example, and the corresponding base fact table named *Sales*, of Example 3. In the *Product* dimension, $\mu = day$. Also assume that there is a fact table $(Price, f_D, price, \mu : month)$, containing the price of each item each month($f_D(t) = \{itemId\}$ for each t).

3.1.1 Simple queries

We begin with queries not involving aggregates.

Example 4 *A query returning the sales for stores in Buenos Aires, on a daily basis, will be expressed in* TOLAP *as:*

```
BASales(p,s,m,t)  ⟵   Sales(p,s,m,t),
                      s  ⟶  city:'BA',
                      t ⟶ month:t₁.
```

In TOLAP, *the query above returns the tuples in* Sales *such that* s *rolls up to BA, where* s *represents an element in the lowest level of the dimension* Store. *This query is expressed in a* point-based *fashion (see Section 3.4 for details).*

We assume a fixed ordering of the attributes in the base fact tables. For instance, in the base fact table *Sales*, the first position from the left will always correspond to dimension *Product*.

3.1.2 Queries with aggregates

In order to address queries involving aggregation, we adapt non-recursive Datalog with aggregate functions [CM90], which, in turn, was based on the approach of Klug's relational calculus with aggregates [Klu82].

Example 5 *Consider the query : "list the total sales per item, region and week," where we want aggregates to be computed using temporally consistent values (i.e., a sale in a given store must be credited to the region that corresponded to that store at the time of the sale).*

$$
\begin{aligned}
\texttt{WS(it,re,w,SUM(m))} \quad &\longleftarrow \quad \texttt{Sales(it,st,m,d),}\\
&\texttt{st} \xrightarrow{mo} \texttt{region:re,}\\
&\texttt{d} \longrightarrow \texttt{month:mo,}\\
&\texttt{d} \longrightarrow \texttt{week:w.}
\end{aligned}
$$

Note that although in Example 5 we made explicit the rollup between the time granularity of the *Sales* and *Store* dimension, (i.e. *day* and *month*), this could be easily avoided, allowing a limited form of "schema independence", as in Schemalog or SchemaSQL. Later examples show the use of variables that range over level names, pushing this independence farther.

Example 6 *We now introduce descriptive attributes of dimension levels. Suppose we want the total sales by store and brand, for stores with more than ninety employees. Assume that level* storeId *is described by an attribute* nbrEmp.

$$
\begin{aligned}
\texttt{SB(br,st,SUM(m))} \quad &\longleftarrow \quad \texttt{Sales(i,s,m,t),}\\
&\texttt{i} \xrightarrow{t} \texttt{brand:br,}\\
&\texttt{t} \longrightarrow \texttt{month:mo,}\\
&\texttt{s} \xrightarrow{mo} \texttt{storeId:st,}\\
&\texttt{s.nbrEmp} \geq \texttt{90.}
\end{aligned}
$$

3.1.3 Metaqueries

We would also like to query the system about the rollup functions themselves, regardless of the facts. Some examples of these kinds of queries are:

- *"Give me the time instants at which store s_1 belonged to the Southern region"*, expressed as:

$$
\begin{aligned}
\texttt{StoreTime(t)} \quad &\longleftarrow \quad \texttt{Store:storeId:`}s_1\texttt{'}\\
&\xrightarrow{t} \texttt{region:`Southern'.}
\end{aligned}
$$

  Note that we must specify the name of the dimension in the atom `Store:storeId:`s_1`'`, because there is no fact table in the body of the rule to bind `s`.

- *"Were products categorized by brands two years ago?"* (this is the query of example (b) of Subsection 1.3).

$$
\texttt{ProdBrand()} \longleftarrow \texttt{Product:X:x} \xrightarrow{1/1/98} \texttt{brand:y.}
$$

  In this example, X is a variable over level names. The expression above means that if any element, in any level in the *Product* dimension rolled up to

an element in level *brand* at the required date, the answer to the query will be '*yes*'.

3.2 Data Warehouse Evolution in $TOLAP$

According to the definitions of Section 2, our model supports evolution of the schema over time (in temporal database terminology, this is called *schema versioning* or *schema evolution*. For instance, suppose in our running example that the bottom level of the *Store* dimension in Figure 1 was, initially *city*, and that, at time d_5, *storeId* was inserted below it. A fact table with attributes *itemId,city, sales,day* is in effect before d_5. After the update, the fact table attributes will be: *itemId,storeId, sales,* and *day*. In $TOLAP$, if an element was not defined at a given instant, it will not contribute to the result. For instance, given the query *"list the total sum of sales by brand and storeId"*, we have:

$$
\begin{aligned}
\texttt{SB(br,st,SUM(m))} \quad &\longleftarrow \quad \texttt{Sales(i,s,m,t),}\\
&\texttt{i} \xrightarrow{t} \texttt{brand:br,}\\
&\texttt{t} \longrightarrow \texttt{month:mo,}\\
&\texttt{s} \xrightarrow{mo} \texttt{storeId:st.}
\end{aligned}
$$

The expression $\texttt{s} \xrightarrow{mo} \texttt{storeId:st}$ means that if an element in any level, which was once a component of a base fact table, rolled up to level *storeId* at time *mo*, it contributes to the aggregation. Thus, the sales made before the month corresponding to d_5 will not contribute to the aggregation in the head (condition $\texttt{s} \xrightarrow{mo} \texttt{storeId:st}$ will not be satisfied). Analogously, a query like *"total sales by store and itemId"* would return exactly the instance of the second fact table above.

Finally, suppose that at time d_9, level *brand* is deleted from the dimension *Product*. The remaining levels would be *itemId,*(bottom level), *itemType, company,* and *All*. The query *"total sales by brand and region"* would read in $TOLAP$:

$$
\begin{aligned}
\texttt{BR(br,reg,SUM(m))} \quad &\longleftarrow \quad \texttt{Sales(i,s,m,t),}\\
&\texttt{i} \xrightarrow{t} \texttt{brand:br,}\\
&\texttt{t} \longrightarrow \texttt{month:mo,}\\
&\texttt{s} \xrightarrow{mo} \texttt{region:reg.}
\end{aligned}
$$

Any sale taking after d_9 will not be considered, as *brand* is not a level of the dimension any more.

3.3 Syntax

In this section we will formally define the syntax of a $TOLAP$ rule. We will first give some definitions which will be used below, and then formalize the concepts introduced in the previous section.

3.3.1 Preliminary definitions

Given a set T, and a discrete linear order $<$, with no endpoints, we define a *point based temporal domain* as the structure $T_P = (T, <)$. Analogously, given $T_P = (T, <)$, we define the set $I(T) = \{(a, b) | a \leq b, a, b \in T \cup \{-\infty, +\infty\}\}$, and let us denote as θ as the set of the usual interval comparison operators. Then, $T_I = (I(T), \theta)$ is an *Interval-based Temporal Domain* corresponding to T_P. These domains will are denoted *Temporal Domains*, and allow us to define the *abstract* and *concrete* rollup functions [Tom97]. We will define the rollup functions over T_P.

3.3.2 Atoms, Terms, Rules, and Programs

Assume $\mathbf{B_s}(\mathbf{D_s}, \mathbf{F_s})$, and $I(\mathbf{B})$ are a multidimensional database schema and instance, respectively, as defined in Section 2. Let $\mathbf{V_L}$ and $\mathbf{V_D}$ be a set of level and data variables, respectively. We have also the sets $\mathbf{C_L}$ and $\mathbf{C_D}$ of level and data constants, respectively. Let $\mathbf{P}$ be a set of intensional and extensional predicate symbols, and $\mathbf{F_F}$ is a set of aggregate function names.

Definition 6 (Terms) *(a) A* data term *is either a variable in* $\mathbf{V_D}$ *or a constant in* $\mathbf{C_D}$*; (b) a* rollup term *is an expression of the form* d:X:x, X:x *or* x, *where* X *is a level name variable in* $\mathbf{V_L}$ *or constant in* $\mathbf{C_L}$*,* x *is a data term, and* d *is a constant in* $\mathbf{C_L}$*; (c) a* descriptive term *is an expression of the form* x.a *where* x *and* a *are data terms (d) an* aggregate term *is an expression of the form* f(d) *s.t.* f *is a function name in* $\mathbf{F_F}$*. A* term *is a data, rollup, descriptive or aggregate* term.

Definition 7 (Atoms) *(a) A* fact atom *is an expression of the form* F(X_1, ..., X_n, M, t)*, where* F *is a fact table in* $\mathbf{F_s}$*, and* X_1, ..., X_n, M *and* t *are data terms; a* rollup atom *is an expression of the form* $X \xrightarrow{t} Y$*, or* $X \longrightarrow Y$*, where* X *and* Y *are rollup terms, and* t *is a data term; (c) a* descriptive atom *is an expression of the form* $x \stackrel{t}{=} y$*, where* x *is a descriptive term, and* y *and* t *are data terms; (d) an* aggregate atom *is of the form* Q(R, ..., Z) *s.t.* $Q \in \mathbf{P}$*, and* R, ..., Z *are data terms s.t. at least one is an aggregate term; (e) an expression* $t_1 \theta t_2$*, where* t_1 *and* t_2 *are data terms, and* θ *is one of* $\{<, =\}$*, is a* constraint atom*; (f) if* $g : N \times .. \times N \rightarrow N$ *is a scalar function,* $g(n_1, ... n_m)$*, where* n_i *are data terms, is a* scalar atom*; (g) an* intensional(extensional) atom *is an expression of the form* p (X, .., Z) *where* X, Y, Z *are data terms, and* p *is an intensional(extensional) predicate symbol.*

An atom is a fact, rollup, descriptive, aggregate, constraint, scalar, intensional or extensional atom. An expression $\neg t_1$*, where* t_1 *is an atom, is a* negated atom.

Definition 8 *(TOLAP rules) A* TOLAP-rule *is a formula of the form* $A \longleftarrow A_1, A_2, ... A_n$*, where* A *is an intensional(possibly aggregate) positive atom, and* A_i*,* $i = 1...n$ *are non-aggregate atoms. A TOLAP rule* Γ *satisfies the following conditions: (a) If a variable appears in the head of the rule, it must also appear in its*

body; (b) every position in a fact atom corresponds to the same dimension, with the rightmost position corresponding allways to the Time dimension. (c) for every level/data variable v, all the rollup terms where v appears are associated to the same dimension; (d) if there is an aggregate atom Q(a_1, ..., a_n) in the head of the rule, for all atoms in the body, of the form $d:X:x \xrightarrow{t} y : a_i$, $d:X:x \longrightarrow y : a_i$, or $x.y \stackrel{t}{=} a_i$, y is a constant data term; (e) if x.a is in the body of Γ, at least one rollup term in the body is of the form d:X:x, X:x or x; (f) every variable which appears in a negated, constraint or predicate atom in the body of a rule, must also appear in a positive rollup or fact atom. A TOLAP Program is a finite set of TOLAP-rules.

From the rules above, it follows that there is a function, call it dim*, that maps each data variable* x *to a unique dimension* dim(x)*, and each level variable* X *to a unique dimension* dim(X)*. Furthermore, there is a function* level*, that maps each instant* t *to a unique level* level(x, t) *of the dimension* dim(x)*, and to a unique level* level(X, t) *of the dimension* dim(X)*.*

3.4 Semantics

We will use point-based semantics [Tom95] for the rollup functions. This means, for instance, that in a dimension such as *Store* of our running example, a value of a rollup function, say, $\text{storeId:s} \xrightarrow{mo} \text{city:c}$, exists for each month.

Let us assume that for each dimension instance we have a pair of relations, call them $\mathcal{R_D}$ and $\mathcal{D_D}$, representing the sets *TRUP* and *TDESC* of Definition 2, respectively. The multidimensional database is defined over three different domains: $\mathcal{D}$, N, T_P, where variables ranging over $\mathcal{D}$ belong to an uninterpreted sort, the ones ranging over N belong to an interpreted sort (numeric), and the temporal variables range over T_P, defined in 3.3.1.

A *valuation* θ for a *TOLAP* rule Γ, is a tuple (θ_s, θ_I), where θ_s is called a *schema valuation*, and θ_I is an *instance valuation*. Valuation θ_s maps the level and attribute variables in Γ to level and attribute names in $\mathbf{B_s}$, while θ_I maps domain variables to values in $I(\mathbf{B})$.

Definition 9 *A* schema valuation *for a rule* Γ*, denoted* $\theta_s(\Gamma)$ *maps level and attribute variables in the atoms of* Γ *as follows: (a) given a rollup atom of the form* $d:X:x \xrightarrow{t} Y:y$*,* θ_s *maps* d *to a dimension name in* $\mathbf{D}_s$*,* t *to a value* $w \in T_P$*, and* X *and* Y *to a pair of values* v, u *s.t.* $v \preceq_w^* u$ *holds in* $d \in \mathbf{D}_s$*; (b) if the rollup atom is of the form* $X:x \xrightarrow{t} Y:y$*,,* θ_s *maps* t *to a value* $w \in T_P$*, and* X *and* Y *to a pair of values* v, u *s.t.* $v \preceq_w^* u$ *holds in* dim(X) $\in \mathbf{D}_s$*; (c) if the rollup atom is of the form* $x \xrightarrow{t} Y:y$*,,* θ_s *maps* t *to a value* $w \in T_P$*, and* Y *to a value* u *s.t.* level(x, w) $\preceq_w^* u$ *holds in* dim(x) $\in \mathbf{D}_s$*; (d) for the rollup atoms of the form*

$X:x \longrightarrow Y:y$, θ_s *maps* X *and* Y *to dimension levels in* $\dim(X)$ *s.t.* v, u *s.t.* $v \preceq^* u$ *holds in* $\dim(X)$; *(e) given a descriptive atom of the form* $x.A \doteq y$, θ_s *maps* t *to a value* $w \in T_P$, *and* A *to an attribute name* $u \in \mathbf{A}$, *s.t.* $u \gg_t \texttt{level(x,w)}$ *in* $\dim(x) \in \mathbf{D}_s$;

Given a rule schema valuation $\theta_s(\Gamma)$ *for a rule* Γ, *an instance valuation is a function* θ_I *s.t.(a) it maps the domain variables* x *and* y *in the rollup atoms defined above, to values in* $\mathcal{R}_\mathcal{D}$ *over levels defined by* θ_s; *(b)* θ_I *maps variable* x *in the descriptive atoms defined as above, to values in* $\mathcal{D}_\mathcal{D}$, *over levels defined by* θ_s; *(c)* θ_I *maps a fact atom* $F(x_1, .., x_n, M, t)$ *as follows: F is mapped to a fact table name in* $\mathbf{F_s}$, *the rightmost term* t *in F, to a value* $w \in T_P$, *each domain variable* x_i *in F to a value in* $dom(\texttt{level(x}_i\texttt{,w)})$, *and the data term* M *in F to a value in* N.

A constraint atom $x \ \{<, =\} \ y$ *evaluates to true whenever* $\theta_I(x) \ \{<, =\} \ \theta_I(y)$. *A negated atom is evaluated using the Close World Assumption. Thus,* $\neg(\ x \stackrel{t}{\longrightarrow} Y:y \ )$ *is true if, given a valuation* θ *s.t.* $\theta(x) = u$, $\theta(t) = w$, $\theta(Y) = l$, *and* $\theta(y) = v$, *then it does not exist a rollup in* $\dim(x)$ *s.t.* $\rho^l_{\texttt{level(x,w)}}[w](u) = v$. *Predicate and function symbols are valuated as in standard datalog.*

Let AGG be the set of aggregate functions, with extension $AGG = \{MIN, MAX, COUNT, SUM\}$, and r a relation. The *aggregate operation* [CM90] $\gamma_{f\ A(X)}(r)$ is the relation

$$\gamma_{f\ A(X)}(r) = \{t \ : \ t \text{ is an XA-tuple}, t[X] \in \pi_X(r), t[A] = f_A(\sigma_{X=t[X]}(r))\},$$

over XA, s.t. $XA \in schema(r), f \in AGG$, and $f_A(r)$ denotes the aggregation of the values in $t[A], t \in r$, using f. Thus, we can now define the semantics of a $TOLAP$ rule Γ of the form $Q(a_1, a_2, \ldots, a_n, AGG(m))$ $\longleftarrow A_1, \ldots, A_m$ as follows: For each level or data variable v_i in the body of Γ, and for a valuation θ of the variables in the rule's body, we have:

$$r_\Gamma = \{< \theta(v_1), \ldots, \theta(v_n) > | \theta \text{ is a valuation of } \Gamma\}.$$
Then
$$Q = \gamma_{AGG_m(a_1, \ldots, a_n)}(r_\Gamma).$$

3.5 Expressive power

In this section we study, somewhat informally, $TOLAP$'s expressive power. We also define an extension to $TOLAP$ which will let us express queries like the fourth one of Section 1.3, which cannot be expressed in basic $TOLAP$.

3.5.1 What can be expressed in $TOLAP$?

Intuitively, it is not hard to see that $TOLAP$ has at least the power of first-order query languages with aggregation. However, in a sense it goes beyond this class. Note that in our data model, only the direct rollups are stored, and their indirect consequences are

left implicit. Thus, to evaluate a rollup atom like $d:X:x \stackrel{t}{\longrightarrow} Y:y$, we effectively need to compute the transitive closure of the rollup functions for dimension d. It is well-known that this cannot be done in first-order, even after adding aggregate functions [LW97]. However, as long as the dimension schema is fixed, this computation can be done in first order, because for a fixed schema, the number of joins needed to transitively close the rollup functions is known in advance.

Not only the structure of a dimension is subject to updates. There are common real-life situations in which the instance of a dimension may be modified in a non-trivial fashion. Suppose for instance, a company considers some country as divided into four regions, *north, south, east, west,* in order to assign representatives; at some time, it is decided that the northern region should be divided into two or more, for any given business reason. We call this change a *split*. As another example, several airlines could become a single one as a result of a corporate fusion, a common situation nowadays. We call this action a *merge* of elements.

Let us suppose the query *"total sales per item and region, using only the currently existing regions(or their descendants)"*. This query cannot be expressed in $TOLAP$. To show this, suppose a region r is split into r_1 and r_2. After that, r_1 is merged with another region r_4. In the meantime, maybe some region could have been deleted. With the tools defined so far, we could not find the "descendants" of r . There are two reasons for this: (a) so far, the model does not keep track of splits and merges, which can be solved by adding such information to the model, which we will do shortly; (b) this, is, again, a transitive closure problem, even if the schema remains fixed, so the extended language we define below is in some sense harder to evaluate than the basic one.

3.5.2 Extending $TOLAP$

We extend $TOLAP$ in order to be able to express the class of queries exemplified above. First, we add two predicates to the data model introduced in Section 2: $split(x, y, L, t)$ and $merged(x, y, L, t)$, with the following meanings: (a) $split(x, y, L, t)$ is true if the element x in level L was split at time t, and y is one of the elements resulting from this splitting; (b) $merged(x, y, L, t)$ is *true* if element x in level L was merged into element y at time t; these are *event* predicates, in the temporal database sense. The formal meaning of these predicates depends on the specification of the update operators *split* and *merge*, given in [HMV99b].

Using the *split* and *merged* predicates, we add to the syntax of $TOLAP$ defined in Section 3.3.2 a new kind of atom, $d : L_1 : x \stackrel{t_1}{\longrightarrow} L_2(t_2) : y$. The valuation of this atom proceeds as in Section 3.4. The interpretation is as follows: the atom evaluates to *True* whenever y

is the element in level L_2 in dimension **d**, to which an element **x** in level L_1 rolled up at time t_2, given that **y** is a successor(if $t_2 > t_1$) or predecessor (if $t_1 > t_2$) of an element **z** in L_2, s.t. **x** rolled up to **z** at time t_1.

In order to clarify the meaning of the expression $\mathbf{d} : \mathbf{L_1} : \mathbf{x} \xrightarrow{t_1} \mathbf{L_2(t_2)} : \mathbf{y}$ let us explain it in terms of datalog with stratified negation expressions. Let us define a predicate $shift(x, y, L, t)$ as follows:

$$
\begin{aligned}
\mathtt{shift(x,y,L,t)} &\longleftarrow \mathtt{split(x,y,L,t).} \\
\mathtt{shift(x,y,L,t)} &\longleftarrow \mathtt{merged(x,y,L,t).} \\
\mathtt{shift(x,y,L,t_2)} &\longleftarrow \mathtt{shift(x,z,L,t_1),} \\
&\qquad \mathtt{merged(z,y,L,t_2), t_2 > t_1.} \\
\mathtt{shift(x,y,L,t_2)} &\longleftarrow \mathtt{shift(x,z,L,t_1),} \\
&\qquad \mathtt{split(z,y,L,t_2), t_2 > t_1.}
\end{aligned}
$$

From predicate *shift* we derive another one, called $shiftPers(x, y, L, t)$, which extends the validity of the *split* or *merge*, to every instant t between updates For instance, if $shift(r, r_1, L, 10)$ and $shift(r_1, r_2, L, 13)$ hold, then, $shiftPers(r, r_1, L, 11)$ and $shiftPers(r, r_1, L, 12)$ also hold. This has been called *Persistence* [BWJ98]. Thus:

$$
\begin{aligned}
\mathtt{shiftPers(x,y,L,t)} &\longleftarrow \mathtt{shift(x,y,L,t).} \\
\mathtt{shiftPers(x,y,L,s(t))} &\longleftarrow \mathtt{shiftPers(x,y,L,t),} \\
&\qquad \mathtt{\neg shift(y,y_1,L,s(t)),} \\
&\qquad \mathtt{y \neq y_1, s(t) \leq} Now, \\
&\qquad \mathtt{\neg deleted(y,L,s(t)).} \\
\mathtt{shiftPers(x,y,L,s(t))} &\longleftarrow \mathtt{shiftPers(x,y,L,t_1),} \\
&\qquad \mathtt{deleted(y,L,t_1),} \\
&\qquad \mathtt{\neg inserted(y,L,t_2),} \\
&\qquad \mathtt{inserted(Y,L,t),} \\
&\qquad \mathtt{t_1 < t_2, t_2 < t.}
\end{aligned}
$$

Here, $s(t)$ stands for the successor of t. Predicates $deleted(y, L, t)$ and $inserted(y, L, t)$ represent the deletion of an element y from a level L containing it, or the insertion of an element into a level, respectively, and can be derived from the available data.

Now, we can define the meaning of $L_1 : x \xrightarrow{t_1} L_2(t_2) : y$ by means of the following datalog rules:

$$
\begin{aligned}
\mathtt{L_1 : x \xrightarrow{t_1} L_2(t_2) : y} &\longleftarrow \mathtt{L_1 : x \xrightarrow{t_1} L_2 : y,} \\
&\qquad \mathtt{L_1 : x \xrightarrow{t_2} L_2 : y.} \\
\mathtt{L_1 : x \xrightarrow{t_1} L_2(t_2) : y} &\longleftarrow \mathtt{L_1 : x \xrightarrow{t_1} L_2 : z,} \\
&\qquad \mathtt{L_1 : x \xrightarrow{t_2} L_2 : y,} \\
&\qquad \mathtt{shiftPers(z,y,L,t_2).} \\
\mathtt{L_1 : x \xrightarrow{t_1} L_2(t_2) : y} &\longleftarrow \mathtt{L_1 : x \xrightarrow{t_1} L_2 : z,} \\
&\qquad \mathtt{L_1 : x \xrightarrow{t_2} L_2 : y,} \\
&\qquad \mathtt{shiftPers(y,z,L,t_2).}
\end{aligned}
$$

We will denote this extension of $TOLAP$ as $TOLAP^+$. The meaning of a $TOLAP^+$ query is analogous to the meaning of a $TOLAP$ one. Now, we can express the query *"total sales per item and region, using only the currently existing regions"*, as:

$$
\begin{aligned}
\mathtt{IR(p,r,SUM(s))} \quad \longleftarrow \quad &\mathtt{Sales(p,st,s,t),} \\
&\mathtt{t \rightarrow month:mo,} \\
&\mathtt{st \xrightarrow{mo} reg(}Now\mathtt{):r.}
\end{aligned}
$$

In order to make things more clear, suppose that a sale such as $(p_1, s_1, 30, 10)$ occurred, and also suppose that at instant "1" store s_1 belonged to region r_2 which no longer exists at time "10", because it was split into r_{21} and r_{22}. After a series of updates(including the deletion of r_{21} and r_{22}), store s_1 currently belongs to region r_5. According to the semantics defined above, this sale will not contribute to the query result, because r_5 is not a descendant of r_1. However, if the rollup $\mathtt{st \xrightarrow{mo} reg(}Now\mathtt{):r}$ were replaced by $\mathtt{st \xrightarrow{Now} reg:r}$, the sale in question would be included in the aggregation. If we wanted this to occur, we must have asked for the *"total sales per item and region, using the current rollups from stores to regions"*, which can also be expressed in $TOLAP$.

4 Implementation

$TOLAP$ could be implemented in at least two different ways: (a) translating $TOLAP$ queries to SQL, or (b) using a temporal query language like TSQL2 [Sno95]. To make these ideas concrete, we use a data structure that encodes the dimensions into one schema relation and a set of instance relations. The schema relation describes all the dimensions in the data warehouse, with structure: $(Dimension, upLevel, loLevel, From, To)$, where $loLevel \preceq_{(From,To)} upLevel$. Although there is one instance relation for each dimension instance, two approaches can be followed: in the first one, the instance relation has the form $(upLevel, loLevel, upVal, loVal, From, To)$, where $\rho^{upLevel}_{loLevel}[(From, To)](loVal) = upVal$. In the second approach, which we will call the "denormalized" representation, a dimension instance is stored as relation with a column for each dimension level, plus two columns $From, To$. This relation is updated every time a dimension update occurs, either at schema or instance level. In this way, the transitive closure of an instance is stored in a single tuple, which allows a more appropriate implementation of the rollup functions.

4.1 Translation into SQL.

The first alternative we analize consists in translating $TOLAP$ queries to SQL, using the data structure defined above. The following example will show that even simple $TOLAP$ queries can have non-trival SQL translations.

Suppose that in our running data warehouse, level *itemId* was deleted from the *Product* dimension at a certain time, causing the fact table schema to change. After that update, the query *"total sales by brand, region and month"* is issued . In $TOLAP$ this query would read:

$$BRM(b,r,mo,SUM(m)) \longleftarrow Sales(it,st,m,t),$$
$$it \xrightarrow{t} brand:b,$$
$$st \xrightarrow{mo} region:r,$$
$$t \longrightarrow month:mo.$$

This *TOLAP* query will yield the following SQL code:

```
SELECT T.month,P.upVal,S2.upVal,SUM(sales)
FROM Sales_1 S, Products P , Store S1,Store S2,
Time T
WHERE S.itemId = P.loVal AND P.loLevel = 'itemId' AND
  P.upLevel = 'brand' AND S.storeId = S1.loVal
  AND S1.loLevel = 'storeId' AND S1.upLevel='city'
  AND S1.upLevel = S2.loLevel
  AND S1.upVal = S2.loVal AND S2.upLevel = 'region'
  AND T.day = S.day AND P.From <= S.day
  AND S.day <= P.To AND S1.From <= T.month
  AND T.month <= S1.To AND S2.From <= T.month
  AND T.month <= S2.To
GROUP BY T.month,P.upVal,S2,upVal
UNION
SELECT T.month,P.loVal,S2.upVal,SUM(sales)
FROM Sales_2 S, Products P , Store S1, Store
S2, Time T
WHERE S.brand = P.loVal AND P.loLevel = 'brand'    AND
S.storeId = S1.loVal AND S1.loLevel = 'storeId'
  AND S1.upLevel='city' AND S1.upVal = S2.loVal
  AND S1.upLevel = S2.loLevel
  AND S2.upLevel = 'region'
  AND T.day = S.day AND P.From <= S.day
  AND S.day <= P.To AND S1.From <= T.month
  AND T.month <= S1.To AND S2.From <= T.month
  AND T.month <= S2.To
GROUP BY T.month,P.loVal,S2.upVal
```

The consequences of the update in the generated query, are shown in italics in the **WHERE** clause. The attribute *P.loVal* in the second SELECT clause is needed because, after the update, *brand* became the bottom level of the dimension, being also one of the aggregation levels. Also note that the composition between levels *storeId* and *region* must be preformed explicitly.

Implementing the "denormalized" alternative delivers a better performance, at the expense of a more sophisticated update procedure. Here, instead of the *level,value* pairs, each column stores the corresponding values for the level it represents. Thus, the query above generates the following SQL code:

```
SELECT T.month,P.brand,S1.region,SUM(sales)
FROM Sales_1 S, Products P , Store S1, Time T
WHERE S.itemId = P.itemId
  AND S.storeId = S1.storeId
  AND T.day = S.day AND P.From <= S.day
```

```
  AND S.day <= P.To AND S1.From <= T.month
  AND T.month <= S1.To
GROUP BY T.month,P.brand,S1.region
UNION
SELECT T.month,P.brand,S1.region,SUM(sales)
FROM Sales_2 S, Products P , Store S1, , Time T
WHERE S.brand = P.brand
  AND S.storeId = S1.storeId
  AND T.day = S.day AND P.From <= S.day
  AND S.day <= P.To AND S1.From <= T.month
  AND T.month <= S1.To
GROUP BY T.month,P.brand,S1.region
```

4.2 Translation into TSQL2

Translating *TOLAP* into TSQL2 seems to be a natural choice, as we can avoid much of the explicit time manipulation, and the generated queries are simpler than their SQL equivalents. However, the translator must deal with the CAST, VALID, and other TSQL2 clauses. For instance, the first term of the query of Subsection 4.1 will look like:

```
SELECT VALID CAST (VALID(S) AS MONTH),P.upVal,
S2.upVal,SUM(sales)
FROM Sales_1 S, Products P , Stores S1, Stores
S2, Time T
WHERE S.ItemId = P.loVal AND S1.loLevel = 'storeId'
  AND P.loLevel = 'itemId' AND P.upLevel = 'Brand'
  AND S.storeId = S1.loVal AND S1.upVal = S2.loVal
  AND S2.upLevel = 'region' AND S1.upLevel='city'
  AND S1.upLevel = S2.loLevel
GROUP BY VALID(S) USING 1 MONTH ,P.upVal, S2.upVal
```

We are currently implementing *TOLAP* at the University of Buenos Aires. We choose the "denormalized" implementation presented in Subsection 4.1, based on the results of early tests performed over prototypes. We have also developed a visual interface which allows the user to visually browse the schema and instance of the dimensions in a multidimensional database, at any given instant . The screen is split into two windows. On the left one, the user browses the different schemas which the dimension goes through over time. In the right window, a tree-view of the rollup fuctions is displayed, synchronized with what is displayed in the other window. A bar in the lower part of the screen shows the validity intervals for these schemas and instances. We are developing using Java , connecting to an Oracle 8 database via JDBC drivers. The figures included in the Appendix will give the reader a better idea about the interface described above

5 Conclusion

We presented a temporal model for multidimensional OLAP, motivated by the observation that ignoring temporal issues leads to impoverished expressive power and questionable query semantics in many real-life scenarios. Our model supports changes both in the instances and in the structure of OLAP dimensions, supporting schema evolution. We also proposed *TOLAP*, a language that supports the model, allowing the expression of *temporal OLAP queries* in an elegant and intuitive fashion. We studied the expressive power of *TOLAP* and introduced an extension that allows transitive closure queries. Finally, we suggested how to translate a *TOLAP* query to different SQL dialects.

Although we presented *TOLAP* using a ruled-based framework, it is straightforward to translate it to an SQL-style if it is considered more expedient. For instance, the query we used as an example in Section 4 could be written as follows.

```
SELECT br, reg, m,SUM(S.sales)
FROM Sales S, Products P , Store ST, Time T
WHERE P.RUP(S.1,Brand,br)
    AND ST.RUP(S.2,Region,reg)
    AND T.RUP(S.time,Month,m).
```

Acknowledgements

This work was partially supported by the Institute of Robotics and Intelligent Systems, the Natural Sciences and Engineering Research Council, and the University of Buenos Aires.

References

[BSSJ98] R. Bliujute, S. Saltenis, G. Slivinskas, and G. Jensen. Systematic change management in dimensional data warehousing. *Time Center Technical Report TR-23*, 1998.

[BWJ98] R. Bettini, S. Wang, and S. Jajodia. Semantic assumptions and their use in databases. *IEEE Transactions on Knowledge and Data Engineering*, 1998.

[CKW89] W. Chen, M. Kifer, and D. S. Warren. Hilog as a platform for database language. In *Proceedings of the 2nd. International Workshop on Database Programming Languages*, pages 315–329, Oregon Coast,Oregon,USA, 1989.

[CM90] M. Consens and A.O. Mendelzon. Low complexity aggregation in Graphlog and Datalog. In *Proceedings of the 3rd International Conference on Database Theory, Lecture Notes in Computer Science n.470*, pages 379–394, 1990.

[CT98] L. Cabibbo and R. Torlone. A logical approach to multidimensional databases. In *EDBT'98: 6th International Conference on Extending Database Technology*, pages 253–269, Valencia, Spain, 1998.

[HMV99a] C. Hurtado, A.O. Mendelzon, and A. Vaisman. Maintaining data cubes under dimension updates. *Proceedings of IEEE/ICDE'99*, 1999.

[HMV99b] C. Hurtado, A.O. Mendelzon, and A. Vaisman. Updating OLAP dimensions. *Proceedings of ACM DOLAP'99*, 1999.

[Kim96] R. Kimball. *The Data Warehouse Toolkit.* J.Wiley and Sons, Inc, 1996.

[Klu82] A. Klug. Equivalence of relational algebra and relational calculus query languages having aggregate functions. *Journal of ACM, p.699-717*, 1982.

[Leh98] W. Lehner. Modeling large OLAP scenarios. In *Proceedings of the 1998 International Conference on Extending Database Technology*, Valencia, Spain, 1998.

[LSS97] L.V.S Lakshmanan, F. Sadri, and I.N. Subramanian. Logic and algebraic languages for interoperability in multidatabase systems. *Journal of Logic Programming 33(2),pp.101-149*, 1997.

[LW97] L. Libkin and L. Wong. On the power of aggregation in relational query languages. In *Database Programming Languages(DBPL'97)*, pages 270–280, 1997.

[PJ99] T.B Pedersen and C. Jensen. Multidimensional data modeling for complex data. *Proceedings of IEEE/ICDE'99*, 1999.

[Sno95] Richard Snodgrass. *The TSQL2 Temporal Query Language.* Kluwer Academic Publishers, 1995.

[Tom95] D. Toman. Point-based vs. interval-based temporal query languages. In *Proceedings of the ACM - PODS Conference*, 1995.

[Tom97] D. Toman. A point-based temporal extension to sql. In *Proceedings of DOOD'97*, Montreaux, Switzerland, 1997.

[YW98] J. Yang and J. Widom. Maintaining temporal views over non-temporal information sources for data warehousing. In *Proceedings of the Sixth International Conference on Extending Database Technology*, Valencia, Spain, 1998.

[YW00] J. Yang and J. Widom. Temporal view self-maintenance in a warehousing environment. *To appear in Proceedings of the Seventh International Conference on Extending Database Technology*, 2000.

Here we show an example of our graphic interface. The left window shows a dimension schema for *Product*, with levels *Brand, Category* and *ItemId*. The window on the right displays the rollup functions, and the instance set of the highlighted level.

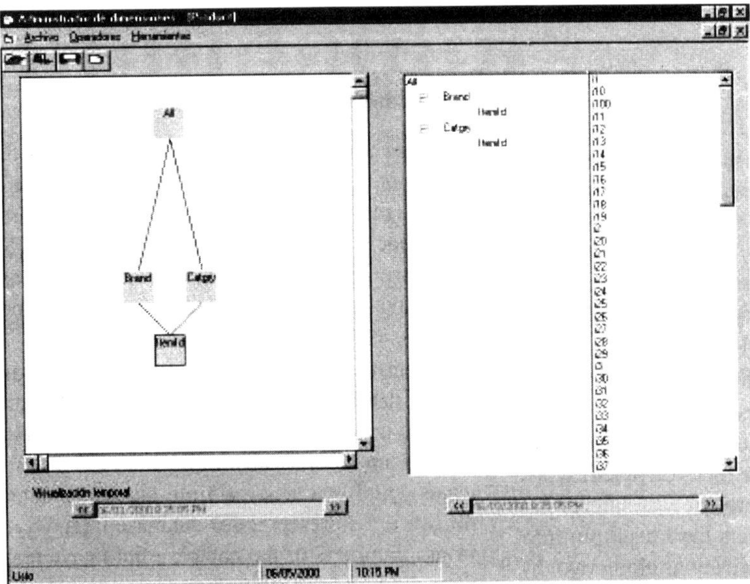

The figure below displays the dimension after a series of updates. We can see how the instances displayed in the right window change according to the schema. The bars on the lower part of the screen allow browsing through time.

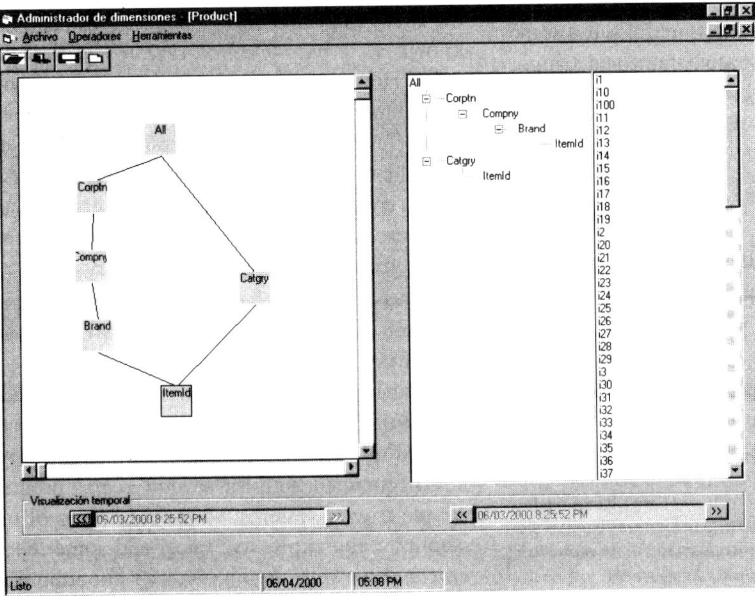

Practical Applications of Triggers and Constraints:
Successes and Lingering Issues

Stefano Ceri*

Politecnico di Milano
ceri@ipmel2.elet.polimi.it

Roberta J. Cochrane

IBM Almaden Research Center
bobbiec@almaden.ibm.com

Jennifer Widom[†]

Stanford University
widom@cs.stanford.edu

1 Introduction

From about the mid-1980's to the mid-1990's there was a flurry of research activity in the area of database triggers and constraints, seeing the development of numerous research proposals and prototypes. Soon thereafter, most mainstream database products ramped up their support for constraints and triggers, with expressive constraint specifications appearing in the SQL-92 standard, and both constraints and triggers in the SQL-99 standard.

We briefly review the emergence of research in constraints and triggers, and we briefly describe standards and current commercial support. We then focus on practical applications of triggers. We describe a variety of interesting and significant ways in which triggers have been put into practice, and we classify trigger applications along two dimensions: *handcrafted* versus *generated*, and *kernel DBMS* versus *DBMS services* versus *external applications*. We also argue that a significant portion of these trigger applications are in fact nothing more than *constraint-maintainers* for various classes of integrity constraints, indicating that our work a decade ago [CW90]—if not itself put into practice directly—was not far off the mark. Finally, we analyze the evolution of trigger applications and discuss some lingering shortcomings in database constraint and trigger systems.

2 Brief Research History

We begin with a very brief description of the emergence and development of constraints and triggers as research topics within the database field.

*Supported in part by the EC under grant P28771 W3I3

†Supported in part by the NSF under grant IIS-9811947

Proceedings of the 26th VLDB Conference,
Cairo, Egypt, 2000.

2.1 Constraints

The idea of *integrity constraints* in relational databases appeared not long after the relational model itself, with several foundational papers in 1975 (the year of the first VLDB conference, incidentally) [EC75, HM75, Sto75]. After this initial work within the research community, database products have steadily provided increasing support for constraints, as discussed in Section 3.1 below.

Integrity constraints also have provided tremendous fodder for database research—we will certainly not attempt to provide a survey here. Suffice it to say that because constraints are theoretically well-grounded (as Boolean predicates), and at the same time are of great practical significance (as preservers of database integrity), researchers from all corners of the database field have made contributions ranging from deep theorems to significant systems.

2.2 Triggers

Shortly after researchers recognized the importance of database integrity constraints, including automatic "reactions" to constraint violations, the idea expanded to the more general concept of *triggers* [Esw76], also now known as *event-condition-action* (*ECA*) *rules* or *active rules*. However, triggers as a research field—or as a feature of commercial database systems for that matter—did not take off nearly as quickly as constraints. One can speculate as to the underlying reasons for the delay; our hunch is that triggers were not as in demand by database users, and as a research topic triggers are not nearly as well-defined or easily grounded as integrity constraints.

It was not until the mid-to-late 1980's that the area of triggers, by then referred to as *active database systems*, truly came alive, and it did so with gusto. A number of significant research efforts were launched, and in the early 1990's there was little doubt that active databases were considered one of the "hot topics" in database research. Interest remained high for several years: products launched simple trigger systems while researchers prototyped more elaborate and expressive ones, and some theoretical work emerged as well. Again, we will not attempt to provide a survey, but we refer the reader to [WC96] for a snapshot of the field in the mid-1990's.

3 Standards and Products

Let us now briefly examine how constraints and triggers have developed in commercial database products, and discuss their standardization. We will go into a bit more depth than in Section 2 since the core topic of this paper is applications built within or upon commercial support, but again, we are not attempting to provide a comprehensive survey or tutorial.

3.1 Constraints

The SQL-92 (and subsequent SQL-99) standard provides several mechanisms for specifying integrity constraints. The most common kinds of constraints—*keys*, *non-null constraints*, and *referential integrity*—each have their own syntax and enforcement mechanisms [UW97]. Of interest in relationship to triggers is the fact that referential integrity constraints can be specified with particular actions to be taken upon violations, such as *cascaded delete* or *set null*.

The more general *check* constraints are associated with a given database table. SQL-like syntax is used to specify conditions that must hold for each tuple of the table, and the conditions are checked on inserts and updates to the table. Although the SQL-92 standard permits subqueries within *check* constraints, thereby enabling *check* constraints to be used for multi-tuple and multi-table constraints, most products do not support this feature. General constraints that are not specific to a single table can be specified by SQL-92 *assertions*, although again many products do not support this level of generality. Finally, *domain* constraints can be specified to constrain all values in all columns of the domain, or any value cast to the domain.

Although constraints are specified declaratively, every constraint implicitly specifies:

- A set of *events* after which the constraint is checked— generally any database operation that could cause the constraint to become violated.

- An *action* to be taken if the constraint is violated— usually raising an error and/or generating a rollback, with some more interesting cases such as referential integrity as described above.

When a constraint is first defined or when new data is loaded, the system verifies the constraint against the data. Thereafter the *events* are monitored and *actions* executed to ensure that the database state always satisfies the constraint as specified.

3.2 Triggers

Although trigger support was not included as part of the SQL-92 standard, triggers were supported by some products already in the early to mid-1990's. The SQL-99 standard has extensive coverage of triggers, and today all major relational DBMS vendors have some support for triggers.

Unfortunately, because the standard was influenced by pre-existing product support, and many products do not do a good job integrating constraints and triggers, most products support only a subset of the SQL-99 trigger standard and most do not adhere to some of the more subtle details of the execution model [CPM96]. Furthermore, some trigger implementations rely on proprietary programming languages for specifying parts of their triggers, which makes portability across different DBMS's difficult.[1]

In contrast to declarative constraints, triggers are explicitly procedural. A trigger is activated whenever a specified *event* occurs, usually an *insert*, *delete*, or *update* on a particular table. Once activated, an optional specified *condition* is checked and, if the condition is true (or omitted), an *action* is executed. There are a number of important details to the specification and execution semantics of triggers, only a few of which are covered here.

Triggers have an *activation time* (either *before*, *after*, or *instead of* the triggering event), and a *granularity* (either *row-level* or *statement-level*). There are some obvious as well as some subtle distinctions in the way triggers behave depending on which settings are selected. Each trigger has access to the old and new values of the row or statement affected by the event, by means of *transition variables* (OLD and NEW) and *transition tables* (OLD_TABLE and NEW_TABLE). Conditions can be arbitrary predicates, and actions are stored procedures which may include SQL statements, control constructs, and calls to user-defined functions. Note that user-defined functions invoked by a trigger action may have side effects that fall outside of DBMS control (including possibly calling the DBMS itself).

Trigger support in DBMS products is variable, with typical deviations from the standard including, e.g., restrictions on predicates in trigger conditions, restrictions on references to transition variables or tables, raising exceptions after a certain number of trigger activations, and trigger actions specified using proprietary languages as discussed above.

3.3 Constraints and Triggers in Products

Products also vary considerably in terms of their integration of constraint and trigger facilities. Historically, some products (e.g., Sybase) offered only triggers, relying on applications to implement any declarative constraints they needed using triggers (perhaps following the methodology of [CW90]). Eventually built-in constraints were added to these products for performance, usability, and to conform to the SQL standard. At the same time, other products (e.g., IBM DB2) initially supported constraints only. Although very expressive declarative constraints were allowed, trig-

---

[1] We expect this last issue to dissolve if the *Persistent Stored Modules* (*SQL-PSM*) language becomes standardized, or if a language such as Java becomes adopted widely for database procedures.

	Embedded in DBMS Kernel	DBMS Services	External Applications
Handcrafted	Metadata management, Internal audit trails	N/A	Business rules, Scheduling, Supply chain management Web applications
Generated	Referential integrity, Materialized views	Replication, Extenders, Audit trails, Migration, Alerters	Workflow management

Figure 1: Classification and examples of trigger applications

gers were added to these products eventually based on application needs, and again to conform to the standard.

The important point to note is that the marketplace has dictated that separate support for both constraints and triggers is appropriate.

4 Trigger Applications

Now that we have reviewed triggers and constraints briefly, both from a research and commercial standpoint, let us take a look at how the functionality has been deployed in real applications.

In Figure 1 we characterize trigger applications along two dimensions. The vertical dimension distinguishes between those triggers that are written by hand for a specific application (*handcrafted*), versus "generic" trigger sets that are produced automatically for a specific purpose, usually parameterized for a given application (*generated*). In the horizontal dimension, on the far right are applications that reside entirely outside of the DBMS, creating triggers and (possibly) responding to trigger actions through the database system's client API. The middle column represents trigger applications that are constructed by the DBMS vendor or a third-party, generally to provide a service or to enhance a specific database functionality. The far left column represents trigger-like behavior built into the kernel of the DBMS. For the last class of applications, the trigger system of the DBMS may be used to prototype the desired functionality, but eventually the behavior is hard-coded into the kernel, in order to circumvent security restrictions, achieve higher performance, or to program declarative behavior that procedural triggers cannot simulate with complete accuracy.

Although not perfect, the dimensions in Figure 1 enable us to classify trigger applications as well as to characterize their evolution. In Sections 5 and 6 we discuss generated and handcrafted trigger applications, respectively. Then in Section 7 we discuss the general evolution of trigger applications, and in Section 8 we attempt to provide a more fine-grained classification than in Figure 1.

5 Generated Triggers

Our own early work established that triggers can be generated automatically for a wide class of applications, including constraint maintenance [CW90], materialized view

maintenance [CW91], and managing semantic heterogeneity [CW93]. An entire database design framework based on trigger generation is presented in [CF97]. The primary idea behind all of this work is that in many cases the desired end result of trigger behavior can be specified declaratively (e.g., *maintain this constraint*, or *keep this view consistent with the base data*), and a set of procedural triggers can be generated automatically from the declarative specifications. This approach can guarantee correctness (which is no minor matter when it comes to triggers), and it frees the user from the detailed and error-prone task of constructing a trigger set by hand. We will argue that a large fraction of useful trigger applications can be approached in this manner—in fact many of them fall into the more specific constraint-maintaining category—even if such triggers are hard-coded today.

5.1 Internal Generated Triggers

As pointed out by Figure 1, two classic instances where triggers can be used to support kernel database functionality are *referential integrity* and *materialized views*. As discussed in Section 3.1, referential integrity is the only built-in constraint type that allows a variety of different actions to occur when the constraint is violated, with the desired actions specified declaratively by the user. Generating a set of triggers to support a single referential integrity constraint with any of the available actions is a straightforward exercise (one that we often assign in our introductory database courses), although there are some subtleties to maintaining multiple referential integrity constraints using triggers [Hor92]. It also is possible to generate a set of triggers that will keep a materialized view consistent with the base data—either naive triggers that recompute the view, or more complicated ones that maintain it incrementally [BDD+98, CW91, LSPC00].

For both referential integrity and materialized views, triggers are a natural and easy mechanism for implementing the desired functionality: with a trigger system in hand, one can provide referential integrity and materialized view support in no time. However, these features also are very intrinsic to database performance, and they are tied up with authorization and transactional issues as well. As a result, most DBMS's will select to implement separate, special-purpose, highly-tuned components for referential integrity and materialized views. It would certainly be nice if trigger systems were fast, scalable, and flexible enough to be used for kernel activities instead of hard-coding them, with no loss of performance or functionality. In the meantime, triggers still provide an excellent means of rapidly prototyping functionality that may end up hard-coded within the kernel of the DBMS.

5.2 Generated Triggers for Services

Moving away from the database kernel, we come to one of the widest and most useful classes of trigger applications: those that can be generated automatically to support a feature or service that enhances the functionality of a database system (second row, middle column of Figure 1). In fact, some purveyors of early "extensible" database systems, which led to today's prevalent object-relational DBMSs, suggested that two of the main features comprising extensibility were objects and active rules [LLPS91, SK91, SRL$^+$90]. Trigger-based services in this class can be designed and implemented by the database system vendor, or provided by third-parties.

Three example applications in this class noted in Figure 1 but not discussed beyond this paragraph are *audit trails*, *migration*, and *alerters*. It should be clear that automatically-generated triggers can easily be used to maintain logs that capture database activity for auditing purposes. In fact, audit trails were one of the earliest suggested applications of triggers, and the ability to generate audit trails still remains a "benchmark" for trigger languages and systems.[2] Triggers also can be used during the process of migrating data from one table or schema (or even DBMS) to another, to ensure consistency when updates occur during the migration process. This application is similar to replication, discussed momentarily in Section 5.2.1. Finally, *alerters* allow users to register for certain database conditions to become true, in which case the user is notified and data may be sent along with the notification, but no action on the database itself is usually taken. Note that in some ways alerters are very similar to integrity constraints, except in the case of alerters a condition becoming true results only in a message being sent, rather than in an error and/or rollback. Furthermore, we expect that alerters may generate orders of magnitude more trigger instances on a given table, as discussed in Section 9 below.

5.2.1 Replication

Most database systems include features for replicating data automatically between tables in a given database schema, across schemas within the same database server, or across servers and even vendors. Tables may be replicated exactly, or the replicated tables may be specified as more complicated expressions (views, essentially) over the source tables

[Tho97]. In all cases, the fundamental operation is to capture changes at source tables and propagate them to replicas. This application shares many obvious similarities with materialized views and can similarly rely on automatically-generated triggers, but it requires interactions outside of the kernel DBMS while materialized views are primarily internal.

Triggers are widely used for the "capture" phase of replication services at a minimum. Triggers also may be used for the "propagate" phase, although because propagation may be decoupled from the transactional semantics of the underlying database systems, in some cases triggers may not be expressive or flexible enough to achieve the desired behavior. For example, in many systems the propagation of updates to replicas is purely time-driven, and most trigger systems currently do not support time-based events.

5.2.2 Extenders

Another widely deployed service supported by triggers is maintaining data structures stored either internally or externally to the database (e.g., specialized indexes) that need to stay consistent with base data stored in the database. Triggers capture changes to the base data and propagate them to the specialized structures. More generally, triggers can provide the "glue" for applying any specialized functions, both internal and external to the DBMS, to specialized data stored in the DBMS. There are numerous *extenders* of this form relying on triggers today, for example we immediately counted eleven that we know of developed by outside vendors to run on IBM's DB2. A few examples are discussed briefly in the next paragraph.

Extenders for multimedia data (image, audio, video, etc.) all use automatically-generated triggers. Triggers are used on insertions to validate multimedia input and generate useful metadata. Other triggers are used subsequently to keep data and metadata synchronized. Triggers are also used heavily in text extenders: When a row is inserted containing a text attribute, a trigger will automatically create a handle for the text, place the text in a specialized external index, and place the handle in the actual base row. Other triggers will ensure that the level of indirection is followed, and will keep the external text index consistent when text data is modified. XML extenders behave similarly, although the trigger actions are more complex. XML documents can be parsed and validated automatically by triggers; document components are then separated and stored in specialized indexes to enable structural searches.

5.3 External Generated Triggers

Generating triggers from declarative specifications is a natural approach to take for DBMS services as discussed in the previous section, since such services tend to be parameterized, only moderately configurable, and relatively simple to specify. For trigger applications that are completely

---

[2]The main issue here is that if one is interested in a complete audit trail (including actions that may ultimately be rolled back), triggers must have the ability to be activated by uncommitted events.

external to the DBMS, automatic trigger generation is less prevalent, although one important example in this class is *workflow management*.[3]

It is interesting to note that workflow management was one of the earliest suggested applications of expressive triggers [DHL90], although initial work did not propose automatic trigger generation. In recent developments in the commercial sector, Oracle's *Workflow Builder* [Ora00] and Informix's *Media360* package [Inf00] both provide tools that generate triggers automatically from higher-level workflow specifications, an approach also suggested in [BBC+97].

6 Handcrafted Triggers

Handcrafted triggers generally support logic that is very specific to the application at hand. In many cases, hand-crafted trigger applications cannot be expressed declaratively. In some cases, even if a declarative specification is possible, it simply may not be worthwhile to write a "trigger generator" if the trigger set will be instantiated only a small number of times. We have found that most hand-crafted trigger applications reside entirely outside of the DBMS, i.e., the upper-right entry in Figure 1, and we were unable to uncover any handcrafted trigger applications providing a DBMS service (the upper-middle entry)—by nature, services tend to be parameterized and simple enough that they can be specified declaratively.

6.1 Internal Handcrafted Triggers

Two uses for handcrafted triggers within the kernel of a DBMS are for *metadata management*, and to maintain customized *internal audit trails* for system administrators. As an example of using internal triggers for metadata management, we are familiar with the details of system catalogs in IBM's DB2 product. For performance, DB2 maintains complex, optimized internal data structures (*descriptors*) that are used during query compilation. These descriptors are derived from the values of other catalog attributes, and they encode (among other things) table statistics. When table statistics are updated, triggers propagate the new statistical values to keep the descriptors consistent. While the function of these triggers is to maintain integrity constraints among catalog data, the details of the data structures are complex, low-level, and subject to adjustments, so it made sense to handcraft a set of triggers to propagate updates in an efficient and correct manner.

6.2 External Handcrafted Triggers

Handcrafted, external triggers are in some sense the most straightforward deployment of triggers, although these ap-

plications also can be the most error-prone. Each trigger or set of triggers is written by an application developer to support application-specific logic that can be managed in part by the DBMS. Often, such triggers are used simply to invoke functions that perform actions external to the DBMS. However, external handcrafted triggers also may be used to maintain auxiliary information within the database that is dependent on the application and may not be easy to specify declaratively. For example, triggers might compute derived columns for each tuple in a table using application-defined "black box" computations, or they might tag inserted and updated rows with a timestamp and/or operation type.

There are a number of broad classes of external handcrafted trigger applications worth noting, as shown in Figure 1: *business rules, scheduling, supply chain management*, and *Web applications*. In each of these classes, although the overall goal may be the same across applications, the specifics of a given application—e.g., the business logic of a particular enterprise, the constraints of a particular scheduling problem—vary enough that a generic system for generating triggers from a declarative specification does not seem feasible.

The fact that handcrafting triggers is difficult has been recognized for quite some time with no broadly applicable solution to date. There is clearly room for trigger programming "wizards" that:

1. Allow the application developer to specify an external trigger-based application in a higher-level language.

2. Translate the specification into triggers.

3. Provide some analysis tools for identifying how the generated triggers will interact.

This approach follows the general approach of [CW90, CW91, CW93], but we are suggesting its use for applications that are somewhat less declarative than the applications discussed in those papers, i.e., the tools would target applications that are nearly always handcrafted today. Some headway has been made in this direction for business rules [Ros97], but primarily applying to business rules that effectively enforce integrity constraints.

We attempted to quantify the number of triggers that are typical in a handcrafted external application, in part to determine whether weak points in trigger scalability are relevant. In one scheduling application that we studied, there were a total of 25 triggers defined over 6 tables. About half of the triggers were defined over two auxiliary tables that were needed to encode the application logic and control the firing of other triggers. Even with this relatively modest number of triggers, they were difficult to write and cumbersome to maintain, and inadvertently contained avoidable recursive logic. By contrast, in a Web application we

---

[3] Admittedly, *business rules* and *scheduling* are similar applications that might use automatic trigger generation, but to date these applications have not done so to the extent of workflow, so we leave business rules and scheduling in the "handcrafted" category.

studied there were over 100 triggers. However, the triggers were spread across nearly 30 tables and served largely to log relevant updates, so trigger interactions were not a serious problem.

7 Evolution of Trigger Applications

Early trigger applications tended to be external and hand-crafted. Trigger systems were touted as the mechanism that would allow databases to become "knowledge bases," with built-in rule-based reasoning capabilities. This claim turned out to be too strong for at least two reasons: trigger performance was not adequate for the large number of rules anticipated in deployed knowledge bases, and trigger interactions were cumbersome and difficult to debug or formally verify.

Our work in the early 1990's [CW90, CW91, CW93] showed that declarative specifications could be used to generate triggers for several useful applications. With this approach, correctness is guaranteed, regardless of the number of (generated) triggers in the application. As trigger applications have "settled out", we see the general trend reflected in Figure 1. Outside of the DBMS kernel, many applications fall into one of two categories: either the triggers are generated automatically for a parameterized service provided in conjunction with the database system (e.g., replication), or the triggers are written by hand for a specific application-dependent task (e.g., scheduling).

Anecdotal evidence suggests that even though triggers have been used to great success for a wide variety of applications as discussed above and shown in Figure 1, it is still the case that a preponderance of trigger applications are simply maintaining relatively straightforward integrity constraints. As a result, scalability in number of triggers has not been a significant concern, with performance efforts devoted instead to scalability in the amount of data that (a small set of) triggers operates over. As triggers become more widely deployed for alerting systems, complex scheduling tasks, and other applications requiring numerous and/or complex triggers, scalability is likely to become a significant concern [BBC+97].

8 Further Classification

We now propose a classification of triggers that is based largely on function and behavior, rather than on the dimensions in Figure 1. The first 8 of these categories are usually generated triggers, while the last are typically handcrafted.

1. **Constraint-preserving triggers:** Signal integrity constraint violations and force rollbacks of the violating transactions.

2. **Constraint-restoring triggers:** Detect integrity constraint violations and modify the database contents in order to restore integrity.

3. **Invalidating triggers:** Signal and mark integrity constraint violations, allowing applications to respond appropriately.

4. **Materializing triggers:** Compute materialized derived information, from simple scaler values to aggregate values to complex views, either by incremental modifications or complete refresh.

5. **Metadata triggers:** Maintain consistency across system catalogs or other metadata (recall Section 6.1).

6. **Replication triggers:** Replicate, migrate, or log information and/or modifications from one table or database (the *primary copy*) to another one (the *secondary copy*).

7. **Extenders:** Manage new types of data (e.g., validate input) and keep specialized external structures consistent with the base data.

8. **Alerters:** Notify or push information to users in the form of messages, typically based on a publish/subscribe model.

9. **Ad-hoc triggers:** Implement business rules, scheduling, workflow, supply-chain management, or other application-specific logic.

We can see that types 5, 6, and 7 are clearly derivatives of type 4, and type 4 itself can be thought of as a specific instance of type 2. In other words, for many trigger applications, the primary purpose is to monitor and maintain some kind of constraint. Furthermore, if we stretch our imagination a bit, other trigger types also can be thought of as constraint maintainers. For example, alerting triggers (type 8) are responding to the abstract constraint that each user must be aware of the information for which he subscribed, perhaps within a certain amount of time.

Once a trigger application can be expressed in the context of maintaining constraints, a framework based on [CW90] may be applicable. In such a framework, trigger generation must enumerate the events that can cause the constraint to be violated, then associate a corrective action for each event. Correctness of the approach is guaranteed if all possible sources of inconsistency are covered. Once triggers for each class of constraints are generated, we might integrate the different types of constraint-maintaining triggers into a coherent framework. For example, we might want to first restore integrity constraints on base data, then update materialized views, then restore integrity constraints on views, then perform replication, and finally execute alerters.

9 Lingering Issues

The 1995 paper by Simon and Kotz-Dittrich [SKD95], which was based on the author's practical experience deploying trigger-based applications, did a good job of summarizing both the benefits and pitfalls of database triggers. To a large extent, the positive and negative aspects brought forth in that paper remain true today. The main recognized advantages of trigger-based applications are still the ability to move shared application logic and business rules into the database (rather than hard-coding the behavior into all applications), and the ability to specify integrity constraints that go beyond the specific types of built-in constraints supported by SQL.

On the negative side, among the problems cited by [SKD95] based on their application-building experience are:

1. Lack of expressive events in the SQL standard, e.g., no event predicates, user-defined events, or conjunction.

2. Product limitations, such as a maximum number of triggers per event type.

3. Lack of uniformity across products—syntactic, semantic, and transactional—resulting in confusion and a lack of portability.

4. Subtle behavior, particularly when mixing different types of triggers, or mixing triggers and built-in constraints.

5. Lack of structuring mechanisms and debugging tools for triggers, making it very difficult to specify and understand how a large number of triggers interact among themselves and with transactions.

6. Performance penalty when compared against hard-coding and optimizing the desired effect.

Let us examine how each of these problem areas has evolved since 1995.

Expressive events

Events are no more expressive, and the now-established SQL-99 standard with only the simplest of event types (*insert*, *delete*, or *update* on one table, possibly restricted to certain columns) virtually guarantees that events will remain simple. However, richer event types as suggested in [SKD95] can largely be encoded using SQL-99 triggers by making trigger conditions more complicated. At that point the issue becomes one of optimization: the triggers are expressible, but they execute inefficiently because of lack of sophistication in the trigger processor. Thus, one important challenge becomes efficient monitoring of triggers with complex conditions. There has been only a smattering initial work in the research community along these lines, e.g., [Han92].

Another class of trigger events not yet supported in products—despite their prominence in several research prototypes—is *time-based events*. Although there are numerous interfaces for specifying and scheduling activities based on time, including database activities, to date we have not seen time-based events incorporated directly into a commercial DBMS trigger system.

Product limitations

Product limitations are being lifted, slowly. The limit on number of triggers per event type has been eliminated in most products, since the limitation was an obstacle even to simple trigger-based services. However, most DBMS's still do not integrate their trigger and constraint systems well [CPM96]. Furthermore, run-time behavior may be unnecessarily restricted (e.g., limits on number of rule activations), and many systems still lack a means of prioritizing when multiple triggers are activated at the same time [ACL91]. All of these issues have been addressed in some detail in the research community [WC96], but not yet adopted in all products.

Uniformity

We expect lack of uniformity to improve somewhat as the SQL-99 standard settles in, although standards never seem to solve uniformity problems fully. For example, the different transactional models supported by different DBMS products can have subtle but significant effects on trigger behavior, even if the semantics of the triggers themselves appear identical.

Subtle behavior

There has been little improvement since 1995, except perhaps in understanding the extent of the subtleties [CPM96]. Even in the presence of well-defined trigger semantics, behavior can be surprising. For example, row-level triggers are activated once for each modified (inserted, deleted, or updated) tuple, but no triggers are activated until the modification statement is complete. Thus, the execution of a row-level trigger effectively enumerates through the modified rows in an undefined order, possibly invoking complex procedural logic (and even database updates) for each row. As another example, if triggers invoke external actions, there is no way for the external actions to know if the triggering transaction committed. Thus, an external action may be invoked multiple times for restarted transactions, and it may perform actions based on changes that do not commit. "Deferred" or "commit" triggers are not supported by most DBMS trigger systems, so programming correct deferred behavior requires a significant amount of effort.

These issues are just examples, but they serve to further underscore the importance of the application development and trigger analysis tools, mentioned next.

Development support

Lack of a support environment for developing handcrafted trigger applications is still a significant problem. Although the research community has produced a number of nice theoretical results and prototype implementations in this area, commercial database systems are void of trigger design support, and introducing such tools may never reach the radar screen for database vendors. Thus, instead of the emergence of fully general trigger analysis and design tools, we see the growth in:

- Automatic generation of trigger sets from declarative specifications, as discussed throughout this paper, and already used in a surprising number of trigger applications (second row of Figure 1).

- An intermediate approach between fully automatic trigger generation and completely handcrafted trigger sets: trigger programming "wizards" as described in Section 6.2 that assist in developing correct trigger sets for a particular application.

Performance

Trigger performance can certainly be a problem, although not uniformly across all applications. There are many cases when a small number of triggers embedded in the DBMS clearly outperforms an approach that hard-codes the same functionality into multiple applications. However, when an application permits a very large number of triggers on the same table (e.g., an alerting system), or when trigger conditions are complex as discussed earlier, performance quickly deteriorates in all deployed trigger systems that we know of. (For example, as mentioned earlier, implementing a rule-based inferencing system using database triggers is infeasible at this time given existing trigger implementations.) Again, there has been some work in the research community, particularly in terms of scaling the number of triggers while maintaining good performance, that has not yet found its way into products.

10 Conclusions

Triggers are being used in a variety of significant ways in today's database systems and applications. The primary use of triggers is still to enforce various integrity constraints driven by the application, and we have argued that more uses of triggers than one might think are in fact maintaining constraints of one sort or another. Meanwhile, there is still work to do in trigger processing for researchers and developers alike, particularly to address performance issues and the lack of application development tools.

Acknowledgements

We are grateful to Jim Gray and Ron Soukop for some initial information on trigger applications to get this paper rolling, to Mike Stonebraker for a useful discussion near the finish line, to Richard Sidle for comments on a draft, and to the following folks at IBM for helpful answers to numerous questions: Qi Cheng, Patrick Dantressangle, Stefan Dessloch, Jing-Song Jang, Beth Hamel, Madhu Kochar, Nelson Mattos, and Calisto Zuzarte.

Stefano and Jennifer are grateful to IBM Almaden for providing a stimulating environment for their joint work in active databases, and to Bruce Lindsay, Hamid Pirahesh, and especially Bobbie Cochrane for all their great work in making constraints and triggers a reality in practice (and in helping us assemble this paper).

References

[ACL91] R. Agrawal, R.J. Cochrane, and B. Lindsay. On maintaining priorities in a production rule system. In *Proceedings of the Seventeenth International Conference on Very Large Data Bases*, pages 479–487, Barcelona, Spain, September 1991.

[BBC+97] P. Bernstein, M. Brodie, S. Ceri, et al. The Asilomar report on database research. *SIGMOD Record*, 27(4):74–80, December 1997.

[BDD+98] R. Bello, K. Dias, A. Downing, et al. Materialized views in Oracle. In *Proceedings of the Twenty-Fourth International Conference on Very Large Data Bases*, pages 659–664, New York, New York, August 1998.

[CF97] S. Ceri and P. Fraternali. *Designing Database Applications with Objects and Rules: The IDEA Methodology*. Addison-Wesley, 1997.

[CPM96] R.J. Cochrane, H. Pirahesh, and N.M. Mattos. Integrating triggers and declarative constraints in SQL database sytems. In *Proceedings of the Twenty-Second International Conference on Very Large Data Bases*, pages 567–578, Mumbai, India, September 1996.

[CW90] S. Ceri and J. Widom. Deriving production rules for constraint maintenance. In *Proceedings of the Sixteenth International Conference on Very Large Data Bases*, pages 566–577, Brisbane, Australia, August 1990.

[CW91] S. Ceri and J. Widom. Deriving production rules for incremental view maintenance. In *Proceedings of the Seventeenth International Conference on Very Large Data Bases*, pages 577–589, Barcelona, Spain, September 1991.

[CW93] S. Ceri and J. Widom. Managing semantic heterogeneity with production rules and persistent queues. In *Proceedings of the Nineteenth International Conference on Very Large Data Bases*, pages 108–119, Dublin, Ireland, August 1993.

[DHL90] U. Dayal, M. Hsu, and R. Ladin. Organizing long-running activities with triggers and transactions. In *Proceedings of the ACM SIGMOD International Conference on Management of Data*, pages 204–214, Atlantic City, New Jersey, May 1990.

[EC75]   K.P. Eswaran and D.D. Chamberlin. Functional specifications of a subsystem for data base integrity. In *Proceedings of the First International Conference on Very Large Data Bases*, pages 48–67, Framingham, Massachusetts, September 1975.

[Esw76]   K.P. Eswaran. Specifications, implementations and interactions of a trigger subsystem in an integrated database system. IBM Research Report RJ 1820, IBM San Jose Research Laboratory, San Jose, California, August 1976.

[Han92]   E.N. Hanson. Rule condition testing and action execution in Ariel. In *Proceedings of the ACM SIGMOD International Conference on Management of Data*, pages 49–58, San Diego, California, June 1992.

[HM75]   M. Hammer and D. McLeod. Semantic integrity in a relational data base system. In *Proceedings of the First International Conference on Very Large Data Bases*, pages 25–47, Framingham, Massachusetts, September 1975.

[Hor92]   B. Horowitz. A run-time execution model for referential integrity maintenance. In *Proceedings of the Eighth International Conference on Data Engineering*, pages 548–556, Phoenix, Arizona, February 1992.

[Inf00]   Informix Software. *Informix Media360*, 2000. Available at http://www.informix.com/media360.

[LLPS91]   G.M. Lohman, B. Lindsay, H. Pirahesh, and K.B. Schiefer. Extensions to Starburst: Objects, types, functions, and rules. *Communications of the ACM*, 34(10):94–109, October 1991.

[LSPC00]   W. Lehner, R. Sidle, H. Pirahesh, and R.J. Cochrane. Maintenance of automatic summary tables. In *Proceedings of the ACM SIGMOD International Conference on Management of Data*, pages 512–513, Dallas, Texas, May 2000.

[Ora00]   Oracle Corporation. *Oracle Workflow Technical Configuration in Oracle Applications Release 11*, 2000. Available at http://www.oracle.com/support/library/supportnews/html/workflow.html.

[Ros97]   R.G. Ross. *The Business Rule Book: Classifying, Defining and Modeling Rules*. Business Rule Solutions Inc., February 1997.

[SK91]   M. Stonebraker and G. Kemnitz. The POSTGRES next-generation database management system. *Communications of the ACM*, 34(10):78–92, October 1991.

[SKD95]   E. Simon and A. Kotz-Dittrich. Promises and realities of active database systems. In *Proceedings of the Twenty-First International Conference on Very Large Data Bases*, pages 642–653, Zürich, Switzerland, September 1995.

[SRL$^+$90] M. Stonebraker, L.A. Rowe, B.G. Lindsay, J. Gray, M.J. Carey, M.L. Brodie, P.A. Bernstein, and D. Beech. Third-generation database system manifesto – The committee for advanced DBMS function. *SIGMOD Record*, 19(3):31–44, September 1990.

[Sto75]   M. Stonebraker. Implementation of integrity constraints and views by query modification. In *Proceedings of the ACM SIGMOD International Conference on Management of Data*, pages 65–78, San Jose, California, May 1975.

[Tho97]   C. Thompson. Database replication. *DBMS Magazine*, 10(5), May 1997.

[UW97]   J.D. Ullman and J. Widom. *A First Course in Database Systems*. Prentice Hall, Upper Saddle River, New Jersey, 1997.

[WC96]   J. Widom and S. Ceri. *Active Database Systems: Triggers and Rules for Advanced Database Processing*. Morgan Kaufmann, San Francisco, California, 1996.

Integrating the UB-Tree into a Database System Kernel

Frank Ramsak[1], Volker Markl[1], Robert Fenk[1], Martin Zirkel[2], Klaus Elhardt[3], Rudolf Bayer[1,2]

[1]Bayerisches Forschungszentrum
für Wissensbasierte Systeme
Orleansstraße 34,
D- 81667 München, Germany

[2]Institut für Informatik
TU München
Orleansstraße 34,
D-81667 München, Germany

[3]TransAction Software GmbH
Gustav-Heinemann-Ring 109,
D-81739 München, Germany

{frank.ramsak, robert.fenk, volker.markl}@forwiss.de, {zirkel, bayer}@in.tum.de, klaus.elhardt@transaction.de

Abstract

Multidimensional access methods have shown high potential for significant performance improvements in various application domains. However, only few approaches have made their way into commercial products. In commercial database management systems (DBMSs) the B-Tree is still the prevalent indexing technique. Integrating new indexing methods into existing database kernels is in general a very complex and costly task. Exceptions exist, as our experience of integrating the UB-Tree into TransBase, a commercial DBMS, shows. The UB-Tree is a very promising multidimensional index, which has shown its superiority over traditional access methods in different scenarios, especially in OLAP applications. In this paper we discuss the major issues of a UB-Tree integration. As we will show, the complexity and cost of this task is reduced significantly due to the fact that the UB-Tree relies on the classical B-Tree. Even though commercial DBMSs provide interfaces for index extensions, we favor the kernel integration because of the tight coupling with the query optimizer, which allows for optimal usage of the UB-Tree in execution plans. Measurements on a real-world data warehouse show that the kernel integration leads to an additional performance improvement compared to our prototype implementation and competing index methods.

Proceedings of the 26th International Conference on Very Large Databases, Cairo, Egypt, 2000

1   Introduction

Various research approaches in the past have shown that multidimensional access methods (MAMs) have a high impact on different database application domains like data warehousing, data mining, or geographical information systems. However, despite the vast research effort MAMs have not made their way into commercial database management systems on a broad scale. This is mostly due to the fact that the integration of these complex data structures into an existing database kernel is fairly complicated. Especially concurrency and recovery issues, which are as important as performance issues for commercial systems, are major obstacles. For most MAMs new solutions to these problems, e.g., locking for R-Trees [KB95, CM98], have to be developed, as the new concepts do not allow reusing standard techniques. This makes the kernel integration of an MAM a very costly task in the range of multiple man-years. As consequence many DBMS producers have not integrated the new technology into their systems, but offer it only as add-on features. So, are MAMs just another nice research gimmick, but commercially not affordable? No, in this paper we will show that there are MAMs, which provide good performance on one side and can smoothly be integrated into a DBMS kernel on the other side. A category of MAMs is based on the combination of one-dimensional index structures and space-filling curves. One prominent example is the UB-Tree [Bay97], which combines the B-Tree and the Z-curve. Together with its sophisticated query processing algorithms it has proven its performance advantages in numerous application domains. Because the UB-Tree is based on the standard B-Tree, which is the basic index structure in almost every commercial DBMS, the task of integrating this MAM into an existing kernel becomes less complex and less costly. The kernel integration of the UB-Tree into TransBase [Tra98] (as part of an ESPRIT project funded by the

European Commission) has been accomplished within one year. TransBase is a full-scale relational database system, which conforms to the SQL-92 standard. TransBase, which handles databases up to 8 Terabyte of data, is used especially in the field of CD-ROM retrieval systems, and has an installation base of well beyond 50,000 sites worldwide.

In this paper, we will present the major issues and problems that have to be tackled and solved for a successful UB-Tree kernel integration. The paper is organized as follows: Section 2 presents the basic concepts behind the UB-Tree and Section 3 deals with the issue of the UB-Tree address representation and the implementation of the standard UB-Tree operations. Section 4 addresses the specific query operation of the UB-Tree and Section 5 tackles the important topic of required optimizer extensions to efficiently support the UB-Tree. Section 6 covers additional enhancements for the UB-Tree and Section 7 presents the performance evaluation. Section 8 summarizes related work and Section 9 concludes the paper.

2 Basic Concept of the UB-Tree

The basic idea of the UB-Tree [Bay97] is to use a space-filling curve to map a multidimensional universe to one-dimensional space. Using the Z-Curve (Figure 2-1a) for preserving multidimensional clustering as good as possible it is a variant of the zkd-B-Tree [OM84].

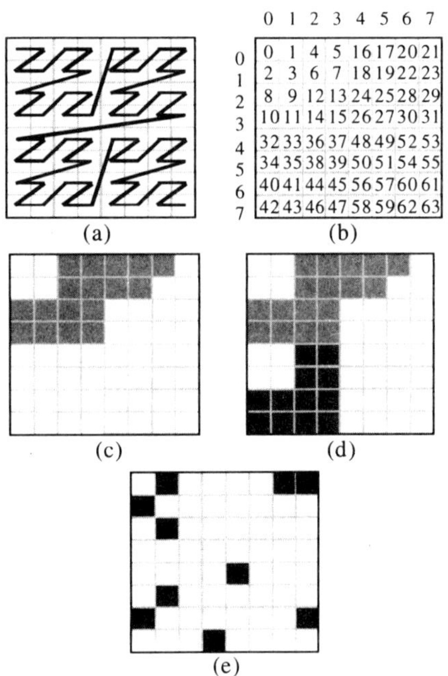

Figure 2-1 Z-Addresses and Z-Regions

A *Z-Address* $\alpha = Z(x)$ is the ordinal number of the key attributes of a tuple x on the Z-Curve, which can be efficiently computed by bit-interleaving (see Section 3.1). A standard B-Tree is used to index the tuples taking the Z-Address of the tuples as keys.

The fundamental innovation of UB-Trees is the concept of *Z-Regions* to create a disjunctive partitioning of the multidimensional space. This allows for very efficient processing of multidimensional range queries (see Section 4). A Z-Region $[\alpha : \beta]$ is the space covered by an interval on the Z-Curve and is defined by two Z-Addresses α and β. We call β the *region address* of $[\alpha : \beta]$. Each Z-Region maps exactly onto one page on secondary storage, i.e., to one leaf page of the B-Tree.

For an 2 dimensional universe of size 8×8, Figure 2-1b shows the corresponding Z-addresses. Figure 2-1c shows the Z-region [4: 20] and Figure 2-1d shows a partitioning with five Z-regions [0 : 3],[4 : 20], [21 : 35], [36 : 47] and [48 : 63]. Assuming a page capacity of 2 points, Figure 2-1e shows ten points, which create the partitioning of Figure 2-1d.

The details of the UB-Tree algorithms are described in the following sections.

3 UB-Tree Address Representation and Standard Operations

For the rest of the paper we will refer to the function computing the Z-Addresses as *UBKEY* and to the keys as *Z-values*. It is important to note that the UB-Tree algorithms can be implemented and integrated without fundamental changes to the query processing of the database kernel. They do not require special tuple handling or other significant modifications, as the following sections show.

3.1 Address Representation and Z-value Computation

An important question for the implementation of the UB-Tree inside the database kernel is how to represent the Z-values. All algorithms for the UB-Tree basically rely on Z-values in the format of variable length bitstrings (trailing zeros are omitted to reduce storage requirements). The operations on Z-values manipulate single bits and copy parts of the bitstring. The UBKEY function can be efficiently implemented, as it requires only reading the specified index attributes bitwise and writing the bits at the corresponding positions in the resulting Z-value. As input the UBKEY function requires a bitstring representation of the attribute values. The natural order $\leq$ of the attribute values in the original domain A has to correspond to the bit-lexicographical order $\leq_{bitstr}$ on bitstrings, i.e.,

$$a_i \leq a_j \Leftrightarrow bitstr(a_i) \leq_{\text{bitstr}} bitstr(a_j),\qquad \text{where}$$

$bitstr : A \rightarrow \{b \mid b \in [0,1]^*\}$ generates the corresponding bitstring. For example, in case of unsigned integers and strings $bitstr := identity$ while for signed integers the $bitstr$ function has to take care of the sign bit.

To compute the Z-value of a tuple, we interleave the bits of the bitstring representation of the key attributes (see Figure 3-1).

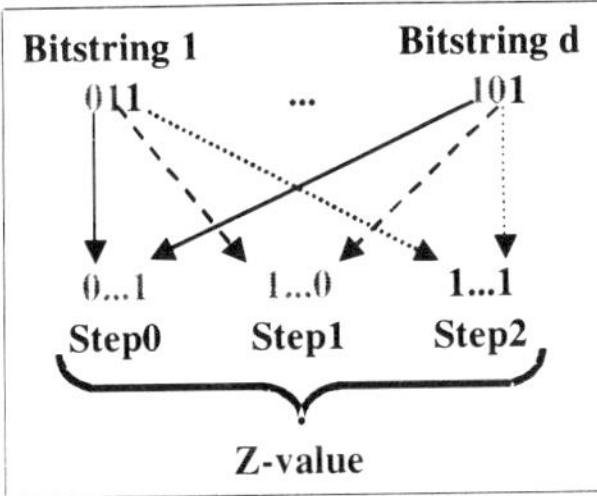

Figure 3-1 Calculation of Z-values by bit-interleaving the transformed attributes

For the following illustration we assume that all bitstrings have the same length *steplength*; $t[i]$ returns the ith attribute of tuple t; $bitstr[i]$ returns the ith bit of the bitstring *bitstr* (the highest order bit has number 0). We partition a Z-value into steps. A *step* consists of all bits from the input bitstrings, which have the same bit ordinal, i.e., step 0 contains the highest order bits from all input values (see Figure 3-1). We require the number of dimensions d (we assume that the key attributes are the first d attributes of the tuple) of the used UB-Tree. Figure 3-2 shows the pseudo code for the basic bit-interleaving algorithm.

```
Z-value UBKEY(Tuple t){
int i,s;
int bp;          //the bit position in the Z-value
Z-value addr;  //the result Z-value
Bitstring bs[dimno];  // bitstring representation of the
//attribute values
//Transformation of the key attributes
for (i=0; i < d; i++) {
// transformation of the attribute to a bitstring depends on the
// attribute type
      bs[i] = TransformAttribute(t[i]);
}
//Bit-interleaving – Calculation of the Z-value
bp=0; //starting with the first bit of the Z-value
//looping first over dimensions then over steps realizes the
//bit-interleaving
for (s=0;s < steplength; s++) {
     for(i=0; i < d; i++) {
          // the bp^th bit of the Z-value is
          // set to the s^th bit of the i^th bitstring
          addr[bp]=bs[i][s];
          bp++; //advance to next bit of Z-value
          }}
return addr;}
```

Figure 3-2: Basic UBKEY Function

It is also possible to use other transformation functions for generating the bitstring for an attribute value, allowing a more powerful semantics, e.g., soundex codes or case insensitive search on strings. As consequence, the *bitstr* function has to be adapted for the individual data types supported by the UB-Tree. If possible, it is useful to normalize attributes to unsigned integers starting with 0 as one step of the transformation, as this allows for a much better space partitioning with shorter Z-values. One example for normalization for complex data types is MHC [MRB99]. Other possibilities for normalization include hashing or more complex non-linear methods.

Note that complex normalization may lead to significant performance overhead, which may then not be neglected any more. Our standard normalization techniques just require a few microseconds of CPU cycles and therefore do not affect the address calculation performance.

3.2 Insertion, Deletion, Update

The basic algorithms of the UB-Tree are handled by the underlying B-Tree. To perform an insertion, deletion or update one just has to compute the Z-value corresponding to the tuple. The underlying B-Tree uses that Z-value to determine the page where the tuple is stored and processes the operation as usual. As consequence, the same performance guarantees as for the basic operations on B-Trees can also be given for the basic operations of the UB-Tree. Figure 3-3 shows the code for insertion, which is similar to deletion and update.

```
Status UBTree_insertTuple(Tuple t)
{
return BTree_insertTuple(UBKEY(t),t); //call to B-Tree
standard insertion algorithm, inserting tuple t with key UBKEY(t)
}
```

Figure 3-3: Insertion Function

3.3 Page Splitting

The split algorithm of the underlying B-Tree handles the page splitting in UB-Trees. Only the calculation of the page separator has to be modified, as the page split (i.e., region split for UB-Trees) strategy is crucial for the range query performance of the UB-Tree by influencing the space partitioning. This modification adds no complexity to the split costs as it is done in $O(n)$ bit operations, where n is the length of the Z-value in bits, and the worst case page utilization of 50% is still guaranteed [Mar99].

The goal of region splitting is to create rectangular regions whenever possible to reduce the number of regions overlapped by a range query. This can be achieved by choosing the *shortest* Z-value (i.e., the Z-value that has as many trailing zero bits as possible) between the two middle tuples s and t as new separator, instead of s, t or another Z-value in the middle of the page. Figure 3-4 shows the split algorithm of UB-Trees.

```
Status UBTree_splitPage(Page P, Tuple s, Tuple
t) {
Z-value sep;
sep=UBTree_calculateSeparator(UBKEY(s),UBKEY(t));
//Calculating the best separator between two Z-values, i.e., the shortest
Z-value between UBKEY(s) and UBKEY(t)
BTree_splitPage(P,s,t,sep);  // Btree_splitPage is the
//standard algorithm of the Btree: It splits page P between the two tuples
// s and t with sep as the separator between the two generated pages
}
```

Figure 3-4 Page Split algorithm of UB-Trees

The advantage of this split strategy is twofold: first, better range query performance on average; second, shorter separators lead to a more compact index part of the UB-Tree, a phenomenon also exploited in Prefix-B-Trees [BU77].

4 Range Query Processing

Processing a multidimensional range query, a UB-Tree retrieves all Z-regions, which are properly intersected by the query box [Mar99]. Due to the mapping of the multidimensional space to Z-values, this results in a set of intervals on the B-Tree storing the Z-values (Figure 4-1).

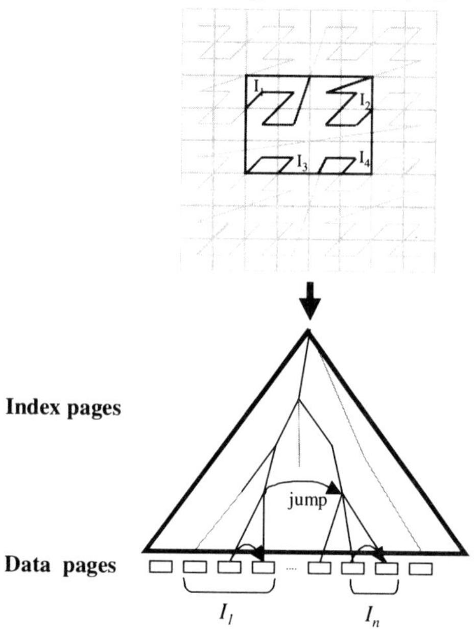

Figure 4-1: How query boxes map to a set of Z-value intervals

A B-Tree answers sets of interval restrictions on its key efficiently by traversing the corresponding intervals of pages directly on the leaf node level. For large B-Trees, i.e., when the index part cannot be completely cached, the processing is improved in TransBase as it supports jumps in the index part of the B-Tree, instead of starting at the root for each interval. Relying on this standard technique, the main task of the UB-Tree range query algorithm is to efficiently calculate the set of one-dimensional intervals of Z-values from one multidimensional interval.

4.1 UB-Tree Range Query Algorithm

One possibility of processing UB-Tree range queries is to compute all Z-value intervals (cf. Figure 4-1) for a query box in advance before accessing the B-Tree. Due to the nature of the Z-curve this may lead to a large set of intervals, many of which may be located in the same Z-Region. This naive approach will either result in multiple accesses to the same B-Tree page or will require calculation effort to identify all intervals belonging to one page. The resulting processing overhead is avoided by constructing the intervals on the fly, processing the query box page-by-page. As a consequence we use the page-by-page approach for the kernel integration. Iteratively constructing the intervals on the fly also has the advantage of providing the first result tuples earlier, which is good

for pipelining. However it requires post filtering of the retrieved pages.

The iterative range query algorithm (see Figure 4-2) for the UB-Tree works as follows. Let the multidimensional range restriction be specified by a query box Q with a starting corner and an ending corner, which are given by the two tuples ql resp. qh (UBKEY(ql) < UBKEY(qh)). First the algorithm computes the Z-values for ql and qh, then the region containing ql is located[1]. Let P, Q be two adjacent pages in the UB-Tree and the Z-value sep be the separator between the two pages with $\forall t \in P, \forall s \in Q : UBKEY(t) \le sep < UBKEY(s)$. We then call sep the *end* or *region address* of the region corresponding to page P. The range query algorithm then iteratively determines all the regions intersected by the query box. This is achieved by calculating the Z-value for the next intersection point of the Z-curve with the query box based on the currently processed region/page (see next section).

```
Status UBTree_Range_Query(Tuple ql, Tuple qh) {
Z-value start = UBKEY(ql);
Z-value end = UBKEY(qh);
Z-value cur = start;
While (1) { //continue as long we are in the query box
    cur = getRegionSeparator(cur); // getting the
address of the region containing cur
    FilterTuples(GetPage(cur), ql, qh); //post-
filtering of the tuples in the region
    if (cur >= end) break; //stop once we covered the
whole query box
    cur = getNextZvalue(&cur, start, end);
//calculation of next region
}}
```

Figure 4-2: Range Query Algorithm

All these steps are performed in $O(n)$ bit operations where n is the length of the Z-value [Mar99]. The separator computation and fetching of the page can be performed by one B-Tree access. After filtering out all matching tuples of a fetched page, they can be piped for further processing by the DBMS.

4.2 Calculating the next intersection point

Calculating the next intersection point is the crucial part of the UB-Tree range query algorithm. In the following we will show that this step only requires bit operations on Z-values and no I/O or B-Tree search is necessary. Starting point for getNextZvalue is the region address cur of the current region. The task now is to find the next intersection point of the Z-Curve with the query box Q. This intersection point $nisp$ is the minimal Z-value larger than the current region address, which is inside Q, i.e.,

$$nisp = \min(\{UBKEY(x) | UBKEY(x) > cur \wedge (x \in Q)\})$$

---

[1] Note: ql and qh do not have to be tuples existing in the database – it is only important to which regions they are mapped according to the space partitioning.

Figure 4-3 illustrates two examples of the next intersection point calculation for the dotted query box Q.

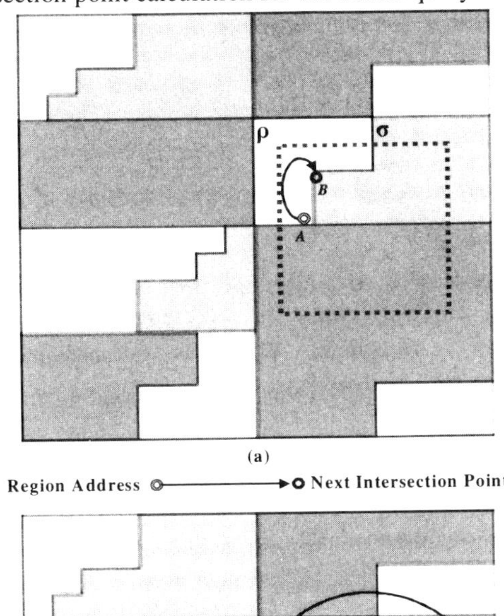

(a)

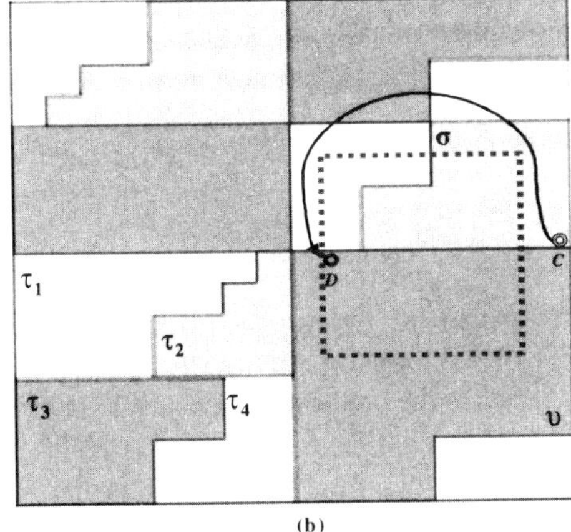

(b)

Figure 4-3 Region Address and Next Intersection Points

In Figure 4-3a, the region address $cur=A$ of region ρ yields B of region σ as the next intersection point with Q. Consequently the range query algorithm will continue with processing region σ. In this case, B is the direct successor of A on the Z-Curve, i.e., $B=A+1$. In Figure 4-3b we are looking for the next intersection point for the region address $cur=C$ of region σ. The call to getNextZvalue yields the Z-value D causing to process region υ next, skipping the four regions τ_1, τ_2, τ_3, and τ_4. Informally, the algorithm determines for the successor of a region address in which dimensions it is not contained in the query box. From this information it identifies the bits that have to be modified to generate the correct next intersection point.

For the detailed description of the algorithm we introduce the following functions: BP(i,s) returns for each bit position/step of a dimension i to which bit position in the resulting Z-value it corresponds; given a bit position bp in a Z-value the functions DIM(bp) and STEP(bp) will return the corresponding dimension resp. step.

The first step is to increment the region address by one, i.e., $nisp=cur+1$. We then test if $nisp$ is in the query box by bitwise comparing with the Z-values of ql and qh – we do not have to transform $nisp$ back to Cartesian coordinates. During the comparison we also determine additional information for each dimension i:

$$flag\,[i]=\begin{cases}-1 & \text{if } nisp \text{ has fallen below the minimum} \\ & \text{of } qb \text{ in dimension } i \\ 0 & \text{if } nisp \text{ is in } qb \text{ in dimension } i \\ 1 & \text{if } nisp \text{ has exceeded the maximum} \\ & \text{of } qb \text{ in dimension } i\end{cases}$$

$outStep\,[i]$ — the step in dimension i where qb has been left; ∞ if $nisp$ in qb in dimension i

$saveMin\,[i]$ — the step in dimension i where the minimum has been exceeded

$saveMax\,[i]$ — the step in dimension i where $nisp$ has fallen below the maximum

If $nisp$ is in qb then we have already found our next intersection point. If not, we have to determine the bits we have to set to 1 and set to 0 to get the correct $nisp$. Let be $outStep = \min(outstep[i])$, and d the corresponding dimension. We have to distinguish two cases: first, if $flag[d]=-1$ then we have found the bit $changeBP=BP(d,outstep)$ that we can safely set to 1 such that $nisp > cur$. Second, if $flag[d]=1$ then we have to find a lower bit position in $nisp$ we can set to 1, because the bit specified by $outstep$ has to be set to 0. In both cases the bits following the changed bit have to be adapted accordingly (see Figure 4-4).

```
BP changeBP=BP(d,outstep);  //we start with the minimal bit
position that has to be changed
int i;
if (flag[d] == 1)  // we cannot set this bit to 1, therefore we
have to find a lower bit position we can safely set
then {
        changeBP=max({bp|bp<changeBP and bp >=
saveMax[Dim(bp)] and Val(nisp,bp)=0});  //maximal
bitposition that is save to set to 1
        saveMin[DIM(changeBP)]=STEP(changeBP);
        flag[DIM(changeBP)]=0;
        }
// now we can change the rest of the Z-value
for(i=0;i<dimno;i++) {  //for each dimension we determine
how to change the bits
if(flag[i]>=0) // we have not fallen below the minimum in this
dimension
then {
    if(changeBP > BP(i,saveMin[i]))
    then "set all bits of dim with bit positions
> changeBP to 0"
    else "set all bits of dim with bit positions
> changeBP to the minimum of the query box in
this dim"
}
else { // if we have fallen below the min in this dimension the lowest
possible value is the min itself
    "set the bits to the minimum of the query
box in this dim"
}}
```

Figure 4-4 Pseudo code for parts of getNextZvalue

5 Query Engine Extensions

One of the major benefits of a kernel integration of the UB-Tree is the tight integration with the query engine. In the following we will discuss the most important issues that enable the query engine to use the UB-Tree in the most efficient way.

5.1 General Extensions

Supporting a new index method usually requires extension of schema information and DDL of the DBMS. For the UB-Tree the database catalog does not have to store additional information except the transformation function for each key attribute. The rest is also required by other index structures, for example, the index attributes, the number of dimensions, the domain of each attribute, etc.

A new storage clause (CLUSTERING UBTREE ON {<set of attributes>}) in the DDL statement for creating a table specifies the creation of a UB-Tree index. Additionally, specifying the actual domains for the attributes indexed by the UB-Tree by check constraints allows for optimal multidimensional clustering. Figure 5-1 shows the creation of a three-dimensional UB-Tree with two additional attributes.

```
CREATE TABLE fact(
date DATETIME [YY:DD] CHECK(date BETWEEN '1997-
1-1' AND '2020-12-31',
region INTEGER CHECK(region BETWEEN 0 AND 2047),
product INTEGER CHECK(product BETWEEN 0 AND
999999),
price NUMERIC (12,2),
quantity NUMERIC(8,2),
PRIMARY KEY (product, date, region),
CLUSTERING UBTREE ON {product, date, region})
```

Figure 5-1 Create statement for a UB-Tree

With the kernel integration the UB-Tree query functionality is hidden by the standard SQL interface, i.e., no extension of the DML is required. The extensions of the query engine, especially of the optimizer, will take care of the appropriate usage of the new index, e.g., processing a multidimensional range query on the UB-Tree if possible.

5.2 Handling Multidimensional Range Queries

One of the big advantages of the UB-Tree is the efficient processing of multidimensional range queries. State-of-the-art query engines usually only extract the most selective predicate from the query to pass it down to the selected index. In case of the UB-Tree the query engine has to take care of generating a suitable query box or a set of query boxes from the query predicate. This requires passing down a more complex structure instead of a single range to the underlying index module. We will specify an optimizer rule that allows for generating a query box from the query. We introduce the physical operator $RQ(R, qb)$ that represents a range query specified by the query box qb on a relation R. Let A be the set of attributes of R with attribute $A_i \in A$ having the domain $[\min_i ; \max_i]$. The query box qb specifies for each attribute the restricted range, i.e.,

$$qb = \begin{pmatrix} \dots & \dots \\ ql_i & qh_i \\ \dots & \dots \end{pmatrix} \text{ for } A_i \in [ql_i ; qh_i]^2.$$ For each

$A_i \in A$, $S(A_i, qb)$ specifies the selectivity of attribute A_i in qb.

Each restriction on a table specified by the predicate Ψ in the WHERE clause is represented by the logical operator $\sigma_\Psi(R)$. This is transformed to $\sigma_\Psi(R) = \sigma_\Xi(\sigma_P(R))$ with P corresponding to the set of multidimensional query boxes on R, i.e., $P = \rho_1 \vee \dots \vee \rho_m$ where $\rho_i = \bigcap_{j=1}^{n} A_j \in [a_j^i ; b_j^i]$, and Ξ corresponding to the restrictions, which cannot be mapped to multidimensional query boxes, e.g., $A_i < A_j$.

We can therefore write: $\sigma_\Psi(R) = \sigma_\Xi(\bigcup_i \sigma_{\rho_i}(R))$.

Example: The SQL statement
    SELECT count(*)
    FROM R
    WHERE A_1 BETWEEN 0 AND 10 AND A_2 IN [3,12,31] AND A_3 BETWEEN 3 AND 9
    leads to the predicate describing 3 query boxes:
    $P = (A_1 \in [0;10] \wedge A_2 \in [3,3] \wedge A_3 \in [3;9]) \vee$
    $(A_1 \in [0;10] \wedge A_2 \in [12,12] \wedge A_3 \in [3;9]) \vee$
    $(A_1 \in [0;10] \wedge A_2 \in [31,31] \wedge A_3 \in [3;9])$

As the example shows, the identification of query boxes from arbitrary predicates is a complex problem by its own the query optimizer needed to be enhanced for. The TransBase optimizer already recognized a special subset of multidimensional intervals, namely those, which can be directly processed by B-Tree intervals. This greatly facilitated the extension of the optimizer to general multidimensional intervals.

Let $P \subseteq A$ be the set of attributes of R, which are specified in ρ_i. We can specify the following rule to create the corresponding query box:

REPLACE $\sigma_{\rho_i}(R)$ BY $RQ(R, qb)$

with $ql_i = \begin{cases} a_i & \text{if } A_i \in P \\ \min_i & \text{otherwise} \end{cases}$ and $qh_i = \begin{cases} b_i & \text{if } A_i \in P \\ \max_i & \text{otherwise} \end{cases}$

---

[2] Note: In this paper we only deal with closed intervals $(\geq, \leq)$ for restrictions. Other restrictions $(>, <)$, which cannot be mapped to closed intervals (e.g., for non-discrete domains), are handled with appropriate post filtering.

Given such a query box, the optimizer then can decide which access method to use to answer the query.

6 UB-Tree Enhancements

This section deals with some enhancements of the UB-Tree and its algorithms, which have not been integrated into the TransBase kernel yet. These improvements are not necessary for a successful integration of the UB-Tree, but they provide further performance optimizations.

6.1 Optimizing Space Partitioning for Range Queries

The UB-Tree range query performance is enhanced by a modification of the page splitting algorithm leading to a better space partitioning. The so-called ε-Split chooses the split point in an interval of ε% of the page capacity around the middle of the page and not directly in the middle.

That is, it chooses the optimal split point according to the space partitioning in a certain range of tuples around the middle of the page, but not only between the two tuples in the middle. The cost for the optimal splitting is the reduced page utilization guarantee of $50\% - \varepsilon\%$. The enhanced split algorithm requires the two tuples, which are $\varepsilon\%$ away to the left and to the right from the middle of the page, whereas the standard version takes just the two tuples to the left and right of the page middle. Figure 6-1 shows the same two-dimensional UB-tree with standard split point calculation and with ε-Split ($\varepsilon = 14\%$): the effect is clearly visible.

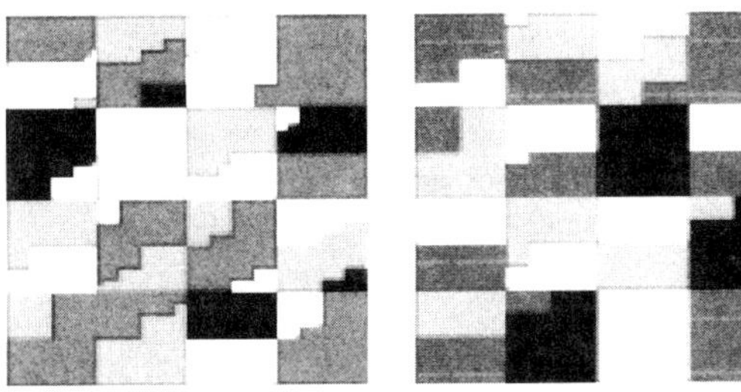

(a) w/o ε-Split   (b) with ε-Split

Figure 6-1: Influence of Epsilon-Split on the Space Partitioning

The optimal choice of ε presents a tradeoff between storage utilization and quality of space partitioning: the higher ε the better the space partitioning and as consequence the range query performance but the lower the worst-case storage guarantee. However, empirical results (Figure 6-2 shows the results of 6-dimensional range queries with varying volume and location on a 6D UB-Tree for growing ε) have shown that already a small ε (around 5%) leads to significant improvement of the space partitioning.

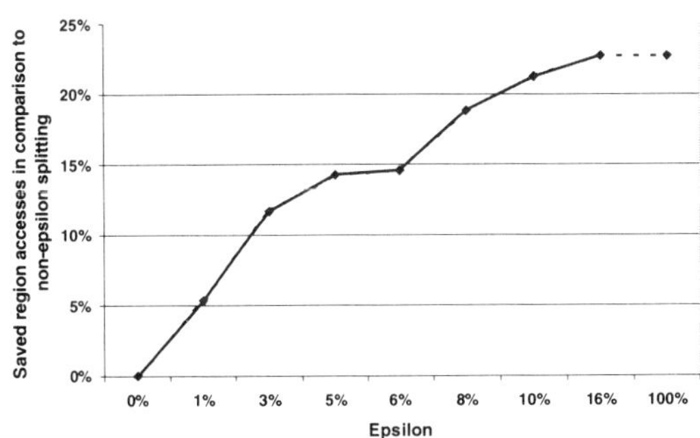

Figure 6-2 Influence of Epsilon Splitting on Range Query Performance

For $\varepsilon > 15\%$ no significant improvements in the space partitioning are observed. It is important to note that the ε-Split has the same complexity as the regular split algorithm, and that for the individual UB-Tree ε is a performance tuning parameter.

6.2 Dealing with multiple query boxes

Often complex queries do not only lead to one query box, but to a set of query boxes on the multidimensional space. Processing the set of query boxes sequentially with the UB-Tree range query algorithm may lead to unnecessary page accesses in the cases where query boxes overlap the same regions. As consequence, performance problems arise if the already accessed page cannot be cached over the total processing of the query box set. The algorithm presented in [FMB99] solves this problem by handling all query boxes simultaneously. It guarantees that each region/page is accessed only once, leading to significant performance improvement over the standard UB-Tree range query algorithm in case of query boxes overlapping many pages together.

6.3 Reducing Post Filtering of the Range Query Algorithm

Post filtering is only necessary for regions not fully contained within the query box. We provide an algorithm similar to getNextZvalue and with the same complexity, which determines for a region if it is completely overlapped by a query box or not. This is an important performance optimization for large query boxes as most regions will be completely inside of the query box.

7 Performance Evaluation

In this section we provide some measurement results that show the performance gains that are achieved by the kernel integration of the UB-Tree into the TransBase database system (called TransBase Hyper Cube, Figure 7-1b). We are comparing with our prototype implementation of the UB-Tree (called UB/API, Figure 7-1a) and the native TransBase B-Tree. Our previous comparisons of the UB-Tree with competing index methods of TransBase and other RDBMSs [MZB99, MRB99], based on the UB/API, yielded significant performance improvements. The speed-up achieved by the kernel integration applies directly to the results of our previous comparisons, yielding a speed-up of several orders of magnitude of UB-Trees compared to the methods used in these papers.

Our prototype implementation of the UB-Tree is realized as an application on top of an existing DBMS using the standard SQL interface (currently TransBase, Oracle, Informix, SQL Server 7, and DB2 are supported). The leaf pages of the UB-Tree are stored as single tuples in a relation and the index part is mapped to the B-Tree index of the underlying system.

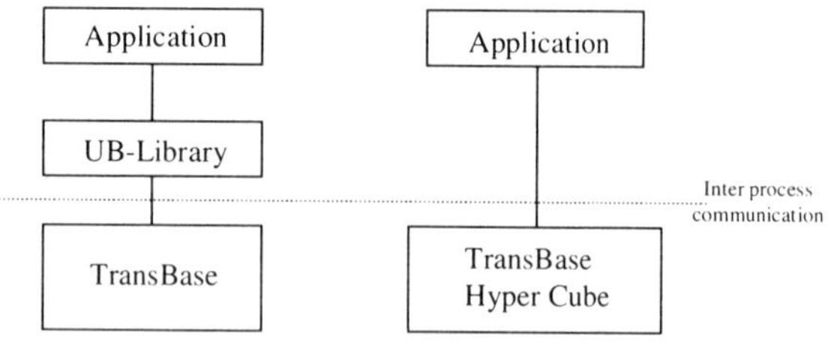

(a) UB/API   (b) TransBase Hyper Cube

Figure 7-1: Implementation as UB/API versus TransBase Hyper Cube

The measurements were conducted on a real world data warehouse provided by one of our project partners, a market research company. The measurements consist of 604 real world reports on a three dimensional (time, products, segments) star-schema with a total of around 4GB of data. The reports represent typical analysis of product hitlists in a given period, market share, market trends, and the like, which result in three-dimensional range queries on the fact table.

We created three instances of the fact table: two indexed by UB-Trees (integrated and external), and one indexed by a compound B-Tree on the three dimension keys. From the reports we only measured the fact table access, as the further processing is identical for all methods. Table 7-1 shows the measurement results over all 604 reports.

On average, the integrated UB-Tree is about 2-3 times faster than UB/API (see Table 7-1). As mentioned above, this speed up applies directly to the performance advantage over both clustering compound B-Trees as well as index intersection of multiple secondary B-Trees or bitmap indexes.

	Speedup Factor UB/API / HCI	Speedup Factor Compound/HCI
Average	2,8	11,5
1. Quartil	2,3	8,5
Max	3,0	5,0
Min	3,0	2,3
3. Quartil	2,8	13,2

Table 7-1 Summary of Report Results (average response times in seconds)

The significant performance improvement of the kernel integration can be explained by the design of UB/API. First, each fetch of a page requires one SQL statement; this leads to heavy client/server communication together with the DBMS overhead of processing the query, which sums up to about 30% of the total processing time of a range query. Second, we had to implement some database functionality, like page and tuple handling, post filtering etc., which causes additional overhead. Putting all together, the above mentioned speedup factor fits our expectation.

8 Related Work

Integrating new index methods into a database kernel is often regarded as a too costly task. On the other side, database vendors have recognized the need for more flexible, powerful indexing methods, often tailored to specific application domains. As consequence, most vendors have extended their standard B-Trees and provide interfaces that allow the users to include their own functions for the index key computation. Some systems even allow the user to implement their own index structures in external modules. We will point out the deficiencies of these approaches in this section.

8.1 Function-based B-Trees

For standard B-Trees the key of the index consists of a subset of the attributes of the underlying table T. A more general idea is to use a function to compute the key values for the tuples $t \in T$. We will refer to this type of B-Trees as *function-based B-Trees* or short B^F-Trees.

Example: A standard B-Tree is a special instance of the B^F-Tree where F is the projection of the key attributes from the tuple. B-Trees storing SOUNDEX codes or case-insensitive keys are other well-known examples.

B^F-Trees were motivated by the need to support indexing on user-defined types in object-relational systems. Commercial implementations are provided for example by function-based indexes in Oracle8i [Ora99], functional indexes in Informix [Inf99], the high level indexing framework of IBM DB2 [CCF+99], or as indexes on computed columns in MS SQL Server 2000 [MS00]. However, B^F-Trees do not allow for the integration of new query algorithms, like the UB-Tree range query algorithm. Therefore, implementing the UB-Tree as a B^F-Tree with UBKEY as F will not lead to the expected performance.

8.2 Extended Index Interfaces

Some commercial database management systems provide even more enhanced indexing interfaces, which allow for implementation of arbitrary index structures by the user in external modules (e.g., Extensible Indexing API by Oracle [ORA99], Informix Datablade API [Inf99]). Analogous to the GiST framework (see next section), the user has to provide a set of functions/operators that are used by the database server to access the index. The index itself can be either stored inside the database (e.g., as an IOT in Oracle) or in external files. The problem of these index interfaces is threefold: performance of the index, optimizer support, and locking and recovery. The performance problem of extended index interfaces has two aspects: first, only non-clustered indexes are supported. Index structures, whose performance is achieved by appropriate clustering, like the UB-Tree that clusters according to multiple dimensions, can therefore not be implemented via these interfaces. In addition, as the DBMS internal modules cannot be used, efficient page and tuple handling has to be implemented. This leads to significant coding effort for the index implementation. The coupling of the external index with the query optimizer is achieved by providing cost functions for the index operations. However, to our knowledge, there is no way to add rules to guide the optimizer with heuristics, which is very important to achieve optimal query plans. Another significant drawback of these 'add-on' approaches is the handling of locking and recovery. The external indexes are not tightly coupled with the DMBS locking and recovery services. As consequence, the index implementation has to take care of recovery issues itself [BSS+99], and the lock granularity is often the complete index itself.

Taking all these aspects into account, in case of the UB-Tree the kernel integration is much more favorable than an implementation as an external index.

8.3   GiST – Framework

The General Search Tree (GiST) approach of [HNP95] provides a single framework for any tree-based index structure. The GiST framework provides the basic functionality for trees, e.g., insertion, deletion, splitting, search, etc. The individual semantics of the index are provided by the user with a key class, which implements six key functions the basic functions rely on. As consequence, the user has only to change a small part of the code to implement various index methods (e.g., B^+-Trees, R-Trees). In general, the UB-Tree fits perfectly into the GiST framework, but efficient implementation would require more user control at two points: search algorithm and splitting. The major drawback of the first GiST approach is the fixed query functionality – the user cannot adapt the search algorithm to the specific indexing technique, which in many application scenarios will lead to significant performance problems. The UB-Tree range query algorithm is one example of such a search algorithm. The extension of [Aok98], which gives the user the control of the tree traversal during search, should suffice for an efficient range query implementation. Putting all together, if the extended GiST framework is available, the benefits described in [Kor99] apply to the UB-Tree integration as well.

9   Summary and Conclusion

Multidimensional access methods are not widely supported by commercial database management systems despite their performance impacts in various application domains. This is mostly due to the fact that a kernel integration of these sophisticated data structures is considered to be a very costly and complex task. In this paper we have shown that this is not the case for the UB-Tree, as it heavily relies on the well-known B-Tree, reducing the complexity of the additional algorithms to a minimum. The UB-Tree was integrated within one year, and by now TransBase Hyper Cube is a commercially available product. Figure 9-1 shows the changes of the individual database kernel modules required by the UB-Tree integration.

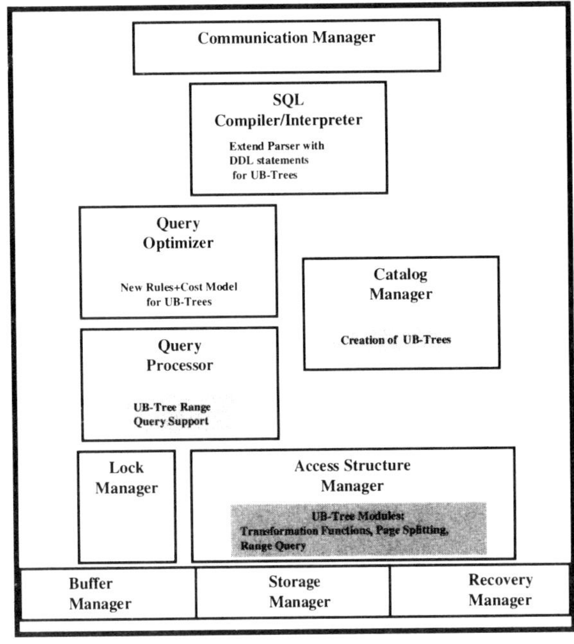

Figure 9-1 Affected Modules of TransBase

The shaded boxes mark the modifications in the single modules, where the darker shading signals the more complex modifications. The performance gains show that the effort of the integration is worth it: with up to a factor of 3 faster than the prototype implementation on top of a DBMS, the kernel integrated UB-Tree provides significantly better performance than traditional access methods in various application domains. The big advantage of the kernel integration in comparison with other approaches is the tight coupling with the query optimizer. This allows for optimal usage of the UB-Tree. As we do not rely on any TransBase specific features for the UB-Tree algorithms, we expect the same integration effort for other database systems as well, as long they provide clustering B-Trees on computed keys.

An issue not addressed in this paper is the question, when to use the UB-Tree for a specific application scenario and which UB-Tree organization (e.g., number of dimensions) is optimal. This problem is addressed in what we call *physical data modeling* and we are in the progress of identifying design rules for optimal indexing strategies with UB-Trees.

Summarizing our experiences, UB-Trees smoothly integrate into the indexing engine and extend the B-Tree concept in order to handle multiple dimensions symmetrically. They are extremely useful for both clustering tables as well as covering secondary indexes (secondary indexes that contain all attributes required by a given query) to speed up multidimensional range queries. Extending the optimizer allows for good combination with single attribute access methods in physical data modeling and query processing, which will lead to efficient and flexible index schemes.

Acknowledgements

We thank our project partners the European Commission, Teijin Systems Technology, and Microsoft Research for funding this research work. We also thank our master student Stephan Merkel for his effort in doing the performance measurements reported in this paper. In addition we thank Goetz Graefe for his constructive comments.

References

[Aok98]   P. M. Aoki. *Generalizing "Search" in Generalized Search Trees*. Proc. of ICDE 1998.

[Bay97]   R. Bayer. *The universal B-Tree for multidimensional Indexing: General Concepts*. World-Wide Computing and Its Applications '97 (WWCA '97). Tsukuba, Japan, 10-11, Lecture Notes on Computer Science, Springer Verlag, March, 1997.

[BSS+99]   R. Bliujute, S. Salentis, G. Slivinskas, and C.S. Jensen. *Developing a DataBlade for a New Index*. Proc. of ICDE 1999.

[BU77]   R. Bayer and K. Unterauer. *Prefix B-Trees*. ACM TODS 2(1), 1977, pp. 11-26.

[CCF+99]   W. Chen, J.-H. Chow, Y.C. Fuh, J. Grandbois, M. Jou, N. Mattos, B. Tran, and Y. Wang. *High Level Indexing of User-Defined Types*. Proc. of 25th VLDB, Edinburgh, Scotland, 1999.

[CM98]   K. Chakrabarti and S. Mehrotra. *Dynamic Granular Locking Approach to Phantom Protection in R-Trees*. Proc. of ICDE, 1998.

[FMB99]   R. Fenk, V. Markl, and R. Bayer. *Improving Multidimensional Range Queries of non rectangular Volumes specified by a Query Box Set*. Proc. of International Symposium on Database, Web and Cooperative Systems (DWACOS), Baden-Baden, Germany, 1999

[HNP95]   J. M. Hellerstein, J. F. Naughton, and A. Pfeffer. *Generalized Search Trees for Database Systems*. Proc. of 21st VLDB, Zurich, Switzerland, 1995.

[HR96]   E.P. Harris, and K. Ramamohanarao. *Join algorithm costs revisited*. VLDB Journal, 5, 1996

[Inf99]   Informix Software Incorporation. *Informix Dynamic Server with Universal Data Option Version 9.1.X Documentation*. 1999.

[LKC99]   J.-H. Lee, D.-H. Kim, C.-W. Chung. *Multi-dimensional Selectivity Estimation Using Compressed Histogram Information*. Proc. of SIGMOD99, Philadelphia, U.S.A., 1999

[KB95]   M. Kornacker and D. Banks. *High-Concurrency Locking in R-Trees*. Proc. of 21st VLDB, Zürich, Switzerland, 1995.

[Kor99]   M. Kornacker. *High-Performance Extensible Indexing*. Proc. of the 25th VLDB, Edinburgh, Scotland, 1999.

[Mar99]   V. Markl. *MISTRAL: Processing Relational Queries using a Multidimensional Access Technique*. Ph.D. Thesis, Technische Universität München, 1999.

[MRB99]   V. Markl, F. Ramsak, and R. Bayer. *Improving OLAP Performance by Multidimensional Hierarchical Clustering*. Proc. of IDEAS'99, Montreal, Canada, 1999.

[MS00]   Microsoft Coperation. *SQL Server 2000 Books Online*. 2000.

[MZB99]   V. Markl, M. Zirkel, and R. Bayer. *Processing Operations with Restrictions in Relational Database Management Systems without external Sorting*. Proc. of ICDE, Sydney, Australia, 1999.

[OM84]   J. A. Orenstein and T.H. Merret. *A Class of Data Structures for Associate Searching*. Proc. of ACM SIGMOD-PODS Conf., Portland, Oregon, 1984, pp. 294-305.

[Ora99]   Oracle Corporation. *Oracle 8i Server, Release 8.1.5 Documentation*. 1999.

[PI97]   V. Poosala, and Y.E. Ioannidis. *Selectivity Estimation Without the Attribute Value Independence Assumption*. Proc of the 23th VLDB, 1997

[Tra98]   TransAction Software GmbH. *TransBase Documentation*. 1998.

[WKW94]   K.Y. Whang, S.W. Kim, G. Wiederhold. *Dynamic Maintenance of Data Distribution for Selectivity Estimation*. VLDB Journal Vol. 3, No. 1, 1994

Multi-Dimensional Database Allocation
for Parallel Data Warehouses

Thomas Stöhr   Holger Märtens   Erhard Rahm

University of Leipzig, Germany
{stoehr | maertens | rahm}@informatik.uni-leipzig.de

Abstract

Data allocation is a key performance factor for parallel database systems (PDBS). This holds especially for data warehousing environments where huge amounts of data and complex analytical queries have to be dealt with. While there are several studies on data allocation for relational PDBS, the specific requirements of data warehouses have not yet been sufficiently addressed. In this study, we consider the allocation of relational data warehouses based on a star schema and utilizing bitmap index structures. We investigate how a multi-dimensional hierarchical data fragmentation of the fact table supports queries referencing different subsets of the schema dimensions. Our analysis is based on realistic parameters derived from a decision support benchmark. The performance implications of different allocation choices are evaluated by means of a detailed simulation model.

1 Introduction

Data warehouses integrate massive amounts of data from multiple sources and are primarily used for decision support purposes. They have to process complex analytical queries for different access forms such as OLAP (on-line analytical processing), data mining, etc. In addition, successful data warehouses tend to be used by many users so that the concurrent execution of multiple complex queries must be supported. Ensuring short query response times in such an environment is enormously difficult and can only be achieved by a combination of different approaches, in particular the use of preaggregated data [12,37], special aggregation operators like cube [13], special index structures such as bitmap indices [22,24] and parallel query processing.

While the first three approaches have been investigated extensively in recent work, surprisingly, parallel query processing tailored for data warehouses has received very little attention in the research community. In particular, we are not aware of research results on data allocation for parallel

data warehouses, which is the main focus of this paper. Of course, basic approaches of traditional parallel databases [7] can be employed for relational data warehouses as well. However, these approaches can only achieve suboptimal performance as they do not utilize specific characteristics of the database organization and query types of data warehouses. Hence, high performance data warehousing should be based not only on specialized index structures but also on tailored approaches for parallel database processing.

We focus on relational data warehouses based on a star schema [5]. The database thus consists of a huge fact table and multiple dimension tables. Dimensions are hierarchically structured, e.g., to group months into quarters, years etc. Queries typically perform aggregations on the fact table based on selections among the available dimension levels (e.g. sales of all products from product group x during quarter y). Such *star (join) queries* can be efficiently supported by bitmap indices but still involve substantial processing and I/O cost. The paper focuses on the design and evaluation of suitable data allocation methods for the fact table and bitmap indices to allow an efficient parallel processing of star queries.

While our data allocation methods are applicable to all major PDBS (parallel database system) architectures, due to space constraints we concentrate on the „Shared Disk" approach [7], which is supported by several commercial DBMS (*IBM DB2/OS390, ORACLE*). Shared Disk is particularly attractive for data warehousing because the read-dominated workloads largely eliminate the need for concurrency and coherency control, which are performance-critical for OLTP [21,28]. Furthermore, there is a high potential for parallel query processing and dynamic load balancing since each processing node has access to all disks allowing it to process any query or subquery [28]. Data allocation for Shared Disk refers to the placement of tables and index structures onto disks; there is no fixed assignment of data partitions to processing nodes. The disk allocation must support parallel processing and load balancing while limiting disk contention.

We propose a multi-dimensional hierarchical fragmentation of the fact table based on multiple dimension attributes. Such an approach permits a significant reduction of processing and I/O overhead for many queries by restricting the number of fragments to be processed for both the fact table and bitmap data. Such savings are achieved not only for the fragmentation attributes themselves but also for attributes at different levels of a dimension hierarchy. The proposed data allocation and processing model also supports parallel I/O and parallel processing as well as load balancing for disks and processors. To find a suitable fragmentation for a given star schema and workload, we determine and analyze critical parameter thresholds to be considered. Furthermore, we have developed a comprehensive simulator of a parallel database system allowing a detailed performance evaluation of the new data allocation methods. Results of several experiments are presented for database and query parameters obtained from the decision support benchmark APB-1. The study leads to several guidelines that can be used by a database administrator or implemented within a tool to determine a physical data warehouse allocation.

The remainder of the paper is organized as follows. In the next section, we mention related work on data allocation and look at the approaches of commercial PDBS. In Section 3, we introduce the APB-1 star schema that has been used in our simulation study and will help illustrate the data allocation methods. We also discuss how bitmap indices are employed for processing of star queries. Section 4 then presents our multi-dimensional data allocation approach and an analysis of major performance factors. After an overview of our simulation approach (Section 5) we present performance results of various experiments for the proposed multi-dimensional database allocation in Section 6. We conclude in Section 7.

2 Related work

In general relational PDBS, data allocation is based on a horizontal fragmentation of tables, typically *round robin, hash,* or *range fragmentation* [7]. Round robin simply distributes rows in their insert order, while hash and range fragmentations are based on a partitioning function applied on the values of a fragmentation attribute. Such a one-dimensional fragmentation permits queries on the fragmentation attribute, which may be a concatenation of several attributes, to be restricted to a subset of the fragments, thereby reducing work. A number of studies analyzed one-dimensional data allocation strategies for Shared Nothing systems, e.g. [4,8,19]. In [9], a multi-dimensional range fragmentation was proposed for scan processing in Shared Nothing environments. Furthermore, there are numerous approaches for multi-dimensional declustering and access methods for spatial data [11]. However, all of these proposals do not exploit the hierarchical structure of dimensions (fragmentation attributes) and the specifics of star queries.

In [34], a multi-dimensional partitioning strategy on fact tables is proposed to achieve load balancing for star queries. The strategy requires exactly 2^k processing nodes and is based on sorting and splitting the fact table on every dimension. Again, Shared Nothing is assumed and hierarchical properties of star schemas are not considered.

Except for our own work, data allocation for Shared Disk systems has hardly been addressed in research papers. In [28,30] we have outlined the increased flexibility of the Shared Disk approach for allocating tables and index structures. In particular, the number of data partitions per table does not impact the communication overhead for query processing as for Shared Nothing. This supports high degrees of declustering even for medium-sized tables. Furthermore, index structures such as B-trees may be partitioned differently from tables (or not at all) without performance loss. In

[31], the impact of simple data allocations on scan performance in single- and multi-user mode was evaluated. In [18], a new approach for declustering large intermediate query results on shared disks was proposed and analyzed. These studies did not consider the specific aspects of data warehousing.

Numerous studies dealt with physical data allocation at the disk level in order to support I/O parallelism, e.g., within disk arrays [17,16,6,32]. Without additional index structures, physical declustering of data does not typically allow the query optimizer to predict which disks have to be accessed for a query. Hence, queries cannot be restricted to a subset of the partitions as for logical fragmentations based on attribute values. Furthermore, employing intra-query parallelism can lead to disk contention between concurrently running subqueries of the same query.

Data allocation in commercial PDBS

Most commercial PDBS have specific support for data warehousing such as bit index structures and processing of star queries, e.g., ORACLE8i [25], *IBM DB2 UNIVERSAL DATABASE (UDB)* [3], RED BRICK WAREHOUSE [29], and the ADVANCED DECISION SUPPORT OPTION of INFORMIX DYNAMIC SERVER [14]. INFORMIX and ORACLE allow choosing a variety of fragmentation options including a multi-dimensional range fragmentation [15,26]. However, it remains unclear to what extent multi-dimensional fragmentation is exploited to reduce query work. Furthermore, the hierarchical structure of fragmentation attributes is not utilized. None of the aforementioned vendors provide sufficient information or even tool support on how to determine an adequate data allocation for star schemas. Some systems such as NCR TERADATA V2R3 [2] and MICROSOFT SQL SERVER 7.0 [10] do not yet support bitmap indices.

Both *DB2 UDB* and *ORACLE8i* can dynamically create and evaluate bitmaps derived from B-tree indices on the fact table. Furthermore, SYBASE ADAPTIVE SERVER IQ [35] employs a completely different data allocation and processing strategy based on vertical partitioning of tables and possible bit-slicing of single attributes (called BIT-WISE INDEXING). Although these approaches have their merits, their consideration is beyond the scope of this paper.

3 Star schema and star queries

While our approaches can be used for any star schema, we make our discussions more specific by using the APB-1 schema, which is presented first. We then discuss the use of bitmap indices for query processing in the central case (no intra-query parallelism). Parallel query processing will be explained in Section 4.

3.1 Star Schema used for evaluation

Figure 1 shows our star schema based on the *Analytical Processing Benchmark APB-1* that was proposed by the OLAP Council to benchmark relational OLAP systems [1]. The schema provides a typical sales analysis environment with one fact table (*SALES*) and the four dimension tables *PRODUCT, CUSTOMER, CHANNEL*[1], and *TIME*. Every attribute of the dimension tables refers to a different hierarchy level.

---

1. We understand the APB-1 dimension CHANNEL to describe distribution channels.

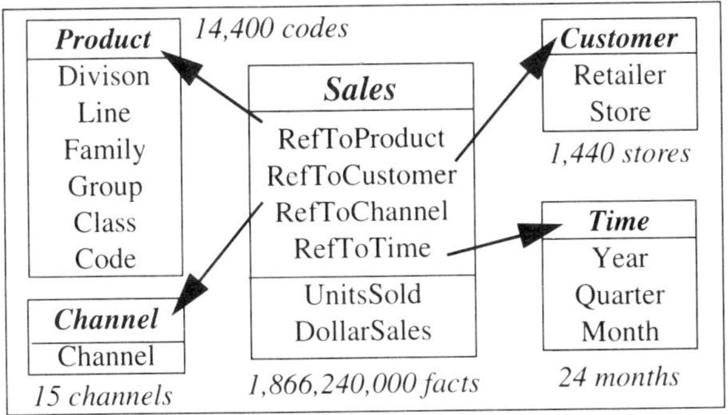

Fig. 1: Considered star schema (derived from APB-1

For instance, we have a 6-level product hierarchy differentiating several product divisions, each consisting of several product lines, each consisting of several product families, etc. Individual products are identified by product codes. As usual for star schemas, dimension tables are denormalized to reduce join overhead. The fact table *SALES* holds the measuring attributes *UnitsSold*, *DollarSales* and *Cost* for calculating aggregations. In addition, there is a foreign key per dimension each referring to the lowest hierarchy level. That is, each sales row refers to a specific product code, customer store, distribution channel and month.

APB-1 assumes a time frame of 24 months and scales the cardinality of the other dimension tables according to the number of channels. Our evaluations are based on a configuration of 15 channels resulting in the dimension cardinalities indicated in Figure 1. The cardinality of the fact table is determined by a *density factor* applied on the maximal number of possible value combinations (product of the dimension cardinalities). We used a density factor of 25% resulting in almost 2 billion fact rows. The benchmark also defines certain ratios between the attribute cardinalities within dimension hierarchies which we follow. Table 1 below shows the respective values for the *PRODUCT* dimension.

We assume typical star queries, also derived from APB-1, aggregating over one or multiple dimensions at different hierarchy levels. Expressed in SQL, a sample query called *1MONTH1GROUP* is

```
SELECT SUM(UnitsSold),SUM(DollarSales)
FROM Sales S, Product P
WHERE     S.RefToTime    = MONTH
AND       P.Group        = PRODUCTGROUP
AND       S.RefToProduct = P.Code
```

1MONTH1GROUP represents a two-dimensional star join query aggregating the measures *UnitsSold* and *DollarSales* for one product group within one month. One-dimensional queries used in our experiments are *1CODE*, *1MONTH* and *1STORE*, each referring to the specified hierarchy level.

3.2 Star query processing with bitmap indices

Such star queries involve a join between the fact table and one or more dimension tables. Standard join implementations such as hash join would require one or more full scans of the fact table. Due to the huge size of the fact table, such full scans are very costly and must be avoided whenever possible even when parallel scans can be utilized. This is also because for most queries, only a small fraction of the fact data is relevant.

Bitmap indices allow a much faster processing of star joins and selections on fact tables [22]. A standard bitmap index contains one bitmap per possible value of a given attribute; the bitmap consists of one bit per row to indicate whether or not that row matches the respective attribute value. A selection for a specific attribute value (e.g., *RefToTime=MONTH* in query *1MONTH1GROUP*) thus has to read only one bitmap to precisely identify all relevant fact rows. A variation are so-called *bitmap join indices* where each bitmap indicates which fact rows match an attribute value of the dimension table (via the respective foreign key). Hence, such bitmaps represent the precomputed result of a join between the fact table and a dimension table. For our sample query, a bitmap join index on product group would be beneficial. The join query can then be processed by reading and intersecting (AND-ing) the two bitmaps for *MONTH* and *PRODUCTGROUP*. The resulting bitmap represents the rows to be read from the fact table. Since the bitmaps are much more compact than the fact table and only the relevant fact rows are to be read, performance can be substantially improved compared to a full scan of the fact table. Of course, the sketched approach can be applied for an arbitrary number of query dimensions and multiple values per dimension; it is supported by several commercial DBMS. Note that more complex queries require additional processing steps (for instance, a join to the *PRODUCT* dimension may still be necessary if aggregation results are to be grouped by the product classes within a selected product group). This will not be considered further because the associated processing cost is typically much smaller than for fact table processing.

Simple bitmap indices become inefficient for high-cardinality attributes resulting in a large number of bitmaps and thus high storage overhead (which may be reduced by compressing the bitmaps). In this case, *encoded bitmap indices* [36] can help by encoding attribute values from a domain of size $|Dom|$ in approximately $\log_2 |Dom|$ bits, thereby reducing the number of bitmaps necessary to represent the index. The trade-off is that selecting a single value in an encoded bitmap index requires finding a specific pattern in *all* of the bitmaps, rather than a single bitmap. This may, however, be ameliorated by an appropriate encoding. Specifically, [36] suggested an encoding scheme that represents individual hierarchy elements of star to support selections on the inner dimension levels.

For our study, we employ encoded bitmap join indices on the higher-cardinality dimensions *PRODUCT* and *CUSTOMER*. We utilize a hierarchical encoding that avoids a separate bitmap index per hierarchy level but only requires one index per dimension. This is illustrated in Table 1 for the *PRODUCT* dimension where we use separate bit sub-patterns to encode *DIVISIONs*, *LINEs* within *DIVISIONs*, *FAMILIEs* within *LINEs* etc. We only need 15 bits to identify a particular product code so that the index only consists of 15 bitmaps instead of 14.400 which would be needed for simple bitmaps. Locating all fact rows of a specific product code thus needs to evaluate 15 bitmaps (which we will access in parallel). The hierarchical encoding reduces the access cost for attributes at a higher level of the dimension hierarchy. For instance, *CODEs* (fact rows) belonging to the same *GROUP*

	DIVISION	*LINE*	*FAMILY*	*GROUP*	*CLASS*	*CODE*	total
#total elements	8	24	120	480	960	14,400	14,400
#elements within parent	8	3	5	4	2	15	
#bits for encoding ($\log_2$)	3	2	3	2	1	4	15
sample bit pattern	ddd	ll	fff	gg	c	oooo	dddllfffggcoooo

Table 1: Hierarchy representation in encoded bitmap join indices

share the same prefix (`dddllfffgg`) of the full bit pattern (`dddllfffggcoooo`) and can be precisely located with access to only 10 of the 15 bitmaps.

The encoded bitmap indices on *PRODUCT* and *CUSTOMER* need 15 and 12 bitmaps, respectively. For the low-cardinality dimensions *TIME* and *CHANNEL* we use simple bitmap indices consisting of up to 34 (24 for month, 8 for quarter, 2 for year) and 15 bitmaps each. This results in a maximum of 76 bitmaps for our configuration. As we will see, our multi-dimensional fragmentation permits eliminating some bitmaps, thus improving storage and access overhead.

4 Data allocation

In this section, we present our fragmentation and allocation strategy for star schemas supporting parallel query processing. We focus on the fact table and its bitmap indices. Dimension tables and their (B*-tree) indices usually cover only a very small fraction of the whole database so that they do not need special treatment. For instance, our four dimension tables only occupy 1 MB and can easily be stored on a single disk. Frequently accessed dimension data will automatically be cached in main memory.

Data allocation of the fact table and bitmap indices is determined in two steps. In the first step, we define a multi-dimensional horizontal fragmentation of the fact table resulting in *n* disjoint *fact fragments*. These fragments are our units for disk placement as well as for query processing. The fact table fragmentation is also to be applied to the bitmap indices meaning that each bitmap of any bitmap index is partitioned into *n bitmap fragments*. This ensures that the bits of a bitmap fragment refer to exactly one fact fragment and allows different fact fragments to be processed inde-

pendently (in parallel). Of course, a bitmap fragment is much smaller than a fact fragment[2]. The second allocation step assigns all fragments onto disks. Typically, the number of fact fragments, *n,* is much higher than the number of disks, *d*, to support high degrees of parallelism and effective load balancing.

Figure 2 illustrates our data allocation approach. A simple round robin allocation of fact fragments to the disks is used. Each of the *k* bitmaps (from all indices) is partitioned into *n* bitmap fragments. We place the *k* bitmap fragments belonging to the same fact fragment onto consecutive disks to enable intra-query parallelism for bitmap processing. For instance, if fact fragment *frag i* is placed on disk *j*, the associated bitmap fragments of all *k* different bitmaps are placed on disk $j, j + 1, .. j + k - 1 (\text{modulo} d)$ [3].

In Section 4.1, we will introduce our approach of multi-dimensional hierarchical fragmentation, followed by a discussion how it reduces query work and bitmap requirements (Section 4.2). After a brief discussion of our parallel processing strategy in Section 4.3, we present some basic thresholds for fragmentation parameters in Section 4.4. Section 4.5 quantifies the I/O cost for different types of queries, and Section 4.6 discusses the physical allocation of table and index fragments to disks. Finally, Section 4.7 lists a set of guidelines for multi-dimensional star schema declustering derived from these considerations.

4.1 Multi-dimensional fragmentation of the fact table

To reflect the inherent multi-dimensional and hierarchical organization of star schema data and queries, we propose a ***multi-dimensional hierarchical fragmentation*** called ***MDHF*** for partitioning the fact table. It allows choosing multiple *fragmentation attributes* from different *hierarchy levels* of the dimension tables. Each fragmentation attribute refers to a different dimension. For each fragmentation attribute – and thus for each dimension – a range partitioning can be specified consisting of disjoint value ranges for the attribute's domain. For completeness, the union of the value ranges must cover the whole domain. As in general multi-dimensional range fragmentation [9], a fragment then consists of all (fact) tuples belonging to one value range per fragmentation attribute.

For simplicity, we will focus on „point fragmentations" where each value range consists of exactly one attribute value of a fragmentation attribute. This approach is feasible for data warehousing due to the well-defined domains of

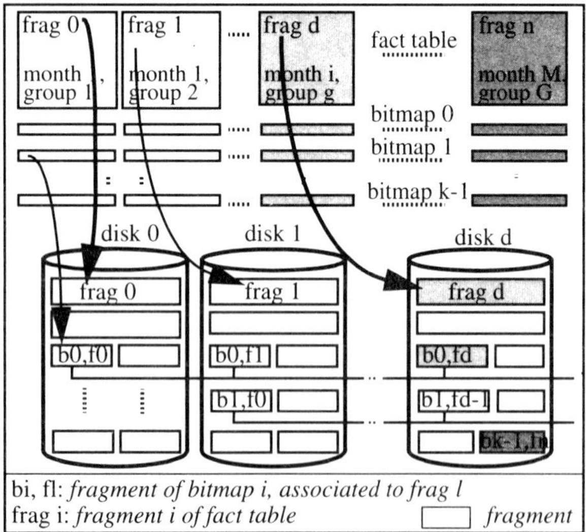

Fig. 2: Fragmentation and allocation of a star schema

2. Bitmaps store 1 bit per fact tuple. Therefore, the size of a fact fragment is $(8 \cdot SizeFactTuple)$ times the size of bitmap fragments. (*SizeFactTuple* denotes the size of a fact tuple in bytes)

3. For Shared Nothing, the bit fragments would have to be allocated to the same processing node as the fact fragment thus restricting the number of disks for allocating bitmaps.

dimensional attributes. Point fragmentations eliminate the need to define value ranges for fragmentation attributes and allow a high number of fragments of reduced size. The number of fragments is simply determined by the product of the fragmentation attributes' cardinalities. Note that point fragmentations still result in range fragmentations at lower levels of the dimension hierarchy because for each value at a specific dimension level, we have an associated value range at the lower levels. For instance, a specific product group covers a range of product classes and product codes.

We denote an m-dimensional (point) fragmentation F by specifying its fragmentation attributes f_i in the form

$$F = \{f_1, f_2, ..., f_m\} \text{ with}$$
$$f_i = 'Dimension_i::Hierarchy\text{-}level_{i,j}'. \; i = 1..m$$

Every fact fragment obtained for such a fragmentation F contains all fact rows with one particular value per fragmentation attribute[4]. For instance, the fragmentation

$$F_{MonthGroup} = \{time::month, product::group\}$$

refers to a two-dimensional fragmentation on product group and month. Each fact fragment of this fragmentation combines all fact rows referring to one particular product group and one particular month. Based on the cardinalities given in Section 3, $F_{MonthGroup}$ results in $24 \cdot 480 = 11,520$ fact fragments. The order in which the fragmentation attributes are specified is irrelevant for the contents of fact fragments. However, we use a specific logical ordering of the dimensions for placing the fragments to disks. For instance, Figure 2 shows an allocation for $F_{MonthGroup}$ for M (= 24) months and G (= 480) groups where we first allocate the G fragments for the first month, followed by the G fragments of the second month etc.

4.2 Reducing query work and bitmap requirements

MDHF not only allows queries on the fragmentation attributes to be confined to a subset of the fragments but also many other query types by utilizing the hierarchical structure of dimensions. We can distinguish the following four basic cases or query types Qi for which such an improvement is possible. Each case has several subcases depending on whether all fragmentation dimensions are involved in the query or only a subset, and on whether attributes not belonging to a fragmentation dimension are additionally to be evaluated.

- *Q1: Queries on the fragmentation attributes*
  Queries referencing all fragmentation attributes can be confined to the minimal number of fragments. For exact-match predicates on all fragmentation attributes we have only 1 fragment to process. This holds for our query *1MONTH1GROUP* from Section 3 and the above fragmentation $F_{MonthGroup}$. Note that every fact row of the selected fragment is relevant for this query so that there is no need to use bitmaps for the query attributes.
  Queries referencing a subset of the fragmentation attributes still can be confined to comparatively few frag-

ments but more than in the previous case. For exact-match queries the number of fragments to be processed increases by the cardinality of the fragmentation attributes not accessed. For instance, if we want to aggregate all facts for one product *GROUP* - over all 24 months - for fragmentation $F_{MonthGroup}$, we have to process 24 fragments. Again, there is no need to access bitmaps for the query attribute because we have to completely process the fragments.
  Bitmap access is only needed for additional query attributes not belonging to any fragmentation dimension. For instance, to aggregate over 1 product *GROUP* and 1 *STORE* we have to process 24 fact fragments but can use a bitmap index on *CUSTOMER* to restrict processing to the relevant fact rows.

- *Q2: Queries on „lower-level“ attributes of the fragmentation dimension*
  Queries accessing attributes from the dimension of a fragmentation attribute but below in the hierarchy can also be restricted to the minimal number of fragments. This is because each value of such an attribute belongs to exactly one value of the fragmentation attribute and is thus confined to a small number of fragments. Ideally, only 1 fragment needs to be accessed when all fragmentation dimensions are involved (e.g. a query *1CODE1MONTH* aggregating over 1 product *CODE* and 1 *MONTH* for $F_{MonthGroup}$). Queries not referencing all fragmentation dimensions need to process a correspondingly larger number of fragments as in the previous case (e.g. query *1CODE* aggregating for 1 product *CODE* and all *MONTH*s involves 24 fragments).
  In contrast to Q1, only a subset of the fragment rows is relevant even if only attributes from the fragmentation dimensions are accessed. Bitmaps may be used within the fragmentation dimension to select the relevant rows (e.g., for product code) and to allow Boolean operations with other bitmaps.

- *Q3: Queries on „higher-level“ attributes of the fragmentation dimension*
  Queries accessing attributes from the dimension of a fragmentation attribute but higher in the hierarchy can also be restricted to a subset of the fragments but to more than in the cases before. This is because each value of such an attribute has multiple associated values of the fragmentation attribute and thus a correspondingly higher number of fragments. For instance, if we want to aggregate a product *GROUP* over a *QUARTER* we have to access three fragments rather than one. Again, the number of fragments increases if only some fragmentation dimensions are involved. For instance if want to aggregate for one *QUARTER* – over all product *GROUP*s – we have to process $480 \cdot 3$ fragments (one eighth of all fragments).
  As in case Q1, all tuples of the selected fragments are relevant (no bitmap access for fragmentation dimension).

- *Q4: „Mixed“ queries on fragmentation dimensions*
  For queries referencing at least two fragmentation dimensions, mixed cases are possible involving both attributes at a lower (or equal) and at a higher (or equal) level than a fragmentation attribute. An example for this case, is a query for a specific product *CODE* and *QUARTER under*

---

4. More formally, a fragment of fact table T, dimension tables D_i, and fragment attributes f_i contains the result of the following relational expression for a specific combination of attribute values w_i ($i = 1 ... m$):

$$\pi_{T\text{-}attributes} \; (\, ... \, ((T \bowtie \sigma_{f_1 = w_1}(D_1)) \bowtie \sigma_{f_2 = w_2}(D_2)) \, ... \bowtie$$
$$\sigma_{f_m = w_m}(D_m) \,)$$

$F_{MonthGroup}$. This query can be restricted to 3 fragments because 1 product *CODE* and 3 *MONTH*s are involved. As for Q2, only a subset of the fact rows of the selected fragments is relevant.

Thus, all queries referencing at least *one attribute of any fragmentation dimension* can be confined to a subset of the fragments. Furthermore, MDHF implies that for selections on fragmentation attributes and on higher-level attributes of a fragmentation dimension all tuples of a fact fragment are relevant so that there is no need to use bitmaps for these attributes (cases Q1 and Q3). This allows us to completely eliminate bitmaps for these attributes (because they would only contain „1" bits) resulting in substantial storage and processing savings. For our fragmentation $F_{MonthGroup}$, we do not need any bitmaps for the *TIME* dimension because for each query on *MONTH*, *QUARTER*, or *YEAR* all rows of the selected fact fragments are relevant. For the product dimension, we do not need bitmaps for product *GROUP* and higher levels, thus saving 10 bitmaps (cf. Table 1). Compared to the maximum of 76 bitmaps (Section 3.2), for $F_{MonthGroup}$ at most 32 bitmaps are thus to be maintained.

4.3 Parallel processing of star queries

We employ two levels of intra-query parallelism for star queries. For each fragment to be processed, we assign a subquery processing the fact fragment and the associated bitmap fragments. Within each subquery, I/O parallelism can be used, e.g. to concurrently access multiple bitmaps. The fragmentation only defines the maximal number of subqueries. The actual degree of intra-query parallelism and the assignment of subqueries to processing nodes is determined by the scheduling and load balancing strategy (see Section 5). To improve sequential I/O performance for both the fact table and bitmaps, we read multiple consecutively stored pages per I/O. Such *prefetch granules* typically range from 1 to 8 pages.

The following steps are performed for processing a star query with respect to a given fragmentation F:

1. Determine fact fragments to be processed based on the query's attributes and the fragmentation attributes of F
2. For each query attribute q_i, determine all associated bitmap fragments. Bitmap access is needed for a q_i, iff
   - the dimension of q_i is not represented in F, or
   - the dimension of q_i is represented in F, but on a higher hierarchy level.
3. Assign a subquery to each fact fragment and its corresponding bitmap fragments
4. For each subquery scheduled for execution
   a) access and process a set of consecutive pages of all relevant bitmap fragments to determine hit rows.
   b) access fact pages containing hits and process aggregation

   Iterate steps 4a and 4b until all pages of the fragment are processed.

4.4 Fragmentation thresholds

As we have seen, both fragmentation and bitmap indices allow identifying which fact data is relevant for a query, thereby reducing processing work. While bitmap indices are effective in many cases they require a substantial storage and processing overhead. For our configuration, each bitmap occupies 223 MB. Since our fragmentation approach eliminates the need for bitmaps for all fragmentation attributes and higher-level attributes of the respective dimension, it seems desirable to choose a fine-grained fragmentation. However, choosing a fragmentation with too many fragments causes a substantial administration overhead and deteriorates I/O performance as we will discuss. On the other hand, the number of fragments must not be too small in order to support a larger number of disks and processors. In particular, there should be at least 1 fragment per fact table disk.

The finest possible fragmentation would be to use all dimensions at the lowest level, i.e. *{time::month, product::code, customer::store, channel::channel}*. This would eliminate all bitmaps but result in more fact fragments (7.5 billion) than fact tuples. The four-dimensional fragmentation *{time::quarter, product::group, customer::retailer, channel::channel}* reduces the number of fact fragments to about 9 million plus about 440 million bitmap fragments. The administration overhead for maintaining such a number of fragments is considered prohibitive. Ideally, the size of the fragmentation information should be small enough to be cached in main memory.

As our simulation experiments have revealed, a high number of fragments can be even more harmful with respect to I/O performance. This holds particularly for queries based on bitmap processing (e.g., for attributes not belonging to a fragmentation dimension). This is because even for huge fact tables a high number of fragments can reduce the average size of a bitmap fragment under the size of a prefetch granule (or even under 1 page). This strongly increases the number of bitmap I/Os and deteriorates I/O times. To ensure a minimal bit fragment size of *Prefetch-Gran* pages (size of prefetch granule) an upper threshold for the number of fragments n_{max} should be observed with

$$n_{max} = \quad N / (8 \cdot PgSize \cdot PrefetchGran)$$

In this formula, N denotes the number of fact tuples and $PgSize$ the page size (in Bytes). For instance, with *Prefetch-Gran* = 4 and $PgSize$ = 4K we get n_{max} = 14,238. For a fact tuple size of 20 B, this corresponds to a minimal fragment size of 2.5 MB.

This is an important threshold eliminating already a substantial number of fragmentation choices. For our sample schema, there are 168 possible fragmentations. As can be seen in Table 2, $1/2$ to almost $3/4$ of these options can be ruled out by demanding a specific minimal bitmap fragment size. In particular, of the 36 possible four-dimensional fragmentations only 1 results in a bitmap fragment size of at least one page and none guarantees at least a size of four pages.

# fragmentation dimensions	minimum bitmap fragment size			
	any	**≥ 1 page**	**≥ 4 pages**	**≥ 8 pages**
1	*12*	*12*	*12*	*11*
2	*47*	*37*	*31*	*27*
3	*72*	*22*	*13*	*9*
4	*36*	*1*	*–*	*–*
total	*167*	*72*	*56*	*47*

Table 2: Number of fragmentation options under size constraints

4.5 I/O cost introduced by a fragmentation

Minimizing the I/O requirements and I/O time of a query is of prime importance for achieving a suitable response time. If a fragmentation F restricts the number of fragments to be processed for a query Q, it as well reduces the number of fact table and bitmap pages that need to be accessed. This is because in this case, all relevant hit rows are co-located within a smaller subset of all pages, increasing the number of hits per page and improving prefetch efficiency. Furthermore, as we have seen, a fragmentation can avoid bitmap access, e.g. if all rows of a fact fragment are relevant for a query.

In order to analytically quantify the I/O performance of different fragmentations, we have developed a set of mathematical formulas estimating the *number of fact table pages containing hit rows* and the *number of bitmap pages* to be accessed for a query. Details on this are provided in [33]. For simplicity, the estimates assume a uniform distribution of query hits within each relevant fragment and page. Furthermore, it is assumed that all pages of a fragment are stored consecutively on disk.

Based on the cases Q1 – Q4 discussed in Section 4.2, we roughly distinguish two classes of queries with respect to their I/O overhead for a given fragmentation. We denote these *I/O overhead classes* as *IOC1* and *IOC2*. In the following, we characterize the I/O behavior of these classes and quantify 2 extreme cases. With $Dim(S)$ we denote the dimensions represented in a set S, $hier(h)$ determines the hierarchy level of an attribute h, $card(h)$ denotes the cardinality of an hierarchy attribute h. Finally, f_q denotes a fragmentation attribute of the *same dimension* of a query attribute q.

***IOC1*: Clustered hits, no bitmap access.** A query of this class achieves near-optimal I/O conditions by not requiring bitmap access and finding all hits optimally located (clustered) within pages of the fact fragments. This is achieved for query types Q1 and Q3 above when only attributes from the fragmentation hierarchies of F are to be accessed. Therefore, in mathematical terms, a query Q is assigned to IOC1, if

$$Dim(Q) \subseteq Dim(F) \wedge \forall q \in Q : hier(q) \geq hier(f_q).$$

A $Q \in IOC1$ has to process all pages of the determined fragments. In the optimal case (subclass *IOC1-opt*), where

$$Dim(Q) = Dim(F) \wedge \forall q \in Q : hier(q) = hier(f_q),$$

queries only have to process one fragment (query type Q1, restricted to F-dimensions). Every dimension f of F that is not referenced in Q increases the number of fragments to be processed with the factor $card(f)$. Accessing an attribute q with $hier(q) > hier(f_q)$ on average increases the number of fragments by a factor of $card(f_q)/card(q)$. An increased number of fragments also reduces the number of hits per page, thereby increasing the number of I/O operations.

***IOC2*: Spread hits and bitmap I/O.** This class contains all remaining queries performing *bitmap access* to determine the hit rows within the fragments. This covers queries of types Q2 and Q4 as well as queries accessing dimensions not represented in F. For these queries, hit rows are spread across more fragments than for *IOC1*. This results in a reduced number of hits per page and prefetching granule introducing worse I/O efficiency and overhead. In the worst case, called *IOC2-nosupp*, a query is not supported at all by the fragmentation, i.e., it does not reference any fragmentation dimension. Hence, all bitmap fragments of all referenced dimensions have to be processed. Assuming more hits than the number of fragments and uniform distribution of hits, every fact fragment has to be accessed.

Quantitative comparison

The formulas developed in [33] allow determining the number of fragments to be accessed as well as the number of fact table and bitmap I/O operations for a given fragmentation and query type. They can thus be used within a tool to quantify the I/O performance of different fragmentation choices for a given query mix to help determine a good fragmentation. Table 3 illustrates the differences in I/O work for the one-dimensional sample query *1STORE* as determined with these formulas. The query belongs to *IOC1-opt* for the optimal fragmentation $F_{opt} = \{customer::store\}$ and to *IOC2-nosupp* for, e.g., $F_{nosupp} = F_{MonthGroup} = \{time::month,\ product::group\}$. We assume a prefetching granule of 8 pages on fact fragments and 5 pages on bitmap fragments (the bitmap fragment size is 4.9 pages for F_{nosupp}). With F_{nosupp}, only every 7th page in a fact fragment contains hits, thus strongly reducing prefetch efficiency. The table shows that a suitable fragmentation permits improvements in I/O performance by several orders of magnitude. Our simulation system allows more detailed performance predictions, in particular with respect to response time, by considering processor and disk contention as well as other factors.

4.6 Physical allocation

Having found a suitable fragmentation, the resulting fact and bitmap fragments have to be allocated onto disks. With respect to the *degree of declustering*, our simulations have confirmed that a full declustering of the fact table utilizing all available disks is the best approach as it supports the maximal degree of parallelism and load balancing. While the minimal number of disks is determined by the capacity requirements to store the fact table, bitmaps and other data, a typically much larger number of disk has to be used – within a reasonable economic range – in order to provide a high degree of I/O rates and I/O bandwidth.

As already indicated in Fig. 2, we use a special round robin allocation called *staggered round robin* to allocate fact fragments and their associated bitmap fragments. In this approach, the bitmap fragments of a fragment are allocated onto consecutive disks so that all bitmap fragments needed for a query can be accessed in parallel during a subquery.

In Section 6.2, we will analyze to which degree this affects query response times. Additionally, fact fragments could also be declustered to support I/O parallelism. We

	F_{opt}	F_{nosupp}
#fragments to be processed	*1*	*11,520*
#fact table I/O [pages]	795	*5,189,760*
#bitmap I/O [pages]	–	*691,200*
total I/O size [MB]	25	*31,075*

Table 3: I/O characteristics for query *1STORE*

store fact tables and bitmap data onto the same disks to allow all disks to be used for the fact table.

As we observed in our simulation experiments, care must be exercised with round robin in order to not artificially restrict parallelism for certain query classes. This is because the p fragments to be accessed by a query can get allocated onto *less than p* disks, introducing sequential disk work. For instance, assume our fragmentation $F_{MonthGroup}$ and $d = 100$ disks. To place the 11,520 fragments on disk, we have to determine an *allocation order* on the fragmentation attributes. Assume that we first assign the 480 fragments for month 1 consecutively, then the next 480 fragments for month 2 and so on. Processing query type $ICODE$ requires access to 24 of these fragments (1 per month) which correspond to every 480th fragment. Due to 480 and 100 having a *greatest common divisor (gcd)* of 20, all relevant fragments for $ICODE$ are located on only 5 disks, thus reducing possible parallelism by a factor of 4.8. If we decide to allocate the other way round, $ICODE$ is optimally supported while, e.g., $IMONTH$ queries are restricted to 25 disks ($gcd = 4$). Hence, we have to find an allocation that reduces the probability of such a clustering as far as possible. A solution is to choose a prime number for the degree of declustering or to use a modified allocation scheme introducing certain gaps to avoid such a clustering.

4.7 Guidelines for data allocation

The conclusion to be drawn from this section is that fragmentation and allocation have a large impact on I/O and query performance. To find a suitable fragmentation, a number of guidelines can be formulated:

- Exclude all possible fragmentations which break at least one of our three thresholds (i) minimal bitmap fragment size, (ii) maximum number of fragments to administer, (iii) maximum number of bitmaps to be materialized. Values for (ii) and (iii) depend on the main memory or disk storage space that can be utilized in a practical environment.
- Limit the dimensionality of fragmentation based on the dimensions typically referenced in the query profile. A broad query mix normally favors a higher number of declustering dimensions. On the other hand, one- or two-dimensional fragmentations may have too few fragments to even use all available disks, which is of course unacceptable.
- Analyze the I/O load introduced by the remaining fragmentations using the analytical formulas of [33]. If no query type is favored, choose a fragmentation that achieves the minimum total amount of I/O work performed by all query types. Otherwise, consider all fragmentations which optimize the favored queries and proceed as above for the rest of the queries on the remaining fragmentation candidates.

5 Simulation system and setup

To test and evaluate the allocation and processing methods described above and to verify our analytical considerations, we designed and implemented a comprehensive simulation system named $SIMPAD$ (*Sim*ulation of *Pa*rallel *D*atabases). It is written in C++ and based on the *CSIM* simulation library [20]. Through a modular design, $SIMPAD$ supports the evaluation of different PDBS and hardware architectures, algorithms, database allocations and workloads. For brevity, we only mention aspects relevant to the study at hand. Major simulation parameters and their settings used in the experiments are listed in Table 4.

For this study, we have modelled a Shared Disk PDBS with a variable number of processing nodes and disks. Processors and disks are explicitly modeled as servers to realistically capture access conflicts and delays. CPU overhead is accounted for in all major query processing steps and communication (Table 4). The disk model calculates varying seek times based on track positions rather than giving constant or stochastically distributed response times. This allows realistic testing of multi-user and parallel processing. A simple buffer manager is used supporting LRU page replacement and prefetching. We maintain separate buffers for tables and indices. An idealized contention-free network model is employed with communication delays proportional to message sizes, so as not to bias simulation results due to a specific choice of a network topology.

Our database model is based on the star schema detailed in Section 3, with a flexible parameterization for the dimension hierarchies and cardinalities as well as the fact table density. Bitmap join indices are provided on the fact table for all dimension keys, with a possible choice of either standard or encoded bitmaps. The dimension tables have B*-tree indices, but these are not relevant to our experiments. The data allocation is determined separately for all tables and indices, each of which can be assigned to an individually defined group of disks. The evaluated fragmentation and allocation of the fact table and its bitmap indices follow the description in the previous sections.

A query generator creates a series of query structures that are passed to the processing module. In this initial study, we restrict ourselves to single-user mode, so queries are issued sequentially with a new query starting as soon as the previous one has terminated. For a single simulation, all queries are of the same type (e.g., $ISTORE$), but specific parameters are chosen at random (e.g., the actual $STORE$ selected).

Parallel processing and load balancing

New queries are first assigned to a randomly selected coordinator node that is responsible for parallelizing the query and scheduling its execution. This coordinator creates a *task list* of all subqueries to be performed, each comprising one fact fragment and its associated bitmap fragments. Based on the query type and fragmentation, the scheduler considers only the relevant fact fragments and bitmaps as outlined in Section 4. The list is sorted in the order in which the fragments were allocated to disks, so that consecutive subqueries can be expected to access different disks. The coordinator assigns subqueries from the task list to available processors in a round-robin manner, where each node receives a maximum of t concurrent tasks (t being a system parameter). As described in 4.2, each subquery processes the required bitmap fragments, reads the associated fact table pages, extracts hit rows, and locally aggregates the measures (e.g., $DOLLARSALES$) found there. When a node finishes a subquery, it returns the partial aggregate to the coordinator and is assigned another task. When all rele-

Parameter	settings	Parameter	settings	Parameter	settings
disk devices		**no. of instructions**		**buffer manager**	
number (d)	100	initiate/plan query	50,000	page size	4 KB
speed-up experiments	1 – 100	terminate query	10,000	buffer size fact table	1000 pages
avg. seek time	10 ms	initiate/plan subquery	10,000	buffer size bitmaps	5000 pages
avg. settle time +	per access 3 ms	terminate subquery	10,000	prefetch size fact table	8 pages
controller delay	+ per page 1 ms	read page	3,000	prefetch size bitmaps	5 pages (var.)
		process bitmap page	1,500		
processing nodes		extract table row	100	**network**	
number (p)	20	aggregate table row	100	connection speed	100 Mbit/s
speed-up experiments	1 – 50	send message	1,000 + #B	message size (small)	128 B
CPU speed	50 MIPS	receive message	1,000 + #B	message size (large)	1 page (4 KB)
subqueries per node	var.				

Table 4: Parameters settings used in simulations

vant data has been processed, the query is terminated and the overall aggregate gathered by the coordinator is returned to the user.

The simulation system considers the CPU and message overhead introduced by this scheduling. Early simulation experiments showed that the overhead is very small compared to the actual processing and the coordinator node can is also be used for processing subqueries. We do, however, count coordination as one task so that the coordinator node will only process $t - 1$ subqueries at a time.

We have devised several additional scheduling techniques that will be explored in a future study.

6 Simulation results

In this section, we present first results of simulation experiments we performed to verify and study our data allocation approach from Section 4. There are three basic simulation series: speed-up tests to verify the scalability of our approach (6.1); experiments on the impact of parallel subqueries and bitmap I/O (6.2); simulations for different fragmentation and allocation strategies (6.3).

6.1 Speed-up experiments

The first series of simulations was designed to investigate the scalability of the allocation approach and fragment-oriented query processing. We used the star schema configuration introduced above with fragmentation $F_{MonthGroup}$ (11,520 fragments) on different hardware configurations as listed in Table 5. The number of disks, d, was varied from 20 to 100; the number of processors, p, ranges from $1/20$ to $1/2$ of the number of disks, resulting in $1 - 50$ processors. For each configuration, we tested two simple query types, *1STORE* and *1MONTH*, to study both disk- and CPU-bound workloads.

We first discuss the performance for query *1STORE*. This query is not supported by the chosen fragmentation and thus requires access to all fragments as well as to all the bitmaps of its encoded index. Figure 3 shows the response time and speed-up curves for this query. We use a fixed number of subqueries per node $t = d/p$ so that the total number of subqueries equals the number of disks which proved sufficient to utilize all disks. As can be seen, response times depend solely on the number of disks used

number of disks (d)	number of processors (p)				
20	*1*	*2*	*4*	*5*	*10*
60	*3*	*6*	*12*	*15*	*30*
100	*5*	*10*	*20*	*25*	*50*

Table 5: Hardware parameters for speed-up experiments

because *1STORE* is heavily disk-bound. The only exception is the data point for 20 disks and 1 processor. That particular experiment suffers from the fact that the single node is also its own coordinator and can only process $t - 1$ (i.e., 19 rather than 20) subqueries at a time (cf. Section 5). The chosen data allocation, processing model and scheduling strategy allow for linear improvement of response times with an increased number of disks. In fact, speed-up with respect to d is slightly superlinear, due to reduced seek times when there is less data on a single disk.

The *1MONTH* query, on the other hand, is optimally supported by our fragmentation. It is confined to the 480 fragments associated with the *MONTH* selected and need not access any bitmap. This query is CPU-bound; as can be seen in Figure 4, its response times depend on the number of processors rather than disks. Again, we achieve optimal speed-up, this time with respect to the number of processors p. The only exception is for the configuration with 100

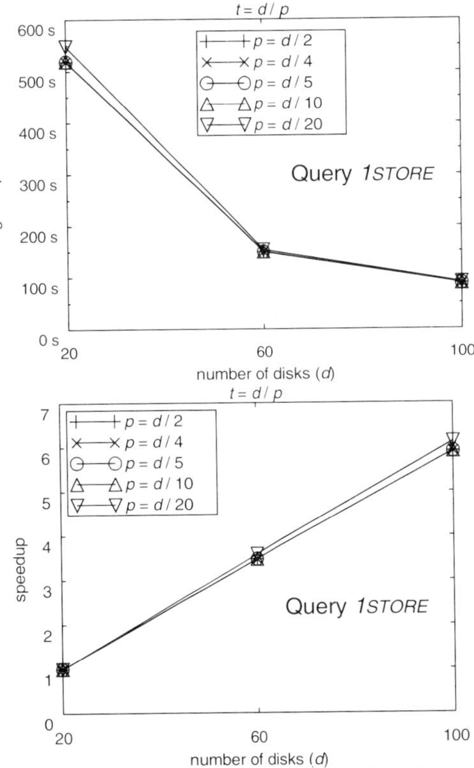

Fig. 3: Response times and speed-up of the *1STORE* query

disks and 50 nodes in the upper end of the curve. Here, a discretization problem occurs: With $t = 4$, which is optimal for most other settings, subqueries will be executed in "batches" of 200 ($t \cdot p = 4 \cdot 50$). For the 480 fragments to be processed, this produces three batches of 200, 200, and 80, the last one being inefficient to process due to the reduced parallelism. Amending the parameter to $t = 5$, we obtain two batches of 250 and 230, which are processed much more efficiently even though a single batch will take longer. Using this result, we can re-establish linear speed-up, as represented by the dotted line in the speed-up graph of Figure 4.

The results confirm that the approaches chosen permit optimal utilization of I/O and processing parallelism. It was demonstrated that linear speed-up can be achieved with respect to either the number of disks or the number of processors, depending on whether the workload is disk- or CPU-bound. In the remaining experiments, we use a fixed hardware configuration of 100 disks and 20 processing nodes.

6.2 Parallel subqueries and parallel bitmap I/O

In this experiment, we investigate the impact of the number of subqueries and the effectiveness of parallel bitmap I/O within a subquery in more detail. The latter is supported by our "staggered" data allocation assigning the bitmap fragments of a fact fragment to separate disks (Section 4.5). A potential problem is increased disk contention, which may harm other subqueries that have to access the same disks. We evaluated this trade-off using the I/O-intensive *1STORE* query type that has to access 12 bitmap fragments for each fact table fragment. Based on the 100-disk, 20-node config-

uration determined above, we tried both parallel and non-parallel bitmap I/O for varying numbers of concurrent subqueries per processor, obtaining the results of Figure 5.

The figure illustrates the importance of using multiple subqueries per node for this I/O bound query type in order to fully utilize all disks. We are able to linearly improve response times up to about 5 subqueries per node where the total number of subqueries reaches the number of disks (100). A higher number of subqueries has only little impact on response time (also influenced by single-user mode). This almost ideal behavior again confirms the scalability and good load balancing achieved with our Shared Disk-oriented scheduling strategy.

Parallel bitmap I/O delivers noticeable response time improvements of up to 13 % despite the concurrent access of subqueries to the same disks and although a larger part of the response time is caused by fact table I/O. The improvements are especially pronounced for a smaller number of concurrent subqueries. For many subqueries, performance of the two alternatives becomes similar due to increased disk contention. However, even in this case parallel bitmap I/O remains slightly ahead.

The conclusion we draw is that parallel bitmap I/O is a good default setting mostly improving system performance. For mixed CPU- and I/O-bound workloads, we expect additional improvements for parallel bitmap I/O due to reduced disk traffic compared to purely I/O-bound cases such as for *1STORE*. Further improvements are likely by utilizing parallel I/O on fact fragments which are larger than the bitmap fragments.

6.3 Implication of the fragmentation strategy for query processing

In this experiment, we quantify our results of Sections 4.4 and 4.5, where we outlined the impact of the fragmentation strategy on query processing. We observed that fine-grained fragmentations allow many query types to be confined to few fragments, thereby increasing I/O efficiency. On the other hand, I/O problems can be introduced if bitmap fragment sizes fall below the size of a prefetch granule. For our experiment on these effects we choose two query types *1STORE* and *1CODE1QUARTER* on three two-dimensional fragmentations $F_{MonthGroup}$, $F_{MonthClass}$ and $F_{MonthCode}$, based on the time and product dimensions. The fragmentations only differ in the selected hierarchy level of the product dimension. Table 6 shows the resulting number of frag-

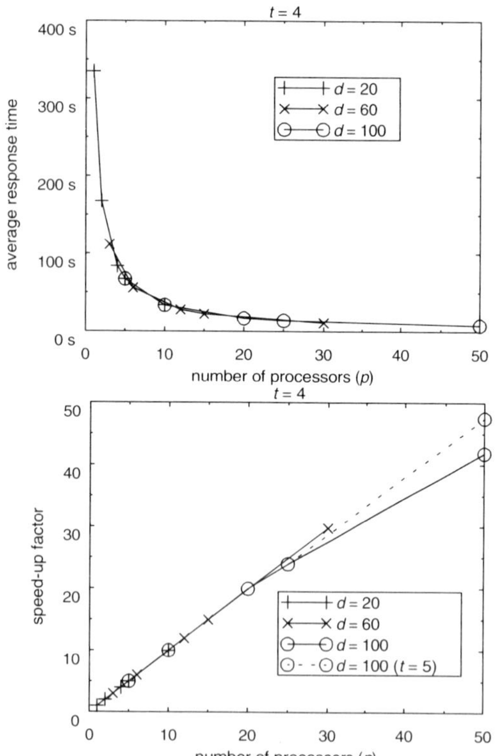

Fig. 4: Response times and speed-up of the *1MONTH* query

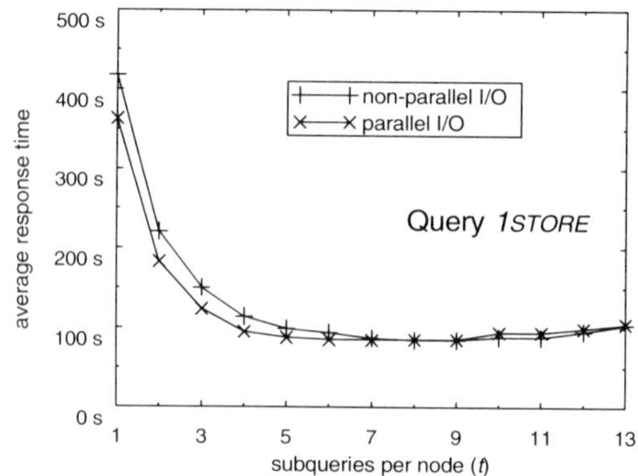

Fig. 5: Response time effects of parallel bitmap I/O

	$F_{MonthGroup}$	$F_{MonthClass}$	$F_{MonthCode}$
number of fragments	*11,520*	*23,040*	*345,600*
bitmap fragment size [pages]	*4.9 (5)*	*2.5 (3)*	*0.16 (1)*

Table 6: Fragmentation parameters for experiment 3

ments and bitmap fragment sizes (numbers in parantheses denote the prefetch granule size). According to Section 4.5, *1STORE* belongs to I/O class **IOC2-nosupp** in any considered case, because the customer dimension is not represented in any of our sample fragmentations, forcing the query to access all fragments. *1STORE* is assigned to the worst case class **IOC2-nosupp** because the customer dimension is not represented in any of our sample fragmentations forcing the query to access all fragments. Due to its query selectivity of 1/1440, and since there are about 200 tuples per fact table page, only 1 in 7 pages of every fragment contains a hit. Query type *1CODE1QUARTER* accesses exactly 3 fragments (one for each month of a quarter), residing on 3 disks regardless of the fragmentation. It has to process only 16,200 rows in total with a sensible processing parallelism of at most 3. For $F_{MonthClass}$ and $F_{MonthGroup}$, bitmap access is introduced so that the query type belongs to class **IOC2** in these cases. For $F_{MonthGroup}$, I/O class **IOC1** is given because the fragments contain only relevant fact rows.

Figure 6 shows the response time behavior of the two queries types for the three fragmentations. The x-axis refers to the total number of subqueries over all (20) processing nodes. For both queries, I/O dominates response times. While *1STORE* has about 80 times more hit tuples than *1CODE1QUARTER* its response time is more than 300 times worse for lower degrees of parallelism. Only for the two better fragmentations and at least 100 subqueries can this query type obtain a response time that is about 80 times higher than for *1CODE1QUARTER* which achieves its optimum for only 3 subqueries. While this leaves many resources unused, in multi-user mode this can be advantageous for other queries.

1CODE1QUARTER benefits from the chosen fragmentations. Within a product group, the selectivity is 1/30 for a certain product. Therefore, every fact page (each containing 200 tuples) of the 3 fragments contains hits regardless of the granule of fragmentation varying from group to code. For fragmentation $F_{MonthClass}$ fragment size halvens compared to $F_{MonthGroup}$ resulting in a corresponding response time improvement because every fragment page is to be read. The best response times are achieved for $F_{MonthCode}$ for which no bitmap access is necessary and fragments only contain relevant tuples (**IOC1**).

1STORE exhibits the inverse behavior with respect to the fragmentations. In particular, the fine-grained fragmentation $F_{MonthCode}$ results in the worst performance. This is especially because the bitmap fragment size drops to only 1/6 of a page resulting in an extreme number of bitmap pages (more than 4 million) to be read for the 12 bitmaps.

This indicates that a fragmentation such as $F_{MonthCode}$ must be avoided, which can be achieved by considering the fragmentation threshold introduced in Section 4. A possibility to improve efficiency for finer fragmentations is to clus-

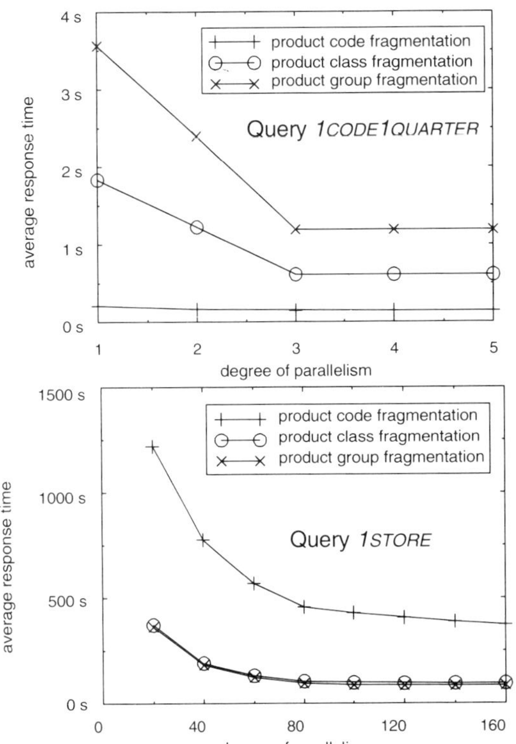

Fig. 6: Response times of *1STORE*, *1MONTH1QUARTER* for different fragmentations

ter together multiple bitmap and fact fragments, respectively, and subsequently assign such *granules* of clustered fragments to consecutive pages and *to one single subquery*. This can especially help to avoid unacceptable bitmap fragment sizes.

7 Conclusions

In this study, we have developed a multi-dimensional hierarchical fragmentation and allocation method for star schemas in a parallel data warehouse environment. The approach called MDHF allows all star queries referencing at least one attribute from any fragmentation dimension to be confined to a subset of the fact table fragments. This clusters hit rows within fewer pages, thereby supporting fewer I/O operations and effective prefetching. Moreover, we can eliminate bitmap indices on the fragmentation dimensions either completely or partially, further saving disk space and I/O load. Our technique uses an analogous fragmentation of fact tables and their associated bitmap indices to enable simultaneous, fragmentwise processing that can be parallelized effectively.

We developed a number of guidelines for finding an appropriate fragmentation. As outlined, we must avoid very fine fragmentations to limit the administration overhead and to avoid only partially filled bitmap index pages that sharply increase I/O load. The guidelines were verified using a detailed simulation model based on the APB-1 decision support benchmark. Together with our analytical formulas calculating star query I/O costs [33], they can be used within a tool to automatically determine suitable fragmentation candidates for a given query mix.

Our approaches assume a Shared Disk PDBS but can be applied to other architectures with minor modifications. The simulation results demonstrated that the flexibility of Shared Disk architectures permits efficient load balancing based on a round robin allocation scheme in combination with intra-processor parallelism. This approach exhibits near-linear scalability with respect to the number of disks and processors. Furthermore, it enables parallel I/O for all bitmap fragments accessed within a given subquery.

We believe that our fragmentation and allocation approaches are directly applicable to commercial PDBS with comparatively little effort. In future studies, we will elaborate on the load balancing properties of star schema processing and examine data skew effects as well as the consequences of multi-user mode. Furthermore, we want to explore how our multi-dimensional hierarchical partitioning can be exploited for the complementary allocation decisions associated with materialized views and caching of query results.

References

[1] *APB-1 OLAP Benchmark, Release II.* OLAP Council, Nov. 1998. www.olapcouncil.org/research/bmarkly.htm

[2] C. Ballinger: *Teradata Database Design 101.* White Paper, NCR Corporation, 1998.

[3] S. Brobst, B. Vecchione: *DB2 UDB: Starburst Grows Bright.* Database Programming & Design, 1998.

[4] G. Copeland et al.: *Data Placement in Bubba.* Proc. ACM SIGMOD Conf., Chicago, 1988.

[5] S. Chaudhuri, U. Dayal: *An Overview of Data Warehousing and OLAP Technology.* SIGMOD Record 26(1), 1997

[6] P. M. Chen et al.: *RAID: High-Performance, Reliable Secondary Storage.* ACM Computing Surveys 26 (2), 1994.

[7] D. J. DeWitt, J. Gray.: *Parallel Database Systems: The Future of High Performance Database Systems.* Comm. ACM 35 (6), 85 - 98, 1992.

[8] S. Ghandeharizadeh, D. J. DeWitt: A *Multiuser Performance Analysis of Alternative Declustering Strategies.* Proc. 6th Int. Conf. on Data Engineering, 1990.

[9] S. Ghandeharizadeh, D. J. DeWitt, W. Qureshi: *A Performance Analysis of Alternative Multi-Attribute Declustering Strategies.* Proc. ACM SIGMOD Conf., 29 - 38, 1992.

[10] G. Graefe, J. Ewel, C. Galindo-Legaria: *Microsoft SQL Server 7.0 Query Processor.* White Paper, Microsoft, 1998.

[11] V. Gaede, O. Günther: *Multidimensional Access Methods.* ACM Comp. Surv. 30 (2), 170 - 231, 1998.

[12] A. Gupta, I. S. Mumick: *Maintenance of Materialized View: Problems, Techniques, and Applications.* Data Eng. Bulletin 18 (2), June 1995.

[13] J. Gray et al.: *Data Cube: A Relational Aggregation Operator Generalizing Group-By, Cross-Tab, and Sub-Totals.* In: U. Fayyad, H. Mannila, G. Piatetsky-Shapiro: Data Mining and Knowledge Discovery 1, 29 - 53, 1997

[14] Informix Corporation: *Informix Decision Support Indexing for the Enterprise Data Warehouse.* White Paper, 1998.

[15] Informix Corporation: *INFORMIX-OnLine Dynamic Server: Administration Guide.* http://www.informix.com/answers/oldsite/answers/pubs/pdf/811xpsu/7624.pdf (June 2000)

[16] R. H. Katz, W. Hong: *The Performance of Disk Arrays in Shared-Memory Database Machines.* Distr. and Parallel Databases 1 (2), 167 - 198, 1993.

[17] E. K. Lee, R. Katz: *An Analytic Performance Model of Disk Arrays,* Proc. ACM SIGMETRICS Conf., 1993.

[18] H. Märtens: *On Disk Allocation of Intermediate Query Results in Parallel Database Systems,* Proc. EURO-PAR Conf., Toulouse, LNCS 1685, Springer 1999. http://dol.uni-leipzig.de/pub/1999-24

[19] M. Mehta, D. J. DeWitt: *Data Placement in Shared-Nothing Parallel Database Systems.* VLDB Journal 6 (1), 1997.

[20] Mesquite Software Inc.: *User's Guide CSIM18 Simulation Engine.* Manual, 1996.

[21] C. Mohan, I. Narang: *Recovery and Coherency-Control Protocols for Fast Intersystem Page Transfer and Fine-Granularity Locking in a Shared Disks Transaction Environment.* Proc. VLDB Conf., 193 – 207, 1991.

[22] P. O'Neil, G. Graefe: *Multi-Table Joins Through Bitmapped Join Indices.* ACM SIGMOD Record 24 (3), 1995.

[23] P. O'Neil: *Model 204 Architecture and Performance.* Proc. 2nd HPTS Workshop, Asilomar, 1987.

[24] P. O'Neil, D. Quass: *Improved Query Performance with Variant Indexes.* Proc. ACM SIGMOD Conf., 1997.

[25] Oracle Corporation: *Star Queries in Oracle8.* White Paper, 1997.

[26] Oracle Corporation: *Oracle 8i Administrator's Guide.* http://www.irm.vt.edu/oracle_816_docs/server.816/a76956/index.htm (June 2000)

[27] E. Rahm: *Empirical Evaluation of Concurrency and Coherency Control Protocols for Database Sharing Systems.* ACM TODS 18 (2), 333 – 377, 1993.

[28] E. Rahm: *Parallel Query Processing in Shared Disk Database Systems.* Proc. 5th HPTS Workshop, Asilomar, 1993. http://www.informatik.uni-leipzig.de/ifi/abteilungen/db/abstr/Ra93.HPTS.ps

[29] Red Brick Systems, Inc.: *Star Schema Processing for Complex Queries.* White Paper, 1998.

[30] E. Rahm, H. Märtens, T. Stöhr: *On Flexible Allocation of Index and Temporary Data in Parallel Database Systems.* Proc. 8th HPTS Workshop, Asilomar, 1999. http://dol.uni-leipzig.de/pub/1999-23

[31] E. Rahm, T. Stöhr: *Analysis of Parallel Scan Processing in Parallel Shared Disk Database Systems.* Proc. EURO-PAR Conf., LNCS 966, Springer 1995. http://dol.uni-leipzig.de/pub/1995-22

[32] P. Scheuermann, G. Weikum, P. Zabback: *Data Partitioning and Load Balancing in Parallel Disk Systems,* VLDB Journal 7 (1), 48 – 66, 1998.

[33] T. Stöhr: *Analytical Evaluation of a Multi-Dimensional and Hierarchical Allocation Strategy for Parallel Data Warehouses.* Technical Report, Univ. of Leipzig, Germany, 2000 (to appear)

[34] J. Sun, W.I. Grosky: *Dynamic Maintenance of Multidimensional Range Data Partitioning for Parallel Data Processing.* Proc. First ACM Intl. Workshop on Data Warehousing and OLAP (DOLAP), Washington D.C., 72 – 79, 1998

[35] Sybase, Inc.: *Adaptive Server IQ.* White Paper, 1997.

[36] M.-C. Wu, A. P. Buchmann: *Encoded Bitmap Indexing for Data Warehouses.* Proc. 14th Proc. Int. Conf. on Data Engineering, Orlando, 1998.

[37] Y. Zhuge, H. Garcia-Molina, J. Hammer, J. Widom: *View Maintenance in a Warehousing Environment.* Proc. ACM SIGMOD Conf., San Jose, 1995.

Oracle8*i* Index-Organized Table and its Application to New Domains

Jagannathan Srinivasan
Eugene Inseok Chong
Ramkumar Krishnan

Souripriya Das
Mahesh Jagannath
Anh-Tuan Tran
Jayanta Banerjee

Chuck Freiwald
Aravind Yalamanchi
Samuel DeFazio

Oracle Corporation
One Oracle Drive, Nashua, NH 03062, USA

Abstract

Primary B^+-tree, a variant of B^+-tree structure with row data in leaf blocks, is an ideal storage organization for queries involving exact match and/or range search on primary keys. Commercially, primary B^+-tree like structures have been supported in DBMSs like Compaq Non-Stop SQL, Sybase Adaptive Server, and Microsoft SQL Server. Oracle's index-organized table is like a primary B^+-tree; however, it differs from its commercial counterparts in the following respects: 1) The storage organization does not require the entire row to be stored in the primary key index. Infrequently accessed columns can be selectively pushed into an overflow storage area to speed up access to columns that are frequently accessed. 2) Secondary indexes on index-organized tables support logical primary key-based row identifiers, and still provide performance comparable to secondary indexes with physical row identifiers by storing and making use of *guess-DBA* (Database Block Address). 3) Support for primary key compression leads to reduced storage requirements. This paper presents the index-organized table storage option in Oracle8*i* with emphasis on the novel aspects mentioned above. The applicability of index-organized tables to new domains such as the Internet, E-Commerce and Data Warehousing is discussed. A performance study is presented, that validates the clustering benefits of Oracle's primary B^+-tree implementation, and characterizes the impact of overflow storage area, guess-DBA use in secondary B^+-tree indexes, and primary key compression.

1 Introduction

A significant number of applications deal with data sets where each individual row is identified by a primary key. The primary key could be a single column such as social security number for employees table in a HR application, or a multi-column entity such as <warehouse, district, order, order line> for orders table in a product sales and distribution business application [TPCC93]. For such applications, if the query workload is dominated by primary-key access, then clustering the rows of the table in the primary key order would be beneficial. In fact, several DBMSs provide a variant of B^+-trees [Com79] with row data in leaf node, also referred to as primary B^+-trees, to speed-up primary key-based access to the table data.

Along the same lines, in Oracle8, a new storage option ORGANIZATION INDEX is introduced. Tables created using this option, referred to as *index-organized tables*[1],

Proceedings of the 26th International Conference on Very Large Databases, Cairo, Egypt, 2000

---

[1] The default storage organization in Oracle is a heap, and we refer to tables created using such an organization as *heap-organized tables.*

include not only the indexed columns, but implicitly also include all the remaining columns of the table in the primary B$^+$-tree. Each row consists of key and non-key columns, and the non-key columns are stored along with the key columns in a B$^+$-tree, making the whole table structure have an *index-organization*. Typically, the entire table data can be held in its primary key index. The benefits of this organization are:

- it provides fast *random* access on the primary key because an index-only scan is sufficient. Once a leaf block is reached, both the key as well as the non-key columns can be retrieved.

- it provides fast *range* access on the primary key because the rows are clustered in primary key order and they contain both key and non-key columns.

- it avoids duplication of primary key columns as in a heap-organized table with a primary key index.

The distinguishing features of index-organized tables when compared to other primary B$^+$-tree implementations are:

- support for a (heap-organized) overflow storage area that provides supplementary storage for columns. This allows controlling the placement of columns in the index vs. overflow storage area and provides the capability for tuning the number of rows that fit in an index leaf. Infrequently accessed non-key columns of the index-organized table can be pushed to the overflow storage area, by (1) specifying the percentage of space reserved for a row in the index block, and/or (2) specifying a column at which a row should be divided into index and overflow portions. This increases the *leaf row density*, that is, the number of index rows that can fit in a leaf block of the B$^+$-tree structure.

- support for secondary indexes with logical primary key-based row identifiers, which include the primary key as well as a database block address (DBA). This DBA, referred to as *guess-DBA*, is treated as a *guess* as to where the row *may* be found in the base table (primary B$^+$-tree). A valid guess will cost only a single block I/O. However, if the guess is invalid, the primary key is used to find the row. Thus, for valid guess-DBAs, the secondary index performance is comparable to that of secondary index with physical row identifiers. At the same time, the logical nature of secondary indexes enables faster reorganization and increased uptime of the base table since they need not be updated during such a reorganization. Support for online guess-DBA fixing allows regaining the guess-DBA based performance.

- support for compressing common (column) prefixes of the primary key. Since the rows are clustered in

the primary key order, there is more likelihood of finding common prefixes.

Index-organized tables in Oracle8*i* have full-table functionality with features such as constraints, triggers, LOB and object columns, and horizontal partitioning. Index-organized tables are key components in several Oracle RDBMS features such as online index creation and rebuild, message queues [OAQ97], nested table columns [OSC97], domain indexes [SMSAD00] and time-series cartridge [OTS97].

Traditionally, primary B+-tree like structures such as index-organized tables have been used in OLTP applications that require fast primary key-based access. However, we argue that such a storage organization, combined with the novel features described above, can be equally useful to several new domains as summarized in Table 1 in Section 3.

Index-organized tables are suitable for order processing applications with 24x7 availability requirements such as for E-Commerce [BSZ98]. Specifically, faster reorganization is achieved due to the logical nature of secondary indexes. Index-based scan performance degradation is avoided through use of guess-DBAs and the guess-DBA based performance is retained by online fixing of any guess-DBAs invalidated during reorganization. Key-compressed index-organized tables are suitable for Internet applications that may require a hierarchical storage organization, such as portals and electronic storefronts. Internet search engines and text databases can implement the inverted index, the fundamental data structure needed for full-text search, as an index-organized table. The need to handle variable length rows in the inverted index [ZMS92] without degrading access to small rows can be met by using index-organized table column placement options. Index-organized tables can also be used for fact tables in data warehousing applications as described in Section 3.5.

1.1 Outline of the Paper

The related work is presented next. Section 2 gives an overview of index-organized table with emphasis on its novel features. Section 3 discusses the applications of index-organized tables to new domains. Section 4 presents experimental results that compare and contrast index-organized table and heap-organized table performance. Section 5 concludes with a summary and outlines future work.

1.2 Related Work

There have been several efforts to build specialized structures to hold table data based upon the primary modes of data access. Oracle RDBMS [OSC97] has traditionally supported *Index-clusters* and *Hash-clusters*. These can be used to cluster one or more tables based on the cluster key. A single data block can hold rows from different tables with the same cluster keys. The primary motivation is to support efficient join-operations on the set of clustered tables.

Non-Stop SQL[2] [Tand87] supports *key-sequenced* tables, which cluster data based on primary keys. Online reorganization of these tables is also supported [Troi96]. However, these tables support rows of only limited size and do not provide the flexibility to control the placement of columns between the index and overflow storage areas. Non-Stop SQL also supports secondary indexes with primary key based row identifiers, but these row identifiers are strictly logical and do not incorporate the guess-DBA mechanism found in secondary indexes for index-organized tables. Thus, they always incur an additional primary B-tree traversal for index-based scan.

IBM DB2 [DB2V5.2] allows the secondary index structure to include additional columns. For example, users can create an index for an employee table on a column, say empno, but also include the column salary into the index. Thus, an index-only scan is sufficient for queries referencing both the columns empno and salary, but this speed-up is achieved at the cost of column duplication.

Sybase Adaptive Server [SYB95] and Microsoft SQL Server 7.0 [MS98] support the concept of a table with single clustered index, which forces the table rows to be maintained in the clustered index key order. However, like Non-Stop SQL, they do not support rows of arbitrarily large size, or flexible column placement between the index and overflow. Secondary indexes for these tables contain physical row identifiers, limiting the online availability of the base table.

Online reorganization of database objects, namely tables and indexes, is increasingly gaining importance and many database systems support some form of online operations. IBM AS/400 [SI96] allows online index (re)construction. Sybase provides capabilities for online resource management [RDC96]. [ZS98] discusses an approach for secondary index maintenance during online reorganization by piggybacking secondary index updates with user transactions. During online reorganization of index-organized tables, secondary indexes need not be maintained due to their logical nature.

2 Index-Organized Tables

This section gives an overview of index-organized tables and then discusses the novel features.

---

[2] Oracle8, Oracle8*i*, DB2, NonStop SQL, Microsoft SQL Server, Sybase Adaptive Server are registered trademarks.

2.1 Overview

Index-organized tables are like conventional tables in Oracle8*i* except for the fact that the data in the table is organized as a B$^+$-tree index built on the primary key for the table. For example, an inverted index which is typically used by a web text-search engine for providing content-based search capability can be implemented using an index-organized table in the following manner:

```
CREATE TABLE inverted_doc ( token CHAR(20),
doc_id NUMBER, token_frequency NUMBER,
CONSTRAINT pk_inverted_doc PRIMARY KEY (token,
doc_id))
ORGANIZATION INDEX TABLESPACE ind_tbs;
```

This creates a table where all the row data, namely the primary key columns plus the remaining columns, are stored in the primary key B$^+$-tree index leaf blocks (Figure 1).

Such a storage organization enables fast primary key-based access to table data for queries involving exact match and/or range search. Once the search has located the target primary key, the remaining columns are present at the same location. This eliminates the need to follow a row identifier to table data, as would be the case with a conventional table and index structure, thereby avoiding an additional I/O. Furthermore storage requirements are reduced as there is no duplication of key columns in the table and the index, and row identifiers are not needed in the primary key B$^+$-tree structure.

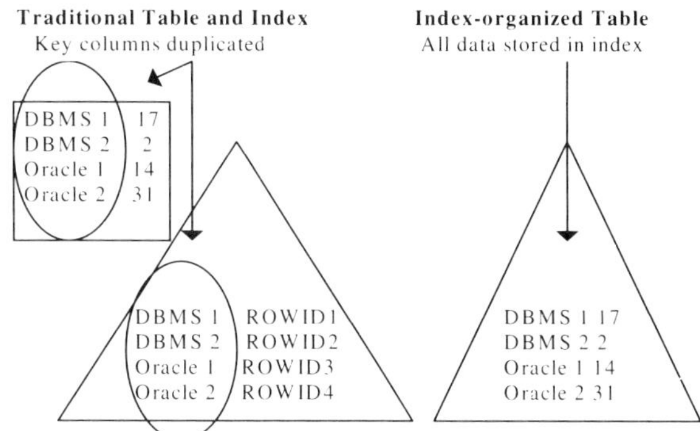

Figure 1: Conventional Table with an Index vs. Index-Organized Table.

Oracle8*i* applications can manipulate the index-organized table just like a conventional table using standard SQL statements.

2.2 Overflow Storage Area and Column Placement Options

Storing all non-key columns in the primary key B$^+$-tree index structure may not always be desirable or possible. Specifically:

- Each additional non-key column stored in the primary key index reduces the leaf row density of the

B^+-tree. To achieve better performance for access to frequently accessed columns, users may want to store only those columns in the index.

- Since a B^+-tree leaf block must hold at least two index rows, placing all non-key columns as part of index row may not always be possible.

To overcome these problems, an *overflow* storage area can be associated with an index-organized table. For example, if an additional column, say *token_offsets* is required for the *inverted_doc* schema, then the table can be created with an overflow storage area as follows:

```
CREATE TABLE inverted_doc ( token CHAR(20),
doc_id NUMBER, token_frequency NUMBER,
token_offsets VARCHAR(512), CONSTRAINT
pk_inverted_doc PRIMARY KEY (token, doc_id))
ORGANIZATION INDEX TABLESPACE ind_tbs
PCTTHRESHOLD 20 OVERFLOW TABLESPACE  ovf_tbs;
```

For such a table, the index row contains a *<key, head row-piece>* pair, where the *head row-piece* contains the first few non-key columns and a row identifier that points to the overflow portion containing remaining column values. Although this approach incurs the storage cost of one row identifier per row, key column duplication is still avoided.

Placement of columns into index and overflow storage area can be controlled by two options described below.

Placement Option for Handling Variable Length Rows

For a table with variable length rows, it is useful to allow each row to occupy not more than certain percentage of the index leaf block. This will ensure a lower bound on the leaf row density and enforce uniformity across rows as far as usage of the leaf block portion is concerned. This tuning is made possible using a percentage threshold parameter.

The PCTTHRESHOLD option, specified as a percentage of the leaf block size, determines the *last* non-key column that should be included in the index *head row-piece* on a per-row basis. The remaining non-key columns are stored in the overflow storage area as one or more row-pieces. Specifically, the last non-key column to be included is chosen such that the index row size (*key + head row-piece*) does not exceed the specified threshold, which in the above example is 20% of the index leaf block.

Such tuning ensures a lower bound of leaf row density which in turn limits the height of the B^+-tree, thereby providing fast access to head row-pieces for all rows. Larger rows, however, incur the cost of additional I/Os required to get to the tail row-pieces stored in the overflow area.

Placement Option for Speeding Up Access to Frequently Accessed Columns

PCTTHRESHOLD option puts a constraint on the index row size, which may translate to different sets of columns being included in the index for different rows. However, many applications may benefit from allowing the *same* set of columns to be included in the index for *all* rows in the table. The motivation here is to speed up access to frequently accessed columns by forcing the infrequently accessed columns out to reside in the overflow storage area. This is achieved by means of the INCLUDING parameter. For example, the following CREATE TABLE statement includes all the columns up to the *token_frequency* column in the index leaf block and forces the *token_offsets* column to the overflow area.

```
CREATE TABLE inverted_doc  . . .       . . .
ORGANIZATION INDEX TABLESPACE ind_tbs
INCLUDING token_frequency
OVERFLOW TABLESPACE  ovf_tbs;
```

Such vertical partitioning of a row between the index and overflow storage areas allows for higher leaf row density, resulting in better query performance for the columns stored in the index. While this approach incurs the cost of one additional block access for columns stored in the overflow, this I/O overhead is no worse than that of a conventional table with an index.

Note that the INCLUDING option only ensures that all columns after the specified column are stored in the overflow area. If this specification is such that the corresponding index row size exceeds the specified threshold, then the last non-key column to be included is determined based on the PCTTHRESHOLD.

The two column placement options discussed above allow breaking the table vertically into two partitions. Vertical partitioning of a table enables user queries to deal with smaller relations, which may result in a smaller number of block accesses [NCWD84, Niam78]. General vertical partitioning, although studied extensively, is typically not supported in most commercial database systems, leaving the task of generating heuristic fragmentation and allocation schemes [HN79] to the application designer. Note that even if such a support is made available, that would require duplication of the key attributes or row identifiers (tuple-ids) in the individual fragments, which is avoided in the limited form of vertical partitioning supported in index-organized tables. An exception to this is the Projection Indexes in Sybase IQ [SYB99], which only holds partitioned column values. However, the column values are not maintained in any index order as in index-organized tables.

2.3 Secondary Index with Guess-DBAs

Secondary indexes can be created on index-organized tables to provide alternate access paths. Unique, non-unique, as well as function-based secondary indexes are supported. However, secondary indexes on index-organized tables differ from indexes on heap-organized tables in several ways:

- They store logical row identifiers instead of physical row identifiers. Thus, a table reorganization operation does not make its secondary indexes unusable.

- The logical row identifier includes primary key columns. Thus, a query involving indexed columns and/or primary key columns can be satisfied by an index-only scan.

While the above properties are desirable, there is one drawback when compared to a secondary index with physical row identifiers. During an index-based scan of an index with physical row identifier, each lookup needs just one extra I/O to fetch the base table columns. But a similar lookup using a secondary index with logical row identifiers requires I/O's equal to the height of the primary key B^+-tree to fetch the base table columns. Such primary key based lookup during index-based scan can degrade the performance substantially.

Guess-DBAs: To mitigate this problem, a 4-byte Database Block Address (DBA) of the primary key index leaf block where the base table row can be found, is stored as part of the logical row identifier. This DBA, referred to as *guess-DBA*, identifies the block where the row is *most likely* to be found for the reasons mentioned below.

The DBAs are populated correctly as part of secondary index creation. Further, DML operations implicitly maintain the guess-DBAs for the rows affected. Specifically, for inserts and updates that do not cause leaf block splits, corresponding rows in the secondary indexes are updated to contain the correct guess-DBAs. However, DML operations may cause a set of rows in the primary key B^+-tree index to move due to a leaf block split. This results in invalidating guess-DBAs stored in the secondary index rows corresponding to the base table rows that moved to a different leaf block.

An argument can be made for fixing the guess-DBAs for the rows that moved to a different leaf block, as part of the DML operation that caused the move. But this scheme was rejected since it would impose an unpredictable performance overhead on the DML. Also, the current design retains the simplicity of traditional B^+-tree index maintenance.

If the table rows do not move, then the guess-DBA will identify the correct leaf block. However, if the guess-DBA is invalid, then the cost of one extra I/O is incurred to fetch the block pointed by guess-DBA, before resorting to a primary key based lookup.

Guess-DBA Quality: To minimize use of invalid guess-DBAs, a statistic called *guess-DBA quality* is maintained for each secondary index. It is defined as percentage of valid guess-DBAs with respect to total number of rows in the secondary B^+-tree index.

The optimizer consults the guess-DBA quality to decide if it should use the guess-DBA or directly fall back to primary key based lookup to access the base table row. This statistic is implicitly set to 100 after the index creation. However, like other index statistics, it gets recomputed as part of the ANALYZE index statement, which analyzes the index and generates statistics for subsequent use by the optimizer.

If the guess-DBA quality drops below a certain threshold, the guess-DBAs can be fixed *online* using an ALTER index statement. Note that a rebuild of the index will also result in fixing the guess-DBAs. However, rebuild of index is typically done when the secondary index itself is fragmented due to large number of inserts and deletes.

The performance of the (logical row identifier-based) secondary index using valid guess-DBAs matches that of the secondary index with physical row identifiers as confirmed by experiments described in Section 4.3. Storing guess-DBAs reduces leaf row density causing extra I/Os for range scans. This overhead, however, is only a small fraction of the overall cost, the larger component being the I/Os needed, one per index row, to access the base table columns.

2.4 Key Compression

Index-organized tables can be compressed by eliminating common primary key column prefixes. Unlike conventional tables, the rows in an index-organized table are naturally clustered in the primary key order and there is a high likelihood of finding common prefixes for the key values.

The salient characteristics of the scheme are:

- Key compression applies to primary B^+-tree with multi-column primary key and specifically to keys in the leaf blocks.

- A key is broken into a prefix entry and a suffix entry at column boundary.

- Compression is achieved by sharing the common prefix entries among all the suffix entries within a leaf block.

Key compression can be enabled by specifying the COMPRESS clause as part of the physical attributes of the table, along with a prefix length (as number of columns) that specifies how the key can be broken into a prefix and a suffix. For example,

```
CREATE TABLE inverted_doc  . . .      . .
ORGANIZATION INDEX TABLESPACE ind_tbs
COMPRESS 1 INCLUDING token_frequency;
```

Here, single column prefixes (that is, token column) will be compressed in the primary key <token, doc_id> occurrences. For the list of primary key values <'DBMS', 1>, <'DBMS', 2>,<'Oracle', 1>, <'Oracle', 2>, the repeated occurrences of 'DBMS' and 'Oracle' are compressed away.

The scheme used provides row-level compression as opposed to block-level compression, which enables index-organized tables and their key-compressed secondary indexes to support the same degree of concurrency as their uncompressed counterparts. Also, our design decision to identify common prefixes at column boundaries avoids the need to reassemble the index row. Specifically, the scheme allows extraction of columns directly from the prefix and suffix entries. Thus, both exact and range scan performance of compressed index-organized tables are comparable to those for uncompressed counterparts as confirmed by the experiments described in Section 4.4.

2.5 Online Reorganization

For index-organized tables, reorganization may be needed more often than conventional tables. The data resides in a B^+-tree structure, which can get fragmented due to large number of inserts, updates, and/or deletes. In the event of such fragmentation, users can either *coalesce* or *rebuild* the primary key B^+-tree structure. These operations can be performed online. Furthermore, secondary index guess-DBAs invalidated by these operations can be fixed online to maintain guess-DBA based access performance. These online operations are discussed below.

Coalesce operation on the primary key B^+-tree coalesces (merges) leaf blocks within the same branch. This is an online operation that locks a few blocks at a time, and quickly frees them as soon as the coalesce on those blocks is completed. For example, the following command will coalesce the primary key B^+-tree index for the *inverted_doc* table.

```
ALTER TABLE inverted_doc COALESCE;
```

Rebuild (also termed *move*) operation on the primary key B^+-tree results in creating a new tree. By default, the table is not available for other operations during the move. However, the logical nature of secondary indexes makes the reorganization window smaller for index-organized table when compared to a conventional table, because the secondary indexes do not have to be updated. This will help in environments which can afford a limited downtime for database maintenance. However, for applications requiring 24x7 availability, the online move is supported which allows DML and query

operations during the actual move operation. For example, the following command rebuilds the *inverted_doc* table online.

```
ALTER TABLE inverted_doc MOVE ONLINE;
```

Key-sequenced tables in Non-Stop SQL also support online move and coalesce operations [Troi96]. However, the analogous operations on index-organized tables differ in their handling of secondary indexes, due to presence of guess-DBAs. In our case, the guess-DBA quality is set to 0 as part of the move operation. This ensures that the optimizer resorts to primary key-based access for rows identified by the index scan, giving a performance comparable to that of key-sequenced tables. However, users can fix the guess-DBAs of the secondary index online by issuing an ALTER index statement. Thus, for index-organized table, the secondary index-based scan performance temporarily falls back to primary key-based access (see Figure 5(a) in Section 4.3) as result of move but improves back to the performance of valid guess-DBA based access (Figure 5(b)) after the online guess-DBA fix-up operation completes.

3 Index-Organized Table Applications

The superior query performance and storage savings of index-organized tables (and primary B^+-tree like structures, in general) have traditionally made them ideal for OLTP applications. However, index-organized tables are equally useful in several new domains. The table below summarizes the applicability of index-organized tables, especially its novel aspects:

App.	Idx	C-Pl.	S-Idx	K-Cmp	O-Reorg
E-Order	√		√		√
I-Search	√	√		√	√
I- Portals	√	√	√	√	
E-Catalog	√			√	
D-Ware	√	√	√	√	
T-Series	√			√	
D-specific	√	*	*	*	*

Table 1: Applicability of Index-Organized Table features (Idx: Index-Organization, C-Pl: Column Placement, S-Idx: Secondary Indexes, K-Cmp: Key Compression, O-Reorg: Online Reorganization, *indicates that applicability is domain-specific)

3.1 Electronic Order Processing

Electronic order processing is quite similar to the scheme described in the TPC-C benchmark [TPCC93]. For example, in an online store such as Amazon.com, an order-entry transaction accepts the order for a book or CD, assigns the order a unique order_id and inserts the order into an orders table with the status as 'confirmed'. The delivery transaction retrieves the order entry by order_id, processes the order by validating if all parameters of the order such as payment, shipping address, etc. are satisfactory, and updates the status of this order entry as 'processed'. The fulfillment transaction retrieves all processed orders by order_id and status, and ships the item, changing the status of the order as 'fulfilled'. Fulfilled orders are periodically moved into a data warehouse. Apart from these state changing DML operations, an order tracking system may also make queries against the table to determine the status of an order.

An index-organized table is an ideal storage structure for the 'orders' table, where the query and DML is predominantly primary-key based. Further, the heavy volume of DML operations is bound to fragment the table, requiring frequent table reorganization. An index-organized table can be reorganized without invalidating its secondary indexes, and moreover, this reorganization can be done online as described in section 2.5, thereby reducing or eliminating the window of non-availability of the orders table. Furthermore, the guess-DBAs invalidated during reorganization of the base table can be fixed online.

3.2 Internet Search Engines

Internet search engines use web crawlers to index contents of the web and provide full-text search capability. The majority of the current search engines and full-text searching in text databases do not employ database technology [Ber+98]. We believe that future systems will be DBMS driven, since they can implicitly benefit from the high availability and scalability characteristics of DBMS.

The fundamental component of a search engine is an inverted index, which can be modeled using an index-organized table as shown in section 2. The example shown maintains one entry per <token, doc-id> pair, that is, the unit of inversion is a document. Since the token occurrence data can be of variable size, we can limit the amount that is stored in the index using the PCTTHRESHOLD column placement option, and thereby ensure a lower bound on the leaf row density. This capability is even more desirable when the unit of inversion is a set of documents or the entire collection. In such cases, the occurrence data can be huge, especially for popular tokens. For a given token, the corresponding inverted index entry can be reached by just traversing the primary B$^+$-tree. In most cases, only a single physical I/O is needed to get to the inverted index row, since the branch blocks will be cached.

The inevitable fragmentation of the inverted index structure due to the huge volume of insertions will mandate frequent reorganization, which means downtime - which is highly undesirable for web sites. Index-organized tables, owing to their support for online reorganization, are suitable for such situations since they can help reduce, or eliminate, downtime.

Although most popular Internet search engines can effectively index content stored in files, they still do not index the vast amounts of information tucked away in *databases*. Database search engines such as Jungle [BBD99] access and advertise databases on the web. Similarly, Infoseek's JavaSeek Search Server [JSEEK] provides full-text search capability for any field in an Oracle database, and uses index-organized tables to store the full-text index.

3.3 Internet Portals

A majority of web sites, including portals, foster online communities. Arsdigita Community System (ACS) is an open source toolkit, based on Oracle8 RDBMS, that can be used to build and manage online communities [Gre99]. One critical function of this toolkit is to track user activity. For example, the User/Content Map module tracks which users have read which pieces of web content. The table holding user/content map is modeled as an index-organized table with <user, page_id> as the primary key. In general, we believe that the toolkits such as ACS, used for building and managing web sites, will have a significant number of database tables with primary keys, which can be best modeled as index-organized tables.

Web applications such as portals and auction sites maintain a database of users. These user tables can be based on index-organized tables. Since only a part of the user information is accessed more frequently than the rest, the flexible column placement options provide the ability to push infrequently accessed data to the overflow storage area.

For queries requiring alternate access paths (based on, for example, zipcode, credit_card_id, etc.), secondary indexes built on these columns perform as well as indexes on conventional tables. This is because the base tables are typically non-volatile and hence help retain the validity of guess-DBAs in the secondary indexes. However, inserts can still cause splits leading to invalidation of guess-DBAs. In such an event, the indexes can be fixed online as described in Section 2.3.

The popularity of Yahoo's directory-like structure among portals confirms that organizing web content hierarchically by categories is, and will remain, the de-facto standard. Index-organized tables are ideal for storing the multi-column primary keys, composed of the category attributes which represent the hierarchy, along with the URL and any additional information. Such tables can also benefit from key compression.

3.4 Electronic Catalogs

Electronic catalogs are essential components of E-commerce. A typical procurement process involves product selection, source selection, negotiation of price, ordering, order fulfillment and finally payment [AK97]. Two types of catalogs are usually needed:

Manufacturer's Catalog: Manufacturers supply several products which might have different sets of attributes, whose diversity can make the task of catalog management very challenging. [Dan98] suggests that the product descriptions be modeled as rows in a table with <product_id, attribute_name, attribute_value> such that there would be one entry per attribute per product. This generalized scheme can easily support addition of entirely new products or addition of new attributes to existing products.

Retailer's Catalog: A retailer selling items from multiple manufacturers needs to group the products into different (buyer-friendly) categories, which may have sub-categories depending on how the vendor, wants to present the products. The retailer can either poll all the manufacturers and build a catalog (Table 2) or the catalog can be a "virtual" one which is dynamically constructed from the manufacturer's catalogs [AK97]. Additionally, the retailer might want to "materialize" the virtual catalog for better performance.

Category	Sub-Category	ItemName	Price
Book	Technical	Oracle8 Tuning	45
Book	Science Fiction	Time Machine	20
...	...	...	...

Table 2: A retailer's catalog constructed by polling manufacturer's catalogs

Assuming a database driven catalog, the resulting structure (Table 2) will have a set of category columns (determined by the retailer) in addition to the attributes retrieved from the manufacturer's catalog. An ideal storage organization should hierarchically cluster these entries on the category columns.

An index-organized table can be used to store these manufacturer catalogs, indexed on <product id, attribute name>, will cluster all attributes of a product together. Similarly, for the retailer's catalog, an index-organized table with a multi-column primary key matching the hierarchy of these categories is a natural fit. Key compression can be used to avoid same <product_id> and <category, subcategory> column value repetitions in the manufacturer's and retailer's catalogs, respectively.

3.5 Data Warehousing

The efforts to speed up data warehousing applications have focused on two areas: supporting ad-hoc queries, and supporting known or expected set of queries. For example, [OQ97] discusses how ad-hoc style queries can be efficiently evaluated using index and clustering techniques, whereas [JLS99] deals with known or given workloads, specifically with the problem of finding optimal ways to cluster records of a fact table to minimize I/Os. We believe that index-organized tables (or other similar primary B$^+$-tree structures) can be used to implement fact tables for the latter class of applications.

Consider a warehouse application illustrated in [JLS99] with relations:

```
location(state, city, lid)
jeans(type, gender, jid)
sales(lid, jid, sale)
```

A typical OLAP query is:

```
SELECT SUM(sales) FROM sales, location, jeans
WHERE  sales.lid = location.lid AND sales.jid
= jeans.jid AND   location.state = NY AND
jeans.type = 'LEVI';
```

Implementing the fact table ('sales') as an index-organized table with primary key <lid, jid> will yield better performance than a conventional table with a primary key index. The join result of <location, jeans> after applying the corresponding filters is used to look-up for <lid, jid> pair in the sales table. This fact table look-up will result in an index-based scan for a conventional table, whereas an index-only scan is sufficient for index-organized table (for the performance characteristics see Section 4.1). The data warehouse applications will also benefit from various novel aspects as indicated in Table 1 with similar reasoning as in Section 3.3.

Support for summary tables and materialized views in Oracle [Bel+98] are being implemented for index-organized tables, and bitmapped secondary indexes will also be available in a future Oracle8 release.

3.6 Time-Series

A time-series is a set of time stamped rows belonging to a single item, such as stock price. Data is accessed through an item identifier such as stock symbol and timestamp. By defining an index-organized table with primary key <stock symbol, timestamp>, the Oracle8 Time Series Data Cartridge [OTS97] is able to efficiently store and manipulate time-series data. Repeated occurrences of the item identifier (e.g., stock symbol) key can be compressed, leading to additional storage savings.

In our experience, individual rows are small in size and hence column placement options are not needed. Data is inserted at the end of subgroups, for example, adding new values for each stock symbol that monotonically increase with time. Deletions are rare. Thus, the primary B$^+$-trees do not tend to fragment, and hence reorganization is usually not required. The use of secondary indexes is also not very common.

3.7 Domain-Specific Indexing

Oracle8*i* introduces the Extensible Indexing Framework [SMSAD00], through which users can add a new access method to the RDBMS engine. Typically, domain-specific indexing schemes need some storage mechanism to hold their index data. Index-organized tables are ideal candidates for such domain index storage. Oracle8 *inter*Media Text Cartridge [OIMT99] has implemented domain-specific indexing schemes that use index-organized tables for storing their index data.

4 Performance Study

This goal of this study is to validate the clustering benefits of primary B$^+$-tree, to illustrate the effect of overflow, to show the effect of logical row identifiers containing guess-DBA, and to illustrate the benefits of key compression.

All the experiments (except key compression) are conducted using Oracle8*i*, Release 8.1.6 configured with 4K database block size, 16MB of database buffer cache on a SunOS 5.6, single CPU Ultra-60 Sparc with 256MB of main memory. The order_line table of TPC-C benchmark [TPCC93], which models a product sales and distribution business, is used as the reference table.

```
CREATE TABLE order_line ( ol_o_id NUMBER,
ol_w_id NUMBER, ol_d_id NUMBER, ol_number
NUMBER,  ol_i_id NUMBER, ol_supply_w_id
NUMBER, ol_quantity NUMBER,  ol_amount
NUMBER(6), ol_delivery_date DATE, ol_dist_info
CHAR(24),
CONSTRAINT pk_orderline PRIMARY KEY (ol_w_id,
ol_d_id, ol_o_id, ol_number));
```

4.1 Performance of Index-organized Table without Overflow

Query and DML execution times are measured for data sizes varying from 100MB (~1.75 million rows) to 500MB (~8.74 million rows). The average and maximum standard deviation (s.d) over 10 iterations are reported. Data for the order_line table is generated in random order. The time for bulk-load into an index-organized table is more than that for the heap-organized table (for example, 28 minutes vs. 17 minutes for 200MB). This can be attributed to larger sort overhead due to inclusion of non-key columns in the sort entries in the case of index-organized table.

Storage requirement for index-organized table is less than that for heap-organized table (for example, 268MB vs. 344MB for 200MB data). The additional storage needed for heap-organized tables can be attributed to duplication of key columns in the table and the primary key index. For the heap-organized table, the primary key index storage required 93MB and the actual table storage required 251MB for 200MB data.

Query Performance

In order to compare the query performance for *random* and *range* access, total time taken to access 1000 random order_line rows and the total time for selecting 100,000 consecutive order_line rows are measured.

The index-organized table shows superior query performance for both random and range scans. The random access on the 100MB table took 0.92 seconds for

index-organized table as compared to 1.16 seconds for the heap-organized table (See Figure 2). The same performance is observed for larger data sets. The faster random access for the index-organized table results from finding both key and non-key columns in the primary key index leaf block. The range scan query performance is consistently faster for index-organized tables (See Figure 2). For the 100MB table, a range-scan on index-organized table took 1.20 seconds as compared to 4.35 seconds for the heap-organized tables. Similar performance is observed for larger data sets. The speed-up can be attributed to the fact that the rows are clustered in primary key order for index-organized tables, plus an additional random I/O per row is avoided.

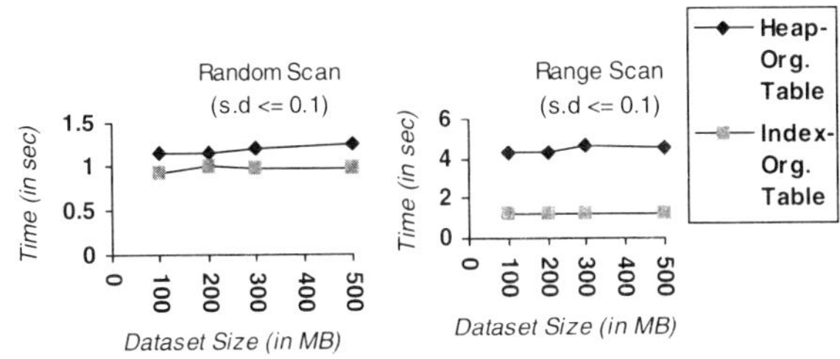

Figure 2: Random and Range Scan Time

DML Performance

Time taken for inserting, updating, and deleting 2000 order_line rows are measured and compared for the two organizations. The update statement involved modification of the delivery_date field. Overall, while insert and update performance of the two table organizations are comparable, delete performs better for index-organized tables (Figure 3). The anomaly in the 200MB case (Figures 3(a) and 3(b)), is because of a larger B$^+$-Tree height for the index-organized table as compared to that for primary key index on heap-organized table (4 vs. 3). Compared to updates where only an extra I/O is incurred, this difference in time is larger for inserts due to branch block splits in the additional level.

Single row updates in both heap and index-organized tables involve finding the target row via primary-key index and then modifying a single structure (table or index, respectively), so it is easy to argue that performance of such updates will be comparable. We focus instead on performance of updating multiple rows with consecutive primary-key values. When compared to just the primary key index of a conventional table, the number of index blocks accessed for selecting the rows that satisfy the where-clause is higher for an index-organized table, since inclusion of non-key columns makes the size of its index rows larger than that of primary-key index rows. However, due to guaranteed clustered placement of consecutive rows, the number of disk block I/Os for accessing and modifying target base table rows is significantly lower, since heap-organized tables generally lack such clustering. The latter reduction in number of blocks is usually sufficient to offset the earlier increase. This is reflected in our results (Figure 3(b)) which shows comparable update performance for index-organized and heap-organized tables. Index-organized tables will usually have better delete performance because only a single structure (index) needs to be modified as opposed to modifying two structures (index and table) for heap-organized tables. This is reflected in our results (See Figure 3(c)).

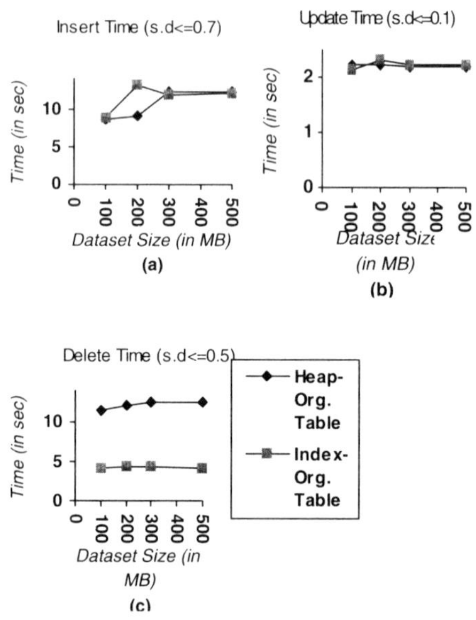

Figure 3: Insert, Update, and Delete Time: without overflow.

4.2 Performance of Index-organized Table with Overflow

This experiment compares the performance of order_line table with column ol_dist_info pushed out to overflow storage area, with that of the table without overflow. Two types of Queries and DML statements were used against 500MB of data: (1) those accessing only *index-resident* columns, that is, columns that have not been pushed out to the overflow, and (2) those accessing the *overflow-resident* column.

Query Performance

Pushing the column ol_dist_info to the overflow results in higher leaf row density as less number of column values per row needs to be stored in the index.

Accessing only index-resident column(s) : Higher leaf row density achieved through the use of overflow leads to improved performance for any query that accesses only index-resident columns. This improvement is particularly evident in the case of range access as less number of index leaf blocks needs to be accessed (Figure 4: 0.98 sec each for exact match, 1.21 sec. vs. 1.01 sec for range scan).

Accessing overflow-resident column(s) : Access to overflow-resident columns requires access to the index leaf block followed by an access to the appropriate overflow block, which in fact is similar to block access sequence needed for heap-organized tables. Thus, in this configuration, both random and range access query performance deteriorates from 0.98 sec to 1.31 sec and from 1.43 sec to 4.75 sec, respectively, which are comparable to query performance for heap-organized table (1.24 sec and 4.78 sec, respectively). The range access query performance for accessing an overflow-resident column improves to 2.09 sec if it follows a table rebuild, since the rebuild clusters overflow row-pieces in primary key order.

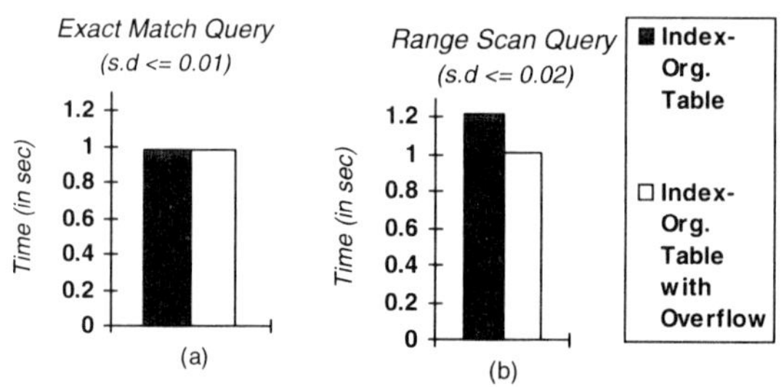

Figure 4: Time for random and range query accessing index-resident column(s) in 500MB index-organized tables.

DML Performance

Insert : Insert performance improves from 12.14 sec to 11.61 sec, mainly because reduction in index row size lowers the frequency of splits during insertion into the B^+-Tree.

Delete : Delete performance however, deteriorates from 4.17 sec to 11.03 sec (approaching delete performance for heap-organized table which takes 12.62 sec) as two structures, index and overflow, need to be modified for deleting the target base table rows.

Update : Higher leaf row density achieved through the use of overflow leads to improved performance for any update that modifies only index-resident columns. On the other hand, any update that modifies an overflow-resident column performs worse because it requires accessing the target index leaf block and also the appropriate overflow block.

4.3 Performance of Secondary Index

This experiment compares the performance of secondary index on a 500MB order_line table, created with index and heap organization. The secondary index is created on the ol_i_id column.

Guess DBA Usage: The *guess-DBA* is stored in the logical row identifier improves the performance of a secondary index-based scan by avoiding the primary key traversal when possible, as confirmed by this experiment. Index-based scan using valid *guess-DBAs* matches the performance of secondary index- based scan on heap-organized tables (Figure 5(b)). The following query is used for this test, and it returns 8000 rows:

```
Q1: SELECT SUM(ol_amount) FROM order_line
WHERE ol_i_id BETWEEN 100001 AND 100050·
```

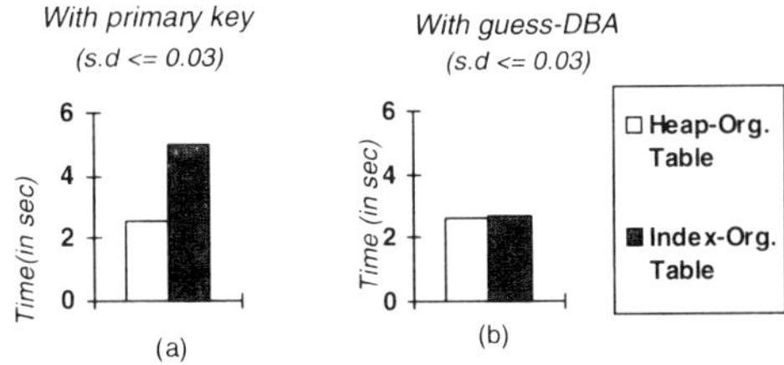

Figure 5: Time for index-based scan

Index Availability: A table reorganization renders the secondary index of a conventional table unusable. Subsequent to the reorganization, this would cause queries (for example, Q1 stated above) that originally required an index-based scan to incur the cost of a full-table scan. However, when an index-organized table is rebuilt, its secondary index remains usable (albeit with invalidated guess-DBAs), thereby allowing an index-based scan for such queries. Thus, for index-organized tables the time for index-based scan after reorganization is significantly better (5.07 sec for index-organized table vs. 74.98 sec for heap-organized table).

Index-Only Scan versus Index-Based Scan: The following query performs an index-only scan, and returns 200000 rows:

```
Q2: SELECT COUNT(*) FROM order_line WHERE
ol_i_id BETWEEN 100001 AND 100500;
```

In this experiment, the leaf row density of the secondary index for the index-organized table is lower, owing to its maintaining the 4-column primary key, when compared to the index on the conventional table. The resulting increase in leaf block fetches explains its poorer performance of index-only scan when compared to

an index on a conventional table (0.7 sec for heap-organized table vs. 1.0 sec for index-organized table).

However, for a query that involves accessing the secondary key and the primary key columns, such as:

```
Q3: SELECT COUNT(*) FROM order_line WHERE
ol_i_id BETWEEN 100001 AND 100500 AND
ol_d_id=10;
```

(which fetches 20000 rows), a secondary index-only scan is sufficient for index-organized tables because the column ol_d_id is available as part of the index row. For a heap-organized table, this would require a secondary index-based scan. This results in significant performance benefit for a secondary index on index-organized table (0.1sec for index-organized table vs. 156.3 sec for heap-organized table).

4.4 Performance of Key-Compressed Index-Organized Table

This experiment compares the performance of a 500MB order_line table with and without compression. The experiment is conducted with Oracle8*i*, Release 2 on a dual CPU Ultra-60 Sparc with 512MB of main memory For the four column primary key, three column prefixes are compressed. The data set typically has the same prefix for 10 order lines. The compression resulted in 12% storage reduction in the primary key index leaf blocks.

Time taken to access 1000 random order_line rows and for selecting 100,000 consecutive order_line rows is measured for the index-organized table with and without compression. The random lookup query took 0.71 and 0.73 seconds for compressed and uncompressed configurations respectively. The additional CPU overhead to process compressed index-organized table did not have any significant impact on the random scan performance.

Range scan query took 0.77 seconds and 0.74 seconds for compressed and uncompressed configurations. For range scan, 12% fewer blocks are needed for the compressed organization when compared to the uncompressed organization. However, the savings in I/Os is offset by the additional CPU overhead incurred to extract the columns from the compressed table. This resulted in comparable range scan performance.

5 Conclusions and Future Work

The primary B$^+$-tree structure, with row data in leaf blocks, is an ideal storage organization for primary key access intensive applications. Traditionally, use of such structures has been limited to OLTP applications. However, we argue that an index-organized table with its support for several additional features, is equally useful in several new domains. Specifically, we discuss its use in Electronic Order Processing, Internet Search Engines,

Internet Portals, Electronic Catalogs, Time-Series, and Data Warehouse applications. The applicability and performance of index-organized tables is enhanced by support for column placement control, use of logical row identifiers with guess-DBAs in the secondary indexes, key compression, and online reorganization.

The performance study demonstrates the superior query performance for both random and range scans for index-organized tables and comparable DML performance to heap-organized tables. The experiment on the effect of overflow demonstrates the benefit of controlling placement of columns between index and overflow storage areas. Secondary indexes on index-organized tables with valid guess-DBAs showed matching query performance with those on heap-organized tables. The key-compression experiment illustrates the storage savings can be achieved without degradation in query performance.

We also plan to support bitmap indexes on index-organized tables to increase its applicability to data warehousing domain. For applications with large primary keys that require several alternate access paths, the current scheme of using primary key based logical row identifiers in secondary indexes is not suitable. For handing such applications, we are investigating an alternate scheme that can optionally fall back to physical row identifiers.

Acknowledgments

We thank Jonathan Klein, Bhaskar Himatsingka, Wei Huang, and Vishwanath Karra for implementing online move support, and their design reviews. For logical ROWID support, we thank Alex Tsukerman. We thank Gopal Krishnan for conducting the initial set of experiments on index-organized tables. Special thanks to Anil Nori and Franco Putzolu for their involvement in defining the index-organized table functionality.

References

[AK97] Keller, A., "Smart Catalogs and Virtual Catalogs," *Readings in Electronic Commerce*, Kalakota, R., Whinston, A.B.(eds.), Chapter 11: 259-274, 1997.

[BBD99] Bohlen, M., Bukauskas, L., Dyreson, C., "The Jungle Database Search Engine," *Proceedings of the ACM SIGMOD Int. Conf. on Management of Data*: 584-586, May 1999.

[Bel+98] Bello, R. G., et al., "Materialized Views in Oracle," *Proceedings of VLDB*, pp. 659-664, 1998.

[Ber+98] Bernstein, P., et al., "The Asilomar Report on Database Research," *SIGMOD Record*, 27(4): 74-80, Dec. 1998.

[BSZ98] Bichler, M., Segev, A., Zhao, J.L., "Component-based E-Commerce: Assessment of Current Practices and Future Directions," *ACM SIGMOD Record*, 27(4): 7-14, Dec. 1998.

[Com79] Comer, D., "The Ubiquitous B-Tree," *Computing Surveys*, 11(2):121-137, Jun. 1979.

[Dan98] Danish, S., "Building database driven electronic catalogs," *ACM SIGMOD Record*, 27(4): 15-20, Dec. 1998.

[DB2V5.2] The SQL Reference. *DB2 Universal Database Version 5.2* Publication.

[Gre99] Greenspun, P., "Philip and Alex's Guide to Web Publishing," *Academic Press/Morgan Kaufmann*, Apr. 1999.

[HN79] Hammer, M., Niamir, B., "A Hueristic Approach to Attribute Partitioning," *Proceedings of the ACM SIGMOD Int. Conf. on Management of Data*, pp.93-101, 1979.

[JLS99] Jagadish, H.V., Lakshmanan, L.V.S.,Srivastava, D., "Snakes and Sandwiches: Optimal Clustering Strategies for a Data Warehouse," *Proceedings of the ACM SIGMOD Int. Conf. on Management of Data*, pp.37-48, May 1999.

[JSEEK] Javaseek Search Server. Available at *http://software.infoseek.com/products/javaseek/applications.htm* .

[MS98] Microsoft SQL Server, *SQL Server 7.0 Storage Engine*, White Paper, Oct. 1998.

[NCWD84] Navathe, S.B., Ceri, S., Wiederhold, G., Dou, J., "Vertical Partitioning of Algorithms for Database Design," *ACM TODS*,pp. 680-710, 1984.

[Niam78] Niamir, B., "Attribute Partitioning in a Self-Aaptive Relational Database System,"*Technical Report 192*, LCS, MIT, 1978.

[OAQ97] *Oracle8 Application Developer's Guide - Advance Queuing*, Oracle Corp., Part # A58241-01, Jun. 1997.

[OIMT99] *Oracle8i interMedia Text Reference, Release 8.1.5*, Oracle Corp., Part No. A67843-01, Feb. 1999.

[OQ97] O'Neil, P., Quass, D., "Improved Query Performance with Variant Indexes," *Proceedings of the ACM SIGMOD Int. Conf. on Management of Data*, pp.38-49, May 1997.

[OSC97] *Oracle8 Server Concepts Volume I & II*: Oracle Corp., Part # A54644-01 & A54646-01, Jun. 1997.

[OTS97] *Oracle8 Time Series Cartridge User's Guide Release 8.1*, Oracle Corp., Part # A64429-01, Jun. 1997.

[RDC96] Rengarajan, T.K., Dimino, L., Chung, D., "Sybase System 11 Online Capabilities," *Data Engineering Bulletin*, pp.18-23, Jun. 1996.

[SI96] Sockut, G.H., Iyer, B.R., "A Survey of Online Reorganization in IBM Products and Research," *Data Engineering Bulletin*, pp.4-11, Jun. 1996.

[SMSAD00] Srinivasan, J., Murthy, R., Sundara, S., Agarwal, N., DeFazio, S., "Extensible Indexing: A Framework for Integrating Domain-Specific Indexing into Oracle8i," *Proceedings of the 16th Data Engineering Conf.*, pp. 91-100, Mar. 2000.

[SYB95] Sybase SQL Server, *Transact-SQL User's Guide*, Document ID:32300-01-1100-02, Dec. 1995.

[SYB99] Sybase Adaptive Server IQ Administration and Performance Guide, Adaptive Server IQ Release 12.0 Collection, Chapter 4, 1999.

[Tand87] The Tandem Database Group, "NonStop SQL: A Distributed, High-performance, High-availability Implementation of SQL," *Proc. 2nd Int. Workshop on High Performance Transaction Systems*, Springer Lecture Notes in Computer Science No. 359, pp60-104, 1987.

[TPCC93] Gray, J. (Editor), The Benchmark Handbook for Database and Transaction Processing Systems, Morgan Kaufmann Publishers, 1993.

[Troi96] Troisi, J., "NonStop SQL/MP Availability and Database Configuration Operations," *Data Engineering Bulletin*, pp.12-17, Jun. 1996.

[ZMS92] Zobel, J., Moffat, A., Sacks-Davis, R., "An Efficient Indexing Technique for Full Text Databases," *Proceedings of VLDB*, pp. 352-362, 1992.

[ZM98] Zou, C., Salzberg, B., "Safely and Efficiently Updating References during On-line Reorganization," *Proceedings of VLDB*, pp. 512-522, 1998.

FALCON: Feedback Adaptive Loop for Content-Based Retrieval

Leejay Wu   Christos Faloutsos   Katia Sycara   Terry R. Payne

Carnegie Mellon University

Abstract

Several methods currently exist that can perform relatively simple queries driven by relevance feedback on large multimedia databases. However, all these methods work only for vector spaces; that is, they require that objects be represented as vectors within feature spaces. Moreover, their implied query regions are typically convex. This research paper explains our solution.

We propose a novel method that is designed to handle disjunctive queries within metric spaces. The user provides weights for positive examples; our system "learns" the implied concept and returns similar objects. Our method differs from existing relevance-feedback methods that base themselves upon Euclidean or Mahalanobis metrics, as it facilitates learning even disjunctive, concave models within vector spaces, as well as arbitrary metric spaces. In addition, our method is completely example-driven, and imposes no requirements upon the user for other aspects such as feature selection.

Our main contributions are two-fold. Not only do we present a novel way to estimate the dissimilarity of an object to a set of desirable objects, but we support it with an algorithm that shows how to exploit metric indexing structures that support range queries to accelerate the search without incurring false dismissals. Our empirical results demonstrate

Proceedings of the 26th VLDB Conference, Cairo, Egypt, 2000.

that our method converges rapidly to excellent precision/recall, while outperforming sequential scanning by up to 200%.

1   Introduction

As the size and diversity of multimedia databases increase, so does the potential complexity of queries. Query concepts such as, "Return all video clips showing any US President speaking", may be be easy to specify, but difficult to perform. Unless comprehensive annotations are provided with every database entry, a multimedia database might be forced to rely on nothing more than query-by-example. In addition, measuring similarity between images then becomes an issue. Should one resort to commercial packages, the result may easily yield – at best – a metric space, as neither the features nor their relevance are known, where a metric space is defined via a distance function which obeys symmetry and the triangle inequality [4]. In this domain, query models demanding vector spaces fail completely. This paper presents a novel approach, *FALCON*, which allows easy specification of complex queries, within both vector and metric spaces, for multimedia and traditional databases.

Many retrieval methods represent database records as vectors, with the assumption that the closer are two vectors, the more similar are the corresponding records [9]. Distance functions are chosen to score dissimilarity between points within this space. Thus, one may query a database by performing either a range query or a nearest-neighbor search relative to a single point or hyper-surface within this space.

However, users may wish to perform more complicated queries. On a real-world database, a user may wish to retrieve a class of objects that does not map to a contiguous region according to the similarity metric. For instance, the aforementioned query regarding US Presidents speaking arguably could map to numerous rather disparate images due to change of venue and personnel – and if the image distances are generated via a black-box function, we now have an unusual query in a metric space. Finding similar objects within this space is related to clustering, which can be done in metric spaces as per [16].

FALCON combines distances and incorporates user feedback in such a way as to "learn" the nature of such queries. This *aggregate dissimilarity* model applies to metric data sets, since it does not use any information about the data itself aside from that returned by a pairwise distance metric. Our experiments demonstrate that FALCON can provide high-quality results in terms of precision and recall after 5 to 20 iterations.

The paper is organized as follows: Section 2 summarizes a sample of existing related systems; the mechanisms underlying FALCON are presented in Section 3; the experiments and corresponding results are detailed in Section 4, and the subsequent analysis is presented in Section 5. The paper concludes with Section 6.

2 Related Work

A number of systems such as the following have been developed to handle example-based queries. Note they handle neither unusual disjoint queries, nor arbitrary metric spaces.

- Rocchio's relevance feedback mechanism [11], which generates hyper-spherical isosurfaces in feature space.

- MARS (Multimedia Analysis and Retrieval System) [10, 12, 13], which includes a query expansion model that can weight features from multiple objects. However, MARS limits the sums of weights, so that when using fixed thresholds it becomes difficult to specify a disjunctive query in which being similar to any one of the examples is sufficient to be considered good.

- MindReader, which uses the Mahalanobis distance to allow arbitrarily oriented ellipsoids [6]. The Mahalanobis distance $M(\vec{x}, \vec{y})$ is defined as $(\vec{x} - \vec{y})^T \times \mathbf{M} \times (\vec{x} - \vec{y})$ where $\vec{x}$ and $\vec{y}$ are n-dimensional column vectors and $\mathbf{M}$ is a $n \times n$ matrix. This corresponds to a weighted Euclidean distance, and permits effective rotation of the axes, but requires many examples to calculate the covariance matrix.

The original assumption behind the earliest systems is that there exists an ideal query vector. One can then try to determine both this vector and the optimal relative weights of the axes. This dependence on a vector space prevents these methods from generalizing to metric spaces.

Later systems, such as current versions of MARS, have query expansion models which permit actual elaboration by weighting the relative importance of different features of multiple positive examples [10]. However, one should note that MARS has been specialized for image databases with features, whereas MindReader generates isosurfaces consisting of single hyper-ellipsoids, and therefore does not handle disjunctive queries.

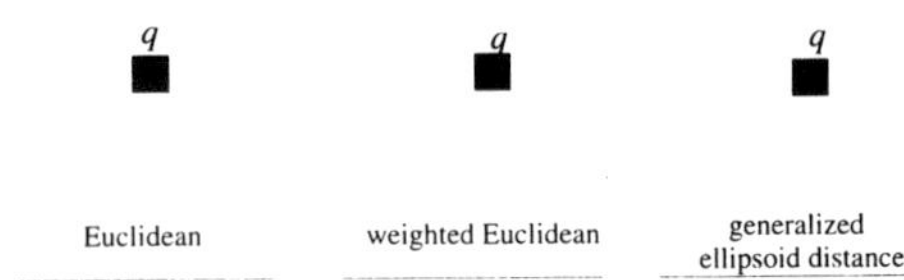

Figure 1: Generic isosurfaces for three previous methods.

See Figure 1 for an illustration of these types of isosurfaces.

Fox and Salton used the L_p metric to surpass fuzzy Boolean methods in the domain of text retrieval, replacing the use of minimum and maximum functions. Our objective is similar, but more complex; we wish to model arbitrarily disjunctive example-based queries in unbounded metric spaces using relevance feedback but lacking specific features [14].

FALCON does not rely on vector spaces, require user input beyond that of relevance feedback and examples, or sacrifice the ability to use disjunctive queries that correspond to arbitrary groupings in metric spaces. In addition, advanced indexing methods can be used to significantly speed up the search process. Spatial indexing methods such as R-trees [5] and R*-trees [1, 2] would serve if we were to limit ourselves to vector domains; M-trees [3] provide fast range-queries in general metric spaces.

3 Proposed Method

This section proposes the underlying mechanisms and assumptions made by FALCON. Table 1 lists the notation used in this section.

Let $\mathcal{X}$ be the set of objects in our metric data set. Then, let $d : \mathcal{X} \times \mathcal{X} \rightarrow \Re$ be the provided distance metric that defines our metric space.

To start each query, the user specifies at least one "desirable" example that is representative of the intended query. This set of "good" examples is denoted by $\mathcal{G}$. Thus:

Problem 1: Query by Multiple Examples	
Given	$\mathcal{X}$, a metric data set
	d, its pairwise distance metric
	$\mathcal{G} = \{g_i\}$, the set of "good objects"
Find	Other desirable objects in $\mathcal{X}$ that are similar to $\mathcal{G}$.

Symbol	Description
$\mathcal{X}$	The set of objects in our data set.
x	Any single object from $\mathcal{X}$.
$\mathcal{G}$	The current set of user-specified "good points".
g_i	A member of $\mathcal{G}$.
$D_{\mathcal{G}}$	The aggregate dissimilarity function based on $\mathcal{G}$.
$D_{\mathcal{G}}(x)$	The aggregate dissimilarity value for object x to the current good set $\mathcal{G}$.
α	A constant that influences how $D_{\mathcal{G}}$ behaves.
d	The pairwise dissimilarity function.

Table 1: Notation used within this paper.

We propose solving Problem 1 by determining a scoring function that models the user's query. Namely, we seek a function $D_{\mathcal{G}} : \mathcal{X} \to \Re$ based on $\mathcal{G}$, such that this function varies inversely with the desirability of x.

3.1 Proposed "Aggregate Dissimilarity" Function

Once we find a function that fulfills our main requirement – ranking objects inversely according to their apparent desirability as compared to $\mathcal{G}$ – the problem of finding relevant objects reduces to that of sorting. We define such a function as follows:

Problem 2: Aggregate Dissimilarity	
Given	$x \in \mathcal{X}$, a candidate $\mathcal{G} = \{g_i\}$, the set of user-selected "good objects" d, pairwise distance metric for $\mathcal{X}$
Determine	$D_{\mathcal{G}}(x)$, its aggregate dissimilarity

We propose that the FALCON aggregate dissimilarity, $D_{\mathcal{G}}(x)$ be computed as the αth root of the arithmetic mean of the αth powers, of the pairwise distances, as expressed by

$$(D_{\mathcal{G}}(x))^\alpha = \begin{cases} 0 \text{ if } (\alpha < 0) \wedge \exists i \, d(x, g_i) = 0 \\ \frac{1}{k} \times \sum_{i=1}^{k} d(x, g_i)^\alpha \text{otherwise} \end{cases}$$

$$(1)$$

If the value of α is very high, the highest distance will have the largest impact on $D_{\mathcal{G}}(x)$, while the reverse is true for very low values of α.

Note that Equation 1 mimics a fuzzy OR if $\alpha < 0$, and a fuzzy AND if $\alpha > 0$.

Since it is not obvious which values of α are the most suitable, we empirically compare results for various values of α. Our upcoming experiments show that $\alpha = -5$ is a reasonable choice for the queries and datasets we selected; however, in specific applications some tuning with subsets may be appropriate.

Were a user to select parrot photos via query-by-example, the following might ensue.

1. The user chooses a data set, $\mathcal{X}$, consisting of bird photos. This data set is paired with a pairwise distance metric d, which relies primarily on coloration when comparing images.

2. The user first chooses the image of a popular green-and-red parrot. This becomes the first member of $\mathcal{G}$.

3. FALCON returns the best matches, according to $D_{\mathcal{G}}$; note that grey parrots might be ranked below cardinals – which are mostly red – and peacocks – which tend to be green.

4. The user adds a picture of a grey parrot to the good set, which alters the aggregate dissimilarity function $D_{\mathcal{G}}$. Other images of grey parrots will now be considered more relevant to the query.

5. Repeat as desired; depending upon the data and the metric, convergence may be fairly rapid.

One useful generalization of the FALCON distance is to allow for weights. Unlike a distance "combination" function that only uses the minimum distance, the FALCON distance is easily modified to accept a positive w_i term for numerical feedback from a user. The proposed extension takes the form:

$$(D_{\mathcal{G}}(x))^\alpha = \frac{1}{\sum_{i=1}^{k} w_i} \cdot \sum_{i=1}^{k} w_i(d(x, g_i))^\alpha \qquad (2)$$

This has the effect that distance to the favored objects is penalized less if α is negative. We do *not* raise the weights to the αth power, as we believe that this – which would have the opposite effect – would be much less intuitive. In addition, we retain the influence of all pairwise distances between candidate and examples in all cases except that of an exact match, unlike a pure minimization function.

3.2 Speed and Completeness

There is the obvious question of speed. Sequential scanning would entail computing aggregate dissimilarity via Equation 1 or 2 for each element of the database, which would require $\Theta(nk)$ given n objects in $\mathcal{X}$ and k in $\mathcal{G}$. Our objective is to return the same results as a sequential scan, with less work on average per search.

Indexing structures which support fast range queries can be used to achieve significant speed-ups. First, we shift focus to the aggregate dissimilarity version of the range query:

Problem 3: Range Query by Multiple Example

Given $\mathcal{X}$, the database
$\mathcal{G} = \{g_i\}$, the set of "good objects"
ϵ, a threshold
d, pairwise distance metric for $\mathcal{X}$

Find Q, such that $Q = \{x : x \in \mathcal{X} \land D_{\mathcal{G}}(x) < \epsilon\}$ quickly

---

Theorem 1 *Consider Problem 3 above. Executing $k = |\mathcal{G}|$ separate range queries with threshold ϵ, will yield k sets, the union of which forms a superset of the actual answer. No object will be falsely discarded as a candidate by such a procedure.*

The proof is omitted for the sake of brevity [15].

This theorem shows that we can use existing indexing methods without fear of false dismissals. A post-processing step can then check every member of the union and discard any whose actual aggregate dissimilarity exceeds the threshold.

The question remains of selecting a suitable ϵ. One method would be to allow the user to flag examples that they consider to be about as dissimilar as they would accept; then, an ϵ can be generated as the maximum $D_{\mathcal{G}}$ for these borderline cases.

4   Experimental Setup

The core parts of FALCON were implemented in C, C++ and Perl, and tested on Intel Pentium II^{TM} workstations under Linux.

We tested FALCON with the intent of answering five central questions.

    (a) Does FALCON "learn" to model concave and disjunctive queries?
    (b) Does FALCON provide satisfactory precision/recall?
    (c) Does FALCON's distance function rapidly converge?
    (d) What is a suitable value of α?
    (e) How fast is FALCON?

Four data sets were used during the experiments, each with exactly one query. Two of the data sets were synthetic, and two consisted of real data. We used the standard Euclidean distance as the pairwise distance metric; with the $2D\_20K$ data set, we also experimented with L_∞.

Vector data sets were used primarily due to ease of generating consistent and objective feedback results; the FALCON system never examined the vectors themselves.

2D_50K: This synthetic data set consists of 50,000 points in 2-dimensional Cartesian space, randomly distributed approximately uniformly within the axis-aligned square (-2,-2) - (2,2).

2D_20K: This synthetic data set was generated using identical rules to that of the 2D_50K data set, but consists only of 20,000 points.

PEN: This database was obtained from the UCI repository [8], and consists of objects that correspond to handwritten digits, with features being the classification of each and the coordinates of spatially resampled points. We used the existing split of 3498 objects in the training set and 7494 in the test set.

STOCKS: Daily closing prices for up to five year periods were collected for 51 stocks from Yahoo's online quote server. They were split into 1856 non-overlapping vectors of length 32, which were then processed via the discrete wavelet transform (DWT). All 32 coefficients for each vector were used for L_2 distance computations.

4.1   Queries

One implicit query was associated with each data set. Queries were reflected via a seed set of five initial "good" objects, and appropriate feedback for each data item. A subset of each data set was selected as training sets, used for query refinement; the rest of the data served only for evaluation. It may in fact be feasible to implement a hierarchical view of a database – perhaps traversing something like an M-tree – in order to allow the user to easily select examples without wading through an entire database at once [3]. In addition, we varied α as there was no *a priori* reason to believe that one particular value would be optimal.

RING: Vectors within the 2D_50K data set were marked as positive examples if and only if they were between 0.5 and 1.5 units from the null vector, inclusive. The training set consisted of 1,000 vectors. 431 in the subset and 19,734 in the full set met this criterion. The five seeds were vectors of magnitude 1.4, with counter-clockwise angles from the positive X axis of 0, 72, 144, 216, and 288 degrees.

This query to tests performance on a contiguous, but non-convex set.

TWO_CIRCLES: Vectors within the 2D_20K data set were marked as positive examples if and only if they were within 0.5 units of either (-1,-1) or (1,1); 1899 points qualified. The subset consisted of 1000 points randomly drawn from the full set, including 99 positive examples. The seeds were randomly generated from within the two circles.

This query tests performance on a disjunctive set.

PEN: Vectors within the PEN data set that were classified as 4's were flagged positive. The existing training and test partition was used. 364 vectors in the training set and 780 in the full set were positive instances. The five seeds were drawn randomly from the positive instances in the training set.

This query tests performance on real data.

STOCKS: Vectors within the STOCKS data set were marked as positive examples if and only if the slopes of their least-squares linear approximations were within the range -0.02 to 0.02. The training set consisted of 500 examples, of which 153 were positive. 540 in the full set were flagged positive. The five seeds were the vectors of DWT coefficients of five perfectly flat lines with y-intercepts of 8, 40, 80, 200 and 400.

This query also tests performance on real data.

4.2 Evaluation Methodology

With each data set and its paired query, we tested with the following values of α: $-\infty$, which scores by minimum distance; -100, which approximates that; -10; -5; -2; 2; and 5.

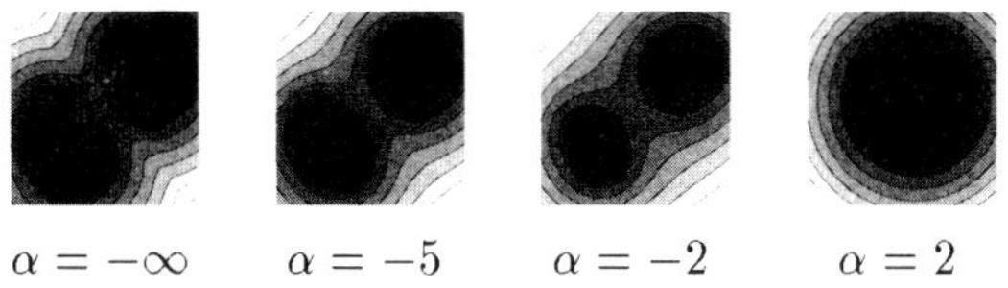

$\alpha = -\infty$ $\alpha = -5$ $\alpha = -2$ $\alpha = 2$

Figure 2: Contour plots for the seeds of the TWO_CIRCLES query.

Figure 2 shows contour plots for four values of α in the TWO_CIRCLES. Note that $\alpha = 2$ reflects only the center of the "good set", even on the TWO_CIRCLES query, and hence is expected to fail on such a disjunctive query.

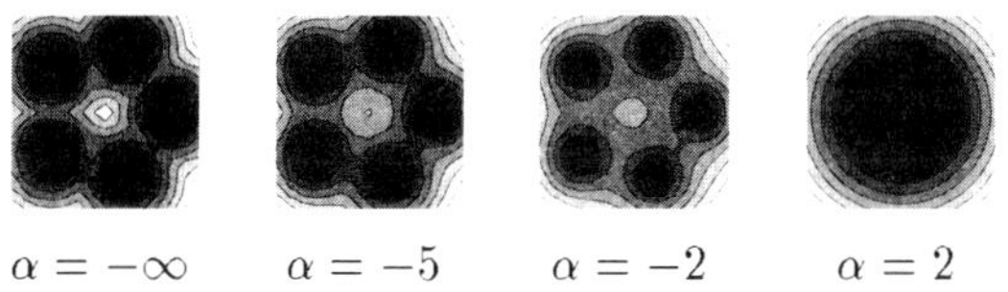

$\alpha = -\infty$ $\alpha = -5$ $\alpha = -2$ $\alpha = 2$

Figure 3: Contour plots for the seeds of the RING query.

Figure 3 shows contour plots for four values of α in the RING. Again, $\alpha = 2$ stands out with contours that are not going to rank the points very well.

FALCON ranks objects by computed score, which permits evaluation via precision/recall. We define recall and precision as follows.

For arbitrary n, consider the n top-ranked objects. Let there be p positive examples among them, out of P positive examples total. Then recall is $\frac{p}{P}$, and precision is $\frac{p}{n}$. We can compute precision for any given level of recall for a full ranking by choosing n appropriately.

With each combination of a query and a value of α, we used the following procedure:

- Start with the seeds as the "good set". Compute precision/recall values over the full set. This gives us a baseline that varies only with the contours generated by α.

- Repeat the following as needed:
  - Find the top twenty which have not yet been picked for feedback. Twenty is arbitrary, but plausible.
  - Add any newly-found positive examples into $\mathcal{G}$.
  - Repeat the precision/recall procedure on the full set.

4.3 Speed

We also ran range-query speed tests. The query and data involved were that of TWO_CIRCLES as described previously. For the indexing structure, we used M-trees [3]. Sequential scanning served as a baseline with which to compare the method described in Theorem 1. We then measured the individual effects of threshold and number of seeds on elapsed time and computational cost. Note that the elapsed time includes everything done on a per query basis, including all range queries as well as the time required for merging and verifying the results.

5 Results and Discussion

We present our analysis of the results, organized with regard to the five central questions.

The following notes apply to the various graphs. For all the figures marked "Precision versus Recall", such as Figures 4, 6, and 9, one line is plotted per charted iteration. Not all iterations were charted, for purposes of readability. Each line is drawn with ten points, each of which shows precision at one level of recall from 10% to 100% at 10% increments. Thus, the general trend of the lines tracks the progress of FALCON as feedback is provided on increasing numbers of points.

Any figure that tracks "Precision versus Iterations", such as Figures 7 and 8, instead focuses on precision at one level of recall, 40%, for multiple values of α. Positive slopes indicate positive progress. 40% was arbitrarily chosen as a level at which it is non-trivial, but also not extremely difficult, to provide good precision.

Figures 10 and 11, labelled "Precision at Multiple Levels of α" also track precision, but after 5 and 20 iterations. The first shows precision at 40% recall; the second, average precision based on all 10 levels of recall.

301

5.1 Concave and Disjunctive Queries

The RING query is concave, but contiguous; the TWO_CIRCLES query is disjunctive. As one sees in Figure 4, FALCON can handle either data set with high levels of precision versus recall. This is a substantial improvement over existing methods such as MARS and MindReader, which would have difficulty with these two.

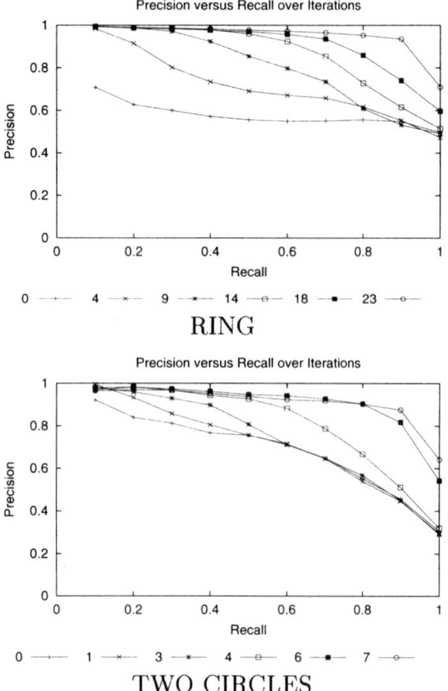

RING

TWO_CIRCLES

Figure 4: Precision versus recall for $\alpha = -5$, for RING and TWO_CIRCLES, using Euclidean pairwise distance.

The numbers in the legend indicate the number of feedback iterations to achieve that level of progress. We observe that in both cases, precision largely stabilizes after the first several iterations – especially for TWO_CIRCLES.

The success on the TWO_CIRCLES query is particularly notable because that set is completely disjunctive; there are two distinct regions of points that deserve high rankings, separated by points that do not. To further test the system, we ran the same query substituting L_∞ for the Euclidean distance as pairwise metric d; Figure 5 shows the resulting precision-recall.

5.2 Quality of Results on Real Data

Both the PEN and STOCKS queries are reasonable queries on real data. Consequently, FALCON's performance on these, as shown in Figure 6, is relevant to any question as to whether FALCON "works" on real data.

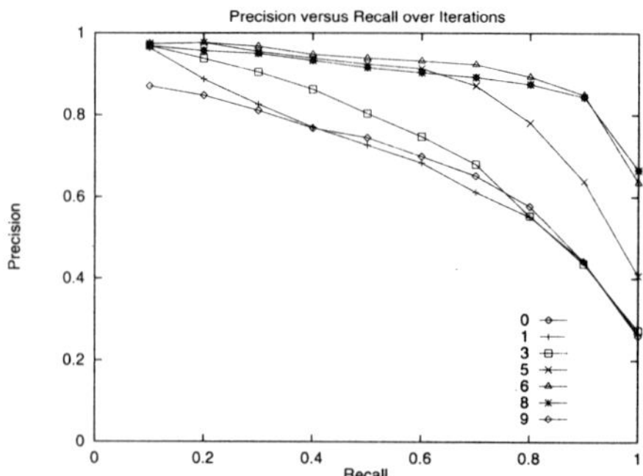

Figure 5: Precision versus recall for $\alpha = -5$, TWO_CIRCLES, and L_∞ as distance metric d

We note that, for the PEN query, convergence at all levels of recall below 100% is rapid; the rest of the iterations after the 4th recall do not add precision except at the highest level of recall. The pattern with the STOCKS query is more interesting, with large gaps between the lines. One plausible explanation is that the positive examples were not evenly distributed in vector space, but instead clustered. The first member of a cluster to be added to $\mathcal{G}$ would immediately cause everything nearby to move upwards in the rankings. This is particularly plausible given that many of the stock vectors were consecutive slivers from the same stock over time, and therefore may have had similar properties.

Figure 6 shows that FALCON provides good precision at almost all levels of recall. In particular, it provides perfect precision at most levels of recall for the PEN data set and query, identifying objects that correspond to 4's. Note also that FALCON provides good precision on the RING and TWO_CIRCLES queries, as shown in Figure 4, as cited above.

5.3 Speed of Convergence

Figures 7 and 8, show precision at 40% recall versus the number of iterations. FALCON can quickly attain high levels of precision over high levels of recall, even with an early $\mathcal{G}$ that has not yet grown to include many of the "good points" in even the training set.

The STOCKS query is unlike other queries. Here, there are very wide gaps in performance until 12 iterations have elapsed; the others show more continuous gains.

Depending upon the complexity of the query and the data set, progress can be very fast (such as in the PEN data set), or slower (as in the RING data set). For 40% recall, precision exceeds 90% after only 4 to 11 iterations for $\alpha = -5$ on all four queries.

There can be overfitting, as seen in the TWO_CIRCLES data set. The law of diminishing returns applies to increasing $|\mathcal{G}|$, suggesting that one does not need to maximize $|\mathcal{G}|$ to attain near-optimal

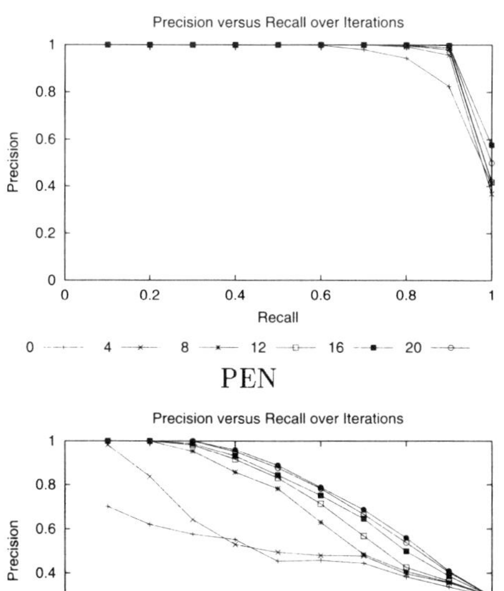

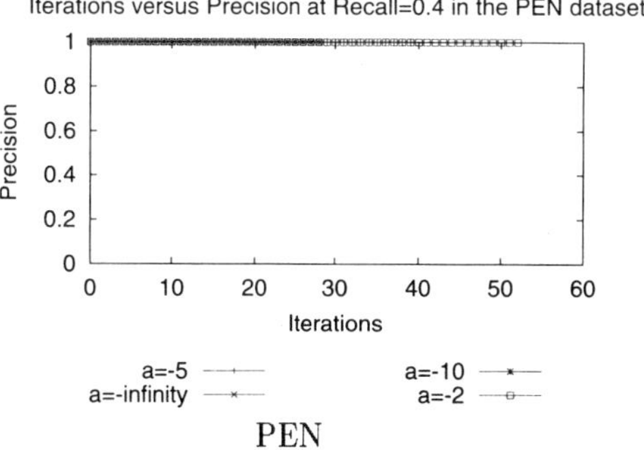

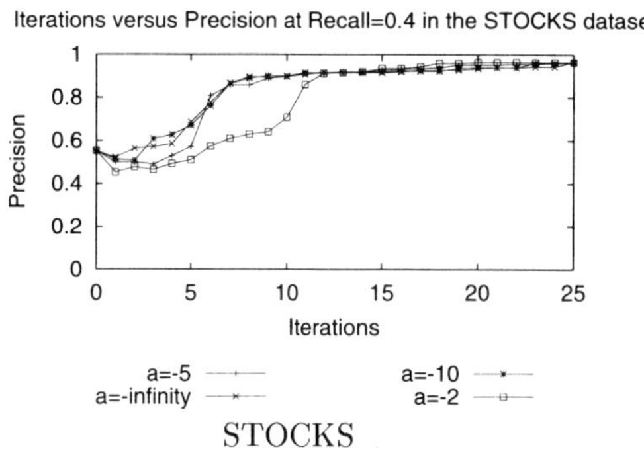

Figure 6: Precision versus recall for $\alpha = -5$, for PEN and STOCKS.

Figure 7: Precision versus iterations at recall=40%.

levels of precision, and therefore sampling can be reasonable.

5.4 Optimal Value of α

We hypothesized that $\alpha = -5$ would be a reasonable choice from our set of possible α's. We found that $\alpha = -100$ generally performed worse due to numerical precision problems, and therefore will not be discussed further.

Figure 9 show precision versus recall for the TWO_CIRCLES data set, using $\alpha = -2$ and $\alpha = -10$. As usual, the numbers in the legend indicate iterations. In both cases, all good points in the sample were added to $\mathcal{G}$ in no more than 9 iterations of feedback. We also note that the progress in precision over multiple levels of recall was fairly steady throughout.

Precision was generally similar for all negative values of α, especially once $\mathcal{G}$ had reached its maximum size. With positive values of α, precision was quite low at most levels of recall; see Figures 10 and 11 for some results.

The first figure shows precision at 40% recall for each level of tested α; each line tracks the precisions yielded by one particular value of α for the different queries. This allows us to compare α both early and late in the process. In the case of TWO_CIRCLES, whose $\mathcal{G}$ stabilized in fewer than 20 iterations, we used the final results. Observe that the differences among the negative values of α largely disappear by the 20th iteration of feedback.

As we can see in the latter figure, difference in average precision over all levels of recall after 20 iterations are a bit more marked than at 40%, but again the negative values of α yield fairly similar average precision.

We still favor $\alpha = -5$, as it provided good performance as empirically observed, and in no case is it significantly inferior. Similar values appear to yield similar results. This may be due to the limited range of values tested, but also reflects the fact that this value permits a significant amount of flexibility, in that this corresponds to a quite fuzzy OR.

5.5 Speed

Empirically, we have found that merging the results of k separate range queries as per Theorem 1 is satisfactory in terms of both the number of distance computations, and the elapsed time. Some of these results may be noted in Figures 12 and 13.

The two graphs in Figure 12 compare the elapsed (real) time and the pairwise distance computation costs incurred in searching the TWO_CIRCLES training data set for points within a variable aggregate dissimilarity threshold from the seeds. These results demonstrate that the k range queries can be merged into one.

We note that the cross-over point where sequential scan performs as quickly as merging occurs at a thresh-

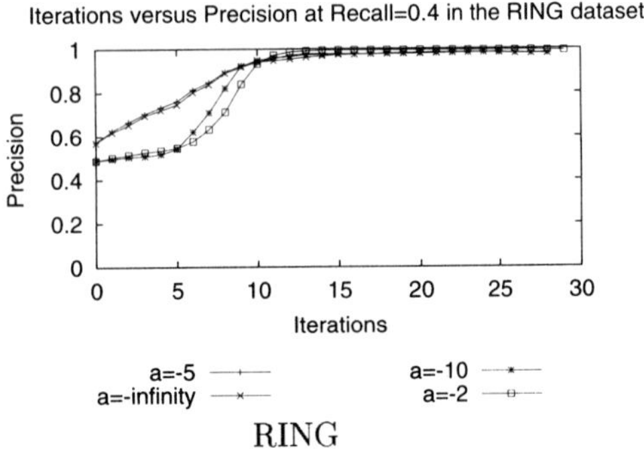

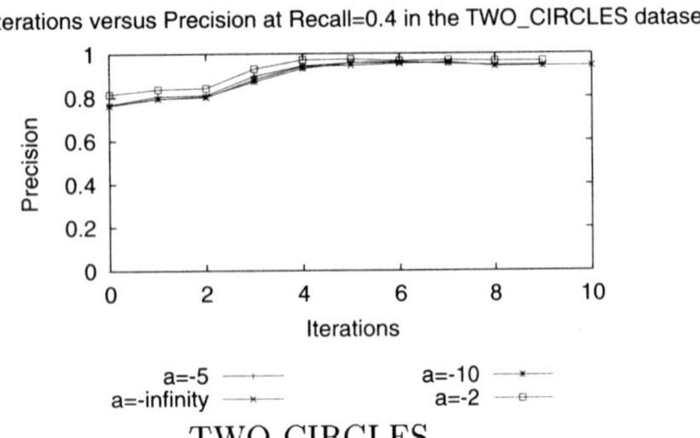

Figure 8: Precision versus iterations at recall=40%

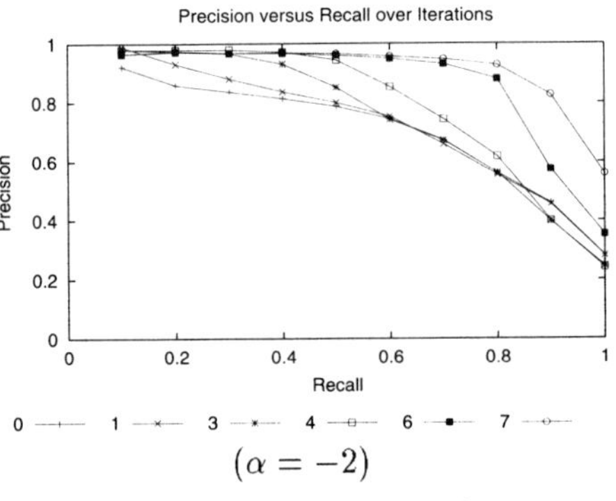

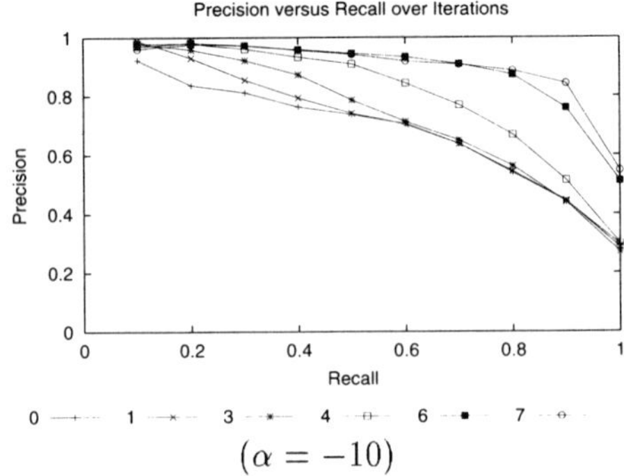

Figure 9: Precision versus recall on the TWO-CIRCLES data set.

old of approximately 0.7; such a threshold accepts approximately 20% of the database. It is our belief that users of large interactive databases will rarely be interested in queries of such scope, and thus the merging method is worthwhile.

As shown in Figure 13, both measurements of performance cost appear to scale with the number of seeds. These results are taken without caching the distance computations from previous searches; these searches were all independent. These two graphs compare the elapsed (real) time and the pairwise distance computation costs incurred in searching the TWO_CIRCLES training data set for points with aggregate dissimilarity less than or equal to 1, varying the number of seeds.

The results for the same test, but with the underlying distance function $d = L_\infty$, are very similar and are not presented here [15].

No direct experimental comparisons are shown with previous methods. This is because our queries were specifically designed to include queries of disjunctive and other highly non-convex behavior in general metric spaces, and thus previous methods simply do not apply.

6 Conclusions

We proposed a method to handle queries by multiple examples, on arbitrary vector or metric databases.

Our method applies to general metric spaces, as the distance combination function depends on only the pairwise distances and not the actual nature of the data. In addition, it handles disjunctive and concave queries that are fundamentally *impossible* for traditional relevance feedback methods. Using our method, a user could, without any domain-specific query language, specify a disjunctive query merely by labelling as "good" objects representative of the different classes. We argue that this combination of general applicability, power and ease-of-use makes this method more valuable than other existing systems today.

The heart of our method is the FALCON aggregate dissimilarity, or $D_\mathcal{G}$, which is able to "learn" disjunctive queries via relevance feedback. Additional contributions include the following:

- Theorem 1, which shows that we can use indexing structures that support range queries, to speed up our search, guaranteeing zero false dismissals.

- Experiments on real and synthetic data, that show that the proposed method ("FALCON") achieves good precision and recall. For instance, with all queries, $\alpha = -5$ yielded at least 80% precision at 50% recall with 10 iterations.

- Experiments that show that FALCON needs at most 10 feedback iterations to reach high precision/recall, and will reach a "steady state" for

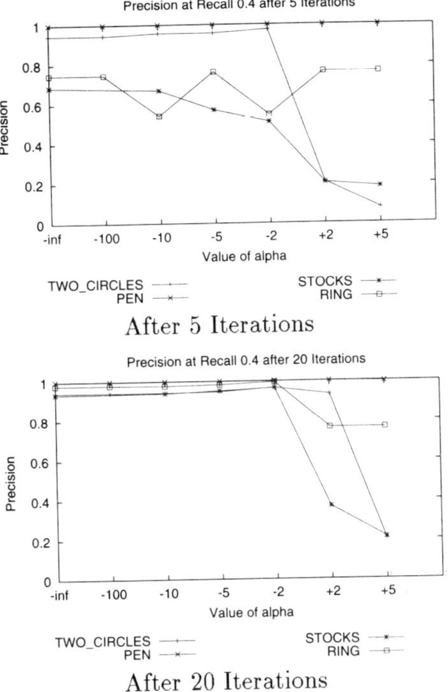

After 5 Iterations

After 20 Iterations

Figure 10: Precision at 40% recall

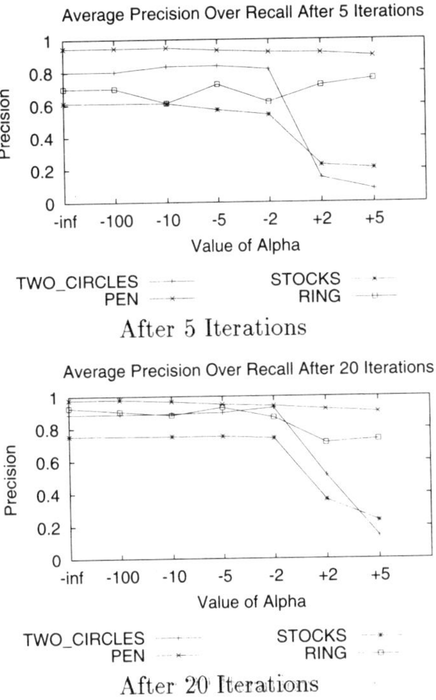

After 5 Iterations

After 20 Iterations

Figure 11: Average precision at multiple values of α.

all levels of recall below 100% within approximately 20 iterations. Beyond 20 iterations, minor progress is made for 100% recall.

- Experiments that show that a good range for α includes -10 to -2; on many queries, the sensitivity of the performance on α is low.

- Experiments that show that we can use the method described by Theorem 1 to gain up to 200% observed performance improvements versus sequential scanning.

Possible avenues for future work include using D_G for other data mining tasks, such as classification and representative selection [7].

Acknowledgements

This research was partially funded by the National Science Foundation under Grants No. IRI-9625428, DMS-9873442, and IIS-9910606; also, by the National Science Foundation, ARPA and NASA under NSF Cooperative Agreement No. IRI-9411299; DARPA/ITO through Order F463, issued by ESC/ENS under contract N66001-97-C-851; and the Office of Naval Research Grant N-00014-96-1-1222. Additional funding was provided by donations from NEC and Intel. Views and conclusions contained in this document are those of the authors and should not be interpreted as representing official policies, either expressed or implied, of the Defense Advanced Research Projects Agency or of the United States Government.

All trademarks are property of their respective owners.

References

[1] N. Beckmann, H.-P. Kriegel, R. Schneider, and B. Seeger. The R*-tree: An efficient and robust access method for points and rectangles. *ACM SIGMOD*, pages 322–331, May 23-25 1990.

[2] Thomas Brinkhoff, Hans-Peter Kriegel, and Bernhard Seeger. Efficient processing of spatial joins using R-trees. In *Proc. of ACM SIGMOD*, pages 237–246, Washington, D.C., May 26-28 1993.

[3] Paolo Ciaccia, Marco Patella, and Pavel Zezula. M-tree: An efficient access method for similarity search in metric spaces. *VLDB*, pages 426–435, 1997.

[4] R.O. Duda and P.E. Hart. *Pattern Classification and Scene Analysis*. John Wiley and Sons, 1973.

[5] A. Guttman. R-trees: A dynamic index structure for spatial searching. In *Proc. ACM SIGMOD*, pages 47–57, Boston, Mass, June 1984.

[6] Yoshiharu Ishikawa, Ravishankar Subramanya, and Christos Faloutsos. Mindreader: Querying

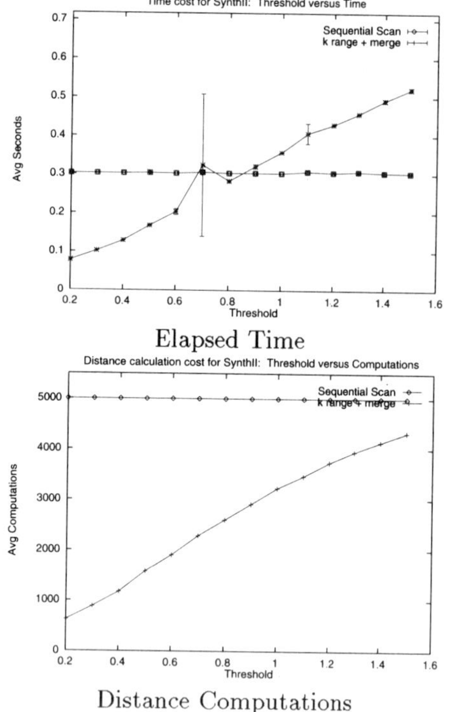

Elapsed Time

Distance Computations

Figure 12: Time and computational cost for TWO_CIRCLES, varying threshold.

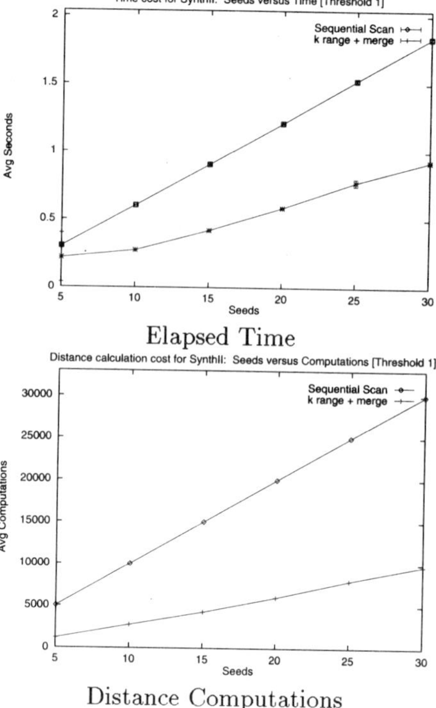

Elapsed Time

Distance Computations

Figure 13: Time and computational cost for TWO_CIRCLES, varying seeds.

databases through multiple examples. Technical report, 1998.

[7] M.V. Boland M.K. Markey and R.F. Murphy. Towards objective selection of representative microscope images. *Biophys. J.*, 1999. in press.

[8] P.M. Murphy and D.W. Aha. UCI Repository of Machine Learning Databases. Department of Information and Computer Science, University of California, Irvine, CA. [http://www.ics.uci.edu/~mlearn/MLRepository.html], 1994.

[9] T.R. Payne. *Dimensionality Reduction and Representation for Nearest Neighbour Learning*. PhD thesis, The University of Aberdeen, Scotland, 1999.

[10] Kriengkrai Prokaew, Sharad Mehrotra, Michael Ortega, and Kaushik Chakrabarti. Similarity search using multiple examples in mars. In *1999 International Conference on Visual Information Systems*, June 1999.

[11] Joseph John Rocchio. Relevance feedback in information retrieval. In Gerard Salton, editor, *The SMART Retrieval System – Experiments in Automatic Document Processing*, pages 313–323. Prentice Hall, Englewood Cliffs, N.J., 1971.

[12] Yong Rui, Thomas S. Huang, and Sharad Mehrotra. Content-based image retrieval with relevance feedback in MARS. In *Proceedings of IEEE International Conference on Image Processing '97*, Santa Barbara, CA, October 1997.

[13] Yong Rui, Thomas S. Huang, and Sharad Mehrotra. Human perception subjectivity and relevance feedback in multimedia information retrieval. In *Proceedings of IS&T and SPIE Storage and Retrieval of Image and Video Databases VI*, San Jose, CA, January 1998.

[14] G. Salton, E.A. Fox, and H. Wu. Extended boolean information retrieval. *CACM*, 26(11):1022–1036, November 1983.

[15] Leejay Wu, Christos Faloutsos, Katia Sycara, and Terry R. Payne. Falcon: Feedback adaptive loop for content-based retrieval. Technical report, Carnegie Mellon University, 2000.

[16] C.T. Zahn. Graph-theoretical methods for detecting and describing gestalt clusters. *IEEE Trans. on Computers*, C-20(1):68–86, January 1971.

User-adaptive exploration of multidimensional data

Sunita Sarawagi

Indian Institute of Technology, Bombay
sunita@it.iitb.ernet.in

Abstract

In this paper we present a tool for enhanced exploration of OLAP data that is adaptive to a user's prior knowledge of the data. The tool continuously keeps track of the parts of the cube that a user has visited. The information in these scattered visited parts of the cube is pieced together to form a model of the user's expected values in the unvisited parts. The mathematical foundation for this modeling is provided by the classical Maximum Entropy principle. At any time, the user can query for the most surprising unvisited parts of the cube. The most surprising values are defined as those which if known to the user would bring the new expected values closest to the actual values. This process of updating the user's context based on visited parts and querying for regions to explore further continues in a loop until the user's mental model perfectly matches the actual cube. We believe and prove through experiments that such a user-in-the-loop exploration will enable much faster assimilation of all significant information in the data compared to existing manual explorations.

1 Introduction

We propose a new method for interactively exploring multidimensional OLAP data cubes [GCB+97] that continuously adapts to what the user knows about the data and uses that to guide him to the parts of the cube that he will find most informative. We provide a method of personalizing OLAP exploration tools so that the user for which it is trained is only shown regions that he will find surprising. Often in large corporations a single OLAP data source is deployed by users at various levels of experience with the cube. There are local store managers who are very familiar with the details of just one store; top executives who know top-level trends but none of the details and recent hire analysts who know nothing about the data but need to subsequently understand a lot of it. Currently, all these three categories of users get the same view of the OLAP data cube which they explore manually using the basic drill-down, rollup, pivot and select operator. Apart from these basic

**Proceedings of the 26th VLDB Conference,
Cairo, Egypt, 2000.**

tools there is little support provided for meaningfully exploring large databases. We propose that users be allowed to navigate a data cube based on information content of the region rather than the current approach of basing it on navigational reachability or random user guesses.

1.1 Overview of the system

The system maintains a profile for each user that has an account with the OLAP system. The profile stores the parts of the cube with which he is already familiar. This profile is built either by the frontend exploration tool monitoring the amount of time the user spends with each view of the cube or by the user explicitly marking a given view of the cube as visited. The system then uses this profile to model the user's expectation about the unvisited parts of the cube. The classical maximum entropy principle is used to provide a unified way of piecing together the information in the scattered visited parts of the cube with which the user is familiar. According to this principle, the best guess expected values are those that maximize the uniformity of the data values while agreeing with all partial sums that the user has seen.

Next we define the information content of an unvisited value as the gap between the actual values and the new expected values if the user had known this value. The user can query this information in a variety of interesting ways to improve his data exploration experience. For instance, during normal exploration, starting from an initial view of the cube the user can query for the most informative path for drilling down further. Or, after having explored the cube for some time, he can ask for the ten most informative cells from anywhere in unvisited data.

As the user explores more regions of the cube, the user's profile gets enhanced and the expected value of unvisited parts is continuously updated. This process of updating the user's context based on visited parts and querying for regions to explore further continues in a loop. In each iteration the user's mental image of the cube gets closer to the actual cube until they both become one and the same. When the user stops the exploration, the context is recorded and digested by the system so that next time when the analyst logs into the cube database, the memory of what parts he has already visited is revoked from the system's log to guide further exploration.

Product	Platform	Geography	Year
Product name (67)	Platform name (43)	Geography (4)	Year (5)
Prod_Category (14)	Plat_Type (6)		
Prod_Group (3)	Plat_User (2)		

Figure 1: Dimensions and hierarchies of the software revenue data. The number in brackets indicate the size of that level of the dimension.

1.2 Illustration

We next illustrate the working of the system using a real-life dataset obtained from International Data Corporation (IDC). The data gives the total yearly revenue in millions of dollars for different software products from 1990 to 1994. The schema as shown in Figure 1 consists of four dimensions Product, Platform, Geography and Time and a three level hierarchy on the Product and Platform dimension.

Consider two kinds of users exploring this dataset. The first user has no prior knowledge of any part of the data and the second user has full familiarity with all the data except for the most recent two years. However, the second user has observed the total revenues for these two years.

Using the existing OLAP exploration operations (like "drill-down" and "roll-up") the first user could launch the process of understanding the data by navigating through subsets of the cube viewed at various levels of aggregation. However, the process of understand data could be long and tedious involving perhaps repeated visits to the same parts of the data. We contrast this with the experience the user would have with the new focussed exploration that this tool provides. Not knowing anything else about the user, the tool starts out modeling the expected value of each non-empty cell to be the same. The user can then query for the most informative views of the cube. The first output (shown in Figure 2) is the Platform dimension showing only ten (out of a total of 43 members) that it found most informative. The remaining are summarized by their average value in the topmost row. A second query for the next informative path returns the product dimension with eight (out of 67) distinctive members as shown in Figure 3. The year dimension shown in Figure 4 has the smallest divergence between member values and is shown last. At all time, a status bar displays how far the user's expectations are from the real values. After showing the aggregates along the four dimensions the status bar would show that 30% of the information in the data is captured. For the remaining 70% the user needs to dig deeper. Depending on the user's interest, he could either quickly ask for the top few informative cells from anywhere in the cube or follow informative paths for drilling down further. Another interesting possibility is to put the system on auto-pilot where he will be driven through the most informative views in the cube in a sequence.

The second more informed user would perhaps use the tool differently. He is already familiar with most of the detailed data except the last two years of 1993 to 1994. The tool has kept track of this fact about the user. Based on previous trends he expects an increase in revenue from 1992 to 1993 to 1994 for each Product,Platform,Geography combination. Therefore, we can directly query the tool for the most informative regions from anywhere in the cube. The results are shown in Figure 6. In the figure, the last column marked "Expected" shows the values that he would see if his extrapolations were correct and the column before it shows the actual values. These are all cases that correspond to a significant drop or increase in 1993 or 1994. For instance, based on prior knowledge the user expected the sales in 1993 for (Other Office Apps, Wester Europe and Multiuser Mainfram IBM) to be 78 whereas the actual was just 3.05. Thus, the second user will only have to concentrate on these few violators which cannot be extrapolated based on his experience of past data and the yearly totals.

1.3 Contents.

The rest of the paper is organized as follows. We present our formulation in terms of the maximum entropy principle in Section 2. In Section 3 we show how we enable practical implementations in large OLAP datasets and validate with experimental results. In Section 4 we present related work and finally conclusions appear in Section 5.

2 Formulation

Our underlying data is a n dimensional cube where each cell is associated with a real value say, total sales or total number of units sold. The user sees different partial views of the data in terms of the sum of values of some subset of the cube. From this partial view he implicitly forms an expectation of the values in the cube. Our goal is to recapture these expected values.

Consider first the case where $n = 1$ and assume that there are 10 total cells along that single dimension. Suppose the user views only the sum of the 10 values in the cell. Let that sum be "1". Knowing nothing else about the data or the user's mindset, what values can we assume for each of these cells? There are an infinite number of possible 10 values that sum up to 1. One possibility is to let the values of the first cell $p_1 = 1$ and the rest of the values p_2 to p_{10} be zero. Another is to let $p_1 = p_2 = 1/2$ and p_3 to p_{10} be zero. Both these alternative make rather bold statements based on the limited knowledge of the data. A safer bet is to let $p_i = 1/10 = 0.1$ for all values.

Suppose if we get another view in the form of the sum of values from p_1 to p_5 to 0.75. What is the best revised guess we can make now? Following the same logic our best guess is for the first half of the values to be 0.15 and the last half 0.05. Again suppose the

PLAT_T	PLATFORM	Act	Exp
(Each)-	(Each)-	1.81	7.7
Unix S.	Each)	2.23	7.7
Wn32	16-bit Windows/DOS	24.7	7.7
Other M.	(Each)-	13.9	7.7
Other M.	Multiuser Mainframe IBM	39.2	7.7
Other M.	Multiuser Windows NT Se	1.23	7.7
Other M.	Multiuser OS/2	1.76	7.7
Other M.	Multiuser Other Server	1.75	7.7
Unix M.	Multiuser UNIX	20.2	7.7
Unix M.	Multiuser UNIX SCO Unix	0.09	7.7
Unix M.	Multiuser UNIX SGI Irix	0.12	7.7
Unix M.	Multiuser UNIX Other Inte	0.06	7.7

Figure 2: Most informative drill-down dimension and its top few informative members.

PROD_CATEG	PRODUCT	ACT	EXP
(Each)-	(Each)-	7.16	7.7
Vertical Apps	(Each)	12.7	7.7
Middleware	(Each)	0.5	7.7
Other	(Each)	0.8	7.7
System SW	(Each)	30.6	7.7
Info. tools	(Each)	3.7	7.7
Develop. tools	DBMS Engines (	15.7	7.7
Develop. tools	Object-Oriented	2.2	7.7
Develop. tools	Object CASE	0.9	7.7

Figure 3: Second most informative dimension.

Year	ACT	EXP
1990	6.54	7.7
1991	6.75	7.7
1992	8.39	7.7
1993	9.58	7.7
1994	7.23	7.7

Figure 4: Least informative of the four dimensions.

Figure 5: Information content of various dimensions. The last column denotes expected value. The "ACT" column represents actual values.

PRODUCT	GEOGRAPHY	PLATFORM	YEAR	ACTUAL	EXPEC
Other Office Apps	Western Europe	Multiuser Mainframe IBM	1993	3.05	78.25
EDA	Western Europe	Multiuser UNIX	1994	19.97	142.41
Operating Systems	United States	Multiuser Other Server	1994	0.22	47.82
Operating Systems	Western Europe	Multiuser Minicomputer O|	1993	3.27	69.74
Middleware	Asia/Pacific	Multiuser Mainframe IBM	1993	185.72	96.10
CASE (Non-Object)	United States	16-bit Windows/DOS	1994	1.77	57.58
DBMS Engines (Non-Object)	United States	Multiuser Mainframe IBM	1994	90.31	315.03
DBMS Engines (Non-Object)	Rest of World	Multiuser Mainframe IBM	1994	11.00	98.92
4GL & Report Writers	Rest of World	Multiuser Mainframe IBM	1993	0.31	42.48
3GLs & Develop. Environments	Rest of World	Multiuser Mainframe IBM	1993	0.62	38.67

Figure 6: Informative regions returned to user who is familiar with the entire cube for years 1990-1992 but unfamiliar with years 1993 and 1994.

user sees a third view of the data consisting of sums of values from p_3 and p_7 and let that sum be 0.5. In this case, it is not all that obvious how we distribute the three partial sums to derive individual values. Fortunately, this is a classical problem with links to biblical times that has found widely accepted answers in the Maximum Entropy principle [BPP96, GS85].

The maximum entropy principle states that given a collection of facts choose a model that is consistent with all the facts but otherwise is as uniform as possible. A mathematical measure of the uniformity of a distribution is provided by entropy defined as $H(p) = -\sum_{i=1}^{m} p_i \log p_i$, where p_i denotes the estimated value or probability of the ith cell. The entropy is bounded from below by zero, the entropy of a model with no uncertainty at all i.e., p_i is either 0 or 1 for all i. It is bounded from above by $\log m$, the entropy of the uniform distribution where all p_i have the same value of $\frac{1}{m}$. Our goal is to choose the distribution p that maximizes $H(p)$ while satisfying the constraints imposed by the partial visited views of the data. A constraint C_i is a restriction on some subset of these m values to sum up to some observed value $\tilde{p}(C_i)$. In the example above we had three such constraints with $\tilde{p}(C_1) = 1$, $\tilde{p}(C_2) = 0.75$ and $\tilde{p}(C_3) = 0.5$. The final optimization problem is:

$$\max_p H(p) = \max_p(-\sum_{i=1}^{m} p_i \log p_i) \quad \text{such that}$$

$$\forall C_i, \sum_j p_j I_{ij} = \tilde{p}(C_i),$$

$$\text{where} \quad I_{ij} = \begin{cases} 1, & \text{if cell } j \text{ is included in } C_i, \\ 0, & \text{otherwise.} \end{cases}$$

This optimization problem is the mathematical essence of the Maximum Entropy philosophy that according to E.T. Jaynes [Jay90] *"agrees with everything that is known, but carefully avoids assuming anything that is not known"*.

2.1 Finding the best values of p

The objective function $H(p)$ always has a unique solution as long as the constraints are consistent [PPL97]. In most cases finding that unique solution through any closed form formula is not possible. However, there are well defined iterative algorithms that are based on the observation that the optimal p values can be expressed in the following product form.

$$p_j^\mu = \mu_0 \prod_{C_i} \mu_i^{I_{ij}} \tag{1}$$

We use p^μ to denote the class of p values that can be expressed in the above product form and p_j^μ is the expected value of the j cell. For each constraint C_i

there is a term μ_i. The term μ_0 is a normalization constant to ensure that the probabilities sum up to 1.

2.1.1 The Iterative scaling algorithm for finding best p

Start with $\mu_i = 1$ for all constraints.
Update μ_0 so probabilities sum to 1
While the μ_is have not converged
    For each constraint C_i
        Update μ_i by scaling with $\tilde{p}(C_i)/p(C_i)$
        Recalculate expected values p using Equation 1
Update μ_0 so probabilities sum to 1

The above algorithm is guaranteed to converge to the optimal solution as long as all constraints are consistent [PPL97].

2.2 Finding informative constraints

The second part of our problem is to find the most informative constraints from unvisited data. We define such a constraint to be the one that reduces the distance between the actual values $\tilde{p}$ and expected values p^μ by the maximum amount. We measure distance using the traditional Kullback-Leibler divergence criteria defined as:

$$D(\tilde{p}||p^\mu) = \sum_j \tilde{p}_j \log \frac{\tilde{p}_j}{p^\mu{}_j}$$

Let p^C denote the expected values after the addition of the first C constraints and let p^{C+f} denote the expected values after adding a new constraint f. Our goal is to pick the f that reduces the distance by the maximum amount, i.e.,

$$f = \operatorname{argmax}_f(D(\tilde{p}||p^C) - D(\tilde{p}||p^{C+f})) \qquad (2)$$
$$= \operatorname{argmax}_f \sum_j \tilde{p}_j(\log p_j^{c+1} - \log p_j^c). \qquad (3)$$

From equation 1 we can write p^C as a product of $|C|$ terms one corresponding to each constraint $c_j \in C$. The values of coefficients μ_j could change due to the new constraint f but for reasons of efficiency we ignore this change and only take into account the change with the addition of the new coefficient μ_{c+1}. Based on this assumption we can write Equation 2 using results from Equation 1 as:

$$f = \operatorname{argmax}_f \sum_j \tilde{p}_j \log \mu_{c+1}^{I_{(c+1)j}} \qquad (4)$$
$$= \operatorname{argmax}_f \sum_j \tilde{p}_j I_{(c+1)j} \log \frac{\tilde{p}(f)}{p^c(f)} \qquad (5)$$

3 Adapting the maximum entropy principle to OLAP data

The main challenge in adapting the maximum entropy principle to OLAP data is handling the scale. Traditional applications have concentrated on small datasets and therefore there is little previous literature on scaling the iterative algorithm and the search for new constraints, both these are computationally expensive procedures. Also our goal is to be able to interactively furnish the next few informative constraints even while the user's context is continually being changed as he navigates around the data. We next discuss a collection of optimizations that we applied on these methods to make them efficient on large OLAP datasets. We also present empirical evidence of their usefulness through experiments on several OLAP datasets. In Section 3.1 we present details of the experimental setup. In section 3.2 we present a number of optimizations for improving the first part of our tool, that is, updating the expected values with the addition of new constraints. In section 3.3 we present optimizations for getting answers to finding the most informative regions. Finally, in Section 3.4 we discuss issues in integrating this tool with a OLAP system.

3.1 Experimental setup

We used the following datasets for our experiments.

Software revenue data: This is a small dataset but is interesting because it is real-life data about the revenues of different software products from 1990 to 1994. We discussed this dataset earlier in Section 1.2.

OLAP Council benchmark [Cou]: This dataset was designed by the OLAP Council to serve as a benchmark for comparing performance of different OLAP products. It has 1.36 million total non-zero entries and four dimensions: Product with a seven hierarchy, Customer with a three level hierarchy, Channel with no hierarchy and Time with a four level hierarchy as shown in the figure below. The numbers within bracket denote the cardinality of that level.

Product	Customer	Channel	Time
Code (9000)	Store (900)	Channel (9)	Month (17)
Class (900)	Retailer (90)		Quarter (7)
Group (90)			Year (2)
Family (20)			
Line (7)			
Divison (2)			

Student data: This data is about the enrollment statistics of a university with dimensions as shown in the table below. The total number of cells at detailed level is 4560 which is very small by OLAP standards. We therefore do not use this dataset for performance studies. However, it is useful for doing a qualitative assessment of our method because the dataset is real.

Student	Sex	Program	Department	Year
Category (9)	Sex (2)	Name (10)	Name (28)	Year (10)
		Category (3)		

Grocery sales data: This is a demo dataset obtained from the Microsoft DSS product [Mic98]. It has 250 thousand total non-zero entries and consists of five dimensions with hierarchies as shown below.

310

Store	Customer	Product	Promotion	Time
Name (24)	City (109)	Name (1560)	Media type (14)	Month (24)
State (10)	State (13)	Subcategory (102)		Quarter (8)
Country (3)	Country (2)	Category (45)		Year (2)
		Department (22)		
		Family (3)		

These experiments were done on a PC with a 333 MHz Intel processor, 128 MB of memory and running Windows NT 4.0. A DB2 ROLAP database was used to process the queries.

Workload We simulate a user's exploration of the data cube using the following model. The user starts at the topmost level where all dimensions are aggregated to a single value. At any time, the user views data in the context of at most two dimensions at a time. Remaining dimensions are either aggregated or selected on a single value at any level of its hierarchy. From one view of the cube the user moves to a neighboring view as follows: Select one dimension d_i from the two dimensions that are currently either row or column and select another dimension d_j from the remaining set to replace d_i. Fix the value of d_i to either one of its members or aggregate it to level "All". This yields a new view of the cube from which the user can move to a neighboring view using the same procedure.

Notation We introduce some notations. Consider a cube with four dimensions A, B, C and D. We use the term *view* to denote the different parts of this cube that the user has visited. A view represents a collection of constraints. For instance, if the user has viewed the totals along dimension A, then the view is said to be A and this view consists of as many constraints as there are members along A. The lower case letter a_i denotes the ith member of dimension A. If the next view the user visits is $a_i B$ i.e., for fixed value a_i of dimension A he is viewing totals along each member of dimension B, then the constraints that they represent have the form $a_i b_j$ where b_j spans over all the members of dimension B. We will sometimes call a view a constraint where the distinction is not important.

3.2 Optimizing the expected value update process

We first present ways of optimizing updates to the expected values of the detailed cube with the addition of a new constraint. Our requirements of long-term memory of the users' context requires an incremental formulation where a persistent storage is used to keep track of the constraints and the partially computed expected values. We maintain two pieces of information for each <cube,user> pair. First is a list of the set of constraint imposed by the user and second is expected values based on the context established so far.

3.2.1 Optimized representation

The first optimization relates to how we store the currently computed expected values. Instead of keeping a separate entry for each detailed cell as implied by the iterative algorithm we group together and keep a single entry for each *contiguous* region that will have the same expected value with the current set of constraints. For instance, if the only constraint that we have is A then all detailed cells with same value of dimension A will have the same expected value, hence we store only as many entries as the domain of A instead of storing the expected value for each detailed cell in $ABCD$. When the user submits a second constraint D all cells with the same value of dimensions A and D will have the same expected value, hence we store the expected values at the AD level.

This optimized representation makes the addition of a new constraint more complicated. Every time a new constraint f is added, we might need to De-aggregate the level to which a region is stored. For instance, in our previous example adding a third constraint $a_i C d_j$ would require us to expand the entry $a_i d_j$ with the new dimension C. From these new regions we remove any region already materialized. More details of this step appear in the expanded version [Sar00a].

The optimized representation not only reduces storage requirements but also improves the iterative algorithm because the iterations are performed over aggregated values.

Improvements achieved on experimental datasets We demonstrate the impact of this optimization by measuring the speed up obtained by the iterative procedure for the datasets and query workload discussed earlier. In the graphs in Figure 10, the X axis represents the constraint in the order in which they are submitted to the system and the Y axis denotes the total time for the constraint propagation. We plot two graphs, one for the optimized representation (marked "opt") and second for the detailed representation where the expected values are at the detailed level (marked "noopt"). From the graphs, we observe a factor of five improvement in total time for the software data and even greater (between factors of 10 and 100) reduction with the larger datasets. This difference is significant because it helps cross the boundary between interactive and batch processing. For the larger datasets, operations that previously required 10 minutes can be completed in half a minute making interactive sessions more feasible.

3.2.2 Optimizing iterative process

We next present optimizations for reducing the number of iterations needed for convergence and also pruning the number of constraints involved in each iteration.

We first introduce some definitions for formalizing the relationships between constraints. A constraint C_i is said to *subsume* another constraint C_j if the sum at C_i includes all elements that are included in C_j. Thus,

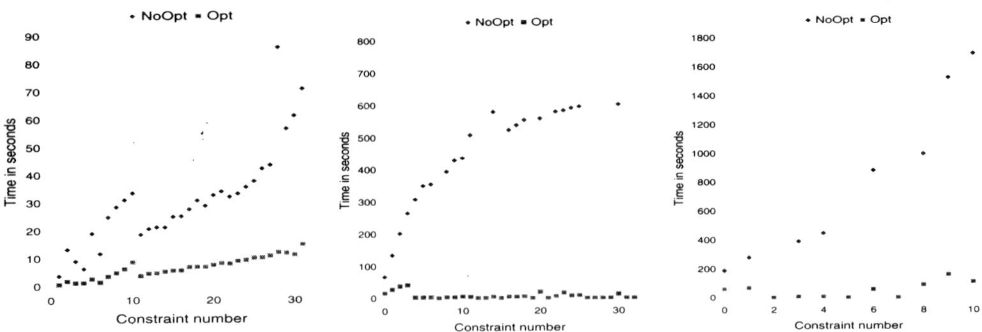

Figure 7: Software revenue data.

Figure 8: Grocery sales data.

Figure 9: Olap benchmark.

Figure 10: Improvement due to optimized representation of expected values. 'Opt' and 'NoOpt' denote total time with and without the optimizations. Y axis is total time in seconds and X axis the number of constraints submitted.

constraint a_i subsumes constraint $a_i c_k$. A view V_i is said to be more detailed than another constraint C_j if V_i aggregates the same set of values as C_j but V_i includes more than one constraint. Thus, view $a_i B$ is *more detailed* than constraint a_i because together they cover all cells where dimension A has value a_i but view $a_i B$ has separate constraints corresponding to different values of B.

We exploit these relationships to speed up the iterative procedure when a new constraint is added.

Minimize overlap between constraints First, when we get a new view say $a_i B c_k$, we find all existing constraints that subsume it (example a_i) and exclude from each of them the subsumed part. For example, an existing constraint, a_i would be replaced by a modified constraint $a_i \overline{c_k}$ that excludes any cell where dimension C has value c_k. Sometimes this might cause an existing constraint like $a_i c_k$ to be eliminated totally. Similarly, from the new view we exclude the constraints that are subsumed by it. For example if there is a constraint $a_i B c_k d_l$ then we modify the new constraint $a_i B c_k$ to be $a_i B c_k \overline{d_l}$.

Rewriting thus significantly reduces the number of iterations because of the reduction in the overlap between constraints. In the modified form $a_i B c_k$ and $a_i \overline{c_k}$ have no cells in common. Therefore, only *one* iteration is needed for convergence with these two constraints.

Prune constraints The algorithm of Figure 2.1.1 cycles through *every* constraint in an iteration. We suggest pruning from the current iteration those constraints whose estimated impact on the expected values is small. When a new constraint is added, we apply it first. Subsequently we apply only those constraints whose estimated change is greater than a small threshold. Clearly, if a constraint has no overlap with any of the constraints before it, it can be safely pruned from the current iteration. For others, we estimate expected change as follows: For each constraint applied before it in the current iteration we

know the maximum change of any expected values due to this constraint. Let δ_j denote this maximum change on a cell due to a constraint C_j. For a constraint C_k at the kth position of the current order of constraints, we calculate the estimated maximum change per cell $\hat{\delta_k}$ as

$$\hat{\delta_k} = \sum_{i=1}^{k-1} \text{influence}(C_i, C_k)\delta_i.$$

and skip those constraints for which this estimated maximum change is smaller than a threshold. We quantify the influence(C_i, C_k) of a constraint C_i on another constraint C_k by the fraction of the aggregated values of C_k that overlap with C_i. For instance, if C_i is a_i and C_j is d_k and there are 100 cells with Dth dimension member d_k and 10 of them have dimension $A = a_i$ then the influence of C_i on C_k is $10/100 = 0.1$. If there is a third constraint $C_l = b_j$ that sums up 1000 entries and 20 of them overlap with C_i, then influence of C_i on C_l will be $20/1000 = 0.02$.

Improvements achieved on experimental datasets We demonstrate the impact of these optimizations on the iterative algorithm. The setup and the axes are the same as in Section 3.2.1. Data is assumed to be stored in the optimized representation of Section 3.2.1. In Figure 14 we show two plots for each datasets. One plot is for the optimized iterative algorithm (marked "order") and the second without these optimizations (marked "opt"). We notice from the graphs that these optimizations give us another around a factor of two reduction in total time. In the initial stages when the number of constraints is small, the improvement is lower as expected and it increases as more constraints get added.

3.2.3 Asynchronous batched computation

A third optimization we propose is batching updates due to multiple constraints. When the user submits a view, the request is queued and the user call returned.

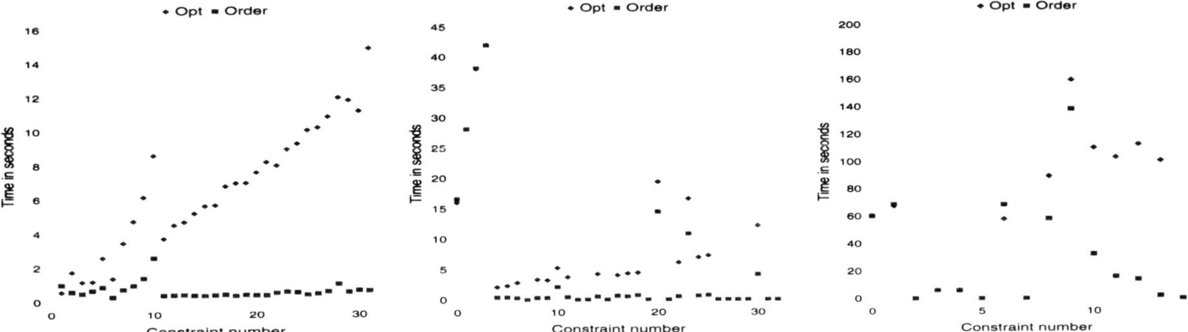

Figure 11: Software revenue data.   Figure 12: Grocery sales data.   Figure 13: Olap benchmark.

Figure 14: Improvement due to removing subsumed constraints and ordering and pruning constraints. 'Order' and 'Opt' denote total time with and without these optimizations respectively. Y axis is total time in seconds and X axis the number of constraints submitted.

The user does not wait for the effect of the new constraints to be propagated. Thus registering a view as visited is instantaneous. A separate thread is used to asynchronously refine the expected values via the iterative process. An offshoot of this architecture is that updates due to multiple constraints can be batched and also redundant constraints removed. For instance, if the user submits a view A followed soon after by another view AB the first view would be removed as redundant. We batch iterations due to multiple constraints as follows. We do not invoke a new round of iterative improvements every single time a constraint is added. Instead, as long as there are new constraints in the queue we apply just that constraint to update the expected value. When no more constraints new constraints are waiting we invoke the iterative algorithm to refine the expected values.

3.3 Optimizing the constraint selection process

Our goal is to use the expected values found in the previous step and the original data cube to report the most informative regions in the data cube. The query for information regions can be posed in a number of different ways as discussed in Section 1.1. These queries can be classified into two broad categories. One class requires the most informative contiguous region starting from some initial view of the cube. The second class requires for the top few informative constraints from anywhere in the cube. We expect the first class of queries to be more frequent at the top levels of the cube when the user is relatively unfamiliar with the rest of the cube. The second class of queries are more likely when a user is familiar with most of the cube and just needs to search for interesting information in detailed data that he might have missed. In terms of computation load, the first class of queries are easier to compute because the user has significantly reduced the portion of the cube to be searched through his

starting context. The second class of queries are more challenging since they require searching the entire cube and also because the constraints could interact with each other in arbitrary ways. Including a constraint of the form $a_i b_j$ changes the information content of constraint $a_i b_j c_k$ and viceversa. Such interactions are not present in the first class of queries because the constraints are all from the same view of the cube and thus cover non-overlapping data. We concentrate on the second class of queries since the first type are straightforward.

The user supplies a parameter N that denotes the maximum number of constraints he is interested in inspecting. We need to return the set of N constraints that are most informative. Using Equation 2 we define the information content of our final set of N chosen constraint as the increase in likelihood due to the new expected values after all the N constraints have been applied to the data. This global objective function is hard to evaluate. When $N = 1$, that is, when we want the single most informative constraint we can simplify Equation 2 to Equation 4 which quantifies the informative content of a constraint as $\sum_j \tilde{p}_j I_{(c+1)j} \log \frac{\tilde{p}(f)}{p^c(f)}$ i.e., the sum over the actual values of all cells included in the constraint multiplied by a scaling factor that is the same for all the cells. One option is therefore to find the most informative constraint first, incorporate its effect on the data, find the next most informative constraint and so on upto N constraints. Not only is this solution computationally expensive, it also does not guarantee optimality. We need a method that finds the N constraints simultaneously and ideally in one pass of the data. The main difficulty is that unlike for the case of $N = 1$ the new expected values p_{c+1} are hard to evaluate in closed form when there are multiple constraints in the final answer affecting it. To enable practical solution, we restrict the class of N constraints to be those that either totally subsume each other or do not overlap at all. We then use the Remove-Subsumed optimization of the previous section to remove from each constraint the part subsumed by some other more detailed subset. Consequently all cells in the cube are now covered by at most one of the N constraint. Even with this restriction finding the optimal solution is non-trivial because of the interactions between subsumed constraints. Including a constraint of the form $a_i b_j$ changes the worth of including a second constraint of the from $a_i b_j c_k$ and viceversa.

In [Sar99] we faced a similar challenge when attempting to find the best N row summary of the difference between two subcubes. We solved the problem by developing an efficient one-pass dynamic programming algorithm that is close to the optimal answer in certain special cases. We directly apply that algorithm. The algorithm starts with a bottom-up scan of the most detailed data and then aggregates tuples to higher levels while at the same time constructing the best solution. More details of the algorithm appear in [Sar99].

3.3.1 Experimental results

We present experimental evaluation of the overall system after including all the optimizations suggested. We evaluate our system along two important metrics: performance and quality of data exploration.

Timing measurements First we show overall response time to the top-N informative feature to demonstrate feasibility in a practical setting. The user interacts with the system in two ways: first by registering part of the constraints as seen and second by querying for informative regions. The response time for the first part is instantaneous because of asynchronous processing. The main concern is about response time of the second part. However, before responding to these queries, we need to ensure that processing on all constraints submitted prior to it has been completed.

For response time measurements we augment the workload in Section 3.1 with timing information. The time spent on one view of the cube is set to be a function of the number of cells in the current view. We assume that per cell the user spends an average of one second distributed randomly from 0 to 2 seconds. Thus, a view with 20 cells would be stared at for twenty seconds before the user navigates to the next neighboring view. Periodically the user queries for the ten most surprising constraints given his current view of the cube. We assume the periodicity to be distributed randomly between one and ten navigation of the cube.

Figure 18 shows the response time for the top-N informative constraints as a function of the number of constraints after which the query is posed. We find that even for the largest data which is the OLAP benchmark with 1.3 million tuples we are able to return the best answer within 2 minutes that makes it possible to deploy our tool in an interactive setting. Our experiments were run on very modest hardware. More powerful servers keeping pace with Moore's bounty can reduce the response time even further. We report performance results on other OLAP databases in the expanded version of this paper [Sar00a].

Exploration quality We measure the rate of information transfer to the user with our new focussed search. For this we measure the gap between the actual and expected values under two scenarios. In the first case, the user marks as visited the constraint that the system returns as the most informative. In the second case, we simulate a random exploration similar to the workload described in Section 3.1. In Figure 22 we plot the relative square error between the actual and expected values against the number of constraints. As expected, in both cases as more and more constraints get added the error reduces. For the student data we notice a remarkable reduction in error where it reduces from 0.9 to 0.18 within just 50 constraints (1% of total data size). In other words 1% of the data captures more than 80% of the information content. Similarly, we notice that for the Software revenue dataset error reduces to 0.73 within 50 constraints (0.2% of total data size). That is, just 0.2% of the total data size can explain 25% of the information content. The Grocery sales data is a synthetic datasets – therefore we notice that they start out with very low information content. Just by including the total sum at the topmost level, we explain 70% of the information in the data. After that we get little improvement with new constraints because of the high randomness in the data.

3.4 Integration with existing OLAP systems

Our goal is to allow persistent storage of the user's context and also to allow immediate refresh of expected values as new constraints get added. Both these requirements, make the underlying OLAP data source a natural choice for storing our intermediate results. For each <cube,user> pair we maintain an Expected-cube that stores the expected values at various aggregate levels using the optimized representation of section 3.2.1. Our tool resides as an attachment to the OLAP system that collects the user interactions and handles all optimization logic. All data intensive tasks are pushed to the OLAP server through dynamically generated queries. For instance, when a new constraint is submitted we need to adjust the expected values using the formulas in 2. This requires first aggregating the Expected-cube up to the level of the constraint to get the scale factor as the ratio of the observed and expected value for each member of constraint. Next we update the Expected-cube by multiplying with the scale factor using a join. Our prototype works on IBM's DB2/UDB's ROLAP features (version 6.1)

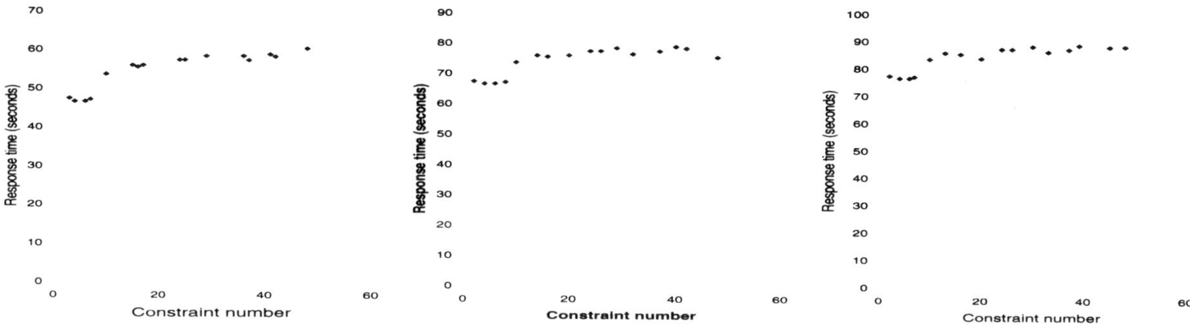

Figure 15: Software revenue data.   Figure 16: Grocery sales data.   Figure 17: OLAP benchmark.

Figure 18: Response time for the N most informative constraints queries. X axis is the number of constraints after which query was posed and Y axis is response time.

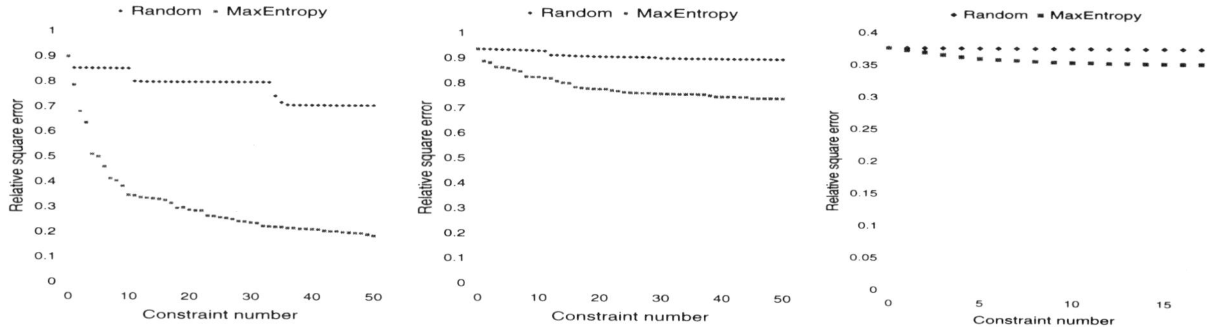

Figure 19: Student data.   Figure 20: Software revenue data.   Figure 21: Grocery sales data.

Figure 22: Change in error as constraints get added. The curve 'Random' shows error for a random set of constraints and the curve 'MaxEntropy' shows error with the most informative constraints

system and Oracle's 8i system – both of which provide advanced indexing and materialized aggregate views for efficient processing of OLAP queries.

4 Related work

The work reported here is part of our continuing $\mathbf{i}^3$project [Sar00b] on taking OLAP to the next stage of interactive analysis where we automate much of the manual effort spent in analysis. Recently, some attempts have been made to enhance OLAP products with mining primitives like decision tree classifiers [Dis, Cor97], clustering [Sof] and association rules [HF95]. In all these cases, the approach is to take existing mining algorithms and integrate them within OLAP products. The approach in the $\mathbf{i}^3$project is to first investigate how and why analysts currently explore the data cube and next automate them using new or previously known operators.

In [SAM98] we presented one such operation that was motivated with the observation that a significant reason why analysts explore to detailed levels is to search for abnormalities in detailed data. We reported as exceptional any value that was significantly different from any value calculated assuming all of its subsets

are known. This method has several differences with our current method of defining information content of a cell. First, the previous method computed exceptions in a batch mode whereas the current setting is online. Consequently, the interest value of a cell was derived assuming all its parents are known whereas in this project we assume only the visited parents are known. Second, the previous method used an intrinsic notion of the information content of a cell by making it a function of its own difference from the expected value. In contrast, in this case we have a more global notion where information content of a cell is measured in terms of how much knowing it bridges the gap between the expected and actual values of the entire cube. Often both definition of interestingness might return the same value but there are important cases where they differ. For instance if an aggregate value v differs significantly from its expected value but otherwise the detailed values underneath it are highly divergent, then by the intrinsic criteria v might qualify as interesting but it will not be so by the extrinsic criteria.

In [Sar99] we automate another area where analysts spend significant manual effort exploring the data: namely, finding reasons to explain why a certain aggregated quantity is lower or higher in one cell v_a compared to another cell v_b. We formulated this as reporting summarized differences between the two isomorphic cubes C_A and C_B that are aggregated to form the observed sums at v_a and v_b. This summarization has close ties with the second part of our tool where we report the top N informative cells from unvisited cube. The expected values cube be thought of as cube C_A and the actual values of cube C_B and we need to report the N constraints that will best summarize the difference. In Section 3.3 we discussed how we used these results.

Another body of related work arises from our use of the Maximum Entropy principle for calculating expected values. This is a classical topic with broad based applications in several areas including physics and chemistry in the pre-computer era and more recent applications in several problems on statistical estimation and pattern recognition. A recent nice tutorial and a computer science application is presented in [BPP96] where maximum entropy is used in natural language processing to model word usage based on prior words used in a passage. In data mining [MPS99] presents a more focussed application of Maximum Entropy to the problem of frequent itemset mining.

5 Conclusion

In this paper we proposed a new method of interactively exploring multidimensional data cubes that guides a user on what is informative after continuously factoring for what the user has already explored. There were two key components of this tool. First, modeling a user's expectation of values in unvisited parts based on what he already knows about the data. Second, attaching a measure of information content to each unvisited part of the cube. We found a unified answer to both these issues in the time-tested philosophy of Maximum Entropy. However, multidimensional data of the scale commonly present in typical OLAP systems are not directly amenable to the expensive iterative procedures required for solving the constrained optimization problem that arises out of the maximum entropy principle. We developed a number of optimizations to make these procedures efficient. Our optimizations lead to one to two orders of magnitude improvement in total time on large OLAP datasets. Another set of experiments on real-life data showed that a guided search can significantly accelerate the understanding of the data — for one dataset just a small 3% of the data captured 80% of the information content in the entire cube. We have implemented a prototype that integrates with existing OLAP systems and capitalizes on their processing power by pushing expensive computations to the OLAP server.

The most compelling future work is providing good visualization of the entire system to visually represent the information content of the various parts of the cube and show it in the context of the user's prior knowledge. Other topics include deleting or fading away constraints and allowing user defined constraints like expected seasonality in sales values.

References

[BPP96] A. Berger, S. Della Pietra, and V. Della Pietra. A maximum entropy approach to natural language processing. *Computational Linguistics*, 22(1):39–71, 1996. `http://www.cs.cmu.edu/afs/cs/user/aberger/www/html/tutorial/tutorial.ht\%ml`.

[Cor97] Cognos Software Corporation. Power play 5, special edition. `http://www.cognos.com/powercubes/index.html`, 1997.

[Cou] The OLAP Council. The OLAP benchmark. `http://www.olapcouncil.org`.

[Dis] Information Discovery. `http://www.datamine.inter.net/`.

[GCB+97] Jim Gray, Surajit Chaudhuri, Adam Bosworth, Andrew Layman, Frank Pellow, and Hamid Pirahesh. Data cube: A relational aggregation operator generalizing group-by, cross-tab and sub-totals. *Data Mining and Knowledge Discovery*, 1(1):29–53, 1997.

[GS85] S. Guiasu and A. Shenitzer. The principle of maximum entropy. *The Mathematical Intelligencer*, 7(1), 1985.

[HF95] J. Han and Y. Fu. Discovery of multiple-level association rules from large databases. In *Proc. of the 21st Int'l Conference on Very Large Databases*, Zurich, Switzerland, September 1995.

[Jay90] E.T. Jaynes. Notes on present status and future prospects. In W.T. Grandy and L.H. Schick, editors, *Maximum Entropy and Bayesian Methods*. Kluwer, 1990.

[Mic98] Microsoft corporation. *Microsoft decision support services version 1.0*, 1998.

[MPS99] Heikki Mannila, Dmitry Pavlov, and Padhraic Smyth. Prediction with local patterns using cross-entropy. In *Proceedings Knowledge discovery in databases*, pages 357–361, 1999.

[PPL97] S. Pietra, V. Pietra, and J. Lafferty. Inducing features of random fields. *In IEEE Transactions on Pattern Analysis and Machine Intelligene*, 19(4):380–393, 1997.

[SAM98] Sunita Sarawagi, Rakesh Agrawal, and Nimrod Megiddo. Discovery-driven exploration of OLAP data cubes. In *Proc. of the 6th Int'l Conference on Extending Database Technology (EDBT)*, Valencia, Spain, 1998. expanded version available from `http://www.almaden.ibm.com/cs/quest`.

[Sar99] S. Sarawagi. Explaining differences in multidimensional aggregates. In *Proc. of the 25th Int'l Conference on Very Large Databases (VLDB)*, 1999.

[Sar00a] S. Sarawagi. User adaptive exploration of olap data cubes. Submission to the VLDB journal: `http://www.it.iitb.ernet.in/~sunita`, 2000.

[Sar00b] Sunita Sarawagi. i[3]: Intelligent, Interactive Investigaton of OLAP data cubes. In *Proc. ACM SIGMOD International Conf. on Management of Data (Demonstration section)*, Dallas USA, May 2000.

[Sof] Pilot Software. Decision support suite. `http://www.pilotsw.com`.

Toward Learning Based Web Query Processing

Yanlei Diao   Hongjun Lu   Songting Chen   Zengping Tian

Department of Computer Science
Hong Kong University of Science & Technology
Hong Kong, China
diaoyl@cs.ust.hk   luhj@cs.ust.hk

Department of Computer Science
Fudan University
Shanghai, China
stchen@fudan.edu.cn   zptain@fudan.edu.cn

Abstract

In this paper, we describe a novel Web query processing approach with learning capabilities. Under this approach, user queries are in the form of keywords and search engines are employed to find URLs of Web sites that might contain the required information. The first few URLs are presented to the user for browsing. Meanwhile, the query processor learns both the information required by the user and the way that the user navigates through hyperlinks to locate such information. With the learned knowledge, it processes the rest URLs and produces precise query results in the form of segments of Web pages without user involvement. The preliminary experimental results indicate that the approach can process a range of Web queries with satisfactory performance. The architecture of such a query processor, techniques of modeling HTML pages, and knowledge for query processing are discussed. Experiments on the effectiveness of the approach, the required knowledge, and the training strategies are presented.

1. Introduction

The Internet and the Web have changed everything. It is estimated that the publicly indexable Web now contains about 600 million pages, encompassing approximately 6 terabytes of text data [15]. The Web has become

Proceedings of the 26th International Conference on Very Large Databases, Cairo, Egypt, 2000

everyone's information source. Each day, a huge number of people search the Web for information of interest, such as news, prices of goods, research papers, etc. With the excitement on electronic commerce growing, the Internet will also become a common platform for conducting business. The usage of the Web therefore will increase more dramatically.

Search engines [4] are widely used to locate information across the Web. Unfortunately for users who are used to retrieving information from database systems, searching from the Web is sometimes frustrating. For example, if they would like to find the lowest price for a certain part in a database, a simple SQL statement does the job. However, it may cost hours to search for the lowest price from the Web, if they have the stamina to find it. One problem of search on the Web is that search engines return very large hit lists with low precision. Users have to sift relevant documents from irrelevant ones by manually fetching and browsing pages. Another discouraging aspect is that URLs or whole pages are returned as search results. It is very likely that the answer to a user query is only part of the page (like one field in a relation). Retrieving the whole page actually leaves the task of search inside a page to Web users. With these two aspects remaining unchanged, Web users will not be freed from the heavy burden of browsing pages and locating required information, and information obtained from one search will be inherently limited.

While the dissimilarity between querying the Web and querying a database is caused by the fundamental differences between the Web and a database system, which will most likely remain, researchers from different disciplines have been trying to improve the situation.

A wide range of research work has been reported in IR to improve the easiness and effectiveness of querying the Web, including developing better classification mechanisms, building more effective indices, using better searching strategies and ranking functions, etc.

Using intelligent agent to help users is originated from the AI community. In the context of querying the Web, such agents can learn user profiles or models from user search behaviors, and then employ the learned knowledge to predicate URLs that may have interesting information, thus providing suggestions to users. Some assistant agents, such as *Syskill & Webert* [20] and *WebWatcher* [13], help users in an interactive mode. Some other assistant agents, *Fab* [3] and *InfoSpider* [17], use heuristics and work autonomously to find interesting pages.

Researchers from the database community take another approach. They view the Web as a large distributed database system and apply database technologies to Web queries. The related efforts include Web query language design and wrapper generation. The Web query languages are classified into two generations [10]. The first generation, including *W3QL* [14] and *WebSQL* [18], aimed to unify content based queries and link structure based queries. The second generation of Web query language, such as *WebOQL* [2] and *StruQL* [9], has the ability to access the structure of the Web objects and to create new complex structures from the query results. Research work on wrapper generation tackles the fundamental difficulty in querying the Web, i.e., Web pages are not well structured and there is no schema that describes the contents of Web pages. It exploits the formatting information on Web pages to hypothesis the underlying structure of a page. With this structure a wrapper that facilitates queries on the page is generated [1, 5, 8, 12, 16, 21].

While there are various issues in Web query processing and different approaches to tackling these issues, we describe in this paper our efforts to build an on-line query processing system that enables users to query the Web with ease and obtain the results in a database-like fashion. By our proposed approach, a user first issues a key word query (probably not precise). It is passed to a general search engine such as *Yahoo!*. The search engine returns URLs of Web pages that might contain requested information. At the beginning, these Web pages are retrieved and presented to the user for browsing. During the browsing, the system records down the segment of a Web page that contains the query result and the sequence of hyperlinks through which the user navigates to find it. Query results and user actions are analyzed. After the user browses a few pages, the system knows what the user exactly wants and becomes capable of scanning Web pages and following links, if necessary, to locate the query results. Finally the system presents to the user the *segments* of Web pages instead of the original Web pages. A segment can be a paragraph in text, a table or a list.

To our knowledge, it is the first query processing system that processes ad hoc queries on HTML pages and automatically extracts segments of pages as query results. Despite the superficial similarity with a large body of related work, this system is unique at the following aspects:

- Unlike information retrieval systems or intelligent agents that return URLs or Web pages as query results, our system returns segments of documents as the query answer (correspondingly in relational databases if a field is the answer, the field but not the whole table is returned).

- The system does not require a prior knowledge about users such as user profiles. Moreover, it does not require preprocessing of Web pages such as generating wrappers either. As a consequence, the system is well suited to processing ad hoc queries that can hardly be handled by static hypertext analysis [5, 6], agents or system using wrappers.

- The system exploits the page formatting and the linkage information simultaneously to automate query processing. Recently there has been a surge of research work either on hyperlinks to help Web search [4, 11, 17] or on internal structure of HTML pages for wrapper generation and *Information Extraction* [7, 8]. However, combining these two in the context of a query processing system is new and poses great challenges.

We call our approach a *learning-based* approach because the system learns about the exact query requirements and the efficient way to locate the information during a query process. As a result of the learning, the system is able to deliver to users the results that better match users' needs in a more concise form. The learning approach brings the following advantages to our query processing system.

- Users can still express their queries in keywords, which is the easiest way for casual Web users. If a user is not familiar with the vocabulary of information suppliers, the query specification may even be vague. To bridge the gap between the issued keywords and the real user requirements, the system learns the precise requirements from users.

- The system has the capability of navigating in the neighborhood of the page where the specified keywords occur. Often the result is not in the page that contains the keywords but is one link or two away. This is especially true when the specified keywords are not very precise. Learning to navigate enables the system to find results that keyword search fails to find.

- Although the learned knowledge is useful to one query, it helps to make 100% use of the hit list returned by a search engine. Users are relieved from browsing dozens or hundreds of Web pages in order to obtain all the required information.

- As a background process of a browser, learning is nearly imperceptible to users and only minimal effort such as clicking and marking in the first few sites is required from them.

A prototype system has been implemented using the approach. The preliminary results are encouraging. User query requirements and navigation heuristics can be

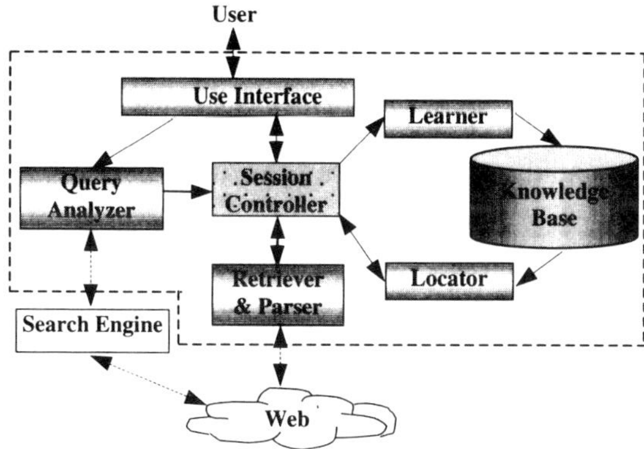

Figure 1: System Architecture

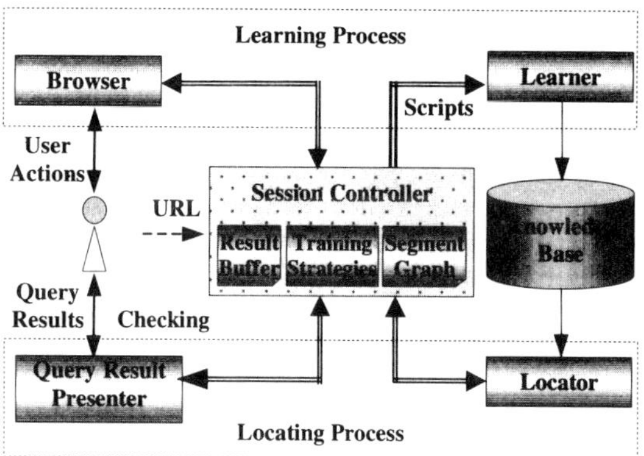

Figure 2: A Query Session

reasonably well captured and stored in a rather simple form. Given a set of about 100 URLs, users need to browse no more than 10 of them to make the system capable of locating the queried segments or denying the Web sites with the correctness rate higher than 80%.

The remainder of the paper is organized as follows. Section 2 describes the learning based Web query processing approach in detail. The knowledge to be learned, its representation and the acquisition process are described in Section 3. Section 4 describes how a user query is processed using the learned knowledge. Experiments conducted to evaluate the approach are presented in Section 5. Section 6 concludes the paper with some discussions on future work.

2. Learning-Based Web Query Processing

In this section, we describe the architecture of a learning-based Web query processing system and explain how a user query is processed.

2.1 A Learning-Based Query Processing System

Figure 1 depicts the reference architecture of a learning-based Web query processing system. It consists of seven major components: *User Interface*, *Session Controller*, *Query Analyzer*, *Learner*, *Locator*, *Retriever & Parser*, and *Knowledge Base*. The User Interface provides users with a friendly environment to work with the system. It accepts user queries and presents results to them. A browser with extended capability to capture user actions is also an important component of it. When a user is browsing Web pages, it records three types of user actions:

- following a hyperlink to browse another page;
- marking a segment that contains the required information; or
- rejecting a site that does not contain the required information.

Query Analyzer analyzes a user query and converts it into a search condition according to the requirement of the search engine that is employed to return URLs from the Web. The set of URLs is passed to Session Controller as the input of the other components in the system.

As a learning-based system, the system can work in two different modes, the *learning mode* and the *processing mode*. When the system works in the learning mode, Learner is activated by Session Controller to generate knowledge from those captured actions and located query results. The learned knowledge is stored in Knowledge Base. When the system works in the processing mode, Locator is activated to apply the knowledge and locate the segment that contains the required information. The two working modes are switched back and forth based on training strategies. The main task of Session Controller is to coordinate the interaction among various components of the system.

Since the result from the search engine is a set of URLs, a Retriever is integrated into the system to retrieve Web pages. The Parser parses each retrieved page and generates an internal data structure that is used later for presentation, learning and query processing.

2.2 A Query Session

To have better understanding of how a query is processed, we describe a query session in detail. As described above, after Session Controller receives the URLs, the system works in either the *learning mode* or the *processing mode*. Corresponding to these two modes, there are two types of processes: the *browsing process* and the *locating process*. Figure 2 depicts the details of the processes and associated data flow (Query Analyzer, and Retriever & Parser are omitted in this figure).

Session Controller activates the processes according to a training strategy stored in its *Training Strategies Module*. A training strategy defines when the learning process should be invoked and how the learning mode and processing mode are interleaved. Three strategies supported by the system are:

Sequential training. It partitions the URLs returned from the search engine into two sets in the original order.

For the first set, the system works in the learning mode. After training, the system processes the second set in the processing mode until the query session is completed.

Random *training*. Similar to sequential training, the system first works in the learning mode and then turns to the processing mode. But it randomly picks a number of sites from the returned URLs for training. The rationale is that the randomly picked sites may be more representative than those on the top of the returned list.

***Interleaved training*.** When interleaved training is used, the system switches back and forth between the learning mode and the processing mode before a stopping criterion is met. It works as follows. At the beginning of a query session, the system is in the learning mode. After a few sites are browsed, the system tries to locate results in the processing mode. As long as the user confirms the results are correct, it remains in the processing mode. When the user finds an incorrect result, the system switches to the learning mode and learns from the incorrectly processed site. This process goes until a stopping criterion for interleaved training (a certain number of browsing processes or an accuracy threshold) is met. After that, the system remains in the processing mode until all sites are processed.

During a browsing process, given a URL, Session Controller first asks Retriever & Parser to retrieve the page and transform it to a segment tree. It adds the tree to the segment graph, an internal data structure maintained by the *Segment Graph Module* (segment tree and segment graph are defined in the next section). Then the controller sends the tree to Browser where the tree is presented for browsing. If the user chooses a link, the system goes to process a new page. The process is repeated until the user marks a query segment or rejects the site. User behaviors, either choosing a link or marking a segment, are recorded on the segment graph. For a successfully located site, the controller generates intermediate files, *knowledge scripts* from the segment graph. The scripts are finally sent to Learner for knowledge generation.

In a locating process, given a URL, Session Controller receives a segment tree from Retriever & Parser and adds the tree to the segment graph. Then it sends the tree to Locator. Locator returns a decision of choosing a link, finding a segment or rejecting the site. If a link is chosen, the system goes to process the new page and asks Locator to make another decision. The process ends when Locator finds a query segment or rejects the site. The located segment is sent to the *Result Buffer Module* that communicates with *Query Result Presenter* in the interface to present the result. When Interleaved training is used and the stopping criteria for training is not met, Query Result Presenter asks the user to check results. If the system returned a wrong result, a browsing process is activated for the current site. The only difference from a normal browsing process is that some pages can be fetched directly from the segment graph.

A query session terminates when all the URLs returned from the search engine are either browsed or processed. If there are too many URLs returned, heuristics can be used to terminate a session.

3. Learning from Users for Query Processing

To facilitate Web query processing, the data on the Web should be properly modeled. Moreover, the system must have the knowledge about how to navigate through the Web to locate information in a page. The most efficient way to obtain such knowledge is to learn from users. This section presents our approaches to these two major issues.

3.1 Modeling A Web Site

The Web consists of a number of Web pages connected by hyperlinks. In order to obtain queried information from a large number of Web pages, both the internal structure of a Web page and the linkage between Web pages need to be captured. We begin with the modeling of a single Web page.

Usually a Web page is an HTML document that contains a sequence of tag delimited data elements. As an atomic element, one that does not contain other elements in it, may not contain enough information to meet the query requirements, *segment* that is a group of elements is used as the unit in our model. In other words, we partition documents into segments each of which serves as a candidate of the answer to a query. Four major segment types are *paragraph*, *table, list* and *heading*. Segments can be nested, that is, a segment can include a number of sub-segments. An HTML document is the largest segment. Each segment has one attribute, *content*, which consists of all textual data in the scope delimited by the start tag and the end tag of the segment, thus including the content of its sub-segments. Content is used to check if a segment meets the query requirements. To facilitate navigation, another attribute, *description*, is designed for each segment (more discussion in § 3.2). It is summarized from the content using certain heuristics. For example, the description of a table segment can be the table caption or the title row. *Hyperlinks*, a special type of elements in HTML pages, can be represented in the same way as segments. The anchor is its description and the URL is its content. To take advantage of the hierarchical structure, each hyperlink is associated with its parent segment, i.e. the smallest segment that contains it[1].

With the notation of segments, a Web page can be modeled as a *segment tree*: The root is the Web page itself; the internal nodes are segments that contain sub-segments; the leaves are atomic segments, the minimal units in this model. Each node has two attributes and is

---

[1] Whether anchor should be included in the parent segment is a technical issue. Currently we include it in if the parent segment contains other text.

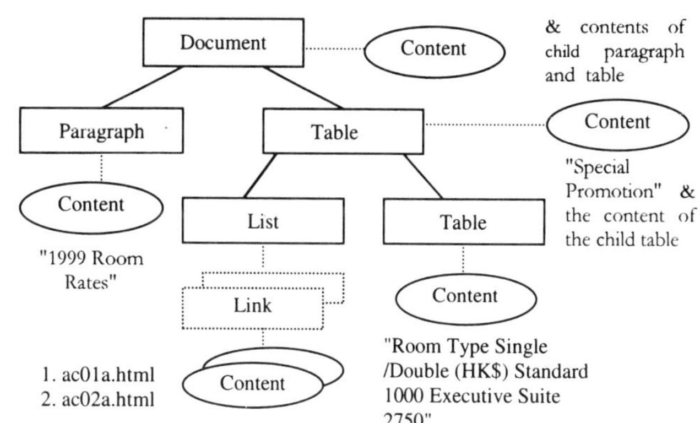

Figure 3: An HTML Document and the Corresponding Segment Tree

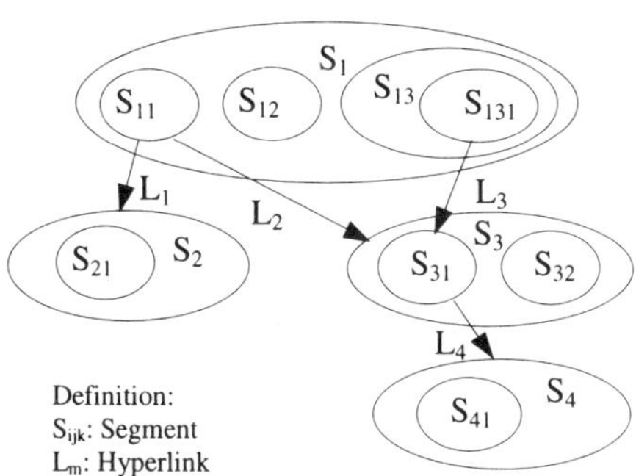

Figure 4: A Segment Graph

associated with hyperlinks it contains. An example of HTML page and the corresponding segment tree is shown in Figure 3 (the attribute, description, is omitted).

Externally, Web pages are connected through hyperlinks. If we view a Web page as a node in a graph and a hyperlink as a directed edge from the page containing it to the pointed page, then Web pages in a site can be represented by a directed graph. If we further ignore backward links, links pointing to one part of the same page, and links pointing to pages outside the current site, a Web site can be modeled as hyperlink-connected segment trees, called *Segment Graph*. The entering page, one pointed by a URL returned form the search engine, is the *root* of the graph. With such a model, *site*, which will be used very often later in this paper, refers to the collection of Web pages that are reachable from the root and of the same base URL as the root. We define the *depth* of a segment is the number of hyperlinks followed to reach the Web page that contains the segment. Note that segments on the same Web page may have different depths along different paths. Segments on the root page have depth 1. The *Level* of a segment is the minimal depth among all hyperlink paths in the segment graph.

We would like to emphasize that it is not our intention to provide a complete and sound model for Web pages and the Web. The sole objective of the above model is to facilitate the retrieval of meaningful query results in the form of segment that is small in size but carries sufficient semantics. The segment graph that combines the intra-document structure with the inter-document linkage can well serve the purpose. An example of such a graph is presented in Figure 4.

3.2 Knowledge for Locating Queried Segments

Let us consider the task of Web query processing. If our system could exhaustively search the segment graph and choose the most relevant segment from all in the graph, the problem would be simplified as hypertext classification. Unfortunately it is not feasible for an on line query processor because a segment graph can be very large. To restrict the search scope, navigation from the root should be terminated if the system finds a segment on a page that meets query requirements well enough or concludes the page is not relevant and will not lead to a relevant document. In other words, on each page, a decision of choosing a link, finding a segment, or giving up this page should be made. Though hyperlinks and internal page structure have been extensively studied by others, they made a decision either among all links or among all segments. A decision made between links and segments is something new and requires these two types of data structures are comparable.

One observation concerns the conventions of composing hypertext documents. Hyperlinks usually convey descriptive information of the pointed documents while segments that meet the query requirements contain both the descriptive information and the query result. For example, we would like to retrieve admission requirements of graduate applicants. The anchor "Admissions" only tells the link points to a page related to admission requirements. The queried segment contains both the descriptive information of admissions and the concrete requirements such as GPA or test scores. Links and segments, two structures presenting different information are hardly comparable by one mechanism.

To make the query system workable, two types of knowledge are designed. One is *Navigation Knowledge* that only concerns descriptive information and helps find a path from a given URL to the queried segment on a Web page. The other type of knowledge examines whether a segment meets the query requirements on both the descriptive information and the result. It is referred to as *Classification Knowledge* because it is in fact used to classify a segment into one of the two classes, containing or not containing the query result.

Attribute content and attribute description are designed for navigation knowledge and classification knowledge, respectively. Note that lengths of links and segments may differ remarkably. We assume the description of a segment can summarize the semantics of the segment and use it in navigation to avoid bias that element lengths bring. Another rationale of using description is that in self-describing languages like *Extensible Markup Language*, element names serve naturally as element descriptions so that our model carries over directly to them.

3.2.1 Navigation Knowledge

Navigation knowledge is generated from user actions of following hyperlinks to locate query results. A path that starts from the entering page of a site and ends at the queried segment is called a navigational path, represented as *(link→)* segment*, where * means any number of occurrences. For example, if segment S_{41} in Figure 4 is a queried segment, one possible navigational path is $L_2{\rightarrow}L_4{\rightarrow}S_{41}$. A hyperlink usually occurs in some segments in a document. Information of those segments also helps determine whether a link should be followed. To capture such information, we extend the navigational path with all segments that contain the links on the path, which is called *extended navigational path*. In our example, the extended navigational path to locate S_{41} is $(S_1{\rightarrow}S_{11}{\rightarrow}L_2) \rightarrow (S_3{\rightarrow}S_{31}{\rightarrow}L_4) \rightarrow (S_4{\rightarrow}S_{41})$. A segment or a link appearing on the extended navigational path is called a *component* of it, e.g. S_{11}, L_4, S_{41}, etc. Extended navigational paths can be easily obtained from segment graphs in browsing processes.

To generate navigation knowledge from an extended navigational path, the first step is to assign a weight, denoted as $W(component)$, to each component on the path. This weight tells how closely a component is related to the query result. One intuition is that the closer to the queried segment, the higher weight the component gets. Then the issue is at what rate the weight of a component decays along the extended navigational path. Instead of hypothesizing the rate, we assume the queried segment is the most closely related to itself (its weight is 1) and let the path length determine the rate. Suppose D to be the depth of a queried segment. On the ith page along the path, N_i is the number of components appearing on the path.

The weight of jth component ($j <= N_i$) on the ith page is given by:

$$W(component_{ij}) = (i-1)/D + 1/D * j/N_i . \qquad (1)$$

The weighting scheme guarantees $(i\text{-}1)/D < i/D$, i.e. the weight of a component on the $i\text{-}1^{th}$ page is less than that on the ith page. The second term of the formula, $1/D * j/N_i$, ensures with the same depth the more specific information a segment conveys, the more weight it gets. In other words, a child segment gets more weight than its parent. A link gets more weight than all segments containing it. Continue with the example in Figure 4. Some components on the path are assigned weights as follows:

Depth: Depth 1   Depth 2   Depth 3
Path: $S_1{\rightarrow}S_{11}{\rightarrow}L_2$ $S_3{\rightarrow}S_{31}{\rightarrow}L_4$ $S_4{\rightarrow}S_{41}$
$W(S_{11})$ =0/3+1/3*2/3=2/9 the 2nd component at depth 1
$W(L_4)$ =1/3+1/3*3/3=2/3 the 3rd component at depth 2
$W(S_{41})$ =2/3+1/3*2/2=1 the 2nd component at depth 3

The next step is to assign weights to terms that describe a component on the path. Since the attribute, *description*, provides such descriptive information, we choose it to represent a component. Then for each component, only words that are in the description and consist of alphabetic letters are selected. A stop list and stemming are further applied to them. The derived words are called terms. In our algorithm, each term in the description of a component is assigned a weight, $w(term)$, which is equal to the weight of the component divided by the number of terms in the description.

The weight of a term tells the term's importance in leading to the queried segment. By our weighting scheme, it is determined by the position of the component that contains the term as well as the number of terms in the component's description. Term weight is accumulated through all browsing processes. The navigation knowledge, represented as a set of (*term*, *weight*) pairs, is stored in the navigation knowledge base.

3.2.2 Classification Knowledge

The task of examining whether a segment meets query requirements is cast in the Bayesian learning framework because it has provided good performance in text and hypertext applications [5, 6]. Two different models, the *multi-variate Bernoulli* model and the *multinomial* model in this framework are reported in [19]. By their report, the multinomial model usually outperforms the multi-variate Bernoulli model. Therefore we adopt the multinomial model. The *classification knowledge* is the knowledge that will be used by the Bayesian classifier.

Classification knowledge takes the form of a set of triplets, (*feature$_i$*, N_{i1}, N_{i2}), where N_{i1} is the number of occurrences of *feature$_i$* in the content of queried segments, and N_{i2} is the number of occurrences of *feature$_i$* in the content of segments that do not meet query requirements.

```
1    Algorithm LocatingProcess ( URL: the URL of a page, QueryResult:
     returned value of the query )
2    begin
3         Stack SegmentStack, LinkStack;
4         Float SegmentMax, LinkMax;
5         Tree SegmentTree;

6         QueryResult := NIL;
7         SegmentTree := Retriever&Parser(URL);
8         Separate(SegmentTree, SegmentStack, LinkStack);
9         if ( StopNavigation( ) == TRUE )
10             PopAll(LinkStack);
11        ApplyNavigation(SegmentStack, LinkStack);
12        while ( ( QueryResult == NIL ) AND (SegmentStack != NIL
                   OR LinkStack != NIL ) ) do
13             SegmentMax := GetMaxScore(segmentStack);
14             LinkMax := GetMaxScore(linkStack);
15             if ( SegmentMax >= LinkMax )
16                  ApplyClassification(SegmentStack, QueryResult);
17                  PopAll(SegmentStack);
18             else
19                  URL := Pop(LinkStack);
20                  if ( Unvisited(URL) == TRUE AND
                        StopNavigatoin( )==FALSE )
21                       LocatingProcess(URL, QueryResult);
22         end while
23   end.
```

Figure 5: The Locating Algorithm

Knowledge generation involves two issues, feature generation and selection of training samples.

Features are extracted from the content of a segment. Unlike most IR systems that only consider English words as features, we also consider values and complex data types. We define five basic feature types, *float, integer, English word* (consisting of alphabetic letters), *special word* (consisting of alphanumeric letters) and *special character*, and four complex feature types, *date, time, email address*, and *telephone number*. A lexical program using regular expressions extracts all these features.

To train the classifier, the user-marked segments are treated as positive samples. As for negative samples, only those segments on the same page as the marked segments are selected. Those pages without marked segments are discarded to avoid excessive negative samples. Then the generation of classification knowledge is straightforward. During the browsing process, when the user marks a queried segment, the system collects $feature_i$ in its content together with the number of occurrences N_{i1}, and $feature_j$ in other segments on the same page together with the number of occurrences N_{j2}. For each feature, numbers of occurrences in both classes are accumulative through all browsing processes.

Since both types of knowledge involve terms, they are organized by *Tries* for efficient access.

4. Query Processing Using Learned Knowledge

In this section, we describe how the learned knowledge is used to locate queried segments in the locating processes.

4.1 Algorithm for Locating Queried Segments

A locating process takes one URL returned from the search engine as the entrance to a site. Then it traverses the segment graph built on the fly. As an online Web query processor, the system will perform badly if general graph searching approaches like breadth-first or depth-first search are used. Considering hyperlinks and segments on a page simultaneously further complicates the search process. The learned knowledge helps the system locate query results efficiently and effectively.

By our approach, the choice between hyperlinks and segments on each page determines the navigation in a site. If a hyperlink is chosen, the locating process goes to the pointed page. If it fails to find a queried segment by following the link, it makes another choice between unvisited hyperlinks and unprocessed segments. If a segment is chosen, classification knowledge is applied to check if it meets the query requirements. If it does, it is returned as the query result and navigation terminates. Otherwise another choice is made between unvisited hyperlinks and not processed segments. If no result is found after all links and segments are processed, the locating process backtracks. The process is running in a recursive fashion.

The key issue is how to make a choice between hyperlinks and segments on a Web page. Navigation knowledge is used. It analyzes the descriptive information of links and segments on the same Web page, and assigns a weight to each of them. This weight uniformly tells how closely one element, either a link or a segment, is related to the query result. Then links and segments, the two different types of data, are sorted by the assigned weights. The element with the highest weight will be chosen for further processing.

Figure 5 presents the locating algorithm. The URL is first passed to *Retriever&Parser* that retrieves the Web page and parses it into a segment tree (line 7). Function *Separate* stores links and segments in *LinkStack* and *SegmentStack*, respectively (line 8). It pushes both atomic segments and segments that contain other segments into the stack. The classifier decides which segment answers the query best. The *ApplyNavigation* function assigns weights to segments and links using the navigation knowledge and sorts them in a decreasing order of the weights in *SegmentStack* and *LinkStack*, respectively (line 11). Each pass inside the *while* loop makes a choice between the link with the highest weight and the segment with the highest weight (line 13-15) as described above. The only change here is that if the weight of the segment is higher, function *ApplyClassification* applies classification knowledge to **all** segments on this page and determines if one of them meets the query requirements (line 16). It is because retrieving a new page on the Internet takes far more time than processing a number of segments on the local machine. Besides, it is reasonable to assume if one segment provides best information about the query result among all links and segments on a page, it is more likely to find the result on this page instead of following a hyperlink. Function *StopNavigation* terminates the navigation if the locating process has already visited a certain number of pages and is still trying to visit more.

4.2 Application of Navigation Knowledge

Function *ApplyNavigation* first assigns weights to segments and links using the navigation knowledge learned during training, and then sorts them by the weights in a descending order.

To assign a weight, W, to a segment or a link, terms are extracted from its description in the way as described in § 3.2.1. Let the terms be t_1, t_2 ... t_n, and their weights be w_1, w_2 ... w_n. W is computed as:

$$W = max \ (topJ \ (w_1, w_2, \ldots, w_n)) \ . \tag{2}$$

Function *topJ* in the equation returns a set of term weights that are top $J\%$ highest in the navigation knowledge base. By considering top $J\%$ of terms only, those segments and links that are remotely related to the query result will be filtered out. When J is reasonably low, *topJ* returns an empty set for segments and links consisting of only terms with low weights. With an empty weight set, W is equal to 0. Those segments will be removed from the stacks later in the sorting process.

Function *max*, is used to keep the most descriptive information in segments and links. Rather than using an average or other function of the weights returned by *topJ*, we choose the max function because the relevance of a segment or a link is often conveyed by very few words. The convention of HTML pages is using short informative sentence fragments [7], which is especially true in lists, headings, hyperlinks, etc. As a result of this function, each segment or link is assigned a weight that is expected to best represent its relevance.

4.3 Application of Classification Knowledge

Function *ApplyClassification* calls a naïve Bayesian classifier to apply classification knowledge to one or multiple segments. The classifier used is adopted from [19] with some modification.

We begin with classification of one segment. For each segment, features are extracted from its content as described in § 3.2.2. The class label C (queried segment, or not in this application) of the segment D', is given by:

$$C = \arg\max_k P(C_k \mid D') = \arg\max_k P(D' \mid C_k)P(C_k)$$
$$= \arg\max_k P(F_1 \mid C_k)...P(F_n \mid C_k)P(C_k) \ , \tag{3}$$

where C_k is a class label ($k = 2$ in this application) and F_i is a feature in the segment.

The estimation of the probability of feature F_i on condition of class k and each class prior are computed using the classification knowledge as follows:

$$P(F_i \mid C_k) = \frac{1 + N_{ik}}{|V| + \sum_{t=1}^{|V|} N_{tk}} \ , \tag{4}$$

$$P(C_k) = \frac{\sum_{t=1}^{|V|} N_{tk}}{\sum_{k=1}^{K} \sum_{t=1}^{|V|} N_{tk}} \ , \tag{5}$$

where N_{ik} comes from the triple (F_i , N_{i1} , N_{i2}) with $k=1,2$ and $\sum_{t=1}^{|V|} P(F_t \mid C_k) = 1$. To handle the probability of features that do not occur in training samples, smoothing of add-by-one is used. $|V|$ is the vocabulary size of the classification knowledge.

To find the queried segment from all segments on a page, the function estimates the confidence of a segment being classified to certain class k, denoted by α_k, where $\sum_k \alpha_k = 1$. For a given segment, α_k ($k=1,2,...,K$) is calculated from the following equations:

$$\frac{E_1}{\alpha_1} = \frac{E_2}{\alpha_2} = \cdots = \frac{E_K}{\alpha_K} \ \text{ and } \ \sum_{k=1}^{K} \alpha_k = 1 \ , \tag{6}$$

where $E_k = P(F_1 \mid C_k)P(F_2 \mid C_k)...P(F_n \mid C_k) \ P(C_k)$. Let C_l denotes the class of queried segments. Given a set of segments D_1, D_2, ..., D_m , function *ApplyClassification* filters segments whose classification confidence α_l is lower than a threshold and chooses a segment D with the largest α_l from all kept segments:

$$D = \arg\max_j \{ \alpha_{jl} \mid \alpha_{jl} > Threshold, j = 1, \ldots m \}, \tag{7}$$

where α_{jl} is the classification confidence α_l with which class label C_l is assigned to segment D_j . If all segments have α_l lower than the threshold, *ApplyClassification* returns no result and the locating process goes on.

5. Performance Evaluation

A prototype of the system has been implemented based on the proposed approach. The system is implemented in Visual C++. *Yahoo!* is used as the external engine. The URLs of Web page matches are used in processing.   A series of experiments were conducted to evaluate the proposed approach and study the related issues. In this section, we describe these tests and discuss the results.

5.1 Evaluation Metrics

For a given query and a URL returned from the search engine, the system either returns a segment or a conclusion that no result is found from the related Web site. We label the first case as *Found* and the latter one *Not Found*. For both cases, we use *Right* or *Wrong* to indicate whether the system makes a correct decision. Using the four terms, a query result belongs to one of the

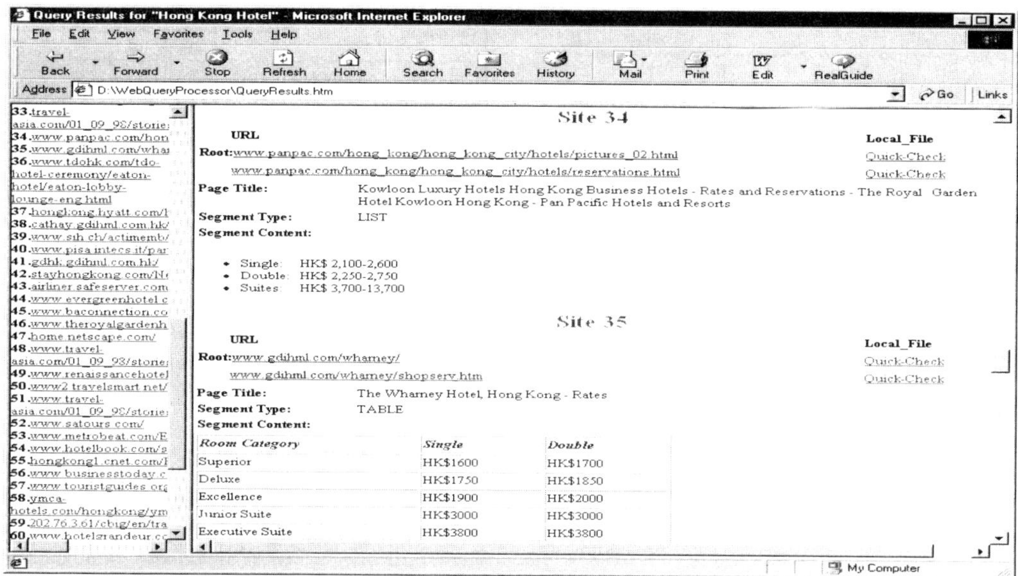

Figure 6: A Sample Output

four categories. A queried segment is a segment that satisfies user query requirements.

Right Found:	The queried segment is found.
Wrong Found:	A segment other than the queried segment or from an irrelevant site is returned.
Right Not Found:	No segment is returned from an irrelevant site.
Wrong Not Found:	The system fails to locate the queried segment that the site contains.

To evaluate *effectiveness*, the following metrics are defined:

> *Precision* = # *Right Found / # Found ,*
> *Recall* = # *Right Found / # Sites Containing Queried Segments ,*
> *Correctness* = # *Right Sites / # Sites Processed .*

In the definition of *correctness*, # *right sites* is the number of the sites for which the system makes correct decisions. That is, it either locates a queried segment, or indicates correctly that a site does not contain a queried segment.

To evaluate efficiency, we take visited pages as the measure because the time of processing a page is insignificant compared to retrieving the page through the Internet. Two measurements are defined. The *absolute path length* is the number of visited pages to locate a queried segment or to conclude that no queried segment can be found for the site. The *relative path length* to locate a queried segment is the ratio between the absolute path length and the level of the queried segment (i.e. the length of the shortest path to locate this segment). The two metrics are presented as:

> *Absolute Path length* = # *Visited pages ,*

> *Relative Path Length* = # *Visited pages / Level of the Queried Segment.*

5.2 The System Capability

Before quantitative analysis of the system performance, we first present sample query results that indicate the capability of the system. A user posted a query consisting of 3 words, *Hong Kong hotel*, with the intention of finding hotel room rates in Hong Kong. The query was passed to *Yahoo!* and a set of URLs was returned, which is shown in the left frame of Figure 6, a snapshot of the system output. The right frame shows the query results after seven successful browsing processes during which the system learned the knowledge about the query. Currently the right frame presents the results located for Site 34 and 35. From the results we can see some of the novel features of the system.

- In addition to URLs and page titles that ordinary search engines can return, our system returns segments of the Web pages that contain queried information. The result of site 34 is a list and of site 35 is a table.
- The query results contain exactly the information that the user is looking for. Note that the segments from site 34 and 35 do not contain any input keyword but meet the requirement of room rates that are not specified in the keyword query. It indicates that the system learned the query requirement from the user.
- Both segments are from pages whose URLs are not directly returned by *Yahoo!*. It indicates that the system learned how to follow hyperlinks to the page that contains a queried segment.

325

Query	URL Selected	URL Used	Train-ing	Test-ing	Irrele-vant	Rele-vant
Q1	100	69	9	60	31	29
Q2	100	71	9	62	24	38

Table 1: URLs Used for Query Processing

Query	Found		Not Found		Correct-ness	Precision	Recall
	R	W	R	W			
Q1	23	7	26	4	81.7%	76.7%	79.3%
Q2	28	4	21	9	79.0%	87.5%	73.7%

Table 2: Basic Performance of the System

5.3 The Effectiveness of the System

In this subsection, we present the results of two queries to illustrate the effectiveness of the system. Two queries used are:

Q1: Hong Kong hotel *room rate,*

Q2: Hong Kong hotel.

The intention of the user was to locate the room rates of hotels in Hong Kong. Processing and usage of the URLs returned from *Yahoo!* is summarized in Table 1. Only 100 top-ranked URLs were chosen for processing. Among them, some URLs were removed. Examples of removed URLs include non-accessible ones, duplicates, URLs pointing to non-HTML documents[2], URLs pointing to non-English documents, etc. The sequential training strategy was used and the number of URLs used for training is shown in column *Training*. The relevancy of a site was determined by examining page contents manually.

The results of the experiments are summarized in Table 2. It can be observed that, with sequential training, the correctness for both queries reaches about 80%. Considering the big discrepancy between the keywords expressed in a user query and the exact requirement, the results are really encouraging. It justifies the basic approach described in the previous sections.

To understand why the system failed to locate some queried segments, we examined the cases where the system chose segments that did not meet query requirements. The major reason is that those returned segments contain much noise, namely the words that are very close to those used to locate queried segments. One returned segment is as follows:

"*QUEEN ELIZABETH 2. Standby fares for the six day transatlantic crossings on this famous ship are available on Nov. 21 (New York to* Southampton) *for $1,199 per person, double occupancy and on the Dec. 14 sailing (Southampton to New York) for $1,099. The single supplement is $350.*"

This segment contains words "*single*" and "*double*", symbol $ and numbers that are important clues to locate segments for room rates of hotels.

---

[2] Processing dynamic Web pages is still under development.

Accuracy	Query 1			Query 2		
	C	P	R	C	P	R
Both Types of Knowledge	81.7%	76.7%	79.3%	79.0%	87.5%	73.7%
Bayesian Only	58.3%	51.2%	69.0%	38.7%	34.0%	42.1%
Navigation Only	36.7%	28.8%	55.6%	29.0%	26.8%	39.5%

* C for correctness, P for precision and R for recall

Table 3: Effects of Using Different Types of Knowledge

Correctness	Query 1: Level=			Query 2: Level=		
	I	1	2	I	1	2
	31/60	27/60	2/60	24/62	12/62	26/62
Both Types of Knowledge	0.838	0.815	0.5	0.875	0.917	0.654
Bayesian Only	0.484	0.704	0.5	0.333	0.75	0.269
Navigation Only	0.212	0.6	0	0.125	0.583	0.308

* I means irrelevant

Table 4: Analysis of Different Types of Knowledge

There are a number of reasons that the system failed to locate a queried segment. Among four such cases of Q1, three of them were caused by the low confidence of being classified as queried segments, which indicates there is deficiency in the generated classification knowledge. Another such case resulted from deprecated use of HTML tags in the original document: A hyperlink uses an image element as the content but leaves the attribute ALT of tag IMG blank. As a result, the system could not find any descriptive information about the link and thus ignored the path that leads to the queried segment.

5.4 Effectiveness of the Knowledge

To verify the effectiveness of using the two types of knowledge, navigation and classification, we modified the system so that it can be configured to apply only one type of knowledge in the process of learning and locating.

Two queries and the testing environment are the same as Table 1. The results are summarized in Table 3. The results of using both types of knowledge are also included for easy comparison.

It can be clearly seen that, the system employing both types of knowledge performs much better than those that employ only one type of knowledge. To analyze the reason for the poor performance of using only one type of knowledge, we classified sites by the level of the queried segment. In Table 4, the title cells specifies the level distribution and the fraction stands for among all test sites, how many of them belong to the level. Usually the coarser the query, the more sites belong to the level above one. The correctness of each group is reported in table cells.

One finding is that the system with one type of knowledge works reasonably only when the queried segment occurs on the first page. Its ability to filter irrelevant sites and to navigate through hyperlinks is very limited. In contrast, employing two types of knowledge manifests good performance of irrelevance filtering and navigation. Even if the queried segment is on the first page, using one type of knowledge is still less accurate then using two types of knowledge. The coordination of navigation knowledge and classification knowledge provides a good way to process Web queries.

5.5 Effects of Training Strategies

Our system supports three training strategies, *sequential training*, *random training* and *interleaved training*. This group of experiments was designed to find out which training strategy provides best performance in terms of both accuracy and efficiency. Besides the training strategies, the training size was another focus of this part. In an online query system, asking users to browse many sites is impractical. In our tests, we varied the training size from 3 to 10 for each training method. For interleaved training, the stopping criterion of training was a pre-defined number of browsed sites, i.e. the training size. The two queries of hotel room rates were used again. Observations are reported as follows. Figures are omitted in the interest of space.

- Random training performs badly in terms of effectiveness and efficiency. Assumption that randomly picked sites are more representative than those on the top of the returned list is not true.

- As the training size increases, the difference between sequential training and interleaved training is enlarged. With 10 training sites, interleaved training beats sequential training by 10% in all effectiveness metrics. The better performance of interleaved training comes from its way of updating knowledge -- updating it when the system makes a mistake.

- In terms of efficiency, interleaved training strategy is also the best. Relative path length for a right "*Found*" segment is in the range of 1.0 to 1.2. That means the system almost always navigates through the shorted path to locate a result. The absolute path length for a right "Not Found" is from 1 to 1.5 pages.

A final note is that, when interleaved training strategy was used with 10 training sites, the number of wrong decisions of Q1 was reduced from 11 to 4 (refer to Table 2). Obviously the knowledge learned by using interleaved training improved greatly.

5.6 Experiments on a Range of Queries

We made some observations of issues related to implementing a Web query processor from two queries concerning room rates of hotels. To better evaluate the effectiveness and efficiency of such a processor, we tested a range of queries on it. Three query requirements with distinct characteristics were selected.

QR1: *room rates of Hong Kong hotels* (included for comparison). It targets at prices, which is well defined and easy to identify by a user during the browsing process. The system is expected to extract the price information during the locating process.

Query Requirement (QR)	Keyword Query (KQ)
QR1: room rates of Hong Kong hotels	KQ11: "Hong Kong hotel room rate"
	KQ12: "Hong Kong hotel"
QR2: admission requirements on graduate applicants	KQ21: "requirements graduate applicant"
	KQ22: "graduate applicant"
QR3: data mining researcher	KQ3: "data mining researcher"

Table 5: Query Requirements and Keyword Queries

Performance	QR1		QR2		QR3
	KQ11	KQ12	KQ21	KQ22	KQ3
Correctness	0.93	0.9	0.84	0.91	0.83
Precision	0.92	0.92	0.85	0.88	0.64
Recall	0.88	0.94	0.94	0.91	0.67
Relative Path Length (Found)	1	1.21	1.08	1.1	1
Absolute Path Length (Not Found)	1.3	1.57	2.5	1.76	1.67

Table 6: Results of A Range of Queries

QR2: *admission requirements*. A user may not know the exact query requirements when she/he issues the keyword query. During the browsing process, she/he makes it clear that the requirements concern concrete items such as degree, GPA, GRE, TOEFL, etc. The system is expected to extract these items as query results. Compared to QR 1, the query results have larger variance because they may contain different sets of items as the need is.

QR3: *data mining researcher*. The query target is in fact a concept. The user wants to extract segments of pages as evidence that a person is a data mining researcher. It is even hard for human readers to tell what these segments should contain and such decision is very subjective. During the browsing process, the user gets to know a data mining researcher can be reflected by research interests, research projects, professional activity, etc. The system is expected to recognize the pieces of the evidence and return the correct segments.

For the first two query requirements, we issued two keyword queries with different precision. All five keyword queries are listed in Table 5. For each keyword query, from the URLs returned by *Yahoo!*, we collected the top 100 and cleaned them for later tests[3]. The interleaved training strategy was used with training size of 10.

The quantitative results are presented in Table 6. Our system works well for the first 4 queries. Accuracy is above 80% and in some queries it reaches 90%. For the last query, precision and recall are not as high as those are in other queries. Fortunately the system is still capable of filtering out irrelevant sites, thus to make the correctness reasonably good. The relative path length to locate a queried segment is close to 1. The absolute path length in an irrelevant site is no more than 2.5 pages.

---

[3] Manual check of each site . . . prevented us from enlarging the URL list. We assume the system will process other URLs with the same performance as it does with the first 100.

Another observation is that the performance of our system is not affected much by how precise the keyword query is. Thus users do not need to worry about the exact words when they issue the queries. In the browsing process they can tell the requirements by their actions. The system will learn them and use them in the locating process.

6. Conclusion

In this paper, we proposed a novel approach for processing queries on the Web. Taking such approach, a user can issue queries in free text sentences and get the results in the form of segments containing the required information. Minimum involvement is required from the user to train the system. To process a query, a general-purpose search engine is employed to get the initial relevant URLs, which are taken as the input of a series of browsing and locating processes. During the browsing processes, the system learns user requirements and the way he navigates through the hyperlinks to locate the segments that meet query requirements. During the locating processes, such learned knowledge is applied to locate the queried segments from a large number of Web pages without interaction of the user. Our preliminary experiments produced encouraging results, which shows that the proposed approach is able to tackle the difficult problem of queries on the Web.

A prototype system has been developed based on the proposed approach. More comprehensive experiments are being conducted. Our future work includes better knowledge representation and more sophisticated algorithms for learning and applying knowledge. To process a wide range of Web queries, HTML page segmentation is another issue that deserves further study.

Acknowledgement

This work is partially supported by a grant from the National 973 project of China (No. G1998030414) and a grant from the Research Grant Council of the Hong Kong Special Administrative Region, China (AOE98/99.EG01)

References

[1] N. Ashish, C. Knoblock. Wrapper Generation for Semi-structured Internet Sources. *SIGMOD Record*, 26(4), pp. 8-15, Dec. 1997.

[2] G. Arocena and A. Mendelzon. WebOQL: Restructuring Documents, Databases, and Webs. In *Proc. of ICDE 98*, pp. 24-33, Feb. 1998.

[3] M. Balabanovic. An Adaptive Web Page Recommendation Service. In *Proc. of 1ˢᵗ International Conference on Autonomous Agents*, pp. 378-385, 1997.

[4] S. Brin, L. Page. The Anatomy of a Large-Scale Hypertextual Web Search Engine. In *Proc. of the 7ᵗʰ WWW Conference*, pp. 107-117, 1998.

[5] M. Craven, D. DiPasquo, D. Freitag, A. McCallum, T. Mitchell, K. Nigam and S. Slattery. Learning to Extract Symbolic Knowledge from the World Wide Web. In *Proc. of AAAI-98*, 1998.

[6] S. Chakrabarti, B. Dom and P. Indyk. Enhanced Hypertext Categorization using Hyperlinks. In *Proc. of ACM-SIGMOD 98*, pp. 307-318, Jun. 1998.

[7] D. DiPasquo. Using HTML Formatting to Aid in Natural Language Processing on the World Wide Web. Senior Honors Thesis, School of Computer Science, CMU, May 1998.

[8] D. Embley, Y. Jiang, Y. Ng. Record-Boundary Discovery in Web Documents. In *Proc. of ACM-SIGMOD* 99, pp. 467-478, May 1999.

[9] M. Fernandez, D. Florescu, Dan Suciu. A Query Language for a Web-Site Management System. *SIGMOD Record*, 26(3), pp. 4-11, 1997.

[10] D. Florescu, A. Levy and A. Mendelzon. Database Techniques for the World Wide Web: A Survey. *SIGMOD Record*, 27(3), pp. 59-74, Sep. 1998.

[11] D. Gibson, J. Kleinberg and P. Raghavan. Inferring Web Communities from Link Topologies. In *Proc. of ACM Hypertext 98*, pp. 225-234, Jun. 1998.

[12] J. Hammer, M. Breunig, H. Garcia-Molina, S. Nestorov, V. Vassalos, R. Yerneni. Template-Based Wrappers in the TSIMMIS System. In *Proc. of ACM-SIGMOD*, pp. 532-535, May 1997.

[13] T. Joachims, D. Freitag, T. Mitchell. WebWatcher: A Tour Guide for the World Wide Web. In *Proc. of the 1997 International Joint Conference on Artificial Intelligence*, pp. 770-775, Aug. 1997.

[14] D. Konopnicki, O. Shmueli. W3QS: A Query System for the World Wide Web. In *Proc. of VLDB 95*, pp. 54-65, 1995.

[15] S. Lawrence and C.L. Giles. Accessibility of information on the Web. *Nature*, 400(8), pp. 107-109, Jul. 1999.

[16] L. Liu, W. Han, D. Buttler, C. Pu, W. Tang. An XML-Based Wrapper Generator for Web Information Extraction. In *Proc.of ACM-SIGMOD 99*, pp. 540-543, May 1999.

[17] F. Menczer, R. Belew. Adaptive Retrieval Agents: Internalizing Local Context and Scaling up to the Web. *Technical Report* CS98-579, University of California, San Diego, 1998. Available: http://www.cse.ucsd.edu/ ~rik/*papers/arachnid/arachnd-mlj.ps*.

[18] A. Mendelzon, G. Mihaila, T. Milo. Querying the World Wide Web. *International. Journal on Digital Libraries*, 1(1), pp. 54-67, 1997.

[19] A. McCallum, K. Nigam. A Comparison of Event Models for Naïve Bayes Text Classification. *Working Notes of AAAI/ICML-98 Workshop on Learning for Text Categorization*, pp. 41-48, 1998.

[20] M. Pazzani, J. Muramatsu, D. Billsus. Syskill & Webert: Identifying Interesting Web Sites. In *Proc. of AAAI-96*, pp. 54-61, 1996.

[21] A. Sahuguet, F. Azavant. Building light-weight wrappers for legacy Web data-sources using W4F. In *Proc. of VLDB 99*, pp. 738-741, Sep. 1999.

Optimizing Queries On Compressed Bitmaps

Sihem Amer-Yahia
AT&T Labs–Research
sihem@research.att.com

Theodore Johnson
AT&T Labs–Research
johnsont@research.att.com

Abstract

Bitmap indices are used by DBMS's to accelerate decision support queries. A significant advantage of bitmap indices is that complex logical selection operations can be performed very quickly, by performing bit-wise AND, OR, and NOT operators. Although they can be space inefficient for high cardinality attributes, the space use of compressed bitmaps compares well to other indexing methods. Oracle and Sybase IQ are two commercial products that make extensive use of compressed bitmap indices.

Our recent research showed that there are several fast algorithms for evaluating Boolean operators on compressed bitmaps. Depending on the nature of the operand bitmaps (their format, density and clusterdness) and the operation to be performed (AND, OR, NOT, ...), these algorithms can have different execution times. We present a linear time dynamic programming search strategy based on a cost model to optimize query expression evaluation plans. We also present rewriting heuristics that encourage better algorithms assignments. Our performance results show that the optimizer requires a negligible amount of time to execute, and that optimized complex queries can execute up to three times faster than unoptimized queries on real data.

Proceedings of the 26th VLDB Conference, Cairo, Egypt, 2000.

1 Introduction

A *bitmap index* is a bit string in which each bit is mapped to a record ID (RID) of a relation. A bit in the bitmap index is set (to 1) if the corresponding RID has property P (i.e., the RID represents a customer that lives in New York), and is reset (to 0) otherwise. In typical usage, the predicate P is true for a record if it has the value a for attribute A. One such predicate is associated to one bitmap index for each unique value of the attribute A. The predicates can be more complex, for example bitslice indices [18] and precomputed complex selection predicates [21].

One advantage of bitmap indices is that complex selection predicates can be computed very quickly, by performing bit-wise AND, OR, and NOT operations on the bitmap indices. Furthermore, the indexable selection predicates can involve many attributes. Let's consider some examples, using a customer database with schema *Customer(Name, Lives_in, Works_in, Car, Number_of_children, Has_cable, Has_cellular)*

- Suppose that we want to select all customers who live in the New York city tri-state area and who drive a car that is frequently purchased in the state in which they live. Then the selection condition is, e.g. *(Lives_in="NJ" AND (Car="Ford Expedition" OR Car="GMC Suburban")) OR (Lives_in="NY" AND (Car="Honda Accord" OR Car="Ford Taurus")) OR (Lives_in="CT" AND (Car="Mercedes 500SL" OR Car="Cadillac Seville")).*

- Suppose that we want to select all customers who work in a state different than the one in which they live, have one or more children, subscribe to a cable service, but do not have a cellular phone. Then the selection condition is *((Lives_in="AL" AND NOT Works_in="AL") OR $\cdots$ OR (Lives_in="WY" AND NOT Works_in="WY")) AND (NOT Number_of_children = 0) AND Has_cable="Y" AND Has_cellular = "N"*

While conventional indices in general cannot handle these types of selections easily, bitmap indices can. These properties of bitmap indices have led to considerable interest in their use in Decision Support Systems (DSS). O'Neil and Quass [18] provide an excellent discussion of the architecture and use of bitmap indices. O'Neil and Graefe [16] show that bitmap indices can be used as join indices for evaluating complex DSS queries on star schemas. O'Neil and Quass [18] point out that bitmap indices not only accelerate the evaluation of complex Boolean query expressions, but can also be used to answer some aggregate queries directly. Several database management system vendors have incorporated bitmap index technology into their products [24, 19]. See [11] for a discussion of the uses of bitmap indexing in Oracle.

A problem with using uncompressed (*Verbatim*) bitmap indices is their high storage costs and potentially high expression evaluation costs when the indexed attribute has a high cardinality. One method for dealing with the problem of using bitmap indices on high-cardinality attributes is to compress the bitmaps. For example, in a secondary index B-tree each unique key value might be shared by many records in a relation. Oracle uses compressed bitmaps to represent these sets of records [19]. A considerable body of work has been devoted to the study of bitmap index compression (see [15]). The use of bitmap compression has many potential performance advantages: less disk space is required to store the indices, the indices can be read from disk into memory faster, and more indices can be cached in memory. Some Boolean operation evaluation algorithms which operate on compressed bitmaps, without having to decompress them, might be faster than same operations on the Verbatim bitmaps. However, the use of bitmap compression can introduce some problems. The data-dependent nature of bitmap compression makes it difficult to apply the existing optimal (uncompressed) bitmap design theory [25, 26, 3, 4]. If the bitmap must be decompressed before performing Boolean operations, the decompression overhead might outweigh any savings in disk space or bitmap loading time.

In a recent research paper [13], we have made a detailed study of the performance of algorithms for compressed bitmap indices. In particular, we analyzed several algorithms for performing Boolean operations between (possibly compressed) bitmaps. We found that the performance of these algorithms varied widely depending on the Boolean operation to be performed and on the properties of the operand bitmaps. No single algorithm was always the best one, and in many occasions there were orders of magnitude difference in the operation execution times.

Bitmap compression presents a number of bitmap index design issues, including 1) optimal bitmap decomposition [3, 4], 2) choosing optimal compression algorithms for storage [13] and 3) optimal evaluation of query expressions (composed of several Boolean operators) over compressed bitmaps.

In this paper, we solve the third problem, of optimizing Boolean query expression evaluation. This problem is the most pressing, because the first two problems can be partially solved with heuristics [4, 13]. Furthermore, choosing an optimal storage method requires an understanding of the Boolean predicate evaluation workload. If we know how to better evaluate a query expression involving several bitmaps, it can help making better decisions about the formats under which these bitmaps should be stored. Therefore, understanding how to optimally evaluate complex Boolean predicates is a necessary prerequisite for solving the other two problems.

Because the bitmaps are used as indices, any query expression optimizer must execute very quickly. We make the following three contributions:
(i) We present an $O(n)$ algorithm to make a globally optimal assignment of operation evaluation algorithms to a fixed query expression parse tree, where n is the number of operations in the tree.
(ii) We create an empirical cost model of Boolean operation evaluation and bitmap format conversion.
(iii) We present fast query expression parse tree rewriting heuristics that work with the global optimizer to further reduce the expression evaluation time.

We implemented a compressed bitmap index and incorporated the expression optimizer. We ran a suite of experiments to show the value of having an optimizer. For example, in the case of one experiment with real data using BBC encoded bitmaps [2, 1], optimizing the evaluation plan results in a two- to five-fold speed improvement, and the improvement increases with increasing attribute cardinality. Our optimizer achieves comparable speedups on complex expressions through the use of multiple operation evaluation algorithms and some query rewrite rules.

The paper is organized as follows. We present in Section 2 previous results about a performance study of compressed bitmaps and explain what influences the evaluation of query expressions in this context. We then present our optimization strategy and cost model (Section 3). We also describe new rewriting rules that we incorporated as heuristics in our optimizer to speed up query expression evaluation. Section 4 briefly presents the main implementation modules. Finally, we give our performance results (Section 5).

2 Bitmap Operation Performance

In a previous paper [13], we measured and analyzed the performance of compressed bitmaps used for data warehousing. In this section, we review these measurements, with a particular focus on factors that affect the performance of evaluating a query expression.

A bitmap is a representation of a set, where each bit represents an element of some common domain. If the bit is set (to one), the element is a member of the set; else the bit is reset (to zero). When used as a bitmap index, the bits represent records in a relation and a bitmap is created for each distinct value of the indexed attributes in the relation. In an index where the bitmap can be compressed and operators can use compressed bitmaps as input, a bitmap (i.e., a set) may have several possible representations or formats. It is always possible to translate a bitmap from one representation to another without loss of information.

Boolean operations on bitmaps can be performed using several algorithms. Each of the algorithms requires the inputs to be in a certain format and produces an output in a given format. The costs of an algorithm depend on the properties of the input bitmaps and the Boolean operation (AND, NOT, ...) to be performed.

The set represented by a bitmap can therefore be stored and manipulated while it is in one of several different formats, some of which bear little resemblance to bitstrings. We might be more precise to say that we work with special set representations rather than bitmaps. However "bitmap" is the established term and we continue to use it.

We first present the different bitmap formats and the Boolean operation evaluation algorithms we are using in this paper. We finish this section by introducing the problem of evaluating a Boolean query expression on bitmaps.

Verbatim: The bitmap is represented as bit string.

Run Length Encoding (RLE): The bitmap is represented as a list of differences in bit positions of successive set bits. These differences are stored as four byte integers (by restricting the size of the bitmap, they can also be stored in two byte integers). In this paper, we use only one-sided RLE codes (i.e., we represent only runs of zeros, not runs of ones).

Gzip: A Verbatim bitmap that has been compressed using zlib [5].

ExpGol: A RLE bitmap that has been compressed using the variable bit length encoding described in [15]. We use only the one-sided ExpGol encoding.

BBC: A Verbatim bitmap that has been compressed using the variable byte length encoding described in [2, 1]. We use only the one-sided BBC encoding.

A wide variety of other bitmap representations have been proposed. For example, one could use two-sided codes, list of set bit positions instead of run length encodings, or variable byte length representations of the run lengths [17]. However, this collection of formats is representative of the best bitmap formats and is sufficient for our optimization study.

There are several algorithms for evaluating a Boolean operation between two operands, each using specific formats for their inputs and having a different cost. The algorithms we use in this paper are the following(for more details, see [13]).

Basic: The two input operands are in the Verbatim format, and the output is also in the Verbatim format. The output is computed by taking the word-size *Boolean_op* between the two inputs. The following code fragment implements the Basic algorithm to compute the OR of bitmaps rbm and lbm, and store the result in lbm (which should be arrays of the largest possible integer type):

```
BitmapLength=MaxLength(lbm, rmb);
for (i=0;i<BitmapLength;i++) lbm[i] |= rmb[i];
```

Inplace: One of the operands is in the Verbatim format, the other can be in RLE, ExpGol or BBC. The second bitmap is applied to Verbatim bitmap in an operation-specific manner. In the case of an OR operation the bits indicated by the second bitmap are set in the Verbatim bitmap. The output is a Verbatim bitmap. The following code fragment implements the OR operation, where lbm is a character array and rbm is an integer array:

```
currpos = -1;
for (i=0;i<NumBitsRhs;i++)
    currpos+=rbm[i];
    bytepos=currpos/8; bitpos=currpos%8;
    lbm[bytepos] |=1 << bitpos;
```

Merge: This algorithm takes input operands in the RLE format and produces an RLE bitmap. The output is created by merging the inputs, and producing an output bit as required by the operation being evaluated. The following code fragment implements the AND operation, where lbm and rbm are the operands, stored as integer arrays, and obm is an integer array that is large enough to store the result:

```
obit = -1; opos = 0; lbit = lbm[0]-1;
lpos = 0; rbit = rbm[0]-1; rpos = 0;
while((lpos<NumBitsLhs)&&(rpos<NumBitsRhs))
    if(lbit == rbit)
        obm[opos++]=lbit-obit; obit=lbit;
        lbit+=lbm[++lpos]; rbit+=rbm[++rpos];
    else if (lbit<rbit) lbit+=lbm[++lpos];
        else rbit+=rbm[++rpos];
```

Direct: The input and output bitmaps are in a compressed format, and the operation is specialized to execute directly on the compressed bitmaps. Antoshenkov [2, 1] presents algorithms for Direct BBC operations (which we use in this paper), and Shoshani et al. [22] present Direct operations for their hybrid bitmap encoding. Because these algorithms are very complex and depend on the format that is used, we refer the reader to [2, 1] and [22] for more details.

Note that in order to use a particular evaluation algorithm, the input bitmaps must be provided in the required format. If the inputs are not in the necessary format, they must be converted before the algorithm can be applied.

It is possible to develop variants of these four evaluation algorithms that use as input or produce as output different formats. For example, the hybrid nature of the BBC encoding allows an especially fast version of the Inplace algorithm that uses as input a Verbatim and a BBC bitmap (which we will refer to as Inplace_BBC). We also developed an Inplace algorithm that uses a bitmap in the ExpGol format instead of the RLE format (which we refer to as Inplace_ExpGol), to save on a transformation step (from ExpGol to RLE).

Boolean Operation Evaluation

Depending on the properties of the operand bitmaps, Boolean operation evaluation algorithms can have orders of magnitude differences in performance. There are two bitmap properties that can have a significant effect on format conversion and algorithm performance : their *density* and their *clusteredness*. The density of a bitmap is defined as the fraction of bits set in the bitmap. The clusteredness, or non-uniformity, or bias, of a bitmap is a measure of the departure from independence of the value of a neighboring bit. Highly clustered bitmaps tend to have all of their set bits in a few small regions of the bitmap. Due to space constraints, all of the experiments in this paper use non-clustered bitmaps (each bit is independent). See [13] for a detailed discussion of the performance effect of bitmap properties on Boolean operation evaluation.

If the output of an operation evaluated with, for e.g., Merge is used as input to an operation evaluated with Basic, the RLE output of the Merge algorithm must be converted to a Verbatim format suitable as input to the Basic algorithm. Similarly, a bitmap stored in BBC format must be converted to RLE format for use in a Merge algorithm and so on. The cost of converting bitmaps can be a significant and determining factor in choosing which algorithms to use to evaluate each operation in a query expression. See [13] for the effect of format conversion.

3 Optimizing Query Expressions

Given the wide variety of bitmap formats and evaluation algorithms, we cannot pick any single format or evaluation algorithm which is always the best one. Instead, we can optimize the evaluation plan and make use of the best bitmap format and evaluation algorithm for every operation. This optimization cannot be performed locally for each operation because the output of one operation (usually) becomes the input of another. If the format of the output is not what the next operation expects as its input, a potentially expensive format conversion is required. Therefore, optimal algorithm assignment (physical optimization) must be global. We present a fast $O(n)$ dynamic programming physical optimization algorithm.

We observed that it is possible to rewrite query expressions to obtain a faster equivalent expression. A wide variety of expression rewritings are possible. For example, one can try to combine common subexpressions. Another option is to use algebraic transformations to reduce the number of operations [25]. One can even use semantic information to obtain more efficient expressions [26]. Because we are optimizing an index structure, a very limited optimization time is available to us. The approach that we choose is to use a small collection of simple heuristic query rewritings that are robust to incorrect assumptions about the properties of the bitmaps involved in the rewritten expressions. These rewritings are inspired from our previous performance evaluation [13] and are designed to let the physical optimizer assign a better collection of algorithms to a portion of a query expression. We present the physical optimization and the cost model first, and the rewrite rules second.

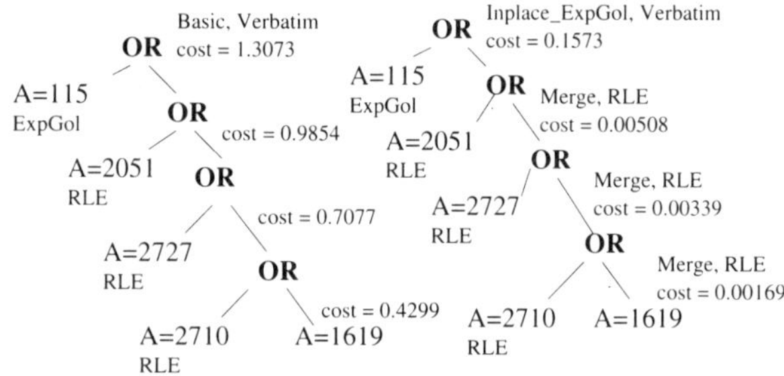

Figure 1 : A simple example

We consider a very simple example where we use a range query on a single attribute A in which each attribute value has a bitmap with density 1/3000. The query expression is the following: (A=115) OR (A=2051) OR (A=2727) OR (A=2710) OR (A=1619). This expression is as a parse tree where leaf nodes are bitmaps and interior nodes are Boolean operations. Each interior node is connected to one (case of NOT) or two subtrees (case of AND or OR). At each leaf, we know the format, density and clusteredness of the corresponding disk-resident bitmap for each value of attribute A. We can propagate this information up to the root node by computing an estimate of these properties at each interior node. For each interior node, we must assign an evaluation algorithm, and make any required format conversions.

Figure 1 shows two different algorithms assignments for the example. In one case, all the nodes are assigned the Basic algorithm and the estimated cost of the query expression is 1.3 seconds and the one. In the other case, the cost is 0.15 seconds. As can be readily seen, the optimization can have a significant effect on performance.

Optimization Algorithm

We have developed an optimization algorithm that is a variant of the well-known dynamic programming algorithm, first presented in [20]. This algorithm uses an *enumerative* search strategy but avoids enumerating all query plans by dynamically pruning suboptimal parts of the space as partial plans are generated.

Given a Boolean operation, an evaluation algorithm and the properties of the operands (format, bit density and clusteredness), we can estimate the time to perform the operation, and make any necessary format conversions (e.g., convert an RLE output to the desired Verbatim output). Therefore, the time to evaluate the whole query expression is the time to evaluate the right subtree (if any) plus the time to evaluate the left subtree (if any), plus evaluation and transformation costs at the root node. Computing the time to evaluate the subtrees is a procedure identical to that for computing the time to evaluate the whole tree. If the subtree is a leaf, the only cost is to transform the bitmap representation into the format expected by the algorithm that will be applied at its parent. Because the only interaction between the evaluation of the root and the evaluation of the subtrees is through the conversion costs, we can develop an efficient dynamic programming algorithm.

Our optimization algorithm decides, in two traversals of the parse tree, which is the best evaluation algorithm at each operation node. The algorithm starts by computing, at each operation node, the lowest cost to evaluate the expression represented by the subtree rooted at the node, for each possible output format. The optimal evaluation algorithm for each output format is also stored. By making a second pass through the tree, we make the algorithm assignments to each node.

In order to give a detailed description of the underlying dynamic programming algorithm, we need to make the following definitions:

n: A node in the query expression tree.

$p(n)$: A number in $[0, 1]$ indicating the fraction of bits set (bit density) in the bitmap output by n.

$c(n)$: A number in $[.5, 1]$ indicating the clusteredness of the bitmap output by n.

$op(n)$: Operation that node n performs. If n is a leaf, the operation is to fetch a bitmap (we set this cost to zero, as it can not be optimized). If n is an interior node, the operation is a Boolean operation.

$lc(n)$: left child of node n. $rc(n)$: right child of node n.

$\mathcal{A}$: Algorithms used to evaluate the Boolean operations. $\mathcal{A}(op)$ a subset of $\mathcal{A}$, contains the set of algorithms that can be used to evaluate op.

$\mathcal{F}$: Collection of bitmap formats.

$F_o(A)$: Output format of algorithm $A \in \mathcal{A}$.

$F_l(A)$: Input format of the left operand of algorithm $A \in \mathcal{A}$.

$F_r(A)$: Input format of the right operand of algorithm $A \in \mathcal{A}$.

$F_i(n)$: Format in which leaf node n is stored.

$conv(F_1, F_2, p, c)$: Time to convert a bitmap with bit density p and clusteredness c from format F_1 to format F_2.

$ev(op, A, p_l, c_l, p_r, c_r)$ is the time to evaluate operation op using algorithm A, where the left operand has bit density p_l and clusteredness c_l, and the right operand has bit density p_r and clusteredness c_r.

$cost(n, F)$: The optimal total time to evaluate the query expression represented by the tree rooted at n and producing output in format F.

We can derive the following equations for $cost(n, F)$ as follows:

$\bullet cost(n, F) = conv(F_i(n), F(n), p(n), c(n))$ if n is a leaf

$\bullet cost(n, F) = min_{A \in \mathcal{A}(op(n))}\{conv(F_o(A), F, p(n), c(n)) + ev(op(n), A, p(lc(n)), c(lc(n))) + cost(F_l(A), lc(n))\}$
if n is unary

$\bullet cost(n, F) = min_{A \in \mathcal{A}(op(n))}\{conv(F_o(A), F, p(n), c(n)) + ev(op(n), A, p(lc(n)), c(lc(n)), p(rc(n)), c(rc(n))) + cost(F_l(A), lc(n)) + cost(F_r(A), rc(n))\}$
if n is binary .

If we precompute $cost(lc(n), F)$ and $cost(rc(n), F)$ for each $F \in \mathcal{F}$, we can evaluate $cost(n, F')$ in $O(|\mathcal{A}|)$ time. We need to evaluate this function for every node n in the expression tree T, and for every format $F \in \mathcal{F}$. Therefore, computing the minimum time to evaluate a query expression requires $O(|T| * |\mathcal{A}| * |\mathcal{F}|) = O(|T|)$ time.

Cost Model

Our optimization algorithm requires a cost model for each Boolean operation evaluation $ev(op, A, p_l, c_l, p_r, c_r)$, a cost model for the transformation costs $conv(F_1, F_2, p, c)$, and a way to estimate the properties of the bitmap produced by each node in the tree.

The execution times of the algorithms are difficult to model analytically. In addition, analytical models can be fragile. Instead, we developed an empirical performance model. We measured the time to perform each operation using each applicable algorithm for a range of the bitmap operand parameters (see [13] for a discussion of the relevant performance parameters). Given a particular function $ev(op, A, p_l, c_l, p_r, c_r)$ to evaluate, we use linear interpolation through the closest measured data points. In a similar manner, we create an empirical cost model to estimate $conv(F_1, F_2, p, c)$. While constructing these models is expensive (several hours of execution time), it only needs to be constructed once per installation site, and is robust to changes in implementation and local conditions.

The cost model needs an estimate of the density and clusteredness of each operand bitmap. The density and clusterdness of the leaf node bitmaps can be computed at compression time. The bitmaps output by the interior nodes are computed dynamically, so we need to estimate their density and clusteredness. One estimator is to assume that bitmaps are uncorrelated, except for bitmaps of values of the same attribute. Let p_l and p_r be the density of the right and left operand bitmaps, and let p_o be the density of the output bitmap. Similarly, let c_l and c_r be the clusteredness of the right and left operand bitmaps, and let c_o be the clusteredness of the output bitmap. Then:

$p_o = p_l + p_r - p_l * p_r$, OR, different attribute

$p_o = p_l + p_r$, OR, same attribute

$p_o = p_l * p_r$, AND, different attribute

$p_o = 0$, AND, same attribute

$c_o = (c_l + c_r)/2$

For a NOT operation, $c_o = c_l$ and $p_o = 1 - p_l$. The bit density and clusteredness can be computed for every node in the expression tree using a simple recursive procedure. In our case, we do it when building the tree.

Rewriting NOT-Free Expressions

Suppose that we have an expression involving only OR operations. If the operands are sparse, then Inplace is a fast evaluation algorithm. The left operand must be Verbatim, the right RLE (or BBC, or ExpGol), and the output is Verbatim. We can minimize the number of conversions into Verbatim by reorganizing the query expression to ensure that the result of an OR (that is in Verbatim) is given as the left operand of the next OR operation. To encourage the physical optimizer to use the Inplace algorithm, we need to convert the tree of OR operations from a bushy tree to a left-deep tree (to minimize the number of conversions to Verbatim), and put the densest bitmap at the leftmost leaf, since making this operand a right operand gives the least performance improvement when using Inplace. This transformation, illustrated in Figure 2, can always be applied because of the commutativity and associativity properties of the OR operation.

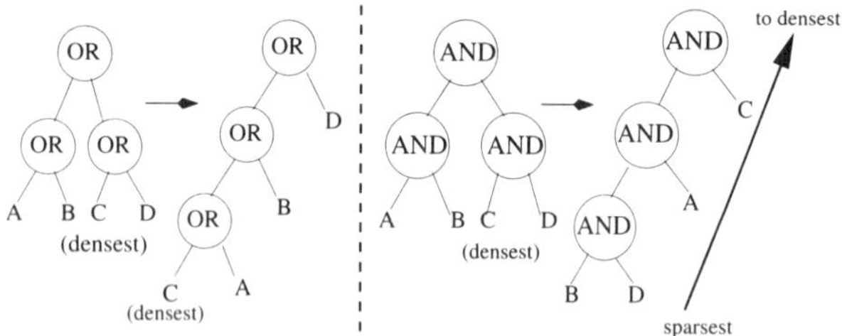

Figure 2 : Transformation of ANDs and ORs

Let us now suppose that we have a query expression involving only AND operations. We know, from our previous experiments, that the Merge and Direct algorithms are the fastest ways to perform the AND operation when the operands are sparse. Merge requires both input operands to be in a RLE format and Direct requires them to be in a BBC format. To encourage the use of these algorithms, we convert a bushy tree of AND operations into a left-deep tree, with the operands sorted from the sparsest on the bottom to the densest at the top. The sparse operands are clustered together and are likely to be evaluated with Merge or Direct. When the density reaches a certain limit, we expect the optimizer to assign a Reverse Inplace algorithm (an Inplace algorithm where the left operand has to be in RLE/BBC/ExpGol and the right one in Verbatim). The format of the result is then Verbatim and the optimizer assigns to the remaining operations an Inplace algorithm. This transformation is also illustrated in Figure 2.

A significant advantage of these transformations is that they tend to be resilient to mistakes in the assumed formats of the operands. Let's consider the case of an OR operation. The Inplace algorithm can take RLE, ExpGol, or BBC as the right operand format. If the right operand is instead supplied as Verbatim, then the reasonably efficient Basic algorithm can be used. With the AND operation, we expect that the format of sparse operands deep in the tree to be in RLE or BBC format. If one or more is instead Verbatim, then the evaluation algorithm switches to Inplace and/or Basic.

Suppose that we have a two level expression, e.g. an AND of OR clauses, or an OR of AND clauses. The OR and AND transformations presented above can still be applied within their own subtrees. These transformations can be applied iteratively because the transformations are not likely to change the format of the output. The output format of an OR subtree that has a sparse result is likely to be RLE or BBC (because the Merge and Direct algorithms are fast for sparse bitmaps), which is what our AND subtree rewriting expects. The output of a sparse AND might be in a Verbatim format, but this does not affect the validity of the OR subtree rewriting.

For three or more levels, the assumptions behind the transformations becomes questionable. However, there will be relatively few operations so far from the leaf level, so most of the expression will benefit from the rewrite.

Creating AND_NOT and OR_NOT

These rewritings aim to reduce the number of operations in a query expression by absorbing the NOT operation into an AND or an OR when it is possible.

a AND NOT b is equivalent to a AND_NOT b.

a OR NOT b is equivalent to a OR_NOT b.

AND_NOT and OR_NOT are two new operations for which we have fast algorithms to evaluate (Oracle uses the AND_NOT operation, calling it MINUS [11]). The benefit of using these operators is not only to reduce the number of operations in the expression, but to allow the use of faster evaluation algorithms that use and accept a wider variety of bitmap formats.

The AND_NOT operator can be evaluated by Inplace, having performance similar to that of the OR operation evaluated by Inplace. The AND_NOT operator can also be evaluated by Merge and Direct, with performance between that of AND and OR evaluated by Merge and Direct. The OR_NOT operator can be evaluated by Inplace, with performance similar to that of the AND operation evaluated by Inplace. However, there is no good implementation of OR_NOT using the Merge or Direct algorithm (assuming one-sided codes).

The AND_NOT and OR_NOT transformations can be integrated with the local AND and OR subtree rewritings. After creating the (AND/OR) left-deep subtree and performing reordering, the NOT operations are absorbed into the parent operations (except for any NOT operation which is the left child of the left-most leaf). There are some considerations for operand reordering when NOT operations are absorbed – the density of a negated operand should be computed as though the NOT operation is not applied (as it will be absorbed). After rewriting the expression, the properties of the nodes in the subtree might have to be recomputed (because they depend upon the properties of their children, which might have changed).

4 Implementation

We built a prototype implementation of a compressed bitmap index that incorporates expression optimization. The index has three major components: a compressed bitmap object, a storage manager, and the optimized plan generator. The compressed bitmap object is a convenient abstraction for handling a bitmap and performing the necessary actions, such as format conversions and operation evaluation. Each bitmap object represents a bitmap of a particular length. Multiple bitmap objects can exist simultaneously.

The storage manager permits the convenient retrieval of bitmaps (i.e., in their disk-resident format), given the attribute name and the attribute value. Because we have assumed that only low to moderate cardinality attributes are indexed, the attribute-value-to-bitmap index is very simple (Oracle uses a more sophisticated index, see [19, 11]). The storage manager also records bitmap density and clusteredness statistics for use by the optimizer. We store all bitmap indices for all attributes in a single file for convenient access during the optimization and evaluation stage. The layout of the index is determined at index creation time. However we have not addressed optimal bitmap layout.

The storage manager breaks each bitmap into fixed size verbatim *bitmap blocks* before compression and disk storage. This horizontal partitioning significantly reduces operation evaluation time by increasing the likelyhood that a bitmap is in the CPU cache when it is used as an operand (e.g., an operand is usually the result of a recent operation, or was recently loaded from disk). For example, we found that performing an operation between two 8 Mbyte verbatim operands takes .91 seconds when an 8Mbyte block size is used, but .088 seconds when a 64 Kbyte block size is used.

The optimizer uses the algorithms we have described to rewrite an expression tree and make an evaluation algorithm assignment at each interior node. We walk this tree inorder traversing the left branch first to generate an evaluation plan. Finally, a simple program uses the bitmap objects and the storage manager to execute the plan.

5 Experiments

To test the beneficial effect of our optimizer, we built bitmap indices on a synthetic data set and a real data set using the Gzip, BBC, and ExpGol compression algorithms and with varying bitmap block sizes. As was suggested in [13], we compressed bitmaps that had a bit density of .05 or less, and stored the denser bitmaps Verbatim.

Data Sets: The synthetic data set has seven attributes, with attribute cardinalities 3, 10, 30, 100, 300, 1000, 3000. Each attribute value is an integer chosen independently and uniformly randomly from the attribute range. This data set is intended to aid in exploring performance trends rather than to model a real data set. Therefore, in addition, we extracted data from an actual data set, which contains information about subscribers to an AT&T service. The real data has seventeen attributes with cardinalities 3, 3, 3, 4, 7, 50, 53, 59, 209, 241, 251, 383, 792, 793, 856, 995, 1079. The attribute values are strings, and the distribution of attribute values of each attribute is highly skewed. Every attribute is indexed in both data sets.

The compressed bitmap indices are fairly space efficient. Their size is not much larger than the size of the data set when compressed. In the case of the synthetic data (16 million tuples, total size of 356 MB, compressed size of 144 MB), the size of the BBC index is 182 MB, the size of the ExpGol index is 144 MB and the size of the Gzip index is 226 MB. For the real data (6 million tuples, total size of 427 MB, compressed size of 86 MB), the size of the BBC index is 110 MB, the size of the ExpGol index is 94 MB and the size of the Gzip index is 127 MB. In the case of the real data, all 17 attributes are indexed with 7.3 bits per tuple per attribute (using the ExpGol compressed index).

We built indices with bitmap block sizes ranging from 8 Kbytes to 64 Kbytes to determine the effect of block size on performance. We found that performance improved as the block size increases (faster queries and smaller indices), but that the improvement is minor after a block size of 32 Kbytes.

Queries: A significant advantage of bitmap indices is their ability to handle complex ad-hoc queries. However, one cannot show trends with ad-hoc queries. Instead, we used the following types of parameterizable queries:

Range: Parameterized by attribute A and range k, a range query is $(A = v_1)$ OR $\cdots$ OR $(A = v_k)$ where v_i's are randomly chosen in the range of A.

Inequality: Parameterized by attributes A, B and range k, an inequality query is $(A = v_1$ AND NOT $B = w_1)$ OR $\cdots$ OR $(A = v_k$ AND NOT $B = w_k)$ where v_i's and w_i's are randomly chosen

Although both of these query types are essentially ranges, the inequality queries are complex conditions difficult to evaluate using conventional indices and difficult to optimize using ad-hoc techniques. Inequality queries will also show the benefit of the NOT rewriting strategy.

Measured Times: In our experiments, we measure only the CPU time to evaluate the Boolean expression, not the time to fetch the compressed bitmaps from disk. This measurement strategy greatly simplified the experiments as we did not need to flush the disk cache between trials. Furthermore, the index loading time depends on the disk-resident bitmap format and the index layout, neither of which we optimize in this paper. Each data point represents the average of 11 trials. To ensure consistent measurements, for each data point we make a first evaluation and throw away the measurement, to ensure that the cache is warm for the remaining trials.

One component of the query evaluation time is the optimization time. However, even for very complex queries (i.e., inequality queries over 200 values) the optimization time was negligible (1/10 of the total time for some complex queries). In the rest of the discussion, we focus on the query evaluation time.

Range Queries: In Figure 3, we show the time to perform a range query over 20 values of an attribute of the synthetic data as the attribute cardinality is varied. For the BBC and the ExpGol compressed bitmaps, we show the two extreme evaluation plans: *Basic*, which performs no rewriting and assigns the Basic evaluation algorithm at each operator node (the default evaluation plan), and *All_opt*, which uses all of the optimization techniques we have discussed. In the case of Gzip bitmaps, *Basic* and *All_opt* are equivalent: the optimizer always assigns the Basic algorithm. The bitmap block size is 64 Kbytes.

We note that Figure 3 is a log-log chart to better show performance trends over a wide range of attribute cardinalities. The optimizer significantly reduces expression evaluation time for the BBC encoded bitmap indices, and for the ExpGol bitmap indices when the attribute cardinality is moderately large. This difference is due to the availability or unavailability of fast

evaluation algorithms. Note also that Gzip encoded bitmaps can evaluate ranges faster than ExpGol encoded bitmaps for attributes with small to moderate cardinalities, indicating that using multiple compression schemes at index creation time can improve performance.

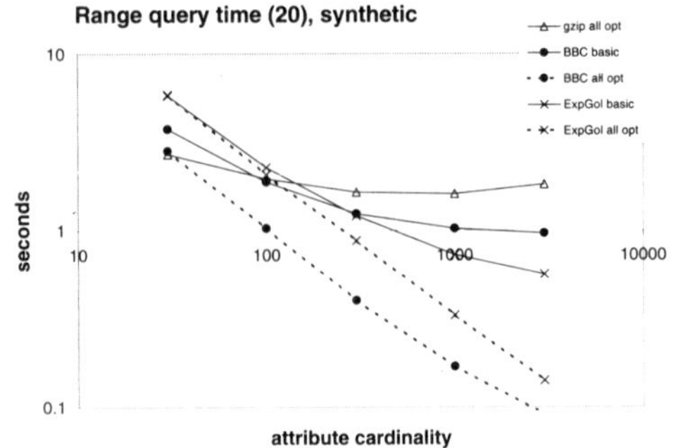

Figure 3 : Time to evaluate a range query over 20 values vs. attribute cardinality (synthetic data)

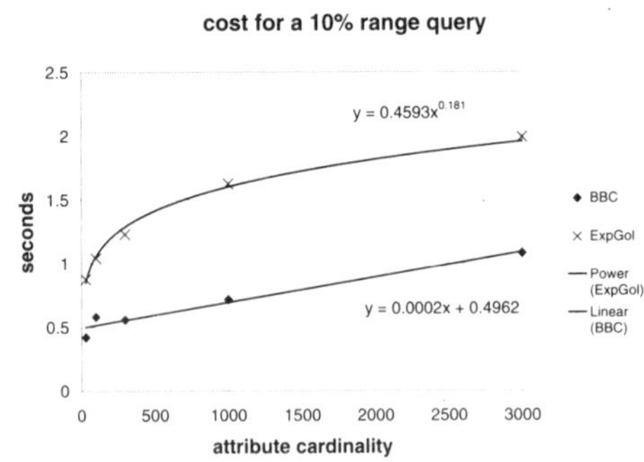

Figure 4 : Range expression evaluation time trends (synthetic data)

We find that the time to evaluate a range query expression is very well fit by a linear regression on the size of the range. By interpolating, we created Figure 4 which shows the time to evaluate a range query over 10% of the attribute values as the attribute cardinality increases. This chart shows that by optimizing the evaluation of the range query, evaluating a range over 300 values of an attribute with cardinality 3000 takes only twice as long as evaluating a range over 3 values of 30. In Figure 4 we fit trend lines to the points, a

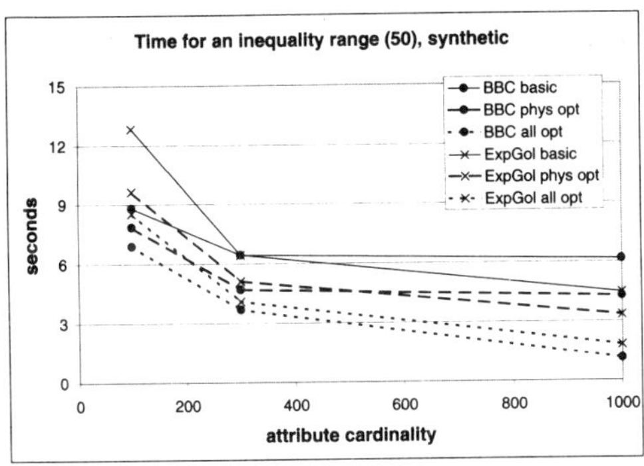

Figure 5 : Time to evaluate an inequality range over 50 values vs. attribute cardinality (synthetic data)

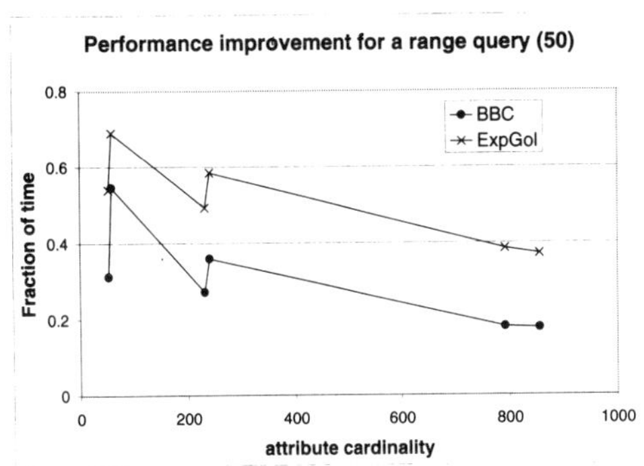

Figure 6 : Time to execute an optimized range query relative to the unoptimized query (50 values, real data)

power regression for the ExpGol encoded bitmap, and a linear regression for the BBC encoded bitmaps.

Inequality Queries: Figure 5 shows the time to evaluate an inequality query over the synthetic data. In addition to showing the time to evaluate the *Basic* plan and the *All_opt* plan, we show the time to evaluate the plan generated using the physical optimizer but with no rewriting (*Phys_only*). The performance improvement is due to absorbing the NOT operators into AND_NOT operators.

Time Ratio for Queries on Real Data: In Figure 6, we show the time to evaluate a range query using the *all opt* plan divided by the evaluation time using the *basic* plan (we change our presentation method to unclutter the charts). Note that the degree of improvement varies considerably as the attribute cardinality increases. The performance of the evaluation algorithms, and thus the optimizer, depends on the characteristics of the bitmaps. The data for these experiments is real data, and thus we cannot precisely tune the bitmap characteristics. However two trends are clear: For the BBC encoded bitmaps, optimizing the evaluation plan results in a two- to five-fold speed improvement. Furthermore, the improvement increases with increasing attribute cardinality. Figure 7 shows similar results for inequality queries over the real data.

On the synthetic data, the NOT-free rewriting has little effect because every attribute value has the same density. In Figure 8, we isolate the performance improvement due to NOT-free rewriting, comparing the performance obtained by the *phys opt* plan with a plan obtained by both rewriting and physical optimization. While not as dramatic as the benefit of the physical optimizer, rewriting does account for a further 4% to 10% performance improvement.

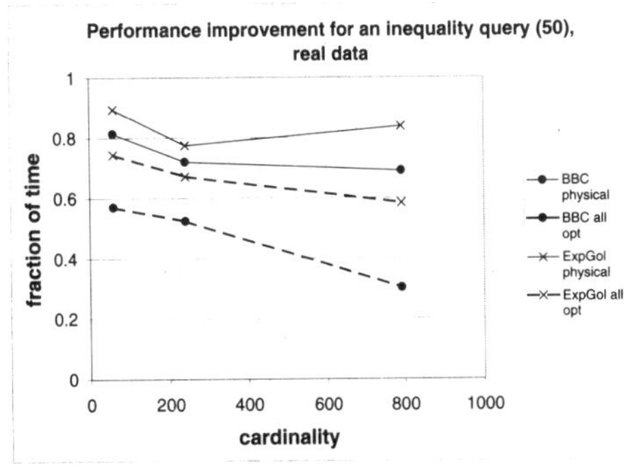

Figure 7 : Time to execute an optimized inequality query relative to the unoptimized query (50 values, real data)

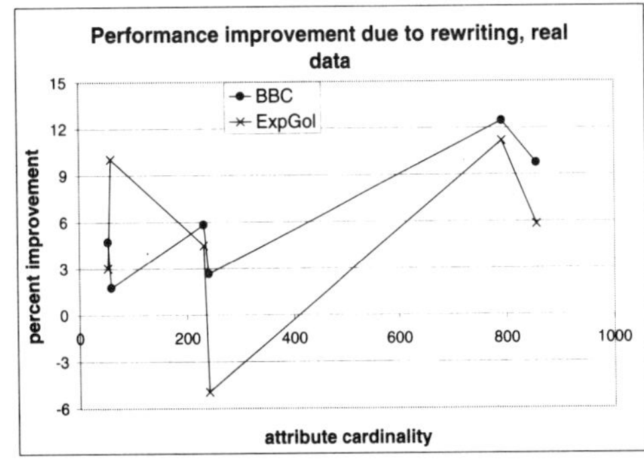

Figure 8 : Performance improvement due to NOT-free rewriting of a range query (50 values, real data)

6 Conclusion

In this paper, we have presented fast and efficient optimization techniques for the evaluation of Boolean query expressions on compressed bitmap indices. We have shown that our optimization algorithm, combined with some simple heuristics, significantly decreases the evaluation time of complex query expressions. We are currently integrating our prototype with the Daytona database system [6] to improve its performance in an OLAP environment. Our optimization algorithm is extensible and can support other Boolean operation evaluation and bitmap compression algorithms. Finally, we are working on extending our techniques to the evaluation of OLAP queries.

References

[1] G. Antoshenkov. Byte-aligned data compression. U.S. Patent number 5,363,098.

[2] G. Antoshenkov. Byte-aligned bitmap compression. Technical report, Oracle Corp., 1994.

[3] C-Y. Chan and Y.E. Ioannidis. Bitmap index design and evaluation. In *SIGMOD '98*.

[4] C-Y. Chan and Y.E. Ioannidis. An efficient bitmap encoding scheme for selection queries. In *Proc. 1999 ACM SIGMOD Conf.*

[5] J-L. Gailly and M. Adler. Zlib home page. http://quest.jpl.nasa.gov/zlib/.

[6] R. Greer. Daytona and the fourth-generation language Cymbal. In *Proc. 1999 ACM SIGMOD Conf.*

[7] T. Ibaraki and T. Kameda. Optimal Nesting for Computing N-relational joins. In *ACM Transactions on Database Systems*, volume 9, September 1984.

[8] Y. E. Ioannidis and Y. Kang. Randomized algorithms for Optimizing Large Join Queries. In *Proc. ACM SIGMOD Conf.*, Atlantic city, NJ, 1990.

[9] Y.E. Ioannidis. Query Optimization. In *Encyclopedia of Computer Science*, 1997.

[10] Y. Ioannidis and E. Wong. Query optimization by simulated annealing. In *Proc. ACM SIGMOD Conf.*, 1987.

[11] H. Jacobsson. Bitmap indexing in Oracle data warehousing. http://WWW-DB.Stanford.EDU/dbseminar/Archive/http://FallY97/slides/oracle.

[12] M. Jarke and J. Koch. Query Optimization in Database Systems. *ACM Comp. Surveys*, 16(2):111–152, June 1984.

[13] T. Johnson. Performance measurements of compressed bitmap indice. In *Proc. Conf. Very Large Data Bases*, 1999.

[14] M.V. Mannino, P. Chu, and T. Sager. Statistical Profile Estimation in Databse Systems. *ACM Comp. Surveys*, 20(3):192–221, September 1984.

[15] A. Moffat and J. Zobel. Parameterized compression of sparse bitmaps. In *Proc. SIGIR Conf. on Information Retrieval*, 1992.

[16] P. O'Neil and G. Graefe. Multi-table joins through bitmapped join indices. *ACM SIGMOD Record*, 24:8–11, 1995.

[17] P. O'Neil, 1998. Personal communication.

[18] P. O'Neil and D. Quass. Improved query performance with variant indices. In *SIGMOD '97*, 1997.

[19] Rdb7: Performance enhancements for 32 and 64 bit systems. http://www.oracle.com/products/servers/rdb/html/fs_vlm.html.

[20] P.G. Selinger and al. Access path selection in a rdbms. In *Proc. ACM SIGMOD Conf.*, Boston, May 1979.

[21] M. Schaller. Reclustering of high energy physics data. In *Proc. Scientific and Statistical Database Management Conf.*, 1999.

[22] Shoshani and et al. Multidimensional indexing and query coordination for tertiary storage management. In *Proc. Scientific and Statistical Database Management Conf.*, 1999.

[23] A. Swami and A. Gupta. Optimization of large join queries. In *Proc. ACM SIGMOD Conf.*, 1988.

[24] Sybase iq indexes. In *Sybase IQ Administration Guide*, Sybase IQ Release 11.2 Collection, Chapter 5., 1997. http://sybooks.sybase.com/cgi-bin/nph-dynaweb/siq11201/iq_admin/1.toc.

[25] M-C. Wu and A.P. Buchmann. Encoded bitmap indexing for data warehouses. In *Int. Conf. on Data Engineering*, 1998.

[26] M-C. Wu. Query optimization for selections using bitmaps. In *Proc. 1999 ACM SIGMOD Conf.*, 1999.

What happens during a Join?
Dissecting CPU and Memory Optimization Effects

Stefan Manegold[1]   Peter Boncz[2]   Martin L. Kersten[1]

[1] CWI, Kruislaan 413, 1098 SJ Amsterdam, The Netherlands; {S.Manegold,M.L.Kersten}@cwi.nl
[2] Data Distilleries B.V., Kruislaan 402, 1098 SM Amsterdam, The Netherlands; P.Boncz@ddi.nl

Abstract

Performance of modern hardware increasingly depends on proper utilization of both the memory cache hierarchy and parallel execution possibilities in todays super-scalar CPUs. Recent database research has demonstrated that database system performance severely suffers from poor utilization of these resources. In previous work, we presented join algorithms that strongly accelerate large equi-join by tuning the memory access pattern to match the characteristics of the memory cache subsystem in the benchmark hardware.

In order to make such algorithms applicable in database systems that run on a wide variety of platforms, we now present a calibration tool that automatically extracts the relevant parameters about the memory subsystem from any hardware. Exhaustive experiments with join-queries demonstrate how a database system equipped with this calibrator can automatically tune memory-conscious database algorithms to their optimal settings.

Once memory access is optimized, CPU resource usage becomes crucial for database performance. We demonstrate how CPU resource usage can be improved by using appropriate implementation techniques. Join experiments with the Monet database system on various hardware platforms confirm that combining memory and CPU optimization can lead to almost an order of magnitude of performance improvement on modern processors.

**Proceedings of the 26th VLDB Conference,
Cairo, Egypt, 2000.**

1   Introduction

As database technology becomes more pervasive, DBMS software is being deployed on an ever wider variety of hardware, that ranges from high-end servers to workstations, PCs, notebooks, and in the near future, portable devices like web pads, palm pilots and even mobile phones. In the previous VLDB conference, we described experiments on an SGI Origin2000 server platform that showed how severely DBMS performance can be impacted by hardware-specific factors. We established through cost modeling and experimentation that a commonly used DBMS algorithm like hash-join runs factors slower than algorithms that are optimally tuned for the specific cache memory subsystem of the benchmark hardware [5]. Several other studies into the behavior of modern hardware on a variety of DBMS query loads corroborate this result, as all report utilization levels on modern super-scalar CPUs that are just a small fraction of their true potential. The sobering truth is that a modern CPU serving a DBMS is typically "stalled" for most of its time (i.e., non-working, waiting for something) [1, 2, 8, 12]. This percentage of CPU under-utilization in DBMS performance is still rising, due to continuing developments in commodity computer hardware. The left table in Figure 1 shows hardware characteristics of a number of popular workstations and PCs of the past decade. The right-hand plot in exponential scale reveals the trend that CPU performance and memory bandwidth[1] have increased with 50% each year (a.k.a. Moore's law), while memory latency has stayed roughly equal. This lack of progress in memory latency means that from the perspective of the CPU, memory access gets more expensive each year at an exponential rate. Therefore, optimal use of the memory caches has become crucial for obtaining good performance, and that is exactly the goal of the cache-conscious DBMS join algorithms we described.

Memory access, however, is not the only cause of under-utilization of modern CPUs. Other factors that are increasingly important have to do with the interaction between CPU and detailed characteristics of ap-

---

[1] We use the STREAM/copy benchmark [10] for characterizing memory bandwidth.

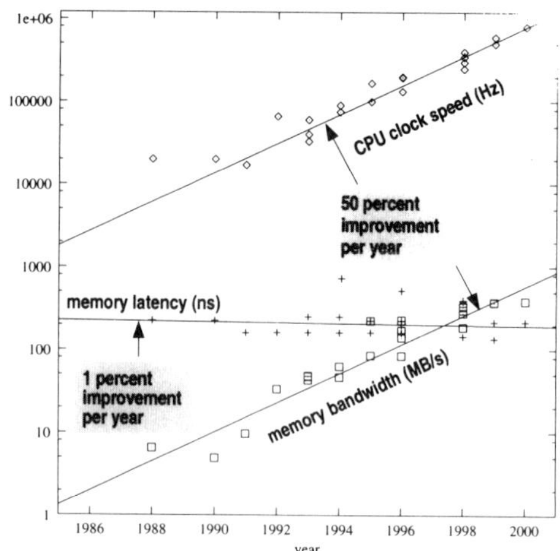

year	computer model	processor				memory	
		type	MHz	#par. units	STREAM/copy (bandwidth)	latency (ns)	
1989	Sun 3/60	68020	20	1	6.5	
1990	Sun 3/80	68030	20	1	4.9	
1991	Sun 4/280	Sparc	17	1	9.6	160
1992	Sun ss10/31	superSparc I	33	3	42.9	
1993	Sun ss10/41	superSparc I	40	3	48.0	
1994	Sun ss20/71	superSparc II	75	3	62.5	870
1995	Sun Ultra1 170	ultraSparc I	167	5	225.2	225
1996	Sun Ultra2 2200	ultraSparc II	200	5	228.5	225
1996	SGI Power Chall.	R10000	195	5	172.7	610
1997	SGI Origin 2000	R10000	250	5	332.0	424
1998	SGI Origin 2000	R12000	300	5	336.0	404
1992	Intel PC	80486	66	1	33.3	
1993	Intel PC	Pentium	60	2	47.1	161
1994	Intel PC	Pentium	90	2	46.4	161
1995	Intel PC	Pentium	100	2	85.1	161
1996	Intel PC	Pentium	133	2	84.4	161
1996	Intel PC	PentiumPro	200	5	140.0	203
1997	Intel PC	PentiumII	300	5	188.2	145
1998	Intel PC	PentiumII	350	5	279.3	145
1998	Intel PC	PentiumII	400	5	304.0	145
1999	Intel PC	PentiumIII	600	5	379.2	135
2000	Intel PC	PentiumIII	733	5	441.9	135
1999	AMD PC	Athlon	500	9	373.5	217
2000	AMD PC	Athlon	800	9	387.9	217

Figure 1: Trends in DRAM and CPU speed

plication program code, like the degree of dependence between instructions. This is explained by another trend in modern CPUs, which is that CPUs get more powerful not only through ever higher clock speeds, but also due to increasing parallelism *inside* the processor. Figure 1 shows that whereas the 80486 and SPARC based systems from the early 1990s still could execute at maximum 1 CPU instruction per clock cycle, an AMD Athlon from 1999 can (in theory) reach a maximum of 9 instructions per clock cycle. For this to happen in practice, aggressive compilers are needed, as well as application code whose inner program loops contain a sufficient substance of independent statements. Only then, the compiler is able to produce code that keeps the parallel units of the CPU busy. Currently, this tends to be the case only in certain scientific computation programs, not in DBMS software.

These issues may seem to drive a DBMS architect into contradictory directions. On the one hand, DBMS technology should be hardware-optimized in order to exploit the cache hierarchy and CPU resources, which could be tackled with all kinds of system-specific optimizations, but on the other hand, that same DBMS technology should be able to run on a very broad spectrum of hardware platforms that each have widely different characteristics. This paper presents important contributions that help to solve this problem.

Road-Map In Section 2, we first briefly explain the basic concepts of modern hardware that determine memory and CPU performance. Then, we recapitulate our partitioned hash-join algorithm [5] that improves join performance by trading extra partitioning CPU work for a strong reduction in memory cache misses. Finally, we summarize the relevant characteristics of our Monet system [4], which we use as experimentation platform.

In Section 3, we present our *calibration tool*, which extracts the most important hardware characteristics like cache line size, number of cache lines, and cache latency from any computer system. This generic tool can be used by any DBMS system that employs cache-conscious algorithms in order to automatically derive the right tuning parameters.[2]

We then describe large main-memory join experiments performed on four different hardware platforms (SGI, Sun, PentiumIII and Athlon) in Section 4. Studying in isolation the two phases of our partitioned hash-join algorithm (the radix-cluster phase and the hash phase), we dissect our experimental results by establishing a link between hot-spots in our DBMS implementation code and detailed split-ups into several CPU and memory cost components. Here, we show how additional factors of improvement, on top of the earlier described gains by memory cost reduction can be gained on all platforms using certain DBMS implementation techniques.

In Section 5, we combine the isolated measurements of the radix-cluster phase and the hash-join phase into full join results. Here, we achieve successful cross-platform validation of the cost models formulated in our earlier work on the SGI architecture, by filling in the hardware parameters derived by our calibrator program for the other hardware platforms into our cost formulas, and comparing the performance predicted by the models with our actual measurements. Finally, we conclude the paper by summarizing our main findings in Section 6.

2 Background

We now describe the technical details of modern hardware relevant for main-memory query performance, introduce our memory-conscious partitioned hash-join algorithm, and describe the Monet system used for experimentation.

---

[2]The software is freely available for download from `http://www.cwi.nl/~monet` and we encourage DBMS designers to incorporate it into their products.

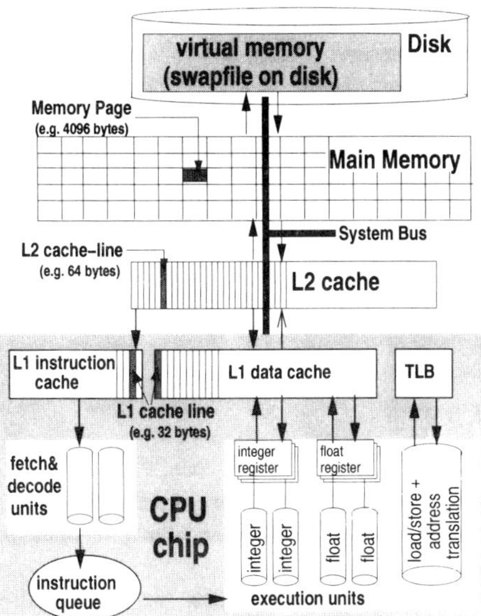

Figure 2: Modern CPU/Memory Computer Architecture

2.1 A Short Hardware Primer

While CPU clock frequency has been following Moore's law (doubling every three years), CPUs have additionally become faster through parallelism *within* the processor. Scalar CPUs separate different execution stages for instructions, e.g., allowing a computation stage of one instruction to be overlapped with the decoding stage of the next instruction. Such a *pipelined* design allows for inter-stage parallelism. Modern *superscalar* CPUs add intra-stage parallelism, as they have multiple copies of certain (pipelined) units that can be active simultaneously. Although CPUs are commonly classified as either RISC or CISC, modern CPUs combine successful features of both. Figure 2 shows a simplified schema that characterizes how modern CPUs work: instructions that need to be executed are loaded from memory by a fetch-and-decode unit. In order to speed up this process, multiple fetch-and-decode units may be present (e.g., the PentiumIII has three, the R10000 two). Decoded instructions are placed in an instruction queue, from which they are executed by one of various functional units, which are sometimes specialized in integer-, floating-point, and load/store pipelines. The PentiumIII, for instance, has two such functional units, whereas the R10000 has even five. To exploit this parallel potential, modern CPUs rely on techniques like *branch prediction* to predict which instruction will be next before the previous has finished. Also, the modern cache memories are *non-blocking*, which means that a cache miss does not stall the CPU. Such a design allows the pipelines to be filled with multiple instructions that will probably have to be executed (a.k.a. *speculative execution*), betting on yet unknown outcomes of previous instructions. All this goes accompanied by the necessary logic to restore order in case of mispredicted branches. As this can cost a significant penalty, and as it is very important to fill all pipelines to obtain the performance potential of the CPU, much attention is paid in hardware design to efficient branch prediction. CPUs work with *prediction tables* that record statistics about branches taken in the past.

Modern computer architectures have a hierarchical memory system as depicted in Figure 2. The main memory on the system board consists of DRAM chips. To narrow the exponentially growing performance gap between CPU speed and memory latency (cf., Figure 1), cache memories have been introduced, consisting of fast but expensive SRAM chips. Cache memories are organized in multiple cascading levels, where the faster and smaller caches are closest to the CPU. Caches consist of *cache lines*, typically 16 to 128 bytes long, which represent the smallest unit of transfer between adjacent cache levels. We assume a typical system with a small on-chip cache called *L1*, and a larger off-chip cache on the system board called *L2*. Our observations and results can be generalized to an arbitrary number of cache levels in a straightforward way.

We identify three aspects that determine memory access costs:

latency Latency is the time span that passes after issuing a data access until the requested data is available in the CPU. In hierarchical memory systems, the latency increases with the distance from the CPU. Accessing data that is already available in the L1 cache causes *L1 latency* (l_{L1}), which is typically rather small (1 or 2 CPU cycles). In case the requested data in not found in L1, an *L1 miss* occurs, additionally delaying the data access by *L2 latency* (l_{L2}) for accessing the L2 cache. Analogously, if the data is not yet available in L2, an *L2 miss* occurs, further delaying the access by *memory latency* (l_{Mem}) to finally load the data from main memory. Hence, the total latency to access data that is in neither cache is $l_{Mem} + l_{L2} + l_{L1}$. As L1 accesses cannot be avoided, we assume in the remainder of this paper, that L1 latency is included in the pure CPU costs, and regard only memory latency and L2 latency as explicit memory access costs.

bandwidth *Memory bandwidth* is a metric for the data volume (in megabytes) that can be transfered between CPU and main memory per second. Bandwidth is usually maximized on a sequential access pattern, as only then all memory words in the cache lines are fully used. In conventional hardware, the memory bandwidth used to be simply the cache line size divided by the memory latency, but modern multiprocessor systems typically provide excess bandwidth capacity.

address translation For data access, logical virtual memory addresses used by application code have to be translated to physical page addresses in the main memory of the computer. In modern CPUs, a Translation Lookaside Buffer (TLB) is used as a cache for physical page addresses, holding the translation for the most recently used pages (typically 64). If a logical address is found in the TLB, the translation has no additional costs. Otherwise, a *TLB miss* occurs. The more pages an application uses (which also depends on the often configurable size of the memory pages), the higher the probability of TLB misses. The actual *TLB miss latency* (l_{TLB}) depends on whether a system handles a TLB miss in hardware or in software.

2.2 Partitioned Hash-Join

The *radix-cluster* algorithm presented in [5] forms a basis for the experiments in this paper. In the following, we briefly recall the principle ideas.

The radix-cluster algorithm divides a relation into H clusters using multiple passes (Figure 3 shows relations R and L both being clustered into 8 clusters using two passes). Radix-clustering on the lower B bits of the integer hash-value of a column is achieved in P sequential passes, in which each pass clusters tuples on B_p bits, starting with the leftmost bits ($\sum_1^P B_p = B$). The number of clusters created by the radix-cluster is $H = \prod_1^P H_p$, where each pass subdivides each cluster into $H_p = 2^{B_p}$ new ones. When the algorithm starts, the entire relation is considered one single cluster, and is subdivided into $H_1 = 2^{B_1}$ clusters. The next pass takes these clusters and subdivides each into $H_2 = 2^{B_2}$ new ones, yielding $H_1 * H_2$ clusters in total, etc. Note that with $P = 1$, radix-cluster behaves like a straightforward clustering algorithm.

The interesting property of the radix-cluster is that the number of randomly accessed regions H_x can be kept low; while still a high overall number of H clusters can be achieved using multiple passes. More specifically, if we keep $H_x = 2^{B_x}$ smaller than the number of cache lines and the number of TLB entries, we totally avoid both TLB and cache thrashing.

Note that a radix-clustered relation is in fact *ordered* on radix-bits (in Figure 3, after radix-clustering relation L, 96 is the first value, as it has radix-bits 000, then come 57,17,81,75, which all have radix-bits 001, etc.). When using this algorithm in the partitioned hash-join, we exploit this property, by performing a merge step on the radix-bits of both radix-clustered relations to get the pairs of clusters that should be hash-joined with each other.

2.3 Monet

We implemented the algorithms described above in Monet, a database kernel developed at CWI, targeted

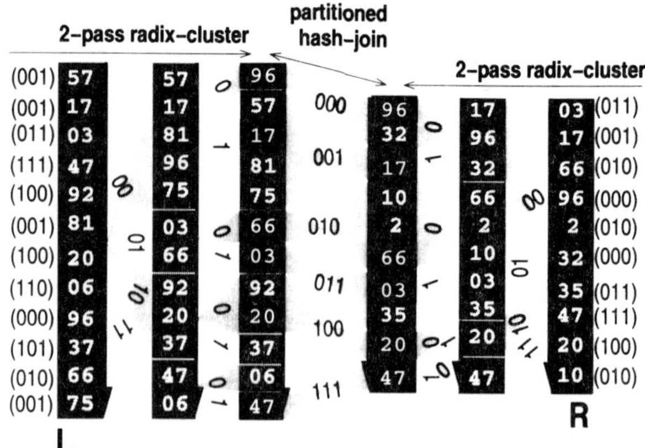

Figure 3: Partitioned Hash-join; black tuples hit (lowest 3-bits of values between parenthesis)

at achieving high performance on *query-intensive* workloads, such as created by OLAP or data mining applications. It uses the Decomposed Storage Model (DSM) [7], storing each column of a relational table in a separate binary table, called a Binary Association Table (BAT). A BAT is represented in memory as an array of fixed-size two-field records [OID,value], or Binary UNits (BUN). The OIDs in the left column are unique per original relational tuple, i.e., they link all BUNs that make up an original relational tuple. The major advantage of the DSM is that it minimizes I/O and memory access costs for column-wise data access, which occurs frequently in OLAP and data mining workloads [6]. The BAT data structure is maintained as a dense memory array, without wasted space for unused slots, both in order to speed up data access (e.g., not having to check for free slots) and because all data in the array is used, which optimizes memory cache utilization on sequential access.

Most commercial relational DBMSs were designed in a time when OLTP was the dominant DBMS application, hence their storage structures, buffer management infrastructure, and core query processing algorithms remain optimized towards OLTP. In the architecture of Monet, we took great care that systems facilities that are only needed by OLTP queries do not slow down the performance of query-intensive applications. We shortly discuss two such facilities in more detail: buffer management and lock management.

Buffer management in Monet is done on the coarse level of a BAT (it is entirely loaded or not at all), hence the query operators always have direct access to the entire relation in memory. The first reason for this strategy is to eliminate buffer management as a source of overhead inside the query processing algorithms, which would result if each operator must continuously make calls to the buffer manager asking for more tuples, typically followed by copying of tuple data into the query operator. The second reason is that all-or-nothing I/O is much more efficient nowadays than random I/O (similarly to memory, I/O bandwidth follows Moore's law, I/O latency does not).

In Monet, we chose to implement explicit transaction facilities, which provide the building blocks for ACID transaction systems, instead of implicitly building in transaction management into the buffer management. Monet applications use the explicit locking primitives to implement a transaction protocol. In OLAP and data mining, a simple transaction protocol with a very coarse level of locking is typically sufficient (a read/write lock on the database or table level). We can safely assume that all applications adhere to this, as Monet clients are front-end programs (e.g., an SQL interpreter, or a data mining tool) rather than end-users. The important distinction from other systems is hence that Monet separates lock management from its query services, eliminating all locking overhead inside the query operators.

As a result, a sequential scan over a BAT comes down to a very simple loop over a memory array with fixed-length records, which makes Monet's query operator implementations look very much like scientific programs doing matrix computations. Such code is highly suitable for optimization by aggressive compiler techniques, and does not suffer from interference with other parts of the system, making it feasible to understand, e.g., what happens during a join? An in-depth discussion of the design and implementation of Monet can be found in [4].

3 Calibration Tool

To achieve their best performance, memory-conscious database algorithms need to be tuned to the characteristics of the very computer system they run on. Preferably, this task should be done by the database system automatically at installation time. For this to be feasible, two requirements have to be fulfilled. On the one hand, the database system has to be provided with appropriate analytical performance models for the algorithms that are to be tuned. In [5], we demonstrate how to create analytical performance models for memory-conscious database algorithms like our radix-cluster algorithm. On the other hand, characteristic parameters of the memory system, including memory sizes, cache sizes, cache line sizes, and access latencies need to be known. In the following, we describe a powerful *calibration tool* to measure the (cache) memory characteristics of an arbitrary machine on the fly.

3.1 Calibrating the Memory System

The idea underlying our calibrator tool is to have a micro benchmark whose performance only depends on the frequency of cache misses that occur. Our calibrator is a simple C program, mainly a small loop that executes a million memory reads. By changing the *stride* (i.e., the offset between two subsequent memory accesses) and the size of the memory area, we

force varying cache miss rates. In principle, the occurrence of cache misses is determined by the array size. Array sizes that fit into the L1 cache do not generate any cache misses once the data is loaded into the cache. Analogously, arrays that exceed the L1 cache size, but still fit into L2, will cause L1 misses but no L2 misses. Finally, arrays larger than L2 cause both L1 and L2 misses. The frequency of cache misses depends on the access stride and the cache line size. With strides equal to or larger than the cache line size, a cache miss occurs with every iteration. With strides smaller than the cache line size, a cache miss occurs only every n iterations (on average), where n is the ratio cache_line_size/stride. Thus, we can calculate the latency for a cache miss by comparing the execution time without misses to the execution time with exactly one miss per iteration. This approach only works, if memory accesses are executed purely sequential, i.e., we have to ensure that neither two or more load instructions nor memory access and pure CPU work can overlap. We use a simple pointer chasing mechanism to achieve this: the memory area we access is initialized such that each load returns the address for the subsequent load in the next iteration. Thus, superscalar CPUs cannot benefit from their ability to hide memory access latency by speculative execution. To measure the cache characteristics, we run our experiment several times, varying the stride and the array size. We make sure that the stride varies at least between 4 bytes and twice the maximal expected cache line size, and that the array size varies from half the minimal expected cache size to at least ten times the maximal expected cache size.

Figure 4 depicts the resulting execution time (in nanoseconds) per iteration for different array sizes on four different machines (see Table 1 for details). Each curve represents a different stride. All curves show two steps, indicating the existence of two cache levels and their sizes. Matching curves mean, that the cache miss frequency has reached its maximum (one miss per iteration), i.e., that the respective stride is equal to (or larger than) the cache line size.

3.2 Calibrating the TLB

We use a similar approach as above to measure *TLB miss costs*. The idea here is to force one TLB miss per iteration, but to avoid any cache misses. We force TLB misses by using a stride that is equal to or larger than the systems page size, and by choosing the array size such that we access more distinct spots than there are TLB entries. Cache misses will occur at least as soon as the number of spots accessed exceeds the number of cache lines. We cannot avoid that. But even with less spots accessed, two or more spots might be mapped to the same cache line, causing *conflict misses*. To avoid this, we use strides that are not exactly powers of two, but slightly bigger, shifted by L2 cache line size.

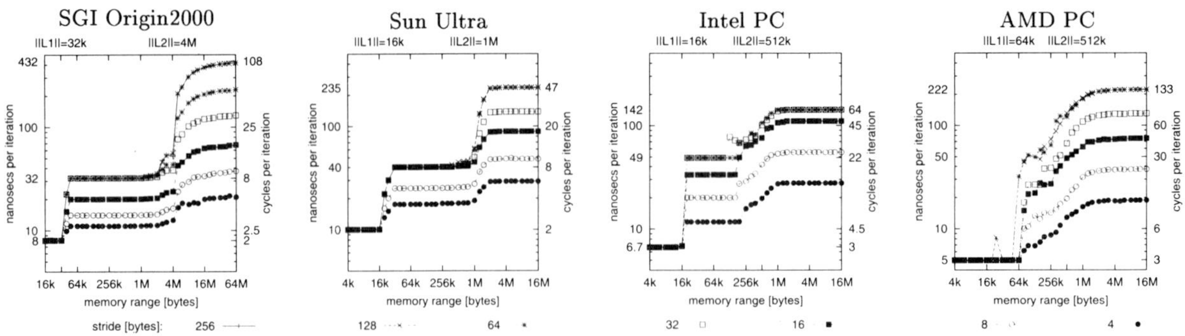

Figure 4: Cache sizes (vertical grid lines), line sizes, and miss latencies (horizontal grid lines)

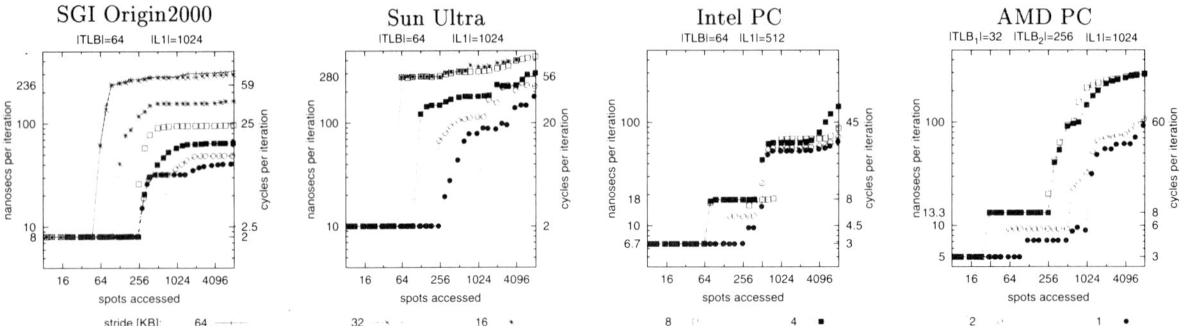

Figure 5: TLB entries (vertical grid lines), page sizes, and TLB miss costs (horizontal grid lines)

Figure 5 shows the results for four machines. The X-axis now gives the number of spots accessed, i.e., array size divided by stride. Again, each curve represents a different stride. For the SGI and the Sun, the curves depict a single distinctive step, indicating a single TLB with 64 entries. The impact of L1 misses when more than 1024 spots are accessed is hardly visible as L1 miss penalty is small compared to TLB miss penalty. On the Intel PC, the first step relates to the 64-entry TLB and the second step relates to L1 misses, which are more expensive than TLB misses on the Intel PC. On the AMD PC, there are two TLBs with 32 and 256 entries, respectively. The third step in the curves again relates to L1 misses. The page sizes can be derived just like the cache line sizes before.

Table 1 gathers the results for all four machines. The PCs have the highest L2 access latencies, probably as their L2 caches are running at only half the CPUs' clock speed. Main-memory access, however, is faster on the PCs than it is on the SGI and the Sun. The TLB miss latency of the PentiumIII and the Athlon (TLB_1) are very low, as their TLB management is implemented in hardware. This avoids the costs of trapping to the operating system on a TLB miss, that is necessary in the software controlled TLBs of the other systems. The TLB_2 miss latency on the Athlon is comparable to that on the R10000 and the UltraSPARC.

The calibration tool and results for a large number of different hardware platforms are available on our web site: http://www.cwi.nl/~monet/.

	SGI Origin2000	Sun Ultra	Intel PC	AMD PC
OS	IRIX64 6.5	Solaris 2.5.1	Linux 2.2.12	Linux 2.2.12
CPU	R10000	UltraSPARC	PentiumIII	Athlon
CPU speed	250 MHz	200 MHz	450 MHz	600 MHz
memory size	64 GB	512 MB	512 MB	384 MB
(local)	(4 GB)			
L1 size	32 KB	16 KB	16 KB	64 KB
L1 line size	32 bytes	16 bytes	32 bytes	64 bytes
L2 size	4 MB	1 MB	512 KB	512 KB
L2 line size	128 bytes	64 bytes	32 bytes	64 bytes
TLB entries	64	64	64	32
TLB_2 entries	-	-	-	256
page size	32 KB	8 KB	4 KB	4 KB
L1 miss	24 ns	30 ns	42 ns	45 ns
latency	6 cycles	6 cycles	19 cycles	27 cycles
L2 miss	400 ns	195 ns	93 ns	172 ns
latency	100 cycles	39 cycles	42 cycles	103 cycles
TLB miss	228 ns	270 ns	11 ns	8 ns
latency	57 cycles	54 cycles	5 cycles	5 cycles
TLB_2 miss	-	-	-	87 ns
latency	-	-	-	52 cycles

Table 1: Calibrated Performance Characteristics

4 Dissecting and Optimizing CPU Utilization

Recent database research demonstrates, that current commercial database systems are not able to exploit the performance potentials of modern CPUs like parallel execution pipelines and speculative execution adequately. Studies on several DBMS products on a variety of workloads [1, 2, 8, 12] consistently show that modern CPUs stall most of the execution time. Lacking access to the source code and insight in implementation details, these studies could not satisfactory answer the question, why the CPUs stall so severely when performing database tasks, nor could they provide any solution for this problem.

In this section, we use the Monet DBMS to analyze the main-memory performance behavior of hash-join algorithms on several modern hardware platform in detail. We demonstrate that once memory access is optimized, CPU utilization becomes crucial. While our original implementations show a similarly poor behavior as described in the previous studies, we present implementation techniques to optimize the CPU utilization significantly. Although we use a specific DBMS as experimentation platform, the observations we make and the improvements we suggest are relevant for any DBMS on any architecture.

4.1 Surgical Instruments

To analyze the performance behavior of our algorithms in detail, we break down the overall execution time into the following major categories of costs:

- *memory access.* In addition to memory access costs for data as described in Section 2.1, this category also contains memory access costs caused by instruction cache misses.

- *CPU stalls.* Beyond memory access, there are other events that make the CPU stall, like branch mispredictions or so-called resource-related stalls.

- *divisions.* We treat integer divisions separately, as they play a significant role in our hash-join.

- *real CPU.* This is the time the CPU is indeed busy executing the algorithms.

We use the four architectures discussed in Section 3 for our investigation. The respective CPUs provide different hardware counters [3] that enable us to measure each of these cost factors accurately. Table 2 gives an overview of the counters used. Some counters yield the actual CPU cycles spent during a certain event, others just return the number of events that occurred. In the latter case, we multiply the counters by the penalties of the events (as calibrated in Section 3). Measuring data TLB misses is not possible on the UltraSPARC and the PentiumIII. We use our analytical models instead [5]. None of the architectures provides a counter for the pure CPU activity. Hence, we subtract the cycles spent on memory access, CPU stalls, and integer division from the overall number of cycles and assume the rest to be pure CPU costs.

In current commercial DBMS, branch mispredictions and instruction cache misses play a significant role [1]. In our experiments, however, we found that in our algorithms, branch mispredictions, instruction TLB misses, and instruction cache misses do not play a role on any tested architecture. The reason is that, in contrast to most commercial DBMSs, Monet's code base is designed for efficient main-memory processing. Monet uses a very large grain size for buffer management in its operators (an entire BAT), processing

category	R10000	UltraSPARC	PentiumIII	Athlon
memory access	L1_data_misses L2_data_misses TLB_misses L1_inst_misses L2_inst_misses	DC_misses[3] EC_misses[4] M_{TLB} stall_IC_miss	DCU_miss_ _outstanding M_{TLB} IFU_mem_stall ITLB_miss	DC_refills_(L2) DC_refills_(sys) L1_DTLB_misses L2_DTLB_misses IC_misses L1_ITLB_misses L2_ITLB_misses
CPU stalls	branch_mispred	stall_mispred stall_fpdep	br_miss_pred ILD_stalled resource_stalls	branch_mispred
divisions	$C * 2 * 35cy$	$C * 2 * 60cy$	cycles_div_busy	$C * 2 * 40cy$

Table 2: Hardware Counters used for Execution Time Breakdown

therefore exhibits much code locality during execution, and hence avoids instruction cache misses and branch mispredictions. Thus, for simplicity of presentation, we omit these events in our evaluation.

4.2 Operating Theatre

In our experiments, we use binary relations (BATs) of 8 bytes wide tuples consisting of uniformly distributed random numbers. Each value occurs three times. Hence, in the join-experiments, the join hit-rate is three. The result of a join is a BAT that contains the [OID,OID] combinations of matching tuples (i.e., a join-index [13]). Subsequent tuple reconstruction is cheap in Monet, and equal for all algorithms, so just like in [11] we do not include it in our comparison. The experiments were carried out on the machines presented in Section 3, an SGI Origin2000, a Sun Ultra, an Intel PC, and an AMD PC (cf. Table 1).

We varied the cardinalities of the relations between 15,000 and 64M tuples, but due to space limits, we only present the results for one cardinality ($C = 8M$). The effects we discuss occur with all relation sizes. For the complete results, we refer the reader to [9].

4.3 Radix Cluster

Original Implementation Figure 6 shows an execution time breakdown for 1-pass radix-cluster on each architecture. The pure CPU costs are nearly constant across all numbers of radix-bits. Memory and TLB costs are low with small numbers of radix-bits, but grow significantly with rising numbers of radix-bits. Only on the Intel PC, TLB thrashing is hardly visible due to its very low TLB miss penalty. The figures clearly reflect the impact of TLB thrashing and cache thrashing on the execution time on all architectures. This confirms that the observations we made in [5] on only one system also hold for other platforms.

Figure 7 depicts the breakdown for radix-cluster using the optimal number of passes. The idea of multi-pass radix-cluster is to keep the number of clusters generated per pass—and thus the memory costs—low,

---

[3] = DC_read - DC_read_hit + DC_write - DC_write_hit.
[4] = EC_ref - EC_hit.

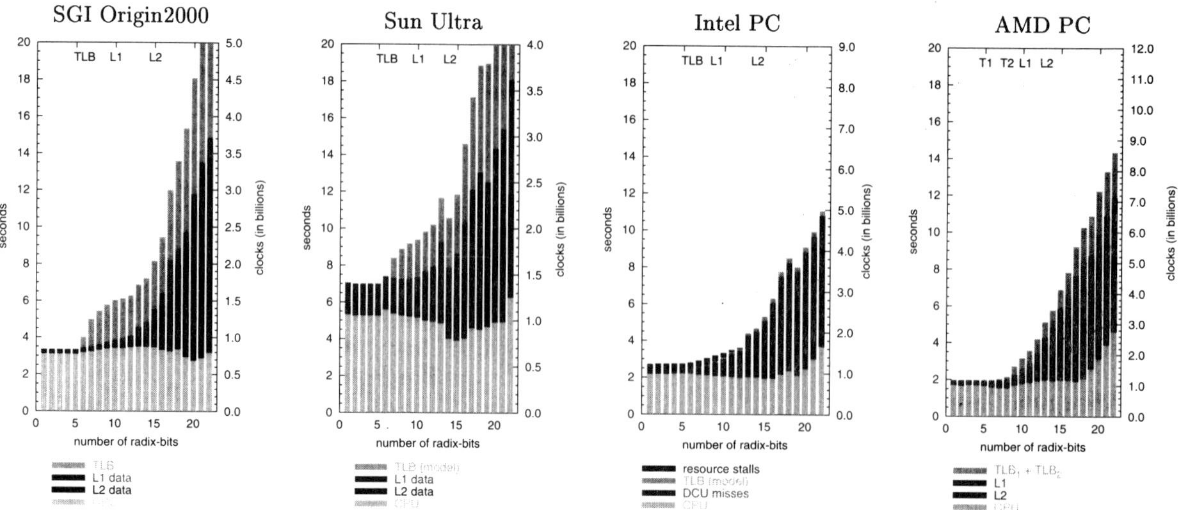

Figure 6: Execution Time Breakdown of Radix-Cluster using one pass

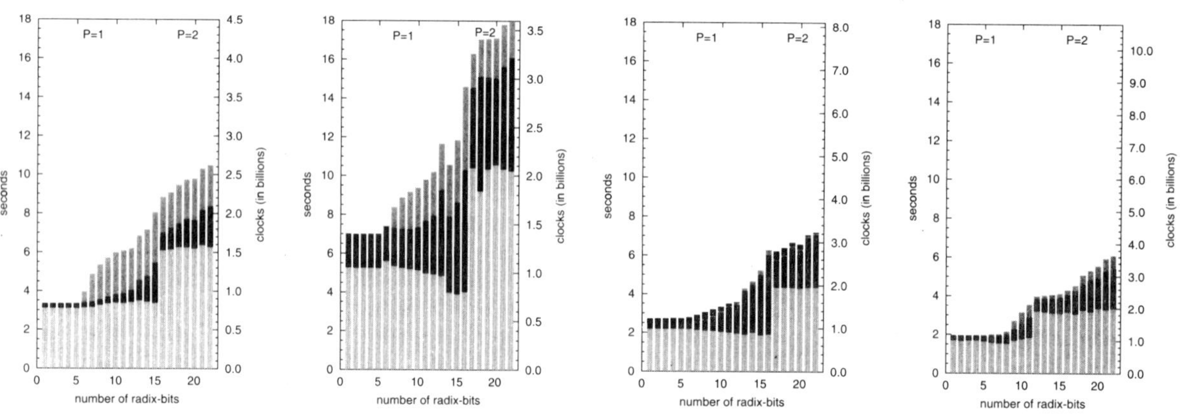

Figure 7: Execution Time Breakdown of Radix-Cluster using multiple passes

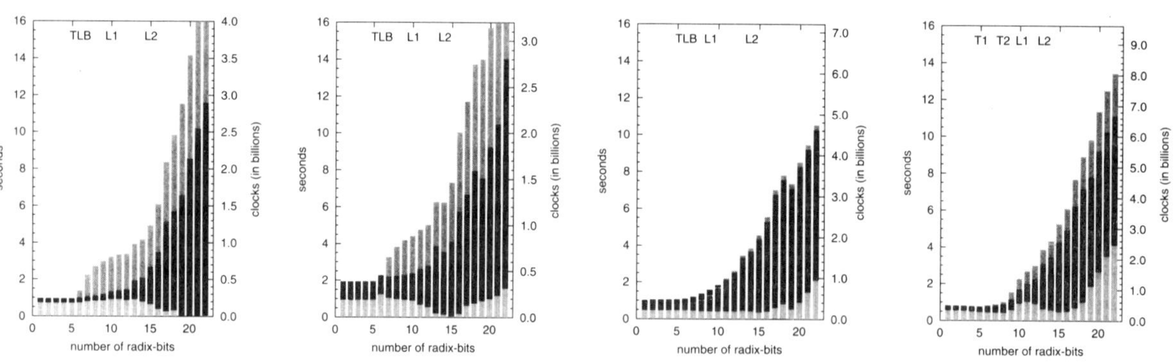

Figure 8: Execution Time Breakdown of optimized Radix-Cluster using one pass

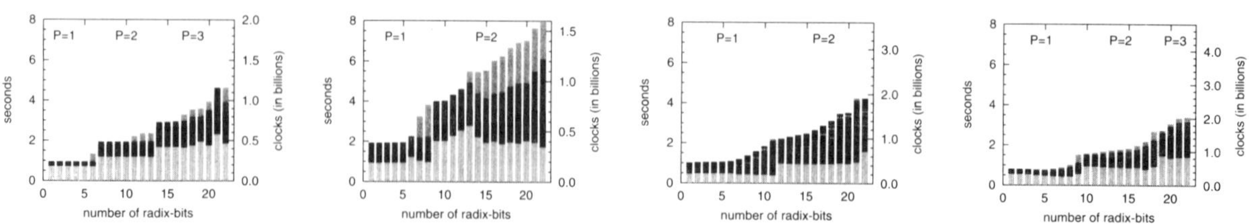

Figure 9: Execution Time Breakdown of optimized Radix-Cluster using multiple passes

346

at the expense of increased CPU costs. Obviously, the CPU costs are too high to avoid the TLB costs by using two passes from 7 radix-bits onward. Only with more than 15 radix-bits—i.e., when the memory costs exceed the CPU costs—two passes win over one pass. Due to the Athlon's high clock speed, two passes outperform one pass already from 11 radix-bits onward.

Optimized Implementation The only way to improve this situation is to reduce the CPU costs, i.e., to optimize the implementation of radix-cluster. Figure 10 shows the source code of our radix-cluster routine. It performs a single-pass clustering on the D bits that start R bits from the right (multi-pass clustering in $P > 1$ passes on $B = P * D$ bits is done by making subsequent calls to this function for pass $p = 1$ through $p = P$ with parameters $D_p = D$ and $R_p = (p-1) * D$, starting with the input relation and using the output of the previous pass as input for the next). As the algorithm itself is already very simple, improvement can only be achieved by means of implementation techniques. We replace the generic ADT-like implementation by a specialized one for each data type.[5] Thus, we can inline the hash function and replace the memcpy by a simple assignment, saving two function calls per iteration.

Figure 8 shows the execution time breakdown for the optimized single-pass radix-cluster. The pure CPU costs have reduced significantly, by factor 4 on the Origin and the Intel PC, by factor 5 on the Sun, and by factor 3.5 on the AMD PC. Replacing function calls has two effects. First, CPU cycles, otherwise needed to copy the parameters to/from the stack and to perform the call itself, are saved. Second, the CPUs can benefit more from their internal parallel capabilities using speculative execution, as the code has become simpler and parallelization options more predictable.

---

[5]The Monet source code is kept small by generating both the optimized and ADT code instantiations with a macro package from one template algorithm. We refer to [4] for a detailed discussion of this subject.

```
#define HASH(v) ((v>>7) XOR (v>>13) XOR (v>>21) XOR v)
typedef struct {
  int v1,v2; /* simplified binary tuple */
} bun;

radix_cluster(
  bun *dst[2^D], bun *dst_end[2^D]  /* output buffers (clusters) */
  bun *rel, bun *rel_end,           /* input relation */
  int R, int D                      /* radix and cluster bits */
){
 int idx, M = (2^D - 1) << R;
 for(bun*cur=rel; cur<rel_end; cur++) {
  idx = (*hashFcn)(cur->v2)&M;      || idx = HASH(cur->v2)&M;
  memcpy(dst[idx],cur,sizeof(bun)); || *dst[idx] = *cur;
  if (++dst[idx]>=dst_end[idx])
    REALLOC(dst[idx],dst_end[idx]);
 }
}
```

Figure 10: C language radix-cluster with annotated CPU optimizations (*right*)

With this optimization, multi-pass radix-cluster is feasible already with smaller numbers of radix-bits (cf. Figure 9). On the Origin, two passes win with more than 6 radix-bits, and three passes win with more than 13 radix-bits, thus avoiding TLB thrashing nearly completely. Analogously, the algorithm creates at most 512 clusters per pass on the AMD PC, avoiding L1 thrashing, which is expensive due to the rather high L1 miss penalty on the Athlon.

4.4 Isolated Join Performance

Original Implementation Partitioned hash-join exhibits increased performance with increasing number of radix-bits. Figure 12 shows that this behavior is mainly caused by the memory costs. While the CPU costs are almost independent of the number of radix-bits, the memory costs decrease with rising number of radix-bits. The smaller the clusters are, the less TLB and cache thrashing occurs. These results confirm that our previous observations hold for all platforms. We point out that division operations significantly contribute to the pure CPU costs on all architectures.

Optimized Implementation Like with radix-cluster, once the memory access is optimized, the execution of partitioned hash-join is dominated by CPU costs. Hence, we apply the same optimizations as above. We inline the hash-function calls during hash build and hash probe as well as the compare-function

```
hash_join(
   bun *dst, bun *dst_end         /* result buffer */
   bun *outer, bun *outer_end,    /* outer relation */
   bun *inner, bun* inner_end,    /* inner relation */
   int R                          /* radix bits */
){
   /* build hash table on inner */
   int pos=0, S=inner_end-inner, H=log2(S), N=2^H;
   int M=(N-1)<<R;
   /* hash bucket array and chain-lists */
   int next[S], bucket[N] = { -1 };
   for(bun *cur=inner; cur<inner_end; cur++){
       int idx = ((*hashFcn)(cur->v2)>>R) % N;
/*     int idx = HASH(cur->v2) & M;                          */
       next[pos] = bucket[idx];
       bucket[idx] = pos++;
   }
   /* probe hash table with outer */
   for(bun *cur=outer; cur<outer_end; cur++) {
       int idx = ((*hashFcn)(cur->v2)>>R) % N;
/*     int idx = HASH(cur->v2) & M;                          */
       for(int hit=bucket[idx]; hit>=0; hit=next[hit]) {
           if ((*compareFcn)(cur->v2, inner[hit].v2)==0) {
/*         if ((cur->v2 == inner[hit].v2)) {                 */
               memcpy(&dst->v1, &cur->v1, sizeof(int));
/*             dst->v1 = cur->v1;                            */
               memcpy(&dst->v2, &inner[hit].v1, sizeof(int));
/*             dst->v2 = inner[hit].v1;                      */
               if (++dst>=dst_end) REALLOC(dst, dst_end);
           }
       }
   }
}
```

Figure 11: C language hash-join with annotated CPU optimizations (*slanted*)

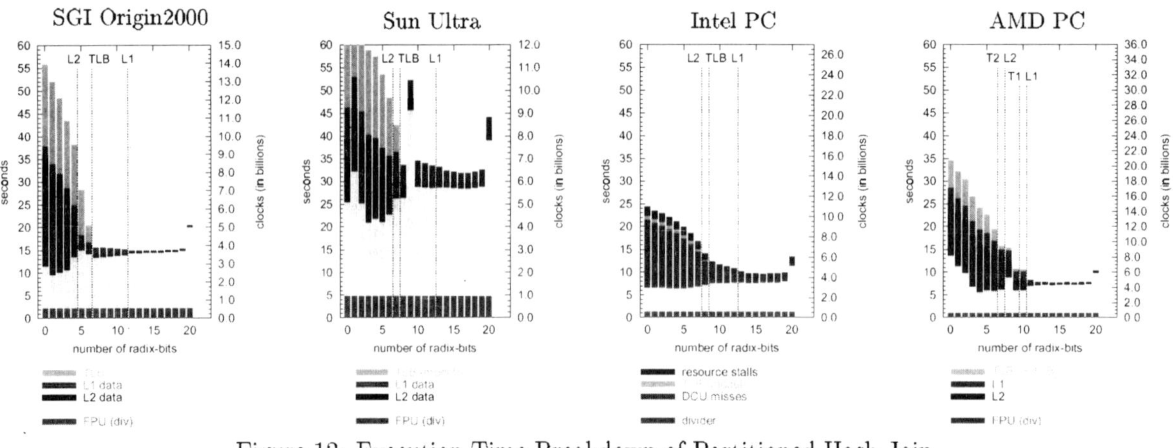

Figure 12: Execution Time Breakdown of Partitioned Hash-Join

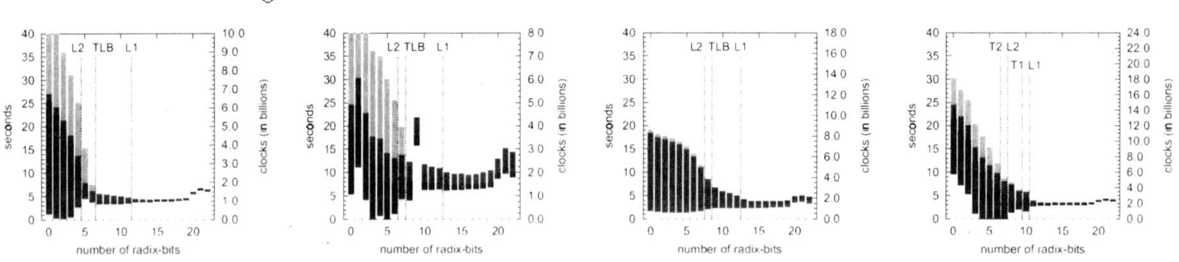

Figure 13: Execution Time Breakdown of optimized Partitioned Hash-Join

call during hash probe and replace two memcpy calls by simple assignments, saving five function calls per iteration. Further, we replace the modulo division ("%") for calculating the hash index by a bit operation ("&"). Figure 11 depicts the original implementation of our hash-join routine and the optimizations we apply.

Figure 13 shows the execution time breakdown for the optimized partitioned hash-join. For the same reasons as with radix-cluster, the CPU costs are reduced by almost a factor 4 on the Origin and the Sun, and by factor 3 on the PCs. The expensive divisions have vanished completely. Additionally, the stalls on the Intel PC have almost disappeared, as well.

It is interesting to note that the 450 MHz PentiumIII and the 600 MHz Athlon outperform the 250 MHz R10000 on non-optimized code, but on CPU optimized code, where the RISC chip executes without any overhead, the R10000 becomes as fast as the PCs.

5 Cross-Platform Validation

Now we turn our attention to the overall join performance, combining both phases. First, we will show that our cost model presented in [5] applies on all architectures. Then, we compare the gains due to CPU and memory optimization on the different platforms.

5.1 Validating Cost Models

In [5], we present an accurate cost model to estimate the performance of our partitioned hash-join algorithm on the Origin2000. The question remaining is, whether this model can be used to estimate the partitioned hash-join performance on other architectures as well.

The cost model mimics the memory access pattern of the algorithm and estimates the number of cache and TLB misses. To reflect platform specifics, we parameterize the model by the machine-specific memory characteristics provided by our calibration tool. Further, we calibrate the pure CPU costs using an in-cache experiment. Due to space limits, we omit the detailed cost formulae, here. The reader is referred to [9].

Figure 14 shows the overall performance for the original and the CPU-optimized versions of our algorithms, using 1-pass and multi-pass clustering on all architectures. The points represent the measured results and the lines represent our model. The model shows to be reasonably accurate on all platforms, correctly reflecting the impact of memory access and implementation techniques on the execution time. We point out that the model accurately predicts the optimal number of passes for clustering and the optimal cluster sizes. Hence, it qualifies for being used to tune memory-conscious algorithms automatically.

The results presented confirm, that the hardware parameters extracted by our calibrator provide sufficient information to capture platform specific memory access behavior. This observation is relevant not only for database cost modeling, but also for database simulators. Further, the results show that calibrating pure CPU costs with an in-cache setup is a reasonable way to capture the impact of implementation techniques and CPU characteristics in cost models.

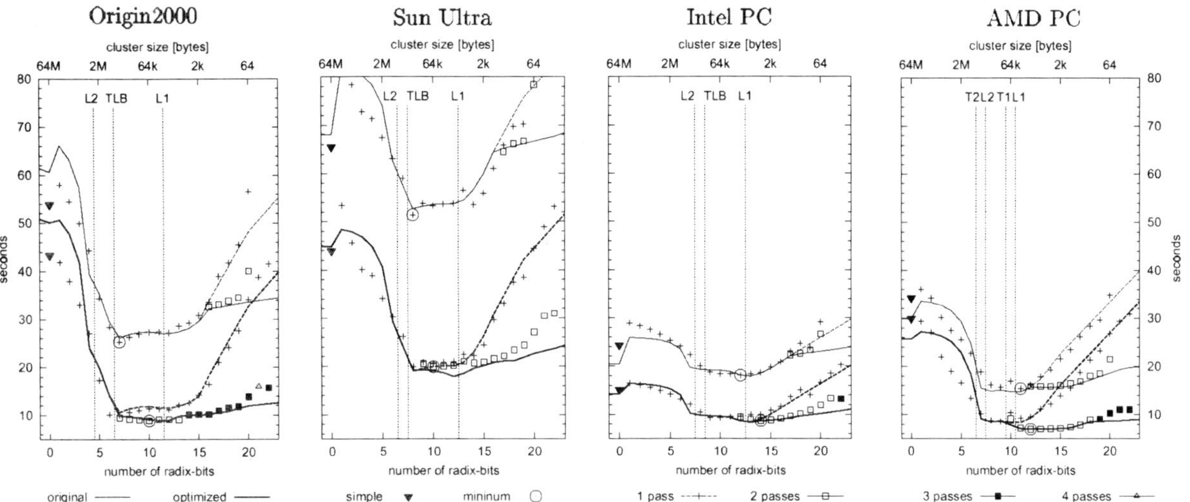

Figure 14: Measured (points) and Modeled (lines) Overall Join Performance

	SGI Origin2000					Sun Ultra					Intel PC					AMD PC				
	def		opt		rel.	def		opt		rel.	def		opt		rel.	def		opt		rel.
C	shj	phj	shj	phj	gain	shj	phj	shj	phj	gain	shj	phj	shj	phj	gain	shj	phj	shj	phj	gain
250k	0.8	0.6	0.4	0.2	3.97	1.7	1.5	1.0	0.4	3.50	0.6	0.4	0.3	0.2	3.01	0.6	0.3	0.4	0.1	3.96
500k	2.2	1.3	1.4	0.4	5.02	3.6	3.0	2.2	1.0	3.62	1.3	1.0	0.8	0.4	2.96	1.5	0.7	1.1	0.3	4.30
1M	5.2	2.7	3.7	0.9	5.74	7.6	6.1	4.8	2.1	3.59	2.7	2.0	1.6	0.9	2.81	3.3	1.5	2.6	0.7	4.59
2M	11.4	5.5	8.6	1.8	6.13	15.7	12.8	10.1	4.5	3.44	5.7	4.2	3.5	2.0	2.77	7.5	3.2	6.3	1.6	4.65
4M	25.0	11.6	19.5	4.1	6.02	32.2	26.2	20.8	9.3	3.45	11.7	8.8	7.2	4.2	2.79	16.1	7.0	13.9	3.4	4.64
8M	53.8	25.2	43.3	8.8	6.05	65.5	51.3	43.9	19.8	3.29	24.3	18.0	15.1	8.6	2.80	34.2	15.3	29.9	6.9	4.94
16M	119.6	53.4	95.1	18.1	6.60															
32M	265.4	113.3	216.7	38.1	6.96															
64M	614.2	234.6	511.4	79.5	7.71															

C:	cardinality	def:	default implementation	shj:	simple hash-join (non memory-optimized)
gain:	overall gain (def_shj/opt_phj)	opt:	CPU-optimized implementation	phj:	phash TLB/L1 (memory-optimized)

Table 3: Overall Join Performance (in seconds) without and with CPU and/or Memory Optimization

5.2 Overall Join Performance

From Figure 14, we derive that cluster sizes just below TLB size achieve the best performance on the RISC architectures. The PCs require even smaller clusters, fitting into the L1 cache. We refer to these settings as *phash TLB/L1*. In all cases, multi-pass radix-clustering is essential to reach the optimal performance.

Table 3 lists the absolute performance of simple hash-join and phash TLB/L1 both without and with CPU optimization applied. The numbers show that CPU and memory optimization support each other and *boost* their effects. The gain of CPU optimization for phash TLB/L1 is bigger than that for simple hash-join ((def_phj−opt_phj) > (def_shj−opt_shj)), and the gain of memory optimization for the CPU-optimized implementation is bigger than that for the non-optimized implementation ((opt_shj−opt_phj) > (def_shj−def_phj)). There are two reasons for the boosting effect to occur. First, modern CPUs try to overlap memory access with other useful CPU computations by allowing independent instructions to continue execution while other instructions wait for memory. In a memory-bound load, much CPU computation is overlapped with memory access time, hence optimizing these computations has no overall perfor-

mance effect (while it does when the memory access would be eliminated by memory optimizations). Second, an algorithm that allows memory access to be traded for more CPU processing (like radix-cluster), can actually trade more CPU for memory when CPU-costs are reduced, reducing the impact of memory access costs even more.

Finally, the "gain"-column in Table 3 shows, that the Origin2000 achieves the best overall performance improvement: factor 6 for 8M tuples and up to almost factor 8 for larger relations. Second is the AMD PC with factor 5, followed by the Sun (factor 3.3) and the Intel PC (factor 2.8).

6 Conclusion

The research presented here shows how the results earlier obtained on one specific platform [5] can be generalized to other hardware, and how cache-conscious query optimization can be generalized and incorporated into existing DBMS technology. A key element for achieving this is the calibrator program we provide, that automatically discovers what the memory subsystem of a computer looks like and derives important cost model parameters like cache line size, numbers of cache lines, and latencies. Combining the parameters derived by the calibrator on a number of new platforms (we additionally tested Sun, Intel and AMD hardware) with the detailed main-memory cost models provided in [5], we were able to successfully predict performance. Hence we conclude that generic optimization of main-memory access costs is both feasible and desirable, as correctly tuned cache-conscious algorithms greatly enhance DBMS performance.

We performed exhaustive experiments on these hardware platforms, in which we dissected the performance of our partitioned hash-join by establishing a clear link between the hot-spots in our code and detailed performance results, split-up into various CPU and memory cost components. This analysis showed that performance can be significantly enhanced even after all memory access has been eliminated. The trend of increasing parallelism inside modern superscalar CPUs makes it ever more crucial for application code that the inner loops of the query processing algorithms contain sufficient (independent) work to keep the parallel units of the CPU busy. We find that performance can be increased by another factor three or four by eliminating all function calls from the inner loops of our algorithms. Interestingly, the memory- and code-optimization seem to boost each other: code-optimization without memory-optimization is much less effective than combined and vice versa. The overall effect of combining both optimizations can yield a performance increase of a factor eight.

Our experimentation platform is the Monet system, developed by our group to support high- performance OLAP and data mining. In previous experiments on the DD Benchmark, we found that Monet was 36 times faster on a data mining query load than a commercial DBMS product that also ran fully memory/CPU bound [6]. The insights gained in this research now tell us that the near 100% CPU utilization achieved by Monet on such tasks makes the crucial difference. The requirements for achieving such high performance lead straight to the core architectural decisions made for a DBMS, hence it will not be easy to repeat these results in already existing DBMS products. We therefore expect Monet to stay in a class of its own for some time to come. Still, we hope that DBMS engineers will pick up the lessons learned and incorporate techniques described here in future DBMS software.

References

[1] A. G. Ailamaki, D. J. DeWitt, M. D. Hill, and D. A. Wood. DBMSs on a Modern Processor: Where does time go? In *Proc. of the Int'l. Conf. on Very Large Data Bases*, pages 266–277, Edinburgh, Scotland, UK, September 1999.

[2] L. A. Barroso, K. Gharachorloo, and E. D. Bugnion. Memory System Characterization of Commercial Workloads. In *Proc. of the Int'l Symp. on Computer Architecture*, Barcelona, Spain, June 1998.

[3] R. Berrendorf and H. Ziegler. PCL - The Performance Counter Library. Technical Report FZJ-ZAM-IB-9816, ZAM, Forschungzentrum Jülich, Germany, 1998.

[4] P. Boncz and M. Kersten. MIL Primitives For Querying a Fragmented World. *The VLDB Journal*, 8(2), October 1999.

[5] P. Boncz, S. Manegold, and M. Kersten. Database Architecture Optimized for the New Bottleneck: Memory Access. In *Proc. of the Int'l. Conf. on Very Large Data Bases*, pages 54–65, Edinburgh, Scotland, UK, September 1999.

[6] P. Boncz, T. Rühl, and F. Kwakkel. The Drill Down Benchmark. In *Proc. of the Int'l. Conf. on Very Large Data Bases*, pages 628–632, New York, NY, USA, June 1998.

[7] G. P. Copeland and S. Khoshafian. A Decomposition Storage Model. In *Proc. of the ACM SIGMOD Int'l. Conf. on Management of Data*, pages 268–279, Austin, TX, USA, May 1985.

[8] K. Keeton, D. A. Patterson, Y. Q. He, R. C. Raphael, and W. E. Baker. Performance Characterization of a quad Pentium Pro SMP using OLTP workloads. In *Proc. of the Int'l Symp. on Computer Architecture*, pages 15–26, Barcelona, Spain, June 1998.

[9] S. Manegold, P. Boncz, and M. Kersten. Optimizing Main-Memory Join On Modern Hardware. Technical Report INS-R9912, CWI, Amsterdam, The Netherlands, October 1999.

[10] J. D. McCalpin. Memory Bandwidth and Machine Balance in Current High Performance Computers. *IEEE Technical Committee on Computer Architecture newsletter*, December 1995.

[11] A. Shatdal, C. Kant, and J. Naughton. Cache Conscious Algorithms for Relational Query Processing. In *Proc. of the Int'l. Conf. on Very Large Data Bases*, pages 510–512, Santiago, Chile, September 1994.

[12] P. Trancoso, J. L. Larriba-Pey, Z. Zhang, and J. Torellas. The Memory Performance of DSS Commericial Workloads in Shared-Memory Multiprocessors. In *Int'l. Symp. on High Performance Computer Architecture*, San Antonio, TX, USA, January 1997.

[13] P. Valduriez. Join Indices. *ACM Trans. on Database Systems*. 12(2):218–246. June 1987.

Set Containment Joins: The Good, The Bad and The Ugly

Karthikeyan Ramasamy[*]
UW-Madison
karthik@cs.wisc.edu

Jignesh M. Patel[†]
UM-Ann Arbor
jignesh@eecs.umich.edu

Jeffrey F. Naughton
UW-Madison
naughton@cs.wisc.edu

Raghav Kaushik
UW-Madison
raghav@cs.wisc.edu

Abstract

Efficient support for set-valued attributes is likely to grow in importance as object-relational database systems, which either support set-valued attributes or propose to do so soon, begin to replace their purely relational predecessors. One of the most interesting and challenging operations on set-valued attributes is the set containment join, because it provides a concise and elegant way to express otherwise complex queries. Unfortunately, evaluating these joins is difficult, and naive approaches lead to algorithms that are very expensive. In this paper, we develop a new partition based algorithm for set containment joins: the Partitioning Set Join Algorithm (PSJ), which uses a replicating multi-level partitioning scheme based on a combination of set elements and signatures. We present a detailed performance study with a complete implementation in the Paradise object-relational database system. Our results show that PSJ outperforms previously proposed set join algorithms over a wide range of data sets.

1 Introduction

The data modeling community has long realized that set valued attributes provide a concise and natural way of modeling complex data [RKS98]. Recently, there has been a resurgence of interest in set-valued

---

[*]Work supported in part by a grant from the Microsoft Corporation

[†]Portions of this research were done while the authors were at NCR Corporation, Madison, WI

**Proceedings of the 26th VLDB Conference,
Cairo, Egypt, 2000.**

attributes from two different perspectives. First, commercial O/R DBMS [Sto96] are beginning to support set-valued attributes, which is likely to lead to their use in "real" applications. Second, the rise of XML as an important data standard increases the need for set-valued attributes, since it appears that set-valued attributes are key for the natural representation of XML data in relational systems [SHT+99]. Unfortunately, although sets have been fairly well studied from a data-modeling viewpoint [Zan83], very little has been published about the efficient implementation of operations on set-valued attributes. In this paper, we consider the implementation of a particularly challenging operation over set-valued attributes, the set-containment join.

Many real world queries can be easily expressed using set containment joins. Consider a simple relation that describes a document and set of hyper-links that point to it.

DOCUMENT(did, {hyper-links-in}, actual-document)

Suppose document d_1 is more important than d_2 if d_1 is linked-to by a superset of the documents that link to d_2. We can find pairs of documents d_1 and d_2 where d_1 is more important than d_2 with the following query:

```
SELECT  d₁.did, d₂.did
FROM DOCUMENT d₁, DOCUMENT d₂
WHERE  d₂.hyper-links-in ⊂ d₁.hyper-links-in
```

The algorithms available for implementing set-containment joins depend upon how set-valued attributes are stored in the database. As described in [KJD00], sets can be stored in the *nested internal representation* (set elements are stored together along with the rest of the attributes) or the *unnested external representation* (set elements are scattered and stored in a separate relation). To the best of our knowledge, current commercial O/R DBMS use the unnested external representation. Since the unnested external representation reduces to standard SQL2 relations under the covers, set containment joins on the unnested external representation can be evaluated by rewriting the queries into SQL2 (with no sets) and evaluating these rewritten queries. On the other hand, with the nested internal representation, the most obvious algorithm for evaluating set-containment joins is nested loops. Two questions immediately arise: (1) Are there better algorithms than nested loops? (2) How do these algorithms compare in efficiency with the rewrite in SQL2 approach that is most logical for the unnested external representation?

This paper attempts to answer these questions by proposing a new partition-based join algorithm for set containment joins, which we call PSJ. Partition-based algorithms certainly dominate join algorithms in scalar and spatial domains, so it is natural to suspect that a partition-based algorithm will be the algorithm of choice for set-containment joins.

This paper makes two main contributions. First, it presents the new algorithm PSJ for set containment joins. Second, it includes an extensive performance study of three set containment algorithms: the traditional SQL approach on the unnested external representation, signature nested loops and PSJ on the nested internal representation. Our experience with an implementation in the Paradise object-relational database system [PYK$^+$97] shows that PSJ yields significant speedup over both the SQL-based approach and signature nested loops. An added benefit of this algorithm is that, like all partition-based algorithms, it is trivially parallelizable. Finally, our results present a strong case for storing sets in the nested internal form, since PSJ and even signature nested loops outperform the rewritten queries over the unnested external representation.

1.1   Related Work

Joins have been studied extensively in relational [MK76], [Bra84], [DKO$^+$84], [DNS91] and spatial domains [LR96], [PD96]. Pointer joins for efficiently traversing path expressions in object-oriented databases has also been studied extensively [DLM93], [SC90]. However, there is very little previous work on set containment joins. The only reported work of which we are aware is the work by Helmer and Moerkotte [HM96], [HM97]. These papers investigate nested loops algorithms for computing a set containment join and propose a new signature based hash join. We discuss these algorithms in Sections 3 and 4.2

1.2   Paper Organization

The rest of the paper is organized as follows. Section 2 defines the problem of set containment and the notation used in the paper. Various storage representations for sets, the SQL approach and signature nested loops joins are explained in detail in Section 3. The partition based set join algorithm is outlined in Section 4.

Section 5 presents a detailed performance study of all the algorithms. The conclusions and future work are presented in Section 6.

2   Problem Definition and Notations

For the rest of the paper, we consider the two relations $R(a, \{b\})$ and $S(c, \{d\})$ containing the set valued attributes $\{b\}$ and $\{d\}$ respectively. Since set is a type constructor, attributes b and d can be of any arbitrary type and we assume that these types provide an equality predicate that compares the equivalence of two set elements. Also we do not assume any order among the set elements. The set containment join, $R \bowtie_{\{b\} \subseteq \{d\}} S$, pairs tuples in relation R and S such that $\{b\}$ is subset of $\{d\}$. Table 1 describes the notation used in the rest of the paper.

3   Previously Proposed Algorithms

Options for algorithms for set containment joins heavily depend on how the set valued attributes are stored in the database. In order to make this paper self-contained, we briefly discuss the options for storing set-valued attributes.

3.1   Storage Representations for Sets

Various representations for sets are possible depending on the following two characteristics: **nesting** (set elements are clustered or scattered) and **location** (set elements are either stored with the rest of the attributes internally or vertically partitioned and stored externally). As outlined in [KJD00], the two main representations for sets are:

- **Nested Internal**: Here the set elements are grouped together and stored with the rest of the attributes in the tuple.

- **Unnested External**: In this representation, the set-valued attribute is stored in a separate relation. For each set-valued attribute in a relation, two relations are created: (1) A base relation that stores the other non set-valued attributes and an identifier, and (2) An auxiliary relation that stores each element of the set-valued attribute as a tuple with the (corresponding) identifier.

3.2   Join Algorithms for Unnested External

If sets are stored in the unnested external representation, set-containment joins can be expressed and evaluated using standard SQL2 constructs. This approach is important to study, because (a) it is the simplest to add to any RDBMS, and (b) perhaps because of (a), to our knowledge the commercial O/R DBMSs all use this approach. As discussed in Section 3.1, in this representation, a relation with a set-valued attribute is decomposed into two relations. A set containment operation can then be expressed using SQL over these

$|R|$	Relation cardinality of R (# of tuples)	$|S|$	Relation cardinality of S (# of tuples)
r_R	Average set cardinality of R	r_S	Average set cardinality of S
σ	Selectivity of $R \bowtie_{\{b\} \subseteq \{d\}} S$	f	False drops as a percent of $\sigma \, |R| \, |S|$
IO_{seq}	Cost of a sequential I/O	IO_{rand}	Cost of a random I/O

Table 1: Notations

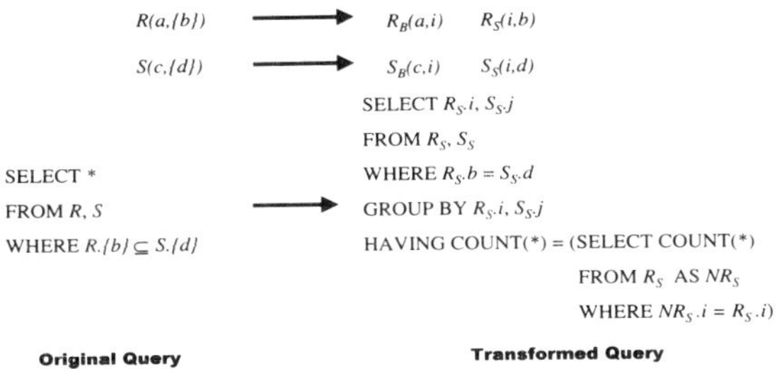

Figure 1: Original and Transformed SQL Queries (excluding final joins for a and c)

decomposed relations. If R and S are the two relations being joined, and R_S and S_S are the corresponding decomposed auxiliary set relations, then the original and transformed queries are shown in Figure 1.

The rewritten query involves a correlated nested sub-query and hence it is expensive to evaluate. A possible optimization is to use magic-sets rewriting [SPL96] and transform the original query into the set of queries shown in Figure 2, thus evaluating the inner query only once (as opposed to once for every tuple produced by the outer block). Our experiments show empirically that even this approach performs very poorly unless the set sizes and relation sizes are small; in fact, in many cases, it is so bad that the algorithm can arguably be called "ugly".

3.3 Signature Nested Loops Algorithm for Nested Internal

The signature nested loops algorithm proposed by [HM97] attempts to reduce the cost of evaluating the containment predicate by approximating sets using signatures and evaluating the join predicate by comparing these signatures. A signature is a fixed length bit vector that is computed by applying a function M iteratively to every element e in the set and setting the bit determined by $M(e)$. If the containment predicate $s \subseteq t$ is to be satisfied for two signatures s and t, then the following condition is necessary: *For all bit positions that are set to 1 in signature s, the corresponding bits in signature t should be set to 1.* However, this condition is not sufficient since signatures are only an approximate representation for the set (unless the signature length is equal to the size of the domain of the set). Hence using signatures to evaluate a predicate will yield false drops. The actual sets must be examined to eliminate these false drops.

The signature nested loops algorithm operates in three phases: the *signature construction phase*, the

probing phase, and the *verification phase*. During the signature construction phase, the entire relation R is scanned, and for every tuple $t_i \in R$, a signature s_i is constructed. A triplet (c_i, s_i, OID_i) is computed and stored in an intermediate relation R_{sig}; here c_i is the set cardinality and OID_i is the physical record identifier (rid) of the tuple. The same process is repeated for the relation S and an intermediate relation S_{sig} is created. Next, the algorithm proceeds to the probing phase, where the tuples of R_{sig} and S_{sig} are joined. For every pair $(c_i, s_i, OID_i) \in R_{sig}$ and $(c_j, s_j, OID_j) \in S_{sig}$, two conditions must be verified (i) $c_i \leq c_j$ and (ii) $s_i \wedge s_j = s_i$, where the wedge represents the bit-wise and of the two signatures. If both the conditions are satisfied, then the pair (OID_i, OID_j) is a possible candidate for the result. During the final verification phase, the tuples referred to in the candidate (OID_i, OID_j) pairs are fetched and the subset predicate is evaluated on the actual set instances, producing the final result.

The main issue in the signature nested loop join algorithm is reducing the number of false drops to minimize the cost of the verification phase. The false drop probability depends on the number of bits used in constructing the signature. The greater the signature length, the smaller will be the false drop probability. However, larger signatures lead to more bit comparisons per signature, thereby increasing the execution time of the probing phase. Hence, it is necessary that the chosen signature size be such that further increases in the number of bits do not significantly reduce the false drop probability. Based on the definition of false drop probability, we derive an equation for the optimal signature length (F) as

$$F = \frac{-r_S}{ln\left(1 - \left(\frac{f\sigma}{1-\sigma(1+f)}\right)^{1/r_R}\right)} \tag{1}$$

The detailed derivation is presented in [KJJK00].

Note that even with the signatures of an ideal length, this algorithm compares signatures for every pair of tuples in the cross product of R and S. If R and S each has one million tuples, there are one trillion comparisons. This is discouraging enough to be considered "bad."

4 Partitioned Set Join (PSJ)

In this section, we propose a new algorithm for the nested internal representation that is based upon partitioning. In general, partition based algorithms for joins (scalar and spatial) attempt to optimize join execution by partitioning the problem into multiple

$$\text{INSERT INTO } R_S Tmp(i, count_i) \qquad \text{INSERT INTO } R_S S_S Tmp(i, j, count_{ij}) \qquad \text{SELECT } R_S S_S Tmp.i, R_S S_S Tmp.j$$

$$\text{SELECT } R_S.i, \text{COUNT}(*) \qquad \text{SELECT } R_S.i, S_S.j, \text{COUNT}(*) \qquad \text{FROM } R_S S_S Tmp, R_S Tmp$$

$$\text{FROM } R_S \qquad \text{FROM } R_S, S_S \qquad \text{WHERE } R_S S_S Tmp.i = R_S Tmp.i$$

$$\text{GROUP BY } R_S.i \qquad \text{WHERE } R_S.b = S_S.d \qquad \text{AND } R_S S_S Tmp.count_{ij} = R_S Tmp.count_i$$

$$\text{GROUP BY } R_S.i, S_S.j$$

| **Count Query** | **Candidate Query** | **Verify Query** |

Figure 2: Magic Sets Rewriting

smaller subproblems using a partitioning function. First, the relation R is partitioned into k partitions, $R_1, R_2, \ldots, R_k$. Similarly, the relation S is partitioned into $S_1, S_2, \ldots, S_k$ using the same function. Note that we are using a generalization of the classical definition of partitioning in that one tuple may be mapped to multiple partitions.

The algorithm proposed in this section, called the Partitioned Set Join Algorithm (PSJ), uses a two level partitioning scheme. It operates in three phases:

- **Partitioning Phase**: Each tuple of R is sent to exactly one partition based on the first level partitioning function h. Each tuple of S, in general, is replicated across multiple partitions using (the same) h.

- **Joining Phase**: Each partition of R is joined with its counterpart in S using a second level partitioning function that operates on signatures. Hence false drops are possible.

- **Verification Phase**: The tuple pairs that the join phase indicates could join, are compared to remove any false drops.

The subsequent sections describe each of the phases in detail.

4.1 Partitioning Phase

This phase uses a partitioning function h that operates on the set elements. The partitioning phase begins by reading the relation R. For each tuple r of R, the following steps are executed

1. A 3-tuple (c_i, s_i, OID_i) is computed, where c_i is the set cardinality, s_i is the signature of the set instance, and OID_i is the OID of the tuple.

2. A random element e_R is picked from $r.\{b\}$.

3. The 3-tuple is sent to the partition determined by $h(e_R)$.

Observe that the 3-tuple for each tuple of R is sent only to one partition. Now the relation S is read. For each tuple s of S, the following steps are executed

1. A 3-tuple (c_i, s_i, OID_i) is computed.

2. *For each* element $e_S \in s.\{d\}$, the 3-tuple is sent to the partition determined by $h(e_S)$.

Note that if $r.\{b\} \subseteq s.\{d\}$ then the partition determined by $h(e_R)$ will contain the 3-tuples corresponding to r and s. Hence the algorithm computes containment correctly.

4.2 Joining Phase

During the joining phase, each partition of R is joined with its counterpart in S. There are various algorithms that could be used in this phase. However, at this point, the tuples in each partition do not carry the actual set instances since they are approximated by signatures. Hence the join algorithm in this phase has to operate directly on signatures. In this phase, we use a partition based in-memory algorithm using signatures.

The joining algorithm works in two steps: the *build step* and the *probe step*. In the build step, an array A of size equal to the number of bits in the signature is constructed. Now the partition R_i is scanned and each 3-tuple (c_i, s_i, OID_i) is read. A bit position m that is set to 1 is chosen randomly from the signature. The 3-tuple is inserted into $A[m]$. At the end of first step, the signatures from partition R_i have been partitioned.

During the probe step, partition S_i is scanned. For each 3-tuple (c_j, s_j, OID_j) the chain of signatures in $A[n]$ is examined whenever bit n is set to 1 in s_j. The containment predicate is evaluated (as in Section 3.3) for each signature encountered in the chain and the candidate pairs (OID_i, OID_j) are inserted into a temporary relation. These candidate pairs potentially satisfy the containment relationship.

This phase of the algorithm is similar to signature hash join (SHJ) proposed in [HM97]. We use a single bit in the signature to determine the array index for R. SHJ in general uses more bits (a partial signature) to determine the array index. For S, SHJ requires all possible subset signatures to be enumerated for a given partial signature to determine the chains to be probed. This enumeration is exponential.

4.3 Verification Phase

In the verification phase, we examine the actual R and S tuples to determine whether they satisfy the join condition. The main issues involved in this phase are speeding up set containment verification and avoiding random seeks while fetching the tuples. Refer to [KJJK00] for a full discussion of the techniques used to accomplish these goals.

4.4 Estimation of Number of Partitions and Signature Size

The performance of PSJ depends two factors: the number of partitions (P_{PSJ}) and the signature size (F_{PSJ}). The desired number of partitions further depends on two parameters: the average set cardinality and the relation cardinality. Even though the speedup is expected to increase as the number of partitions is increased, in practice, the overhead associated with each partition prevents such unbounded speedup.

In order to estimate the desired number of partitions, we employ a detailed analytical model which accounts for the overheads. Based on this model, we estimate the ideal number of partitions as

$$P_{PSJ} = \left(\frac{|R||S|\left(1 - \left(1 - \frac{1}{F}\right)^{r_S}\right)}{Z} \right)^{1/3} \qquad (2)$$

where $Z = 2IO_{rand} + 2IO_{seq} + H$

The derivation of this equation is presented in [KJJK00]. The fudge factor H accounts for various system dependent factors. The fudge factor is likely to vary across systems. For a given system, H can be determined by choosing a sample set of data and running the algorithm for various partitions.

Since partitioning avoids many redundant comparisons, one can expect the signature size to be lower (when compared to Sig-NL). Also, as the number of partitions is increased the signature size is expected to get lower. We derive an equation for signature size.

$$(1 - e^{-r_S/F_{PSJ}})^{r_R} - \frac{f\sigma P_{PSJ}}{\left(1 - \left(1 - \frac{1}{F_{PSJ}}\right)^{r_S}\right) - \sigma P_{PSJ} - f\sigma P_{PSJ}} = 0 \qquad (3)$$

We use bisection method to solve this equation. There is a cyclic dependency between equations (2) and (3). Hence both the equations have to be solved simultaneously. We use these equations to determine the appropriate combination of partitions and signature size in our experiments for PSJ. As we shall see in Section 5.8 and Section 5.9, fortunately the performance curves as a function of the number of partitions and signature size are rather flat. So these equations do not have to be exact for reasonable performance.

5 Performance Evaluation

In this section, we evaluate the performance of the three set containment algorithms: the SQL approach for the unnested external representation (**SQL**), and the signature nested-loops (**Sig-NL**) and **PSJ** algorithms for nested internal. As a special case, we also ran PSJ with one partition which we call **PSJ-1**. The special case of one partition is important when applicable, because it has no partitioning overhead. We first describe our implementation of these algorithms and then present results from various experiments designed to investigate the performance of these algorithms under various conditions.

5.1 Implementation

Paradise is a shared nothing parallel object-relational system developed at the University of Wisconsin-Madison [PYK+97]. We implemented sets using the ADT mechanism in Paradise. The set ADT implements a number of set-oriented methods, including: create-iterator, which returns an iterator over the elements of the set; and set operators which are implemented by type specific methods invoked by the query engine when comparison and assignment are performed on sets. For more details on the implementation, refer to [KJD00], [RPN].

We implemented signature-nested loops (Sig-NL) and PSJ as join algorithms in the system, and extended the optimizer to recognize set containment join operations in queries. For the SQL approach, magic set optimization was used to rewrite the correlated nested query as shown in Section 3.2. In order to ensure that the optimizer did not choose bad plans, optimal physical plans for each query were fed into the system rather than the queries themselves.

5.2 Experimental Setup and Data Generation

In our experiments, the total size of the non set-valued attributes in a tuple was 68 bytes. The average size of each set element was 30 bytes. We ran the experiments on an Intel 333 MHZ Pentium processor with 128MB of main memory running Solaris 2.6. We used a 4GB disk for storing the database volume. The disk was mounted as a raw device. It provided an I/O bandwidth of 6 MB/sec. Paradise was configured with a 32MB buffer pool. Though this buffer pool size may seem small compared to current trends in memory, we used this value since we wanted to test data sets that were much larger than the buffer pool. As will be seen in the following sections, with this buffer pool size, some experiments take many days to run. Each experiment was run against a cold buffer pool to eliminate the effect of file caching. The data generator for the BUCKY benchmark [CDN+97] was modified to generate data synthetically. The data generator takes as input the cardinality of the relations R and S, the average cardinality of the set valued attributes in the two relations, the size of the domain from which the set elements are drawn, and a correlation value. For each tuple, the set-valued attribute is generated as follows. First, the data generator divides the entire domain into 50 smaller sub-domains. The set elements are drawn from these sub-domains. Set elements are correlated if they are drawn from the same sub-domain. Correla-

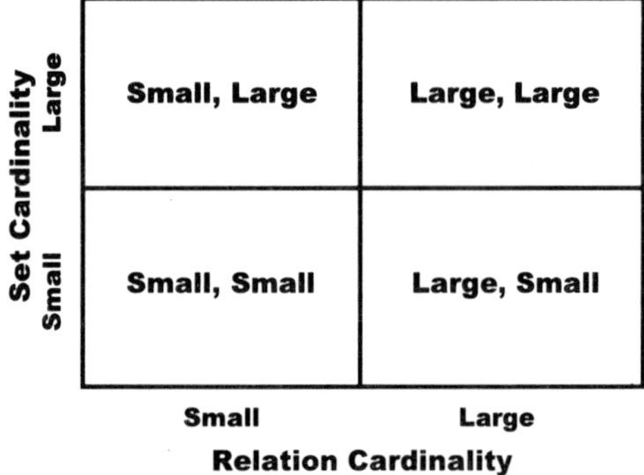

Figure 3: Taxonomy of Set Distributions

tion of a set instance is defined as the percentage of the set elements that are drawn from a single sub-domain. For example, if the set cardinality is 10, a correlation of 90% implies that 9 set elements are picked from one sub-domain and 1 element is randomly chosen from one of the remaining 49 sub-domains. All the experiments used a correlation of 10% unless otherwise specified. Joining tuples were generated such that every R tuple joins with exactly one S tuple.

5.3 Set Distributions

There are many distributions involving set valued attributes because there are many degrees of freedom:

- Average set cardinality of relation R and S
- Relation cardinality of R and S
- Size of domain from which the set elements are drawn
- Degree of correlation among the elements.

Each parameter can influence the performance of the containment algorithm. In an effort to reduce the problem space, we restricted ourselves to varying the relation and set cardinalities. Based on these two parameters we have four possible quadrants as shown in Figure 3 and the experiments explore each of the quadrant in detail. We chose the response time as our performance metric.

5.4 Varying Relation Cardinality

In this set of experiments, we investigated the effect of varying the relational cardinality. The domain size was fixed at 10000. Since the join was not symmetric, we further refined the experiments based on different cardinalities of R and S :

- The relation cardinalities of R and S are varied together and the values are kept the same.
- The relation cardinality of S is kept constant at a large value and that of R is varied.
- The relation cardinality of R is kept constant at a large value and that of S is varied.

5.4.1 Vary Relation Cardinalites of R and S

In this experiment, the relation cardinality was varied for two values of set cardinality: 20 and 120. The results of these experiments are plotted in Figure 4. The numbers for the SQL approach for relation cardinalities greater than 20000 are not included in the figure since these runs took more than 24 hours. The main observation is that PSJ outperforms (or performs as well as) other algorithms consistently over the entire space of relation cardinality. On the other hand, the SQL approach starts getting worse from 10000 onwards. Section 5.5 discusses why the SQL approach performs poorly. Sig-NL and PSJ are analyzed in Section 5.6.

5.5 Performance of the SQL Approach

As seen from Figure 4, the SQL approach performs reasonably well at very small relation and set cardinalities. However, as the relation sizes increase (note the peak at 10000), the response time increases rapidly. The cost breakdown of the SQL approach shows that most of the time is dominated by candidate generation query.

- The input to the joins are two large set relations R_S and S_S.
- The number of intermediate tuples generated as a result of the join is also large.
- The number of groups generated from the aggregate operator is also large.

For a detailed cost breakdown of SQL approach, refer the expanded version of the paper [KJJK00]. Because of the aforementioned problems and consequent performance degradation, the SQL approach is not considered in the remaining sections.

5.6 Sig-NL Vs PSJ

The individual cost breakdown of these algorithms is shown in Figure 5, Figure 6 and Figure 7.

In general, the cost of these algorithms consists of three components: partitioning cost, comparison cost and verification cost. The cost of Sig-NL and PSJ-1 do not have any partitioning cost. The cost of Sig-NL can be broken down into signature creation cost (labeled as Rsig-creat and Ssig-creat in the graphs), join cost (labeled as Sig-join) and sort and verify costs (labeled as Sort and Verify). The cost of PSJ-1 is broken down into build cost (labeled as R-build), probe cost (labeled as S-probe), and sort and verify costs (labeled as Sort and Verify). The cost of PSJ is broken into partition creation and deletion cost (labeled as Part-creat and Part-delete), partition cost (labeled as Spart-time and Rpart-time), join cost (labeled as Part-join) and sort and verify costs (labeled as Sort and Verify). The comparison cost is high in Sig-NL. It decreases in PSJ-1 and is least in PSJ.

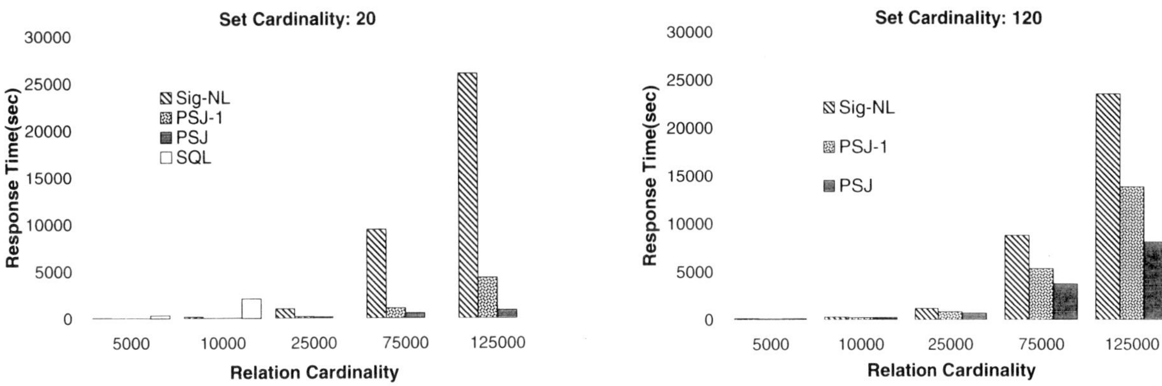

Figure 4: Varying Relation Cardinalities

The first observation is that PSJ outperforms PSJ-1 and Sig-NL consistently as seen from Figure 4. Sig-NL spends most of its execution time in comparing the signatures (see Figure 5), whereas the execution time of PSJ-1 is dominated by the signature probing cost (see Figure 6). Looking at Figure 7, we observe that the cost in PSJ is distributed across the partitioning, signature joining and the verification costs. Partitioning reduces the signature comparisons, but requires a partitioning phase. For PSJ to perform well the reduction in the number of comparisons from partitioning should be significant, and the partitioning cost should not be too high. The reduction in number of comparisons is dominant at higher relation cardinalities as seen in Figure 6 and Figure 7 (compare Part-Join in PSJ with S-probe in PSJ-1 and Sig-Join in Sig-NL). Hence PSJ consistently performs better at higher relation cardinalities. For lower relation cardinalities, the cost gained by avoiding unnecessary comparisons is not high.

The second observation is that the gap between PSJ and the rest is smaller for set cardinality of 120. This is because the partitioning cost is higher for larger set cardinalities. In addition, the comparison cost also increases because of replication. Another contributing factor is the requirement of large signature sizes for lower set cardinalities of R. This unexpected phenomenon occurs because the probability that a given set instance in R joins with some set instance in S increases as its cardinality decreases. Hence in order to keep the false drops minimum, an increase in the signature size is required. For example, in Sig-NL when the relation cardinality of R (and S) was 25000, the required signature size was 181 bits for a set cardinality of 20 while it was 104 bits for a set cardinality of 120. This larger signature size has a much greater impact on Sig-NL and PSJ-1. Note however that as the average set cardinality of S increases, the signature size increases as expected.

The third observation is that PSJ-1 outperforms Sig-NL consistently. This is expected since several unnecessary comparisons are eliminated. Quantitatively, for a set cardinality of 20 and relation cardinality of 25000, Sig-NL requires 625 million comparisons whereas PSJ-1 requires only 80 million comparisons. When the set cardinality is 120, the number of comparisons increases since the expected number of bits set to 1 in the signature increases thereby causing more chains to be examined for a given set of S. Hence the performance gap between the two decreases.

We also conducted experiments where the cardinality of one relation was fixed and the other was varied. The trends observed were the same.

5.7   Varying Set Cardinality

In this experiment, we varied the set cardinality for two different relation cardinalities: 20000 and 100000 to explore the quadrants of small and large relation cardinalities. The signature size for Sig-NL and PSJ-1 and the number of partitions for PSJ were chosen using equations (2) and (3). The domain size was set at 10000. The results are plotted in Figure 8 and the cost breakdown of PSJ-1 and PSJ are shown in Figure 9 and Figure 10.

For a given relation cardinality, as the set cardinality increases, the gap between PSJ and the rest diminishes. In fact for a relation cardinality of 20000 when the set cardinality is 160, PSJ-1 marginally outperforms PSJ. This is because the partitioning cost increases rapidly with increasing set cardinality as seen in Figure 10. This happens because more partitions are required and replication is higher. At the larger relation cardinality of 100000, the set cardinality threshold beyond which PSJ-1 outperforms PSJ increases as expected.

5.8   Effect of Signature Size

In this experiment, we study the effect of signature size on the performance of Sig-NL and PSJ. Both algorithms use signatures for producing an intermediate

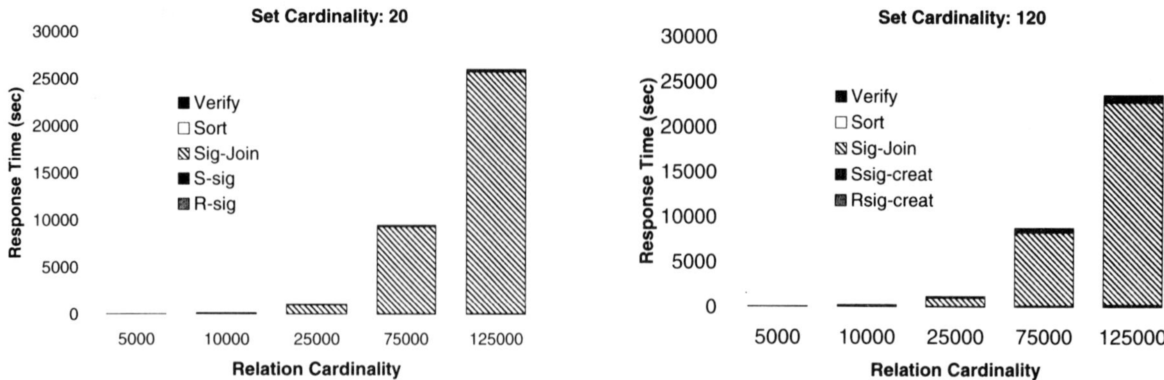

Figure 5: Cost Breakdown for Sig-NL

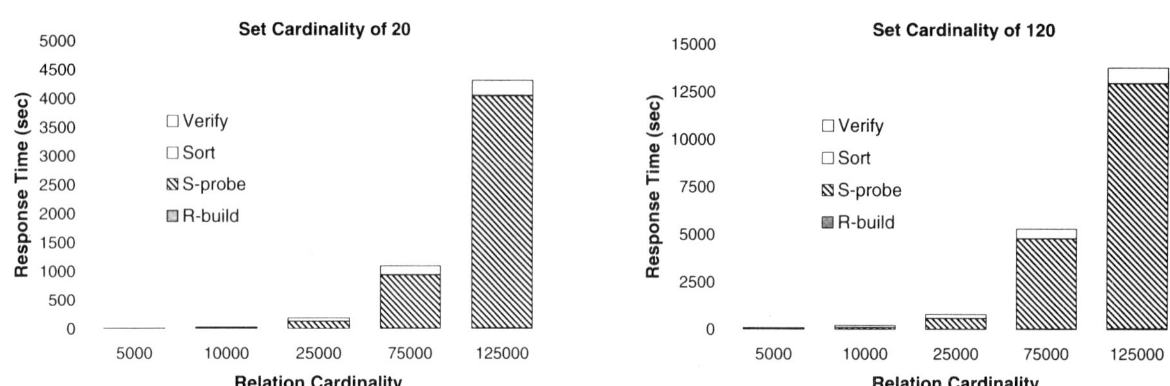

Figure 6: Cost Breakdown for PSJ-1

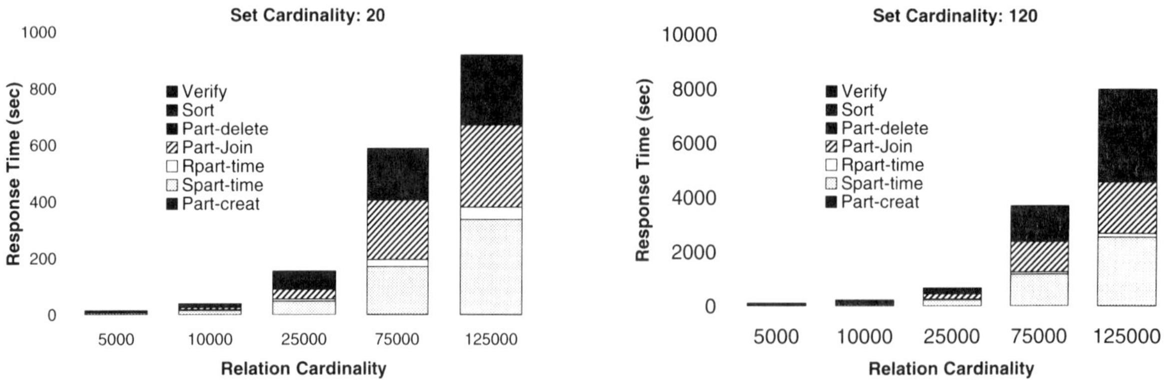

Figure 7: Cost Breakdown for PSJ

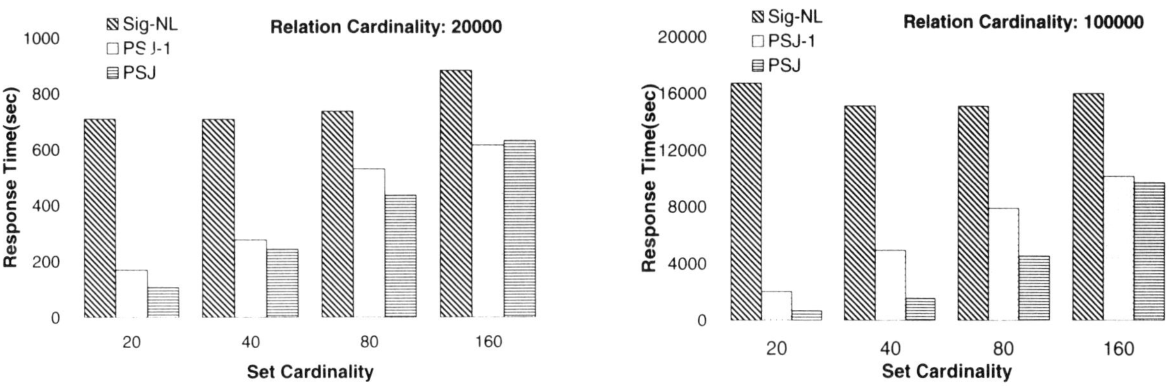

Figure 8: Varying Set Cardinality

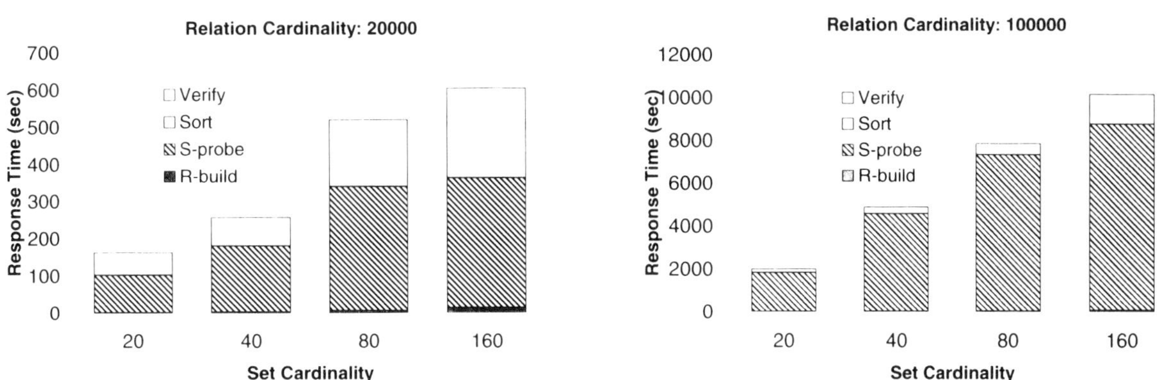

Figure 9: Cost Breakdown for PSJ-1

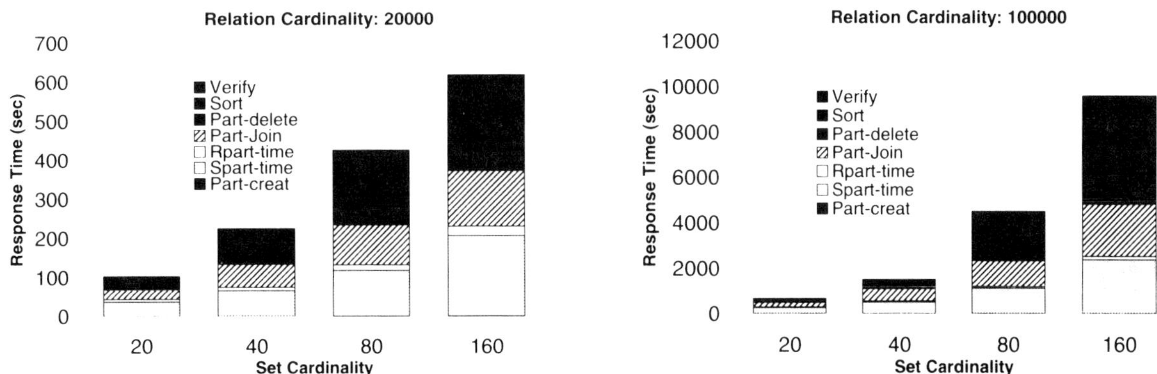

Figure 10: Cost Breakdown for PSJ

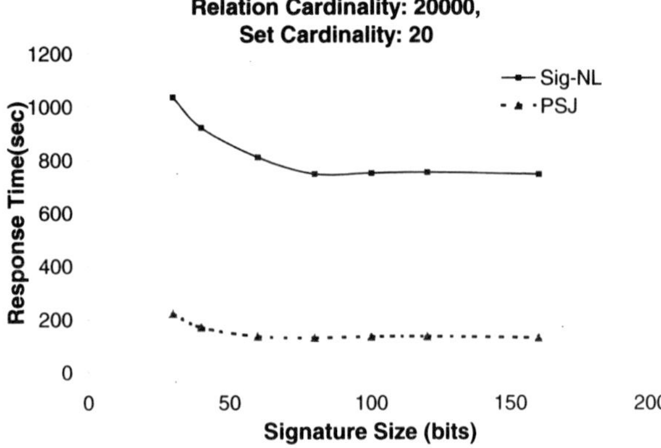

Figure 11: Effect of Signature Size

candidate set of result. As noted in Section 3.3, the number of false drops in the candidate set is influenced by the size of the signature. Hence the choice of signature size is important both in Sig-NL and PSJ. For this experiment, we used a relation cardinality of 20,000 for both R and S, an average set cardinality of 10 for R, and average set cardinality of 20 for S. The size of domain was fixed at 10,000. For PSJ, we used the optimal number of 42 partitions, as predicted by equation (2). The result of this experiment is plotted in Figure 11.

The first observation is that for smaller signature sizes, Sig-NL is very expensive. This is because many elements in the domain hash to the same bit, thereby increasing the false drops. Such an increase in the false drops increases the time of the verification phase. As the signature size increases, the number of false drops reduces and hence the performance of Sig-NL improves. However, after a signature size of 80, increasing the signature length does not cause any significant improvement in the performance of Sig-NL. The second observation is that PSJ is relatively immune to the signature size. This is because partitioning reduces the number of false drops.

For this data set, the signature size for Sig-NL predicted by equation (1) was 173 bits. For PSJ with 42 partitions, the signature size predicted by equation (3) was 116 bits. Given the flatness of the PSJ curve, it is not important to get the signature size exactly right.

5.9 Effect of Increasing Partitions in PSJ

In this experiment, we study the effect of the number of partitions on the performance of PSJ. The relation cardinality of both relations was set at 20,000 and the set cardinality was set at 120. The set elements are drawn from a domain size of 10000. An appropriate combination of partitions and signature size was used as determined by equations (2) and (3). The results of this experiment is shown as the first graph in Figure 12. It shows the breakdown of total cost: partition creation and deletion times (the time to create and delete the

partition files in SHORE, the storage manager used in Paradise), partition time (the time taken to insert tuples into the partition files), join time, sort time and verification time. From this figure, we observe that PSJ has three phases: the first phase, in which the total cost decreases gradually as the number of partitions is increased; the second phase in which the total cost is approximately constant; and the third phase in which the total cost starts increasing as the number of partitions becomes very large.

In order to further investigate the sharp increase in partitioning overhead, we plot both the total number of pages generated by the algorithm and the actual number of pages that the system uses (see the second graph in Figure 12. The actual number of pages generated by the system counts the number of disk pages that were created by the algorithm. This number is higher than the number of pages generated by the algorithm as it includes the per-tuple overhead, and the overhead due to fragmentation. The storage manager allocates pages in extents (a group of pages) and fragmentation occurs when there are unused pages in the extent. The graph shows that as the number of partitions increases, there is a corresponding increase in the size of the data generated (because of the increased replication of S tuples). However, the replication of each tuple is bounded by the set cardinality, and, consequently the increase in the amount of data generated slows down after 64 partitions. However, the actual number of pages required still continues increasing rapidly because of fragmentation. In addition, other costs like the the number of buffer pool pins and unpins, the cost of creating and deleting the partitions also increases with the number of partitions. Thus, the partitioning overhead increases sharply when the number of partitions is large. This experiment shows that the number of partitions has a critical impact on the performance of PSJ. The equation (2) can be used to estimate a reasonable number of partitions. For set cardinality of 120, the number of partitions chosen by the equation was 70.

5.10 Disk Space Requirements

Here we investigate the size of the intermediate space required for Sig-NL and PSJ. We do not consider PSJ-1 since it is an in-memory algorithm. We ran two experiments to examine the disk space requirements. In the first experiment, we set the relation cardinalities to 100,000 and varied the set cardinality, and in the second experiment, we set the set cardinality to 120 and varied the relation cardinalities. The results of these two experiments are plotted in Figure 13 and Figure 14 respectively. In these two figures, we plot the number of pages generated by each algorithm (labeled as Sig-NL-Gen and PSJ-Gen in the graphs) and the actual number of pages created on disk (labeled as Sig-NL-Actual and PSJ-Actual). The main observation

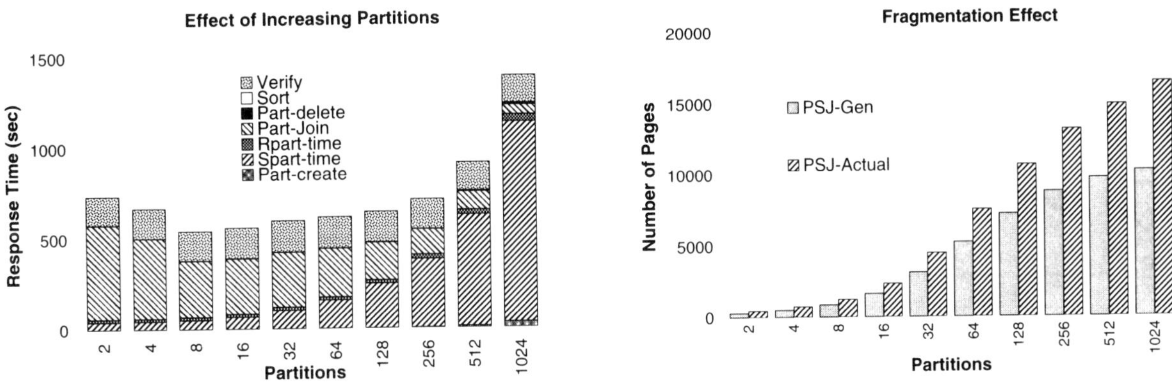

Figure 12: Effect of Increasing Partitions and Fragmentation for Set Cardinality of 120

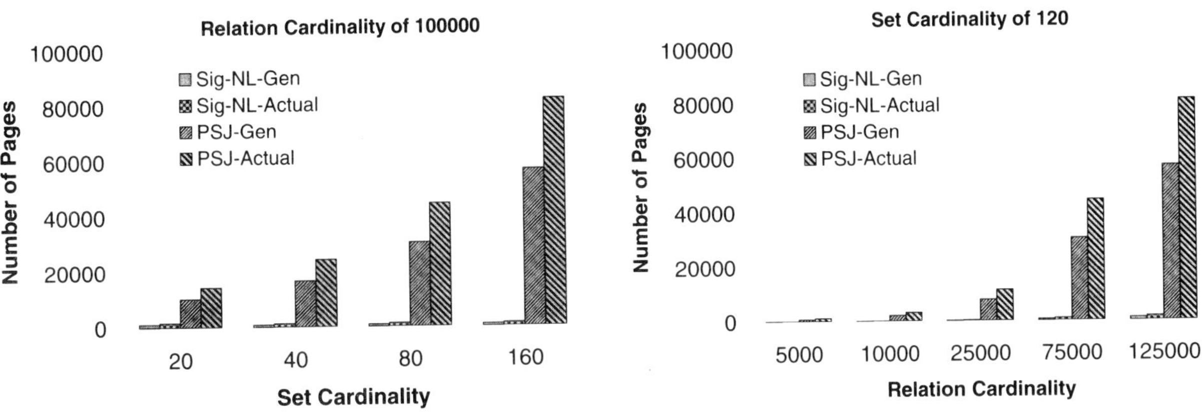

Figure 13: Disk Space, Varying Set Cardinality

Figure 14: Disk Space, Varying Relation Cardinality

is that Sig-NL requires much less storage than PSJ as expected. The number of pages required by Sig-NL varies slightly because of the variation in signature size. Since the number of pages required by Sig-NL is so low, there is a high probability that these pages will remain in the buffer pool during the operation of the algorithm. PSJ on the other hand requires a large amount of intermediate storage that steadily increases as the cardinality increases. This behavior in PSJ is caused by the following two factors: a) the number of times the 3-tuple (as described in section 4.1) is replicated increases as set cardinality increases and b) the number of tuples per partition increases as the relation cardinality increases.

For large data sets, the memory requirement for PSJ-1 is very high since the entire set of R signatures has to be accommodated. On the other hand, Sig-NL and PSJ adapt themselves to available amount of memory. Hence they are well suited to a multi-user environment.

6   Conclusions and Future Work

This paper investigates algorithms for computing a set containment join. These algorithms cover two possible implementations of set valued attributes: the unnested external representation and the nested internal representation. The unnested external representation is used by commercial O/R DBMSs for implementing set-valued attributes. In this case, set containment join is implemented using a standard SQL2 query. For the nested internal representation, this paper considers two algorithms. The first is a variation of nested loops (Sig-NL) that uses signatures to speed up the evaluation of the join predicate. The second algorithm is PSJ, a new partition based algorithm that is proposed in this paper. This algorithm is based on a two level partitioning scheme by using set elements to partition relation R and replicate relation S. Within each partition, it uses an in-memory algorithm based on partitioning of signatures.

This paper also presents a detailed performance study of the three algorithms. The performance space of these algorithms is summarized in Figure 15. For small data sets and small set cardinalities, PSJ works well. The SQL approach and Sig-NL performs reasonably well for extremely small data sets and small set cardinalities; however, as the relation or the set cardinality size increases the performance degrades very

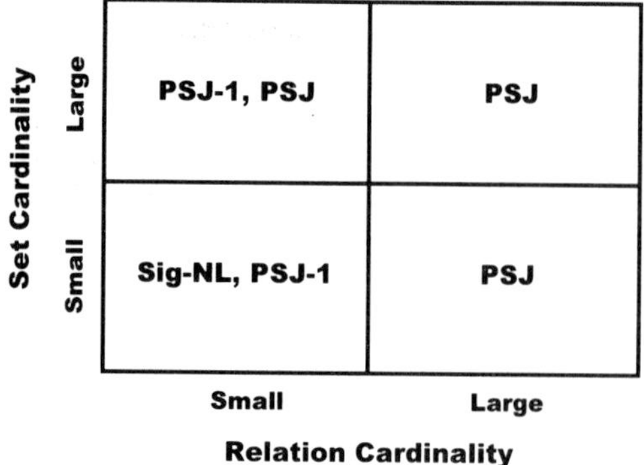

Figure 15: Performance Space of Set Containment Algorithms

rapidly. PSJ with one partition is usable at higher set cardinalities provided there is enough memory. Elsewhere, PSJ is the algorithm of choice.

Since the native SQL approach performed so poorly, we are investigating how the benefits of PSJ can be achieved even in systems that use the unnested external set representation. One obvious approach would be to execute the join by: (a) converting the inputs from the unnested external format to a temporary nested internal approach, (b) doing the join, (c) reconverting the output. In this way the nested internal approach is just an internal data structure of the join algorithm. Clearly this will be much faster than the native SQL over unnested external approach (which took days in some of our tests.) In future work we plan to investigate this and other alternatives.

References

[Bra84] K. Bratbergsengen. Hashing methods and relational algebra operations. In *Proceedings of International Conference on Very Large Databases (VLDB)*, pages 323–333, 1984.

[CDN+97] M. Carey, D. Dewitt, J. F. Naughton, M. Asgarian, P. Brown, J. E. Gerke, and D. N. Shah. The bucky object-relational benchmark. In *Proceedings of the ACM SIGMOD Conference on Management of Data*, 1997.

[DKO+84] D. Dewitt, R. Katz, F. Ohlken, L.Shapiro, M.Stonebraker, and D. Wood. Implementation techniques for main memory database systems. In *Proceedings of the ACM SIGMOD Conference on Management of Data*, pages 1–8, 1984.

[DLM93] D. Dewitt, D. Lieuwen, and M. Mehta. Pointer-based join techniques for object-oriented databases. In *PDIS*, 1993.

[DNS91] D. Dewitt, J. Naughton, and D. Schneider. Parallel sorting on a shared-nothing architecture using probabilistic splitting. In *PDIS*, Miami Beach, 1991.

[HM96] S. Helmer and G. Moerkotte. Evaluation of main memory join algorithms for joins with set comparison join predicates. Technical report, University of Mannheim, 1996.

[HM97] S. Helmer and G. Moerkotte. Evaluation of main memory join algorithms for joins with set comparison join predicates. In *Proceedings of International Conference on Very Large Databases (VLDB)*, Athens, Greece, 1997.

[KJD00] K.Ramasamy, J.Naughton, and D.Maier. High performance implementation techniques for set valued attributes. Technical report, Computer Sciences Department, University of Wisconsin, Madison, 2000.

[KJJK00] K.Ramasamy, J.Patel, J.Naughton, and K.Raghav. Set containment joins: The good, the bad and the ugly. Technical report, Computer Sciences Department, University of Wisconsin, Madison, 2000.

[LR96] M. Lo and C. Ravishankar. Spatial hash-joins. In *Proceedings of ACM SIGMOD Conference on Management of Data*, Montreal,Quebec, May 1996.

[MK76] M.W.Blasgen and K.P.Eswaran. On the evaluation of queries in a relational database system. Technical report, IBM, 1976.

[PD96] J. Patel and D. DeWitt. Partition based spatial merge join. In *Proceedings of ACM SIGMOD Conference on Management of Data*, Montreal,Quebec, May 1996.

[PYK+97] J. Patel, J. Yu, N. Kabra, K. Tufte, B. Nag, J. Burger, N. Hall, K. Ramasamy, R. Lueder, C. Ellman, J. Kupsch, S. Guo, J. Larson, D. DeWitt, and J. Naughton. Building a scalable geo spatial dbms: Technology, implementation and evaluation. In *Proceedings of ACM SIGMOD Conference on Management of Data*, Tucson, Arizona, May 1997.

[RKS98] M. Roth, H. Korth, and A. Silberschatz. Extending relational algebra and calculus for nested relational databases. *ACM Transactions on Database Systems*, 13(4):389–417, December 1998.

[RPN] K. Ramasamy, J. Patel, and J. Naughton. Efficient pairwise operations for nested set valued attributes. Working paper.

[SC90] E. J. Shekita and M. J. Carey. A performance evaluation of pointer based joins. In *Proceedings of ACM SIGMOD Conference on Management of Data*, pages 300–311, 1990.

[SHT+99] J. Shanmugasundaram, G. He, K. Tufte, C. Zhang, D. DeWitt, and J. Naughton. Relational databases for querying xml documents: Limitations and opportunities. In *Proceedings of International Conference on Very Large Databases (VLDB)*, Scotland, 1999.

[SPL96] P. Seshadri, H. Pirahesh, and T.Y. C. Leung. Complex query decorrelation. In *Proceedings of IEEE Conference on Data Engineering(ICDE)*, pages 450–458, 1996.

[Sto96] M. Stonebraker. *Object-relational DBMS: The Next Great Wave*. Morgan Kaufmann, 1996.

[Zan83] Carlo Zaniolo. The database language gem. In *Proceedings of 1983 ACM SIGMOD Conference on Management of Data (SIGMOD)*, San Jose, California, May 1983.

Identifying Representative Trends in Massive Time Series Data Sets Using Sketches

Piotr Indyk
Stanford University
indyk@cs.stanford.edu

Nick Koudas
AT&T Laboratories
koudas@research.att.com

S. Muthukrishnan
AT&T Laboratories
muthu@research.att.com

Abstract

Many data stores, including scientific and financial databases, business warehouses and network repositories, contain time series data. Time series data depict trends for an observed value e.g., value of a stock, number of bytes sent on a router interface, etc., as a function of time. Analysis of the trends over different time windows is of great interest.

In this paper, we formalize problems of identifying various "representative" trends in time series data. Informally, an interval of observations in a time series is defined to be a representative trend if its distance from other intervals satisfy certain properties, for suitably defined distance functions between time series intervals. Natural trends of interest such as periodic or average trends are examples of representative trends.

We present efficient algorithms for analyzing massive time series data sets for representative trends over arbitrary windows of interest. Our algorithms are highly processor and IO efficient; they are approximate but provide probabilistic guarantees for the approximations achieved. Our approach for identifying representative trends relies on a dimensionality reduction technique that replaces each interval by a "sketch" which is a low dimensional vector. We present efficient algorithms to construct such sketches using a pool of select sketches that we precompute using polynomial convolutions. Using such sketches, we can compute representative trends accurately.

**Proceedings of the 26th VLDB Conference,
Cairo, Egypt, 2000.**

Finally, we present results of a detailed experimental study of our technique on very large real data sets. Our results show that, compared to approaches that determine representative trends exactly, our approach shows significant performance gains with only a small loss in accuracy.

1 Introduction

Many data sources are observations that evolve over time leading to time series data. For example, financial databases depict stock prices over time which is a common example of a time series. Reporting meteorological parameters such as the temperature over time gives rise to a time series in the area of scientific databases. Telecommunications and network databases represent many different time series data derived from the usage of various networking resources over time such as the total number and duration of calls, number of bytes or electronic mails sent out from one ISP to another, amount of web traffic at a site, etc. Business warehouses represent time series such as the sale of a specific commodity over time. Therefore, time series data abound in various databases.

Time series data depict the trends in the observed value over time, and hence, capture valuable information that users may wish to analyze and understand. For example, users may wish to know for a given time window, the "typical" trend of values or an "outlier" trend, in the intuitive sense of these words; or, as a dual, users may wish to find the time window such that most trends are as similar as possible or clustered. Finding such trends, what we will call "representative trends", will have many uses. For example, representative trends may be used in lieu of the entire data for quick approximate analysis; this maybe thought of as Data Reduction [2], specifically for the time series domain. In addition they can be used for identifying and detecting anomalous behavior or intrusion and for prediction.

We formalize the problems of finding various "representative" trends in time series data. In general, an interval of observations in the time series is defined to be a representative trend if its distance to other intervals satisfy certain properties, for suitable distance functions defined between intervals. However, the intervals, properties and distance functions can vary and this leads to many different notions of representative trends. Another aspect of our study here is the focus on massive time series data. For example, AT&T collects around 500GB of data per year about one of the services it provides. Aggregate statistics about a single attribute (say usage of that service for every second) over a year results in a time series of size approximately 250MB, containing more than 31 million values. Running a quadratic algorithm for data analysis to analyze, say 5 years worth of data, would be prohibitively time consuming. The situation is aggravated if one wishes to perform analysis over a longer window of time or over a refined time scale.

In this paper, we formulate the problems of finding representative trends and focus on designing processor and I/O efficient algorithms for identifying them in large time series databases. In Section 2 we present examples of representative trends. In Section 3 we formally define various representative trends. Section 4 presents exact algorithms for identifying representative trends. These are expensive but exact. Section 5 presents our overall approach as well as our techniques for preprocessing time series data, which will be suitable for finding different representative trends. Section 6 presents how these techniques can be used to search for relaxed periods and average trends, presenting efficient algorithms for this task. Our algorithms will be very efficient, but will only be approximate; we provide guarantees on the accuracy. Section 7 contains the results of a detailed experimental evaluation of the proposed technique and algorithms, using real data sets, analyzing various tradeoffs. Section 8 discusses other notions of representative trends and application of our techniques to solve them. Section 9 presents related work and finally Section 10 presents concluding remarks.

2 Examples of Representative Trends

In this section, we describe two examples of representative trends in some detail, namely, relaxed periods and average trends, in order to motivate our more formal study in the later sections.

Relaxed Periods. The notion of a period of a time series is well understood[17]. Given a time series V, its period is T if $V = T^\ell T'$ where T' is a prefix of T and ℓ is some positive integer (typically taken to be at least 2). Informally, V is a repetition of non-overlapping copies of T. For example, 113 is a period of 11311311311311. However, rarely do time series data have exact period as defined above. So, in reality, one needs a relaxed notion of a period. We define a relaxed period of V to be T' if the sequence generated by repeating T' to the extent needed results in a sequence

V' whose distance from V is the smallest possible in some distance measure, say, in sum of squares distance, for concreteness. (This will be formally defined in Section 3). According to this notion, the relaxed period of 213123213132213 will be 213. If there was a period for T, that will also be its relaxed period. ∎

Finding the Average Trend. Consider a time series $V[1\cdots n]$ and a length l. V consists of $\lceil \frac{n}{l} \rceil$ disjoint subsequences of length l (except possibly the last one which may be shorter). One may ask which is the subsequence whose total distance to all the other subsequences is the smallest; again, we can fix the sum of squares as the distance function. We will call such a subsequence the average trend. For example, if $V = 113123213132113$ and $l = 3$, then we have 5 subsequences of interest, namely, 113, 123, 213, 132 and 113. The average trend is 123 which has a smaller total sum of squares distance than the others. ∎

Both relaxed period and average trend will be instances of representative trends we study in this paper. Representative trends suitable in different applications may differ, and many different notions of representative trends may be formalized and studied. For example, representative trends may not be global at all, but rather occur locally in significant ways and indeed our formulation below will enable us to express such variations. Our study will therefore be general, encompassing the many different notions of representative trends.

3 Definitions

Let $V[1,\ldots n]$ be a time series of length n. We adopt a vector notation and we refer to the time series V as a vector $\vec{V}$. We denote the i-th element of this vector by $V[i]$. For some integer T, we define $V(T) = \{\vec{v_i}\} = \{(V[iT+1], V[iT+2], \ldots V[iT+T])\}, 0 \le i \le \frac{n}{T} - 1$; if T does not divide n, the final subvector is not considered. Let $D(\vec{v}, \vec{u})$ be the distance between two vectors. In this paper, we will focus on L_2 which is a natural measure of distance between two vectors. We define

$$C^i(V(T)) = \sum_{j=0}^{\frac{n}{T}-1} D(\vec{v_i}, \vec{v_j}).$$

Definition 1 *Given a vector $\vec{V}$ and integers l and u, the relaxed period of $\vec{V}$ in range $[l, u]$ is the T, $l \le T \le u$ such that $C^0(V(T))$ is minimized.*

Definition 2 *Given vector $\vec{V}$ and integers l and u, the average trend of $\vec{V}$ in the range $[l, u]$ is the subvector $\vec{v_i}$ such that $C^i(V(T))$ is minimized for $l \le T \le u$.*

Both relaxed periods and average trends are examples of representative trends. In both these definitions, we have an interval $[l, u]$ of interest which specifies the length of the trend of interest. Note that if

$C^0(V(T)) = 0$, then T is the exact period of the sequence as is well understood [17]. Other variants of representative trends will be of interest as well.

4 Exact Algorithms

Let $\vec{V}$ be a time series and $[l, u]$ a range of interest in $\vec{V}$. Let us consider the exact algorithms to identify relaxed periods and average trends. Let $V(T) = \{\vec{v_i}\}$ be a set of vectors as defined in section 3, for $l \leq T \leq u$ and $0 \leq i \leq \frac{n}{T} - 1$. The brute force algorithm for identifying relaxed periods exactly is an $O(n^2)$ algorithm: for each T from l to u, for each i from 0 to $n/T - 1$, determine the minimum value of $D(\vec{v_0}, \vec{v_i})$. It can be implemented efficiently for large time series data, by assuming that for every $T \in [l, u]$ two vectors of size T can be stored in memory at any time and $u - l + 1$ counters can be maintained in memory. Under these assumptions the computation can be performed by a single pass on $\vec{V}$, and is likely to be processor bound for realistic sizes of $\vec{V}$ and $[l, u]$.

The brute force algorithm for identifying average trends exactly, is as follows: for each T from l to u, for each i from 0 to $n/T - 1$, for each j from 0 to $n/T - 1$, determine the minimum value of $D(\vec{v_i}, \vec{v_j})$. It is an $O(n^3)$ algorithm. In the worst case, we have to scan the data set for every value of $T \in [l, u]$ and every $i, 0 \leq i \leq \frac{n}{T} - 1$. In the best case, $\vec{V}$ fits in memory and for every value of T a quadratic number of evaluations of the distance function $D(.)$ between vectors of length T has to take place.

Application of the above algorithms in large scale time series data sets is formidably time consuming. Even for vectors of a few thousand points the above algorithms are very inefficient. In the next section, we introduce a technique than can lead to the design of efficient solutions for both problems even for very large data sets.

5 Sketching Approach

We will develop algorithms for finding relaxed periods and average trends which will be faster than the algorithms in the previous section, but will only provide an approximate answer. This is based on a sketch based approach which (1) is general and it applies to other notions of representative trends as will be discussed in Section 8, (2) gives guaranteed approximation performance, with high probability, as we prove. We will present our overall approach in steps:

1. First, we will define the *sketch* of a vector and state its properties. This will be useful in computing the distance between two subvectors efficiently.

2. We will then present an algorithm for finding the sketch of all subvectors of a given width T efficiently. This step will rely on polynomial convolutions.

3. We will then show how to determine the sketch of all subvectors of width in a given range. In order to do this efficiently, this will involve preprocessing the given vector into a pool of sketches for a chosen subset of subvectors, and then we will show how to extract the sketch of any subvector from the pool efficiently.

4. We will show how to find the representative trends of our interest using sketches. This will show the improvement in performance over the exact algorithms in the previous section as well as the guarantee on the loss in accuracy.

5.1 Sketch of a Vector

Given a vector $\vec{t} = t[1 \cdots \ell]$, we present an algorithm to construct its *sketch* vector $\vec{S}(t)$. $\vec{S}(t)$ is of size k. We generate $S(t)[i]$ as follows. We pick a random vector $v_i[1 \cdots \ell]$ by picking each component $v_i[j]$ to be an independent random variable with normal distribution $N(0, 1)$ and the entire vector $\vec{v_i}$ is normalized to 1 in magnitude. We define

$$\vec{S}(t)[i] = \vec{t} \cdot \vec{v_i} = \sum_j t[j].v_i[j]$$

This is the well known inner product between two vectors.

Example 5.1 Say $\vec{t} = (2, 1, 3, 1)$ and suppose we wish to construct a sketch vector of size two. We choose two vectors $\vec{v_1} = (-0.45, -0.09, 0.10, 0.87)$ and $\vec{v_2} = (-0.19, 0.73, -0.61, 0.21)$ and compute the inner product. The sketch vector $S(t)$ is $(0.18, -1.28)$. ∎

The sketch of a vector has many nice properties of which the one that interests us the most is the following which follows from the Johnson-Lindenstrauss Lemma [11]; hence we do not include its proof here.

Lemma 5.1 *For any given set L of vectors of length ℓ, for fixed $\epsilon < 1/2$, if $k = \frac{9 \log |L|}{\epsilon^2}$, then for any pair of vectors $\vec{u}, \vec{w} \in L$*

$$(1 - \epsilon)||\vec{u} - \vec{w}||^2 \leq ||\vec{S}(u) - \vec{S}(w)||^2 \leq (1 + \epsilon)||\vec{u} - \vec{w}||^2$$

with probability $1/2$. Here $||U - V||^2$ is the L_2 distance between two vectors U and V.

This lemma has the additional property that by increasing k, one can increase the probability of success as needed.

5.2 Fixed Window Sketches

In this section, we focus on computing the sketch for each subvector of a given length ℓ in $T[1 \cdots n]$. That is, we need to compute the sketch of $\lceil \frac{n}{\ell} \rceil$ vectors: $\vec{t}_1 = T[1 \ldots \ell], \vec{t}_2 : T[2 \ldots \ell + 1], \ldots, \vec{t}_{n-\ell+1} = T[n - \ell + 1, \ldots, n]$. Let us fix our attention on one of components, say, $S(t_i)[j]$ for each such vector $\vec{t}_i$.

The straightforward method would be as follows. We first generate random vector $\vec{v}_j$. We then consider each of the vectors $\vec{t}_i$ and compute $T[i, \ldots, i + \ell - 1] \cdot \vec{v}_j[1 \cdots \ell]$ directly. This takes $O(n\ell)$ time since there are $n - \ell + 1$ such vectors and for each we perform $O(\ell)$ work computing the inner product. Now we can repeat the whole procedure for the other components of the k sized sketch, in all taking $O(n\ell k)$ time all together. While this algorithm is practical for small ℓ, later, we will need sketches for rather large time windows, that is, large ℓ up to $O(n)$. For such cases, the straightforward algorithm above takes time $O(n^2 k)$ which is prohibitive for large n such as the ones we consider in our applications.

Our key observation here is that we can compute all such sketches fast by using Fast Fourier Transforms. Again, let us focus on one of the components of the sketch, say, $S(t_i)[j]$ for all i. The key observation is that *the problem of computing the sketches of all subvectors of length ℓ simultaneously is precisely the problem of computing the polynomial convolution of the two vectors $\vec{t}$ and $\vec{v}_j$.* This observation is evident when one considers the definition of the polynomial convolution.

Definition 3 *Given two vectors $A[1 \cdots a]$ and $B[1 \cdots b]$, $a \geq b$, their convolution is the vector $C[1 \cdots a + b]$ where $C[k] = \sum_{1 \leq i < b} A[k - i] \times B[i]$ for $2 \leq k \leq a + b$, with any out of range references assumed to be 0.*

For example, if $A = [1, 10, 2, 4]$ and $B = [7, 2]$, we have $C = [7, 72, 34, 32, 8]$. Polynomial convolution of two vectors can be computed in $O(a \log b)$ time using Fast Fourier Transforms. Here, we observe that

Lemma 5.2 *Sketches of all subvectors of length ℓ can be computed in time $O(nk \log \ell)$ using polynomial convolution.*

Proof. Consider reversing $\vec{v}_j$ and performing the polynomial convolution of $\vec{t}$ and $\vec{v}_j$. The output we are interested in is precisely $C[b + 1] \cdots C[a + 1]$ of the convolution. Repeat for all k components of the sketch. ∎

Figure 1 presents an example of the use of convolutions to compute sketches. A vector $(2, 1, 3, 1)$ is convolved two times with normalized normal vectors and the same coordinates of all three sketches of length two are computed at the same time.

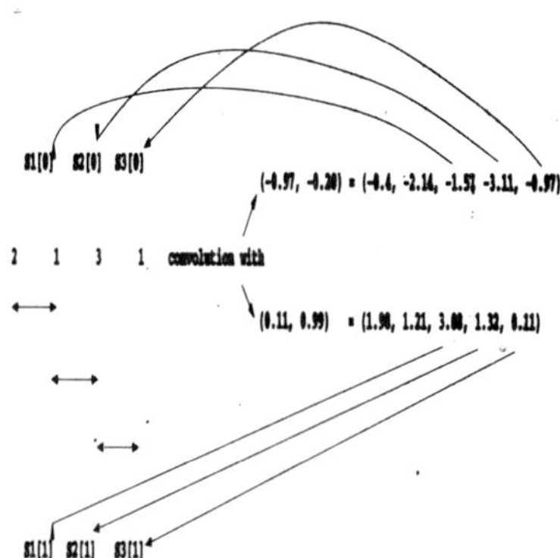

Figure 1: Using convolutions to compute sketches

5.3 Computing Sketches for Range of Subvectors

In this section, we consider the most general problem of computing the sketch for any subvector of length between l and u, of a given long vector. The most straightforward approach would be to consider all possible subvectors, and compute the sketch of each directly. There are $O(\sum_{l \leq i \leq u} \frac{n}{i})$ such subvectors. In the worst case, this is $O(n^2)$ subvectors and the majority of them are of size $\Theta(n)$, hence, the entire algorithm will take time $O(n^3)$ which is prohibitive. A less straightforward approach would be to apply our algorithm from the previous section with all possible values of ℓ. Since there are $O(u - l)$ possible values of ℓ, this algorithm will take $O(n^2 \log^2 n)$, which is better, but still prohibitive. In this section, we propose an algorithm to perform this task significantly more efficiently.

Our algorithm has the following structure. We will carefully construct a *pool* of sketches which we will store; this will be a small subset of the set of all sketches we need. Following this preprocessing, we will be able to determine the sketch of any subvector in the original vector in $O(1)$ time fairly accurately. In what follows, we will explain this procedure in more detail.

First we focus on the preprocessing. We choose $l \leq \ell \leq u$ such that ℓ is a power of 2. For each such ℓ, we compute the sketch of all subvectors of $\vec{t}$ of that length using our algorithm in Section 5.2. In fact, we compute *two* versions of sketches, each using different random variables; they are called S^1 and S^2. The resulting set of sketches is what we call the *pool*. This is of size $O(n \log(u - l)k)$ altogether and it takes time $O(n \log u \log(u - l)k)$ to compute; this is $O(n \log^3 n)$ in the worst case, hence, this algorithm scales well with the input size.

Second, we focus on determining the sketch for any subvector $\vec{t}_i$. Let us fix a particular component, say, $S(t_i)[j]$ for now. Two possibilities exist:

- $L = 2^r$, in which case, we have the sketches for this subvector in our pool, so we merely lookup

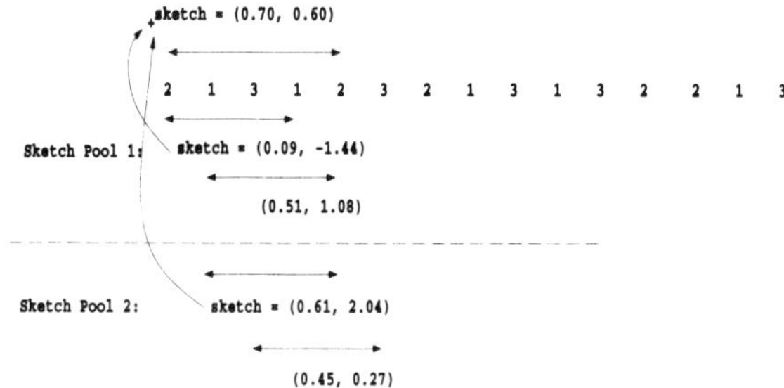

Figure 2: Synthesizing sketches for a subsequence of length 5 from sketches of subsequences of length 4 the desired sketch.

- $2^r < L < 2^{r+1}$. In that case, we compute as follows: $S'(T[i, \ldots, i+L-1])[j] = S^1(T[i, \cdots, i+2^r-1])[j] + S^2(T[i+L-2^r, \ldots, i+L-1])[j])$ (both the terms on the right belongs to our pool). See Figure 2 for an example.

We claim that S' satisfies a property very similar to the one in Lemma 5.1, namely:

Theorem 5.1 *For any given set L of vectors of length ℓ, for fixed $\epsilon < 1/2$, if $k = \frac{9 \log |L|}{\epsilon^2}$, then for any pair of vectors $\vec{u}, \vec{w} \in L$*

$$(1 - \epsilon)\|\vec{u} - \vec{w}\|^2 \leq \|\vec{S'}(u) - \vec{S'}(w)\|^2 \leq 2(1 + \epsilon)\|\vec{u} - \vec{w}\|^2$$

with probability $1/2$.

Note the additional factor 2 in the second inequality.

Proof. The idea of the proof is to use *stochastic dominance*. Recall that for two random variables X and Y we say that Y *dominates* X (or $X \leq Y$), if for any z we have $Pr[Y > z] \geq Pr[X > z]$. The dominance relation is known to be preserved under monotone functions, i.e., if $X_1 \leq Y_1, \ldots, X_l \leq Y_l$, then $f(X_1, \ldots, X_l) \leq f(Y_1, \ldots, Y_l)$ if f is a monotone function. We will also use the additive property of the normal distribution, namely if $X_1, \ldots, X_l$ are independent variables with $N(0,1)$ distribution, then for any sequence $a_1, \ldots, a_l$ of real numbers the variable $X = \sum_i a_i X_i$ has distribution $N(0, \sum_i a_i^2)$. Finally, for any interval $I \subset \{1 \ldots l\}$, define 1_I to be a vector of length l containing 1's at positions belonging to I and zeros elsewhere.

We are now ready to prove the theorem. Define $I_1 = \{i, \ldots, i+l-1\}$ and $I_2 = \{i, \cdots, i+2^r-1\}$. Note that $1_{I_1} + 1_{I_2}$ contains only 1's and 2's (no zeros), since $I_1 \cup I_2 = \{1, \ldots, l\}$. Let v_i^b be the vectors used for sketch S^b. Let $x = u - w$ and observe that $S'(u) - S'(w)][i] = S'(x)[i] = v_i^1 \cdot x + v_i^2 \cdot x = (v_i^1 + v_i^2) \cdot x$. By additivity property, the jth coordinate of $v_i^1 + v_i^2$ has distribution $N(0,2)$ if $j \in I_1 \cap I_2$ and $N(0,1)$ otherwise. Thus $S'(x)[i]$ has distribution $N(0,D)$, where $D = \sum_j (1_{I_1} + 1_{I_2})[j](x[j])^2$. For comparison, note that $S(x)[i]$ (as in Lemma 5.1) has distribution $N(0, \sum_j (x[j])^2)$ and $\sqrt{2}S(x)[i]$ has distribution $N(0, 2\sum_j (x[j])^2)$. Therefore (by monotonicity)

$\|S(x)\| \leq \|S'(x)\| \leq \sqrt{2}\|S(x)\|$. The theorem then follows from Lemma 5.1. ∎

5.4 Using Sketches to Compute Representative Trends

In this section, we will show how to compute the representative trends of our interest, namely, relaxed periods and average trends, using sketches.

Let us first consider finding relaxed periods. First, we will preprocess the given vector $\vec{V}$ as in the previous section so that the sketch of any subvector can be computed in $O(1)$ time. This takes time $O(n \log(u - l)k \log u)$ if we know $[l, u]$ or $O(nk \log^2 n)$ in the worst case. As in the exact algorithm, we will now consider all T, $l \leq T \leq u$, and for each T, we compute $C^0(V(T))$ by considering each $\vec{v}_i$ in turn and computing $D(\vec{v}_0, \vec{v}_i)$. The key is that we can now estimate $D(\vec{v}_0, \vec{v}_i)$ in $O(k)$ time by determining the sketch of $\vec{v}_0$ and $\vec{v}_i$. This process takes time $O(\sum_T \frac{n}{T} k) = O(nk \log n)$ time in the worst case (here we have used the harmonic series summation formula). Choosing $k = \frac{9 \log n}{\epsilon^2}$ from Lemma 1, it follows that the relaxed period we find will be at most a factor of $2 + \epsilon$ away from the true relaxed period with high probability (this probability can be made essentially as high as we need by choosing larger k, for example, by picking k to be twice as much, the probability that we find a relaxed period more than $2 + \epsilon$ away from the true relaxed period is at most $1/n$, a tiny quantity!).

The algorithm for computing the average trend using sketches is a similar modification to that of finding exact average trend: wherever $D(\vec{v}_i, \vec{v}_j)$ is needed, we use the estimate for that distance derived from the sketch of $\vec{v}_i$ and $\vec{v}_j$. Again, we will find a $(2 + \epsilon)$ approximation with very high probability.

6 Implementation Issues

Making our proposed sketching technique practical involves addressing important issues such as constraints in main memory size, efficient retrieval of sketches from the pool, and the impact of these constraints on the overall performance of our technique.

6.1 Computing Sketches

Assume the data set consists of n points, the sketch window is ℓ and the size of each sketch is k points. If no main memory constraints exist, an application of our technique would involve reading the data set of N points in memory, allocating $k * (n - \ell + 1)$ space for the sketches and performing k convolutions to compute the sketches each requiring time $O(n \log n)$. With realistic data sizes and a fixed memory size, it is unlikely that the data set will fit in main memory. In that case, we have to read the data set in pieces, compute a batch of sketches each time and insure that we have enough space to keep both the computed batch of sketches as well as the data points of the data piece we are working on, in memory.

Let B be the total memory available for our approach. Let M be the size of the data piece that we have to read from disk. Applying our sketching on M points will produce $M - \ell + 1$ sketches, each of size k. Thus, we have to guarantee that $M + k*(M - \ell + 1) \leq B$ and the value of M can be derived. Once the first batch of sketches is computed in main memory we can write it to disk and continue, by reading the next piece and constructing the next sketch batch. This process is repeated until we read the entire data set. A data piece of size M is loaded into memory and the sketches are computed for each subsequence of size k. Notice that construction of the first batch of sketches can be performed independently from the construction of the second batch. We only need to maintain the last $k - 1$ points from the first piece of size M, in memory, and continue with the construction of the second batch, Thus, sketches can be computed with a single scan of the underlying data set. The fact that sketch batches can be computed almost independently, makes sketching ideal for a parallel implementation, either on an SMP or distributed memory environment. Only a small amount of information needs to be communicated across processors.

6.2 Retrieving Sketches from the Pool

Once sketches are computed and the sketch pool is materialized on disk, we have to access the pool and retrieve sketches required for computing sketches of sequences in suitable range $[l, u]$. We discuss the following two cases:

Relaxed Periods. Under the assumption that we have space in memory to store two vectors of size at most u as well as $u - l + 1$ counters in memory, we can compute the corresponding clustering for every length in the range with a single pass of the sketch pool. Clustering C^0 evaluates the distance of the first sketch to all the others, so we only need to maintain the first sketch for each length in the range in memory and accumulate the value of the clustering for each length in memory.

If this assumption does not hold, we have to perform random disk accesses and retrieve the required sketches from secondary storage. However, clusterings for a number of consecutive lengths in the range can be evaluated at the same time. More specifically for $l \leq m \leq m + 1 \leq u$ the offsets of required sketches are at j sketches away for the case of the first sketch pool and $j + 1$ away for the case of the second, $0 \leq j \leq \frac{N}{m}$. Thus, if for each value of m and j we prefetch j $(j+1)$ sketches from the first (second) pool we would be able to compute the sketches for the sequence of length $m + 1$ entirely in memory, saving the disk accesses. Thus, by employing selective prefetching between successive values of m we can reduce the total number of disk accesses by half. Subsequently, additional IO savings are possible if one is willing to prefetch more aggressively. The amount of prefetching depends on the memory constraints which in turn determine the number of successive values of m one can evaluate simultaneously. This observation provides a nice trade-off between main memory usage and disk access time.

Average Trend. Evaluating average trends involves application of C^i clustering. A single scan of the pools is not enough, as all pairwise evaluations of distance between sketches corresponding to sequences of the same length is necessary. Constructing sketches by random accesses for every length is needed. This way, we are able to bring all sketches corresponding to a specific length in memory and evaluate C^i entirely in memory. Prefetching can be applied in this case as well, to save disk accesses by devoting more memory to store sketches.

7 Experimental Evaluation

We implemented the proposed sketching technique as well as the proposed algorithms to check for various kinds of representative trends and in this section we present detailed experimental results evaluating our approach. We begin our description of the experiments by describing the data used in our evaluation and then we continue with the presentation of experimental results from each of the classes of experiments we performed. With the experiments in this section we are interested in evaluating the time to construct sketches as well as the time to compute relaxed periods and average trends. In all experiments in this section whenever we retrieve sketches from the pool to synthesize sketches we do so by **random IO** accesses to the sketch pool. Our experiments were run on a SUN sparc Ultra Enterprise 8 processor SMP. The IO transfer rate in our configuration was approximately 10MB/sec.

Due to space limitations only a small subset of our experimental evaluation is presented. More discussion is available elsewhere [9].

7.1 Description of Datasets

All the datasets used in our performance study are real, extracted from one of the warehouses we maintain at AT&T Labs. All the data sets are time series containing utilization information of one of the services AT&T provides to customers. The performance data are collected in the granularity of a second and we range the time duration from a month (approximately 16MB of data) to a year (approximately 256MB).

7.2 Evaluating Time to Compute Relaxed Periods

We compare the performance of the proposed sketching technique, as applied in the identification of relaxed periods, with that of the brute force algorithm. Our treatment of the brute force algorithm is favorable since we assume that given a range of length p, we have the space to store two vectors of size up to p as well as space to maintain p variables, all in main memory. Thus we can simultaneously evaluate the clustering for all candidate relaxed periods in memory with a single scan of the time series.

In Figure 3(a), we search for the best relaxed period using our proposed sketching technique. The data set size is 16MB and we are interested in finding the best relaxed period, within specified ranges of values. The impact of our approach is most evident when ranges are large enough, so we start at offset 512 in the sequence. We vary the range from 512 to 128K. Thus, the first range is [512,1024], the second, [512, 1536] etc. Figure 3(a) presents the results of two experiments. The first one uses a sketch size equal to the logarithm of the number of data points in the data set and the second uses a sketch twice that size. For each range of values we compute the sketches necessary, from scratch. We present, for each range, the time required to construct all the necessary sketches plus the time to search for the best relaxed period within that range. For example, checking for the best relaxed period in the range [512,1536] consists of constructing sketches with a window of 512 points, using these sketches to check the lengths in the range [512,1023], and then constructing sketches with a window of 1024 points, and checking the lengths in range [1024,1536]. As we increase the size of the sketch, the time to perform the computation increases as is evident in Figure 3(a). This is because, the number of required convolutions doubles, and thus the required processor time.

Figure 3(b) presents the results of a scalability experiment plotting the total time to search for the best relaxed period in a range of size 8K as the size of the data set increases. The total time includes the time to construct the sketches on a suitable sketch window and the time to search for the best relaxed period in that range. Again, we report two experiments, using sketches of size $\log(n)$ and $2 * \log(n)$ were n is the number of points in each data set. Our sketching approach requires time linear to the size of the data set. Moreover, the time approximately doubles by doubling the data set size. This is expected as the number of sketches almost doubles by doubling the data set size and thus the processor time required for their construction. In addition more time is spent reading the data set, but IO time is only a small fraction of the computation.

As a comparison, figure 4(a) presents the total time (in minutes) requested by the brute force algorithm to compute the best relaxed period in a range p as the range increases from 512 to 128K for a 16MB data set. The time to read the data is constant for each of the ranges since the computation for the entire range is performed by a single scan of the time series. Thus, the computation performed by the brute force algorithm is processor bound. In figure 4(b) we present the time to compute the best relaxed period for a range of 8K, as the data size increases from 16MB to 256MB.

From the experiments in this section, it is evident that the proposed sketching technique offers important savings during the search for the best relaxed period, when compared with a brute force approach. Contrasting figures 4(a) and 3(a) two major performance trends are evident. First, as the range of lengths increases the performance benefits of our sketching approach become continuously better. For the 0.5K range, the time required by our sketching algorithm is slightly higher than that of brute force, when sketches are computed from scratch. Sketching is not beneficial for testing relaxed periods, in very small ranges, if sketches have to be constructed from scratch, since the overhead of constructing them becomes higher than the time required by the brute force algorithm to perform the exact computation. This observation makes sketching the method of choice for larger ranges. The exact performance cross over point between the two approaches is difficult to quantify since it depends of the machine characteristics. In our case, for any length above 512 points, sketching is always beneficial. Second, by increasing the sketch size, the cross over point essentially moves to the right, but again quickly sketching becomes the method of choice. For the range of values shown in the figure, sketching becomes almost an order of magnitude faster. The performance benefits increase as larger ranges are considered.

Contrasting figures 4(b) and 3(b) one can make a similar observation. Sketching appears 4 times faster than brute force for a sketch size of $\log(n)$ and almost 2 times faster for $2 * \log(n)$ sketch size. These performance benefits will increase when a larger range of lengths in considered, than the 8K range in the figures. In particular the performance benefits of sketching approximately double by doubling the range of lengths over which we search.

The application of the proposed technique to the identification of average trends offers much larger performance benefits when compared to brute force. Details are available elsewhere [9].

7.3 Evaluating the accuracy of the approximation

The proximity of the resulting approximation to the optimal relaxed period or average trend depends on the sketch size. We showed analytically the exact dependency of the sketch size to the approximation value ϵ. In this section we experimentally evaluate the influence of the sketch size to the resulting approximation. We conducted the following experiment: for a specific data set, we determine using the brute force algorithm

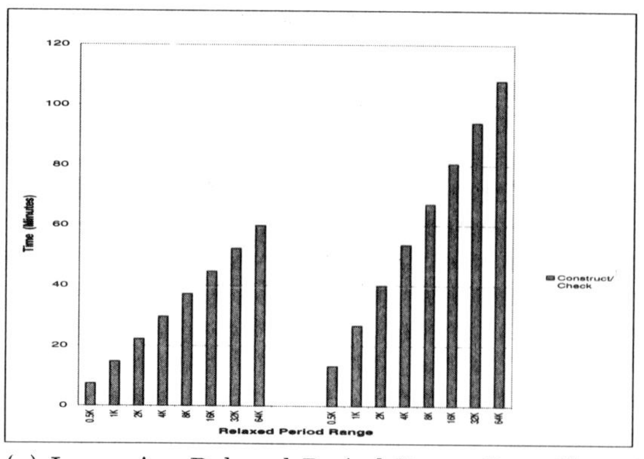 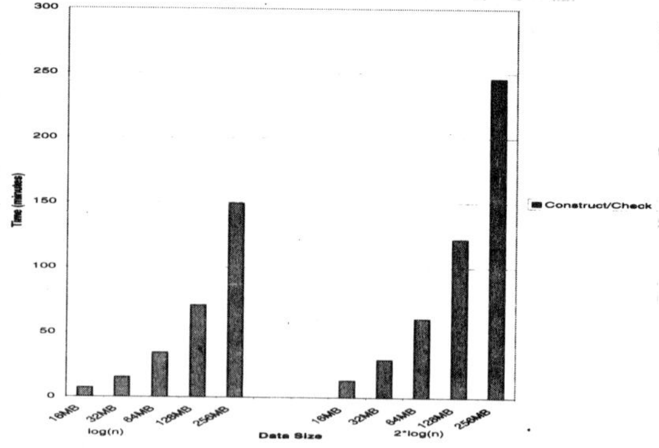

(a) Increasing Relaxed Period Range Data Size 16MB(b) Increasing Data size, window size 8K

Figure 3: Approximate relaxed period computation

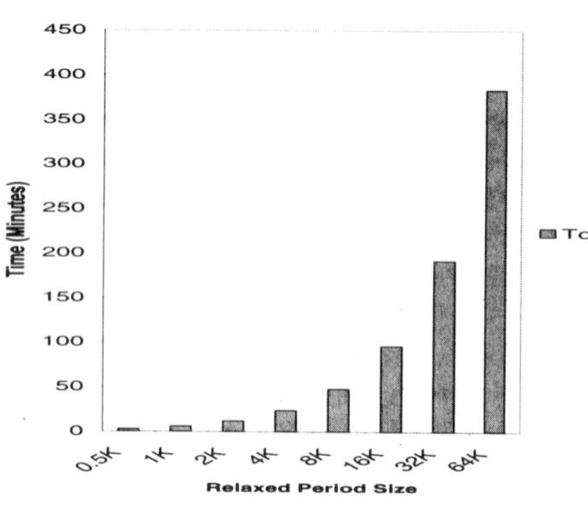 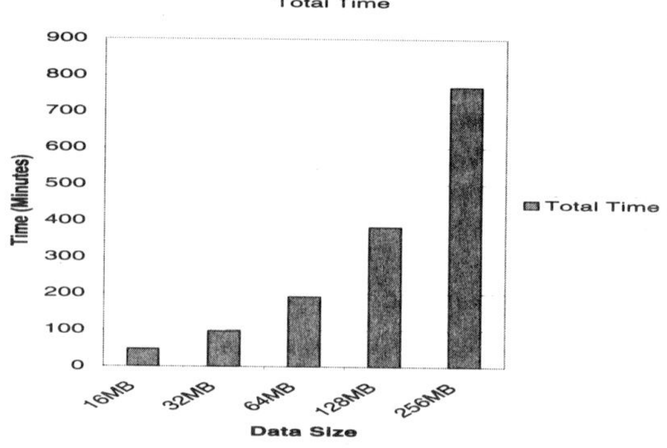

(a) Increasing Relaxed Period Size, Data Size 16MB(b) Increasing Data size, range 8K

Figure 4: Brute Force Algorithm

the optimal relaxed period and the corresponding L_2 error. We then use our technique to find the best relaxed period as the sketch size increases and we measure the absolute relative error between that of the optimal L_2 value and the L_2 value resulting from our approximation. Let O be the optimal L_2 value and O' the approximated. The absolute relative error (ARE) is defined as:

$$ARE = \frac{|O - O'|}{O} \qquad (1)$$

Figure 5 presents the results of this experiment. It shows the results for two data sets containing 1M points, representing utilization information of an AT&T service. We include the results for two data sets with different statistical characteristics. Let n be the size of the data set. In both cases we can observe that using a sketch size between $\log(n)$ or $2\log(n)$ provides reasonable accuracy, close to the optimal value. This behavior was consistent over a large collection of data sets we used in our experiments and we experimentally recommend these values. If guaranteed accuracy is required, one should select the sketch size according to Theorem 5.1 as a function of ϵ, the error one is willing to tolerate.

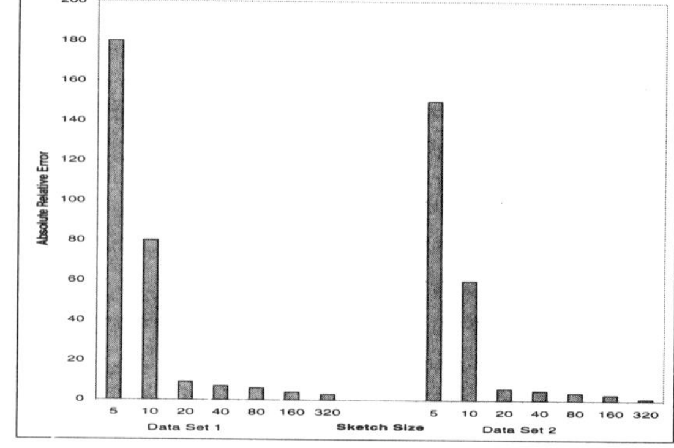

Figure 5: Evaluating the accuracy as a function of the sketch size

7.4 Comparison with Fourier Transform Based Approach

In the context of times series data, the use of fourier transform has been proposed in the community for dimensionality reduction and subsequent query processing [5]. This approach consists of the following steps: (a) compute the fourier transform of the time series segment, (b) maintain a number of fourier transform coefficients (usually the first few coefficients), and (c)

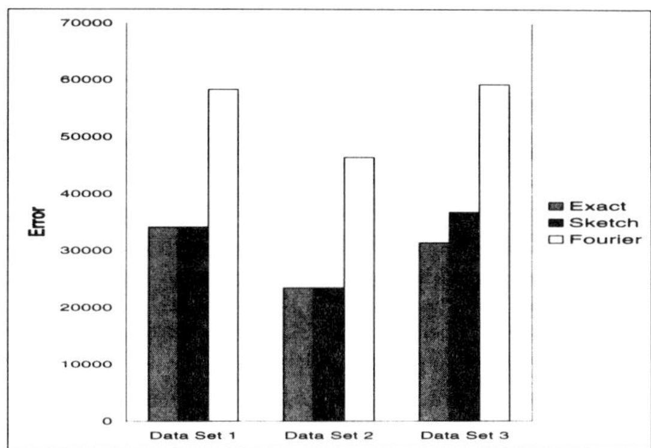

Figure 6: Error for exact relaxed period, relaxed period based on sketches, and relaxed period based on fourier coefficients

use the coefficient vector during query processing. Notice that performing such a fourier analysis of the time series data does not provide us with relaxed periods or average trends directly. However, a natural way to employ this approach for finding representative trends is to use fourier transforms as sketches. A major technical hurdle for this approach is that we are not aware of a method to combine fourier coefficients (in the spirit of Theorem 5.1 for our proposed sketching approach) and derive the fourier coefficients of a larger time series segment. This means that fourier-transforms based approach, at least in its natural version, will be inefficient since we need to recompute the fourier transform for every sketch window. Nevertheless, in order to understand the relative merits of fourier transform based approach for finding representative trends, we focused only on comparing the accuracy of the two methods (our approach vs the fourier transform based approach) without regard to their respective efficiency. We performed the following experimental study. For the case of fourier transform, for each sketch window, we computed the fourier transform and maintained as many leading coefficients as the size of the sketch. (Notice that we explicitly compute the fourier transform for each sketch window). For all the experiments we performed, our proposed sketching technique, was almost always able to identify correctly the relaxed period of the average trend in contrast with the use of fourier coefficients that failed consistently to do so. In the cases that the proposed sketching technique failed to identify the exact relaxed period, the relaxed period returned was more accurate than the one returned with the use of fourier coefficients. Results for three sample datasets are presented in figure 6.

7.5 Experimental Observations on Real Datasets

We used the proposed sketching technique to analyze large time series data sets in order to identify relaxed periods and average trends. Our analysis revealed several unexpected findings. For example in some data sets, over a very large period of time, the relaxed period was at the granularity of a week. Moreover, in other data sets, the relaxed period was at the granularity of a month. We also discovered data sets, having both a relaxed period and an average trend at the granularity of a single day. Different services that provided the data sets had particular bias: day, week or month, etc. While one expects the "periods" to be aligned with the natural time, it is intriguing why some data sets align with days and others with weeks or months.

8 Extensions

The approach of using sketches is quite powerful. We can formulate many other notions of representative trends and compute them using sketches; the results will of course be an approximation, but guaranteed to be a small factor (such as $2 + \epsilon$) with a very high probability. The idea in all such applications is that instead of using the distance $D(\vec{v}_i, \vec{v}_j)$, we can use its estimate from the sketch for $\vec{v}_i$ and $\vec{v}_j$. The process is extremely efficient because we can compute these sketches in $O(1)$ time after a preprocessing step of $O(n \log^2 n)$ in the worst case. As an example we can find local relaxed periods rather than global ones, that is, we can find all subvectors which have at least as many period repetitions as specified by a threshold, for a given window size T. In particular the framework presented in [7, 8] for partial periodic patterns, can be expressed using sketches on subsequences.

9 Related Work

A number of dimensionality reduction techniques have been proposed in the database literature including FastMap [4], applications of fourier transforms [1, 5], Singular Value Decomposition [16, 12], wavelet transforms [14, 18], and the cosine transform [13]. However, none of the above techniques has the property of our sketching technique, as proved in Theorem 5.1. This property is crucial for the algorithmic framework we presented in this paper. Indyk and Motwani [10] and Gionis et. al., [6] provide a framework based on lemma 5.1 for nearest neighbor search in multiple dimensions.

Identifying representative trends in a time series database is a problem that, to the best of our knowledge, has not been addressed in the database literature. In the case of identifying relaxed periodic patterns, one can imagine the possible application of techniques based on fourier transforms [15]. Our work, specifically, for the problem of identifying relaxed periods, offers the following advantages: (a) it guarantees that the identified relaxed period is the best *internal* (consisting of a part of the data set) relaxed period, as opposed to, a sinusoidal approximation of it (b) it identifies relaxed periods under various metrics, as opposed to only L_2 as is the case for fourier transforms (c) since time series are approximately periodic (noisy signals) an application of fourier transform will involve filtering of the time series before processing to guarantee accuracy. Even with state of the art filtering techniques, and even assuming that no phase shifts have occurred, fourier transforms cannot offer the type of approximation guarantees that the approach presented herein offers.

Han et. al., [8, 7] in their pioneering work, defined notions of partial periodicity in time series and proposed IO efficient algorithms to identify partial periods in time series datasets. Let p be a user specified period in a time series of length n. Han et. al., [8] defined partial periodicity as the existence of $f * \frac{n}{p}$ (f a user specified parameter) similar subsets (one for each of the $\frac{n}{p}$ segments), of maximum size p. Similarity between two subsets is defined in terms of equality in the corresponding elements. Subsequently, Han et.al., [7] generalized their framework to search for partial periods without specifying the period in advance. Our framework for partial periodicity is related to that of Han et.al. We do not consider similar subsets however, but similar subsequences. Two subsequences are considered similar if their distance (under some metric) is smaller than a user specified threshold. Been less strict in our definition of partial periodicity, we are able to scale our algorithms to massive datasets in an approximate way.

Techniques based on Hidden Markov Models [3] could be applied towards the type of time series analysis considered in this paper. We plan to investigate the relationship further in the future.

10 Concluding Remarks

We introduced the problem of identifying representative trends in massive time series data sets. Our work makes the following specific contributions. We presented processor and IO efficient algorithms to search for relaxed periods and average trends in large time series data bases. Our algorithms are based on a sketching technique where we showed how to efficiently construct a pool of sketches and combine them in a specific way such that other sketches can be derived from this combination efficiently. Our experiments with real data sets of realistic size showed that sketching is a fast approach for these problems and significant performance benefits are attainable. To the best of our knowledge our work is the first that addresses this important problem and provides efficient solutions for it. Given the flexibility sketching offers for approximate computations, it will be worthwhile to offer its applications to other problems of interest in time series analysis.

11 Acknowledgments

We wish to thank the referees for their comments and Dennis Shasha for overseeing the preparation of the final manuscript.

References

[1] R. Agrawal, C. Faloutsos, and A. Swami. Efficient Similarity Search in Sequence Databases. *Proc. of the 4th Int'l Conference on Foundations of Data Organization and Algorithms*, pages 69–84, Oct. 1993.

[2] D. Barbara, C. Faloutsos, J. Hellerstein, Y. Ioannidis, H. V. Jagadish, T. Johnson, R. Ng, V. Poosala, K. Ross, and K. Sevcik. The new jersey data reduction report. *Data Engineering Bulletin*, Sept. 1996.

[3] R. Durbin, S. Eddy, A. Krogh, and G. Mitchison. *Biological Sequence Analysis: Probabilistic Models of Proteins and Nucleic Acids*. Cambridge University Press, 1998.

[4] C. Faloutsos and D. Lin. FastMap: A Fast Algorithm for Indexing, Data Mining and Visualization of Traditional and Multimedia Data Sets. *Proceedings of ACM SIGMOD, San Jose California*, pages 163–174, June 1995.

[5] C. Faloutsos, M. Ranganathan, and I. Manolopoulos. Fast Subsequence Matching in Time Series Databases. *Proceedings of ACM SIGMOD*, pages 419–429, May 1994.

[6] A. Gionis, P. Indyk, and R. Motwani. Similarity Search in High Dimensions via Hashing. *Proceedings of VLDB, Endiburgh, England*, Sept. 1999.

[7] J. Han, G. Dong, and Y. Yin. Efficient Mining of Partial Periodic Patterns in Time Series Databases. *Proceedings of ICDE*, pages 106–115, Mar. 1999.

[8] J. Han, W. Gong, and Y. Yin. Mining Segment-Wise Periodic Patterns in Time Series Databases. *KDD*, pages 214–218, Aug. 1998.

[9] P. Indyk, N. Koudas, and S. Muthukrishan. Identifying Representative Trends In Massive Time Series Data Sets Using Ske tches. *AT&T Labs Technical Report*, Feb. 2000.

[10] P. Indyk and R. Motwani. Approximate Nearest Neighbors: Towards Removing the Curse of Dimensionality. *30th Symposium on the Theory of Computing*, Sept. 1998.

[11] W. B. Johnson and J. Lindenstrauss. Extensions of Lipshitz mapping into Hilbert Space. *Contemporary Mathematics, Vol 26*, pages 189–206, May 1984.

[12] K. V. R. Kanth and A. Singh. Dimensionality Reduction For Similarity Searching In Dynamic Databases. *Proceedings of ACM SIGMOD*, pages 97–105, June 1998.

[13] J. Lee, D. Kim, and C. Chung. Multi-dimensional Selectivity Estimation Using Compressed Histogram Information. *Proc. of the 1999 ACM SIGMOD Intern. Conf. on Management of Data*, June 1999.

[14] Y. Matias, J. S. Vitter, and M. Wang. Wavelet-Based Histograms for Selectivity Estimation. *Proc. of the 1998 ACM SIGMOD Intern. Conf. on Management of Data, Jun e 1998*.

[15] A. Oppenheim and A. Willsky. *Signals and Systems*. Prentice Hall, Signal Processing Series, Aug. 1992.

[16] V. Poosala and Y. Ioannidis. Selectivity Estimation Without the Attribute Value Independence Assumption. *Proceedings of VLDB, Athens Greece*, pages 486–495, Aug. 1997.

[17] D. Sankoff and J. Kruskal. *Time Warps, String Edits and Macromolecules: The Theory and Practice of Sequence Comparison*. Addison-Wesley, Reading, Mass.,, 1983.

[18] J. Vitter and M. Wang. Approximate Computation Of Multidimensional Aggregates On Sparse Data Using Wavelets. *Proceedings of SIGMOD*, pages 193–204, June 1999.

Decision Tables: Scalable Classification
Exploring RDBMS Capabilities

Hongjun Lu
Department of Computer Science
Hong Kong University of Science & Technology
Hong Kong, China
luhj@cs.ust.hk

Hongyan Liu
School of Economics and Management
Tsinghua University
Beijing, China
liuhy@em.tsinghua.edu.cn

Abstract

In this paper, we report our success in building efficient scalable classifiers in the form of decision tables by exploring capabilities of modern relational database management systems. In addition to high classification accuracy, the unique features of the approach include its high training speed, linear scalability, and simplicity in implementation. More importantly, the major computation required in the approach can be implemented using standard functions provided by the modern relational DBMS. This not only makes implementation of the classifier extremely easy, further performance improvement is also expected when better processing strategies for those computations are developed and implemented in RDBMS. The novel classification approach based on grouping and counting and its implementation on top of RDBMS is described. The results of experiments conducted for performance evaluation and analysis are presented.

1. Introduction

Classification is a process of finding the common properties of data objects that belong to the same *class*. It has a wide range of applications, such as credit approval, customer group identification, medical diagnosis, etc. The problem has been studied extensively by researchers in various fields, such as statistics, machine learning, and neural networks [WK91]. During the recent surge of KDD research, classification becomes one of the most studied data mining problems [AIS93b]. Techniques developed earlier were re-examined in the new context [AGI+92, LSL95, MAR96, SAM96, WIV98, LHM98]. Since classification algorithms developed in machine learning and statistics assume that the training set resides in memory, most of the recent work is devoted to develop scalable classifier for training set whose size is much larger than the size of memory.

The work reported in this paper is motivated by the following observations.

First, most existing scalable classification algorithms [MAR96, SAM96, WIV98] are decision tree based [Quin93]. Decision tree based algorithms consist of two phases: *tree building* and *tree pruning*. During the tree-building phase, the training set is split into two or more partitions using an attribute (the *splitting attribute*). This process is repeated recursively until all (or most of) the examples in each partition belong to one class. Both the selection of the splitting attribute and the splitting points involve operations with high computational cost such as scanning the data, sorting and subset selection. Furthermore, since such operations are required at each internal node, they become the performance bottleneck of scalable classification [MAR96].

Second, although most work on scalable classification algorithms originated from the database researchers, the database technology developed during the past decades has not been fully explored in developing efficient scalable classifiers. Recently, researchers have started to focus on issues related to integrating data mining with databases. Agrawal *et. al.* addressed issues of tightly coupling a mining algorithm with a relational database system from the system point view [AS96]. They propose to use user-defined functions (UDFs) in SQL statement to push parts of the computation required by data mining algorithms into the database system. Wang, Iyer and Vitter reported their experience in mining classification rules in relational databases using UDFs [WIV98]. Since UDFs are not native functions to DBMS, the performance benefit that the relational DBMS can provide may still be limited.

Finally, in order to meet the challenge posed by on-line analytical processing (OLAP) of large volume of data, efficient processing of data aggregation and summarization has been a research hit in recent years. Extensions to RDBMS functionality, operations and the related process strategies have been proposed [GCB+97, AAD+96, ZDN97]. The results have been quickly integrated into the commercial products. For example, IBM DB2 extended the traditional GROUP BY functions to include GROUP BY GROUPING SETS, GROUP BY CUBE, GROUP BY ROLLUP [Cham98]. Although such data aggregation and summarization are basic operations of a classification process, those new developments have not attracted much attentions from the data miners yet.

Based on the above observations, we developed a new approach, *GAC (Grouping And Counting)*, for scalable classification. Like any classification process, the input of *GAC* is a training set, a set of objects with known classes, often in the form of $(n+1)$-tuples, $(a_1, a_2, ..., a_n, c_k)$, where a_i is a value from the domain of attribute A_i, $A_i \in \{A_1, A_2, ..., A_n\}$, and $c_k \in \{c_1, c_2, ..., c_m\}$ is the class label. The output of *GAC*, a *GAC*-classifier, is a table, *decision table* with $n+3$ columns, $(A_1, A_2, ..., A_n, Class, Sup, Conf)$. Each row in the table, $(a_{1i}, a_{2i}, ..., a_{ni}, c_i, sup_i, conf_i)$, represents a classification rule

    if $(A_1 = a_{1i})$ and $(A_2 = a_{2i})$ and ... and $(A_n = a_{ni})$

    then *class* = c_i ($sup_i, conf_i$)

where sup_i and $conf_i$ give the *support* and *confidence* of the rule. The support of the rule denotes how popular is the rule and the confidence of the rule is the conditional probability, $P(class = c_i \mid (A_1 = a_{1i}) \wedge (A_2 = a_{2i}) \wedge ... \wedge (A_n = a_{ni}))$. The value of a_{ki}, $(1 \leq k \leq n)$, could be a *"don't care"* value, denoted by a special token *ANY* in our paper. In such case, term $(A_k = a_{ki})$ can be dropped from the rule.

The process of generating the decision table is rather simple and can be implemented using the powerful grouping and counting facilities provided by modern relational DBMS, such as IBM's DB2. After proper grouping and counting, the statistical information about class distribution over attribute values is obtained in a candidate decision table. The final decision table is obtained by pruning the entries in the candidate table.

The unique features of our approach include the following.

1. Compared to existing scaleable classifiers, the new approach not only provide as high classification accuracies as other approaches, such as naïve Bayesian classifier [DH73], Bayesian classifiers [FGG97], decision trees [Quin93], and classifiers based on associations

[LHM98,MW99], but also improves the classification speed in the order of magnitudes. It also achieves the linear scalability with respect to the number of training samples within the tested range up to ten millions samples. We are able to obtain such drastic performance gain because we shifted away from the traditional record-at-a-time paradigm to the set-oriented relational paradigm. The main computation required, the grouping and counting over a large data set can be completed by executing a single SQL statement. With the current technique, such SQL statement can be executed rather efficiently even for large training set.

2. Our approach, GAC, can be implemented using standard data aggregation and summarization functions supported by RDBMS. As such the speed of building a decision table mainly depends on how the underlying DBMS process those operations. Whilst our experimental results indicate the current implementation such as in DB2 provides surprisingly good results, further performance improvement can be expected when better processing algorithms are developed and implemented in DBMS. Another benefit of avoiding UDFs is that the implementation becomes much easier. This can be seen clearly if we compare our implementation with MIND, a scalable miner for database implemented using user defined functions [WIV98].

3. Although our approach bears some similarities with those association rule based classification algorithms [AMS97, Bay97, LHM98, MW99], our approach avoids the Apriori-based frequent rule set finding [AIS93a], which requires to transform the training data into to transactional database and to scan the data repeatedly. The performance comparison with CBA [LHM98] indicates that our approach is more than 10 times faster.

The remainder of the paper is organized as follows. Section 2 describes the grouping and counting based classification approach in general. Section 3 presents the detailed implementation of the approach on top of relational database management systems. The results of our performance evaluation are presented in Section 4. A brief discussion on related work is presented in Section 5. Section 6 concludes the paper.

2. Decision Table and Its Generation

In this section, we introduce a new type of classifier, the *decision tables* and a grouping-and-counting based approach that generate decision tables for given data sets. The related issues will also be discussed.

2.1 An Illustrative Example

Before we formally describe the grouping and counting based classification approach, we use a mini-training data about car insurance shown in Table 2.1 to illustrate the basic idea. The table consists of three columns, two attributes, *age-group* and *car-type*, and a class label *risk*.

The objective of the classification problem is to find the rules that can be used to determine the class of a customer based on their age group and the types of cars they own.

Table 2.1: An example training set

age-group	car-type	risk
young	family	high
young	sport	high
middle	sport	high
old	family	low
middle	family	low

From the training samples in Table 2.1, we can obtain the class population for each combination of attribute values by grouping and counting as shown in Column 2 – 5 of Table 2.2. For easy reference, we added the row number as the first column. Column 6 and 7 are derived from Column 2- 5 and will be explained later. In this table, the grouping attributes of each row consist of one or more attributes and the class label. Row 1-4, 5-7 and 8-12 are grouped on *(age-group, risk)*, *(car-type, risk)*, and *(age-group, car-type, risk)*, respectively. Column 5, *c-count* (class count), contains the total number of tuples whose attribute values are the same as the grouping attribute values. For example, *c-count* = 2 for Row 1 means that there are two tuples with *age-group = "young"* and *risk = "high"* in the training set; and *c-count* = 1 for Row 2 means that there are only one tuple with *age-group = "middle"* and *risk = "high"*, and so on.

Table 2.2: Results of grouping and counting

row No.	age-group	car-type	risk	c-count	g-count	conf
1	young		high	2	2	1.00
2	middle		high	1	2	0.50
3	middle		low	1	2	0.50
4	old		low	1	1	1.00
5		Family	high	1	3	0.33
6		Family	low	2	3	0.67
7		sport	high	2	2	1.00
8	young	Family	high	1	1	1.00
9	young	sport	high	1	1	1.00
10	middle	sport	high	1	1	1.00
11	middle	Family	low	1	1	1.00
12	old	sport	low	1	1	1.00

From Column 2-5, two additional columns, *g-count* (*group count*) and *conf* (*confidence*), can be computed: Column *g-count* contains the number of tuples in the same group, i.e., tuples with the same attribute values (exclusive of class label). For example, *g-count* = 2 in Row 1 means that there are two tuples with *age-group="young"* and *g-count=1* of Row 8 indicates that there is only one tuple with *age-group="young"* and *cat-type="family"*. Note that if the original table is sorted on grouping attributes, the value of *g-count* can be obtained after reading all the rows in the same group. The figures in the last column, *conf*, is obtained by dividing the two

counts, *conf = c-count/g-cou*nt. That is, the value of represents the conditional probability for a tuple having the indicated class label given its attribute values. In our example, *conf* =1.00 for Row 1 means that, if the value of attribute *age-group* of a tuple is *young*, the probability that the tuple belongs to class *risk="high"* is 100%. In other words, rows in Table 2.2 can be interpreted as classification rules with certain level of *support* and *confidence*. For example, the first row in Table 2.2 represents the following rule:

$$age\text{-}group = \text{"}young\text{"} \rightarrow risk = \text{"}high\text{"}$$

with 100% confidence and 40% (2/5) support from the training data in Table 2.1.

The confidence of certain row is quite low. For example, the confidence of second row is only 0.50. That is, given a tuple with age-group = "middle", we are not able to tell the class labels. There is another type of rows, such as Row 8. It represents the following rule

$$(age\text{-}group=\text{"}young\text{"}), (car\text{-}type = \text{"}family\text{"}) \rightarrow risk = \text{"}high\text{"}$$

with confidence equal to 1.00. However, this rule is redundant since if we already have the rule generated from Row 1.

Table 2.3: The decision table for the sample data

age-group	car-type	risk	sup	conf
young	*ANY*	high	0.40	1.00
ANY	sport	high	0.40	1.00
old	*ANY*	low	0.20	1.00
middle	family	low	0.20	1.00

If we delete all those rows in Table 2.2 with confidence less than 1.0 and rows that represent redundant rules, we obtained Table 2.3. The first three columns are the attributes and class label as in the training data. Column *sup* is the support of the rule represented by the row, obtained by dividing the *c-count* in Table 2.2 by the total number of tuples in the training data, 5 in our example. Last column is the confidence explained above. We name the table as a *decision table*, as each row in the table represents a rule that can be used to determine the class of a sample with given attribute values. In our example, the table contains the following rules.

age-group = "young" → *risk = "high"* (40%, 100%)
age-group = "old" → *risk = "low"* (40%, 100%)
car-type = "sport" → *risk = "high"* (20%, 100%)
(age-group ="middle"), (car-type = "family")
　　　→ *risk = "low"* (20%, 100%)

2.2 Decision Tables

In this subsection, we define decision table and discuss how it can be used to classify unknown sample.

Definition. *Decision table* for data set D with n attributes A_1, A_2, ..., A_n is a table with schema R (A_1, A_2, ..., A_n , *Class, Sup, Conf*). A row $R_i = (a_{1i}, a_{2i}, ..., a_{ni} , c_i, sup_i, conf_i)$ in table R represents a classification rule, where a_{ij} $(1 \leq j \leq n)$ can be either from $DOM(A_i)$ or a special value ANY, $c_i \in \{ c_1, c_2, ..., c_m \}$, $minsup \leq sup_i \leq 1$, and $minconf \leq conf_i \leq 1$ and $minsup$ and $minconf$ are predetermined thresholds. The interpretation of the rule is **if** $(A_1 = a_1)$ and $(A_2 = a_2)$ and ... and $(A_n = a_n)$ **then** *class* $= c_i$ **with probability** $conf_i$ **and having support** sup_i, where $a_j \neq ANY$, $1 \leq j \leq n$.

Example: Table 2.3 is the decision table for data given in Table 2.1 with $minsup = 0.20$ and $minconf = 1.00$.

Since a row in a decision table represents a classification rule, we will use these two terms interchangeably in this paper.

Definition. A tuple $t = (a_1, a_2, ..., a_n, c_k)$ *matches* $R_i = (a_{1i}, a_{2i}, ..., a_{ni}, c_i, sup_i \, conf_i)$ if for all a_j $(1 \leq j \leq n)$, either $a_{ji} = ANY$ or $a_j = a_{ji}$. If tuple t matches R_i and $c_k = c_i$ we say that tuple t *is covered* by R_i, or R_i *covers* t.

Example: (*young, family, high*) matches and is covered by (*young, ANY*, high, *sup, conf*).

Given $R_i = (a_{1i}, a_{2i}, ..., a_{ni}, c_i, sup_i, conf_i)$ and $R_j = (a_{1j}, a_{2j}, ..., a_{nj}, c_j, sup_j, conf_j)$, we say R_j is *redundant* if all the tuples covered by R_j are covered by R_i.

Lemma. Given two rules, $R_i = (a_{1i}, a_{2i}, ..., a_{ni}, c_i, sup_i, conf_i)$ and $R_j = (a_{1j}, a_{2j}, ..., a_{nj}, c_j, sup_j, conf_j)$, If (1) $c_i = c_j$, and (2) $a_{lj} = a_{li}$ for all $1 \leq l \leq n$ if $a_{li} \neq ANY$, then rule R_j is redundant.

Proof: Let $(a_{1k}, a_{2k}, ..., a_{nk}, c_k)$ be a tuple covered by R_j. Based on the definition, we have $a_{lk} = a_{lj}$ for all $1 \leq l \leq n$ if $a_{lj} \neq ANY$ and $c_k = c_j$.

(1) Since we are given $c_i = c_j$, we have $c_i = c_j = c_k$.

(2) Since $a_{lj} = a_{li}$ for all $1 \leq l \leq n$ if $a_{li} \neq ANY$, we have $a_{lk} = a_{lj} = a_{li}$ for all $1 \leq l \leq n$ if $a_{li} \neq ANY$.

Therefore, $(a_{1k}, a_{2k}, ..., a_{nk}, c_k)$ is covered by R_i. Since any tuple covered by R_j is covered by R_i, R_j is redundant.

Example: Given (*young, ANY, high*), (*young, family, high*) becomes redundant.

2.3 *GAC*: Generating Decision Table by Grouping and Counting

In this subsection, we describe *GAC*, a decision table generation algorithm based on grouping and counting. The input is a training data set, D, consisting of N tuples, each of which is an $(n+1)$-tuple, $(a_1, a_2, ..., a_n, c_k)$, where a_i is a value from the domain of attribute A_i, $DOM(A_i)$ and $A_i \in \{A_1, A_2, ..., A_n \}$, and $c_k \in \{ c_1, c_2, ..., c_m \}$ is the class label. We assume that all the attributes are categorical. Those non-categorical attributes are discretized using any appropriate existing discretization algorithms [FI93]. The output of *GAC* is a decision table. *GAC* consists of two major steps: *grouping and counting* and *table pruning*.

2.3.1 Grouping and counting

With a given training data set D $(A_1, A_2, ..., A_n, Class)$, the grouping and counting phase generates a table that contains all possible entries in the decision table. We call this table a *candidate decision table*. In addition to the original columns in the data set, the candidate decision table has one more column, *count*, whose value is the number of tuples in the training data covered by the corresponding row in the table. That is, the candidate decision table has schema $(A_1, A_2, ..., A_n, Class, Count)$.

The computation in this phase is rather straightforward. Tuples in the training data set are grouped based on their attribute values and class labels. For each grouping, the number of tuples that belong to each class is counted and recorded in the *count* column. For those non-grouping attributes, we use a special value ANY in the candidate decision table.

2.3.2 Table pruning

The size of the candidate decision table is usually large. Not all its rows should be used to form rows in the decision table. A row in the candidate table will be pruned if the classification rule it represents

    1. is not statistically significant; or
    2. has low confidence; or
    3. is redundant.

The significance of a rule is measured by its support. With the given training data, the support of a rule, *sup*, is the number of tuples covered by the rule divided by the size of the data set. For a rule to be statistically significant, its support should be greater than a threshold, *minsup*, a parameter set by the system or user. Setting proper support threshold can prevent the problem of overfitting and increase the ability to handle noise data. If the threshold is set to less than $1/N$, where N is the total number of tuples in the training data, then every tuple can be a classification rule even as it correctly classifies at least one sample. However, some tuple with very low support could be noise in the data.

Confidence of a rule represents the conditional probability of a tuple having the specified class label given its attribute values. By accepting a rule with confidence larger than a threshold, *minconf*, we actually allow that among a group of tuples with the same set of attribute values, (1-*minconf*) percentage of them have their class labels different from the class label for the group. That is, the threshold reflects our requirement of class purity. The appropriate value of *minconf* also depends on the application. For example, if training data contain noise, high *minconf* may result in no qualifying classification rules.

The third type of rows to be pruned from the candidate decision table is redundant rows, that is, the rows covered by the others in the table.

The main computational task for the second phase is to calculate the support and confidence for each row in the candidate decision table and remove entries that belong to the above three categories. Since the candidate decision table contains the counts for the number of tuples covered by a row in the table, the support is easy to calculate. Let's define a group as the tuples with the same non-*ANY* attribute values but different class labels. Then, we need only count the number of tuples of a group in order to calculate the confidence for the tuples in the group. Let the candidate decision table be sorted on (A_1, A_2, ..., A_n, *Class*) in ascending order; and the special value ANY is the minimum among all possible attribute values. It is obvious that a tuple can be only covered by tuples in the same group or the tuples in the previous groups in the sorted order. The decision table can be generated group by group as follows

(1) Tuples in the same group are read from the candidate decision table. The total number of tuples in the group is counted.

(2) The support and confidence for each tuple is calculated by definition.

(3) Tuples whose support or confidence is less than the specified threshold are discarded.

(4) Tuples with sufficient large support and confidence are checked against tuples already in the decision table. Redundant tuples are discarded. None redundant tuples are inserted into the decision table.

(5) Continue with the next group until all the tuples in the candidate decision table are processed.

2.3.3 An optimization

To reduce the size of the candidate decision table, we introduce one extra-step to determine the first attribute of the rules using methods that are used to determine the splitting attribute in decision tree based algorithms. Information gain is used as the goodness function of selecting the splitting attribute.

Assume attribute A has k distinct values. We will have k groups, D_1, D_2, ..., D_k, if we group the training data tuples based on the values of A. The *information gain* for such a grouping is

$$I_A = E(D) - \sum_{i=1}^{k} \frac{|D_i|}{|D|} E(D_i)$$

$$E(X) = -\sum_{i=1}^{m} \frac{count(c_i, X)}{|X|} \bullet \log \frac{count(c_i, X)}{|X|}$$

where $E(X)$ is the *entropy* of a set of tuples, $count(c_i, X)$ is the number of tuples in X that belong to class c_i, $1 \leq i \leq m$, and $|X|$ is the total number of tuples in X. We choose among all the attributes the one that gives the largest information gain as the splitting attribute. In the first phase, we group and count tuples for groups with this attribute and others. That is, if there are four attributes, A, B, C, and D and C is the attribute giving the largest information gain among them, we only count for groups based on the values of (C, A), (C, B), (C, D), (C, A, B), (C, A, D), (C, B, D), and (C, A, B, D). Other groups, such as (A, B), (A, B, D), etc. will not be considered.

2.4 The Algorithm

Based on previous discussion, our algorithm, *GAC*, can be summarized as in Figure 2.1. The algorithm takes *TrainD*, the training data, and two thresholds, *minsup* and *minconf*, as input. The best splitting attribute is obtained by calling function *BestSplitAttr* that selects the best splitting attribute using information gain. Function *CandidateDTable* takes the training data and the splitting attribute as its input and generates the candidate decision table. The candidate decision table is pruned to form the decision table by calling function *PrunDTable* that takes

---

Algorithm GAC (TrainD: table, *minsup*, *minconf*: real)

```
1    begin
2        bestSplitAttr := BestSplitAttr (TrainD);
3        candDTable := CandidateDTable (TrainD,
                            bestSplitAttr);
4        decisionTable := PrunDTable (candDTable,
                            minsup, minconf);
5    end.
```

Figure 2.1: The main algorithm that generates the decision table for a given data set.

---

minsup and *minconf* as input parameters.

2.5 Classification Using Decision Tables

The decision table generated is to be used to classify unseen data samples. To classify an unseen data sample, u (a_{1u}, a_{2u}, ..., a_{nu}), the decision table is searched to find rows that matches u. That is, to find rows whose attribute values are either *ANY* or equal to the corresponding attribute values of u. Unlike decision trees where the search will follow one path from the root to one leaf node, searching for the matches in a decision table could result in *none*, *one* or *more* matching rows.

One matching row is found: If there is only one row, r_i(a_{1i}, a_{2i}, ..., a_{ni} , c_i, sup_i, $conf_i$) in the decision table that matches u (a_{1u}, a_{2u}, ..., a_{nu}), then the class of u is c_i .

More than one matching row is found: When more than one matching rows found for a given sample, there are a number of alternatives to assign the class label. Assume that k matching rows are found and the class label, support and confidence for row i is c_i, sup_i and $conf_i$, respectively. The class of the sample, c_u, can be assigned in one of the following ways.

(1) based on confidence and support: $c_u = \{c_i \mid conf_i = \max_{j=1}^{k} conf_j\}$. If there are ties in confidence, the class with highest support will be assigned to c_u. If there are still ties, one randomly picked from them will be assigned to c_u.

(2) based on weighted confidence and support:
$c_u = \{c_i \mid conf_i * sup_i = \max_{j=1}^{k}(conf_j * sup_j)\}$. The ties are treated similarly.

Note that, if the decision table is sorted on (*Conf, Sup*), it is easy to implement the first method. We can simply assign the class of the first matching row to the sample to be classified. In fact, our experiments indicated that this simple method provides no worse performance than others.

No matching row is found: In most classification applications, the training samples cannot cover the whole data space. The decision table generated by grouping and counting may not cover all possible data samples. For such samples, no matching row will be found in the decision table. To classify such samples, the simplest method is to use the default class. However, there are other alternatives. For example, we can first find a row that is the nearest neighbour (in certain distance metrics) of the sample in the decision table and then assign the same class label to the sample. The drawback of using nearest neighbour is its computational complexity.

Recall that we calculated class population for individual attributes in function *BestSplitAttr* to determine the best split attribute. With such information, we can use a Naïve-Bayesian based approach to determine the class as follows. Let u (a_{1u}, a_{2u}, ..., a_{nu}) be an uncovered sample, and $P(c_k \mid u)$ be the probability that u belongs to class $c_k \in \{c_1, c_2, ..., c_m\}$. According to Bayes theorem, we have

$$P(c_k \mid u) = \frac{p(c_k)p(u \mid c_k)}{P(u)}$$

That is,

$$P(c_k \mid u) \propto p(c_k)p(u \mid c_k)$$

With independence assumption we have

$$P(c_k \mid u) \propto p(c_k)\prod_{i=1}^{n} p(a_{iu} \mid c_k) = \frac{\prod_{i=1}^{n} p(a_{iu} \wedge c_k)}{p(c_k)^{n-1}}$$

since

$$p(a_{iu} \mid c_k) = \frac{p(a_{iu} \wedge c_k)}{P(c_k)}$$

For a given training data set, D, $P(a_{iu} \wedge c_j)$ and $P(c_j)$ can be approximate by the number of occurrences:

$$P(a_{iu} \wedge c_j) = \frac{count(a_{iu} \wedge c_j)}{|D|} \qquad P(c_j) = \frac{count(c_j)}{|D|}$$

Note that $count(a_{iu} \wedge c_j)$ and $count(c_j)$ have been obtained in computing the information gain and determining the best splitting attribute. Therefore we can classify u into class c_k such that $P(c_k \mid u)$ is the maximum for $1 \leq k \leq m$. Experiments conducted indicated that classifying samples that do not have matches in the decision table using this approach provides higher classification accuracy than other ways listed.

3. Implementing GAC on Top of RDBMS

The approach described in Section 2 was motivated by the recent extensions of RDBMS capabilities. Traditionally, relational database management systems provide aggregate functions (MIN(), MAX(), AVG(), SUM(), COUNT()) and the GROUP BY operator to produce aggregates over a set of tuples. With applications of relational databases in on-line decision support systems, more complex aggregate functions and operators are required and proposed [GCB+97]. For example, recent releases of IBM DB2 provide a more powerful GROUP BY operator, which makes it possible to build a *GAC* classifier using SQL query language for the required major computation – the grouping and counting. In this section we describe in detail how SQL can be used to implement a classifier.

3.1 GROUP BY Operator In DB2

The traditional GROUP BY operation operates on a set of attributes. The semantics of the GROUP BY operator is to partition a relation (or sub-relation) into disjoint sets based on the values of the grouping attributes, the attributes specified in the GROUP BY clause. Aggregate functions are then applied to each of such sets. For example, SQL query

    SELECT risk, count(*) **FROM** insurance
    GROUP BY risk

partitions the relation insurance based on the values of *insurance.risk*, and counts the number of each partitions and produces a table with two columns, *risk* and the *count*. If the relation contains instances as shown in Table 2.1, the query will produce an output relation with two tuples (*high*, 3), (*low*, 2).

DB2 extended the GROUP BY operator to allow complex grouping requirements with *grouping-sets* and *super-groups*. A grouping-sets specification allows multiple grouping clauses to be specified in a single statement. By applying query

    SELECT age-group, car-type, risk, count(*) as count
    FROM insurance
    GROUP BY GROUPING SETS (age-group, car-type), risk

to our sample *insurance* table. We can obtain the following table:

age-group	car-type	risk	count
middle	-	high	1
middle	-	low	1
old	-	low	1
young	-	high	2
-	family	high	1
-	family	low	2
-	sport	high	2

For super-grouping, DB2 supports two super-groups, ROLLUP and CUBE. A CUBE grouping is the n-dimensional generalization of the GROUP BY operator. It can be viewed as a series of grouping-sets, i.e., all permutations of attributes in the GROUP BY CUBE clause are computed along with the grand total. Therefore, the n elements of a CUBE translate to 2^n grouping-sets. For example, a GROUP BY CUBE (*age-group*, *car-type*, *risk*) query computes 8 grouping-sets: (*age-group*, *car-type*, *risk*), (*age-group*, *car-type*), (*age-group*, *risk*), (*car-type*, *risk*), (*age-group*), (*car-type*), (*risk*), and (), where GROUP BY () computes the aggregate function over the entire table. In addition to simple grouping-sets and super-groups, DB2 also supports the combination of such simple grouping. When simple grouping attributes are combined with other groups, they are "appended" to the beginning of the resulting grouping sets. When super-groups are combined, they operate like multipliers on the remaining groups, forming additional grouping set entries according to the definition of the super groups. For instance, GROUP BY *age-group*, CUBE (*car-type*, *risk*) will produce groups (*age-group*, *car-type*, *risk*), (*age-group*, *car-type*), (*age-group*, *risk*), and (*age-group*).

3.2 Building Decision Tables Using GROUP BY Operators

With the above introduction, we can see that the grouping and counting over the training data can be fully implemented using GROUP BY operator provided by DB2. However, GROUP BY CUBE is an expensive operation, especially when the number of attributes of the cube is large. More importantly, resource requirement for the computation is high. On the other hand, most classification rules do not involve all attributes A_1, A_2, ..., and A_n. In order to improve efficiency, the basic algorithm shown in GAC is modified in such a way that the decision table is constructed in iterations. In each iteration, a number of attributes are used to generate entries in the decision table. To control the number of attributes used in cube computation, two system parameters, *initCubeSize* and *maxCubeSize*, are introduced to denote the number of attributes used in the first iteration and the maximum number of attributes to form cubes, respectively. The first parameter provides a mechanism to

adjust the training speed. Intuitively, with large *initCubeSize*, less number of iterations will be required for training but each iteration takes longer time since large cube is to be computed. The second parameter is mainly determined by the system resource. The training process ends when the desired classification accuracy is achieved, or the predetermined training time limit is reached.

The algorithm is outlined in Figure 3.1. We assume that the discretized training data set is stored in a relational database as a table with schema (A_1, A_2, ..., A_n, *class*). Two input parameters, *minsup* and *mincof* are given based on the application and the quality of the data. Another parameter minerror is used to control the training process. First, the attributes are sorted based on the information gain (line 2). The first attribute in the list, the one with highest information gain is chosen as the splitting attributes. Function *SelectAttrs* selects a set of attributes to generate decision table entries in each iteration (line 4). The decision table entries are generated as described in the previous section (line 5-6). The up-to-date decision table is applied to the training data set to check the error rate (line 7). The process repeats until the error is smaller than the required minimum error, or training time limit is reached (line 8). In the following subsections, we explain the details of the major functions.

Algorithm GAC-RDB (TrainD: table, *minsup, minconf, minerror*: real)

1. **begin**
2.   *sortedAttrList:= SortAttr* (TrainD);
3.   **repeat**
4.   *curAttrs:= SelectAttrs* (*sortedAttrList*);
5.   *candDTable := CandidateDTable* (TrainD, *curAttrs*);
6.   *decisionTable := PrunDTable* (*candDTable, minsup, minconf*);
7.   *error := EstimateError*(TrainD, decisionTable);
8.   **until** *error* $\leq$ *minerror* **or** *timeout*
9. **end.**

Figure 3.1: *GAC-RDB*: A decision table generation algorithm.

3.2.1 Determining the first splitting attribute

As in algorithm *GAC*, we select an attribute as the splitting attribute based on information gain to reduce one attribute in the computation of cube, which is an expensive operation. We also use entropy to facilitate attribute selection in each iteration. Therefore, we sort the attributes on their entropy in descending order. The first attribute on the list is chosen as the split attribute explained in the previous section. The algorithm is outlined in Figure 3.2. The major computation is to calculate the class population among different attribute values. The SQL statement (line 3-6) performs this task. After obtaining these counts, entropy for partitioned data using each of the attributes is compared (line 7-8). The

```
Function SortAttr (TrainD: relation);
1.    begin
2.        obtain the class population for each attribute values
          by executing SQL query
3.        SELECT    A_1, A_2, ..., A_n, class, count(*)
4.        FROM      TrainD
5.        GROUP BY GROUPING STES
              ( (A_1, class), (A_2, class), ..., (A_n, class))
6.        ORDER BY A_1, A_2, ..., A_n
7.        for each attribute A_i ∈ { A_1, A_2, ..., A_n} do
8.            Compute entropy E(A_i);
9.            Sort attributes on E(A_i) into sortedAttrList ;
10.       return sortedAttrList;
11.   end.
```

Figure 3.2: Function *SortAttr* that sorts attributes
in the order of entropy.

attributes are then sorted in the descending order of their entropy.

As discussed in Section 2, the query results, i.e., the class population of each attribute value is saved to classify samples uncovered by decision table entries.

3.2.2 Selecting attributes

Given *initCubeSize* and *maxCubeSize*, Function *SelectAttrs* (line 4 in Figure 3.2) selects attribute set, *curAttrs*, for generating decision table entries as follows:

1. For the first iteration, top *initCubeSize* attributes in the *sortedAttrList* are selected as *curAttrs*.

2. After each iteration, attributes that contribute to decision table entries are inserted into a set, denoted as *relevantAttrs*, whose size is denoted as R

3. When R is smaller than *initCubeSize*, *RelevantAttrs* and top (*initCubeSize* - *R*) attributes in the *sortedAttrList* form the set of *curAttrs*. If R is larger than *initCubeSize*, *curAttrs* will be formed by the *relevantAttrs* and next attribute in *the sortedAttrList*.

4. After R reaches *maxCubeSize*, *curAttrs* will be formed by the top *maxCubeSize* of attributes in *relevantAttrs* and next attribute in the *sortedAttrList*.

That is, the current set of attributes used in each iteration is selected in the greedy fashion based on the entropy of attributes. The number of attributes selected is limited to (*maxCubeSize*+2).

This process is indeed a type of feature selection process [LM98]. However, it selects relevant features for a subspace defined by *curAtts* in each iteration, while most feature selection algorithms select relevant features based on entire training data. In most cases, not all classification rules involve all relevant features. Therefore, we can generate the whole decision table iteratively using different set of attributes.

3.2.3 Generating candidate decision table

Function CandidateDTable (line 5 in Figure 3.2) generates the candidate decision table with schema of (A_1,

A_2, ..., A_n, *class*, *count*) by executing the following SQL query:

```
SELECT    A_1, A_2, ..., A_n, class, count(*)
FROM      TrainD
GROUP BY A_k, CUBE (A_1, A_2, ..., A_{k-1}, A_{k+1}...,
          A_n), class
ORDER BY A_1, A_2, ..., A_n
```

where A_k is the splitting attributes. Since the results obtained from the SQL query in Figure 3.2, line 3-6, may also be candidate classification rules, they are inserted into the candidate decision table. Since the candidate decision table will be processed by *PrunDTable,* it need not be stored on the disk. It can stay in the SQL common area.

3.2.4 Pruning the decision table

Implementation of Function *PrunDTable* is quite straightforward as described in the previous section. The decision table has one more field, *conf*, than the candidate decision table, with values equal the count of the rule divided by the sum of all counts of the rules from the same group. Therefore, the tuples in the candidate decision table are processed group by group. If a new tuple read is covered by the current group, it is inserted into the current group for processing and the count for the group is increased. When a tuple starts a new group, the old group is processed, i.e., tThe confidence of each rule in the group is computed. If the support and confidence of the rule are above the thresholds, and the rule is not covered by any other rules, the rule is inserted to the final decision table with its confidence.

4. A Performance Study

A comprehensive performance study has been conducted to evaluate the approach and our implementation. In this section, we describe those experiments and their results. All experiments reported in this section were performed on an HP Omnibook 3000 notebook computer with 233MHZ CPU running Microsoft Windows NT 4.0 and IBM DB2 version 5.0.

4.1 Classification Accuracy

Classification accuracy is one of the basic performance metrics for any classification algorithms. In their recent paper Meretakis and Wüthrich compared the classification accuracy of a set of classification methods [MW99] using a set of data from the UCI Repository [MM96]. We tested our system using the same data sets. The continuous attributes are discretized using the *MLC* discretizer based on entropy discretization [FI93, KJL+94]. To be comparable with the other methods, the size of training set and testing set follow what given in [MW99]. In most cases, 10-fold cross-validation is used. The results of our system are shown in Table 4.1, along with other five other classifiers with different approaches:

Table 4.1: Classification accuracy of GAC and other classifiers as given in [MW99]

Data set	Properties				Accuracy					
	#attrs	#classes	# train	# test	C4.5	NB	TAN	CBA	LB	GAC
Australian	14	2	690	CV-10	0.843	0.857	0.852	0.855	0.857	**0.883**
Chess	36	2	2,130	1,065	**0.995**	0.872	0.921	0.981	0.902	0.944
Diabetes	8	2	768	CV-10	0.717	0.751	0.765	0.729	0.767	**0.767**
Flare	10	2	1,066	CV-10	0.812	0.795	0.826	0.831	0.815	**0.843**
German	20	2	1,000	CV-10	0.717	0.741	0.727	0.732	0.748	**0.768**
Heart	13	2	270	CV-10	0.767	0.822	0.833	0.819	0.822	**0.838**
Letter	16	26	15,000	500	0.777	0.749	**0.857**	0.518	0.764	0.800
Lymph	18	4	148	CV-10	0.784	0.819	0.838	0.773	**0.846**	0.839
Pima	8	2	768	CV-10	0.711	0.759	0.758	0.730	0.758	**0.780**
Satimage	36	6	4,435	2,000	0.852	0.818	**0.872**	0.849	0.839	0.847
Segment	19	7	1,540	770	**0.958**	0.918	0.935	0.935	0.942	0.943
Splice	60	3	2,126	1,064	0.933	0.946	0.946	0.700	0.946	**0.956**
Shuttle-small	9	7	38,661	934	0.995	0.987	0.996	0.995	0.994	**0.998**
Vehicle	18	4	846	CV-10	0.698	0.611	**0.709**	0.688	0.688	0.681
Voting Records	16	2	435	CV-10	**0.957**	0.903	0.933	0.935	0.947	0.956
Waveform-21	21	3	300	4,700	0.704	0.785	0.791	0.753	**0.794**	0.761
Yeast	8	10	1,484	CV-10	0.557	0.581	0.572	0.551	**0.582**	0.574
AVERAGE					0.810	0.807	0.831	0.787	0.824	**0.834**

(1) *C4.5*, Quinlan's decision tree classifier C4.5 [Quin93], (2) NB: a Naïve Bayes classifier [DH73], (3) TAN, a state of the art Bayesian network classifier that relaxes the independence assumptions of Naïve Bayes by taking into account dependencies among pairs of non-class attributes [FGG97], (4) CBA, a classifier based on association rules [LHM98], and (5) LB, a naïve Bayes classifier using long items [MW99].

From Table 4.1, we can summarize the relative performance of GAC as follows:

Ranking	1	2	3	4	5	6
# Data Sets	8	5	1	2	1	0

that is, comparing with other five classifiers, *GAC-RDB* performs the best for 8 data sets and the second best for 5 data sets. It never performs worst in other cases. Astute readers may argue that the absolute accuracy rates listed in Table 4.1 may not precisely reflect the performance since they were not obtained using the same training and testing data sets. However, from those figures, we are confident to claim that *GAC-RDB* can provide at least the same level of accuracy as other popular classifiers.

4.2 Execution Speed And Scalability with Respect to Number of Training Samples

The second set of experiments investigates the execution speed and the scalability with respect to the number training samples. This set of experiments used the synthetic data and classification functions defined in [AIS93b]. Each record in the data set consists of 9 attributes, including *salary, commission, age, elevel, car, zipcode, hvalue, hyears* and *loan.*. There are 10 classification functions defined on these 9 attributes. To compare with the results reported in the literature, we present the execution speed on two functions, Function 5 and 10.

Function 5

Class A: $((age<40) \wedge (((50k \leq salary \leq 100k))$?
$(100k \leq loan \leq 300k) : (200k \leq loan \leq 400k)))) \vee$
$((40 \leq age<60) \wedge (((75k \leq salary \leq 125k))$?
$(200k \leq loan \leq 400k) : (300k \leq loan \leq 500k)))) \vee$
$((age \geq 60) \wedge (((25k \leq salary \leq 75k))$?
$(300k \leq loan \leq 500k) : (100k \leq loan \leq 300k))))$

Function 10:

$hyears < 20 \Rightarrow equity=0$
$hyears \geq 20 \Rightarrow equity=0.1 \times hvalue \times (hyeares-20)$
$disposable = (0.67 \times (salary +commission) -$
$5000 \times elevel + 0.2 \times equity -10k)$

Class A: disposable >0

Since *GAC-RDB* works with categorical attributes, the non-categorical attributes are discretized first. We used a simple equi-width method for discretization. As mentioned earlier, feature selection algorithms are usually used to select the relevant features before classification. Since Function 10 has 5 relevant attributes (salary, commission, ed_level, hyear, hvalue), we use data sets consisting of these 5 attributes for both tests. The number of training samples was varied from 0.5 to 10 million. The elapsed time measured is shown in Figure 4.1.

From the figure, we can see that linear scalability is achieved with respect to the number of training sample

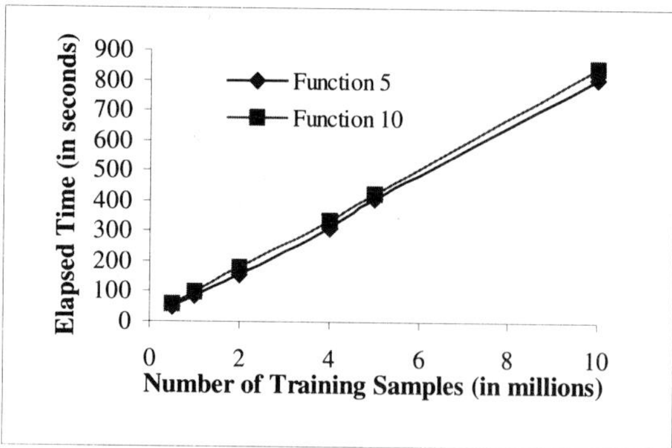

Figure 4.1: Elapsed time for Function 5 and 10

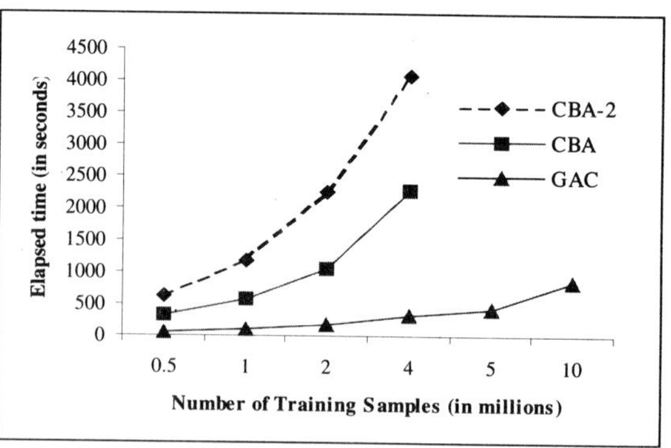

Figure 4.2: Comparison with CBA

within the range tested. To see how the execution speed compare to other algorithms, we obtained a copy of the executable code of *CBA* [LHM98] and run Function 10. By checking the log of *CBA* execution, we realized that the time reported by the program, indicated by curve *CBA* in Figure 4.2, is only the sum of scanning the data set. Furthermore, it does not include the time of transforming the data set into transactional database, which takes more than 300 seconds for 0.5 million tuples. It is reasonable to assume that the transformation is linear to the number of samples in the data set, the total elapsed time will then be at least as what shown by the curve *CBA-2* in Figure 4.2. We can see that *GAC-RDB* is actually more than 10 times faster than *CBA*. Moreover, *CBA* failed to complete its execution for the data set of 5 and 10 million tuples in the notebook we conducted the tests.

To compare with other scalable classifiers reported in the literature, we reproduced the two performance figures appeared in papers in Figure 4.3. Figure 4.3 (a) depicts the performance of SLIQ with two functions, Function 5 and 10 [Mar96]. Figure 4.3 (b) is scalability results of MIND for Function 2 reproduced according to Wang *et. al.* [WIV98]. While our results on Function 5 and 10 are given in Figure 4.1, the results on Function 2 are presented in Figure 4.3 (c).

Since performance figures for SLIQ, MIND and SPRINT were obtained running on IBM RS/6000

workstations running AIX, it is difficult to compare the absolute numbers. We would like to point out one important property of *GAC-RDB*. The classification speed of *GAC-RDB* is independent on the complexity of classification functions, as the major operation of *GAC-RDB*, grouping and counting only depends on the number of attributes, number of distinct values for each attribute and number of tuples. Comparing Function 5 and 10, we can see that Function 10 is non-linear which is more complex than Function 5 where the hyperplanes separating the classes are parallel to axis. With complex classification functions, the decision-tree will usually have more levels. Since the execution time of decision-tree based algorithms is directly related to the number of levels of the tree, classification of those functions requires longer time. This is clearly shown in the SLIQ performance for Function 5 and 10. On the other hand, performance of *GAC-RDB* is not affected by the classification functions.

Function 2 reported in MIND is the simplest function among 10 classification functions: A sample belongs to class *if* ((*age*<40) ^ (50k≤*salary* ≤100k)) ∨ ((40≤*age*<60) ^ (75k≤*salary*≤125k)) ∨ ((*age*≥60) ^ (25k≤*salary* ≤75k)). Again, we can see that *GAC-RDB* performs well, comparing to other two algorithms.

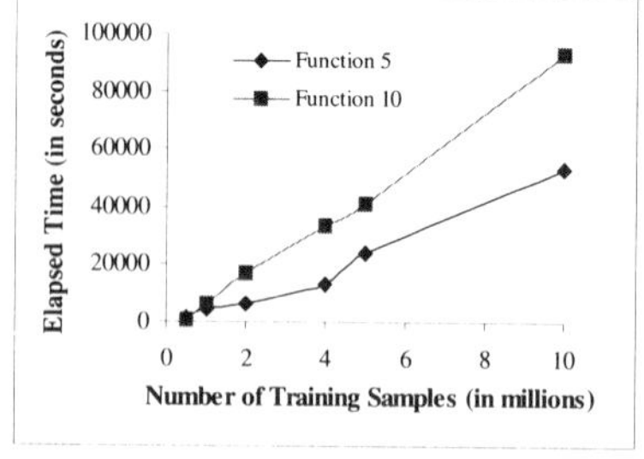

(a) Results from SLIQ [MAR96]

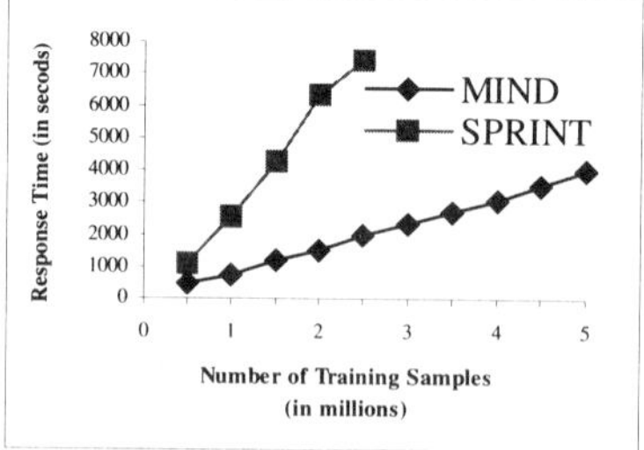

(b) Results reported in [WIV98]

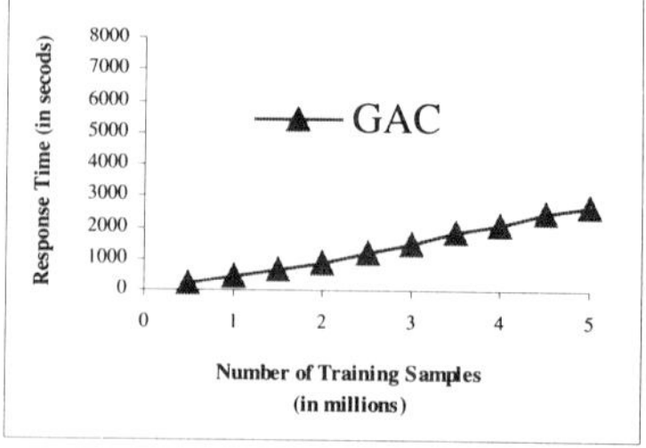

(c) Performance of GAC-RDB

Figure 4.3: Comparison with other scalable classifiers.

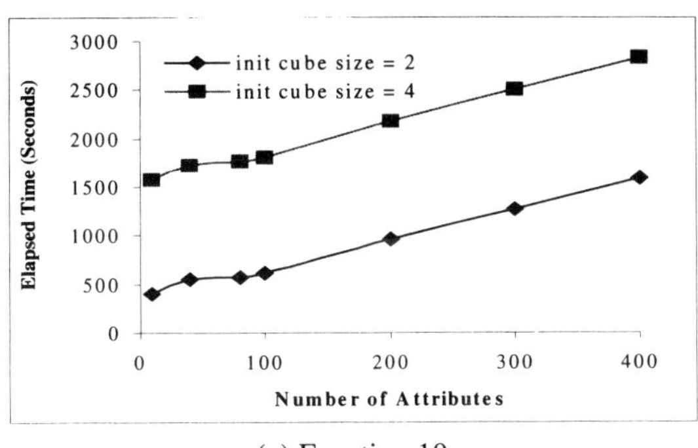

(a) Function 10   (b) Function 5

Figure 4.4: Scalability with respect to number of attributes.

4.3 Scalability With Respect to Number of Attributes

The third set of experiments was conducted to investigate the scalability of GAC-RDB with respect to the number of attributes. Function 5 and 10 were used in the experiments. The training data and testing data contain 100,000 and 10,000 samples, respectively. The number of attributes was varied from 9 to 400 by introducing extra attributes into the data set. Although the classification functions do not change when the number of attributes increases, the tuple length of the data increases. More importantly, with large number of attributes, it requires more time to locate the relevant attributes. Therefore, the training time is expected to increase. Figure 4.4 (a) and (b) depicts the elapsed time when the number of attributes increases from 9 to 400 for Function 10 and 5, respectively. For each case, we used two initial cube sizes, 2 and 4. The maximum cube size was set to 6.

We can see that, when the number of attributes increases, the elapsed time also increases. Comparing two data sets, the elapsed time for Function 5 increases much faster than that for Function 10 when the number of attributes increases from 9 to 400. However, for both functions, *GAC-RDB* provides near linear scale-up with respect to the number of attributes of training data.

In Figure 4.4, we also present the effects of the initial cube size on the training speed when the number of attributes increases. It is interesting to notice the different behavior of two functions. For Function 10, two curves for the initial cube size of 2 and 4 are in parallel. With large initial cube size, the cube to be computed at the beginning is large and it requires more computation time. When a data set contains large number of attributes, another factor will affect the speed of training. That is, the iterations need to include all relevant attributes into the decision tables. This can be seen from Figure 4.4 (b). With small number of attributes, setting small initial cube size has some advantage. However, when the number of attributes becomes large, larger initial cube size (4) leads to better performance. This also gives us some heuristics in setting the parameter of initial cube sizes.

One last note is that, all the experiments reported in this section were conducted on a notebook computer, which is not a really appropriate environment for large-scale computation tasks. For example, the resources are too limited to compile SQL queries with CUBE computation on large number of attributes. With more resources, *GAC-RDB* is expected to perform better.

5. Conclusions

Classification is a classical problem. It has been well studied by researchers from different areas. The book by Weiss and Kulikowski [WK91] gives the mosi comprehensive summary of the work in 1980s or earlier. A paper by Agrawal *et. al.* [AGI+92] trigged another round of interests in the classification problem, especially in the context of knowledge discovery and data mining. Since then, a large amount of work has been reported on building scalable classifiers and integrating classification into database systems to address the scalability problem. Recently, classification algorithms based on association rule mining were also introduced.

In this paper we described a novel approach to build efficient scalable classifiers by exploring the capability of relational database management systems that support powerful data aggregation and summarization functions. The approach is an elegant integration of all the recently developed techniques. As the result, it is scalable with respect to both the number of training samples and the number of attributes. Furthermore, with more sophisticate and efficient implementation of such data aggregate and summarization functions in relational DBMS, even better performance and scalability can be expected.

We are currently further refining the approach and carrying on more comprehensive performance evaluation. The issues related to feature selection, missing value and noise handling will also be addressed.

Acknowledgement

This work is partially supported by a grant from the National 973 project of China (No. G1998030414) and a grant from the Research Grant Council of the Hong Kong Special Administrative Region, China (AOE97/98.EG05)

References

[AAD+96] S. Agrawal, et. al., On the computation of multidimensional aggregates, In *Proceedings of the 22nd International Conference on Very Large Databases*, Mumbai (Bombay), India, September 1996, 506-521.

[AGI+92] R. Agrawal, S. Ghosh, T. Imielinski, B. Iyer, and A. Swami. An interval classifier for database mining applications. In *Proceedings of the 1992 International Conference on Very Large Databases*, Vancouver, Canada, August 1992, 560--573.

[AIS93a] R. Agrawal, T. Imielinski, and A. Swami. Mining association rules between sets of items in large databases. In *Proceedings of ACM SIGMOD International Conference of Management of Data*, Washington D.C., May 1993, 207-216.

[AIS93b] R. Agrawal, T. Imielinski, and A. Swami. Database mining: A performance perspective. *IEEE Transactions on Knowledge and Data Engineering*, 5(6), December 1993.

[AMS97] K. Ali, S. Manganaris, and R. Srikant, Partial classification using association rules. In *Proceedings of 3rd International Conference on Knowledge Discovery and Data Mining*, 1997.

[AS96] R. Agrawal and K. Shim. Developing tightly-coupled data mining applications on a relational database system. In *Proceedings of the 2nd International Conference on Knowledge Discovery in Databases and Data Mining*, August 1996.

[Bay97] R.J. Bayardo, Brute-Force mining of high confidence classification rules. In *Proceedings of 3rd International Conference on Knowledge Discovery and Data Mining*, 1997.

[CFB99] S. Chaudhuri, U.M. Fayyad, and J. Bernhardt. Scalable classification over SQL databases. In *Proceedings of the 15th International Conference on Data Engineering*, Sydney, Australia, March 23-26 1999, 470-479.

[Cham98] D.D. Chamberlin. *A Complete Guide to DB2 Universal Database*. Morgan Kaufmann Publishers, 1998.

[DH73] R.Duda and P.Hart, *Pattern Classification and Scene Analysis*, John Wiley & Sons, 1973.

[FGG97] N. Friedman, D.Geiger, and M. Goldszmidt, Bayesian network classifier, *Machine Learning*, 29, 1997, 131-163.

[FI93] U.M. Fayyad and K.B. Irani, Multi-Interval discretization of continuous-valued attributes for classification learning, In *Proceedings of the 13th International Joint Conference on Artificial Intelligence*, 1993, 1022-1027.

[GCB+97] J. Gray, S. Chaudhuri, A. Bosworth, A. Layman, D. Richart, M. Venkatrao, F. Pellow, and H. Pirahesh. Data Cube: A relational aggregate operator generalizing group-by, cross-tab, and sub-totals, *Data Mining and Knowledge Discovery*, 1(1), 1997, 29-54.

[KJL+94] R. Kohavi, G. John, R. Long, D. Manley, and K. Pfleger, MLC++: a machine learning library in C++, *Tools with Artificial Intelligence*, 1994, 740-743.

[LHM98] B. Liu, W. Hsu, and Y. Ma. Integrating classification and association rule mining. In *Proceedings of the Fourth International Conference on Knowledge Discovery and Data Mining*, New York, USA, 1998, 80-86.

[LM98] H. Liu and H. Motoda, Feature extraction, construction and selection: A data mining perspective. Kluwer Academic Publisher, 1998.

[LSL95] H. Lu, R. Setiono, and H. Liu. NeuroRule: A connectionist approach to data mining. In Proceedings of *the 21th International Conference on Very Large Databases*, Zurich, Switzerland, September 11-15 1995, 478-489.

[LSL96] H. Lu, S.Y. Sung, and Y. Lu. On pre-processing data for effective classification, *ACM SIGMOD '96 Workshop on Research Issues on Data Mining and Knowledge Discovery*, Montreal, Canada, June 1996.

[MAR96] M. Mehta, R. Agrawal, and J. Rissanen. SLIQ: A fast scalable classifier for data mining. In Proceedings of the 5th International Conference on Extending Database Technology, Avignon, France, March 1996.

[MM96] C.J. Merz and P. Murphy, *UCI repository of machine learning databases*, 1996. (http://www.cs.uci.edu/~mlearn/MLRepository.html)

[MW99] D. Meretakis and B. Wüthrich. Extending naïve Bayes classifiers using long itemsets. In *Proceedings of 5th International Conference on Knowledge Discovery and Data Mining*, San Diego, California, August 1999.

[Quin93] J.R. Quinlan. *C4.5: Programs for Machine Learning*. Morgan Kaufmann, 1993.

[SAM96] J. C. Shafer, R. Agrawal, and M. Mehta. SPRINT: A scalable parallel classifier for data mining. In *Proceedings of the 22nd International Conference on Very Large Databases*, Mumbai (Bombay), India, September 1996.

[WIV98] M. Wang, B. Iyer, and J.S. Vitter. Scalable mining for classification rules in relational databases. In *Proceedings of the 1998 International Database Engineering and Applications Symposium*, Cardiff, Wales, U.K., July 8-10, 1998.

[WK91] S.M. Weiss and C.A. Kulikowski. *Computer Systems that Learn: Classification and Prediction Methods from Statistics, Neural Nets, Machine Learning, and Expert Systems*. Morgan Kaufman, 1991.

[ZDN97] Y. Zhao, P.M. Deshpande and J.F. Naughton. An array-based algorithm for simultaneous multidimensional aggregations. In *Proceedings of the 1997 ACM-SIGMOD International Conference on Management of Data*, Tucson, Arizona, June 1997, 159—170.

Fast Time Sequence Indexing for Arbitrary $\mathcal{L}_p$ Norms

Byoung-Kee Yi[*]
Dept. of Computer & Info. Science
New Jersey Institute of Technology
kee@cis.njit.edu

Christos Faloutsos[†]
Dept. of Computer Science
Carnegie Mellon University
christos@cs.cmu.edu

Abstract

Fast indexing in time sequence databases for similarity searching has attracted a lot of research recently. Most of the proposals, however, typically centered around the Euclidean distance and its derivatives. We examine the problem of multimodal similarity search in which users can choose the best one from multiple similarity models for their needs.

In this paper, we present a novel and fast indexing scheme for time sequences, when the distance function is any of arbitrary $\mathcal{L}_p$ norms ($p = 1, 2, \ldots, \infty$). One feature of the proposed method is that only one index structure is needed for all $\mathcal{L}_p$ norms including the popular Euclidean distance ($\mathcal{L}_2$ norm). Our scheme achieves significant speedups over the state of the art: extensive experiments on real and synthetic time sequences show that the proposed method is comparable to the best competitor for $\mathcal{L}_2$ and $\mathcal{L}_\infty$ norms, but significantly (up to 10 times) faster for $\mathcal{L}_1$ norm.

1 Introduction

Time sequences of real-values arise in many applications such as stock market, medicine/science, and multimedia.

[*]This work was partly done while this author was at the University of Maryland, College Park.

[†]This material is based upon work supported by the National Science Foundation under Grants No. IRI-9625428, DMS-9873442, IIS-9817496, and IIS-9910606, and by the Defense Advanced Research Projects Agency under Contract No. N66001-97-C-8517. Additional funding was provided by donations from NEC and Intel. Any opinions, findings, and conclusions or recommendations expressed in this material are those of the author(s) and do not necessarily reflect the views of the National Science Foundation, DARPA, or other funding parties.

Proceedings of the 26th VLDB Conference,
Cairo, Egypt, 2000.

Retrieval of these sequences is based on *'similarity'* as opposed to *exact equality*. For instance, a financial analyst may be interested in such queries as:

- *"Find all stocks whose prices moved similarly to that of a company over the last two months."*

- *"Find all companies which have similar patterns of revenue growth to that of another company for the last decade."*

- *"Find all currencies whose prices w.r.t. US Dollar have changed similarly to the price of gold for a specific period of time.*

Results of the queries can be used for further analysis of the market trends and/or key factors behind certain market events.

Similarity-based search in large collections of time sequences has attracted a lot of research recently in database community, including [1, 9, 11, 2, 19, 24], to name just a few. Main focus has been fast indexing techniques to improve performance when a particular similarity model is given. Typically, sequences of fixed length are mapped to points in an N-dimensional Euclidean space and, then, multi-dimensional access methods such as R-tree family [12, 21, 3] can be used for fast access of those points.

Since, however, time sequences are usually long, a straightforward application of the above approach suffers from performance degradation due to a phenomenon known as *'dimensionality curse.'* [4] To address the problem, several dimensionality-reduction techniques have been proposed. *Discrete Fourier Transform* (DFT) was the most popular and used in [1, 9, 11, 19] and, more recently, *Discrete Wavelet Transform* (DWT) was also proposed [15]. The basic idea is to approximate original time sequences with a few transform coefficients and, hence, map them into low-dimensional points. These methods guarantee that every qualifying sequence will be retrieved (*no false dismissals*). Some non-qualifying sequences may be retrieved, but can be removed in the post-processing stage. Other techniques include *piece-wise constant* approximation [7], and *FastMap* [8, 24].

Another issue in the area has been the choice of similarity models. *Euclidean* distance ($\mathcal{L}_2$ norm) was the most heavily used one [1, 9, 11, 19]. Linear correlation co-eff. [15] is closely related to the normalized Euclidean distance [8]. We investigated the *Time Warping* distance in [24]. Infinity norm ($\mathcal{L}_\infty$) was proposed in [2] as part of a more complex similarity model. Other similarity models are also possible and have been proposed, but due to the space limitation we do not discuss them any further.

We note the following limitations in the previous approaches.

- **Multi-Modality Support:** No single model of similarity is suitable for every application. Sometimes several similarity models may be required for the same database of sequences, depending on different perspectives of different users. (Even a single user may want to have multiple models.) No previous work has proposed a single framework to support this *multi-modal* query processing for time sequences. To support it, we are forced to implement different techniques for different models into a DBMS, which is not efficient and only add complexity to the system, making it hard to build core DBMS components such as query optimizer, since different techniques may require different access methods and storage organizations *etc.*

- **Feature Extraction:** Proposed feature extraction (dimensionality reduction) methods are either (a) only suitable for a particular similarity model, or (b) have other shortcomings. For example, DFT as well as DWT has been shown very effective when the given distance function is Euclidean, but its effectiveness is questionable for other similarity models. FastMap may be used for a wider class of models, but it does not guarantee '*no false dismissal.*' Piece-wise constant approximation does not allow for indexing due to its irregularity.

In this paper, we address the above problems and propose a new similarity-based query processing scheme for time sequences. We focus on arbitrary $\mathcal{L}_p$ norms, since they have been widely used in real applications and can be used as basic building blocks for more complex similarity models as in [2].

We propose a new feature extraction method based on *segmented means*. We divide each time sequence into a fixed number, say 's', equal sized segments and take the mean of each segment to form a feature vector. It has a nice mathematical property such that we can decrease the given search range without affecting the correctness of the query results. Moreover, the proposed method provides a single unified framework in which,

- multiple similarity models are supported simultaneously,

- indexing for fast retrieval is supported, and,

- the same index structure can be re-used for different models.

Symbol	Definition
DFT	Discrete Fourier Transform
DWT	Discrete (Haar) Wavelet Transform
$\vec{x}$	a time sequence
x_i	the i-th value of $\vec{x}$ ($1 \leq i \leq L$)
$|\vec{x}|$	length of $\vec{x}$
s	number of segments
l	length of each segment ($= \lceil L/s \rceil$)
P_j^x	the j-th segment of $\vec{x}$ ($1 \leq j \leq s$ and $|P_j^x| = l$)
F_s^x	feature vector of $\vec{x}$
ϵ	search tolerance
w	sliding window size for the subsequence matching

Table 1: List of symbols

We will demonstrate the efficiency of the method via extensive experiments based on *whole-sequence* and *subsequence* matching queries against a stock price dataset as well as a synthetic dataset.

Organization of the paper In Section 2, we survey related work. In Section 3, we present our proposed method in detail as well as how to use existing techniques. Section 4 reports experimental results to compare the proposed method and the competitors. Finally, Section 5 discusses the key contributions of the paper. In Table 1, we list the symbols and their definitions that we use in the rest of the paper.

2   Related Work

Similarity-based matching of time sequences has been studied extensively in the signal processing area, and specifically in speech processing [18]. However, the usual assumptions are a small dataset (*e.g.*, a few tens of phonemes) so that the primary concern is precision rather than efficiency in the presence of large datasets.

Performance is the main focus in the recent database work on sequence matching. They differ in what type of distance function is used and what type of matching they aim at. In [1], Agrawal *et al* examined the whole matching problem when the given dissimilarity function is the Euclidean distance, and suggest using the Discrete Fourier Transform (DFT). They argued that most of real signals need only a few DFT coefficients to approximate them. They proposed an indexing mechanism called *F-Index* which takes a few of the first coefficients and regards them as a point in the Euclidean space. Hence it makes possible to use any of readily available multidimensional access methods. The proposed method may allow a few false alarms which can be removed in the post-processing stage, but guarantees no false dismissals. In [9], authors generalized the approach for subsequence matching. Follow-up work by Goldin and Kanellakis [11] suggested that we normalize the sequences first, to allow for differences in level and scale. Agrawal *et al* [2] introduce a new distance function for time sequences, aiming to capture the intuitive notion that two sequences should be considered similar if they have enough non-overlapping time-ordered pairs of similar subsequences. The model allows

Table 2: Comparison of different approaches

Ref.	Dist.	Features	Matching	Index	Transformations
[1]	$\mathcal{L}_2$	DFT	whole	yes	none
[9]	$\mathcal{L}_2$	DFT	subseq	yes	none
[11]	$\mathcal{L}_2$	DFT	whole	yes	offset translation, amplitude scaling
[2]	$\mathcal{L}_\infty$ based	none	subseq	yes	offset translation, amplitude scaling, gaps allowed
[19]	$\mathcal{L}_2$	DFT	whole	yes	moving average, time scaling
[15]	Corr. Coeff.	DFT or DWT	subseq	no	offset translation, amplitude scaling
[7]	$\mathcal{L}_2$ variant	piece-wise constant	whole	no	regional add
[24]	Time Warping	FastMap	whole	yes	none
[13]	$\mathcal{L}_2$	PAA	whole	yes	weighting

the amplitude of one of the two sequences to be scaled by any suitable amount and its offset adjusted appropriately. It also allows non-matching gaps in the matching subsequences. Rafiei and Mendelzon [19] extend previous work by proposing techniques to handle moving average and time scaling (*i.e.*, globally stretching or shrinking of the time axis), but not time warping. In [15], authors proposed a hierarchical scanning method based on the linear correlation coefficient as a similarity measure. Faloutsos *et al* [7] proposed a generic framework for similar time sequences. It takes advantage of piece-wise constant approximations as signatures for fast comparison of sequences and allows for *regional add* transform. We proposed efficient techniques when the similarity measure is defined by the time warping distance [24]. Keogh and Pazzani [13] proposed a feature extraction method which is coincidently vey similar to ours, but their focus was on $\mathcal{L}_2$. These approaches are summarized in Table 2. We compared them in terms of the distance metrics, the features, the type of matching, the possibility of indexing and the allowed transformations.

3 Indexing Time Sequences for $\mathcal{L}_p$ Norms

Different dissimilarity measures have been discussed in the literature. Among others, $\mathcal{L}_p$ norm is the most popular class of dissimilarity measures and defined as follows:

$$\mathcal{L}_p(\vec{x} - \vec{y}) = \left(\sum_{i=1}^{L} |x_i - y_i|^p \right)^{\frac{1}{p}}$$

It is called the *city-block* or the *Manhattan* norm when $p = 1$, and the *Euclidean* norm when $p = 2$. In the extreme case when $p = \infty$, it is called the *maximum* norm and can be reformulated as follows:

$$\mathcal{L}_\infty(\vec{x} - \vec{y}) = \max_{i=1}^{L} |x_i - y_i|$$

It is known that $\mathcal{L}_2$ norm is optimal (in the Maximum Likelihood sense) when measurement errors are additive, *i.i.d.* (independent, identically distributed) Gaussian [22]. It has been the most popular dissimilarity measure in similar time sequence matching [1, 9, 11, 19]. Linear correlation coefficient was used in [15], but it can be effectively converted to $\mathcal{L}_2$ norm without loss of information [8].

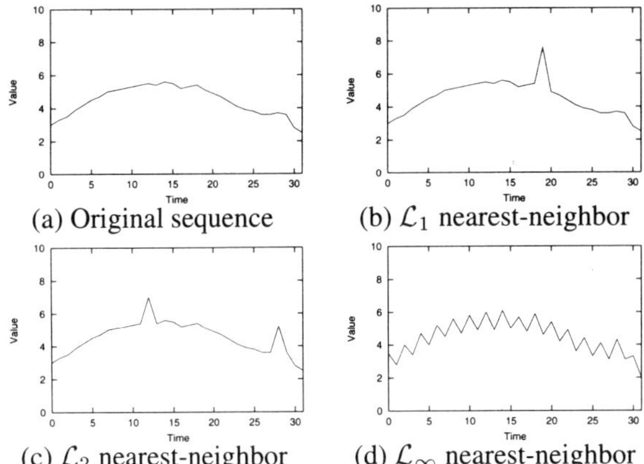

Figure 1: Different characteristics of $\mathcal{L}_1$, $\mathcal{L}_2$, and $\mathcal{L}_\infty$

$\mathcal{L}_1$ norm is optimal when measurement errors are additive, *i.i.d.* Laplacian (or Double Exponential), hence more robust against impulsive noise [22]. $\mathcal{L}_1$ has been used in the context of robust (parametric or non-parametric) regression [14, 20, 22] for many applications including time sequences [14, 6]. More recently, it was also used in [10] for their hashing-based similarity search technique.

$\mathcal{L}_\infty$ was used for atomic matching in a more complex dissimilarity measure in [2]. The measure proposed in [2], however, only decides whether two sequences are similar or not and ranking of query result is not possible.

Figure 1 illustrates the characteristics of different $\mathcal{L}_p$ norms. All sequences are of length 32. The original sequence is in (a). We added a single impulse of size 2.5 in (b), two impulses of size 1.5 in (c). In (d), we added and subtracted 0.5 alternately at each time spot. Then the closest sequences to the sequence (a) with respect to $\mathcal{L}_1$, $\mathcal{L}_2$, and $\mathcal{L}_\infty$, are (b), (c), and (d), respectively. This example clearly shows the different notion of similarity each norm offers.

Effective feature extraction functions such as DFT and DWT are available only for $\mathcal{L}_2$ because they are rotation-based (orthonormal transformations) and do not preserve distance for $\mathcal{L}_1$ and $\mathcal{L}_\infty$ in the feature space. Thus, in case of $\mathcal{L}_\infty$, they were forced to search in high dimensional space [2], rather than low dimensional feature space as in [1, 9].

We believe the choice of appropriate dissimilarity measures is highly application dependent and up to application engineers. Since, however, the perspectives of different users can vary even on the same dataset, some form of *multi-modality* is required. In such an environment, a DBMS for similarity-based retrieval of time sequences must provide a single unified framework which supports:

- multiple similarity models simultaneously,

- indexing for fast retrieval, and,

- re-use of the same index structure for multiple models.

In this regard, our first goal is to provide a general indexing scheme which can be used for any of $\mathcal{L}_p$ norms

$(p = 1, 2, \ldots, \infty)$. We specifically support the following two types of queries.

Problem 3.1 ($\mathcal{L}_p$-based Whole Sequence Matching)
Given a query sequence $\vec{q}$ and a set of sequences SEQ ($|\vec{q}| = |\vec{x}|$, for all $\vec{x} \in$ SEQ), find all sequences $\vec{x}$ in SEQ such that $\mathcal{L}_p(\vec{q} - \vec{x}) \leq \epsilon$, for any value of $p = 1, 2, \ldots, \infty$.

Problem 3.2 ($\mathcal{L}_p$-based Subsequence Matching) *Given a query sequence $\vec{q}$ and a set of sequences SEQ ($|\vec{q}| \leq |\vec{x}|$, for all $\vec{x} \in$ SEQ), find all subsequences $\vec{x}'$ of all $\vec{x}$ in SEQ such that $|\vec{q}| = |\vec{x}'|$ and $\mathcal{L}_p(\vec{q} - \vec{x}') \leq \epsilon$, for any value of $p = 1, 2, \ldots, \infty$.*

While we are primarily concerned with *whole* and *subsequence* matching, we note that a fast method for both types of matching is also essential for more complex matching such as the one proposed in [2], in which *atomic* matching is in fact whole matching based on $\mathcal{L}_\infty$.

Some transformations can be allowed before sequences are compared. These include *offset translation, amplitude scaling* [11, 2, 15], and *time scaling* [19]. Offset translation subtracts/adds a certain offset value (usually mean) from each element of a sequence. Amplitude scaling multiplies a normalization factor to the element such that either the amplitude is within a fixed range or the sample variance is 1. Time scaling is to enlarge the time axis by a certain amount so that two sequences of different lengths can be matched. They provide a certain degree of flexibility in the notion of similarity. Our next goal is to support these transformations in our scheme.

Problem 3.3 (Transformations) *Support efficiently 'offset translation', 'amplitude scaling', and 'time scaling' in our indexing scheme.*

3.1   Proposed Method – Segmented Means

Suppose we have a set of sequences of length L. The basic idea of our proposal consists of two steps. First we partition each time sequence into s segments of equal length l. We assume $L = s * l$. Otherwise, we add zeros at the end of sequences. Note that it does not affect query results. Next, we extract simple features from each segment. We propose to use *mean* as a feature for all $\mathcal{L}_p$ norms.

Formally, let $\vec{x} = \langle x_1, \ldots, x_L \rangle$ be a sequence of length L. Let s and l be two numbers such that $L = s * l$. Then $\vec{x}$ can be divided into s segments of length l. Let P_j^x denote the j-th segment of $\vec{x}$, i.e.,

$$P_j^x = \langle x_{(j-1)l+1}, \ldots, x_{j \cdot l} \rangle.$$

We define a feature vector of $\vec{x}$ as follows. (See Figure 2 for an example.)

Definition 3.1 (Segmented-Mean Feature) *Given a sequence $\vec{x} = \langle x_1, \ldots, x_L \rangle$ and the number of segments $s > 0$, define the feature vector $\vec{F_s^x}$ of $\vec{x}$ by,*

$$\vec{F_s^x} = \langle f_1^x, \ldots, f_s^x \rangle = \langle mean(P_1^x), \ldots, mean(P_s^x) \rangle$$

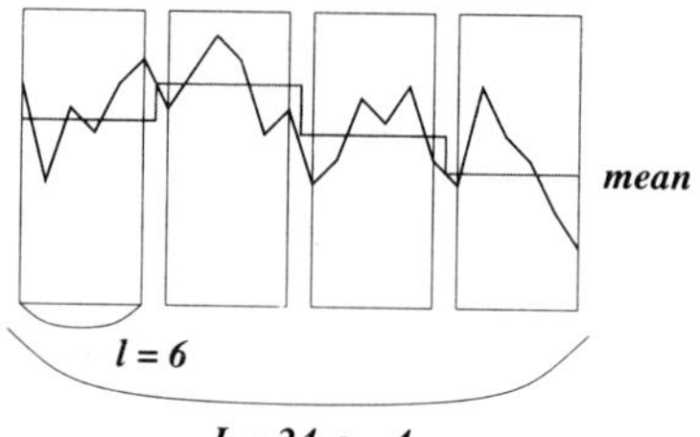

Figure 2: Example of Segmented Means

The algorithm to compute $\vec{F_s^x}$ is fairly obvious and omitted in this paper. To avoid the possibility of false dismissals, we must show that the distance between feature vectors lower-bounds that of original sequences. It is not very hard to see that it is indeed the case, *i.e.*, for all $p = 1, \ldots, \infty$,

$$\mathcal{L}_p(\vec{F_s^x}) \leq \mathcal{L}_p(\vec{x})$$

In practice, however, $\vec{F_s^x}$ is a poor approximation of $\vec{x}$, since it is essentially a down-sampling of $\vec{x}$. Much of the information would be lost and, consequently, too many false alrams would occur.

Our goal is to find a way to compensate the loss of information so that we could reduce the number of false alarms. More specifically, we seek a factor $\alpha_p > 1$ such that,

$$\alpha_p \cdot \mathcal{L}_p(\vec{F_s^x}) \leq \mathcal{L}_p(\vec{x})$$

We claim that there exists such a factor, thanks to the nice mathematical property of $\vec{F_s^x}$, and we will take advantage of it for efficient query processing. There is a well-known mathematical result on *convex* functions. We borrow the following theorem from [17, p.379].[1] (See Figure 3 for an intuitive example.)

Theorem 3.1 *Suppose that $x_1, \ldots, x_L \in \mathcal{R}$, and $\lambda_1, \ldots, \lambda_L \in \mathcal{R}$ such that $\lambda_i \geq 0$ and $(\sum_{i=1}^{L} \lambda_i) = 1$. If f is a convex function on $\mathcal{R}$, then*

$$f(\lambda_1 x_1 + \cdots + \lambda_L x_L) \leq \lambda_1 f(x_1) + \cdots + \lambda_L f(x_L)$$

where $\mathcal{R}$ is the set of real numbers.

It is clear that $f(\cdot) = |\cdot|^p$ is a convex function on $\mathcal{R}$ for $1 \leq p < \infty$. Hence, as a direct consequence of Theorem 3.1 by taking $\lambda_i = \frac{1}{L}$, we have the following corollary.

Corollary 3.2 *For any sequence $\vec{x} = \langle x_1, \ldots, x_L \rangle$ and $1 \leq p < \infty$, the following holds.*

$$L \cdot |mean(\vec{x})|^p \leq \sum_{i=1}^{L} |x_i|^p$$

Or, equivalently, for each segment of $\vec{x}$, we have, for $1 \leq j \leq s$,

$$l \cdot |mean(P_j^x)|^p \leq \sum_{i=(j-1)l+1}^{j \cdot l} |x_i|^p$$

---

[1] The definitions of convex sets and functions are beyond the scope of the paper and are found in [17, pp.373-376]. Note also that we modified it such that we only consider $\mathcal{R}$ rather than $\mathcal{R}^d$.

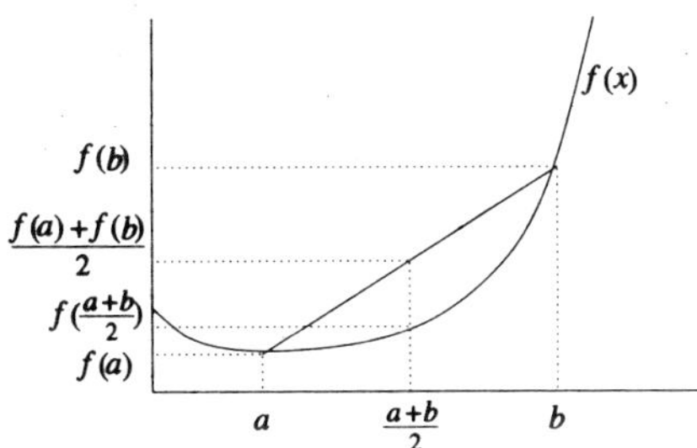

Figure 3: Illustration of convex function theorem

Now we have our main theorem as follows.

Theorem 3.3 *For any sequence* $\vec{x} = \langle x_1, \ldots, x_L \rangle$ *and* $1 \leq p \leq \infty$, *the following holds.*

$$\sqrt[p]{l} \cdot \mathcal{L}_p(\vec{F_s^x}) \leq \mathcal{L}_p(\vec{x})$$

Proof: We first consider when $p \neq \infty$. By the definitions of $\mathcal{L}_p$ and $\vec{F_s^x}$,

$$l \cdot \mathcal{L}_p(\vec{F_s^x})^p = l \cdot \sum_{j=1}^{s} |\text{mean}(P_j^x)|^p$$

$$\text{By Corollary 3.2,} \quad \leq \sum_{j=1}^{s} \left(\sum_{i=(j-1)l+1}^{j \cdot l} |x_i|^p \right)$$

$$= \sum_{i=1}^{L} |x_i|^p$$

$$= \mathcal{L}_p(\vec{x})^p$$

By taking p-th root on both sides, we prove the theorem. If $p = \infty$, then

$$\mathcal{L}_\infty(\vec{F_s^x}) = \max_{j=1}^{s} |\text{mean}(P_j^x)|$$

$$\leq \max_{j=1}^{s} \left(\max_{i=(j-1)l+1}^{j \cdot l} |x_i| \right)$$

$$= \max_{i=1}^{L} |x_i| = \mathcal{L}_\infty(\vec{x})$$

Since $\sqrt[\infty]{l} = 1$, it completes the proof. $\square$

3.1.1 Query Processing

Thanks to Theorem 3.3, we can efficiently handle ϵ-range queries with segmented-mean feature vectors. Suppose we are to compare two sequences $\vec{x}$ and $\vec{y}$. By the theorem, we know that $\mathcal{L}_p(\vec{x} - \vec{y}) \leq \epsilon$ implies $\mathcal{L}_p(\vec{F_s^x} - \vec{F_s^y}) \leq \epsilon/\sqrt[p]{l}$. (The converse does not hold in general.) Therefore, any $\mathcal{L}_p$-based ϵ-range queries against a set of sequences $\vec{x}$ can be correctly converted to $\mathcal{L}_p$-based $(\epsilon/\sqrt[p]{l})$-range queries against a set of the corresponding feature vectors $\vec{F_s^x}$ without worrying about the possibility of false dismissals. This is an improvement to the plain usage of the feature vectors, since we have reduced the search range by a factor of $\sqrt[p]{l}$.

We summarize a general strategy for the whole-sequence matching (Problem 3.1) as follows:

1. Extract feature vectors $\vec{F_s^x}$ for all $\vec{x} \in$ SEQ. The number of segments, s, is a system tuning parameter as the number of Fourier coefficients in [1]. (Trailing zeros are padded if necessary.)

2. Build an index structure on $\vec{F_s^x}$ using any of the readily available multi-dimensional access methods such as the R-tree.

3. For each $\mathcal{L}_p$-based ϵ-range query with a query sequence $\vec{q}$, extract $\vec{F_s^q}$ and convert the query to an equivalent $(\epsilon/\sqrt[p]{l})$-range query with $\vec{F_s^q}$ in the feature space, and perform search on the index. $(l = \lceil L/s \rceil)$

4. Filter out false alarms.

Processing subsequence matching queries (Problem 3.2) is more complex. The basic idea is fairly the same as in [9]. We assume that all sequences including query sequences are longer than a predetermined minimum length 'w'. (In this case, however, the length of each individual sequence can vary.) Then, our strategy is the following:

1. A sequence $\vec{x}$ is divided into $(|\vec{x}| - w + 1)$ sliding windows of fixed length w and extract the segmented-mean features from them. We use the same value of s as in the case of whole-sequence matching.

2. The feature vectors form a trail in the s-dimensional feature space. To reduce the storage overhead and enhance the system performance, we divide them into a few sub-trails based on the '*marginal cost*' criterion defined in [9], and compute their minimum bounding rectangles (MBRs).

3. We repeat the above steps for each $\vec{x} \in$ SEQ.

4. Build an index structure on the MBRs using any of the readily available multi-dimensional access methods such as the R-tree.

5. For each $\mathcal{L}_p$-based ϵ-range query with a query sequence $\vec{q}$,

    (a) Divide $\vec{q}$ into $p(= \lfloor |\vec{q}|/w \rfloor)$ non-overlapping subsequences, $\vec{q_k}, 1 \leq k \leq p$. (Note that we can ignore the remaining $(|\vec{q}| - p \cdot w)$ elements without compromising the correctness of the query results.)

    (b) For each feature vector of $\vec{q_k}$, perform $(\epsilon/\sqrt[p]{l \cdot p})$-range search on the index and 'OR' the query results.

6. Filter out false alarms.

3.1.2 Transformations - Data Preprocessing

We have shown how to efficiently process $\mathcal{L}_p$-based queries using the proposed feature extraction method. We now turn to our next goal. As for offset translation and amplitude scaling, let $\vec{y} = a \cdot \vec{x} - b$ with 'a' for the scaling factor

```
Algorithm HaarWaveletCoefficients
  Input:   X[1,...,L], L = 2^n for some n
  Output:  H[1,...,L], Haar wavelet coeff.  for X[]

  H[1,...,L] := X[1,...,L];
  For (len := L; len >= 2; len := len/2) {
    For (i := j := 1; i < len; i := i+2, j := j+1) {
      S[j] := (H[i] + H[i+1]) / √2;
      D[j] := (H[i] - H[i+1]) / √2;
    }
    For (i := 1; i <= len/2; i := i+1) {
      H[i]        := S[i];
      H[i+(len/2)] := D[i];
    }
  }
  Return H[1,...,L];
End Algorithm
```

Figure 4: Algorithm to compute Haar wavelet coefficients

and 'b' for the offset value. That is, $\vec{y}$ is the translated and rescaled version of $\vec{x}$. Then the feature vector of $\vec{z}$ can be computed as follows:

$$
\begin{aligned}
\vec{F_s^y} &= \langle \mathrm{mean}(P_1^y), \ldots, \mathrm{mean}(P_s^y) \rangle \\
&= \langle (a \cdot \mathrm{mean}(P_1^x) - b), \ldots (a \cdot \mathrm{mean}(P_s^x) - b) \rangle \\
&= a \cdot \vec{F_s^x} - b
\end{aligned}
$$

Thus, once we have the feature vectors, it is almost straightforward to compute the translated and rescaled versions.

As for time scaling, since extending time axis does not change the mean, the mean feature vector is *invariant* under time scaling. Let $\vec{z}$ is an extended version of $\vec{x}$ by 'c' times for an integer c. That is, $z_i = x_{\lceil i/c \rceil}$. Then,

$$
\begin{aligned}
\vec{F_s^z} &= \langle \mathrm{mean}(P_1^z), \ldots, \mathrm{mean}(P_s^z) \rangle \\
&= \left\langle \frac{c \cdot \mathrm{mean}(P_1^x)}{c}, \ldots, \frac{c \cdot \mathrm{mean}(P_s^x)}{c} \right\rangle \\
&= \vec{F_s^x}
\end{aligned}
$$

Thus, we can reuse the same feature vector *as-is* for the time-extended version. We believe other transformations such as *moving-average* [19] can be easily handled likewise.

3.2 An Alternative–How to use DWT

As an alternative, we can use the existing feature extraction methods based on orthogonal linear transforms such as DWT and DFT. In this paper, we focus on DWT, especially '*Haar*' DWT, since it has been widely used as a state-of-the-art method for various database applications recently [16, 23]. We present an algorithm to compute 1-d Haar wavelet coefficients in Figure 4. (For the theory of wavelets, readers are referred to [5].)

Since DWT as well as DFT is an orthogonal linear transform, it rotates the data distribution in a predetermined way. As such, $\mathcal{L}_2$ norm is perfectly preserved by the transform, since it is invariant under rotations. Other $\mathcal{L}_p$ norms for

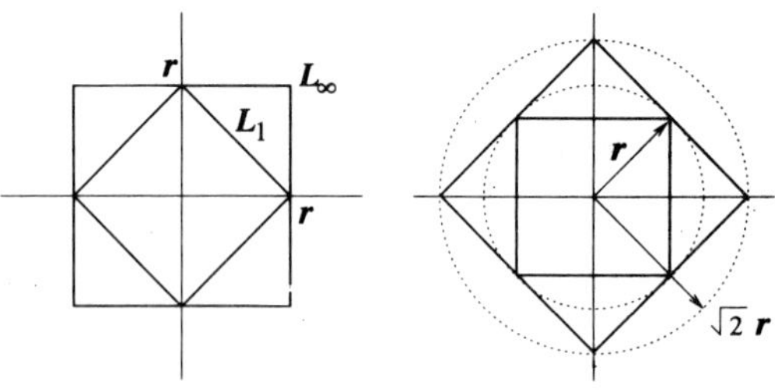

(a) Before rotation   (b) After rotation

Figure 5: Example of adjusting ranges for rotated points

$p \neq 2$ are not preserved. Therefore, we can not use the DWT-based feature vectors for arbitrary $\mathcal{L}_p$-based query processing.

One way to fix the problem is to adjust the search range such that all qualifying sequences are included within the search boundary. Suppose $\vec{x}'$ and $\vec{y}'$ are the rotated versions of two sequences $\vec{x}$ and $\vec{y}$ of length L, respectively. Then, it is not hard to see the following translation rules hold: (Figure 5 describes the idea in the 2-d plane, *i.e.*, $L = 2$.)

$$
\begin{aligned}
\mathcal{L}_1(\vec{x} - \vec{y}) \leq \epsilon &\implies \mathcal{L}_2(\vec{x}' - \vec{y}') \leq \epsilon \\
\mathcal{L}_\infty(\vec{x} - \vec{y}) \leq \epsilon &\implies \mathcal{L}_2(\vec{x}' - \vec{y}') \leq \sqrt{L} \cdot \epsilon
\end{aligned}
$$

Similar rules are possible for $\mathcal{L}_p$ norms for $3 \leq p < \infty$.

We convert each $\mathcal{L}_1$- and $\mathcal{L}_\infty$-based ϵ-range queries to $\mathcal{L}_2$-based queries with search ranges according the above conversion rules, and then perform search on the index built on top of the DWT feature vectors. Note that, this way, we can guarantee no false dismissals. As we will see in the next section, however, it is not very efficient except for $\mathcal{L}_2$ norm.

3.2.1 The Haar DWT vs the Segmented Means

The two types of feature vectors produced by the proposed method and the Haar DWT are closely related to each other. More specifically, we have the following theorem.

Theorem 3.4 *Let $\vec{H_s^x}$ denote a feature vector of $\vec{x}$, composed of the first s Haar wavelet coefficients. We further assume $|\vec{x}| = 2^n$ ($n > 0$) and $s = 2^m$ ($n \geq m \geq 0$). Then, the following equality holds.*

$$
\mathcal{L}_2(\sqrt{l} \cdot \vec{F_s^x}) = \mathcal{L}_2(\vec{H_s^x})
$$

where $l = |\vec{x}|/s = 2^{n-m}$.

Proof: By definition,

$$
\begin{aligned}
\sqrt{l} \cdot \vec{F_s^x} &= \langle \sqrt{l} \cdot \mathrm{mean}(P_1^x), \ldots, \sqrt{l} \cdot \mathrm{mean}(P_s^x) \rangle \\
&= \langle \mathrm{sum}(P_1^x)/\sqrt{l}, \ldots, \mathrm{sum}(P_s^x)/\sqrt{l} \rangle
\end{aligned}
$$

Note that, if we take the Haar DWT of the above vector, we get $\vec{H_s^x}$. Since the Haar DWT is invariant under $\mathcal{L}_2$, we have,

$$
\begin{aligned}
\mathcal{L}_2(\sqrt{l} \cdot \vec{F_s^x}) &= \mathcal{L}_2(\mathrm{DWT}(\sqrt{l} \cdot \vec{F_s^x})) \\
&= \mathcal{L}_2(\vec{H_s^x})
\end{aligned}
$$

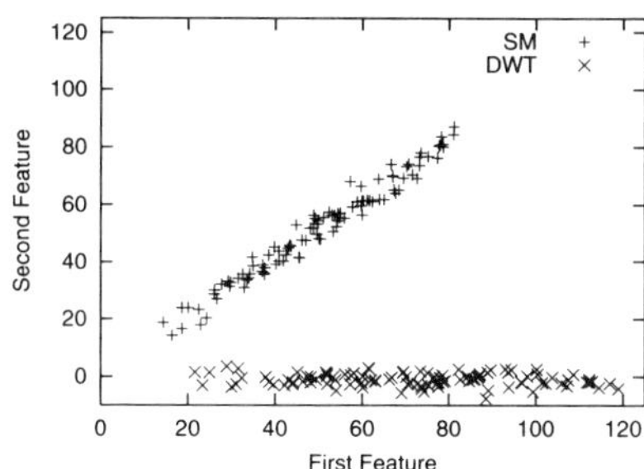

Figure 6: Examples of $\mathcal{S}_{SM}$ and $\mathcal{S}_{DWT}$

Hence, the theorem holds. $\qquad\square$

Let $\mathcal{S}_{\text{SM}}$ and $\mathcal{S}_{\text{DWT}}$ be two feature spaces defined by $\sqrt{l} \cdot \vec{F}_s^x$ and $\vec{H}_s^x$, respectively. The above theorem tells us that if the dimension of feature space is some power of 2 (*i.e.*, $s = 2^m$), then the $\mathcal{S}_{\text{SM}}$ is a rotated version of $\mathcal{S}_{\text{DWT}}$ and *vice versa*. In Figure 6, we present examples of $\mathcal{S}_{\text{SM}}$ and $\mathcal{S}_{\text{DWT}}$ of 100 time sequences ($s = 2$). We observe that they are indeed rotated versions of each other. In terms of indexing, however, $\mathcal{S}_{\text{DWT}}$ seems a little bit better since its minimum bounding rectangle (MBR) is smaller as we can see in the example. Therefore, for $\mathcal{L}_2$-based queries, we expect slightly better performance from $\mathcal{S}_{\text{DWT}}$ and, as we will see later, the experimental results prove this point.

4   Experimental Results

To verify the effectiveness of the proposed method, we performed experiments on real time sequences (daily stock prices) and synthetically generated time sequences. Our experiments were based on ϵ-range queries for both whole- and subsequence matching. We compared the proposed method and the DWT-based method as well as the sequential scanning method as a sanity checker. All methods were implemented in the C programming language. For R-tree, we used DR-tree (v2.5) library developed at the Univ. of Maryland with some modifications to handle $\mathcal{L}_p$-based search. As a measure of success, we recorded the wall clock time with the UNIX `time` command. All experiments were performed on a dedicated Sun UltraSparc-1 workstation with a 143MHz CPU, 64MB of memory and SCSI disks (Seagate ST410800N), running SunOS version 5.5 operating system.

We present more specific information on the experimental setting in the following subsection.

4.1   Experimental Setting

For the experiment, we prepared two datasets of sequences. Samples of these time sequences are plotted in Figure 7.

- STOCK: The stock dataset contains 675 stocks, each with varying number of daily closing prices. The average length is 1,187. For the whole-sequence matching, we generated fixed length sequences with 128 samples each. The sample windows overlap by 1/3 of the window size. For subsequence matching, we used the dataset as-is.

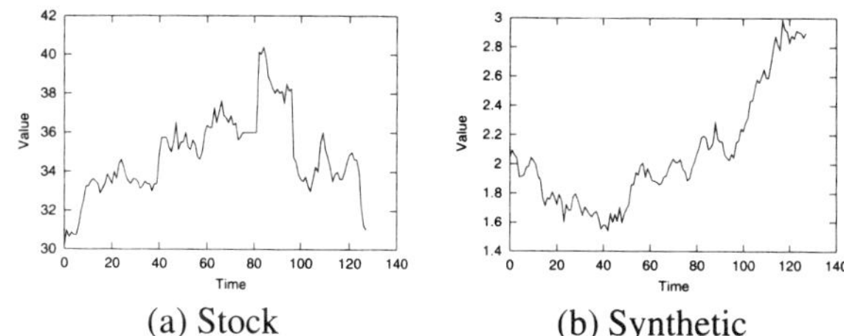

(a) Stock (b) Synthetic

Figure 7: Sample Time Sequences

Dataset	Num. of Seq.	(Avg.) Seq. Len.	Feature Dim.
STOCK	675	1,187	4
SYNTH	30,000	128	4

Table 3: Summary of the Experimental Setting

- SYNTH: Additional 30,000 synthetic sequences, with 128 samples each, were generated using the *random-walk* model following [1]. More specifically, each sequence was generated by the following formula.

$$x_t = x_{t-1} + \alpha \cdot z_t$$

where $x_0 \sim \text{Uniform}(2, 10)$, $z_t \sim \text{Normal}(0, 1)$, and $\alpha = 0.06$, for $t = 1, \ldots, 128$.

We compared the following 3 methods:

- SM: Our proposed method based on the segmented means.

- DWT: The alternative method based on the Haar wavelet transform.

- SCAN: The naive sequential scanning method.

An important parameter is the dimension of the feature space, *i.e.*, the length of feature vectors. In general, the optimal value depends on the datasets, the feature extraction methods to use, and the distance functions ($\mathcal{L}_p$ norms). We fixed it as 4 because of the following two reasons:

- The value was good enough for both SM and DWT methods, a little more in favor of DWT, regardless of the datasets.

- Since one of our goals is to re-use the same index structure for all $\mathcal{L}_p$ norms, we need to fix it for all values of p.

Table 3 summarizes the experimental setting.

4.2   Whole Sequence Matching Queries

We first performed $\mathcal{L}_p$-based whole-sequence matching queries. We took 100 sequences randomly from each dataset and used them as the query sequences. We measured the average response time (including both the search time and the post-processing time). Search ranges were chosen such that the average selectivity of query results be

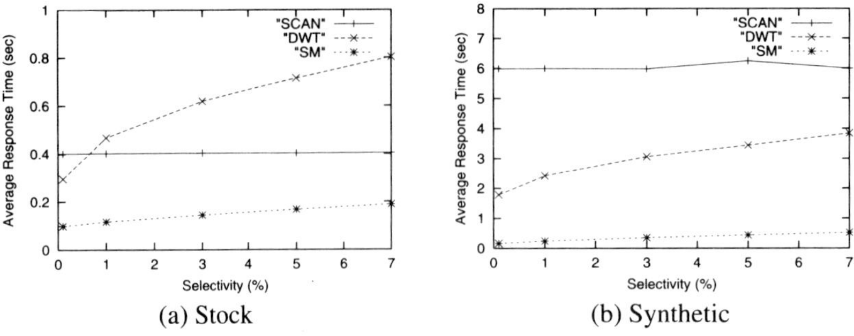

(a) Stock   (b) Synthetic

Figure 8: $\mathcal{L}_1$-based whole-sequence matching

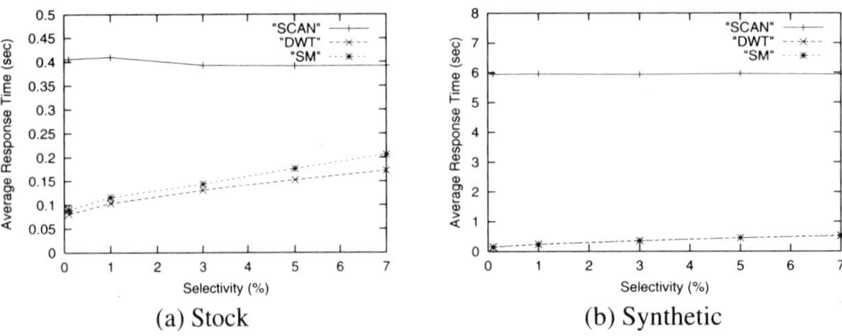

(a) Stock   (b) Synthetic

Figure 9: $\mathcal{L}_2$-based whole-sequence matching

0.1%, 1%, 3%, and 7%, for each value of $p = 1, 2, \infty$ and for each dataset.

The results of $\mathcal{L}_1$-based whole matching queries are presented in Figure 8. The proposed method is the clear winner for both datasets. Interestingly, DWT method was even slower than the SCAN method on the stock dataset. For the synthetic dataset, the proposed method achieved 10 time speedup over the DWT method and 50 time speedup over the naive method at the selectivity of 0.1%.

In the case of $\mathcal{L}_2$-based queries (see Figure 9), the DWT method was slightly faster than the proposed method for the stock dataset. It is, however, expected because DWT is highly optimized for $\mathcal{L}_2$ norm. For the synthetic dataset, it is almost impossible to distinguish between the proposed method and the DWT method and they both scaled up very well.

Figure 10 presents the results from $\mathcal{L}_\infty$-based queries. Again, the proposed method is the winner for both datasets, although the difference between the proposed method and the DWT method is small in the stock dataset. For the synthetic dataset, they both scaled very well and the proposed method consistently outperformed the competitor.

As a summary, we conclude that the proposed method is the clear winner in all cases except for $\mathcal{L}_2$-based queries against the stock dataset. But the DWT method performed very poorly for $\mathcal{L}_1$-based queries.

4.3 Subsequence Matching Queries

We next performed $\mathcal{L}_p$-based subsequence matching queries. For the stock dataset, we re-used the same query sequences that had been used for the whole matching queries. For the synthetic dataset, we used the first 64 values of the query sequences from the whole matching experiment. Hence the ratios between the query length and the data length are 128:1187 for the stock dataset and 64:128 for the synthetic dataset. The search ranges were chosen in the same way as in the previous experiment.

In Figure 11, presented are the results from $\mathcal{L}_1$-based subsequence queries. We observed that, again, the proposed method is the clear winner for both datasets and it scales very well even at the relatively hight selectivity (7%). The DWT performed poorly for both datasets. At highest selectivity, it almost converged to the naive method.

In Figure 12, $\mathcal{L}_2$-based query results are shown. Yet gain, the DWT method performed slightly better than the proposed method on the stock dataset, but the difference was small. For the synthetic dataset, the proposed method outperformed the DWT method just a little after 1% of selectivity. On both datasets, they scaled very well.

In the case of $\mathcal{L}_\infty$ (Figure 13), the results are not much different from the other cases and the proposed method consistently outperformed the competitor.

Summary In Table 4, we present the relative response time of the proposed method *w.r.t.* the DWT-based method for the 3%-selectivity queries. For $\mathcal{L}_1$-based queries, the proposed method outperforms the DWT-based method by big margins, in all datasets. For $\mathcal{L}_2$-based queries, the DWT-based is slightly faster as we anticipated. Note, however, the proposed method outperforms in subsequence queries against the synthetic dataset. For $\mathcal{L}_\infty$-based queries, the proposed method consistently outperforms by the competitor by up to 30% margin. Overall, we conclude

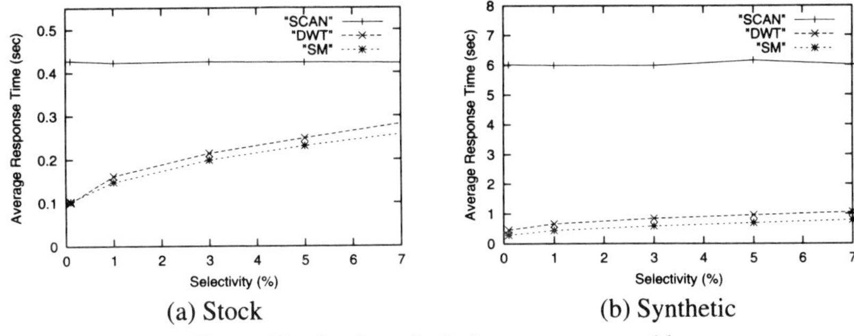

(a) Stock   (b) Synthetic

Figure 10: $\mathcal{L}_\infty$-based whole-sequence matching

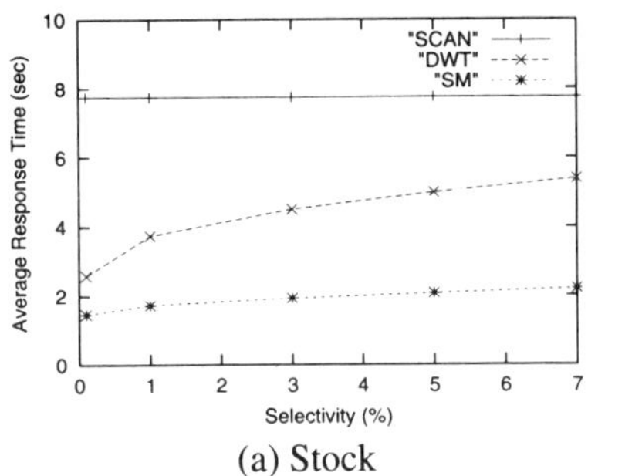

(a) Stock   (b) Synthetic

Figure 11: $\mathcal{L}_1$-based subsequence matching

Dataset	Whole			Subsequence		
	$\mathcal{L}_1$	$\mathcal{L}_2$	$\mathcal{L}_\infty$	$\mathcal{L}_1$	$\mathcal{L}_2$	$\mathcal{L}_\infty$
STOCK	0.23	1.1	0.93	0.43	1.05	0.88
SYNTH	0.12	1.03	0.7	0.18	0.95	0.74

Table 4: Relative response time (T_{SM}/T_{DWT}) for 3%-selectivity queries

that the proposed method is the winner in the competition.

5 Conclusion

The major contribution of the paper is two-folds:

- **Multi-modality Support:** No single model of similarity is suitable for every application. Sometimes several similarity models may be required for the same database of sequences, depending on the different perspectives of different users. We addressed this problem by supporting arbitrary $\mathcal{L}_p$ norms for any value of $p = 1, 2, \ldots, \infty$, because they are the most popular class of dissimilarity measures and, also, they can be used as the building blocks for more complex ones. No previous work has proposed a single framework to support this *multi-modal* query processing for time sequences.

- **Efficient Indexing:** For efficient query processing, we proposed a new unified indexing scheme which provides the following advantages over previous approaches.

  - All $\mathcal{L}_p$ norms are supported simultaneously.
  - Indexing for fast retrieval is supported.
  - The same index structure can be re-used for different $\mathcal{L}_p$ norms.
  - It is easy to incorporate such data preprocessing techniques as 'offset translation', 'amplitude scaling', and 'time scaling'.

We showed the soundness of our method mathematically. We also explained in detail how to efficiently process both the whole-sequence and the subsequence matching queries in our unified indexing scheme. Through extensive experiments, we verified that our method is very efficient. Our method achieved up to 10 time speedup over the DWT-based state-of-the-art method and scaled up very well for all $\mathcal{L}_p$ norms on both the real and the synthetic datasets. Further research will focus on extending the proposed method to a broader class of similarity models.

References

[1] R. Agrawal, C. Faloutsos, and A. Swami. Efficient similarity search in sequence databases. In *Proc. of the FODO Conf.*, Evansotn, IL, October 1993.

[2] R. Agrawal, K.-I. Lin, H. S. Sawhney, and K. Shim. Fast similarity search in the presence of noise, scaling, and translation in time-series database. In *Proc. of the VLDB Conf.*, Zürich, Switzerland, 1995.

[3] N. Beckmann, H.-P. Kriegel, R. Schneider, and B. Seeger. The R*-Tree: an Efficient and Robust Access Method for Points and Rectangles. In *Proc. ACM SIGMOD Conf.*, pages 322–331, Atlantic City, NJ, May 1990.

[4] S. Berchtold, D. A. Keim, and H.-P. Kriegel. The X-tree: An Index Structure for High-Dimensional Data. In *Proc. VLDB Conf.*, Bombay, India, 1996.

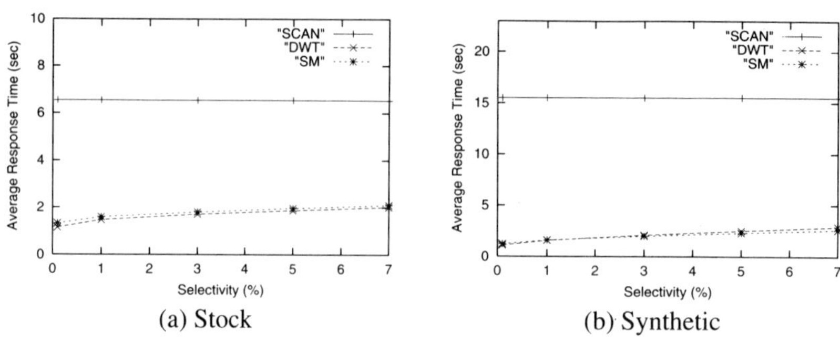

(a) Stock   (b) Synthetic

Figure 12: $\mathcal{L}_2$-based subsequence matching

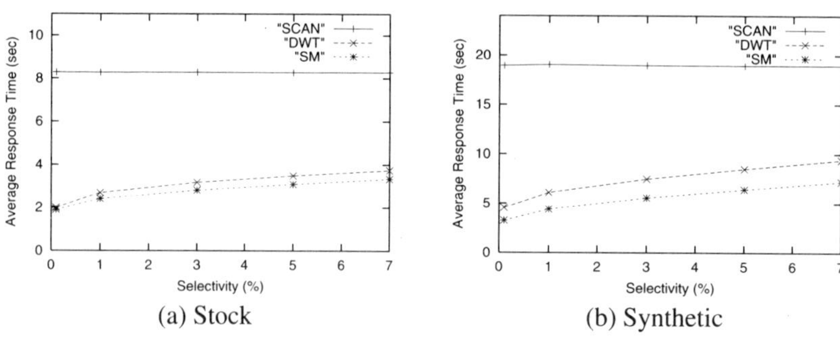

(a) Stock   (b) Synthetic

Figure 13: $\mathcal{L}_\infty$-based subsequence matching

[5] I. Daubechies. *Ten Lectures on Wavelets*. Capital City Press, Montpelier, Vermont, 1992. Society for Industrial and Applied Mathematics (SIAM), Philadelphia, PA.

[6] Y. Dodge, editor. L_1-*Statistical Procedures and Related Topics*. Institute for Mathmatical Statistics, Hayward, CA, 1997.

[7] C. Faloutsos, H. V. Jagadish, A. O. Mendelzon, and T. Milo. A signature technique for similarity-based queries. In *Proc. of SEQUENCES'97*, Salerno, Italy, June 1997.

[8] C. Faloutsos and K.-Ii. Lin. FastMap: a Fast Algorithm for Indexing, Data-Mining and Visualization of Traditional and Multimedia Datasets. *Proc. of ACM-SIGMOD*, pages 163–174, May 1995.

[9] C. Faloutsos, M. Ranganathan, and Y. Manolopoulos. Fast Subsequence Matching in Time-Series Databases. In *Proc. of the ACM SIGMOD Conf.*, May 1994.

[10] A. Gionis, P. Indyk, and R. Motwani. Similarity Search in High Dimensions via Hashing. In *Proc. of VLDB Conf.*, Edinburgh, Scotland, 1999.

[11] D. Q. Goldin and P. C. Kanellakis. On similarity queries for time-series data: Constraint specification and implementation. In *Proc. of Constraint Programming 95*, Marseilles, France, September 1995.

[12] A. Guttman. R-Trees: a Dynamic Index Structure for Spatial Searching. In *Proc. ACM SIGMOD Conf,*, pages 47–57, Boston, Mass, Jun 1984.

[13] E. J. Keogh and M. J. Pazzani. A simple dimensionality reduction technique for fast similairity search in large time series databases. In *Proc. of the 4th Pacific-Asia Conf. on Knowledge Discovery and Data Mining*, Kyoto, Japan, 2000.

[14] K. D. Lawrence and J. L. Arthur, editors. *Robust Regression*. Dekker, 1990.

[15] C.-S. Li, P. S. Yu, and V. Castelli. HierarchyScan: A Hierarchical Similarity Search Algorithm for Databases of Long Sequences. In *Proc. of ICDE*, pages 546–553, New Orleans, LA, 1996.

[16] A. Natsev, R. Rastogi, and K. Shim. WARLUS: A Similarity Retrieval Algorithms for Image Databases. In *Proc. of ACM SIGMOD Conf.*, pages 395–406, Philadelphia, PA, 1999.

[17] M.H. Protter and C.B. Morrey. *A First Course in Real Analysis*. Springer-Verlag, 1977.

[18] L. Rabiner and B.-H. Juang. *Fundamentals of Speech Recognition*. Prentice Hall, 1993.

[19] D. Rafiei and A. Mendelzon. Similarity -based queries for time series data. In *Proc. of the ACM SIGMOD Conf.*, Tucson, AZ, May 1997.

[20] P. Rousseeuw and A. Leroy. *Robust Regression and Outlier Detection*. John Wiley, New York, 1987.

[21] T. Sellis, N. Roussopoulos, and C. Faloutsos. The R+ Tree: a Dynamic Index for Multi-Dimensional Objects. In *Proc. VLDB Conf.*, pages 507–518, 1987.

[22] N. D. Sidiropoulos and R. Bros. Mathematical Programming Algorithms for Regression-based Non-linear Filtering in R^N. *IEEE Trans. on Signal Processing*, Mar 1999.

[23] J. S. Vitter and M. Wang. Approximate Computation of Multidimensional Aggregates of Sparse Data Using Wavelets. In *Proc. of ACM SIGMOD Conf.*, pages 193–204, Philadelphia, PA, 1999.

[24] B.-K. Yi, H.V. Jagadish, and C. Faloutsos. Efficient Retrieval of Similar Time Sequences under Time Warping. In *IEEE Proc. of ICDE*, Feb 1998.

Novel Approaches to the Indexing of
Moving Object Trajectories[*]

Dieter Pfoser

Dept. of Computer Science
Aalborg University
Denmark
pfoser@cs.auc.dk

Christian S. Jensen

Dept. of Computer Science
Aalborg University
Denmark
csj@cs.auc.dk

Yannis Theodoridis

Computer Technology Institute
Patras, Greece

ytheod@cti.gr

Abstract

The domain of spatiotemporal applications is a treasure trove of new types of data and queries. However, work in this area is guided by related research from the spatial and temporal domains, so far, with little attention towards the true nature of spatiotemporal phenomena. In this work, the focus is on a spatiotemporal sub-domain, namely the trajectories of moving point objects. We present new types of spatiotemporal queries, as well as algorithms to process those. Further, we introduce two access methods this kind of data, namely the Spatio-Temporal R-tree (STR-tree) and the Trajectory-Bundle tree (TB-tree). The former is an R-tree based access method that considers the trajectory identity in the index as well, while the latter is a hybrid structure, which preserves trajectories as well as allows for R-tree typical range search in the data. We present performance studies that compare the two indices with the R-tree (appropriately modified, for a fair comparison) under a varying set of spatiotemporal queries, and we provide guidelines for a successful choice among them.

1 Introduction

Space and time are two properties inherent to any object in the real world. If modeled in a database (Spaccapietra et al. 1998, Tryfona and Jensen, 1999), efficient ways to query these kinds of data have to be provided. Research efforts in the fields of spatial and temporal databases to index the respective data are numerous, and as we shall see later on in this work, serve as the basis for a more far-reaching effort into spatiotemporal data. It is sometimes not enough to take the "best" of both worlds to obtain a satisfying solution to a given spatiotemporal problem. In our context the problem is the indexing and querying of spatiotemporal information. More specifically, in this work we focus on data stemming from the *movement of spatial point objects*. We consider point objects, since in many applications, the size and shape of an object is of no importance—only its position matters. Examples include navigational systems, but also the thriving developments in mobile computing (Barbará 1999).

The data obtained from moving point objects is similar to a "string," arbitrary oriented in 3D space, where two dimensions correspond to space and one dimension corresponds to time. By sampling the movement of a point object, we obtain a polyline, instead of a "string," representing the trajectory of the moving point object. In pure geometrical terms, this object movement is termed a *trajectory* (cf. Figure 1). In the sequel, we will use "movement" and "trajectory" interchangeably.

When designing an access method, we not only have to be aware of the nature of the data, but must also know the types of queries, the method is to be used for. Typical queries in spatial and temporal databases are range (window/interval) queries. Queries for spatiotemporal data are often more demanding due to the extra semantics involved. An object's trajectory can be treated as spatial (3D) data itself, and thus may besupported by a spatial access method.

In the literature, the following taxonomy exists: (a) work on indexing the present positions of objects and asking future queries (Kollios et al. 1999, Saltenis et al. 2000) and (b) work on indexing the past positions of objects and asking historical queries. Within the latter category, into which the present work also belongs, most approaches deal with spatial data changing discretely over time and do not take continuous changes into account. Examples include R-trees for multimedia data (Theodoridis et al. 1996), overlapping Quadtrees (Tzouramanis et al. 1998) and R-tree variations for spatial data (Nascimento et al. 1999).

A problem not addressed by using any of the above access methods is the *preservation* of trajectories. Related

[*] Research partially supported by the CHOROCHRONOS project, funded by the European Commission DG XII, contract no. ERBFMRX-CT96-0056. The first and the second author were additionally supported by the Nykredit Corporation.

Proceedings of the 26th International Conference on Very Large Databases, Cairo, Egypt, 2000

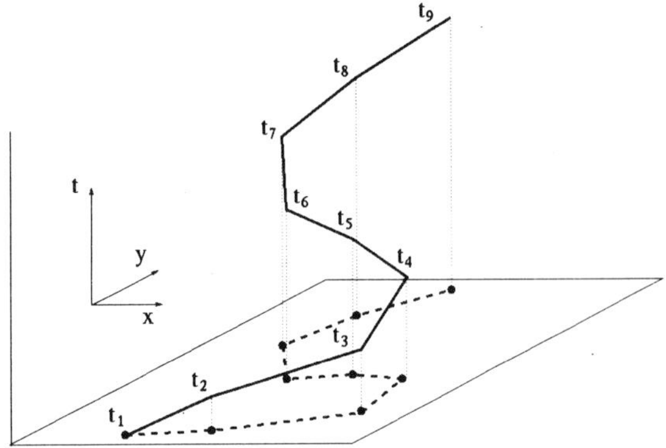

Figure 1: The movement of a spatial object and the corresponding trajectory

work treats data merely as a set of line segments, regardless of whether some belong to the same trajectory. Line segments are grouped together merely according to spatial properties such as proximity. This is not optimal, since certain types of queries require access to parts of the whole trajectory. Further, the presented spatiotemporal data has another particularity; it is considered to be append-only with respect to time, i.e., data grows mainly in the temporal dimension (Theodoridis et al. 1998).

To capture the particularities of spatiotemporal data and queries, we propose two access methods. The first, the Spatio-Temporal R-tree (hereafter called STR-tree), organizes line segments not only according to spatial properties, but also by attempting to group the segments according to the trajectories they belong to. We term this property *trajectory preservation*. The second, the Trajectory-Bundle tree (hereafter called TB-tree), aims only for trajectory preservation and leaves other spatial properties aside.

The outline of the paper is as follows. Section 2 describes the nature of the data as well as the type of queries encountered in applications with moving point objects. Section 3 presents the algorithms comprising the proposed access methods. Section 4 presents query-processing algorithms. Section 5 gives performance studies that compare both methods with the "classic" R-tree, appropriately modified to take gain of the knowledge that the entries to be indexed are line segments. Finally, Section 6 gives conclusions and directions for future research[1].

2 Moving Objects: Data and Queries

In this section, we discuss spatiotemporal data by giving a motivating example. We further introduce sampling as a method to measure positions over time. Also, we introduce a set of queries that are of importance in the given application context.

2.1 Trajectories

The optimization of transportation, especially in highly populated areas, is a very challenging task that may be supported by an information system. A core application in this context is fleet management. Vehicles equipped with GPS devices transmit their positions to a central computer using either radio communication links or mobile phones. At the central site, the data is processed and utilized. In order to record the movement of an object, we would have to know the position at all times, i.e., on a continuous basis. However, GPS and telecommunications technologies only allow us to sample an object's position, i.e., to obtain the position at discrete instances of time, such as every few seconds.

A first approach to represent the movements of objects would be to simply store the position samples. This would mean that we could not answer queries about the objects' movements at times in-between those of the sampled positions. Rather, to obtain the entire movement, we have to interpolate. The simplest approach is to use linear interpolation, as opposed to other methods such as polynomial splines (Bartels et al. 1987). The sampled positions then become the endpoints of line segments of polylines, and the movement of an object is represented by an entire polyline in 3D space. The solid line in Figure 1 represents the movement of a point object. Space and time coordinates are combined to form a single coordinate system. The dashed line shows the projection of the movement on the 2D plane (Pfoser and Jensen 1999). Figure 2 illustrates the spatiotemporal workspace (the cube in solid lines) and several trajectories (the solid polylines). Time moves in the upward direction, and the top of the cube is the time of the most recent position sample. The wavy-dotted lines at the top symbolize the growth of the cube with time.

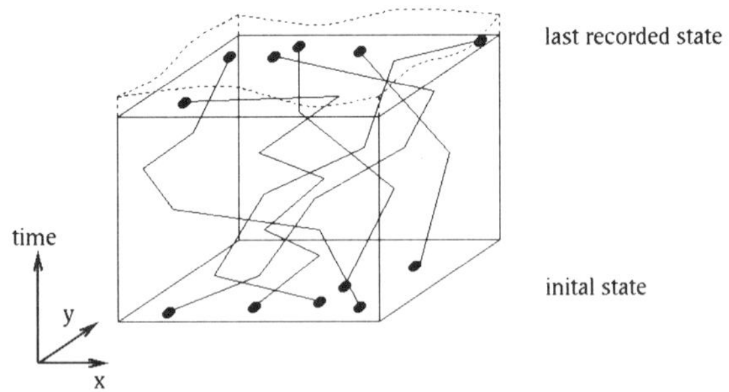

Figure 2: Trajectories of moving point objects in spatiotemporal workspace

Semantically, the temporal dimension is different from the two spatial dimensions. In classical spatial databases, only positional information is available. In our case, however, we have also *derived information*, e.g., speed, acceleration, traveled distance, etc. Consequently, information is derived from the combination of spatial and temporal data. Further, we do not only store a number of

---

[1] Although in the sequel we consider objects moving on a 2D plane, extending to 3D space (e.g. movement of planes) is straightforward.

spatial objects in the index, i.e., line segments, but rather have entries that are parts of larger objects, the trajectories. As we will see in the next section, these differences create interesting new and inherently spatio-temporal types of queries.

2.2 Queries

A typical search on sets of objects' trajectories includes a selection with respect to a given range, a search inherited from spatial and temporal databases. Queries of the form *"find all objects within a given area (or at a given point) some time during a given time interval (or at a given time instant)"* or *"find the k-closest objects with respect to a given point at a given time instant"* (Theodoridis et al. 1998) remain very important. A query type important in temporal databases is the time-slice query, i.e., in the spatiotemporal context, to determine the positions of (all) moving objects at a given time point in the past (Theodoridis et al. 1996). Using the 3D representation presented in Section 2.1, the time-slice query constitutes a special case of a range query with a query window of *zero extent in the temporal dimension.*

In addition, novel queries become important due to the specific nature of spatiotemporal data. The so-called trajectory-based queries are classified in *"topological"* queries, which involve the whole information of the movement of an object, and *"navigational"* queries, which involve derived information, such as speed and heading.

As such, we distinguish between two types of spatiotemporal queries:

- *coordinate-based queries*, such as point, range, and nearest-neighbor queries in the resulting 3D space, and
- *trajectory-based queries*, involving the topology of trajectories (topological queries) and derived information, such as speed and heading of objects (navigational queries).

Both types of queries will be involved in our performance study in Section 5 while in the sequel we discuss the latter ones in more detail.

2.2.1 Topological Queries

Topological queries involve the whole or a part of the trajectory of an object. They are deemed very important, but also rather expensive. Unfortunately, a definition of a well established set of predicates, such as the 9-intersection model (Egenhofer and Franzosa 1991) for spatial data and the 13 relations between intervals (Allen 1983) for temporal data is not yet available for spatiotemporal data. In one of the first approaches, Erwig and Schneider (1999) discuss extending SQL with the spatiotemporal versions of the basic spatial predicates, *disjoint*, *meet*, *overlap*, *equal*, *covers*, *contains*, *covered-by*, and *inside*, defined by the 9-intersection model as well as composite predicates based on the basic ones, namely *enter* (and its reverse, *leave*), *cross*, and *bypass*.

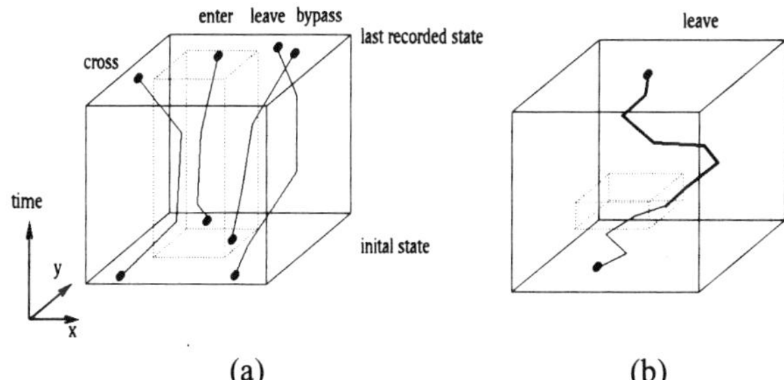

Figure 3: (a) Topological and (b) combined queries

Whether an object *enters*, *crosses*, or *bypasses* a giver area can be determined only by examining more than one segment of its trajectory. For instance, an object *entered* into an area with respect to a given time horizon, if the start point of its least recent segment (respectively, the endpoint of its most recent segment) was outside (respectively, inside) the given area. "Recent" here refers to time, e.g., a point is less recent, if its time stamp is older in time. Similar definitions hold for the *leave*, *cross*, and *bypass* predicates, which are also illustrated in Figure 3(a).

2.2.2 Dynamic Information and Navigational Queries

Dynamic information is not explicitly stored, but has to be derived from the trajectory information. The average or top *speed* of an object is determined by the fraction of traveled distance over time. The *heading* of an object is computed by determining a vector between two specified positions. Also, the *area* an object covers is computed by considering the convex hull of its trajectory. From these definitions, it is evident that each property is unique, but depends on the *time interval* considered. For example, the heading of an object in the last ten minutes may have been strictly East, but considering the last hour, it may have been Northeast. The same is true for speed; at the moment, the speed of an object might be 100 mph, but during the last hour, it might average out to 30 mph.

Queries involving speed or heading are expected to be very important in real-life applications. Let us discuss the following examples: *"At what speed does this plane move? What is its top speed?"* (Güting et al. 2000). The former considers the *now* instance as the time horizon, whereas the second one is an aggregation over a longer time period. But again, to compute the result, we have to examine a set of line segments that belong to the same trajectory, as opposed to lie within a spatiotemporal range.

Table 1 summarizes the spatiotemporal query types. We adopt a signature-like notation as presented in (Güting et al. 2000). The "operation" column lists the operations used for several query types and the "signature" column presents the involved types, e.g., a coordinate-based query uses the inside operation to determine the segments within the specified range. The notation {segments} simply refers to a set, it does not capture that this set constitutes one or more trajectories.

Query Type		Operation	Signature
Coordinate-based Queries		overlap, inside, etc.	range × {segments} → {segments}
Trajectory -based Queries	Topological Queries	enter, leave, cross, bypass	range × {segments} → {segments}
	Naviga-tional Queries	traveled distance, covered area (top or average), speed, heading, parked	{segments} → int {segments} → real {segments} → bool

Table 1: Types of spatiotemporal queries

2.2.3 Combined Queries

An important issue in dealing with spatiotemporal queries is to extract information related to (partial) trajectories, i.e., we have to (a) select the trajectories and (b) select the parts of each trajectory we want to return. Selection of trajectories can occur (i) by querying the trajectory identifier, (ii) by selecting a segment of the trajectory using a spatiotemporal range, (iii) by using a topological query, and/or (iv) by using derived information. In the previous examples, we left the identity of the taxi unspecified; it can either be selected by an identifier, e.g., "*taxi no. 120*," or by spatiotemporal selection, e.g., "*a taxi at the corner of 5th Avenue and Central Park South between 7 a.m. and 7:15 a.m. today.*"

In the following we show a more complicated example of combined search: "What were the trajectories of objects after they left Tucson between 7 a.m. and 8 a.m. today, in the next hour?" This query uses the range, "Tucson between 7 a.m. and 8 a.m. today" to identify the trajectories while, "in the next hour" gives a (temporal) range to delimit the parts of the trajectories that we want to retrieve. Figure 3(b) illustrates this principle. The dotted cube represents the spatiotemporal range used when selecting the trajectories, and the polyline stands for a selected trajectory of a moving object. The bold part of the polyline represents the part of the trajectory that is returned (e.g., in the next hour).

Along these lines, one can construct various query combinations that are plausible in the spatiotemporal application context.

3 The Access Methods

Having described the types of data and queries, the following section defines the two access methods proposed for those types of data and queries. Before that, we will give a short overview of the R-tree (Guttman 1984). The R-tree is a height-balanced tree with the index records in its leaf nodes containing pointers to actual data objects. Leaf node entries are of the form (*id, MBB*), where *id* is an identifier that points to the actual object and *MBB* (Minimum Bounding Box) is an *n*-dimensional interval. Non-leaf node entries are of the form (*ptr, MBB*), where *ptr* is the pointer to a child node and *MBB* is the

covering *n*-dimensional interval. A node in the tree corresponds to a disk page. Every node contains between *m* and *M* entries.

The insertion of a new entry into the R-tree is done by traversing a single path from the root to the leaf level. The path is chosen with respect to the least enlargement criterion (ChooseLeaf algorithm by Guttman (1984)) and covering MBBs are adjusted accordingly. In case an insertion causes splitting of a node, its entries are reassigned to the old node and a newly created one (according to one of the three alternative algorithms, Exhaustive, QuadraticSplit or LinearSplit, proposed by Guttman (1984)). To delete an entry from the R-tree, a reverse insertion procedure applies, i.e., covering MBBs are adjusted accordingly. In case the deletion causes an underflow in a node, i.e., node occupancy falls below *m*, the node is deleted and its entries are re-inserted. When searching an R-tree, we check whether a given node entry overlaps the search window (assuming a range query). If so, we visit the child node and thus recursively traverse the tree. Since overlapping MBBs are permitted, at each level of the index there may be several entries that overlap the search window.

In the context of spatiotemporal data this technique proves to be inefficient. Figure 4(a) shows that in approximating the line segments with MBBs, we introduce large amounts of "dead space." It is evident that the corresponding MBB covers a large portion of the space, whereas the actual space occupied by the trajectory is small. This leads to high overlap and consequently to a small discrimination capability of the index structure.

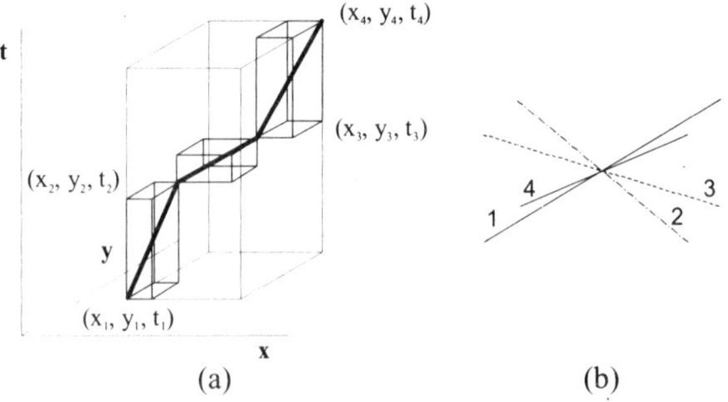

Figure 4: (a) approximating trajectories using MBBs, and (b) mapping of line segments in a MBB

Another aspect not captured in R-trees is the knowledge about the specific trajectory a line segment belongs to. To smoothen these inefficiencies (and provide an as fair as possible performance comparison later in Section 5), we modify the R-tree as follows: As can be seen in Figure 4(b), a line segment can only be contained in four different ways in an MBB. This extra information is stored at the leaf level by simply modifying the entry format to (id, MBB, orientation), where the orientation's domain is {1,2,3,4}. Assuming we number the trajectories from 0 to *n*, a leaf node entry is then of the form (id, trajectory#, MBB, orientation).

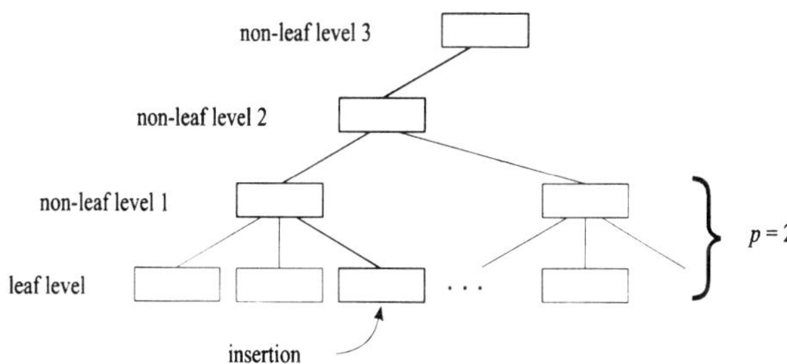

Figure 5: Insertion into the STR-tree

Algorithm Insert(N,E)
INS1 Invoke FindNode(N,E)
INS2 IF node N' found,
    IF N' has space,
        insert E
    ELSE
        IF the *p*-1 parent nodes are full,
            invoke **ChooseLeaf(N'',E)** on a tree, pointed to by
            N'', which excludes the current branch.
        ELSE invoke **Split(N')**.
    ELSE ChooseLeaf(N,E).

Algorithm FindNode(N,E)
FN1 IF N is NOT a leaf,
    FOR EACH entry E' of N whose MBB intersects with the
    MBB of E,
        invoke **FindNode(N',E)**, where N' is the childnode of
        N pointed to by E'.
    ELSE
        IF N contains an entry that is connected to E,
        RETURN N.

Figure 6: STR-tree insert algorithm

Although these suggestions are simple to implement and improve the efficiency of the R-tree to index line segments as parts of trajectories of moving points, we argue that this is not enough and query processing is still problematic. Therefore, we propose two novel approaches in indexing trajectories, the STR-tree and the TB-tree.

3.1 The STR-tree

The STR-tree is an extension of the (appropriately modified, as discussed previously) R-tree to support efficient query processing of trajectories of moving points. The two access methods differ in their insertion/split strategy.

3.1.1 Insertion Algorithm

The insertion process is considerably different from the procedure known from the R-tree. As already mentioned, the insertion strategy of the R-tree is based on the (purely spatial) least enlargement criterion. On the other hand, insertion in the STR-tree not only considers *spatial closeness,* but also partial *trajectory preservation,* i.e., we try to keep line segments belonging to the same trajectory together. As a consequence, when inserting a new line segment, the goal should be to insert it as close as possible to its predecessor in the trajectory. Thus, insertion in the

STR-tree involves a new algorithm, FindNode, which returns the node that contains the predecessor. As for the insertion, if there is room in this node, the new segment is inserted there. Otherwise, we have to apply a node split strategy. In Figure 5, we show a sample index in which the node returned by FindNode is marked with an arrow.

The ideal characteristics for an index suitable for object trajectories would be to decompose the overall space according to time, the dominant dimension in which "growth" occurs, while simultaneously preserving trajectories. In the following, we describe the Insert algorithm shown in Figure 6, which includes an additional parameter, called the *preservation parameter, p,* that indicates the number of levels we "reserve" for the preservation of trajectories. When a leaf node returned by FindNode is full, the algorithm checks whether the *p*-1 parent nodes are full (in Figure 5, for *p* = 2, we only have to check the node drawn in bold at non-leaf level 1). In case *one of them is not full,* the leaf node is split. In case *all of the p-1 parent nodes are full,* Insert invokes ChooseLeaf on the subtree including all the nodes further to the right of the current insertion path (the gray shaded tree in Figure 5). In the sequel, the so-called ChooseLeaf and QuadraticSplit algorithms will be used without further details, since they are identical to Guttman's original algorithms.

The extended version of this paper (Pfoser et al. 2000) experimentally established that the best choice of a preservation parameter is *p* = 2. A smaller *p* decreases the trajectory preservation and increases the spatial discrimination capabilities of the index. The converse is true for a larger *p*.

3.1.2 Split Algorithm

Since the goal is to preserve trajectories in the index, splitting a leaf node requires an analysis of what kinds of segments are contained in a node. Any two segments in a leaf node may belong to the same trajectory or not, and, suppose they belong to the same trajectory, may have common endpoints or not. Thus a node can contain four different types of segments:

- *disconnected* segments, i.e., segments not connected to any other segment in the node,
- *forward-* (respectively, *backward-*) *connected* segments, i.e., the top (respectively, bottom) endpoint, in other words, the more (respectively, less) recent endpoint, of such a segment is connected to the bottom (respectively, top) endpoint of another segment belonging to the same trajectory,
- *bi-connected* segments, i.e., both (top and bottom) endpoints of such a segment are connected to the (bottom and top, respectively) endpoint of two other segments belonging to the same trajectory.

With this, we can distinguish the three split scenarios of Figure 7. In case (a), where all segments are *disconnected*, the QuadraticSplit algorithm is invoked to determine the split. In case (b), where not all but at least

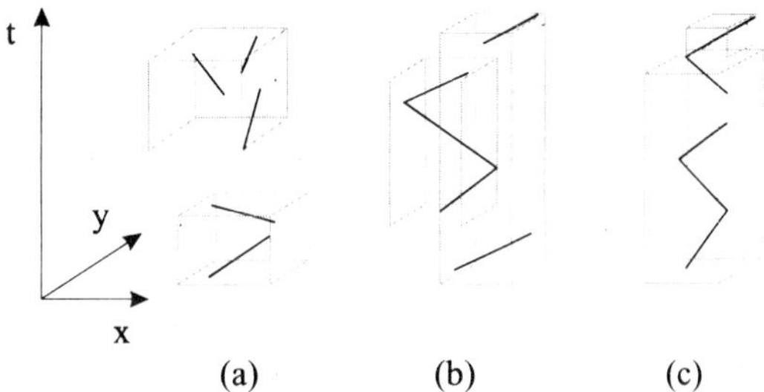

(a)   (b)   (c)

Figure 7: Different split scenarios

Algorithm Split(N)
S1 IF node is a non-leaf node,
    invoke **SplitNon-leafNode(N)**.
    ELSE invoke **SplitLeafNode(N)**.

Algorithm SplitNon-leafNode(N)
SNN1 Put the new entry into a new node and keep the old one
    as it is

Algorithm SplitLeafNode(N)
SLN1 IF entries in node are all disconnected segments,
    invoke **QuadraticSplit(N)**.
    ELSE IF node contains disconnected, and other types of
segments,
        put all disconnected segments in a new node.
    ELSE IF node contains single and disconnected
segments,
        put the newest single connected segment in new node

Figure 8: STR-tree split algorithm

one segment is *disconnected*, the *disconnected* segments are placed into the newly created node. Finally, in case (c) where no *disconnected* segments exist, the most recent (i.e., with respect to time) *backward-connected* segment is placed in the newly created node.

Figure 8 summarizes the split algorithm. The general idea is to put newer and thus more recent segments into new nodes. Consequently, new segments are much likelier inserted into these nodes, i.e., these nodes have a higher "insertion potential" than the ones containing older nodes. This potential allows us also to relax the constraint of minimum node capacity m, known from the R-tree, when splitting a node. Finally, splitting non-leaf nodes is simple, in that we only create a new node for a new entry. Using this insertion and split strategy, we obtain an index that preserves trajectories and considers time as the dominant dimension when decomposing the occupied space.

3.2 The TB-Tree

The TB-tree is fundamentally different from the previously presented access methods. The STR-tree introduces a new insertion/split strategy to achieve trajectory orientation, while not compromising the space discrimination capabilities of the index too much. Apart from this, the STR-tree is an R-tree based access method. The TB-tree takes a more radical step. An underlying assumption when using the R-tree is that all inserted geometries are independent. In our context this translates

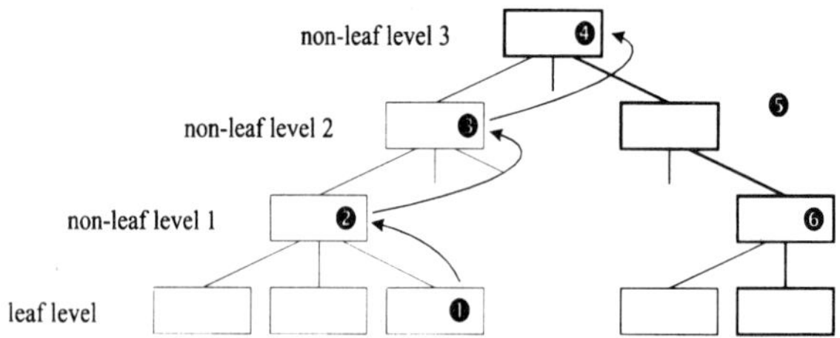

Figure 9: Insertion into the TB-tree

Algorithm Insert(N,E)
INS1 Invoke **FindNode(N,E)**
INS2 IF node N' is found,
    IF N' has space,
        insert new segment.
    ELSE
        create new leaf node for new segment
  ELSE
    create new leaf node for new segment

Figure 10: TB-tree insert algorithm

to all line segments being independent. However, line segments are parts of trajectories and this knowledge is only implicitly maintained in the R-tree and the STR-tree structures. With the TB-tree, we aim for an access method that *strictly preserves trajectories* such that a leaf node only contains segments belonging to the same trajectory, thus the index is best understood as a *trajectory bundle*. This approach is only possible when making some concessions to the most important R-tree property, node overlap or spatial discrimination. As a drawback, line segments independent from trajectories that lie spatially close will be stored in different nodes. As the overlap increases, the space discrimination decreases, and, thus, the classical range query cost increases. However, by giving up on space discrimination, we gain on trajectory preservation. As we shall see later, this property is important for answering "pure spatiotemporal" queries[2].

3.2.1 Insertion Algorithm

The goal is to "cut" the whole trajectory of a moving object into pieces, where each piece contains M line segments, with M being the fanout, i.e., a leaf node contains M segments of the trajectory. Figure 9 illustrates the insertion procedure. Important stages throughout the procedure are marked with black, circled numbers 1-6.

The insertion algorithm is formally shown in Figure 10. To insert a new entry, we simply have to find the leaf node that contains its predecessor in the trajectory. We start by traversing the tree from the root and step into every child node that overlaps with the MBB of the new line segment. We choose the leaf node containing a

---

[2] Both the (modified) R-tree and the STR-tree store entries of the format (*id, trajectory#, MBB, orientation*) at the leaf level. Since the TB-tree does not allow segments from different trajectories to be stored in the same leaf node, the *trajectory#* is assigned to the node rather than to each entry. Thus, the format of a leaf node entry is (*id, MBB, orientation*) while *trajectory#* can be stored once in the header of the leaf node

segment connected to the new entry (stage 1 in Figure 9). The finding of a segment is summarized in the FindNode algorithm, which is identical to that of the STR-tree. In case the leaf node is full, a *split* strategy is needed. Splitting a leaf node would violate our principle of total trajectory preservation. Thus, we instead create a new leaf node. In our example, we step up the tree until we find a non-full parent node (stages 2 through 4). We choose the right-most path (stage 5) to insert the new node. If there is room in the parent node (stage 6), we insert the new leaf node as shown in Figure 9. In case it is full, we split it by creating a new node at (non-leaf) level 1 that has the new leaf node as its only descendant. If necessary, the split is propagated upwards. Illustratively, the TB-tree is growing from left to right, i.e., the left-most leaf node was the first and the right-most was the last, we inserted.

3.2.2 Trajectory Preservation

At this point one might argue that this strategy leads to an index with a high degree of overlap. This would certainly be the case if it were arbitrary 3D data that was indexed. However, in our case, we only "neglect" two out of three dimensions, the spatial dimensions, with respect to space discrimination. The temporal dimension offers a given space discrimination, in that data is inserted in an append-only fashion (Theodoridis et al. 1998).

As such, the structure of the TB-tree is actually a set of leaf nodes, each containing a partial trajectory, organized in a tree hierarchy. In other words, a trajectory is distributed over a set of disconnected leaf nodes. As we shall see later on when discussing about query processing, it is necessary to be able to retrieve segments based on their trajectory identifier. A simple solution we have implemented is to connect leaf nodes by a superimposed data structure. We choose a doubly linked list that connects leaf nodes including parts of the same trajectory in a way that preserves trajectory *evolution*. Figure 11 gives a part of a TB-tree structure and a trajectory illustrating this approach. For clarity, the trajectory is drawn as a band rather than a line. The trajectory symbolized by the gray band is fragmented across six nodes, c1, c3, etc. In the TB-tree these leaf nodes are connected through a linked list.

By visiting an arbitrary leaf node, these links allow us to retrieve the (partial) trajectory at minimal cost: Considering a fanout f at a leaf node, the size of the partial trajectory contained in the leaf node is f. Among the segments stored and assuming that $f \geq 3$, it is by definition that f-2 segments are *bi-connected*, one is *forward-connected* and one is *backward-connected*. To find the remaining segments of the same trajectory, one has just to follow the pointers of the linked list to the next and previous leaf nodes.

4 Query Processing

Section 2 described various types of queries as they occur in spatiotemporal applications. In this section, we present

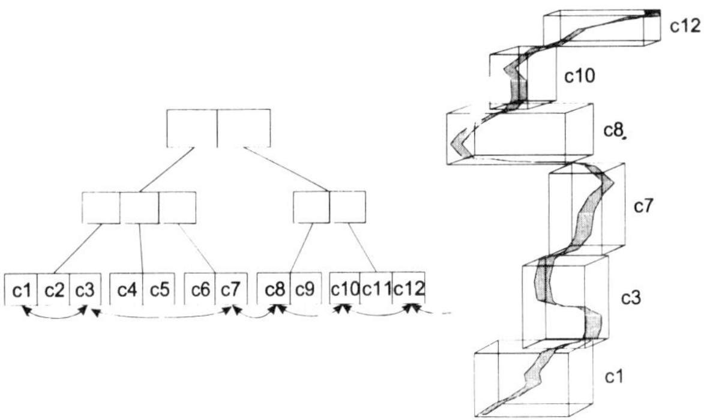

Figure 11: The TB-tree structure

the algorithms for processing those queries using the three access methods. The queries and algorithms can be classified as *coordinate-based*, *trajectory-based*, or *combined* (cf. Section 2).

The processing of coordinate-based queries is a straightforward extension of the classical range query processing using the R-tree; the idea is to descend the tree with respect to coordinate constraints until the entries are found in the leaf nodes. Trajectory-based queries comprise topological and navigational queries. Due to space limitations, we omit the presentation of topological query processing (and the corresponding discussion in the performance section); for details, please refer to Pfoser et al. (2000).

Algorithms for combined queries are different in that not only a spatial, but also a combined search, is performed, i.e., we not only retrieve all entries contained in a given sub-space (range query), but retrieve entries belonging to the same trajectory.

We will devise separate algorithms, on one hand, for the R-tree and the STR-tree and, on the other hand, for the TB-tree. The algorithm for the TB-tree is different because this method provides the data structure of a linked list to retrieve partial trajectories.

4.1 Combined Search in the R-Tree and the STR-Tree

The first step in processing combined queries is to retrieve an initial set of segments based on a spatiotemporal range. We apply the range-search algorithm used in the R-tree. The idea is to descend the tree with respect to intersection properties until the entries are found in the leaf nodes. In Figure 12, we search the tree using the cube c_1 and retrieve two segments of trajectory t_2 (labeled 1 and 2), and four segments of trajectory t_1 (labeled 3 to 6). The six segments are shown in darker gray contained in cube c_1. This completes the first stage of the combined search.

In the second stage, we extract partial trajectories. We now take each of the found segments and try to find its connecting segment, first, in the same leaf node, and, second, in other leaf nodes. Consider segment 1 of trajectory t_2. We find two segments, one connected to the top endpoint (forward connected) and one connected to the bottom endpoint (backward connected).

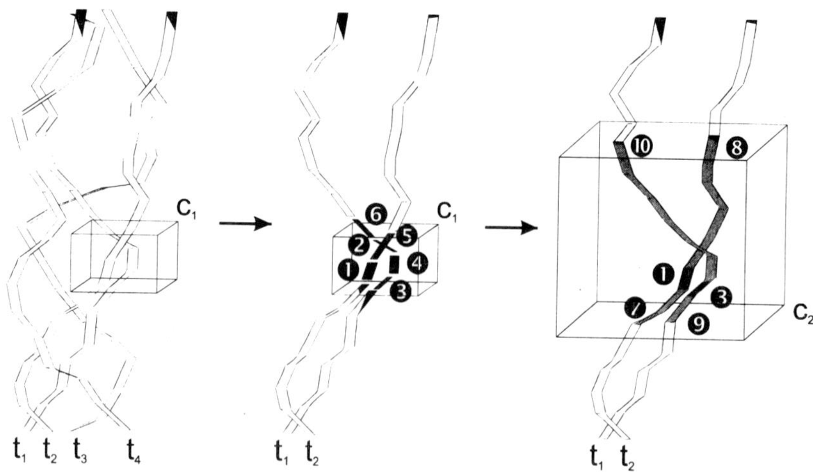

Figure 12: Stages in combined search

We may find those segments in the same leaf node, or we may have to search in other leaf nodes. Searching in other leaf nodes is conducted as a range search, with the endpoint of the segment in question as a predicate. Arriving at the leaf level, the algorithm checks whether a segment is connected to the segment in question in the specified way. Using this recursive approach, we retrieve more and more segments of the trajectory. The algorithm continues until a newly found segment is outside cube c_2. The last segments returned for segment 1 are segments 7 and 8.

Figure 13 outlines the combined search algorithm. One problem remains, namely that of not retrieving the same trajectory twice. The initial range search retrieves two segments, 1 and 2, of trajectory t_2. By using both segments as a starting point, we will retrieve the same trajectory twice. To avoid this, we store the *trajectory#* once it is retrieved and check before querying a new trajectory whether it was retrieved already. In our example, if we use segment 1 first to retrieve a partial trajectory t_1 and store this information, we omit retrieving it again for segment 2.

4.2 Combined Search in the TB -Tree

The combined search algorithm of the TB-tree is similar to the one presented above. The difference lies in how the partial trajectories are retrieved. The R-tree and the STR-tree structures provide little help in retrieving trajectories, i.e., connected segments, but offer only a modified range search algorithm. The linked lists of the TB-tree allow us to retrieve connected segments without searching.

The first stage in combined searching is the same as before. Here, for the seed segments—in our example segments 1 and 2 for t_2 and segments 3 to 6 for t_1—we have to retrieve a partial trajectory contained in the outer range c_2. Again, we have two possibilities: a connected segment can be in the same leaf node or in another node. If it is in the same, finding it is trivial. If it is in another

node, we have to follow the next (previous) pointer to the next (previous) leaf node (cf. Section 3.2.2).

Although the approach to retrieve partial trajectories is different, we have to take care not to retrieve the same trajectory more than once (cf. Section 4.2). Once a partial trajectory is retrieved, we store its id, and, before retrieving another trajectory, we check whether it was retrieved already.

Figure 14 contains the updates to the combined search algorithm as presented in Figure 13.

5 Performance Comparison

In this section, we aim at comparing the three access methods and establishing conditions, which are optimal for each one. This allows us to delimit the situations in which each access method is useful. Thus, we compare the access methods under varying sets of data and queries. The performance studies were conducted using C implementations of the three access methods. For the parameters in the experiments, we have chosen the page size for the leaf and non-leaf nodes to be 1024 bytes. With this page size, the R-tree and the STR-tree fanout is 28 and 36 for leaf and non-leaf nodes, respectively. Since the leaf node structure of the TB-tree is different, the fanout is 31 and 36 for leaf and non-leaf nodes, respectively.

5.1 Datasets

Unlike spatial data, where there exist several popular real datasets for experimentation purposes (e.g., the TIGER-Line files of geographic features, such as roads, rivers, lakes, boundaries covering the entire United States), well-known and widely accepted spatiotemporal datasets for experimental purposes are missing. Due to the lack of real data, our performance study consists of experiments on synthetic datasets. We utilize the GSTD generator of spatiotemporal datasets (Theodoridis et al. 1999) to create trajectories of moving objects under various distributions. GSTD allows the user to generate a set of line segments stemming from a specified number of moving objects.

402

Algorithm CombinedSearch(N,range1,range2)
CS1 IF N is NOT a leaf,
    FOR EACH entry E' of N whose MBB intersects with range1,
        invoke **CombinedSearch(N',E)**, where N' is the childnode of N pointed to by E'.
    ELSE
        for all entries E that satisfy range1 AND whose trajectory was not yet retrieved,
            invoke **DetermineTrajectory(N,E)**

Algorithm DetermineTrajectory(N,E,range2)
DT1 Loop through N and find segment E' that is fwd connected to E
DT2 WHILE found AND E' is within range2
    Add E' to set of solutions,
    Loop through N and find segment E' that is connected to the new E
DT3 IF not found (but within range)
    invoke **FindConnSegment(root,E,forward)**
    repeat from DT1
DT4 the same as above for bwd connected

Algorithm FindConnSegment(N,E,direction)
FCS1 IF N is NOT a leaf,
    FOR EACH entry E' of N whose MBB intersects with the MBB of E,
        invoke **FindConnSegment(N',E,direction)**, where N' is the childnode of N pointed to by E'.
    ELSE
        IF N contains an entry that is direction connected to E, RETURN N.

Figure 13: R-tree and STR-tree: CombinedSearch algorithm for trajectory-based queries

Algorithm FindConnSegment(E,N,direction)
FCS1 Set N to be the node pointed to be the direction pointer

Figure 14: TB-tree: CombinedSearch algorithm update

Probability functions are used to describe the movement of the objects as a combination of several parameters. More precisely, the user can specify the initial positional distribution of the objects in the unit workspace $[0, 1)^2$ as well as the stepping in time and space for each movement using either uniform, Gaussian, or skewed probability functions.

The parameters of the generator are given the following values: The initial distribution of points is Gaussian, i.e., all points are distributed around the center of the workspace. The movement of points is always ruled by a random distribution of the form `random(-x,x)`, thus achieving an unbiased spread of the points in the workspace. The number of different possible snapshots (i.e., the temporal resolution) is held constant at 100K. Finally, the number of moving objects (i.e., trajectories) varies between 10 and 1000, resulting in datasets consisting of between 15K and 1500K entries (i.e., line segments).

5.2 Space Utilization and Index Size

An aspect often neglected when comparing access methods is the *size* of the created index structures. Table 2

lists the sizes of the three different indices and the corresponding space utilization.

The average space utilization for the R-tree is between 55% and 60%, whereas it approaches 100% in case of the STR-tree and the TB-tree. The reason is that the R-tree construction strategy does not take the unilateral growth of the data in the temporal dimension into account.

The R-tree is roughly twice as big as the other two indices. For example, for datasets of 1000 objects (i.e., consisting of 1500K line segments), the R-tree size is about 95 MB, while the other two indices size about 57 MB. This difference is mainly due to the R-tree's smaller space utilization. The TB-tree is smaller than the STR-tree. The two indices have similar space utilization, but the TB-tree's fanout is larger. For a ten times larger dataset, the index size increases by the same factor for the STR-tree and the TB-tree. The increase is only approximate in the case of the R-tree, since its space utilization can fluctuate.

	R-tree	STR-tree	TB-tree
Index size	~ 95 KB per object	~ 57 KB per object	~ 51 KB per object
Space utilization	55%-60%	~100%	~100%

Table 2: Index sizes and space utilization

5.3 Range Queries

Range queries are important for spatial data as well as spatiotemporal data. In this section, we compare the three access methods for processing range queries. As already mentioned, we use datasets stemming from 10 to 1000 moving objects. We use three sets of query windows with a range of 1%, 10%, and 20% of the total range with respect to each dimension, i.e., 0.0001%, 0.1%, and 0.8% of the total space. Each query set includes 1000 query windows.

Figure 15 shows the number of total node accesses for various range queries and datasets. Do note that both axes are of logarithmic scale, the x-axis is to the base of 2, and the y-axis is to the base of 10. We observe the following trends. For a small number of moving objects, the STR-tree and the TB-tree show superior range query performance over the R-tree. The break-even point at which this trend is reversed depends on the query size. In case of a 1% range per dimension, the break-even point with respect to the R-tree for the STR-tree is at 30 moving objects, and for the TB-tree at 60 moving objects (cf. Figure 15(a)). For a larger, 10% range size per dimension, the break-even point for the STR-tree is at 25 moving objects and for the TB-tree at 200 moving objects (cf. Figure 15(b)). In case of an even larger range, e.g., 20% per dimension, the break-even points increase to 50 and over 1000 moving objects for the STR-tree and the TB-tree, respectively (cf. Figure 15(c)). Both, the TB-tree and the STR-tree, are trajectory oriented. For a smaller number of trajectories the total dataset (line segments) is more oriented along time than it is with respect to space. We term this property the *temporal discrimination*, as the dataset grows only with respect to the temporal dimension. Thus, for such a dataset, the spatial discrimination capabilities of the index are of no importance. However, if the number of trajectories increases, more segments exist at a given point in time. Thus, the spatial discrimination becomes important. Otherwise, the overlap between the nodes increases.

The R-tree does not "know" about the natural discrimination of the data. Its sole purpose is to group objects according to spatial characteristics, i.e., spatial proximity. For a small number of trajectories, this ambition turns out to be a "boomerang." In this case, the spatial discrimination is of minor importance. The TB-tree puts connected segments in the same node and does not consider spatial discrimination. It thus exploits the temporal discrimination of the data. As the results show, this approach is better up to a certain number of segments. The STR-tree adopts an approach in-between the two extremes. However, although this index performs better than the R-tree for a small number of trajectories, it is always worse than the TB-tree. The STR-tree, too, is heavily dedicated to trajectory preservation. This explains its performance with respect to the R-tree. However, because of its R-tree properties, it is worse than the TB-tree for a small number of trajectories.

5.4 Time Slice Queries

In several applications it is useful to determine the positions of (all) moving objects at a given time point in the past (Theodoridis et al. 1996). This query type constitutes a special case of a range query with a query window of *zero extent at the temporal dimension*. The size of the query window in the spatial dimensions can be arbitrary. In the performance studies we choose 1%, 10%, and 100% of the respective range in each spatial dimension. This corresponds to three sets, each comprising of 1000 individual queries.

The results shown in Figure 16 are similar to what could be seen in the previous section. For each set of queries (Figure 16(a)-(c)), there exists a break-even point in terms of number of moving point objects when the number of node accesses for the R-tree is smaller than for the STR-tree and the TB-tree, respectively. The break-even point moves from 60 moving objects (1% range) to 500 moving objects (100% range). This trend can also be observed in the case of range queries. However, there the TB-tree always outperforms the STR-tree. In Figure 16(a)-(c), we observe that the gap between the two indices decreases with an increasing range until the STR-tree outperforms the TB-tree (Figure 16(c)).

The nature of a time slice query is to retrieve all positions of moving objects at a given instance in time. In other words, this query favors particularly an index that organizes its content based on its spatial aspects (R-tree and STR-tree) rather than relying on the temporal discrimination capabilities of the data (TB-tree). For smaller ranges (Figure 16(a)), this phenomenon is not as apparent as for larger ranges.

5.5 Combined Queries

What follows is a performance study related to the algorithms for combined searching as presented in Section 2.2.3. We use datasets stemming from a varying number of moving objects. As for the queries, the size of the inner and the outer range is 1% (0.0001%) and 10% (0.1%), and 1% (0.0001%) and 20% (0.8%) in each dimension (of total space). Each set of queries consists of 1000 individual queries.

The results in Figure 17 show that the TB-tree is in all cases superior to the STR-tree and the R-tree, up to one order of magnitude with the gap increasing in proportion to the number of objects. Apart from the (partial) trajectory preservation in each node, it is also the additional data structure (a linked list) for retrieving neighbor nodes that contribute to this result. Thus, the numbers of node accesses in case of the TB-tree are only slightly larger than the numbers from the range query experiments in Figure 15(a). Comparing the STR-tree with the R-tree, they only differ in the index structure itself, but have the same combined search algorithms. Just as we have observed a break-even point between those two methods for range queries, it also exists here. For the first experiment, shown in Figure 17(a), the break-even point is at about 300 moving objects. For the second experiment, involving a larger secondary range, the break-even point is at 500 moving objects.

5.6 Summary

The TB-tree supports trajectory-based queries much more efficiently than the R-tree does. At the same time, it is worth to be mentioned that its performance on typical range queries is competitive to the R-tree. As shown in the experiments, for combined queries, the TB-tree's performance is closely connected to the "number of moving objects" of the dataset. The relative gap between the R-tree and the TB-tree increases with an increasing number of moving objects. As for the STR-tree, although designed to combine the benefits of the TB-tree and the R-tree, it usually performs worse than the TB-tree, with the only exception being time slice queries.

6 Conclusions and Future Work

Work in spatiotemporal query processing has dealt with range queries. However, spatiotemporal data, in the context of trajectories of n-dimensional moving objects, is somewhat different from $(n+1)$-dimensional spatial data due to the peculiarity of the temporal dimension (Theodoridis et al. 1998). This paper presents a set of pure spatiotemporal queries, the so called trajectory-based (topological and navigational) queries, as well as combined (coordinate- and trajectory- based) queries.

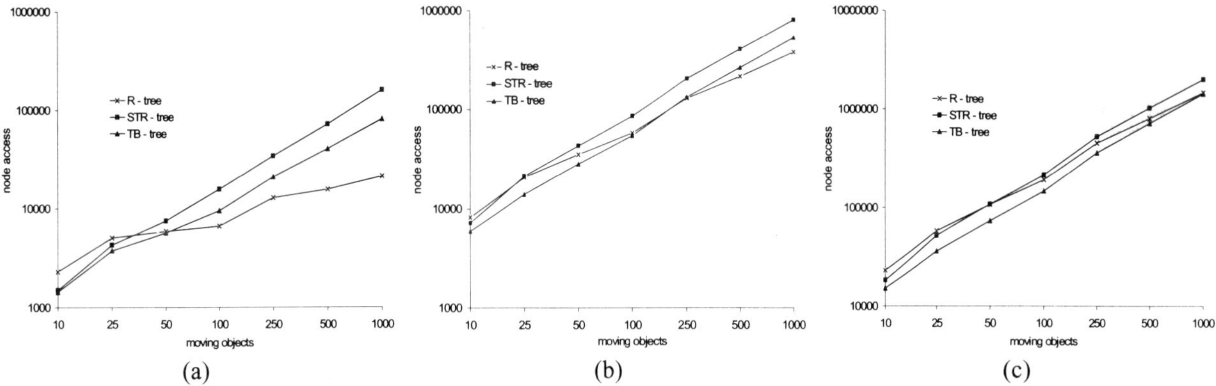

(a)   (b)   (c)

Figure 15: Range queries: varying range, (a) 1%, (b) 10% and (c) 20% in each din ension

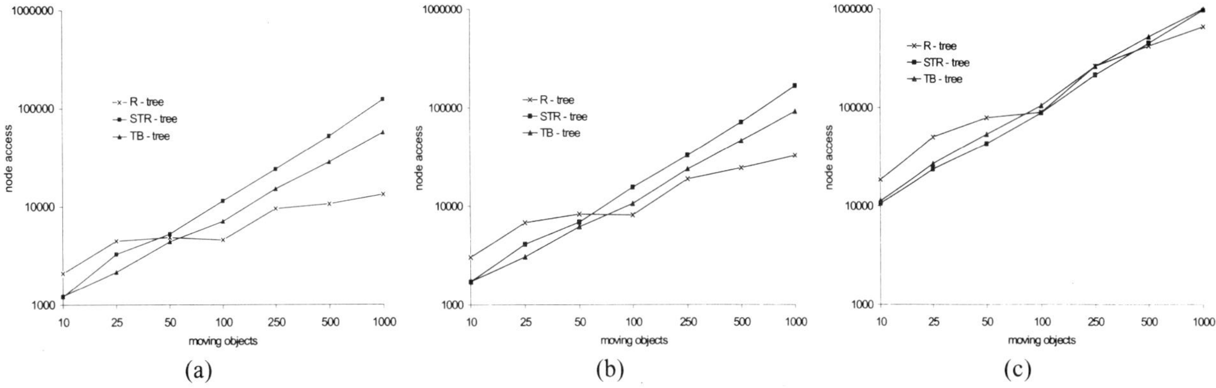

(a)   (b)   (c)

Figure 16: Time slice queries: varying spatial range, (a) 1%, (b) 10% and (c) 100% in each dimension

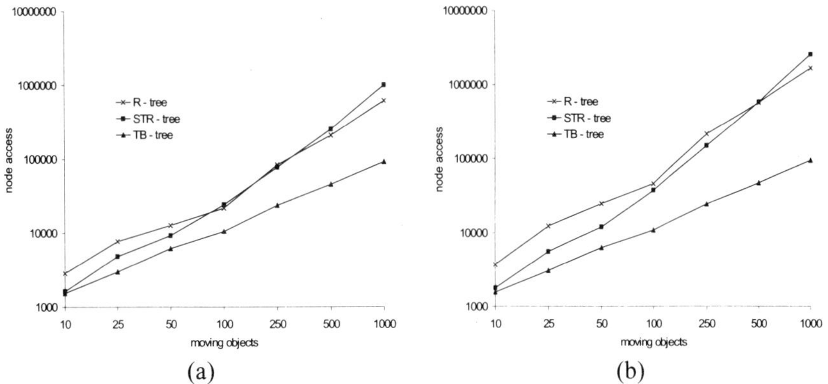

(a)   (b)

Figure 17: Combined queries: (a) 1% inner- 10% outer range and (b) 1% inner- 20% outer range, in each dimension

Efficient processing of those queries requires indices and access methods for spatiotemporal data; a simple modification to the R-tree as well as two new access methods, namely the STR-tree and the TB-tree, are proposed for indexing the trajectories of moving point objects.

First, trajectory data and a set of queries are defined to derive requirements. Trajectory data is obtained by discretely sampling the movement of point objects in time. Linear interpolation is considered in-between the samples. The set of queries is then presented. Subsequently, the paper discusses the R-tree to determine the shortcomings of this method with respect to spatiotemporal data and queries, and introduces modifications to overcome these limitations. Then the STR-tree and the TB-tree, both tailored to the requirements of trajectory data and spatiotemporal queries, are proposed. They can also easily be implemented on top of the R-tree, which is already adopted in commercial extensible database systems.

The performance study presents results from experiments involving spatial range queries, as well as experiments related to navigational and combined queries. The TB-tree proves to be an access method well suited for trajectory-based queries, and also has a good spatial search performance. The STR-tree performance stays behind the

TB-tree. Although designed to combine the "best of both worlds," it seems that the STR-tree is rather a weak compromise. The "pure" concepts of the R-tree and the TB-tree seem to be far superior in their respective domains.

Although recent literature includes related work on indexing trajectories of moving objects by maintaining the complete history of object movement (Theodoridis et al. 1996, Tzouramanis et al. 1998, Nascimento et al. 1999), the work presented in this paper is the first to

- propose an access method (namely, the TB-tree) clearly addressing the requirements and peculiarities of this context by considering *trajectory preservation*,
- propose and implement specific modifications to the "classic" R-tree in order to overcome (some of) its inefficiencies with respect to trajectories, and
- present novel algorithms for "pure" spatiotemporal searching apart from the typical range querying.

This work points to several future research directions. The present work only presents first algorithms to process navigational and topological queries. Derived from the requirements from real spatiotemporal applications, e.g., fleet management, these algorithms can be refined in more detail. Furthermore, not only novel queries, such as the previous ones, but also known though expensive spatial queries deserve more attention in the spatiotemporal domain; examples include neighbor searching (Roussopoulos et al. 1995) and joins (Mamoulis and Papadias 1999). Finally, investigating geometric shapes other than MBBs as approximations for moving objects' trajectories deserves further research; for instance, extending related work on indexing line segments (Bertino et al. 1998).

References

Allen, J.F.: Maintaining Knowledge About Temporal Intervals. *Communications of the ACM*, 26(11), pp. 832-843, 1983.

Barbará, D.: Mobile Computing and Databases – a Survey. *IEEE Transactions of Knowledge and Data Engineering*, 11(1), pp. 108-117, 1999.

Bartels, R., Beatty, J., and Barsky, B.: *An Introduction to Splines for Use in Computer Graphics & Geometric Modeling*. Morgan Kaufmann Publishers, Inc., 1987.

Bertino, E., Catania, B., and Shidlovsky, B.: Towards optimal indexing for segment databases. In *Proc. of Int'l Conference on Extending Database Technology*, pp. 39-53, 1998.

Egenhofer, M. and Franzosa, R.: Point-Set Topological Spatial Relations. *Int'l Journal of Geographic Information Systems*, 5(2), pp. 161-174, 1991.

Erwig, M. and Schneider, M.: Developments in Spatio-Temporal Query Languages, In *Proc. of DEXA Workshop on Spatio-Temporal Data Models and Languages*, 1999

Güting, R., Böhlen, M., Erwig, M., Jensen, C. S., Lorentzos, N., Schneider, M., and Vazirgiannis, M.: A Foundation for Representing and Querying Moving Objects. *ACM Transactions on Database Systems*, to appear, 2000.

Guttman, A.: R-trees: a Dynamic Index Structure for Spatial Searching. *In Proc. of ACM-SIGMOD Conference on the Management of Data*, pp. 47-57, 1984.

Kollios, G., Gunopulos, D., and Tsotras, V.: On Indexing Mobile Objects. In *Proc. of the 18th ACM Symposium Principles of Database Systems*, pp. 261-272, 1999.

Mamoulis, N. and Papadias, D.: Integration of Spatial Join Algorithms for Processing Multiple Inputs. In *Proc. of ACM-SIGMOD Conference on Management of Data*, pp. 1-12, 1999.

Nascimento, M., Silva, J., and Theodoridis, Y.: Evaluation of Access Structures For Discretely Moving Points. in *Proc. of Int'l Workshop on Spatio-Temporal Database Management*, pp. 171-188, 1999.

Papadias, D., Theodoridis, Y., Sellis, T., and Egenhofer, M.: Topological Relations in the World of Minimum Bounding Rectangles: A Study with R-trees. In *Proc. of ACM-SIGMOD Conference on Management of Data*, pp. 92-103, 1995.

Pfoser, D. and Jensen, C.: Capturing the Uncertainty of Moving-Object Representations, In *Proc. of the 6th Int'l Symposium on Spatial Databases*, pp. 111-132, 1999.

Pfoser, D., Jensen, C. S., and Theodoridis, Y.: Novel Approaches In Query Processing For Moving Objects. CHOROCHRONOS Technical Report, CH-00-3, 2000.

Roussopoulos, N., Kelley, S., and Vincent, F.: Nearest Neighbor Queries. In *Proc. of ACM-SIGMOD Conference on Management of Data*, pp. 71-79, 1995.

Saltenis, S., Jensen, C. S., Leutenegger, S., and Lopez, M.: Indexing the Positions of Continuously Moving Objects. In *Proc. of ACM-SIGMOD Conference on Management of Data*, pp. 331-342, 2000.

Spaccapietra, S., Parent, C., and Zimanyi, E.: Modeling Time from a Conceptual Perspective. In *Proc. of Int'l Conference on Information and Knowledge Management*, pp. 432-440, 1998.

Theodoridis, Y., Sellis, T., Papadopoulos, A., and Manolopoulos, Y.: Specifications for Efficient Indexing in Spatiotemporal Databases, In *Proc. of the 10th Int'l Conference on Scientific and Statistical Database Management*, pp. 123-132, 1998.

Theodoridis, Y., Silva, R., and Nascimento, M.: On the Generation of Spatiotemporal Datasets. In *Proc. of the 6th Int'l Symposium on Spatial Databases*, pp.147-164, 1999.

Theodoridis, Y., Vazirgiannis, M., and Sellis, T.: Spatio-Temporal Indexing for Large Multimedia Applications. In *Proc. of the 3rd IEEE Int'l Conference on Multimedia Computing and Systems*, pp. 441-448, 1996.

Tryfona, N. and Jensen, C. S.: Conceptual Data Modeling for Spatiotemporal Applications, *Geoinformatica*, 3(3), pp. 245-268, 1999.

Tzouramanis, T., Vassilakopoulos, M., and Manolopoulos, Y.: Overlapping Linear Quadtrees: A Spatio-Temporal Access Method. In *Proc. of the 6th Int'l Symposium on Advances in Geographic Information Systems*, pp. 1-7, 1998.

Managing Intervals Efficiently in Object-Relational Databases

Hans-Peter Kriegel
University of Munich
Institute for Computer Science
kriegel@informatik.uni-muenchen.de

Marco Pötke
University of Munich
Institute for Computer Science
poetke@informatik.uni-muenchen.de

Thomas Seidl
University of Munich
Institute for Computer Science
seidl@informatik.uni-muenchen.de

Abstract

Modern database applications show a growing demand for efficient and dynamic management of intervals, particularly for temporal and spatial data or for constraint handling. Common approaches require the augmentation of index structures which, however, is not supported by existing relational database systems. By design, the new Relational Interval Tree[1] (*RI-tree*) employs built-in indexes on an as-they-are basis and is easy to implement. Whereas the functionality and efficiency of the RI-tree is supported by any off-the-shelf relational DBMS, it is perfectly encapsulated by the object-relational data model.

The RI-tree requires $O(n/b)$ disk blocks of size b to store n intervals, $O(\log_b n)$ I/O operations for insertion or deletion, and $O(h \cdot \log_b n + r/b)$ I/Os for an intersection query producing r results. The height h of the virtual backbone tree corresponds to the current expansion and granularity of the data space but does not depend on n. As demonstrated by our experimental evaluation on an Oracle8i server, competing dynamic interval access methods are outperformed by factors of up to 42 for disk accesses and 4.9 for query response time.

1 Introduction

There is a growing demand for database applications that handle temporal and spatial data. Intervals occur as transaction time and valid time ranges in temporal databases [SOL 94] [Ram 97] [BÖ 98], as line segments on a space-filling curve in spatial applications [FR 89] [BKK 99], as inaccurate measurements with tolerances in engineering databases, for hierarchical type systems in object-oriented databases [KRVV 93] [Ram 97], or for handling interval and finite domain constraints in declarative systems [KS 91] [KRVV 93]

Proceedings of the 26th International Conference on Very Large Databases, Cairo, Egypt, 2000

[HP 94]. Particularly for industrial or commercial applications, the integration into RDBMS or ORDBMS is essential.

The *Relational Interval Tree*[1] (*RI-tree*) is a new method to efficiently support intersection queries, i.e. reporting all intervals from the database that overlap a given query interval. Rather than being a typical external memory data structure, the RI-tree follows a new paradigm in being a *relational storage structure*. The basic idea is to manage the data objects by common relational indexes rather than to access raw disk blocks directly. While exploiting the availability, robustness and high performance of built-in index structures in existing systems, the advantages for the RI-tree are in detail:

- Built-in indexes are used on an *as-they-are* basis without any augmentation of the internal data structure. Thus, no interface below the SQL level is required, and any arbitrary off-the-shelf RDBMS immediately supports the technique.

- A proper integration with existing RDBMS is an essential aspect for most industrial or commercial applications. By using built-in relational index structures, their strong robustness, performance and integration into transaction management (including recovery services and concurrency control) is for free. Thus, a lot of implementation efforts and code maintenance is avoided by a relational storage structure in contrast to typical external memory solutions.

- The efficiency of the RI-tree is due to the logarithmic I/O complexity of the underlying relational system for one-dimensional range queries on point data. Almost all RDBMS qualify for this quite weak requirement since they typically have implemented the popular B+-tree. By virtualizing the backbone structure of the original main-memory method and storing the intervals in relational indexes, a high efficiency for the RI-tree is achieved.

- In addition to its efficient support by any off-the-shelf RDBMS, the RI-Tree perfectly fits to the object-relational facilities of modern DBMS including the Oracle8i Server [Ora 99a], the Informix Universal Server [Inf 98] or the IBM DB2 Universal Database [IBM 99]. These systems support integrating the RI-Tree with the declarative SQL level as well as with the relational query optimizer.

---

[1] Patent pending [KPS 00]

Internally, the RI-tree manages intervals by two relational indexes. Storing n intervals occupies $O(n/b)$ disk pages, and inserting or deleting an interval requires $O(\log_b n)$ I/O operations where b denotes the disk block size as in [MTT 00]. For reporting the r intervals that intersect a given query interval, $O(h \cdot \log_b n + r/b)$ I/Os are required. The height h of the virtual backbone reflects the current expansion and granularity of the data space but does not dependend on the number n of intervals. On top of a good analytical complexity, also the empirical performance is superior to competitors.

The paper is organized as follows: Section 2 surveys related work for interval management in databases. In Section 3, we introduce the structure of the new Relational Interval Tree, whereas the algorithms for query processing are presented in Section 4. Section 5 discusses the integration into an ORDBMS. After an experimental evaluation in Section 6, the paper is concluded by Section 7.

2   Related Work

A variety of methods has been published concerning interval management in databases, most of them addressing temporal applications. The following sections intentionally survey interval handling in general. Specialized work e.g. on append-only structures for transaction time intervals is omitted due to lack of space.

2.1   Main Memory Structures

In the context of computational geometry, several data structures that support 1D interval data have been developed [PS 93] [Sam 90a]. Among them the *Segment Tree* of Bentley, the *Priority Search Tree* of McCreight and the *Interval Tree* of Edelsbrunner are the most popular. More recent developments include the *Interval Skip List* and the *IBS-Tree* of Hanson et al. [HJ 96].

As major limitation, the main memory resident data structures do not meet the characteristics of secondary storage. In a disk-oriented context, access is block-oriented and only small portions of a structure may reside in main memory at a given time. The concept of *Segment Indexes* [KS 91] is a way to overcome the problem by combining optimal interval structures with efficient disk-oriented indexing techniques. Our approach follows this paradigm and, moreover, uses existing index structures the way they are rather than to extend them what is typically required for custom secondary storage structures.

2.2   Secondary Storage Structures

A variety of secondary storage structures for intervals has been presented in the literature [TCG+ 93] [MTT 00]. Since they typically are based either on the augmentation of existing indexes or on the definition of new structures, most of them share the limited support for an integration into existing systems. When being committed to a commercial ORDBMS, the structures cannot be integrated as the built-in indexes are not extensible by the user.

The *Time Index* of Elmasri, Wuu and Kim [EWK 90] is an index structure for valid time intervals. A set of linearly ordered indexing points is maintained by a B+-tree, and for each point, a bucket of pointers refers to the associated set of intervals. Since an interval may be registered with several indexing points, the space requirement is $O(n^2)$ for n stored intervals [HJ 96]. Due to this redundance, the time complexity is $O(n)$ for insertion and deletion and $O(n^2)$ for interval intersection query processing [AT 95].

The *Interval B-tree* (*IB-tree*) of Ang and Tan [AT 95] has been developed to overcome the weaknesses of the time index. It can be regarded as an implementation of Edelsbrunner's interval tree [Ede 80] using an augmented B+-tree rather than a binary tree. The original main memory model is thus transformed to an efficient secondary storage structure while preserving the optimal space and time complexity. As a disadvantage that we avoid in our approach, the complex three-fold structure of the interval tree is retained, and a dedicated structure of its own is used for each level. More seriously, the augmentation is not supported by commercial ORDBMS's.

The *Interval B+-tree* (*IB+-tree*) of Bozkaya and Özsoyoglu [BÖ 98] is a secondary storage model of the interval tree of [CLR 90] that differs from Edelsbrunner's interval tree by the fact that it uses the lower bounds of the intervals as primary keys. As a result, queries referring to the upper bounds of intervals such as *meets* or *after* are not supported well. The I/O complexity for insertions or deletions as well as for finding a single intersecting interval for a query is $O(\log_b n)$. Retrieving all r intersecting intervals, however, may result in a scan of the internal nodes covered by the query range. Thus, the worst case time complexity is $O(n)$ rather than the minimum $O(\log n + r)$ which Edelsbrunner's interval tree guarantees. The concept of time splits is introduced as a successful heuristics to avoid large fruitless scans. Again, the augmentation is an obstacle for the integration into commercial systems.

The *TP-Index* of Shen, Ooi and Lu [SOL 94] is based on a transformation of intervals into a triangular 2D space. Duplicates are avoided and the index is well suited for appending intervals since the data space may grow dynamically at the upper bound. The access method is highly specialized to the suggested mapping, and an integration into existing ORDBMSs is not supported. A similar mapping organized by a grid file is presented in [LT 98].

The *External Memory Interval Tree* of Arge and Vitter [AV 96] is an externalization of Edelsbrunner's interval tree where the fan-out of the backbone tree is increased from 2 to $\sqrt{b}$ for disk blocks of size b. The intervals are stored in slab lists and multislab lists. The structure requires $O(n/b)$ pages for n intervals, supports insertions and deletions in $O(\log_b n)$ I/Os and requires $O(\log_b n + r/b)$ I/Os to answer a stabbing query reporting r results, which is the optimal complexity. Unfortunately, no experiments demonstrate the performance and, again, the integration into existing systems is not supported.

Beside originally one-dimensional interval index structures even multi-dimensional index structures can be employed for the task of managing 1D intervals. In general, however, spatial access methods such as Guttman's *R-tree* [Gut 84] and its variants including R^+-*tree* [SRF 87] and *R*-tree* [BKSS 90] may not behave well for one-dimensional intervals. Particularly the long durations and high overlaps of intervals in many temporal applications induce severe performance problems [EWK 90] [GLOT 96]. Two particular solutions are sketched in the following.

The *Segment R-tree* (*SR-tree*) of Kolovson and Stonebraker [KS 91] is a combination of the main memory-based segment tree with the secondary storage-oriented R-tree. The split algorithm cuts long intervals into spanning portions and remnant portions thus producing some redundance. The authors recommend to combine the SR-tree with a *Skeleton Index* that performs a pre-partitioning of the data space in order to improve query processing performance. The SR-tree performs similar to the R-tree, and particularly the skeleton version yields an improvement. Just as the IB-tree and IB+-tree are augmentations of the B+-tree, implementing the SR-tree requires an adaption of the R-tree structure provided there exists any R-tree in the target DBMS at all. Another approach that supposes a specialized multi-dimensional index structure is suggested by Fenk et al. [FMB 00].

2.3 Relational Storage Structures

Very few methods immediately meet our core requirement to use built-in index structures the way they are rather than to augment indexes or to introduce new structures whose integration is typically not supported by existing RDBMS.

The *Window-List* technique of Ramaswamy [Ram 97] is a static solution for the interval management problem and employs built-in B+-trees. The optimal complexity of $O(n/b)$ space and $O(\log_b n + r/b)$ I/Os for stabbing queries is achieved. Unfortunately, updates do not seem to have non-trivial upper bounds, and adding as well as deleting arbitrary intervals can deteriorate the query efficiency of this structure to $O(n/b)$. Despite the practicability of the approach, no experimental results are demonstrated.

The *Tile Index* approach provided by the Oracle8i Spatial Product [RS 99] is a relational implementation of the multi-dimensional *Linear Quadtree* [Sam 90b]. Spatial objects are decomposed and indexed at a user-defined fixed quadtree level. Each resulting fixed-sized tile contains a set of variable-sized tiles as a fine-grained representation of the covered geometry. Intersection queries are performed by an equijoin on the indexed fixed-sized tiles, followed by a sequential scan on the corresponding variable-sized tiles. When applied to one-dimensional data, the *Tile Index* technique maps an interval to a set of fixed-sized segments to be stored in a built-in B+-tree. Finding a good fixed level for the expected data distribution is crucial, as with the fixed level set too high, too much redundancy emerges due to small fixed-sized tiles, whereas a low fixed level causes too much overhead for scanning the large variable-sized tiles. Therefore, an inappropriate setting causes the response time to degenerate vastly [Ora 97] [Ora 99b]. Unfortunately, the fixed level can only be set at index creation time, and adapting it to changing data and query distributions requires bulk-loading the whole dataset anew. This major drawback is not shared by our *RI-Tree*.

The *Interval-Spatial Transformation* (*IST*) of Goh et al. [GLOT 96] is based on encoding intervals by space-filling curves called *D-*, *V-* and *H-ordering* that map the boundary points into a linear space. No redundancy is produced, and space complexity is $O(n/b)$. Whereas the expansion of the data space at the upper bound is an explicit feature of the method, the expansion at the lower bound which is supported in our solution remains unclear. Unfortunately, no experimental performance results are reported in the paper. The I/O complexity of the query algorithm linearly depends on the resolution of the space whereas our method guarantees a logarithmic dependency on the resolution. A dynamic refinement of the resolution is not supported by the *IST*. A closer look at the structure reveals a strong correspondence to relational composite indexes. Aside from quantization aspects, the D-ordering is equivalent to a composite index on the interval bounds (*upper*, *lower*), and the V-ordering corresponds to an index on (*lower*, *upper*). For intersection queries, however, these indexes reveal a poor query performance if the selectivity relies on the "wrong" bound, i.e. the secondary attribute in the index. Thus, intersection queries have a worst case I/O complexity of $O(n/b)$. The H-ordering simulates an index on (*upper – lower*, *lower*), thus particularly supporting queries referring to the interval length. The *MAP21* approach of Nascimento and Dunham [ND 99] behaves very similar to the IST while the composite index (*lower*, *upper*) is implemented by a single-column index. A static partitioning by the interval lengths is introduced, but intersection query processing still requires $O(n/b)$ I/Os if the database contains many long intervals.

2.4 Custom Access Methods in ORDBMS

Modern commercial ORDBMS such as the Informix Universal Server [Inf 98], the Oracle8i Server [Ora 99a] or the IBM DB2 Universal Database [IBM 99] support the logical embedding of custom indextypes into the database system. Though the developer may use an extensibility framework to seamlessly bind a new access method to the query language, optimizer and query processor, there is no application program interface to the physical layer of the database engine, e.g. to the block manager. In the absence of any generalized search tree framework in the sense of [HNP 95], the developers have the option to store their custom index structure in external files. Of course, this technique allows excellent performance results, but as external files do not participate in the transaction management of the database server, the developers have to implement and maintain their own block manager including "industrial strength" concurrency control and recovery services.

Alternatively storing the index as a single Large Object (LOB) in the database also requires extensive implementation and maintenance efforts, particularly because the built-in locking mechanism on entire LOBs is far too coarse in a multi-user environment [BSSJ 99]. A natural way to avoid these technical problems is to exploit as much functionality of the database server as possible by mapping the index structure to a fine granular relational schema organized by built-in access methods. We follow this approach in the present paper and propose an efficient index structure for interval data that is designed to operate as logical indextype on top of the relational query language of the DBMS. The code can be implemented and maintained with minimum effort. Nevertheless our technique provides "industrial strength" stability and transaction semantics, while still showing a logarithmic worst case I/O complexity for interval intersection queries and while demonstrating the best experimentally measured performance compared to previous approaches.

3 The Relational Interval Tree

In this section, we introduce the new *Relational Interval Tree*, which efficiently implements Edelsbrunner's interval tree on top of any relational database system.

3.1 Original Interval Tree Structure

Edelsbrunner's interval tree [Ede 80] [PS 93] is an optimal data structure for intervals. Since the registered intervals are not decomposed as in the segment tree, no redundancy is produced and the space complexity is $O(n)$. The three-fold structure is illustrated in Figure 1: The backbone tree or primary structure is a balanced binary search tree that organizes the values of all bounding points of the intervals. Each of the inner nodes w is associated with two lists $L(w)$ and $U(w)$ that form the secondary structure. $L(w)$ and $U(w)$ contain, respectively, sorted lists of the lower and upper bounds of the intervals that are associated to w. An interval (l, u) is registered at the highest node it overlaps, i.e. the first node w for which $l \leq w \leq u$ holds when descending the tree. The tertiary structure is an additional binary tree that supports fast range scans by linking the nodes w whose lists $L(w)$ and $U(w)$ are nonempty.

3.2 Structure of the Relational Interval Tree

The basic idea of our technique relies on the following observations:

- For many applications, the *primary structure* does not need to be materialized at all. First, the nonempty nodes are linked by the tertiary structure as well. Second, even dynamic data spaces can be managed without a physical tree structure as we will show below. Only a few system parameters occupying $O(1)$ space are required.

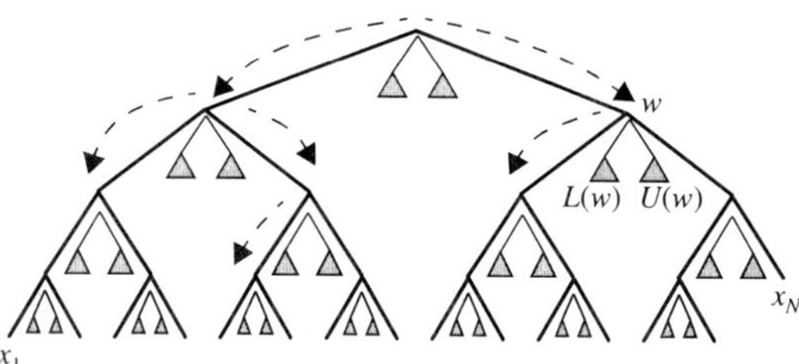

Figure 1: Three-fold structure of an interval tree.

- The *secondary* and *tertiary structure* can be combined to a relational representation that highly fits to the strength of built-in composite indexes as provided already by an RDBMS. As desired, the space complexity is $O(n/b)$ for n intervals.

The secondary structure is mapped to a relational schema as follows: Let $L(w) = \{l_1, ..., l_{n_w}\}$ denote the list of lower bounds of the n_w intervals that are registered at node w. The same information is represented by the set of tuples $\{(w, l_1), ..., (w, l_{n_w})\}$. The union over all nodes w yields a relation (*node, lower*). Analogously, the lists $U(w) = \{u_1, ..., u_{n_w}\}$ of upper bounds correspond to $\{(w, u_1), ..., (w, u_{n_w})\}$ and yield a relation (*node, upper*). Together, the relations exactly reflect the information of the secondary structure.

In an RDBMS, the two relations (*node, lower*) and (*node, upper*) are efficiently organized by built-in composite indexes. These indexes typically own a robust and highly tuned implementation, e.g. a B+-tree; they already obey the transaction semantics and are hardly outperformed by user-defined structures. Key compression techniques avoid redundancy for equal node values w. Since the indexes only manage the nonempty nodes, they already comprise the tertiary structure.

The resulting relational schema contains the attributes (*node, lower, upper, id*) and is supported by two composite indexes (*node, lower*) and (*node, upper*). Thus, a given interval relation is prepared for the RI-tree by adding a single attribute *node* and two indexes. Figure 2 presents the respective DDL statements in SQL. Alternatively, the artificial attribute *node* may be omitted from the base table and encapsulated by index-organized tables for the two indexes.

CREATE TABLE Intervals (node int, lower int, upper int, id int);
CREATE INDEX lowerIndex ON Intervals (node, lower);
CREATE INDEX upperIndex ON Intervals (node, upper);

Figure 2: SQL statements to instantiate an RI-Tree.

3.3 Updates in Relational Interval Trees

Whereas the registered intervals are completely managed by the relational schema, the remaining task of the primary structure is to organize the data space in order to manage insertions and query processing. The original interval tree is

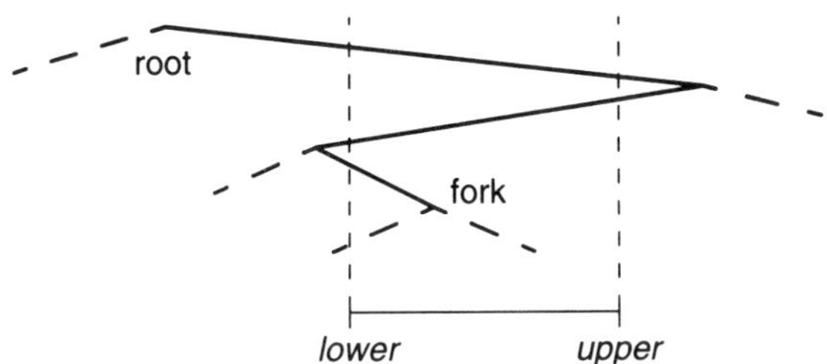

Figure 3: Fork node of an interval in the tree.

built on a static set of bounding points for the intervals. In a dynamic context, however, intervals are inserted and deleted whose actual bounding points are not known in advance. Moreover, temporal applications require an ongoing expansion of the data space. For this reason, a general and adaptable technique is required.

Our solution is as simple as effective: Rather than materializing any set of nodes, the primary structure is managed purely virtually. Thus, the bounding points of the intervals are not restricted to given values but the entire range $[1, 2^h-1]$ is supported for some $h \geq 0$. Moreover, no reorganization of any structure is necessary when inserting or deleting intervals.

In the basic version, the root node is set to 2^{h-1}, and the tree is traversed recursively via bisection, i.e. using simple integer arithmetics but consuming no I/O operations. As already mentioned, an interval (l, u) is registered at the topmost node w for which $l \leq w \leq u$ holds, called the *fork node* (Figure 3). As an extension of the original interval tree, intervals may begin and end also at inner nodes rather than only at leaves. Points p are represented by degenerate intervals (p, p). A procedure to determine the fork node is provided in Figure 4. For computational reasons, the recursion is controlled by a decreasing step width rather than the depth in the tree.

```
FUNCTION int forkNode (int lower, int upper) {
   int node = root;
   for (int step = node/2; step >= 1; step /= 2)
      if (upper < node) node -= step;
      elsif (node < lower) node += step;
      else break;
   return node;
}
```

Figure 4: Computing the fork node of an interval.

Once the fork node is computed, inserting the interval into the relational indexes is efficiently performed by the DBMS itself. Only a single SQL statement needs to be executed (Figure 5) which also holds for the deletion of an interval. Todays RDBMS typically perform both operations by $O(\log_b n)$ I/Os on a database containing n intervals.

```
INSERT INTO Intervals
   VALUES (forkNode(:lower, :upper), :lower, :upper, :id);
```

Figure 5: Insertion of an interval (lower, upper, id).

3.4 Dynamic Expansion of the Data Space

In the basic version, the data space is fixed to a range of 2^h-1 values yielding a tree of height h. Whereas the I/O complexity for updates is $O(\log_b n)$ and thus independent of h, the CPU time complexity linearly grows with h.

We suggest a solution that combines various aspects: First, the tree height is adjusted to the actual data distribution. Second, the data space may be expanded dynamically at the upper bound; this requirement is typical for temporal applications. On top of this, even expansions of the data space at the lower bound are supported.

The tree height is affected by two parameters: The value of the root node at which searches in the tree start, and the depth down to which algorithms have to descend in the tree. In order to control the minimum tree height, we introduce the system parameters *root*, *offset*, *leftRoot*, *rightRoot* and *minstep*.

Root. Dynamically adapting the parameter *root* yields two advantages: The tree height is kept minimal, and the data space may be expanded at its upper bound as new intervals arrive. A root value of 2^h is sufficient to manage intervals with $0 < lower$ and $upper < 2^{h+1}$, and $h = \lfloor \log_2(\max\{upper\}) \rfloor$ is adjusted at every insertion without affecting the existing entries, i.e. in $O(1)$.

Offset. The optimality of the root height clearly holds for an actual data space starting at 1. The intervals, however, may be located in a range $[x_1, x_N]$ with $x_1 \gg 1$, i.e. far away from the origin. The resulting tree height is $\lfloor \log_2(x_N) \rfloor$ whereas a height of $\lfloor \log_2(x_N - x_1) \rfloor$ would be sufficient for a data range of length $x_N - x_1$. By shifting the intervals such that 1 becomes the lower bound of the data space, the optimal root height $h_{opt} = \lfloor \log_2(\max\{upper\} - \min\{lower\}) \rfloor$ is obtained. The amount of shift is stored in the parameter *offset*.

LeftRoot and RightRoot. Changing the *offset* parameter would cause a recalculation of all node values stored in the tree. To avoid such an unnecessary $O(n/b)$ I/O effort, *offset* is fixed after having inserted the first interval. The interval that leftmost begins in the data space, however, is not guaranteed to arrive at first to be inserted. Therefore, the space needs to be expanded at the lower bound as well as at the upper bound.

In our solution, we use 0 as global root value and manage a left and a right subtree for negative and positive node values, respectively. Instead of the single parameter *root*, two parameters *leftRoot* and *rightRoot* are maintained that manage the expansion of the data space at the lower bound and at the upper bound independently.

Minstep. The parameter *minstep* traces the lowest level i_{min} at which insertions of intervals have taken place with level 0 as the leaf level. Obviously, a query algorithm does not need to descend deeper than to level i_{min} since the secondary structures of all nodes in lower levels are empty. An estimation of i_{min} is obtained from the interval lengths:

> **Lemma.** An interval (l, u) is not registered below the level $i_{min} = \lfloor \log_2(u - l) \rfloor$, i.e. the largest cardinal i with $2^i \leq u - l$.

> **Proof.** Assume an interval (l, u) registered at a level $j < \lfloor \log_2(u - l) \rfloor$. Then there are two successive multiples $k \cdot 2^j$ and $(k+1) \cdot 2^j$ for which $l \leq k \cdot 2^j < (k+1) \cdot 2^j \leq u$. Since one of the multiples is also a multiple of 2^{j+1}, the interval (l, u) had to be registered not lower than level $j+1$ which contradicts the assumption.

Figure 6 presents the final insertion procedure including the update of the persistent tree parameters. Only the artificial node value is shifted by *offset*; the lower and upper bounds of the intervals are stored without modification. The parameters *leftRoot* and *rightRoot* are initially set to 0, and *minstep* is initialized by infinity. The minimum value of 0.5 for minstep will not be stored and, thus, the implementation by an integer works well.

```
PROCEDURE insertInterval (int lower, int upper, int id) {
    // initialize offset and shift interval
    if (offset = NULL) offset = lower;
    int l = lower – offset, u = upper – offset;

    // update leftRoot and rightRoot
    if (u < 0 and l <= 2*leftRoot)  leftRoot = –2^⌊log₂(–l)⌋;
    if (0 < l and u >= 2*rightRoot) rightRoot = 2^⌊log₂(u)⌋;

    // descend the tree down to the fork node
    int node, step;
    if (u < 0) node = leftRoot;
    elsif (0 < l) node = rightRoot;
    else /* 0 is fork node */ node = 0;

    for (step = abs(node/2); step >= 1; step /= 2) {
        if (u < node) node –= step;
        elsif (node < l) node += step;
        else /* fork reached */ break;
    } // now node is fork node

    if (node != 0 and step < minstep) minstep = step;

    INSERT INTO Intervals VALUES (:node, :lower, :upper, :id);
}
```

Figure 6: Insertion of an interval and update of the tree parameters *offset*, *leftRoot*, *rightRoot* and *minstep*.

3.5 Analysis of the Tree Height

The parameters *offset*, *leftRoot*, *rightRoot* and *minstep* form an $O(1)$ representation of the primary structure that is dynamically adjusted to the cardinality m of the current data space. Including the global root 0, the resulting tree height is $\log_2(m) + 1$ with m given by the following formula where the minimum value of 0.5 for minstep may occur:

$$m = \max\{-leftRoot, rightRoot\} / minstep$$

In terms of data characteristics, the tree height is determined as follows: The range from *leftRoot* to *rightRoot* reflects the expansion of the data space from $\min\{lower\}$ to $\max\{upper\}$ over all currently registered intervals, and *minstep* indicates the granularity of the data space, i.e. the smallest interval length, $\min\{upper - lower\}$. We increase this value by 1 to proper handle points which are represented by degenerate intervals. Nevertheless, *minstep* could be greater than $\min\{upper - lower + 1\}$ since even small intervals can be registered at high nodes, e.g. at the root node. In any case, the tree height does not depend on the number of intervals. In terms of the interval bounds, the tree height is $O(\log_2 m)$ where m obeys the following complexity:

$$m = O\left(\frac{\max\{upper\} - \min\{lower\}}{\min\{upper - lower + 1\}}\right)$$

4 Query Processing

Having presented the internal structure of the relational interval tree in the preceding section, we now introduce the algorithms for query processing.

4.1 Original Intersection Search

Let us shortly review the algorithm for intersection query processing in the original interval tree. For any query interval $(lower, upper)$, the primary structure is descended as follows:

(1) Descend from the root node down to the node preceding the fork node of the query interval. Each node w on this path lies either to the left or to the right of the query interval. Suppose $w < lower$, then intervals (l, u) registered at w intersect the query interval exactly if $lower < u$. To report these r_w intervals, the sorted list $U(w)$ of upper bounds is scanned in $O(r_w)$ time. Analogously, $L(w)$ is scanned for intervals fulfilling $l < upper$ in the symmetric case $upper < w$.

(2) Descend from the fork node down to the node that is closest to *lower*. For each node w on this path, two cases are distinguished: If $w < lower$, $U(w)$ has to be scanned as before to report the intersecting intervals registered at w. Otherwise, if $lower \leq w$, the query interval is known to intersect all intervals registered at the node w. In addition, all intervals from the right subtree of w are reported except if w is the fork node.

(3) Descend from the fork node down to the node closest to *upper*. Analogously to step (2), the lists $L(w)$ have to be scanned, and all registered intervals from the respective nodes are reported.

Note that the algorithm even works for degenerate intervals, i.e. $lower = upper$, thus supporting point queries as efficient as interval queries. Figure 7 provides an illustration of the algorithm. Only the nodes of the tree which are affected by the search are depicted. The symbols indicate the

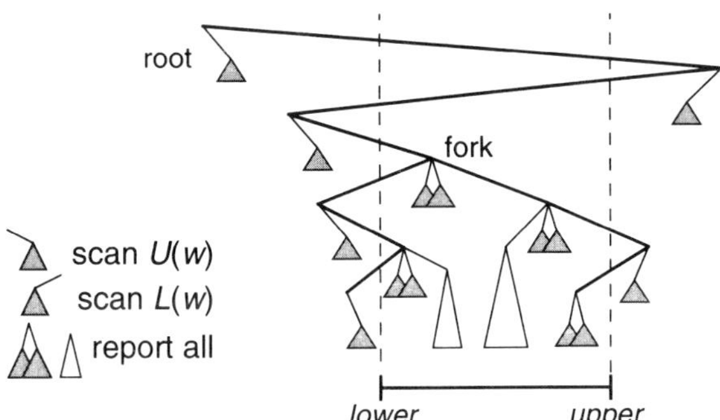

Figure 7: Query processing in the interval tree.

nodes for which $U(w)$ or $L(w)$ are scanned, and the nodes for which all entries have to be reported. Note that the latter are exactly the nodes w that are covered by the query interval, i.e. $lower \leq w \leq upper$.

4.2 Translation into a Single SQL Query

The basic idea of our approach is to exploit the efficiency of built-in relational indexes. Scanning the lists $U(w)$ and $L(w)$ immediately translates to an index range scan over the attributes $(node, upper)$ and $(node, lower)$, respectively. These attribute combinations are managed by the *upperIndex* and *lowerIndex* as defined above. Scanning the nodes w between *lower* and *upper* is supported by any of the two indexes.

Rather than immediately scanning the lists $U(w)$ and $L(w)$ while descending the tree, in our algorithm the respective nodes are collected in transient lists *leftNodes* and *rightNodes* both obeying the unary relational schema $(node)$. These transient relations are managed in the transient session state thus causing no I/O effort. As for interval insertion (Figure 6), the virtual primary structure is descended by integer arithmetics without any I/O operation. Finally, a single SQL query suffices to retrieve all intersecting intervals from the database. A basic version of the query is shown in Figure 8.

```
SELECT id FROM Intervals i, leftNodes left, rightNodes right
WHERE (i.node = left.node AND i.upper >= :lower)
   OR (i.node = right.node AND i.lower <= :upper)
   OR (i.node BETWEEN :lower – offset AND :upper – offset);
```

Figure 8: Prelim. SQL query to retrieve intersecting intervals.

As illustrated in Figure 7, the nodes from *leftNodes*, from *rightNodes*, and the nodes between *lower* and *upper* are distinct from each other. The three OR-connected conditions in the WHERE clause therefore specify disjoint interval sets, and the DISTINCT option is omitted from the SELECT clause since no duplicates have to be eliminated.

4.3 Simplified SQL Query

The first transformation typically performed by relational optimizers is to split the complex OR-query into a set of three simpler queries connected by UNION ALL. The sub-

queries concerning *leftNodes* and *rightNodes* are efficiently supported by the respective indexes *upperIndex* and *lowerIndex* and cannot be intermixed. The third subquery that only addresses the attribute node, however, is supported by any of the two indexes. Hence, in order to reduce the cost for internal query management, we combine this subquery with the *leftNodes* subquery according to the following lemma which analogously holds for the *rightNodes* subquery.

Lemma. (*i*) The condition '*i.node = left.node*' may be substituted by the equivalent condition '*i.node BETWEEN left.min AND left.max*' if *left.node = left.min = left.max* without loss of efficiency for an index scan.

(*ii*) The condition '*i.node BETWEEN :lower – offset AND :upper – offset*' is not restricted by adding the constraint '*i.upper >= :lower*'.

Proof. (*i*) The equivalence is obvious. An index scan searches the first hit by testing *left.min $\leq$ i.node* and proceeds while testing the condition *i.node $\leq$ left.max*.

(*ii*) Since by definition, *i.node $\leq$ i.upper – offset* holds for any interval i in the tree, the condition *:lower – offset $\leq$ i.node* implies *:lower $\leq$ i.upper*.

In detail, the modifications of the query are as follows: The transient relation *leftNodes* now obeys the binary relational schema (min, max) instead of the unary schema $(node)$. When descending the tree, a node w is inserted into *leftNodes* as a pair (w, w) rather than as a single value (w) as before. Finally, to include the original BETWEEN subquery, the pair $(lower – offset, upper – offset)$ is inserted into *leftNodes*. The lemma guarantees that no intervals are missing after the transformation. Figure 9 presents the resulting two-fold SQL query for intersection search still producing no duplicates.

```
SELECT id FROM Intervals i, leftNodes left
   WHERE i.node BETWEEN left.min AND left.max
      AND i.upper >= :lower
UNION ALL
SELECT id FROM Intervals i, rightNodes right
   WHERE i.node = right.node AND i.lower <= :upper;
```

Figure 9: Final SQL statement for intersection queries.

Figure 10 shows the execution plan for the query as generated by an Oracle8i server. Most RDBMS provide an easy way ('hints') to guarantee this query plan to be chosen by the optimizer. For this example the attribute *id* was included in the indexes.

4.4 Analysis of the Algorithm

In Section 3.5, we already observed that the tree height of $h = O(\log m)$ only depends on two parameters that determine the quotient m, i.e. the extension of the intervals in the data space and the minimal interval length. It does not depend on the number n of intervals registered in the tree. The tree height is an upper bound for the number of entries in the transient relations *leftNodes* and *rightNodes*. For each of the

413

```
SELECT STATEMENT
  UNION-ALL
    NESTED LOOPS
      COLLECTION ITERATOR
      INDEX RANGE SCAN UPPER_INDEX
    NESTED LOOPS
      COLLECTION ITERATOR
      INDEX RANGE SCAN LOWER_INDEX
```

Figure 10: Execution plan for an intersection query in Oracle.

$O(\log m)$ entries in the transient relations, an index range scan on *upperIndex* or *lowerIndex* is performed. Such an index range scan consists of two phases. In a search phase, the beginning of the range ρ is located, and in a scan phase, the r_ρ resulting objects from the range are reported. Typical index structures such as the B+-tree in relational database systems require $O(\log_b n)$ I/O operations for the search phase on a database containing n objects, and $O(r_\rho/b)$ I/Os in the scan phase to report the r_ρ results for the range ρ.

> **Theorem** (*Complexity of Query Processing*).
> An intersection query on a Relational Interval Tree of height h that returns r results from the n intervals in the tree has an I/O complexity of
> $$O(h \cdot \log_b n + r/b)$$

Proof. For each of the $O(h)$ entries in the transient relations *leftNodes* and *rightNodes*, an index search of $O(\log_b n)$ I/O complexity is performed. Scanning and reporting the total of r results requires $O(r/b)$ operations.

We conjecture that this complexity is optimal for managing intervals by relational storage structures.

4.5 General Topological Queries

In addition to the intersection query predicate, there are 13 more fine-grained temporal relationships between intervals [BÖ 98]. Obviously, also queries based on these specialized predicates are efficiently supported by the Relational Interval Tree. For some of them, there is an additional potential for optimization since they only refer to the lower bound as in *meets* or in *before*, or they only refer to the upper bound as in *met-by* or in *after*. Competing methods such as the IB+-tree [BÖ 98] or the IST [GLOT 96] efficiently support only queries referring to one of the two interval bounds, i.e. *lower* for the IB+-tree or the V-ordering and *upper* for the D-ordering. Using these techniques, queries referring to the opposite bound are processed with a poor performance since $O(n)$ comparisons are required in the worst case.

4.6 Handling Temporal Intervals

In the context of temporal databases, the special values *now* and *infinity* occur as upper values of valid time intervals [BÖ 98]. The straightforward solution to manage these intervals in separate indexes, however, yields the major disadvantage that additional SQL (sub-)queries have to be executed. This overhead is avoided by managing appropriate values for the fork nodes thus achieving a very natural integration into the Relational Interval Tree.

Infinity. In a first attempt, we set the fork node of an infinite interval to MAXINT but do not further modify the algorithms. Thus, the tree becomes very high but it is almost empty close to the root. A slight but very effective extension avoids the resulting overhead for query processing: An artificial exclusive value *fork*$_\infty$ is assigned to the attribute *node* of an infinite interval. At query processing time, *fork*$_\infty$ is inserted into the transient list *rightNodes*. Thus, the lower bounds of intervals ending at *infinity* are tested against the upper bound of the query interval as desired. Note that if choosing *fork*$_\infty$ = NULL, the condition '*i.node = right.node*' in Figure 9 is not evaluated correctly whereas our choice to set *fork*$_\infty$ = MAXINT avoids any modification of the SQL statement thus yielding a perfect integration.

Now. Whereas *infinity* is constant over time, intervals ending at *now* continuously change their upper bound. Aiming at a correct positioning of now-relative intervals within the tree at any time requires permanent modifications of the node values and, therefore, of the tree. Our solution completely avoids such an overhead and, again, uses an artificial exclusive node value, e.g. *fork*$_{now}$ = MAXINT − 1, which is assigned to *now*-ending intervals when being inserted. At query processing time, *fork*$_{now}$ is inserted into the transient table *rightNodes* exactly if *lower* $\leq$ *now*, i.e. if the query interval begins in the past. As desired, the SQL query then tests the lower bounds of the *now*-ending intervals against the upper bound of the query interval.

5 Object-Relational Wrapping

The Relational Interval Tree may be easily implemented on top of *any* relational DBMS featuring a procedural query language like the Oracle8i Server with PL/SQL or the Informix Universal Server with SPL. A persistent data dictionary provides a convenient way to store index specific system parameters such as *root* or *minstep*, whereas the *leftNodes* and *rightNodes* query tables can be efficiently managed in the transient user session state. As mentioned in Section 3.3, the insertion and deletion of a new interval requires only a single SQL statement. The computation and storage of the fork node and the update of the index parameters can be performed automatically by database triggers. Whereas the complete index maintenance therefore may be managed by a trigger mechanism, query processing has to be started manually by invoking the appropriate stored procedure.

Modern object-relational DBMS provide a solution to preserve the declarative paradigm of SQL even at query time, because all maintenance and access procedures of a custom index structure are completely hidden from the user. An extensible indexing framework allows the developer to package the implementation of the access method and the corresponding index data into a user-defined indextype [Inf 98] [Ora 99a] [IBM 99]. As the object-relational database server automatically triggers the maintenance and scan of custom indexes, end users can use the Relational Interval Tree just like a built-in index. With a cost model registered at the optimizer, the server is able to generate efficient execution plans for queries on interval data types.

6 Experimental Evaluation

6.1 Experimental Setup

To evaluate the performance of our approach, we have integrated the Relational Interval Tree into the Oracle Server Release 8.1.5 using PL/SQL and packaged stored procedures. All experiments have been executed on a Pentium Pro/180 server having 128 MB main memory and an U-SCSI hard drive. The database block cache was set to the default value of 200 database blocks with a block size of 2 KB. We have evaluated the performance of interval intersection queries on various interval databases with different data distributions and cardinalities (cf. Table 1). The bounding points of all intervals lie in the domain of $[0, 2^{20}\text{-}1]$. For the distributions D_3 and D_4, we assume transaction time or valid time intervals where the arrival of temporal tuples follows a Poisson process. Thus the inter-arrival time is distributed exponentially.

Name	Starting point distribution	Duration distribution
$D_1(n,d)$	uniform in $[0, 2^{20}\text{-}1]$	uniform in $[0, 2d]$
$D_2(n,d)$		exponential in $[0, \infty]$, mean $= d$
$D_3(n,d)$	poisson process in $[0, 2^{20}\text{-}1]$	uniform in $[0, 2d]$
$D_4(n,d)$		exponential in $[0, \infty]$, mean $= d$

Table 1: Sample interval databases with cardinality n.

As mentioned in Section 2.3, among the wide range of existing interval access methods only the static Window-List approach [Ram 97], the Tile Index [RS 99] and the Interval-Spatial Transformation technique [GLOT 96] are designed to use existing B+-trees on an as-they-are basis, i.e. without any internal modifications or augmentations. Therefore, we restrict our performance comparison to these techniques.

Window-List. In our experiments, queries on Window-Lists produced twice as many I/O operations than on the dynamic RI-tree. As the Window-List technique is a static storage structure, we do not further investigate it in the following evaluation of dynamic structures.

Tile Index (*T-index*). In our experiments, we have used the recommended hybrid indexing method of fixed- and variable-sized tiling as it is documented in [Ora 97] and [Ora 99b]. To ensure comparability to the other techniques, we have reimplemented the hybrid indexing package for one-dimensional data spaces. Our version is less complex and shows a significant performance gain over the original two-

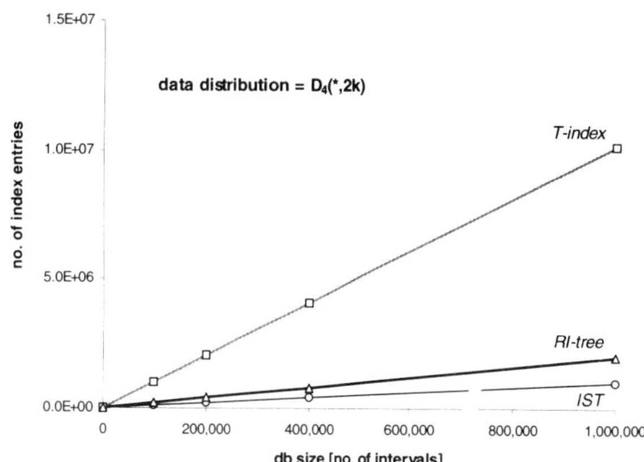

Figure 12: Number of index entries for varying database size.

dimensional implementation. When we use the Tile Index for the interval domain of $[0, 2^{20}\text{-}1]$, the fixed level parameter may be set to a value between 0 and 20. For our experiments, we took a representative sample of 1,000 intervals from each individual data distribution and determined the optimal setting for the fixed level. In most cases, the optimum for the query performance was found at the level 7, 8 or 9.

Interval-Spatial Transformation (*IST*). For the following experiments we have implemented the Interval-Spatial Transformation with *D-order* as proposed by [GLOT 96]. For integer interval bounds [*lower, upper*], the D-order index is equivalent to a composite index on the attributes (*upper, lower*) and therefore has identical performance characteristics. Range queries on D-ordered intervals can be expressed in a simple SQL statement by just testing the upper and lower bounds for intersection with the query range, as presented in Figure 11.

```
SELECT id FROM Intervals i
    WHERE (i.upper >= :lower AND i.lower <= :upper);
```

Figure 11: A range query for the Interval-Spatial Transformation (*IST*) on a D-ordered index.

Relational Interval Tree (*RI-tree*). We have implemented the Relational Interval Tree as it is described in the previous sections. As each data distribution of Table 1 contains intervals with length 0 (i.e. points), the granularity of the respective data space is maximal. Therefore, the *minstep* system parameter always reaches its minimum value of 1 upon index creation and the virtual backbone tree is expanded to a height of 20, unless noted otherwise.

6.2 Storage Occupation

We performed several experiments to compare the *RI-tree* with the *IST* and the *T-index*. An illustration of the storage occupation of the three techniques is given in Figure 12 for a $D_4(*,2k)$ distribution. As the *IST* technique produces no redundancy, the number of index entries is equal to the num-

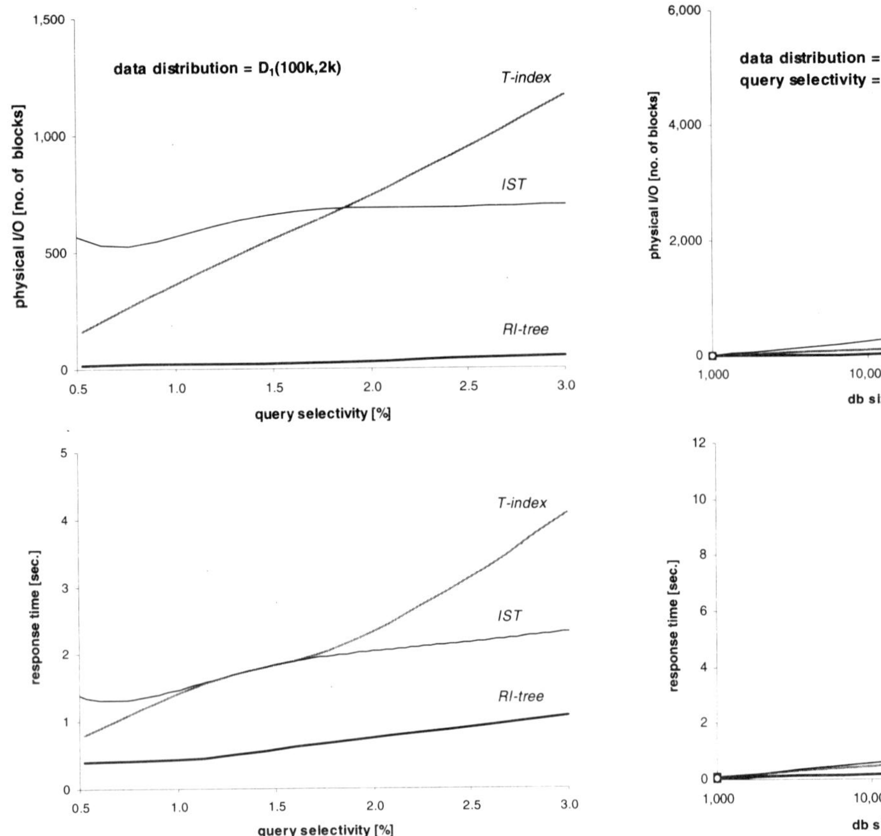

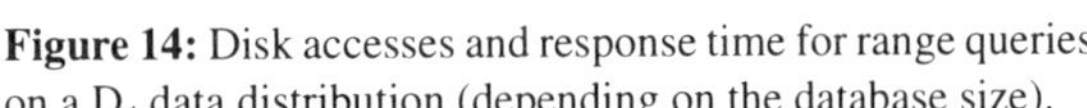

Figure 13: Disk accesses and response time for range queries on a D_1 data distribution (depending on query selectivity).

Figure 14: Disk accesses and response time for range queries on a D_4 data distribution (depending on the database size).

ber of indexed intervals. The *RI-tree* requires two index entries for each stored interval (for the lowerIndex and the upperIndex, cf. Figure 2). In our example, the *T-index* needs a redundancy factor of 10.1 to index the decomposed intervals accurately. As we have experienced in our evaluation, this causes major performance and storage problems for very large interval databases.

6.3 Query Processing

All query experiments given in this subsection have been performed with query intervals following a distribution which is compatible to the respective interval database. Our first experiment compares the number of physical disk block accesses and the response time of the three access methods depending on the selectivity of the range queries. Figure 13 depicts polynomially interpolated results of 100 range queries on a D_1(100k,2k) distribution. At a query selectivity of 0.5%, the *RI-tree* clearly outperforms the other techniques by a factor of 10.8 (*T-index*) and 46.3 (*IST*) for the disk accesses. At a 3.0% selectivity, the speedup factor is 22.8 (*T-index*) and 13.6 (*IST*). Thus the Relational Interval Tree shows a superior performance for both high and low query selectivities. The fast response times of *T-index* and *IST* (e.g. 500 I/Os in two seconds) are caused by the good clustering

properties of the bulk loaded indexes and will deteriorate in a dynamic environment. For D_2(100k,2k), D_3(100k,2k), and D_4(100k,2k) datasets we measured similar results.

Figure 14 compares the scaleup of the three techniques for D_4(*,2k) datasets growing from 1,000 to 1,000,000 stored intervals. For each database size, the average number of disk accesses and the average response time of 20 range queries is presented. Both the *T-index* and the *IST* demonstrate their linear scaleup whereas the *RI-tree* scales sublinearly and shows a significant performance gain over the other access methods. The speedup factor from the *T-index* to the *RI-tree* increases from 2 to 42 (disk access) and from 2.0 to 4.9 (response time). We observed a similar improvement for the same experiments on D_1(*,2k), D_2(*,2k), and D_3(*,2k) data distributions.

The next set of experiments investigates the influence of the dataspace granularity on the query performance of the *RI-tree*. For this experiment, we restricted the domain for the interval lengths of a D_3 distribution from [0, 4k] to [500, 3.5k], [1k, 3k], and [1.5k, 2.5k], respectively. With increasing minimum interval length, fewer levels of the virtual backbone have to be traversed due to larger *minstep* values. As shown in Figure 15, the response time is almost indepen-

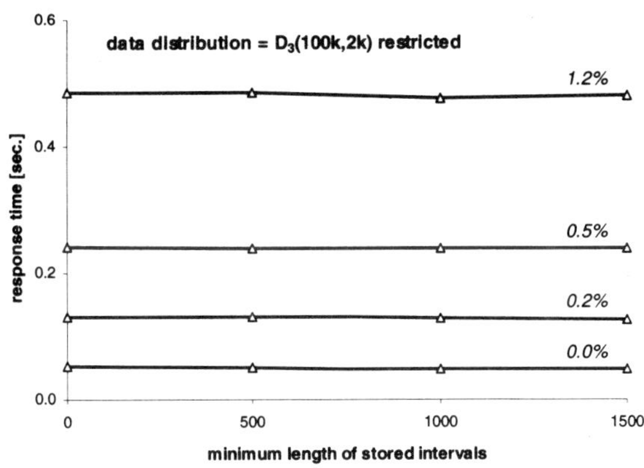

Figure 15: Response time for range queries with different selectivities on an *RI-tree* for restricted D_3 databases.

dent of the minimum length of the stored intervals. So the resulting height h of the virtual backbone has only little empirical significance. The response times for the different selectivities illustrate also the desired property that the performance of queries is largely bound to the number of results.

The next series of experiments compares the influence of the mean of interval duration on the query performance of the different techniques. Figure 16 depicts the average results for a sample of 20 range queries on various $D_4(100k,*)$ datasets with increasing average length of intervals. The *T-index* and the *RI-tree* require about the same response time for range queries, if the average length of the indexed intervals is very low. As short intervals do not suffer from the spatial decomposition, the redundancy caused by the *T-index* tiling approach decreases from 10.1 to 1 when the mean value of interval duration is reduced from 2,000 to 0. Even for a pure point database, the *RI-tree* performs slightly better than the *T-index*. The benefit of the *RI-tree* becomes obvious for a higher mean of duration. Both the *RI-tree* and the *IST* perform better as longer intervals are stored in the database.

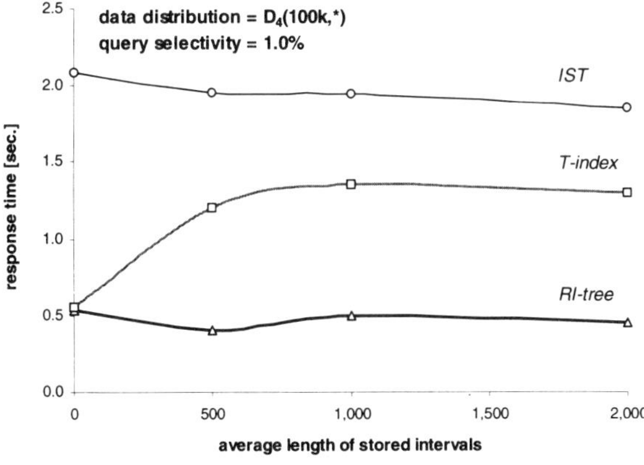

Figure 16: Response time on a D_4 data distribution with varying mean of interval length. Even for small intervals, the *RI-tree* outperforms the *T-index* approach.

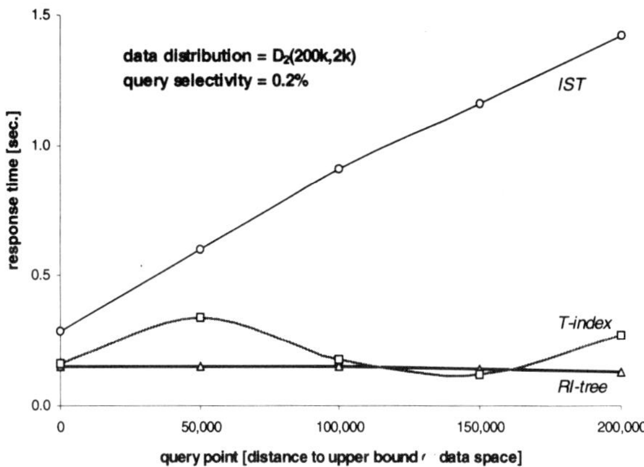

Figure 17: Response time for a "sweeping" point query on a D_2 data distribution. The *IST* degenerates with higher distance to the upper bound of the data space.

As expected, the location of the query range with respect to the data domain exerts a strong influence on the performance of the *IST*. In Figure 17 we illustrate this effect by 'sweeping' a query point starting at the upper bound of the data space where the bound index on (*upper, lower*) benefits the most from the high selectivity in the first indexed column. The comparison between the *RI-tree* and *T-index* reveals another interesting aspect of this experiment: Although for point queries the *T-index* performs at its best as it retrieves no duplicates caused by redundancy, the *RI-tree* is still slightly better on the average. We obtained these results as well for the other interval data distributions D_1, D_3 and D_4.

7 Conclusions

In this paper, we presented the Relational Interval Tree which is a new access method for interval data. It can be created for any relational or object-relational table containing intervals. As we have shown, the main design goals for our new approach have been fulfilled:

- *Integration.* The RI-tree is not a stand-alone concept. It can easily be implemented on top of any relational DBMS. As much functionality as possible of built-in indexes is exploited and no changes or additions to the internal layer of the database server are made. Therefore the effort of code development and code maintenance is minimal. For modern database servers featuring an object-relational application program interface, a natural and seamless integration can be achieved while preserving the declarative paradigm of SQL.

- *Performance.* Our analytical and experimental evaluation of the RI-tree shows superior performance characteristics compared to previous approaches. This is achieved by introducing the virtual primary structure. Although the structure is space-oriented, the storage of intervals is object-driven and, thus, no storage space is wasted for empty regions in the data space.

- *Extensions.* Our basic concept supports a wide range of efficient application specific extensions. We have illustrated this by the dynamic expansion of the data space, by handling the special temporal variables *now* and *infinity*, and by discussing fine-grained topological query types.

The flexibility and extensibility of the RI-tree concept opens up a number of interesting research problems and applications. A promising extension is the application of the Skeleton Index technique to the RI-tree, because a partial materialization of the primary structure can be adapted to the expected data distribution and, for example, the management of string intervals is supported.

References

[AT 95]   Ang C.-H., Tan K.-P.: *The Interval B-Tree.* Information Processing Letters 53(2): 85-89, 1995.

[AV 96]   Arge L., Vitter J. S.: *Optimal Dynamic Interval Management in External Memory.* Proc. 37th Annual Symp. on Foundations of Computer Science, 560-569, 1996.

[BKK 99]   Böhm C., Klump G., Kriegel H.-P.: *XZ-Ordering: A Space-Filling Curve for Objects with Spatial Extension.* Proc. 6th Int. Symp. on Large Spatial Databases, LNCS 1651, 75-90, 1999.

[BKSS 90]   Beckmann N., Kriegel H.-P., Schneider R., Seeger B.: *The R*-tree: An Efficient and Robust Access Method for Points and Rectangles.* Proc. ACM SIGMOD Int. Conf. on Management of Data, 322-331, 1990.

[BÖ 98]   Bozkaya T., Özsoyoglu Z. M.: *Indexing Valid Time Intervals.* Proc. 9th Int. Conf. on Database and Expert Systems Applications, LNCS 1460, 541-550, 1998.

[BSSJ 99]   Bliujute R., Saltenis S., Slivinskas G., Jensen C.S.: *Developing a DataBlade for a New Index.* Proc. IEEE Int. Conf. on Data Engineering, 314-323, 1999.

[CLR 90]   Cormen T. H., Leiserson C. E., Rivest R. L.: *Introduction to Algorithms.* Cambridge, MA: MIT-Press, 1990.

[Ede 80]   Edelsbrunner H.: *Dynamic Rectangle Intersection Searching.* Institute for Information Processing Report 47, Technical University of Graz, Austria, 1980.

[EWK 90]   Elmasri R., Wuu G. T. J., Kim Y.-J.: *The Time Index: An Access Structure for Temporal Data.* Proc. 16th Int. Conf. on Very Large Databases, 1-12, 1990.

[FMB 00]   Fenk R., Markl V., Bayer R.: *Management and Query Processing of One-Dimensional Intervals with the UB-Tree.* PhD Workshop, 7th Conf. on Extending Database Technology, Konstanz, Germany, 7-10, 2000.

[FR 89]   Faloutsos C., Roseman S.: *Fractals for Secondary Key Retrieval.* Proc. 8th ACM Symp. on Principles of Database Systems, 247-252, 1989.

[GLOT 96]   Goh C. H., Lu H., Ooi B. C., Tan K.-L.: *Indexing Temporal Data Using Existing B+-Trees.* Data & Knowledge Engineering, Elsevier, 18(2): 147-165, 1996.

[Gut 84]   Guttman A.: *R-trees: A Dynamic Index Structure for Spatial Searching.* Proc. ACM SIGMOD Int. Conf. on Management of Data, 47-57, 1984.

[HJ 96]   Hanson E., Johnson T.: *Selection Predicate Indexing for Active Databases Using Interval Skip Lists.* Information Systems, 21(3): 269-298, 1996.

[HNP 95]   Hellerstein J. M., Naughton J. F., Pfeffer A.: *Generalized Search Trees for Database Systems.* Proc. 21st Int. Conf. on Very Large Databases, 562-573, 1995.

[HP 94]   Hellerstein J. M., Pfeffer A.: *The RD-Tree: An Index Structure for Sets.* Technical Report #1252, University of Wisconsin at Madison, Oct. 1994.

[IBM 99]   IBM Corp.: *IBM DB2 Universal Database Application Development Guide, Version 6.* Armonk, NY, 1999.

[Inf 98]   Informix Software, Inc.: *DataBlade Developers Kit User's Guide.* Menlo Park, CA, 1998.

[KRVV 93]   Kanellakis P. C., Ramaswamy S., Vengroff D. E., Vitter J. S.: *Indexing for Data Models with Constraints and Classes.* Proc. 12th ACM Symp. on Principles of Database Systems, 233-243, 1993.

[KPS 00]   Kriegel H.-P., Pötke M., Seidl T.: *Relational Interval Tree.* EPO patent application, 2000.

[KS 91]   Kolovson C. P., Stonebraker M.: *Segment Indexes: Dynamic Indexing Techniques for Multi-Dimensional Interval Data.* Proc. ACM SIGMOD Int. Conf. on Management of Data, 138-147, 1991.

[LT 98]   Lee C., Tseng T.-M.: *Temporal Grid File: A File Structure for Interval Data.* Data & Knowledge Engineering, Elsevier, 26(1): 71-97, 1998.

[MTT 00]   Manolopoulos Y., Theodoridis Y., Tsotras V. J.: *Advanced Database Indexing.* Chapter 4: *Access Methods for Intervals.* Boston, MA: Kluwer, 2000.

[ND 99]   Nascimento M. A., Dunham M. H.: *Indexing Valid Time Databases via B+-Trees.* IEEE Trans. on Knowledge and Data Engineering 11(6): 929-947, 1999.

[Ora 97]   Oracle Corp.: *Oracle8 Spatial Cartridge User's Guide and Reference, Rel. 8.0.4.* Redwood City, CA, 1997.

[Ora 99a]   Oracle Corp.: *Oracle8i Data Cartridge Developer's Guide, Rel. 8.1.5.* Redwood City, CA, 1999.

[Ora 99b]   Oracle Corp.: *Oracle8i Spatial User's Guide and Reference, Rel. 8.1.5.* Redwood City, CA, 1999.

[PS 93]   Preparata F. P., Shamos M. I.: *Computational Geometry: An Introduction.* 5th ed., Springer, 1993.

[Ram 97]   Ramaswamy S.: *Efficient Indexing for Constraint and Temporal Databases.* Proc. 6th Int. Conf. on Database Theory, LNCS 1186, 419-431, 1997.

[RS 99]   Ravada S., Sharma J.: *Oracle8i Spatial: Experiences with Extensible Databases.* Proc. 6th Int. Symp. on Large Spatial Databases, LNCS 1651, 355-359, 1999.

[Sam 90a]   Samet H.: *The Design and Analysis of Spatial Data Structures.* Reading, MA: Addison-Wesley, 1990.

[Sam 90b]   Samet H.: *Applications of Spatial Data Structures.* Reading, MA: Addison-Wesley, 1990.

[SOL 94]   Shen H., Ooi B. C., Lu H.: *The TP-Index: A Dynamic and Efficient Indexing Mechanism for Temporal Databases.* Proc. IEEE Int. Conf. on Data Engineering, 274-281, 1994.

[SRF 87]   Sellis T., Roussopoulos N., Faloutsos C.: *The R^+-Tree: A Dynamic Index for Multi-Dimensional Objects.* Proc. Int. Conf. on Very Large Databases, 507-518, 1987.

[TCG+ 93]   Tansel A. U., Clifford J., Gadia S., Jajodia S., Segev A., Snodgrass R.: *Temporal Databases: Theory, Design and Implementation.* Redwood City, CA, 1993.

Optimizing Multi-Feature Queries for Image Databases

Ulrich Güntzer
University of Tübingen
guentzer@informatik.uni-tuebingen.de

Wolf-Tilo Balke
University of Augsburg
balke@informatik.uni-augsburg.de

Werner Kießling
University of Augsburg
kiessling@informatik.uni-augsburg.de

Abstract

In digital libraries image retrieval queries can be based on the similarity of objects, using several feature attributes like shape, texture, color or text. Such multi-feature queries return a ranked result set instead of exact matches. Besides, the user wants to see only the k top-ranked objects. We present a new algorithm called Quick-Combine (European patent pending, nr. EP 00102651.7) for combining multi-feature result lists, guaranteeing the correct retrieval of the k top-ranked results. For score aggregation virtually any combining function can be used, including weighted queries. Compared to Fagin's algorithm we have developed an improved termination condition in tuned combination with a heuristic control flow adopting itself narrowly to the particular score distribution. Top-ranked results can be computed and output incrementally. We show that we can dramatically improve performance, in particular for non-uniform score distributions. Benchmarks on practical data indicate efficiency gains by a factor of 30. For very skewed data observed speed-up factors are even larger. These performance results scale through different database sizes and numbers of result sets to combine.

1 Introduction

In universal database systems the handling of multimedia data such as images, video or audio files poses an increasingly demanding problem. The query evaluation model typically does not retrieve a set of exact matches but rather a ranked result set, where an aggregated score is attached to each object returned. Only a few top-ranked results are normally of interest to the user. Imagine a traditional image archive where every image is labeled with captions like name, registration number and related information like the photographer's name or the image's size. To retrieve images this meta-information has to be known for each search. In times of digitization, these archives are increasingly replaced by modern image databases, but most systems still only focus on the related text information for retrieval instead of allowing users intuitively to describe the desired retrieval result. A natural query would for example ask for the top 10 images from the database that are most similar to a fixed image in terms of color, texture, etc.; a query type which is often referred to as 'query by visual example'.

Query optimization needs to be adapted to this essentially different query model for multimedia data. Some systems have already been implemented, e.g. visual retrieval systems like IBM's QBIC [FBF+94] or Virage's VIR [BFG+96]. Database applications and middlewares like GARLIC [CHS+95], VisualHarness [SSPM99], HERMES [SAB+99] or the HERON project [KEUB+98] have already started to use the capabilities of visual retrieval. A major challenge in all of these systems is that similarity between different objects cannot be defined precisely. To handle queries on similarity different kinds of information on the multimedia objects have to be stored. For example in the case of images this could be color histograms, features on textures and layout or related fulltext information describing the object. As similarity cannot be measured exactly, the form of the retrieval result likewise has to be adapted to the user's needs. Consider the following query returning only the top four objects from the HERON-database [KEUB+98], ranked according to their aggregated similarity score (cf. figure 1):

```
SELECT   top(4, images)
FROM     repository
RANK BY  average_color(images)
    SIMILAR TO average_color(ex1.pic)
  AND texture(images)
    SIMILAR TO texture(ex2.pic)
```

Queries on similarity do not have to focus on one single feature. In general multimedia queries will refer to at least some different features simultaneously. According to a potentially weighted combining function for each database object an *aggregated score value* is computed. The results are then sorted according to their scores and are returned with a *rank number* – the top-ranked object has the best score value of the entire database collection and so on. A

**Proceedings of the 26th VLDB Conference,
Cairo, Egypt, 2000.**

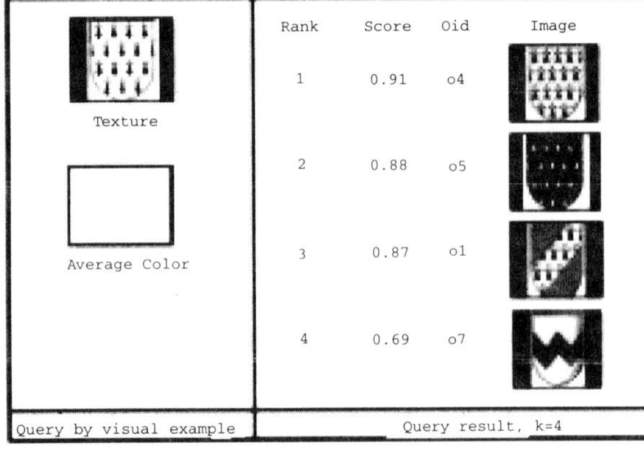

	Rank	Score	Oid	Image
Texture	1	0.91	o4	
	2	0.88	o5	
Average Color	3	0.87	o1	
	4	0.69	o7	
Query by visual example		Query result, k=4		

Figure 1: Query on color and texture with top 4 results

query focusing on only one feature is called *atomic*. Any complex multimedia query can be seen as a combination of atomic subqueries.

One optimization challenge is to combine the ranked results of atomic queries in order to determine the k overall best objects from the database. A naive approach would calculate the aggregated score for all database objects according to a given combining function. With growing size of the database, this obviously results in unacceptable response times, requiring a linear scan of the entire database. But as only the k top objects have to be returned, not all database objects have to be accessed. In this paper we will focus on efficient query combinations of atomic subqueries. We aim on solutions that guarantee a correct result set and at the same time minimize the number of objects to be accessed. Previous significant work in this area is due to Fagin [Fag96, Fag98], who gives an algorithm that guarantees a correct result set. This algorithm is asymptotically optimal in terms of database size with arbitrarily high probability, however only for uniform score distributions – which very rarely occur in practice.

The next section introduces the basic version of our new algorithm, called Quick-Combine. Section 3 extends Quick-Combine to cope with skewed data, which is ubiquitous in practice. In section 4 we will prove analytical results for the worst-case behavior of Quick-Combine. Section 5 reports the speed-up gain of Quick-Combine for skewed data, implying that a real performance breakthrough is achievable. The last section will give a summary of our results and an outlook on parallel work for query combination in heterogeneous environments.

2   A New Test of Termination

In [Fag96] an approach has been presented to process a complex query consisting of several atomic subqueries that may use any monotonous combining function, as for example the maximum or arithmetical mean. This algorithm correctly retrieves the k best objects in the database for any such combination of atomic queries. We will use Fagin's

algorithm as a yardstick throughout this paper.

In general atomic queries can be posed in two ways:

- The first type is searching the database and retrieving the objects in the database ordered by descending score for a single feature, which we refer to as enlarging an *atomic output stream* or *sorted access*.

- On the other hand a specific object's score in each atomic output stream could be of interest. This case is referred to as *random access*.

2.1   The Quick-Combine Algorithm (Basic Version)

Fagin's algorithm proceeds in two phases: The first producing atomic output streams and the second consisting of random accesses. Though both phases are necessary, the number of necessary accesses can be minimized with a new test of termination. For this new test we do not only use the information of ranks in output streams, but also the scores which are assigned to all objects in each output stream and the specific form of the combining function.

The following algorithm returns the top answer $(k = 1)$ to any combined query consisting of n atomic subqueries $q_1, ..., q_n$ aggregated using a monotone combining function F. Let x be an object and $s_i(x)$ be the score of x under subquery q_i. An object occuring in the result set of subquery q_i on rank j will be denoted $r_i(j)$.

Algorithm Quick-Combine (basic version):

1. For each subquery compute an atomic output stream consisting of pairs $(x, s_i(x))$ in descending order based on score and get some first elements.

2. For each object output by a stream that has not already been seen, get the missing scores for every subquery by random access and compute its aggregated score $S(x) = F(s_1(x), \ldots, s_n(x))$.

3. Check if the present top-scored object o_{top} is the best object of the database:

   Compare the aggregated score $S(o_{top})$ to the value of F for the minimum scores for each subquery that have been returned so far. Test:

$$S(o_{top}) \geq F(s_1(r_1(z_1)), \ldots, s_n(r_n(z_n))) \qquad (1)$$

   where z_i is the lowest rank that has already been seen in the output stream of q_i.

4. If inequality 1 holds, according to theorem 1 o_{top} can be returned as top object of the whole database. If inequality 1 does not hold, more elements of the output streams have to be evaluated. Therefore get the next elements of the streams and proceed as in step 2 with the newly seen objects.   □

2.2 Examples and Correctness

Consider the sample results of our query by visual example (cf. fig. 1). The following example will show how to get the top-scored object of the database ($k = 1$) using Quick-Combine:

s_1 : query on texture			
rank	1	2	3	...
score	0.96	0.88	0.85	...
object	o1	o2	o3	...

s_2 : query on avg. color			
rank	1	2	3	...
score	0.98	0.93	0.79	...
object	o4	o5	o6	...

The atomic output streams s_1 and s_2 are evaluated alternately. As objects in both streams are collected one after another, their aggregated score has to be calculated using for instance the arithmetical mean as combining function $F(s_1(o), s_2(o)) = \frac{s_1(o)+s_2(o)}{2}$. Therefore random accesses have to be made:

	object	o1	o4	o2	o5	...
random	output	s_2	s_1	s_2	s_1	...
accesses	stream					
	score	0.78	0.84	0.40	0.83	...

Now the test of termination can be performed using the lowest scores seen in each output stream. Due to the sorting of the streams these scores are the scores of the object that has been seen last in each stream:

test of termination				
last object seen	o1	o4	o2	o5
agg. score	0.87	0.91	0.64	0.88
$F(lowest\ scores)$	-	0.965	0.94	0.905
o_{top}	o1	o4	o4	o4

After accessing the fourth object the evaluation of streams can already be stopped as inequality (1) holds: $0.91 = S(o_{top}) \geq F(s_1(o2)), s_2(o5)) = 0.905$. Now o4 - the best object seen - can be returned as top-scored object of the entire database. Note that none of the objects accessed has been seen by sorted access in both streams.

Quick-Combine is applicable for every monotonous combining function, even in the case of maximum and minimum. In this case Fagin presents two special algorithms differing from his general approach. To show that Quick-Combine's test of termination will definitely return the most relevant object from the database the following theorem is stated:

Theorem 1 (Correctness of results)
If the output streams are evaluated until inequality 1 holds, the object providing the best aggregated score for all objects in any output stream so far has the best aggregated score of all objects in the database. (Proof omitted)

3 Efficiency Improvements for Skewed Data

Now we focus on a further gain of efficiency. We show that evaluating the test of termination twice can save random accesses. We also create a control flow that takes advantage of the distribution of scores in each stream, and address weighted queries. Then we generalize the test of termination to return the k best objects from the database and present the complete algorithm. After proving Quick-Combine's correctness at the end of this section, we will see that the top-scored objects can be successively returned, while the algorithm is still running.

3.1 Reducing the Number of Random Accesses

Without loss of generality we also focus on the case that only the best object of the database will be returned ($k = 1$). Taking a closer look at formula 1, it is obvious that the inequality may become true:

1. If its *right side is reduced*, i.e. any query stream q_j is enlarged and $s_j(r_j(z_j))$ is replaced by $s_j(r_j(z_j+1))$.

2. If its *left side is increased*, i.e. a newly seen object has a maximum aggregated score, sufficient to terminate the algorithm.

In Quick-Combine stream q_j is enlarged first, providing the new score $s_j(r_j(z_j + 1))$. If a new object has been seen, random accesses on $(n-1)$ score values are needed to calculate its aggregated score. The next theorem will show that, if according to case 1 formula 1 already holds before the random accesses are made, the aggregated score of the newly seen object can never be larger than the maximum score of the objects which have already been seen before enlarging q_j. Thus $(n - 1)$ random accesses can be saved, if the test of termination is performed not only after the random accesses, but also before.

Theorem 2 (Saving random accesses)
Let L be the set of objects that have already been seen and whose aggregated scores have been calculated. The aggregated score of any object o_{new} occurring in stream q_j at rank $z_j + 1$ that has been seen last by enlarging query stream q_j, will be less or equal to the maximum aggregated score of objects in L, if formula 1 holds by substituting $s_j(r_j(z_j))$ with $s_j(r_j(z_j + 1))$. (Proof omitted)

3.2 Control Flow for Evaluation of Streams

Quick-Combine considers the top-ranked element of each output stream before proceeding to the next ranked elements. As Quick-Combine uses not only ranks but also scores, a control flow based on the distribution of scores relative to the ranks on which they occur will decrease the number of objects accessed until termination. Of course this distribution has not to be the same in every atomic output stream. We present a heuristic approach to determine in which order streams with different distributions should be evaluated to gain a maximum effect. As a heuristic measure of efficiency a simple rule can be stated:

Accessing less objects to make formula 1 hold means less database accesses and thus results in a more efficient algorithm.

Obviously, there are two ways to make formula 1 hold:

- Initializing the algorithm with some first ranks of each stream helps to *increase the left side.* An object that has been seen later in any output stream generally has to do better in at least one other stream to get the maximum aggregated score, i.e. the chance that it has already been seen on the first few ranks in a different output stream is getting more and more probable. Thus, before a certain query stream should be preferred for further evaluation, it is advisable to analyze some first objects of each stream.

- To *decrease the right side* quickly consider the distribution of scores relative to the ranks on which they occur. This distribution can totally differ in each output stream. Though in all output streams the scores are falling monotonously with declining ranks, there may be streams where the scores only slightly change with decreasing ranks. Streams starting with high score values but declining rapidly may exist or even output streams with scores not changing at all. As we want to force the decline of the right side, streams showing a behavior of declining scores most rapidly relative to the ranks should be preferred for evaluation.

For a more efficient combining algorithm a control mechanism preferring the evaluation of rapidly declining output streams is needed. An obvious measure is the derivative of functions correlating score values to the ranks on which they occur for each output stream. Since these functions are discrete, their behavior can be estimated using the difference between the pth last and the last output score value assuming that there are at least p elements in the stream. Of course the same p has to be used for any stream to provide comparability. A larger value for p better estimates an output stream's global behavior, small values detect more local changes in a stream.

The above considerations are not only useful for equally weighted queries. An indicator for streams with low weights should naturally be regarded less important than indicators for highly weighted streams which should get prior evaluation. As the weights can be expressed in the combining function F (e.g. a weighted arithmetical mean), a simple measure for the importance of each stream q_i is the partial derivative of the combining function $\frac{\partial F}{\partial x_i}$. Thus in the weighted case an indicator for any stream q_i containing more than p elements can be calculated as follows:

$$\Delta_i = \left| \frac{\partial F}{\partial x_i} \right| \cdot (s_i(r_i(z_i - p)) - s_i(r_i(z_i))) \qquad (2)$$

3.3 The Quick-Combine Algorithm (Full Version)

Now we generalize Quick-Combine to a result set containing the k best matches for any $k \in \mathbb{N}$ and implement

our control flow. Under the assumption that there are at least k objects in each stream, it returns the top k answers to any complex query consisting of n atomic subqueries $q_1, ..., q_n$. For each subquery a ranked result set consisting of pairs $(x, s_i(x))$ in descending sorted order based on score is computed where x is an object and $s_i(x)$ is the score of x under subquery q_i.

Algorithm Quick-Combine (full version):

0. *Initialization:* Get the first p results for each subquery, where p is a suitable natural number. Compute an indicator Δ_i for each query stream q_i according to equation 2.

1. *Random access for new objects:* For each new object output by any stream that has not already been seen previously, get the missing scores for every subquery by random access. For each new object there are $(n - 1)$ random accesses necessary. Objects that have already been seen before can be ignored.

2. *Calculation of aggregated scores:* For any new object x that has been seen compute the aggregated score $S(x) = F(s_1(x), \ldots, s_n(x))$.

3. *First test of termination:* Check if the k top-scored objects are already in what has been seen so far: Compare the aggregated score of the present k top-scored objects to the value of the combining function with the lowest scores seen for each feature. Check if there are at least k objects whose aggregated score is larger or equal than the aggregated minimum scores per feature:

$$|\{x|S(x) \geq F(s_1(r_1(z_1)), .., s_n(r_n(z_n)))\}| \geq k \quad (3)$$

If inequality 3 holds, according to theorem 3 the k top-scored objects can be returned as top objects of the whole database.

4. *Enlarging an atomic output stream:* If inequality 3 does not hold, more elements of the atomic output streams have to be evaluated. Therefore get the next element of the stream having the maximum Δ (if the maximum Δ is reached for two or more streams any of them can be chosen randomly).

5. *Second test of termination:* Check if inequality 3 holds using the new object's score. If the inequality holds, return the k top-scored objects.

6. *Indicator computation:* Calculate a new Δ for the enlarged stream. Proceed as in step 1 with the newly seen object. $\qquad \square$

As a control mechanism the indicator Δ approximates the local behaviour of the distribution of absolute score values relative to the ranks on which they appear. Again we will have to show that no relevant database object is missed by Quick-Combine:

Theorem 3 (Correctness of Results)
If the output streams are evaluated until inequality 3 holds, the k objects providing the best aggregated scores that appeared in any output stream so far have the best aggregated score of all objects in the database.

Proof: *It is to show that no object that has not been seen can have a larger aggregated score than the top k objects that have been seen.*

Let inequality 3 hold, x be any of the top k objects and o be an object from the database that has not been seen yet in any of the output streams. Then due to the sorting of the streams the atomic scores of o satisfy

$$s_1(o) \leq s_1(r_1(z_1)), \ldots, s_n(o) \leq s_n(r_n(z_n))$$

and therefore due to the monotony of F and formula 3:
$$\begin{aligned} S(o) &= F(s_1(o), \ldots, s_n(o)) \\ &\leq F(s_1(r_1(z_1)), \ldots, s_n(r_n(z_n))) \\ &\leq F(s_1(x), \ldots, s_n(x)) = S(x). \end{aligned} \qquad \square$$

Theorem 3 shows that the first found object satisfying inequality 3 always is the top-scored object of the whole collection. Thus it can be delivered to the user as soon as it is found, which of course also applies to all following ranks up to k, when the algorithm finally terminates. If the user is already satisfied by the first few ranks, the query execution for large values of k can be stopped during processing. We therefore state the following corollary to theorem 3:

Corollary 1 (Successive Output of Results)
Since Quick-Combine will run until k objects that satisfy formula 3 are successively found, for $k > 1$ the first objects can already be returned while the algorithm is still running.

4 Complexity for Uniform Distributions

In this section we focus on the efficiency of Quick-Combine compared to Fagin's algorithm. In particular we will show that Quick-Combine's complexity is upper-bounded by the complexity of Fagin. We give a general geometrical interpretation of efficiency issues and present improvement factors even in the rare case of uniform distribution of score values.

4.1 Worst Case Complexity

The following theorem will show that Quick-Combine will never access more distinct objects than Fagin's algorithm. To this end the number of distinct objects that Fagin's algorithm collects in its first phase is compared to the number of distinct objects collected by Quick-Combine.

Theorem 4 (Upper-Bounding)
Given n atomic output streams sorted in descending order. Formula 3 holds, if all streams have been evaluated at least as far enough that Fagin's algorithm terminates, i.e. that there is a set L of k objects delivered by all streams.

Proof: *Let $o_1, \ldots, o_k \in L$ be k different objects that have been output by each stream and F be any monotonous combining function. Due to the descending order of scores in every stream any atomic score $s_i(o_j)$ $(1 \leq i \leq n, 1 \leq j \leq k)$ satisfies:*

$$s_1(o_j) \geq s_1(r_1(z_1)), \ldots, s_n(o_j) \geq s_n(r_n(z_n))$$

and thus due to the monotonocity of F:

$$\begin{aligned} S(o_j) &= F(s_1(o_j), \ldots, s_n(o_j)) \geq \\ &F(s_1(r_1(z_1)), \ldots, s_n(r_n(z_n))) \end{aligned}$$

for each of the objects $o_1, \ldots, o_k$, i.e. equation 3 holds. $\square$

4.2 Geometrical Interpretation

According to [PF95], a geometrical model for combining query results could be as shown in figure 2 for the case $n = 2$. If each atomic subquery is mapped onto an axis divided into score values from 0 (no match) to 1 (exact match), each object in the database can be represented by a point in n-dimensional space.

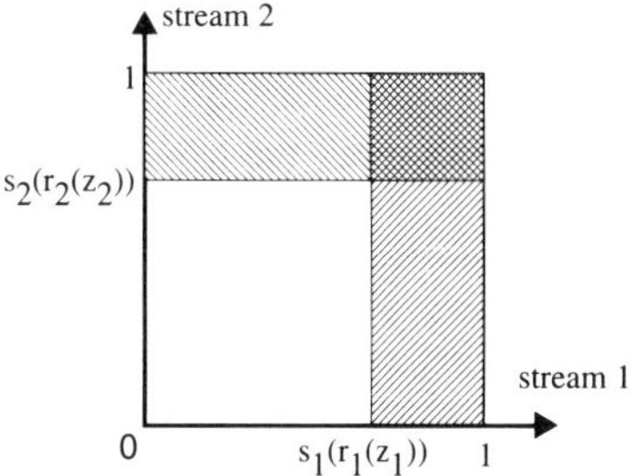

Figure 2: Combining two atomic output streams

Evaluating results of an atomic subquery by ranks can be represented by moving a hyperplane orthogonal to its axis from 1 downwards to 0. The order in which objects are collected by the hyperplane can exactly be mapped onto the ranks on which they occur. For example consider figure 2 and assume that output stream i for subquery i has been evaluated for all objects o that satisfy $s_i(o) \geq s_i(r_i(z_i))$, i.e. all objects have been retrieved from stream i, whoses scores is larger or equal to the score of the object occurring on rank z_i in stream i $(i = 1, 2)$. The areas evaluated from stream 1 and stream 2 have an intersection containing the top-scored objects already seen in both streams. Fagin's algorithm in its first phase collects k objects that occur in the dark-shaded area. Of course all the objects collected in the shaded areas need random accesses, as they all have been seen in the first phase.

Evaluations of aggregated scores by a *monotonous* combining function can also be represented by moving a hypersurface collecting objects while moving over the area. As the k objects collected first should have the top aggregated scores and thus can be returned as correct retrieval result, the hypersurface has to be orthogonal to the optimal direction starting at the optimal level.

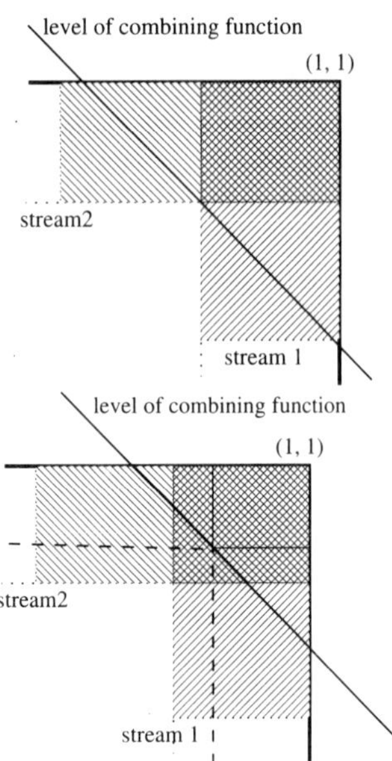

Figure 3: The arithmetical mean as combining function for Fagin's algorithm (upper) and Quick-Combine (lower)

To return a correct result the hypersurface has to collect the first k objects. Since Fagin's algorithm insists that there are at least k objects in the dark-shaded area, the hypersurface only sweeps objects with already calculated aggregated scores. Thus no relevant object can be missed. But depending on the combining function the area and thus the number of objects in Fagin's algorithm, for which aggregated scores are calculated, might be far too large. Consider for example figure 3 (left) showing the arithmetical mean as combining function. The hypersurface can collect any object till the lower left corner of the dark-shaded area, as all objects in this area have been seen and also all aggregated scores for these objects have been calculated.

There are at least k objects in the dark-shaded area, but also all the objects in the two light-shaded triangles between the hyperplane and the dark-shaded area are collected. For e.g. uniform distributions a triangle with the same area as the dark-shaded area would also guarantee the correctness of results, but would minimize the calculations of aggregated scores and the random accesses needed, cf. figure 3 (right). Unlike Fagin's algorithm Quick-Combine only concentrates on this minimized area. As shown in figure 3 (right) for the case $n = 2$, in Quick-Combine streams 1 and 2 would only be enlarged down to the dashed lines.

4.3 Improvement Analysis for Uniform Distributions

Fagin has proven the important result that his algorithm is expected to be asymptotically optimal for independent output streams under uniform score distribution. Though uniform distributions rarely occur in practice, it can be stated that also in this case Quick-Combine improves Fagin's algorithm by minimizing the number of object accesses.

For the analysis our geometrical interpretation is used. With growing dimension, i.e. the number of atomic subqueries to be combined, the dark-shaded area in our model evolves to a high dimensional cuboid whose volume determines the number of objects to calculate aggregated scores for. Depending on the combining function also in high dimensional cases this cuboid is contained by a geometrical figure guaranteeing correctness for more than k objects.

Consider the n-dimensional case with the arithmetical mean as combining function and the output streams evaluated down to score s. Then the triangles of figure 3 have to be generalized to polyhedra $S_{n,s}$, the dark-shaded square to a n-dimensional cube $W_{n,s}$ and the light-shaded rectangles to n-dimensional cuboids. The polyhedron $S_{n,s}$ is formed by the set of all points on or above the combining function's hypersurface $\frac{1}{n} \sum_{i=1}^{n} x_i = s$. The next theorem shows that the cube's volume shrinks rapidly with growing dimensions in proportion to the polyhedron's volume.

Theorem 5 (Ratio between Cube and Polyhedron)
Let W_n be the n-dimensional cube in $[0,1]^n$ with $W_n = \{(x_1, \ldots, x_n) \mid 0 \leq x_i \leq \frac{1}{n}$ for $i = 1, \ldots, n\}$ and $Vol(W_n)$ be its volume. Let further S_n denote the polyhedron $S_n = \{(x_1, \ldots, x_n) \mid 0 \leq \frac{1}{n} \sum_{i=1}^{n} x_i \leq \frac{1}{n}\}$ and $Vol(S_n)$ be its volume.
Then the ratio $\frac{Vol(W_n)}{Vol(S_n)}$ is equal to $\frac{n!}{n^n}$. (Proof omitted)

To get a more precise impression of the efficiency gain one has to compare the total number of objects accessed by Fagin's algorithm and Quick-Combine. Therefore the volume of the dark- and light-shaded areas (cf. figure 2) of Fagin's algorithm has to be compared to the corresponding areas needed by Quick-Combine using a polyhedron of the same volume as Fagin's cube. Increasing volumes of the cuboids obviously causes more necessary object accesses and the ratio between these volumes is also the improvement factor for the number of objects accessed.

Theorem 6 (Improvement for Uniform Distributions)
The total number of objects accessed by Quick-Combine using the polyhedron $\tilde{S}_n$, which has the same volume as the cube W_n needed by Fagin's algorithm, is $\left(\frac{n}{\sqrt[n]{n!}}\right)$ times smaller than the number of objects accessed by Fagin's algorithm for uniformly distributed scores. (Proof omitted)

With Stirling's formula the improvement factor is asymptotically equal to $\frac{n}{\sqrt[n]{n!}} \approx \frac{e}{\sqrt[n]{\sqrt{2\pi n}}} \overset{(n \to \infty)}{\longrightarrow} e$. Quick-Combine thus results in an efficiency gain of 2.72 with increasing n. As not only visual features determine a multimedia query, but also ranked results from text retrieval, typical values for n are between five and ten. Table 1 shows improvement factors for some practical values of n:

n	3	4	5	6	7	8	9
	1.64	1.81	1.92	2.01	2.07	2.13	2.17

Table 1: Improvement factors for object accesses in the uniformly distributed case.

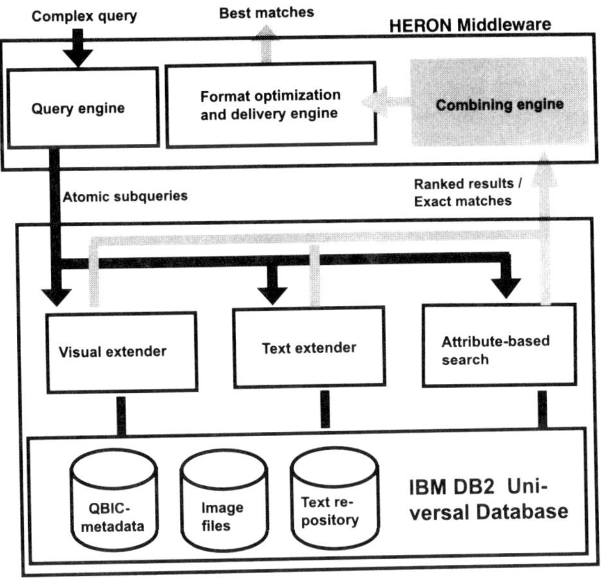

Figure 4: Architecture of the HERON system

5 Speed-up Results for Skewed Data

Fagin's optimality results – plus the improvements of Quick-Combine – are only valid for the very unlikely case of uniform score distributions. In practice, however, skewed data is prevalent. Thus the name of the game is about efficiency speed-ups for such practical, skewed data. We will first report performance results from practical data, followed by extensive synthetic benchmarks.

5.1 Benchmark Results for Practical Data

The HERON system [KEUB+98] has been used to process a set of atomic queries on heraldic images. Besides components for query composition, user specific image delivery and efficient format conversions, it features a combining engine that can use different visual retrieval systems and databases (cf. fig. 4). The combining engine implements Quick-Combine. For our experiments we used IBM DB2 V 5.2 and QBIC technology [FBF+94] for visual retrieval.

To measure the gain of efficiency the number of objects to be retrieved was compared to the average number of objects which the combining algorithm had to access. As described in section 4 the number of objects accessed determines the number of random accesses that are needed to calculate aggregated scores and thus forms the main computational costs. To be exact, Fagin's algorithm will not need random accesses for all the objects, but as k objects have already been seen in all atomic output streams, their aggregated values can directly be calculated. Nevertheless, those small number of random accesses have proven to be rather negligible even in the case $n = 3$.

We set up a scenario for the combination of three atomic subqueries over a repository of 230 heraldic images from the HERON database. The randomly chosen subqueries focused on the image's average color, textures and color histograms, i.e. $n = 3$; as combining function we chose the arithmetical mean and used an indicator computation for $p = 3$. Figure 5 shows the average experimental results for 30 different queries. The output streams were statistically independent as e.g. the color of an object is not supposed to be related to its shape or texture.The number of objects accessed is plotted against the number of objects k to be returned. Since the scores are *not distributed uniformly*, Fagin's algorithm accesses far more objects. Obviously, the early use of the combination function's composition and the use of our control flow in Quick-Combine results in a higher gain of efficiency especially for larger values of k. For practical values of k ($k \leq 50$) Quick-Combine even accesses *30 times less objects* than Fagin's algorithm.

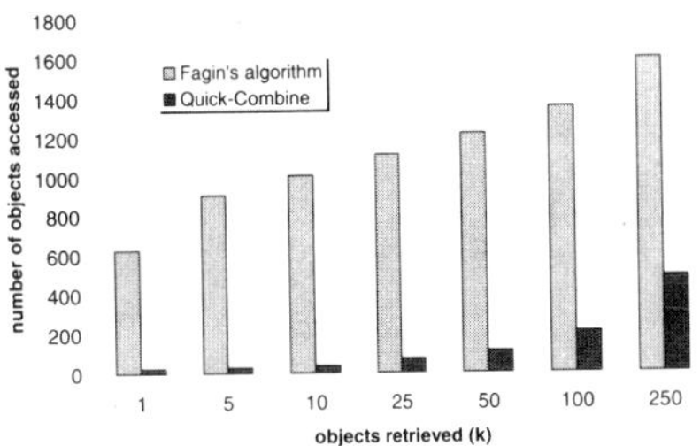

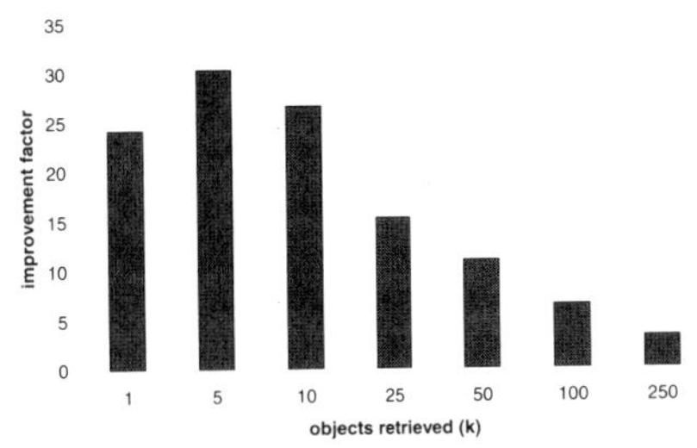

Figure 5: Benchmark results on real data

5.2 Benchmark Results for Synthetic Data

From our practical tests we gained insight into distributions that really occur in image retrieval. We argue that typical distributions from visual retrieval systems are a low percentage of objects having high and medium score values and a high percentage having very low scores. If text retrieval is included the percentage having high and medium scores even decreases. We extensively tested these types of distributions on synthetic data for two databases with $N = 10000$ and $N = 100000$ objects generating different score distributions. The performance of Quick-Combine changes with variations of the number k of objects to return, the number n of streams to combine, the database size N and the skewedness of the distribution. The results of Quick-Combine are always compared to the result of Fagin's algorithm. The efficiency measures to compare are threefold: The number of distinct database objects accessed, the number of necessary sorted accesses and the number of necessary random accesses.

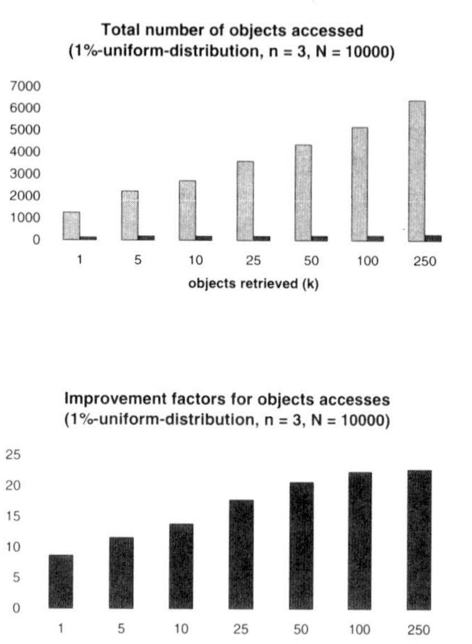

Figure 6: Average number of object accesses for skewed distributions

Our first test scenario focused on a slightly skewed score distribution typical for content-based image retrieval. One percent of database objects have high or medium score values (uniformly distributed), the rest shows values smaller than 0.1. On the smaller database ($N = 10000$) we combined three streams ($n = 3$). As can be seen in the diagrams (Fig.6, Fig.7 and Fig.8) we measured the number of accesses of different objects and the number of sorted and random accesses for varying values of k. Fagin's algorithm (light columns) on the average always needs to access far more objects than Quick-Combine (dark columns). On the right diagram the respective average improvement factors can be seen. For all three types of accesses they range between 10 and 20. Obviously the improvement scales with varying k as for $k = 250$ already 2.5% of the entire database size is retrieved.

Observation: In *all our experiments* the ratio of sorted and random accesses between Fagin's algorithm and Quick-Combine was nearly the same as the respective ratio of distinct object accesses. Thus in the further analysis we will concentrate on these accesses and omit the diagrams for sorted and random accesses.

The next experiments focused on even more skewed score distributions (Fig. 9). A score distribution of 0.1% high and medium scores and 99.9% of low scores was generated. Here average improvement factors around 100 can be observed for $k \leq 25$ as Quick-Combine adopts itself to the specific distribution. The improvement for $k \geq 50$ in

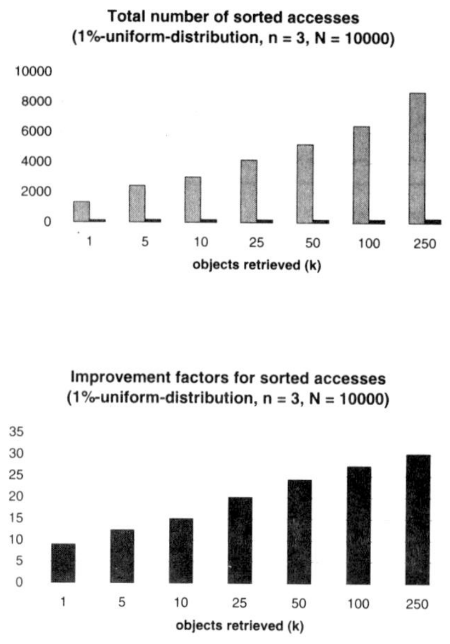

Figure 7: Average number of sorted accesses for skewed distributions

this case is minimal since with $N = 10000$ and $n = 3$ there are only 30 objects in the database having noticable scores.

The next diagram (Fig.10) shows the scalability to large databases. A database with $N = 100000$ was generated showing the same score distribution as above. Note that for the retrieval of 0.25% of database size Quick-Combine accesses little objects, whereas Fagin's algorithm already accesses a third of the entire database objects. Average improvement factors in this case range from 50 to 120.

The last experiment (Fig. 11) analyzes the scalabilty of Quick-Combine, if a varying number n of streams is combined. We combined up to 10 different streams using the same database size and score distribution as in our first experiment. Here we observed average improvement factors ranging from 10 to 20. Note that Fagin's algorithm accesses almost all database objects if more than 5 output streams are combined.

5.3 Discussion of Overall Performance Results

As stated in [Fag96] Fagin's algorithm is expected to access $k^{\frac{1}{n}} N^{(1-\frac{1}{n})}$ objects. As shown before Quick-Combine is expected to access $\left(\frac{\sqrt[n]{n!}}{n}\right)$ less objects in the uniformly distributed case. But this case is very rare in practice. To get an impression on practical efficiency issues the experiments on real or synthetic data with more practical score distributions had to be compared.

- In all our experiments with real and synthetic data the number of objects Fagin's algorithm accesses is by far higher than the number accessed by Quick-Combine.

- The number of sorted and random accesses in Fagin's

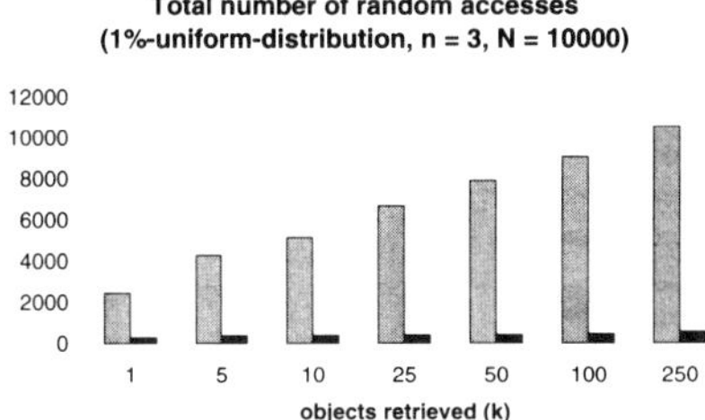

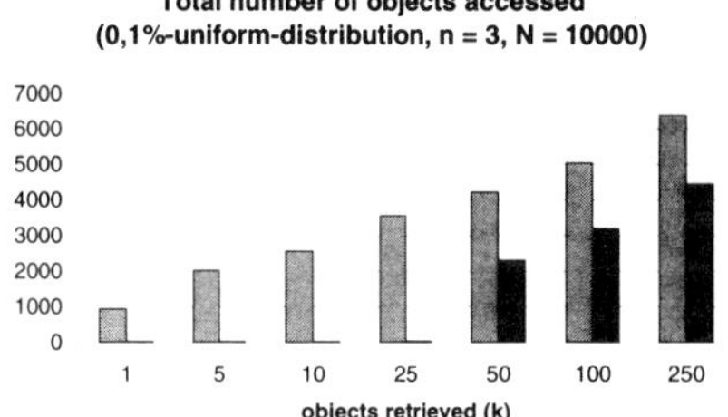

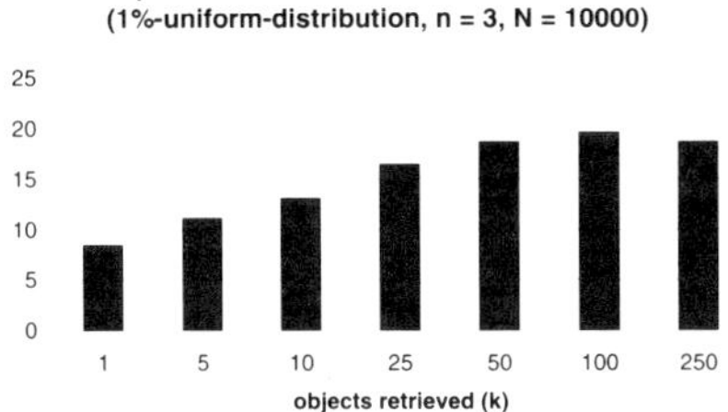

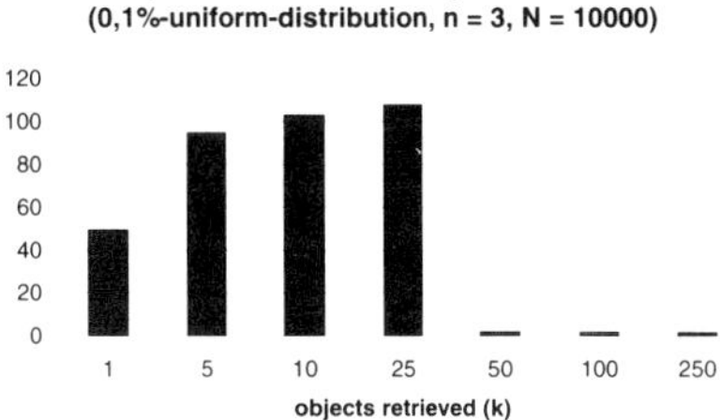

Figure 8: Average number of random accesses for skewed distributions

Figure 9: Average number of object accesses for very skewed distributions

algorithm is also always considerably higher than in Quick-Combine.

- Quick-Combine scales both with growing values for k and with increasing number n of streams to combine.

- Quick-Combine is very efficient even for large database sizes.

- Quick-Combine is also highly efficient for very skewed score distributions.

Fagin's work also strongly influenced statistical approaches as [CG97], for which experimental results show that the number of objects retrieved can be considerably smaller than in Fagin's algorithm. However, such approaches gain performance in exchange of a guaranteed correctness of results. With Quick-Combine we can get both: High performance and correct results.

6 Summary and Outlook

In this paper we proposed an algorithm – called Quick-Combine – to combine multi-feature queries that are typical for the use in modern digital libraries and digital image archives. We examined previous work in this area and compared our approach to Fagin's algorithm presented in [Fag96]. Quick-Combine efficiently retrieves the k most relevant database objects with guaranteed correctness for every monotonous combining function. Measuring the number of necessary database accesses, our theoretical analysis as well as experimental results indicate that Quick-Combine is considerably more efficient than Fagin's algorithm. This speed-up of Quick-Combine compared

to Fagin's algorithm increases with growing skewedness of score distributions from a factor around 2 towards one or two orders of magnitude. A real live benchmark with heraldic images showed speed-up factors around 30.

These remarkable benchmark results suggest that with Quick-Combine a real performance breakthrough for content-based image retrieval in large image databases is achievable. Definitely so, high-speed iterators for sorted accesses (relying on efficient multi-dimensional indexes) and fast access methods for random accesses are essential. Parallel execution of several sorted streams (e.g. by Java threads) can be done in addition. Given all of that fast Internet access to very large image databases, like commercial digital photo archives, is in sight now.

Acknowledgements

We are grateful to Matthias Wagner, Thomas Birke and Achim Leubner for helpful comments and suggestions. The HERON-project is funded by the German Research Foundation DFG within the strategic research initiative "Distributed Processing and Exchange of Digital Documents". The European patent is supported by the DFG Ideenwerkstatt. The database software applied in the HERON system is granted within IBM's program "DB2 For Educational Purpose".

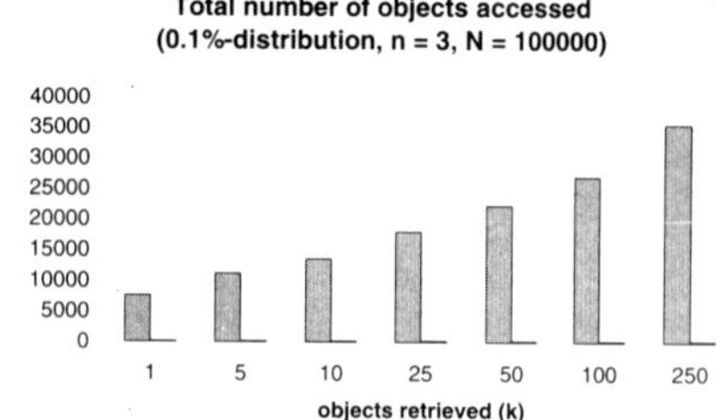

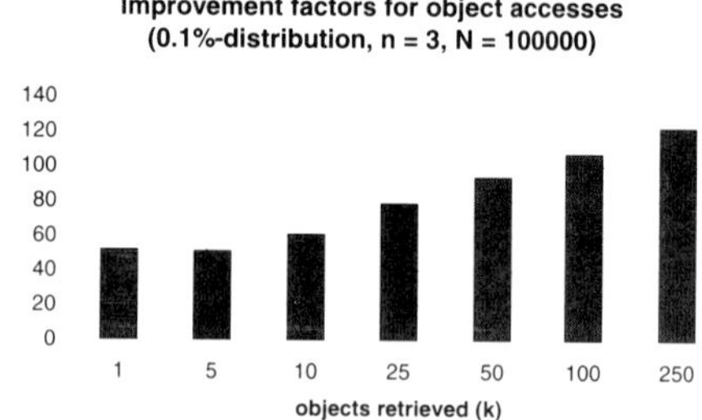

Figure 10: Average number of object accesses for large databases

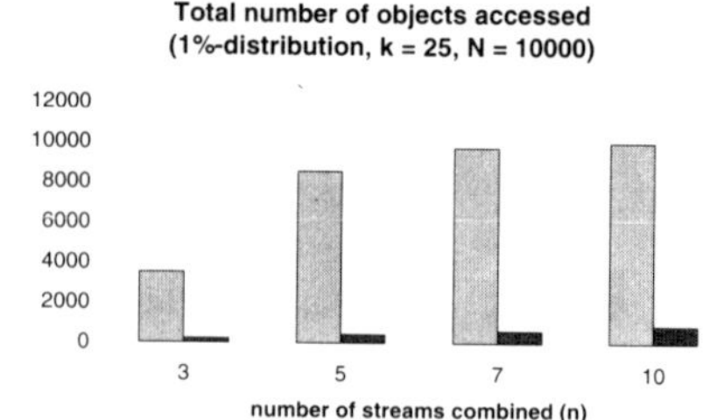

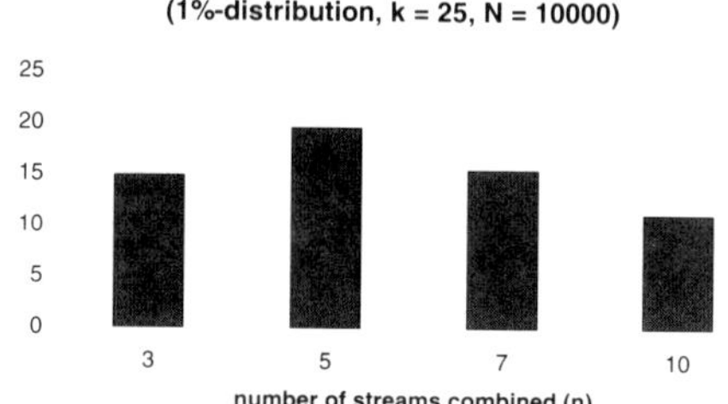

Figure 11: Average number of object accesses with varying number of streams to combine

References

[BFG+96] J. Bach, C. Fuller, A. Gupta, A. Hampapur, B. Horowitz, R. Humphrey, R. Jain, and C-F. Shu. Virage image search engine: An open framework for image management. In *Storage and Retrieval for Image and Video Databases (SPIE) 1996*, pages 76–87, 1996.

[CG97] S. Chaudhuri and L. Gravano. Optimizing queries over multimedia repositories. In *16th ACM Symposium on Principles of Database Systems*, pages 91–102, Tucson, 1997. ACM.

[CHS+95] M. Carey, L. Haas, P. Schwarz, M. Arya, W. Cody, R. Fagin, M. Flickner, A. Luniewski, W. Niblack, D. Petkovic, J. Thomas, J. Williams, and E. Wimmers. Towards heterogeneous multimedia information systems: The GARLIC approach. In *5th Intern. Ws. on Research Issues in Data Engineering: Distr. Object Management*, pages 124–131. IEEE-CS, 1995.

[Fag96] R. Fagin. Combining fuzzy information from multiple systems. In *15th ACM Symposium on Principles of Database Systems*, pages 216–226, Montreal, 1996. ACM.

[Fag98] R. Fagin. Fuzzy queries in multimedia database systems. In *17th ACM Symposium on Principles of Database Systems*, pages 1–10, Seattle, 1998. ACM.

[FBF+94] C. Faloutsos, R. Barber, M. Flickner, J. Hafner, W. Niblack, D. Petkovic, and W. Equitz. Efficient and effective querying by image content. *Journal of Intelligent Information Systems*, 3:231–262, 1994.

[KEUB+98] W. Kießling, K. Erber-Urch, W.-T. Balke, T. Birke, and M. Wagner. The HERON project — multimedia database support for history and human sciences. In J. Dassow and R. Kruse, editors, *Proc. of the GI Annual Conf. INFORMATIK'98*, pages 309–318. Springer, 1998.

[PF95] U. Pfeifer and N. Fuhr. Efficient processing of vague queries using a data stream approach. In *18th Annual International ACM SIGIR Conference on Research and Development in Information Retrieval*, pages 189–197, Seattle, 1995. ACM.

[SAB+99] VS. Subrahmanian, S. Adali, A. Brink, J. Lu, A. Rajput, T. Rogers, R. Ross, and C. Ward. HERMES: Heterogeneous reasoning and mediator system. Technical report, University of Maryland, 1999.

[SSPM99] A. Sheth, K. Shah, K. Parasuraman, and S. Mudumbai. Searching distributed and heterogeneous digital media: The VisualHarness approach. In *8th Conf. on Database Semantics - Semantic Issues in Multimedia Systems*, pages 311–330. Kluwer, 1999.

Contrast Plots and P-Sphere Trees: Space vs. Time in Nearest Neighbor Searches

Jonathan Goldstein

Microsoft Research

`jongold@microsoft.com`

Raghu Ramakrishnan

Department of Computer Sciences University of Wisconsin-Madison

`raghu@cs.wisc.edu`

Abstract

In recent years, many researchers have focused on finding efficient solutions to the nearest neighbor (i.e. NN) problem. While there have been many efforts to find faster than linear scan processing strategies for these tasks, there has been no success at solving the problem for high dimensionality.

While previous work shows that the problem can't be solved efficiently in general, we present a technique for either in-memory or secondary storage that is guaranteed to perform well in the "good" situations previously described. Furthermore, it is the first NN strategy that allows a database administrator to easily trade space for execution time. In addition, the space/time performance for a particular dataset can be easily predicted by examining one characteristic the data. Finally, there are variants of the strategy that perform far better than the tested alternative techniques in all tested scenarios.

1   Introduction

In recent years, many researchers have focused on finding efficient solutions to the *nearest neighbor (NN)* problem, defined as follows: *Given a collection of data points and a query point in a d-dimensional metric space, find the data point that is closest to the query point.* Particular interest has focused on solving this problem in high dimensional spaces, which arise from techniques that approximate (e.g., see [32]) complex data—such as images (e.g., [18, 37, 38, 28, 38, 30, 34, 21, 4]), sequences (e.g., [3, 2]), video (e.g., [18]), and shapes (e.g., [18, 39, 34, 29])—with long "feature" vectors. Similarity queries are performed by taking a given complex object, approximating it with a high dimensional vector to obtain the query point, and

determining the data point closest to it in the underlying feature space.

While there have been many efforts to find faster than linear scan processing strategies for these tasks, there has been no success at solving the problem for arbitrary high dimensional workloads. The reasons for this lack of success have, in the past several years, become more clearly understood.

Indeed, in [13], we prove that there is no faster than linear scan processing strategy to solve the problem for a wide variety of high dimensional workloads. We also establish workload based performance bounds for the problem itself. They show that a performance limiting feature of the problem is the tendency, in high dimensionality, of data and query points to all become equidistant. This effect can be summarized visually by examining the distribution of the distances between data points and a typical query point. We will call such distributions **contrast distributions** and graphs of such distance distributions **contrast plots**.

This paper introduces several NN processing techniques. These techniques are all predicated on a very important requirement: that a random sample of the query distribution is available at index build time. Exploiting this requirement, we create a class of NN processing techniques with new properties and capabilities. For instance, the techniques presented in this paper have performance that is easy to characterize in terms of contrast distributions. In addition, having sample query points allows us to integrate redundancy into the index itself to easily trade space for time; a tradeoff that is necessary to overcome problems associated with dimensionality for range queries ([23]). This redundancy, when used with a non-deterministic (but highly accurate) variant of the techniques presented here, allows unparalleled search performance on the "hard cases" identified in [13]. Our techniques can be used with any distance metric and speed up NN processing over both in memory and disk based data.

The nature of the easily characterizable behavior of our techniques has an interesting repercussion. With the additional assumption that query distribution follows data distribution, we can prove that contrast distribution spread is the primary performance limiting feature of the nearest neighbor problem. We do this by relating the behavior of the strictly worst performing variant of our techniques to the theoretical performance bounds established in [13] for the problem.

In [13], we showed that as the spread of the contrast distribution for a particular workload narrows, a sub linear NN strategy for processing that workload becomes harder

---

[0] **Proceedings of the 26th VLDB Conference, Cairo, Egypt, 2000.**

and harder to find, until a threshold is reached at which there is no sub linear NN strategy. The strategy described in this paper can be viewed as a constructive proof of the implication proven in [13] going the opposite direction. When combined, the two results create an "if and only if" relationship between contrast distribution spread and attainable performance. There are two important aspects of this result, the first is that it establishes contrast as not only *a* limiting factor, but *the* primary limiting factor of NN processing techniques in situations where data and query distributions are equivalent. The second is that it shows that the techniques presented in this paper perform according to the inherent difficulty of the problem (i.e. there is no unnecessary "bad" behavior).

This paper is divided into 7 sections. Section 2 describes the two simplest and worst performing variants of the algorithm. The better performing of these variants allows one to trade some user controlled level of accuracy for improved performance. Section 3 contains the highlights of our theoretical analysis of the worst performing of the algorithm variants. Section 4 contains a description of the best performing variant of our NN processing strategy. Section 5 contains a performance analysis of all variants of the algorithm presented in the previous sections while Section 6 discusses related work. This paper finishes with the conclusions in Section 7.

2 P-Sphere Trees

The query processing strategy presented in this paper involves building and searching a structure called a P-Sphere tree (probabilistic sphere tree). This structure is built using the entire dataset and assumes that a set of sample query points Q is available at index build time.

Note that in situations where query distribution follows the data distribution, we can use a random sample of the data points themselves as our sample query points. This is frequently a valid assumption for high dimensional similarity/matching problems. For instance, if we are trying to match fingerprints or retina prints for building security, queries will typically be a random sample of the people that work in the building, whose fingerprints were used to generate the database in the first place.

The structure will be built in such a manner that approximately some user specified percentage of the time, a search of the structure will yield a provably (at query run time) correct answer. More precisely, the user can specify the 95% confidence interval for the percentage of the time that a search of the structure yields a provably correct answer. The narrower the interval, the longer index construction takes. From now on, we will describe the accuracy of such trees as $u_{95\%}$ accurate since the user can control a 95% confidence interval around some desired level of accuracy u.

When a search of the structure doesn't yield a provably correct answer, the next best strategy (possibly a linear scan) will be performed. Thus, while we may sometimes need to perform a search using some alternate, worse performing technique, assuming there is acceptable contrast, on average we will get much better performance.

2.1 The Anatomy of a P-Sphere Tree

All P-Sphere trees have the same basic two level structure (see Figure 1). The top level is a single large node that contains a series of <*sphere descriptor, leaf page pointer*> pairs. Each leaf of the index contains **all** data points that lie within the sphere described in the corresponding sphere descriptor from the top level. All leaves cover the same amount of data (not the same amount of hypervolume). For instance, each sphere in Figure 1 covers LS data points.

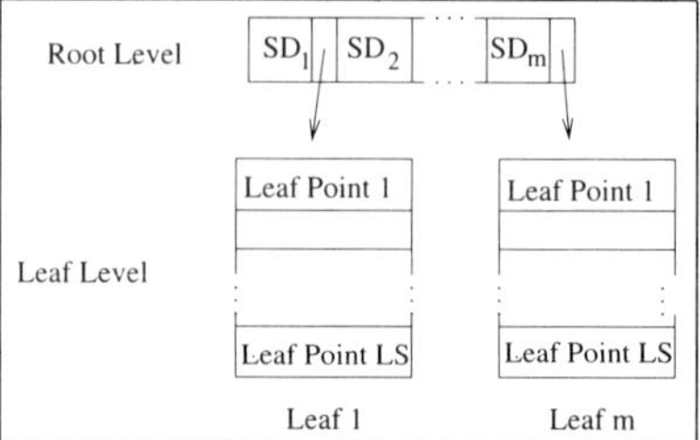

Figure 1: Anatomy of a P-Sphere Tree

Note that since each leaf contains all points that lie within a spherical subsection of the data space, spatial overlap amongst the leaves may lead to redundancy. Also, there is no guarantee that the entire data space will be covered by the sphere descriptors in the top level. As a result, there is no guarantee that all data points of the original data set will be in the generated P-Sphere tree.

2.2 Searching P-Sphere Trees

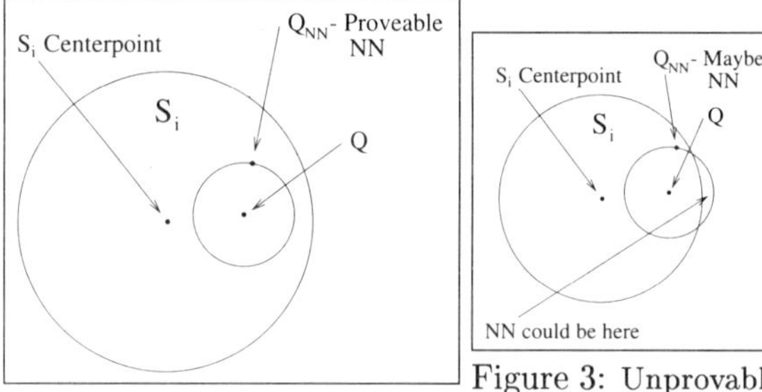

Figure 2: Provable NN

Figure 3: Unprovable NN

The search algorithm for P-sphere trees is very simple and involves finding the closest point to the query point in the sphere whose center is closest to the query point. More precisely:

1. Search the root node for the sphere/pointer pair $< S_i, LP_i >$ whose centerpoint is closest to the query point Q.

2. Return the point Q_{NN} in leaf L (pointed to by LP_i) that is closest to Q.

In order to determine with certainty that the point generated from the algorithm above is the correct one, we determine if S_i contains the sphere C with centerpoint Q and radius $Distance(Q, Q_{NN})$. If S_i contains C, then we know that there is no closer point in the dataset or it would have been in L (See Figures 2 and 3). More precisely, the final search algorithm is shown in Figure 4

2.3 Creating a P-Sphere tree

This section describes the manner in which a P-sphere tree is generated from a dataset such that some specified $u_{95\%}$

1. Search the root node for the sphere/pointer pair $<S_i, LP_i>$ whose centerpoint is closest to the query point Q.

2. Find the point Q_{NN} in leaf L (pointed to by LP_i) which is closest to Q.

3. If S_i contains the sphere with centerpoint Q and radius $Dist(Q, Q_{NN})$, return Q_{NN}.

4. Otherwise return the result using the next best strategy.

Figure 4: Deterministic P-Sphere Tree Search Algorithm

accuracy during search is met. Note that the width of the CI is controlled by one of the algorithm inputs, $|Q|$, and that the relationship between $|Q|$ and CI is presented in Section 2.3.1.

There are three parameters to adjust in the tree: the fanout of the root, the centerpoints in the sphere descriptors, and the leaf size. We will fix the fanout of the root to be some constant greater than one. While we assume in this section that the fanout is constant, it is, in fact, a parameter that must be determined at index build time. Chapters 3 and 5 contain a further discussion on the choice of fanout. The centerpoints will be generated by taking a random sample of the data set. This is useful for theoretical analysis as it implies that the sphere centerpoint distribution follows the data distribution. Note that the only parameter to determine is the leaf size. This parameter is the most difficult to determine. The problem of determining leaf size can be summarized as follows:

Given a data set, sample query points, user specified $u_{95\%}$ accuracy, and fanout and centerpoints of the final P-Sphere Tree, determine the leaf size of the P-Sphere tree such that the user specified $u_{95\%}$ accuracy is met.

The strategy we employ to determine leaf size involves "reverse engineering" our tree to work correctly for query distributions like the one we set aside from the original data set. This is done by observing that for every query, there is an associated leaf size that is just large enough, given the centerpoints of the P-sphere tree, to return the provably correct answer when searching the resulting tree. In other words, there is an associated distribution of leaf sizes for a given workload such that the area under the curve between 0 and a given leaf size LS is the expected accuracy of the P-Tree with leaf size LS. We use our queries to sample this leaf size distribution. Based on this sample and our accuracy goal, we decide on an appropriate leaf size.

More precisely, the algorithm in Figure 5 empirically samples the implicit leaf size distribution using the query points as the basis of those samples. Note that the number of queries determines the number of samples taken of the distribution of leaf sizes and is the basis for the 95% confidence interval for accuracy established in Section 2.3.1.

The first loop simply calculates the nearest neighbor of every query in a manner that insures we make only 1 pass over the data. This is useful in reducing I/O if your query points and their nearest neighbors fit in memory, which is typically the case.

The second loop determines, for each query, the leaf that would have been searched had that query been run on the P-Sphere tree being constructed. In addition, the algorithm determines the minimum radius of the found leaf needed to ensure that the leaf, when searched, contains the provably nearest neighbor for that query.

The last loop simply counts, for each query, the number

1. Initialize all Q_{NN}

2. For each data point D

    (a) For each query point Q

        i. If Q_{NN} is further from Q then D

            A. $Q_{NN} = D$

3. For each query Q

    (a) Q_{Center} = the center point of the leaf closest to Q

    (b) $Q_{Radius} = Dist(Q_{Center}, Q) + Dist(Q, Q_{NN})$

4. For each data point D

    (a) For each query Q

        i. If Q falls inside the sphere described by Q_{Center} and Q_{Radius}

            A. Increment the $Q_{Leafsize}$

Figure 5: Determining Leaf Size Distribution

of data points that lie within the sphere whose centerpoint is Q_{Center} and radius Q_{Radius}. Once again, the loop is performed such that one pass over the data is all the I/O typically needed to perform the computation.

Upon termination of the algorithm, there is associated with each query a leaf size ($q_{Leafsize}$) which when divided by the number of data points, is a sample of the leaf size distribution discussed above. To meet the accuracy goal, we determine the correct leaf size of our P-Sphere tree by sorting the calculated leaf sizes and picking the one whose percentile matches the user defined level of correctness. For instance, if there were 100 queries, and the user wanted 90% accuracy, we would sort the 100 leaf sizes and pick the $90th$ leaf size in the list.

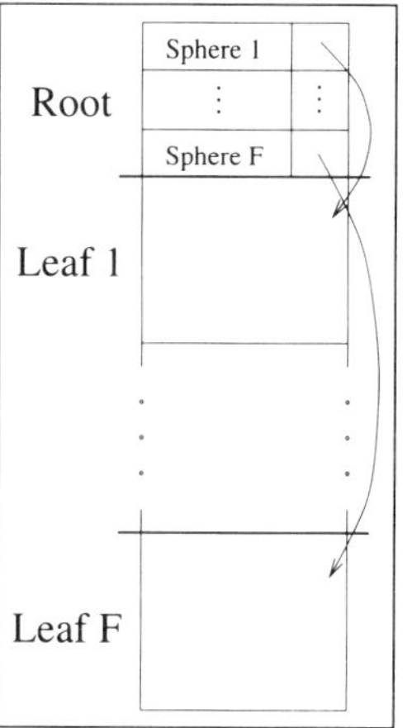

Figure 6: Layout of a P-Sphere Tree in a File

We now have all the parameters needed to build our P-Sphere Tree. The first level of the tree is trivial to build since it simply consists of $<$centerpoint, pointer$>$ pairs. The pointers to appropriate size chunks of disk space can be set up ahead of time since the sizes of the chunks are known in advance (See Figure 6).

Setting up the second level is harder. Since each leaf must contain the LS closest data points to that leaf's centerpoint, a scan of the data must be made in order to calculate that list. In addition, we want to avoid as many disk I/Os as possible since the entire tree is not likely to fit in memory. As a result, we must calculate these leaves a group at a time, such that for each group, one pass is made over the data set. During these passes, a priority queue for each leaf with LS entries is used to keep track of the LS closest points encountered during the pass. The number of leaves calculated during each pass is chosen to minimize construction time. More precisely, Figure 7 shows how the tree is constructed from its parameters.

The full algorithm (making use of the previously listed algorithms) for computing the P-Sphere tree is given in

1. Write out the first level

2. For each group of leaves

   (a) Populate the priority queues associated with the current group's leaves with the first $LeafSize$ data points

   (b) For each data point D beyond the first $LeafSize$ data points

      i. For each leaf L within the current group

         A. If D is closer to the centerpoint of L than the furthest point in the associated priority queue Q
- Remove the furthest point from Q
- Insert D into Q

   (c) Write out the priority queues to the appropriate places on disk

Figure 7: Building the Actual P-Sphere Tree

Figure 8.

1. Set aside some random number of data points to be query points, removing them from the data point list.

2. Randomly sample the data points to determine leaf centerpoints

3. Determine, for each query, $Q_{Leafsize}$ (see Figure 5)

4. Make a sorted list $LeafSizeList$ out of all $Q_{Leafsize}$

5. $LeafSize = LeafSizeList[UserAccuracy * ListSize]$

6. Write out the tree (see Figure 7)

Figure 8: Full Algorithm for P-Sphere Tree Construction

2.3.1 Determining the Number of Queries

One important parameter to the P-Sphere tree algorithm is the number of query points $|Q|$ used to build the tree. This number determines the confidence interval for the accuracy of the resulting P-Sphere tree. This confidence interval is established by mapping the problem into a classic problem in probability theory.

This mapping is the result of thinking of every query as a coin flip, where the coin comes up heads if the P-Sphere tree search algorithm results in a provably correct answer, and comes up tails if it doesn't produce a provably correct answer. We can then think of the confidence interval for the P-Sphere tree accuracy as the confidence interval for the bias of a coin which was flipped as many times as we have queries, and resulted in the user specified accuracy percent heads.

Another way to state the problem is that we want a confidence interval on the p-value of a Bernoulli process that was independently sampled as many times as we have queries. More precisely, if $\widehat{p}$ is the user specified accuracy goal (and also, as a result, the estimator for the likelihood of success for the coin flip), the 95% confidence interval for the actual accuracy is approximately

$$\widehat{p} \pm 2\sqrt{\frac{\widehat{p}(1-\widehat{p})}{|Q|}} \qquad [14] \qquad (1)$$

Note that this analysis will apply to all variants of P-Sphere trees.

3 Theoretical analysis of Deterministic P-Sphere Trees

This section contains highlights from the theoretical analysis of deterministic P-Sphere trees found in [22]. For ease of reading, all references in this section to P-Sphere trees are, more specifically, deterministic P-Sphere trees. In this analysis, the overall behavior of P-Sphere trees is described by examining the effect of datasets on the parameters of P-Sphere trees that have a known level of accuracy (not just a CI). Among the qualities examined are run time and space requirements as well as various upper and lower bounds. Note that these results apply equally to both CPU and disk costs.

3.1 Contrast Plots

The contrast plot of a query with respect to a dataset is a histogram of distance between points in the dataset and that query point. A plot of the integral of the function in a contrast plot is the cumulative contrast plot. Normalized contrast plots are contrast plots where distances are normalized so that the distance to the nearest neighbor is 1. For instance, the normalized contrast plot displayed in Figure 9 indicates that half the points in the dataset are less than twice as far as the nearest neighbor.

Note that contrast plots are constructed about a *particular* query point and are therefore unique to each query. As a result, every workload has an associated distribution of contrast plots. This distribution is implicitly sampled in P-Sphere tree construction by using multiple queries to determine leaf size. It is useful to note, however, that [13] shows that as the workload becomes harder and harder to index, the distribution of contrast plots converge to the same constant distribution.

3.2 Analysis of the P-Sphere Tree with Respect to Contrast Plots

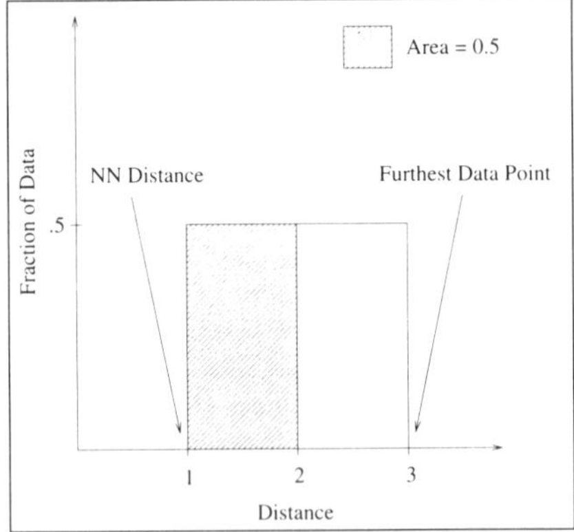

Figure 9: Sample Contrast Plot

Interestingly, if we make the simplifying assumption that all queries have a contrast plot identical to some "typical" contrast plot, the contrast plot is enough to precisely determine the median space and time behavior of P-Sphere trees applied to that workload. While such an analysis is not strictly accurate (because of the simplifying assumption), it lends much insight into the conditions under which this algorithm does and does not perform well. In addition, the upper and lower bounds described in this paper are completely accurate (the simplifying assumption is not needed).

3.2.1 General Space and Time Analysis

Since the fanout of the P-Sphere Tree is fixed at index construction time, the only parameter that determines space and time is the leaf size. Determining the leaf size is the purpose of Lemma 1. In this lemma, we assume that we are given the top level of a P-sphere tree, and a level of accuracy that we meet exactly (not a CI), and wish to determine leaf size.

In this lemma, we construct a cumulative distribution $F(x)$, which is the percent of data which is at most x distance away from a particular query point. Note that this function corresponds to a cumulative contrast plot. As mentioned earlier in this chapter, we will make the simplifying assumption that all random query points Q produce identical contrast plots, and therefore, $F(x)$ is independent of Q. While this is not generally true, the resulting analysis gives us insight into the relationship between contrast plots and leaf sizes. The fact that different queries have different contrast plots is a second order averaging effect that happens "on top of" the one described in this analysis. Furthermore, experimental results in [13] found that, in practice, contrast plots do not vary widely amongst query points.

Lemma 1 *Given:*

- *A dataset D with n datapoints.*

- *A P-Sphere tree T over D with fanout m (we assume in this proof that each of the m centerpoints were sampled with replacement) which returns the provably correct answer $(u*100)\%$ of the time and whose leaf size is S percent of the entire dataset.*

- *A random query point Q.*

- *A set of cumulative distributions $F_Q(x)$, such that for a particularly query point Q, $F_Q(x)$ equals the percent of data which is at most x distance away from Q. Because of an assumption we make later, $F_Q(x)$ is identical for any assignment of Q. We will therefore refer only to $F(x)$, which is the distribution for any assignment of Q.*

- *A random variable B_C, or nearest bucket centerpoint, which is, by definition of the P-Sphere tree algorithms, the closest of m points sampled from the original dataset.*

- *NN, the nearest neighbor of Q, which is $DMIN$ distance away from Q.*

and assuming that Q and $F(x)$ are independent, the leaf size S of T as a fraction of the total dataset is

$$F(F^{-1}(1 - [1 - u]^{(1/m)}) + DMIN) \qquad (2)$$

With the above lemma, we can now produce the main result of this theoretical analysis, which is the following theorem about the behavior of P-Sphere Trees:

Theorem 1 *Given all assumptions and symbol definitions of Lemma 1, the space/time (tree search time) requirements (as a fraction of linear scan space/time) for the P-Sphere tree (disregarding space/time overhead incurred by storing/reading pointers in the root) are:*

$$Space = \frac{m}{n} + S * m, \ Time^1 = \frac{m}{n} + S, \qquad (3)$$

$$S = F(F^{-1}(1 - [1 - u]^{(1/m)}) + DMIN) \qquad (4)$$

Furthermore, the best possible space/time (tree search) behavior of P-Sphere trees over all datasets (assuming no duplicates) is:

$$Space = \frac{m}{n} + S * m, \ Time = \frac{m}{n} + S, \ S = 1 - [1 - u]^{(1/m)} \qquad (5)$$

Also, the worst possible space/time behavior of P-Sphere trees over all datasets is:

$$Space = \frac{m}{n} + m, \ Time = \frac{m}{n} + 1, \ S = 1 \qquad (6)$$

3.2.2 Leaf Size and Contrast Plots

It is clear from the above theorem that leaf size is the determining factor of overall P-Sphere Tree behavior. It is interesting to note that the formula for leaf size,

$$S = F(F^{-1}(1 - [1 - u]^{(1/m)}) + DMIN) \qquad (7)$$

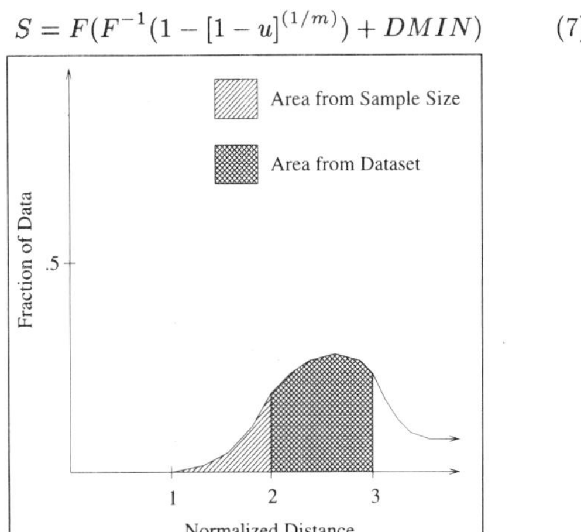

Figure 10: The affect of DMIN on Leaf Size

can be intuitively understood in terms of normalized contrast plots. One way of interpreting the above expression is that the leaf size is $1 - [1 - u]^{(1/m)}+$ the area under the curve of the normalized contrast plot from $1 - [1 - u]^{(1/m)}$ into the plot and spanning the subsequent interval of size 1(See Figure 10).

For instance, an example contrast plot that would result in the minimum possible leaf size, $1 - [1 - u]^{(1/m)}$ is shown in Figure 11.

In this example, the data is divided into clusters. There is the cluster which contains the query point that corresponds to the first bump in the plot. The rest of the clusters are contained in the second larger bump. There are two interesting properties of these bumps:

---

[1]Note that this equation is tree search time only and does not include the time for using an alternative strategy when necessary.

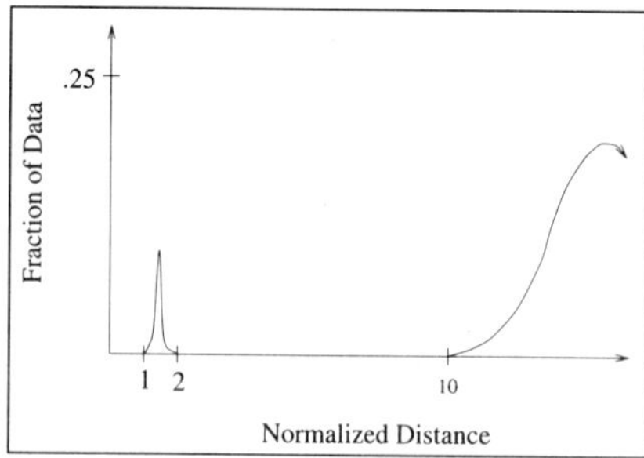

Figure 11: Contrast Plot of Clustered Data

- The first bump has area under the curve $1 - [1 - u]^{(1/m)}$.

- The distance between bumps is larger than 1.

As a result of the above two properties, the addition of $DMIN$ to $F^{-1}(1 - [1 - u]^{(1/m)})$ has no effect on the value of F, which is unchanging in the interval between the 2 bumps.

Overall, it is easy to see that the determining factor of leaf size is the area under the curve of the normalized contrast plot of a certain interval of size 1. Thus, the leaf size is determined by the spread of the normalized contrast plot in that region.

3.3 ND P-Sphere Trees

The P-Sphere trees discussed above find the provably correct answer with $u_{95\%}$ accuracy. While this approach is useful if one always needs the correct answer, there are many cases where the exact answer is not always needed. In these cases, it is enough to know that with $u_{95\%}$ accuracy, the algorithm returns the correct answer, but correct and incorrect answers can not be distinguished by the search algorithm.

For instance, if we are solving an approximate matching problem such as identifying matching fingerprints, we can compare the actual fingerprints as part of a postprocessing step to determine correctness outside the algorithm. Furthermore, if we're performing some kind of similarity heuristic (document, image, sound), being correct most of the time is typically sufficient.

We will refer to P-Sphere trees which return the unprovably correct answer close to some specified percentage of the time as ND (non-deterministic) P-Sphere Trees. The method of construction is straightforward. The only difference between the construction of deterministic P-Sphere trees and ND P-Sphere Trees is that, for each query, we determine the leaf size needed to return the correct answer, not the provably correct answer. Thus, in terms of the algorithm in Figure 5, Q_{Radius} should be just large enough to include Q_{NN}, but no larger. Thus, $Q_{Radius} = Dist(Q_{Center}, Q_{NN})$. The rest of the algorithm remains unchanged.

The only change to the search algorithm is that we remove the verification step that determines if the answer is provably correct and the subsequent alternate strategy.

Observe that every deterministic P-Sphere tree is also an ND P-Sphere tree with differing accuracy and vice-versa. This is obvious when one considers that deterministic P-Sphere trees frequently return correct answers that can't be proven correct. In addition, ND P-Sphere trees will sometimes return the provably correct answer, but not very often. In fact, the only difference between the two types of P-Sphere trees is the size of the leaves. ND P-Sphere trees of some given accuracy have smaller leaves than a deterministic P-Sphere tree of the same accuracy. Thus the space and time performance of ND P-Sphere trees is strictly better than P-Sphere trees given the same level of accuracy over the same data.

Note that since this strategy is a strict performance improvement over deterministic P-Sphere trees, all the theoretical statements we made about deterministic P-Sphere trees are upper bounds for ND P-Sphere trees.

4 Pk-Sphere Trees

While P-Sphere trees are simple, and as a result, lend themselves to analysis, there are variants of the basic algorithm that are more complex but are strictly and significantly more efficient. The particular variant of deterministic and non-deterministic P-Sphere trees discussed in this section involves maintaining the $u_{95\%}$ accuracy discussed in the previous section using a slightly different search algorithm.

4.1 ND Pk-Sphere Trees

In the original ND search algorithm, we simply returned the closest point in the closest leaf. In the ND Pk-Sphere tree search algorithm, we instead return the closest point in the k closest leaves where k is a given constant. More precisely, the search algorithm becomes:

1. Search the root node for the k sphere/pointer pairs $< S_i, LP_i >$ whose centerpoints are closest to the query point Q.

2. Return the point Q_{NN}, the point closest to Q amongst the points in the leaves pointed to by the entries found in the previous step.

While the change in the search algorithm is simple, the resulting changes in the tree construction are more complex. In particular, the algorithm shown in Figure 5, which determines, per query, the leafsize needed to return the correct answer for that query is significantly more complicated. The new version of this algorithm will now determine, for each query, the size of the leaf, amongst the k closest, that can best accommodate the nearest neighbor of the current query. More precisely:

1. Initialize all Q_{NN}

2. For each query point Q

   (a) $Q_{Leafsize} = n$

   (b) For each of the k closest leaves L

      i. $L_{Radius} = Dist(L_{Center}, Q_{NN})$

      ii. If (leafsize of L assuming radius L_{Radius}) $< Q_{LeafSize}$

         • $Q_{LeafSize} =$ Size of L assuming radius L_{Radius}

Of course, there is one aspect of this algorithm that is more complex than it appears. Calculating the size of L assuming radius L_{Radius} is a very compute intensive task.

We will therefore create, for each leaf, a histogram of the dataset with respect to distance from the leaf. These histograms are used to estimate leafsizes given radii. A more precise description of the search algorithm can be found in Figure 12.

---

1. Initialize all Q_{NN}

2. For each leaf L

    (a) Create a histogram L_{Hist} of distance to L_{Center} of the dataset.

3. For each query point Q

    (a) $Q_{Leafsize} = n$

    (b) For each of the k closest leaves L

        i. $L_{Radius} = Dist(L_{Center}, Q_{NN})$

        ii. If (estimated (using L_{Hist}) leafsize of L assuming radius L_{Radius}) $< Q_{LeafSize}$

            • $Q_{LeafSize}$ = estimated size of L assuming radius L_{Radius}

Figure 12: Determining Leafsize Distribution for ND Pk-Sphere Trees

5 Performance Analysis

This section contains a series of experiments that test the behavior of P-Sphere trees and the variants described in this paper. These experiments are used to obtain an understanding of the following issues:

- The effect of fanout for all P-Sphere tree variants on space/time performance.

- The effect of k for PK-Sphere tree variants on space/time performance.

- The performance of the fastest P-Sphere tree variants on low contrast data.

- How the variants of P-Sphere trees compare to existing techniques on real data.

To address the first three issues, we used synthetic datasets. For these datasets, we intentionally chose the most difficult datasets to index. All datasets were created using identical and independently distributed dimensions, which is a very difficult case to handle ([13]). The data set size was 100,000 tuples. Note that larger datasets perform better than smaller ones ([13]), so the really difficult datasets to handle are the smallest ones. In all experiments, various parameters of the various types of trees were tested, and dimensionality of the dataset was varied. Space and search time numbers were collected for each combination of variables.

To address the last issue, we measured the performance of P-Sphere trees as compared to the performance of the SR-Tree([25]) for two real datasets. One of these datasets was also used to evaluate density based indexing in [24]. We therefore include their results in this paper. In these experiments, we were able to beat both alternative strategies' query times by approximately a factor of 20.

For experiments using synthetic data, in memory query times were measured (although the number of seeks if these had been I/O times is easily predicted as the number of leaf pages searched+1), while I/O times were measured for the real datasets. This allowed us to examine the affect

of seeks (frequently the dominating component of I/O performance) independently from the affect of contrast on leaf sizes.

5.1 Varying the fanout of P-Sphere Trees

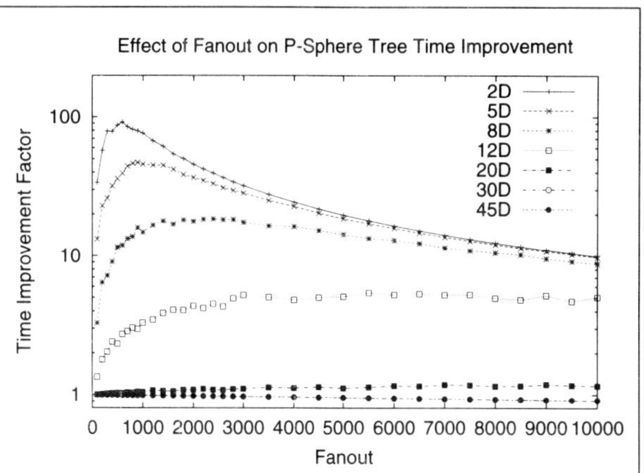

Figure 13: Effect of fanout on time for P-Sphere Trees

The experiments in this section were designed to test the effect of varying fanout for deterministic and nondeterministic P-Sphere Trees. In these experiments, an accuracy goal of 95% was used for 1000 queries. Note that performance in this section is in terms of in-memory performance. The only difference between in-memory and disk performance is the addition of a seek plus latency for each leaf being searched (assuming the root stays in memory). Note that a linear scan of the data on disk also results in one seek plus latency.

While the experiments on deterministic P-Sphere trees indicate that using deterministic P-Sphere trees for medium to high dimensionality is impractical, they are presented to highlight the effectiveness of the nondeterministic algorithms as well as the value of searching multiple leaves. The importance of P-Sphere trees lies in their theoretical value. They provide upper bounds (for all P-Sphere tree variants) that follow the inherent difficulty of the indexing problem.

Figures 13 and 14 show the effect of varying fanout on nondeterministic P-Sphere trees on time and space respec-

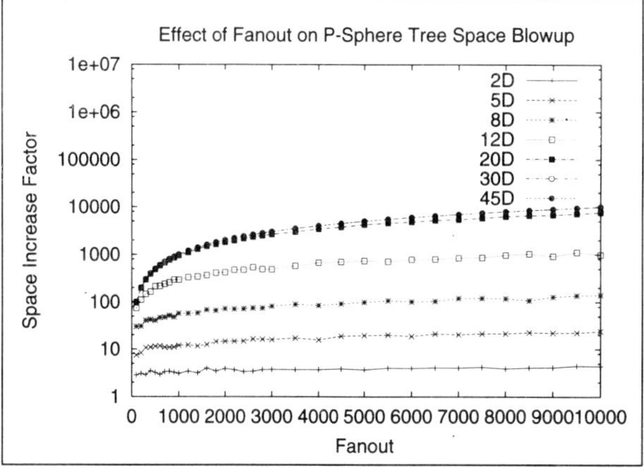

Figure 14: Effect of fanout on space for P-Sphere Trees

tively. There are several interesting features.

In Figure 13, which shows time improvement relative to linear scan, increasing leafsize helps for a while, but begins to have a negative impact after a certain point. This is especially true for lower dimensionality. At first, this seems odd since we know that increasing the fanout will reduce the leafsize, and hence the subsequent scan of the leaf. But we must remember that, especially for low dimensionality, the leaf sizes are very small, and begin to be dominated by the time to search the root, which grows linearly with leaf size. the highest dimensions are less affected since the leaves are very large in all cases, and the root only grows in these experiments to one tenth the size of the dataset.

Figure 14, which shows space blowup relative to the original dataset, is very easy to interpret. Basically, increasing fanout always increases overall size, although very slowly in low dimensionality and very quickly in high dimensionality.

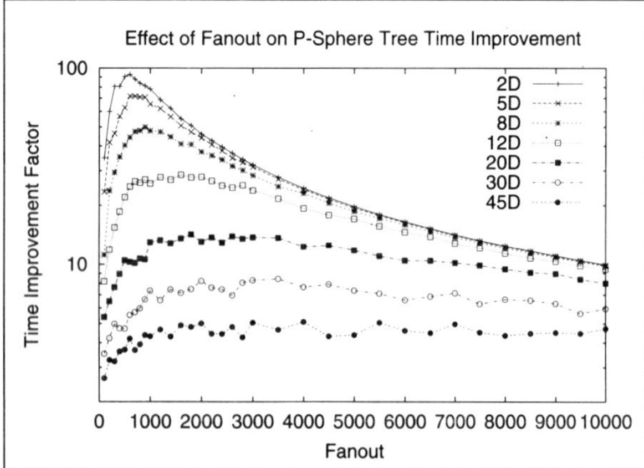

Figure 15: Effect of fanout on time for ND P-Sphere Trees

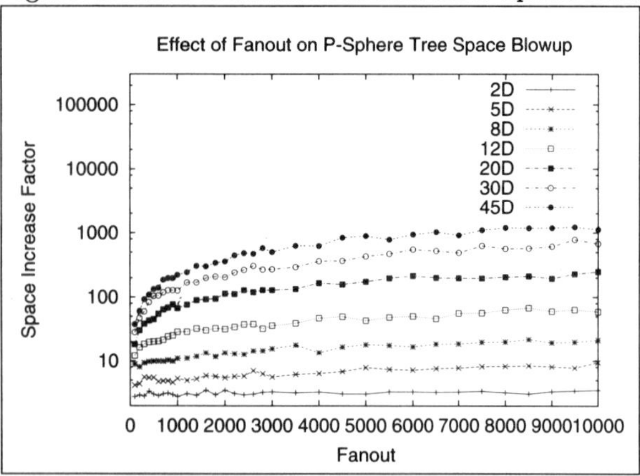

Figure 16: Effect of fanout on space for ND P-Sphere Trees

Figures 15 and 16 show corresponding graphs to the previous two for ND P-Sphere trees. Note that the overall behavior is identical, except that both space and time are considerably improved for higher dimensions. In particular, examine the time improvement of the 30 dimensional case in Figure 15. In this case, we are actually still achieving a factor of 8 speedup over linear scan! Even for the 45 dimensional case, we still achieved a factor of 3 speedup over linear scan. This is very impressive considering that other techniques fail to beat linear scan at around 10 di-

mensions.

For instance, [40] provides us with information on the performance of both the SS tree and the R* tree in finding the 20 nearest neighbors. Conservatively assuming that linear scans cost 15% of a random examination of the data pages, linear scan outperforms both the SS tree and the R* tree at 10 dimensions in all cases. In addition, in [25], linear scan vastly outperforms the SR tree for all synthetic datasets of dimensionality greater than 10. Lastly, in [15], performance numbers are presented for NN queries where bounds are imposed on the radius used to find the NN. While the performance in high dimensionality looks good in some cases, in trying to duplicate their results we found that the radius was such that few, if any, queries returned an answer.

While the degree to which we beat other techniques in query time is impressive, there is a down side. Unfortunately, time improvement isn't the only factor. Examine the blowup in space for the same 30 dimensional case (Figure 16). There is approximately a 100 to 200 times increase in storage requirements to achieve this 8 fold increase in performance. The 45 dimensional case is even worse, with a space blowup of nearly 800. Fortunately, the best performing variant of P-Sphere Trees, ND Pk Sphere Trees, will address this issue.

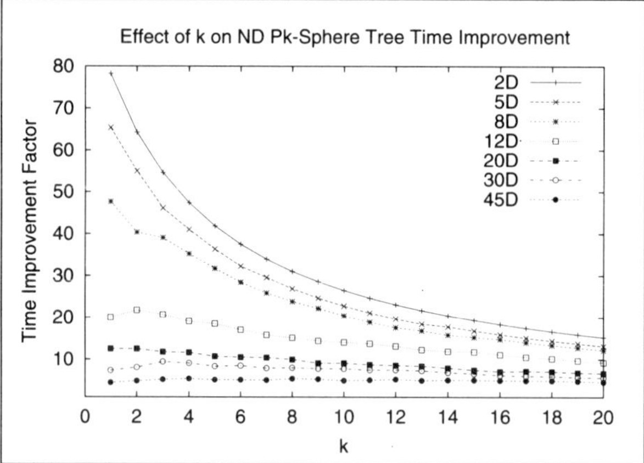

Figure 17: Effect of k on time for ND Pk-Sphere Trees with Fanout 1000

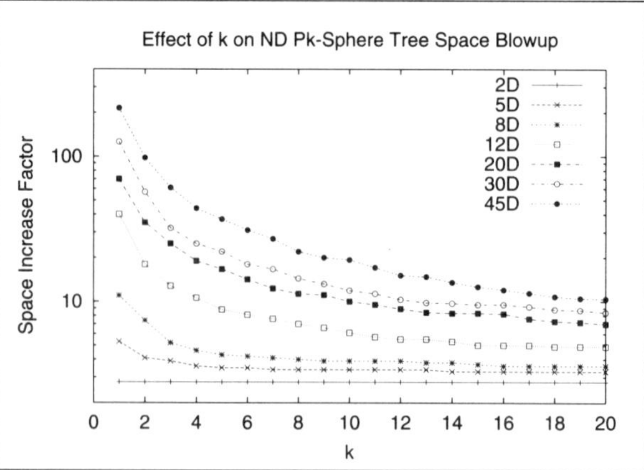

Figure 18: Effect of k on space for ND Pk-Sphere Trees with Fanout 1000

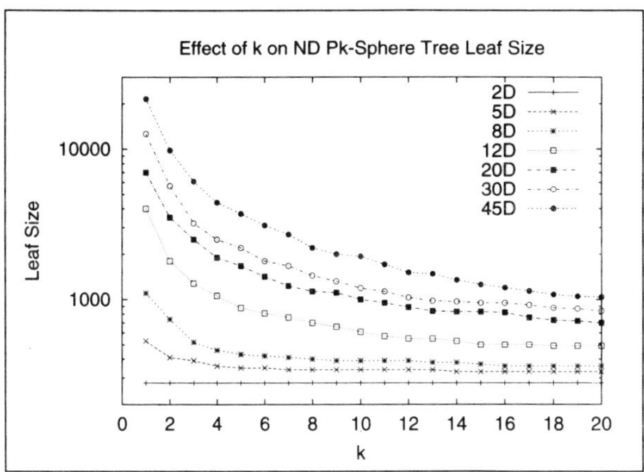

Figure 19: Effect of k on Leaf Size for ND Pk-Sphere Trees with Fanout 1000

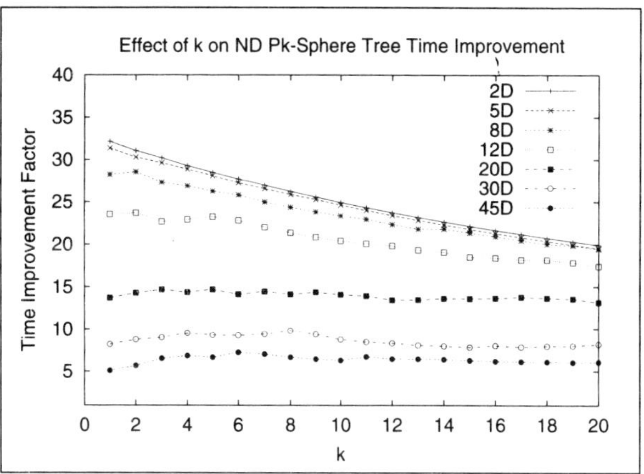

Figure 20: Effect of k on time for ND Pk-Sphere Trees with Fanout 3000

5.2 The Performance of Pk-Sphere Trees

This section examines the performance of ND Pk-Sphere trees, the best performing NN technique described in this paper. The experiments involved varying fanout and k. Since the overall effect of fanout on these trees was identical to the P-Sphere trees described in the previous section, we will simply show the effect of varying k for two different settings of fanout.

The results for the first setting of fanout, 1000, are shown in Figures 17 and 18, which show the impact of k on time and space respectively. Note that for low dimensionality, k has little impact on space while having a detrimental impact on time. As dimensionality increases, however, the detrimental impact that k has on time becomes much diminished. In addition, for higher dimensionality, k has an extremely beneficial effect on space.

The reasons behind such behavior are more obvious when one considers Figure 19, the effect of k on leaf size. While in low dimensionality, increasing k has little effect on leaf size, in high dimensionality, increasing k dramatically reduces leaf size. As a result, in low dimensionality, increasing k has little impact on space, but requires us to search more leaves, resulting in poor search times. In higher dimensionality, however, increasing k dramatically reduces leaf size. As a result, searching additional leaves incurs little penalty since the leaves become smaller, but overall space becomes greatly reduced.

The results for a fanout of 3000, shown in Figures 20, 21, and 22 are very similar to those for a fanout of 1000, except that the larger fanout resulted in smaller leaf sizes. For low dimensionality, the savings in space and time due to smaller leaves was dominated by the increase in the number of leaves and the increase in the size of the root respectively. As a result, neither overall space nor total query time improved. For higher dimensions and high values of k, however, the increase in fanout resulted in a noticeable improvement in time with a slight penalty for space, resulting in a better overall space/time tradeoff.

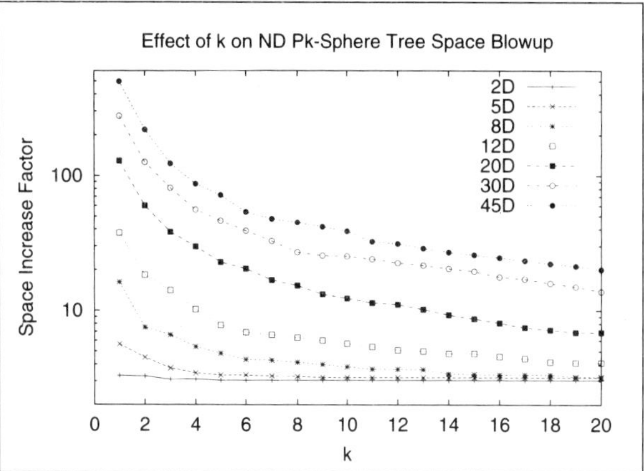

Figure 21: Effect of k on space for ND Pk-Sphere Trees with Fanout 3000

5.3 P-Sphere Tree Performance on Real Data

This section describes the performance of the three variants of P-Sphere trees on two real datasets. In each case, the space and time performance were measured against data set size and linear scan respectively. Note that time performance in this section refers to the I/O time (including seeks) for running the queries cold. In all experiments, an accuracy level of 95% was used with 1000 queries. Note that the number of queries used was enough to obtain very close to 95% accuracy ($\pm$ 1.5%). The obtained results are also compared to the SR-Tree [25] applied to the same dataset.

To determine the best setting of root fanout, all settings of fanout between 1000 and 3000 were tested at intervals of 100. The results of varying k are discussed individually for each dataset.

The first dataset was the astronomy dataset used with the probabilistic nearest neighbor processing technique described in [24]. As a result, we show their performance results for an accuracy level of 95%. This dataset is a 29 dimensional dataset with over half a million rows. The results are shown in Figure 23. Note that the speedups over linear scan are considerable. In addition, ND P-Sphere trees beat both alternative strategies by a factor of 20 to

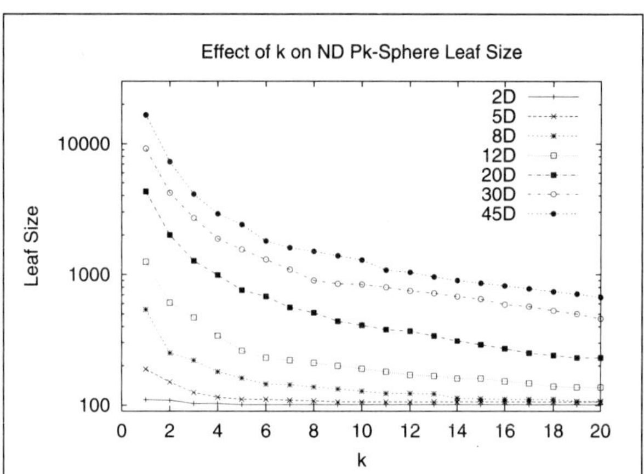

Figure 22: Effect of k on Leaf Size for ND Pk-Sphere Trees with Fanout 3000

30 for query time.

Technique	Blowup	Speedup over LS
P-Sphere	40	52
ND P-Sphere k=1	8	120
Density Based Indexing	1	6.6
SR-Tree	1.4	6.4

Figure 23: Performance Results for Astronomy Data

Technique	Blowup	Speedup over LS
P-Sphere	98	7.5
ND P-Sphere k=1	13	27
ND P-Sphere k=2	9	19
ND P-Sphere k=3	8	15
ND P-Sphere k=4	7	12
SR-Tree	1.5	.84

Figure 24: Performance Results for Color Histogram Data

The second dataset was a dataset derived from color histograms of images. This dataset is a publicly available dataset available from the University of California at Irvine Machine Learning Repository. This dataset has 32 dimensions and nearly 70,000 tuples. As we can see from the results in Figure 24, this is a difficult dataset to index. This is obvious from the space blowup versus query speedup of the deterministic P-Sphere tree. Despite this, we still achieved nearly a factor of 30 speedup over linear scan, and more than a factor of 30 over the SR-Tree.

Observe that the SR-Tree was outperformed by linear scan. It is interesting to note that the SR-Tree managed to prune the search space to less than 10% of the dataset, but that the cost of performing one seek per node visited so dominated the cost expression, that the pruning was irrelevant. As the gap between sequential versus random disk throughput widens (as it has dramatically done for the last 10 years), the tendency for the number or seeks to determine disk throughput will strengthen.

The color histogram dataset clearly shows the benefits of using a probabilistic search algorithm. Both space and time were improved considerably over the deterministic case. In addition, increasing k leads to an overall reduction in both space blowup and speedup. The decrease in speedup was caused by the domination of the seek associated with accessing each leaf. In this particular case, the actual amount of data accessed as k increased hardly changed. Thus, for a larger sample of this dataset, where the cost of scanning the leaf dominates the seek, increasing k would have little effect on speedup for small k. For this particular sample of this dataset, one should use the lowest setting of k for which the space blowup is acceptable.

While it is difficult to determine exactly how other techniques such as X-Trees([11]) and R*-Trees([7]) would have performed on these datasets, it is worth noting that the color histogram dataset was an example of a low contrast dataset, and was roughly equivalent in contrast to a 15 dimensional 1 million tuple iid uniform dataset. Alternative techniques are known to perform poorly on such datasets. In addition, the performance studies in [25] and [11] present evidence that R*-Trees perform significantly worse than both SR-Trees and X-Trees, and that SR-Trees and X-Trees are within a factor of 2 of one another. It is therefore likely that we would have beaten both X-Trees and R*-Trees by at least an order of magnitude.

6 Related Work

There are many processing strategies from the database community for tackling the high dimensional nearest neighbor problem. These include [40, 11, 25, 15, 10], all of which were designed with low contrast situations (high dimensionality) in mind. By making use of the assumption that sample query points are available at index construction time, the algorithms presented in this paper far outperform these strategies (for low contrast cases), all of which are beaten by linear scan around 10 dimensions ([13], [36]). Also, none of them provide asymptotic optimality guarantees for the important case where query distribution follows data distribution.

[16] is of interest in that they provide informal arguments that unnormalized contrast plots are important in evaluating the difficulty of NN processing on a given dataset. They also introduce a NN processing strategy for in-memory NN query processing. They significantly reduce the number of distance computations in medium to low contrast situations, but point out that the technique is not really suitable for disk based searching. This seems likely given that the behavior of the stucture would be very seek time dominated.

A processing strategy called the VA-File ([36]) achieves improvements over linear scan, even on low contrast datasets, by using a lossy compression technique on the entire dataset. Note that this strategy is complementary to ours and could be used on each leaf in a P-Sphere tree to further improve performance.

There has recently been interest in hashing based techniques for determining approximate nearest neighbors ([33] and [1]). Unfortunately, all available experimental results are for relatively high contrast situations, providing no insight into the cases that are truly difficult to index. In addition, their notion of approximation requires the user specified error criteria to decrease with contrast to maintain a constant level of discrimination between data points. For instance, if we used their hashing technique to determine one of the five closest data points to a random query point, the necessary level of user specified error would decrease with contrast. Thus there is a dependence between contrast and user specified error that is not made explicit in their theoretical statements about overall behavior.

The nearest neighbor processing technique presented in [31] is noteworthy in that they use a notion of approximation (returning the correct answer some percentage of the time) similar to the one presented in this paper. Unfortunately, they present no precise way of controlling or predicting the level of accuracy for a particular dataset. A precise comparison between the effectiveness of their techniques and ours is difficult since they do not present any information about the behavior of their techniques on identical and independently distributed data.

[24] also uses a notion of approximation similar to the one presented in this paper. Their approach consists of modeling the data as a mixture of Gaussians. This model guides the construction of their data subdivision (distribution based rather than space based), and ultimately guides their search algorithm. In many ways, the difference between our approaches can be summarized as sampling (our approach) versus modeling. There are, however, further important differences between their work and ours. For instance, we leverage redundancy to improve performance. In addition, dataset distribution does not affect the confidence interval for our accuracy. We also relate our results to theoretical bounds established on the overall problem [13], and not just to a specific kind of workload ([24] evaluate their approach for clustered datasets). Finally, for the same dataset with the same level of accuracy, ND P-Sphere trees were nearly 20 times faster with a space blowup of 8.

The computational geometry community has also been interested in the nearest neighbor problem and has discovered various query processing strategies [5, 6, 9, 12]. Unfortunately, none of these techniques were designed with low contrast (high dimensionality) in mind. As a result, while some of them perform quite well and are well understood in 2 or 3 dimensions, they perform very poorly in higher dimensionality. In cases where upper and lower bounds are available, there are constants that scale exponentially with dimensionality. One noteworthy technique from this community was published in [17]. Like P-Sphere trees, they use redundancy and a random sample of query points at index build time. Their structure is, however, quite different and would require many more seeks than P-Sphere trees while searching. They also show that for *fixed* dimensionality, their technique scales logarithmically with the number of data points. But like other techniques from the computational geometry community, there are constants in the bounds that scale exponentially with dimensionality. It is worth mentioning that their search time bounds become asymptotically linear as the spread of the contrast distribution becomes negligible. However, since there are no published performance results for this technique, it is impossible to compare their strategy directly to ours.

There has been much work recently on trying to capture the properties of a high dimensional dataset that makes various forms of query processing, including nearest neighbor, difficult [20, 8, 19, 27, 13]. Of these, only principal components analysis, which led to the TV-Tree ([27]), has resulted in any new query processing techniques. It is easy to find situations, however, where principal components analysis fails to recognize properly whether datasets are hard to index. As a result, the TV-Tree is not guaranteed to perform well in all situations that P-Sphere Trees are guaranteed to perform well. An interesting piece of concurrent related work, ([26]), relates fractal dimensionality, a concept very similar to contrast, to the performance of NN queries on R-Trees. They show that under certain conditions, the performance of the queries is directly related

to the fractal dimensionality.

Perhaps the most relevant piece of related work is [13], which introduced the concept of contrast plots. In addition, they established asymptotic bounds on the overall problem that match the behavior of our own strategy. This is powerful evidence that the type of strategy presented in this paper is a promising new approach to the problem in general. [35] is notable in that it further develops the ideas in [13] by relating contrast to concentration of measure.

7 Conclusions

This paper has introduced several exciting new nearest neighbor query processing techniques, that by making use of the assumption that a random sample of the query distribution is available at index build time, have the following properties:

- They allow the data administrator to easily trade redundancy for time.

- Performance improvements apply equally to CPU and disk. The techniques are therefore suitable for both in-memory and secondary storage applications

- They can be applied to any scenario where the distance function is a metric.

- We present variants of the basic algorithm that offer excellent performance, if the user is willing to accept the fact that a small (user-specified) percentage of the time, the returned answer is not the nearest neighbor. These variants are particularly effective in low contrast situations. For instance, for 30 dimensional (identically distributed independent dimensions) uniform data, one of the techniques presented in this paper achieves about an 8 fold increase in speed (relative to linear scan) with about an equal blowup in space (relative to the dataset). It is well established that other techniques fail to beat linear scan at around 10 dimensions ([13], [36]) for the same datasets.

- P-Sphere trees consistently beat two alternative strategies' (SR-Tree [25], Density based indexing [24]) query times by a factor of 20 to 30 on the real datasets they were tested on.

- The theoretical results presented in this paper establish that dimensionality in and of itself is irrelevant to the performance of this structure, and instead relate the performance to a simple aspect of the workload, contrast distribution. This form of analysis greatly simplifies the task of describing overall behavior and leads to surprisingly simple and precise statements about how we can expect particular workloads to perform.

- For situations in which the query distribution follows the data distribution, the theoretical results presented in this paper, when combined with the results in ([13]) establish contrast as *the* performance limiting feature of sub linear strategies for NN query processing. A corollary of this is that the techniques presented in this paper are asymptotically optimal in the sense that their performance scales with the inherent difficulty of the problem.

Interesting future work includes theoretical studies that lead to tighter upper bounds for ND P-Sphere Trees, deterministic PK-Sphere Trees, and ND PK-Sphere Trees. In addition, a more thorough performance study comparing the techniques presented in this paper to a wider variety of NN processing techniques would definitely be useful. Handling updates and K-NN searches are also important extensions to this work.

References

[1] R. Motwani A. Gionis, P. Indyk. Similarity search in high dimensions via hashing. In *VLDB*, 1999.

[2] R. Agrawal, C. Faloutsos, and A. Swami. Efficient similarity search in sequence databases. In *FODO*, 1993.

[3] S. F. Altschul, W. Gish, W. Miller, E. Myers, and D. J. Lipman. Basic local alignment search tool. *Journal of Molecular Biology*, 215, 1990.

[4] Y. H. Ang, Zhao Li, and S. H. Ong. Image retrieval based on multidimensional feature properties. In *SPIE vol. 2420*, 1995.

[5] S. Arya. *Nearest Neighbor Searching and Applications*. PhD thesis, Univ. of Maryland at College Park, 1995.

[6] S. Arya, D. M. Mount, N. S. Netanyahu, R. Silverman, and A. Wu. An optimal algorithm for nearest neighbor searching. In *Proc. 5th ACM SIAM Symposium on Discrete Algorithms*, 1994.

[7] N. Beckmann, H.-P. Kriegel, R. Schneider, and B. Seeger. The R*-Tree: An efficient and robust access method for points and rectangles. In *SIGMOD*, 1990.

[8] A. Belussi and C. Faloutsos. Estimating the selectivity of spatial queries using the 'correlation' fractal dimension. In *VLDB*, 1995.

[9] J. L. Bentley, B. W. Weide, and A. C. Yao. Optimal expected-time algorithms for closest point problem. *ACM Transactions on Mathematical Software*, 6(4), 1980.

[10] S. Berchtold, C. Böhm, B. Braunmüller, D. A. Keim, and H.-P. Kriegel. Fast parallel similarity search in multimedia databases. In *SIGMOD*, 1997.

[11] S. Berchtold, C. Böhm, and H.-P. Kriegel. The X-Tree: An index structure for high-dimensional data. In *VLDB*, 1996.

[12] M. Bern. Approximate closest point queries in high dimensions. *Information Processing Letters*, 45, 1993.

[13] K. Beyer, J. Goldstein, R. Ramakrishnan, and U. Shaft. When is nearest neighbors meaningful? In *ICDT*, 1999.

[14] G. Box, W. Hunter, and J. Hunter. *Statistics for Experimenters*. Wiley and Sons, 1978.

[15] T. Bozkaya and M. Ozsoyoglu. Distance-based indexing for high-dimensional metric spaces. In *PODS*, 1997.

[16] S. Brin. Near neighbor search in large metric spaces. In *VLDB*, 1995.

[17] K. Clarkson. Nearest neighbor queries in metric spaces. In *STOC*, 1997.

[18] C. Faloutsos et al. Efficient and effective querying ny image content. *Journal of Intelligent Information Systems*, 3(3), 1994.

[19] C. Faloutsos and V. Gaede. Analysis of n-dimensional quadtrees using the Housdorff fractal dimension. In *SIGMOD*, 1996.

[20] C. Faloutsos and I. Kamel. Beyond uniformity and independence: Analysis of R-trees using the concept of fractal dimension. In *PODS*, 1994.

[21] U. M. Fayyad and P. Smyth. Automated analysis and exploration of image databases: Results, progress and challenges. *Journal of intelligent information systems*, 4(1), 1995.

[22] J. Goldstein. *Improved Query Processing and Data Representation Techniques*. PhD thesis, University of Wisconsin - Madison, 1999.

[23] J. M. Hellerstein, E. Koutsoupias, and C. H. Papadimitriou. On the analysis of indexing schemes. In *PODS*, 1997.

[24] D. Geiger K. Bennett, U. Fayyad. Density-based indexing for approximate nearest-neighbor queries. In *Density-Based Indexing for Approximate Nearest-Neighbor Queries*, San Diego, California, 1999.

[25] N. Katayama and S. Satoh. The SR-tree: An index structure for high-dimensional nearest neighbor queries. In *PODS*, 1997.

[26] Philip Korn. Deflating the dimensionality curse using multiple fractal dimensions. In *ICDE*, San Diego, CA, February 2000.

[27] K.-I. Lin, H. V. Jagadish, and C. Faloutsos. The TV-Tree: An index structure for high-dimensional data. *VLDB Journal*, 3(4), 1994.

[28] B. S. Manjunath and W. Y. Ma. Texture features for browsing and retrieval of image data. In *IEEE Trans. on Pattern Analysis and Machine Learning*, volume 18(8), 1996.

[29] R. Mehrotra and J. E. Gary. Feature-based retrieval of similar shapes. In *ICDE*, 1992.

[30] H. Murase and S. K. Nayar. Visual learning and recognition of 3D objects from appearance. *Int. J. of Computer Vision*, 14(1), 1995.

[31] U. Shaft N. Megiddo. Efficient nearest neighbors indexing based on a collection of space filling curves. Technical Report RJ 10093(91909), IBM Almaden Research Center, November 1997.

[32] S. A. Nene and S. K. Nayar. A simple algorithm for nearest neighbor search in high dimensions. In *IEEE Trans. on Pattern Analysis and Machine Learning*, volume 18(8), 1996.

[33] R. Motwani P. Indyk. Approximate nearest neighbor - towards removing the curse of dimensionality. In *STOC*, 1998.

[34] A. Pentland, R. W. Picard, and S. Scalroff. Photobook: Tools for content based manipulation of image databases. In *SPIE Volume 2185*, 1994.

[35] Vladimir Pestov. On the geometry of similarity search: dimensionality curse and concentration of measure. *Information Processing Letters*, To Appear.

[36] S. Blott R. Weber, H.-J. Schek. A quantitative analysis and performance study for similarity-search methods in high-dimensional spaces. In *VLDB*, 1998.

[37] M. J. Swain and D. H. Ballard. Color indexing. *Inter. Journal of Computer Vision*, 7(1), 1991.

[38] D. L. Swets and J. Weng. Using discriminant eigenfeatures for image retrieval. In *IEEE Trans. on Pattern Analysis and Machine Learning*, volume 18(8), 1996.

[39] G. Taubin and D. B. Cooper. Recognition and positioning of rigid objects using algebraic moment invariants. In *SPIE Vol. 1570*, 1991.

[40] D. A. White and R. Jain. Similarity indexing with the SS-Tree. In *ICDE*, 1996.

Temporal Integrity Constraints with Indeterminacy

Wes Cowley
Department of Computer Science and Engineering
University of South Florida
wcowley@acm.org

Dimitris Plexousakis
Department of Computer Science
University of Crete
dp@csd.uch.gr

Abstract

Temporal integrity constraints specify the way in which a temporal database may be updated in order to maintain semantic integrity with respect to temporal and non-temporal data elements as these change over time. Temporal indeterminacy evolves from uncertainty in the measurement of time and from changes to or differences in the granularity of temporal elements under consideration. We introduce an algebra for indeterminate time intervals and define the semantics of potential satisfaction of temporal integrity constraints. We propose a temporal integrity constraint framework which supports temporal indeterminacy by employing a novel representation for indeterminate time intervals and discuss the optimization of integrity maintenance by the compilation and simplification of constraints.

1 Introduction

Database integrity constraints provide a mechanism for specifying rules in regards to which facts may legally be stored in the database [10]. They specify the legal database states as well as the allowable database state transitions. Although database management systems have traditionally provided support for a small class of mainly structural integrity constraints, there are great benefits stemming from the support of semantic constraints: in its absence, constraints must be implemented at the application level. This results in the integrity constraints being implemented in several application programs with the expected code

**Proceedings of the 26th VLDB Conference,
Cairo, Egypt, 2000.**

consistency and maintenance issues. Centralizing integrity constraints at the database level ensures that all programs accessing the database will respect the same constraints. Furthermore, there are potential efficiency gains available when constraints reference data that would not otherwise be retrieved by a given program. Integrity constraints have been an ongoing area of research in the database community for many years.

Another long standing area of database research is temporal support. Typically databases maintain only the current state of the facts stored therein and provide little support for temporal data. The aim of temporal database research is to equip DBMSs with a higher level of support for temporal data, specifically the ability to maintain the history of updates to the database as well as to maintain the history of values which an attribute has had in the modeled domain [26, 17].

With temporal databases comes the need to maintain the integrity of the temporal data through temporal integrity constraints. This is a relatively recent area of research [24, 16, 21, 5, 22, 13]. Temporal integrity constraints must take into account not only the valid values of the temporal attribute themselves, but also the allowable ways in which all attributes, including non-temporal ones, may change over time. Therefore, temporal integrity constraints must potentially take into account the entire history of the database's evolution over time. The problem of constraint expressibility also becomes more complicated because of the need to involve temporal information in the constraint specification language.

Temporal indeterminacy is an inherent problem which arises in maintaining attribute values at different time periods in the modeled domain [11, 18, 14, 9, 4]. It may not always be clear at exactly which point in time an attribute's value changes. This indeterminacy may stem from inherent uncertainty in the modeled reality or from granularity changes. Hence, a recent area of research has focused on how to handle temporal indeterminacy in databases.

Given that there is a need to support both temporal integrity constraints and temporal indeterminacy in temporal databases, it is reasonable to assume that there is a need for temporal integrity constraints to take into account temporal indeterminacy. In this paper, we discuss a novel method of representing, manipulating, and comparing indeterminate time intervals as well as what we believe is the first proposed method for incorporating indeterminacy into a temporal integrity constraint enforcement mechanism.

Providing support for temporal indeterminacy with temporal integrity constraints has a number of benefits. In general, more flexibility is allowed in how constraints are specified in the presence of temporal indeterminacy. Specific application areas where temporal indeterminacy and hence the concept of potential satisfaction of temporal integrity constraints are useful include planning, archaeology, astronomy, and genealogy. To the best of our knowledge this is the first work to account for indeterminacy within the context of temporal integrity maintenance.

The remainder of this paper is organized as follows. Section 2 reviews research in temporal integrity constraint specification and the problem of dealing with temporal indeterminacy in databases. Section 3 presents a representation of indeterminate temporal intervals using valid interval stamps, defines an algebra for manipulating valid interval stamps and characterizes the complexity of operations on intervals. That section also includes a brief discussion of the relationships between indeterminate intervals [7]. Section 4 introduces the notion of potential satisfaction of integrity constraints and the integration of temporal indeterminacy into a constraint maintenance framework. Finally, section 5 concludes the paper with a discussion of further research directions.

2   Related Work

The temporal integrity constraint method proposed here is extended from that previously presented for determinate time [22, 23, 21]. There have been several proposals for implementing temporal integrity constraint checking. The work begun by Gertz, Lipeck and Saake appears to be the earliest [24, 13]. They use active rules to monitor progress through a transition graph generated from a Future Temporal Logic (FTL) specification. Chomicki and Toman propose a method based on generating triggers for active RDBMSs from Past Temporal Logic (PTL) [5]. Sistla and Wolfson's method uses Condition/Action rules to implement an and/or graph for evaluating constraints specified in either FTL or PTL [25]. Gal, Etzion, and Segev propose an active database language which includes temporal integrity constraints [12]. Martín and Sistac show a method for deductive databases using SLDNF resolution [19]. Doucet, et al, base their approach on a bitemporal version database [8]. The method we describe here has been developed within the context of the Telos KBMS [20]. We believe it is the first to incorporate temporal indeterminacy.

Dyreson and Snodgrass have shown the most extensive results in temporal indeterminacy [9]. They describe a timestamp with a probability function for describing indeterminacy at the point and interval levels. Their method for representing and manipulating indeterminate timestamps is both more flexible and more complex than that described here. Anger, et al. handle indeterminacy by storing interval constraints between tuples in a temporal constraint network (TCN) [2]. Griffiths and Theodoulidis' method also stores interval relationships between tuples in a TCN [14] and uses Allen's constraint propagation algorithm to check local consistency and derive new relationships [1]. Koubarakis' work represents temporal indeterminacy by local and global constraints on variables representing the end points of the intervals [18]. Gadia, et al. propose a set oriented representation which supports both indeterminacy and incompleteness with a three-valued logic [11]. Their work is the closest to the indeterminate intervals described here, but provides a different set of operators. They do not describe a method for translating between interval constraint notation and their representation, while our work does not examine temporally missing values.

3   Valid Interval Stamps

3.1   Motivation

Indeterminate time may arise in a number of ways and is nearly unavoidable when dealing with the valid time of facts in a database. We are interested in associating a valid time period with tuples in order to support a temporal integrity constraint implementation [22, 23] in which constraints include combinations of the thirteen interval relationships [15, 1]. As such, it is appropriate that the valid time periods are also specified using interval relationships. Because most of these relationships do not precisely constrain the time periods involved, the resulting time stamps are indeterminate. Thus, we must be able to derive indeterminate valid time stamps from interval constraints, manipulate those indeterminate intervals, and translate the results back to interval constraints.

3.2   Points and Intervals

We assume a linear discrete time line [3] bounded by the range of the underlying integer type in which temporal points are represented. For our purposes, we assume that the underlying type is unbounded with respect to the range of the temporal domain being modeled. In practice, overflows will need to be addressed by allowing the granularity to be changed or by changing to a type with a larger range. We do not address either of these solutions in this paper. We further assume distinct elements ∞, $-\infty$, and `nil`. With the exception of the incomparable element `nil`, points are totally ordered by $<$. The relationships $<$, $=$, and $\leq$ between two points, p_1 and p_2, carry the expected meaning. More formally, we will assume a temporal structure $\mathcal{T}$ where $\mathcal{T}$ is characterized by a set of points $\mathcal{P}$, $\mathcal{P} = \{\ldots, p_{-1}, p_0, p_1, \ldots\}$, and a relation $<$.

The set $\mathcal{P}' = \mathcal{P} \cup \{-\infty, \infty, \mathtt{nil}\}$ is isomorphic to the set $\mathcal{Z}' = \mathcal{Z} \cup \{-\infty, \infty, \mathtt{nil}\}$. We define a one-to-one, onto, and invertible mapping function, $\iota : \mathcal{P}' \to \mathcal{Z}' : \mathcal{Z}' \to \mathcal{P}'$, as follows:

$$\iota(p) = \begin{cases} p & \text{if } p = -\infty, \infty, \text{ or } \mathtt{nil} \\ i & \text{for } p_i, \ i \in \mathcal{Z} \end{cases}$$

The relation $<$ between members of the set $\mathcal{P}$ is defined as $p_1 < p_2 \Leftrightarrow \iota(p_1) < \iota(p_2)$ and can be extended to the special elements $-\infty$ and ∞ by observing that $\forall p \in \mathcal{P} \ -\infty < p < \infty$. Finally, $<$ is undefined if either operand is $\mathtt{nil}$. Similar translations give the meanings for $=$ and $\leq$. Note that from the definition of ι, $p_i = p_j \Rightarrow i = j$.

In several places in the sequel we will need to determine the relative order of a pair of points on the time line. The functions to do so are defined next.

Definition 1. The functions $\min_{\mathrm{p}}$, $\max_{\mathrm{p}}$, $\min_{\mathrm{vp}}$, $\max_{\mathrm{vp}} : \mathcal{P}' \times \mathcal{P}' \to \mathcal{P}'$ are defined as follows:

$$\min_{\mathrm{p}}(p_1, p_2) = \begin{cases} \mathtt{nil} & \text{if } p_1 = \mathtt{nil} \vee p_2 = \mathtt{nil} \\ p_1 & \text{if } p_1 < p_2 \\ p_2 & \text{otherwise} \end{cases}$$

$$\max_{\mathrm{p}}(p_1, p_2) = \begin{cases} \mathtt{nil} & \text{if } p_1 = \mathtt{nil} \vee p_2 = \mathtt{nil} \\ p_1 & \text{if } p_2 < p_1 \\ p_2 & \text{otherwise} \end{cases}$$

$$\min_{\mathrm{vp}}(p_1, p_2) = \begin{cases} \mathtt{nil} & \text{if } p_1 = \mathtt{nil} \wedge p_2 = \mathtt{nil} \\ p_1 & \text{if } p_2 = \mathtt{nil} \vee p_1 < p_2 \\ p_2 & \text{otherwise} \end{cases}$$

$$\max_{\mathrm{vp}}(p_1, p_2) = \begin{cases} \mathtt{nil} & \text{if } p_1 = \mathtt{nil} \wedge p_2 = \mathtt{nil} \\ p_1 & \text{if } p_2 = \mathtt{nil} \vee p_2 < p_1 \\ p_2 & \text{otherwise} \end{cases}$$

$\min_{\mathrm{p}}$ ($\max_{\mathrm{p}}$) chooses the earliest (latest) operand if both are not $\mathtt{nil}$. $\min_{\mathrm{vp}}$ and $\max_{\mathrm{vp}}$ treat the case where exactly one of the operands is $\mathtt{nil}$ by returning the other point. All four operators are commutative, reflexive, and associative.

Given a point p, we need to refer to its next and previous points on the time line.

Definition 2. The functions previous and next, each with signature $\mathcal{P}' \to \mathcal{P}'$, are defined as follows:

$$\mathrm{previous}(p) = \begin{cases} p & \text{if } p \in \{-\infty, \infty, \mathtt{nil}\} \\ \iota^{-1}(\iota(p) - 1) & \text{otherwise} \end{cases}$$

$$\mathrm{next}(p) = \begin{cases} p & \text{if } p \in \{-\infty, \infty, \mathtt{nil}\} \\ \iota^{-1}(\iota(p) + 1) & \text{otherwise} \end{cases}$$

In order to discuss periods of time, as opposed to instants, we use intervals.

Definition 3. A *convex interval* is a set of consecutive points. An interval I can be represented by its lowest and highest points $\langle I_s, I_e \rangle$, $I_s \leq I_e$, $I_s = \mathtt{nil} \Leftrightarrow I_e = \mathtt{nil}$. We say that $p \in I$ iff $I_s \leq p \leq I_e$. The empty interval, which contains no point, is represented by $\langle \mathtt{nil}, \mathtt{nil} \rangle$ or $\emptyset$. We say that a convex interval is *infinite* if one or both endpoints is ∞ or $-\infty$. $\mathcal{I}$ refers to the set of all convex intervals. Points may be implicitly converted to intervals by the function *interval*: $\mathcal{P} \to \mathcal{I}$, defined as $\mathrm{interval}(p) = \langle p, p \rangle$.

We will use the 13 basic interval relationships [15, 1] for comparing intervals for ordering and inclusion. The concept of intersection of convex intervals is important. This carries the same meaning as in set theory, namely that there is at least one point in common. Note that the empty interval, $\langle \mathtt{nil}, \mathtt{nil} \rangle$ does not intersect with any interval due to the incomparability of $\mathtt{nil}$. The infinite interval, $\langle -\infty, \infty \rangle$ intersects with all non-empty intervals. We also need the concept of adjacency of convex intervals, which is defined next.

Definition 4. We say that two intervals I_1 and I_2 are *adjacent* if $\mathrm{next}(I_{1_e}) = I_{2_s} \vee \mathrm{next}(I_{2_e}) = I_{1_s}$.

We will also need the concept of non-convex intervals to talk about sets of non-consecutive points. These are defined simply as a set of convex intervals I_i which neither intersect nor are adjacent.

3.3 Valid Interval Stamps

A *valid interval stamp* (VIS) is an extension of the interval concept. A VIS describes the set of points which are definitely in the interval as well as those which *may* be in the interval. Through this we can represent the indeterminacy inherent in interval constraints.

Definition 5. A *convex valid interval stamp* (CVIS) is a 4-tuple $\langle I_s, D_s, D_e, I_e \rangle$ associated with a fact in a database. D_s, D_e, if not $\mathtt{nil}$, are time stamps marking the end points of the determinate interval D; that period of time during which the associated fact is true. I_s and I_e, if not $\mathtt{nil}$, represent the extended period of time before and after the determinate interval, respectively, during which the associated fact *may* be true. The indeterminate interval then is the non-convex interval $I = \{I_L, I_H\}$ where I_L and I_H are derived from the CVIS V as follows:

$$I_L = \begin{cases} \emptyset & \text{If } I_s = \mathtt{nil} \\ \langle V.I_s, V.I_e \rangle & \text{If } D = \emptyset \\ \langle V.I_s, \mathrm{previous}(V.D_s) \rangle & \text{otherwise} \end{cases}$$

$$I_H = \begin{cases} \emptyset & \text{If } I_e = \mathtt{nil} \vee D = \emptyset \\ \langle \mathrm{next}(V.D_e), V.I_e \rangle & \text{otherwise} \end{cases}$$

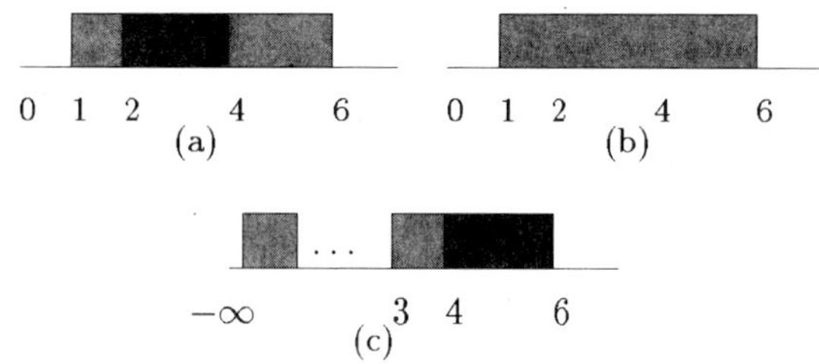

(a)   (b)   (c)

Figure 1: Three examples of CVISs

A CVIS for which both I_s and I_e are `nil` is called *fully determinate*, while one with both D_s and D_e being `nil` is called *fully indeterminate*. The empty VIS is represented as $\langle \texttt{nil}, \texttt{nil}, \texttt{nil}, \texttt{nil} \rangle$ or $\emptyset$. We will use $\mathcal{CV}$ to refer to the set of all CVISs. An interval I can be converted implicitly to a CVIS with the function $\mathrm{cvis} : \mathcal{I} \to \mathcal{CV}$, defined as $\mathrm{cvis}(I) = \langle \texttt{nil}, I_s, I_e, \texttt{nil} \rangle$.

Example 1. Figure 1a shows the CVIS $\langle 1, 2, 4, 6 \rangle$. This contains the points $\{2, 3, 4\}$ in the determinate region and $\{1, 5, 6\}$ in the indeterminate region. Figure 1b shows the same period of time covered by the fully indeterminate interval $\langle 1, \texttt{nil}, \texttt{nil}, 6 \rangle$. Finally, figure 1c shows the left infinite CVIS $\langle -\infty, 4, 6, \texttt{nil} \rangle$ which has no upper indeterminate region.

We will often need to obtain the earliest and latest points in a CVIS independently of whether that point is determinate or not.

Definition 6. We define the functions *upper* and *lower*: $\mathcal{CV} \to \mathcal{P}$ as $\mathrm{upper}(V) = \max_{\mathrm{vp}}(V.D_e, V.I_e)$ and $\mathrm{lower}(V) = \min_{\mathrm{vp}}(V.D_s, V.I_s)$.

We will also need to know the latest point at which a CVIS V can start and the earliest point at which it can end. To understand these functions, observe that if V has a determinate region then the interval will start no later than $V.D_s$ and end no earlier than $V.D_e$. On the other hand, if V is fully indeterminate then it may start as late as $V.I_e$ and end as earlier as $V.I_s$.

Definition 7. We define two functions, *maxlo* and *minup*: $\mathcal{CV} \to \mathcal{P}$ as $\mathrm{maxlo}(V) = \min_{\mathrm{vp}}(V.D_s, V.I_e)$ and $\mathrm{minup}(V) = \max_{\mathrm{vp}}(V.I_s, V.D_e)$.

The following extends the definition of membership in an interval. We will also use $p \in V.D$ to represent p's determinate inclusion in V and $p \in V.I$ to represent p's indeterminate inclusion in V.

Definition 8. We denote membership of a point p in a CVIS V as $p \in V$ and define that membership as $p \in V \Leftrightarrow \mathrm{lower}(V) \leq p \leq \mathrm{upper}(V)$.

Next we extend the concept of intersection.

Definition 9. Two CVISs, V_1 and V_2 *intersect* if: $\mathrm{lower}(V_1) \leq \mathrm{upper}(V_2) \wedge \mathrm{lower}(V_2) \leq \mathrm{upper}(V_1)$. We say V_1 and V_2 *determinately intersect* if $V_1.D \neq \emptyset \wedge V_2.D \neq \emptyset \wedge V_1.D$ intersects $V_2.D$.

The concept of adjacency can be extended to convex valid interval stamps as follows.

Definition 10. We say that two CVISs, V_1 and V_2 are *adjacent* if $\mathrm{next}(\mathrm{upper}(V_1)) = \mathrm{lower}(V_2) \vee \mathrm{next}(\mathrm{upper}(V_2)) = \mathrm{lower}(V_1)$. We say that V_1 and V_2 are *determinately adjacent* if $V_1.D \neq \emptyset \wedge V_2.D \neq \emptyset \wedge V_1.D$ adjacent $V_2.D$. Note that two CVISs which are determinately adjacent may intersect but will not determinately intersect.

Details on how to translate from interval constraints of the form $\mathcal{R}\ I$, where $\mathcal{R}$ is an interval relationship and I is a determinate interval, to a convex valid interval stamp can be found in [6].

We will also need to consider non-convex valid interval stamps.

Definition 11. A *non-convex valid interval stamp* (NVIS) is a finite set of CVISs which meet two conditions. 1) No two CVISs may intersect. 2) If any two CVISs are adjacent, then both must have a definite interval and they must not be determinately adjacent. $\mathcal{NV}$ refers to the set of all NVISs. A CVIS can be implicitly converted to an NVIS with the function *nvis*: $\mathcal{CV} \to \mathcal{NV}$, defined as $\mathrm{nvis}(C) = \{C\}$.

Definition 12. $\mathcal{V} = \mathcal{CV} \cup \mathcal{NV}$ denotes the set of VISs.

3.4 Operators on Valid Interval Stamps

There are a number of operators on VISs which correspond to the similarly named ones on Boolean expressions and sets. Specifically, we will define conjunction, intersection, union, and difference of VISs below. To avoid confusion, we will annotate the usual operators to emphasize that they carry different semantics than the familiar ones. For example, we use $\overset{v}{\cup}$ for the union of VISs. When operands are known to be convex (non-convex) VISs, we will use $\overset{cv}{\cup}$ ($\overset{nv}{\cup}$). When the familiar semantics from logic or set theory are sufficient, we will use the unannotated operators. The algorithms and correctness proofs are omitted for space reasons and are presented elsewhere [6].

3.4.1 Conjunction

There are times when a single interval constraint may not adequately express the knowledge one has about a fact's valid time. For that we must conjoin multiple constraints. We will do this by way of the VIS conjunction operator[1]: $\overset{v}{\wedge}$. The effect of $\overset{v}{\wedge}$ is to produce

---

[1] The term *conjunction* refers to the operation on interval constraints which $\overset{v}{\wedge}$ supports. It might be more appropriate to

444

a determinate region which includes the determinate region of both operands and an indeterminate region which includes only points in the indeterminate region of both operands. The operator uses the knowledge expressed by two VISs in order to increase the accuracy to which the valid time of a fact is known.

In order to compute the resulting VIS, V_r, from the conjunction of two existing CVISs, V_1 and V_2, we must first ensure that the conjunction is satisfiable. For example, there are no dates which satisfy the condition "contains Jan-98 and during Mar-98". On the other hand, "contains Jan-98 and after Nov-97" can be satisfied. Each operand restricts the range of the other.

Definition 13. Two CVISs, V_1 and V_2, are *conjunction compatible*, denoted $V_1 \wedge_{\text{comp}} V_2$, if 1) V_1 intersects V_2, 2) $V_2.D \neq \emptyset \Rightarrow (\text{lower}(V_1) <= V_2.D_s \wedge V_2.D_e <= \text{upper}(V_1))$, and 3) $V_1.D \neq \emptyset \Rightarrow (\text{lower}(V_2) <= V_1.D_s \wedge V_1.D_e <= \text{upper}(V_2))$. We extend this definition to NVISs by saying that two NVISs are *conjunction compatible* if $\forall V_{1_i} \in V_1 \exists V_{2_j} \in V_2$ such that $V_{1_i} \wedge_{\text{comp}} V_{2_j}$ and $\forall V_{2_j} \in V_2 \exists V_{1_i} \in V_1$ such that $V_{2_j} \wedge_{\text{comp}} V_{1_i}$. It should be clear from this definition that $\wedge_{\text{comp}}$ is symmetric and reflexive.

Conjunction compatibility ensures that the indefinite region of each interval encloses the definite region of the other. Otherwise, there would be a point which is in the definite region of one operand but not in the other operand at all. That is the condition which results from inconsistent interval constraints.

Definition 14 ($\overset{v}{\wedge}$). If V_1 and V_2 are VISs such that $V_1 \wedge_{\text{comp}} V_2$ we define their conjunction, denoted by $V_1 \overset{v}{\wedge} V_2$, as the VIS V_r such that $V_r.D = \{p | p \in V_1.D \vee p \in V_2.D\}$ and $V_r.I = \{p | p \in V_1.I \wedge p \in V_2.I\}$. If $\neg(V_1 \wedge_{\text{comp}} V_2)$ then $V_1 \overset{v}{\wedge} V_2 = \emptyset$.

Example 2. Suppose we wish to conjoin the three VISs shown in figure 2:

$$V_1 = \langle -\infty, 14, 21, \infty \rangle$$
$$V_2 = \langle -\infty, 17, 19, 23 \rangle$$
$$V_3 = \langle -\infty, 9, 12, \infty \rangle$$

We will arbitrarily start with $V_1 \overset{cv}{\wedge} V_2$. It's clear that they intersect and that each interval's determinate region falls within the indeterminate region of the other. Hence, they are conjunction compatible. Further, we can see that they determinately intersect. We compute the intermediate result to be $V_r = \langle -\infty, 14, 21, 23 \rangle$. The final valid interval is then $V_r' = V_r \overset{cv}{\wedge} V_3$. We note that V_r and V_3 are conjunction compatible but neither determinately intersect nor are determinately adjacent. The result then is:

$$V_r' = \{\langle -\infty, 9, 12, \texttt{nil} \rangle, \langle 13, 14, 21, 23 \rangle\}$$

think of the effect on a VIS as *strengthens*.

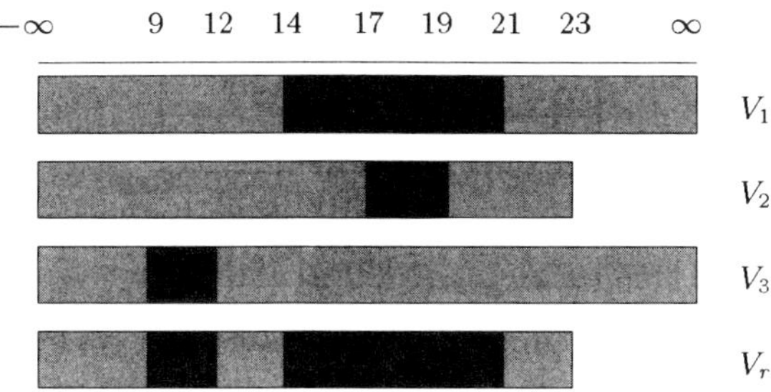

Figure 2: A Graphical Representation of Example 2

Because the order of the interval constraints in a valid time specification should not matter, it is important that the order of VISs with respect to $\overset{v}{\wedge}$ not matter. It can easily be shown that $(\mathcal{V}, \overset{v}{\wedge})$ forms a commutative monoid with identity $\langle -\infty, \texttt{nil}, \texttt{nil}, \infty \rangle$.

3.4.2 Intersection

The intersection of two CVISs is defined similarly to conjunction. The precondition is not as restrictive. It is simply necessary that the intervals intersect by definition 9. On the other hand, the result of intersection is more restrictive than that of conjunction. Specifically, the determinate region produced by conjunction includes the determinate regions of both operands. If a point is determinate in only one of the operands, it is determinate in the result. For intersection, the determinate region includes only those points determinately in *both* operands. If a point is determinately in one operand but indeterminately in the other, the intersection contains that point indeterminately.

Definition 15 ($\overset{v}{\cap}$). We define the intersection of two VISs, V_1 and V_2, denoted by $V_1 \overset{v}{\cap} V_2$, as the VIS V_r such that $V_r.D = \{p | p \in V_1.D \wedge p \in V_2.D\}$ and $V_r.I = \{p | p \in V_1 \wedge p \in V_2 \wedge (p \in V_1.I \vee p \in V_2.I)\}$.

It is straightforward to show that $(\mathcal{V}, \overset{v}{\cap})$ forms a commutative monoid with identity $\langle \texttt{nil}, -\infty, \infty, \texttt{nil} \rangle$.

3.4.3 Union

When an insert operation is performed for a tuple whose non-temporal attributes are the same as an existing tuple either the operation is treated as a new insert, resulting in a pair of tuples which are duplicated except in their valid interval stamps; or the valid interval stamp of the existing tuple is updated to include the valid time specified for the insert. We choose the latter semantics, provided by the union operator.

The union of two VISs is somewhat more complicated than conjunction and intersection. This is because the union of two NVISs may contain overlapping regions on the time line, which must be merged or split

Operator	Complexity
$\wedge_{\text{comp}}$	$O(|V_1||V_2|)$
$\overset{nv}{\wedge}$	$O(|V_1||V_2|)$
$\overset{nv}{\cap}$	$O(|V_1||V_2|)$
$\overset{nv}{\cup}$	$O((|V_1||V_2|)^2)$
$\overset{nv}{-}$	$O(|V_2|^4|V_1|)$

Table 1: Complexity of Operators over NVISs

in order to satisfy the definition. There are also no restrictions on the VISs which can be combined by $\overset{v}{\cup}$.

Definition 16 ($\overset{v}{\cup}$). We define the union of two VISs, V_1 and V_2, denoted by $V_1 \overset{v}{\cup} V_2$, as the VIS V_r such that $V_r.D = \{p | p \in V_1.D \vee p \in V_2.D\}$ and $V_r.I = \{p | p \notin V_r.D \wedge (p \in V_1.I \vee p \in V_2.I)\}$.

Again, it is easy to show that $(\mathcal{V}, \overset{v}{\cup})$ forms a commutative monoid with identity $\langle nil, nil, nil, nil \rangle$.

3.4.4 Difference

When performing a deletion or update operation where the valid time specified is only a portion of the valid time for the affected tuples, we will need to produce the difference of two valid interval stamps. In general, this results in a non-convex interval. Observe that when deleting an interval V_d from another interval V, the resulting non-convex interval contains two portions of V. One is the section of V occurring before V_d, the other is the section occurring after V_d. If either V or V_d is indeterminate, then so is the resulting interval.

Definition 17 ($\overset{v}{-}$). We define the difference of two VISs, V_1 and V_2, denoted by $V_1 \overset{v}{-} V_2$ as the VIS V_r such that $V_r.D = \{p | p \in V_1.D \wedge p \notin V_2\}$ and $V_r.I = \{p | (p \in V_1.D \wedge p \in V_2.I) \vee (p \in V_1.I \wedge p \notin V_2.D)\}$.

Note that $\overset{v}{-}$ is neither commutative nor associative. There is, however, an identity element: $\emptyset$.

3.5 Complexity of VIS Operators

The basic operators on CVISs: $\wedge_{\text{comp}}, \overset{cv}{\wedge}, \overset{cv}{\cap}, \overset{cv}{\cup}$, and $\overset{cv}{-}$, are all constant time. This should be clear from their definitions, which depend solely on the values of the end points and not the duration of the intervals. For an NVIS V, we will use $|V|$ to indicate the number of CVISs $V_i \in V$. Based on an analysis of the algorithms developed to implement the operators, we have the results in table 1 for NVISs. Proofs of these results can be found with the algorithms [6].

3.6 Indeterminate Intervals Relationships

Having defined a representation for indeterminate intervals, we need a way of comparing intervals for ordering and inclusion. We propose an extension of the thirteen relationships between determinate intervals. For each relationship between determinate intervals we have two corresponding relationships, potential and definite, between indeterminate intervals. The following principles give the basis for defining the definite and potential relationships. The specific definitions for each of the twenty-six relationships can be found in previous work [7].

Principle 1. For V_1 definitely $\mathcal{R}$ V_2 to hold, where $\mathcal{R}$ is an interval relationship, we must have: $\nexists V_1', V_2'$ such that $V_1 \wedge_{\text{comp}} V_1' \wedge V_2 \wedge_{\text{comp}} V_2' \wedge \neg((V_1 \overset{cv}{\wedge} V_1').D \, \mathcal{R} \, (V_2 \overset{cv}{\wedge} V_2').D)$. If this principle is met, it is not possible to conjoin any compatible interval constraint to either V_1 or V_2 such that $\mathcal{R}$ will not be satisfied.

Principle 2. For V_1 potentially $\mathcal{R}$ V_2 to hold, where $\mathcal{R}$ is an interval relationship, we must have: $\exists V_1', V_2'$ such that $V_1 \wedge_{\text{comp}} V_1' \wedge V_2 \wedge_{\text{comp}} V_2' \wedge (V_1 \overset{cv}{\wedge} V_1')$ definitely $\mathcal{R}$ $(V_2 \overset{cv}{\wedge} V_2')$. This ensures that it is possible, via the conjunction of additional interval constraints with V_1 and V_2 to arrive at a pair of intervals which definitely satisfy $\mathcal{R}$ by principle 1[2].

Previous work has shown some interesting observations about the compatibility of the various interval relationships [7]. First, we note that the interval relationships between determinate intervals are mutually exclusive. This observation extends to the definite relationships between valid interval stamps. We cannot make the same conclusion regarding potential relationships, however. It is easy to show that, for indeterminate interval V_1, V_2 and indeterminate relationships $\mathcal{R}_1, \mathcal{R}_2$, V_1 potentially $\mathcal{R}_1$ $V_2 \not\Rightarrow \neg(V_1$ potentially $\mathcal{R}_2$ $V_2)$. Finally, we can see from Principles 1 and 2 that, as expected, a definite relationship implies a potential one.

4 Potential Temporal Integrity Constraint Satisfaction

4.1 Constraint Satisfaction

We now examine what it means for a database to satisfy an integrity constraint in the presence of temporal indeterminacy. Definitions for constraint satisfaction have previously been given for the case of determinate intervals [21, 22, 23]. We extend those definitions to allow for temporal indeterminacy as supported by the VIS. In what follows, the notations $r(i_1, i_2)$ and $i_1 \, r \, i_2$ where r is an interval relationship and i_1, i_2 are valid interval stamps will be used interchangeably. First, we define the contents of the knowledge bases (databases) which underlie the integrity constraints.

---

[2] Note that either or both of V_1', V_2' may be the identity.

Definition 18. A *knowledge base, KB,* comprises a set of propositions, KB_P, defining the validity of predicates over possibly indeterminate time intervals, as well as a set, KB_R, of deductive rules and a set, KB_I of integrity constraints.

We will need the concepts of both object and temporal variable substitution.

Definition 19. An *object variable substitution* σ is a function mapping a variable x_i of sort S_i to an instance of the corresponding class C_i so that $instanceOf(\sigma(x_i), C_i, t) \in KB_P$ for some VIS t. A *temporal variable substitution* τ is a function mapping a temporal variable t of sort *Time* to an interval in $\mathcal{V}$.

The next definition forms the core of the extension of the temporal integrity constraint method to indeterminate intervals. We show how to determine whether a knowledge base satisfies, either definitely or potentially, a temporal formula. In this definition and the following, we will require a shorthand notation for a common disjunction of interval relationships. We will use the term *covers* as the disjunction between *finishes, starts, during,* and *equals,* prefixing with *potentially* or *definitely* as appropriate. We will use *covered-by* as the disjunction of the inverses of those four relationships.

With the introduction of temporal indeterminacy, one may not be able to determine with certainty whether a knowledge base KB satisfies a formula or not. In the case where KB may or may not satisfy a formula because of temporal indeterminacy, we will use the symbol $\overset{p}{\vDash}$ for potential satisfaction. The traditional $\vDash$ will be used for definite satisfaction.

Definition 20. For base predicates P and Q, object substitution σ and temporal substitution τ:

- If P is ground and of the form $r(i_1, i_2)$ for a determinate interval relationship r and intervals i_1, i_2 then $(KB, \sigma, \tau) \vDash P$ iff $(KB, \sigma, \tau) \vDash$ definitely $r(i_1, i_2)$. Similarly, $(KB, \sigma, \tau) \overset{p}{\vDash} P$ iff $(KB, \sigma, \tau) \vDash$ potentially $r(i_1, i_2)$.

- If P is ground, then $(KB, \sigma, \tau) \vDash P$ and $(KB, \sigma, \tau) \overset{p}{\vDash} P$ iff $P \in KB_P$.

- $(KB, \sigma, \tau) \vDash P(x, t)$ iff $\exists t' \in \mathcal{V}$ such that $\tau(t)$ definitely covered-by $\tau(t') \wedge (KB, \sigma, \tau) \vDash P(\sigma(x), \tau(t'))$.

- $(KB, \sigma, \tau) \overset{p}{\vDash} P(x, t)$ iff $\exists t' \in \mathcal{V}$ such that $\tau(t)$ potentially covered-by $\tau(t') \wedge (KB, \sigma, \tau) \overset{p}{\vDash} P(\sigma(x), \tau(t'))$.

- $(KB, \sigma, \tau) \vDash \neg P(x, t)$ iff $\not\exists t' \in \mathcal{V}$ such that

$\tau(t)$ potentially covered-by $\tau(t') \wedge (KB, \sigma, \tau) \overset{p}{\vDash} P(\sigma(x), \tau(t'))$.

- $(KB, \sigma, \tau) \overset{p}{\vDash} \neg P(x, t)$ iff $\not\exists t' \in \mathcal{V}$ such that $\tau(t)$ definitely covered-by $\tau(t') \wedge (KB, \sigma, \tau) \vDash P(\sigma(x), \tau(t'))$.

- $(KB, \sigma, \tau) \vDash P(x, t_1) \vee Q(x, t_2)$ iff $(KB, \sigma, \tau) \vDash P(x, t_1) \vee (KB, \sigma, \tau) \vDash Q(x, t_2)$. Similarly, $(KB, \sigma, \tau) \overset{p}{\vDash} P(x, t_1) \vee Q(x, t_2)$ iff $(KB, \sigma, \tau) \overset{p}{\vDash} P(x, t_1) \vee (KB, \sigma, \tau) \overset{p}{\vDash} Q(x, t_2)$.

- $(KB, \sigma, \tau) \vDash \forall x/C \ P(x, t)$ iff $(KB, \sigma[x/d], \tau) \vDash P(x, t)$ for all d such that $instanceOf(d, C, T)$ for some interval T, T definitely covered-by $\tau(t)$.

- $(KB, \sigma, \tau) \overset{p}{\vDash} \forall x/C \ P(x, t)$ iff $(KB, \sigma[x/d], \tau) \overset{p}{\vDash} P(x, t)$ for all d such that $instanceOf(d, C, T)$ for some interval T, T potentially covered-by $\tau(t)$.

- $(KB, \sigma, \tau) \vDash \forall t/Time \ P(x, t)$ iff $\forall T \in \mathcal{V} (KB, \sigma, \tau[t/T]) \vDash P(x, t)$.

- $(KB, \sigma, \tau) \overset{p}{\vDash} \forall t/Time \ P(x, t)$ iff $\forall T \in \mathcal{V} (KB, \sigma, \tau[t/T]) \overset{p}{\vDash} P(x, t)$.

If P is a derivable predicate defined by a set of deductive rules with bodies $R_1, \ldots, R_k$ and respective time intervals $T_1, \ldots, T_k$, $T_i \in \mathcal{V}$, then:

- $(KB, \sigma, \tau) \vDash P(x, t)$ iff $(KB, \sigma, \tau) \vDash \bigvee_{i=1}^{k} R_i \wedge$ (t definitely covered-by T), where $T = \bigcap_{i=1}^{k} T_i$.

- $(KB, \sigma, \tau) \overset{p}{\vDash} P(x, t)$ iff $(KB, \sigma, \tau) \overset{p}{\vDash} \bigvee_{i=1}^{k} R_i \wedge$ (t potentially covered-by T), where $T = \bigcap_{i=1}^{k} T_i$.

The intuition behind the cases for $(KB, \sigma, \tau) \vDash \neg P(x, t)$ and $(KB, \sigma, \tau) \overset{p}{\vDash} \neg P(x, t)$ is that if there is some time interval t' which potentially covers t during which KB potentially entails P then we cannot say that KB definitely entails P's negation. Likewise, we can say that KB may entail the negation of P during some interval t only if there is no time interval t' which definitely covers t during which P is definitely entailed by KB.

The satisfaction of temporal integrity constraints follows from definition 20.

Definition 21. If the temporal variables $t_1, \ldots, t_k$ occur in the constraint C with history time[3] T, then:

- $(KB, \sigma, \tau) \vDash C \, [\text{at } T]$ iff $(KB, \sigma, \tau) \vDash C'$, where $C' \equiv C \wedge \bigwedge_{i=1}^{k} (t_i \text{ definitely covered-by } T)$.

---

[3] In the context of Telos, history and belief time refer to the same concepts as valid and transaction time, respectively.

- $(KB, \sigma, \tau) \overset{p}{\vDash} C\,[\text{at } T]$ iff $(KB, \sigma, \tau) \overset{p}{\vDash} C'$, where $C' \equiv C \wedge \bigwedge_{i=1}^{k} (t_i \text{ potentially covered–by } T)$.

4.2 Compilation and Simplification

In this paragraph, we will discuss an extension of temporal integrity constraint compilation algorithm previously given in [21, 22, 23] to handle valid interval stamps. First, we define what is meant by an update and transaction in the context of the Telos language [20].

Definition 22. An *update* is an instantiated literal whose sign determines whether it is an insert or a deletion. A *transaction* is an arbitrary set of updates.

Next, we define how to determine updates possibly affecting the validity of a constraint.

Definition 23. Let t and T be VISs. An update $U(\,\_,\,\_,\,\_, t)$ is an *affecting update* for a constraint $C\,[\text{at } T]$ if and only if there exists a literal $L(\_,\,\_,\,\_)$ in C such that L unifies with the complement of U, and the indeterminate intersection $(\overset{v}{\cap})$, $t * T$, of intervals t and T is non-empty. A transaction $X = \{U_1, \ldots, U_m\}$ is called an *affecting transaction* for a constraint $C\,[\text{at } T]$ if and only if at least one of $U_1, \ldots U_m$ is an affecting update for the constraint.

The notion of dependence between constraints and deductive rules, defined next, does not depend on the temporal intervals involved.

Definition 24. A literal L *directly depends* on a literal K if and only if there exists a rule of the form $\forall x/C_1 \ldots \forall x_n/C_n \,(F \Rightarrow A)$ such that there exists a literal in F unifying with K with most general unifier θ and $A\theta = L$. A literal L *transitively depends* (or, simply, depends) on literal K if and only if it directly depends on K or depends on a literal M that directly depends on K.

The concerned class of a literal is used to narrow the set of constraints to be checked at runtime for each update. This is not strictly necessary for constraint checking, but is used as an optimization.

Definition 25. A *concerned class* for a literal L is a most specialized class CC such that inserting or deleting an instance of CC can affect the truth of L and the time intervals of L and CC are potentially unifiable[4]. The *concerned set* for a literal L is the set of distinct concerned classes for L.

Now we arrive at the compiled form of a constraint, the Parameterized Simplified Structure (PSS).

----

[4]By *potentially unifiable* we mean that there is some assignment which can be made to the intervals such that they are potentially equal.

Definition 26. Given a temporal constraint $C\,[\text{at } T]$ expressed in DNF and a literal L occurring positively (negatively) in C, the *parameterized simplified structure* of C with respect to L is a 6-tuple $(L, Params, CS, T, T', SF)$ where $Params$ is the list of instantiation variables of L, CS is the concerned set of L, T and T' are the history and belief time intervals of the constraint respectively, and SF is the simplified form of the constraint that suffices to be evaluated when a deletion from (insertion to) L takes place. SF is derived by replacing instantiation variables with parameters, conjoining history time variables with potentially during(t_i, T), conjoining belief time variables with potentially during(t_i, T'), replacing L with *True* when the update is an insertion or *False* when the update is a delete, applying first order logic absorption rules, and applying temporal simplification rules.

Example 3. As an example of the application of the above definition to integrity constraints, consider the following dynamic constraint expressing the property that "salaries should never decrease".

$$\forall p/\texttt{Employee} \; \forall s, s'/\texttt{Integer} \; \forall t_1, t_2/\texttt{Time}$$
$$(salary(p, s, t_1) \wedge salary(p, s', t_2) \wedge$$
$$\texttt{potentially before}(t_1, t_2)$$
$$\Rightarrow (s \le s')) \; (\texttt{at } 02/01/99..*)$$

The constraint is expressed in the assertion language of Telos [20], a many-sorted first-order language with classes corresponding to sorts (e.g., the class **Employee**). **Time** is a built in class of time intervals. The example serves to convey the idea behind compilation and simplification of constraints.

Applying the simplification steps of definition 26 to this constraint will generate the following simplified form (capitalized variables denote parameters):

$$\forall s/\texttt{Integer} \; \forall t_1/\texttt{TimeInterval}$$
$$(salary(p, s, t_1) \wedge$$
$$(t_1 \; \texttt{potentially during } 02/01/1999..*) \wedge$$
$$(t_1 \; \texttt{potentially before } T_2)$$
$$\Rightarrow (s \le S'))$$

4.3 Temporal Simplification

The last phase of the constraint compilation algorithms is temporal simplification. Consider a conjunction of the form potentially during$(t, i_1) \wedge r_1(t, i_2)$ where r_1 is one of the interval relationships or the negation of one of the relationships and i_1, i_2 are known intervals. Such a constraint often arises from the building of the PSS. Using the derived interval relationship, r_2, between i_1 and i_2 one can in some cases either show that the conjunction is unsatisfiable or find a simpler form of the conjunction, $r(t, i_3)$ where r and i_3 are derived from a simplification table. The simplification tables as well as details on their development have been omitted for space reasons. They can be found in [6].

Example 4. Suppose we have the temporal constraint:

$$C = \text{potentially during}(t, i_1) \wedge \text{potentially starts}(t, i_2)$$

where $i_1 = \langle 10, 20, 30, 40 \rangle$ and $i_2 = \langle 5, 20, 35, \texttt{nil} \rangle$. In [7], definition 20 gives the *potentially finishes* relationship as:

$$V_1.I_e = \texttt{nil} \wedge V_2.I_e = \texttt{nil} \wedge V_1.D_e = V_2.D_e \wedge$$
$$V_2.D_s < \text{lower}(V_1)$$

From this we can see that i_1 potentially finishes i_2. From C we see that r_1 is potentially starts. By consulting the simplification table we find the simplification rule:

Let $i_1' = \langle \texttt{nil}, \text{next}(\text{lower}(i_1)), \text{upper}(i_1), \texttt{nil} \rangle$
and $i_3 = i_1' \overset{cv}{\cap} i_2$.
If $\text{lower}(i_3) < \text{upper}(i_3)$ then
    $C' = \text{potentially starts}(t, i_3)$
otherwise inconsistent

and we proceed as follows:

$$i_1' = \langle \texttt{nil}, 11, 40, \texttt{nil} \rangle$$
$$i_3 = i_1' \overset{cv}{\wedge} i_2 = \langle \texttt{nil}, 11, 35, \texttt{nil} \rangle$$
$$C' = \text{potentially starts}(t, i_3)$$

4.4 Graph Construction and Run Time Evaluation

The remainder of the integrity constraint compilation algorithms, specifically the construction of the dependency graph, the computation of its transitive closure, and the incremental maintenance of both, do not require changes from the original definition [23] to handle indeterminate intervals. Graph construction proceeds by assigning each PSS to a vertex and drawing directed arcs from a vertex v_1 to a vertex v_2 when the integrity constraint or deductive rule associated with v_2 directly depends on the deductive rule associated with v_1. Definition 24 does not rely on the valid time interval of the rules.

The time intervals associated with the rules and the associated literals come into play during the run time evaluation of the dependency graph. The original evaluation algorithm [23] does not need to be changed to incorporate indeterminate intervals except for the choice between definite or potential constraint satisfaction semantics. The algorithm assumes that before each update all constraints are satisfied. When an update is made to the database the algorithm identifies each PSS in the graph associated with a literal which unifies with a literal involved in the update. All integrity constraints which are associated with these PSSs are potentially affected and must be evaluated using definition 21.

Complexity results and a performance analysis for the dependency graph maintenance and constraint evaluation phases have been previously produced for the determinate version of the algorithms [23]. Because the operations used in the extension to indeterminate intervals have a constant time complexity it is not expected that these results will be significantly different for the extension.

5 Conclusions and Future Directions

By using a novel representation for indeterminate intervals and an extension of the interval relationships to indeterminate time, a previously proposed method for temporal integrity constraint enforcement has been extended to accommodate temporal indeterminacy. Potential integrity constraint satisfaction allows a constraint designer more flexibility in specifying integrity constraints so as to delay violation until it is certain that no series of updates can be made which will cause the database to satisfy the constraints under definite constraint satisfaction semantics. We believe that for applications in which temporal indeterminacy is inherent this flexibility will prove important. To the best of our knowledge this is the first work to account for indeterminacy within the context of temporal integrity maintenance.

As far as complexity is concerned, the operations on valid interval stamps which are involved in the potential constraint satisfaction semantics are constant time, so should not increase the previously presented complexity results for determinate temporal integrity constraints.

There are several directions for further research. Foremost will be to produce an implementation of both the determinate version of the temporal integrity constraint algorithms, as well as the extension presented here. From a more theoretical standpoint, it would be interesting to examine whether the indeterminate interval relationships could be applied to an extension of Allen's constraint propogation algorithm [1] and to reformulate the indeterminate interval relationships without reference to the endpoints. The determinate interval relationships can be stated in terms of *before* or *meets*, for example. Finally, it is worth investigating how the complexity and expressiveness of potential constraint satisfaction would change if the indeterminate intervals had an associated probability function, similar to Dyreson and Snodgrass [9] and also to fuzzy logic based approach of Bouzid and Mouaddib [4].

References

[1] James F. Allen. Maintaining knowledge about temporal intervals. *Communications of the ACM*, 26(11):832–843, 1983.

[2] Frank D. Anger, Ramon A. Mata-Toledo, Robert A. Morris, and Rita V. Rodriguez. A re-

lational knowledge base with temporal reasoning. In *Proceedings of the Florida AI Research Symposium*, pages 147–151, 1988.

[3] Johan van Benthem. *The Logic of Time*. Kluwer Academic Publishers, Dordrecht, Holland, 1991.

[4] Maroua Bouzid and Abdel-Illah Mouaddib. Uncertain temporal reasoning for the distributed transportation scheduling problem. In *Proceedings of the 5th Int. Workshop on Temporal Representation and Reasoning*, pages 21–28, 1998.

[5] Jan Chomicki and David Toman. Implementing temporal integrity constraints using an active DBMS. *IEEE Transactions on Knowledge and Data Engineering*, 7(4):566–582, 1995.

[6] Wes Cowley. Temporal integrity constraints with temporal indeterminacy. Master's thesis, University of South Florida, November 1999.

[7] Wes Cowley and Dimitris Plexousakis. An interval algebra for indeterminate time. In *Proceedings of the Seventeenth National Conference on Artificial Intelligence (AAAI-2000)*. To appear.

[8] Anne Doucet, Marie-Christine Fauvet, Stéphane Gançarski, Geneviève Jomier, and Sophie Monties. Using database versions to implement temporal integrity constraints. In *Proceedings of the Int. Workshop on Constraint Databases*, pages 219–233, 1997.

[9] Curtis E. Dyreson and Richard T. Snodgrass. Supporting valid-time indeterminacy. *ACM Transactions on Database Systems*, 23(1):1–57, 1998.

[10] J. Florentin. Consistency auditing of databases. *Computer Journal*, 17(1):52–58, 1974.

[11] Shashi K. Gadia, Sunil S. Nair, and Yiu-Cheong Poon. Incomplete information in relational temporal databases. In *Proceedings of the 18th Int. Conference on Very Large Databases*, pages 395–406, 1992.

[12] Avigdor Gal, Opher Etzion, and Arie Segev. A language for the support of constraints in temporal active databases. In *Proceedings ILPS'95–Workshop on Constraints, Databases and Logic Programming*, pages 42–58, 1995.

[13] M. Gertz and U.W. Lipeck. Deriving optimized integrity monitoring triggers from dynamic integrity constraints. *Data and Knowledge Engineering*, 20(2):163–194, 1996.

[14] Antony Griffiths and Babis Theodoulidis. SQL+i: Adding temporal indeterminacy to the database language SQL. In *Proceedings of the British National Conference on Databases*, pages 204–221, 1996.

[15] C. L. Hamblin. Instants and intervals. In J. T. Fraser, F. C. Haber, and G. H. Müller, editors, *The Study of Time*, pages 324–331, New York, NY, USA, 1972. Springer-Verlag.

[16] K. Hulsmann and G Saake. Theoretical foundations of handling large substitution sets in temporal integrity monitoring. *Acta Informatica*, 28(4):365–407, 1991.

[17] Christian S. Jensen, et al. A consensus glossary of temporal database concepts. *ACM SIGMOD Record*, 23(1):52–64, March 1994.

[18] Manolis Koubarakis. Database models for infinite and indefinite temporal information. *Information Systems*, 19(2):141–174, 1994.

[19] Carme Martín and Jaume Sistac. Applying transition rules to bitemporal deductive databases for integrity constraint checking. In *LID '96*, pages 111–128, 1996.

[20] John Mylopoulos, Vinay Chaudhri, Dimitris Plexousakis, Adel Shrufi, and Thodoros Topaloglou. Building knowledge base management systems. *VLDB Journal*, 5(4):238–263, 1996.

[21] Dimitris Plexousakis. Integrity constraint and rule maintenance in temporal deductive knowledge bases. In *Proceedings of the 19th Int. Conference on Very Large Databases*, pages 146–157, 1993.

[22] Dimitris Plexousakis. Compilation and simplification of temporal integrity constraints. In *Proceedings of the 2nd Int. Workshop on Rules in Database Systems*, pages 260–274, 1995.

[23] Dimitris Plexousakis. *On the Efficient Maintenance of Temporal Integrity in Knowledge Bases*. PhD thesis, University of Toronto, 1996.

[24] G. Saake and U. Lipeck. Foundations of temporal integrity monitoring. In C. Roland et al., editor, *Temporal Aspects in Information Systems*, pages 235–249. North Holland, 1988.

[25] A. Prasad Sistla and Ouri Wolfson. Temporal triggers in active databases. *IEEE Transactions on Knowledge and Data Engineering*, 7(3):471–486, 1995.

[26] A. U. Tansel, J. Clifford, S. Gadia, S. Jajodia, A. Segev, and R. Snodgrass, editors. *Temporal Databases: Theory, Design, and Implementation*. Benjamin/Cummings, Redwood City, Cal., 1993.

The BT-Tree: A Branched and Temporal Access Method

Linan Jiang, Betty Salzberg *
College of Comp. Sc., Northeastern Univ.
Boston, MA 02115
{linan, salzberg}@ccs.neu.edu

David Lomet
Microsoft Research
One Microsoft Way Bldg 9
Redmond, WA 98052
lomet@microsoft.com

Manuel Barrena †
Universidad de Extremadura
Cáceres, Spain
barrena@unex.es

Abstract

Temporal databases assume a single line of time evolution. In other words, they support time-evolving data. However there are applications which require the support of temporal data with *branched* time evolution. With new branches created as time proceeds, branched and temporal data tends to increase in size rapidly, making the need for efficient indexing crucial. We propose a new (*paginated*) access method for branched and temporal data: the BT-tree. The BT-tree is both storage efficient and access efficient. We have implemented the BT-tree and performance results confirm these properties.

1 Introduction

There are many database applications that require the support of time-evolving data. Temporal database systems model explicitly the temporal behavior of data, thus providing the ability to store and query temporal data efficiently [9].

Conventional temporal databases assume a single line of time evolution. As an example, consider an architect's design of a new house (say Joe's house). The house design starts from scratch and evolves over time. Figure 1 shows the design of Joe's house along a single line of time evolution starting from January. A temporal database captures the evolution of this design. Queries such as "Find Joe's house design in February" are supported by the database.

While conventional temporal databases work well for many temporal database applications, they are not sufficient for applications that require the support of tempo-

---

†This work was partially supported by NSF grant IRI-93-03403 and IRI-96-10001 and by a grant for hardware, software and research from Microsoft Corp.

†This work was partially supported by DGES grant PR95-426.

**Proceedings of the 26th VLDB Conference,
Cairo, Egypt, 2000.**

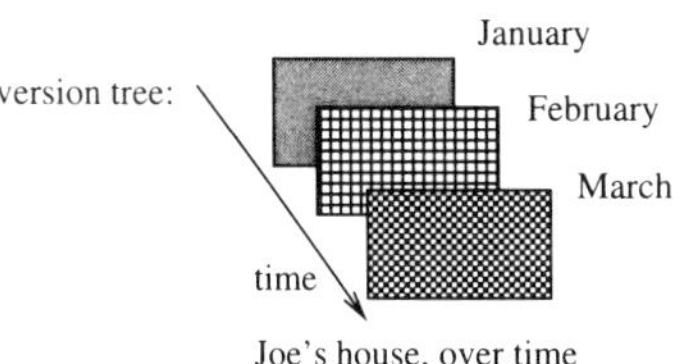

Figure 1: House design with a single line of time evolution.

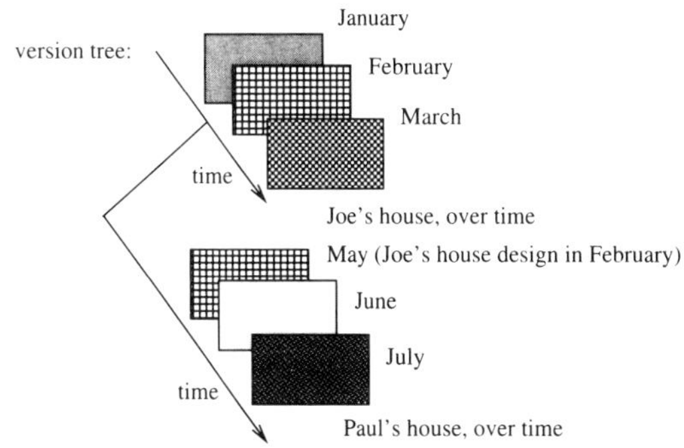

Figure 2: House design with branched time evolution.

ral data with *branched* time evolution, called **branched-and-temporal data**. Branched and temporal data arises in several important areas, such as software configuration control and engineering design. An example application is given in [4]. In our running example, consider the case where, at some time in May, the architect begins a new house design (say Paul's house). Instead of starting from scratch, the architect may choose to start from Joe's house design in February, which is already stored in the database. Joe's house design in February is modified to suit Paul's requirement later on. As time proceeds, Paul's house design can be viewed as a new time evolution branch which starts in May with Joe's house design in February as its initial design. Figure 2 captures the process of temporal house design with branched time evolution. Graphs as shown in Figure 1 and Figure 2 describing the evolution of the history of different branches are called **version trees**.

A branched and temporal database, such as the house design database, has three dimensions: data space, branch, and time. In our example, the *data space* contains different parts of a house such as the kitchen and the bedroom. The *branch* corresponds to the full design product, say "Joe's house". *Time* reflects the changes made in the design as it evolves. This is illustrated in Figure 3. A (Branch, Time) pair, say Joe's house in February, noted as *(Joe's house, Feb.)*, is called a **version**.

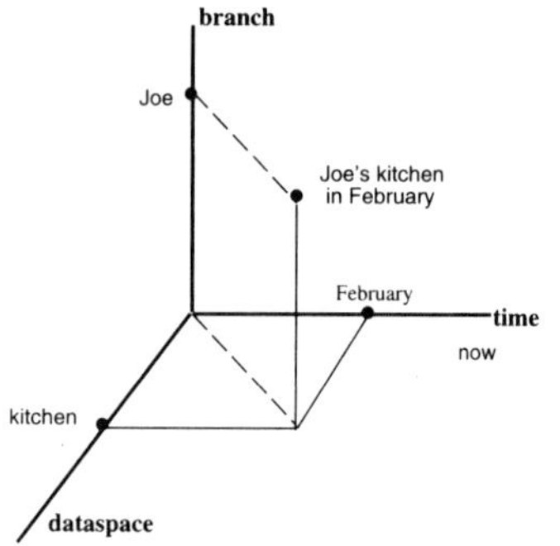

Figure 3: Design database dimensions.

Given a specific branch B, branches that are derived from branch B are called **descendent branches** of B. For example, "Paul's house" is a descendent branch of "Joe's house". Analogously, for a specific version (B, T), versions that are derived from (B, T) are called **descendent versions** of (B, T). For example, *(Paul's house, June)* is descendent version of *(Paul's house, May)*. If a branch $B1$ (version $(B1, T1)$) is a descendent branch (descendent version) of branch $B2$ (version $(B2, T2)$), we say that branch $B2$ (version $(B2, T2)$) is an ancestor branch (ancestor version) of branch $B1$ (version $(B1, T1)$).

With new branches created as time proceeds, branched and temporal data tends to increase in size rapidly, making the need for efficient indexing crucial. A branched-and-temporal index method not only needs to support version slice queries, such as "show me the design for Joe's house in March.", but also needs to support historical queries [4], including horizontal queries and vertical queries, which arise because of branching. A typical horizontal query is "Find all the house designs for a given branch, say "Joe's house", or one of its *descendent* branches, in June". This shows what has evolved from Joe's house. A typical vertical query is "Find all the house designs for a given branch, say "Paul's house", or one of its *ancestor* branches, in July." This shows how Paul's house has evolved differently from its ancestors.

Simply concatenating branch and key, and using temporal access methods for branched-and-temporal data does not consider the ancestor/descendent relationship among versions, hence won't be able to support historical queries efficiently. Even for version slice queries the data would not be clustered efficiently with concatenation since ancestor branches contribute to the version slices of their descendent branches. For example, some of Joe's house design is shared by Paul's house in May.

Our perspective on how to index a branched and temporal house design database is motivated by (1) keeping the total amount of disk space small and (2) making the number of disk accesses for typical queries, such as the version slice query and the historical query, minimal. Therefore, in designing the BT-tree, we focus on exploiting the sharing property of data records across different versions to save space, meanwhile clustering data records according to versions (for version slice queries) and versions with ancestor/descendent relationship (for historical queries) to achieve query efficiency. Our solution to the problem provides a reasonable trade-off between space and access time.

To save space, we exploit how data is shared between versions. Data records consist of a invariant part (usually called the **key**), which describes the part of the data space they cover, and a varying part which contains the branch identifier, a time stamp, and the rest of the data (in a house design, this might include the type and size of cabinets or the color of the paint.) When Joe's house design in February did not change the kitchen design from its January's version, we say that the data record with key "kitchen" and version *(Joe's house, Jan.)* is shared between two versions *(Joe's house, Jan.)* and *(Joe's house, Feb.)*. Later on if Paul's house design in May created from Joe's house design in February also did not change the kitchen design, the same data record will be shared by version *(Paul's house, May)* as well.

Disk pages which contain data records are called **data pages**. Data records in a data page are shared among different versions as much as possible. Data page splitting policies will cause some copying of data records, requiring some extra space for duplication, but resulting in more efficient search. Other pages, which direct searches, are called **index pages**.

Assuming that our house only consists of a kitchen and a bedroom, an example of the structure capturing the branched evolution in Figure 2 is shown in Figure 4. The index page in Figure 4 indicates that if you are searching for any data derived from version (Paul's house, June) you look in data page 2, otherwise you look in data page 1.

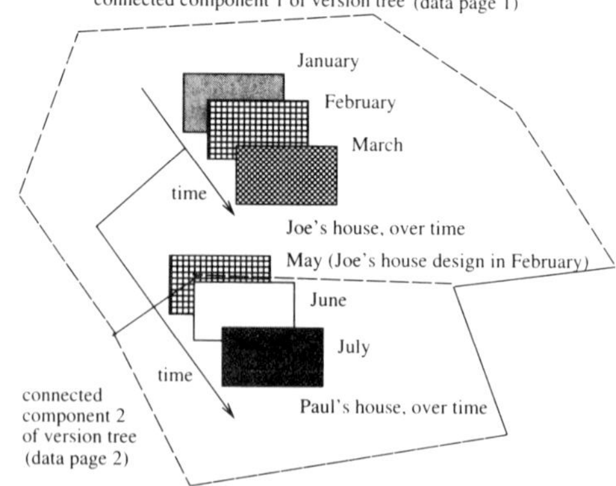

Figure 4: Data pages and index pages in the proposed structure.

Figure 5: A version tree is divided into subtrees.

To efficiently support typical queries, the version tree is divided into connected components, each of which is rooted at a certain version. For example, Figure 5 shows that the version tree in Figure 2 is divided into two connected

452

components with one rooted at version *(Joe's house, Jan.)* and another one rooted at version *(Paul's house, June)*. The data space is divided into key ranges. Each disk page in our structure, whether an index page or a data page, will correspond to a connected component of the version tree and a key range. For example, data page 1 in Figure 4 corresponds to the connected component 1 in Figure 5 and the entire data space [bedroom, kitchen]. Data page 2 in Figure 4 corresponds to the connected component 2 in Figure 5 and the entire data space [bedroom, kitchen]. The index page in Figure 4 corresponds to the entire version tree and the data space.

The index page in Figure 4 only contains one version node *(Paul's house, June)* and two pointers. The right pointer channels all the searching for data records in version *(Paul's house, June)* and its descendent versions. The left pointer channels all the searching for data records in the set of versions that are not descendents of version *(Paul's house, June)*, for example *(Joe's house, Jan.)*.

Data records of versions that are not descendents of version *(Paul's house, June)* are all stored in data page 1. From the version tree shown in Figure 2 or Figure 5, we know that these versions include three versions of Joe's house in January, February and March separately, and Paul's house in May. Considering the assumption that each house contains only two keys: bedroom and kitchen, data page 1 should store information about 8 data records in total. However only 5 data records are stored in data page 1. This is because some of the data records are shared among different versions. For example, Joe's kitchen in January is shared among three versions: *(Joe's house, Jan.)*, *(Joe's house, Feb.)* and *(Paul's house, May)*.

Data page 2 contains data records in two versions of Paul's house in June and July. June's version has the bedroom of Paul's house in May which is a record that is copied to data page 2 from data page 1 through data page splitting policies, while data record "Paul's kitchen in June" is shared between two versions *(Paul's house, June)* and *(Paul's house, July)*.

Figure 4 shows a simple case of our structure where only version information is needed inside the index page. We will also need to distinguish the different key ranges covered by data pages.

The access structure with data pages and index pages as outlined above is called a **BT-tree (Branched and Temporal Tree)**. The rest of the paper describes the BT-tree in detail.

1.1 Background and Previous Work

Branched-and-temporal indexing is a relatively unexplored area. However, many access methods (for example, [3], [1], [6], [10] and [7]) have been proposed for temporal data. A survey and comparison of these access methods can be found in [8]. These methods have effectively solved the problem of providing access to versioned record sets where the versioning is actually linear, i.e, no branching.

Other approaches to managing versioned data are less closely related. Work on "version management," for example, in software engineering, does not consider efficient use of disk pages. The paper [4] does not consider pagination and, although the structure is "branched," only a current version can be split into branches. Old versions can not be

modified. Driscoll et al. [2] develop techniques for making linked data structures (e.g. binary search trees) fully persistent (all versions can be read and updated).

Perhaps closest to our work is that of Lanka and Mays [5], which is based on ideas from [2]. Lanka and Mays' "fully persistent $B+$-tree" maintains multiple versions of B+-trees. The Fully persistent $B+$-tree is a *branched-only* access method. Branched-only data structures can be used for branched-and-temporal data if the versions are made to correspond to a branch and a timestamp. Lanka and Mays did not suggest this. There is no access method in the literature explicitly proposed for branched-and-temporal data. In addition, fully persistent $B+$-trees have extra "version block" nodes in the search path making them less efficient than our BT-tree. Their data nodes also store some redundant information, making the total space usage greater than ours. Furthermore we provide an ancestor determination method which exploits the lesser amount of branching found in a branched-and-temporal database. The paper [5] maintains a full version tree for ancestor determination. This is too space-and-compute expensive for our case.

1.2 Organization of This Paper

The rest of the paper is organized as follows. Section 2 contains the description of the BT-tree including the ancestor determination method, the structure of data pages and index pages, the splitting algorithm and the consolidation algorithm. Performance results are presented in section 3.

2 The BT-tree

For the purpose of this paper, time is assumed to be discrete, described by a succession of nonnegative integers. Each branch is assigned a unique branch id, which is represented by a positive integer. A combination (B, T) of a branch identifier B and a time stamp T is called a **version**. A branch typically has a large number of versions, one for each time stamp when a change was made in that branch.

The first problem we encounter in designing such a branched and temporal index method is that the versions (B, T) in the structure are only partially ordered. The lack of a linear ordering on versions makes navigation through a representation of a fully persistent BT-tree structure problematic. We need to be able to decide whether or not one version is a descendent or ancestor of another.

2.1 Ancestor Determination

Ancestor determination methods used in [2] and [5] for branched data use $O(n)$ space. Their methods are not suitable for branched-and-temporal case where the number of timestamps is large (hence the corresponding total number of the versions is large). Our approach of solving the ancestor problem is designed for the case when the number of branches is small although the number of timestamps may be large.

Let us we define the version tree first. Unlike the version tree in the branched case, where every node corresponds to a branch, every node of the version tree here corresponds to a pair (B, T). An edge from node (B, T) to node (B', T') exists if version (B', T') is obtained by updating version (B, T). Figure 6 shows an example of version tree where only one branch exists.

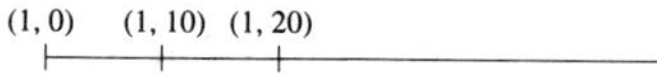

Figure 6: An example of version tree where only one branch exists.

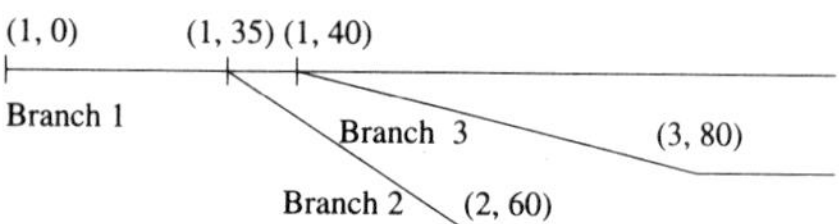

Figure 7: The version tree corresponding to the branch table in Table 1 below.

The main idea is to use a branch table, which contains one entry for each branch. Each entry consists of four items: a branch id, the branch id of its ancestor branch, the start time of this branch and the share time which is the time when this branch shares information with its ancestor branch. For example, the branch table entry for branch 2 is $(2, 1, 60, 35)$. This means that branch 2 is created out of version $(B, T) = (1, 35)$ at time 60. Given the branch table entry for branch 2, a version $(2, T)$ is valid only if $T \geq$ start_time=60. An example of branch table with three branches is shown in Table 1.

Branch id	Ancestor branch id	Start time	Share time
1	1	0	0
2	1	60	35
3	1	80	40

Table 1: Branch table for the running example.

When a new branch i is created out of version (j, T) at time T', a new entry (i, j, T', T) is generated and appended at the end of the branch table. Each branch table defines a subset of a version tree, indicating only the branching. Not all versions are listed as entries, since a version which is created as an update of a current version (with the same branch number, but a new time stamp) is not listed. This is why the large number of versions in a branched-and-temporal structure can be captured in a small table. A version tree containing only branching information corresponding to the branch table in Table 1 can be found in Figure 7.

Definition 2.1.1 *The branch id of the ancestor branch found in the branch table entry of branch i is called* **Direct_ancestor(i)**. *The share_time found in the branch table entry of branch i is called* **Share_time(i)**. *The start_time found in the branch table entry of branch i is called* **Start_time(i)**.

For example, given the branch table shown in Table 1, Direct_ancestor(2)=1, Share_time(2)=35 and Start_time(2)=60.

Definition 2.1.2 *Given two versions (B_1, T_1) and (B_2, T_2) with $B_1 \leq B_2$, (B_1, T_1)* **is an ancestor of** *(B_2, T_2) if $(B_1 = B_2$ and $T_1 \leq T_2)$ or (B_1, T_1) is an ancestor of version $(Direct\_ancestor(B_2), Share\_time(B_2))$. If (B_1, T_1) is an ancestor of (B_2, T_2), then (B_2, T_2)* **is a descendant of** *(B_1, T_1).*

This definition is used to develop the following algorithm **Ancestor(v1,v2)** for ancestor determination. **Ancestor(v1,v2)** returns true if $v1 = (B1, T1)$ is an ancestor of $v2 = (B2, T2)$.

```
If B1=B2 then { if  T2<T1 then return FALSE
                      else return TRUE }
If B2<B1 then return FALSE
else return(Ancestor(v1,
        (Direct_ancestor(B2), share_time(B2))))
```

This algorithm requires following the direct ancestor path of a version $(B2, T2)$ upwards in the branch table until it can be determined whether or not $(B1, T1)$ is an ancestor. Since the total number of branches is small, the number of ancestors of a given branch is small and this search will be fast.

Definition 2.1.3 Ancestor(B,T) *is the collection of versions which are ancestors of version (B, T). i.e, if $(B_1, T_1) \in Ancestor(B_2, T_2)$, then (B_1, T_1) is an ancestor of (B_2, T_2).*

2.2 Overview of the BT-tree

The structure of the BT-tree is a directed acyclic graph of pages, including index pages and data pages. Fully persistent structures are traditionally called "trees" because the restriction to one version is a tree. In addition, there is one distinguished page called *the root* and a set of *leaf pages* which are those pages with no outgoing edges. Leaf pages are data pages and they are the furthest pages from the root. Furthermore, all leaves are the same distance from the root. Hence the BT-tree is balanced.

Data pages contain branched-and-temporal data while index pages contain a small binary tree channeling search to lower level pages. Initially the BT-tree starts from one index page and one data page, where the data page is empty and the index page contains only one node pointing to the data page. As time proceeds, data records are continuously added to the data page. At some point when there is no additional space to insert new data into the data page, a *data page overflow* happens.

Data page overflow needs special handling: a split is performed on the overflowed data page. One or two new data pages will be created and a small portion of data from the overflowed data page will be copied to the new data page(s). Information about the data page split will be posted up to the upper level index page to direct future searches to either the old overflowed data page or the newly created page(s).

As new data is added to data pages, more and more data pages overflow and are therefore split, consequently more and more information is posted to upper level index pages to record the splitting history of data pages. At some point *index page overflow* happens.

Index page overflow needs special handling: a split is performed on the overflowed index page. One or two new index pages will be created from the index page splitting. A tree will be extracted and copied to the new index page(s). The tree copied to the new index page(s) points to old pages as well as new pages therefore making the BT-tree a directed acyclic graph of pages instead of a tree of pages. An example will be given in the index page splitting section.

As a result of the index split, information will be posted to upper level index pages to record the split history. The split may percolate up as needed. A new root will be created when the root index page is split.

Now we give a detailed explanation of data pages and index pages and their splitting algorithms.

2.3 Data Pages

Data pages contain branched-and-temporal data. Our data consists of **record variants**. For our purpose a **record variant** is characterized by four entries: a time-invariant part called a **key**, a branch id, a time stamp and an information field. For example, $(a, 3, 80, info)$ is a record variant with key $= a$, branch id $= 3$, time stamp $= 80$ and $info$ representing the data content of this record variant.

A page is identified with a key range and a connected component of version tree. For example, the data page $D2$ shown in Figure 10 is identified with key range $[a, d]$ and the connected component of version tree enclosed in the bigger dotted boundary, denoted as $V1$-20, in the right side of the figure. Version tree components are named with the branch (in this case branch 1) and the time stamp (in this case 20) of their root.

Definition 2.3.1 *A record variant $(k, b, t, info)$ is said to be* **alive in a connected component of version tree and a key range** *if*

- *k is within the key range and*
- *either*

    - *(b, t) is within the connected component of the version tree or*
    - *Let version (B', T') be the root of the connected component of the version tree. Then $(b, t) \in Ancestor(B', T')$, and $\forall$ record variants $(k', b', t', info)$ with $k' = k$ and $(b', t') \in Ancestor(B', T')$, $t \geq t'$.*

The second condition in Def 2.3.1 implies that either the version (b, t) is contained in the connected component of the version tree or it is the most recent ancestor of the root of the connected component of the version tree on a record variant with the same key. In our example, the connected component of the version tree is $V1$-20, from Figure 10. Let's consider the only two record variants in the database with key d: $(d, 1, 2, info)$ and $(d, 1, 3, info)$. The root of $V1$-20 is $(1, 20)$. Record variant $(d, 1, 2, info)$ is *not* alive in the connected component of version tree $V1$-20 and key range $[a, d]$ because $(d, 1, 3, info)$ has the same key and has a version which is a more recent ancestor of $(1, 20)$. Record variant $(d, 1, 3, info)$ is alive in $V1$-20 and $[a, d]$ because its version *is* the most recent ancestor of $(1, 20)$ for key $= d$. Record variant $(a, 2, 60, info)$ is alive in $V1$-20 and $[a, d]$ because its version is contained in $V1$-20.

Each data page contains copies of all the record variants alive in a connected component of version tree and a key range. For example, data page $D2$ in Figure 10 corresponds to the component $V1$-20 and the key range $[a, d]$. $D2$ contains record variants $(d, 1, 3, info)$ and *not* $(d, 1, 2, info)$ because $(d, 1, 3, info)$ is alive in $V1$-20 and $[a, d]$ while $(d, 1, 2, info)$ is *not* alive in $V1$-20 and $[a, d]$.

Data pages partition the entire version tree and data space for which the database is defined. For example, in Figure 10, both data pages cover the key range $[a, d]$ and the two connected components of the version tree, $V1$-0 (corresponding to page D1) and $V1$-20 (corresponding to page $D2$) are disjoint and cover the version tree.

Record variants in a data page are ordered by key, branch and time stamp inside a data page. When a new record with key k is added to the data page at time t ($=$ current time) by branch i, a new record variant of the form $(k, i, t, info)$ is created and inserted in a proper position so that the all data variants are in order. When a data page becomes full, a data page splitting occurs.

2.4 Data Page Splitting

We distinguish **updates**, which create a new record variant for an existing key and **inserts**, which create a new record variant with a new key. When a new update or insertion, say $(k, i, T, info)$ (T is current time,) into a data page causes the page to become over-full, it will be split at (i, T) with one or two new data pages allocated. Information about the split will be posted to the parent page that channeled the search to the split data page.

Definition 2.4.1 *A record variant $(k, j, t, info)$ in a data page is said to be* **alive at version** (i, T) *with $T =$ current time if $(j, t) \in Ancestor(i, T)$ and $\forall$ record variant $(k', j', t', info)$ in the data page with $k' = k$, and $(j', t') \in Ancestor(i, T)$, $t \geq t'$.*

For example, in Figure 10, record variant $(a, 3, 83, info)$ in data page $D2$ is alive at $(3, T)$ (say T is current time 90), while the same record variant is not alive at $(2, T)$ because $(3, 83)$ is not an ancestor of $(2, T)$.

To split a data page at (i, T), only alive record variants at (i, T) are copied to the new pages. Copying the alive record variants into *one* new page is called a **version split**.

If there are not many alive record variants in the full page (because in this page, most of the record variants are old variants of alive record variants) only one new page is needed. If there are many alive record variants or (considering variable-length records) if the space occupied by alive record variants is too large, two new pages are allocated and a B^+-tree-like key split is made among the alive record variants being copied. This is called a **version-and-key split**. We define a threshold utilization U for alive record variants. When alive record variant utilization exceeds U, we do a version-and-key split. When alive record variant utilization is less than or equal to U, we do a version split. A typical value for U is about .66, which guarantees that a new data page will be at least one third full of current data.

BT-tree data page splitting is illustrated in Figure 8, Figure 9, Figure 10, and Figure 11. The database starts with an empty data page $D1$. Figure 8 shows the insertion of 6 record variants in data page $D1$ up to current time $T = 19$. Only branch 1 is created so far and data page $D1$ is full. At time 20, in order to insert record variant $(a, 1, 20, info)$, a version split occurs to data page $D1$. Consequently, data page $D2$ is created, as shown in Figure 9. Only those record variants in data page $D1$ which are alive at $(1, 20)$ are copied to the new page, data page $D2$. The new record variant is also inserted into the new data page $D2$.

Figure 10 shows that branch 2 is created and a new record variant $(a, 2, 60, info)$ is inserted into data page $D2$ at time 60. At time 80, branch 3 is created and a new record variant $(a, 3, 80, info)$ is inserted into data page $D2$. At time 83, the insertion of another record variant into data page $D2$ by branch 3 makes the data page $D2$ a full data page. The version tree grows as new branches are created.

In Figure 11, as we are trying to insert record variant $(b, 3, 85, info)$ into the data page $D2$ which is already full, data page $D2$ has to be split. A version-and-key split at version $(3, 85)$ and key c occurs here generating two new pages $D3$ and $D4$ corresponding to same connected component of the version but different key ranges.

A data page could be split more than once if it is already full and new branches are created from some version in its version-tree component. This cannot happen in temporal (not branched) structures.

2.5 Index Pages

Index pages also represent connected components of version tree and key ranges, with a full partition of the version-key space at each level of the tree. Within each BT-tree index page is information that identifies the connected component of version tree and key range for each child page, and hence channels searches to its children pages.

A **split history** tree or **sh-tree** is used within each index page. The sh-tree is a small binary tree. The sh-tree, describing the history of the splits of its children, contains three types of nodes: **vsh** nodes, **ksh** nodes and **leaf** nodes. A vsh node contains a branch id and a time stamp (indicating a *version*), a ksh node contains a key value while a leaf node contains a disk page address of a child page in the next lower level of the BT-tree.

Initially the BT-tree only has one index page I, with one leaf node as shown in Figure 12(a), referencing the only data page $D1$ in Figure 11. As new data is added into the data page $D1$, $D1$ becomes full and a data page split occurs. Whenever a data page split occurs, the sh-tree in the parent index page is changed so that it reflects the splitting history of its children.

In case of a version split of a data page at (i, T) (T is current time,) the parent's reference to the old page is replaced by a new vsh node (i, T). This node has one child referencing the old page while the other references the new page. Figure 12(b) shows that the vsh node $(1, 20)$ is posted to index page I (which is also root index page of this BT-tree) when data page $D1$ is split and data page $D2$ is generated as shown in Figure 9.

In case of version-and-key split at (i, T) (T is current time) and key k, the parent page's reference to the old page is also replaced by a new sh-tree vsh node (i, T). This node has its left child referencing the old page while the right child is a ksh node with key value k referring to the two new pages. Figure 12(d) shows how posting happens when data page $D2$ is version-and-key split at version $(3, 85)$ and key c generating data pages $D3$ and $D4$ as shown in Figure 11.

A vsh node (b, t) in an index page divides the lower level BT-tree rooted at (b, t) into two parts, with the right subtree of the vsh node containing everything which is a descendent of (b, t) while the left subtree of the vsh node contains everything which is not a descendent of (b, t). Similarly, a ksh node k divides the lower level BT-tree rooted at k into two parts, with the right subtree of the ksh node containing record variants with key value greater than or equal to k while the left subtree of the ksh node contains record variants with key value less than k. The search algorithm for a single point (K, B, T) in a BT-tree is in Figure 13.

1. Start at the root page of the BT-tree.

2. BT-tree index page has been reached: Start at the root node of the sh-tree in this BT-tree page.

3. Sh-tree node has been reached: Test the type of sh-tree node.

    (a) ksh: If $K \geq$ key value in ksh, go right, else go left. Go to step 3.

    (b) vsh (B', T'): If $(B', T') \in Ancestor(B, T)$, go right, else go left. Go to step 3.

    (c) sh-tree leaf: Fetch the disk page P in the sh-tree leaf. If P is another index page, go to step 2. Otherwise continue.

4. BT-tree data page has been reached: Find the record variant in this data page with key value K and alive at version (B, T).

    - If there is none, return indicating the search is unsuccessful.

    - If this is a deletion record variant, the record did not exist in the database at time T for version B. Return indicating the search is unsuccessful.

    - Otherwise, return the record variant and indicate that the search is successful.

Figure 13: Search in the BT-tree for (K, B, T), a record variant with key K alive at version (B, T).

2.6 Index Page Splitting

An index page records the split history of data pages by getting one (in case of version-split) or two (in case of version-and-key split) index node(s) posted whenever a child data page splits. Index page splitting happens when an index page overflows. Only disk addresses of children (leaf nodes) **alive at the splitting version** and the key boundaries separating them are copied.

Definition 2.6.1 *A child (leaf) of an sh-tree in an index page is* **alive at (B, T)** *(T= current time) if (B, T) is in the connected component of the version tree associated with the child page whose disk address recorded in the leaf node of the sh-tree.*

Consider a BT-tree with root index page in Figure 12 (d) and four data pages in Figure 11. Suppose the current time is 90. To find children (leaves) of the sh-tree in Figure 12 alive at $(3, 90)$, we look at the connected components of version trees in Figure 11. Since $(3, 90)$ is in the connected component of the version tree corresponding to $D3$ and $D4$, leaves $D3$ and $D4$ in the sh-tree in Figure 12 (d) are alive at $(3, 90)$. However $(3, 90)$ is not in the connected component of version trees corresponding to $D1$ and $D2$, hence leaves $D1$ and $D2$ are not alive at $(3, 90)$.

If there are too many alive children found when splitting an index page, a key split is also made. Split information is posted to the parent as usual. When a root page is split, a new root page is allocated to hold the split information, as

456

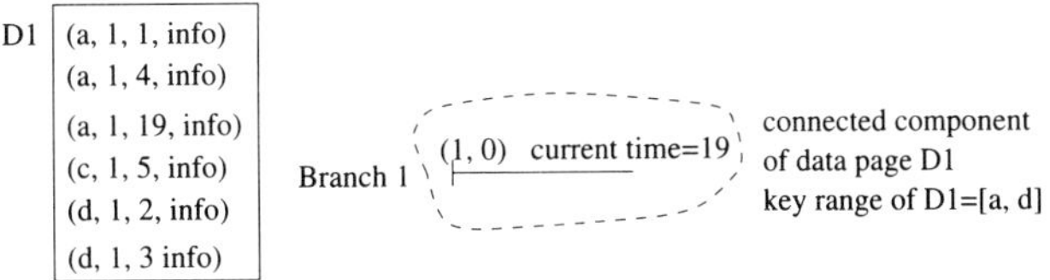

Figure 8: Data page $D1$ is full at this point.

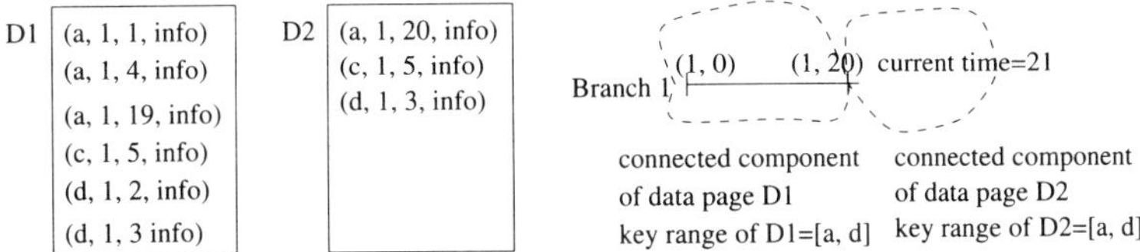

Figure 9: In order to insert a new record variant $(a, 1, 20, info)$, data page $D1$ has to be version split. Data page $D2$ is generated.

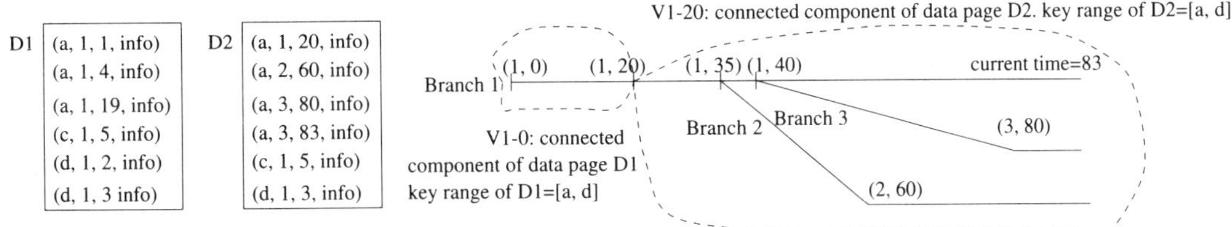

Figure 10: Branch 2 and 3 are created and new record variants are inserted into data page $D2$ causing it to become full at time 83.

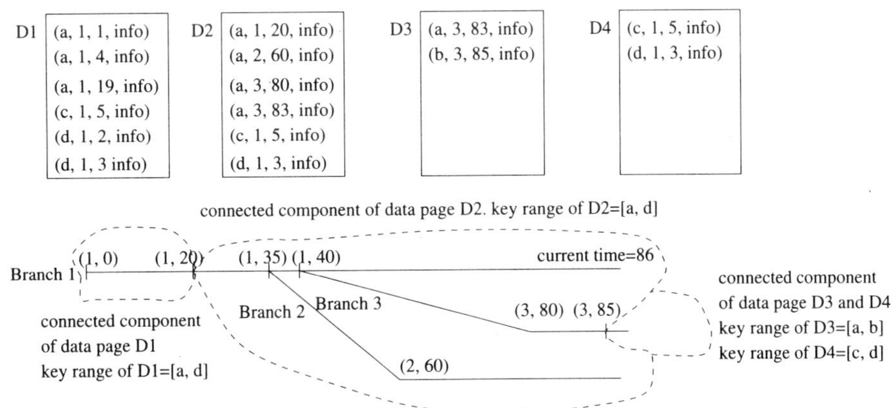

Figure 11: Data page $D2$ is version-and-key split at $(3, 85)$ as new record variant $(b, 3, 85, info)$ is attempted to be inserted into data page $D2$.

Figure 12: The evolution of index page I corresponding to data pages in (a) Figure 8; (b) Figure 9; (c) Figure 10; (d) Figure 11. The connected component of index page I is the entire version tree and the key range of index page I is [a, d].

in the B^+-tree. Root-page splits thus increase the height of the BT-tree.

When we version split an index page, the new index page has a sh-tree which only has ksh nodes. The algorithm for BT-tree index-page split (split an index page at version (B, T) (T is current time)) is in Figure 14. The effect of this algorithm is to obtain one (in case of version-split) or two (in case of version-and-key-split) binary search tree(s) on key only referring only to the *alive* children.

---

1. Start at the root of the sh-tree of the full index page.

2. If a vsh (B', T') is encountered, do not copy the vsh.

   (a) If $(B', T') \in Ancestor(B, T)$, go right.

   (b) Otherwise, go left.

3. If a ksh is encountered, copy the ksh to the new index page and process both subtrees recursively.

4. When a new sh-tree is constructed in the new index page, the key ranges and their corresponding disk addresses are known. Construct a balanced sh-tree with these key ranges. If two such trees are needed, for two new sh-tree index pages, split at the middle key range and construct two balanced sh-trees, one for each new sh-tree index page.

Figure 14: Algorithm for splitting a BT-tree index page at version (B, T) (T is current time.)

Figure 15 illustrates the resulting index page I, evolved from the index page I shown in Figure 12(d), after page $D2$ had a version split at version $(2, 88)$, and page $D3$ had a version-and-key split at version $(3, 95)$ and key b. Assume that index page I is about full at this point. At time 98, branch 3 inserts or updates a record variant in data page $D4$ causing it version-and-key split at version $(3, 98)$ and key d. While attempting to post the sh-tree shown in Figure 15 to index page I, the index page I overflows. Therefore index page I is version split at version $(3, 98)$, as shown in Figure 16, creating a new index page with four children. Vsh node $(3, 98)$ is posted up to the new root page created.

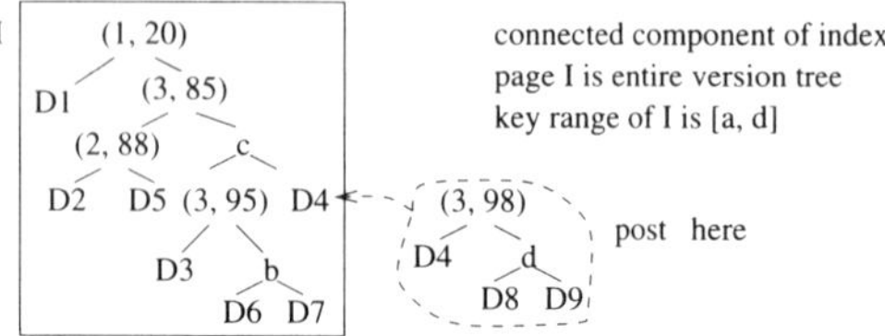

Figure 15: This is the index page I, shown in Figure 12(d), after $D2$ had a version split at version $(2, 88)$ and page $D3$ had a version-and-key split at $(3, 95)$ and key b. Now data page $D4$ are having a version-and-key split at version $(3, 98)$ and key d. When attempting to post the vsh node and the ksh node up to index page I, we find that the page is full.

2.7 Discontinued Record Variants

Record variants are never physically deleted. When the most recent record variant with a given key is to be discontinued, a new record variant is inserted with the key, the branch id, say B, of the branch in which the record vari-

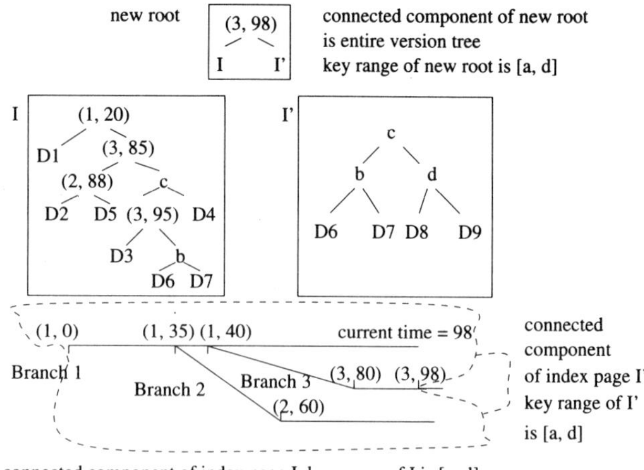

Figure 16: Version split index page I at version $(3, 98)$ creating new page I'. A new root is created and vsh node $(3, 98)$ is posted.

ant is deleted, the time stamp, say T, of the delete, and a **delete marker** indicating it is marking the end time of the most recent previous variant within certain branch. Delete marker record variants are necessary in data pages which include the key in their key range and include the version (B, T) in the corresponding connected component of version tree. This is the only way to tell that a record variant has been discontinued by branch B at time T, i.e. that its prior record variant is no longer alive. That is, the delete marker record variant bounds the time interval of the preceding record variant existing in a specific branch.

If a page where a delete marker record variant is version-split, we can choose to treat the delete marker record variant like any other record variant and copy it to the new page. This permits us easily to answer queries about the history of record variants with a given key. However, if deletes are common, this dilutes the number of actual record variants that a page can hold. Hence, here we choose not to copy the record variants with delete markers. Version queries will still be correct. Say a record variant with key value k is deleted at version (B, T). We have a data page D that every version within the connected component of version tree corresponded to data page D is a descendent of version (B, T). The absence of a record variant with key value k in such a page indicates that the record is not alive at that time within version B.

2.8 Page Consolidation

When a version query finds only a small number of record variants satisfying the query in each visited data page, query performance is poor. Low density of correct variants for a given version is caused by deletion. Consolidation guarantees good version query performance for the BT-tree.

A data page is **sparse at version** (B, T) when the space occupied by *alive variants* at version (B, T), not including delete marker variants, falls below a threshold. To consolidate a page P sparse at (B, T), both P and a sibling page are version split at (B, T). (A **consolidating sibling** must be a page whose corresponding segment of the version tree contains (B, T) and which has the same parent as

P and an adjacent key range.[1]) Copies of the alive record variants at version (B, T) from both the sparse page and its consolidating sibling are combined in a new page or, should that result in an over-full page, we then key-split the new consolidated page. This is similar to consolidation in [5]. Since more copies are made, page consolidation degrades space utilization in order to improve query performance. A page consolidation threshold of t "guarantees" that the space occupied by record variants alive at any given query version in any given data page will not fall below t.[2]

Non-root index pages can also be consolidated. This can be done when posting information about a lower level consolidation at version (B, T) results in the index page having too few alive children in the same version. The index page is version split at (B, T) and combined with a sh-tree copy resulting from a version split of one of its siblings at (B, T).

3 Performance

We present some results of our performance study on the BT-tree. The parameters of the system are described first. Graphs and explanations follow.

3.1 System Parameters

We assume all record variants, including delete marker record variants, have the same size. A transaction is either an insertion of a record variant with a new key, an update of an existing record variant or a delete of an old record variant (in one branch and with current time).

The database system starts up with only one branch. Other branches are created gradually after a number of transactions occurred in the first branch. Transactions are randomly assigned to existing branches.

Let the number of branches in the system be denoted "B". The maximum number of variants per page is b. In our case, b is 35. R is the total number of non-redundant record variants, including delete marker record variants. R includes different variants of records with the same key. R is 50,000 here. $K(i)$ is the number of record variants alive at version (i, T) (T is current time.) K does not include records that have been deleted. Let N be the total number of data pages in the BT-tree and let $N_c(i)$ be the number of data pages containing record variants alive at version (i, T) (T is current time) in this BT-tree.

We measure total space cost by **multiversion total utilization(MVTU)**. Keeping every distinct record variant (including delete marker record variants) is needed to support arbitrary version slice queries and historical queries. MVTU measures the fraction of the total data space occupied by distinct record variants.

$$MVTU = \frac{R}{N \times b}$$

Every version was once the current version in a branch and every version query will access only those data pages, which were current at that time in that branch. Hence,

version query cost is captured by **single version current utilization** for branch i (**SVCU(i)**) (the fraction of a branch's data pages containing record variants alive at version (i, T) (T is current time) occupied by these alive record variants).

$$SVCU(i) = \frac{K(i)}{N_c(i) \times b}$$

The value of SVCU may vary from one branch to another. **Average SVCU ($\overline{SVCU}$)** is the average SVCU value across different branches. $\overline{SVCU}$ measures the average version slice query efficiency.

$$\overline{SVCU} = \frac{\Sigma_{i=1}^{B} SVCU(i)}{B}$$

3.2 Performance Results

In order to study the performance of the system under different circumstances, three sets of experiments were carried out. The first set of experiments measures performance as the number of branches increase. The second set of experiments measures performance as the ratio of updates versus insertion varies (no deletes are allowed). The third set of experiments allows deletes and examines the effect of consolidation. Because of space limitation, we only present the second set of experiments.

The number of branches is fixed to be 10. All branches other than the first are randomly created between the 10,000th and 20,000th transaction with a randomly selected ancestor version (other branch creation profiles were also implemented, but since their results were similar, they are not presented here.) The key range of the first branch is $[0, 800,000)$. All other branches are allowed to modify versioned records in key range $[0, 600,000)$. We vary the fraction of updates versus insertions. No deletes are allowed. In this experiment, the height of the BT-tree never rose above 3.

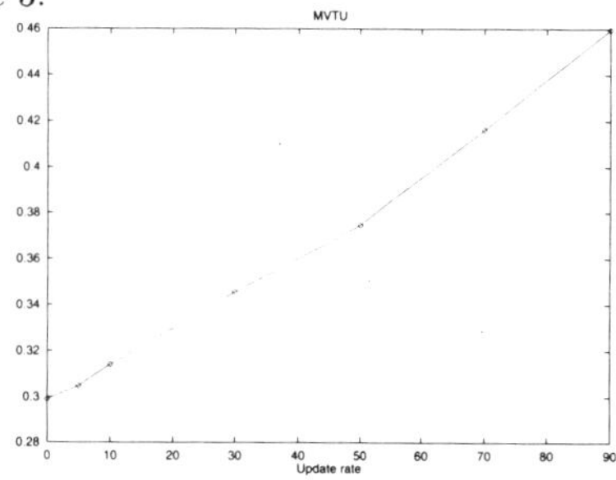

Figure 17: No Deletes: MVTU for early branch creation.

Figure 17 shows the $MVTU$ curves for early branch creation profile. We first remark on the general property of the BT-tree $MVTU$ curves. As the update rate increases, the $MVTU$ value of the BT-tree increases. In other words, the total amount of space occupied by 50,000 records decreases. The reason is as follows. When the update rate increases, we have more transactions updating existing record variants instead of inserting new record variants with different key values. Therefore, considering one data page, there will be a smaller number of distinct key values as the update rate increases. Consequently, when this data page is full and split, there will be fewer record variants copied to

---

[1] In the case that the key range of the parent equals the key range of the child, a page has no consolidating sibling, making page consolidation impossible. This does not impact search correctness as page consolidation is needed only for performance.

[2] Disregarding the case when page consolidation is impossible.

459

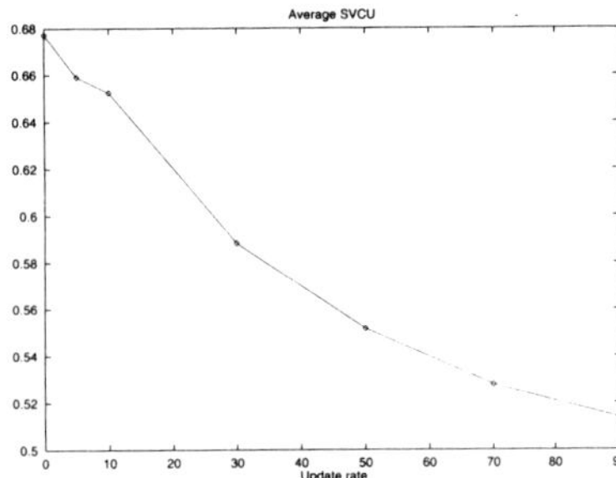

Figure 18: No Deletes: $\overline{SVCU}$ for early branch creation.

the new page. When the total number of record variants copied is less, the $MVTU$ value is higher.

The space needed is at worst three times the minimal amount when the update rate is low, i.e. mostly insertions of record variants with new keys, and at best about twice the minimal amount when there are mostly updates of existing record variants.

Figure 18 shows the $\overline{SVCU}$ curve. As the update rate increases, the $\overline{SVCU}$ value decreases. The reason is as follows. When the update rate increases, distinct key values in a data page decrease. Therefore record variants alive at current versions are not compactly clustered, making the version slice query less efficient. The percent of the found data pages which is occupied by answers to the version slice query is at worst near 50% when there is a high update rate. In this case, much of the other space is occupied by record variants which are not alive in the query version. At best, it is around 68% when the update rate is 0, similar to the B-tree.

4 Conclusions

There are many database applications that require the support of branched and temporal data. Since branched and temporal data increases in size as time proceeds, efficient indexing is important.

In this paper, we have presented the BT-tree, a new paginated method for storing and accessing branched and temporal data. Each data page and index page in BT-tree corresponds to a connected component of the version tree and a key range. At each level of the tree, the pages partition the version-data space so that each point (K, B, T) (key, branch, time stamp) is in exactly one page. Performance results show that the BT-tree provides a reasonable trade off between space and access time.

References

[1] Bruno Becker, Stephan Gschwind, Thomas Ohler, Bernhard Seeger, and Peter Widmayer. On optimal multiversion access structures. In *Porc. Symp. on Large Spatial Databases, in Lecture Notes in Computer Science, Vol. 692*, pages 123–141, Singapore, 1993.

[2] James R. Driscoll, Neil Sarnak, Daniel D. Sleator, and Robert E. Tarjan. Making data structures persistent. *Journal of Computer and System Sciences, 38*, pages 86–124, 1989.

[3] M. C. Easton. Key-sequence data sets on indelible storage. *IBM J. Res. Development*, 30(3):230–241, 1986.

[4] Gad M. Landau, Jeanette P. Schmidt, and Vassilis J. Tsotras. Historical queries along multiple lines of time evolution. *VLDB Journal, 4*, pages 703–726, 1995.

[5] Sitaram Lanka and Eric Mays. Fully persistent B+-trees. In *Proceedings of the ACM SIGMOD conference on Management of Data*, Denver, CO, 1991.

[6] David Lomet and Betty Salzberg. The performance of a multiversion access method. In *Proceedings of the ACM SIGMOD conference on Management of Data*, pages 354–363, 1990.

[7] Peter Muth, Patrick O'neil, Achim Pick, and Gerhard Weikum. Design, implementation, and performance on the LHAM log-structured history data access method. In *Proceedings of the 24th VLDB Conference*, pages 452–463, New York, 1998.

[8] Betty Salzberg and Vassilis J. Tsotras. A comparison of access methods for time evolving data. *Computing Surveys*, March 1999.

[9] R. Snodgrass and I. Ahn. Temporal databases. *IEEE computer*, pages Vol. 19, No. 9, pp 35–42, 1986.

[10] Vassilis J. Tsotras and Nickolas Kangelaris. The snapshot index: An I/O-optimal access method for timeslice queries. *Information Systems 20(3)*, pages 237–260, 1995.

Performance Issues in Incremental Warehouse Maintenance[*]

Wilburt Juan Labio, Jun Yang, Yingwei Cui, Hector Garcia-Molina, Jennifer Widom

Computer Science Department, Stanford University

{wilburt,junyang,cyw,hector,widom}@db.stanford.edu

Abstract

A well-known challenge in data warehousing is the efficient incremental maintenance of warehouse data in the presence of source data updates. In this paper, we identify several critical data representation and algorithmic choices that must be made when developing the machinery of an incrementally maintained data warehouse. For each decision area, we identify various alternatives and evaluate them through extensive experiments. We show that the right alternative leads to dramatic performance gains, and we propose guidelines for making the right decisions under different scenarios. All of the issues addressed in this paper arose in our development of WHIPS, a prototype data warehousing system supporting incremental maintenance.

1 Introduction

Data warehousing systems integrate and store data from remote sources as *materialized views* in the warehouse [11, 3]. When source data changes, warehouse views need to be *maintained* so that they remain consistent with the source data. Commercial data warehousing systems typically recompute all warehouse views periodically to keep them up to date, but this process can be very expensive for large views. In contrast, with *incremental* maintenance, only the portions of the views that have changed are actually modified [6]. Because of the potential performance advantage, incremental view maintenance has recently found its way into commercial systems, e.g., [4, 1, 2].

In this paper we experimentally study various options for incremental maintenance when the warehouse data is stored in an off-the-shelf commercial database system (DBMS). For instance, we investigate how views are best stored in the DBMS, how aggregate views should be maintained, how deletions can be handled by the DBMS, how parameters such as memory and base relation size impact our choices, and several other issues. To illustrate the types of questions we address, we briefly introduce one of the options faced by the warehouse implementor: how to represent views.

* This work was supported by the National Science Foundation under grant IIS-9811947, by NASA Ames under grant NCC2-5278, and by Sagent Technology Inc.

Example 1.1 A warehouse often must support bag (duplicate) semantics. For instance, to efficiently maintain complex views involving aggregates, we also need to maintain supporting (auxiliary) views that may contain duplicates. Furthermore, bag semantics can simplify incremental maintenance, as we will see below. How should views be represented when bag semantics are called for? If view V contains three copies of tuple t, should we explicitly store those three copies? Or should we add a *dupcnt* attribute to V to record the number of copies of t? For each case, how should the DBMS insert or delete new tuples?

To illustrate, consider a concrete but *very simple* example. Consider a source table $R(K, A_1, A_2, ..., A_n)$ with key attribute K, and a simple warehouse view $V(A_1, A_2, ..., A_n)$ defined over R which projects out the key of R. Without bag semantics, maintaining V would be expensive: when a tuple $\langle k, a_1, a_2, ..., a_n \rangle$ is deleted from R, we cannot decide whether to delete $\langle a_1, a_2, ..., a_n \rangle$ from V without querying R, because there might exist another tuple $\langle k', a_1, a_2, ..., a_n \rangle$ in R which also derives $\langle a_1, a_2, ..., a_n \rangle$ in V. On the other hand, if duplicates are preserved in V, we should always delete one tuple from V for each tuple deleted from R, and no R queries are required.

Suppose that we implement bag V by keeping explicit copies of tuples. Suppose further that based on the deletions from R we have computed $\bigtriangledown V$, a bag of tuples to be deleted from V. To apply $\bigtriangledown V$ to V, one might be tempted to use the following:

```
DELETE FROM V WHERE (A_1, A_2, ..., A_n) IN
    (SELECT * FROM ▽V)
```

Unfortunately, this statement does not work because SQL `DELETE` always removes *all* tuples satisfying the `WHERE` condition. If V has three copies of a tuple t and $\bigtriangledown V$ contains two copies of t, the above statement will delete all three copies, instead of correctly leaving one. To properly apply $\bigtriangledown V$, we need to use a cursor on $\bigtriangledown V$ (details will be provided later). However, a cursor-based implementation forces $\bigtriangledown V$ to be processed one tuple at a time.

Given this problem with deletions, we may want to consider the *dupcnt* approach, where we store only one copy for each tuple, together with an extra attribute to record the number of duplicates for that tuple. Under this representation, $\bigtriangledown V$ can be applied in batch with two SQL statements (again, details will be given later). Besides the obvious advantage of being more compact when the number of duplicates is large, how does this count representation compare with the default duplicate representation? In particular, does it speed up overall view maintenance? Are SQL statements really better than a cursor loop for applying $\bigtriangledown V$? □

In this paper we study several issues like the ones illustrated in Example 1.1. For each issue we propose various alternatives, including interesting new variations for aggregate view maintenance that turn out to have important advantages over previous algorithms. In many of the decision areas we discuss, making a wrong decision can severely hamper the efficiency of warehouse maintenance. For example, the time required to install changes into a view can vary by orders of magnitude depending on how maintenance is implemented: as data volumes grow, picking the right strategy can mean the difference between a few minutes and many hours of warehouse maintenance time. Based on the results of our experiments, we provide guidelines for making the right decisions under different scenarios.

For our experiments we use WHIPS (*W*are*H*ouse *I*nformation *P*rocessing *S*ystem), a prototype data warehousing system at Stanford [14]. (In fact, most of the design issues we consider in this paper arose in the design and implementation of WHIPS.) Because WHIPS is representative of warehousing infrastructures built using commercial DBMS, we believe that our results have applicability well beyond WHIPS—they should prove helpful to any implementation of incremental warehouse maintenance either within or on top of a commercial DBMS.

In closing our introduction, we make two points. First, even though incremental maintenance has enjoyed considerable attention from the research community [6], very little research to date covers practical implementation issues backed up by thorough experiments. Thus we believe that our paper makes a unique contribution in this regard. Second, experimental evaluations always raise many questions, especially if the evaluations involve commercial products. Was "enough" memory used? Were the databases studied "big enough?" Should the query optimizer be hand-tuned to maximize performance? Will next year's DBMS invalidate the conclusions because it has a snazzy new feature? As questions like these arise in our paper, keep in mind that our goal is *not* to make absolute performance predictions, but rather to understand the choices and tradeoffs involved. We study incremental maintenance in a realistic, off-the-shelf scenario, and we have varied many of the parameters involved (e.g., memory size). Of course, there are other interesting scenarios and more questions that can follow our initial study.

The rest of the paper is organized as follows. In Section 2, we give an overview of the WHIPS architecture, which sets the stage for later discussions. In Section 3, we focus on the component of WHIPS responsible for warehouse maintenance and discuss the various choices in building its view maintenance machinery. In Section 4, we conduct experiments to evaluate each alternative and present guidelines for making the best choices. Finally, we discuss related work in Section 5 and conclude in Section 6.

2 WHIPS Architecture

The warehouse views incrementally maintained by WHIPS are derived from one or more independent and usually remote data sources. Data in the warehouse is modeled conceptually using a *view directed acyclic graph* (*VDAG*). Each node in the graph represents a materialized view stored at the warehouse. An edge $V_j \rightarrow V_i$ indicates that view V_j is defined over view V_i. A node with no outgoing edges represents a view that is defined over source data. WHIPS requires that each warehouse view V is defined either only over source data, or only over other warehouse views, because views defined over source data require special algorithms for ensuring their consistency [15]. We call views defined over source data *base views*, and views defined over other warehouse views *derived views*. (In a typical OLAP-oriented data warehouse, fact tables and dimension tables would be modeled as base views, while summary tables would be modeled as derived views.) In WHIPS, each base view is defined over source data using a single SQL SELECT-FROM-WHERE (SFW) statement. This simple base view definition language allows the warehouse designer to filter and combine source data using appropriate selection and join conditions in the WHERE clause. Currently, aggregation is not permitted in base view definitions because it is difficult to ensure the consistency of aggregates over remote source relations [15]. Each derived view is defined over other warehouse views using one or more SQL SELECT-FROM-WHERE-GROUP-BY (SFWG) statements, where aggregation is permitted. Multiple SFWG statements may be combined using UNION ALL.

Example 2.1 As a concrete example, let us suppose that there are three remote information sources S_1, S_2, and S_3, exporting the tables *Lineitem*, *Order*, and *Customer*, respectively. The schema of these tables is loosely based on the TPC-D benchmark [13], but simplified for succinctness of presentation. (All our experiments in Section 4 strictly follow the TPC-D schema.) Base views V_1, V_2, and V_3 at the warehouse could be defined as projections over $S_1.Lineitem$, $S_2.Order$, and $S_3.Customer$ as follows:

```
CREATE VIEW V₁ AS
    SELECT orderID, partID, qty, cost FROM S₁.Lineitem
CREATE VIEW V₂ AS
    SELECT orderID, custID, date FROM S₂.Order
CREATE VIEW V₃ AS
    SELECT custID, name, address FROM S₃.Customer
```

Of course, selection and join operations may be used in base view definitions as well. Derived view V_4 could be defined to count the number of orders each customer has made in 1998:

```
CREATE VIEW V₄ AS
    SELECT custID, COUNT(*) FROM V₂, V₃
    WHERE V₂.custID = V₃.custID AND
    V₂.date>='1998-01-01' AND V₂.date<'1999-01-01'
    GROUP BY custID                                □
```

Three types of components comprise the WHIPS system: the *Extractors*, the *Integrator*, and the *Warehouse Maintainer*. As mentioned previously, WHIPS also relies on a commercial relational DBMS to store and process warehouse data. The WHIPS components, along with the

DBMS, are shown in Figure 1 (most figures appear at the end of the paper). We discuss the components by walking through how warehouse data is maintained when source data changes. Each *Extractor* component periodically detects *deltas* (insertions, deletions, and/or updates) in source data. One Extractor is used for each information source. For instance, in Figure 1, the Extractor assigned to S_1 detects the changes to the *Lineitem* table which resides in S_1. The *Integrator* component receives deltas detected by the Extractors, and computes a consistent set of deltas to the base views stored in the warehouse. The Integrator may need to send queries back to the sources to compute base view deltas. For details, see [14, 15]. The *Warehouse Maintainer* component receives the base view deltas from the Integrator and computes a consistent set of deltas to the derived views. The Warehouse Maintainer then updates all of the warehouse views based on the provided and computed deltas. To compute the derived view deltas and update the materialized views, the Warehouse Maintainer sends a sequence of Data Manipulation Language (DML) commands to the DBMS. These DML commands include SQL queries for computing the deltas, as well as modification statements (e.g., INSERT, DELETE, cursor updates) for updating the materialized views.

The remainder of the paper focuses on the Warehouse Maintainer component. We refer readers to [8] and [15] for extended discussions of the Extractors and the Integrator.

3 The Warehouse Maintainer

The Warehouse Maintainer is the component responsible for initializing and maintaining the warehouse views. There are many possible ways of representing the warehouse views and performing incremental maintenance on them. In Sections 3.1 and 3.2, we identify specific important decision areas. For each decision area, we propose several alternatives and analyze them qualitatively. Quantitative performance results will be presented in Section 4. We have decided to separate the performance results from the discussion of the decision areas (rather than mixing them), because some of the decision areas are interrelated and it is important to have a complete overview of the issues before we delve into the detailed performance analysis.

3.1 View Representation and Delta Installation

Views in WHIPS are defined using SQL SFWG statements (for derived views) and SFW statements (for base views) with bag semantics. There are two ways to represent a bag of tuples in a view. One representation, which we call the DUP representation, simply keeps the duplicate tuples, as shown in Table 1 for a small sample of data in view V_1 from Example 2.1. Another representation, which we call the CNT representation, keeps one copy of each unique tuple and stores the number of duplicates in a special *dupcnt* attribute, as in Table 2. Let us denote a view V's DUP representation as V^{DUP} and its CNT representation as V^{CNT}. Next, we compare the two representations in terms of their storage costs and implications for queries and view maintenance.

orderID	partID	qty	cost
1	a	1	20
1	b	2	250
1	a	1	20

Table 1: V_1^{DUP}.

orderID	partID	qty	cost	dupcnt
1	a	1	20	2
1	b	2	250	1

Table 2: V_1^{CNT}.

3.1.1 Storage Cost and Query Performance

The CNT representation of a view V has lower storage cost if there are many duplicates in V and if the tuples of V are large enough that the storage overhead of having a *dupcnt* attribute is not significant. The reduction in storage achieved by using V^{CNT} instead of V^{DUP} may speed up selection, join, and aggregation queries over V by reducing I/O. However, projections may be slower when the CNT representation is used. Consider the following simple operation of listing the *orderID*'s in V_1:

```
SELECT orderID FROM V_1
```

If we operate directly on the CNT representation V_1^{CNT} (Table 2), the answer to the above query will not remain in the CNT representation. We need to group the tuples with matching *orderID*'s and sum up their *dupcnt* values:

```
SELECT orderID, SUM(dupcnt) AS dupcnt
    FROM V_1^{CNT} GROUP BY orderID
```

In general, whenever projection is used in a query, aggregation may be necessary to produce an answer in the CNT representation.

3.1.2 Deletion Installation

If V has no duplicates, then the deletions from V, denoted $\triangledown V$, can be installed using a single DELETE statement. For example, to install $\triangledown V_1$ in our working example, we use:

```
DELETE FROM V_1 WHERE (V_1.orderID, V_1.partID) IN
    (SELECT orderID, partID FROM ▽V_1)
```

The above statement assumes that $\{orderID, partID\}$ is a key for V_1. The WHERE clause can be modified to handle keys with any number of attributes, where in the worst case, all attributes of the view together form a key. Unfortunately, when V_1 has duplicates and hence no key, the above statement is incorrect because it may delete more tuples than intended, as discussed in Example 1.1.

In general, care must be taken when installing $\triangledown V$ in the presence of duplicates. Under the DUP representation, a cursor on $\triangledown V^{\mathrm{DUP}}$ is required. For each tuple t in $\triangledown V^{\mathrm{DUP}}$ examined by the cursor, we delete one and only one tuple in V^{DUP} that matches t. Doing so generally requires another cursor on V^{DUP}. However, if the DBMS provides some mechanism of restricting the number of rows processed by a statement (such as allowing statements to reference row counts or tuple ID's), we can avoid the cursor on V^{DUP}.

Under the CNT representation, each deleted tuple t in $\triangledown V^{\mathrm{CNT}}$ results in either an update to or a deletion from V^{CNT}. If $t.dupcnt$ is less than the *dupcnt* value of the tuple in V^{CNT} that matches t, we decrement the matching V^{CNT} tuple's *dupcnt* value by $t.dupcnt$. Otherwise, we delete the matching tuple from V^{CNT}. This procedure can be implemented with a cursor on $\triangledown V^{\mathrm{CNT}}$. Alternatively, the entire $\triangledown V^{\mathrm{CNT}}$ can be processed in batch with one UPDATE statement and one `DELETE` statement, but both statements contain potentially expensive correlated subqueries. The `DELETE` statement is illustrated below. The `UPDATE` statement is twice as long, with one correlated subquery in its `WHERE` clause and one in its `SET` clause. We omit the details due to space constraints.

```
DELETE FROM V^CNT
WHERE EXISTS (SELECT * FROM ▽V^CNT
             WHERE ▽V^CNT.orderID = V^CNT.orderID
             AND   ▽V^CNT.partID  = V^CNT.partID
             AND   ▽V^CNT.dupcnt >= V^CNT.dupcnt)
```

We could eliminate the `DELETE` statement by using a row-level trigger that automatically deletes any tuple in V with *dupcnt* less than or equal to 0. Under this approach, we only need one `UPDATE` statement to decrement the *dupcnt* values of all V tuples with matching $\triangledown V^{\text{CNT}}$ tuples. The trigger is fired for each updated tuple that satisfies the trigger condition.

3.1.3 Insertion Installation

Under the DUP representation, we can install the insertions into V^{DUP}, denoted $\triangle V^{\text{DUP}}$, using a single straightforward SQL `INSERT` statement. Under the CNT representation, we can install $\triangle V^{\text{CNT}}$ with a single `INSERT` statement only if we know that V never contains any duplicates. In general, however, each tuple t in $\triangle V^{\text{CNT}}$ results in either an update or an insertion to V^{CNT}. If there is a tuple in V^{CNT} that matches t, we increment the matching V^{CNT} tuple's *dupcnt* value by $t.dupcnt$. Otherwise, we insert t into V^{CNT}. Again, this procedure can be implemented with a cursor on $\triangle V^{\text{CNT}}$, or we can process the entire $\triangle V^{\text{CNT}}$ in batch with one `UPDATE` statement and one `INSERT` statement, but again, both statements contain potentially expensive correlated subqueries.

3.1.4 Discussion

Intuitively, for a warehouse view that never contains any duplicates (i.e., it has a known key), the DUP representation should outperform the CNT representation in all metrics (storage cost, query performance, and delta installation time) because the DUP representation does not have the overhead of one *dupcnt* attribute per tuple. On the other hand, for a view with many duplicates, we would expect the CNT representation to be preferable because it is more compact. For WHIPS, we are interested in knowing, quantitatively, which representation is better as we vary the average number of duplicates in a view. We also would like to quantify the overhead of the CNT representation for views with no duplicates.

Another issue we wish to investigate is the strategy for delta installation. As discussed earlier in this section, delta installation becomes much simpler if we know that the view will not contain duplicates. Let KEYINSTALL denote the method of installing deltas that exploits a lack of duplicates (i.e., a known key), and let GENINSTALL denote the general method that does not. It is easier for the Warehouse Maintainer component to support only GENINSTALL because it works for all views with or without keys. However, warehouse views frequently do have keys. For instance, dimension tables and fact tables, which are modeled as base views,

usually have keys. Summary tables often perform GROUP-BY operations, and the GROUP-BY attributes become the keys of the summary tables. If KEYINSTALL consistently outperforms GENINSTALL for these common cases, the Warehouse Maintainer should support KEYINSTALL as well.

Finally, we also need to evaluate different implementations of GENINSTALL under the CNT representation. As discussed earlier, GENINSTALL under the CNT representation can be implemented with a cursor loop, with two SQL statements, or with one SQL statement and a trigger. (Under the DUP representation, GENINSTALL must be implemented with a cursor loop.) With a cursor loop or a row-level trigger, we have better control over the execution of the installation procedure, so we can optimize it by hand according to our knowledge of the warehouse workload. On the other hand, the SQL statements are optimized by the DBMS, armed with a more sophisticated performance model and statistics. Although traditional DBMS optimizers were not designed originally for data warehousing, modern optimizers have added considerable support for warehouse-type data and queries [3]. It is interesting to determine whether the SQL-based delta installation procedure can be optimized adequately by the DBMS we are using. In Section 4.1, we present answers to all of the questions discussed above based on the experiments we have conducted.

3.2 Maintaining Aggregate Views

Given deltas for base views, the Warehouse Maintainer needs to modify the derived views so that they remain consistent with the base views. A simple approach is to recompute all of the derived views from the new contents of the base views, as many existing warehousing systems do. WHIPS, on the other hand, maintains the derived views incrementally for efficiency. The Warehouse Maintainer first computes the deltas for the derived views using a predefined set of queries called *maintenance expressions*, and then it installs these deltas into the derived views. The maintenance expressions of views defined using SQL SFW statements (without subqueries) are well studied, e.g., [5], and we do not discuss them here. For views defined using SFWG statements (i.e., views with GROUP-BY and aggregation), we introduce and contrast four different maintenance algorithms through a comprehensive example.

In this example, let us suppose that view V_1 contains the tuples shown in Table 3. A view *Parts* is defined over V_1 to group the V_1 tuples by *partID*. The *revenue* of each part stored in *Parts* is computed from V_1 by summing the products of *qty* and *cost* for each order for that particular part. *Parts* also records in a *tuplecnt* attribute the number of V_1 tuples that are used to derive each *Parts* tuple. The SQL definition of *Parts* is as follows:

```
CREATE VIEW Parts AS
    SELECT partID, SUM(qty*price) AS revenue,
           COUNT(*) AS tuplecnt
    FROM V_1 GROUP BY partID
```

The tuples in *Parts* are shown in Table 4. We use the DUP representation for *Parts* since *Parts* has a key (*partID*)

orderID	partID	qty	cost
1	a	1	20
1	b	2	250
2	a	1	20
3	c	1	500

Table 3: V_1.

partID	revenue	tuplecnt
a	40	2
b	500	1
c	500	1

Table 4: *Parts*.

orderID	partID	qty	cost
1	a	2	20
4	c	1	500
4	d	1	30

Table 5: $\triangle V_1$.

orderID	partID	qty	cost
1	a	1	20
1	b	2	250

Table 6: $\bigtriangledown V_1$.

and hence contains no duplicates. Note that the *tuplecnt* attribute differs from the *dupcnt* attribute used under the CNT representation since *tuplecnt* does not reflect the number of duplicates in *Parts*. Nevertheless, like *dupcnt*, *tuplecnt* helps incremental view maintenance by recording the number of base view tuples that contribute to each derived view tuple: The *tuplecnt* attribute is used to determine when a *Parts* tuple t should be deleted because all of the V_1 tuples that derive t have been deleted from V_1. In fact, had *tuplecnt* not been included in *Parts*'s definition, WHIPS would automatically modify the view definition to include *tuplecnt* so that *Parts* could be maintained incrementally.

Now suppose that the tuples shown in Table 5 are to be inserted into V_1, and the ones shown in Table 6 are to be deleted. (Note that tuples $\langle 1, a, 1, 20 \rangle$ in $\bigtriangledown V_1$ and $\langle 1, a, 2, 20 \rangle$ in $\triangle V_1$ together represent an update in which the *qty* of a parts purchased in the first order ($orderID = 1$) is increased from 1 to 2.) Next we illustrate how we can maintain *Parts* given the deltas $\bigtriangledown V_1$ and $\triangle V_1$, using four different algorithms.

3.2.1 Full Recomputation

Full recomputation (FULLRECOMP) is conceptually simple and easy to implement. First, we install the base view deltas $\bigtriangledown V_1$ and $\triangle V_1$ into V_1. Then, we delete the entire old contents of *Parts* and compute its new contents from V_1.

3.2.2 Summary-Delta With Cursor-Based Installation

The original *summary-delta* algorithm (SDCURSOR for short) for incremental maintenance of aggregate views [12] has a *compute phase* and a cursor-based *install phase*. In the compute phase, the net effect of $\triangle V_1$ and $\bigtriangledown V_1$ on *Parts* is captured in a *summary-delta* table, denoted $Parts_{SD}$ and computed as follows:

```
SELECT partID, SUM(revenue) AS revenue,
       SUM(tuplecnt) AS tuplecnt FROM
 ((SELECT partID, SUM(qty*price) AS revenue,
   COUNT(*) AS tuplecnt FROM △V₁ GROUP BY partID)
 UNION ALL
  (SELECT partID, -SUM(qty*price) AS revenue,
   -COUNT(*) AS tuplecnt FROM ▽V₁ GROUP BY partID))
GROUP BY partID
```

The summary-delta applies the GROUP-BY and aggregation operations specified in the definition of *Parts* to $\triangle V_1$ and $\bigtriangledown V_1$ and combines the results. Note that the aggregate values computed from $\bigtriangledown V_1$ are negated to reflect the effects of deletions on the SUM and COUNT functions. Given the $\triangle V_1$ and $\bigtriangledown V_1$ shown in Tables 5 and 6, the summary-delta $Parts_{SD}$ is shown in Table 7.

In the install phase, SDCURSOR instantiates a cursor to loop over the tuples in the summary-delta $Parts_{SD}$. For each $Parts_{SD}$ tuple, SDCURSOR applies the appropriate change to *Parts*. For instance, tuple $\langle a, 20, 0 \rangle$ affects *Parts* by incrementing the a tuple's *revenue* by 20 and *tuplecnt* by 0. This change reflects the effect of updating the *qty* of a parts in the first order (see $\bigtriangledown V_1$ and $\triangle V_1$). The *tuplecnt* is unchanged because the update does not change the number of V_1 tuples that derive the a tuple in *Parts*. Tuple $\langle b, -500, -1 \rangle$ in $Parts_{SD}$ affects *Parts* by decrementing the b tuple's *revenue* by 500 and *tuplecnt* by 1, which reflects the effect of deleting $\langle 1, b, 2, 250 \rangle$ from V_1 (see $\bigtriangledown V_1$). Moreover, the b tuple is then deleted from *Parts*, since its *tuplecnt* becomes zero after it is decremented. Tuple $\langle c, 500, 1 \rangle$ increments the c tuple's *revenue* by 500 and *tuplecnt* by 1, reflecting the effect of inserting $\langle 4, c, 1, 500 \rangle$ into V_1 (see $\triangle V_1$). Finally, tuple $\langle d, 30, 1 \rangle$ results in an insertion, since there is no existing tuple with the same *partID*.

3.2.3 Summary-Delta With Batch Installation

The summary-delta algorithm with batch installation (SDBATCH) is a variation we propose in this paper on the original summary-delta algorithm from [12] described above. The idea is to do more processing in the compute phase in order to speed up the install phase, since views must be locked during installation. In the compute phase of SDBATCH, we first compute the summary-delta $Parts_{SD}$ as before. From $Parts_{SD}$, we then compute the deletions $\bigtriangledown Parts$ and insertions $\triangle Parts$ to be applied to *Parts*. $\bigtriangledown Parts$ contains all the *Parts* tuples that are affected by $Parts_{SD}$:

```
SELECT * FROM Parts WHERE partID IN
   (SELECT partID FROM Parts_SD)
```

$\triangle Parts$ is the result of applying $Parts_{SD}$ to $\bigtriangledown Parts$:

```
SELECT partID, SUM(revenue) AS revenue,
       SUM(tuplecnt) AS tuplecnt
FROM ((SELECT * FROM ▽Parts) UNION ALL
      (SELECT * FROM Parts_SD))
GROUP BY partID HAVING SUM(tuplecnt) > 0
```

Notice that we filter out those groups with *tuplecnt* less than one because they no longer contain any tuples after $Parts_{SD}$ is applied. Given the $Parts_{SD}$ shown in Table 7, the resulting $\bigtriangledown Parts$ and $\triangle Parts$ are shown in Tables 8 and 9.

In the install phase of SDBATCH, we first apply $\bigtriangledown Parts$, and then $\triangle Parts$, to *Parts*. Because of the way we compute $\bigtriangledown Parts$ in the compute phase, every $\bigtriangledown Parts$ tuple always results in a true deletion from *Parts*, instead of an update that decrements the *revenue* and *tuplecnt* attributes of an existing *Parts* tuple. Since *Parts* is an aggregate view and hence contains no duplicates, the entire $\bigtriangledown Parts$ can be applied in batch using KEYINSTALL with a simple DELETE (Section 3.1.2). Once $\bigtriangledown Parts$ has been applied to *Parts*, every $\triangle Parts$ tuple always results in a true insertion into *Parts*, instead of an update that increments the *revenue* and

partID	revenue	tuplecnt
a	20	0
b	-500	-1
c	500	1
d	30	1

Table 7: $Parts_{\mathrm{SD}}$.

partID	revenue	tuplecnt
a	20	1
b	500	1
c	500	1

Table 8: $\triangledown Parts$.

partID	revenue	tuplecnt
a	40	1
c	1000	2
d	30	1

Table 9: $\triangle Parts$.

tuplecnt attributes of an existing tuple. Therefore, $\triangle Parts$ can be applied in batch using KEYINSTALL with a simple INSERT.

3.2.4 Summary-Delta With Overwrite Installation

Both SDCURSOR and SDBATCH update *Parts* in place, which requires identifying the *Parts* tuples affected by the $Parts_{\mathrm{SD}}$ tuples. To avoid this potentially expensive operation, we introduce a new summary-delta algorithm with overwrite installation (SDOVERWRITE). SDOVERWRITE completely replaces the old contents of *Parts* with the new contents, just like FULLRECOMP. However, SDOVERWRITE differs from FULLRECOMP in that SDOVERWRITE does not recompute *Parts* from scratch; instead, it uses the summary-delta $Parts_{\mathrm{SD}}$ and the old contents of *Parts* to compute the new *Parts*. The SQL statement used here is similar to the one used to compute $\triangle Parts$ in SDBATCH:

```
SELECT partID, SUM(revenue) AS revenue,
       SUM(tuplecnt) AS tuplecnt
FROM ((SELECT * FROM Parts) UNION ALL
      (SELECT * FROM Parts_SD))
GROUP BY partID HAVING SUM(tuplecnt) > 0
```

One technicality remains: there is no easy way to replace the contents of *Parts* with the results of the above SELECT statement since the statement itself references *Parts*. To avoid unnecessary copying, we store the results of the above query in another table, and then designate that table as the new *Parts*. Therefore, compared to the other three algorithms, SDOVERWRITE requires additional space roughly the size of *Parts*.

3.2.5 Discussion

Although the example in this section only shows how the various algorithms can be used to maintain a specific aggregate view, it is not hard to extend the ideas to handle views with arbitrary combinations of SUM, COUNT, and AVG aggregate functions. For views with MAX or MIN, SDCURSOR, SDBATCH, and SDOVERWRITE are not applicable in general, since we cannot perform true incremental maintenance when a base tuple providing the MAX or MIN value for its group is deleted.

To summarize, we have presented four algorithms for maintaining SFWG views. FULLRECOMP recomputes the entire view from scratch. Intuitively, if the base data is large, FULLRECOMP can be very expensive. SDCURSOR, SDBATCH, and SDOVERWRITE avoid recomputation by applying only the incremental changes captured in a summary-delta table. These three algorithms differ in the ways they apply the summary-delta to the view.

In WHIPS, we are interested in knowing which algorithm is best under different settings. We also wish to compare how long the different algorithms must lock the view for

update. This measure is important because once a view is locked for update, it generally becomes inaccessible for OLAP queries. FULLRECOMP needs to lock while it is regenerating the view. SDCURSOR and SDBATCH only need to lock the view during their install phases. SDOVERWRITE does not lock the view at all, because it computes the new contents of the view in a separate table. In fact, with an additional table, we can eliminate the locking time of FULLRECOMP, SDCURSOR, SDBATCH, or any maintenance algorithm in general, since we can work on a copy of the view while leaving the original accessible to queries. In this case, it is useful to know how much locking time we are saving in order to justify the additional storage cost. In Section 4.2, we experimentally compare the performance and locking time of the four algorithms.

So far, we have focused on how WHIPS maintains a single view. In practice, WHIPS maintains a set of views organized in a VDAG (Section 2). When a view V is modified, other views defined over V need to be modified as well. In order to maintain the other views incrementally, we must be able to capture the incremental changes made to V. Among our four algorithms for aggregate view maintenance, only SDBATCH explicitly computes the incremental changes to V as delta tables $\triangledown V$ and $\triangle V$. Although the summary-delta V_{SD} in a way also captures the incremental changes to V, using V_{SD} to maintain a higher-level view is much harder than using $\triangledown V$ and $\triangle V$, especially if the higher-level view is not an aggregate view. For this reason, we might prefer SDBATCH as long as it is not significantly slower than the other algorithms.

4   Experiments

Section 3 introduced several areas in which we must make critical decisions on warehouse view representation and maintenance, and provided some qualitative comparisons of the alternatives. For each decision area, we now quantitatively compare the performance of various alternatives through experiments.

The base views used in the experiments are from TPC-D [13], often including fact tables *Order* and *Lineitem*, which we call O and L for short. The derived views vary from one experiment to the next. Contents of the base views and their deltas are generated by the standard dbgen program supplied with the TPC-D benchmark. A TPC-D scale factor of 1.0 means that the entire warehouse is about 1GB in size, with L and O together taking up about 900MB. The commercial DBMS we use is running on a dedicated Windows NT machine with a Pentium II processor.[1] The database buffer size is set at 6.4MB. We have chosen

---

[1] We are not permitted to name the commercial DBMS we have used (nor the second one we are using to corroborate some of our results), but both are state-of-the-art products from major relational DBMS vendors.

466

a small database buffer in combination with relatively small TPC-D scale factors in order to limit the duration and the storage requirement of repeated experiments. To study scalability issues we have explored wide ranges of buffer sizes and scale factors for some of our experiments, and found the performance trends to be consistent with the results presented. An example will be shown in Section 4.2.1.

Recall that the WHIPS Warehouse Maintainer sends a sequence of DML statements to the DBMS to query and update views in the data warehouse. In the experiments, we measure the wall-clock time required for the DBMS to run these DML commands, which represents the bulk of the time spent maintaining the warehouse. We have specifically avoided hand-tuning the DBMS optimizer for our experiments because improvements are very sensitive to the workload and to the expertise of the person doing the tuning. We believe it is more instructive to study performance with an "out of the box" DBMS (system parameters at their default values), under the assumption that all of the results we present could probably be improved somewhat in some cases by careful tuning.

4.1 View Representation and Delta Installation

In Section 3.1.4 we identified three decisions that need to be made regarding view representation and delta installation: (1) whether to use DUP or CNT as the view representation; (2) whether to use GENINSTALL or KEYINSTALL to install deltas when the view has a key; (3) whether to use a cursor loop, SQL statements, or a SQL statement and a trigger to implement GENINSTALL under the CNT representation. In this section, we present performance results that help us make the best decisions for all three areas. The results are presented in reverse order, because we need to choose the best GENINSTALL implementation for CNT (decision area 3) before we can compare CNT with DUP (decision area 1).

4.1.1 GENINSTALL Under CNT: Cursor vs. SQL

In the first experiment, we compare the time to install deltas for base view L^{CNT} (view L using the CNT representation) using a cursor-based implementation versus a SQL-based implementation for GENINSTALL. It would be interesting to compare the performance of a trigger-based implementation as well, but unfortunately the DBMS we are using does not allow a row-level trigger to modify the table whose update caused the trigger to fire.

For this experiment, a TPC-D scale factor of 0.1 is used. Normally, L has a key $\{orderkey, linenumber\}$ and therefore contains no duplicates. We artificially introduce duplicates into L so that on average each L tuple has two other duplicates (i.e., L has a *multiplicity* of 3). We also vary the update ratio of L from 1% to 10%. An update ratio of $k\%$ implies $|\bigtriangledown L| = |\bigtriangleup L| = (k/100) \cdot |L|$, i.e., $(k/100) \cdot |L|$ tuples are deleted from L and $(k/100) \cdot |L|$ tuples are inserted. Finally, we assume L^{CNT} has an index on $\{orderkey, linenumber\}$, since $\{orderkey, linenumber\}$ functionally determine all other 13 attributes of L. In general, if there are no nontrivial func-

tional dependencies to exploit, we would have to equate all 15 attributes of L instead of only *orderkey* and *linenumber* when matching L tuples with $\bigtriangledown L$ and $\bigtriangleup L$ tuples. We performed experiments where no functional dependencies were exploited, and our results (not shown here) reveal that in this case all implementations of GENINSTALL become slower by almost an order of magnitude. Nevertheless, the overall performance trends remain identical to the results presented in this section.

Fig. 2 plots the time it takes for the two GENINSTALL implementations to process $\bigtriangledown L$ and $\bigtriangleup L$. Recall from Section 3.1 that cursor-based GENINSTALL processes a delta table one tuple at a time, similar to a nested-loop join between the delta and the view with the delta being the outer table. As a result, the plots of cursor-based GENINSTALL for $\bigtriangledown L$ and $\bigtriangleup L$ are linear in the size of $\bigtriangledown L$ and $\bigtriangleup L$ respectively.

SQL-based GENINSTALL is optimized by the DBMS. To ensure that the optimizer has access to the most up-to-date statistics, we explicitly ask the DBMS to gather statistics after L, $\bigtriangledown L$, and $\bigtriangleup L$ are populated (and the time spent in gathering statistics is not counted in the delta installation time). If the optimizer were perfect, SQL-based GENINSTALL would never perform any worse than cursor-based GENINSTALL, because the cursor-based plan is but one of the many viable ways to execute SQL-based GENINSTALL. Unfortunately, we see in Fig. 2 that SQL-based GENINSTALL is consistently slower than cursor-based GENINSTALL for deletion installation. This phenomenon illustrates the difficulty of optimizing DELETE and UPDATE statements with correlated subqueries, such as the second DELETE statement shown in Section 3.1.2. The way these statements are structured in SQL leads naturally to an execution plan that scans the entire view looking for tuples to delete or update. However, in an incrementally maintained warehouse, deltas are generally much smaller than the view itself, so a better plan is to scan the deltas and delete or update matching tuples in the view, assuming the view is indexed. Evidently, the state-of-the-art commercial DBMS used by WHIPS missed this plan, which explains why the plots for SQL-based GENINSTALL go nowhere near the origin. We expect this behavior may be typical of many commercial DBMS's today, and we have confirmed this expectation by replicating some of our experiments on another major relational DBMS.

On the other hand, the DBMS is more adept at optimizing SQL-based GENINSTALL for insertions, presumably because INSERT can be optimized similarly to regular SELECT queries and more easily than DELETE. As shown in Fig. 2, SQL-based GENINSTALL is faster than cursor-based GENINSTALL for insertion installation when the update ratio is higher than 1%. To summarize, at TPC-D scale factor 0.1 and update ratio between 1% and 10% on the DBMS we are using, cursor-based GENINSTALL is preferred for deletion installation and SQL-based GENINSTALL is preferred for insertion installation under the CNT representation.

In the next experiment, we investigate how the size of

the views might affect this decision. We fix the size of $\triangledown L$ and $\triangle L$ at about 2.6MB each while varying the TPC-D scale factor from 0.04 to 0.36. The update ratio thus varies from 9% to 1%. The results in Fig. 3 indicate that the running time of cursor-based GENINSTALL is insensitive to the change in $|L|$, while the running time of SQL-based GENINSTALL grows linearly with $|L|$. Thus, we should use cursor-based GENINSTALL to process both deletions and insertions for large views with low update ratios.

4.1.2 Delta Installation: KEYINSTALL vs. GENINSTALL

In the following experiment, we seek to quantify the performance benefits of using KEYINSTALL instead of GENINSTALL when the view has a key and hence no duplicates. In this case, we are only interested in the DUP representation since DUP should always be used instead of CNT when the view contains no duplicates (Section 3.1.4). Furthermore, under the DUP representation, insertion installation requires one simple INSERT statement, which is the same for both KEYINSTALL and GENINSTALL. Therefore, our task reduces to comparing KEYINSTALL and GENINSTALL for deletion installation under the DUP representation.

In Fig. 4, we plot the time it takes for KEYINSTALL and GENINSTALL to install $\triangledown L$ in base view L, which contains no duplicates and has an index on its key attributes. We fix the TPC-D scale factor at 0.1 and vary the update ratio from 1% to 10%. At first glance, the results may seem counterintuitive: KEYINSTALL is slower than GENINSTALL when the update ratio is below 5%. However, recall from Section 3.1.2 that KEYINSTALL uses a simple DELETE to install $\triangledown L$, while GENINSTALL requires a cursor loop. Clearly, the DBMS has failed again to take advantage of the small $\triangledown L$ and the index on L when optimizing the DELETE statement. Given this limitation of the DBMS optimizer, we cannot justify implementing KEYINSTALL in addition to GENINSTALL in the Warehouse Maintainer from a performance perspective.

4.1.3 View Representation: DUP vs. CNT

We now evaluate the performance of DUP and CNT representations in the case where the view may contain duplicates. In Fig. 5, we compare the the time it takes to install $\triangledown L$ and $\triangle L$ under DUP and CNT representations. Again, the TPC-D scale factor is fixed at 0.1 and the update ratio varies from 1% to 10%. The multiplicity of L in this first experiment is close to 1, i.e., L contains almost no duplicates. We create indexes for both L^{DUP} and L^{CNT} on $\{orderkey, linenumber\}$, even though $\{orderkey, linenumber\}$ is not a key for L^{DUP} because of potential duplicates. For the CNT representation, we use cursor-based GENINSTALL to install $\triangledown L^{\text{CNT}}$ and SQL-based GENINSTALL to install $\triangle L^{\text{CNT}}$, as decided in Section 4.1.1 for scale factor 0.1. The results plotted in Fig. 5 indicate that delta installation (insertions and deletions combined) under the CNT representation is about twice as expensive as delta installation under the DUP representation.

	DUP representation	CNT representation
$\triangledown$ (deletion)	$1.94\,ms$ / tuple	$\frac{2.49\,ms}{\text{multiplicity}}$ / tuple
$\triangle$ (insertion)	$0.57\,ms$ / tuple	$\frac{4.48\,ms}{\text{multiplicity}}$ / tuple

Table 10: Per-tuple delta installation costs.

In the next experiment, we increase the multiplicity of L from 1 to 3, thereby tripling the size of L^{DUP}, $\triangledown L^{\text{DUP}}$, and $\triangle L^{\text{DUP}}$. On the other hand, the increase in multiplicity has no effect on the size of L^{CNT}, $\triangledown L^{\text{CNT}}$, and $\triangle L^{\text{CNT}}$. As Fig. 6 shows, installing $\triangledown L^{\text{DUP}}$ becomes more than twice as slow as installing $\triangledown L^{\text{CNT}}$, but installing $\triangle L^{\text{DUP}}$ is still three times faster than installing $\triangle L^{\text{CNT}}$. Overall, delta installation under the DUP representation is slightly slower than under the CNT representation. By comparing Fig. 5 and 6, we also see that the delta installation time under the DUP representation increases proportionally with multiplicity, while the time under CNT remains the same.

To study the effect of view size on delta installation time, we conduct another experiment in which we fix the size of the deltas and vary the TPC-D scale factor from 0.04 to 0.36. Multiplicity of L is set at 3. For the CNT representation, we use the best GENINSTALL implementation (either cursor-based or SQL-based, depending on the scale factor; recall Section 4.1.1). The results are shown in Fig. 7. Notice that all four plots become nearly flat at large scale factors: when the view is sufficiently large, the cost of installing a delta tuple into the view approaches a constant for each delta type and each view representation. Thus, measured once, these per-tuple costs can be used to estimate the delta installation time in a large data warehouse. Table 10 shows the per-tuple installation costs measured under our experimental settings.

All experiments so far have focused on delta installation. In the next experiment, we compare the time to compute deltas for derived views under DUP and CNT representations. We define one derived view LO_1 as an equijoin between L and O, with a total of 24 attributes. Another derived view LO_2 is defined as the same equijoin followed by a projection which leaves only two attributes. In Fig. 8, we plot the the time it takes to compute $\triangledown LO_1$ and $\triangledown LO_2$ given $\triangledown L$ under both DUP and CNT representations. We choose an update ratio of 5% and increase the multiplicity of L from 1 to 5. When the multiplicity of L is close to 1 (i.e., L contains almost no duplicates), DUP and CNT offer comparable performance for computing derived view deltas. The overhead of the extra *dupcnt* attribute and the extra aggregation required for doing projection under the CNT representation (discussed in Section 3.1.1) turns out to be insignificant in this case. As we increase the multiplicity, computing derived view deltas under DUP becomes progressively slower than CNT because CNT is about m times more compact than DUP, where m is the multiplicity.

To summarize, the CNT representation scales well with increasing multiplicity and carries little overhead for computing derived view deltas. However, in the common case where the average number of duplicates is low (e.g., multiplicity is less than 3), the DUP representation is preferable because it is faster in installing deltas, especially insertions, which are common in data warehouses.

4.2 Maintaining Aggregate Views

In Section 3.2 we presented aggregate view maintenance algorithms FULLRECOMP and SDCURSOR, as well as two new variations SDBATCH and SDOVERWRITE. This section compares their performance in terms of the total time required for maintaining aggregate views. We also compare the install phase lengths of SDCURSOR and SDBATCH. Recall from Section 3.2.5 that we want to minimize the length of the install phase in a data warehouse because during this phase the view is locked for update.

We consider two types of aggregate views. A *fixed-ratio* aggregate over a base view V groups V into $\alpha \cdot |V|$ groups, where α is a fixed *aggregation ratio*. The size of a fixed-ratio aggregate increases with the size of the base view. On the other hand, a *fixed-size* aggregate over a base view V groups V into a small and fixed number of groups. We will see that the four aggregate maintenance algorithms behave differently for these two types of aggregates.

4.2.1 Maintaining Fixed-Ratio Aggregates

In the first experiment, we use a fixed-ratio aggregate V_{large} which groups the base view L by *orderkey* into approximately $0.25 \cdot |L|$ groups. First, we study the impact of the update ratio on the maintenance time of V_{large} by fixing the TPC-D scale factor at 0.1 and varying the update ratio from 1% to 10%. Fig. 9 shows that the update ratio has no effect on FULLRECOMP at all. However, the total maintenance time increases (gradually) with the update ratio for the three summary-delta-based algorithms. Among them, SDCURSOR is most sensitive to the change in update ratio, and SDOVERWRITE is least sensitive. Fig. 9 also shows that FULLRECOMP is far more expensive than the others. SDBATCH is the fastest when the update ratio is small, while SDOVERWRITE becomes the fastest when the update ratio is higher than 10%. In Fig. 10, we further compare SDCURSOR and SDBATCH in terms of the install phase. By doing more work in its compute phase, SDBATCH has a much shorter install phase than SDCURSOR. This shorter install phase gives our new algorithm SDBATCH an edge in applications where data availability is important.

Fig. 11 and 12 show the results of repeating the same experiment with the size of the database buffer set to 240MB instead of 6.4MB (the default in our experiments). Despite the large disparity in buffer size, the performance trends revealed by Fig. 11 and 12 are remarkably similar to those revealed by Fig. 9 and 10. We have repeated this experiment with a number of different buffer sizes, and found that even though performance is improved by extra memory (though not linearly), the relative performance of the schemes remains the same.

To study the impact of base view size on aggregate maintenance, we fix the size of $\bigtriangledown L$ and $\bigtriangleup L$ and vary the scale factor of L from 0.04 to 0.36. Fig. 13 shows that the performance of FULLRECOMP deteriorates dramatically as $|L|$ increases, because FULLRECOMP is recomputing the aggregate over a larger L. Although SDOVERWRITE and SDBATCH are not affected by $|L|$

as much as FULLRECOMP, their running time still increases because $|V_{large}|$ grows with $|L|$. On the other hand, SDCURSOR is almost unaffected by the increase in $|L|$. The reason is that SDCURSOR uses an index on V_{large} to find the matching V_{large} tuples for each tuple in the summary-delta table, and the lookup time of the index remains constant for the range of $|V_{large}|$ in this experiment. Fig. 13 also shows that FULLRECOMP is much slower than the other algorithms. SDBATCH is the fastest algorithm for smaller base views, while SDCURSOR is the fastest for larger base views.

Fig. 14 compares the time of the install phase for SDCURSOR and SDBATCH. The install phase of SDCURSOR is not affected by the size of the base view, for the same reason discussed above. The install phase of SDBATCH takes much less time than that of SDCURSOR for relatively small base views, but it increases as the base view becomes larger. Once again, the explanation lies with the limitation of the DBMS optimizer. When executing the SQL DELETE statement to install $\bigtriangledown V_{large}$, the DBMS fails to make use of the index on V_{large}; instead, it scans V_{large} looking for tuples to delete, which requires time proportional to $|V_{large}|$, or $0.25 \cdot |L|$.

4.2.2 Maintaining Fixed-Size Aggregates

We now compare the performance of the four algorithms for a fixed-size aggregate view V_{small}, which groups the base view L by *linenumber* into exactly seven groups, regardless of the size of L. Fig. 15 shows the impact of the update ratio on the maintenance of V_{small}. Again, the performance of FULLRECOMP does not change much as the update ratio increases. Plots of the other three algorithms, although somewhat noisy due to inconsistent DBMS behavior on such a small table, show that the total maintenance time increases at about the same rate for all three algorithms. The reason is that the time it takes to compute the summary-delta table (which is used by all three algorithms) increases with the update ratio. On the other hand, the size of the summary-delta is usually fixed for a small fixed-size aggregate such as V_{small}, because any base view delta of reasonable size will likely affect all groups in the aggregate. The type of work after computing the summary-delta varies from one algorithm to another, but for each algorithm, the amount of work depends only on the size of the aggregate and the size of the summary-delta, which are both fixed in this case. Fig. 16 further indicates that SDBATCH has a shorter install phase than SDCURSOR, and neither is affected by the update ratio because V_{small} is a fixed-size aggregate. In this case the install phase does not take a significant portion of the total maintenance time, but as we have discussed, the length of the install phase is still an important measure of warehouse availability.

Finally, Fig. 17 and 18 plot the total maintenance time and installation time of V_{small} respectively as we fix the size of the base view deltas and vary the size of the base view. We see in Fig. 17 that FULLRECOMP becomes dramatically slower as the base view becomes larger. However, the other three algorithms are not affected, again because the size of

	fixed-ratio aggregate		fixed-size aggregate	
	base view delta size	base view size	base view delta size	base view size
FULLRECOMP	0	3	0	3
SDOVERWRITE	1	2	1	0
SDBATCH	2	1	1	0
SDCURSOR	3	0	1	0

Table 11: Sensitivity of aggregate view maintenance algorithms.

the aggregate and the size of the summary-delta remain constant despite the increasing base view size. Fig. 18 also shows that the install phase of SDCURSOR and SDBATCH is not affected by the increasing base view size. Furthermore, SDBATCH has a faster install phase than SDCURSOR.

4.2.3 Summary

Based on our experiments, we learn that the aggregate maintenance algorithms behave differently on different types of aggregate views. In addition, two other factors—the size of the base view and the size of the base view deltas—also affect the performance of aggregate view maintenance, and different maintenance algorithms react differently to these factors. Table 11 summarizes the sensitivity of each algorithm to various factors using a scale of 0 (insensitive) to 3 (very sensitive). In conclusion, the following guidelines may be used to choose an aggregate view maintenance algorithm for a given scenario:

- Algorithms based on summary-delta tables (SDBATCH, SDCURSOR, and SDOVERWRITE) are much faster than FULLRECOMP, especially for relatively large base views.

- For fixed-ratio aggregates, SDCURSOR is preferred for large base views with small deltas, while SDOVERWRITE is preferred for small base views with large deltas. SDBATCH is a compromise between the two.

- For fixed-size aggregates, all three algorithms based on summary-delta tables perform equally well.

- SDBATCH generally has a shorter install phase than SDCURSOR. However, in the case of fixed-ratio aggregates this advantage of SDBATCH could diminish as the size of the base view increases if the DBMS is unable to optimize DELETE statements effectively.

5 Related Work

There has been a significant amount of research devoted to view maintenance; see [6] for a survey. However, there has been little coverage of the important details of view maintenance that are the focus of this paper. For instance, reference [9] assumes there is an *Inst* operation for installing deltas into a view, but does not cover the details on how to implement *Inst*. Reference [12] proposes the summary-delta algorithm for aggregate maintenance, but does not consider the various alternatives for applying the summary delta to the aggregate view. In this paper, we have presented three possible implementations of the view maintenance procedure, and evaluated their performance through experiments.

Reference [7] assumes that materialized views use the CNT representation. On the other hand, reference [5] assumes the DUP representation. To our knowledge, our paper is the first to investigate in detail the pros and cons of the two representations for view maintenance, and to present supporting experiments.

We also briefly described the WHIPS system. Although significant research has been devoted to both view maintenance and data warehousing, only a few systems focus on incremental view maintenance the way WHIPS does. The extended version of this paper [10] discusses in detail how WHIPS relates to the other systems.

As mentioned in Section 1, incremental warehouse maintenance has also found its way into commercial systems, such as the Red Brick database loader [4], Oracle materialized views [1], and DB2 automatic summary tables [2]. The results in this paper should be especially useful to the vendors for improving the performance of these systems, since we have conducted all of our experiments on a commercial DBMS as well.

6 Conclusion

This paper has addressed performance issues in incrementally maintained data warehouses, with our own WHIPS prototype serving as a framework for experimenting with a variety of techniques for efficient view maintenance. We identified several critical data representation and algorithmic decisions, and proposed guidelines for making the right decisions in different scenarios, supported by our experimental results. From the results of our experiments, we can see that making the right decision requires considerable analysis and tuning, because the optimal strategy often depends on many factors such as the size of views, the size of deltas, and the average number of duplicates. Ideally, some of the decisions can and should be made by the DBMS optimizer, since it has access to most relevant statistics. However, because of current limitations of DBMS optimizers, many decisions still need to be made by an external agent, such as the Warehouse Maintainer in WHIPS or a human warehouse administrator. As DBMS vendors continue to introduce more data warehousing features, we hope that view maintenance, especially delta installation, will receive an increasing level of support.

Acknowledgements

We are grateful to past WHIPS project members Reza Behforooz, Himanshu Gupta, Joachim Hammer, Janet Wiener, and Yue Zhuge, and to all of our colleagues in the Stanford Database Group who have contributed to WHIPS.

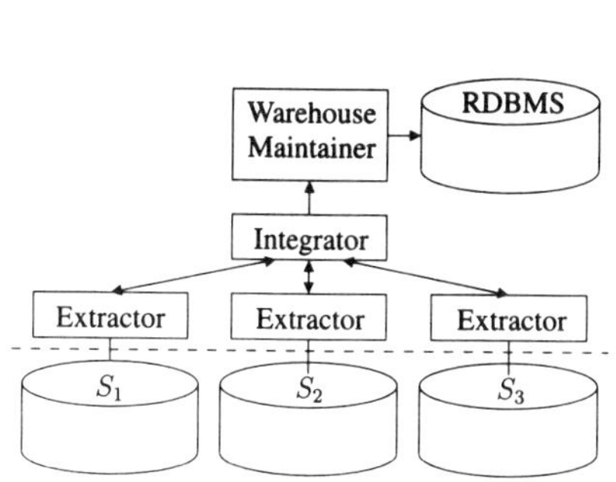

Fig. 1: WHIPS components.

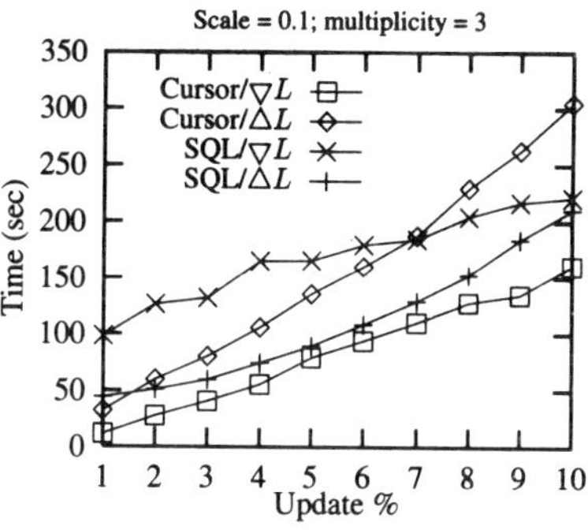

Fig. 2: GENINSTALL under CNT.

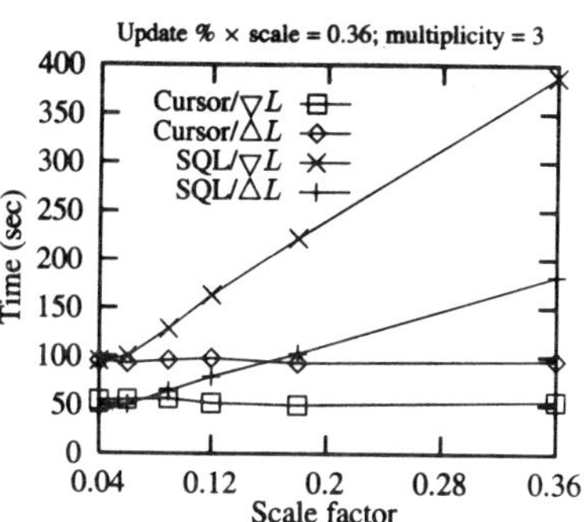

Fig. 3: GENINSTALL under CNT.

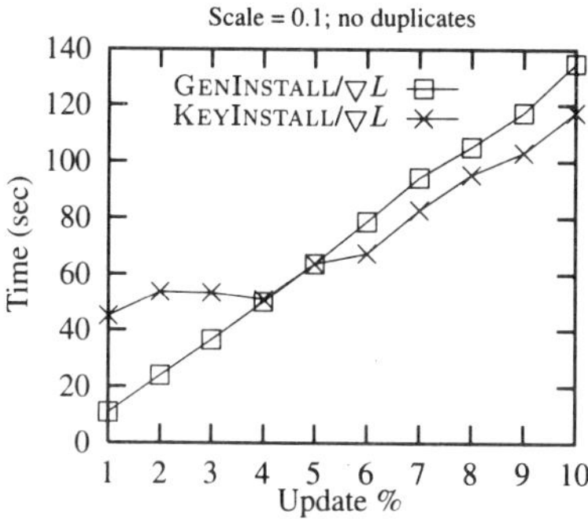

Fig. 4: KEYINSTALL vs. GENINSTALL.

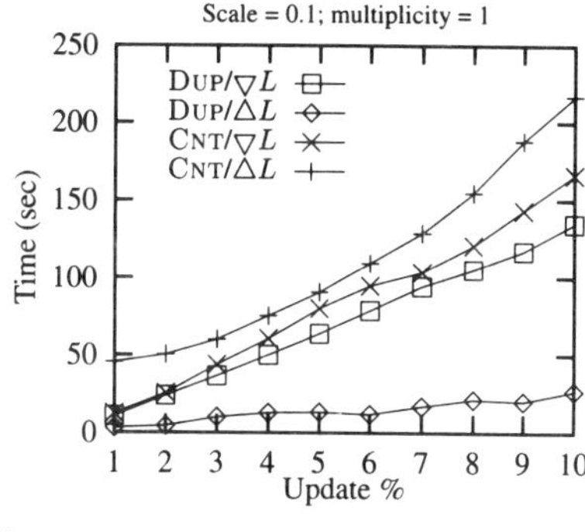

Fig. 5: DUP vs. CNT for delta installation.

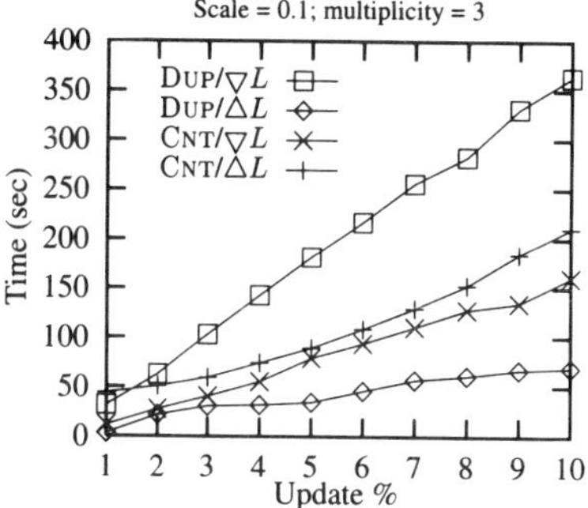

Fig. 6: DUP vs. CNT for delta installation.

References

[1] R. G. Bello, K. Dias, A. Downing, J. Feenan, W. D. Norcott, H. Sun, A. Witkowski, and M. Ziauddin. Materialized views in Oracle. In *Proc. of the 1998 Intl. Conf. on Very Large Data Bases*, pages 659–664, August 1998.

[2] S. Brobst and D. Sagar. The new, fully loaded, optimizer. *DB2 Magazine*, 4(3):23–29, September 1999.

[3] S. Chaudhuri and U. Dayal. An overview of data warehousing and OLAP technology. *SIGMOD Record*, 26(1):65–74, March 1997.

[4] P. M. Fernandez and D. A. Schneider. The ins and outs (and everthing in between) of data warehousing. In *Proc. of the 1996 ACM SIGMOD Intl. Conf. on Management of Data*, page 541, June 1996.

[5] T. Griffin and L. Libkin. Incremental maintenance of views with duplicates. In *Proc. of the 1995 ACM SIGMOD Intl. Conf. on Management of Data*, pages 328–339, May 1995.

[6] A. Gupta and I. S. Mumick. Maintenance of materialized views: Problems, techniques, and applications. *IEEE Data Engineering Bulletin*, 18(2):3–18, June 1995.

[7] A. Gupta, I. S. Mumick, and V. S. Subrahmanian. Maintaining views incrementally. In *Proc. of the 1993 ACM SIGMOD Intl. Conf. on Management of Data*, pages 157–166, May 1993.

[8] W. J. Labio and H. Garcia-Molina. Efficient snapshot differential algorithms for data warehousing. In *Proc. of the 1996 Intl. Conf. on Very Large Data Bases*, pages 63–74, September 1996.

[9] W. J. Labio, R. Yerneni, and H. Garcia-Molina. Shrinking the warehouse update window. In *Proc. of the 1999 ACM SIGMOD Intl. Conf. on Management of Data*, pages 383–394, June 1999.

[10] W.J. Labio, J. Yang, Y. Cui, H. Garcia-Molina, and J. Widom. Performance issues in incremental warehouse maintenance. Technical report, Computer Science Department, Stanford University, 1999. `www-db.stanford.edu/pub/papers/whips-wm.ps`.

[11] D. Lomet and J. Widom, editors. *Special Issue on Materialized Views and Data Warehousing, IEEE Data Engineering Bulletin*, 18(2), June 1995.

[12] I. S. Mumick, D. Quass, and B. S. Mumick. Maintenance of data cubes and summary tables in a warehouse. In *Proc. of the 1997 ACM SIGMOD Intl. Conf. on Management of Data*, pages 100–111, May 1997.

[13] Transaction Processing Performance Council. *TPC-D Benchmark Specification, Version 1.2*, 1996. `www.tpc.org`.

[14] J. L. Wiener, H. Gupta, W. J. Labio, Y. Zhuge, H. Garcia-Molina, and J. Widom. A system prototype for warehouse view maintenance. In *Proc. of the 1996 ACM Workshop on Materialized Views: Techniques and Applications*, pages 26–33, June 1996.

[15] Y. Zhuge, H. Garcia-Molina, J. Hammer, and J. Widom. View maintenance in a warehousing environment. In *Proc. of the 1995 ACM SIGMOD Intl. Conf. on Management of Data*, pages 316–327, May 1995.

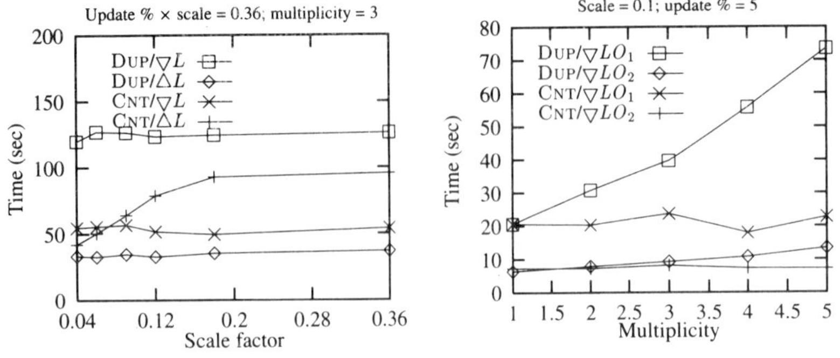
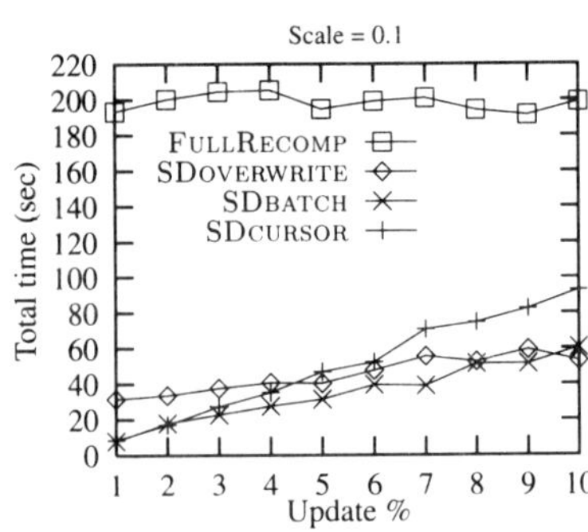

Fig. 7: DUP vs. CNT for delta installation. Fig. 8: DUP vs. CNT for delta computation.

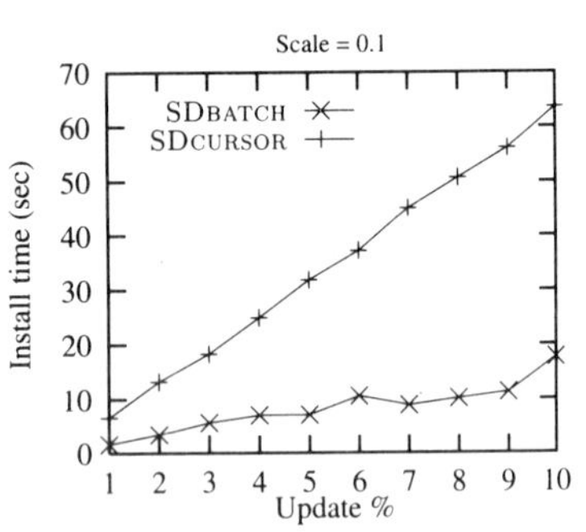
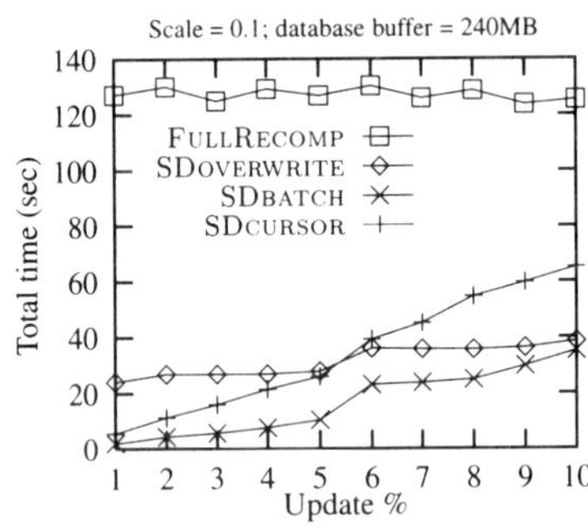
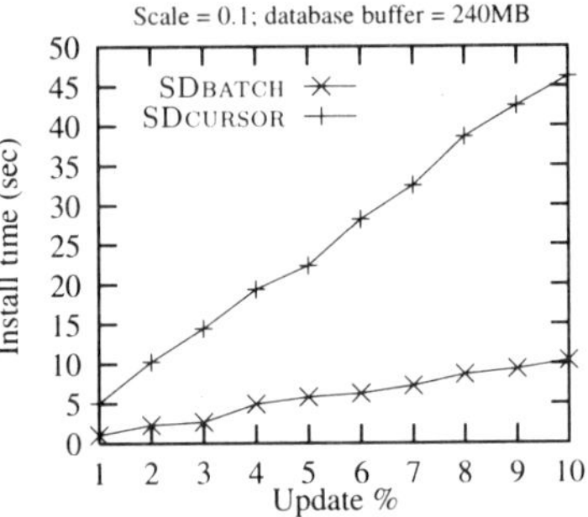

Fig. 9: Maintaining V_{large}.

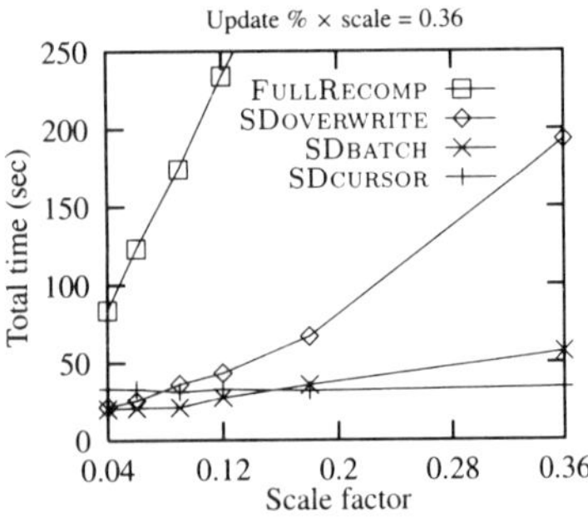
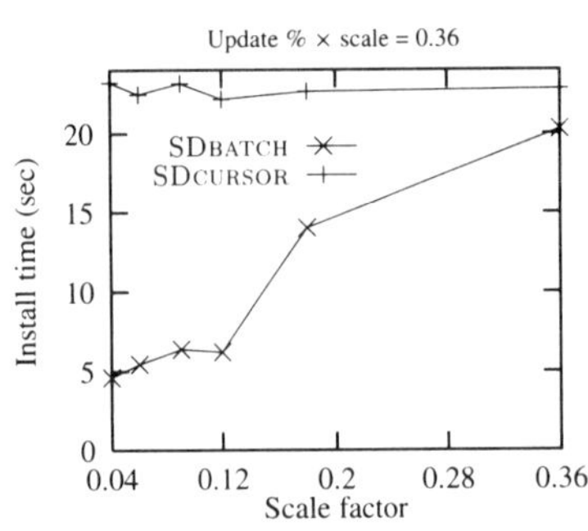
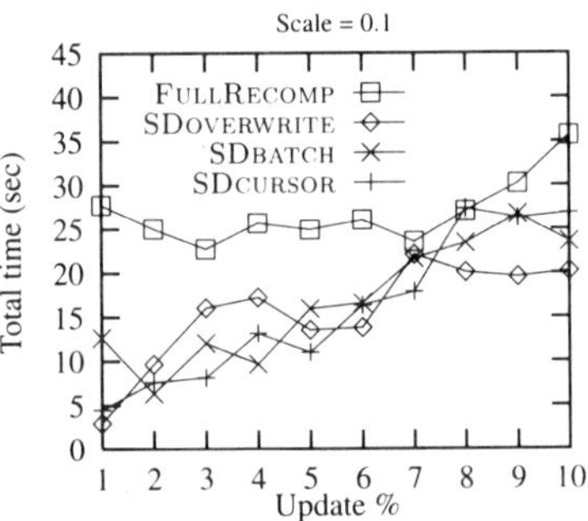

Fig. 10: Installing deltas for V_{large}. Fig. 11: Maintaining V_{large}. Fig. 12: Installing deltas for V_{large}.

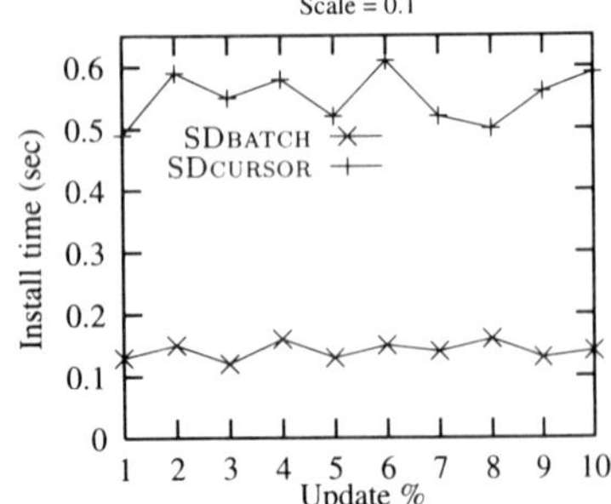
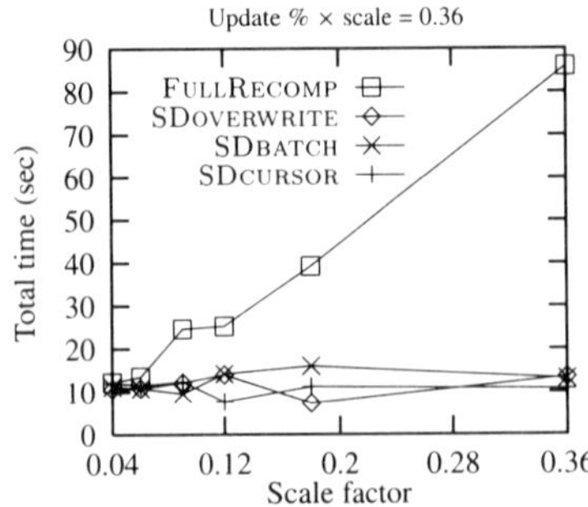
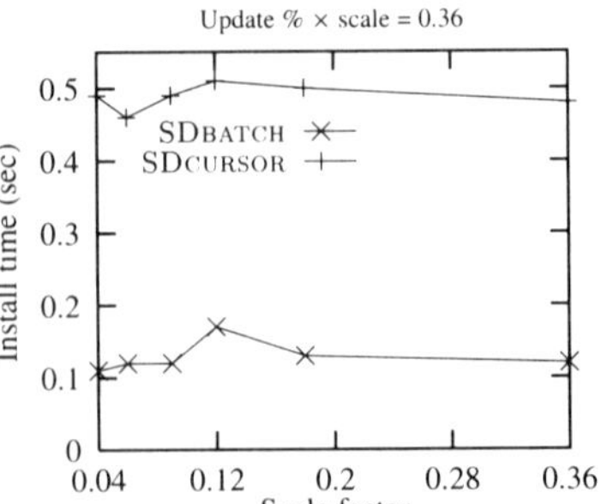

Fig. 13: Maintaining V_{large}. Fig. 14: Installing deltas for V_{large}. Fig. 15: Maintaining V_{small}.

Fig. 16: Installing deltas for V_{small}. Fig. 17: Maintaining V_{small}. Fig. 18: Installing deltas for V_{small}.

472

The Challenge of Process Data Warehousing

Matthias Jarke [1,2]   Thomas List [1]   Jörg Köller [1]

[1] RWTH Aachen, Informatik V (Information Systems), Ahornstr. 55, 52056 Aachen, Germany
{jarke,list,koeller}@informatik.rwth-aachen.de

[2] GMD-FIT, Schloss Birlinghoven, 53754 Sankt Augustin, Germany

Abstract

The management of organizational knowledge is becoming a key requirement in many engineering organizations. In many cases, it is difficult to capture this knowledge directly, as it is hidden in the way-of-working followed by networks of highly qualified specialists. Moreover, much of this knowledge is strongly context-dependent, so rules to be followed must be augmented by adequate situation analysis. Hardware and software tools used to support these processes are strongly heterogeneous, involving significant effort of usage and very different kinds of data.

In this paper, we propose *process data warehouses* as a means to remedy these problems. A process data warehouse, according to our approach, is centered around a knowledge-based metadata repository which records and drives a heterogeneous engineering process, supported by selected materialized instance data. We follow a concept-centered approach expanding ideas from the European DWQ project and illustrate our solution with a prototypical process data warehouse for chemical engineering design developed within the Collaborative Research Centre IMPROVE at Aachen University of Technology.

1. Introduction

Data warehouses have established themselves in the information flow architectures of business organizations for

Proceedings of the 26th International Conference on Very Large Databases, Cairo, Egypt, 2000

two main reasons: firstly, as a *buffer* between operational and transactional tasks on the one hand, and analytical strategic tasks on the other. Secondly, to capture the *history* of business transactions for purposes of archiving, traceability, experience mining and reuse.

In this paper, we claim that the same basic arguments apply to engineering applications. In these applications, the *buffer function* of data warehousing may be even more important. Research results are often obtained by expensive simulations or even more expensive laboratory experiments, such that analytic processing on demand from information sources is only possible with exceptional effort.

Similarly, from the viewpoint of *history management*, many engineering organizations complain that simulations and experiments are repeated unnecessarily, or at least, that too few lessons for analogous cases concerning promising or useless simulation/experimentation are drawn beyond the experiences of individual engineers. Several organizations are therefore embarking on large-scale traceability or process-capture programs [Ros98, Ram98]; other organizations pursue the introduction of large-scale document management systems [GSS99] (e.g. the Documentum product) that make at least a coarse-grained representation of products and processes available electronically.

This trend is particularly strong in the research-intensive and law-suit prone process industries (chemicals, oil, food, pharmaceuticals, biotechnology) where global competition with many mergers is largely decided by timely and cost-effective invention of novel products with high market potential. In these industries, data exchange standards, interoperation standards, web-based information distribution and portals, groupware and workflow are being developed within companies and on a scale of worldwide cooperation and competition. However, few (if any) coherent approaches have emerged.

Process data warehousing is proposed as a solution strategy for some of these issues. We define a process data warehouse (PDW) as a data warehouse which stores histories of engineering processes and products for experience reuse, and provides situated process support. According to our approach, a PDW synchronizes features from document management systems, engineering databases, and traceability tools through active repository technology. To make the idea more precise, we report in this paper about a research effort in which we extend a recent approach to the design of data warehouses (developed in the European DWQ project [JaVa97]) to the case of process data warehousing in the domain of chemical engineering. This research is carried out in the context of the IMPROVE Collaborative Research Center at RWTH Aachen [NaWe99] which investigates IT support for cooperative chemical engineering, and the European CAPE-OPEN initiative in which the chemical industries worldwide are attempting to standardize open interfaces for process simulation software [Bra*99]. We are aware of at least two major German organizations in the chemical and pharmaceutical industry where similar systems are in progress, in part based on earlier research results of ours. It has to be stressed that our experiences are still preliminary and point out more challenges than actual solutions – therefore the title of the paper.

The paper is structured as follows: In section 2, we summarize the DWQ method for concept-driven data warehouse development. In section 3, we point out the major extensions required for process data warehousing in the chemical engineering domain and describe the principle solution strategies followed in the above-mentioned projects. These strategies are illustrated, in section 4, by a demonstration scenario we have implemented in the IMPROVE environment. Lessons learned and a summary of the remaining challenges conclude the paper.

2. The DWQ Approach

A large body of literature addresses the problems introduced by the data warehouse approach, such as the trade-off between freshness of data warehouse data and disturbance of OLTP work during data extraction; the minimization of data transfer through incremental view maintenance; and a theory of computation with multi-dimensional data models. For an overview, see [JLVV99].

The goal of the European DWQ project [JaVa97] was to study a systematic methodology for data warehouse design by developing, prototyping and evaluating comprehensive Foundations for Data Warehouse Quality, delivered through *enriched metadata management facilities* in which specific analysis and optimization techniques are embedded.

The main difference of the DWQ architecture to the standard data warehouse architecture in the literature [CGH+94] is the addition of an explicit *conceptual perspective* according to which the goals of the data warehouse, the quality of the available sources, and the interests of the clients can be characterized. Such a concept-driven architecture is of particular relevance in our proc-

ess engineering context where data representations differ so widely that their interrelationships can only be described at a conceptual level.

The DWQ method consists of the six steps shown in figure 1. In this figure, the dark-grey boxes indicate logical data objects, such as relations, queries, or materialized (possibly multi-dimensional) views. The light-grey boxes describe conceptual models; in DWQ, these are externally represented as extended Entity-Relationship models, internally modelled using Description Logic formalisms from artificial intelligence to allow for subsumption reasoning. The two ovals describe related support at the operational level which we do not discuss further in this paper: aggregate query optimization and view refreshment. The whole process is administered through a metadata repository which has been implemented using the ConceptBase system [JGJ+95].

In the following subsections, we briefly describe the main steps and point to literature where more details about the underlying theory or applications can be found.

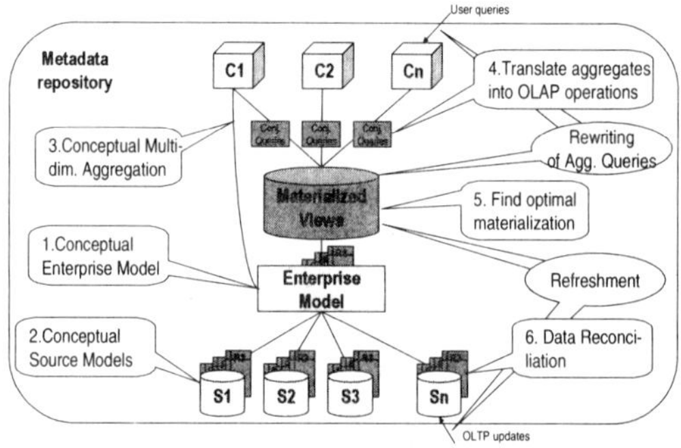

Figure 1: DWQ Data Warehouse Development Process

2.1 Source Integration (Steps 1 and 2)

The DWQ approach to source integration is incremental: Whenever a new portion of a source is taken into account, the new information is integrated with an "Enterprise Model", and the necessary new relationships are added. The main concepts used in DWQ source integration are shown in figure 2 (a corresponding mapping exists on the client side of the data warehouse):

- The *Enterprise Model* is a conceptual representation of the global concepts and relationships that are of interest to the data warehouse application. It provides a consolidated view of the concepts and relationships that are important to the enterprise, and have so far been analysed. Such a view is subject to change as the analysis of the information sources proceeds. The Description Logic formalism we use is general enough to express the usual database models, such as the Entity-

474

Relationship Model, and the Relational Model [CDL+99]. Inference techniques associated with the formalism allow for carrying out several reasoning services on the representation. The formalism is hidden from the user of the DWQ tools who only uses a graphical interface.

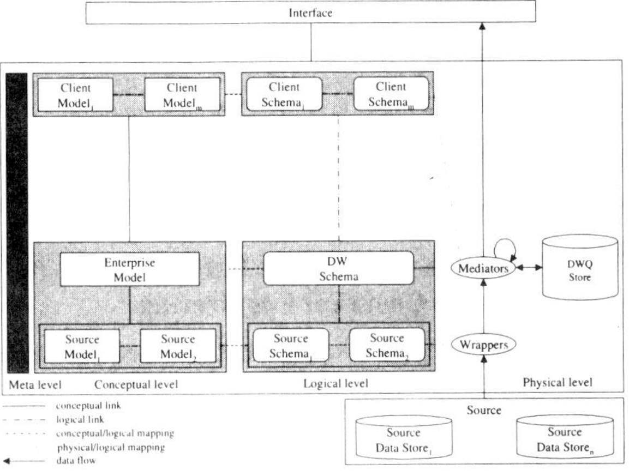

Figure 2: DWQ Architecture for Data Integration

- For a given information source S, the *Source Model* of S is a conceptual representation of the data residing in S. Again, the approach does not require a source to be fully conceptualized. Source Models are expressed by means of the same formalism used for the Enterprise Model.

- Integration does not simply mean producing the Enterprise Model, but rather being able to establish the correct relationships both between the Source Models and the Enterprise Model and between the various Source Models. We formalize the notion of interdependency by means of *intermodel assertions* [CL93]. An intermodel assertion states that one object (i.e., class, entity, or relation) belonging to a certain Model (either the Enterprise or a Source Model) is always a subset of an object belonging to another Model. This simple declarative mechanism has been shown to be extremely effective in establishing relationships among different database schemas (see also [Hul97]). We use a logic-based formalism to express intermodel assertions, and the associated inference techniques provide a means to reason about interdependencies among models.

- The logical content of each source S, called the *Source Schema*, is provided in terms of a set of definitions of relations, each one expressed as a query over the Source Model of S. The logical content of a source represents the structure of data expressed in terms of a logical data model, such as the Relational Model. The logical content of a source S, or of a portion thereof, is

described in terms of a view over the Source Model associated with S (and, therefore, of the Conceptual Data Warehouse Model). Wrappers map physical structures to logical structures.

- The logical content of the materialized views constituting the Data Warehouse, called the *Data Warehouse Schema*, is provided in terms of a set of definitions of relations, each one expressed in terms of a query over the Conceptual Data Warehouse Model. How a view is actually materialized starting from the data in the sources is specified by means of *Mediators*.

The following tasks work on this structure within steps 1 and 2 of figure 1:

- *Enterprise and Source Model construction.* The Source Model corresponding to the new source is produced, if not available. Analogously, the conceptual model of the enterprise is produced, if not available.

- *Source Model integration.* The Source Model is integrated into the Conceptual Data Warehouse Model. This can lead to changes both to the Source Models, and to the Enterprise Model. Moreover, intermodel assertions between the Enterprise Model and the Source Models and between the new source and the existing sources are added to the Conceptual Data Warehouse Model. The designer can specify such intermodel assertions graphically, and can invoke various automated analyses supported by the Description Logic formalization.

- *Source and Data Warehouse Schema specification.* The Source Schema corresponding to the new source (or, corresponding to a new portion of the source) is produced. On the basis of the new analysed source, an analysis is carried out on whether the Data Warehouse Schema should be restructured and/or modified.

In all these tasks, the metadata repository stores the values of the quality factors involved in source and data integration, and helps analyse the quality of the design choices. The Quality Factors of the Conceptual Data Warehouse Model and the various schemas are evaluated and a restructuring of the Models and the schemas is accomplished to match the required criteria.

2.2 Multidimensional Aggregation and OLAP Query Generation

The next two steps consider the client side, symmetric to the source integration; they will therefore be described in less detail.

Step 3 in Figure 2: The conceptual modeling language underlying the enterprise and source models, and the corresponding modeling and reasoning tools, have been extended to the case where concepts are organized into aggregates along multiple dimensions with multi-hierarchy structure [FS99]. Data warehouse designers can thus define multi-dimensional and hierarchical views over the enterprise conceptual model in order to express the interests of certain DW client profiles, without losing the advantages of consistency and completeness checking as well as semantic optimisation provided by the conceptual modeling approach.

Step 4: The thus defined "conceptual data cubes" can either be implemented directly by MOLAP data models, or supported by a ROLAP mapping to relations. Faithful representation of client views requires a careful design of an OLAP relational algebra, together with the corresponding rewritings to underlying star schemas [Vass98].

2.3 Design Optimization and Data Reconciliation

Step 5: Viewed from the logical level, our conceptually controlled approach to source integration has created a schema of relations implementing the enterprise model. This schema could be implemented directly as an operational data store (ODS). In a data warehouse with lots of updates and completely unpredictable queries, this would be the appropriate view materialization.

Conversely, the mapping of multi-dimensional aggregates to ROLAP queries creates a set of view definitions (queries). The materialization of these queries would be the optimal solution (storage space permitting!) in a query-only data warehouse with hardly any updates.

Typical data warehouses have less extreme usage patterns and therefore require a compromise between the two view materialization strategies. The DWQ project has investigated solutions to this combinatorial optimisation problem [ThSe97, LiTS98].

Step 6: The physical-level optimisation is fully integrated with the conceptual modeling approaches because it works on their outcomes. Conversely, the resulting optimal design is now implemented by data integration and reconciliation algorithms, semi-automatically derived from the conceptual specifications. The views to be materialized are initially defined over the ODS relations. There can be several qualitatively different, possibly conflicting ways to actually materialize these ODS relations from the existing sources. These ways are generated by a further set of rewritings that can be derived from the source integration definitions [CDL+99].

The problem of data reconciliation arises when data passes from the application-oriented environment to the Data Warehouse. During the transfer of data, possible inconsistencies and redundancies are resolved, so that the warehouse is able to provide an integrated and reconciled view of data of the organization. In the DWQ methodology, data reconciliation is based on (1) specifying through Interschema Assertions how the relations in the Data Warehouse Schema are linked to the relations in the Source Schemas, and (2) designing suitable mediators for every relation in the Data Warehouse Schema. In step (1), interschema correspondences are used to declaratively specify the correspondences between data in different schemas (either source schemas or data warehouse

schema). Interschema correspondences are defined in terms of relational tables, similarly to the case of the relations describing the sources at the logical level. [CDL+99] distinguish among three types of correspondences, namely Conversion, Matching, and Reconciliation Correspondences. By virtue of such correspondences, the designer can specify different forms of data conflicts holding between the source, and can anticipate methods for solving such conflicts when loading the Data Warehouse. In step (2), the methodology aims at producing, for every relation in the Data Warehouse Schema, a specification of the corresponding mediator, which determines how the tuples of such a relation should be constructed from a suitable set of tuples extracted from the relations stored in the sources.

3. Extensions for Process Data Warehousing: The Case of Chemical Engineering

The DWQ approach assumes a business data warehouse setting with a coherent conceptual model and limited heterogeneity in the data sources and client applications, based on relational or possibly semi-structured data models.

In this section, we discuss the extensions we found necessary to support process data warehousing in the chemical engineering domain. These extensions are mainly twofold. At the conceptual level, the "enterprise model" of the DWQ approach has to be split into a set of loosely connected partial models which look at different facets of the chemical engineering process. Coherence between these partial models is achieved through the so-called process flowsheet, a data structure (and visualization) which turns out to be the central communications medium between the different kinds of specialists cooperating in a design process. This is the key access structure to heterogeneous sources and documents.

At the logical and physical level, heterogeneity of the process engineering tools is far greater than traditionally considered in OLTP data sources. Therefore, an intermediate standardization step is necessary, not only at the level of data but also at the level of services; this is due to the fact that often the data of engineering tools are not sensibly accessible directly but only via the tool services.

3.1 Partial Models in Chemical Process Engineering

Chemical engineering is the combination of physical, chemical, biological, and informational operations on a chemical plant with the aim of transforming input materials in a manner that a material product with desirable properties concerning type, behaviour, and composition results. Besides this main goal, the chemical engineering process is heavily influenced by considerations of cost and time, but also by environmental side effects, such as energy consumption, detrimental side products, water heating or pollution, and the like.

Process engineering encompasses the handling of these processes in all stages from the early design phase to the operation of a plant. The overall development of a chemical process is a complex task that starts with the conceptual design. It does not end with the mapping to physically available equipment for operation and control, but accompanies the whole lifecycle, often over decades.

The decisions made in the different design steps depend on various factors: Chemical properties of the materials involved in the process (reactions, temperature, pressure,...), technical feasibility, environmental and safety issues, cost and time. To assess all these properties, mathematical simulation models are built and calculated in the design phase. These models may differ widely in complexity and the kind of data they produce or need. Hence, the tools involved in the design process are highly heterogeneous. This includes flowsheeting tools for conceptual design, process simulators for predicting the reactions and behaviour of the chemical components in a process or numerical solvers for the large non-linear problems typically occurring in this context.

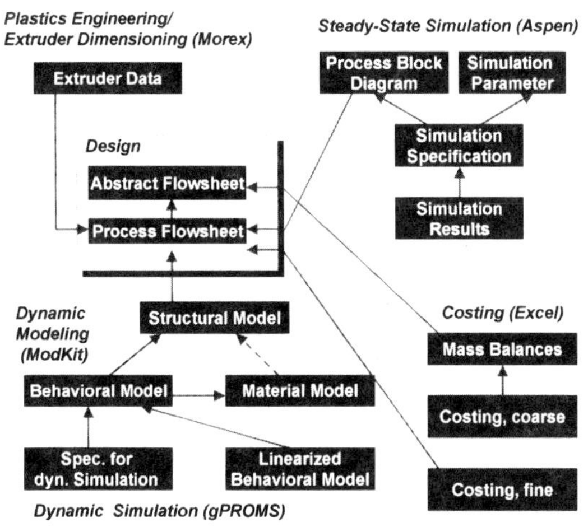

Figure 3: Partial Models and Tools

At the conceptual level considered in the DWQ approach, this heterogeneity implies that a coherent "enterprise model" cannot easily be built. Instead, a multitude of partial information models is being considered with poorly understood interconnections. In IMPROVE, such information models are being systematically developed for the important process engineering perspectives [BaSM99]. However, empirical studies of process engineering work demonstrate that one family of closely related sub-models, visualized through flowsheets of the chemical process, has a clearly dominating role in the communication between different designers. Our modeling strategy, described in more detail in [JLW99], has

therefore been to use a conceptual model of flowsheeting as the kernel of a metadata model to which all other information models are related. To illustrate the central role of the flowsheet, figure 3 shows the partial models (and related tools) considered in the IMPROVE demonstrator.

In the simplest case, a flowsheet looks like a kind of data flow diagram with a lot of fancy graphical types for different kinds of devices (corresponding to processes) and connections (corresponding to dataflows). However, this simple analogy is complicated by at least three factors. These factors are illustrated in figure 4 that instantiates some aspects of figure 3.

Firstly, flowsheets may describe very complex processes and evolve in complex refinement structures, including operations such as enrichment of object definitions, decomposition of functions, specialization of choices, and realization of functions by (combinations of) device types. This can be seen in the middle of figure 4.

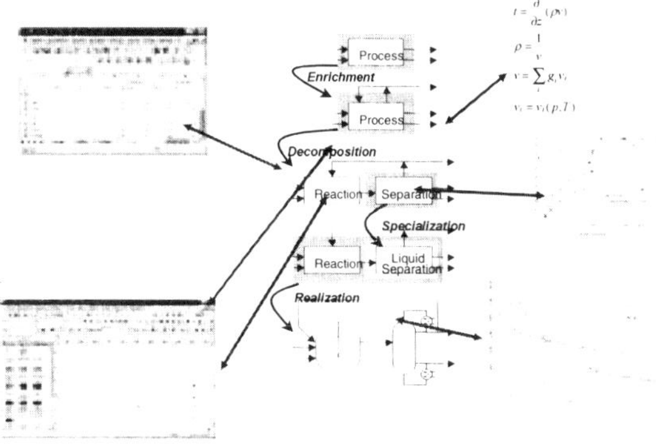

Figure 4: Flowsheet Hierarchy connected to Heterogeneous Data

Second, process synthesis decisions are made under uncertainty about their impact. A complete analysis of all design choices is impractical due to the high effort in setting up simulations or laboratory experiments. However, decisions under uncertainty may mean backtracks in the engineering process, especially if not accompanied by deep experience or available theory. The heterogeneity of representations required is illustrated in the figures surrounding the conceptual model hierarchy in figure 4.

Last not least, there is a huge and continuously growing number of different devices, connections, and specialized functions that can be used in chemical engineering; estimates speak about roughly 50.000 types to be considered. The information models of a meta database for process data warehousing must therefore be easily extensible by new product and process knowledge, and cannot be mapped one-to-one in tool functionality. Indeed, even the storage, search and consistency analysis of such large schemata becomes a problem [BaJa99, Satt98].

Summarizing, the requirements of the process engineering domain strongly support the case of a concept-driven approach as proposed in DWQ. They also require further refinements of metadata handling concerning information model integration, structural and behavioural refinement, the interplay of design and analysis, and the extensibility with a growing body of knowledge. In section 4, these issues are demonstrated through an "extended situation analysis" function where only basic structural knowledge is hard-coded in design tools such as a flowsheet editor. Detailed domain knowledge is available in declarative form in the metadata repository of the process data warehouse. The situation knowledge required for context-adequate application of the domain knowledge is collected from either the PDW itself or by callback queries to other engineering tools.

3.2 Dealing with Heterogeneity at the Technical Level

The diversity of information models at the conceptual level is exacerbated by diversity of data formats and service accessibility at the technical level of chemical engineering tools and materials databases. Current process engineering environments often hide this problem through monolithic software architectures with fixed means of access. These make it close to impossible to include company-specific knowledge or home-grown specialist tools.

The European process industries have therefore embarked on the CAPE-OPEN initiative [BJM+99, GCO00] in order to accomplish a standardization of simulation interfaces, such that a component-based approach can be followed. This standard has been defined at the conceptual level through UML models – semi-formal source models in the sense of the DWQ approach. At the implementation level, the standard is defined in both DCOM [MS00] and CORBA [Vin97,OMG]. In IMPROVE, we are using the CORBA version. Both the conceptual aspect and the tool service integration are illustrated below, focussing on the aspect of heterogeneous process simulation as an example.

Process simulators are complex software systems designed for creating mathematical models of manufacturing facilities for processing and/or transforming materials. Simulation allows the chemical engineer to interactively predict the behaviour of an existing or proposed chemical process. It enables the assessment of process alternatives with respect to economic, safety, and environmental performance without actually building a plant, thereby reducing cost and speeding up the design phase of the plant. Process simulators follow different internal architectures, e.g. block modular systems, equation based systems and simultaneous modular systems. Surveys of current approaches for process modeling and simulation can be found in [PB94, Maq95, JM96].

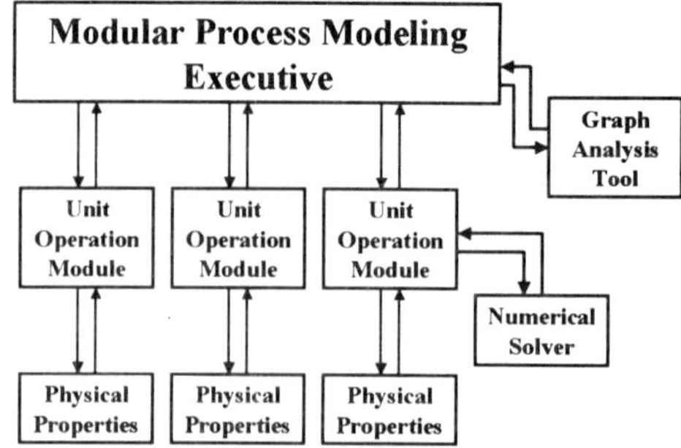

Figure 5: CAPE-OPEN Standard Components

As illustrated in figure 5, CAPE-OPEN has identified the following standard components of a process simulator from a conceptual point of view [CO98]:

- **Unit Operation Modules,** often just termed units, represent the behavior of physical process steps (e.g. a mixer or a reactor). They are linked to the simulation flowsheet which represents an abstraction of the plant structure. They compute the quality of a material stream of their outlet ports if the according information is given at the inlet ports. The simulation models are assembled from predefined libraries of unit operation modules into a flowsheet which represents the overall plant.

- **Physical Properties (Thermodynamics) Packages:** An important functionality of a process simulator is its ability to calculate thermodynamic and physical properties of materials (e.g. density or boiling point). Thermodynamic packages are complex and highly optimized pieces of software. Typically, they consist of a database containing a lot of simple properties for a set of chemical species. Based on these such packages offer FORTRAN or C programs to calculate more complex properties using the properties in the database.

- **Numerical Solvers:** The mathematical process models of a unit operation or a complete plant are large and highly non-linear. An analytical solution is impossible. Therefore iterative, numerical approaches are used to either solve the equations of a single unit operation module or to solve the overall flowsheet.

- **Simulator Executive:** This is the simulator's core which controls the set-up and execution of the simulation, i.e. analyzing the flowsheet and calculate the units. Furthermore, it is responsible for a consistent flowsheet set-up and error checking.

Figure 6 shows the set-up of a prototypical CORBA-based CAPE-OPEN compliant simulator we built jointly with Aachen's process engineering group. The distributed objects communicate via the CORBA object bus using the CAPE-OPEN standard interfaces.

478

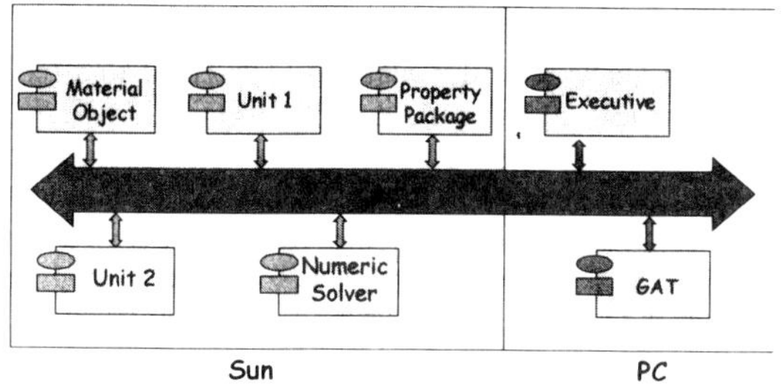

Figure 6: CAPE-OPEN CORBA Prototype Set-Up

Two different units are linked by a flowsheet in the executive component. To solve the flowsheet, i.e. run the simulation, the executive calls the graph analyzer (GAT) component to determine the order of unit calculations to be done. Then all unit simulation models are called in the order calculated by the GAT. To enable the units to calculate themselves, the executive has to configure them and to provide input values. It sends CORBA references for property packages and numerical solvers to the units which it has obtained from a component repository provided by the CORBA system. Now the units are ready to perform thermodynamic calculations (using the properties package) and solve their internal mathematical models.

Before a unit actually can be calculated it has to know what chemical components are at its input ports. This information is also provided by the Executive by creating a Material Object and handing over its reference to the unit. The Material Object is the central mechanism of exchanging complex data between the different CAPE-OPEN components and encapsulates all kind of chemical properties data. It is also used for data exchange to a property package. After the unit calculation is finished the unit creates new material objects carrying information about the materials at the units output ports. Then this material object is handed over by the executive as input data for the next unit in the flowsheet.

The example implies that the use of CAPE-OPEN components in a process data warehouse requires explicit representations of the material object, the units, and the property packages. In section 4, we show how these components can be conceptually embedded in our approach.

3.3 A Metadata-Driven Architecture

As an additional complication over the basic DWQ approach, chemical engineering tools often cover aspects from more than one partial model within the enterprise model. The mapping between logical and conceptual representations becomes considerably more complex. It is not even clear whether we have a data-to-data mapping at all, or whether it is more appropriate to think of engineering tools as document-producing and document-consuming objects, such that process data warehousing becomes an issue of content extraction from document histories rather than a data model mapping with incremental updates.

Indeed, traceability reference models drawn from studies in large software organizations – a vaguely similar domain – indicate that, when capturing an engineering process, we must model three main aspects [RJ00]: how the engineering product evolves through decisions made on content objects, in what media and with which persistence and legal value this is documented, and what is the contribution structure of stakeholders and analysts who made the content-oriented and administrative decisions. The resulting highest-level meta model of a process data warehouse is shown in figure 7.

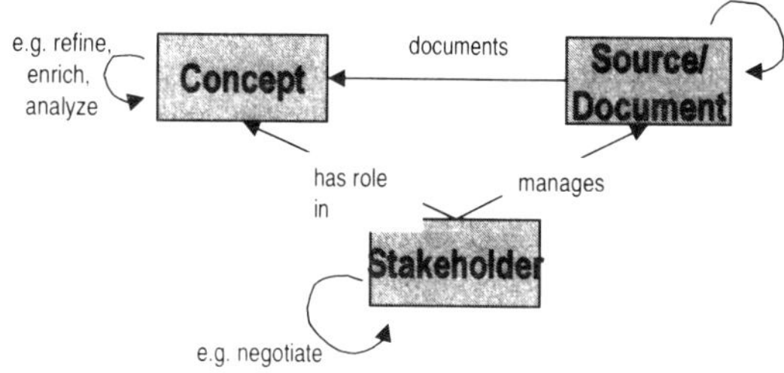

Figure 7: Meta Meta Model of Process Data Warehouse

Our implementation strategy foresees to integrate commercial tools available for data management (e.g. an object relational database or specialized engineering databases such as Comos Pt [Inn00]), document management (e.g. Lotus Notes, Documentum), and trace/dependency management (e.g. DOORS, SLATE) with the wrapped and mediated tool data via a knowledge-based metadata repository. The implementation of this full architecture is still in progress. In the prototype illustrated in the next section, only a product database and a couple of chemical engineering tools have been interfaced with the metadata repository, while others have been emulated by putting example instances in the metadata repository itself.

4. Application example

In this section, we present an example that shows how the standard interfaces from CAPE-OPEN supplement the process data warehouse in the chemical engineering domain. Our prototype combines techniques for integrating the highly heterogeneous information sources in the application domain with the standard interfaces for unit operations and physical properties packages. The process data warehouse client that operates on the prototype (called "cross-tool situation analysis") uses the domain knowledge captured in the meta database to give guidance to the chemical engineer via a process-integrated flowsheet tool [JLW99], by analysing the current development situation via the product state of several source database or tools.

4.1 Scenario

In the early conceptual design stage a chemical engineer draws a flowsheet of the plant. The blocks in the flowsheet (called devices) represent functions, such as mixing, reaction or separation. These devices are then further decomposed and realized in concrete apparatuses.

Figure 9: Conceptual Flowsheet of the example

As a (very simple) example, we consider the flowsheet in figure 9. Two of the three devices (mixer and CSTR - continuous stirred tube reactor) are already given through unit operations that realize specific functions (mixing and reaction). The developer's task is to find a suitable realization for the third device (Separation). This realization can range from a single device to a complex combination of different devices, with or without backflow into earlier devices. The detailed setting is: Two input streams feed an initial mixer. The substances A and B are fed through the streams into a mixing device. The mixture is then fed into a reactor of type CSTR. The result is the product C and the (unwanted) by-product D. These substances now have to be separated. Assume that the mixing device is completely specified. The unit to simulate the reactor is known (including the equations for the reaction). Now the task of the chemical engineer is to find a useful realization for the separation unit.

The extended situation analysis function of the process data warehouse is able to provide some hints of which unit operations should be considered for this task if some of the properties of the reactor's output stream (containing C and D) are known: temperature and pressure of the mixture in the stream, the fraction of each substance in the stream and its boiling temperatures.

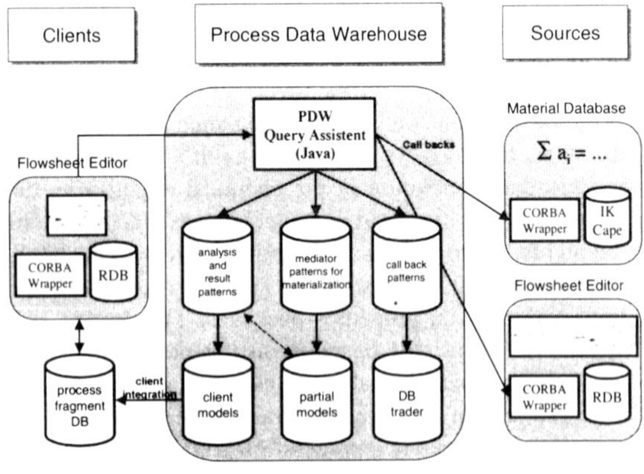

Figure 10: Architecture of the Process Data Warehouse

Figure 10 describes the functionality of the cross-tool situation analyser of the warehouse. A client tool (here: the flowsheet editor) calls the PDW Query Assistant, a Java-based control program. The call contains an identifier for the selected flowsheet element (the separation device) and an operation to be executed on the device (realize). The warehouse itself contains several sub-meta databases that are queried during the processing of the call:

- **Call back patterns** are used to determine which additional information is needed to answer the request.
- The **DB trader** contains information from which tool or database and how this information can be accessed. The calling client will be one of the tools that are accessed. In the example, a larger part of the flowsheet is needed to classify the context of the call.
- The **mediator patterns for materialization** are then used to materialise the additional data into the data warehouse such that they become instances of the **partial models** of the data warehouse. See section 4.3 for details of these integration steps.
- The **analysis and result patterns** are now applied to calculate useful results for the original query.
- The presentation of the results is highly dependent on the client tool that initiated the query. The **client model** is used to transform the result in a suitable form. The special process integrated features of the flowsheet tool can be used to directly insert a proper refinement of the separation into the flowsheet. Details on the flowsheet tool and its interaction with the process data warehouse can be found in [JLW99].

These databases are not accessed sequentially but in a nested way so that only these information sources are accessed that are needed to answer the specific query.

The call back queries used in these steps are not purely queries to source databases. For example, the needed simulation results of the reactor are results of an aggregation function. In this sense the results are the results of a (highly complex) query on the data warehouse store. As simulating is a time consuming and expensive task we also store the results in the data warehouse for reuse. To gain access to the units the DB trader contains meta information about the CAPE-OPEN components. As a result of the usage of the CAPE-OPEN compliant units we do not need to handle very different simulators such as Aspen-Plus, Pro/II or gProms but we have to create the CAPE-OPEN objects used by units. This is especially the material object for each substance contained in the input ports of the unit. The process data warehouse produces these CORBA objects and is then able to start the simulation of the unit.

4.2 Applying the DWQ approach

For the example application the partial models *plant* (for the flowsheet) and *material concept* (for the material properties) are of interest (Fig. 11 & 12, we omit most of the attributes and the specializations of `ProcessStep`). The results of the simulation of the reactor have the form of material objects and thus refer to the material concept partial model. More complex simulations than those of a single unit would be represented in an own partial model for simulation results. The two partial models are connected via the *abtract plant model* that states that `Stream` is an aspect of an `abstract_stream` and therefore can contain a `material_concept`. The EER-models form a part of the conceptual enterprise model in figure 2.

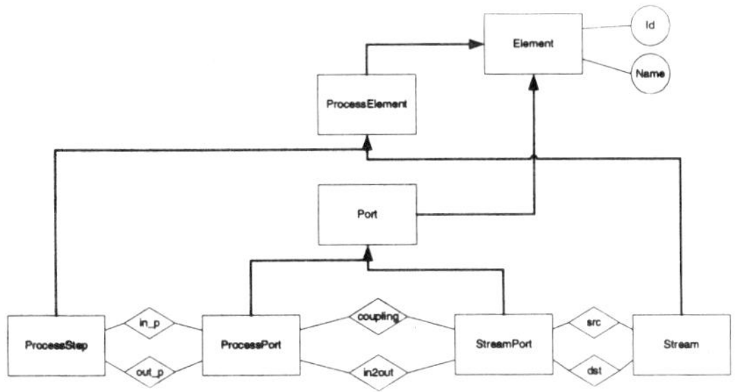

Figure 11: The Plant Partial Model

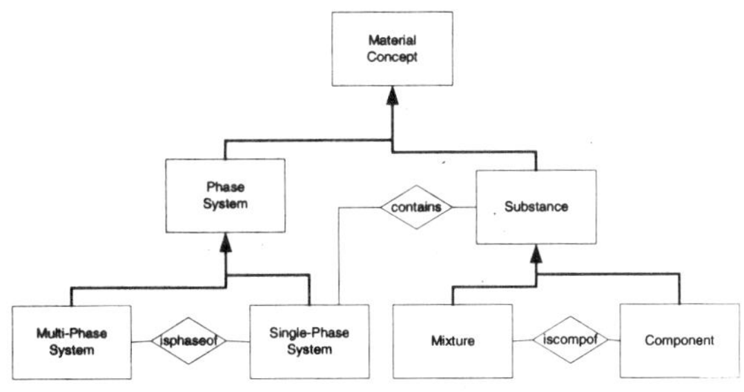

Figure 12: The Material Concept Partial Model

4.3 Source Integration

The first step in integrating data sources (such as the flowsheet editor) into the data warehouse is to reverse engineer the conceptual model from the data source. As the flowsheet editor is not a relational database but a technical tool, we built a CORBA-wrapper to access its data. This wrapper simplifies the internal data structure used by the tool by suppressing some constructs only needed for implementation purposes. The CORBA IDL now reflects some relational structure that can be reverse engineered to the EER diagram in figure 13. This diagram shows that the data in the flowsheet editor covers (parts of) both partial models from figure 11 and figure 12.

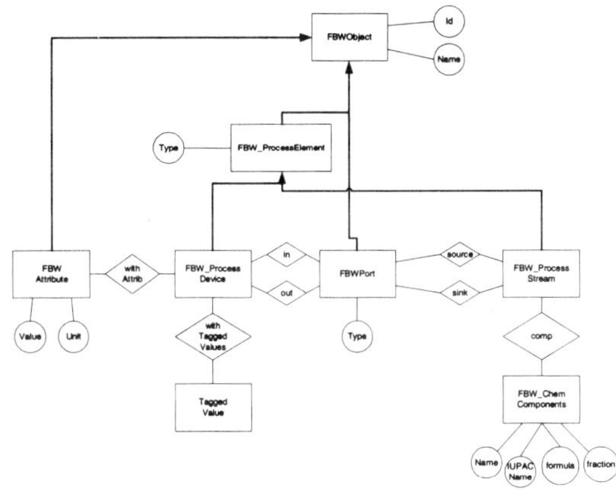

Figure 13: Conceptual Model of the Flowsheet Editor

In addition the flowsheet structure is different. There are no stream ports – these are important if a tool regards streams as decomposable objects, which the flowsheet editor doesn't. The flowsheet editor simply uses tagged values instead of a specialization hierarchy to specify the type of flowsheet devices (*FBW_ ProcessDevice*). The domain knowledge coded into the flowsheet editor was intentionally kept low because of the volatility of domain knowledge. The conceptual model is now transformed into a description logic formalism [CDL+98] and enriched through the definition of intramodel assertions that define some constraints not captured by the EER diagram.

The other information source – the physical properties package of the CAPE-OPEN standard – is seen as a collection of *material objects*. The EER model of that source consists of exactly one entity and a set of attributes. This data source in special in the way that it calculates some of its data on demand. This fact is hidden by the wrapper!

We specify the relations of the data sources in terms of adorned Datalog-like queries [CDL+99]. This step is needed because the mapping from the EER model to the relational model is ambiguous. Figure 14 shows an extract from the mapping of the flowsheet editor. The query for `FBWStream_R` is an example where several relationships and entities are mapped onto a single relational table.

```
FBWObject_R(I,N) <-
    FBWObject(X),Id(X,I),Name(X,N) |
        identify([I],X), I::ObjIDs,N::ObjNames

FBWPort_R(I,T) <-
    FBW_Port(X),Id(X,I),PortType(X,T) |
    identify([I],X), I::ObjIDs, T::PortTypes

FBWProcessElement_R(I,T) <-
    FBW_ProcessElement(X),Id(X,I),
    ElementType(X,T) |
    identify([I],X), I::ObjIDs,
    T::ProcessElementTypes
```

```
FBWDevice_R(I) <-
FBW_ProcessDevice(X),Id(X,I) |
identify([I],X), I::ObjIDs

FBWStream_R(I,SOURCE_PORT,SINK_PORT,
   SOURCE_DEV,SINK_DEV) <-
   Source(S,P1),Sink(S,P2),Out(D1,P1),
   In(D2,P2),Id(S,I),Id(P1,SOURCE_PORT),
   Id(P2,SINK_PORT),Id(D1,SOURCE_DEV),
   Id(D2,SINK_DEV)
      OR
   Stream(S),
   NOT Source(S,P),Sink(S,P2),In(D2,P2),
   Id(S,I),SOURCE_PORT=NULL,Id(P2,SINK_PORT),
   SOURCE_DEV=NULL,Id(D2,SINK_DEV)
      OR
   Stream(S), Source(S,P1),NOT Sink(S,P),
   Out(D1,P1),Id(S,I),Id(P1,SOURCE_PORT),
   SINK_PORT=NULL,Id(D1,SOURCE_DEV),
   SINK_DEV=NULL
      OR
   FBW_Port(P),FBW_Port(PP),NOT Source(S,P),
   NOT Sink(S,PP),Id(S,I),SOURCE_PORT=NULL,
   SINK_PORT=NULL,SOURCE_DEV=NULL,
   SINK_DEV=NULL |
   identify([I],S), I::ObjIDs,
   identify([SOURCE_PORT],P1),
      SOURCE_PORT::ObjIDs,
   identify([SINK_PORT],P2),
      SINK_PORT::ObjIDs,
   identify([SOURCE_DEV],D1),
      SOURCE_DEV::ObjIDs,
   identify([SINK_DEV],D2),
      SINK_DEV::ObjIDs
```

Figure 14: The logical Flowsheet Editor Model

The same formalism is used to specify the relations of the data warehouse in terms of the conceptual data warehouse model. The difference between these two steps is that on the source level it is a reverse engineering task, on the data warehouse level the relations are designed from the conceptual model.

The mapping of the source model onto the data warehouse model have to be given as intermodel assertions on the conceptual part and as interschema correspondences on the logical part. The intermodel assertions are constructs similar to the intramodel assertions of the conceptual source model [CDL+98]. The interschema correspondences build the basis for the generation of the mediators that actually load the data into the data warehouse. The correspondences in figure 15 demonstrate how the "missing" stream port of the flowsheet model can be specified.

```
convert_1([I,SRC_P],[PID,T]) <-
   FBW_ProcessStream(X),Id(X,I),Source(X,P),
   Id(P,SRC_P),StreamPort(P2),Id(P2,PID),
   T == 'Source'
   THROUGH new_src(I,PID)

convert_2([I,SNK_P],[PID,T]) <-
   FBW_ProcessStream(X),Id(X,I),Sink(X,P),
   Id(P,SNK_P),StreamPort(P2),Id(P2,PID),
   T == 'Sink'
   THROUGH new_sink(I,PID)
```

Figure 15: Interschema Correspondences

The small programs `new_sink` and `new_src` are used to create new identifiers for the relations in the data warehouse. They are supplemented by a code fragment that converts identifiers used in the source databases into data warehouse identifiers and makes use of a global hash table for the mapping. Similar rules specify how the device type coded as tagged value in the flowsheet editor is transferred into an instance of a subclass of `ProcessStep` (figure 11). These interschema correspondences look like this:

```
convert_reactor([I],[PID]) <-
   FBW_ProcessDevice(X),Id(X,I),with_tag(X,T),
   Reactor(R),Id(R,PID), Tag(T,'Type'),
   Value(X,'Reactor')
   THROUGH convert_device([I],[PID])
```

This correspondence is accompanied by an intermodel assertion that states that process devices of the flowsheet editor can be transformed into a reactor.

Mediators that load the data instances into the data warehouse can now be generated using the data reconciliation too [CDL+99]. So the mediators are constructed from small, partly reusable software constructs, combined with declarative specification of the tools and its models.

5. Conclusions

The move from business data warehouses to process data warehouses mirrors the historical development of operational databases in the 70s and 80s. Early databases, evolving around the relational model, focused on business applications. A few years later object-oriented databases came up mostly as a proposal to handle engineering data. Nowadays, semi-structured data models á la XML provide a complementary source of technologies which, also in our context, is becoming important for document analysis and distributed information delivery. We hope to profit from work such as [GSN99] on the generation of XML wrappers for a wide range of media which may appear as interfaces to process engineering tools.

Summarizing the experiences so far, the concept-centred approach to data warehouse design proposed in projects such as Information Manifold and DWQ appears even more important in the process engineering context. This is due to the greater syntactic variations of engineering tools which can only be bridged by semantic modeling approaches with strong formal support. This conceptual modeling approach also enabled us to make operational an extensible body of method knowledge. In the past such growing knowledge either had to remain in the heads of engineers, or led to an growing complexity and unmaintainable engineering tools. Domain standards such as CAPE-OPEN emerge as an indispensible prerequisite for our approach which assumes open tool interaction, with much of the changing body of knowledge captured in the process data warehouse and its metadata repository.

As discussed earlier, the network of tools we have linked to our PDW prototype is still limited in comparison to the richness of chemical engineering reality. Moreover, the number of experimental uses is far too small to see whether case-based method reuse (quite successful in the mechanical service domain) has a real future here. However, it is encouraging to see that one of the largest chemical engineering departments worldwide is indeed setting up a major PDW according to a simplified version of our approach, albeit only for the product perspective. In order to include the process aspect, and to broaden the scope of PDW usability beyond the initial engineering process, a key research challenge will be to understand the interplay between a document-oriented management view of process engineering and plant administration, and the concept-oriented database-like approach pursued in this work.

Acknowledgments. This work was supported in part by the European Commission under BRITE-EURAM project Global CAPE-OPEN, and by DFG under Collaborative Research Center IMPROVE (SFB 476). Thanks are due to the partners in these projects, especially Maurizio Lenzerini, Panos Vassiliadis, Klaus Weidenhaupt, Manfred Nagl, Bertrand Braunschweig, Wolfgang Marquardt, Birgit Bayer and Christoph Quix.

6. References

[BaJa99] M. Baumeister, M. Jarke: Compaction of large class hierarchies in databases for chemical engineering. *Proc. BTW 99 (Freiburg, Germany).* Springer 1999, 343-361.

[BaSM99] B. Bayer, R. Schneider, W. Marquardt: Product Data Modeling for Chemical Process Design. In *Proc. European Concurrent Engineering Conference*, Erlangen, Germany, April 1999.

[BJM+99] B. Braunschweig, M. Jarke, J. Köller, W. Marquardt, L .v. Wedel: CAPE-OPEN - experiences from a standardization effort in chemical industries. *Proc. Intl. Conf. Standardization and Innovation in Information Technology (SIIT99)*, Aachen 1999.

[Bra*99] B. Braunschweig , M. Jarke, A. Becks, J. Köller, C. Tresp: Designing Standards for Open Simulation Environments in the Chemical Industries: A Computer-Supported Use-Case Approach. *Proc. of the 9th Annual Int. Symposium of the Int. Council on Systems Engineering*, Brighton, England, June, 1999.

[CDL+98] D. Calvanese, G. De Giacomo, M. Lenzerini, D. Nardi, R. Rosati: Description Logic Framework for Information Integration, *In Proc. 6th Intl. Conf. on Principles of Knowledge Representation and Reasoning (KR'98)*, Trento, Italy, 1998, pp. 2-13.

[CDL+99] D. Calvanese, G. De Giacomo, M. Lenzerini, D. Nardi, R. Rosati: A principled approach to data integration and reconciliation in data warehousing. *Proc. Int. Workshop on Design and Management of Data Warehouses (DMDW'99)*. Heidelberg, Germany, 1999.

[CGH+94] S. Chawathe, H. Garcia-Molina, J. Hammer, K. Ireland, Y. Papakonstantinou, J. Ullman, J. Widom: The TSIMMIS project: Integration of heterogenous information sources. In *Proc. IPSJ Conference*. Tokyo, Japan, 1994, pp. 7-18.

[CL93] T. Catarci, M. Lenzerini: Representing and using interschema knowledge in cooperative information systems. *Intelligent and Cooperative Information Systems*, **2**(4), 375–398, 1993.

[CO98] CAPE-OPEN, Conceptual Design Document 2. *http://www.global-cape-open.org/ CAPE-OPEN_standard.html*, 1998.

[FS99] E. Franconi, U. Sattler: A data warehouse conceptual data model for multidimensional aggregation. In *Proc. Int. Workshop Design and Management of Data Warehouses (DMDW'99)*, Heidelberg, Germany, 1999.

[GCO00] Global CAPE-OPEN Web Site http://www.global-cape-open.org, 2000.

[GSN99] G. Gardarin, F. Sha, T.D. Ngoc: XML-based componetnes for federating multiple heterogeneous data sources. Proc. Conceptual Modeling – ER 99, Paris 1999, 506-519

[GSS99] J. Gulbins, M. Seyfried, H. Strack-Zimmermann: Dokumenten-Management. Springer-Verlag, 2nd edn. 1999

[Hul97] R. Hull: Managing semantic heterogeneity in databases: A theoretical perspective. *Proc. 16th ACM Symp. Principles of Database Systems (PODS)*, Tucson, AZ, pp. 51–61, 1997.

[Inn00] Comos Pt product description. http://www.innotec.de, 2000.

[JaVa97] M. Jarke, M. Vassiliou: Foundations of data warehouse quality: An overview of the DWQ project. *Proc. 2nd International Conference on Information Quality*, Cambridge, MA, 299–313, 1997.

[JGJ+95] M. Jarke, R. Gallersdörfer, M. Jeusfeld, M. Staudt, S. Eherer: ConceptBase – a deductive object base for meta data management. *Intelligent Information Systems*, **4**(2), 167–192, 1995.

[JLVV99] M. Jarke, M. Lenzerini, Y. Vassiliou, P. Vassiliadis: *Fundamentals of Data Warehouses.* Springer 1999.

[JLW99] M. Jarke, T. List, K. Weidenhaupt: A Process-Integrated Conceptual Design Environment for Chemical Engineering. In *Proc. 18th Int. Conference on Conceptual Modeling (ER 99)*, Paris, France; 1999, 520-537.

[JM96] Jarke, M., Marquardt, W. Design and evaluation of computer-aided process modeling tools. *International Conference on Intelligent Systems in Process Engineering* (Snowmass, Co, July 1995), AIChE Symposium Series, vol. 92, 1996, 97-109.

[LiTS98] S. Ligoudistianos, D. Theodoratos, T. Sellis: Experimental Evaluation of Data Warehouse Configuration Algorithms. In *Proc. 9th DEXA Workshop (DEXA'98)*. Vienna, Austria, August 1998.

[Maq95] Marquardt, W. Trends in Computer-Aided Process *Modeling. Computers and Chemical Engineering*, 1995.

[MS00] Microsoft DCOM Web Site http://www.microsoft.com/com/tech/DCOM.asp , 2000

[NaWe99] M. Nagl, B. Westfechtel (Hrsg.): Integration von Entwicklungssystemen in Ingenieuranwendungen. Springer 1999.

[OMG] OMG CORBA Web Page http://www.omg.org/corba

[PB94] Pantelides, C.C; Britt, H.I.: Multipurpose process modelling environments. In: *Proc. Conf. on FOCAPD '94.* CACHE Publications, 1994.

[Ram98] B. Ramesh: Factors influencing requirements traceability practice. *Comm. ACM* 41, (12) 1998, 37-44.

[RJ00] Ramesh, B., Jarke, M.: Towards reference models of requirements traceability. *IEEE Transactions on Software Engineering*, July 2000, vol. 26, no. 7.

[Ros98] T. Rose: Visual Assessment of Engineering Processes in Virtual Enterprises. *Comm. ACM* 41, (12) 1998, 45-52.

[Satt98] U. Sattler: Terminological Knowledge Representation Systems in a Process Engineering Application. *Dissertation*, RWTH Aachen, 1998.

[ThSe97] D. Theodoratos, T. Sellis: Data warehouse configuration. In *Proceedings of the 23rd International Conference on Very Large Databases (VLDB)*, 126–135, Athens, Greece, August 1997.

[Vass98] P. Vassiliadis: Modeling multidimensional databases, cubes and cube operations. In *Pro.s 10th Intl Conf. Scientific and Statistical Database Management (SSDBM)*, 53–62, Capri, Italy, 1998.

[Vin97] S. Vinoski: CORBA: Integrating Diverse Applications Within Distributed Heterogeneous Environments. *IEEE Communications Magazine*, 35, 2., Feb 1997.

A Scalable Algorithm for Answering Queries Using Views[*]

Rachel Pottinger
University of Washington
rap@cs.washington.edu

Alon Levy
University of Washington
alon@cs.washington.edu

Abstract

The problem of answering queries using views is to find efficient methods of answering a query using a set of previously materialized views over the database, rather than accessing the database relations. The problem has received significant attention because of its relevance to a wide variety of data management problems, such as data integration, query optimization, and the maintenance of physical data independence. To date, the performance of proposed algorithms has received very little attention, and in particular, their scale up in the presence of a large number of views is unknown.

We first analyze two previous algorithms, the bucket algorithm and the inverse-rules algorithm, and show their deficiencies. We then describe the MiniCon algorithm, a novel algorithm for finding the maximally-contained rewriting of a conjunctive query using a set of conjunctive views. We present the first experimental study of algorithms for answering queries using views. The study shows that the MiniCon algorithm scales up well and significantly outperforms the previous algorithms. Finally, we describe an extension of the MiniCon algorithm to handle comparison predicates, and show its performance experimentally.

[*]Thanks to Daniela Florescu, Marc Friedman, Zack Ives, Ioana Manolescu, Dan Weld, and Steve Wolfman for their comments on earlier drafts of this paper. This research was funded by a Sloan Fellowship, NSF Grant #IIS-9978567, a NSF Graduate Research Fellowship, and a Lucent Technologies GRPW Grant

1 Introduction

The problem of answering queries using views (a.k.a. rewriting queries using views) has recently received significant attention because of its relevance to a wide variety of data management problems [20]: query optimization [6, 21, 36], maintenance of physical data independence [35, 33, 27], data integration [22, 9, 18, 19], and data warehouse and web-site design [16, 32]. Informally speaking, the problem is the following. Suppose we are given a query Q over a database schema, and a set of view definitions $V_1, \ldots, V_n$ over the same schema. Is it possible to answer the query Q using *only* the answers to the views $V_1, \ldots, V_n$, and if so, how?

There are two main contexts in which the problem of answering queries using views has been considered. In the first context, where the goal is query optimization or maintenance of physical data independence [35, 33, 6], we search for an expression that uses the views and is *equivalent* to the original query. Here it is usually assumed that the number of views is on the same order as the size of the schema. The second context is that of data integration, where views describe a set of autonomous heterogenous data sources. A user poses a query in terms of a mediated schema, and the data integration system needs to reformulate the query to refer to the data sources. In a subsequent phase, the queries over the sources are optimized and executed. The reformulation problem can be solved by algorithms for answering queries using views, though in this context, we usually cannot find a rewriting that is equivalent to the user query because of the data sources' limited coverage. Instead, we search for a *maximally-contained rewriting*, which provides the best answer possible, given the available sources. When the query and views are conjunctive (i.e., select-project-join) without comparison predicates, the maximally-contained rewriting is a union of conjunctive queries over the views. The key challenge in this context is to develop an algorithm that scales up in the number of views.

We consider the problem of answering conjunctive queries using a set of conjunctive views in the presence of a large number of views. In general, this problem is NP-Complete because it involves searching through a possibly exponential number of rewritings [21]. Previous work has mainly considered two algorithms for this purpose.

The bucket algorithm, developed as part of the Information Manifold System [22], controls its search by first considering each subgoal in the query in isolation, and creating a bucket that contains only the views that are relevant to that subgoal. The algorithm then creates rewritings by combining one view from every bucket. As we show, the combination step has several deficiencies, and does not scale up well. The inverse-rules algorithm, developed primarily in the InfoMaster System [29, 8], considers rewritings for each database relation independent of any particular query. Given a user query, these rewritings are combined appropriately. We show that the rewritings produced by the inverse-rules algorithm need to be further processed in order to be appropriate for query evaluation. Unfortunately, in this additional processing step the algorithm must duplicate much of the work done in the second phase of the bucket algorithm.

Based on the insights into the previous algorithms, we introduce the MiniCon algorithm, which addresses their limitations and scales up to a large number of views. The key idea underlying the MiniCon algorithm is a change of perspective: instead of building rewritings by combining rewritings for each query subgoal or database relation, we consider how each of the *variables* in the query can interact with the available views. The result is that the second phase of the MiniCon algorithm needs to consider drastically fewer combinations of views. Hence, as we show experimentally, the MiniCon algorithm scales up much better. The specific contributions of the paper are the following:

- We describe the MiniCon algorithm and its properties.
- We present a detailed experimental evaluation and analysis of algorithms for answering queries using views. The experimental results show (1) the MiniCon algorithm significantly outperforms the bucket and inverse-rules algorithms, (2) the MiniCon algorithm scales up to hundreds of views, thereby showing for the first time that answering queries using views can be efficient on large scale problems. We believe that our experimental evaluation in itself is a significant contribution that fills a void in previous work on this topic.
- We describe an extension of the MiniCon algorithm to handle comparison predicates and experimental results on its performance.

This paper focuses on the problem of answering queries using views for select-project-join queries under set semantics. While such queries are quite common in data integration applications, many applications will need to deal with queries involving grouping and aggregation, semi-structured data, nested structures and integrity constraints. Indeed, the problem of answering queries using views has been considered in these contexts as well [15, 31, 7, 13, 26, 4, 10, 14]. In contrast to these works, our focus is on obtaining a scalable algorithm for answering queries using views and the experimental evaluation of such algorithms. Hence, we begin with the class of select-project-join queries.

The paper is organized as follows. Section 2 presents the problem formally, and Section 3 discusses the limitations of the previous algorithms. Section 4 describes the MiniCon algorithm, and Section 5 presents the experimental evaluation. Section 6 describes an extension of the MiniCon algorithm to comparison predicates. Section 7 discusses related work and Section 8 concludes.

2 Preliminaries

Queries and views: We consider the problem of answering queries using views for *conjunctive queries* (i.e., select-project-join queries). A *conjunctive query* has the form:

$$q(\bar{X}) :\text{-} e_1(\bar{X}_1), \ldots, e_n(\bar{X}_n)$$

where q and $e_1, \ldots, e_n$ are predicate names. The atoms $e_1(\bar{X}_1), \ldots, e_n(\bar{X}_n)$ are the *subgoals* in the body of the query, where $e_1, \ldots, e_n$ refer to database relations. The atom $q(\bar{X})$ is called the *head* of the query, and refers to the answer relation. The tuples $\bar{X}, \bar{X}_1, \ldots, \bar{X}_n$ contain either variables or constants. We require that the query be *safe*, i.e., that $\bar{X} \subseteq \bar{X}_1 \cup \ldots \cup \bar{X}_n$ (that is, every variable that appears in the head must also appear in the body). The variables in $\bar{X}$ are the *distinguished* variables of the query, and all the others are *existential* variables. We denote individual variables by lowercase letters. We use $Vars(Q)$ $(Subgoals(Q))$ to refer to the set of variables (subgoals) in Q, and $Q(D)$ to refer to the result of evaluating the query Q over the database D.

Note that unions can be expressed in this notation by allowing a set of conjunctive queries with the same head predicate. A *view* is a named query. If the query results are stored, we refer to them as a materialized view, and we refer to the result set as the *extension* of the view. In Section 6 we consider queries that contain subgoals with comparison predicates $<, \leq, \neq$. In this case, we require that if a variable x appears in a subgoal of a comparison predicate, then x must also appear in an ordinary subgoal.

Example 2.1 Consider the following schema that we use throughout the paper. The relation cites(p1,p2) stores pairs of publication identifiers where p1 cites p2. The relation sameTopic stores pairs of papers that are on the same topic. The unary relations inSIGMOD and inVLDB store ids of papers published in SIGMOD and VLDB respectively. The following query asks for pairs of papers on the same topic that also cite each other. Note that join predicates in this notation are expressed by multiple occurrences of the same variables.

q(x,y):- sameTopic(x,y), cites(x,y), cites(y,x)   □

Query containment and equivalence: The concepts of query containment and equivalence enable us to compare between queries and rewritings. We say that a query Q_1 is *contained* in the query Q_2, denoted by $Q_1 \sqsubseteq Q_2$, if the answer to Q_1 is a subset of the answer to Q_2 for *any* database instance. We say that Q_1 and Q_2 are *equivalent* if $Q_1 \sqsubseteq Q_2$ and $Q_2 \sqsubseteq Q_1$.

Containment mappings provide a necessary and sufficient condition for testing query containment. A mapping

τ from $Vars(Q_2)$ to $Vars(Q_1)$ is a containment mapping if (1) τ maps every subgoal in the body of Q_2 to a subgoal in the body of Q_1, and (2) τ maps the head of Q_2 to the head of Q_1. The query Q_2 contains Q_1 if and only if there is a containment mapping from Q_2 to Q_1 [5].

Given a partial mapping τ on the variables of a query, we extend it in the obvious manner to apply to sets of variables and to subgoals of the query (when all the variables of the subgoal are in the domain of τ). A conjunctive query is said to be *redundant* if it is possible to remove some of its subgoals and obtain an equivalent query.

Answering queries using views: Given a query Q and a set of view definitions $\mathcal{V} = V_1, \ldots, V_m$, a rewriting of the query using the views is a query expression Q' whose body predicates are either $V_1, \ldots, V_m$ or comparison predicates.

We distinguish between two types of query rewritings: *equivalent rewritings,* that are used in the contexts of query optimization and the maintenance of physical data independence, and *maximally-contained rewritings,* that are used in the context of data integration.

Definition 2.1 (equivalent rewriting) Let Q be a query, and $\mathcal{V} = V_1, \ldots, V_n$ be a set of views, both over the same database schema. The query Q' is an equivalent rewriting of Q using $\mathcal{V}$ if for any database D, the result of evaluating Q' over $V_1(D), \ldots, V_n(D)$ is the same as $Q(D)$. $\square$

Example 2.2 Consider the query from Example 2.1 and the following views. The view V1 stores pairs of papers that cite other, and V2 stores pairs of papers on the same topic and each of which cites at least one other paper.

Q(x,y):- sameTopic(x,y), cites(x,y), cites(y,x)
V1(a,b):- cites(a,b), cites(b,a)
V2(c,d) :- sameTopic(c,d), cites(c,c1), cites(d,d1)

The following is an equivalent rewriting of Q:

Q'(x,y):- V1(x,y), V2(x,y) .

To check that Q' is an equivalent rewriting, we unfold the view definitions to obtain Q", and show that Q is equivalent to Q", using a containment mapping (in this case the identity mapping except for x1 $\rightarrow$ y, y1 $\rightarrow$ x).

Q"(x,y):- cites(x,y), cites(y,x), sameTopic(x,y),
       cites(x,x1), cites(y,y1) $\square$

Data Integration: One of the main uses of algorithms for answering queries using views is in the context of data integration systems that provide their users with a uniform interface to a multitude of data sources [22, 18, 12, 19]. Users pose queries in terms of a *mediated schema,* which is a set of relations designed to capture the salient aspects of the application. The data, however, is stored in the sources. In order to be able to translate users' queries into queries on the data sources, the data integration system needs a description of the contents of the sources. One of the approaches to specifying such descriptions is to describe a data source as a view over the mediated schema, specifying which tuples can be found in the source. For example,

in our domain, we may have two data sources, S1 and S2, containing pairs of SIGMOD (respectively VLDB) papers that cite each other. The sources can be described as follows:

S1(a,b):- cites(a,b), cites(b,a), inSIGMOD(a),
      inSIGMOD(b)
S2(a,b):- cites(a,b), cites(b,a), inVLDB(a),
      inVLDB(b)

Given a query Q, the data integration system first needs to reformulate Q to refer to the data sources, i.e., the views. There are two differences between this application of answering queries using views and that considered in the context of query optimization. First, the views here are not assumed to contain *all* the tuples in their definition since the data sources are managed autonomously. For example, the source S1 may not contain all the pairs of SIGMOD papers that cite each other. Second, we cannot always find an equivalent rewriting of the query using the views because there may be no data sources that contain all of the information the query needs. Instead, we consider the problem of finding a maximally-contained rewriting, as illustrated below.

Example 2.3 Continuing with our example, assuming we have the data sources described by S1, S2 and V2 and the same query q, the best rewriting we can generate is:

q'(x,y):- S1(x,y), V2(x,y)
q'(x,y):- S2(x,y), V2(x,y)

Note that this rewriting is a union of conjunctive queries, describing multiple ways of obtaining answer to the query from the available sources. The rewriting is not an equivalent rewriting, since it misses any pair of papers that is not both in SIGMOD or both in VLDB, but we don't have data sources to provide us such pairs. Furthermore, since the sources are not guaranteed to have all the tuples in the definition of the view, our rewritings need to consider different views that may have similar definitions. For example, suppose we have the following source S3:

S3(a,b):- cites(a,b), cites(b,a), inSIGMOD(a),
      inSIGMOD(b)

The definition of S3 is identical to that of S1, however, because of source incompleteness, it may contain different tuples than S1. Hence, our rewriting will also have to include the following in addition to the other two rewritings.

q'(x,y):- S3(x,y), V2(x,y) $\square$

Maximally-contained rewritings are defined w.r.t. a particular query language in which we express rewritings. Intuitively, the maximally-contained rewriting is one that provides all the answers possible from a given set of sources. Formally, they are defined as follows.

Definition 2.2 (maximally-contained rewriting) The query Q' is a maximally-contained rewriting of a query Q using the views $\mathcal{V} = V_1, \ldots, V_n$ w.r.t. a query language $\mathcal{L}$ if

1. for any database D, and extensions $v_1, \ldots, v_n$ of the views such that $v_i \subseteq V_i(D)$, for $1 \le i \le n$, then $Q'(v_1, \ldots, v_n) \subseteq Q(D)$ for all i

2. there is no other query Q_1 in the language $\mathcal{L}$, such for every database D and extensions $v_1, \ldots, v_n$ as above (1) $Q'(v_1, \ldots, v_n) \subseteq Q_1(v_1, \ldots, v_n)$ and (2) $Q_1(v_1, \ldots, v_n) \subseteq Q(D)$, and there exists at least one database for which (1) is a strict subset. $\qquad\square$

Given a conjunctive query Q and a set of conjunctive views $\mathcal{V}$, the maximally-contained rewriting of a conjunctive query may be a union of conjunctive queries (we refer to the individual conjunctive queries as *conjunctive rewritings*). When the queries and the views are conjunctive and do not contain comparison predicates, it follows from [21] that we need only consider conjunctive rewritings Q' that have at most the number of subgoals in the query Q.

Remark 1 It is important to emphasize at this point that the definitions considered in this section only ensure that the rewriting of the query obtains as many answers as possible from a set of views, which is the main concern in the context of data integration. We are not considering here the problem of finding the rewriting that yields the *cheapest* query execution plan over the views, which would be the main concern when using algorithms for answering queries using views for query optimization and maintenance of physical data independence. In the concluding section we revisit this issue. In addition, we do not consider here the issue of ordering the results from the sources. $\qquad\square$

3 Previous Algorithms

The theoretical results on answering queries using views [21] showed that when there are no comparison predicates in the query, the search for a maximally-contained rewriting can be confined to a finite space: an algorithm needs to consider every possible conjunction of n or less view atoms, where n is the number of subgoals in the query. Two previous algorithms, the bucket algorithm and the inverse-rules algorithm, attempted to find more effective methods to produce rewritings that do not require such exhaustive search. In this section we briefly describe these algorithms and point out their limitations. In Section 5 we compare these algorithms to our MiniCon algorithm and show that the MiniCon algorithm significantly outperforms them. We describe the algorithms for queries and views without comparison subgoals.

3.1 The Bucket Algorithm

The bucket algorithm was developed as part of the Information Manifold System [22]. The key idea underlying the bucket algorithm is that the number of query rewritings that need to be considered can be drastically reduced if we first consider each subgoal in the query in isolation and determine which views may be relevant to a particular subgoal.

We illustrate the bucket algorithm with the following query and views. Note that the query now only asks for a set of papers, rather than pairs of papers.

Q1(x) :- cites(x,y),cites(y,x),sameTopic(x,y)
V4(a) :- cites(a,b), cites(b,a)
V5(c,d) :- sameTopic(c,d)
V6(f,h) :- cites(f,g),cites(g,h),sameTopic(f,g)

In the first step, the bucket algorithm creates a bucket for each subgoal in Q1. The bucket for a subgoal g contains the views that include subgoals to which g can be mapped in a rewriting of the query. If a subgoal g unifies with more than one subgoal in a view V, then the bucket of g will contain multiple occurrences of V. The bucket algorithm would create the following buckets:

cites(x,y)	cites(y,x)	sameTopic(x,y)
V4(x)	V4(x)	V5(x,y)
V6(x,y)	V6(x,y)	V6(x,y)

Note that it is possible to unify the subgoal cites(x,y) in the query with the subgoal cites(b,a) in V4, with the mapping x → b, y → a. However, the algorithm did not include the entry V4(y) in the bucket because it requires that every distinguished variable in the query be mapped to a distinguished variable in the view.

In the second step, for each element of the Cartesian product of the buckets, the algorithm constructs a conjunctive rewriting and checks whether it is contained (or can be made to be contained) in the query. If so, the rewriting is added to the answer. Hence, the result of the bucket algorithm is a union of conjunctive rewritings.

In our example, the algorithm will try to combine V4 with the other views and fail (as we explain below). Then it will consider the rewritings involving V6, and note that by equating the variables in the head of V6 a contained rewriting is obtained. Finally, the algorithm will also note that V6 and V5 can be combined. Though not originally described as part of the bucket algorithm, it is possible to add an additional simple check that will determine that the resulting rewriting will be redundant (because V5 can be removed). Hence, the only rewriting in this example (which also turns out to be an equivalent rewriting) is:

Q1'(x) :- V6(x,x)

The main inefficiency of the bucket algorithm is that it misses some important interactions between view subgoals by considering each subgoal in isolation. As a result, the buckets contain irrelevant views, and hence the second step of the algorithm becomes very expensive. We illustrate this point on our example.

Consider the view V4, and suppose that we decide to use V4 in such a way that the subgoal cites(x,y) is mapped to the subgoal cites(a,b) in the view, as shown below:

$$\text{Q1(x) :- cites(x,y),cites(y,x), SameTopic(x,y)}$$
$$\downarrow \qquad\quad \downarrow \qquad\qquad\qquad ?$$
$$\text{V4(a) :- cites(a,b)cites(b,a)}$$

However, the variable b does not appear in the head of V4, and therefore, if we use V4, then we will not be able to apply the join predicate between cites(x,y) and SameTopic(x,y) in the query. Therefore, V4 is not usable for the query, but the bucket algorithm would not discover this.

Furthermore, even if the query did not contain Same-Topic(x,y), the bucket algorithm would not realize that if it uses V4, then it has to use it for *both* of the query subgoals. Realizing this would save the algorithm exploring useless combinations in the second phase.

As we explain later, the MiniCon algorithm discovers these interactions. In this example, MiniCon will determine that V4 is irrelevant to the query. In the case in which the query does not contain the subgoal SameTopic(x,y), the MiniCon algorithm will discover that the two cite subgoals need to be treated atomically.

3.2 The Inverse-Rules Algorithm

Like the bucket algorithm, the inverse-rules algorithm [29, 8] was also developed in the context of a data integration system. The key idea underlying the algorithm is to construct a set of rules that *invert* the view definitions, i.e., rules that show how to compute tuples for the database relations from tuples of the views. Given the views in the previous example, the algorithm would construct the following inverse rules:

R1: cites(a, f1(a)) :- V4(a)
R2: cites(f1(a), a) :- V4(a)
R3: sameTopic(c,d) :- V5(c,d)
R4: cites(f, f2(f,h)) :- V6(f,h)
R5: cites(f2(f,h), h) :- V6(f,h)
R6: sameTopic(f, f2(f,h)) :- V6(f,h)

Consider the rules R1 and R2; intuitively, their meaning is the following. A tuple of the form (p1) in the extension of the view V4 is a witness of two tuples in the relation cites. It is a witness in the sense that it tells that the relation cites contains a tuple of the form (p1, Z), for some value of Z, and that the relation also contains a tuple of the form (Z, p1), for the *same* value of Z.

In order to express the information that the unknown value of Z is the same in the two atoms, we refer to it using the functional Skolem term f1(Z). Note that there may be several values of Z in the database that cause the tuple (p1) to be in the self-join of cites, but all that we know is that there exists at least one such value.

The rewriting of a query Q using the set of views $\mathcal{V}$ is simply the composition of Q and the inverse rules for $\mathcal{V}$. Hence, one of the important advantages of the algorithm is that the inverse rules can be constructed ahead of time in polynomial time, independent of a particular query.

The rewritings produced by the inverse-rules algorithm, as originally described in [8], are not appropriate for query evaluation for two reasons. First, applying the inverse rules to the extension of the views may invert some of the useful computation done to produce the view. Second, we may end up accessing views that are irrelevant to the query. To illustrate the first point, suppose we use the rewriting produced by the inverse-rules algorithm in the case where the view V6 has the extension { (p1, p1), (p2,p2) }.

First, we would apply the inverse rules to the extensions of the views. Applying R4 would yield cites(p1, f2(p1,p1)), cites(p2, f2(p2,p2)), and similarly applying R5 and R6 would yield the following tuples:

cites(p1, f2(p1,p1)),
cites(f2(p1,p1),p1),
cites(f2(p2,p2),p2),
sameTopic(p1,p1),
sameTopic(p2,p2).

Applying the query Q1 to the tuples computed above obtains the answers p1 and p2. However, this computation is highly inefficient. Instead of directly using the tuples of V6 for the answer, the inverse-rules algorithm first computed tuples for the relation cites, and then had to re-compute the self-join of cites that was already computed for V6. Furthermore, if the extensions of the views V4 and V5 are not empty, then applying the inverse rules would produce useless tuples as explained in Section 3.1.

Hence, before we can fairly compare the inverse-rules algorithm to the others, we need to further process the rules. Specifically, we need to expand the query with every possible combination of inverse rules. However, expanding the query with the inverse rules turns out to repeat much of the work done in the second phase of the bucket algorithm.

In the experiments described in Section 5 we consider an extended version of the inverse-rules algorithm that produces a union of conjunctive queries by expanding the definitions of the inverse rules. We expanded the subgoals of the query one at a time, so we could stop an expansion of the query at the moment when we detect that a unification for a subset of the subgoals will not yield a rewriting (thereby optimizing the performance of the inverse-rules algorithm). We show that the inverse-rules algorithm can perform much better than the bucket algorithm, but the MiniCon algorithm scales up significantly better than either algorithm.

4 The MiniCon Algorithm

The MiniCon algorithm begins like the bucket algorithm, considering which views contain subgoals that correspond to subgoals in the query. However, once the algorithm finds a partial mapping from a subgoal g in the query to a subgoal g_1 in a view V, it changes perspective and looks at the variables in the query. The algorithm considers the join predicates in the query and finds the minimal additional set of subgoals that need to be mapped to subgoals in V, given that g will be mapped to g_1. This set of subgoals and mapping information is called a *MiniCon Description* (MCD), and can be viewed as a generalization of buckets. In the second phase, the algorithm combines the MCDs to produce the rewritings. It is important to note that because of the way we construct the MCDs, the MiniCon algorithm does not require containment checks in the second phase, giving it an additional speedup compared to the bucket algorithm. Section 4.1 describes the construction of MCDs, and Section 4.2 describes the combination step. The proof of correctness of the algorithm is omitted for lack of space, but is described in the full version of this paper [28].

4.1 Forming the MCDs

We begin by introducing a few terms that are used in the description of the algorithm. Given a mapping τ from $Vars(Q)$ to $Vars(V)$, we say that a view subgoal g_1 *covers* a query subgoal g if $\tau(g) = g_1$.

A MCD is a mapping from a subset of the variables in the query to variables in one of the views. Intuitively, a MCD represents a fragment of a containment mapping from the query to the rewriting of the query. The way in which we construct the MCDs guarantees that these fragments can later be combined seamlessly.

As seen in our example, we need to consider mappings from the query to specializations of the views, where some of the head variables may have been equated (e.g., V6(x,x) instead of V6(x,y) in our example). Hence, every MCD has an associated *head homomorphism*. A head homomorphism h on a view V is a mapping h from $Vars(V)$ to $Vars(V)$ that is the identity on the existential variables, but may equate distinguished variables, i.e., for every distinguished variable x, $h(x)$ is distinguished, and $h(x) = h(h(x))$. Formally, we define MCDs as follows.

Definition 4.1 (MiniCon Descriptions) A MCD C for a query Q over a view V is a tuple of the form $(h_C, V(\bar{Y})_C, \varphi_C, G_C)$ where:

- h_C is a head homomorphism on V,
- $V(\bar{Y})_C$ is the result of applying h_C to V, i.e., $\bar{Y} = h_C(\bar{A})$, where $\bar{A}$ are the head variables of V,
- φ_C is a partial mapping from $Vars(Q)$ to $h_C(Vars(V))$
- G_C is a subset of the subgoals in Q which are covered by some subgoal in $h_C(V)$ and the mapping φ_C (note: not all such subgoals are necessarily included in G_C). □

In words, φ_C is a mapping from Q to the specialization of V obtained by the head homomorphism h_C. G_C is a set of subgoals of Q that we cover by the mapping φ_C. Property 1 below specifies the exact conditions we need to consider when we decide which subgoals to include in G_C. Note that $V(\bar{Y})_C$ is uniquely determined by the other elements of a MCD, but is part of a MCD specification for clarity in our subsequent discussions. Furthermore, the algorithm will not consider all the possible MCDs but only those in which h_C is the least restrictive head homomorphism necessary in order to unify subgoals of the query with subgoals in a view.

The mapping φ_C of a MCD C may map a set of variables in Q to the same variable in $h_C(V)$. In our discussion, we sometimes need to refer to a representative variable of such a set. For each such set of variables in Q we choose a representative variable arbitrarily, except that we choose a distinguished variable whenever possible. For a variable x in Q, $EC_{\varphi_C}(x)$ denotes the representative variable of the set to which x belongs. $EC_{\varphi_C}(x)$ is defined to be the identity on any variable that is not in Q.

The construction of the MCDs is based on the following observation on the properties of query rewritings.

procedure **formMCDs**$(Q, \mathcal{V})$
/* Q and $\mathcal{V}$ are conjunctive queries. */
   $\mathcal{C} = \emptyset$.
    For each subgoal $g \in Q$
      For view $V \in \mathcal{V}$ and every subgoal $v \in V$
      Let h be the least restrictive head homomorphism on V
        such that there exists a mapping φ, s.t. $\varphi(g) = h(v)$.
      If h and φ exist, then add to $\mathcal{C}$ any new MCD C
        that can be constructed where:
        (a) φ_C (resp. h_C) is an extension of φ (resp. h),
        (b) G_C is the minimal subset of subgoals of Q such that
          G_C, φ_C and h_C satisfy Property 1, and
        (c) it is not possible to extend φ and h to an MCD that
          covers fewer subgoals than G_C.
   Return $\mathcal{C}$

Figure 1: First phase of the MiniCon algorithm: Forming MCDs. Note that condition (b) minimizes G_c *given* a choice of h_C and φ_C, and is therefore not redundant with condition (c).

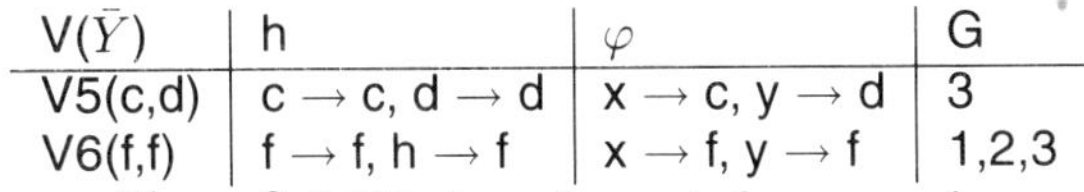

$V(\bar{Y})$	h	φ	G
V5(c,d)	c → c, d → d	x → c, y → d	3
V6(f,f)	f → f, h → f	x → f, y → f	1,2,3

Figure 2: MCDs formed as part of our example

Property 1 *Let C be a MCD for Q over V. Then C can only be used in a non-redundant rewriting of Q if the following conditions hold:*

C1. For each head variable x of Q which is in the domain of φ_C, $\varphi_C(x)$ is a head variable in $h_C(V)$.

C2. If $\varphi_C(x)$ is an existential variable in $h_C(V)$, then for every g, subgoal of Q, that includes x (1) all the variables in g are in the domain of φ_C, and (2) $\varphi_C(g) \in h_C(V)$

Clause C1 is the same as in the bucket algorithm. Clause C2 captures the intuition we illustrated in our example, where if a variable x is part of a join predicate which is not enforced by the view, then x must be in the head of the view so the join predicate can be applied by another subgoal in the rewriting. In our example, clause C2 would rule out the use of V4 for query Q1 because the variable b is not in the head of V4, but the join predicate with Same-Topic(x,y) has not been applied in V4.

The algorithm for creating the MCDs is shown in Figure 1. Consider the application of the algorithm to our example with the query Q1 and the views V4, V5, and V6. The MCDs that will be created are shown in Figure 2.

We first consider the subgoal cites(x,y) in the query. As discussed above, the algorithm does not create a MCD for V4 because clause C2 of Property 1 would be violated (the property would require that V4 also cover the subgoal sameTopic(x,y) since b is existential in V4). For the same reason, no MCD will be created for V4 even when we consider the other subgoals in the query.

In a sense, the MiniCon algorithm shifts some of the work done by the combination step of the bucket algorithm to the phase of creating the MCDs. The bucket algorithm will discover that V4 is not usable for the query when combining the buckets. However, the bucket algorithm needs to discover this many times (each time it considers V4 in conjunction with another view), and every time it does so, it uses a containment check, which is much more expensive. Hence, as we show in the next section, with a little more effort spent in the first phase, the overall performance of the MiniCon algorithm outperforms the bucket algorithm and the inverse-rules algorithm.

Remark 2 *(covered subgoals)* When we construct a MCD C, we must determine the set of subgoals of the query G_C that are covered by the MCD. The algorithm includes in G_C only the *minimal* set of subgoals that are necessary in order to satisfy Property 1. To see why this is not an obvious choice, suppose we have the following query and views:

Q1'(x) :- cites(x,y),cites(z,x), inSIGMOD(x)
V7(a) :- cites(a,b),inSIGMOD(a)
V8(c) :- cites(d,c),inSIGMOD(c)

One can also consider including the subgoal inSIGMOD(x) in the set of covered subgoals for the MCD for both V7 and V8, because x is in the domain of their respective variable mappings anyway. However, our algorithm will not include inSIGMOD(x), and will instead create a special MCD for it.

The reason for our choice is that it enables us to focus in the second phase only on rewritings where the MCD cover *mutually exclusive* sets of subgoals in the query, rather than overlapping subsets. This yields a more efficient second phase. □

4.2   Combining the MCDs

Our method for constructing MCDs pays off in the second phase of the algorithm, where we combine MCDs to build the conjunctive rewritings. In this phase we consider combinations of MCDs, and for each valid combination we create a conjunctive rewriting of the query. The final rewriting is a union of conjunctive queries.

The following property states that the MiniCon algorithm need only consider combinations of MCDs that cover pairwise disjoint subsets of subgoals of the query:

Property 2 *Given a query Q, a set of views $\mathcal{V}$, and the set of MCDs $\mathcal{C}$ for Q over the views in $\mathcal{V}$, the only combinations of MCDs that can result in non-redundant rewritings of Q are of the form $C_1, \ldots, C_l$, where*
D1. $G_{C_1} \cup \ldots \cup G_{C_l} = Subgoals(Q)$, and
D2. for every $i \neq j$, $G_{C_i} \cap G_{C_j} = \emptyset$.

The fact that we only need to consider sets of MCDs that provide partitions of the subgoals in the query drastically reduces the search space of the algorithm. Furthermore, even though we do not discuss it here, the algorithm can also be extended to output the rewriting in a compact encoding that identifies the common subexpressions of the conjunctive rewritings, and therefore leads to more efficient query evaluation. We note that had we chosen the alternate strategy in Remark 2, clause D2 would not hold.

procedure **combineMCDs**($\mathcal{C}$)
/* $\mathcal{C}$ are MCDs formed by the first step of the algorithm. */
/* Each MCD has the form $(h_C, V(\bar{Y}), \varphi_C, G_C, EC_C)$. */
   Given a set of MCDs, $C_1, \ldots, C_n$, we define the function
     EC on $Vars(Q)$ as follows:
     If for $i \neq j$, $EC_{\varphi_i}(x) \neq EC_{\varphi_j}(x)$, define $EC_C(x)$ to be
      one of them arbitrarily but consistently across all y for which
      $EC_{\varphi_i}(y) = EC_{\varphi_i}(x)$

   Let $Answer = \emptyset$
   For every subset $C_1, \ldots, C_n$ of $\mathcal{C}$ such that
     $G_{C_1} \cup G_{C_2} \cup \ldots \cup G_{C_n} = subgoals(Q)$ and
     for every $i \neq j$, $G_{C_i} \cap G_{C_j} = \emptyset$ then
      Define a mapping Ψ_i on the $\bar{Y}_i$'s as follows:
      If there exists a variable $x \in Q$ such that $\varphi_i(x) = y$
       $\Psi_i(y) = x$
      Else
       Ψ_i is a fresh copy of y
      Create the conjunctive rewriting
       $Q'(EC(\bar{X})) :\text{-} \ V_{C_1}(EC(\Psi_1(\bar{Y}_{C_1}))), \ldots,$
                $V_{C_n}(EC(\Psi_n(\bar{Y}_{C_n})))$
     Add Q' to $Answer$.
   Return $Answer$.

Figure 3: Phase 2: combining the MCDs.

Given a combination of MCDs that satisfies Property 2, the actual rewriting is constructed as shown in Figure 3.

In the final step of the algorithm we tighten up the rewritings by removing redundant subgoals as follows. Suppose a rewriting Q' includes two atoms A_1 and A_2 of the same view V, whose MCDs were C_1 and C_2, and the following conditions are satisfied: (1) whenever A_1 (resp. A_2) has a variable from Q in position i, then A_2 (resp. A_1) either has the same variable or a variable that does not appear in Q in that position, and (2) the ranges of φ_{C_1} and φ_{C_2} do not overlap on existential variables of V. In this case we can remove one of the two atoms by applying to Q' the homomorphism τ that is (1) the identity on the variables of Q and (2) is the most general unifier of A_1 and A_2. The underlying justification for this optimization is discussed in [21], and it can also be applied to the bucket algorithm and the inverse-rules algorithm.

We note that even after this step, the rewritings may still contain redundant subgoals. However, removing them involves several tests for query containment.

In our example, the algorithm will consider using V5 to cover subgoal 3, but when it realizes that there are no MCDs that cover either subgoal 1 or 2 without covering subgoal 3, it will discard V5. Thus the only rewriting that will be considered is
Q1'(x) :- V6(x,x).

The following theorem summarizes the properties of the MiniCon algorithm:

Theorem 4.1 *Given a conjunctive query Q and conjunctive views $\mathcal{V}$, both without comparison predicates, the MiniCon algorithm produces the union of conjunctive queries that is the maximally-contained rewriting of Q using $\mathcal{V}$.*

It should be noted that the worst-case asymptotic running time of the MiniCon algorithm is the same as that of the bucket algorithm and of the inverse-rules algorithm after the modification described in Section 3.2. In all cases, the running time is $O(n\,m\,M)^n$, where n is the number of subgoals in the query, m is the maximal number of subgoals in a view, and M is the number of views.

The next section describes experimental results showing the differences between the three algorithms in practice.

5 Experimental Results

The goal of our experiments was twofold. First, we wanted to compare the performance of the bucket algorithm, the inverse-rules algorithm, and MiniCon algorithm in different circumstances. Second, we wanted to validate that MiniCon can scale up to large number of views and large queries. Our experiments considered three classes of queries and views: (1) chain queries, (2) star queries and (3) complete queries, all of which are well known in the literature [25].

To facilitate the experiments, we implemented a random query generator which enables us to control the following parameters (1) the number of subgoals in the queries and views, (2) the number of variables per subgoal, (3) the number of distinguished variables, and (4) the degree to which predicate names are duplicated in the queries and views. The results are averaged over multiple runs generated with the same parameters (at least 40, and usually more than 100). An important variable to keep in mind throughout the experiments is the number of rewritings that can actually be obtained.

In most experiments we considered queries and views that had the same query shape and size. Our experiments were all run on a dual Pentium II 450 MHz running Windows NT 4.0 with 512MB RAM. All of the algorithms were implemented in Java and compiled to an executable.

5.1 Chain queries

In the context of chain queries we consider several cases. In the first case, shown in Figure 4(a), only the first and last variables of the query and the view are distinguished. Therefore, in order to be usable, a view has to be identical to the query, and as a result there are very few rewritings. The bucket algorithm performs the worst, because of the cost of the query containment checks it needs to perform (it took on the order of 20 seconds for 5 views of size 10 subgoals, and hence we do not even show it on the graph). The inverse-rules algorithm and the MiniCon algorithm scale linearly in the number of views, but the MiniCon algorithm outperforms the inverse-rules algorithm by a factor of about 5 (and this factor is independent of query and view size). In fact, the MiniCon algorithm can handle more than 1000 views with 10 subgoals each in less than one second.

The difference in the performance between the inverse-rules algorithm and the MiniCon algorithm in this context and in others is due to the second phases of the algorithms. In this phase, the inverse-rules algorithm is searching for a

unification of the subgoals of the query with heads of inverse rules. The MiniCon algorithm is searching for sets of MCDs that cover all the subgoals in the query, but cover pairwise disjoint subsets. Hence, the MiniCon algorithm is searching a much smaller space, because the number of subgoals is smaller than the number of variables in the query. Moreover the MiniCon algorithm is performing better because in the first phase of the algorithm it already removed from consideration views that may not be usable due to violations of Property 1. In contrast, the inverse-rules algorithm must try unifications that include such views and then backtrack. The amount of work that the inverse-rules algorithm will waste depends on the order in which it considers the subgoals in the query when it unifies them with the corresponding inverse rules. If a failure appears late in the ordering, more work is wasted. The important point to note is that the optimal order in which to consider the subgoals depends heavily on the specific views available and is, in general, very hard to find. Hence, it would be hard to extend the inverse-rules algorithm such that its second phase would compare in performance to that of the MiniCon algorithm.

In the second case we consider, shown in Figure 4(b), the views are shorter than the query (of lengths 2, 3 and 4, while the query has 12 subgoals). In this case the MiniCon algorithm stills scales linearly while the inverse-rules algorithm grows faster. For example, for 90 views, the MiniCon algorithm runs 3 times faster than the inverse-rules algorithm, and for 180 views it runs 6 times faster.

Finally, though not shown here, we also considered another case in which all the variables in the views are distinguished. In this case, there are many rewritings (often more than 1000), and hence the performance of the algorithms is limited because of the sheer number of rewritings. Since virtually all combinations produce contained rewritings, any complete algorithm is forced to form an exponential number of rewritings. The MiniCon algorithm still performs better than the inverse-rules algorithm by anywhere between 10% better and a factor of 2, but with queries and views with 5 subgoals, the algorithms take on the order of 10 seconds for 10 views. It should be emphasized that the difference in performance between the MiniCon algorithm and the inverse-rules algorithm in this case is only due to the smaller search space being considered by the MiniCon algorithm.

5.2 Star and complete queries

In star queries, there exists a unique subgoal in the query that is joined with every other subgoal, and there are no joins between the other subgoals. In the cases of two distinguished variables in the views or all view variables being distinguished, the performance of the algorithms mirrors the corresponding cases of chain queries. Hence, we omit the details of these experiments. Figure 5(a) shows the running times of the inverse-rules algorithm and the MiniCon algorithm in the case where the distinguished variables in the views are the ones that do not participate in the joins. In

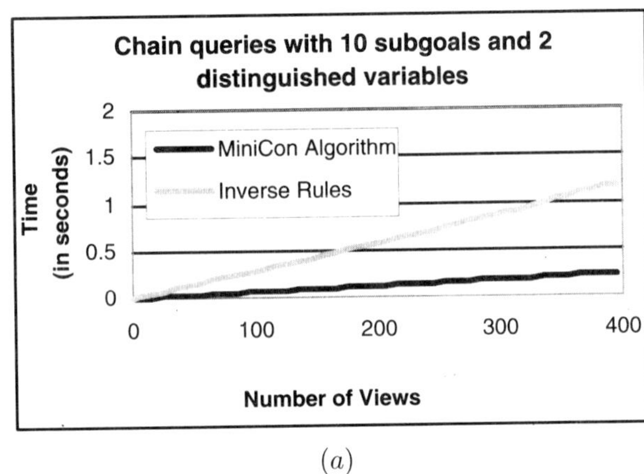 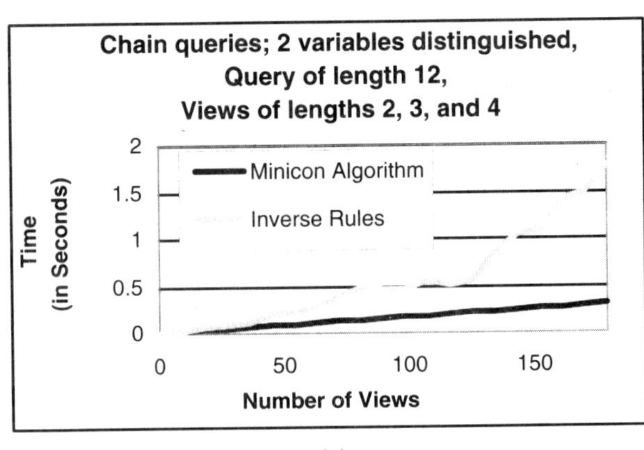

Figure 4: Experimental results for chain queries. The graph on the left considers two distinguished variables in the views, and shows that the MiniCon algorithm and the inverse-rules algorithms both scale up to hundreds of views. The MiniCon algorithm outperforms the inverse-rules algorithm by a factor of 5. In the right graph, the views are of lengths 2, 3 and 4, and the query has 12 subgoals. In this case the MiniCon algorithm still scales linearly, while the inverse-rules algorithm does not.

this case, there are relatively few rewritings. We see that the MiniCon algorithm scales up much better than the inverse-rules algorithm. For 20 views with 10 subgoals each, the MiniCon algorithm runs 20 times faster than the inverse-rules algorithm. Here the explanation is that the first phase of the MiniCon algorithm is able to prune many of the irrelevant views, whereas the inverse-rules algorithm discovers that the views are irrelevant only in the second phase, and often it must be discovered multiple times.

An experiment with similar settings but for complete queries is shown in Figure 5(b). In complete queries every subgoal is joined with every other subgoal in the query. As the figure shows, the MiniCon algorithm outperforms the inverse-rules algorithm by a factor of 4 for 20 views, and by a factor of 6 for 50 views, which is less of a speedup than with of star queries. The explanation for this is that there are more joins in the query, and thus the inverse-rules algorithm is able to detect useless views earlier in its search because failures to unify occur more frequently. Finally, we also ran some experiments on queries and views that were generated randomly with no specific pattern. The results showed that the MiniCon algorithm still scales up gracefully, but the behavior of the inverse-rules algorithm was too unpredictable (though always worse than the MiniCon algorithm), due to the nature of when the algorithms discover that a rule cannot be unified. Additional experiments are needed in order to draw any conclusion as to how the algorithms perform for completely random queries.

5.3 Summary

In summary, our experiments showed the following points. First, the MiniCon algorithm scales up to large numbers of views and significantly outperforms the other two algorithms. This point is emphasized by Table 1, where we tried to push the MiniCon algorithm to its limits. The table considers number of subgoals and number of views that the MiniCon algorithm is able to process given 10 seconds. In

Query type	Distinguished	# of subgoals	# of views
Chain	All	3	45
Chain	All	12	3
Chain	Two	5	9225
Chain	Two	99	115
Star	Non Joined	5	12235
Star	Non Joined	99	35
Star	Joined	10	4520
Star	Joined	99	75

Table 1: The number of views that the MiniCon algorithm can process in under 10 seconds in various situations

some cases, the algorithm can handle thousands of views, which is a magnitude that was clearly out of reach of previous algorithms.

Second, the experiments showed that the bucket algorithm performed much worse than the other two algorithms in all cases. More interesting was the comparison between the MiniCon algorithm and the inverse-rules algorithm. In all cases the MiniCon algorithm outperformed the inverse-rules algorithm, though by differing factors. In particular, the performance of the inverse-rules algorithm was very unpredictable. The problem with the inverse-rules algorithm is that it discovers many of the interactions between the views in its second phase, and the performance in that phase is heavily dependent on the order in which it considers the query subgoals. However, since the optimal order depends heavily on the interaction with the views, a general method for ordering the subgoals in the query is hard to find. Finally, all three algorithms are limited in cases where the number of resulting rewritings is especially large since a complete algorithm must produce an exponential number of rewritings.

6 Comparison predicates

The effect of comparison predicates on the problem of answering queries using views is quite subtle. If the views

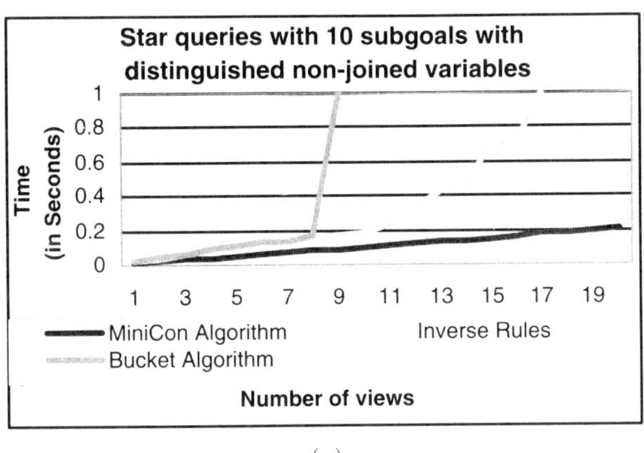 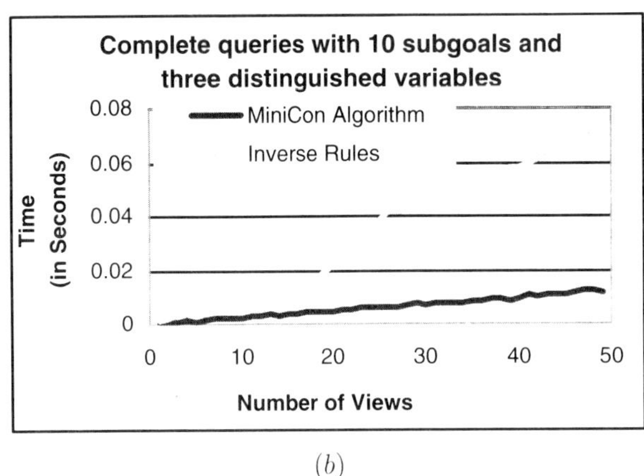

(a) (b)

Figure 5: The left figure shows the running times for star queries, where the distinguished variables in the views are those not participating in the joins. The graph on the right shows running times for complete queries with a similar setting. In both cases the MiniCon algorithm significantly outperforms the inverse-rules algorithm.

contain comparison predicates but the query does not, then the MiniCon algorithm without any changes still yields the maximally-contained query rewriting. On the other hand, if the query contains comparison predicates, then it follows from [1] that there can be no algorithm that returns a maximally-contained rewriting, even if we consider rewritings that are recursive datalog programs (let alone unions of conjunctive queries).

In this section we present an extension to the MiniCon algorithm that would (1) always find only correct rewritings (2) find the maximally-contained rewriting in many of the common cases in which comparison predicates are used, and (3) is guaranteed to produce the maximally-contained rewriting when the query contains only *semi-interval* constraints, i.e., when all the comparison predicates in the query are of the form $x \leq c$ or $x < c$, where x is a variable and c is a constant (or they are all of the form $x \geq c$ or $x > c$). We show experiments demonstrating the scale up of the extended algorithm. Finally, we show an example that provides an intuition for which cases the algorithm will not capture.

In our discussion, we refer to the set of comparison subgoals in a query Q as $I(Q)$. Given a set of variables $\bar{X}$, we denote by $I_{\bar{X}}(Q)$ the subset of the subgoals in $I(Q)$ that includes (1) only variables in $\bar{X}$ or constants and (2) contains at least one existential variable of Q. Intuitively, $I_{\bar{X}}(Q)$ denotes the set of comparison subgoals in the query that *must* be satisfied by the view, if $\bar{X}$ is the domain of a MCD. We assume without loss of generality that $I(Q)$ is logically closed, i.e., that if $I(Q) \models g$, then $g \in I(Q)$. We can always compute the logical closure of $I(Q)$ in time that is quadratic in the size of Q [34].

We make three changes to the MiniCon algorithm to handle comparison predicates. First, we only consider MCDs C that satisfy the following conditions:

1. If $x \in Vars(Q)$, $\varphi_C(x)$ is an existential variable in $h_C(V)$ and y appears in the same comparison atom as x, then y must be in the domain of φ_C.

2. If $\bar{X}$ is the set of variables in the domain of the mapping φ_C, then $I(h_C(V)) \models \varphi_C(I_{\bar{X}})$.

The first condition is an extension of Property 1, and the second condition guarantees the comparison subgoals in the view logically entail the relevant comparison subgoals in the query. Note that because of the second condition, the only subgoals in $I_{\bar{X}}(Q)$ that may not be satisfied by V must include only variables that φ_C maps to distinguished variables of V. As a result, such a subgoal can simply be added to the rewriting after the MCDs are combined.

The second change is that we disallow all MCDs that constrain variables to be incompatible with the variables they map in the query. For example, if a query has a subgoal $x > 17$ and a MCD maps x to a view variable a, and $a < 5$ is in the view, then we can ignore the MCD.

The third change we make to the MiniCon algorithm is the following: after forming a rewriting Q' by combining a set of MCDs, we add the subgoal $EC'(g)$ for any subgoal of $I(Q)$ that is not satisfied by Q'.

Example 6.1 Consider a variation on our running example, where the predicate year denotes the year of publication of a paper.

Q2(x) :- inSIGMOD(x), cites(x,y), year(x,r1),
   year(y,r2), r1 $\geq$ 1990, r2 $\leq$ 1985
V7(a,s1) :- inSIGMOD(a), cites(a,b), year(a,s1),
   year(b,s2), s2 $\leq$ 1983
V8(a,s1) :- inSIGMOD(a), cites(a,b), year(a,s1),
   year(b,s2), s2 $\leq$ 1987

Our algorithm would first consider V7 with the mapping $\{x \rightarrow a, y \rightarrow b, r1 \rightarrow s1, r2 \rightarrow s2\}$. In this case, the subgoal r2 $\leq$ 1985 is satisfied by the view, but r1 $\geq$ 1990 is not. However, since s1 is a distinguished variable in V7, the algorithm can create the rewriting:
Q2'(x) :- V7(x,r1), r1 $\geq$ 1990
When the algorithm considers a similar variable mapping to V8, it will notice that the constraint on r2 is not satisfied, and since it is mapped to an existential variable in V8, no MCD is created. $\square$

Example 6.2 The following example provides an intuition for which rewritings our extended algorithm will not discover. Consider the following query and view:

Q(u) :- e(u,v), u ≤ v
V1(a) :- e(a,b), e(b,a)

The algorithm will not create any MCD because the subgoal $u \leq v$ in the query is not implied by the view. However, the following is a contained rewriting of Q.

Q'(u) :- V1(u)

In order to show that the query contains the rewriting, we need to consider two different containment mappings, depending on whether $a \leq b$ or $a > b$ [17]. In each of these mappings, the subgoal $e(u, v)$ is mapped to a different subgoal. Our algorithm will only find rewritings in which the target of the mapping for a subgoal in the query is the same for any possible order on the variables. □

Figure 6 shows sample experiments that we ran on the extended algorithm in the case of chain queries. In the experiments, we added to the queries and views a number of comparison subgoals of the form $x < c$ or $x > c$.

The experiments show that the same trends we saw without comparison predicates appear here as well. In general, the addition of comparison predicates reduces the number of rewritings because more views can be deemed irrelevant. This is illustrated in Figure 6(b) where all of the variables in the views are distinguished and therefore without comparison predicates there would be many more rewritings. However, since the comparison predicates reduce the number of relevant views, the algorithm with comparison predicates scales up to a larger number of views. In Figure 6(a), the number of rewritings is very small, and the extra overhead of processing the comparison predicates causes slow down of a factor of 4. This factor can be decreased with further optimizations of our comparison predicate code that we did not explore.

7   Related Work

Algorithms for rewriting queries using views are surveyed in [20]. Most of the previous work on the problem focused on developing algorithms for the problem, rather that on studying their performance. In addition to the algorithms mentioned previously, algorithms have been developed for conjunctive queries with comparison predicates [35], queries and views with grouping and aggregation [15, 31, 7, 13], OQL queries [11], and queries over semi-structured data [26, 4]. The problem of answering queries using views has been considered for schemas with functional and inclusion dependencies [10, 14], languages that query both data and schema [23], and disjunctive views [2]. Clearly, each of the above extensions to the basic problem represents an opportunity for a possible extension of the MiniCon algorithm. Mitra [24] developed a rewriting algorithm that also captures the intuition of Property 1, and thus would likely lead to better performance than the bucket algorithm and the inverse-rules algorithm.

Several works discussed extensions to query optimizers that try to make use of materialized views in query processing [33, 6, 3, 27, 36]. In some cases, they modified the System-R style join enumeration component [33, 6], and in others they incorporated view rewritings into the rewrite phase of the optimizer [36, 27]. These works showed that considering the presence of materialized views did not negatively impact the performance of the optimizer. However, in these works the number of views tended to be relatively small. In [27], the authors consider a more general setting where they use a constraint language to describe views, physical structures and standard types of constraints. Unlike our algorithm, the above works are designed to produce a *single* conjunctive rewriting that is equivalent to the query and has the least cost, whereas we search for the maximally-contained rewriting.

8   Conclusions

This paper makes two important contributions. First, we present a new algorithm for answering queries using views, and second, we present the first experimental evaluation of such algorithms. We began by analyzing the two existing algorithms, the bucket algorithm and the inverse-rules algorithm, and found that they have significant limitations. We developed the MiniCon algorithm, a novel algorithm for answering queries using views, and showed that it scales gracefully and outperforms both existing algorithms. As a result of our work, we have established that answering queries using views can be done efficiently for large-scale problems. Finally, we described an extension of our algorithm to handle comparison predicates. As we show in the extended version of the paper, the MiniCon algorithm can also be extended in a straightforward fashion to deal with access-pattern limitations [30] in the same spirit of [10].

An interesting direction of future research is to extend the MiniCon algorithm to the context of using materialized views for query optimization and to consider bag semantics. In this context, we are interested in the *cheapest* rewriting of the query. Conceivably, it is possible as in [33, 6] to modify the second phase of the MiniCon algorithm such that it combines the MCDs in a bottom-up dynamic programming style, and hence saves only the cheapest rewriting. However, for the algorithm to guarantee finding the cheapest rewriting, we now need to consider rewritings that contain logically redundant subgoals.

Example 8.1 Suppose we have the following query and views:

Q(x,y) :- e1(x,z), e2(z,y)
V1(x,y) :- e1(x,y)
V2(z,y) :- e2(z,y)
V3(x) :- e1(x,z), e2(z,y)

If the join of e1 and e2 is very selective, the rewriting of the query that will yield the cheapest query execution plan may be:

q'(x,y) :- v3(x), v1(x,y), v2(z,y).

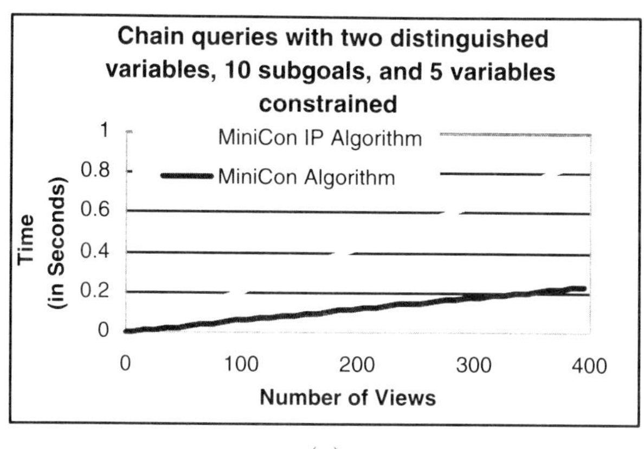

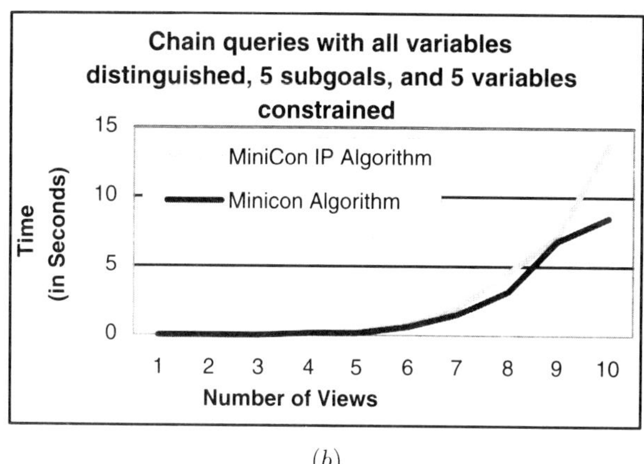

(a) (b)

Figure 6: Experiments with the MiniCon algorithm and comparison predicates. The left graph shows the same case as in Figure 4(a) and shows that adding comparison predicates only slows down the running time by a factor of 4. The graph on the right shows the running times when all of the variables in the views are distinguished.

However, the MiniCon algorithm would not create a MCD that includes V3, because it would violate Property 1, and would hence miss this rewriting. $\square$

Hence, to extend the MiniCon algorithm to this context we need to establish a bound on the size of rewritings that need to be considered, and to relax the definition of MCDs.

References

[1] S. Abiteboul and O. Duschka. Complexity of answering queries using materialized views. In *PODS*, 1998.

[2] F. Afrati, M. Gergatsoulis, and T. Kavalieros. Answering queries using materialized views with disjunctions. In *ICDT*, 1999.

[3] R. Bello, K. Dias, A. Downing, J. Feenan, J. Finnerty, W. Norcott, H. Sun, A. Witkowski, and M. Ziauddin. Materialized views in oracle. In *VLDB*, 1998.

[4] D. Calvanese, G. D. Giacomo, M. Lenzerini, and M. Vardi. Rewriting of regular expressions and regular path queries. In *PODS*, 1999.

[5] A. Chandra and P. Merlin. Optimal implementation of conjunctive queries in relational databases. In *Proceedings of the Ninth Annual ACM Symposium on Theory of Computing*, pages 77–90, 1977.

[6] S. Chaudhuri, R. Krishnamurthy, S. Potamianos, and K. Shim. Optimizing queries with materialized views. In *ICDE*, 1995.

[7] S. Cohen, W. Nutt, and A. Serebrenik. Rewriting aggregate queries using views. In *PODS*, 1999.

[8] O. M. Duschka and M. R. Genesereth. Answering recursive queries using views. In *PODS*, 1997.

[9] O. M. Duschka and M. R. Genesereth. Query planning in infomaster. In *Proceedings of the ACM Symposium on Applied Computing*, 1997.

[10] O. M. Duschka and A. Y. Levy. Recursive plans for information gathering. In *IJCAI*, 1997.

[11] D. Florescu, L. Raschid, and P. Valduriez. A methodology for query reformulation in cis using semantic knowledge. *Int. Journal of Intelligent & Cooperative Information Systems, special issue on Formal Methods in Cooperative Information Systems*, 5(4), 1996.

[12] M. Friedman and D. Weld. Efficient execution of information gathering plans. In *IJCAI*, 1997.

[13] S. Grumbach, M. Rafanelli, and L. Tininini. Querying aggregate data. In *PODS*, 1999.

[14] J. Gryz. Query folding with inclusion dependencies. In *ICDE*, 1998.

[15] A. Gupta, V. Harinarayan, and D. Quass. Aggregate-query processing in data warehousing environments. In *VLDB*, 1995.

[16] V. Harinarayan, A. Rajaraman, and J. D. Ullman. Implementing data cubes efficiently. In *SIGMOD*, 1996.

[17] A. Klug. On conjunctive queries containing inequalities. *Journal of the ACM*, pages 35(1): 146–160, 1988.

[18] C. T. Kwok and D. S. Weld. Planning to gather information. In *AAAI*, 1996.

[19] E. Lambrecht, S. Kambhampati, and S. Gnanaprakasam. Optimizing recursive information gathering plans. In *IJCAI*, pages 1204–1210, 1999.

[20] A. Y. Levy. Answering queries using views: A survey, 2000. Manuscript available from www.cs.washington.edu/homes/alon/views.ps.

[21] A. Y. Levy, A. O. Mendelzon, Y. Sagiv, and D. Srivastava. Answering queries using views. In *PODS*, 1995.

[22] A. Y. Levy, A. Rajaraman, and J. J. Ordille. Querying heterogeneous information sources using source descriptions. In *VLDB*, 1996.

[23] R. J. Miller. Using schematically heterogeneous structures. In *SIGMOD*, 1998.

[24] P. Mitra. An algorithm for answering queries efficiently using views. Stanford University Technical Report, Stanford, CA, USA, 1999.

[25] M. Steinbrunn, G. Moerkotte, and A. Kemper. Heuristic and randomized optimization for the join. *VLDB Journal*, 6(3):191–208, 1997.

[26] Y. Papakonstantinou and V. Vassalos. Query rewriting for semistructured data. In *SIGMOD*, 1999.

[27] L. Popa, A. Deutsch, A. Sahuguet, and V. Tannen. A chase too far? In *SIGMOD*, 2000.

[28] R. Pottinger and A. Levy. A scalable algorithm for answering queries using views. Technical Report UW-CSE-2000-06-01, University of Washington Department of Computer Science and Engineering, 2000.

[29] X. Qian. Query folding. In *ICDE*, pages 48–55, New Orleans, LA, 1996.

[30] A. Rajaraman, Y. Sagiv, and J. D. Ullman. Answering queries using templates with binding patterns. In *PODS*, 1995.

[31] D. Srivastava, S. Dar, H. V. Jagadish, and A. Y. Levy. Answering SQL queries using materialized views. In *VLDB*, 1996.

[32] D. Theodoratos and T. Sellis. Data warehouse design. In *VLDB*, 1997.

[33] O. G. Tsatalos, M. H. Solomon, and Y. E. Ioannidis. The GMAP: A versatile tool for physical data independence. *VLDB Journal*, 5(2):101–118, 1996.

[34] J. D. Ullman. *Principles of Database and Knowledge-base Systems, Volumes I, II*. Computer Science Press, Rockville MD, 1989.

[35] H. Z. Yang and P. A. Larson. Query transformation for PSJ-queries. In *VLDB*, 1987.

[36] M. Zaharioudakis, R. Cochrane, G. Lapis, H. Pirahesh, and M. Urata. Answering complex SQL queries using automatic summary tables. In *SIGMOD*, 2000.

Automated Selection of Materialized Views and Indexes for SQL Databases

Sanjay Agrawal
Microsoft Research
sagrawal@microsoft.com

Surajit Chaudhuri
Microsoft Research
surajitc@microsoft.com

Vivek Narasayya
Microsoft Research
viveknar@microsoft.com

Abstract

Automatically selecting an appropriate set of materialized views and indexes for SQL databases is a non-trivial task. A judicious choice must be cost-driven and influenced by the workload experienced by the system. Although there has been work in materialized view selection in the context of multidimensional (OLAP) databases, no past work has looked at the problem of building an industry-strength tool for automated selection of materialized views *and* indexes for SQL workloads. In this paper, we present an end-to-end solution to the problem of selecting materialized views and indexes. We describe results of extensive experimental evaluation that demonstrate the effectiveness of our techniques. Our solution is implemented as part of a tuning wizard that ships with Microsoft SQL Server 2000.

1. Introduction

In addition to indexes, today's commercial SQL database systems also support creation and use of materialized views. The presence of the right materialized views can significantly improve performance, particularly for decision support applications. However, to realize this potential, a judicious selection of materialized views is crucial.

Conceptually, both indexes and materialized views are physical structures that can significantly accelerate performance. An effective physical database design tool must therefore take into account the interaction between indexes and materialized views by considering them together to optimize the physical design for the workload on the system. Ignoring this interaction can significantly compromise the quality of recommendations. Despite a large number of recent papers in this area, most of the prior work considers the problems of index selection and materialized view selection in isolation.

Although indexes and materialized views are similar, a materialized view is much richer in structure than an index since a materialized view may be defined over multiple tables, and can have selections and GROUP BY over multiple columns. In fact, an index can logically be considered as a special case of a single-table, projection only materialized view. This richness of structure of materialized views makes the problem of selecting materialized views significantly more complex than that of index selection. We therefore need innovative techniques for dealing with the large space of potentially interesting materialized views that are possible for a given set of SQL queries and updates over a large schema. Previous papers on materialized view selection typically ignore this problem. Rather, they focus only on the "search" problem of picking an attractive set of materialized views from a given set. Thus, they implicitly assume that the given set is the set of all potentially interesting materialized views for the workload. Such an approach is simply not scalable in the context of SQL workloads. Finally, to be an effective solution, it is important to ensure that the solution to this problem is robust and takes into account the complexities of full SQL as a query language, as well as pragmatic issues such as the fact that in today's commercial database systems, it is often the case that the language of materialized views is a restricted subset of the language of queries. For example, a materialized view may not be allowed to contain nested sub-queries.

In this paper, we present an architecture and novel algorithms for addressing each of the above problems. Our work leverages previous work we did in building an index selection tool for Microsoft SQL Server [4,5], but requires several significant innovations. We establish that in order to pick a physical design consisting of indexes and materialized views, it is critical to search over the combined space of indexes and materialized views (Section 5). We quantify the impact on quality of *not* enumerating this space together, particularly in the presence of storage constraints or updates. Second, we present a principled way to identify a much smaller set of *candidate* materialized views such that searching over the reduced space of candidate materialized views preserves most of the gains of searching the entire space of possible

Proceedings of the 26th International Conference on Very Large Databases, Cairo, Egypt, 2000

materialized views, at a fraction of the enumeration cost (Section 4). We introduce two key techniques that form the basis of a scalable approach for candidate materialized view selection. First, we show how to identify *interesting sets of tables* such that we need to consider materialized views only over such sets of tables. Next, we present a *view merging* technique that identifies candidate materialized views that while not optimal for any single query, can be beneficial to multiple queries in the workload. The techniques presented in this paper are designed to be robust for handling the generality of SQL as well as other pragmatic issues arising in index and materialized view selection. These techniques have enabled us to build an industry-strength physical database design tool that can determine an appropriate set of indexes, materialized views (and indexes on materialized views) for a given database and *workload* consisting of SQL queries and updates. This tool is now part of Microsoft SQL Server 2000's upcoming release. The extensive experimental results in this paper (Section 6) demonstrate the value of our proposed techniques. This work was done as part of the AutoAdmin [1] research project at Microsoft, which explores novel techniques to make databases self-tuning.

2. Architecture for Index and Materialized View Selection

An architectural overview of our approach to index and materialized view selection is shown in Figure 1. We assume that we are given a representative workload for which we need to recommend indexes and materialized views. One way to obtain such a workload is to use the logging capability of modern database systems to capture a trace of queries and updates faced by the system. Alternatively, customer or organization specific benchmarks may be used. As in our previous work on index selection [4], the key components of the architecture are: *syntactic structure selection, candidate selection, configuration enumeration,* and *configuration simulation and cost estimation.*

Given a workload, the first step is to identify *syntactically relevant* indexes, materialized views and indexes on materialized views that can potentially be used to answer the query. For example, consider a query **Q**: SELECT Sum(Sales) FROM Sales_Data WHERE City = 'Seattle'. For the query **Q**, the following materialized views (among others) are syntactically relevant: v_1: SELECT Sum(Sales) FROM Sales_Data WHERE City = 'Seattle'. v_2: SELECT City, Sum(Sales) FROM Sales_Data GROUP BY City. v_3: SELECT City, Product, Sum(Sales) FROM Sales_Data GROUP BY City, Product. Optionally, we can consider additional indexes on the columns of the materialized view. Like indexes on base tables, indexes on materialized views can be single-column or multi-column, clustered or non-clustered, with the restriction that a given materialized view can have at most one clustered index on it. In this paper, we focus on the class of single-block materialized views consisting of selection, join, grouping and aggregation. The workload however, may consist of arbitrary SQL statements. In this paper, we do not consider materialized views that can be exploited using back-joins by the optimizer.

As mentioned in the introduction, searching the space of all syntactically relevant indexes and materialized views for a workload is infeasible in practice, particularly when the workload is large or complex. Therefore, it is crucial to eliminate spurious indexes and materialized views from consideration early, thereby focusing the search on a smaller, and interesting subset. The *candidate selection* module is responsible for identifying a set of traditional indexes, materialized views and indexes on materialized views for the given workload that are worthy of further exploration. Efficient selection of candidate materialized views is a key contribution of our work. For the purposes of this paper, we assume that candidate indexes have already been picked. For details on how candidate indexes may be chosen for a workload, we refer the reader to [4].

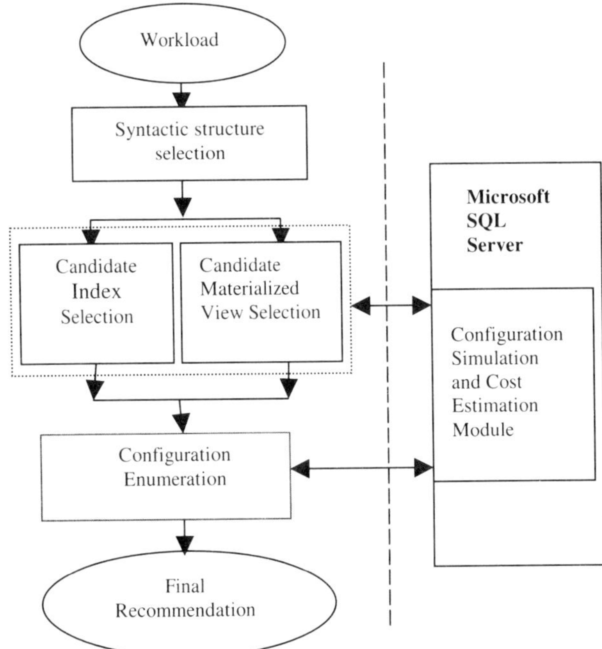

Figure 1. Architecture of Index and Materialized View Selection Tool

Once we have chosen a set of candidate indexes and candidate materialized views, we need to search among these structures to determine the ideal physical design, henceforth called a **configuration**. In our context, a configuration will consist of a set of traditional indexes, materialized views and indexes on materialized views. In this paper we will not discuss issues related to selection of indexes on materialized views due to lack of space. Despite the remarkable pruning achieved by the *candidate selection* module, searching through this space in a naïve fashion by enumerating all subsets of structures is infeasible. We adopt the same greedy algorithm for *configuration enumeration* as was used in [4]: Greedy(m,k). This algorithm returns a configuration consisting of a total of k indexes and materialized views. It first picks an optimal configuration of size up to m ($\leq$ k) by exhaustively enumerating all configurations of size up to m. It then picks the remaining (k-m) structures greedily. As will be shown in Section 6.2.4, this algorithm works well even when the set of candidates contains materialized views in addition to indexes. An important characteristic of our approach is that *configuration enumeration* is over the *joint* space of indexes and materialized views.

The configurations considered by the *configuration enumeration* module are compared for quality by taking into account the expected impact of the proposed configurations on the sum of the cost of queries in the workload. The *configuration simulation and cost estimation* module is responsible for providing this support. We have extended Microsoft SQL server to simulate the presence of indexes and materialized views that do not exist (referred to as "what-if" indexes and materialized views) to the query optimizer, and have also extended the optimizer costing module, so that given a query Q and a configuration C, the cost of Q when the physical design is the configuration C, may be computed. A detailed discussion of simulation of what-if structures is beyond the scope of this paper (see [5]). Finally, we note that index and materialized view maintenance costs are accounted for in our approach by the inclusion of updates/inserts/deletes statements in the workload.

3.   Related Work

Recently, there have been several papers on selection of materialized views in the OLAP/Data Cube context [9,10,11,12,18]. These papers assume that the set of candidate materialized views is identical to the set of syntactically relevant materialized views for the workload[1]. As argued earlier, such a technique is not scalable for reasonably large SQL workloads since the space of syntactically relevant materialized views is very large. The focus of the above papers is almost exclusively on the *configuration enumeration* problem. In principle, their proposed enumeration schemes may be adopted in our architecture by simply substituting Greedy(m,k). Thus, we view the work presented in the above papers to be complementary to the work presented in this paper. Although one of the papers [11] studies the interaction of materialized views with indexes on materialized views, none of the papers consider interaction among selection of indexes on base tables and selection of materialized views. Thus, they implicitly assume that indexes are either already picked, or will be picked after selection of materialized views. As will be shown in this paper, both these alternatives severely impact quality of the solution.

The work by Baralis et al. [3] is also set in the context of OLAP/Data Cube and does not consider traditional indexes on base tables. For a given workload, they consider materialized views that exactly match queries in the workload, as well as a set of additional views that can leverage commonality among queries in the workload. Our technique for exploiting commonality among queries in the workload for candidate materialized view selection (Section 4.3) is different. Further, our techniques can also deal with arbitrary SQL workloads and materialized views with selection.

In the context of SQL databases and workloads, the work by [22] picks materialized views by examining the

plan information of queries. However, since the plan is an artifact of the existing physical design, such an approach can lead to sub-optimal recommendations. The paper also suggests an alternative of examining all possible query plans of a query. However, the latter technique is not scalable for even moderately sized workloads.

There is a substantial body of work in the area of index selection that describes how to pick a good set of indexes for a given workload [4,8,16]. More recently, other commercial systems have also added support for automatically picking indexes [14,20]. The architecture adopted in our scheme is in the spirit of [4]. However, as noted above, the candidate materialized view selection as well as the comparison of alternative strategies to pick indexes on base tables along with materialized views, constitute novel and important contributions of this paper. Rozen [15] presents a framework for choosing a physical design consisting of various "feature sets" including indexes and materialized views. The space of materialized views considered in Rozen's thesis is restricted to single-table aggregation views with GROUP BY, whereas we allow materialized views to consist of join selection, grouping and aggregation operators,

Some commercial systems (e.g., Redbrick/Informix [16] and Oracle 8i [14]) provide tools to tune the selection of materialized views for a workload. As with the body of the work referenced above, these tools exclusively recommend materialized views. In contrast, we present an integrated tool that can recommend indexes on base tables as well as materialized views (and indexes on them) by weighing in the impact of both on the performance of the workload. Finally, our paper is concerned with selection of materialized views but not with techniques to rewrite queries in the presence of materialized views.

4.   Candidate Materialized View Selection

Considering all syntactically relevant materialized views for a workload in the *configuration enumeration* phase (see Figure 1) is not scalable since it would explode the space of configurations that must be searched. The space of syntactically relevant materialized views for a query (and hence a workload) is very large, since in principle, a materialized view can be proposed on any subset of tables in the query. Furthermore, even for a given *table-subset* (a table-subset is a subset of tables referenced in a query in the workload.), there is an explosion in the space of materialized views arising from selection conditions and group by columns in the query. If there are m selection conditions in the query on a table-subset T, then materialized views containing any subset of these selection conditions are syntactically relevant. Therefore, the goal of *candidate materialized view selection* is to quickly eliminate materialized views that are syntactically relevant for one or more queries in the workload but are never used in answering any query from entering the *configuration enumeration* phase.

We observe that the obvious approach of selecting one candidate materialized view per query that exactly matches each query in the workload does not work since in many database systems the language of materialized views may not match the language of queries. For example, nested sub-queries can appear in the query but may not be part of the materialized view language.

---

[1] Typically, these are aggregation views over subsets of dimensions. For each subset of dimensions, multiple aggregate views are possible in the presence of dimension hierarchy.

Moreover, in storage-constrained environments, ignoring commonality across queries in the workload can result in sub-optimal quality. This problem is even more severe in large workloads. The following simplified example of Q_1 from the TPC-H benchmark illustrates this point:

Example 1. Consider a workload consisting of 1000 queries of the form: SELECT l_returnflag, l_linestatus, SUM(l_quantity) FROM lineitem WHERE l_shipdate BETWEEN <Date1> and <Date2> GROUP BY l_returnflag, l_linestatus. Assume that each of the 1000 queries has different constants for <Date1> and <Date2>. Then, rather than recommending 1000 materialized views, the following materialized view that can service all 1000 queries may be more attractive for the entire workload: SELECT l_shipdate, l_returnflag, l_linestatus, SUM(l_quantity) FROM lineitem GROUP BY l_shipdate, l_returnflag, l_linestatus.

A second observation that influences our approach to candidate materialized view selection is that there are certain table-subsets such that, even if we were to propose materialized views on those subsets it would only lead to a small reduction in cost for the entire workload. This can happen either because the table-subsets occur infrequently in the workload or they occur only in inexpensive queries.

Example 2. Consider a workload of 100 queries whose total cost is 10,000 units. Let T be a table-subset that occurs in 25 queries whose combined cost is 50 units. Then even if we considered all syntactically relevant materialized views on T, the maximum possible benefit of those materialized views for the workload is 0.5%.

Furthermore, even among table-subsets that occur frequently or occur in expensive queries, not all table-subsets are likely to be equally useful.

Example 3. Consider the TPC-H 1GB database and the workload specified in the benchmark. There are several queries in which the tables, lineitem, orders, nation, and region co-occur. However, it is likely that materialized views proposed on the table-subset {*lineitem, orders*} are more useful than materialized views proposed on {*nation, region*}. This is because the tables *lineitem* and *orders* have 6 million and 1.5 million rows respectively, but tables *nation* and *region* are very small (25 and 5 rows respectively). Hence, the benefit of pre-computing the portion of the queries involving {*nation, region*} is insignificant compared to the benefit of pre-computing the portion of the query involving {*lineitem, orders*}.

Based on these observations, we approach the task of *candidate materialized view selection* using three steps: (1) From the large space of all possible table-subsets for the workload, we arrive at a smaller set of interesting table-subsets (Section 4.1). (2) Based on these interesting table-subsets, we propose a set of materialized views for each query in the workload, and from this set we select a configuration that is best for that query. This step uses a cost-based analysis for selecting the best configuration for a query (Section 4.2). (3) Starting with the views selected in (2), we generate an additional set of "merged" materialized views in a controlled manner such that the merged materialized views can service multiple queries in the workload (Section 4.3). The new set of merged materialized views, along with the materialized views selected in (2) is the set of candidate materialized views that enters *configuration enumeration*. We now present the details of each of these steps.

4.1. Finding Interesting Table-Subsets

Our goal is to find "interesting" table-subsets from among all possible table-subsets for the workload, and restrict the space of materialized views considered to only those table-subsets. Intuitively, a table-subset T is interesting if materializing one or more views on T has the potential to reduce the cost of the workload significantly, i.e., above a given threshold. Thus, the first step is to define a metric that captures the relative importance of a table-subset.

Consider the following metric: $TS\text{-}Cost(T)$ = total cost[2] of all queries in the workload (for the current database) where table-subset T occurs. The above metric, while simple, is not a good measure of relative importance of a table-subset. For example, in the context of Example 3, if all queries in the workload referenced the tables *lineitem*, *orders*, *nation*, and *region* together, then using the $TS\text{-}Cost(T)$ metric, the table-subsets T_1 = {*lineitem, orders*} would have the same importance as the table-subset T_2 = {*nation, region*} even though a materialized view on T_1 is likely to be much more useful than a materialized view on T_2. Therefore, we propose the following metric that better captures the relative importance of a table-subset: $TS\text{-}Weight(T)$ = $\sum_i Cost(Q_i)*$(sum of sizes of tables in T)/ (sum of sizes of all tables referenced in Q_i)), where the summation is only over queries in the workload where T occurs. Observe that $TS\text{-}Weight$ is a simple function that can discriminate between table-subsets even if they occur in exactly the same queries in the workload. A complete evaluation of this and alternative functions, and their relationship to cost estimation by the query optimizer is part of our ongoing work.

1.   Let S_1 = {T | T is a table-subset of size 1 satisfying $TS\text{-}Cost(T) \geq$ **C**}; i = 1
2.   **While** i < MAX-TABLES and $|S_i| > 0$
3.   i = i + 1; S_i = { }
4.   Let G ={T | T is a table-subset of size i, and $\exists$ s $\in$ S_{i-1} such that s $\subset$ T}
5.   **For** each T $\in$ G
         If $TS\text{-}Cost$ (T) $\geq$ **C** **Then** S_i = $S_i \cup$ {T}
6.   **End For**
7.   **End While**
8. $S = S_1 \cup S_2 \cup \dots S_{\text{MAX-TABLES}}$
9. $R = \{T \mid T \in S$ and $TS\text{-}Weight(T) \geq$ **C**}
10. **Return** R

Figure 2. Algorithm for finding interesting table-subsets in the workload.

Although $TS\text{-}Weight(T)$ is a reasonable metric for relative importance of a table-subset, there does not appear to be an obvious efficient algorithm for finding all table subsets whose $TS\text{-}Weight$ exceeds a given threshold. In contrast, the $TS\text{-}Cost$ metric has the property of "monotonicity" since for table subsets T_1, T_2, $T_1 \subseteq T_2 \Rightarrow TS\text{-}Cost(T_1) \geq TS\text{-}Cost(T_2)$. This is because in all queries where T_2 occurs, T_1 (and likewise all other subsets of T_2)

---

[2] The cost of a query (or update statement) Q, denoted by $Cost(Q)$ can be obtained from the *configuration simulation and cost estimation* shown in Figure 1.

also occur. This monotonicity property of *TS-Cost* allows us to leverage efficient algorithms proposed for identifying frequent itemsets, e.g., as in [2], to identify all table-subsets whose *TS-Cost* exceeds the specified threshold. Fortunately, it is also the case that if *TS-Weight(T)* $\geq$ **C** (for any threshold **C**), then *TS-Cost(T)* $\geq$ **C**. Therefore, our algorithm (shown in Figure 2) for identifying interesting table-subsets by the *TS-Weight* metric has two steps: (a) Prune table-subsets not satisfying the given threshold using the *TS-Cost* metric. (b) Prune the table-subsets retained in (a) that do not satisfy the given threshold using the *TS-Weight* metric. We note that the efficiency gained by the algorithm is due to reduced CPU and memory costs by not having to enumerate all table-subsets.

In Figure 2, we define the *size* of a table-subset T to be the number of tables in T. MAX-TABLES is the maximum number of tables referenced in any query in the workload. A lower threshold **C** leads to a larger space being considered and vice versa. Based on experiments on various databases and workloads, we found that using **C** = 10% of the total workload cost had a negligible negative impact on the solution compared to the case when there is no cut off (**C** = 0), but was significantly faster (see Section 6.2.1 for details).

4.2. Exploiting the Query Optimizer to Prune Syntactically Relevant Materialized Views

The algorithm for identifying interesting table-subsets presented in Section 4.1 significantly reduces the number of syntactically relevant materialized views that must be considered for a workload. Nonetheless, many of these views may still not be useful for answering any query in the workload. This is because the decision of whether or not a materialized view is useful in answering a query is made by the *query optimizer* using cost estimation. Therefore, our goal is to prevent syntactically relevant materialized views that are not used in answering any query from being considered during *configuration enumeration*. We achieve this goal using the algorithm shown in Figure 3, which is based on the intuition that if a materialized view is not part of the best solution for even a single query in the workload, then it is unlikely to be part of the best solution for the entire workload. This approach is similar to the one used in [4] for selecting candidate indexes. For a given query Q, and a set S of materialized views (and indexes on them) proposed for Q, Step 4 of our algorithm assumes the existence of the function *Find-Best-Configuration*(Q, S) that returns the best configuration for Q from S. *Find-Best-Configuration* has the property that the choice of the best configuration for a query is cost based, i.e., it is the configuration that the optimizer estimates as having the lowest cost for Q. Any suitable search method can be used in this function, e.g., the Greedy(m,k) algorithm described in Section 2. We also see that in the presence of updates or storage constraints, we may need to pick more than one configuration for a query (e.g., the **n** best configurations) in Step 4 to maintain quality, at the expense of increased running time during *configuration enumeration* [4].

Next we discuss the issue of which syntactically relevant materialized views should proposed for a query Q_i in Step 3. Observe that among the interesting table-

subsets that occur in Q_i, it is not sufficient to propose materialized views only on the table-subset that exactly matches the tables referenced in Q_i. One reason for this is that the language of views may not match the language of queries, e.g., the query may contain a nested sub-query whereas the view cannot. Also, for complex queries the query optimizer performs algebraic transformations of the query to find a better execution plan. In such cases, determining which of the interesting table-subsets to consider requires analysis of the structure of the query as well as knowledge of the transformations considered by the query optimizer. We also note that due to the pruning of table-subsets in previous step (Section 4.1), the table-subset that exactly matches the tables referenced in the query may not even be deemed interesting. In such cases, it again becomes important to consider smaller interesting table-subsets that occur in Q_i. Fortunately, due to the effective pruning achieved by the algorithm for finding interesting table-subsets (Figure 2), we are able to take the simple approach of proposing syntactically relevant materialized views for a query Q_i on *all* interesting table subsets that occur in Q_i.

1.   M = {} /* M is the set of materialized views that is useful for at least one query in the workload W*/
2.   **For** i = 1 to |W|
3.   Let S_i = Set of materialized views proposed for query Q_i.
4.   C = *Find-Best-Configuration* (Q_i, S_i)
5.   M = M $\cup$ C;
6.   **End For**
7.   **Return** M

Figure 3. Cost-based pruning of syntactically relevant materialized views.

For each such interesting table-subset T, we propose (in Step 3): (1) A "pure-join"[3] materialized view on T containing join and selection conditions in Q_i on tables in T. (2) If Q_i has grouping columns, then a materialized view similar to (1) but also containing GROUP BY columns and aggregate expression from Q_i on tables in T. It is also possible to propose additional materialized views on a table-subset that include only a *subset* of the selection conditions in the query on tables in T, since such views may also apply to other queries in the workload. However, in our approach, this aspect of exploiting commonality across queries in the workload is handled via view merging (Section 4.3). For each materialized view proposed, we also propose a set of clustered and non-clustered indexes on the materialized view. We omit the details of this discussion due to lack of space. Our experiments (see Section 6.2.3) show that the above algorithm is not only efficient, but it dramatically reduces the number of materialized views that need to be considered in *configuration enumeration* (Figure 1).

4.3. View Merging

We observe that if the materialized views that enter *configuration enumeration* are limited to the ones selected

---

[3] In principle, such a "pure-join" materialized view can also be generated via view merging (Section 4.3). We omit this discussion due to lack of space.

by the algorithm presented in Section 4.2, then we can get sub-optimal recommendations for the workload when storage is constrained (see Example 1). This observation suggests that we need to consider the space of materialized views that although are not optimal for any individual query, are useful for multiple queries, and therefore may be optimal for the workload. However, proposing such a set of syntactically relevant materialized views by analyzing multiple queries at once could lead to an explosion in the number of merged materialized views proposed. Instead, our approach is based on the observation that M, the set of materialized views returned by the algorithm in Figure 2 (Section 4.2), contains materialized views selected on a cost-basis and are therefore sure (or very likely) to be used by the query optimizer. This set M is therefore a good starting point for generating additional "merged" materialized views that are derived by exploiting commonality among views in M. The newly generated set of merged views, along with M, are our candidate materialized views. Our approach is significantly more scalable than the alternative of generated merged views starting from all syntactically relevant materialized views.

An important issue in view merging is characterizing the space of merged views to be explored. In our approach, we have decided to explore this space using a sequence of pair-wise merges. Thus, the two key issues that must be addressed are: (1) determining the criteria that govern when and how a given pair of views is merged (Section 4.3.1), and (2) enumerating the space of possible merged views (Section 4.3.2). Architecturally, our approach for view merging is similar to the one adopted in our prior work on *index merging* [7]. However, the algorithm for merging a pair of views needs to recognize the fact that views (unlike indexes) are multi-table structures that may contain selections, grouping and aggregation. These differences significantly influence the way in which a given pair of views is merged.

4.3.1. Merging a Pair of Views

Our goal when merging a given pair of views, referred to as the *parent* views, is to generate a new view, called the *merged* view, which has the following two properties. First, all queries that can be answered using either of the parent views should be answerable using the merged view. Second, the cost of answering these queries using the merged view should not be significantly higher than the cost of answering the queries using views in M (the set obtained using algorithm in Figure 2). Our algorithm for merging a pair of views, called *MergeViewPair*, is shown in Figure 4. Intuitively, the algorithm achieves the first property by structurally modifying the parent views as little as possible when generating the merged view, i.e., by retaining the common aspects of the parent views and generalizing only their differences. For simplicity, we present the algorithm for SPJ views with grouping and aggregation, where the selection conditions are conjunctions of simple predicates. The algorithm can be generalized to handle complex selection conditions as well as account for differences in constants between conditions on the same column.

Note that a merged view v may be derived starting from views in M through a sequence of pair-wise merges.

We define Parent-Closure(v) as the set of views in M from which v is derived. The goal of Step 4 in the *MergeViewPair* algorithm is to achieve the second property mentioned above by preventing a merged view from being generated if it is much larger than the views in Parent-Closure(v). Precisely characterizing the factors that determine the value of the size increase threshold (x) requires further work. In our implementation on Microsoft SQL Server, we have found that setting x between 1 and 2 works well over a variety of databases and workloads.

<table>
<tr><td>1.</td><td>Let v_1 and v_2 be a pair of materialized views that reference the same tables and the same join conditions.</td></tr>
<tr><td>2.</td><td>Let $s_{11}, \ldots s_{1m}$ be the selection conditions that occur in v_1 but not in v_2. Let $s_{21}, \ldots s_{2n}$ be the selection conditions that occur in v_2 but not in v_1.</td></tr>
<tr><td>3.</td><td>Let v_{12} be the view obtained by (a) taking the union of the projection columns of v_1 and v_2 (b) taking the union of the GROUP BY columns of v_1 and v_2 (c) pushing the columns $s_{11}, \ldots s_{1m}$ and $s_{21}, \ldots s_{2n}$ into the GROUP BY clause of v_{12} and (d) including selection conditions common to v_1 and v_2.</td></tr>
<tr><td>4.</td><td>If $((|v_{12}| > $ Min Size (Parent-Closure $(v_1) \cup$ Parent-Closure $(v_2)) * \mathbf{x})$ Then Return Null.</td></tr>
<tr><td>5.</td><td>Return v_{12}.</td></tr>
</table>

Figure 4. MergeViewPair algorithm

We note that in Step 4, *MergeViewPair* requires estimating the size of a materialized view. One way to achieve this is to obtain an estimate of the view size from the query optimizer. The accuracy of such estimation depends on the availability of an appropriate set of statistics for query optimization [6]. Alternatively, less expensive heuristic techniques have been proposed in [19] for more restricted multidimensional scenarios.

<table>
<tr><td>1.</td><td>R = M</td></tr>
<tr><td>2.</td><td>While (|R| > 1)</td></tr>
<tr><td>3.</td><td>Let M' = The set of merged views obtained by calling MergeViewPair on each pair of views in R.</td></tr>
<tr><td>4.</td><td>If M' = { } Return (R–M)</td></tr>
<tr><td>5.</td><td>R = R $\cup$ M'</td></tr>
<tr><td>6.</td><td>For each view v $\in$ M', remove both parents of v from R</td></tr>
<tr><td>7.</td><td>End While</td></tr>
<tr><td>8.</td><td>Return (R–M).</td></tr>
</table>

Figure 5. Algorithm for generating a set of merged views from a given set of views M

4.3.2. Algorithm for generating merged views

Our algorithm for generating a set of merged views from a given set of views is shown in Figure 5. As mentioned earlier, we invoke this algorithm with the set of materialized views M (obtained using the algorithm in Figure 3). We comment on several properties of the algorithm. First, note that it is possible for a merged materialized view generated in Step 3 to be merged again in a subsequent iteration of the outer loop (Steps 2-7). This allows more than two views in M to be combined into one merged view even though the merging is done pair-wise. Second, although the number of new merged views explored by this algorithm can be exponential in the size of M in the worst case, we observe that much fewer merged materialized views are explored in practice (see Section 6.2.3) because of the checks built into Step 4 of *MergeViewPair* (Figure 4). Third, the set of merged views returned by the algorithm does not depend on the exact sequence in which views are merged (we omit the proof due to lack of space). Furthermore, the algorithm is guaranteed to explore all merged views that can be generated using *any* sequence of merges using *MergeViewPair* starting with the views in M. The algorithm in Figure 5 has been presented in its current form for simplicity of exposition. Note however, that if views v_1 and v_2 *cannot* be merged to form v_{12}, then no other merged view derived from v_1 *and* v_2 is possible, e.g., v_{123} is not possible. We can leverage this observation to increase efficiency by using techniques for finding frequent itemsets, e.g., as in [2]. Finally, we can ensure that merged views generated by this algorithm are actually useful in answering queries in the workload, by performing a cost-based pruning using the query optimizer (similar to the algorithm in Figure 3).

5. Trading Choices of Indexes and Materialized Views

Previous work in physical database design has considered the problems of index selection and materialized view selection in isolation. However, both indexes and materialized views are fundamentally similar – both are redundant structures that speed up query execution, compete for the same resource – storage, and incur maintenance overhead in the presence of updates. Not surprisingly, indexes and materialized views can interact with one another, i.e., the presence of an index can make a materialized view more attractive and vice versa. Therefore, as described in Section 2, our approach is to consider joint enumeration of the space of candidate indexes and materialized views. In this section, we compare our approach to alternative approaches and quantify the benefit of joint enumeration.

There are two alternatives to our approach of jointly enumerating the space of indexes and materialized views. One alternative is to pick materialized views first, and then select indexes for the workload given the materialized views picked earlier (we denote this alternative by **MVFIRST**). The second alternative reverses the above order and picks indexes first, followed by materialized views (**INDFIRST**). We have implemented these alternatives on Microsoft SQL Server 2000, and conducted extensive experiments to compare their quality and efficiency. These experiments (see Section 6.2.5) support the hypothesis that joint enumeration results in significantly better quality solutions than the two alternatives, and also shows the scalability of our approach.

5.1. Selecting one feature set followed by the other

In both MVFIRST and INDFIRST, if the global storage bound is S, then we need to determine a fraction **f** ($0 \le$ **f** ≤ 1), such that a storage constraint of **f***S is applied to the selection of the first feature set. After selecting the first feature set, all the remaining storage can be used

when picking the second feature set. This raises the issue of how to determine the fraction **f** of the total storage bound to be allocated to the first feature set? In practice, the "optimal" fraction **f** depends on several attributes of the workload including amount of updates, complexity of queries; as well as the absolute value of the total storage bound. In our empirical evaluation of MVFIRST and INDFIRST we found that the optimal value of **f** changes from one workload to the next. Furthermore, even at this optimal data point, the quality of the solution is inferior in most cases compared to our approach (JOINTSEL). Another problem relevant to both INDFIRST and MVFIRST is redundant recommendations if the feature selected second is better for a query than the feature selected first. This happens since the feature set selected first is fixed and cannot be back-tracked subsequently.

A further drawback of MVFIRST is that selecting materialized views first can adversely affect the quality of candidate indexes picked. This is because for a given query, the best materialized view is likely to be more beneficial than the best index since a materialized view can pre-compute (parts of) the query (via aggregations, grouping, joins etc.). Therefore, when materialized views are chosen first, they are likely to preclude selection of potentially useful candidate indexes for the workload.

5.2. Joint Enumeration

The two attractions of joint enumeration of candidate indexes and materialized views are: (a) A graceful adjustment to storage bounds, and (b) Considering interactions between candidate indexes and candidate materialized views that are not possible in the other approaches. For example, consider a query Q for which indexes I_1, I_2 and materialized view v are candidates. Assume that I_1 alone reduces the cost of Q by 25 units and I_2 reduces the cost by 30 units, but I_1 and v together reduce the cost by 100 units. Then, using INDFIRST, I_2 would eliminate I_1 when indexes are picked, and we would not be able to get the optimal recommendation $\{I_1, v\}$. We use the Greedy(m,k) algorithm for enumeration, which allows us to treat indexes, materialized views and indexes on materialized views on the same footing. We demonstrate the quality and scalability of this algorithm for index and materialized view selection in Section 6.2.4.

6. Experiments

We have implemented the algorithms presented in this paper on Microsoft SQL Server 2000. In the first set of experiments, we evaluate the quality and running time of our algorithm for selecting *candidate materialized views* (Section 4). We demonstrate that: (1) Our algorithm for identifying interesting table-subsets for a workload (Section 4.1) does not eliminate useful materialized views, while substantially reducing the number of materialized views that need to be proposed. (2) The application of our view merging algorithm (Section 4.3) significantly improves quality of the recommendation specially when storage is at a premium.

Our second set of experiments is related to the architectural issues in this paper. We show that: (1) Our *candidate selection* module (Figure 1) significantly reduces the running time compared to an exhaustive scheme that does not use this module, while maintaining high quality recommendations. (2) Our *configuration enumeration* module Greedy(m,k) gives results comparable to an exhaustive algorithm that enumerates over all subsets of candidates, and runs significantly faster. (3) Our approach for joint enumeration over the space of indexes and materialized views (JOINTSEL) gives significantly better solutions than MVFIRST or INDFIRST.

6.1. Experimental Setup

The experiments were run on two Dell Precision 610 machines with 550 Mhz CPU and 256 MB RAM. The databases used for our tests were stored on an internal 16.9 GB hard drive.

Databases: The algorithms presented in this paper have been extensively tested on several real and synthetic databases as part of the shipping process of the tuning wizard for Microsoft SQL Server 2000. However, due to lack of space and the intrinsic difficulty of comparing our algorithms with "optimal" algorithms on large workloads, we limit our experiments to relatively small workloads on the TPC-H [20] 1GB database as well as one real-world database used within Microsoft to track the sales of products by the company. Therefore, the experiments presented should be interpreted as illustrative rather than exhaustive empirical validation.

Name	#queries	Remarks
TPCH-22	22	TPC-H benchmark
TCPH-UPD25,	25	25 % update statements
TCPH-UPD75	25	75% update statements
WKLD-4-TBL,	100	Max 4-table queries
WKLD-8-TBL	100	Max 8-table queries
WKLD-VM	50	Real-world workload
WKLD-SCALE (n)	n = 25, 50, 75, 100, 125	Workloads of increasing size

Table 1. Summary of workloads used in experiments.

Workloads: The workloads used in our experiments are summarized in Table 1. We created the synthetic workloads using a program that can generate Select, Insert, Delete and Update statements. The queries generated by this program are limited to Select, Project, Join queries with Group By and Aggregation. Nested sub-queries connected via an EXISTS clause can also be generated. In all experiments we use the cost of the workload for the recommended configuration as a measure of the *quality* of that configuration.

6.2. Experimental Results

6.2.1. *Evaluation of algorithm for identifying interesting table-subsets*

In this experiment, we evaluate the reduction in number of syntactically relevant materialized views proposed by our algorithm (see Section 4.1) and its impact on quality compared to an approach that exhaustively proposes all syntactically relevant materialized views. We carry out this comparison for three workloads: TPCH-22 (the original benchmark), WKLD-4TBL, and WKLD-8TBL (see Table 1). We used a threshold of **C**=10%. Figure 6 shows that across all three workloads, our algorithm achieves significant pruning of the space of syntactically relevant materialized views. Furthermore, as seen in Figure 7, we see a small drop in quality. This experiment shows that our pruning is effective and yet does not miss out on important table-subsets.

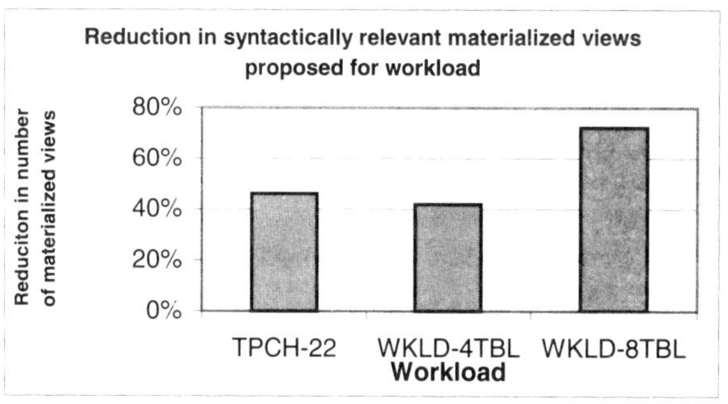

Figure 6. Reduction in syntactically relevant materialized views proposed compared to Exhaustive

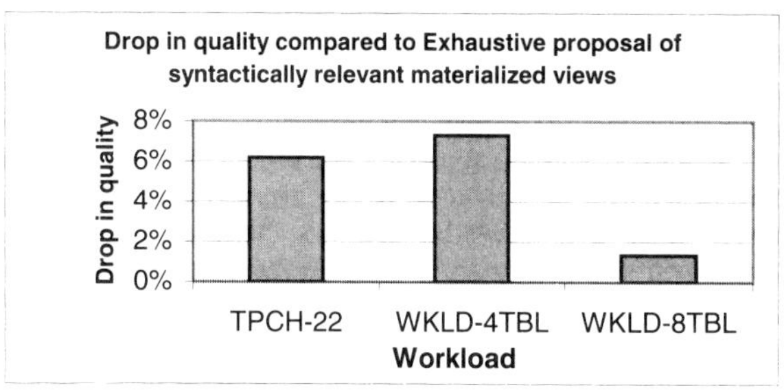

Figure 7. Comparison of quality of our algorithm to Exhaustive.

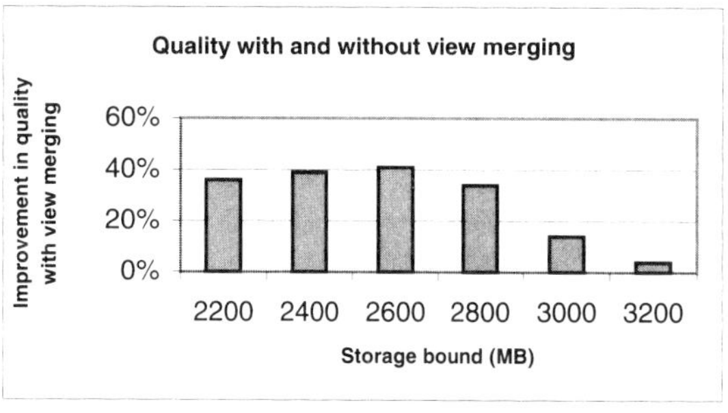

Figure 8. Quality vs. storage bound with and without view merging.

6.2.2. *Evaluation of view merging algorithm*

Next, we illustrate the importance of view merging (Section 4.3) using workload WKLD-VM (see Table 1), which consists of 50 real-world queries (SPJ with grouping and aggregation). We compare two versions of our algorithm – with and without our view merging module. Figure 8 shows the improvement in quality of the solution as the total storage bound is varied from 2.2GB to 3.2 GB. We see that at low storage constraints the version with view merging significantly outperforms the version without view merging. As expected, when the storage bound is increased, the two versions converge to the same solution. For the above workload the number of additional merged views proposed was about 19%, and the increase in running time due to view merging was about 9%. Finally, we note that yet another positive aspect of view merging is that it produces more compact recommendations (i.e., having fewer materialized views).

Workload	Ratio of running time	% improv. in quality *Without*	% improv. in quality *With*
TPC-H queries Q_1, Q_2, Q_3	64	98.1%	97.6%
TPC-H queries Q_4, Q_5	13	93.6%	93.6%
TPC-H queries Q_6, Q_7, Q_8	31	73.4%	73.4%
TPC-H queries Q_9, Q_{10}, Q_{11}	14	66.6%	60.1%

Table 2. Comparison of schemes *with* and *without* the candidate selection module.

6.2.3. *Evaluation of Candidate Selection*

Table 2 compares the running time and quality of our approach to an exhaustive approach in which the *candidate selection* step (Section 4) is omitted, i.e. all syntactically relevant materialized views and indexes are considered in the *configuration enumeration*. In both cases, we use Greedy(m,k) as the algorithm for *configuration enumeration*. Due to the large running time of the version without *candidate selection*, we restrict each workload to a small subset of the TPC-H workload. The table shows that *candidate selection* not only reduces the running time by several orders of magnitude, but the drop in quality resulting from this pruning is very small. This experiment emphasizes the importance of restricting enumeration to a set of candidates rather than all syntactically relevant indexes and materialized views. In Figure 9 we evaluate the scalability of our candidate materialized view selection technique (Section 4) as the workload size (using workloads WKLD-SCALE(n)) is increased from 25 to 125. We see that the number of candidate materialized views grows approximately linearly with the workload size.

6.2.4. *Evaluation of Enumeration algorithm*

In this experiment, we show that the Greedy(m,k) algorithm for *configuration enumeration* over the space of candidate indexes and materialized views: (a) performs well with respect to quality of recommendation compared to an exhaustive algorithm that enumerates over all subsets of candidates and (b) is significantly faster than the exhaustive approach. Table 3 shows that the Greedy(m,k) algorithm (with m=2) gives a solution that is comparable in quality to exhaustive enumeration, while it runs about an order of magnitude faster on both workloads.

6.2.5. *JOINTSEL vs. MVFIRST vs. INDFIRST*

We first compare the quality and running time of our architecture for selecting indexes and materialized views, JOINTSEL (Section 5.2), with the two alternative architectures MVFIRST and INDFIRST (Section 5.1). We study the quality of these alternatives when they are not subject to any storage constraint (i.e., storage = ∞). Table 4 shows that even with no storage constraint the quality of solution using MVFIRST is significantly worse than the quality of JOINTSEL, particularly in the presence of updates in the workload. This confirms our intuition that picking materialized views first adversely affects the subsequent selection of indexes (see Section 5.1) even in a query only workload (TPCH-22). In the presence of updates, the solution of MVFIRST degenerates rapidly (TPCH-UPD25) compared to JOINTSEL. We therefore drop this alternative from further experiments. We note that the quality of INDFIRST is comparable to JOINTSEL on TPCH-22 when storage is not an issue. In the presence of updates (TPCH-UPD25) however, the INDFIRST recommendations are inferior compared to JOINTSEL.

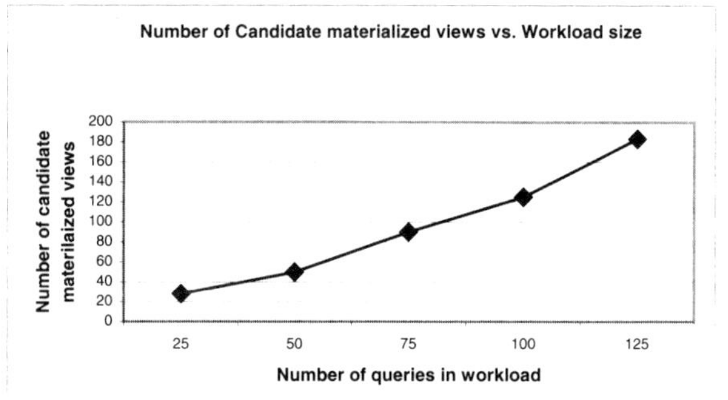

Figure 9. Scalability of candidate materialized view selection with workload size

Workload	Ratio of Running Time: Exhaustive to Greedy (m, k)	% improv in quality with Exhaustive	% improv in quality *withGreedy (m, k)*
TPCH-22	11	83%	81%
TPCH-UPD25	9	79%	77%

Table 3. Comparison of Greedy(m,k) and exhaustive enumeration algorithms.

Workload	Drop in quality of **MVFIRST** compared to **JOINTSEL**	Drop in quality of **INDFIRST** compared to **JOINTSEL**
TPCH-22	8%	0%
TPCH-UPD25	67%	11%

Table 4. Comparison of alternative schemes without storage bound (i.e., storage = ∞)

Next, we compare the quality of JOINTSEL and INDFIRST with varying storage. INDFIRST (**f**) denotes that fraction **f** of the total additional storage space is available for indexes. (with **f** = 0.25, 0.50, 0.75). We vary the additional storage allowed (**s**) between 25% of the current database size to 100% of the current database size. Figure 10 shows that JOINTSEL consistently outperforms INDFIRST for the TPCH-22 workload. In addition, we observe that for **s**=1, **f**=0.75 is the optimal partitioning fraction whereas for **s**=0.5, **f**=0.50 is the right fraction. *For a given database and a workload, the optimal storage partitioning varies with the storage constraint.* Finally, we study the behavior of INDFIRST vs. JOINTSEL for three workloads and a fixed total storage, as the fraction of storage allotted to indexes (**f**) is varied. Figure 11 shows that the best allocation fraction is different for each workload, e.g., **f** = 0.25 is best for TPC-H and TPCH-UPD25 but **f** = 0.50 is optimal for TPCH-UPD75. *For a given database and a storage space, the "right" partition varies with the workload.* In contrast, we see the consistently high quality of JOINTSEL across various workloads. We also note that the running time of JOINTSEL and INDFIRST are comparable to one another (within approximately 10% of each other for the workloads we experimented with). For example, for the data point where additional storage allowed = 100%, for the TPCH-22 workload, JOINTSEL is slightly faster than INDFIRST (**f**=0.50) by about 4% whereas for the TPCH-UPD25 workload, INDFIRST is faster by about 6%.

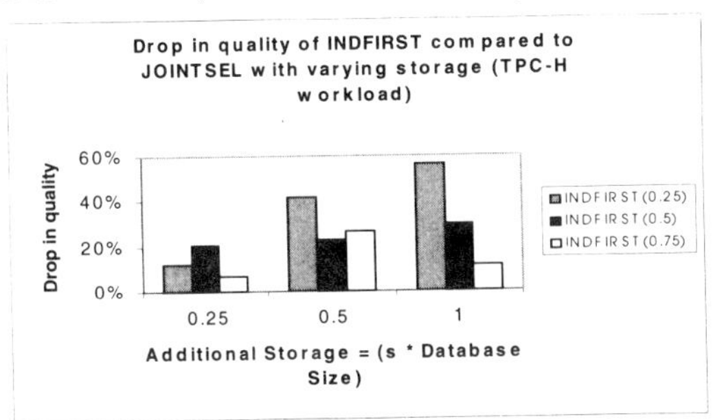

Figure 10. Quality of INDFIRST vs. JOINTSEL with varying storage bound.

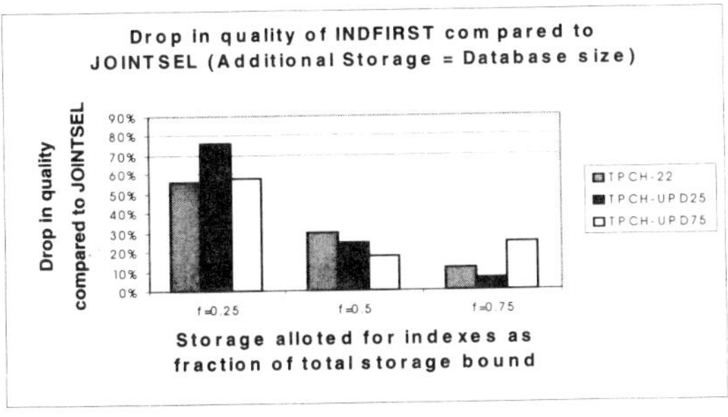

Figure 11. Quality of INDFIRST vs. JOINTSEL with varying storage partitioning (f).

7. Conclusion

The architecture and novel algorithms presented in this paper are the foundation of a robust physical database design tool for Microsoft SQL Server 2000 that can recommend both indexes and materialized views. In a recent paper, Kotidis et al.[13] present a technique for OLAP databases to dynamically determine which materialized views should be maintained. Extending this paradigm to SQL workloads is a significantly more complex problem, but is worth exploring. Another challenging task is developing a theoretical framework and appropriate abstractions for physical database design that is able to capture complexities of the physical design problem, and thus enables us to compare properties of alternative algorithms. Finally, note that indexes and materialized views are only a part of the physical design space. In the context of the AutoAdmin project [1], we continue to pursue our long-term goal of a complete physical design tool for SQL databases.

8. Acknowledgments

We thank Gautam Das for his help in analyzing the main algorithms presented in this paper. We thank the Microsoft SQL Server team with their help in providing the necessary server-side support for our implementation.

9. References

1. AutoAdmin project, Microsoft Research. http://www.research.microsoft.com/dmx/AutoAdmin
2. Agrawal R., Ramakrishnan, S. Fast Algorithms for Mining Association Rules in Large Databases, VLDB 1994.
3. Baralis E., Paraboschi S., Teniente E., Materialized View Selection in a Multidimensional Database, VLDB 1997.
4. Chaudhuri S., Narasayya V., An Efficient Cost-Driven Index Selection Tool for Microsoft SQL Server. VLDB 1997.
5. Chaudhuri S., Narasayya V., AutoAdmin "What-If" Index Analysis Utility. ACM SIGMOD 1998.
6. Chaudhuri S., Narasayya V., Automating Statistics Management for Query Optimizers. ICDE 2000.
7. Chaudhuri S., Narasayya V. Index Merging. ICDE 1999.
8. Finkelstein S, Schkolnick M, Tiberio P. Physical Database Design for Relational Databases, ACM TODS, Mar. 1988.
9. Gupta H., Selection of Views to Materialize in a Data Warehouse. ICDT, 1997.
10. Gupta H., Mumick I.S. Selection of Views to Materialize Under a Maintenance-Time Constraint. ICDT 1999.
11. Gupta H., Harinarayan V., Rajaramana A., Ullman J.D., Index Selection for OLAP, ICDE 1997.
12. Harinarayan V., Rajaramana A., Ullman J.D., Implementing Data Cubes Efficiently, ACM SIGMOD 1996.
13. Kotidis Y., Roussopoulos N. DynaMat: A Dynamic View Management System for Data Warehouses. ACM SIGMOD 1999.
14. http://www.oracle.com/
15. Rozen S. Automating Physical Database Design: An Extensible Approach, Ph.D. Dissertation. New York Univeristy, 1993.
16. http://www.informix.com/informix/solutions/dw/redbrick/vista/
17. Rozen S., Shasha D. A Framework for Automating Physical Database Design, VLDB 1991.
18. Shukla A., Deshpande P.M., Naughton J.F., Materialized View Selection for Multidimensional Datasets. VLDB 1998.
19. Shukla A., Deshpande P.M., Naughton J.F., Ramaswamy K., Storage Estimation for Multidimensional Aggregates in the Presence of Hierarchies. VLDB 1996.
20. TPC Benchmark H (Decision Support) Revision 1.1.0. http://www.tpc.org/
21. Valentin G., Zuliani M., Zilio D., Lohman G., Skelley A. DB2 Advisor: An Optimizer Smart Enough to Recommend Its Own Indexes. ICDE 2000.
22. Yang J., Karlapalem K., Li Q., Algorithms For Materialized View Design in Data Warehousing Environment. VLDB 1997.

What is the nearest neighbor in high dimensional spaces?

Alexander Hinneburg[†] Charu C. Aggarwal[‡] Daniel A. Keim[†]

[†]Institute of Computer Science, University of Halle
Kurt-Mothes-Str.1, 06120 Halle (Saale), Germany
{hinneburg, keim}@informatik.uni-halle.de

[‡]IBM T. J. Watson Research Center
Yorktown Heights, NY 10598, USA
charu@watson.ibm.com

Abstract

Nearest neighbor search in high dimensional spaces is an interesting and important problem which is relevant for a wide variety of novel database applications. As recent results show, however, the problem is a very difficult one, not only with regards to the *performance issue* but also to the *quality issue*. In this paper, we discuss the *quality issue* and identify a new generalized notion of nearest neighbor search as the relevant problem in high dimensional space. In contrast to previous approaches, our new notion of nearest neighbor search does not treat all dimensions equally but uses a quality criterion to select relevant dimensions (projections) with respect to the given query. As an example for a useful quality criterion, we rate how well the data is clustered around the query point within the selected projection. We then propose an efficient and effective algorithm to solve the generalized nearest neighbor problem. Our experiments based on a number of real and synthetic data sets show that our new approach provides new insights into the nature of nearest neighbor search on high dimensional data.

1 Introduction

Nearest neighbor search in high dimensional spaces is an interesting and important, but difficult problem. The traditional nearest neighbor problem of finding the nearest neighbor x_{NN} of a given query point $q \in \mathbb{R}^d$ in the database $D \subset \mathbb{R}^d$ is defined as

$$x_{NN} = \{x' \in D | \forall x \in D, x \neq x' :$$
$$dist(x',q) \leq dist(x,q)\}.$$

Finding the closest matching object is important for many applications. Examples include similarity search

**Proceedings of the 26th VLDB Conference,
Cairo, Egypt, 2000.**

in geometric databases [14, 12], multimedia databases [8, 17], and data mining applications such as fraud detection [11, 6], information retrieval [3, 16] among numerous other domains. Many of these domains contain applications in which the dimensionality of the representation is very high. For example, a typical feature extraction operation on an image will result in hundreds of dimensions.

Nearest neighbor problems are reasonably well solved for low dimensional applications for which efficient index structures have been proposed. Starting with the work on the R-Tree [10], a wide variety of multidimensional indexes have been proposed which work well for low dimensional data (see [9] for a comprehensive overview). These structures can support a wide range of queries such as point queries, range queries, or similarity queries to a predefined target. Many empirical studies have shown that traditional indexing methods fail in high dimensional spaces [5, 22, 4]. In such cases, almost the entire index is accessed by a single query. In fact, most indexes are handily beaten by the sequential scan [19] because of the simplicity of the latter.

However, as recent theoretical results [5] show, questions arise as to whether the problem is actually meaningful for a wide range of data distributions and distance functions. This is an even more fundamental problem, since it deals with the *quality issue* of nearest neighbor search, as opposed to the *performance issue*. If the nearest neighbor problem is not meaningful to begin with, then the importance of designing efficient data structures to do it is secondary. This paper is positioned to deal with the quality issue of nearest neighbor search, and examines several theoretical and practical aspects of performing nearest neighbor queries in high dimensional space.

There can be several reasons for the meaninglessness of nearest neighbor search in high dimensional space. One of it is the sparsity of the data objects in the space, which is unavoidable. Based on that observation it has been shown in [5] that in high dimensional space, all pairs of points are almost equidistant from one another for a wide range of data distributions and distance functions. In such cases, a nearest neighbor query is said to be *unstable*. However, the proposition of [5] is not that the difference between the distance of the nearest and the farthest data point to a given query point approaches zero with increasing dimensionality, but they proved that this difference does not increase as fast as the distance from the query point to the nearest points when the dimensionality goes to infinity. It is still an open question whether and when nearest neighbor search in high dimensional spaces is meaningful. One objective of this paper is to qualify the results reported in [5].

It is useful to understand that high-dimensional nearest neighbor problems often arise in the context of data mining or other applications, in which the notion of similarity is not firmly pre-decided by the use of any particular distance function. Currently often used is an instance of the L_p metric ($p = 1$, manhattan; $p = 2$, euclidian) based on all dimensions. In this context, many interesting questions arise as to whether the current notion of NN search solves the right problem in high dimensions. If not, then what is the nearest neighbor in high dimensions? What is the meaning of the distance metric used? One of the problems of the current notion of nearest neighbor search is that it tends to give equal treatment to all features (dimensions), which are however not of equal importance. Furthermore, the importance of a given dimension may not even be independent of the query point itself.

In this paper, we report some interesting experiments on the impact of different distance functions on the difference between the nearest and farthest neighbor. As we will see, our findings do not contradict the findings of [5] but provide interesting new insights. We discuss why the concept of nearest neighbor search in high dimensional feature spaces may fail to produce meaningful results. For that purpose, we classify the high dimensional data by their meaning. Based on our discussion and experiments, we introduce a new generalized notion of nearest neighbor search which does not treat all dimensions equally but uses a quality criterion to assess the importance of the dimensions with respect to a given query. We show that this generalized notion of nearest neighbor search, which we call *projected nearest neighbor search*, is the actually relevant one for a class of high dimensional data and develop an efficient and effective algorithm which solves the problem.

The projected nearest neighbor problem is a much more difficult problem than the traditional nearest neighbor problem because it needs to examine the proximity of the points in the database with respect to an a-priori unknown combination of dimensions. Interesting combinations of dimensions can be determined based on the inherent properties of the data and the query point which together provide some specific notion of locality. Note that the projected nearest neigh-

bor problem is closely related to the problem of projected clustering [1, 2] which determines clusters in the database by examining points and dimensions which also define some specific notion of data locality.

This paper is organized as follows. In the next section, we discuss the theoretical considerations on the meaningfulness issues for nearest neighbor search in high dimensional spaces and qualify some of the earlier results presented in [5]. In section 3, we provide a discussion of practical issues underlying the problems of high dimensional data and meaningful nearest neighbors. Our generalized notion od nearest neighbor search and an algorithm for solving the problem are presented in section 4. Section 5 discusses the empirical results and section 6 discusses the conclusions and summary.

2 Nearest Neighbor Search in high-dimensional Spaces

The results of [5] show that the relative contrast of the distances between the different points in the data set decreases with increasing dimensionality. In this section we first present some interesting theoretical and practical results which extend the results presented in [5]. The results are very interesting since – despite the pessimistic results of [5] – the results show that meaningful nearest-neighbor search in high dimensions may be possible under certain circumstances.

2.1 Theoretical Considerations

Let us first recall the important result discussed in Beyer et. al. [5] which shows that in high dimensions nearest neighbor queries become unstable. Let $Dmin_d$ be the distance of the query point[1] to the nearest neighbor and $Dmax_d$ the distance of the query point to the farthest neighbor in d-dimensional space (see Table 1 for formal definitions).

The theorem by Beyer et al. states that under certain rather general preconditions the difference between the distances of the nearest and farthest points ($Dmax_d - Dmin_d$) does not increase with the dimensionality as fast as $Dmin_d$. In other words, the ratio of $Dmax_d - Dmin_d$ to $Dmin_d$ converges to zero with increasing dimensionality. Using the definitions given in Table 1, the theorem by Beyer et al. can be formally stated as follows.

Theorem 1
If $lim_{d \to \infty} var \left(\frac{\|X_d\|}{E[\|X_d\|]} \right) = 0$, then

$$\frac{Dmax_d - Dmin_d}{Dmin_d} \to_p 0.$$

---

[1] For our theoretical considerations, we consistently use the origin as the query point. This choice does not affect the generality of our results, though it simplifies our algebra considerably.

d	Dimensionality of the data space
N	Number of data points
$\mathcal{F}$	1-dim. data distribution in $(0,1)$
$\mu_{\mathcal{F}}$	Mean of $\mathcal{F}$
X_d	Data point from $\mathcal{F}^d$, each coordinate follows $\mathcal{F}$
$dist_d(\cdot,\cdot)$	Sym. dist. func. in $[0,1]^d$, with $dist_d(\cdot,\cdot) \geq 0$ and triangle inequality
$\|\cdot\|$	Dist. of a vec. to the origin $(0,\ldots,0)$
$Dmax_d$	max. dist. of a data point to origin
$Dmin_d$	min. dist. of a data point to origin
$P[e]$	Probability of event e
$E[X]$	Expected value and
$var[X]$	variance of a random variable X
$Y_d \to_p c$	A sequence of vectors $Y_1,\ldots$ converges in probability to a constant vector c if: $\forall \epsilon > 0 \ lim_{d\to\infty} P[dist_d(Y_d,c) \leq \epsilon] = 1$

Table 1: Notations and Basic Definitions

Proof: See [5]. ■

The theorem shows that in high dimensional space the difference of the distances of farthest and nearest points to some query point does not increase as fast as the minimum of the two. This is obviously a problem since it indicates poor discrimination of the nearest and farthest points with respect to the query point.

It is interesting however to observe that the difference between nearest and farthest neighbor ($Dmax_d - Dmin_d$) does not necessarily go to zero. In contrast, the development of ($Dmax_d - Dmin_d$) with d largely depends on the distance metric used and may actually grow with the dimensionality for certain distance metrics. The following theorem summarizes this new insight and formally states the dependency between ($Dmax_d - Dmin_d$) and the distance metric used. It allows to draw conclusions for specific metrics such as the Manhattan distance (L_1), Euclidean metric (L_2), and the general k-norm L_k.

Theorem 2

Let $\mathcal{F}$ be an arbitrary distribution of two points and the distance function $\|\cdot\|$ be an L_k metric. Then,

$$lim_{d\to\infty} E\left[\frac{Dmax_d^k - Dmin_d^k}{d^{(1/k)-(1/2)}}\right] = C_k,$$

where C_k is some constant dependent on k.

Proof: see Appendix. ■

We can easily generalize the result for a database of N uniformly distributed points. The following theorem provides the result.

Theorem 3

Let $\mathcal{F}$ be an arbitrary distribution of n points and the distance function $\|\cdot\|$ be an L_k metric. Then,

$$C_k \leq lim_{d\to\infty} E\left[\frac{Dmax_d^k - Dmin_d^k}{d^{(1/k)-(1/2)}}\right] \leq (N-1)\cdot C_k,$$

Metric	$Dmax - Dmin$ converges against
L_1	$C_1 * \sqrt{(d)}$
L_2	C_2
$L_k, k \geq 3$	0

Table 2: Consequences of Theorem 2

where C_k is some constant dependent on k.

Proof: If C is the expected difference between the maximum and minimum of two randomly drawn points, then the same value for N points drawn from the same distribution must be in the range $[C, (N-1)\cdot C]$. ■

A surprising consequence of theorem 2 is that the value of $Dmax_d - Dmin_d$ grows (in absolute terms) as $d^{(1/k)-(1/2)}$. As a result, $Dmax_d - Dmin_d$ increases with dimensionality as $\sqrt{d}$ for the Manhattan metric (L_1 metric). The L_1 metric is the only metric for which the absolute difference between nearest and farthest neighbor increases with the dimensionality. It is also surprising that for the Euclidean metric (L_2 metric), $Dmax_d - Dmin_d$ converges to a constant, and for distance metrics L_k for $k \geq 3$, $Dmax_d - Dmin_d$ converges to zero with increasing d. These consequences of theorem 2 are summarized in Table 2.

2.2 Experimental Confirmation

We performed a series of experiments to confirm these theoretical results. For the experiments we used synthetic (uniform and clustered) as well as real data sets. In Figure 1, we show the average $Dmax - Dmin$ of a number of query points plotted over d for different metrics. Note that the resulting curves depend on the number of data points in the data set. These exper-

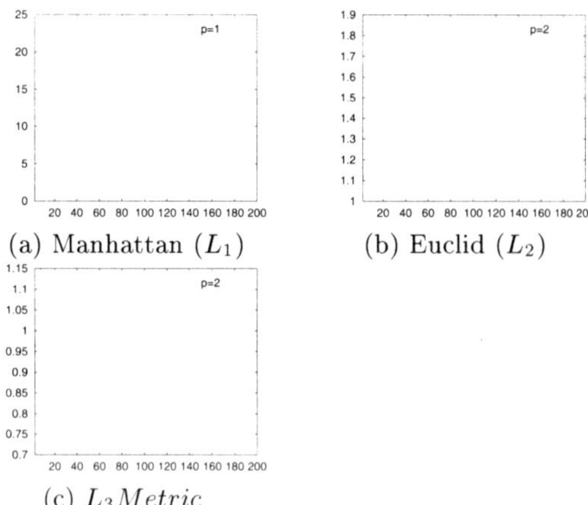

Figure 1: $|Dmax - Dmin|$ depending on d for different L_k metrics (uniform data)

imental results are no contradiction to the results of [5]. The reason that even for the L_1 and L_2 metrics $\frac{Dmax_d - Dmin_d}{Dmin_d} \to_p 0$ is that $Dmin_d$ grows faster with

d than $Dmax_d - Dmin_d$. In case of the L_1 metric, $Dmin_d$ grows linearly with d and in case of the L_2 metric, $Dmin_d$ grows as $\sqrt{d}$ with d. As a result, for the L_1 metric $lim_{d\to\infty} \frac{\sqrt{d}}{d} = 0$ and for the L_2 metric $lim_{d\to\infty} \frac{C_2}{\sqrt{d}} = 0$.

The theoretical and experimental results of this section show that for L_k metrics with $k \geq 3$, nearest neighbor search in high dimensional spaces is meaningless while for the L_1 and L_2 metrics the distances may reveal important properties of the data.

3 Problems of high dimensional data and meaningful nearest neighbor

In one- or two-dimensional spaces, it is usually relatively easy to understand the properties of the data and identify the data distribution. It is safe to assume that all dimensions are equally relevant and that a standard (Euclidean) metrics provides meaningful results. In general, this is not true in the high-dimensional case.

To get a deeper understanding of the nature of high dimensional data, it is important to uncover the meaning of the dimensions. High dimensional data points or feature vectors are typically derived from complex real world objects like products, images, CAD data, etc. In considering the different types of data, we identified three main methods to derive a high dimensional feature vector from a complex real world object:

- enumerating some properties of the object (irreversible transformation),

- determining histograms which describe some statistical properties of the object (irreversible transformation) or

- transforming the full description of the object into a feature vector (reversible transformation).

In the following, we examine the impact of the three potential sources of high dimensional data to the meaningfulness of the nearest neighbor problem.

1. Enumeration of Properties: We use an example in order to elucidate this case. For our example, we assume that we want to compare cars. Comparing cars is often done by deriving various properties of the cars such as motor power, equipment, design and so on. Each measurement forms a dimension which is only related to the other measurements of the same object. When users query the car data base, they can select or weight the importance of the different properties, and in that way each user is able to form his own meaningful distance metric. The reason why a user can easily perform a meaningful nearest neighbor search is that the dimensions are directly interpretable by the user. By omitting some of the dimensions and by weighting them the user can control the degree of abstraction for

the nearest neighbor search. In our experience, the dimensionality of such data is in the medium range (10 to 50). The dimensionality can be reduced by pooling dimensions together to a single categorical dimension and forming a hierarchy for the new dimension.

2. Determination of Histograms: Histograms are often used to produce high dimensional data because they allow a flexible description of complex properties of real world objects. Examples are color histograms [20], word counts for document retrieval and text mining [13, 16] and census data [15]. Each bin of the histogram is taken as a single dimension. The information transformation from the real world object into the histogram is an irreversible process which means that some information about the object is lost. The user of a histogram data base has to be aware of this. The goal of the query has to match the reduced information of the transformed object. On the other hand the histogram may contain information about aspects (for instance the background in an image) the user wants to abstract from. In that case, the information in the histogram must be reduced to the relevant portion. However, in contrast to the enumeration method the users are generally not able to specify the reduction because they usually do not know the underlying transformation. Another difference to the previous method is that it is not useful to group the dimensions independently from the users and the query points. In general, all possible groupings are potentially meaningful. First approaches to deal with this problem of query specification are reported in [8, 18]. In general, the connection between the information in the histograms and the semantic information of the objects is weak. The dimensionality of such data can vary from the medium to large range (10 to 1000).

3. Full Feature Description: The third method is to use the description of complex a object directly as a feature vector. The advantage is that all information about the object is stored in the feature vector and that the object is reconstructible from the vector. However, often the real world objects do not allow a representation as a feature vector with fixed length. Examples for data which allow such a representation are molecular biology data [7]. Like the histogram data, it is also not meaningful to group the dimensions to sensible units independently from the query point and/or the user. Due to the possibility of reconstruction, the semantic aspects are strongly connected to the information stored in the feature vectors.

The three types of high dimensional data relate to different aspects of *meaningfulness*. In general there is not a single meaningful nearest neighbor for a query, but the user has to select the desired aspects. For the first category of high dimensional data, the user is able to specify his/her notion of 'meaningfulness' (the actual relevant aspects) by his knowledge about the real world objects. This procedure is similar to analytical querying in an OLAP environment. To deal with the second and third types of data, the user needs help from the data creator or the database system to specify the 'meaningful' aspects. But how does a specification assistance for the relevant aspects may look like? For certain applications, there exist data dependent methods which use interaction in the selection process [8]. In this paper, we focus on a method which selects the relevant dimensions automatically by extracting and rating additional information about the data distributions.

As a second question, we investigate how good a single metric can serve as a similarity measure for the second and third type of data. We already mentioned that for those types of data the relevant dimensions (attributes) depend on the query point and the intention of the user. If the meaningfulness of a metric depends on the query point, then a metric can not serve as a measure of similarity between the query object and all other objects. In other words, a metric which is only based on the relevant attributes (which are assumed to be a subset of all attributes) can only serve as a criterion for similarity in a local environment of the query point. Objects (or data points) outside of this environment are incomparable to the query object, because they may have other relevant attributes. In summary, one can say that for the second and third types of data, the relationship between the metric and the intended similarity becomes weaker with increasing distance to the query point. As a consequence, meaningful metrics for high dimensional data spaces have to be varied according to the considered query point and the data objects under consideration. Our generalized notion of nearest neighbor search which is presented in the next section provides an automatic adaptation of the similarity measure in order to allow a meaningful nearest neighbor search in high dimensional space.

4 Generalized NN Search

In the previous sections, we have seen that the problem of finding a meaningful nearest neighbor in high dimensional spaces consists of the following two steps: First, an appropriate metric has to be determined, and second, the nearest neighbor with respect to this metric has to be determined. The first step deals with selecting and weighting the relevant dimensions according to the users intention and the given query point. This step is obviously rather difficult since it is difficult to select and weight the relevant dimensions among all combinations of hundreds of dimensions. The basic idea of our approach is to automatically determine a combination of relevant dimensions for a given query point based on the properties of the data distribution. Although our approach can not guess the users intention, the data distribution contains highly relevant information and allows a much better and more meaningful nearest neighbor search.

4.1 Definition

In this section, we propose a generalization of the nearest neighbor search problem which remains meaningful in high-dimensional spaces. The basic idea of our new notion of nearest neighbor search is to use a quality criterion to dynamically determine which dimensions are relevant for a given query point and use those dimensions to determine the nearest neighbor[2]. The space of all combinations of dimensions can also be seen as the space of axes-parallel projections of the data set, and the problem can therefore be defined as an optimization problem over the space of projections. In the following, we formalize our generalized notion of nearest neighbor search. First, we formally introduce a quality criterion which is used to rate the usefulness of a certain combination of dimensions (projection).

Let $D = \{x_1, \ldots, x_n\}$, $x_i \in \mathbb{R}^d$ be a database of d-dimensional feature vectors, $x_q \in \mathbb{R}^d$ the query point, $p : \mathbb{R}^d \to \mathbb{R}^{d'}$, $d' \leq d$ a projection, and $dist(\cdot, \cdot)$ a distance function in the projected feature space.

Definition 1 (Quality Criterion)
The **quality** **criterion** *is a function* $C(p, x_q, D, dist) \to \mathbb{R}$, $C \geq 0$ *which rates the quality of the projection with respect to the query point, database, and distance function. In other words, the quality function rates the meaningfulness of the projection p for the nearest neighbor search.*

In section 4.3, we develop a useful quality criterion based on the distance distribution of the data points to the query point within a given projection.

Let P be the space of all possible projections $p : \mathbb{R}^d \to \mathbb{R}^{d'}$, $d' \leq d$ and $\forall x \in \mathbb{R}^d : p(p(x)) = p(x)$. To find a meaningful nearest neighbor for a given query point x_q we have to optimize the quality criterion C over the space of projections P.

Definition 2 (Generalized NN Search)
A meaningful nearest neighbor for a given query point $x_q \in \mathbb{R}^d$ *is the point*[3]
$$x_{NN} = \{x' \in D | \forall x \in D, x \neq x' :$$
$$dist(p_{best}(x'), p_{best}(x_q)) \leq dist(p_{best}(x), p_{best}(x_q))\};$$
$$p_{best} = \{p \in P | \underset{p:\mathbb{R}^d \to \mathbb{R}^{d'}, d' \leq d}{MAX} \{C(p, x_q, D, dist)\}\}.$$

Solving the generalized nearest neighbor problem problem is a difficult and computation intensive task. The space of all general projections P is infinite and even the space of all axes-parallel projections is exponential. In addition, the quality function C is apriori

---

[2]Note that the nearest neighbor determined by our approach may be different from the nearest neighbor based on all dimensions.

[3]Note that our definition can be easily generalized to solve the k-nearest neighbor problem by fixing the selected projection and determining the k nearest neighbors.

unknown and therefore, it is difficult to find a general and efficiently computable solution of the problem. In the next section, we develop an algorithm which provides a general solution of the problem.

4.2 Generalized Nearest Neighbor Algorithm

The most important but difficult task in solving the generalized nearest neighbor problem is to find the relevant projections. As mentioned in the previous subsections, this decision is in general query and data dependent which makes the problem computationally difficult. For our following considerations, we restrict the projections to the class of axes-parallel projections, which means that we are searching for meaningful combinations of dimensions (attributes). The restricted search space has still an exponential size with respect to dimensionality, which makes enumeration impossible for higher dimensionalities.

In order to keep our algorithm generic and allow different quality criterions (cf. subsection 4.3), our first approach was to use general optimization algorithms such as random search, genetic and greedy optimization, for which the implementations can be made largely independent of the specific problem structure. In random search, simple random combinations of dimensions are evaluated in terms of the quality criterion, and the best projection is returned. The genetic algorithm uses multiple populations which are mutated and combined based on the quality criterion, and the greedy algorithm directly uses the best one-dimensional projections which are combined into higher-dimensional ones. All three algorithms are sketched in pseudo code (see figures 3, 4 and 5).

The results of the first experiments showed that none of the three algorithms was able to find the relevant subset of dimensions. Even for synthetic data, for which the relevant subset of dimensions is known.only a subset of the relevant dimensions was found. Random search was found only useful to check whether a given quality criterion is effective on a specific data set or not. If the random search does not find any projection with good quality, both genetic and greedy algorithm are likely to fail in finding a good projection as well. However, in cases when random search does not fail, the genetic search provides much better results. The greedy algorithm assumes that the influence of a dimension on the quality is independent from other dimensions. In general, this assumption is not true for real data sets. A crucial problem is that one-dimensional projections of high dimensional data usually do not contain much information and so the greedy algorithm picks the first dimensions randomly and is therefore not useful for selecting the first dimensions. It turned out, however, that the greedy algorithm can be used effectively to refine results from random or genetic search.

Our algorithm to determine the relevant subset of

p_nn_search $(x_q, d_{tar}, D, C, dist)$
$d_{tmp} := 3$ to 5
$no\_iter := 10$ to 20
$p_{tmp} := $ genetic_search$(x_q, d_{tmp}, D, C, dist, no_iter)$
$p_{best} := $ greedy_search$(x_q, d_{tar}, D, C, dist, p_{tmp})$
$x_{NN} := $ p_nn_search$(x_q, D, dist, p_{best})$
return (x_{NN})

Figure 2: Generalized Nearest Neighbor Algorithm

random_search $(x_q, d_{tar}, D, C, dist, no\_iter)$
$p_{best}.quality := 0$
for $i := 0$ **to** no_iter **do**
  $p := $ generate_random_projection(d_{tar})
  $p.quality := C(p, x_q, D, dist)$
  if $p_{best}.quality < p.quality$ **then** $p_{best} := p$
end do
return (p_{best})

Figure 3: Random Optimization

genetic_search $(x_q, d_{tar}, D, C, dist, no\_iter)$
$population := \emptyset, pop\_size = 100, elite := 10, child := 80$
for $i := 0$ **to** pop_size **do**
  $p := $ generate_random_projection(d_{tar})
  $p.quality:=C(p, x_q, D, dist)$
  $population.insert(p)$
end do
for $i := 0$ **to** no_iter **do**
  $new\_pop := \emptyset$
  insert the $elite$ best projection into new_pop
  for $j := elite$ **to** $elite + child$ **do**
    // projections with high quality have higher
    // probability to be selected for cross-over
    $parent1:=$randomly select a projection from old_pop
    $parent2:=$randomly select a projection from old_pop
    $child := $ gen. a new proj. by comb. $parent1, parent2$
    $child.quality := C(p, x_q, D, dist)$
    $new_pop.$insert$(child)$
  end do
  qualify and insert $pop\_size - (elite + child)$ random
  projections into new_pop
  $population := new\_pop$
end do
select the best projection p_{best} and return it

Figure 4: Genetic Optimization

greedy_search $(x_q, d_{tar}, D, C, dist, p_{tmp})$
set of selected dimensions $S := \emptyset$ or from p_{tmp}
for $i := 0$ **to** dim_{tar} **do**
  pick the dimension $k_i \notin S$ such that the quality of the
    projection based on $S \cup \{k_i\}$ is maximal
  $S := S \cup \{k_i\}$
end do
return $(p_{best}(S))$

Figure 5: Greedy Optimization

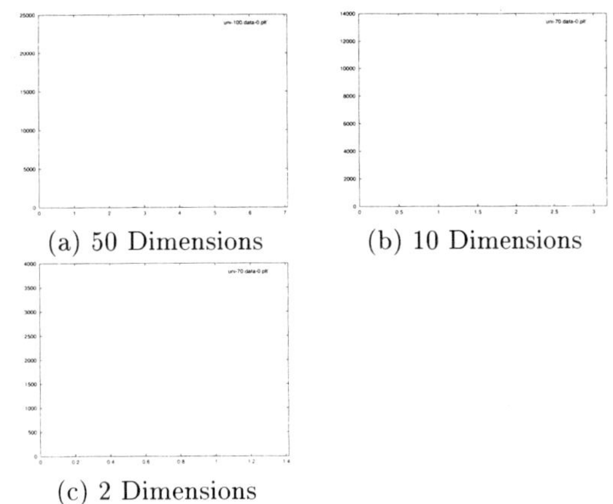

(a) 50 Dimensions   (b) 10 Dimensions

(c) 2 Dimensions

Figure 6: Distance Distribution of Uniform Data

dimensions is therefore based on a combination of the genetic and the greedy algorithm. For determining the first three to five dimensions, we use a genetic algorithm and for extending the result to more dimensions we use a greedy-based search. Figure 2 shows the pseudocode of the algorithm. For controlling the degree of abstraction and improving the efficiency, we use the target dimensionality $d_{tar} = d' \leq d$ as a parameter of the algorithm. If the genetic algorithm determines the first five of the relevant dimensions and the greedy algorithm the remaining ones, the complexity of our algorithm is

$$O((5 \cdot \#(Iterations) \cdot PopulationSize + d \cdot (d_{tar} - 5)) \cdot O(\text{Quality Determination})).$$

4.3 Distance Distributions

In this section we develop a quality criterion based on the distance distribution with respect to the query point. The distance distribution of a data set D with respect to a query point x_q is the distribution of distances of the data points $x \in D$ from x_q. More formally, we have to consider the probability that the distance of a query point x_q to another data point is smaller than a threshold $dist_t$:

$$\Phi(dist_t) = P[dist(x_q, x) < dist_t], x \in D, dist_t \in \mathbb{R}$$

The corresponding probability density is

$$f(dist_t) = \Phi'(dist_t).$$

Note that $\Phi(dist_t)$ is not continuous and therefore we can only estimate the probability density $f(dist_t)$. In this subsection, we use simple histograms for approximating the frequency of the distances of the data points from the query points.

To examine how typical distance distributions look like, we examine the distance distribution for different dimensionalities. Let us first consider the case of high-dimensional uniform data. We know that in this case

the distances are meaningless. Figure 6 shows typical distance distributions[4] of a 50-dimensional data set consisting of 100,000 data points uniformly distributed in $[0,1]^d$. Figure 6 (a)-(c) show typical projections[5] onto randomly chosen 50, 10, and 2 dimensions. The distance distribution has always one peak which means that all data points are basically in one big distance cluster from the query point. As a consequence from the theorem in [5] the peak gets sharper as the distance to the query point grows. We neglect this effect for our quality criterion by estimating the density only in the range $[d_{min}, d_{max}]$, because this effect is common to mostly all distributions and from section 2 we conclude that this effect does not necessarily tell something about the meaningfulness of the nearest neighbor. From the discussion in section 3 we assume that a meaningful distance distribution should show two peaks. The nearer peak is formed by the points which are comparable to the query point (the metric is related to a type of similarity). The other peak – in most cases the larger one – is formed by those points which are incomparable to the query point because other attributes are relevant for those data objects. However, with respect to the currently used attributes they are assumed to behave like uniformly distributed data.

How to detect a two peak distance distribution? Our idea is to use kernel density estimation (see [21] for an introduction) to smooth the distribution and suppress random artifacts. To measure the quality we increase the kernel width (smoothing factor) until the smoothed distribution yields only two maxima. The obtained kernel width is h_1. Then we increase the kernel width further until the distance distribution yields only one maximum. This results in the kernel width h_2. We use the difference between the smoothing factor for one maximum and for two maxima $h_2 - h1$ as our quality criterion to measures the similarity of a current distance distribution with a distance distribution that yields two significant peaks. To get rid of possible disturbances in the tail of the distribution, which may also result in two maxima, we use only the k nearest percent of the data. Figure 7 shows distance distributions of data, which contains full uniformly distributed data and a projected cluster, which means that these points follow a Gaussian distribution in some dimensions and a uniform distribution in the others. Figure 7(a) shows the distance distribution in a projection where all dimensions are relevant, which means that all selected dimensions are used in the definition of the projected cluster. In Figure 7(b), one relevant dimension is replaced by a non-relevant and in Figure 7(c) two relevant dimensions are replaced by non-relevant ones. In 7(c) the two peak structure is hard to recognize and the quality criterion gives no

---

[4] In case of uniform data, the distance distribution is always similar independent of the chosen query point.

[5] In case of uniform data, the distance distribution always looks the same independent of the chosen projection.

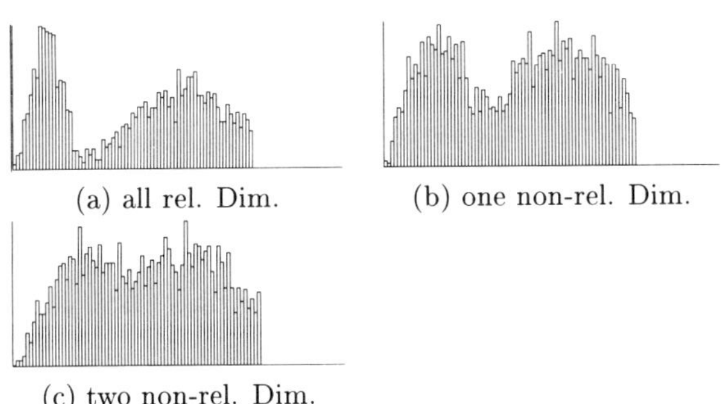

(a) all rel. Dim.   (b) one non-rel. Dim.

(c) two non-rel. Dim.

Figure 7: Distance Distribution of Data

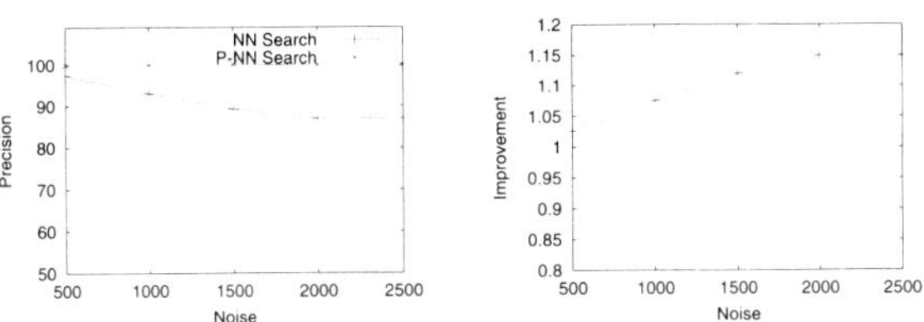

Figure 8: Generalized Nearest Neighbor Classification (Synthetic Data)

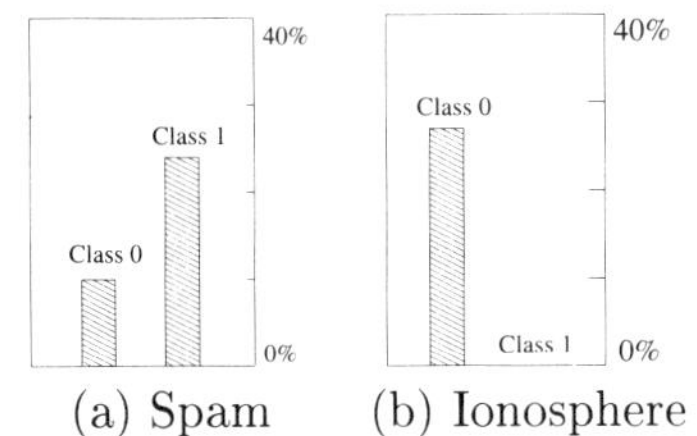

(a) Spam   (b) Ionosphere

Figure 9: Improvement (Real Data)

Database	Class	NN	P-NN	Improv.
Ionosphere	0	0.52%	0.66%	27%
	1	0.95%	0.94%	0%
Spam	0	0.77%	0.85%	10%
	1	0.64%	0.79%	23%

Table 3: Generalized Nearest Neighbor Classification (Real Data)

hint on the hidden relevant dimensions. From these observations we can conclude that the genetic algorithm can only optimize projections with a dimensionality of 3-5. If the dimensionality is higher the quality criterion degenerates to an oracle and the algorithm can only guess a good projection – and the probability to guess a good projection in high dimensional data is rather low.

5 Experiments

In this section we report experiments, to show the effectiveness of our quality function and the generalized notion of nearest neighbor search. Note that in real world application the quality function have to be modified due to the data dependency of the term 'meaningful'. In our experiments we focused on improving the effectiveness of the nearest neighbor search in general and omitted as far as possible dependencies of the quality function from the data.

First we compared the effectiveness of the generalized k-nearest neighbor search with the full k-nearest neighbor search. For this purpose we used synthetic labeled data, consisting of two types of data. The first and relevant part follows a normal distribution in some of the dimensions, but are uniformly distributed with respect to the other dimensions. The second not relevant part is uniformly distributed in the whole feature space. In the experiments with the synthetic data we used only query points from the first part. For the effectiveness we measured the percentage of relevant data in the result of a k-nearest neighbor search(precision). For all experiments we set $k = 20$. Figure 8 shows the results for the compar-

ison of the generalized nearest neighbor search with the full nearest neighbor search. The data sets consist of a projected cluster of 200 relevant points (normaly distributed in 7 of 30 dimensions) and 500 to 2500 not relevant points (uniformly distributed). The improvement over the full nearest neighbor search is up to 14%.

We also applied our method to labled real data sets from the UCI Machine Learning Repository (*www.ics.uci.edu/mlearn/*). We used the Ionosphere Database and the Spambase Database. The Ionosphere Database consists of 351 instances with 34 numeric attributes and contains 2 classes, which come from a classification of radar returns from the ionosphere. The Spambase Database is derived from a collection of spam and non-spam e-mails and consists of 4601 instances with 57 numeric attributes. In both cases we used a target dimensionality of $d_{tar} = 10$ for the generalized nearest neighbor. The results are averages over 20 randomly selected queries. Our generalized nearest neighbor search shows an improvement of up to 27% (figure 9).

To adopt our generalized nearest neighbor search to other applications like image retrieval or document search we suggest to use a fast k-nearest neighbor search on all dimensions with large k or a key word search as a filter step.

To show the applicability of our method we examined the search time depending on the number of data points (figure 10). In our implementation we did not use any index structure, but used a simple linear scan to calculate our quality function and the query results. The experiments were measured on a Pentium III, 500 MHz with 200 MB RAM.

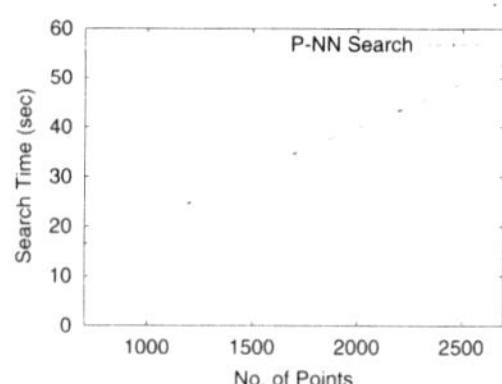

Figure 10: Search Time (Synthetic Data)

6 Conclusion

In this paper, we developed a generalized notion of nearest neighbor search in high dimensional spaces. We show that our new notion is highly relevant in practical applications and improves the *effectiveness* of the search. The basic idea is to determine a relevant subset of dimensions depending on the query point and the data distribution by an optimization process which rates the distance distribution for the selected subset of dimensions according to an elaborate quality criterion. Our new technique for solving the generalized nearest neighbor problem is not only valuable for allowing a more meaningful and effective nearest neighbor search in high dimensional spaces but it also provides a better understanding of the data and the relevant notion of proximity. The experimental results show the high potential of our new technique which is likely to extent the common full-dimensional nearest neighbor search in most applications that deal with high dimensional data. Futher research on similarity search applications should elaborate the observation that the notion of similarity often depend from the data point and the users intentions and so could be not uniquely predefined. High dimensional data may contain different aspects of similarity. Open research questions include: how to find appropriate quality criterias for the meaningfulness of similarity search; what can be done using automated algorithms; when are interactive techniques to determine the meaningfulness of similarity search more effective than automated algorithms?

References

[1] Aggarwal C. C. et al.: Fast Algorithms for Projected Clustering,*Proc. of the ACM SIGMOD Conf.*, 1999, pp 407-418.

[2] Aggarwal C. C., Yu P. S.: Finding Generalized Projected Clusters in High Dimensional Spaces, *Proceedings of the ACM SIGMOD Conference*, 2000, pp. 70-81.

[3] Altschul S. F., Gish W., Miller W., Myers E. W., Lipman D. J.: A Basic Local Alignment Search Tool, *Journal of Molecular Biology*, Vol. 215, No. 3, 1990, pp. 403-410.

[4] Berchtold S., Keim D. A., Kriegel H.-P.: The X-Tree: An Index Structure for High-Dimensional Data, *Proc. Int. Conf. on Very Large Databases (VLDB'96)*, Bombay, India, 1996, pp. 28-39.

[5] Beyer K., Goldstein J., Ramakrishnan R., Shaft U.: When is Nearest Neighbors Meaningful?, *Proc. of the Int. Conf. Database Theorie*, 1999, pp.217-235.

[6] Bonchi F., Giannotti F., Mainetto G., Pedreschi D.: Using Data Mining Techniques in Fiscal Fraud Detection, *First Int. Conf. on Data Warehousing and Knowledge Discovery* , 1999, pp. 369-376.

[7] X. Daura, B. Jaun, D. Seebach, W. F. van Gunsteren, A. E. Mark.: Reversible peptide folding in solution by molecular dynamics simulation, *Journal of Molecular Biology*, 280, 1998, pp. 925-932.

[8] Faloutsos C., Barber R., Flickner M., Hafner J., et al.: Efficient and Effective Querying by Image Content, *Journal of Intelligent Information Systems*, 1994, Vol. 3, pp. 231-262.

[9] Gaede V., Günther O.: Multidimensional Access Methods, *ACM Computing Surveys*, Vol. 30, No. 2, 1998, pp. 170-231.

[10] Guttman, A.: R-Trees: A Dynamic Index Structure for Spatial Searching, *Proc. of the ACM SIGMOD Conf.*, 1984, pp. 47-57.

[11] He H., Graco W., Yao X.: Application of Genetic Algorithm and k-Nearest Neighbour Method in Medical Fraud Detection, *Asia-Pacific Conf. on Simulated Evolution and Learning*, SEAL'98, 1998, pp. 74-81.

[12] Korn F., Sidiropoulos N., Faloutsos C., Siegel E., Protopapas Z.: Fast Nearest Neighbor Search in Medical Image Databases, *Proc. 22nd Int. Conf. on Very Large Data Bases*, Mumbai, India, 1996, pp.215-226.

[13] Kukich K.: Techniques for Automatically Correcting Words in Text, *ACM Computing Surveys*, Vol.24, No. 4, 1992, pp.377-440.

[14] Mehrotra R., Gary J.: Feature-Index-Based Similar Shape Retrieval, *Proc. of the 3rd Working Conf. on Visual Database Systems*, March 1995, pp. 46-65.

[15] Openshaw S.:*Census User Handbook*, Pearson Professsional Ltd., Cambridge, 1995.

[16] Salton G.: *Automatic Text Processing: The Transformation, Analysis, and Retrieval of Information by Computer*, Addison-Wesley.

[17] Seidl T., Kriegel H.-P.: Efficient User-Adaptable Similarity Search in Large Multimedia Databases, *Proc. of the 23rd Int. Conf. on Very Large Databases*, Athens, Greece, 1997, pp. 506-515.

[18] Ankerst M., Kriegel H.-P., Seidl T.: A Multi-Step Approach for Shape Similarity Search in Image Databases, *IEEE Trans. on Knowledge and Data Engineering (TKDE'98)*, Vol. 10, No. 6, 1998, pp. 996-1004.

[19] Shaft U., Goldstein J., Beyer K.: Nearest Neighbor Query Performance for Unstable Distributions, *Technical Report TR 1388*, Department of Computer Science, University of Wisconsin at Madison.

[20] Shawney H., Hafner J.: Efficient Color Histogram Indexing, *Proc. Int. Conf. on Image Processing*, 1994, pp. 66-70.

[21] Silverman B.W.: *Density Estimation*, Chapman & Hall 1986.

[22] Weber R., Schek H.-J., Blott S.: A Quantitative Analysis and Performance Study for Similarity-Search Methods in High-Dimensional Spaces, *Proc. of 24rd Int. Conf. on Very Large Data Bases (VLDB'98)*, New York, 1998, pp. 194-205.

Appendix

Theorem 2

Let $\mathcal{F}$ be an arbitrary distribution of two points and the distance function $\|\cdot\|$ be an L_k metric. Then,

$$lim_{d\to\infty} E\left[\frac{Dmax_d^k - Dmin_d^k}{d^{1/k-1/2}}\right] = C_k,$$

where C_k is some constant dependent on k.

Proof: Let $A_d = (P_1 \ldots P_d)$ and $B_d = (Q_1 \ldots Q_d)$ with P_i and Q_i being drawn from $\mathcal{F}$. Let $PA_d = \{\sum_{i=1}^{d}(P_i)^k\}^{1/k}$ be the distance of A_d to the origin using the L_k metric. Let $PB_d = \{\sum_{i=1}^{d}(Q_i)^k\}^{1/k}$.

We assume that the kth power of a random variable drawn from the distribution $\mathcal{F}$ has mean $\mu_{\mathcal{F},k}$ and standard deviation $\sigma_{\mathcal{F},k}$. This means that:

$$PA_d^k/d \to_p \mu_{\mathcal{F},k}, PB_d^k/d \to_p \mu_{\mathcal{F},k}.$$

We express $|PA_d - PB_d|$ in the following numerator/denominator form:

$$|PA_d - PB_d| = \frac{|(PA_d)^k - (PB_d)^k|}{\sum_{r=0}^{k-1}(PA_d)^{k-r-1}(PB_d)^r} \quad (1)$$

Dividing both sides by $d^{1/k-1/2}$, expanding the numerator in terms of P_i and Q_i, and regrouping on right-hand-side provides

$$\frac{|PA_d - PB_d|}{d^{1/k-1/2}} = \frac{|\sum_{i=1}^{d}((P_i)^k - (Q_i)^k)|/\sqrt{d}}{\sum_{r=0}^{k-1}\left(\frac{PA_d}{d^{1/k}}\right)^{k-r-1}\left(\frac{PB_d}{d^{1/k}}\right)^r} \quad (2)$$

Since each $P_i^k - Q_i^k$ is a random variable with zero mean and finite variance, the expected value of the numerator is a constant because of the central limit theorem. The denominator converges to the constant $k \cdot (\mu_{\mathcal{F},k})^{(k-1)/k}$ because of the convergence behavior of PA_d^k/d and PB_d^k/d and Slutsky's theorem. The result follows. ∎

The A-tree: An Index Structure for High-Dimensional Spaces Using Relative Approximation

Yasushi Sakurai[†]   Masatoshi Yoshikawa[§]   Shunsuke Uemura[§]   Haruhiko Kojima[†]

† NTT Cyber Solutions Laboratories
sakurai@marsh.hil.ntt.co.jp,
kojima@aether.hil.ntt.co.jp

§ Graduate School of Information Science
Nara Institute of Science and Technology
{yosikawa, uemura}@is.aist-nara.ac.jp

Abstract

We propose a novel index structure. A-tree (Approximation tree), for similarity search of high-dimensional data. The basic idea of the A-tree is the introduction of Virtual Bounding Rectangles (VBRs), which contain and approximate MBRs and data objects. VBRs can be represented rather compactly, and thus affect the tree configuration both quantitatively and qualitatively. Firstly, since tree nodes can install large number of entries of VBRs, fanout of nodes becomes large, thus leads to fast search. More importantly, we have a free hand in arranging MBRs and VBRs in tree nodes. In the A-trees, nodes contain entries of an MBR and its children VBRs. Therefore, by fetching a node of an A-tree, we can obtain the information of exact position of a parent MBR and approximate position of its children. We have performed experiments using both synthetic and real data sets. For the real data sets, the A-tree outperforms the SR-tree and the VA-File in all range of dimensionality up to 64 dimension, which is the highest dimension in our experiments. The A-tree achieves 77.3% (77.7%, resp.) savings in page accesses compared to the SR-tree (the VA-File, resp.) for 64-dimensional real data.

**Proceedings of the 26th VLDB Conference,
Cairo, Egypt, 2000.**

1 Introduction

1.1 Data Retrieval in High-Dimensional Space

Fast content-based retrieval is a core function to provide high-quality human interface for large-scale multimedia databases. In content-based retrieval, usually. feature vectors extracted from multimedia data are used as keys. For instance. the features extracted from images include color. texture. structure and so on. In the balance of the reduction of computational cost and the raise of object recognition ratio. feature vectors of which dimensionality is ten or tens are used in many recognition methods[12][13] or systems[17]. Since retrieving high-dimensional feature vectors incurs high cost for large data sets. new spatial indices and search methods that offer efficient data retrieval are required. Various spatial indices[16][6] have been proposed so far. This paper introduces a new index structure, named A-tree (Approximation tree). that offers remarkably higher search performance than existing indices.

1.2 Related Work

The conventional approach to supporting similarity search in high-dimensional vector space can be broadly classified into two categories. The first approach is using data-partitioning index trees. Neighbor vectors are covered by MBRs (Minimum Bounding Rectangles) or MBSs (Minimum Bounding Spheres). which are organized in a hierarchical tree structure. Many index trees have been proposed so far. They include the R-tree[8], the R*-tree[2], the Hilbert R-tree[10] and the SS-tree[19]. Also. nearest neighbor search methods using such indices have been proposed[14][9]. Two recently proposed indices, the X-tree[5] and the SR-tree[11], are reported to offer good performance. The X-tree[5] introduces the notion of supernode, and outperforms the R*-tree. The SR-tree[11] has a unique feature in that it uses both MBRs and MBSs, and is reported to outperform both the R*-tree and the SS-tree. The second approach is the use of approximation files. Among others, the VA-File (Vector Approximation File)[18] is a simple yet powerful scheme. The VA-File divides the data space into cells and allocates a bit-string to each cell. The vectors inside a cell are approximated by the cell, and the VA-File itself is simply an array of these geometric approximations. For search, the entire VA-File is scanned to select candidate vectors. Those candidates are then verified by visiting the vector files. In [18], Weber et al. have reported that the VA-File outperforms both the R*-tree and the X-tree when the dimensionality is high ($\geq$ around 6.) To sum up, among access methods for high-dimensional vector space search, the SR-tree and the VA-File are two methods which are not reported to be outperformed by other methods[1] .

In the field of spatial search for high-dimensional data, the well-known problem, the "curse of dimensionality" looms large before us. Of late, search methods which present an approximate answer [1] [7], have been proposed to avoid the influence of the problem. Although these works are useful, the goal of our work to overcome the problem by providing a search method which gives an exact answer.

1.3 The Introduction of the A-tree

In this paper, we propose a new index structure, the A-tree. The introduction of the A-tree is motivated by the comparison and analysis of the SR-tree and the VA-File. Since no result on the comparison between these two access methods is available, we first performed experiments comparing the two access methods. Based on the experiments, we have developed a new tree index structure, A-tree, and search and update algorithms. The basic idea of the A-tree is the introduction of Virtual Bounding Rectangles (VBRs), which contain and approximate MBRs and data objects, respectively. VBRs can be represented rather compactly, and thus affect the tree configuration both quantitatively and qualitatively. Firstly, since tree nodes can install large number of entries of VBRs, fanout of nodes becomes large, thus leads to fast search. More importantly, we have a free hand in arranging MBRs and VBRs in tree nodes. In the A-trees, nodes contain entries of an MBR and its children VBRs. Therefore, by fetching a node of an A-tree, we can obtain the information of exact position of a parent MBR and approximate position of its children.

We evaluate the performance of the A-tree using both synthetic and real data. The results demonstrate the effectiveness of the A-tree in high-dimension search. The mechanism of the A-tree is remarkably successful, especially for non-uniformly distributed

data sets such as real data sets. For both real data sets and synthetic clustered data sets, the A-tree outperforms the SR-tree and the VA-File in all dimensionality ranges up to 64 dimensions, the highest dimension examined in our experiments. The A-tree achieves 77.3 % (77.7 %, resp.) savings in page access compared to the SR-tree (the VA-File, resp.) for real data with 64-dimensions. As far as we know, 64 is the highest dimension of real data used for performance evaluation in high-dimensional access methods with the only exception of 100-dimensional EigenFace data used in [19].

The remainder of this paper is organized as follows. In Section 2, the summary of the comparison and analysis of the SR-tree and the VA-File is given. Based on the summary, the motivation and design principles of the A-tree are presented. Section 3 describes the definitions and algorithms of the A-tree. Section 4 presents the results of a performance evaluation of the A-tree and conventional access methods. Finally, Section 5 concludes the paper.

2 Motivation: An Introduction of Approximation Mechanism in Tree Structure

In this section, we summarize the result of performance evaluation of the SR-tree and the VA-File. Based on the summary, we present the design philosophy of the A-tree, and shows the uniqueness of the A-tree among the proposed indices for high-dimensional data.

2.1 Properties of the SR-tree and the VA-File

We have performed extensive experiments to analyze the SR-tree and the VA-File. The details of the experiments are described in [15]. The result revealed that both indices have their own drawbacks. The evaluation result can be summarized as follows:

(1) For non-uniformly distributed data such as real data and synthetic clustered data, the SR-tree offers better performance than the VA-File. Since the tree structure changes flexibly according to the distribution of data sets, the SR-tree exhibits higher search performance for non-uniformly distribute data sets. In the VA-File, vector data are approximated based on absolute positions. Since the approximation of absolute vector positions is independent of data distribution, a large number of dense data tend to be approximated by same value. Hence, the absolute approximation leads to large approximation errors for skew data. Thus, the VA-File is not effective for non-uniformly distributed data which are commonly found in real applications.

(2) However, in the SR-tree, like many other indices in the R-tree family, the size of entries in a node

---

[1] Recently, Berchtold et al. have reported that the IQ-tree outperforms the VA-File in the range of dimensionality up to 16 [4].

is directly proportional to dimensionality. Hence, as dimensionality increases, the fanout of nodes becomes small. This causes the increase of backtracks of non-leaf nodes; thus degrades search performance.

(3) Increasing node page size leads to the increase of fanout. With real data, the SR-tree provides the lowest search cost at one page per node, and the structures for larger node size require higher cost. However, larger fanout contributes to the reduction of the number of node accesses.

(4) In the SR-tree, as dimensionality increases, the frequency of the usage of MBSs decreases since MBSs occupy much larger volume than MBRs. Hence the contribution of MBSs in node pruning is small in high-dimensional spaces.

2.2 The Design Philosophy of the A-tree

By analyzing the experimental results, we have developed a new index data structure, A-tree, which is based on the following design philosophy:

- **Tree Structure:** From the evaluation result (1), we adopt a tree index.

- **Relative Approximation:** To overcome the problem of tree indices identified in the evaluation result (2), we introduced a new notion, relative approximation, which is a simple yet powerful approximation method utilizing the hierarchy of tree indices. In relative approximation, bounding regions or data points are approximated by their relative positions in terms of parent's bounding region. Relative approximation has the following benefits:

  - Unlike the absolute approximation in the VA-File, approximation values of the relative approximation change in accordance with the data distribution. By this flexibility, the approximation error in the relative approximation is considerably smaller than that of the VA-File. This feature is especially effective for non-uniformly distributed vectors, commonly found in real applications.

  - Since approximation values can be compactly represented, the size of entries in an index node becomes small, which implies larger fanout. This leads to the reduction of the number of node accesses as shown in evaluation result (3).

  - Compact representation of approximated bounding regions allows wider design options of tree configuration freed from traditional tree indices. More concretely, each index node of the A-tree contains representation

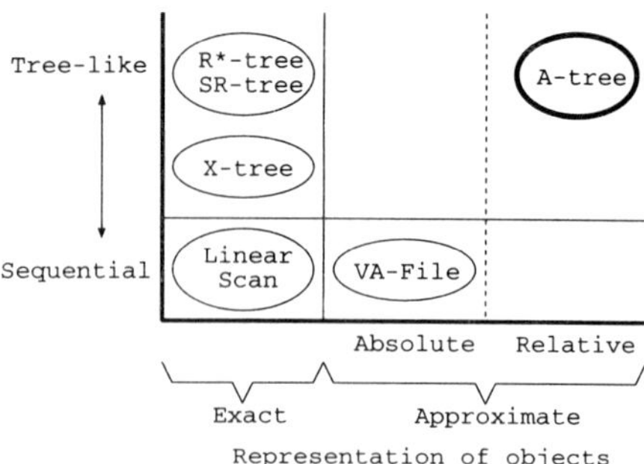

Figure 1: Classification of spatial access methods.

of i) exact position of a bounding region B; and ii) relative approximation of B's children. Therefore, by fetching a node of an A-tree, we can obtain the (partial) information on bounding regions in two generations. This configuration is also useful for efficient handling of update operations.

As a negative side, approximation error may cause the degradation of the power of pruning subtrees in searching. From the performance evaluation presented in Section 4, we have confirmed the benefits of relative approximation well compensate the approximation error.

- **Partial Usage of MBSs:** Since the SR-tree is one of the best indices among the tree indices proposed so far, the SR-tree is used as a start point in the design of the A-tree. However, as shown in the evaluation result (4), the effect of MBSs is limited in search of high dimensional data. Hence, MBSs are not stored in the A-tree, but the centroid of data objects in a subtree is used only for insertion and deletion.

In all, the A-tree is a new index which applied the notion of the relative approximation to the hierarchical structure of the SR-tree. However, this application is not simple; the configuration of the A-tree is unique in that 1) each node contains an MBR and representation of relative approximation of its children; and 2) centroid of data objects are used only for update.

2.3 Classification of Indices

Figure 1 shows a classification of spatial access methods from two viewpoints: representation of spatial objects and index structure. Conventional spatial access methods can be roughly classified into the following three categories: (1) linear scan; (2) the VA-File, a sequential file of absolute approximation of feature vectors; and (3) R-tree family which has tree structures. R-tree family can be further classified into "pure" tree-structured indices such as the R*-tree and the SR-tree, and "hybrid" of tree and sequential structure such as the X-tree, which, with the notion of supernode, shows stronger property of sequential scan as dimensionality increases. The A-tree does not belong to any of these categories and is unique in that i) the A-tree is a tree-structured index; and ii) the representation of MBRs and data objects is based on approximation relative to their parent MBRs.

3 The Data Structure and Algorithms of the A-tree

In this section, we first give the definitions of **VBR (Virtual Bounding Rectangle)**, which is representation of relative approximation of an MBR or a data object in the A-tree. Then we describe the structure of the A-tree. Also, algorithms for searching and updating are presented. The nearest neighbor search algorithm is guaranteed to return exact answers, that is, the A-tree finds the desired objects without omission.

3.1 Virtual Bounding Rectangle

A VBR is a rectangle that contain and approximate an MBR or a data object. In the A-tree, children MBRs and data objects are approximated as VBRs by the relative position in terms of their parent MBR.

A rectangle A in n-dimensional space is represented by the two endpoints a and a' of its major diagonal: $A = (a, a')$, where $a = [a_1, a_2, \ldots, a_n]$, $a' = [a'_1, a'_2, \ldots, a'_n]$, and $a_i \leq a'_i$ for $i \in \{1, 2, \ldots, n\}$. Let $B = (b, b')$ ($b = [b_1, b_2, \ldots, b_n]$, $b' = [b'_1, b'_2, \ldots, b'_n]$) be a rectangle contained in A. Hence, $a_i \leq b_i \leq b'_i \leq a'_i$ ($i = 1, 2, \ldots, n$) holds. The basic idea of relative approximation is to quantize the start value b_i and the end value b'_i of the interval (b_i, b'_i) relatively to the interval (a_i, a'_i). The quantization functions for the start and end values are similar but slightly different.

We will define the quantization functions more specifically. Let q (≥ 1) be an integer. The quantization function Q_s for start values is defined as follows:

$$Q_s(b_i) = a_i + \frac{(a'_i - a_i)h_s(b_i)}{q}$$

where

$$h_s(b_i) = \begin{cases} q - 1 & \text{(if } b_i = a'_i) \\ \left\lfloor \left(\frac{b_i - a_i}{a'_i - a_i}\right) \cdot q \right\rfloor & \text{(otherwise)} \end{cases}$$

Similarly, the quantization function Q_e for end values is defined as follows:

$$Q_e(b'_i) = a_i + \frac{(a'_i - a_i)h_e(b'_i)}{q}$$

where

$$h_e(b'_i) = \begin{cases} 1 & \text{(if } b'_i = a_i) \\ \left\lceil \left(\frac{b'_i - a_i}{a'_i - a_i}\right) \cdot q \right\rceil & \text{(otherwise)} \end{cases}$$

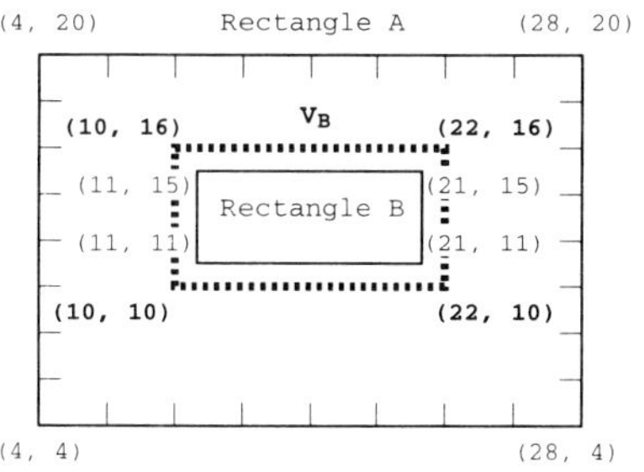

Figure 2: An example of spatial representation using VBR.

Note that $h_s(b_i) \in \{0, 1, \ldots, q - 1\}$, and $h_e(b'_i) \in \{1, 2, \ldots, q\}$. Also, it is easy to verify that the following property holds:

$$a_i \leq Q_s(b_i) \leq b_i \leq b'_i \leq Q_e(b'_i) \leq a'_i \qquad (1)$$

The **virtual bounding rectangle** (**VBR** for short) of B (in A with radix q) is the rectangle

$$V_B = (v, v')$$

where

$$v = (Q_s(b_1), Q_s(b_2), \ldots, Q_s(b_n))$$
$$v' = (Q_e(b'_1), Q_e(b'_2), \ldots, Q_e(b'_n))$$

From the property (1), B is contained in V_B, and V_B is contained in A. Let C be a data object contained in a rectangle A. Since a data object can be regarded as a special rectangle of which two diagonal endpoints coincide, the VBR of C (in A with radix q) can be similarly defined. Figure 2 shows an example of VBR. In this figure, V_B is the VBR of B in A with radix 8.

The VBR V_B of B (in A with radix q) can be represented by $2n$ integers $h_s(b_i)$, $h_e(b'_i)$ ($i = 1, 2, \ldots, n$). Since the number of possible values of $h_s(b_i)$ is q, $h_s(b_i)$ can be represented by a binary code of length l ($= \lceil \log_2 q \rceil$). The same discussion applies to $h_e(b'_i)$. More specifically, we define the binary representation of $h_s(b_i)$ be $[h_s(b_i)]_2$. Also, the binary representation of $h_e(b'_i)$ be $[h_e(b'_i) - 1]_2$. Here, $[x]_2$ is the binary number of an integer x. We call the binary code of length $2nl$, which are obtained by concatenating these $2n$ binary codes of length l, as the **subspace code** of V_B (in A with radix q). For a data object C, the VBR V_C of C (in A with radix q) can be represented by n integers $h_s(b_i)$ ($i = 1, 2, \ldots, n$). Hence, the subspace code of V_C (in A with radix q) is of length nl. For example, for the V_B in Figure 2, $h_s(b_1) = 2$, $h_e(b'_1) = 6$, $h_s(b_2) = 3$, and $h_e(b'_2) = 6$. Hence, 010101011101, which is the concatenation of four binary codes $[2]_2$, $[6 - 1]_2$, $[3]_2$, $[6 - 1]_2$ of length 3 ($= \lceil \log_2 8 \rceil$), is the subspace code of V_B in A with radix 8. The subspace code of a VBR V is denoted by $sc(V)$.

Obviously, there is a tradeoff between the length of subspace code and the approximation error. We will discuss this tradeoff in Section 4.

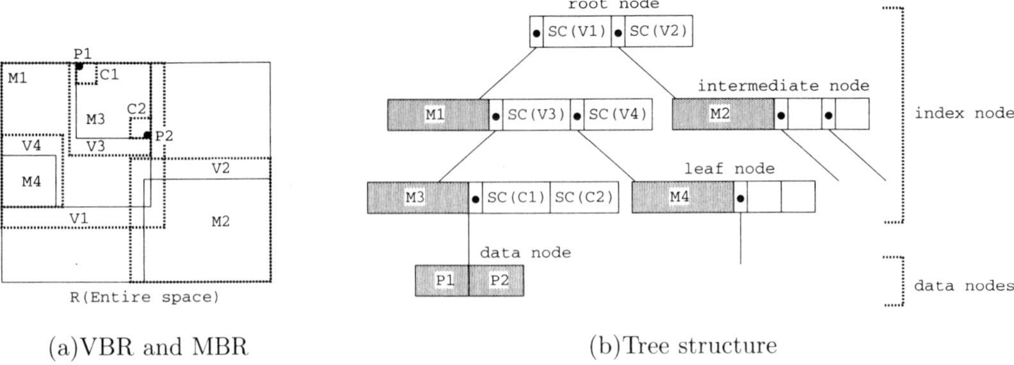

(a)VBR and MBR   (b)Tree structure

Figure 3: The A-tree structure.

3.2 Index Structure

Besides MBRs and data objects, subspace code of VBRs are included in the structure of the A-tree. Figure 3 shows an example of this structure. In Figure 3(a), the rectangle R represents the entire space. $M1$ and $M2$ represent rectangles in R. $M1$ is the MBR of $M3$ and $M4$. $M3$ is the MBR of data objects P_1 and P_2. In this structure, $V1$, $V2$, $V3$ and $V4$ are the VBR of $M1$ in R, the VBR of $M2$ in R, the VBR of $M3$ in $M1$, and the VBR of $M4$ in $M1$, respectively. Also, $C1$ and $C2$ are the VBRs of $P1$ and $P2$ in $M3$, respectively.

As shown in Figure 3(b), A-trees consist of index nodes and data nodes. Index nodes other than the root in A-trees contain exactly one MBR, say M, and subspace codes of VBRs of MBRs in children nodes. M is the MBR of MBRs (or data objects) contained in children nodes. In the root node, no MBR is contained; instead, the entire data space is assumed. When creating A-trees, subspace codes of children VBRs in a node can be calculated from the information of their parent MBR in the same node and the children MBRs (or data objects). In case of the root node, subspace codes of children VBRs are calculated from the information of the entire data space and the children MBRs. Inversely, when searching data objects, the absolute positions of children VBRs of a node can be calculated from the parent MBR and subspace codes of those VBRs stored in the node. Therefore, a node in A-trees contains partial information of MBRs in two consecutive generations; namely the exact position of an MBR and approximate positions of its children MBRs. The search algorithm of the A-tree effectively uses these VBRs for node pruning.

In A-trees, index nodes are classified into leaf nodes, intermediate nodes and the root node. The configuration of each type of nodes is described below:

1. Data nodes:

   A data node has a list of entries (P_1, o_1), (P_2, o_2), $\ldots$, (P_m, o_m), where P_i $(i = 1, 2, \ldots, m)$ is the spatial vector of a data object, and o_i $(i = 1, 2, \ldots, m)$ is the pointer to the data object description record. The number of entries in a leaf, m, is bounded by predefined minimum and maximum.

2. Leaf nodes:

   There is a one-to-one correspondence between data nodes and leaf nodes. The leaf node corresponding to a data node $N((P_1, o_1), (P_2, o_2), \ldots, (P_m, o_m))$ has i) a rectangle M, which is the MBR of $P_1, P_2, \ldots, P_m$. ii) a pointer to N; and iii) a list of entries $sc(V_1), sc(V_2), \ldots, sc(V_m)$, where V_i is the VBR of P_i in M $(i = 1, 2, \ldots, m.)$

3. Intermediate nodes:

   An intermediate node, which is an index nodes other than the root node and leaf nodes, contains i) a rectangle M, which is the MBR of children nodes' MBRs. ii) a list of entries, each of which is a quadruplet $(ptr, sc(V), \omega, P_{centroid})$. where ptr is the pointer to a child node C. V is the VBR of the MBR contained in C, ω is the number of all data objects contained in the subtree rooted by C, and $P_{centroid}$ is the centroid of the data objects in the subtree.

   As explained in Section 2.2, in the A-trees, MBS radius is not stored in non-leaf nodes. ω and $P_{centroid}$ is used only for the insertion or deletion of data objects. Since the search algorithm uses only M, ptr and $sc(V)$, the data of ptr and $sc(V)$ is clustered together in the implementation. This method of implementation allows larger fanout of $ptrs$ and faster access to the necessary data in searching.

4. The root node:

   The root node has entries of the form: $(ptr, sc(V), \omega, P_{centroid})$, where ptr is the pointer to a child node C, V is the VBR of the MBR contained in C, ω is the number of all data objects contained in the subtree rooted by C, and $P_{centroid}$ is the centroid of the data objects in the subtree.

3.3 Full Utilization

For data-partitioning index trees, the number of entries is less than the maximum number of entry slots in most of the nodes.[2] That is, there are many empty slots in index nodes. We present a new technique, **full utilization**, which fully uses all disk pages in an A-tree structure. With this technique, blank disk space is equitably distributed among all entries in a node. The distributed space is then unevenly assigned to each dimension in an entry. The amount of assigned space in an entry depends on the edge length of the parent MBR. Dimensions along which the MBR has longer edge have higher priority and a large number of bits are assigned to the dimensions. This assignment reduces the approximation error.

Let e_{max} be the maximum number of entry slots in a node. A node has available space of size $l \cdot n \cdot e_{max}$ for entire entry slots, where l is the length of subspace code and n is the dimension of the space. In the full utilization, this space is evenly shared by entries. Hence, if e is the number of stored entries in a node, each entry is assigned a space of the length:

$$L_{entry} = \frac{l \cdot n \cdot e_{max}}{e}$$

Note that the code of length L_{entry} is equitably assigned to each entry. If E_i is the edge length of a parent MBR on the i-th dimension ($i = 1, \ldots, n$), the code length for approximating the i-th position coordinate in an entry is determined as:

$$L_i = \log_2 \left(E_i \cdot \sqrt[n]{\frac{2^{L_{entry}}}{\prod_{j=1}^{n} E_j}} \right)$$

Code length is calculated in every accessed node for the search and the updating of an A-tree with full utilization.

3.4 Searching

Figure 4 shows the k-nearest neighbor search algorithm for the A-tree, which is an improvement on the algorithm in [9]. In the algorithm of [9], which uses traditional tree structures, MINDIST (i.e. minimum distance) between MBRs in a node and a given query point are calculated and kept in a priority queue. The priority queue is sorted in the ascending order of MINDIST. Nodes are visited from the top of the queue until the queue becomes empty. Also, a list is maintained to keep k-nearest objects found during the execution of the algorithm. The priority queue is pruned

---

[2] The exception is the Hilbert R-tree [10]; this method can utilize about 100 % page space.

```
Procedure search(point query, integer k)
1.  enqueue(a_pointer_to_the_root, 0);
2.  for i = 1 to k,
              NNOL[i] := (node : dummy, dist : ∞);
3.  for i = 1 to k, NNVL[i] := ∞;
4.  while emptyQueue() = false do
5.     N := dequeue();
6.    if N is a data node then
7.       for each entry ∈ N do
8.          if DIST(query, entry.vector) ≤
                               NNOL[k].dist then
9.             NNOL[k].node := entry.oid;
10.            NNOL[k].dist :=
                       DIST(query, entry.vector);
11.            sort NNOL by dist;
12.            pruneQueue(NNOL[k].dist);
13.         endif
14.      enddo
15.    else         // N is an index node
16.       for each entry ∈ N do
17.         vbr := decode(N.MBR, entry.sc(VBR));
18.         if MINDIST(query, vbr) ≤ NNOL[k].dist
            and MINDIST(query, vbr) ≤ NNVL[k]
            then
19.            enqueue(entry.ptr, MINDIST(query, vbr));
20.            if N is a leaf node and
               MAXDIST(query, vbr) ≤ NNVL[k] then
21.               NNVL[k] := MAXDIST(query, vbr);
22.               sort NNVL;
23.               pruneQueue(NNVL[k]);
24.            endif
25.         endif
26.      enddo
27.    endif
28.  enddo
29.  output(NNOL);        // output the result
```

Figure 4: k-nearest neighbor search algorithm.

by eliminating nodes whose distance to the query is longer than that of the k-th nearest neighbor object in the list.

In the priority queue of the search algorithm of the A-tree, pairs of a pointer to a node and a distance are kept. The queue is sorted in the ascending order of the distance. Since the sort of queue incurs high CPU cost if a substantial amount of data is stored in the queue, the search algorithm performs filtering using two nearest neighbor lists. One is the usual nearest neighbor list created using the algorithm of [9]. Candidate data objects and their distance from the query point are stored in this list. It is called the **NNOL** (Nearest Neighbor Object List) in this paper. The other list stores the maximum distance from the query point to VBRs of data objects, and is called the **NNVL** (Nearest Neighbor VBR List.)

In Procedure *search* (see Figure 4), as an initialization, the pair of a pointer to the root and 0 is stored in the priority queue (step 1). In step 5, the function dequeue() dequeues the pair from the top of the priority queue, extracts a pointer to a node from the pair, traverses the extracted pointer, and fetch a node. If a fetched node is an index node, the positions of VBRs are calculated from the MBR of the node and the subspace codes for all entries by the function `decode()` (step 17). If the distance between *query* and a VBR is less than or equal to the k-th distance in NNOL (and the k-th distance in NNVL), the function `enqueue()` inserts the pair of the pointer to the corresponding child node and the distance into the queue, then sort the queue in the ascending order of the distance. (steps 18 and 19). In steps 20 to 24, `MAXDIST`(*query*, *vbr*), the maximum distance from *query* to each VBR, is calculated. Moreover, if the distance is less than or equal to the k-th distance in NNVL, NNVL is updated and the function `pruneQueue()` is executed. This function reduces the queue size by eliminating pairs in the queue whose distance to *query* is longer than the argument.

If the extracted node is a data node, data objects in the node are examined (steps 6 and 7). If the distance between *query* and the data object is less than or equal to the k-th nearest neighbor object found so far, the data object together with its distance is stored in NNOL as a nearest neighbor candidate (steps 8, 9, 10), and NNOL is sorted (step 11). Furthermore, queue filtering is performed using NNOL (step 12).

We explain the search algorithm using Figure 3(a) as an example. First, VBRs $V1$ and $V2$ are calculated from the position coordinates of R, $sc(V1)$ and $sc(V2)$. If the distance from the query point to $V1$ is less or equal to the distance to the k-th nearest neighbor, the node which contains $M1$ is fetched, then VBRs $V3$ and $V4$ are calculated from $M1$, $sc(V3)$ and $sc(V4)$. Similarly, the calculated VBRs are compared to the k-th nearest neighbor. If $V3$ is not subject to pruning, the node which contains $M3$ is fetched, then the VBRs $C1$ and $C2$ are calculated from $M3$, $sc(C1)$ and $sc(C2)$, and the calculated VBRs are compared to the k-th nearest neighbor. Moreover, `MAXDIST` from the query point to $C1$ and to $C2$ are stored in NNVL. If $C1$ is not subject to pruning, $P1$ is accessed.

3.5 Updating

The update algorithm of the A-tree is based on that of the SR-tree. Starting from data object insertion or deletion, it propagates upward while adjusting MBRs and centroids in non-leaf nodes. The difference between the A-tree and the SR-tree is that the A-tree algorithm needs to calculate and update the codes of VBRs. Concretely, the A-tree structure is updated as follows:

(1) Let N be a data node, and M be the MBR of N. Then, M is stored in the parent node of N. If a data object insertion or deletion occurs in N, adjust M and the centroid of all data objects contained in N.

(2) If M is unchanged, calculate the code of the VBR that approximates the inserted object from M, and update. Otherwise, update the codes of all VBRs stored in the parent node of N.

(3) Let N be an index node, and M be the MBR of N. If a data object insertion or deletion occurs in the subtree whose top node is N, update the centroid of all data objects contained in the subtree, which is stored in the parent node of N. Moreover, if the insertion or deletion causes a change in a child MBR, adjust M.

(4) If M is unchanged, calculate the code of the VBR that approximates the updated child MBR from M, and update. Otherwise, update the codes of all VBRs stored in the parent node of N.

On structures with full utilization, code length for approximating MBRs or data objects in each node varies according to circumstances. Therefore, if the MBR or the number of entries in a node is changed, the codes for all entries in the node must be calculated. Concretely, the A-tree with full utilization performs (2') and (4') instead of (2) and (4):

(2') If M and the number of entries in N are unchanged, calculate the code of the VBR that approximates the inserted object, and update. Otherwise, calculate the code length assigned to each dimension for approximating all data objects from M and the number of entries, and update the codes of all VBRs stored in the parent node of N.

(4') If M and the number of entries in N are unchanged, calculate the code of the VBR that approximates the updated child MBR, and update. Otherwise, calculate the code length assigned to each dimension for approximating all children MBRs, and update the codes of all VBRs stored in the parent node of N.

4 Performance Test

To verify the effectiveness of the A-tree, we implemented the algorithm and compared our proposed method with the VA-File and the SR-tree. The experiments used three data sets:

(1) Uniformly distributed data sets
Random point sets uniformly distributed in the range [0.1) in each dimension.

(2) Real data sets
Feature vectors of Hue histograms extracted from color images.

(3) Cluster data sets
For cluster data sets, the number of clusters is 100 in each data set and the center of cluster is

Table 1: Maximum number of entry slots in SR-trees.

Dimensionality	4	8	16	24	32
Non-leaf	73	39	20	13	10
Leaf	227	120	62	41	31
Dimensionality	40	48	56	64	
Non-leaf	8	7	6	5	
Leaf	25	21	18	15	

Table 2: Maximum number of entry slots in A-trees.

Dimensionality	4	8	16	24	32
Root	818	511	292	204	157
Intermediate	812	503	283	195	147
Leaf	2706	1342	660	433	319
Dimensionality	40	48	56	64	
Root	127	107	93	81	
Intermediate	117	97	82	71	
Leaf	251	205	173	149	

distributed uniformly in the range [0.10). In addition, as the number of objects is N, $N/100$ objects are gathered according to Gaussian distribution around the center of cluster.

In our evaluation, the dimensionality for synthetic and real data is varied from 4 to 64. The size of all data sets is 100,000. The page size is 8KB. For the A-tree and the SR-tree, one node occupies one page (i.e. 8KB) because both indices give the best search performance under this configuration. In assessing search performance, the page access number and CPU-time were measured by the average of 1.000 queries. Query points were generated randomly and independently of data points in indices. 20-nearest neighbor queries are used. CPU-time was measured on a SUN UltraSPARC-II 296MHz. The search performance of the SR-tree was measured using the algorithm presented in [9], which outperforms the branch-and-bound R-tree traversal algorithm [14] as shown in [3]. As for insertion, the average cost for 1,000 insertions was measured; 1,000 objects not included in the indices were inserted into the data sets. The maximum number of entry slots in SR-trees is shown in Table 1. For the A-tree, the most superior structure from among five variants, $l = 4$, $l = 6$, $l = 8$, $l = 10$ and $l = 12$, was chosen. The maximum number of entry slots in A-trees of code length $l = 6$, is shown in Table 2 as an example.

4.1 Search Performance

Figure 5 shows a comparison of the A-tree with the VA-File and the SR-tree. The comparison used code lengths of $l(\in \{4, 6, 8, 10, 12\})$ of the A-tree because these values yield the best search performance for the different levels of dimensionality. The optimum code length for uniformly distributed data sets was $l = 12$ for 4 dimensions, and $l = 4$ for dimensions from 8 to 64. For real data sets, the code lengths selected were $l = 12$ for 4 dimensions, $l = 8$ for 8 dimensions, $l = 6$ for dimensions from 16 to 64. Also, for clustered data sets, the optimum code length was $l = 12$ for 4 dimensions, $l = 6$ for dimensions from 8 to 64. For the comparison shown in Figure 5, we selected the best code length for each dimension. Also, for the VA-File, the most superior approximation file from among three variants, $l = 4$, $l = 6$ and $l = 8$, was chosen according to [18].

As shown in Figure 5, in all data sets ranging in dimensionality from 4 to 64, the effectiveness of the A-tree is obvious. The A-tree is almost equal to the VA-File with uniform data sets, and greatly outperforms the other structures for non-uniformly distributed data sets such as real data sets. The A-tree is extremely effective for non-uniformly distributed data sets in particular. For example, the A-tree needs 77.3 % (77.7 %) fewer accesses than the SR-tree (the VA-File) for real data sets with 64 dimensions.

Figure 6 shows the effectiveness of full utilization. Although both A-trees have the same organization, their coding differs. Since full utilization distributes blank disk space among all entries in a node for coding, the approximation errors of VBRs are reduced. Accordingly, this technique decreases the search cost of the A-tree.

The experimental results in the rest of the paper are based on real data sets.

4.2 Superiority of the A-tree

4.2.1 Comparison of the A-tree with the SR-tree

Figure 7 shows the number of page accesses to index nodes of the A-tree and non-leaf nodes of the SR-tree. Also, Figure 8 shows the page accesses to data nodes of the A-tree and leaf nodes of the SR-tree. As shown in these figures, the A-tree requires remarkably fewer accesses to both index nodes and data nodes compared with the SR-tree. Moreover, the difference between the two curves increases with dimensionality. Confirming the position stated in Section 2.1, one of the most significant problems with the SR-tree is its high search cost for non-leaf node accesses because both MBRs and MBSs are stored in non-leaf nodes. Since the A-tree is based on relative approximation, the cost of storing VBRs is small. This property leads to higher performance.

4.2.2 Approximation Error with Variable Length Code

VBRs include approximation error which could degenerates the search performance of the A-tree. There is a tradeoff between approximation error and the length of subspace code. We measured the approximation

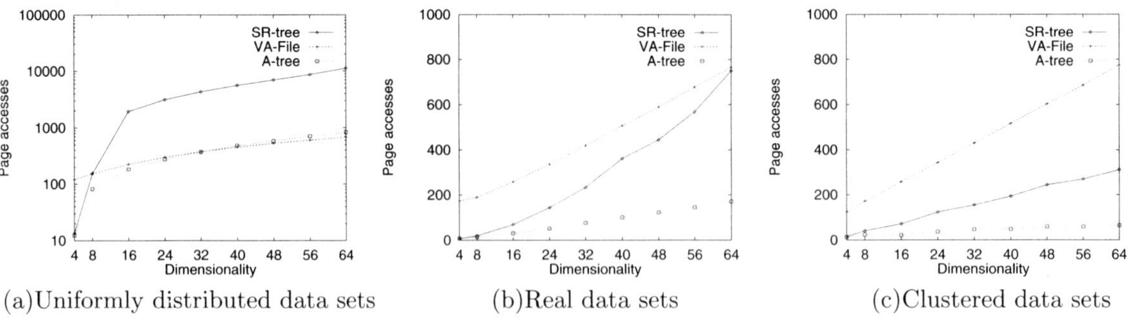

(a)Uniformly distributed data sets   (b)Real data sets   (c)Clustered data sets

Figure 5: Number of page accesses versus dimensionality.

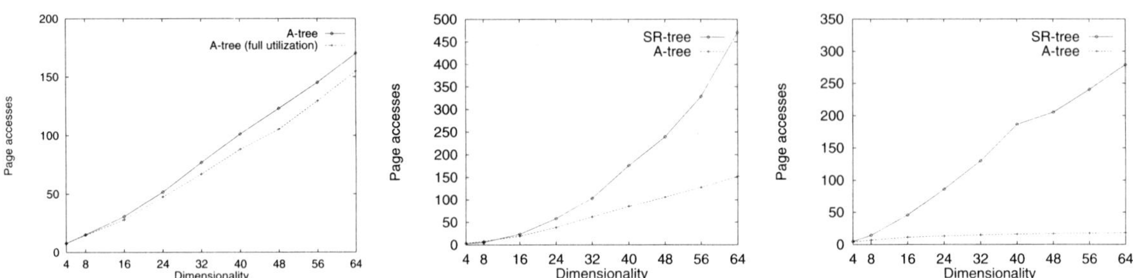

Figure 6: Number of page accesses for the structure with full utilization.

Figure 7: Number of page accesses to index nodes of the A-tree and non-leaf nodes of the SR-tree.

Figure 8: Number of page accesses to data nodes of the A-tree and leaf nodes of the SR-tree.

error of the distance between query points and visited VBRs in the root and intermediate nodes during search. Figure 9 plots the error of MBR approximation against dimensionality for different code lengths. Note the logarithmic scale of the vertical axis in this figure. We defined the approximation error ϵ of the distance as follows:

$$\epsilon = (1 - r) \cdot 100, \quad r = \frac{1}{S} \sum_{i=1}^{S} \frac{\|\boldsymbol{p}, V_i\|}{\|\boldsymbol{p}, M_i\|}$$

where $\boldsymbol{p}$ is a query point and S is the number of visited VBRs in the root and intermediate nodes during search. V_i are the visited VBRs, and $\|\boldsymbol{p}, V_i\|$ is the distance between $\boldsymbol{p}$ and V_i. M_i are the MBR corresponding to V_i. ϵ was measured by the average of 1,000 queries.

Figure 9 shows that the approximation errors versus dimensionality for the A-trees with $l = 4$, $l = 6$ and $l = 8$. In the structures with $l = 4$, $l = 6$ and $l = 8$, the distance decreases by about 10 %, 2 % and 0.7 %, respectively. The approximation error decreases significantly as the length of the code increases. However, on the other hand, longer codes cause smaller fanout of nodes, thus could degenerate search performance. Hence, there is an optimum code length in terms of search performance. As described in Section 4.1, in our experimental setting, the optimum code length changes from $l = 4$ to 12 depending on the di-

mensionality and distribution of data sets. In A-trees with optimum code length, the effect of reducing the entry size outweighs the influence of VBR error; consequently, fewer node accesses are required.

4.2.3 Comparison of the A-tree with the VA-File

This section explains why the A-tree is superior to the VA-File. Although both the A-tree and the VA-File employ a common idea of approximating position coordinates, their data structures and algorithms are completely different. In the A-tree, the approximation is calculated in terms of a parent MBR. Therefore, as the level of nodes goes down to the leaves, smaller VBRs are used for approximation. This property is in clear contrast to the approximation computed by the entire space in the VA-File. The difference of data structures causes the difference in accuracy of data object approximation. Figure 10 shows the average edge length of VBRs for data objects. In the VA-File, the edge of each cell occupies the interval 2^{-l}. When compared with the VA-File, the A-tree provides high accuracy for VBRs as shown in the figure. Consequently, fewer data object accesses are required and the search cost is reduced. Figure 11 gives the number of object accesses as a function of dimensionality. As expected, the difference in data object access number between the A-tree and the VA-File is significant.

524

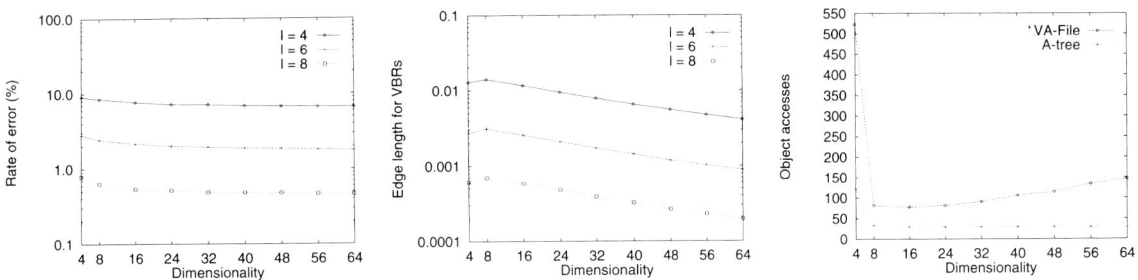

Figure 9: Approximation error in the distance between query points and VBRs in root and intermediate nodes.

Figure 10: Edge length of VBRs in leaf nodes.

Figure 11: Number of object accesses versus dimensionality.

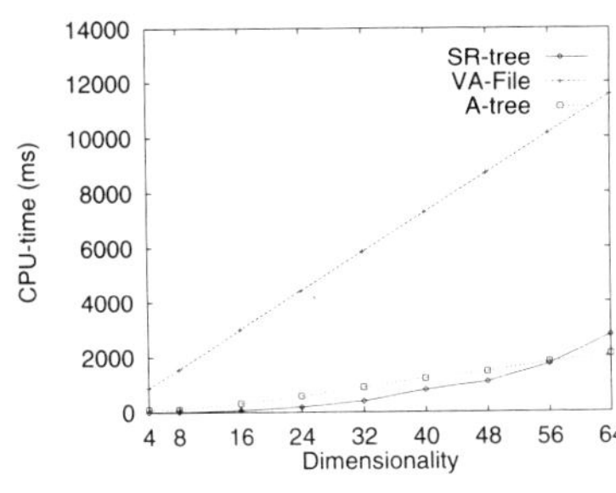

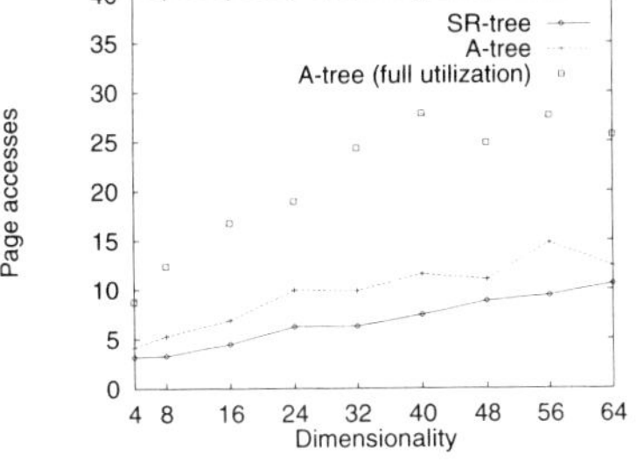

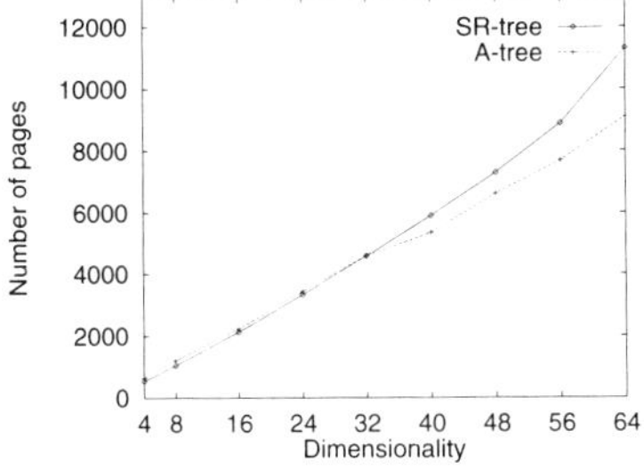

Figure 12: CPU time for search.

Figure 13: Page accesses for insertion.

Figure 14: Storage cost.

4.3 Evaluation of CPU-time

Figure 12 shows the CPU-time measured for the VA-File, the SR-tree, and the A-tree. CPU-time was measured using the same conditions used in Figure 5(b). The figure indicates that the A-tree is superior in terms of CPU-time. For 64 dimensions, the performance of the A-tree is almost equal to that of the SR-tree, and it outperforms the VA-File by 81.8 %.

Since the VA-File must calculate the approximated position coordinates for all objects, its CPU-time is much higher than the A-tree as shown in Figure 12. On the other hand, although the A-tree needs to calculate VBRs, the CPU-time of the A-tree is lower than that of the VA-File for the following reason. Since the number of node accesses is extremely low, calculation and comparison of the distances from the query point are reduced. Therefore, the A-tree requires less CPU time even though it must calculate VBRs. In addition, the search algorithm filters the queue using two nearest neighbor lists in order to lower CPU cost. This filtering lowers queue length and provides a valuable contribution to the reduction in CPU-time. As a result, the A-tree provides reasonable CPU cost.

4.4 Insertion Cost

Figure 13 compares the A-tree with the SR-tree in terms of insertion cost under the same conditions as used in Figure 5(b). Insertion cost was measured as the average cost of inserting 1.000 randomly-selected objects. Random objects were used because inserted objects are usually unpredictable in practical situations.

Since the A-tree must access VBRs in addition to MBRs and data objects to maintain the structure, the A-tree incurs larger insertion cost than the SR-tree. However, the increase in cost for the A-tree without full utilization is modest. On the other hand, the A-tree with full utilization considerably increases insertion cost. Since full utilization provides lower search cost, this method is suitable for static data set.

4.5 Storage Cost

Figure 14 compares the storage cost of the A-tree to that of the SR-tree under the same conditions as used in Figure 5(b). The A-tree and the SR-tree incur similar storage costs for 4 to 32 dimensions, but the A-tree incurs 19.5 % less cost for 64 dimensions. The storage cost of the A-tree is low even though it includes VBRs. There are two reasons for this. First, VBRs need only small storage volumes. Second, the number of index nodes in the A-tree is extremely small due to its larger fanout.

5 Conclusions

This paper has presented the A-tree (approximation tree) which offers excellent performance in searching for data in high-dimensional spaces. First, we analyzed the VA-File and the SR-tree, existing structures used for high-dimensional searching, and discussed their problems. Based on this analysis, we developed the A-tree to overcome the problems and so achieve higher search performance.

The A-tree achieves high performance due to its use of relative approximation. Since the A-tree index nodes contain VBRs, whose storage size is low, the volume of entries in the nodes is reduced which yields improved search performance. Although VBRs include approximation error in terms of size, the error is reduced by the mechanism of relative approximation. By using this mechanism, A-tree bests the alternative search methods, the VA-File and the SR-tree.

The mechanism of the A-tree is remarkably efficient, especially for non-uniformly distributed data sets such as real data sets. For non-uniformly distributed data sets, the A-tree outperforms the SR-tree and the VA-File in all dimensions up to 64, which is the highest dimension examined in our experiments. The A-tree requires 77.3 % (77.7 %) fewer page accesses than the SR-tree (the VA-File) for real data with 64-dimensions.

We also present a new technique, full utilization, which fully uses all disk pages in an A-tree structure. This technique provides higher search performance since the approximation errors of VBRs are reduced.

VBRs approximate MBRs and data objects, however, searches yield exact solutions, that is, the A-tree finds the desired objects without omission. The search performance of the A-tree is greatly improved, and its storage cost is low. Thus, this method well supports practical applications.

References

[1] S. Arya, D. M. Mount, N. S. Netanyahu, R. Silverman, and A. Y. Wu. An Optimal Algorithm for Approximate Nearest Neighbor Searching. In *Proc. of ACM-SIAM Symposium on Discrete Algorithms*, pp. 573–582, 1994.

[2] N. Beckmann, H. P. Kriegel, R. Schneider, and B. Seeger. The R*-tree: An Efficient and Robust Access Method for Points and Rectangles. In *Proc. ACM SIGMOD Conf.*, pp. 322–331, Atlantic City, NJ, May 1990.

[3] S. Berchtold, C. Böhm, D. A. Keim, and H.-P. Kriegel. A Cost Model For Nearest Neighbor Search in High-Dimensional Data Space. In *Proc. ACM Symp. on Principles of Database Systems*, pp. 78–86, March 1997.

[4] S. Berchtold, C. Böhm, H. V. Jagadish, H.-P. Kriegel, and J. Sander. Independent Quantization: An Index Compression Technique for High-Dimensional Data Spaces. In *Proc. of IEEE 16th International Conference on Data Engineering*, pp. 577–588, 2000.

[5] S. Berchtold, D. A. Keim, and H.-P. Kriegel. The X-tree: An Index Structure for High-Dimensional Data. In *Proc. of the 22nd International Conference on Very Large Data Bases (VLDB)*, pp. 28–39, Bombay, September 1996.

[6] V. Gaede and O. Günther. Multidimensional Access Methods. *ACM Computing Surveys*, Vol. 30, No. 2, pp. 170–231, June 1998.

[7] A. Gionis, P. Indyk, and R. Motwani. Similarity Search in High Dimensions via Hashing. In *Proc. of the 25th International Conference on Very Large Data Bases (VLDB)*, Edinburgh, Scotland, September 1999.

[8] A. Guttman. R-Trees: A Dynamic Index Structure for Spatial Searching. In *Proc. ACM SIGMOD Conf.*, pp. 47–57, Boston, MA, June 1984. Reprinted in M. Stonebraker, Readings in Database Sys., Morgan Kaufmann, San Mateo, CA, 1988.

[9] G. R. Hjaltason and H. Samet. Ranking in Spatial Databases. In *Proceedings of the 4th Symposium on Spatial Databases*, pp. 83–95, Portland, Maine, August 1995.

[10] I. Kamel and C. Faloutsos. Hilbert R-tree: An Improved R-tree using Fractals. In *Proceedings of the Twentieth International Conference on Very Large Databases*, pp. 500–509, Santiago, Chile, 1994.

[11] N. Katayama and S. Satoh. The SR-tree: An Index Structure for High-Dimensional Nearest Neighbor Queries. In *Proc. ACM SIGMOD International Conference on Management of Data*, pp. 369–380, May 1997.

[12] H. Murase and S. Nayar. Visual Learning and Recognition of 3-D Objects from Appearance. *International Journal of Computer Vision*, Vol. 14, No. 1, pp. 5–24, 1995.

[13] A. Pentland, B. Moghaddam, and T. Starner. View-Based and Modular Eigenspaces for Face Recognition. In *Proc. IEEE Conf. on CVPR*, pp. 84–91, Seattle, Washington, June 1994.

[14] N. Roussopoulos, S. Kelley, and F. Vincent. Nearest Neighbor Queries. In *Proc. ACM SIGMOD International Conference on Management of Data*, pp. 71–79, May 1995.

[15] Y. Sakurai, M. Yoshikawa, S. Uemura, and H. Kojima. The A-tree: An Index Structure for High-Dimensional Spaces Using Relative Approximation. Technical report, Nara Institute of Science and Technology, 2000.

[16] T. K. Sellis, N. Roussopoulos, and C. Faloutsos. Multidimensional Access Methods: Trees Have Grown Everywhere. In *Proc. of the 23rd International Conference on Very Large Data Bases (VLDB)*, pp. 13—14, Athens, August 1997.

[17] H. D. Wactlar, T. Kanade, M. A. Smith, and S. M. Stevens. Intelligent Access to Digital Video: Informedia Project. *IEEE Computer*, Vol. 29, No. 5, pp. 46–52, May 1996.

[18] R. Weber, H.-J. Schek, and S. Blott. A Quantitative Analysis and Performance Study for Similarity-Search Methods in High-Dimensional Spaces. In *Proc. of the 24th International Conference on Very Large Data Bases (VLDB)*, pp. 194–205, New York City, NY, August 1998.

[19] D. A. White and R. Jain. Similarity Indexing with the SS-tree. In *Proc. of IEEE 12th International Conference on Data Engineering*, pp. 516–523, 1996.

Focused Crawling Using Context Graphs

M. Diligenti[†], F. M. Coetzee, S. Lawrence, C. L. Giles and M. Gori[*]

NEC Research Institute, 4 Independence Way, Princeton, NJ 08540-6634 USA
[†]Dipartimento di Ingegneria dell'Informazione, Università di Siena
Via Roma, 56 - 53100 Siena, Italy
{diligmic,gori}@dii.unisi.it, {coetzee,lawrence,giles}@research.nj.nec.com

Abstract

Maintaining currency of search engine indices by exhaustive crawling is rapidly becoming impossible due to the increasing size and dynamic content of the web. Focused crawlers aim to search only the subset of the web related to a specific category, and offer a potential solution to the currency problem. The major problem in focused crawling is performing appropriate credit assignment to different documents along a crawl path, such that short-term gains are not pursued at the expense of less-obvious crawl paths that ultimately yield larger sets of valuable pages. To address this problem we present a focused crawling algorithm that builds a model for the context within which topically relevant pages occur on the web. This context model can capture typical link hierarchies within which valuable pages occur, as well as model content on documents that frequently co-occur with relevant pages. Our algorithm further leverages the existing capability of large search engines to provide partial reverse crawling capabilities. Our algorithm shows significant performance improvements in crawling efficiency over standard focused crawling.

1 Introduction

The size of the publicly indexable world-wide-web has provably surpassed one billion (10^9) documents [1] and as yet growth shows no sign of leveling off. Dynamic content on the web is also growing as time-sensitive materials,

Proceedings of the 26th VLDB Conference,
Cairo, Egypt, 2000.

such as news, financial data, entertainment and schedules become widely disseminated via the web. Search engines are therefore increasingly challenged when trying to maintain current indices using exhaustive crawling. Even using state of the art systems such as AltaVista's *Scooter*, which reportedly crawls ten million pages per day, an exhaustive crawl of the web can take weeks. Exhaustive crawls also consume vast storage and bandwidth resources, some of which are not under the control of the search engine.

Focused crawlers [2, 3] aim to search and retrieve only the subset of the world-wide web that pertains to a specific topic of relevance. The ideal focused crawler retrieves the maximal set of relevant pages while simultaneously traversing the minimal number of irrelevant documents on the web. Focused crawlers therefore offer a potential solution to the currency problem by allowing for standard exhaustive crawls to be supplemented by focused crawls for categories where content changes quickly. Focused crawlers are also well suited to efficiently generate indices for niche search engines maintained by portals and user groups [4], where limited bandwidth and storage space are the norm [5]. Finally, due to the limited resources used by a good focused crawler, users are already using personal PC based implementations [6]. Ultimately simple focused crawlers could become the method of choice for users to perform comprehensive searches of web-related materials.

While promising, the technology that supports focused crawling is still in its infancy. The major open problem in focused crawling is that of properly assigning credit to all pages along a crawl route that yields a highly relevant document. In the absence of a reliable credit assignment strategy, focused crawlers suffer from a limited ability to sacrifice short term document retrieval gains in the interest of better overall crawl performance. In particular, existing crawlers still fall short in learning strategies where topically relevant documents are found by following off-topic pages.

We demonstrate that credit assignment for focused crawlers can be significantly improved by equipping the crawler with the capability of modeling the context within which the topical materials is usually found on the web. Such a context model has to capture typical link hierarchies within which valuable pages occur, as well as describe off-topic content that co-occurs in documents that are frequently closely associated with relevant pages. We present a general framework and a specific implementation of such a context model, which we call a Context Graph. Our algorithm further differs from existing focused crawlers in that it leverages the capability of existing exhaustive search engines to provide partial reverse crawling capabilities. As a result it has a rapid and efficient initialization phase, and is suitable for real-time services.

The outline of the paper is as follows: Section 2 provides a more detailed overview of focused crawling. Section 3 describes the architecture and implementation of our approach. Comparisons with existing focused crawling algorithms on some test crawls are shown in Section 4, and we conclude by discussing extensions and implications in Section 5.

2   Prior Work in Crawling

The first generation of crawlers [7] on which most of the web search engines are based rely heavily on traditional graph algorithms, such as breadth-first or depth-first traversal, to index the web. A core set of URLs are used as a seed set, and the algorithm recursively follows hyper links down to other documents. Document content is paid little heed, since the ultimate goal of the crawl is to cover the whole web.

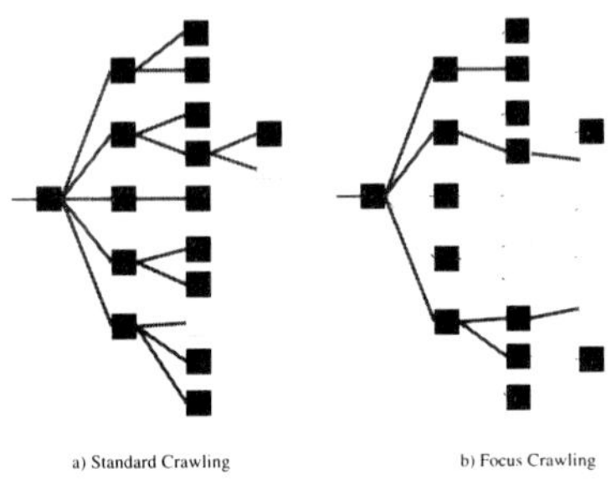

Figure 1: a) A standard crawler follows each link, typically applying a breadth first strategy. If the crawler starts from a document which is i steps from a target document, all the documents that are up to $i-1$ steps from the starting document must be downloaded before the crawler hits the target. b) A focused crawler tries to identify the most promising links, and ignores off-topic documents. If the crawler starts from a document which is i steps from a target document, it downloads a small subset of all the documents that are up to $i-1$ steps from the starting document. If the search strategy is optimal the crawler takes only i steps to discover the target.

A focused crawler efficiently seeks out documents about a specific topic and guides the search based on both the content and link structure of the web [2]. Figure 1 graphically illustrates the difference between an exhaustive breadth-first crawler and a typical focused crawler. A focused crawler implements a strategy that associates a score with each link in the pages it has downloaded [8, 9, 10]. The links are sorted according to the scores and inserted in a queue. A best first search is performed by popping the next page to analyze from the head of the queue. This strategy ensures that the crawler preferentially pursues promising crawl paths.

The simplest focused crawlers use a fixed model of the relevancy class, typically encoded as a classifier, to evaluate the documents that the current document links to (henceforth referred to as children) for topical relevancy [2, 3, 11]. The classifier is either provided by the user in the form of query terms, or can be built from a set of seed documents. Each link is assigned the score of the document to which it leads. More advanced crawlers adapt the classifier based on the retrieved documents, and also model the within-page context of each hyperlink. In the most common adaptive crawlers decision directed feedback is used, where documents that are marked as relevant by the classifier are also used to update the classifier. However, ensuring flexibility in the classifier, without simultaneously corrupting the classifier, is difficult.

A major problem faced by the above focused crawlers is that it is frequently difficult to learn that some sets of off-topic documents often lead reliably to highly relevant documents. This deficiency causes problems in traversing the hierarchical page layouts that commonly occur on the web. Consider for example a researcher looking for papers on neural networks. A large number of these papers are found on the home pages of researchers at computer science departments at universities. When a crawler finds the home page of a university, a good strategy would be to follow the path to the computer science (CS) department, then to the researchers' pages, even though the university and CS department pages in general would have low relevancy scores. While an adaptive focused crawler described above could in principle learn this strategy, it is doubtful that the crawler would ever explore such a path in the first place, especially as the length of the path to be traversed increases.

To explicitly address this problem, Rennie and McCallum [12] used reinforcement learning to train a crawler on specified example web sites containing target documents. The web site or server on which the document appears is repeatedly crawled to learn how to construct optimized paths to the target documents. However, this approach places a burden on the user to specify representative web sites. Initialization can be slow since the search could result in the crawling of a substantial fraction of the host web site. Furthermore, this approach could face difficulty when a hierarchy is distributed across a number of sites.

An additional difficulty faced by existing crawlers is that links on the web are uni-directional, which effectively restricts searching to top-down traversal, a process that we call "forward crawling" (Obtaining pages that link to a particular document is referred to as "backward crawling"). Since web sites frequently have large components that are organized as trees, entering a web site at a leaf can result in a serious barrier to finding closely related pages. In our example, when a researcher's home page is entered, say via a link from a list of papers at a conference site, a good strategy would be for the crawler to find the department member list, and then search the pages of other researchers in the department. However, unless an explicit link exists from the researcher's page to the CS department member list, existing focused crawlers cannot move up the hierarchy to the CS department home page.

Our focused crawler utilizes a compact context representation called a *Context Graph* to model and exploit hierarchies. The crawler also utilizes the limited backward crawling [13, 14] possible using general search engine indices to efficiently focus crawl the web. Unlike Rennie and McCallum's approach [12], our approach does not learn the context within which target documents are located from a small set of web sites, but in principle can back crawl a significant fraction of the whole web starting at each seed or on-topic document. Furthermore, the approach is more efficient in initialization, since the context is constructed by directly branching out from the good set of documents to model the parents, siblings and children of the seed set.

3 The Context Focused Crawler

Our focused crawler, which we call the *Context Focused Crawler* (CFC), uses the limited capability of search engines like AltaVista or Google to allow users to query for pages linking to a specified document. This data can be used to construct a representation of pages that occur within a certain link distance (defined as the minimum number of link traversals necessary to move from one page to another) of the target documents. This representation is used to train a set of classifiers, which are optimized to detect and assign documents to different categories based on the expected link distance from the document to the target document. During the crawling stage the classifiers are used to predict how many steps away from a target document the current retrieved document is likely to be. This information is then used to optimize the search.

There are two distinct stages to using the algorithm when performing a focused crawl session:

1. An initialization phase when a set of context graphs and associated classifiers are constructed for each of the seed documents

2. A crawling phase that uses the classifiers to guide the search, and performs online updating of the context graphs.

The complete system is shown in Figure 2. We now describe the core elements in detail.

3.1 Generating the Context Graphs

The first stage of a crawling session aims to extract the context within which target pages are typically found, and encodes this information in a context graph. A separate context graph is built for every seed element provided by the user. Every seed document forms the first node of its associated context graph. Using an engine such as Google,

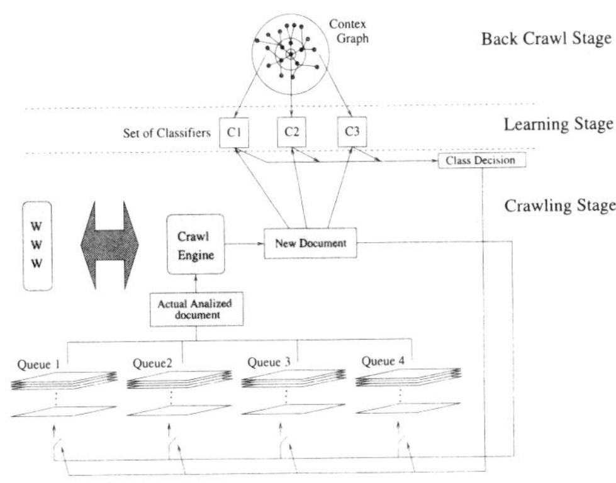

Figure 2: Graphical representation of the Context Focused Crawler. During the initialization stage a set of context graphs are constructed for the seed documents by back-crawling the web, and classifiers for different graph layers are trained. During the crawling stage the crawl engine and the classifiers manage a set of queues that select the next page on which to center the crawl.

a number of pages linking to the target are first retrieved (these pages are called the parents of the seed page). Each parent page is inserted into the graph as a node and an edge is established between the target document node and the parent node. The new nodes compose *layer* 1 of the context graph. The back-crawling procedure is repeated to search all the documents linking to documents of layer 1. These pages are incorporated as nodes in the graph and compose layer 2. The back-linking process is iterated, until a user-specified number of layers have been filled. In practice the number of elements in a given layer can increase suddenly when the number of layers grow beyond some limit. In such a case a statistical sampling of the parent nodes, up to some system dependent limit, is kept. To simplify the link structure, we also use the convention that if two documents in layer i can be accessed from a common parent, the parent document appears two times in the layer $i + 1$. As a result, an equivalent induced graph can be created where each document in the layer $i + 1$ is linked to one and only one document in the layer i.

We define the *depth* of a context graph to be the number of layers in the graph excluding the level 0 (the node storing the seed document). When N levels are in the context graph, path strategies of up to N steps can be modeled. A context graph of depth 2 is shown in Figure 3.

By constructing a context graph, the crawler gains knowledge about topics that are directly or indirectly related to the target topic, as well as a very simple model of the paths that relate these pages to the target documents. As expected, in practice, we find that the arrangement of the nodes in the layers reflect any hierarchical content structure. Highly related content typically appears near the center of the graph, while the outer layers contain more general pages. As a result, when the crawler discovers a page

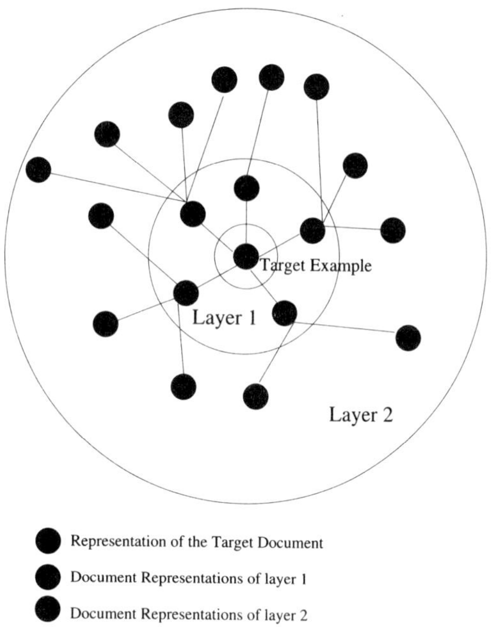

Figure 3: A context graph represents how a target document can be accessed from the web. In each node a web document representation is stored. The graph is organized into layers: each node of layer i is connected to one (and only one) node of the layer $i-1$ (except the single node in layer 0). There are no connections between nodes at the same level. The seed document is stored in layer 0. A document is in layer i if at least i steps (link followings) are needed to reach the target page starting from that document.

with content that occurs higher up in the hierarchy, it can use its knowledge of the graph structure to guide the search towards the target pages. Returning to our example of looking for neural network pages, the context graph will typically discover a hierarchy where levels correspond to researcher home pages, research group pages, and ultimately department and university home pages.

Once context graphs for all seed documents have been built, the corresponding layers from the different context graphs are combined, yielding a layered structure that we call the *Merged Context Graph*.

3.2 Learning Classifiers for the Context Graph Elements

The next stage in initialization builds a set of classifiers for assigning any document retrieved from the web to one of the layers of the merged context graph, and for quantifying the belief in such a classification assignment.

The classifiers require a feature representation of the documents on which to operate. Our present implementation uses keyword indexing of each document using a modification of TF-IDF (Term Frequency Inverse Document Frequency). TF-IDF representation [15] describes a document as a vector relative to a basis of phrases that define a vocabulary V. Each element in the vector represents the frequency of occurrence of the phrase in the document, weighted according to the discrimination implied by the presence of the phrase within a reference corpus. This discrimination is approximated by the phrase frequency in the reference corpus. If two phrases have the same number of occurrences in a document, the TF-IDF value of the less common phrase will be higher. The TF-IDF score $v(w)$ of a phrase w is computed using the following function:

$$v(w) = \frac{f^d(w)}{f^d_{max}} log \frac{N}{f(w)} \qquad (1)$$

where $f^d(w)$ is the number of occurrences of w in a document d, f^d_{max} is the maximum number of occurrences of a phrase in a document d, N is the number of documents in the reference corpus and $f(w)$ is the number of documents in the corpus where the phrase w occurs at least once.

We implement TF-IDF using the following steps. All the documents in the seed set, as well as optionally, the first layer, are concatenated into a single master document.

1. All *stop-words* such as "by", "and", or "at" are removed from the master document

2. Word stemming is performed to remove common word transformations, such as plurals or case changes [16];

3. TF-IDF computation is performed using a reference corpus derived from an exhaustive web crawl.

The resulting set of phrases form the vocabulary V. When a document is retrieved, the TF-IDF score for phrases in V that occur in the document are computed and placed in a vector. We then truncate the vector representation to include only the forty highest scoring components by zeroing out the remaining components. This processing, yielding a representation which we will refer to as reduced TF-IDF representation, ensures numerical stability and high speed of the classifiers.

Given a representation procedure, we next construct the classifiers. Our goal is to be able to assign any web document to a particular layer of the merged context graph. However, if the document is a poor fit for a given layer, we wish to discard the document, and label it as one of the category "other". The major difficulty in implementing such a strategy using a single classifier mapping a document to a set of $N+2$ classes corresponding to the layers $0, 1, \ldots N$ and a category "other", is the absence of a good model or training set for the category "other". To solve this problem we use a modification of the *Naive Bayes Classifier* for each layer. This classifier architecture provides reasonable performance, high speed, meets the requirement of our system that a likelihood estimate be provided for each classification, and is well studied [17, 18, 12].

Assume that we have a document d_i represented by the vector corresponding to the reduced TF-IDF representation relative to the vocabulary V. Documents from class c_j, defined to correspond to layer j, are assumed to have a prior probability of being found on the web which we denote $P(c_j)$. The probability that a vector element w_t occurs in documents of class c_j is $P(w_t|c_j)$. To classify a page, we first wish to find the class c_j such that $P(c_j|d_i)$ is maximized. The solution is given by Bayes rule

$$P(c_j|d_i) \propto P(c_j)P(d_i|c_j) \propto P(c_j)P(w_{d_i,1} \ldots w_{d_{i,N}}|c_j) \quad (2)$$

where $w_{d_{i,k}}$ is the k-th feature of the document d_i. The Naive Bayes assumption ignores joint statistics and formally assumes that given the document class the features occur independently of each other, yielding the final solution

$$P(c_j|d_i) \propto P(c_j)P(d_i|c_j) \propto P(c_j)\prod_{k=1}^{N_{d_i}} P(w_{d_{i,k}}|c_j) \quad (3)$$

where N_{d_i} indicates the number of features in the document d_i. If N denotes the maximum depth of the context graphs, then $N+1$ discriminant functions $P(c_j|d_i)$ are built corresponding the layers $j = 0, 1, \ldots N$.

The discriminant functions allow for a given page d_i to first be assigned to one of the layers of the merged context graph, by finding the layer j^* for which the discriminant function $P(c_j|d_i)$ is maximized. Subsequently, by computing the likelihood function $P(c_{j^*}|d_i)$ for the winning layer j^*, and comparing this likelihood to a threshold, it is possible to discard weakly matching pages. These pages are effectively marked as "other", which avoids the need for construction of an explicit model of all documents not in the context graph. In effect, we build a set of parallel two-class Naive Bayes classifiers, one for each layer, and select the winning layer by maximizing the *a-posteriori* likelihood of the layer based on the context graph.

In training the classifiers, the documents that occur in layer j of all of the seed document context graphs are combined to serve as a training data set D_j. The phrase probabilities $P(w_t|c_j)$ are computed on the sets D_j by counting the occurrences of the feature w_t and then normalizing for all the words in the documents of class c_j:

$$P(w_t|c_j) = \frac{1 + \sum_{d_i \in D_j} N(w_t, d_i)P(c_j|d_i)}{|V| + \sum_{d_i \in D_j} \sum_{s=1}^{|V|} N(w_s, d_i)P(c_j|d_i)} \quad (4)$$

where $N(w_t, d_i)$ is the number of occurrences of w_t in the document d_i and $|V|$ is the number of phrases in the vocabulary V [17, 18, 12].

The parameters $P(c_j)$ can be calculated by estimating the number of elements in each of the layers of the merged context graph. While useful when the layers do not contain excessive numbers of nodes, as previously stated practical limitations sometimes prevent the storage of all documents in the outermost layers. In these cases the class probabilities $P(c_j)$ are set to a fixed constant value $1/C$, where C is the number of layers. This corresponds to maximum likelihood selection of the winning layer. In our experience, performance is not severely impacted by this simplification.

The classifier of layer 0 is used as the ultimate arbiter of whether a document is topically relevant. The discriminant and likelihood functions for the other layers are used to predict for any page how many steps must be taken before a target is found by crawling the links that appear on a page.

3.3 Crawling

The crawler utilizes the classifiers trained during the context graph generation stage to organize pages into a sequence of $M = N + 2$ queues, where N is the maximum depth of the context graphs. The i-th class (layer) is associated to the i-th queue $i = 0, 1, \ldots N$. Queue number $N + 1$ is not associated with any class, but reflects assignments to "other". The 0-th queue will ultimately store all the retrieved topically relevant documents. The system is shown graphically in Figure 2.

Initially all the queues are empty except for the dummy queue $N + 1$, which is initialized with the starting URL of the crawl. The crawler retrieves the page pointed to by the URL, computes the reduced vector representation and extracts all the hyperlinks. The crawler then downloads all the children of the current page. All downloaded pages are classified individually and assigned to the queue corresponding to the winning layer, or the class "other". Each queue is maintained in a sorted state according to the likelihood score associated with its constituent documents.

When the crawler needs the next document to move to, it pops from the first non-empty queue. The documents that are expected to rapidly lead to targets are therefore followed before documents that will in probability require more steps to yield relevant pages. However, depending on the relative queue thresholds, frequently high-confidence pages from queues representing longer download paths are retrieved.

The setting of the classifier thresholds that determine whether a document gets assigned to the class denoted "other" determines the retrieval strategy. In our default implementation the likelihood function for each layer is applied to all the patterns in the training set for that layer. The confidence threshold is then set equal to the minimum likelihood obtained on the training set for the corresponding layer.

During the crawling phase, new context graphs can periodically be built for every topically relevant element found in queue 0. However, our focused crawler can also be configured to ask for the immediate parents of every document as it appears in queue 0, and simply insert these into the appropriate queue without re-computing the merged context graph and classifiers. In this way it is possible to continually exploit back-crawling at a reasonable computational cost.

4 Experimental Results

The core improvement of our focused crawler derives from the introduction of the context graph. We therefore com-

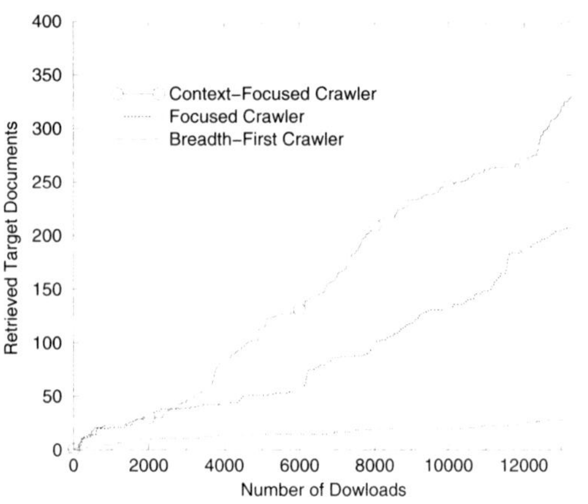

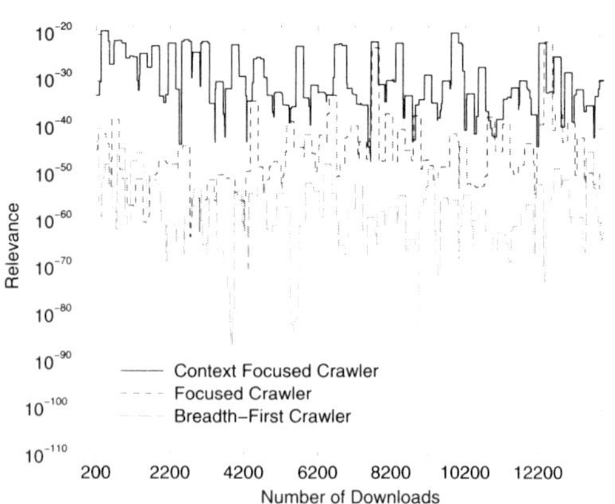

Figure 4: Both the Context Focused Crawler and the standard focused crawler are orders of magnitude more efficient than a traditional breadth-first crawler when retrieving "Call for Papers" documents. The Context Focused Crawler outperforms the standard crawler, retrieving 50 – 60% more "on-topic" documents in a given period.

Figure 5: The average relevance of the downloaded documents computed using a sliding window of 200 downloads, illustrating the improved capability of the Context Focused Crawler to remain on-topic.

pare the efficiency of our Context Focused Crawler to two crawlers:

- a breadth-first crawler, using the classifier constructed by the Context Focused Crawler on the seed set;

- a traditional focused crawler which does not use the context to search targets. This crawler evaluates all children of the current document using the same classifier used by the Context Focused Crawler for the seed set, and schedules crawls based on the document with the highest score.

As a test set we performed a focused crawl for conference announcements, and, in particular, for the "Call for Papers" section. We used ten examples as a seed set and constructed ten context graphs of depth four. We limited the number of documents in a single layer of the context graph to 300 . The resulting data was used to learn the 5 Naive Bayes classifiers associated with the five queues.

To evaluate our algorithm we used the accepted metric of measuring the fraction of pages that are on-topic as a function of the number of download requests. The results are shown in the Figure 4. Both of the focused crawlers significantly outperform the standard breadth-first crawler. However the Context Focused Crawler has found on average 50-60% more on-topic documents than the standard focused crawler on the "Conference" task.

The ability of the crawlers to remain focused on "on-topic" documents can also fruitfully be measured by computing the average relevance of the downloaded documents. The relevance of a document is equated to the likelihood that the document has been generated by the Naive Bayes model of the seed set. In Figure 5 we show the average relevance using a sliding window of 200 downloads. In

each case the Context Focused Crawler maintains a significantly higher level of relevance than either of the other two crawlers, reflecting the ability of the crawler to use off-topic paths to find new sets of promising documents.

Our experiments showed that the overhead due to the initialization stage is negligible, especially when the overall higher efficiency of the crawler is taken into account.

The improvement that results from querying for the parents of every on-topic document when it is discovered can be seen in Figure 6. This approach shows bursts of rapid retrieval when back-crawling from a target document yields a hub site. We note that for general use we ration the number of back-link requests to avoid over-taxing the search engines.

Figure 7 shows a different category, "Biking", for which our focused crawler showed the least average performance improvement over standard focused crawling (although it still significantly outperforms the standard crawler over most of the trial). We found that such difficult categories are those where target content is not reliably co-located with pages from a different category, and where common hierarchies do not exist or are not implemented uniformly across different web-sites. It is therefore to be expected that the context graph provides less guidance in such cases. However, due to our architecture design, and as illustrated by Figure 4 and Figure 7, the performance will at worst approach that of the standard focused crawling approach.

5 Discussion

We presented a focused crawler that models the links and content of documents that are closely linked to target pages to improve the efficiency with which content related to a desired category can be found. Our experiments show that the Context Focused Crawler improves the efficiency of traditional focused crawling significantly (on average about

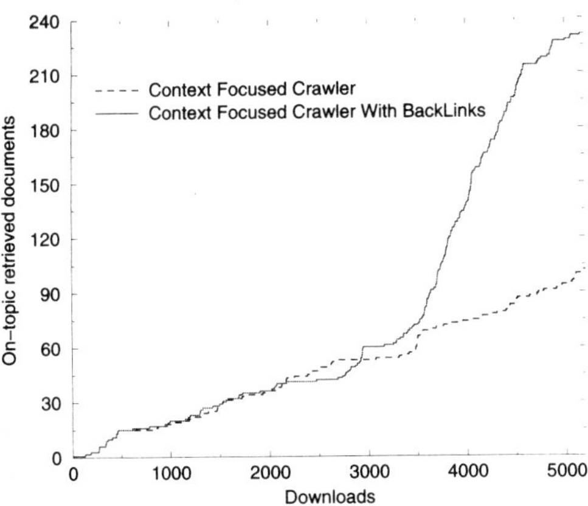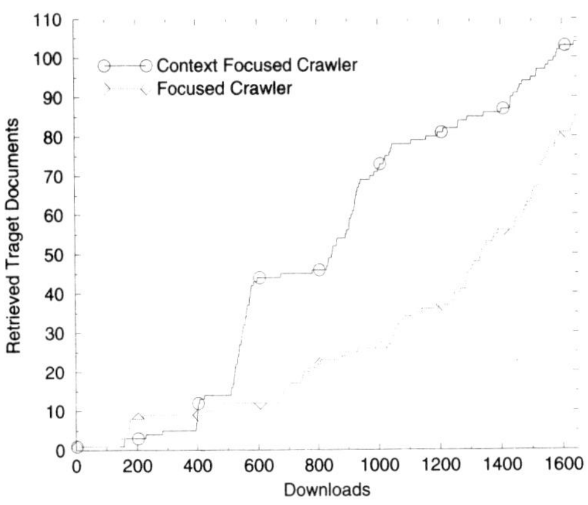

Figure 6: Performance of Context Focused Crawler as compared to Context Focused Crawler with BackLinks, where parents of each on-topic document are obtained from the search engines immediately after the document is discovered. The task is retrieval of "Call for Papers" documents on the web.

Figure 7: Performance of focused crawlers on the category "Biking".

50-60%), and standard breadth-first crawling by orders of magnitude.

The major limitation of our approach is the requirement for reverse links to exist at a known search engine for a reasonable fraction of the seed set documents. In practice, this does not appear to be problem. However, even when no seed documents have yet been indexed by search engines, the approach can be bootstrapped. In this case a content model of the seed set is extracted and other high-confidence target data can be found using query modifications on a search engine. The indexed target data pages returned by the search engine can then be used to build context graphs. The system can also start with a breadth-first crawl and a set of example documents for training the level 0 classifier, with context graphs being built once a minimum number of target documents have been recovered.

The architecture we presented already yields very good performance, but can be fruitfully improved. Major improvements should result from more sophisticated approaches for setting the confidence thresholds of the classifiers. We are currently investigating other machine learning algorithms for setting these thresholds. A promising approach maintains a graph representation of the current crawl, which a separate on-line process uses to quantify the effect of different queue thresholds.

Other areas of interest are the extension of the feature space to include page analysis of HTML structure, using the statistics gained during the search to develop ranking procedures for presenting results to the user, and performing online classifier adaptation. At present adaptation in our system is restricted to periodically incorporating the context graphs of newly discovered target documents that are found in queue 0, and re-building the classifier (the tests in this paper did not use this feature, to avoid introducing another parameter). Online parameter updating of the classifiers using the EM approach [19] should result in more efficient continuous optimization of the classifier performance.

Not only can our approach be used for background gathering of web material, the computational and bandwidth requirements of the crawler are sufficiently modest for the crawler to be used in an interactive session over a DSL or cable modem connection on a home PC. The focused crawler can therefore be used as a valuable supplement to, and in some cases a replacement for, standard search engine database queries. We have no doubt that further improvement of focused crawling will soon make crawling not only the privilege of large companies that can afford expensive infrastructures, but a personal tool that is widely available for retrieving information on the world wide web.

References

[1] "Web surpasses one billion documents: Inktomi/NEC press release." available at http://www.inktomi.com, Jan 18 2000.

[2] S. Chakrabarti, M. van der Berg, and B. Dom, "Focused crawling: a new approach to topic-specific web resource discovery," in *Proc. of the 8th International World-Wide Web Conference (WWW8)*, 1999.

[3] J. Cho, H. Garcia-Molina, and L. Page, "Efficient crawling through URL ordering," in *Proceedings of the Seventh World-Wide Web Conference*, 1998.

[4] A. McCallum, K. Nigam, J. Rennie, and K. Seymore, "Building domain-specic search engines with machine learning techniques," in *Proc. AAAI Spring Symposium on Intelligent Agents in Cyberspace*, 1999.

[5] A. K. McCallum, K. Nigam, J. Rennie, and K. Seymore, "Automating the construction of internet por-

tals with machine learning," *To appear in Information Retrieval.*

[6] M. Gori, M. Maggini, and F. Scarselli, "http://nautilus.dii.unisi.it."

[7] O. Heinonen, K. Hatonen, and K. Klemettinen, "WWW robots and search engines." Seminar on Mobile Code, Report TKO-C79, Helsinki University of Technology, Department of Computer Science, 1996.

[8] S. Chakrabarti, B. Dom, P. Raghavan, S. Rajagopalan, D. Gibson, and J. Kleinberg, "Automatic resource compilation by analyzing hyperlink structure and associated text," in *Proc. 7th World Wide Web Conference, Brisbane, Australia*, 1998.

[9] K. Bharat and M. Henzinger, "Improved algorithms for topic distillation in hyperlinked environments," in *Proceedings 21st Int'l ACM SIGIR Conference.*, 1998.

[10] J. Kleinberg, "Authoritative sources in a hyperlinked environment." Report RJ 10076, IBM, May 1997, 1997.

[11] S. Chakrabarti, M. van den Berg, and B. Dom, "Distributed hypertext resource discovery through examples," in *VLDB'99, Proceedings of 25th International Conference on Very Large Data Bases, September 7-10, 1999, Edinburgh, Scotland, UK* (M. P. Atkinson, M. E. Orlowska, P. Valduriez, S. B. Zdonik, and M. L. Brodie, eds.), pp. 375–386, Morgan Kaufmann, 1999.

[12] J. Rennie and A. McCallum, "Using reinforcement learning to spider the web efficiently," in *Proc. International Conference on Machine Learning (ICML)*, 1999.

[13] K. Bharat, A. Broder, M. Henzinger, P. Kumar, and S. Venkatasubramanian, "The connectivity server: Fast access to linkage information on the web," *WWW7/ Computer Networks 30(1-7)*, pp. 469–477, 1998.

[14] S. Chakrabarti, D. Gidson, and K. McCurley, "Surfing backwards on the web," in *Proc 8th World Wide Web Conference (WWW8)*, 1999.

[15] G. Salton and M. J. McGill, *An Introduction to Modern Information Retrieval*. McGraw-Hill, 1983.

[16] M. Porter, "An algorithm for suffix stripping," *Program*, vol. 14, no. 3, pp. 130–137, 1980.

[17] T. M. Mitchell, *Machine Learning*. McGraw-Hill, 1997.

[18] K. Nigam, A. McCallum, S. Thrun, and T. Mitchell, "Text classification from labeled and unlabelled documents using EM." To appear in Machine Learning, 1999.

[19] A. Dempster, N. Laird, and D. Rubin, "Maximum likelihood from incomplete data via the EM algorithm," *J. R. Statist. Soc. B*, vol. 39, pp. 185–197, 1977.

Approximating Aggregate Queries about Web Pages via Random Walks [*]

Ziv Bar-Yossef[†]   Alexander Berg   Steve Chien[‡]   Jittat Fakcharoenphol[§]

Dror Weitz[¶]

Computer Science Division
University of California at Berkeley
387 Soda Hall #1776, Berkeley, CA 94720-1776
U.S.A.
{zivi,aberg,schien,jittat,dror}@cs.berkeley.edu

Abstract

We present a random walk as an efficient and accurate approach to approximating certain aggregate queries about web pages. Our method uses a novel random walk to produce an almost uniformly distributed sample of web pages. The walk traverses a dynamically built regular undirected graph. Queries we have estimated using this method include the coverage of search engines, the proportion of pages belonging to .com and other domains, and the average size of web pages. Strong experimental evidence suggests that our walk produces accurate results quickly using very limited resources.

1 Introduction

Timely and accurate statistics about web pages are becoming increasingly important for academic and commercial use. Some relevant questions are: *What percent of web pages are in the .com domain? How many pages are indexed by a particular search engine? What is the distribution of sizes, modification times, and content of web pages?* These questions can be written as either aggregate queries or selection queries. We present a method for efficiently and accurately approximating the results of these and other similar queries.

In order to answer these questions we need to estimate the size of certain sets of web pages. In particular, given a user defined boolean predicate, p, we want to estimate the fraction of all web pages that would satisfy a selection query using p. We also want to estimate the results of aggregate queries about all web pages. For example we might estimate the average number of bytes in a web page.

We present an efficient solution, requiring small amounts of computing power, storage space, and network bandwidth. Starting from scratch, we can accurately estimate results for the previously mentioned queries in as little as a few days using one PC with a modest connection to the Internet. Furthermore, given additional time and network bandwidth, our method can produce increasingly accurate results.

It is important to understand that there is no complete, current index of the web. The web is a hypertext corpus connected by a link structure, and it is possible to traverse (crawl) this link structure in order to obtain an index of the web. Unfortunately even the fastest crawls require 3 to 4 months to visit a large fraction of the web, and must utilize significant computer and network resources. When combined with the fact that thousands of pages are added, modified, and deleted every day this means that an index of the web generated by a crawl will be neither current nor complete.

---

[*] This work used the Berkeley Now machines, supported by grant CDA-9401156

[†] Supported by NSF Grant CCR-9820897

[‡] Supported by NSF Graduate Research Fellowship

[§] Supported by the Faculty of Engineering Kasetsart University Scholarship and by the Fulbright Scholarship

[¶] Supported by the University of California Regents Fellowship

**Proceedings of the 26th VLDB Conference,
Cairo, Egypt, 2000.**

1.1 Our Solution: Random Walks for Uniform Sampling

In order to estimate the results of aggregate queries or the fraction of all web pages that would satisfy a selection query for a given predicate, we will use random sampling. First, a uniformly distributed sample of web pages will be produced. It will then be used to estimate the quantities in question. The fraction of sampled web pages that satisfy a predicate is an estimate for the fraction of all web pages that would satisfy the predicate.

It is important to note that the accuracy of the random sampling technique depends on the selectivity of the predicate. In particular if a large fraction of all web pages satisfy the predicate, then the estimate will be more accurate than if a very small fraction of all web pages satisfy the predicate.

In order to produce a uniformly distributed sample of web pages without an index of all web pages, we will use ideas from the theory of random walks. It is well known that random walks on regular [1] undirected graphs can provide a close to uniformly distributed sample of nodes. Unfortunately the web is neither undirected, nor regular. We present a method to simultaneously walk the web and a dynamically generated graph G. The graph G has a node for each web page discovered on the web, but is regular and undirected. As the walk progresses it produces a close to uniformly distributed sample of web pages.

The next important question is how quickly our process can produce a close to uniformly distributed sample of web pages. The answer to this question is related to the structure of the generated graph G. We have analyzed the structure of the web obtained from a large Alexa [1] crawl circa 1996 to conclude that such a walk can converge extremely fast. We also demonstrate that, in fact, the walk we implement quickly finds an apparently close to uniformly distributed set of pages from this crawl.

Our random walk strategy is finally validated by results on the web today. In section 4 we compare our estimate for the distribution of web pages by domain (.com .edu .net .org, etc.), to that published by Inktomi as a result of a recent and extensive crawl over a period of four months. We also compare estimates for the size of the search engines FAST and AltaVista. In the first case the approximations we obtain from our approach in one to two days are consistent with those of Inktomi's extensive crawl. The coverage estimates for FAST and AltaVista are also consistent with various other estimates. These results provide strong evidence that our walk performs well.

---

[1] A graph is regular if all its nodes have an equal number of incident edges.

1.2 Outline

We begin by describing an ideal but unrealizable random walk on the web in Section 2. We then describe our random walk, a close approximation of the ideal one, in Section 3. We present strong experimental evidence that our walk works well and applications of our walk to aggregate queries about the current web in Section 4. Section 5 discusses related work and Section 6 concludes.

2 Ideal Random Walk on the Web

In this section we develop an idealized random walk on the web. This ideal random walk will be provably accurate and efficient, but unfortunately cannot be implemented. Nevertheless, it provides a useful model for our actual random walk, described in Section 3.

2.1 The Indexable Web

Before explaining our random walk on the web, we must first define what we mean by "the web". A recent experiment [12] suggests that the structure of the web is similar to that shown in Figure 1. According to this model the web graph divides into four parts of roughly equivalent size:
(1) A giant strongly connected component (the largest subset of nodes from which every pair of nodes are mutually reachable from one another by following links).
(2) A "right" side containing pages reachable from (1), but which cannot reach (1) in return.
(3) A "left" side whose pages can reach (1), but are not reachable from (1) in return.
(4) All the rest (other small connected components, or pages that link to the right side or are linked from the left side).

We refer to the union of (1) and (2) as the "indexable" web, since this is the part that is easily explored by most users and search engines, and that arguably contains most of the meaningful content of the web. Our random walk and experiments are conducted mainly on this part of the web.

2.2 Random Walks on Graphs

In its most general form a random walk on a graph is simply what its name suggests. Let $G = (V, E)$ be a (directed or undirected) graph, where $V = \{v_1, v_2, \ldots, v_N\}$ is the set of vertices and E the collection of edges. A random walk is then a stochastic process that iteratively visits the vertices of the graph. The next vertex of the walk is chosen by following a randomly chosen outgoing edge from the current one. The nodes visited by a random walk can be written as a sequence $x_0, x_1, x_2, \ldots$. Furthermore, since the walk is random, it makes sense to describe the state of a random walk after t steps as a probability distribution X_t over the graph's vertices, described as a vector of length N.

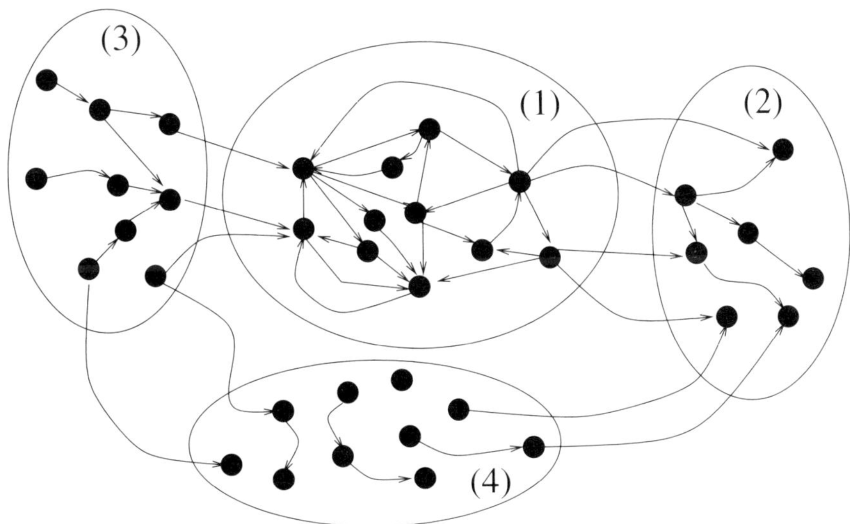

Figure 1: Web Graph Structure

The web can be naturally described as a graph W with pages as vertices and hyperlinks as directed edges, and for the remainder of this paper it will be convenient to identify vertices with pages and edges with links.

Our goal was to develop a random walk on the web's graph structure that satisfies two criteria: first, the walk's state (X_t) should approach the uniform distribution, and second, the number of steps required for the walk to approach this distribution should be reasonably small.

It turns out that the web's graph structure is unwieldy and the straightforward random walk of randomly choosing a link from the current page will not work. The straightforward walk will have a heavy bias towards high-degree nodes, may become trapped in leaves, and requires too many steps to run.

We now describe the ideal (and unattainable) scenario in which such a simple scheme would perform well, and discuss our approximation of it in Section 3.

2.3 The Ideal Walk: Uniform Distribution

Ideally, our random walk will be a Markov chain on a connected, undirected, regular graph. Walks with these properties can be proven to eventually approach a uniform distribution over the vertices of the graph.

A Markov chain is a memoryless walk over a graph in that the choice of the next vertex depends only on the current vertex and not the previous history of the walk. In our case, from its current vertex, the walk will choose the next vertex by following an outgoing edge chosen uniformly at random.

A Markov chain can be described entirely by its transition matrix P, describing one step of the Markov chain as $X_{t+1} = X_t P$. This simplicity makes it relatively easy to analyze specific Markov chains, including

our ideal random walk.

In particular, when the underlying graph is connected, undirected, and regular, we can show that our first desired property is satisfied: our random walk will converge to the uniform probability distribution. (The connectedness property ensures that the random walk has a limiting distribution, and undirectedness and regularity guarantee that this distribution is uniform.)

Unfortunately the natural web graph W initially meets none of these three conditions, but we can modify it to satisfy them. We first make each edge in W undirected, meaning that our random walk can now follow links either forwards or backwards. This makes the graph undirected. (It is connected because we consider only the indexable web.) It is still not regular, since some pages will have higher degree than others. This can be fixed by adding a different number of self-loops to each page so that every page ends up with the same number of links as the original vertex of maximum degree. We will denote this maximal degree as d.

The final graph W' thus fits all three requirements and our random walk over this graph will approach a uniform distribution. Since our walk is a Markov chain, we can associate it with a transition matrix $P_{W'}$. See Figure 2 for a complete description of the ideal walk.

2.4 The Ideal Walk: Feasibility

We now need to determine the ideal walk's *mixing time*, or the number of steps the walk must make before reaching a distribution acceptably close to uniform. A well known convergence theorem from the theory of Markov chains shows that for our case, the mixing time is bounded by $O(\frac{1}{\epsilon}\log N)$ steps, where N

537

```
Ideal_Visit(v) {
   I := all in-neighbors of v

   O := all out-neighbors of v

   w := d - |I ∪ O|

   Compute the number of self loop steps
   spent at v (distributes geometrically
   with parameter 1 - w/d)

   Select a random u ∈ I ∪ O

   Ideal_Visit(u)
}
```

Figure 2: Ideal Walk's Visit Function

is the total number of pages in W'. Here ϵ is the *eigenvalue gap* of our Markov chain, or $|\lambda_1| - |\lambda_2|$, where λ_1 and λ_2 are the eigenvalues of $P_{W'}$ with largest and second largest absolute value. The eigenvalue gap is a measure of the conductance of the Markov chain; a large eigenvalue gap indicates that there are few bottlenecks or isolated parts of the graph. In this case the walk will avoid becoming trapped and approach the uniform distribution rapidly.

It is impractical to compute the eigenvalue gap of $P_{W'}$, since this would require complete knowledge of the web's structure. We do have access to a large crawl of the indexable web from 1996, however, and were able to use brute force to determine that the eigenvalue gap for the undirected regular graph there was $\epsilon = 10^{-5}$. If a similar figure is still true today, and estimating the current size of the web as approximately 10^9, the convergence theorem above shows that the mixing time of the ideal random walk is on the order of 3,000,000 steps. We will denote the mixing time as τ.

The prospect of our walk performing this many web accesses would seem a little daunting, but we are saved by the observation that most of the steps of the ideal walk are self-loops, which do not require a web access. Furthermore, we do not need to simulate each self-loop step separately. The number of consecutive self-loops our ideal walk takes at each page can be modeled by a geometric random variable, so that one calculation can simulate many steps of the actual walk. In fact, on the undirected regular 1996 graph, each page had a degree of 300,000, but an average of only ten links which were not self-loops. Thus only 1 in 30,000 steps of the random walk is not a self-loop and requires a web access, meaning that a 3,000,000 step walk requires only 100 actual web accesses, a very feasible number.

2.5 Subset Sampling Procedure

The above ideal random walk meets our initial requirements: it produces nearly uniform samples from the web and runs in a small amount of time. We now show how we can apply this to one of our main applications, estimating the relative size of subsets of the web. (We will also use the same procedure to estimate the results of aggregate queries.)

Suppose we have a subset A of all web pages V_W (with $|V_W| = N$) whose relative size we wish to estimate. The most obvious method would be to repeatedly run the walk T times for τ steps to obtain a nearly uniform distribution, and then choose the walk's current page as a sample point. While workable, this approach is not ideal. Aldous [10] proposes a more efficient sampling procedure: Instead of running T walks of length τ Aldous suggests we run only one walk of length $\tau + k$, and use the last k nodes as the sample points, disregarding the first τ steps as *sample delay*. Gilman [13] and Kahale [16] prove that $k = O(\frac{1}{\epsilon} \frac{1}{\beta^2 \frac{|A|}{N}} \log \frac{1}{\delta})$ steps are sufficient to obtain a (β, δ) approximation. This means that after this many steps, we will have $Pr[(1 - \beta)\frac{|A|}{N} \leq \frac{s}{k} \leq (1 + \beta)\frac{|A|}{N}] \geq 1 - \delta$, where s is the number of sample pages that belong to A. This allows us to save a factor of $\log N$ random walk steps over the naive approach.

With the above estimates of the eigenvalue gap ϵ and the size of the web N, this result shows that if we wish to estimate the size of a subset A that comprises at least 20% of the web to within 10% accuracy with 99% confidence, we will need 350,000,000 random walk steps, of which only about 12,000 will not be self-loops.

2.6 Lessons from the Ideal Walk

What all of this demonstrates is that the ideal walk, if we could realize it, would provide a reliable and excellent tool for uniform random sampling and subset estimation on the web. Unfortunately we cannot implement this walk, since we cannot follow links backwards, a crucial step in our design. We now describe how our actual walk approximates this model, and the results we obtain from it.

3 WebWalker - Realization of a Random Walk on the Web

Realization of the ideal random walk scheme described in Section 2.3 requires the following primitives:

1. Determining the degree of a given page v (i.e., the number of incoming and outgoing links it has).

2. Given a page v and an index $i \in \{1, \ldots, d\}$, selecting the ith neighbor of v.

The first primitive is needed for computing the self loop weight of v, and the second for choosing a random neighbor of v. A straightforward solution for both is to retrieve the list of all incoming and outgoing links of v, and then infer from this list the degree of v and the chosen random neighbor. Obtaining all the outgoing links of v is easy: we just have to extract the links from its HTML text. Getting the list of incoming links is, however, more intricate. We can acquire incoming links from two sources:

1. The walk itself - if the walk visits a page u with a link to v before it visits v, it can know of this link at the time it visits v.

2. Search engines - some search engines (AltaVista [2], Go [4], Google [5], HotBot [6], and Lycos [8]) allow one to retrieve all the pages they index that contain a link to a given page v.

These two sources of incoming links are not sufficient to implement the primitives mentioned above. First, they might miss some of the incoming links. Suppose there exists a link $u \rightarrow v$. If the walk does not visit u before it visits v and none of the search engines indexes u, then the walk will not be aware of the link $u \rightarrow v$ at the time it visits v. Second, the search engines return at most 1000 links for each queried page. Thus, for pages with a much larger number of incoming links we have access to only a small fraction of these links.

The inability to obtain all the incoming links of a page v, or even to know their exact number, prevents us from fully realizing the above primitives. This means that there is no obvious way to realize the ideal undirected regular random walk on the web. We now describe *WebWalker* - a new random walking process that attempts to come close to the ideal random walk, given only limited knowledge of incoming links.

3.1 WebWalker Specification

WebWalker performs a regular undirected random walk while exploring the web, using the above mentioned link resources (i.e., the HTML text, the walk itself, and the search engines). As WebWalker traverses the web it builds a d-regular undirected graph that is used to determine the next step of the walk. Each time WebWalker visits a new page it adds a corresponding node v to the graph. At this point we will determine and fix for the remainder of the walk the d edges (possibly including self-loops) incident to v. More explicitly, denote by $N(v)$ the set of v's neighbors that are available from the above resources the first time WebWalker visits v. WebWalker considers only pages in $N(v)$ to be neighbors of v throughout the walk. If it happens to discover a new link $u \rightarrow v$ later, it ignores this link and does not add u to $N(v)$. This is done in order to ensure *consistency* in the graph on which WebWalker walks: we want to make sure that the exact same set of neighbors is available to WebWalker every time it visits v. The importance of this feature will become apparent in Section 3.2.

The self loop weight assigned to v is $d - |N(v)|$. Each time WebWalker visits v, it first calculates the number of self loop steps spent at v, and then picks a random page in $N(v)$ to be visited next. Figure 3 specifies the Visit function run by WebWalker when it visits a page v.

```
WebWalker_Visit(v) {
    If v was already visited, skip to SELF

    I := r random in-neighbors of v from the
         ones returned by the search engines

    O := all out-neighbors of v

    For all u ∈ (I ∪ O) \ N(v) do {
        if u was not visited yet {
            add u to N(v)
            add v to N(u)
        }
    }

SELF:
    w := d - |N(v)|
    Compute the number of self loop steps
    spent at v (distributes geometrically
    with parameter 1 - w/d)

SELECT:
    Select a random u ∈ N(v)
    If u is ``bad'' go back to SELECT
    WebWalker_Visit(u)
}
```

Figure 3: WebWalker's Visit Function

We also choose the following implementation parameters for WebWalker:

- WebWalker's starting point is an arbitrary page in the largest strongly connected component of the web. We usually start from www.yahoo.com.

- WebWalker uses AltaVista and HotBot as sources for incoming links. For each visited page it retrieves up to 20 links from AltaVista and up to 100 links from HotBot.

- From the set of candidate in-neighbors of v returned by the search engines, WebWalker picks only r at random (r is a parameter of Web-Walker). This is done in order to reduce bias towards pages covered by the search engines (see Sections 3.2 and 4.1 for details).

- The degree d with which WebWalker computes the self loop weight of each visited node needs to bound the web's maximal degree. Note that choosing a loose upper bound makes no difference, since it only increases the number of self loop steps. Therefore, we pick a crude overestimate of $d = 10,000,000$.

- We consider a page u to be "bad" (in which case we do not visit it, even if it is selected) in one of the following cases: (1) it is not a static HTML page, (2) we cannot establish a connection to it within 3 minutes, or (3) its URL address is longer than 300 characters.

3.2 WebWalker Analysis

We next analyze WebWalker's performance. We show that WebWalker is a Markovian random walk not on the web graph itself, but rather on a subgraph of the web. This subgraph is built on the fly as WebWalker explores the web. Since this subgraph is designed to be connected, undirected, and regular, WebWalker converges to a uniform stationary distribution over its nodes.

We then show that this subgraph always covers the whole indexable web, which means WebWalker can generate uniform samples from the indexable web. We finally address the question of how long it takes WebWalker to converge to the uniform stationary distribution. We do not have a satisfactory theoretical answer to this question, but we point out the factors that influence the mixing time. We show that in early stages of the walk WebWalker might suffer from biases towards high degree pages and pages covered by the search engines. Experiments (described in Section 4) show that in practice, these biases are small.

Assume we could run WebWalker infinitely long. Let G be a subgraph of the web that contains all the nodes visited and all the edges traversed by WebWalker during this run. We call G the *induced subgraph* of WebWalker's run.

G does not necessarily contain all the edges of the web. At the first time WebWalker visits a page v, it fixes its neighbor set $N(v)$, and ignores any further links to v it encounters later. Thus, only edges of the form (v, u) for $u \in N(v)$ will be traversed by WebWalker, and therefore included in G.

The subgraph G depends on the random choices made by WebWalker. For example, if v is a page that is not covered by any of the search engines and $v \rightarrow u$ is an outgoing edge from v, then only if WebWalker happens to visit v before it visits u, is $v \rightarrow u$ included in G. We conclude that G is a *random variable* that depends on the walk itself. Different runs of WebWalker may yield different induced subgraphs.

WebWalker behaves as a Markovian random walk on G. Furthermore, by definition G is connected, undirected, and regular. Therefore, WebWalker is guaranteed to converge to a uniform stationary distribution over its nodes. There are two questions left open: (1) what fraction of the web is G guaranteed to cover? and (2) how fast does WebWalker approach the uniform distribution over the nodes of G? The following proposition provides an encouraging answer to the first question.

Proposition 1 *In any infinite run of WebWalker, G covers the whole indexable web.*

Proof: Let v be some node in the indexable web. Thus, there exists a directed path $v_0, \ldots, v_k = v$ of "good" (i.e., not "bad") pages from WebWalker's starting point v_0 to v (since v_0 belongs to the largest strongly connected component). We prove by induction on i ($i = 0, \ldots, k$) that $v_i \in G$. It follows that in particular $v = v_k$ belongs to G.

The base case $i = 0$ is easy: WebWalker starts from v_0, therefore $v_0 \in G$. Assume $v_0, \ldots, v_i \in G$. Consider the edge (v_i, v_{i+1}). Since $v_i \in G$, v_i is visited by WebWalker. Let t be the first time WebWalker visits v_i. v_{i+1} will not be included in $N(v_i)$ only if it was visited before. But in this case v_{i+1} already belongs to G, and we are done.

Therefore, assume $v_{i+1} \in N(v_i)$. Since the graph G on which WebWalker walks is finite, undirected, and connected, in any infinite run WebWalker visits each node in G (and in particular, v_i) infinitely often. Since $N(v_i)$ is finite, all the nodes in $N(v_i)$ will be picked to be visited next at some point. When v_{i+1} is picked by WebWalker it is also visited, since v_{i+1} is a "good" page. Hence, $v_{i+1} \in G$. $\square$

Note that G may also contain parts of the non-indexable web, if the search engines index these parts.

In order for WebWalker to be useful for sampling from the indexable web, we need to make sure that with high probability it converges quickly to the uniform stationary distribution over the vertex set of G. The eigenvalue gap analysis made for the web graph (see Section 2.4) does not hold for G, since G is only a subgraph of the web. If G misses many edges from the web its eigenvalue gap may be much smaller, implying a long mixing time for WebWalker. Unfortunately, we currently do not have any theoretical analysis of the mixing time of WebWalker as a random walk on the graph G.

We suspect that during its early stages WebWalker might be biased towards certain kinds of pages. We identified three sources of potential bias:

(1) Bias towards high degree nodes. The walk will tend to discover high degree nodes earlier than low degree nodes, because high degree nodes have many more short paths leading to them from the walk's starting point than low degree nodes.

(2) Bias towards nodes covered by the search engines. Since WebWalker uses some search engines as a source of incoming links, it is more likely to visit pages covered by these search engines than ones that are not.

(3) Bias towards the neighborhood of the walk's starting point.

The lack of theoretical foundation compels us to resort to experimental evaluation of WebWalker's convergence rate. Section 4.1 presents the results of such experiments, in which we ran WebWalker on a copy of the web from 1996. We use the above potential biases as indicators for evaluating how close WebWalker is to the uniform distribution (small biases indicate convergence).

4 Experiments

We performed experiments using WebWalker to estimate the size of certain subsets of webpages, and to estimate the answer to various aggregate queries about web pages. These experiments were run in February 2000. In addition we also ran WebWalker on a graph created from a large crawl of the web performed in 1996. Because we had access to all the nodes in the graph we can quantitatively evaluate WebWalker's performance and biases on the 1996 web graph.

4.1 Evaluation Experiments

In order to observe WebWalker's effectiveness and bias, we performed a 100,000 page walk on the 1996 web graph. Ideally the samples from this walk, when weighted by self-loops, would be uniformly distributed over all nodes. In order to see how close the samples were to uniform, we compared them to a number of known sets. The sets we considered were: 10 sets each containing one decile of nodes ordered by degree, 10 sets each containing one decile of nodes in breadth first search order from the starting node for WebWalker, and the set of nodes contained in the search engine (see below) used for incoming links.

As discussed in Section 3.2, WebWalker may suffer from biases at early stages of the walk. The experiments were designed to address three sources of possible bias: (1) bias towards nodes with high degree in the web graph, (2) bias towards the neighborhood of WebWalker's starting page, and (3) bias towards nodes indexed by the search engine(s) used for incoming links.

An obstacle to running WebWalker on the 1996 web graph is that we do not know which of the 1996 pages were covered by the search engines at that time. Instead, we designate an arbitrary subset of the nodes as the search engine index. Thus, the incoming edges WebWalker discovers come from nodes already visited and from nodes in the designated search engine subset. Unless stated otherwise the experiments in this section used 50% of the 1996 web graph as the search engine set.

The experimental results shown in this section also show the effect of changing r, the number of incoming links we take from the search engine for each visited

page (see Section 3.1). WebWalker was run using $r = 0$, $r = 3$, and $r = 10$.

Figure 4 shows the distribution of nodes from two walks accumulated into bins by degree. The nodes in the 1996 web graph are sorted by degree and then separated into 10 deciles, each containing 10% of the nodes. For each decile the bar chart shows the percentage of nodes in a walk that had a degree in the range specified. More or fewer than 10% of the nodes in the walk in a particular range shows a bias in the walk. From this graph we see that 24% of the walk with $r = 0$ was spent in the top 10%, an overestimate of 14%. By taking $r = 3$ we see that the bias towards the top 10% of nodes is decreased to an overestimate of 9%. We also notice for both walks that the bias is concentrated in the top 10% of nodes by degree. There is relatively little bias in the other deciles, and even the nodes in the lowest decile are estimated well.

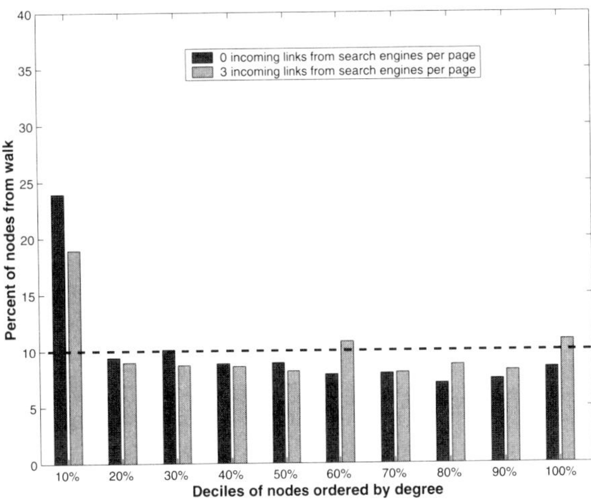

Figure 4: Percent of nodes in two walks on the 1996 web graph by decile of the nodes ordered by degree. For example, the leftmost bar indicates that 24% of the pages in the walk using $r = 0$ were among nodes ranked in the top 10% by degree in the 1996 web graph.

Figure 5 shows the nodes of two walks divided into neighborhoods of WebWalker's starting point. The two walks shown use parameters $r = 0$ and $r = 3$, respectively. All the nodes in the 1996 web graph are ordered by a BFS starting at WebWalker's initial node. They are then divided into 10 equal sized, consecutive sets. The small variations from a uniform distribution indicate that WebWalker has little bias toward its starting neighborhood.

Figure 6 shows the percent of nodes from each of six walks that were also in the search engine for each walk. The first three use 30% of the 1996 web graph as a search engine, and various values for r. The last three use 50% of the 1996 web graph as a search engine. We see from the results that there is a small bias toward

541

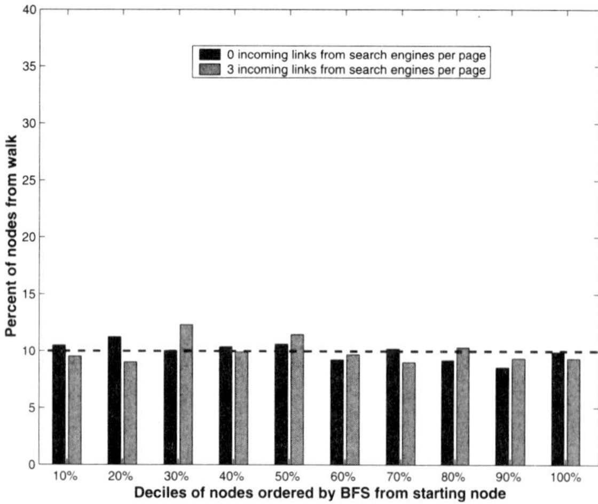

Figure 5: Percent of nodes in the walk on the 1996 web graph by decile of nodes ordered by breadth first search distance from the walk's starting node. For example, the leftmost bar indicates that 10.5% of the nodes in the walk using $r = 0$ were among the first 10% of all nodes when ordered by a BFS starting with WebWalker's initial node.

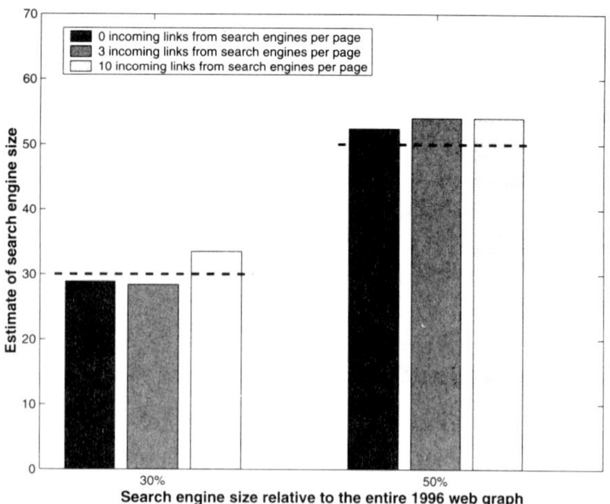

Figure 6: Percent of nodes in six walks that are also contained in the search engine used for incoming links in those walk. For example, the leftmost bar indicates that 28.9% of the nodes in the $r = 0$ walk were actually in the search engine comprised of 30% of all nodes in the 1996 web graph.

the search engine, and that the bias increases as more incoming links are taken from the search engine.

We have observed in our experiments that increasing the number of links taken from a search engine *increases* the bias toward that search engine, an undesirable effect. At the same time increasing the number of incoming links taken from search engines *decreases* the bias toward high degree nodes. Based on the experiments on the 1996 web graph we found $r = 3$ to be a good compromise.

We conclude that from the biases we examined that only the bias towards the highest degree nodes is significant.

4.2 Subset Size and Aggregate Query Approximation Experiments

Next, we show a flavor of the approximations of web subsets one can perform using WebWalker. We ran WebWalker on the current web (February 2000) and tried to approximate the relative size of the following subsets:

(1) The pages that can be returned as query results by AltaVista [2]. WebWalker uses AltaVista as a source for incoming links. We wished to check the effect this has on the approximation of AltaVista.

(2) The pages that can be returned as query results by the FAST search engine [3] (formerly called "All the Web") WebWalker does not use FAST as a source for incoming links.

(3) The overlap of AltaVista and FAST (pages that are covered by both).

(4) The pages that contain inline images.

In order to check whether a given sample page belongs to a search engine (e.g., FAST or AltaVista) we extract a list of features from the page (its URL and title and the list of phrases it contains) and repeatedly query the search engine for pages that contain one of these features. We determine that the page is covered by the search engine if we find the exact URL (after normalization) of the page in the results of one of these queries. Note that if the search engine keeps only one copy for mirrored sites, this method might determine that a page is not included in the search engine index, although it actually is (it is simply not returned by the search engine as a result of a query). Therefore, the actual coverage of the search engine might be somewhat larger than what is reflected by our approximations.

The approximations we obtained for the relative size of FAST, AltaVista, their intersection, and the image set are presented in Table 1. Reports for the FAST and AltaVista indexes [9] were about 300 million pages and 250 million pages respectively. This means that the ratio between them should be about 1.2. Our approximations come close with a ratio of 1.14. This may indicate that the bias of WebWalker towards AltaVista (compared to FAST) is not significant. These results were obtained from three walks with a total of 41,384 page accesses.

In addition we wanted to evaluate the following aggregate queries about the web:

(1) The distribution of pages according to the last part of their domain name (com, edu, org, and others)

(2) The average size of static HTML pages.

(3) The average number of hyperlinks in static HTML pages.

Set	Size Approximation
FAST	39.97%
AltaVista	35.46%
FAST ∩ AltaVista	21.13%
Images	72.60%

Table 1: Web Subset Approximations

The approximations we obtain for domain name distributions are based on a combination of 21 runs of WebWalker, with a total of 146,133 page accesses. To validate the accuracy of the resulting approximations we compare them against similar tests made in February, 2000 by Inktomi [7], which based their estimations on an extensive 1 billion page index of the web.[2]

The 14 largest domains (and .mil) together with their relative sizes are presented in Table 2. We give the corresponding Inktomi approximations, when available, for reference.

Domain	Our Approximation	Inktomi Approximation
.com	49.15%	54.68%
.edu	8.28%	6.69%
.org	6.55%	4.35%
.net	5.60%	7.82%
.de	3.67%	
.jp	2.87%	
.uk	2.75%	
.gov	2.08%	1.15%
.ca	1.58%	
.au	1.37%	
.us	1.12%	
.fr	1.01%	
.se	0.98%	
.it	0.94%	
...		
.mil	0.19%	0.17%

Table 2: Largest Internet Domains

The average page size and the average number of links in a page are presented in Table 3.

Query	Approximation
Average size (in bytes)	11,655
Average number of hyperlinks	9.56

Table 3: Aggregate Query Approximations for Static HTML Pages

5 Related Work

Several recent attempts have been made to estimate the size and/or quality of various search engines' indexes. All of this previous work requires obtaining a sample of pages in some way. In some cases the idea is to obtain a uniformly distributed sample, while in others it is to find a sample weighted by a particular metric.

Henzinger et al. [15] used a large number of random walks designed to converge to Google's [5] *page rank* distribution over the nodes walked. This distribution favors popular pages. They then attempt to remove the bias by sampling pages from the walk based on the inverse of an estimate for the page rank of each page. They used a random graph model for the web, and produced data showing a clear bias towards high degree nodes. This bias is difficult to compare with our own since the random graph model used did not exhibit many properties of the 1996 web graph we used. For instance the 1996 web graph has significantly higher maximum degree, which could potentially cause a much larger bias in their walk. Their results on the web also indicate a bias towards Google, possibly the result of a bias toward pages with a high page rank. Their approach seems to require many more page accesses to get approximations than the one presented in this paper. This work was carried out independently to our own, over a similar time-frame, and is an extension of their previous work on approximating page rank using random walks [14].

Bharat and Broder [11] attempted to generate random pages in a search engine index by constructing random queries. These pages were then used to estimate the relative size and overlap of various search engines. Their queries were based on a dictionary of words collected from Yahoo!, and the resulting sample was therefore biased towards English language pages. Also, because they combined several terms in their queries, they note a bias towards content rich pages.

Lawrence and Giles [17, 18] report the sizes of several search engines based on the number of pages returned in response to 1,050 actual queries. They note that the resulting pages are not uniformly distributed and use the results to discuss what might be called the useful size of a search engine, instead of measuring the total number of pages indexed. In addition

---

[2]Note that in order to generate this index, Inktomi needed powerful computational and network resources and four months of work.

they attempted to approximate the size of the web by estimating the number of web servers (via sampling random IP addresses and querying for a server) and multiplying by an estimate for the number of pages per site. They note, as do others, that the distribution of pages per server has a very high variance, and that their estimates are susceptible to inaccuracy as a result.

6 Conclusions

We have presented an efficient and accurate method for estimating the results of aggregate queries on web pages in the indexable web. We achieve this by performing a carefully designed random walk to produce a close to uniformly distributed sample of web pages. We have validated the walk in extensive experiments on the web today as well as on a large portion of the web from 1996 obtained by an ALEXA crawl. Furthermore, our technique is extremely efficient, and can produce uniformly distributed web pages quickly without significant computation or network resources. In fact, our estimates are reproducible on a single PC with a modest connection to the Internet in as little as one to two days.

One particularly interesting application of our technique is estimating the fraction of web pages covered by a particular search engine. This can be extended to a less biased mechanism for comparing search engine coverage. Furthermore, with accurate knowledge of the absolute size of a search engine, we can estimate the size of the web.

This technique opens up many new interesting questions. We would like to obtain stronger theoretical analysis of WebWalker's mixing time to support our experimental results. In addition, we would like to further reduce the bias towards high degree nodes and pages indexed by the search engine.

Acknowledgements

Sridhar Rajagopalan introduced us to this subject, provided us with the 1996 copy of the web, and gave us his constant support.

Thanks also to Alistair Sinclair and David Gibson for helpful discussions, and to Randy Huang and David Gibson for technical assistance.

References

[1] Alexa. `http://www.alexa.com`.

[2] AltaVista. `http://www.altavista.com`.

[3] fast. `http://www.alltheweb.com`.

[4] Go. `http://www.go.com`.

[5] Google. `http://www.google.com`.

[6] HotBot. `http://www.hotbot.com`.

[7] Inktomi. `http://www.inktomi.com`.

[8] Lycos. `http://www.lycos.com`.

[9] Search Engine Watch. `http://searchenginewatch.com`.

[10] D. Aldous. On the Markov chain simulation method for uniform combinatorial distributed and simulated annealing. *Probability in the Engineering and Informational Sciences*, 1:33–46, 1987.

[11] K. Bharat and A. Broder. A technique for measuring the relative size and overlap of public Web search engines. In *Proceedings of the 7th International World Wide Web Conference (WWW7)*, pages 379–388, April 1998.

[12] A. Broder, R. Kumar, F. Maghoul, P. Raghavan, S. Rajagopalan, R. Stata, A. Tomkins, and J. Wiener. Graph structure in the web: experiments and models. In *Proceedings of the 9th International World Wide Web Conference (WWW9)*, May 2000.

[13] D. Gilman. A Chernoff bound for random walks on expander graphs. *SIAM J. on Computing*, 27(4):1203–1220, 1998.

[14] M.R. Henzinger, A. Heydon, M. Mitzenmacher, and M. Najrok. Measuring index quality using random walks on the Web. In *Proceedings of the 8th International World Wide Web Conference (WWW8)*, pages 213–225, May 1999.

[15] M.R. Henzinger, A. Heydon, M. Mitzenmacher, and M. Najrok. On Near-Uniform URL Sampling. In *Proceedings of the 9th International World Wide Web Conference (WWW9)*, pages 295–308, May 2000.

[16] N. Kahale. Large deviation for Markov chains. *Combinatorics, Probability and Computing*, 6:465–474, 1997.

[17] S. Lawrence and C.L. Giles. Searching the World Wide Web. *Science*, 5360(280):98, 1998.

[18] S. Lawrence and C.L. Giles. Accessibility of information on the web. *Nature*, 400:107–109, 1999.

Computing Geographical Scopes of Web Resources

Junyan Ding
Computer Science Department
Columbia University
dingjy@cs.columbia.edu

Luis Gravano
Computer Science Department
Columbia University
gravano@cs.columbia.edu

Narayanan Shivakumar
Gigabeat, Inc.
shiva@gigabeat.com

Abstract

Many information resources on the web are relevant primarily to limited geographical communities. For instance, web sites containing information on restaurants, theaters, and apartment rentals are relevant primarily to web users in geographical proximity to these locations. In contrast, other information resources are relevant to a broader geographical community. For instance, an on-line newspaper may be relevant to users across the United States. Unfortunately, current web search engines largely ignore the *geographical scope* of web resources. In this paper, we introduce techniques for automatically computing the geographical scope of web resources, based on the textual content of the resources, as well as on the geographical distribution of hyperlinks to them. We report an extensive experimental evaluation of our strategies using real web data. Finally, we describe a geographically-aware search engine that we have built to showcase our techniques.

1 Introduction

The World-Wide Web provides uniform access to information available around the globe. Some web sites such as on-line stores and banking institutions are of "global" interest to web users world-wide, while many web sites contain information primarily of interest to web users in a geographical community, such as the Bay Area or Palo Alto. Over the past few years, web users have been discovering web sites using web search engines such as AltaVista [1] and Google [2]. In practice, these engines are ineffective for identifying *geographically scoped* web pages. For instance, finding restaurants, theaters, and apartment rentals in or near specific regions is a difficult task with these web search engines.

Now consider the scenario in which we have a database with the geographical scope (e.g., a city, a state) of all "resources" (e.g., restaurants, newspapers) with a web presence. We can then exploit such information for a variety of applications, including the following:

- **Personalized searching:** Consider the case a resident in Palo Alto searches for "newspapers." A geographically-aware search engine would first identify where the user is from (e.g., using a profile at my.yahoo.com or my.excite.com). The search engine then uses this information to return newspapers that are relevant to the user's location, rather than returning references to newspapers all over the world. For instance, the engine might recommend The New York Times as a "globally relevant" newspaper, and the Stanford Daily as a local newspaper. Note that this strategy is not equivalent to the user querying the search engine for "newspaper AND Palo Alto," since such a query would miss references to The New York Times, a newspaper that is published in a city not in the vicinity of Palo Alto. This newspaper even has the name of a specific city ("New York") in its name, but is nevertheless geographically relevant to the entire United States.

- **Improved browsing:** Web portals like Yahoo! already classify web resources *manually* according to their geographical scope [3]. The techniques that we present in this paper will make it possible

Proceedings of the 26th VLDB Conference, Cairo, Egypt, 2000.

---

[1] http://www.altavista.com
[2] http://www.google.com
[3] http://dir.yahoo.com/Regional/

to conduct such hierarchical categorization efforts automatically, improving their scalability.

It is easy to build geographically aware applications such as the above if we are supplied with a table that lists the geographical scope of each resource. Unfortunately, no such table exists for web resources. In this paper, we consider how to mine the web and automatically construct such a table using web hyperlinks and the actual content of web pages. For example, we can map every web page to a location based on where its hosting site resides. Then, we can consider the location of all the pages that point to, say, the Stanford Daily home page [4]. By examining the distribution of these pointers we can conclude that the Stanford Daily is of interest mainly to residents of the Stanford area, while The Wall Street Journal is of nation-wide interest. We can draw the same conclusion by analyzing the geographical locations that are mentioned in the pages of the Stanford Daily and in those of The Wall Street Journal.

The primary contributions of this paper include:

1. **Algorithms to estimate geographical scope:** We propose a variety of algorithms that automatically estimate the geographical scope of resources, based on exploiting either the distribution of HTML links to the resources (Section 3) or the textual content of the resources (Section 4).

2. **Measures to evaluate quality of algorithms:** We introduce evaluation criteria for our estimation algorithms, based on traditional information-retrieval metrics (Section 5).

3. **Experimental study of techniques:** We empirically evaluate our algorithms using real web data (Section 6).

4. **Implementation of a geographically aware search engine:** We also discuss how we used our algorithms in the implementation of a geographically aware search engine for on-line newspapers, which is accessible at `http://www.cs.-columbia.edu/~gravano/GeoSearch` (Section 7).

Related Work

Traditional information-retrieval research has studied how to best answer keyword-based queries over collections of text documents [14]. These collections are typically assumed to be relatively uniform in terms of, say, their quality and scope. With the advent of the web, researchers are studying other "dimensions" to the data that help separate useful resources from less-useful ones in an extremely heterogeneous environment like the web. Techniques for text-database selection [3, 8, 13, 10] decide what web databases to use to answer a user query, basing this decision on the textual contents of the web databases.

Recent research has started to exploit web links for improving web-page categorization [4] and for web mining [6, 9, 5]. Notably, search engines such as Google [1] and HITS [6, 12] estimate the "importance" of web pages by considering the number of hyperlinks that point to them. The rationale for their heuristics is that the larger the number of web users who made a hyperlink to a web page, the higher must be the importance of the page. In essence, this work manages to capture an additional dimension to the web data, namely how important or authoritative the pages are. Unlike the new techniques that we introduce in this paper, HITS and Google ignore the *spatial distribution* of incoming links to a web resource.

In this paper, we propose to extract yet another crucial dimension of the web data, namely the geographical scope of web resources. This new dimension can then be used to complement traditional information retrieval techniques and those used by Google and HITS to answer web queries in more effective ways. Some commercial web sites already *manually* classify web resources by their location, or keep directory information that lists where each company or web site is located (e.g., see `http://www.iatlas.com`). Quite recently, the NorthernLight search engine [5] has started to extract addresses from web pages, letting users narrow their searches to specific geographical regions (e.g., to pages "originated" within a five-mile radius of a given zip code). Users benefit from this information because they can further filter their query results. In reference [2], we discussed how to map a web site (e.g., `http://www-db.stanford.edu`) to a geographical location (e.g., Palo Alto), and we also presented a tool to visualize such geographical web data. In this paper, we extend this preliminary work to a harder problem: how to *automatically* estimate the geographical *scope* of a web resource? That is, which data is targeted towards residents of a city as opposed to the country, or the world?

2 Geographical Scopes of Web Resources

Web resources are built with a target audience in mind. Sometimes this audience is geographically enclosed in some neighborhood (e.g., the target audience of the web page of a local pizzeria that delivers orders to houses up to 2 miles away from the store). Some other times, the target audience of a resource is distributed across the country (e.g., the target audience of the web page of the USA Today newspaper). In this section,

---

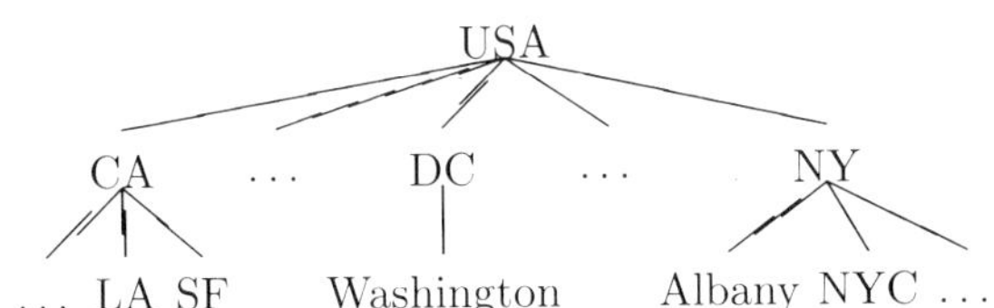

Figure 1: Portion of the hierarchy of geographical locations for the United States.

we introduce the notion of the *geographical scope* of a web resource, which captures the geographical distribution of the target audience of a web resource. This notion is a subjective one, the same way that the information-retrieval notion of *document relevance* is subjective [14].

Definition 1: *The **geographical scope** of a web resource w is the geographical area that the creator of w intends to reach.*

Using this informal definition, the geographical scope of our pizzeria above is the neighborhood where the pizzeria resides, whereas the geographical scope of the USA Today newspaper is the entire United States.

For concreteness, in the rest of the paper we focus on how to approximate the geographical scope of web resources within the United States. For this, we will view the United States as a three-level location hierarchy (Figure 1). The root of the hierarchy corresponds to the entire country. The next level down the hierarchy has one node for each of the 50 states, plus one node for the District of Columbia. Finally, the leaf level in the hierarchy has one node for each city in the country. Using this hierarchy, a human expert might specify that the geographical scope of the USA Today newspaper is the whole USA. In contrast, the geographical scope of The Arizona Daily Star Online is the state of Arizona, since this state is the target audience of this newspaper. Finally, the geographical scope of yet another newspaper, The Knoxville News-Sentinel, has the city of Knoxville as its geographical scope. Of course, this three-level hierarchy can be extended to span all the countries in the world, as well as to further localize resources in cities, to counties and boroughs. However, for simplicity this paper focuses only on the three levels listed above.

Given our three-level hierarchy of geographical locations in the United States, we can choose to define the geographical scope of web resources in different ways. For example, instead of indicating that the geographical scope of the USA Today newspaper is the top node in the hierarchy (i.e., the whole United States), we could list all 50 states plus Washington D.C. as comprising this geographical scope. Although it could be argued that this state-level formulation expresses the same information as the country-level one, we will

always express geographical scopes using nodes that are "as high" as possible in our three-level hierarchy. Thus, instead of aggregating the information that the USA Today is a national newspaper out of the list of states of its geographical scope, we will state this fact directly, and simply specify its scope to be the United States as a whole.

As mentioned above, the notion of geographical scope is subjective. To capture this notion accurately, we could hand-classify each web resource according to its intended geographical scope. (Incidentally, this is the way that web portals like Yahoo! operate.) In this paper, we study scalable ways to *automatically* approximate the resources' geographical scopes. Sections 3 and 4 describe two ways in which we can estimate the geographical scope of a web resource. Later, Section 6 will report the experiments that show that our automatically-computed approximations closely match the "ideal," subjective definition.

3   Exploiting Resource Usage

In this section, we show how we can estimate the geographical scope of web resources by exploiting the link structure of the web. (We will present an alternative estimation method that exploits the *contents* of the web resources in Section 4.)

Consider a web resource whose geographical scope is the entire United States (e.g., the USA Today newspaper). Such a resource is likely to then attract interest across the country. Our assumption in this section is that this interest will translate in web pages across the country containing HTML links to this web resource. [6] Conversely, a resource with a much more limited geographical scope will exhibit a significantly different link distribution pattern across the country. Hence a promising way to estimate the geographical scope of a resource is to study the geographical distribution of links to the resource. More specifically, two conditions that a location ℓ will have to satisfy to be in the geographical scope of a resource w are:

- A significant *fraction* of ℓ's web pages contain links to w (Section 3.1).

- The web pages in ℓ that contain links to w are distributed *smoothly* across ℓ (Section 3.2).

Below we show how to estimate the geographical scope of a web resource w by identifying a set of candidate locations ℓ that satisfy the two conditions above. This process results in the estimated geographical scope of w. Our experiments of Section 6 will show that these

---

[6] Of course, if we knew who *accesses* each web resource we could use this information for our problem. Unfortunately, web access logs for all resources whose geographical scopes we would like to characterize are not easily available.

estimates are often a good approximation of the subjective geographical scopes that we discussed in Section 2.

3.1 Measuring Interest: *Power*

Intuitively, a location ℓ that is in the geographical scope of a web resource w should exhibit relatively high "interest" in w among its web pages. In other words, a relatively high fraction of the web pages originated in ℓ should contain links to resource w. $Power(w, \ell)$ measures the relative interest in w among the pages in location ℓ:

$$Power(w, \ell) = \frac{Links(w, \ell)}{Pages(\ell)} \tag{1}$$

where $Links(w, \ell)$ is the number of pages in location ℓ that contain a link to web resource w, and $Pages(\ell)$ is the total number of web pages in ℓ. (We explain how we compute these numbers in Section 6.1.)

3.2 Measuring Uniformity: *Spread*

Geographical locations can be decomposed into several sub-locations. As an example, the United States consists of 50 states plus the District of Columbia, while the state of New York, in turn, comprises a number of cities (e.g., Albany, New York City). As we discussed in the previous section, to include a location ℓ (e.g., the state of New York) in the geographical scope of a web resource w, there should be a sufficiently high "interest" in resource w in location ℓ (i.e., $Power(w, \ell)$ is high). In addition, we need to ask that this interest be spread smoothly across the location. Thus, a resource with an unusually high number of links originating, say, in New York City, but with no links coming from other New York state cities should not have the state of New York in its geographical scope, but perhaps just New York City instead.

To determine how uniform the distribution of links to a web resource w is across a location ℓ, we introduce a second metric, *Spread*. Intuitively, $Spread(w, \ell)$ will be high whenever $Power(w, \ell_i) \sim Power(w, \ell_j)$ for all "sub-locations" ℓ_i, ℓ_j that are children of ℓ in the location hierarchy of Section 2. In what follows, we provide three alternative definitions of *Spread*. These definitions are all built on this intuition, but will compute the value of $Spread(w, \ell)$ using techniques borrowed from different fields. In Section 6 we experimentally compare how these three definitions perform relative to each other.

For our three definitions of *Spread*, $Spread(w, \ell)$ will have the maximum possible value (i.e., a value of 1) in the following two special cases:

- ℓ is a leaf node of our location hierarchy: In this case, by definition, the distribution of *Power* across ℓ is completely uniform, because we regard

ℓ as an "atomic" location. In this paper, these atomic locations are the United States cities.

- $Power(w, \ell)=0$: In this case, there is no "interest" at all in resource w across location ℓ. Since *Spread* measures the uniformity of this interest across ℓ, $Spread(w, \ell)$ is trivially maximum in this case.

Next, we give three alternative definitions for $Spread(w, \ell)$ for the case when ℓ is not a leaf node in our location hierarchy and $Power(w, \ell) > 0$. In the definitions below, $\ell_1, \ldots, \ell_n$ are the children of ℓ in the hierarchy. Also, we associate with location ℓ vector $\vec{Pages} = (p_1, \ldots, p_n)$, which lists the number of pages $p_i = Pages(\ell_i)$ of each child ℓ_i of ℓ. A second vector associated with ℓ, $\vec{Links} = (l_1, \ldots, l_n)$, lists the number of pages $l_i = Links(w, \ell_i)$ that have a link to resource w at location ℓ_i, for $i = 1, \ldots, n$. Finally, vector $\vec{Power} = (r_1, \ldots, r_n)$ lists the value of *Power* $r_i = Power(w, \ell_i)$ for each sub-location of ℓ.

Vector-Space Definition of *Spread*

The first definition of *Spread* is inspired in the vector-space model from information retrieval [14]. Intuitively, we will compute how "similar" vectors $\vec{Pages}$ and $\vec{Links}$ are by computing the cosine of the angle between them. If the fraction of pages with links to w is mostly constant across all of ℓ's children $\ell_1, \ldots, \ell_n$, then $\vec{Pages}$ and $\vec{Links}$ will be roughly scaled versions of one another, and the cosine of the angle between these vectors will be close to 1:

$$
\begin{aligned}
Spread(w, \ell) &= \vec{Pages} \odot \vec{Links} \\
&= \frac{\sum_{i=1}^{n} p_i \times l_i}{\sqrt{\sum_{i=1}^{n} p_i^2} \cdot \sqrt{\sum_{i=1}^{n} l_i^2}}
\end{aligned}
\tag{2}
$$

Relative-Error Definition of *Spread*

Let $R = (\sum_{i=1}^{n} l_i)/(\sum_{i=1}^{n} p_i)$. If the distribution of interest in w were perfectly smooth, then $r_i = R$ for all i. To measure how far we are from this perfectly smooth distribution, we compute how much each r_i deviates from the "target" value R. We can then give a definition of *Spread* based on computing the "relative error" for each ℓ_i with respect to R:

$$Spread(w, \ell) = \frac{1}{1 + \frac{1}{\sum_{i=1}^{n} p_i} \sum_{i=1}^{n} p_i \cdot \frac{|R - r_i|}{R}} \tag{3}$$

Entropy Definition of *Spread*

Our third and final definition for *Spread* is based on the notion of entropy from information theory [11]. To give this definition, we assume that there is an "information source" associated with web resource w and geographical location ℓ. The information source generates symbols representing the different children of

ℓ, namely $\ell_1, \ldots, \ell_n$. Moreover, we assume that this information source generates its symbols by infinitely executing three steps:

1. Randomly select an ℓ_i.

2. Randomly select a web page located in ℓ_i.

3. If the web page has a link to web site w, then generate a symbol representing ℓ_i.

Intuitively, when $r_i = Power(w, \ell_i)$ is uniform across the ℓ_i sub-locations, the information source will achieve the maximum entropy available at geographical location ℓ, which is $\log n$. To make this definition comparable across geographical locations with different numbers of sub-locations, we define $Spread$ as follows:

$$Spread(w, \ell) = \frac{-\sum_{i=1}^{n} \frac{r_i}{\sum_{j=1}^{n} r_j} \cdot \log(\frac{r_i}{\sum_{j=1}^{n} r_j})}{\log n} \quad (4)$$

3.3 Estimating Geographical Scopes

The previous sections showed metrics to measure the strength ($Power(w, \ell)$) and uniformity ($Spread(w, \ell)$) of the interest in a web resource w at a location ℓ. In this section we define how we can use $Power$ and $Spread$ to estimate what locations we should include in the geographical scope of a given web resource.

As a first step to estimate the geographical scope of a web resource w, we identify the locations ℓ in our hierarchy of Section 2 with $Spread(w, \ell) \geq \tau_c$, for some given threshold $0 \leq \tau_c \leq 1$. These are the locations with a relatively smooth distribution of links to w across their sub-locations. Furthermore, we only include in $CGS(w)$, the *candidate geographical scope* for w, those locations that have no ancestor ℓ' with $Spread(w, \ell') \geq \tau_c$. In other words, $CGS(w)$ contains locations with smooth distribution of links for w such that are not "subsumed" by any other ancestor location also in $CGS(w)$:

Definition 2: *The **candidate geographical scope** $CGS(w)$ of a web resource w is a set of nodes in the geographical hierarchy. A location ℓ is in $CGS(w)$ if it satisfies the following two conditions, given a fixed threshold τ_c:*

- *$Spread(w, \ell) \geq \tau_c$.*

- *For all ℓ' that is an ancestor of ℓ, $Spread(w, \ell') < \tau_c$.*

Given a web resource w, we can compute $CGS(w)$ with a simple algorithm that recursively visits the nodes in the location hierarchy top-down. [7]

---

[7]We have investigated an alternative, "stricter" definition of $CGS(w)$. According to this definition, $\ell \in CGS(w)$ if *every* location ℓ' in the location subtree rooted at ℓ has $Spread(w, \ell') \geq \tau_c$. Our experimental results showed that the weaker definition that we give above outperformed this stricter definition. For space constraints, we then do not discuss this stricter version further.

The candidate geographical scope of a resource w, $CGS(w)$, contains locations exhibiting relatively smooth interest in w. However, as we discussed earlier, this interest could be quite small in some cases. In particular, a location ℓ with $Power(w, \ell)=0$ (e.g., a leaf node) might be included in $CGS(w)$, which is clearly undesirable. Consequently, we need to prune our candidate geographical scopes to only include locations with high enough $Power$ in the final estimated geographical scope of a resource:

Definition 3: *The **estimated geographical scope** $EGS(w)$ of a web resource w is a set of locations obtained from $CGS(w)$ using one of the following scope pruning strategies:*

- **Top-k pruning:** *Given an integer k, $EGS(w)$ consists of the top-k locations in $CGS(w)$, in decreasing order of their $Power$.*

- **Absolute-threshold pruning:** *Given a threshold τ_e, $EGS(w) = \{\ell \in CGS(w) | Power(w, \ell) \geq \tau_e\}$.*

- **Relative-threshold pruning:** *Given a percentage p, $EGS(w) = \{\ell \in CGS(w) | Power(w, \ell) \geq max\_Power(w) \times p\}$, where $max\_Power(w) = \max\{Power(w, \ell) | \ell \in CGS(w)\}$.*

4 Exploiting Resource Contents

So far, we have used the distribution of links to a resource to estimate the resource's geographical scope. A natural question, however, is whether we can instead just examine the resource's contents to accomplish this task. In this section we explore this idea, and discuss how to use the resources' text to estimate their geographical scope.

Consider a resource whose geographical scope is, say, the state of New York. We may argue that the text in such a resource is likely to mention New York cities more frequently than locations corresponding to other states or countries. This is our main assumption in this section. (Section 6 experimentally compares the resulting technique with our link-based strategy of Section 3.) Hence an interesting direction to explore to estimate the geographical scope of a resource is to study the distribution of locations that are *mentioned* in the resource. More specifically, two conditions that a location ℓ will have to satisfy to be in the geographical scope of a resource w are:

- A significant *fraction* of all locations mentioned in w are either ℓ itself or a sub-location of ℓ.

- The location references in w are distributed *smoothly* across ℓ.

Next, Section 4.1 shows that we can use the location references in the contents of a web resource to define a variation of the *Power* and *Spread* metrics of Section 3. We then estimate the geographical scopes completely analogously as we did for the link-based strategy. Later, Section 4.2 addresses a fundamental step in our content-based approach, namely how we can effectively extract the location names from the text of a resource.

4.1 Estimating Geographical Scopes

To estimate whether a location ℓ is part of a resource w's geographical scope we will proceed exactly as in Section 3 and compute (modified versions of) $Power(w, \ell)$ and $Spread(w, \ell)$. For this, we need to extract from w two numbers. The first one, $Locations(w)$, is the number of references to geographical locations in w's text. The second one, $References(w, \ell)$, is the number of references to ℓ mentioned in w's text. [8] Given these counts, we can adapt our definition of *Power* from Section 3.1 in the following way:

$$Power(w, \ell) = \frac{References(w, \ell)}{Locations(w)} \quad (5)$$

To adapt the definition of *Spread* of Section 3.2, we now define the following three vectors for a web resource w and a location ℓ with children $\ell_1, \ldots, \ell_n$. First, vector $\vec{Locations} = (p_1, \ldots, p_n)$ is a vector with every element having the same value $p_i = Locations(w)$, which is the number of references to geographical locations in w's text. Second, vector $\vec{References} = (l_1, \ldots, l_n)$ lists the number of references to each sub-location ℓ_i in w's text, i.e., $l_i = References(w, \ell_i)$. Finally, vector $\vec{Power} = (r_1, \ldots, r_n)$ lists each sub-location's *Power* value $r_i = Power(w, \ell_i)$. These vectors will play a role that is completely analogous to those of the $\vec{Pages}$, $\vec{Links}$, and $\vec{Power}$ vectors of Section 3, respectively, for defining $Spread(w, \ell)$. We can now use exactly the same definitions for *Spread* that we used in Section 3 and calculate the estimated geographical scope $EGS(w)$ for a web resource w.

4.2 Extracting and Processing Location References

To estimate the geographical scope of a web resource w as in the previous section, we need to extract all of the locations that are mentioned in the textual contents of w. Furthermore, the technique above expects the list of *cities* that are mentioned in the text of the web resources. In this section, we discuss the main problems involved in such an extraction process.

---

[8] We will discuss in Section 4.2 how we map references to, say, an entire state to references to individual cities within the state, which is what we count in *References* and *Locations*.

Extracting Location Names from Plain Text

State-of-the-art named-entity taggers manage to identify entities like people, organizations, and locations in natural-language text with high accuracy. For the experiments that we report in Section 6 we used the Alembic Workbench system developed at MITRE [7].

Normalizing and Disambiguating Location Names

After the tagging phase in which we identify the locations (e.g., "New York City," "California") mentioned in w, we should map each location to an unambiguous city-state pair. Problems that arise when completing this task include:

- **Aliasing:** Different names might be commonly used for the same location. For example, San Francisco is often referred to as SF. It is relatively easy to address this problem at the country or state level. (These aliases are indeed quite limited, and we compiled a list of them by hand.) For cities, though, we resorted to a web-accessible database of the United States Postal Service (USPS) [9]. For each zip code, this service returns a list of variations of the corresponding city's name. For example, if we use Columbia University's zip code, 10027, we obtain a list of names for New York City, including New York, Manhattan, New York City, NY City, NYC, and, interestingly enough, Manhattanville. (Incidentally, the USPS standard form for this city is New York.) By repeatedly querying the USPS database with different zip codes, we can build a list of city-name aliases, together with the corresponding "normal form" for each group.

- **Ambiguity:** Another problem when processing a given city name is that it can refer to cities in different states. For example, four states, Georgia, Illinois, Mississippi, and Ohio, have a city called Columbus. A reference to such a city without a state qualification is inherently ambiguous, unless of course we could understand the context in which the reference was made. We have developed heuristics for managing this kind of ambiguous location references. Our technique starts by identifying the unambiguous location references in the web resource at hand w, and uses them to disambiguate the remaining references. Intuitively, if w mentions mostly locations in the state of New York, for example, we will assume that a reference to "Manhattan" is a reference to New York City, not to Manhattan, Kansas. More specifically, if w mentions an ambiguous city name C m times, and C can refer to a city in a number of

---

[9] http://www.usps.gov

states $S_1, \ldots, S_k$, then we "distribute" the m occurrences of C among the k states proportionally to the distribution of unambiguous cities in these states. Suppose that in our example 90% of the unambiguous cities that are mentioned in resource w are in the state of New York, and the remaining 10% are in the state of Kansas. Then, if w refers to Manhattan five times, we will assume that 4.5 of these references correspond to New York, NY, and only 0.5 of them to Manhattan, KS.

Mapping Locations to City Names

A location name can refer to a city, a state, or a country, for example. Our technique to estimate geographical scopes analyzes the distribution of *cities* that are mentioned at a web resource w. Consequently, we need a way to map references to, say, states to city references that our technique can use. For this, we simply "push down" references to high-level locations in our location hierarchy (Section 2). This way, a reference to the state of New York will be pushed down as a reference to every city in the state. When we propagate these references down, we also scale their *weight* by some constant α. (A value of $\alpha = 0.1$ worked best in our Section 6 experiments.)

5 Evaluating the Quality of the Estimated Geographical Scopes

In the previous sections we discussed two approaches to estimating the geographical scope of resources. Of course, other approaches are possible (e.g., a "hybrid" strategy combining our two techniques). We now propose measures to evaluate the quality of any such algorithm for estimating a web resource's geographical scope.

To evaluate the quality of our estimated geographical scopes, we need to compare them against the ideal, subjective scopes. We could base our comparison on metrics commonly used for classification tasks: for example, we could just compute the number of web resources in our testbed for which we managed to identify their geographical scope *perfectly*. Such a metric would not fully capture the nuances of our problem. For example, if the geographical scope of a resource w is {California} and we compute $EGS(w)$ as, say, {California, New York City}, this metric would mark our answer as completely wrong. Similarly, consider the case where our $EGS(w)$ computation consists of, say, 90% of the California cities, but does not include California as a whole state, which would have been the perfect answer. Traditional classification accuracy metrics would also consider our estimate as completely wrong, even when our technique managed to identify only cities in the right state as part of the geographical scope of w.

With these observations in mind, we adapt the precision and recall metrics from the information retrieval field to yield metrics that we believe are appropriate for our problem. More specifically, we will define *precision* and *recall* for our problem as follows, after we introduce an auxiliary definition. Given a set of locations L, we will "expand" it by including all locations under a location $\ell \in L$. Thus, $Expanded(L) = \{\ell'$ location $\mid \ell' \in L$ or ℓ' is in the location subtree of some $\ell \in L\}$. Now, let w be a web resource, *Ideal* be its "expanded" geographical scope, and *Estimated* be our expanded estimate, $Expanded(EGS(w))$. Then:

$$Precision(w) = \frac{|Ideal \cap Estimated|}{|Estimated|}$$

$$Recall(w) = \frac{|Ideal \cap Estimated|}{|Ideal|}$$

Intuitively, precision measures the fraction of locations in an estimated geographical scope that are correct, i.e., that are also part of the ideal geographical scope. (Perfect precision might be trivially achieved by always returning empty geographical scopes.) Recall measures the fraction of the locations in the ideal geographical scope that are captured in our estimated geographical scope. (Perfect recall might be trivially achieved by always including all locations in the geographical scopes.) Finally, to simplify the interpretation of our experiments, we combine precision and recall into a single metric using the F-measure [15]:

$$F(w) = \frac{2 \times Precision(w) \times Recall(w)}{Precision(w) + Recall(w)}$$

6 Experimental Evaluation

Section 2 defined the "ideal," subjective geographical scope of a web resource w. Later, we showed how we can automatically calculate the estimated geographical scope $EGS(w)$ by analyzing the geographical distribution of HTML links to w (Section 3), or, alternatively, by analyzing the distribution of location names from the textual contents of w (Section 4). In this section, we experimentally evaluate how well our different techniques can approximate the ideal geographical scopes using the evaluation criteria we discussed in Section 5. We describe our experimental setting in Section 6.1. We then report the results of our experiments, which involved real web resources, in Section 6.2.

6.1 Experimental Setting

In this section we explain the main aspects of our experimental setting. In particular, we describe the real web resources that we used, and highlight some of the challenging implementation issues that we had to address to carry out our study.

Web Resources

Ideally, to evaluate our techniques of Sections 3 and 4 we should use a set of real web resources, each with its corresponding geographical scope, as determined by a human expert. (Analogously, the information retrieval field relies on human relevance judgments to evaluate the performance of search-engine algorithms [14].) For our experiments, we needed a list of web resources whose intended geographical scope was self-apparent and uncontested. Furthermore, we wanted our list to cover the different levels of our location hierarchy of Section 2. In other words, we wanted resources who would have the United States as their geographical scope, but we also wanted resources whose geographical scope was at the state and city levels. Finally, the resources that we picked needed to have a sufficiently large number of HTML links directed to them, so that we can apply our technique of Section 3. (We discuss how to handle resources with not enough references to them in Section 8.) With the above goals in mind, we collected a list of 150 web resources whose geographical scopes span the three levels of our location hierarchy:

- **National level:** 50 of our web resources have the United States as their geographical scope. These resources are the 50 most heavily cited Federal Government web sites listed in the FedWorld web site [10]. (We determined the 50 most cited pages by querying AltaVista to obtain the number of pages with links to each of these resources.) These web sites have the whole United States as their intended audience, and include the web sites of NASA [11] and the National Endowment for the Arts [12], for example.

- **State level:** 50 of our web resources have a state as their geographical scope. These resources are the official web site of each state in the United States (e.g., `http://www.state.ny.us` (state of New York)), and have their corresponding state as their geographical scope.

- **City level:** 50 of our web resources have a city as their geographical scope. These resources are the 50 most cited among the US cities' official web sites (e.g., `http://www.ci.sf.ca.us` (San Francisco)), and have their corresponding city as their geographical scope. (We obtained a list of the US cities' official web sites from Piper Resources' "State and Local Government on the Net." [13])

Implementation Issues

We now describe some interesting tasks that we had to perform to run our experiments:

[10]`http://www.fedworld.gov/locator.htm`
[11]`http://www.nasa.gov`
[12]`http://www.arts.endow.gov`
[13]`http://www.piperinfo.com/state/states.html`

- **Mapping web pages to city names:** Our technique of Section 3 requires that we find all pages with HTML links to a given web resource w. After identifying these pages, we need to place their location so that we can study their geographical distribution and estimate w's geographical scope. This is a challenging task, because we really need the location of the *author* of a page, which might be quite different from the location of the site that hosts the page. For example, web pages with links to w from, say, the `aol.com` domain are hardly useful for our task: If we examine just the location of the web site where these pages reside, we would most likely be misguided in determining w's geographic scope. (We elaborated on these issues further and outlined alternative approaches to "placing web pages on the map" in [2].) A key observation that we exploit for our experiments is that it suffices for our Section 3 technique to have a reasonable *sample* of the pages with links to resource w to estimate w's geographical scope. Following this observation, we focussed on web pages whose author's location we could determine reliably, and that would span the entire United States. More specifically, we analyzed link information from pages originating only in educational domains (e.g., from web sites with a `.edu` suffix, like `www.columbia.edu`). Given such a page, we query the `whois` service to map the page's web site into its corresponding zip code. After this, we query the USPS zip-code server and obtain the standard city name associated with the zip code.

- **Refining our location hierarchy:** Our experimental setting considers links originating only in educational institutions. Unfortunately, not all cities have one such institution. Hence, we refined our location hierarchy to include only cities with a university with a `.edu` web site. We further pruned our list by eliminating every city hosting fewer than 500 pages in `.edu` web sites, so that we analyze only cities with a significant web presence in `.edu` domains. At the end of this process, we are left with a location hierarchy consisting of 673 cities as leaf nodes, the 50 states and the District of Columbia as intermediate nodes, and the entire United States as the root node.

- **Computing** $Pages(\ell)$ **and** $Links(w, \ell)$**:** For each city ℓ in our location hierarchy, we need to obtain the number of pages from `.edu` domains that are located in it. To get this number, we query AltaVista and obtain the number of pages that each educational institution in location ℓ hosts. By adding these numbers for each institution in ℓ we compute $Pages(\ell)$, which we need in Section 3. Similarly, we can identify how many of these pages have links to a specific web resource

w to compute $Links(w, \ell)$.

- **Obtaining the textual contents of a web resource** w**:** For our content-based technique of Section 4, we download the full-text contents of the 150 web sites of our testbed, using Gnu's `wget` web crawler. We then use the `lynx` browser to eliminate the HTML tags in the web pages and extract the plain-English text in them. As explained in Section 4, after this we run the Alembic named-entity tagger [7] to extract the location names that are mentioned in the plain text. Finally, we resolve aliasing and ambiguity issues, map locations to city names, and estimate the geographical scopes as outlined in Section 4. [14]

6.2 Experimental Results

In Table 1 we summarize the algorithms we now evaluate. In addition to the three different definitions of *Spread* we discussed in Section 3.2, we also consider the following two simple "baseline" algorithms for computing candidate geographical scopes. The first one, *AllLeaves*, always defines the candidate geographical scope $CGS(w)$ of a web resource w as consisting of all of the cities in our location hierarchy. In contrast, the second baseline technique, *OnlyRoot*, always defines $CGS(w)$ as consisting of the United States only. The candidate geographical scope, obtained by any baseline technique or *Spread* definition, is then pruned by one of the three scope-pruning strategies to produce the estimated geographical scope as described in Section 3.3. Table 1 also summarizes the parameters involved with each of the different algorithms. For example, recall that k is a tunable parameter in the *TopK* scope-pruning strategy of Section 3.3.

We comprehensively evaluated the above algorithms to understand the impact of the different tunable parameters on precision, recall, and the *F*-measure. Due to lack of space, we present a few sample results to highlight some of our key observations. Specifically, we present our results for the relative-threshold pruning strategy *RelThr*. We evaluated our results for the *TopK* and for the *AbsThr* strategies as well, and observed similar trends. Hence we do not discuss these further.

In Figure 2, we show the impact of parameter p on the average *F*-measure for the link-based approach using the relative-threshold pruning strategy *RelThr*. (We use the values of τ_c that are specified in Table 2.) Notice that all the *Spread* definitions perform very well, especially as p increases, and the *Spread* definitions have a much higher average *F*-measure compared to the strawman *AllLeaves* and *OnlyRoot* tech-

---

[14]We only used 142 of the 150 web resources in our testbed to evaluate the content-based technique of Section 4: out of the remaining eight web resources, either `wget` could not crawl their pages, or the named-entity tagger that we used, Alembic, could not find any location name in their pages.

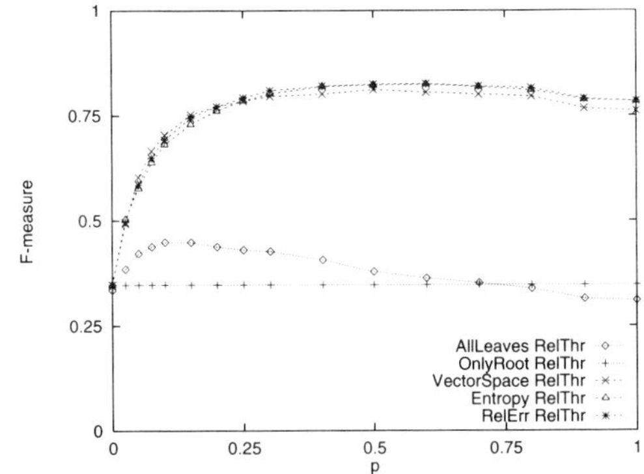

Figure 2: Average *F*-measure for the link-based strategy of Section 3 as a function of p (*RelThr* pruning strategy).

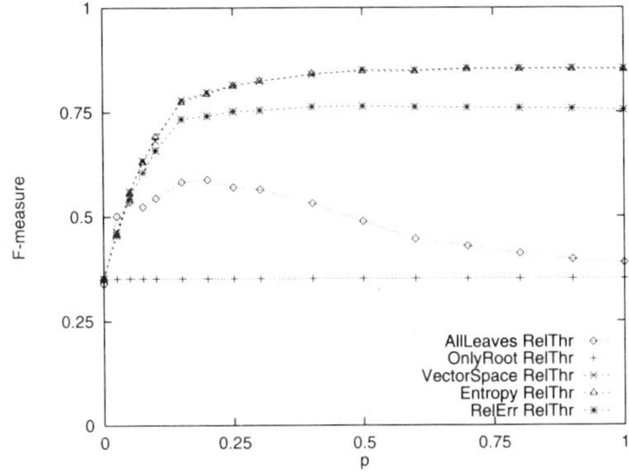

Figure 4: Average *F*-measure for the content-based strategy of Section 4 as a function of p (*RelThr* pruning strategy).

niques. Figure 3 shows the average precision and recall for *RelErr*, with the *RelThr* pruning strategy. Our techniques have more than 75% average precision and recall for several settings of the p parameter, which translates into the correspondingly high average *F*-measure values of Figure 2.

So far we have evaluated our link-based techniques for different parameter settings. We now discuss similar results for our content-based techniques of Section 4. In Figure 4 we report the impact of p on the average *F*-measure for the content-based approach on our entire data set, using the values of τ_c specified in Table 3. We observe similar results to our link-based approach in that our techniques have high average F values, especially for $p > 0.2$, compared to the strawman techniques.

Table 2 summarizes our results from the previous graphs for the link-based approach, and reports the "best" (i.e., highest average F value) parameter values

	Label	Description	Associated Parameter
Baseline	*AllLeaves*	Scope consists of all USA cities	–
Techniques	*OnlyRoot*	Scope consists of just USA	–
Spread	*VectorSpace*	Vector-space definition of *Spread*	τ_c
Definition	*Entropy*	Entropy definition of *Spread*	τ_c
(Section 3.2)	*RelErr*	Relative-error definition of *Spread*	τ_c
Scope-Pruning	*TopK*	Top-k pruning	k
Strategies	*AbsThr*	Absolute-threshold pruning	τ_e
(Section 3.3)	*RelThr*	Relative-threshold pruning	p

Table 1: The variations of our techniques that we use in our experiments, together with their associated parameters.

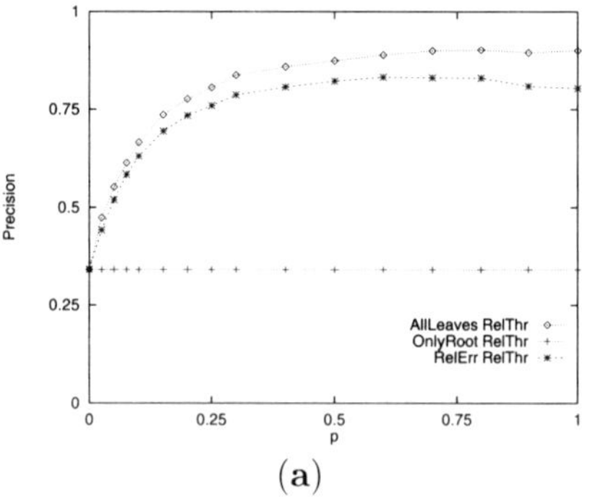

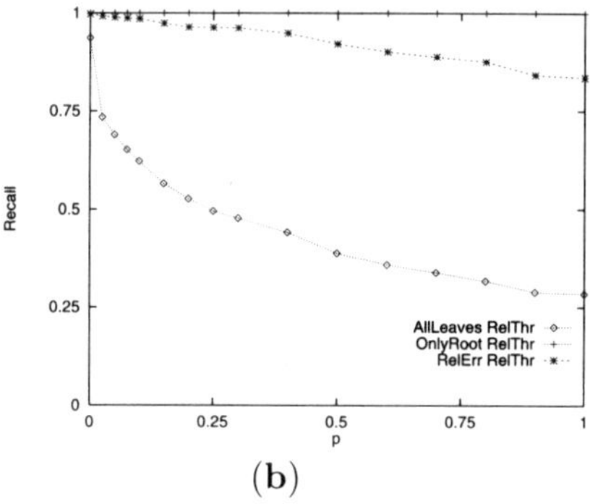

Figure 3: Average precision (**a**) and recall (**b**) for the link-based strategy of Section 3 as a function of p ($\tau_c = 0.57$ for *RelErr*; *RelThr* pruning strategy).

for each of our *Spread* definitions and scope-pruning strategies. In Table 3, we report similar results for the content-based approach. In general, we see that the relative-threshold strategy to pruning scope works best in practice. In our data set, the content-based approach has a slight advantage over the link-based approach. However, we should regard these two approaches as complementary to each other for the following reasons, which we already touched on in Section 6.1. Often, web sites restrict robots from crawling their site (e.g., this is the case for The New York Times newspaper). In such cases, we cannot apply our content-based approach for estimating geographical scope, while we can still resort to the link-based approach. In other cases, the number of incoming links to a web site may be limited. In these cases, we should use our content-based approach, as long as any useful geographical information can be extracted from such resources that are not heavily cited.

7 A Geographically Aware Search Engine

Based on the techniques we developed in the previous sections, we have implemented a geographically aware search engine that downloads and indexes the full contents of 436 on-line newspapers based in the United States. Our search engine estimates the geographical scope of the newspapers using the link-based technique of Section 3 with the *Entropy* definition for *Spread* and the *RelThr* scope-pruning strategy. This search engine is available at `http://www.cs.columbia.edu/-~gravano/GeoSearch`.

Our search engine automatically pre-computes the geographical scope of the 436 newspapers that it indexes. When users query the engine, they specify their zip code in addition to their list of search keywords. Our system first uses just the keywords to *rank* the newspaper articles on those keywords using a standard, off-the-shelf text search engine called Swish. Our system then filters out all pages coming from newspapers whose geographical scope does not include the user's specified zip code. Furthermore, our engine recomputes the score for each surviving page and returns the pages ranked in the resulting order. A page's new score is a combination of the Swish-generated score for the page and the *Power* of the location in the geographical scope of the page's newspaper that encloses the user's zip code. Figure 5 shows the results for query "startups business" with zip code 94043, which corresponds to Mountain View, California. The first article is from The Nando Times, a national online newspaper. Our system has determined that this newspaper's geographical scope is the whole country, hence the coloring of the map next to the correspond-

	TopK			AbsThr			RelThr		
	F	τ_c	k	F	τ_c	τ_e	F	τ_c	p
AllLeaves	0.34	–	∞	0.51	–	0.0007	0.45	–	0.1
OnlyRoot	0.35	–	1	0.35	–	0	0.35	–	0
VectorSpace	0.76	0.7	1	0.52	0.9	0.0007	**0.81**	0.7	0.5
Entropy	0.78	0.8	1	0.51	0.8	0.0007	**0.82**	0.8	0.6
RelErr	0.78	0.57	1	0.52	0.67	0.0007	**0.83**	0.57	0.6

Table 2: Best average F-measure results for different *Spread* definitions (Section 3.2) and scope-pruning strategies (Section 3.3), using the link-based strategy of Section 3.

	TopK			AbsThr			RelThr		
	F	τ_c	k	F	τ_c	τ_e	F	τ_c	p
AllLeaves	0.37	–	1	0.42	–	0.0007	0.59	–	0.2
OnlyRoot	0.35	–	1	0.35	–	0	0.35	–	0
VectorSpace	**0.85**	0.6	1	0.82	0.6	0.1	**0.86**	0.6	0.7
Entropy	**0.85**	0.8	1	0.82	0.8	0.1	**0.85**	0.8	0.7
RelErr	0.76	0.57	1	0.72	0.50	0.1	0.76	0.57	0.5

Table 3: Best average F-measure results for different *Spread* definitions (Section 3.2) and scope-pruning strategies (Section 3.3), using the content-based strategy of Section 4.

ing article. The second article returned is from the San Jose Mercury News, a newspaper based in San Jose, California, whose technology reports have followers across the country. Our search engine has classified this newspaper as having a national geographical scope. The last article returned originated in a newspaper whose geographical scope consists of the entire state of California, which is marked with a solid color on the map, plus a few cities scattered across the country, indicated by placing a dot in their corresponding states.

8 Conclusion

In this paper, we discussed how to estimate the geographical scope of web resources, and how to exploit this information to build geographically aware applications. The main contributions of this paper include automatic estimation algorithms based on web-page content and HTML link information, metrics to evaluate the quality of such algorithms, a comprehensive evaluation of these techniques in a realistic experimental scenario, and an implementation of a geographically aware search engine for newspaper articles. One of the key observations of this paper is that the content-based techniques and the link-based techniques have specific advantages and disadvantages, and in fact can be used as complementary estimators of the scope of web resources. In effect, some sites might not allow us to "crawl" their contents, preventing us from using our content-based techniques. Some other sites might have a low number of incoming HTML links, preventing us from using our link-based techniques reliably. By combining these two approaches we can accurately estimate the geographical scope of many web resources, hence capturing a crucial dimension of web data that is currently ignored by search engines.

Acknowledgments

This material is based upon work supported by the National Science Foundation under Grants No. IIS-97-33880 and IRI-96-19124. We also thank Jon Oringer for implementing the search engine of Section 7, and Jun Rao and Vasilis Vassalos for useful comments on the paper.

References

[1] S. Brin and L. Page. The anatomy of a large-scale hypertextual web search engine. In *Proceedings of the Seventh International World Wide Web Conference (WWW7)*, Apr. 1998.

[2] O. Buyukkokten, J. Cho, H. García-Molina, L. Gravano, and N. Shivakumar. Exploiting geographical location information of web pages. In *Proceedings of the ACM SIGMOD Workshop on the Web and Databases (WebDB'99)*, June 1999.

[3] J. P. Callan, Z. Lu, and W. B. Croft. Searching distributed collections with inference networks. In *Proceedings of the Eighteenth ACM International Conference on Research and Development in Information Retrieval (SIGIR'95)*, July 1995.

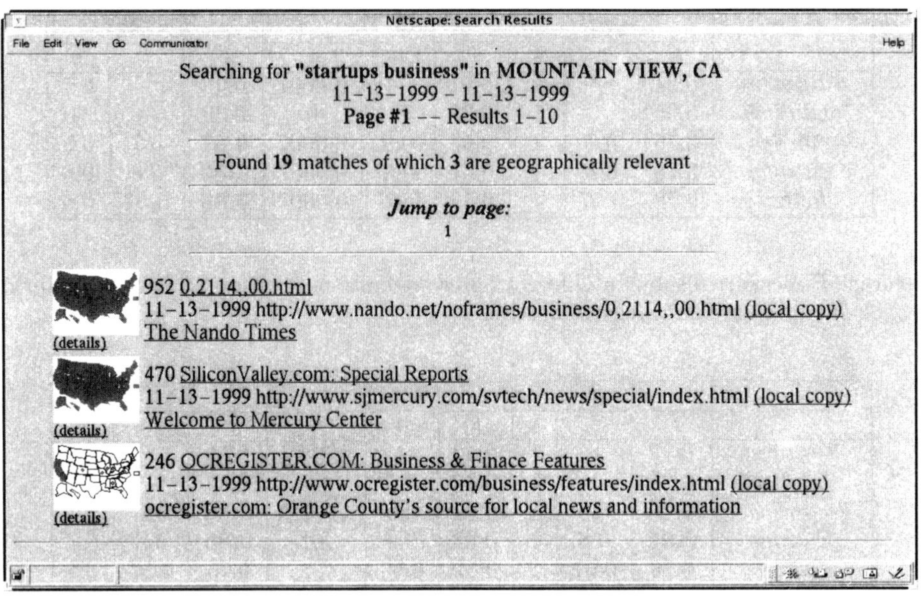

Figure 5: Search results from our geographically-aware search engine.

[4] S. Chakrabarti, B. Dom, and P. Indyk. Enhanced hypertext categorization using hyperlinks. In *Proceedings of the 1998 ACM International Conference on Management of Data (SIGMOD'98)*, June 1998.

[5] S. Chakrabarti, B. Dom, S. R. Kumar, P. Raghavan, S. Rajagopalan, A. Tomkins, D. Gibson, and J. Kleinberg. Mining the web's link structure. *IEEE Computer Magazine*, 32(8):60–67, 1999.

[6] S. Chakrabarti, B. Dom, P. Raghavan, S. Rajagopalan, D. Gibson, and J. Kleinberg. Automatic resource compilation by analyzing hyperlink structure and associated text. In *Proceedings of the Seventh International World Wide Web Conference (WWW7)*, Apr. 1998.

[7] D. Day, J. Aberdeen, L. Hirschman, R. Kozierok, P. Robinson, and M. Vilain. Mixed-initiative development of language processing systems. In *Proceedings of the Fifth ACL Conference on Applied Natural Language Processing*, Apr. 1997.

[8] J. C. French, A. L. Powell, C. L. Viles, T. Emmitt, and K. J. Prey. Evaluating database selection techniques: A testbed and experiment. In *Proceedings of the Twentyfirst ACM International Conference on Research and Development in Information Retrieval (SIGIR'98)*, Aug. 1998.

[9] D. Gibson, J. Kleinberg, and P. Raghavan. Inferring web communities from link topology. In *Proceedings of the Ninth ACM Conference on Hypertext and Hypermedia*, pages 225–234, June 1998.

[10] L. Gravano, H. García-Molina, and A. Tomasic. *GlOSS*: Text-source discovery over the Internet. *ACM Transactions on Database Systems*, 24(2), June 1999.

[11] R. W. Hamming. *Coding and Information Theory*. Prentice-Hall, 1980.

[12] J. Kleinberg. Authoritative sources in a hyperlinked environment. In *Proceedings of the Ninth Annual ACM-SIAM Symposium on Discrete Algorithms*, pages 668–677, Jan. 1998.

[13] W. Meng, K.-L. Liu, C. T. Yu, X. Wang, Y. Chang, and N. Rishe. Determining text databases to search in the Internet. In *Proceedings of the Twenty-fourth International Conference on Very Large Databases (VLDB'98)*, Aug. 1998.

[14] G. Salton. *Automatic Text Processing: The transformation, analysis, and retrieval of information by computer*. Addison-Wesley, 1989.

[15] C. J. Van Rijsbergen. *Information Retrieval*. Butterworths, 1979.

A Case-Based Approach to Information Integration

Maurizio Panti[a]   Luca Spalazzi[a]   Alberto Giretti[b]

[a]Istituto di Informatica, University of Ancona, via Brecce Bianche, 60131 Ancona, Italy
[b]IDAU, University of Ancona, via Brecce Bianche, 60131 Ancona, Italy
{panti,spalazzi}@inform.unian.it   giretti@idau.unian.it

Abstract

Information integration is the problem of taking information from distributed, heterogeneous, and often dynamic sources and making them work together as a whole. A number of ideas concerning information integration are based on the notion of rewriting queries. In this paper we propose a distributed case-based approach to the problem of rewriting queries. According to this approach we use a case memory instead of static views, i.e. views that are defined a priori. As a consequence, the mediated schema is dynamically updated, strongly influenced by the queries submitted by a consumer. This approach allows a mediator to face systems where consumers may change their customization needs and information sources may become unavailable, may be added, or may modify their schemas.

1   Introduction

Nowadays, information systems can be thought as collections of *information producers* (i.e., information sources) and *information consumers* (i.e., users that perform transactions) that are often *distributed* in world-wide networks. This means that producers and consumers can be autonomous and, as a consequence, are often *heterogenous* and *dynamic*. Information sources are heterogenous due to discrepancies

**Proceedings of the 26th VLDB Conference,
Cairo, Egypt, 2000.**

at the physical level (different DBMSs, legacy applications, software and hardware platforms), logical level (different data models), and conceptual level (different schemas, concept and relation names). Moreover autonomous information sources are dynamic. Basically this is due to the fact that they may be added to the system, or become (temporarily or definitively) unavailable. Sometimes, they may also vary their conceptual schemas. Information consumers are heterogeneous and dynamic as well. Indeed new consumers can be inserted or removed. Furthermore, each consumer may have different customization needs due to distinct business objectives and these needs can change very often. In this work, we focus on information integration in distributed, heterogeneous, and dynamic information systems, i.e., constructing answers to query from consumers. The problem consists on rewriting a consumer's query into queries to specific information sources. In this paper we present a distributed case-based approach to the problem of rewriting queries. According to this approach we have a dynamic mediated schema instead of a static one, i.e., a schema that is defined a priori.

2   Related Work

Up to now, several approaches have been proposed for information integration in distributed, heterogeneous, and dynamic information systems.

Classic Approach [30, 32, 1, 23]. This approach relies on building a single global schema to encompass the differences among multiple local source schemas. The mapping from the global schema to each local schema is often expressed in a common SQL-like language (e.g., HOSQL [1] and SQL/M [23]). The enforcement of a single global schema through data integration yields full transparency for uniform access to distributed and heterogeneous information sources. Nevertheless this approach does not fit well in the case of dynamic producers since the global schema is statically built a priori. Moreover, a single global schema does not support different needs of heterogeneous and dynamic consumers.

Federated Approach [33]. This approach improves the previous approach dealing with consumer heterogeneity. Indeed it relies on multiple integrated schemas. However, the heterogeneity problems are resolved at the schema integration stage and integrated schemas are static. This approach cannot scale well when new sources or consumers need to be added or removed. Moreover, source schemas or consumer requirements cannot be upgraded without a revision of the integrated schemas.

Distributed Object Management Approach [27, 28, 8]. This approach generalizes the federated approach by modeling distributed and heterogeneous databases as collections of objects in a distributed object space. It is based on a common object model and a common object query language (e.g., the ODMG standard [8]). Nevertheless, this approach does not yield full transparency for uniform access to sources that are heterogeneous at the conceptual level.

Intelligent Information Integration (I^3) Approach [35, 19]. This approach relies on the so called *mediator architecture*: a three-layers system architecture for information integration. A layer is devoted to information consumers, another layer is devoted to information producers, the middle layer deals with mediation, i.e., the original query is reformulated in a set of queries, each targeted at a selected source. There are two basic approaches to intelligent information integration: the procedural approach and the declarative approach. In the *procedural* approach (e.g., TSIMMIS [19], Squirrel [37], and WHIPS [21]), mediators integrate information from sources through ad-hoc procedures defined with respect to a set of predefined information needs. When such needs or sources change (i.e., we have a dynamic information system), a new mediator must be generated. In the *declarative* approach (e.g., Carnot [11], SIMS [2], Information Manifold [24], Infomaster [16], and CDLNR [7]), mediators use suitable mechanisms to rewrite queries according to source descriptions. Intuitively, a rewritten query would be equivalent to the original query (i.e., denote the same set of instances). Nevertheless, often this is not possible. As a consequence, "in information-integration applications, [query] containment appears to be more fundamental than equivalence" [34]. Query containment has been related to information integration via an approach called *synthesizing queries from views* [36, 9, 34, 3, 17]. According to this approach, a query reformulation problem becomes the problem of finding a solution (in terms of views) that must be contained in the original query.

Related to the declarative approach is the use of *description logics* [5, 4, 6] (see Appendix A) as a data modeling language and as a query language. This is the approach followed by several authors, see for example [2, 3, 7, 24, 34]. Indeed, description logics offer an interesting tradeoff between complexity and expressive power. In this perspective, it is worth to notice that the problem of query containment corresponds to the subsumption problem. Subsumption is a tractable problem for most of the description logics [6, 4] while query containment without any restriction is undecidable [3].

Among declarative based I^3 projects, only a few have dealt with dynamic information producers and consumers. For example Information Manifold [24], SIMS [2], and Infomaster [16] do not allow automatic adaptation of source descriptions even if the authors claim that a new (view of a) source can be easily added by writing its description without redefining the mediator. For example, this is the case when a consumer's need change and thus it cannot be satisfied by the given views.

Case-Based Approach. Case-based reasoning is a problem solving methodology which is based on previously experienced, concrete problem situations [26]. According to this approach, a system learns by experience how problems can be solved, therefore it is appropriate for dynamic application domains, when it is impossible to have predefined solution. Nevertheless, as far as we know, its application to information integration is a novel approach. The closest applications are in information retrieval [13, 31] (i.e., the extraction of information from non-structured data) and associative query answering [18, 10] (i.e., associating relevant additional information to a query answer). Even if these systems deal with queries, usually they do not deal with distributed information sources. A noteworthy example of distributed computing by means of case-based reasoning is the so called *distributed case-based reasoning* (DCBR). In DCBR there are several agents; each agent has its own case memory since it could have acquired its own independent problem-solving experiences. A new problem is solved through agent cooperation. Indeed each agent reuses the local past case that best contributes to the overall case. For example, CBR-TEAM [29] has a negotiation-driven case retrieval algorithm applied to distributed mechanical design problems.

Description logic is applied to case-based reasoning as well [25, 22, 12, 20]. Indeed, in case-based reasoning, subsumption becomes a powerful tool to automatically derive case hierarchies that can be used in case retrieval and case retention.

3 Work Overview

Our goal is to build an information system capable of interconnecting information consumers and producers. Previous approaches solve several problems concerned with distributed, heterogeneous information systems. Their main limitation is related to the capability of evolving according to dynamic information systems. We propose a system (see also [15]) which is based on a mediator architecture in order to support customizable information integration across distributed, heterogeneous, and dynamic information sources. Source heterogeneity at the physical level is removed by suitable **wrappers**. Indeed each information source has its own management system and query language, it can use a very recent technology or be a legacy system. As a consequence, it is needed a sort of interface (a wrapper) between a source and the rest of the system. Wrappers translate queries in the local format and answers from the local format in the common language. Source heterogeneity at logical and conceptual levels is removed by **mediators** and their mediated schemas. Consumer heterogeneity is removed by the presence of several mediators since each of them is related to a consumer (or a class of consumers). Finally, the effects of dynamic sources and consumers are removed by mediators since they are able to dynamically update their schemas. Indeed when a mediator does not have enough local knowledge to reformulate a query, it can cooperate with sources (to access their original schemas) and other mediators (to access their mediated schemas).

Mediators capability to face heterogeneous and dynamic systems relies on a thesaurus and a distributed case-based reasoning. Each mediator has its own *thesaurus* in order to solve name heterogeneity. A thesaurus is composed by a set of classes of synonyms. Each element of a class has the reference to the information sources that use it as term. Every time a new query arrives, its terms are translated in standard terms by means of the thesaurus. The reverse process occurs when the rewritten query must be sent to information sources. The thesaurus must be dynamically updated when a change in the system occurs. The classes of the thesaurus are modified by means of clustering. The explanation of this technique is out of the scope of the paper, for more details we remind to [14]. Each mediator has also its own *case-based reasoner* in order to solve heterogeneity of schemas and consumer's needs. Each case contains a query and its reformulation, and it is stored in the mediator's case memory. When a new query from the consumer arrives, the mediator looks for a past query similar to the new one and adapts the corresponding solution in order to obtain a reformulation of the new query. This means that the mediated schema of a mediator is strongly influenced by the queries submitted by consumers (mediator's experience). When this experience does not help, the mediator interacts with other mediators and/or information sources. This approach allows the mediator to update its schemas and therefore to take into account changes in information sources and consumer's needs. This is called distributed case-based reasoning.

The rest of the paper is organized as follows. A running example is introduced in Section 4. Section 5 describes how cases are represented. Local and distributed query rewriting are discussed in sections 6 and 7, respectively. Finally, some conclusions are given in Section 8.

4   A Running Example

We consider an information system which contains computer science bibliography data, namely information about articles and their authors. This information system is composed by several sources, consumers, and mediators. Figure 1 depicts three information sources of the system. Since the description of the thesaurus is out of scope of this paper, we consider that all the (concept and role) names have been already translated and thus no name heterogeneity occurs. Nevertheless, their conceptual schemas are different. The source w_1 (Figure 1.a) contains a set of authors and a set of articles classified according their publication type, i.e., *journal*, *conference*, etc. The source w_2 (Figure 1.b) contains a set of authors and a set of articles on database classified according their topic, i.e., *object_oriented* databases, *active* databases, *federated* databases, etc. Finally, the source w_3 (Figure 1.c) contains a set of authors and a set of articles on artificial intelligence classified according their topic as well, i.e., *planning*, *cbr*, *agents*, etc.

5   Query Representation

Generally speaking, a case is an arbitrary set of features (attribute-value pairs). Some features are devoted to represent a problem (in our application the query to be reformulated) in order to make easier the retrieval of a past problem similar to the current situation. The rest of features are devoted to represent the problem solution (the reformulated query and information sources where the reformulated query has been sent) to reuse it in the current problem. Furthermore, the problem of rewriting queries has a fundamental condition that must be satisfied: *the rewritten query must be contained in the original query* [3, 34]. We use a description logic as a language for representing queries and thus cases. The subsumption relation is used as query containment and thus for case retrieval. According to above considerations we define a case as follows:

Definition 5.1 (Case) *Let* $w_1, \ldots, w_n$ *be information sources. Let* $Q_1, \ldots, Q_n$ *be queries to* $w_1, \ldots, w_n$ *respectively. Let* $Sol(Q)$ *be a query obtained by an arbitrary combination of* $Q_1, \ldots, Q_n$. *Let* Q *be a query such that*

$$Sol(Q) \sqsubseteq Q \qquad (1)$$

Then $Sol(Q)$ *is a rewriting of the query* Q *and* $\langle Q, Sol(Q), \langle (Q_1, w_1), \ldots (Q_n, w_n) \rangle \rangle$ *is a case.*

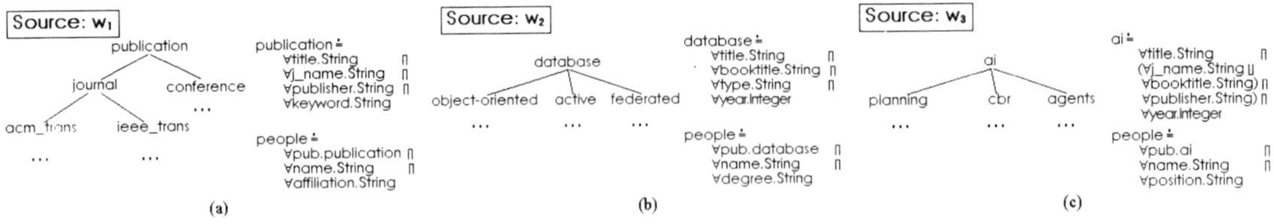

Figure 1: An example of information sources.

A collection of cases is called **case memory**. A **terminology** (i.e., a set of concept definitions and their relations) is always associated to a case memory. $\top, \bot$ represent the boundaries of the terminology w.r.t. the subsumption relation.

Example 5.1 In the example presented in Section 4 let us consider a mediator that has the following cases:

$$\dots\dots$$
$$\langle H, (\forall pub.conference \sqcap \forall pub.db) \sqcup \forall pub.cbr,$$
$$\langle (\forall pub.conference, w_1), (\forall pub.db, w_2), (\forall pub.cbr, w_3) \rangle \; \rangle$$
$$\langle I, \forall pub.acm\_trans \sqcup$$
$$\forall pub.(ai \sqcap \forall j\_name.String \sqcap$$
$$\forall publisher.\{``ACM"\})$$
$$\langle (\forall pub.acm\_trans, w_1),$$
$$(\forall pub.(ai \sqcap \forall j\_name.String \sqcap$$
$$\forall publisher.\{``ACM"\}), w_3) \rangle \qquad \rangle$$
$$\langle J, \forall pub.journal \sqcup \forall pub.ai,$$
$$\langle (\forall pub.journal, w_1), (\forall pub.ai, w_3) \rangle \qquad \rangle$$
$$\langle K, \forall pub.\exists keyword.\{``Agents"\} \sqcup \forall pub.agents,$$
$$\langle (\forall pub.\exists keyword.\{``Agents"\}, w_1), (\forall pub.agents, w_3) \rangle \; \rangle$$
$$\dots\dots$$

and the corresponding terminology:

$$\{\dots journal \dot{\leq} \top \,, \; acm\_trans \dot{\leq} journal \,,$$
$$acm\_trans \doteq \forall publisher.\{``ACM"\} \,,$$
$$ai \dot{\leq} \top \,, \; agents \dot{\leq} ai \,, \; cbr \dot{\leq} ai \,, \; db \dot{\leq} \top \,,$$
$$A \doteq \neg journal \sqcap db \,, \; H \doteq \forall pub.(A \sqcup cbr) \,,$$
$$I \doteq \forall pub.acm\_trans \,, \; J \doteq \forall pub.(journal \sqcup ai) \,,$$
$$K \doteq \forall pub.agents \qquad \qquad \dots \}$$

A pictorial view of the terminology is given in Figure 2. For example the evaluation of $Sol(H)$ consists on querying sources w_1, w_2, and w_3 with $\forall pub.conference$, $\forall pub.db$, and $\forall pub.cbr$ respectively, and integrating the related answers. The semantics of concepts helps us on integrating the answers. Let $I_{w_1}(\forall pub.conference)$, $I_{w_2}(\forall pub.db)$, and $I_{w_3}(\forall pub.cbr)$ be answers from w_1, w_2, and w_3 respectively, then the answer to $\forall pub.(A \sqcup cbr)$ is: $(I_{w_1}(\forall pub.conference) \cap I_{w_2}(\forall pub.db)) \cup I_{w_3}(\forall pub.cbr)$. Notice that this is just one possible answer, another mediator with a different case memory may rewrite the query in a different way and thus return a different answer.

6 Local Query Retrieval and Reuse

Every time a new query arrives, it is inserted in the terminology and classified by means of subsumption. If there exists a past problem equal to the new query, then its solution can be used as solution for the new query. Otherwise, the solutions of the past problems that are subsumed by the new query can be used as solution for the new problem. The closest to the new query the retrieved cases are, the best the solutions are. This drives us to the notion of problems maximally contained in the new query [3, 34]. This notion allows the definition of the retrieval function $M_{inf}(Q, \mathcal{P})$ as a set of conjunctions of concepts $(\sqcap_{i \geq 1} X_i)$ of the given terminology $(\mathcal{P})$. For each conjunction of concepts there does not exist another conjunction of concepts of the same terminology $(\sqcap_{j \geq 1} Y_j)$ such that $\sqcap_{i \geq 1} X_i \sqsubseteq \sqcap_{j \geq 1} Y_j \sqsubseteq Q$.

Example 6.1 Let us suppose to have $Q \doteq \forall pub.ai$ as input query in Example 5.1. Applying the retrieval function we obtain: $M_{inf}(Q, \mathcal{P}) = \{K, H \sqcap J\}$

Now, we can obtain two different reuse methods depending on whether or not the original query is decomposed before the application of the retrieval methods. In the first approach, the system retrieves a solution if and only if the new query subsumes some past problems, if so past solutions are simply replied. The algorithm is reported below.

$$\mathcal{S}_{inf}(Q, \mathcal{P}) \doteq \begin{cases} \bigsqcup_{\sqcap_i X_i \in M_{inf}(Q, \mathcal{P})} \sqcap_i Sol(X_i) \\ \qquad \qquad \text{if } M_{inf}(Q, \mathcal{P}) \neq \emptyset \\ \bot \qquad \qquad \text{if } M_{inf}(Q, \mathcal{P}) = \emptyset \end{cases} \qquad (2)$$

Example 6.2 Applying the basic reuse algorithms to case memory and input case of Example 6.1 we obtain: $\mathcal{S}_{inf}(Q, \mathcal{P}) = Sol(K) \sqcup (Sol(H) \sqcap Sol(J))$

The second approach is based on the combination of past solutions according to the new query structure. It is based on a decomposition algorithm that exploits the algorithm 2. The resulting algorithm is described in Figure 3. Notice that $Dual\_\mathcal{D}$ is the dual algorithm of $\mathcal{D}$. It retrieves concepts that minimally contain the given query. Moreover, when an unsuccessful termination occurs, the algorithm backtracks and stops the query decomposition to a higher level.

Example 6.3 Let us suppose to have $Q' \doteq \forall pub.ai \sqcap \forall pub.acm\_trans$ as input query in Example 5.1. Applying the algorithm of Figure 3 we obtain:

$$\mathcal{D}(Q', \mathcal{P})$$
$$= \mathcal{S}_{inf}(\forall pub.ai, \mathcal{P}) \sqcap \mathcal{S}_{inf}(\forall pub.acm\_trans, \mathcal{P})$$
$$= (\; Sol(K) \sqcup (Sol(H) \sqcap Sol(J)) \;) \; \sqcap \; Sol(I)$$

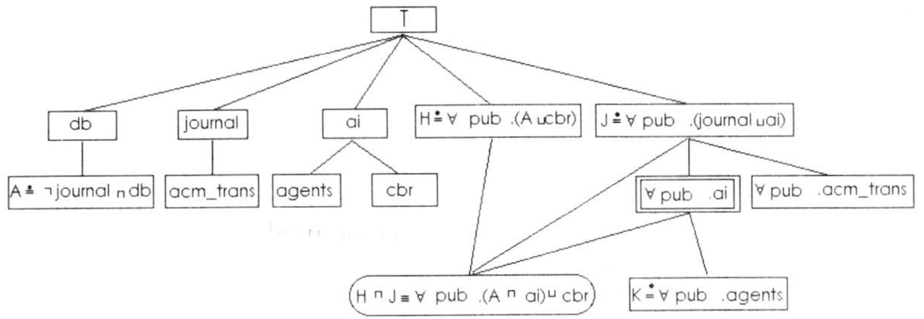

Figure 2: An example of terminology.

```
Function   𝒟(Q : concept; 𝒫 : terminology) : concept;
begin
     if        Q is a primitive condition or  Q ∈ 𝒫 then return  𝒮_inf(Q, 𝒫)
     elseif  Q ≡ C ⊔ D      then if  𝒟(C, 𝒫) ≠ ⊥ and  𝒟(D, 𝒫) ≠ ⊥
                                   then return  𝒟(C, 𝒫) ⊔ 𝒟(D, 𝒫)
                                   else return  𝒮_inf(Q, 𝒫)
     elseif  Q ≡ C ⊓ D      then if  𝒟(C, 𝒫) ≠ ⊥ and  𝒟(D, 𝒫) ≠ ⊥
                                   then return  𝒟(C, 𝒫) ⊓ 𝒟(D, 𝒫)
                                   else return  𝒮_inf(Q, 𝒫)
     elseif  Q ≡ ¬C          then if  𝒟(C, 𝒫) ≠ ⊥
                                   then return  ¬Dual_𝒟(C, 𝒫)
                                   else return  𝒮_inf(Q, 𝒫)
     elseif  Q ≡ ∀R.C       then if  𝒟(C, 𝒫) ≠ ⊥
                                   then return  ∀R.𝒟(C, 𝒫)
                                   else return  𝒮_inf(Q, 𝒫)
     elseif  Q ≡ ∃R.C       then if  𝒟(C, 𝒫) ≠ ⊥
                                   then return  ∃R.𝒟(C, 𝒫)
                                   else return  𝒮_inf(Q, 𝒫)
     elseif  Q ≡ ≤ nR        then return  (∀R.𝒮_inf(⊤, 𝒫)) ⊓ (≤ nR)
     elseif  Q ≡ ≥ nR        then return  (∀R.𝒮_inf(⊤, 𝒫)) ⊓ (≥ nR)
     elseif  Q ≡ (R_1 = R_2) then return  (∀R_1.𝒮_inf(⊤, 𝒫)) ⊓ (∀R_2.𝒮_inf(⊤, 𝒫)) ⊓ (R_1 = R_2)
     else return  ⊥
end;
```

Figure 3: The decomposition algorithm.

Notice that Condition (1) is preserved by above reuse methods since it is easy to prove (by induction) that the following theorem holds.

Theorem 6.1 *Let Q be a query. Let $\mathcal{P}$ be the terminology of a given case memory. Then*

$$\mathcal{S}_{inf}(Q, \mathcal{P}) \sqsubseteq Q \qquad\qquad \mathcal{D}(Q, \mathcal{P}) \sqsubseteq Q$$

Notice that in general $\mathcal{S}_{inf}(Q, \mathcal{P}) \neq \mathcal{D}(Q, \mathcal{P})$. As a consequence, we can combine the above methods in order to obtain a wider solution, i.e., $Sol(Q) \doteq \mathcal{S}_{inf}(Q, \mathcal{P}) \sqcup \mathcal{D}(Q, \mathcal{P})$

7 Distributed Query Retrieval and Reuse

A *local failure in query reuse* occurs when a mediator is not able to rewrite a given query Q, i.e., $Sol(Q) = \perp$[1]. This means that the mediator's case memory contains no past cases that can be used to reformulate Q. Usually this is due to the fact that it is the first time that the consumer formulates such a query, i.e., the consumer has a new information need.

Example 7.1 Let us consider the case memory of Example 5.1 and the query $Q'' \doteq \forall pub.ai \sqcap \exists affiliation.\{``Stanford"\}$. The mediator is not able to rewrite the query. Indeed, we have

$$\mathcal{D}(Q'', \mathcal{P}) = (\ Sol(K) \sqcup (Sol(H) \sqcap Sol(J))\ ) \sqcap \perp = \perp$$

Furthermore a *local failure in query evaluation* occurs when a mediator send a rewritten query to related sources and receives at least an empty answer. This means that the case memory of the mediator is not updated. Typically, an information source has been removed from the system or changed its schema.

Example 7.2 Let us suppose that source w_1 has been (perhaps temporarily) removed, then the evaluation of the reformulated query in Example 6.3 fails. Indeed $I_{w_1}(\forall pub.conference) = I_{w_1}(\forall pub.acm\_trans) = I_{w_1}(\forall pub.journal) = I_{w_1}(\forall pub.\exists keyword.\{``Agents"\}) = \emptyset$

Even if a local failure (in query reuse or evaluation) occurs, the system has still a possibility of solving the

---

[1] Notice that $I(\perp) = \emptyset$.

problem by means of distributed query retrieval and reuse. Notice that this provides the system the most important way of learning. Indeed, if the query is reformulated, the new rewritten query and/or the new sources can be stored as a new case. In such a way the mediator can support dynamic information systems. Furthermore, it does not need to maintain consistent its case memory every time something changes, but only when a consumer sends a query that fails. This allows us to avoid of overloading the distributed information system with consistency maintenance operations, that usually are time consuming. Distributed query retrieval and reuse is based on cooperation with other mediators and sources. Cooperation strategies can be classified according to three parameters: partners, queries, and answers.

- **Partners.** When a mediator (say M) fails, it can cooperate with other *mediators* asking them to rewrite a query according to their own case memories. If they succeed, M can store the result as a new case in its case memory. The mediators involved in this strategy can be all the mediators of the system or just mediators that have never been in touch with M. The mediator M can directly cooperate with information sources as well. It can involve all the sources (it is very expensive), sources responsible of the local failure (this strategy takes into account changes of schemas), or recently added sources (this strategy takes into account new sources). Each source processes the query with an algorithm based on maximally contained rewriting (it is the Algorithm 2, but the schema is static instead of dynamic) and returns the answer.

- **Queries.** Cooperation strategies can also be classified according to the query. Indeed M can send the original query or the reformulated query (if any). In the latter case the "approximation of the solution grows". For example, let us suppose that Q is the original query and $Q' = Sol_M(Q)$ is the query rewritten by M. Let N be the mediator or source that cooperates with M and thus receives Q' as input query. Let us suppose that $Q'' = Sol_N(Q')$ is the query rewritten by N. The Theorem 6.1 states that $Q'' \sqsubseteq Q' \sqsubseteq Q$. As a consequence, Q'' is more distant from Q than Q'

  Cooperation strategies can also be classified depending on the fact that the query can be sent as it is or be decomposed in basic components.

- **Answers.** Finally, cooperation strategies can be classified according to the answer. M can ask for rewriting the query. Its goal is to update its case memory with a rewritten query obtained from its collaborators. M can also ask for data that answer the query. In such a situation, it stores in the case memory the addresses of the mediators/sources that answered.

Let us focus on two of the possible strategies.

As a first strategy, let us consider a mediator M that cooperates with the others mediators, sends them the original query, and asks for receiving the rewritten query. A possible disadvantage of such a strategy is that asymptotically all the mediators may have the same case memory. This result is a consequence of the following theorem.

Theorem 7.1 *Let M, N be two mediators such that M interacts with N when M fails. Let $C_n(M)$ be the case memory of M after n interactions with N. Let $C(N)$ be the case memory of N such that it does not change while N interacts with M. Then*

$$\lim_{n \to \infty} \frac{card(C_n(M) \cap C(N))}{card(C(N))} = 1 \tag{3}$$

The above theorem is quite straightforward to prove and states that the case memory of M converges to the case memory of N when M cooperates with N.

As a second strategy, let us consider a mediator M that directly cooperates with information sources, sends them the original query, and receives both the rewritten query and the data. This strategy guarantees a given consumer that the mediator M converges to the consumer's information need (i.e., the recall ratio converges to 1). Indeed it is possible to prove the following theorem.

Theorem 7.2 *Let $S_1, \ldots, S_n$ be n information sources. Let $\mathcal{V}$ be a view of $S_1, \ldots, S_n$. $\mathcal{V}$ is represented as a case memory that does not change. Let M be a mediator such that M interacts with $S_1, \ldots, S_n$ when it fails. Let $C_n(M)$ be the case memory of M after n interactions with $S_1, \ldots, S_n$. Then*

$$\lim_{n \to \infty} \frac{card(C_n(M) \cap \mathcal{V})}{card(\mathcal{V})} = 1 \tag{4}$$

The theorem above states that if the information need of a consumer is represented by $\mathcal{V}$, then the mediator will asymptotically satisfy such a need. Let us demonstrate the utility of this strategy with an example.

Example 7.3 In the situation of Example 7.2, let us suppose that the mediator chooses to look for new sources and cooperate with them. Let us suppose that w_4 is a new information source which contains ACM publications and has the following schema:

$$\ldots$$

$$acm\_tods \doteq \forall j\_name.\{"TODS"\} \sqcap \forall publisher.\{"ACM"\}$$
$$acm\_tocl \doteq \forall j\_name.\{"TOCL"\} \sqcap \forall publisher.\{"ACM"\}$$
$$acm\_tois \doteq \forall j\_name.\{"TOIS"\} \sqcap \forall publisher.\{"ACM"\}$$

$$\ldots$$

The mediator decomposes the query Q' and sends each component to w_4. For example, when w_4 receives $\forall pub.acm\_trans$, it looks for maximally contained concepts and obtains $M_{inf}(\forall pub.acm\_trans, \mathcal{P}) = \{\forall pub.acm\_tods, \forall pub.acm\_tocl, \forall pub.acm\_tois\}$. When the mediator receives the answer, retains as new case:

$$\langle\ \forall pub.acm\_trans\ ,\quad \forall pub.acm\_tods \sqcup \forall pub.acm\_tocl$$
$$\sqcup\ \forall pub.acm\_tois\ ,$$
$$\langle\ (\forall pub.acm\_tods, w_4)\ ,$$
$$(\forall pub.acm\_tocl, w_4)\ ,$$
$$(\forall pub.acm\_tois, w_4)\ \rangle\qquad\qquad \rangle$$

8 Conclusions

We considered the problem of rewriting queries by means of distributed case-based reasoning. As far as we know, this is a novel approach. We showed that the notion of maximally contained rewriting of a query can be also applied to a case memory (what we call local query retrieval). This allows us to have dynamic mediated schemas instead of static ones. We also showed that a real dynamic mediator is obtained by means of distributed query retrieval and reuse, i.e., cooperation with other mediators and sources. Thanks to this approach, the mediator is able to be updated when sources and consumers are added/removed or change their schemas/needs. This operation is performed only when a consumer sends a query that fails and not every time something changes. This allows us to avoid of overloading the distributed information system with consistency maintenance operations, that usually are time consuming. In distributed case-based reasoning, the choice of the right cooperation strategy is crucial. We hinted several possible strategies and sketched a discussion about their advantages. We also demonstrated by examples the utility of this approach. Finally, notice that the choice of an appropriate description logic can reduce the algorithm complexity for query retrieval and reuse. For example, if we choose core–CLASSIC [3], we have that the maximally-contained rewriting can be computed in polynomial time.

Acknowledgement

This work was partially supported by M.U.R.S.T. under Project INTERDATA. We thank J. Mylopoulos for suggestions and useful discussions about the topics presented in this paper. Comments by P. Coupey, C. Diamantini, and L. Penserini are also greatly appreciated.

A Description Logic

A description logic is composed by symbols taken from the alphabet of Concept Names, the alphabet of Role Names, and the alphabet of Individual Names (or Individuals). It also includes a set of constructors that permit the formation of Concepts and Roles (see Table 1). Its formal semantics (e.g., [6]) is the structure $\mathcal{I} = (\Delta, I())$. It consists of a nonempty set Δ (the domain of $\mathcal{I}$) and a function $I()$ (the interpretation function of $\mathcal{I}$) that maps every individual to an element of Δ, every concept to a subset of Δ, and every role to a subset of $\Delta \times \Delta$ (see Table 1). We say that C is subsumed by D iff $I(C) \subseteq I(D)$ for every interpretation $\mathcal{I}$. A *terminology* has statements about concepts (see Table 1) and intuitively describes the conceptual schema of a database.

References

[1] Ahmed and et al. The Pegasus heterogeneous multidatabase system. *IEEE Computer*, 24(12), 1991.

[2] V. Arens, C. Y. Chee, C-N. Hsu, and C. A. Knoblock. Retrieving and integrating data from multiple information sources. *International Journal on Intelligent and Cooperative Information Systems*, 2(2):127–158, 1993.

[3] C. Beeri, A. Y. Levy, and M.-C. Rousset. Rewriting Queries Using Views in Description Logics. In *Proc. of the 16th ACM Symposium on Principles of Database Systems (PODS)*, pages 99–108, New York, NY, May 12–14, Tucson, Arizona 1997. ACM Press.

[4] A. Borgida and P. F. Patel-Schneider. A Semantics and Complete Algorithm for Subsumption in the CLASSIC Description Logic. *Journal of Artificial Intelligence Research*, 1:277–308, 1994.

[5] R.J. Brachman and J.G. Schmolze. An Overview of the KL-ONE Knowledge Representation System. *Cognitive Science*, 9:217–260, 1985.

[6] M. Buchheit, F. M. Donini, and A Schaerf. Decidable Reasoning in Terminological Knowledge Representation Systems. *Journal of Artificial Intelligence Research*, 1:109–138, 1993.

[7] D. Calvanese, G. De Giacomo, M. Lenzerini, D. Nardi, and R. Rosati. Information integration: Conceptual modeling and reasoning support. In *Proc. of the 6th International Conference on Cooperative Information Systems (CoopIS'98)*, pages 280–291, 1998.

[8] R.G.G. Cattell. *The Object Database Standard ODMG-93*. Morgan Kaufmann, San Mateo, CA, 1993.

[9] S. R. Chaudhuri, S. R. Krishnamurthy, S. Potamianos, and K. Shim. Optimizing queries with materialized views. In *International Conference on Data Engineering*, 1995.

Constructor Name	Syntax	Semantics
concept name	A	$I(A) \subseteq \Delta$
top	$\top$	Δ
bottom	$\bot$	$\emptyset$
conjunction	$C \sqcap D$	$I(C) \cap I(D)$
disjunction	$C \sqcup D$	$I(C) \cup I(D)$
negation	$\neg C$	$\Delta \setminus I(C)$
universal quantification	$\forall R.C$	$\{s \mid \forall t.(s,t) \in I(R) \rightarrow t \in I(C)\}$
existential quantification	$\exists R.C$	$\{s \mid \exists t.(s,t) \in I(R) \wedge t \in I(C)\}$
number restrictions	$\leq nR$	$\{s \mid card(\{t \mid (s,t) \in I(R)\}) \leq n\}$
	$\geq nR$	$\{s \mid card(\{t \mid (s,t) \in I(R)\}) \geq n\}$
equality restriction	$Q = R$	$\{s \mid \{r \mid (s,r) \in I(Q)\} = \{t \mid (s,t) \in I(R)\}\}$
role name	P	$I(P) \subseteq \Delta \times \Delta$
role chain	$Q \circ R$	$\{(s,t) \mid \exists r.(s,r) \in I(Q) \wedge (r,t) \in I(R)\}$

Statement Name	Syntax	Semantics
Concept Specification	$A \dot{\leq} C$	$I(A) \subseteq I(C)$
Concept Definition	$A \doteq C$	$I(A) = I(C)$

where A is a concept name, C, D are concepts, P is a role name, and Q, R are roles.

Table 1: Syntax and semantics of description logics.

[10] W. W. Chu and G. Zhang. Associative query answering via query feature similarity. In *International Conference on Intelligent Information Systems (IIS'97)*, The Bahamas, 1997.

[11] C. Collet, M. N. Huhns, and W.-M. Shen. Resource integration using a large knowledge base in Carnot. *IEEE Computer*, 24(12):55–62, 1991.

[12] P. Coupey, C. Fouqueré, and S. Salotti. Formalizing partial matching and similarity in CBR with a description logic. *Applied Artificial Intelligence*, 12(1):71–112, 1998.

[13] J. J. Daniels and E. L. Rissland. A Case-Based Approach to Intelligent Information Retrieval. In *Proc. of the SIGIR'95 Conference*, pages 238–245, Seattle, WA, 1995. ACM.

[14] C. Diamantini and M. Panti. A Conceptual Indexing Method for Content-Based Retrieval. In A. M. Tjoa, A. Cammelli, and R. R. Wagner, editors, *Tenth International Workshop on Database and Expert Systems Applications (DEXA'99)*, Florence, Italy, 1–3 September 1999. IEEE Computer Society.

[15] C. Diamantini, M. Panti, L. Spalazzi, and S. Valenti. Federated Information System Architectures for Local Public Administration. In M. Khosrowpour, editor, *Information Resource Management Association International Conference (IRMA'99)*, Hershey, PA, May 1999. Idea Group.

[16] O. M. Duschka and M. R. Genesereth. Infomaster - An Information Integration Tool. In *Proc. of the International Workshop on Intelligent Information Integration*, Freiburg, Germany, September 1997.

[17] O. M. Duschka and M. R. Genesereth. Query Planning with Disjunctive Sources. In *Proc. of the AAAI Workshop on Artificial Intelligence and Information Integration*, Madison, WI, July 1998.

[18] G. Fouqué, W. W. Chu, and H. Yau. A case-based reasoning approach for associative query answering. In *Proc. of the 8th International Symposium on Methodologies for Intelligent Systems*, pages 183–192, Charlotte, N.C., October 1994.

[19] H. Garcia-Molina, Y. Papakonstantinou, D. Quass, A. Rajaraman, Y. Sagiv, J. Ullman, V. Vassalos, and J. Widom. The TSIMMIS approach to mediation: data models and languages. *Journal of Intelligent Information Systems*, 8:117–132, 1997.

[20] A. Giretti and L. Spalazzi. ASA: A Conceptual Design-Support System. *Engineering Application of Artificial Intelligence*, 10(1):99–111, January 1997.

[21] J. Hammer, H. Garcia-Molina, J. Widom, W. Labio, and Y. Zhuge. The Stabford data warehousing project. *IEEE Bull. on Data Engineering*, 18(2):3–18, 1995.

[22] G. Kamp. Using Description Logics for Knowledge Intensive Case-Based Reasoning. In *Proc. of th 3rd European Workshop on Case-Based Reasoning*, volume 1168 of *Lecture Notes in Artificial Intelligence*, Berlin, Germany, 1996. Springer-Verlag.

[23] W. Kim and et al. On Resolving Semantic Heterogeneity in Multidatabase Systems. *Distributed and Parallel Databases*, 1(3), 1993.

[24] T. A. Kirk, A. Y. Levy, Y. Sagiv, and D. Srivastava. The Information Manifold. In *AAAI Spring Symposium on Information Gathering*. AAAI, 1995.

[25] Jana Koehler. An Application of Terminological Logics to Case-based Reasoning. In Pietro Torasso, Jon Doyle, and Erik Sandewall, editors, *Proceedings of the 4th International Conference on Principles of Knowledge Representation and Reasoning*, pages 351–362, Bonn, Germany, May 1994. Morgan Kaufmann.

[26] D. Leake, editor. *Case-Based Reasoning : Experiences, Lessons, & Future Directions*. AAAI Press / The MIT Press, 1996.

[27] F. Manola and et al. Ditributed object management. *International Journal of Intelligent and Cooperative Information Systems*, 1(1), March 1992.

[28] T. Ozsu, U. Dayal, and P. Valduriez. *Distributed Object Management*. Morgan Kaufmann, San Mateo, CA, 1993.

[29] M. V. N. Prasad, V. R. Lesser, and S. E. Lander. Retrieval and reasoning in distributed case bases. *Journal of Visual Communication and Image Representation, Special Issue on Digital Libraries*, 7(1):74–87, March 1996.

[30] S. Ram. Special issue on heterogenous distributed database systems. *IEEE Computer Magazine*, 24(12), December 1991.

[31] C. Ramirez. Case-based reasoning applied to information retrieval. In *IEEE Coloquium on Case-Based Reasoning: Prospects for Application*, London, February 1995. IEE.

[32] A. Sheth. Special Issue in Multidatabasem Systems. *ACM SIGMOD Record on Management of Data*, 20(4), December 1991.

[33] A. Sheth and J. Larson. Federated Database Systems for Managing Distributed, Heterogeneous, and Autonomous Databases. *ACM Transaction on Database Systems*, 22(3), 1990.

[34] J. D. Ullman. Information Integration Using Logical Views. In *Proceedings of the International Conference on Database Theory*, pages 19–40, 1997.

[35] G. Wiederhold. Mediators in the Architecture of Future Information Systems. *IEEE Computer Magazine*, 25:38–49, March 1992.

[36] H. Z. Yang and A. Larson. Query transformation for PSJ queries. In *Proc. of the International Conference on Very Large Data Bases*, pages 245–254, 1987.

[37] G. Zhou, R. Hull, and R. King. Generating data integration mediators that use materializations. *J. of Intelligent Information Systems*, 6:199–221, 1996.

Approximate Query Translation
Across Heterogeneous Information Sources [*]

Chen-Chuan K. Chang
Electrical Engineering Department

Hector Garcia-Molina
Computer Science Department

Stanford University
{kevin,hector}@db.stanford.edu

Abstract

In this paper we present a mechanism for approximately translating Boolean query constraints across heterogeneous information sources. Achieving the best translation is challenging because sources support different constraints for formulating queries, and often these constraints cannot be precisely translated. For instance, a query [score > 8] might be "perfectly" translated as [rating > 0.8] at some site, but can only be approximated as [grade = A] at another. Unlike other work, our general framework adopts a customizable "closeness" metric for the translation that combines both precision and recall. Our results show that for query translation we need to handle interdependencies among both query conjuncts as well as disjuncts. As the basis, we identify the essential requirements of a rule system for users to encode the mappings for atomic semantic units. Our algorithm then translates complex queries by rewriting them in terms of the semantic units. We show that, under practical assumptions, our algorithm generates the best approximate translations with respect to the closeness metric of choice. We also present a case study to show how our technique may be applied in practice.

1 Introduction

To enable interoperability, mediator systems [1, 2] must integrate heterogeneous information sources with different data representations and search capabilities. A mediator presents a unified context for uniform information access, and consequently must translate *original* user queries from the unified context to a *target* source for native execution. This translation problem has become more critical now that the wide range of disparate sources are just "one click away" across the Internet. Achieving the best translation is challenging because sources use different constraints for formulating queries, and often these constraints cannot be precisely translated. This paper presents a framework that finds perfect mappings if possible, or in general the "closest" approximations, taking into account differences in attribute names, operators, and data formats.

Example 1: Consider a mediator that integrates online shopping sites for books, audio, and videos. (This example is based on our case study in Section 6.) In particular, the mediator presents a unified view Media(name, format, $\cdots$). Suppose a user wants to find the "VHS" items by some actor "Harrison." Let us consider translating the corresponding constraints $v =$ [format = vhs] and $n =$ [name contains Harrison].

The mediator will find perfect mappings whenever possible (*e.g.*, it will translate n to [au contains Harrison] for source fatbrain.com, and v as is for amazon.com). However, in many cases such perfect mappings simply do not exist. For instance, for source *EB* at www.evenbetter.com, neither v nor n can be translated precisely.

Consequently, some schemes focus on "minimal-superset" mappings [3], which will return all the potential answers but with as few unwanted answers as possible. In particular, the mediator will map v to [type = movies] (*i.e.*, searching the "movies" category) for *EB*, returning VHS as well as DVD items. Unfortunately, for n the only superset mapping at *EB* is *True* (*i.e.*, returning the entire source database), which is often unacceptable.

However, in many cases, good approximations do exist, and they may be more favorable. For instance, *EB* can approximate n as [star = "Harrison"] to match Harrison as a last name. (Note that *EB* requires at least a last name for star.) It will miss those answers with Harrison as the first name, *e.g.*, Ford, Harrison. However, since most users will actually mean last names (e.g., Harrison, George) in such a name query, this mapping may be better than *True*.

In fact, even v may need a different approximation, say if [type = movies] returns a huge number of DVDs and very few VHS items. Alternatively, mapping [desc contains vhs] simply looks for vhs in the textual descriptions. This mapping may return a lot less data than [type = movies], but may perhaps miss a few VHS items (that do not mention vhs in desc). If the "false negatives" are acceptable, then the alternative mapping may be more attractive. ∎

[*] This material is based upon work supported by the National Science Foundation under Grant NSF IIS 9811992.

Proceedings of the 26th VLDB Conference,
Cairo, Egypt, 2000.

We can view a query as a Boolean expression of constraints of the *selection* form [attr1 op value] or the *join* form [attr1 op attr2]. (While not discussed here, we stress that our approach can generally handle join constraints as well; see [4].) These constraints constitute the query "vocabulary," and must be transformed to "native" constraints understood by the target source. For example, constraint [score > 8] may have to be mapped to [grade = A]. In this process, attributes have to be mapped (*e.g.*, score to grade), values have to be converted (*e.g.*, score 8 to grade A), and operators have to be transformed (*e.g.*, ">" to "="). Reference [3] provides more details on how we generally model this constraint-mapping problem in the common mediation architecture [1, 2].

After we first studied query translation in an earlier work [3], and implemented that machinery, we soon realized that *approximate translation* is critical for "real-world" applications. Our earlier work focused on minimal-superset mappings as the "correct" translations, because the *exact* results can be recovered by post-processing their supersets. As just illustrated, in many cases only approximations exist, and they might be even more practical than the strictly correct ones. (Analogously, a concurrent system with strict serializability may result in undesirable low concurrency.) In fact, in our case study of a "real-world" scenario (Section 6), we informally estimated that 70% of the translations must rely on approximation.

Furthermore, different mediation applications need different "correctness" or *closeness* criteria for mappings. It is thus essential for a translation system to flexibly support a wide range of closeness metrics. This paper presents such a framework, where the best approximate translations can be found under virtually *any* reasonable metric. In particular, the framework supports minimal-superset, maximal-subset (when extra-answers must not be returned), and other "hybrid" criteria in between. Our customizable criteria allows one to quantify "false positives" and "false negatives" that are expected to occur in a translation, in an analogous fashion to how the conventional IR parameters of precision and recall quantify "errors" in executing a single query.

Our results show that, under such flexible metrics, one must cope with *interdependencies* among both query conjuncts and disjuncts (Section 4). It is thus critical to note that query mapping is not simply a matter of translating each constraint separately. Some interrelated constraints can form a "semantic unit" that must be handled together. This discovery is surprising since our previous study [3] showed that query disjunctions can be translated separately, significantly simplifying the translation process. Now, in an approximate translation scenario, interrelation depends on the particular closeness metric, as we next illustrate.

Example 2: Let us continue our movie search example. Suppose that the user is looking for both VHS and DVD formats with the query $Q = v \vee d$, where $d =$ [format = dvd]. (Recall that $v =$ [format = vhs].) Let us denote the closest mapping (for some closeness metric) of query Q as $\mathcal{S}(Q)$.

Suppose that the mediator adopts the minimal-superset metric, under which it will generate $\mathcal{S}(v)$ and $\mathcal{S}(d)$ both as

[type = movies] (Example 1). In this case, to translate Q, the mediator can separately map the disjuncts v and d, *i.e.*, $\mathcal{S}(Q) = \mathcal{S}(v) \vee \mathcal{S}(d) =$ [type = movies], which indeed precisely translates Q, *i.e.*, $Q \equiv \mathcal{S}(Q)$.

To contrast, assume that the mediator is concerned about large result sizes, so as illustrated earlier, uses the mappings $\mathcal{S}(v) =$ [desc contains vhs] and $\mathcal{S}(d) =$ [desc contains dvd]. (That is, given the mediator's closeness metric, these are the best approximate translations.) Now $\mathcal{S}(v) \vee \mathcal{S}(d) =$ [desc contains vhs] $\vee$ [desc contains dvd]. This mapping is not as good as [type = movies], which in our example exactly gets all VHS and DVD titles. Thus, for the closeness metric in use, translating $\mathcal{S}(v)$ and $\mathcal{S}(d)$ separately leads to a suboptimal mapping, and hence disjunction Q is not "separable." ∎

Query translation must rely on human expertise to define what constraints may be interrelated, and how to translate basic semantic units. For instance, in Example 2 we need a rule for translating the single-constraint pattern [format = F] such as v and d. But do we need a rule for composite queries, *e.g.*, $(v \vee d)$? What kind of queries must constitute such "semantic units"? In this paper we will answer these questions, identifying the essential requirements for a translation rule system.

Based on rules, our challenge is to translate arbitrary queries as Boolean expressions of constraints (we currently do not handle negation). Our approach is to *divide-and-conquer*. We present Algorithm *NFB* to "decompose" an original query into its semantic units, which can then be translated by the given rules. Note that there are many decompositions, but not all of them will lead to the closest mapping. In our running example, suppose that we are given translation rules for the semantic units (n), (v), (d), and $(v \vee d)$, and we wish to translate query $nv \vee nd$. We can decompose the query as $(n)(v) \vee (n)(d)$, or with some rewriting, as $(n)(v \vee d)$. On which expression should we apply the rules to obtain the best mapping? Is the best solution unique? How is the optimality of translation guaranteed? Again, we will answer these questions in this paper.

In summary, we make the following main contributions for approximate query translation:

- We propose a general *framework*, and we define the notion of translation closeness. Our framework can adopt different closeness metrics for different applications.

- We present an *algorithm* for systematically finding the best translation with respect to a given closeness metric. Algorithm *NFB* will find a *unique* best-mapping in the practical cases when semantic units do not "interlock."

- We develop fundamental theorems on the separability of query components, and safeness of decompositions. These results are critical for the development of any algorithm that attempts approximate query translation.

- We study how to estimate the precision and recall parameters of a translation, and we show that reasonable formulas do exist for such estimation.

We briefly discuss related work in Section 2, and then start in Section 3 by defining closeness criteria that combine precision and recall. Section 4 studies a basic assumption on compositional monotonicity and our results on compositional separability. In Section 5 we present our framework and Algorithm *NFB*. Finally, Section 6 concludes with a case study to show how our approach may be applied in practice. Note that, due to space limitations, we leave the details of some important results (that support but are not directly used by our algorithms) and their formal proof to an extended report [5].

2 Related Work

Information integration has been an active research area [1, 2, 6, 7]; however, we believe that our focus on the *constraint mapping* problem is unique. Many integration systems have dealt with source capabilities, *e.g.*, Information Manifold [8, 9], TSIMMIS [10, 11], Infomaster [12, 13], Garlic [14, 15], DISCO [16], and others [17, 18, 19]. These efforts have mainly focused on generating query plans that observe the *grammar* restrictions of native queries (such as allowing conjunctions of two constraints, or disallowing disjunctions).

Our work complements these efforts by addressing the semantic mapping of constraints, or analogously the translation of *vocabulary* (of native constraints). In particular, the output of our semantic mapping (which uses the constraint vocabulary understood by the target source) can be the input to the capability mapping that others have analyzed. See reference [3] for additional details of what distinguish our focus on the constraint mapping problem from other integration efforts and how our approach can be applied in the common mediation architecture [1, 2].

There has also been much work on data translation and schema integration. The main focus of these related efforts (*e.g.*, [20, 21, 22, 23, 24, 25]) is to unify data representations across mismatched domains by transforming data to a unified context, where queries can be performed. In contrast, our complementary goal is to map queries to the native domain where data reside. We believe our approach is especially well suited for autonomous sources containing large volumes of data, such as found on the Web (where it is not economical or feasible to transform all data). In addition, note that in our constraint mapping problem we must consider both data conversion and query capability mapping (as Section 1 discusses). Furthermore, we consider translation errors and closeness, which as far as we know are not considered in traditional schema and data translation work.

Surprisingly, while approximation is critical for query mapping (Section 1), we have seen virtually no translation efforts that stress this notion. However, approximation has been studied for query processing: First, some work aims to reduce processing cost through approximation. For instance, references [26, 27] study the approximate fixpoints of Datalog predicates, and [28] uses approximate predicates as filters for expensive ones. Second, several researchers have explored accelerated but approximated query answering to reduce response time [29, 30, 31, 32]. Third, reference [33] develops a framework for representing approximate complex-objects and supporting queries over them. Finally, CoBase [34] explored query relaxation for approxi-

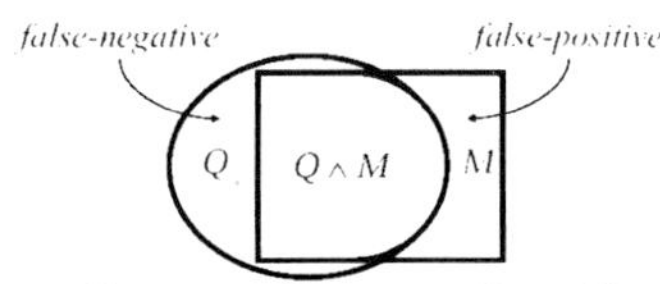

Figure 1: Venn diagram of a query Q and its mapping M.

mate answering.

We define our translation metrics based on the parameters of precision and recall. Both classic notions have been commonly used for quantifying respectively false-positives and false-negatives, most notably for information retrieval [35, 36]. In addition, some single-valued measures for IR effectiveness have also been proposed, such as the well-known E-measure [35] (see Section 3).

Finally, the approximate translation discussed in this paper was motivated by our previous work [3]. As Section 1 mentioned, our earlier model of "exact" mappings significantly simplifies the translation process, but unfortunately cannot accommodate general closeness metrics. In contrast, this paper specifically explores the notion of *approximation*, and deals with mappings under virtually *any* reasonable closeness metric.

3 Query Approximation: Accounting for Precision and Recall

Our goal for query mapping is to find the closest translation for an original query, which may not be fully expressible at the target. To quantify how closely a mapping M approximates the original query Q, we use a *closeness criterion* $\mathcal{F}[M, Q]$ that returns a normalized "rating" in $[0 : 1]$ as the *closeness* between M and Q. The higher the rating is, the closer M approximates Q. Our framework allows a wide variety of closeness functions (we will discuss some intuitive and important ones). We say that a mapping M is the *closest mapping* for Q with respect to the closeness criterion $\mathcal{F}$, if for any other mapping M' of Q, $\mathcal{F}[M, Q] \geq \mathcal{F}[M', Q]$ (with ties broken arbitrarily). We denote the closest mapping of Q by $\mathcal{S}(Q)$.

An approximation may erroneously introduce *false-positives* or *false-negatives*, as compared to the original query. Figure 1 illustrates these errors using a Venn diagram for the result sets of a query Q and its mapping M. To quantify (and ultimately minimize) these errors, we define the following metrics. The *precision* measures the proportion of the mapping results that are correct:

$$\mathcal{P}[M, Q] = \frac{|Q \wedge M|}{|M|}. \tag{1}$$

(We denote the size of the result set of query X by $|X|$.) This parameter captures the false-positive component in the approximation error. As Figure 1 suggests, precision will increase as we reduce the number of false-positives.

In contrast, *recall* measures the proportion of the correct results that are retrieved by the mapping, *i.e.*,

$$\mathcal{R}[M, Q] = \frac{|Q \wedge M|}{|Q|}. \tag{2}$$

As the dual of precision, recall captures the false-negatives, *i.e.*, higher recall corresponds to fewer false-negatives. Note that both the $\mathcal{P}$ and $\mathcal{R}$ parameters are normalized in $[0 : 1]$.

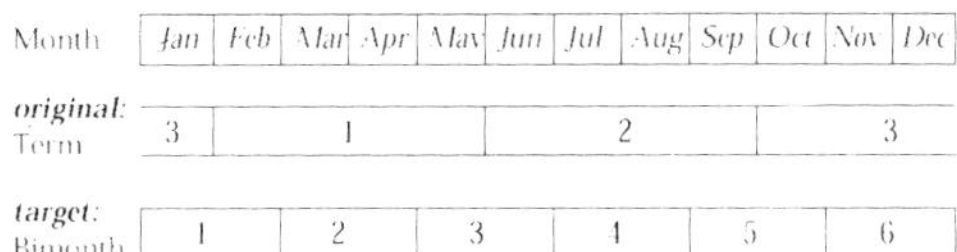

(a) Correspondence of **term** and **bimonth**.

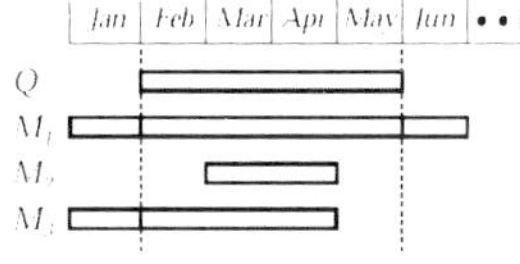

(b) Mappings for $Q = [\text{term} = 1]$.

Figure 2: Mapping **term** constraints to **bimonth** constraints.

Example 3 (Precision & Recall): Consider translating between two different calendar systems. As the time unit, the original context uses the **term** attribute, while the target uses **bimonth**. Figure 2(a) shows the correspondence. In the original context a year consists of three terms (*i.e.*, trimesters); *e.g.*, constraint [**term** = 1] represents *Feb* through *May*. In contrast, the target divides a year into six bimonths; *e.g.*, [**bimonth** = 1] matches *Jan* and *Feb*. We illustrate some mappings for query $Q = [\text{term} = 1]$ (see Figure 2(b)).

First, consider M_1:[bimonth = 1:3] (bimonth 1 to 3). Note that Q covers (*Feb, Mar, Apr, May*), while M_1 covers *Jan* and *Jun* in addition. Thus, M_1 incurs no false-negatives, but does have false-positives. By Eq. 2, as $Q \wedge M_1 = Q$, the recall is *perfect*, *i.e.*, $\mathcal{R}[M_1, Q] = 1$. Furthermore, according to Eq. 1, we can estimate $P[M_1, Q] = 4/6 = .67$ since $M_1 \wedge Q$ covers four out of the six months of M_1 (assuming that each month has equal likelihood).

In contrast, M_2:[bimonth = 2] is a subset of Q ($M_2 \subseteq Q$). As Figure 2(b) shows, $P[M_2, Q] = 2/2 = 1$; as a dual of the superset mapping, a subset mapping implies a perfect precision (*i.e.*, no false-positives). The high precision comes at the cost of a lowered recall, *i.e.*, $\mathcal{R}[M_2, Q] = 2/4 = .5$.

Finally, a mapping may have neither perfect precision nor perfect recall. For M_3:[bimonth = 1:2], we can similarly compute $P[M_3, Q] = 3/4 = .75$ and $\mathcal{R}[M_3, Q] = 3/4 = .75$. Note that M_3 incurs both false-positives (*Jan* is extra) as well as false-negatives (*May* is missed). ■

To quantify translation closeness, a reasonable metric must account for the two *competing* goals of precision and recall. We thus define our closeness criterion $\mathcal{F}[M, Q]$ as a function of the precision and recall between M and Q. For instance, some applications may want to focus on precision while requiring a recall threshold. We denote this important class of closeness functions as *RThresh*. Given a threshold θ, we define *RThresh*(θ) as follows:

$$RThresh(\theta) : \mathcal{F}(P, \mathcal{R})[M, Q] = \mathcal{F}(P[M, Q], \mathcal{R}[M, Q]) =$$
$$\begin{cases} P[M, Q] & \text{if } \mathcal{R}[M, Q] \geq \theta \\ undefined & \text{otherwise} \end{cases} \quad (3)$$

Example 4: Consider the mappings in Example 3 for $\mathcal{F} = RThresh(.7)$. The closeness for M_1 is $\mathcal{F}[M_1, Q] = \mathcal{F}(P = .67, \mathcal{R} = 1) = .67$. Similarly $\mathcal{F}[M_3, Q] = \mathcal{F}(.75, .75) = .75$. Since M_2 has an unqualified recall ($.5 < .7$), its closeness is *undefined*, *i.e.*, M_2 is an *invalid* mapping. For our illustration, assume that M_1, M_2 and M_3 represent *all* the relevant mappings for Q. M_3 is thus the best mapping, *i.e.*, $\mathcal{S}(Q) = M_3$, because it has the highest closeness w.r.t. *RThresh*(.7). ■

We similarly define *PThresh*(θ) as follows:
$$PThresh(\theta) : \mathcal{F}(P, \mathcal{R})[M, Q] = \mathcal{F}(P[M, Q], \mathcal{R}[M, Q]) =$$
$$\begin{cases} \mathcal{R}[M, Q] & \text{if } P[M, Q] \geq \theta \\ undefined & \text{otherwise} \end{cases} \quad (4)$$

The *PThresh* and *RThresh* classes represent many intuitive and important closeness metrics. We stress two special instances typically adopted for query mapping, namely *RThresh*(1) and *PThresh*(1). First, some applications may require perfect recall and hence *RThresh*(1), where M subsumes Q, *i.e.*, $M \supseteq Q$. The goal here is to find the most precise mapping (with the highest P) that subsumes the query (with $\mathcal{R} = 1$), usually referred to as the *minimal subsuming mapping* [3] or the *tight upper envelope* [26, 27]. We designate *RThresh*(1) as *MinSup*, since M will retrieve a *minimal superset* of what Q does.

As the dual, other applications may instead require that a mapping return only precise answers, *i.e.*, $M \subseteq Q$. We can implement this closeness criterion as *PThresh*(1) with perfect precision. Unlike *MinSup*, the goal now is to find the *maximal subsumed mapping* or the *tight lower envelope* [26, 27]. We thus refer to *PThresh*(1) as *MaxSub*.

Example 5: Different closeness criteria will determine different mappings as the closest. Example 4 showed that in our calendar application $\mathcal{S}(Q) = M_3$ w.r.t. $\mathcal{F} = RThresh(.7)$. To contrast, consider $\mathcal{F} = MinSup$: We obtain $\mathcal{F}[M_1, Q] = \mathcal{F}(.67, 1) = .67$, $\mathcal{F}[M_2, Q] = \mathcal{F}(1, .5) = undefined$, and $\mathcal{F}[M_3, Q] = \mathcal{F}(.75, .75) = undefined$. Thus instead $\mathcal{S}(Q) = M_1$ under *MinSup*. Furthermore, if we adopt *MaxSub*, both $\mathcal{F}[M_1, Q]$ and $\mathcal{F}[M_3, Q]$ will be *undefined*, and thus $\mathcal{S}(Q) = M_2$. ■

In addition to the above intuitive metrics, many other reasonable criteria are possible. For instance, if we need a function that is defined for every P and R, we can adopt the averages such as the arithmetic average $\mathcal{F}(P, \mathcal{R}) = (P + \mathcal{R})/2$ (corresponding to the error measure of [27]) or the harmonic mean $\mathcal{F}(P, \mathcal{R}) = 2P\mathcal{R}/(P + \mathcal{R})$. The latter actually corresponds to the *E-measure* [35], a conventional single-valued measure for information retrieval.

Finally, we stress that our general framework (Section 5) does not assume particular metrics. However, we do require that the closeness criterion be *monotonic*: If $P_1 \leq P_2$ and $R_1 \leq R_2$ then $\mathcal{F}(P_1, R_1) \leq \mathcal{F}(P_2, R_2)$. That is, if mapping M_2 (with parameters P_2 and R_2) is better than M_1 (with P_1 and R_1) in both parameters, then M_2 must be an overall better mapping. Because precision and recall capture both false-positive and false-negative errors, clearly any *reasonable* closeness metric (such as the sample functions just discussed) must satisfy monotonicity. (Monotonicity supports our framework through the "separability" theorems, which we discuss in [5] due to space constraint.)

4 Query Compositions

In this section we address two fundamental questions, whose answers will help us build our approximate query translation machinery. The first question (Section 4.1) is about compositional monotonicity. For instance, if we wish to translate query $Q = A \wedge B$ as $\mathcal{S}(A) \wedge \mathcal{S}(B)$, can we compute $\mathcal{S}(A)$, the best translation for A, independently from that for B? Or will somehow the best translation for A depend on the fact that it will be eventually intersected with $\mathcal{S}(B)$? Furthermore, the second question (Section 4.2) is whether in general it is possible to find the best translation for a query like $Q = A \wedge B$ by separately translating its components A and B.

4.1 Compositional Monotonicity

Consider a query composition $Q = Q_1 \odot \cdots \odot Q_n$, where operator $\odot$ is either $\wedge$ or $\vee$. The following assumption reduces our search space when looking for a best translation.

Assumption 1 (Compositional Monotonicity): For a query composition $Q = Q_1 \odot \cdots \odot Q_n$, let $\mathcal{S}(Q_i)$ be the closest mapping of Q_i with respect to some closeness criterion $\mathcal{F}$. For every mapping $\mathcal{M}_i$ of Q_i:

$$\mathcal{F}[\mathcal{M}_1 \odot \cdots \odot \mathcal{M}_n, Q] \leq \mathcal{F}[\mathcal{S}(Q_1) \odot \cdots \odot \mathcal{S}(Q_n), Q]. \quad \blacksquare$$

This assumption tells us that, if we wish to search for the best way to decompose a query, we can focus on using the "local optimals" as the building blocks, *i.e.*, the mapping $\mathcal{S}(Q_1) \odot \cdots \odot \mathcal{S}(Q_n)$, with the best mappings for each Q_i. In other words, the search for the best translation for each Q_i will not be affected because Q_i appears with other terms in Q. Note, however, that this assumption does *not* tell us if decomposition is the right strategy, *i.e.*, it does not tell us if $\mathcal{S}(Q_1) \odot \cdots \odot \mathcal{S}(Q_n)$ is as good as $\mathcal{S}(Q)$. (We study this "separability" issue in Section 4.2.) It only says that $\mathcal{S}(Q_1) \odot \cdots \odot \mathcal{S}(Q_n)$ is the best of the mappings for Q that use decomposition.

Under certain closeness metrics, such as *MinSup* and *MaxSub*, we can formally verify Assumption 1 (see [5]). We do not have a proof for the general case, but we believe it holds in all cases where we need to use the assumption. That is, when Q_i's are "semantically independent," their individual best-mappings should lead to an overall better mapping, and Assumption 1 should be valid. Otherwise, when Q_i's are indeed interrelated, the closest mapping $\mathcal{S}(Q)$ probably cannot be constructed by separating the components. For such "inseparable" compositions (Section 4.2), our algorithm will not use Assumption 1 and thus it is harmless. Finally, we stress that, even for the rare exceptional cases, $\mathcal{S}(Q_1) \odot \cdots \odot \mathcal{S}(Q_n)$ clearly remains at least a *good* mapping for Q.

4.2 Compositional Separability

When translating a query composition $Q = Q_1 \odot \cdots \odot Q_n$, can we handle the subqueries separately? We say that Q is *separable* if $\mathcal{S}(Q) = \mathcal{S}(Q_1) \odot \cdots \odot \mathcal{S}(Q_n)$, in which case we can obtain the overall mapping simply by translating the components individually. It turns out that separability depends on the particular closeness metric chosen. Our results indicate that disjunctions are *always* separable *for and only*

$\mathcal{S}(t_1)$	$\mathcal{S}(t_2)$	$\mathcal{S}(t_1 \vee t_2)$	$\mathcal{S}(t_1 \wedge t_2)$
[bimonth = 1:3] $(\mathcal{P}, \mathcal{R}) = (.67, 1)$	[bimonth = 3:5] $(\mathcal{P}, \mathcal{R}) = (.67, 1)$	[bimonth = 1:5] $(\mathcal{P}, \mathcal{R}) = (.8, 1)$	*False* $(\mathcal{P}, \mathcal{R}) = (1, 1)$

(a) $\mathcal{F}(\mathcal{P}, \mathcal{R}) = $ *MinSup*.

$\mathcal{S}(t_1)$	$\mathcal{S}(t_2)$	$\mathcal{S}(t_1 \vee t_2)$	$\mathcal{S}(t_1 \wedge t_2)$
[bimonth = 2] $(\mathcal{P}, \mathcal{R}) = (1, .5)$	[bimonth = 4] $(\mathcal{P}, \mathcal{R}) = (1, .5)$	[bimonth = 2:4] $(\mathcal{P}, \mathcal{R}) = (1, .75)$	*False* $(\mathcal{P}, \mathcal{R}) = (1, 1)$

(b) $\mathcal{F}(\mathcal{P}, \mathcal{R}) = $ *MaxSub*.

Figure 3: Closest mappings for t_1 and t_2 (Example 6).

for MinSup (*i.e.*, $RThresh(1)$, which requires a perfect recall threshold). As a dual result, conjunctions are *always* separable *for and only for MaxSub* (*i.e.*, $PThresh(1)$, which requires a perfect precision threshold). Due to space limitations, please refer to reference [5] for our formal results. Here we simply illustrate with an example.

Example 6 (Separability): Consider query t_1:[term = 1] and t_2:[term = 2] (for the calendar systems in Example 3). We will compare if their disjunction $(t_1 \vee t_2)$ and conjunction $(t_1 \wedge t_2)$ are separable under *MinSup* and *MaxSub*.

(a) *MinSup*: Figure 3(a) shows the closest mappings $\mathcal{S}(t_1)$, $\mathcal{S}(t_2)$, $\mathcal{S}(t_1 \vee t_2)$, and $\mathcal{S}(t_1 \wedge t_2)$ under *MinSup* (*e.g.*, Example 5 shows how we determined $\mathcal{S}(t_1)$). It turns out that for *MinSup* disjunctions are separable, but not conjunctions: We can verify that $\mathcal{S}(t_1 \vee t_2) = \mathcal{S}(t_1) \vee \mathcal{S}(t_2)$ (*i.e.*, [bimonth = 1:5] = [bimonth = 1:3] $\vee$ [bimonth = 3:5]). In contrast, $\mathcal{S}(t_1 \wedge t_2) \neq \mathcal{S}(t_1) \wedge \mathcal{S}(t_2)$, because $\mathcal{S}(t_1 \wedge t_2) = $ *False*, while $\mathcal{S}(t_1) \wedge \mathcal{S}(t_2) = $ [bimonth = 3].

(b) *MaxSub*: We obtain the opposite results: First, the conjunction is separable, since $\mathcal{S}(t_1 \wedge t_2) = \mathcal{S}(t_1) \wedge \mathcal{S}(t_2) = $ *False* (see Figure 3(b)). Second, the disjunction is not separable: $\mathcal{S}(t_1) \vee \mathcal{S}(t_2) = $ [bimonth = 2] $\vee$ [bimonth = 4], but $\mathcal{S}(t_1 \vee t_2) = $ [bimonth = 2:4]. $\quad \blacksquare$

In general, for any metric other than *MinSup* or *MaxSub*, neither conjunctions nor disjunctions are always separable. Therefore, a general framework for more flexible approximation metrics must cope with the potential inseparability for both types of compositions, as we will discuss next.

5 Framework and Algorithm

This section presents our framework and the associated algorithm for approximate translation. Section 5.1 first defines a translation rule system for codifying the mappings of basic semantic units. Based on the given rules, our algorithm will rewrite an original query using the semantic units to construct the closest mapping. As we just discussed, the rewriting must respect compositional separability to ensure mapping optimality; Section 5.2 presents such an algorithm.

5.1 Semantic Translation Rules

Query translation must be based on human expertise to resolve semantic heterogeneity. This section identifies the essential requirements of a rule system that codifies human expertise. We will illustrate with a "reference rule system," which is based on our mechanism designed earlier specifically for minimal-superset mapping [3]. We adapt this

```
R₁)  [format = F] ↦ emit: [desc contains F]                                              // (P,R) = (1.0, 0.8)
R₂)  [format = F1] ∨ [format = F2]; FormatPair(F1,F2) ↦ T = TypeOfPair(F1,F2);  emit: [type = T]   // (P,R) = (1.0, 1.0)
R₃)  [term = T] ↦ (B1,B2) = TermToBimonth(T) ;  emit: [bimonth = B1:B2]                   // (P,R) = (.75, .75)
R₄)  [term = T1] ∨ [term = T2] ↦ (B1,B2) = TermToBimonth(T1,T2) :  emit: [bimonth = B1:B2]   // (P,R) = (0.8, 1.0)
R₅)  [fn = F] ↦ emit: [review contains F]                                                // (P,R) = (0.9, 0.7)
R₆)  [ln = L] ↦ A = LnFnToName(L, "*"):  emit: [name = A]                                 // (P,R) = (1.0, 1.0)
R₇)  [ln = L] ∧ [fn = F] ↦ A = LnFnToName(L, F);  emit: [name = A]                        // (P,R) = (1.0, 1.0)
R₈)  [price in P1:P2] ↦ emit: [price ≥ P1] ∧ [price ≤ P2]                                 // (P,R) = (1.0, 1.0)
R₉)  [subject = S] ↦ K = SubjKwds(S); emit: [review contains K]                          // (P,R) = (0.9, 0.7)
R₁₀) [title = T] ↦ W = WordsIn(T); emit: [title contains W]                              // (P,R) = (0.9, 1.0)
```

Figure 4: Example mapping specification K_{med} with respect to $\mathcal{F} = RThresh(.7)$.

mechanism (to handle semantic units that can be complex queries) for general approximate translation.

We stress that our contribution is *not* the rule system itself, but its integration with a general query mapping scheme. The "reference" rule system is rather simple (*e.g.*, it has no recursion and negation). However, note that our algorithm can work with any rule mechanism that satisfies our soundness and completeness requirements (see later). For instance, if necessary, our framework can adopt more sophisticated rules that support recursive query patterns (*e.g.*, a conjunction of arbitrary number of conjuncts). Nevertheless, we believe that our simple system is well suited to most query translation tasks, as we will demonstrate through a case study in Section 6.

Figure 4 shows a *mapping specification* K_{med} consisting of rules $R_1, \ldots, R_{10}$ for translating queries that search for media items of books, audios, and videos (based on a real scenario that Section 6 will study). Our discussion assumes $\mathcal{F} = RThresh(.7)$. Each rule defines the closest mapping (with respect to $\mathcal{F}$) of the matching query patterns, as we next illustrate. (Note that, as Section 6 will discuss, we typically only need a rule for a query "pattern" rather than every "instance.") Figure 4 also shows the estimated $(\mathcal{P}, \mathcal{R})$ for the particular mappings. We stress that our algorithm will not require these numeric values to compute the best mappings. However, if we want to quantify the actual closeness of an output mapping, we can estimate it based on the $\mathcal{P}$ and $\mathcal{R}$ of the rules (using the technique in [5]).

Example 7 (Mapping Rules): We illustrate rule R_1 and R_2 for translating media format. Suppose that the original context expects formats `hardcover` and `softcover` (for books), `cassette` and `disc` (for audios), and `vhs` and `dvd` (for videos). In contrast, the target accepts media type of `book`, `audio`, and `video`.

First, consider a format constraint such as $v = $ [format = vhs]. As an atomic constraint, it needs a rule to define its mapping. To illustrate, we have at least two choices: First, consider $M_1 = $ [type = video]. Since M_1 will access both VHS and DVD titles, it has $(\mathcal{P}, \mathcal{R}) = (.5, 1)$ (assuming VHS accounts for 50% of videos). With $\mathcal{F} = RThresh(.7)$ (see Eq. 3), M_1 has a closeness of $\mathcal{F}(.5, 1) = .5$. Alternatively, mapping $M_2 = $ [desc contains vhs] simply looks for the keyword in desc (a textual description of the media). Suppose that about 80% VHS descriptions mention the word, and on the other hand only VHS items do, M_2 will have $(\mathcal{P}, \mathcal{R}) = (1, .8)$ or $\mathcal{F}(1, .8) = 1$. Thus M_2 is the closest mapping with respect

to $RThresh(.7)$, *i.e.*, $\mathcal{S}(v) = M_2$ (assuming no other relevant mappings exist). Rule R_1 simply matches any format constraint f (as a *matching*) at the left side and defines $\mathcal{S}(f)$ with respect to $\mathcal{F}$ at the *emit*: clause of the right side.

Furthermore, we notice that a query asking for a pair of formats (such as $v \vee d$, where $d = $ [format = dvd]) can map perfectly to a particular type (*e.g.*, [type = video]). Since we cannot construct this perfect (and thus the closest) mapping from the components, such a query forms a new semantic unit and thus Rule R_2 defines its translation. At the left side, R_2 will match a disjunctive pattern [format = F1] ∨ [format = F2] for those F1 and F2 that satisfy the condition `FormatPair(·)` as a pair of formats. For a matching m (*e.g.*, $m = v \vee d$), the right side then finds the corresponding type with function `TypeOfPair(·)` and emits $\mathcal{S}(m)$. Note that we assume that conditions and functions are both implemented externally with some programming language (*e.g.*, our implementation uses Java). ∎

Our discussion will assume an original query $Q_{med} = t(h \vee c)(v \vee d)$ as a running example. (Referring to Figure 5(a), we are querying the VHS or DVD titles by Tom Hanks or Tom Cruise. Note that we omit the ∧ operator for notational simplicity.) To map a query, we begin by matching it to the rules to find the subqueries for constructing the overall mapping, as we next illustrate.

Example 8 (Rule Matching): Consider matching Q_{med} against rules K_{med}; *i.e.*, we want to find the subqueries of Q_{med} that match a pattern described by some rule in K_{med}. Since a matching can be any complex query (with conjunctions, disjunctions, or both), we perform the matching on some normal form, say, DNF (Disjunctive Normal Form). (We could have instead chosen CNF or Conjunctive Normal Form. The choice is not critical, but it does affect how we structure the algorithm, as Section 5.2 will discuss.)

Specifically, we write Q_{med} in a DNF to compare it with the DNF patterns of the rules. Note that a DNF has the form $\hat{D}_1 \vee \cdots \vee \hat{D}_n$. (Note that we write $\hat{X}$ to stress that it is a conjunction; we will similarly use $\check{X}$ for a disjunction). For Q_{med} we have $\hat{D}_1 = (thv), \ldots, \hat{D}_4 = (tcd)$ (see Figure 5). As our framework also assumes, each rule specifies a DNF pattern of the form $\hat{d}_1 \vee \cdots \vee \hat{d}_m$: *e.g.*, rule R_2 has pattern P_2 with $\hat{d}_1$:[format = F1] and $\hat{d}_2$:[format = F2].

We next determine if the rule pattern matches some subquery of Q_{med}. To see if a pattern P represents a *subquery*, we check if every $\hat{d}_j$ in P is "simpler" than some differ-

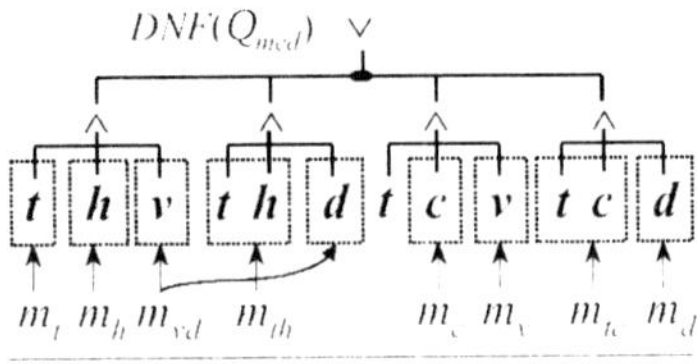

t - [fn - tom]
h - [ln - hanks] c - [ln - cruise]
v - [format - vhs] d - [format - dvd]

(a) Matchings in query DNF.

rule	matching	rule output	(P,R)
R_1	m_v :v	$\overline{m_v}$:[desc contains vhs]	(1...8)
R_1	m_d :d	$\overline{m_d}$:[desc contains dvd]	(1...8)
R_2	m_{vd}:$v \lor d$	$\overline{m_{vd}}$:[type = video]	(1..1.)
R_5	m_t :t	$\overline{m_t}$:[review contains tom]	(.9..7)
R_6	m_h :h	$\overline{m_h}$:[name = "hanks,*"]	(1..1.)
R_6	m_c :c	$\overline{m_c}$:[name = "cruise,*"]	(1..1.)
R_7	m_{th}:th	$\overline{m_{th}}$:[name = "hanks,tom"]	(1..1.)
R_7	m_{tc}:tc	$\overline{m_{tc}}$:[name = "cruise,tom"]	(1..1.)

(b) Matchings and their mappings.

Figure 5: Example query $Q_{med} = t(h \lor c)(v \lor d)$ and its matchings with respect to K_{med}.

ent $\hat{D}_i$ in the query. Note that, since both $\hat{D}_i$ and $\hat{d}_j$ are a simple conjunction, we say that $\hat{d}_j$ is *simpler* than $\hat{D}_i$ (or $\hat{D}_i$ is *more complex* than $\hat{d}_j$) if $\hat{d}_j$ matches some part of $\hat{D}_i$. For instance, consider pattern $\hat{d}_1 \lor \hat{d}_2$ of R_2: Since $\hat{d}_1$ can match v (with F1 bound to constant vhs), it is simpler than $\hat{D}_1$ (among others). Similarly $\hat{d}_2$ can match d (with F2 = dvd) and is thus simpler than $\hat{D}_2$. Thus R_2 matches subquery $v \lor d$ (or m_{vd} in Figure 5) of Q_{med}, *i.e.*, $v \lor d$ is a matching to R_2.

We repeat this process for every rule to find all the matchings. Figure 5(a) indicates these matchings as subtrees of Q_{med}'s DNF. Figure 5(b) then summarizes each matching m, the rule output for m (denoted by $\overline{m}$), and the estimated (P, R) (from Figure 4). (As noted, our algorithm does not need these parameter values for computing mappings.) ■

To enable query translation, we assume two essential requirements for semantic rules. *First*, we require that each rule define the closest mappings of the matching queries with respect to $\mathcal{F}(P, R)$— which we refer to as the *soundness* requirement (*i.e.*, a rule generates sound mappings). To determine such mappings, we can use source statistics (or perform sample queries) to estimate the precision and recall for different mappings (as Example 7 showed) and choose the one with the highest $\mathcal{F}(P, R)$. In fact, we can also simply make *intuitive* choices; *i.e.*, in practice a closeness function is *not* explicitly required when defining mapping rules, which Section 6 will discuss.

Second, we require that there be one rule for every semantic unit— which we refer to as the *completeness* requirement, since it enforces necessary rules be supplied. A *semantic unit* (*e.g.*, v and $v \lor d$ in our example) is a query whose closest mapping cannot be constructed from that of its subqueries. Since a semantic unit is "atomic" in query translation, its mapping must be manually defined with a

rule (and thus this requirement). Note that any individual constraint (such as v) is clearly a semantic unit; *e.g.*, R_1 and R_3 in K_{med} both describe such single-constraint units.

Moreover, a semantic unit can be a composite query (such as $v \lor d$). Our separability results (Section 4.2) show that query compositions can be inseparable (and thus form a unit) depending on the particular $\mathcal{F}(P, R)$. For instance, since for $\mathcal{F} = RThresh(.7)$ disjunctions are not always separable (see [5] for the formal results), a semantic unit *may* contain disjunctions, *e.g.*, as in R_2 and R_4. (Obviously we only need a rule for interrelated disjuncts; *e.g.*, we do not need one for [ln = hanks] $\lor$ [format = dvd].) Similarly, we may expect a semantic unit with conjunctions [5], *e.g.*, R_7.

In fact, as Section 4.2 discussed, for any closeness metric other than *MinSup* and *MaxSub*, neither disjunctions nor conjunctions are always separable, and thus a semantic unit may be just any complex queries. Although in many cases a unit might be no more complex than simple disjunctions or conjunctions (as in K_{med}), our algorithm can generally handle any complex units.

We stress that our soundness and completeness requirements together enable the analogously *divide-and-conquer* approach. Given an original query Q, if Q can match a rule, then itself is a semantic unit. We simply fire the rule to compute $\mathcal{S}(Q)$. Suppose $\overline{Q}$ denotes the rule output after matching Q, the soundness requirement ensures that $\mathcal{S}(Q) = \overline{Q}$. For instance, since $(v \lor d)$ will match rule R_2, it follows that $\mathcal{S}(v \lor d) = $ [type = video] as given by R_2.

On the other hand, if Q does not match any rule, then by the completeness requirement Q is *not* a semantic unit. In other words, we can construct $\mathcal{S}(Q)$ with the semantic units that are subqueries of Q. For instance, since Q_{med} contains the matching subqueries shown in Figure 5, these semantic units will be the *building blocks* for constructing $\mathcal{S}(Q_{med})$. Such construction of complex mappings thus becomes the main challenge of our framework, which we next discuss.

5.2 Algorithm *NFB*: Normal-Form Based Algorithm

This section presents the core algorithm of our query translation framework. Based on the rule system just discussed, Algorithm *NFB* will construct the mapping of a given query from the semantic units that it contains.

To construct a complex mapping, we are essentially looking for a rewriting using the semantic units. For instance, consider our example query Q_{med}. As we will see, we can construct its mapping from that of the units m_{th}, m_{tc}, and m_{vd} (see Figure 5): *i.e.*, $\mathcal{S}(Q_{med}) = (\overline{m_{th}} \lor \overline{m_{tc}})(\overline{m_{vd}})$. (Recall that $\overline{m}$ denotes the rule output for a matching m.) In other words, we rewrite Q_{med} into a Boolean function of these units: $B_1(m_{th}, m_{tc}, m_{vd}) = (m_{th} \lor m_{tc})(m_{vd})$. (Note that as a rewriting B_1 is logically equivalent to Q_{med}.) We refer to such a rewriting as a *decomposition*, since it breaks the query into the semantic units. Based on decomposition B_1 (but not others), we can simply construct $\mathcal{S}(Q_{med}) = B_1(\overline{m_{th}}, \overline{m_{tc}}, \overline{m_{vd}})$.

There exist *many* decompositions for a given query:*e.g.*, $B_2 = (m_{th} \lor m_{tc})(m_v \lor m_d)$ is another one for Q_{med}. For query mapping we want to find a *safe decomposition*, in which *every* composition (conjunction or disjunc-

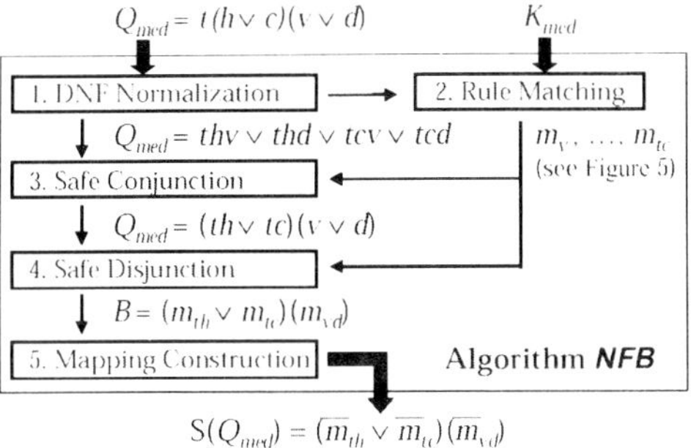

Figure 6: Illustration of Algorithm **NFB** for query Q_{med} with respect to rules K_{med}.

tion) is guaranteed to be separable. The optimal mapping can then be constructed straightforwardly from such a decomposition: We simply separate every composition, and thus only deal with the semantic units by their rules. To demonstrate, note that B_1 is such a safe decomposition (which can be shown by our results in [5] for determining such *safety*). Because $Q_{med} \equiv B_1$, we can obtain $S(Q_{med})$ or $S(B_1)$ as $[S(m_{th}) \vee S(m_{tc})]S(m_{vd})$ (by separating every composition since B_1 is safe). Applying the rules for the units (Figure 5), we can construct the mapping form B_1, i.e., $S(Q_{med}) = (\overline{m_{th}} \vee \overline{m_{tc}})\overline{m_{vd}} =$ ([name = "hanks,tom"] $\vee$ [name = "cruise,tom"]) $\wedge$ [type = video].

Therefore, the main challenge for mapping a query is to find its safe decomposition. Our results (as we will see in Theorem 1) show that, in practical cases, there exists exactly *one* safe decomposition (among many possible rewritings) for a query. Our Algorithm **NFB** (Figure 7) will find such a unique decomposition to construct the closest mapping.

Given a query Q and mapping rules K, **NFB** will output the closest mapping of Q with respect to the closeness metric $\mathcal{F}(\mathcal{P}, \mathcal{R})$ that K is defined upon. Referring to Figure 7, **NFB** first formulates the safe decomposition in Step (1) through Step (4), and finally Step (5) constructs $S(Q)$ accordingly. We will illustrate by translating Q_{med} using K_{med}, which defines the mappings under $\mathcal{F} = RThresh(.7)$. Figure 6 summarizes this process, showing the input and output for each step.

Algorithm **NFB** (for *Normal-Form-Based*) is essentially based on Boolean normal forms to systematically rewrite a query into a safe decomposition. As Figure 6 shows, **NFB** starts by normalizing the input query into a DNF (of the constraints) in Step (1) and finally formulates the safe decomposition B as a CNF (of the semantic units) in Step (4). Note that we could have instead structured a *dual* algorithm that starts with a CNF and concludes at a DNF.

As an overview, we now summarize how **NFB** works (Figure 6). Step (1) first normalizes Q_{med} into a DNF, on which Step (2) performs rule matching. Section 5.1 discussed these steps, resulting in the matching units in Figure 5. **NFB** will then rewrite Q_{med} into a safe decomposition B in a CNF (as just mentioned), a simple *two-level* tree with a root conjunction and some leaf disjunctions. To ensure that such CNF rewriting is safe, Step (3) focuses on forming a separable conjunction (or a *safe* conjunction)

at the root, and similarly Step (4) will form separable disjunctions (or *safe* disjunctions) at the leaves. Specifically, as Example 9 below explains, Step (3) will rewrite Q_{med} into a conjunctive form (see Figure 6) that is separable, i.e., $S(Q_{med}) = S(th \vee tc)S(v \vee d)$. Step (4) then further rewrites each resulted conjunct into a separable disjunction of the semantic unit: i.e., the first conjunct as $(m_{th} \vee m_{tc})$ and the second as (m_{vd}), which Example 10 will illustrate. We have thus formulated the safe decomposition in a CNF: $B = (m_{th} \vee m_{tc})(m_{vd})$. Finally, Algorithm **NFB** simply constructs $S(Q_{med})$ from B as just discussed.

Example 9 (Safe Conjunction): We explain Step (3) of Algorithm **NFB**, which uses function *SafeConj* to rewrite an input query into a conjunction that is guaranteed to be separable. As a basis, to determine whether a conjunction is separable, we have developed the sufficient conditions (called the *safety* conditions) that imply the separability. Due to space limitations, we will leave to reference [5] the safety formalism. We simply stress here that the conjunction that Step (3) formulates will satisfy our formal safety conditions in [5] and thus must be separable.

Intuitively, to eventually form a safe decomposition of Q_{med} using the semantic units (see Figure 5), we first form a safe decomposition for every conjunction in the former using that in the latter. Note that, since both Q_{med} and the units are written in DNF, all their conjunctions are explicit at the leaves (of the query tree); e.g., Q_{med} has (thv), (thd), (tcv), and (tcd) as Figure 6 shows. In particular, we can rewrite (thv) as $(t)(h)(th)(v)$ with the four "sub-conjunctions" from units m_t, m_h, m_{th}, and m_{vd}. We can then omit (t) and (h), since they are subexpressions of (th) and are thus redundant (i.e., they will not contribute to the next step). Consequently, we have rewritten $Q_{med} = (th)(v) \vee (th)(d) \vee (tc)(v) \vee (tc)(d)$ or $\vee\{(th)(v), (th)(d), (tc)(v), (tc)(d)\}$.

Our goal here is to formulate a conjunction (at the root of the query tree). Since the above rewriting is disjunctive, Step (b) of *SafeConj* simply distributes the outer disjunction over the inner conjunctions (using the standard Boolean algebra). Omitting any redundancies, we will obtain a conjunctive form $Q_{med} = C_1 C_2$ with two conjuncts $C_1 = (th \vee tc)$ and $C_2 = (v \vee d)$. (In [5] we show that the conjunction is safe and thus separable.)

Finally, Step (c) of *SafeConj* determines if every such conjunct is ready for Step (4) of Algorithm **NFB**, or else it needs further rewriting. In other words, we want to test if C_i can be written as the sum of the contained units (which is essentially the safe disjunction that Step (4) will formulate). In particular, referring to Figure 5, C_2 contains units m_v, m_d and m_{vd}. Since we can indeed write C_2 as their sum (i.e., $C_2 \equiv m_v \vee m_d \vee m_{vd}$), it does not need further rewriting, and similarly neither does C_1. ∎

In general, while not shown in the above example, any resulted conjunct that cannot be written as a sum-of-units will be further "decomposed." In other words, such C_i will be rewritten, by recursively calling *SafeConj*, into simpler conjuncts. To illustrate, consider a query $wx \vee yz$, and suppose that the matching units are $m_1 = wx \vee y$, $m_2 = w$,

Algorithm *NFB*: Normal-Form Based Query Mapping
Input: • Q: an arbitrary query in the original context.
• K: the constraint mapping specification for a target system T *w.r.t.* a closeness criterion $\mathcal{F}$.
Output: $\mathcal{S}(Q)$, the closest mapping of Q for T *w.r.t.* $\mathcal{F}$.
Procedure:

(1) DNF Normalization:
- convert Q into DNF: $DNF(Q) \leftarrow \sum_{l=1}^{m} \hat{D}_l$, where $\hat{D}_l$ is a simple conjunction of constraints.

(2) Rule Matching:
- if Q itself matches a rule: $\mathcal{S}(Q) \leftarrow \overline{Q}$; output $\mathcal{S}(Q)$ // *fire the rule for Q as a semantic unit.*
- else: find all the matchings $m_1, \ldots, m_u$ of Q *w.r.t.* K; note m_i is in DNF: $m_i = \sum \hat{d}_{ij}$

(3) Safe Conjunction: // *rewrite $DNF(Q)$ into a safe conjunction $Q \equiv \wedge(\mathcal{C})$, such that*
- $\mathcal{C} = \{\check{C}_1, \ldots, \check{C}_n\} \leftarrow SafeConj(DNF(Q))$ // *every conjunct $\check{C}_k$ can then form a safe disjunction.*

(4) Safe Disjunction:
- for all $\check{C}_k \in \mathcal{C}$: rewrite $\check{C}_k = \hat{x}_1 \vee \cdots \vee \hat{x}_m$ into $\check{C}_k \equiv \sum m_i$, for all matchings m_i s.t.:
  - every $\hat{d}_{ij}$ in m_i appears as some $\hat{x}_l$ in $\check{C}_k$ // *i.e., m_i can be found in $\check{C}$ and $m_i \subseteq \check{C}$.*
  - // *omit m_i if $m_i \subseteq m_{i'}$ for some $m_{i'}$, and thus m_i is redundant because of $m_{i'}$.*
  - $\not\exists\, m_{i'}$ s.t. $m_i \subseteq m_{i'}$, i.e., m_i covers only a subset of $\hat{x}_l$ terms that $m_{i'}$ does
- $B(m_1, \ldots, m_u) \leftarrow \prod_{k=1}^{n} \check{C}_k$ // *the safe decompositon in terms of the matchings as units.*

(5) Mapping Construction:
- compute $\overline{m_i}$ for each m_i actually used in B // *fire rules for the relevant matchings.*
- $\mathcal{S}(Q) \leftarrow B(\overline{m_1}, \ldots, \overline{m_u})$; output $\mathcal{S}(Q)$ // *construct the mapping from B.*

Function $SafeConj(DNF(Q) = \sum_{l=1}^{m} \hat{D}_l)$: // *rewrite a query in DNF into a safe conjunction in CNF.*

(a) *Conjunction Rewriting:* // *rewrite each $\hat{D}_l$ using the DNF disjuncts of any matching m_i found in Q.*
- for all $\hat{D}_l$: rewrite $\hat{D}_l \equiv \prod \hat{d}_{ij}$ for all $\hat{d}_{ij}$ (a disjunct of $DNF(m_i)$; see Step (2) above) s.t.:
  - $\hat{d}_{ij} \supseteq \hat{D}_l$, i.e., $\hat{d}_{ij}$ is a subconjunction of $\hat{D}_l$ // *as simple conjunctions, $\hat{d}_{ij}$ is simpler than $\hat{D}_l$.*
  - $\not\exists\, \hat{d}_{i'j'}$ s.t. $\hat{d}_{ij}$ is a subconjunction of $\hat{d}_{i'j'}$ // *omit $\hat{d}_{ij}$ that is simpler than other $\hat{d}_{i'j'}$.*

(b) *CNF Formulation:* // *standard Boolean algebra to convert Q into a conjunctive form.*
- rewrite Q in CNF (in terms of the $\hat{d}_{ij}$'s), i.e., $Q \equiv \prod \check{C}$, for all $\check{C}$ s.t.
  - $\check{C} = \hat{x}_1 \vee \cdots \vee \hat{x}_m$, where every $\hat{x}_l$ denotes some $\hat{d}_{ij}$ from $\hat{D}_l$ as formulated in (a)
  // *omit $\check{C}$ if $\check{C}' \subseteq \check{C}$ for some $\check{C}'$, and thus $\check{C}$ is redundant in the CNF of Q.*
  - $\not\exists\, \check{C}' = \hat{x}'_1 \vee \cdots \vee \hat{x}'_m$ s.t. $\forall \hat{x}'_j, \exists \hat{x}_i, \hat{x}'_j \subseteq \hat{x}_i$

(c) *Recursive Rewriting:*
- $\mathcal{C} \leftarrow \phi$ // *to store the formulated conjuncts.*
- for all $\check{C} = \hat{x}_1 \vee \cdots \vee \hat{x}_m$ formulated in (b):
  - $M \leftarrow \{m_i \mid$ every $\hat{d}_{ij}$ in m_i appears as some $\hat{x}_l$ in $\check{C}\}$ // *all m_i found in $\check{C}$ s.t. $m_i \subseteq \check{C}$.*
  - if every $\hat{x}_l$ in $\check{C}$ appears as $\hat{d}_{ij}$ in some m_i in M: // *i.e., $\check{C} \equiv \vee(M)$.*
    - $\mathcal{C} \leftarrow \mathcal{C} \cup \{\check{C}\}$ // *a safe disjunction of Step (4) can be formed; no need for further rewriting*
    - else: $\mathcal{C} \leftarrow \mathcal{C} \cup SafeConj(\check{C})$ // *recursively perform further rewriting of $\check{C}$.*
- return $\mathcal{C}$ // *$DNF(Q)$ is rewritten safely into $\wedge(\mathcal{C})$.*

Figure 7: Algorithm *NFB* for approximate query translation.

$m_3 = x$, $m_4 = y$, and $m_5 = z$. Given $wx \vee yz$ as input, *SafeConj* will first rewrite it into $(wx \vee y)(wx \vee z)$. Conjunct $(wx \vee y)$ can be written as sum-of-units simply as m_1, but the latter conjunct cannot. Consequently, a recursive call *SafeConj*$(wx \vee z)$ will further rewrite the latter into $(w \vee z)(x \vee z)$, where the new conjuncts can be written as $(m_2 \vee m_5)$ and $(m_3 \vee m_5)$ respectively.

This recursive process will eventually terminate and produce a separable conjunction: Intuitively, every recursion will derive strictly simpler subqueries as just illustrated. Eventually, *SafeConj* will terminate with the simplest form (if not earlier), *i.e.*, a disjunction of atomic constraints (*e.g.*, $w \vee z$), which is trivially a sum of single-constraint units. Please refer to reference [5] for a formal proof that the conjunctions so formulated are separable.

After forming the safe conjunction in Step (3) as just shown, Algorithm *NFB* will then focus on the disjunctions in Step (4), as the following example illustrates.

Example 10 (Safe Disjunction): Continuing our example, Step (4) will next rewrite each conjunct $\check{C}_i$ into a safe disjunction. (Like our discussion for conjunctions, the resulted disjunctions will satisfy the formal safety conditions in reference [5] and thus must be separable.) As just illustrated, Step (3) ensures that every $\check{C}_i$ can be written as the sum of the contained units, *e.g.*, $\check{C}_2 \equiv (m_v \vee m_d \vee m_{vd})$. Removing the redundant terms (*i.e.*, $m_v \subseteq m_{vd}$ and $m_d \subseteq m_{vd}$), we obtain $\check{C}_2 \equiv m_{vd}$. Similarly, we can rewrite $\check{C}_1 \equiv (m_{th} \vee m_{tc})$. (We show in [5] that the disjunction is indeed safe).

It turns out that, when semantic units are not "interlocking," the disjunctions so formulated will be safe and thus separable. As we will see, in the rare interlocking cases, a safe decomposition may not exist and thus Step (4) may not form safe disjunctions. For the majority of cases, as in this example, the resulted disjunctions (and thus the decomposition overall) are safe. ∎

By constructing a safe decomposition, Algorithm *NFB* will generate the best translation, as we have illustrated. Essentially, based on the optimal mappings for semantic units (as given by sound rules), and by respecting constraint dependencies (as the units indicate) to preserve optimality through query rewriting, *NFB* guarantees the overall optimal mappings. Our results below show that, in the vast majority of cases, namely when no semantic units "interlock" (defined below), a query will have a *unique* safe decomposition. Consequently, Algorithm *NFB* will find this unique decomposition and thus construct the closest mapping. Please refer to reference [5] for a proof.

Theorem 1 (Unique Safe Decomposition): Given a query Q and a mapping specification K *w.r.t.* some closeness criterion $\mathcal{F}$, if Q has no interlocking semantic units by matching K, then

- there exists a *unique* safe decomposition of Q, from which $\mathcal{S}(Q)$ *w.r.t.* $\mathcal{F}$ can be constructed, and
- Algorithm *NFB* will find the safe decomposition and output $\mathcal{S}(Q)$.

Otherwise, when there are interlocking units, a safe decomposition for Q may not exist. ■

On the other hand, Theorem 1 also states that, when a query involves interlocking units, it may *not* have a safe decomposition. Note that Q still have a best mapping, but $\mathcal{S}(Q)$ must instead be found among the unsafe decompositions. (Our completeness requirement in Section 5.1 asserts that $\mathcal{S}(Q)$ can be constructed from *some* decomposition using its semantic units.) We formally define interlocking below, and then illustrate with Example 11.

Definition 1 (Interlocking Units): A set of semantic units $\mathcal{U}$ is *interlocking*, if for some $m \in \mathcal{U}$, there exist $m_1, \ldots, m_n$ also in $\mathcal{U}$ such that the following hold:

(1) Let $DNF(m) = \sum \hat{d}_k$ and $DNF(m_i) = \sum \hat{d}_{ij}$. (a) Every m_i has some $\hat{d}_{ij}$ that overlaps with but is not strictly simpler than some $\hat{d}_k$; at least one such $\hat{d}_{ij}$ is strictly more complex than the corresponding $\hat{d}_k$. (b) m is simpler than $(m_1 \vee \ldots \vee m_n)$.

(2) Let $CNF(m) = \prod \check{c}_k$ and $CNF(m_i) = \prod \check{c}_{ij}$. For some $\check{c}_k$, $\check{c}_k \subseteq \sum_{i=1}^{n} \check{c}_{ij_i}$ but $\check{c}_k \not\subseteq \check{c}_{ij_i}, \forall i$. ■

Example 11 (Interlocking Units): Consider query $Q = xy \vee z$. Suppose that (by matching rules) Q has semantic units (written in DNF): $m_{x \vee z} = (x) \vee (z)$, $m_{xy} = (xy)$, $m_x = (x)$, $m_y = (y)$, and $m_z = (z)$. Note that these units are interlocking: Intuitively, an interlock exists because x is involved in both conjunction m_{xy} and disjunction $m_{x \vee z}$.

More formally, we show the interlocking by Definition 1. Let $m = m_{x \vee z}$, $m_1 = m_{xy}$, and $m_2 = m_z$. First, Condition (1) will hold: Term (xy) of m_1 satisfies (a) with respect to term (x) of m, and similarly term (z) of m_2 with respect to term (z) of m. In addition, term (xy) of m_1 is also strictly more complex than (x) of m. Because m is indeed a subexpression of $m_1 \vee m_2$, (b) is also satisfied. Second, since $CNF(m) = (x \vee z)$, $CNF(m_1) = (x)(y)$, and $CNF(m_2) = (z)$, Condition (2) also holds because $(x \vee z) \subseteq (x) \vee (z)$ while $(x \vee z) \not\subseteq (x)$ and $(x \vee z) \not\subseteq (z)$.

Consequently, Q may not have a safe decomposition (by Theorem 1) because of the interlocking. Intuitively, to rewrite Q using the semantic units, we must separate *either* the disjunction (between xy and z) *or* the conjunction (between x and y). (Otherwise, Q remains monolithic.) However, *neither* will be safe— The former, such as in $B_1 = m_{xy} \vee m_z$, will break the dependency between x and z (as indicated by $m_{x \vee z}$) and thus is not safe (*i.e.*, it will fail the safety conditions in [5]). Similarly, the latter will break m_{xy}, such as in $B_2 = m_{x \vee z}(m_y \vee m_z)$, which is also unsafe (by the safety conditions in [5]). ■

We believe that such interlocking cases will be rare in practice. As we intuitively noted above, interlock occurs between such "overlapping" units as m_{xy} and $m_{x \vee z}$. That is, interlocking will happen only when a constraint (*e.g.*, x in our example) participates in *both* a conjunction unit (*e.g.*, m_{xy}) *and* a disjunction unit (*e.g.*, $m_{x \vee z}$). If x appears in only simple-disjunction units, like $(x \vee y)$ and $(x \vee z)$, no interlocking will form. (Similarly, no simple-conjunction units can interlock.) Because a semantic unit represents interdependencies among its constraints, such complex interlocking is very unlikely in practice. In fact, in our case study of real mapping systems (see Section 6), we have indeed observed no instances of such an "anomaly."

When interlocking does occur, because no safe decomposition exists, Algorithm *NFB* will not be able to construct $\mathcal{S}(Q)$. We can address these exceptional cases in two ways: First, we may simply require these interlocking queries (*e.g.*, $xy \vee z$) be defined by rules. Alternatively, we can find all the unsafe decompositions, estimate the closeness of each corresponding mapping, and select the best as $\mathcal{S}(Q)$. Note that it is possible to estimate the $\mathcal{P}$ and $\mathcal{R}$ parameters and thus the closeness of a constructed mapping; we show such estimation technique in [5] due to space limitations.

Finally, we conclude by analyzing the running time of Algorithm *NFB*. First, in Step (1) and Step (3) (*i.e.*, subroutine *SafeConj*), *NFB* will perform DNF and CNF conversion respectively. Such a conversion is in general exponential in the number of query constraints (because the Boolean satisfiability problem is NP-complete [37]). However, this conversion has been well studied and practical algorithms have been proposed in the literature [38]. Therefore, for queries of practical sizes, we believe this normalization can be reasonably efficient.

Furthermore, the other steps of Algorithm *NFB* are quite efficient and actually run in linear time of the input size: Consider a query Q and rules K as input (note that they are all in DNF after Step (1)). Let D_Q and N_Q be the number of disjuncts and constraints-per-disjunct in the DNF of Q; similarly, let D_R and N_R be those of the DNF query pattern in a rule. Let R be the number of rules in K. With these input size parameters, Step (2) will take time $O(N_Q N_R D_Q D_R R)$: That is, the algorithm will match each pair of constraints (thus the factor $N_Q N_R$), for each pair of query and rule disjuncts (thus the factor $D_Q D_R$), and for each rule (thus the factor R). Step (4) will then run in $O(C_Q M)$ time, where C_Q is the number of CNF conjuncts of Q (thus an upper bound of what Step (3) can generate) and M is the number of matchings found in Step (2). Finally, Step (5) will simply take time of $O(M)$.

6 Practical Implications: A Case Study

To verify that our framework makes sense in practice, we explore several sources on the Web. We wish to study how to "program" our general framework for a specific mapping system. That is, we will demonstrate the mapping rules for a representative scenario. Through this concrete example, we also want to understand practical issues such as the ease of composing rules, the number of rules typically required, and whether approximation is essential in practice. This case

```
Target Source: BN at www.barnesandnoble.com
B₁) [title O T] ↦ W = WordsIn(T); emit: [title contains W]
B₂) [fn = F] ↦ emit: [keyword contains F]
B₃) [ln = L] ↦ A = LnFnToName(L, null); emit: [author = A]
B₄) [ln = L] ∧ [fn = F] ↦ A = LnFnToName(L, F); emit: [author = A]
B₅) [subject O S1]; EqualsOrStarts(O) ↦
        S2 = MapSubjHeading(S1); emit: [subject = S2]
B₆) [subject contains W] ↦
        S = SubjKwdToSubjHeading(W); emit: [subject = S]
B₇) [format = F1] ↦ F2 = MapFormat(F1); emit: [format = F2]

Target Source: Socrates at socrates.stanford.edu
S₁) [title O T] ↦ [title O T]
S₂) [A = N]; LnOrFn(A) ↦ emit: [au contains N]
S₃) [subject O S1]; EqualsOrStarts(O) ↦
        S2 = MapSubjHeading(S1); emit: [subject = S2]
S₄) [subject contains W1] ↦
        W2 = MapSubjKwd(W1); emit: [subject contains W2]
S₅) [format = F] ↦ [keyword contains F]
S₆) [format = hardcover] ∨ [format = paperback] ↦ True

Target Source: EB at www.evenbetter.com
E₁) [title O T] ↦ W = WordsIn(T); emit: [title contains W]
E₂) [fn = F] ↦ emit: [keyword contains F]
E₃) [ln = L] ↦ A = LnFnToName(L, null); emit: [author = A]
E₄) [ln = L] ∧ [fn = F] ↦ A = LnFnToName(L, F); emit: [author = A]
E₅) [subject O S] ↦ W = WordsIn(S); emit: [keyword contains W]
E₆) [format = F] ↦ emit: False
E₇) [format = hardcover] ∨ [format = paperback] ↦ True
```

Figure 8: Rules for mapping *Amazon* to different sources.

study is based on a similar scenario that is available online for demonstrating our translation server (see Section 7).

6.1 A Book-Search Mediator

Let us consider building a book-search mediator that integrates online sources *Amazon* at `www.amazon.com` and *BN* at `www.barnsandnoble.com` (both are online bookstores), *EB* at `www.evenbetter.com` (a comparison shopping service), and *Socrates* at `socrates.stanford.edu` (Stanford library online catalog, currently not publicly accessible). Our scenario assumes that the mediator integrates these sources by adopting *Amazon*'s query context and thus needs translation for the other sources.

We will thus demonstrate constraint mappings from *Amazon* to respectively *BN*, *EB*, and *Socrates*. For each target source, we compare its constraint vocabulary (*i.e.*, supported constraints as described in the specific query interface and the documentations) with that of *Amazon* and define the mapping rules. As Figure 8 shows, we need seven rules for *BN*, six rules for *Socrates*, and seven rules for *EB*. As Section 5.1 discusses, each rule gives the best mapping for the matching semantic unit with respect to the closeness metric, which we assume to be $\mathcal{F} = PThresh(.7)$. In fact, in practice it is *not* required to explicitly consider the closeness function, as we will discuss in Section 6.2.

For instance, rules $B_1, \ldots, B_7$ map the constraints on attributes title, ln, fn, subject, and format in the *Amazon*[1] context to ones on title, keyword, author, subject, and format in the *BN* context. Note that when defining mapping rules, we only need to focus on the corresponding *clusters* of attributes in either contexts. For instance, cluster {ln, fn} at *Amazon* corresponds to {author, keyword} at *BN*, whose

mappings are given by B_2, B_3, and B_4. In addition, note that *True* (a trivial superset) and *False* (a trivial subset) are both possible mappings (when no better ones exist, as in rules S_6, E_6, and E_7), which will effectively remove the matching units from the translated query.

6.2 Observations

Our case study shows that the query-mapping framework that we have presented can be easily applied in practice. The number of mapping rules are small: Observe that constraint dependencies exist only within a cluster of attributes (*e.g.*, {ln, fn} as in B_4 and {format} as in S_6) and are typically simple. Thus we will only need a few more rules (that describe compositional units) than the number of atomic constraint patterns in the original context. In addition, note that we only need a rule for a query *pattern* (*e.g.*, [subject O S1] of B_5) when its *instantiations* (*e.g.*, [subject = "web design"] and [subject starts "web"]) share the same way of mapping, which we found to be true in our study. Furthermore, it is often possible to reuse mapping rules for different sources as they share some common constraints; *e.g.*, E_2, E_3, and E_4 are reused from B_2, B_3, and B_4.

Furthermore, we indeed observed no instances of interlocking units (as Section 5.2 discussed). Note that semantic units essentially indicate the correspondence of attributes, such as the *conjunction* of ln and fn versus author (or similarly month and year versus date) and the *disjunction* of format versus type. We have observed no attributes involved in *both* types of correspondence, without which interlocking simply cannot occur (Section 5.2). Our algorithm will thus generate the unique best mappings in the practical cases.

While our framework is formally supported by the notion of closeness, a closeness function is *not* explicitly required when defining a mapping rule. That is, given a semantic unit, we can *intuitively* choose its best mapping when there are competing choices (without explicitly computing their closeness with a metric as in Example 7). Such mappings are thus defined with some *implicit* metric that corresponds to the "intuition" we may have in mind. However, we stress that, as Theorem 1 states, our algorithms will preserve the optimality with respect to any closeness metrics that the mapping rules conform to– be it explicitly or implicitly.

Furthermore, our case study shows that the general notion of approximation (as this paper specifically introduces) is truly essential for a "usable" query-mapping framework. Observe that, among the twenty rules in Figure 8, only six (B_3, B_4, B_7, S_1, E_3, E_4) are perfect mappings, a ratio of 30% – the other 70% is not possible without approximation. Moreover, we need a general framework that can deal with *all* types of approximation, *i.e.*, supersets (*e.g.*, B_1, S_2), subsets (*e.g.*, E_6), and hybrid mappings that contain both false-positives and false-negatives (*e.g.*, B_2, B_5). The approximate translation technique presented in this paper can thus be very helpful in practice. We have studied additional scenarios to the one presented here, and in all cases we have found our observations to hold.

7 Conclusion

In this paper we have presented a framework and the associated algorithm for approximate query translation. Our

---

[1] Since *Amazon* distinguishes the first and last names in author attribute, we separate it into ln and fn in translation.

framework is robust under virtually any reasonable closeness metric that combines both precision and recall. We also intuitively presented our results on the separability and safety of query compositions (and we cover the full details in [5]). These results are critical for the development of any algorithm that attempts approximate query translation. Our Algorithm *NFB* will generate a unique best-mapping in the practical cases when semantic units do not "interlock."

While our algorithm generates the closest mappings, it does not compute the actual "closeness," in terms of the precision and recall parameters. (In fact, our algorithm does not explicitly use the parameter to compute the best mappings.) While not essential for the operation of our algorithm, in some cases it may be desirable to estimate the $\mathcal{P}$ and $\mathcal{R}$ (or the corresponding closeness) of a mapping. As a complement to our translation machinery, we have developed simple formulas for such estimation, and it is covered in [5].

Although we present our approach specifically for translating queries across contexts, we believe its generality can support much broader heterogeneous problems. For instance, the framework can be applied to map *data* and queries across *ontologies*. In fact, we have studied in [25] how to model data as conjunctive queries and thus apply the minimal-superset algorithms [3] for data translation.

We have implemented the approximate query translation mechanism described in this paper in the Stanford Digital Libraries Project. Our implementation of an online translation server is available for demonstration. While the back-end translation server is generic, we program it (by defining specific mapping rules) to demonstrate a particular translation scenario of online media search (whose simplified version is presented in Section 6). The server is available at `http://www-db.stanford.edu/~kevin/aqt`.

References

[1] G. Wiederhold. Mediators in the architecture of future information systems. *IEEE Computer*, 25(3):51–60, Mar. 1992.

[2] J. D. Ullman. Information integration using logical views. In *Proc. of the 6th ICDT*, Jan. 1997.

[3] C.-C. K. Chang and H. Garcia-Molina. Mind your vocabulary: Query mapping across heterogeneous information sources. In *Proc. of the 1999 ACM SIGMOD Conf.*, pages 335–346, Philadelphia, Pa., June 1999. ACM Press, New York.

[4] C.-C. K. Chang and H. Garcia-Molina. Mind your vocabulary: Query mapping across heterogeneous information sources (extended version). Technical Report SIDL-WP-1998-0095, Stanford Univ., 1999. Accessible at `http://www-diglib.stanford.edu`.

[5] C.-C. K. Chang and H. Garcia-Molina. Approximate query translation across heterogeneous information sources (extended version). Technical Report SIDL-WP-1999-0115, Stanford Univ., 1999. Accessible at `http://www-diglib.stanford.edu`.

[6] R. Hull. Managing semantic heterogeneity in databases: A theoretical perspective. In *Proc. of the 16th ACM PODS*, pages 51–61, 1997.

[7] M. A. Hearst. Trends & controversies: Information integration. *IEEE Intelligent System*, 13(5):12–24, Sept. 1998.

[8] A. Y. Levy, A. Rajaraman, and J. J. Ordille. Querying heterogeneous information sources using source descriptions. In *Proc. of the 22nd VLDB Conf.*, pages 251–262, Bombay, India, 1996.

[9] A. Y. Levy, A. Rajaraman, and J. J. Ordille. Query-answering algorithms for information agents. In *Proc. of the 13th National Conf. on Artificial Intelligence, AAAI-96*, Portland, Oreg., Aug. 1996.

[10] Y. Papakonstantinou, H. Garcia-Molina, and J. Ullman. Medmaker: A mediation system based on declarative specifications. In *Proc. of the 12th Intl. Conf. on Data Engineering*, New Orleans, La., 1996.

[11] Y. Papakonstantinou, H. Garcia-Molina, A. Gupta, and J. Ullman. A query translation scheme for rapid implementation of wrappers. In *Proc. of the 4th Intl. Conf. on Deductive and Object-Oriented Databases*, pages 161–186, Singapore, Dec. 1995. Springer, Berlin.

[12] O. M. Duschka. *Query Planning and Optimization in Information Integration*. PhD thesis, Stanford Univ., Dec. 1997.

[13] M. R. Genesereth, A. M. Keller, and O. M. Duschka. Infomaster: An information integration system. In *Proc. of the 1997 ACM SIGMOD Conf.*, Tucson, Ariz., 1997. ACM Press, New York.

[14] L. M. Haas, D. Kossmann, E. L. Wimmers, and J. Yang. Optimizing queries across diverse data sources. In *Proc. of the 23rd VLDB Conf.*, pages 276–285, Athens, Greece, Aug. 1997.

[15] M. T. Roth and P. M. Schwarz. Don't scrap it, wrap it! a wrapper architecture for legacy data sources. In *Proc. of the 23rd VLDB Conf.*, pages 266–275, Athens, Greece, Aug. 1997.

[16] O. Kapitskaia, A. Tomasic, and P. Valduriez. Dealing with discrepancies in wrapper functionality. Tech. Report RR-3138, INRIA, 1997.

[17] H. Garcia-Molina, W. Labio, and R. Yerneni. Capability sensitive query processing on internet sources. In *Proc. of the 15th Intl. Conf. on Data Engineering*, Sydney, Australia, Mar. 1999.

[18] A. Rajaraman, Y. Sagiv, and J. D. Ullman. Answering queries using templates with binding patterns. In *Proc. of the 14th ACM PODS*, pages 105–112, San Jose, Calif., May 1995.

[19] A. Y. Levy, A. Rajaraman, and J. D. Ullman. Answering queries using limited external query processors. In *Proc. of the 15th ACM PODS*, pages 27–37, Montreal, Canada, June 1996.

[20] L. G. DeMichiel. Resolving database incompatibility: An approach to performing relational operations over mismatched domains. *IEEE Trans. on Knowledge and Data Engineering*, 1(4):485–493, 1989.

[21] E. Sciore, M. Siegel, and A. Rosenthal. Using semantic values to facilitate interoperability among heterogeneous information systems. *Trans. on Database Systems*, 19(2):254–290, June 1994.

[22] P. Buneman, S. Davidson, K. Hart, C. Overton, and L. Wong. A data transformation system for biological data sources. In *Proc. of the 21st VLDB Conf.*, Zurich, Switzerland, 1995.

[23] S. Abiteboul, S. Cluet, and T. Milo. Correspondence and translation for heterogeneous data. In *Proc. of the 6th ICDT*, 1997.

[24] S. Cluet, C. Delobel, J. Simon, and K. Smaga. Your mediators need data conversion! In *Proc. of the 1998 ACM SIGMOD Conf.*

[25] C.-C. K. Chang and H. Garcia-Molina. Conjunctive constraint mapping for data translation. In *Proc. of the Third ACM Intl. Conf. on Digital Libraries*, pages 49–58, Pittsburgh, Pa., June 1998.

[26] S. Chaudhuri. Finding nonrecursive envelopes for datalog predicates. In *Proc. of the 12th ACM PODS*, Washingtion, D.C., 1993.

[27] S. Chaudhuri and P. G. Kolaitis. Can datalog be approximated? In *Proc. of the 13rd ACM PODS*, Minneapolis, Minn., 1994.

[28] N. Shivakumar, H. Garcia-Molina, and C. Chekuri. Filtering with approximate predicates. In *Proc. of the 24th VLDB Conf.*, pages 263–274, New York City, USA, 1998. VLDB Endowment, Saratoga, Calif.

[29] K.-L. Tan, C. H. Goh, and B. C. Ooi. On getting some answers quickly, and perhaps more later. In *Proc. of the 15th Intl. Conf. on Data Engineering*, pages 32–39, Sydney, Austrialia, 1999.

[30] V. Poosala and V. Ganti. Fast approximate query answering using precomputed statistics. In *Proc. of the 15th Intl. Conf. on Data Engineering*, page 252, Sydney, Austrialia, 1999. ACM Press, New York.

[31] M. J. Carey and D. Kossmann. On saying "enough already!" in SQL. In *Proc. of the 1997 ACM SIGMOD Conf.*, Tucson, Arizona, 1997.

[32] M. J. Carey and D. Kossmann. Reducing the braking distance of an SQL query engine. In *Proc. of the 24th VLDB Conf.*, pages 158–169, New York City, USA, 1998. VLDB Endowment, Saratoga, Calif.

[33] P. Buneman, S. B. Davidson, and A. Watters. A semantics for complex objects and approximate answers. *Journal of Computer and System Sciences*, 43(1):170–218, Aug. 1991.

[34] W. W. Chu, M. A. Merzbacher, and L. Berkovich. The design and implementation of cobase. In *Proc. of the 1993 ACM SIGMOD Conf.*, pages 517–522, Washington, D.C., 1993. ACM Press, New York.

[35] C. J. V. Rijsbergen. *Information Retrieval, 2nd edition*. Butterworths, London, 1979.

[36] G. Salton. *Automatic Text Processing*. Addison-Wesley, 1989.

[37] A. V. Aho, J. E. Hopcroft, and J. D. Ullman. *The design and analysis of computer algorithms*. Addison-Wesley, Reading, Mass., 1974.

[38] E. J. McCluskey. *Logic Design Principles*. Prentice Hall, 1986.

Design & Development of a Stream Service in a Heterogeneous Client Environment

N. Pappas   S. Christodoulakis

Laboratory of Distributed Multimedia Information Systems and Applications
(MUSIC) - Technical University of Crete (TUC)
E-mail: {nikos, stavros}@ced.tuc.gr

Abstract

Most research in the area of designing and implementing continuous media servers, which support delay-sensitive data like audio and video, has assumed either clients with very small memory sizes for buffering and no secondary storage (thin clients) or a homogeneous client environment where all clients have exactly the same performance characteristics. Both assumptions are radically changing due to the availability of inexpensive storage, as well as the great diversity of clients that exist now and will exist in the future. In this work we look more closely at the implications that the existence of clients with diverse performance characteristics may have in the server design. Our approach is experimental. We use conventional hardware for servers and clients and examine bottlenecks and optimization options systematically, in order to reduce jitter and increase the maximum number of clients that the system can support. We show that the diversity of client performance characteristics can be taken into account, so that all clients are well supported for delay-sensitive retrieval in a heterogeneous environment. We also show that their characteristics can be exploited to maximize server throughput under server memory constrains.

Proceedings of the 26th International Conference on Very Large Databases, Cairo, Egypt, 2000

1   Introduction

In recent years the research community and the computer industry have focused their attention on the management of multimedia data such as audio and video and on the provision of advanced multimedia services in the workplace, at home and on the road. The management of multimedia data and their delivery over telecommunication lines presents difficult problems that arise from the nature of the data. These problems are related to the management of very large volumes of data, high bandwidth requirements for the delivery of data that have to be consumed in output devices on high average rate, and the requirements for small variance in data delivery due to the delay-sensitive nature of the data.

The above problems have drawn research in the areas of storage media ([1], [2]), secondary storage parallelism ([3]-[8]), storage hierarchies ([9]-[12]), scheduling and delay-sensitive data support ([13]-[23]). Some studies focus on the overall system architecture trying to identify server bottlenecks. In environments where clients are thin it has been shown that main memory space requirements are very high and they form a system bottleneck [24]. Recent studies have focused on environments where the clients have enough main memory to buffer significant amount of data during the delivery process, in order to alleviate the load of the server [25]. These studies however are analytical in nature and necessarily treat the clients as if they were uniform. In addition, they can not easily accommodate very significant performance metrics, such as the transmission jitter.

Access to multimedia services through telecommunication lines becomes rapidly widespread and the variety of devices attached to the network extends continuously. A heterogeneous mix of clients varying from very powerful ones with excessive memories, to thinner ones with less CPU, as well as mobile devices receiving video and audio (through newer standards like UMTS (up to 2Mbps) or Bluetooth (up to 20Mbps)), will be the rule rather than the exception. In the future, secondary storage devices of the clients will radically increase their sizes at a low cost, allowing their use for buffering purposes to alleviate server bottleneck.

The work presented in this paper is a first effort to study some of the problems that appear in heterogeneous client environments and the implications to the server architecture. The approach is necessarily experimental since there are too many interdependent parameters involved in the overall system design, which are difficult to model. The experiments involve off-the-shelf hardware components and give a picture of the technology and the design choices as they are now. We show that the diversity of client performance characteristics can be taken into account, so that all clients are well supported for delay-sensitive retrieval in a heterogeneous environment. We also show that their characteristics can be exploited to maximize server throughput under server memory constrains. The results of the study are easily extendible to clusters of workstations acting as multimedia server.

In sec.2 we present the design parameters and we proceed with experiments that were performed on both server and client systems. Sec. 3 is a brief description of the architecture of our stream service where we present the developed scheduling mechanisms and report the experimental results. In the following sections we focus on buffer space requirements in the server (sec.4), we discuss the support of heterogeneous clients and system scalability issues (sec. 5, 6) and finally we summarize our work (sec. 7).

2 Designing the stream service

The development of a multimedia management system relies on a storage subsystem that takes into account the special characteristics of stream data and guarantees real time delivery. In addition, such a multimedia system must be able to control effectively the processing of a large number of different tasks. These tasks include device management, data storage management, and request processing, buffer and transmission management.

The challenge in our development of the stream service was to design a complete scheduling mechanism, that would be capable of guiding and synchronizing the different tasks, while at the same time it would provide real time service guarantees.

Before we proceed presenting the design of the stream service, we analyze the requirements that arise during the operation of such a system experimentally.

2.1 Hardware architecture

The stream service (in the experiments that will follow) runs on an Ultra-1 workstation with two (2) SCSI-2 controllers and four (4) disks (SEAGATE ST51080N), two in each controller. The data is transmitted through an ATM card (Fore SBA-200-155Mbps) over the local ATM network. Experimental clients run on a Sparc-20 and two (2) Sparc-4 workstations connected to the local ATM network (with an ATM switch) and three (3) PCs connected with an Ethernet switch.

2.2 Data transmission & retrieval experiments

We studied the behavior and the capabilities of our transmission server, running several experiments on different machines. The aim of those experiments was to identify the maximum transmission throughput (independently of the stream server) and the processing demands for this task.

We used the UDP/IP protocol stack for the delivery of stream data to client sites. During the experiments the transmission server assumes that the stream data is available in its buffers on time. We used three different workstations that were connected to the local ATM network with the same device.

The experiments showed us that using small UDP packet sizes resulted in reduced performance. Using the maximum packet size the transmission server achieved 56 Mbps on a Sparc-4 machine, using 100% of its processing power. Running the same experiment on a Sparc-20 and Ultra-1 workstation, we monitored throughput 100Mbps with 100% CPU usage and 122 Mbps with 96% CPU usage respectively.

It is obvious from the above that data transmission tasks have high processing demands and that the system throughput depends both on the network infrastructure and the available processing power. Thus, CPU becomes a critical resource and careful scheduling of the execution of different tasks is needed.

Several experiments were also carried out to identify the real capabilities of the storage subsystem that would support the stream service. The experiments showed that the current storage subsystem (4 disks, 2 SCSI controllers) was capable of supporting from 70-90 MPEG-1 (1.5Mbps) clients, varying the retrieval block size from 192KB to 8MB.

The results of all those experiments (transmission and retrieval) were useful, because we were able to compare the performance of the complete system with the performance that each subsystem (I/O, network) could independently achieve with the same hardware configuration, and thus to evaluate the operation of the whole system at various stages of the design.

2.3 Data reception experiments

In this section we describe some experiments that took place using heterogeneous client systems. The aim of those efforts was to identify the requirements that the stream server should satisfy, in order to provide acceptable quality of service at the client side. The experiments that follow were performed on different computers and under diverse conditions. Later in this paper we will see how such experiments can be applicable in a real system as part of a client configuration phase.

We ran the transmission server on an Ultra-1 workstation and we used 7 different packet sizes (1KB-64KB). In the experiment the server starts with the smaller packet and transmits data increasing the rate in steps. In figures 1,2 we present the results we monitored in two different clients (Sparc-20, Ultra-1) that were equipped with the same network devices. During the experiments we recorded the percentage of packet loss relatively with the packet size and the transmission rate.

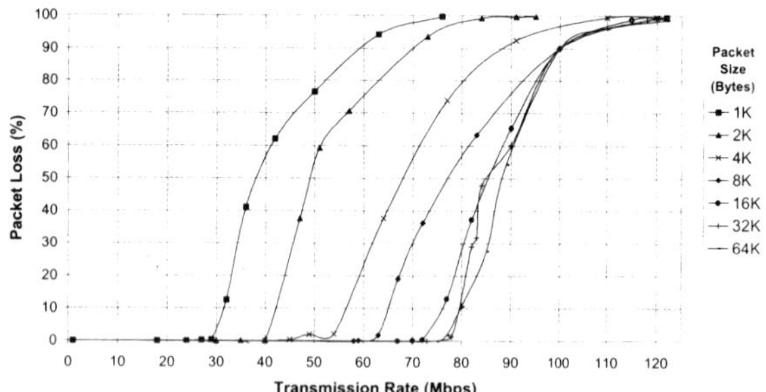

Figure 1: Packet loss (%) vs. transmission rate for various packet sizes (Sparc-20 client, ATM)

Figures 1,2 show that the use of small packets leads to significant packet loss problems. Comparing the two figures we can also observe that the more powerful client (Ultra-1) succeeded in accepting data without losses at higher rates than the Sparc-20 client in all cases.

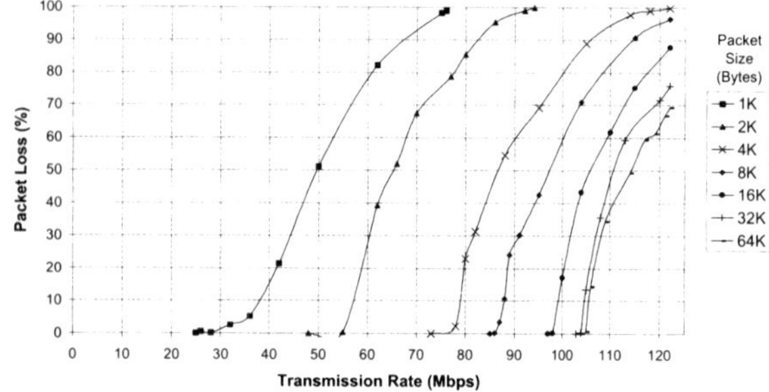

Figure 2: Packet loss (%) vs. transmission rate for various packet sizes (Ultra-1 client, ATM)

Trying to monitor what is happening in a thin client system during data reception activity, we used one PC with Intel Pentium 166 MHz processor, connected through a 10Mbps Ethernet channel with the server (the PC was connected with an Ethernet switch, which was connected to the ATM switch). We forced the server to send data starting at 1Mbps rate and increasing it gradually up to 10Mbps. At the client side, we measured the usage of the CPU and the percentage of packet loss. The results are presented in figure 3 and show that the client faced the problem of packet loss for transmission rates over 4 Mbps. In addition, we observed that high data

arrival rates reserved significant percentage of the CPU time in the client (up to 90% for 9Mbps transmission rate).

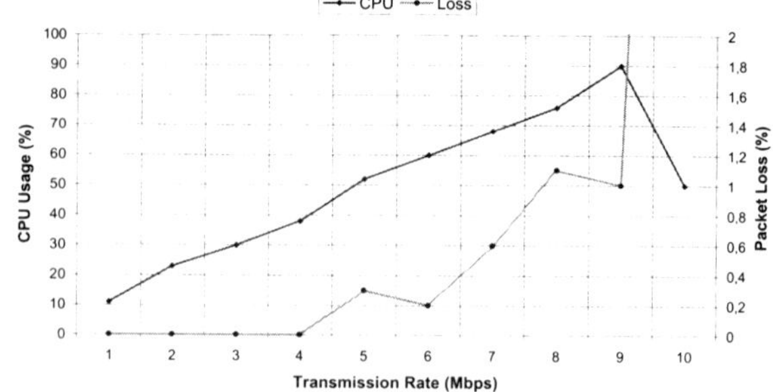

Figure 3: CPU usage and packet loss measurements during data reception (PC client – Intel Pentium Pro 233Mhz, Ethernet)

As it is expected, using a more powerful client system (Intel Pentium II 433Mhz) the data is received without losses at higher rates, while at the same time a much smaller portion of the available processing power of the client is used (figure 4).

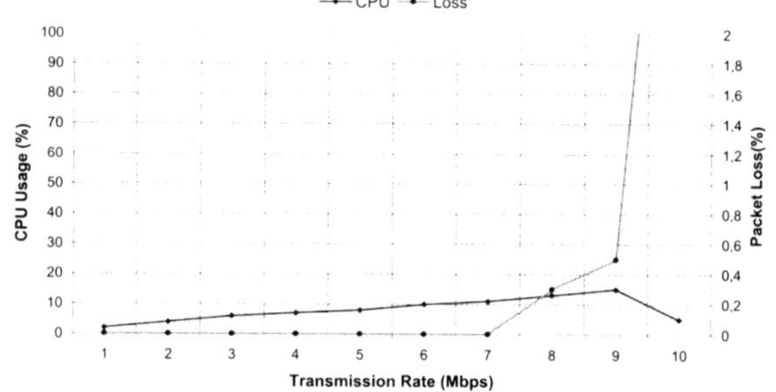

Figure 4: CPU usage and packet loss measurements during data reception (PC client – Intel Pentium II 433Mhz, Ethernet)

In the previous experiments the client's CPU was processing only data reception tasks. In real multimedia applications the client's software is responsible of performing several other tasks.

For example a simple MPEG VoD client subsystem includes software modules for receiving data over the network, storing data in buffers or storage media, decoding the MPEG data and finally displaying them on output devices. Naturally, all these tasks reserve portions of CPU time (especially MPEG decoding, if it is not supported by hardware), affecting the overall client ability in data reception. To prove this, we run a complete client application that accepts data from the server, stores them in a local disk, decodes and displays the requested media. At the same time, we monitor at the client side the display frame rate and the packet loss percentage for different data transmission rates of the server. The results running the client on an Ultra-1 machine are presented in figure 5. As we can see, data transmission rates over 10Mbps result in noticeable display frame rate degradation thus reduced quality of service. From the experimental results we conclude that the data reception tasks are consuming much CPU time. Therefore, a client with a fast network infrastructure must also have increased processing capabilities, in order to accept data at high rates and succeed to perform other necessary jobs simultaneously.

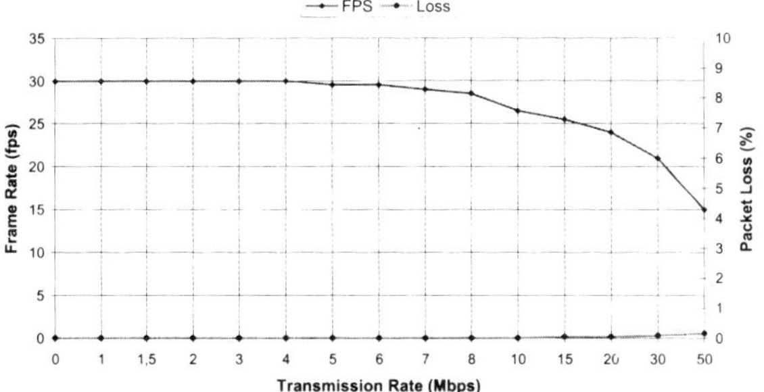

Figure 5: Display frame rate and packet loss (%) vs. transmission rate (Ultra-1 client, ATM)

Since we are interested in supporting heterogeneous client systems we ran the same experiments using different network infrastructure (Ethernet) and client systems (Windows NT, PCs). Figures 6,7 show the results of these experiments using 2 PCs, one Pentium Pro 233Mhz and one Pentium II 433Mhz.

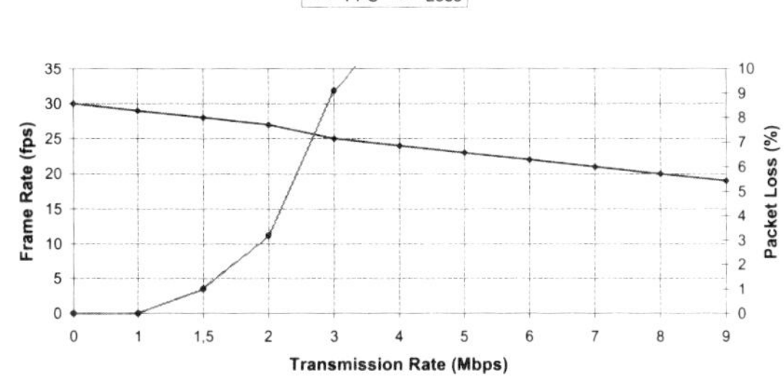

Figure 6: Display frame rate and packet loss (%) vs. transmission rate (PC client-Pentium Pro 233Mhz, Ethernet)

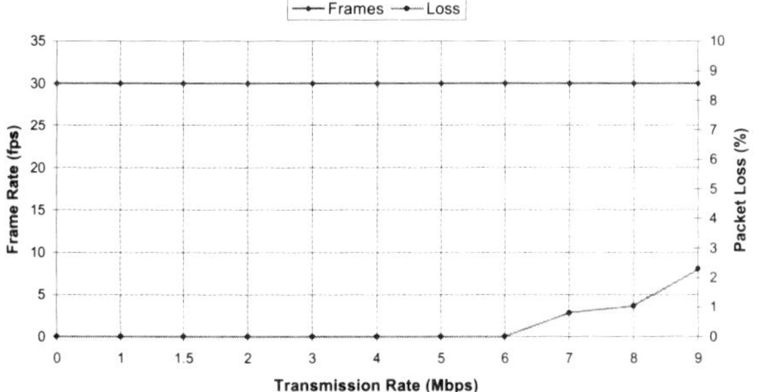

Figure 7: Display frame rate and packet loss (%) vs. transmission rate (PC client - Pentium II 433Mhz, Ethernet)

The first client faced difficulties while it was trying to display the video object and at the same time receive the video data at 1.5 Mbps. When we forced the server to send data at higher rates we observed noticeable reduction at presentation frame rate and substantial increase in packet losses. On the contrary, in the second client we did not monitor any changes in display frame rate even at high transmission rates. Studying the graphs we can conclude that clients with smaller CPU power (figure 6) need special attention by the server, since they require stable data rate transmission with low jitter in order to receive services at satisfactory levels.

On the other hand, powerful clients (figure 7) that can accept and store data at high rates can be exploited by the server for better results, as we describe later.

3   The system architecture

In order to develop a high performance system, such as the stream service, the choice of the software development tools and techniques is an important and substantial factor. Based on our previous experience in system development ([24], [25], [26]), we wanted to avoid the existence of many processes, which can lead in excessive IPC overhead and implement an immediate data flow path through the subsystems. Having the above in mind and trying to exploit the benefits of the multithreading technology we present the architectural design of the stream service.

The basic tasks that the stream service must take care and are logically independent are the following. (1) The request management task is the input gate of the system. Tasks such message acceptance, decoding, and storing in appropriate data structures are included in this category. (2) Every new service that a new client requests from the system forms a different new task. (3) Another independent category of tasks is associated with the storage media. It is obvious that the operation of a disk drive can be viewed as an autonomous execution flow or in other words the management of a disk drive resembles of a micro-server. (4) Finally one more task that must be handled by the stream service is the data transmission to the client sites. The existence of a central software scheduler module is necessary for managing the access to critical resources, synchronizing multiple storage media and defining the timing execution order of different system tasks. If we map each one of the different tasks that we mentioned above with an independent execution flow, thus with a different thread, we have the first step in our multithreading design that is graphically showed in figure 8. Each ellipse in the figure corresponds to an independent thread of execution. Next we briefly describe the responsibilities of each thread.

Stream Service Interface: This thread is the front end of the stream service. It is permanently at a waiting stage to accept, decode new messages from clients and exchange information with them.

Main Scheduler: The scheduler thread holds the responsibility of central processing for request execution scheduling. It gathers the necessary information from the appropriate subsystems, checks the ability of the system to serve new requests and is always informed about the status of each request service. Whenever a new request must be processed, the main scheduler fires a new thread

(Process Request Thread), which works independently and returns the results to the scheduler.

RT-Controller: The real-time controller is a special thread that aims to provide timing information to internal modules of the system. The RT-Controller periodically and in small intervals takes time stamps from the system clock and drives the scheduling, synchronizes the storage media and guides the operation of the transmission server (Xmt-Server).

D-Servers: Each one of these threads is responsible of managing the operation of one disk drive. The disk server thread (D-Server) reads the appropriate disk sub-requests, executes them and transfers the retrieved data to the system buffer.

Xmt-Server: This server thread with the appropriate scheduling mechanism takes over the transmission of stream data over the network to the clients that requested service. The scheduling mechanism that must be applied to the transmission of packets is a critical factor for the overall system performance.

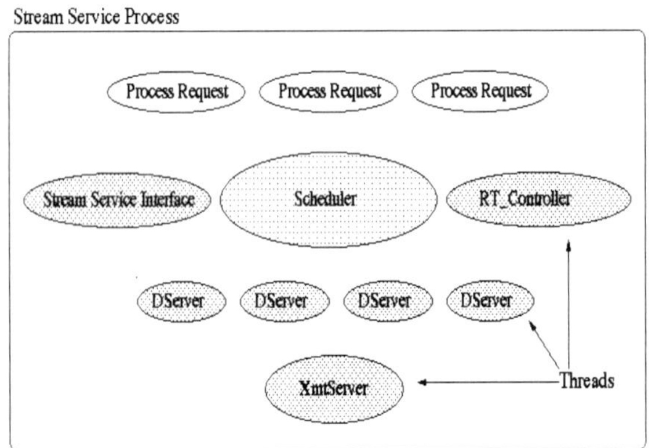

Figure 8: Threads executing different tasks in the stream service

The next step in the design is the attentive tuning and the appropriate synchronization of thread execution. For example the response of each thread must be within certain time limits, depending on how critical the execution of each task is for the system performance.

3.1 The scheduling mechanism for data retrieval

The scheduling mechanism that was developed for stream retrieval implements a scheme of servicing requests in rounds. This technique is often used and follows the periodic nature of stream data. In each service round, data blocks for each stream are retrieved from storage devices and are transmitted over the network to clients.

The RT-Controller thread continuously watches the system clock and helps in keeping the system rounds accurate. The main scheduler determines the tasks that must be performed during a service round, processes all active streams and produces the appropriate disk retrieval subrequests. These subrequests are written in a special memory space shared among the threads that is called DSR-Channel (D-Server Request channel). The system

round is stable and common for all D-Servers. For performance reasons we store the stream data in such a way so that each data block (that must be retrieved in one round) is stored physically in contiguous storage. The above model of retrieval operation is graphically presented in figure 9 and is an open approach since the appropriate data placement and scheduler operation allows the easy application of both coarse and fine striping techniques, as well as priority and prefetching schemes.

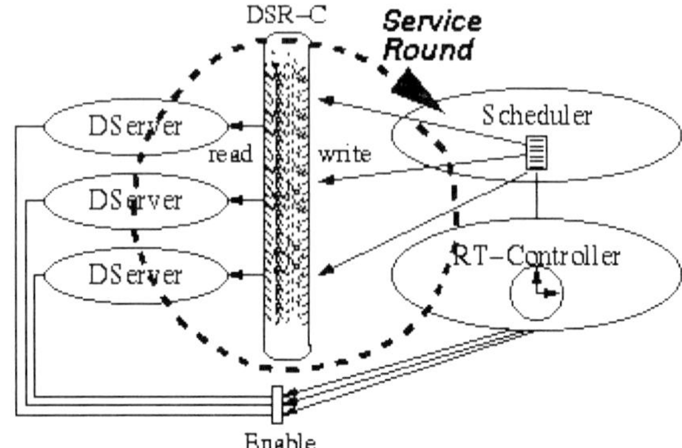

Figure 9: The scheduling mechanism of data retrieval

3.2 The scheduling mechanism for stream data transmission

One of the most important goals of a stream server is to provide quality of service, and at the same time to maximize its throughput. Therefore, the task of delivering the retrieved stream data to clients is critical since it immediately affects the way each client is served.

For the experiments that follow in this section, we isolated the storage subsystem (supposing that data retrieval is done on time) and focused on the transmission subsystem, trying to apply different scheduling policies for packet transmission and to monitor the results at the client side.

We assume that several MPEG1 video streams (CBR-1.5Mbps) are stored (in data blocks of 192Kbytes) in the server, which is running on an Ultra-1 machine connected to the local ATM network. For the delivery of data the server sends each retrieved block continuously in FIFO order (among the blocks), using 48KB packets. During the experiment we monitored the first client (Sparc-20, ATM) that requested a video playback and we measured the data arrival rate, while at the same time new clients were inserted in the system. The results are shown in figure 10 and as we can see the monitored client is served poorly, since the measured data arrival rate is below the expected one for satisfactory service. The obvious reason for this is that due to bursty transmission of data blocks, the client faces a great amount of packet losses.

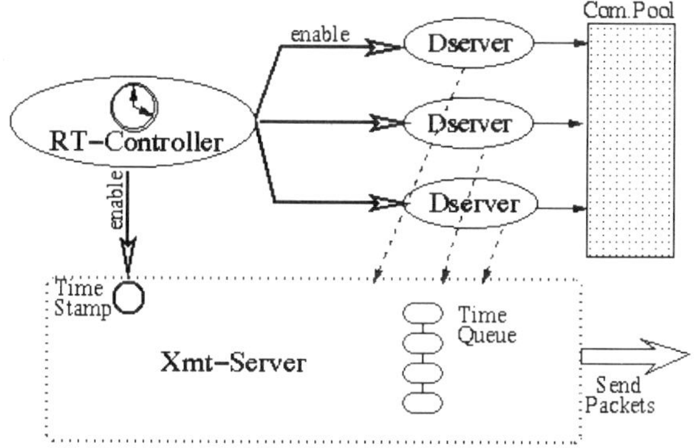

Figure 10: The scheduling mechanism of data transmission

Trying to improve the service of clients, we apply the EDF scheduling policy in the transmission process. A deadline is dynamically assigned to each new packet, based on the bite rate that each client must receive data (in this experiment we assume 1.5Mbps for all clients). The transmission server multiplexes data packets for different clients and keeps a deadline queue sending each time the packet with the earliest deadline that is available.

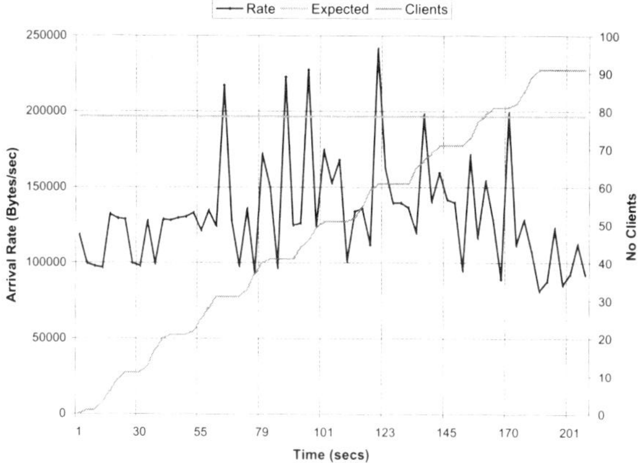

Figure 11: Arrival data rate at first client vs number of active clients in server (Scheduling scheme: transmission of data blocks in FIFO order)

We repeated the experiment by applying the EDF policy and from figure 11 we conclude that multiplexing and prioritizing the stream packets during transmission gives better service to the clients. This is due to the fact that packet multiplexing creates delays in the transmission of successive packets for the same client resulting in a more smooth arrival rate. However it is worth noticing that when the number of clients that are served by the system is small, these delays are not enough, so we face again packet loss problems.

Defining jitter as the variations of the packet arrival times from the expected ones for smooth transmission rate, we graph the jitter measured at the client side during the same experiment (figure 12). From this graph we observe that the transmission jitter is reducing as new clients are inserted in the system.

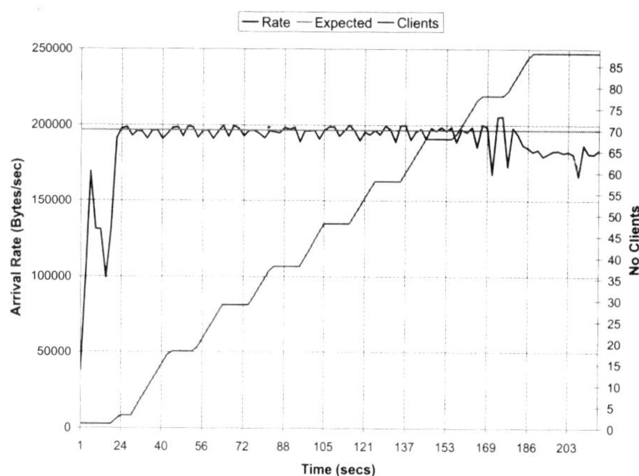

Figure 12: Arrival data rate at first client vs. number of active clients in server (Scheduling scheme: transmission of data packets with the EDF policy)

Taking into account the above results and those from the transmission experiments that we performed in heterogeneous clients, we conclude that the stream server should transmit the data to each client with specific maximum rate, which depends on the hardware configuration and the processing power of the clients.

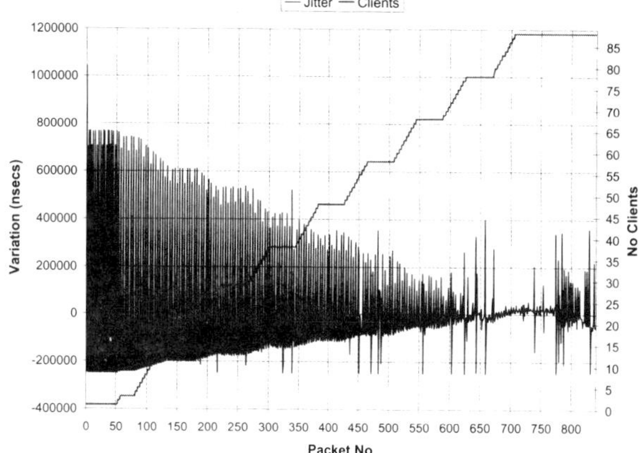

Figure 13: Transmission jitter monitored at first client side (Scheduling scheme: transmission of data packets with the EDF policy)

Figure 13 describes how the transmission of stream data is performed in the server. The scheduling mechanism is a non work-conserving approach. Each time a new stream block is retrieved in the buffer (Communication Pool), the D-Servers inform the Xmt-Server that new data is available for delivery. The Xmt-Server forms the transmission packets (each client may accept different packet sizes) and assigns the appropriate deadlines. The RT-Controller periodically enables the execution of Dservers with period the service round. In subdivisions of this round, the RT-Controller continuously takes time stamps and informs the Xmt-Server about the current time. A deadline queue (a min-heap tree) is maintained. The nodes of the tree point to data packets. The Xmt-Server starts sending the packets, the deadlines of which are near to the current time. When the deadline of the next packet is far enough that can be serviced in the next subround, it blocks its execution and waits the RT-Controller to wake it up with the next time stamp.

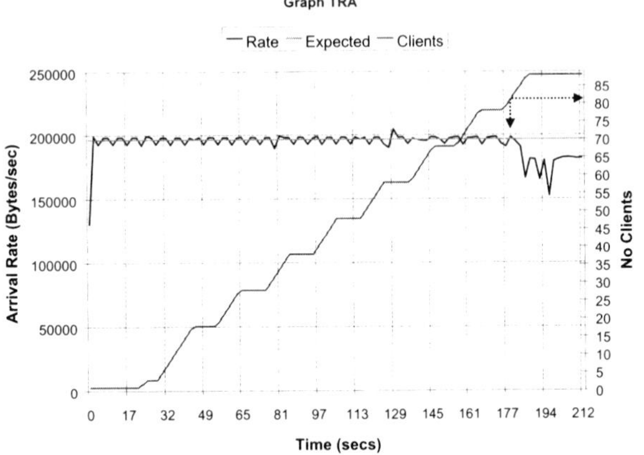

Figure 14: Arrival data rate at first client vs. number of active clients in server

With this technique we exploit the benefits of multiplexing different stream packets, while at the same time we insert delays when this is necessary. The application of the above mechanism leads to stable transmission rates with low jitter, as it is shown in the next experiment, and the mechanism was embodied in the stream server. We ran the transmission server with the new scheduling scheme and we measured (at the first client) the arrival rate, which was near the expected one without any packet loss problems. From figure 14, it can be seen that the maximum throughput of the transmission server is 81 clients (121.5 Mbps), which approximates the maximum transmission throughput (122 Mbps) of the system measured in the experiments in section 2.2.

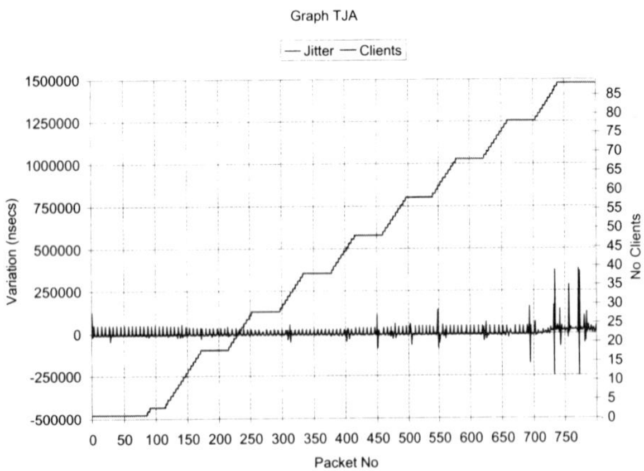

Figure 15: Transmission jitter monitored at first client side

The graph in figure 15 shows that the application of our transmission mechanism led to low jitter even under heavy load conditions. This has a positive impact to clients resulting in satisfactory service quality without packet loss problems.

The previous experimental results showed that this transmission mechanism is capable of supporting the delivery of multiple data streams by properly adjusting the transmission rate to network and client capabilities, if they are known.

3.3 The complete system architecture

In sections 3.1 and 3.2 we presented the scheduling mechanisms of data retrieval and transmission. In figure 16 is shown the complete multi-threaded architecture of the stream service with all the task threads, the software modules that support them, as well as the way they interact and cooperate with each other.

The stream service interface thread accepts the requests and stores them in a waiting queue. The scheduler (through the executor module) fires threads to process new requests and the processed results are returned back to the scheduler's appropriate table (processed request table). The scheduler keeps the necessary information for request service (active streams table) and is supported by several managers and the stream storage system (which manages the storage of streams in disks and maintains the necessary indexing information). Finally the RT-Controller drives the operation of the D-Servers and the Xmt-Server proceeding in time rounds.

Several experiments were performed using the architecture shown below that are not presented here due to lack of space. Although the results were satisfactory at the client side, the overall system performance appeared reduced, compared to the performance that the transmission and storage subsystems achieved independently. It is obvious that the combination of all tasks running in real conditions was not optimal and possibly time critical tasks were being delayed by other non-critical. We have made an effort to overcome such problems by fine-tuning the system design, focusing in thread scheduling and real time response of critical tasks.

3.4 Improving system performance

The first step in trying to fine tune the stream service, was to assign priorities to threads dynamically. Two levels of priorities were used, one low priority level which indicates that the current thread is not as critical, and a high one which indicates that the fast processing of the thread is important for system performance.

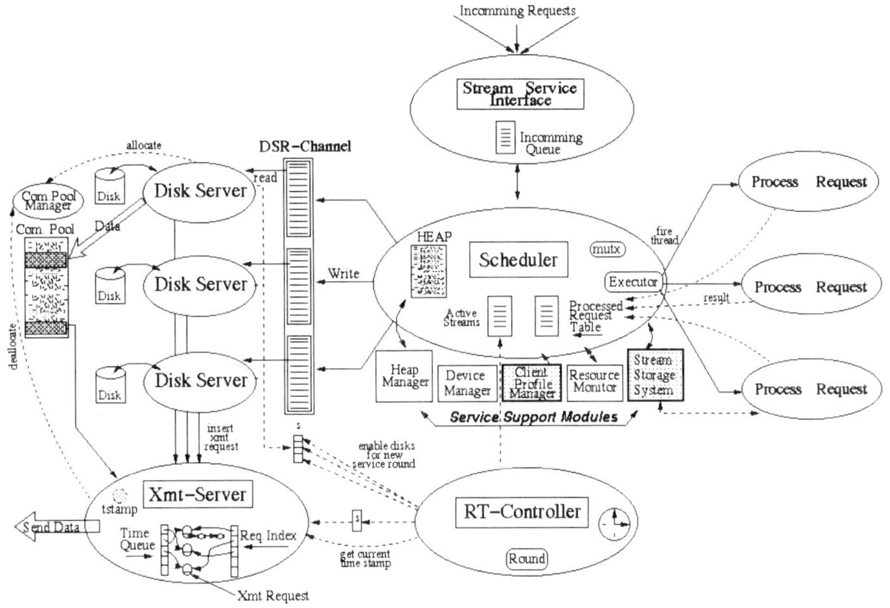

Figure 16: The complete architecture of the stream service

A high priority thread is favored by the operating system during the reservation of an available lightweight process (LWP) in the kernel (a LWP can be considered as a bridge between user-level and kernel level threads). But this is not enough, especially when we have to deal with time critical tasks such as packet transmission and retrieval of stream data. These tasks should have special treatment at kernel level for better results. In order to achieve this goal we tried to exploit the real time services of the Solaris 2.x operating system, on which we developed the stream service. The Solaris operating system permits privileged users to run their processes in the real-time (RT) scheduling class and thus have the highest possible software dispatch priority in the system (even higher than the system tasks), and at the same time the OS guarantees bounded dispatch latency for RT processes. This fact is very important and it helped us to built a stream server capable of providing real time service guaranties.

Figure 17 shows in more detail the changes that took place to exploit the real-time benefits of the OS. Time critical threads (RT-Controller, Dservers, Xmt-Server) were bounded to a LWP for exclusive use. By doing this, it was possible to change the scheduling class of the bounded threads to the RT class. As we can see in the figure, the scheduling of critical threads is now performed at the kernel level with high priority, while the rest of the threads remain under the applied user-level scheduling scheme. Proper synchronization techniques and blockage for system service prevent RT threads from monopolizing the CPU resource.

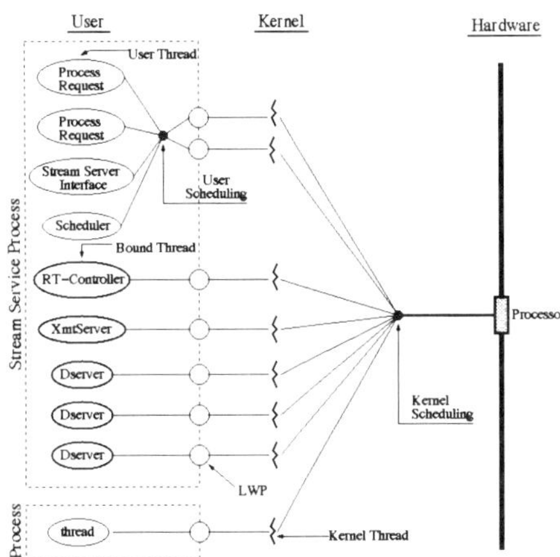

Figure 17: The thread-scheduling scheme applied in the stream service

By running experiments with the new complete system (all subsystems active), we had encouraging results. Figure 18,19 show the arrival rate of stream data and the monitored jitter in the first client, while new clients were continuously inserted in the system. The stream server succeeds to serve 70 clients, since the storage subsystem appeared to be the bottleneck with the current experiment configuration (with a data retrieval block size of 192KB).

One of the interesting characteristics of the system was that it experimentally proved to have also the same performance under heavily loaded processing conditions (running at the same time other CPU consuming processes together with the stream server). This fact drives us to the conclusion that the system is capable of providing real time service guarantees.

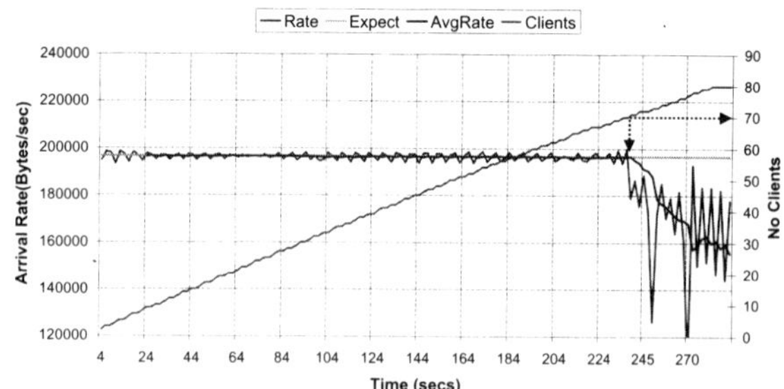

Figure 18: Arrival data rate at first client side using the complete system vs the number of active clients in server

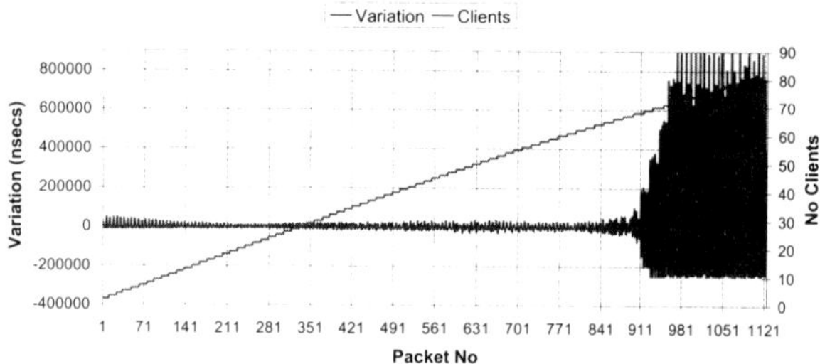

Figure 19: Transmission jitter monitored at first client side running the complete system

The same experiments were run many times for other random users (not only the first), in order to check that service quality was stable for all clients, and all gave similar results.

4 Buffer Space Requirements

In the development of the stream service we embodied a well-known and widely accepted scheduling scheme for disk data retrieval in which the service of streams is performed in rounds and in each round the SCAN policy is applied in order to minimize disk seek overhead.

Memory management is an important issue in stream server operation [CM97]. Assuming that S bytes are retrieved for each stream in each round, eventually we need the double buffer space (2S) due to the round-SCAN scheme. Thus, the stream server in order to serve N clients should reserve 2NS space using a double buffering scheme.

On the other hand in order to improve the storage media performance to approach maximum device throughput, we have to use very large retrieval data block sizes. This method, as expected, leads to excessive memory space requirements. Thus, the system designers are often forced to under-utilize the storage subsystem, in order to reduce the buffering demands.

In the previous experiments we used a retrieval block size of 192KB and system round 1sec. If we run the server with the same configuration, inserting gradually up to 70 clients, and we measure the space that is dynamically reserved during the experiment we will see that the highest values (bytes of memory reserved) are equal to

26.25MB (2NS) that corresponds to the double buffering scheme. If we increase the block size to 1MB, in order to improve the performance of the storage subsystem so as to serve 80 clients, the server will need 160MB of buffer space. Following the same technique if we want to fully exploit our storage subsystem and support 90 clients we have to use 8MB block size, resulting in memory requirements of 1440MB.

The allocation-deallocation scheme that is used in our system to manage the buffer space is presented graphically in figure 20 (steps 1-5).

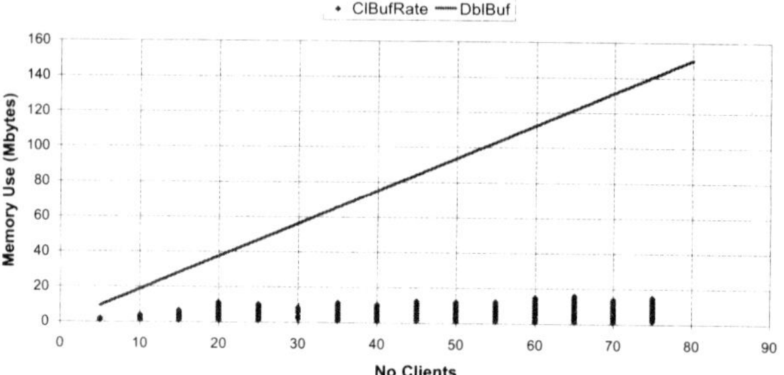

Figure 20: Buffer space reservation measurements using double buffering scheme (DblBuf) or exploiting the client capabilities (ClBufRate)

One solution to reduce the memory size needed is to exploit the buffering and data reception capabilities of powerful clients. Due to the round-SCAN scheme, the transmission of the first block is delayed (in the server) until the end of the current round. Instead of forcing the server to buffer and delay the transmission, we could send immediately the first block and force the client to buffer the data and delay the presentation of media. It is easily understood that this action could save half of the buffer space at the server side. If we also assume that a set of powerful clients is available, which can receive data with high transmission rates without problems, then the server can take advantage of it by sending the available data to clients with the maximum rate. Thus, it would succeed to free space in buffers faster than the normal scheduling scheme. We experimentally proved that the above technique leads to drastic reduction of memory space requirements (figure 21, ClBufRate). In the experiment we used data block size 1MB and we assumed that a set of powerful ATM clients able to receive data at 100Mbps were available. The experimental results show that the system accomplished to serve up to 79 clients with less than 20MB of buffer space. The stream server in this experiment exploited 100% of the CPU, 97,13% of the network equipment and 87,7% of the storage subsystem, according to performance values we recorded from independent tests to each subsystem (section 2.2). This is an encouraging result, since it shows that the integrated system schedules many tasks efficiently and succeeds to approximate the maximum throughput that the physical configuration allows.

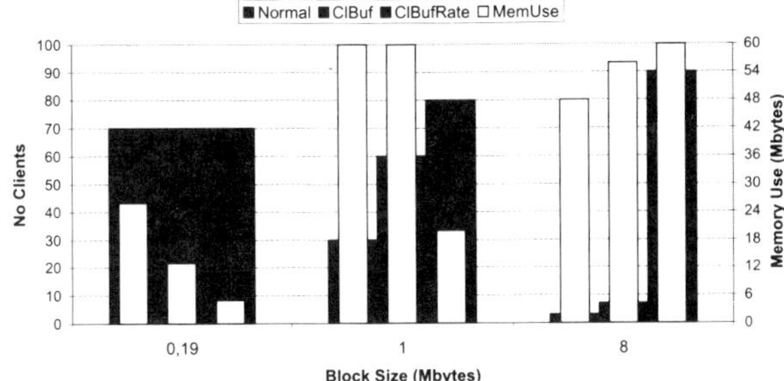

Figure 21: System throughput comparison under limited buffer space (60MB) and different scheduling approaches (Normal, ClBuf, ClBufRate)

Assuming that we solved the CPU and network bottleneck (by using a faster or multiprocessing machine and additional network cards), we ran an experiment using 60MB of buffer size and three different versions of servers. One that follows the normal round-SCAN scheduling scheme (Normal), one that exploits client's buffer space capabilities (ClBuf) by forcing it to delay the presentation of the first block and one that exploits both buffer space and data reception capabilities of powerful clients (ClBufRate).

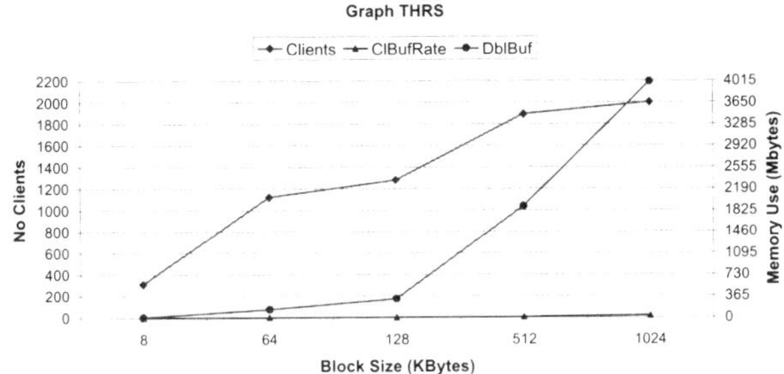

Figure 22: Number of audio clients supported for various retrieval block sizes and memory space requirements using double buffering or exploiting client capabilities

In figure 22 we compare the three schemes and observe large performance variations when we increase the retrieval block size. From the figure it becomes evident that the last technique maximizes system throughput since it significantly reduces the memory size requirements.

In fact the first two approaches (normal, ClBuf) result in system throughput reduction due to the memory space constrains. On the contrary, the last technique (ClBufRate) presents high performance, since it exploits the increase in storage device throughput (large blocks), by reducing the buffer space requirements.

The memory requirements are significantly increased when we have to deal with audio clients. In this case the stream data demands are reduced but the system has to support a much greater number of clients. Trying to utilize the storage devices, the memory space requirements grow rapidly to unacceptable sizes for conventional server machines (DblBuf line, figure 23). If we assume that a set of clients (capable of receiving data

at 10Mbps max) is available, then the stream server can apply the same technique previously described to reduce memory space demands by exploiting their capabilities. In figure 23 is shown experimentally that the stream server (ClBufRate) succeeded in supporting 2000 audio clients (64Kbps) using extremely low buffer space, compared to the normal approach (DblBuf) that would need several Gbytes of memory for the same task.

5 Supporting heterogeneous clients

One of the conclusions of the work we presented so far is that heterogeneous clients have different demands and the scheduler of the stream server must be informed of client configuration and processing capabilities, in order to serve properly thin clients and exploit powerful ones.

The first step in the effort to support many clients efficiently is to collect the characteristics of clients that wish access to the server.

We could face the following cases: (1) clients with large memory capacity (disks or buffers), (2) clients with small buffer space, (3) clients with different network hardware, and (4) clients with different processing power.

According to the experimental results, the server must send the data packets with a maximum rate specific for each client; otherwise the possibility of packet losses is increased. It is obvious that the system scheduler must be aware of these rates for all the clients it serves.

This can be accomplished if each client that wishes to be serviced downloads a small application and runs it locally. Through this application the user inserts the hardware characteristics of his system and asks the server for registration. A special thread is fired at the server side and takes over the client configuration process. During this process small tests are ran to identify the reception capabilities of the new client in real conditions. All the necessary info, which is gathered during configuration, is stored in the client profile manager (figure 13).

The client profile manager helps the scheduler to drive properly the stream data retrieval and transmission process for each client, through the scheduling mechanisms we described in this paper (section3.2).

The knowledge of client characteristics gives also the opportunity to the server to decide whether is going to apply prefetching mechanisms or techniques to reduce the buffer requirements, with main goal to maximize its throughput.

6 Scalability

Multimedia servers must be developed to be flexible and independent from resource limits, so that can guarantee scalability, while keeping the response times, availability and reliability within satisfactory levels.

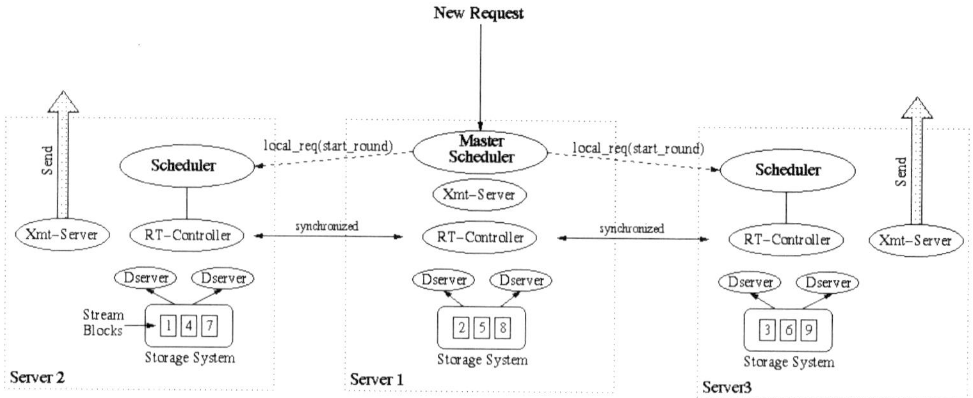

Figure 23: An example of scaling stream service using a cluster of three servers

The multithreaded design of the stream service that was presented in this paper gives the capability of effective system scaling after the addition of new resources (new disks, CPUs, network devices). The scaling of the server in shared-memory multiprocessing environments is straightforward, since the addition of new storage media or network devices can be handled by new threads that will run on different processors.

The system is also able to scale over a distributed environment, using a cluster of workstations. On each machine we can run an instance of the stream service. In such a scheme we can use replication techniques or we can apply striping methods on network level to achieve load balancing across server nodes.

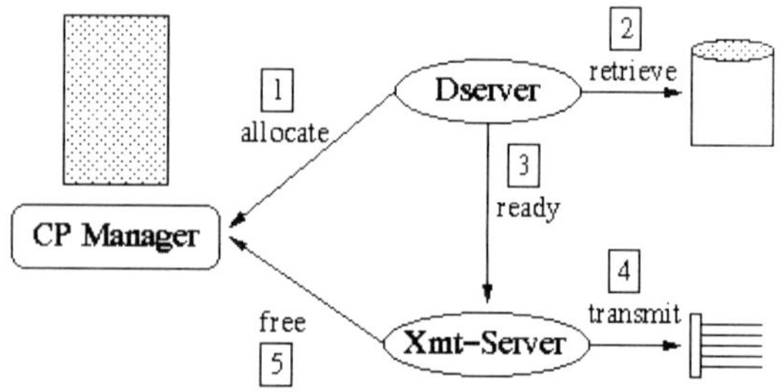

Figure 24: Allocation and deallocation of space in CP during system operation

The architecture of the system uses the RT-Controller thread, which is responsible for providing timing information that drives the system operation. By synchronizing these threads of the different server nodes over the network (using existing network time synchronization protocols), each node can operate independently without the overhead of passing media data to other nodes or circulating synchronization messages, as we see in other approaches in the literature. In figure 24 we present graphically an example of scaling the system using a cluster of three servers. If we assume that a stream object is stored striped across the servers in round-robin manner, then each node can operate independently retrieving and transmitting the stream data at the proper intervals (based on the assumption that the server nodes are accurately synchronized). Some preliminary experiments that were performed using the above schema of multiple servers, produced encouraging results. More experimentation and research on this scalable schema is in our future plans.

7   Summary and conclusions

In this paper we presented the process of designing and developing a real stream server system, which is capable of providing stream services to a great number of clients.

We have tried to identify the impact that the need of supporting heterogeneous clients would impose on server system design. We performed a large number of experiments both at client and server side, using different hardware, configurations and conditions. Thin clients with limited processing capabilities and small buffer capacities, need an attentive data delivery with the appropriate rate and low jitter, in order to be serviced with acceptable quality. On the other hand, the existence of clients with large storage capabilities, fast network equipment and powerful processors can be exploited by the server in order to reduce the internal memory demands, utilize the storage subsystem and maximize its throughput. Thus, the server should be informed about the profiles of the clients.

Experiments showed that data transmission needs increased processing power, so CPU becomes a critical resource and careful scheduling of task execution is necessary.

Finally, we described the design and the process of developing of the stream service, and tested experimentally the performance of the embedded complete scheduling mechanism that have the following characteristics:

- Exploit the multithreading technology and real time services of the OS
- Synchronize the execution of different tasks from the retrieval to data transmission

- Drive the transmission server for supporting multiple data streams over network with the appropriate rate and low jitter.
- Provide real time service guarantees
- Experimentally achieve the maximum performance that the system configuration and the hardware limits allow
- Change their scheduling strategy based on the characteristics of their client mixes, in order to serve heterogeneous client environment
- Exploit client capabilities in order to reduce buffer space demands
- Have the ability to scale using cluster of servers

Summarizing, we believe that as the diversity of devices that are attached to the network increases, proper execution of a stream service demands knowledge of the configuration and the processing power of the clients. The client profile information can be used to optimise the throughput of the server. Considerably more work is needed in this area for supporting the great variety of clients and networks that will be attached to the network in the future.

8 References

[1] Reummler, C. and Wilkes, J. "An Introduction to Disk Drive Modeling". *IEEE Computer* 27(3): 17-28, 1994.

[2] Ghandeharizadeh, S., Stone, J. and Zimmermann, R. "Techniques to Quantify SCSI-2 Disk Subsystem Specifications for Multimedia", *Technical Report* USC-CS-TR95-610, University of Southern California, 1995.

[3] Tobagi, F.A., et. al. "Streaming RAID: A Disk Array Management System for Video Files", In *Proceedings of the ACM Conference on Multimedia*, August 1993.

[4] Berson, S., Muntz, R., Ghandeharizadeh, S. and Ju, X. "Staggered Striping in Multimedia Information System", In *Proceedings of the SIGMOD Conference*, May 1994.

[5] Vin, H.M., Shenoy, P. and Rao, S. "Analyzing the Performane of Asychronous Disk Arrays for Multimedia Retrieval". In *Proceedings of the 1ˢᵗ ISMM International Conference on Distributed Multimedia Systems and Applications*, August 1994.

[6] Ghandeharizadeh, S. and Kim Seon H. "Striping in Multi-Disk Video Servers", In *Proceedings of High-Density Data Recording and Retrieval Technologies SPIE Vol. 2604*, October 1995.

[7] Oezden, B., Rastogi, R. and Silberschatz, A. "Disk Striping in Video Server Environments", In *Proceedings of the IEEE International Conference on Multimedia Computing and Systems (ICMCS)*, June 1996.

[8] Scheuermann P., Weikum, G., Zabback, P. "Data Partitioning and Load Balancing in Parallel Disk Systems", *VLDB Journal* 7(1):48-66, 1998.

[9] Golubchik, L., Muntz, R., Watson, R.W. "Analysis of Striping Techniques in Robotic Storage Libraries", In *Proceedings of the 14ᵗʰ IEEE Symposium on Mass Storage Systems*, November 1994.

[10] Ghandeharizadeh, S. and Shahabi, C. "Personal Computers and Hierarchical Storage Systems", On Multimedia Repositories, *In Proceedings of the ACM Multimedia Conference*, 1994.

[11] Kienzle, M.G., Dan, A., Sitaram, D., and Tetzall, W. "Using Tertiary Storage in Video-on-Demand Servers", *COMPCON'95 Digest of Papers*, IEEE-CS, 1995.

[12] Christodoulakis, S., Triantafillou, P., Zioga, F. "Principles of Optimally Placing Data in Tertiary Storage Libraries", In *Proceedings of the 23ʳᵈ International Conference on Very Large Data Bases*, August 1997.

[13] Gemmell, D., Christodoulakis, S. "Principles of Delay Sensitive Multimedia Data Storage Servers", *ACM Transactions on Information Systems* 10(1): 51-90, 1992.

[14] Vin, H.M., Rangan, P.V. "Designing a Multi-User HDTV Storage Server", *IEEE Journal on Selected Areas in Communications* 11(1), 1993.

[15] Gemmell, D., Han, J., Beaton, R.J., Christodoulakis, S. "Delay-Sensitive Multimedia on Disks", *IEEE Multimedia* 1(3): 56-67, 1994.

[16] Gemmell, J. and Han, J. "Multimedia Network File Servers: Multi-channel Delay Sensitive Data Retrieval", *Multimedia Systems* 1(6):240-252, 1994.

[17] Gemmell, J., et. al. "Multimedia Storage Servers: A Tutorial", *IEEE Computer* 28(5): 40-49, 1995.

[18] Oezden, B., Rastogi, R. and Silberschatz, A. "On the design of a low-cost video-on-demand storage system", *Multimedia Systems* 4(1): 40-54, 1996.

[19] Bolosky, W.J., et. al. "The Tiger Video Fileserver", In *Proceedings of the 6ᵗʰ International Workshop on Network and Operating Systems Support for Digital Audio and Video (NOSSDAV)*, April 1996.

[20] Gemmell, J. "Disk Scheduling for Continuous Media", *Multimedia Information Storage and Management*, S.M. Chung, Ed., Kluwer Academic Publishers, Boston 1996.

[21] Shenoy, P.J., Goyal, P., Rao, S.S., Vin, H. "Symphony: An Integrated Multimedia File System", In *Proceedings of SPIE/ACM Conference on Multimedia Computing & Networking (MMCN)*, 124-138, 1998.

[22] Zimmerman, R., Ghandeharizadeh, S. "Continuous Display Using Heterogeneous Disk Subsystems", In *Electronic Proceedings ACM Multimedia*, 1997.

[23] Johnson, T.V., Zhang, A. "Dynamic Playout Scheduling Algorithms for Continuous Multimedia Streams". *Multimedia Systems* 7(4): 312-325, 1999.

[24] Chang, E., Garcia-Molina, H. "Effective Memory Use in a Media Server", In *Proceedings of the 23ʳᵈ International Conference on Very Large Data Bases*, 496-505, 1997.

[25] Christodoulakis, S. and Zioga, F. "Data Base Design Principles for Placement of Delay-Sensitive Data on Disks", *IEEE Transactions on Knowledge and Data Engineering* 11(3): 425-447, 1999.

[26] Christodoulakis, S., Pappas, N. et. al. "The KYDONIA multimedia information server". In *Proceedings of the European Conference on Multimedia Applications Services and Techniques (ECMAST)*, May 1997.

[27] Mavraganis, Y., Maragoudakis, Y., Pappas, N., Kyriakaki, G. "The SICMA multimedia server and the virtual museum application", In *Proc. of the European Conf. on Multimedia Applications Services & Techniques*, 1998.

[28] Maragoudakis, Y., Mavraganis, Y., Meyer, K., Pappas, N. "The SICMA Teleteaching Trial on ADSL and Intranet network". In *Proc. of the 4ᵗʰ European Con.e on Multimedia Applications Services & Techniques*, 1999.

SemanticAccess: Semantic Interface for Querying Databases

Naphtali Rishe
Shu-Ching Chen
Alexander Vaschillo

Jun Yuan
Xiaoling Lu
Artyom Shaposhnikov

Rukshan Athauda
Xiaobin Ma
Dmitry Vasilevsky

High-performance Database Research Center
School of Computer Science
Florida International University
University Park, Miami, FL 33199
USA
{rishen, yuanj, rathau01, chens, lu01, ma01, avasch01, shaposhn, dvasil01}@cs.fiu.edu

Abstract

Semantic Binary Object-oriented Data Model (Sem-ODM) provides an expressive data model (similar to Object-oriented Data Models) with a well-known declarative query facility - SQL (similar to relational databases). Advantages of using Sem-ODM include (i.) friendlier and more intelligent generic user interfaces; (ii.) comprehensive enforcement of integrity constraints; (iii.) greater flexibility; (iv.) substantially shorter application programs; and (v.) easier query facility. SemanticAccess is a set of tools developed to provide a semantic interface to Semantic Binary Object-oriented Databases (Sem-ODB) as well as relational databases. This presentation focuses on the system architecture of SemanticAccess including Semantic Binary Object-oriented Data Model, Semantic SQL query language, Semantic Binary Database and a wrapper developed for relational databases.

Proceedings of the 26th International Conference on Very Large Databases, Cairo, Egypt, 2000

1. Purpose

Semantic Binary Object-Oriented Data Model (Sem - ODM) [4] combines the advantages of relational and object-oriented data models. Sem-ODM provides expressive data modeling capabilities, similar to object-oriented data model, but also has the simplicity of constructs similar to relational data model (which provides only one construct, namely *table*). Sem-ODM consists of *category*, which may be inherited and *relation*, which is a relationship between categories. Detailed discussion on Sem-ODM can be found in [4]. One of the major advantages contributing to relational databases' success is the standard query language, SQL, which is declarative in nature. Object-Oriented Database (OODB) query languages are usually correlated with an Object-Oriented Programming Language (OOPL) [1] and/or are procedural in nature [3]. We have adapted SQL (SQL-92) for Sem-ODM (called Semantic SQL), thus providing a well-known declarative query language for Sem-ODM. We, at HPDRC [8], have developed a fully functional Semantic Binary Object-Oriented Database System (Sem-ODB). Due to the above-mentioned features, Sem-ODB has many advantages including friendlier and more intelligent generic user interfaces, comprehensive enforcement of integrity constraints, greater flexibility, substantially shorter application programs and easier query facility. We have been able to successfully deploy Sem-ODB for non-traditional applications such as Geographic Information System (GIS) [2] at the NASA Regional Application Center at Florida International

University. In order to propagate the advantages of Sem-ODM and its query facilities to access various databases, we have developed SemanticAccess – a set of tools to access both relational and semantic databases, which is the focus of our discussion in this paper.

2. System Architecture

SemanticAccess is a set of tools developed for accessing semantic and relational databases using Semantic Binary Object-Oriented Data Model and Semantic SQL query language. It consists of three major components: Query Coordinator, Relational Site and Semantic Site. Figure 1 depicts the overall architecture of the system.

- Query Coordinator: This component is responsible for collecting schemas from different databases and dispatching the users' queries to the appropriate sites. It contains a catalog of schemas stored in a Sem-ODB. This component uses CORBA based architecture for communication and query distribution to other components.

- Relational Site: This component (SemWrap [7]) wraps relational databases to provide a Sem-ODB interface. It contains a knowledge base and a reverse-engineering tool (KDBTool) for schema translation and storage. The relational schema is loaded into the knowledge base and a corresponding semantic schema is generated. This conversion process is a bottom-up methodology similar to the reverse order of conversion described in [5]. The DBA can create complex semantic schema with the use of KDBTool and Knowledge Base thereafter. We used Sem-ODB as the storage medium of the knowledge base in the relational site. Translator module implements a query translation algorithm from Semantic SQL to relational SQL. Currently, this module is capable of wrapping any commercial relational database system, which has an appropriate ODBC driver.

- Semantic Site: This module implements the Semantic Database Engine (Sem-ODB [6]) and Semantic SQL interpreter. Sem-ODB engine is a multi-platform fully functional client-server database system (platforms include Solaris, HPUX, Linux, and various versions of Windows). Clients running on any platform can interact with one or more database servers running on the same or different platforms. Moreover, database files are fully compatible across platforms at binary level. Multiple clients can access server through network protocols such as TCP/IP or NETBIOS while some other clients can run locally as threads within the server process. While the database is suitable for large applications storing terabytes of data, it is also appropriate for small embedded applications because the database engine has very low memory requirements. Its footprint in main memory is about 2 Megabytes including code and auxiliary structures, plus the amount allocated for

cache which could be specified by database administrator. A 2 Megabytes cache is enough for a wide class of embedded applications, which means that the database can efficiently run in 4 Megabytes of total memory. The size of the database server executable is about 1Mb.

In addition to the SQL-level access provided by Semantic SQL interpreter, the database engine (architecture shown in Figure 2) provides a native C++ and Java API for elementary database access, similar to procedural access in an OODB. This is the API which controls three modules that work closely together. **Vocab** controls database schema, **SetQuery** provides functionality for cursors, and **Elementary Queries** module is the main module which provides the functionality of the elementary database access. It uses several logical data types (and correspondingly named modules) to represent data: **Fact Data**, **Record Data**, and **Index**. Furthermore, data is stored using one of three physical data storage types which are **B-Tree**, **Bit-Scale**, and **Raw Data**. All three go through **Memory manager** and **Cache Manager** to access disk files through the file system. Cache Manager module includes version control and concurrency control to provide complete transaction isolation and optimistic concurrency. Binary data can be stored using **Parallel Binary Server** which can be a part of the system or run as a separate process on a different server. It uses several Disk Servers for physical storage, which can use either an underlying file system or raw disks to store data. This server is capable of storing huge amounts of binary data such as pictures and other multimedia data distributed over a TCP/IP network.

SemanticAccess was implemented in C++. The source code for the database engine itself is about 75,000 lines. In addition to that, the source code of SQL server is about 40,000 lines. KDBTool was implemented in VC++ 6.0 with the use of Microsoft Foundation Classes (MFC) for the implementation of graphical user interfaces to interact with the DBA, while the translator module was implemented in C++. The source code of this module is about 45,000 lines. The Query Coordinator was implemented in C++ as well.

3. Demonstration

We will demonstrate Semantic Database Technology emphasizing its advantages. We focus on Semantic Binary Object-Oriented Data Model, Semantic Binary Object-Oriented Database, Semantic SQL query language and Semantic Wrapper for relational databases. Following are some highlights of our demonstration:

- Sem-ODM and database interoperability: SemanticAccess provides Sem-ODM access to both

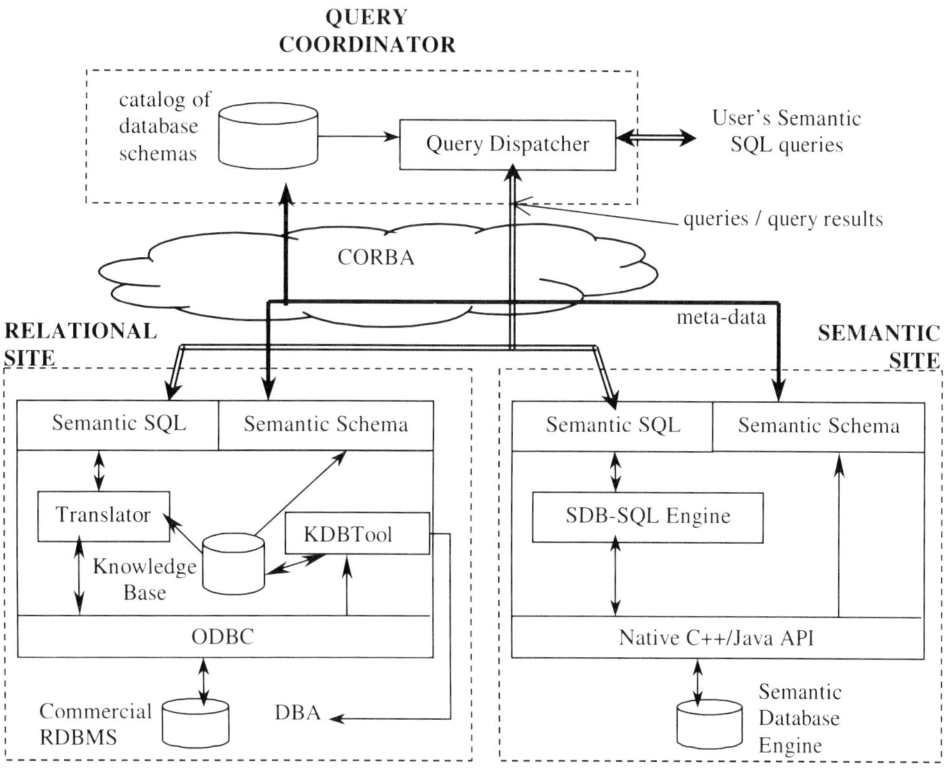

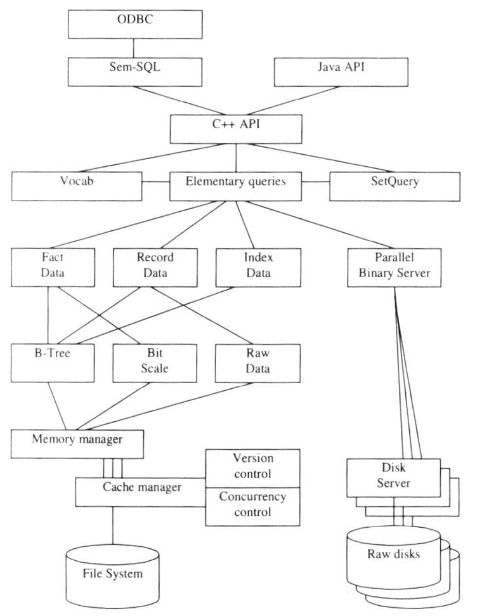

Figure 1. Overall architecture of SemanticAccess

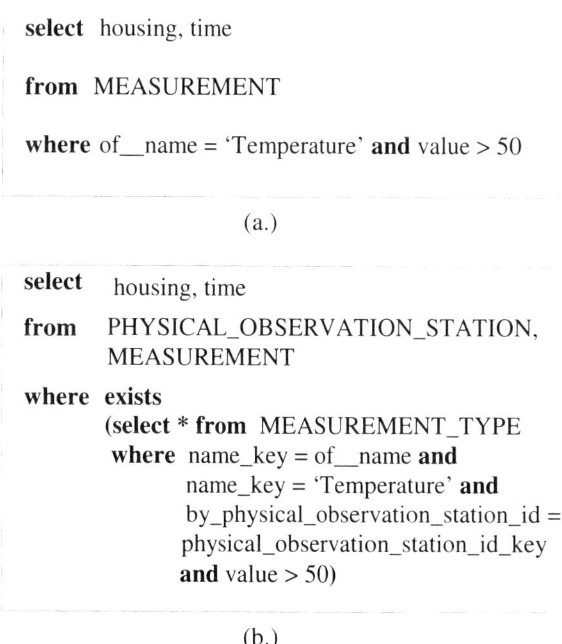

Figure 2. Sem-ODB Engine architecture

select housing, time

from MEASUREMENT

where of__name = 'Temperature' **and** value > 50

(a.)

select housing, time

from PHYSICAL_OBSERVATION_STATION,
MEASUREMENT

where exists
(**select** * **from** MEASUREMENT_TYPE
where name_key = of__name **and**
name_key = 'Temperature' **and**
by_physical_observation_station_id =
physical_observation_station_id_key
and value > 50)

(b.)

Figure 3. (a.) Semantic SQL query based on a semantic schema   (b.) Equivalent relational SQL query for (a.) based on a relational schema

semantic and relational databases. Hence, we can gain the advantages of a more expressive data model than relational data model while providing a well-known query facility, namely SQL.

- Semantic SQL query language: Semantic SQL is SQL language adopted for Sem-ODM. The syntax of Semantic SQL is identical to standard SQL (SQL-92). However, we have extended the semantics of SQL when posing a query to a Sem-ODM schema. The queries are posed on virtual tables, which is determined by examining the query complexity and semantic schema on which the query is posed. Due to the availability of relationships between categories in a semantic schema, explicit joins need not be specified, as in the case of relational schemas. Hence, we have achieved easier and less complex query facilities. A Semantic SQL query based on a semantic schema is shorter and less complex than a relational SQL query posed on an equivalent relational schema. An example is illustrated in Figure 3.

- Sem-ODB and native APIs: We will demonstrate Sem-ODB including its expressive data model capabilities such as inheritance, relations (1:m relations, m:m relations, multi-valued attributes), capability of objects to belong to multiple categories and other features (including native APIs that provides basic database access). Also, Semantic SQL interpreter for Sem-ODB will be demonstrated.

- Semantic Wrapper: We will demonstrate the KDBTool module which is used in creating complex semantic schemas (including inheritance, m:m relations and multi-valued attributes, which is not inherent in the relational schema). The Translator module will be demonstrated with a comparison of Semantic SQL queries and the corresponding translated relational SQL queries. Semantic Wrapper module preserves database autonomy. That is, installation of the wrapper does not effect the existing relational database or its applications. Thus, new applications can be built on top of the wrapper, which provides a more expressive data model and easier query facilities, without affecting the existing applications. Also, the wrapper module is easily installable on any existing commercial relational database with an appropriate ODBC Driver.

Sem-ODB technology is suitable for non-traditional database areas such as GIS, multi-media databases, where relational databases are inadequate. Also, the expressive data model, easier query facility and interoperability architecture of SemanticAccess can be exploited in application areas such as federated/multidatabase environments and data-warehousing environments. We plan to extend the SemanticAccess to access semi-structured and unstructured data sources as well.

Acknowledgements

This research was supported in part by NASA (under grants NAGW-4080, NAG5-5095, NAS5-97222, and NAG5-6830) and NSF (CDA-9711582, IRI-9409661, HRD-9707076, and ANI-9876409).

4. References

[1] Blakeley J., "OQL[C++]:Extending C++ with an Object Query Capability". *Modern Database Systems: The Object Model, Interoperability, and Beyond*, ACM Press, pp.69-88, 1995.

[2] Chen S.-C., N. Rishe, X. Wang, M. Weiss, "A User-Friendly Multimedia System for Querying and Visualizing of Geographic Data". To appear in *The 4th World Multiconference on Systemics, Cybernetics and Informatics*, July, 2000.

[3] Krieger D., T. Andrews, "C++ Bindings to an Object Database". *Modern Database Systems: The Object Model, Interoperability, and Beyond*, ACM Press, pp. 89-107, 1995.

[4] Rishe N., *Database Design: The Semantic Modeling Approach*, McGraw-Hill, 1992.

[5] Rishe N., "A Methodology and Tool for Top-down Relational Database Design". *Data and Knowledge Engineering*, Vol. 10, pp 259-291, 1993.

[6] Rishe N., A. Vaschillo, D. Vasilevsky, A. Shaposhnikov, S.-C. Chen, "A Benchmarking Technique for DBMS`s with Advanced Data Models". To appear in *ACM SIGMOD ADBIS-DASFAA Symposium on Advances in Databases and Information Systems*, September, 2000.

[7] Rishe N., J. Yuan, R. Athauda, X. Lu, X. Ma, "SemWrap: A Semantic Wrapper over Relational Databases, with Substantial Size Reduction of User's SQL Queries". In *Proceedings of the 7th International Conference on Extending Database Technology - Software Demonstrations Track*, pp. 13-14, March, 2000.

[8] Rishe N., W. Sun, D. Barton, Y. Deng, C. Orji, M. Alexopoulos, L. Loureiro, C. Ordonez, M. Sanchez, A. Shaposhnikov, "Florida International University High Performance Database Research Center". *SIGMOD Record*, Vol. 24, No. 3, pp. 71-76, 1995.

The TreeScape System: Reuse of Pre-Computed Aggregates over Irregular OLAP Hierarchies

Torben Bach Pedersen   Christian S. Jensen

Department of Computer Science,
Aalborg University, DK–9220 Aalborg Ø, Denmark,
{tbp,csj}@cs.auc.dk

Curtis E. Dyreson

School of Information Technology,
Bond University, Gold Coast, QLD 4229,
Australia, cdyreson@bond.edu.au

Abstract

We present the TreeScape system that, unlike any other system known to the authors, enables the reuse of pre-computed aggregate query results for irregular dimension hierarchies, which occur frequently in practice. The system establishes a foundation for obtaining high query processing performance while pre-computing only limited aggregates. The paper shows how this reuse of aggregates is enabled through dimension transformations that occur transparently to the user.

1 Introduction

In order to improve query performance, modern On-Line Analytical Processing (OLAP) systems use a technique known as *practical pre-aggregation*, where *select* combinations of aggregate queries are materialized and re-used when computing other aggregates; full pre-aggregation, where all combinations of aggregates are materialized, is infeasible, as it typically causes a blowup in storage requirements of 200–500 times the size of the raw data [3, 5]. Normally, practical pre-aggregation requires the dimension hierarchies to be regular, i.e., to be balanced trees, but this is quite often not the case in real-world systems.

The TreeScape system presented here enables practical pre-aggregation even for irregular hierarchies, based on techniques described previously by the authors [4]. We show how to achieve practical pre-aggregation through transformations of the dimensions and how the transformations can be accomplished transparently to the user. The

**Proceedings of the 26th VLDB Conference,
Cairo, Egypt, 2000.**

system enables the achievement of fast query response time while saving huge amounts of storage compared to current OLAP systems and techniques. The prototype implementation of TreeScape demonstrates that these benefits may be achieved with standard technology. While this demonstration uses a particular RDBMS, it's ODBC driver, and particular relational OLAP tool, TreeScape is not dependent on any specific suite of products[1], making the solution flexible and useful.

2 Normalizing Hierarchies

We use a small case study concerning patients and their diagnoses for illustrating the workings of the system. Diagnoses have three different levels of precision, depending on how accurate a patient's condition can be described. The most precise diagnoses are *low-level diagnoses*, which are grouped into *diagnosis families*, which, in turn, are grouped into diagnosis groups. The example data consists of 9 diagnoses and their hierarchical relationship, along with patient counts. The data can be seen in Table 1 and to the left in Figure 1.

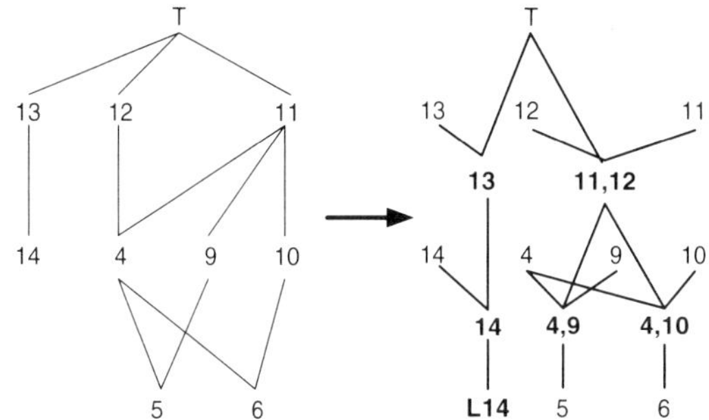

Figure 1: Dimension Transformations

The hierarchy is irregular. For example, it is unbalanced because the diagnosis "Lung cancer" (14) has no low-level diagnoses associated with it. The hierarchy is non-strict because, e.g., diagnosis 4 ("Diabetes during pregnancy")

---

[1] The solution assumes that an ODBC interface is available for the RDBMS, a requirement that is met for all commercial RDBMSs.

ID	Text	Type
4	Diabetes during pregnancy	Family
5	Insulin dependent diabetes during pregnancy	Low-Level
6	Non insulin dependent diabetes during pregnancy	Low-Level
9	Insulin dependent diabetes	Family
10	Non insulin dependent diabetes	Family
11	Diabetes	Group
12	Pregnancy related	Group
13	Cancer	Group
14	Lung cancer	Family

Diagnosis

ParentID	ChildID
4	5
4	6
9	5
10	6
11	9
11	10
12	4
13	14

Grouping

DiagID	Count
5	1

Patient

Table 1: Case Study Tables

has several parents. As a result, problems occur when pre-aggregated data at lower levels is used to compute new values at higher levels. For example, if we pre-aggregate the number of patients at the low-level diagnosis level and want to aggregate to the diagnosis family level, we cannot deduce what the value should be for "Lung Cancer" (14). If we pre-aggregate at the diagnosis family level, patients with diagnoses 5 or 6 will be counted for both of the diagnoses 4 and 9, and 4 and 10, respectively, leading to wrong results when we aggregate to the diagnosis group level.

A solution of the problems with pre-aggregation is to render the hierarchies well-behaved by *normalizing* them. Informally, the normalization process introduces new *placeholder* values where the hierarchy is unbalanced, and introduces *fused* values that represent *sets of* parent values when child values have multiple parents. The result of normalizing the hierarchy described above is seen to the right in Figure 1. For example, value "L14" representing "Lung Cancer" at the low-level diagnosis level, and value "4,9" representing the set of diagnoses $\{4, 9\}$ are introduced by the normalization. In the figure, all boldface values and links have been added by the normalization process. The normalization technique is described in detail elsewhere [4].

The normalized hierarchy supports practical pre-aggregation. For example, it is possible to store counts of patients at the low-level diagnosis level, and then re-use these to compute the counts for diagnosis families and diagnosis groups. With the example data (one patient with diagnosis 5), this will only require the storage of the one value versus six values being required for *full* pre-aggregation (one value for low-level diagnosis 5, two values for diagnosis families 4 and 9, two values for diagnosis groups 11 and 12, and one value for ⊤, which represents the total for all diagnoses).

The example is somewhat indicative of the storage savings achieved within a single dimension. When several dimensions are combined, the total space saved (with respect to full pre-aggregation) is the product of the savings in each dimension, resulting in savings factors of 100 or more in practice. The savings occur because of *multidimensional sparseness* [3, 5], the phenomenon of the multidimensional space being very sparse for the lower levels in the dimen-

sions, while quickly becoming more dense at higher levels. The query response time using the normalization approach will not be quite as fast as using full pre-aggregation, but will most likely be comparable, i.e., within an order of magnitude. This is much faster than computing the results from the base data, as would be required with *no* pre-aggregation.

3   System Architecture

While the hierarchy transformations enable practical pre-aggregation, they also have the undesired side-effect of introducing new values into the hierarchies that are of little meaning to the users. Thus, the transformations should remain invisible to the users. This is achieved by working with two versions of each user-specified hierarchy and by using a query rewrite mechanism. This is described in detail in Section 4. The overall system architecture is seen in Figure 2.

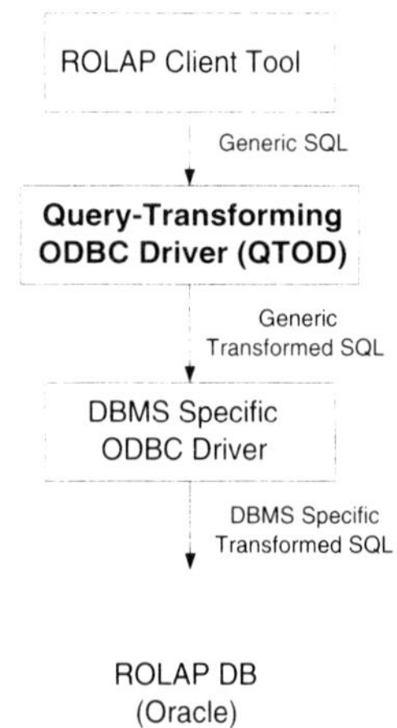

Figure 2: System Architecture

The ROLAP client tool , in this case the ROLAP tool Synchrony which originated from Kimball's Startracker tool [1], makes SQL requests to the ROLAP database, in this case the Oracle8 RDBMS, using the ODBC standard. We have implemented a special, query-transforming ODBC driver (QTOD) that, based on case-specific metadata, trans-

DiagID	Lowlevel	Family	Group
5	Insulin dependent diabetes during pregnancy	Diabetes during pregnancy	Diabetes
5	Insulin dependent diabetes during pregnancy	Diabetes during pregnancy	Pregnancy related
5	Insulin dependent diabetes during pregnancy	Insulin dependent diabetes	Diabetes
6	Non insulin dependent diabetes during pregnancy	Diabetes during pregnancy	Diabetes
6	Non insulin dependent diabetes during pregnancy	Diabetes during pregnancy	Pregnancy related
6	Non insulin dependent diabetes during pregnancy	Non insulin dependent diabetes	Diabetes
100	!Lowlevel!Lung Cancer	Lung cancer	Cancer

Table 2: DDiagnosis Dimension Table

forms the SQL requests into requests that hide the transformations from the users, returning the query results that the user would expect based on the original hierarchies. A transformed request is submitted to the OLAP DB using an RDBMS-specific ODBC driver. The QTOD component is common to all RDBMSs, so Oracle8 may be replaced by another RDBMS such as IBM DB2, Informix, or MS SQL Server. Another ROLAP tool may also be used, making the solution quite general and flexible.

We have chosen to base the prototype on an RDBMS (Oracle8) since RDBMSs are the most commonly used platform for Data Warehouse and OLAP applications. Additionally, the major RDBMSs now, like dedicated multidimensional DBMSes (MDDBs), use pre-aggregated data for faster query responses [6]. However, the approach could also be implemented using multidimensional technology, e.g., based on the Microsoft OLE DB for OLAP standard [2].

The transformation algorithms are implemented in Oracle's PL/SQL programming language. The transformations are relatively fast, taking at most a few minutes, even for large dimensions. Once the dimension hierarchies have been transformed, the QTOD transforms queries and results between the original and transformed hierarchies. The QTOD is a thin layer and adds very little overhead to queries. It is implemented using GNU Flex++/Bison++ scanner/parser generators and the MS Visual C++ compiler.

4 Implementation Specifics

Studies have shown that queries on a data warehouse consist of 80% *navigational* queries, which explore the dimension hierarchies, and 20% *aggregation* queries, which aggregate the data at various levels of detail [1]. These two types of queries are treated differently to give the user the illusion that the dimension hierarchies have their original form.

The multidimensional data is captured in a *star schema* [1]. The dimension table for the Diagnosis dimension is given in Table 2, which has one column for the low-level diagnosis ID in addition to columns for the textual descriptions of low-level diagnoses, diagnosis families, and diagnosis groups.

The hierarchy captured in the table is *partially normalized*, i.e., placeholder values have been introduced to balance the hierarchy (but it remains non-strict). Specifically,

the "!Lowlevel!Lung Cancer" placeholder value has been inserted into the Low-level Diagnosis level. We prefix such values with a "!" and their level to indicate that they are inserted by the transformation process. Note the multiple occurrences of lower-level values caused by the non-strictness of the hierarchy. This is the table that will be used for user navigation in the hierarchy. Its name is prefixed with a "D" to distinguish it from another "Diagnosis" dimension table (described below), to be used for aggregation queries.

We now describe how to achieve transformation transparency for *navigational queries*. The query below retrieves all low-level diagnosis names.

SELECT DISTINCT `Lowlevel`
FROM `Diagnosis`

Navigational queries issued by ROLAP tools have exactly this format. The query is transformed by the QTOD into the query below, which operates against the table DDiagnosis. The transformed query returns the result seen in Table 3.

SELECT DISTINCT `Lowlevel`
FROM `DDiagnosis`
WHERE `Lowlevel` **NOT LIKE** `'!%'`

Lowlevel
Insulin dependent diabetes during pregnancy
Non insulin dependent diabetes during pregnancy

Table 3: Navigational Query Result

Due to the use of `DISTINCT` as a quantifier, duplicates are not returned. The `NOT LIKE` predicate removes the placeholder values inserted into the hierarchy to balance it, which in this case is the value "!Lowlevel!Lung Cancer." As desired, the result is unaffected by the translations.

For *aggregation queries*, it is also possible to achieve transformation transparency, although this is more difficult. For dimensions with non-strictness, a special dimension table is introduced that holds only the part of the normalized hierarchy that does *not* contain non-strictness. In the normalized hierarchy to the right in Figure 1, this part is the Low-level Diagnosis category and the two special categories introduced by the normalization process to hold *sets of diagnosis families* and *sets of diagnosis groups*, respectively. This part of the hierarchy is implemented in the Diagnosis dimension table seen in Table 4.

DiagID	Lowlevel	Family	Group		Group	SGroup
1000020	!Low-level Diagnosis!Lung cancer	14	13		Cancer	13
5	Insulin dependent diabetes during pregnancy	4,9	11,12		Diabetes	11,12
6	Non insulin dependent diabetes during pregnancy	4,10	11,12		Pregnancy Related	11,12
	Diagnosis				SGroup	

Table 4: Dimension and Group Tables for Aggregation

The "Lowlevel" column contains the normal textual diagnosis description, whereas the special "Family" and "Group" columns contain comma-separated ordered lists of the IDs of the sets of values that are represented by the column values. For example, value "4,9" represents the set $\{4,9\}$.

We need to capture the remaining part of the hierarchy, which consists of non-strict mappings from a "set-of-X" category to the "X" category, e.g., the mapping of the "set-of-Diagnosis Group" category to the "Diagnosis Group" category to the right in Figure 1, which maps $\{13\}$ to 13 (Cancer) and $\{11,12\}$ to 11 (Diabetes) and 12 (Pregnancy Related). This is done by introducing a special table for each such mapping, named by the category prefixed with an "S" (for Set-of). For example, for the Diagnosis Group category, table "SGroup" in Table 4 maps sets of diagnosis groups to the individual diagnosis groups in the sets. The "Group" column represents the diagnosis group, while the "SGroup" column represents the associated set of diagnosis groups.

With these tables available, it is possible to obtain transformation transparency for aggregation queries. A ROLAP aggregation query has the format of the query below that computes the number of patients per diagnosis group.

```
SELECT Diagnosis.Group, SUM(Patient.Count)
FROM Diagnosis,Patient
WHERE Diagnosis.DiagID=Patient.DiagID
GROUP BY Diagnosis.Group
```

This is transformed into the query given next.

```
SELECT SGroup.Group, SUM(QQQQQQQ.Count)
FROM Sgroup,
  (SELECT Diagnosis.Group,
        SUM(Patient.Count) AS Count
   FROM Diagnosis,Patient
   WHERE Diagnosis.DiagID=Patient.DiagID
   GROUP BY Diagnosis.Group) QQQQQQQ
WHERE  QQQQQQQ.Group=SGroup.SGroup AND
        SGroup.SGroup NOT LIKE '!%'
GROUP BY SGroup.Sgroup
```

The transformed aggregation query has two parts. The nested table expression computes the number of patients per *set of diagnosis group*, making this available via correlation name QQQQQQQ. This part of the hierarchy is a balanced tree, so the RDBMS can safely use pre-aggregated data for optimizing the query performance. The result of the nested table expression is used in the outer query, which aggregates the last part of the way up to the diagnosis groups using the "SGroup" table. The outer query also

filters out any placeholder values inserted by the normalization process (prefixed with a "!"). As a result, the client OLAP tool will retrieve the expected result.

Good query performance without the use of excessive storage for pre-aggregated data is obtained by using practical pre-aggregation for the "nice" part of the hierarchy captured in the "Diagnosis" dimension table. The query transformation exemplified here can be performed for all ROLAP aggregation queries, making the solution quite general.

5 Demonstration

Based on concrete data from a real-world case study, the demonstration will initially show snapshots that illustrate the hierarchy normalization process. Next, query processing will be demonstrated by means of concrete navigational and aggregation queries. This includes a description of how the queries are transformed to hide the hierarchy transformations from the user, as well as the evaluation of the queries on concrete data. Finally, the demonstration will compare the query execution times for the queries and the amount of storage required for pre-aggregated data with the two alternatives to our approach, namely *no* pre-aggregation, which gives very long query response times, and *full* pre-aggregation, which requires unrealistically large amounts of storage for pre-aggregated data.

Supporting material in the form of slides and posters will be used in the demonstration.

References

[1] R. Kimball. *The Data Warehouse Toolkit*. Wiley Computer Publishing, 1996.

[2] Microsoft Corporation. OLE DB for OLAP Version 1.0 Specification. Microsoft Technical Document, 1998.

[3] The OLAP Report. *Database Explosion*. <www.olapreport.com/DatabaseExplosion.htm>. Current as of February 18, 2000.

[4] T. B. Pedersen, C. S. Jensen, and C. E. Dyreson. Extending Practical Pre-Aggregation in On-Line Analytical Processing. In *Proc. VLDB*, pp. 663–674, 1999. Extended version available as TR R-99-5004, Dept. of Comp. Sci. Aalborg University, <www.cs.auc.dk/~tbp/articles/R995004.ps>, 1999.

[5] A. Shukla et al. Storage Estimation for Multidimensional Aggregates in the Presence of Hierarchies. In *Proc. VLDB*, pp. 522–531, 1996.

[6] R. Winter. Databases: Back in the OLAP game. *Intelligent Enterprise Magazine*, 1(4):60–64, 1998.

OLAP++: Powerful and Easy-to-Use Federations of OLAP and Object Databases

Junmin Gu

Lawrence Berkeley National
Laboratory, Berkeley,
CA 94720, USA.
jgu@lbl.gov

Torben Bach Pedersen

Department of Computer
Science, Aalborg University,
9220 Aalborg Ø, Denmark.
tbp@cs.auc.dk

Arie Shoshani

Lawrence Berkeley National
Laboratory, Berkeley,
CA 94720, USA.
shoshani@lbl.gov

Abstract

We describe the OLAP++ system for federating OLAP and object databases. The system allows users to easily pose OLAP queries that reference external object databases. This enables very flexible and fast integration of object data in OLAP systems without the need for prior physical integration.

1. Introduction

On-Line Analytical Processing (OLAP) systems provide good performance and ease-of-use when retrieving summary information from very large amounts of data. However, the complex structures and relationships inherent in related non-summary data are not handled well by OLAP systems. In contrast, object database systems are built to handle such complexity, but do not support summary querying well.

This paper presents OLAP++, a flexible, federated system that enables OLAP users to exploit simultaneously the features of OLAP and object database systems. In a previous paper [1], we have defined a comprehensive framework for handling federations of OLAP and object databases, including the SumQL++ language that allows OLAP systems to naturally support queries that refer to and retrieve data from object databases. The OLAP++ system allows data to be handled using the most appropriate data model and technology: OLAP systems for summary data and object database systems for the more complex, general data. Also, the need for physical integration of data is reduced considerably. We present a case study based on the Transaction Processing Council (TPC) TPC-R benchmark [3]. The system is implemented in C++ on top of the Object Protocol Model (OPM) system [4] and the Microsoft SQL Server OLAP Services system [2].

2. Federations of OLAP and Object Databases

OLAP systems use a *multidimensional* view of data that typically categorizes data as being measurable *facts* (measures) or *dimensions*, which are mostly textual and characterize the facts. Dimensions are structured using *categories* (levels) that correspond to the required levels of detail. Object systems use the familiar concepts of *classes*, *attributes*, and *relationships* between classes. A *federation* between an OLAP and an object database is defined by specifying a *link* between a category in the OLAP database and a class in the object database.

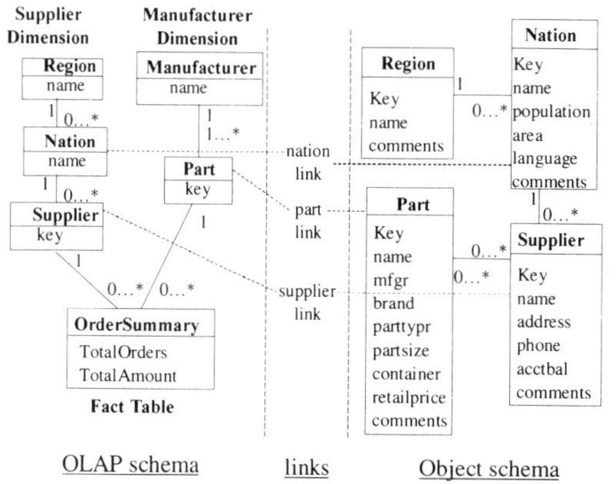

Figure 1: Schema of the Federation

Figure 1 shows an example schema of a federation in UML notation. The schema is based on the TPC-R benchmark [3], but has been divided into an OLAP part and an object part. The measured facts in the OLAP schema are the *total number of orders* and the *total cost amount* for the orders. The facts are characterized by a *Supplier dimension* and a *Manufacturer dimension*. The Supplier dimension has *Customer, Nation,* and *Region* categories that allow the facts to be summarized to the required level of detail. The Manufacturer dimension has the categories *Part* and *Manufacturer*. The object part of the schema has *Region, Nation, Supplier,* and *Part* classes and relationships between them. Link *nationlink* connects the Nation category in the OLAP part to the Nation class in the object part as indicated by the dotted lines. Links *supplierlink* and *partlink* connect the Supplier category and class, and the Part category and class, respectively. Below is an example SumQL++ query for the schema.

SELECT TotalAmount **INTO** testdb
BY_CATEGORY Manufacturer, Nation
FROM OrderSummary
WHERE (Region = "ASIA") **AND**
Nation.nationlink.[Nation].population > 100,000,000

The above query gets the total cost amount for the two-dimensional cross product of nation and manufacturer where the nations have populations beyond 100 million and are in the Asian region. This query uses the link "nationlink" to go from the OLAP schema to the object schema. The class name in the square brackets is optional and is only specified here to indicate the class reached by going through the link.

3. System Architecture

The overall architecture of the federated system is seen in Figure 2. The object part of the system is based on the OPM tools [4] that implement the Object Data Management Group's (ODMG) object data model [5] and the Object Query Language (OQL) [5] on top of a relational DBMS, in this case the ORACLE RDBMS. The OLAP part of the system is based on Microsoft's SQL Server OLAP Services using the Multi-Dimensional eXpressions (MDX) [2] query language. The GUI is implemented as Java classes running in a standard Web browser for optimal flexibility.

When a SumQL++ query is received by the Federation Coordinator (FC), it is first parsed to identify the measures, categories, links, classes and attributes referenced in the query. Based on this, the FC then queries the metadata to get information about which databases the object data and the OLAP data reside in and which categories are linked to which classes.

Based on the object parts of the query, the FC then sends OQL queries to the object databases to retrieve the data for which the particular conditions hold true. This data is then put into a "pure" SumQL statement, i.e., without object references, as a list of category values. This SumQL statement is then sent to the OLAP database layer to retrieve the desired measures, grouped by the requested categories. The SumQL statement is translated into MDX by a separate layer, the "SumQL-

to-MDX translator", and the data returned from OLAP Services is returned to the FC.

The reason for using the intermediate SumQL statements is to isolate the implementation of the OLAP data from the FC. As an another alternative, we have also implemented a translator into SQL statements against a relational "star schema" design.

The system offers good query performance even for large databases while making it possible to integrate existing OLAP data with external data in object databases in a flexible way that can adapt quickly to changing query needs.

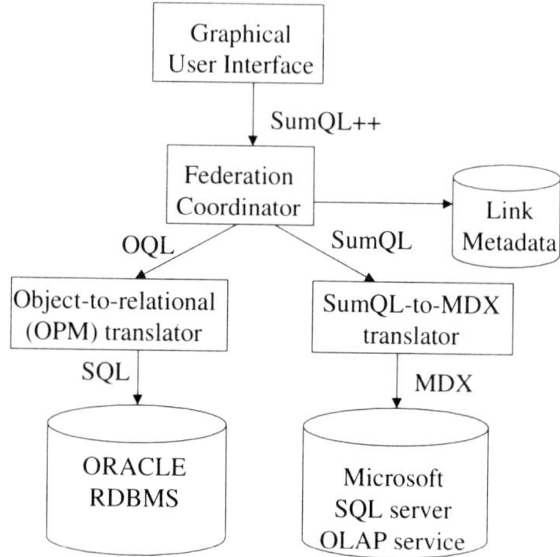

Figure 2: Architecture of the Federated System

4. The Demonstration

The demonstration will show the specification of, and query processing for, specific queries on a large TPC-R-based database. First, the use of the system will be demonstrated. Second, we will describe the details of query processing in the system. In the demonstration, we will also show how new federations can be specified "on-the-fly" and used immediately. Supporting material in the form of slides and posters will be used in the demonstration.

4.1 User Interface

The web screen interface shown in Figure 3 below shows how the user perceives the specification of a SumQL++ query. Figure 3 shows the selection of the summary measure "TotalAmount". This is followed by the section with the category attributes "Manufacturer" and "Nation". Note that each category can be selected from a "category hierarchy". In the figure, "Nation" was selected from the "Region-Nation-Supplier" category hierarchy. The order of the category grouping

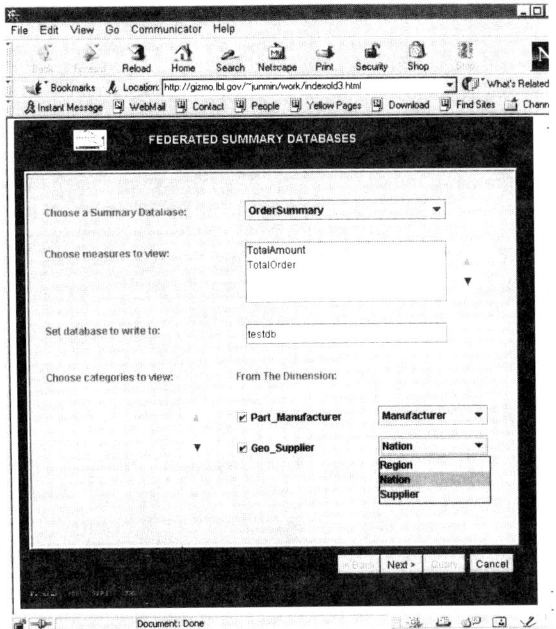

Figure 3: Selection of Measures and Categories

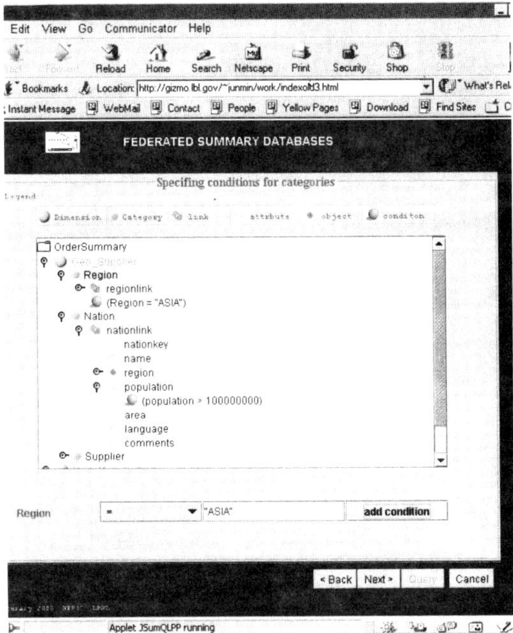

Figure 4: Specification of Query Conditions

can be specified in this screen as well by switching the dimension positions.

Figure 4 shows the specification of query conditions. Initially, each dimension is shown with its categories and links to the object database. If a category is selected, a category condition can be entered. In the figure, Region= "ASIA" was selected. If a link is clicked on, then the attributes of the object linked to are shown. The user can select an attribute to specify a condition. In the figure, the condition "population > 100 Million" was selected through the "nationlink". The result of the above selections is a concise SumQL++ query (the same query as the example in Section 1), as shown next.

SELECT TotalAmount **INTO** testdb
BY_CATEGORY Manufacture, Nation
FROM OrderSummary **WHERE** (Region = "ASIA")
AND (Nation.nationlink.population > 100000000)

The result of this query is then displayed on the user's screen, as shown in Figure 5.

4.2 Query Processing

We now proceed to describe the steps in the query processing in more detail.

After the query is generated, the system parses the query to determine the OLAP and object parts. For the example above the result of the parsing is:

SELECT TotalAmount **INTO** testdb
BY_CATEGORY Manufacturer, Nation
FROM OrderSummary
[AND]
    predicate: CATEGORY = Region
        no object path
        -------> = "ASIA"
    predicate: CATEGORY = Nation
        LINK = nationlink
        PATH = .
        ATTR = population
        -------> > 100000000

Each link predicate is then evaluated by the object system. For example, the following OQL query is passed to the object DB system to find the nations with a population of more than 100 million:

SELECT name = @n001
FROM @n000 **IN** tpcr:NATION,
    @n001 **IN** @n000.name
WHERE @n000.population > 100000000;

After the results are returned, they are used in the OLAP part of the system to generate the following SumQL query that retrieves the desired data.

SELECT TotalAmount **INTO** testdb
BY_CATEGORY Manufacturer, Nation
FROM OrderSummary **WHERE**
(Region = 'ASIA' **AND** Nation **IN** ('BRAZIL', 'INDIA',
'INDONESIA', 'JAPAN', 'CHINA', 'RUSSIA',
'UNITED STATES'))

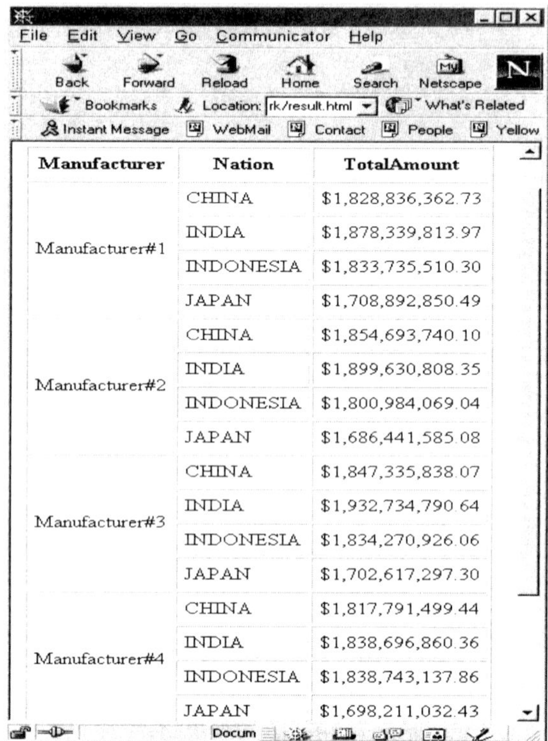

Figure 5: Query Result

This, in turn, gets translated into MDX as follows.
SELECT {[Measures].[L ExtendedPrice] } **ON**
COLUMNS, INTERSECT
(**CROSSJOIN**([Part_Manufacture].[P
Mfgr].**MEMBERS, DESCENDANTS**([R Region
Name].[ASIA],[N Nation Name],**SELF**)),
CROSSJOIN([Part_Manufacture].[P
Mfgr].**MEMBERS**, {[N Nation Name].[BRAZIL],[N
Nation Name].[INDIA],[N Nation
Name].[INDONESIA],[N Nation Name].[JAPAN],[N
Nation Name].[CHINA],[N Nation
Name].[RUSSIA],[N Nation Name].[UNITED
STATES]})) **ON ROWS FROM** OrderSummary

The result is then stored in the Oracle database "testdb,"
to make it available for further processing, and
converted to HTML for presentation to the user.

This section was intended to illustrate the amount of
work that a user will have to go through without the aid
of the user interface and the federated translation tools.
In particular, we wish to emphasize the usefulness of
the OLAP-object database links to generate the
combined result.   Also, the users are spared the
verbosity of MDX (which is hidden from them). It is
optional to display the concise SumQL++ expression to
the user, as a way to verify the correctness of the query.
Due to space constraints, we do not describe the
specification of new links in this paper. However, this
will be shown at the demonstration.

References

1. T. B. Pedersen, A. Shoshani, J. Gu, and C. S.
    Jensen. Extending OLAP Querying to External
    Object Databases. Submitted for publication.
2. Microsoft Corporation, OLE DB for OLAP
    Version 1.0 Specification. *Microsoft Technical
    Document*, 1998.
3. Transaction Processing Council. The TPC-R
    Benchmark. *URL: <www.tpc.org>*. Current as of
    June 1, 2000.
4. I-Min A. Chen, Victor M. Markowitz: An
    Overview of the Object-Protocol Model (OPM)
    and OPM Data Management Tools. *Information
    Systems* 20(5): 393-418 (1995).
5. R. G. G. Cattell et al. (editors). *The Object
    Database Standard: ODMG 2.0.* Morgan
    Kaufmann, 1997.

Memex: A browsing assistant for collaborative archiving and mining of surf trails

Soumen Chakrabarti   Sandeep Srivastava   Mallela Subramanyam   Mitul Tiwari

Indian Institute of Technology Bombay

`soumen,sandy,manyam,mits@cse.iitb.ernet.in`

Abstract

Keyword indices. topic directories. and link-based rankings are used to search and structure the rapidly growing Web today. Surprisingly little use is made of years of browsing experience of millions of people. Indeed. this information is routinely discarded by browsers. Even deliberate bookmarks are stored in a passive and isolated manner. All this goes against Vannevar Bush's dream of the *Memex*: an enhanced supplement to personal and community memory.

We propose to demonstrate the beginnings of a 'Memex' for the Web: a browsing assistant for individuals and groups with focused interests. Memex blurs the artificial distinction between browsing history and deliberate bookmarks. The resulting glut of data is analyzed in a number of ways at the individual and community levels. Memex constructs a topic directory customized to the community. mapping their interests naturally to nodes in this directory. This lets the user recall topic-based browsing contexts by asking questions like "What trails was I following when I was last surfing about *classical music?*" and "What are some popular pages in or near my community's recent trail graph related to *music?*"

1 Motivation

Three paradigms have emerged for exploring the Web: keyword search. directory browsing. and following links. Popular search engine and directory sites are visited tens of millions of times per day. We speculate that the total number of clicks per day is orders of magnitude larger. This third source of information. the browsing history of millions of Web users over several years. an information source that dwarfs the scale of the Web itself. is almost entirely discarded by browsers as 'history'. Deliberate 'bookmarks' are preserved. but passively. in browser-dependent formats: this separates them from the dominant world of HTML hypermedia. even if their owners were willing to share them (as they are, in our experience. with all but a small section of their browsing activity).

In 1945. Vannevar Bush dreamt of *Memex*: an enhanced. intimate supplement to personal and community memory [2]. Assisted by a Memex for the Web, a surfer can ask:

- What was the URL I visited about six months back regarding compiler optimization at Rice University?

- What was the Web neighborhood I was surfing the last time I was looking for resources on classical music?

- Are their any popular sites. related to my (Web) experience on classical music. that have appeared in the last six months?

- How is my ISP bill divided into access for work. travel. news. hobby and entertainment?

- What are the major topics relevant to my workplace? Where and how do I fit into that map? How does my bookmark folder structure map on to my organization?

- In a hierarchy of organizations (by region. say) who are the people who share my interest in recreational cycling most closely and are not likely to be computer professionals?

Since Bush proposed Memex, the theme of a 'living' hypermedia into which we "weave ourselves" has been emphasized often. e.g.. by Douglas Engelbart[1] and Ted Nelson[2]. and of late by Tim Berners-Lee[3] and Jim Gray[4]. Indeed. the current cost/volume ratio of storage makes it unnecessary to delete *anything* from one's Web surfing experience. provided we can make fruitful use of it.

We propose an architecture of a 'Memex' for the Web which can answer the above questions. Memex is a large project involving hypertext data mining. browser plug-in and applet design. servlets and associated distributed database architecture. and user interfaces. We have validated the design using a prototype implementation that we describe here. Memex is currently implemented on Netscape 4.5+. We are currently testing Memex with the help of local volunteers. The Memex service will be made

**Proceedings of the 26th VLDB Conference,
Cairo, Egypt, 2000.**

---

[1] `http://jefferson.village.virginia.edu/elab/hfl0035.html`

[2] `http://www.sfc.keio.ac.jp/~ted/`

[3] `http://www.w3.org/1999/04/13-tbl.html`

[4] `http://research.microsoft.com/~gray/papers/MS_TR_99_50_TuringTalk.pdf`

publicly accessible[5]. Further details about Memex have been reported elsewhere [4].

2   Client architecture overview

Memex should run on popular browsers. It should be possible to distribute updates and new features effortlessly to users. Hence the Memex client has been designed as an applet. In view of secure firewalls, proxies, and ISPs' restrictions on browser setups, the client should communicate with the server over HTTP. The data transfered should be encrypted, if desired, to preserve privacy.

The user can log on to a Memex server at the level of a department, organization, interest group, ISP, nation or the world. The architecture makes no assumptions about the logical community level at which Memex might be deployed. At any time, the user can choose not to archive surfing actions, archive for private use, or archive for use by the community (Figure 1). If permitted, Memex taps the browser to get the current location and passes this on to the server, which then processes it in many ways.

Apart from a standard full-text search over all pages visited, the Memex client has several function tabs to assist topic-based mining. The editable **folder tab** (Figure 1) provides topic management: this is the means by which users exemplify their interests. Existing bookmarks from Netscape or Explorer can be imported into Memex's editable tree-structured topic view; conversely Memex can export back to these browsers. Apart from implicit history logging, bookmarks can be added to folders while surfing. A user will typically assign a bookmark explicitly to a topic. These assignments are analyzed by the server, which then **classifies** all surfed pages automatically into these folders. The folder tab can also be used to reinforce or correct the classifier. Memex also uses unsupervised **clustering** to propose a topic hierarchy [6] over a set of links that the user may want to reorganize. Periodically, the server consolidates all users' public folders and browse history into a topic directory tailored to the needs of that specific community (see §4 and Figure 4).

Users surf on many topics with diverse priorities. Because browsers have only a transient context (one-dimensional history list), surfers frequently lose context when browsing about a topic after a time lapse. Studies have shown that visiting Web pages is best expressed using spatial metaphors: your context is "where you are" and "where you are able to go" next [9]. Memex's topic classifier also helps render the topic-focused **trail tab** (Figure 2). In the trail tab, the left panel shows the user's topic folders. Selecting a folder replays the hypertext graph of recent pages publicly surfed by the community which are most likely to belong to the selected topic, and thus recreates the user's browsing context.

3   Server architecture overview

On the server side, the system should be robust and scalable. It is important that the server recovers from network and programming errors quickly, even if it has to discard a few client events. The server consists of servlets that perform various archiving and mining functions as triggered by client action, or continually as demons. We prefer servlets to CGI scripts because the client-server interactions exchange complex objects and sometimes have state. We prefer HTTP tunneling also because direct JDBC connections may be refused by many firewalls.

Server state is managed by two storage mechanisms: a relational database (RDBMS) such as Oracle or DB2 for managing metadata about pages, links, users, and topics, and a lightweight Berkeley DB[6] storage manager to support fine-grained term-level data analysis for clustering, classification, and text search. Storing term-level statistics in an RDBMS would have overwhelming space and time overheads.

An interesting aspect of the Memex architecture is the division of labor between the RDBMS and the lightweight storage manager. Planning the architecture was made non-trivial by the need for asynchronous action from diverse modules. There are some user interface-related events that must be guaranteed immediate processing. Typically these are generated by a user visiting a page, or deliberately updating the folder structure. With many users concurrently using Memex, the server cannot analyze all visited pages, or update mined results, in real time. Background demons continually fetch pages, index them, and analyze them w.r.t. topics and folders. The data accesses made by these demons have to be carefully coordinated. This would not be a problem with the RDBMS alone, but maintaining some form of coherence between the metadata in the RDBMS and several text-related indices in Berkeley DB required us to implement a loosely-consistent versioning system on top of the RDBMS, with a single producer (crawler) and several consumers (indexer and statistical analyzers). Figure 3 shows a block diagram of the system.

4   Mining algorithms overview

The stream of data from surfers has to be analyzed in various ways. Some parts of the processing, such as keyword indexing, are mundane. Other parts constitute new algorithms or novel implementations.

For clustering we started with a bottom-up hierarchical agglomerative approach [6]. For classification we started with a Bayesian classifier [3]. Although these simple text-based techniques work reasonably well for

---

[5]http://www.cse.iitb.ernet.in/~soumen/memex/

[6]http://www.sleepycat.com

average Web pages, bookmarked URLs offer special challenges: people tend to bookmark many "front pages" with less text and more graphics compared to typical Web documents. Surfers may also place two URLs in the same folder for functional reasons, even if the corresponding documents are syntactically dissimilar.

We have implemented two new learning algorithms for Memex. For classification we use a new technique that combines features from text, hyperlink and folder placement to offer significantly boosted accuracy, increasing from a mere 40% accuracy for text-only learners to about 80% with our more elaborate model.

We generalize clustering to finding a new notion of **themes** among the bookmarks. In principle, each user need not design his/her own topic hierarchy, given there are 'standard' ones like Yahoo![7] and the Open Directory[8]. In practice, these 'universal' hierarchies are neither necessary nor sufficient for individual surfers and focused communities, they are too specialized in most topics, and not sufficiently specialized in the areas in which the community is deeply interested. We propose a new formulation for discovering a topic hierarchy specifically expressing and addressing the interests of the community, refining topics where needed and coarsening where possible. Details of the new classification and theme discovery algorithms are reported elsewhere [4] (also see Figure 4).

Once topic hierarchies for the user community are determined, automatic resource discovery is undertaken by demons to update users about recent and/or authoritative sources, organized by topic [5]. 'Normalizing' all members of the community to themes also lets us represent surfers' interests in a *canonical form*: roughly speaking, a user profile is a set of weights associated with each node of a theme hierarchy; this gives us a means of comparing profiles that is far superior to overlap in sets of URLs. We intend to use this for better collaborative recommendation [10].

5   Related work

Our work is closest in spirit to two well-known systems, PowerBookmarks[9] and the Bookmark Organizer [8].

PowerBookmarks is a semi-structured database application for archiving and searching bookmark files via explicit CGI programs. PowerBookmarks uses Yahoo! for classifying the bookmarks of all users. In contrast, Memex preserves each user's view of their topic space, and reconciles these diverse views at the community level. Furthermore, PowerBookmarks does not use hyperlink information for classification or for synthesizing themes. The Bookmark Organizer is a client-side solution for personal organization, but does

not provide community-level themes or topical surfing contexts. Purple Yogi[10] is a client-side software which logs pages visited and clusters them into folders. Then it tunes in on the Purple Yogi server to collect additional related material. No community-level mining is involved; Purple Yogi explicitly guarantees that user-specific data is stored locally on the user's desktop and never shipped out. Thus scope for valuable collaboration is lost and surfing history becomes inaccessible from other places from which the user might browse.

Other Internet start-ups have been quick to discover the annoyance of surfers maintaining multiple bookmark files and the opportunity of a central, networked bookmark server. We can list several sites which, using Javascript or a plugin, import existing Netscape or Explorer bookmarks and thereafter lets the surfer visit their Web site and maintain it using CGI and Javascript: Yahoo Companion[11], YaBoo[12], Baboo[13], Bookmark Tracker[14], and Backflip[15] are some examples. Some services like Third Voice[16] enables surfers to attach public or private annotations to any page they visit. These are essentially glorified FTP services with none of our extensive server-side analysis.

Several visualization tools have been designed recently that explore a limited radius neighborhood and draw clickable graphs. These are often used for site maintenance and elimination of dead links. Mapuccino and Fetuccino from IBM Haifa are well known examples [7, 1]. Our context viewer could benefit from better hypertext rendering techniques.

References

[1] I. Ben-Shaul, M. Herscovici, M. Jacovi, Y. S. Maarek, D. Pelleg, M. Shtalheim, V. Soroka, and S. Ur. Adding support for dynamic and focused search with Fetuccino. In *8th World Wide Web Conference*. Toronto, May 1999.

[2] V. Bush. As we may think. *The Atlantic Monthly*, July 1945. Online at http://www.theatlantic.com/unbound/flashbks/computer/bushf.htm.

[3] S. Chakrabarti, B. Dom, R. Agrawal, and P. Raghavan. Scalable feature selection, classification and signature generation for organizing large text databases into hierarchical topic taxonomies. *VLDB Journal*, Aug. 1998. Invited paper, online at http://www.cs.berkeley.edu/~soumen/VLDB54_3.PDF.

[4] S. Chakrabarti, S. Srivastava, M. Subramanyam, and M. Tiwari. Archiving and mining community web browsing experience using Memex. In *9th International World Wide Web Conference*, Amsterdam, May 2000.

[5] S. Chakrabarti, M. van den Berg, and B. Dom. Focused crawling: a new approach to topic-specific web resource discovery. *Computer Networks*, 31:1623–1640, 1999. First appeared in the 8th International World Wide Web Conference[17],

[7] http://www.yahoo.com
[8] http://dmoz.org
[9] http://www.ccrl.neclab.com/webdb/

[10] http://www.purpleyogi.com
[11] http://www.yahoo.com/r/cm
[12] http://www.yaboo.dk
[13] http://www.baboo.com
[14] http://www.bookmarktracker.com
[15] http://www.backflip.com
[16] http://www.thirdvoice.com
[17] http://www8.org

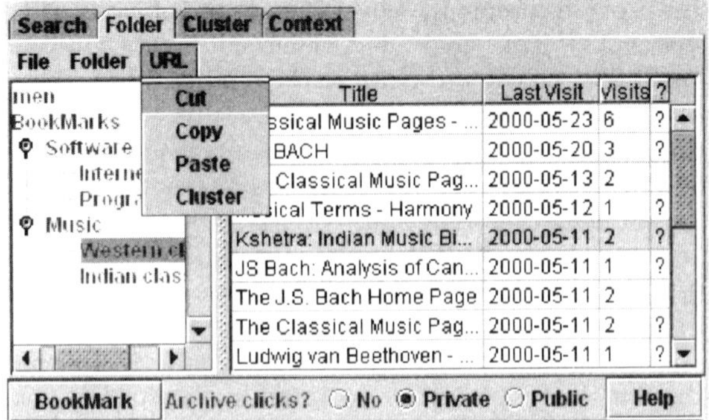

Figure 1: Each user has a personal folder/topic space, which is usually initialized by importing existing browser-specific bookmark folders. The classification demon then classifies all subsequent history elements, marking its guesses by '?'. The user can correct or reinforce the classifier using cut/paste, thus continually improving Memex's models for the user's topics of interest.

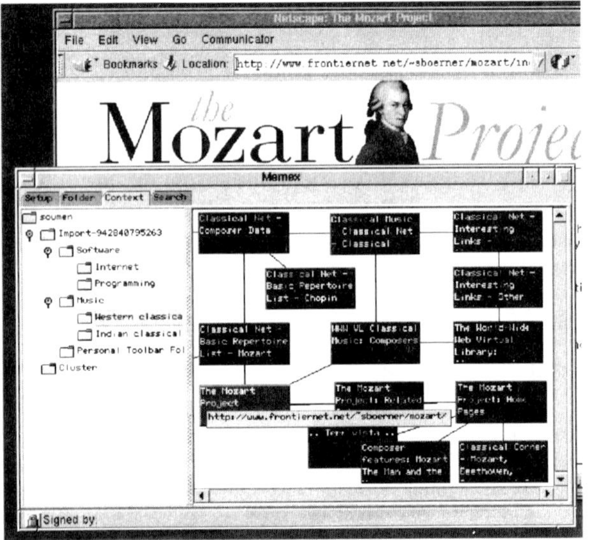

Figure 2: The trail tab shows a read-only view of the user's current folder structure. When the user selects a folder, Memex replays recently browsed pages which belong to the selected (or contained) topic(s), reminding the user of the latest topical context. In the screen-shot above, the chosen folder is */Music/Western Classical*. The user can now resume browsing and the display is updated with additional resources related to the topic.

Toronto, May 1999. Available online at `http://www8.org/w8-papers/5a-search-query/crawling/index.html`.

[6] D. R. Cutting, D. R. Karger, and J. O. Pedersen. Constant interaction-time scatter/gather browsing of very large document collections. In *Annual International Conference on Research and Development in Information Retrieval*, 1993.

[7] M. Hersovici, M. Jacovi, Y. S. Maarek, D. Pelleg, M. Shtalheim, and S. Ur. The Shark-Search algorithm-an application: Tailored web site mapping. In *7th World-Wide Web Conference*, Brisbane, Australia, Apr. 1998. Online at `http://www7.scu.edu.au/programme/fullpapers/1849/com1849.htm`.

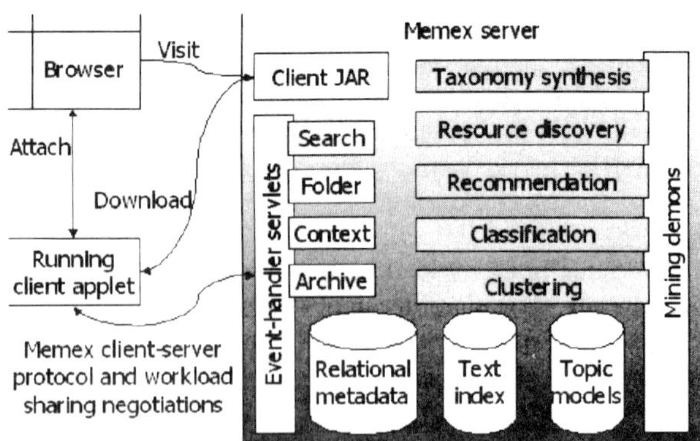

Figure 3: Block diagram of the Memex system, showing the client-server interface, the UI event handlers, the mining demons, and the loosely synchronized data repositories.

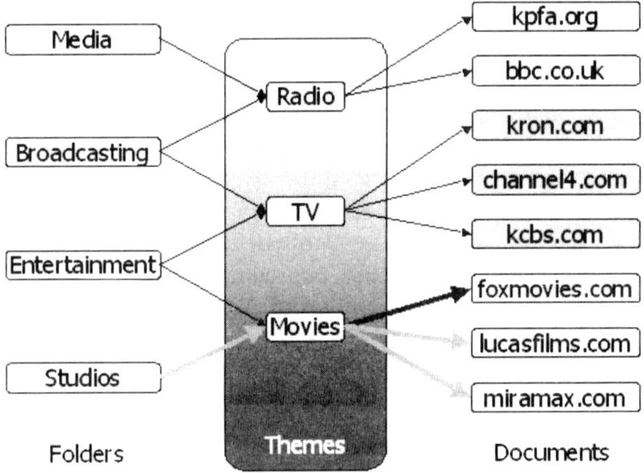

Figure 4: Memex computes, from the document-folder associations of multiple users, a topic taxonomy specifically tailored for the interests of that user population. The taxonomy consists of *themes* which capture common factors in people's interests when they can, while maintaining individuality when they must. Once computed, they can be used to guide resource discovery and collaborative recommendation.

[8] Y. S. Maarek and I. Z. Ben Shaul. Automatically organizing bookmarks per content. In *Fifth International World-Wide Web Conference*, Paris, May 1996.

[9] P. P. Maglio and T. Matlock. Metaphors we surf the Web by. In *Workshop on Personalized and Social Navigation in Information Space*, Stockholm, Sweden, 1998.

[10] L. H. Ungar and D. P. Foster. Clustering methods for collaborative filtering. In *AAAI Workshop on Recommendation Systems*, 1998. Online at `http://www.cis.upenn.edu/~ungar/papers/clust.ps`.

Building and Customizing Data-Intensive Web Sites using Weave

Khaled Yagoub, Daniela Florescu, Valérie Issarny, Cezar Andrei[*]

INRIA-Rocquencourt

Domaine de Voluceau, 78153 Le Chesnay Cédex, France

{firstname.lastname}@inria.fr

1 Overview

We call a *data-intensive* Web site a Web site that provides access to large numbers of pages whose content is dynamically extracted from a database. In this context, producing a Web page may require costly interaction with the database system for connection and querying. The database interaction cost adds up to the non-negligeable base cost of Web page delivery, thereby increasing much the client waiting time.

Various solutions have been proposed to improve Web performance by reducing the waiting time for a page. These solutions include predictive prefetching, caching of Web objects, and architecting the network and Web servers for scalability and availability [1]. Among these works, Cao et al. [3] introduce cache applets, which enable Web servers to attach a piece of Java code to each dynamic document. This code is run whenever a request for a cached document is received. A cache applet can either rewrite the cached document and return it, or request the cache to either fetch or regenerate the document. Close to this work, Barnes et al. [2] propose a domain-specific programming language, CacheL, for defining customizable caching policies. The language allows defining how objects are cached, replaced, and kept consistent. While these solutions present benefits, they remain insufficient to improve the Web latency of pages built from database content when the query execution cost dominates.

We demonstrate Weave[1], a data-intensive Web site management system developed at INRIA. The system addresses the performance problem of accessing dynamic Web pages in the case of sites whose content is derived from relational databases.

**Proceedings of the 26th VLDB Conference,
Cairo, Egypt, 2000.**

In a previous research, we addressed the problem of runtime management of data-intensive Web sites [4]. The proposed solution was to cache in the database the results of parameterized queries, under the form of relational tables, and reuse the results for subsequent requests. This improves performance of handling database queries, allows for efficient update propagation, and enables caching of data that are shared among various pages. However, this solution can alter the Web site's performance in the case of a low hit ratio or when the query execution time is not the most prominent cost (every cache action access the database via expensive SQL statements).

In the current version of Weave, we generalize this work. Our goal is to reduce the response time for serving page requests through an appropriate *customizable* cache system. Our solution enables data caching at various levels of data elaboration within the site. The system allows to cache the results of *database queries*, intermediate *XML fragments* and *HTML files*. In addition, it provides a *declarative language* (*WeaveL*) for specifying Web site structure and content, and an extension of this language for specifying the customized cache management policy within the site.

2 System description

Figure 1 depicts the architecture of the Weave system. In the following, we briefly discuss the key features and the corresponding components of Weave.

Declarative Web site specification. Weave [4] adopts the XML graph data model to describe the structure and the content of the Web site independently of its graphical representation (different models can be seen in [1]). An instance of this data model corresponding to a particular Web site is an *XML site graph*, which is a directed labeled graph with two types of nodes: internal nodes corresponding to Web pages, and leaf nodes corresponding to data values attached to pages. Links between pages are modeled as arcs between the internal nodes representing them in the graph. An XML site graph is defined *intensionally*, via an *XML site schema*, rather than extensionally (i.e., one Web page/XML fragment at a time). Therefore, a site schema represents nothing else than an XML view definition over a database. In this view, the Web pages are classified into

[1] http://www-caravel.inria.fr/Eprototype_WEAVE.html

homogeneous collections called *site classes*. Applying the site schema to a particular instance of the database results in a complete XML site graph. The graphical representation of the site is described using XSL style sheets.

Two components are fundamental in the Weave system: the XML Generator, which applies the definition of the site schema to the underlying data and produces (fragments of) the XML site graph, and the HTML Generator, which applies XSL style sheets to XML fragments, resulting in browsable HTML pages.

The WeaveL language. XML site schemas are described using the WeaveL language. A WeaveL program consists of a set of site class specifications. Each class specification contains the declaration of the parameters identifying an instance of the class, the SQL query whose result gives all possible instances for the above parameters (describing how to produce all instances of the class), the specification of the data contained in an instance, and the specification of the hyperlinks from an instance of the respective class.

Suppose we want to produce a browsable version of the data contained in the TPC/D benchmark [4]. A fragment of a program written in WeaveL is presented bellow. It describes Supplier pages, where each such page contains the name of the supplier, a set of links to the pages of his customers, and a form allowing a user to search information about the parts the supplier produces. The query given in the clause instances specifies how to obtain from the database all the possible values of the parameter $SK. This information is needed for the static evaluation of the Web site.

```
define class Supplier($SK)
{instances using Q0}
{
      data name using Q1;

      link customer to Customer($CK) using Q2);

      form parts
        input $partname text
        link to PartList($partname);

}
// where Q1, Q2,... are (parameterized) SQL queries defined as:

define query Q0 as
     select s.s_suppkey as $SK from Supplier s ;

define query Q1 as
     select s.s_name as name
     from Supplier s
     where s.s_suppkey = $SK ;
```

In order to support page components modeling, the link clause can be prefixed with the keyword embedded. In the example, if the clause **link** *customer* was prefixed by embedded, the system would compute all the customers pages related to the given supplier and embed them in the supplier page instead of creating links to these pages. Moreover, for performance purpose, a link clause can be prefixed with the keyword **prefetch**. In our example, if **prefetched** was used, a request for a **Supplier** page would trigger a

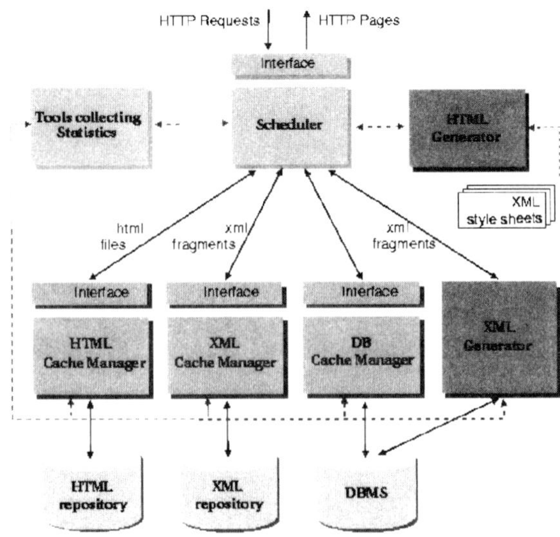

Figure 1: Architecture of the Weave system.

self (artificial) request to Weave for all the customer pages reachable via the given supplier page.

The XML Generator is responsible for the evaluation of the queries in the site schema and producing the corresponding XML data. Given a particular binding for the parameter $SK of the class Supplier, the XML generator produces the XML fragment corresponding to the Web page. For example given $SK=421, the following XML fragment is generated:

```
<XML_fragment id=" Supplier_421 ">
<class> Supplier </class>
<parameter> 421 </parameter>

<data_fragment name=" name ">
 <data_value> Supplier#000000421 </data_value>
<data_fragment>

<link_fragment name=" customer ">
 <link_item>
   <XML_fragment id=" Customer_2 ">
     <class> Customer </class>
     <parameter> 2 </parameter>
   </XML_fragment>
   <anchor> Customer#000000002 </anchor>
 </link_item>
 ...
</link_fragment>

<form_fragment name=" parts ">
   <XML_fragment>
     <class> PartList </class>
     <input> $partname </input>
   </XML_fragment>
   <input type=" text"> $partname </input>
</form_fragment>

</XML_fragment>
```

Three-level caching architecture. For performance sake, Weave can cache data at three levels of abstraction: tables, XML, and HTML. As in [4], the DB cache manager controls caching and lookahead computation within the database system. It interfaces with the system, and offers additional capabilities such as the pooling of database connections.

Compared to the HTML cache, which caches HTML files on disk, the XML cache has the advantage of storing less data and allows for carefully controlling the granularity of the cached data, ranging from the entire page to fragments of the page. Moreover, it allows diminishing the load generated on the database by the Web server.

The architecture (Figure 1) includes a manager for each individual cache and a cache scheduler. The cache managers share the same interface and implement standard cache operations for data retrieval like addition and removal. These operations are triggered by events such as HTTP requests and data invalidations. The scheduler coordinates the execution of cache managers. It interacts with one or more of the individual caches according to the caching policy set for the given page.

The system architecture is modular and can easily be distributed. The replication of components on proxies and clients is also possible.

Customized cache management. Our final goal is to automatically compile a declarative specification of a Web site into a customizable *runtime policy*. A runtime policy controls the runtime behavior of the Web site so to make optimal usage of the caches according to the users' access patterns and the update frequency of the data. It specifies which data to prefetch or to cache (HTML pages, XML fragments, relational tables, or any combination of those), which particular items to prefetch or cache (e.g, which particular HTML pages or XML fragments), and which actions to perform under different events, such as page requests, data updates or environmental changes.

So far our system does not support such an automatic generation of runtime policies. However, to ease the task of the Web site administrator, we introduce *WeaveRPL*, a high level language for the abstract specification of the cache system's behavior (the specification is similar for each cache). The language is based on event-condition rules. It enables to explicitly specify the global policies implemented by an individual cache manager for setting overall features such as the maximum cache size, and the actions to be carried out upon a global event such as a cache overflow. Furthermore, it builds upon the declarative Web site specification, and allows the definition of per-site-class customized caching (basically, how to handle events related to data retrieval, addition, removal, and staleness).

In the following example, the HTML cache is configured as a single container, named **HTML_CONT**, which stores instances of classes Supplier, Customer, and Part. The container can be used to cache all Part instances and only instances of the Supplier and Customer classes that satisfy the following constraints: instances of Supplier must have a size less than 2KB, and instances of Customer must have an access frequency that is greater than 0.3. Upon initialization (handling of the onInit event), the HTML cache is fed with all the instances of class Part, and only with the instances of class Supplier, whose value of key SK is less than 100 and which meet the aforementioned constraint on size over cached instances. The content of the cache

is refreshed every 30 minutes using the onTimer event, removing all the stored instances whose age is greater than 10 minutes. Whenever the cache is full (onFull event), a traditional LRU algorithm is applied for the replacement of the instances.

```
Cache HTML
{
  //Container definitions
    define container HTML_CONT as
    select Supplier where size <= 2KB,
      Customer where frequency >= 0.3,
      Part;
  //ECA rules
    onInit compute Part, Supplier(SK) where SK<100;
    onTimer(30mn) remove all where age>10mn;
    onFull(200M) applay LRU;
}
```

The XML cache specified in the example below also contains a single container (XML_CONT).

```
Cache XML
{
  //Container definitions
    define container XML_CONT as
      select Customer : fragments{name, supplier};
  //ECA rules
    onInit compute all;
    onTimer(120mn) reinit;
}
```

As opposed to its HTML counterpart, the XML cache container is used only to cache the fragments corresponding to the name of a given Customer and the set of links to his suppliers' pages. We assume that these fragments are not frequently updated and worth being cached. The other fragments, which are links to orders' pages of a Customer, are supposed to be frequently updated and therefore should be built on demand. The container is refreshed every 2 hours by removing and recomputing all the instances (reinit action).

Even in the absence of an automatic way to generate runtime policies, a high level language for specifying such policies does ease the production of data intensive Web sites, compared to existing approaches. By using our system, a Web site administrator is only requested to abstractly describe the desired cache management. Besides this language, Weave provides also an *API* for Web application programs to explicitly control the content of the caches.

3 Demonstration

The main focus of the demonstration is on Weave's ability of improving the performance of Web sites through a customized cache management. To this end, we compare different runtime policies with a Web site derived from the

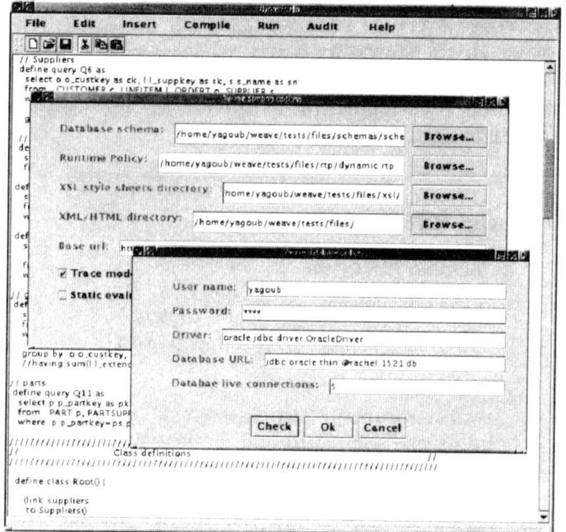

Figure 2: Weave configuration window.

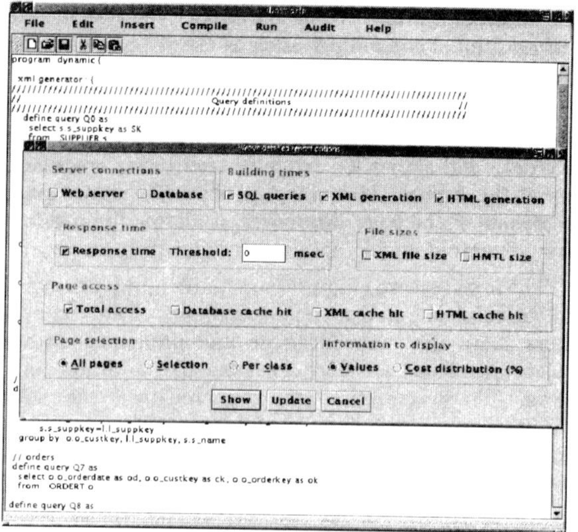

Figure 3: Execution reports main window.

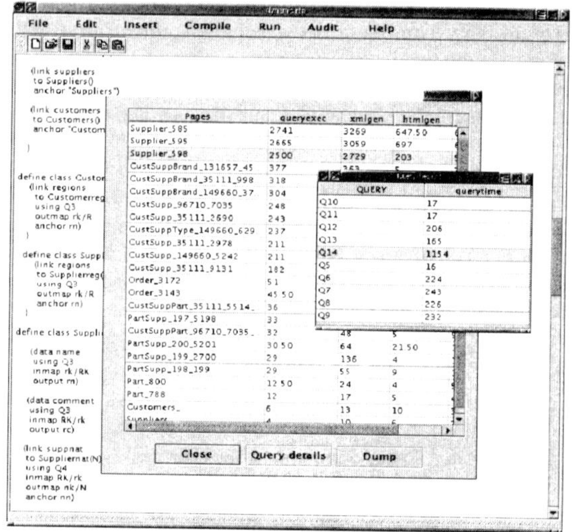

Figure 4: Query execution time report.

TPC/D benchmark database. The data is loaded into the Oracle8 DBMS.

Figure 2 shows the Weave user interface that allows a Web administrator to edit, modify and compile a WeaveL program or a runtime policy. The administrator can also set the execution parameters of Weave like the selected runtime policy and the maximum number of reusable database connections through this interface.

The demonstration starts by showing how to specify the Web site using the WeaveL language and a set of XSL style sheets. Then, we automatically run the Web site under two extreme conditions: when the entire site is precomputed before the pages are requested (purely static evaluation) and when each page is computed on the fly (purely dynamic evaluation). We show that it is immediate to derive from the declarative specification each of the above extreme approaches. In doing so, we run the Web site according to a particular trace (which can be given or generated based on a certain probability distribution).

For each execution (Figure 3), the system can be configured to generate reports containing information about the distribution of the various execution costs (database access, XML generation, HTML generation), the average total response time and the average XML and HTML file size. This information can be generated per page or per site class. Figure 4 shows an example of a Weave report obtained after browsing the TPC/D Web site. The report also displays the details of the execution time for all of the queries involved in building a particular page (see Figure 4).

Based on the results of the execution reports, the Web site administrator can tailor a specific caching strategy aimed at performance improvement. We show how complex caching strategies can be expressed in our formalism by simply using high level runtime policies. Given a particular runtime policy, the Web site can be rerun; the system will interpret the runtime policy and utilize the caches appropriately. Finally, by comparing the execution reports obtained from various runtime policies we show that a mixed strategy (caching data at different levels) is generally optimal, and therefore desirable.

References

[1] http://caravel.inria.fr/~yagoub/webdbase.html.

[2] J. F. Barnes and R. Pandey. Providing dynamic and customizable caching policies. In *Proc. of USENIX Symp. on Internet Technologies and Systems*, 1999.

[3] P. Cao, J. Zhang, and K. Beach. Active cache: Caching dynamic contents (objects) on the Web. In *Proc. of Middleware*, 1998.

[4] D. Florescu, V. Issarny, P. Valduriez, and K. Yagoub. Caching strategies for data-intensive Web sites. In *Proc. of the Int. Conf. on Very Large Data Bases (VLDB)*, 2000.

Information Integration: the MOMIS Project Demonstration

D. Beneventano[1],[*] S. Bergamaschi[1,*], S. Castano[2], A. Corni[1,*],

R. Guidetti[1], G. Malvezzi[1], M. Melchiori[3], M. Vincini[1]

(1) Università di Modena e Reggio Emilia, DSI-Via Campi 213/B, 41100 Modena
(2) Università di Milano, DSI-Via Comelico 39 - 20135 Milano
(3) Università di Brescia DEI-Via Branze 38 - 25123 Brescia

e-mail : {domenico.beneventano,sonia.bergamaschi,corni.alberto,maurizio.vincini}@unimo.it
castano@dsi.unimi.it, melchior@bsing.ing.unibs.it

1 Overview

The goal of this demonstration is to present the main features of a Mediator component, *Global Schema Builder*, of an I3 system, called MOMIS (Mediator envirOnment for Multiple Information Sources) [1]. MOMIS[1][2] has been conceived to provide an integrated access to heterogeneous information stored in traditional databases (e.g., relational, object-oriented) or file systems, as well as in semistructured sources. The demonstration is based on the integration of two simple sources of different kind, structured and semi-structured, wich will be described in Section 2.

Like other integration projects [2, 3], MOMIS follows a "semantic approach" to information integration based on the conceptual schema, or metadata, of the information sources, and on the following functional elements:

---

[2] MOMIS is a joint project among the Università di Modena e Reggio Emilia, the Università di Milano, and the Università di Brescia within the national research project INTERDATA, theme n.3 "Integration of Information over the Web", coordinated by V. De Antonellis, Università di Brescia.

1. a common data model, ODM_{I^3}, which is defined according to the ODL_{I^3} language, to describe source schemas for integration purposes. ODM_{I^3} and ODL_{I^3} have been defined in MOMIS as subset of the corresponding ones in ODMG, following the proposal for a standard mediator language developed by the I^3/POB working group [4]. In addition, ODL_{I^3} introduces new constructors to support the semantic integration process;

2. one or more wrappers, to translate metadata descriptions into the common ODL_{I^3} representation;

3. a mediator which is composed of two modules: the *Global Schema Builder* (GSB) and the *Query Manager* (QM). The GSB module processes and integrates ODL_{I^3} descriptions received from wrappers to derive the integrated representation of the information sources. The QM module performs query processing and optimization. In particular, it generates the OQL_{I^3}[3] queries for wrappers, starting from a global OQL_{I^3} query formulated by the user on the global schema. Using Description Logics techniques, the QM component can generate in an automatic way the translation of the generic OQL_{I^3} query into different sub-queries, one for each involved local source.

The original contribution of MOMIS is related to the

---

[3]OQL_{I^3} is a subset of OQL-ODMG.

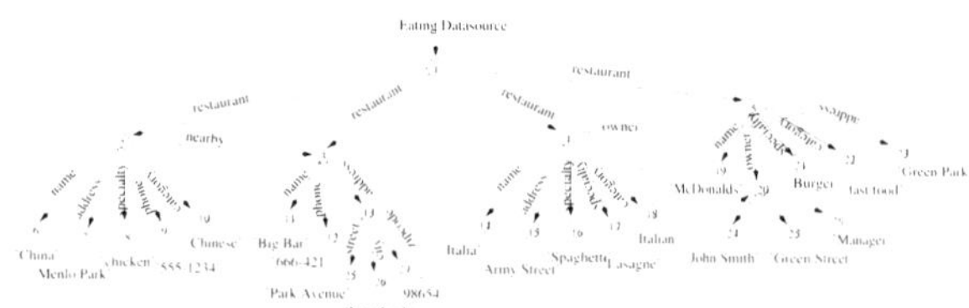

Figure 1: Eating Data Source (ED)

```
Restaurant-pattern =
      (Restaurant,{name,address, phone*,
      specialty,category,nearby*,owner*})
Owner-pattern = (Owner,{name,address,job})
Address-pattern =
      (Address,{street,city,zipcode})
```

Figure 2: Object patterns for the source ED

availability of a set of techniques for the designer to face common problems that arise when integrating pre-existing information sources, containing both semistructured and structured data. MOMIS provides the capability of explicitly introducing many kinds of knowledge for integration, such as integrity constraints, intra- and inter-source intensional and extensional relationships, and designer supplied domain knowledge. MOMIS supports information integration in a way automated as much as possible and performs revision and validation of the various kinds of knowledge used for the integration. To this end, MOMIS combines reasoning capabilities of Description Logics with affinity-based clustering techniques, by exploiting a common ontology for the sources constructed using lexical knowledge from WordNet and validated integration knowledge.

2 Demonstration

2.1 Running example

In order to illustrate how the MOMIS approach works, we will use the following example of integration in the Restaurant Guide domain, involving two different datasources that collect information about restaurants. The first datasource is the Eating Datasource guidebook (ED), containing semistruc-

```
Steakhouse(s_code, name, street, pers_id,
      special_dish)
Bistro(s_code, type, pers_id)
Person(pers_id, first_name, last_name,)
      qualification)
Brasserie(b_code, name, address)
```

Figure 3: Food Guide Database (FD)

tured objects about restaurants of the west coast with information about menu, specialties, category, and so on. Fig. 1 illustrates a portion of the ED datasource (with a notation similar to the one of the OEM model [5, 6]).

We use the notion of *object pattern* to represent at intensional level all different objects that describe the same concept in a given semistructured source. Object patterns for all the objects in our semistructured source are shown in Fig. 2 (where the symbol "*" denotes optionality). Three object patterns are defined: Restaurant, containing information about restaurants; Owner, containing information about people involved; Address, containing information about addresses. Each Restaurant has an atomic name, category, and specialty. Furthermore, some Restaurant objects have an atomic address and some other a complex address, a phone, a complex object nearby, specifying the nearest restaurant, and an owner, specifying the name, the address and the job of the restaurant's owner.

The second datasource is the Food Guide Database (FD), a relational database containing information about USA restaurants. The FD is composed of four relations, namely Steakhouse, Bistro, Person, and Brasserie (see Fig. 3). Information related to restaurant is maintained into the Steakhouse relation. Bistro instance is a subset of Steakhouse instance and contains information about the small informal restaurants that serve wine. Each Steakhouse and Bistro is managed by a Person. Information about places where drinks and snacks are served on, are stored in Brasserie relation.

2.2 Demonstration Architecture

The *Global Schema Builder* (GSB) is the mediator component which processes and integrates ODL$_{I3}$

source descriptions received from wrappers to derive the integrated representation of the datasources, that is, the Global Virtual Schema. It is composed mainly by a GUI (the SI-Designer module), a data repository, and a coordination module (GlobalSchema module) and a set of services (service level) used during the integration (see Figure 4). All such modules are available as CORBA objects and interact using established `idl` interfaces. Datasources to be integrated are reachable by *wrapper modules* that are also CORBA objects (with a very simple common interface).

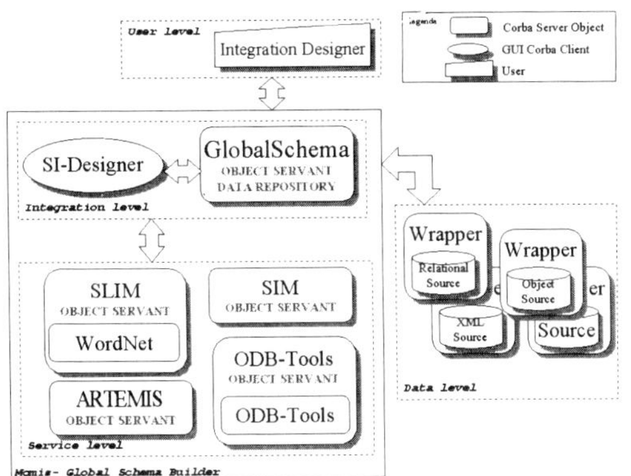

Figure 4: Demonstration architecture

The designer performs the integration process in a semi-automatic way, following the steps suggested by the (**SI-Designer**). Each step is characterized by a graphical form (see Figure 5) and each form "talks directly" with the *GlobalSchema* object (the `idl` interface between *GlobalSchema* and *SI-Designer* is strictly modular) retrieving data and saving new information provided by the designer in the Common Thesaurus, a common ontology among sources.

For the integration phase, GSB uses the following services: **SIM** (*Source Integrator Module*): it extracts intra-schema intensional relationships on the basis of the source structures; **SLIM** (*Schemata Lessical Integrator Module*): it extracts inter-schema intensional relationships between attribute and class names, exploiting the Wordnet lexical system [7]; In this case, synonyms, hypernyms/hyponyms, and related terms can be automatically proposed to the designer, by se-

lecting them according to relationships predefined in the lexical system. **ARTEMIS** tool environment [8], which uses terminological relationships in the Common Thesaurus to assess the level of *affinity* between ODL_{I3} classes by interactively computing a set of affinity coefficients, that take into account both ontological and structural knowledge about ODL_{I3} classes. Furthermore, ARTEMIS classifies ODL_{I3} classes by affinity levels using hierarchical clustering techniques; **ODB-Tools**, a tool based on the OLCD Description Logics [9] inference techniques, such as *incoherence* detection and *subsumption* computation, which performs ODL_{I3} schema validation and evaluates implicit inter-schema *isa* relationships.

The integration process is subdivided in two phases (**1**) *Common Thesaurus* generation, (**2**) Global Virtual Schema generation.

To build the Global Virtual Schema, the following sequence of interactions is performed:

- **SIM**, to extract intra-schema relationships;
- **SLIM**, to extract inter-schema intensional relationships between attribute and class names, exploiting the Wordnet lexical system [7]). At each interaction the extracted relationships are shown to the designer who can confirm them or not and can provide further information.
- **ARTEMIS**, to compute *affinity* coefficients between ODL_{I3} classes, to evaluate their level of matching.

As a result of these interactions, ODB-Tools performs checking and validation to come up with a *Common Thesaurus*. Once the *Common Thesaurus* has been built, the ARTEMIS tool is invoked from within **SI-Designer** to perform clustering and identify clusters of classes with a given *affinity* threshold value. Affinity clusters of ODL_{I3} classes interactively selected by ARTEMIS are passed to ODB-Tools to construct the Global Virtual Schema of the mediator. In particular, an integrated global ODL_{I3} class is interactively defined for each selected cluster. ODB-Tools is exploited for a semi-automatic generation of the global ODL_{I3} classes. The set of global ODL_{I3} classes defined constitutes the Global Virtual Schema of the MOMIS mediator to be used for posing queries against the sources.

The **GlobalSchema** (see Figure 4) is the information repository and acts as coordination object for an integration session. A GlobalSchema object exists for each *integration process*. Such object is characterized by a *status* that spaces between the value *uninitialized* to the value *complete*, corresponding to having a completely modeled Global Virtual Schema. A GlobalSchema object constitutes the input for the *Query Manager* object that will manage queries on the integrated schema.

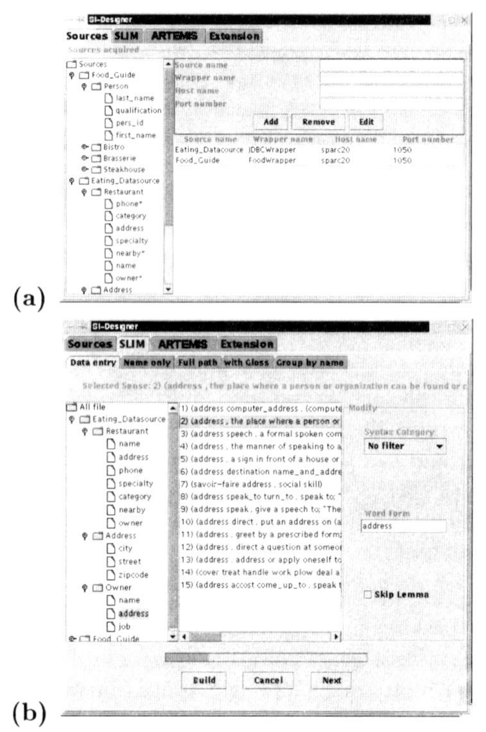

Figure 5: Example: (a) Source binding interface and (b) SLIM interface

References

[1] S. Bergamaschi, S. Castano, and M. Vincini. Semantic integration of semistructured and structured data sources. *SIGMOD Records*, 28(1), March 1999.

[2] Y. Arens, C.Y. Chee, C. Hsu, and C. A. Knoblock. Retrieving and integrating data from multiple information sources. *International Journal of Intelligent and Cooperative Information Systems*, 2(2):127–158, 1993.

[3] M.T. Roth and P. Scharz. Don't scrap it, wrap it! a wrapper architecture for legacy data sources. In *Proc. of the 23rd Int. Conf. on Very Large Databases*, Athens, Greece, 1997.

[4] P. Buneman, L. Raschid, and J. Ullman. Mediator languages - a proposal for a standard, April 1996. Available at ftp://ftp.umiacs.umd.edu/pub/ ONRrept/medmodel96.ps.

[5] S. Abiteboul, D. Quass, J. McHugh, J. Widom, and J. Wiener. The lorel query language for semistructured data. *Journal of Digital Libraries*, 1(1), 1996.

[6] Y.Papakonstantinou, H.Garcia-Molina, and J.Widom. Object exchange across heterogeneous information sources. In *Proc. of ICDE95*, Taipei, Taiwan, 1995.

[7] A.G. Miller. Wordnet: A lexical database for english. *Communications of the ACM*, 38(11):39–41, 1995.

[8] S. Castano and V. De Antonellis. A schema analysis and reconciliation tool environment for heterogeneous databases. In *IEEE Proc. of IDEAS'99 Int. Database Engineering and Applications Symposium*, Montreal, 1999. ARTEMIS home page: http://bsing.ing.unibs.it/*sim*deantone/ interdata_tema3/Artemis/artemis.html.

[9] D. Beneventano, S. Bergamaschi, S. Lodi, and C. Sartori. Consistency checking in complex object database schemata with integrity constraints. *IEEE Transactions on Knowledge and Data Engineering*, 10:576–598, July/August 1998.

Telcordia's Database Reconciliation
and Data Quality Analysis Tool

Francesco Caruso, Munir Cochinwala , Uma Ganapathy, Gail Lalk, Paolo Missier

Telcordia Technologies
445 South Street
Morristown, NJ
U.S.A.
caruso@research.telcordia.com

Abstract

This demonstration illustrates how a comprehensive database reconciliation tool can provide the ability to characterize data-quality and data-reconciliation issues in complex real-world applications. Telcordia's data reconciliation and data quality analysis tool includes rapid generation of appropriate pre-processing and matching rules applied to a training set created from samples of the data. Once tuned, the appropriate rules can be applied efficiently to the complete data sets. The tool uses a modular JavaBeans-based architecture that allows for customized matching functions and iterative runs that build upon previously learned information. Telcordia has been able to provide significant insights to clients who recognize that they have data reconciliation problems but cannot determine root causes effectively when using currently available off-the-shelf tools. A description of the analysis of a duplicate-record problem in a set of taxpayer databases is included in this report to illustrate the effective use of the tool.

1. Introduction

Data reconciliation is becoming increasingly important due to the mergers of companies, one-stop shopping for services (each service used to have its own database) and the popularity of warehouses for decision support. One of the fundamental problems of data reconciliation is the problem of identifying duplicates in databases. [1,2,3] Duplicate identification can be further split into exact matching techniques and approximate matching techniques.

At Telcordia, case studies that have been done using a prototype data reconciliation and analysis tool have shown that in a typical large database matching problem involving several million records in each database, the number of exact matches is about 3%-5%. The necessity for approximate matching is clear. The focus at Telcordia in this area is on building a tool and methodology that facilitates approximate matching and also allows users the flexibility to define their own rules for pre-processing, matching and testing/refining the results on a training set. The rules generated from the training set are applied to the (usually much larger) complete data set.

Telcordia's data reconciliation tool has been applied to several real database reconciliation problems. In one case study, where the goal was simply to improve the matching percentage on customer addresses between two databases, Telcordia's tool improved the matching percentage by 30% over off-the-shelf tools. In another case study, described in detail below, one of the goals was to find potential duplicate records among two databases. The client was already aware of a certain number of records that had been verified to be duplicates. The Telcordia tool improved the identification of the number of likely duplicates by nearly a factor of 2 and, more importantly, the tool was used to classify the likely causes of duplication, which helped significantly narrow-down the number of records that would require a manual verification.

Specifically, in addition to the known duplicates (4.4% on a 600,000 records sample), the tool identified another

Proceedings of the 26th International Conference on Very Large Databases, Cairo, Egypt, 2000

"

1.8% of the remaining records (excluding the training set) which are suspect duplicates. 1.5% are automatically classified as duplicates with high confidence, while only 0.3%, or about 1,700 records, are expected to require further analysis. The benefits of this analysis are twofold: the reduction in the number of records that needs to be manually inspected significantly reduces the cost of maintaining data quality in this application and the identification of the additional duplicate records improves the overall quality of the data.

2. Data Reconciliation Process

A general process for data reconciliation among pairs of records can be summarized in the following steps:

- **Development of Training Set:**
  A training set is a set of records drawn from the larger dataset being analyzed that can be used to rapidly generate pre-processing and matching rules. A training set is typically generated by sampling the larger data sets and manually verifying the matching conditions applying domain knowledge of the larger dataset.

- **Preprocessing:** Preprocessing includes the elimination of stopwords, special characters, and blanks, and the reduction of known, common words to a canonical form. This step is usually highly domain dependent. For instance, in the context of Italian street addresses, the notation "vle" is expanded to "Viale" ("avenue"), "p.zza" to "Piazza", and so forth.

- **Parameters space:** The tool is parametric, with the main types of customizable parameters being the set of distance measures to perform approximate matching, and the set of descriptors for the data records under comparison.[4] Both these sets are extensible. Common definitions of string-based distance measures include Hamming distance and edit or alignment distance. Customized algorithms can be used in the tool to implement specific distance functions. Typical record descriptors include field lengths, last update, and source of record.

- **Matching Rule Generation:** This consists of selecting an algorithm to generate matching rules. The validity of the matching rules will be tested using the training set. The algorithm will typically evolve as domain knowledge is achieved through successive passes on the data. The parameter space can be pared down to include only parameters that contribute significantly to the matching process. Machine learning and statistical techniques can be used to reduce the amount of manual analysis that is required at this stage.

- **Application of Pruned Parameter Rule:** Once the improved matching rule has been developed on a training set, it can be applied to the original (larger) datasets. The pruning of the parameter space carried out in the previous step will have significantly reduced the complexity of the matching process.

3. Data Reconciliation and Data Quality Tool

Telcordia's data-reconciliation and data-quality tool consists of three basic stages: data source selection, pre-processing, and matching. The tool is able to process complex data analysis flows in which the results of the match between two data sources are used as input for a match on a third source. This flexibility allows one to analyze problems that involve more than two data sources, and to compute multiple matching functions on a dataset. The tool is written using a JavaBeans-based architecture. New pre-processing or matching functions are encapsulated into Java classes and can be dynamically added to the tool.

The first processing stage enables the selection of the files or database tables to be compared. The tool can accept files with fixed-width columns or variable-width columns with delimiters. One can specify the headings for each column or let the tool determine the headings based on the contents of the first record. After specifying the file type and format, the tool enables the user to view the contents of the files. At this stage, there is an option to select only a sample of the database of interest. The ability to sample the data allows for rapid generation of pre-processing and matching rules.

The second stage allows the user to select the columns that are of interest and to perform pre-processing functions on the data. These functions modify columns in each record to bring them to a consistent format. Examples of pre-processing functions include the elimination of special characters, replacing name aliases, removal of parenthesis in telephone numbers and removal of dashes in dates. Some of these functions also have data associated with them (e.g. list of aliases) which can be changed at run time. Default pre-processing rules can be specified for particular data types (e.g. address, name, numeric data). This streamlines the labor involved in selecting pre-processing rules for repetitive runs on similar data sets. After pre-processing rules have been selected and applied to the data, one can view the data and see highlighted cells where data has been modified. The pre-processing functions can be iterated until the user is satisfied with the effect the rules have on the data.

The final stage in the process is the matching stage where matching functions are applied to the pre-processed data. The matching is between one or more columns from a record in one data source and one or more columns from a record in the other data source. The modularity built into the tool allows the user to select from a variety of matching functions including the following:

- Identification of records that have an exact or approximate match in specified columns
- Identification of records in a data source that have no match in the other data source
- Identification of records that match on one column and mismatch on another column
- Identification of duplicate records within a data source
- Classification of mismatched records based on a measure such as edit distance
- Filtering of particular data from the matching process, such as blank fields.

One of the advantages of this tool is the ability to create new matching functions that may be application-specific. Traditional edit distance (based on a weighted calculation of character deletions, additions, or transpositions), for example, may not be a sufficient measure of the differences between fields in which the mismatches are the result of word permutations and non-standard abbreviations. It has been demonstrated that the ability to easily modify the matching functions can assist in providing a useful characterization of the root causes of data reconciliation problems.

4.0 Case Study – Data Reconciliation of Taxpayer Data

Telcordia's data reconciliation and data quality methodology and tool have been successfully used to perform data analysis and reconciliation on a number of real-life cases. Discussed here is a case study centered on the analysis of Public Administration data, in the context of work done for a foreign Government. The data resides in a large legacy database, in which taxpayers' personal and residence data have been accumulating over many years. At different times, various official and unofficial data sources contributed to the database, inserting and updating data in a way that depended more on the intricacies of tax laws than on a rational design for data acquisition. In this situation, format consistency, value accuracy and data currency arise as the most common problems. Specifically, various data sources have been providing data in different formats. Address formats differ, according to local conventions that change in time, resulting in multiple versions for the same real address. Access to a directory of official addresses, when defined

at all, was not an option. Personal data also follows local conventions, with multiple spellings of the same names. Most of the records are fed to the database by processes in which one or more steps include manual data entry, without any automatic cross-reference to logically related data. This accounts for a predictably low accuracy for the majority of the data values at the time they are inserted into the database. Furthermore, those records are only occasionally updated, either when an error is detected, or when they are run through an ad hoc validation batch job. The main problem appears to be that the central Administration is a user, not a steward, of (personal and residence) data whose responsibility in terms of accuracy rests with other local administrations. Because communication with the periphery is difficult and occasional, the update pattern for this data is erratic, resulting in a large fraction of potentially stale records.

To compound the problem, an interesting data duplication issue arises because of the peculiar nature of the definitions of the record keys. As it turns out, one individual may be represented by multiple records in the database, and be assigned multiple keys (equivalent to the Social Security Number in the U.S.), with an obvious negative impact on the tax administration. Telcordia's tool has been used successfully to identify the possible record duplicates, and, using appropriate reference data, to determine the actual correctness and currency levels of personal and address information.

4.1 Duplicate Record Analysis

To illustrate the methodology supported by the tool, the duplicate detection problem is described in detail. In this scenario, the database is populated with the taxpayers' vital and address data. For each record, encoding part of the first and last name, the place and date of birth, and the gender generates a key. Keys generated in this way are unique: if two records yield the same encoding, one of the two keys is modified in order to differentiate between them. Problems may arise when the same individual is entered multiple times in the database, each time with slightly different values for the fields that contribute to the encoding. This can happen for a variety of reasons that can be traced to the nature of the processes that feed the database, and are well known in the data quality community. When these errors go undetected, an individual is assigned multiple, slightly different keys, all formally valid. Our task was to detect as many of these errors as possible, and to correctly classify suspect records pairs as duplicates (representing the same individual). Notice that this is an instance of the well-known object-identity problem, and that it is in general not possible to determine with certainty that two records represent the same object, without asking the Data Steward.

In this case study, a number of such duplicates had already been detected by the owners of the database, so that a small fraction of all record pairs was correctly labelled as duplicates. Those records can therefore be used as a training set. The main strategy, then, is to determine a set of heuristic classification rules for the record pairs (the only classes being duplicate/non-duplicate), with the goal of maximizing the number of classified pairs while minimizing the number of false positives, i.e., the number of pairs incorrectly labelled as duplicates. First, for each pair, a set of derived attributes is computed, including various versions of edit distances among corresponding pairs of attributes in the two records. The first step in rules generation is to create a taxonomy of the types of mismatches that cause each pair to be classified as duplicate, along with a frequency distribution of the records by type of mismatch.

Telcordia's tool is used to produce the sets of derived attributes and the taxonomy automatically. For instance, it calculates the frequency of record pairs for which the edit distance on the last name field lies in a given range, for different ranges. Distributions based on more than one attribute can be used also. The term "taxonomy" indicates a hierarchical classification: first, a subset of pairs that exhibit a particular type of mismatch (e.g. edit distance on last name between 1 and 4) is selected. Then, the distribution of members of this set with respect to additional properties is computed. For instance, one may determine the fraction of pairs, among those that mismatch slightly on last name, for which the gender information disagrees. Again, the tool automates this process. The resulting taxonomy, annotated with distribution frequencies, can then be used to infer classification rules. The rules are tested and tuned on the training set (notice that rules are not generated using the training set, hence potential problems of rules overfitting are largely avoided), and finally applied to the main dataset.

This analysis groups the set of record pairs by type(s) of mismatch, with reference to the taxonomy mentioned above. Furthermore, it classifies each such group as duplicate/nonduplicate, with a specified confidence level. This provides both classification and problem explanation. The resulting output consists of one group of records, each labeled according to the type of mismatch they exhibit, that are duplicates with high confidence; a second group of high-confidence non-duplicates; and a group of borderline cases that require further analysis. Specifically, in addition to the known duplicates (4.4% on a 600,000 records sample), the tool identified another 1.8% of the remaining records (excluding the training set) which are suspect duplicates. Out of these, 1.5% are automatically classified as duplicates with high confidence, while only 0.3%, or about 1,700 records, are expected to require further analysis. This further investigation inevitably requires manual intervention (it is often necessary to check with the Data Steward or contact the individual directly to resolve the case), absorbing the bulk of the costs. This approach has resulted in a significant reduction on the cost of manual inspection, compared with previous studies on the same domain. In this respect, one of the main and most appreciated results achieved using Telcordia's tool has been to reduce the undecided set to a manageable size.

5.0 Summary

Telcordia's data reconciliation and data quality tool has been demonstrated on several complex real-world data sets including customer address matching in several industries and duplicate identification in government administrative data. The flexibility the tool provides the user to define customized pre-processing and matching rules combined with the capability to iterate through sample data sets allows for improved matching accuracy and root-cause analysis of defects.

4. References

[1] Bitton, D. and DeWitt, D.J.H., "Duplicate record elimination in large data files" *ACM Transactions on Database Systems*, 8(2):255-65, 1983.

[2] Hernandez, M. and Stolfo, S., "The merge/purge problem for large databases" *Proceedings of the ACM SIGMOD International Conference on Management of Data*, pages 127-138, May 1995.

[3] Burch, George, *Building, Using and Managing the Data Warehouse,* Edited by Barquin, Ramon, and Edelstein, Herb, New York, Prentice Hall, 1997.

[4] Gusfield, D., *Algorithms On Strings, Trees And Sequences,* Cambridge, Cambridge University Press, 215-225, 1997.

[5] Newcombe, Howard B., Kennedy, J.M., Axford, S. J. and James, A.P., "Automatic linkage of vital records", *Science*, 130;954-959, October 1959.

Rainbow: Distributed Database System for Classroom Education and Experimental Research

Abdelsalam (Sumi) Helal and Hua Li

Computer & Information Science & Eng. Department
University of Florida
Gainesville, FL 32611-6120, USA
{helal,huli}@cise.ufl.edu

1. Overview

Rainbow is a Java and web-based distributed database system designed for academic purposes, and serves as an exercise to understand concepts of distributed transactions and transaction management including concurrency control, atomic actions, data replication, and fault tolerance.

The motivation for the Rainbow project is twofold. First, Rainbow can be used as a teaching tool. Graduate students taking Distributed Database (or Database Implementation courses) can gain a better understanding and experience of issues involved in transaction processing in a distributed environment [1][2][4]. The second motivation is to use Rainbow as a research tool to conduct scientific experiments on distributed database and transaction processing. To achieve these goals, Rainbow allows the user to configure and program the distributed environment, transactions, and transaction management protocols, and to observe local as well as global executions (history and measured behavior and performance). Rainbow also lends itself as an open system that can be easily changed and extended by students and researchers.

2. Rainbow Architecture and Design

Rainbow consists of three tiers: the graphical user interface (GUI), the Web middle tier, and the Rainbow core (Figure 1).

Proceedings of the 26th International Conference on Very Large Databases, Cairo, Egypt, 2000

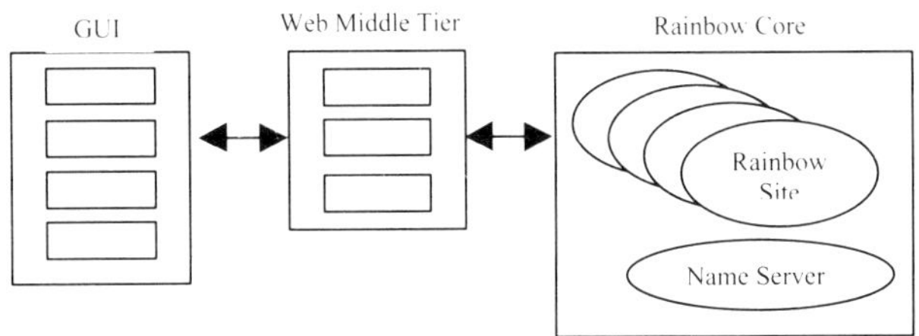

Figure 1. Rainbow architecture with functional mapping

Rainbow GUI allows the user to: a) configure a network simulation; b) configure a name server, Rainbow sites, database items, and select and configure protocols; c) manually or automatically configure and dispatch transactions; d) inject network and site failures and recoveries; and d) monitor the execution state, progress, and measure the performance resulting from executing a Rainbow instance.

The Rainbow core is comprised of the name server and a number of Rainbow sites. The name server stores metadata of all Rainbow sites, such as the id and end point specifications. Also maintained in the name server are the database fragmentation, replication and distribution schema. Any site can query the name server to get pertinent information. Each site can freely communicate with each other. Any site has the capability to concurrently process multiple transactions.

The Web middle tier serves as a fast and reliable bridge between Rainbow GUI and the Rainbow core. This tier consists of Java servlets, which are located at two levels, with level one being at the Rainbow home host and level two at the hosts where the Rainbow core resides. Even though Rainbow GUI applet can only communicate with the Rainbow home host, servlets do not have such restrictions. This means that the servlets residing at the Rainbow home can communicate freely with any other host in the network. Thus, the two-level arrangement of servlets provides Rainbow GUI applet the freedom of reaching any host in a Rainbow domain.

The detailed architecture is presented in Figure 2.

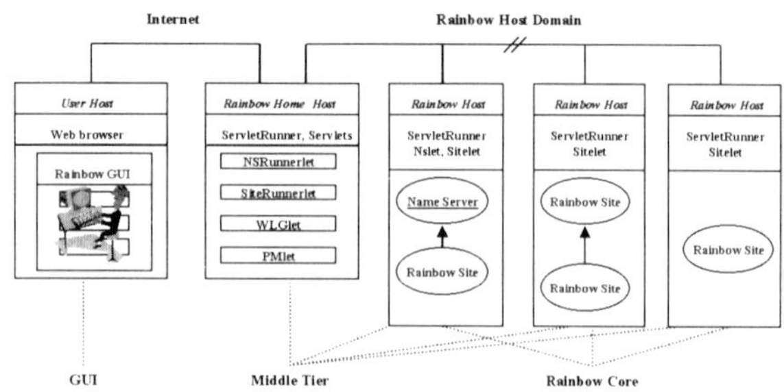

Figure 2. Rainbow architecture with physical mapping.

In this architecture, the user interacts with the Rainbow GUI via a Web browser in the user host. Rainbow GUI is downloaded to the user host as a Java applet when the user clicks a Web universal resource locator (URL) link to the Rainbow home. This URL has the following form:

http://RainbowHomeHost:8080/RainbowDemo.html

where RainbowHomeHost is the IP of the Rainbow home host, 8080 is the listening port of the Web server in this host. The Web page *RainbowDemo.html* contains the Rainbow access authorization and Rainbow GUI applet.

Rainbow GUI applet communicates with Java servlets living in the Rainbow home host. Java servlets are server-side programs (Java threads) living inside a servlet enabling Web server process. The Web server at the Rainbow home host is such a servlet enabling Web server. Rainbow chooses the Java™ Servlet Development Kit Version 2.1 (JSDK) Web server for its lightweight and ease of use. For convenience, we call this Web server the "ServletRunner", which in fact is its former name. Obviously every host in the Rainbow host domain needs a ServletRunner because it requires servlets to function properly. It is for this reason that light-weight of ServletRunner becomes very desirable.

The middle tier consists of a number of servlets, i.e. server side threads living in the ServletRunner. The servlets are: NSRunnerlet, NSlet, SiteRunnerlet, Sitelet, WLGlet, and PMlet. NSRunnerlet and NSlet are responsible for starting the Rainbow name server in the Rainbow host domain and later transferring user request to it. Similarly, SiteRunnerlet and Sitelet are responsible for creating Rainbow sites in the Rainbow host domain and later bringing user requests to them.

WLGlet transfers transaction processing related requests (WLG refers to workload generator) to Rainbow sites in cooperation with Sitelets. PMlet brings progress related requests (PM stands for progress monitor) to and

results back from both the name server and the Rainbow sites by working closely with NSlet and Sitelet.

The system requires that the Rainbow home host must have the following servlets: NSRunnerlet, SiteRunnerlet, WLGlet, and PMlet. The reason is that the Rainbow GUI Applet can only communicate with the host it is downloaded from, i.e. the Rainbow home host. The four resident servlets serve as jump-off points for Rainbow GUI to the other hosts in the Rainbow host domain.

NSlet is only needed in the host that the name server lives in. There is only one name server per a Rainbow instance. If there is only one Rainbow instance running, one NSlet is all that is needed. If there are multiple instances running and the name servers are in different hosts, then one NSlet for each distinct host. Similarly, a Sitelet is needed in every host that Rainbow sites live. If multiple sites are created in one host, they share the same Sitelet. It may not be apparent tier from Figure 3 that the middle tier actually involves all Rainbow domain hosts, not just the Rainbow home host.

The Rainbow core consists of the name server and the Rainbow sites, which can live anywhere in the Rainbow host domain including the Rainbow home host. Thus like the middle tier, the Rainbow core may also involve all hosts in the Rainbow domain.

2.1 Transaction Processing Protocols

Rainbow supports 1) replication control protocols (RCP) including Read one write all (ROWA) and Quorum consensus (QC); 2) Concurrency Control Protocols (CCP) including Two-phase locking (2PL) and Timestamp ordering and 3) Two-phase commit (2PC) as the Atomic Commit Protocol (ACP). Rainbow protocols are implemented with minimum interdependencies and assumptions in order to facilitate their replacement (e.g., by students) with minimum system-wide modifications.

The following scenario demonstrates the RCP, ACP, and CCP interactions during the course of transaction processing, in a given Rainbow configuration. When a new transaction arrives at a Rainbow site, the site dedicates one thread to process it. The thread immediately invokes the RCP. The default protocol for RCP in Rainbow is QC. QC starts by building a quorum (read or write) for the first operation of the transaction. To do this, QC needs first to find a set of sites from whom the quorum can be built. QC then sends each site in the set a request for that site's local copies. At that site, copies are read (returning their current value) or pre-written (returning their current version number) through CCP. When a quorum is built for an operation, the next operation is considered. When all operations of a transaction are processed by the RCP, the home site initiates a two-phase commit session, the default ACP in Rainbow. When commitment terminates, the transaction is complete and the thread finishes.

3. Use of Rainbow in Experimental Research

Rainbow is an effective tool to conduct scientific experiments. It has been successfully used in studying the quorum consensus behavior and message traffic in quorum-based systems [3]. It could be used by other researchers when it is made publicly accessible. Rainbow supports experimentation through the following facilities:

- A workload generator component
- A network simulator and fault/recovery injector
- A GUI support in automating experiments and visual rendering of the results.

The performance of transaction processing and several dynamics of the distributed database system can be monitored and measured. Rainbow offers an extensible set of output statistics including:

- Number of committed transactions
- Number of aborted transactions (and rate) due to RCP, ACP, and CCP
- Transaction commit rate
- Transaction abort rates for each type of aborts
- Total number of messages generated per time unit
- Transaction throughput and response time measures
- Other parameters such as number of orphan transactions, round trip messages and other load balance/imbalance indicators.

4.   A Brief Tour of the Rainbow Demo

4.1 Setting Up

From any Web browser, the user first downloads the Rainbow GUI downloading applet using a well-known URL[1], where *RainbowHomeHost* is the Rainbow home host, which is controlled by the Rainbow system administrator (Figure 3). Upon successful login, the Rainbow GUI is downloaded to the user machine and is activated. If the user is the administrator, he is able to access Administrator menus to configure the Rainbow host domain and the Rainbow name server. Otherwise, the user is ready to start a Rainbow session.

4.2 Running Rainbow

When a new session starts, the user should first configure Rainbow and then submit a workload. Rainbow configuration includes Rainbow sites, transaction processing protocols, database items, and database replication scheme, in that order (Figure 4). If networking simulation is desired, then it should be

---

[1] *"http://RainbowHomeHost:8080/RainbowDemo.html*

configured first. The configuration data can be saved for reuse in another session.

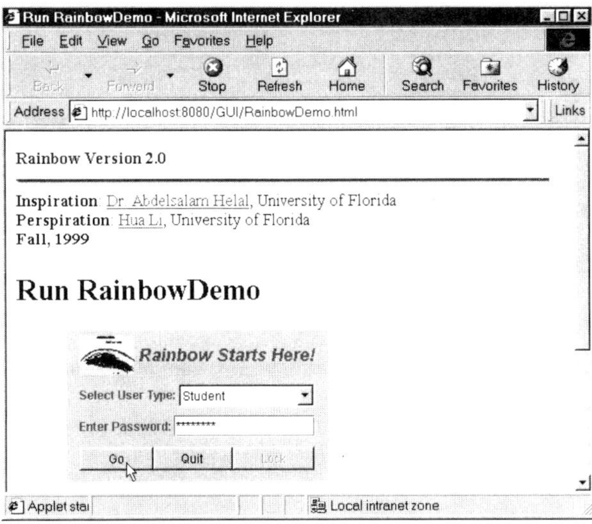

Figure 3. A screenshot of Rainbow GUI downloading applet.

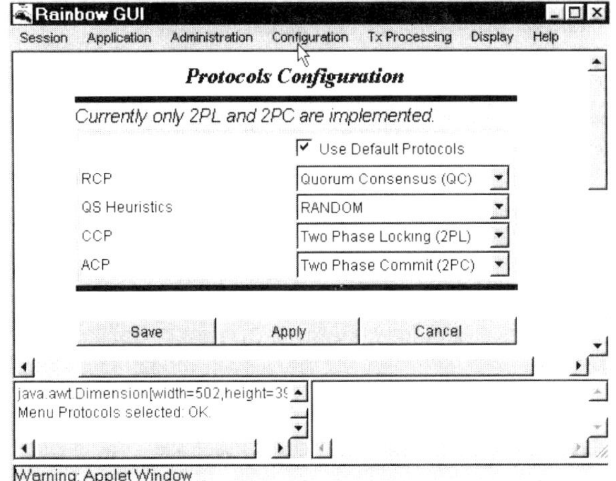

Figure 4. A screenshot of Protocols Configuration window.

Once the configuration is complete, the user can use either the manual or the simulated workload generation panel to compose and submit transactions to Rainbow. The results of transaction processing are feeding back to the user in real time and displayed in the Rainbow GUI. The user can view the final outputs graphically via the Display menu and Tx processing statistics via the Tx Processing menu (Figure 5).

5.   The use of Rainbow in the Classroom

The Teaching Assistant (TA) or the Rainbow Administrator is responsible for the following tasks:

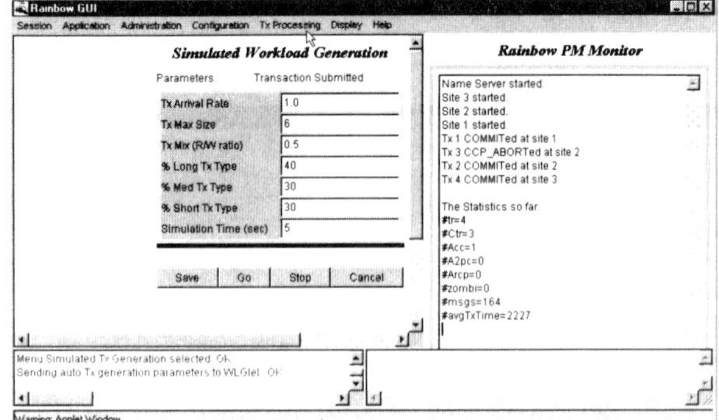

Figure 5. Transaction processing output in a Rainbow session.

- The installation of the Rainbow software on potential Rainbow domain hosts.
- Startup of the dedicated Web server, ServletRunner, on each Rainbow domain host. It is essential that the Rainbow home host must have the ServletRunner running at all times.
- Configuration of the Rainbow Domain. This is done by logining into Rainbow as the administrator and then use the Administration menu.
- Rainbow Name Server Configuration. The administrator can access the submenu "Name Server Configuration", under the Administration menu to configure the parameters and the location of the Rainbow name server.

As soon as the TA has done her work setting up Rainbow, students can download Rainbow and login as Student. The students need to do two basic things. First, they need to configure Rainbow sites, transaction processing protocols (RCP, ACP, and CCP), and the database. Second, they need to generate transactions either manually or using the simulation mode. They can then sit back and examine the results of the execution of the submitted transactions. Homework and lab assignments can be designed around Rainbow. The code can be distributed to students so they can gain hands-on experience on how to implement transaction processing and distributed database concepts. Term projects can be based on modifying Rainbow by adding a protocol (e.g. replacing two phase commit by three-phase commit, basic timestamp ordering by multi-versioning TSO, etc.)

6. References

[1]   Bell, D., Grimson, J., *Distribtued Database Systems*, Addison-Wesley, Reading, MA, USA, 1992.

[2]   Ceri, S., Pelagatti, T., *Distributed Database: Principle and Systems*, McGraw-Hill Book Company, New York, NY, USA, 1984.

[3]   Helal, A., Srinivasan, J., Bhargava, B., *SETH: a quorum-based database system for experimentation with failures*, Proceedings of the 5th IEEE International Conference on Data Engineering, Los Angeles, CA, USA, 1989.

[4]   Özsu, M.T., Valduriez, P., *Principles of Distributed Database Systems*, 2nd edition, Prentice Hall, Upper Saddle River, NJ, USA, 1999.

7. Appendix

In the following, we include screen dumps of additional Rainbow GUI windows and dialogue boxes.

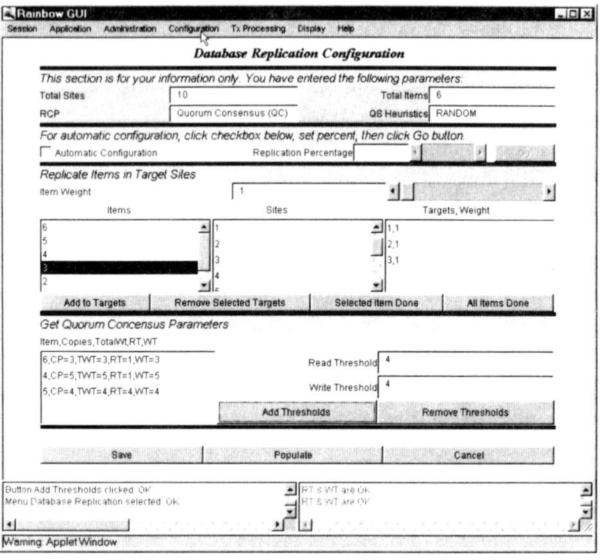

Figure A-1: Database Replication Configuration panel.

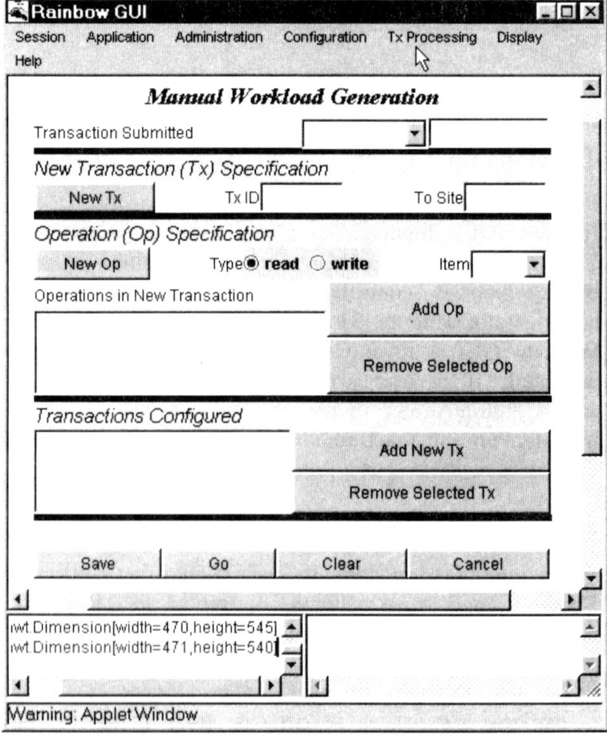

Figure A-2: Manual Workload Generation panel.

Agora: Living with XML and Relational

Ioana Manolescu, Daniela Florescu, Donald Kossmann, Florian Xhumari, Dan Olteanu[*]

{Ioana.Manolescu, Daniela.Florescu, Florian.Xhumari, Dan.Olteanu}@inria.fr

kossmann@informatik.tu-muenchen.de

1 Introduction

There has been a significant body of research in the last fifteen years dedicated to integration of data from various repositories, exhibiting heterogeneous formats, and sometimes access restrictions; for a survey of such systems see, for example, [12]. The main technical issues to be addressed in a mediation system are: how to semantically unify heterogeneous data formats and schemas, and how to use query processing capabilities of participant data sites and that of the mediator in order to answer a particular query.

Systems like the Information Manifold, and Garlic from IBM have chosen the relational and respectively the object-oriented model as the integration model. Given the popularity of XML as a data description format, more and more DBMS manufacturers have added to their systems the capability to export relational or object-oriented data to an XML format; other data formats (flat data files, regular HTML, PowerPoint presentations, annotated text) are also easily converted to XML. XML has become somehow a *de facto* standard for information exchange.

While XML has clear advantages as a description format, state-of-the-art query optimization and query processing algorithms for data integration still rely on the relational model. This is the case, for example, of the existing algorithms for answering queries using views [9]. Given the richness of the semistructured model (and the peculiarities of XML as a data model), algorithms of equivalent efficiency and ease-of-use, but *designed for XML*, are more difficult to find. Recent projects like [1] and [4] put XML in the center of query processing, describing data sources in XML and evaluating queries over

---

[*]The permanent address of this author is the CS Department of the Polytechnic University of Bucharest, Romania. This work was done while the author was in INRIA Rocquencourt

Proceedings of the 26th VLDB Conference, Cairo, Egypt, 2000.

a tree-structured model; optimization is ignored or reduced to a few simple heuristics. As a consequence, performance might degrade whenever an XML data source joins a set of relational sources, that we were able to integrate efficiently.

The Agora System. The particularity of our data integration system is that it employs XML as the user interface format, while all data flows inside the query processor consist of relational tuples. Queries are posed using an XML query language and the results are formatted as XML documents, making the underlying relational engine transparent to the user.

Agora is implemented on top of the Le Select data integration system [8], developed in the Caravel project, at INRIA Rocquencourt. Our goal in designing Agora was to investigate the feasibility and the attainable performance of a system that processes XML queries based on relational technology. Besides being intelectually interesting, we find this approach particularly tempting, given the strength acquired in the research and industrial communities in the field of query processing for relational data. We demonstrate the particular techniques that we have implemented in Agora to complement Le Select's functionalities, namely:

- how to define a generic, relational, virtual integration schema, that describes the content of XML documents

- how to translate queries from a query language dedicated to XML to the relational integration schema, and how to rewrite the resulting query using view definitions that describe the XML documents

- how query optimization extends to cope with access pattern limitations, when constructing query plans over heterogeneous sources

- how a text index (implemented by a few relational tables) improves performance and helps formulating user queries over the semistructured part of the data.

2 Adding XML Value into a Relational Data Integration System

We will now briefly describe the architecture of the Le Select relational integration system, that provides the relational framework that Agora is based on; we will then

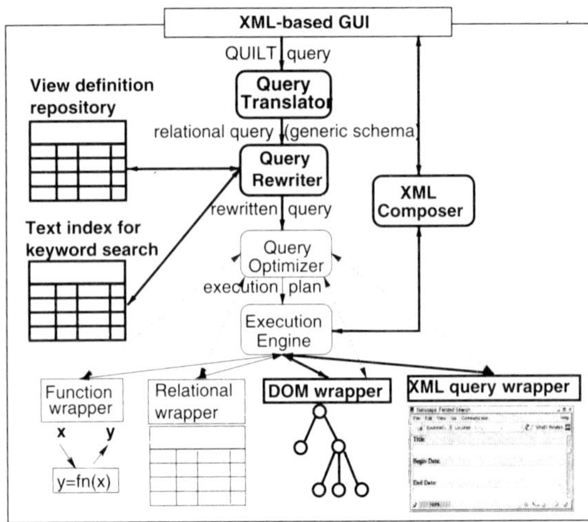

Figure 1: General architecture of the Agora system.

detail our technical contributions. Agora, as well as Le Select, is meant to function on several servers running identical code, each server owning and sharing data and programs. The complete architecture of a single Agora server is depicted in Figure 1. The components inherited from Le Select are detailed in 2.1 and are shown in the figure in thin lines; the novel components that we add are described under 2.4 and are shown with bold lines and fonts. Solid lines describe data flow during query processing; dotted lines represent the flow of statistic informations provided to the optimizer by the data and program wrappers.

2.1 Le Select

This system offers a framework for publishing and querying relational data and programs. A network of connected servers share their data and programs and collaborate in answering users queries posed against any server. Relational data and programs are published via specific wrappers. For some frequent data formats, like native relational and formatted files data, pre-defined wrappers can be easily configured. Query optimization is done on the site the query, while query execution is distributed among the sites. Wrappers export statistics about their data, like cardinalities, available access patterns, and, for functions, cost of executing them. They also export information about their query processing capabilities, in terms of evaluation of arithmetic expressions, capacity of performing a join, an equality test etc.

The query optimizer of the query site consults the wrapper capabilities and constructs an execution plan that distributes the work to be done among the wrappers of the data and program sources, their corresponding sites, and the site of the query. The optimizer is cost-based; repartitioning of tasks on different locations is made with the goal of minimizing the global cost (an important part of which is the cost of data transfers). The optimizer has a built-in treatment of access patterns, in order to deal with access restrictions and with functions, as described in [7]; this makes Le Select a suitable candidate for extension to XML. The execution engine contains an efficient implementation of bind joins, that minimizes data transfers, if the size of the attribute(s) to be passed across the join is important. More details on its functioning can be found under [8].

2.2 Motivating Example.

We consider integrating nutritional information (what food ingredients are recommended/forbidden for people with a certain ailment) with patient medical records and a collection of cooking recipes, to help a nutritional expert advise his patients on how and what to eat. Independent of the native storage, all information is available via an XML interface.

The nutritional information is stored in a relational database; the simplified relational schema consists of two tables:

    Recommendations(illness, recFood)
    Interdictions(illness, intFood)

The relational data is available to the data integration system as a virtual XML source. We use for this purpose a mapping like the one described in the Xperanto project [3]. Hence, this data will appear to the user as the following (virtual) XML file:

```
<Recommendations>
    <tuple>
        <illness>some illness</illness>
        <recFood>some food</recFood>
    </tuple>
    ...
</Recommendations>
<Interdictions>
    <tuple>
        <illness>some illness</illness>
        <intFood>some food</intFood>
    </tuple>
    ...
<Interdictions>
```

The structure of the patients medical records tends to be irregular, and these records are stored in a proprietary format. The logical interface that they export to the data integration system is also based on XML, as in the example shown below, and the only access methods it supports are based on the Document Object Model (DOM) API:

```
<patient_rec patientID="1000" sex="M">
    <pers_rec>
        <dob>12/6/1965</dob>
        <illness>Calcium deficiency</illness>
        <ilness>Pneumonia in 1969</illness>
    </pers_rec>
</patient_rec>
```

Finally, the cooking recipes can be obtained from a website that only allows searching its database by keyword search over the ingredient field of the recipes. As an example, a query searching for recipes using salmon as an ingredient produces as a result the following XML document:

```
<recipe recID="epicurious124">
    <plate>"Potato and salmon casserole"</plate>
    <ingredient qty="14oz">pink salmon, drained</>
    <ingredient qty="2 1/2 pounds">russet potatoes</>
    <ingredient qty="1/2cup">chopped green onions</ >
```

```
<ingredient qty="2 pc">large eggs</>
<directions>Preheat oven to 400F. Separate salmon>
    into chunks...</>
</recipe>
```

A data integration query can extract and combine
data from all three sources. As stated before, the query
interface visible to the users, and, subsequently, the
query language are completely based on XML. In the
absence of a standard XML query language, we will use
in the demonstration (a subset of) the Quilt query language [10]. To get a first glimpse at the language, consider the following query, asking for the medical records
of all patients whose personal records contain "illness"
and "calcium defficiency":

```
for $p in document("medicalRecords.xml")//patient_rec
where contains($p,"calcium deficiency") and
    contains($p,"illness")
return $p
```

In a Quilt query, the for clause binds variable by iter-
ating over collections of XML nodes, the where clause
specifies selection conditions (much like in traditional
query languages like OQL and SQL), and the return
clause constructs the result (this can involve construction of element hierarchies etc).

2.3 Modeling XML data sources

Generic Relational Schema. The particularity of our
system resides in the fact that even if the *external* data
model (i.e. as seen by the user formulating the queries)
is XML, the *internal* data model (i.e. used for the data
flowing inside the execution engine) is still relational.
Hence, the first step to acomplish is to map the XML
view of the data into the relational model. XML data
sources are modeled in our system by a generic relational schema [5], which is independent of any particular XML data instance. The tables that we propose to
add are shown in figure 2.3. The tables Element, Elem-
Content, Attribute, ElemAttribute, Tag and Value fully
describe the contents of the XML elements. The Value
table stores all the string values found in the document,
either attribute values or contents of text nodes.

Describing Access and Storage by Views. The
generic relational schema is used to logically describe
the content of data sources; in order to specify the actual
storage and the access patterns supported by the sources,
Agora allows for defining views with binding patterns
(in a manner similar to that described in [11]. The view
definitions can be arbitrarily complex, and by consulting
them, the query processor is informed of the alternative
ways to access the data, as well as the costs involved.
As an example, let us consider the DOM method call
retrieving all elements with a specific tag within a given
document:

```
{y} = x.getElementByName(z)
```

This API call can be modeled as a view over the
generic relational schema. Note that since the document
and the tag must be known in order to make this call,
there are inherent constraints on consulting this view,
that we model by the view's binding pattern (note that
the document and the tag are bound variables in the
view definition):

$$V(x^b, y^f, z^b) \text{:-} ElemDoc(y, x^b), Element(y, t), Tag(t, z^b)$$

The advantage of the logical modelisation of XML by
a collection of generic relational tables is twofold. First,
these tables can be added to any relational mediation
system, regardless of its mechanism for defining a global
schema (or even if there is no such schema). Second,
arbitrarily complex structures and physical access methods can be easily described as views with binding patterns over this generic schema, as in the example we
have shown; thus, the system can take full advantage of
optimized access paths, materialized views etc.

2.4 Query Processing Methodology.

We sketch here the main steps of a query scenario with
our system.

Formulating the Quilt query. There are two ways
of posing a query to the system. Expert users that
are familiar with the data structure can write full Quilt
queries, while novice users can use the GUI that allows for browsing the data, and progressively refine their
query, exclusively via the GUI. In the case of our sample application, a novice user would have to discover,
for example, the structure of recipe and Recomandation
elements and pose the join condition between the two.

Translating the Quilt query into SQL. The Quilt
query will be then translated into a set of correlated,
parameterized SQL queries over the relational generic
schema. These queries are equivalent with the original Quilt query; instead of producing as result an XML
document they produce the equivalent instance of the
generic relational schema. For example, the sample Quilt
query shown in section 2.2 can be rewritten into the following equivalent one[1]:

```
calciumDefPatient(patRec):-Document(docID,_)
    ElemDoc(docID, patRec),ElemDoc(docID,e2).
    Element(e1,t1),Tag(t1,"patient_rec"),
    ElemContent(e1,e2,null,_ ,Element(e2,t2).
    Tag(t2,"pers_rec"),contains(e2,"calcium",depth,tag).
    contains(e2,"deficiency",depth,tag).
    contains(e1,"illness",depth2,tag2).
```

The support for this translation phase is an underlying
algebraic model close to the one described in [2].

Query rewriting using views. The relational
query obtained in the previous step is then rewritten into
an equivalent relational query which uses only the views
modeling the real access patterns to the native XML
data, as well as to the actual access path to relational
data (that was referred to under its XML interface in
the query). We use a simple rewriting query using views
algorithm which produces equivalent rewritings of the
relational query, with respect to bag semantics[9].

Rewriting the previous query using the view V thus
defined would yield:

```
Result(patRec):-Document(docID,_),
    V(docID,patRec,"patient_rec"),
    ElemContent(e1,e2,null,_),V(docID,e2,"pers_rec"),
    contains(e2,"calcium",depth,tag),
    contains(e2,"deficiency",depth,tag).
```

---

[1] We use Datalog instead of SQL for simplicity.

Document	(**docID**, docURL)	Element	(**elID**, tagID)
Value	(**valID**, value)	ElemContent	(**parentID, childID**, valID, index)
Tag	(**tagID**, valID)	ElemAttribute	(**elID**, attID, valID)
Attribute	(**attID**, valID, type, isRequired)	ElemDoc	(**elemID, docID**)
Word	(**wordID**, word)	Contains	(elID, wordID, depth, tag)

Figure 2: Generic relational schema

Support for Keyword Search. We now explain the purpose of the last two generic tables, Word and Contains. The user might not know the particular structure of the documents or might have only some partial knowledge about it. For example, when querying the medical records for calcium-deficient patients, she might ignore if names of the maladies are to be found under illness tag, nested within the consultation tag, or directly under the pers_rec tag.

A text index at the granularity of XML elements can be used to retrieve all the XML elements that contain the words "calcium deficiency", at a specific nesting depth, in the content (as opposed to in the data tags). This index can be used as a help for novice users to "browse" the information content available, or as a filter for more structured queries. For the purpose of query optimization and execution, this type of index will be modeled as a relational table (see 2.3) with binding patterns limitations. More details on the usage and possible implementations of such an XML index can be found in [6].

Query Optimization and Execution. The rewritten query is optimized in a cost-based manner, following the optimization principles of LeSelect, that we described in 2.1; see also [7]. The result of the execution is a set of tuples.

Assembling the Result in XML. The tuples thus obtained are then grouped and organized into XML documents, that are presented to the user. We complete the illusion of an "all-XML" system.

3 Implementation and Scenarios

All the implementation (Le Select as well as the top layer for query rewriting, full-text indexing etc.) is done in Java; we use Oracle 8i as the DBMS that stores the text index and the index on metadata. The demonstration will be shown on a PC under Windows NT. Our scenario is close to the motivating example. We will use real life data collections, namely several collections of cooking recipes available on the Web (that we will replicate on the demonstration machine for the purpose of the demo), a relational source of nutritional information, and a set of XML medical files (corrupted for the sake of confidentiality). We plan to show:

- how to register the relational and XML data sources on several distict servers, and how to create instances of pre-defined wrappers for these sources;

- how to pose queries on one server, with the help of the GUI interface; how the full-text index is used to help the user discover the structure of available data and reformulate queries;

- how query rewriting operates using the available view definitions that describe XML and relational sources, by tracing the rewriting, optimization and execution of the same query;

- what is the influence of wrapper configuration and data localization on the final distributed execution of the query.

- what are the performances that can be achieved by the system.

The demonstration will build a case for what we consider to be an interesting, solid, and efficient alternative to pure-XML mediation.

References

[1] C. K. Baru, A. Gupta, B. Ludäscher, R. Marciano, Y. Papakonstantinou, P. Velikhov, and V. Chu. XML-based information mediation with MIX. In *Proc. of ACM SIGMOD Conf. on Management of Data*, pages 597–599, 1999.

[2] C. Beeri and Y. Tzaban. SAL: An algebra for semistructured data and XML. In *Proceedings of the International Workshop on the Web and Databases, Philadelphia, Pennsylvania*, 1999.

[3] M. Carey, D. Florescu, Z. Ives, Y. Lu, J. Shanmugasundaram, E. Shekita, and S. Subramanian. XPERANTO: Publishing object-relational data as XML. In *WebDB Workshop, in conj. with ACM Sigmod*, 2000.

[4] V. Cristophides, S. Cluet, and J. Simeon. On wrapping query languages and efficient XML integration. In *Proc. of ACM SIGMOD Conf. on Management of Data*, 2000.

[5] D. Florescu and D. Kossmann. Storing and querying XML data using an RDMBS. In *IEEE Data Engineering Bulletin*, volume 22(3), pages 27–34, 1999.

[6] D. Florescu, D. Kossmann, and I. Manolescu. Integrating keyword search into XML query processing. In *Proc. of the Int. WWW Conf.*, 2000.

[7] D. Florescu, A. Levy, I. Manolescu, and D. Suciu. Query optimization in the presence of limited access patterns. In *Proc. of ACM SIGMOD Conf. on Management of Data*, pages 311–322, 1999.

[8] http://www-caravel.inria.fr/Eaction_Le_Select.html.

[9] A. Y. Levy. Answering queries using views: a survey. submitted to publication, available at http://www.cs.washington.edu/homes/alon/.

[10] J. Robie, D. Chamberlin, and D. Florescu. The Quilt query language for semistructured data and XML. In *Proceedings of the International Workshop on the Web and Databases, Dallas, Texas*, 2000.

[11] O. G. Tsatalos, M. H. Solomon, and Y. E. Ioannidis. The GMAP: A versatile tool for physical data independence. In *Proc. of the Int. Conf. on Very Large Data Bases (VLDB)*, pages 367–378, Santiago, Chile, 1994.

[12] J. D. Ullman. Information integration using logical views. In *Proc. of the Int. Conf. on Database Theory (ICDT)*, Delphi, Greece, 1997.

Publish/Subscribe on the Web at Extreme Speed

João Pereira*
INRIA Rocquencourt
Joao.Pereira@inria.fr

Françoise Fabret
INRIA Rocquencourt
Francoise.Fabret@inria.fr

François Llirbat
INRIA Rocquencourt
Francois.Llirbat@inria.fr

Radu Preotiuc-Pietro[†]
"Politehnica" University of Bucharest
rady@ss.pub.ro

Kenneth A. Ross[†]
Columbia University
kar@cs.columbia.edu

Dennis Shasha[‡]
Courant Institute of Mathematical Sciences
New York University
shasha@cs.nyu.edu

1   Introduction

This demonstration presents *Le Subscribe* an event notification system for the Web.

It is widely accepted that the majority of human information will be on the Web in ten years. As pointed out in [6], besides systems for searching, querying and retrieving information from the Web, there is a need for systems being able to capture the dynamic aspect of the web information by notifying users of interesting events. This functionality is crucial for web users (or applications) who want to exploit highly dynamic web information such as stock markets updates or auctions. A tool that implements this functionality must be scalable and efficient. Indeed, it should manage millions of user demands for notifications (i.e. subscriptions); It should handle high rates of events (several millions per day) and notify the interested users in a short delay. In addition, it should provide a simple and expressive subscription interface and efficiently cope with high volatility of web user demands (new subscriptions, new users and cancellations). Finally, it should facilitate integration of similar kinds of information issued by different publishers (e.g. new auctions coming from

distinct auction sites).

The classical approach for query subscription is a mediator system where queries are periodically evaluated against static data. This static approach does not scale for high rate of events and a large number of volatile subscriptions, since it requires the storage of large event histories between two successive computations and requires repeated complex multi-query optimization. In Le Subscribe we adopt a different approach where events are processed on-the-fly to discover matching subscriptions. Our main contributions in Le Subscribe are:

- A semi-structured event model which is well suited for the information published on the Web, and flexible enough to support easy integration of publishers.

- A subscription language which is designed to be simple while supporting the most usual queries on event notifications.

- An efficient matching algorithm for processing events in real time which can handle a large number of volatile subscriptions and supporting high event rates.

- Simple interfaces for publishing and subscribing which enable an easy integration of the system in the Web. The system supports both HTTP protocol and Java RMI.

The demonstration consists of an application whose goal is to notify interested users of items put up for auction. These items are captured by Le Subscribe from a set of *auction Web sites*, e.g. ebay [5], amazon [2] or yahoo [16], or can be transmitted to our system using a web interface. Every day, the system has to handle a large number of items. For example, ebay publishes about 560000 new auction items per day.

*Founded by "Instituto Superior Técnico" - Technical University of Lisbon and by a JNICT fellowship of Program PRAXIS XXI (Portugal)

[†]The work of R. Preotiuc-Pietro and K. Ross was performed while visiting INRIA. The work of K. Ross was partly supported by grant 9812014 of the United States National Science Foundation.

[‡]The work of D. Shasha was partly supported by grant 9531554 of the United States National Science Foundation.

**Proceedings of the 26th VLDB Conference,
Cairo, Egypt, 2000.**

2 Overview of the system

The main characteristics of our system are its event model, its subscription language and its matching algorithm.

2.1 Event Model

The event model supported by Le Subscribe is in the spirit of the LDAP [12] data model. It consists of a set of attributes, and a set of event types. Each attribute has a domain that may be *numeric*, *string*, *enumerated* or *hierarchical*. The *hierarchical* domain is specific to our model: it is an *enumerated* domain where the elements are organized according to a hierarchy. Hierarchical domains are useful to depict categories and sub-categories. For example, a hierarchical domain ranging over furniture categories can be organized in bedroom, dining room, outdoor categories and sub-categories like table, chair, $\cdots$. An event type is always associated with a set of attributes each of them being either mandatory or optional. For example, an item of type *antiques* is described by three mandatory attributes *price*, *period* and *quantity*. An item of type *furniture* can be described using three mandatory attributes: Attributes *price* and *quantity* are in common with the *antiques* event type; Attribute *furniture_category* has a hierarchical domain ranging over furniture categories. Furniture description could be enriched with the optional attribute *material*.

An event instance can be associated with several event types. It is defined by a set of (attribute, set of values) pairs. Among these pairs there is always a pair of the form ($event\_type$, T) where $event\_type$ is a distinguished attribute and T is a set of event types. An event instance definition has to include a non-empty set of values for each attribute that is a mandatory attribute of at least one event type in T, values for other attributes are optional. Let us point out that our model permits publishers to present a given event from several points of view by associating several event types with this event. For example, using event types *antiques* and *furniture*, a publisher can present a table of the Louis XVI period as furniture, as antique or as both. In the last case the event instance definition will associate two event types (*antiques* and *furniture*) to the distinguished attribute and will provide values for attributes *price*, *quantity*, *period* and *furniture_category*, plus possibly for attribute *material*.

2.2 Subscription Language

A *subscription* is defined as a conjunction of elementary predicates. The language provides predicates of the form $X\theta y$, where X is an attribute name, y is a value belonging to the domain of X and θ is a comparison operator. In the case of hierarchical domains $\leq$ and $<$ operators are semantically equivalent to the standard *is a kind of* relationship. In addition, the language supports X *contains* y predicates. Such predicate is true for an event instance e, if value y occurs in the set of values associated with attribute X in e. For example [(*event_type contains antiques) and (furniture_category < dining table)*] describes a subscription for all the new auctions concerning any antique which belongs to any sub-category of *dining table*.

An event instance e matches a subscription s if e provides a binding for every attribute occurring in s and all predicates of s are true with respect to this binding. A subscription is satisfied by any matching event instance.

2.3 Matching Algorithm

We have implemented several main memory matching algorithms from the literature (Hanson et al[11], NEONRules[15], Gough et al[9] and Aguilera et al[1]) and have arrived at a synthesis that fits better with the *Web* context. The algorithm is predicate based. Its global optimization strategy exploits predicate redundancy and predicate dependencies among subscriptions to reduce the number of predicate evaluations. Such a strategy is particularly efficient in the *Web* context where a lot of attributes have enumerated domains ranging over a limited number of values. Our matching algorithm can easily be adapted to a multi-processor environment for performance enhancement. Experiments have shown the efficiency of our algorithm even at high event rates, large number of subscription and frequent subscriptions modifications. A detailed description of the matching algorithm, a performance analysis and a comparison with existing matching algorithms can be found in [7, 8].

3 Overview of the demonstration

To show the main features of our system, we have developed an application that uses Le Subscribe. This application notifies interested users of items put up for auction on the *Web*. These items can be extracted from real auction sites (e.g. ebay and amazon) or can be directly published in our system.

The items published by auction sites are represented by *generic_auction* event type. This type has the attributes *description* (string), *category* (hierarchical) and *price* (numeric). The *description* attribute is a set of keywords that describe the item in a summary way. Auction sites classify the items according to their *category*. The existing categories form a hierarchy, e.g. category *Antiques* (which gathers antique items) has the subcategories *Books & Manuscripts*, *Ceramics*, *Furniture*, $\cdots$. The *category* attribute identifies the item's category. Finally, the *price* attribute specifies the starting price of the auction. For the demonstration, we have designed a *Web* site for Le Subscribe which describes the event types, attributes and domains currently defined in the system. We will show that this site can be modified in real time to incorporate new event types, attributes or domains added by publishers. Subscribers browse through this *Web* site as an aid to define their subscriptions.

General architecture

The general architecture of the application is shown in Figure 1. This application consists of three types of entities: *subscribers*, *Le Subscribe* system and *publishers*. Subscribers interact with Le Subscribe through its *subscription* interface. In the demonstration, subscribers send HTML requests to Le Subscribe and receive HTML pages as answer. Publishers publish their events through the publication interface of Le Subscribe. We consider the existence of two kinds of publishers: users publishing events through a *web* browser and auction sites. The former publish events through the HTML interface. The latter publish events via wrapper components (one wrapper per auction site). A wrapper component polls its auction site periodically to get the HTML pages that describe the new items. Next, it parses these pages and translates each item into the event format corresponding to *generic_auction*. Finally, it communicates the events to the system using Java RMI.

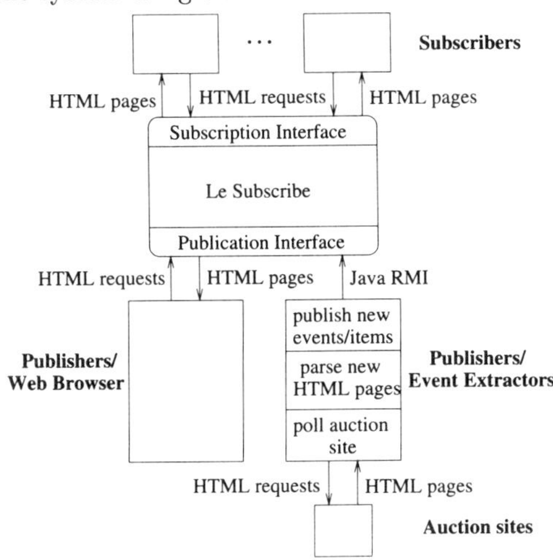

Figure 1: The architecture of the application.

Web subscription interface

Figure 2 shows the *subscription* page used by subscribers interested in events belonging to the *generic_auction* event type. The page has two parts. One part allows to define the predicates and the other to name the subscription[1] and to specify the notification mode. There are three *notifications* modes, *push*, *pull* and *email*. In the *push* mode, for each new notification, the system updates a HTML page that the user has loaded in his browser. In the *pull* mode, the

---

[1] The name is used afterwards in notifications to refer the subscriptions which were matched by the notified event.

notifications are stored in the system, and are sent on demand to subscribers (in a HTML page). Finally, in the *email* mode, notifications are sent to subscribers by email.

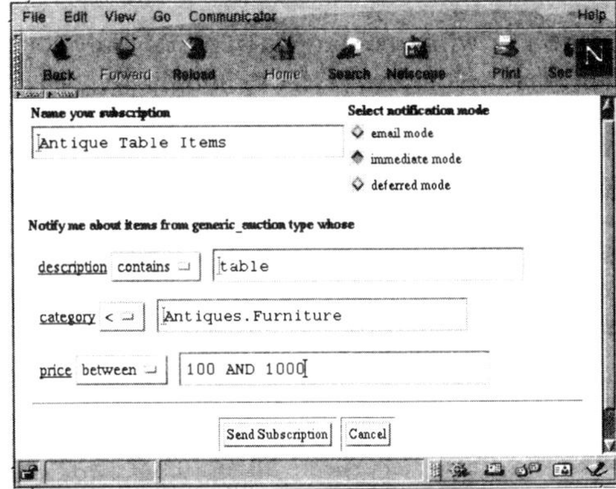

Figure 2: The HTML *subscription* page for *generic_auction* event type.

Demonstration scenario

During the demonstration we will run various scenarios that illustrate some nice features of Le Subscribe:

- The efficiency of our real time matching algorithm will be shown using a scenario with a large number of subscriptions (1000000) and with a high rate of events (400 events per second). If an internet connection is available we will use new auction items extracted on real time from existing *Web* auction sites. We will also subject our system to frequent changes of the set of subscriptions (cancellation and insertion of subscriptions) and show how slightly the system performance is affected.

- Event types and attributes can be defined on-the-fly. They are immediately taken into account by the system. To demonstrate the responsiveness of our system we will show the following scenario: We consider a new auction publisher who is specialized in antiques and wants to offer to interested subscribers a more complete description of antique auction items. To do this the publisher defines (through the publication interface) a new event type, *antiques*, that contains attributes *period*, *style*,···. The publisher can immediately publish event instances which include attributes values for both *antiques* and *generic_auction* types. We show that all the subscriptions on *generic_auction* items of category antiques will benefit immediately from the additional information. Moreover, new defined attributes are automatically made visible to subscribers via the *Web* site. This way, subscribers that imperatively want information about the period and style of antiques can subscribe to the *antiques* type.

- We also show that our system can take advantage of the filtering capabilities of publishers. To do this we extend our wrapper functionality with a subscription interface where categories of relevant new items can be specified. Thanks to this interface, wrapper components look only for new auctions belonging to the required categories and reduce the number of HTML pages loaded from the remote web sites. By using this interface to push predicates toward the wrapper components, the system behaves as a subscriber with regard to the wrappers. This optimization significantly improves performance when all users are interested in a same (small) set of categories.

4 Related work and conclusions

To our knowledge Le Subscribe is the first proposal for using an event notification (or publish/subscribe) service on the web to deal with highly dynamic Web information. A lot of event notification services have been already developed as middleware for gluing together distributed applications or systems. These systems differentiate from each other by their filtering capabilities, the efficiency of their matching algorithm and additional features like QoS guarantees[2].

There are two kinds of publish/subscribe systems: *subject-based* and *content-based*. In subject-based systems, events are classified by groups and can be filtered only according to their group. Examples of such systems are TIB/Rendezvous[4] and OrbixTalk[13]. Content-based systems are an emerging type of publish/subscribe system where events are filtered according to their attribute values. Le Subscribe is a content-based system. We can cite other content-based systems, like Gryphon[3], NEONet[14], or READY[10] and publish/subscribe mechanisms integrated in commercial DBMS products like Oracle8i, SQL Server 7.0, or Sybase. Compared to subject-based systems, content-based systems offer more subscription expressiveness. The cost of this gain in expressiveness is an increase in the complexity of the matching process: the more sophisticated the constructs, the more complex the matching process. This complexity combined with a large number of subscriptions may severely degrade the matching efficiency. So, systems devoted to support a large number of subscriptions as Le Subscribe system does, have to face a tradeoff between the subscription language sophistication and matching efficiency. In Le Subscribe we designed an expressive language that lends itself to very efficient matching.

The subscription languages of Gryphon and NEONet are quite similar to our language. Their matching algorithm do not exploit predicate redundancy nor dependencies (as Le Subscribe does). The READY system[10] has a more expressive subscription language supporting grouping constructs, compound

event matching and event aggregation. Its matching algorithm uses only local optimizations unlike Le Subscribe which intensively exploits global optimization opportunities. Commercial DBMS products use SQL as their subscription language, and these products are designed for contexts where the number of subscriptions is relatively small, as might occur in the context of enterprise application integration.

References

[1] Marcos K. Aguilera, Robert E. Strom, Daniel C. Sturman, Mark Astley, and Tushar D. Chandra. Matching events in a content-based subscription system. In *Eighteenth ACM Symposium on Principles of Distributed Computing (PODC '99)*, 1999.

[2] Amazon.com, Inc. *http://www.amazon.com*.

[3] G. Banavar, T. D. Chandra, B. Mukherjee, J. Nagarajarao, R. E. Strom, and D. C. Sturman. An efficient multicast protocol for content-based publish-subscribe systems. In *International Conference on Distributed Computing Systems*, 1999.

[4] Arvola Chan. Transactional publish/subscribe: The procative multicast of database-changes. In *SIGMOD'98*, page 521, 1998.

[5] eBay Inc. *http://www.ebay.com*.

[6] Phil Bernstein et al. The asilomar report on database research. *ACM Sigmod record*, 27(4), 1998.

[7] F. Fabret, F. Llirbat, J. Pereira, and D. Shasha. Efficient matching for content-based publish/subscribe systems. Technical report, INRIA, 2000. http://www-caravel.inria.fr/~pereira/matching.ps.

[8] F. Fabret, F. Llirbat, J. Pereira, and D. Shasha. Efficient matching for web-based publish/subscribe systems. In *Proc. of Fifth International Conference on Cooperative Information Systems*, 2000.

[9] K J Gough and G Smith. Efficient recognition of events in distributed systems. In *Proceedings of ACSC-18*, 1995.

[10] R. E. Gruber, B. Krishnamurthy, and E. Panagos. The architecture of the ready event notification service. In *Proceedings of the 19th IEEE International Conference on Distributed Computing Systems Middleware Workshop*, 1999.

[11] Eric N. Hanson, Moez Chaabouni, Chang-Ho Kim, and Yu-Wang Wang. A predicate matching algorithm for database rule systems. In *SIGMOD'90*, pages 271–280, 1990.

[12] T. A. Howes, M. C. Smith, and G. S. Good. *Understanding and Deploying LDAP Directory Services*. Macmillan Technical Publishing, 1999.

[13] IONA Technologies. *OrbixTalk http://www.iona.com/products/messaging/index.html*.

[14] New Era of Networks Inc. *NEONet http://www.neonsoft.com/products/NEONet.html*.

[15] New Era of Networks Inc. *NEONRules http://www.neonsoft.com/whitepapers/MQSIRules.html*.

[16] Yahoo! Inc. *http://auctions.yahoo.com*.

---

[2]In Le Subscribe we do not consider these additional features.

Demonstration: Enabling Scalable Online Personalization on the Web

Kaushik Dutta
Georgia Tech
gte314q@prism.gatech.edu

Anindya Datta
Chutney Technologies
and Georgia Tech
adatta@cc.gatech.edu

Debra VanderMeer
Chutney Technologies
and Georgia Tech
deb@cc.gatech.edu

Krithi Ramamritham
University of Massachusetts
and IIT, Bombay
krithi@cs.umass.edu

Helen Thomas
Chutney Technologies
and Georgia Tech
helen@cc.gatech.edu

1   Introduction

Given the current hyper-competitive nature of the e-commerce marketplace, coupled with razor-thin margins, online personalization is of great interest to e-companies. The attractiveness of online personalization technologies derives from the claim by consumer behaviorists that a personalized experience leads to increased *buy probabilities* on the part of e-shoppers [11].

Virtually all personalization technologies are based on the idea of storing as much historical customer session data as possible, and then querying the data store as customers navigate through a web site. The holy grail of on-line personalization is an environment where fine-grained, detailed historical session data can be queried based on current on-line navigation patterns to formulate real-time responses. The problem, of course, is one of *scale* – it is extremely difficult to track tens of thousands of e-shoppers in real time, and even more difficult to access a database online to provide real-time responses. As a result, virtually all web-based customer interaction schemes use *static profiling* techniques, and provide either *delayed* or *canned* responses to users.

Real-time interaction management, the focus of our work, uses *dynamic profiles* to incorporate users'

changing interests and needs over time. For example, a user who purchases Physics textbooks for his daughter from an online seller later returns to the site, looking for books for himself. After a few clicks the system should recognize that the user is not interested in Physics books in his current visit, and suppress its knowledge regarding his past behavior and instead adjust its current responses to be in tune with his more recent behavior.

We have developed the a system that (1) tracks a large number of users (potentially tens of thousands) in real time as they navigate through a site, (2) performs retrievals from a large data warehouse in real time, and (3) delivers an appropriate user response, in real time, based on the system's knowledge of the user's current behavior and the information retrieved from the data warehouse. To achieve our goals, we store three basic types of data: (1) navigational (i.e., where users go in the site), (2) transactional (e.g., what customers purchase), and (3) third-party data, e.g., demographic data. This knowledge is encoded simply as a set of rules of the type generated by standard data mining techniques. The foundation of this system is the *eGlue Server*, the subject of this demonstration proposal.

2   Architecture

eGlue Server is a component-based system which works with readily available web server and e-commerce application server systems. Figure 2 shows a graphical depiction of an "end-to-end" e-commerce system architecture, including the eGlue Server component. A full description of the system can be found in [16]. Perhaps the best way to de-

Proceedings of the 26th VLDB Conference, Cairo, Egypt, 2000.

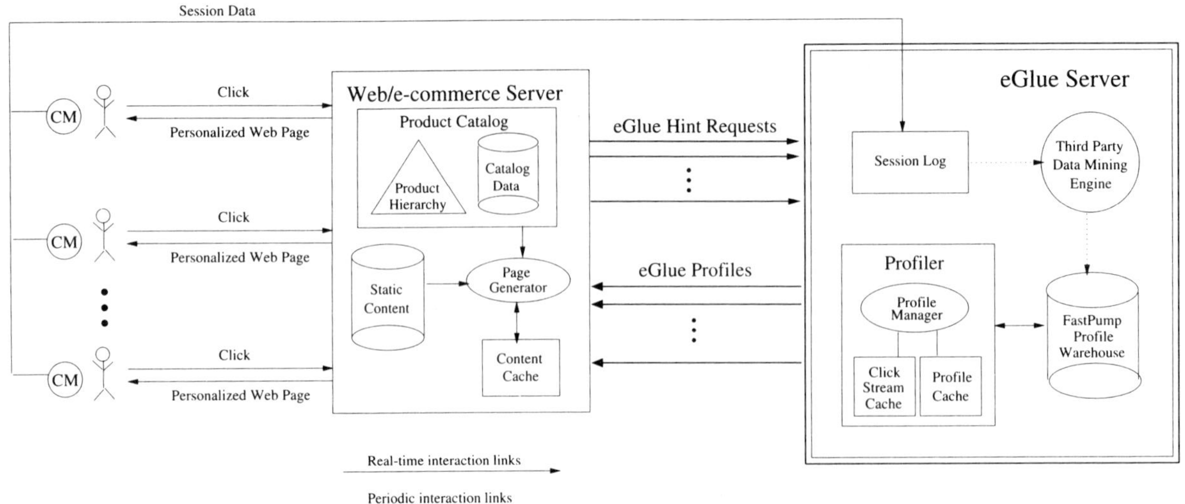

Figure 1: Real-Time Personalization System Architecture

scribe the overall workings of the system is to provide an example. Consider a user U, who clicks in an eGlue enabled e-commerce site. This causes an HTTP request to be sent to the *Web/E-commerce Server* (WES). (Note that, although the e-commerce and web servers are actually separate components, we describe them as a single component here for convenience). When the WES receives an HTTP request from U, it forwards U's click information to the *eGlue Server* (eGS) in the form of a *Profile Request* (HR). Upon receiving U's click information, the eGS performs two tasks.

1. *The eGS updates U's clickstream.*

2. *The eGS generates a profile.* A *profile* is simply a set of *action-probability pairs* (APPs), where the APPs represent actions U is likely to take, along with the corresponding probability that U will choose the action, given his current clickstream.

When the WES receives a *profile* from the eGS, it uses the profile to generate a customized web page for U. Precisely how the WES uses the profile to generate a personalized web page for a user is dependent on the needs of the web site.

3 The eGlue Server Components

Here, we provide an overview of the interaction of the components of the eGS, which is the primary focus of this demo. The *Profiler* consists of a set of data structures and algorithms designed to provide profile as to users' next actions on a site *in real time*, enabling a variety of interaction management applications, such as the delivery of customized

pages or the prefetching of high-probability content from disk.

The Profiler consists of three components: (1) a *Clickstream Cache* (CC), which stores current clickstream information (of maximum length CSL) for each user in the system, (2) a *Profile Cache* (PC), which stores recently-used profiles, and (3) a *Profile Manager* (PM), which generates profiles for the WES.

To illustrate the mechanics of the profile-generation process, we return to our user U. Consider a situation where the WES has submitted a *hint request* to the eGS for U's i^{th} click. The PM first checks the CC to find U's previous clickstream (if any), and updates that to include U's latest reported action.

After determining U's current clickstream, the PM checks the PC for a profile matching U's clickstream (i.e., a profile whose RA matches the observed clickstream). If such a profile is found, the PM sends it to the WES. If, at this point, another user, say U', were to follow on the same path as U, the reader can easily see that the needed profile would be in the PC (assuming U' follows U closely enough that the profile has not been replaced by a newer profile).

If a matching profile is not found in the PC, the PM requests the information from the *FastPump Profile Warehouse* (FP) (described below). After FP returns the profile information, the PM sends it to the WES. This profile will also now reside in the PC until a decision is made to discard it.

The *FastPump* data warehouse engine, described in detail in [8] is an extremely fast storage and retrieval engine. Within the context of the eGlue server, FP serves as a *profile warehouse*, storing historical and navigational data in the form of rules, and retrieving this data in response to queries.

The rules stored in FP are generated by a *Third Party Data Mining Engine*. The data mining engine takes a *Session Log*, i.e., clickstream and transaction information generated by various clients clicking in the web site, as input, and generates a set of rules as output. Click and transaction data is added to the session log in real time (as noted by the solid lines in Figure 2), while the mining of the session log and update of the Profile Warehouse takes place offline (shown by the dotted lines in Figure 2).

4 eGlue Demonstration

We demonstrate our system by showing an eGlue-enabled e-commerce site. This demo has two objectives: (A) to demonstrate the workings of eGlue software, with special emphasis on scalability, and (B) to demonstrate the importance of the underlying database, i.e., FastPump, which was specifically designed for eGlue (as opposed to using a commercial data warehousing system, e.g., Oracle).

In the demo, we introduce two types of visitors concurrently into an e-commerce site: real (i.e., foreground) visitors and simulated (i.e., background) visitors. These visitors will navigate the demo catalog of the e-commerce site.

For foreground visitors, the demo will show various personalization features of the eGlue Server, e.g., ad targeting. The demo will allow the demonstrator to control the behavior of a foreground user, i.e., to "become" the visitor. Here, the demonstrator will be able to choose the visitor's navigation through the site, and see the eGlue profiles generated for each click, as well as the page generated in response to that click. The purpose of adding simulated background users is to show the scalability of the system. To this end, the demo shows each simulated user's current position, updated as users move through the site.

We show the performance of the system in two ways. First, we replace FastPump with a commercial data warehousing system, e.g., Oracle, to show the effect of the underlying database on the system. Second, we remove the Profiler, thus showing the performance of the system using the only web server's own cache.

5 Related Work

Within the academic literature, web personalization is emerging as a major field of research. We review some of the important literature in this field here, and mention a few commerical products. At present, there are two main approaches to personalization: collaborative filtering and data mining for user behavior patterns.

Collaborative filtering [12] is a means of personalization in which users are assigned to groups based on similarities in rankings of content of web pages, i.e., users with similar interests will rank the same pages in the same way. [5] presents an analysis of predictive algorithms for collaborative filtering. [7] describes a non-invasive method of collecting user interest information for collaborative filtering.

Much work has been published in the area of user navigation pattern discovery based on web logs, e.g., [6, 13]. A great deal of this work in web navigation and usage mining is based on fundamental work in data mining for association rules [2] and sequential patterns [3, 14]. This type of work is quite complementary to our work; in fact, we base our navigation pattern discovery methods on some of the ideas found in these papers.

On the commercial side, several companies offer products in the Internet Personalization space. The two functions supported are *recommendations*, (i.e., static, predetermined responses to actions) based on collaborative filtering techniques [12] and *reporting* (i.e., analysis of a web site's traffic). Recommendation products include Net Perceptions Recommendation Engine [9], Engage Technologies [15], and LikeMinds [4]. Personify [10] and Accrue [1] offer analysis and reporting based on log data.

While the general philosophy of our work is similar to that of the above personalization products in that we use a database and cache to store and retrieve our information, we depart from current personalization efforts in two key ways: (1) We do not use static profiles; rather, we make *dynamic decisions* based on the information available at the time a user clicks; and (2) We merge historical information with knowledge of a user's current behavior in order to make these dynamic decisions, as opposed to delivering canned responses to pre-determined actions.

6 Contribution & Conclusion

We demonstrate a component-based system to address the problem of real-time user interaction by generating *profiles*, which profile predictive information as to a user's future actions on the site, thus enabling a vast array of customization or prefetching applications on a site.

The foundation of this system consists of two components: FastPump, an extremely fast storage and retrieval engine; and the Profiler, an efficient profile caching mechanism. Perfomance studies indicate that our system gives an order of magnitude performance gain over an implementation using off-the-shelf database back end without the Profiler.

References

[1] Accrue. Accrue technologies. www.accrue.com, 1999.

[2] R. Agrawal, T. Imielinski, and A. Swami. Mining association rules between sets of items in large databases. In *Proceedings of the 1993 ACM SIGMOD International Conference on Management of Data*, pages 207–216, May 1993.

[3] R. Agrawal and R. Srikant. Mining sequential patterns. In *Proceedings of the Eleventh International Conference on Data Engineering*, pages 3–14, March 1995.

[4] Andromedia. Likeminds. www.andromedia.com/products/likeminds, 1999.

[5] J.S. Breese, D. Heckerman, and C. Kadie. Empirical analysis of predictive algorithms for collaborative filtering. In *Proceedings of the Fourteenth Conference on Uncertainty in Artificial Intelligence*, pages 43–52, July 1998.

[6] A.G. Buchner, M. Baumgarten, S.S. Anand, M.D. Mulvenna, and J.G. Hughes. Navigation pattern discovery from internet data. In *Proceedings of WEBKDD'99: Workshop on Web Usage Analysis and User Profiling*, 1999. http://www.acm.org/sigs/sigkdd/proceedings/webkdd99/toconline.htm.

[7] P.K. Chan. A non-invasive approach to building web user profiles. In *Proceedings of WEBKDD'99: Workshop on Web Usage Analysis and User Profiling*, 1999. Available at http://www.acm.org/sigs/sigkdd/proceedings/webkdd99/toconline.htm.

[8] A. Datta, H. Thomas, and K. Ramamritham. Curio: A novel solution for efficient storage and indexing in data warehouses. In *Proceedings of 25th International Conference on Very Large Data Bases*, pages 730–733, 1999. NB: Curio is the former name of the FastPump data warehouse.

[9] Net Perceptions. Net perceptions recommendation engine. www.netperceptions.com, 1999.

[10] Personify. Personify technologies. www.personify.com, 1999.

[11] F.F. Reichheld and W.E. Sasser. Zero defections: quality comes to services. *Harvard Business Review*, 68:105–7, September-October 1990.

[12] U. Shardanand and P. Maes. Social information filtering: algorithms for automating "word of mouth". In *Conference proceedings on Human factors in computing systems*, pages 210–217, May 1995.

[13] M. Spiliopoulou, L.S. Faulstich, and K. Winkler. A data miner analyzing the navigaitional behavior of web users. In *International Conference of ACAI'99: Workshop on Machine Learning in User Modelling*, 1999.

[14] R. Srikant and R. Agrawal. Mining sequential patterns: Generalizations and performance improvements. In *Advances in Database Technology - EDBT'96, 5th International Conference on Extending Database Technology*, pages 3–17, March 1996.

[15] Engage Technologies. Engage e-commerce product suite. www.engage.com, 1999.

[16] D. VanderMeer, K. Dutta, A. Datta, K. Ramamritham, and S. Navathe. Enabling scalable online personalization on the web. Technical Report CER-0004, Chutney Technologies, Atlanta, GA, 2000.

INSITE: A Tool for Real-Time Knowledge Discovery from Users Web Navigation[*]

Cyrus Shahabi   Adil Faisal   Farnoush Banaei Kashani   Jabed Faruque

Integrated Media Systems Center
University of Southern California
Los Angeles, CA 90089, USA
{shahabi, faisal, banaeika, faruque}@usc.edu

Abstract

The major challenges in web mining are a) tracking the data accurately (as not everything is reported to the web server), b) real-time acquisition of the huge volume of data (435 Million visits to yahoo per day, 2-4 GB clickstream data per hour), c) real-time interpretation of the data without compromising the privacy of the user (order of seconds for personalization and targeting information), and d) visualization of the data to facilitate policy making. To address these challenges, we demonstrate an integrated software platform, called INSITE – a) to accurately track users interactions with a web space with minimum overhead and no voluntary user participation, b) to generate individual and aggregate user profiles in real time (or off-line) through the use of a unique Connectivity Matrix Model (CM-model), c) to show the efficacy and scalability of the CM-model in capturing the essence of the users' participatory attributes in the context of the web, d) to visualize the result of clustering of users navigation paths in real time by leveraging on the CM-model, and e) to execute a suite of queries (including temporal ones) and prove the utility of the captured data in making meaningful decisions about user interaction with a web site.

Proceedings of the 26th International Conference on Very Large Databases, Cairo, Egypt, 2000

1. Introduction

Understanding and modelling users' behaviour by analysing users' interactions with digital environments, such as web sites, is a hot topic that has resulted in vast recent commercial interests. Commercial products such as Personify.com^{TM}, Verbind^{TM}, WebSideStory^{TM}, and BlueMartini^{TM}, and acquired companies such as Matchlogic^{TM}, Trivida^{TM}, Andromedia^{TM}, Rightpoint^{TM}, and DataSage^{TM} are all witnesses of such interests. Meaningful interpretation of the users' digital behaviour is necessary in the disparate fields of e-commerce, distance education, online entertainment and management for capturing individual and collective profiles of customers, learners and employees; for targeting customized/personalized commercials or information, and for evaluating the information architecture of the site by detecting the bottlenecks in the information space.

Several researches in various industrial and academic research centres are focusing on this topic. Among them, Lee's et al. [1] have deployed a *parallel coordinate* system for interpretation and analysis of user clickstream data of online stores; they define "micro-conversion rates" as metrics in web merchandising analysis to understand effectiveness of marketing and merchandising efforts. Heckerman et al. [2] take a model-based approach and use a mixture model to predict behaviour of user clusters and visualize the classification of users. Mobasher et al. [3] propose a hybrid approach to real-time web personalization by combining web usage mining and context- based mining, in a try to overcome the inabilities of each approach individually.

** This research has been supported in part by NASA/JPL contract nr. 961518, and unrestricted cash/equipment gifts from Intel, NCR and NSF grants EEC-9529152 (IMSC ERC) and MRI-9724567.*

With INSITE, we have developed a system for knowledge discovery from users web site navigation in a real-time, adaptive and scalable fashion. INSITE consists of the following layers: a) tracking of user interaction, b) acquisition of the data, c) analysis of the data (includes extraction of navigation paths and clustering of the paths), d) interpretation, and e) visualization of the result of analysis. Our system is novel because it demonstrates a) accurate, unobtrusive tracking of users navigation through a web site, b) real-time, scalable and adaptive clustering of navigation paths by leveraging on a new path/cluster model, and c) a role-based recommendation engine that allows the web site to react to the user in real time with customized information (e.g. target advertisement). In Section 2, we introduce the ideas behind the layers of INSITE. Section 3 discusses the features of INSITE that are demonstrated in this presentation. Finally, in Section 4 we present our conclusions.

2. INSITE: Research Issues

In this section we introduce three out of five layers of INSITE and describe the novel ideas behind each layer. The other two layers, acquisition and visualization, mostly involve implementation issues and are discussed in Section 3.

2.1 Tracking

Tracking is defined as following and recording user interactions with a web site. We keep track of both selected hyperlinks and visited pages. The major challenges in tracking are being accurate and unobtrusive.

As for accuracy, in [4] we proposed the utilization of an agent in the client side to detect and log user interactions in place and send the collected data to an agent server for further analysis. This approach enables us to track the exact time of user interactions. With server-side tracking, in contrast, we have to rely heavily on time approximations because profiler is located at the server, far away from client in the network. In addition, our agent reports visiting of cached pages (whether at the proxy or at the browser) to the server, which results in more accurate tracking as compared with what recorded at server logs. Finally, tracking is performed unobtrusively: no modification is needed to the browser and/or current HTTP, and no collaboration required from users.

2.2 Analysis

To make the analysis layer scalable, we need to cluster similar paths in order to reason about clusters as opposed to paths. There are a handful of clustering algorithms such as CLARANS[5], BIRCH[6], CLUDIS[7], and K-Means that we can use for this purpose. However, regardless of what clustering algorithm we choose, we have to model both path and cluster, and we have to define a distance function to quantify similarity between paths and clusters. In [8], we introduced a unique model to represent both paths and clusters denoted as *Connectivity Matrix Model (CM-Model)*. Via this model, we represent a path/cluster by a set of matrices, each representing a spatial or temporal navigational attribute of the path/cluster. The attributes we are considering in our system are Hit, Sequence, Time and Frequency. The choice of attribute is application-dependent and our model is open to deployment of any other suitable attribute. We aggregate each attribute of the path/cluster into its corresponding matrix in the CM-Model of the path/cluster. Moreover, we introduced a new similarity measure in [4], which suffers from overestimating the similarity between two paths. This is due to the fact that the base sub-paths of the two compared paths that are used for computing their inner product are not orthogonal. To overcome this problem, we have proposed a new similarity measure termed *Vector Angel (VA)*. To find out how similar a path is to a cluster in context of each specific attribute, we consider the corresponding matrices of the attribute in their CM-Models as two vectors, and find the angle between these two vectors:

$$VA(\vec{u}, \vec{v}) = Cos <\vec{u}, \vec{v}> = \frac{\vec{u}.\vec{v}}{|\vec{u}||\vec{v}|}$$

The smaller the value of VA, the more similar the path to the cluster. The final distance between a path and a cluster is computed as the weighted average of VA values over all the attributes. Note that although we are still using the inner product of vectors to define this new similarity measure, the base vectors (unit vectors) are now orthogonal. To be able to make real-time decisions, it is possible to treat the similarity measure as Member Probability (MP), which denotes the probability of a path belonging to a cluster.

Another challenging question with clustering is that should we update the clusters as new paths become available (i.e. more users visit the site)? While updating the clusters makes them adaptive to user behaviour changes, it increases the time complexity of the clustering process drastically. One approach is to apply the clustering algorithm periodically to regenerate or update the existing clusters. In popular web sites such as Yahoo, with Terra-bytes of logged data, this approach will be non-affordably costly. As an alternative, we might be able to cluster the paths in a dynamic manner as follows. When a new path is extracted, its model is compared with current model of all clusters and will be assigned to the closest one. If the new path is not close enough to any cluster, a new cluster is generated with the same model as the path. Once the new path is assigned to its cluster, we use the path attributes represented by the path CM-Model to update the cluster attributes in the cluster CM-Model dynamically. Thus, the cluster model will reflect both the attributes of the newly added path as well as those of the old paths that had already joined that cluster. This second approach has been implemented within INSITE and will be demonstrated.

2. 3 Interpretation

In [9], we defined a methodology to measure the correlation between the structure of the web site and the user profile by borrowing the concept of channel mutual information from the field of *Information theory*. If there is a strong correlation of the users personal profile with his/ her navigation path, we can statistically predict the answer of the user to a given question (i.e. predict the users behaviour in a certain context) from his/ her interaction with the web site. With INSITE, the soft memberships of the users' paths to the clusters (computed as member probability, MP, in Section 2.2) help generate a footprint for the user in real time. The footprint consists of the clusters that the user may belong to with certain probabilities. By associating each cluster with a set of users' behavioural characteristics with certain probabilities we can predict the behaviour of the user. If the user path belongs to cluster C1 with probability p1 (dynamic, determined in real time), and if anyone associated with cluster C1 is supposed to belong to a certain behavioural group (static, determined in training session) with probability p2, then the user is playing the particular role with a probability of p1 x p2. Thus, the role of the user can be extracted without compromising his/ her privacy. Note that if the same user plays different roles at different times s/he will be clustered into different clusters. This is unlike the approach taken by cookies, which generates static profiles of the users.

3. INSITE: Implementation issues

3.1 Tracking

To make a web site trackable by INSITE, we should embed the INSITE applet agent in each page of the web site. The embedding procedure itself is automated. The agent can be embedded in the dynamic pages by minor modification to the script code and can also be automated. Here, we shall demonstrate tracking of static pages only.

Whenever a visitor views a page, the agent is downloaded in the client machine. Whenever the visitor stops viewing the page (switch to another one or closes the window), the agent sends a single line of text to a java server. Irrespective of where the page is retrieved from (web server, cache or proxy), the agent tracks the page the user is viewing. Agent uses TCP socket to communicate with the server. The agent records the viewing time and the

time stamp (of visitation) associated with each page. Each page is identified by a unique combination of its own id and the id of the context to which it belongs. Each user is identified by the host name of the machine s/he is using. For scalability, the server should not be executed in the same machine as the web server. The server buffers the data and periodically stores it in the database as the INSITE log.   INSITE tracking is already deployed in three public web sites (digimuse.usc.edu, www.ascusc.org/jcmc/, www.bluesincolor.com). The complete functionality of the INSITE tracking (from user navigation to INSITE log generation and storage) is demonstrated.

3.2 Acquisition

The INSITE log is periodically read into the database. The data is sorted first by host name and then by the timestamp of each entry. Paths are time delimited i.e. two consecutive entries from the same host that are separated by a certain threshold in time indicates the beginning of a new path. Paths are thus readily extractable from the sorted data. Each path goes through a transformation filter [10] that yields the CM-Model of the path. We demonstrate the real time extraction of the CM-Models of the paths from the INSITE log (generated by live navigation of a web site).

3.3 Analysis

Each path is then subjected to a dynamic clustering algorithm that decides the soft membership of the path. Each cluster is represented by a unique CM-Model. We are now testing a number of distance functions to choose the best similarity measure between the CM-Models of a path and a cluster. Experimental validation of the dynamic clustering technique is also underway. However, our preliminary results prove our approach to be very effective in handling the paths and finding their membership to the clusters in real time [10]. Once the membership of a path is decided, the CM-Model of the path updates the CM-Model of the cluster. It also updates the footprint of the user with the id of the cluster with which s/he has been associated. Since a cluster represents certain behaviour, the weighted update of the cluster helps capture the finer changes in a users behaviour (role) within the larger context of the cluster. A persistent, new behaviour from the users gives birth to new clusters. By keeping periodic snapshots of the clusters, we can capture the gradual changes in user behaviour. The database is kept current with the updated CM-Models of the clusters. Due to the very finite number of clusters and the sparse nature of the matrices in the CM-Models, most of the data is kept in memory and does not degrade the performance of the dynamic clustering technique noticeably.   We demonstrate the dynamic clustering of the paths and also the generation of a new cluster in response to new user behaviour.

3.4 Interpretation

The footprint of the user is handed over to the INSITE recommendation engine. The engine queries the database to decide on the salient features of the cluster (most popular pages by hit count, by viewing time, by time stamps etc.) and target the user with customized information accordingly. In our implementation, we have not used the association rules as suggested in [9]. We rather use more straightforward approach of basing our decisions on the salient features of the clusters. During a single session, a visitor can play multiple roles, each captured by the presence of a representative cluster in his/her footprint. We shall demonstrate the feature of extraction of roles by a target advertising application. The footprints are kept in memory. In case of registered users, we can store the footprints in the database for future references.

3.5 Visualization

To facilitate the policy making, INSITE provides the administration and the site owner with a web-based interface for querying the database about the clusters and users (or rather their footprints). We demonstrate this utility through a suite of queries like a) show the clusters that capture the visitors interested in product X and related products, b) show the most (least) recently updated or newborn clusters (also shows the salient features of the clusters), c) show the history of the cluster over a period T, d) show the footprint of all users who have spent over T time on product X, etc.

In our demonstration, the web site is hosted in an apache web server. We use two different browsers (IE and Netscape). The backend database is Oracle. We use a canned version of a public web site for the demonstration.

4. Conclusion

In summary, INSITE tracking captures substantially more information (including accurate temporal information) than the traditional approaches; INSITE acquisition extracts and stores the essence of the captured information in real time by leveraging on the Connectivity matrix model; INSITE analysis possess memory through preserving persistent user behaviors in CM-Models of clusters. Our approach does not compromise the privacy of users; rather it identifies the user through the role s/he is playing. Lastly, our approach is equally applicable to static and dynamic web spaces and works seamlessly with the state of the art load balancing appliances, caching appliances and content mirroring.

5. References

[1] Gomory, S., R. Hoch, J. Lee, M. Podlaseck, and E. Schonberg. Analysis and Visualization of Metrics for Online Merchandizing. In *Proccedings of WEBKDD'99 Workshop on Web Usage Analysis and User Profiling*, San Diego, CA, USA, August,1999.

[2] Cadez, I., D. Heckerman, C. Meek, P. Smyth, and S. White. Visualization of Navigation Patterns on a Web Site Using Model Based Clustering. In *Technical Report MSR-TR-00-18*, Microsoft Research, Microsoft Corporation, Redmond, WA, USA. March 2000.

[3] Mobasher, B., H. Dai, T. Luo, Y. Sun, and J. Zhu. Combining Web Usage and Content Mining for More Effective Personalization. In *Proceedings of the International Conference on E-Commerce and Web Technologies (ECWeb2000)*, Greenwich, UK, September 2000.

[4] Shahabi, C., A. Zarkesh, J. Adibi, V. Shah. Knowledge Discovery from Users Web-Page Navigation. In Proceedings of the IEEE RIDE97 Workshop, Apr. 1997.

[5] Raymond, T. Ng. and J. Han. Efficient and effective clustering methods for spatial data mining. In *Proc. of VLDB Conf.*, pages 144-155, September 1994.

[6] Zhang, T., R. Ramakrishnan, and M. Livny. Birch: An efficient data clustering method for very large databases. In *SIGMOD '96*, pages 103-114, Montreal, Canada, June 1996.

[7] Ester, M., H.P. Kriegel, and X. Xu. Knowledge discovery in large spatial databases: Focusing techniques for efficient class identification. In *Proc. of 4th International Symposium on Large Spatial Databases*, 1995.

[8] Faisal, A., C. Shahabi, M. McLaughlin, F. Betz. INsite: Introduction to a generic paradigm for interpreting user-web space interaction. In *Proceedings of the ACM WIDM*, 1999.

[9] Zarkesh, A., J. Adibi, C. Shahabi, R. Sadri, V. Shah. Analysis and Design of Server Informative WWW-sites. In *Proceedings of the ACM CIKM*, 1997.

[10] Shahabi, C., A. Faisal, F. Banaei Kashani, J. Faruque. A Formal Approach Towards Real-time (and off-line) Analysis of User-Web Space interactions With INSITE. Submitted for publication.

Model-Based Information Integration in a Neuroscience Mediator System

Bertram Ludäscher[*]   Amarnath Gupta[*]   Maryann E. Martone[‡]

[*]San Diego Supercomputer Center, UCSD   {gupta,ludaesch}@sdsc.edu
[‡]Department of Neurosciences, UCSD   mmartone@ucsd.edu

1 Overview

We present the information mediator prototype called KIND[1] [GLM00], recently developed as part of an integrated Neuroscience workbench project at SDSC/UCSD within the NPACI[2] project. The broad goal of the workbench is to serve as an environment where, among other tasks, the Neuroscientist can query a mediator to retrieve information from across a number of information sources, and use the results to perform her own analysis on the data.

The KIND mediator is an instance of a novel *model-centered* mediator architecture that extends current XML-based mediator approaches by incorporating a semantic *model* of an information source as an integral part of the mediation process. Thus, by model we mean a combination of (i) a *conceptual model* of the source data, for example a UML or EER model, and (ii) any additional conceptual-level *knowledge* about the source as expressed through IDB (intensional database) rules. While current mediators for information integration address and solve the problems of *syntactic* and *structural* heterogeneities amongst sources using a semistructured data model like XML [GMPQ+97, CDSS98, GMW99], the *semantic* integration problem remains and a mediation engineer has to come up with integrated view definitions on top of the different XML views and DTDs exported by sources. In contrast to this structure-centered approach, the model-centered mediator architecture provides a framework to the mediation engineer in which the integrated domain model (i.e., both its conceptual schema and data instances) can be defined in terms of the domain-level semantic models of sources using a high-level declarative language.

Our development of a model-based mediator was driven by the need to integrate scientific databases like those of the Neuroscience workbench, where source data comes from different "semantic worlds", often sharing few if any attributes. Thus, in contrast to the more traditional "one world" integration scenario (say integrating information from online book-shops) where despite differences in the local schemas, the sources share the same domain of discourse, here we need to integrate across different domains like *neuroanatomy*, *protein properties* and *ion-currents in nerves*. Since

Proceedings of the 26th VLDB Conference, Cairo, Egypt, 2000.

[1] *Knowledge-based Integration of Neuroscience Data*

[2] *National Partnership for Advanced Computational Infrastructure*, http://www.npaci.edu

these sources are scientifically related in the physical world through (expert and common) knowledge, the integration process using a mediator becomes feasible if those associations between objects from different domains are definable at the level of the domain model.

The system we demonstrate includes the following salient features:

- We use XML as the uniform format for exchanging instance data (relational, object-oriented, semistructured) and *model data* (like UML and EER schemas). In particular UML models of sources are represented in XML using XMI [XMI99].

- The model-integration language is F-Logic (short: FL) [KLW95], a rule-based, object-oriented language that allows to represent, query, and reason with not only semistructured data like XML trees but also conceptual-level information, i.e., object-oriented data and *schema*. Query evaluation at the mediator level is based on the FLORA engine [LYK99, YK00], enabling a *virtual integrated view* approach, and on the MIXm system for querying XML-enabled sources via the XML query language XMAS [BGL$^+$99, LPV00].

- For sources that export a conceptual model CM (in XMI) to the mediator, a semantics-preserving DTD$_{CM}$ is derived. At runtime, the mediator can automatically construct CM (i.e., populate the classes of CM and validate against the integrity constraints of CM) and then integrate across different CMs, provided the sources export XML data which is valid wrt. DTD$_{CM}$. Otherwise, declarative FL rules are used to map instances from the source-specific DTD to DTD$_{CM}$ and thus again to instances of CM. In this way, sources are not only queryable as labeled ordered trees (as is the case with pure XML-based query languages), but as *domain-level object-bases*; in

particular information about *generalizations* (class hierarchy), *properties of relationships* (cardinalities, relationship types like aggregation and composition), and *application-specific integrity constraints and rules* all become accessible for defining the integrated view at the mediator.

2 Demonstration

The demonstration presents a Neuroscience application where the KIND mediator integrates three data sources and two domain knowledge sources (cf. Figure 1). The central component of the architecture is the KIND mediator which uses the FLORA system [LYK99] for executing the integration rules. The mediator has several "plug-in" modules for interfacing with the runtime environment. For example, the module XML$_2$FL maps XML to equivalent FL objects. For sources like CAPROT which export a conceptual model CM, there is a XMI$_2$FL plug-in, which takes the conceptual model CM(S) of source S and produces an FL model of it. As we will show in the demo, the plug-in can generate from CM(S) (which is here given in the XMI syntax for UML) the FL equivalent of CM(S), i.e.,

- a *class signature* augmented with a set of *integrity constraint rules* for capturing the semantics of CM(S), and

- a set of *instantiation rules* which are used at runtime to populate CM(S) from the XML data exported by S.

For sources that do *not* export a CM, the mediation engineer has to reverse-engineer the CM from the exported XML DTD. Based on this, the instantiation rules for CM are derived. The integrated view INSM (Figure 1) is exported to the user or application as XML; it is defined in the declarative FL rule language on top of the CMs of all involved sources. It is important to notice that the mediator does *not* materialize the complete CMs but computes the relevant CM instances on the fly at query evaluation time, based on the user query against the integrated view. This *virtual integration approach* results from the use of the top-down query evaluation engine FLORA. In addition, for integration scenarios where materialization of CM(S) is advantageous, we may use the bottom-up FL engine FLORID [FLO, LHL+98].

XML sources are accessed through the MIX*m* mediator system which can evaluate complex XML queries expressed in XMAS[3]. The "structure-level" XML mediator MIX*m* is mainly used to produce *on demand* virtual XML views on top of potentially huge XML sources [LPV00]. Here, "on demand" means that the construction of the virtual XML view is driven by the navigation of the client (i.e., the KIND mediator) within the view.

The demonstration involves the following sources:

- PROLAB stores results of image analysis from protein labeling experiments performed on one or more regions of the brain. They contain measurements of protein concentration in different *segments* of light and electron microscope images. Segments are organized into collection objects called *anatomical structures*. An anatomical structure may contain other anatomical structures.

- DENDREC is a database of volumetric reconstructions of nerve compartments called *dendritic spines* and *dendritic shafts*. The database records a number of measurements performed on these volumetric objects. As in PROLAB, dendritic shafts and spines are spatially composed into larger volumetric objects called *dendrites*. Both PROLAB and DENDREC are implemented on an ORACLE8i database and wrapped to produce XML output.

- CAPROT is a Web-accessible database of calcium binding proteins.[4] In contrast to PRO-

LAB and DENDREC whose conceptual models had to be reverse-engineered, CAPROT publishes a conceptual model (EER) of its data which we have mapped into an UML/XMI encoding so it is accessible to the mediator through the FL$_2$XMI plug-in. CAPROT contains protein properties, the organisms and tissues and cells where they are found, as well as the known functions of the proteins.

- TAXON is a database containing the scientific classification of the animal kingdom, along with the common names of the animals. This database is an example for a knowledge source that allows to eliminate "semantic holes" of otherwise unrelated source models. Here, it bridges the gap between the scientific names used in CAPROT and the common names used in the other data sources. As shown in the demonstration, this also allows users to query on animals by higher order group names (e.g, mammals instead of humans and mice).

- Finally, ANATOM defines a hierarchy of biological organ names starting from the brain down to cells and subcellular components. It also contains a set of rules defining different groupings and classification hierarchies of organs. For example, it states how the set of brain regions can be grouped structurally and functionally. It also specifies transitive properties of *is-a* and *has-a* relations which are beyond the expressive power of most XML query languages.

An example user query spanning different sources (and which, therefore, could not be answered without the mediator) is:

- *"Find the cerebellar distribution of all rat proteins with more than 90% amino acid homology with the human NCS-1 protein"*, or

- *"Like before, but give the distribution of this protein or its homologs in other rodents."*

---

[3] ***XML Matching And Structuring Language*** [BGL+99]
[4] `http://structbio.vanderbilt.edu/cabp_database`

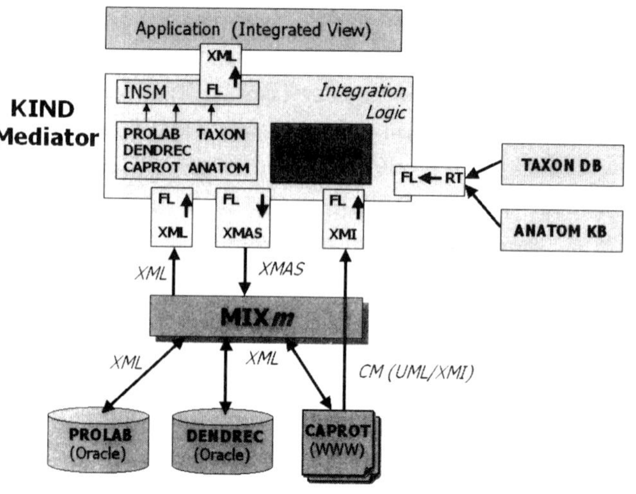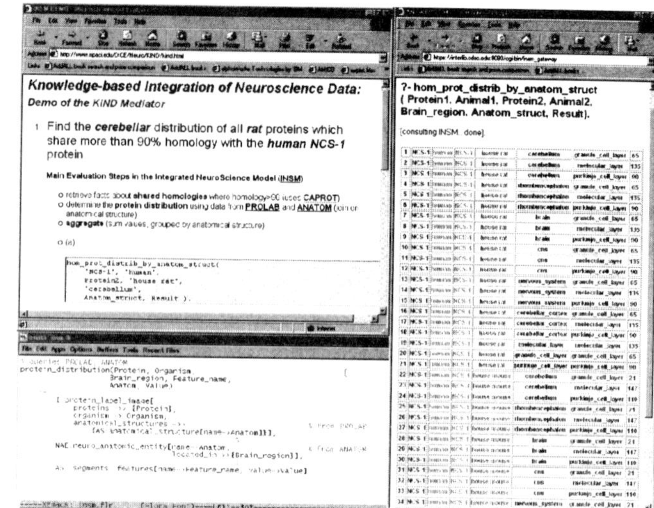

Figure 1: **left:** architecture of the KIND mediator; **right:** snapshot of the Web interface

As part of the demonstration, we will show the different system components involved in the evaluation of such queries, along with the corresponding data and schema definitions and the mappings between them. A screenshot of the current Web interface is shown on the right in Figure 1.

References

[BGL+99] C. Baru, A. Gupta, B. Ludäscher, R. Marciano, Y. Papakonstantinou, P. Velikhov, and V. Chu. XML-Based Information Mediation with MIX. In *ACM Intl. Conference on Management of Data (SIGMOD)*, Philadelphia, PA, 1999. exhibition program.

[CDSS98] S. Cluet, C. Delobel, J. Simeon, and K. Smaga. Your Mediators Need Data Conversion! In *ACM Intl. Conference on Management of Data (SIGMOD)*, pp. 177–188, 1998.

[FLO] FLORID Homepage. `www.informatik.uni-freiburg.de/~dbis/florid/`.

[GLM00] A. Gupta, B. Ludäscher, and M. E. Martone. Knowledge-Based Integration of Neuroscience Data Sources. In *12th Intl. Conference on Scientific and Statistical Database Management (SSDBM)*, Berlin, July 2000. IEEE Computer Society.

[GMPQ+97] H. Garcia-Molina, Y. Papakonstantinou, D. Quass, A. Rajaraman, Y. Sagiv, J. Ullman, V. Vassalos, and J. Widom. The TSIMMIS Approach to Mediation: Data Models and Languages. *Journal of Intelligent Information Systems*, 8(2), 1997.

[GMW99] R. Goldman, J. McHugh, and J. Widom. From Semistructured Data to XML: Migrating the Lore Data Model and Query Language. In *ACM SIGMOD Workshop on the Web and Databases (WebDB)*, pp. 25–30, Philadelphia, 1999.

[KLW95] M. Kifer, G. Lausen, and J. Wu. Logical Foundations of Object-Oriented and Frame-Based Languages. *Journal of the ACM*, 42(4):741–843, July 1995.

[LHL+98] B. Ludäscher, R. Himmeröder, G. Lausen, W. May, and C. Schlepphorst. Managing Semistructured Data with FLORID: A Deductive Object-Oriented Perspective. *Information Systems*, 23(8):589–613, 1998.

[LPV00] B. Ludäscher, Y. Papakonstantinou, and P. Velikhov. Navigation-Driven Evaluation of Virtual Mediated Views. In *Intl. Conference on Extending Database Technology (EDBT)*, LNCS 1777, Konstanz, March 2000.

[LYK99] B. Ludäscher, G. Yang, and M. Kifer. FLORA: The Secret of Object-Oriented Logic Programming. Technical report, State University of New York, Stony Brook, June 1999. see also `www.cs.sunysb.edu/~sbprolog/flora/`.

[XMI99] XML Metadata Interchange (XMI). `www.omg.org/cgi-bin/doc?ad/99-10-02`, 1999.

[YK00] G. Yang and M. Kifer. FLORA: Implementing an Efficient DOOD System Using a Tabling Logic Engine. In *6th International Conference on Rules and Objects in Databases (DOOD)*, 2000.

Push Technology Personalizatiom
Through Event Correlation

Asaf Adi, David Botzer, Opher Etzion, Tali Yatzkar-Haham

IBM Research Laboratory in Haifa

{(Adi / Botzer / Opher / Tali)@il.ibm.com}

Abstract

"Push Technology" stands for the ability to transfer information as a reaction to event occurrence. This demonstration proposal describes Amit, a middleware framework that resolves a major problem in this area: the gap that exists between events that are reported by various channels, and the actual cases in which the user needs to react to, hereby called; *reactive situations*. These situations are composition of events or other situations (for example, "when atleast four events of the same type occurred") or content filtering on events (for example, "only events that relate to IBM stocks") or both ("when atleast four purchases of more than 50,000 shares have been performed on IBM stocks in a single week"). This paper describes the generic application development tool, the middleware architecture and framework, and describes the demo.

1. The problem

Reactive applications are those that include components that respond to the detection of events by triggering alerts or other actions (active databases is an example of it). The importance of reactive applications has increased in the recent years with the emergent of e-commerce applications (stock market, business opportunities, sale alerts), as well as system management applications, command and control applications, and customer relationship management applications. Many tools in different areas have been built to detect events, and to couple their detection with appropriate actions. These tools exist in products that implement active databases, event management systems, the "publish/subscribe" protocol, real-time systems and similar products.

Most current tools enable the application to respond to a **single event**. A major problem in many reactive applications is the gap between the events that are supplied by the event source, and the situations to which the clients are required to react, which can be (possibly complex) predicates on the event history. In order to bridge this gap in contemporary systems, the client must monitor all the relevant events, and apply an ad hoc decision process in order to decide if the conditions for reactions have been met.

Some examples of situations that need to be handled are:

- The client wishes to activate an automatic "buy or sell" program if, for any stock that belongs to a predefined list of stocks that are traded in two stock markets, there is a difference of more than 5 percent between the values of the same stock in distinct stock-markets, where the time difference of the reported values is less than 5 minutes ("arbitrage").

- The customer relationship manager wishes to receive an alert if a request was reassigned by different agents at least three times.

- A groupware user wishes to start a session when there are 10 members of the group logged in to the groupware server.

In most current implementations, the clients need to store and process all the events. For example, in the arbitrage case, the client has to subscribe to quotes in different stock markets, accumulate the events, correlate them and decide when to operate the "buy or sell" program (in the second case). This may be impossible in some cases, such as "thin" clients without significant storage and processing capabilities. Even if it is possible, the solution that requires a client to process single events may result in a substantial overhead (ad-hoc programming efforts, communication traffic is significantly increased, redundant storage). The problem is intensified due to the many-to-many relationships that exist between the event sources, and the target clients. For example: many stock traders may subscribe to the information services of multiple stock markets.

The goal of the active middleware framework is to personalize push technology through event correlation and enable each client to detect customized situations without the need to be aware of the occurrence of the basic events, or their source.

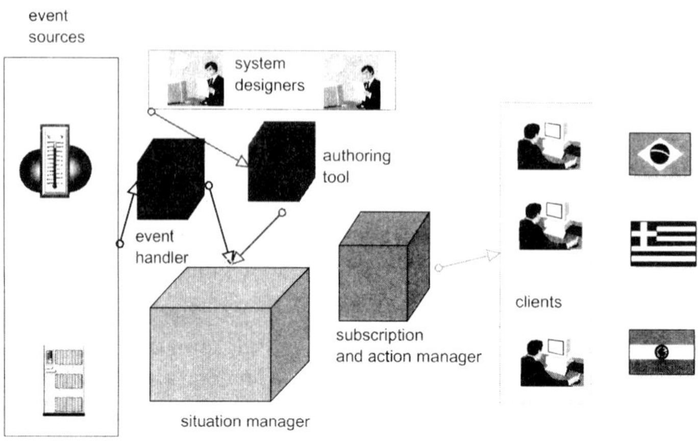

2. The Architecture

Figure 1 illustrates the implementation's architecture. The architecture consists of the following components:

2.1. Event sources:

The "push" style of event reporting is typical for many information notification applications.
An example is a stock market reporting application.

2.2. Event handler:

This component consists of two sub-components:

Event adapters: programs that convert the reported events to a standard format;

Event base: a data store (implemented on top of a DBMS or a file system) that stores the event instances that are reported by the event sources.

2.3. The authoring tool:

The authoring tool is the system designer's vehicle to define metadata for situations and actions' definitions. All the definitions are phrased as XML propositions, while the meta-meta-data is defined as DTD. The metadata resides in a data store.

2.4. The situation manager:

This is the middleware engine. Its goal is to detect the desired situations.

The situation manager receives two types of input:

- The metadata, which is a collection of parsed XML propositions that guide the situation manager.

- The event instances that are being submitted from the sources using the event adapters.

The situation manager employs composition operators and content filtering on the basic events, and detect situations. Each detected situation is detected as an event, a feature that enables the definition of nested situations. The architecture may vary from a totally centralized solution of having a single situation manager, to a totally distributed solution, in which each subscriber has its own situation manager. In other cases there are multiple instances of the situation manager, that are either subject base, or peers that are aimed at improving the scalability. Each enterprise can choose its own architecture.

2.5. The Subscription and Action controller

This component uses the metadata definitions to decide what to do when the situation is detected. This information has two components:

- Who are the subscribers to this situation?

- What action should be taken for each subscriber (e.g., real-time alert notification, Email message, putting a message on a message queue, triggering a software module)?

2.6. Subscribers:

The clients that subscribe to the information or action. The action can be performed at the client's site, or at the middleware's site.

3. The Actual Demo

The Demo will show the following items:

- Definition of metadata (events and situations) using XML editing GUI (new applications can be written on-the-fly).

- Run-time reaction to simulated events file.

- Run-time trace of situation detection.

- Post-mortem graphical representation of the situation detection

The Demo will show a variety of applications. Examples are:

- E-brokerage application of personalized subscription to situations related to the stock market.

- System management application of personalized subscription to problems and other events.

- Reactive coordination application such as the 2 Phase Commit protocol.

References

[1] S. Chakravarthy & D. Mishra - Snoop: an expressive event specification language for active databases. Data & Knowledge Engineering, 13(3), Oct 1994.

[2] C. Collet, T. Coupaye, T. Svenson - NAOS - Efficient and modular reactive capabilities in an object-oriented database system. In Proceedings. VLDB'94.

[3] S. Gatziu, K. Dittrich - Detecting composite events in active database systems using Petri

Nets. Proceedings IEEE RIDE'94.

[4] N.H. Gehani, H.V. Jagadish, O. Shmueli - Composite event model specification in active databases: model and implementation. Proceedings VLDB'92.

[5] G. Kappel, S. Rausch-Schott, W. Retschitzegger - A Tour on the TriGS active database system - architecture and implementation. Proceedings ACM SAC'98.

[6] Nebula white paper:
http://www.linmor.com/library/white_pa/nms_wp.html

[7] Nervecenter white paper:
http://www.seagatesoftware.com/nervecenter/

[8] K. R. Sheers - HP OpenView Event Correlation Services. HP Journal. Oct 1996.

[9] S. Yemini et al.- High Speed and Robust Event Correlation. IEEE Communications Magazine, May 1996.

[10] D. Zimmer, R. Unland, A. Meckenstock - A General model for event specification in active database management systems. In Proceeding 5th DOOD, 1997.

XPERANTO: A Middleware for Publishing Object-Relational Data as XML Documents

Michael Carey[*]   Jerry Kiernan   Jayavel Shanmugasundaram[+]

Eugene Shekita   Subbu Subramanian

IBM Almaden Research Center
650 Harry Road
San Jose, CA 95120
carey@acm.org, kiernan@almaden.ibm.com, jai@cs.wisc.edu,
shekita@almaden.ibm.com, subbu@us.ibm.com

Abstract

The eXtended Markup Language (XML) is quickly emerging as the universal format for publishing and exchanging data on the World Wide Web. As a result, data sources, including object-relational databases, are now faced with a new class of users and applications; customers and programs that would like to deal directly with XML data rather than being forced to deal with the data source's particular (e.g., object-relational) schema and query language. The goal of the XPERANTO middleware project is to support this new class of users and applications. XPERANTO does this by providing query-able "XML Views" over the underlying object-relational database. Users can then query and (re)structure XML data using an XML query language, without having to deal with the underlying SQL tables and query language. The XPERANTO system translates XML-based queries into SQL requests, receives the tabular query results, converts them into XML, and then returns XML documents to the system's users and applications.

1. Motivation and Introduction

XML [2][4] is emerging as the standard for publishing and exchanging data on the World Wide Web. As a result, many "e-businesses" want to publish their existing data as XML documents so that their business partners can process them. For example, an online wholesale bookstore may want to make its inventory available in XML form so that retail merchants can process this information over the Internet. It is also important to provide query capability over such XML data because, for instance, a retail merchant may want to check whether the wholesale bookstore has a particular book in stock (this is a selection query over the inventory XML document).

The goal of the XPERANTO project [3] at the IBM Almaden Research Center is to publish *object-relational data* as XML documents. XPERANTO operates as a middleware on top of existing (object-)relational database systems and provides query-able "XML Views" over them. In doing so, it shields users of XPERANTO from the underlying database and language (SQL) and allows them to create and query XML data using an an XML query language (currently XML-QL [5]). Thus, businesses that have large amounts of important business data stored in existing (object-)relational databases can use XPERANTO to make this data available on the Internet in query-able XML form.

XPERANTO differs from other similar systems that we are aware of [6] in the following ways. First, XPERANTO is based on a "pure XML" philosophy – users and developers do no need to know or learn SQL.

---

[*]Currently at Propel, 2350 Mission College Blvd., Santa Clara, CA 95054.

[+]Also at the University of Wisconsin, Madison, WI 53706.

Proceedings of the 26th International Conference on Very Large Databases, Cairo, Egypt, 2000

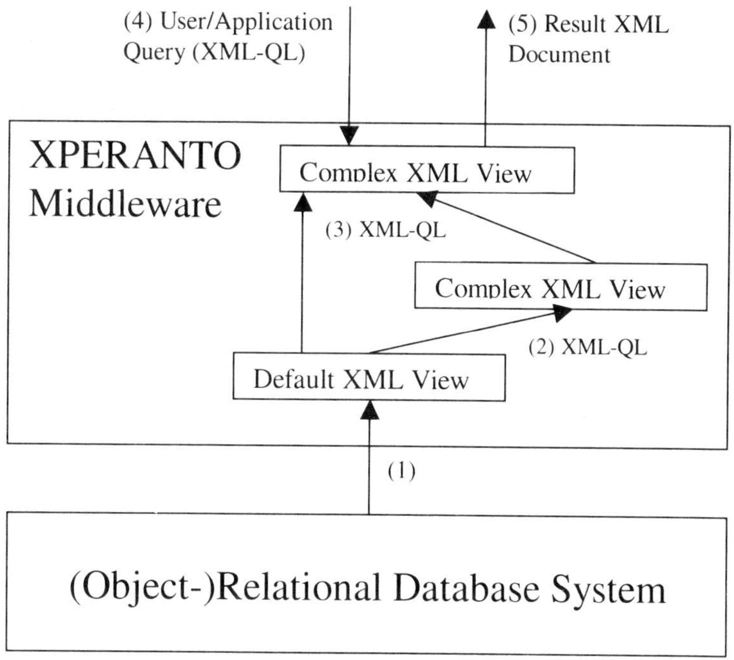

Figure 1: XPERANTO Architecture

Second, XPERANTO attempts to push as much processing down to the relational engine as possible for more efficient query execution [7]. Third, XPERANTO handles object-relational structures in addition to flat relational structures. Finally, XPERANTO enables the seamless querying of relational data (such as column values) and meta-data (such as column names).

For the remainder of this demo proposal, we outline the architecture of the XPERANTO system and show it can efficiently support query-able XML views by doing smart XML query rewrites and by harnessing the sophisticated processing capability of the underlying (object-)relational engine.

2. The XPERANTO High Level Architecture

As mentioned earlier, XPERANTO is a middleware system that works on top of existing (object-)relational database systems. Figure 1 shows the high level architecture of the XPERANTO system. XPERANTO starts by providing a default virtual view of a given (object-)relational database (step 1). XML application developers can then create more complex or specialized views (which are also virtual) on top of this default view (step 2) by using an XML query language (currently XML-QL). These tailored views can then be made available to other applications and/or user groups, who can in turn create more complex view over the existing views (step 3). The views can then be queried using the same XML query language used to define them (step 4) and XPERANTO returns the result XML document (step 5). XPERANTO clients use an XML-based RPC facility –

Simple Object Access Protocol [1] – to communicate with the XPERANTO middleware for creating and querying XML views and retrieving the XML results.

Note that XPERANTO takes a "pure XML" approach to the problem of publishing (object-)relational data as XML - i.e., developers interact with XPERANTO using only XML (and an XML query language); they do not have to use or learn SQL.

An interesting and novel aspect of XPERANTO is that it provides a uniform framework that allows users to use XML as a way to seamlessly query over both relational data and relational metadata. This power stems from the fact that the XPERANTO default XML view of a relational database does not distinguish between data (such as column values) and metadata (such as column names). In this sense, XPERANTO provides users and applications a more powerful query capability than SQL.

3. XPERANTO Internals

We now describe the internals of the XPERANTO system and show how it supports query-able XML views over relational sources. As Figure 2 shows, when an user or applications poses an XML-QL query over an XML view, it is first parsed and translated into an internal representation called XQGM (Xml Query Graph Model). The representation is designed to be language neutral (i.e., not tied to the XML-QL query language) so that XPERANTO can be easily modified to support the standard XML query language when one becomes available.

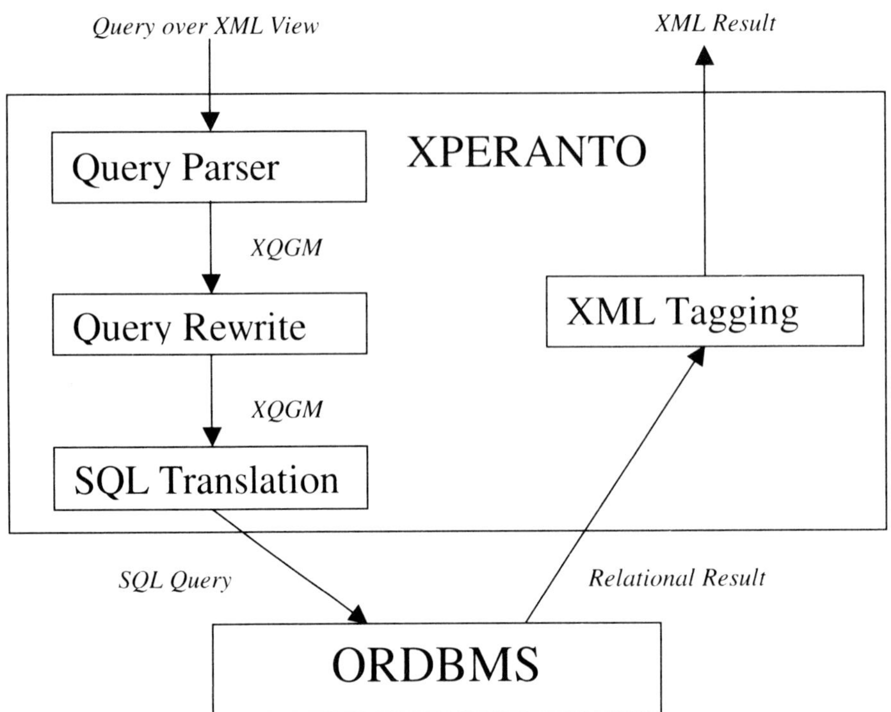

Figure 2: XPERANTO Internals

Once the query parser creates XQGM for a user query, the XPERANTO rewrite engine performs XML view composition in the middleware layer (i.e. outside of any database system) and produces simplified XQGM that is semantically equivalent to the original XQGM. The SQL generator component then converts this simplified XQGM representation to SQL queries that generate the content of the XML document. A typical XML query over an XML view will result in just one SQL query being issued, thus harnessing the query processing capabilities of the underlying relational engine [7]. The relational query results are then tagged in the XPERANTO middleware layer in order to produce the result XML document.

One attractive aspect of the XPERANTO approach is that it can work with any existing relational database system since the XPERANTO system generates regular SQL and tags the results outside the database engine.

4. The Demo

In this demo, we will illustrate the "pure XML" approach by presenting how the XPERANTO system automatically creates a default XML view over an (object-)relational database system. We will then show how developers can create more complex XML views on top of the system's default view. We will demonstrate how views are composed on top of other views, how queries on these views are translated into SQL queries, and how the results are converted into XML in the XPERANTO middleware layer.

5. References

[1] T. Box, D. Ehnebuske, G. Kakivaya, A. Layman, N. Mendelsohn, H. Nielson, S. Thatte, D. Winer, "SOAP: Simple Object Access Protocol," http://www.w3.org/TR/SOAP.

[2] T. Bray, J. Paoli, C.M. Sperberg-McQueen, "Extensible Markup Language (XML) 1.0", http://www.w3.org/XML/1998/06/xmlspec-report-19980910.htm.

[3] M. Carey, D. Florescu, Z. Ives, Y. Lu, J. Shanmugasundaram, E. Shekita, S. Subramanian, "XPERANTO: Publishing Object-Relational Data as XML," *Workshop on the Web and Databases (Informal Proceedings), May 2000.*

[4] R. Cover, "The SGML/XML Web Page," http://www.oasis-open.org/cover/xml.html.

[5] A. Deutsch, M. Fernandez, D. Florescu, A. Levy, D. Suciu, "XML-QL: A Query Language for XML," *Proceedings of the 8th International World Wide Web Conference, Toronto, May 1999.*

[6] M. Fernandez, W. Tan, D. Suciu, "SilkRoute: Trading Between Relations and XML," *Proceedings of the 9th International World Wide Web Conference, Amsterdam, May 2000.*

[7] J. Shanmugasundaram, E. Shekita, R. Barr, M. Carey, B. Lindsay, H. Pirahesh, B. Reinwald, "Efficiently Publishing Relational Data as XML Documents", *Proceedings of the VLDB Conference, Egypt, September 2000.*

Building Scalable Internet Applications with Oracle 8i Server

Julie Basu, Jose Alberto, Fernandez, Olga Peschansky

Java Platform Group

Oracle Corporation

jbasu@us.oracle.com

This paper was not available at the time of publication.

This proceedings and additional presentations will be available through www.vldb.org

Social, Educational, and Governmental Change Enabled Through Information Technology

Krithi Ramamritham
University of Massachusetts, USA and IIT Bombay, India – krithi@cs.umass.edu
Yehia El Atfi
National Number Database, Egypt – yatfy@idsc.gov.eg
Carlo Batini
Authority for Information Systems in Public Administration, Italy – batini@aipa.it
Michael Eitan
Information Technology & Internet committee of the Knesset, Israel – meita@netvision.net.il
Valerie Gregg
National Science Foundation, USA – vgregg@nsf.gov
D. B. Phatak
School of Information Technology, IIT Bombay, India – dbp@it.iitb.ernet.in

1 Introduction

The ability to store, access and disseminate large amounts of data has altered the social, educational, and governmental landscape throughout the world. The developments in technology, policy, and the economics of computing have been observed by some governments as providing a means to make government agencies more responsive to each others' as well as citizens' needs and also make government actions transparent and accountable to citizens. This panel brings together technocrats who are at the forefront of decision making, creating visions for the future, and exploiting the new technologies. After a brief look at what has been accomplished already, panelists will discuss the challenges that lay ahead from their respective perspectives.

In this panel statement, we shall try to give a glimpse of the various activities that some of the governments around the work have embarked upon in order to harness the power of information technology. This statement does not intend to provide uniform treatment to the various uses of IT, nor does it attempt to paint a picture pertaining to the different geographical regions of the world using similar brush strokes. Instead, its goal is to give the reader a feel for the types of activities governments around the world are focusing on and the dynamics that drive some of these activities.

Realizing that information is key to socioeconomic development, many governments have committed themselves to comprehensively develop modern information repositories. We discuss some of these efforts in Section 2. Most countries are also aiming to use IT to streamline the management of internal governmental processes. We discuss such efforts in Section 3. Section 4 concludes the paper by discussing some of the challenges that lie ahead.

2 Enhancing the Availability of Information

Modern information repositories can be exploited by governments to provide timely and accurate information (about population registry, company registers, motor vehicle database, property registry, etc.) for planning, monitoring and operational activities. This information can be used by all sectors of the society to achieve a multitude of goals. For example, government agencies can use the information about population distributions in order to plan for services such as education and medical care. It can help provide a clear, accurate and up-to-date picture of the society, allow personal, family and statistical information to be made available to individuals as well as public and private organizations to aid in planning, administra-

**Proceedings of the 26th VLDB Conference,
Cairo, Egypt, 2000.**

tion and identification issues related to socioeconomic development, and in improving the services provided by government agencies to individual citizens.

Allowing government agencies and citizens to access basic information relieves the pressure of information requests on government, firms and citizens; Beyond this, it will be valuable to provide for the automatic distribution of information to government departments and interested citizenry by triggered "live events" such as changes in civil status, judicial events, etc.

2.1 Egypt's Civil Information System

In Egypt, the Civil Status Organization (CSO) provides services in registration birth, marriage, divorce and death and also handles transactions for change residence and of occupation. Based on its records the CSO issues identification cards to persons above 16 years of age. In addition it furnishes statistical and aggregate information to a number of Government Organizations for their own use. But, because of the limited resources available to CSO and the increasing population of the country, the manual system was becoming cumbersome, slow, inaccurate and incomplete. Hence, Egypt has begun to upgrade the organization functions and services by employing modern information technologies. For example, the manually issued id cards are being upgraded to create a unique identification (numbers and cards) for citizens to be used in all their dealings with society in order to facilitate identification and exchange of information across different organizations.

In order to achieve these goals, Egypt has begun a number of specific actions geared towards satisfying the following immediate objectives:

- Build a national database for civil information that contains personal information that is continuously updated to reflect any changes in the society through birth, marriage, divorce, death and other events.

- Build an integrated automated system for maintaining the national civil information database and managing its use.

- Create a comprehensive system for producing reports for individuals, groups such as families, voting blocks, etc. and for the population at large.

2.2 India's National Information Repository

The Indian government set up the National Informatics Center (www.nic.in) in 1975. Its charter was to bring the benefits of information technology and networking to serve the needs of the government and of the nation at large. Towards this end, NIC developed the NICNET, a satellite-based computer communication network with over 1400 nodes connecting the National Capital, the State Capitals and the District Headquarters to one another. Using NICNET, NIC helps the government collect information of various types, from weather to crop yields. Thus, NIC serves as an information provider to more than fifty ministries in the central as well as state governments for planning and forecasting. NIC is also charged with the collection and analysis of India's population census and in handling the complex task of managing India's general elections.

GISTNIC (General Information Service Terminal - National Informatics Centre, www.nic.in/gist) is an on-line database service of NICNET. GISTNIC offers on-line retrieval of information pertaining to the Indian economy, population, village amenities, rural technologies, tourism, district profiles, universities and colleges, as well traditional sciences and technologies of India. For example, the database that monitors the economy provides a detailed monthly review of the Indian economy in the form of a time series of over 10000 parameters, covering both the state level and national level, and sectors such as agriculture, infrastructure, industries, health, education, employment, housing, and public finance. At the other end of the spectrum, the database on traditional sciences and technologies of India provides details of over 5000 items in over one hundred subject areas such as traditional Indian medicine, yoga, medicinal plants of India, traditional Indian practices and methodologies, architecture, town planning, metallurgy, agriculture, irrigation, and textiles. Most provincial governments are now making information more readily available through special portals.

2.3 The Federal Statistics Repository of the United States

More than 70 agencies in the United States Federal Government produce statistics of interest to the public. The Federal Interagency Council on Statistical Policy maintains a portal (www.fedstats.gov/) to provide easy access to the full range of statistics and information produced by these agencies for public use. From this portal one can obtain vast amounts of raw as well as aggregate information.

For instance, it is possible to obtain a statistical abstract of the United States from the National Data Book. It contains a collection of statistics on social and economic conditions in the United States. Selected international data are also included. The abstract serves as a guide to sources of other data from the census bureau, other Federal agencies, and private organizations. The State and Metropolitan Area Data Book contains a collection of statistics on social and economic conditions in the United States at the State and metropolitan area levels. Selected data for component counties and central cities of metropolitan areas are also included.

3 Enhancing Government Processes

3.1 Unitary Network of the Italian Government

In 1993, the Italian government created a new agency named Autorit' per l'Informatica nella Pubblica Amministrazione (Authority for IT in the Public Administration, or AIPA – www.aipa.it). AIPA's charter was to promote technology innovation in the information systems of the government, and define criteria for planning, implementing, managing and maintaining them. AIPA designers preferred not to force administrations to carry out a specific re-engineering strategy against their legacy information systems. So, an Integration approach was chosen so that it allowed access to legacy data by integrating old and new applications without requiring substantial modifications. This was achieved by adopting a three-tier client/server architecture to model the "business" relationships among domains.

AIPA's main communication infrastructure, the Unitary Network, was initiated by the Italian Government in 1995. Rete Unitaria della Pubblica Amministrazione (Unitary Network of the Italian Government) or RUPA, was set up to provide administrations with a single point of provision of network services at a lower cost. The RUPA is the government Intranet which caters to most of the internal and external networking needs of administrations, enabling them to co-operate. The RUPA network model is designed as a confederation of highly autonomous and heterogeneous co-operating systems. Projects aimed at workflow automation, integrating the main government Geographical Information Systems, building a network of registry offices, improving personnel information systems, particularly for human resource management, and developing norms for digital signature usage are being conducted under the auspices of AIPA.

The Italian experience has demonstrated that the concept of a federation of interoperable and cooperating information systems can be used to reform public administration with modest financial resources, with the potential for immediate progress. It has shown the feasibility of redesigning interdepartmental working procedures and automated information flows using available interoperability services.

3.2 Israel's Direct Democracy Project

With the view of advancing information technology in Israel and with the idea of experimenting with *direct democracy*, a pilot project has begun in Israel with the goal of bringing the proceedings of Israel's Knesset to the public and allowing citizens to be active participants in the proceedings, where possible. The website being constructed (www1.knesset.gov.il/itcommittee) for this purpose is based on the following principles:

- All the Knesset Committees' activities, including internal administrative activities, will be carried out digitally and "paperlessly".

- All the Committee's activities will be carried out over the Internet and, with the exception of matters relating to individual privacy and/or security limitations, will be totally visible to the public. (Actual Committee meetings will occur only rarely and will be presented online, in real-time on the Committee's website, allowing online responses to the discussions).

- The public will have the opportunity of actively participating in the work of the Committee and special tools have been developed for this purpose.

- The Committee and the website draw their strength from the Knesset and are bound by the Knesset charter and the constraints resulting from the safeguarding of the rights of the Members of the Knesset and its factions.

Using appropriate tools, members and incidental visitors to the web site can submit background material or opinion, queries, or motions for legislation, and participate in polls and chat rooms devoted to various topics. The tools will be simple and and based on existing popular applications. The real innovation is the amalgamation of these tools in the work of the Knesset and the willingness to put these tools at the disposal of the public and through them to bring the work of the Knesset to every home in Israel, not in the form of single directional media, which presents de facto details, but rather by means of an invitation to a process of joint and mutually fruitful work between the elected and the electorate.

Will the Israeli public actually respond to an invitation from the legislative body and actively participate in the managing of the affairs of state? It must be remembered that only 12% of the Israeli public has access to the Internet, a fact that in itself creates disproportionality in many areas, and will influence the volume of participation. The world will be watching!

3.3 India's Emerging IT Strategy

As a developing economy, India in recent years has been attempting to use the modern Information Technology as a core around which to build a modern nation. It has formulated an IT strategy that hopes to capitalize on the high global demand of IT services and products. The strategy also envisages a much larger usage of this technology within the country to create an information-enabled society. E-Commerce, e-governance, IT-based education and services are expected to become the corner stones of future national development. For these advances to be useful, the Indian society must create the necessary infrastructure as also an ethos of information usage that will permit proper absorption of these technologies at all levels. As a starting point, the necessary telecom and networking infrastructure is being rapidly put into place by the federal government as well as most state governments. Furthermore, the recently formulated Indian IT strategy calls upon all Government and public sector organizations to spend a minimum of one per cent of their annual budget on IT enabled systems. These strategic measures are expected to fuel a rapid growth of IT industry in the country and along with it the exploitation of IT towards better governance at the federal as well as provincial levels.

3.4 The Digital Government Program of the United States

Today, the United States government has embraced the IT infrastructure in a big way. Examples include Thomas, the Congress' Web site, and the US Internal Revenue Service's interfaces for electronic tax filing. Looking into the future potential of IT, the US National Science Foundation's Digital Government Program (www.digitalgovernment.org/) aims to support innovative projects that effectively and broadly address through research the potential improvement of agency, interagency, and intergovernmental operations and/or government/citizen interaction. Such research is expected to enable the generation and use of a continuous stream of advanced information technologies for early adoption and integration into the government information systems community.

4 Conclusions and Challenges

IT Education and Human Resource Development:

A very rapidly burgeoning IT industry will make highly skewed demands on human resource development: For example, India by itself estimates that from the current work force of about 200,000 people, it will need over 2.5 million IT professionals by the year 2008. There are several hurdles in this ambitious road map including the production and nurturing of such a large pool of professionals. While computer science graduates alone can not be produced in sufficient numbers, schemes for converting bright students of other disciplines to the field of IT, as also continued education programs to constantly update and upgrade the knowledge base of working professionals, will need to be addressed adequately. Fortunately, the Cyberspace and the e-commerce world do appear very exciting and have been greatly hyped in the recent years. Because of the adverse demand supply ratio, the IT industry routinely absorbs, and is able to absorb, good students from other branches of learning. The Indian educational System at the school level is known to be highly competitive and fairly rigorous. The basic mathematical abilities coupled with English medium for university education permit students to migrate to IT with comparative ease.

Finally, quality in CS and IT related mass education needs a corresponding number of high grade teachers and academicians. This is a very major problem and does not seem to currently offer any easy solution. The problem is exacerbated by two phenomena: the large gap in salaries, especially in developing countries, between academics and industry; and, the huge demand for CS and IT trained faculty and professionals in developed countries.

The IT Divide: The proliferation of IT has created a new *divide* of information-haves and have nots. This is particularly significant for developing countries. Thus it is of utmost important that education systems in schools be significantly spruced up using IT as the modern enabler. In addition to this, Internet spread in all but a few countries is currently at a low level, the only solace being that it is growing exponentially in almost all parts of the world. Together with the free-market competition that is increasingly spreading in developing countries, the basic infrastructure and operational efficiencies should soon achieve a world class status.

Also, given that the internet is growing fast, there is a great need to create contents on the net that are in native languages and which cater to the local needs of school and college students. fg This should be in addition to good internet access at reasonable prices. India, for example, has formulated a proposal for an "Indian-Internet", combining the above features, but that is workable under existing legal service provisions.

Privacy and Authentication Issues: For citizens to feel comfortable about contributing to government-managed information repositories, high levels of privacy and security must be guaranteed with respect to civil information by ensuring proper authorized access to different types of data and by implementing measures against the destruction or loss of data. Several steps are being contemplated, for example, through out the world, laws defining the legality and technological context for digital signature have been enacted. The salient aspects of the laws developed, for example, in Italy last year include full legal value of electronic signature, use of open standards for digital certificates, clear conformance requirements for signing devices (including smart cards), and co-existence of multiple certification authorities subject to public registration.

In spite of these seemingly un-surmountable difficulties, the world at large has clearly seen the tremendous wealth generation potential that IT has, and hence feels highly optimistic about addressing these issues. It has also seen and sensed that a more comfortable and honorable life style is possible through the effective use of IT in all aspects of human life. So even countries which missed the fruits of the industrial revolution are now ready to firmly embrace the emerging cyber world.

A 20/20 VISION OF THE VLDB-2020?

S. M. Deen [Moderator]
University of Keele, England
deen@cs.keele.ac.uk

Anant Jhingran
IBM Almaden, USA
anant@us.ibm.com

Sham Navathe
Georgia Inst. Tech, USA
sham@cc.gatech.edu

Erich J Neuhold
GMD, Germany
erich.neuhold@gmd.de

Gio Wiederhold
Stanford University, USA
gio@cs.stanford.edu

1. Introduction : Moderator

A 20/20 vision in ophthalmology implies a perfect view of things that are in front of you. The term is also used to mean a perfect sight of the things to come. Here we focus on a speculative vision of the VLDB in the year 2020. This panel is the follow-up of the one I organised (with S. Navathe) at the Kyoto VLDB in 1986, with the title: "Anyone for a VLDB in the Year 2000?". In that panel, the members discussed the major advances made in the database area and conjectured on its future, following a concern of many researchers that the database area was running out of interesting research topics and therefore it might disappear into other research topics, such as software engineering, operating systems and distributed systems. That did not happen.

However, in the last 15 years the database research has not been unquestioned. Some concern about its future research is expressed in the Asilomar report [Sigmod Record, Vol (27:4), 1998, p74], as well as by some eminent researchers who fear that the excitement has gone. We must take these criticisms seriously. As we are in the year 2000, this is the right time to look again at database research and to ponder on its future growth over the next 20 years.

To date the database technology has provided large sharable persistent reliable and quality controlled storage and management of data. For many years the focus of the DB research in the VLDB series was dedicated to improving

Proceedings of the 26th International Conference on Very Large Databases, Cairo, Egypt, 2000

this core technology, which is recently being extended to include the infrastructure for information system development. However, over the last 30 years, the relational model has dominated this technology. By 2020, the 50th anniversary year of that model, we are likely to see many new rich approaches and middleware brought about by the challenge of the Internet/Web, new application domains and new hardware technology.

Additionally, storage and handling in the next 20 years will include data, processes, execution strategies quality of service, relevance and ease of search, in addition to the traditional concerns of reliability and optimisation. There will be a growing need to interact with thousands of databases in the Internet/Web, requiring a database capability to cooperate and negotiate to reach compromises based on preferences. Associated with this, there will be an enhanced need for security, semantics and interoperability, as already being encountered in many distributed applications. There is also likely to be an impact of newer technologies, such as molecular computing and quantum computing.

The 1986 panel identified relational model as the only major achievement in data modelling, without any parallel. SQL was viewed as a great success, eclipsing many other offerings of that time. Many research trends current at that time were predicted to continue as rewarding (rather than dry) topics of investigation (as they actually did), but the expectation of great advancement in information (including data, images, sound) bases, "intelligent" and natural-language processing and image queries have not been materialised. Furthermore, the enthusiastic (encouraged by the Japanese Fifth Generation project next door) forecast of ever increasing cooperation between AI and database research has remained as elusive as ever. None of us foresaw interoperability (1989[*]), legacy systems (1989[*]), middleware (1993[*]), data mining (1992[*]), data warehousing (1992[*]) or Internet (1997[*]) as future hot topics – although the ability to retrieve information of all kinds from diverse

Topic Name	80	81	82	83	84	85	86	87	88	89	90	91	92	93	94	95	96	97	98	99	00	Total	F3	L3
AI & Deductive DB		3		3	1	6	9	5	3	1	9	3	3	3	4		1					54	1	
DB Machines		4					3			1	3											11	1.33	
Concurrency Control	4	3	3	7		3		1				3				3						27	3.33	
DDBs	3		3	7	3		4	3	1		3		6	3	3		6	9	3	6	4	67	2	4.33
Data Modelling	9	6	4	11	1		6	3	4	3	3	9	6		4	3			3	3	2	80	6.33	2.67
DB Theories	3	6	4		8	4		6	3			3		2								39	4.33	
DB Trans		3			4			5	6	5	15	3	4	9	3	6	2	3				68	1	
Query Proc	3	5			6	5	12	9	8	8	3	6	3	6	3	6	8	9	12	13	9	134	2.67	11.33
Views & Der.Rel		3			3					2		1									1	10	1	0.33
Languages									1	3	3	1		3	3							14		
DB Sys Perf		2			3	6		3	5			6	3		3	3	3		3	6	1	47	0.67	3.33
DB Search					3				1	2						3			6			15		2
DB Design	10	5	8	9	7	6	8	3	2		3				3	3	1	3			4	75	7.67	1.33
DB Storage	3	6	3		4	6	3	3	5	2	6	3	5	8	10	5		6	4	8	7	97	4	6.33
Multimedia		3		1	3	3		3				1				3		3	2			22	1	0.67
Info Retrieval			1										1			3	3		3	6	5	22	0.33	4.67
Object Tech							3			7	6	1	4	5	7	6	4	2			2	47		0.67
Design/Image			1	1	4	3		6		1					3		1				1	21	0.33	0.33
Spatial DBs										1	3	1			3	2	3	4	4			21		1.33
Scientific & Stat DBs			4	1	1					3				3				1				13	1.33	
Security		2						1								1						4	0.66	
Time Dimension					1		3	3		2	3	3	3	1	1		3		1	2	3	29		2
User Interfaces	3		3	4		3			3	3												19	2	
Active DB										2		6	3	3	1	1	1					17		
Parallel DB												3	3	1	3	3	3			3	2	21		1.67
Data Mining													3		1	6	4	3	10	6	3	36		6.33
C\S & Middleware																1	1				1	3		0.33
Data Warehousing													3				3	3	4	1	2	16		2.33
Workflows																1						1		
Internet																		3		3	6	12		3
Agent Tech																						0		
Total	38	51	34	44	52	45	52	53	42	46	60	50	49	51	54	56	48	55	52	57	53	1042	41	54

sources all over the world was anticipated [*apparent first reference in a VLDB conference]. As an *aside*, Cobol was predicted to survive the Century as it indeed has done.

In the remainder of this position paper, we shall present the individual contribution of each panelist on the 2020 vision, preceded by a brief analysis database in `the past as represented by the VLDB papers.

2. **Analysis of the Past:** Moderator

At this point it might be interesting to look at the rise and fall of topics in the VLDB conference over the last 20 years (21 including this year). In the table above, I have included only the research papers and grouped them into rough subject categories based on paper titles, choosing from various possible alternatives. The session titles were not always helpful, as they were meant to define sessions, but not necessarily subjects. There was also a question of how many categories I should make. I started with 10 and ended up with about 30, quite arbitrarily as a sort of a canonical basis; but a broader picture can be gleaned from different combinations of related subjects.

The reader might find it interesting to examine the last two columns, F3 the average for the first three years (1980-82) and L3 the average for the last three years (1998-2000), which capture the change over the last 21 years. I make the following observations:

- Some topics are less popular today [AI, Database Machines,...]
- Some important topics had too few papers, but will perhaps come back [Security, Workflows, User Interfaces].
- Some topics are always popular – bread and butter topics [Queries, Transactions, Data modelling, Theories, Performance, ...]
- Some topics are very new [Data mining, Data warehousing, Internet/Web, ...] (today's hot topics?)

It seems there were too few papers on User Interfaces, given its importance. Equally surprising is the presence of only one paper on workflows, not to speak of a complete absence of any paper in the category of agent technology. In fact I have not seen any paper title with the word agent in it.

3. S. M. Deen: Agents are Green

Green is a sign for Go. It also implies environmentally friendly, and hence preferable. I argue here provocatively to consider agents as the most appropriate vehicles (and hence preferable) to deliver the goodies in a user-friendly environment from the Internet/Web based complex distributed systems of the future, expected to be commonplace by the year 2020. In addition, I also make some other general points on the future research direction.

The Asilomar Report identifies the forces that will shape database research as being: (i) Internet/Web, (ii) ever complex applications and (iii) advances in hardware. It predicted that multitudes of databases and "trillions of Gizmos" over the Internet/Web would provide special challenges to be overcome with new distributed architectures with ability to provide an interoperable environment. Undoubtedly this is an area of exciting research, which is likely to flourish and bear fruits over the next 20 years on many topics. The anticipated highly distributed environment will in particular need to support open interfaces and complex queries, both of which I think can benefit from the application of agent technology as a means of delivery as claimed below. By complex queries I mean queries from multiple sources, but without a single answer – the "best" answer to be determined by preferences with negotiation and compromises.

Since agents support dynamically changing user-contexts and preferences (with the ability to cooperate negotiate, coordinate and adapt), they should be able integrate multiple (including new) applications that can interface and collaborate with synergy. Such agents should be able to negotiate dynamically on software interfaces forming super applications during the runtime, thus offering scalability and cost effectiveness in an environment where a multitude of databases and "gizmos" are involved. On the other hand the autonomy and use of partial knowledge, which makes agents effective, could also cause severe side-effects, such as poor-decision-making, excessive use of resources, non-convergence and eventually loss of control – all of which could open up new topics for investigation.

Returning to the more general theme, the database research in the first 20 years seems to have culminated in the establishment of the relational model as the central plank, and the single major achievement of the last 20 years is arguably the development of a transaction model, with all its variations.

In the next 20 years, we shall probably be looking at the extensive growth in the middleware technology for handling multitude of information bases distributed over the Internet/Web. Search, navigation, optimization and security will become important topics, often implemented via agent technology, which should also provide platform (middle-ware) independent, dynamically adjustable interfaces and semantic interoperability. How to control emerging group behaviour of agents from their individualised behaviours will be another important topic of study. There will also be richer queries permitting complex retrievals (from disparate sources over the Internet/Web) based on not only constraints but also negotiations and preferences.

Our current concern on distributed data consistency will probably be subsumed within a greater concern on the correctness of behaviour, the consistency of results and timely termination - the problems of complex distributed systems. I suspect User Interfaces will always remain an important topic distinguished by too few VLDB papers.

Finally a highly speculative prediction on new technology: By the year 2020, we should see a paper on quantum processing and/or nano-optimisation in a VLDB conference.

4 . A. Jhingran: Porkbellies of the future

It is impossible to predict 20/20, since the changes in the world happen through small transformations connecting the dots towards a larger trend, and interpolation from the first few dots is all but incorrect. However, a 20/10 vision (even better than 20/20!) is much more realistic, and here is my attempt to extrapolate from a few dominant trends.

1. While the PC Installed base will remain stuck in the 600 - 800 million devices, there will be more than 1.2 billion mobile phones by 2010. Data Access will dominate Data Processing.
2. Boundaries of enterprises will transform significantly, with considerable outsourcing of non-strategic functions, including, but not restricted to I/T. Infinite bandwidth will speed up this trend. Consequently, data warehousing will be passe.
3. The network will become much more intelligent, again shifting data and processing away from the enterprise model that we are used to today, but in spite of that Distributed databases and models will not become important. However, "service level agreements" (like QoS) and economic models would become far more important.
4. Value will continue to shift upwards in the food chain, commoditizing database engines (making them like porkbellies -- a thriving business, but most would not care). Application Enabling will be the buzzword for our domain.
5. E-Business will continue to reward those who utilize data for business advantage
6. Moore's Law will continue to work, hence performance will not be a major story

5. E. J. Neuhold: Knowledge and Databases – A Vision of the VLDB 2020

Recently I had an interesting discussion with some people from DARPA. One of the challenges to information and knowledge handling and therefore to Very Large Data Bases they see is in a device to directly and continuously dump the contents of our brain, i.e. our personal memory, into some database and retrieve parts again directly into our brain whenever they are needed. Such a device - well known in science fiction literature - would give us perfect memory and as a consequence a much wider base for knowledge, decision making, creativity and wisdom.

Concentrating on the data base aspects of such a device it is very easy to see that the ongoing discussion of the relational model, object oriented approaches, XML databases, or image, video and audio storage mechanisms, even when extended with meta data and semantics will not solve that problem. They are all too far removed from the way our memory is organized, handled, increased, and used. In addition the (partial) reloading of such dumped memory and integrating it with the newly acquired knowledge will compose formidable challenges.

By the way, whenever we dump our knowledge into a computer or other device it will become data/ information and not remain knowledge. We have a tendency to forget that only after we will be able to construct self-aware machines will they be able to say - I know. Without such awareness they will just store data/information and will give back to us that same information or the result of processing these data/information components

6. S. Navathe: Databases and DBMSs for Ubiquitous computing in 2020.

Database technology has been evolving for the last 35+ years ever since it was first made available for commercial consumption through DBMS products like IBM's IMS and Honeywell's IDS. In some ways, it has gone a circular route by revisiting concepts that were used in the past by giving them new twists and solving new demands for data. A couple of examples of this circular process stand out that include going from CODASYL network model through relational, back to Object Models which are again graph oriented. The recently popularized XML has the idea of hierarchical organization and access, which was the hallmark of DBMS like IMS and languages like DL/1 based on tree-structured organization of information.

Databases also went through an evolution from centralization to decentralization and distribution to compromise client-server architecture and are coming back to a central theme with data warehousing. From these experiences, it is very obvious that database technology has

not necessarily always invented new concepts to meet new challenges, but is likely to revisit, modify and integrate concepts from the past in the next two decades that will address new issues and new applications. In this context, the following four points are particularly relevant:

A. Future databases will have to integrate sensors in them attached to external stimuli and they must incorporate the notion of signal processing together with data processing. This will bring with it concomitant problems of sampling, fuzzy matching and pattern understanding that are new as far as basic DB functionality goes. We foresee a very dynamic new research domain that will include EE topics of DSP (digital signal processing) and sensor fusion and domain transforms that aim at handling sampled values from streams for detecting and extracting information, to be coupled with the "standard" notions of query processing and information retrieval.

B. Adaptability to users is an area of future development, which will call for models of user behavior based on their psychological underpinnings. User interaction data will have to be archived and processed with technologies such as clustering, classification and data mining at large, which will allow us to understand the users better and adapt the content and display of information in real time.

C. The footprint of databases will have to be reduced so that entire databases reside within portable devices, appliances, and gadgets of all types. Rulebases will store rules on user preferences, the understanding of the environment and context under which data need to be processed. Instead of the simple ECA (event-condition-action) rules, we will have a rich repertoire of rules that include economical, psychological and system configuration oriented aspects that must be taken into account before a query is processed or an update is installed in a database.

D. It is conceivable that as a "standard" repertoire of functions, database systems may have to offer information requests that require processing of "looks like", "feels like", or "smells like" type of processing. This requires a lot more progress in areas like natural language and speech understanding, understanding of a variety of image formats from a range of application domains. The field of "intelligent databases" seems wide open and is only limited by the types and forms of intelligence we may want to bring into the database functionality.

The exact nature of database management in 2020's is hard to speculate, but it will be a result of some of the pragmatic integration of research from a variety of disciplines together with orders of magnitude advances in storage capacities, bandwidths, and processor speeds with appropriate architectures. Global connectivity and availability of a variety of input/output media will make every individual a database client and every electrical/electronic device a database processor by 2020!

7. G. Wiederhold: Will database research really support decision-making?

Although database systems have been promoted by their developers as supporting decision- makers we find very few instances where databases are used directly by the decision-makers. The primary computer-based tool used today by actual decision-makers is the spreadsheet, which appears to provide satisfactory interaction. Even when spreadsheet data and formulas have been initialized by an intermediary specialist, the decision-maker can easily plug in parameters to evaluate alternate futures, an essential aspect of planning.

In planning, the decision-maker does not only need data about the past, as provided by databases and data warehouses, but also information that provides projections into possible futures. The future is in part determined by actions the decision-maker can take, and in part by reactions and independent events that may occur in the world. Is the database community interested in providing services to meet such requirements? I would like to assume so, but it will require an expansion of the database researchers' mindsets.

Many concepts from databases will remain valuable, such as schema-driven execution, query languages, distributed access, temporal functions, attached procedures, and caching to gain performance.. But additional concepts will be needed and must be formalized and integrated to build a new generation of information system. Predictions are often based on substantial computations, which may be best supplied by remote processors. Many intermediate results will have associated uncertainties, and these must be aggregated with their data. There will not be a single correct timeline, representing the past, but a bush of future alternatives. Queries must be able to return multiple sets of values for a future point-in-time, and these value sets must be labeled with the actions and assumptions that led to them.

The space needed for all results obtainable for all future situations is immense, and cannot be stored, so that it becomes essential to provide execution-time linkages to computations. The results of these computations must be seamlessly integrated with results derived from databases. Results from planning sciences can help in combining uncertainties and pruning unlikely or low-value alternatives to keep the information volume presented to a decision-maker modest.

Set-based a'gebras from databases may be combined with ranking schemes from web-based searches. Interpolation is needed to provide values at arbitrary future points in time. The simplest approach is to assume a linear function to estimate the intermediate values, although other more involved approaches can sometimes be required.

The benefit of being able to interpolate for missing values is not limited to the predictive system capabilities. Anywhere where functions are naturally continuous interpolation has benefits, since data in a database are always associated with discrete points, or are means over an interval bounded by discrete points. For instance, observations at temporal and spatial points rarely match the query. We may want to the temperature and wind speed and direction at Gizeh, but have data only for major cities, say Cairo, Port Said, Alexandria, etc. Interpolation is also important in computer-aided design, to find optimal materials satisfying stress, flex, lifetime, and environmental conditions. Satellite data are not directly linked to points known to geographers or politicians, and require interpolation.

Architecturally there are a number of questions to be resolved. How much of these support functionalities belong inside the database systems and which are best served by external services? Where should caching take place? How will schemas handle computed elements and their identification? The research issues are broad, and it will be interesting to see where new research efforts will take place.

Summary and Remarks

In addition to the Introduction and Review, this position paper includes contributions from all Panel members expressing their differing individual visions of the database research of the future, using the year 2020 as target.

In this Deen has focused on requirements of complex distributed systems with agent technology playing a significant role, while Jhingran depicted the operational environment in terms of both the infrastructure facility and core technology. Neuhold considered future databases as holders of not only information but also real knowledge (including human knowledge) as data with connection to the human brain. Navathe has explored the role of databases in ubiquitous computing which in the future should offer a wide range of facilities including individualized *touchy*, *feely* and even *smelly* services. On the other hand, Wiederhold pondered on research needed, and likely to be carried out in the next two decades, to extend the database facility to the actual decision--makers.

These presentations were not meant to offer a comprehensive coverage of future directions of database research, nor to provide mutually consistent and non-controversial visions, but to provoke and stimulate discussion at the Panel meeting.

Acknowledgement:

Thanks to Thomas Neligwa of Keele for struggling painstakingly with MS Word and the VLDB page format, and finally getting everything neatly into five pages.

Panel: Is Generic Metadata Management Feasible?

Philip A. Bernstein

Microsoft Corporation
One Microsoft Way, Redmond, WA 98052-6399
philbe@microsoft.com

1. Panel Overview

The database field has worked on metadata-related problems for 30 years. Examples include data translation and migration, schema evolution, database design, schema / ontology integration, XML wrapper generation, data scrubbing and transformation for data warehouses, message mapping for e-business, and schema-driven web site design. Tools that address these problems are strikingly similar in their design. Arguably, we are making very little progress, since we keep reapplying the same old 1970's techniques of data translation [9] and views to one new problem after another, without getting much leverage from each succeeding step. Despite all the research on the above tools, we have so far been unable to offer general-purpose database technology that factors out the similar aspects of these tools into generic database infrastructure.

This panel addresses the following questions:

- Is it feasible to develop a generic infrastructure for managing models? If so, what would it need to do, beyond what's offered in the best object-oriented databases and repositories?

- Can we devise a useful generic notion of model that treats all popular information structures as specializations (SQL schemas, ER diagrams, XML DTD's, object-oriented (OO) schemas, web site maps, make scripts, etc.)?

- Can we produce a generic model manipulation algebra that generalizes transformation operations developed for data integration and translation, such as union, match, difference, and merge? What about generic operations on mappings between models, such as invert and compose?

- What is the role of an expression language that captures the semantics of models and mappings, not only for design but also for run-time execution?

- Does a generic approach offer any advantages for model manipulation areas of current interest, such as data integration and XML?

If the skeptics are right that a generic approach to model management is unachievable pie-in-the-sky, are writers of metadata-driven applications doomed forever to writing special-purpose object-at-a-time code for navigating their information structures? If so, what is the leverage that the database field can offer for these problems?

2. Panelists

- Dr. Laura Haas, IBM Research is working on a tool that can (semi-)automatically produce mappings between two data representations. She has been working on various aspects of data integration since starting the Garlic project in 1994.

- Prof. Matthias Jarke, GMD-FIT and Aachen University of Technology, led the ConceptBase project, a model management system that combines semantic modeling and deductive database technology.

- Prof. Erhard Rahm, University of Leipzig, works on the evaluation of metadata management for data warehouses and web portals. He is currently investigating the applicability of generic model management operations to these areas.

- Prof. Gio Wiederhold, Stanford University, has worked on integration of data and knowledge bases for over 20 years [10]. He has proposed a generic ontology algebra that can be used, among other things, for constructing "articulation" models that link and therefore allow integrated access to existing models, without having to integrate them completely.

3. A Case for Model Management

The metadata-related applications listed in Section 1 all involve the manipulation of models and mappings between models. By "model," we mean a complex discrete structure that represents a design artifact, such as an XML DTD, web-site schema, interface definition, relational schema, database transformation script, workflow definition, semantic network, software configuration or complex document. One way to make DBMSs easier to use for metadata-related applications is to make *model* and *mapping* first-class objects with high-level operations that simplify their use. We call this capability *model management* [2].

A possible representation for models and mappings is directed graphs. This amounts to representing them as interconnected sets of objects, which is how most model management applications work today. What's different in the approach proposed here is that an entire graph (i.e., a model or mapping) can be manipulated as a single object, something that no OO database currently does.

To make it easier to build applications, we need to raise the level of abstraction of operations on models and mappings — something much higher level than navigating object structures. Some candidate operators are:

- Match -- automatically create a mapping between two models.

- Merge – merge two models into a third, or merge one model into another based on a mapping.

- Compose – return the composition of two mappings (if map_1 relates model M_1 to M_2, and map_2 relates model M_2 to M_3, then return map_3 that relates M_1 to M_3).

- Invert – reverse the direction of a mapping.

- Set operations – union, intersection, difference

- Project and Select – comparable to relational algebra.

- Bulk operations on models, such as Apply (apply a function to all objects in a model) and Delete (delete all objects in a model).

Several research projects in the data integration field have used graph-oriented representations with high-level algebraic operations like those listed above [1][3][4][5][8]. However, they haven't been generalized to make them applicable to a broad range of model management problems. Other researchers have developed similar operations using sets, rather than graphs, as the representation of models [6].

Graphs and sets can describe the syntax of models and mappings. However, to capture semantics, an expression language is needed, such as some form of logic (predicate calculus, description logic), algebra (relational algebra, arithmetic), or formal language (regular expressions, BNF). To be truly general-purpose, a model management facility would need to factor out the inferencing engine module that can manipulate these expressions, so that one could plug different inferencing engines into the facility. For example, when executing the Compose operation, the model management facility would send the expressions associated with the two mappings being composed to the inferencing engine, which would return the composition of those expressions.

There are many research areas whose technology is potentially worth including in a model management facility, such as deductive databases, answering queries using views, transitive closure and recursive queries, differencing, schema and graph matching, and data translation. This past work gives us some confidence that a generic model management facility is feasible. There is much work to build on.

4. Reasons for Skepticism

The proposed approach to generic model management consists of the following generalizations of problem-specific approaches:

- a single data structure representation for models,

- generic operations on that data structure representation, and

- a generic interface for plugging in inference engines for various expression languages.

These are big steps, given that the state of the art for model management applications is to:

- customize the data structure representation for a particular type of model for a given class of application

- augment a predicate calculus query language (e.g., SQL, OQL) with object-at-a-time code for navigating object structures

- hard code the mapping logic for the problem at hand, rather than use a generic inference engine.

There are many ways to represent the semantics of models and mappings. Moreover, there are many semantic ambiguities in models, which often are quite application-specific. So is there any reason to believe that a generic data model can be defined that meets the needs of these diverse semantic representations and includes operations that correctly interpret subtle ambiguities?

5. Counterpoint

A counter-argument is to identify small, tractable steps. For example, one could do detailed walkthroughs of practical model manipulation problems, showing how generic operations can be used to solve them. This could be done by looking at hard examples solved by some of today's tools for database design, schema mapping, or schema integration. Then one could implement a few generic algebraic operations and apply them to several model manipulation problems, to prove that it's possible to define generic operations that solve practical problems. For example, all of the panelists are currently applying high level operations to internet-oriented data integration problems. In some cases, the operations are partly customized to the application. Whether these operations generalize to other areas is somewhat problematic, but the similarity of operations developed in different research projects gives some reason for hope. In other cases, operations allow for a human in the loop to interpret subtle semantics. But this is hardly a show-stopper, since most metadata management problems involve a human designer anyway, to ensure that models match the real world requirements.

Integration of heterogeneous web-based data sources and e-commerce sites is the latest and most pressing metadata management problem. But it is hardly unique. Many, perhaps most, of the hardest and most pervasive problems facing data management involve the manipulation of models. Yet applications that manipulate models are complicated and hard to build. The best hope for speeding up and reducing the cost of developing such applications is to significantly raise the level of abstraction of model manipulation functions that these applications rely on. This is the goal of generic model management. If successful, it could improve programmer productivity for model management applications by an order of magnitude. It is feasible? There are few database research questions for which there is as much at stake.

6. References

[1] Bergamaschi, S., S. Castano and M. Vincini, "Semantic Integration of Semistructured and Structured Data Sources," *SIGMOD Record* 28, 1, March 1999.

[2] Bernstein, P.A.., A. Y. Levy, and R.A. Pottinger. A Vision for Management of Complex Models. Technical Report MSR-TR-2000-53, http://www.research.microsoft.com/pubs/, June 2000.

[3] Jannink, Jan, Prasenjit Mitra, Erich Neuhold, Srinivasan Pichai, Rudi Studer, and Gio Wiederhold. An Algebra for Semantic Interoperation of Semistructured Data. In *1999 IEEE Knowledge and Data Engineering Exchange Workshop (KDEX'99)*, Nov. 1999.

[4] Milo, Tova and Sagit Zohar. Using Schema Matching to Simplify Heterogeneous Data Translation. In *Proc. 24th VLDB*, pp. 122-133, 1998.

[5] Mitra, Prasenjit, Gio Wiederhold, and Martin L. Kersten. A Graph-Oriented Model for Articulation of Ontology Interdependencies. In *EDBT 2000*, Springer Verlag LNCS 1777, pp. 86-100.

[6] Mylopoulos, John and Renate Motschnig-Pitrik. Partitioning Information Bases with Contexts. In *Proc. 3rd CoopIS*, Vienna, pp. 44-54, May 1995.

[7] Nissen, Hans W. and Matthias Jarke, "Repository Support for Multi-Perspective Requirements Engineering," *Information Systems 24, 2* (1999), Special Issue on Meta-Modelling and Methodology Engineering, pp. 131-158.

[8] Palopoli, Luigi, Domenico Sacca, and Domenico Ursino. Semi-Automatic Semantic Discovery of Properties from Database Schemas. In *IDEAS* 1998, pp. 244-253.

[9] Shu, N.C., B.C. Housel, R.W. Taylor, S.P. Ghosh, and V.Y. Lum. EXPRESS: A Data EXtraction, Processing and REStructuring System. *ACM TODS* 2,2: 134-174, June 1977.

[10] Wiederhold, Gio, and Ramez Elmasri. Data Model Integration Using the Structural Model. In *ACM SIGMOD Conf.*, pp. 191-202. 1979.

Panel: Future Directions of Database Research - the VLDB Broadening Strategy, Part 1

Hans-Jörg Schek

ETH Zurich
8092 ETH-Zentrum, Zurich,
Switzerland
Schek@inf.ethz.ch

Abstract

This panel introduces and explains the "future directions" and "broadening" discussions at the VLDB Endowment. Panelists are Michael Brodie, Stefano Ceri, Umesh Dayal, John Mylopoulos, and Hans Schek. We report on the steps that are being implemented at the upcoming VLDB Conferences (Mylopoulos). The main objective of the future direction and broadening discussions is to ensure that database technology remains vital. It should keep its pivotal role as infrastructure for application development for data-intensive, central and distributed applications. In a first part we explain the announcement that has been published through DBWorld (Schek). In a second part we report on statistics taken over the last conferences and on first experiences in the implementation of the broadening strategy this year (Brodie). We continue with steps that are undertaken for the upcoming Rome Conference (Ceri) and we conclude with further perspectives on future directions and broadening (Dayal)

1. Future Directions of Database Research - Changes in the VLDB Conference PC Structure

The following text is taken from [VLDB] after some minor editing. For other other interesting observations on the evolution of database research the reader is referred to documents such as [Si+96] and references given there.

Proceedings of the 26th International Conference on Very Large Databases, Cairo, Egypt, 2000

1.1 Background

At the New York VLDB Endowment meeting, concerns were expressed that the area of database research may lose the pivotal role it now plays among information system technologies. It was agreed that the Endowment should maintain a watch on trends and future directions in the general area of information management to ensure that database research in general, and the VLDB conferences and journal in particular remain current and relevant. It was decided to set up a small "future directions" working group which maintains an ongoing dialogue with key researchers in the DB community and reports back to the Endowment Board. Working group members were Rakesh Agrawal, Michael Brodie, Michael Carey, Umesh Dayal, Jim Gray, Yannis Ioannidis, John Mylopoulos, Hans Schek, Kyu-Young Whang and Jennifer Widom.

1.2 Situation

The main observation of the working group was the following: While database technology has achieved a high standard in research and development, its future role in a globally distributed information network is less central. Considering the central role of databases in the past in providing a platform for application development, the members strongly felt that actions must be taken. Of course, it is true that databases still do a great job as storage managers for many applications. However, it was felt that the distance to applications and application development has grown substantially during the past decade. Among others, the following examples of application development and application areas were discussed as evidence for the need to act: Managing components, application services, Distributed client/middleware/server computing, Application frameworks, ERPs, XML, e-commerce. To bring such topics into the fold of database conferences, the working group proposed to distinguish between the two main research directions: (1) core database technology and (2) infrastructure for information system development

While (1) is well established and will be further developed worldwide by the international DB research and development community, the infrastructure direction (2) is under-developed and under-represented at conferences. In all examples given above, the database role of providing a storage manager, i.e. core DB technology remains central. However, client application development takes place on other platforms provided by middleware technologies. Or client applications are obtained by customizing pre-fabricated ERP systems. The focus of our community should turn to the investigation of how core technology can become more widespread and usable, by concentrating on the description of new application areas, on the methods and tools for data analysis, design and integration, on the technologies for data deployment in modern architectures (middleware, wireless technology, the WEB), and in general on all the problems and challenges which are due to the need of using very large databases in new contexts.

1.3 Action

In order to evolve into these directions the Endowment has decided in its 1999 Board meeting in Edinburgh to take actions with regard to the selection of tutorials, panels and invited speakers for future VLDB conferences. Most important for the community is the following change in the VLDB Conference PC structure: While in the past there were two PCs for the scientific and industrial tracks tof the program, in future VLDB conferences a new track called "IS infrastructure and applications" will be added. Therefore in future Calls-for-Papers for VLDB conferences, three subcommittees will be distinguished, responsible respectively for papers on:

- Core DB technology
- IS infrastructure and applications
- Industrial applications and experience

The new strategy will be fully implemented in the year 2002 but efforts are undertaken to realize it earlier in the upcoming VLDB conferences in Cairo and Rome. The strategy for VLDB2000 and experiences are summarized in [Bro00].

2. Additional remarks and related observations

When relational database systems have been introduced twenty years ago, they have been considered as infrastructure and main platform for development of data-intensive applications. Data independence was considered to be a breakthrough: Programmers were freed from low-level details, e.g., how to access shared data efficiently and correctly, given concurrent access. But by now, the prerequisites for application development have changed dramatically. For instance, communication has become fairly cheap, and the internet dominates modern information infrastructures. Consequently, the role of database concepts must be re-visited and newly determined.

Carey, Hellerstein and Stonebraker [Regr] observe that all current databases have been designed with the technology of twenty years ago. They state that due to a three-tier architecture, data are at the bottom and application code is away from data in the middle tier. They also state that databases are "bloated" by object-relational features, by stored procedures and triggers, and by warehouse features. They conclude that we should rethink everything.

In a keynote speech Brodie [Bro99] states that states that "the database era nears its end" because DBMSs, in their current form, cannot adequately deal with current heterogeneity and interoperability demands let alone the vast increases in data and transaction volumes of next generation applications. Architectural complexity is another issue in view of the many engine and repository types with ad-hoc solutions for warehousing and mining.

The database group at ETH Zurich [AHST97], [Sch+00], in order to move into new directions, strives for „higher order data independence" in its hyperdatabase projects. A hyperdatabase is a database over databases and other specialized components. A hyperdatabase applies database technology at a higher level.

2. References

[AHST97] Alonso, G., Hagen, C., Schek, H.-J., Tresch, M.: *Distributed Processing over Stand-alone Systems and Applications*, In: Proc. of 23rd International Conference on Very Large Data Bases (VLDB'97), Athens, Greece

[Bro00] Brodie, M.L.: *Future Directions of Database Research – the VLDB Broadening Strategy, Part 2*, this Proceedings

[Bro99] Brodie, M.L.: *Que Sera, Sera: The Coincidental Confluence of Economics, Business, and Collaborative Computing*, Proc. of the 15th International Conference on Data Engineering, Sydney, Australia, March 1999, pp. 2-3

[Regr] Carey, M.,., Hellerstein, Stonebraker, M.: Seminar talk *"A sketch of Regres"*, http://www.cs.berkeley.edu/~gribble/-summaries/talks_seminars/regres.html

[Sch+00] Schek et al. : *Hyperdatabases,* In: Proc. of the WISE2000 Conference, Hongkong, June 2000.

[Si+96] Silberschatz, A. et al.: *Strategic directions in database systems – breaking out of the box.* ACM Computing Surveys, Vol. 28, No. 4, Dec. 1996, pp. 764-778.

[VLDB] http://www.vldb.org/

Panel: Future Directions of Database Research—
The VLDB Broadening Strategy, Part 2

Michael L. Brodie

GTE Laboratories Incorporated
40 Sylvan Road, Waltham, MA, USA
Brodie@gte.com

1. Broadening the Database Field

1.1 The Challenge

Over its 40-year history, database research has made major contributions to developing core database management systems technology, which now lies at the heart of every conventional application. Whereas the database field should contribute to the full scope of data management—its applicability, its challenges, and its future directions—this has not happened. The database field now faces two challenges. First, fundamental data management assumptions do not apply to the data requirements of the next generation of applications. Long-standing data application challenges, such as semantic interoperability, inhibit data-centric solutions, thus leading to solutions in other domains. New computing environments, such as the WWW, require a rethinking of core database technology in all areas, e.g., architecture and query/search techniques. Second, new application domains typically do not appeal to the database field to address new data management problems. Over the past decade, other new or established areas have addressed data-intensive problems (e.g., the role of data in the Web, e-commerce, digital libraries, and knowledge management/discovery). As the Internet, gizmos, e-applications, ubiquitous computing, and other trends revolutionize computing (which is accompanied by an explosive growth of data and transaction volumes), database technology is relegated to its conventional forms. The database field is being narrowed to core database technologies used by conventional applications.

As we embrace the largest revolution in computing history, the database community should face the full scope of data management challenges in the next generation of computing, that is, all forms of data in all applications. Data, which is one of the three pillars of computing, is critical to current and future computing. Data volumes and database transactions are growing to astronomical levels. Yet data and its management are not first-class citizens with process/logic, communications, or presentation. New areas with critical data components do not turn to the database community for ideas, advice, or technology. In turn, the database community does not adequately reach out to these new domains. The database community has much more to offer the current and next generation of computing than is currently offered or requested. This must change. The database community must broaden its scope to all aspects of data in all contexts and to take its proper role in developing the next generation of computing.

1.2 A Role for VLDB

In addition to presenting database research results and current industry challenges, database conferences provide an opportunity to push the boundaries of database research to meet new requirements. Invited talks, panels, and industrial sessions are intended to introduce new challenges, directions, and ideas to the VLDB community. On average, 90% of papers in past VLDB conferences dealt with core database technology, including many high-quality "delta" papers. This remarkable strength contributed to the worldwide $10 billion (US) annual DBMS market. However, there is much more to the world of data than core technology. The VLDB Endowment has attempted to expand the scope of VLDB conferences beyond core database technology, by introducing paper categories and a Broadening Strategy.

In 1996, the VLDB Endowment added the Experience/Application submission category to the conventional Research category. In 1998, the Vision category was added. These categories, defined in [Bro00-1], were introduced to encourage the submission of such papers, with the promise that these papers would be recognized as different from Research papers and be evaluated accordingly. To date, categories have been only modestly successful. Research papers dominate (i.e., between 86% and 98% of accepted papers). Vision and Experience/Application papers are increasing, but much too slowly. In 1996 and 2000, the acceptance rates for Experience/Application papers far exceeded those for Research papers. The submission and acceptance rate for Vision papers is unacceptably low. Since categories have not had the desired effect, the Broadening Strategy was introduced for VLDB2000.

1.3 The Broadening Strategy

The strategy attempted to encourage Broadening by soliciting papers that were (1) on a broader range of topics than those considered by previous database conferences; (2) on riskier and more novel challenges, as opposed to incremental improvements on existing results; (3) from a broader range of contributors (e.g., from across the spectrum of developing and deploying database technology and from those outside the field who pose new requirements and challenges); and (4) in novel formats such as reports on case studies, systems development and testing, and product evaluations relative to new application requirements.

A VLDB submission was considered to contribute to broadening the database field if it addressed issues beyond conventional database topics and technology. It must contribute to expanding database technology or methods beyond conventional databases and applications to the full scope of data management—its applicability, its challenges, and its future directions. The program committee evaluated Broadening on a three-point scale.

- **Strong**: Papers that produce new, substantial results related to issues that clearly contribute to Broadening data management beyond core topics (e.g., address new, advanced application challenges or Broadening issues such as the impacts of data management on new applications or business processes, or vice versa).

- **Modest**: Papers that explicitly address and contribute to a Broadening topic or issue or apply exciting or new solutions to a topic or issue that is beyond core data management.

- **Little or none**: Applies to most VLDB papers in the past, which have generally dealt with core data management technologies or topics. Papers may mention or reference applications requirements or contexts or Broadening issues but not contribute to the Broadening objectives, as defined for VLDB2000.

The Broadening Strategy objectives were that (1) 30% of VLDB2000 papers, 50% of keynotes and demos, and 67% of panels and industrial sessions contribute to Broadening; (2) the quality of those contributions be comparable to the standards set by previous VLDBs; and (3) the database community (e.g., VLDB attendees and subsequent readers) be encouraged to expand the scope of the work to include all relevant aspects of data. The objective of increasing the accepted Broadening papers from between 2% and 19% to 30% was not dramatic. The strategy was defined to the community in calls for papers, in announcements in *DBWorld,* and in a document [Bro00-1] that defined the Broadening Strategy, its objectives, and its implementation, including examples of Broadening contributions in past VLDBs (1996–1999). A VLDB first was to publish the paper review form and the instructions to reviewers.

The strategy was initially resisted by those who, although they agreed with the objectives, felt that they did not understand Broadening or its implementation. Quality was a typical concern. Research methodologies for conventional database topics are well established. This leads to high-quality standards for papers on those topics. Research methods and standards for Broadening papers, those that go beyond conventional topics, are much less settled. This leads to novelty and innovation and to risk due to a lack of adequate quality measures. The VLDB Endowment unanimously accepted this risk in order to broaden the database field, at least in VLDB conferences. However, program committees tend to be very conservative (see the Appendix). In the past, papers submitted on advanced topics were rejected because they did not match the quality established by papers on core database technology. To ensure the acceptance of contributions that contribute to Broadening and to maintain the quality of core papers, quotas were established. At least as many core papers were to be accepted as in the past, while at least 20 Broadening papers were to be accepted. This required adding a fourth parallel session to the conference.

1.4 Broadening Strategy Results

An informal evaluation of contributions in recent VLDB conferences (see the Appendix) indicated that prior to VLDB2000, few research papers contributed to Broadening, (i.e., from 2% in 1998 to 19% in 1997). Other sessions contributed more (i.e., from a range of 25%–83% in 1995 to a range of 35%–100% in 1998). After Broadening was defined, encouraged, and incorporated into the VLDB2000 submission and review processes [Bro00-1], the program committees evaluated 78% of submitted papers and 89% of the accepted papers as contributing to Broadening. All other sessions increased the Broadening range to 56%–100%. The acceptance rate for Broadening papers (17.3%) was more than double that for non-Broadening papers (7.7%). The quality of these papers was on par with or exceeded that of core papers. In fact, the papers with the highest overall scores also had the highest Broadening scores. Moreover, there was no shortage of Broadening papers to fill the broadening quota—something that was initially a concern. Indeed, the Broadening quotas were exceeded in part by strong core papers that included Broadening content.

1.5 Future Directions

Two Broadening Strategy objectives were achieved, while the third is an ongoing challenge. It was a very successful step. The ultimate success of the Broadening Strategy will be when the scope of the database field is broadened to encompass all data-related topics in all relevant contexts and when database work is expressed with adequate context—applications, technical, business, policy, political, etc. This will take time. Success will require that all participants—contributors, program committee members, and chairs—share a common understanding of Broadening and its objectives. Contributors must plan, execute, and report their work to fit categories and to contribute to Broadening. Reviewers and program committee chairs must understand and apply the appropriate criteria consistently in evaluating papers and be willing to accept innovations related to the strategies over research papers on core technology. This was not the case for VLDB2000 and is not yet the case in the database field.

What can the database community do to broaden the database field to its full scope and to take its proper role in developing the next generation of computing? SIGMOD has recently adopted a strategy with objectives similar to VLDB's Broadening Strategy. The purpose of this panel is to provide an open forum to discuss these challenges and to identify effective directions for future VLDB conferences.

1.6 Grand Challenges

To leap beyond conventional data management requires a depth of understanding of specific domains before the solutions can be generalized. Hence, researchers should choose an application domain within which to investigate new challenging data management requirements. Biodiversity is an ideal domain in which database researchers, in cooperation with biodiversity experts, could contribute to good computer science and significantly contribute to improving the world for all living creatures. Such multidisciplinary work requires significant time and effort to understand the domain requirements and the potential that data management could bring. Biodiversity and biodiversity informatics were chosen as themes of VLDB2000 to illustrate the Broadening Strategy. Biodiversity involves a worldwide network of people, computers, and information bases that are vastly more effective used cooperatively than separately. The Biodiversity keynote by Dr. Ebbe Nielsen, the Biodiversity Domain Session, and the Applications Industrial Session pose relevant challenges to the database community.

Over its 50-year history, computer science has produced an amazingly rich and powerful set of general-purpose tools. As general-purpose tools, they are somewhat sterile. It may now be time for computer scientists to apply these tools in specific domains to attempt to address the Grand Challenges of Man that arise in those domains. Computer science today is much like mathematics at the turn of the century. Advances in mathematics paved the way for solving major problems in physics, chemistry, astrophysics, engineering, pharmaceuticals, etc. Computing is now in position to enable progress toward solutions to the Grand Challenges of Man as long as the relevant domains are fully understood.

2. References

[Bro00-1] Brodie, M.L.: Paper Reviewer Guidance. http://www2.aucegypt.edu/vldb2000, February 2000.

Submission and Acceptance Statistics from Recent VLDB Conferences

Submitted Papers	Research	Vision	Experience/ Application	Total Over Categories	Little or No Broadening	Modest Broadening	Strong Broadening	Total Over Broadening Score	Modest or Strong Broadening Score	% Modest or Strong Broadening Score
Americas	156	11	17	**184**	41	85	58	184	143	78%
Europe, Africa, and the Middle East (two research papers withdrawn)	94	5	14	**113**	27	58	26	111	84	76%
Far East, Asia, and Australia	51	0	3	**54**	10	32	12	54	44	81%
Total	**301**	**16**	**34**	351	**78**	**175**	**96**	349	271	78%
Accepted Papers										
Americas	22	1	4	**27**	4	12	11	27	23	85%
Europe, Africa, and the Middle East	16	0	2	**18**	2	7	9	18	16	89%
Far East, Asia, and Australia	8	0	0	**8**	0	3	5	8	8	100%
Total	**46**	**1**	**6**	53	**6**	**22**	**25**	53	47	**89%**
Paper Acceptance Rate								Average Broadening Score	Acceptance Rates	
Americas	4.10%	9.09%	23.53%	14.67%	9.76%	14.12%	18.97%	1.77	16.08%	
Europe, Africa, and the Middle East	7.02%	0.00%	14.29%	15.93%	7.41%	12.07%	34.62%	1.85	19.05%	
Far East, Asia, and Australia	5.69%	0.00%	0.00%	14.81%	0.00%	9.38%	41.67%	1.85	18.18%	
Total	.28%	**6.25%**	**17.65%**	**15.10%**	**7.69%**	**12.57%**	**26.04%**	**1.81**	**17.34%**	

Figure 2000-1: VLDB2000 Paper Submission and Acceptance by Category and Broadening

VLDB Sessions	Submitted	Solicited	Total	Target / Accepted	Acceptance Rate	Broadening Score	Modest or Strong Broadening Score	% Modest or Strong Broadening Score
Papers	349	0	349	53	15.19%	1.81	47	89%
Demonstrations	33	0	33	16	48%	1.81	9	56%
Panels	3	3	6	3	50%	2.67	3	100%
Tutorials	13	3	16	5	38%	2.40	4	80%
Industry/Domain Presentations	6	18	24	18	75%	2.25	13	72%
10-Year Award	0	1	1	1	N/A	2.00	1	100%
Keynotes	0	6	6	2	**N/A**	2.50	2	100%

Figure 2000-2: VLDB2000 Contribution Submission and Acceptance Statistics

Program Committee Statistics	Americas	Europe, Africa, and the Middle East	Far East, Asia, and Australia	Total
PC Size	44	39	22	105
PC Papers	43	26	16	85
Reviewer Load (3/Paper)	13.5	9	8	10
Late Papers Rejected	1	1	1	3
Submission Problems	5	6	0	11
PDF Printing Problems	5%	2%	20%	9%
Abstracts Submitted	230	137	64	431
Papers Submitted	184	111	54	349
% Abstracts Only	20%	19%	16%	19%

Figure 2000-3: VLDB2000 Program Committee Statistics

Submitted Papers	Research*	Vision*	Experience/ Application*	Total
Americas				**210**
Europe, Africa, and the Middle East				**116**
Far East, Asia, and Australia				**60**
Total				**386**
Accepted Papers				
Americas				**33**
Europe, Africa, and the Middle East				**15**
Far East, Asia, and Australia				**8**
Total				**56**
Acceptance Rates (%)				
Americas				15.71%
Europe, Africa, and the Middle East				12.93%
Far East, Asia, and Australia				13.33%
Total				**14.51%**

*VLDB99 used three categories. The General PC Chair did not provide statistics, feeling that the use of categories was not significant.

Figure 99-1: VLDB99 Paper Submission and Acceptance by Category

VLDB Program Components	Submitted	Solicited	Total	Accepted	Acceptance Rate	Modest or Strong Broadening Score	% Modest or Strong Broadening Score
Papers	387	0	387	57	14.73%	8	14%
Demonstrations	16	0	16	8	50%	2	25%
Panels	2	1	3	1	33%	0	0%
Tutorials (1/2 day)	6	4	10	5	50%	5	100%
Industrial Sessions	0	9	9	9	100%	5	56%
10-Year Award	0	1	1	1	N/A	0	0%
Keynotes	0	2	2	2	N/A	2	100%

Figure 99-2: VLDB99 Contribution Submission and Acceptance Statistics

Submitted Papers	Research	Vision	Experience/ Application	Total	Industrial Sessions
Americas/Australia	154	11	15	**180**	19
Africa/Asia/Europe	140	1	7	**148**	6
Total	**294**	**12**	**22**	328	25
Accepted Papers					
Americas/Australia	27	1	0	**28**	13
Africa/Asia/Europe	22	0	1	**23**	5
Total	**49**	**1**	**1**	51	18
Acceptance Rates (%)					
Americas/Australia	18%	9.09%	0.00%	15.56%	68.42%
Africa/Asia/Europe	15.71%	0.00%	14.29%	15.54%	83.33%
Total	**16.67%**	**8.33%**	**4.55%**	**15.55%**	**72.00%**

Figure 98-1: VLDB98 Paper Submission and Acceptance by Category

VLDB Program Components	Submitted	Solicited	Total	Accepted	Acceptance Rate	Modest or Strong Broadening Score	% Modest or Strong Broadening Score
Papers	328	0	328	51	15.55%	1	2%
Demonstrations	N/A	N/A	N/A	N/A	N/A	N/A	N/A
Panels	3	?	3	2	66.67%	3	100%
Tutorials (1/2 day)	26	0	26	7	26.92%	6	86%
Industrial Sessions	25	0	25	18	72.00%	6	35%
10-Year Award	0	1	1	1	N/A	0	0%
Keynotes	0	2	2	2	N/A	2	100%

Figure 98-2: VLDB98 Contribution Submission and Acceptance Statistics

Submitted Papers	Research*	Total
Americas	170	170
Europe, Africa, and the Middle East	110	110
Far East, Asia, and Australia	75	75
Total	355	355
Accepted Papers		
Americas	29	29
Europe, Africa, and the Middle East	18	18
Far East, Asia, and Australia	6	6
Total	53	53
Acceptance Rates (%)		
Americas	17%	17.06%
Europe, Africa and the Middle East	16.36%	16.36%
Far East, Asia, and Australia	8.00%	8.00%
Total	14.93%	14.93%

*VLDB 97 had Research and Experience/Application categories but received only three Experience/Application papers.

Figure 97-1: VLDB97 Paper Submission and Acceptance by Category

VLDB Program Components	Submitted	Solicited	Total	Accepted	Acceptance Rate	Modest or Strong Broadening Score	% Modest or Strong Broadening Score
Papers	355	0	355	53	14.93%	5	9%
Demonstrations	N/A	N/A	N/A	N/A	N/A	N/A	N/A
Panels	2	1	3	2	67%	1	50%
Tutorials (1 day)	23	0	23	6	26%	4	67%
Industrial Sessions	20	4	24	12	50%	10	83%
10-Year Award	0	1	1	1	N/A	0	0%
Keynotes	0	2	2	2	N/A	1	50%

Figure 97-2: VLDB97 Contribution Submission and Acceptance Statistics

Submitted Papers	Research	Experience/ Application	Total
Asia/Australia	93	0	**93**
Americas	143	9	**152**
Europe	104	0	**104**
Total	**340**	**9**	349
Accepted Papers			
Asia/Australia	10	0	**10**
Americas	18	4	**22**
Europe	16	0	**16**
Total	**44**	**4**	48
Acceptance Rates (%)			
Asia/Australia	10.8%	0.0%	10.8%
Americas	12.6%	44.4%	14.5%
Europe	15.4%	0.0%	15.4%
Total	**12.9%**	**44.4%**	**13.8%**

Figure 96-1: VLDB96 Paper Submission and Acceptance by Category

VLDB Program Components	Submitted	Solicited	Total	Accepted	Acceptance Rate	Modest or Strong Broadening Score	% Modest or Strong Broadening Score
Papers (Research, Experience)	349	0	349	48	13.8%	9	19%
Demonstrations	N/A	N/A	N/A	N/A	N/A	N/A	N/A
Panels	4	2	6	3	50%	1	33%
Tutorials	31	0	31	7	23%	5	71%
Industrial Sessions	0	6	6	6	100%	6	29%
10-Year Award	N/A	1	1	**1**	N/A	0	0%
Keynotes	N/A	2	2	**2**	N/A	2	100%

Figure 96-2: VLDB96 Contribution Submission and Acceptance Statistics

Submitted Papers	Research
Asia/Australia	49
Americas	146
Europe	102
Total	297
Accepted Papers	
Asia/Australia	9
Americas	25
Europe	18
Total	52
Acceptance Rates (%)	
Asia/Australia	18.37%
Americas	17.12%
Europe	17.65%
Total	17.51%

Figure 95-1: VLDB95 Paper Submission and Acceptance Statistics

VLDB Program Components	Solicited	Submitted	Accepted	Acceptance Rate
Papers	0	297	52	18%
Demonstrations	N/A	N/A	N/A	N/A
Panels	2	4	3	25%
Tutorials	?	?	7	?
Industry/Application Papers	3+	3+	4	67% +
10-Year Award	1	0	1	N/A
Keynotes/Invited Talks	3	0	3	N/A
Solicited Vendor Papers	12	0	10	83%

Figure 95-2: VLDB95 Contribution Acceptance Statistics

An Ultra Highly Available DBMS

Svein-Olaf Hvasshovd, Svein Erik Bratsberg, Øystein Torbjørnsen
Clustra AS, 7485 Trondheim, Norway
svein-olaf.hvasshovd@clustra.com

1 Introduction

Mainstream database management systems are designed for general use. Various compromises have been done to satisfy the most common users and the largest markets. One application which has been mostly ignored, is the network equipment made for the telco operators.

The equipment used in the telco industry has requirements differing from traditional database applications with respect to availability and real-time performance. This has caused the telco manufacturers to develop their own hardware, operating systems and programming languages.

The Internet market is starting to demand the same reliability as the telco industry has provided for decades, thus the market for such equipment is growing rapidly. The telco industry and Internet world are melting together as they are fighting each other for market shares. The growth of the Internet increases the market for database management solutions based on standard computer equipment, but designed for the *requirements* of the telco market:

Availability should be at least 99.999%, corresponding to average 5 minutes unavailability per year including all maintenance work, e.g. SW and HW upgrades.

Real-time response times should be in range of one to ten milliseconds for a specified percent of the transactions (say 98%).

Throughput rates In average thousand subscribers generate one call per second. The large network components today serve one million subscribers, thus handling one thousand calls per second. In average a call can lead to from one to ten transactions.

Scalability Typical for services today is that they start out as small trial services. If it becomes a success, it grows rapidly to huge dimensions. The service provider does not want to buy big and expensive equipment before he knows the service will be successful. On the other hand, he does not want to throw out the initial investment when upgrading to a system handling the growing load.

Open interfaces The DBMS must use open interfaces as SQL, ODBC and Java to ensure interoperability with other data sources and applications.

Run on commodity HW/SW

For today's mainstream database management systems several of these requirements are not satisfied. Although claiming high availability, the systems can only achieve an availability which is one or two orders of magnitude worse than the requirements. The main obstacles for this are system maintenance and long takeover times in the case of failures.

Another requirement not satisfied by mainstream systems is the response times for update transactions. They all synchronous write the log to disk before committing, and combined with a group commit strategy, transaction response times are highly variable and in the range of 50 milliseconds or higher for update transactions.

2 The Clustra Parallel Data Server

This presentation covers basic software and hardware architecture for a high availability DBMS, including interconnect and disk solutions. Basic transaction execution strategies for parallel systems will be discussed.

Special focus will be made on fault-tolerance mechanisms, including replication, take-over, recovery and repair. We will also go through methods for on-line system maintenance, including on-line backup and restore, software and hardware upgrades and schema changes.

The Zero Latency Enterprise

Dave Liles

Compaq Computer Corporation
1295 Stonegate Rd
Algonquin, Il
USA
Dave.Liles@Compaq.com

Abstract

Today's Internet economy has primed customers to expect immediate access and immediate results. But instant results are difficult to achieve when your customers want up-to-the-minute information about themselves: account balances, detailed transactional histories across all products, immediate problem resolution, and recommended advice on future purchases. Their expectation is that they will get the same interaction with your company whether they communicate with you via telephone, the web, a kiosk, or e-mail. To retain customers and make better decisions, businesses must step up the pace. Customers and systems need access to events – like orders, shipments, and payments – the moment they occur. They need to be able to act on events automatically, in real time. The prescription: a "Zero Latency Enterprise".

1. The ZLE Challenge

From an IT perspective, the challenge is twofold: integrating customer and product information scattered in disparate systems throughout the enterprise, and acting on it in real time.

The first challenge, integrating customer and product

information scattered in disparate systems throughout the enterprise, focuses on enterprise application integration (EAI). EAI instantaneously transform decisions and information into operational changes by "pushing" information to where it is needed. The second challenge, instant access, analysis, and reaction to information, has been addressed traditionally by using business intelligence technologies, such as data marts, data warehouses, and operational data stores (ODS). Of particular need is a data-centric ODS that is a central, operations-focused data store fed in near real time by all of the other databases in the enterprise. This ODS could provide a central repository from which users and applications "pull" information as needed.

The problems with these traditional approaches is that they don't address the challenge of minimizing the lag, or information float, between when the data is captured in one place and when it can be used somewhere else. Each approach has its limitations; most organizations require a combination of the two – a real time ODS combined with EAI.

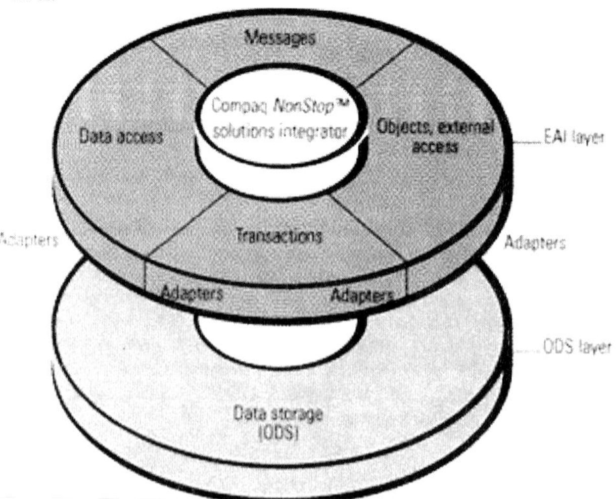

"

However, combining the two approaches has been considered impractical because of technology limitations in providing a single zero latency solution that could:

- Provide 24*366 service availability
- Loading and updating massive event volumes without disrupting the service
- Extracting data from transactional systems without impacting their performance
- Ensuring consistency of data collected from multiple fragmented source systems
- Scalability in terms of supporting a large, active user base executing a wide variety of both response time sensitive transactions as well as large scale queries
- Very large database manageability

2. World's Largest Zero Latency Enterprise Proof-point

2.1 The customer challenge

A large telecommunications customer approached Compaq with this exact challenge. They asked Compaq to demonstrate a Zero Latency Solution that would provide real time call and network utilization management, enterprise application integration of event data, and real time customer relationship management. They had a 5 terabyte database which was expected to increase in size to 25 terabytes. They wanted to make sure that their platform of choice could handle the expected growth in terms of database size as well as users. They also wanted to mirror the data for reliability.

2.2 Compaq's response

Compaq upped the ante. Compaq decided to build a telecommunication proof-point that would handle the combined business support functions for the equivalent of *the five largest telecommunications companies* in the world! That is, a proof-point that would handle:

- Over 1.2 billion call detail records (CDRs) per day, over 12,000 per second
- An 90 day ODS, over 100 billion events
- Over 45 terabytes of raw data, 90 terabytes mirrored, 111 terabytes of disk storage
- A customer care call center of over 40,000 agents
- Over 20 million customers

2.3 The Zero Latency Applications

Applications that use the ODS include service business processes for real time surveillance of called numbers, customer service inquiries by 40,000 agents, EAI integration processes providing downstream data mart feeds for credit verification, large adhoc business intelligence queries, customer usage analysis (data mining), and system management services via statistics displays.

2.4 The Zero Latency Platform

The center of the Zero Latency Enterprise Solution runs on a Compaq *NonStop* ™ Himalaya Server with 128 processors, 256 GBs of memory, and 111 terabytes of disk storage. An Compaq *AlphaServer* GS 140 with 1 terabytes of disk storage was utilized for data warehousing. A combination of multiple Compaq *Proliant* servers were used as simulation drivers, data mining servers, and statistical display servers.

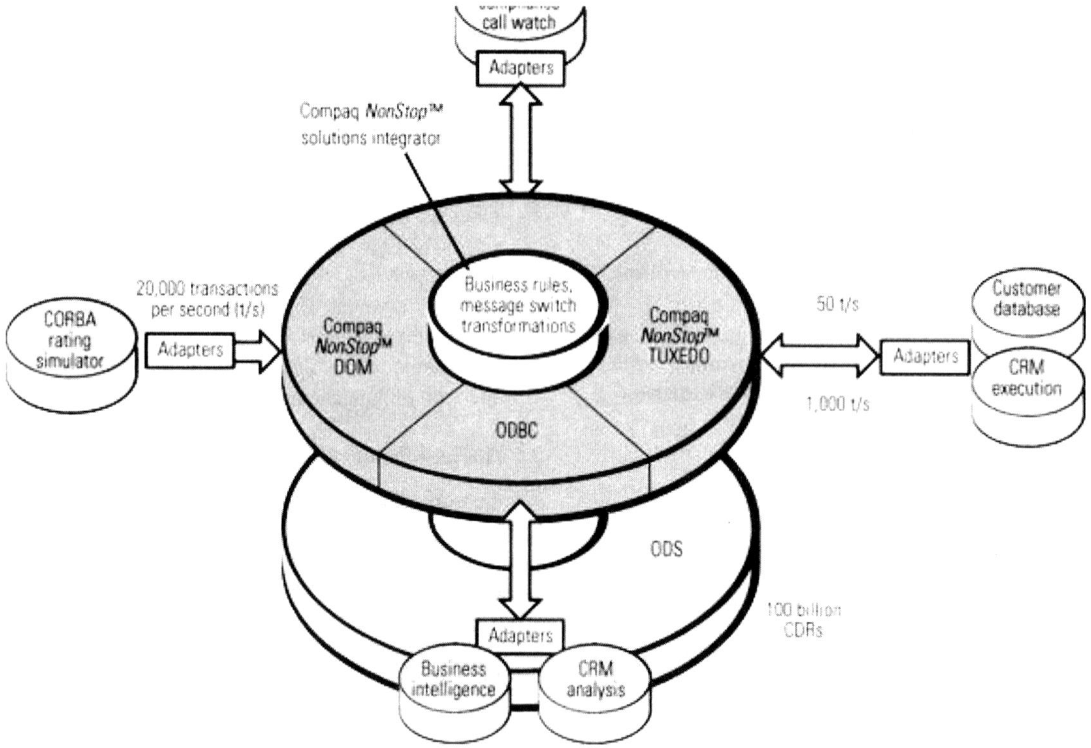

2.5 The Zero Latency Solution Integrator

At the center of the demonstration is Compaq's *NonStop™* solutions integrator, based on BEA, Java based Blaze (for dynamic rules-based decision making), and CORBA technologies. Message transport services are provided by is Compaq's *NonStop™* Tuxedo transaction manager and Compaq's *NonStop™* DOM CORBA. Application adapters provide connectivity to outside servers such as Oracle Data Mart Suite, a data mining cluster, and other applications such as SAP. The ODS is based on Compaq *NonStop™* SQL database. Large queries against the ODS are performed with Microstrategy's DSS Web tool.

3. ZLE Proof-point Results

The proof-point implementation retains over 100 billion CDRs, a 90 day history. Each day, 1.2 billion CDR's are deleted. At peak operation, it accepts up to 50,000 random transactional inserts per second through the CORBA-based application and handles more than 100,000 customer service agents performing more than 3,000 transactions per second in the TUXEDO environment. It also processes 100 customer profile updates per second, physical de-fragmentation of CDR tables, trickle feed to the data mart, and batch extracts to the mining cluster and the massive ad hoc parallel query.

4. Conclusion

Compaq's proof-point implementation has exceeded every industry specification and expectation and has confirmed Compaq's revolutionary new concept for achieving zero latency. The Compaq *NonStop™* solutions integrator concept has been validated by customers to serve as a dynamic integrator for applications and a central database for caching data, as well as providing zero latency throughout the enterprise. With our solution, customer profiles and marketing models can be generated dynamically in real time, with up-to-the-second data, in a fraction of the time required by conventional solutions.

This zero latency solution was made possible because the Compaq's *NonStop™* Himalaya ODS provides:

- Unprecedented scalability – the shared nothing hardware and software architecture is unique in it's ability to scale incrementally and virtually unlimited in size and bandwidth
- Mixed workload capabilities – the unique capabilities of Compaq's *NonStop™* SQL DBMS in combination with Compaq's *NonStop™* Software provides for the *simultaneous* execution of demanding transactions, queries, event capture, and application integration
- World renowned availability – patented hardware and software fault tolerance
- Very large DMBS support - *NonStop™* SQL DBMS industry leading support for very large tables, online database manageability, and parallel and granular operations

High Performance and Scalability through Application-Tier, In-Memory Data Management

The TimesTen Team
TimesTen Performance Software
1991 Landings Drive
Mountain View, CA 94043
info@timesten.com

Abstract

TimesTen Performance Software's Front-Tier product is an application-tier data cache that inter-operates with disk-based relational database management systems (RDBMSs) to achieve breakthrough response time and throughput, scalability in transaction load, high availability, and ease of administration and deployment. Front-Tier caches frequently used subsets of the corporate database on multiple servers in the application tier and supports SQL queries and updates to the caches. The caches may or may not be overlapping, are kept synchronized with the corporate database and with each other, and may be dynamically reconfigured to contain different subsets of the corporate database. Front-Tier provides the fundamental bridge between the corporate database and high-performance, scalable application servers. It eliminates the main barrier to application server scalability and high performance, namely the sole reliance on a centralized corporate database server for data management.

1. Introduction

Three-tier and multi-tier computing architectures have been popular for several years, having first been accepted as the standard architectures for enterprise computing, and more recently as the standard architectures for Internet computing. These architectures separate the presentation logic, hosted in the tier closest to the end user, from the application tier where all the business logic is implemented, and finally from the data management tier where the corporate database is centrally managed and administered. While these architectures have been suitable for enterprise computing, they are not as suitable for data-intensive, high-performance Internet applications. With the former, the number of users is limited and the interactions are well defined while with the latter, the number of users keeps increasing and low and predictable response times are a competitive differentiator. The separation of data management from the application tier imposes a performance overhead in accessing the required data, and a scalability barrier in forcing all queries and updates through the database tier.

This paper examines these traditional architectures, their advantages and drawbacks, and describes a new approach to data management that greatly improves the performance of data-intensive Internet applications.

2. Internet Computing Systems

Computing systems that service Internet requests consist of multiple tiers of systems that include web servers, application servers, and backend corporate DBMS server(s). The web servers handle incoming requests, routing them to the appropriate application server. Application servers implement the logic required to service requests. They execute the business logic and periodically query or update the corporate database. Finally, the database server hosts one of the popular disk-based RDBMSs and handles requests to the corporate database. Web servers and application servers may be scattered around the corporate Intranet, while the database server is typically consolidated in a centralized server(s).

These architectures have the benefit of providing somewhat scalable architectures since increasing the

Proceedings of the 26th International Conference on Very Large Databases, Cairo, Egypt, 2000

number of web servers and application servers can accommodate increases in number of users. They also have the benefit of consolidating all data management in the database server; thus simplifying the management and administration of the corporate database and avoiding issues of replicated or partitioned data management. Even in geographically dispersed and heavily accessed Intranets, it is seldom the case that the corporate database is either replicated or partitioned at multiple sites because of the complexity of synchronizing, managing, backing up and archiving multiple copies of the corporate database. But, the centralization of data management poses scalability problems. As the number of users increases, the number of requests to the database server increases. Eventually, the throughput of the database server is reduced thus degrading performance or requiring the upgrade of the database server to a faster, larger, more expensive multi-processor machine. Even if throughput problems are resolved, response time remains a problem because each access to the database server requires network messages.

Application developers and application server vendors have recognized these problems and have used a number of approaches to reduce contention on the database server and improve performance. These approaches are described in section 3.1. Each of these approaches has some drawbacks as described in sections 3.1 and 3.2. What application servers need is a lightweight, high-performance DBMS that is easy to install and maintain, has a small-enough footprint to reside in the application tier, and provides the bridge between the application tier and the backend database server.

TimesTen's Front-Tier™ product [3,4] is an application tier data cache that provides the following functionality and advantages:

1. It caches frequently-used subsets of the corporate database in the application tier. This improves response time by reducing network overhead to the database server, and increases throughput by reducing contention on the database server.

2. It services data management requests in the application tier in an in-memory DBMS that delivers unprecedently low response time and high throughput.

3. It supports declarative SQL queries and updates through the standard ODBC and JDBC APIs [3,4,5]. This reduces development time as it offers the same familiar APIs as the database server.

4. It synchronizes updates to the cache with the corporate database.

5. It supports caching in multiple application servers with potentially overlapping caches. Overlapping caches provide high availability and enable load balancing. Non-overlapping caches are used to partition the workload among application servers.

6. It provides an infrastructure for detection and notification of failed replication components to support fail-over and auto-restart.

7. It does not modify the corporate database schema, thus preserving the advantages of centralized corporate data management and administration.

3. Data Caching with Front-Tier

3.1 Reducing Contention on the Database server

Application developers and application server vendors have used a number of approaches to reduce contention on the database server, and improve response time. These approaches include:

- *Result Set Caching.* This approach consists of caching some of the results obtained from the database server in the application tier, and reusing them if they happen to process requests identical to the ones whose results have already been cached. This caching technique is severely limited because:
  - ❖ It lacks query processing capability. The only queries that can be answered from the cache are queries whose results were previously cached.
  - ❖ The caches cannot be shared or updated. They are typically read-only caches with no concurrency control. Furthermore, multiple application servers running on the same machine do not typically share caches among themselves. The result is duplicate data that consumes resources unnecessarily on the application server.

- *Disk-Based RDBMS Replication.* With this approach, subsets of the corporate database are replicated in the application tier. While this approach does provide transaction management and complex query processing in the application tier, it is too heavy weight, because disk-based RDBMSs are fairly demanding in their resource requirements. Furthermore, they do not provide the performance advantages of in-memory data management.

- *Disk-Based RDBMS Partitioning.* This approach consists of partitioning the corporate database into several databases; each managed by a disk-based RDBMS that resides in the database tier. This approach reduces contention over a single database server by distributing it over several database servers, but presents several disadvantages:
  - ❖ Response time remains an issue, as each database access requires network messages.
  - ❖ The advantage of a consolidated repository of corporate data for analysis and report generation is lost.
  - ❖ The corporate database is harder to administer, as it becomes spread over several servers. Furthermore, scaling by adding more database servers poses the challenge of having to repartition the corporate database.
  - ❖ Some transactions may require distributed transaction management support and will suffer from its accompanying performance overhead.

3.2 Front-Tier: In-Memory Data Management in the Application Tier

Front-Tier manages an organization's frequently-used data in the application tier, using TimesTen's in-memory database technology. Unlike disk-optimized RDBMSs that have been designed to reduce disk I/O through the buffering of disk data in main memory, Front-Tier relies on the memory residence of data to eliminate much of the overhead associated with disk-based RDBMSs. For example, Front-Tier does not have to maintain, manage, or search a buffer pool since all data is always in memory. Similarly, Front-Tier uses index structures optimized to reduce CPU processing and memory consumption. The result is a system that is an order of magnitude faster than fully cached disk-based RDBMSs. In addition to high performance, Front-Tier offers the standard capabilities found in disk-based RDBMSs such as data sharing, transaction management and SQL functionality. Front-Tier's architecture is lightweight, easy to embed, and can be deployed on a range of application tiers and computing platforms. TimesTen Performance Software's in-memory database technology has been described in [1,2].

Managing frequently-accessed data in the application tier reduces contention on the backend database server thus improving overall throughput, and brings data close to the application, thus improving response time by avoiding network overhead. These advantages, coupled with the inherent performance advantages of in-memory data management, provide a powerful boost to response time, throughput, and overall system scalability. Front-Tier's approach has the added benefit of not modifying the schema of the corporate database, which can remain centralized and whole, thus permitting global data analysis and ease of administration.

The approaches described in section 3.1 and the Front-Tier approach are summarized in the following table, together with their advantages:

<table>
<tr><th rowspan="3"></th><th rowspan="3"></th><th colspan="4" align="center">Approach</th></tr>
<tr><th>Result set caching</th><th>Disk-Based RDBMS repl.</th><th>Disk-based RDBMS part.</th><th>Front-Tier</th></tr>
<tr><td>SQL support</td><td>No</td><td>Yes</td><td>Yes</td><td>Yes</td></tr>
<tr><td rowspan="8">F
E
A
T
U
R
E
/
B
E
N
E
F
I
T</td></tr>
<tr><td>Transaction mgmt support</td><td>No</td><td>Yes</td><td>Yes</td><td>Yes</td></tr>
<tr><td>Lightweight</td><td>Yes</td><td>No</td><td>NA</td><td>Yes</td></tr>
<tr><td>Ease of admin of corp DB</td><td>Yes</td><td>Yes</td><td>No</td><td>Yes</td></tr>
<tr><td>Reduced resp time</td><td>Yes</td><td>Somewhat</td><td>No</td><td>Yes</td></tr>
<tr><td>Improved Throughput</td><td>Yes</td><td>Yes</td><td>Yes</td><td>Yes</td></tr>
</table>

3.3 Defining the Content of a Cache

To define what is to be cached, Front-Tier provides a Web-based easy-to-use tool called the *Front-Tier Administrator*. Through the Front-Tier Administrator, the application designer may view the schema of a chosen corporate database. From that schema, the user chooses the sub-schema that should be cached using the concept of Cache Groups. A *Cache Group* is a set of Front-Tier tables that corresponds to a set of related and frequently used tables in the corporate database. SQL syntax is used to define Cache Groups and may be used to further qualify which columns and rows from a set of related tables belong to a cache. The Front-Tier Administrator assists the user in defining Cache Groups and automatically generates the appropriate SQL syntax. Users may also define Cache Groups programmatically using SQL syntax.

Example:

Assume that the following tables exist in the corporate database:

    Customer (CustId, Name, Age, Gender,
        StreetAddress, State, ZipCode, PhoneNo)
    Order (CustId, OrderId, PurchaseDate, Amount)
    CustInterest (CustId, Interest)

An application may want to cache the profiles of customers who have placed one or more purchase orders worth more than $500 since January 1, 2000. To that end, it may define the following two cache groups:

```
CREATE CACHE GROUP PacificCustomers
SELECT CustId, Name, Age, Gender, Interest
FROM Customer, Order, CustInterest
WHERE Customer.CustId = CustInterest.CustId
AND Customer.CustId = Order.CustId
AND Customer.State IN ('WA', 'OR', 'CA',    'NV')
AND Order.PurchaseDate >= 'JAN 1 2000'


CREATE CACHE GROUP MountainCustomers
SELECT CustId, Name, Age, Gender, Interest
FROM Customer, Order, CustInterest
WHERE Customer.CustId = CustInterest.CustId
AND Customer.CustId = Order.CustId
AND Customer.State IN
        ('MT', 'ID', 'UT', 'AZ', 'WY', 'CO', 'NM')
AND Order.PurchaseDate >= 'JAN 1 2000'
```

where the Cache Groups PacificCustomers and MountainCustomers are to be cached on different application servers.

Two tables will be cached in Front-Tier. They are:
    Customer (CustId, Name, Age, Gender)
    CustInterest (CustId, Interest)
They can be used to answer any queries over these tables for the columns listed above. (Note that there is no need to cache the Order table.)

An additional concept used by Front-Tier is that of a Cache Instance. A *Cache Instance* is a complex object or a collection of related records that are uniquely identifiable. Cache Instances form the unit of cache loading and cache aging as will be described in section 3.4. In the example above, all records in the Customer and CustInterest tables that belong to a given customer id belong to the same Cache Instance.

When data is cached into Front-Tier, types must be converted from the corporate database types to Front-Tier's data types. The Front-Tier Administrator assists the user in recommending the Front-Tier data types that most closely match the corporate database types.

3.4 Caching Data and Managing the Cache

Once a Cache Group has been defined, the data that it describes can be loaded all at once from the corporate database into Front-Tier for processing. Alternatively, Cache Instances may be faulted into Front-Tier, or loaded, on demand, from the corporate database. Data that has been loaded into Front-Tier is available for SQL processing through JDBC or ODBC. The user may choose to periodically refresh Cache Groups from the corporate database, unload Cache Groups, and/or load different Cache Groups. This may be accomplished programmatically while the application is running.

Note that Front-Tier enables developers to create indexes on cached data. Front-Tier indexes may match the indexes in the corporate database or may be different. The application designer can use the flexibility of Front-Tier to create multiple indexes on the same table and may define indexes over multiple columns.

Cache Instances are automatically aged out of the cache when the cache capacity is exceeded. Aging is based on last time of access, and uses an LRU scheme by default. In addition, Front-Tier provides applications with a number of cache-aging options. An application may set up different durations for different Cache Groups as well as for different Cache Instances. Furthermore, the application may specify that certain Cache Groups should never be aged out. For example, the application may want to keep catalog information in the cache all the time, while a user's profile is only relevant while the user is connected to the application.

3.4 Synchronization

During normal processing, applications read and update data cached in Front-Tier. Applications residing on the same machine can share caches. Furthermore, different caches of the same corporate database may reside on the same machine or on different machines. These caches may be identical or may contain different subsets of the corporate database. For example, an application tier may consist of several servers each dedicated to serve a subset of subscribers. The subscribers may be partitioned according to zip code, area code, user identifier, etc. With such a scheme, the data cached on each server will contain a different subset of the corporate database.

Read-only transactions do not require communication with the corporate database. However, when the application completes a transaction that has modified the database, Front-Tier first commits the transaction in the corporate database, and then in Front-Tier. This technique allows the corporate database to apply any required logic related to the data before it is committed in Front-Tier. As a result, the corporate RDBMS always reflects the latest image of the data.

Similarly, if the content of caches overlap in different application servers, Front-Tier's replication keeps the content of the caches consistent.

4. Conclusion

TimesTen Performance Software's Front-Tier product is an in-memory application-tier data cache targeted at high-performance, data-intensive Internet applications. In contrast to simple result cache mechanisms, Front-Tier can process new SQL queries over cached data. Front-Tier caches can be shared among different applications. Updates can be applied to the caches, and the caches are kept consistent with the backend corporate database. Front-Tier is also superior to disk-based RDBMS replication schemes that replicate parts of a corporate database in the application tier because it provides better performance and because it is lightweight and therefore requires fewer resources on the application server. Finally, Front-Tier is superior to schemes that partition the corporate database into multiple disk-based databases because it preserves the centralized management and administration of the corporate database.

By bringing data closer to the application, and by processing queries in an in-memory RDBMS, Front-Tier reduces response time significantly. By offloading some of the data processing work from the database server, Front-Tier improves overall throughput without interfering with the centralized management and administration of the corporate database.

4. References

[1] The TimesTen Team. In-Memory Data Management for Consumer Transactions: The TimesTen Approach. *Proc. of the Int. Conf. on Management of Data*, June 1999.

[2] The TimesTen Team. In-Memory Data Management in the Application Tier. *Proc. of the 16th Int. Conf. on Data Engineering*, February 2000.

[3] *Front-Tier JDBC Developer's Guide*. TimesTen Performance Software. http://www.timesten.com.

[4] *Front-Tier ODBC Developer's Guide*. TimesTen Performance Software. http://www.timesten.com.

[5] *Front-Tier SQL Reference Manual*. TimesTen Performance Software. http://www.timesten.com.

Asera: Extranet Architecture for B2B Solutions

Anil Nori

Asera, USA

anori@asera.com

This paper was not available at the time of publication.

This proceedings and additional presentations will be available through www.vldb.org

Linking Businesses to Deliver Value: A Data Management Challenge

Anand Deshpande

Persistent Systems Private Limited
Panini, 2A Senapati Bapat Road
Pune
India
anand@pspl.co.in

Abstract

Internet based eCommerce is expected to grow at a phenomenal rate. As businesses rapidly move to deploy business-to-business eCommerce solutions, systems designers are likely to face new challenges while integrating and managing data.

In this presentation, I propose to discuss some of the new business models and the impact on data management in the context of these evolving eCommerce scenarios.

1. Introduction

As enterprises start to conduct serious business on the Internet, business practices and models as we know today will dramatically change and newer business models will replace existing ones.

In this presentation we discuss different business models that are likely to evolve as enterprises figure out innovative ways of transacting business in the Internet Economy. We discuss technologies that will evolve to enable these transactions to happen seamlessly. We believe that with the growth of broadband and wireless capabilities and the standardization offered by XML, Internet infrastructure will evolve to a data-oriented network offering services where businesses would plug-in for data access. Falling costs of appliances and cost of communicating data will enable new appliances to be part of this plug-and-play Internet economy.

With changes in business processes and technologies, it is quite clear that challenges for managing data are only likely to grow. The amount of data being managed by organizations is growing exponentially and this trend is likely to continue. Data is no more stored in any one database but enterprises deal with data scattered all over the Internet. Businesses will want to be far more flexible about sharing data with others at different times. While making all these changes, investments in existing systems will have to be protected

The deployment of Internet e-Commerce is likely to happen very rapidly over the next three to five years. As businesses start to deploy business-to-business e-commerce over the next few years, application developers will have to address these challenges as they come. In this dynamic world, it is appropriate for the database research community to anticipate the evolution of new business practices in the Internet economy and work on finding solutions to these problems. In this talk we will identify some of data management challenges that must be addressed for a smooth transition to the new economy.

2. Data Management Challenges

In this section, we list some areas that database researchers could help enable business-to-business eCommerce.

2.1 Security

The notion of "insiders" and "outsiders" has changed. Companies have limited duration partnerships of where they are interested in sharing information on a need basis. Defining policies and other mechanisms that allow businesses to share precise information for a specified period is essential. At the same time, adequate access

Proceedings of the 26th International Conference on Very Large Databases, Cairo, Egypt, 2000

control mechanisms would have to ensure that the privacy of data is not compromised.

2.2 Document-based Data Model

The granularity of objects in a relational database system is typically tables, attributes etc. The granularity of data exchange in the B2B eCommerce scenario is likely to be at the level of business objects such as a Purchase Order or an Invoice. While it is possible, to map data from such documents into base tables, we need better abstractions in the data management layer that permit interaction that is consistent with the requirements of the business.

2.3 XML: getting beyond the hype

XML is evolving as the de-facto standard for data interchange. While efforts to standardize XML are important, the real value of b2b eCommerce is possible only if business interchange documents are standardized. While document exchange systems hold promise, metadata repositories and other associated infrastructure would have to evolve before XML can have serious impact.

2.4 Data Extraction

Businesses already have data in multiple diverse data sources. Extracting data from these diverse sources to allow interoperability would be essential for the success of the new eCommerce infrastructure. These data sources are likely to be databases, documents on the web and various legacy systems. The problem is significantly complicated because raw data as stored in databases is not entirely useful and one needs to have the necessary wrappers to extract information from these applications.

2.5 Wireless and Mobile Devices

Wireless devices are getting popular. Wireless devices such as cell phones typically have very small screens and very small caches. The transfer speeds are also quite low. A model with caches distributed with service providers at various locations on the network make it possible to design interesting applications that include mobile devices as part of the eCommerce systems. Voice activated eCommerce through cell-phones and other mobiledevices is also likely to create interesting challenges.

2.6 Distributed Data

Data is already distributed all over the network. It is a challenge to present to the user an appropriately unified view of data despite the distribution of the data over distant geographic locations.

2.7 Caching and Performance

As more and more business is transacted over these networks, performance will be a primary concern. Research in replication and caching would be essential to improve performance in these distributed data framework. As there is far too much data to cache and innovative application sensitive caching will be necessary to provide improved performance.

2.8 Data Overload

We are already living in a world of data overload; marketplaces and other eCommerce environments are going to enable us to get access to more data than we would want to. Significant opportunities exist in terms of creating tools and services to sift through large volumes of data would be an important challenge. Data mining tools and other visualization tools that make it easier for end-users to make sense out of their data would be essential.

2.9 More forgiving data models

Database models are based on fairly rigid assumptions. Business models in the real world are more forgiving and account for certain delays and permit retries in the business processes. It is not essential at the macro level to have the same level of transaction support as is common in relational databases. Models that use redundancy and can handle failure gracefully need to evolve.

2.10 Zero Administration and Reduced Deployment Resources

Most businesses have had very high IT spending over the last five years due to Year 2000 and ERP implementations. Companies do realize that they need to adopt new technologies but are uncomfortable with systems that require very high customization and deployment resources. There is an acute shortage of programmers and businesses are looking for solutions that do not require large armies of programmers.

3. Conclusion

These are interesting times for both the business and the software community. E-Commerce solutions will have significant impact on how we do business and business models will evolve to suit the evolution of technology.

It is quite clear that data management will remain an important challenge and it is up to the database community to evolve to suit these new requirements.

Evolution of Groupware for Business Applications:
A Database Perspective on Lotus Domino/Notes

C. Mohan, R. Barber, S. Watts, A. Somani, M. Zaharioudakis

IBM Almaden Research Center, 650 Harry Road, San Jose, CA 95120, USA
{mohan, barber, somani, markos}@almaden.ibm.com, swatts@us.ibm.com
www.almaden.ibm.com/u/mohan/, www.almaden.ibm.com/u/barber/

Abstract

In this paper, we first introduce the database aspects of the groupware product Lotus Domino/Notes and then describe, in some more detail, many of the logging and recovery enhancements that were introduced in R5. We discuss briefly some of the changes that had to be made to the ARIES recovery method to accommodate the unique storage management characteristics of Notes. We also outline some of the on-going logging and locking work in the Dominotes project at the IBM Almaden Research Center.

1. Introduction

Over a decade ago, Iris Associates, now a subsidiary of IBM's Lotus, pioneered the concept of groupware and released the product Lotus Notes in 1989. It was based on a research prototype, called PLATO Notes, which was built by some of the Iris founders while they were students at the University of Illinois in Urbana Champaign (a lengthier description of the product's historical evolution can be found in http://www.notes.net/history.nsf/). Notes provides a feature-rich application development and deployment environment [Moore95]. Over the years, more and more of the functionality that used to be in other products complementary to Notes have been folded into Notes itself (e.g., calendaring, scheduling, high-level workflow process definition capabilities). Notes lets program scripts be defined by users and be stored in the

Proceedings of the 26th VLDB Conference, Cairo, Egypt, September 2000.

Notes DB. Triggers, which are valuable for implementing workflow applications, are supported via the notion of agents. While Notes was initially designed as a workgroup product for use by a small number of users working collaboratively, subsequently it has been enhanced extensively with functionality and infrastructure improvements, allowing it to be successfully deployed as a platform for business applications in numerous large enterprises. Currently, it has an install base of over 55 million seats. Without relying on a DBMS, Notes does its own persistent storage management. Our aim here is to provide a database (DB) perspective on this product.

Since the time Notes was enabled for the internet a few years ago, the name *Domino* has been used to refer to the server and the name *Notes* to the client. Because the DB functionality supported in the client and the server is almost identical, we use the two names interchangeably.

2. Semi-Structured Data Management

Since its first release in 1989, long before the topic became fashionable in the DB and web research communities, Lotus Notes had been targeted at the management of semi-structured data. Notes supports the storage and manipulation of documents (*notes*) that contain structured as well as unstructured data (e.g., audio, video). *Views* can be used for the presentation of a subset of the data in the documents of a DB in a structured way. View columns can have collation options associated with them. From the GUI, *forms* can be used to create, view and update documents. The Notes API can be used by programs for performing these and other operations. Document sizes could vary widely. Every document in a Notes DB could potentially be structured differently (e.g., with respect to number and types of fields) compared to every other document in the same DB. Document structure could evolve easily over time. At anytime, existing fields in a document could be deleted or their types could be modified, and new fields could be added. A document can point to another document, in the same or different DB, via a *DocLink*. Parent-child relationships could exist between documents. In addition, documents could be classified along category hierarchies. Querying of a DB's contents can be done using a fairly high-level query language, although the latter is not as sophisticated as the recently proposed query languages for semi-structured DBs and XML data. Since Notes does not have an RDBMS-style query optimizer, choice of an access path to process a query needs to be made by the user.

3. Storage Architecture

All user data and metadata belonging to a Notes DB is stored in a single file dedicated to that DB. A server or a client can manage any number of DBs. Data is stored on disk in a machine-independent format so that binary copying of a DB file across dissimilar machine architectures (e.g., PC and RISC) does not require any conversions to be performed before the DB becomes accessible on the target system. Because of the unstructured nature of the supported data model, DBs as well as individual documents within them are stored in a completely location independent and self-describing format. Storage management is done differently for structured fields versus multimedia or rich text fields (e.g., attachments). Within a DB (e.g., when an index entry points to a document), a document is identified using a short *NoteID* and across DBs (e.g., for replication purposes) it is identified using a longer *UNID* (Universal Note ID).

Sophisticated (hierarchical and ranked) B⁺-trees are used for managing views. The latter are like the indexes or materialized views of RDBMSs. With each view, an expression can be associated to determine which documents in the DB qualify to be included in the view. Unlike RDBMS indexes, Notes views are not maintained synchronously as the underlying documents are updated. Timestamps contained in documents and in tombstones of deleted documents are exploited to efficiently update the views. Not using a log for this purpose poses an interesting problem since the old values of a modified document's fields are not available to compute and remove the old key. This has been resolved by maintaining for each view an inverse NoteID to key mapping.

Full text indexes are managed differently from view indexes and are maintained in files external to a Notes DB file. A single so-called Domain Index can be used to index multiple Notes DBs to allow uniform searching across those DBs.

4. Replication

From its first release, support for replication and disconnected operation has been one of the most significant and innovative features of Notes. The replication mechanism is very flexible with respect to with which server(s) and when to synchronize. With each replica of a DB, an expression can be specified to determine which documents should be included in that replica, thereby supporting selective replication. One can also restrict only a subset of the qualifying documents' fields to be replicated. Initially, concurrent updates to the same document were checked for conflicts at document granularity [KBHOG92]. Subsequent enhancements have made it possible to do conflict checking at field granularity. As in the case of views, document timestamps are relied upon to identify changed documents. Sequence numbers associated with individual fields are used to support the optional field-level conflict checking functionality. Notes DB can also be replicated with PDAs like the Palm Pilot.

5. High Availability

In order to provide high availability in the event of server failures, Domino allows the clustering of a collection of servers for supporting automatic failover. The clustered servers manage replicated DBs that are synchronized more often and differently than in the case of normal replication. The switchover of a client from one server in the cluster to another can be made to happen even if the first server is not responsive enough, thereby providing load balancing functionality.

6. Security

Sophisticated access control features and very early support of RSA public key technology for authentication have been the hallmarks of the product. Field level encryption of documents is also supported. These security features are exploited in business applications, especially when role-based workflows are involved. In the web context, Domino's features can be exploited to dynamically create highly personalized web pages.

7. Heterogeneous Data Access

Through companion products like NotesPump and DECS (Domino Enterprise Connection Services), it is possible to integrate data from Notes and other sources (e.g., RDBMSs, SAP R/3). Notes applications can be written as if all the data comes from a Notes DB itself when in fact some of the data may be dynamically or periodically materialized from other sources. This is one way to integrate backend enterprise data using Notes on the desktop. Domino can be accessed from not only Notes but also web browsers and CORBA clients. Similarly, Notes can be used to access not only Domino but also CORBA, SMTP and POP3 servers.

8. ARIES for Semi-Structured Data

Through the joint efforts of Iris Associates and IBM Almaden's Dominotes project, one of the major features that was introduced in the latest release (R5) of Lotus Domino is a traditional DBMS-style, write-ahead logging-based recovery scheme [Mohan99]. This optional feature can be enabled at the granularity of a DB. At anytime, logging can be turned on or off by an administrator. When logging is on, each Notes API call is implicitly treated as an ACID transaction. Even with this restriction, a single transaction could run for a long time by manipulating multiple documents and/or multiple DBs in a single API call. Since Notes had not been originally designed with log-based recovery in mind, adding this sophisticated technology required significant design work. This is because enhancements had to be made to our ARIES recovery method [MHLPS92] to deal with the fact that storage management in Notes is done in very unconventional ways. We call this version of our recovery method **ARIES/SSD** (ARIES for Semi-Structured Data).

Notes stores persistently in a DB file numerous kinds of data structures - different kinds of hash-based search structures, lists of NoteIDs, B-trees, bit vectors, objects, tables, ... Some of these structures are paginated while others are not. Different page sizes are used by different structures. Over time, these data structures might also be moved around within the file in arbitrary ways. Since some of the data structures might contain attachments like audio, video, etc., internally logging had to be made optional at the data structure level also.

File Caching Some of the recovery complications also come from the fact that Notes relies on file caching being done by the file system of the operating system. In other words, Notes does not provide raw device support. Under certain conditions (e.g., when some metadata is changed), Notes issues a *file sync* call to the operating system to force the file cache contents to be written to disk immediately. This is an expensive operation and with our logging enhancement in R5 we have been able to improve performance by reducing the number of times such a call needs to be issued.

Recover_LSN Tracking Until R5, Notes did not have a full-blown buffer manager (BM). Unlike an RDBMS BM, the Notes BM has to manage variable sized pages in a single buffer pool (BP) since the Notes DB contains structures with many different page sizes. Even with the new BM in place, the non-paginated data structures are managed outside of the buffer pool. This fact, coupled with the existence of the file cache in the operating system that might contain some recently written data means that the *Recover_LSN* information tracked by BM in ARIES for checkpointing and restart redo recovery purposes needs to be supplemented with additional such information relating to the data not in BP. We now have a table in virtual storage which tracks Recover_LSNs for non-paginated structures of a DB which are manipulated outside BP. We also track a global Recover_LSN for the file cache on a per DB basis. This value is computed based on the Recover_LSNs of the recently written pages and other non-paginated structures. File sync calls cause this value to be reset. This resetting has to be done carefully since writes to the file cache may occur while a sync is in progress.

Analysis and Redo Passes Accommodating the storage management characteristics of Notes has required changes to the analysis and redo passes of ARIES. We could not rely on an LSN (Log Sequence Number) field that was created at a certain offset in the DB file continuing to be at that same offset after a while. This is because pages might be migrated (within a DB) or deallocated and later some user data might be stored at that LSN location. For such reasons, in ARIES/SSD, the analysis pass gathers information about space allocations. The latter is used during the redo pass to skip processing some log records whose LSNs, in ARIES, might have been compared with LSNs on corresponding DB pages. Whenever possible, ARIES/SSD does logical logging and LSN-based recovery. Otherwise, it does physical logging and non-LSN-based recovery.

DB Migrations Notes users frequently move or replicate DBs by doing file copying via the operating system. This can cause a logged version of a DB to be overlaid with an older or newer replica of that DB from another system. Attempting to apply the log records to the wrong version of a DB can cause major problems. We track extra information in the DB header to deal with such situations. When we detect that a DB had been migrated from one system to another, we reset the LSN fields in that DB since the logs at the 2 systems may be growing at different rates. In particular, the LSNs being assigned in the new system may be lower than the LSNs already assigned by the old system. For a number of reasons, we did not adopt the solution of [MoNa94] where a similar problem arose because DB pages could migrate from client to client and the logger was at the server but an LSN had to be assigned locally in a client machine, while producing a log record, without communicating with the server.

Backup and Restore Prior to R5, backup and restore of a Notes DB were not supported directly in the product itself. Notes administrators had to rely on file system utilities for accomplishing those functions. Starting with R5, APIs are provided for backup vendors to use to get a transaction-consistent copy of a DB, while still permitting concurrent updates to the DB as the copying is done. This approach is very different from the one implemented in DB2 [MoNa93].

Methods to deal with partial writes to disk have been added [Mohan95a]. Due to lack of time, in R5, we did not enhance the view index manager with support for logging. Just as we exploited the *Nested Top Actions* feature of ARIES extensively in ARIES/IM [Mohan95b, MoLe92], ARIES/LHS [Mohan93] and ARIES for MQSeries [MoDi94], in ARIES/SSD also we have benefited tremendously from it. It has permitted us to improve performance and increase concurrency. By using a single log for logging the changes made to all the DBs managed by a server, we have been able to gain performance advantages even if no single DB encounters significant update activity.

9. Current Work and Conclusions

We are currently enhancing Notes to expose the transaction API calls (Begin, Commit, Rollback) to users, thereby allowing a transaction to span multiple Notes API calls. We are also improving the granularity of locking. This is requiring significant work to be done since the earlier coarse granularity of locking had been taken advantage of in many unobvious ways. The new enhancements are now forcing us to address space reservation problems to handle rollbacks correctly [MoHa94]. We are exploiting the Commit_LSN technique [Mohan90] in a number of places to improve pathlengths. By exploiting some of the logical logging techniques of [MoLe92, Mohan95b], we are in the process of adding logging to the view index manager.

In R5, with the changes made to some of its core storage structures, scalability of the product has been enhanced significantly. Without logging support, recovering from a failure took time that was proportional to the size of an affected DB. Implementing logging-based recovery has enabled restart from a failure to be much faster. Apart from the introduction of such industrial-strength features, Notes, which has been much more than merely a messaging system from its very beginning, is now evolving more and more with knowledge management capabilities also.

Acknowledgements: We would like to thank our past colleagues in the Dominotes project at IBM Almaden Research Center and our partners in Iris Associates. Our joint work gave us deep insights into the internals of the product and led to significant enhancements to its DB infrastructure/functionality.

10. References

[KBHOG92] Kawell, L., Beckhardt, S., Halvorsen, T., Ozzie, R., Greif, I. *Replicated Document Management in a Group Communication System*, In **Groupware: Software for Computer-Supported Cooperative Work**, IEEE Computer Press, 1992.

[MHLPS92] Mohan, C., Haderle, D., Lindsay, B., Pirahesh, H., Schwarz, P. *ARIES: A Transaction Recovery Method Supporting Fine-Granularity Locking and Partial Rollbacks Using Write-Ahead Logging*, **ACM Transactions on Database Systems**, Vol. 17, No. 1, March 1992.

[MoDi94] Mohan, C., Dievendorff, R. *Recent Work on Distributed Commit Protocols, and Recoverable Messaging and Queuing*, **Data Engineering**, Vol. 17, No. 1, March 1994.

[MoHa94] Mohan, C., Haderle, D. *Algorithms for Flexible Space Management in Transaction Systems Supporting Fine-Granularity Locking*, **Proc. 4th International Conference on Extending Database Technology**, Cambridge, March 1994.

[Mohan90] Mohan, C. *Commit_LSN: A Novel and Simple Method for Reducing Locking and Latching in Transaction Processing Systems*, **Proc. 16th International Conference on Very Large Data Bases**, Brisbane, August 1990.

[Mohan93] Mohan, C. *ARIES/LHS: A Concurrency Control and Recovery Method Using Write-Ahead Logging for Linear Hashing with Separators*, **Proc. 9th International Conference on Data Engineering**, Vienna, April 1993.

[Mohan95a] Mohan, C. *Disk Read-Write Optimizations and Data Integrity in Transaction Systems Using Write-Ahead Logging*, **Proc. 11th International Conference on Data Engineering, Taipei, March 1995.**

[Mohan95b] Mohan, C. *Concurrency Control and Recovery Methods for B^+-Tree Indexes: ARIES/KVL and ARIES/IM*, In **Performance of Concurrency Control Mechanisms in Centralized Database Systems**, V. Kumar (Ed.), Prentice Hall, 1995.

[Mohan99] Mohan, C. *Repeating History Beyond ARIES*, **Proc. 25th International Conference on Very Large Data Bases**, Edinburgh, September 1999.

[MoLe92] Mohan, C., Levine, F. *ARIES/IM: An Efficient and High Concurrency Index Management Method Using Write-Ahead Logging*, **Proc. ACM SIGMOD International Conference on Management of Data**, San Diego, June 1992.

[MoNa93] Mohan, C., Narang, I. *An Efficient and Flexible Method for Archiving a Data Base*, **Proc. ACM SIGMOD International Conference on Management of Data**, Washington, D.C., May 1993. A *corrected* version of this paper is available as IBM Research Report RJ9733, IBM Almaden Research Center, March 1993.

[MoNa94] Mohan, C., Narang, I. *ARIES/CSA: A Method for Database Recovery in Client-Server Architectures*, **Proc. ACM SIGMOD International Conference on Management of Data**, Minneapolis, May 1994.

[Moore95] Moore, K. *The Lotus Notes Storage System*, **Proc. ACM SIGMOD International Conference on Management of Data**, San Jose, May 1995.

Process Automation as the Foundation for E-Business

Fabio Casati and Ming-Chien Shan

Hewlett-Packard Laboratories
1501 Page Mill road
Palo Alto, CA
USA
[casati,shan]@hpl.hp.com

Abstract

E-business is becoming the trademark of the 2000s. Companies are using the Web to communicate with their partners, connect with their back-end systems, and perform e-commerce transactions. However, the transition from traditional business to e-business requires a fundamental re-implementation of their business operational systems. Many companies have focused their transitions on developing web-based interfaces to their legacy applications. However, the backend infrastructure is often inadequate to support the offering, not only for established corporations but also, surprisingly, for many newly formed dotcoms.

On the other hand, successful e-business companies have identified workflow as the key technology for connecting front-end and back-end applications, for integrating, automating, and monitoring business and e-commerce processes, and for providing on-line service delivery. In this paper we discuss the benefits of workflow automation and we show why workflow is a key technology for building the foundation for e-business. We will demonstrate these concepts by presenting an example of a very successful e-business startup that has placed HP Changengine at the core of its e-business platform.

Proceedings of the 26th International Conference on Very Large Databases, Cairo. Egypt, 2000

1. Behind the Web Façade

E-Business is transforming corporations, markets, and the global economy. The Web is affecting the business transactions are performed: It makes it easy to find products and services as well as providers and suppliers, compare prices and qualities, and trade, buy, and get products and services quickly delivered to us. Customers are getting used to nice and friendly user interfaces, targeted advertisement, up-to-date product catalogues, and personalized stores.

However, the web façade hides huge inefficiencies, manual and error-prone operations, and slow, complex, inflexible, and unmanageable systems. Indeed, quite surprisingly, in many e-commerce applications the execution of business processes still involves a lot of human intervention in several aspects of business process execution such as (repeated) data entry, monitoring of process executions (that often requires tracking the process over several system in order to find out its current advancement state), exception handling, and even the scheduling of the different activities that are part of the process.

Inefficiencies in e-commerce processes result in high operating costs that, combined with the low margins required in order to provide competitive offers, are strongly affecting the profits of the large majority of e-businesses (see Fig. 1). To compete successfully, enterprises are demanding effective ways to implement e-business and deliver e-services over the Internet.

Most e-business applications are characterized by a web front-end, typically powered by a personalization engine, an application server that supports dynamic generation of web content and links the front-end to business applications, and a set of back-end systems that manage inventory, procurement, billing, payment, shipment, and all the functions required for performing e-commerce transactions.

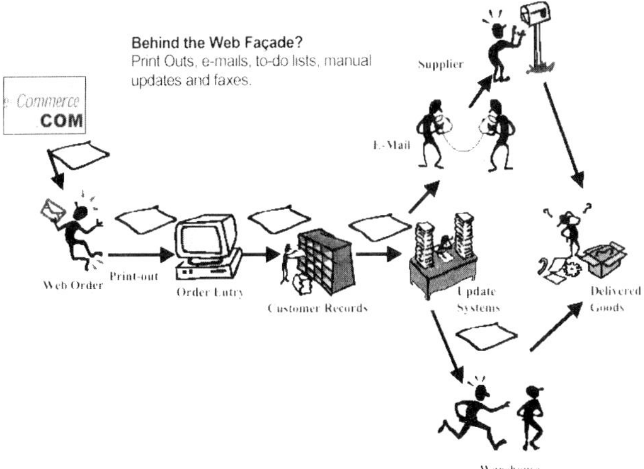

Figure 1. Behind the Web façade, processes are carried out manually

Currently, no product or vendor can effectively provide the functionality required to support e-business. While some vendors, such as Broadvision, ATG, and Vignette, provide excellent solutions in the front-end space, the back-end side is dominated by ERP and DBMS vendors such as Oracle, SAP, or PeopleSoft. Despite huge efforts by many of them aiming at covering the whole spectrum, none of them has yet provided a complete and satisfactory solution to all the challenges raised by e-business. Therefore, top-class solutions are typically characterized by a number of different software applications provided by different vendors.

While the adoption of best-of-breed applications is a must in order to stay competitive, it also raises significant technical challenges. In fact, most e-business processes require functionality not typically provided by a single application. Hence, they need to span across several software systems. For instance, the process of ordering a product involves checking the inventory, allocating the goods from the stock (and/or procuring them), dispatching the goods, and verifying their shipment, in addition to the customer credit verification, billing, payment, and update of customer information for personalized advertisement campaigns.

The need of accessing several applications to perform a business function generates a lot of issues, ranging from understanding and accessing the different APIs with the appropriate communication protocol, to managing the different security requirements, data formats, programming models, and transmission models (e.g., publish/subscribe, request/reply). To further complicate the picture, different systems often run on top of heterogeneous hardware and software platforms.

A partial solution to this problem is provided by Enterprise Application Integration (EAI) platforms. Integrators such as Tibco Tib/rendezvous, ActiveSoftware's ActiveWorks, STC eGate, or BEA eLink, ease the daunting task of connecting different applications, by providing uniform access to heterogeneous systems and by offering design tools that help system integrators in appropriately accessing the different applications and managing their results. However, while EAI solutions are useful and even necessary to manage complexity given by heterogeneity, they still do not solve the problem of managing e-commerce processes and making them more efficient.

Typically, attempts to automate processes are based on writing ad-hoc code to execute the flow logic. While this approach does provide advantages over human-driven execution and allows for larger throughput and reduced latency, it still does not address many crucial issues:

- *Rapid process development and change management*: one of the most important requirements in the e-business world is the ability of quickly introducing new services as soon as the need for them is recognized. Therefore, suppliers and service providers must be able to easily and rapidly develop and deploy the corresponding business processes. In addition, the business and IT environment changes very often; hence, processes must transparently adapt as much as possible to such changes, and process modifications should be supported in those cases where human intervention is needed.

- *Process monitoring*: ad-hoc solutions usually lack process monitoring and tracking capabilities, especially when processes span across many systems, and it is difficult to "locate" which process step is currently in execution for a given instance.

- *Process management*: it is often necessary to intervene on running process instances in order to manage unexpected situations and perform the required corrective actions.

- *Performance and the "ilities"*: performance, scalability, reliability, and high availability are key issues in e-commerce applications. Indeed, the costs (in terms of loss of customers and of business transactions) due to poor performances and downtimes are too high to be tolerated for any company that does its business on the Web. Therefore, any e-business process solution must provide the appropriate performance level as well as the "ilities".

In fact, trying to automate business processes by hard-coding the process flow is a classic mistake: it makes e-commerce processes - and the overall system itself - difficult to design, deploy, monitor, and modify. In addition, the time-to-market for introducing new services is often very high. Indeed, according to several technology marketing research groups, the main reason for the April 2000 crash in the Internet stock market is due to the lack of a suitable e-business backbone that efficiently connects the back-end enterprise applications and streamline e-commerce processes. Many dotcoms have been victims of their own success, being unable to sustain the overwhelming responses to their offerings.

2. Process Management Support for E-Business Applications

Business processes are at the heart of every e-business operation. Correspondingly, business process management systems (or Workflow Management Systems, WfMSs) should be at the heart of any e-business solution.

State-of-the-art WfMSs, such as HP Changengine [1], address all the issues listed above. In particular, they allow the model-driven design, analysis, and simulation of business processes, which can be designed from scratch or from templates that support rapid application development, as shown in Fig. 2. They also provide features for monitoring the execution of individual process instances (or sets of process instances) and for automatically reacting to exceptional situations.

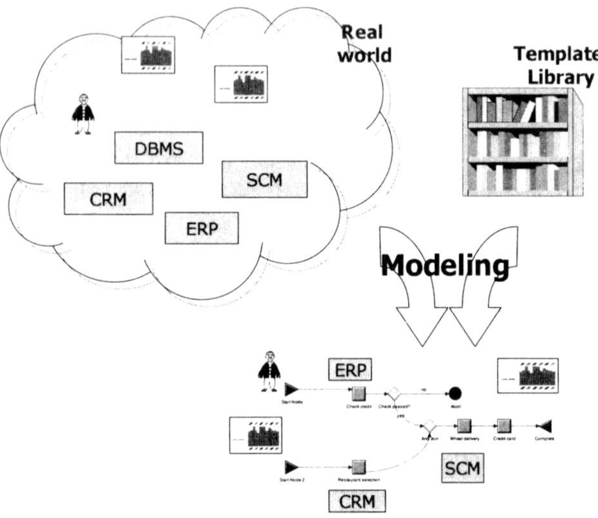

Figure 3. Changengine processes are designed from scratch or through templates

The integration of WfMSs with EAI tools (such as in the case of Changengine and ActiveSoftware [2], depicted in Fig. 3) further increases the effectiveness of these systems, and enable them to handle the two crucial aspects of process automation: end-to-end process flow management and interaction with the (heterogeneous) invoked applications. Finally, WfMSs are designed to deliver the required performance and to be scalable, reliable, and highly available to sustain the needs of e-commerce applications.

WfMSs allow for incremental and controlled process and process management automation. Typically, in the first stages of their introduction, WfMSs are only used to schedule and monitor the work, but the process is still carried out by using the same "old" technology, such as e-mails or manual data entries. Subsequently, the different steps in the process can be progressively automated, possibly by implementing the interaction with external systems through the integrated EAI tool. Once a process has been designed and automated, it can be measured and incrementally improved, as shown in Fig. 4.

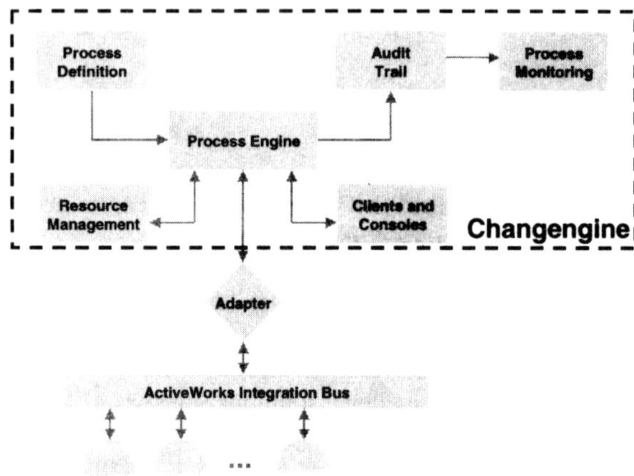

Figure 3. Changengine can access any business application through the ActiveWorks EAI tool.

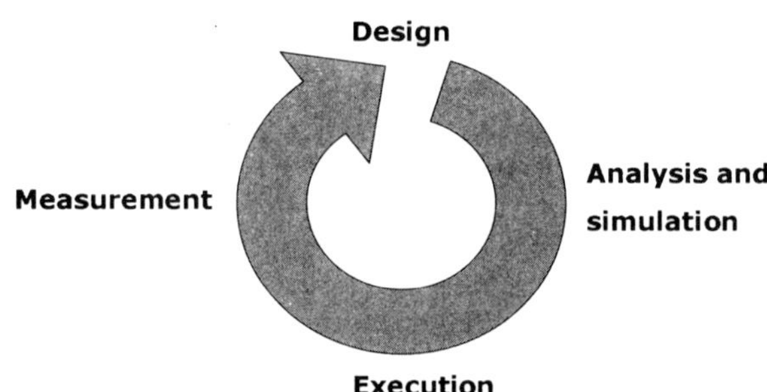

Figure 4. Process lifecycle

Indeed, successful e-business companies build their e-commerce applications on top of state-of-the-art process management tools. One of the most amazing and shining examples is the case of *LetsBuyIt.com*, an e-commerce site that provides branded goods at discounted prices through the concept of co-buying: Buyers interested in the same product can join their efforts on *LetsBuyIt.com* in order to achieve more purchasing power.

LetsBuyIt.com was founded in April 1999, and has already become the leading e-commerce site in Europe.

They have achieved this position in such an incredible short time through an excellent customer service provided at extremely low operating costs.

There are a lot of web sites offering branded goods at competitive prices. They all have nice and friendly front-ends, but the weak part is often the integration between front- and back-end systems and among the different back-end systems themselves. Hence, they suffer from excessive delays and unreliable and untraceable order management. On the contrary, *LetsBuyIt.com* achieves an effective and flexible integration of the different components of the e-business application by exploiting the many features of Changengine.

The process management and automation achieved through Changengine allows the successful Stockholm-based company to drastically reduce costs, improve quality of service and time to market, and respond to the ever-changing business environment. In addition, in an environment where customer service is crucial, Changengine provides the key ability of tracking the status of any process. For instance, *LetsBuyIt.com* uses Changengine for managing the Promotions Management process, which is critical for securing better goods at lower prices and for ensuring that they are in stock when required by customers, even upon sudden surge in the demand due to special promotions.

3. Still Ahead

Despite the great benefits that WfMSs can provide today, there is still much work to be done in order to better support the development and management of e-business solutions. We list some of the issues below:

- *Adaptive and dynamic process flows*: the business and IT scenario changes constantly in the Internet age. It is necessary to minimize the need for human intervention in order to cope with such changes and with the need of the different, individual customers. WfMSs provide some support in this area, but there is still much work to be done in order to enable the design of adaptive flows. In addition, WfMSs must improve their capability of handling dynamic changes, i.e., modifications applied to running process executions.
- *Transaction management*: current WfMSs provide poor support for transactional properties (such as atomicity and isolation) at the business process level. Such properties are very useful in order to properly handle concurrent executions and to cope with failures in a more effective way.
- *Configurable systems*: different WfMSs users require different features. It often happens that a user only needs a subset of the features provided by a WfMS. For this reason, it is important that the WfMS is configurable, so that users only get the features they need, and therefore can use a version of the product which is lightweight compared to the full-fledged one.
- *Process Knowledge Management*: no WfMS offers functionality for analyzing process logs and automatically identifying which processes can be improved and how. We foresee that process knowledge management will be an important differentiator for WfMS solutions, especially in an rapidly evolving environments, where reactions to changes need to be very quick and effective.

At HP we are working on addressing these issues, focusing in particular on composition of e-services. Preliminary results of our efforts can be found in [4,5].

Another key application of business process management technology will very likely be within *E-Hubs*, i.e., web sites that handle e-commerce and e-service transactions, by directly fulfilling them or by redirecting them to the appropriate supplier or service provider. E-Hubs provide facility for flow-through process management, business process knowledge management, security, and various CRM, ERP, and supply chain management applications, in order to be able to satisfy all the e-business requirements of customers that want to host their applications on the E-Hub.

4. References

[1] Hewlett-Packard Corp. Changengine Process Design Guide. 2000.
     Available from http://www.ice.hp.com

[2] Hewlett-Packard Corp. Process Integration Architecture: Process automation with HP Changengine. 2000
     Available from http://www.ice.hp.com

[3] Hewlett-Packard Corp. LetsBuyIt.com Case Study. 2000.
     Available from http://www.ice.hp.com

[4] F. Casati, S. Ilnicki, L.J. Jin, and M.C. Shan. eFlow: an Open, Flexible, and Configurable Approach to Service Composition. In *Proceedings of WECWIS2000*, pp. 125-132, June 2000.

[5] F. Casati, S. Ilnicki, L.J. Jin, V. Krishnamoorthy, and M.C. Shan. Dynamic and Adaptive Service Composition in eFlow. In *Proceedings of CAiSE2000*, pp. 13-31, June 2000.

Media360 workflow - Implementing a Workflow Engine Inside a Database

Carsten Blecken

Informix
4100 Bohannon Drive
Menlo Park, CA 94025
USA
Carsten.Blecken@informix.com

Abstract

I describe a Workflow Management System, where the workflow engine is implemented inside a database. The focus here is on the architectural approach and on the lessons learned from a commercial implementation in the workflow component of the Informix Media 360 content management solution.

Conceptually, the two main primitives of workflow are activities, which represent the work items of a larger process (containing either predefined or user-defined logic) and transitions, which describe the flow logic – in essence in what order and under what conditions the activities are being executed.

Existing workflow systems are typically implemented with an n-tier architecture. The flow logic necessary to execute the workflow , user-defined logic and pre- and post-activity logic is all usually implemented in a middle tier, although the workflow-relevant data is stored in a back-end database.

However, it is rather straightforward to use features of a modern Object Relational Database Management Systems like Informix Internet Foundation.2000 to implement a workflow engine completely inside a database. The flow logic can be implemented using the trigger concept, which 'fires' an appropriate transition to execute the next activity. User-defined logic, and pre- and post-activity logic are implemented using database functions or routines, which are a common extensibility feature of any ORDBMS. There is a wide array of programming languages available to express user-defined logic.

The principal advantage of such an approach is that the workflow logic is kept directly where the workflow data resides, resulting in a more efficient, simpler and more compact system design. It also aids with the embedding of database-centric workflow into a larger framework application, since a DBMS is part of all enterprise applications.

Finally, I discuss the advantages and disadvantages of this conceptual approach, and show how additional common workflow features can be added to the current architecture of the Informix Media360 workflow component.

Proceedings of the 26th International Conference on Very Large Databases, Cairo, Egypt, 2000

Work and Information Practices
in the Sciences of Biodiversity

Geoffrey C. Bowker

Department of Communication
University of California, San Diego
La Jolla, CA 92093
USA
bowker@ucsd.edu

Abstract

This paper provides an introduction to data practices in biodiversity science. This is an area where multiple scientific domains are in constant interaction, and use data from multiple sources in that process. There is a consequent huge proliferation of technical standards in the field. Further, datasets used in the biodiversity sciences often extend over several decades — and thus attention must be paid to changing standards and the development of new storage media. Finally, the classification systems used in many of the contributing sciences are in a constant state of flux as more information is gathered. I describe the main categories of data development and use in the field of biodiversity, paying particular attention to work processes both in the generation and in the analysis of data.

1. The Age of Biodiversity Information

Diana Crane [2] claims that in scientific literature "The 'life' of a paper is very short, with the exception of a few classics. Papers published five years ago are 'old'. Papers published more than fifteen years ago are almost useless in many scientific fields". In this paper, I will examine a field of science in which this is emphatically not the case — the field of biodiversity science. Crane's model works best in physics, where there is no assumption that information collected in the early nineteenth century will still be of interest to the current generation of field theorists. There is the assumption [6, for example] that new theories will reorder knowledge in the domain effectively and efficiently; and since Kuhn [5] most would accept that a major paradigm change in, say, the understanding of 'gravity' renders previous work on incline planes literally incommensurable — not to mention technical improvements making the older work too imprecise. Astronomers trawl back further in time, seeking traces of supernovae in ancient manuscripts — but sporadically; they are just as likely to look at monastery records as at Tycho Brahe's original data.

Biodiversity information is fundamentally historical in three different ways. First, the sciences of biodiversity are trying to build up a picture of life on the planet since its inception up to the present. In the absence of the time and analytic ability to carry out experiments on complex ecological systems over tens to thousands of generations, the only real information about biodiversity comes from the history of life on this planet. Second, key work practices, especially in the field of systematics, require the recording of accurate information about publication place and date for publications extending back to the mid eighteenth century — a scope of interest unimaginable for any other scientific endeavour (and for few other academic endeavours). Third, the sciences of biodiversity more than other sciences depend on being able to triangulate between multiple disparate datasets produced by different agencies for different motives. The history of the dataset itself is a key to understanding the contribution it can make to the history of life.

Proceedings of the 26th International Conference on Very Large Databases, Cairo, Egypt, 2000

In this paper I shall briefly explore each of these three temporal aspects of biodiversity information with respect to work practices in biodiversity science. Be it noted that I am not thereby underplaying the vital role of issues of spatial scope and scale in biodiversity science — indeed I shall return to this issue in the conclusion.

2. Biodiversity Research and the History of Life

Doing good biodiversity research entails the collection and manipulation of massive datasets. All information about life on earth is potentially useful: from satellite photos through aerial photos and biodiversity inventories of forests down to minute descriptions of a square foot of soil and advances in molecular biology. No-one claims that it is easy to work these all into a single vast dataset: however to truly understand life on this planet we need to produce viable means for sharing information between these varied information sources.

There are two main models for understanding biodiversity, each with their own sets of information needs (and each with their own imperative to articulate with the other). The first is the view that life on earth can basically be understood informationally — there is a given amount of information in a gene pool, for example, and as the gene pool shrinks information is lost until a species becomes non-viable because it cannot react to changing conditions. By this view, the kind of data that we need in order to design good biodiversity policy is a fully ramified 'tree of life' which enables us to recognize key branch points and to identify specific species which carry a maximal amount of genetic information. The second is the view that biodiversity can best be understood ecologically: species develop in interaction with other species, and the basic unit of concern is the deme (an 'economically' active population group) rather than the gene. Although these views place their emphases differently, and sometimes lead to conflicting policy advice, they are not in principle irreconcilable.

Complicating the equation, is the fact that in the world of biodiversity research, difficult decisions need to be taken immediately on imperfect data. For example, at the current rate of completion, we could be well into the second half of this millennium before the various national floras are complete. Taxa are disappearing at a much faster rate; and decisions that in principle require the entire flora need to be taken now.

3. Biodiversity Research and Publications

In the field of biodiversity research, there are multiple needs for extensive manipulable online versions of publications dating back two hundred and fifty years. This is partly a technical issue of nomenclature: the rules of zoological and botanical nomenclature require that naming priority be given to the first published instance of a name. There are innumerable cases in the literature of plants and animals receiving multiple names (and there is natural reluctance on the part of a given community to change the names that they are used to), so this adjudicatory mechanism holds quite an important place. However, this need goes further, in that we need very long datasets in general in the field of biodiversity research: historical observations of a given community can have immediate relevance for underbanding their current structure and nature. Much of this information might be hidden in obscure journals in different fields and a variety of languages, each using their own naming conventions. Some of the earliest incunabula are botanical and zoological field guides; and there is an enormous wealth of locally-generated material since about the flora and fauna of most countries.

4. Datasets in Biodiversity Research

4.1 Nomenclature and Systematics

The current dogma, accepted in most parts of the world except Kansas, is that there is a single origin for life as we know it; and the work of systematists involves producing an hierarchical classification system that more or less accurately reflects the history of life. In the best of all possible worlds, one would imagine assigning a single identifier to flora and fauna found over the world using a facetted classification system that permitted easy 'on the fly' ordering of classifications when new data (e.g. the discovery of new species) demands. This is far from being workable, for a number of reasons. The first is that not all users have the same need or desire to keep up with the latest classification — a change in the genus of the tomato (recently approved) would cost nurserymen millions of dollars if they instituted it; a change in the name of a wild orchid might well remove it from legal protected status in a given country [4]. Second is that some agencies will follow their own name list, which often conflicts with other local, state, national and international lists — GAP analysis is a good example here [3].

One could multiply the reasons but the effect is clear. Although in principle one wants to have single identifiers for all taxa, in fact this is not achievable. Naming conventions will vary by group and discipline, and it will always be difficult to reconcile the different datasets. I should note that there are a number of national and international initiatives (some conflicting with each other) to bring some order into the field; however is is clear from the history of such attempts at order that they will generate their own local differences: this is not a fault of the field but a fact about the maintenance of global classification systems [1].

4.2 Regional and Temporal Variation

Many individual scientists or teams of scientists specialize both temporally (studying the fauna of the Eocene period for example) and spatially (studying the flora or fauna of a particular region). In principle this division of labor is efficient and in practice it is frequently effective. However, when one tries to aggregate data from a set of regions or from a series of tranches of the fossil record, one has difficulties Naming conventions differ from region to region, and from tranche to tranche. Thus simply fitting the pieces together to make a global overview does not work: there needs to be a process of negotiation at the same time between local specialists about their processes of identification and naming in order to prevent an artificial reification of contingent modern differences — Koch points to the possibility of tracing the Austro-Hungarian empire on the floral map of Europe, because of the differing naming conventions between the Austro-Hungarian and British Empires!

4.3 Range of Metadata Needs

Information about species tends to rely on a very small sample. In the case of plants, for example, a 'type specimen' is held by a herbarium in folders on library shelving. When a researcher wants to verify that such and such a species described in the literature is the same as another one described elsewhere, then he or she has to either visit the herbaria where the two desiccated type specimens are held or request that it be sent out through the mail. In some cases, even this impoverished material basis is not present, and the 'type specimen' is taken to be the description of the specimen in a published article. The type specimens carry their own context with them: in the form of annotations, lists of previous consultants, date and time of collection and so forth. The dispersed nature of the collections of type specimens means that reconciliation of the holdings of different herbaria is extremely difficult — thus when conjuring these data into electronic form there is a need to maintain sufficient flexibility in order to merge and disaggregate certain species.

Further, there is a need to preserve information about the precise details of a given measurment technique. Thus if an ecological measurement entails collecting lake water samples which are then measured for carbon dioxide content, it makes a difference to the measurement whether or not it is done immediately at lakeside or on return to the laboratory — perhaps later that day. In the short term, local research communities know and understand their own practices. However, over time this information is lost — in general when a scientific paper was published in the past, the accompanying dataset gradually decayed, and people forgot the full details of data collection (no scientific paper is long enough to be complete on these details). In practical terms, this means that there needs to be good and easy provision within biodiversity databases for the recording of as much contextual information as possible — both immediately and retrospectively. Research in the field has repeatedly shown that scientists will not have the time to fill in complex forms which record data that is not immediately relevant to their purposes. However, in the case of biodiversity science, later interest focuses often less on the paper and its conclusion than on the dataset and its construction. There needs to be a dual effort to on the one hand educate domain scientists about the nature of this shift and its implications for their work practices and on the other to design systems which make it truly easy to enter the maximum amount of contextual data.

4.4 Interdisciplinary Communication

Biodiversity work in general entails communication between multiple overlapping scientific disciplines. In general, each discipline has grown up with its own information infrastructure and information standards. This is true at a very mundane level: some scientific communities use almost exclusively Macintoshes, others rely on Unix boxes. It is also true at many other levels. For example, there are a number of different geological timelines available for paleoecological work. Any one subcommunity might be using a different, slightly conflicting timeline. This will not make a difference when there is no need to integrate information across disciplines: however this form of integration is of the essence of biodiversity research.

More generally, a slight lack of fit between models in different disciplines only becomes apparent when one is trying to integrate information across them. Thus, in a study I am doing of work to map the environmental hydrology of the Mississippi River Basin (work that has direct implications for the preservation of biodiversity in that region) there are inconsistencies between the atmospherical, groundwater and river flow models. The negotiation of these inconsistencies is occurring precisely at the time when a team of computer scientists are trying to build up a general model of the whole water cycle in the region. My point here is that a major part of the task of building robust databases in biodiversity is facilitating interdisciplinary communication — this communication cannot just be a desired outcome, it must be designed into the data collection and representation work that is being done. In the case I have described, and in innumerable others, this communication work is not receiving the attention it deserves.

4.5 Computer Science and Biodiversity Science

It is unclear what the career trajectory is for someone in computer science who turns to biodiversity science; or vice versa of someone in biodiversity science who turns to computer design. It is certainly clear in this regard that the interests of the two communities taken separately are not the same. A computer scientist often wants to use the latest database techniques in order to produce a maximally effective and flexible tool. Indeed she has to, since without this she will not get promotion within her university department. However, the biodiversity scientist is aware that much of the work in the field is being done by relatively untrained parataxonomists, say, who have little or no access to computing equipment. For them, the simplest and most basic database form is the only one that they can use. Perhaps, as suggested by Schnase in an accompanying paper in these proceedings, these two fields must develop together over time to become truly synergistic.

5. Conclusion

I started this paper by talking about the importance of history in the design of good databases for biodiversity research. I could equally have talked about issues of space; and then walked this theme through an analogous set of issues. In both cases, the central lessons would be the same:

- Biodiversity research increasingly requires the generation of very large scale easily manipulable datasets.
- The creation of suitable database structures necessarily entails attention being paid to local work practices — in both the developing and developed world — with respect to both access to computing and modes of data collection.
- The creation of such databases is a site at which genuine interdisciplinary communication occurs — and so the role of databases in making such communication possible should be recognized at the moment of design. This can be done both through sensitising designers to different scientific cultures and carrying out studies of work practice concurrent which can feed into the design process.

Biodiversity research relies fundamentally on database design; and the present is a great opportunity for designing database structures which can further research through facilitating interdisciplinarity and can thus make a major contribution to the development of workable biodiversity policy.

6. References

[1] Bowker, Geoffrey C., and Susan Leigh Star. *Sorting Things Out: Classification and its Consequences.* Cambridge, MA: MIT Press, 1999.

[2] Crane, Diana. *Invisible colleges; diffusion of knowledge in scientific communities.* Chicago: University of Chicago Press, 1972.

[3] Edwards, Thomas C., Collin G. Homer, Scott D. Bassett, Allan Falconer, R. Douglas Ramsey, and Doug W. Wight. *Utah GAP analysis: An Environmental Information System.* Logan, UT: National Biological Service, Utah Cooperative Fish and Wildlife Research Unit, Utah State University, 1995.

[4] Klemm, Cyrille de, International Union for Conservation of Nature and Natural Resources, and World Wide Fund for Nature. *Wild plant conservation and the law.* Gland, Switzerland: IUCN-The World Conservation Union, 1990.

[5] Kuhn, Thomas S. *The Structure of Scientific Revolutions.* Chicago: University of Chicago, 1970.

[6] Poincaré, Henri. *Science and Hypothesis.* New York: The Science Press, 1905.

Research Directions
in Biodiversity Informatics

John L. Schnase

Earth and Space Data Computing Division
NASA Goddard Space Flight Center
Greenbelt, MD 20771
USA
schnase@gsfc.nasa.gov

Abstract

This paper provides an introduction to the major research directions in biodiversity informatics. The biodiversity enterprise is a vast and complex information domain. I describe the need to build infrastructure for this domain, major research thrusts needed to improve its work practices, and areas of research that could contribute to the advancement of the field. I emphasize that the science of biodiversity is fundamentally an information science, worthy of special attention from the computer and information science communities because of its distinctive attributes of scale and socio-technical complexity.

1. Biodiversity

The most striking feature of Earth is the existence of life, and the most striking feature of life is its diversity. This biological diversity — or *biodiversity* — provides us with clean air, clean water, food, clothing, shelter, medicines, and aesthetic enjoyment. Biodiversity, and the ecosystems that support it, contribute trillions of dollars to national and global economies, directly through industries such as agriculture, forestry, fishing, and ecotourism and indirectly through biologically-mediated services such as

Proceedings of the 26th International Conference on Very Large Databases, Cairo, Egypt, 2000

plant pollination, seed dispersal, grazing land, carbon dioxide removal, nitrogen fixation, flood control, waste breakdown, and the biocontrol of crop pests. And biodiversity — the species richness of habitats *per se* — is perhaps the single most important factor influencing the stability and health of ecosystems [2, 3].

It is not surprising, then, that information about biodiversity forms the basis of one of our most important knowledge domains, vital to a wide range of scientific, educational, commercial, and government uses. Unfortunately, most biodiversity information now exists in forms that are not easily accessed or used. From traditional paper-based libraries to scattered databases of varying size and physical specimens preserved in natural-history collections throughout the world, our record of biodiversity is uncoordinated and poorly integrated, and large parts of it are isolated from general use. We lack the technologies needed to effectively gather, analyze, and synthesize these data into new discoveries. As a result, this information is not being used as effectively as it could by scientists, resource managers, policy-makers, or other potential client communities. The good news is that research activities are being conducted around the world that could improve our ability to manage biodiversity information, and the emerging field of biodiversity informatics is attempting to meet the challenges posed by this domain.

2. Biodiversity Informatics

Until recently, little attention has been paid to computer and information science and technology research in the biodiversity domain. Those working in the field of biodiversity informatics — many cross-trained or cross-teamed in computer science and biology — are attempting to change that. If we are to keep pace with our need for quality information about the living systems of our planet, we must produce mechanisms that can efficiently manage petabytes of a whole new generation of high-resolution, Earth-observing satellite data. We must understand how to integrate these new datasets with traditional biodiversity data, such as specimen data held in natural history collections, and genomic data from cellular- and molecular-level work. We must be able to make correlations among data from these and even more disparate sources, such as ecosystem-scale global change and carbon cycle data, compile those data in new ways, analyze and synthesize them, and present the results in an understandable and usable manner.

Despite encouraging advances in computation and communication performance in recent years, we are able to perform these activities only on a very small scale. It is only recently, for example, that IBM announced plans to build the world's fastest supercomputer — *Blue Gene* — which will attempt to compute the three-dimensional folding of human protein molecules. Given the thousands of proteins that are produced by the unknown millions of species on this planet, and given too that many of these molecules may have potentially significant economic value, we are clearly just embarking on a whole new world of computer-mediated exploration. We can, however, make rapid progress if the computer and information science and technology research community becomes focused on the challenges posed by the biodiversity research community.

3. Managing Complexity

The single most important factor influencing the nature of work in biodiversity informatics is the problem of complexity. Living systems are complex, and they are complex at many levels. The computational challenges associated with work on cellular processes — such as decoding the structure of DNA — are enormous. But DNA-level functions are only part of an elaborate web of biotic and abiotic interactions that span from molecules to cells, and from organisms to populations and entire ecosystems. Knowledge about biodiversity is a vast and complex information domain.

This complexity arises from two sources. The first of these is the underlying biological complexity of the organisms themselves. There are millions of species, each of which is highly variable across individual organisms, populations, and time. Species have complex chemistries, physiologies, developmental cycles, and behaviors resulting from more than three billion years of evolution. There are hundreds, if not thousands, of ecosystems, each comprising complex interactions among large numbers of species and between those species and multiple abiotic factors.

The second source of complexity in biodiversity information is sociologically generated. The sociological complexity includes problems of communication and coordination — among agencies, among divergent interests, and among groups of people from different regions, different backgrounds (academia, industry, government), and with different views and requirements. The kinds of data humans have collected about organisms and their relationships vary in precision, accuracy, and in numerous other ways. Biodiversity data types include text and numerical measurements, images, sound, and video. The range of other databases with which biodiversity datasets must interact is also broad, including geographical, meteorological, geological, chemical, physical, and genomic datasets. The mechanisms used to collect and store biodiversity data are almost as varied as the natural world that they document. In addition, biological data can be politically and commercially sensitive and can entail conflicts of interest. User's skill levels are highly variable, and training in this field is not well developed.

Because of these complexities, humans still play a crucial role in the processing of biological data. Biological information is not as amenable to automatic correlation, analysis, synthesis, and presentation as many other types of information, such as that in radioastronomy, where there is more coherent global organization and the problems being studied are often conducive to automatic analysis. In biodiversity research, people act as sophisticated filters and query processors— locating resources on the Internet, downloading datasets, reformatting and organizing data for input to analysis tools, then reformatting again to visualize results. This process of creating higher-order understanding from dispersed datasets is a fundamental intellectual process in the biodiversity sciences, but it breaks down quickly as the volume and dimensionality of the data increase. Who could be expected to "understand" millions of cases, each having hundreds of attributes? Yet problems on this scale are common in biodiversity and ecosystem research.

4. Research Directions

4.1 Information Infrastructure

The total volume of biodiversity and ecosystem information is almost impossible to measure. We do know that whatever the total, only a fraction has been captured in digital form. The natural history museums in the US alone, for example, contain at least 750 million specimens, the vast majority of which have not been recorded in databases. The same holds for the published record, where most biodiversity and ecosystem information still resides in paper-based journals, books, field notes, and the like. Clearly, one of the most important infrastructure issues is to move the biodiversity enterprise into a digital world — to create the content for a global biodiversity digital library — by digitizing the existing corpus of scholarly work on a large scale.

Such an infrastructure would place challenging demands on network hardware services and on software services related to authentication, integrity, and security. Needed are both a fuller implementation of current technologies and consideration of tools and services in a broader context related to the use of online biological resources. Since biodiversity research is a global enterprise, this infrastructure must be designed to detect and adapt to various degrees of accessibility of resources connected to the Internet.

A fully digital, interactive biodiversity information service will require substantial computational and storage resources. Many information-retrieval and data mining techniques are intensive in their computational and input-output demands as they evaluate, structure, and compare large databases in a distributed environment. Distributed database searching, resource discovery, automatic classification and summarization, visualization, and presentation are also computationally intensive activities common to this field. As described earlier, large storage capacities are required for the myriad new datasets being populated by an expanding array of sensors.

In an accompanying paper in these proceedings, Cotter and Bauldock describe some of the capacity-building activities that are currently underway, the most prominent of which are work on the US National Biological Information Infrastructure (NBII) program and the international effort to create a Global Biodiversity Information Facility (GBIF). Importantly, both infrastructure efforts propose programs of basic and applied research in biodiversity informatics.

4.2 Process Improvement

New approaches to data management must be developed to handle biodiversity information. Massive datasets can lead to the collapse of traditional approaches in database management, statistics, pattern recognition, personal-information management, and visualization. Many of the interesting questions that users of biodiversity information would like to ask are "fuzzy," and the data needed to answer them must come from multiple sources that will be inherently different in structure and conceptually incompatible, and the answers might be approximate.

Major advances are needed in methods for knowledge representation and interchange, database management and federation, navigation, modelling, and data-driven simulation; in approaches to describing large, complex networked information resources; and in techniques to support networked information discovery and retrieval in large-scale distributed systems. In addition to near-term operational solutions, new approaches are needed to longer-term issues, such as the preservation of digital information across generations of storage, processing, and representation technology. Traditional information-science skills, such as thesaurus construction and indexing, must be elaborated upon and scaled to accommodate large information sources.

Also much needed are software applications that provide more natural interfaces between humans and databases than are now available. We must refine and augment the interactions between people and machines, expand the role of agentry in information systems, and discover more powerful and more natural ways of navigating this complex scientific record.

4.3 Process Reinvention

Biologists have identified approximately 1.5 million living species of all kinds of organisms, but vast arrays of species remain to be discovered. The grand total for all life is currently estimated to fall somewhere between 10 and 100 millions species [3]. There is little doubt that the Earth's biodiversity is declining. By all estimates, we are in the midst of the sixth major extinction event of the planet's history, this one the primary result of human modifications to the environment. The Nature Conservancy has estimated that one-third of the plant and animal species in the US are now at risk of extinction. The problem is a monumental one, and forces us to consider how we should respond.

Given this context, it is disturbing to realize that the fundamental work practices of the biodiversity sciences — largely unchanged over the past two centuries — are utterly unable to keep pace with rate of habitat destruction and species loss. Species discovery is still largely a manual activity requiring field collection of specimens, months or years of laboratory analysis, and time-consuming publishing activities. Conservation practices alone cannot solve the problem. If we hope to ever fathom the Earth's biodiversity, the biodiversity enterprise must reinvent itself — develop wholly new approaches to dealing with global-scale problems in a rapidly-changing, information age. Herein lies some of the most interesting informatics research challenges. There are at least three broad categories of research of particular relevance to this reinvention effort.

Collaboration In-the-Large — Bowker, in an accompanying paper in these proceedings, has described how deeply interdisciplinary and collaborative work in the biodiversity sciences can be. As an example, the Flora of North America (FNA) project is attempting to produce a comprehensive study of all the naturally occurring species of plants in North America. Surprisingly, such a study of North American plants has never been done before. FNA is a long-term publishing project involving as many as 1000 botanists distributed across North America and Europe. The result will be 30-plus printed volumes produced by Oxford University Press and an online version of the flora. FNA is an example of one of the largest coordinated, scientific publishing activities ever funded by the National Science Foundation.

The point here is that collaboration — often among very different scientific communities — is an important feature of work in the biodiversity sciences and presents an opportunity to do fundamental research on collaborative systems that is deeply embedded in real-world activities. The major task of building robust databases in biodiversity is facilitating interdisciplinary communication — and this communication cannot just be a desired outcome, it must be designed into the data collection and representation work from the outset. Both the biodiversity and computer and information sciences domains have much to gain by paying attention to collaborative systems research in this area.

Instrumented Species Discovery — An important open question is the extent to which we might be able to instrument the discovery and monitoring of biodiversity. Think for a moment of how weather and climate prediction have been revolutionized by the capacity to detect, analyze, and inform scientists — as well as the general public — about salient attributes of the Earth's atmosphere on an ongoing, real-time basis. A similar capability for detecting and monitoring the status of biodiversity could likewise revolutionize this science.

I can only speculate about the candidate technologies that might make this possible. Certainly there is a role for mobile computing and the enhanced *in situ* collection of data about organisms in their habitats. MEMS sensors — microelectromechanical systems — offer the prospect of low-cost, high-resolution detection of a potentially unlimited range of environmental attributes, including temperatures, rainfall, chemicals, and sounds. The algorithms and software architectures required to manage dense MEMS arrays or mobile computers in exotic settings have yet to be invented, and this is quickly becoming the focus of much research.

Space-based remote sensing is entering a new era with the deployment of high-resolution optical instruments, hyperspectral sensors, and laser- and radar-based sensors. We really do not understand the full capacity of these instruments and how they might help the biodiversity community, but some interesting prospects are emerging. For example, Ritchie and Olff [1] have developed a synthetic theory of biodiversity that predicts relations between species richness and productivity more effectively than previous models. Their mathematical rules are based entirely on spatial scaling laws and notions about how organisms acquire resources in space. Is this a potential "hook" that would allow us to measure the carrying capacity — or perhaps even the species richness — of an ecosystem from space? After all, we can compute the fractal dimension of landscapes using satellite data. It is too early to tell, but clearly new areas of investigation are opening up that could have profound implications for the enterprise.

Computational Exploration — Biology is a science strongly influenced by historical events. Unlike much of physics or chemistry, one cannot predict what happens at time $t+1$ by knowing only the conditions at time t. Evolution and environmental history impose "ecological memory" on living communities, introduce time lags in ecological processes, and constrain the trajectories of community composition in ways that are poorly understood. Ecological memory is encoded in the genetic structure of species and the current structure of biological communities. It affects how communities assemble, and it may affect the likelihood that they can be restored once dissembled. These attributes reveal a fundamental property of living systems: they are computational systems, encoding and storing data and programs in biopolymers (such as DNA) and executing the genetic algorithm against elements in a complex biotic and abiotic context.

The implication here, I believe, is that the dominate mode of discovery for the biodiversity enterprise must increasingly become model- and computation-driven. We cannot get a handle on these processes any other way, because they are simply too complex. We need a unified way of incorporating the spatial and temporal context of ecological interactions. This suggests an important role for research on artificial life systems, evolutionary computation, and adaptive and complex systems approaches to exploring biodiversity. The research opportunities here are unlimited.

5. Conclusion

In this paper, I have basically tried to make the point that the science of biodiversity is fundamentally an information science, and one worthy of special attention from the computer and information science communities because of its distinctive attributes of scale and socio-technical complexity. At almost every turn, scale, complexity, and urgency conspire to create a particularly wicked set of problems. Working on these problems will undoubtedly advance our understanding and use of information technologies, and, even more important, give us the tools to protect and manage our natural world so as to provide a stable and prosperous future.

6. References

[1] Ritche, Mark E. and Han Olff. Spatial Scaling Laws yield a Synthetic Theory of Biodiversity. *Nature* 400: 557, 1999.

[2] Schnase, John L., Meredith A. Lane, Geoffrey C. Bowker, Susan Leigh Star, and Abraham Silberschatz. Building the Next-Generation Biological-Information Infrastructure. In *Nature and Human Society: The Quest for a Sustainable World*. Washington: National Academy Press, 2000.

[3] Tilden, David. Causes, Consequences, and Ethics of Biodiversity. *Nature* 405: 208, 2000.

[4] Wilson, Edward O. *The Diversity of Life.* Cambridge: Belknap Press, 1992.

Biodiversity Informatics Infrastructure:

An Information Commons for the Biodiversity Community

Gladys A. Cotter

U.S. Geological Survey
300 National Center
Reston, VA   20192
USA
gladys_cotter@usgs.gov

Barbara T. Bauldock

U.S. Geological Survey
300 National Center
Reston, VA   20192
USA
barbara_bauldock@usgs.gov

Abstract

This paper provides an overview of efforts to create an informatics infrastructure for the biodiversity community.   A vast amount of biodiversity information exists, but no comprehensive infrastructure is in place to provide easy assess and effective use of this information. The advent of modern information technologies provides a foundation for a remedy. Biodiversity informatics infrastructures are being called for at national, regional, and global levels, and plans are in place to coordinate these efforts to ensure interoperability. The paper reviews some essential requirements and some challenges related to building this infrastructure.

1. Introduction

A vast amount of information on biological resources (plants, animals, and ecosystems) exists throughout the world today.   It has been collected by government agencies, universities, museums, and private organizations. This information is diverse and includes biological specimens, journal articles, videos, numeric data, satellite images, and audio files. Some of the information such as biological specimens were collected by early explorers and scientists and are maintained in natural history museums. Journal articles exist in libraries throughout the world, often in paper format. Other information such as numeric and visual representations are maintained at high performance computer facilities and are fully digitized. A significant portion of the information remains in the hands of the scientists who originated it. The fact that biodiversity information is collected and stored in diverse forms, formats and locations has proved a serious obstacle to our ability to correlate and synthesize the information to create new knowledge.

The biodiversity information which exists today has economic value and represents an investment of billions of dollars worldwide. Unfortunately, a comprehensive infrastructure that would allow this information to be easily accessed and effectively used so that society can reap a return on its investment does not yet exist. Often, people who need help to answer a question or solve a problem are unable to ascertain if the information required even exists. Therefore questions go unanswered, problems go unsolved, or money is wasted re-collecting information that already exists but is not accessible.

The advent of the Internet and the World Wide Web has created a technological environment in which it is possible to link people and information in unprecedented ways. We have the opportunity to apply this technology to develop an information infrastructure that will enable us to unlock the wealth of biodiversity information that exists around the world. We can in effect choose to create an interoperable global biodiversity information "Commons" that will bring together people, information, and analytical capabilities that can accelerate the process of knowledge discovery, deliver answers to natural resource management and research questions, and affect the quality of life on earth for the good.

Proceedings of the 26th International Conference on Very Large Databases, Cairo, Egypt, 2000

2. Community Calls to Action – National, Regional, Global

The opportunities that technological advancements have laid before us to create a biodiversity information infrastructure complement the calls to action from different sectors of the community to create this infrastructure. In 1996, the Megascience Forum of the Organization for Economic Cooperation and Development (OECD) established a Working Group on Biological Informatics to further the vision of interconnected, interoperable, global biological informatics. Biodiversity informatics was a prime focus of this Group which recommended the establishment of a Global Biodiversity Information Facility (GBIF). GBIF will comprise the expertise and products of efforts going on in all participating countries and will facilitate the development of standards including an electronic catalog of the names of known organisms.

Also globally, the United Nations' Convention on Biological Diversity has established a Clearing-House Mechanism (CHM) on the World Wide Web, which provides an opportunity for nations to share biodiversity information and technology.

We hear calls to action at hemispheric levels as well. For example, development of an Inter-American Biodiversity Information Network (IABIN) is an initiative resulting from the 1996 Summit of the Americas on Sustainable Development. IABIN's goal is to promote greater coordination among Western Hemisphere countries in the collection, communication, and exchange of biodiversity information to support decision-making and education.

At a sub-hemispheric level, groups of countries are getting together as in the case of the North American Biodiversity Information Network (NABIN), an initiative of the North American Commission for Environmental Cooperation which seeks to promote open access to biodiversity data and collaborations among scientists.

At the national level, national academies of science, presidential committees, and natural resource groups are calling for a commitment to build a biodiversity information infrastructure. In its report, "Teaming with Life: Investing in Science to Understand and Use America's Living Capital," the President's Committee of Advisors on Science and Technology (PCAST) stated:

> The economic prosperity and, indeed, the fate of human societies are inextricably linked to the natural world. Because of this, information about biodiversity and ecosystems is vital to a wide range of scientific, educational, commercial, and governmental uses. Unfortunately, most of this information exists in forms that are not easily used. ... There exists no comprehensive technological or organizational framework that allows this information to be readily accessed or used effectively by scientists, resource managers, policy makers, or other potential client communities [1].

The Committee called for the development of a next-generation National Biological Information Infrastructure (NBII), the goal of which would be to promote the use of biodiversity and ecosystems information in management decisions, in education and research, and by the public. Similar activities are occurring in countries around the globe.

Perhaps most encouraging are the community-building activities that are coming from the biodiversity community itself – the universities and non-governmental organizations, the museums, the government agencies, the private sector, and the public citizens who have started working together and who share a vision to make the biodiversity informatics Commons a reality.

3. Essential Elements for the Global Commons

In order to implement this global "Commons" for the biodiversity information community, we need to work together on several critical, interrelated pieces. Content – the biodiversity information itself – is the most important piece. Schemas for organizing available information, technologies to enable its use, and rules of conduct to protect its value are the other components which must be addressed collaboratively to realize the benefits of our global association.

3.1 Content

Biodiversity information exits in both digital and non-digital forms and is held in a variety of institutions and agencies worldwide. The first step in building content for our commons, then, is to discover what data and information are already available in the community and to work toward incorporating them into the knowledge base. As the integrated knowledge base grows, gaps in the information required to support biodiversity activities will become apparent. These gaps then become challenges to the research community and may help individuals and institutions direct their research initiatives to areas of potential high return on research dollar investment. Knowing where our knowledge or understanding falls short may also suggest areas where multi-institutional collaborations on a particular biodiversity issue might be most appropriate.

3.2 Knowledge Organization

Knowledge flowing into our biodiversity commons must be organized in useful ways to facilitate the discovery and retrieval of a comprehensive selection of information pertinent to the question at hand. Library science has a long history of the development and maintenance of schemas for the organization of information, and the lessons of that discipline should guide us as we sort through, discuss, and choose for adoption the various ways of organizing electronically accessible information.

Biodiversity information can be organized thematically, such as by taxon, issue, etc., or geospatially, such as by region or ecosystem. It can be organized chronologically, to show trends over time or provide historical snapshots. Fortunately, digital technologies allow us to store information in ways such that all of these organizational approaches can be applied to our knowledge space concurrently, allowing users to select the schema most appropriate for their requirements.

Knowledge organization requires tools to facilitate information discovery and retrieval. Controlled vocabularies in general, and standard taxonomies in particular, allow information seekers to "speak the same language" – literally – as information providers, which increases retrieval precision. Much work remains to be done, however, in the area of thesauri development to agree on a set of terms to describe the various parameters central to discussions of biodiversity and to provide multi-lingual access to those terms.

Standard taxonomies, including scientific names, synonyms, common names in various languages, and information about the authorities on which the standard taxonomies are based, are central to the identification and retrieval of biodiversity information by species. IT IS, the Integrated Taxonomic Information System, is an example of such a standard system. ITIS was first developed by a group of U.S. Federal government agencies for internal use. Now ITIS has been expanded to include other institutions and agencies as partners. The system has been incorporated into biodiversity networks in Canada and Mexico and represents a substantial contribution to the Species 2000 global taxonomic information system initiative.

Metadata provide standardized descriptions of the biodiversity databases, datasets, and information products in our knowledge base. These descriptions convey concisely such things as subject matter; how, when, where, and by whom the data were collected; how to access the database or information product; and person(s) or institution(s) to contact for more information. Use of a consistent metadata format allows users to compare and contrast different distributed data and information sources quickly and easily and to locate and choose those which best meet their needs.

We must examine metadata standards currently in use and determine or develop a recommended standard for biodiversity information. Because much of the information of interest to the biodiversity community is geo-referenced, our community should build on the standards work of the spatial data community. In the United States, for example, we have developed a biological extension to the Geospatial Metadata Content Standard developed by the Federal Geographic Data Committee. This standard, including the biological extension, is currently being considered for adoption by the International Standards Organization.

3.3 Information Technology Tools

Information technologies are advancing rapidly and provide us with many of the capabilities required to implement our vision. Information technology provides us with tools to digitize information and store it in accessible systems; discover and retrieve data pertinent to the issue at hand; analyze data from diverse, distributed databases; input these data to decision-support, modelling or other management systems; and promote interaction among colleagues through collaboratoria, Internet-based communications facilities which enable discussion, document development and revision, and decision-making in real time. The biodiversity community must assess the IT tools available and customize them as necessary for our particular requirements. We must also develop an IT research agenda for the biodiversity infrastructure. Both of these efforts would be most effectively addressed through multi-institutional and multi-national collaborations.

3.4 Rules of Conduct

A final aspect which we must address collectively might be termed "Rules of Conduct" for the community. Digital technologies allow data and information to come together in ways not previously possible. Internet-based technologies enable not only the scientific community but the global public at large, sometimes a mixed blessing. Open access is a fundamental principle in most biodiversity networking initiatives; however, in many areas, some agreement must be made concerning the level of detail of information which will be generally available through our networks. Locations of endangered species is an obvious example.

We must also seek concurrence on rules for the protection of privacy, intellectual property rights, and the value of information, and we must consider the impact of existing and proposed national and international law touching on these areas. In many instances, these legal and institutional issues may be greater barriers to information-sharing than the technical issues.

4. Complementary Networking Initiatives

Implementation of a global biodiversity information Commons as envisioned here is already underway through a series of nested networking initiatives. The "nest" of initiatives in which an institution participates varies from country to country or region to region. In the United States., biodiversity informatics is included in our NBII effort. NBII has been developed through collaboration among Federal, state and local governments, academic institutions, non-governmental organizations, inter-agency groups, and commercial enterprises to provide increased access to the nation's biological resources.

4.1 NBII's Role in Other Networking Initiatives

The NBII then is the U.S. component in regional and global information networks including NABIN, IABIN, CHM, and the proposed GBIF. Each of these multi-national network initiatives had a different genesis, but all share common principles: open access to scientifically credible biodiversity information; interoperable data systems linking geographically dispersed resources; data ownership remaining with the data providers; and respect for intellectual property rights in the data.

By recognizing the shared goals and by designating the NBII as a focal point for these various initiatives, the United States seeks to ensure complementary development and elimination of duplicate effort in the creation of information, tools and policies relevant to all of these initiatives. Furthermore, through collaboration across networks, scarce network implementation resources can be leveraged to meet the objectives of more than a single initiative.

4.2 The "Species Analyst" Collaboration

An excellent example of such a multi-network initiative is the development and promulgation of Species Analyst, an Internet-based query system (search engine) which accesses dozens of databases compiled by universities, natural history museums, conservation organizations, and other groups and agencies. Species Analyst, developed by the University of Kansas, allows concurrent searching of databases of specimen information from collections located throughout the world and subsequent analysis of these data using computer applications such as Microsoft Excel and ESRI's ArcView GIS. The system will be linked to the San Diego Supercomputer Center, which will be able to perform predictive and geospatial analysis of the data. The resulting distributional maps are used to make educated guesses about the whereabouts of rare or poorly known species, or where an invasive species might gain a foothold in a new area.

The Species Analyst began as a project of NABIN, sponsored by the Commission on Environmental Cooperation. The U.S. National Science Foundation provided funding for the development of a prototype and additional enhancements. The University of Kansas and the World Bank subsequently provided funding to train IABIN participants on the tool, thereby expanding its use from North America to the Western Hemisphere. An effort is now underway to apply Species Analyst to a multi-national invasive species project. Efforts continue to recruit additional institutional participants worldwide. The Species Analyst success story shows the value of coordination and collaboration within the community.

5. The Way Ahead – Two Success Factors

New information technologies will enable us to accomplish extraordinary things by working in a distributed but coordinated information paradigm. But realization of the vision for a global biodiversity Commons is dependent upon the continuing desire of the biodiversity community to bring it into being. It is critical that the community stay together, keep growing, express its requirements with a unified voice, and develop innovative partnerships among all sectors of society to work toward this common goal.

Funding for this venture is also a critical need and must be identified soon. Although some requirements can be met through partnerships among existing efforts, there is a need for new funding targeted at priority gaps in content, technology, and infrastructure identified by the community. The PCAST report referenced earlier points out that the investment needed to create a biodiversity information infrastructure is small compared to expenditures on data gathering, and that failure to create the infrastructure will result in missed opportunities to generate new knowledge from existing data. The recent conference summary, "Weaving a Web of Wealth, Biological Informatics for Industry, Science, and Health," asserts that biological informatics can result in the generation of wealth [2]. But the investment must precede the harvest.

Although there is a growing acknowledgement in many sectors of society that a biodiversity information infrastructure needs to be funded, the debate continues on how, when, and from where this funding will appear. We must work together to articulate and demonstrate through our fledgling efforts toward a biodiversity informatics Commons the value that such a capability will provide not only to scientists and researchers but to decision-makers, educators, and the general public, those constituencies to which our potential funding sources are accountable. By supporting the efforts of the biodiversity informatics community, those most directly responsible for stewardship of the earth's natural resources support their own efforts to preserve and protect the living capital of the planet.

6. References

[1] President's Committee of Advisors on Science and Technology, PCAST Panel on Biodiversity and Ecosystems. *Teaming with Life: Investing in Science to Understand and Use America's Living Capital.* Washington, DC: Executive Office of the President of the United States, 1988.

[2] Lane, Meredith. *Biological Informatics: Weaving a Web of Wealth for Industry Science and Health.* Canberra: Australian Academy of Science, 1998.

A Database Platform for Bioinformatics

Sandeepan Banerjee

Oracle Corporation
500 Oracle Pkwy
Redwood Shores, CA
USA
sabanerj@us.oracle.com

Abstract

In recent years, new developments in genetics have generated a lot of interest in genomic and proteomic data, investing international significance (and competition) in the fledgling discipline of bioinformatics. Researchers in pharmaceutical and biotech companies have found that database products can bring a wide range of relevant technologies to bear on their problems. Benefiting from a number of new technology enhancements, Oracle has emerged as a popular platform for pharmaceutical knowledge management and bioinformatics.

We look at four powerful technologies that show promise for solving hitherto intractable problems in bioinformatics: the extensibility architecture to store gene sequence data natively and perform high-dimensional structure-searches in the database; warehousing technologies and data mining on genetic patterns; data integration technologies to enable heterogeneous queries across distributed biological sources, and internet portal technologies that allow life sciences information to be published and managed across intranets and the internet.

1. Introduction

As the mapping of the human genome draws to a close, there is increasing realization that the 'life' sciences are dependent, as never before, on computing. The atlas of the human genome promises to revolutionize medical

practice and biological research for the next millennium: all human genes will eventually be found, accurate diagnostics will be developed for all heritable diseases, animal models for human disease research will be more easily developed, and cures developed for many diseases. Many of these developments will occur, not inside test-tubes in biologists' laboratories, but on high-performance computing platforms, with massive storage systems to store genomic data, databases to search through the data, identifying similarities and patterns, as well as integration software to unify the slices of knowledge developed at globally distributed institutions.

The primary goal of the public and private genomic projects is to make a series of descriptive diagrams maps of each human chromosome at increasingly finer resolutions [1]. This involves dividing the chromosomes into smaller fragments that can be isolated, and ordering these fragments to correspond to their respective locations on the chromosomes. After ordering is completed, the next step is to determine the sequence of bases A,T, C & G in each fragment. Then, various regions of the sequenced chromosomes are to be annotated with what is known of their function. Finally differences in sequences between individuals may be catalogued on a global scale. Correlating sequence information with genetic linkage data and disease gene research will reveal the molecular basis for human variation. Any two individuals differ in about one-thousandth of their genetic material, i.e. about 3 million base pairs [1]. The global population is now about 6 billion. A catalogue of all sequence differences, which will be necessary in the future to find all rare and complex diseases, would run to 18×10^{15} entries.

2. Database Support for Sequence Data

As the sequencing community sharply increases its activities to pile up As, Ts, Cs and Gs, it is clear that the goals above need industrial-strength database products as well as innovations in underlying database technologies. Databases have, so far, been used largely for managing simple business data – numbers, characters or dates. Few databases have had a native ability to deal with complex data -- whether multimedia, text, spatial data, or gene sequence data. Most databases find it hard to handle high-dimensional data, such as performing similarity queries on gene sequences, spatial queries on locations, or 'looks-like' queries on images. For the specific case of genomic data, we should be able to search for:

- Properties: What are the human sequences that are longer than 10 Kb, and have a specific annotation associated with them?
- Structural similarity: Given a particular sequence, what other sequences resembling this sequence exist in the database – for this organism and for other organisms? (The 'resemble' operation must be able to find sequences that share, say, only isolated regions of similarity, and also score the returned results.)
- Location: Given a gene or a sequence, what are the neighbouring genes/sequences?

Unless databases can treat complex data natively, specialized applications have to be used as custom middle-tiers to perform sequence searches or spatial searches. BLAST (Basic Local Alignment Search Tool) [2] is a set of similarity search programs that can apply a heuristic algorithm to detect relationships between sequences, and rank the 'hits' statistically. However, such loosely integrated specialty middle-tiers have several disadvantages: applications become too large, too complex, and far too custom-built. Even though these mid-tier products can exploit special algorithms to manipulate complex data, they run outside the database server, causing performance to degrade as interactions with the database increase.

Further, optimizations across data sources cannot be performed efficiently. Since BLAST-like servers know nothing about textual annotations, one cannot search for similarity AND annotation efficiently. For example, given a (pseudo) query *'Find the names of all sequences where GappedSearch('IKDLLDTTLVLVNAI++LSS D') returns a score less than 2, AND any annotation associated with the sequence contains the keyword 'Swiss Protein''*, we do not know which of the two clauses in the predicate is more restrictive, and therefore important to evaluate first during query execution.

Finally, each specialty server comes with its own utilities and practices for administering data, making the overall system hard to manage. Since processing for complex data is beset with problems when done outside the database, we have to ask what the best way is to support specific types of complex data inside databases. As it is not clear what constitutes a full set of such types, it seems inefficient to provide, on an ad hoc basis, support for each new type that comes along. In other words, unless all possible complex types can be accommodated in some comprehensive architecture, they will continue to be devilled by issues in re-engineering, cross-type query optimization, uniform programmatic access and so on.

3. Extending Databases

We approached the complex data problem from the standpoint of creating such an architecture. Databases must be made inherently *extensible* to be able to efficiently handle various rich, application-domain-specific complex data types. Extensibility is the ability to provide support for any user-defined datatype (structured or unstructured) efficiently without having to re-architect the DBMS. Such types – which can be plugged into the database to extend its capabilities for specific domains – are also called *data cartridges* [3].

An extensible database system needs support for:

- user-defined types -- the ability to define new datatypes corresponding to domain entities like sequence,
- user-defined operators -- like `Resembles()` or `Distance()` to add domain-specific operators that can be called from SQL,
- domain-specific indexing - support for indexes specific to genomic data , spatial data etc., which can be used to speed the query, and
- optimizer extensibility - intelligent ordering of query predicates involving user-defined types, especially for multi-domain queries.

3.1 User-defined Types

The Oracle Type System (OTS) [4] provides a high-level SQL-based interface for defining types. The behaviour for these types can be implemented in Java, C/C++ or PL/SQL. The DBMS automatically provides the low-level infrastructure services needed for input-output, heterogeneous client-side access for new data types, and optimisations for data transfers between the application and the database and on. Two central constructs in OTS are *object types*, whose structure is fully known to the database, and *opaque types* whose structure is not.

An *object type*, distinct from native SQL data types such as NUMBER, VARCHAR or DATE, is user-defined. It specifies both the underlying persistent data (called 'attributes' of the object type) and the related behaviour ('methods' of the object type). Object types are used to extend the server's modelling capabilities. You can use object types to make better models of complex entities in the real world by binding data attributes to semantic behaviour. There can be one or more attributes in an object type. The attributes of an object type can be the native data types, other object types, 'large objects' or LOBs, or reference types. We also provide collections of native types, objects types, LOBs or references. Object types can have methods to access and manipulate their attributes, and these methods can be run within the execution environment of the database server. In addition, methods can be dispatched to run outside the database. With OTS, it is possible to (i) create database abstractions for sequence, gene, annotation etc., (ii) program behaviour for these abstractions – say `Size()` for a sequence, (iii) create collections of sequence to yield aggregations like chromosome and so on.

The *opaque type* mechanism provides a way to create new fundamental types in the database whose internal structure is not known to the DBMS. The internal structure is modelled in some 3GL language (such as C). The database provides storage for the type instances. Type methods or functions that access the internal structure are external methods or external procedures in the same 3GL language used to model the structure.

The benefit of opaque types arises in cases where there is an external data model and behaviour available to store or manipulate sequences – say as a C library. For instance, object models for genomic use have been devised as part of the Life Sciences Research Domain Special Interest Group (LSR-SIG) under the Object Management Group (OMG) umbrella [5]. Implementing these objects as opaque types enables them to store genomic data persistently in the database, but at the same time call on behaviour implemented external to the database for purposes of insert, updates, deletes or queries on the data.

3.2 User-defined operators

Typically, databases provide a set of pre-defined operators to operate on built-in data types. Operators can be related to arithmetic (`+`, `-`, `*`, `/`), comparison (`=`, `>`, `<`), Boolean logic (`NOT`, `AND`, `OR`), string comparison (`LIKE`) and so on. We have also found it useful to add to Oracle the capability to define domain-specific operators. For example, it is possible to define a `Resembles()` operator for comparing sequences. The actual implementation of the operator is left to the user, and he can choose to bind them to functions, type methods, packages, external library routines and so on. User-defined operators can be invoked anywhere built-in operators can be used — i.e., wherever expressions can occur. User-defined operators can be used in the select list of a `SELECT` command, the condition of a `WHERE` clause, the `ORDER BY` clause, and the `GROUP BY` clause. After a user has defined a new operator, it can be used in SQL statements like any other built-in operator. For example, if the user defines a new operator

`Contains()` which takes as input a decoded DNA fragment and a particular sequence, returning `TRUE` if the fragment contains the specified sequence, then we can write a SQL query as

```
SELECT ID FROM DNATABLE WHERE
Contains(fragment,
'GCCATAGACTACA');
```

This ability to increase the semantics of the query language by adding domain-specific operators is akin to extending the query service of the database.

When an operator is invoked, the evaluation of the operator is transformed to the execution of one of the functions bound to it. Just as databases use indexes to efficiently evaluate some built-in operators (a B+Tree index is typically used to evaluate comparison operators), in Oracle user-defined domain indexes (see below) can be used to efficiently evaluate user-defined operators.

3.3 Extensible Indexing

Typically, databases have supported a few standard access methods (B+Trees, Hash Indexes) on the set of built-in data types. As we add the ability to store complex domain data, there arises a need for indexing such data using domain-specific indexing techniques. For simple data types such as integers and small strings, all aspects of indexing can be easily handled by the base database. For gene sequences, however, we would need special indexes to efficiently perform 3-D structural comparison, similarity or substructure search, 'distance' evaluation and so on.

The framework to develop new index types is based on the concept of cooperative indexing where a user-supplied implementations and the Oracle server cooperate to build and maintain indexes for complex types such as genetic, text or spatial data. The user is responsible for defining the index structure, maintaining the index content during load and update operations, and searching the index during query processing. The index structure itself can either be stored in the Oracle database, or externally (e.g. in operating system files), though most implementers find it desirable to have the physical storage of domain indexes within the database for reasons of concurrency control and recovery.

To this end, Oracle introduces the concept of an Indextype. The purpose of an Indextype is to enable efficient search and retrieval functions for complex domains such as text, spatial, image, and genomics. An Indextype is analogous to the sorted or bit-mapped index types that can be found built into the Oracle server, with the exception that the former depends on user implementation.

With such 'extensible' indexing, the user:

- Defines the structure of the domain index as a new Indextype
- Stores the index data either inside the Oracle database (in the form of tables) or outside the Oracle database
- Manages, retrieves, and uses the index data to evaluate user queries.

In the absence of such user-defined domain index capabilities, many applications -- such as the aforementioned BLAST -- maintain separate memory- or file-based indexes for complex data. A considerable amount of code and effort is required to:

- maintain consistency between external indexes and the related database data
- support compound or multi-domain queries (involving tabular values, or data from other domains)
- manage the system (backup, recovery, allocate storage, etc.) with multiple forms of persistent storage (files and databases)

By supporting extensible indexes, the Oracle server significantly reduces the level of effort needed to develop solutions involving high-performance access to complex data types.

3.4 Extensible Optimizer

A typical optimizer generates an *execution plan* for a SQL statement. Consider a SELECT statement. The execution plans for such a statement includes (i) an access method for each table in the FROM clause, and (ii) an ordering (called the join order) of the various tables in the FROM clause. System-defined access methods include indexes, hash clusters, and table scans. The optimizer chooses a plan by generating a set of join orders or permutations, computing the cost of each, and selecting the one with the lowest cost.

For each table in the join order, the optimizer estimates the cost of each possible access method using built-in algorithms. Databases collect and maintain statistics about the data in tables – such as the number of distinct values, the minimum and the maximum, histograms of distribution and so on, to help the optimizer in its estimations.

As discussed earlier, extensible indexing functionality enables users to define new operators, index types, and domain indexes. For such user-defined operators and domain indexes, the extensible optimizer gives developers control over the three main inputs used by the optimizer: statistics, selectivity, and cost. The extensibility of the optimiser lies in the user's ability to collect domain-

specific statistics, and, based on such statistics, predict the selectivity and cost of each domain-specific operation. The user's inputs are 'rolled up' with the rest of the optimizer's heuristics to generate the optimal execution plan.

Whenever a domain index is to be 'analysed', a call is made to a user-specified statistics collection function. The representation and meaning of these user-collected statistics is not known to the database, but are to be used later by the user in estimating the cost or selectivity of a domain operation. In addition to domain indexes, user-defined statistics collection functions are also supported for individual columns of a table and data types (whether built-in or user-defined).

The *selectivity* of a predicate or a clause is the fraction of rows in a table that will be chosen by the clause or predicate; it is used to determine the optimal join order. By default, the optimizer uses a built-in algorithm to estimate the selectivity of selection and join predicates. However, since algorithm has no intelligence about functions, type methods, or user-defined operators, the presence of these may result in a poor choice of join order – i.e. a very expensive execution plan. So, if we were to build a domain index for sequences and implement a Contains() operator based on this index, we would also specify the selectivity of the operator. This could be based on the arguments it receives (a very long sequence is likely quite selective, whereas a short sequence like 'GCT' is not selective at all), or on the actual distribution of sequence data based on analysed statistics. Thereafter, if a user executed a query of the form

```
SELECT * FROM DNATABLE WHERE
Contains(fragment,
'GCCATAGACTACA') AND id > 100;
```

then the selectivity of the first clause of predicate could computed by invoking the user supplied implementation, and an execution plan generated to determine whether the Contains operator should be applied before the > operator or vice-versa.

A similar consideration applies to *cost*. The optimizer also estimates the cost of various access paths while choosing an optimal plan. For example, it may compute the cost of using an index as well as a full table scan in order to be able choose between the two. However, for user-defined domain indexes with user-specified internal structre, cost cannot be estimated easily. For proper optimization, the cost model in Oracle has been extended to enable users to define costs for domain indexes, user-defined functions, type methods etc. The user-defined costs can be in the form of default costs that the optimizer simply looks up, or can be full-blown cost functions based on user-collected statistics, which the optimizer calls at run time.

4. Mining Sequence Data

The current approach for finding genes has a large experimental component. Any small increase in the accuracy of computer classification of genes can result in substantial time and cost savings. Oracle has developed a suite of software tools that analyse large collections of data to discover new patterns and forecast relationships [6]. This process of sifting through enormous databases to extract hidden information is called 'data mining'. Mining sequence data can help discover relationships between genes, discover gene expression, discover drugs based on functional information and so on. Oracle's data-mining tool -- Darwin -- has been utilized for bioinformatics. Darwin was built to address the terabyte databases found in genomics databases. In fact, various parallelism technologies built into Darwin ensure that there is no limit to the size of data it can mine. Darwin currently provides classification and regression Trees (C&RT), neural networks, and k-nearest neighbours algorithms, k-means Naïve-Bayes and enhanced clustering (self-organizing maps or SOM) algorithms.

A simple case of mining genetic data could be to classify cancers based solely on gene expression. Classifiers are first trained on the genes in a training set, and then applied to the remaining genes to assign them to specific clusters. Thence, Darwin's algorithms can be used to help identify new clusters. This suggests a general stratagem for predicting cancer classes for other types of cancer, creating new biological knowledge [7].

Another use of mining relates to predicting which sections of a piece of DNA are 'active' and which are not. Chromosomes have coding sequences (exons), interspersed with non-coding sequences (introns.) It has recently been discovered through mining that a non-linear correlation statistic for DNA sequences, called the Average Mutual Information (AMI) [8], is very effective at distinguishing exons from introns. The AMI is a non-linear function based on a vector of 12 frequencies each dependent on the positions of the bases A, C, T & G. The inductive process of mining helps us arrive at such complex insights, which deductive analyses have little hope of unearthing.

When terabytes of data are involved, traditional data mining relies on analysts trying to guess which small subset of the information in a database is relevant. Because of their limited capacity for data, traditional methods often operate on only 1-2% of the data available in every record. Yet discarded variables often contain key information: correlations that aren't obvious, patterns one wouldn't expect, or significant fluctuations that are normally overshadowed by larger trends. Darwin, on the other hand, can afford to look at every bit of data in each

record because of its parallel architecture. This architecture is shown in Fig 1.

Darwin's architecture is based on a distributed-memory SPMD (single program multiple data) paradigm. This shared-nothing approach facilitates scalability in performance by reducing inter-processor communications and making optimal use of local memory and disk resources. The processors work on their local section of the dataset and all inter-processor communication is achieved by the use of a message-passing library called MPI, which provides the basic programming and process model. The main architectural component of the server is a unified data access and manipulation library: StarData, which provides most of the data access and transformation infrastructure that supports the machine learning modules StarTree, StarNet, StarMatch etc. A

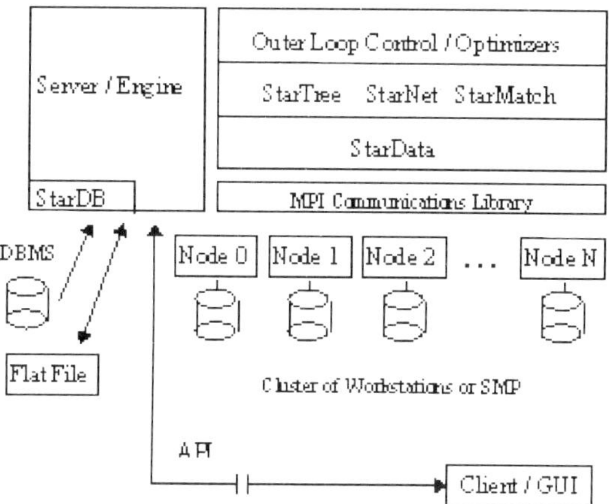

Figure 1: Darwin Data Mining Architecture

toolset provides a client/API to support general or application specific graphical user interfaces (GUIs). The API also allows the toolset to be integrated with, or embedded into, other products. This API can also be called from the member functions of object- or opaque-types, making it possible to integrating the data mining functionality with the data modelling aspects.

Mining of sequence data is still in its infancy because the methodologies are much more involved, and because a large number of tools have to be integrated before progress can be made. However, this area has a potential of yielding rich dividends in the years to come.

5. Integrating Heterogeneous Data

Not all bioinformatics data will exist in the same database. Sequence data for the human genome is likely to end up spread across a handful of public or private databases. Sequence data for other organisms will also be distributed, across hundreds of institutions. Annotations to this data will make it change and grow all the time.

Pharmaceutical companies will have their own private data. Researchers everywhere will like to integrate all sorts of heterogeneous data sources.

Oracle's 'gateway' technologies make it possible for informatics applications to access and manipulate non-Oracle system data. Researchers can query any number of non-Oracle systems from an Oracle database in a heterogeneously distributed environment. Generic connectivity enables connectivity using industry standards such as ODBC and OLEDB. Gateways extend distributed capabilities to a heterogeneous environment – so distributed transactions as well as distributed queries, joins, inserts, deletes can be performed easily. Gateways make the data's location, SQL dialect, network and operating system transparent to the end user, making it easy to implement in a heterogeneous environment.

6. Portal Technologies

While it is important to query on sequences, mine sequence data and so on, it is also important for database platforms to support the dispersion of information over the Internet and intranets. Oracle has emerged as a crucial 'back-end' for commercial web sites – because of new features that enable records to be published directly to browsers as dynamic HTML or XML, server-based Java execution, support for web-based secure transactions, connection pooling etc., coupled with traditional high-availability, scalability and reliability features. While portals related to genomics and bioinformatics need many of the features that commercial horizontal or vertical industry portals do, there are some additional requirements in this domain that are worth discussing.

6.1 'Soft Goods' Sales

Bioinformatics marketplaces buy and sell information rather than 'hard goods'. Portals in this area must be able to measure the usage of soft goods (e.g. the number and complexity of queries against a sequence database, or amount of data downloaded by a subscriber.) Oracle provides a wide array of server-based features as well as application packages to enable soft goods transactions over the Internet.

6.2 Visualization

It is not only important for a bioinformatics portal to serve sequence, aggregate or annotation data, but it is also important for the user to be able to visualize such data. Oracle enables the publishing of graphical data in formats such as the Vector Markup Language (VML) that can be used to display sequences. It is possible to generate XML from the database, and transform this to VML using XSL transformation capabilities. It is also possible to display aggregated or processed data – say scatter plots resulting

from mining – as charts or plots using a number of popular charting packages.

6.3 Security & Access Control

Organizations searching against sequence stores want to protect not only the results of their queries, but also the nature of queries themselves. To this end, Oracle provides comprehensive PKI-based security to protect information on data as well as user-sessions.

7. Acknowledgements

Over the years a number of individuals at Oracle have contributed to the gradual building of this platform. Anil Nori, Vishu Krishnamurthy, Jayanta Banerjee, S. Muralidhar, Jags Srinivasan, Ravi Murthy, Nipun Agarwal, Seema Sundara and others have contributed to database extensibility. Pablo Tamayo and others have set the direction of mining sequences. Benny Souder and others have created the 'gateway' and data integration technologies.

8. References

[1]   Human Genome Program, *Primer on Molecular Genetics*, Washington D.C, U.S. Department of Energy, 1992.
See http://www.ornl.gov/hgmis/publicat/primer/intro.html
[2]   Altschul, S.F., Gish, W., Miller, W., Myers, E.W. & Lipman, D.J, Basic local alignment search tool, *J. Mol. Biol.* 215:403-410, 1990.
See http://www.ncbi.nlm.nih.gov/BLAST/
[3]   Oracle Corp., *Oracle8i Data Cartridge Developer's Guide: Release 8.1.5   (Part No.   A68002-01)* Redwood Shores, Oracle Corp., 1999.
[4]   Oracle Corp., *Oracle8i Concepts: Release 8.1.5 (Part No. A67781-01)* Redwood Shores, Oracle Corp., 1999.
[5]   Life Sciences Research Group, Genomic Maps RFP, Philadelphia, Object Management Group, 1999.
See http://lsr.lbl.gov/
[6]   Oracle Corp., *Darwin: Release 3.6.1   (Part No. A83710-01)* Redwood Shores, Oracle Corp., 2000.
[7]   T.R. Golub, D.K. Slonim, P. Tamayo, C. Huard, M. Gaasenbeek, J.P. Mesirov, H. Coller, H. Loh, J.R. Downing, Molecular Classification of Cancer: Class Discovery and Class Prediction by Gene Expression Monitoring, *Science, Oct 15 1999:531-537*, 1999. M.A. Caligiuri, C.D. Bloomfield, and E.S. Lander.
[8]   I. Grosse, K. Marx, S. Buldyrev, G. Grinstein, H. Herzel, P. Hoffman, A. Li, C. Meneses, and H.E. Stanley. Data Mining of Large Gene Datasets Using the Mutual Information Function. to appear in *Journal of Biomolecular Structure and Dynamics.*

Data Mining in the Bioinformatics Domain

Shalom Tsur
SurroMed, Inc.
Palo Alto, CA., USA
tsur@surromed.com

Abstract

Bioinformatics, the study and application of computational methods to life sciences data, is presently enjoying a surge of interest. The main reason for this welcome publicity is the nearing completion of the sequencing of the human genome and the anticipation that the knowledge derived from this process will have a great impact on modern medicine. The pharmaceutical industry, which expects to utilize the knowledge for new drug design, has a particular interest in bioinformatics.

The structure of data in this domain has its own characteristics which set it apart from data in other domains. While genomic data have a well-known representation as sequences taken from the {A,C,G,T} alphabet, there is no clear model for data representing the expression products of genes: proteins and higher forms of organisms e.g., cells and the multitude of forms they assume in response to environmental challenges.

Data collected at these levels of information can be often thought of as "broad": meaning that for a relatively small number of records representing biological samples, a very large number of attributes, representing measurements or observations is collected per sample. In contrast, typical data used for mining are "long" i.e., consist of a large number of records in which each record is characterized by a relatively small number of attributes.

**Proceedings of the 26th VLDB Conference,
Cairo, Egypt, 2000.**

Mining broad data presents a new and unique challenge. The presentation will elaborate on some of the issues in this domain.

1   Introduction

In the biological enterprise, biological samples e.g., blood, are collected from donors or study subjects and are subjected to an array of different measurements. These measurements can be quantitative, to determine the purity or concentration of some substance such as a protein in the sample, or can be qualitative to merely detect the presence of some substance. Measurements of the former type are referred to as assays. The process and conditions under which these samples are processed, the timing and the characterization of the participating subjects, are specified in a study or clinical protocol.

Biology draws a distinction between the *genotype* and *phenotype* of an organism. The genotype is determined by its genetic makeup and is invariant over the organism's life. The phenotype on the other hand, is determined by a set of observable characteristics of the organism that in turn, are determined by its genotype *and* by the environment. Thus, a certain protein is the expressed product of a gene. The measured concentration of this protein in the blood may be the result of a disease burden, taking a certain drug, a diet, exposure etc. The phenotype is thus a set of time varying quantities. Tracing a phenotype over time may provide a longitudinal record of e.g., the evolution of a disease and the response to a therapeutic intervention. By analogy, the code making up a software system (assuming we do not change it) would be its genotype. The dynamic execution behavior of the system, which is dependent on the code, the operating system, the input data and the user-interaction with it, would be its phenotype. It is worth noting that portions of this code may never be executed and hence, will not contribute to the dynamic behavior. Likewise, the biological genome contains large portions of DNA that are considered "junk" and seemingly do not serve any purpose.

From the clinical perspective, subjects interact with

physicians who collect their own observations on their patients. A measure of interest in this context is that of a *clinical endpoint*: a set of characteristics that directly measure how well a patient feels, functions or survives. Examples would be a patient's blood pressure, the time required to climb 5 stairs or simply, the response to the question "how do you feel?" Often these measures offer only vague and imprecise information and worse, whenever they become clearer it is often too late: the disease has advanced and at best, can be arrested at the present state, rather than having prevented it at an early stage. There is a strong need therefore to come up with better predictive information that would support the clinical practice.

Lastly, the patient him/herself is the most reliable source of information about his own wellness. Especially since the physician has only a very limited opportunity for interaction and given the constraints he operates under, is unable of forming a complete and reliable picture of the patient's health. Tools for systematically assisting patients in assessing their own health form thus an important complement to the information already collected.

The sources we mentioned here, measurements on biological samples, clinical information and patient's self-assessment define all of the characteristics required for a comprehensive determination of human phenotype. In the future, integrated data warehouses containing these sources will be created and will be used to derive knowledge of interest to a variety of different consumers: the patient herself, the physician/care giver, health insurers, the pharmaceutical industry and lastly, to the academic research community. We will elaborate on some of this knowledge in the sequel. Perhaps, the biggest payoff these integrated data will yield is that of enabling *personalized medicine*—care giving that is based on the individual's genotype and phenotype.

2 Biological Markers

According to the NIH Definitions Working Group, a Biological Marker (or Biomarker) is defined as:

> A characteristic that is measured and evaluated as an indication of normal biologic processes, pathogenic processes or pharmacological responses to therapeutic intervention

There exist today a few but well-known examples of biomarkers: elevated levels of Cholesterol (LDL, HDL) are biomarkers for Cardiovascular disease, reduced counts of CD4+ T-cells is a biomarker for HIV, and high PSA (Prostate Specific Antigen) concentration is a biomarker for Prostate Cancer. These characteristics serve only as indicators—they are not necessarily the cause of the disease. In other words, they correlate with the disease but do not form a causal link; eliminating these symptoms does not necessarily influence the course of the disease. The value of this knowledge is therefore in its predictive potential in that the characteristics can be observed a long time before the disease manifests itself to the extent it is observed by the physician in normal clinical practice. Biomarkers serve therefore as an early warning signs, which hopefully enable preventative therapeutic intervention.

Other applications of biomarkers include:

- Determine susceptibility to disease and enable early diagnosis.

- Predict disease severity and outcome

- Predict and monitor response to therapeutic interventions.

We noted that the pharmaceutical industry has a particular interest in this knowledge. The biggest problem facing this industry today is the so called "Clinical Bottleneck:" advances in modern science have created a situation in which potential leads for drugs are generated at a rate that vastly outperforms the ability to evaluate these during clinical trials. The total time from lead identification to completion of trials has therefore tremendously grown, the risk of failure is very high and today, the total cost of a successful launching of a new drug is on the order of \$M300–600. Any information that would reduce the time or the risk involved in this process is of great value to the industry and biomarkers are expected to play a critical role in this respect. They could serve to stratify patient populations i.e., classify them into smaller, better-defined sub-populations of patients suffering from some disease. A drug could then be developed for only a particular sub population. This would reduce the risk and cost involved and would ease the FDA licensing requirements that must be met.

3 Databases for Biological Information

Databases, or more appropriately data warehouses constructed to support the goals described in the previous sections, accumulate data from a multitude of different sources that are combined to represent the phenotype. For example, in the case of SurroMed Inc., a warehouse is under construction containing measurements obtained using a multitude of bioanalyis techniques: cellular assays to measure populations of cells having certain identifiable antigenic characteristics, immunoassays to measure concentrations of small molecules in the blood, and the results of mass spec measurements to obtain more information about proteins and small organic molecules in the blood. These data are combined with the responses obtained from test subjects to a detailed questionnaire assessing their state of health. A simple data model representing these sources would be:

$$phenotype(Subject, Sample, Time, C_1, \ldots, C_n:$$
$$S_1, \ldots, S_m; P_1, \ldots, P_k; H_1, \ldots, H_w)$$

where the C, S and P components represent the cellular, immunoassay and mass spec measurements respectively, obtained from *Sample* and the H region represent the health-related information obtained from *Subject*. The data are partially ordered by *Time* and represent multiple measurements obtained from the same subject over time i.e., they represent the results of longitudinal studies. A multitude of different dependencies and correlations exist between these components, often in ways that are not completely understood. The H region is essentially a long vector of categorical values representing answers to health related questions.

The model represents an array of N samples by M attributes representing measurements or observations. N is on the order of 100's and M is on the order of 1000's. In this model $M \gg N$ and furthermore, as the measurement technology develops, the ratio M/N is expected to increase rapidly. We are thus presented with a *broad data model*. This model is very different from the "typical" data set used in a mining application e.g., a set of credit card transactional records, in which the number of records is very large and the number of attributes is small. Hence $M \ll N$ and we refer to this model as a *long data model*. The model presented here forms the tip of the iceberg in the sense that the model components at this level are the results of a considerable data reduction process at lower levels during which the raw, uninterpreted measurement results were condensed into the the top level parameters. For example, tens of thousands measured cellular events are first clustered into populations and the resulting population statistics are presented at the top level. Performing this data reduction process requires deep domain expertise and the model is a summary of results spanning the biology, chemistry and the medical domains of expertise. The most challenging task is to horizontally interpret this broad model so as to infer from it information of relevance to bio markers.

4 Data Mining: Using the Phenotype for Predictive Purposes

We are interested in creating predictive models that would enable us to use a small subset of measured parameters, collected from the C, S and P regions of the model to predict the state of health of a subject. Specifically, assume that we can use the H information (responses to a detailed medical questionnaire, used for self assessment)to partition the subject population into classes. The classes will be determined by an unsupervised clustering method. Denote the vector of health responses of subject i by $\vec{H}_i$. The

distance between two response vectors $\vec{H}_i$ and $\vec{H}_j$, obtained from subjects i and j will be denoted by $d_{ij}; d_{ij} = f(\vec{H}_i, \vec{H}_j)$. The objective is to define a distance measure d such that the intra-cluster distance among responses that are "similar" is much smaller than the inter-cluster distance among responses belonging to different clusters. The quality of the clustering clearly depends on the distance measure used. Ideally, the measure maximizes some function (e.g., the average) of the inter-cluster distances and minimizes the intra-cluster distances. Thus, we seek a measure d such that:

$$min\{\frac{1}{N}\sum_{i,j} d_{ij}\} \quad i,j, \ in \ the \ same \ cluster$$

$$max\{\frac{1}{N}\sum_{i,j} d_{ij}\} \quad i,j, \ not \ in \ the \ same \ cluster$$

The method, which does not assume any a-priori knowledge about the subjects, has one drawback: there is no objective way to evaluate the quality of the clustering; we cannot determine from the clustered information how similar the state of health of respondents within the same cluster really is. Nor can we label the cluster and associate it with a known state of health. We need therefore an independent method for the verification of the results. The most promising verification method is to link the information with an electronic medical record (EMR) independently obtained about the subject from his/her physician.

Once we have a subject classification we can use it, in a supervised learning mode, to infer a classifier that uses a subset of the measurements (C, S and P regions of the model) as an input vector and which maps this input into one of the subject classes. We seek thus to learn a function $g : [X_1, \ldots, X_k] \rightarrow Y$ where $X_1, \ldots, X_k$ are taken from the measurement regions and Y is a subject class.

The learning methodology of g proceeds by dividing the data in two sets: a training set and a test set. For each of the record of the training set we associate the known subject class. We train the learning algorithm and test the result on the remaining test set. There exist a multitude of different machine learning methods, the Support Vector Machine method [Nell00] appears to be a very promising technique. Different input vectors will produce different classification results. In a broad data model like ours there is a danger of overfitting the data: using large input vectors it is easy to infer a classifier that will produce perfect results for the training points but will perform poorly for any other input data. The big issue is thus to select the smallest input vector to produce high quality classification results. This is a complex combinatorial problem. At this stage the data mining strategy sketched out here is untested and is a subject of ongoing research. It is possible that ultimately, a systematic search for the best input vector in the measurement space may be the only feasible approach to this problem.

5 Conclusion

In this short paper we have provided the background and an overview of the emerging domain of Bioinformatics. This area presents a set of new problems that hitherto have not been addressed by the data mining community and it can reasonably be assumed that these problems will become central with the rapid advances of modern biology. Given the space constraints of this paper it is impossible to provide a complete exposition of the field and therefore, only a few challenging problems, of particular interest, were exposed. Nevertheless, it is hoped that this will be sufficient to create more interest in an area that until now was largely hidden from the database community.

References

[Nell00] Nello Cristiani, John Shawe-Taylor. *Suport Vector Machines*, Cambridge University Press, 2000

DB-Prism: Integrated Data Warehouses and Knowledge Networks for Bank Controlling

Elvira Schäfer [1]   Jan-Dirk Becker [1]   Matthias Jarke [2]

[1] Global Technologies & Services, Deutsche Bank AG, Prior-Str. 11, 65936 Frankfurt, Germany

[2] GMD-FIT, Schloss Birlinghoven, 53754 Sankt Augustin, Germany

Abstract

DB-Prism is an integrated data warehouse system developed for distributed financial and management controlling (data collection, processing, and reporting) at Deutsche Bank. It combines fine-granular availability of historical data with high-actuality reporting and planning facilities. Major components of interest include an OLAP system in the Terabyte range, and a meta database responsible for the whole process from heterogeneous data selection to individual OLAP report positions and back via drill-through to the individual business activity. For these purposes, control workbenches have been developed both at the user –level and at the metadata level.

1 Introduction

The Controlling Warehouse System DB-Prism is a knowledge-driven network of database, processing, and reporting subsystems. Its full functional spectrum is currently used in the controlling of Deutsche Bank AG, the online bank DB 24 AG, and further German subsidiaries including DB Trust, DB Lübeck etc. The system is used in financial accounting, e.g. for creation of balance sheets and profit/loss statements, for information of the bank regulation agencies, and for daily internal status reports. In management accounting, the system is used e.g. for assessments of business units, business areas, and sales evaluation in the commercial banking sector.

Proceedings of the 26th International Conference on Very Large Databases, Cairo, Egypt, 2000

The DB-Prism project was motivated by challenges concerning data quality factors [WSF95], such as integrity and transparency/traceability of data. Besides a heterogeneous hardware/software landscape, different principles of modelling and aggregation of multidimensional financial data were followed, targeted to the business goals of individual business units or simply resulting from history. Rule systems were not only heterogeneous but often also hidden in program code. Moreover, data often went through different parts of various controlling systems before ending up in a report. As a consequence of this semantic heterogeneity and knowledge structures hidden both in individual transformation programs and in the overall controlling workflow paths, analysts spent a lot of time reconciling seemingly contradictory information in reports.

The main design goal of DB-Prism has therefore been to clarify this heterogeneity at the conceptual, logical, and physical level, such that integrity of the data is improved, relationships between the different data source and reporting perspectives are made explicit (thus improving transparency and traceability), and reporting as well as refreshment of data are highly efficient. This has been achieved on the one hand by capturing sophisticated domain and systems knowledge about the information network in a metadata repository, on the other by employing and tailoring an efficiently scalable multi-dimensional OLAP system. As a result, heterogeneity is now consolidated into a uniform data warehouse environment based on a uniform historical business data store.

2 DB-Prism Architecture

The system has been tuned for efficient mass data processing and fast reporting. The database is refreshed with current changes on a daily bases, as well as the client-oriented sub-data cubes and reports. Fine-granular historical data are maintained in full detail for four years. The warehouse comprises 1200 GB, of which 250 GB are base data of the controlling warehouse (GDH) stored in flat files and 150 GB in DB2 relations; note that these amounts reflect the relatively short operation history of the system and can be expected to grow further. The biggest part and the most important analysis instrument comprises 800 GB of interlinked data cubes stored as collections of sparse matrices in a multidimensional OLAP system called Matplan/b2brain [GMI00].

In the remainder of this paper, we describe the individual components of the DB-Prism architecture shown in figure 1. In the lower part of this figure, we show the basic Controlling Warehouse (GDH) which provides a common cleaned base store integrated from heterogeneous data sources, and the Controlling Workbench CBM which allows the Controller to operate on the GDH; more details can be found in section 3. In the middle of the figure on the right, we find the OLAP environment Matplan/b2brain which contains data cubes extracted and re-organised from the GDH according to various client interests, indicated by the Analyst in the middle; details are described in section 4. GDH/CBM with their underlying data sources (not shown) on the one hand, and OLAP-based analysis on the other, are interconnected in a metadata-driven manner. Metadata, defined and evolved in the CDR workbench for controlling dimensions and reports, are held in a meta database MetaDB. This is described in section 5.

In terms of the traditional data warehouse architecture, as described e.g. in [JLVV99], GDH/CBM roughly correspond to an integrated, cleaned, and historised, but not-yet-aggregated Operational Data Store, whereas Matplan/b2brain corresponds to a MOLAP warehouse and client environment. MetaDB/CDR comprise a significant enrichment of the metadata facilities available in other data warehouses, mostly due to the semantic richness and heterogeneity at the levels of concepts, logical data models, physical efficiency and safety.

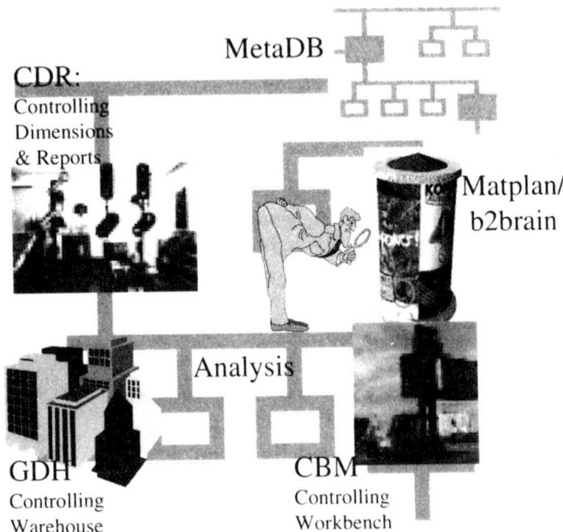

Fig. 1: DB-Prism Components

3 Basic Controlling Warehouse

As stated earlier, data from heterogeneous sources are cleaned, integrated, and historised in a Controlling Warehouse (GDH) supported by the CBM Controlling Workbench which does not only support generic versions of the above operations but also domain-specific operations for Financial and Management Controlling.

3.1 GDH (Controlling Warehouse)

GDH is based on detailed account-level information and is designed for mass data storage needs. GDH consists of five components: import, transformation, storage, access methods and export, following these key ideas:

- *Standard import and export interfaces.* Data are imported from many heterogeneous operative systems, statistics archives and controlling applications mainly through standard interface files. The delivery system does not need any special GDH know-how, as files are created exclusively by GDH modules. For calling up these modules, standardised file interfaces are available. They are generated from the MetaDB and are tailored to the individual delivery system. Also data export takes place only through standard interfaces which are supplied by GDH access.

- *Transformation and ‚cleaning‘* of import data achieve a consistent data base with *uniform data meaning.* Transformation comprises restructuring, redefinition, filtering, derivation, extrapolation and aggregation of data and data registers. Keys and data fields from heterogeneous delivery systems are harmonised, current and historical data undergo the same sort of structural processes.

- *Homogeneous storage of current and past data, methods of storage synchronised with access requests.* There are a variety of access requirements placed on the GDH: insertion of mass data, exchange and deletion of whole data groups, access to individual deals and data groups, processing of all individual deals. Such varied access requirements necessitate varying storage methods if the data availability and response times are to remain acceptable. This requires accepting redundancies in the data storage. As long as the integrity of the redundancies is inherently ensured within the system, such redundancies are useful.

- *Data access with ‚licensed‘ access modules only.* The GDH appears to the external users as a black box. Data access is provided by access functions. The encapsulation of the GDH strictly separates logical and physical aspects. This allows flexible data administration and storage with respect to extensibility of structures or changes in the physical data base.

Further important features include:

-   *Possibility of flexible and efficient repetitions.* The GDH components for import, transformation, storage and export can be efficiently and flexibly, even retroactively, repeated. A repetition is executed down to the smallest delivery inventory level and all affected warehouse levels. Repetition needs are recognised and processed automatically.
-   *Integrated workflow and control management.* The GDH programs and modules work universally through a common steering and control center. A universal MetaDB records all processing steps and status evaluations by subsequent programs. Thus, event- and result-oriented processing is achieved.
-   *Scalability.* The structures in the GDH are constructed flexibly and permit subsequent expansion (variable container concept). Structural changes can therefore be implemented relatively quickly and cost-effectively on all relevant components. It is no problem to incorporate new GDH data inventories into the GDH administration.

3.2 CBM (Controlling Workbench)

CBM is a central workbench for controllers to work on the GDH. It supports additions of relevant information, corrections, interim account shifts and bookings, and plausibility checks. CBM therefore has access to the individual accounts and topic fields of GDH.

4 Matplan/b2brain (Multi-dimensional OLAP System)

Matplan/b2brain is the multidimensional database and OLAP system within the b2brain environment developed and marketed by GMI, a software house based in Aachen, Germany [GMI00]. Matplan/b2brain allows very flexible OLAP functionality (e.g. drill down and roll up between different dimensions and aggregation levels) and provides different application modules for planning, consolidation, data mining, data integration via XML, dynamic pricing & revenue management.

In DB-Prism, Matplan/b2brain is used as the standard instrument for reporting and analysis. Being an end-user task-oriented system, interactive, complex and multidimensional analyses can be carried out.

Matplan/b2brain is based on aggregated reporting data constructed from the Controlling Warehouse (GDH). Main features in the context of DB-Prism include:

-   *full integration of Matplan/b2brain in the metadata concept.* All Matplan/b2brain report data taken from GDH are known in the meta database. Their dimensions, source, meaning, structure and composition are recorded. All metadata relevant for the structure of the multidimensional data cubes and all report definitions for data viewing are administered in the MetaDB.
-   *Drill through functionality.* The user has the ability to call up as a trace for analysis the basis for the aggregated Matplan/b2brain report data, the GDH individual deals. For a focused analysis, selection criteria for data analysis can be defined (dimensions and their characteristics, cut-offs).
-   *Scalability & storage capacity.* In the interest of unlimited analytical possibilities, it might appear useful to declare all dimensions as orthogonal, i.e. to define all data divisible intrinsically by all dimensions at all aggregation levels. However, this would require a storage capacity of 8.56×10^{26} cells; all the computers in the world would be insufficient. For this reason, there are several interlinked data cubes of various dimensions and scales. These data cubes constitute a logical hypercube such that all possibilities of multidimensional navigation (e.g. drill-down/ roll-up, slice & dice) remain fully available for the overall system.
-   *Scalability & performance.* DB-Prism needs to move a very high volume of current data to make a fully refreshed data warehouse available every day. Matplan/b2brain allows flexible scaling by switching freely between pre-aggregation in batch windows, and dynamic online aggregation. The possible time delay associated with dynamic online aggregation is largely avoided by the usage of efficient hashing techniques.

5 Metadata Management

As stated earlier, semantic heterogeneity with domain rules hidden in program code was one of the main motivations for the DB-Prism project. Thus, as postulated in [JJQV99], a conceptual perspective documenting the meaning of data and their relationships has been a critical success factor of the system. However, the mapping of this conceptual approach to the logical level – i.e. the incremental creation of basic GDH data from various sources and the restructuring of GDH data into numerous cube formats and report structures – has been equally important. Given the size and complexity of the system, it is not surprising that physical-level optimisation is also very important. For example, major surmounted challenges at the physical level include the scheduling of join operations in data integration for GDH production and the decision when to pre-materialize cubes and when to do dynamic aggregation.

These aspects cannot be considered independently, but are closely interlinked. The precise documentation and, where possible, automation of these tasks is the goal of the metadata management facilities in DB-Prism; analogous to GDH/CBM, they comprise the meta database MetaDB and an associated workbench called CDR.

5.1 MetaDB

The DB-Prism meta database brings together knowledge about a wide range of heterogeneous application and system aspects. MetaDB describe data from the viewpoints of their origin, structure, meaning, use and relationships; it is the knowledge base for the whole system and for the interaction of its components. As an active knowledge networking system, MetaDB knows, steers and drives the processes within the system as a whole not only at the conceptual but also at the logical and physical level. This way, transparency, integrity, quality, standardisation, consistency and flexibility are ensured. Figure 2, following the steps of the DB-Prism operational processes from source import via GDH and OLAP cube creation up to drill-through back to the operational data, gives an indication of the richness of knowledge covered by the MetaDB.

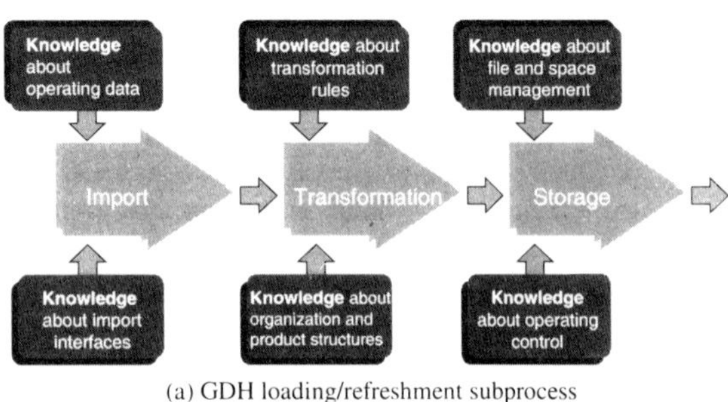

(a) GDH loading/refreshment subprocess

(b) multidimensional aggregation subprocess

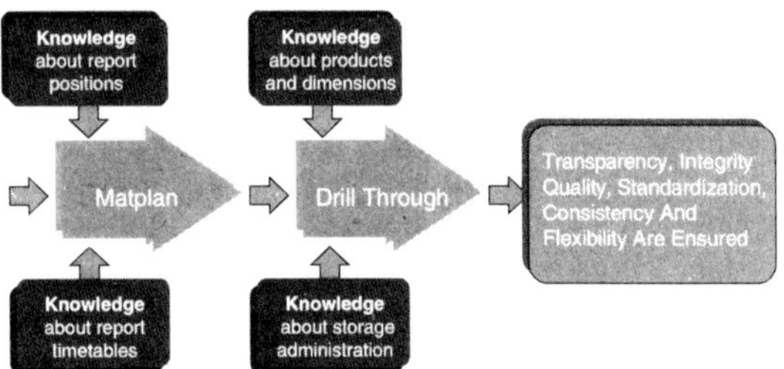

(c) multidimensional analysis subprocess with drill-through

Fig. 2: Knowledge networking in the DB-Prism process

5.2 CDR Tool (Controlling Dimensions & Reports)

CDR is the central user tool for Controllers and system people to manage the MetaDB. Dimensions, products, hierarchies, delivery interfaces and report positions can be defined and adjusted. Processing is carried out online on the operational MetaDB. After an integrated program driven integration and extensive quality checks, changes can be released for real-time effectiveness. Additional important CDR features include:

- time & status concept for defining the scheduling and monitoring policies for operational data flows such as shown in figure 2.
- online status control from data import through GDH creation to data export
- metadata export functionality to automatically or interactively evolve the structure of external systems such as Matplan/b2brain.

6   Conclusions

The DB-Prism system in the form described here has been in operation for about a year. It has had a significant impact on the organisation by achieving the quality goals of integrity, coherence across controlling pathways and reporting systems, currency and availability of data, evolvability and efficient handling of massive amounts of heterogeneous data both at the source and client side.

Primary success factors include the highly efficient and flexible facilities for multidimensional databases provided by Matplan/b2brain, and a metadata model and environment that supports domain-specific quality aspects from the conceptual perspective of bank accounting knowledge in addition to the more traditional logical data transformations and physical data transport and manipulation facilities. Thus, DB-Prism provides an interesting example of a quality-oriented, concept-centred data warehouse architecture as researched in the European DWQ project [JJQV99]. Ongoing work concerns the extension to further parts of the organisation as well as broadened accessibility on the client side.

Acknowledgments. Thanks are due to the people from GMI in Aachen and Frankfurt who contributed significantly to the success of the system described here.

References

[GMI00] GMI mbH. Matplan and b2brain product description (in German). http://www.gmi-mbh.de/nav/produkte.html, June 2000.

[JJQV99] Jarke, M., Jeusfeld, M., Quix, C., Vassiliadis, P. Architecture and quality in data warehouses: an extended repository approach. Special Issue Advanced Information Systems Engineering (Pernici/ Thanos, eds.), *Information Systems 24*(3):229-253, 1999.

[JLVV99] M. Jarke, M. Lenzerini, Y. Vassiliou, P. Vassiliadis: *Fundamentals of Data Warehouses*. Springer-Verlag 1999.

[WSF95] Wang, R.Y., Storey, V., Firth, C.P. A framework for analysis of data quality research. *IEEE Trans. Knowledge and Data Eng.* 7(4):623-640, 1995.

Integration of Data Mining and Relational Databases

Amir Netz, Surajit Chaudhuri, Jeff Bernhardt, Usama Fayyad[*]
Microsoft, USA

Abstract

In this paper, we review the past work and discuss the future of integration of data mining and relational database systems. We also discuss support for integration in Microsoft SQL Server 2000.

1. Introduction

Data mining techniques, based on statistics and machine learning can significantly boost the ability to analyze data. Despite the potential effectiveness of data mining to significantly enhance data analysis, this technology is destined be a niche technology unless an effort is made to integrate this technology with traditional database systems. This is because data analysis needs to be consolidated at the warehouse for data integrity and management concerns. Therefore, one of the key challenges is to enable integration of data mining technology seamlessly within the framework of traditional database systems [7].

2. Related Work in Data Mining Research

In the last decade, significant research progress has been made towards streamlining data mining algorithms. There has been an explosion of work (e.g., [1]) in *scaling* many major data mining techniques to work with large data sets, i.e., ensuring that the algorithms are "disk-aware" and more generally, conscious of memory hierarchy, instead of making the assumption that all data must reside in memory. Another direction of work that has been pursued is to consider if data mining algorithms may be implemented as traditional database applications. Such implementations ensure that the data mining

---

Proceedings of the 26th International Conference on Very Large Databases, Cairo, Egypt, 2000

implementations are not only disk-aware but also "SQL-aware", i.e., the implementations take advantage of the functionality provided through the SQL Engine and the API, e.g., [2]. Efforts to implement mining algorithms on top of database systems have also led to primitives such as sampling to ease the task of data mining on relational systems, e.g., see the proposal in [3].

3. Representing Mining Models in Databases

The progress in data mining research has made it possible to implement several data mining operations efficiently on large databases. While this is surely an important contribution, we should not lose sight of the final goal of data mining – it is to enable database application writers to construct *data mining models* (e.g., a decision tree classifier, regression model, segmentation) from their databases, to use these models for a variety of predictive and analytic tasks, and to share these models with other applications. Such integration is a precondition to make data mining succeed in the database world.

Recognizing the above fact, it is obvious that a key aspect of integration with database systems that needs to be looked into is how to treat data mining models as first class objects in databases. Unfortunately, in that respect, data mining still remains an island of analysis that is poorly integrated with database systems. Recall that a data mining model (e.g., classifier) is obtained via applying a data mining algorithm on a training data set. Although a mining model may be derived using a SQL application implementing a training algorithm, the database management system is completely unaware of the semantics of mining models since *mining models* are *not explicitly represented* in the database. But, unless such explicit representation is enabled, the database management system capabilities cannot be leveraged for sharing, reusing and managing mining models in a rich way. In particular, even if several mining models have been created, there is no way for a user or an application to search the set of available models based on its properties, indicate that a certain model should be applied to predict a column of an unknown data set and then to query the result of the prediction, e.g. to compare the results of predictions from two models.

In order to effectively represent data mining models in relational databases, we need to capture *creation* of data mining models using *arbitrary* mining algorithms, *browsing* of such models (examining their structure or contents), and *application* of a selected model to an ad-hoc data set for analysis tasks such as *prediction*. Furthermore, for a column that is the result of the prediction, sufficient meta-data must be available with the predicted column so that analysis tools can interpret properties of prediction, e.g., its accuracy.

Relational database systems understand and support only relations as first class objects and so if we are to represent a data mining model in databases, it must be viewed as a "table-like" structure. However, at a first glance, a model is more like a graph, with a complex interpretation of its structure, e.g., a decision tree classifier. Thus, trying to represent a mining model as a table (or a set of rows) appears unnatural. Fortunately, this need not be the stumbling block. The key steps in the lifecycle of a mining model are to *create and populate* a model via an algorithm on a training data source, and to be able to use the mining model to *predict* values for data sets. If we can capture these steps using SQL metaphors then it would ensure that database developers are able to leverage data mining functionality without a shift in their paradigm for application development. In the next section, we outline an approach to accomplish this goal.

3. OLE-DB for Data Mining

OLE-DB is a well-known programming interface that allows an application to connect to and consume information from any relational data source (need not be a SQL database). This generality makes OLE-DB an ideal candidate API to extend with data mining capabilities based on the design philosophies outlined in the previous section. Microsoft has proposed OLE-DB for DM to enable data mining functionality on OLE-DB providers. The details of this specification is available online [4] and we only provide a short overview here.

The OLE DB for DM interface allows client applications to explore and manipulate the existing mining models and their properties through an interface similar to that used for exploring tables, views and other first class relational objects. All mining models are represented as table-like objects with columns, data types and extended meta-information that is needed for data mining algorithms.

Before we discuss how one can view mining models as tables, we need to recognize the data representation needs related to mining. Traditional statistical learning algorithms prefer to view a data set to consist of (attribute, value) pairs representing "cases" (observations) on a certain entity, e.g., customer. Effective data mining often requires that these cases in the training consolidate all the information relevant to the entity. Since in relational databases data is often scattered over multiple normalized tables, this creates a conceptual mismatch. In particular, cases are far better represented as nested records than flat records[1]. Traditional SQL representation also falls short is in capturing metadata on columns. To effectively derive and use a mining model, we must be able to identify properties of an attribute (e.g., discrete vs. continuous) and relationships among attributes. Accordingly, we have enabled a column in a rowset (representing a set of cases) of the four **content types**: *key, attribute, relationship, and qualifier*. The notion of key and attributes are traditional, i.e., a key uniquely identifies the case and an attribute is a property of the case. More interesting are the column types relationship and qualifier. A relationship column qualifies/classifies an attribute, e.g., a column "product type" classifies the attribute "product name". Thus, the column "product type" can be recorded as *related to* "product type". A qualifier represents a column that provides additional information on value of another attribute that can be interpreted by an OLE-DB provider. For example, a column may represent the probability associated with a predicted attribute, distribution information, domain types (discrete/continuous) etc. Such information can be invaluable in data analysis. We describe how the key steps on a mining model are supported in OLE-DB for DM:

CREATE: A client application can create (define) a new mining model simply by executing a *CREATE MINING MODEL* statement. This statement is very similar in style and semantics to that of a CREATE TABLE statement but contains more meta-information about the columns as indicated above. An example is presented below:

```
CREATE MINING MODEL  [Age Prediction](
[Customer ID]LONG          KEY,
[Gender]   TEXT    DISCRETE,
[Age]      DOUBLE DISCRETE PREDICT,
[Product Purchases] TABLE(
[Product Name]   TEXT    KEY,
[Quantity]DOUBLE NORMAL CONTINUOUS,
[Product Type]   TEXT    DISCRETE    RELATED
TO [Product Name]))
USING [Decision_Trees_A]
```

Note that each column has an additional meta-data specification that identifies its column type. For example, Product Type is marked as related to Product Name. The training algorithm is indicated using the USING clause. The columns that are being predicted are indicated by use of the keyword PREDICT.

INSERT: Once the mining model was created, it functions as an empty table, i.e., its structure could be

---

[1] Microsoft Data Access Components support hierarchical rowsets using the Shape Provider. See [4] for details.

browsed but queries will always return empty data. In order to be able to execute prediction using a mining model, it must be *trained* with known cases by using the *INSERT* statement that will point to the source of the training data (like source of input rows in SQL). The behavior of this INSERT statement is somewhat different than that of the traditional INSERT operation on a table. The training cases (i.e. rows) being "inserted" into the mining model are not persisted in the mining model as it is. Instead, the mining model *analyzes* the rows and builds the mining model, which could be a set of decision trees or clusters, as per the schema specified in the CREATE statement used to define the model. Once the training rows are consumed, the mining model is marked "trained" and could be used for prediction queries. Usually the physical the size of the model is quite small as it contains only the data summarization of the model rather than the original set of cases used the training.

SELECT: The content of the model could be browsed in various ways. In particular, the schema rowset associated with the mining model may·be obtained via the following statement (see [4] for description of the mining model schema rowset):
*SELECT * FROM <my model>.CONTENT*
It is also possible to retrieve the content in XML representation consistent with the proposed PMML specification.

PREDICTION JOIN: Performing prediction is a simple matter of issuing SQL queries to the data-mining engine, enabled by extensions, notably the *PREDICTION JOIN* and statistics retrieval functions. Thus, the result of a prediction may be viewed as a "join" between the table representing the mining model and a data set. The following example illustrates the syntax:
SELECT <columns to predict> FROM <data mining model> PREDICTION JOIN <new data> ON <conditions>.
The *ON* clause ties up correspondences between a column in a data mining model with a column in the data set[2]. The result of a prediction join is always a relational result set that could be either retrieved by the client application for navigation and presentation, persisted in a table within the relational database or could be used for subsequent relational operations within the same statement.

4. Data Mining in SQL Server 2000

Microsoft SQL Server 2000 integrates for the first time Data Mining capabilities together with relational and OLAP database engines. The Analysis Services component of SQL Server 2000 contains a data-mining engine that is exposed through an OLE DB for DM

---

[2] The heterogeneous query processor of SQL Server allows queries to span both relational table and data mining models using the OPENROWSET function.

interface. The data-mining engine is integrated in both the server component of analysis services, which includes also the OLAP engine, as well as on the client component. The data-mining engine provides two classes of scalable algorithms based on work done in Microsoft Research [5,6]: classification and segmentation (clustering). Future releases of the product will extend the repertoire of algorithms. The product provides a full GUI based console for the administration of the data-mining model including the creation, training, browsing of content and access security management. While the detailed aspects of the UI are not the central focus of this paper, the UI serves as a natural way to introduce a user to how data mining can be done naturally within the SQL Server framework. However, it should be noted that the primary contribution of our proposal is the backend components that support this UI and understand the semantics of data mining.

Creation of data mining model is done through the "Mining Model Wizard" that guides the user through four easy steps for building the basic data mining model: the selection of the table containing the cases, the selection of the algorithm (classification/clustering), the identification of the case-key column and the selection of the predictable columns and the input columns (Figure 1).

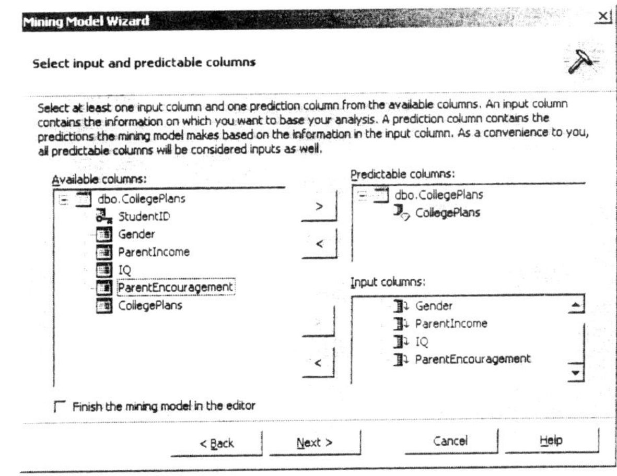

Fig 1: Mining Model Wizard

After the mining model has been defined and named, it is trained by simply executing the appropriate SQL statements as defined by the OLE DB for DM specification through a simple UI. Once the training is done, the user is led to a full-blown mining model editor (see Figure 2) that allows the user to enhance the basic model defined in the wizard and manipulate the properties of the model.

At this point the user can elect to browse the content of the trained model including rules and statistics by selecting the content tab where the various rules and statistics could be browsed and manipulated. Figure 3 displays a view of a classifier.

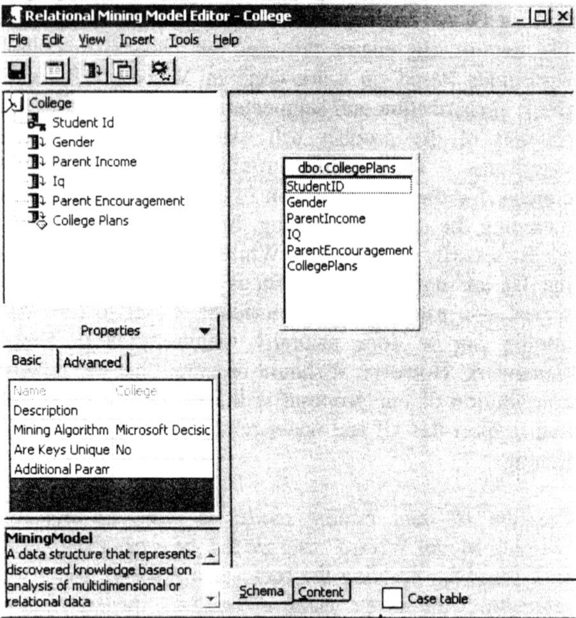

Fig 2: Model Editor

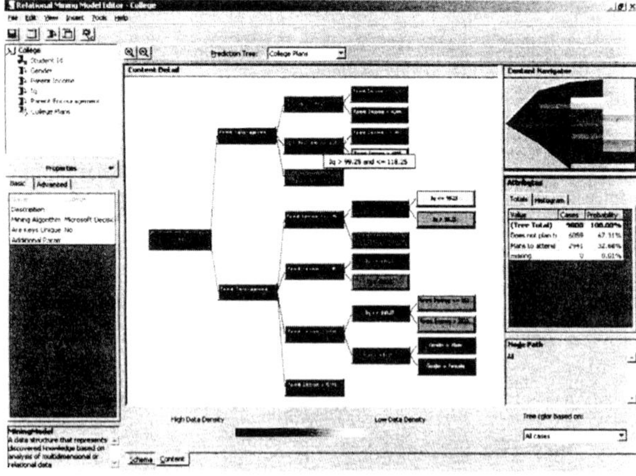

Fig 3: Model Browsing

The object on the upper right corner indicates the distribution of population among classes via the degree of shade in color. Since the mining model can support multiple predicted attributes, each mining model can result in multiple decision trees. A special Bayesian Dependency Network browser can be used to view the relationships among the attributes across all of the decision trees. The browser allows identification of prediction relationships and enables the user to manipulate the relationship strength slider to better identify the most important relationships.

In summary, SQL Server 2000 provides a comprehensive and open platform for the development of embedded data mining applications. The OLE DB for DM interface fits well into the relational framework and allows developers to leverage their familiarity with the SQL language and the OLE DB interfaces to facilitate application development using the data-mining technology. The easy to use administration tools ease the burden of managing the repository of data mining models and the scalable data-mining algorithms supported in the product enable the applicability of the technology to potentially a wide range of scenarios and applications.

5. Outstanding Challenges

OLE-DB for DM takes a significant step forward in proposing an approach that can make it easy to support the data mining process. Our proposal emphasizes the importance of being able to generate and reuse mining models effectively. While this must indeed be the first priority, it is also important to support interfaces that enable providers of data mining technologies to be able to register and integrate effectively a variety of data mining algorithms to create mining models.

Finally, there is still the issue of efficient *implementation* of data mining algorithms on the relational engine to optimize execution of integrated querying and mining [7]. Complexity of modern relational engines require us to determine judiciously the functionality that needs to be pushed down into the engine vs. the functionality that can be layered on top of the relational engine.

6. References

[1] Rakesh Agrawal et al.: Fast Discovery of Association Rules. Advances in Knowledge Discovery and Data Mining 1996: 307-328

[2] Sunita Sarawagi, Shiby Thomas, Rakesh Agrawal: Integrating Association Rule Mining with Relational Database Systems: Alternatives and Implications. Data Mining and Knowledge Discovery 4 (2/3).

[3] John Clear et al.: NonStop SQL/MX Primitives for Knowledge Discovery. *KDD 1999*: 425-429.

[4] Introduction to OLE-DB for Data Mining: http://www.microsoft.com/data/oledb/dm.

[5] Surajit Chaudhuri, Usama M. Fayyad, Jeff Bernhardt: Scalable Classification over SQL Databases. ICDE 1999: 470-479

[6] Paul Bradley, Usama Fayyad, Cory Reina: Scaling Clustering Algorithms to Large Databases. *KDD-98*, pages 9-15.

[7] Surajit Chaudhuri: Data Mining and Database Systems: Where is the Intersection? Data Engineering Bulletin 21(1) 1998.

E.piphany Epicenter Technology Overview

Sridhar Ramaswamy

E.piphany, USA

sridhar@epiphany.com

This paper was not available at the time of publication.

This proceedings and additional presentations will be available through www.vldb.org

Concurrency in the Data Warehouse

Dr. Richard Taylor

Informix Software Inc.
485 Alberto Way
Los Gatos
USA
richard.taylor@informix.com

Abstract

When a data warehouse is loaded at night and queried during the day, there is no requirement for concurrent update and querying. However there are a number of situations where concurrency is needed: trickle feed applications, correcting exception data from the nightly load, the narrowing load window. The end point of the narrowing load window is a data warehouse that is available 7x24. Query Priority Concurrency is the concurrency mechanism implemented by the Informix Red Brick Decision Server. It is called Query Priority Concurrency because it uses versioning to achieve the goal that query performance is unaffected by concurrent loads. The paper discusses the differing requirements for concurrency in a data warehouse, explains why versioning is appropriate, gives a sketch of the implementation and discusses the 6 lock modes that are needed to achieve concurrency and serialised execution. Finally, the frozen query feature is described. This allows users to query the current published version of the data warehouse while the administrators go through all the steps of loading and verifying new data to create the next issue of the warehouse for publication.

1. Introduction

The common data warehouse cycle is to load the data warehouse at night with a day's worth of transactions, and to query the data warehouse during the day. In this regime, there is no need for concurrent querying and update. However, the increasing demands on data warehousing creates situations where concurrency is needed.

One situation is a trickle feed application that has a small amount of critical data that needs to be continuously loaded during the day. Trickle feed is commonly found in financial applications where stock prices or currency exchange rates that change during the day are loaded as they change. Another situation where concurrency is convenient is to allow corrections and exception data from the nightly load to be reloaded during the day. Also, it may be convenient to update dimensional data as soon as a new version of the customer or product master file becomes available.

Companies spread across many time zones, stores and offices that stay open late, increased business volume and other similar causes are causing the nightly load window to narrow. The narrowing load window means that the data warehouse may not be completely loaded by the time it is needed for querying. At the end point of the narrowing load window are the global companies and e-commerce enterprises that never sleep. These companies want their data warehouse to be available 7x24.

2. Concurrency Requirements

The requirements for concurrency in a data warehouse are very different from those of an OLTP system. As most database systems have been designed to support OLTP, they do not match the requirements of a data warehouse.

Consider the transaction. An OLTP transaction typically uses indexes to directly select a small number rows and perhaps update some of them. In a data warehouse a typical query may access multiple tables through several indexes, join the results, hopefully with the aid of a multi-table join index and then perform some aggregation to produce a result. The other type of transaction in a date warehouse is a bulk load, which needs to build several indexes including join indexes and may need to check referential integrity and if necessary automatically generate rows to maintain referential integrity.

In an OLTP system, having a transaction lock individual rows works most of the time, and where there are hot spots that prevents locking from working, special techniques can be used. One special technique is versioning where the unit of data being versioned can be a row or even a data item. In a data warehouse, locking individual rows is not useful for either queries that roam over large amounts of data or for the bulk loader. Versioning is a useful technique for allowing bulk loads to proceed in parallel with queries, but the versioning system has to be able to handle versioned data on a far larger scale than is ever envisioned by the implementers of an OLTP system.

2. Query Priority Concurrency

The Informix Red Brick Decision Server implements concurrency using versioning. This concurrency mechanism is called **Query Priority Concurrency** because it is specifically designed for data warehousing with the goal that query performance is unaffected by concurrent modifications of the database. A query sees a consistent snapshot of the database. This snapshot is called a **revision**. A transaction that modifies the database makes a new revision of the database. Each new revision is assigned a monotonically incrementing number.

The implementation of Query Priority Concurrency is straightforward. When a data block is modified, the new version of the block is written to a special segment called the **version log**. Whenever a block is fetched from disk, the transaction checks an in-memory index called the **version log index** to see whether the block should be fetched from the database or from the version log. There may be multiple versions of a block in the version log associated with different revisions. The version log index ensures that the correct block is selected. Finally, when it is safe to do so, blocks from the version log are merged back into the database by a **vacuum cleaner daemon**.

The transaction manager keeps a table of active revisions that is used to determine when the vacuum cleaner daemon should clean a revision. When a query starts, it is assigned a revision R to read. R is always the latest committed revision, except in the case of the frozen query revision feature, which is described later. When the transaction finishes and the transaction manager determines that no other transaction is accessing R or any previous revision, the vacuum cleaner is alerted that it can start cleaning. The vacuum cleaner cleans all revisions in the version log up to and including the latest active revision. This protocol means that when modifications to the database have completed and the queries that access older revisions finish, the vacuum cleaner daemon can clean out the entire version log.

A transaction that updates the database reads the current revision of the database when it starts. Modified blocks are written to the version log, but the blocks are not assigned a revision number until the transaction commits. This means that many transactions can be modifying different tables the database concurrently and the order in which they can commit is not predetermined.

Another important optimisation is that new blocks are written to the database directly. The only blocks that are written to the version log are blocks that are modifications of existing blocks. Thus in a load of new data, we expect the data blocks to be written to directly to the database while most of the changes to indexes will be modifications of existing blocks, and therefore go to the version log. The flip side of this optimisation is that bulk deletes create new versions of blocks that are completely empty. Users are suggested to use non-versioning deletes when they roll-off data to create space.

3. Locking

As has been discussed, fine granularity locking is not appropriate for data warehousing. The Red Brick server only implements table locks, and these locks are used to ensure that there is only one transaction that is modifying a table at one time. While a transaction is creating a new revision of a table, other transactions can read the previously created revisions of the table. However, there is a potential for problems if these other transactions are also modifying other tables in the database system.

For example, a transaction could be reading a fact table to create an aggregate table, while at the same time, another transaction could be loading new data into the fact table. If this were allowed, when both of these transactions commit, the aggregate table will not reflect the contents of the fact table. Another example is that a transaction could be loading a fact table and checking referential integrity by reading a dimension table while at the same time another transaction could be deleting rows from the dimension table. If this were allowed, when both transactions committed, referential integrity of the fact table would be broken.

To overcome these problems, new lock modes are required. The Red Brick server implements 6 lock modes as shown in Table 1.

Table 1. Lock Modes

RO	Read Only	Normal read lock, used by queries. Compatible with versioned writes.
RK	Read Key	Indicates that the key should not change. Used for referential integrity checking
RD	Read Data	Not compatible with versioned writes, used by a transaction that read existing tables to modify another table.
WD	Write Data	Used by versioning operations that do not change the existing key column in a table: versioned inserts and non-key column updates.
WK	Write Key	Used by versioning operations that change the key column: versioned deletes and updates to key columns.
WB	Write Only	Non-versioned modifications to the table. Not compatible with any other lock.

The lock compatibility matrix is shown below.

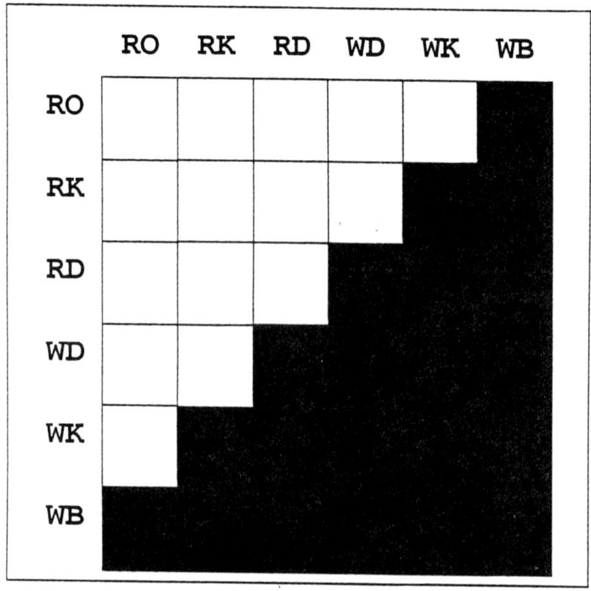

The compatibility matrix shows that a RK lock is compatible with a WD lock but not a WK lock. Thus, a transaction can insert rows into a table that is being used for referential integrity checking, but the transaction cannot delete rows from the table.

By default, a transaction that does an INSERT ... SELECT ... gets a RD lock because it is both reading tables and writing a table. The RD lock is not compatible with any versioning write locks. This behaviour can be overridden by setting the transaction isolation level to repeatable read, in which case an RO lock is used.

The RK lock and its associated WK lock can be thought of as a special case of the RD lock that allows greater freedom while checking referential integrity. In practice this is important in the Red Brick server, which relies heavily on referential integrity for maintaining the coherence of its join indexes and algorithms.

4. Periodic Commit

Query Priority Concurrency provides a simple transaction atomicity mechanism. When a transaction aborts, all that is needed to rollback the transaction is to throw away the blocks in the version log that have been created by the transaction. Similarly, crash recovery is just a matter of restoring the version log metadata and then restarting the vacuum cleaner, which will proceed to clean all the committed blocks in the version log.

Statement atomicity is an essential characteristic of a transaction. However it is sometimes convenient to have sub-statement atomicity. **Periodic Commit** is a feature in the Red Brick loader that implements sub-statement atomicity. The concept is that a load statement can be specified to commit after a number of rows have been loaded, or that the commit occurs after a specified time interval or either depending on which comes first.

The time interval is used to implement trickle feed applications. In a trickle feed application, a low volume stream of data is loaded continuously while the data warehouse is being queried. To implement trickle feed, the periodic commit timer is set to a suitable interval, for example 15 minutes. Then, every 15 minutes, the date loaded since during the interval is committed and immediately becomes visible to any new queries that access the database.

Another use of periodic commit is to save having to restart a bulk load from the beginning when the load aborts. In this case the loader is set to commit after loading a specific number of rows, say for example, every 10 million rows in a 100 million row bulk load. If the load does abort, at most 10 million rows needs to be reloaded, rather than an average of 50 million rows that would have to be reloaded without using periodic commit.

5. Frozen Query Revision

The process for creating a data warehouse involves a number of steps. Data is extracted from operational systems transformed into a suitable form and loaded into the data warehouse. First the dimension tables are loaded and then the fact tables. If there are load problems such as referential integrity failures, these need to be fixed up. Next aggregate tables and their indexes need to be loaded. Finally a few test queries may be run to verify that the data warehouse is complete and consistent. When the data warehouse is ready, it is published to the user community for querying. Creating the next version of the data warehouse repeats the cycle.

Frozen Query Revision allows the administrator to create the next version of the data warehouse while users are querying the published version. A frozen query revision is created with an alter database statement that specifies the current revision as the frozen revision. Normally with versioning, when a query starts it is assigned to access the current revision of the database. When a frozen revision exists, a query is accesses the frozen revision by default.

After publishing the data warehouse by creating a frozen query revision, the administrator uses versioning operations to create the next version of the database for publication. While the frozen query revision exists, all modifications of the database must be versioned, because non-versioned operation would modify the underlying database and change the frozen revision. The frozen query revision is read only, it cannot be modified.

Modifications to the database must be made in the context of the latest revision. For example, a query that creates an aggregate table must see the latest version of the base table. A flag is set in the administrator session so that transactions in that session access the latest revision. Each versioned operation such as a load creates a new revision when it commits. If the load fails, only that statement is rolled back. When the next version of the data warehouse is ready to be published, the administrator issues an alter database statement to remove the frozen revision, and all new queries access the latest revision which is the newly published revision.

6. Conclusions

Query Priority Concurrency is a versioning mechanism that is designed specifically for data warehousing. For that reason it is different from versioning that has been implemented in other database systems. In the Red Brick server, the unit of versioning is the block. Other versioning schemes version pages, rows or even the individual data item. This aspect of the design matches the data warehouse regime where database modifications are almost always bulk operations.

In the Red Brick server, the new data is written to the log, from where it may be accessed, and the database retains the old version of the data. In other database systems, the new version of the data typically is written to the database and older versions of the data may be accessed from the database, or from an exception file or from the pre-image log. This aspect of the design comes from the requirement that query performance is unaffected by modifications to the database.

Finally, most versioning systems have a tight limit on the number of versions that are kept around. In Red Brick, the default is to allow for 5000 active revisions, and much larger numbers have been used.

Biodiversity Informatics:

The Challenge of Rapid Development, Large Databases, and Complex Data

Meredith A. Lane
Academy of Natural Sciences
1900 Benjamin Franklin Pkwy
Philadelphia, PA 19103
USA
lane@ansp.org

James L. Edwards
National Science Foundation
4201 Wilson Blvd
Arlington, VA 20560
USA
jledward@nsf.gov

Ebbe S. Nielsen
CSIRO Entomology
GPO Box 1700
Canberra ACT 2601
Australia
ebben@ento.csiro.au

Abstract

There are high expectations in all sectors of society for immediate access to biological knowledge of all kinds. To fully exploit and manage the value of biological resources, society must have the intellectual tools to store, retrieve, collate, analyze, and synthesize organism-level and ecological scale information. However, it currently is difficult to discover, access, and use biodiversity data because of the long history of "bottom-up" evolution of scientific biodiversity information, the mismatch between the distribution of biodiversity itself and the distribution of the data about it, and, most importantly, the inherent complexity of biodiversity and ecological data. This stems from, among many factors, numerous data types, the nonexistence of a common underlying (binary) language, and the multiple perceptions of different researchers/data recorders across spatial or temporal distance or both. The challenge presented to the computer science and information technology community by the biodiversity and ecological information domain is worthy of all the time and talent that can be

Proceedings of the 26th International Conference on Very Large Databases, Cairo, Egypt, 2000

brought to bear, because the continued existence of the species *Homo sapiens* depends upon gaining an understanding of this spaceship Earth and our fellow passengers upon it.

1. Introduction

The economic prosperity and, indeed, the fate of human societies are inextricably linked to the natural world. Because of humanity's dependence on natural systems, information about biodiversity and ecology is vital to a wide range of scientific, educational, commercial, and governmental uses. Biodiversity (in the sense of the totality of all species) and ecosystems are themselves interdependent. Ecosystems and the diversity of species they support underpin our lives and our economies in very real, though often underappreciated, ways. The living things with which we share the planet provide us with clean air, clean water, food, clothing, shelter, medicines, and aesthetic enjoyment. Yet, increasing human populations and their activities are disturbing species and their habitats, disrupting natural ecological processes, and even changing climate patterns on a global scale. These are greater stresses on the natural world than humanity has ever generated in the past. Since biodiversity is arguably the most precious resource on Earth, it is becoming more and more important that we actively conserve biodiversity and protect natural ecosystems in order to preserve the quality of human life. As human populations and their demands on the natural world grow, our accumulated knowledge about biodiversity and the environment will become ever more important in the effort to develop a sustainable world.

Recognition of this has led to the National Biological Information Infrastructure in the United States, to the Environmental Resources Information Network in

Australia, and to a number of regional biodiversity information networks (NABIN, IABIN, EIOnet, and others). Indeed, the recommendation by an international working group established by the Global Science Forum (formerly Megascience Forum) of the Organization for Economic Cooperation and Development (OECD) that the nations of the world establish and maintain a Global Biodiversity Information Facility (GBIF), which is poised to become a reality in early 2001, is a direct outgrowth of both concern about the environment and the economy, and the acknowledgment that the complexity of biodiversity and ecological datasets reflects the complexity of natural systems. It has become apparent that practitioners in the computer science and information technology fields must become as invigorated by and invested in the biodiversity and ecological information domain as are the biologists, who collect, generate, query, and interpret the data.

2. Biodiversity and Ecology Information

Biodiversity itself is distributed all over the Earth, with concentrations primarily in developing countries. In contrast, scientific biodiversity knowledge is concentrated in major centers in developed countries. To be useful in the management and use of biodiversity, biodiversity information should be available when and where it is needed. At present, it is more likely that information on the plants of a particular part of Africa is stored in an herbarium in Europe, for example. Because it is not immediately at hand, biodiversity information is often not applied in policy or management decisions that affect the organisms involved. At present, scientists and others find it is difficult to discover, access, and use biodiversity data because of the long history of "bottom-up" evolution of scientific biodiversity information, the mismatch between the distribution of biodiversity itself and the distribution of the data about it, and, most importantly, the inherent complexity of biodiversity and ecological data. This complexity stems from inclusion of multiple data types, the nonexistence of a common underlying (binary) language, and the multiple perceptions of different researchers/data recorders across spatial or temporal distance or both. In contrast, in disciplines that have emerged very recently, such as genomics (which has a history measured in mere decades in comparison to the centuries of history of biodiversity science), researchers have been able to capitalize on modern information technology to capture the data in digital form and make the data more readily accessible from the very beginning of their science.

In order to comprehend and sustainably utilize the biodiversity resources of the world, humankind must learn how to exploit massive data sets, learn how to store and access them for analytic purposes, develop methods to cope with growth and change in data, and make it possible to "repurpose" previously existing data. Many issues· surround efforts to make biodiversity and ecological information electronically accessible and usable. We must unlock the knowledge and economic power lying dormant in the masses of biodiversity data that we have on hand that is stored in static media (for the most part in print, on paper). We need to bring the results of a great deal of earlier research that are now only found in static media into electronic format. We need information science research that is focused on biodiversity and ecosystems datasets and information—their structures, their complexity, their fuzziness, and their clarity.

3. Biological Informatics

There are high expectations in all sectors of society for immediate access to biological knowledge of all kinds. The desire to call upon the data in these databases, collate the information from various sources, analyze the combined data, and make predictions and correlations is growing exponentially. Therefore, one of the greatest needs in biology (and between biology and related sciences) lies in the area of information management and provision over networks; that is, biological informatics.

Biological informatics integrates biological, computational, networking, and organizational research, and is concerned with the development, sharing, and analysis of biological datasets, which are usually very large and complex. Examples of such datasets include results from the Human Genome Project, from research in biotechnology and medicine (including pharmaceuticals and neurobiology), and from environmental research such as biodiversity and ecosystem ecology. To date, "bioinformatics" as a term has been recognized as important mostly in the area of genome research. However, as genome data are accumulated, it will become more and more apparent that those data, without the context of all sorts of other information about the organism (physiological, ecological, etc.) from which the genome was sampled, will be limited in their usefulness. In the context of the full informational milieu, however, the usefulness of each of the several different kinds of data will be increased. To fully exploit and manage the value of biological resources, society must have the intellectual tools to store, retrieve, collate, analyze, and synthesize organism-level and ecological scale information. In short, biodiversity and ecological informatics inevitably will become increasingly important.

4. Biodiversity and Ecological Informatics

If all the biodiversity information that we currently have stored on static media were digitized and as freely available online as is that from the Hubble telescope or GenBank, biodiversity informatics would be more similar to astronomy and molecular biological informatics in its present capabilities. This would lead to economic benefits from mining biodiversity itself for currently unknown and therefore untapped resources, as well as those benefits that can be derived from mining existing data.

A major challenge within ecological informatics is extrapolation from data sampled from an ecosystem to the totality of that ecosystem, about which queries may be posed. Generalizations are critical to ecological analyses, because thorough, complete-coverage data collection, given paltry funding levels compared to astronomy, medicine, or other fields, would be prohibitively expensive. Meeting this challenge has allowed ecological informatics to enable integration of traditional field ecology with modern technology. Thus, it is now possible consistently to link scientific research to ecological planning and management. Diverse sources of information, from field ecology to satellite images, are beginning to be brought to bear on a host of practical problems, from land use planning to global change.

Environmental informatics may be viewed as a merging of biodiversity and ecological informatics with geographic information systems (GIS) and other environmental data. Using information sources and software algorithms developed in Australia and elsewhere, it is possible to generate predictive models of environmental change. Increases in functionality, automation, and refinement of predictive capabilities are much needed.

One issue that is particularly critical to biological informatics is the establishment of data standards, and the development of metadata standards. This is true within all disciplines, but biodiversity and ecology are particularly far behind in this area. There are hardware technologies that are also needed, but the development of these is more nearly keeping pace with demand, with the exception of network bandwidth. Discipline-specific data exchange, interdisciplinary and requirements for data exchange, and the computer science of data exchange and integration, along with the definition of scientific and technical metadata issues (as well as the anticipation of future needs in these areas), are important challenges. Major advances are needed in methods for knowledge representation and interchange, database management and federation, navigation, modelling, and data-driven simulation; in effective approaches to describing large, complex networked information resources; and in techniques to support networked information discovery and retrieval in extremely large-scale distributed systems.

A major scientific consideration in biodiversity science is the need to bring 25 decades' worth of accumulated information into an electronically available format. The data labels on hundreds of millions of specimens (probably as many as three billion) in natural history collections around the world must be digitized, and hundreds of years' worth of scientific publication (unlike many fields of science, data and information—unless false or otherwise disproven—never go out of date) must be prioritized and brought online. Rapid means of data entry must be designed and implemented to capture all of this from static media or to rescue it from the unscrupulous. It is important to reuse data derived from earlier studies. Not only is it impractical to recreate the research projects that resulted in data published in print, but many of those studies cannot be replicated because anthropogenic modifications have severely disturbed the habitat of the organisms involved, driven the study populations or species to extinction, or both.

In addition, new kinds of data are being generated by satellite imagery and other measures of nonbiological, global phenomena—phenomena that have significant influence upon biodiversity. Great forward strides could be made in the understanding of the biological world, for instance, if informatics techniques were developed to make it possible to correlate historical information with newly collected satellite data; if molecular genetic datasets could be linked to species-documentation datasets such as those held by natural history collections; and if neurobiological, physiological, chemical, and other sorts of datasets could be correlated with taxonomic and ecological ones.

To index it all, a catalogue of the names of known organisms is a critical element that must be developed. No complete listing of all the names for organisms exists. The information necessary to compile such a list does exist, but it is scattered throughout millions and millions of pages of printed journals and books. A database of this type would be useful in and of itself, but it is absolutely critical to the progress of biodiversity and ecological informatics. This is because the scientific name of an organism has been handled as the index marker for that organism for hundreds of years. Searching the literature for information on the breeding habits of the yellow-naped parrot will avail the researcher little unless s/he knows that the scientific name is *Amazona ochrocephala* ssp. *auropalliata*; in addition, to garner all the information that might be available, it is important to know that the same creature has also been called *Amazona auropalliata*, because some publications might have used that synonym. The electronic catalogue must make it possible for even the naïve user of a biodiversity and ecological information system to retrieve all information relevant to a query, even if that query is incompletely or poorly structured.

Critical thought must be given to mechanisms for across-scale computing. That is, we need to be able to pose queries that will require combinations and correlation of data that have been measured at scales that may differ by orders of magnitude. One such query might be: *What is the likelihood of survival of the red knot (a bird species that yearly migrates from the Southern tip of South America to the northern reaches of North America and back again) given the diminishment of the Delaware Bay horseshoe crab population?* The answer to this question will require combination and correlation of (among other datasets) data on single specimens of red knots, the horseshoe crabs on whose eggs they feed mid-migration; NEXRAD data along the migration route; remote sensing data on the 30-meter scale; vegetational and faunal community sample data; trend data on accumulation of excess nitrogen and phosphorus, heavy metals, and pesticides over watershed and local scales over a multiyear period; and gene sequence data from population-size samples of birds, crabs, and other creatures that are part of the Delaware Bay ecosystem. This question might be followed by: *How great would be the positive effect (for the horseshoe crabs and therefore for the red knots) if the states of Pennsylvania, Maryland, and Delaware severely or moderately restricted the application of pesticides or fertilizers during the migration season? Banned it altogether? The year before?* The answers to these latter questions, of course, require additional input from datasets not initially included in the analysis. Users ultimately will require on-the-fly flexibility, so that they can reshape and redirect queries depending on initial results.

All of this informatics capability is needed because we are losing, at an ever-increasing rate, both species that we know (there are probably 1.8 million known, named species) and (approximately) ten times as many that we don't know. These species live and interact within communities; each interaction is multifactorial. Those interactions are the source of the emergent properties of ecological systems. Emergent properties then give rise to further interactions; there are an unknown number of levels of interactions and emergent properties in ecosystems. Datasets that contain measurements of ecosystem elements probably don't (yet) reflect the interactions, even though the dataset size may be enormous. We need to find ways to incorporate the living nature of the natural system within our information systems. This challenge is worthy of the attention of all the computer science and information technology talent that can be brought to bear, because the continued existence of the species *Homo sapiens* depends upon gaining an understanding of this spaceship Earth and our fellow passengers upon it.

6. References

[1] Lane, M. A. 1999. *Weaving a Web of Wealth: Biological Informatics for Industry, Science and Health.* Report from the Australian Academy of Science, Canberra, Australia. 40 pp.

[2] President's Committee of Advisors on Science and Technology Panel on Biodiversity and Ecosystems. 1998. *Teaming With Life: Investing in Science to Understand and Use America's Living Capital.* 96 pp. http://www.whitehouse.gov/WH/FOP/OSTP/Environment/html/teamingcover.html

[3] Web site for the Global Biodiversity Information Facility (GBIF) http://www.gbif.org/

Toto, We're Not in Kansas Anymore: On Transitioning from Research to the Real World

Michael Carey

Propel
2350 Mission College Blvd., Suite 1200
Santa Clara, CA 95054, USA

Abstract

Over the past five years or so, I've moved from academia to industrial research and now to an Internet startup. In this talk, I'll share some of the experiences I've had and some of the things that I've observed and learned along the way. Among the issues to be discussed are some of the technical and nontechnical "real-world constraints" that I've bumped into in trying to apply research-y thinking in practice. I'll also share some thoughts on where database systems may or may not be headed as a result. I'll close by describing some of what we're doing in "database space" at Propel, including how we're using database systems as off-the-shelf parts in assembling what we like to think of as "the e-commerce platform of the future."

Index of Authors

Index of Authors